# THE DICTIONARY OF BIBLE AND RELIGION

# THE
# DICTIONARY
## OF
# BIBLE AND
# RELIGION

## William H. Gentz
## General Editor

ABINGDON/NASHVILLE

*Project Editor*
Carey J. Gifford

*Designer:*
John R. Robinson

*Editorial Assistant for Reference Books:*
Joyce A. King

*Input Specialists:*
Mary Lou Allen, Kathy Harding, and Marcia Ryan

*Project Assistants:*
Jackie Glancy and Polly Thompson

*This book is printed on acid-free paper.*

**Library of Congress Cataloging in Publication Data**

THE DICTIONARY OF BIBLE AND RELIGION.
  1. Theology—Dictionaries. 2. Bible—Dictionaries. 3. Religion—
Dictionaries. 4. Religions—Dictionaries.
I. Gentz, William H., 1918–
BR95.D46      1986      203'.21      85-15011

ISBN 0-687-10757-1
*(alk. paper)*

MANUFACTURED BY THE PARTHENON PRESS AT
NASHVILLE, TENNESSEE, UNITED STATES OF AMERICA

# MAPS, TABLES, CHARTS

# CONTRIBUTORS

JOHN CHARLES COOPER
Professor of Religion; Chairman, Department of Philosophy and Religion, Susquehanna University, Selinsgrove, Pennsylvania

CHARLES B. COUSAR
Professor of New Testament, Columbia Theological Seminary, Decatur, Georgia

KEITH CRIM
Editorial Director, The Westminster Press, Philadelphia, Pennsylvania

MARTIN CRIM
Free-lance Writer, Durham, North Carolina

IRIS V. CULLY
Alexander Campbell Hopkins Professor of Christian Education, Emeritus, Lexington Theological Seminary, Lexington, Kentucky

ROBERT S. ELLWOOD
Bishop James W. Bashford Professor of Oriental Studies, School of Religion, University of Southern California, Los Angeles

PAUL LESLIE GARBER
Professor of Bible and Religion, Emeritus, Agnes Scott College, Decatur, Georgia

WILLIAM H. GENTZ
Free-lance Editor and Writer; General Editor, Dictionary of Bible and Religion

JUSTO L. GONZALEZ
Associate for International Relief and Development, Presbyterian Church (USA); Visiting Professor of Theology, Interdenominational Theological Center, Atlanta, Georgia

NANCY A. HARDESTY
Church Historian and Author of *All We're Meant to Be* and *Women Called to Witness*

JOHN H. HAYES
Professor of Old Testament, Candler School of Theology, Emory University, Atlanta, Georgia

RUSSELL T. HITT
Author and Editor, Emeritus, *Eternity* Magazine

BARBARA JURGENSEN
Assistant Professor of Ministry and Contextual Education, Trinity Seminary, Columbus, Ohio

HOWARD CLARK KEE
William Goodwin Aurelio Professor of Biblical Studies; Chairman, Graduate Division of Religious Studies, Boston University

T. J. KLEINHANS
  Senior Editor, Aid Association for Lutherans; Retired Air Force Chaplain

LIONEL KOPPMAN
  Jewish Educator, Temple Isaiah, Forest Hills, New York; Public Information Director, Jewish Welfare Board, New York, New York

J. KENNETH KUNTZ
  Professor, School of Religion, University of Iowa, Iowa City, Iowa

JAMES C. LIVINGSTON
  Professor of Religion, The College of William and Mary, Williamsburg, Virginia

JOHN MACQUARRIE
  Lady Margaret Professor of Divinity and Canon of Christ Church, University of Oxford, England

CLYDE L. MANSCHRECK
  Chavanne Professor of Religious Studies, Rice University, Houston, Texas

RALPH P. MARTIN
  Professor of New Testament; Director of Graduate Studies Program, Fuller Theological Seminary, Pasadena, California

CHARLES S. McCOY
  Robert Gordon Sproul Professor of Ethics, Pacific School of Religion/Graduate Theological Union, Berkeley, California

JOHN R. McRAY
  Professor of New Testament and Archaeology, Wheaton College Graduate School, Wheaton, Illinois

JAMES D. NEWSOME, Jr.
  Professor of Old Testament Language, Literature, and Exegesis, Columbia Theological Seminary, Decatur, Georgia

JAMES L. PRICE
  Professor of Religion, Duke University, Durham, North Carolina

DAVID M. SCHOLER
  Dean of the Seminary; Julius R. Mantey Professor of New Testament, Northern Baptist Theological Seminary, Lombard, Illinois

W. SIBLEY TOWNER
  The Reverend Archibald McFadyen Professor of Biblical Interpretation, Union Theological Seminary, Richmond, Virginia

F. BRUCE VAWTER
  Professor of Old Testament; Chairman, Religious Studies Department, DePaul University, Chicago, Illinois

# EDITOR'S PREFACE

THE DICTIONARY OF BIBLE AND RELIGION (DBR) can best be explained as an expanded Bible dictionary—expanded to include information from four other areas of religious knowledge: the history of Christianity, systematic theology or Christian doctrine, world religions, and contemporary religions. The dictionary is a lay-oriented, alphabetically arranged compendium of religious information. Entries vary in length from less than 50 to more than 3,000 words. A total of over 880,000 words on more than 2,800 subjects contains information on a comprehensive list of subjects that run the gamut of religious knowledge in all fields.

There is an extensive system of cross references contained in the book for those interested in finding information on related subjects. Where duplication of material was unwarranted, the reader is referred to another entry. Also, within entries, words in capital letters indicate that the dictionary also contains separate entries on these subjects. Readers will also find "see" or "compare" references at the close of some entries as well as a For Further Study section of other sources of information in the back of the book.

Although the majority of the 28 writers are teachers or experts in the field in which they write, a concerted effort has been made to avoid complicated or technical terms and to present the material in language that can be readily understood by readers not trained in theological disciplines. Foreign language terms are translated wherever possible.

The dictionary is ecumenically Christian in origin and outlook, though including articles on personal religion in other traditions. Due to its principal origins and authorship in America and a number of practical limitations, its ecumenical thrust is focused on, but not limited to, Protestant and Catholic Christianity. The dictionary also includes articles on Jewish and other non-Christian traditions, thus broadening the ecumenical horizon. It is ecumenical in another, more informal sense, in that it incorporates representative liberal and conservative viewpoints from within the historic churches and denominations. Also, the authors have been selected from several different backgrounds and denominations.

This book is entitled a dictionary, rather than an encyclopedia or handbook, to emphasize the fact that it is intended to provide fast, direct access to information. The alphabetical arrangement of the topics, the inclusion of definitions, and the fact that a fairly large number of topics of short or intermediate length are included, gives the dictionary its practical efficiency and usability.

Articles are intended to strike a balance between objective and inclusive presentations of material, on the one hand, and individual insight, judgment, and opinion, on the other. The articles present current knowledge and practice objectively and bring supportive and corrective effects of research to bear on the topic involved.

Obviously not every religious subject is included here, but the publisher, writers, and editor have attempted to bring to the reader as comprehensive a source of information as is possible within the limits of the space available. Photos, illustrations, maps, and charts have been included to enhance the understanding of the subject by visual as well as verbal means.

We are grateful for the concerted efforts of all of the writers, editors, proofreaders, designers, and others involved in the process of publishing to make the dictionary the best possible vehicle of religious information available.

William H. Gentz
*General Editor*

# Aa

**AARON.** The elder brother of MOSES (Exod. 7:7) and of MIRIAM, siblings born of Amram and Jochebed (Num. 26:59). He is represented as having been appointed Moses' "prophet," that is, his spokesman, to compensate for Moses' lack of eloquence or persuasiveness in dealing with the Pharaoh of Egypt and securing the release of the Israelites from bondage (Exod. 7:1-4). This note, together with the major role attributed to him and his charismatic powers in the subsequent Exodus chronicle and the character ascribed to him as the first of Israel's priesthood (Exod. 28), argue in favor of the reminiscence of a genuine historical personage within the tradition. The tendency of the tradition was to ascribe to Moses everything that was formative of Israel: its judiciary, its prophecy, its law, its tribal organization, its very salvation from Egypt. That important, even essential, functions in this process should have been attributed to one other than Moses could indicate that history rather than convenient legend had guided the tradition.

Aaron appears in the biblical tradition under various and, in part, conflicting guises. (1) As indicated above, he is Moses' surrogate and, at times, his superior in the process that led to Israel's liberation from Egypt. (2) He also appears, along with his sister Miriam, as Moses' opponent on significant occasions. (3) He appears, finally, as a high priest and image of a priesthood to come, which Moses could not institute but could inaugurate according to divine decree (*see* Exod. 28ff.; Lev. 8–10).

Repeatedly, from Exodus 5:1 on, it is Moses *and Aaron* who are credited equally as the human agents through whom God obtained the release of the people from bondage in Egypt. In Exodus 4:2ff. the rod or "magic wand" wielded by Moses is identified as the first instrument in Israel's liberation and is thereafter associated with the two brothers. But ultimately it is "*Aaron's* rod" and his alone that stands as lasting testimonial to the Exodus (Num. 17:10).

There seems to be no doubt that tradition has smoothed over many inconsistencies in what was remembered of the Exodus. Aaron and Miriam opposed their brother Moses (Num. 12), but according to Numbers 16–19 a revolt took place against all three. This latter story may be the reworking of what was originally recorded as a rebellion against the domination of the clerical caste of the Levites. In any case, the ultimate tradition has worked to exculpate Aaron from any blame: he was a man deceived and misled. (*See* AARONITE[S].)

B.V.

**AARONITE(S).** Male descendants of AARON and according to Exodus 28ff. and Leviticus 8–10 the sole legitimate priesthood of Israel. The Aaronites formed one family within the larger class of LEVITES, who in the older tradition (compare the Deuteronomic expression, "Levitical priests," Deut. 18:1) had been the professional priestly class. The centralization of the cult in Jerusalem (II Kings 23) and restriction to its priesthood doubtless lies behind this prerogative of the Aaronites.

B.V.

**AB.** See HEBREW CALENDAR.

**ABBA.** An Aramaic word for "father," which is transliterated into Greek in Mark 14:36, Romans 8:15, and Galatians 4:6. The term was the intimate one used by children, as mishnaic and modern usage indicate. This fact makes all the more remarkable Jesus' use of it to address God in the midst of his passion in Gethsemane.

W.S.T.

**ABBASSID CALIPHS.** (MUSLIM dynasty, A.D. 750–1258.) Remembered for their patronage of the arts, music, and literature. They deposed the Umayyad dynasty with the aid of discontented Muslims, especially non-Arabs, although the Abbassids themselves were Arabic and claimed descent from MUHAMMAD. In the West, the best-known Abbassid is Harun al-Rashid (A.D. 764–809), hero of many of the stories in the *Arabian Nights*. The dynasty fell when the Mongols sacked Baghdad in 1258.

K./M.C.

**ABBE, ABBESS, ABBEY, ABBOT.** Terms derived from the French language referring to the clergy and clerical institutions and positions. Abbe is a common title for the secular clergy; in France anyone in clerical garb is called an abbe. An abbess is the superior of the community of nuns in the BENEDICTINE tradition, although the title is also used in other orders, such as the Poor Clares. An abbess is elected by the choir sisters. She wears a ring of office and carries a staff on ceremonial occasions. An abbey is a major community of MONASTICISM within a religious order, male or female, of regular canons, monks, or nuns. An abbot is the superior of a major monastery in the Benedictine tradition. He oversees the temporal and spiritual affairs of the order. Only a monk with ten years profession, above the age of thirty, may be an abbot.

J.C.

**ABBOTT, LYMAN** (1835–1922). Minister, editor, and author, Abbott was born December 18 in Roxbury, Massachusetts. He graduated from New York University as a lawyer in 1853 and married Abby Frances Hamlin in 1855. Inspired by HENRY WARD BEECHER to become a minister, he served first in Terre Haute, Indiana.

Abbott joined Beecher in 1876 in editorship of the *Christian Union*, which became *The Outlook* in 1893. He became Beecher's successor at Plymouth Congre-gational Church in Brooklyn (1890-99) and retired to devote himself to the editorship of *The Outlook*.

He wrote forty books including *The Theology of an Evolutionist* (1897), *The Evolution of Christianity* (1892), illustrating how the SOCIAL GOSPEL mediated between orthodoxy and science, and *The Spirit of Democracy* (1910).

N.H.

**ABEL.** See CAIN AND ABEL.

**ABELARD, PETER** (1079–1142). One of the main forerunners of SCHOLASTICISM. He studied under the most famous teachers of his time and showed his contempt for them, thus making the first of a long series of enemies. He taught in Paris and attracted such a large number of students that he could be regarded as the founder of the University of Paris. His success and career there were curtailed because of a love affair with Heloise, a niece of Fulbert, canon of Notre Dame, who employed Abelard to supervise her education. The wrath of Fulbert forced Abelard to seek refuge at the monastery of Saint-Denis in 1118. Three years later, the Council of Soissons condemned his doctrine of the Trinity and burned one of his books on the subject. He then infuriated the monks at Saint-Denis by declaring that the monastery could not have been founded by Dionysius the Areopagite, and he had to leave the monastery. By 1136 he was again teaching in Paris. But then Bernard of Clairvaux accused him of heresy, and he was once more condemned by the Council of Sens in 1141. Eventually reconciled to Bernard, Abelard died in 1142.

He left his mark on the Scholastic method through his book *Sic et non (Yes and No)*, in which he showed that biblical and Patristic authorities could be cited in support of seemingly contradictory positions. He was also one of the clearest exponents of what historians call the "subjective" or "moral" theory of ATONE-MENT. On the question of UNIVERSALS he took a position between the extremes of realism and nominalism.

J.G.

**ABIATHAR** ("the father [God] is abundant"). This son of Ahimelech and (as a descendant of Eli) member of the priestly line of Shiloh was one of two leading priests under David. Later Solomon banished him for having supported Adonijah, Solomon's rival to the throne.

*Abiathar and David.* When Saul ordered the slaughter of the priests of Nob, Abiathar, the sole survivor, took the oracular ephod and fled to David at Adullam (I Sam. 22:20-23; 23:6). David, who received Abiathar warmly, consulted the oracle during his outlaw days, and as religious adviser, Abiathar provided its interpretation (23:9-12; 30:7-8). After David had become king, captured Jerusa-lem, and moved the ark of the covenant there,

Abiathar, along with Zadok, was appointed priest of the new tent shrine in which the ark was kept. The two presumably coexisted as leading priests in David's cabinet (II Sam. 20:25). During Absalom's rebellion, when David was required to return to a fugitive existence, Abiathar rendered the king faithful service (15:24, 29, 35-36; 17:15).

*Abiathar and Solomon.* When Adonijah, David's oldest living son, competed with Solomon for the nhrone during David's last days, the priestly and military leadership were split. Zadok and Benaiah supported Solomon, but Abiathar and Joab backed Adonijah (I Kings 1). To steady his position, the ultimately victorious Solomon deposed Abiathar from the Jerusalem priesthood and banished him to Anathoth, his ancestral home. The priestly rule of the house of Eli was thereby regarded as finished (2:27), and the earlier prophecy predicting the fall of Eli's house (I Sam. 2:27-36) was seen as fulfilled. Solomon might have treated Abiathar more harshly were it not for his previous loyalty to David (I Kings 2:26). As one of "the priests who were in Anathoth" (Jer. 1:1), Jeremiah may have descended from Abiathar.

J.K.K.

**ABIB.** *See* HEBREW CALENDAR.

**ABIGAIL.** The beautiful wife of the churlish NABAL of Carmel. According to I Samuel 24, David nearly incurred blood-guilt in his anger at Nabal ("fool") for refusing to repay with food the kindness earlier shown him by David. Only the intervention of Abigail with gifts of food and wine and earnest entreaties to David not to seek vengeance prevented a massacre of Nabal and his men. David blessed Abigail for her discretion in restraining him. After Nabal died about ten days later, David took Abigail to be the second of his many wives. According to I Chronicles 3:1, she bore him a son, Daniel.

First Chronicles 2:15-17 reports that David also had a sister named Abigail, who became the mother of Amasa. Abigail's sister, Zeruiah, was Joab's mother. According to II Samuel 19:13, Amasa temporarily displaced his cousin Joab as David's chief of staff, but in the end he was assassinated by Joab (II Sam. 20:4-10).

W.S.T.

**ABIHU.** The second of the four sons of AARON (Exod. 6:23) who, with his brother NADAB, suffered a strange fate. As priestly sons of Aaron, they were permitted to eat and drink in Yahweh's presence on Sinai on the occasion of the ratification of his covenant with Israel (Exod. 24:1-11; compare 28:1). However, in the aftermath of the original burnt offering made by their father (Lev. 9:22-24), they permitted themselves to burn incense before the Lord in a way that was not commanded (Lev. 10:1-3). As a punishment for offering this "unholy fire," they were burned with holy fire. This account may reflect a polemic alive at the time in which the Priestly source (*see* P DOCUMENT) was written regarding the status of various priestly families, or it may even reflect some judgment on the use of incense as an offering. It also preserves the motif of the displacement of the elder brother(s) by the younger, which frequently recurs in OT narratives.

W.S.T.

**ABIJAH.** As many as nine OT figures bear this name, which means "[My] father is Yahweh." These include: (a) the wicked younger son of Samuel (I Sam. 8:1-9); (b) a descendant of Aaron who was identified with the eighth of the twenty-four priestly divisions that rotated duty in the Temple (I Chr. 24:10); (c) the son of JEROBOAM I, ruler of the northern kingdom of Israel, whose death as retribution for the apostasy of his father was pronounced by the prophet AHIJAH (I Kings 14:1-18).

The Abijah of greatest historical significance, however, was the son of the first ruler of the southern kingdom of Judah, REHOBOAM; Abijah reigned following Rehoboam (II Chr. 13:1-22; see also I Kings 15:1-8 where, probably because of a scribal error, Abijah is called Abijam). The simple report of I Kings that "there was war between Abijam and Jeroboam" (15:7) is expanded by the Chronicler into a lengthy account of a border engagement pitting Ahijah's 400,000 troops against the 800,000 of his opponent! Following a vigorous condemnation of the cultic apostasy of the northern kingdom, Abijah, announcing that "God is with us at our head," turned the tide of battle against the Israelites, slaughtered half a million of them, and captured Bethel and other towns of Ephraim. This highly exaggerated claim, which reflects the Chronicler's own anti-northern bias, is rounded out with the notice that Abijah managed to run a household consisting of fourteen wives, twenty-two sons, and sixteen daughters.

W.S.T.

**ABILENE.** A district in the central Anti-Lebanon mountains bordering the Barada (ancient Abadna) River, which descends from there into Damascus eighteen miles to the southeast. The chief town, Abila (the legendary site of the tomb of Abel), is today the Syrian village of Suq Wadi Barada. In his *Antiquities,* Josephus reports that the Roman emperor Caligula gave Abila to the Jewish king Agrippa I in A.D. 37. This donation was confirmed by Claudius on his accession in A.D. 41, thus making Agrippa the ruler of all the lands from Judea to the northern slopes of Mount Hermon. Josephus also confirms the only information about Abilene contained in the Bible (Luke 3:1), namely that the district had been the tetrarchy of one Lysanias in the days of Herod the Great (about 34 B.C.). From A.D. 53 to 100 the territory was ruled by Agrippa II, after which it reverted to the Roman province of Syria.

W.S.T.

**ABIMELECH.** Other than the probably erroneous reference in the title of Psalm 34, this name, which means "Melech [the name of a Canaanite deity] is father," is attached to two biblical figures.

(1) The first Abimelech was the king of Gerar, a city halfway between Beersheba and Gaza, who, according to the Elohist (see E DOCUMENT), was the victim of a plot by Abraham to pass Sarah off to the king as his sister (Gen. 20). An earlier version of the same story is told in Genesis 26 by the Yahwist, who uses Isaac and Rebekah as the Israelite protagonists. (In Gen. 12:10-20, the entire event takes place in Egypt, and Pharaoh, not Abimelech, is the dupe.) In the more sophisticated of the accounts, Genesis 20, Abimelech is presented as a man of integrity, whom God saved from mortal sin with Sarah, even though he had taken her as a wife. God ordered Abimelech to restore Sarah to Abraham, which he did with generous compensation but not without the complaint that Abraham had deceived him. Abraham's excuse was that because there was "no fear of God at all in this place" (20:11), he felt sure that someone would kill him in order to take his wife. Furthermore, he claimed for the one and only time that Sarah really was his half sister (20:12). Abraham subsequently dwelt in Abimelech's territory, once even settling a dispute over a desert watering place with a peaceable covenant ceremony. The place came to be known as Beersheba, "well of the oath" (Gen. 21:25-34).

(2) The second Abimelech of biblical fame was one of the seventy-two sons of Jerubaal, also known as Gideon. His mother was a concubine in Shechem (Judg. 8:31), whose name is never given. Although his father, Gideon, had firmly refused to be made king over Israel (Judg. 8:23), Abimelech actively promoted his own kingship over Shechem through the good offices of his mother's family. Using "hired knives," he confirmed his election by killing seventy of his brothers. Only his youngest half brother, Jotham, escaped the purge (Judg. 9:1-6). This Jotham stood on the top of Mount Gerizim overlooking Shechem and pronounced the curse preserved in his renowned parable of the trees, saying to the city, in effect, If you have acted in good faith with Gideon's house, rejoice in Abimelech; but if not, let fire come out and devour both the citizens of Shechem and Abimelech (9:7-20). As the tortuous history recounted in the remainder of Judges 9 draws to an end, the curse is effectuated. Abimelech turned on Shechem after he had ruled Israel for three years, and he burned its tower fortress down over the heads of one thousand of its people (9:49). Subsequently God requited Abimelech's crimes against him (9:56) when a woman of Thebez brained him with a millstone while he was besieging that city.

W.S.T.

**ABISHAG** ("my father has wandered"?). A lovely Shunammite maiden employed as a concubine to warm David and restore his virility in old age (I Kings 1:1-4, 15). That Adonijah requested her for himself following David's death was interpreted by Solomon as evidence that Adonijah still coveted the crown (2:22). This stratagem cost Adonijah his life.

J.K.K.

**ABISHAI.** The Hebrew term meaning "father exists." A son of David's sister Zeruiah and brother of Joab and Asahel (I Chr. 2:16). He commanded a third of David's army during Absalom's rebellion (II Sam. 18:2) and was head of David's "mighty men" known as the "Thirty" (II Sam. 23:18-19; I Chr. 11:20-21).

*In the Wilderness of Ziph.* Abishai moved with David into Saul's camp by night. Finding Saul and his men asleep, Abishai sought David's permission to kill the king. David would not condone such violence against "the Lord's anointed" and elected instead to sneak away with Saul's spear and jar of water (I Sam. 26:5-12).

*At the Pool of Gibeon.* After a military tournament, which found Abner's forces overcome by Joab's, Abner fled and was relentlessly pursued by Asahel. When the latter refused to desist, Abner speared him to death (II Sam. 2:12-23). Joab and Abishai soon killed Abner in cold blood at Hebron, thereby avenging their brother (3:26-30).

*In Ammon.* Israel waged a retaliatory campaign against the Ammonites for their shameful treatment of David's envoys who had visited their king Hanun. With select troops Joab fought off interfering Syrian mercenaries who came to Ammon's aid, and charged Abishai to oversee the remainder of the army in its movements against the Ammonites. Both brothers tasted victory (II Sam. 10:9-14).

*Near Jerusalem.* When David was required to flee from Jerusalem due to Absalom's uprising, he was met by Shimei, who cursed him thoroughly. Abishai asked permission to slay this rude Benjaminite. Believing that Shimei was doing Yahweh's bidding, David restrained him (II Sam. 16:5-14). After Absalom's death, when Shimei met David at the Jordan and profusely apologized for his disrespectful conduct, Abishai enthusiastically recommended Shimei's death and was again overruled by David (19:16-23).

*Other Exploits.* Abishai dauntlessly rescued the weary David from the hands of the Philistine giant, Ishbibenob, whom he killed (II Sam. 21:15-17). With Joab he suppressed the Benjaminite revolt of Sheba against David (20:1-22), and presumably joined Joab and David in leading Israel's successful campaign against the Edomites (II Sam. 8:13-14; I Kings 11:15-16; I Chr. 18:12-13). Although Abishai sometimes made David feel uneasy, his loyalty to the king was unswerving.

J.K.K.

**ABLUTIONS.** Washing of the hands before MASS, before the canon, and after distributing Communion outside of Mass by a priest of ROMAN CATHOLICISM.

After Communion, the celebrant washes out the CHALICE with wine, and his fingers with wine and water. These ablutions are drunk by the priest.

J.C.

**ABNER.** A name meaning "father is a lamp." This man was a kinsman of SAUL and commander-in-chief of his army (I Sam. 14:50). He also was the mainstay behind Saul's ineffectual son, Ish-baal, during his two-year reign following his father's death.

*Abner and Saul.* Abner distinguished himself militarily under Saul's rule. As head of the Israelite army in the Philistine war, Abner introduced David to Saul after the former's triumph over Goliath (I Sam. 17:55-58). Moreover, Abner joined Saul in his frantic pursuit of David. Abner's inattentive watch over the sleeping Saul, however, afforded David opportunity to enter the king's tent and to reprove Abner for negligence in protecting Yahweh's anointed (26:5-16).

*Abner and Ish-baal.* After Saul's death, Abner led Ish-baal to Mahanaim in trans-Jordan and proclaimed him king. This refugee government secure from Philistine aggression failed to attract the tribe of Judah, which now looked to David (II Sam. 2:8-10). After Abner and his forces lost to Joab and his forces in a war game staged at the Pool of Gibeon, Abner fled and was relentlessly pursued by Joab's brother Asahel. When the latter refused to desist, Abner speared him to death and then returned to Mananaim (2:12-29).

Later Ish-baal berated Abner for having visited Saul's concubine, Rizpah, a sign that Abner himself coveted the throne. The enraged Abner inflicted on Ish-baal an intimidating speech in which he announced his intention to transfer his allegiance to David at Hebron (II Sam. 3:7-11).

*Abner and David.* Abner's overtures struck David favorably. After winning the Israelite elders to his position that a united monarchy under David would benefit everyone, the triumphant Abner took a diplomatic team to Hebron to lay final plans (II Sam. 3:12-21). Soon the ruthless Joab, unknown to David, murdered Abner in private, thereby avenging Asahel's death and ensuring that he would not be supplanted as commander-in-chief of David's army (3:26-27). The incensed David convinced the people of his own innocence by thoroughly cursing Joab, participating in Abner's funeral, and voicing a moving dirge (3:33-34), which bemoaned Abner's untimely end. He was buried in Hebron. On his deathbed, David challenged Solomon to avenge Joab's crime against this undisputably capable Benjaminite (I Kings 2:5-6).

J.K.K.

**ABOLITIONISM.** *See* SLAVERY.

**ABOMINATION.** Anything considered culturally, ritually, or ethically repugnant or loathsome to God or human beings. A wide range of matters and conditions are called abominations in the OT. Four different Hebrew words are so translated although frequently the same terms are translated as "detestable thing," "abhorrence," or "foul thing." The cultural reference can be seen in the statements for the Egyptians that eating with Hebrews and the presence of shepherds were abominations (Gen. 43:32; 46:34). Most frequently mentioned in the Bible are ritual abominations, including prohibited foods or unclean animals (Lev. 7:21), sacrifices (Deut. 17:1), flesh eaten with blood in it (Isa. 65:4), idols (Deut. 7:25-26), and magic and divination (Deut. 18:10-12). The ethical dimension denotes moral faults (Deut. 25:14-16), reversal of sex roles in clothing (Deut. 22:5), sexual irregularities (Lev. 18:22), and various practices unacceptable to Israelite religion (Lev. 18:27). The idea that certain things and acts are abominations is based on a world view in which sharp distinctions are drawn between the normal and acceptable and the abnormal and unacceptable. The latter are abominations. Because of Israel's specific food restrictions focusing on the difference between CLEAN AND UNCLEAN and special sacrificial laws, numerous conditions could thus be classified as abnormal.

J.H.

**ABOMINATION OF DESOLATION.** A foreign feature introduced into the Temple of Jerusalem probably during the reign of ANTIOCHUS IV (175–164 B.C.). Four texts in the book of Daniel refer to this feature but the same Hebrew terminology does not appear throughout: 8:13—"the transgression that makes desolate," 9:27—"upon the wing of abominations shall come one who makes desolate," 11:31—"the abomination that makes desolate," and 12:11—"abomination that makes desolate." Presumably all of these refer to the same feature. Because of the cryptic language, uncertainty exists about how the terms should be translated and what the abomination refers to. The Hebrew term translated desolate is *sh-m-m*, which can mean "be deserted, desolate," "be removed from," "appall, horrify," or "be mad."

In all probability, the author of Daniel was referring to the altar placed in the Temple by the Seleucid king Antiochus IV Epiphanes, the Macedonian ruler over Syria, which during his day included Jerusalem. First Maccabees 1:54-59 reports that the Seleucids erected a "desolating sacrilege upon the altar of burnt offering" in the Jerusalem Temple in 167 B.C. This appears to have been a smaller altar set up on the regular temple altar to be used for sacrifices to a god worshiped by the Seleucids. Thus "abomination of desolation" would be the name given this altar by the Jews. As a nickname or byname, it might be translated "the abomination that makes desolate" (that empties the temple of orthodox Jews), "the abomination of the madman" (Antiochus Epiphanes, who was nicknamed Epimanes, which

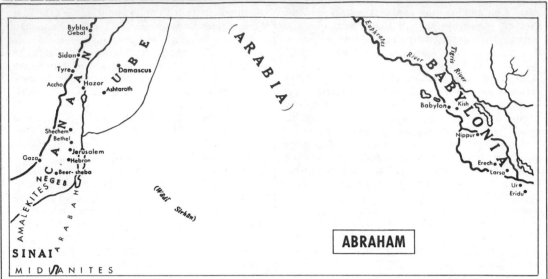

ABRAHAM

Adapted from *The Westminster Historical Atlas to the Bible,* revised. Edited by G. Ernest Wright and Floyd V. Filson. Copyright © The Westminster Press.

means "madman"), or "the abomination that horrifies." In all likelihood, however, the Hebrew phrase *shiqqus shomem* is a play on the name of the Seleucid god *baʿal shamem,* "Baʿal or Lord of the Heavens," who was identified with the Greek god Zeus Olympios. Thus *shiqqus* ("abomination") was substituted for *baʿal* ("Lord") and *shomem* ("the one making desolate") was a pun on *shamem* ("heavens"). Thus "abomination of desolation" (or "the one making desolate") refers to the pagan altar and the services associated with it that were introduced into the Jerusalem Temple.

Similar terminology is found in the NT (Mark 13:14 and parallels in Matt. 24:15; Luke 21:20) where the "desolating sacrilege" seems to refer to the presence of Gentiles (Romans) or their religious emblems in the Temple. These NT texts probably refer to the presence of Roman standards, which were the objects of religious veneration set up in the Temple after its capture in A.D. 70.

J.H.

**ABRAHAM.** The son of Terah, husband of SARAH, and father of ISAAC, whose noble example as Israel's first patriarch made him the father of the faithful in Judeo-Christian tradition. The name "Abram" and its dialectical variant "Abraham" may both be rendered "the [my] father is exalted" or "exalted father."

*Abraham and Archaeology.* (a) Textual evidence. Though the epigraphic material unearthed by Near Eastern archaeologists is extensive, we know nothing about Abraham except what the Bible discloses. The EBLA tablets (about 2500 B.C.) and First Dynasty Babylonian texts (about 1830–1530 B.C.) attest the name "Abram." Hurrian legal sanctions disclosed by the fifteenth-century B.C. NUZI texts in the east Tigris vicinity make intelligible Abraham's anxiety that his slave Eliezer might be his heir (Gen. 15:1-4) and

Sarah's desire to deliver her maid Hagar to Abraham as a concubine (16:1-4). Abraham's striking mobility meshes well with what eighteenth-century Mari texts convey. While such documents confer some credibility on the patriarchal legends of Genesis, they do not speak directly of Abraham.

(b) Dating proposals. Contemporary biblical scholarship knows no single date for Abraham. Presumed affinities with Eblaite material led D. N. Freedman to posit a mid-third millennium date (early Bronze Age), but C. H. Gordon assigns Abraham to the late Bronze Age (about 1550–1200 B.C.) owing to parallels he deduces in Nuzi and RAS SHAMRA texts (fifteenth and thirteenth centuries B.C. respectively). Certain Genesis nomenclature (for example, Arameans, Philistines) and mention of domesticated camels induce T. L. Thompson and J. Van Seters to shift Abraham to the Iron Age (about 1200–300 B.C.). Most scholars, however, identify these elements as anachronistic. The prevailing view, advanced by R. de Vaux and J. Bright, places Abraham in the middle Bronze II Age (about 2000–1550 B.C.) on the assumption that, as a seminomadic clan chief, Abraham belonged to the sweeping movement of Amorites (Northwest Semites) felt throughout much of the Near East early in the second millennium. Yet, even here, caution is required.

*Abraham According to J.* (a) The issue. Abraham's story (Gen. 11:27–25:18) derives from several originally independent traditions that have been united into a semblance of biographical wholeness. Apart from Genesis 14, these are attributed to the primary strata of Genesis—J, E, and P. Though all three reflect on Abraham's journey of faith, J dominates. Its author, commonly termed the Yahwist and perhaps a contemporary of Solomon (about 961-922 B.C.), emphasized two motifs. These were Yahweh's persistent promise of progeny and land to God's chosen patriarch and the latter's capacity to believe in its fulfillment. As more recent writers, E and P build on the work of J. Highlights in the J, E, and P portrayals of Abraham invite inspection.

(b) Abraham's call and aftermath (Gen. 12:1-20). In his hometown of Haran (mention of Ur in 11:28 is textually suspect), Abraham was commanded by YAHWEH to abandon his country and kindred and move to a yet unidentified destination. Concomitantly the Deity promised that from Abraham a great nation would emerge that would richly benefit humankind (vv. 2-3). When the obedient Abraham reached Shechem, Yahweh again appeared and pledged, "To your descendants I will give this land" (v. 7). Abraham responded faithfully by erecting an altar. Yet in an emergency sojourn to Egypt (vv. 10-20), he implicitly questioned the promise of divine protection. To guarantee his own security, he fabricated a lie about his wife Sarah (v. 13).

(c) Further affirmation and denial of the promise. When the herdsmen of Abraham and his nephew Lot strove in the Canaanite-inhabited region of Bethel so that Lot's separation from Abraham commended itself, Abraham's faith in Yahweh's promise shone brightly. He gave Lot first choice, who providentially preferred the fertile Jordan Valley to the Land of Promise (13:11). Yahweh's pledge to Abraham was renewed (13:14-18). J portions in Genesis 15 instruct that Abraham "believed the Lord; and he reckoned it to him as righteousness" (v. 6). Indeed, God was voluntarily bound in solemn promise to the patriarch through ancient covenant ritual (vv. 7-12, 17-21).

Then despairing that Yahweh had abandoned the promise of progeny, Abraham and Sarah hastened to actualize its fulfillment through Sarah's maid Hagar (16:2, 4-6). The outcome was abysmal; Sarah became jealous and Hagar was brutally expelled. Yahweh's mysterious visit to Abraham and Sarah at Mamre (Gen. 18) and restatement of the promise evoked doubt only in Sarah (v. 12), and for remaining faithful, God confided to Abraham the intention to destroy Sodom. This permitted the patriarch to assume an intercessory role in behalf of non-Israelites (affirming the promise of 12:2-3). Ultimately Sarah bore Isaac (21:2), and when it was time for this child of promise to marry, Abraham acted faithfully by sending his majordomo to obtain a suitable (non-Canaanite) wife for Isaac among his kinsfolk in Haran, thereby sparing Isaac the necessity of vacating the Land of Promise (Gen. 24).

*Abraham According to E.* Like the Yahwist, the Elohist (E) narrates God's twofold promise to Abraham (15:5, 13-16), the patriarch's faith-doubt response, and his positive relation to non-Israelites. Again exhausted in faith, Abraham deceived Abimelech about Sarah (20:2); but then Abraham as prophet interceded for this non-Israelite king whose innocence was established (v. 17). Also E tells of Hagar's expulsion (21:8-14), but with two variants. The incident happened after the births of Ishmael and Isaac, and Abraham conceded to Sarah's demand, but only after securing divine approval. Then by his treaty with Abimelech (21:22-34), Abraham faithfully shared his blessing with non-Israelites. Abraham's supreme test of faith involved his having to place Isaac, at God's inscrutable command, on a sacrificial altar (22:2). The laconic prose of this gripping narrative (22:1-19) portrays Abraham in a position of faithful surrender. Willing to yield this child of promise, Abraham won him back and triumphantly qualified as a model of faith.

*Abraham According to P.* Though the Priestly writer (P) minimized the faith-doubt tension in his rendering of Abraham (but see Gen. 17:17-18), he reaffirmed the earlier motif of promise and fulfillment. The main contribution of P consists of several chronological notices and two extended narratives. The first (chap. 17) centers on the Deity's covenant with Abraham, which culminates in the institution of circumcision. Here the ongoing relationship between the transcendent Deity and the patient, listening patriarch is formalized with a dual interest in divine promise and solemn procedure. The other narrative (chap. 23), anchored in earlier Hebraic tradition, involves Abraham's purchase of the cave of Mechpelah from Ephron the Hittite following Sarah's death. By so claiming this corner of the Land of Promise, Abraham decisively demonstrated his faith in God's promise.

*Abraham's Impact on Biblical Thought.* Above all, Abraham is remembered as the father of all who are faithful, be they Jew or Gentile. Israel consistently perceived Abraham's unconditional trust in divine promise and guidance as its own appropriate response to divine election. Abraham's struggles were not forgotten, and even as the prototype of believing Israel, he was rightly spared a sainthood status. Nevertheless, this "friend" of God (Isa. 41:8; Jas. 2:23) and colossus of faith showed both the old and new Israel how to live well before God and to embrace the world with a spirit of Universalism.

J.K.K.

**ABRAHAM'S BOSOM.** A place of special status for the good in the world of the dead. This phrase occurs only once in the Bible, in Jesus' story of Lazarus and the rich man (Luke 16:19-31). In the story, Lazarus, the poor man, dies and is carried by angels to Abraham's bosom (Luke 16:22). Here he is separated by a chasm from the rich man tormented in Hades. Apparently in Jewish thought at the time of Jesus, not all the dead were believed to go to the same place. Sheol seems to have been divided into places where those judged righteous were already at rest and those judged unrighteous were already tormented before the final judgment. Abraham's bosom would have been the place—like Paradise in Luke 23:43—where the righteous found rest. Since "bosom" represents intimacy and Abraham was the ideal patriarch, then to be found in Abraham's bosom was to be granted a special place. In some Jewish texts of the time, the patriarchs Abraham, Isaac, and Jacob were viewed as those who welcomed the elect to the world beyond. Not only the intimate association with the patriarchs was stressed but also the meal enjoyed with them in the world beyond (see Matt. 8:11), although no reference is made to the meal in the Lazarus story.

J.H.

**ABSALOM.** In I Kings 15:2 called Abishalom (both in Hebrew meaning "[god] the father is peace, perfection"), the third son of DAVID. His mother was Maacah, daughter of Talmai, the king of Geshur (II Sam. 3:3). After his sister Tamar was raped by AMNON, their half brother, Absalom harbored vengeance against him, bided his time, and eventually had him slain by treachery. Thereupon he took refuge with his mother's kinsmen in Geshur (II Sam. 13). The story of Absalom graphically illustrates David's shortcomings as a father. David knew of Amnon's crime but did nothing about it, and subsequently he proved himself to be totally inept in handling Absalom.

The Absalom story likewise reveals, by implication, the precarious state of David's rule over his kingdom, at least in his latter years. After Joab, David's commander and the prop of his throne, brought about a reconciliation between David and Absalom (II Sam. 14), the latter experienced no difficulty in quickly presenting himself as a populist alternative to his father (II Sam. 15:1-6). The subsequent narrative of II Samuel 15:7–17:29, which describes Absalom's successful rebellion and usurpation of the throne, is the chronicle of a bewildered and ineffectual David, prey to the long suppressed hatreds of his enemies and supported now largely only by mercenaries and allies from bygone days. Absalom fails by overextending himself and following advice that appeals to his vanity. David regains his kingdom by force of arms—significantly, Absalom's opposing forces are termed "the men of Israel"—but only as a bystander in a battle waged by his generals. It is Joab who recognized that Absalom must be executed, contrary to David's wishes, and it is Joab who forces David to resume kingly responsibilities and who reconsolidates the kingdom after the revolt (II Sam. 18–19).

Absalom had three sons and a daughter named Tamar according to II Samuel 14:27. According to I Kings 15:2, 10 and II Chronicles 11:20 there was another daughter (or granddaughter) Maacah, the wife and mother of Judahite kings.

B.V.

**ABSOLUTE.** The word "absolute," used as an adjective, is the opposite of "relative" and means that which is unconditioned and dependent on nothing else. Some philosophers have used the noun "The Absolute" to designate the ultimate Reality. It is a more inclusive term than "God" and accords rather with PANTHEISM or panentheism than with traditional theism.

J.M.

**ABSOLUTION.** In the Catholic sacrament of PENANCE, it is the forgiveness of sins. The priest announces the pardon of the sinner in the name of Christ while forgiveness is effected by the sacrament itself. Absolution rests on the priest's power to forgive sins and the recipient's repentance, demonstrated in CONTRITION, CONFESSION, and satisfaction.

In early ROMAN CATHOLICISM absolution was given by the bishop when he declared peace to worshipers who did public penance. This was followed by HOLY COMMUNION. Thomas Aquinas stressed that true forgiveness was granted in penance only when the sinner was genuinely contrite (sorry for sin), confessed wrongs done, and attempted to put wrongs right (that is, made satisfaction for sins). Other liturgical churches, such as the Lutheran and the Episcopalian, also include confession, which concludes with absolution or the announcement of forgiveness to the truly contrite, as part of the Holy Communion service or as separate confessional services.

J.C.

**ABSTINENCE.** The practice of self-control, of restraint, and refraining from certain activities, habits, foods, and drink. Many religions teach abstinence from one or more activities, foods, and beverages. In Judaism, one is enjoined to refrain from foods declared unclean by the Mosaic code (including pork). Islam teaches abstinence from pork, alcohol, and drugs. In the Roman Catholic church, abstinence from sexual relations is required of priests as a clerical obligation (CELIBACY). Among many pietistic Protestants (see PIETISM) abstinence from alcohol is stressed ("teetotalism"). In Hinduism abstinence from meat is taught in many sects, and beef-eating is rejected by all.

J.C.

**ABYSS.** The word is derived from the Greek *abyssos*, meaning "bottomless." It was used to describe the lowest part of the underworld in the ancient cosmology and occurs several times in the NT. The legion of demons possessing the Gerasene demoniac beg Jesus not to send them into the abyss (Luke 8:31), and there is also mention of Abaddon (Greek, Apollyon), ruler of the abyss (Rev. 9:11). The word is used in quite a different sense among the mystics. Their most intense experience of God is strangely ambiguous. God is known as that which is real above everything else, yet so wholly different from everything else that in comparison this reality is also nothing, the ineffable. This pure essence of God, indescribable in human language, can also be called darkness or the wilderness. The doctrine of creation out of nothing is interpreted by some mystics to mean the emanation of the world out of the divine abyss.

J.M.

**ABYSSINIAN CHURCH.** The ancient COPTIC Christian church of Abyssinia (modern Ethiopia). Abyssinia lies in East Africa and is the only historic Christian country in Africa. Before the breakup of European colonialism, Abyssinia was the only independent country in Africa, although it was conquered, briefly, by Fascist Italy.

Abyssinia lies between the Blue Nile and the Red Sea, southeast of the Sudan. It was founded early by missionaries from Egypt and has many affinities to the Coptic church in Egypt. For example, it never affirmed the decisions of Nicea and is monophysite in its Christology.

The Abyssinian church has two sacraments: baptism and the Lord's Supper. There are many feast days in the year, and the Jewish Sabbath as well as the Christian Sunday is observed. There is a complicated angelology in its worship life, with the archangel Michael playing a leading role. The Virgin Mary and the saints are also venerated.

J.C.

**ACCAD.** An ancient city of Shinar (Babylonia) mentioned once in the OT as part of the kingdom of Nimrod (Gen. 10:10), and the equivalent of Sumerian "Agade" and Semitic "Akkad" in cuneiform texts. When SARGON I, an aspiring politically minded Semite, won mastery over all the land of Sumer (about 2360 B.C.), he moved his residence from Kish to nearby Akkad. From there he, two sons, and a grandson, Naramsin, conducted energetic military campaigns throughout the Near East.

The impressive dynasty Sargon established is often celebrated as the head of history's first true empire. Nevertheless, it sometimes found a worthy competitor in the empire of Ebla. In time the name "Akkad" came to denote an entire region, not just the city. Presumably Akkad met destruction when the Sargon dynasty expired, about 2180 B.C. Though the site of ancient Akkad has never been identified, its name continued to enjoy mention in the phrase "the land of Akkad and Sumer," a common inscriptional designation for Babylonia.

J.K.K.

**ACCURSED.** *See* ANATHEMA.

**ACHAIA.** Originally a district on the north coast of the Peloponnesus, the peninsula which forms the southern part of the Greek mainland. The Achaeans seem to have invaded Greece in prehistoric times, and were the leaders in the formation of a democratic league of Greek cities, the Achaean League, which figured importantly in the struggles for control of GREECE from the third century B.C. through the time

of the coming of the Romans in the middle of the second century.

The Romans gave the name Achaia to the whole of central Greece where they established a province in 140 B.C. with its capitol at Corinth. In Acts (18:12, 27) and in the letters of Paul (I Cor. 16:15; II Cor. 1:1), this is the name given to central and southern Greece, as distinct from the northeastern section, Macedonia (Acts 16:9, 10) and the northwestern section, Illyricum (Rom. 15:19). When Paul wants to refer to all the churches in Greece, he uses the term "Achaia and Macedonia" (Rom. 15:26; II Cor. 9:2; 11:9-10; I Thess. 1:7, 8).

H.K.

**ACHAN.** A Judahite who broke religious taboos during warfare and thus, along with his family and possessions, was put to death. The story of Achan is found in Joshua 7. When the Israelites were trying to capture the city of Ai, Achan had taken some valuables from the enemy—clothing, silver, and gold—which had been devoted to God (7:21), that is, what belonged to the enemy had been promised to Yahweh and was not to be available for personal use. Achan's wrong led to the defeat of the Israelites because of God's anger. When Achan was discovered, probably through the use of sacred lots, he confessed his sin and disclosed the hiding place of the consecrated goods in his tent. His confession was seen as a way to "give glory to the Lord God of Israel, and render praise to him" (7:19). Achan, after his confession, along with his family, livestock, tent, and all his possessions, was stoned and burned, thus illustrating that things devoted to God must not be used for ordinary purposes and that such abuse brings God's judgment. That Achan's family and possessions were destroyed suggests the belief that the presence of the consecrated items contaminated everything connected with the culprit and thus had to be eradicated. That Achan's name (given as Achar in I

Chr. 2:7) is also connected with the Valley of Achor ("trouble"), where the event was set, may suggest that the story originated to explain the name.

J.H.

**ACHISH.** The king of the Philistine city of Gath with whom David had a tenuous relationship during the last years of Saul's reign in Israel. Their first encounter occurred when David sought sanctuary with Achish outside Saul's domain (I Sam. 21:10-15). Achish proved too dangerous to be David's suzerain at that time, evidently because he sensed that David—who had "slain . . . his ten thousands"—was too dangerous to be his vassal. After several close encounters, however, David once again sought asylum among the Philistines (I Sam. 27:1-12). Achish awarded him the city of Ziklag, and there David dwelt for a year and four months. Achish considered David a loyal vassal, and was prepared to consider him an ally in the great campaign against Israel that finally claimed the lives of Saul and his son Jonathan. Achish even appointed David his personal bodyguard (I Sam. 28:1-2). Other Philistine commanders were suspicious of David, however, and finally forced his return to Ziklag (I Sam. 29). That development both saved David from fratricidal conflict against his own people and enabled him to rescue the women, children, and booty of Ziklag from the clutches of marauding Amalekites (I Sam. 30).

W.S.T.

**ACHOR.** The name of a valley in lower Palestine, not easily identifiable in modern geography, probably on the border of Judah and Benjamin (Josh. 15:7), possibly in the vicinity of JERICHO and QUMRAN. In the later Israelite tradition Achor was the proverbial starting place for the beginning of the Israelite "conquest" of the land of Canaan (Josh. 7:24-26). Hence Hosea 2:15, envisaging a new and eschatological inheritance of the Promised Land by a redeemed Israel, plays on a popular etymology of the name Achor ("trouble, misery") stating that in the latter days it will be instead a gateway of hope to the people (similarly Isa. 65:10).

In Joshua 7 the name of the valley of Achor is fancifully derived from that of Achan, the Judahite leader who withheld booty from the sack of Jericho and became therefore legendarily responsible for Yahweh's anger and Israel's consequent initial defeat at Ai. The legend undoubtedly underlies the popular etymology of the later tradition.

B.V.

**ACOLYTE.** In both Protestant and Catholic churches, one who serves the altar with the minister. Among Protestants, the acolyte's duties are lighting and extinguishing the candles and handling the offering. Historically, the acolyte was a member of the highest of the MINOR ORDERS of the Roman Catholic Church.

J.C.

**ACROPOLIS.** The word literally means "the higher part of a city." The Greeks preferred to build cities at a site where a hill with steep sides could be fortified for protection against attacks. The best-known of these was in ATHENS, where the Acropolis was crowned with a temple (the Parthenon) to the patron goddess, Athena, and overlooked the central market area and other shrines and public gathering places on the lower slopes adjoining.

When Paul visited Athens, according to Acts 17, he addressed the intellectual and civic leaders gathered on or near the AREOPAGUS, the Hill of Ares (Mars), below the Acropolis. Paul's comment on how very religious the Athenians were (Acts 17:22) was wholly appropriate at this spot, with shrines of various traditional Greek gods visble all around, and with the magnificent temple of Athena towering above all else on the summit of the Acropolis.

H.K.

> **A fish (in Greek, ΙΧΘΥΣ)**
>
> Ι = Ἰησοῦς = **Jesus**
> Χ = Χριστός = **Christ**
> Θ = Θεοῦ = **God's**
> Υ = Ὑιός = **Son**
> Σ = Σωτήρ = **Savior**

*The Greek acrostic for "fish," which means "Jesus Christ, God's Son, Savior." The inscribed fish, with such a hidden meaning, was frequently found in the catacombs of the early Christians.*

**ACROSTIC.** A literary composition so arranged that the first letter of each of the lines forms a word or meaningful pattern. In the book of Psalms, the Hebrew writer has developed an acrostic in Psalms 25 and 34. Psalm 119 is arranged in brief sections, each of which is headed by all the successive letters of the Hebrew alphabet (see POETRY, HEBREW). Some editions of the Bible indicate this by the heading at the beginning of each of the twenty-two sections of the Psalm. In the Middle Ages, monks and other poets wrote pious poetry in acrostic form.

The best-known acrostic of early Christianity was formed by a grouping of the names and titles of Jesus, here given in a form transliterated from the Greek:

> Iesous - Jesus
> CHristos - Christ
> THeou - of God
> Uios - the Son
> Soter - Savior

As noted by the church father Lactantius and by the church's first true historian, Eusebius (A.D. 260-340), the initial letters spell in Greek the word "fish":

I-CH-TH-U-S. This word, which had links with Jesus' call of fishermen to become "fishers of men" (Mark 1:17; Matt. 4:19), as well as his sharing bread and fish with his followers (Mark 6:38-44; John 21:6-11) served as a powerful symbol of his continuing presence with his followers in worship and in mission.

H.K.

## ACTS, APOCRYPHAL.

Among documents that survive from the early centuries of the church and from the NT APOCRYPHA (that is, books purportedly apostolic and which enjoyed some status of authority before being rejected and excluded from the CANON of sacred writings) is a group of "Acts." There are five outstanding books.

The earliest title, the *Acts of John,* about A.D. 150, professes to record the miracles and speeches of the apostle John in Asia. It is gnostic and ascetic in outlook, as indeed are most other examples of this genre, and is biographical, suggesting the close union between Jesus and his disciple. The *Acts of Paul* contains a section dealing with Thecla, a girl in Asia who refused to marry, because of Paul's insistence that she should be celibate, and became a loyal worker in Paul's missionary endeavors. The *Acts of Peter,* also second century, centers on Peter's encounter with the magician Simon Magus (see Luke's Acts 8). This document contains the *Quo Vadis?* story, where Peter is fleeing from martyrdom but is rebuked, and returns to be crucified head-down. The *Acts of Thomas* is famous for the Hymn of the Pearl, a saga of gnostic redemption, where the soul of man is set free from the corruption of matter. The *Acts of Andrew* is possibly third century, and biographical and hagiographic in tone and temper.

R.M.

## ACTS OF THE APOSTLES, BOOK OF THE.

The second volume of a two-part work, Luke-Acts, written by the third evangelist, but now separated from volume I (the Gospel of LUKE) and arranged in the NT order as the fifth book. According to its superscription (Acts 1:1), it forms the sequel to all Jesus did and taught that Luke recorded in the Gospel. As such a sequel, or continuation of the story of the early church, Acts demonstrates the spread of the gospel from Palestine to Rome.

Internal evidence, as well as the similar superscriptions to both Luke and Acts, makes the common authorship of both books a certainty. The traditional belief that Luke-Acts was written by "Luke, the beloved physician," the companion of Paul, is not necessarily proved by the internal evidence of Acts, however. Acts does not present us with a portrait of or a rendition of Paul's teachings that accords well with the Paul of the undoubtedly genuine letters of Paul. Above all, Luke abandons the keen expectation of the imminent end of the age and assumes, in his narrative, that the ongoing work of the church, which is still under way as Acts closes, is proof that God's plan of salvation is working out through the church set in the here and now of human history. The story, then, of God's gracious dealing with humankind stretches from Galilee to Jerusalem (Luke) to the coming of the Holy Spirit at PENTECOST (chaps. 1–2).

Luke's conception of the mission of the church to the whole world begins in the Gospel (Luke 2:29-30), where the coming of the Messiah is said to be a light to enlighten the Gentiles, and continues on through the book of Acts, turning on the Pentecost experience where people from every nation of the Mediterranean area "hear them [the apostles] telling in our own

Courtesy of Edward P. Blair

*Excavated area at the harbor city of Miletus, where Paul addressed the elders from Ephesus (Acts 20:17 ff.)*

tongues the mighty works of God" (2:11). The theme of expansion of the COVENANT relationship to include the Gentiles is central to Acts, with the story of the Roman soldier CORNELIUS and his conversion standing at the center of the book. From Cornelius' conversion, Luke moves on to show how the gospel is responded to in faith by non-Jews in Asia Minor and in Europe. A strong minor theme is the reasonableness and moral legitimacy of the gospel, for none of the judges and other authorities who hear Paul and other Christians find them guilty of anything wrong.

Luke's outline for Acts is given in 1:8: The gospel is preached in Jerusalem, in Judea and Samaria, and to the ends of the earth. The preaching of the apostles and other evangelists, like Philip and Stephen, forms a large part of Luke's record. Scholarship generally agrees that Luke has 'shaped the early Christian preaching in the manner that other ancient historians shaped speeches by prominent persons to illustrate the meaning of historical events. We cannot, therefore, think of Peter's or Paul's speeches as precisely what Peter or Paul may have said. Indeed, Paul's speeches are not very like the teachings of Paul in his letters, for according to Acts, both PAUL and PETER preached essentially the same thing, while Galatians 1–2 suggests disagreements between the two. Contemporary scholars generally agree that Acts does not accurately reflect either the life or teachings of Paul. They attribute Luke's presentation to an irenic desire, that is, the wish to stress the unity of the church in its exposure to the non-Christian world.

A prominent feature of Acts is the "we" passages (16:10-17; 20:5–21:18; 27:1–28:16), which suggest that the author was a traveling companion of Paul. Some suggest, on the basis of these passages, that the author was "the man of Macedonia" who asked Paul to come over to Europe.

J.C.

**ACTUALITY.** That which is the case at this moment. The actual does not necessarily coincide with the real, for someone might hold that reality includes past and future as well as the present actuality, or that there is an invisible or eternal reality transcending what is actual.

J.M.

**ADAM AND EVE.** The first human couple, from whom all humanity descended. Foremost, Adam and Eve is a generic phrase meaning "humankind" (for example, Gen. 1:27).

*In GENESIS.* According to the Yahwist's tenth-century B.C. narrative (Gen. 2:4b–3:24), Yahweh shapes man from earth's dust, and by breathing into his nostrils the breath of life, he makes him into an animated creature. The man is placed in the primeval Garden of Eden to tend it. On penalty of death, he is commanded not to eat of the tree of knowledge of good and evil. The man shares in the creation of the animals by naming them. To alleviate the man's

loneliness, Yahweh forms Eve from his rib. The two live harmoniously. They are innocent of their nakedness, until the woman, with intellect awakened, yields to the serpent's tempting and the man joins her in eating the forbidden fruit. Immediately Yahweh confronts the couple to issue punishments—pain in childbirth and subordinate status for the woman, and a cursed ground aggravating man's existence as laborer. Thereupon the couple is driven from the garden.

According to the Priestly sixth-century B.C. history (Gen. 1:1–2:4a), God creates man along with the animals on the sixth day. Man is created in the divine image as male and female. Blessing accompanies their unique creation as does the mandate to multiply and exercise dominion over the earth.

*In Intertestamental Literature.* Adam plays a vital role in the Apocrypha and Pseudepigrapha. In Ecclesiasticus 49:16 Adam is honored "above every living being in the creation," and in II Enoch 30:8-9 he is lauded for being made from seven substances. The *Testament of Levi* (18:10) promises that after opening the gates of paradise, the Messiah will "remove the threatening sword against Adam." In IV Ezra 7:118, Adam is told that the Fall is not only his, "but ours also who are thy descendants" (compare 3:21; 4:30). Second Baruch 54:19, however, counters that man's sin results from his own action, not Adam's.

*In the New Testament.* As a historical figure, Adam is twice mentioned in genealogical contexts (Luke 3:38, as "the son of God," and Jude 14). Far more crucial are Paul's Adam-Christ typologies, which maintain that all humanity experiences the impact of both Adam and Christ. In Romans 5:12-21, Paul avers that if the world knows death through Adam's sin, it also knows justification and life through Christ's obedience. In I Corinthians 15:21-22, the certainty of the Resurrection is dramatically expressed in Adam-Christ typology. Some verses later (45-49) Paul claims that whereas Christians in their flesh resemble the first Adam "from the earth," in the Resurrection they resemble Christ, the last Adam and "man of heaven."

Eve appears twice in the NT, in I Timothy 2:11-15 within a statement advocating the submissive status of women in the church, and in II Corinthians 11:3 to illustrate how easily one can be led astray.

J.K.K.

**ADAMS, SARAH FLOWER** (1805–48). The author of the hymn "Nearer, My God, to Thee" (1841) though it is sometimes erroneously attributed to HARRIET BEECHER STOWE. The text is based on Jacob's vision of a ladder between earth and heaven (Gen. 28:10-22). Adams was born on February 22 in Great Harlow, Essex, England, a daughter of writer Benjamin Flower. Her sister Eliza often set her poems to music. Married to William Bridges Adams in 1834, she was a member of a Unitarian congregation in London. She contributed thirteen hymns to

W. J. Fox's *Hymns and Anthems* (1841). Her other works include the hymn "He Sendeth Sun, He Sendeth Shower," a translation of Fenelon's "Living or Dying, Lord, I Would Be Thine," *Vivia Perpetua, a Dramatic Poem* (1841), and *The Flock at the Fountains,* a catechism and hymns for children (1845). She died August 14, 1848.

N.H.

**ADAR.** *See* HEBREW CALENDAR.

**ADDISON, JOSEPH** (1672–1719). English hymn writer, essayist, poet, and statesman. Best known for "The Spacious Firmament on High" and "When All Thy Mercies, O My God," first published in 1712 in *The Spectator.* He also wrote "How Are Thy Servants Blest, O Lord," "The Lord My Pasture Shall Prepare," and "When Rising from the Bed of Death." Born May 1, 1672, near Amesbury, Wiltshire, England, Addison was the son of Jane Gulston and the clergyman and writer Lancelot Addison, who once served as dean of Lichfield. Educated at Charterhouse and Queen's and Magdalen colleges at Oxford, Addison received the B.A. in 1691, the M.A. in 1693, and served as a fellow from 1697–1711. He read law and devoted himself to politics, performing duties in a number of government posts before becoming chief secretary for Ireland. His essays from *The Spectator* and *The Tatler* are often anthologized alongside those of his friend Richard Steele. Addison married the Countess of Warwick in 1716. He died on June 17.

N.H.

**ADIAPHORA.** A Greek term meaning "things indifferent," or vestments and ceremonies not commanded by the Bible and thus not necessary for salvation. Adiaphoron are nonessentials in worship.

J.C.

**ADLER, ALFRED** (1870–1937). Austrian psychoanalyst who founded individual psychology and is best known for his concepts of "inferiority feeling" and the "will to power." He was born in Penzing, Austria, on February 7, 1870, and was trained as an ophthalmologist at the University of Vienna Medical School in 1895. He became an associate of SIGMUND FREUD in 1902, but by 1908 he began to argue that the aggressive rather than the sexual drive is primary. He chaired the Vienna psychoanalytic circle when he broke with Freud and wrote one of his most popular works, *Study of Organ Inferiority and Its Psychical Compensation* (1917).

His other important contribution was *The Neurotic Constitution* (1917), in which he argued that the principal human motivation is a striving for perfection, which can become a neurotic striving for superiority. He was keenly aware of social as well as individual perspectives.

In 1921 he established the first of thirty child guidance clinics in Vienna. In 1927 he was a visiting professor at Columbia University, New York City, and the Long Island School of Medicine in 1932.

N.H.

**ADLER, FELIX** (1851–1933). Founder and lecturer of the Society for ETHICAL CULTURE. Born in Germany, Adler came to America when he was six. After graduating from Columbia University in 1870 he went to Germany for further study and received his doctorate at the age of twenty-three. In May 1876, he formed the Society for Ethical Culture, which invited people of all faiths to join in a commitment to a moral excellence as the highest duty of the human being. It was to have no prayers, ceremonies, or rituals. Its meetings were to be discourses on moral and ethical living.

The movement spread quickly throughout the United States and Europe. Its advanced educational methods for children were studied by educators from all parts of the world. Adler established the first free kindergarten for poor children.

Expecting to succeed his father as rabbi of New York's Temple Emanu-El, erected in 1929, Adler preached sermons expounding the more radical theories of REFORM JUDAISM. He angered the congregation and was not offered the post. He authored a number of books, including *Creed and Deed* (1877), *An Ethical Philosophy of Life* (1918), and *The Reconstruction of the Spiritual Ideal* (1924).

L.K.

**AD MAJORAM DEI GLORIAM** (A.M.D.G.). Latin for "to the greater glory of God." A frequent expression in the writings of IGNATIUS OF LOYOLA, founder of the Society of Jesus (JESUITS). This motto is often inscribed on altars, stained-glass windows, and other objects dedicated to God's work through the church.

J.C.

**ADONAI.** An honorific title of God. The term is based on the general Hebrew word *Adon*, which means "lord" and was employed when an inferior addressed a superior. *Adon* was frequently used in addressing gods in the Near East and the Syrians worshiped a dying-rising vegetation god called Adonis. Adonai is a special form of the word *Adon* actually meaning "my Lord." In later Judaism, the term functioned almost as a name for God being used instead of the earlier name YAHWEH. (See JEHOVAH.)

J.H.

**ADONIJAH.** A name (Hebrew meaning "Yahweh is Lord") which was probably very common in OT times but which appears in the Bible rarely (Neh. 10:16, as a contemporary of NEHEMIAH; II Chr. 17:8, as a Levite of the time of King Jehoshaphat of Judah) aside from its reference to the fourth son of DAVID, born to him by his wife Haggith (II Sam. 3:4).

The story of Adonijah in I Kings 1–2 offers a fascinating view into the palace politics of the last days of David's senility and of the circumstances that eventually led to the accession of SOLOMON. With David's demise imminent and his senior brothers also deceased, Adonijah apparently assumed, in the absence of contrary indications, that the kingship was his by right of succession. In this assumption he was supported by Joab, the long-time military mainstay of the Davidic throne, and by Abiathar, representative of the official priesthood. Accordingly he had himself proclaimed king at En-rogel, on the border of Judah and Benjamin (I Kings 1:9), probably a symbolic place of the United Kingdom that had emerged from the ancient conflict of Saul and David.

Adonijah reckoned without the influence on David of Nathan the seer/prophet, of Zadok (representing a rival priesthood to Abiathar's), of Benaiah the son of Jehoiada (a rival to Joab in the military role), and of Bathsheba, the mother of Solomon. Whether or not David had ever in an idle moment designated the son of Bathsheba with whom he was besotted to be his successor (I Kings 1:17, 30), he honored the alleged promise. Solomon was anointed king at David's direction with all due solemnity at Gihon, a place peculiarly associated with Jerusalem and the Davidic conquest (II Sam. 5:8) and rode there on David's mule (I Kings 1:33), the vehicle of royalty.

Adonijah survived the attempted coup d'etat and was merely sentenced to house arrest. He was not included in the chilling will of vengeance that David bequeathed to Solomon (I Kings 2:1-9). However, according to I Kings 2:13-25, Adonijah doomed himself by asking for Abishag, the virgin consort of the senile David, to be his wife. This request was judged by Solomon to be a pretense to royalty. The request was made through Bathsheba (with her cynical encouragement?). Adonijah was therefore put to death by Benaiah. But this death was only one by which Solomon consolidated his kingdom (I Kings 2:13-46).

B.V.

**ADONIKAM.** One of the Jewish exiles whose descendants returned to Jerusalem from Babylon after the edict of restoration issued by Cyrus in 538 B.C. According to Ezra 2:13, the Adonikam clan numbered 666 at their return; Nehemiah 7:18 gives the figure of 667. Nearly a century later, three other Adonikites returned with Ezra (compare Ezra 8:13).

W.S.T.

**ADONIS.** A Greek god, originally a young man so handsome that he was loved by the goddess APHRODITE. When Adonis was slain by a bear while hunting, Aphrodite reacted with such grief that the gods allowed his remains to be kept on earth most of the year and only a portion of it in HADES. Generally, the term means "a handsome young man."

J.C.

**ADONIZEDEK.** An Amorite king of Jerusalem in the era of the Israelite conquest. When news of Joshua's victories over Jericho and Ai reached him, he organized a coalition of five Amorite kings of the hill country to meet the Israelite troops at Gibeon, six miles northwest of Jerusalem (Josh. 10:1-5). The Gibeonites, who had capitulated to Joshua only a short time before (9:1-27), appealed for help. Supported by a great hailstorm on the ascent of Beth-horon, Joshua routed the coalition (10:6-11). Indeed, a ballad sings that Joshua made the sun stand still on that day until the slaughter was completed (10:12-14). The five kings were penned in the cave at Makkedah in which they had taken refuge. Only when his victory was complete did Joshua kill Adonizedek and the others (10:16-27) and seal their bodies in the cave with great stones, which "remain to this very day" (10:27).

W.S.T.

**ADOPTION.** The establishment, whether by legal process or not, of a relationship modeled on one which exists by nature. An adopted child acquires within a family the title, rights, and privileges he or she would otherwise have possessed by birth. Within a larger society or nation an alien can be adopted ("naturalized") and so acquire the prerogatives of a born citizen.

*In the OT*. There was no provision in the Mosaic law for familial adoption, though the practice was widespread in the ancient Near East. Inheritance and property disposition, which largely motivated laws governing adoption, were handled by other means in the simpler society of Israel. Some of the earlier Israelite traditions (for example, Gen. 15:2) seem to recall adoption as a practice of ancient times. Also, but only from a work of late Hellenistic times (Esth. 2:7), an elder Jewish cousin adopted an orphaned girl as his daughter.

Legalities aside, there is no doubt that the concept of adoption was operative in Israelite religious thought. Israel itself, alternatively figured as a son or a daughter, had been adopted by the Lord (Exod. 4:22; Ezek. 16; Hos. 11:1-2) and had thus become the Lord's particular possession. Also, the mystique of royalty shared with other Near Eastern cultures dictated that the king, as representative and incarnation of the presence of the national Deity, be considered the adopted son of God (Ps. 2:7; II Sam. 7:14).

*In the NT*. In Greco-Roman law *hyiothesia* was a technical term for adoption. In Romans 9:4 Paul applies the word "adoption of sons/children," in a religious sense to signify the privilege that Israel had acquired as God's chosen. The same term is applied by him to the new Israel of faith, the Christian community, which had received the Spirit of God by which it knew itself to have been freed from sin and therefore capable of calling upon God as its Father (Rom. 8:15).

The NT concept of the Christian as the adopted child of God is based on the belief that the Christian has been incorporated into Christ, who by his redemptive act has been constituted the firstborn of many brethren (Rom. 8:29). Christ's own sonship in relation to God is construed by the NT in various ways. In any case, faith in him renders the Christian assimilated to him as God's child in a spiritual and adoptive relationship of rebirth (John 1:12-13).

B.V.

**ADOPTIONISM.** The doctrine, declared heretical by several councils, which claims that Jesus is the Son of God, not by nature, but by adoption. It was held in early times by the EBIONITES, and in the third century by PAUL OF SAMOSATA, who declared that Jesus was a "mere man" whom God adopted as Son. More recently, several liberal theologians (see LIBERALISM) have held similar views.

In the eighth century, there arose in Spain another doctrine, which was also called "adoptionism." This was based on a radical distinction between the humanity and the divinity of Jesus, similar to that proposed earlier by Nestorius (see NESTORIANS). The Spanish "adoptionists," led by bishops Elipandus of Toledo and Felix of Urgel, held that Jesus, "according to His human nature," is the adopted Son of God. The Word of God incarnate in Jesus is the Son of God "by nature," but the man Jesus is such only "by adoption." These views, condemned by a synod gathered at Frankfort in 794, were later revived by other medieval theologians and repeatedly rejected as heretical.

These two forms of "adoptionism" are very different. While one declares that Jesus is a "mere man" whom God adopted, the other affirms that the Word of God that was incarnate in Jesus is indeed the Son of God by nature, but that the same cannot be said of the humanity of Jesus.

J.G.

**ADORATION OF THE MAGI.** *See* MAGI.

**ADULTERY.** In the Bible, the violation of marital sexual rights and commitments. Both lists of the Ten Commandments prohibit adultery (Exod. 20:14; Deut. 5:18) but no texts give a full explanation of what constituted adultery. It was not equated with all sexual intercourse outside the marriage relationship. Apparently a man could commit adultery against another marriage than his own but a woman only against her own. If a woman was married or betrothed, the husband or male had the right to sole sexual possession, which assured that her children were his. When a man had sex with another man's wife, both were subject to the death penalty (Lev. 20:10; Deut. 22:22). Intercourse of a married male with a female slave, even a betrothed one, or with a virgin was not a capital offense and probably was not classified as adultery. In the former case, a sacrifice

was required, and in the latter, the man was expected to marry the female or pay a money equivalent (Lev. 19:22; Exod. 22:16-17; Deut. 22:28-29). If a husband suspected his wife of adultery, she could be subjected to an ordeal (Num. 5:5-31).

Outside OT law, adultery was considered a serious offense. In fact, most Near Eastern cultures considered it a heinous sin or the "great sin" (see Gen. 20:9; Job 31:11). Proverbs warns against the adulteress and adultery (Prov. 7:6-23). For the prophets, Israel's disloyalty to Yahweh was viewed as adulterous infidelity (Hos. 4:12-14; Jer. 3:8-9; Ezek. 16; 23).

In the sayings of Jesus in the NT, lustful looks are identified with adultery (Matt. 5:28), and marriage to a divorced woman is called adultery (Matt. 5:32; Mark 10:11-12; Luke 16:18). Nonetheless, Jesus refused to condemn the woman taken in adultery (John 7:53–8:11). As in the OT, adultery is used to speak of religious infidelity (Rev. 2:22).

J.H.

**ADVENT.** The first or opening season of the church year, usually beginning four Sundays before Christmas. Advent was formally instituted at the end of the fifth century as a preparation for the celebration of the Nativity of our Lord, or Christmas. Advent also refers to the SECOND COMING OF CHRIST and the final judgment that accompanies the coming of the kingdom of God. Historically, Advent is a time of fasting and repentance, yet it has strong overtones of joy as the Christmas season approaches. The liturgical color of the season is violet or purple, symbolizing the coming of the King and his Kingdom.

J.C.

**ADVENTISTS.** Throughout the history of the church various groups have stressed the doctrine of the SECOND COMING OF CHRIST. Indeed both the OT and the NT constantly reiterate the note of God's program for the future. The old covenant people of Israel were promised a messianic kingdom, and the early church was told that "this Jesus . . . will come in the same way as you saw him go into heaven" (Acts 1:11). In the earlier centuries of the church those sounding the Second Advent theme included such eminent church fathers as Polycarp and Justin Martyr, as well as the Montanists.

Adventism was revived particularly among the eighteenth-century Pietists (see PIETISM) on the Continent and a number of groups in early nineteenth-century Britain, such as the Plymouth Brethren and the Irvingites. Adventist teaching was embraced in America by the MORMONS, JEHOVAH'S WITNESSES, SHAKERS, and the Millerites (see WILLIAM MILLER), forerunners of the Seventh-Day Adventists. British influence on such men as DWIGHT L. MOODY and CYRUS I. SCOFIELD introduced the teaching to a wide span of U.S. Protestantism, which crystallized into the Fundamentalist movement (see FUNDAMENTALISM). There is a close relationship between MILLENARIANISM, which teaches that there will be a future one-thousand-year period when Christ will reign on earth, and Adventism.

Besides Fundamentalism, the largest remnant of nineteenth-century Adventist movement is the SEVENTH-DAY ADVENTISTS, who came into being after William Miller, a Baptist preacher, had predicted Christ would return in 1844. When his prediction proved to be erroneous, Miller gave up on his mission. Others, however, refused to relinquish Advent teaching. Hiram Edson said he experienced a vision of Christ entering the heavenly sanctuary to cleanse it on the date predicted by Miller. The full implementation of the Second Advent would occur at some future date.

Another follower of Miller was Ellen Gould White, whose visions were regarded as true prophecy and established her as the most prominent leader of the new movement. Mrs. White also determined by visions the necessity of keeping the seventh day as the Sabbath.

There are several smaller Adventist groups in the United States, such as the Advent Christian Church, the Church of God General Conference (Oregon, Illinois), and the Primitive Advent Christian Church.

R.H.

**AESTHETICS.** The study within philosophy pertaining to the understanding of beauty. The term is also used in a less technical sense as referring to the affective qualities of the human being as differentiated from the rational or cognitive. Thus, in theology, one can speak of the aesthetics of worship, or of the manifestation of symbolic form in church architecture.

I.C.

**AFFINITY.** Affinity denotes the lines between a woman and her husband's blood relations or between a man and his wife's blood relations, as distinguished from the relationships of blood which tie one to others (consanguinity). Canon and civil law in countries where large numbers of the population are Christians frequently prescribe the permissibility of marriage between persons related by affinity as well as between blood relations.

I.C.

**AFFLICTION.** In the RSV, the terms "afflict" and "affliction" are used to translate several Hebrew and Greek words, although most suggest abnormal hardships, calamities, and suffering, sometimes imposed on one by others, sometimes self-imposed or the consequence of one's actions, and at other times divinely imposed.

Affliction imposed by others appears throughout the Bible, especially with reference to the Hebrew suffering in Egyptian slavery (Exod. 3:7). Bread eaten at Passover celebrating the escape from Egypt could be called the bread of affliction (Deut. 16:3). Paul

speaks frequently of his hardships and the afflictions he suffered (II Cor. 1:4, 8). In addition, prayers in the Psalms ask that God remember the people's afflictions (Pss. 25:18; 107:10). Disease was also considered a form of affliction (Lev. 13:9).

Sometimes afflictions were self-imposed. Part of the ritual of the DAY OF ATONEMENT required self-affliction (Lev. 16:29, 31), that is, fasting and a break with normal activity. Afflictions could be seen as the result of one's actions (Job 5:6) or the consequence of one's iniquities (Ps. 107:17).

Some afflictions are traced to divine action. God afflicted Pharaoh with plagues (Gen. 12:17). Hannah's barrenness was an affliction because God had closed her womb (I Sam. 1:5, 11). Affliction could be sent as divine testing (Ps. 66:11). The suffering servant was afflicted by God (Isa. 53:4, 7) as vicarious suffering.

Paul admonishes those afflicted to endure and even to find joy in their afflictions, which are momentary (II Cor. 4:8, 17; 7:4). Those in affliction should be aided (I Tim. 5:10).

J.H.

**AFRICAN METHODIST EPISCOPAL CHURCH.** *See* METHODIST CHURCHES.

**AFRICAN METHODIST EPISCOPAL CHURCH ZION.** *See* METHODIST CHURCHES.

**AFTERLIFE.** *See* IMMORTALITY.

**AGABUS.** The name of Agabus appears twice in the Acts of the Apostles. On both occasions he is associated with prophecy in the form of foretelling the future (Acts 11:27-28; 21:10-11). From the first text we learn that Agabus was a prophet, a charismatic preacher associated evidently with the Judean church. Agabus arrived at Antioch, where he predicted "a great famine over all the world" in the days of the emperor Claudius (A.D. 41–54). The closest independent evidence gets to this prediction is the statement in Suetonius (*Claudius* 18) that there were frequent dearths in the emperor's reign.

The second oracle of Agabus was more specific. Set in Caesarea it was accompanied by an acted symbolism, which was typical of the OT prophets (I Kings 11:29ff.; Isa. 20:2ff.; Jer. 13:1ff.; Ezek. 4:1ff.). Agabus warned Paul not to go to Jerusalem, where he would be delivered to the Gentiles. Agabus' oracle was rejected by Paul, who pursued his course and went to Jerusalem.

Later tradition made Agabus one of the Seventy (Luke 10:1) and a Christian martyr.

R.M.

**AGAG.** A king of the Amalekites, whose name may have been derived from an Amalekite tribe (compare Num. 24:7; Esth. 3:1). In I Samuel 15, Yahweh ordered Saul into holy war against the Amalekites.

That meant death to every living thing. Saul, however, spared King Agag and the choicest of the flocks, only to be confronted by Samuel with a word of judgment from the Lord. The same day Saul was rejected from being king over Israel. Samuel then said to Agag, "As your sword has made women childless, so shall your mother be childless among women" (I Sam. 15:33). Then Samuel hewed him in pieces before the Lord!

W.S.T.

**AGAPE.** In contrast to English language usage, which has one word for LOVE, Greek has several terms in addition to *agapē*. For example, EROS and PHILIA. In classical Greek the verb *agapaō* is a neutral term, with a generalized meaning, "to be fond of," "to treat with respect," "to express pleasure" in something, or "to welcome." The last named definition seems to be the root sense of the word.

In the Greek OT, *agapē*, with its verb equivalent (which is more often used) renders a Hebrew verb *ahēb*, used of human relationships but more importantly of God's love for the special people in choosing Israel and establishing the covenant with them. This idea plays an important role in fixing the NT use of *agapē*, meaning "divine love" based on self-giving favor shown to undeserving people.

R.M.

**AGE OF REASON.** See ENLIGHTENMENT, CHRISTIANITY IN THE.

**AGGIORNAMENTO.** From the Italian *Aggiornore,* for "updating." The term was used by POPE JOHN XXIII for the modernization of the Roman Catholic Church by the SECOND VATICAN COUNCIL. It signifies new beginnings in ecumenical relations, the defense of the poor and oppressed, and the translation of the Mass into the local language of the people.

J.C.

**AGNOSTIC.** From the Greek "not know," signifying the unknown or unknowable. The term was coined by THOMAS HENRY HUXLEY in an 1889 essay that said that a person cannot have knowledge of phenomena that are not apprehended by the senses. The agnostic neither affirms nor denies the existence of GOD or the unseen world, but declares that the evidences for belief are inconclusive. The viewpoint is polemical in insisting that the limits of knowledge must affect belief about the nature of God. But agnosticism is not identical to ATHEISM.

I.C.

**AGNUS DEI.** From the Greek for "Lamb of God" (John 1:29, 36); an ancient liturgical formula in the Communion service. The Second Trullan Council in A.D. 692 declared that it was forbidden to represent Christ as a lamb, and Pope Sergius I reacted by ordering all priests to sing the Agnus Dei at Communion. This expressed the opposition of the Roman Catholic Church to the iconoclasm of Second Trullan Council. From the eleventh century the priest beat his breast, bowed, and recited the Agnus Dei three times before taking Communion. The formula is widely used in liturgical services today.

J.C.

**AGONY IN THE GARDEN.** See GETHSEMANE, GARDEN OF.

**AGRAPHA.** The term *agrapha* is Greek, meaning "things that are not written." It refers to words, usually "sayings of Jesus" not found in the Bible's four Gospels, which have been preserved in other sources. There are three specimens calling for comment.

There is one example of a "word of Jesus" in the NT outside the Gospels—in Acts 20:35. Less likely I Thessalonians 4:15 falls into this category.

Then there are *agrapha* that are found in one or more—but not all—textual traditions of the Greek NT. The longest example is in Mark 16:9-20, printed in the KJV but relegated to the footnotes or margins of all modern editions in view of the poor textual attestation of this "longer ending." More problematical is the text of Luke 22:19*b*-20, which contains a fuller account of Jesus' words at the Last Supper, and is currently given credence as authentic in spite of the double mention of the cup at the meal. Luke 6 illustrates another textual peculiarity. In some manuscripts, verse 5 follows verse 10, and in its place there is the *agraphon*: "On the same day he saw a man working on the Sabbath and said to him, 'Man, if you know what you are doing, you are blessed; but if you do not know, you are accursed and a transgressor of the law.'"

Finally, papyri documents discovered in the sands of Egypt, at Oxyrhynchus and more recently at NAG HAMMADI, have brought to light a fund of *agrapha*, whether as isolated sayings or collected to form a document (for example, *The Gospel of Thomas,* which has 114 "sayings" of Jesus, gnostic in outlook). Among these sayings are such well-known words, attributed to Jesus, as "Raise the stone, and you will find me; cleave the wood, and I am there." (*See* APOCRYPHA, NT.)

R.M.

**AGRIPPA I and II.** "HEROD" was a family name of a succession of rulers in Israel in NT times. Herod the Great (40-4 B.C.) had a grandson born to his son Aristobulus, who was executed in 7 B.C.; thereafter this son was brought to Rome and lived as part of the imperial family. He quarreled with the emperor Tiberius and was imprisoned. Later released on Tiberius' death, he was favored by the next Roman emperor Gaius (or Caligula), who gave him the title of "king," a term that is found in Acts 12:1. This is Herod Agrippa I.

Herod's kingdom was gradually enlarged after A.D. 41, when Claudius became emperor, until the domain extended over an area about the same in size as his grandfather's, who was also named Herod. He was moderately popular with the Jews because of his connection with the Hasmoneans, who in turn had been associated with the patriotic Maccabees in the second century B.C. This favor is seen in his action regarding the early Christians. He killed James and had Peter incarcerated (Acts 12), but a sudden death in A.D. 44 (Acts 12:20-23) is seen by Luke as a divine judgment on his opposition to the church. A parallel account of his horrible death is related by Josephus in his *Antiquities*.

Herod left one son to succeed him. Herod Agrippa II was born in A.D. 27 and so was a mere youth on his father's death in A.D. 44, a fact which prevented his claiming the title immediately. In A.D. 50 he was acknowledged by Claudius with the title of "king"—a courtesy honor, to be sure, since Rome would tolerate no rival emperors in the provinces such as Judea and Syria. The emperor Nero, who ruled from A.D. 48 to A.D. 66, added more territory in the north of Palestine to his dominion in A.D. 56. At the latter date, Jewish opposition to Roman rule and Herod's client status welled up in armed revolt at the outbreak of the Jewish war (A.D. 66–72). This led to Jerusalem's destruction in A.D. 70, but Herod lived on in loyalty to Rome until A.D. 100.

His character is best studied from Acts 25–26, where he encountered Paul during the latter's Caesarean imprisonment. Especially interesting and revealing is the snatch of dialogue (in Acts 26:26-29), where Agrippa is confronted by Paul's challenge.

R.M.

**AHAB.** Seventh king of the northern kingdom of Israel, about 869–850 B.C. He was the son of OMRI and husband of JEZEBEL, daughter of the king of Tyre.

Neither the Deuteronomic historian nor his sources have dealt kindly with Ahab. Whereas his father, Omri, undoubtedly one of Israel's most capable kings, is dismissed with only a few lines (I Kings 16:23-28), however, considerable space is given to Ahab. The reason for this is Ahab's considerable involvement in the prophetic stories, principally those about ELIJAH, which were all important source material for this historian. His judgment, always negative with regard to the kings of Israel, is especially severe of Ahab, who is characterized as having provoked the Lord more than all the other kings who preceded him (I Kings 16:29-34).

Nevertheless, the sources contain enough data to inform us about the positive as well as the negative aspects of Ahab's career, some of the former being also indicated by extra-biblical sources. The Deuteronomist states that Ahab built an altar to Baal in Samaria and worshiped him. This may be quite true, but the names of Ahab's children AHAZIAH and ATHALIAH are Yahwistic. There is no doubt that Yahweh was the national god of Israel as well as of Judah and no reason to think that Ahab departed from the national religion, but in preexilic times this was not the theoretical monotheism of the prophets. Ahab's involvement with Baal was bound up with his marriage to Jezebel, and this was part of the Omrides' policy of cementing good relationships with neighboring peoples. The same policy is evidenced in the giving of Ahab's daughter Athaliah in marriage to the king of Judah.

Archaeology has confirmed the great building program conducted by Ahab at Samaria and elsewhere (I Kings 22:39). Internal organization and stabilization were accompanied by the securing of Israel's borders and astute international alignments. Though committed to a policy of accommodation with the Arameans, whose yoke his father Omri had been unable to shake off, when finally provoked beyond endurance he engaged them in combat and humbled them (I Kings 20:1-30a). His benign treatment of the conquered enemy, the act of a shrewd politician, was condemned by an unnamed prophet as betrayal of true belief (I Kings 20:30b-43). In a later campaign to enforce Aramean reparations he was less successful, however, even though he evidently dominated his ally Judah in this venture. A chance arrow shot ended his life at the siege of Ramoth-gilead, where he died bravely, encouraging his forces to the last (I Kings 22:1-36).

The celebrated Stela of Mesha the king of Moab (the MOABITE STONE, between 840–820 B.C.) testifies that Moab was kept in subjugation to Israel during Ahab's reign. Two years before Ahab's death, "Ahab the Israelite" is listed in an inscription of SHALMANESER III of Assyria as one of an alliance of twelve kings who (apparently successfully) resisted his initial probing at the vulnerability of the West. Israel is credited there with having mounted against Assyria the second largest force.

To Ahab's discredit the Bible makes mention principally of the episode of Naboth's vineyard (I Kings 21:1-24), coveted by Ahab, acquired by him by more than questionable means, and made by Elijah a symbol of his doom. If the story is read attentively, it is evident that the biblical author actually attributes to Jezebel the flagrant disregard of traditional Israelite rights, which Ahab would otherwise have respected, however reluctantly. As in so much else, Ahab is an opportunist and a pragmatist, willing to be instructed in non-Israelite ways if they are to his advantage, but not an inherently evil man.

B.V.

**AHASUERUS.** A legendary king of Persia who is a protagonist of the book of ESTHER. After he had banished his first wife Vashti, Ahasuerus selected from his harem the beautiful Jewish maiden Esther to be his queen. Esther could thus intercede with the king on behalf of her people when a high official of the empire, the wicked Haman, sought to eliminate Esther's stepfather, MORDECAI, and all other Jews. Her intervention was a success, and Haman was hanged on the very gallows on which he had intended to hang Mordecai. The Jews enjoyed the king's favor ever after. The Ahasuerus of the book of Esther is often identified with Xerxes (486–465 B.C.), although Ezra 4:4-6 would make Darius I eligible for consideration as well. Daniel 9:1 knows him as the father of "Darius the Mede," of whose existence history has no other record.

W.S.T.

**AHAZ.** A shortened form of Jehoahaz (II Chr. 21:17) meaning "Yahweh has taken [my] hand." The shortening is doubtless due to the reluctance of a biblical author to attribute a Yahwistic name to a king who was remembered as an idolater. Ahaz was the twelfth king of Judah after Solomon and reigned about 735–715 B.C.

On his accession to the throne Ahaz was immediately caught up in the power politics of the Near East. A newly aggressive Assyrian empire under TIGLATH-PILESER III was being opposed in the West by a coalition of small Palestinian and Aramean states. The refusal of Ahaz to join the coalition precipitated an invasion of Judah by the forces of Israel and Damascus (II Kings 16:5; Isa. 7:1-9); and possibly Edom and Philistia as well (II Chr. 28:16-18), which sought to substitute for Ahaz a more malleable chief of state who would favor the anti-Assyrian alliance. Ahaz was supported in his refusal by the prophet Isaiah, and he proved in this instance to have adopted a prudent course, since the inevitable sequel to the coalition was the Assyrian subjugation of Damascus and large parts of Israel (II Kings 15:29; 16:9).

The price Ahaz paid for immunity from Assyrian devastation was, however, a high one. He became the vassal of the Assyrian king and paid him tribute (II Kings 16:7-9). Then he proceeded to carry this subservience to its logical conclusion by adopting the religion of his suzerains and introducing the cult of their gods into the Jerusalem temple, the citadel of the national religion (II Kings 16:10-18; II Chr. 28:22-25). This policy was definitely not supported by the prophet Isaiah (compare Isa. 7:10-17) and was obviously regarded by the biblical historian as total apostasy from the traditional religion of Israel (II Kings 16:17-18).

Whether connected or not with the preceding events, Ahaz is singled out as having sacrificed his children in the bloody rites associated with a "king god" (Adrammelech and Anammelech in II Kings 17:31) in the notorious valley of Hinnom on the outskirts of Jerusalem (II Chr. 28:3). This site, also called Topheth (II Kings 23:10; Jer. 7:31-32), witnessed human sacrifices all through preexilic times, despite their condemnation in prophetic religion. It is even possible that the "king god" Melek

or Molech was, in the popular mind, identified with Yahweh "the king" (I Kings 11:7; Jer. 32:35).

The geography of Isaiah 7:3 may indicate that the prophet met the king on the latter's return from sacrificing in the valley of Hinnom. If so, a special poignancy is added to the succeeding prophecies.

B.V.

**AHAZIAH.** The same name as Jehoahaz, which means "Yahweh has taken [my] hand."

1. The son of AHAB, king of Israel about 850-849 B.C., eighth in succession and third of the Omride line. Like his father he was not exclusively devoted to the national Yahwistic religion (I Kings 22:51-53), and in II Kings 1:2-16 he is physically hurt and calls in mortal need on "Baal-zebub, the god of Ekron." There is doubtless in this latter text a dissimulation of background history. Baal-zebub ("lord of flies") is a deliberate Hebrew corruption of Baal-zebul ("Baal the prince"), the title of the aboriginal fertility god of Canaan (compare I Kings 22:53) who only incidentally had been adopted as a patronal deity by the hated Philistines of Ekron.

Ahaziah was not a memorable king. He died without royal issue (II Kings 1:17). During his short reign the kingdom of Moab, which had been subject to Israel in the time of Omri and Ahab, successfully regained its independence (II Kings 1:1; the Stela of Mesha). A joint mercantile venture with Judah in which he was involved seems to have had disastrous results (I Kings 22:48-49; II Chr. 20:35-37).

2. The son of Jehoram and ATHALIAH, called Jehoahaz in II Chronicles 20:17, king of Judah about 842 B.C. He is represented as being influenced by his Israelite-Phoenician ancestry (II Kings 8:26-27; II Chr. 22:2-5), and indeed he joined with his uncle JORAM, king of Israel, in an unsuccessful assault against the Arameans at Ramoth-gilead, where Joram was grievously wounded (II Kings 8:28-29). When Joram was recuperating from his wounds at Jezreel and Ahaziah was attending him, both were caught up in the rebellion of Jehu against the house of Omri that had been stirred up by the prophet Elisha (II Kings 9). In the ensuing massacre both Joram and Ahaziah were slain, the latter under circumstances that are variously detailed by II Kings 9:27-28 and II Chronicles 22:7-9.

Ahaziah's youth and untimely demise left the throne of Judah vulnerable to the machinations of the queen mother, Athaliah, who seized power and ruled for six years in the Phoenician manner supporting the cult of the Canaanite Baal. Eventually she was assassinated in a Yahwistic palace rebellion, and Ahaziah's seven-year-old son Jehoash (Joash), who had been hidden from his grandmother's murderous designs, was proclaimed king (II Kings 11; II Chr. 24:1).

B.V.

**AHIJAH.** This name, which means "Yahweh is a brother" (also spelled Ahiah), is borne by six OT figures, including the father of the third king of Judah, Baasha (I Kings 15:27 ff.), and persons mentioned only in passing (I Chr. 2:25; 11:36; 26:20; and Neh. 10:26). The most significant Ahijah, however, was the prophet of Shiloh, whose work is recounted in I Kings 11; 14 and II Chronicles 9:29; 10:15. This Ahijah arranged to encounter JEROBOAM, the son of Nebat, a young supervisor of Solomon's forced labor gangs, while the latter was walking on a country road. Ahijah took the new garment that he was wearing, tore it into twelve pieces and handed ten to Jeroboam with the charge that he become ruler over the ten northern tribes of Israel. In a speech redolent of Deuteronomic theology, Ahijah justified this insurrection as a divine retribution against Solomon for worshiping foreign deities (I Kings 11:29-39).

Not long afterward, Jeroboam sounded the clarion call, "To your tents, O Israel" (I Kings 12:16), and the division of the kingdom was effected. But his subsequent decision to erect calves of gold, dedicated with the words "Behold your gods, O Israel, who brought you up out of the land of Egypt" (I Kings 12:28), was judged by the prophet to be apostasy. For this sin, Ahijah announced the death not only of ABIJAH, Jeroboam's son (I Kings 14:12), but the utter elimination of the house of Jeroboam. This judging work of God was carried out in due course, though unwittingly, by Baasha, king of Judah (I Kings 15:29-30).                                    W.S.T.

**AHIMAAZ.** A name translated "brother is counselor." Two persons bear this name in the OT.

(1) Father of Ahinoam, Saul's wife (I Sam. 14:50).

(2) A son of ZADOK, high priest in David's cabinet (II Sam. 15:27). During ABSALOM's rebellion, Ahimaaz and Jonathan, Abiathar's son, maintained communication between the fugitive David and his Jerusalem supporters (15:27-28, 36). When this espionage activity, which kept David informed about Absalom, was discovered, Ahimaaz and Jonathan fled and eluded Absalom's search party by hiding in a well at Bahurim. Thereupon they told David about Ahitophel's anti-Davidic counsel and remained with him (17:17-21).

Later when Ahimaaz eagerly volunteered to carry word about Absalom's defeat to David, he was turned down by Joab, who instead sent a Cushite slave to convey grim tidings of the prince's death. With renewed effort Ahimaaz obtained Joab's permission. By outrunning the Cushite, Ahimaaz was the first to inform David of the victory. Evasive about Absalom, Ahimaaz left it to the Cushite to impart the worst (II Sam. 18:19-32). Subsequently, this Ahimaaz, or another, was Solomon's son-in-law and commissioner in the district of Naphtali (I Kings 4:15).                            J.K.K.

**AHIMELECH.** ("The brother [God] is king.")

(1) Son of Ahitub and chief priest at NOB. In his flight from Saul, David visited Ahimelech and falsely claimed that he was on a royal assignment. Ahimelech gave the famished David "the bread of the Presence" from Yahweh's sanctuary, which, according to law (Lev. 24:5-9), was the sole property of priests. Also he delivered to this unarmed outlaw the sword of Goliath (I Sam. 21:1-9). As witness to these proceedings, Doeg the Edomite informed Saul, who read this as evidence that the eighty-five priests of Nob were treacherously seeking his demise. Summarily he commanded their execution. When Saul's retainers refused to obey this outrageous order, Doeg freely complied. Abiathar, the sole survivor and son of Ahimelech, fled to and obtained asylum with David (22:9-23).

(2) Son of Abiathar, who escaped the slaughter at Nob, and grandson of Ahimelech, son of Ahitub. This assumes the accuracy of I Chronicles 24:3, 31, since the names of Abiathar and Ahimelech are presumably transposed in II Samuel 8:17 and I Chronicles 18:16; 24:6.

(3) A Hittite who served David (I Sam. 26:6).
                                                        J.K.K.

**AHIMSA.** Non-injury, the basis of traditional Indian ethics and the inspiration for the nonviolent resistance of MOHANDAS GANDHI (1869–1948).

In early HINDUISM, ahimsa was understood as emphasizing the unity of life. The animal sacrifices prescribed in the VEDAS were seen as being in accord with ahimsa, because these sacrifices united the people with the gods.

JAINISM rejected this view from the beginning and saw ahimsa on the personal level instead. The Jains expect each individual to practice ahimsa—that is, to avoid injuring any living being. They have always interpreted ahimsa in the strictest possible sense. Therefore Jain monks beg all their food, search it carefully for animal content, sweep the road ahead of them to avoid crushing any insect, and wear a cloth over the mouth to prevent insects from entering.

BUDDHISM has always sought the middle path between indulgence and asceticism. So too, it practices a more relaxed version of ahimsa. Buddhists do not count a death as a breach of ahimsa unless it was intentional. For Buddhists, ahimsa is more positive than negative, more directive than binding.

Most Hindus today place some emphasis on ahimsa. Most practice vegetarianism, in partial adherence to ahimsa. Those who seek purification or enlightenment (MOKSHA) practice a more strict ahimsa. Ahimsa received international attention in this century because of Gandhi. Through passive resistance, civil disobedience, and hunger strikes he led India to independence and weakened many of the CASTE divisions in Indian society. (See KARMA.)
                                                        K./M.C.

**AHURA MAZDA.** In ZOROASTRIANISM the supreme deity, creator, and leader of the forces of good

Courtesy of the Oriental Institute, University of Chicago

*Ahura Mazda, the Persians' winged god*

against those of evil. In Avestan, the language of the Zoroastrian Scriptures, the name means "Wise Lord." Certain schools of Zoroastrian thought have come close to DUALISM, making Ahura Mazda and Angra Mainyu, or Ahriman, the principle of evil, virtually equal, and eternal antagonists. But the most ancient Zoroastrian teachings seem to agree with modern adherents of the faith in viewing Ahura Mazda as a supreme, MONOTHEISTIC god who will in due course triumph utterly over evil, which derives from a lesser source.

R.E.

**AI.** A Canaanite city, "beside Bethel" (Josh. 12:9), identified with a modern site called et-Tell, about ten miles north of Jerusalem. Joshua 7 recounts an initial abortive raid upon Ai from their base at Jericho by Joshua's forces. The setback and casualties suffered by the Israelites led to the discovery of corruption within their own ranks, for Achan, the son of Carmi, had kept some of the "devoted things" of Jericho, namely, booty that had been reserved by Yahweh for sacred purposes. As soon as Achan and his entire household had been stoned and burned with fire in the valley of Achor, the battle against Ai was resumed. Joshua 8:1-29 recounts Joshua's strategy against the city. He began by sending an ambush of thirty thousand men by night to hide west of Ai. Joshua, with the bulk of the Israelite force, feigned an attack against Ai from the north two days later, then deliberately retreated, drawing the Ai defense force out of the city in pursuit. The ambush was thus able to enter the city and put it to the torch and then join Joshua's men in slaughtering the confused populace of twelve thousand people. The conclusion suggests that the story

was told partly in order to explain the existence of a heap of ruins, which remains "to this day" (v. 28), and a great heap of stones (under which the king of Ai was buried), "which stands there to this day" (v. 29).

The likelihood that the account in Joshua is a historically accurate depiction of the demise of Ai is diminished by the fact that archaeology cannot demonstrate that the town existed between about 2500 B.C. and a date somewhat after the Israelite conquest of Palestine. This fact has led some to suggest that the story really recalls the conquest of Bethel, about a mile to the west, which was destroyed by fire in the thirteenth century B.C.—about the time of the Israelite conquest.

W.S.T.

**AILLY, PIERRE D'** (1350–1420). French cardinal, theologian, and prominent advocate of a council to reform the church and end the Great Schism (1378–1417). Born in Compiègne, France, Pierre d'Ailly was educated at the University of Paris, and in 1389 he became its chancellor. Skilled in nominalist philosophy (see NOMINALISM) and theological debating, he was skeptical about reason finding truth, but accepted church dogma on faith. In this way he influenced Martin Luther's view of reason. For years he worked to resolve the Great Schism, which divided Christendom between rival popes at Avignon and Rome. With the University of Paris and others he tried to persuade both popes to resign, and he eventually joined the cardinals of both in calling the Council of Pisa, 1409. Pisa elected a third pope, Alexander V—succeeded within ten months by Pope John XXIII, but popes Gregory XII and Benedict XIII refused to step down. Pope John XXIII made Pierre a cardinal in 1411 and sent him to Germany as papal legate in 1413. Yet Pierre worked to have the Council of Constance (1414–18) depose all three popes. It did, and elected Martin V. Pierre fought to keep the cardinals from losing their traditional election role and helped to condemn JOHN HUSS.

C.M.

**AKBAR THE GREAT** (1542–1605). The wisest of the Mogul emperors of India; one of the most celebrated Oriental emperors of modern times. He succeeded to the throne in the Punjab in 1556 but was under a regency until 1560. The first seven years of his reign were occupied with warfare, in which he established his authority in several provinces until he ruled the greater part of India. He is chiefly remembered for his wonderful administrative ability and tolerance of other religious beliefs. He studied all religions and adopted for himself a pure deism, embracing them all. A patron of the arts, Akbar established schools throughout the empire where Muslims, Hindus, and others might study together. Because of his tolerance and sympathy of others he gained for himself the title of "guardian of mankind."

W.G.

**AKHENATON** ("the splendor of Aton"). The later name of Amenophis IV, an Eighteenth Dynasty Pharaoh (about 1364–1347 B.C.) who temporarily transformed Egyptian culture and religion by rigorously promoting the sun-god Aton at the expense of the established imperial deity Amon.

Brooklyn Museum, Charles Edwin Wilbour Fund

*Akhenaton (left) with his wife, Nefertiti (right); sculptor's limestone model found at Akhenaton (Tell el-Amarna)*

*Domestic Policy.* When Amenophis IV succeeded his father, Amenophis III (about 1403–1364), he boldly replaced the cult of Amon with that of Aton. Lacking earthly visible form, this one god was the Solar Disk which, with its life-giving power, was claimed worthy of human veneration. In his fifth year, Amenophis IV broke with the powerful priesthood of Amon by leaving Thebes and establishing a new capital at Akhetaton ("the Horizon of the Solar Disk"), near modern Tell el-Amarna. Contending that he was the one mediator available between the Aton and humankind, Amenophis changed his name to Akhenaton.

Aton was celebrated as the sole deity and creator of all. A near approximation of monotheism was achieved, but its impact on the emerging Israelite faith less than a century before Moses was negligible. Under Akhenaton's direction, Amon's name was systematically removed from Egyptian monuments. Also Egyptian literature and art were channeled to give the new religion compelling expression. Akhenaton was largely motivated by a political desire to curb the influence of the Amon clergy and to unify the empire under a new form of worship. Although this upstart religion produced a superb hymn to the Aton, it fostered no substantive theology or ethic.

Akhenaton's reform was short-lived. He was succeeded by his son-in-law, Tut-ankh-aton (about 1347–1338), who was obliged to make peace with the Amon priesthood. Without delay he reestablished the cult of Amon, changed his name to Tut-ankh-amon, and returned the court to Thebes. Soon all Egypt regarded Akhenaton's religious innovations as heretical.

*Foreign Policy.* Akhenaton's preoccupation with domestic concerns led to indifference and incompetence in external affairs. Nearly four hundred AMARNA letters excavated at Akhenaton's capital attest that Egypt's influence in Asia deteriorated rapidly at this time. Mainly written by Akhenaton's vassals in Palestine and Phoenicia, this correspondence reveals a chaotic environment wherein city-kings unassisted by Egypt engaged in a life and death struggle to maintain their own positions. Owing to Akhenaton's complacency, the advantage now fell to the Hittites. Only with the emergence of the Nineteenth Dynasty (about 1306-1200) was the trend reversed.

J.K.K.

**AKIBA, RABBI** (also AKIVA) (A.D. 50–132). Scholar and religious martyr who inspired the revolt against the Romans. Originally an illiterate shepherd, Akiba was encouraged by his wife, Rachel, to study the TORAH. He began his studies when he was forty. He became the most prominent teacher of the MISHNAH and Jewish leader of his time. Akiba personally intervened in Rome in behalf of his suffering people. As the Roman rule stiffened, he urged Bar Kokhba and other Jewish patriots to rebel against their oppressors.

In his interpretation of Jewish law, Akiba advocated democratic procedures, urging that decisions be rendered in accordance with the views of the majority of leading scholars and not on the basis of personal authority. In the last moments of his life, when tortured by his Roman executioner, Akiba calmly recited, without showing any sign of physical pain, the prayer that begins, "Hear, O Israel, the Lord our God, the Lord is One."

L.K.

**AKKADIAN.** *See* ASSYRIA AND BABYLONIA.

**ALAND, KURT.** Born in 1915, Aland completed his theological studies at Berlin. He has held professorial appointments in the fields of NT and church history at Berlin, Halle, and is currently professor at Muenster in West Germany. His major scholarly contributions have been as editor of the world-standard critical edition of the Greek New Testament, *Novum Testamentum Graece* (25th ed.) and as a member of the international team that prepared the United Bible Societies' *Greek New Testament* (1966).

H.K.

**ALB.** A basic clerical VESTMENT, adapted from the ancient Roman tunic. Its name is from the Latin *alba,* or "white." The alb was—and is today in many churches—worn for Holy Communion. A wide, white linen robe with sleeves, it is covered with the stole and sometimes with the chasuble.

J.C.

**ALBAN.** The first British martyr, perhaps killed during the persecution of DIOCLETIAN, early in the fourth century. BEDE says that he was a pagan who hid a fugitive Christian priest. The latter converted him, and when the authorities arrived, Alban took the priest's clothes and was killed in his stead.

J.G.

**ALBERTUS MAGNUS.** Dominican theologian of the thirteenth century, noted for his studies of ARISTOTLE and of natural sciences, and for having been the teacher of THOMAS AQUINAS. He outlived his famous disciple, whom he then defended against charges of heresy.

His main contribution to the field of theology—as well as to his disciple Thomas—was his openness to the philosophy of Aristotle. For centuries, the Platonic tradition had dominated philosophy in Western Europe (see PLATONISM). In Albertus' time, works of Aristotle previously unknown among Latin-speaking Christians were being translated. As a commentary on Aristotle, the works of AVERROES, a Muslim philosopher, were also translated. On the basis of these writings, some philosophers, particularly at the University of Paris, began taking positions that many deemed heretical. These philosophers—the "Latin Averroists"—held, for instance, that reason is independent of faith, and that the world is eternal. Reacting to such views, most theologians held that reason must be guided by faith in all philosophical inquiry, and that the doctrine of the eternity of the world is an example of how reason proceeding by itself errs.

Albertus rejected both extremes by distinguishing between philosophy and theology. Philosophy seeks truth on the basis of reason, apart from revealed truth. Theology is grounded on revealed truth, which reason alone cannot discover. Philosophy then is autonomous as long as it remains within its proper sphere, but errs when it goes beyond the limits of reason. Reason, for instance, can prove neither the eternity of the world nor its creation out of nothing. This is a matter for theology to discuss, since it falls in the realm of revealed truth, and not of autonomous reason.

J.G.

**ALBIGENSES.** A heretical group that gained many adherents in southern France late in the twelfth and early in the thirteenth centuries. They were named after the town of Albi, where they were particularly numerous. Often also called CATHARS, they held doctrines very similar to those of MANICHAEISM, although it is difficult to prove any connection between the two movements. It seems that they derived their teachings from the Bogomils of Bulgaria.

They were extreme dualists, holding that there are two eternal principles—one good and one evil. In the present world, spirits are the creation of the good principle, whereas matter is evil. Therefore, "true believers" must lead a life of extreme asceticism, rejecting the temptations of the body. Although mere "believers" were not expected to do this, the "perfect" sometimes starved themselves to death in a rite called endura. Worship must be purely spiritual, with no material elements such as those used in the sacraments of the church. Since matter is evil, they also denied the physical INCARNATION of God in Jesus and the final RESURRECTION of the body.

In southern France, their doctrines soon became involved in the resistance of Langedoc to be incorporated into France. After several unsuccessful attempts to convert them, INNOCENT III proclaimed a crusade against them. Under the leadership of Simon de Montfort, this was an exceedingly cruel affair, punctuated by massacres. The failure of Catholics to convert the Albigenses contributed to DOMINIC's decision to found a new Order of Preachers, commonly known as Dominicans. By the fifteenth century, the last traces of the Albigenses had disappeared.

J.G.

**ALBRIGHT, WILLIAM F.** (1891–1971). World-renowned scholar and teacher in Semitic languages (Johns Hopkins University) and biblical archaeology (American School of Oriental Research, Jerusalem). His linguistic skills shed new light on Hebrew language and biblical history, and his archaeological methods made more precise the datings of ancient sites and events. His best-known works include *From the Stone Age to Christianity,* (1940, 1957) and *The Archaeology of Palestine* (1949, 1964).

H.K.

**ALCHEMY.** A prescientific body of practices, which were thought to produce long life and immortality and to transmute base metals into gold. Chinese alchemists conducted experiments with recipes derived from the Taoist sacred writings (*see* TAOISM) and the system of the I CHING. Yang, the male principle, was the symbol for mercury, and yin, the female principle, for lead; their fusing was supposed to yield gold. By using an elixir made from that gold, the alchemist would attain immortality.

Western alchemy followed a similar theory of using transmuted gold for purification. It began in Alexandria around the time of Christ and used mystical and Aristotelian thought as the basis of its experiments. Because Western alchemists looked forward to immortality after death, they did not seek it in the physical world. However, interest in longevity from elixirs of gold and silver remained strong at least until the sixteenth century. Understood metaphorically, alchemy can symbolize the purification of the practitioner, the death and resurrection of Christ, or, as the psychologist C. G. Jung saw it, the process of becoming an individual.

K./M.C.

**ALCUIN** (735–804). A native of York, England, and one of the key figures in the Carolingian Renaissance. After serving as head of the cathedral school in York, he moved to the Frankish kingdom, where he became CHARLEMAGNE's personal tutor and adviser in religious matters. He is mostly responsible for the revival of learning during Charlemagne's reign.

J.G.

**ALDERSGATE.** *See* WESLEY, JOHN.

**ALEXANDER, ARCHIBALD** (1772–1851). An American Presbyterian minister. Alexander served as president of Hampden-Sydney College from 1796 to 1804. Moving to a prominent pastorate in Philadelphia, he urged the General Assembly to found a seminary at Princeton. They did so in 1812. As a leader of Old School Presbyterianism, he thus helped found Princeton Theological Seminary and was its first president.

N.H.

**ALEXANDER, CECIL FRANCES** (1818–95). Author of more than four hundred hymns, including "All Things Bright and Beautiful," "Once in Royal David's City," "Jesus Calls Us O'er the Tumult," and "There Is a Green Hill Far Away." She is also the translator of St. Patrick's hymn, "I Bind unto Myself Today."

Born in Ireland to the mayor of Miltown House, County Tyrone, she was married in 1850 to William Alexander, bishop of Derry (1867-93), archbishop of Armagh, and primate of all Ireland (1893 till death). Alexander published four books: *Verses for Holy Seasons* (1846), *Hymns for Little Children* (1848), *Narrative Hymns for Village Schools* (1853), and *Poems on Subjects in the Old Testament* (1854, 1857). Other of Alexander's hymns that appear in modern hymnals, are "Saw You Never, in the Twilight," "His Are the Thousand Sparkling Rills," and "He Is Risen, He Is Risen."

N.H.

**ALEXANDER, FRANZ GABRIEL** (1891–1964). Born in Budapest on January 22. He studied medicine at Göttingen and later taught at the Berlin Psychoanalytic Institute. His 1924-25 lecture series, published as *The Psychoanalysis of the Total Personality* (1927; Eng. trans. 1930) developed Freud's theory of the SUPEREGO or CONSCIENCE. In 1928 he was invited to the University of Chicago, and in 1929 collaborated at Boston on a study of delinquency, published as *The Roots of Crime* (1933). Alexander returned to Chicago in 1932 to found the Chicago Institute for Psychoanalysis, which he also directed, serving concurrently in the Department of Psychiatry of the University of Illinois medical school.

Alexander and his students engaged in research on the relationship between emotional disturbances and physical illnesses, advancing the theory that psycho-somatic disease is not an attempt to express emotional conflict (Freud), but a physical expression of a constant or recurring state. He has been called the Father of Psychosomatic Medicine. In 1956 he established a research program in psychiatry and psychosomatic medicine at Mount Sinai Hospital, Los Angeles, exploring the effect of the therapist's personality on treatment.

I.C.

**ALEXANDER THE GREAT.** Alexander III, son of Philip II of Macedonia, is called "the great" because of his vast conquests in Europe, Asia Minor, the Middle East, Egypt, Persia, and Southwest Asia as far as the Indus River in India. He was born in Pella, capital of Macedonia, in 356 B.C. His father was a military genius who made himself master of Greece and the Balkans, laying the foundation for Alexander's greater empire.

Alexander was educated by the philosopher Aristotle, who drilled the concept of Greek superiority into his pupil. Upon the death of Philip II, Alexander invaded Persia—that ancient threat to Greece—with a copy of *The Iliad* by his side.

First Alexander had to subdue the tribes and city states that revolted against Macedonian rule. This he completed by 334 B.C. and crossed the Hellespont, beginning a series of campaigns from which he would not return.

Alexander first fought the Persians at the Granicus River (May-June 334 B.C.) and defeated them. During the winter western Asia Minor was conquered. At Issus, Alexander routed the Persians and turned south into Syria. At Tyre, it was necessary to lay a long siege, but the city fell in July 332 B.C. In November 332 B.C. Egypt surrendered and greeted him as pharaoh. In July 331 B.C. Alexander was in the Middle East, on the Euphrates River. The war was won when Alexander defeated the Persians on the plain of Gaugamela.

The emperor Darius was killed by traitors in 330 B.C., and Alexander had him buried with honors. He advanced eastward to the Caspian Sea and on into Afghanistan, campaigning until 328 B.C. In the summer of 327 B.C. Alexander moved into India. By spring, 326 B.C., he crossed the Indus River and fought his last battle at the Hydaspes River. When Alexander attempted to go on, his army revolted; Alexander turned back. He left India in September 325 B.C., marching across the Baluchistan Desert back to Persia.

Alexander sought to combine the Greek and Persian nobility into one great ruling force. HELLENISM applies to this marriage of East and West. While camped on the Tigris River, Alexander fell ill after an orgy, dying on June 13, 323 B.C. His empire split into several parts under various generals.

Alexander was a paradox—brave and loyal, intelligent and kind; he could also fall into drunkenness and cruelty. It must be admitted though that he did change history.

J.C.

**ALEXANDRIA.** A city in Egypt founded by ALEXANDER THE GREAT in 331 B.C. and subsequently turned into the major intellectual and cultural center of the Hellenistic world by his successors in Egypt, the PTOLEMIES. Constructed on a strip of land between Lake Mareotis and the Mediterranean Sea, the city was provided with excellent harbors and became a major commercial meeting place for Africa, Asia, and Europe.

The Ptolemies made the city into their capital. They referred to it as "Alexandria beside Egypt" to distinguish their Hellenistic (Greek) culture from the local Egyptian. After his early death, Alexander the Great's body was enshrined in the city. Lavish building projects and the city's cultural, educational, and commercial attractions made it second only to Rome in size and splendor.

The city was famous for many of its buildings, including the world-renowned *Pharos* (lighthouse), one of the seven wonders of the ancient world. Two other structures are worthy of note since they helped make Alexandria the chief intellectual center of the time. (1) The so-called Museum was like a modern university where literature, arts, and sciences were studied and state-supported professors lectured. (2) The library, founded by Ptolemy I (323–285 B.C.), eventually housed over 500,000 manuscripts collected from throughout the Greco-Roman world and even from as far away as India. Major portions of the main structure of the library and its contents appear to have been destroyed during Caesar's Egyptian campaign in 48 B.C. According to some ancient sources, Mark Antony later presented the Royal Library of Pergamum to Cleopatra to help replace the loss. The exact date of the library's final destruction remains uncertain. Scholars attribute its destruction to either Bishop Theophilus (A.D. 391) or the Muslim caliph Omar (A.D. 641). Its great splendor and use had declined years before either of these dates however.

Alexandria had a diverse population estimated at almost a million people at its zenith. Many Jews settled in the city, where they were treated as a rule with tolerance and participated in many facets of the city's life. Tradition traces the first Greek translation of the Hebrew Torah to Alexandria. Numerous outstanding Jewish scholars worked in the city. Here Aristobulus and Philo, the latter a contemporary of Jesus, labored to integrate Greek thought and philosophy with the Hebrew scriptures and Judaism. In the early Christian centuries, a famous catechetical school flourished in the city, numbering among its teachers Clement and Origen.

J.H.

**ALEXANDRIAN THEOLOGY.** A theological tradition which, although centered in Alexandria, Egypt, was widely influential throughout the Greek-speaking church, at least until the time of the Arab conquests. It combined elements of the PLATONIC tradition with others from Scripture, as had been done in the first century by the Jewish philosopher PHILO. Its most important early teachers were CLEMENT OF ALEXANDRIA and ORIGEN. But it was in the controversies regarding Christology, beginning in the fourth century, that it came to the foreground as the main rival of ANTIOCHENE THEOLOGY.

Alexandrian theology emphasized the divinity of Jesus and the union between that divinity and his humanity. The Christology of the APOLLINARIANS, condemned at the Council of Constantinople, was typically Alexandrian. At the Council of Ephesus, Cyril of Alexandria won a victory for this type of theology by having the Nestorians condemned. Finally, extreme Alexandrian theology, in the form of MONOPHYSITISM, was condemned by the COUNCIL OF CHALCEDON, and much later, as Monothelitism (the theological doctrine of the MONOTHELITES), by the Third Council of Constantinople.

J.G.

**ALFORD, HENRY** (1810-71). Best known as the author of "Come, Ye Thankful People, Come," Alford also devoted twenty years to producing a five-volume definitive edition of the Greek New Testament. Born on October 7 in London to an Anglican rector and his wife, Alford was educated at Charmouth, Ilminster, and Trinity College, Cambridge, and was ordained deacon at Exeter Cathedral in 1833 and priest at St. Margaret's, Westminster, on November 6, 1834. From 1841 to 1857 he was examiner in logic and moral philosophy at the University of London. He became dean of Canterbury Cathedral in 1857 and served there until his death.

Other Alford hymns in contemporary collections are "Forward! Be Our Watchword," and "Ten Thousand Times Ten Thousand." Alford translated and compiled hymns, and he wrote books on other subjects.

N.H.

**ALIENATION.** The phenomenon of alienation has received attention from philosophers, sociologists, psychologists, theologians, and many others. In theology, it has been chiefly theologians of existentialist background, such as BULTMANN and TILLICH, who have used the notion of alienation or ESTRANGEMENT to explain the concept of sin. In classical theology, SIN was held to be the state of being turned away from God (*aversio a Deo*). Theologians have seen this as the basic form of alienation and have claimed that it is correlated with other forms—alienation from nature or the sense of not being at home in the world; alienation from other people who, in the absence of God, no longer have a "family relationship"; and even alienation from oneself, for if we are creatures or children of God, then a relation to God is necessary for our well-being.

Many atheistic philosophers would dispute this correlation. In the last century, FEUERBACH argued that it is precisely belief in God that alienates us from our own humanity, because we project all the desirable human qualities upon God and attribute to ourselves only what is weak and base in human nature. MARX followed him in teaching that religion causes us to revolve around a false sun (God) to the neglect of our own human well-being, though he disagreed that religion is the fundamental cause of alienation, seeing it rather as a symptom of alienation in the area of work and production. NIETZSCHE and SARTRE have both taught that belief in a transcendent God is inimical to a true humanity, for if everything in the long run is decided by God, human freedom and transcendence are illusory. All of these atheistic philosophers have considered God to be an oppressive power and have believed that the abolition of God is a necessary step in the liberation of humanity for a more truly human existence.

It can hardly be denied that some theologians have presented God in oppressive terms. On the other hand, atheism as we have known it in the past hundred and fifty years or more is so far from having abolished alienation that it has rather intensified it. Theologians may have been too ready to suggest that alienation from God leads to other forms of alienation, but it is even less plausible to claim that these alienations stem from belief in God.

J.M.

**ALI ĪBN ABĪ TĀLIB.** Cousin of MUHAMMAD and husband of Muhammad's daughter Fatima; fourth caliph of the SUNNITES and first imam of the SHI'ITES. He embraced ISLAM about the age of ten and is considered the first Muslim after Muhammad's wife Khadīja. The Shi'ites give him a place of pivotal importance alongside God and the Prophet Muhammad. His tomb, near Kufa, Iraq, is an important pilgrimage center.

K./M.C.

**ALLAH.** The general name for God among Arabic speaking people. Before MUHAMMAD's time, Allah was worshiped in the Arabian peninsula as one among many deities. Most scholars say that he had an important position, perhaps as the god of weather. Muhammad charged that people of MECCA neglected Allah, the One, supreme God, in favor of lesser deities, who they hoped would intercede for them with Allah. Muhammad denied that Allah had any partners or offspring and rejected all mediators, although he apparently accepted the reality of the lesser gods.

Muhammad affirmed Allah as a jealous and personal God and as a just, yet merciful, judge. Allah is the absolute creator, sustainer, ruler, destroyer, and restorer. The QUR'AN, which MUSLIMS believe was written by Allah and revealed verbatim to Muhammad, gives many titles or qualities of God. These and others were collected to form the "ninety-nine beautiful names of God." The set of names can be divided into two groups: those emphasizing God's power and wrath, and those emphasizing God's compassion and providence. Some names show the influence of Greek philosophy: "The Existing" and "The Necessarily Existing."

Since Muhammad's death, the major influence on the understanding of Allah has been the tension between the frequently anthropomorphizing literal view and Greek-based rationalism. That conflict has produced three schools of thought: traditionalism, rationalism, and mysticism. Traditionalism teaches the acceptance of doctrine because the Prophet taught it, but rejects logical inferences from the Qur'an. For example, traditionalists reject the view that God has eyes, while affirming the Qur'an's teaching that God sees. Rationalists also reject such conclusions, but they take the opposite position from the traditionalists. For rationalists, passages in the Qur'an that speak of God as sitting on a throne or seeing are purely metaphorical. Rationalists define God through negatives; God does not have a body, God is not in only one place, God is not bound by anything. Mystics reject both traditionalism and rationalism as irrelevant and teach an intuitional, direct understanding of God. For them, Allah is pure will, not intellect. The theologian AL-GHAZZALI (A.D. 1058-1111) systematized this view, which has enjoyed wide popularity since Islam's early centuries. Ghazzali remains Islam's greatest theologian, comparable in influence to Augustine in Christianity.

K./M.C.

**ALLEGORY.** Two uses of the term are found in theology.

*Literary.* As a literary form allegory means "a figurative expression by which something is said other than what the word used normally means" (the Greek *allēgoroō* means "to say something other than" the obvious; see Gal. 4:24). Allegory can be understood as an extended metaphor or a sustained imaginative story in which characters represent virtues and vices (Spenser's *Fairie Queene* and Bunyan's *Pilgrim's Progress* are good popular examples). Parts of the OT share this literary form, namely, Judges 9:8-15; II Kings 14:9; Ezekiel 17:3-8; 31:3-14; and Song of Solomon is usually taken in this sense. At least one of Jesus' parables (Mark 12:1-11) has allegorical features in its final edition.

*Hermeneutical.* Under this head, allegory refers to a method of biblical interpretation. The key to the meaning of words is sought in their symbolic or pedagogical sense. This way of understanding a story or text goes back to pre-Christian times, as the Greek myths of the gods were spiritualized. Applied to the OT narratives by PHILO of Alexandria, it came over into the church through Paul (in a limited way, in Gal. 4:21-31) and the Letter to the Hebrews. AUGUSTINE found his authority for treating texts allegorically in II Corinthians 3:6, and he laid the foundation for the medieval "fourfold" sense of Scripture: the literal teaches what actually occurred; the allegorical what is to be believed; the moral how to behave; and the anagogical the direction to take in life.

The Reformers, especially LUTHER, opposed the allegorical method on the principle, "Do not import a meaning into scripture, but draw it out"; and modern biblical scholarship, Roman Catholic and Protestant, has accepted this caution, though with some qualification as when a "fuller sense" is found in historical detail or typology is recognized.

R.M.

**ALLELUIA.** *See* HALLELUJAH.

**ALLEN, ETHAN** (1738–89). Revolutionary War leader of the Green Mountain Boys, Allen became famous for his controversial religious and philosophical views expressed in *Reason the Only Oracle of Man* (1784), which defended DEISM and attacked the Bible and "priestcraft." Born in Litchfield, Connecticut, January 10, 1738, he scored a major victory for the American patriots by leading an expedition, joined by a small force led by Benedict Arnold, in the capturing of Fort Ticonderoga on May 10, 1775.

N.H.

**ALLEN, ROLAND** (1868–1947). Anglican clergyman and missions enthusiast. Allen was sent to China in 1895, but returned for health reasons in 1904 to take over an English parish church. He spent World War I as a chaplain on a hospital ship and in the 1920s became active with others in the stimulation of interest in foreign missions. He traveled widely to mission fields but was best known for his writings on behalf of changes in missionary methods. He urged indigenization of the churches, use of voluntary clergy, and other ideas that were quite revolutionary for his time.

W.G.

**ALLPORT, GORDON.** (1897–1967). Born on November 11, in Montezuma, Indiana. Allport was appointed a social science instructor at Harvard in 1924, he became professor of psychology in 1930, later holding an office in social ethics. His important introductory work was *Personality—A Psychological Interpretation* (1937). His basic theory was that while adult motives develop from infantile drives, adults are independent of those drives. He stressed a functional, personal autonomy in motives and structure. Thus he examined a social concern in *The Nature of Prejudice* (1954) and the religious dimension in *The Individual and His Religion: A Psychological Interpretation* (1950). He died on October 9 in Cambridge, Massachusetts.

I.C.

**ALL SAINTS' DAY.** A feast day celebrated on November 1, in memory of all martyrs and, by extension, all deceased Christians. The feast probably originated with the dedication of the oratory in St. Peter's built by Pope Gregory III, in which, according to tradition, the bodies of the apostles and martyrs were buried.

J.C.

**ALL SOULS' DAY.** A feast day celebrated on November 2, memorializing all people who have died in the Christian faith without suffering martyrdom (*see* MARTYR). The feast was established by Odilo of Cluny around A.D. 988 for the members of his order. It was later extended to celebrate all those who have departed with the sign of faith.

J.C.

**ALMS.** A Greek word used only in the NT. Philanthropy, the "haves" sharing with the "have nots," is an almost universal practice, often regarded as a religious duty. In some societies, the beggar, who makes opportunity for almsgiving, is considered a holy person. The strong providing for the weak helps the whole group survive. Pity is another motive for almsgiving.

Among the Hebrews, almsgiving, or care for the needy and hospitality to the STRANGER, was regarded as a virtue from early times. Blameless and upright Job "delivered the poor," "the fatherless," "the widow," "the blind" and "the lame." Conversely, Isaiah 32:6 calls "the fool" one who deprives "the thirsty of drink" and leaves "the craving of the hungry unsatisfied." Giving mutual care came to be characteristic of Hebrew homelife (Prov. 31:20) and kinship (Ruth 2:9, 14-16; Esth. 2:7). The Hebrew traditions of philanthropy may relate to their memories of wanderings in the desert, a hostile physical and social environment where care for one another was essential to survival.

In the OT law, almsgiving as philanthropy is related to SACRIFICES, OFFERINGS, and TITHES. Tithes to Yahweh, regarded somewhat as rent to be paid to the landlord, were collected in products of the land, which were then distributed to the poor (Deut. 14:28-29). In OT thought, there is a distinctive motivation for pity, compassion, and almsgiving. Reported in the Pentateuch, the Prophets, and the Psalms is the injunction to remember that "you were a slave in Egypt" (Exod. 13:8, 14; Lev. 23:43; Deut. 10:19; 16:2, 12). Remembering Yahweh's compassionate "mighty acts" that released the people from bondage was to prompt the Hebrews to be as compassionate to the needy as Yahweh had been to their forefathers.

In later Judaism, with the Temple no longer standing, the duty of almsgiving took the place of the obligations to provide sacrifices. Good deeds to the poor deliver one from death (Prov. 11:4; Tob. 4:10-11), bring happiness (Prov. 14:21), lengthen social tranquility (Dan. 4:27) and individual life (Tob. 12:8-9).

Jesus assumed that his Jewish followers would continue their giving of alms (Matt. 6:2). He was not as concerned with the amount given (Mark 12:41-44; Luke 21:1-4) as with the spirit and manner of the giving (Matt. 6:1-4; Mark 12:41-44; Luke 11:4; 12:35). Recognizing "how hard it is for those who have riches to enter the kingdom of God" (Luke 18:24), Jesus recommended giving as a way to follow him, thus, to escape servitude to mammon (Matt. 6:24; Luke 16:13). Giving, Jesus taught, brings rewards in this life (Luke 6:38) and "a treasure in the heavens" (Luke 12:33; Matt. 25:31-46). In fact "there is more happiness in giving than in receiving" (Acts 20:35 TEV).

Paul urged "cheerful" almsgiving (II Cor. 9:7) to benefit fellow Christians near at hand (Gal. 6:2, 5) and also those far away; such as the "saints at Jerusalem" (Acts 24:17). Barnabas (Acts 4:37), Dorcas (Acts 9:36, 39), and Cornelius are among those commended in the NT for their charity.

In Christian ethics, and also in Christian theology, giving has a special place. The emphasis in John 3:16 falls on the verb "gave" (compare I John 5:11). Paul wrote of Christ as being rich but choosing to become poor "so that by his poverty you might become rich" (II Cor. 8:9; see also Phil. 2:6; Gal. 1:4; 2:20; Eph. 5:2, 25; I Tim. 2:6; Tit. 2:14). In Christian thought, almsgiving is less a duty than a life-style, an emulation of the self-sacrificing way of God in Christ and God's love (I Cor. 13:3).

P.L.G.

*Alpha and Omega*

**ALPHA AND OMEGA.** The first and last letters of the Greek alphabet, thus a phrase signifying "the beginning and the end." Revelation 1:8; 21:6; 22:13 present Christ declaring, "I am the Alpha and the Omega, the first and the last, the beginning and the end." This echoes Isaiah 44:6 and 48:12, where God declares, "I am He, I am the first, and I am the last." The phrase asserts the eternal divine nature of Christ.

J.C.

**ALTAR.** A place or structure for the purpose of making various forms of sacrificial offerings. The Hebrew word for altar, *mizbe'ah,* derived from the root *zbh,* meaning "to slaughter," suggests that originally the altar was the place where the slaughter of animals for sacrifice occurred (see Gen. 22:9). In

*A reconstruction of the altar of burnt offering*

the Bible, however, animals are never slaughtered on the altar, but offerings of things not slaughtered (grain, wine, incense) were made on altars. Altars, like sacrificial offerings, were common features in practically all ancient religions. Many examples have been unearthed in archaeological excavations. Altars were sometimes given names (El-Elohe-Israel—the God of Israel, Gen. 33:20; The LORD is Peace, Judg. 6:24).

*Construction.* Three types of material were utilized for building altars: earth, stone, and metal. The law on altars in Exodus 20:24-25 stipulates three conditions about their construction. (a) They are to be built of earth or stone. (b) If from stone then it must be from unworked not "hewn stones; for if you wield your tool upon it [the stone] you profane it." (c) Altars were also to be built without steps "that your nakedness be not exposed on it." Descriptions of the tabernacle and some narratives have references to bronze altars, but no OT laws mention altars constructed from metal (see the next section).

Although altars of earth are spoken of in the OT, no description of these is given; perhaps they were simply constructed of artificial mounds of earth. When the Syrian general Naaman returned home from Israel, he requested two mule-loads of earth since he had promised that "your servant [Naaman] will not offer burnt offering or sacrifice to any god but the LORD" (II Kings 5:17). This suggests the use of earthen altars. Stone altars could be natural formations (Judg. 13:19-20; I Sam. 6:14; 14:33-35; I Kings 1:9), hastily made artificial heaps (Gen. 31:46-54; Exod. 24:4; Josh. 4:1-8; I Kings 18:31-32), or well-built constructions (II Kings 16:10-16). Although no OT reference notes such construction, earth and stone were utilized to build the Israelite altar excavated at the site of ancient Arad. Horns or upraised corners seem to have been a feature of well-built altars (Exod. 27:2; 29:12; I Kings 2:28). The exact functions of such horns are unknown, though one function was probably to prevent the offering and burning material from rolling off the top.

*Descriptions of Specific Altars.* Two altars were in the Jerusalem Temple complex. Their counterparts are presented as part of the tabernacle as well. The altar of burnt offering associated with the tabernacle was 5 x 5 x 3 cubits, made of acacia wood, and overlaid with bronze (Exod. 27:1-8; 38:1-7). It was conceived as being hollow and portable, perhaps to be filled with stones and earth when in use. The incense altar, used within the sacred tent, was 1 x 1 x 2 cubits and overlaid with gold (Exod. 30:1-10; 37:25-28).

Reference is made to these two altars in conjunction with Solomon's Temple. The incense altar, located within the Temple, is described (I Kings 6:20-22; 7:48) but, surprisingly, no description is given in I Kings of the bronze sacrificial altar, which stood in front of the Temple (see I Kings 8:64; 9:25; II Kings 16:14-15). It is stated earlier that David built an altar on the site of the future Temple (II Sam. 24:18-25). Second Chronicles 4:1 says this altar was 20 x 20 x 10 cubits in size, which would certainly have required steps or a ramp (see Exod. 20:26; 28:42-43).

In the second half of the eighth century B.C., King Ahaz replaced the bronze altar before the Temple with a new altar, apparently of stone, based on a type he had seen in Damascus (II Kings 16:10-15), which required steps or a ramp (II Kings 16:12). The bronze altar was set aside for the private use of the king (II Kings 16:15).

In the description of the new Temple in Ezekiel, there is a description of the altar in the prophet's vision (Ezek. 43:13-17). The altar, with four graduated tiers, was twelve cubits, or twenty and a half feet tall (here the long cubit of twenty and one-half inches is used [Ezek. 43:13] rather than the normal cubit of eighteen inches). The incense altar, of wood, is also described (Ezek. 41:22).

The altars in the Temple of Herod are described in rabbinic sources (the Mishnah and Talmud). Consisting of four graduated tiers, the sacrificial altar was 32 x 32 cubits at the base and ten cubits high (50 x 50 x 15 according to JOSEPHUS, *Wars,* v. 225). The top of the altar was reached by a ramp thirty-two cubits long and sixteen cubits wide. The incense or gold altar is said to have stood in the center of the sanctuary.

*Uses of Altars.* Altars were used for several purposes: for the burning of sacrifices, both animal and grain; for rituals involving animal blood, which was smeared on the horns or thrown on the sides or the base of the altar; and for the burning of incense. Altars were also places of asylum. One could claim "sanctuary" rights by fleeing to the altar or by grasping its horns (Exod. 21:14; I Kings 1:50-51; 2:28-34). An altar could also serve as witness to group relations (Gen. 31:46-54; Josh. 22:21-27) and oaths could be sworn by it (Matt. 23:18-20).

*Theological Aspects.* Altars possessed a special sanctity and were considered most holy (Exod. 29:37). In the Temple complex in Jerusalem, the altar was part of the center of the universe, according to priestly theology. The sanctity of the altar was exceeded only by the sanctity of the Holy of Holies.

Only priestly personnel could approach the altar although non-priests could view the courtyard altar. It was upon the altar where the purifying and purging sacrifices were made, where life symbolized by blood was given back to God, its origin, and where the presence of the Divine and the affairs of the human met. It was in the rituals of the altar that mediation between the heavenly and the earthly worlds occurred in a concentrated manner.

In some expressions of early Christian thought, the significance of the altar is retained although spiritualized. Revelation 6:9 speaks of the heavenly altar in the heavenly sanctuary where the souls of the martyrs await vindication. Here the angel of God mingles incense with the prayers of the saints to be presented to the Divine (Rev. 8:3-4) and from this altar fire is flung upon earth (Rev. 8:5). Hebrews 13:10-15 claims that the (heavenly?) altar excels that of the old altar and that the fruit of the lips is the sacrifice of praise. After the destruction of the Temple, Judaism also preserved and spiritualized some of the imagery and importance of the altar by seeing one's deeds of charity and lovingkindness as forms of sacrifice, by interpreting the everyday table as the replacement of the altar, and by understanding the Jewish community as a temple. (*See* SACRIFICES, TEMPLES.)

J.H.

**ALTHAUS, PAUL** (1886–1966). A Lutheran theologian. He held professorial posts in Germany, notably at Erlangen. While his initial interests were in Gospel studies, he gained fame as a systematic theologian, writing a major book surveying the entire range of Christian doctrine (*Die christliche Wahrheit,* eighth ed. 1969). In his last years his chief preoccupation was with LUTHER's theology and eschatology.

R.M.

**ALVARS.** From TAMIL meaning "one who has dived" or "one who is immersed." Twelve poets and saints of South India who lived about A.D. 650–940 celebrated for their utter "immersion" in the love of God in the form of VISHNU. They did much to advance the growing BHAKTI or devotionalist movement, providing passionate and moving poetic vehicles for its fervent love of God modeled on the raptures and vicissitudes of human love.

The *Alvar Tirumankai* (800–870), for example, sings of the anguish of separation from the divine Lord in the language of a lover parted from the beloved, while *Vittucittan* focused on the life of the infant KRISHNA, believed to be an AVATAR or human appearance of Vishnu. His daughter Kotai wrote with deep romantic feeling of the youthful Krishna, sublime lover of the gopis or milkmaids, whose fervent love for the handsome god was in turn the model of the devotee's. The Alvars did much to develop the cultural, literary, and religious self-consciousness of the South Indian. The ranks of these wandering singers included outcasts and both sexes; in this they demonstrated the potential universalism of the Bhakti way.

R.E.

**AMALEK/AMALEKITES** (meaning "warlike," or "dwellers in the vale"). Amalek is listed in Genesis 36:12, 16, as the son of Eliphaz and the grandson of Esau, whose descendants are the Edomites (Deut. 2:4). The Amalekites, a nomadic tribe, known from the age of the patriarchs (Gen. 14:7), wandered throughout the Transjordan, Negeb, and Sinai deserts (I Sam. 15:5; 27:8). At one time they had a king named Agag (I Sam. 15:8; Num. 24:7) and a "city of Amalek" in the Negeb (I Sam. 15:5).

Moses commanded Israel to establish friendly relations with the Amalekites, "your brethren" (Deut. 2:4-6) but, historically, the Amalekites, along with the EDOMITES, were prominent among the enemies of Israel (Ps. 83:7), beginning with the Exodus' battle of Rephedim (Exod. 17:8-9), a treacherous attack (Deut. 25:17-19; Judg. 10:12; I Sam. 15:2). The abortive attempt by Israel to enter Canaan from the south was repelled by Canaanites supported by the Amalekites (Num. 14:45). The Amalekites were particularly troublesome during the time of the Judges. They defeated Israel and took "the city of palms" (Jericho? Judg. 3:13). Along with the camel-nomads, the Midianites, the Amalekites threatened Israel at the time of Gideon (Judg. 6:3, 33; 7:12). Saul ruthlessly destroyed Agag's people (I Sam. 15:7), and Amalekites wounded him in a battle before he fell upon his own sword (I Sam. 31:3-5; II Sam. 1:8).

David conducted raids against the Amalekites (I Sam. 27:8-10; 30:1-20). Once, in the time of Hezekiah, Judah was victorious over the Amalekites (I Chr. 4:43). Some Amalekites may have been among the Idumeans who, from the Maccabean period to the time of Herod the Great, were pushed out of Edom by the Nabateans into southern Judah.

P.L.G.

**AMANA COMMUNITY.** A production and marketing cooperative in Iowa, descended from the Amana Society or Community of True Inspiration. Incorporated in 1859, it covered seven villages on 26,000 acres on the Iowa River, southwest of Cedar Rapids. Community members were followers of a pietistic sect from the rural Rhineland of Germany, founded in 1714 by a tailor, Michael Krausent; a carpenter, Christian Metz; and a domestic, Barbara Heinemann. Calling their group the New Community, they rejected the institutional church and based their ideas on the Bible, interpreted by dreams, visions, and revelations. Community of goods or communism was adopted in their first American settlement, called Ebenezer, established by Metz in 1843 near Buffalo, New York. The group of eight hundred migrated to Iowa in 1855 in search of more land. They finally became a secular corporation in 1932, producing kitchen appliances.

N.H.

**AMARNA, TELL EL.** The modern name of ruins on the east bank of the Nile River, 190 miles south of Cairo, Egypt. The site is that of the city of AKHETATON, built about 1375 B.C. by Iknaton (Amenophis IV) as the nation's capital in place of Thebes. He and his lovely queen, Nefertiti, had abandoned the worship of Amon as the national deity and erected a new city, Akhetaton, on virgin soil, which they dedicated to the sole worship of Aton, the sun-god, as the official religion of Egypt.

Archaeologists, beginning in 1891 and following, thoroughly excavated this one-level site, which stretches five miles along the Nile. Its center, a great, open-air temple, nearly one-half mile long by three hundred yards wide, was connected by a ceremonial bridge to the royal palaces. These consisted of rooms around a central court. The walls were decorated with colorfully painted, lively scenes of everyday life. Each had a temple to Aton and a landscaped garden around a pool.

A chance find from the records office yielded about three hundred clay tablets written in cuneiform script, first-hand documents from the Amarna period (1379–1362 B.C.). Included were letters to the pharaoh from vassal princes of the empire, from Syria and Palestine as well as from kings of Assyria, Babylonia, and Mitanni. These have shed much light on those times.

At Iknaton's death, his revolutionary religion was repudiated. Akhetaton was abandoned; the capital was returned to Thebes. Some have thought that in Moses' Egyptian education, he may have learned something about Iknaton's monolatrous religion.

P.L.G.

**AMASA** (meaning "burden bearer"). A son of Jether (or Ithra) the Ishmaelite, and Abigail, David's sister (II Sam. 17:25-26; I Chr. 2:17).

(1) Absalom, David's son, appointed his cousin Amasa, David's nephew, head of a rebel army (II Sam. 17:25). David forgave Amasa and, in an apparent effort to appease Absalom's former supporters after the rebellion was quelled, David gave Amasa command of the national army, replacing Joab, another of David's nephews. Amasa was ordered to assemble the army in three days, but he failed to do so (II Sam. 20:4-5). Joab found Amasa, and treacherously and brutally murdered him. David did not forget this. On his death bed, he condemned Joab and charged Solomon that, after David's death, Solomon should condemn (I Kings 2:5) and then execute Joab, which was done (I Kings 2:32).

(2) Son of Hadlai, an Ephraimite chief. In the time of Ahaz, following Pekah's victory over Judah,

officers of the Israelite army proposed to take the Judean prisoners to Samaria and make them slaves. Oded, the prophet, rebuked them. Other officers, including Amasa, clothed and outfitted them from the war spoils and reunited them with their families at Jericho (II Chr. 28:8-15).

P.L.G.

**AMBROSE OF MILAN.** Bishop of Milan, A.D. 374–97, and one of four theologians counted as the great "DOCTORS" of the Western church—the others are Jerome, Augustine, and Gregory the Great. He was a civil official in Milan and not yet baptized, although a believer, when he was unexpectedly elected bishop. A defender of orthodoxy against ARIANISM and of the powerless against the powerful, he clashed with Empress Justina, who defended Arianism, and with Emperor Theodosius, whom he excommunicated for ordering a massacre. Several of the hymns that he composed are still used in Christian worship, as is the ATHANASIAN CREED, which some scholars attribute to him. He was instrumental in the conversion of Augustine, and also in promoting Eastern theology and monasticism in the West, which he probably owed to his knowledge of Greek.

J.G.

**AMEN.** A Hebrew word meaning "to trust," showing assent to an oath, acceptance of an utterance, or approval of a course of action. Jesus used the word according to the Gospels, and early Christians used it regularly to mean "yes." Its use denotes faithfulness, assurance, assent, certainty, and trust.

J.C.

**AMENHOTEP IV.** *See* AKHENATON.

**AMERICAN BAPTIST CHURCHES IN THE U.S.A.** *See* BAPTIST CHURCHES.

**AMERICAN BIBLE SOCIETY.** A non-profit association founded in 1816 to promote the circulation and reading of the Bible. The ABS makes special efforts to make available free copies of the Scriptures to the poor, to members of the armed forces, and to prisoners and others who might not have access to the Holy Scriptures. For almost 170 years, the ABS has faithfully supplied the Scriptures to hundreds of thousands of people in at least one hundred translations and editions, worldwide. Before 1816, there were 128 Bible societies in the United States. The society was incorporated in 1841 although overseas work began in 1836.

J.C.

**AMERICAN BOARD OF COMMISSIONERS FOR FOREIGN MISSIONS.** The first foreign mission board founded in the United States, organized at Bradford, Massachusetts, by the Massachusetts General Association (Congregational) in response to a petition from four Andover Seminary students. Predominantly Congregational, the board avoided the term in its name and thus served as the foreign missionary agency for the Presbyterian and Dutch Reformed churches until they formed their own missionary boards. Barely able to provide passage, the board sent its first five missionaries to India in 1812. A stirring of interest and support in the churches, however, soon made it possible for the board to send missionaries to several other countries. Committed to an institutional as well as evangelistic approach, the ABCFM rendered outstanding service in the founding of colleges and schools. In 1961 the ABCFM merged into the United Church Board for World Ministries of the recently founded United Church of Christ.

W.G.

**AMERICAN COUNCIL OF CHRISTIAN CHURCHES.** An organization of ultra-Fundamentalist sects formed in 1941, to oppose what Fundamentalists consider the apostasy of other churches. The ACCC was formed on September 17, 1941, in New York by the Bible Presbyterian Church and the Bible Protestant Church. The guiding spirit in its foundation and throughout its history has been the Reverend Carl McIntyre, an opponent of the National Council of Churches and the World Council of Churches. Essentially polemic, the ACCC has no authority over its members—now grown to fifteen sects—but serves as a voice in affairs where joint witness and united action are felt to be required. In actual practice, the ACCC is mainly preoccupied with making critical pronouncements on the NCC and the WCC. In fact, the ACCC often holds "shadow" conferences in the cities where the NCC and WCC hold their meetings, and at the same time.

J.C.

**AMERICAN ETHICAL UNION.** The Ethical Culture movement was begun in New York City in 1876 by FELIX ADLER (1851–1933). He considered Judaism and Christianity mistaken in making ethics dependent on religious dogma. Inspired by IMMANUEL KANT, Adler promoted the betterment of human life based on neither theism nor atheism.

Adler's original goals included sexual purity, help for the working classes, and continued intellectual development. Ethical Culture was promoted similarly to a religion through Sunday meetings with music, readings, and an address, plus rituals for marriage and death.

The society was prominent in promoting social reforms and founding workingmen's schools, settlement houses, visiting nurses' programs, legal aid, and model tenements. In 1886 Stanton Coit, who had taken the movement to London, also founded University Settlement on New York's lower East Side. John Lovejoy Elliot founded the Hudson Guild, the Henry Booth House in Chicago, and Southwark Neighborhood House in Philadelphia.

Today the American Ethical Union is the national organization of about thirty societies in the U.S. It trains ministers or Ethical leaders, publishes literature, supports national programs on race relations, ecology, nontheistic conscientious objection, separation of church and state, and the protection of civil liberties.

N.H.

## AMERICAN FRIENDS SERVICE COMMITTEE.

An organization, founded by the Society of FRIENDS (QUAKERS) that endeavors to promote programs of social service and public information in the areas of peace, disarmament, environmental issues, social justice, and world hunger. Founded in 1917, by American Quakers, the AFSC aims to relieve human suffering and to find new approaches to world peace and to nonviolent social change.

The AFSC works overseas in refugee relief, rehabilitation, peace education, and development of self-help community programs. At home, the organization offers programs on minority group problems in employment, housing, and civil rights.

In 1947, the AFSC and the British Friends Service Council shared the Nobel Peace Prize for their humanitarian efforts. The AFSC is a major promoter of peace in the world and strongly supports campaigns for a nuclear freeze bill in the United States Congress.

J.C.

## AMERICAN SCHOOLS OF ORIENTAL RESEARCH (ASOR).

An association of scholars working in archaeological, historical, and biblical fields, as well as interested laypeople, founded in 1900 to initiate, encourage, and support research on the peoples and cultures of the Near East and to promote public understanding of the area and its peoples. ASOR has a staff of 25 and 2,447 members. Its work consists of offering fellowships, visiting professorships, study and travel grants, and conducting archaeological research into the culture and peoples of the Near East. The association maintains libraries in Amman, Jordan; Nicosia, Cyprus; and Jerusalem. It publishes several journals and newsletters, including its quarterly bulletin, the *Biblical Archeologist*, the Annual (a monograph series), and *The Journal of Cuneiform Studies* (semiannually). Many colleges, universities, theological seminaries, libraries, and research institutes maintain membership in the ASOR. The association maintains data bases for research and sponsors student competitions. There is one major ASOR committee on archaeological policy.

J.C.

## AMERICAN STANDARD VERSION.

The decision of British authorities to revise the KING JAMES VERSION of the Bible in 1870 resulted in the production of the REVISED VERSION (RV) or English Revised Version (ERV) of 1881-85. American scholars, however, preferred to make additional changes, and these were included in the American Standard Version (ASV) of 1901. Both the British and American versions tended to be stilted in style, probably because the translators had been mandated to retain as much of the KJV as possible, and also because they were committed to a literal translation of the Greek and Hebrew texts. Except for a few scholars, most readers spurned both the RV and ASV. This probably can be explained by this statement of the British revisers: "In regard to the language of the Authorized Version, the Revisers have thought it no part of their duty to reduce it to conformity with modern usage, and have therefore left untouched all archaisms, whether of language or construction, which though not in familiar use cause a reader no embarrassment and lead to no misunderstanding." (*See also* BIBLE TRANSLATIONS, ENGLISH.)

R.H.

## AMERICAN TRACT SOCIETY.

In 1814 the New England Tract Society was founded in Boston. Nine years later it became the American Tract Society and in 1825 became truly national through a merger with a New York society. It blanketed the growing nation with evangelical tracts, magazines, and books, particularly for children.

N.H.

## AMES, EDWARD SCRIBNER (1870–1958).

Philosopher and liberal theologian, Ames was born April on April 21 to Lucius Bowles and Adaline Scribner Ames in Eau Clair, Wisconsin. After graduating from Drake University (1889, 1891) and Yale Divinity School (1892), he became, like his father, a Disciples of Christ minister.

The first recipient of a Ph.D. from the University of Chicago philosophy department, he taught there from 1900 to 1935. From 1900 to 1940 he was minister at the Disciples' University Church, and from 1937 to 1945 he was dean of the Disciples' Divinity House. He wrote *The Psychology of Religious Experience* (1910), *Religion* (1929), and his autobiography *Beyond Theology* (1959).

N.H.

## AMES, WILLIAM (1576–1633).

English Puritan theologian. He received the B.A. and M.A. from Christ's College, Cambridge. A moderate non-Separatist, he emigrated to Holland. He was present for the SYNOD OF DORT. After successful debates with the Arminian Nicolaas Grevinckhoven (*see* ARMINIANISM) he became professor of theology at the University of Franeker in Friesland, 1622–32.

His *Marrow of Sacred Divinity* (1642) became the prime theological text for New England PURITANS. Equally important was his *Cases of Conscience* (1639), a book on moral theology. He was about to leave for America when he died in Rotterdam on November 14.

N.H.

**AMICE.** A liturgical VESTMENT that covers the head of priests and brothers on the way to and from MASS. It is an oblong linen cloth, placed on the head and fastened about the neck with cords. It originated as a head cover for the priest in the eighth century.

J.C.

**AMISH.** Followers of Jacob Amman (1644?–1730?), a MENNONITE preacher in Berne, Switzerland, who about 1693 began to urge stricter observance of earlier practices, particularly the shunning of excommunicated members. His teachings also attracted followers from Alsace-Lorraine and the Palatinate. Under persecution they decided to emigrate to America and began arriving in Pennsylvania as early as 1727. Large numbers arrived in the 1740s. They settled first in Berks and Lancaster counties of Pennsylvania, but also spread to Ohio, Indiana, and Ontario, Canada. The most conservative, or Old Order, refuse to use electricity or automobiles, preferring horses and buggies. They total more than 80,000 members in 535 congregations in the U.S. and about 700 members in 14 congregations in Canada. The Beachy Amish, or followers of Moses Beachy, decided in 1927 to allow members to drive cars and to have meetinghouses. Their membership is nearly 5,000 in 77 congregations in the U.S.

The Amish are noted for their conservative manners, dress, and language. Opposed to church buildings or formal organization, the Old Order meets in houses or barns. They have no colleges or denominational structures. Recently they have had difficulties with the government and have been the source of much controversy concerning their desire to educate their own children rather than send them to public schools and their resistance to paying Social Security taxes because they care for their own elderly.

N.H.

**AMMON/AMMONITES.** A Semitic people occupying central trans-Jordan along the headwaters of the Jabbok, who for seven centuries (about 1250–580 B.C.) enjoyed political autonomy and regularly affected the history of biblical Israel.

*Origins.* Although hard facts about Ammonite origins are scant, Israelite tradition presents Ammon as a hostile (Amos 1:13-15; Zeph. 2:8-11; Jer. 49:1-5; Ezek. 25:1-7), yet kindred people who descended from Ben-ammi, the second son of Lot, Abraham's nephew (Gen. 19:38). Commonly called the "sons of Ammon" *(benê 'ammôn),* they dispossessed the Zamzummim, an unknown prehistoric people (Deut. 2:20). The territory of the Ammonites undoubtedly overlapped that of the Amorites with whom they were closely related (Num. 21:21-24).

*Ammon and Early Israel.* In the mid-thirteenth century B.C., the Ammonites consisted of small tribal groups clustered around Rabbath-Ammon (modern Amman), their subsequent capital. Thus, in the era of the conquest, Israel bypassed this settlement (Deut.

2:37). Soon the Ammonites expanded into an organized state, first recognized in the story of temporary Benjaminite enslavement under Eglon, king of Moab, who employed Ammonite allies (Judg. 3:12-13).

The Ammonites next tried to penetrate northward into Gilead. Resident Israelites rallied around Jephthah and successfully curbed the aggression (Judg. 11:4-10, 29-33). Ammon still entertained expansionist dreams. In about 1020 B.C. the Ammonites, under King Nahash, besieged Jabesh-gilead and disgraced its citizens with repugnant terms of surrender (I Sam. 11:1-3). The city was magnificently liberated by Saul (11:8-11), who dealt Ammon a stunning defeat.

*Ammon and Monarchic Israel.* Unlike Saul, David befriended Nahash (II Sam. 10:2). But the odious behavior of Nahash's successor, Hanun, toward Israelite ambassadors made renewed warfare inevitable. Though Aramean allies assisted Ammon, Israelite troops won the first campaign (10:13-14). A non-decisive victory, however, required a second campaign whereupon Israel overtook Rabbah, the Ammonite capital, and reduced the Ammonites to vassalage (12:26-31). Later, when Absalom's rebellion necessitated David's flight to Mahanaim, Hanun's brother, Shobi, aided David, perhaps as a deputy appointed by David to govern Ammon (17:27). During Solomon's reign, friendly relations persisted. Among the king's Ammonite wives was Naamah, the future mother of Rehoboam, who succeeded Solomon (I Kings 14:21). To meet his wives' religious needs, Solomon constructed a sanctuary for Milcom (MOLECH), the chief Ammonite deity (11:7).

Following the collapse of the united Israelite monarchy (922 B.C.), Ammon regained independence. In 853 Ammon joined other western states (including Israel), which in the Battle of Qarqar checked Assyria's westward expansion under Shalmaneser III. Two strong eighth-century Judean monarchs, Uzziah and Jotham, exacted tribute from Ammon (II Chr. 26:8; 27:5-6). When Jehoiakim rebelled against Babylon in about 600 B.C. (II Kings 24:2), Nebuchadnezzar unleashed Ammonite guerrillas to harass Judah. Nevertheless, Ammonite representatives soon participated in a Jerusalem meeting of western states to discuss anti-Babylonian strategies (Jer. 27:3).

*Ammon and Post-monarchic Israel.* Following Jerusalem's destruction (587 B.C.), Baalis, king of Ammon, successfully dispatched Ishmael, a Judean refugee, to assassinate Gedaliah, whom Nebuchadnezzar had appointed as governor of Judah (Jer. 40:14). Presumably Baalis aspired to bring the Judean remnant within the orbit of Ammonite sovereignty. While Ammon soon fell victim to Arab invasions, order again prevailed under Persian rule. In about 440 B.C. Tobiah, leader of a Jewish colony in Ammon, joined Sanballat, the Samarian governor, in opposing

Nehemiah's efforts to rebuild Jerusalem (Neh. 2:19; 4:7-8). But Nehemiah prevailed and soon censured Judean-Ammonite intermarriages (13:23-27), as did Ezra (Ezra 9:1-2). Subsequently, Ammon was overrun by the Nabateans and then claimed by the Egyptian Ptolemies following the conquest of Alexander the Great.

J.K.K.

Courtesy of the Metropolitan Museum of Art. Gift of Edward S. Harkness, 1926

*Statuette of the Egyptian god Amon*

**AMON-RE.** Egyptian sun deity esteemed as "king of the gods." Egyptian legend celebrated the sun-god RE as Egypt's first ruler. Thus the pharaoh was regarded as the "son of Re," emanating from his body at birth and returning thereto at death. Re's home, Heliopolis, was a significant religious center in Egypt. During the second millennium B.C., Re was amalgamated with other important deities, one of which was Amon. With his sanctuary at the Egyptian capital of THEBES, the air-god Amon (the "Hidden One") was manifested in both wind and vital breath. Despite their functional fusion as the supreme national god, Amon-Re, they remained separate air

and sun deities. The Egyptian urge toward MONO-THEISM was therefore limited.

J.K.K.

**AMORITES.** From the Akkadian word *Amurru* meaning "westerner." Ancient Semitic inhabitants of a large, indeterminate territory situated west of Mesopotamia which likely encompassed Syria and portions of Palestine.

*Extra-biblical Evidence.* Mesopotamian cuneiform texts dating to the latter half of the third millennium B.C. yield the earliest mention of the Amurru as a diverse body of northwest Semitic-speaking stock breeders and the region they occupied. Having originated from the Arabian desert, these Amorites dominated all Mesopotamia after the collapse of the (Sumerian) Third Dynasty of Ur (about 1950 B.C.). Amorite leadership centered in the city-state of Mari (Tel Hariri) on the upper Euphrates, whose monarch Zimri-lim (about 1730–1697) was most effective. Later it moved to Babylon during the rule of Hammurabi (about 1728–1686), the best known of the Amorite kings of the First Dynasty of Babylon. By 1750 the Amorites had so thoroughly disrupted ongoing life in Syro-Palestinian territory and so fully taken over that it had become the main segment of its Canaanite population. This original Amorite stock probably counted among its descendants many of the Hebrews and Arameans of the OT.

*Biblical Evidence.* Presumably the term "Amorite" was originally applied to Palestinian inhabitants who, prior to the Israelite conquest, occupied the territory east of the River Jordan (Num. 21:13; Deut. 4:46; Josh. 24:8). The term eventually included inhabitants living in mountainous regions west of the Jordan (Deut. 1:7, 19-20), if not the whole of cis-Jordan (Josh. 24:15; Judg. 6:10). Jerusalem was likely an Amorite city in pre-Israelite days (Ezek. 16:3) as were Hebron and Lachish (Josh. 10:5). Two Transjordanian Amorite kingdoms are of particular interest in biblical tradition—Heshbon, ruled by Sihon, and Bashan, ruled by Og (Num. 21:21-35; Josh. 2:10; 9:10; compare Jdt. 5:15). Both fell to the Israelites as they migrated toward the Land of Promise.

Reference to the Gibeonites as "the remnant of the Amorites" (II Sam. 21:2) demonstrates that whereas the pre-Israelite population of Palestine is often designated in the Bible as Canaanite, this is not always so. In Numbers 13:29 the Amorites and Canaanites are distinguished respectively as inhabitants of the highlands and coastal plain (compare Josh. 5:1), and once the Amorites are even located in the plain (Judg. 1:34-35). Owing to their reputed descent from the Rephaim (giants), the Amorites are presented in a few OT passages as a race of extraordinarily tall and strong people (Deut. 3:11; Amos 2:9). This legendary element, however, fails to advance our present-day quest for the Amorites of history.

The Israelite conquest did not rid Palestine of all Amorite elements (Judg. 1:34-36). In Samuel's day they lived peaceably with Israel (I Sam. 7:14), and in Solomon's day they were a useful source of conscripted brawn for royal building projects (I Kings 9:20-21).

J.K.K.

**AMOS.** The earliest of all the biblical prophets to leave a book in his own name (*see* AMOS, Book of). The only biographical information about Amos available is that supplied by his book. Its superscription (Amos 1:1) places Amos' ministry during the reigns of JEROBOAM II in Israel (786–746 B.C.) and UZZIAH in Judah (783–742 B.C.). Though he was "among the shepherds of Tekoa," a village that lay about five miles south of Bethlehem in the southern kingdom of Judah, his prophetic ministry carried him to the central royal sanctuary at BETHEL (7:13) in the heart of the northern kingdom of Israel. There he threatened the nation with exile and King Jeroboam with death by the sword (7:11).

In defending his mission to Amaziah, the priest of Bethel, Amos dissociated himself from other prophets: "I am no prophet, nor a prophet's son; but I am a herdsman, and a dresser of sycamore trees" (7:14). This suggests that he belonged to no band of charismatic "prophets" (see I Sam. 10:9-13), prophetic school (II Kings 2:15-18), or association of cult prophets (Mic. 3:5-12), but had unexpectedly received his own fresh summons from God to leave the flock and to undertake his dangerous errand.

W.S.T.

**AMOS** (Book of). The third of the twelve shorter prophetic writings of the Hebrew Bible, and the earliest in point of time. Although the 146 verses of the book can be read aloud in less than half an hour, the book contains all we know of the life work of the prophet AMOS, who preached at the royal sanctuary at BETHEL (7:13) in the northern kingdom of Israel during the latter years of the reign of JEROBOAM II (786–746 B.C.).

Following a short introduction (1:1-2), the book falls into four parts: 1:3–2:16, oracles against the nations, including Judah and Israel; 3:1–6:14 and 8:4–9:10, oracles of judgment against Israel; 7:1–8:3, visions and biographical information; and 9:11-15, a promise of restoration. As this outline indicates, judgment predominates in the prophet's message. Running like a scarlet thread through all of it is the theme of the day of the Lord. Amos radicalizes this formerly benign notion of a day of Yahweh's victory for the people; now it becomes a threat to Israel (5:20). On that day the wrath of Yahweh will fall upon Israel, above all because of the unjust exploitation of the poor by the rich and powerful (5:11-13; 4:1-3; 6:4-7; 8:4-8). This indictment contrasts sharply with the message of Amos' contemporary prophet, HOSEA, for whom cultic

malpractice and the fertility rites of BAAL were the sins that demanded God's judgment upon Israel.

The uniqueness of Amos 9:11-15, the single "promise" oracle in Amos, has led many to challenge its authenticity; however, it provides for Amos the balance between judgment and salvation that is typical of the prophetic canon as a whole.

W.S.T.

**ANABAPTISTS.** *See* RADICAL REFORMATION.

**ANALECTS OF CONFUCIUS.** A collection of short sayings and anecdotes about CONFUCIUS (551–479 B.C.). It was put together by Confucius' followers a century after his death and is our best source of information about him. It is generally agreed that some parts of the *Analects* are later additions. The book became a standard throughout the Far East for how to live a life of morality and service. (*See also* CONFUCIANISM.)

K.C.

**ANALOGY.** A similarity between things otherwise unlike. The use of analogy in theology derives from a fundamental problem central to theistic belief. Theists wishing to speak about God appear faced with two unacceptable choices. One is to apply attributes or predicates to God as we apply them to creatures (univocally). Goodness is *the same* when applied to God and humans. But to speak of God in human terms (univocally) is to fall into ANTHROPOMORPHISM.

Alternatively, one can apply predicates to the Creator in an entirely different way (equivocally) than we apply them to creatures. Goodness does *not* have the same meaning when applied to God as it has when applied to humans. What meaning, then, does it have? We can't be sure. Equivocal language about God leads to AGNOSTICISM, the belief that nothing certain can be known about God. Finding neither of these alternatives acceptable, theologians—especially in the Roman Catholic tradition—have resorted to that form of analogy which holds that, while two things may be different, they may also have a relation of likeness, an analogy of being (*analogia entis*).

Since the time of THOMAS AQUINAS (1225–74), Catholic theology has distinguished between two kinds of analogy. The analogy of *proportion* or *attribution* relates things in such a way that one (the prime analogate) possesses the attribute in a "formal," intrinsic sense, while the other analogate possesses the attribute in a secondary or *virtual* sense. Applied to the analogy between God and man, our actual experience of goodness in humans (the prime analogate) suggests that God, being the creator of humans, possesses goodness in whatever manner is necessary to produce goodness in humans. Goodness, then, exists virtually in God. But this leaves us ignorant of the actual, intrinsic nature of God's goodness. The analogy of attribution appears to fail.

The analogy of proportionality maintains that both analogates hold the attribute in question, for example, goodness, intrinsically *but* in the mode appropriate to each analogate. This protects God's infinite otherness, but the irreducible disparity *between* finite and infinite goodness holds. The analogy thus remains uninformative. KARL BARTH denounced the *analogia entis* and proposed an analogy of faith (*analogia fidei*) derived from biblical revelation.

J.L.

**ANALYTICAL PHILOSOPHY.** A dominant philosophical influence especially in the English-speaking countries since the time of World War II. The analyst holds that philosophy has no specific subject-matter of its own (thus rejecting the traditional metaphysical concern with such topics as God, freedom, and immortality) but has for its business the logical examination of the language used in the sciences and other intellectual disciplines. It asks about the signification of terms, the meaning and reference of propositions, the coherence of arguments, and so on. When combined with extreme empiricism, analytical philosophy took the form of LOGICAL POSITIVISM. In this form, it declared theological language to be meaningless.

However, there were too many unexamined assumptions in logical positivism itself, and analytical philosophy has tended to become more neutral in its assessment of the language of religion. Few would now say that the language of religion is meaningless, though the charge of incoherence is still occasionally heard. On the other hand, some theologians have welcomed analytical philosophy as a challenge to clean up and clarify the frequently obscure language of their discipline, and to explain how religious language functions.

J.M.

**ANANIAS.** Three people in the Apostolic church are known by this name.

First, there is the early Jerusalem member with his wife, Sapphira (Acts 5:1-11). The story of their deceit and its attempted cover-up is told in some detail. At a time when the wealthier Christians were contributing funds for the relief of the poor and as a token of a shared common life (Acts 2:24-27; 4:32-37), this couple offered the price of their property, pretending to have given all when in fact they had retained a part of the proceeds for themselves. This was the essence of their sin, according to the record: they tried to deceive both the apostles and God. A summary judgment fell on Ananias, whose death was quickly followed by that of his wife, who died on the spot after hearing of her husband's swift demise. Luke narrates the story without comment, but it was evidently intended as a warning in the later church and a sign of God's "terrible presence" in the congregation ("church" is first mentioned in the narrative at Acts 5:11).

Then, by contrast, Ananias is a name borne by another Jewish Christian at Damascus, known for his exemplary character (Acts 9:10-19). In a later speech given by Paul, tribute is paid to him as "a devout man according to the law" (Acts 22:12). At his hands Paul received his sight, the gift of the Spirit, and (just as important) a ready welcome into the church fellowship at Damascus at a time when Ananias had to believe that he was a genuine convert and not a spy infiltrating the Christian community, a fear voiced in the dialogue of Acts 9:13-16. Later church tradition made Ananias one of the Seventy (Luke 10:1), a bishop in Damascus, and a Christian martyr.

Third, there is a Jewish Sadducean high priest called by this name (Acts 22:30–23:5). This Ananias was in office from A.D. 47 to 58 and was the presiding officer of the Sanhedrin, the Jewish Council, when Paul was summoned to appear before it. He was ill-reputed on account of his greed and was hated for his pro-Roman sympathies. Not surprisingly, he was assassinated by the nationalist Zealots at the outbreak of the Jewish war in A.D. 66.

R.M.

**ANATHEMA.** From the Greek meaning something "devoted" or "given over to destruction." The term appears in the NT in Romans 9:3; I Corinthians 16:22 KJV; and Galatians 1:8, 9, where it means "devoted to" or "given over to destruction." It thus means "damned" and corresponds to the Hebrew term *herem* or "ban" as in Leviticus 27:28, 29 and Joshua 6:17; 7:1. Romans 9:3 uses anathema in the sense of "accursed," as does I Corinthians 12:3 and Galatians 1:8, 9. This is in reference to anyone who would change the gospel of Christ, that is, it is the Christian's response to HERESY.

The anathema developed in the history of Christianity was a formal declaration that some person, doctrine, or activity was theologically and morally wrong. For example, in A.D. 1054, the Roman Catholic Church excommunicated (or anathematized) the Eastern Orthodox Church, when the Byzantine emperor closed Latin churches in Constantinople (*see* EXCOMMUNICATION).

Again, POPE LEO X, in 1520, wrote a BULL (or papal declaration) of condemnation against the reforming work of Martin Luther. The anthema is therefore synonymous with excommunication or separation from the reception of Holy Communion and fellowship with the church.

Paul, in I Corinthians 16:22 uses the form "anathema, maranatha," interpreted as "let him be accursed. Our Lord, come!" in reference to persons who do not love the Lord, and who are destined to condemnation at the SECOND COMING of Christ, when he will judge the earth and separate believers from nonbelievers.

J.C.

**ANATTA.** In BUDDHISM, Anatta (Pali) or Anatman (Sanskrit) refers to the doctrine of "No Self." Anatta contains the notion that a human being, like the universe itself and all its parts, does not possess a permanent, unchanging essence—a "soul" or separate selfhood—but is a composite and transitory creature in a universe of flux. The concept is related to the Buddhist emphasis on desire or attachment as the root of suffering. From this bondage, the Buddha's teaching offers liberation.

R.E.

## ANCESTOR VENERATION.

The ritual worship or honoring of the spirits of the dead by their descendants. The ancestors are seen as benefiting from the offerings and ritual and as protecting the family in return. In some societies, the ancestors are thought to watch over and judge the behavior of the descendants. Accidents are thought to be punishment for bad behavior. In many societies, spirits not honored by sacrifice can cause mischief or calamity in the house of the descendant. In other societies, forgotten spirits only weaken and die. Ancestor veneration is never found as the sole religion in any area; rather it exists alongside religions almost everywhere. In the modern world, only those religions with Judaic influence—JUDAISM, Christianity, ISLAM, and SIKHISM—lack strong ancestor cults. Even there, however, saints and great leaders—who are sometimes also ancestors—are venerated.

Ancestor veneration serves other purposes besides protection from mishap. It unites a group through shared ritual and kinship. It assures the old of continuing respect and existence after death. It establishes the leader of the family—the one who performs the ritual. The funeral ritual and continuing veneration mark the end of the life cycle and also preserve the continuity of the lineage.

In most societies, ritual centers around some material symbol of the deceased: engraved tablets in China, carved sticks or stools in Africa, statues of the dead in ancient Rome, the ancestor's skull in the Manus tribe in the Pacific. Some societies believe that the ancestor is in some way present in the symbol. Food and drink are ritually offered to these symbols, and petitions are made for protection from evil spirits or natural calamities, and perhaps for ill fortune to befall an enemy.

K./M.C.

## ANCHORITE.

A person living in solitary contemplation and asceticism. Originally most common in the East, during the Middle Ages anchoritism took its characteristic form in the West, where the term was applied specifically to those who were willingly enclosed for life, often with their own casket.

J.G.

## ANCIENT OF DAYS.

An Aramaic expression portraying God as judge of the world (Dan. 7:9, 13, 22). Equivalent with "advanced in years" in contemporary English idiom, this title highlights God's sovereignty, wisdom, and especially God's eternity within the eschatological scene unfolding in Daniel's first vision (chap. 7). Confident belief in God's changeless nature (compare Ps. 90:1-2) thereby counterbalances a turbulent human existence that is thoroughly outlined by the book of Daniel.

J.K.K.

## ANDREW.

This man whose name in Greek means "manly" has the distinction of being the first one to be called as a member of the twelve disciples (John 1:40). Initially he is described as a follower of John the Baptist and lived in his hometown of Beth-saida in Galilee (John 1:44). SIMON PETER was his brother, and his father's name is given as John (John 1:42; 21:15-17). Jesus met Andrew and his brother Simon Peter by the Sea of Galilee where they were engaged in the fishing industry (Matt. 4:18), gaining a certain affluence.

The initial summons to discipleship, given in the Fourth Gospel, led to a call to full-time allegiance (Matt. 4:18-20; Mark 1:16-18). In this way Andrew became one of the twelve APOSTLES (Matt. 10:1-2; Mark 3:13-18; Luke 6:12-14). Andrew stands out in the gospel tradition as a person of some resourcefulness. He directed attention to the presence of the lad with his lunch basket (John 6:8-9) as a prelude to the feeding of the five thousand. In John 12:21-22 Philip turned to Andrew for advice in response to the Hellenes who came to interview Jesus. He is mentioned again as one of the four who questioned Jesus (Mark 13:3-4) on the Mount of Olives—traditionally understood as the place of final revelation according to Zechariah 14. This questioning was the incentive for Jesus' apocalyptic speech on the fate of Jerusalem. Acts 1:13 also notes that Andrew was in the company of the other apostles.

The Apocryphal Acts (see APOCRYPHA: OT and NT) contain the *Acts of Andrew,* which relate how Andrew died by crucifixion in Achaia (southern Greece). This is a second-century source, referred to by Eusebius (*Church History* 111.25.6). In the *Gospel of Mary* (part of the recently found and edited library from Nag Hammadi) Andrew and Peter play the role of champions of orthodoxy who oppose and accuse Mary of gnostic teaching.

The relics of Andrew were found in Constantinople in the time of the emperor Justinian, and part of the cross on which he was crucified is held in veneration at the Vatican. His memory was cherished in Scotland, where he has become the patron saint.

R.M.

## ANDROGYNY.

From the Greek roots for male/female, the word denotes a uniting of the physical characteristics and the natures of both sexes. Earlier the term was used in a derogatory sense, suggesting a hermaphroditic being and denoting sexual ambivalence. Today the term has positive significance in suggesting that men and women need the freedom to develop as full human beings. Studies concerning the two hemispheres of the brain indicate that the development of the intuitive and rational aspects of personality could be influenced by societal patterns. And, if encouraged to do so, men could develop the intuitive, emotional characteristics more fully and women those of the logical and rational.

Textual biblical studies indicate that *adham* (Hebrew) includes male and female, and that our being "made" in the image of God . . . male and female" (Gen. 1:27) suggests the androgynous character of God. The Bible portrays God in traditionally male roles (king, God of battles) and in female roles (pitying, feeding). Jesus assumed authority in male roles (commanding, pronouncing), and also, in a female allusion, gathered the people "as a hen gathers her chickens." Paul writes that in Christ there is neither male nor female. This also suggests that verbs may describe God more suitably than do nouns, and images that are not sex-specific may better describe the activity of God.

In this perspective people should be encouraged to develop a new kind of wholeness, exhibiting a variety of characteristics. This requires a restructuring of values in a society so that the traditional male/female competition disappears, hierarchical structures are reshaped, and patriarchialism is renounced. In theory this might lead to a "unisex," in which a recombining of male/female traits leads to the disappearance of sexual differences. Or it could indicate a transcending of sex-specific characteristics for the fuller self-actualization of each person. It has been pointed out that some of the classical saints fit this description: TERESA OF AVILA was an able administrator who reached the heights of mystical unity with God, and FRANCIS OF ASSISI, who founded an order, was renowned for gentleness and self-effacement.

I.C.

**ANGELS.** In biblical and most ancient nonbiblical Jewish and Christian texts, angels are spiritual or divine beings superior to humans in power and knowledge. Angels in the OT are generally viewed as in the service of God, but in later literature some angels are depicted as opponents of God.

*Terminology.* The Hebrew word *mal'ak* and the Greek word *angelos* are the biblical terms commonly translated as "angel." Both of these words basically mean "messenger," and the terms themselves provide no clue as to whether a divine or human messenger is intended. Only in Latin *(angelus)* and subsequent Western languages is the word "angel," in its biblical usage, taken for granted as referring to divine beings. Sometimes in the biblical text uncertainty exists about whether a figure is human or superhuman (compare Gen. 32:24-25 with 32:30; see Josh. 5:13-14) and about whether God or a messenger is involved (compare Gen. 16:7 with 16:13; Exod. 3:2 with 3:4). The OT speaks of the "angel of Yahweh" (Gen. 16:7 and frequently elsewhere) although this phrase could be used of humans also (Hag. 1:13; Mal. 2:7). Divine beings subordinate to God are also called "sons of God" (Gen. 6:2; Job 1:6) or "holy ones" (Ps. 89:7; Job 5:1). Seraphim and cherubim also appear (Isa. 6:1-6; Gen. 3:24; Ezek. 10), but they presumably were considered, unlike angels, as nonhuman in form.

*Functions of Angels.* The general impression one is inclined to receive about angels from the Bible is that as a king would be surrounded by attendants and subordinates who praise, serve, and carry out orders, so God is surrounded by such a body of heavenly beings, the sons of God, the divine council, or angels who perform these functions for God. In the earlier portions of the OT, the appearance of angels is reasonably sporadic. Here they function primarily in the following ways: (a) as divine messengers, (b) as protectors and guides for the people (see Ps. 91:11), and (c) as troublers of the people's enemies in battle (see Ps. 35:5-6). Angels are shown preventing Abraham from offering his son Isaac as a sacrifice (Gen. 22:11-12), reassuring Jacob (31:11), encountering Moses in the burning bush (Exod. 3:2), announcing the births of Ishmael and Samson (Gen. 16:11; Judg. 13:3-5), leading the Hebrews in the wilderness and into the Promised Land (Exod. 14:19; 23:20-23; 33:2), directing the actions of Balaam (Num. 22:22-35), feeding Elijah in the wilderness (I Kings 19:5), and creating disaster for the Assyrians attacking Jerusalem (II Kings 19:35; Isa. 37:36).

In the later OT, noticeable shifts appear, not only in the nature and roles of angels, but also in the frequency and importance of their appearance. In Ezekiel (see 40:3), Zechariah, and Daniel (see chaps. 7–12), angels reveal secrets about the future, interpret dreams and visions, and aid in interpreting scripture. Unlike the role and power he possessed in the presentation in Job, SATAN, a "son of God," becomes more of an anti-God power (see Zech. 3:1-2; I Chr. 21:1). In Daniel, angels have proper names, such as Gabriel and Michael (8:16; 9:21; 10:13, 21; 12:1).

Between the OT and NT, the following developments reflected in the Pseudepigrapha and Dead Sea Scrolls can be seen in Jewish angelology: (a) angels become associated with various phenomena such as stars, the seasons, and so forth, and are involved in the governance of the world; (b) names for many angels appear; (c) evil angelic powers hostile to God appear and are named; (d) angels are often pictured in a hierarchy, thus giving rise to the concept of archangels; (e) angelic armies, both good and bad, are mentioned; (f) angels function as intercessors and carry humans' prayers to the Divine; (g) different angels are associated with different nations (already reflected in Daniel); (h) angels are present in worship (see I Cor. 11:10); (i) the guardian role of angels becomes more important (see Acts 12:15); (j) stories are told in which angels play special roles (see the book of TOBIT); and (k) angels are considered to have been the mediators of the Law at Mount Sinai (see Acts 7:53; Gal. 3:19).

The NT reflects the angelology of the world of its day. Angels as messengers announce the births of John the Baptist and Jesus (Luke 1:11-20; Matt. 1:18-25) and herald Jesus' birth (Luke 2:8-15). They offer assurance and protection (Matt. 1:18-25; 2:13; Acts 12:6-9). Angels serve Jesus in the wilderness and in the ordeal before the Crucifixion (Matt. 4:11; Mark 1:12; Luke 22:43). Angels appear at the tomb (Matt. 28:1-7; Mark 16:5-7; Luke 24:4). Angels are said to surround the throne of God, and in the book of Revelation, where the primary actions are set in heaven, angels play dominant roles in world history and the events of the end of days. Jude 6 alludes to the primeval rebellion of angelic powers. Angels are assigned roles in the world (Rom. 8:38; Acts 5:19; Gal. 4:3; Col. 2:8; Eph. 3:10) but are considered inferior to Jesus the Son (Heb. 1:4-13). While angels are said to appear at the final judgment (Matt. 13:39-43; 24:29-31; Mark 13:24-27), Paul declares that Christians shall judge the angels (I Cor. 6:3).

J.H.

**ANGELUS.** A Catholic prayer recited three times a day, at 6:00 A.M., noon, and 6:00 P.M. It is a series of three versicles and responses, each of which is followed by a HAIL MARY and a prayer. The Angelus began in the sixteenth century.

J.C.

**ANGLICAN CHURCHES.** The worldwide association of churches in communion with the Church of England (see CANTERBURY), including the Episcopal Church in the U.S.A. To be in official relationship with the Anglican Communion, churches must "uphold and propagate the catholic and apostolic faith and order as they are generally set forth in the BOOK OF COMMON PRAYER . . . they are particular or national churches, and, as such, promote within each of their territories a national expression of Christian faith, life and worship"; and "are bound together not by a central legislative and executive authority, but by mutual loyalty sustained through the common council of bishops."

This was the statement issued by the 1930 LAMBETH CONFERENCE. Since 1867 these conferences have been the rallying point of Anglicanism and are convened every ten years at Lambeth Palace, the London residence of the archbishop of Canterbury. He serves as the chairman of these consultative and non-legislative meetings. Currently some 365 dioceses are represented at the conferences by their respective bishops.

Recent revisions of the Book of Common Prayer in several national churches since the 1930 Lambeth Conference have not materially changed the basis for membership in the Anglican Communion. Actually one of the recognized characteristics of Anglicanism is the freedom member churches possess in determining theology and liturgical practice.

Anglicanism is an outgrowth of the Church of England into various parts of the world through colonization and missionary endeavor, beginning with the Society for the Propagation of the Gospel in 1701 and later through church-related missionary societies.

It is not known when Christianity first came to Great Britain, but British bishops were present at the Council of Arles in 314. Rome sent St. Augustine on a mission to Britain in 597. This gave impetus to the ongoing growth of the church. In 1529 KING HENRY VIII, quarreling with the Vatican, initiated the break from the Roman Catholic Church. But it was QUEEN ELIZABETH who really organized the Church of England and gave it the character it has maintained to the present day. Anglicans have always insisted that they did not form a new church but implemented reforms in the ecclesiastical body that had existed for at least a thousand years.

Anglicanism has always adhered to an episcopal system of church government, that is, rule by the bishops, who along with priests (presbyters) and deacons serve as the ministers. The historic episcopate embodies the concept that bishops are consecrated by the laying on of hands of other bishops in a continuing succession since the first bishops were ordained by the apostles (see APOSTOLIC SUCCESSION).

The doctrinal basis of the church includes the simple statement that Holy Scriptures contain all things necessary to salvation and are the supreme authority for the faith and life of the church. Three historic creeds—APOSTLES', NICENE, and ATHANASIAN—are held as proper expositions of scriptural doctrine. Anglicans also attest to the teaching of four COUNCILS of the early church: Nicaea, Ephesus, Constantinople, and Chalcedon (see each council). The THIRTY-NINE ARTICLES (1563) reflect the mediating position the church took between Rome and the ultra-Protestant position in the sixteenth century, but they are not authoritative today.

Since its origin Anglicans have been involved in the ECUMENICAL MOVEMENT, which emphasizes the unity of the universal church. Yet they often display ambivalence in relationships with non-Anglican communions. The High Church party in recent years has favored reconciliation with the Roman Catholic Church, and the evangelical wing has favored merger with the free churches of Protestantism. All provinces are members of the World Council of Churches, and four Anglican dioceses have become an integral part of the Church of South India.

R.H.

**ANGLO-CATHOLIC (ANGLICANS).** The most traditionalist segment of the HIGH CHURCH party of the Church of England. The term Anglo-Catholic has been used since the Oxford movement to describe two trends in Anglicanism: a revival of Roman Catholic sacramental theology and the development of more complex, traditional liturgies.

J.C.

**ANGST.** *See* ANXIETY.

**ANIMISM.** The belief that animals, plants, places, and people have similar souls or spirits. This soul is physical, not metaphysical. It is often equated with the breath, blood, name, or shadow of the object or creature. The term "animism" was coined by the nineteenth-century anthropologist Edward Tylor to denote the first stage of the evolution of religion. Culturally, animism was linked to what Tylor called "savagery"—that is, hunter-gatherer societies. Tylor claimed that as a culture rose to "barbarism" (chiefdoms) and then "civilization," its religions leaned toward polytheism and then to monotheism.

Tylor saw the origin of animism as an attempt to account for fainting, dreams, and death. He proposed that early humans rationally explained these conditions as products of the activity of the "soul" and that early humans extended this "soul" to animals, plants, and other objects (*see* TOTEM). Later anthropologists have rejected the validity of his concept as a generalization and an evolutionary scheme. They admit, however, that many primitive cultures share certain common beliefs: the soul animates the body; it can be attacked or protected by MAGIC (witchcraft); it is strengthened by passages through the proper LIFE CYCLE RITES; if the rituals are performed correctly, the souls of nature and the dead will protect the living; if the rituals are neglected, the spirits will do harm (*see* ANCESTOR VENERATION). Some societies believe that the soul comes back to the lineage in a new body (*see* REINCARNATION).

K./M.C.

**ANNAS.** A high priest and titular head of the priestly party in Jerusalem in the time of Jesus. He was appointed in A.D. 6 and deposed in A.D. 15. Yet he is described as high priest after his deposition and the succession of his son-in-law Caiaphas (John 18:13). The Jews, however, seem to have regarded the office, at least in its title, as one for life, and Luke (3:2) may be using a source that paid tribute to Annas' continuing influence *ex officio*. We know Annas did have powerful prestige, which carried over to the succeeding holder of the office of high priest.

At the trial of Jesus, Annas played a role by conducting a preliminary inquiry, according to John 18:13-24. Jesus had opposed the priestly (Sadducean) aristocracy, especially in his cleansing the Temple, whose forecourt was a profitable money exchange and emporium for the sale of sacrificial animals. This fact may well have had repercussions in leading Annas bitterly to resist Jesus and condemn him in the Jewish court. In Acts 4:5-12 Annas appears in a hostile role, opposing the followers of Jesus in apostolic times.

R.M.

**ANNUAL CONFERENCE.** The yearly meeting of all United Methodist parishes within a conference, held under the direction of the bishop. All ministers (elders and deacons) must attend, and representatives from each congregation attend. Ministers are assigned to congregations for the coming year (or other set period) at the conference.

J.C.

**ANNUNCIATION.** The announcement by an angel, GABRIEL, to MARY that she is going to have a son as reported in Luke 1:26-35. Since she was a virgin she was puzzled and fearful. Joseph, to whom she was engaged, was of the lineage of David, so his sons would be possible heirs to the Davidic throne of Israel. Mary was astonished at the angelic report, but was assured that her pregnancy was a sign of divine favor, and that her child—though not the physical offspring of Joseph—would indeed obtain the throne of David. Furthermore, he would reign forever, just as God had promised David, according to II Samuel 7:13.

The angel also told Mary that the child is to have the title of "Son of the Most High" or "Holy, Son of God," in keeping with the divine acclaim of Israel's ruler in Psalm 2:7. His name will be Jesus, which in Hebrew means "Yahweh saves (his people)." Mary is promised that this miraculous birth will take place, not by human means, but by God's spirit and power.

H.K.

**ANOINTED.** The English equivalent of the Hebrew word *meshiah* (messiah) and Greek *christos* (Christ). The anointed in ancient Israel was the designation of the king. David, for example, refused to injure or kill King Saul because he was "the Lord's anointed" (I Sam. 24:6). In later times, "the anointed" also became a designation of the high priest when rituals and functions of the king were assumed by the holder of this office.

The Hebrews used two different words for anoint. One *(suk)* related to the normal rubbing of the body with oil. The other *(mashah)* was employed primarily with reference to the act by which a person or thing was consecrated by the pouring or smearing of sacred oil. The latter type of anointing was a special religious act setting aside the anointed for divine service. Thus sacred pillars (Gen. 31:13), the altar (Exod. 29:36), the tabernacle and its furnishings (Lev. 8:10; Num. 7:1), special bread (Exod. 29:2), and other things were anointed.

The ritual of anointment was especially associated with the king (I Sam. 10:1; II Sam. 2:4; 5:3; I Kings 1:39) and thus his title "the anointed." Similar royal inauguration rituals were practiced in Canaan before the time of Israel so the ritual is not unique to the Bible. A single biblical text refers to the anointment of a prophet (I Kings 19:16). Anointment not only set aside and consecrated the object but was also believed to transfer to the recipient something of the holiness and strength of the deity.

In post-biblical times, the anointed (Messiah) was one of the designations given to the expected

redeemer figure. "Christ," the Greek translation of Messiah, tended to become as much a name (Jesus Christ) as a title since special anointing was not part of royal rituals in the Greco-Roman world. The use of the word Christ in the sense of Messiah or "the anointed one" can be seen in such NT passages as Mark 8:29.

J.H.

**ANSELM.** Archbishop of Canterbury from 1093 to 1109, famous for his ONTOLOGICAL ARGUMENT for the existence of God and for his theory of substitutionary ATONEMENT.

A native of Italy who had become abbot of a monastery in Normandy, he was called to England by the Norman King William II. But the question of investitures, as well as other issues of church and state, led to conflicts between the archbishop and the throne (see INVESTITURE CONTROVERSY). Due to these conflicts with William II, and later with Henry I, Anselm spent many years in exile from England. He finally reconciled with Henry I through compromise in 1107, but died three years after having been restored to his see.

His argument for the existence of God, which is developed in the *Proslogion,* can be stated quite briefly: God is "that-than-which-no-greater-can-be-thought," and this idea includes in itself the notion of existence. A nonexistent being cannot be declared to be "that-than-which-no-greater-can-be-thought," for in that case an existing being would be greater than it. This would contradict the very notion of "that-than-which-no-greater-can-be-thought." Therefore, this greatest of beings, God, can only be thought of as existing. This argument, which can be stated so succinctly, is usually called the ontological argument and has given rise to numerous diverging interpretations. To this day philosophers and logicians debate its meaning and significance.

Anselm developed his theory of substitutionary atonement in his treatise *Cur Deus Homo?—Why God-man.* There he argued that, since sin is an offense against the infinite God, its penalty must be infinite. But, since sin is a human offense, its penalty must be paid by humankind. Hence there would be the need for God made human, Jesus Christ, who pays in our stead. This theory gained such acceptance that to this day many regard it as the only correct understanding of atonement.

Anselm's theological method consisted of seeking to understand by reason what he already knew by faith—the existence of God, the saving work of Christ, and so on. By the use of this method, he became one of the founders of medieval SCHOLASTICISM.

J.G.

**ANTE-NICENE FATHERS.** The collective name given to Christian authors who wrote before the Council of NICEA in 325, excluding, on the one hand,

the books of the NT and, on the other, those which were declared heretical from a very early date.

The earliest of these writings are grouped under the title APOSTOLIC FATHERS. Then came the APOLOGISTS, who were mostly second-century authors who wrote in defense of Christianity during times of persecution. IRENAEUS, late in the second century, wrote a voluminous work against Gnosticism, and a shorter one expounding the basics of Christianity for the benefit of recent converts. In Alexandria, CLEMENT and ORIGEN sought to build bridges between Christian theology and pagan philosophy. Since Greek was the common language of the eastern Mediterranean basin, all the aforementioned authors wrote in Greek.

The first Christians to write extensively in Latin were the apologist Minucius Felix and the North African TERTULLIAN, who was so influential that he has been called the Father of Latin Theology. In the third century, the most significant Latin theologian was CYPRIAN, also from North Africa.

J.G.

**ANTHEM.** A sacred vocal (solo or choral) composition, accompanied by instruments, sung by a choir in the language of the people. The anthem originated in the early Anglican church. It is generally a composition for two or more voices. The text may be biblical but usually is not drawn from the liturgy.

J.C.

Courtesy of the Metropolitan Museum of Art, Rogers Fund, 1920

*Saint Anthony Tormented by Demons, by Martin Schongauer*

**ANTHONY OF EGYPT.** One of the earliest Christian hermits, reputed by some to be the founder of Egyptian MONASTICISM. After many years of total solitude, in which he is said to have fought with constant temptations, he found peace in the assurance that God was always with him. Later, others joined him in the desert, where he founded a closely knit community of hermits. After CONSTANTINE's conversion, as the powerful gained an increasing voice in the church, many flocked to the desert in protest, and Anthony became their model. When ARIANISM came to the foreground, Anthony intervened in the controversy, supporting ATHANASIUS and his followers. The *Life of Anthony,* which Athanasius wrote after the hermit's death, was very influential in the spread of monasticism.

J.G.

**ANTHONY OF PADUA.** One of the early Franciscans, renowned for his preaching. He was born in Lisbon to a noble family in 1195 and soon joined the Augustinian Canons. He spent most of his early years in study, but then he decided to join the Franciscans in order to go as a missionary to North Africa. When he was forced to return to Europe for reasons of health, the Franciscans suddenly discovered his wisdom and eloquence and named him to a series of teaching posts. But he was particularly famous for his preaching, which achieved the conversion of many ALBIGENSES. One of his main themes was the rights of the poor and the sins of greed and usury. He died in 1231, and was canonized a year later.

J.G.

**ANTHROPOCENTRIC.** Defines the tendency to measure all things by human standards and to regard the human situation as one of AUTONOMY. This is in contrast to allowing God to be central (the theocentric view). Yet theologians stress that only a true understanding of the value of human personality can permit humankind to know the reality of God as creator and savior. Anthropocentric and theocentric, therefore, are not strictly terms in opposition.

I.C.

**ANTHROPOMORPHISM.** Derived from the Greek words *anthropos* (human being) and *morphe* (form). It refers to the process whereby God's nature is expressed in terms of human attributes or abilities. In the OT, although no one ever sees God with eyes, God is portrayed as having form and substance, so that God feels, acts, and even breathes and smells like us. The INCARNATION, too, in a sense is a form of anthropomorphism, for God is conceived as having been fully present in the human Jesus.

I.C.

**ANTICHRIST.** *Biblical.* "Who is the liar but he who denies that Jesus is the Christ? This is the antichrist, he who denies the Father and the Son" (I John 2:22).

The term "antichrist" is heard often in the late-twentieth century. Some evangelists identify the social, moral, and international ills of the times with the dark days foreseen by the writer of II Thessalonians 2:3-4. Here, Paul speaks of the coming again of the Lord, and Christians are warned: "that day will not come, unless the rebellion comes first, and the man of lawlessness is revealed, the son of perdition, who opposes and exalts himself against every so-called god or object of worship, so that he takes his seat in the temple of God, proclaiming himself to be God."

The "son of perdition" is generally taken to equal the Antichrist of John's Epistles. Antichrist occurs in the Bible only in the Johannine Epistles (in I John 2:18, 22; 4:3; II John 7). The "son of perdition/man of lawlessness" phrase occurs only in II Thessalonians 2. Nevertheless, the concept of the Antichrist has excited Christian imaginations since the earliest days of the church.

Just as darkness is meaningless without light, the Antichrist is meaningless apart from Christ. First, there is the faith of the church that Christ will return to earth, to overthrow evil and establish his Kingdom. Dependent upon this is the idea of the writer of II Thessalonians, that the Lord will not return until the Antichrist is revealed and the forces of evil have done their worst to destroy humanity. Second Thessalonians 2 implies that Christ's return is not yet ready to occur because this "man of lawlessness" has not appeared. Historical forces, evidently directed by God, restrain the "mystery of lawlessness," but that will not be forever. The lawless man will reveal himself and be destroyed by the appearance of Christ (II Thess. 2:8).

The "little apocalypse" of Mark 13, given as a discourse of Jesus, generally is believed to refer to the Antichrist, also. This material is duplicated in Matthew 24 and Luke 21. Interestingly, the phrase used in the Synoptic Gospels is "false Christs" and "false prophets" (Mark 13:22; cf. Matt. 7:15; Luke 6:26). In this case, also, the appearance of the "desolating sacrilege set up where it ought not to be" (Mark 13:14; cf. Daniel 9:27; 11:31; 12:11) is connected to the return of Christ to gather his elect into the Kingdom (Mark 13:27).

Ezekiel 38–39 speaks of GOG AND MAGOG, who will fight terrible battles, and Zechariah 14:2 ff. speaks of the destruction of Jerusalem before God saves the people. Daniel 7:21-27; 9:24-27; and chap. 11 seem to visualize the fourth beast in the SON OF MAN vision as an ultimate demonstration of the powers of evil, similar to the "man of lawlessness" of II Thessalonians 2.

The Revelation to John also contains poetic material that Christian tradition has assimilated to the Antichrist motif. The twelfth chapter of Revelation speaks of the "great red dragon, with seven heads and ten horns, and seven diadems upon his heads" (v. 3) that persecutes the woman and her child, which is evidently a reference to the Virgin

Mary and the Christ child (Rev. 12:4-6). Revelation 13:2-9 presents the beast who wars on the saints, and Revelation 13:11-18 shows another beast who forces humans to worship the first beast. Revelation 19:11-16 proclaims the SECOND COMING OF CHRIST—the warrior from heaven on a white horse who fights the evil beasts and their earthly followers, overcoming them and imprisoning SATAN for one thousand years. Revelation 20:4, 7 show the freeing of Satan, who seeks to destroy the earth; but Christ destroys evil, and the DAY OF JUDGMENT dawns. The similarity of this mystical account to the "man of lawlessness" scenario of II Thessalonians 2 is quite close.

*Historical.* There are three schools of interpretation of the Antichrist throughout Christian history. The *past* interpretation depicts the Antichrist as a personage who has already lived (as, for example, NERO). The *present* interpretation looks for the "man of lawlessness" who pretends to be God among contemporary figures (as, for example, LUTHER's identification of the PAPACY as the Antichrist, or some twentieth-century Christians' identification of Hitler as the "man of lawlessness"). The *future* interpretation presents a vigil for signs of the coming of the Antichrist in the near future (as, e.g., some contemporary FUNDAMENTALISTs' proclamations of Communist leaders as possible candidates for the Antichrist).

The *past* interpretation is often given by Bible scholars who point out that the Revelation (as well as II Thess.) was written in a time of persecution. Roman emperors, like Nero, who claimed to be divine and tried to destroy the church were good candidates to be identified (in a disguised way) as the arch foes of Christ.

The *present* interpretation has always enjoyed currency among some Christians. Sectarians persecuted by the Roman Church, such as the WALDENSES, the HUSSITES, the WYCLIFFITES, and the LOLLARDS readily identified the Pope as the Antichrist in their times. When Martin Luther found himself condemned and a deaf ear turned to his call for a council to reform the church, he, too, denounced the office of the Pope as the Antichrist in harsh words. Some Protestants still make this identification, even in this time of Christian acceptance across confessional lines.

The *future* interpretation of the Antichrist has had the largest following. Since most Christians have considered Christ's return to be in the far future, the arising of the Antichrist is seen as a future event.

*Contemporary.* The last half of the twentieth century has witnessed a revival of interest in the Revelation to John, the Son of man visions of Daniel, and other apocalyptic portions of Scripture. The emphasis of popular evangelists—not least those preachers with access to radio and television—on the imminence of the Second Coming has also stirred interest in the identification of the Antichrist either in the present or the near future. Generally, the Antichrist is identified as a political leader of the Communist or Arab worlds.

J.C.

**ANTI-DEFAMATION LEAGUE.** An organization that seeks "to stop the defamation of the Jewish people," and "to secure justice and fair treatment for all citizens alike." An arm of the service organization B'NAI B'RITH, the ADL was founded in 1913 as a reaction to the trial by prejudice of Leo Frank, accused of rape and murder in Atlanta, Georgia, and subsequently lynched.

L.K.

**ANTILEGOMENA.** *See* CANON; PSEUDEPIGRAPHA.

**ANTINOMIAN.** A term describing those in the early church who claimed that after the gospel's promulgation, obedience to the Law became abrogated. The belief led to some excesses in behavior condemned by Paul (compare I Cor. 5:6; 9:21). The church repudiated the antinomian view by insisting that free justification did not erase the moral principles inherent in the Law.

I.C.

**ANTIOCHENE THEOLOGY.** A type of theology that was influential in Syria and Asia Minor at least until the time of the Arab conquests. Its main rival was ALEXANDRIAN THEOLOGY and, although there were many differences between the two, the main point of conflict was CHRISTOLOGY. Alexandrian theology emphasized the divinity of Jesus and the close union between that divinity and the humanity of the Savior. It is therefore called a "unitive" Christology. Antiochene theology feared that this would lead to a denial of the full humanity of Jesus, which would be obscured by the divinity. Therefore, it tended to stress the distinction between the "two natures" of the Savior—the divine and the human. For this reason it has often been described as holding to a "disjunctive" Christology.

Antiochene theologians were instrumental in the condemnation of the APOLLINARIANS in A.D. 381, at the Council of Constantinople. But fifty years later the Antiochene Nestorius (see NESTORIANS), who was patriarch of Constantinople, was condemned at the COUNCIL OF EPHESUS for declaring that Mary was "bearer of Christ"—CHRISTOKOS—and not "bearer of God"—THEOTOKOS. Nestorius meant that the distinction between the divinity and the humanity of Christ does not allow one to speak as if the divinity had been borne by Mary. In 451, at the COUNCIL OF CHALCEDON, Antiochene theology, with the support of Pope Leo, gained a victory in the condemnation of MONOPHYSITISM, an extreme form of Alexandrian theology. But the conflict continued, and in A.D. 553, at the Second Council of Constantinople, three of the great figures of Antiochene theology were condemned.

J.G.

**ANTIOCH ON THE ORONTES; ANTIOCH OF PISIDIA.** Seleucus I (312–281 B.C.), founder of the Seleucid dynasties in Syria, Asia Minor, and Mesopotamia following the death of Alexander the Great, named sixteen cities in honor of his father, Antiochus; two of these Antiochs are mentioned in the NT. Antioch in Syria lies near the northeast corner of the Mediteranean, just upstream from where the Orontes empties into the sea. It was the capital of Syria in Hellenistic and Roman times, the site having been chosen where Alexander had erected an altar to Zeus, near a fine spring. Major trade routes pass the site; archaeological evidence goes back to Neolithic times.

The city was laid out in gridiron fashion, with the main street colonnaded in Roman times. Daphne, a fine suburb to the south, was filled with groves and springs. A stadium and a theater were provided by Roman rulers, beginning with Augustus. The population of the city was about a half million, including a large Jewish community, in addition to Syrians, Greeks, and Romans. The Antiochians' interest in religion was proverbial, so that Juvenal, a Roman satirist (A.D. 60–140) wrote that the Orontes had overflowed and flooded the Tiber, that is, with superstition (*Satire* 111.62). The city regarded itself, however, as the intellectual rival of Athens and Alexandria.

In Acts 11:2-26 Antioch is said to be the first place where Jesus' followers were called Christians; it was at this Antioch that the gospel was first preached to Gentiles who lacked any connections with Judaism. There Christian prophets chose Barnabas and Saul to launch the Gentile mission (Acts 13:1-3), and Paul returned there more than once in the course of his missionary career (Acts 14:27; 18:22).

From this Antioch, Paul's missionary journey penetrated Asia Minor as far north as Antioch in Pisidia (Acts 13:13-52), high on the Anatolian plateau. There Paul preached first in a synagogue, but then Jewish hostility led him to turn to direct evangelization of Gentiles.

H.K.

**ANTIOCHUS III-VII.** In 200 B.C. Antiochus III, Seleucid king, defeated Ptolemy V, and Palestine became dominated by Seleucids. By this time, the Seleucids had to accommodate to the rising power in the West, Rome. Out of the power struggle, Antiochus IV came to the throne, announcing himself as the manifestation of Olympian Zeus and taking the title Epiphanes. In order to unify the kingdom behind him, he insisted that all subject peoples honor him alone as divine. The Jews were forbidden to practice circumcision or to offer the sacrifices required by their law, but were to pay him divine honors at an altar he ordered erected in the Temple at Jerusalem. This was viewed by Jews as the "abomination of desolation" mentioned in Daniel. When royal officers were brought in to enforce the decree of Antiochus, a priest

by the name of Mattathias led the Jews in revolt, organizing a surprisingly successful guerrilla army. Leadership in the Jewish independence movement passed to Judah (Judas) the Maccabee, whose schemes and exploits are told in I and II Maccabees.

From *Atlas of the Bible* (Thomas Nelson & Sons Limited)

*Antiochus III*

The Temple was cleansed in 164 B.C., as celebrated in the Feast of Hanukkah. At the death of Antiochus IV, leadership passed to Lysias, who was regent for Antiochus V and who, after narrowly failing to recapture Jerusalem, signed a treaty with the Jews. The struggle of the brothers of Judas to extend and confirm their control of Palestine was complicated by the rise of several men fighting for the Seleucid throne. Among these competing claimants was Antiochus VI, whose chief supporter was Trypho, skilled in military and diplomatic contests. The third and last of the sons of Mattathias to assume leadership over the Jewish independence movement was Simon, who was officially acknowledged by the Seleucids as high priest and governor. Antiochus VII, also called Antiochus Sidetes, sought to remove Simon from power, since he had cooperated with a pretender to the throne, Demetrius II. But Simon's troops defeated Sidetes' army in a crucial battle. Although

Simon was betrayed and murdered, his son John Hyrcanus succeeded him in his joint role as military, political, and priestly leader of the Jews. Antiochus VII placed Jerusalem under siege, but was ordered by Rome (with which the Maccabees had a treaty, I Macc. 12:1-23) to withdraw the troops and reach an accommodation with John Hyrcanus. In 128 B.C., when Demetrius II defeated and killed Antiochus VII, John Hyrcanus was able to gain control of more cities, including some in Samaria and east of the Jordan. From this point on, the Seleucids never again exercised effective control over Palestine.

H.K.

**ANTIPAS, HEROD.** *See* HEROD.

**ANTI-SEMITISM.** The expressed hatred and persecution of Jews. In the Bible, Haman tells the king: "There is a certain people scattered abroad and dispersed among the peoples in all the provinces of your kingdom; their laws are different from those of every other people, and they do not keep the king's laws, so that it is not for the king's profit to tolerate them" (Esth. 3:8).

This is a classical expression of animosity toward the Jews. It contains the traditional aspects of anti-Semitism: (1) dispersion and homelessness of the Jews; (2) suspicions aroused by their different laws and customs which give rise to "the dislike of the like for the unlike"; and (3) the accusation that they are potentially harmful to the state.

Much of the early hatred was based on the rejection by Jews of the many gods of the pagans. The Jewish refusal to worship images led to a series of clashes with the Hellenistic and Roman authorities. The first serious manifestation of anti-Semitism in history was the concentrated attack on the Jewish religion in the days of ANTIOCHUS IV (175-164 B.C.). He was also called Antiochus Epiphanes.

In the Christian world anti-Semitism assumed tragic proportions. The Jews were persecuted both because of the alleged crime of deicide and the nonacceptance of the divinity of Jesus. Jews were gradually forced out of every sphere of political influence and deprived of civil and political rights. The church's attempts to erect barriers between Jews and non-Jews were translated into legislation affecting all aspects of Jewish life. Conversion to Judaism was punishable by death. A movement for the destruction of synagogues and forced conversion of Jews was intense from the fifth century on. Religious anti-Semitism reached its first climax in the period of the CRUSADES. The Fourth Lateran Council (1215) passed a series of anti-Jewish measures. The blood libel and *The Protocols of the Elders of Zion,* a proven forgery, generated vicious attacks against Jews. Anti-Semitism reached its height with the rise of Hitler and the Nazi HOLOCAUST.

Responsible contemporary church leaders, realizing the dangers of anti-Semitism as well as the common ground of people of all faiths, have condemned anti-Semitism and are making efforts to promote tolerance and understanding.

L.K.

**ANXIETY.** (German, *Angst*) A phenomenon that has been the subject of much study by existentialist philosophers (see EXISTENTIALISM). Many of their reflections have been taken over by theologians. The importance of anxiety is that it is an ontological emotion, that is to say, a feeling or state of mind which reveals in a fundamental way the being of the person who experiences it (see ONTOLOGY).

A classic discussion of anxiety is found in KIERKEGAARD's *Concept of Anxiety,* which discusses the origin of sin. What makes sin possible, or how does a human being pass from innocence to sin? Kierkegaard answers this question by pointing to anxiety. He does not mean the concrete anxieties that we experience from day to day but a profound malaise or feeling of uneasiness, already present in innocence. He gives as an illustration the awakening of sexuality and sensuality in the individual. There is an uneasiness that finally issues in the sensual act, and so in the loss of innocence one experiences a changed quality of existence.

We are aware too of anxiety in the exercise of freedom. It is like a dizziness as we look into the abyss of possibilities opening before us. Kierkegaard also speaks of anxiety in connection with the task of becoming a person—what he calls the synthesis of body and soul. In all these cases, we are aware both of the finiteness of our human constitution and of the tremendous responsibilities laid upon us. However, Kierkegaard also sees anxiety as a preparation for faith. To experience anxiety is to know the reality of the human condition and so to acknowledge the need for grace.

Later existentialists acknowledge their debt to Kierkegaard, but develop their understanding of anxiety in a different manner. HEIDEGGER claims that anxiety gives us "one of the most far-reaching and primordial possibilities of disclosure." It brings humans face to face with themselves. We have a tendency to veil from ourselves the human condition, so we lose ourselves in mass existence or we let ourselves become absorbed in the day-to-day business of getting and spending. The mood of anxiety summons us back to ourselves. Again, this mood is nothing concrete—it is not like the fears we experience, which are fears of some identifiable object or eventuality. Anxiety is indefinite and arises from the human condition as a whole.

Heidegger also describes anxiety as a mood in which all the things that concern us in the world seem to sink into a kind of grayness, and we are thrown back on ourselves as beings constituted by both freedom and finitude. We try to repress anxiety, but from time to time it breaks in. Likewise we try not to think about death, the final threat to existence.

Though he does not speak of faith, Heidegger, like Kierkegaard, thinks that anxiety makes us free for an authentic existence, in which we are delivered from illusions and take upon ourselves the burden of our freedom. According to SARTRE, Kierkegaard sees anxiety in the face of freedom, while Heidegger sees it as the apprehension of nothingness. In a sense, both of these aspects belong to anxiety in the face of the conjunction in the human person of the polarities of freedom and finitude. Sartre too believes that anxiety—and, indeed, all emotional moods—has ontological significance and has to be faced and endured. We are tempted to escape from anxiety by submerging ourselves in the conventional patterns of society, but that is "bad faith" and a betrayal of our authentic humanity.

Something comparable to the phenomenon of anxiety is found in the philosophy of JASPERS, who makes much of "limit-situations"—junctures of life where individuals come to the end of their resources, confronted perhaps by guilt or death. Such situations have a revelatory quality, lighting up not only the individual's own situation but also what Jaspers calls "Transcendence," the environing reality. Many theologians of the twentieth century have made use of such ideas. Bultmann's interpretation of the NT—especially the theology of Paul, which is expounded as an anthropology in which we trace the course from sin to the new life in Christ—has many parallels to the philosophical views discussed above. Paul Tillich has much to say about anxiety and finitude, the shock of possible nonbeing, the need to overcome the polarities and ambiguities of the human situation. His whole METHOD OF CORRELATION takes its rise from the anxiety-producing human predicament. We may note, however, that there has been a strong reaction in theology against the major role given to anxiety by Tillich and others.

BONHOEFFER began this reaction by questioning whether the Christian theologian should approach humanity at the point of its weakness rather than of its strength. Since his time, Roman Catholic theology, as represented by RAHNER and others, has developed a different anthropological approach, stressing human transcendence rather than anxiety, while among Protestants MOLTMANN has developed a theology of hope. It may be worth recalling that although Heidegger made much of the themes of anxiety and death introductory to the question of the meaning of being, he also says that this question can be raised by joy. RICOEUR goes further and suggests that the only ontological emotion is joy. But no doubt joy and anxiety belong together and indicate the ambiguities and oscillations of human destiny (see DESPAIR).

J.M.

**APHRODITE.** A Greek goddess, in Homer's pantheon, who combined in her person many traits as a patron of love, beauty, and fertility. Her name,

connected with the Greek word for "foam," gave rise to the myth that she rose from the sea as a daughter of Zeus. Her maritime connections made her popular among sailors, though her cult was widespread throughout the ancient world.

Her primary role was as a deity of generation and the sexual instinct. Prostitutes claimed her as their patroness, especially at Corinth where sacred prostitution flourished, and according to the geographer Strabo, at her temple on Acrocorinthus, overlooking the city. Strabo speaks of Corinthian sexual laxity, with Aphrodite's temple served by a thousand female slaves and prostitutes. Corinth was a seaport, standing at the isthmus of the two stretches of water—the Gulf of Corinth and the Saronic Gulf—and this was an added reason for Aphrodite's popular appeal in that city, when elsewhere in the Greek world she was known for her austere demeanor. In Latin literature she is called Venus.

R.M.

**APOCALYPSE.** *See* REVELATION, BOOK OF.

**APOCALYPSES** (Apocryphal). Not all apocryphal literature is apocalyptic, but most apocalypses are apocryphal.

Jewish apocalyptic literature includes the book of Enoch, the Assumption of Moses, IV Ezra (II Esdras), Testaments of the Twelve Patriarchs (partly with Christian supplementation), the Sibylline Oracles (pagan in origin, imitated and amplified by Jews and later by Christians), II and III Baruch (the latter reworked by Christians), the book of Jubilees, and various apocalypses of Abraham, Elijah, and others. Some of these works are known only by reference made to them by later authors, and those preserved have usually been so only in translation and fragmentarily. The Jewish sectaries of QUMRAN evidence an acquaintance with some of the works above and also, as an apocalyptic group, have handed on others of their own, which until the twentieth century were still unknown, such as the War Scroll.

Besides the amplifications of Jewish apocalypses just mentioned, early Christianity created some of its own, such as the Ascension of Isaiah, developed from a non-apocalyptic Jewish apocryphon. Most Christian apocalypses, some of which have been fairly well preserved, were developed in imitation of the Revelation of John: for instance, the apocalypses of Peter, Paul, Thomas, Stephen, Mary, and others. (*See* APOCALYPTICISM, PSEUDEPIGRAPHA, and APOCRYPHA.)

B.V.

**APOCALYPTICISM.** Apocalyptic literature is characterized by most or all of the following traits. (1) Its perspective is of a definitive end time, the transition from this historical age into a world to come. (2) It adopts the literary forms of prophecy as a guise, pretending that the present and imminent end time with which it is concerned was predicted long ago. This trait frequently entails pseudonymity or attribution of the pretended prophecy to some famous figure of the past. (3) Its vehicle of communication is an imitation of prophetic vision which, however, tends to be highly complex and allegorical, frequently requiring an involved "interpretation," whereas authentic prophetic vision was generally concerned with the spiritual significance of very routine natural events. (4) Part and parcel of the apocalyptic "vision," which is the burden of its message (*apokalyptein*, meaning "reveal [what is to come]"), is a proliferation of symbolism and deliberately esoteric imagery. The symbolism is sometimes apparently sought for its own sake, but more normally could be explained as what would be expected of a consolation literature, which was also the resistance literature of a persecuted people who would be keyed into the nationalistic meaning of what might appear innocuous maunderings to the uninitiated. The time of the apocalyptic literature is roughly from the beginning of the second century B.C. to the end of the second century A.D. (5) This literature more than any other was, somewhat paradoxically, willing to incorporate into itself ideas and motifs (angelology, ethical or physical dualism, etc.), which derive not from native Israelite tradition but from foreign influences, particularly Persian and Hellenistic.

In the OT the only full-fledged apocalyptic work is the book of DANIEL. At least Daniel 7–12 has the traits of pseudonymity, pseudo-prophecy, lush imagery, and allegorical vision. This passage also encompasses an evident relation to the circumstances of its composition—the Seleucid oppression in Palestine shortly prior to the MACCABEAN REVOLT. The earlier chapters of Daniel are more closely related to works like Esther, Ruth, Judith, and Tobit, which are not apocalyptic in form but serve one of apocalyptic's purposes which was to reassure the faithful in their beliefs. The furthering of this purpose was one of the functions of Israelite WISDOM, which is also one of the possible sources of apocalypticism.

Other OT passages that can with greater or less probability be called apocalyptic are Isaiah 24–27 ("the apocalypse of Isaiah"), a very late addition to the Isaianic collection; Ezekiel 38–39, whether or not the work of the prophet Ezekiel, depicting a final victory over eschatological enemies by God's people; and parts of Joel and Zechariah, partly pseudonymous and partly allegorial, more imitative of than natural to prophecy.

The NT church was formed during the dominance of the apocalyptic mentality, and therefore it would be expected that we should find in the NT more apocalyptic literature than in the OT. (Most of the Jewish apocalyptic literature appears in the intertestamental apocryphal APOCALYPSES.) However, most of the NT writings, of which the Pauline letters are the earliest, date from a time when apocalyptic fervor had cooled and former apocalyptic thoughts were being recast in terms of a recognition that the church was destined to live in a world of continuing history. Apocalyptic utterances are to be found in I Thessalonians 4:13–5:11; II Thessalonians 2:1-12; and Mark 13 with Synoptic parallels. The only pure form of apocalyptic to be found in a NT book is the last work: REVELATION.

B.V.

**APOCRYPHA.** A term, deriving from the common Greek word *apokryphos,* meaning "hidden," which has come to be used especially by Protestants to refer to a particular collection of writings, many of which are accepted as canonical Scripture by Roman Catholics and other Christians.

*Usage of the Term.* Originally, when applied to writings, the term denoted that their content was either not to be made available to the general public or else was obscure and difficult to understand. The term "apocrypha" subsequently came to be used in various ways in the church. In its early usage, it was apparently a rather neutral term. II ESDRAS 14:44-46 speaks of ninety-four books whose content was reproduced by Ezra. Twenty-four of these (the Hebrew CANON) were to be made available for all, but seventy were to be given only "to the wise among your people." Although the term "apocrypha" is not used in this text, the seventy books were to be "hidden" or "kept secret" from the general public. No list is given of these seventy esoteric books for the wise.

Later the Christian scholar ORIGEN referred to "apocryphal" books as a group over against the books to be read in public worship. The term subsequently came to be used in a negative sense since non-orthodox groups often utilized "secret" or "hidden" writings. JEROME used the word to refer to those writings accepted as authoritative by Christians but not found in the Hebrew canon. This usage corresponds to its neutral modern usage meaning "noncanonical." Since there are wide differences among the Christian canons—ranging from the sixty-six books in the Protestant Bible to the eighty-one in that of the COPTIC (Egyptian) church—exactly what the term "Apocrypha" refers to is often uncertain.

*Old Testament Apocrypha.* When Protestants speak of the Apocrypha, they generally refer to the books of I and II ESDRAS, TOBIT, JUDITH, the ADDITIONS TO THE BOOK OF ESTHER, the WISDOM OF SOLOMON, ECCLESIASTICUS (or the Wisdom of Jesus the Son of Sirach), BARUCH, the LETTER OF JEREMIAH, the PRAYER OF AZARIAH and the SONG OF THE THREE YOUNG MEN, SUSANNA, BEL AND THE DRAGON, the PRAYER OF MANASSEH, and I and II MACCABEES. Some of these writings are actually additions to existing books (Esther and Daniel) rather than separate works. None of these was ever a part of the Hebrew canon. The early church, in the councils of Hippo (393) and Carthage (397, 419), accepted as canonical a larger OT than the Hebrew canon. At the

Reformation, the Protestants reverted to a shorter OT canon, which included, but in a slightly different order, only those works in the Hebrew Bible. At the Council of Trent (1546), Catholics affirmed an OT canon that included all the above works except I and II Esdras and the Prayer of Manasseh. In Catholicism, these seven works (Tobit, Judith, Wisdom of Solomon, Ecclesiasticus, Baruch [with the Letter of Jeremiah], I and II Maccabees) as well as the longer forms of Esther and Daniel (the latter including the Prayer of Azariah and the Song of the Three Young Men, Susanna, and Bel and the Dragon) are frequently referred to as Deuterocanonical Books since their canonicity has not been undisputed. As a consequence, when Catholics speak of the OT Apocrypha, they are frequently referring to what Protestants call the OT PSEUDEPIGRAPHA. The Eastern Orthodox Church, at the Synod of Jerusalem in 1672, declared Wisdom of Solomon, Tobit, Judith, I and II Maccabees, and Ecclesiasticus to be canonical. For this confession, therefore, "Apocrypha" generally denotes the remainder of the books noted above plus III and IV Maccabees and Psalm 151. This expanded Apocrypha appears in the 1977 edition of the RSV.

The attitude of Protestants toward the OT Apocrypha has varied over the centuries. In Luther's 1534 translation of the Bible, they are placed between the Testaments with the heading: "Apocrypha: these are books which are not held equal to the Sacred Scriptures and yet are useful and good for reading." Most early English translations, although not that of WYCLIFF (1382), included the Apocrypha, generally between the Testaments. After much controversy, the British and Foreign Bible Society in 1827 decided to suspend "circulation of those books or parts of books which are usually termed Apocryphal." Only in recent years have these writings been included in editions of the Bible and a less polemical attitude been taken toward the Apocrypha by Protestants.

*New Testament Apocrypha.* There also exists what, on the analogy of the OT, has come to be called the NT Apocrypha. These are works produced by early Christians, which are similar both in content and form to NT writings. Among these are gospels, epistles, apocalypses, and "acts" of the various apostles. Although some of these were used by certain groups in the early church, there is no evidence that they were widely circulated or ever given authority outside of very limited circles and thus never enjoyed canonical status.

J.H.

## APOLLINARIANS/APOLLINARIUS. A fourth-century bishop and theologian, and the followers of his views on CHRISTOLOGY. Apollinarius was a leader of the opposition to ARIANISM who, in his attempts to defend the Nicene faith, proposed a view that was soon rejected by the church at large. What he suggested was that in Jesus the eternal Word took the

place of the human spirit. In Jesus there was a human body and "soul"—that which makes the body live—but no human spirit or "rational soul." Simply stated, in his physical life Jesus was a man; but in his mental and spiritual life he was God.

This view, which to Apollinarius seemed quite reasonable, was soon rejected. A synod in Rome in 374 condemned it, and several others concurred, until their actions were definitively upheld by the COUNCIL OF CONSTANTINOPLE in 381. By then, the Apollinarians had left the communion of the church and established their own worship services. On the basis of the council's action, such services were forbidden by the empire, and Apollinarianism eventually died out.

Those who condemned the doctrines of Apollinarius were convinced that his theories undercut the very purpose of the Incarnation. God assumed humanity, they argued, so that humanity could be saved. Therefore, "that which is not assumed, is not saved." In Apollinarius' scheme, God assumed a human body, and thus saved human bodies; but, in not assuming a human "rational soul," God left our rational souls in subjection to sin.　　J.G.

Herbert G. May

*Ruins of the temple of Apollo at Corinth; seven of the thirty-eight monolithic Doric columns, about twenty-four feet high, still stand*

**APOLLO.** An ancient Greek god who had both a terrifying side and a gentle side. He could make people feel their guilt, and even the other gods feared him. But he was also the god of music, poetry, and dance. He was believed to speak through his oracle at DELPHI.　　K.C.

**APOLLOS.** A Jew from ALEXANDRIA (Acts 18:24) who played a prominent part in the early Christian movement. He is described as having knowledge of the story of Jesus (from disciples of John the Baptist?) before he came to Ephesus in A.D. 52. There he was brought into touch with the Christian couple AQUILA

AND PRISCILLA, who instructed him in the complete Christian message (Acts 18:26). As a result Apollos added a new dimension to his natural eloquence and scriptural learning—an experiential knowledge of the Holy Spirit. His fresh understanding and experience of the messianic faith showed itself in his enthusiasm in a mission to the Jews in southern Greece (Acts 18:27-28).

His coming to Corinth, however, led to some unforeseen consequences. A group sprang up in the church there, whether with his consent or not, claiming him as a patron and mentor (I Cor. 1:12; 3:4). The basis of this claim was evidently Apollos' eloquence as a rhetorician and exponent of the OT in the tradition of PHILO, that is, adopting an allegorizing technique. Paul, however, saw the danger of a reliance on human wisdom (I Cor. 1:18—2:10). He went out of his way to stress the unity of purpose between himself and Apollos (I Cor. 3:5-23), and so denied the reason for this party spirit and rivalry (I Cor. 4:6). Apollos took the hint and never returned to Corinth, where his presence could have made matters worse (I Cor. 16:12). He did engage in some (later?) travels, according to Titus 3:13.

R.M.

**APOLOGETICS.** Apologetics traditionally has signified that branch of theology concerned with a reasoned defense of the Christian religion. Recently it has also referred to the general defense of a religious or theistic world view, including arguments for the existence of God, theodicies, and the refutation of atheist or materialist views. In this latter sense, apologetics is akin to NATURAL THEOLOGY. Christian apologetics is more specifically concerned with the rational defense of biblical revelation. In countering objections brought against Christian belief, apologetics does not itself determine the doctrines requiring defense. These are imposed by the criticisms, either explicit or implicit, advanced by the unbeliever or critic. Therefore, because of fresh challenges brought by rival religions or by changes in secular knowledge, the apologetic task must be undertaken anew in every age.

Christianity's claim to absoluteness and universality and the biblical demand that believers be prepared always to give an accounting to those who ask to know the grounds of Christian hope (I Pet. 3:15) have made the apologetic task imperative. The early Christian church, challenged by pagan religions and Hellenistic philosophy, produced the great apologies of Paul and JUSTIN MARTYR, ORIGEN's *Contra Celsum,* and AUGUSTINE's several works against the Manichaean religion (see MANICHAEISM). In the Middle Ages, THOMAS AQUINAS defended Christianity in his *Summa Contra Gentiles* against a resurgent Islam. The most important modern apologetic works include Bishop JOSEPH BUTLER's *Analogy of Religion* (1736) against the DEISTS; SCHLEIERMACHER's *Speeches on Religion* (1799), addressed to the "cultured despisers" of Christianity; and REINHOLD NIEBUHR's *Nature and Destiny of Man* (1940), a profound critique of modern naturalism, idealism, and Marxism and defense of the biblical doctrine of man and history.

Since LUTHER, Protestant theology has occasionally rejected the apologetic task on the grounds that it is the Christian's task, not to argue about or to attempt to prove Christianity but, rather, simply to confront persons with the gospel of God's judgment and mercy. Some NEO-ORTHODOX theologians took this position between 1920 and 1960. The view that there is no "point of contact" between Christian revelation and human reason and experience nevertheless runs against the main current of Christian thought since apostolic times.

J.L.

**APOLOGIA PRO VITA SUA.** *See* NEWMAN, JOHN HENRY CARDINAL.

**APOLOGISTS** (Greek). The collective name given to those early Christian writers, mostly in the second century, who wrote in defense of the faith. The earliest was Quadratus, who wrote in Asia Minor around A.D. 124. His work is probably lost, although some scholars think it may be the one known to us as the EPISTLE TO DIOGNETUS. Others are Aristides, JUSTIN MARTYR, his disciple TATIAN, ATHENAGORAS, and Theophilus of Antioch. Most of them showed great respect for Greco-Roman culture, although a few, such as Tatian, mocked the customs and beliefs of the Greeks and praised the wisdom of the Hebrew "barbarians."

The main task of the Apologists was to refute the accusations, both popular and cultured, leveled against Christians. Among the populace, it was widely believed that Christians ate children, practiced incest, and worshiped an ass. Such notions the Apologists usually rejected with a flat denial. Among the more cultured, it was felt that Christians were an ignorant lot, and that their faith was good only for the ignorant. Against such views, the Apologists sought to show the accord between Christianity and the best of pagan culture—particularly Greek philosophy. In so doing, they were the first to seek to cast the Christian message in a philosophical mold, and therefore some have dubbed them—rather inaccurately—the first systematic theologians of the church.

J.G.

**APOSTATE.** A person who by choice separates from a body to which he or she belongs, whether that be a national or a church community. This means the repudiation of those tenets one has previously professed in the light of new or radically different commitments, or sometimes without adopting any substitute allegiance. In Roman Catholic Canon law one can become an apostate from the faith, from holy orders, or from the monastic state.

I.C.

**A POSTERIORI.** Literally "from that which comes after." It is a term referring to that aspect of thinking or reasoning that moves from effects to causes, from observable results to prior principles, from experience to formative factors. It is the opposite of A PRIORI, which begins with causes. "Inductive" is a possible synonym.

I.C.

**APOSTLE.** Our word comes from the Greek *apostolos,* which means a person to whom responsibility has been assigned or delegated. The apostle carries the authority of the one who did the sending and is commissioned to carry out a transaction or task. The closest followers of Jesus are called apostles in the Gospel tradition (Matt. 10:2; Luke 9:10; Mark 6:30) when he commissioned them to preach and to perform healings and exorcisms. Mark uses the noun "apostle" (6:30), but he prefers the related verb *apostello,* "to send or commission." An essential qualification for being apostles was that they had "been with Jesus" (Mark 3:14).

Paul, on the other hand, identifies himself as an apostle at the opening of several of his letters (Rom. 1:1; I Cor. 1:1; II Cor. 1:1; Gal. 1:1), and that tradition is continued in the later writings attributed to Paul (Col. 1:1; I Tim. 1:1; II Tim. 1:1; Tit. 1:1). Paul offers what amounts to a definition of the role of apostle in I Corinthians 15:7-9, where having seen the Risen Christ and having been commissioned by him are what constitute apostleship. Not every one of the "more than five hundred" to whom the resurrected Lord appeared were numbered among the apostles, but all the apostles had seen him, as Paul implies by his questions in I Corinthians 9:1. What seems to be sharply different between Paul and the Gospels, however, is that at least two of the apostles had not been followers of the earthly Jesus: Paul and James, the brother of Jesus (I Cor. 15:7, 9). One way to reconcile this apparently contradictory evidence is to assume that those who were originally commissioned by Jesus at the outset of his ministry formed the core of those designated by him in his post-resurrection appearances to carry forward his work. It was this larger, more inclusive group commissioned by him to whom this designation of apostle was given. And since it became a familiar title, it was understandably read back into the record of Jesus' initial dealings with his disciples.

Since there had been an original group of twelve (Mark 3:14-16; Matt. 10:2; Luke 6:13) chosen as the inner circle of his followers, and since this number recalled that of the sacred tribes of Israel (Matt. 19:28; Luke 22:30), the central group of apostles after the Resurrection was also twelve in number. It was essential to preserve the Twelve, so that Matthias is reported as chosen to replace Judas, now disgraced and dead (Acts 1:15-26). Not surprisingly, it is also in Acts that the Twelve gather to render formal judgments, as in the case of (1) the assignment of new

responsibilities for administration of welfare in the church (6:2), (2) the approval of the work of Paul among Greek-speaking people (9:26-30), and (3) the recognition of Gentiles as Christians, even though they do not observe Jewish purity laws (chap. 15). In sharp contrast to this authoritative view of the apostles, Paul merely consulted with them and agreed to offer them financial support from the Gentile churches (Gal. 1:15–2:10). He is quite explicit that he neither sought nor gained official approval from "those who were apostles before me" (Gal. 1:17). At the same time, Paul does exercise authority in the churches under his control, as in the incident of aspostlicexpulsion of the incestuous member of the Corinthian church (I Cor. 5). Yet he does not appeal in that incident to his own apostolic office.

In the later Pauline literature, however, the authority of the apostolic office is made explicit: the apostles are the foundation of the church (Eph. 2:20); they are holy men (Eph. 3:5), and are the guarantors of true doctrine and proper moral behavior (II Pet. 3:2). Clearly the process is under way that led to the designation in the second and third centuries of the apostles and their successors as the basic ecclesiastical authority in all matters of faith and practice.

H.K.

**APOSTLES' CREED.** The most commonly used creed in Western churches, both Protestant and Catholic, although unknown in Eastern churches. In its full form, it reads as follows:

> I believe in God the Father Almighty, maker of heaven and earth;
> And in Jesus Christ his only Son our Lord: who was conceived by the Holy Spirit, born of the Virgin Mary, suffered under Pontius Pilate, was crucified, dead, and buried; he descended into hell; the third day he rose from the dead; he ascended into heaven, and sitteth at the right hand of God the Father Almighty; from thence he shall come to judge the quick and the dead.
> I believe in the Holy Spirit, the holy catholic Church, the communion of saints, the forgiveness of sins, the resurrection of the body, and the life everlasting.

The legend that has this creed as the joint composition of the apostles as they prepared to leave Jerusalem has no basis in fact. Actually, the core of the Apostles' Creed seems to have appeared in Rome in the middle of the second century and to have been directed specifically against the teachings of Marcion. Marcion held that matter was evil, that Jesus was not born, and that the gospel includes no word of judgment, but only grace. He also held that the Creator was not the same as the Father of Jesus Christ. A careful reading of the Apostles' Creed will show that such views are rejected by it.

To the core, which was prepared against Marcion, other elements were added through the years. These are particularly the DESCENT INTO HELL, which some churches today do not include in the creed, and most of the final clauses of the creed. Several clauses were added in the course of later controversies, in order to exclude various heresies.

This creed became dominant in the West as a result of the FILIOQUE controversy, which centered on an interpolation in the NICENE CREED. The East rejected that interpolation, and the Franks insisted on it. In order to avoid the issue, the popes began using the so-called Apostles' Creed instead of the Nicene.

J.G.

**APOSTOLIC COUNCIL.** The meeting of early church leaders in Jerusalem according to Acts 15. The immediate occasion was evidently the success attending Paul's mission to the Gentiles, in which many non-Jews had been won over to the faith without having received the Jewish initiatory rite of CIRCUMCISION. News of this event had reached the Jerusalem church, where alarm was felt.

The discussion (Acts 15:2) centered on the conditions to be imposed on Gentile converts. The strict Jewish Christians were insisting on circumcision (15:1, 5), whereas Paul and Barnabas stood for a liberal attitude. The issue was not the admission of the Gentiles, but the terms on which they were to be admitted. The danger of a split in the early church with two centers, one in Jerusalem, the other in Antioch—which was the headquarters of Paul's missionary endeavors—was present.

The chief speakers were Peter, who rehearsed God's dealings with him leading to the conversion of Cornelius (Acts 10–11), who received the Spirit without mention of circumcision, and James, the leader in Jerusalem who contributed the point that the reception of Gentiles was already promised in the OT, based on Amos 9:11 (and following) in the Greek Bible. The verdict passed went in favor of Paul's mission (Acts 15:19). Yet James wished to safeguard the Jewish position by imposing a "decree" (Acts 15:20; 21:24-25) that regulated table fellowship between the two wings of the church and insisted on Gentile believers restricting their diet to kosher foods. Whether Paul actually accepted this ruling is uncertain since he never quotes the decree in his correspondence with the church when he might have done so (I Cor. 8, 10).

R.M.

**APOSTOLIC FATHERS.** The collective name of the earliest Christian writings apart from those in the NT. These usually include: (1) The *Epistle to the Corinthians* of CLEMENT OF ROME, dealing mostly with the need for unity among Christians; (2) the DIDACHE or *Doctrine of the Twelve Apostles*, dealing with issues of worship and church order; (3) the seven letters which IGNATIUS OF ANTIOCH wrote on his way to martyrdom; (4) a letter which POLYCARP of Smyrna wrote to the Philippians asking for news of Ignatius; (5) the remaining fragments of the *Exposition of the Sayings of the Lord* by PAPIAS OF HIERAPOLIS; (6) the EPISTLE OF BARNABAS, which is really a sermon by an unknown author, dealing with the relationship between Christianity and Judaism; (7) the *Shepherd of*

HERMAS, who was concerned with the forgiveness of post-baptismal sins; (8) the EPISTLE TO DIOGNETUS, which in truth should be counted among the APOLOGISTS. To these are often added other related writings, such as the *Martyrdom of Polycarp* and the *Second Epistle of Clement,* which is not his. The Apostolic Fathers are very valuable as our main source for the life of the church after NT times. Some were included in the NT before the CANON was fixed.

J.G.

**APOSTOLIC SEE.** The administrative center of the Roman Catholic Church, including the POPE and the ROMAN CURIA (see ROMAN CATHOLICISM). "See" is derived from the Latin term *sedes,* a chair, and refers to the seat or residence of a bishop. The office of bishop is symbolized by the seat or chair occupied by the bishop during worship and rituals.

J.C.

**APOSTOLIC SUCCESSION.** A term denoting an authentic, unbroken ministry from the apostles to the present, guaranteed by the bishop's laying on of hands at ordination. In the early church it symbolized true teaching as well as valid leadership. Plagued by second-century teachers like Valentinus (see VALENTINIAN GNOSTICISM) and MARCION, and believing that disunity threatened the church's survival, the early church argued that only those bishops with a direct line to Christ and his teachings through the apostles were authentic bearers of Christianity. Only such bishops were endowed by the Holy Spirit to ordain and to teach. Rome, Jerusalem, Ephesus, Antioch, and others supported this view. Rome boasted a double descent through Peter and Paul, and assumed a place of primacy as early as Clement I in A.D. 96. However, ordination became the focal point in apostolic succession.

The Roman Catholic and Greek Orthodox churches accept each other's orders, despite disputes. The Greeks accept Anglican orders, but Rome does not. Rome disputed Archbishop Parker's descent and consecration, and in 1896 Pope Leo XIII declared Anglican orders null and void. The fact of continuous descent is often questioned. Protestants generally do not acknowledge the necessity of apostolic succession, and today it is a primary barrier to ecumenicity.

C.M.

**APOTHEOSIS.** From the Greek word *apotheou,* meaning "to deify" or "to create a god", from the ancient Greek polytheistic idea in which there are many gods of various ranks, with divine men or heroes representing human beings who become divine. At times even living men, like Alexander's father, Philip II of Macedon, and, later, Alexander the Great, were worshiped as gods.

J.C.

**A PRIORI.** Literally "from what is before," referring to such concepts as God, freedom, and immortality.

Such are considered to be innate in human perception, rather than the result of human experience. Friedrich Schleiermacher preferred "to be conscious of oneself as being in relation to God." In contrast, this phrase has been used by philosophers such as KANT to refer to objective reality not dependent on our experience. (*See* A POSTERIORI.)

I.C.

**APSE.** An arc, a semicircular enclosure, in which the aisles and choir of cathedrals and churches end. Within the apse lie the altar and the bishop's throne, as well as benches or pews for the clergy, arranged on both sides. This style was not used until after the fifth century A.D.

J.C.

**AQUILA AND PRISCILLA.** Two people, husband and wife (her name is shortened to Prisca in some texts, chiefly in Paul's letters), who met Paul in Corinth (Acts 18:1-3), and were drawn to him because they shared his occupation as tentmaker (or worker in leather). Their home was in Pontus in northeast Asia Minor. They had been in Rome but were expelled by CLAUDIUS' edict driving out all Jews in A.D. 49. They visited Ephesus when Paul left for that city (Acts 18:18-28), and a church was formed in their home there (I Cor. 16:19). After Claudius' expulsion order lapsed, they returned to Rome (Rom. 16:3, if this chapter is an integral part of the Letter to the Romans, and not an appendix added onto a copy of the letter Paul sent to Ephesus, as some scholars believe). Their stay in Ephesus is attested in II Timothy 4:19—if that letter is genuinely addressed to Timothy in Ephesus.

The picture we glean from these itinerary references is that of a Christian couple who jointly exercised a teaching office (Acts 18:24-26), and moved around the churches with a considerable degree of mobility. Their home was a gathering place for believers. The fact that Priscilla's name often appears first in sequence has led to the speculation that she was an influential woman, and even a writer of one of our NT books (Harnack's theory), namely, the Letter to the Hebrews. On surer ground we may certainly applaud the courage of this couple and their fidelity to Paul, whose commendation of them is eloquent (Rom. 16:3).

R.M.

**AQUINAS, THOMAS.** Dominican theologian of the thirteenth century, whose work marks the high point of SCHOLASTICISM. He was born in Italy near the outskirts of Naples, probably in 1224. His family was aristocratic, and his brothers and sisters eventually became persons of eminence in Italian social circles. Thomas, the youngest, had been destined by his parents to an ecclesiastical career. Consequently he was placed in the monastery of Montecassino when he was five years old. At fourteen, he went to the University of Naples, where he first came in contact with the Aristotelian philosophy, which was being reintroduced into western Europe. With such training and the support of his family, a brilliant career was open to him.

But in 1244 young Thomas decided to join a recently founded organization—the DOMINICAN Order of Preachers. Many viewed with contempt the Dominicans' practice of living on alms. Fearing that Thomas would ruin his career, his family kidnapped him and kept him a prisoner for over a year. During this time they tried to dissuade him from joining the Dominicans.

He escaped, became a Dominican, and was sent to study at Cologne, where ALBERTUS MAGNUS was teaching. His genius was not apparent to his classmates, who called him "the dumb ox" because of his size and paucity of speech. But soon Albertus and others recognized his ability and directed him toward an academic career. He spent most of that career at the University of Paris.

Like all university professors at that time, he commented on various books of Scripture as well as on the *Sentences* of PETER LOMBARD. These commentaries, along with his *Summa contra gentiles* and his *Summa theologia* (or *Summa theologica*), are his most important theological works. He also wrote about philosophy, especially commentaries on ARISTOTLE. He died in 1274, and his former teacher Albertus Magnus became the champion of his work, which many considered heretical.

The great challenge to theology in Thomas' time was the philosophy of Aristotle, which was being brought into western Europe by means of new Latin translations. Many philosophers, particularly at the University of Paris, claimed that on the basis of the newly translated works, philosophy must come to a number of conclusions that contradicted generally accepted doctrine—conclusions such as that matter has always existed, and that all souls ("active intellects") are one. In reaction, many church leaders declared that the traditional Platonic and Augustinian philosophy (see PLATONISM and AUGUSTINIANISM) was the only true one, and banned the study and discussion of certain elements of Aristotelian philosophy.

Thomas took up the challenge, and set out to show that Christian faith is compatible with Aristotelian philosophy, as long as one understands the proper field and methodology of both theology and philosophy. His commentaries on Aristotle often sought to prove that the opinions attributed to the Philosopher were not his own, but rather the result of mistaken interpretations. But it was the *Summa theologica*, more so than any of his previous works, that showed that it was possible to interpret the Christian faith in a perfectly orthodox way while making use of Aristotelian philosophy.

THOMISM—the name given to Thomas' system— came under attack from both extreme Aristotelians and traditional theologians. There were repeated charges against the innovations of Thomas. In 1277, three years after the death of Thomas, the bishop of Paris issued a condemnation of 219 Aristotelian propositions, several of which had been held by Thomas. Similar steps were taken at Oxford. But slowly, with the staunch defense of many Dominicans, Thomism gained acceptance. In 1323 John XXII canonized Thomas, and in 1567 Pius V declared him a "Universal Doctor of the Church."

J.G.

**ARABIA/ARABIANS.** The world's largest peninsula, located in southwest Asia, whose inhabitants, consisting of various groups of Semitic peoples, receive the general label "Arabians." Ordinarily the OT designates the Arabians by such group names as Ishmaelites, Midianites, and Sabeans.

*Geography.* This basically rectangular peninsula encompasses almost one million square miles of predominantly desert terrain (roughly one-third the size of the continental United States). It is bounded on the north by modern Jordan, Syria, and Iraq; on the east by the Persian Gulf; on the south by the Indian Ocean; and on the west by the Red Sea. Following Ptolemy, the second-century A.D. geographer of Alexandria, classical geographers assigned Arabia a three-part division: Arabia Petrea in the northwest, including Sinai, Edom, Moab, and east trans-Jordan; Arabia Deserta, comprising the Syrian Desert; and Arabia Felix, the southern section. (Today most of the peninsula is claimed by Saudi Arabia.) Sporadic rainfall doomed the land to limited fertility, and a coastline with few harbors discouraged the emergence of sizable settlements. Understandably, a nomadic life-style was the norm for Arabia's inhabitants.

*Arabians in Biblical Tradition.* Among the earliest Arabians mentioned are the Ishmaelites (Gen. 37:25) and Midianites (37:28) of the second millennium B.C. who actively engaged in wide-ranging caravan trade. In the twelfth century B.C. the Midianites, Amalekites, and Bene Qedem (people of the East), advantaged by the domesticated camel, terrorized Gideon's tribe of Manasseh (Judg. 6–7). In the ninth century the Arabs carried away the family and property of Jehoram, king of Judah (II Chr. 21:16-17, though II Kings contains no parallel), and four centuries later Nabatean Arabs frustrated Nehemiah's efforts to rebuild Jerusalem (Neh. 2:19; 4:7-8; 6:1-6). Moreover, the list of traditional enemies offered by Psalm 83 includes the Ishmaelites (v. 6).

Other texts, however, show Israel prospering from Arabian contacts. In the tenth century Solomon engaged in successful caravan trade with the Sabeans (presumably stimulating the queen of Sheba's visitation, I Kings 10:1-10). A century later the Arabians awarded Jehoshaphat, king of Judah, tribute of livestock (II Chr. 17:11, again without

parallel in II Kings). Arabian resources of frankincense, gold, livestock, and textiles regularly arrived in Israel by camel caravan (Jer. 6:20; II Chr. 9:14; Isa. 60:6-7; Ezek. 27:20-21). Luke reports that Arabians were among those assembled in Jerusalem at Pentecost (Acts 2:11), and Paul, in reflecting on his apostolic commission, mentions his Arabian sojourn in Nabatean territory southeast of Damascus (Gal. 1:17).

J.K.K.

**ARAD.** (1) A Canaanite city in the NEGEB, whose king took some Israelites captive as they headed toward Mount Hor near the end of the wilderness era (Num. 21:1-3). Under Joshua that king or his successor, along with his city, was overtaken by Israel (Josh. 12:14). Nomadic Kenites reoccupied the site (Judg. 1:16). Excavations at Tell Arad, sixteen miles south of Hebron, have uncovered an impressive Israelite sanctuary constructed in the tenth century B.C. and vacated in the seventh, when the centralization of Israelite worship at Jerusalem intensified.

(2) Son of Beriah, a Bejaminite (I Chr. 8:15).

J.K.K.

**ARAM.** (1) Son of Shem and grandson of Noah in the Table of Nations (Gen. 10:22; compare I Chr. 1:17).

(2) Son of Kemuel and grandson of Nahor, Abraham's brother (Gen. 22:21). These names point to the vicinity of Haran and reflect the keen sense of kinship that the Israelite patriarchs had to the Arameans.

(3) Son of Shemer in the Asher genealogy (I Chr. 7:34).

(4) Primarily a collective designation for the ARAMEANS who dwelt in scattered settlements in a plain stretching from the Lebanon Mountains to beyond the Euphrates. When "Aram" is compounded with another noun, a more precise location is achieved. Thus Aram-naharaim ("Aram of the rivers") refers to a region between the Tigris and Euphrates in which Paddan-aram was located (Gen. 28:5), the ancestral home of the patriarchs. During the era of the monarchy, the concentration of Aramean power in Damascus sometimes proved troublesome for Israel (for example, I Kings 22:1-38). Damascus succumbed to Assyrian aggression in 732 B.C., a mere decade before Israel's own fall.

J.K.K.

**ARAMAIC.** A general term used to refer to a group of closely related Semitic dialects. In the OT, Ezra 4:8–6:18; 7:12-26; Daniel 2:4b–7:28, and a single verse in Jeremiah (10:11) are written in Aramaic. The NT contains several Aramaic expressions: *Talitha cumi* (Mark 5:41), *Ephphatha* (Mark 7:34), *Elo-i, Elo-i, lama sabach-thani* (Mark 15:34), and *Maranatha* (I Cor. 16:22 KJV).

Aramaic derives its name from its earliest users, the ARAMEANS, who are first noted in an inscription of the Assyrian king Tiglath-Pileser I (about 1115-1077 B.C.). Scholars speak of four phases in the use of the Aramaic language. The first, Old Aramaic (about 925–700 B.C.), is represented by several inscriptions, including international treaties, as well as a text about the figure Balaam discovered at the site of Tell Deir Alla in Transjordan. In the second phase, Official or Imperial Aramaic (about 700–200 B.C.) became an international language in the Near East. This widespread use of Aramaic developed during Assyrian domination (see ASSYRIA). The negotiations between King HEZEKIAH and the officials of the Assyrian king SENNACHERIB (in 701 B.C.) illustrate the diplomatic use of Aramaic (see II Kings 18:26-27). In later periods, and especially under the Persians, Aramaic became the international language in a vast region from Egypt and Asia Minor in the south and west, to India in the east. The Aramaic in Ezra and Daniel belongs to this Imperial Aramaic.

During the third phase, Middle Aramaic (200 B.C.–A.D. 200), Aramaic was replaced by Greek as the international language. But Aramaic continued as the everyday language in many regions. This Aramaic was the common language in Palestine at the time of Jesus and the early church. From this period also come some of the early Aramaic translations (the TARGUMS) of portions of the OT, as well as numerous inscriptions and other texts. Various dialects of Aramaic, such as Palestinian, Nabatean, Palmyrene, and early Syriac, existed during this period. Mark 15:70 and Matthew 26:73 may suggest that different dialects of Aramaic were spoken in Galilee and Judah.

Finally, Late Aramaic (from A.D. 200 on), with its various dialects, is reflected in the Jewish Targums and TALMUDS, the Syriac translation of the Bible (the PESHITTA), Samaritan texts, and other documents. Even today, various forms of Aramaic are spoken by Jews and Christians in several areas of the Near East.
                                                                                                 J.H.

**ARAMEAN.** A term designating an ARAMAIC speaker and/or a native of Aram. The term "Aramean(s)" or "Aram" occurs frequently in the Hebrew OT but is generally translated, following early Greek practice, as "Syrians(s)" or "Syria" (see, for example, II Sam. 8:5-6).

The territory of Aram is rather ill-defined in both biblical and nonbiblical texts but generally denotes the region of the upper Tigris-Euphrates (Mesopotamian) valley and Syria (see MESOPOTAMIA). The biblical texts locate Arameans both east and west of the Euphrates River.

Old Testament texts closely associate the ancestors of Israel with the Arameans. Deuteronomy 26:5 describes one of the Israelite patriarchs (probably Jacob) as "a wandering Aramean." The wife of Isaac and the wives of Jacob (Gen. 24:1-61; 28:1–30:13) came from the region of Aram in northern Mesopotamia, and their fathers-in-law, Bethuel and Laban, are referred to as Aramean (Gen. 25:20; 28:5; 31:20, 24).
                                                                                                 J.H.

**ARARAT.** The biblical equivalent of Urartu, an ancient non-Semitic kingdom roughly identifiable with the classical Armenia north of Mesopotamia, now politically divided between Turkey and the Soviet Union. It is mentioned in II Kings 19:37 and Isaiah 37:38 as the place where the Assyrian king SENNACHERIB's assassins took refuge. In Jeremiah 51:27 it is referred to as simply a kingdom.

In Genesis 8:4 the ark of Noah is said to have come to rest "upon the mountains of Ararat." Not one mountain is singled out in the biblical narrative (in distinction to the Mesopotamian Flood Epic of GILGAMESH, which identified the site as Mount Nisir in the vicinity of Lake Van). Nevertheless, through the centuries there has been a persistent desire, born of a pious quest of "holy places," to pinpoint the location of Mount Ararat. The present contender for the title, which it has won through a variety of considerations, including the political and the relative facility of access by explorers, is the mountain known in Turkish as Ağri Daği, which stands 16,950 feet (about 5166 meters) high. The tradition identifying this as *the* "Mount" hardly dates from before the eleventh century A.D.
                                                                                                 B.V.

**ARCHAEOLOGY.** Archaeology is the systematic description and analysis of the material remains of ancient cultures, both written and "silent." Biblical archaeology, in contrast to such regionally specialized fields as Egyptian, Mesopotamian, and even Syro-Palestinian archaeology, continues to pursue the original quest of all Near Eastern archaeology to reconstruct a cultural and historical matrix in which to place the literature of the Bible.

*History and Scope.* At its beginning, archaeology was basically a treasure hunt. However, by the turn of the nineteenth century, the collection and study of antiquities was moving onto a scientific basis. A major step was taken when the young French scholar Champollion broke the code of the hieroglyphics by using the ROSETTA STONE found in 1799 in Egypt. Soon there followed Botta's excavations of the Assyrian city at Khorsabad, Layard's work at Nineveh, and Schliemann's dramatic find of the buried treasure of Troy. Archaeological work in the Holy Land proper did not begin until Sir Flinders Petrie excavated Tell el-Hesi in 1890.

Since then, biblical archaeology has given us great gifts, chief of which is a significantly clearer picture of the religious, linguistic, and historical contexts out of which our Bible came. It has made clear that the full story of biblical faith is not to be found exclusively in Israel and the early church. It has made possible an assessment of the relative maturity of biblical thought by recovering theological literature from other cultures with which to compare it. In many instances,

# BIBLICAL ARCHAEOLOGY TIME-LINE

*(Entries in bold are discussed in article)*

| PALESTINE | DATES | SYRIA, MESOPOTAMIA, EGYPT | AGE |
|---|---|---|---|
| Great tower at Jericho<br>Pottery | 8,000 B.C.<br>4,500 B.C. | | NEOLITHIC (Late Stone) |
| Copper tools<br>Writing & art | 3,150 B.C. | | CHALCOLITHIC ("Copper/Stone") |
| **Canaanite Sanctuaries—Ai** ←Amurru→ | 2,200 B.C. | Sumerian & Akkadian city-states<br>**Ebla** | EARLY BRONZE |
| The Patriarchs? ◄<br>Canaan | 1,550 B.C. | | MIDDLE BRONZE |
| | 1,200 B.C. | **Uggarit**<br>Akh-en-Aton **Tell el-Amarna**<br>Ramses II | LATE BRONZE |
| Israel & Moses ◄<br>Sea Peoples<br>**Hazor destroyed** Conquest (Joshua) | 1,000 B.C. | | IRON I |
| David and Solomon<br>**Solomonic Architecture**<br>**Samaria**<br>**Siloam tunnel**<br>Jeremiah<br>**Lachish ostraca** | 586 B.C. | Assyria<br><br><br><br><br>Babylon | IRON II |
| Exile<br>Temple rebuilt | 332 B.C. | Cyrus, King of Persia<br>Alexander the Great | IRON III (Persian Period) |
| | 37 B.C. | | HELLENISTIC |
| Herod the Great<br>**Temple reconstructed**<br>**Caesarea**<br>Jesus<br>**Masada**<br>Paul<br>Dead Sea Scrolls | A.D.70 | | ROMAN I (Herodian) |

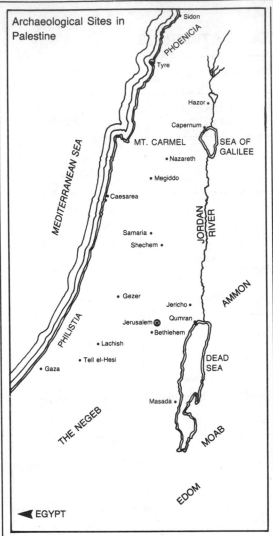

Archaeological Sites in Palestine

language family of which Hebrew is a later descendant.

The transition from early to middle Bronze Age was marked by disruptions all over the Middle East and Egypt, evidently due to the incursion of the Amurru (Amorites), a nomadic group that spoke a west Semitic language. Archaeologists and historians usually associate the movement of the patriarchs (Gen. 12:50) with these Amurru.

During the late Bronze Age, Canaanite culture flourished. Archaeology has produced a rich store of Canaanite texts from the ancient site of UGARIT (Ras Shamra) on the Mediterranean coast of Syria. These fourteenth-century B.C. texts, first deciphered in 1930, make it clear that the religion of Israel was profoundly indebted to the religion of Canaan. The poetry of Ugarit has affinities to our Psalter, and the language itself is quite similar to Hebrew. On the other hand, the religion was of the polytheistic fertility variety; the cult of its god Baal existed everywhere Canaanite culture was found, including in Israel. The late Bronze Age was also a period of Egyptian domination of Palestine. At Tell el-'AMARNA, the desert capital of the pharaoh Akh-en-aton (Amenophis IV), were found letters from Egyptian vassals in Palestine and elsewhere complaining of raids by brigands and outlaws called "Apiru." The connection of this term with Hebrew, while obvious, is not fully understood.

With the Iron Age also arrived two new peoples in Palestine: the Sea Peoples (some of whom later became known as the Philistines) from the west, and the Israelites from the south and east. Archaeology has not, however, been able either to confirm or to deny the account of Israel's conquest of Palestine contained in the book of Joshua. For example, almost none of late Bronze-early Iron Age Jericho is extant, and what little does remain suggests a destruction at the beginning of the thirteenth century B.C. at the latest. If the exodus from Egypt took place, as most scholars think it did, around 1250 B.C., during the reign of Rameses II, Jericho simply would not have been around to destroy twenty to forty years later. On the other hand, Hazor was indeed destroyed in a violent conflagration not too long after 1300 B.C. (Josh. 11:10-13).

In terms of linkages to the biblical text, the most important period of Palestinian archaeology quite understandably is Iron II, the period of the Israelite monarchy. Although no trace of the Temple of Solomon remains in Jerusalem, very substantial Solomonic structures have come to light at Hazor, Gezer, Megiddo, and elsewhere. These are all characterized by such architectural details as casemate city walls and three-roomed gates. The affinity of many buildings with Phoenician architecture fits well with the biblical record that Solomon received assistance in his construction projects from Hiram, king of Tyre (I Kings 5:5-6). Some time after the separation of the kingdom of Israel from Judah, Omri

the historical records uncovered by archaeology have provided independent, secular verification of the historical data of the biblical text—even though it will always be the case that the religious truth claims of the biblical text can neither be validated nor invalidated by archaeological discovery.

*The Emerging Archaeological Picture of the World of the Bible.* The earliest archaeological era to have direct bearing on the biblical text is the early Bronze Age (see the time line). In that millennium, the Canaanite inhabitants of Palestine began to erect fortified cities. In a number of these, substantial high places and sanctuaries have been identified, including one at Ai, which displays the same three-part floor plan used in Solomon's temple fifteen hundred years later. The recent discovery of EBLA at Tell Mardikh in the Syrian desert promises to expand our knowledge of the end of the early Bronze Age. It is already clear that the fourteen thousand or more tablets found there are written in an early form of the same northwest Semitic built a new capital at Samaria (I Kings 16:24). Excavations at the site confirm that the town was begun in the Iron II period. In addition to well-built structures, Samaria has also yielded ostraca—potsherds upon which messages and records are written in ink. These are among the earliest Hebrew inscriptions anywhere.

Carved ivory furniture ornamentation has also been found, confirming the allusions to the wealth of that community in I Kings 22:39 and in Amos 6:4-7. Elaborate water systems also typify Iron II; they are found at Megiddo, Hazor, and the very significant Siloam tunnel in Jerusalem itself (II Kings 20:20; II Chr. 32:30).

Iron II ends with the conquest of the southern kingdom of Judah by the Neo-Babylonian king Nebuchadnezzar in 587 B.C. It was his total destruction of Jerusalem that forever erased the original city of David and nearly all evidences of the Davidic dynasty there. Nevertheless, a poignant reminder of that conquest survives in the twenty-one LACHISH OSTRACA. These are messages from the defenders of that fortified city southwest of Jerusalem, some of which report that they can no longer see the signals of other outposts, presumably because they have been taken by the Babylonians.

In the Roman I period, nearly three centuries later, archaeology throws striking light on the pluralism of Judaism in the time of Jesus. Above all, of course, mention should be made of the massive platform wall of the Temple of Herod the Great, which remains today on the west side of the sacred enclosure in Jerusalem upon which stands the Islamic shrine, the Dome of the Rock. This is the Wailing Wall, or "Western Wall," of such great significance in Jewish life. Nothing of Herod's Temple as such remains; but other Herodian monuments in Jerusalem, Samaria, Masada, and especially Caesarea on the Mediterranean coast, pay tribute to the thoroughly Roman architectural taste, if not the moral caliber, of the man.

Finally, from this same period emerged one of the most extraordinary archaeologial finds of all time—the DEAD SEA SCROLLS—from the ancient communal settlement at QUMRAN on the west shore of the Dead Sea. This monastic community was founded in the first century B.C. and survived earthquakes and the rigors of desert life for nearly two centuries. Although the buildings were destroyed in A.D. 68 by the tenth Roman legion under Titus, who was in Palestine to suppress the first Jewish revolt, those scrolls that had been deposited by the sectarians in caves around the site survived for nearly two millennia. It was not an archaeologist but a Bedouin shepherd boy who had the privilege of discovering them there in 1947.

W.S.T.

**ARCHANGEL.** *See* MICHAEL, THE ARCHANGEL.

**ARCHDEACON.** A diocesan office in existence since the third century, although the title dates from the fourth century. An archdeacon is a priest who

supervises a fixed territory, assisting the bishop in liturgical and administrative functions. In ancient times, the archdeacon had the right of succession to the SEE.

J.C.

**ARCHDIOCESE.** A territorial division of the Roman Catholic church ruled by a bishop in his own right. It is called an eparchy in the Orthodox church. An archdiocese is usually the same area as a civil political division. It is usually named after the city in which the bishop lives.

J.C.

**AREOPAGUS.** The place-name (found only in Acts 17:22) derives from *Areios pagos* in Greek, meaning "the hill of Ares," the god of war whom the Romans called Mars. Hence "Mars' Hill" in the KJV of the above text.

Topographically it refers to a small hill northwest of the ACROPOLIS in ATHENS. The term "Areopagus" also is used to denote the Council of the Areopagus, a judicial body, which used to meet in later times not on Mars' Hill but in the market-place at Athens, in the "Royal Portico" *(stoa basileios).*

There are two views as to the precise location of Paul's meeting with philosophers in Athens, according to the narrative in Acts 17:16-34. One interpretation is that Paul was called to an official investigation to defend his teaching, and the court met either on the hill or in the *stoa basileios.* The other view thinks more of an informal gathering of philosophers on the Areopagus hill. The weight of opinion is on the side of the second reconstruction since there is little suggestion in the text that Paul was called to a legal arraignment. The reference to Dionysius the Areopagite (Acts 17:34) may suggest that the council did meet informally, and it has been cogently argued that the group met in or in front of a colonnade of the market-place.

Paul's speech exploited his interest in both groups—Stoics and Epicureans—in his audience, as he valiantly made an appeal to their cherished beliefs. But in vain; when he touched on distinctively Christian matters, they dismissed him, with the sole exception of one of the council members, Dionysius.

R.M.

**ARIANISM/ARIUS.** The doctrine that the Word or Son of God is not eternal, but is rather the first of all creatures. This view was proposed by Arius, a presbyter of Alexandria, Egypt, early in the fourth century. The slogan, "there was a time when he [the Word] was not" expressed Arius' position in a nutshell. To this, his opponents countered that the Word is divine and therefore eternal. Arius and his teachings were condemned at the COUNCIL OF NICEA in A.D. 325. But then, through a series of political circumstances, Arianism enjoyed a revival, until the

COUNCIL OF CONSTANTINOPLE, in A.D. 381, reaffirmed and expanded the decisions of Nicea. These debates were the occasion for the formulation of the doctrine of the TRINITY. The controversy was also important for CHRISTOLOGY, for it was the Council of Nicea that categorically affirmed the divinity of the Son. The key word affirming this in the Creed of Nicea was HOMOOUSION, "of the same substance," meaning that the Father and the Son are both equally divine.

Arius himself died shortly after the Council of Nicea. His more extreme followers, however, continued insisting on the radical difference between God and the Son or Word. For this reason they were called *anomoeans,* from a Greek word meaning "different." Others straddled the fence by declaring that the Son was "similar" to the Father, and not clarifying the matter any further. These were called *homoeans,* from a word meaning "similar." Many who sought to safeguard the divinity of the Son, but who feared that the term *homoousios* was capable of an interpretation that erased all distinction between the Father and the Son, preferred to use the term *homoiousion*—of a similar substance. The great opponents of Arianism, particularly ATHANASIUS and the CAPPADOCIAN FATHERS, managed to allay the fears of the homoiousians and thus prepared the way for the final condemnation of Arianism in A.D. 381.

By that time, however, several of the tribes north of the Danube, particularly the Goths and the Vandals, had been converted to Christianity in its Arian form. These tribes later invaded the West, and Arianism had a brief revival in areas such as Italy, Spain, and North Africa.                                                    J.G.

**ARIMATHEA.** A city and district northwest of Jerusalem, which was added to Judah during the Hasmonaean period (mid-first century B.C.). Control of this territory, located about twenty miles due east of Joppa (present-day Tel Aviv), helped assure Jewish access to the sea. Joseph, who arranged for Jesus to be buried in his private tomb (Mark 15:43; Matt. 27:57; Luke 23:51; John 19:38) was from Arimathea.
                                                                        H.K.

**ARISTOTLE.** Aristotle (384-322 B.C.) was not only one of the greatest Greek philosophers but one of the very greatest ever produced by any nation. His legacy is discernible in virtually every branch of Western learning. This is partly because of his own encyclopedic investigations in numerous fields—biology, physics, psychology, metaphysics, ethics, politics, literature, and others. Equally important was his pioneering work in logic and EPISTEMOLOGY, so that he set up patterns of thought and argument, and categories of understanding which were destined to hold their place in the West for generations, and even now have not been left behind.

Not the least has his influence been felt in Christian theology, for although in the patristic and early medieval periods PLATONISM and NEOPLATONISM were the strongest influences in theology, the rediscovery of Aristotle in the thirteenth century brought his ideas into the theological mainstream, through the work of AQUINAS and others. It could indeed be claimed that among philosophical conceptions of God, it is the Aristotelian one that best corresponds to the transcendent God of the Bible. Though he began as a disciple of Platonism, Aristotle became a realist (*see* REALISM) in opposition to the IDEALISM of Plato; that is to say, he rejected Plato's belief that reality belongs to the timeless invisible forms or ideas, and held that these forms do not exist independently but only as manifested in the concrete individual things that make up the world. These things are the real beings or substances. Each of them is composed of matter and form. Matter is mere potentiality that is dependent upon form to have actuality. However, there is a hierarchy of forms, each of which may be the matter for a higher form. But there is not an infinite regress of forms. One comes eventually to a pure form (something like Plato's idea of the good), which cannot itself be matter for any higher form. This pure form Aristotle calls the "Unmoved Mover." He seems to conceive its relation to the world in terms of final rather than efficient causation. The Unmoved Mover draws the finite beings of the world after itself. But although Aristotle's conception of God is monotheistic and transcendent, it appears also to be purely intellectual and impersonal. God's activity is pure thinking of God's own thought.

The form/matter schema is also applied to the human being. The soul is the form of the body. Here too there is a hierarchy of forms. There is a vegetative soul, concerned with merely biological functions; an animal soul, which rises to sentience; and at the head of this hierarchy is the rational soul, which gives to human beings their distinctive status ("the rational animal"), and this rational element in the soul is the immortal part of a human being. The Aristotelian ethic is derived from these fundamental conceptions. The good for humanity is happiness, but this is not just good fortune, but rather the development of character according to reason. In his detailed treatment of the individual virtues, Aristotle seeks to show that these are the rational means between extremes—courage, for instance, is the mean between rashness and cowardice. Although his views, both on metaphysics and ethics, may seem distant from Christianity at many points, THOMISM has shown the possibility of synthesis.
                                                                        J.M.

**ARK, NOAH'S.** *See* NOAH.

**ARK OF THE COVENANT.** A box made of acacia wood overlaid with gold and crowned with two golden cherubim bending over the cover or "mercy seat," which ancient Israel believed to have been

God's throne or footstool. It is said to have contained only the two tablets of the Law that Moses brought down from HOREB. In the earliest tradition the ark preceded Israel in its journey through the wilderness and was carried into battle with the cry, "Arise, O Lord, and let thy enemies be scattered" (Num. 10:33-36). During the conquest, it was the ark, carried by the Levitical priests, that opened the Jordan River to allow Israel to pass through (Josh. 3) and that brought down the walls of Jericho (Josh. 6).

Holand-Garber model of Solomon's Temple, Agnes Scott College, Decatur, Georgia

*A model of the Ark of the Covenant*

The function of the ark as a locus of oracles is evident in Judges 20:27 and becomes more dramatic after the ark is installed at the central Israelite sanctuary at SHILOH. There before the ark Samuel received his prophetic call (I Sam. 3). When the Philistines captured the ark, Israel believed that the luminous presence ("glory") of God had departed from Israel (I Sam. 4:19-22). However, the Philistines found it too hard to cope with because they were afflicted with boils and their god DAGON fell flat on his face in ASHDOD. So they returned it to Israel by oxcart. After a brief stay in Beth-shemesh (I Sam. 6), the ark ultimately reached the town of Kiriath-jearim, where it remained until David brought it up to Jerusalem (II Sam. 6). There Solomon built his Temple in order to provide a permanent home for it (I Kings 8).

The most elaborate descriptions of the ark and its rich golden ornamentation were actually written after the ark was lost in the destruction of Jerusalem by Nebuchadnezzar in 587 B.C. They were written by the Priestly writers who worked during and after the Babylonian exile and are found in Exodus 25:10-22; 37:1-9; and chapter 40.

Apart from a dramatic passage in Psalm 132:6-10, which seems to provide us a liturgical reenactment of the bringing of the ark to Jerusalem, the rest of the Bible pays remarkably little attention to it. Jeremiah even dismisses it as unnecessary for the coming age of restoration (Jer. 3:16).

W.S.T.

**ARMAGEDDON.** This geographic place name (in Hebrew) apparently means "mountain of Megiddo" (*har-megiddon; har-magedon* in Greek), though there is no certainty that this is what is intended in the sole biblical reference to Armageddon (Rev. 16:16). In that verse the place is the meeting point of the kings of the world who gather for apocalyptic judgment dispensed by God Almighty. Perhaps the seer of

REVELATION intended the name to be symbolic. If so, we should inquire what Megiddo came to represent in OT history.

At MEGIDDO Israel defeated Sisera the Canaanite (Judg. 5:19), and here, too, Josiah was brought to his end by Pharaoh Neco (II Kings 23:29-30; II Chr. 35:22). The place name is therefore appropriate for the final engagement between good and evil—an idea already implied in Ezekiel 39:1-4.

R.M.

**ARMENIAN CHURCH.** Two branches of the ancient Armenian Apostolic Church have been established in the United States. They trace their roots to the See of Etchmiadzin, which was organized about A.D. 301 by St. Gregory, the Illuminator, in what is now a part of Soviet Armenia, not far from Mount Ararat.

The North American branch was founded by Armenian immigrants in Worcester, Massachusetts, in 1889. In 1933 a division occurred within the American diocese over the condition of the church in Soviet Armenia. One group, now officially known as the Diocese of the Armenian Church in America, maintained its ties with Etchmiadzin. The other, which calls itself the Armenian Apostolic Church of America—colloquially known as the Prelacy—remained independent until 1957 when it came under the jurisdiction of the See of Celicia, which has its headquarters in the suburbs of Beirut, Lebanon. Despite the existence of two dioceses in North America, they have functioned as one church in dogma and liturgy.

Starting in the fourteenth century, a portion of the Armenian church united with the Roman Catholic church, joining with others of the UNIAT rite who have retained their own liturgies and rites. Churches of this connection have been established in the United States and Canada. An even smaller segment of the ancient church turned to Protestantism in 1846, when the Armenian Evangelical church was formed in Istanbul. Congregations of the Evangelical church may be found in various parts of the United States and in other countries where there are Armenian communities.

R.H.

**ARMINIANISM.** Arminianism stands for a variety of liberal religious views. The term developed out of the struggle with strict CALVINISM of Jacobus Arminius (1560-1609), a Dutch theologian. Arminius studied Calvinism at Geneva and Basel under BEZA and Grynaeus, but years later found he could not accept the belief that before all time God chose who should be saved and who should be damned. Appointed professor at the University of Leiden in 1603, he clashed with Franciscus Gomarus, an ardent Calvinist, on unconditional election and irresistible grace. After Arminius' death, his followers expanded his views in their "Remonstrances" of 1610. They asserted five points: (1) all who believe in Christ and persevere shall be saved, (2) Christ's atonement is universal, and so all can be saved, (3) without God's grace one cannot be saved, (4) God's grace is not irresistible, and (5) whether grace once received can be lost needs further study. Fierce controversy ensued; churches divided. The SYNOD OF DORT, 1618-19, reasserted ultra-Calvinism. Over two hundred Remonstrant preachers lost their pulpits, and many were banished.

English Calvinistic PURITANS accepted the Synod of Dort, labeled their opponents "Arminian," and officially condemned them in the House of Commons, 1641. However, Arminianism was characteristic of Anglicanism in the second half of the 1600s. In the following century JOHN WESLEY separated himself from the strict Calvinism of GEORGE WHITEFIELD and insisted that Christ died for all. In 1778 Wesley founded a journal and deliberately named it *The Arminian Magazine*.

Arminianism now connotes free response to God, rationalism, and a repudiation of ultra-Calvinism. It has leavened much theology (*see* PELAGIANISM).

C.M.

**ARMSTRONG, HERBERT W. AND GARNER, TED.** *See* WORLDWIDE CHURCH OF GOD.

**ARNDT, JOHANN** (1555–1621). German Lutheran theologian and mystic. In the conflict among Lutherans he sided with the Calvinists, who taught that Christ was present in the Lord's Supper in power but not spatially. His best-known writings are four books about *True Christianity* and *Little Paradise-Garden of All the Christian Virtues*.

H.K.

**ARNDT, WILLIAM F.** Born in 1880, Arndt was professor of NT at Concordia Seminary in St. Louis until his death in 1957. His earlier writings addressed problems of faith and biblical authority. His major work was the translation (with F. W. Gingrich) of Walter Bauer's great lexicon of the NT, *Griechisch-Deutsches Wörterbuch zu den Schriften des Neuen Testaments . . .* , which was first published in 1957 under the title, *A Greek-English Lexicon of the New Testament and Other Early Christian Literature*.

H.K.

**ARNOLD, GOTTFRIED** (1666–1714). A German Lutheran church historian, mystic, and hymnist. He influenced church history by insisting that heretics and Separatists be examined anew rather than summarily rejected (*see* SEPARATISM). During his theological studies at Wittenberg he independently read early church history. Recommended by PHILIPP SPENER, in 1689 he tutored at Dresden and later at Quedlinburg. At this time he studied mysticism and wrote *Die erste Liebe* (Superior Love), praising the early church's simple virtues. In 1697 he became professor

of history at Giessen, but annoyed by routine duties he quit the following year and returned to Quedlinburg. His large, four-volume *Unparteiische Kirchenund Ketzer-Histoire* ("Unbiased History of Church and Heresy") 1699–1700, drew directly on sectarian and heretical sources. Controversy erupted, causing him to retreat to mysticism and hymnwriting. As a pastor and church inspector during his last ten years he became reconciled to Lutheran orthodoxy.

C.M.

**ARNOLD, MATTHEW** (1822–88). An English Victorian poet second only to Tennyson and Browning, cultural critic, educator, and observer of religion. He was among the first to apply literary criticism to the Bible. Schooled primarily under his father, Thomas Arnold, at Rugby, he entered Oxford in 1840, and became professor of poetry there, 1857–67. To earn money he worked as a government school inspector, 1851–86. His unusual annual reports attracted wide attention and led to reforms.

Arnold had no contemporary equal in criticism. He believed literary and cultural criticism should promote perfection by promoting the best the world has known. He stressed personal conduct as primary for Christians, emphasized natural truth over dogma, and praised the Bible as literature. His best books on religion include *Culture and Anarchy*, 1869; *St. Paul and Protestantism*, 1870; *Literature and Dogma*, 1873; and *God and the Bible*, 1875. Virtually all aspects of culture were touched by this man's critical essays.

C.M.

**ARTHINGTON, ROBERT** (1823–1900). Wealthy British Quaker whose life and fortune were spent in the support and propagation of missionary efforts. He became interested in foreign missions in 1850, and although extremely wealthy he lived like the poor. Even though he had given generously to several Christian causes, his wealth continued to multiply far beyond his knowledge. He had a prejudice against the institutionalization of missionary work. He considered the primary task evangelization. When he died, his fortune of nearly one million pounds was designated for the aid of foreign missionary societies. Those responsible for the distribution of the money bore in mind his wishes and principles. No endowments were created, but some money went to the support of hospitals and schools. The major share continued to be used for pioneer work on the frontiers of Christian mission. The trust was brought to an end in 1936, but for twenty-five years the Protestant missionary enterprise felt the stimulus of "Arthington's million."

W.G.

**ART, HISTORY OF CHRISTIAN.** When one speaks of Christian art, one speaks of content rather than form. One may be describing the finished work of art and/or the artist's personal piety. Christian art then is that which has been used to convey the Christian message and to express and nourish Christian spirituality.

Jewish and Islamic artists have been generally suspicious of pictoral images and decorated their places of worship with abstract design and color. The early Christians drew on OT and NT stories, plus the legacy of Greek art. Thus, catacomb art has references to Noah, Abraham, and Moses. Because Christianity was also not yet socially acceptable, Christians represented their faith in symbols—the vine, dove, wind, water, fire, shepherd and sheep, boat. The fish became a universal Christian symbol in part because the letters of the ACROSTIC *ichthus* in Greek are the initial letters of the words for "Jesus Christ, Son of God, Savior."

After Constantine adopted Christianity, the grandeur of Byzantine art was at its disposal. The great churches such as HAGIA SOPHIA in Constantinople and the churches of Ravenna, Italy, were decorated with luminous mosaics depicting the majesty of Christ, the PANTOCRATOR. Ivory carvings, metal book covers decorated with enamel and pearls, as well as the mosacis, celebrated OT stories, the life of Christ, and the martyrs. The Iconoclast Edict in 730 prohibited the images of divine and holy personages, which resulted in the destruction of many works of art. But after about a hundred years Byzantine art flourished again. The Basilica of St. Mark in Venice is a twelfth-century example.

In northern Europe the Christian faith was illustrated by carvers and book illuminators steeped in Celtic design. The massive crosses of Ireland were carved in the manner of runic stones. The *Book of Kells* and the Lindisfarne Gospels of the eighth century express faith and artistic vision. Other artists worked in enamel (Limoges) and precious stones to cover the books. Most were anonymous, except for Gislebertus, who carved his name into the scene of the Last Judgment at Autun in the twelfth century.

Romanesque architecture gave way to GOTHIC, and art and architecture became one piece in the incredible CATHEDRALS of the thirteenth and fourteenth centuries—Notre Dame, Reims, CHARTRES. The soaring vaults framed brilliant scenes in stained glass. Architecture was miniaturized in jeweled reliquaries. The enthroned Christ gave way to the suffering savior, writhing on the cross. Central to the vision was the Blessed Virgin. Despite the vision of pain and suffering, playful animals and fantastic gargoyles also decorated the cathedrals.

The sixteenth century brought the Renaissance and the Reformation. The term "Renaissance" meant "a renewal of Greek realism and an emphasis on the human as well as the divine." Illustrating the discovery of the individual, artists began to be known by their names.

Giotto's frescoes in the Arena Chapel at Padua, at the beginning of the fourteenth century, show real people in human situations, even though the scenes depict biblical stories. Whereas Gothic spirituality had been visionary and symbolic, the new art visualized a more realistic spirituality.

The high point of the Renaissance and the history of Christian art can be seen in the work of two men. Leonardo da Vinci combined both the natural and the supernatural, the scientific and the spiritual, sculpture and painting. MICHELANGELO concentrated entirely on the human figure. The results are sculptures such as the Pieta in ST. PETER'S Cathedral and the scenes on the ceiling of the SISTINE CHAPEL. In the *Creation of Adam* one sees a balance between the new humanism and the old faith.

Until this point, most artistic work, indeed all Christian art, had been done under patronage, often by or for the church. With the Renaissance came both secular patronage and independent artists. Thus artistic themes became more secular—revival of Greek literary themes and a celebration of the everyday. Secularization began to influence art. Tintoretto, in the sixteenth century, could still make Christian themes profound in his *Crucifixion* and *Temptation of Christ* at San Rocco and yet paint tributes to physical beauty for the Ducal Palace.

Just as the Reformation degenerated into scholastic orthodoxy, Christian art in the last three-quarters of the sixteenth century devolved into mannerism and baroque. Skill and charm remained, but the inner message was lost to some extent. Protestantism was suspicious of, if not hostile to, art. Indeed, many works of medieval art were destroyed. Thus, in Protestant countries artists tended to develop secular genres of landscape, portraiture, and still life. The church was no longer the patron of the arts it once was.

However, Rubens, having visited Rome and Venice, poured the energy and heroic opulence of his style into the *Deposition* for Antwerp Cathedral 1611-14. Rembrandt was one of the last artists with the gift for taking ordinary people and making them parties of eternal mystery. His *Deposition* is not a study in diagonals, as is Ruben's, but the compelling image of a grief-stricken crowd. He portrayed the facts of the biblical record, not the symbolic content.

In contrast the Council of Trent in 1563 reasserted for Roman Catholics the didactic value of art, and Ignatius of Loyola restated the spiritual value of images. From this fertile soil grew the lavishness of baroque art.

In the modern period, which has produced much great art, fewer artists have chosen religious themes. During the Romantic period, WILLIAM BLAKE's mystical drawings offered a heavenly vision. G. F. Watts painted *Eve Tempted,* and among the Pre-Raphaelites, Rossetti illustrated the *Annunciation,* using his sister Christina as a model for the Virgin. In the twentieth century, British painter Stanley Spencer offered his personal interpretation of Christian themes using the people of Cookham-on-Thames. For the rebuilding of Coventry Cathedral, Graham Sutherland created a tapestry of *Christ in Glory in the Tetramorph,* giving modern expression to a vision reminiscent of the Byzantine mosaics. Henri Matisse designed all elements of a chapel at Venice. Perhaps most forceful are the paintings of Rouault in his Miserere series of 1922–27. Marc Chagall has painted both Jewish and Christian scenes. Their work provides a glorious heritage of religious art.

N.H.

**ARTICLES OF FAITH.** Concise statements of Christian belief or confessions considered basic to theology. Thomas Aquinas and other scholastic theologians said the APOSTLES' CREED expressed revealed truths organic to Christian teaching. Various Reformation Articles of Faith expressed truths organic to the development of confessional theologies, for example, the AUGSBURG CONFESSION (Lutheranism) and the THIRTY-NINE ARTICLES (Anglicanism).

C.M.

**ARTICLES OF RELIGION.** Refers to the *Thirty-nine Articles of Religion* of the ANGLICAN CHURCH (1563) and to the *Twenty-five Articles of Religion* (1784) JOHN WESLEY drew from them for Methodists in America (see METHODIST CHURCHES). They were preceded by the *Thirteen Articles* (1538) when Henry VIII attempted an alliance with the Lutherans and by the strongly Calvinistic *Forty-two Articles* (1553) by CRANMER, KNOX, and others (see LUTHERAN CHURCHES; CALVINISM).

The *Thirty-nine Articles* rejected papal authority and sought to join Lutheran and REFORMED doctrines. Wide interpretations resulted. Wesley modified some Calvinistic aspects for American Methodists. Today neither set of articles strictly binds either church.

C.M.

**ASA.** The Hebrew term meaning "physician" or a contraction for "Yahweh has healed." King of Judah about 913–873 B.C. and ABIJAH's son and successor.

*Asa's Religious Reform.* Asa halted the syncretism that had been in vogue during the reign of his immediate predecessors—AHIJAH, REHOBOAM, and SOLOMON. In particular, he "put away the male cult prostitutes out of the land, and removed all the idols that his fathers had made" (I Kings 15:12). Also Asa deposed Maacah (his mother) as queen mother because she sponsored an image for Asherah, the Canaanite goddess of fertility. Though Asa destroyed that image (15:13) and upended various Judean altars (II Chr. 14:5), his people did not completely desist from sacrificing to Yahweh on high places (I Kings 15:14). Despite exaggerated elements in the Chronicler's account (II Chr. 15:1-15), which elevate Asa's reform to the level of those of Hezekiah and Josiah, Asa's efforts did reduce the appeal that the pagan cults had for the Judean populace.

*Asa's Military Strategy.* (a) Confrontation with Zerah. When Zerah the "Ethiopian" and his mercenaries invaded Judah from the south, they were defeated by Asa's forces near the frontier fortress of Mareshah. Judah's army chased the aggressor to Gerar and plundered its environs (II Chr. 14:9-15). Though the size of Zerah's army is exaggerated (one million soldiers), this encounter is undoubtedly historical, reflective of Egypt's desire to maintain influence in Palestine.

(b) Confrontation with Baasha. As Asa's contemporary, this strong Israelite king moved his army far south into Benjamin. Seizing and fortifying Ramah, Baasha successfully blockaded northern approaches into Jerusalem. Thereupon Asa successfully bribed Ben-hadad, king of Syria, to transfer his allegiance from Israel to Judah. Ben-hadad dispatched an army to ravage northern Galilee, which necessitated Baasha's withdrawal. Immediately Asa used Baasha's building material to fortify Geba and Mizpah, thereby extending his territory northward and ensuring Jerusalem's safety (I Kings 15:16-22). The Chronicler adds that Asa was reproved by the seer Hanani for preferring Ben-hadad's support to Yahweh and Asa responded by consigning Hanani to prison (II Chr. 16:7-10). Asa's stubborn opposition was thus offered as justification for the foot disease he suffered in old age (16:12).

The OT attests another Asa, a Levite, son of Elkanah, who resided in a village of the Netophathites (I Chr. 9:16).

J.K.K.

*Francis Asbury*

**ASBURY, FRANCIS** (1745–1816). A METHODIST bishop, Francis Asbury was born near Birmingham, England, to Joseph and Elizabeth Rogers Asbury. At age fourteen he was converted and began attending

Methodist meetings. Soon designated as a lay preacher, he went to London at age twenty-one and was admitted to the Wesleyan Conference.

Sent to America by JOHN WESLEY in 1771, he was the only one of Wesley's English preachers who stayed during the Revolution. A citizen of Delaware, he became a leader of northern Methodists at the Baltimore Conference of 1782. In 1784 Wesley appointed him and THOMAS COKE joint superintendents of the American work. Sensing the American spirit, Asbury instead received his appointment from the Christmas Conference in Baltimore in 1784. On successive days he was ordained deacon, elder, and superintendent (he called himself bishop despite Wesley's expressed disapproval).

Coke's frequent absences left Asbury in charge of the American church, which he ruled with skill. He traveled on horseback more than three hundred thousand miles, encouraging Methodism to become America's fastest-growing denomination. He died March 31, 1816. His *Journals* rival Wesley's in importance for American Methodists.

N.H.

**ASCENSION.** At the climax of Jesus' earthly ministry, in Luke's account, he was "received up" to God's presence (Mark 16:19 KJV; Luke 9:51) in a dramatic episode (Luke 24:51, according to one textual reading; Acts 1:4-11). Luke places this event at the close of a forty-day period after Easter, though Luke 24:50-53 apparently locates ASCENSION DAY on Easter Day (compare Barnabas 15:9 for a similar telescoping of events).

The consequences of the Ascension, if not the actual description of Jesus' "going up," are woven into the fabric of early Christian teaching, as is clear from the following references: John 6:62; 16:5-11; Acts 2:33-34; 3:21; Rom. 8:34; 10:6-7; I Thess. 1:10; Phil. 2:9-11; Eph. 1:20; 4:8-10; Heb. 4:14; 8:1, 9:24; I Pet. 3:21-22; Rev. 3.21. In sum total these diverse allusions agree on several points. (1) The close of Jesus' work was marked by an act of installation as world-ruler and enthronement (based possibly on a Near Eastern kingly acclamation, as the monarch is acknowledged as all-powerful; see Matt. 28:18-20; I Tim. 3:16; Heb. 1:1-3); (2) Jesus' visible presence was withdrawn to another sphere of existence called God's presence or glory. Glimpses of that heavenly order are found, however, for example in Stephen's vision of the ascended SON OF MAN in Acts 7:54-60; and (3) Christian apologetics needed the Ascension to give a response to the question, Where is the body of Jesus, claimed to be raised to life after death? The answer was that the body was taken up into the divine presence, where Jesus acts as exalted intercessor (Heb. 7:25) and from which he was expected to come again (Heb. 9:28).

R.M.

**ASCENSION DAY.** A feast day celebrated on the fortieth day after EASTER, observed on the Thursday of the sixth week after Easter. Ascension day is, thus, the end of the Easter season. The festival dates from the fourth-century Jerusalem church. It is a holy day of obligation in the Roman Catholic Church.

J.C.

**ASCETICISM.** *See* MONASTICISM.

**ASHDOD.** Best known as the chief of the five cities of the Philistine pentapolis (after the twelfth century B.C.), though it had enjoyed a former thousand-year-old history as a prosperous port and trading center in Egyptian-dominated Canaan.

Despite Joshua 15:46-47, it does not appear that Ashdod ever formed a part of the early Israelite domination of Palestine. It figures largely in the story of the Philistine wars (I Sam. 5-6) and was a proverbial enemy power on Israel's borders in the eighth century B.C. (compare Amos 1:6-8). For the most part it maintained a precarious and relative autonomy throughout Israelite history by subjecting itself to the successive Assyrian and Chaldean hegemonies in the Near East.

For postexilic Judaism, Ashdod remained a center of alien culture and language (Neh. 13:23-24). During the Maccabean wars it was repeatedly sacked by the Jews (I Macc. 5:68; 10:84; 11:4), but in 63 B.C. it was reconstituted as a free city by Pompey as part of the *pax romana* imposed on Palestine. It formed part of the kingdom of Herod the Great established by the Roman Senate and was inherited by his successors.

In the NT Ashdod (Azotus) was evangelized by the Hellenist Philip (Acts 8:40). The name has been preserved in the modern Isdud, half-way between Jaffa and Gaza on the Palestinian coast. The port of Ashdod was at the nearby Tell el-Kheidar.

B.V.

**ASHER.** Jacob's eighth son, for whom one of the twelve tribes was named. Born of Leah's maid Zilpah (Gen. 30:12-13), Asher was Gad's younger brother and is consistently listed after him (Gen. 35:26; 46:16-17; Exod. 1:4; I Chr. 2:2).

*Geographical Setting of the Tribe.* Stretching about sixty miles northward from Carmel, Asher's territory was bounded on the west by the Mediterranean and on the east by the holdings of Zebulun and Naphtali (Josh. 19:24-31). A maritime tribe, Asher took advantage of its proximity to northern Phoenician mercantilism centered at Tyre. The blessing of Jacob attests the fertility of Asher's territorial allotment ("Asher's food shall be rich, and he shall yield royal dainties," Gen. 49:20; compare Deut. 33:24). This region boasted of substantial olive harvests—and still does.

*Involvement in Israelite History.* The Song of Deborah (Judg. 5:17) questions Asher's motives when a lucrative business with foreign clients rendered her unwilling to respond to inner Israelite need. Residing on the fringe of that region most endangered by

Canaanite threat, Asher ignored Deborah's battle cry against Sisera and his coalition. Even so, Asher assisted Gideon in ousting the Midianites from the Esdraelon Plain (6:35; 7:23). Following Saul's death, Asher immediately acknowledged the refugee monarchy of Ish-baal (Ish-bosheth) in Gilead (II Sam. 2:9, reading "Ashurites"). Though Asher is listed as a district in Solomon's reorganization of the land (I Kings 4:16), the Chronicler's failure to mention Asher in his account of David's military and civic administration likely denotes Asher's political unimportance (I Chr. 27:16-22).

*Asher in the New Testament.* Twice mentioned, Asher is home for Anna, the prophetess (Luke 2:36), and Asher follows Gad in a listing of those favored by divine protection (Rev. 7:6).

J.K.K.

From *Atlas of the Bible* (Thomas Nelson & Sons Limited)

*Palestinian coast near ruins of ancient Ashkelon*

**ASHERAH.** A Semitic goddess venerated throughout the ancient Near East and the cult object symbolizing her.

Known as Ashratum in early Babylonian texts and Ashirta in the Amarna letters of Egypt, this mother-goddess is best described in fourteenth-century B.C. Canaanite epic literature from RAS SHAMRA, where her name is Athirat. There she functions as El's consort, the mother of seventy deities, including Baal, the most visible member of the Canaanite pantheon. The designation "holiness" (qdš) predicated to Athirat may imply identity with Qudšu, a nude Egyptian goddess.

Though the goddess and her cult object are not always distinguished, the goddess is regularly linked with Baal in localized Canaanite fertility worship, which ensnared various Israelites (Judg. 3:7). Asherah's pole symbol, constructed of wood, stood upright beside the altar of Baal (6:28). In Elijah's day, Ahab, king of Israel, tolerated Jezebel's support of four hundred Asherah prophets (I Kings 18:19), and Manasseh, king of Judah, introduced an Asherah image into the Jerusalem Temple (II Kings 21:7). Two other Judean kings, Asa and Josiah, are fondly remembered for their determination to annihilate this alien element from Yahweh worship (I Kings 15:13; II Kings 23:4, 7).

J.K.K.

**ASHKELON.** One of the five leading Philistine cities (Pentapolis) on the Mediterranean seacoast about twelve miles north of Gaza.

*In Old Testament Times.* The Execration Texts (about 1850 B.C.), reporting Ashkelon's rebellion against Egypt constitute its earliest literary mention. Though the Amarna letters (about 1375–1350 B.C.) attest Egyptian loyalty, Rameses II and Marniptah curbed rebellion there in the thirteenth century B.C. Soon the Philistines overtook Ashkelon and adjacent territory, which had eluded Joshua (Josh. 13:3). Ashkelon is unmistakably a Philistine city of Israelite traditions, focusing on Samson (Judg. 14:19) and the ark of the

covenant (I Sam. 6:11, 17) and in David's lament over Saul and Jonathan (II Sam. 1:17-20). Woe oracles in Jeremiah 47:5, 7; Amos 1:8; Zephaniah 2:4, 7; and Zechariah 9:5 also mention Ashkelon.

Assyria under Tiglath-pileser III claimed Ashkelon in 733 B.C., and Sennacherib quelled rebellion there in 701 B.C. The Babylonians destroyed Ashkelon in 604 B.C. for its resistance against Nebuchadnezzar. Subsequently, the city welcomed the Hellenistic advances of Alexander the Great; yet relations with Maccabean Jews were friendly (I Macc. 10:86; 11:60).

*In Later Times.* Ashkelon is said to be the birthplace of Herod the Great, who embellished it with baths and colonnades, and his sister Salome lived there. In their war against Rome (A.D. 66), the Jews partially destroyed Ashkelon, but in a second phase of battle they sustained heavy losses. Crusaders captured Ashkelon in 1153, and Muslims reclaimed it in 1187.

J.K.K.

**ASHKENAZIM.** From the Hebrew *Ashkenazi,* meaning "Germany," a term given to Jews who formed an early community along the Rhine River, now applied to their descendants, about 80 percent of the world's Jews. Their counterpart, the SEPHARDIM—Jews from Spain, differ in ritual, speech, culture, writing, and outlook. YIDDISH, a mixture of German, Slavic, and Hebrew, became a mark of the Ashkenazim.

Persecution and trade prompted heavy migration of Ashkenazim to Slavic countries (Poland, Hungary, Russia) during the Middle Ages and especially in the fifteenth and sixteenth centuries. However, massacres in east Europe, particularly in Poland in 1648, dispersed the Ashkenazim throughout Europe, the United States, Canada, South Africa, and Australia. The Nazi Holocaust sharply reduced their numbers in World War II. The state of Israel originally was heavily Ashkenazim, but the Sephardim increased by birth and immigration and currently outnumber them. Rabbis of the "two models" in Judaism share equally in Israel's chief rabbinate.

Historically, the Ashkenazim absorbed aspects of their surrounding cultures, and tended to produce Conservative and Reform congregations, although they are not without their Orthodox. Rigorist biblical and Talmudic studies, liturgy, mystical piety, poetry, contemplation, and martyrdom form parts of their tradition.

C.M.

**ASHTAROTH.** Plural form of Ashtoreth, the Hebrew designation of the Canaanite fertility goddess Astarte, and name of a city in north trans-Jordan, about twenty miles east of the Sea of Galilee.

*Canaanite Divinity.* Ashtaroth presumably encompasses diverse local embodiments of Astarte in the same way that "Baalim" (or "Baals") embraces varied manifestations of the fertility god Baal. In Judges 2:13 Israelite defection from her ancestral faith in God is portrayed in general terms as a cultic affirmation of the Baalim and Ashtaroth (compare Judg. 10:6; I Sam. 12:10). Samuel admonishes the people to resist such idolatry just prior to Saul's election as Israel's first king at Mizpah (I Sam. 7:3).

*The City* (Tell Ashtarah). Originally claimed by Og, king of Bashan, as his capital (Deut. 1:4; Josh. 9:10; 12:4), Ashtaroth was subsequently captured by the Israelites, assigned to "the people of Machir the son of Manasseh" (Josh. 13:31), and designated as one of the Israelite cities of refuge (I Chr. 6:71; compare Josh. 21:27). As Ashteroth-karnaim, the city is mentioned in Genesis 14:5 as inhabited by the Rephaim (prehistoric Canaanite settlers), who fell victim to Chedorlaomer's punitive campaign against Transjordan. As Carnaim, the city, along with its Astarte sanctuary, was destroyed by Judas during his second-century B.C. liberation of the Jews (I Macc. 5:43-44).

J.K.K.

**ASHTEROTH KARNAIM.** A locale about twenty miles east of the Sea of Galilee occupied by the Rephaim (prehistoric Canaanite inhabitants), which fell to Chedorlaomer during his punitive campaign against Transjordan (Gen. 14:5). Ashteroth Karnaim is assuredly Ashtaroth (Tell Ashtarah), capital of Bashan (Deut. 1:4), which has been equated with nearby Karnaim (Sheikh Saad) first mentioned in Amos 6:13. Judas Maccabeus destroyed Karnaim during his second-century B.C. liberation of the Jews (I Macc. 5:43-44; II Macc. 12:26).

J.K.K.

**ASHTORETH.** The intentional Hebrew misvocalization of the name of the Canaanite fertility goddess, Astarte. Following the analogy of Ish-bosheth (II Sam. 2:8) for Ish-baal or Esh-baal (I Chr. 8:33), the name is vocalized with the vowels of the noun *bōsheth* ("shame"). As a singular form, Ashtoreth is found merely three times in the OT (I Kings 11:5, 33; II Kings 23:13), though the context in I Samuel 31:10

also invites it. The plural "Ashtaroth" is more frequently met within comprehensive allusions to Israelite idolatry.

If in the tenth century B.C. the cult of Ashtoreth won the support of the religiously pluralistic Solomon (I Kings 11:5, 33), three centuries later it evoked the wrath of the zealous Josiah in his forthright promotion of the ancestral covenant faith (II Kings 23:13). In both instances, Ashtoreth is linked with the Sidonians of Phoenicia. Also in both, the veneration of Ashtoreth is associated with that of the Ammonite deity, Milcom, and in the latter text, the Moabite deity, Chemosh, is likewise mentioned. If Milcom and Chemosh were local manifestations of the Venus star, Athtar (Babylonian Ishtar), Ashtoreth may have been Athtar's female consort.

Rather than advertising Ashtoreth's astral function, extant Canaanite texts and figurines present her as a fertility goddess. Canaanite epic literature from Ras Shamra shows Baal's sister, Anath, overtaking Ashtoreth in that capacity, yet further south (in southern Syria and Palestine) Ashtoreth mainly remained intact.

J.K.K.

**ASHURBANIPAL.** The son and successor of the Assyrian monarch ESARHADDON and the last important ruler of the Assyrian Empire. His reign began in 668 B.C., but the date of the end of his rule is uncertain, probably 627 or 626 B.C. During his rule, Judah was under Assyrian domination. There is no certain reference to Ashurbanipal in the Bible, although he is generally identified with the Osnapper mentioned in Ezra 4:10 as having settled foreigners in the cities of Samaria.

Ashurbanipal pursued the vigorous policies of his father and succeeded in establishing dominance over Egypt and capturing Thebes (Nah. 3:8). The inscriptions of both Esarhaddon and Ashurbanipal note the submission of the Judean king Manasseh to their authority and his support in their campaigns.

His father had established arrangements for Ashurbanipal to serve as primary Assyrian king and for his brother Shamash-shum-ukin to reign as king in Babylon. Eventually warfare broke out between the two, lasting for four years (652–648 B.C.) and greatly weakening Assyrian authority.

Ashurbanipal prided himself on his literacy and spent time assembling and copying various and sundry ancient documents and inscriptions. His library in Nineveh was partly excavated by the British and provides one of the richest sources of ancient Near Eastern texts.

J.H.

**ASH WEDNESDAY.** The first day of LENT, the forty-day season of preparation and repentance before EASTER. The name derives from the custom of burning the palm branches from the previous PALM SUNDAY. These ashes are dabbed on the foreheads of believers, in the sign of the cross, by the minister or priest. In the Roman Catholic Church they are burned before MASS, with a prayer of blessing. The ashes are sprinkled on the altar three times, then priests apply them to their own foreheads before marking the communicants. The ashes signify the sorrow of believers as they meditate on the sacrifice of Christ.

J.C.

**ASIA.** A geographical term of uncertain origin whose usage among some ancient geographers was inclusive of the continent of Asia or major portions thereof. The term does not occur in the OT, but in the Apocrypha it still denotes a large eastern territory generally considered equivalent to the kingdom of the Seleucids. In Roman and NT times, the term was primarily applied to the Roman province of Asia located in what later was called Asia Minor.

The broader usage of the term with reference to a large portion of the Asian continent appears in II Esdras 15:46; 16:1, one of the later books of the Apocrypha. The books of Maccabees describe the Seleucid monarch as "king of Asia," probably drawing on an earlier Persian designation and speak of pretenders seeking to acquire the throne of Asia (I Macc. 8:6; 11:13; 12:39; 13:32; II Macc. 3:3). Since the Seleucids ruled territory extending from Egypt to the Iranian Plateau and most of Asia Minor, such references must be seen in fairly broad terms.

In the NT, Asia is used in a much more restricted sense denoting primarily the Roman province of Asia, located in western Asia Minor, with its capital first in Pergamum and then Ephesus. This province was created some years after the Attalid king of Pergamum willed his kingdom to the Romans at his death in 133 B.C. This narrower reference for the term Asia is found throughout Acts (for example, 2:9; 6:9; 16:6), and in Paul's letters he speaks of the first convert in Asia (Rom. 16:5) and of the churches in Asia (I Cor. 16:19; see also II Cor. 1:8; II Tim. 1:15; I Pet. 1:1). The book of Revelation shows a special interest in seven churches in Asia, all of which were located in the western region of the Roman province (Rev. 1:4). The author highlights three of the major cities of this region: Ephesus, Smyrna, and Pergamum (Rev. 1:11).

J.H.

**ASIARCHS.** The only reference to these people is in Acts 19:31. They were the administrators of a confederation of cities in the Roman province of Asia (modern Turkey) and were centered in Ephesus where the scene of Acts 19 is laid. Their religious functions concerned the protection of the cult of *dea Roma* (involving "Rome and the emperor"), and this cult was located at Pergamum, also in Asia. The Asiarchs were elected annually from among the leading and wealthiest citizens of the province.

The interest in the story of Acts 19 is that these high-placed aristocrats called Paul a friend, came to his aid in a crisis, and gave him advice not to venture into the amphitheater of Ephesus, dedicated to the goddess Artemis. The one text that mentions Asiarchs is a window through which we see at least a glimpse of Paul's social contacts and the appeal of his message to the upper strata of Greco-Roman society.

R.M.

**ASOKA.** Emperor of the Mauryan dynasty who ruled over north India and Afghanistan around 269–232 B.C. Asoka ranks as one of the great humanitarian rulers of world history, and was as well a sovereign whose support of BUDDHISM did much to set that faith on the path to becoming a major world religion.

Asoka spent the first eight years of his reign expanding his domains through the usual sanguinary military means. But the suffering his warlike policies entailed moved him to great remorse. Renouncing conquest, he turned to the study of Buddhism and devoted himself to promulgating its gentle ethical principles and the alleviation of suffering throughout his realm. This he saw as the following of DHARMA, righteousness, which embraced such virtues as truthfulness, nonviolence, compassion, and non-acquisitiveness. Asoka sent envoys to kings near and far to convey to them the dharma message, and in his own realm bespoke it in inscriptions on pillars—the "pillar edicts"—and rock walls and caves. By his command hospitals and way stations were built, roadside trees planted, wells dug, and the quantity of animals killed for meat greatly reduced. The emperor and his leading ministers actively traveled throughout the land dispensing justice, especially to women and the powerless.

Asoka patronized the Buddhist sangha, or order, built Buddhist places of worship, and according to tradition sent out missionaries, including those who converted Ceylon (Sri Lanka). But while his preference for Buddhism is not in doubt, he also endowed Vedic rites, and above all inculcated tolerance and respect for all faith through his example. His edicts treat only matters of ethics, not doctrine, and nowhere enjoin upon his subjects the religious practice of Buddhism. But Buddhism's strength and influence grew rapidly under his benevolent rule.

R.E.

**ASSEMBLIES OF GOD.** *See* PENTECOSTAL CHURCHES.

**ASSUMPTION OF MARY.** A festival of Roman Catholicism honoring the bodily assumption of the BLESSED VIRGIN MARY into heaven after her death; a parallel to the Ascension of Christ (Acts 1:9). Around A.D. 600, the emperor Maurice set the feast on August 15, but Pope Gregory the Great set it on January 18. The term "assumption" was once applied to receptions of martyrs directly into heaven. It is now used only to refer to the Virgin Mary. The Assumption of Mary was declared an article of faith by the First VATICAN COUNCIL in 1870. It is based on tradition since no mention is made of it in the NT.

J.C.

**ASSURANCE.** The sense of confidence and trust that the believer and the faithful have toward the promises, fidelity, and pledges of God. Although the actual term "assurance" is rare in the RSV, the concept is frequent, especially in the NT and the Letter to the Hebrews. The concept is closely allied to what is implied in the concept of FAITH and denotes the subjective attitude of trust, which the believer possesses.

Something of what assurance means can be seen in negative form in Deuteronomy 28:58-67, which describes the distressful situation that accompanies lack of obedience and trust in God. Deuteronomy 28:66 describes the situation where there is no assurance as "your life shall hang in doubt before you; night and day you shall be in dread, and have no assurance of your life." Lack of assurance produced uncertainty, anxiety, and discontent with life.

The presence of assurance produces the opposite attitude, namely confidence and certainty. Acts 17:31 points to the objective basis of Christian assurance, namely the sign that produces the believer's confidence: "he has given assurance to all men by raising him from the dead." Assurance is a special theme of Hebrews. In Hebrews 11:1, the author describes faith as "the assurance of things hoped for." The Greek term employed here (*hypothasis*) describes the subjective confidence of the believer who, like the faithful ancients of old (Heb. 11:4-31), can act on the certainty that what God has promised about the future can be trusted. The same term occurs in Hebrews 3:14 (RSV, "first confidence"), where it refers to the initial assurance that the believer had. Hebrews 3:14 also, however, seems to imply that assurance can be lost just as it suggests that the believer can become an unbeliever, and the saved become unsaved (6:1-8). The book, on the other hand, has as one of its purposes the encouragement of that inner placing of confidence in salvation that has been wrought and will be fully realized in the future (19:25). Assurance is thus a disposition that is not a once-for-all given state but an attitude to be constantly renewed in living out of and by faith.

J.H.

**ASSYRIA AND BABYLONIA.** Designation of the two Mesopotamian civilizations that flourished between the mid-third and late first millennia B.C. Their names derive from Asshur and Babylon, their capital cities.

*Land and People* (a) *The land.* Basically, Babylonia encompassed the alluvial territory between the Euphrates and Tigris rivers, from Baghdad south to the Persian Gulf. Occasionally flatlands extending east of the Tigris toward the Zagros Mountains and territory upstream on the Euphrates likewise be-

longed to Babylonia. Assyria's original holdings were almost entirely limited to land east of the middle Tigris, but much land to the north and west was ultimately taken.

As Mesopotamia's most outstanding geographical feature, the Tigris and Euphrates directly affected agricultural pursuits with their annual flooding. Autumn rains and melting winter snow in the Armenian Mountains produced spring floods useful to adjacent fields so long as dikes had been established to control the amount of water spill. The inevitable silting up of canal systems, however, necessitated frequent relocation of agricultural pursuits.

(b) *The people.* The Babylonians and Assyrians, who may be collectively designated as the Akkadians after the seat of their first empire (Akkad), were Semitic peoples. They originated in the movements of nomadic tribes that left the Arabian Desert for better conditions in the Tigris-Euphrates plain. By the mid-third millennium they were arriving with increasing force. Speaking the Semitic language of Akkadian, these newcomers appropriated the cuneiform, syllabic script of the Sumerians whom they invaded. Also they adopted the Sumerian pantheon while adding gods of their own. For many decades the mingling of intruding Semite and settled Sumerian was peaceful. The Sumerians organized no monolithic empire since their relatively small city-states flourished independently. Sumerian continued as a literary and sacred language, while Akkadian, involving two dominant dialects, Babylonian and Assyrian, increasingly became the spoken language of Mesopotamia's residents. Eventually the Semites actively sought political dominance over Mesopotamia. This was realized under Sargon, who in about 2360 B.C. founded Akkad, history's first great empire.

*Babylonian History.* Various king lists, date lists, court chronicles, and royal inscriptions offer scholars source material, which permits the writing of Mesopotamian history.

(a) *Early ascendancy and downfall* (about 2360–1950 B.C.). With Sargon's triumph over Sumerian opponents in about 2360, the empire at Akkad (near the later Babylon) was founded. This energetic imperialist gave to Mesopotamia a unification hitherto unknown. He was succeeded by two sons and his grandson, Naramsin, who likewise achieved military brilliance. The rulers of Akkad controlled vast territories, but they met a worthy opponent in the EBLA Empire of northern Syria. Ebla's triumph over Akkad following Sargon's death, however, was temporary, for Naramsin brought Ebla to its knees.

Akkad's sway over the Near East quickly deteriorated after Naramsin's death. In about 2180 B.C., the Semitic Empire succumbed to northeastern Guti invasions. But these barbarians were incapable of firm rule. Consequently, under the Third Dynasty of UR (about 2060–1950), Sumerian culture underwent a renaissance, especially in jurisprudence and art.

Nevertheless, the Sumerians in their self-contained city-states were enjoying their last years of independence.

Once Elam overtook Ur (about 1950), numerous Amorite peoples, all speaking dialects of northwest Semitic, systematically dominated lower Mesopotamia. Although the Amorite-controlled city-states of Isin and Larsa first emerged as significant political rivals, the First Dynasty of Babylon (about 1830–1530, also Amorite) eventually won command.

(b) *Old Babylonian period* (about 1830–1530 B.C.). In Hammurabi (about 1728–1686), the First Dynasty boasted its most effective monarch. The surrounding kingdoms of Larsa, Eshnunna, and Mari were all the worse for having to face his political and military strategies. Having led Babylon to a far more secure position in international affairs, HAMMURABI moved his city toward new cultural heights. This was a busy era of pseudoscience (for example, magic and astrology), literary productivity, and a well-articulated religion that promoted Marduk, Babylon's patron god, to the pinnacle of the Mesopotamian pantheon. Best known of Hammurabi's achievements was the promulgation of his law code, which masterfully subjected previously existing legal traditions to needful national order.

Following Hammurabi's death, Babylon soon lost significant ground, though the dynasty persisted for another 150 years. Weakened by invading Kassites, who arrived from the Iranian Mountains, it ultimately succumbed to intrusive Hittite forces entering from the west. Yet these visitors from distant Anatolia (Asia Minor) failed to consolidate their military gains. Consequently, a Kassite dynasty took control of Babylon for the next four centuries.

*Cylinder seal depicting animals and heroes*

(c) *Middle Babylonian period* (about 1530–1150 B.C.). Though knowledge about the Kassite rulers is scant, they apparently weathered border warfare with Assyria and had some dealings with Egypt. Intermarriages involving the Kassite royal family with those of Assyria, Hatti, and Egypt improved Babylon's international position. The Kassite dynasty, which kept Babylonian culture basically intact, ruled less authoritatively during its last decades when land grants to various officials became commonplace. Finally it succumbed to Elamite invaders in the mid-twelfth century.

*Glazed brick relief of a lion from the royal processional, Babylon (sixth century* B.C.*)*

(d) *Neo-Babylonian period* (626–539 B.C.). Babylonian recovery was painfully slow in the ensuing years when Assyria regularly dominated the Mesopotamian landscape. Nevertheless, Babylonia benefited from extensive long-distance trade contact with northern Assyria. The brief meteoric Neo-Babylonian or Chaldean period opened with the rule of NABOPOLASSAR (626–605), who, as an ally of the Medes, conquered Nineveh (612), thereby terminating the Assyrian Empire. This Babylonian success was buttressed by the westward campaigns of NEBUCHADNEZZAR (605–562), who dealt the Egyptians a stunning defeat at Carchemish in northeast Syria in 605 and subsequently devastated Jerusalem in 587 (II Kings 25:1-21). As Babylon's last monarch, NABONIDUS (556–539) foolishly tried to supplant Marduk with the moon-god Sin of whom he was a devotee. The citizenry of Babylon loathed his religious policies, and the infuriated Marduk priesthood even helped Cyrus the Persian to conquer Babylon (539). With the transformation of the city into a Persian administrative center, Babylonian sovereignty expired.

*Assyrian History.* (a) *Old Assyrian period* (about 1900–1600 B.C.). Following the collapse of the Third Dynasty of Ur, Asshur asserted its political independence and became a busy commercial center. The Cappadocian Texts (nineteenth century B.C.) disclose that sophisticated trade relations with Anatolia enabled Asshur to obtain tin for the production of bronze. Commercial expansion, not military conquest, was Assyria's goal, and it was realized by astute Assyrian merchants. But some crisis halted this venture shortly after 1800 B.C. Under the Amorite, Shamshi-adad I (about 1750–1718), Assyria briefly dominated upper Mesopotamia. Shamshi-adad resumed trade with Anatolia and claimed the Amorite city-state of Mari. His kingdom, however, rapidly disintegrated after his death, permitting MARI to reach its zenith under Zimri-lim (about 1730–1697). Thrown into confusion by many peoples on the move in upper Mesopotamia during the seventeenth century, Assyria eventually experienced western annexation by the Hurrian kingdom of Mitanni.

(b) *Middle Assyrian period* (about 1350–1075 B.C.). When Mitanni fell prey to the Hittites in the

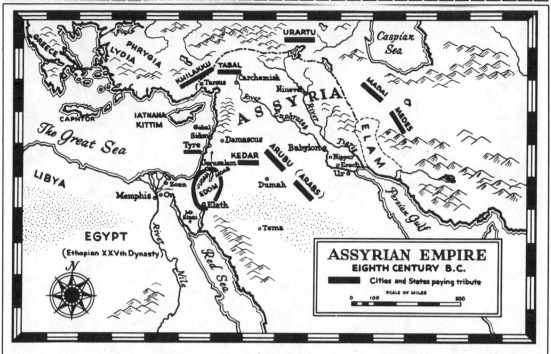

ASSYRIAN EMPIRE
EIGHTH CENTURY B.C.
■■■ Cities and States paying tribute
SCALE OF MILES
0      100                    500

mid-fourteenth century, Assyria recovered under Asshur-uballit I (about 1356–1321). During the tenure of three strong thirteenth-century kings—Adad-nirari I (about 1297–1266), Shalmaneser I (about 1265–1235), and Tukulti-Ninurta I (about 1234–1197)—Assyria pushed westward to wrest Mittani from Hittite control, and under Tukulti-Ninurta she momentarily conquered Babylon. Conversely, Assyria sustained a cultural invasion from Babylonia at this time. Subsequent Aramean pressure ushered Assyria into more than two centuries of weakness. This was only temporarily alleviated by the military accomplishments of Tiglath-pileser I (about 1116–1078), who bequeathed to Assyria more territory than she was able to consolidate.

(c) *Neo-Assyrian period* (930–612 B.C.). Beginning with Asshur-dan II (935–913), the first of the Neo-Assyrian monarchs, Assyria steadily arose to political prominence. Under Ashurnasirpal III (884–860), Shalmaneser III (859–825), and Adad-nirari III (811–784), Assyria waged numerous campaigns west of the Euphrates to search out prized timber, minerals, and new commercial opportunities. Although the western states, including Israel, successfully checkmated Shalmaneser at the Syrian site of Qarqar (853) and benefited from a four-decade interval of Assyrian weakness (about 785–745), Tiglath-pileser III (745–727) emerged to initiate a century of imperial rule. Under the name of Pul (II Kings 15:19), he assumed governorship of Babylonia. To ensure that his westward conquests would be permanent, he engaged in the wholesale relocation of conquered people, a policy that his successor, SHALMANESER V (726–722), reaffirmed when he conquered the Israelite capital of Samaria (722; II Kings 17:1-6). While SARGON II (721–705) spent much of his reign addressing the anti-Assyrian rebellion, which erupted following Shalmaneser's death, he did conquer numerous Syro-Palestinian cities and seize the Babylonian throne. Similarly, SENNACHERIB (704–681) was required to crush rebellion before pursuing a militaristic agenda leading to the near sack of Jerusalem (II Kings 18:13–19:37) and destruction of Babylon.

Assyrian expansion achieved its climax under ESARHADDON (680–669), who took possession of Egypt in 671. For a brief interval, the entire Fertile Crescent was united in one empire. ASHURBANIPAL (668–627) was Assyria's last great king. His triumph over numerous foes, including Egypt and Babylon, allowed him to undertake peaceful pursuits, including the gathering of an extensive library of ancient Babylonian myths and epics. But Ashurbanipal's death sealed Assyria's fate. In the nation's last two decades no leader was capable of holding the massive empire together. When the Medes joined the Babylonians in upending Nineveh in 612, Assyria met certain death.

*Religion.* (a) *Prominent deities.* The three cosmic Sumerian deities—Heaven, Atmosphere, and Earth—reappear with the same names in the Babylonian and Assyrian pantheon: Anu, Enlil, and Ea (Enki). The Sumerian astral trinity—the moon, the sun, and Venus—is likewise affirmed but with different names: Sin, Shamash, and Ishtar. Clearly, the superior, though politically weaker, culture provided useful models for the Akkadian newcomers. In Marduk and Asshur, Babylonia and Assyria

Courtesy of the Metropolitan Museum of Art

*Lamassu (guardian spirits of the gate); palace of Ashurnasirpal II at Nimrud, one of the Assyrian royal capitals*

respectively identified its national deity. Though Marduk was one of the younger deities, the enviable political stature of his city, Babylon, elevated him to the head of the pantheon, where he was glorified as the creator and organizer of the cosmos early in the second millennium. Asshur bore the same name as Assyria's capital. His pronounced warlike character reflected the basic tenor of his people. During those periods when Assyria's imperial strength was most evident, Asshur was honored as father of the gods and creator of the universe.

To some degree, the gods could be differentiated according to age. The most regal of the gods, Anu (Heaven), was the oldest deity, whose realm was the remote celestial sphere. As one of the older gods, Enlil (Atmosphere) shared some of Anu's royalty and remoteness. Though lord of the earth, Enlil's attitude toward humankind was ambivalent. He was responsible for sending the great flood. As the wise patron god of exorcism and other human crafts, Ea claimed the water surrounding the earth as his abode. Among the astral deities, Ishtar was noted for both militant

*The sun-god; dynasty of Akkad*

and fertility capacities. Shamash was affirmed as judge of heaven and earth who supported the poor and oppressed.

(b) *Divine-human encounter.* The Akkadian deities were experienced as awesome beings whose radiance terrified the beholder. This feature was also attributed to numerous Assyrian kings who overwhelmed their opponents on the battlefield. Day-to-day contact with the gods was realized through the temple cult. On analogy with the king who inhabited his palace, the god for whom an Akkadian temple had been built was understood to occupy the sanctuary. The image in which the deity was regarded present was placed in the temple's main room. Just as servants awakened, washed, clothed, and fed the king, specific temple priests similarly ministered to the divine image. Only ritually pure food was passed on platters and in jars before the image, which was thought to devour it by looking at it through eyes of precious stone. Solely of human shape, these images were ordinarily constructed of valuable wood, plated with gold, and covered with magnificent garments suiting the ritualistic occasion.

The gods moved with their images. Accordingly, the average layperson, who was not admitted into the temple, could relate with the gods on such a solemn occasion as the New Year festival, when the images were carried in procession beyond the temple. This fusion of god and image also fostered in the Akkadians a belief that if the enemy stole the image, the god in question must have grown angry with his city and voluntarily departed. Undoubtedly, non-priestly individuals mainly interacted with divinity through abundantly available Akkadian mythology.

(c) *Divination.* Akkadian religion put humanity in touch with natural phenomena in the hope that believers might partially control a hostile universe. As they pursued an admittedly precarious existence, the Akkadians regularly wed religion with magic. Many ills were attributed to demons, which originated from souls of the dead who had received improper burial. If one's sinful deeds might evoke demonic intervention, upright deeds would not necessarily protect one against malevolent forces.

Thus it was vital that priests inflict exorcism formulas upon the demons. With the support of priestly divination, individuals and groups might influence future events. The scrutiny of animal livers

was a popular method of divination. Archaeologists have uncovered many clay models of livers. These have been meticulously marked out according to their parts and their significance annotated. Some divination helped astronomy to develop, since the location of the stars was thought to affect the future of the newborn. Moreover, divination was practiced when the king consulted the oracle before departing for battle.

The apprehensive Akkadians were singularly intent on trying to influence fate's dreary course. Their grim religious perspective on life colored their view of the hereafter. Beneath the earth was the dark abode of the dead, which offered its inhabitants a miserable existence. Only offerings made by the living, when they remembered, would alleviate the customary diet of dust and dirty water.

*Literature.* (a) *Akkadian poetry.* The Tigris-Euphrates region witnessed the production of brief religious lyrics of high literary merit as well as longer epics that engage the imagination. In the former category are hymns glorifying specific deities (for example, "Hymn to Shamash," "Hymn to Ishtar") and penitential prayers linked with sacrificial ritual. The two most celebrated epics are *Enuma elish,* named after its opening phrase, which presents Marduk's ordering of the cosmos, and the EPIC OF GILGAMESH, which narrates the longings and adventures of the previously known Sumerian hero.

*Cylinder seal showing Shamash enthroned*

At the center of *Enuma elish* lies the conflict between primordial chaos, personified by the monster-goddess Tiamat, and cosmic order, manifested in the god Marduk. The poem tells how the body of Tiamat is split by the triumphant Marduk to form the earth below and the firmament above. Marduk's task involves not the production of chaotic matter but its structuring into cosmic order. His efforts continue with the setting up of astral constellations and the creation of humanity, which is charged with serving the gods and their temples. Finally, the assembled deities in their newly formed heaven acknowledge Marduk's supremacy by reciting his fifty honorific names.

Through rich description and vivid dialogue, the Epic of Gilgamesh presents its hero in numerous situations. The whole poem turns, however, on the

Courtesy of the Oriental Institute, University of Chicago

*Painting showing the city of Babylon and the Tower of Babel*

issue of human mortality. Despite his magnificent physical strength and political clout as king of Erech, Gilgamesh is haunted by the fear that death will conquer him as it does all mortals. After an adventurous but futile search for immortality, he returns home resigned with the knowledge that only the gods do not die. Similarly, the Akkadian Adapa myth portrays its priest-hero as one who enjoys wisdom but not immortality, which lies just beyond his grasp.

Poetic wisdom literature includes the Akkadian Counsels of Wisdom, which dispatch advice on such practical issues as cultivating disciplined speech and avoiding bad company. More elaborate Babylonian wisdom texts project a rigorous pessimism. Though "I Will Praise the Lord of Wisdom" (often called The Babylonian Job) offers hymnic thanksgiving to Marduk for personal deliverance from mortal danger, it swarms with skepticism about divine justice and one's ability to know what the gods really want. In "The Babylonian Theodicy" the sufferer raises many questions about the meaning of life. These questions, however, are poorly answered by an orthodox friend.

(b) *Akkadian prose.* This classification includes detailed royal annals, inscriptions on commemorative stelae, administrative documents recording palace transactions, letters imparting the king's decision about overland commercial activities, diverse linguistic texts, scientific writings on mathematics and astronomy, and legal documents governing private transactions and public policy. The best-known prose text is the CODE OF HAMMURABI, with its piecemeal legislation about such matters as false testimony,

marriage, adoption, loans, property rights, and slavery.

*Artistic Dimensions.* (a) *Architecture.* Temples were often constructed of lengthy brick walls with recurring recesses and buttresses to break the monotony. Attention was also paid to level. The temple was erected on an elevated terrace, and its cella, housing the divine image, was set at a still higher elevation. Emerging well above the temple complex was the tower or ZIGGURAT, an Akkadian word meaning "pinnacle." Designed to facilitate human contact with the gods who resided on the mountains, these towers were built both beyond the temple compounds (Babylonia) and within (Assyria).

(b) *Art media.* Palace murals, animal statuary, relief carvings, ivories, and enameled brick all invited Akkadian artists to display their talents. In Assyria the rooms of the great palaces hosted colorful mural decorations, which mainly extolled the king's military and hunting achievements. Scenes involving the slaughter of the defeated and the presentation of tribute were vividly executed. Though humans were depicted stiffly, animal figures were naturally presented. Here the hunting scenes in Ashurbanipal's palace are superb.

Animal statuary maintained realistic levels, and in Assyria a variant form, the orthostat, manifesting dual characteristics of statuary and relief carving, was popular. At the entrance gate of the palace, an animal statue was inserted into the wall to perform a guardian function. In addition to lions and bulls there were fantastic winged bulls with human heads.

Akkadian artists excelled in relief carvings. Commemorative stelae appearing with some regularity conferred a sense of movement on their human figures, something unattested in Sumerian art. The four-sided obelisk was a variation of the stelae. Truly impressive is the black obelisk of Shalmaneser III, exhibiting carved reliefs and inscriptions that celebrate the monarch's military achievements.

At Nimrud was found a superb collection of carved and engraved ivories, which excelled in its realistic depiction of the female figure and various animals. Moreover, in the Neo-Babylonian Era, enameled brick was used in gates and along streets as a pleasing exterior decoration. At regular intervals stood the repeated figure of a lion, bull, or awesome dragon. This was set against a blue brick background and framed by geometric designs. The famed Babylonian Ishtar gateway is an outstanding example.

J.K.K.

**ASTARTE.** *See* ASHTORETH.

**ASTROLOGY.** The art and pseudo-science of divination through the study of the stars and other celestial phenomena. It is to be distinguished from astronomy, the science which deals with the physical universe.

Astrology has enjoyed a long history, and in every age it has been modified by the prevailing world view.

It has been a part of science and religion in many places and was not distinguished from astronomy until the rise of modern science in the sixteenth and seventeenth centuries. The three branches of ancient astrology were: (1) the reading of celestial omens; (2) the charting of a person's destiny, based on the positions of the stars and planets at the time of birth; and (3) the study of the influence of the stars on human affairs. Horoscopes (charts developed by the second branch) are always spoken of as being "cast," a term that brings to mind other forms of divination, such as casting dice, lots, or sticks. Additional forms of divination popular in ancient times were the reading of animals' entrails, the interpretation of the flight of swallows, and the consulting of oracles. Astrology was often seen as the most refined method for divination.

*Early History.* The earliest known astrology was developed in Mesopotamia. The casting of horoscopes did not begin until the fifth century B.C., by which time branches 1 and 3 were already old. In the late fifth century B.C. astronomers divided the ecliptic (the apparent orbit of the sun around the earth) into twelve "houses," and they calculated tables of the movement of the moon and planets. The stars were seen by astrologers as messages from the gods. Each of the seven "planets" (Saturn, Jupiter, Mars, the Sun, Venus, Mercury, and the Moon) was considered both a deity and a personified number. Each ruled over a day of the week.

The Greeks and Ptolemaic Egyptians developed both astrology and astronomy well above the level of the Babylonians. The Greeks included astrology in their larger scheme of sciences and pseudo-sciences, such as alchemy, botany, medicine, minerology, zoology, and so forth. The zodiac was interpreted in terms of these fields, and vice versa. The Greeks associated the planets and signs with colors, metals, animals, stones, plants, and parts of the body, a practice which continues today.

*Astrology and Religion.* In the second century A.D. mathematical and scientific astronomy declined in favor of astrology, as mystery cults, GNOSTICISM, and other anti-rational forces gained momentum. Astrology found a respectable ally in STOICISM, which shared its essentially fatalistic outlook. Their alliance proved important in the revival of astrology in the Renaissance.

Astrology spread east with the Greek conquest of India, and made its way from there to China, Japan, and Korea with the spread of Buddhism. Hinduism and Jainism also adopted Greek astrological ideas and combined them with fresh speculations about the universe.

The rise of Christianity put an end to astrology for a time, but Islam, in many ways the heir to Greek thought, reestablished it. Muslim astrologers also drew on Persian (Zoroastrian) and Indian texts. Whereas Christianity often acknowledged the reality of astrological prediction, but rejected it as traffick-ing with demons, Islam accepted it as dealings with djinn. Arabic astrologers cast three types of horoscopes: (1) an answer to a specific question; (2) determination of the right time for an undertaking; and (3) determination of an individual's fate through examination of the constellations supposed to be visible at the time of birth or conception.

"Astrology," by which was meant astronomy, was part of the general medieval education in Europe wherever and whenever Latin was taught. In the Renaissance, as Greek and Arabic texts became known throughout Europe, astrology, magic, and other forbidden activities were revived. The church, in turn, revived its opposition to these matters, using arguments from the theologians of the early church. This time, however, astrology became firmly established among the learned.

*Astrology in the Modern World.* With the increasing acceptance of the modern world view, astrology began to lose popularity among the educated. Copernicus (1473–1543) advanced the idea that the earth was a planet that revolved around the sun. This attacked the foundations of astrology, first by removing the sun and the moon from the category of planets, and second by reducing the significance of the earth. Galileo (1563–1642) used the telescope to show that the moon, far from being an unblemished creation (as medieval cosmology had said), was scarred. He also showed that other heavenly bodies were imperfect: Jupiter had satellites, Saturn a ring, and Venus went through phases like the moon. Kepler (1571–1630) and Newton (1642–1727) proposed laws of motion and gravity that removed the hand of God from its previous direct involvement in the heavens and also removed the significance of the planets. It was hard for anyone to believe that a body moving around the sun in an elliptical path had any influence on a person's life.

In the twentieth century, astrology has been most popular with the uneducated, but, unlike UFOs and psychic healing, it has not formed any significant part of the study of the paranormal. On the other hand, like biorhythms, it has provided some basis for the investigation of self-fulfilling prophecies and the effects of wishful thinking. Although it has long been lacking a supporting cosmology, astrology continues today. It continues to assume, now on faith alone, that the constellations in the sky at the time of birth are of some importance to an individual's life, and that the astrological month of birth affects (or even determines) the individual's personality.

In our age, astrology has remained a pretender to the status of a science, because careful, unbiased studies have yet to turn up any significant evidence to support it. No uniform correlation has been reliably shown between an astrological sign and a personality trait. Yet astrologers have continued to make and publish studies that claim to show, for example, that great leaders, or movie stars, or astronauts are mostly of one or another sign. The most common fault with these findings is that in any small group there is bound to be some random grouping of birthdates. Astrologers examine birthdates and then explain why so many of the group are of one sign. A scientific astrologer would first predict that group *x* is of sign *y*, and then examine the data. However, this would prove unfruitful, since astrological predictions, like psychic predictions, mostly fail. Predictors point to their few vaguely worded successes, but hide the percentage of their predictions that fail.

Astrologers' popularity is not unlike that of the one-arm bandit, whose occasional payoff justifies the gambler's loss over the long haul. One favorite rationale for failure is to say that there must have been some unknown (and unknowable) feature that threw the prediction off. The argument is strikingly similar to the shaman's excuse, when a spell fails, that counter-witchcraft must be working against the spell.

K./M.C.

**ASURA.** From the Sanskrit word for "titan" or "demon." In the earliest VEDIC literature, the term is applied to such gods as Varuna and INDRA, but later comes to be applied to beings associated with the underworld, darkness, and death, who are eternal antagonists of the DEVAS, or great gods of sky, light, and life. The chief asura is Vrtra, the dragon who was defeated by Indra, hero of the devas.

The famous myth of the churning of the milk ocean gives an explanation of the antipathy between devas and asuras. It tells us that the two classes of beings cooperated to churn the ocean and produce amrit, the nectar of immortality. But afterward they quarreled, and the devas cheated the asuras out of most of the precious drink, thus growing in power while their rivals diminished.

The trickery to which the devas resorted suggests that, while their function may be to fight on the side of light and life, they are not necessarily superior morally to their dark opponents. However, in the later mythology of the great saving gods who transcend the devas, asuras become more distinctly evil demons defeated by such AVATARs of VISHNU as Rama and KRISHNA.

R.E.

**ATHALIAH.** The name of the only queen ever to rule Judah in her own right. A granddaughter of Omri, king of Israel, and his Tyrian wife Jezebel, Athaliah had been given in marriage to Jehoram, king of Judah (II Kings 8:18, 25-26). After the deaths of her husband Jehoram (842 B.C.) and their son Ahaziah, who ruled Judah for less than one year, Athaliah herself assumed the throne (842–837 B.C.). To do so, she was obliged to murder all other members of the royal family (II Kings 11:1); however, a son of Ahaziah, Joash (11:2), also called Jehoash (11:21), was secretly saved by opponents of the queen. After six years, Jehoiada, the priest, gathered the captains of the guard and introduced the

seven-year-old prince to them (11:21). He then crowned the boy, and the guard cried, "Long live the king!" (11:12). Athaliah cried, "Treason!" when she heard and saw what had happened, but it was too late. She was executed, and the trappings and practices of Baalism, which she had introduced, were rooted out (11:13-20).

A nearly identical account is given in II Chronicles 22:10–23:21. I Chronicles 8:26 mentions in passing another Athaliah, a son of Jeroham a Benjaminite. Also a third person by the same name is listed among the returned exiles in Ezra 8:7.

W.S.T.

**ATHANASIAN CREED.** A doctrinal statement traditionally attributed to ATHANASIUS and sometimes called *Quicunque Vult,* after its first two words—"whoever wishes." It was not used in the Eastern churches until fairly recent times and was originally written in Latin rather than Greek. These and other reasons have led scholars to doubt that it was indeed written by Athanasius and to suggest such possible authors as AMBROSE OF MILAN, Vincent of Lerins, and others. The first half of the creed deals with the TRINITY and is addressed against ARIANISM. The latter part deals with CHRISTOLOGY, and its chief target is the views of the APOLLINARIANS.

J.G.

**ATHANASIUS.** Bishop of Alexandria from 328 to 373 and the chief opponent of ARIANISM. As a deacon and secretary to Bishop Alexander of Alexandria, he was present at the Council of Nicea, although not a member of the assembly. Even before the outbreak of the controversy, he had written a treatise *On the Incarnation,* which showed that his faith was grounded on the divinity of the one who became incarnate in Jesus, and that therefore he would find the views of Arius and his followers repugnant.

Probably of Coptic stock, he was so short and dark that his enemies called him the Black Dwarf. His contacts with the monks of the Egyptian desert, which may have begun at an early age, were extensive and repeatedly served him well, for there was a time when he hid among the monks from the authorities that sought to arrest him. He in turn contributed to the spread of the monastic idea with his *Life of Anthony* (*see* ANTHONY OF EGYPT).

His staunch defense of the Nicene faith and his refusal to buckle before civil authorities caused him to be exiled by CONSTANTINE, twice by Constantius, and then again by Julian and Valens. But he was not an inflexible man, and through careful theological negotiation and clarification he was eventually able to allay the fears of many who rejected the decisions of Nicea because they feared an extreme interpretation of the term HOMOOUSION. Against Macedonius of Constantinople, who denied the divinity of the Spirit, Athanasius held the divinity of all three persons of the TRINITY. And, by rejecting the views of Apollinarius, he played an important role in the early controversies regarding CHRISTOLOGY.

                                                                J.G.

**ATHEISM.** The denial that any reality is designated by what the religions call "God." More generally, one might say that atheism denies that the ultimate reality is personal, intelligent, purposive, or endowed with any of the attributes that have been traditionally ascribed to God or the gods.

Atheism had already emerged in ancient Greece, where Leucippus and Democritus taught that the final reality is "atoms and the void." However, it is in modern times that atheism has become a major force. It forms part of the official philosophy of Marxist countries and is also widespread in Western countries. Just as there have been many ideas of God, so there have been many forms of atheism, depending on what particular God is denied. This has led to some ambiguities. Both SOCRATES and some of the early Christians were charged with atheism because they were judged to have called in question the gods of classical religion, but they had their own belief in God and were certainly not "godless."

There are in fact intermediate positions between a thoroughgoing atheism and a fully developed belief in God. There is even the possibility of a religious atheism, a view which denies any personal God or spiritual Absolute, but which retains a feeling of reverence for the universe (Haeckel is a good exemplar of this point of view, though it would seem to be leaning toward PANTHEISM). The rise of modern atheism parallels the rise of science from the Renaissance onward. Modern science incorporates what has sometimes been called a methodological atheism; that is to say, it seeks to explain events within the world in terms of other events within the world, without appeal to any supernatural agency, such as God. Among the early scientists, a few inexplicable phenomena were still ascribed to divine intervention, but increasingly it was seen that the ideal of science must be to treat the world of nature as a self-regulating system to be explained on immanentist principles. This point of view is now virtually universal among educated people, and it is agreed that if there is a function for God, it cannot be that of a *deus ex machina* called in to explain some recondite phenomenon of nature. In any case, this would be a very undignified role for God.

But atheism has gone beyond a methodological assumption, and throughout the nineteenth century the atheistic critique was extended to all forms of theistic religion. God might be explained as a projection of human ideals or even of the human father (FEUERBACH and FREUD). Or religion might be accounted for as a by-product of social and economic conditions (MARX and his followers). Or the idea of a transcendent God was held to be an obstacle to human freedom and transcendence, and it was pointed out that the human condition had been improved by

science and human effort rather than by reliance on God (NIETZSCHE and SARTRE). These intellectual arguments for atheism combined with certain emotional feelings of rebellion against God. For some, the sheer evil and injustice of much that goes on in the world seemed a disproof of God's existence and called for "metaphysical rebellion" (CAMUS). It cannot be denied that many points in the atheistic critique have in fact touched on weaknesses and distortions in the ways people have thought about God and call for a radical rethinking of the concept of God, just as did the Hebrew prophets in their day.

Yet atheism is far from having established its case. It seems highly improbable that our universe owes its origin to a "chance collocation of atoms." The crude materialism on which nineteenth-century atheism was based has long since been discredited. As has been argued from PLOTINUS to WHITEHEAD, out of that kind of beginning no structured world could ever evolve.                                                        J.M.

**ATHENAGORAS.** One of the Christian APOLOGISTS of the second century (about 177). Two of his works are extant, *A Plea for the Christians* and *On the Resurrection of the Dead.* Although he was not as profound as JUSTIN MARTYR, his Greek style is the best of all Christian writers of the second century.

                                                                J.G.

*The Parthenon at Athens*

**ATHENS.** An important city in classical times located in southern Greece, and the cultural center of Greek philosophical thought and life from the time of SOCRATES, PLATO, and ARISTOTLE (fifth through fourth centuries B.C.). With the Roman conquest of Greece, Athens maintained its independence and had special treaty relations within the empire, retaining the judicial authority to decide its own affairs. Its status as a university city was acknowledged throughout the empire, though its intellectual life was on the decline at the time of the birth of Christianity. Nonetheless, it lived on its past heritage and its architectural glories, seen in the vast array of temples, statues, and monuments, which made it a good place to visit.

Courtesy of the American School of Classical Studies, Athens

*General air view of Athens; the Agora is in the foreground, and the Acropolis is in the background.*

Courtesy of the American School of Classical Studies, Athens

*The Erechtheion on the Acropolis at Athens*

Courtesy of the American School of Classical Studies, Athens

*Temple of the Greek god Hephaestus at Athens*

Courtesy of the American School of Classical Studies, Athens

*The Acropolis at Athens, viewed from the west, with the Areopagus (Mars' Hill) in the foreground*

Pausanias' *Description of Greece*, written in the second century A.D., still contains a lot of important information as to what the ancient city looked like in his day and served as a traveler's guidebook. In particular, Pausanias' descriptions of the *agora* (market place), the *odeion* (place for musical performances), and the *stoa* (or covered walkway) of Attalus II, where Peripatetic philosophers met and conversed, have all been confirmed by recent archaeological discoveries.

The attention of NT readers is drawn to the account of Acts 17:15-34, which describes Paul's visit to

Courtesy of the American School of Classical Studies, Athens

*Athens from the southwest, showing the ruins of the Agora, with the restored Stoa of Attalus*

Athens. The two sites specifically mentioned are the *agora* (17:17) and the AREOPAGUS (17:19), known from the KJV as Mars' Hill. There Paul met and spoke to an audience of popular philosophers. Recent discovery has made it more probable that this encounter took place at the scene of the northwest corner of the *agora,* near the Painted Colonnade *(stoa poikile)* from which the philosopher Zeno and his friends derived their name, the Stoics.

Paul's speech directed to Epicurean and Stoic philosphers is given in such a way as to show the appeal of the Christian message to Hellenistic thought. That God does not lack anything and has no need of human service is exactly what the Epicureans held. The Stoics would have applauded the teaching that the Divine is the source of all life. Paul is said even to have cited the poet Aratus for the axiom that men are the "offspring of God" (17:28) and that idolatry is to be rejected. But to no avail. The offensive claim (to Greek ears) was the resurrection of Jesus, which sounded no different to his hearers from a credulous belief in the resuscitation of a dead corpse. The irony is that on that very site in Athens, Apollo had been made to say (in Aeschylus' play cycle): "But when the earth has drunk up a man's blood / Once he is dead, there is no resurrection." Paul moved on to Corinth, leaving behind a few converts but no settled congregation.    R.M.

**ATHOS, MOUNT.** A community of twenty monasteries inhabited by GREEK ORTHODOX monks. It is located on a promontory, which juts out from the

Courtesy of Religious News Service

*Mount Athos*

Macedonian mainland into the Aegean Sea. Many art treasures and ancient and medieval manuscripts are preserved there. The first monastery was founded in A.D. 963. No women or female animals are allowed into the monasteries.

K.C.

**ATMAN.** A fundamental Hindu philosophical term referring to the most profound substratum or constituent of personality, the pure essence of consciousness and being prior to mental content or activity of KARMA. In VEDANTA thought the atman is said to be one with BRAHMAN, the universal consciousness and absolute. Though rejected by some, this idea has had very great influence.

R.E.

**ATONEMENT.** A central doctrine in both biblical theology and the formulation of the Christian message. In its essence the Anglo-Saxon work (*at-one-ment*, that is, making "at one") refers to the restoration of harmonious relations between God and humankind, fractured by reason of human disobedience and alienation. The term is akin to RECONCILIATION (the restoring of mutual friendship), but with the extra dimension that atonement also suggests the procedures by which God and humankind are reunited.

*Atonement in the Old Testament.* The main Hebrew idea is contained in the verb "to cover" *(kpr)*, which is usually translated "atone" (for example, Lev. 16:11, 20). The offending matter, which must be covered, is human transgression of the divine ordinance. Sometimes such ordinances are cultic and ceremonial, but the best OT insights go deeper and search out the basic flaw in human nature. This is discovered in humanity's disobedience to God's moral commands, which are designed for humankind's well-being both individually and in society. Above all, sin for the prophets of Israel in particular is that which displeases God (Jer. 44:4), and so transgression takes on a more personal aspect of what humans are and do as wayward children and rebellious sons or daughters (Hosea's prophecy is full of such echoes; see also Isa. 1:2-3).

Atonement, therefore, is needed because of humanity's persistent and incorrigible desire to go their own way (Isa. 53:6). What is needed specifically is for sin to be covered from God's righteous and holy eyes (Hab. 1:13), and the provider of such a covering is none other than God, as the important wording of Leviticus 17:11 makes plain. These summary statements may be said to epitomize the essential teachings of the OT writers, with the exception that in the postexilic period Israel's consciousness of national guilt and failure increased, and there was a tendency to spell out that failure in terms of cultic infraction rather than personal relationship with Israel's God.

*Atonement in the New Testament.* As background to the NT teaching, we should observe the contribution

of intertestamental writers who influenced the thinking of the Jewish rabbis in the first century A.D. Jewish scholars promised that Atonement could be achieved by four methods: repentance, sacrifice, suffering, and death. All these words became part of the NT vocabulary as its writers sought to explain what had happened in the divine purpose at the cross of Jesus where Atonement for Christians is without exception located.

REPENTANCE is made the prerequisite to Atonement and is a token of a person's sincerity and desire to turn from sin and start on a new way of life. John the Baptist emphasized the seriousness of the nation's wrongs and the need to start over again (Matt. 3:7-12). Jesus picked up on this theme in his call, though with more stress on the good news that accompanied the call, namely that since God is gracious and willing to save, men and women should *want* to turn to him ("turning to God" is the essence of repentance for later NT writers; see Acts 2:38; 3:19; 11:18; 20:21; 26:20; II Tim. 2:25; 26; II Pet. 3:9).

Sacrifice is the key idea in Christian Atonement theology, and the cultic-ceremonial flavor is seen notably in Paul's allusions (I Cor. 5:7-8; I Pet. 2:4-10). But the chief writer to explore the Christianized teaching on sacrifice is the author of Hebrews. For this author Christ's one offering on the altar of the cross has brought an end to all Levitical sacrifices offered to restore humanity to God's favor (see Heb. 9:11-28). The Hebrew idea of "covering" is replaced by sin's final removal, already foreshadowed in Jeremiah 31:31-34 (cited in Heb. 8). Yet a person's gratitude and desire to live for God are matching responses, and it is possible that eucharistic ideas are part of what Hebrews 13:10, 15 teaches as human acceptance of Christ's sacrifice. Certainly in the later centuries "sacrifice" became a regular understanding of what the Eucharist celebrates.

Suffering and death are the focuses of Atonement for all the NT writers, with reference to Christ's death on the cross. The early credal statement (I Cor. 15:3-5) is but one answer to the question: Why did Jesus die? It responds, "He died for our sins," whether in the sense of the suffering servant of Isaiah 53, who vicariously bore the sins of the many, or of martyrs who gave their lives in a representative way for the nation's good (an idea from 4 Maccabees, sometimes believed to be in view at Mark 10:45). All the NT literature, with diverse emphases, agrees that Christ's passion (a theme in I Pet. that says often, "Christ suffered," as an exhortation to a suffering church) and death are the ground of human forgiveness and divine reconciliation, whereby the past record of failure and coming short of divine standards is put away. The death of Christ is the ground on which God is both righteous and the one who sets sinners in right relationship with themselves (Rom. 3:24-26). And with a single voice the various writers state exultantly that this Atonement derives from God's heart of love (Rom. 5:1-10; I John

4:712), and it must evoke an answering response of love and faith (Gal. 5:6), leading to new life (Rom. 6:1-23).

R.M.

**ATONEMENT, DAY OF.** *See* DAY OF ATONE-MENT.

**ATONEMENT, THEORIES OF.** The doctrine of atonement gives expression to the belief that the saving work of Christ, especially his passion and death, has overcome the ALIENATION between God and the human race. Thus this doctrine implies that Christ's saving work has obtained FORGIVENESS of sins and effected RECONCILIATION.

The doctrine has always had a central place in Christian theology, but it has been expressed in a variety of ways. For a thousand years, the classic or dramatic theology of atonement prevailed. On this view, the cross was the climax of Christ's struggle against the demonic forces which, since the FALL, had held the world in subjection. Christ's cross and resurrection broke the power of the demons and liberated the human race from sin and death. This is the teaching found in IRENAEUS and other patristic writers. GREGORY OF NYSS elaborated the theory into the idea that the death of Christ was a ransom paid to the devil as the price of human liberation.

These ancient views were challenged by ANSELM in the eleventh century. He introduced a new theology of atonement, based on legal concepts and strictly argued. The honor of God had been infringed by human sin. Even if humans repented and turned away from sin, this would not effect reconciliation, for the past affront to God would remain. In no way could this be put right from the human side, for it would require a "satisfaction" which humans could not give. This legal term "satisfaction" is at the center of Anselm's view, and it means an extra payment or compensation. God alone could provide this satisfaction, but since it was owed by humans, Anselm argued to the necessity of a God-human. It was his belief that only such a one would have the power to offer satisfaction and at the same time belong to the human race, which owed satisfaction. Christ, being sinless, had no need to die, so his death is that extra payment to God, satisfying God for the sins of the world.

Ansated cross

Latin cross

Papal cross

Patriarchal cross

Chi-Rho monogram

Russian cross

St. Anthony's cross

Crusaders' cross

Jesus Christ
the Conqueror
Monogram

Greek cross

St. Andrew's cross

Orb
and
Cross

Jesus
Monogram

*Various Historic Crosses*

A new shift in the doctrine took place at the time of the Reformation. The concepts were still legal, but the death of Christ was now seen as a punishment that he took upon himself in place of sinful humankind. This is the view known as "penal substitution." CALVIN expressed it by writing that Christ "bore the weight of God's vengeance." The sins of humanity were imputed to him, while his righteousness was imputed to us. Not long after the time of Anselm, an alternative view of atonement was expressed by ABELARD in a commentary on Romans; but this alternative was left unheeded until modern times when it atracted the attention of liberal theologians. In Abelard's view, the death of Jesus is to be understood as a supreme manifestation of love, designed to kindle love in human hearts, consequently bringing them to God. Among modern exponents of this so-called "moral influence" theory may be mentioned Hastings Rashdall.

A distinctive understanding of atonement was developed in the nineteenth century by John McLeod Campbell, some of his ideas being later taken up by R. C. Moberly. Campbell was dissatisfied with the legalism and harshness of the Calvinist teaching, and tried to find personal categories instead. He shifted attention from the physical death of Christ on Calvary to his mental agony in Gethsemane, which he interpreted as a perfect act of contrition and penitence for the sins of the world. Campbell also stressed what he called the "prospective aspect" of atonement as a present ongoing reality, in opposition to the view that it was a "once-for-all" event of the past. This enabled him to move away from the idea of Christ as a substitute to the more fruitful thought that he is a representative or pioneer who opens up a way of penitence and reconciliation which human beings can then follow themselves.

This in turn points toward existential views of atonement (see EXISTENTIALISM) as found in such twentieth-century writers as BULTMANN, who speaks of "making Christ's cross one's own." Though these different theologies of atonement have been regarded in the past as rival theories, they are more likely today to be considered as alternative forms of imagery, though one may still argue about which imagery is the most adequate.

J.M.

## ATTRITION.
In Catholic theology a preparation for the grace of love that brings forth CONTRITION, or genuine sorrow for sin. Attrition is a state of unease over one's sinful conduct, motivated by fear of God's punishment. Attrition is not a deep enough sorrow for the wrongs done to prompt amendment of life.

J.C.

## AUGSBURG CONFESSION.
The first confessional writing prroduced during the age of the REFORMATION of the sixteenth century. Written by PHILIP MELANCHTHON as a summary, in irenic form, of the teachings of MARTIN LUTHER, the Augustana represents the common belief of those who accepted Luther's theology. It was prepared in 1530 for presentation at the Diet of Augsburg, on June 25, a diet that Luther could not attend because he was under the ban of the Holy Roman Empire. The subject of much debate and some misunderstandings among early PROTESTANTS, the Augustana is the fundamental confessional platform of world Lutheranism (see LUTHERAN CHURCHES).

In January 1530, the emperor CHARLES V invited the German Diet to assemble at Augsburg to begin discussions that might end the religious struggles in the empire. Luther had been declared a heretic by the DIET OF WORMS in 1521; but Duke Frederick of Saxony, and later Duke John, protected Luther. Charles wanted to compose the differences outstanding in a peaceful way because the Turks were threatening his empire.

When the diet was called, the Protestants felt that they should clearly state their beliefs and the grounds of their dispute with the Roman church. Duke John ordered Melanchthon and other theologians to draw up a statement. Later, Melanchthon drafted a preface to the "Torgau articles" (dealing with abuses) and the "Schwabach articles" (written by Luther), which confessed the Protestant faith. This became the Augsburg Confession, after revisions were made to include all the Protestant territories that embraced Luther's teaching. They requested the right to sign the Augsburg Confession also. The text faithfully reflects the teaching of Martin Luther and other Lutheran theologians and not simply Melanchthon's alone.

The Augsburg Confession is in two parts. The first deals with the traditional Catholic doctrines confessed by the Lutherans (Articles I-XXI), and the second discusses the abuses in Roman church practice that Protestants believed should be corrected (Articles XXII-XXVIII). Throughout the Confession there is a conciliatory spirit that holds open the hope that Rome and Wittenberg may join in reforming the whole church to the glory of God and the benefit of all parties.

J.C.

## AUGUSTINE/AUGUSTINIANISM.
One of the most influential theologians in the entire history of Western Christianity, and the theology and philosophy patterned after his thought.

He was born in A.D 354 in the small town of Tagaste, in North Africa. His mother, MONICA, was a Christian who prayed constantly for the conversion of her son. After some studies at nearby Madaura, he went to Carthage, which was then the intellectual and economic center of North Africa. There he continued his studies and took a concubine, who gave him a son and with whom he continued a relationship until Monica practically forced him to leave her many years later. In Carthage he was attracted to MANICHAEISM,

The Pierpont Morgan Library (Manuscript No. 399, Folio No. 299 v)

*Augustine of Hippo*

whose doctrines seemed more rational than those of Christianity, but he never went beyond the level of a "hearer" in the Manichaean community. Eventually, he decided that Manichaeism did not really solve his innermost quest and left it. His career as a teacher of rhetoric then took him to Rome and later to Milan. During this period he became interested in NEOPLATONISM, which solved his doubts regarding the origin of evil and the nature of God and the soul.

In Milan, the preaching of AMBROSE dissolved his last doubts. He was then ready to become a Christian but found that he did not have the strength of will to follow the Christian life. It was then that, in a garden in Milan, he heard the voice of a child crying, "take up and read." Reading a text from Romans, he felt that he now had the strength to give up his former life and become a Christian. After having been baptized by Ambrose, he returned to North Africa with his son and some close friends. His mother died as they were preparing to leave Italy. In North Africa, Augustine and his friends lived in a monastic community, devoted to meditation and contemplation. Then, against his will, he was made a presbyter in the town of Hippo Regius and later a bishop. He died in A.D. 430, as the Vandals were besieging the city.

Augustine's theology is a combination of the earlier teachings of the church with Neoplatonism. In its concrete content, it was deeply influenced by his polemics against Manichaeism, PELAGIANISM, and Donatism. Also, the fall of Rome in 410 led him to write *The City of God,* in which he sought to refute the claim of some pagans that Rome had fallen because it had become Christian.

From Neoplatonism Augustine derived his doctrine of God, whom he conceived in terms of the Neoplatonic "ineffable One," as well as his theory of the incorporeity of the soul. This latter view, which later became commonplace among Christians, was at first rejected by many as an unbiblical innovation. Also from the Neoplatonists, he derived his view of evil as not a substance but rather a deprivation of good. Every creature is in itself good, for it is made by God. But the corruption of the goodness of a creature is what we call evil.

Against the Pelagians, Augustine developed his doctrine of GRACE and PREDESTINATION. He felt that their view of human capabilities was too positive. Although before the "Fall" humans were free both to sin and not to sin, in our fallen condition we are free only to sin. It is the grace of Jesus Christ that restores in us the freedom not to sin, which will be the only freedom we shall have in the Kingdom. This means that fallen humans cannot of themselves decide to do good, to believe in God, or to receive grace. In our fallen state, God's grace must *operate* in us the will to accept it. And, once we do, it must *cooperate* with our will so that our works may be good. Since this grace does not depend on our will, Augustine concludes that it is irresistible, and this in turn leads him to the doctrine of predestination. This, however, does not mean that he holds to predeterminism, nor that he denies the existence of free will. On the contrary, he rejected Manichaean DETERMINISM and insisted that within its limits in each of our various stages as human beings, our will is free to determine itself. As he would put it, "the will is its own cause."

Against the DONATISTS, Augustine developed his understanding of the church and of the validity of the sacraments, quite apart from the worthiness of the person who administers them. Also, against the more extreme Circumcellion, he developed the theory of the just war, which would be very influential in later discussions on issues of war and peace.

The meaning of the term "Augustinianism" varies according to its context. It can be applied first of all to those who defended Augustine's teachings immediately after his death, when his views on the incorporeity of the soul were rejected by many and when the Semi-Pelagians questioned his doctrines of grace and predestination. At a later time, particularly after the reintroduction of Aristotle into western Europe in the thirteenth century, it was applied to those who held to the more traditional views, particularly on issues of epistemology. Finally, in Protestant circles, and particularly among Calvinists, it means those who affirm irresistible grace, unconditional predestination, and human depravity. It has also been used in a similar manner by those within Roman Catholicism who have held similar views, particularly the Jansenists. The truth of the matter is that neither Catholics nor Protestants have ever held to the entirety of Augustine's teachings on salvation, for while Catholics have rejected his views on irresistible grace and its consequences, Protestants have rejected his understanding that we are saved by doing good works with the cooperation of grace.

J.G.

**AUGUSTINE OF CANTERBURY.** Missionary sent to England in A.D. 596 by Pope Gregory the Great. Although Christianity had existed in Britain during Roman times and continued to exist, it had lost most of its contact with the Continent. Thus, although Augustine won the conversion of King Ethelbert of Kent and this became the base of operations for missions to other kingdoms, the significance of the work of Augustine and his successors lies mostly in his having brought British Christianity into conformity with the rest of the Western church. Augustine was made archbishop of CANTERBURY in Kent, which consequently became the main episcopal see in England.

J.G.

**AUGUSTUS** (63 B.C.–A.D. 14). The surname conferred by the Roman senate upon Caius Julius Caesar Octavianus, on January 17, A.D. 27, for his eminent services in restoring the Roman republic. The great-uncle of Octavian was Julius Caesar (102–44 B.C.), a connection that cleared the way for his rapid advancement. After Caesar's assassination Octavian learned that the dictator had made him his heir and adopted him, whereby he acquired the title Gaius Julius Caesar Octavianus.

Courtesy of the American Numismatic Society

*Coin with head of Augustus*

In the struggle to fulfill his destiny, Octavian made skillful use of competitors for power, while assisting none. After Mark Anthony's dalliance with Cleopatra, the decisive battle was fought at Actium in 31 B.C., which made Octavian "the master of all." In the East, Herod's support of Anthony made his position precarious, but Octavian recognized Herod's abili-

ties, appointed him *rex socius* (an allied king), and extended Herod's territories to the limits held by David and Solomon a thousand years earlier. It was Augustus who divided Herod's kingdom among his sons and denied Archelaus the title king, ordering his deportation in A.D. 6.

The political contexts of Paul's missions were established by Augustus in his reorganization of the Roman provinces. Luke reports that the apostle worked at the *Colonia Augusta Iulia Philippensis*, was arraigned before its chief magistrates (*praetors*), and beaten by its police (*lictors*) (Acts 16:12, 22, 35).

J.P.

**AULÉN, GUSTAF** (1879–1977). With ANDERS NYGREN the foremost leader of the influential Swedish LUNDENSIAN THEOLOGY. Aulén served as professor of theology at Uppsala (1907–13), at Lund (1913–33), and as bishop of Strängnäs (1933–52). His two most influential works are *The Faith of the Christian Church* (U.S. ed. 1948) and *Christus Victor,* a classic study of the Atonement.

J.L.

**AURICULAR CONFESSION.** Oral confession, made to a priest in the Roman Catholic Church. It was ordered by Pope Leo the Great in place of public confession. The Fourth Lateran Council made it obligatory for all Catholics every year. To neglect it is to court excommunication and loss of Christian burial.

J.C.

**AUROBINDO** (1872–1950; full name Sri Aurobindo Ghose). Scholar, political activist, and spiritual philosopher. In all stages of Aurobindo's life the dominant issue was response to the overwhelming reality confronting one of his time and place, the meeting of East and West. He responded to the presence of the West in his native India as an assiduous student of its lore, as a revolutionary resister, and finally as a philosophical synthesizer.

Born in Calcutta, Aurobindo enjoyed a brilliant academic career both in India and England, culminating in a professorship at Baroda College. Beginning around 1902, he embarked on a campaign of agitation against British rule, which led to his imprisonment for sedition in 1908. While in jail, Aurobindo pursued the study of YOGA. Upon his release, he retired to the French enclave of Pondicherry in south India, where he established an ashram, or spiritual community, and devoted himself entirely to yoga and philosophy.

Aurobindo's prolific writings, of which the *Life Divine* is the most important, present a complex philosophy of spiritual evolution. Souls of divine essence have evolved through the worlds of matter, life, and mind to become humans on their long trek back to God. Now, with the help of yoga and divine enlightenment from above, we must evolve on to the planes of super mind and pure spirit. Both individuals and humanity as a whole are making this toilsome but all-important journey. Aurobindo's thought, which has been compared to that of HEGEL and TEILHARD DE CHARDIN, represents a significant meeting of Western evolutionism and Eastern spirituality.

R.E.

**AUTHORITY, RELIGIOUS.** In any community of faith, there must be some recognized authority that has the power to pronounce about matters of belief and practice and to settle disputes about such matters. Most religions claim to go back to some original REVELATION by God that would be authoritative for the religion in its subsequent history. But since such revelations were given in the more or less remote past, they have to be mediated in one way or another. Christianity claims to be founded in the revelation of God in Christ and acknowledges Christ as the head of the church. God's word would therefore be authoritative, but that word has to be mediated through some secondary authority.

The authority of the BIBLE comes in at this point, since it testifies to Christ and to the whole Judeo-Christian experience of God. So if the Bible reports that Jesus forbade divorce, that is taken by many as authoritative. But the Bible is ambiguous on many points (including Christ's teaching on divorce) so it is in fact supplemented by tradition. Though in the Protestant churches the Bible has sometimes had sole authority, in Catholicism TRADITION ranks alongside the Bible. Since Vatican II, however, tradition is not regarded as a separate mediation of the revelation, but is rather considered as the church's own elucidation of the same revelation as is found in the Bible.

In the Roman Catholic church the *magisterium* of the church, that is to say, its present teaching, especially the teaching of the POPE, has a high degree of authority unparalleled in Protestant churches. Reliance on external authority has been breaking down in every field of human activity since the ENLIGHTENMENT, and the new attitude found expression in matters of religion through the work of SCHLEIERMACHER. He made experience the final court of appeal. If we accept a doctrine or practice, it is because the experience of the believing community has demonstrated its salvific value, not because it is prescribed by the Bible or the tradition. It is important to note that Schleiermacher's appeal is to corporate experience and is quite different from the individualistic experience of the enthusiast who claims some inward spiritual illumination that overrides all other authorities. Perhaps we could not ascribe any authority or even meaning to the Bible and the tradition were there not something in our own experience that confirms their teaching. Perhaps too we could not accept their teaching if it went against the deliverances of our own reason and conscience.

Yet this is not to say that the traditional sources of authority are superseded. It does however suggest that in religious matters, as already in secular matters, authority should be composite and diffused, rather than monolithic. Neither the Bible nor the pope nor reason nor the opinions of scholars can be decisive separately. These different sources of authority have to be allowed to check one another if we are to arrive at a balanced decision on doubtful questions.

J.M.

**AUTHORIZED VERSION (AV).** *See* KING JAMES VERSION.

**AUTOCEPHALIC.** A self-governing Orthodox church with the right to name its bishops and the head of the church. The Canon demands that the church originate in a previously independent church, be located in a country independent from the mother church, and have a heirarchy of three duly appointed bishops.

J.C.

**AUTONOMY** (*autos* "self" + *nomos* "law"). Having or making one's own laws, independence, and self-governance. In religion, autonomy is associated with the revolt, in the eighteenth-century ENLIGHTENMENT, against the authority of the established churches. IMMANUEL KANT called for "man's release from his self-incurred tutelage," meaning "man's inability to make use of his understanding without direction from another." The duty of autonomy meant refusing to entertain any belief that was not warranted by rational evidence and personal experience. Opposed to autonomy is HETERONOMY (*heteros* = "other") or the imposition of authority or sanctions upon oneself from another—for example, the Bible or the church—which one would not impose if one were truly free and rational. More recently PAUL TILLICH has used autonomy and heteronomy in his theological analysis of culture. He contrasts them to *theonomy* or autonomous reason, which is realized in obedience to the very law and ground of its being or God. THEONOMY is, then, the quest for revelation.

J.L.

**AV.** *See* HEBREW CALENDAR.

**AVALOKITESVARA.** A BODHISATTVA who is especially loved and worshiped in Tibet, China, Korea, and Japan. This Sanskrit name means "Lord who looks down [to hear and answer prayer]," and it was translated into Chinese as Kwan Yin.

Since a bodhisattva is a being who has lived many lifetimes and has moved beyond the distinction between self and others, Avalokitesvara's mind can move freely through all things without being distracted. Avalokitesvara is especially known for great compassion, and worshipers can call him to their aid by reciting a MANTRA. In PURE LAND BUDDHISM the Avalokitesvara assists Amida Buddha in welcoming souls into the Pure Land, or Western Paradise.

By the twelfth century A.D. Chinese Buddhists had come to think of Avalokitesvara as a feminine figure, and from that time on paintings and statues usually show her as radiant, gracious, and serene. She has often been called the Goddess of Mercy, and throughout the Far East women give her special attention. They call on her in times of trouble and ask her for protection in childbirth and for other blessings.

Many statues show the bodhisattva wearing royal garments and holding a lotus blossom in one hand. Others show the figure with six or more arms, symbolizing the power to save, or with multiple heads and eyes, symbolizing the power to see all and to know all. Statues may be in a standing or seated position.

K.C.

**AVARICE.** One of the seven cardinal or "deadly" sins, consisting of an excessive love of wealth or possessions. Like the other CARDINAL SINs, avarice, or greed, is a distorted form of love. It is opposed to the virtue of liberality. The NT often speaks of the dangers of inordinate concern for wealth and possessions. Jesus taught that "a man's life does not consist in the abundance of his possessions" (Luke 12:15) and warned that "it is easier for a camel to go through the eye of a needle than for a rich man to enter the kingdom of God" (Matt. 19:24). One cannot serve God and mammon (Matt. 6:24). Avarice calls to mind the image of the rich but insecure and reclusive miser, fingering his gold. It is not a coincidence that the Latin *miser,* meaning a greedy, stingy person, comes from the same root as "miserable." A miser is a miserable, wretched person—a Scrooge.

Avarice is making an idol of wealth and possessions and is sinful because such excessive possessiveness, by subordinating all else to its achievement, corrupts the moral life. It is the sin that the avaricious confessed to Dante: "Our eyes would never seek the height, / Being bent on earthly matters"; so that "love of all true good was quenched in us / By avarice, and our works were left undone." The inordinate love of possessions may not, however, be an end in itself. It may be a means to secure fame, power, popularity, or pleasure. Thomas Aquinas believed avarice to be a sin of the practical man rather than of the philosopher or the theoretically inclined person.

However, in our highly commercial, acquisitive society few would seem to be free of its temptations. Psychologists tell us that unbridled economic competition, with its attendant insecurity and fear of failure, leads to an intensified quest for possessions. One of the evils of being "possessed by the love of possessions" is a self-absorption that closes a person off from one's neighbor in real need. The fruit of avarice is "hardness of heart" toward the widow, the orphan, and the poor. The needy are forgotten and unnecessary poverty and suffering are allowed to persist. The sins of avarice often are the sins of omission. Like the other deadly sins, avarice is self-love in one of its most dangerous forms.

J.L.

**AVATARS.** From the Sanskrit word for "descent." In HINDUISM, the appearances of gods in the world in animal or human form to instruct, to awaken devotion, and, typically, to defeat some particular demonic evil that is present. The concept first appears in the BHAGAVAD GITA, where KRISHNA declares that "whenever DHARMA declines," he takes a body to enter the world and rectify matters. Avatars are most commonly associated with VISHNU. Vaishnava (Vishnuite) mythological literature presents a widely accepted list of ten avatars, including several animal and semi-human forms. This list culminates in Rama, Krishna, the BUDDHA (here seen however as a strange sort of avatar whose business was to lead the weak into a false religion, thus maintaining the purity of Hinduism), and the coming avatar, Kalki, who will appear as a triumphant king at the end of our age.

Hindu thought tends to hold that the bodies of avatars are made of a pure, transcendent substance, or are even illusory projections, and so they cannot be deemed incarnations in a strict sense. On the other hand, many modern Hindus are prepared to broaden the concept to include any great person through whom God has been revealed to the world, and speak freely of such men as JESUS, GANDHI, or RA-MAKRISHNA as avatars.

R.E.

**AVE MARIA.** Latin for "Hail, Mary." The Ave Maria is based on the salutation of the angel to Mary in Luke 1:28, when she is told she is to become the mother of Christ. The Hail Mary is a prayer to the Virgin MOTHER OF GOD, often repeated in the Roman Catholic Church. The prayer developed between the sixth and the sixteenth centuries, becoming a standard prayer in the eleventh century. It was not until the thirteenth century, however, that the prayer was generally adopted throughout Western Christendom.

The usual words of the prayer are: "Hail, Mary, full of grace, the Lord is with you. Blessed are you among women, and blessed is the fruit of your womb, Jesus. Holy Mary, Mother of God, pray for us sinners now and at the hour of our death. Amen." Although sometimes sung as an anthem in Protestant churches, this prayer is not usually used by Protestants.

J.C.

**AVERROES** (Ibn-Rushd). The foremost Muslim philosopher of the Middle Ages, whose views conflicted both with orthodox Islam and with orthodox Christianity. Born in Cordoba, Spain, in

1126, late in his life he was banished because of his unorthodox views. A devoted student and follower of ARISTOTLE, he wrote commentaries on the works of the great philosopher, and later generations knew him as the Commentator.

His views conflicted with Muslim and Christian orthodoxy on three main points. First, he insisted on the autonomy of reason to pursue philosophical inquiry, apart from any guidance by faith. Second, he declared the world to be eternal and thus contradicted the doctrine of creation out of nothing. Finally, by affirming the "unity of the active intellect"—that is, of all rational beings—he contradicted the doctrine of individual life after death. His views, introduced from Spain to Christian Europe, created quite a stir, particularly at the University of Paris, where theologians such as BONAVENTURE and THOMAS AQUINAS sought to refute the views of the Latin Averroists. He died in Morocco in 1198, having been reconciled with the authorities, and was buried in Cordoba.

J.G.

**AVESTA.** The principal sacred book of the Zoroastrians. It is a collection of hymns, prayers, invocations, and instructions for ritual and moral practice.

Hymns called Gathas are probably the oldest portion of the Avesta. They have been accepted as the most reliable record we have of the beliefs and practices of the prophet Zoroaster, who lived around 600 B.C. (see ZOROASTRIANISM). They present a demand for righteousness (although that is not clearly defined) and tell of the reward for righteousness at the end of the age. They also tell us about the god AHURA MAZDA.

The text of the Avesta has gone through a long process of transmission. It probably took its present form between the third and seventh centuries A.D. Tradition indicates that there was a fuller version in ancient times, but it was lost when Alexander the Great conquered Persia in 331 B.C.

K.C.

**AVICENNA.** A Persian philosopher and physician (980-1037) whose works, translated into Latin in the twelfth and thirteenth centuries, were influential in late medieval philosophy and theology. In his philosophy he combined elements taken from ARISTOTLE with others derived from NEOPLATONISM. He distinguished between the necessary being, whose existence belongs to its essence, and contingent beings, whose existence is an accident. But then, arguing that creation is an act of the necessary being, and that nothing in that being is contingent, he came to the conclusion that created beings, although contingent in themselves, are necessary results of the necessary being, and therefore he affirmed eternal creation. His arguments were used by the Latin Averroists of Paris in the thirteenth century. J.G.

**AVIDYA.** From the Sanskrit word for "not seeing." In philosophical HINDUISM and BUDDHISM, ignorance in the sense of not rightly perceiving the true nature of Reality. This ignorance is the root impediment to salvation or liberation. Its opposite, VIDYA ("seeing") or *jnana* ("knowledge" or "wisdom") is not simply correct factual information, but profoundly experienced spiritual insight that discriminates aright between illusion and Reality.

In the earlier VEDAS, avidya refers merely to ignorance of the correct performance of rites. In the UPANISHADS, the philosophical meaning begins to appear; among other references, we are told that those lost in avidya are like dreamers. In the classic Advaita Vedanta (non-dualist) philosophy of Shankara, any supposed knowledge based upon distinctions (for example, between subject and object, God and the world) is declared to be avidya, not conducive to realization that BRAHMAN (God) is the sole Reality and the ground of all being. In Buddhism, avidya is the first of the twelve stages in the chain of causation by which one falls into egocentricity, birth, desire, and suffering. It is thus their ultimate cause.

R.E.

**AVIGNON.** A city in southern France that belonged to the popes, and where the PAPACY resided from 1305-78. When the papacy returned to Rome, rival popes were set up at Avignon, and thus began the GREAT SCHISM. The last of the popes of Avignon, Benedict XIII, died in exile in 1423.

J.G.

**AXIOLOGY.** From the Greek *axios,* "value or worth," the term is used in modern philosophy to designate the theory or study of value. Axiology has been used in a confusing variety of ways, from a study of goodness or value in general, to a discussion of various realms of value, to a more narrow application to specific types of ethical analysis. In the eighteenth century the term "value" was principally associated with political economy, for example in Adam Smith's use of exchange value. In the late nineteenth century the term value began to be used more widely, but also more variously, by philosophers like Hermann Lotze and F. NIETZSCHE. A. RITSCHL made value judgments the key to his theology, distinguishing them from scientific judgments of fact. According to Ritschl, causal or scientific judgments and value judgments proceed simultaneously, and both are indispensable to knowledge.

W. M. Urban popularized value theory in America, his *Valuation, Its Nature and Laws* (1909) being the first treatise on the subject in English. Another important early work on the subject was Ralph Barton Perry's *General Theory of Value* (1926). The analysis of value or the good has produced numerous distinctions, for example, between extrinsic or instrumental value (as a means) and intrinsic value, or value as an end in itself; between hedonistic and non-hedonistic value; between subjective (because it is valued) and objective value (because it has value independent of human interest); or between the cognitive or factual and noncognitive status of value judgments. Noncognitivists, such as A. J. Ayer and Bertrand Russell, regard value judgments as expressions of emotion or desire, while other noncognitivists, such as R. M. Hare, hold that value judgments are essentially prescriptions or recommendations.

Philosophers have given a variety of answers to the question of what is ultimately or intrinsically good. A hedonist, such as Epicurus or J. S. Mill would say it is pleasure; Kant, a good will; Augustine and Aquinas, the vision of God; Nietzsche, power; while a pragmatist would locate it in growth or adjustment itself. Many philosophers, from Plato to G. E. Moore, are "pluralists" in that they regard many things to be valuable or good in themselves, including knowledge, beauty, freedom, friendship, and virtue.

J.L.

**AXIOM.** That which is self-evident, unnecessary to belabor a point to prove, and commending itself to reason. An axiom is a principle universally accepted, hence a statement of a truth. In logic it refers to any proposition, regardless of whether it be true. In mathematics, as well as in some philosophy, it is a proposition that does not have to be proved but is immediately accepted as valid or true.

I.C.

**AYATOLLAH.** In SHI'ITE ISLAM a scholar of religious law who on his own authority issues rulings on religious belief and practice. The broader term for such a scholar is "mujtahid." A mujtahid who attracts a large following can take the title of ayatollah (literally "sign of God"). His followers regard him as the most learned person of his age, an example of righteousness and piety. His authority rests on that of the infallible Shi'ite IMAM, or supreme leader. The imam is not usually accessible. He may have withdrawn from this world entirely, or he may be living concealed in the present world because of the hostility of God's enemies.

In the Iranian revolution of the late 1970s several ayatollahs were prominent. The most important of them was Ayatollah Khomeini. His followers often addressed him as Imam.

K.C.

**AZARIAH, VEDANAIAKAM SAMUEL** (1875–1945). A native leader of the Christian movement in India. Azariah was born the son of a village pastor and a mother who greatly influenced his faith. He was affected in his public life by Sherwood Eddy, a United States Christian leader. After years of work with the YMCA, he accepted Anglican ordination and in 1912 became the first Indian bishop of the Anglican church. The church grew under his leadership, and he represented younger churches at many ecumenical and international gatherings. His book, *Christian Giving*, originally written in Tamil, has been translated into fifty languages.

W.G.

# Bb

*B*

BAAL (meaning "master," "lord," "husband," and signifying ownership).

The term "Baal" often appears in the OT in combination with the names of places, such as Baal-peor (Num. 25:3, 5; Deut. 4:3) and Baal-hermon (Judg. 3:3). Baal is sometimes coupled with characteristic functions, such as Baal-berith, "lord of the covenant" (Judg. 8:33; 9:4) and Baal-zebub, "lord of the flies" (II Kings 1:2; compare Matt. 10:25). Some Baals were given individual names, such as Dagon (Judg. 16:23; I Sam. 5:2), Hadad, and Melqart of Tyre, probably the Baal whom Jezebel worshiped (I Kings 16:31).

In the Ugaritic tablets, the youthful Baal has the name Hadad, god of winter rains, most prominent in the fertility cults. He bears the title "rider of the clouds" (compare Ps. 104:3). His chief enemy is Mot (death), god of the rainless season and the nether

From *Atlas of the Bible* (Thomas Nelson & Sons Limited)

*View of the Great Court of the Altar or Parthenon of the Acropolis at Baalbek*

world. El, the senior god, was supreme in social and moral matters, according to the Ugaritic mythology.

In Canaan, Baal was associated with ASHERAH (plural, Asheroth; Greek, Astarte), wife of El and mother of the gods. At Ras Shamrah, Baal-Hadad's sister-consort was Anath (or Anat), the cruel goddess of sex and war. Mount Cassius, north of Ugarit, was the Canaanite Olympus, home of the gods.

The sensuous Baal fertility cult, with its lasciviousness, was uniformly condemned by all the prophets from Elijah to the exile (Hos. 2:17; Jer. 19:5). The influence of Baal worship appears to have been strong in the period of the Judges, the times of Ahab and Jezebel (I Kings 18), and in the eighth century (Hos. 2). Hezekiah and Josiah suppressed the practices, but mention of Baalism continues into the early days of the exile (as Tammuz, Ezek. 8:14) and in the Persian period (Zech. 12:11).

The statues of Baal from Ugarit and Phoenicia represent him as a young man posed almost in the posture of Zeus at Olympia. His helmet bears horns; the bull is his special animal. He wears a short kilt and carries in his left hand a stylized lightning bolt for a spear and in his right hand a mace or club, the thunderstick (compare "thy rod and thy staff," Ps. 23:4). On his pedestal, there are wavy lines representing mountains (compare Yahweh "treads on the heights of the earth," Amos 4:13; Mic. 1:3). HIGH PLACES were sacred worship places for both Canaanites and Israelites. Or, the wavy lines may represent waters, either the sea or the rains Baal was thought to bring, so necessary to abundant crops in Syria-Palestine.

At some point, Baal's pagan connotations led to changes in personal names, such as Esh-baal (I Chr. 8:33) to Ish-bosheth (II Sam. 2:8), and, Merib-baal (I Chr. 8:34) to Mephibosheth (II Sam. 4:4), "bosheth" meaning shame or shameful thing. (Compare also BEL.)

P.L.G.

**BAALZEBUB.** The BAALS were the local deities of Cannanite towns, thought to be responsible for the growth of crops and the fertility of flocks and human beings. Baalzebub (also spelled BEELZEBUB) is the god of Ekron in the OT. In Hebrew it means "Lord of the Flies" or "Lord of Dung" but in the original Canaanite probably meant "Lord of rulers."

J.C.

**BAASHA.** The name of the third king of Israel (900-877 B.C.), son of Ahijah, of the tribe of Issachar. Baasha became king by murdering his predecessor, Nadab, son of Jeroboam. Soon thereafter, Baasha killed every surviving member of the house of Jeroboam (I Kings 15:27 ff.).

Baasha made war on ASA, king of Judah, "all their days" (I Kings 15:16, 32). He attempted to fortify Ramah in order to stop all traffic between Israel and Judah (II Chr. 16:1). As a defense against Baasha's possible attacks, Asa dug a large cistern in Jerusalem (Jer. 41:9). With funds taken from the Temple and palaces, Asa bribed Ben-hadad, king of Syria, to attack northern Israel. This forced Baasha to stop the work at Ramah to meet the challenge (II Chr. 16:2-5).

Jehu had prophesied the destruction of the house of Baasha just as he had destroyed Jeroboam's (I Kings 16:1-4). Baasha seems to have died a natural death (I Kings 16:6). His son Elah tried to succeed him (877-876 B.C.) but was assassinated by one of his officers, Zimri, who, during his seven days as king, killed all the house of Baasha and "his friends" (I Kings 16:11). Jehu's prophecy was that retribution would come upon Baasha for destroying the house of Jeroboam and for "all the evil that he did" (I Kings 16:7).

P.L.G.

**BABCOCK, MALTBIE DAVENPORT** (1858–1901). Author of the hymn "This Is My Father's World," Babcock was born August 3 in Syracuse, New York, to James and Emily Maria Maltbie.

He was graduated from Syracuse University in 1879 and from Auburn Theological Seminary in 1882. Ordained July 13, 1882, he was called to serve First Presbyterian Church of Lockport, New York. On October 4, 1882, he married Katherine Eliot Tallman. From Lockport they moved to Brown Memorial Church in Baltimore, Maryland, and in 1899 Babcock succeeded Henry van Dyke at Brick Presbyterian Church in New York City.

An active sportsman, Babcock was a proficient vocal and instrumental musician and an excellent preacher with a magnetic personality. In Lockport he had suffered a bout of depression, which returned in 1901 when, on a tour of the Middle East, he contracted Mediterranean fever. While confined to a hospital in Naples, he committed suicide. N.H.

**BABEL** (meaning "gate of God"). The Hebrew name of an ancient city in the land of Shinar (that is, Babylonia or Chaldea), a city in the kingdom of Nimrod, the mighty hunter (Gen. 10:10). According to the account in Genesis 11:4, this city's people, wanting to "make a name for ourselves," and to keep from being "scattered abroad upon the face of the whole earth," determined to build a city "of brick" as a lasting memorial and "a tower with its top in the heavens." Assyrian and Babylonian kings prided themselves on the size of buildings and temple towers or ZIGGURATS they erected. To desert Semites, any of a number of the Shinar cities could have fit the Genesis description of Babel. BABYLON was such a walled city and had a ziggurat, probably as high as a four- or five-story modern building, built of sun-dried bricks held together with "mud" (bitumen). At its top, there was a sacred shrine, used on special occasions. It was called "bab-il," gate of God. Thus, by a play on words, it was simple to relate Babel, from the Hebrew verb "to confuse," with the

Courtesy of the Oriental Institute, University of Chicago

*Model of the ziggurat of Babylon (Tower of Babel)*

name Babylon, locale of the captivity. The association characterized Babylon's prehistoric ancestors as people made objectionably proud and self-sufficient through their new-found technology of brickmaking. Also, here was a theological explanation of why people who descended from one couple speak in different (confused) languages.

P.L.G.

**BABYLON.** The name of the ancient city and nation of Mesopotamia that was the most influential outside source on Hebrew life and thought. Babylon was also a tyrannical military empire that threatened the destruction of Israel and Judah on several occasions, a threat that the Neo-Babylonian Empire carried out in 586 B.C. Thereupon, the upper classes of Judah were taken into exile in Babylon, until their release by Cyrus the Great in 539 B.C. This historical background caused the apocalyptic writers of the NT era to use the name "Babylon" to refer to tyranny and opposition to God in their own times. The REVELATION to John (the Apocalypse) in particular uses "Babylon" as a symbol for a world power hostile to the true God, which put itself forward as an anti-God, destroying the saints by persecution and demanding that believers worship "the beast" (Satan) instead. For the author of the Revelation, that power was Rome.

There are a number of sound reasons for identifying Rome as the real enemy symbolized by "Babylon." The first is the occasion of the writing. Under the emperor DOMITIAN (A.D. 81–96), Christians in Asia Minor (the area where Revelation was written) were threatened by an imminent persecution because their faith forbade them to offer divine honors to the emperor. The Revelation was written to encourage the church to be faithful unto death.

Another reason is the fact that the notorious "number of the beast," 666, is a numerical code for "Neron Caesar" (Rev. 13:18), under whose unjust administration even more terrible persecutions had been inflicted on the church. "Babylon," in Revela-

tion, is called the great whore and mother of harlots and is said to be drunk with the blood of the saints. Harlotry is readily understood as idolatry, in the same way that the prophets spoke of idolatrous Israelites "playing the harlot." The use of this symbol for Rome shows that the strand of early Christianity represented by John the Elder saw the Roman Empire as evil, the enemy of God.

J.C.

**BABYLONIAN CAPTIVITY, OLD TESTAMENT.** *See* EXILE.

**BABYLON, OLD TESTAMENT.** *See* ASSYRIA AND BABYLONIA.

**BACH, JOHANN SEBASTIAN** (1685–1750). The German composer and organist was born March 21 in Eisenach, Thuringia, the youngest child of Johann Ambrosius and Elizabeth Lämmerhirt Bach, a very musical family. By 1695 both his parents were dead. He was reared by his elder brother Johann Christoph (1671–1721), an organist who taught him the keyboard.

In 1700 his voice secured him a place in a choir of poor boys in Lüneburg, which furthered his musical education. At age eighteen he was appointed organist for a new organ at the Neukirche in Arnstadt, where he stayed until 1707, synthesizing northern and southern German styles of music. He once walked a great distance to study with Dietrich Buxtehude. He married his cousin Maria Barbara Bach on October 17, 1707.

At Mühlhausen (1707–1708) Bach wrote several cantatas including "God Is My King." From 1708 to

Courtesy of the Bettmann Archive

*Johann Sebastian Bach*

1717 he was court organist and orchestra concertmaster at Weimar, writing a cantata a month. Here he became very interested in the music of Italian composers, especially that of Antonio Vivaldi.

Bach moved to Köthen, where he was musical director to Prince Leopold (1717–23). Here he wrote the Brandenburg Concertos. His first wife died July 7, 1720, and he married Anna Magdalena Wilcken on December 3, 1721. Of his twenty children, ten survived; four sons also became musicians and composers.

The first version of Bach's *Magnificat* was written in Leipzig soon after his arrival in 1723 as director of church music for the city's parishes. In 1724 he published the *St. John Passion* and in 1723 the Sanctus for the *Mass in B Minor,* which was finished in 1733. The *Goldberg Variations* were completed in 1742, and the *St. Matthew Passion* also dates from this period.

Incredibly prolific, Bach is probably best known to churchgoers for his harmonizations of a number of familiar hymn tunes for such standards as "O Sacred Head, Now Wounded," "Jesus, Priceless Treasure," "Come, Holy Spirit, God and Lord," "Deck Thyself, My Soul, with Gladness," "God of the Living, in Whose Eyes," "Lord of All Majesty and Might," "O God, Our Faithful God," "Wake, Awake, for Night Is Flying," "Break Forth, O Beauteous Heavenly Light," and "The Day Is Past and Over."

N.H.

**BAECK, LEO** (1873–1956). One of the foremost Jewish theologians of the twentieth century. He was born and grew up in Imperial Germany and received his doctorate from the University of Berlin. At that time, Harnack was the most famous member of the faculty of theology in the university. Harnack's lectures on the essence of Christianity (Eng. trans. *What Is Christianity?*), given in 1899, had stressed the originality of Jesus' teaching and minimized the connection with Judaism, a fashion that had begun in German religious thought at least as early as Kant's *Religion Within the Limits of Reason Alone.* Baeck responded with *The Essence of Judaism* (1948), asserting the debt of Christianity to Judaism, a view upheld by subsequent scholarship. Baeck found room in his thinking for both the religious and the ethical aspects of Judaism. He claimed there is no conflict between transcendence and immanence. He survived imprisonment in a concentration camp and spent his last years in England.

J.M.

**BAHA'I.** An eclectic faith that declares that God is one and that all religions are true and agree in essentials. Baha'i developed from Babism, which was begun in Shiraz, Iran (Persia), in 1844 by Mirza Ali Muhammad (1819–50). The "Bab," as he was known, wrote one hundred books expounding his teachings. Baha'i has a liberal, progressive outlook. Mirza called upon world rulers to peacefully form a world government, before the middle of the nineteenth century. Baha'i establishes its beliefs on the doctrine of God's continuing and progressive revelation.

Among Baha'i's teachings are the oneness of the human race, the need for a world without borders and a truly open society, peace through universal disarmament, and the evolution of humanity to a higher stage of personal and cultural development. The equality of the sexes, the desire for equality of opportunity, and the need to freely search for truth are high Baha'i ideals. True worship is work that serves these ideals and improves the harmony and happiness of the human race.

The chief center of Baha'i in the United States is a beautiful temple in Evanston, Illinois. Since the Iranian Revolution, Baha'ists have been mercilessly persecuted by the MUSLIM fundamentalists who support the Ayatollah Khomeini. Thousands of believers have been killed, their villages and homes destroyed; their places of worship and even their cemeteries have been broken up and desecrated. Protests from international organizations have not stopped this savage attack on a peaceful, idealistic people.

J.C.

**BALAAM.** The son of Boer and a SEER summoned by Balak king of Moab to invoke a curse upon Israel's tribes as they entered Canaan. Instead, Balaam pronounced a blessing and predicated Israel's future preeminence (Num. 25:5–24:25; Deut. 23:4-5; Josh. 13:22; 24:9-10). Balaam's story is a unique tale of a non-Israelite Mesopotamian who was attentive to the commands of the God of Israel. The story of Balaam's talking ass and the story of the talking serpent in Genesis 3, are the only two stories of talking animals in the OT. Balaam's story also depicts the universal scope of the power of Israel's God and the power that the OT attributed to the spoken word. New Testament references to Balaam (II Pet. 2:15; Jude 11; Rev. 2:14) are not flattering.

W.G.

**BALM.** A gum or resin associated with Gilead, as "balm in Gilead" (Jer. 8:22). No specific botanical identification of the tree or shrub that produced balm has been made yet. Balm was prized for medicine (Jer. 8:22; 46:11; 51:8), cosmetics, and embalming. It was, apparently, a staple in caravan trade (Gen. 43:11; Ezek. 27:17), named along with gum and myrrh (Gen. 37:25).

P.L.G.

**BALSAM.** Only found in the RSV and always associated with trees; in the KJV, balsam is referred to as mulberry trees (II Sam. 5:23-24; I Chr. 14:14-15; I Macc. 6:34). Botanically the balsam trees could be the black or red mulberry trees, *Morus nigra L,* which grow abundantly in Palestine. From the "sound of marching" in the tops of the balsam trees (I Chr. 14:15), the trees could be a type of aspen or poplar (Hos. 4:13), through whose leaves a blowing wind makes a particular kind of sound (*compare* BALM)

P.L.G.

**BALTIMORE CATECHISM.** The doctrinal standard used for generations for Roman Catholic parochial school children. Written in 1885 in standard question-and-answer format, it contained 421 questions divided into thirty-seven chapters covering the creed, the sacraments, prayer, the commandments, and last things. Revised in 1941 by the Confraternity of Christian Doctrine, it remains a summary of traditional pre-Vatican II American Roman Catholic theology.

N.H.

**BALTIMORE, COUNCILS OF.** From 1789 to 1808 all American Roman Catholics were part of the Diocese of Baltimore. The city became the preeminent see. Three early "general chapters of the clergy" were held near there (1783–84, 1786, 1789). JOHN CARROLL held his only general synod there in 1791. The term "Councils of Baltimore" more properly refers to the first seven provincial councils (1829, 1833, 1837, 1840, 1843, 1846, 1849) and the three plenary councils (1852, 1866, 1884). All ten of these were held there.

N.H.

**BAPTISM.**

*Antecedents.* The use of water in religious purifications and cleansings is an age-old custom. Christianity has followed suit and has incorporated a water rite into its visible expression from the beginning. Baptism has been an integral part of Christianity from the first, but the church's understanding of baptism has been diversified and its practice threatened in several ways. As early as Paul's writing of I Corinthians we can see evidence of division over baptism (I Cor. 1:13-17) and of misunderstanding of the apostolic practice (I Cor. 10:1-13). There have been strange incrustations that have gathered around baptismal procedures (I Cor. 15:29). Hence the appeal to baptism as a focal point among Christians (I Cor. 12:12-13), which was needed at Corinth to set matters right in Paul's eyes. In later centuries the place of controversy in baptism centered on the role of faith, exercised by the subject to be baptized, and the mode of administration, whether it was to be immersion or sprinkling (see *Didache* 7:1-4 for this diversity).

The origins of Christian baptism are unclear. We can, however, be certain that early Christian proclamation dated the commencement of the KERYGMA, or announced good news, from the activity of Jesus' cousin, known invariably as John "the baptizer." The title suggests that there was something distinctive about John's practice of baptizing men and women in the Jordan River. If John's practice was based on proselyte baptism practiced by Gentile converts to Judaism, the novelty lay in the fact that John insisted on a radical change, or repentance, on the part of fellow Jews in preparation for the coming of God's rule which he heralded (see Luke 7:29-30). If John was doing what the ESSENES at QUMRAN did, according to the DEAD SEA SCROLLS, then he was offering a new beginning of cleansing in anticipation of a divine visitation or judgment on the ungodly in Israel. At all events John came to make ready for Jesus (Luke 16:16) and to point forward to him who would in turn "baptize with the Holy Spirit" (Mark 1:8; cf. John 1:33; Acts 19:4).

Jesus received baptism at the hands of his cousin (Matt. 3:13-17), which raises some unresolved questions as to why a sinless Jesus *needed* to be baptized. Presumably Jesus regarded baptism as the start of his public ministry and an identification with the people. What Jesus meant by baptism has to be gleaned from his occasional use of the term in his reported teaching (Mark 10:38-39; Luke 12:49ff.). John seems to have looked forward to a Messiah who would judge and condemn sinners. Jesus reinterpreted baptism as a picture of his suffering endured vicariously for others with whom he was closely identified in both his death and new life beyond the cross. He would save them by associating with them in their sins, and would emerge to a risen life, bringing his people with him. If this is the correct view of Jesus' own baptism, it leads us to the threshold of Paul's baptismal theology in Romans 6:1-11.

*Apostolic Practice.* The first Christian sermon (in Acts 2) closed, we are told, with a call to "repent and be baptized." These terms, or their equivalents, recur repeatedly in the stories of conversion in the Acts of the Apostles (2:38, 41; 8:12f.; 16:14f., 33f.; 18:8; 19:2-5; 22:16), thus making baptism a decisive step that publicly associated the new convert with his or her fellow believers as an open profession. "In the name of Jesus" as a formula suggests a passing under the lordship of Jesus Christ, whose "name" (or authority) was invoked in the rite. At a later time the baptism was administered in the name of the Trinity (Matt. 28:19-20, *Didache* 7:1, 3) as baptismal practice took on a more confessional coloration and became part of the church's creedal position over against the non-Christian world.

As far back as we are able to trace Christian origins, becoming and being a Christian has always been understood as receiving the gift of the Holy Spirit (Rom. 8:9). But how was the Spirit received? No clear answer is possible from the documents of the apostolic church; yet it does seem evident that the act of baptism was in some way connected with the receiving of the Spirit (Acts 2:38; 8:14-17; 9:17-18; 10:44-48; 19:5, 6. No one set pattern was known to Luke).

Paul's contribution to baptismal teaching was built on what he inherited as part of the tradition he took over (Rom. 6:1-14, which clearly reflects his use of pre-Pauline material). The key to Paul's distinctives is in his describing baptism as a new creation rather than as a washing from sin's stain. His emphasis falls on dying and rising with Christ as the gateway to a new existence set within the fellowship of Christ and his church. That new life is likened to putting off the old ways as a suit of clothes and putting on a new life-style, a figure appropriate to what occurred literally in baptism (Gal. 3:27). Baptism marked the entry to a corporate life (I Cor. 12:12-13) and is predicated on a faith-response (Col. 2:11-13) as befits the missionary and first-generation character of Paul's own situation as evangelist, apostle, and church builder. The same close connection of preaching/believing/receiving baptism and so entering on a new life in the Christian community is shared by all the writers after Paul (in the Pastorals, I Peter, and the Johannine church).

*Post-apostolic Developments.* From the mid-second century onward the rite of initiation took on fresh meaning as it became the kernel around which many formulas and ceremonies with preparatory and explicatory significance gathered. Beginning with postbaptismal anointing, the laying on of hands, and "signing" with the cross preparatory to admitting to first communion—a sequence found in Tertullian and the *Apostolic Tradition* of Hippolytus—other rites and customs followed. The chief of these were fasting and exorcism with a renouncing of Satan, on the negative side, and the use of symbols (candle, white robe, kiss of peace, partaking of milk and honey as a sign of entry to the Promised Land), on the positive. It is important to note that the ceremonies referred to can only be applied after a lengthy period of teaching and training; and this procedure may well have continued in the Western church, had it not been for one decisive new development, namely the popularity of infant baptism.

Infant baptism owes much of its influence as a church practice to Augustine's reversal of a trend found in Tertullian. The latter argues that little children are innocent and do not need baptismal cleansing. Augustine contended for exactly the opposite viewpoint on the strength of his doctrine of original guilt according to which children inherit Adam's sin and enter upon life handicapped by the guilt of Adam's disobedience and share in his fallen nature. It is imperative that the stain of birth-sin should be cleansed at the earliest opportunity and baptism should not be delayed. Thus the practice of infant baptism, already in vogue in Cyprian's time, was given a theological rationale; and it became part and parcel of medieval Catholicism.

*The Reformers.* Two quite different solutions to what the Reformers regarded as an unsatisfactory state of affairs appeared in the sixteenth century. The Reformers were anxious to retain the idea of baptismal

instruction as children were admitted to the school of Christ, and they were equally adamant in retaining the belief that Christian families are sharers in the covenant of God stretching back to Abraham. Only the left-wing Reformers, beginning with Swiss reformer Grebel in A.D. 1525, reverted to what they believed was NT precedent. They withdrew infants from baptism and practiced only the "baptism of believers," even if it involved a "second baptism" (hence the name ANABAPTISTS) subsequent to infant baptism.

Yet the Reformers' heavy emphasis on faith posed a problem. Obviously newborn infants could not respond openly to the call of the gospel. So "faith" was given several different nuances. Luther believed that infants *do* believe, based on the sacrament's power to evoke faith. Calvin stressed the covenantal relationship of children in a Christian household, and argued for vicarious faith transferred to infants' account and later to be exercised, as circumcision was applied to the children of Jewish households. The Anglican Reformers left the question in abeyance, but the 1662 Prayer Book used the promise of the child's godparents or sponsors as proleptic or anticipatory "until he come of age to take it upon himself." The net effect was to accentuate the importance of CONFIRMATION as a "rite of completion" when the initiation was fully carried through. The Anabaptist protest, however, was picked up by English and then American Baptists who insisted that faith by definition is personal and incorporates a consciously made decision; hence they refused to baptize any but professed believers.

*Modern Proposals.* Concern over indiscriminate infant baptisms that never get "completed" in confirmation in a post-Christian society and an alarm over the superstition that can gather around infant baptism have led to some serious questioning of infant baptismal practice. It is being asked whether it would be more honest and adequate to admit infants to a catechumenate in the hope of their future baptism at such a time as they can voluntarily ask for it. On the other side, those who practice infant baptism are reluctant to give up their cherished belief in the church as composed of believers and their children seen as "children of promise" and "heirs of the covenant." This is really the sticking point in the baptismal debate; and little real progress has been made to get through the impasse, except the notable experiment of the North India scheme, 1970, of including *both* types of baptism, with conversion-confirmation acting as a necessary hinge linking them.

R.M.

**BAPTISMAL FONT.** A pedestal or base, usually of marble or other stone, supporting a large basin that contains the water used in baptism. Generally, the basin, or font, is about three feet high. The baptismal font, historically, was located at the entrance or west end of the church building. This symbolized the entering of the church by way of baptism. Later, in Protestant churches, the font was often located at the front or chancel end of the church to show the equality of the sacrament of baptism to the sacrament of the Lord's Supper. It may also stand at the south end of the chancel. The font is usually protected by a close-fitting cover made of the same material as the font itself.

J.C.

**BAPTISM FOR THE DEAD.** One of the most baffling passages in the Bible is I Corinthians 15:29, where Paul refers to a custom in which early Christians, apparently, received baptism on behalf of the dead. Actually, this is not presented as a direct statement, or a recommendation of the practice, but occurs as two rhetorical questions designed to underscore the reality of the Resurrection. Many questions have been raised throughout Christian history about this practice, for if such rituals did take place they would reflect a superstitious understanding of the gospel unworthy of the faith. Much of this questioning centered on why Paul would have passed over this subject without condemning it. However, a strict reading of the reference does not reveal an approval of the practice by Paul. His questions simply recognize that some such practice was observed, along with taking advantage of the practice as a further proof that the church did, indeed, believe firmly in the physical resurrection of Christ, and the coming physical resurrection of all believers.

The church fathers (Tertullian and Chrysostom) tried to explain Paul's reference as referring to the baptism of our bodies, which are dying, so that baptism gives eternal life to our mortal bodies. The reformers also sought to put an orthodox construction on the passage. Luther interpreted the passage to refer to an early Christian practice of administering baptism at the tombs of the martyrs. Calvin said it referred to the administering of "deathbed baptism," that is, to baptism of the dying.

J.C.

**BAPTISM OF THE SPIRIT.** In Pentecostalism and the HOLINESS MOVEMENT, the doctrine of the "second blessing" or subsequent reception of the Holy Spirit distinct from conversion or justification. This reception is generally marked by "signs of the Spirit," usually speaking in tongues (GLOSSALALIA). In Holiness doctrine this experience signifies entire sanctification.

J.C.

**BAPTIST CHURCHES.** One of the largest groups of evangelical Christians. Their name is derived from their emphasis on baptizing only those who have made a conscious personal commitment to Jesus Christ as Lord and Savior.

The Baptist World Alliance, which includes most of the autonomous conventions and unions of Baptists from all parts of the world, estimates that there are more than 33 million Baptists. However, since many congregations are unregistered in Communist lands or are unrelated to denominational bodies in Western countries, the Baptist population of the world is probably much larger than the Baptist World Alliance figure. Baptist membership in the United States in 1981 totaled 27 million. Southern Baptists alone listed 13.6 million.

Although some historians seek to trace Baptist origins to apostolic times, the movement came into being in the wake of the Protestant REFORMATION. John Smyth (about 1554–1612), an English Puritan preacher who first served an Anglican church at Lincoln, then a Separatist congregation at Gainsborough, became the first Baptist. Because of persecution in his homeland, Smyth and a group of followers fled to Amsterdam. There he came under the influence of Mennonites, descendants of the ANABAPTISTS. Imbued with their distinctive teaching that only believers should be baptized, Smyth reorganized his Separatist congregation and it became the first English Baptist congregation in 1609. Smyth baptized himself first, then the others of his exile church, which became the first of those later to be known as General Baptists. They subscribed to the ARMINIANISM's belief that the atonement of Christ was not limited to the elect but was general, open to all. In 1611 or 1612 some of the members of the Amsterdam congregation, under the leadership of Thomas Helwys, returned to London and established a Baptist church there.

Meanwhile another band of Separatists—Puritans who separated themselves from the Church of England—founded the first Particular Baptist congregation in Southwark in 1633. They held to the Calvinistic concept that only the elect were to be baptized. In 1644 a group of seven Particular Baptist congregations developed a creedal statement that included the requirement not only of believers' baptism but that the mode was to be by immersion.

The late Ernest F. Kevan, a British scholar, pointed out that it is a mistake to think that the chief concern of Baptists is the administration of baptism. They are primarily concerned with the spiritual nature of the church, and believers' baptism becomes a corollary of that teaching. Baptists, from their beginnings, repudiated the Anglican sacramental and the Presbyterian covenantal view of infant baptism. Baptists stress the idea of the "gathered church," members of which are joined by God into a communion of life and service under the lordship of Christ.

The local church of believers looms large in Baptist thinking. Each congregation is autonomous. Baptists repudiate the connectional concepts of other ecclesiastical bodies. Therefore, it is wrong to speak of the Southern Baptist "Church" or the American Baptist "Church." Yet since their earliest days Baptists have voluntarily joined themselves in unions, associations, and conventions. None of these bodies possesses the ecclesiastical authority uniquely attributed to the local congregation.

Baptists are not reticent about voicing their distinctive claims. In the 1936 issue of the *United States Census, Religious Bodies,* their spokesman declared: "It is a distinct principle with Baptists that they acknowledge no human founder, recognize no human authority, and subscribe to no human creed. For all these things Baptists of every name and order go back to the New Testament."

Despite a strong and persistent adherence to an anti-creedal position on the part of many Baptists, they have, nonetheless, developed a number of creeds. Besides the creedal affirmation of the Particular Baptists in 1644, there have been several subsequent confessions of faith. Probably the best known of these in America is the *New Hampshire Confession* of 1833. This statement is silent on the doctrine of the universal church and is therefore heartily espoused by those who emphasize the authority and independence of the local congregation. The Southern Baptist Theological Seminary of Louisville, Kentucky, adopted the *Abstract of Principles* in 1859, portions of which reflect the *Second London Confession of 1677* and the *Philadelphia Confession of 1742.* Some regard the latter as a Baptist interpretation of the Westminster Confession (1646). The Southern Baptist Convention issued a statement of the *Baptist Faith and Message* in 1925.

Repudiating the concept of an established church, Baptists have always emphasized the principle of church-state separation. When Baptists moved from the atmosphere of Puritan England to the American colonies and the emerging nation, they tended to emphasize the principle even more.

While Baptists have made a continuing impact on Britain, it was in the New World that the movement exploded and eventually became the largest segment of American Protestantism. The English Baptist ROGER WILLIAMS came to Massachusetts in 1632, but it was not long before the Puritans, soon to become the religious establishment of New England, forced him to flee to Rhode Island, where in 1639 he formed the first Baptist church in America.

The Baptists did not make great headway in the new land until the Revolution. Presbyterians and Congregationalists, stirred by the Great Awakening, undoubtedly influenced the Baptists. They were soon moving, first southward, then westward, and, along with the Methodists, took over the revivalistic task of frontier evangelism.

The Baptists of Britain, starting with WILLIAM CAREY in 1792, were deeply involved in the modern missionary movement. England and Scotland also gave the world Baptist preachers such as CHARLES HADDON SPURGEON and Alexander Maclaren, and Wales produced Christmas Evans. In the New World, Adoniram Judson, a Congregationalist

turned Baptist, became a pioneer missionary, first to India and later to Burma.

Because of the outreach of both British and American missionaries, the Baptist faith was carried to Europe and Russia, and today perhaps the largest force of Baptists after those of the United States is found in the Soviet Union. There is a large Baptist testimony in Brazil, as well as in other countries of Latin America, Africa, and Asia.

Except for the Baptist Union of Great Britain and Ireland and the American Baptist Churches in the United States, most Baptist bodies have been unallied with the ecumenical movement. In a rare exception, Baptists in India have joined with non-Baptists to form the Church of North India.

These listings may be helpful in identifying the wide variety of Baptist groups in the United States. Note the following definitions:

*Regular Baptists* claim to hold to the position of the original English Baptists before the distinction between Particular and General Baptists.

*Particular Baptists* are those who believe in a particular atonement in which Christ died only for his elect people. The greater percentage of Baptists are found in this category.

*General Baptists* are Arminian in theology, believing in a universal atonement and free will.

*American Baptist Association,* not to be confused with the American Baptist Churches in the U.S.A., is a fellowship of regular and independent missionary Baptist churches whose greatest strength is in the South. Known sometimes as "equality" Baptists, they stress that only local congregations have the authority to conduct missionary work. Separatists, they claim a unique type of Baptistic "apostolic succession" called LANDMARKISM. They believe that since the days of the early church, immersed believers have maintained the true Baptist succession to the present day.

*American Baptist Churches in the U.S.A.* From 1907 to 1950 they were known as the Northern Baptist Convention and from 1950 to 1972 as the American Baptist Convention. For about two hundred years the Baptists of the northern states did not grow as did their counterparts in the South. Yet they did found the American Baptist Foreign Mission Society in 1814, their publication society in 1824, and the Home Mission Society in 1832. Theological diversity developed in the northern and (later) western Baptist churches now associated in the ABC. Indeed polarization of its liberal and conservative wings forced Northern Baptists into the Modernist-Fundamentalist controversies of the 1920s, causing the secession of groups that became the General Association of Regular Baptists and the Conservative Baptist Association. The ABC, though not participating in the CONSULTATION ON CHURCH UNION, has been the most ecumenical of all United States Baptist groups.

*Baptist General Conference.* Beginning as an ethnic communion in the mid-nineteenth century, this collection of churches, first known as the Swedish Baptists, organized as a conference in 1879. Now a virile movement, it has extended its ministry to individuals and families beyond its racial roots, and supports both Bethel College and Bethel Theological Seminary, St. Paul, Minnesota.

*Baptist Missionary Association.* This is a group of Regular Baptist churches organized in 1950 as the North American Baptist Association, which had no relationship to the North American Baptist Conference, or German Baptists. The present name was adopted in 1969. In theology these churches are evangelical, missionary-oriented, and premillennial in eschatology.

*Conservative Baptist Association of America.* This is an association of churches that broke away from the Northern Baptist Convention (now known as American Baptist Churches), and was organized in 1947. They recognize the OT and the NT as the divinely inspired Word of God. Each local church is independent and autonomous. They support the Conservative Baptist Theological Seminary of Denver, and Western Conservative Baptist Seminary, of Portland, Oregon.

*Duck River (and Kindred) Association of Baptists.* This is a group of Baptist associations located in Tennessee, Alabama, Georgia, Kentucky, and Mississippi. They practice foot washing, the Lord's Supper, and baptism by immersion. Their doctrinal position is similar to that of the Separate Baptists.

*Free Will Baptists.* This group originated in two lines of Arminian Baptists. The southern branch was first organized in North Carolina in 1727. A similar movement was organized in 1780 in New Hampshire. A remnant of the northern group joined with the southern in 1935 to form the National Association of Free Will Baptists.

*General Association of General Baptists.* This is an Arminian group of Baptists that first arrived in the New World in 1714. The movement was revived by Benoni Stinson in 1823 in Indiana.

*General Association of Regular Baptists.* This group was founded in 1932 in Chicago by a group that had withdrawn from the Northern Baptist Convention. They subscribe essentially to the New Hampshire Confession of Faith.

*General Six Principle Baptists.* This group was organized in Rhode Island in 1653, drawing its name from Hebrews 6:1-2 KJV.

*National Baptist Convention of America.* This is known as the "unincorporated" body of black Baptists, which withdrew from the parent body in 1915 following a dispute over the adoption of a charter and the ownership of a publishing house.

*National Baptist Convention, U.S.A., Inc.* In colonial days black slaves attended the churches of their white masters. However, the first black Baptist church in America was organized at Silver Bluff, South Carolina, in 1773. But the disruption of two main groups of black Baptists occurred in 1915. This group, known as the "incorporated" convention, traces its beginning to the Foreign Mission Baptist Convention of 1880, as does the National Baptist Convention of America. Baptists make up the largest segment of black Christians.

*National Primitive Baptist Convention of the USA.* This group of black congregations hold basically to the same doctrinal position as the white Primitive Baptists. Both are opposed to all forms of church organization; yet the black Primitive Baptists have local associations and a national convention. Since the beginning of the twentieth century they have established aid societies, conventions, and Sunday schools.

*North American Baptist Conference.* Congregations of German immigrants formed this conference, which in some communities still conduct bilingual services. The churches of this conference have a firm belief in CALVINISM.

*Primitive Baptists.* This is a grouping of Baptist congregations, chiefly in the South, who have never organized as a denomination. They are opposed to any ecclesiastical organization including Sunday schools and missionary societies because they are not specifically mentioned in Scripture. Known sometimes as "Hard Shells," this group of Baptists are strongly Calvinistic. Some congregations practice foot washing and some eschew the use of musical instruments in worship.

*Progressive National Baptist Association, Inc.* This is a group of black Baptist congregations that organized in 1961 after breaking away from the two older black Baptist denominations, principally the National Baptist Convention, U.S.A., Inc.

*Reformed Baptists.* This is a small communion of strongly Calvinistic Baptists who have banded together without a formal central ecclesiastical structure. Active since 1955 these churches reflect the doctrinal position of the London Confession (1689) and the Philadelphia Confession (1742).

*Separate Baptists in Christ.* This group, found in Indiana, Ohio, Kentucky, Tennessee, Illinois, and North Carolina, traces its origins to the Separatist movement of the English Reformation (see SEPARATISM). The first association was formed in 1758 in North Carolina.

*Seventh Day Baptist General Conference.* Originating in England in 1617, the Seventh Day Baptists organized their first church in the colonies in 1672 at Newport, Rhode Island. Their doctrines are similar to those of all Calvinistic Baptists except that Saturday, not Sunday, must be observed as the Sabbath. William Miller, spiritual forebear of the Seventh-Day Adventists, originally belonged to this group.

*Southern Baptist Convention.* More than half of all Baptists in the United States belong to this denomination, which broke with northern brethren over the slavery question, and formed its own convention in 1845. Although it is still a regional group, churches have been formed in every one of the fifty states. Southern Baptists are generally conservative in doctrine, committed to evangelistic work at home and missionary endeavors abroad. They have resisted efforts to draw them into the ECUMENICAL MOVEMENT.

*United Free Will Baptists.* This is a group of black Baptists whose theology is similar to that of the white Free Will Baptists. Both groups teach the doctrines of free grace, free salvation, and free will.

There are many independent Baptist churches, unrelated to any organization. They are generally separatistic and fundamentalistic in doctrine.

R.H.

**BAPTISTERY.** A special structure, generally separate, but sometimes part of the church, used for baptisms in ancient times and still in use in some areas today. As baptism was celebrated en masse at certain holy seasons like Lent, large chapels were needed for the ceremony. Immersion, practiced in the fourth-century church, also required a large baptismal pool. Baptisteries were generally circular or polygonal in shape. The baptismal pool was surrounded by pillars and topped with a dome. As the baptism of adults passed out of practice, after the pagans in the Roman Empire were converted in the fourth century, and was replaced by the baptism of the children of Christians, baptisteries were replaced by BAPTISMAL FONTS in rooms built into church buildings.

J.C.

**BAR-.** An Aramaic prefix to the father's name meaning "son of _____." The Hebrew equivalent is "Ben-." Bar- is used more in the NT, for instance, Bar-nabas, Bar-sabbas, Bar-jona, and Bar-jesus.

P.L.G.

**BARABBAS.** The criminal chosen by the crowd (Matt. 27:15-26; John 18:38-40) to be released at Passover instead of Jesus. According to some Greek manuscripts, Barabbas was his surname; his first name was Judas or Jesus. Barabbas is said to be a robber (John 18:40) in most translations, but the term probably means a bandit or revolutionary. Mark 15:7 and Luke 23:19 declare that Barabbas was a revolutionary fighter against the occupying Romans. He was involved in a riot in which a murder occurred and was in prison for that crime when Jesus was arrested. Pilate apparently considered Barabbas so clearly guilty of murder that he felt the crowd (even if it were disturbed by Jesus) would have no difficulty rejecting Barabbas and freeing Jesus. Since the crowd chose Barabbas, the suggestions of some commentators that the crowd was composed mainly of supporters of Barabbas, is given some weight.

J.C.

**BARBARIAN.** The Greek word *barbaros,* from which our English term is taken, is an onomatopoeic expression, that is, the sound of the word betrays its significance. To Greek ears, all those who did not speak their language sounded as if they were uttering nonsense syllables that came over as *"bar-bar."* But this was not a verdict on the civilization or culture of the speaker in the original context of the word. Luke reverts to the original, neutral sense of *"barbaros"* in Acts 28:2-4, which pays tribute to the kindness of the Maltese, who spoke a Phoenician dialect.

The idea of "barbarian" as uncouth and lacking Greek civilization is seen in Colossians 3:11, where the term is a partner to "Scythian," a wild race that bordered the Black Sea. The problem of communication from one language to another lies behind I Corinthians 14:11 (the English versions have "foreigner" for Paul's *barbaros*); and in Romans 1:14 the term is coupled with "Greek" to take in the totality of humankind as the audience for Paul's universal gospel message (Rom. 1:16).

R.M.

**BARCLAY, WILLIAM** (1907–78). Scottish minister, theologian, professor of biblical criticism, and prolific, popular author on biblical topics. Born in Wick, Caithness, Scotland, Barclay died in Glasgow, Scotland, on January 24. He was known as "the common man's theologian" as he appealed to great numbers of people in the United Kingdom through his books and radio and television talks. He was famed as an extraordinary communicator. Not as conservative as some of his colleagues, he was, nonetheless, more successful in reaching the masses

Courtesy of The Westminster Press

*William Barclay*

than any other Christian thinker of his day. An ordained minister of the Church of Scotland, Barclay served Trinity Church, Renfrew, 1933–46; and as lecturer in NT language and literature, 1946–63, and professor of divinity and biblical criticism, 1963–74, at the University of Glasgow. He was a member of the joint committee for the *New English Bible,* authored the NT section of the *Daily Study Bible,* and was made a commander of the Order of the British Empire.

J.C.

**BARING-GOULD, SABINE** (1834–1924). The author of the hymns "Onward, Christian Soldiers" and "Now the Day Is Over" was born January 28 in Devon, England. Educated at Clare College, Cambridge, he received a B.A. in 1857 and an M.A. in 1860. He was ordained in the Church of England in 1864.

In his day he was best known for his books. His fifteen-volume *Lives of the Saints* was published from 1872–77. He also wrote *Curious Myths of the Middle Ages,* two series, 1866–68, and a two-volume work on *The Origin and Development of Religious Belief* (1869–80).

Other of Baring-Gould's hymns found in contemporary hymnals are "Daily, Daily, Sing the Praises" and "On the Resurrection Morning." Baring-Gould translated "Through the Night of Doubt and Sorrow," by Bernard Severin Ingemann, and is credited with the familiar tune "Eudoxia."

N.H.

**BARMEN DECLARATION.** A German Protestant manifesto of 1934 presented by Christians who formed the confessing church in opposition to the Nazi-controlled Office of Church Affairs and the German Christians movement that supported Hitler's racial and imperialistic policies. The German Christians were given control of the religious offices of the nation when Hitler came to power in 1933. They elected Ludwig Müller as chief bishop of the newly united German Evangelical Church. The German Christians used the church structure to advance Nazi political aims. Young people in church organizations were recruited for the Hitler youth; faithful pastors were intimidated by Nazis. A pastors' union to oppose this was formed by a hero of World War I, Martin Niemöller.

The Swiss theologian KARL BARTH, who was teaching in Germany, took the lead in writing the courageous manifesto. It went beyond any previous church platform in stressing the independence of the church from state control. As it states, there is one Word of God which all are to hear, trust, and obey, and that is Jesus Christ. There is no other source of revelation. In life or death, Christians must cling to Christ alone and obey him rather than human authorities.

J.C.

Courtesy of the American Jewish Archives of the Hebrew Union College—Jewish Institute of Religion

*A bar mitzvah celebrant reads the Torah as his father and the rabbi look on*

**BAR MITZVAH.** Term applied to a Jewish boy on his thirteenth birthday, considered the age of religious responsibility when he is duty bound to follow God's laws. Bar Mitzvah means "Son of the Commandment." The Bar Mitzvah has certain prerogatives, such as the right to be called up to the reading of the Torah and to be counted in the *minyan,* the quorum of ten mature males required for public prayers. He is held to account for his own sins and is commanded to fast on the Day of Atonement. One reason given for the age of thirteen as the age of religious responsibility is that Abraham is said to have rejected the idolatry of his father when he was thirteen.

The Bar Mitzvah ceremony, usually held in the synagogue on the Sabbath following the Bar Mitzvah's thirteenth birthday, consists of three parts: (1) the blessing by the Bar Mitzvah's father, the calling up of the Bar Mitzvah to the reading of the Torah and his reading a portion from the Prophets; (2) the address to the congregation by the initiate; and (3) the festive meal. The Bar Mitzvah ceremony serves to motivate a period of training, which leads to an individual's intelligent acceptance of responsibility as a member of the Jewish people. (*Compare* also BAT MITZVAH.)

L.K.

**BARNABAS.** An early Christian leader in both the Jerusalem church and Paul's missionary party. This man, otherwise called Joseph (Acts 4:36), was given the descriptive name Barnabas, literally "son of encouragement," possibly in view of his speaking ability, though the exact derivation of Barnabas is uncertain. We find Barnabas exercising a type of exhortative ministry in Acts 11:23.

He was a Levite, deriving from a Jewish-Cypriot priestly family. His other family link was with a cousin—John MARK (Col. 4:10). Both men had homes in Jerusalem, since Acts 12:12 tells us Mark's mother lived there; and Acts 4:36-37 informs us of Barnabas selling a property to contribute to the common fund for the relief of the poor.

As to his character Luke is unstinting in his praise of Barnabas, commencing with the designation "a good man, full of the Holy Spirit and of faith" (Acts 11:24). Thereafter his sterling worth is seen in four episodes in which he played a significant role.

(1) He befriended the newly converted Saul and spoke for him to the leaders of the Jerusalem mother church in witness to Saul's integrity (Acts 9:27).

(2) The mission of his compatriots from Cyprus led to the founding of a church in Syrian Antioch. Barnabas was delegated to investigate this piece of mission preaching directed to Gentiles as the Jerusalem leaders were evidently suspicious or at least cautious in giving it their blessing (Acts 11:19-24). This task Barnabas performed well; and he sought out Saul to consolidate the gains (Acts 11:25-26). But he was not as fully convinced concerning Gentile freedom as Paul was, and the latter does not shrink from pointing to Barnabas' immaturity under pressure (Gal. 2:9, 13).

(3) However, Paul's confidence in him did not prevent his including Barnabas in the first mission to Asia in accord with the Spirit's prompting (Acts 13:1-3). At this juncture he began to take second place to Paul, who henceforth is named first in the duo (see Acts 13:13) and became the evident leader.

(4) At the Council of Jerusalem (about A.D. 50) Paul enlisted Barnabas' support (Acts 15:2) and received the approval of the council's edict for a *modus vivendi* (working agreement) between Jewish Christians and converted Gentiles (Acts 15:25-26). There was increasing tension, however, between Barnabas, whose sympathies may well have lain with his home church, and Paul, who saw his life's mission to carry the message to the pagan world of Greco-Roman society. The split described in Acts 15:36-41 sealed the differences of opinion, leaving Barnabas free to enlist John Mark's help and return to Cyprus as a Christian leader.

At a later time he visited Corinth, where he was known (I Cor. 9:6). Luther and Calvin saw Barnabas referred to anonymously in II Corinthians 8:18 (NIV) as the "brother who is praised by all the churches." Tertullian gave him an even more important role as the author of the Letter to the Hebrews. The so-termed Epistle of Barnabas is one of the apostolic Fathers and has no identifiable connection with the man of the Acts. His martyrdom in Cyprus is part of later tradition.

R.M.

**BARNABAS, EPISTLE OF.** A document, probably written around A.D. 135 in or near Alexandria, Egypt, and usually included among the APOSTOLIC FATHERS. It enjoyed great prestige in Alexandria, where Clement of Alexandria ascribed it to Barnabas, and Origen quoted it as Scripture. Its twenty-one chapters can be divided into two distinct sections, for the first seventeen are doctrinal in nature, whereas chapters eighteen through twenty-one contain moral teachings. This last section is so similar to parts of the *Didache* that scholars suppose that both authors must have used a common source, which they call the Document of the Two Ways.

The doctrinal section deals mostly with the interpretation of the OT as pointing to Christianity. This is done both through allegorical and through typological interpretations. Pseudo-Barnabas carries allegory to the point of claiming that many commandments of the OT, such as those referring to circumcision, were never intended literally, and that it was an evil angel that led Jews to take literally what was intended to refer to the circumcision of the heart and ears. Such allegorical interpretation, so highly valued by ALEXANDRIAN THEOLOGY, may be one of the reasons why Clement and Origen ascribed great authority to this document.

J.G.

**BARTH, KARL** (1886–1968). Barth must be reckoned as possibly the major Protestant theologian since SCHLEIERMACHER. Born at Basel, he received his education in Switzerland and Germany, and for twelve years served as pastor in two Swiss industrial parishes. It was at this time that he developed his radical political views and also became dissatisfied

Courtesy of Wm. B. Eerdmans Publishing Company

*Karl Barth*

with the current liberal theology. In 1919 he published his famous commentary on Romans, inaugurating a new era in theology. In place of the liberal attempt to bridge the distance between God and humanity, Barth emphasized the otherness of God whose word comes as judgment upon all human institutions and strivings. Between 1921 and 1935, Barth taught successively in the German universities of Göttingen, Münster, and Bonn. During these years he and some like-minded theologians vigorously pursued the attack on liberal theology and developed in its place a theology of the Word. A highlight of this period was his controversy with HARNACK, the most distinguished of the old liberals.

In 1933 Hitler had come to power in Germany, and Barth identified himself with the Confessing Church, which sought to resist Nazi encroachments. He was the main influence behind the BARMEN DECLARATION of 1934. He believed that his own dogmatic theology of transcendence was the only appropriate answer to the dogmatism of Nazi ideology, and, in retrospect, REINHOLD NIEBUHR was probably unjust in accusing Barth of "transcendental irrelevance." In 1935 Barth was forced to give up his chair at Bonn. He returned to Switzerland and became a professor at Basel. He had already begun *The Church Dogmatics,* and it continued to occupy him for more than thirty years and was still unfinished at his death. The first volume treats of "the Word of God." There is no way from the human side to the divine, so there can be no natural theology. Theology is made possible only because God has spoken a word, and that word is the starting point behind which we cannot go. Theology is an autonomous science based on the word and has no need to harmonize its findings with secular inquiries.

Among the many topics that Barth treats as he moves through his gigantic work may be noted the following: the critique of religion as the illegitimate human attempts to grasp at God, an attempt which can end only in idolatry; revelation (and this means exclusively "the biblical revelation") as the opposite of religion, for this is God's movement toward humans; the critique of analogy as the attempt to confine God within finite categories; the radical restatement of the doctrine of predestination, which Barth interprets as meaning that the whole human race has been elected from eternity in Jesus Christ; the sensitive treatment of the reconciling work of Jesus Christ, where Barth seems to recognize a real condescension on the part of God, difficult to reconcile with the stark otherness and transcendence ascribed to God in the early writings, but undoubtedly truer to a Christian concept of God.

Barth began to speak too of the "humanity" of God, and although this relieves the problems occasioned by his insistence on God's otherness, it was not meant to be the slightest concession to natural theology or "religion" in Barth's sense of the term. In the course of expounding his own theology, Barth

carries out a critical commentary on most of the important theological movements, both ancient and modern, so that to read his *Dogmatics* is like a complete education in Christian theology, though admittedly from a very definite point of view. His influence has been enormous and is likely to be felt for a long time to come.

J.M.

BARTHOLOMEW. One of the original twelve disciples of Jesus, known as the APOSTLES. Under the name Bartholomew nothing is recorded of his ministry in the NT. Nonetheless, it is possible that Bartholomew is the same man as Nathanael, who is mentioned in John 1:45-51. Nathanael is listed with Peter, Thomas, James, and John in John 21:2. In the Synoptic Gospels, Bartholomew is mentioned in association with Philip, and the Fourth Gospel nowhere mentions an apostle named Bartholomew. To clinch this reasoning, the Synoptic Gospels never mention Nathanael. Bartholomew is a family name meaning "the son of Tolmia," and so he could have had a first name. If this identification is correct, then we know a good deal more about this otherwise unknown Apostle.

According to early church tradition, recorded in Eusebius and Jerome, Bartholomew preached in India. Other legends associate him with evangelistic work in Armenia, where he is supposed to have been flayed alive and crucified upside down. The martyr's body was then supposed to be miraculously transported to Benevento. The feast day of Bartholomew is traditionally August 24, but at Rome it is celebrated on August 25. There is an Apocryphal "Gospel of Bartholomew," which is included in the Apocryphal NT.

J.C.

BARUCH. The most important OT personage to bear the name Baruch ("blessed") is the prophet Jeremiah's secretary. This Baruch, son of Neriah, is first introduced when JEREMIAH placed into his safekeeping the deeds to the field that he had purchased in Anathoth (Jer. 32:12-16). He is the principal actor in Jeremiah 36, where, at the prophet's dictation, he writes on a scroll all the words of the Lord spoken through Jeremiah. He then reads this scroll publicly, first to the people of Jerusalem and Judah at the Temple entrance (Jer. 36:10) and then to princes of Judah in the king's own house (vv. 11-19). Ultimately the scroll is read to King Jehoiakim, who burns two or three columns at a time. This dramatic scene is enlarged upon, and lyrical words of comfort to Jerusalem are appended to it in the apocryphal book of BARUCH, generally dated sometime between 160 and 60 B.C. A Jewish pseudepigraphical Apocalypse of Baruch (known as II Baruch) also claims descent from Jeremiah's scribe.

W.S.T.

**BARUCH** (Apocrypha). Son of Neriah, brother of Seraiah (Jer. 51:59 ff.), grandson of Mahseiah (Jer. 32:12), member of a prominent Judean family. Baruch (meaning "blessed") was secretary, close friend, and strong supporter of JEREMIAH.

Baruch witnessed Jeremiah's purchase of a field in Anathoth (Jer. 32:12-16). From Jeremiah's dictation, Baruch transcribed the "oracles of destruction" (Jer. 36:4) and then read them publicly in several different places (Jer. 36:10). This was the scroll that King Jehoiakim had read to him and immediately burned (Jer. 36:23). Along with Jeremiah, Baruch was taken by force from Jerusalem to Egypt (Jer. 43:6). Jeremiah 45 discloses Baruch's agony over the fall of Jerusalem.

The name of noble and faithful Baruch is attached to late Jewish writings: (1) *Apocalypse of Baruch,* part of the OT pseudepigrapha, written in Hebrew, but preserved in Greek and dated about A.D. 70–100. (2) *The Book of Baruch,* part of the OT APOCRYPHA, claims to have been written in Babylon during the exile and sent to Jerusalem as a confession of sin to be read on feast days "and at appointed feasts" (1:14). In its preserved form, the book, written in Hebrew but soon thereafter translated into Greek, is dated between 160 and 150 B.C.

P.L.G.

**BASEL, COUNCIL OF.** One of the councils called at the high point of CONCILIARISM in order to reform the church. It began its sessions in 1431, and among its leaders were such distinguished theologians as NICHOLAS OF CUSA and Aeneas Sylvius Piccolomini, later to become PIUS II. It clashed with Pope Eugenius IV and seemed assured of victory until the emperor and the patriarch of Constantinople, fearing the Turks, offered to unite with Rome. To accommodate them, the pope ordered the council to move to Ferrara. Since some obeyed and some did not, there were now two rival councils. The success of the Council of Ferrara-Florence in obtaining a nominal union with the Byzantines spelled the defeat of the Council of Basel, which became increasingly radical as its most moderate leaders left it. After moving to Lausanne, the last remnant of the Council of Basel was dissolved in 1449. This marked the end of conciliarism as a rival to the authority of the popes.

J.G.

**BASHAN** (meaning "fruitful plain" or "without stones"). Bashan is the name given to the northernmost district of the region east of the Jordan, generally considered to lie south of Mount Hermon, north of the Yarmuk, east of the Sea of Galilee, and west of Jebel Druze. The territory is part of that traditionally allotted to the tribe of Manasseh.

A fertile, tableland highlands (1600-2300 ft. above sea level), Bashan was famous for wheat, cattle (Ps. 22:12; Amos 4:1), grapes (Deut. 32:14), and groves of oak trees (Isa. 2:13; Ezek. 27:6). Its preconquest king was Og of Ashtaroth, whose huge "bedstead of iron" (Deut. 3:11) was exhibited long after his time in Rabbah of the Ammonites (Deut. 3:11; II Sam. 12:26; 17:27; Jer. 49:2; Ezek. 21:20).

P.L.G.

**BASIL THE GREAT.** One of the CAPPADOCIAN FATHERS, bishop of Caesarea in Cappadocia from 370 until his death in 379, and a staunch opponent of ARIANISM. He received an excellent education in Caesarea, Constantinople, and Athens. Among his fellow students were Gregory Nazianzus, with whom he established a lasting friendship, and Prince Julian, later known as the Apostate. On his return to Caesarea, he boasted of his education and rhetorical ability, until the death of one of his brothers and the entreaties of his sister Macrina led him to abandon the pomps of the world for the monastic life.

The community that he founded and the instructions he gave it were so influential that he has been called the father of Eastern MONASTICISM. In 370 he became bishop of Caesarea. As such, he clashed with the Arian emperor Valens. His work on the subject of the TRINITY centered on clarifying the meaning of "ousia" and "hypostasis," and on convincing the Homoiousians that they should not fear the formula HOMOOUSION, which had become the trademark of the decisions of the Council of Nicea. His efforts were crowned at the COUNCIL OF CONSTANTINOPLE, shortly after his death. He was also noted for his defense of the poor against the encroachments of the rich and for his care for the sick, the strangers, and others in need.

J.G.

**BATES, KATHERINE LEE** (1859–1929). The author of "America the Beautiful" was born August 12 in Falmouth, Massachusetts, to the Reverend William and Cornelia Frances Lee Bates, the youngest of their five children. Her father, a Congregational minister, died within a month of her birth.

She received her B.A. in 1880 from Wellesley College, where she soon returned to teach English until her retirement in 1925. After a year's study at Oxford University in England in 1891, she was awarded an M.A. by Wellesley. She published eight volumes of poetry as well as travel, children's, and text books.

"America the Beautiful" was written in Colorado in the summer of 1893, inspired by the view from the summit of Pike's Peak. It was originally published July 4, 1895, in the *Congregationalist.* A revised version appeared in 1904 in the *Boston Evening Telegraph,* and it was revised slightly again several years later. Bates died on March 28.

N.H.

**BATHSHEBA.** A Hebrew name meaning "daughter of abundance." The daughter of Eliam, the wife of Uriah the Hittite, and later, David's wife. Captivated by Bathsheba's beauty, DAVID seduced her, and, with Joab's help, orchestrated Uriah's death so that he might claim her as his wife (II Sam. 11). Later, Bathsheba bore SOLOMON (12:24).

When David was in his dotage, Bathsheba and the prophet Nathan successfully obtained from the king his assurance that Solomon, rather than Adonijah, would succeed him as king (I Kings 1:11-31). Soon after Solomon's enthronement, Bathsheba conveyed to Solomon Adonijah's rash petition that Abishag, David's concubine, be given to him to be his wife. This incident cost Adonijah his life (2:13-25).

J.K.K.

**BAT MITZVAH.** A Jewish girl who has reached the age of religious responsibility (according to Jewish law, twelve years and a day) and who is therefore obligated to perform God's commandments. Unlike the BAR MITZVAH ceremony, the Bat Mitzvah rite is an American innovation. It is observed in Conservative, Reform, and Reconstructionist synagogues.

L.K.

**BAUER, WALTER** (1904–60). This Göttingen (West Germany) NT scholar has two claims to fame. Among his many contributions to early Christian history is a commentary on the Gospel of John in which he sought to establish connections between John and the sect of the Mandaens, a Syrian Gnostic group whose texts had been published by R. Bultmann about the time Bauer's commentary appeared. Of far greater and lasting value was Bauer's work as a lexicographer of NT Greek, whose language he systematically and scientifically studied over several decades. The result is his definitive *A Greek-English Lexicon of the New Testament and Other Early Christian Literature,* whose fourth edition (1952) was translated by W. F. Arndt and F. W. Gingrich in 1957, with a revised and augmented translation, edited by Gingrich and F. W. Danker in 1979. Bauer died in 1960, two years after his fifth edition of the *Lexicon.*

R.M.

**BAUR, FERDINAND C.** (1762–1860). His name is inseparably linked with the University of Tübingen, West Germany, where his teaching and influence were centered. The "Tübingen School" looks to him as its founder.

His chief contribution lay in a historical reconstruction of early Christianity according to the principle that each NT document and piece of early Christian writing was motivated by a desire to represent a distinctive point of view. The upshot was seen in his configuration of the early church, which was set by two opposing groups—a Jewish party led by Peter and a Gentile movement under Paul's inspiration. Luke's Acts came later as an attempt to effect a synthesis and led to the rise of the early Catholic church of the second century. Baur thus anticipated many of the more recent trends in NT

study, notably in tracing a move away from early apostolic enthusiasm to institutionalized Christianity in the later NT documents.

R.M.

**BAXTER, RICHARD** (1615–91). The founding father of English nonconformity was born November 12 in Rowton, Shropshire. Largely self-educated, he was ordained in 1638 by the Presbyterian party.

A "peacemaker at the center of all disputes in a contentious time," he served as chaplain to OLIVER CROMWELL and yet worked to restore King Charles. Along with a thousand other PURITANS, he was ousted on St. Bartholomew's Day in 1662, from his parish. He had served at Kidderminster since 1641. Persecuted over the next twenty years, he was imprisoned in 1685 for eighteen months.

In the midst of turmoil and despite ill health, he managed to write about two hundred works. *The Reformed Pastor* is a textbook for parish ministry, stressing the importance of personal counseling as well as preaching. While slowed down because of illness in 1647 and anticipating death, he wrote the devotional classic *The Saints' Everlasting Rest.* Also widely reprinted is *A Call to the Unconverted.* His celebrated autobiography, *Mr. Richard Baxter's Narrative of the Most Memorable Passages of His Life and Times,* was published in 1696. He once said he preached as "a dying man to dying men."

He died in London on December 8.

N.H.

*BAY PSALM BOOK.* Titled *The Whole Booke of Psalmes,* it was the first book published in British North America. This metric version of the Psalms was prepared by the PURITAN leaders of the Massachusetts Bay Colony and printed by Stephen Day in Cambridge, Massachusetts, in 1640.

N.H.

**BEAST.** Though the precise meaning of "beast" is not always evident, the biblical reference might be to any mammal, a wild animal or a domesticated animal. Undifferentiated animals appear in such texts as Job 35:11 (comparing the wisdom of "beasts of the earth" with that of "birds of the air"), Ecclesiastes 3:18-21 (declaring that "the sons of men" and "beasts" meet the same fate), and Psalm 50:10 (affirming that God owns "every beast of the forest").

Nevertheless, wild beasts and domesticated animals are often distinguished. Jacob assumes that a "wild beast" has devoured his favorite son, Joseph (Gen. 37:33). Goliath taunts David by saying, "I will give your flesh . . . to the beasts of the field" (I Sam. 17:44). And Jesus dwells among "wild beasts" during his temptation experience (Mark 1:13). Domesticated animals are obviously referred to in the prohibition against sodomy (Lev. 20:15-16), the narrative reporting that the Israelites smote Benjaminite "men and beasts" (Judg. 20:48), and the aphorism that a righteous man treats "his beast" considerately (Prov. 12:10).

Beasts appear symbolically in the apocalyptic books of Daniel and Revelation (see APOCALYPTICISM) to denote worldly kingdoms that oppose God and God's people. In Daniel's first vision, four beasts emerge from the watery chaos (Dan. 7:2-7). An angel instructs Daniel that the lion, bear, leopard, and ten-horned monster respectively symbolize the Babylonian, Median, Persian, and Seleucid kingdoms. All four transient powers must yield to the establishment of God's eternal, universal kingdom.

These four beasts have been combined into one composite monster in Revelation 13:1-10 to symbolize godless worldly power, now culminating in the Roman Empire. Emerging from the sea, this beast is incited to persecute God's saints. A second beast in Revelation, bearing lamb's horns, emerges from the earth. As it engages in false priestly and prophetic functions, God's sovereignty is challenged and Roman emperor worship advanced (13:11-18).

J.K.K.

**BEATIFICATION.** A process in the Roman Catholic Church which ends with a papal decree that allows a diocese, nation, or religious order to honor as blessed (that is, as certainly being in heaven), a deceased person who had a reputation for holiness. A public declaration may later be made, after investigation, that the blessed person practiced heroic virtues or was martyred, and after death was instrumental in interceding with God so as to work miracles. Strong evidence of at least two miracles is required generally for beatification to be conferred, although this may be waived for a martyr.

J.C.

**BEATIFIC VISION.** Seeing God directly, in God's own essence; a theophany or manifestation of the Divine. Such a vision is attainable only by the deeply pious, aided by divine grace. There is said to be no mediation or image in this final experience of human happiness, the blessed Holy Trinity.

J.C.

**BEATITUDES.** The series of statements of Jesus reported in Matthew 5:3-12 and Luke 6:20-23, in which he pronounces the benefits bestowed by God on the faithful, are commonly known as the Beatitudes. In each case these appear in the context of an address by Jesus: in Matthew, the SERMON ON THE MOUNT; in Luke the address to his followers spoken on a plain (Luke 6:17). The basic Jesus tradition drawn upon by both evangelists derives from the Q SOURCE, but has been modified and adapted in each case.

The term "blessed" or "happy" is a familiar one from the Psalms and wisdom literature, for example, Psalms 1:1; 32:1; 41:1; 84:5; 119:1; Proverbs 8:34. The basic meaning of the Hebrew root is "straight,"

or "in the right direction," so that the word implies that one is in right relationship to God and to God's will for humanity. What distinguishes the Beatitudes of Jesus from those in the Jewish wisdom tradition are (1) the assurance to those who are presently deprived that God has not abandoned them, and (2) the promise of vindication by God at the end of the present age.

The older form of the tradition is found in Luke, who reports the Beatitudes as addressed by Jesus directly to his hearer: "Blessed are you. . . ." By contrast, Matthew reports Jesus as making more general statements in the third person: "Blessed are *the* poor. . . ." Furthermore, Luke's version of the saying is addressed to those in immediate, practical need: "*You* poor" (6:20), "*You* that hunger" (6:21*a*), "*You* that weep" (6:21*b*). But in Matthew these difficulties are represented as in the spiritual or strictly religious realm: "the *poor in spirit*" (5:3); "those who hunger and thirst *for righteousness*" (5:6). Further, the Lukan form of these sayings makes a sharp contrast between present deprivation and future divine vindication, while Matthew places more emphasis on the present. The now/then contrast is explicit in Luke 6:21 (twice) and in 6:25. The hatred experienced by Jesus' hearers is the consequence of their fidelity to the Son of man (6:22), whose triumphant return and exaltation is awaited "in the day" (6:23). The reward awaiting the faithful—according to both Matthew's and Luke's versions—is already stored up in heaven awaiting its bestowal by God in the day of future judgment.

Luke has provided a set of "Woes" to match the Beatitudes (6:24-26). These warnings of judgment are addressed to those who possess precisely what the "blessed" lack: wealth, abundance of food, laughter, good popular reputations. Thus Luke highlights the practical concerns that permeate his Gospel and Acts. For him the gospel is preeminently for "the poor" (Luke 4:18; as is for Isaiah, 61:1).

Matthew's version of the Beatitudes has generalized and spiritualized them. The "poor in spirit" are those aware of their spiritual needs, just as those who "hunger and thirst for righteousness" are those who long for their lives to be fully consonant with the will of God. Their mourning, their meekness, their role as peacemakers give evidence of their dependence upon God, of their refusal to take the initiative in their own defense, and of their eagerness to share in the work of reconciling to God their fellow creatures (5:4, 5, 9). Having assumed this stance toward God and the world, they are warned to expect hatred, suffering, and persecution for the sake of the righteous life in obedience to God to which they are committed (5:11). In proclaiming their understanding of God's purpose by their words and deeds of reconciliation they are inviting upon themselves the hatred and denunciation that the prophets of ancient Israel experienced. Indeed, they have now taken over the prophetic role, as is implied in their being differentiated from "the prophets who were before you" (5:12).

In both versions of the Beatitudes, Jesus is represented as summoning his followers to a new mode of life, with values and objectives so different from those of their religious contemporaries that the latter reject them and their message. The hope of the faithful rests not in popular acclaim, however, but in the assurance of ultimate vindication by God.

H.K.

**BECKET, THOMAS** (about 1118–70). English chancellor, archbishop, and martyr was born in Cheapside, London. Educated at Merton priory and in Paris, he began his career as a city clerk and accountant.

Archbishop Theobald sent him to study civil and canon law in Bologna and Auxerre. In 1154 Theobald appointed him archdeacon of Canterbury and within three months also recommended him as chancellor to Henry II. Fifteen years older than the king, he served as a paternal friend and devoted administrator.

However, after Theobald's death in 1161, Henry insisted on naming Thomas archbishop of CANTER-BURY. Thomas transferred his allegiance to the church, becoming devout, austere, and completely embracing the Gregorian reforms, which included free election of clergy, inviolability of church property, freedom of appeal to Rome, and clerical immunity from secular courts.

He resigned the chancellorship, opposed Henry's tax proposals, and excommunicated a leading baron. The crisis came in January 1164 when Henry demanded blanket assent to the Constitutions of Clarendon, which gave the king the right to punish lesser clerics and forbade appeals to Rome. Thomas resisted and was tried at the Council of Northampton, October 6-13, 1164. He lived in exile in France from November 2, 1164, to December 2, 1170.

When Henry had the archbishop of York crown his son co-king, Thomas and the pope excommunicated all participants. Fearing interdict, Henry allowed Thomas to return to Canterbury and restored Thomas' confiscated possessions. However, four knights murdered Thomas in the cathedral on December 29, 1170.

His tomb immediately became a place of pilgrimage, and in order to pacify his people and his conscience, Henry did penance there in 1174. Henry VIII despoiled the shrine, burned his bones, and erased his name from the service books, making him a symbol for Catholics.

N.H.

**BECOMING.** A philosophical term meaning "to enter into existence, to emerge." The term conveys a sense of process and the possibility of fulfillment or completion. To become involves growth, through which the essence or nature of being is made known. Becoming can also mean to develop significance.

Becoming is contrasted with ESSENCE, which suggests a state of being that is static. Classical philosophies referred to essence as the ultimate reality. Existentialist thinkers, like process thinkers, prefer dealing with a dynamic situation. They would say that the reality of personhood lies not in mere "essence," which is basic to all, but in becoming or existence, which is the quality of living in time and space, confronting a world that may be unfriendly, indifferent, or inimical—a situation that confronts one with choices and decisions.

I.C.

**BEDE, THE VENERABLE.** English monk, scholar, and historian, best known for his *Ecclesiastical History of the English Nation,* although he also wrote a number of works of biblical exposition, as well as treatises on scientific subjects. He was probably born after 672, and died sometime around 735. The reason he was known as the Venerable from an early time—perhaps less than a century after his death—is not altogether clear. Although at present he is known mostly for his historical works, as one of the main sources for our knowledge of early English history, in earlier times he was most admired for his sanctity and for his expositions of Scripture.

J.G.

Courtesy of the Scribner Art File

*Three Beechers: Lyman, with his daughter Harriett and son Henry Ward*

**BEECHER, HENRY WARD** (1813–87). The pastor of Plymouth Congregational Church, Brooklyn, was born to Lyman and Roxanna Foote Beecher, at Litchfield, Connecticut. He attended Mt. Pleasant Classical Institute of Amherst, Amherst College, and Lane Seminary. In 1837 he was licensed by the Cincinnati Presbytery and called to Lawrenceburg, Indiana. That same year he married Eunice White Bullard. Ordained November 9, 1838, he served eight years in Indianapolis, where he wrote his famous *Seven Lectures to Young Men* (1844).

On October 10, 1847, he was called to Plymouth Church in Brooklyn. From 1870 to 1881 he served as editor of the *Christian Union*. His career was marred in the 1870s, however, by scandal. He was accused of adultery, though both ecclesiastical and civil courts acquitted him. His writings include *Life of Jesus the Christ* (1871), *Norwood, or Village Life in New England* (1867), *Yale Lectures on Preaching* (1872–74), and *Evolution and Religion* (1885). He died on March 8.

N.H.

**BEECHER, LYMAN** (1775–1863). The Presbyterian revivalist and seminary president was born in New Haven, Connecticut, to David and Esther Lyman Beecher. At Yale he was strongly influenced by TIMOTHY DWIGHT. In 1799 he was ordained to the Presbyterian Church of East Hampton, Long Island. On September 19, 1799, he married Roxanna Foote, and they had nine children including Catherine, Harriet, and Henry Ward. He married Harriet Porter in 1817, and after her death, Lydia Beals Jackson.

In 1810 he moved to Litchfield, Connecticut, and gained fame as a revivalist, temperance advocate, leader in the Home Missionary, American Bible, and American Colonization societies. In 1826 he was called to Hanover Street Church, Boston, to battle Unitarianism. In 1831 his anti-Roman Catholic sermons resulted in the sacking of the Ursuline Convent in Charlestown, Massachusetts. In 1832 he became president and professor of theology at Lane Theological Seminary and pastor of Second Presbyterian Church in Cincinnati. He retired in 1850 and died on January 10.

N.H.

**BEELZEBUL/BEELZEBUB.** The name given "the prince of demons" in the NT, used interchangeably with SATAN (compare Matt. 12:24 with Matt. 12:27). Beelzebul is the form of the name used in the RSV, although ancient Latin and Syriac versions used the form "Beelzebub." The foes of Jesus declared that he worked miracles because he was possessed by Beelzebub, or was actually Beelzebub himself. Jesus made fun of the idea that the devil would give him power to cast out demons, demolishing that charge (Matt. 12:22-29). From Jesus' response to the Pharisees, it appears that the name was used for Satan. The Hebrew background of the term Satan means "adversary, accuser, slanderer." Beelzebul (or, properly Beelzebub, in the original) may carry the same meaning, but probably means "the lord of the flies" or "the lord of dung," sarcastic Hebrew references to false gods or idols. Jesus' enemies may have used this old-fashioned term in order to express their horror and contempt of Jesus' person and works.

J.C.

**BEER-SHEBA.** The meaning of the word is undetermined, but it may mean "well of the seven" (Gen. 21:25-31), "of the oath" (Gen. 21:31; 26:32-33), perhaps "well of (the city of) Sheba" (Josh. 19:2; Job 6:19; Ps. 72:10, 15; Isa. 60:6; Jer. 6:20; Ezek. 27:22; 38:13). For topographical reasons, Beer-sheba was and is the unique crossroads and center of population of the Negeb. It was a sacred place (Gen. 21:33; 46:1-5; Amos 8:14) and the traditional southernmost limit of Judah, as in "from Dan to Beer-sheba" (Judg. 20:1; I Sam. 3:20).

Tel Beer-sheba, about four miles east of the modern city, has been excavated by Y. Aharoni and others, beginning in 1969. A well-planned, walled city from the time of David and Solomon was uncovered, having a complex of storehouses, a large, disassembled stone altar, the foundations of a temple(?), and, in front of the city gate, a well, excavated to a depth of sixty-five feet, possibly the well of the patriarchs.

P.L.G.

**BEHAVIORISM.** The term first referred to the work of a Russian psychologist, I. P. Pavlov, who published the results of his experiments (1927) in what is now referred to as "classical" conditioning. His objective was to demonstrate the relationship between a stimulus and the response. He wondered if another stimulus could be substituted that would bring the same response. Pavlov concluded that there are physiological connections within the brain that call forth specific responses to particular stimuli. (You smell a fragrance from the oven and begin to feel hungry; the smell signals "dinner.") Such conditioning can be used to establish emotional reactions in one person to another person or situation.

The present emphasis of the term is on operant or instrumental conditioning. This refers to the fact that the objective of conditioning is to form habits or teach skills, thereby changing behavior. All learning proceeds gradually through successive steps. Specific learning will take place when a particular stimulus evokes a desired response. But practice alone will not cause a person to remember. The key to learning is reinforcement.

There are two forms of reinforcement. The most effective one is a positive reinforcement, reward. A teacher demonstrates to a pupil the first step in learning a new skill. The learner repeats this step in imitation of the teacher. If the learner has succeeded, the teacher says "well done" and may give a tangible reward, indicating approval. After this step has been repeated a number of times, the habit pattern will usually have become established. Repetition at longer intervals helps retention. Highly motivated people may seem to wait a long time for positive reinforcement, but in fact they may be receiving this through the sense of satisfaction that comes from believing that they are on the right track, or because of their determination to succeed.

Negative reinforcement, punishment, has another effect. The person whose incorrect answer or incomplete performance is received with disparaging words or a sharply worded "that's wrong" will become anxious or angry. These emotions inhibit learning. The learner's attention has shifted from the task to the personal discomfort. There are some situations in which potential danger makes it necessary to use punishment (or "aversive" conditioning)—if, for example, a person might be hurt or do damage.

Reward needs to follow immediately upon the giving of the correct answer, otherwise the pupil makes no direct connection between the answer and the affirmation. Reinforcement theory is connected with the name of Harvard psychologist B. F. Skinner. He has applied these principles to all forms of learning.

A child talks because adults encourage this. Children respond in love because someone evidences love to them. Creativity is encouraged when a person wins approval by thinking in novel ways. If, however, a person is ridiculed for trying the unusual, that person learns to conform to such expectations. In the religious sector, attitudes toward doctrine, Scripture, authority, or life-styles are influenced by what the religious group deems acceptable behavior. The responses to a worship service, whatever the form, become habitual.

Conditioned learning has had various applications. Programmed learning is a method by which an objective is analyzed into specific steps. The learner is reinforced at the completion of each step until the whole procedure is learned. Conditioning has also been used as a method for behavior therapy, a departure from classical techniques because it ignores the patient's past and concentrates on the immediate problem. It has been used to help brain-damaged children learn motor skills.

Through conditioning psychologists hope to develop tools for predicting and controlling behavior. It is admitted that there are so many variables involved in the responses people make that such prediction is difficult, although computers have been used in the process. It is also recognized that conditioning can be abused. People can be trained to do evil as well as to do good.

Philosophically, behaviorism raises the question of DETERMINISM versus FREE WILL. Behavioristic psychology has tended to be deterministic. If specific conditions encourage people to make particular responses, can there be a freely willed response? B. F. Skinner has addressed the question in more than one book and seems to answer that good conditioning is freedom.

I.C.

**BEHEMOTH** (a plural noun meaning "dumb beasts"). Behemoth is a poetic noun referring, presumably, to one of the "great sea monsters," probably the hippopotamus or a similar river-marsh dwelling mammoth, created on the fifth day of creation (Gen. 1:21).

Job 40:15-24 gives a lengthy description of the beast, "the first of the works of God," its frightening appearance, and its remarkable behavior. The "cattle (behemoth) on a thousand hills" (Ps. 50:10) probably should be thought of as "dumb beasts." In Jewish lore, Behemoth became a female sea BEAST, whose male counterpart, LEVIATHAN (Job 41:1-11), is a land beast (Apoc. of Baruch 29:4). In the Revelation, reference is made to a "beast rising out of the sea" (13:1) "with seven heads and ten horns" (17:7), and to a second "beast which rose out of the earth" (13:11). (Compare Dan. 7:3, "four great beasts came up out of the sea.")

P.L.G.

**BEING AND NONBEING.** These terms have been discussed by philosophers from the beginning. That which has being is real. For PLATO, reality belongs to eternal essences—ideas, values, mathematical entities, etc. The sensible world of becoming lies between being and nonbeing. For ARISTOTLE, on the contrary, the reality consists of individual existent entities. A third view is found in PLOTINUS—the ultimate reality is not itself something that is (a being) but the mysterious ground and begetter of beings, so that paradoxically it can be called a "nonbeing." It should be noted that the Greeks distinguished two meanings of nonbeing: *ouk on* is sheer nothingness, *me on* is potentiality.

Theologians connected these speculations with the name of God in Exodus: I am that I am. So Aquinas held that the most appropriate name for God is *Qui est,* "He who is." What is not clearly resolved in Aquinas is the problem of whether God is a being, albeit of a different order from created beings. Mystical theologians in the tradition of NEOPLATONISM were clear that God is not *a* being and could even call God nothing. This view was also held by the German Dominican theologian, mystic, and preacher, Meister Eckhart. These questions have been revived in recent times. HEIDEGGER speaks of the ontological difference between being and beings, while TILLICH holds that while God is being itself, God does not exist as a being.

J.M.

**BEL** (meaning "one who rules," that is, Lord; an Akkadian title similar to the Hebrew title BAAL, Bel is used in the Bible only by Isaiah (46:1) and Jeremiah (50:2; 51:44) as a designation for the chief god of Babylon and Babylonia—MARDUK. From before Hammurabi (about 1800 B.C.), Marduk was worshiped. In Babylonian thought, the gods chose him to be supreme after his victory over Tiamat, goddess of chaos. Thereafter Marduk made humans and gave them civilization.

P.L.G.

**BEL AND THE DRAGON.** An addition to the book of Daniel contained in the APOCRYPHA. It offers two entertaining stories dating to about 130 B.C., which polemicize against idols by subjecting them to ridicule. The first story portrays Daniel's success in convincing King Cyrus that the great statue of Bel (Bel-Marduk), Babylon's patron deity, is merely inanimate and his priests fraudulent. The second story reports that a monstrous Babylonian dragon is slain by the peculiar diet (pitch, fat, and hair) Daniel feeds it. In both, Daniel, who resolutely trusts in "the living God" (vv. 5, 25), survives life-threatening circumstances.

J.K.K.

**BELIAL.** A noun of obscure mythological origin denoting that which threatens cosmic, social, and cultic order. Its etymology has been variously explained. If the noun derives from the Hebrew root *bāla* ("to swallow"), it would signify a devouring abyss (Sheol) or personify an enemy (mythological). But if Belial is a Hebrew neologism consisting of the particle *beli* ("not") plus a verb of positive expression, two meanings are plausible. First, *beli* may combine with *'ālah* ("to ascend") to denote that which does not ascend ("what is unsuccessful?") or the underworld from which ascent is impossible. Second, *beli* may combine with *yā'al* ("to profit, benefit") to denote what is worthless, base, or destructive.

The poetic Hebrew text of Psalm 18:4 ("the torrents of perdition") and Psalm 41:8 ("a deadly thing") demonstrates the capacity of Belial to symbolize mythological powers of chaos that bring sickness or death. A threatened social order is attested in the noun's use in Deuteronomy 15:9 to indicate "a base thought" inducing mistreatment of the poor, and in Proverbs 19:28 to portray "a worthless witness" mocking justice. Mention of "base fellows" advocating the worship of foreign gods (Deut. 13:13) and "worthless men" (Eli's priestly sons) who hold ritualistic requirements in contempt (I Sam. 2:12) illustrates the use of Belial to convey a threatened cultic order.

The Dead Sea Scrolls personify Belial as the leader of the children of darkness against the children of light, and in the Pseudepigrapha, Belial (frequently miswritten "Beliar") is mainly the tempter enticing humanity to sin. The NT attests Belial but once, in a personification synonymus with SATAN (II Cor. 6:15).

J.K.K.

**BELIEF.** *See* FAITH.

**BELLARMINE, ROBERT** (1542–1621). A cardinal and JESUIT theologian, Bellarmine was a leader of the COUNTER-REFORMATION. Born on October 4 in Montepulciano, Tuscany, Italy, he entered the Society of Jesus in 1560. He studied in Rome, Mondovi, Padua, and finally Louvain, where he was ordained in 1570 and then taught theology. While teaching in Rome, he was named a cardinal in 1599 by Clement VIII. He became archbishop of Capua in 1602.

Bellarmine was the first to critique the writings of GALILEI. His own writings included a series of lectures against heresies (1568–93), the Clementine edition of the Vulgate (1591–92), an influential catechism (1597), a book on the pope's power (1610), and an autobiography (1675). Bellarmine died September 17, 1621, was canonized in 1930, and named a doctor of the church in 1931.

N.H.

**BELOVED DISCIPLE.** The designation "the disciple, whom Jesus loved" occurs five times in the Fourth Gospel, and nowhere else in the NT. Moreover, he appears only in the latter part of that Gospel, from chapter 13 to 21 (13:23; 19:26; 20:2; 21:7, 20). Various suggestions have been made as to his identity: John, Mark, Lazarus, an "ideal disciple" and—traditionally—John the apostle. Of these options the last-named has the strongest claim to credibility, though distinguishing him from the author or final editor of the Gospel. Rather he is one of the sources embodying the Johannine tradition that is built into this multi-layered Gospel.

R.M.

**BELSHAZZAR.** An Akkadian name, meaning "O Bel, guard the king," which was given to the last king of Babylon (556–539 B.C.; Dan. 7:1; 8:1), the crown prince, son, and regent of Nabonidus. In Assyriological sources, the death of Belshazzar is not mentioned. In the Bible, Belshazzar is remembered for his great "feast" (Dan. 5). This festal occasion Belshazzar arranged in Babylon. In the midst of the revelry, a hand appeared and wrote on the plastered wall of the king's palace words that Daniel interpreted as forecasting the king's death. "That very night Belshazzar, the Chaldean king, was slain" (Dan. 5:30), and Babylon fell into the hands of the Medes (Dan. 5:31).

P.L.G.

**BEN-** The Hebrew equivalent of the Aramaic BAR-. A prefix to a father's name meaning "son of ———," regularly so translated in English versions. Ben- also appears in combination with a word related to the circumstances of birth, such as, Ben-jamin, son of fortune, and Ben-oni, son of my sorrow (Gen. 35:18).

P.L.G.

**BENEDICT/BENEDICTINES/RULE OF ST. BENEDICT.** Benedict of Nursia (about 480–543) founded the Benedictines, and through his Rule influenced virtually all subsequent MONASTICISM. Born in Nursia and educated in Rome, he sought at an early age to escape the gross immoralities of his day by retreating to the Abruzzi mountains. Many visitors sought his advice, and some nobles sent children to him for instruction. Nearby monks made him their abbot, and then rejected him for imposing strict discipline. Eventually he established twelve monasteries with twelve monks each around Rome, and served as their abbot. Contentions forced him to leave. About 520, he and some followers founded the monastery at Monte Cassino. There he wrote his Rule. Our scant biographical data comes from *The Dialogues* of GREGORY I (590–604).

The Benedictines are monks, nuns, other clergy, and laity in Roman Catholicism who follow St. Benedict's Rule. Their monasteries and houses are relatively autonomous, being only loosely joined regionally and nationally. When the Lombards overran Monte Cassino, 580-90, Benedict's followers found refuge in Rome and thrived under Gregory I, the first of fifty Benedictine popes. In 596 Gregory sent AUGUSTINE OF CANTERBURY and a group of monks to Britain. The Rule was later carried back to the mainland by Benedictines from England, particularly Boniface, who in 751 crowned Pepin king of the Franks. By 1100 there were over three thousand Benedictine monasteries in Europe. During the Middle Ages their self-contained establishments became centers of learning, liturgy, art, and hospitality. Their numbers steadily increased in the Middle Ages but declined sharply during the Renaissance-Reformation. In France and Germany during the seventeenth century they contributed substantially to scholarly research. Now worldwide, the Benedictines have regained much of their former strength.

The Rule of St. Benedict was written to govern monastic living at Monte Cassino. It organized the monks' lives around the Divine Office *(Opus Dei)*, dividing each day into worship, work, study, and sleep. The Rule reflected Benedict's experience but drew on the rules of BASIL THE GREAT and PACHOMIUS. By not disdaining material things or encouraging ascetic poverty, the Rule had wide appeal and provided a base for works of mercy. Meriting heaven through good deeds was primary. An abbot chosen by the group guided and disciplined the community. To him each monk swore loyalty and obedience, but the abbot was considerate of needs and sought counsel from others.

The Benedictines owned everything in common. Personal articles were gifts for use and were returned when others were issued. Their clothing was cheap and simple, only what the weather required. Seven times each day they formally praised God. During their two daily meals a brother read aloud, thus affording an education. Food per day was a pound of bread, a pint of wine, two cooked vegetables, and fruit in season. Only the sick received meat. Silence was enjoined at all times. Guests were treated well whether rich or poor. Disobedient monks could be severely disciplined and expelled. Readmission was possible only after repentance, but not more than three times. Monasteries were self-contained, and the Rule was read frequently.                    C.M.

**BENEDICT XIV, POPE.** Born Prospero Lambertini, in Bologna, Italy, 1675. He was one of the most accommodating, respected, and intelligent popes of the eighteenth century (1740–58). Highly educated, a scholar all his life, he rose in ecclesiastical ranks to become cardinal, 1728; archbishop of Bologna, 1731; and pope in 1740 after 254 ballots.

Admired for his administration, he settled mixed marriage disputes, regulated Indian and Chinese rites, restrained the INDEX OF PROHIBITED BOOKS, fostered science, and wrote numerous letters. Voltaire was among his correspondents. In the papal states he lowered taxes, promoted commerce, and improved agriculture. His concessions to secular powers aroused criticism. He relinquished patronage, rights of nominations to vacant sees, and some jurisdiction. However, he was highly regarded and heightened the papacy's moral image. His writings include *On Sacrifice in the Mass, On the Beatification and Canonization of Saints, On Mixed Marriages,* and *On Canon Law,* plus numerous bulls and encyclicals. He died in Rome in 1758.

C.M.

**BENEDICTION.** A blessing, in Protestant churches, a parting prayer or invocation of the Lord at the end of a worship service. In the Roman Catholic Church, it communicates divine powers by purifying or blotting out sins of omission and the temporal punishment for sins. Supernatural powers are believed to be communicated by the benediction.

J.C.

**BENEDICTUS.** A poem or canticle spoken as a prophecy by Zechariah, father of John the Baptizer, at John's circumcision (Luke 1:68-79). It is called the Benedictus from the first word of the poem in Latin, "Praise be (to the God of Israel)." This poem closely resembles the MAGNIFICAT of Mary, recorded in Luke 1:46-55, for Zechariah, like Mary, thanks and praises God for divine grace. God's liberation of the oppressed is also stressed (vv. 73 ff.), as it is in the Magnificat (vv. 50-53). The language and the poetic parallelism of the Benedictus point to a Hebrew original, which was either translated by Luke or quoted from an existing Greek translation. The poem is strongly oriented to a Messianic expectation and makes many references to the salvation history recorded in the OT. The last part of the poem specifies that John will be the prophet of God and the forerunner of God's Messiah (vv. 76-77).

J.C.

**BEN-HADAD.** A Hebrew name meaning "son of (the god) Hadad"; the name of three kings of Aram-Damascus.

Courtesy of the National Museum in Aleppo

*Stele of Ben-hadad, son of Tabrimmon, king of Damascus, from Aleppo, bearing Aramaic dedicatory inscription of the god Baal Melqart*

(1) Ben-hadad I was the son of Tabrimmon, who was the son of Hezion, king of Syria (I Kings 15:18). He reigned as king about 885–870 B.C. When BAASHA, king of Israel (900–877), and ASA, king of Judah (913–873), disputed their common boundary across the hill country, Ben-hadad was persuaded to intervene for Judah's benefit. Baasha sought to strengthen Israel's position by blockading Judah's capital on its northern side (I Kings 15:16-22). His forces penetrated southward into Benjamin, where they overtook and began to fortify Ramah, a city only five miles north of Jerusalem. Striving to defend his endangered capital, Asa bribed Ben-hadad to annul his already existing alliance with Baasha and support Judah. Ben-hadad's forces ravaged territories north of the Sea of Galilee, whereupon Baasha abandoned Ramah and terminated his Jerusalem blockade. Moreover, by his display of strength in northern Israel, Ben-hadad protected a vital Galilean caravan route, linking Damascus with the Mediterranean coast.

(2) Ben-hadad II, whose personal name presumably was Hadadezer, reigned about 870–842 B.C. Increas-ingly, biblical scholarship suspects that the reign of Ben-hadad I was briefer than once supposed, and that the Israelite kings, AHAB (869–850) and Jehoram (849–842), interacted with a different Damascus ruler than did Baasha. At issue is the interpretation of a five-line inscription displayed on a basalt stele discovered near Aleppo and dating to about 850 B.C. Dedicated to the Phoenician deity Melqart (Mel-carth), it appears to celebrate Syria's victory over the Assyrian monarch, Shalmaneser III (859–825), which was secured by a ruler other than the one presented in the preceding paragraph.

Though Israel felt uneasy about the northern presence of Aram-Damascus, the relationship that developed between Ahab and Ben-hadad II was bittersweet. Probably early in Ahab's reign, Ben-hadad II sought to thwart Israelite resurgence. Besieging Samaria, he demanded Israel's full-scale submission (I Kings 20:3, 5-6). With the general support of his people (20:8) and endorsement from Yahweh's prophets (20:13-14, 22), Ahab prepared for battle. Twice Damascus met defeat at Ahab's hand, and Ben-hadad II was captured (20:16-21, 26-33). Ahab magnanimously released his opponent on the conditions that the border cities Aram had taken from Omri be restored to Israel and that Israel be allowed a trading street in Damascus (20:34).

Assyria's goal of westward expansion under Shalmaneser III stimulated Ben-hadad II and Ahab to become serious allies. According to his annals, Shalmaneser tangled with an anti-Assyrian coalition at Qarqar in 853 B.C. Among the dozen western kings listed were Hadadezer of Damascus and Ahab of Israel. Since Shalmaneser opposed the same coalition in 849, 848, and 845, Israel and Aram must have maintained their friendship. At some juncture, however, Ahab sought to wrest Ramoth-gilead from Ben-hadad II. Damascus triumphed, and Ahab was slain (I Kings 22:29-37). Subsequently, Ben-hadad was murdered by his officer, Hazael, upon being told by Elisha that he would succeed the ailing king (II Kings 8:7-15).

(3) Ben-hadad III, Hazael's son and successor (about 806–? B.C.; II Kings 13:24). Ruling over a kingdom weakened by Assyrian invasions, Ben-hadad III was defeated three times by Jehoash, king of Israel (802–786; II Kings 13:14-19, 25). This allowed Israel to recover territories previously lost to Ben-hadad's father, Hazael (about 842–806; II Kings 10:32-33). Moreover, Ben-hadad III was devastated by the heavy tribute that the Assyrian monarch Adad-nirari (811–784) imposed on him.

J.K.K.

**BENJAMIN/BENJAMINITES.** A Hebrew name meaning, strictly, "son of the south, southerner," but in folk etymology, "son of the right hand [fortune]").

(1) Son of JACOB and Rachel (Gen. 35:18) and the eponymous ancestor of one of the twelve tribes. At his birth, his dying mother despairingly called him

Ben-oni ("son of my sorrow"), but Jacob named him Benjamin. He was the one full brother of Joseph and the only son of Jacob born in Palestine (near Bethlehem). Being the son of Jacob's autumn years and the offspring of Rachel, his favorite wife, Benjamin was greatly loved by his father, who only reluctantly permitted his departure to Egypt with his brothers in search of food (Gen. 43:1-15). Joseph's affection for Benjamin was likewise strong (43:29-34). Moreover, the Blessing of Moses (tenth century B.C.?) portrays Benjamin as a special recipient of God's love and protection (Deut. 33:12). Eventually, through Benjamin's offspring, his tribe came into existence (Gen. 46:21; Num. 26:38-41; I Chr. 7:6-12; 8:1-40).

(2) The tribe of Benjamin and its territory. Biblical scholars searching for the origins of this Israelite tribe are fascinated with mention of the Banû-yamîna ("sons of the south") in eighteenth-century B.C. cuneiform inscriptions discovered at Mari on the Middle Euphrates near Haran (Abraham's point of departure; Gen. 12:4). Their association with the Banû-simal ("sons of the north") has removed any misgivings about the meaning of their name. Most significant of all the peoples attested in these inscriptions, the Banû-yamîna are portrayed as a fierce, non-sedentary group that regularly assaulted territories over which Mari's king, Zimri-lim, ruled (about 1730-1697 B.C.). Their turbulent manner readily accords with the depiction of Benjamin as "a ravenous wolf" in the tenth-century B.C. (?) Blessing of Jacob (Gen. 49:27) and with the tribe's violent behavior in Judges 19-21. Nevertheless, the resemblance between the "southerners" of Mari and Israel may involve little more than their shared name.

"Southerner" Benjamin settled in the fertile hill country south of Ephraim, the tribe it accompanied across the Jordan River when penetrating central Palestine. Basically, Benjamin's modest territorial holding (presumably appropriate for the descendants of Jacob's *youngest* son) was circumscribed by these boundaries: a line from Bethel to Jericho on the north, the river Jordan on the east, a line from the Dead Sea to Beth-horon on the south, and a line from Kirjath-jearim to Beth-horon on the west. This territory, extending about twenty-eight miles in an east-west direction and twelve miles in a north-south direction, hosted such important towns as Jerusalem, Jericho, Bethel, Gibeon, and Mizpah (Josh. 18:11-28). Benjamin's smallness may account for the tribe's eighteen-year enslavement under Eglon, the king of Moab, until Ehud delivered his tribespeople (Judg. 3:12-30). And for protecting bestial men of Gibeah who had raped the Levite's concubine, the tribe was almost obliterated in the intertribal warfare that ensued (Judg. 20-21).

Israel's first king, Saul, chosen by prophetic designation and popular acclamation (I Sam. 10:1-2; 11:14-15), was a Benjaminite who governed the people from Gibeah, his hometown. Intense Benja-minite loyalties to Saul's house sometimes proved troublesome to David, who followed Saul on the throne (II Sam. 16:5-8; 20:1-2). Even so, when the ten northern tribes withdrew from Judah under Jeroboam's lead, Benjamin remained true to the Davidic house (I Kings 12:21). In fact, "Judah and Benjamin" are typically treated as one unit by later authors (for example, II Chr. 11:1; 15:2; 34:9; Ezra 4:1). Among the better known Benjaminites mentioned in the Bible are Jeremiah (Jer. 1:1), Mordecai (Esth. 2:5), and Paul (Rom. 11:1; Phil. 3:5).

(3) Jacob's great-grandson, through Benjamin, Jediael, and Bilhan (I Chr. 7:10).

(4) A son of Harim, who followed Ezra's mandate and divorced his Gentile wife (Ezra 10:31-32).

(5) A priestly contemporary of Nehemiah (Neh. 12:34), presumably identical with the Benjamin who helped repair Jerusalem's walls (3:23).          J.K.K.

## BENTHAM, JEREMY (1748–1832).

UTILITARIAN philosopher, Bentham was born in London on February 15. Educated at Westminster School, he received the B.A. from Queen's College, Oxford, in 1763. He then studied law at Lincoln's Inn.

His 1789 book, *An Introduction to the Principles of Morals and Legislation,* declared that the object of all legislation should be to provide for the "greatest happiness of the greatest number." His ethical HEDONISM recognized two basic human motives: pain or evil and pleasure or good. To help make ethical decisions, he developed a "hedonistic calculus" to measure an action's potential pain or pleasure.

A critic of judicial and political institutions, he fostered a number of reforms, such as a circular panopticon model for prisons in which a guard can see all the prisoners from a central position. His 1817 *Catechism of Parliamentary Reform* advocated annual elections, equal electoral districts, wider suffrage, and the secret ballot. In 1823 he helped found the *Westminster Review.* He died in London on June 6.

N.H.

## BERDYAEV, NIKOLAI (1874–1948).

Widely regarded as one of the most profound and important spiritual philosophers of this century. He is appropriately spoken of as an advocate of Christian EXISTENTIALISM, although his thought was influenced by many sources and is not easily categorized. Berdyaev was born into a noble Russian family in Kiev, where he attended the university. In 1894 he embraced Marxism and for a time participated in revolutionary activities. He was arrested in 1898, spent two years in prison and three more years in exile in Vologda province. Upon his return to Kiev he met SERGIUS BULGAKOV, who was instrumental in his transition from Marxism to Christianity. The writings of DOSTOEVSKY played an even greater role in Berdyaev's conversion, and his study of the Russian novelist is among the best interpretations of Dostoevsky's religious views.

In 1922 Berdyaev was banished from Russia and settled in Paris, where he lived until his death. He organized meetings of Orthodox, Catholics, and Protestants and became a leading critic of communism and spokesman for the Russian emigrés.

For a quarter century Berdyaev published a score of works touching on various aspects of his philosophy of "spiritual Christianity." His criticism of the institutional church and his unorthodox religious views caused him to be denounced by some Russian Orthodox churchmen. Nevertheless, works such as *Freedom and the Spirit* (Eng. trans. 1935), *The Destiny of Man* (Eng. trans. 1937), *Solitude and Society* (Eng. trans. 1938), and *Spirit and Reality* (Eng. trans. 1939) were published in several European languages and established Berdyaev as not only an influential Christian thinker but a preeminent twentieth-century philosopher of human freedom and the life of the spirit.

J.L.

**BERENGER OF TOURS.** An eleventh-century theologian and professor at Tours who opposed the growing tendency toward the doctrine of TRANSUBSTANTIATION. He objected to Lanfranc's assertion that the body of Christ descends from heaven and is physically present at COMMUNION. His views, mostly derived from a treatise by Ratramnus of Corbie, which he attributed to JOHN SCOTUS ERIGENA, are not as clear as is his criticism of Lanfranc. The general direction of his argument, based on the theory of UNIVERSALS, is that the body of Christ, which is in heaven, does not descend to earth, but rather is present at Communion in a manner similar to that in which universals are present in particulars, that is, "ideally." His use of this term has led some to interpret him as holding to a symbolic presence of Christ in Communion. But this is probably a misrepresentation. Repeatedly condemned by ecclesiastical authorities, Berenger died a lonely and broken man in 1088.

J.G.

**BERGSON, HENRI** (1859–1941). A French philosopher considered one of the most original thinkers of this century. He is associated especially with the doctrines of vitalism and creative evolution. Bergson studied at the École Normale Superieure, where, in 1889, he submitted his provocative essay *Time and Free Will* for the doctorate. He held the chair of the history of philosophy at the Collège de France from 1900 to 1924; was elected to the French Academy in 1914; and honored with the Nobel Prize in 1927.

In *Time and Free Will* (Eng. trans. 1910), Bergson sought to show the self-evidence of human freedom, and in *Matter and Memory* (Eng. trans. 1911) he demonstrated that consciousness is not identical with the physical activity of the brain. In *Creative Evolution* (Eng. trans. 1911), Bergson portrayed the evolutionary process as the work of a creative, spiritual life-force (élan vital) whose movement is novel and unpredictable. *The Two Sources of Morality and Religion* (Eng. trans. 1935) distinguished between closed and open moralities and religions, the former being static, the latter progressive and creative—the work of the great prophets and mystics.

Bergson's ideas have attracted many religious thinkers, including the Roman Catholic Modernist Eduard LeRoy and GEORGE TYRRELL, PIERRE TEILHARD DE CHARDIN, and several theologians associated with PROCESS THEOLOGY.            J.L.

**BERKELEY, GEORGE** (1685–1753). Bishop and idealist philosopher, Berkeley was born March 12 in County Kilkenny, Ireland. Educated at Kilkenny College and Trinity College, Dublin, he received the B.A. in 1704. Ordained in 1710, he left Ireland in 1713 for London.

In 1724 he was named dean of Derry, and in 1728 he married Anne Forster. After living in Newport, Rhode Island, 1728–31, he became bishop of Cloyne in Dublin in 1734. He was a benefactor to both Harvard and Yale.

Influenced by the empiricism of JOHN LOCKE, Berkeley argued that "to be is to be perceived." One cannot conceive, much less prove, an independent world of matter. To do so would also set up such a world co-eternal with God and thus limit the deity.

Among Berkeley's most significant works are *An Essay Towards a New Theory of Vision* (1709), and *A Treatise Concerning the Principles of Human Knowledge* (1710). Berkeley died in Oxford on January 14.

N.H.

**BERKHOF, LOUIS** (1873–1957). Dutch-American Calvinistic theologian, minister of the Christian Reformed Church, professor of dogmatics, and president of Calvin Theological Seminary, Grand Rapids, Michigan. Born in Holland, Berkhof was brought to America as a child. He graduated from Calvin Theological Seminary, studied at Princeton, was a pastor for a short while, and then taught for thirty years at Calvin Theological Seminary. Berkhof's speciality was SYSTEMATIC THEOLOGY. He produced a three-volume *Reformed Dogmatics* in 1932 and a *Manual of Reformed Doctrine* in 1933. His *Systematic Theology* (1941) is still studied by orthodox Reformed pastors. His last book was *The Second Coming of Christ* (1953). Berkhof stood in the line of the Free University of Amsterdam's orthodox Reformed theologians, Kuyper and Bavinck, and the Americans CHARLES HODGE and B. B. WARFIELD. His writings are still popular among American evangelicals. Berkhof rejected the hyper-Calvinism popular among some American Dutch Reformed pastors in the 1920s.            J.C.

**BERKOUWER, GERRIT CORNELIUS** (1903– ). Professor of theology at the Free University of Amsterdam and Dutch Reformed theologian of the dissenting Gereformeerde Kerken, a nineteenth-century schism from the established Hervorme Kerk. A gymnasium teacher's son, Berkouwer was educated at the Christian Gymnasium and the Free University of Amsterdam, receiving the doctorate in theology, *cum laude*, in 1934. He served as a parish pastor, first in Friesland, then in Amsterdam, from 1927 to 1945. In the latter year, Berkouwer was elected to the chair of dogmatics at the Free University. He began a steady but unsystematic series of monographs, publishing one every other year. He also wrote a number of other books, including the widely read *The Triumph of Grace in the Theology of Karl Barth* (1956). Berkouwer contributed articles almost every week to the *Gereformeerde Weekblod* and the newspaper *Trouw*. In 1961 he was invited to be an official observer at the Second Vatican Council.

Berkouwer is well known in neo-Fundamentalist and Fundamentalist circles in the United States. Despite his rejection of theological speculation and his gradual movement toward the positions of Karl Barth, he is fundamentally a scholastic theologian dealing in the debates of the seventeenth century concerning predestination and election. Berkouwer's teachings on ELECTION begin with his dissatisfaction with the orthodox (SYNOD OF DORT) belief in the comprehensive decree of God to save some and to condemn others from before the foundation of the earth. He covered these issues in *Divine Election* (1955), *Man, the Image of God* (1957), and *Een Halve Eeuw Theologie Motieven Stromigen Van 1920 tot Heden* (1974). Berkouwer emphasizes the practical implications of the doctrine of election, which he stresses as a comfort and consolation to the believer, not as a threat. He downgrades the idea of synergism—human cooperation with God—since synergism is not the attitude of the believer according to the Bible. He also seeks to show that election does not mean God is arbitrary. It is his belief that Christians can receive certainty of election only as they respond to Christ. This certainty is made stronger as the believer grows in grace. In his most liberal development, Berkouwer denies the double predestination of the Synod of Dort. He does not believe in reprobation, God's "negative election" of some to be condemned to show the glory of God.                                              J.C.

**BERNADETTE OF LOURDES** (1844–79). The woman whose mystical visions led to the founding of the shrine at LOURDES, France, was the eldest child of the poverty-stricken Frances and Louise Soubirous.

In frail health after a bout of cholera in 1854 and with chronic asthma, at age fourteen she had a series of eighteen visions of the VIRGIN MARY between February 11 and July 16, 1858. Appearing to her in a cave above the Gave de Pau River outside Lourdes, the Virgin told her, "I am the Immaculate Conception." The Lady also told her to drink from a spring, which miraculously appeared, and to build a chapel in the place.

Coutesy of Religious News Service

*Bernadette of Lourdes*

To escape increasing public attention, Bernadette became a resident at a local school run by the Sisters of Charity of Nevers. In 1866 she became a novitiate at the mother house, where she lived out her life in increasing sickness and pain. She died April 16, 1879, and is buried in St. Gildard convent chapel in Nevers. Miracles of healing began almost immediately at the spring and shrine. Bernadette was canonized by Pope Pius XI in 1933, and Lourdes remains a center of healing.

N.H.

**BERNARD OF CLAIRVAUX** (1091–1153). Most renowned of the CISTERCIAN monks, greatest churchman of his time, mystic, preacher, and moralist. Born a noble near Fontaine-les-Dijon, France, he became disgusted with easy living at twenty-two and experienced a conversion. In 1113, with thirty companions, he joined the reform Cistercian monastery at Citeaux, France, a strict Benedictine order. His exemplary discipline and excessive austerity warranted his being chosen in 1115 to found and be abbot of a branch monastery at Clairvaux. His ascetic practices, integrity, mystical contemplation, preaching, and outspokenness against injustice won him acclaim as Europe's conscience. The Cistercians grew phenomenally. Nobility, popes, and commoners sought his advice.

In the struggle for the papal throne (1130–38), Bernard's moral status shifted the balance from Anacletus II to Innocent II. Bernard strove to express his mystical relationship to God in practical piety and love. The greatest stage of love was not quietism but love of self for God's sake, to do God's work in the world. He zealously guarded the faith. He opposed PETER ABELARD's dialectical rationalism, and influenced the Council of Sens to condemn Abelard for heresy in 1140. In 1146 he protected Germany's Jews from church persecutors. He persuaded Pope Eugenius III and King Louis VII of France to undertake the unsuccessful Second Crusade (1147–49), which he preached against the Turks. He wrote a book of ascetic counsels for Pope Eugenius II, *De Consideratione (Some Considerations)*. He was canonized saint, 1173, and made a Doctor of the Church, 1830.

C.M.

**BERNARD OF CLUNY** (ca. 1100–56). A Benedictine monk and poet who satirized medieval immoralities. At CLUNY during the time of Peter the Venerable, he attacked monastic corruptions in the Latin poem *De Contemptu Mundi (On Contempt of the World)*, approximately 1140. Though little known, his writings include over three thousand verses, many sermons, and hymns. "Jerusalem the Golden," "The World Is Very Evil," and "For Thee, O Dear, Dear Country" are hymns translated from his Latin poems by John Mason Neale.

C.M.

**BETHANY.** The name of a village two miles east of Jerusalem, on the eastern side of the Mount of Olives and on the road to Jericho. It was the home of the family of Lazarus with his sisters Mary and Martha according to John 11:1. The village also figures in the Synoptic Gospels as the place to which Jesus retired when he came to Jerusalem on Palm Sunday (Mark 11:11 and parallels) and where he was anointed by an unnamed woman (Mark 14:3-9 and parallels).

At John 1:28 there is a well-attested reading of "Bethany," a place where John was baptizing. Origen preferred Bethabara (KJV) to this reading because he was unable to locate a Bethany by the Jordan River. But the reading "Bethany" should be accepted as original, though we have no knowledge of its exact whereabouts.

R.M.

**BETHEL.** An ancient city, identified with present-day Beitin, located ten miles north of Jerusalem on the Benjamin-Ephraim border. Bethel hosted a near continuous occupation from about 2000 B.C. until the Christian Era, and apart from Jerusalem is the most frequently mentioned city in the OT (seventy-two times).

*Archaeological Background.* Ceramic evidence indicates that occupation began soon after the demise of neighboring Ai. Hyksos occupation (about 1750–1550 B.C.) produced a superb defense system, and prior to Israel's takeover the house masonry was first-rate. Israel's conquest of Bethel is summarily reported in Judges 1:22-26 and at greater length in Joshua 8, assuming, as many scholars do, that Bethel, not Ai, was the city originally mentioned. Bethel's extensive thirteenth-century B.C. destruction is ordinarily attributed to Israel since a complete break is attested and a much poorer culture followed. Repeated twelfth- and eleventh-century B.C. destructions invite the thesis that Bethel was temporarily held by Benjamin (Josh. 18:22), reclaimed by the Canaanites, and later taken by Ephraim (I Chr. 7:28 lists Bethel as Ephraimite property). Formerly named Luz (Gen. 28:19), the city boasted a Canaanite sanctuary dedicated to El who headed the Canaanite pantheon.

*Bethel in Premonarchic Israel.* The city is first linked with Abraham, who erected an altar there (Gen. 12:8). At Bethel, Yahweh extended the dual promise of land and progeny to Jacob, who responded with a pledge of loyalty (Gen. 28:10-22). Deborah's judgeship had its locus near Bethel (Judg. 4:5), and the city was included in Samuel's itinerary of towns he visited as an Israelite judge (I Sam. 7:16).

*Bethel in Monarchic Israel.* Saul recruited a detachment of soldiers who were with him near Bethel (I Sam. 13:2), and David dispatched there a portion of war booty (30:27). As monarch of the northern kingdom, Jeroboam I made Bethel a royal sanctuary to rival the Jerusalem Temple (I Kings 12:26-33). Here the Deuteronomist denounced as idolatrous his choice of fertility-oriented golden calves as pedestals upon which Yahweh was invisibly enthroned. Amaziah, the priest of Bethel, scolded Amos for his harsh criticism of king (Jeroboam II) and cult (Amos 7:10-17). Where Jehu failed, Josiah succeeded in destroying Bethel's sanctuary (II Kings 10:29; 23:15). Razed in the interim between Babylonian and Persian rule, Bethel was resettled by a small group returning from Babylonian exile (Ezra 2:28). In the Hellenistic and early Roman periods, Bethel was more prosperous though it is never mentioned in the NT.

J.K.K.

**BETHESDA.** An alternative name is Bethzatha, according to different textual traditions in John 5:2 and accepted by the RSV, J. B. Phillips, and Good News Bible. The NEB and NIV prefer the standard reading, but there is no certainty. Also the name stands for either the Sheep-Pool itself (RSV) or a building near the Sheep-Pool (NEB, a location many recent commentators accept, ever since the archaeological work carried on at the site in the northeast corner of the Temple area, near the present St. Stephen's Gate in Jerusalem).

If Bethesda is the correct name—and the latest evidence from the Dead Sea Scrolls *may* suggest that this is so—the meaning is "house of two springs" rather than "house of mercy." Two pools near the Temple area were known to Eusebius in the fourth century and to the Bordeaux pilgrim on his visit. The existence of such a twin pool, separated by several cisterns that held water for sheep washing, was confirmed in an archaeological discovery. These reservoirs, divided into two sections, were bounded by colonnades (John 5:2, "five porticoes") on four sides and along the central partition. The supply of water came from underground springs, a feature that may explain the movement of the water in John 5:7.

R.M.

**BETH-HORON.** This place-name refers to two sites in biblical times, one located about ten miles northwest of Jerusalem, the other about twelve miles in the same direction. Today there are two villages to mark these spots, called in the OT Upper Beth-horon and Lower Beth-horon. A distance of seven hundred feet in elevation separates these adjacent villages.

In OT history both towns played an important role, being on the main trade route between Gibeon and the Valley of Aijalon on the east and the coast plain to the west. Both were border towns marking off the tribal boundaries of Benjamin and Ephraim (Josh. 16:3-5; 18:13ff.).

Beth-horon was one of the Levitical "cities of refuge" (Josh. 21:22; I Chron. 6:68). Solomon rebuilt both sites after Pharaoh's destruction (II Chron. 8:5). Here too was the scene of the famous OT battle (Josh. 10:6-15), when Joshua and five Canaanite kings engaged in conflict. In the intertestamental period, the story of how Holofernes attacked Beth-horon is told (Judith 4:4), and in the Maccabean revolt Judas was twice successful in battle at Beth-horon (I Macc. 7:15-26, 39-43).

R.M.

**BETHLEHEM.** Two Israelite towns carry this name. The one of lesser importance is located in the tribal region of Zebulun, seven miles northwest of Nazareth (Josh. 19:15). It has little significance in biblical history.

The more important Bethlehem (whose name means "house of bread," corresponding to the Arabic name of the village on the site, Bayt Lahm) is situated six miles southwest of Jerusalem, near the main trade route joining Hebron and the South with the capital city of DAVID. In fact, Bethlehem came into prominence with David, though the locale has a long history stretching back to the fourteenth century, since it is referred to in the Amarna letters. It was also known then as Ephrath (Gen. 35:19), the traditional place of Rachel's tomb until the present day. It is

From *Atlas of the Bible* (Thomas Nelson & Sons Limited)

*Bethlehem as viewed from the south*

From *Atlas of the Bible* (Thomas Nelson & Sons Limited)

*Bethlehem. Between the bell towers in the center is the site of the basilica built by Constantine about* A.D. *325 (but no longer there).*

mentioned in the book of Judges (Judg. 19). But it is in connection with David's influence that Bethlehem took on special importance. Through David Bethlehem gained an aura as the birthplace of the future Messiah of Israel (Mic. 5:2; Matt. 2:1-12). The story of the massacre of the children in Bethlehem is Matthew's way of appealing to OT prophecy (Matt. 2:16-18).

The Davidic link begins with the tradition underlying the book of Ruth. Naomi's return to Bethlehem from Moab with the book's heroine, and the latter's subsequent marriage to Boaz, point forward to the future king of Israel (Ruth 4:11). David is so identified as "the son of an Ephrathite of Bethlehem in Judah, named Jesse" (I Sam. 17:12).

Because of this cluster of associations, both in Jewish expectation and Christian thought and piety, Bethlehem has long been venerated. The emperor Constantine's mother, Helena, built a church here in A.D. 325; this edifice was enlarged by the emperor Justinian in the sixth century. This is the site of the church of the Nativity, which tourists visit today.

R.M.

**BETHPHAGE.** The name of a village not far from Bethany on or near the road from Jerusalem to Jericho. The name means "house of unripe figs" (Matt. 21:18-19; Mark 11:12-14, 20-24). Bethphage is mentioned only in the account of Jesus' "triumphal entry" into Jerusalem (Matt. 21:1; Mark 11:1; Luke 19:29). In this vicinity, the disciples procured a young donkey, upon which Jesus made his way into the city. The route took him one-half mile up the ascent of the Mount of Olives where, in full view of the old city of Jerusalem, according to popular belief, the Messiah would appear. Origen, in the third century, refers to Bethphage as "the house of

triumph," "of the meeting," and "of the mounting of the ass." The Talmud states that "Beth Page" marked the city limits of Jerusalem. It was here that the city of JERUSALEM began (Isa. 62:11; Zech. 9:9).

P.L.G.

**BETH-SAIDA** (meaning "house of the fishers"). The name of a Galilean city (Luke 9:10; John 1:44) or village (Mark 8:26). Two sites are associated with Beth-saida. (1) et-Tell, or Bethsaida-Julias, is situated on the Jordan River, two miles from where the river empties into the Sea of Galilee. About 2 B.C., this crossroads of the region was made a city by Herod Philip, named Julias in honor of Julia, the daughter of Augustus. (2) el-Araj is the name of a natural harbor on the sea just east of the mouth of the Jordan. This place has the remains of a town wall, an ancient mosaic, and a strong spring nearby. This may have been the fishermen's settlement of Bethsaida-Julias. Traces of a Roman road and aqueduct have been found, which join the two places.

Beth-saida was the natal city of the apostles Philip, Andrew, and Peter, all Greek names. Jesus' ministry in Beth-saida was disappointing (Mark 8:22-26; Matt. 11:21; Luke 10:13). The healing of a blind man (Mark 8:22-26) took place at Beth-saida. Jesus and his disciples must have gone near or through Beth-saida en route to Caesarea Philippi, where, it is thought, Peter's confession and the Transfiguration took place (Mark 8:27 ff. and parallels).

P.L.G.

**BETH-SHAN.** An ancient city located where the Jezreel and Jordan valleys intersect. It is sometimes called Beth-shean and Scythopolis. According to the biblical references (Judg. 1:27; Josh. 17:16; I Sam. 31:10) and the Egyptian records, the city was in the valley of JEZREEL, near Mt. Gilboa. In the excavations of Tell el-Husan, one of the largest tells in Palestine, two fifteenth-century B.C. hieroglyphic texts have been found that include the name Beth-shan.

The site lies at the junction of trade routes from Egypt to Damascus and the East. It has a subtropical climate, five hundred feet below sea level, with abundant water and cultivatable soil. From excavation the site is known to have been occupied since 3000 B.C., perhaps earlier. The early settlement, without walls, followed the arts of pottery, basketry, and weaving. Dates and grapes were the principal crops.

The Egyptian influence began after Thutmose III's victory at Megiddo (1468 B.C.). For three centuries, Egypt maintained control in order to protect its trade with the North and East. In this period, city walls and a number of temples were built. It was on the city walls (I Sam. 31:10) that the Philistines, then in charge, hanged the bodies of Jonathan and Saul after the battle on Mount Gilboa. They put Saul's armor in the temple of Ashtaroth (I Sam. 31:10). David probably took Beth-shan, for the name appears in the list of Solomon's fifth administrative district (I Kings 4:12).

In NT times, Beth-shan was called Sythopolis. It was captured in 107 B.C. by John Hyrcannus, who dealt generously with its mixed population of Jews and Gentiles (I Macc. 12:29). Until the Arab conquest (A.D. 636), Beth-shan was a member—Josephus claimed it was one of the largest—of the Decapolis League.

P.L.G.

**BETH-SHEMESH.** Meaning "house of the sun," the name of an old settlement, sometimes a walled city, in northeast Shephelah (the Valley of Sorek, Judg. 16:4), over 12½ miles west of Jerusalem. The ancient site is identified with Tel er-Rumeilah, just west of an Arab village, 'Ain Shems, a name that recalls the ancient name. Located on a ridge, 825 feet above sea level, between two valleys, Beth-shemesh experienced several destructions, notably the invasions of Shishak (about 925 B.C.), Sennacherib (about 701 B.C.), and Nebuchadnezzar (588–587 B.C.).

Excavations have disclosed two periods of the city's prosperity: (1) The end of the fifteenth century through early fourteenth century, when industry flourished and numerous plastered cisterns were dug that provided for a sizable population. Oil and wine production was the chief industry, together with metalworking and the growing of wheat (I Sam. 6:13). Late in the thirteenth century, its destruction took place, presumably by the Israelites. (2) After their victory over Israel at Ebenezer (about 1050 B.C., I Sam. 4:1-11; 5:1), the Philistines politically and culturally dominated Beth-shemesh's considerable Israelite population. It was during this time that Joash of Israel captured Amaziah of Judah at

Beth-shemesh (about 790 B.C., II Chr. 25:22). The Philistines appear to have sacked the city around 735 B.C.

P.L.G.

**BEULAH** (meaning "married"). A "new" name for redeemed Zion found in Isaiah 62:4 (KJV; RSV marg.; compare Isa. 54:1), signifying Yahweh's wife. Such an expression, though rare in the OT, appears in Hosea 2:16, 19; Jeremiah 2:2; and Ezekiel 16:32. In the NT Christ's bride is the church (Eph. 5:23-27) and the New Jerusalem (Rev. 21:2, 9 ff.).

P.L.G.

**BEZA, THEODORE** (1519–1605). French Reformed theologian who succeeded CALVIN at Geneva. Born into Burgundian nobility, he was educated in law and humanism; his humanist mentor was Melchoir Wolmar. Licensed in law, 1539, he practiced in Paris and studied classics, a lifelong interest, before undergoing a physical-spiritual crisis and renouncing Catholicism in 1548. He journeyed to Geneva, where Calvin publicly performed his marriage to Claudine Denosse. At Lausanne, he taught Greek and wrote extensively for ten years. Beza defended the burning of Servetus in *The Punishment of Heretics by the Civil Magistrate,* 1554, and issued an annotated Latin translation of the NT, 1556.

Calvin invited him to Geneva in 1558 to teach Greek. He became rector of the Genevan Academy, 1559. Skilled in negotiations, he represented French Protestants at numerous gatherings and served as chaplain to Huguenots Condé and Coligny. He succeeded Calvin in 1564 and belligerently defended Calvin's doctrines. Besides completing Marot's translations of the Psalms, he did biblical textual work, presided over the Huguenot synod at LaRochelle, 1571, and argued the right of lesser magistrates to revolt in *On Rights of Magistrates,* 1572.

C.M.

**BHAGAVAD GITA.** From the Sanskrit word for "Song of the Lord." A book of seven hundred verses, probably composed about A.D. 100, which has had immense influence on the subsequent thought and life of HINDUISM. The *Bhagavad Gita* is actually a section of the great epic, the MAHABHARATA, which deals with the rivalry of two branches of a royal house for the throne. As the *Gita* opens, Arjuna, the king whose claim is presented as just, is riding his chariot into battle at the head of his army against the forces of his kinsmen. His charioteer is KRISHNA—God come into the world in human form as an AVATAR. As Arjuna is about to join with the foe, he suddenly holds back, overcome with doubt and remorse at what he is about to do.

Arjuna tells Krishna that, even though the adversaries are evil, to fight them would bring greater evil, the disruption of family and social order. He throws down his bow and refuses to proceed. Most of the remainder of the book consists of Krishna's answers to the king, telling him how he can and must do the duty that his station has laid upon him, in the process offering passages of exceptional power on the classic Hindu view of humanity, God, and their relationship. While it may seem surprising that a spiritual masterpiece should take the form of an injunction to war, the *Gita*'s insights go far beyond the occasion, and it can be interpreted on several levels. For one as committed to nonviolence as MOHANDAS K. GANDHI it was a peerless inspiration. He read Arjuna's war as an allegory of the eternal struggle of righteousness against evil, a battle in which bloodless weapons are best, but in which none can rightly be noncombatant.

Krishna's first response is to point out that one should not truly grieve the dead in battle, for the real self, the spirit, neither slays nor is slain, but changes from one body to another as one casts aside a worn-out garment and takes a new one. But while the spirit is eternal, it must play its part in the drama of the world. Krishna reminds Arjuna that, as a member of the Kshatriya caste, the caste of rulers and warriors, it is his duty to lead his army into battle.

Moreover, one can find liberation in the midst of such activity. Spiritual liberation is freedom from the shackles of egocentric desire, and if one works for good, without personal attachment to the fruits of the labor, one can be as free in the midst of work as in meditation. This is karma-yoga, a major aspect of Krishna's message in the *Gita*.

The climax of the book is Krishna's stupendous self-revelation of himself as infinite God embracing the multitudinous forms of the universe. With it are associated exhortations to BHAKTI, devotional worship of God as personal, a way to liberation through faith, love, and divine grace. There is a darker side, however. God seen as personal is also God as Time, the destroyer. Arjuna as warrior would be only doing his work.

The *Bhagavad Gita* has been an immensely important source for modern Hindu thinkers and spiritual leaders. While its traditional interpretation has often been conservative, seeing it as a bulwark of the caste system, many moderns have viewed it as a rallying-point in the struggle for justice through social change and even revolution. Others have made it basic to new meditation and bhakti movements.

R.E.

**BHAKTI.** In HINDUISM, bhakti is the path of devotionalism, of the loving worship of the great gods and goddesses. Ordinarily, a bhakta, or follower of this way, will be a special devotee of only one such deity, his or her "chosen ideal." Bhakti teaches that if the devotee worships the deity with true fervor and selflessness, love will melt away all sin and bad KARMA; god and worshiper will become mystically united; and the latter will enjoy a rapturous eternity in a paradise reserved for true lovers of the divine.

The origins of bhakti are obscure, but undoubtedly lie in folk religion. By the time of the BHAGAVAD GITA (about A.D. 100), however, it was capable of forceful intellectual expression. Devotional theism, in which intention and love count for much, was made preferable to sacrifice or yogic techniques. In the early centuries A.D. bhaktic movements grew apace, aided by the patronage of rulers such as those of the Gupta dynasty, and countenanced by the BRAHMINS, who saw in it an antidote to such heresies as BUDDHISM and a means of Hinduizing tribal groups. The works of the bhaktic sage Narada, the PURANAS (books presenting myths of the gods), and the passionately devotional verse of such poets as the ALVARS in the early Middle Ages all gave voice to the movement. Many great Hindu temples, associated with bhakti and its gods, were built in this period as well.

Bhakti properly makes much of its way as a spiritual path equally accessible to all, high or low, learned or illiterate, of any caste, whether proficient in such techniques as yoga or not. It demands nothing but the simple service of a loving heart. Nonetheless bhakti is much more than folk religion or uncouth religious enthusiasm. Its exposition has attracted some of India's best theological minds. Ramanuja (twelfth century A.D.), for example, a Vaisnava (devotee of Vishnu), powerfully countered Advaita (non-dualism or monism) with arguments for a personal god not wholly identified with creation or with the human soul—prerequisites for the bhakti relation of love, rather than simple oneness between God and humans.

The major bhaktic gods include VISHNU, his main AVATARS Rama and KRISHNA, their consorts, SHIVA, and his consort who goes under many names, from Parvati to Durga and KALI. Bhaktas are usually Vaisnavas, worshipers of a deity in the Vishnu lineage, or Saivas, devotees of Shiva or his mate. The great majority of Hindus are practitioners of some forms of bhakti, though not necessarily in an exclusive or highly committed sense.

Bhakti worship includes puja, presentation of simple offerings at a home or temple shrine, and *kirtanas* or *bhajans,* singing of fervent hymns sometimes accompanied by ecstatic dancing and other gestures of intense feeling. Bhakti worship characteristically puts more emphasis on feeling than form and gives all devotees ample opportunity for participation.

R.E.

**BIBLE.** The Holy Scriptures include the writings, regarded as the inspired record of divine REVELATION, both to Israel, the ancient people of God, and to Christians, the people of the New Covenant.

The Christian church accepts both the books of the OT and NT as authoritative and divinely inspired, while the Jewish Bible consists of the record of the covenant or "testament" God made with the people and revealed to Moses on Mt. Sinai and to the prophets and other "holy men" of subsequent times. Essentially, the OT is the record of Israel's prophets, while the NT contains the books written by the apostles and other disciples of Jesus Christ.

The word "Bible" comes from the Greek word (neuter plural) meaning "books." As the collection of Holy Scriptures increasingly was regarded as a unity, the transliterated *Biblia* came to be understood as a feminine singular word—"Bible," in English.

The Jews divided their holy Scriptures into three groups: (1) the Law (TORAH) consisting of the PENTATEUCH or first five books of Moses; (2) the PROPHETS, which were subdivided into two groups—the Former Prophets (Joshua, Judges, I and II Samuel and I and II Kings) and the Latter Prophets, including Isaiah, Jeremiah, Ezekiel, and the twelve so-called Minor Prophets; and (3) the Writings, comprised of all the other books of the OT.

In Christ's day these writings were universally regarded by the Jews as divinely inspired and authoritative. Certainly Christ treated the OT as the record of God's self-revelation, even though human beings were employed in its authorship (Luke 24:44-47; Matt. 19:4; 22:29).

While virtually all NT references to the "scriptures" meant the OT books, at least one (II Pet. 3:16) places Paul's writings on the same level of inspiration and authority as "the other scriptures."

Both the OT and the NT were written over a period of many centuries, but in time those recognized as sacred scriptures became known as the CANON of Scripture. The canon of Jewish scripture was not established until action was taken by a council of rabbis at Jamnia (JABNEEL), a town on the northern border of Judah, in A.D. 90.

About two hundred years earlier, Greek-speaking Jews had made a Greek translation of the Hebrew religious books that became known as the SEPTUAGINT (from the Latin word for "seventy.") Some seventy-two Jewish translators produced this translation for Ptolemy II for his library at Alexandria.

Roman Catholic and Eastern Orthodox OT's contain thirteen books known as the APOCRYPHA. These are books that were a part of the Septuagint but were not regarded as canonical by the learned Jewish elders at Jamnia. The first Latin Bibles, including Jerome's VULGATE, were translated from the Greek Septuagint rather than from the Hebrew text. In 1548 the Council of Trent recognized the Apocrypha, except for I and II Edras and the Prayer of Manasses, as being canonical. However, the Reformers repudiated the Apocrypha. As a result, Protestants generally follow in that tradition. Anglicans place some value on the Apocrypha but not for establishing doctrine.

The NT, better translated "new covenant" since the term is based on the prophecy of Jeremiah 31:31-34, which declares that God would make a new covenant with people, does not have the canonical problems of the OT. The apostolic church believed God had made the new covenant in Christ. As the church grew, the apostles and those associated with them wrote the twenty-seven books now accepted as the NT. Toward the end of the second century all NT books except Hebrews, James, II Peter, II and III John, Jude, and Revelation were widely accepted by the church. The canon, as universally received by all of the church today, was first announced in Athanasius' Easter letter in A.D. 367.

Shortly after the end of the fourth century, Jerome had produced the Latin Vulgate, which soon became the most widely used version in the West. And so it continued to be popular for centuries. The first book printed in Europe, the famed Gutenberg Bible of 1456, was an edition of the Vulgate.

The Reformation sparked the need for vernacular publications in the principal languages of Europe. One of the greatest was Luther's translation, which brought the Bible to life in German.

(*See* BIBLE TRANSLATIONS (English); BIBLICAL CRITICISM; BIBLE, TEXT OF.)

R.H.

**BIBLE, TEXT OF.** With few exceptions, the oldest copies of any parts of the Bible in the original languages (Hebrew, Aramaic, and Greek) date from long after the original writing. The oldest known manuscript containing a portion of the Bible is a fragment of the book of Exodus found in the Dead Sea caves and dating from the third century B.C. The oldest copy of any part of the NT, however, is from the early second century A.D.; it contains John 18:31-33. This fragmentary manuscript of John was written within thirty to fifty years of the time of the composition of that Gospel. Copies of parts of the later OT books found at QUMRAN—Daniel, Ecclesiastes, and the Wisdom of Sirach—date from within a hundred years of their literary origin.

In spite of the time gap, and in spite of the thousands of differences in details among the biblical manuscripts, the text of the Bible as a whole is better attested and more carefully preserved than that of any other literature from antiquity. The copies of the Bible from Qumran vary so widely in the style of writing, age, and even in details of content that it has been conjectured that they were brought to Qumran by incoming members of the community, who pooled them as part of the resources of the entire group. Until the discovery of the DEAD SEA SCROLLS, which included more than one hundred copies of smaller and larger portions of what we know as the OT, copies of the Hebrew Bible were known almost solely from medieval manuscripts, preserved in ancient synagogues and libraries. One exception was a document containing brief selections from the OT, including the Ten Commandments and some verses from Deuteronomy. Dating from about 150 B.C. it is known as the Nash Papyrus. Papyrus is a fragile writing material made from reeds that grow in Egypt.

It was exported widely, including huge quantities shipped to Syria. Although it may have been used in Palestine in ancient Israel, by the time of Jeremiah (seventh/sixth centuries B.C.) writing was usually done on leather scrolls, with the subject matter arranged in columns, as Jeremiah 36 attests.

Hebrew was originally written only in consonants, with the reader supplying the vowels in the course of reading aloud. By the ninth century, and perhaps even earlier, copyists began to include vowel markings and punctuation to aid the reader with what was, even then, an archaic language. The oldest dated copy of a text with the vowels supplied is from an ancient synagogue in Cairo and is dated to the equivalent of A.D. 895. These aids to pronunciation of the Hebrew Bible, which are found in the medieval manuscripts, vary considerably. By the tenth century the dominant method was one developed by Ben Asher and his family at Tiberias in Palestine, which had for centuries been a center for rabbinic and scriptural studies.

In the late nineteenth century, other ancient copies of the Hebrew Scriptures, including the Wisdom of Sirach (or Ecclesiasticus), were found in the storeroom of a synagogue also in Cairo. Following the excavations of Qumran, other caves and ancient sites near the Dead Sea were excavated, which resulted in the discovery of portions of the Psalms and the Torah at the fortress of Masada, as well as another copy of Sirach in Hebrew. At other nearby sites copies of the OT in both Hebrew and in Greek translations were found. These documents, dating from the early second century A.D., show that by that time the consonantal text of the Hebrew Bible was fixed—a practice that probably dates from A.D. 70 or shortly thereafter, when the Pharisees, with Roman encouragement, sought to move Judaism away from nationalistic revolt toward religious unity and structure. The premedieval copies of the Hebrew Bible were all in scroll form, rather than codices (a codex is written on separate sheets, bound at the edge, as in our modern books). Some of the earliest fragments of the Greek NT were written as a codex, however, and all the complete ancient copies of the NT (from the fourth century A.D. forward) are codices.

*Style of Writing.* Until a century or so before the birth of Jesus, Hebrew scribes copied the biblical text in one of two types of script: (1) an ancient alphabet, borrowed from the Canaanites, the Semitic tribes whose lands the invading Israelites began occupying in the thirteenth century B.C.; (2) the squarish letters used for writing Aramaic, a Semitic language long and widely used throughout the Near East in antiquity. ARAMAIC and GREEK had largely replaced HEBREW as the common language of Jews in the Hellenistic and Roman periods (see LANGUAGES OF THE ANCIENT NEAR EAST, AND OF THE BIBLE). Some of the Qumran manuscripts are written in the Aramaic script, except that the sacred, unpronounce-able name of God, YHWH, was written in the archaic script. The ancient script was originally pictographic; that is, the letter *Beth* (which means "house") was shaped like a house, and the letter *Mem* (or *Mayim,* meaning "water") was represented by wavy lines.

There were also different ways of writing Greek. One, resembling our printed capital letters, is called *uncials* or *majuscules;* the other, which is similar to modern connected script, is called *cursive* or *minuscule.* The great Greek uncial codices of the NT, which derived from the fourth and fifth centuries and which remain the chief base for the critical reconstruction of the text, were written on PARCHMENT. Their testimony to the ancient text of the NT was importantly supplemented in the late nineteenth and twentieth centuries by the discovery in Egypt of portions of the NT written on PAPYRUS. These documents, which date from the second and third centuries, contribute to the analysis of the Greek text, just as the Hebrew discoveries at the Dead Sea have done more recently for an analysis of the OT text.

*Recovery of the Original Hebrew Text.* The most important witnesses to the Hebrew text of the Bible are contained in these early medieval manuscripts, which seem to have originated through the Tiberias School or one of its rivals. Among them is the Cairo manuscript (dated A.D. 895), mentioned above, which included some of the historical books (Joshua, Judges, Samuel, Kings) and all the prophetic books. A somewhat later document that was taken to Aleppo in Syria by the Crusaders, is now in Jerusalem. A still later copy in the tradition of Tiberias is in Leningrad. These and related manuscripts are largely in agreement on the consonantal text, but it is in the vowels supplied in the so-called "Pointed text" that they differ. The pointing was done in order to assure that the reader would understand the consonantal text in the same way that the scribe (or his tradition) did.

Although rival systems of pronunciations, and hence of interpretation, were produced and have survived, it was with the invention of printing that the Hebrew text became fixed permanently. Unfortunately, the earlier forms of the printed text were based on manuscripts of mixed quality. An edition printed in Venice in 1524, edited by Jacob ben Chayyim, though based on textually unreliable manuscripts, became the standard Hebrew text up to modern times. It was only in the present century that editors of the Hebrew biblical text turned from their basic copy back to the Tiberian tradition of the ninth and tenth centuries. The major breakthrough on this critical matter was made by Gerhard Kittel in the third edition of his *Biblia Hebraica* (in 1937), which he based on an eleventh-century manuscript preserved in Leningrad and to which he in subsequent editions brought the insights and alternate readings of the Dead Sea manuscript finds. An elaborate critical edition is presently in process of preparation at the Hebrew University in Jerusalem, based on the recently acquired Aleppo manuscript mentioned earlier. This edition will take into account a comprehensive range of textual evidence from various traditions, including ancient translations of the Hebrew Bible into various languages.

*The Evidence from Ancient Translations.* Of importance for the reconstruction of the Hebrew text are the translations and paraphrases of Scripture that have survived to the present, but which may be traced back to older archetypes of the Bible than those preserved in the medieval manuscripts on which most recent work on the Hebrew text is so heavily dependent. Among these ancient versions are the Samaritan, the Syriac, the TARGUMS (paraphrases in Aramaic), and the Greek (usually identified as the Septuagint). Comparative studies of the OT text go back at least as far as ORIGEN of Alexandria (third century A.D.), who in an effort to make responsible choices among the various translations of the OT into Greek available in his day aligned the versions in parallel columns together with the Hebrew text and a Greek transliteration of the Hebrew. In developing this six-column work (known as the HEXAPLA) he seems to have used different Hebrew editions available to him, so that his work shows in detail how varied the forms were in which the Hebrew was preserved, both in the original language and in the translations used by Origen.

The Samaritan edition of the Hebrew Pentateuch (which was all of the Bible that the Samaritans regarded as authoritative), is presumably based on a form of the text that is four hundred years older than the Jewish standard text. In thousands of instances, the Samaritan edition is closer to the one that underlies the Greek translations than it is to the Jewish authoritative text. At the same time that the standard Jewish text was being shaped and given authority by the traditionalist scribes (known as MASORETES), the centuries-long custom of having a paraphrase in Aramaic in the synagogues immediately following the reading of the Hebrew original began to be codified in the Targums. Different editions of the Targums appeared in Palestine and in Babylonia, where large numbers of Jews had remained even after many returned to Judea from the exile at the end of the sixth century B.C. The two best-known Targums are those linked with Onkelos and Jonathan, both of which are now known in forms edited in Babylonia in the fifth century A.D. Also important is the Targum of the Pentateuch, usually known as Pseudo-Jonathan. The oldest Targums extant are those found in fragmentary form at Qumran, including one on Job and another on Genesis, usually called the Genesis Apocryphon. Although all these are free paraphrases in most passages, they do point to a Hebrew text, which on occasion is significantly different from the Masoretic standard.

The Syriac-speaking Christians by the middle of the second century A.D. had made a translation, not only of the Greek NT, but also of the Hebrew Bible.

Since Syriac is a language closely akin to Aramaic, the Syriac version shows the influence of the Targums, as well as of the Greek version so widely used by the early Christians. Indeed, different sources seem to have been used for different books of the OT. Later on, other Syriac versions were prepared by different sects of the Syriac church.

*The Primary Translation for the Christians: The Greek Old Testament.* The versions of the OT most significant for both Jews and Christians are those in Greek, some of which date back to the third century B.C. Long before the time of Origen, the Hebrew text of the Bible was being transliterated into Greek for Jews whose basic language was Greek, but who wanted to hear the Bible as nearly as possible in the sound of the original Hebrew. Later legend (in the Letter of Aristeas) reported that Ptolemy II of Egypt (285-246 B.C.) had responded to mounting interest in the Jewish Bible among his subjects by arranging for a team of seventy-two translators to come from Palestine (six from each of the twelve tribes) to prepare a definitive translation of their Bible into Greek. The number was later rounded off at seventy, which in its Latin form, SEPTUAGINTA (LXX), became the common designation of the dominant Greek version of the Bible. Historically it is more likely that different books were translated at different times and only later assembled in the complete LXX.

Copies of the Bible in Greek have been found that go back as early as the second century B.C. Copies from the second century A.D. and later have been found in both Egypt and Palestine, so that a base is provided for a broad and detailed analysis of what became the standard Greek version of the OT. Significant variations from the LXX appear, however, as in a fragment from Qumran Cave 4, in which the name of God is transliterated from the Hebrew as IAO, rather than being replaced by the title *Kyrios* ("Lord"), which is standard in the LXX. Some scholars assess this new evidence as proving that there was indeed an original Greek translation, as the Septuagint legend implies, but that it was later modified and paraphrased in subsequent usage. Others think that there was a free range of translations into Greek available in the centuries before and after the birth of Jesus. According to this second theory, it was only in the hands of the Christians—who adopted the Greek version as their official OT—that it developed into the standard form we now know as the LXX. One could point to the various Christian translations (by Aquila, Symmachus, and Theodotion in the second century A.D.) and Origen's effort to sort through this evidence as supporting the second theory. But the Hexapla of Origen could as well be interpreted to be Origen's attempt to recover the original of the LXX.

Similar problems arise in relation to the various Old Latin translations, which were carried out in dependence on the LXX. They were widely used prior to Jerome's production in the late fourth century A.D.

of the Common Version, known as the VULGATE, which he based directly on the Hebrew.

*Recovering the Original Greek Text of the New Testament.* The evidence for the reconstructing of the Greek NT overlaps in some degree that for the Hebrew Bible, but it is far more extensive. W. G. Kümmel, in his *Introduction to the New Testament* (1975) gives the following statistics on NT manuscripts: 85 papyri; 268 majuscules; 2,792 minuscules. In addition to the latter group, in which the text is written in unbroken sequence as in our modern translations, there are 2,193 manuscripts in lection-ary form, broken up into smaller units for public reading in the context of worship. The division of the NT into the chapters that we now use was done about A.D. 1200. Three hundred years later a Parisian edition marked off the present system of verses.

In addition to the John Rylands Library fragment of John mentioned earlier there are papyrus manuscripts of two of the Gospels, Matthew and Luke, which date from around A.D. 200. From the second and third centuries is a series of papyri, including the Gospels and Acts; all the letters of Paul, plus Hebrews; and part of Revelation. Other papyri from

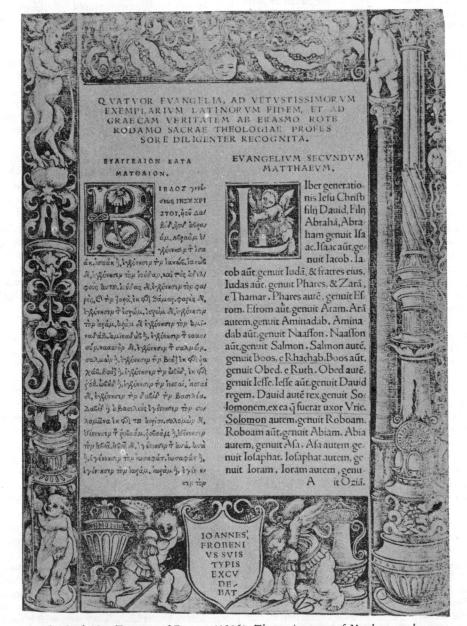

*The Greek New Testament of Erasmus (1516). The opening verses of Matthew are shown.*

the third century include copies of John, the letters of Peter and Jude, Luke and John, all of which give general and detailed support to the type of Greek text found in the early majuscules (or uncials), to which we now turn.

As the church became more affluent and more solidly grounded culturally, handsome manuscript copies of the entire NT on parchment were produced. Written in elegant calligraphy, probably in Egypt, they have been carefully preserved—at first in churches or monasteries and now in museums. Before evaluating the textual testimony of these imposing documents, however, it is essential to consider the system of classification of the types of text of the NT preserved in this array of manuscript witnesses. It was only in the nineteenth and twentieth centuries that this sorting out of text types was carried out on a broad basis. What had happened with the Hebrew and Greek OT—the drive to overcome the difficulties presented by the diverse forms of the biblical text through the shaping of a single, standardized, "Received Text"—is apparent in the transmission of the text of the NT as well. By far the majority of the manuscripts that have survived to the present do embody a text that includes expansions and modifications of the Greek text, which are absent in the demonstrably older manuscripts.

There was, therefore, a RECEIVED TEXT, without it being so designated. In the sixteenth century, however, under the impact of the Protestant movement, with its emphasis on the Bible and its accessibility to all believers, it was determined to prepare a standard printed version of the Greek Text. This was undertaken by ERASMUS, a scholar engaged by a printer in Basel, Switzerland. Unfortunately, he used as his base late flawed manuscripts, which included passages that are clearly later additions (such as Mark 16:9-20). They also lacked some verses from Revelation, but Erasmus took care of that by making his own (clumsy) translation from the Latin back into Greek. Not only was this the edition used by Luther in his monumental German translation and by the translators of the King James Version of the Bible into English, but it became the standard Greek Text of the NT well into the nineteenth century.

There was, however, no single alternative Greek Text that was generally recognized as preferable to the Received Text. Beginning with Karl Lachmann in 1831, however, scholars began to compare and assess the textual evidence, not only from the oldest available manuscripts, but also from the testimony to be derived from the ancient translations of the NT and from the quotations of it in the writings of the fathers of the church. Konstantin von Tischendorf, who had managed to bring back to Europe the monks' most prized NT manuscript, from St. Katherine's Monastery on Mount Sinai, proceeded to use the Codex SINAITICUS as the base for his reconstruction of the Greek Text. In Britain, B. F. Westcott and F. J. A. Hort had used Codex Vaticanus as their primary

textual standard, and referred to their results as "the Neutral Text," by which they meant that it was free from the errors that had crept into other manuscripts. Both Vaticanus and Sinaiticus, which date from the fourth century, differ from the later majuscules and most of the later minuscules, which represent the inclusive version that corresponds to the Received Text and are accordingly of little value in the effort to recover the original form of the text.

Although some of the translations of the Greek NT into other languages (such as Syriac and Latin) are older than many of the Greek manuscripts, they are only occasionally helpful in recovering the purer form of the text, since they are not literal translations and since they tend to be based on the eclectic Received Text.

Although Westcott and Hort's classification scheme for the manuscripts has not found universal support, it has dominated the discussion in a useful way. They distinguished the following text types: (1) the Syrian Text, which is basically the Received Text and is represented by many of the majuscules and nearly all the minuscules; (2) the Western Text, for which the chief representatives are Codex Bezae (comprising two bilingual manuscripts, in Latin and Greek) and the type of text used by several Western church fathers (for example, Justin, Irenaeus, Tertullian); (3) the Neutral Text, represented by Vaticanus and less accurately by Sinaiticus, though both seem to have escaped extensive alteration from the supposedly original form; (4) the Alexandrine Text, used by Origen and the Coptic (Egyptian) versions, and similar to the Neutral Text.

After this scheme was proposed, however, it was perceived that the so-called Western Text had actually been used by writers in the Eastern churches as well, and further, that the "Western" text types vary so widely from manuscript to manuscript as to call into question the designation of a Western text type at all. This group of manuscripts may evidence nothing more than a free-wheeling text tradition that developed concurrently with the more conservative Egyptian type best represented by Vaticanus and Sinaiticus. Yet in individual cases, the textual evidence from the Western type manuscripts must be taken into account in the effort to reconstruct the original text.

Still useful is the critical rule drawn up in the nineteenth century: "The preferred reading is the difficult one; the shorter reading is the more significant." While it is important that sifting of textual evidence continues, it is useful to remember that the proportion of the Greek NT about which there is critical agreement is astonishingly large, while the number of seriously disputed passages is surprisingly few.        H.K.

**BIBLE TRANSLATIONS** (English). While no complete Bible version was translated into Anglo-Saxon, some portions of Scripture in that tongue have been discovered. There were also versions of certain books produced in English during the thirteenth century.

Some historians have credited JOHN WYCLIFFE, of the fourteenth century, with being the first translator of the Bible in English, but later research does not seem to confirm this. Possibly Wycliffe may have contributed to one of two "Wycliffe" versions, but they undoubtedly were the work of two of his followers. The first translation from the Latin VULGATE by Nicholas of Hereford was published at the end of the fourteenth century. The second version, said to be in more idiomatic English, was the work of John Purvey, Wycliffe's secretary. Shortly after their appearance, the two versions were proscribed by the church, and orders went out prohibiting translations made "without diocesan or synodical" permission.

A number of factors paved the way for the publication of the milestone version of WILLIAM TYNDALE: (1) the invention of printing, which resulted in the production of the GUTENBERG (Vulgate) Bible in 1456; (2) the spread of Greek learning and the publication of Erasmus' Greek NT (1516); (3) the Latin translation of the Hebrew Bible by Santes Pagninus, an Italian Dominican scholar (1528); and (4) the spread of the Protestant Reformation and particularly the publication of Luther's German vernacular NT in 1522 and complete Bible in 1534.

Tyndale, who had studied Greek at Cambridge, had heard of Erasmus' call for Bibles in the vernacular. Knowing that the church forbade unauthorized translations, Tyndale decided to conduct his work on the Continent. After a start at Cologne, Tyndale moved to Worms, where the first printed edition of the English NT was completed in 1526. There is evidence that he was greatly influenced by Luther's rendering of the German NT.

Tyndale began work on the OT, completing the Pentateuch in 1530 and Jonah in 1531. George Joye, another Englishman, joined Tyndale on the Continent and worked with him for a while, but he ultimately betrayed Tyndale by running off with a pirated edition of the NT. Undaunted, Tyndale produced a second NT version (1534), which had a strong influence on the phrasing of the KING JAMES VERSION. Tyndale was arrested near Brussels in 1535, and was strangled and burned at the stake in 1536. He had not completed a translation of the entire Bible.

Meanwhile the situation had been changing in England. The church had broken with Rome, creating a better climate for Bible translations. In 1534 the Canterbury Convocation asked permission of Henry VIII to translate the entire Bible into English. MILES COVERDALE, a British scholar who had worked with Tyndale in Germany and Antwerp, was chosen for the task. Depending heavily on Tyndale's labors, Coverdale's Bible was published in 1535 with royal approval.

In 1537 another English translation appeared, which purported to be the work of Thomas Matthew. This undoubtedly was the work of John Rogers, a former assistant of Tyndale. Actually the so-called Matthew's Bible was essentially a compilation of Tyndale's work including portions that had not reached print. It also contained some of the work of Coverdale and others. It is ironic that this approved translation, largely the work of Tyndale, appeared in print a year after his death.

These versions of Scripture were followed by the Great Bible of 1539, in reality Coverdale's revision of Matthew's Bible. The Great Bible had the advantage of royal approval, and orders were given that copies of it be provided to parish churches throughout the land. Because this version contained a preface by the archbishop of Canterbury, Thomas Cranmer, it came to be called Cranmer's Bible.

The *Geneva Bible* (1560) was produced by William Whittingham, an Oxford graduate, and other Protestant exiles in Geneva. This is the first English translation to divide the text into verses or numbered paragraphs. Since the Geneva Bible was dedicated to Elizabeth, it was circulated without difficulty. It soon became the Bible of Protestant homes.

Courtesy of the American Bible Society

*The Geneva Bible of 1560*

Churchmen who objected to the Reformed slant of the Geneva Bible ordered the publication of a version known as the Bishops' Bible, published in 1568. But it never had the impact of the Geneva Bible, which was the Bible of Shakespeare and the pilgrim fathers. Excerpts from it were employed in Cromwell's soldier's pocket Bible.

During Elizabeth's reign Roman Catholic exiles developed their version of Scripture. The chief translator (from the Vulgate) was Gregory Martin, who lived in exile in Flanders. This came to be known as the DOUAY-RHEIMS BIBLE.

But probably the greatest Bible in English was the King James Version, published in 1611 and still popular today after more than three centuries. At the Hampton Court Conference convened by James I in 1604 "for the hearing, and for the determining of things pretended to be amiss in the Church," John Reynolds, president of Corpus Christi College, Oxford, and a Puritan, made the motion that a new translation of Scriptures be made. The king seized upon the suggestion and the project was approved immediately. Consequently six companies of scholars were appointed, ostensibly to revise the Bishops' Bible. However, the translators turned to the Hebrew and Greek original texts in making a faithful translation. The majestic cadences of this great version have never been surpassed. Although Tyndale had set a standard for beautiful language, which continued in this version, the KJV has had unparalleled influence on English literature. Although it is known as the Authorized Version in Britain, the evidence that it was ever authorized by order in council cannot be proved. However, it gained acceptance by its essential character.

With the growth of biblical scholarship in the succeeding centuries and the discovery of a number of ancient manuscripts that were not known to the KJV translators, scholars began to see the need for a major revision.

In 1870 a proposal for such a version was made at the Centerbury Convocation. Certain principles were to be followed, such as adherence as much as possible to the language of the KJV. When changes were made, they were to be noted in the margins of the revised text.

The REVISED VERSION of the NT was published simultaneously in London and New York in 1881. The OT segment followed in 1885. Appendices indicated instances where British and American translators disagreed. The AMERICAN STANDARD VERSION, which was an independent work of the American revisers, was published in 1901.

Toward the end of the nineteenth century and throughout the twentieth century a spate of translations have been produced.

J. N. DARBY, an Irish clergyman who became the prominent leader of the Plymouth Brethren, translated the Bible into both French and German before rendering it into English. His New Translation was one of several attempts at literal translation that sought to be faithful to the Greek and Hebrew text but were lacking in English style.

The Twentieth Century NT (1901) was produced by a group of anonymous translators, none of whom had wide acceptance as scholars, it was later revealed.

The noted British classical scholar, Arthur S. Way, translated a portion of the NT, calling it *Letters of St. Paul to Seven Churches and Three Friends* (1901). Another classicist, Richard F. Weymouth, produced the NT in Modern Speech, which was published in the year of his death (1903). JAMES MOFFAT's New Translation of the NT appeared in 1913 and the complete Bible in 1928 and 1935. In the same period came The NT: An American Translation by EDGAR J. GOODSPEED (1923). Goodspeed started work on the OT translation but delegated its completion to J. M. P. Smith for publication in 1935.

Helen Barrett Montgomery, an American Greek scholar, produced The New Testament in Modern Speech, which was published in 1924 to celebrate the centenary of the American Baptist Publication Society of Philadelphia.

A leader of the Jehovah's Witnesses, A. E. Knoch, with several colleagues prepared *The Concordant Bible* (1921 and 1926). Since Knoch was self-taught in Greek, his translation has not had great acceptance beyond the bounds of his special constituency.

J. B. Phillips, an Anglican clergyman, issued his *Letters to Young Churches* in 1947. This was followed by *The Gospels* in 1952, the *Young Church in Action* in 1955, and *The Book of Revelation* in 1957. The NT IN MODERN ENGLISH, and appealing paraphrase, was published in 1958.

Under the sponsorship of the International Council of Religious Education, which later became a part of the National Council of the Churches of Christ in the U.S.A., a committee of American and Canadian scholars set to work on an official revision of the American Standard Version. Because of its sponsorship by the NCC, this REVISED STANDARD VERSION was spurned by many American ultraconservatives even though the new version was promoted vigorously by the major United States denominations as a sort of official translation. But its superior scholarship won it acclaim in Great Britain and other countries of the English-speaking world. Roman Catholics also found it to be a worthy translation. The NT was published in 1946, the entire Bible in 1952, and the Apocrypha in 1957. It can properly claim to be a legitimate descendant of both Tyndale's Bible and the King James Version.

British scholars, not to be outdone by their American counterparts, decided it was time that a Bible that would render the original languages into "timeless English" needed to be produced. A Joint Committee on the New Translation of the Bible was formed, and its general director was the learned biblical scholar Charles Harold Dodd. Oxford University Press and Cambridge University Press became the joint publishers. On the 350th anniversary of the publication of the King James Version (1961), the NT of the NEW ENGLISH BIBLE appeared. The complete Bible, with the Apocrypha, was published in 1970.

Roman Catholics, besides publishing a Catholic translation of the RSV in 1966, were concerned about translations that were not bound by the limitations of the Latin Vulgate. In 1941 the Confraternity of Christian Doctrine published a NT translation, a revision of the Challoner Douay-Rheims Version (1750). THE NEW AMERICAN BIBLE "translated from the original languages" appeared in 1970.

Both Protestants and Catholics have embraced THE JERUSALEM BIBLE published in English in 1966. It was based upon the labors of French scholars who had worked at the Dominican Biblical School in Jerusalem. Under the general editorship of Pére Roland de Vaux, La Bible de Jerusalem had first appeared in French in 1961.

Jewish scholars have also been concerned about producing readable translations of their scriptures. The first rendering in English was accomplished by Isaac Leeser in 1853. The Jewish Publication Society (JPS) of America produced its first translation in 1917. In 1962 the JPS published the Torah, a new translation of "the Holy Scriptures according to the Masoretic Text." Volumes on the Prophets and Writings have followed.

Even so with so many substantial translations available to them, the urge to publish new versions of the Bible in contemporary English seems to have no end. The Berkeley Version in Modern English, under the editorship of Gerrit Verkuyl, was published in 1945 (NT) and 1959 (entire Bible). In England, E. V. Rieu's Four Gospels and C. H. Rieu's the Acts of the Apostles appeared in 1952 and 1957. The Basic English Bible, which confined itself to one thousand commonly employed words, was published in 1940 (NT) and 1949 (entire Bible). C. R. Williams followed with the Plain English Version.

Earlier in the United States, another Williams (Charles B.), an American scholar, had produced The New Testament: A Translation in the Language of the People (1937). William F. Beck, a Lutheran, was the scholar responsible for The Holy Bible in the Language of Today. The NT appeared in 1963 and the full Bible in 1976. William Barclay, the noted Scottish biblical scholar and commentator, produced The New Testament: A New Translation in 1968 and 1969. The Lockman Foundation of LaHabra, California, sponsored the anonymous translation, The Amplified Bible (1954–64). The same Lockman organization also sponsored the NEW AMERICAN STANDARD VERSION of the Scriptures (1960–75), which, like the Revised Standard Version, is considered in the same family as the KJV and the ASV. This Bible (NASV) has appealed to conservative evagelicals who have felt that the NCC-sponsored volume reflects liberal scholarship. Its competitors in the marketplace are The Living Bible and the New International Version.

THE LIVING BIBLE was the project of Kenneth Taylor, who began it as a means of making the Scriptures comprehensible to his children. Because his work did not find acceptance with publishers who felt the modern idiom Bible market was surfeited, Taylor launched his own publishing concern in Wheaton, Illinois. After a slow start The Living Bible soon saw sales soar to the multiple millions. The Living Bible set records in a market that experts felt was saturated. Honestly labeled as a paraphrase, Taylor's unique venture of rendering the Bible in colloquial American speech has had unparalleled acceptance. Adoptions have been produced in many languages around the world.

THE NEW INTERNATIONAL VERSION of the Bible was translated by more than one hundred evangelical scholars. The project had its beginning in 1965, after several years of exploratory study by committees from the Christian Reformed Church and the National Association of Evangelicals. In 1967 the New York Bible Society, later renamed the International Bible Society, provided the financing. Starting out with the Gospel of John in 1970, other books of the Bible were translated until the NT made its appearance in 1973 and the complete Bible in 1978. From the start the NIV has met with success, and already millions of the new version have been sold.

THE GOOD NEWS BIBLE (Today's English Version) was a translation project of the American Bible Society. Under the guideline of using "common English," this work of Robert E. Bratcher, former missionary to South America, produced The New Testament in Today's English Version, which was first published in 1966. Known widely as the TEV, the entire Bible was released in 1976 as The Good News Bible—The Bible in Today's English Version. From the start this popular contemporary version of the Scriptures met with wide acceptance. Today, similar Bibles, based on the same philosophy of translation, have appeared in a number of modern languages.

The Anchor Bible, which is more a commentary than a translation, began to appear in 1964 and will continue until its thirty-eight volumes are completed. The publishers of Reader's Digest sponsored a condensation of the Revised Standard Version in 1982. It was designed to encourage the reading of the entire Bible from cover to cover. The publishers insist it is a condensation, not an abridgment.

R.H.

**BIBLE VERSIONS** (Non-English). Western Christians generally think of the church moving out from its birthplace in Palestine into what was then called Asia, now a part of Turkey. From thence the missionary journeys of Paul and his companions are properly credited with introducing the gospel to Europe.

However, the gospel evidently also moved out in other directions, to the Parthian Empire east of the Euphrates and ultimately as far east as India and China. Other emissaries of the risen Lord moved south into Africa and to the land around the

Mediterranean. The faithful itinerant witnesses universally carried with them the scriptures of the OT—if not scrolls, certainly in their minds and hearts.

As we know, there were "Parthians and Medes and Elamites, and the dwellers in Mesopotamia" included among the throngs who gathered for that first Christian Pentecost in Jerusalem. The records that verify this eastward movement after Pentecost have not yet been found. But we have evidence that before the end of the first century, Christianity had reached the Arbela district to the east of the Tigris and east of Nineveh. Actually many in those parts, most of whom spoke Aramaic, were first converted to Judaism. Before long Christianity was established in Upper Mesopotamia, and the city of Edessa became the chief center for disseminating the gospel in those parts as well as on into the Far East. The Syriac church became the major conduit of the redemptive message. Syria was the name given to Christian Aramaic.

Probably the first Bible translated from the original Hebrew of the OT was the Syriac OT. Theodore of Mopsuestia wrote in A.D. 400 that "the Bible had been translated into the tongue of the Syrians," but he did not know who undertook that linguistic task or when it occurred. But it was well before his time apparently.

The PESHITTA, or simple version of the Syriac OT, may have been a Jewish or Christian translation. In any case this Peshitta was in use among Christians by the beginning of the third century. The Peshitta NT was completed sometime in the fifth century, but the DIATESSARON, a harmony of the Four Gospels, was compiled by Tatian about A.D. 170.

Meanwhile, the Western world was influenced by the translation of the Bible into Latin. Jerome's VULGATE, "common" or "popular" version, became the Bible of western Europe, and even today it is a most revered translation of the Roman Catholic Church. For centuries it was the one and only official version of the Roman church.

There had been a bewildering variety of Latin texts before Jerome under the bidding of Pope Damasus, bishop of Rome, worked from A.D. 386 to 404 to complete this landmark translation of the Scriptures. By that time Latin had superseded Greek as the official language of the civilized world. It was Jerome's Vulgate that formed the text of the GUTENBERG Bible in 1456—the first Bible printed in Europe. WYCLIFFE and his disciples first translated the Bible into English from Jerome's Vulgate.

In the early centuries of the Christian Era the Bible was translated into Armenian, Georgian, Sogdianese, an Indo-Iranian language, Coptic, Ethiopic, Arabic, and even Gothic. The Goths who sacked Rome in 410 had already been Christianized. Their bishop Ulfilas, the "Apostle of the Goths," translated their Bible in the part of Europe now known as Bulgaria. By the ninth century the Slavonic peoples had their own Scriptures.

Courtesy of the British Library

*Arabic manuscript of the book of Job, written in the first half of the ninth century* A.D. *(British Museum add. 26116), showing Job 22:12 ff.*

There are three epochs in the work of Bible translation: (1) the period between A.D. 150 and 450; (2) the Reformation age, which gave us Luther's German Bible (1522–34), the French versions of Lefevre and Olivetan (1534, 1535), the Spanish and Czech translations of 1602, Diodati's Italian translation of 1607, and most important to us the English translations of TYNDALE and his successors; (3) the missionary revival period beginning early in the nineteenth century.

The Reformation's emphasis on biblical rather than ecclesiastical authority inevitably promoted vernacular translations of Holy Scripture. The invention of the printing press aided the movement that made Bibles available to the general Christian public. When Luther, under the ban of the church and the empire, retreated to Wartburg Castle, he devoted himself to translating Erasmus' Greek NT into German. It was a significant milestone of the Reformation, and it set a standard soon duplicated in other countries, including England.

When the Protestant missionary movement sent heralds of the gospel to hitherto unreached countries of the world in the eighteenth century, these sturdy evangelists also became linguists. For example, WILLIAM CAREY arrived in India in 1794 and rapidly mastered the language. Soon he was translating the Scriptures into Bengali. Thereafter he learned Sanskrit and Marathi, and in his lifetime supervised and edited translations of the Bible into thirty-six languages.

The Pietists in Germany were pioneers in founding the Van Canstein Bible Society in 1710. The wave of missionary fervor inspired the founding of the British and Foreign Bible Society in 1804, and the AMERICAN BIBLE SOCIETY in 1816. Both societies aggressively pursued the translation and distribution of the Scriptures in many foreign tongues. Because of a duplication of efforts, it became apparent that a worldwide coordinating agency needed to be formed. This occurred after World War II when the UNITED BIBLE SOCIETIES was established. Today, all of the major languages of the world—Mandarin, English, Hindi, Spanish, Russian, German, Japanese, Malay, Bengali, French, Portuguese, and Italian—possess Bibles.

Missionaries working in obscure tribes recognized that there were many smaller language groups without their own translations of Scripture. Two American missionaries to Latin America, L. L. Legters and W. Cameron Townsend, realized the enormousness of the task of reaching the many tribal peoples of the world. In 1934 they conducted a summer school in descriptive linguistics for pioneer missionaries at "Camp Wycliffe" in Arkansas. Soon this fledgling operation began to work in the Indian tribes of Mexico. In 1942 they organized two parallel organizations—Wycliffe Bible Translators and the Summer Institute of Linguistics, SIL representing the scientific, linguistic, and cultural fields as a non-sectarian entity. These organizations took on the tasks of making contacts with foreign governments and conducting summer training programs in several contributing countries. WBT was assigned the work of enlisting Christian linguists and seeking financial support from churches. Today the Wycliffe organization has become the largest force of Bible translators in the world.

The United Bible Societies published in 1975 its first listing of the languages in which at least some portion of the Scriptures has been translated. By 1974 the list included 1,549 languages. Since then the numbers have escalated. To bring vernacular translations to all the peoples of the world is a formidable task even though the science of linguistics has leaped forward. In 1960 Wycliffe workers published the book *Two Thousand Tongues to Go.*

Through the efforts of the Bible societies and other organizations, contemporary translations of Scripture have been rendered in most of the major languages. The American Bible Society has been promoting equivalent foreign versions of the Good News Bible, and Living Bibles International is rendering colloquial translations comparable to the popular American paraphrase, the Living Bible. (*Compare* BIBLE TRANSLATIONS.)

R.H.

**BIBLICAL CRITICISM.** Under the influence of the Renaissance commitment to the freedom of the human mind from ecclesiastical dogma and the surge of interest in the reappropriation of human intellectual and cultural achievements in past ages, theological scholarship began in the mid-seventeenth century to raise critical questions about the Bible. These lines of inquiry were stimulated by the philosophical movements of the eighteenth century in England and Germany (Deism and the Enlightenment), which shifted attention from the remote God to the immanent activity of the human mind. Biblical criticism, as it came to be called, asked the same questions about the Bible and its origins that classical scholars were asking about the ancient documents with which they were concerned: How and why were these books written? What was the original text? What were the sources used by the writer? What historical factors can be discerned from work behind and within the documents? What were the special aims of the writer and the special interests of his intended audience? What social and cultural factors—acknowledged or unacknowledged—helped to shape the material as we now have it?

*Textual Criticism.* The Jewish scholars gathered at the so-called Council of JAMNIA at the end of the first century A.D. not only formulated the official list of Hebrew scriptures called the CANON, but also sought to determine the definitive Hebrew TEXT of the Bible. In the sixteenth century an official rabbinic edition of the Bible was published in Venice, the Biblia Rabbiniea, which became the norm, and is in use down to the present day. It included not only the consonants in which Hebrew is written, but also the stylized diacritical marks, which indicate the vowels to be read with the consonants. In 1678, however, a Roman Catholic priest named Richard Simon published his *Critical History of the Old Testament,* in which he sought to show that behind the written documents can be discerned earlier, oral sources, and that Moses did not write the first five books of the Bible, which had been traditionally attributed to him.

Although Simon's work was rejected by the church initially, it elicited interest in England and Germany, where work was undertaken in analysis of the OT to determine what its original text was, drawing not only on the Hebrew evidence but using the ancient Greek version, the Septuagint, as well. Furthermore, other Semitic languages were studied with the aim of determining more precisely the meanings of biblical words and place names, for which the lexicon of WILLIAM GESENIUS (1786–1842) became an enduring standard reference.

The preparation in Basel of a printed text of the Greek NT, which set the standard for the so-called *Textus Receptus,* was marred by the fact that Erasmus used inferior manuscript resources in preparing this edition, and at some points translated from the standard Latin text what he thought the Greek ought to have said. The efforts by German scholars to determine rules by which one might decide among differences within the manuscript evidence (especially J. J. Griesbach, 1745–1812) and the discovery of new ancient manuscript copies of the NT (the most notable being that found by C. von Tischendorf at Mount Sinai and published by him in 1862) combined to prepare for the publication of carefully edited critical editions of the Greek NT. Of these the dominant editions were, in Britain, that of B. F. Westcott and F. J. A. Hort (1881–82) and the German tradition linked with the names of B. Weiss, E. Nestle, and KURT ALAND (1894 to the present). Some scholars think, however, that these widely used editions do not reflect adequately the evidence from other ancient sources: the early translations of the NT into Syriac, Armenian, and Georgian, for example.

The process of textual reconstruction for the OT has been greatly aided by the discovery of the DEAD SEA SCROLLS, copies of many parts of the Hebrew scriptures in the first-century library at QUMRAN. The result of this research and these discoveries is that the textual criticism, and, therefore, textual reconstruction of the Bible, rests on the broadest basis and the most fully examined principles of any literary document from the ancient world. Nearly all the modern translations of the Bible not only take into account the manuscript discoveries and the careful textual analyses that have been carried out, but they also frequently indicate the variations in meaning derived from this evidence through variants that are given in notes with which the translations are interspersed.

*Historical Criticism.* The discovery of abundant literary and archaeological evidence contemporary with the events reported in the Bible and with the writing of these books sacred to Jews and Christians raises two basic questions: How accurate as historical documents are the biblical narratives? What credence is to be given to the extraordinary events reported in the Bible, including accounts of direct divine action in human affairs and the performance of miracles by human beings? An overarching question would be, Of what historical worth is the Bible? Two of the leading figures who led off the development of historical criticism were J. D. Michaelis (1717–91), whose work in Semitic languages and archaeology enabled him to explain and interpret the Bible in light of historical setting, and J. S. Semler (1721–92), who insisted that the importance of a biblical writing lay in the insight that it provided human beings rather than in any divinely imposed authority, as was implied by the concept of canon.

The historical method developed on down into the eighteenth century in two distinct ways: one group of scholars emphasized the aesthetic and humane values that are present in the biblical writings, especially in the poetic passages (as in J. G. Herder, 1744–1803), while J. G. Eichhorn (1752–1827) sought to combine the historical and contextual features of Semler's work with the romantic appeal of Herder. It was the latter interest that was developed and made more precise by W. M. L. de Wette (1780–1849), who worked to reconstruct the circumstances of the writing of the biblical books, including both the historical setting and the literary styles and methods employed. This method of illuminating the meaning of Scripture by comparing and contrasting it with what other cultures were doing, thinking and saying in the ancient world contemporary with the Bible has proved to be an enormously helpful and illuminating enterprise. It makes possible sensitive understanding of what human aspirations and anxieties were, how people felt oppressed or threatened by the political and social forces that shaped their lives, and how the divine promise gave them hope of release and renewal.

Ironically, the freeing of scriptural interpretation from the dogmatic authority of the church was soon matched by the scholars adopting certain hypotheses about the movement of history and arranging the historical picture to conform to those assumptions. In nineteenth-century Germany, where the intellectual life was dominated by the theory of G. W. F. HEGEL (1770–1831) and his notion that the course of history is determined by the forces and counterforces of history out of which a new third possibility emerges inevitably (thesis—antithesis—synthesis), the history of the NT period was forced into the following pattern: first there was Paul's system of a law-free gospel; then came a type of Christianity in the name of the disciples of Jesus which sought to make Christians subject to Jewish law; from this emerged the universal Christianity of the post-apostolic period. A comparable system has been imposed on the NT evidence in the present century through the writings of RUDOLF BULTMANN (1884–1976). Building on the work of his predecessors in the so-called History-of-Religions School of thought, R. Reitzenstein (1861–1931) and W. Bousset (1865–1920), Bultmann represented the first century in NT times as a period in which Paul and the leaders of the Gentile churches used an allegedly widespread myth of a heavenly redeemer figure who comes to earth to achieve human redemption, and thereby they created a Hellenistic mystery cult centered upon Jesus. The second phase came in a reaction to this construct on the part of Jewish Christians, who sought to depict Jesus along more Jewish lines, especially drawing on apocalyptic imagery. This conflict of theological viewpoints brought the third stage: the church became institutionalized, and its freedom in thought and action was transformed into a dogmatic, authoritative system. In variant forms, this construction of NT history continues to have its adherents down to the later twentieth century, even though the Gnostic myth cannot be demonstrated before the second century A.D., and the evidence must be coerced in order to fit the pattern.

Major contributions to the providing of material with which the people of the Bible could be compared and contrasted were made by W. F. ALBRIGHT and A. DEISSMANN. Albright's encyclopedic works included the exploration of archaeological evidence and the study of literary and inscriptional materials from all over the Middle East, with the result that there was available a vast array of comparative evidence for the historical analysis of life in Bible times. Deissmann's study of the language and the contents of a great mass of letters and other documents from Egypt, in the centuries before and after the birth of Jesus, shed light on the common Greek language of the period, as well as on patterns of social and economic life at that time. The latter study has been carried further through the lexical work of W. BAUER and G. KITTEL—projects that have been translated and adapted in English. The discoveries at QUMRAN and in the Gnostic library at NAG HAMMADI have greatly enhanced our historical knowledge of this period from the first down into the second and third centuries.

*Literary Criticism.* The need for identifying the sources behind the biblical writings was noted by the earliest historical critics, but the results of that undertaking became evident and useful only in the nineteenth century. Building on the work of his teachers, J. WELLHAUSEN (1844–1918) propounded what is referred to as the DOCUMENTARY HYPOTHESIS, the theory that there are four literary strands that underlie the first five books of the Bible: J (in which the God of Israel is called "Yahweh," or in common usage, Jehovah); E (in which God is called Elohim); D, which is the reworking of older material from the point of view represented in Deuteronomy; P, which represents another editing from the point of view of the priests.

On the NT side, questions raised as to which Gospel was written first and whether the original language was Greek or Aramaic continue to be debated, but the following consensus has emerged: that there was a period of oral transmission of the tradition now included in the Gospels that continued after the Gospels were written; that the First Gospel was Mark, which was used as a basic source by Matthew and Luke; that the latter two Gospels also drew upon a source called Q (from the German word for source, *Quelle*), which consisted chiefly of sayings of Jesus; that the Gospel writers were not bound by the tradition, but adapted it to serve the needs of the particular community of Christians that was addressed in each Gospel. John is the example of the freest modification of the tradition and of the inclusion of a structure and a style that has no counterpart in the other three Gospels. As an important part of the detailed analysis of the Gospels,

scholars have noted the ways in which the writers also adapted, for their own purposes, the literary styles and patterns (or genres) in use in their time, such as letters, biography, narrative style, romances, apocalypses, and liturgical forms.

*Form-criticism.* This analytical method (which literally translated from its German origins would be form-history) seeks to identify and to analyze the small patterns of speech and narrative that lie behind the written documents of the Bible, which share certain cultural features with other writings of biblical times and which can be shown to have fulfilled certain specific functions for the writer and his community. In the OT, these forms would include patterns of prophetic speech, narrative, and psalms (H. GUNKEL, 1862–1932). Scandinavian scholars responded to this method by emphasizing the sociological (J. Pedersen) and cultic (S. Mowinckel) functions of this formal material.

In NT studies, form-criticism emerged as an important method through the work of K. L. Schmidt (1891–1956), whose study of Mark showed the importance of the connecting passages in the Gospel, which linked what was likely unorganized, free-floating material in the oral tradition, and did so to serve the needs of instruction and worship within the life of the Markan community. M. DIBELIUS (1883–1947) and R. Bultmann developed their studies of the Gospel tradition along similar lines. Each gave attention to the life-situation (SITZ-IM-LEBEN) of Jesus, of the church that preserved the tradition, and of the evangelist who incorporated it into his account. Dibelius was more interested in literary classification of material, while Bultmann used the method to demonstrate the expansion and adaptation of it to serve the changing needs of the church. Their categories were simplistic, however, so that they were content to classify the tradition as suited for worship or instruction, as arising in the Jewish or the Greek-speaking church—as though most Jews of this epoch did not in fact speak Greek and were not powerfully influenced by Hellenistic culture, as Martin Hengel's study of *Judaism and Hellenism* has shown was indeed the case.

Another serious flaw in the form-critical approach is that it fails to take adequate account of the way that a tradition undergoes basic change when it shifts from the freely adaptive oral stage to the fixed form of a written document. W. Kelber and E. Güttgemans have correctly drawn attention to this fault in form-criticism.

*Redaction-criticism.* One of the chief contributions of form-criticism, however, is that it enables the interpreter of a composite document like a Gospel to discern how the author has adapted and modified the material he is drawing upon to serve his own specific aims. The Gospel writers are seen, therefore, not as inept editors (as Dibelius depicted them) but as creative thinkers who draw on tradition to address the situation in their own community. The focus, therefore, is not on the components, but on the work as a whole. Thus Mark seems to be addressing a community that is living in a situation of urgency and threat of persecution, which he speaks to by pointing to the model of Jesus' vindication by God in consequence of his obedience. Luke develops the tradition to portray the ministry of Jesus as already inclusive of the Gentiles and other religious outsiders. Matthew lays emphasis on the authority of Jesus, which has been transmitted to the disciples/apostles who carry on in his absence. John may be seen to build on such models as the personified Jewish wisdom and the saving acts of Hellenistic deities, such as Isis and Asclepius, in his effort to portray Jesus as the agent of God in establishing a community that is open to all who are in need and come seeking divine help.

*Canon-criticism.* Another type of critical study, which likewise seeks to understand the books of the Bible, canon-criticism considers each writing in relation to its role as a part of the collection of writings acknowledged by church or synagogue as authoritative.

*Sociological and Structuralist Criticism.* Under the influence of C. Lévi-Strauss and other cultural anthropologists, some biblical scholars seek to abstract from the diversity of material in the Bible to certain underlying structures of human life and thought, which they regard as universal. Although this approach can be illuminating, one must bear in mind that the attempt to discern universal patterns must always be balanced by acknowledgment of the unique specific features of any historical situation. Following the lead of MAX WEBER, a more responsible undertaking than a rigid system of classifying data is the identification of certain "ideal types" which sociologists note in human societies, and which can be used as norms for discovering what is shared by a historical phenomenon with other cultures in the biblical period, and what is distinctive about it as well. This sociological approach to biblical life and thought gives promise of providing new insights for the kind of analysis and interpretation of the Bible that has been sought after since the rise of critical methods in the post-Renaissance period.

H.K.

**BIBLICAL REALISM.** The social and ethical outlook of REINHOLD NIEBUHR and other Neo-Orthodox social commentators. Rather than the unabashed optimism of pre-World War I LIBERALISM or the social inactivity based on pessimism about the world of FUNDAMENTALISM, Niebuhr and other biblical realists stressed the tragic dimension of history occasioned by original sin, and the call of the covenant God for people to act responsibly to limit evil and promote human good.

J.C.

**BIBLICAL THEOLOGY.** The term does not refer simply to a theology based on the Bible. It refers rather to a method of study, that of approaching theology from a biblical rather than a philosophical point of view. As currently used, the term "biblical theology" refers to the discipline of studying theology from the perspective of contemporaneity with biblical authors, seeking an understanding of the text consistent with what it might have meant or should have meant to its first readers. In comparison, SYSTEMATIC THEOLOGY is not simply the effort to systematize biblical thought, but in modern times has come to mean the study of biblical thought from the perspective of contemporaneity with modern exegetes and along the lines of philosophical rather than historical methodology.

At issue is the relation of the biblical writings to modern society. Are documents written so long ago applicable today (or in any time subsequent to their composition), and if so in what way? Thus the issue of both HERMENEUTICS and canonical history are involved, and the primary problem becomes the "distance between the centuries," or the "conversation" between past and present.

Until the Reformation the biblical sources were primarily appealed to on the basis of reason, either literally or allegorically, and the resultant exegesis reflected a hermeneutic consisting fundamentally of logic. Such was the basis, for example, of Augustine's *Enchiridion,* Calvin's *Institutes of the Christian Religion,* and Thomas Aquinas' *Summa Theologica.* Texts were chosen and exegeted to undergird dogmatic positions. Therefore, neither the historical positions of the original authors, conditioned by time and place, nor any overall system of "biblical theology" was reflected in the writings of these exegetes. Not until late in the eighteenth century were real efforts made at writing biblical theology, and those that were done were more philosophical than theological in their presuppositions and methodologies. The nineteenth century saw the ultimate extension of this orientation in the rise of a liberal theology that placed its emphasis on the modern end of this "distance between the centuries," insisting that an existential value of the sources made the question of historical meaning irrelevant. Over against this arose, largely as the product of a new trend in LITERARY CRITICISM in Germany, a history of religions school of thought, led by the university of Tübingen, which replaced the theological interest with a historical and biblical one. The relation of Israel to her neighbors was viewed from the perspective of the assumed evolutionary development of Israelite religion, and the progress of the early Christian church was charted on the framework of Hegelian dialectic. Theology had given way to history of religion. The present was ignored if not forgotten. The sources were relevant for a study of historical backgrounds and cultural interrelationships but of little or no importance for the perception of revelation through faith.

The limited appeal of such a purely historical study of the Bible and the development of the science of archaeology eroded the impact of the historical school by the twentieth century, reviving an interest in the question once more of how the twentieth century could be meaningfully related to the ancient sources. Even if the Bible were to be considered a repository of theological truth rather than a mere source of ancient history and cultural anthropology, the question of how that theology was to be extracted became the focus of attention and remains so. The focus on the historical ramifications of placing the books of the Bible in their proper cultural setting naturally leads to an interest in descriptive theology, that is, answering the question as to what the Bible meant to those who first received its books and read them. Biblical theology is, after all, interwoven in the history of Israel and the story of Jesus Christ. But, as we have learned, unless that theology has direct and significant bearing on modern people, they are going to find little more than historical interest in pursuing its study. Thus the appeal of systematic theology is based primarily on a philosophical approach to people's needs and seeking to find in the ancient sources only those truths that speak universally and timelessly to the human heart. Philosophy may pose the questions, and theoloy may provide the answers, but how? Systematic theology says by seeking answers, not to the question, What did the text mean to those who first heard it, but to the question, What does it mean to those who hear it now?

Such was the approach of KARL BARTH, who felt that Paul spoke in the first century and modern people hear. Thus the "distance between the centuries" is bridged immediately because the subject matter Paul deals with is common to people of all time and in every place. It is, therefore, always relevant. Another approach that takes seriously the source matrials, though not for their historical value, is that of RUDOLPH BULTMANN. The "distance bridge" is spanned for Bultmann by the fact that issues of EXISTENTIALISM, those that force people to investigate themselves and that lead to faith, are raised in the Bible and become relevant wherever and whenever people confront them. Modern people are scientifically oriented, however, and recognize that the Bible, being an ancient and prescientific collection of books, is written in mythological and cosmological terms that are incomprehensible to them today. Therefore such ideas as the virgin birth, resurrection, miracles, and so forth must be removed (DEMYTHOLOGIZATION) from the text and do not constitute historical reality. It is not historical reality, anyway, but existential confrontation that is ultimately important. A third position is represented by OSCAR CULLMANN, who approaches theology as descriptive rather than systematic. He sees theology as a religious philosophy of history, quite unlike the nonhistorical existential philosophy of Bultmann. Time and history are important for Cullman. That which the NT states about Christ is set forth in the reality of time and history. While these must be taken seriously, they are to be studied not merely for historical interest but for

theological content as well. How this content is relevant to modern people is not as clear in Cullman, however, as it is in the other two systems.

Perhaps it would be well to remind ourselves at this point that the tendency to extremes is better avoided. Preoccupation with history belongs to the historian, while the evaluation of people's ongoing psychological and philosophical responses to their environment belongs to the psychologist and philosopher. But not entirely. Common sense dictates that any historical document should be studied with an appreciation for the historical circumstances in which it was produced, and that any responses contemporary people make to such documents must be based on those eternal and universal truths that transcend any particular period of history. Such is the task of the theologian. While one may argue from common sense in realizing the nature of the task, it is not equally clear what methodology most appropriately, and therefore, most successfully fulfills that task.

Biblical theology will not have fulfilled its task if it merely describes and categorizes the various topics on which the several biblical authors touch. Thus, it cannot adequately do without proper regard for the historical, cultural, and linguistic milieu in which the biblical books were produced. Nor will it be sufficient for the biblical theologian to ignore the pressing concerns of human nature as they relate to the implications inherent in the concept that the Bible is Holy Scripture. The question of the application of historical documents to modern people is inherent in the philosophical presuppositions of any historically based religion. The myth that the biblical theologian deals with historical materials but the systematic theologian relates to contemporary people is just that, a myth. All systematic theology presupposes an understanding of biblical theology, just as biblical theology finds its justification as foundation for systematic thought. (*Compare* BIBLICAL CRITICISM.)

J.M.

**BICKERSTETH, EDWARD HENRY** (1825–1906). Best known for his hymns "Peace, Perfect Peace," "Till He Comes," and "Come Ye Yourselves Apart," Bickersteth was the son of hymn writer Edward Bickersteth and nephew of hymn writer John Bickersteth. Educated at Walton and Trinity College, Cambridge, he received a B.A. with high honor in 1847 and the M.A. in 1850. Ordained in 1848, he served a number of smaller parishes before being named dean of Gloucester in 1885. That same year he became bishop of Exeter. The author of numerous poems, hymns, and books, his most lasting contribution was editing *The Hymnal Companion to the Book of Common Prayer* (1870). He authored nearly thirty books.

N.H.

**BIGAMY.** *See* MARRIAGE.

**BILDAD** (meaning "the Lord has loved" [?]. Bildad is mentioned in Job (2:11; 8:1; 18:1, 25:1; 42:9) as "the Shuhite," and is regularly the second speaker of Job's friends. Bildad is thought to be younger than Eliphaz and older than Zophar. His thinking is traditional and conventional. Through Job's intercession, his "folly" is forgiven.                          P.L.G.

**BILHAH** (meaning "unconcerned"[?]). LABAN'S maid, given to RACHEL when she married Jacob (Gen. 29:29). Following custom, and thinking she herself was barren, Rachel gave Bilhah to Jacob as a concubine. Through this, Rachel thought to become legally a mother (Gen. 30:3). Bilhah bore Dan and Naphthali. Reuben, son of Leah, had intercourse with Bilhah (Gen. 35:22), for which the dying Jacob publicly rebuked him (Gen. 49:4; see Deut. 27:20).                          P.L.G.

**BINDING AND LOOSING.** These terms denote actions either forbidden ("bound") or permitted ("loosed"), according to the determination of the Jewish teachers, the scribes. Several areas are covered by such decisions, chiefly to do with Jewish theology, but also relating to moral questions. In these matters the twin terms came to be associated with the disciplinary procedures of the synagogue in its function as a "house of judgment" (Hebrew *beth din*), that is, a law court. This is the way in which "binding" and "loosing" became synonymous with both expulsion from the synagogue and a receiving back of penitent Jews.

In a third way the terms became used in connection with magical practices. A person was said to be "bound" by coming under the power of a demon or god, while his release from such power by exorcism was his being "loosed." This last-named collocation of terms is found in the Synoptic Gospels (for example, Luke 13:10-17), and is part of the overall teaching on the kingdom of God present in Jesus' earthly ministry (Luke 11:20). He came to set the prisoners free (Luke 4:18) and to release men and women from bondage to legalistic religion (Matt. 11:28-30).

Matthew's Gospel, however, reflects a dual strain of teaching. While it celebrates God's free favor to all people in the coming of Jesus, it evidently is cautious in not allowing liberty to degenerate into license and disregard of moral sanctions. In this light we should understand Matthew 16:19, with its Jewish Christian exaltation of Peter as apostolic leader to whom was entrusted the "power of the keys," that is, the authority to decide what Christians in those times should regard as indispensable for faith and practice. The tension underlying this passage is seen in Galatians 2:11-21.                          R.M.

**BIOETHICS.** A field of applied ETHICS developed over the past quarter century that deals with the capability to keep terminally ill (or injured) patients alive with elaborate life support systems and to transplant vital organs, and the knowledge that makes these activities possible. Since medical science now has this knowledge and capacity, and more, questions naturally arise about the ethical nature of such activities. Ought we to keep the brain-dead patient alive by respirators? Should we implant the hearts of baboons in infants with malformed hearts? Ought we to tamper with the sex of human embryos? Are we moral if we produce "test tube babies"? These and similar kinds of questions are the domain of bioethics. Such issues involve basic human VALUES, and the decisions made, even by, or especially by, "experts" affect the quality of life of everyone in society.

Bioethics seeks, above all, to be rational, to avoid causing unnecessary evil (prevention of evil), and to apply the same standards to everyone, everywhere, all the time (universality). It generally does not speak of the promotion of good, since the good of one person may conflict with or contradict another's conception of one's own good. Rather, it seeks the avoidance of evils, such as pain, death, disability, and discrimination.

Bioethics includes medical ethics, but is a larger field of concern, that is, in relation to questions about manipulation of the DNA chain or the possibility of producing genetic "clones" of people. Medical ethics, as an applied ethical area that sooner or later touches everyone's life, is of great importance and interest to the general public. For example, does cutting off a respirator when a patient is "brain dead" constitute killing? Is refusal to start "heroic" medical measures to keep the heart of an old, exhausted, "terminal" patient beating an act of manslaughter? Such issues and questions appear in the press daily, and several classic court cases have involved precisely these elements.

Bioethics may, therefore, be seen as the standard or everyday morality of ordinary, decent people, applied to the critical, and often tragic, situations that can and do arise in hospitals and in experimental laboratories. A frequently asked question is, "We *can* do this (for example, put an animal's organ into a human), but *ought* we to do so?" The realm or area of concern sometimes called the bio-realm of bioethics is far wider than medical ethics, and much more complex than our usual day-to-day ethical problems involving honesty and respect of other's rights, but it is directly related to ordinary ethical values.

With reference to the far-reaching possibilities of medical science, that is, to correct defects in the unborn child, we encounter the ethical problem of lack of informed consent. While it seems morally unobjectionable to tamper with the fetus so as to prevent it being born crippled, is it as clear that the scientist has the right to alter the sex or personality of the fetus? Is not such a tactic the manipulation of a human being by the standard of a "good" he or she has not fully understood and freely consented to?

Another area of bioethics involves the rights (if any) of animals. Many people have sympathized with the helplessness of animals before the technology of science, but in recent years the issue has grown larger. Of course, the various physical and medical sciences would not be capable of making their discoveries without the use of experimental subjects, chiefly rats, dogs, and monkeys, but also sheep, horses, pigs, and a wide array of other animals. The concern to protect the environment, the forests, oceans, streams, lakes, and even the sky ("acid rain") is also an area in contemporary bioethics.

J.C.

**BIRETTA.** A stiff, square hat with three or four ridges pointing upward and a tassel in its center, worn by cardinals, bishops, or priests. As priests in the Middle Ages were tonsured, that is, had the top of their heads shaved, a hat was needed for protection from the elements. Birettas are found in the colors red, purple, or black to correspond to the rank of the church officials.

J.C.

**BISHOP.** From the Greek *episkopos* or "overseer"; the spiritual leader of a church or churches in the NT and in various traditions of Christianity up to the present day. In the NT, the term appears five times, once clearly applied to Christ as the head of the church (I Pet. 2:25 KJV) and the rest designating church officials (Acts 20:28; Phil. 1:1; I Tim. 3:2; and Titus 1:7). Possibly the office of bishop may have been the same office designated by the term "ELDER." Acts 20:17 and Titus 1:5-7 seem to make that identification.

By the time of Ignatius in the second century A.D., the bishop was recognized as the supreme church officer. The Roman Catholic church, holding to a polity derived from the "early Catholic" period of church development, sees the bishop as supreme in the hierarchical government of the church. Bishops do not constitute a separate order of ministry, but rather, alone, possess the full powers of the Christian priesthood, including the power to confirm and to ordain. Catholic bishops are thus the chief pastors of their dioceses.

The Anglican and Episcopal churches practice a similar polity. Other Protestant churches also have bishops, notably the Lutheran and Methodist communions. The powers of bishops in these churches is considerably less than those of Catholic or Anglican bishops, however. Other, less traditionally ordered Protestant bodies assign the bishop's classic functions of spiritual oversight to assemblies of pastors and lay representatives, as in the case of the presbytery in Presbyterian and Reformed churches.

J.C.

**BLACK FRIARS.** *See* DOMINIC/DOMINICANS.

**BLACK LETTER DAYS.** An expression traditional in the Anglican communion for a lesser Sunday or festival in the church year. The term derives from the use of red letters to mark major church festivals on announcement boards. Thus black letter days are less significant than red letter days.      J.C.

**BLACK MONKS.** *See* BENEDICT/BENEDICTINES.

**BLACK MUSLIMS.** A religious movement among American blacks first begun in 1930 by W. D. Fard, who proclaimed that Christianity was a slave religion foisted on black people by white people, and that ISLAM was the proper religion for self-respecting blacks.

Fard's movement gained followers who responded to his message, which stressed economic and political power for blacks, promoted Afro-American culture, and called for black unity. Fard took the name Farrad Muhammad and was an unusual man, who eventually disappeared. Before that time, he became known as the Prophet. The movement came under the leadership of Elijah Poole, who took the name ELIJAH MUHAMMAD. Elijah brought growth and an unorthodox understanding of Islam, which declared the white race to be devils. He stressed black power in a radical way, earning the fear of many police officials. He moved the headquarters from Detroit to Chicago and began to recruit members among the large black prison population. Elijah taught a strict Islamic morality, which was the salvation of many alcohol and drug-abusing black urban men. His theology was a reverse racism that exalted the black race and declared the white race to have been created by an evil scientist (or devil). This teaching seemed to offer some consolation to the depressed poor of black urban slums.

In the 1950s, a prisoner named Malcolm Little was converted to Elijah's doctrine and took the name Malcolm X. This X was adopted by all black Muslims who rejected their European "slave names." At first radical, Malcolm in time became more moderate. He urged more normal Muslim beliefs, including the brotherhood of man, even with white people. Malcolm and Elijah became estranged over this, and Malcolm was assassinated by Black Muslims in 1965.

Upon Elijah's death, his son, Walter D. Muhammad, assumed control. He is bringing the group's theology more into line with Orthodox Islam. Black Muslims, since the time of Malcolm X, have become progressively more positive as a force in the inner city and in prisons. Their emphasis on personal morality, sobriety, and family unity is a force for good among urban blacks today.      J.C.

**BLACKS, CHRISTIANITY AND.** *See* PLURALISM.

**BLACK THEOLOGY.** A contemporary theological movement of diverse viewpoints that arose among black religious leaders in the United States during the

1960s. Of course, black theology had a history, stretching back into the nineteenth-century struggle against slavery and including the many religious experiments of the black community, from rural revivalism to the urban origins of the BLACK MUSLIMS in Detroit and elsewhere. The most immediate causes of the rise of black theology, which declared the struggle of American blacks for justice and equality against racism to be equivalent to Moses calling Israel out of Egyptian slavery or Jesus' liberation of sinners from the bondage of sin, were MARTIN LUTHER KING, JR's leadership of the civil rights movement during the fifties and early sixties; a book, *Black Religion,* written by Joseph Washington in 1964; the black nationalistic movement sparked by Malcolm X; and the Black Power movement. More remote, but influential, were the early thinkers, Henry McNeal Turner, who declared "God is a Negro" in 1894, and Marcus Garvey (1887–1940), who spoke of a black Jesus.

The major proponents of black theology include James Forman, who made the demand for reparations from white churches and synagogues at Riverside Church in May 1969; James Cone, who declared "Christ is Black, baby"; Joseph Washington, another militant of the 1960s; Deotis Roberts, a more moderate spokesman; Albert Cleage, who affirms a black Messiah; and Major Jones, who found elments of Jurgen Moltmann's theology of hope helpful for blacks.

Black theology expresses a radical but profound belief that God is on the side of the oppressed, whom black theologians identify with the black poor in America. Some thinkers claim that blacks are God's chosen people, and that because of their experiences of slavery and contemporary racism, blacks are the only people qualified to understand Christianity. Other thinkers believe the African background of blacks enables them to better embody the original life-style and attitudes of Christianity. There is much creative disagreement among black theologians. William Jones has criticized black thinkers for not taking the problem of sin and evil seriously. More moderate blacks have attacked the reverse racism of radical claims that whites are not Christians—or even are evil in essence. Major Jones and others have stressed the universalism of Christianity—that it is for all, regardless of race. Warner Traynham, as early as 1973, pointed out that black theology must learn from and make common cause wih other LIBERATION theologies, especially the thought and practice developed in Latin America and among FEMINIST theologians. More recently, meetings between Latin Americans, feminists, and black theologians have taken place.

Black theology has been opposed by many conservative churchmen in America, the same ones who oppose feminist and Latin American liberation theologies. Without doubt, many radical statements have been made by some proponents of black theology, nonetheless, the reasons for even extreme claims are humanly understandable. The parallels between Israel in Egyptian bondage and blacks in American slavery forms the heritage of blacks in America for three hundred years. The parallel between Moses and Martin Luther King, Jr., a leader recognized as one in the true prophetic mold by people of all races, is more than symbolic. The claim that God is on the side of the oppressed cannot be disputed by anyone who reads the NT closely. The Magnificat, which proclaims that God puts down the mighty from their thrones and exalts those of low degree in the Incarnation; the Pauline hymn of Christ's kenosis, his humbling of himself to become fully human (Phil. 2:5-11); and the story of Jesus' lowly birth and humble life are far more radical than any contemporary theological statements.

J.C.

## BLACKWOOD, ANDREW WATTERSON

(1882–1966). A minister and educator, Blackwood was born on August 5 in Clay Center, Kansas, to Thomas and Bella Watterson. He graduated from Franklin College (1902), Harvard (1905), and Xenia Theological Seminary (1908).

Ordained in the United Presbyterian Church in 1908, he pastored three churches before becoming a professor at Presbyterian Theological Seminary, Louisville, Kentucky, in 1925. From 1930 to 1950 he taught homiletics at Princeton, and at Temple University School of Theology until 1958. He authored twenty-two books on religion, preaching, and pastoral care.

N.H.

## BLAKE, WILLIAM (1757–1827).

Engraver, poet, painter, and perhaps the most imaginative Christian visionary of the nineteenth century. Sent to drawing school in London at age ten, he began a seven-year apprenticeship as an engraver at fourteen. At twenty-one he exhibited water colors at the Royal Academy. Later he painted biblical illustrations as well as powerful symbolic drawings, which he engraved for his own works. From 1790 on, Blake published a series of illuminated visionary, apocalyptic works including *The Marriage of Heaven and Hell,* depicting a revolutionary Christian humanism; *The Book of Urizen* (1794); and *Jerusalem* (1818–20), in which the union of God and humans leads to God's annihilation and resurrection as the Great Humanity Divine.

Blake saw himself as a Christian, but his unique spirituality was radically personal and heterodox, influenced by the Bible, SWEDENBORG, J. BOEHME, and Jewish cabbalistic writings. Blake's influence is evident in the writings of some "death of God" theologians.

J.L.

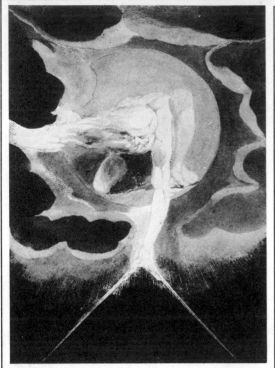

*The Ancient of Days, an etching by William Blake*

**BLASPHEMY.** From the Greek noun meaning "to speak evil of God," and the Hebrew word "to curse the name of the Lord" (Lev. 24:16). It is snyonymous in Hebrew with "reviling" (Ezek. 35:2) and "cursing" (Lev. 24:11); in Greek "to utter blasphemy" (Rev. 13:1 ff.; 17:3). The penalty among the Hebrews for willful SIN (Num. 15:30, "with a high hand") was stoning to death (Lev. 24:16). Blasphemy could be in deed, as in Ezekiel 20:27 ("dealing treacherously"), and practicing IDOLATRY (Isa. 65:7).

Jesus was charged with blasphemy because he claimed authority to forgive sins (Matt. 9:3; Luke 5:21) and to be the Christ, the Son of God (Matt. 26: 63-65; Mark 14:61-64; John 10:29, 36). Stephen spoke "blasphemous words against Moses and God" (Acts 6:11) and was stoned to death. The NT considers it blasphemous to revile Christ (Matt. 27:39; Mark 15:29; Luke 22:65; 23:39), to oppose the gospel (Acts 26:11; I Tim. 1:13), and to discredit Christianity (Rom. 2:24; I Tim. 6:1; Tit. 2:5; Jas. 2:7; II Pet. 2:2).

In a somewhat less serious form, it is blasphemy to mock, revile, or slander spiritual authorities, since they represent Christ (Acts 13:45; 18:6; II Pet. 2:10-12; Jude 8-10). Blasphemy against the Holy Spirit is called the unforgivable or "eternal sin" (Matt. 12:31-32; Mark 3:28-30; Luke 12:10). This represents willful rejection of God and refusal of God's redemptive work to the extent of giving credit for God's "mighty acts" not to God but to another.
P.L.G.

**BLESS/BLESSING.** A double sense is given to these terms in biblical literature. When used of God, "to bless" is to acknowledge the divine person and worth, usually in the light of what God has done or has given to people. Less often, material objects are said to be "blessed," as when Jesus took bread in the Upper Room and BLESSED it, according to Mark 14:22 and parallels. But clearly for Jewish readers this would imply not that the object was blessed, rather God was being thanked as the giver.

The same understanding is to be seen in Paul (I Cor. 10:16) and later NT writers (see I Tim. 4:3-5). The other sense of "bless" is found in those instances where humans are the recipients of blessing, that is, from God, or just occasionally from one another (Gen. 27:41; Lev. 25:21; James 3:9, 10). Such bestowals are both material goods and property (Deut. 11:26; Prov. 10:22; 28:20) and spiritual enrichments. The Psalms are particularly rich in the latter category, even when adversity comes (Ps. 94:12), a theme expounded in the NT (Rom. 5:3-5; II Cor. 1:3-7; James 1:2).

The NT picks up the spiritual dimension, centering chiefly on the theme of God's blessing on people through Christ and the gospel. Doxologies and liturgical expressions (for example, Eph. 1:3-10; I Pet. 1:3-9; Rev. 5:1-10) suggest that such ways of praising God arose in scenes of the church at worship when hymns and confessions chanted Christian praise. The Eucharist took its rightful place as the focal point of thanksgiving to God for divine blessings (I Cor. 10:16, based on Jesus' actions recorded in 11:24), though as a counterblast to Gnostic depreciation in the material world Christians saw God's hand in the common mercies of life (I Tim. 4:3-5; Heb. 13:4). The offering for the Jerusalem poor is described under terms of "blessing" (II Cor. 9:8) suggesting that the NT knows that we praise God, not in word only but by practical assistance to the needy (I John 3:1, 18; compare James 2:14-26).
R.M.

**BLESSED.** This term is most frequently found in both OT and NT with God as the implied object. "Blessed be God!" is a typical liturgical expression in the Psalter and in synagogue worship. Family worship in Judaism celebrates God as the giver of food and drink by the use of such formulas.

When applied to human beings, "blessed" refers to their state of happiness and well-being (Hebrew *shalom*) under divine favor, for example Psalm 1:1. BEATITUDE is the state of bliss enjoyed now in a Christian context and reaching out to the vision of God, which consummates that blessedness. Matthew 5:3-11 (parallel Luke 6:20-26) summarizes the qualities of such life in the kingdom of God, present and future.
R.M.

**BLESSED VIRGIN MARY** (BVM). MARY, THE MOTHER OF JESUS Christ, called the MOTHER OF GOD (*Theotokos*) by the ancient church. In Roman Catholic theology, the greatest of the saints. Mary, by virtue of her IMMACULATE CONCEPTION and her motherhood through the agency of the Holy Spirit, is elevated above all other human beings and is second only to her son, Jesus, in holiness. In the Catholic practice, Mary is specially venerated with a devotion greater than the honors paid to the saints, but less than the reverence given to the Holy Trinity alone.

By the Immaculate Conception, Catholic theology means Mary was "conceived without sin," as a preparation for her divine motherhood. This freedom from sin was not merited but was given as a special gift of God—an exception to the universal incidence of sin among humankind.

Catholic theology, following Augustine, declares that Mary, as the Blessed Virgin, lacked personal sin. Her perpetual virginity is understood as including the conception of Jesus without concupiscence and without the agency of a human male, the delivering of Jesus without damage to her physical virginity, and a lifelong preservation of her virginity. Because of these beliefs, the Fifth Council of Constantinople declared Mary to be perpetually virgin, following Augustine's phrase: "A virgin conceived, a virgin gave birth, a virgin remained."

Later theology held that Mary was infused by the Holy Spirit and filled with all the theological and moral virtues. These virtues give the Blessed Virgin the power to work miracles, such as healing. All such supernatural deeds are said to be in accord with the inspiration of the Holy Spirit.

The ancient church also believed that the Blessed Virgin, at death, was bodily assumed into heaven (the ASSUMPTION) on the order of the miracle attached to Elijah in the OT. After the Assumption, Mary participates in the vision of God—although she does not share the omniscience of the godhead. Her knowledge remains less than that possessed by the human nature of Christ.

Mary's role in Christian theology, both Protestant and Catholic, is an important one. Paul's declaration that Christ was "born of a woman" in Galatians, and the confession "born of the virgin Mary" in the ancient creeds stand as refutations of GNOSTIC speculation that Christ was purely spirit and was not a real human being at all. By his birth from Mary, Jesus is shown to be fully human as well as fully divine (the doctrine of two natures in one person). As Athanasius observes, "Whatever was not assumed (by Christ) was not redeemed," therefore it was necessary that the Christ be like all other humans are, yet without sin.

Since the efficacy of the atonement depends on the birth of Jesus from Mary, the Blessed Virgin has been highly venerated since the sub-Apostolic Age. Above all other considerations, Mary is reverenced as the Mother of the Redeemer. Although Jesus had no human father, his true humanity is established by Mary's humble acceptance of the divine commission at the visitation (Luke 2). Just as the analogy of Paul in Romans (5:12-21) states that the first Adam brought sin and death into the world (Gen. 3), so the second Adam (Christ) brought forgiveness and eternal life. Mary is sometimes called the new (or second) Eve. God's plan for the world was confounded by the Fall, instigated by Eve, and now Mary introduces the agent of redemption into the world in whom God's plan is restored and completed.

In the Catholic liturgical year, there are many feast days dedicated to Mary, including the Feast of the Annunciation, and the Purification of the Virgin.

J.C.

**BLISS, PHILIP P.** (1838–76). The well-known gospel songwriter was born on July 9 in Clearfield County, Pennsylvania. In 1864 he went to Chicago to work with musician and educator George F. Root. Originally a Methodist, about 1871 Bliss became choirmaster at First Congregational Church, Chicago, and superintendent of its Sunday school. In 1874 he joined Major D. W. Whittle in evangelistic work.

Inspired by news items, ministers' anecdotes, and overheard conversations, he composed a large number of hymns, both words and music. His *Gospel Songs* (1874) was a bestseller. Among his many familiar songs (known by titles or the first line of their choruses rather than the first line of the verse) are "Almost Persuaded," "Dare to Be a Daniel," "Hallelujah, He Is Risen," "Hallelujah, 'tis Done!" "Hallelujah, What a Savior," "I Know He Is Mine," "I Know Not the Hour," "I Will Sing of My Redeemer," "Jesus Loves Even Me," "Look and Live," "The Light of the World Is Jesus," "Once for All," "Whosoever Heareth," "Brightly Beams Our Father's Mercy," and "Sing Them Over Again to Me."

Bliss died in a tragic railroad accident on December 30 near Ashtabula, Ohio. On a monument erected to his memory in Rome, Pennsylvania, is the title of his most popular song during his lifetime, "Hold the Fort."

N.H.

**BLOOD.** The viewpoint of the OT writers on blood is essentially based on observation and experience. Hence a person's life-force (Hebrew *nephesh*) is seen to depend on the blood within the person's body (Lev. 17:11); and when the blood flows out onto the ground, one's life goes with it, and one dies (Gen. 4:10). The same is true for animals (Gen. 9:4; 37:31; etc.), and it is natural therefore to associate the taking or shedding of human blood with the crime of murder (Gen. 9:6; Hab. 2:12; Matt. 27:24; Luke 13:1). So far the witness of both the OT and the NT is clear, and at a surface level it might explain the phrase "blood of Christ" to mean simply his death, that is, when his life left him, as in John 19:34 where, however, a symbolic meaning is certainly intended by the evangelist.

The use of blood in a series of manipulative acts in the Levitical sacrificial system and the exposition of the cross of Jesus by using this sacrificial idiom further complicates the picture. Two theories are debated. On the one side, it is maintained that "blood" represents the release of the life-force of both animals and humans so that such an offering may be then presented to God as an act of dedicated service. Something similar to this line of reasoning lies behind the Epistle to the Hebrews, it is said, where Jesus offered his "blood" (that is, sacrificed life) in death, and thereafter that offering was found acceptable to God as part of Christ's high priestly ministry (see Heb. 9:11-28; 10:19 for a clearer view). This understanding is usually tied in with his Eucharistic sacrifice as an offering made both historically and representatively in his heavenly work, whose "sign" is seen at the Communion altar.

On the other side, it seems statistically more plausible to argue that "blood" (found 362 times in the OT, with the preponderance of references to do with violent death) is a metonymy not for the release and re-offering of life, but for the life itself laid down or taken away in death. In sacrificial cultus it speaks of the animals' role as bearing the sin of the people in atonement. This conclusion has important relevance for on the NT teaching regarding ATONEMENT wrought by the cross.

Atonement enters the theological lexicon of the church as a distinctively Anglo-Saxon loanword from the sixteenth century. In Shakespeare it describes reconciliation as two estranged parties who are brought together in amity and friendship with their hostility ended. The NT teaching has this situation in view as it describes how God and humankind are alienated by reason of human sin (see Rom. 5:1-11; KJV retains "atonement" in verse 11, where the Greek is "reconciliation," as in the RSV). God has taken effective steps to remedy this estrangement and has done so at great cost. Hence the text, usually set in a liturgical and cultic context, speaks of Christ's blood as the means by which sin is forgiven and the sinner is returned to harmony with the Creator and Redeemer (see representative illustrations in Mark 14:24 reverting to the scene of Exodus 24; Rom. 3:25; 5:9; Col. 1:20; Eph. 1:7; Acts 20:28; I Pet. 1:2; Rev. 5:9; I John 1:7). In all these cases, in spite of diverse backgrounds, what is the common thread seems apparent; the cost of human redemption is expressed by relating it to the violent and sacrificial death of Jesus as God's Son, whose self-offering made an end of sin as an estranging barrier between the holy God and sinful humanity. Thus he effected atonement (literally, at-one-ment, that is, he brought God and the world together in a cosmic, social, and personal reconciliation, as in Eph. 2:13-18, a hymnic celebration of this multifaceted act).

Elsewhere "blood" carries several other shades of meaning, of which we may single out for special mention those places where it refers to Christ's incarnation. He became human by taking our human nature and becoming one with us as a sharer in "flesh and blood" (Heb. 2:14).

R.M.

**B'NAI B'RITH.** Oldest and largest Jewish fraternal service organization. Founded in 1843 in New York as a purely fraternal organization that provided health insurance and sick benefits for its members, B'nai B'rith today is international. B'nai B'rith means "sons of the Covenant." It has established orphans' homes, homes for the aged, and hospitals. Under its wing are the ANTI-DEFAMATION LEAGUE, which fights ANTI-SEMITISM and promotes better relations between Jews and non-Jews; Hillel Foundations, which conduct cultural, religious, and social programs for Jewish college students at major universities; B'nai B'rith Youth Organization (incorporating Aleph Zadik Aleph and B'nai B'rith Girls) for Jewish teen-agers; B'nai B'rith Women; and Career and Counseling Services. B'nai B'rith programs include communal service, social action, and public affairs with emphasis on preserving Judaism through projects in and for Israel, for Soviet Jewry, and adult Jewish education.

L.K.

**BOANERGES.** According to Mark 3:17, which is the only NT text to report this name, the title was given as a surname to two of the disciples of Jesus, James and John. Its meaning is unclear, but it seems to be derived from a Hebrew expression meaning "sons of thunder" *(bene regesh)*. The designation is thought to betoken the violent nature of the disciples, for which there is some evidence (Luke 9:54-56).

R.M.

**BOAZ** (meaning "strength" or "might").

(1) The prosperous and righteous Bethelehem farmer, kinsman of Elimelek and Naomi, who married RUTH, the Moabitess, a widowed daughter-in-law of Naomi (Ruth 2:1; 4:13). He became the great-grandfather of David (Ruth 4:22; I Chr. 2:12-15) and an ancestor of Jesus (Matt. 1;5; Luke 3:32.) The book of Ruth emphasizes Boaz's sense of family responsibilities, his resourcefulness and care in obeying laws and customs, and his generosity to his workers, especially to gleaners and to a non-Israelite proselyte.

(2) The term is used of one of the twin, free-standing columns that stood on either side of the doorway to Solomon's Temple. R. B. Y. Scott suggests that the name Boaz, like JACHIN, may have had a dynastic reference as "In thy *strength* the king rejoices" (Ps. 21:1), and "*Strength* and beauty [Jachin] are in his sanctuary" (Ps. 96:6b).

P.L.G.

**BODE, JOHN ERNEST** (1816–74). Author of "O Jesus, I Have Promised," Bode was educated at Eton, Charterhouse, and Christ Church College, Oxford, obtaining his B.A. in 1837 and an M.A. in 1840. From 1841 to 1847 he was a tutor in the college. Ordained deacon in 1841 and priest in 1843, he held several parish posts. His *Hymns from the Gospel of the Day* (1860) also included "God of Heaven, Enthroned in Light" and "Spirit of Truth, Indwelling Light."

N.H.

**BODHI.** "Enlightenment," the perfect clarity of mind achieved by Gautama BUDDHA through meditation. In this meditation he first remembered each of his past lives. Then he grasped the meaning of SAMSARA, the cycle of birth and death. Finally he perceived the FOUR NOBLE TRUTHS.

When he became enlightened, Gautama was sitting under a bo tree, or bodhi tree, the *ficus religiosa*. Like the Banyan tree, it branches indefinitely and has thick prop roots that support the branches. (*See* BUDDHISM.)

K.C.

**BODHISATTVA.** A being who sets out on the quest for enlightenment (BODHI). In early BUDDHISM the term is used of earlier Buddhas before their enlightenment and also of the Buddha who is yet to come, Maitreya (see below). Gautama Buddha had been a bodhisattva in earlier lifetimes. In Mahayana the bodhisattva is so close to full enlightenment as to be able to enter NIRVANA but stays behind to help others on their quest.

*Three Ways of Buddhahood.* There have been three traditional ways of achieving Buddhahood: the bodhisattva, the pratyeka Buddha, and the arhant. The pratyeka Buddhas attained enlightenment on their own without forming a group of followers. The arhants, beginning with the disciples of Gautama himself, achieved salvation through following the career of a disciple. In Mahayana the arhants (known in Chinese as lohans) were regarded as selfish because they sought only their own salvation and not that of others. Far Eastern art portrays them as strange figures, even grotesque, and sometimes comic. The LOTUS SUTRA is probably the most influential Buddhist scripture in the Far East. It says that there is only one real way of salvation, that of the bodhisattva.

*Becoming a Bodhisattva.* The person who sets out to become a bodhisattva must show the proper disposition—a desire for enlightenment without a desire for gain for oneself. There is a traditional bodhisattva vow that shows the sense of compassion of a true seeker: (a) Living beings are countless, and I vow to save them all. (b) Passions cannot be extinguished, but I vow to extinguish them. (c) The truths of the faith (DHARMA) cannot be measured, but I vow to master them all. (d) The way of Buddhahood cannot be excelled, and I vow to attain it. This vow can be made in the presence of someone believed to be a "living Buddha," or in the presence of another person who has taken the vow. It can also be made in the awareness of the presence of all Buddhas and bodhisattvas.

Much has been written in detail about the career of a bodhisattva. One must go through various stages and show personal discipline in a way that agrees with the ideal.

*The Great Bodhisattvas.* For art and popular piety there are a number of important and widely known bodhisattvas. AVALOKITESVARA (known in Chinese as Kwan Yin) is sometimes called the Goddess of Mercy, and is generally, though not always, pictured as female.

Maitreya has been known from the time of earliest Buddhism. Having successfully completed many previous lives, he now waits in the Tushita heaven, an intermediate realm. When the end is near, he will be born on earth as a sort of Messianic figure. He is important in Theravada (Buddhism), but in Mahayana other figures have become more popular.

MANJUSRI is the bodhisattva who personifies wisdom. Pictures and statues show him holding a book of wisdom in one hand, and in the other a sword with which he slays ignorance. According to one tradition the name of Manchuria is derived from his name.

KSHITIGARBA is known as one who has vowed to save all beings living between the time of the Buddha and the coming of Maitreya. This led to the belief that he has power over the Buddhist hells. In Japan he is especially popular and is known as Jizo, the Japanese translation of his name. He is usually portrayed as a monk, holding in his right hand a staff with six rings. The rings are symbols of the six realms into which a being can be reborn (the realm of the gods, of humans, of hungry ghosts, of animals, of demons, and of hell). In addition to helping the dead, he is a guide to the living and protects travelers.

In MANDALAS, diagrams of the way to enlightenment, a specific bodhisattva is usually paired with a Buddha. For example, Avalokitesvara and Amita Buddha are usually thought of together and worshiped together.

K.C.

**BODY.** Basically a noun denoting physical objects that can be seen and touched, though it can be used in a metaphorical capacity to represent crucial theological concepts.

*Body in the Old Testament.* Since the ancient Hebrews usually referred to individual parts of the body, their need for a noun denoting the body in its entirety was slight. The nearest comprehensive term is *bāśār* ("FLESH"). Accordingly, the visible part of the body is at issue in legislation on the consecration of Levites requiring that a razor go over "all their body" (Num. 8:7) and on the diagnosis of leprosy, which distinguishes between the skin and hair of the body (Lev. 13:2-4). When the psalmist states, "My bones cleave to my flesh" (Ps. 102:5), he is complaining that he has disintegrated into "skin and bone." The entire body is of concern in Proverbs 4:20-22, with its portrayal of wisdom as a person's medication that induces "healing to all his flesh." The disclosure in Psalm 119:120, "My flesh trembles for fear of thee," demonstrates the Hebrew affirmation of human existence in the body. Clearly, bodily and psychic life are perceived in organic oneness.

*Body in the Gospels.* Although the Greek noun *sarx* ("flesh") is often used in the NT in ways resembling the Hebrew word *bāśār,* as a metaphor it acquired theological meaning. This is likewise the case with *sōma,* the NT Greek noun for "body." When Jesus broke bread and distributed it to his disciples at that eschatological farewell meal known as the Last Supper, he said, ". . . this is my body" (Matt. 26:26; Mark 14:22; Luke 22:19). This image deftly denotes Jesus' sacrificial giving of himself for his disciples. He was declaring, "This bread represents me." As Jesus' followers henceforth ate bread together, they would remain in fellowship with him.

*Body in Paul's Letters.* Paul's mention of "body" (*sōma*) is imaginatively diverse. At the same time he speaks of the body as being sinful and redeemed. If it is a sinful "body of death" (Rom. 7:24), it is likewise redeemed in Christ (6:11), especially through baptism (Gal. 3:27), enabling the believer's body and Christ's to experience spatial union. Paul affirms the body's immortality. Against his opponents, Paul insists that Christ's bodily resurrection ensures the bodily resurrection of believers united to him through baptism into everlasting heavenly fellowship (I Cor. 15:42-54). Here the "lowly" human body will be spiritually transformed into Christ's "glorious body" (Phil. 3:21). Moreover, Paul perceives the Christian community (the church) as the multi-membered body of Christ (Rom. 12:5), with Christ exercising sovereignty as its head (Col. 1:18).

J.K.K.

**BODY OF CHRIST.** The starting point for NT thought concerning the body of Christ is the INCARNATION—whether John's "the Word became flesh" (1:14), the Synoptics' birth narratives (Matt. 1:18-25; Luke 2:1-20), or Paul's "(He) being born in the likeness of men" (Phil. 2:7). The physical body of Christ was important to the early church. "Every spirit which confesses that Jesus Christ has come in the flesh is of God" (I John 4:2). The physical body of the incarnate Jesus had every characteristic of human, physical bodies, for example, it was subject to birth and death, and could act, be acted upon, be anointed (Matt. 26:12; Mark 14:8), and be laid in a tomb (Luke 23:53; 24:3; John 19:38, 40; 20:11-12).

What was done in salvation through the crucified body of Christ made the body a symbol of Christ's atoning work: "We have been sanctified through the offering of the body of Jesus Christ once for all" (Heb. 10:10), "you have died to the law through the body of Christ" (Rom. 7:4), "he himself bore our sins in his body on the tree, . . ." (I Pet. 2:24).

Compare the familiar Eucharistic language in the Pauline account (I Cor. 11:23-25) with the Gospel records (Matt. 26:26-29; Mark 14:22-25; Luke 22:17-19; John 13:21-30). Jesus identified the Passover bread as "my body," broken for the benefit of his followers, and to be eaten by them as a body together.

Paul told members of the Corinthian church, taken as a whole, "Now you are the body of Christ" (I Cor. 12:27). This semimystical concept appears exclusively in the writings of Paul and constitutes a major theme in his thought (Rom. 12:4, 5; I Cor. 6:15, 19; 10:16, 17; 12:13, 27; Eph. 1:23; 2:16; 4:12, 16; 5:23, 30; Col. 1:18, 29; 2:19; 3:15).

There is no exact OT parallel to this idea, yet it may be reflected in Israel's self-awareness as God's "chosen" people, tribe, or family: "Once you were no people but now you are God's people; . . ." (I Pet. 2:10). "There is one body and one Spirit" (Eph. 4:4). "Christ is head of the church" (Eph. 5:23), who enlivens the Christian community as its Spirit.

The resurrected and ascended body of Christ is referred to in Philippians 3:21 as having been made "glorious" by God the Father.

P.L.G.

**BOEHME, JAKOB** (1575–1624). Protestant, Lutheran mystic, and one of Germany's greatest thinkers. Born near Görlitz, he received little education but studied Scripture. A vision of future greatness brought loss of his cobbler's apprenticeship, and he wandered for a year, greatly disturbed by quarreling Protestant sects. In 1599 he married and lived quietly in Görlitz. After two visions revealing the harmony of everything, he hurriedly wrote *Aurora, or Morning Redness* (1612). It was printed without his consent, and he was forbidden to write further. But by 1619 he was writing again, eventually producing thirty-one books.

His works combine mystical insight into reality with traditional Christian beliefs and practices: primordial Being (God) undergirds all being, embraces all opposites, and is the source of all energy; existing things are signatures of God—the divine will and love manifested. Boehme felt that all would be harmonious except that single elements attempt to be God, thus introducing sin, disharmony, and evil. In Christ, God restores and regenerates all things to their proper harmony. His best works include *The Signature of All Things,* 1621, and *Mysterium Magnum, or An Exposition of Genesis,* 1623. Boehme's followers in England are called Behmenists. His influence extends to Schelling, Hegel, Schopenhauer, and Tillich.

C.M.

**BOETHIUS.** One of the greatest scholars and philosophers of the early Middle Ages, whose works were widely used until modern times. He lived in

Italy, and under the Ostrogothic King Theodoric he held a high civil post. But Theodoric and the Ostrogoths were followers of ARIANISM and therefore suspected that the population over which they ruled, which held to the doctrines of Nicea, would conspire with the Byzantines against them. For these reasons Boethius, who was orthodox and part of the earlier Italian population, came under suspicion, and Theodoric had him arrested. In prison, he wrote his most famous work, *Consolation of Philosophy,* in which he spoke of the soul's ascent to the vision of God. Although Boethius was a Christian and had written several works on theology, this particular treatise is mostly philosophical. He was executed, by order of Theodoric, about the year 524, and was soon regarded as a martyr.                                    J.G.

**BOHEMIAN BRETHREN.** *See* MORAVIANS.

**BOISEN, ANTON** (1876–1965). A pioneer in CLINICAL PASTORAL EDUCATION. He graduated from the University of Indiana, completed studies at Union Theological Seminary (NY) in 1908, and was pastor at several small churches. Months spent at the Boston Psychiatric Hospital after a personal breakdown brought a realization of the need for a ministry to people in mental hospitals. He then became chaplain at Worcester State Hospital. In 1930 he founded the Council for the Clinical Training of Theological Students. He also established a training center at Elgin State Hospital (IL) in 1932 and taught at Chicago Theological Seminary from 1937 until retirement in 1942.                                    I.C.

**BONAR, HORATIUS** (1808–89). The noted author of poems, hymns, and devotional books was born on December 19 in Edinburgh, Scotland, heir to a long line of Church of Scotland clergy. Educated at the University of Edinburgh, he was ordained in 1837 as minister of North Parish Church in Kelso.

He left during the "Disruption" of 1843 but remained a minister of the Free Church of Scotland, serving in 1883 as its moderator. From 1866 to the end of his life he was pastor of Chalmers Memorial Church in Edinburgh. He died July 31, 1889.

Bonar's hymns include "Blessing and Honor and Glory and Power," "Fill Thou My Life," "Go, Labor on; Spend, and Be Spent," "Here, O My Lord, I See Thee Face to Face," "I Heard the Voice of Jesus Say," "Not What I Am, O Lord," "O Love That Casts Out Fear," and "This Is the Hour of Banquet and of Song." He also translated many from Greek and Latin. His series of three *Hymns of Faith and Hope* (1857–66) were popular. His prose works include *God's Way of Holiness, Prophetical Landmarks,* and several missionary biographies.                                    N.H.

**BONAVENTURE** (1221–74). The most important figure in the history of the Franciscans after the death of FRANCIS OF ASSISI, both for his administrative

leadership and for his theological work. A Franciscan from an early age, he studied at Paris under Alexander of Hales and in 1248 began teaching at the university. He was one of the main targets of those in the university who opposed the MENDICANT FRIARS and in response wrote in defense of poverty. On the question of the proper place of Aristotle in theology, he accepted some Aristotelian tenets but remained basically a believer in the philosophy of AUGUSTINE, thus differing from both Thomas Aquinas and the Latin Averroists. In 1257 he was elected Minister General of the Franciscans. As such he took firm action against the Spirituals and against the views of Joachim of Fiore. He was made a cardinal in 1273 and died a year later. In later times, his mysticism, as seen in his *Itinerarium Mentis in Deum,* would be more influential than his systematic theology.

J.G.

*Dietrich Bonhoeffer*

**BONHOEFFER, DIETRICH** (1906–45). German theologian and Christian martyr. The writings he produced while in a Nazi concentration camp introduced to a wide public the concept of a nonreligious form of Christianity. Bonhoeffer was born in Breslau, Germany, into a culturally upper-class, but religiously indifferent, Lutheran family. His father was a prominent psychiatrist and professor at the University of Berlin. Bonhoeffer began his study of theology at Tübingen (1923) but settled in at the University of Berlin the following year. In 1927 he defended his dissertation on "The Communion of Saints: A Dogmatic Inquiry into the Sociology of the Church." The following year Bonhoeffer served as an assistant pastor of a German-speaking church in Barcelona. Upon his return to Berlin he became an assistant to a professor of theology and in 1930 defended a thesis entitled "Act and Being," which qualified him for university teaching. A year's leave was spent at Union Theological Seminary in New York. The experiences in Spain and in New York gave Bonhoeffer valuable perspective on the German church and nation as well as on his own rather privileged bourgeois life.

In August 1931, Bonhoeffer began teaching in the theological faculty at Berlin, and the same year he accepted the ecumenical post of Youth Secretary for the World Alliance for Promoting International Friendship Through the Churches. In November 1931, he was ordained. As Bonhoeffer was beginning to immerse himself in his professorial duties, Germany was turning from the Weimar Republic to the totalitarianism of national socialism. In 1933, the year Hitler became chancellor of the Third Reich, Bonhoeffer joined with Martin Niemöller in the Pastor's Emergency League, which sought to resist Nazi influence over the German churches. In July 1933, Bonhoeffer accepted a call to be pastor of a German parish in London where he remained until April 1935. He used this opportunity to make known to ecumenical gatherings the Nazi heresy of the "German Christians" and the opposition of the newly formed Confessing Church. On his return to Germany, Bonhoeffer took charge of a seminary of the Confessing Church at Finkenwalde. It was closed by the Gestapo in October 1937, a month before Bonhoeffer published his most widely read book, *The Cost of Discipleship*.

By early 1939 Bonhoeffer was in close contact with leaders of the Resistance movement. On April 5, 1943, he was arrested by the Gestapo and sent to Tegel prison. After the attempt on Hitler's life in July 1944, the Gestapo discovered the extent of Bonhoeffer's activity as a counteragent for the Resistance. He was sent to the concentration camp at Buchenwald in February 1945, and then to the camp at Flossenburg, where he was hanged on April 9 on special orders from Himmler.

There are many accounts of his courage, serenity, and helpfulness during his imprisonment. It was during this time that he wrote the letters that made up the posthumous *Letters and Papers from Prison* (1953; 1977), in which he calls for a "religionless Christianity." Bonhoeffer believed that the world had "come of age" and that the time of "religion" was over. By religion Bonhoeffer meant a purely inward, individualistic piety, which abandons the world or a special province of life, such as churchgoing. Religion

conceives of God as a *deus ex machina,* brought in only when our human powers give out or to provide solutions to our problems. Bonhoeffer, on the contrary, speaks of God as a this-worldly transcendence, discovered in concrete living for others— hence in the life of the Crucified. The only difference between Christians and nonbelievers is that Christians combine a true worldliness with a secret spiritual discipline by means of which they participate in the sufferings of God at the hands of a godless world. The church's task is, then, "to exist for others." Discipleship is always modest but *costly* and must be kept *worldly* to avoid all forms of religious escapism. Critics, such as K. Barth, find Bonhoeffer's fragmentary ideas only mystifying. Others believe that these revolutionary thoughts point to Christianity's authentic message for this modern, secular age.

J.L.

**BONIFACE VIII, POPE.** Pope from 1294 to 1303. His reign was marked by high claims of authority over secular rulers. But these claims coincided with the decline of the PAPACY, which would eventually lead to its control by France and its move to AVIGNON. Celestine V, whom Boniface succeeded, was a Franciscan of great humility, and therefore Boniface's haughtiness was all the more noticeable. Soon after his election, stories began circulating that he had forced Celestine to abdicate and that his election had been irregular. In spite of this, he enjoyed great prestige during the early years of his reign.

His bull *Clericis laicos* of 1296 barred ecclesiastics from paying taxes to the state and was resented and resisted by several sovereigns. But through it and other means he managed to force peace between Edward I of England and Philip IV, "the Fair," of France. Scotland became a fief of the popes. The "jubilee" of 1300 brought pilgrims, wealth, and prestige to Rome. The bull *Unam Sanctam* of 1302 declared that the Pope could stand in judgment over secular sovereigns, but that only God could judge the pope. In 1303, however, agents of Philip IV, whom Boniface threatened with excommunication, captured the pope at Anagni, struck him, and humiliated him publicly, while the populace sacked his palace and the palaces of his relatives. Although freed by his supporters, Boniface never recovered and died shortly thereafter. This marked the beginning of French hegemony over the papacy.                    J.G.

**BOOK AND FORMULA OF CONCORD.** *The Book of Concord* is the chief confessional symbol of the Lutheran Church throughout the world, made up of about seventy million Christians. *The Formula of Concord* (written in 1577, thirty-one years after LUTHER's death), ended the various disputes among theologians over the correct understanding of Luther's teaching. *The Book of Concord,* made up of six confessional books—the unaltered AUGSBURG CONFESSION, the Apology for the Augsburg Confession, the Smaldkald Articles, Luther's Small Catechism and Luther's Large Catechism, and the Formula of Concord (with the three ecumenical creeds)—was published on the fiftieth anniversary of the Augsburg Confession (1580).

The *Book of Concord* ensured the doctrinal loyalty and unity of the various state Lutheran churches and brought peace ("concord") in the theological dimension of German Protestant life. The acceptance of the *Book of Concord* enabled the Lutheran churches to maintain their independence from Calvinism and actually expressed the consensus on doctrine that existed among followers of Luther at that time. It also marked the political system (or polity) of Lutheranism for centuries to come. The various state or territorial churches were dominated by princes and ultimately by the Prussian kaiser, until recent times.

The central teachings of the *Book of Concord* include justification by faith in Jesus Christ, Luther's distinction between law and gospel, emphasis on Scripture as authoritative in the church, and on the real presence of Christ in Holy Communion. These basic tenets of the REFORMATION were interpreted differently by other Protestants or were disputed by the Catholics.

J.C.

**BOOK OF COMMON PRAYER.** The authorized liturgical service book of the Church of England used also by all churches in the worldwide ANGLICAN communion. The Book of Common Prayer has had a long history of revision, since it, rather than theological confessions, forms the essential core of the unity of Anglicanism. It contains the morning and evening prayers, Holy Communion services, the Psalms, and rituals for the administration of the sacraments and other prayers. It also contains the ORDINAL for conferring holy orders. Family prayers and the Thirty-Nine Articles of religion, along with various special orders, are found in appendices.

THOMAS CRANMER, the great English reformer, derived the materials for the Book of Common Prayer from the earlier Roman BREVIARY and MISSAL books. Changing emphases in doctrine, as the Reformation advanced or waned in England, caused the several revisions of the book. The 1549 version of Edward VI removed the concept of the Mass as a sacrifice. The 1552 version moved the church closer to the Reformed tradition of the Continent by removing reference to the real presence of Christ in the Eucharist, rejecting TRANSUBSTANTIATION. Suppressed by Queen Mary in 1553, the book was restored by Elizabeth I in 1559. Only the British Parliament can decree a modification or change in the Book of Common Prayer in the Church of England, as Anglicanism is the state church of England, with the queen as its temporal head.

There are modern revisions of the book, most notably in the Episcopal Church in the United States. This move toward contemporary English usage (and

away from the Elizabethan language shared by the Book of Common Prayer and the Authorized Version or King James Bible) has stirred up much controversy in Episcopal circles and even led to the withdrawal of some bishops, priests, and congregations from the denomination. These contemporary struggles over the venerated prayer book are only recent outcroppings of tensions and dissension that have marked the book's history since 1549. When the act of uniformity and mandatory use of the Book of Common Prayer was enforced by Elizabeth I and her successors, the Puritans (later Presbyterians, Congregationalists, and sectarians) rebelled against the "Catholic" nature of the prayer book's rituals. The Parliament of Westminster abolished use of the prayer book (and the order of bishop) in 1645. However, at the restoration of the monarchy in 1662, Charles II also reinstated the Book of Common Prayer.

The prayer book was revised and the new form proposed to Parliament in 1928, but Parliament rejected the revision in 1929. Other Anglican churches, such as those in the United States and Canada, nevertheless adopted revised versions. The current, new revision of the Book of Common Prayer, used in the Episcopal Church in the United States, is a further modernization of the revised prayer book of 1928. The newest edition shares much with the contemporary Roman Catholic missal in English and the Lutheran *Book of Worship* developed in the United States and Canada.

J.C.

**BOOK OF MORMON.** A book published by JOSEPH SMITH, founder of the CHURCH OF JESUS CHRIST OF LATTER-DAY SAINTS (LDS), or Mormons, in 1830, and accepted as divinely inspired by that group. The origin of the book is surrounded by controversy, and several theories disputing Smith's authorship are now current. In 1823, Smith claimed a vision of the angel Moroni (hence the name "Mormon") appeared to him and showed him where some golden plates were buried on a hill he called Mount Cumorah, near Palmyra, New York. Moroni said he buried the plates there about one thousand years earlier, at the close of a disastrous war between groups descended from the ten lost tribes of Israel. A set of spectacles, called Urim and Thummim, were discovered with the plates, and by wearing these, Smith was able to translate the "Reformed Egyptian" characters on the plates. Smith proceeded to do this translation, dictating to a secretary, while he sat behind a screen. The book purports to be a history of peoples who inhabited ancient America from 600 B.C. to A.D. 400. Moroni declared that the ascended Jesus appeared to one of these people, the Nephites, and founded his church in the new world. Smith established the Latter-day Saints as a restoration of the church Jesus established, according to Moroni's history.

Along with other writings of Joseph Smith, the Book of Mormon is looked upon as sacred scripture by the Latter-day Saints. Critics believe that anachronisms in the text show that it could not be from the fifth century A.D. They also point out that there is no archaeological or historical support for the belief that ancient Israelites came to the New World. Certain scholars believe Smith may have used a fictional biblical novel circulating in the early nineteenth century as the basis for his text. J.C.

## BOOK OF THE DEAD.

A text in Tibetan BUDDHISM and Egyptian religion that is concerned with the time between a person's death and the time the person enters another incarnation. This intermediate state is known in Tibetan Buddhism as the bardo state, and the Book of the Dead is known as the *Bardo Thodol* ("liberation by hearing while in the bardo state"). *The book instructs those who attend the dying person about the bardo state and the ways for seeking liberation from the cycle of birth and death.*

The Book of the Dead is used in rituals at the time of death and for as long as forty-nine days after death. A monk sits near the head of the dying person and reads the instructions for obtaining liberation. The corpse is usually present for the first four days, and after that the book is read before a picture or an effigy of the dead person.

Courtesy of the Oriental Institute, University of Chicago

*Egyptian papyrus of the Book of the Dead, showing the weighing of the heart of the deceased*

The forty-nine days are divided into three parts. The first lasts up to four days, and the dead person, if assisted properly, may obtain immediate liberation. Only a few are so fortunate.

The next period lasts fourteen days. During this time the person meets the peaceful deities and the wrathful deities. These are not beings on a higher plane, but are projections of the forces of KARMA that bind the person. If one recognizes that they are projections, it is possible to give up all desire and fear.

In the third stage the chance for liberation is slight. The person has visions of the six realms of rebirth and is drawn into a womb to start life over again. CARL G. JUNG and others have interpreted this book psychologically. They say that it identifies what it is that we fear—the self when it confronts itself, and that the book provides a way of overcoming this fear. In Tibet, however, its main use has been as a ritual text. K.C.

## BOOTH, WILLIAM AND CATHERINE. *See* SALVATION ARMY.

## BOOTHS, FEAST OF. *See* SUKKOTH.

## BORN AGAIN.

A popular phrase for the experience of CONVERSION, of a turning away from SIN and a drawing closer to God through Christ. The phrase is based on Jesus' word to Nicodemus that he must be "born again" or (in the Greek) "born from above" (John 3). The notion of rebirth, of a dying to one's old life and the beginning of a new life, is common to all religion, from shamanism and the ancient Greek and Middle Eastern mysteries to modern "Televangelism." In ancient religions (and in surviving forms of shamanism), rebirth is accomplished through ordeals, trials, tests, journeys, and quests, but especially through visions and dreams. Perhaps it is not surprising, then, that contemporary emphases on being "born again" are generally emotional, and the experience is usually one that occurs in large crowds stirred by music and long sieges of prayer and preaching. Interestingly, in John, Jesus connects the "birth from above" with the action of the Holy Spirit, which brings the experience about at his own good pleasure ("the wind blows where it wills"), thus making a premeditated attempt to induce the new birth unnecessary. In traditional churches, the new birth is associated with baptism, either of the infant or the adult.

J.C.

## BORNKAMM, GÜNTHER (1905– ).

A living NT scholar whose literary output and influence continue to the present. His early interest was in Gnosticism, which led to his academic career under Julius Schniewind at Königsberg. Prior to World War II, he was identified with the theological school at Bethel until it was closed by the Nazis in 1939. He served as a pastor at Münster and Dortmund until 1943, when he became a soldier in the German army. At the cessation of hostilities he taught at Göttingen, and since 1949 he has been linked with the University of Heidelberg, West Germany.

Bornkamm's claim to attention, on the theological scene, came with the publication of an essay on "End-Expectation and Church in Matthew," which is credited with signaling the advent of redaction criticism as a NT method of interpretation. The method, which sees the Gospel writers not simply as handers-on of the tradition to do with Jesus' ministry but the first theological commentators on that tradition, found expression in his well-known book, *Tradition and Interpretation in Matthew* (Eng. trans. 1963), in which he was joined by his pupils, G. Barth and H. J. Held. His most popular book, however, was *Jesus of Nazareth*, 1956 (Eng. trans. 1960), which had an unprecedented sale for a religious publication in Germany. This title marks a new phase in the "quest of the historical Jesus," and Bornkamm was more positive in his evaluation of the historical data of the Synoptic Gospels than Bultmann, his teacher, had been. Other books, on *Paul* (1971) and *Early Christian Experience* (1970) have followed, serving to establish his reputation as a lucid thinker and writer.

R.M.

**BOSSUET, JACQUES** (1627–1704). French bishop of Meaux and one of the great pulpit orators in the history of the church. He was prepared for ordination (1652) by St. Vincent de Paul (1576–1660), whose influence was decisive. Bossuet's oratorical gifts, intellectual acuteness, and moral power were recognized early. He was a frequent preacher before the French court and was tutor to the Dauphin for eleven years. During this time he published some of his most important books, including the *Discourse on Universal History*. Many of his publications were directed against Protestantism, including *History of the Variations in the Protestant Churches*.

Bossuet's piety and moral fervor attracted him to JANSENISM. In his late years he became a bitter opponent of Madame Guyon and QUIETISM. A leader of moderate GALLICANISM, he authored the famous Gallican Articles of 1682, which were rejected by Pope Innocent IX. Bossuet's *Meditations on the Gospel* is a devotional classic, as are his *Funeral Orations* classics of pulpit oratory. Bossuet was truly the voice of France in the age of Louis XIV.

J.L.

**BOWELS.** Both in Hebrew and Greek the words refer to the intestines, thought of as the seat of the human emotions, whether of compassion or affection (Jer. 31:20; Phil. 1:8; Col. 3:12; I John 3:17; all from the KJV) or more generally of a deeply felt emotional response (Ps. 22:14; Jer. 4:19; both KJV). It is a description that can be used also of God's attitude of mercy to creatures (Isa. 63:15 KJV) as well as of a human feeling. The Revised Standard Version usually renders by "heart," interpreting the psychosomatic term by this more elegant translation. One reference is to be understood literally, namely to the manner of Judas' demise (Acts 1:18, where RSV retains "bowels").

R.M.

**BOWRING, SIR JOHN** (1792–1872). Author of "In the Cross of Christ I Glory," "Watchman, Tell Us of the Night," and "God Is Love; His Mercy Brightens," Bowring was born in Exeter, England, on October 17. In 1825 he became editor of the *Westminster Review.* He served two terms in Parliament (1835–37, 1841–49) and was noted for his efforts to repeal the Corn Laws, reform the penal system, and abolish flogging in the army.

His diplomatic career began in 1849 when he became British consul to Canton, serving as superintendent of all trade to China and as plenipotentiary from 1853 to 1857. In 1854 he also became governor of Hong Kong. In 1855 he visited Siam to negotiate a commercial treaty, and in 1861 he was sent as a commissioner to Italy. He was knighted for his work in 1854.

A brilliant linguist, he wrote books on the poets of Russia, Spain, Holland, Poland, Bohemia, and Hungary. A Unitarian, he was also friend and literary executor of Jeremy Bentham, publishing his eleven-volume *Life and Works* (1838-43). His own two-volume *Autobiographical Recollections* were published posthumously by his son in 1877.

N.H.

**BRADBURY, WILLIAM B.** (1816–68). Sometimes called the father of popular Sunday school music, Bradbury was born on October 6 in York, Maine, to David and Sophia Chase Bradbury, both skilled musicians. At seventeen he went to Boston to study with Sumner Hill and Lowell Mason. In 1841 he became organist at First Baptist Church, New York City. Following Mason's practice of free singing classes, he conducted festivals with as many as a thousand children participating. He encouraged the introduction of music into the public schools. Altogether he published fifty books for young church choirs and a number of popular cantatas. In 1854 he helped found the Bradbury Piano Company, which eventually merged with Knabe Piano Company.

Bradbury is best known for his tunes to such favorite gospel songs as "Just As I Am," "Savior, Like a Shepherd Lead Us," "He Leadeth Me, O Blessed Thought," "My Hope Is Built," "Sweet Hour of Prayer," and "'Tis Midnight; and on Olive's Brow."

N.H.

**BRAHMA.** From a Sanskrit root meaning "to swell, grow." A Hindu god regarded as creator, and also as the source of wisdom, guardian of the VEDAS, and special patron of the priestly BRAHMIN caste, Brahma first comes into prominence in the Vedic scriptures called the BRAHMANAS. He was thus closely connected with the sacrifice, and indeed in one place in those scriptures is said to have been born of the priestly sacrifice, and then "though mortal, he created the immortals." He is elsewhere said to arise first in each new cycle of the universe, and then to create the gods and the three worlds (heavens, middle, and lower). Each cycle is a kalpa or day of Brahma, though 4,320 million years to us. At the end of that "day" the god sleeps, and the universe reverts to darkness and chaos, to be created anew when he awakes.

In the later mythology of the PURANAS, Brahma is associated with VISHNU. Here, we are told, that deity reclines between universes, and when it is time for a new one to come into being, a lotus grows from his navel, and Brahma appears—self-created, though drawing power from Vishnu—in its heart, and sets about the job of creation.

Brahma dwells in the highest heaven, and his consort is Sarasvati, the popular goddess of culture and learning. He is portrayed with four (or five) heads, seated on a lotus or riding a goose or swan. But though formally a member of the Hindu Trimurti or "trinity" of Brahma, Visnu, and SHIVA, he has enjoyed few shrines and little devotional worship since the rise of BHAKTI, unlike the other two gods. In Vedantic thought Brahma has been regarded as a personification of BRAHMAN, the impersonal Absolute.                                                              R.E.

**BRAHMAN.** From a Sanskrit root meaning "to swell, grow." A neuter form of the same expression is found in BRAHMA, the creator god of HINDUISM, and BRAHMIN, the Hindu priestly caste. Brahman meant (1) in Vedic times, the holy power generated by sacrifice, and (2) in the UPANISHADS and VEDANTA philosophy, the universal Spirit, ultimate Reality, or Absolute.

In the earlier Vedas, Brahman is a life-force, ill-defined but of great potency, which exists throughout nature but is especially invoked or created by the sacrifices of the Brahmin priests. It is said to have been produced by Prajapati, the creator, just after he made sacrifice. It is the force that gives the gods immortality and enables them to defeat demons. It is the sacred words of the ritual and the magical spell they spread to sustain the universe or accomplish the ends for which the sacrifice is done. It also has, like MANA, the quality of making objects and places taboo and should not be approached by the unprepared.

Later, the observation becomes more and more pronounced, that Brahman is greater than the gods, giving them their power, and underlies the universe itself. In the Upanishads, Brahman becomes the One, the sole Reality, of which all seemingly separate entities are but manifestations, like one flame taking many different shapes. Brahman emanated the world like a spider producing its web out of itself. He (or better, it) permeates that world like the invisible but all-pervasive salt in salt water. Finally, the great message of the Upanishads is "Thou art That," as the Chandogya Upanishad has it. The ATMAN, the inner life or "soul" of every human being, is none other than Brahman, the universal life and soul. By turning through meditation away from outer things, from desires and superficial feelings, one can know the Atman, and know it as Brahman, the Infinite. In the Chandogya we again read, "Only in the Infinite is there joy." Brahman is not known through reason or learning, for it is not an object of thought but the ground of consciousness. The Upanishads tell us that knowledge of Brahman comes through spiritual realization resulting from renunciation and meditation, under the guidance of a teacher who has attained that knowledge.                                              R.E.

**BRAHMANAS.** A portion of the Vedic scriptures of HINDUISM, the Brahmanas were produced approximately 900–700 B.C., and consist of prose commentaries on the earlier RIG VEDA and other of the largely poetic Samhita, or first stratum of Vedic literature. Focusing on the sacrifice, the Brahmanas offer detailed directions for their performance, but also present valuable speculative and mythological material. Emphasis is placed on the sacrifice in all its various implements and ritual gestures as having correspondence with the aspects of the cosmos. The rite is thus a "miniaturization" of the universe by which it can be regulated and controlled. The priest is the powerful "knower" at the center of both worlds, the large and the small. The Brahmanas represent a stage in development from the "primal naïveté" of the Rig Veda to the philosophical "interiorization" of sacrifice, and BRAHMAN or divine power and presence, of the Upanishads.

R.E.

**BRAHMANISM.** *See* VEDIC RELIGION.

**BRAHMIN.** Conventional anglicized spelling of the Sanskrit *Brahmana* and *Brahman* referring to the priestly caste of HINDUISM. Of ancient Indo-European background, the Brahmins have traditionally been the custodians of Hinduism's most sacred learning, especially the VEDAS, and the officiants of its oldest and holiest rites, particularly the Vedic fire sacrifices and other rituals involving recitation of Vedic texts.

R.E.

**BRAZEN SERPENT.** *See* BRONZE SERPENT.

**BREAD OF THE PRESENCE.** *See* SHOWBREAD.

**BREVIARY.** The service book of the Roman Catholic church containing the DIVINE OFFICE or services for the CANONICAL HOURS. The breviary is to be prayerfully used in times of quiet and meditation by the priest so that the apostolic command, "to pray without ceasing" may be realized.

The breviary is arranged as a collection of prayers with brief passages of Scripture interspersed, along with passages from the CHURCH FATHERS and the texts of classic Christian hymns. The canonical hours are prime (6:00 A.M.); terce (9:00 A.M.); sext (noon); none (3:00 P.M.) and vespers (6:00 P.M.). There is also a MATINS service, divided into three parts, and LAUDS. Most of the hourly material is from the Psalms. Collects or prayers, additional prayers, responses, and versicles complete the collection.

The breviary is divided into four parts, modeled on the four seasons. The festivals of the church and the commemorations of the saints are also included. The book concludes with the office for the dead, GRADUALS and PENITENTIAL PSALMS, prayers for the dying, prayers for travelers, and graces for before and after meals. It is a beautiful and useful collection of devotional material designed to enrich the lives of all those who use it.

J.C.

## BRIDGES, MATTHEW (1800–1894).

The author of "Crown Him with Many Crowns" and "Behold the Lamb" was born in Essex on July 14, 1800. Reared in the Church of England, he later became Roman Catholic. The last years of his life were spent in Quebec, Canada.

His other hymns include "My God, Accept My Heart This Day," "There Is an Everlasting Home," "Rise, Glorious Conqueror, Rise," and "Soil Not Thy Plumage, Gentle Dove." He also wrote *Hymns of the Heart* (1848).

N.H.

## BRIDGET OF SWEDEN (about 1303–73).

Variously called Brigid, Birgitta, Birgit, she is the patron saint of Sweden, a mystic, and founder of the Brigittine Order. The daughter of Birger Persson, governor of Uppland, she had visions from childhood. In 1316 she married Ulf Gudmarsson, later governor of Nesicia, to whom she bore eight children, including Catherine. At her husband's death in 1344, she retired to Alvastra on Lake Vetter.

In one of the *Revelations* she was commanded to found an order, for which she received papal permission in 1370. She had gone to Rome in 1350 with Catherine, and spent the remainder of her life there, serving the poor and working to return the pope from Avignon. She died July 23, 1373, and was canonized by Pope Boniface IX on October 7, 1391.

N.H.

## BRIGGS, CHARLES A. (1841–1913).

Controversial Presbyterian Old Testament scholar born on January 15 in New York City, to Alanson and Sarah Mead Berrian Briggs. He married Julia Valentine Dobbs in 1865.

Having studied at the University of Virginia and Union Theological Seminary in New York, he spent four years in Berlin, where he embraced HIGHER CRITICISM. After pastoring a Presbyterian church in New York, he was appointed in 1874 as professor of Hebrew and cognate languages at Union. In 1890 he became the Edward Robinson professor.

He was tried for heresy in 1892 by the presbytery of New York. There he was acquitted, but on appeal to the General Assembly, he was condemned and suspended from the ministry. He later took Episcopal orders.

Thoroughly conservative theologically, except for his higher critical views of Scripture, he was founder and for ten years editor of the *Presbyterian Review*. His two hundred titles include the Hebrew Lexicon and a two-volume commentary on the Psalms (1906–1907). He also edited two influential series, the International Critical Commentary and the International Theological Library.

N.H.

## BRIGHTMAN, EDGAR (1884–1953).

American philosopher and leading exponent of PERSONALISM. He studied at Boston University under Borden Parker Bowne, the foremost early advocate in America of a theistic personalism. Brightman taught at Nebraska Wesleyan University (1912–15), Wesleyan University (1915–19), and Boston University from 1919 until his death.

Brightman's METAPHYSICS is best described as pluralistic IDEALISM. It is idealist in that it holds that "everything that exists is in, of, or for a mind on some level." Being is personal. Furthermore, reality is a society of persons: God the ultimate, uncreated Person and humans finite, created persons. Brightman's most distinctive thought was his revision of the idea of God. God, if genuinely personal, cannot be timeless. Neither, Brightman taught, can God's goodness square with omnipotence. The power of God is limited by nonrational conditions (the Given) within God, which the Divine neither created nor approves—hence suffering, evil, and loss are real. Through his long teaching career, Brightman had great influence on the liberalizing of Methodist theology. His form of personalism is now, however, in eclipse. The development of Brightman's position is best known through the writings of Peter Bertocci, his successor at Boston University. Brightman's works include *The Problem of God* (1930); *Personality and Religion* (1940); and *Person and Reality* (ed. by P. Bertocci, 1958).

J.L.

## BRITISH COUNCIL OF CHURCHES.

A union of British denominational groups formed in 1942–43, from churches that had carried on interdenominational work since the conferences at Oxford and Edinburgh in 1937. The BCC is similar to the WORLD COUNCIL OF CHURCHES in its theological platform, that is, as a "fellowship of churches which accept Jesus Christ as God and Saviour" but qualify this by saying, "any body which has hitherto been represented on the commission shall continue in membership of the council, if so willing, even though it does not itself accept this basis."

The BCC has 118 members who represent the Church of England, Scotland, Wales and Northern Ireland, the Salvation Army, the Society of Friends (Quakers), the Unitarian Church, the various Free churches, five interdenominational agencies, and some twenty other religious groups. The BCC exists to promote four purposes embraced by all the participating churches and agencies: to facilitate concerted action in evangelism and to promote the sense of social responsibility, to facilitate common action, to promote cooperation in the studies of the World Council of Churches, and to nourish the growth of ecumenicity.

J.C.

## BRITISH MORALISTS.

The term applied to that distinguished tradition of British moral and political philosophy that includes RICHARD HOOKER (1554–

1600), Thomas Hobbes (1588–1679), JOHN LOCKE (1632–1704), Shaftesbury (1671–1713), Bernard Mandeville (1670–1733), Francis Hutcheson (1694–1746), JOSEPH BUTLER (1692–1752), and DAVID HUME (1711–76). Recently the term has been broadened to include social critics and moralists from Thomas Carlyle and Matthew Arnold to F. R. Leavis in this century.

J.L.

**BROAD CHURCH.** Originally a designation of the liberal or inclusive wing of the Church of England in the nineteenth century. It interpreted the THIRTY-NINE ARTICLES so as to include people of many different religious outlooks in the church. The Broad Church movement deemphasized episcopal polity and ancient ritual.

J.C.

**BRONZE SERPENT.** In Numbers 21:4-9, the people of Israel grumbled over the hardships of the Exodus through the wilderness. The people had craved meat (Num. 11); Miriam and Aaron had spoken out foolishly (Num. 12); the people were defeated at Hormah (Num. 14); and Moses had sinned by striking a rock to get water. Now the people complained that they would starve and die of thirst. The Lord then sent fiery serpents who bit the people and many died. This brought about fear and repentance (Num. 21:7), and Moses prayed for their deliverance. The Lord told Moses to make a serpent of bronze and mount it on a pole. People bitten by a serpent needed only to look at the bronze serpent and they would live (Num. 21:9).

According to II Kings 18:4, this bronze (or brasen in the KJV) serpent was preserved and kept in the temple, where people burned incense before it. It was named Nehushtan and obviously was a relic of superstition, or even of idolatry. Hezekiah, who sought to return to the covenant relationship with Yahweh and to cleanse Jewish worship of pagan practices, cut down the fertility pillars of Baal and Asherah and broke the bronze serpent in pieces (II Kings 18:1-6).

In the NT, Jesus "lifted up" on the cross at Calvary is likened to the bronze serpent that Moses "lifted up" (John 3:14). The healing that came when the Israelites looked at the bronze serpent in faith is said also to be true of Jesus, for "so must the Son of man be lifted up, that whoever believes in him may have eternal life" (John 3:14-15). Thus the brazen serpent in the OT can be seen as a "type" or image of Christ, who redeemed the world by being lifted, but who is effective only in the lives of those who look to him in faith.

J.C.

**BROOKS, PHILLIPS** (1835–93). The well-known Episcopal bishop and author of "O Little Town of Bethlehem," was born December 13 to William Gray

Courtesy of Religious News Service
*Phillips Brooks*

and Mary Ann Phillips Brooks. On his mother's side he was heir to a long line of Massachusetts ministers, and the founders of Phillips Exeter and Phillips Andover academies and Andover Theological Seminary. He was the second of six sons, four of whom became ministers.

Baptized at First Church (Unitarian), Boston, he was four when the family joined St. Paul's Episcopal Church. He studied at Harvard, taught at his alma mater Boston Latin School, and entered seminary in Alexandria, Virginia. There he was ordained deacon July 1, 1859. In August he went to the Church of the Advent in Philadelphia, and in January 1863 became rector of Holy Trinity Church. His famous carol was written for that church's Sunday school and first sung on Christmas 1868.

On October 31, 1869, he began his ministry at Trinity Church, Boston. When fire destroyed the church in 1872, the congregation rebuilt on Copley Square.

Brooks was a masterful speaker. His prayer at an 1865 Harvard memorial service for those who had died in the Civil War overshadowed the speaker. His *Yale Lectures on Preaching* (1877) were widely read. He preached at Westminster Abbey in 1880 and was the first American to preach for Queen Victoria. In 1879 he gave the Bohlen Lectures on *The Influence of Jesus*. In 1891 he was elected bishop of Massachusetts but served only two years before he died January 23, 1893.

N.H.

**BROTHERHOOD, BROTHERLY LOVE.** One of the first descriptions Christians used of one another was "brother." There is precedent for this in the OT, where "brother" often means fellow Israelite or Jewish neighbor (Lev. 19:17, 18). Jesus' teaching widened the scope of the term "neighbor" as in the parable of the kind Samaritan (Luke 10:25-37), and in a similar way the parable of Matthew 25:31-46 lifts the meaning of "these my brethren" to include all who suffer and are in need as believers. See also Matthew 12:46-50 for what is clearly revolutionary teaching that universalizes the scope of "brother" to include all who "do the will of God," irrespective of ethnic origins.

"Brotherhood" also received a new dimension from the role of Christ as "elder brother" in the family of God (Rom. 8:29; Heb. 2:11, 17; see John 20:17). It was therefore a natural consequence for the early Christians to call themselves by this title (Acts 1:15, 16; I Cor. 1:11; James 2:1, 5, 14); and indeed to use the term, in a nonsexist way, to mean all the members of the church (I Thess. 5:25-27). The implication is that all Christians belong to the same divine family under one Father, who is both Father of Jesus his firstborn (Col. 1:15; compare Luke 2:7) and of believers (Rom. 8:14-16).

In that family circle the hallmark is a life of love. Hence the call to "love as brothers" (I Thess. 4:9; I Pet. 3:8). "Brotherly love" (Greek *philadelphia*) is a fairly frequent term in the NT (Rom. 12:10 KJV; Heb. 13:1; I Thess. 4:9 KJV), and it describes the ethos of those who belong to the Christian "brotherhood" (I Pet. 2:17; 5:9) as that way of life appropriate to a fellowship in Christ. Its marks are unity (Rom. 12:16; 15:5) and practical concern to help those in need (I John 3:17).

R.M.

**BROTHERS OF THE COMMON LIFE.** Monastic groups founded in the Netherlands by Gerhard Groote (1340–84) and Florentius Radewin (1350–1400). They stressed *devotio moderna*—simple, sincere, religious living, without permanent vows. Their Deventer house became famous for teaching. THOMAS À KEMPIS was a noted member, and they influenced ERASMUS and LUTHER.

C.M.

**BROWNE, ROBERT** (1550–1633). Controversial PURITAN Separatist and early advocate of congregational polity. Born in Tolethorpe, Rutland (England), and educated at Corpus Christi, Cambridge, Browne urged further reform in Anglicanism. With Robert Harrison he started an independent church in Norwich, 1581, and was imprisoned briefly. He then emigrated to Holland, where in 1582 he published *Reformation Without Tarrying for Any,* and *A Booke Which Sheweth the Life and Manners of All True Christians.*

He denounced Puritans who were waiting for Queen Elizabeth I to reform the church. He said rulers should neither compel nor control in religious matters. Rather, the only true church is an autonomous, voluntary covenant body of believers united to Christ and directed by his laws. Ministers have a special task but are subject to the congregation. Browne returned to England and Anglicanism, 1585, and spent his final years conforming outwardly to the Anglican ministry.

C.M.

**BRUNNER, EMIL** (1889–1966). Swiss theologian and influential leader of the movement variously known as NEO-ORTHODOXY, DIALECTICAL THEOLOGY, or the Theology of Crisis, in the years between the two world wars. Drawing on a fresh reading of the Bible, the Reformers Luther and Calvin, and Kierkegaard, Brunner—with K. Barth, F. Gogarten, and E. THURNEYSEN—attacked the prevailing nineteenth-century tradition of Protestant liberal theology from Schleiermacher to Harnack. In *The Theology of Crisis* (1929), Brunner faulted the emphasis in liberal theology on the immanence of God and stressed, instead, God's mystery and otherness, the crisis of belief, and the radically paradoxical nature of Christian faith.

Brunner was born and educated in Switzerland, attending the University of Zurich. Early influences included the south German pastor Christoph Blumhardt (1842–1919), Herman Kutter (1863–1931), a disciple of Blumhardt, and Leonhard Ragaz (1868–1945), Brunner's teacher at Zurich. From 1916 to 1922 Brunner was pastor in the mountain village of Obstalden. In 1922 he was made *Privatdozent* in theology at the University of Zurich and, two years later, he was appointed professor of systematic and practical theology, a post he held until 1953. Brunner did not have a great influence on German theology, although he wrote in that tongue. This was due, in part, to the fact that his books were banned by the Nazis.

His influence on Anglo-American theology, however, was considerable. Brunner traveled and lectured extensively in Britain and the United States in the twenties and thirties. In 1938–39 he was professor of systematic theology at Princeton Seminary. His many books, translated into English, were widely known in the United States in the thirties and forties. During this period Brunner also was active in the Faith and Order and Life and Work movements, which led to the ecumenical World Council of Churches. Later he became a theological advisor to the worldwide YMCA. In that post he traveled extensively through Asia in 1949. In 1953 he became professor of Christian ethics and philosophy at the International Christian University, Tokyo, Japan. In 1955 Brunner returned to Zurich as preacher at the Fraumünster Church, where for many years he had preached to overflowing congregations.

*Emil Brunner*

Brunner's first major work in Christian doctrine was *The Mediator* (1927), a study in Christology. The book rejected the liberal view of Jesus of Nazareth as a religious genius. Comparisons between Jesus and other religious visionaries is impossible. "We are confronted," Brunner asserts, "with an absolutely incomparable new fact . . . a new category which transcends history"—the incarnate Word of God. While upholding the ancient creedal definitions of God and Christ, Brunner nevertheless continually warned against overly intellectual approaches to theological knowledge. For Brunner, God is known only in personal encounter. This is the theme of *The Divine-Human Encounter* (1937), a work that reflects the profound influence of M. Buber's *I and Thou*.

Brunner maintained throughout his writings that God is revealed, though imperfectly, in and through the natural world and the events of history. That is, despite the FALL there remains a "point of contact" between God and natural humanity, an ongoing divine revelation in the Creation. However, Brunner also asserted that genuine *saving* knowledge of God is found *only* in Christian revelation. This position satisfied neither those in favor of natural theology nor K. Barth, who, in a pamphlet entitled *Nein!*, charged Brunner with being tainted by Catholic natural theology and denying the exclusive revelation of God

in Christ. This dispute led to a tragic personal break between the two theologians, but it also sparked a lively theological debate on the nature of divine revelation.

Brunner wrote important works on the Christian doctrine of human existence, *Man in Revolt* (1937), and on Christian ethics, *The Divine Imperative* (1947). His other works include the Gifford Lectures, published as *Christianity and Civilization* (1948), *Revelation and Reason* (1947), *Eternal Hope* (1954), and the three volumes of his *Dogmatics: The Christian Doctrine of God I* (1950), *The Christian Doctrine of Creation and Redemption II* (1952), and *The Christian Doctrine of the Church, Faith, and the Consummation III* (1960).

J.L.

**BUBER, MARTIN** (1878–1965). One of the greatest Jewish thinkers of this century. Born in Vienna, Buber grew up in Lemberg in Galicia in the home of his grandfather Solomon Buber, a brilliant rabbinic scholar. Here young Buber imbibed both genuine piety and sound learning. At eighteen Buber entered the philosophy faculty at the University of Vienna. In the next few years he also studied in Leipzig, Berlin, and Zurich. One of his earliest publications was on the mystical writers of the Renaissance and Reformation periods. In Leipzig Buber founded a local Zionist group, and in 1901 he became editor of the Zionist journal *Die Welt* in Vienna. He soon left, however, because of differences with THEODOR HERZL, leader of the movement. With friends he founded the Jewish publishing firm *Judische Verlag* in 1902, which helped create a Jewish national movement in central Europe. In 1904 Buber received his doctoral degree from Vienna.

Soon, however, he withdrew from his Zionist and editorial activities and for five years, from 1904 to 1909, devoted himself to a study of the traditions and writings of the Hasidic movement of Jewish mystical piety. HASIDISM was the most formative influence on Buber's life and work. The fruit of these years of study was a series of books on the Hasidic legends. In 1913 Buber resumed interest in Zionism and, from 1916 to 1924, edited *Der Jude,* an effort to further the spiritual and cultural dimensions of the Zionist movement. In the 1920s Buber joined with Franz Rosenzweig in a number of cultural and educational activities, including work on a German translation of the Hebrew Bible and the establishment of the Free Jewish Academy in Frankfurt am Main. This educational work left an important mark on German Jewry.

In 1923 Buber was appointed professor of Jewish history of religion and ethics at Frankfurt University. That same year he published *I and Thou,* his best-known and most influential work. In 1933 Buber was deprived of his teaching post by the Nazis, and in 1938 he left Germany for Israel. There he served as professor of sociology at the Hebrew

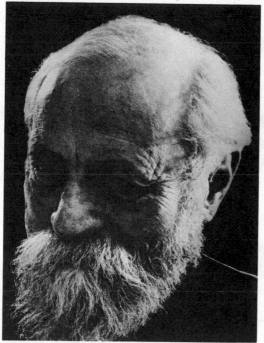

Courtesy of Religious News Service

*Martin Buber*

University of Jerusalem until his retirement in 1951. His many writings include *Tales of the Hasidim, The Legends of the Baal-Shem, Daniel, Between Man and Man, Two Types of Faith, Israel and the World,* and *Eclipse of God.*

Buber's greatest contribution to thought is his "philosophy of dialogue," developed in *I and Thou* but implicit in much of his other work, including the studies of Hasidism. "In the beginning," writes Buber, "is relation." All real life is meeting. The self of each person comes into being in one of two primary relations: the I-It or the I-Thou. The usual way of relating to other persons is to treat them as an It: by experiencing and using them. It is an objective and instrumental mode of relation, exemplified in the experimental or scientific method. It is a form of relation that is indispensable to the ordering and maintaining of human life.

However, it is not the primary relationship, for it lacks genuine mutuality; that is found in the relationship of I-Thou. According to Buber, real knowledge of another requires openness, participation, empathy—genuine encounter and mutuality. Thus real knowledge of another can come only as a free gift, and such knowledge always remains finally ineffable. Because I-Thou relations cannot be coerced or sustained, they are rare, intense, fleeting revelations of new depths of meaning. It follows that human beings cannot live continuously in the world of I and Thou. However, Buber insists, one who lives in the

world of I-It relations alone is not fully human. What has happened in the modern world is an abdication before the world of the It, which has made impossible a genuine spiritual life. Our lives are divided between the worlds of external institutions and private feelings. Both worlds deny real meeting and community.

Just as we cannot really know another person in terms of I-It, neither can we know God objectively. Only in openness, risk, and surrender is God or the Eternal Thou revealed. For Buber, meeting the Eternal Thou occurs in the hallowing of the everyday activities of life. The "filled present," which comes through such encounters with the Eternal Thou, is what Buber calls revelation. Revelation is not a "content" or a "solution" but, rather, a confirmation of meaning and a call to action. "Meet the world in the fullness of your being and you shall meet Him."

Buber's criticism of traditional Jewish religious practice has reduced his influence within orthodox Judaism, and many Zionists consider him utopian and unrealistic. Buber's historical interpretation of Hasidism also has been severely criticized by Jewish scholars. Nevertheless, his philosophy of dialogue has had wide influence not only on JUDAISM but also on the work of Christian theologians such as F. GOGARTEN, K. Heim, E. BRUNNER, and P. TILLICH.

J.L.

**BUCER, MARTIN** (1491–1551). Protestant reformer of Strasburg and leading Reformed Church theologian after ZWINGLI. At fourteen he joined the Dominicans and later studied both ERASMUS' and LUTHER's writings at Heidelberg. In 1521 he gained release from his monastic vows, married, and in 1523 was excommunicated for preaching Lutheranism. Bucer's Lutheran ideas were modified by his strong Erasmian humanism, nonviolence, and hope for religious unity. Throughout his life he sought to ease Protestant differences and heal Catholic-Protestant hatreds with ambiguous words. He sided with Zwingli at Marburg, 1529, yet signed the Wittenberg Concord, 1536, with Luther affirming the REAL PRESENCE of Christ in the Eucharist. Under him Strasburg became Protestant and was a haven for religious refugees, but Anabaptists were still persecuted. In 1548 he opposed the Augsburg Interim and fled to England, welcomed there by King Edward VI and Thomas Cranmer. He taught briefly at Cambridge and wrote *De Regno Christi (On the Kingdom of Christ),* his greatest work, a model for making all of life conform to God's will. He did not speak English but influenced Anglicanism through his students. He was buried at Cambridge. When Mary became queen, he was declared a heretic, and his body exhumed and burned, 1557.

C.M.

**BUCHMAN, FRANK.** *See* OXFORD GROUP.

*The Great Buddha of Kamakura, Japan*

**BUDDHA, GAUTAMA.** The person known as the Buddha and honored as the founder of BUDDHISM. He was born in what is now Nepal about 560 B.C. and died somewhere around eighty years later. These dates are based on modern historical research. Many Buddhist sects (including the Nichiren sects) follow a tradition that the Buddha died in 949 B.C. In the Far East his birthday is observed on April 8.

The earliest texts that give information about his life were written in Sri Lanka (Ceylon) as late as 89–77 B.C. The first biography was the *Buddhacarita,* written by Ashvaghosha in Sanskrit late in the first century A.D. It contains much legendary material, but is widely accepted as giving valid information about the historical Buddha.

*Birth and Early Years.* His family name was Gautama (Gotama, in the Pali language in which the earliest scriptures were written), and his given name was Siddhartha. He was born to King Suddhodana of the Shakya clan, and his consort, Maya. Buddha is thus widely known as Shakyamuni—the Sage of the Shakyas. It is by this title that he is most frequently adored and venerated in the Far East.

Legend tells that in a dream Maya saw a white elephant entering her womb and impregnating her. Her son was born in a pleasant grove, with fountains, flowers, and fruit trees. He at once spoke a prophecy that he would become enlightened, and that this was his last birth in the cycle of birth and death.

Various signs were found on his body, indicating

his future destiny. Three signs that are easily seen in images of the Buddha are a bulge on the top of his skull, a sign of supernatural mental powers; a hair in the middle of his forehead, represented in images by a jewel; and elongated ear lobes.

When his parents heard prophecies that he would leave his heritage of wealth and power to lead a religious life, they were frightened and tried to shield him from the world. He married a beautiful princess named Yashodhara, and she bore him a son. They named him Rahula, meaning "hindrance." Rahula later became one of his father's disciples and is honored as one of the most important arhants.

*Beginnings of His Religious Life.* The gods were displeased with Siddhartha's sheltered life and arranged for him to see four disturbing sights. On three successive trips outside the palace, accompanied by his charioteer, he saw a man overcome with old age, a man afflicted by disease, and a corpse. He was greatly troubled to learn that this is the common destiny of humans, and that the world is unconcerned.

Gautama then began to meditate on what he had observed. When he was able to become passionless and detached, the fourth sight, a man dressed as a begging monk approached him. A brief conversation convinced Gautama that he too should become a wandering monk. His parents vigorously opposed this decision and tried to distract him with worldly pleasures, including dancing girls. But he saw them only as impure and loathsome. In the silence of the night, he slipped away from home and family.

After many wanderings during which he almost starved himself to death, he concluded that tormenting the body achieved nothing. He accepted some food from a girl who was passing by. Then he determined to sit in meditation until he achieved a knowledge of the truth.

*Enlightenment.* Gautama sat cross-legged under the BODHI tree, resisting furious temptations from Mara the Tempter. He recalled all his previous lives, seeing that ignorance leads to old age and death, and death leads to rebirth and repetition of the cycle. He realized he could break the chain of causation if he once destroyed attachment to persons and things and the craving to possess them. Thus he became enlightened. For seven days he sat there contemplating the truth he had found.

Not content to find liberation only for himself, the now Enlightened One, the Buddha, set out for the city of Varanasi (Benares). There he met five wandering monks whom he had known during his period of near starvation. They were prepared to treat him with contempt, because he had given up the life of self-torment, but his person was now so powerful that they knelt before him. There in a place known as the Deer Park, he preached his first sermon and made the five monks his first disciples.

*Teachings.* Gautama's first sermon consisted of the FOUR NOBLE TRUTHS and the EIGHTFOLD PATH OF BUDDHA—the basic insights he had gained in his enlightenment. Ever since then they have constituted the central core of Buddhist beliefs and the basic guide to Buddhist practice. Essentially the Buddha taught a middle path between the one extreme of the indulgence of our desires and the other extreme of total asceticism. As the Enlightened One he had the freedom to teach or not teach; that is, he could remain detached from the sufferings of others. But because he could see with the eyes of a Buddha, he felt great compassion for all those whose minds are confused by false views, greed, and hatred. Since their problem is an inward or mental one, changing their outward conditions is in itself no help. Only by teaching and preaching can a real change be brought about.

The teachings are known as DHARMA, or the cosmic law of righteousness. The goal is, first, wisdom, and then, as the result of enlightenment, NIRVANA, where the cycle of birth and death ceases, and all individual identity is lost.

Since beings can be reborn not only as humans, but as animals, ghosts, gods, and dwellers in heaven or hell, compassion must be extended to them all. Killing animals, eating meat, using leather or silk are thus all wrong. Heaven and hell are temporary stages, and the gods are also subject to birth and death. The most favorable realm for achieving enlightenment is the human realm.

Until the age of eighty, Gautama traveled about India teaching and preaching. Then, surrounded by followers, he lay down on his right side and died. This was his *Parinirvana*—great entry into Nirvana.

K.C.

**BUDDHISM.** The religion of "enlightenment" (BODHI), that is, understanding that the world we experience is unreal and impermanent. Enlightenment leads one to escape from this world of suffering and illusion into NIRVANA. There passions and ignorance are extinguished and individual human existence is ended.

Buddhism had its origin in northern India. The founder, Siddhartha Gautama (about 560-480 B.C.), came to be the BUDDHA, or "Enlightened One." From its start Buddhism was a protest against HINDUISM and especially the Hindu ideas of CASTE, ASCETICISM, and an immortal soul that is in reality part of the world soul.

Over the following centuries Buddhism spread to Sri Lanka, Burma, Thailand, Laos, and Cambodia in a form known as Theravada ("Tradition of the Elders," see below). It also spread north into central Asia, China, Korea, and Japan, where a new form, Mahayana ("Greater Vehicle"), became dominant. Beginning in the eighth century A.D., another form arose in Tibet (see below). Some of the most important developments took place in China and Japan. There is so much variety among the various schools and sects that at times Buddhism seems more like a family of religions than a single religion.

The earliest sacred writings are in Pali, a language that had developed from Sanskrit. When Buddhism expanded into new areas, Sanskrit came to be used, since it was a more widely understood language. The first missionaries to China (first century A.D.?) used Sanskrit and translated their teachings from it into Chinese. It was necessary to find or invent Chinese vocabulary to do this, and the choice of terms deeply influenced the meaning of many of the teachings. The Buddhist scriptures in Chinese have been used in neighboring lands where Chinese culture is influential: Korea, Japan, and Vietnam.

*General Concepts.* Buddhism is rich in profound concepts, and the following are those which are most important to understand.

(a) *The four noble truths.* When Gautama became enlightened he perceived four truths about human existence. The first of these is the truth of suffering. Human existence is unsatisfactory. We suffer physically through sickness, old age, etc., and mentally by being with those we dislike or separated from those we love. In medical terms, this is the symptom of our problem. The second truth is that our suffering is caused by craving, lust, and greed. This is the diagnosis of our problem. Third, it is possible to put an end to this craving that brings suffering—the prognosis. And fourth, there is an eightfold path that makes it possible to put an end to suffering—the prescription.

(b) *The eightfold path.* The eight parts of this path are not successive steps, but are to be practiced at the same time, even though some parts can be achieved before others. The first two parts, right understanding and right thoughts, involve wisdom. The next three, right speech, right action, and right means of earning a living, involve morality. The last three, right effort, right mindfulness, and right concentration, lead to singleness of mind, and finally to Nirvana.

(c) *Dukkha.* This is the term for the suffering that we learn about in the first of the Four Noble Truths. It may be mental or physical suffering that we experience consciously, or it may be suffering that results from our psychological makeup, which is constantly changing. It may also be connected with the next two items in this list, *anicca* and *anatta*. In that case it is the suffering that is involved in all things that are pleasant, because they cannot last, but change and disappear.

(d) *Anicca* ("impermanence"). The fact of change is obvious to every observer. Plants, animals, and human beings are born, live a while, and die, and the earth on which they live is changing, surely though sometimes slowly. Buddhists hold that we are only a procession of changes, always in flux, never ceasing. Even a giant tree or a human being cannot be said to "exist." We are at most a changing proportion of the elements that make us up. It would be foolish to attach ourselves to these changing objects or persons.

(e) *Anatta* ("no-self"). In a reaction against the doctrine of an undying self (ATMAN) in Hinduism, early Buddhism taught that there is no permanent self. We are a temporary collection of "heaps" or separate parts; form, sensation, perception, predispositions, and consciousness. A wagon can be divided into its separate parts, and instead of a wagon we have only a pile of those parts. Just so, death ends the connection of our separate "heaps" with each other, and what we thought was a self is gone forever. Wanting to cling to the illusion of a "self" is a mistake. It leads to sorrow and suffering.

(f) *Karma* (the results of our thoughts and acts). Even though there is no permanent self, the results of what we do and think are carried over to a new life. This teaching is hard to explain, if there is no self that continues. The passing of good or bad karma to the next life has been compared to the passing of energy from a lighted candle to an unlighted one. Or it is said to be like a teaching process in which pupils memorize the truths the teacher gives them.

(g) *Samsara* (the repeated process of birth and death). We are destined to be born and die over and over again, and both birth and death bring sorrow and suffering. By following the Four Noble Truths and the Eightfold Path a person can eventually escape. In the meantime, however, a being may live many lifetimes and pass through various realms of existence, such as human life, animal life, hell, the realm of the gods, the realm of hungry ghosts, and the realm of demons.

(h) *Sunyata* ("emptiness"). Everything and any independent being in this world are empty of lasting value. Therefore nothing here is worthy of our ultimate commitment. To realize that this is true, the believer must meditate. Finally, with full realization, one is free from entanglements.

*Ways to Enlightenment.* (a) *Buddhahood.* It is the goal of every believer to become a Buddha, even though this may require many lifetimes. Soon after Gautama's death the belief arose that there had been other Buddhas before him. There also came to be a distinction between different kinds of Buddhas. Some, like Gautama, had entered Nirvana and could not be reached by prayers. Others, like Amida, had become enlightened, not on earth, but in a heavenly realm, and so could be reached by prayer.

(b) *Bodhisattva* ("Buddha to be"). This is the last stage before the final birth and death, when one enters Nirvana. Gautama had been a BODHISATTVA before becoming a Buddha. Because of compassion for those who suffer, a person can take a vow to help all beings to salvation. This means that he or she will stop at the bodhisattva stage and not enter Nirvana until everyone else can be saved too. Thus a bodhisattva can hear and answer prayer. The most popular bodhisattva in the Far East is AVALOKITESVARA (called Kwan Yin in Chinese). Kwan Yin is usually thought of as feminine and often called the Goddess of Mercy. She can help people with everyday problems or help them get to the Western Paradise, a "Pure Land" of beauty and delight ruled over by Amida Buddha.

(c) *Arhat or lohan* ("learner, disciple"). Most early arhats were disciples or close followers of Gautama Buddha. In Mahayana (see below) the Chinese equivalent of the term "arhat" is *lohan*. Lohans are considered selfish, because they do not try to save others. Statues and pictures of bodhisattvas are beautiful and tranquil, while lohans are often given a grotesque form, at times even comic. Some of them are in an inferior Nirvana, and some remain behind in the world in order to protect the DHARMA, the true teaching.

(d) *The triple body*. This is a Mahayana teaching that says the Buddha has three distinct modes of existing. The first is the dharmakaya, or body of dharma, which is absolutely unlimited in nature. Many sects believe everyone is a manifestation of the dharmakaya, and therefore everyone is worthy of life and will eventually be saved. The second is the Buddha body on the worldly plane, and the third is the Buddha body in a heavenly form. A worshiper can move from the contemplation of the earthly Buddha body to the heavenly, and finally to the dharmakaya.

*Monasticism.* From earliest times the followers of the Buddha were organized in a monastic order, or sangha. Special organizations for nuns soon developed. A monk or nun pledges to take refuge in the Buddha, in the dharma, or teaching, and in the sangha. These three are known as the "three jewels." The monastic life is regarded as closer to the ideal life, and therefore it is easier for a monk or nun to be reborn in a favorable realm in the next life than it is for a lay person.

Monasteries developed into self-sufficient communities, often with large holdings of land or other property. At times their wealth brought persecution from envious governments. In China there was fierce persecution in A.D. 845, after which Buddhism went into a slow decline. Monasteries were destroyed, gold and silver images were melted down, and monks and nuns were forced back into secular life. Throughout Buddhist lands monasteries have buildings of great beauty and preserve priceless art treasures. They continue to be centers of devotion and have enormous impact on culture and society, especially in Japan.

*Scriptures.* The earliest collection of Buddhist scriptures is called the Tripitaka, literally "three baskets," after its three major divisions. The first "basket" contains writings governing the conduct of monastic life. The second contains discourses on the basic ideals and teachings of the Buddha. One of these discourses is the DHAMMAPADA, which is especially popular with lay persons. It sums up the teachings in a clear and simple way, and it is easy to memorize. The third basket deals with theological controversies and is only of academic interest.

Many other scriptures, usually known as "sutras," took shape over the centuries, especially in Mahayana. They set forth distinctive Mahayana teachings.

Because they often do not agree with one another, great scholars tried to develop ways of including them all in one system of thought. The Tendai school (see below) was especially successful in this.

*Aids to Meditation and Worship.* (a) *Mantra.* A word or phrase that is recited over and over as an aid to meditation or to call on a supernatural being for help. In Tibet the syllable *om* is especially used. The name of a specific Buddha or bodhisattva often forms the core of a mantra, for example, "Namu Amida Butsu" (Japanese), meaning, "I adore Amida Buddha."

(b) *Mandala.* A diagram with symmetrically arranged circles within larger concentric circles. It is arranged around a central Buddha figure, surrounded by other Buddhas and bodhisattvas. Basically it is regarded as a diagram of the universe, and thus as a sort of map of the way to salvation. Some mandalas are very elaborate and colorful.

(c) *Mudra.* A ritual gesture, in which the hands are placed in specific positions. Each mudra has a separate meaning, and many are associated with a specific Buddha or bodhisattva.

(d) *Paintings and images.* In earliest times no images of the Buddha were made. A tree or other symbol represented his presence. Later a great variety of figures and symbols came to be used to portray Buddhas, bodhisattvas, lohans, and saints. Paintings range from the simple and austere to the elaborate and colorful. Statues range from small household images to giant images several stories high.

(e) *Stupa.* A commemorative monument that may contain relics of a holy being. A pilgrim may bring offerings to the stupa, chant scriptures there, and walk around it repeatedly. In China the stupa took the form of a multi-storied wooden watchtower, often called a pagoda. Throughout the Far East stupas of wood or stone range in size from a meter or two to tens of meters in height.

*Theravada.* "Tradition of the Elder" is the form of Buddhism found in Sri Lanka, Burma, Thailand, and other countries in Southeast Asia. It is the closest to the earliest forms of Buddhism. Emphasis is on the practices that individuals perform to achieve salvation for themselves. Merit acquired in this way cannot be transferred to others. The ideal is to become an arhant (see above), and only a monk can do so. Critics of Theravada call it "Hinayana," or "Lesser Vehicle (for salvation)."

*Tibetan Buddhism.* Buddhism reached Tibet comparatively late. In A.D. 747 Padma-Sambhava introduced into Tibet a form of Buddhism known as Tantric or esoteric, that is, containing secret practices and doctrines. Some of these involve sexual practices designed to bring home the point that there is no duality, but everything is basically one. Art, scriptures, and worship developed to a high level of sophistication.

To aid a dying person to come back in a favorable realm in his or her next rebirth, Tibetan Buddhists developed a guidebook to the period of time between death and rebirth. It is popularly known as the BOOK OF THE DEAD.

*Mahayana.* The "Greater Vehicle (to salvation)," so called because of its emphasis on helping others to salvation in contrast to "Hinayana" (Theravada; see above).

(a) *Origins and emphases.* The basic idea of Mahayana is that every being possesses the Buddha nature and is therefore capable of becoming a Buddha. Since the path to Buddhahood is now open to everyone, there must be simpler means of traveling it. This can be done by faith and devotion to the Buddha and by love and compassion for all living beings. Faith in Amida Buddha and calling on his name even once may be enough to assure one of salvation. A great variety of

sects and schools developed, but many of them are now only of historical interest. Among the many scriptures, the Lotus Sutra is the most influential.

(b) *Tendai* (in Japanese), *T'ien T'ai* (in Chinese). This school arose in China in the sixth century A.D. on T'ien T'ai Mountain in eastern Chekiang Province. In the preceding centuries scholars had translated large numbers of scriptures into Chinese. They represented conflicting teachings, so it was hard to accept them all as the literal sermons of the Buddha while he was on earth. The solution was to divide the Buddha's life into five periods. During these periods he moved from simple teachings to higher teachings suitable to those mature enough to understand them. The LOTUS SUTRA was the highest teaching of all. Tendai also

## Buddhism in China

● Place having a substantial Buddhist presence before A.D. 400.
▲ Mountain having an important Buddhist monastery
△ Mountain having early Buddhist presence
★ Other places having important monuments or monastaries

Reprinted with permission of Macmillan Publishing Company, from *Historical Atlas of the Religions of the World*, edited by Isma'il Ragi al Faruqi and David E. Sopher. Copyright © 1974 by Macmillan Publishing Company

developed a complex philosophy that continues to have great influence today, especially in PURE LAND and NICHIREN Buddhism.

(c) *Pure land buddhism.* A number of sects, especially in Japan, take their name from the "Pure Land," or "Western Paradise," of Amida Buddha. They stress faith in Amida, recitation of his name, and the goal of being reborn in paradise as of more immediate importance than entering Nirvana. The Pure Land is rich in pleasures and delights, and the scriptures give glowing accounts of it.

Pure Land Buddhism has accepted and followed many of the teachings of Tendai. Today Pure Land sects have more followers than any other Buddhist group in Japan. Its practices have spread to other sects as well.

(d) *Nichiren buddhism.* Unlike other sects, which have their roots in India or China, this branch of Buddhism began with the dramatic career of the monk Nichiren in thirteenth-century Japan. He drew on the Tendai teachings and stressed the importance of the Lotus Sutra. Nichiren taught that we are living in the final age of Buddhism (*Mappo,* literally "end of the Dharma"), and that in this age people can achieve salvation only through him. He rejected as false all forms of Buddhism except his own. Those who worship Amida are "Hell," and Zen (see below) is "a devil." This attitude has been continued in the present century by Nichiren Shoshu, a sect that has grown phenomenally since 1945 and has spread to America. Here some of its extreme demands have been modified. Nichiren Shoshu has had its largest growth, not through the activities of monks, but under lay leadership in a parallel organization called Soka Gakkai. From a handful of believers in 1945 it has grown to perhaps fifteen to twenty million in the 1980s. It also has a political party, the Komeito, a strong middle-of-the-road force in Japanese politics.

A less aggressive form of lay Buddhism in the Nichiren tradition is known as RISSHO KOSEIKAI, with about five million members. Its leader, Kikkyo Niwano, is active in international, interfaith movements. Their distinctive practice is called *hoza* ("circle of harmony"), a circle of twelve persons who gather to share mutual concerns for their spiritual and physical welfare.

(e) *Zen (literally "meditation").* The best known and most popular form of Buddhism in the West. Its aim is enlightenment (*satori* in Japanese), which requires great discipline. Satori can be achieved more than once, with varying degrees of intensity. Zen's origins are traced to the semilegendary figure of Bodhidharma in fifth-century China. He taught that there is a special transmission of truth outside of scripture. There should be no dependence on words or writings or on images, but instead a direct pointing to the human soul. As a result one will be able to see into his or her own nature and attain Buddhahood.

Zen was shaped by the Chinese practical approach to life. Unlike monks in other Buddhist schools, Zen monks did physical labor and as a result were widely respected. In China the movement borrowed practices from other schools, but developed its own distinctive methods. Anecdotes about teachers formed the basis of later koan—sayings used to force students to give up traditional ways of thinking. Teachers also use shouts, slaps, questions, and symbolic actions to trigger the experience of satori. Sitting in meditation (*zazen*) is a basic practice.

After a long history in Japan, Zen experienced a decline until it was revived by Hakuin Ekaku, who died in 1768. He reorganized the discipline and training, and made new and creative use of the koan. He also left a rich heritage in art.

Zen has always emphasized the arts. In addition to ink painting and calligraphy, the masters have practiced and taught martial arts, the tea ceremony, flower arrangement, the temple rock garden, and the Haiku form in poetry.

Since World War II, Zen has enjoyed great popularity outside Japan. The writings of D. T. SUZUKI have had a major influence in this development. Most Americans seem to appreciate the aesthetic elements of Zen, but avoid the monastic discipline.

K.C.

## BULGAKOV, SERGIUS

**BULGAKOV, SERGIUS** (1871–1944). One of the formost Russian theologians and spiritual philosophers of this century. After studying law at the University of Moscow he became, in 1901, professor of political economy at the Polytechnic Institute at Kiev and, in 1906, lecturer at the University of Moscow. A Marxist in his youth, in *Capitalism and Agriculture* (1900) he seriously questioned Marxist theory. The influence of KANT and the break with MARX are reflected in *From Marxism to Idealism* (1904). There followed a move away from IDEALISM. Bulgakov's return to the ORTHODOX CHURCH was influenced by Vladimir Soloviev's and Pavel Florensky's doctrine of SOPHIA or Divine Wisdom. The concept of Sophia, or "Sophialogy," became henceforth the all-embracing center of Bulgakov's theological writing.

In 1918 Bulgakov was ordained an Orthodox priest. His conversion was related in his last purely philosophical writing, *The Unfading Light* (1917). Banished from Russia by the Soviet government in 1922, he fled first to Prague. In 1925 Bulgakov settled in Paris and took part in the founding there of the Orthodox Theological Institute of St. Sergius. He remained at the Institute as dean and professor of dogmatic theology until his death. Bulgakov's theological works are difficult and speculative, and his "Sophialogy" was condemned by the Moscow patriarchate. He submitted, however, to the Metropolitan Eulogius of Paris and declared his belief in Orthodox dogma.

J.L.

BULLINGER, HEINRICH (1504–75). Swiss reformer and ZWINGLI's successor. Son of a priest, he was born at Bremgarten and was educated by Brothers of the Common Life and at Cologne University. He studied the Reformers and was especially drawn to Zwingli. He taught several years in the Cistercian monastery at Kappel, and in 1529, the year of his marriage, he followed his father as pastor at Bremgarten. He turned the congregation to Protestantism.

Often called the second founder of the German Reformed Church, he assisted Zwingli in several disputations and succeeded him as pastor at Zurich in 1531. He helped write the First HELVETIC CONFESSION, 1536, hoping in vain to achieve unity with the Lutherans on the Eucharist. He and CALVIN achieved harmony with the *Consensus Tigurinus,* 1549, and in 1566 he authored the Second Helvetic Confession to unify other scattered Reformed churches. He corresponded with royalty of England, France, Denmark, and Germany, and heightened his influence in England by aiding exiles during Queen Mary's reign. He condoned Servetus' execution in Geneva. His biblical expositions and sermons won him wide acclaim. A chronicled *History of the Reformation* stands as one of his most significant works.

C.M.

BULL, PAPAL. A decree by the pope, declaring a doctrinal decision binding on all Catholics. The Bull follows a set pattern, naming the Pope and the date according to the Roman and Christian calendars and the year of the Pope's reign. "Bull" is from the Latin *bulla* or seal.

J.C.

BULTMANN, RUDOLPH (1884–1966). One of the most influential NT scholars of the twentieth century. Both his development of critical methods for the study of the Gospels and his own reconstruction of NT theology profoundly affected study in his field, and had an enduring impact on biblical scholarship.

*Biographical Information.* Born in a village in the grand duchy of Oldenburg (now in East Germany), Bultmann was the son of an Evangelical-Lutheran pastor and grandson of a missionary to Africa. After completing his preparatory schooling in his native district, he entered Tübingen University in 1903. In the German fashion, he spent some semesters of study at the universities in Marburg and Berlin, as well. Among the professors who influenced him most were the historian ADOLF VON HARNACK, the systematic theologian WILHELM HERMANN, and the NT scholar Johannes Weiss. From Harnack, Bultmann seems to have derived his ability to reduce complex detail to a simple formula; from Hermann, he gained his sense of theology as concerned with experience rather than merely concepts. And from Weiss he learned rigorous historical, critical method. After completing his

Courtesy of Religious News Service

*Rudolf Bultmann*

doctorate under Weiss, he taught briefly at Marburg, and then in Breslau, where he completed his monumental analysis of the components and stages of development of the Gospels, *The History of the Synoptic Tradition* (first published in 1920; Eng. trans. in 1963). In 1921 he returned to Marburg University, where he remained until his retirement in 1951 and his death in 1966.

*Major Writings.* Although Bultmann's dissertation was a study of the influence of the Cynic-Stoic rhetorical style on Paul's preaching, most of his writings concentrated on the Gospels. In addition to his basic study mentioned above, a more popular work, *Form Criticism* (Eng. trans. 1934), contributed to what was then a new method of studying the Gospels. On the assumption that what was reported about Jesus' teaching and activities was originally transmitted orally, Bultmann sought to discern behind the written Gospels the brief patterns (forms) of instruction and narrative as they must have existed at the oral stage. By distinguishing between older material and the editorial framework in which the Gospel writers had placed it, Bultmann believed it was possible to trace, as his title implies, the history of the Synoptic tradition. In addition, he thought he could identify the original setting in the life of the church, either in Palestinian Christianity or the Gentile world, of each of these forms—preaching, instruction, or worship.

His *Theology of the New Testament* (Eng. trans. 1955) and his *Gospel of John* (Eng. trans. 1971) employ critical methods, but are chiefly concerned with setting forth the basic theological insights of the major NT writings. Significantly, however, the *Theology* makes no place for the first three Gospels. Rather the focus is on Paul and John. Both these writers are interpreted as setting forth the essence of the message of Jesus, which Bultmann had earlier distilled from the Jesus of the Gospel tradition in a small book known in its English version as *Jesus and the Word* (Eng. trans. 1934).

*Theological Position.* A powerful influence on Bultmann at Marburg had been the existentialist philosopher MARTIN HEIDEGGER, who had viewed life as consisting of a sequence of situations in which people are called to make decisions that open the way either to what he called "authentic existence" or to meaninglessness. Bultmann was convinced that that was the essence of the message of Jesus, of Paul, and of John. All three of them used language whose imagery was burdened by mythological symbols and pre-scientific assumptions. But when the myth was stripped away by the interpreter, the call to authentic existence could be discerned behind the archaic language. That interpretive thesis was set forth by Bultmann in *Jesus Christ and Mythology* (1958).

This demythologizing enterprise is reminiscent in method to the reductionist scheme of Harnack, who saw the essence of Christianity in "the fatherhood of God, the Kingdom of God, and the infinite worth of the human soul." By means of this method of DEMYTHOLOGIZATION Bultmann was able to display his profound learning in the analysis of the NT material against its ancient background and concurrently extract from it a religious essence, which for him was unaffected and uncontaminated by the mythological language and world view in which it was expressed. H.K.

BUNYAN, JOHN (1628–88). The great Puritan minister and writer was born in Elstow, Bedfordshire. His father, Thomas, was a tinker, and John followed the trade. He was converted one Sunday at age fourteen when he heard a voice while playing ball.

For Bunyan the year 1644 was eventful. His mother died in June, his younger sister Margaret in July, and in August his father remarried. In November Bunyan became a soldier in CROMWELL's Parliamentary army and served until July 1647. Sometime between 1647 and 1649 he married. The Bunyans had four children. Although daughter Elizabeth was baptized in 1654 in the Church of

Courtesy of the American Antiquarian Society

*John Bunyan*

England, her father had already been immersed as a member of a Bedford INDEPENDENT congregation.

His adult awakening was a gradual process from 1650 to 1655. He regularly attended the established church and gradually gave up what he considered sinful recreations. For several years he wrestled with temptation and spiritual despair, until he felt all was lost. Yet from that state of spiritual darkness, he emerged into an integrated faith and selfhood. He united with the church in 1655 and became a lay preacher by 1657.

In 1660, however, RESTORATION brought an end to the Separatists' twenty years of freedom. On November 12 Bunyan was charged with Nonconformity and in January 1661 imprisoned at Bedford. Though his second wife, Elizabeth, whom he wed in 1659, tried to get him released, he spent the next twelve years there. In 1666 he wrote *Grace Abounding to the Chief of Sinners,* an autobiographical account of his inner life. He probably also wrote much of *Pilgrim's Progress,* published in February 1678, following a second six-month imprisonment in 1677. His classic allegory of Christian's pilgrimage to the Celestial City gave a map to PURITAN spirituality.

While pastoring churches, he continued to write: *The Life and Death of Mr. Badman* (1680); *The Holy War* (1682), a second allegory of conversion and backsliding, fall and redemption; *The Pilgrim's Progress . . . Second Part* (1684), the story of Christian's wife, Christiana, and their children. Bunyan's last ten years were devoted to a number of doctrinal and controversial works plus poems for adults and children. He died August 31, 1688, in London, and is buried in Bunhill Fields. N.H.

**BURNING BUSH.** A flaming, thorny (?) bush of unknown species through which Yahweh's mysterious presence was imparted to Moses during the inaugural theophany at Mount Horeb (Exod. 3:2-4). Older interpreters understood the bush as a symbol of profane Israel, and the fire that did not consume it as the holy Deity, who dwelt among the Israelites without destroying them. The text itself simply states that on the occasion of Moses' call, Yahweh chose to be manifest through this striking visual element. Indeed, fire typically denotes God's actual presence in OT discourse (for example, Exod. 13:21; Deut. 4:12; I Kings 18:24; Ezek. 1:27). Multiple mention of the noun "bush" (*sene*) may symbolically anticipate the great theophany of MOUNT SINAI (Exod. 19).

J.K.K.

**BUSHIDO.** From the Japanese word for "way of the warrior." A code of values and behavior developed for the samurai or military class in medieval and early modern Japan. The ideals of Bushido had immense impact on Japanese education and militarism at least until the end of the Pacific War in 1945. Bushido drew from the Taoist-related martial arts, SHINTO nationalism, and the ZEN virtues of concentration and fearlessness in the face of punishment and death. But its heart was the CONFUCIANISM which, in Japan, stressed above all integrity and loyalty to one's house and feudal lord. Bushido thus inculcated bravery, honesty, simplicity of life, indifference to suffering and death, eternal preparedness, and supreme loyalty to one's lord and one's obligations. Failure in one's duty could be redeemed only by *seppuku (hari-kiri)* or ritual suicide, which in such circumstances was a noble deed.

While originating in the Kamakura period (1185–1333) with its many samurai wars, Bushido was not fully systematized until the more peaceful Tokugawa Era (1600–1867), when the samurai actually had little fighting to do. Its leading exponent was Yamaga Sokō (1622–85), whose writings summarize and explicate Bushido precepts.

R.E.

**BUSHNELL, HORACE** (1802–76). The Father of American Religious Liberalism, best known for *Christian Nurture* (1847), was born on April 14, the son of Ensign and Dotha Bishop Bushnell, in Bantam, Connecticut. He "owned the covenant" at age nineteen in the New Preston Church.

He received the B.A. from Yale University in 1827 and studied law before an 1831 revival motivated him to study theology at Yale with NATHANIEL W. TAYLOR. He was ordained a Congregationalist May 22, 1833, in North Church, Hartford, which he served until his retirement in 1861. He married Mary Apthorp on September 13, 1833.

Conservative on matters of science, women's rights (*Women's Suffrage; The Reform Against Nature*, 1869),

slavery, and immigration, he was deeply influenced by the ROMANTICISM of COLERIDGE and SCHLEIERMACHER in theology. In *Christian Nurture,* the foundation of modern Christian education, he stressed the organic view of family, church, and nation. Revivals and sudden conversion are unnecessary where nurture has steadily evoked the child's natural goodness.

His own "clear knowledge of God," experienced in a mystical way in February 1849, became the basis for *God in Christ. Christ in Theology* (1851) was followed by *Nature and the Supernatural* (1858), which defined the supernatural as all that has life beyond mechanical causality. In *The Vicarious Sacrifice* (1866), Bushnell favored ABELARD's moral influence theory of the Atonement. He died on February 17.

N.H.

**BUTLER, JOSEPH** (1692–1752). Among the greatest English theologians and moralists of the modern period. Raised a Presbyterian, he entered the Church of England before going up to Oriel College, Oxford, in 1714. Ordained in 1718, Butler served as preacher at the Rolls Chapel, London (1718–26). The product of this assignment was *Fifteen Sermons* (1726), which made his reputation and established him as one of the preeminent BRITISH MORALISTS. Butler was successively rector of Houghton and of Stanhope ("not dead but buried"); clerk of the closet to Queen Caroline; bishop of Bristol; dean of St. Paul's Cathedral, London; clerk of the royal closet to George II; and bishop of Durham.

Butler is best known as the author of *The Analogy of Religion* (1736). Little discussed in his own time, the book was widely studied in the nineteenth century and had a profound influence on such figures as JOHN HENRY NEWMAN and Prime Minister W. E. Gladstone. The *Analogy* is addressed to those DEISTS who, conceding the existence of God as a moral governor, were skeptical of the particular claims of Christianity. Their chronic complaint was that if God's will had been revealed in the Bible God would not have allowed for such contradictions and moral ambiguities. Butler attempts to show that the Deist belief in God—the author and moral governor of nature, when viewed in the light of nature's puzzling confusion and seeming misery—faces difficulties comparable to those found in Christian revelation.

Butler, nevertheless, argues that in the case of both natural and revealed religion one can discern inferences and analogies that support reasonable belief. On the basis of his analogical arguments, Butler defends the immortality of the soul, future rewards and punishments, miracles, and God's moral governance of the world. For Butler neither nature nor the Bible offers unquestionable proof of the claims of theism. For our finite minds, "probability is the very guide of life." Butler was, in Leslie Stephen's words, "honest enough to admit the existence of doubts, and brave enough not to be paralyzed by them."

J.L.

**BUTTRICK, GEORGE ARTHUR** (1892–1980). Presbyterian preacher and scholar, born in Seaham Harbour, Northumberland, England, on March 23. Buttrick was a spellbinding sermonizer and an exponent of liberalism against fundamentalism. He began his ministry as a Congregationalist, and was a graduate of Victoria University and the Lancaster Independent Theological Seminary. He emigrated to the United States and served parishes in Quincy, Illinois; Rutland, Vermont; and Buffalo, New York; until he was called at age thirty-four as pastor of the Madison Avenue Presbyterian Church in New York City. He remained pastor there until 1954.

Buttrick was president of the Federal Council of Churches, 1939–41. From 1954 to 1960, he was preacher and professor at Harvard and later at Union Seminary, Garrett Seminary, Presbyterian Seminary, and Southern Baptist Seminary in Louisville. He was editor for *The Interpreter's Bible* and the *Interpreter's Dictionary of the Bible;* and author of *The Parables of Jesus; The Christian Fact and Modern Doubt; Christ and Man's Dilemma; Faith and Education; Jesus Came Preaching; God, Pain, and Evil;* and *The Power of Prayer Today.*

J.C.

**BYZANTINE RITE.** Historically, the worship form or rite of the Byzantine Empire, derived from early Christian practice in Jerusalem and Antioch. One of five major rites used by Eastern Catholics (in communion with Rome) and the Eastern Orthodox Church. It is a beautiful, elaborate mass often concelebrated by several priests.

J.C.

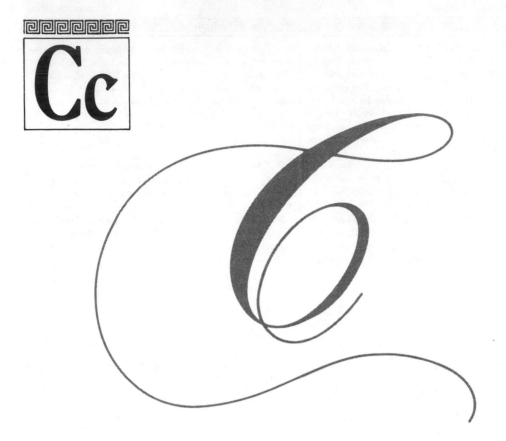

# Cc

**CABBALA.** *See* KABBALA.

**CAESAR, GAIUS JULIUS.** Illustrious Roman soldier, dictator, historian. Born of a patrician family about 102 B.C., who traced its ancestry to Venus and Anchises, Caesar's early manhood was effected by the rise and fall of a political party with which he identified his interests, the *popularis*. As *praetor* in 61 B.C., Caesar supported proposals in Pompey's favor, which aroused violent opposition in the Senate, but upon this great general's return from the East, Caesar was recognized as his ally. While campaigning in Syria, Pompey had "arbitrated" a dispute between the Hasmonean brothers, and claimed Roman hegemony over Judea. Julius Caesar was to confer upon Antipater, father of Herod the Great, the title procurator of Judea. With Pompey and Crassus, Caesar formed the first triumvirate. For all practical purposes constitutional government ceased to exist.

While Caesar fought the Gallic wars (58–51 B.C.), his prestige in the Senate was eclipsed by Pompey's. Civil war ensued and Caesar followed Pompey to Alexandria, where it was learned that Pompey had been murdered (Pss. of Sol. 17:8-15). In the year 29 B.C., Caesar received the dictatorship for a period of ten years, a title renewed in 48 B.C. and again in 46 B.C. This position granted him the sole right of making war and peace and disposing of the finances of the state. On March 15, 44 B.C., Caesar was murdered in the Senate house at the foot of Pompey's statue.

The first emperors of Rome belonged to the Julian house: AUGUSTUS, TIBERIUS, Gaius (CALIGULA), CLAUDIUS, and NERO. The Flavian dynasty was founded by VESPASIAN. J.L.P.

**CAESAREA.** A major seaport and Roman political capital of NT Palestine. It lay on the "Way of the Sea" highway, about twenty-two miles south of Mount Carmel, and twenty-eight miles north of JOPPA, where a highway led through the Megiddo Pass. Near ancient ruins called Strato's Tower, Herod the Great began a grandiose Greco-Roman city in 21 B.C., which he completed twelve years later and named to honor Caesar Augustus.

The geometrically planned, semicircular shaped city was walled. The beach side was a mile long. The city had many noteworthy features: a well-protected harbor, larger than that at Piraeus, decorated with lofty towers and colossal statues; a temple of Augustus, visible far out at sea, with great statues of Rome and the emperor; a drainage system flushed by the tides; aqueducts, one that was eight miles long; a hippodrome; an amphitheater seating twenty thousand; a theater where the name Pontius Pilate was found recently; and other magnificent structures. Three thousand Roman soldiers were assigned there.

Among the significant NT events that took place in Caesarea are: the baptism of Cornelius (Acts 10), repeated visits by Paul to the Caesarean Christian community, Paul's trial and two years' imprisonment (Acts 23), followed by his journey under guard to Rome (Acts 23).

P.L.G.

**CAESAREA PHILIPPI.** A regional center and resort city on the southwest flank of Mount Hermon, occupying a terrace over eleven hundred feet above sea level, wooded and with luxurious mountain vegetation, and having a wide view of the Jordan Valley. The city's pilgrimage center was a grotto from which a perennial stream emerged, the most abundant source of the Jordan River. In ancient times, some nature-god (Baal-Hermon), was, perhaps, venerated here. The Romans called it Paneas for the god Pan (Banias).

In 20 B.C. Augustus gave the place to Herod the Great, who built a white marble temple and dedicated it to the emperor. Herod's son, Philip, inherited the city in 4 B.C. He enlarged and beautified it and named it for Tiberius Caesar and for himself.

Matthew 16:13 and Mark 8:27 locate Peter's confession in the area of Caesarea Philippi (compare Luke 9:18 ff.). The place of Jesus' transfiguraton is not named (Matt. 17:1-8; Mark 9:2-8; Luke 9:28-36), but since this account follows that of Peter's confession, it is thought the TRANSFIGURATION took place near Caesarea Philippi. Others hold that this event occurred on Mount Tabor.

P.L.G.

**CAESAROPAPISM.** The control of the church by secular rulers. This system of church-state relations was characteristic of the Byzantine Empire and led to repeated clashes with the West, which objected particularly to the attempts by the emperors to intervene in doctrinal matters.

J.G.

**CAIAPHAS.** A high priest for about eighteen years from roughly A.D. 18 to A.D. 36. The Gospels and Acts mention Caiaphas as high priest in the trial of Jesus (Matt. 26:57–27:2; Mark 14:53–15:1; Luke 22:54–23:1) and the trial of the apostles (Acts 5:12-42). The text relates Caiaphas to Annas, high priest from about A.D. 6 to A.D. 15. Precisely what that relation was cannot now be determined. John 18:13 states that Annas was the father-in-law of Caiaphas and that, after Jesus' arrest, he was taken first to Annas before Caiaphas had an opportunity to examine Jesus (vv. 13, 19). Annas had been deposed by the Romans in A.D. 15, but may have continued to exercise powerful influence. Caiaphas, his five sons, and one grandson of Annas, were in the succession of high priests. Thus, when, as in Acts 4:6, Annas is called "the high priest," it may be a recognition of his *de facto* political power, an honorary rather than a legal title (Luke 3:2; John 18:19).

When Saul was sent to Damascus to persecute the Christians, he went with letters to the synagogues there from "the high priest" in Jerusalem (Acts 9:2; 22:5; 26:12). The high priest then in office was Caiaphas, who was unaware of the role he played in the conversion of Saul. Nothing further is known concerning Caiaphas except that in some Christian circles a legend arose that he became a Christian.

P.L.G.

**CAIN AND ABEL.** Abel, possibly meaning "breath," but more probably "human kind." Cain, meaning "smith" or "metal worker," related in name only to the Kenites. Cain and Abel were sons of ADAM AND EVE, brothers, but not necessarily twins; the firstborn of the human race (Gen. 4:1-16).

Abel became "a keeper of sheep," whose offerings to Yahweh of "the firstlings of his flock and of their fat" was acceptable to the Lord (Gen. 4:4). The account does not say why. Perhaps, this is because meat sacrifices were prominent later at the tabernacle and temple (Heb. 11:4 attributes Abel's acceptance to faith). "Innocent" (RSV) and "righteous" (KJV) Abel was murdered by Cain, his brother (Matt. 23:35), a significant event that is memorialized in the phrase "the blood of Abel" (Luke 11:51).

Cain followed Adam's occupation as "a tiller of the ground" (Gen. 3:23; 4:2). His offering to Yahweh was "the fruit of the ground" (Gen. 4:3). "For Cain and his offering, he [Yahweh] had no regard" (Gen. 4:5). This made Cain "very angry, and his countenance fell," and he killed Abel. Why was Cain's sacrifice not regarded? Perhaps it had to do

Courtesy of the Fogg Art Museum, Harvard University

*Sacrifice of Cain and Abel. A twelfth-century Romanesque pilaster capital from Moutier-Saint-Jean*

with the later secondary rank of bloodless sacrifices, but also, as shown by what follows, it had to do with Cain's temper and his lack of concern for his brother, "Am I my brother's keeper?" (Gen. 4:9). There is no connection between the descendants of Cain and their fate and the Canaanites who descended from Ham, the son of Noah (Gen. 10:6, 15-19).

P.L.G.

**CALEB** (meaning "dog"). (1) Caleb (Num. 13:6; I Chr. 4:15), the son of Jephunneh, represented Judah among the men who spied out Kadesh (Num. 13:1–14:10). Only JOSHUA and he returned with encouraging reports, and he alone of the twelve lived to enter Canaan (Num. 14:38). In contrast to the ten, Caleb is said to have had "a different spirit" and to have followed Yahweh "wholly" or "fully" (Num. 14:24; Deut. 1:36).

In the division of the land, Yahweh, through Joshua, gave Caleb the town of Hebron, from which he had to drive out "the three sons of Anak" (Josh. 15:13 ff.). Othniel, Caleb's nephew, captured neighboring Debir (Tell Beit Mirsim), and thereby won as wife Achsah, Caleb's daughter (Josh. 15:18). Associated with the name Caleb is a territory south of Judah called the Negeb of Caleb (I Sam. 30:14). The Chronicler, in recording Caleb's genealogy, attempted to give him a place in the tribe of Judah, but his father is known to be a Kenizite (Num. 32:12). However, Caleb is remembered for contributing numerous progeny to the people and for having been a man of fearless courage and of strong faith in Yahweh's promises of a land for Israel.

(2) Caleb, son of Hezron, a member of the tribe of Judah (I Chr. 2:18, 24). The name Ephrathah (Bethlehem, see Mic. 5:2) is given to Caleb's step-mother, whom he married, after his father's death.

These two Calebs may be the same person. The OT accounts do not make this clear.

P.L.G.

**CALENDAR, LITURGICAL.** *See* CHRISTIAN YEAR.

**CALF, GOLDEN.** A gold-plated or molded figure of a young bull (I Kings 12:28; II Kings 10:29), first used in Israelite worship at Mt. Sinai, and, later, at Dan and Bethel. Because of its impressive physical strength and sexual virility, the bull was associated closely, as a representation or throne-pedestal, with the gods throughout the ancient Near East from Egypt, Syria-Palestine, Asia Minor to Crete.

After the SINAI, solemn blood-ceremony in which the people of Israel had covenanted to do "all that the Lord has spoken" (Exod. 24:1-8), Moses left them for forty days and nights (Exod. 24:9-18; Deut. 9:13-21). The people concluded that Moses was not coming back. They demanded that Aaron "make us gods" to guide them out of the wilderness. Aaron

collected their gold earrings, melted them, and formed a calf-like figure, which the people acclaimed to be the god who had brought them out of Egypt (Exod. 32:4-35; Deut. 9:16, 21; Neh. 9:13). The next morning, sacrifices were made to the calf figure, "a feast to the Lord," (Exod. 32:5) with eating, drinking, and sexual relations ("play" Exod. 32:6). (See Baal-peor, Num. 25:1-9 KJV.) The entire episode was regarded as a serious breach of the covenant and as idolatry: "having other gods before [or besides] me" (Exod. 20:3, 4). The punishment was the execution of three thousand men (Exod. 32:28, 35).

When the kingdom was divided, JEROBOAM, first king of Israel, made Shechem his residence and capital (I Kings 12:25)—but what could be his "Mount Moriah" (II Chr. 3:1)? He selected two ancient pilgrimage places, southern Bethel and northern Dan (I Kings 12:29, 32). Unable to duplicate the Ark of the Covenant, he made a calf of gold for each sanctuary (I Kings 12:28). His original intention may have been that these would be, like the ark, empty thrones or pedestals for Yahweh. This practice was not unknown in the ancient Near East (*see* BAAL). Jeroboam appointed priests for the shrines and instituted a calendar of festivals and feasts.

The biblical historians, who wrote from a Judean perspective, used the expression "the sins of Jeroboam, the son of Nebat" (II Kings 10:29, 31; 15:24, 28) to refer to Jeroboam's religious practices, thus linking these to the making of the golden calf at Sinai. It would appear, however, that Jeroboam attempted to be a Yahwist. He named his son Ahijah, meaning "my father is Yahweh."

Twelve bull-calves formed the base of the brazen sea at Solomon's Temple. These were not idols, but may have been understood as Yahweh symbols. The I Kings account of the shrines in Israel lacks elements of Canaanite worship. It may be that, in some sense, the bulls at Dan and Bethel were intended originally to be representative of or connected with Yahweh, despite how they may have come to be regarded in later history (Hos. 8:5-6; 13:2; II Kings 10:29; 17:16; II Chr. 11:15; 13:18).

A serious matter for NT Christians was, "Has God rejected his people," the Jews? Paul's answer was, "By no means!" (Rom. 11:1). Stephen concluded his address at a Jerusalem synagogue, "You stiff-necked people, . . . you always resist the Holy Spirit" (Acts 7:51). He cited as evidence the Exodus' making and worshiping of the calf. He compared that apostasy to the Crucifixion, the rejection, and the murder of Jesus (Acts 7:52).

P.L.G.

**CALIGULA** (A.D. 12–41). Roman Emperor from A.D. 37 to 40; successor to his granduncle, Tiberius. During childhood Gaius inherited the popularity of his late father, Germanicus, and became a darling of the military establishment, nicknamed by the soldiers caligula ("Little Boots"). The first half-year of his reign augured well for the future, but a serious illness caused a change of personality. Josephus writes that "with the passage of time he no longer thought of himself as an ordinary man, but was driven by the greatness of his power to deify himself."

Gaius cruelly persecuted Jews of Alexandria who refused him divine honors and, after offenses by Jews at Jamnia, he ordered the installation of his statue in Jerusalem's Temple. This dreadful sacrilege was prevented by the intervention of his life-long friend, Herod Agrippa. Gaius was assassinated by military tribunes of the Praetorian Guard.

J.L.P.

**CALLING.** The divine summons to an individual or group to enter into a meaningful fellowship with God and participate in the divine plan for human salvation. God consistently takes the initiative in summoning those who are chosen. Realizing that they are claimed as God's own possession, they understand that a specific historical destiny awaits them.

*Calling in the Old Testament.* The separation of individuals from presumably mediocre existence to direct involvement in God's own saving purpose begins with Abraham (Gen. 12:1-3). Suddenly Abraham is invited to embark on a pilgrimage that ushers him from the known security of his settled existence into the unknown. Abraham's call is confirmed in a promise of offspring and land that is frequently repeated in the OT. He will father a great people who will eventually claim the land of his present sojourning. (Though Gen. 12 lacks the verb "to call," it is present in Isa. 51:2 and Heb. 11:8, which refer to this event.)

A series of call-narratives is introduced by Exodus 3:1–4:17, with its portrayal of God's summons of Moses. "Called" from the burning bush (3:4), Moses is drawn into a dramatic encounter with the Holy involving visual and auditory perception. Moses is charged with the mission of delivering the Israelites from Egyptian bondage. Though he tries to resist the call by raising four objections (3:11, 13; 4:1, 10), God's sovereignty prevails. Thereupon the divinely empowered Moses labors to assist in his people's rescue. Subsequently, Moses is divinely "called" to Sinai's summit (Exod. 19:20) to receive the Law that will appreciably define Israel's existence and its relation with the Deity. Once the Israelites have tenuously settled into Canaan, their drive for liberation from oppressive forces (hostile neighbors) continues under the charismatic leadership of various judges who are divinely summoned and favored with God's spirit (for example, Othniel, Judg. 3:9-10; Gideon, 6:11-24, 34; Jephthah, 11:29). The leadership of Saul, Israel's first king, is similarly perceived (I Sam. 11:5-7).

Reports about the visions of Amos (7:1-9; 8:1-3; 9:1-4), Isaiah (6:1-13), Jeremiah (1:4-19), and

Ezekiel (1:4-28) attest to the divine summons of prophets into public vocations of far-reaching significance. Amos' sudden discovery of divine presence resembles Abraham's, and Jeremiah's resistance to God's initiative resembles Moses'. The prophets are called not to promote national deliverance but to speak messages of stern judgment so that God's rebellious people might return with renewed faith and obedience.

That God's calling reaches beyond isolated individuals to encompass the entire nation is clear from Hosea's interpretation of the Exodus as the people's vocational summons: "Out of Egypt I called my son" (11:1). Moreover, Second Isaiah affirms that Israel is called by God in such manner that even the welfare of other nations is addressed (41:9; 42:6; 48:15; 49:1; 54:6).

*Calling in the New Testament.* The Gospels affirm that certain people were called to a special vocation of following Jesus during his earthly ministry. Thus Matthew explains how Peter, Andrew, James, and John accepted the invitation to discipleship (4:18-22). Paul's first-person account of his call (Gal. 1:13-17) is paralleled by Luke's third-person narrative of Saul's conversion (Acts 9:1-22). Jesus' disclosure that he "came not to call the righteous, but sinners" (Mark 2:17) shaped earliest Christianity's approach to potential converts (Acts 2:38-39). In his letters Paul emphasizes that the Christian "upward call" (Phil. 3:14) into God's "kingdom and glory" (I Thess. 2:12) is based on freely offered divine grace (Gal. 1:6, 15). The hope this offers struggling humanity is best expressed in Paul's statement that "in everything God works for good with those who love him, who are called according to his purpose" (Rom. 8:28). (*Compare* ELECTION.)

J.K.K.

**CALVARY.** *See* GOLGOTHA.

**CALVIN, JOHN/CALVINISM.** John Calvin, in French Jean Chauvin or Caulvin (1509–64), one of Protestantism's greatest theologians, author of the *Institutes of the Christian Religion,* PROTESTANTISM's most influential systematic theology.

Born in Noyon, France, Calvin studied at colleges de la Marche and de Montaigu in Paris. He was given Roman Catholic benefices at ages twelve and eighteen and seemed headed for a church career. However, his father sent him to the University of Orléans in 1528 to study law. About the same time, Calvin encountered evangelical ideas through his cousin Robert Olivetan, Melchior Wolman, Theodore Beza, and Lutheran books. When his father died in 1531, Calvin returned to Paris to pursue Greek, Hebrew, and Reformation ideas. His first book, *On Mercy,* 1532, reflected religion only obliquely.

In 1533 he received his Doctor of Law degree, experienced a "sudden conversion," and for helping Nicholas Cop spread evangelical ideas at the

Courtesy of the Presbyterian Historical Society

*John Calvin*

University of Paris had to flee the city. He resigned his benefices, became a wandering scholar, 1534–36, and in 1536 at Basel published his *Institutes,* a vigorous religious statement to inform Francis I of France that his Protestant subjects were truly following the gospel of Jesus Christ and that his persecution was in defiance of God's will. When Calvin visited Geneva that same year, Guillaume Farel urged him to stay. There he promoted the Protestant cause, 1536–38, until he and Farel were forced by political opponents to leave the city. Calvin lived as an exile in Strasburg, pastored a French refugee congregation, married Idelotte de Bure, became a friend of MARTIN BUCER, and represented Strassburg at conferences in Worms and Ratisbon.

Called back in 1541 to quell Geneva's political-religious disorders, Calvin insisted on more authority for the church, a theocratic form of government, and an externally pure church. He dominated the city until his death, though not without opposition from Roman Catholic sympathizers, the Libertines, and individuals with different religious views. Between 1542 and 1546 Calvin's stern disciplinary demands brought banishment to seventy-six people and death to fifty-eight. Geneva's *Ecclesiastical Ordinances* and *Little Treatise on the Lord's Supper,* 1541, second *Catechism of the Church of Geneva,* 1542, *Treatise on Free Will* and *Necessity for Reforming the Church,* 1545, new editions of the *Institutes,* and numerous commentaries on biblical books rapidly increased his fame and set the tone of Geneva's theocracy. The Second *Catechism,* the last edition of the *Institutes,* 1559, and the *Gallican Confession,* 1559, became standard doctrine

for most of Europe's Reformed (as distinguished from Lutheran) churches. Calvin's most famed controversy was with MICHAEL SERVETUS, a Spanish theologian, primarily over the nature of the Trinity. Servetus could not accept the divinity of the Son on either rational or biblical grounds. Servetus' execution in Geneva, 1553, climaxed a long feud between Calvin and Servetus and tested and clinched Calvin's control of the city.

Although Calvin departed from LUTHER on the Lord's Supper, stressing a spiritual rather than physical presence of Christ, Calvin's basic theology derived heavily from Luther. But Calvin organized and systematized his views with different emphases. The SOVEREIGNTY OF GOD and ELECTION anchored Calvin's theology. Luther stressed justification by faith and forgiveness of sins. Calvin's aim was not salvation; God had already determined that in election. Rather it was to glorify God. God controls everything, is all-knowing, all-powerful, and present everywhere. God is pure, merciful, and just. Human beings are sinful, depraved by original and actual sin. They deserve condemnation, but God in mercy chooses some for election and leaves others to the damnation they deserve. No one knows the elect for sure, but faith, upright living, and participation in the sacraments are signs of election for Calvin. Scripture, unfolded through the Holy Spirit, is the source of divine truth. Faith is an act of God assuring humans of forgiveness and new life. Strict discipline and good works are means of glorifying God. Consequently Calvin sought to control Geneva in accordance with God's will in the entire Bible. The state is ordained by God to order society and to protect the church, but Calvin thought of both ministers and magistrates as servants of God and of the entire community in Geneva as the church. He wanted the godly to control governmental functions (*see* THEOCRACY), but insisted that church discipline belongs to the church. He eventually won the right to excommunicate through the consistory.

With church and state equated as the holy community, nonbelievers were invited to leave Geneva. Refugees devoted to Calvin replaced them, increasing the population by 50 percent to about nineteen thousand—a bastion of strength for Calvin. Lutheranism developed into territorialism with the state dictating in religion and education; Calvinism became an international model; God was to be glorified everywhere. Calvinism also provided a basis for resistance to ungodly regimes, exemplified in leaders like Admiral Coligny, William the Silent, and Oliver Cromwell. Calvin was not ordained. His only child died shortly after birth, 1542; his wife died seven years later. In 1559 Calvin established the Genevan Academy, which became the University of Geneva, a center for training thousands of clergy for the Reformed churches.

Calvinism refers to the religious influence of Calvin. His views inspired the HUGUENOTS in

France; the PRESBYTERIANS in Scotland; the PURI-TANS in England and America; the BAPTISTS; and REFORMED CHURCHES in the Netherlands, Poland, Hungary, and parts of Germany. THEODORE BEZA continued Calvin's work in Geneva and JOHN KNOX promoted his doctrines in Scotland. The Church of England felt the influence of Calvin, particularly in the Puritan attempt to rid Anglicanism of Catholic vestiges, but reaction developed along opposite lines. Disputes over election resulted in ARMINIANISM in both Anglicanism and Methodism. Calvin's *Institutes* provided the doctrinal base for Calvin's influence; and the WESTMINSTER CATECHISMS and Confession of Faith, 1647-48, provided the most widely accepted formal statements of Calvinism.

C.M.

**CAMBRIDGE PLATFORM.** This document, the foundation of American Congregationalism, was written by the Cambridge Synod, which met a few times between 1646 and 1648, and included most of the PURITAN churches of the Massachusetts Bay Colony. Theologically it committed the churches to the WESTMINSTER CONFESSION.

It defined church polity as "the communion of churches with one another" in contrast to those strains of Puritanism that preferred Presbyterian or Baptist forms. Councils and synods were given advisory and admonitory powers but no coercive legal authority.

N.H.

**CAMBRIDGE PLATONISTS.** A small group of philosophical divines who played a mediating role in the turbulent religious life of seventeenth-century England. The group flourished at Cambridge University between 1633 and 1688. All but one had some association with Emmanuel College, Cambridge, a center of Puritanism. Although from PURITAN backgrounds, the Cambridge Platonists rejected dogmatic Calvinism. They represented a position between the Puritans and the High Church Anglicanism associated with Archbishop Laud (1573–1645). They were liberal and LATITUDIN-ARIAN in that they rejected fanatical ENTHUSIASM as well as theological dogmatism and believed in liberty of conscience, toleration, and charity.

Unlike the Puritans, the Cambridge Platonists did not stress the utter "fallenness" of humanity. God created humans in the divine image, endowed with reason. Benjamin Whichcote delighted in saying that "the spirit of man is the candle of the Lord," and they sought to keep the lights of faith and reason in balance. They believed that the test of Christian belief is in the exercise of virtues such as modesty, humility, obedience to God, and charity to one's neighbor. The Cambridge Platonists included, in addition to Whichcote (1609–83), Nathanael Culverwel (1618–51), John Smith (1616–52), Ralph Cudworth (1617–88), and Henry More (1614–87).

J.L.

Courtesy of Bethany College
*Alexander Campbell*

**CAMPBELL, ALEXANDER** (1788–1866). Founder of the Christian Church (Disciples of Christ) and the Churches of Christ. Campbell was born in County Antrim, Ireland, on September 12 to Thomas and Jane Corneigle Campbell. His father was a Scotch Irish schoolmaster, his mother a French Huguenot.

In 1809, after a year of study at the University of Glasgow, Campbell arrived in America. He began preaching in 1810, and after organizing a church at Brush Run, Pennsylvania, he was licensed to preach. In 1811 he married Presbyterian Margaret Brown, but with the birth of their first child, they decided against infant baptism. They were immersed by local Baptists, and the Brush Run church affiliated with the Redstone Baptist Association.

Campbell came to believe that baptism was necessary for the remission of sins and began publishing the *Christian Baptist* in 1823. The Baptists excluded him in 1826, so he became independent. In 1827 he published a new translation of Scripture and in 1828 a hymnal. In 1830 he began publishing the *Millennial Harbinger*. Eventually he allied with James O'Kelley's Republican Methodists, Abner Jones' group of Baptists, and Barton Stone's Presbyterian followers to form the "Christian Connection." His chief work was *The Christian System* (1839).

N.H.

**CAMP MEETING.** A prominent feature of the Second GREAT AWAKENING, particularly in the South, camp meetings were religious gatherings in the woods for several days or a week. From the sacramental seasons at Gasper River (1800) and CANE RIDGE, Kentucky (1801), they became occasions for REVIVALS. Camp meetings were characteristic of the Holiness Movement. The National Camp Meeting Association for the Promotion of Christian Holiness was formed in 1866. Today they continue at various summer campgrounds around the country.

N.H.

**CAMUS, ALBERT** (1913–60). French writer and philosopher of EXISTENTIALISM, born in Algeria while it was a French *département*. He came to believe that human life has to be lived in an alien universe, so that it is essentially absurd, frustrating, and self-stultifying. But he combined with this pessimistic view a passionate belief in human dignity and moral values, however inconsistent that combination may have been. This led him to the doctrine of "metaphysical rebellion," a form of protest atheism. His views are expressed in the philosophical essays, *The Myth of Sysiphus* (Eng. trans. 1955) and *The Rebel* (Eng. trans. 1954), and in such novels as *The Plague* (Eng. trans. 1948).

J.M.

**CANA.** A village in Galilee mentioned only in John's Gospel (2:1, 11; 4:46; 21:2). The name means "place of reeds." Cana in Galilee was the location of two "signs" or miracles: (1) The changing of water into wine at a wedding (2:1-12). (Jesus' mother seems familiar with the family; perhaps the town was near Nazareth.) (2) The healing of a *basilikos'* son (4:46-54). (The word *basilikos* means a "relative of the royal [Herodian] family" or a royal, military, or tax gathering official.) The father's exemplary faith in Jesus points to Jesus' universal saviorhood.

Cana has several possible sites. (1) Joshua 19:28 mentions Kanah, a town with a brook (Josh. 16:8) in northern Palestine. This may be the Kanah Josephus mentions as being near Tyre. (2) The Arabic *Qana-el-Jelil* (Cana of/in Galilee) refers to ruins five miles north of Sephhoris, overlooking a marshy plain where reeds grow abundantly. (3) Although the etymology of Kefr Kenna fails to support the claim, that modern village, four miles beyond Nazareth on the road to Capernaum and Bethsaida, is widely accepted as Cana. The location was convenient for pilgrims. This may account for its popularity as Cana in Galilee.

P.L.G.

**CANAAN/CANAANITES.** Canaan was the ancient name of the eastern Mediterranean coastal region from the northern borders of present-day Lebanon to the end of the arable land south of Gaza. Most ancient texts construe it as reaching no further inland than the Great Rift Valley.

*Canaan in the Ancient Near Eastern Context.* Linguistically and culturally, Canaan belonged to the world of greater SYRIA. Its language was a dialect of northwest Semitic and was closely akin to the languages of UGARIT on the Syrian coast, the inland city of Ebla, Phoenicia, Moab, and Israel itself. Similarly, its culture did not differ materially from that of Ugarit to the north. The Ugaritic texts from the fourteenth century B.C. have given us a rich insight into the religion of Phoenicia and Canaan. Centering on worship of the dying and rising god BAAL, it was a fertility religion suitable for an agricultural people settled in arable lowland areas. Phoenician texts coming from a much later time but from the same region refer to a hero named Canaan as the first Phoenician. The original name of Beirut was, according to a second-century B.C. Phoenician text, "Laodicea in Canaan."

The Tell el-Amarna texts of Egypt (about 1375–1345 B.C.) make clear that Canaan of the late Bronze Age was a collection of small principalities, each centered around a city, governed by indigenous kings under Egyptian overlordship. The Canaanites had to contend always with nomads who filtered in through the network of city-states and at times clashed with them. In the Amarna texts, some of these nomads are known as *hapiru,* a word that many scholars link with the term "Hebrew." Toward the end of the late Bronze Age, Egyptian texts begin to mention larger national entities that had evolved out of the earlier, more fragmentary city-state environment. Moab is mentioned during the time of Ramses II (about 1285 B.C.), Edom and Israel are mentioned by the pharaoh Mer-ne-Ptah (about 1224–1211 B.C.), and the Philistines appear in Egyptian records during the reign of Ramses III, who claims to have defeated them about 1175 B.C. All of this suggests that Canaan had begun to be absorbed into larger political units, each of which had its own dynastic rulership, and one of which was Israel. Except as a general geographical designation, Canaan ceased to exist around the turn of the first millennium B.C.

*Canaan from the Point of View of Israel.* Canaan is first mentioned in the Hebrew Bible not as a country but as a person. In Genesis 9:18 he is a grandson of Noah and the son of Ham; later in that chapter Canaan is cursed by Noah to be a slave to Shem and Japheth (vss. 25-27).

Although Abram went forth to the land of Canaan (Gen. 12:5) and successfully took up residence there among the native peoples of the place, the patriarchal narratives as a whole seem to have relatively vague notions of exactly who occupied the land. A more concrete early memory of Canaan is that found in Judges 5:19, in the so-called Song of Deborah (often dated as early as the twelfth century B.C.). It is a hostile memory—the very stars supported Deborah and Barak in their fight against a coalition of the kings of Canaan led by Sisera, the general of the army of Jabin, king of Canaan, who reigned in Hazor (Judg. 4:2). Although they worked in the seventh century B.C., the Deuteronomic historians drew upon older sources to recount the victories of Joshua over Jericho, Ai, and the whole of Canaan (Joshua 1–12). To them the Canaanites represented a profound threat to the integrity of Israel as a people of Yahweh, and in the name of the survival of Israel and of Yahwism they idealized the story of the acquisition of the land of

— 176 —

Canaan by the people of Israel into a holy war (compare Deut. 7:1-2). More realistic accounts, however, such as Judges 1:1–2:5, make clear that Israel did not conquer all of Canaan at the time of Joshua's victories, and in fact, for good or for ill, lived alongside the Canaanites for centuries.

*The Israelite Conquest of Canaan.* That Israel came into possession of the land of Canaan is a manifest fact, but the process by which that occurred has been the subject of much recent scholarly debate.

(a) *Conquest.* Archaeologists such as W. F. Albright, G. E. Wright, and Paul Lapp argue that Israel conquered the whole of Palestine with a swift military sweep much like that described in Joshua. These scholars point to evidences of massive destruction and subsequent reoccupation by a different people at sites such as Bethel (Judg. 1:22-26), Hazor (Josh. 11:1-15), and Lachish (Josh. 10:31-32). The problem with this position lies in the fact that at some of the key sites supposedly conquered by Joshua, such as Jericho, Ai, Arad, and Heshbon, neither an occupation nor a destruction layer exists at the end of the late Bronze Age. Furthermore, even at those sites that do show destruction layers, it is not possible to say for certain that Israel inflicted the destruction.

(b) *Gradual occupation.* German scholarship, particularly centering around the work of A. Alt and M. Noth, has generally taken the view that the Israelite occupation of Palestine was a gradual process of infiltration and settlement in the thinly populated hill country, with the gradual assimilation of the local Canaanite communities. Though occasional military conquests might have occurred, such as at Bethel, on the whole Israel moved only slowly toward a unified national identity. The account of Judges 1:1–2:5 conforms much more closely to this model, for it records local tribal conquests and by no means reflects a unified all-Israel outlook.

*A Hapiru Uprising.* The most recent theory regarding the conquest of Canaan is associated with the name of the American scholar George Mendenhall, and is favored by John Bright as well. According to this model, the nomads that were troubling the Canaanite city-states in the Tell el-Amarna texts were really dispossessed bands of indigenous people living on the margins of the Canaanite city-state system. When a new band of *hapiru* arrived from across the Jordan with an account of the Exodus and of a covenant with a sovereign God, Yahweh, the marginals were galvanized into action. In cases such as Hazor and Lachish, they overcame Canaanite cities, and in other cases they simply absorbed their populaces. Both of the latter two theories about the Israelite triumph over Canaan have in their favor the high likelihood that an all-Israel perspective emerged only after what had once been weak and scattered tribes had coalesced into a unified nation.

W.S.T.

**CANE RIDGE REVIVAL.** "Sacramental season" in Bourbon County, Kentucky, in August 1801, noted for its unusual emotional and physical manifestations. Presbyterian BARTON W. STONE, converted under James McGready and an observer at the July 1800 revival at his Gasper River Church, adopted McGready's methods and called the meeting at Cane Ridge. Presbyterian, Methodist, and Baptist ministers preached to twenty-five thousand people for a week. It became both a symbol and an impetus for the Second GREAT AWAKENING.

N.H.

**CANON.** A priest on the staff of a cathedral or collegiate church. Secular canons are clergymen who live together under a rule or discipline and provide the worship leadership for the cathedral. Regular canons live together near the church in a monastic life-style. All Anglican canons are secular.

J.C.

**CANON.** *Old Testament Canon and Authority.* The term "canon" transliterates a Greek term meaning rule, originally a carpenter's measuring stick. An older Hebrew term with virtually the same spelling designated a measuring reed about nine feet long. Since the fourth century the term has come to be used in reference to that collection of books recognized by the church as its authority but most often designated simply as the BIBLE, that is, the Book. Every book in the canon was considered authoritative but not every authoritative book was in the canon. In the history of Judaism the Law has always held the place of preeminent authority, followed by the Prophets and then the Writings. Christians recognized the entire OT as their Bible from the ealiest of times. Modern Christianity is divided in its attitude toward the canon as authority. Catholic Christianity sees the canon as an important source of authority along with the TRADITION of the church, while Protestant and evangelical Christianity tends to view the canon as the sole authority.

*Old Testament Canon.* The formation of the Jewish canon was hundreds of years in process. The oldest portions of the Pentateuch are regarded by some as having been written in the ninth century B.C. and by others as early as the fourteenth. Some regard the latest portions to be the postexilic prophets written in the fifth century B.C., while others consider Daniel to be as late as the second century B.C. The book of Psalms seems to reflect this extremely long process of canonization spanning a thousand years from the Psalm attributed to Moses (90) to that written during the Babylonian exile (137). It is significant that the people later called Israel do not claim to have produced any writings from the time of Abraham to that of Moses, although we now know that writing existed in highly sophisticated form since before the time of Abraham (as the recently discovered Ebla tablets have shown).

Nothing is known of the process of canonization itself except that the PENTATEUCH was considered uniquely authoritative from the beginning, and other books were collected through the centuries as they were produced and determined to be inspired and useful. A number of books are mentioned in the OT that are not preserved in the canon, such as the Book of Jasher (Josh. 10:13) and the book of the acts of Solomon (I Kings 11:41; see also Num. 21:14 and I Chr. 29:29). About fifteen such books are mentioned throughout the OT. The oldest list of OT books accepted in the Jewish canon comes from Melito, a bishop of Sardis in A.D. 170. His list omits Esther, Lamentations, and Nehemiah, although Lamentations may have been regarded as a part of Jeremiah, and Nehemiah as a part of Ezra. His order of books also differs from that found in modern English Bibles.

Differences exist today in the order and content of the OT, not only among Catholics and Protestants, but also in the Hebrew, Greek, and Latin texts from which the translations are made. The modern English Protestant Bible follows the order of the Latin VULGATE and the content of the Hebrew Bible. The Catholic Bible follows the Vulgate in both content and order of books, thus including the APOCRYPHA. The following chart shows the differences that exist in the content and order of the original texts:

*Hebrew*

Law—Genesis–Deuteronomy

Prophets—Former: Joshua–II Kings
           Latter: Major—Isaiah, Jeremiah, Ezekiel
                   Minor—Hosea–Malachi

Writings—Poetry and Wisdom: Psalms, Job, Proverbs
           Rolls: Ruth, Song of Solomon, Ecclesiastes, Lamentations, Esther
           History: Daniel, Ezra, Nehemiah, I and II Chronicles

*Greek Septuagint* (includes the Apocrypha)

Taken from Codex Vaticanus (fourth century)
Law—Genesis–Deuteronomy
History—Joshua–II Chronicles
Poetry and Wisdom—Psalms, Proverbs, Ecclesiastes, Song of Solomon, Job
Additional—Esther
Minor Prophets—Hosea-Malachi
Major Prophets—Isaiah, Jeremiah, Lamentations, Ezekiel, Daniel

Taken from Codex Alexandrinus (fifth century)
Law—Genesis–Deuteronomy
History—Joshua–II Chronicles
Minor Prophets—Hosea–Malachi
Major Prophets—Isaiah, Jeremiah, Ezekiel, Daniel
Additional—Esther
Poetical and Wisdom—Psalms, Job, Proverbs, Ecclesiastes, Song of Solomon

Taken from Codex Sinaiticus (fourth century)
The OT listing is mutilated.

*Latin Vulgate*
Has the same order as modern English Bibles.
Includes the Apocrypha interspersed throughout.

It will be evident from a reading of this chart that there is no uniformity of order in the Greek OT, either in terms of individual books or of categories of books. The Hebrew does not contain the Apocrypha, while both the Greek and the Latin do. It has been argued that the OT canon's third division, the Writings, was not closed until the Pharisaic gathering of rabbis at Jamnia in A.D. 90, thus remaining open while most of the NT was being written. However, the meeting at Jamnia did not discuss the canon as such and, at any rate, had no decision-making authority. Jewish authorities have always considered the canon to have been closed with the last of the prophets in the days of Malachi. Thus, they have never accepted the Apocrypha.

*New Testament Canon and Authority.* The various books and letters that make up the NT canon, although considered authoritative at the time of their composition, were not appealed to as sources of authority by early church writers until late in the second century. The question of their canonicity was not discussed until this time, and extant lists were not compiled of NT canonical books until the fourth century (assuming the Muratorian Canon is not second century in date). Authority and canonicity were two independent issues in the early history of Christianity. By the fourth century everything canonical was considered authoritative, but in earlier centuries the question of authority was closely connected to living apostolic tradition. The earliest writers, the APOSTOLIC FATHERS, who lived in the latter part of the first century and the beginning of the second, write in the generation of living apostles or men who had known them, and these Fathers consider themselves to be also authoritative. They make no appeal to NT books for the purpose of establishing authority for their message. They write from the perspective of co-authorities. The early APOLOGISTS, who wrote their defenses of Christianity in the early and mid-second century, make no appeal to NT books for sources of authority either. The reason is that they are arguing from a philosophical point of view to a non-Christian audience that would not acknowledge the authority of the NT books if they were appealed to. It is only in the later Apologists, toward the close of the second century, that NT books begin to be employed as sources of authority, and it is only at this time that questions of canonicity begin to arise. The primary reason is the emergence of GNOSTICISM as a literary force that challenges mainline Christianity on its interpretation of Scripture, and both make their appeal to the authority of the text. Naturally questions of canon arise at this time. The Gnostics began to produce their own books of Scripture, giving greater impetus to the mainline church to determine which books are to be regarded as Scripture.

*New Testament Canon.* More books are mentioned in the NT than appear in the canon itself. Paul mentions a prior letter to the Corinthians in I Corinthians 5:9, and a letter to the Laodiceans is referred to in Colossians 4:16. Christian history has never claimed documents from more than three of the original twelve aposles (Peter, John, and Matthew). It is not unreasonable to assume that the others wrote some material that never became a part of the canon. Such a belief formed the basis of third-century apocryphal NT books. As with the OT, the process of theformation of the NT canon is hidden in obscurity. No lists of the canon have yet been found from the third century, but a number appear in the fourth. The earliest list of only our twenty-seven books was produced in A.D. 367 by Athanasius of Alexandria, but, unlike ours, it places Hebrews after II Thessalonians. The first list to correspond exactly to our NT in both order and content comes from Amphilocius of Iconium in A.D. 380. He introduces the list by saying, "I shall tell you each of the inspired books," and after listing the twenty-seven mentions that some say Hebrews and the Revelation of John are spurious. Distinctions among accepted, unaccepted, and doubtful books become prominent in the fourth century and are clearly evidenced in the writings of Eusebius of Caesarea.

It is clear from extant NT manuscripts and the writings of the early church authors that each locality had its own collection of books. Alexandria, for example, as seen in Codex Alexandrinus, used I and II Clement in addition to the twenty-seven. When viewed together these differing local canons had a number of books in common. This group of commonly held books eventually became, by definition, a general canon, that is, one acknowledged by all. Local canons continued to differ for centuries, because local texts continued to differ, but the general canon tended to become uniform with the passing of time. Some of this may have had to do with the standardization of the Byzantine text of Lucian in the fourth century. The activity of the Holy Spirit in this process has been maintained by Christian churches throughout its history.

There was no uniform order of books in the early church. The four Gospels, however, appear in the order Matthew, Mark, Luke, and John in most of the ancient sources. More than twenty different arrangements of the Pauline corpus have been found in Greek, Latin, and Coptic manuscripts, and more than 284 different sequences of scriptural books appear in Latin manuscripts alone. Until recently, most modern editions of the Greek NT placed the Pauline corpus after the General Epistles.

J.R.M.

**CANON CRITICISM.** *See* BIBLICAL CRITICISM.

**CANONICAL HOURS.** Set hours of the day devoted to prayer and meditation, ordained by the church on the basis of apostolic tradition. The early church probably followed the Jewish custom of prayer three times a day, at the third, sixth, and ninth hours. The canonical hours generally are observed by readings from the Psalms, the use of other scriptural selections, and collects and prayers.

J.C.

**CANONIZATION.** The process of declaring a deceased Christian believer to be a "saint," that is, certainly saved and now in heaven with the Lord. The cult or veneration of the saints developed in both the Roman Catholic and Eastern Orthodox churches, although Vatican II severely reduced the "calendar" of saints.

J.C.

**CANON LAW.** In the polity of the Roman Catholic church, a body of legal regulations that are no longer exercised by the ecclesiastic hierarchy. These laws are, in the modern world, exercised by the state and secular courts. The provisions of canon law are inoperative, although the church still claims these laws to be valid. Canon law deals with relations of church and state, the legal rights of heretics, the church's jurisdiction over its priests and their exclusion from secular legal sanctions, and other matters over which the church has lost control since the sixteenth century.          J.C.

**CANTERBURY.** County and cathedral city in Kent, England, archepiscopal SEE of the PRIMATE of the Church of England. On the Stour River, fifty-four miles east-southeast of London, it is one of England's oldest cities; called *Cantwaraburh,* "town of the Kentish people," in the sixth century. AUGUSTINE OF CANTERBURY, a missionary sent with forty companions to Britain by Pope Gregory I, made Canterbury his residence in A.D. 597. He became archbishop in 601, and on the site of an ancient Roman Basilica, presented to him by King Ethelbert, Augustine consecrated the primitive edifice of England's later magnificent Canterbury Cathedral.

England's archbishops traditionally have been crowned on Augustine's chair in Corona Chapel, on the east end of the cathedral. Lanfranc, the first Norman archbishop, built a grander church in the eleventh century—enlarged by his successor Anselm and then destroyed by fire in 1174. Over the next three centuries, William of Sens, and other architects restructured and restored the cathedral, though damaged repeatedly by fire and military action. In 1942 it suffered damage in a German air raid. The various stages of the present 522-feet-long cathedral, with a nave measuring 178 by 71 feet, can still be

Courtesy of Religious News Service

*Canterbury Cathedral*

traced. In 1170 Archbishop THOMAS Á BECKET was murdered in the cathedral. His tomb became a mecca for thousands of pilgrims, vividly described in Geoffrey Chaucer's fourteenth-century *Canterbury Tales.* Henry VIII ravaged Becket's shrine in Trinity Chapel in 1538, confiscated its treasured relics, and burned his bones.                                    C.M.

**CANTICLE OF THE SUN.** *See* FRANCIS OF ASSISI.

**CANTICLES.** Hymns or songs used liturgically that are derived from Scripture other than the Psalms.

They are usually similar to the Psalms, for example, the BENEDICTUS (of Zechariah), the MAGNIFICAT (of Mary), and the NUNC DIMITTIS (of Simeon). Portions of the OT are also used as canticles in Roman Catholic services.                    J.C.

**CANTICLES.** *See* SONG OF SOLOMON.

**CANTOR.** A choir member who intones the psalms and other chants in a liturgical service in Roman Catholic, Episcopal (Anglican), and Lutheran services. Before the fourth century, this was done by the clergy, but the rise of complex liturgies led to specialization. A cantor performs similar services in Jewish liturgies.

J.C.

**CAPERNAUM.** A lakeside Galilean city where, according to the Synoptic Gospels, so much of Jesus' ministry took place that Matthew (9:1) called it "his own city." (Compare Mark 2:1, "at home.")

Capernaum has one of the best-preserved synagogues, a two-story building, sixty-five feet long, carefully studied and partly restored in the 1920s. The third-century A.D. structure was built of limestone brought from some distance and erected on a foundation of basalt, the local, black, volcanic rock. The foundation may be that of the synagogue in which Jesus taught. The decorations are elaborate and varied—geometric, floral, and vegetative. The rabbis held that Capernaum was the seat of the "Minim" sectaries. Recently an octagonal building, probably a fourth-century A.D. church, has been uncovered and is said to enclose Peter's house, where Jesus often stayed. An inscription was found on a pillar reading: "Alpheus, son of Zebedee, son of John, made this column. On him be blessing."

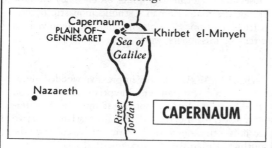

Capernaum was an important regional city, a home port for a commercial fishing fleet, and a distribution point for surrounding, rich, agricultural lands. It lay on a major highway going east three miles, to the mouth of the Jordan River and Bethsaida and on to Damascus. Westward, the road mounted the hills of Galilee, through Cana and Nazareth and the Esraelon, to Ptolemais-Accho, the Mediterranean port (modern Acre).

It is understandable that in Capernaum there would have been Roman centurions (Matt. 8:5; Luke 7:1-2) and Roman "tax offices," where Matthew (Levi) worked and where there were "sinners" of many sorts (Matt. 9:9-10). Andrew, Peter, James, and John lived in Capernaum (Mark 1:6-20). The people of Capernaum witnessed many of Jesus' healing miracles, even raisings from the dead. The Sermon on the Mount was delivered nearby; also Jesus' day-long teaching and the feeding of thousands. Even so, Jesus commented on the failure of Capernaum to repent. He said, "It shall be more tolerable on the day of judgment for the land of Sodom than for you" (Matt. 11:24; compare Luke 10:13-15).

P.L.G.

**CAPITAL SINS/CAPITAL VIRTUES.** *See* CARDINAL SINS/CARDINAL VIRTUES.

**CAPPADOCIAN FATHERS.** The joint name usually given to BASIL THE GREAT, his brother GREGORY OF NYSSA, and their friend GREGORY NAZIANZUS. They were among the dominant theological figures of the fourth century and played important roles in the controversies regarding the Trinity (in which they refuted ARIANISM) and Christology (in which they opposed the views of the APOLLINARIANS). Often forgotten is Basil's older sister, Macrina, who was the force behind his decision to follow the monastic life and whom Gregory of Nyssa called the Teacher.

J.G.

**CAPTIVITY.** *See* EXILE.

**CAPUCHINS.** One of several orders born in attempts to reform the Franciscans, returning to the original practices of St. Francis. The Capuchin movement began within the Observant Franciscans in the sixteenth century and was constituted as an independent order in 1619.

J.G.

**CARDINAL.** Ecclesiastical official ranking just below the pope in the Roman Catholic heirarchy. The COLLEGE OF CARDINALS elects a new pope upon a vacancy in that office. Cardinals are created by the pope and selected by standards similar to those for selecting bishops, although no one of illegitimate birth may be made a cardinal. The candidate for cardinal must also have held ORDERS (even if minor orders) in the church for at least one year and have no children or grandchildren, even by a former, lawful marriage. He must not be closely related to any other cardinal. Cardinals serve for life, although since Vatican II those of advanced age are not permitted to take part in papal elections. Cardinals are divided into three orders: cardinal deacons, cardinal priests, and cardinal bishops. The ranking cardinal bishop is dean of the Sacred College. When the papacy is vacant, the cardinals administer the church.

J.C.

**CARDINAL SINS/CARDINAL VIRTUES.** Cardinal sins are the capital sins, which show a strong inclination to selfishness, debauchery, sensualism, hedonism, and lasciviousness. The seven cardinal virtues concern virtuous living, and by a negative parallelism the seven cardinal sins concern actions that lead to indecent, gross, and shameless living.

Cardinal or capital sins are vices that lead a person on to other sins. The term "capital" applied to these sins is understood by Thomas Aquinas to come from the Latin *caput* or source. Such vices are, therefore, the source of many other sins.

Traditionally, the cardinal sins are called the seven deadly sins. They are usually enumerated as pride, covetousness (or avarice), lust, anger, gluttony, envy, and acedia (or sloth). These seven sins were much more emphasized before the Reformation than they have been since. Cardinal sins endanger a person's virtue and are the fountainhead of a life-style that leads to a multitude of sins.

Cardinal virtues are the chief moral virtues: prudence, justice, fortitude, and temperance. Prudence enables the Christian to form correct judgments about what we must do or not do. Justice disposes the believer to give to all what is due to them. Fortitude helps the Christian to do what is right in spite of all difficulties. Temperance guides the believer to control desires and prevents the abuse of lawful pleasures. To these four cardinal virtues are sometimes added the three theological virtues of faith, hope, and love. The three theological virtues are said in Catholic theology to be infused into the soul in baptism. Taken together, the theological and cardinal virtues are seven great virtues.        J.C.

**CAREY, WILLIAM** (1761–1834). A Baptist missionary to India. Born on August 17 in Paulerspury, Northamptonshire. Baptized as an infant in the Church of England, he became a Baptist about 1783 and served as pastor in Moulton, along with teaching school and making shoes. In 1789 he transferred to the Baptist church in Leicester and in 1792 wrote *An Enquiry into the Obligations of Christians to Use Means for the Conversion of the Heathens,* which led to the founding of the Baptist Missionary Society.

He and Dr. John Thomas were its first missionaries, arriving in Calcutta in 1793. The next year Carey became self-supporting as superintendent of an indigo plant. In 1800 he and his family moved to the Danish territory of Frederiksnagar. In 1801 he was appointed to teach Bengali, Sanskrit, and Marathi at Fort William College.

An incredible linguist, he translated the Bible into six languages, parts of it into twenty-nine more, wrote seven grammars, and compiled three dictionaries. He also fought infanticide and suttee. He died on June 9.        N.H.

**CARLSTADT, ANDREAS** (1480?–1541). Senior colleague and volatile friend-foe of LUTHER at Wittenberg. He studied at Erfurt, Cologne, and Wittenberg, where he became professor of philosophy. Influenced by Luther, he rejected Thomistic thought and attacked the papacy. He helped Luther at Leipzig, 1519, and was condemned in the bull against Luther in 1520. While Luther was at the Wartburg, 1521–22, Carlstadt married, celebrated mass in peasant's garb, urged the laity to help themselves to bread and wine, criticized education, lived as a peasant, and upheld personal revelation as superior to written Scripture. Luther disapproved.

Carlstadt adopted a memorial view of the Lord's Supper and was forced twice to leave Wittenberg. He ended his career teaching at Basel.
        C.M.

**CARMELITES.** A religious order founded on Mount Carmel early in the thirteenth century. At first they were strictly eremitical (of, relating to, or befitting a hermit), following the example of Elijah, whom they later claimed as their founder. When conditions in Palestine became unsafe, they moved to western Europe, where they eventually followed the example of the Franciscans (*see* FRANCIS OF ASSISI) and DOMINICANS, and thus joined the ranks of the Mendicants. In 1452, a feminine branch was added to the order. By the sixteenth century, much of the original fervor and rigor had been lost, and a reform movement began under the leadership of St. TERESA OF AVILA. She recruited the help of St. JOHN OF THE CROSS to reform the masculine branch of the order. The result was the separate order of the Discalced Carmelites—so called because they wore sandals instead of shose. This became a formal order in 1593. Fifty years later, the movement of the Strict Observance reformed the older order. They are now one of the main Roman Catholic monastic orders, particularly among women, and are involved in extensive missionary work.
        J.G.

**CARMEL, MOUNT.** An impressive wooded elevation referred to in ancient Egyptian, Assyrian, and Israelite texts. Jutting northwest into the Mediterranean Sea, it splits the Palestinian coastland into two sections—the northward Plain of Acco and the southward plains of Sharon and Philistia.

Mount Carmel heads a thirteen-mile mountain range on which it has conferred its name. Consisting of hard porous limestone, it attains a maximum elevation of 1,742 feet at its southeastern extremity and falls to an elevation of 470 feet at its northwestern promontory. Its base comes within 600 feet of the Mediterranean. Thus, commercial and military traffic ordinarily traversed the Carmel range on inland passes rather than risk using the shore road to become the easy target of hostile forces commanding Carmel's slopes. Contained within Asher's southern territorial limit (Josh. 19:26), Mount Carmel was sparsely inhabited in historical times. Caves in its lower western slope at Wadi el-Mugharah, however, have yielded Stone Age skeletons.

Since the lists of three Egyptian pharaohs (Thutmosis III, Ramses II, and Ramses III) mention Mount Carmel under the name Rosh Qidshu ("holy cape"), its character as an ancient sanctuary is implied. The designation of Mount Carmel as Ba'li-ra'si ("Baal of the promontory") in the Assyrian annals of Shalmaneser III certifies its sacral significance. While he camped there in 841 B.C., he received tribute from Israel's king Jehu. Recognized by

Shalmaneser as the border between Israel and Tyre, this holy terrain hosted Elijah's triumphant contest against the prophets of Baal that established Yahweh's sovereignty at Baal's expense (I Kings 18:19-40). Elisha is also linked with Carmel (II Kings 2:25; 4:25).

Mount Carmel is famous for beautiful orchards cultivated on its slopes, and its fertility is celebrated in the imagery of Song of Solomon 7:5; Isaiah 35:2; and Jeremiah 50:19. Yet three prophetic texts portending judgment (Isa. 33:9; Amos 1:2; Nah. 1:4) figuratively speak of Carmel's vegetation as being victimized by drought.

J.K.K.

**CARMICHAEL, AMY** (1867–1951). The famed poet and missionary to India was born on December 16, the eldest of seven children of David and Catherine Jane Filson Carmichael. She was baptized a Presbyterian in Millisle, County Down, Northern Ireland, on January 19, 1868.

Influenced by the Keswick Movement, she arrived in India on November 9, 1895, under the Church of England Zenana Missionary Society and the Keswick Missionary Committee. She served without furlough until her death on January 18.

In 1901 she began her work rescuing girls who had been "married to the gods" by their parents. In 1918 she began accepting boys also. Eventually in 1926 her work became an independent faith mission known as Dohnavur Fellowship. She wrote a total of thirty-five books, thirteen of them after a fall in 1931 rendered her an invalid. Most are poetry.

N.H.

**CARROLL, JOHN** (1735–1815). The first American Roman Catholic bishop was from a distinguished Maryland family. The fourth of seven children of Daniel and Eleanor Darnall Carroll, he was educated by his mother and at Bohemia Manor on the Pennsylvania border.

He entered St. Omer's, a school for English Catholics, in France in 1748. Beginning in 1753 he spent two years as a JESUIT novice in Watten, France, and then studied in Liège for three years, before returning to teach at St. Omer's in 1758. He was ordained at Liège about 1767. Wishing to see his mother and realizing that the Americans were about to declare their independence, he returned to Maryland in 1774 after Pope Clement XIV had suppressed the Jesuits on August 16, 1773.

Carroll's *Address to the Roman Catholics of the United States of America* (1784) was well received, and he was named prefect-apostolic and superior of the American Jesuit Mission on June 9, 1784, by Pope Pius VI. He was elected bishop on November 14, 1789, and consecrated August 15, 1790. In 1791 he presided over the first American synod. In 1808 he became archbishop. Firm in his attachment to Rome and orthodoxy, yet progressive in practical matters, he

Courtesy of Georgetown University

*John Carroll*

advocated a vernacular liturgy and an Americanized church. In 1791 he established Georgetown University to educate American men.

N.H.

**CARTER, JIMMY** (1924– ). James Earl Carter, Jr., the thirty-ninth president of the United States (1977–81) was born in Plains, Georgia, on October 1. A former governor of Georgia, Carter was little known nationally before being chosen the Democratic candidate in 1976. He was, while in office, and remains, a modest but sincere and attractive Protestant Evangelical with a strong social conscience. In 1976, he attracted a large vote from the rising political Evangelical wing, but proved too moderate for the increasingly vocal and right-wing leadership of the Moral Majority and similar religious movements who voted for Ronald Reagan over Carter in the 1980 election.

Carter graduated from the U.S. Naval Academy and after service in nuclear submarines resigned his commission in 1953. He became a successful peanut farmer before entering politics. Carter's service as a Georgia state senator and governor established a record of financial conservatism and social liberalism. He was a strong supporter of racial justice and a leader in creating the "new South," in which blacks were integrated into state government. Carter married

Rosalyn Smith on July 7, 1946, and they have four children, John, James, Jeffrey, and Amy. A member of the Baptist church, Carter remains active in church programs.

J.C.

**CARTESIAN.** *See* DESCARTES, RENÉ.

**CARTHUSIANS.** One of the strictest of Roman Catholic monastic orders, founded by St. Bruno, who in 1084 began a small monastic community in the valley of Chartreuse, near Grenoble, France. The name of the order is derived from "Chartreuse," and to this day its main house is La Grande Chartreuse, whose prior, elected by the monks of that particular house, is the general of the entire order. There is also a general chapter, with representatives from all the houses, which meets annually. English Carthusian monasteries are also called Charterhouses, after the Grande Chartreuse. There is a feminine branch, although it is much smaller than its male counterpart.

The Carthusians are vowed to silence, except in common worship and on great feast days, when there are set periods of conversation. They spend most of their time in their cells, where they study, pray, sleep, and eat in private. Their food, prepared by lay brothers whose rule is not as strict, is usually served through a window in their cells. On feast days there are common meals, but never any meat. In general, their life has changed very little from the time of their founding.

J.G.

**CARTWRIGHT, PETER** (1785–1872). The famed Methodist circuit rider was born on September 1 in Virginia to Justinian and Mrs. Wilcox Cartwright. In 1793 they settled in Kentucky, where at sixteen Peter was converted. He was given an exhorter's license in 1802 and became an itinerant in 1803.

He was ordained deacon (1806) and elder (1808) by FRANCIS ASBURY. In 1808 he married Frances Gaines. He was presiding elder in Illinois. He wrote his *Autobiography* (1857) and *Fifty Years as a Presiding Elder* (1871).

N.H.

**CARY, ALICE** (1820–71). With her sister Phoebe Cary (1824–71), she became known as a writer of hymns and novels. Alice was born on April 26 and Phoebe on September 4 near Cincinnati, Ohio. They were two of nine children of Robert and Elizabeth Jessup Cary.

The *Poems of Alice and Phoebe Carey* (sic) were published in 1849. Shortly thereafter the sisters moved to New York City, where their Sunday evening receptions became popular. Alice published five volumes of poetry, plus short stories and sketches of life in Ohio (*Clovernook*, 1852; *The Clovernook Children*, 1855; and *Pictures of Country Life*, 1859) and novels (*Hagar*, 1852; *Married, Not Mated*, 1856; and

*The Bishop's Son*, 1867). Both were active in abolition and "woman's" rights.

Alice's best-known works are the "Dying Hymn," and "Earth with Its Dark and Dreadful Ills." Phoebe's hymn "One Sweetly Solemn Thought" is most often reprinted. Alice died on February 12 and Phoebe on July 31, of the same year.

N.H.

**CASSOCK.** A long, narrow robe with long sleeves, buttoned down the front and generally black, worn by clergy under a surplice when conducting worship. In the Catholic church, the pope wears a white cassock, and cardinals wear scarlet ones. Bishops wear purple cassocks, and choir members, robes of various colors.

J.C.

**CASTE.** The social system of South Asia, rooted in HINDUISM. Caste is actually two things: (1) *varna* (color)—the broad division of society into categories of descending purity; they are Brahmin (priest), Kshatriya (warrior), Vaishya (merchant), Shudra (laborer), and Outcaste (traditionally known as "untouchable," but now often called "Harijan," meaning literally "children of God"); and (2) *jāi*, or birth group. Every *varna* contains many *jāti*. Each *jāti* has a set of occupations, rituals, customs, and dietary laws that set it apart. Subcastes, or groups of *jāti*, are ideologically and economically related to one another, but do not intermarry.

The ideology of caste is rooted in the Hindu belief in KARMA (psychic product of action) and REINCARNATION. Everyone has already lived many lives and will live many more. How well one follows the DHARMA, or law of one's present existence, determines one's karma. Good actions generate good karma and assure rebirth in a better caste; bad actions produce bad karma and rebirth lower in the caste system, in hell, or as an animal or ghost. The dharma of a Brahmin is to be a priest, the dharma of a Kshatriya is to fight and rule, and so on. Myth relates that the castes were made from parts of a giant's body; the first Brahmin from the mouth, the first Kshatriya from the arms, the first Vaishya from the thighs, and the first Shudra from the feet. The actual heritage of the castes comes from India's early history. In the latter part of the second millennium B.C., Aryan invaders speaking Sanskrit conquered India and its Dravidian peoples, who had built the Indus Valley civilization. Recent research has uncovered great Dravidian contributions to the subsequent civilization of India. Dravidian culture influenced much of the religious system, including Sanskrit, the sacred language. The invaders' name for themselves, *ārya*, lost some of its racial connotations as Dravidians were assimilated into all parts of the caste system. Still, modern high-caste Indians identify themselves and their light skin with the Aryan invaders.

Subsequent history affected the caste system, but did not displace it. BUDDHISM arose as a reform of

Hinduism and rejected caste, but the new religion died out in India. Later converts to ISLAM, SIKHISM, Christianity, and Buddhism formed separate groups, which Hindus regard as castes.

Today ideas and attitudes toward caste are changing. *Jāti* related by dietary or religious customs have discussed intermarriage, and many younger Indians have some say in choosing a mate. Younger Indians especially are experiencing conflict between the dictates of their caste and their loyalties to class or nation. The old ideology of caste purity is giving way to notions of race, and members of higher castes believe themselves to be genetically superior.

K./M.C.

CASTOR AND POLLUX. Also called the Dioscuri, meaning "the Twin Brothers" (RSV). The word is used once in the Bible (Acts 28:11) as the "sign" (KJV) or "figurehead" (RSV) of a ship from Alexandria, probably a grain carrier. Paul was a passenger on it from Malta to Puteoli en route to Rome. To Romans, the Dioscuri were twin sons of Jupiter by Leda. Sailors claimed Castor and Pollux as their own particular deities, holding that they could be seen in heavenly transformation as the constellation of Gemini or the twins. Phosphoric lights playing on masts and sails were regarded as appearances of the twins. Sacrifices were made to them to obtain fair winds and rescue in case of shipwreck.

P.L.G.

CASUISTRY. In theology casuistry refers to the bearing of general moral principles upon specific and unique cases—for example, killing or lying. The obligatory practice of confession of sin in the late Middle Ages made the study of casuistry especially imperative in the training of priests. The sixteenth and seventeenth centuries saw the appearance of highly technical manuals for dealing with particular cases of conscience. They often were logically brilliant but highly abstract and had little relationship to real life. Moral reflection too often was reduced to logical hairsplitting and casuistry received a bad name ("finding good reasons for approving bad actions"). Among the most important systems of casuistry is that known as PROBABILISM, advocated by St. Alphonsus Liguori in the eighteenth century. Defenders of situation ethics reject moral casuistry as too rigorous and legalistic. However, when its proper limitations are recognized, most moral theologians, Catholic and Protestant, consider casuistry to be indispensable to moral reflection and guidance.

J.L.

CATACOMBS. A word of unknown origin applied to early subterranean cemeteries, particularly those built by Christians in the outskirts of ROME. The custom of burial in niches carved in the rock of underground galleries was probably already practiced in Rome by Jews, and therefore the Christian catacombs were patterned after the earlier Jewish ones. At first, these burial places were fairly small; but as the Christian community grew, galleries were extended, and sometimes others were dug at different levels, so that there are catacombs with up to four different stories.

The common notion that the catacombs were essentially places where Christians hid for worship is erroneous. Christians did celebrate Communion at the tombs of MARTYRS on the anniversary of their death, and therefore such services did take place in the catacombs. But the existence of the catacombs was known to Roman authorities, and in any case their narrow corridors would make it very difficult to celebrate large services in them. On occasion, some Christians did hide in the complex galleries of the catacombs, but this was not the general practice. Abandoned in the early Middle Ages, the catacombs were unknown until 1578, when the first of them was uncovered. Today, they are particularly valuable because their frescoes are the oldest existing early Christian art.

J.G.

CATECHISMS. Catechisms are writings used to teach the basic content of the Christian faith. The earliest materials in existence are the Catechetical lectures of CYRIL OF JERUSALEM. Designed for use during LENT for those preparing for baptism, the lectures embrace three basic components: the APOSTLES' CREED, which each will affirm at the baptismal liturgy; the TEN COMMANDMENTS as a rule for Christian living; and the LORD'S PRAYER, the prayer of the church by which Christians are taught how to pray.

Centuries later, when western Europe had become Christian and infant baptism was the custom, there was less demand for catechetical instruction. The form took on new importance after the Reformation. The Protestant traditions wanted to enunciate their understandings, and the Roman Catholic church wanted to reaffirm its interpretation of the faith. LUTHER's Shorter Catechism took the form of the earlier lectures. Like Cyril, he affirmed the creed to be a statement that we believe *in* (a confession of faith) rather than what we believe *about* (a statement of belief). Other catechisms were couched in question-and-answer form: the WESTMINSTER (Presbyterian), the HEIDELBERG (Reformed), and the Anglican Articles of Instruction. American Roman Catholics learned about the faith through the BALTIMORE CATECHISM. Frequently viewed as a recitation of doctrine to be memorized, the catechism was meant to be a simple statement through which people could learn the reasons for faith, thereby making it easier to affirm these reasons in the life of faith.

I.C.

CATECHUMEN. A person being instructed by the church in preparation for baptism. In the early church, catechumens were allowed to be present during the early part of the service, which consisted mostly of the reading and exposition of Scripture. But they were dismissed before the service of Communion proper was begun. For this reason, the earlier part of the service came to be called "mass of the catechumens." At first, the period between conversion and baptism was very brief. But as the number of Gentile converts increased, the church found it necessary to allow more time to instruct them in matters that the earlier Jewish converts already knew. By the time of Constantine, it had become customary to delay baptism in some cases until the moment before death. Thus arose the distinction between the masses of catechumens and those who were actually preparing to receive baptism. Later, as infant baptism became the norm, the catechumenate declined and eventually disappeared, to be revived in modern times, particularly in missionary lands.

J.G.

**CATEGORICAL IMPERATIVE.** KANT took the view that an action has worth only if it is done from a sense of duty, that is to say, in obedience to the moral law. An action cannot be justified by appeal to an external authority (HETERONOMY) or to desirable consequences that may flow from it (utilitarianism) (*see* UTILITARIANS). Its rightness is perceived by the autonomous rational agent, and this rightness is intrinsic to itself.

It is this sense of unconditional, moral obligation that finds expression in the categorical imperative. It is formulated thus: "I ought never to act except in such a way that I can also will that my maxim should become a universal law." This principle of morality, he believed, rests entirely on the rational nature of the moral agent. It may seem a very austere and even legalistic view of morality, but it can be expressed in another way that introduces concepts of a more personal kind. "Act so as to treat humanity never only as a means but always also as an end." Kant is not saying that we should never treat another human being as a means, for obviously we all do this, but a human being can never be regarded as *merely* a means—human beings possess in their rationality an inherent dignity, which makes them also an end. Kant also introduces the concept of respect, though he claims that respect is primarily for the law and only derivatively for persons. Many people have the opinion that the defect of Kant's teaching is his lack of an adequate concept of a human person. (*Compare* GOLDEN RULE.)

J.M.

**CATHARS/CATHARI.** A term derived from a Greek word meaning "pure," and applied at various times to different heresies. In the twelfth century, it was used in Germany for those known in France as ALBIGENSES, and that is still its common usage.

J.G.

**CATHEDRALS.** Larges churches, the principal places of worship of Catholic or Anglican DIOCESES, which contain the bishop's cathedra or "chair." It is the bishop's seat, where he exercises his preaching and teaching ministry. In the basilicas built by Constantine, the chair or throne was put at the rear of the apse, centered behind the altar. Later, the chair was placed on the north side of the chancel. From his chair the bishop presides at Holy Communion and preaches. Due to the honor paid to the bishop's teaching and governing function, the cathedral came to be the mother-church of the whole diocese.

The chair generally is placed atop three steps and is covered by a canopy, showing the dignity of the bishop's office. Originally, the cathedral was in or near the bishop's palace and he and his assistants served it. Later, administrative duties prevented his leading worship very often, so a "chapter" of clergy was founded to serve the cathedral. This chapter had the right to elect a new bishop when the bishop died or was "translated" elsewhere.

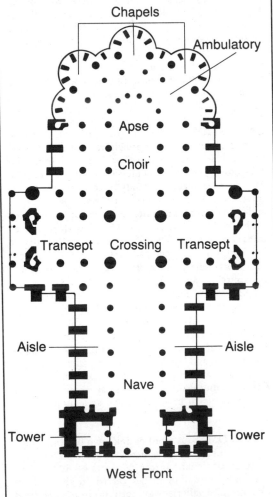

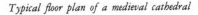

*Typical floor plan of a medieval cathedral*

Cathedrals, especially in the Middle Ages, came to be fine examples of the architecture of the period in which they were built. They contained the bishop's throne, a choir, a nave, a baptistery (sometimes in a separate building), the bishop's palace, a bell tower, and a monastery for the chapter clergy serving the church. As only a bishop in residence in his diocese can establish a cathedral, there is generally only one church designated by the term in a diocese. The location of a cathedral can be changed. There are examples of co-cathedrals, where the bishop maintains a chair in two churches. A procathedral is a church used by a bishop until a finer church is built.

The building of cathedrals is governed by canon law, which holds that a cathedral is to be dedicated in a solemn service of consecration. Ordinations and the synod meeting of the diocese are held there. Canon law permits a bishop to be buried in his cathedral.

J.C.

**CATHERINE OF ALEXANDRIA.** A legendary MARTYR supposed to have died during the persecution of Maxentius, after confounding her persecutors with her learning. Her symbol is a wheel, for she is said to have been tied to a wheel and tortured before being beheaded. According to an even later legend, her body was carried by angels to the monastery of St. Catherine on the Sinai.

J.G.

**CATHERINE OF SIENA.** A mystic who was influential in the return of the papacy from Avignon to Rome, and one of only two women on whom the Roman Catholic church has bestowed the title of DOCTOR OF THE CHURCH. Born in Siena in 1347, she joined the Third Order of Dominicans when still in her teens and shortly thereafter had the experience of a "mystical marriage" with Jesus. Around her gathered a group of followers, several of them learned theologians, who came to learn of the life of devotion and MYSTICISM. She was also known for her service to the poor and the sick. In 1376, spurred by a vision, she went to Avignon and persuaded Gregory XI to return to Rome. When the GREAT SCHISM followed, she devoted her remaining years to the cause of the Roman papacy. She died in 1380, was declared a saint in 1461, and a Doctor of the Church in 1970.

J.G.

**CATHOLIC.** A transliteration of the Greek word, *katholikos,* meaning "universal" or "general." Throughout Christian history the word has expressed various nuances of meaning. During the early patristic period it conveyed the idea of "universal," as in the expression by Ignatius, "Wherever Jesus Christ is, there is the catholic church." Here the universal church is contrasted with the local congregation.

It is also applied to the faith of the entire church. Thus in the "holy catholic church" of the Apostles' Creed, it expresses the sense of universality and unity.

The Catholic Epistles of the NT were so designated to indicate they were intended for the whole church.

"Catholic" came to mean "orthodox." Vincent of Lerins, in his *Commonitorium* says, "What all men have at all times and everywhere believed must be regarded as true." Thus the concepts of universality and orthodoxy are joined.

After the schism of the Eastern and Western churches in 1054, the Western church was referred to as "catholic" and the Eastern church as "orthodox."

In the Reformation period the churches that adhered to the papacy rather than the Protestant cause were known as "catholic." The Anglican Church insisted on the right to use the term "catholic" in describing the continuum between it and the apostolic church. Rome claimed the appelation uniquely on the ground of its organizational continuity.

Often Anglicans and Old Catholics employ the term to include themselves, the ROMAN CATHOLIC CHURCH, and Eastern ORTHODOX churches as those communions related to the undivided pre-Reformation church.

Today, the term is used to describe Christians who claim to be in the historical and continuous tradition of faith and practice, as opposed to PROTESTANTISM, which centers its faith on an authoritative Bible.

R.H.

**CATHOLIC EPISTLES.** Refers to seven NT letters, James, I and II Peter, I, II, and III John, and Jude, as "general" in the sense: (1) they are not addressed to any single church, in contrast to most other NT letters, and (2) they are addressed not only to a wider audience but also they are concerned with matters of more general or ecumenical nature. The term does not appear in the NT but seems to have developed within the first four Christian centuries. Origen (about A.D. 250) states that in his time, I Peter and I John were universally accepted as canonical scripture, but that there was strong opposition by many, but not by him, to the other five.

P.L.G.

**CATHOLIC REFORMATION.** A move toward renewal within Roman Catholicism dominated by reactions to sixteenth-century Protestantism. During the BABYLONIAN CAPTIVITY (1309–77) with the papacy at Avignon, and the GREAT SCHISM (1378–1417) with two and then three popes vying for supremacy, calls for reform "in head and members" resounded in Roman Catholicism. The COUNCIL OF CONSTANCE (1414–18) achieved some reform only to have Pope Pius II in 1460 condemn even an appeal to a council. Nepotism, worldliness, immorality, and abuses mounted alarmingly within the papal hierarchy. These conditions prompted the basis for the founding of numerous new orders dedicated to living genuine Christianity—Oratory of Divine Love, Theatines, Barnabites, Sommaschi, Capuchins,

Brothers of Mercy, Ursulines, Angelicals, Daughters of Mary, Brothers of the Good Death, and others. Hospitals, orphanages, the sick, prayer, preaching, mass, fasting, and asceticism all received their attention. Humanists like ERASMUS and Contarini criticized the church's hypocrisy and ignorance. Cardinal XIMENES began a religious revival in Spain, and IGNATIUS LOYOLA founded the SOCIETY OF JESUS (Jesuits), 1534.

When the Protestant Reformation erupted and attracted converts, Roman Catholicism sought to recover members and territories by redefining its doctrines. This was done in the COUNCIL OF TRENT, 1545–63. It reaffirmed every dogma questioned by the Protestants. Trent made scripture and tradition equal sources for faith and morals, sanctioned the APOCRYPHA, adopted JEROME's VULGATE Latin Bible as official, defined justification to include meritorious good works, reaffirmed TRANSUBSTAN-TIATION and the seven sacraments, withheld the cup from the laity, extolled celibacy as more excellent than marriage, said souls could be helped in PURGATORY, and upheld relics and INDULGENCES. In 1564 Pope Pius IV issued a Tridentine creed for Catholics to sign as a personal confession. Four subsequent popes implemented Trent and pushed moral reform: Pius V, Gregory XIII, Sixtus V, and Paul V. Trent provided basic guidelines for Catholicism until VATICAN COUNCIL II (1962–65). St. Teresa of Avila established thirty CARMELITE branches. The Jesuits promoted education and missions. PALESTRINA reformed church music. ROBERT BELLARMINE and Peter Canisius defended Catholic doctrines and practices.

To stop heresy and untruth the Catholic Reformation also resorted to force—against individuals with a renewed INQUISITION (1542), and with military might against the Lutherans in Germany, Calvinists in Holland, HUGUENOTS in France, and the Anglicans in England. By the seventeenth century a reformed Roman Catholicism had curbed Protestantism and recovered much of its lost prestige. (See REFORMATION and PROTESTANTISM.)

C.M.

**CELEBRANT.** The priest or minister who actually presides at the consecration of the bread and wine at Holy Communion or the Mass, in either Catholic or Protestant worship services. When several clergy take part in a service, it is the presiding minister who is in actual charge of the celebration of the Eucharist.

J.C.

**CELIBACY.** The permanently unmarried state and restraint from any sexual activity demanded of the clergy (major ORDERS) and of both men and women in religious (monastic) orders in the Roman Catholic Church. Recipients of such orders vow to remain permanently unmarried, and chaste in thought and act. Luther and the other Reformers protested against the church's rules of celibacy for the priesthood and began the marriage of pastors in Protestant churches. The Council of Trent, however, confirmed the church's teaching on celibacy for priests and the religious. Indeed, the rules of celibacy hold that once a person takes major orders or a monastic vow as brother or nun, any future marriage he or she may enter is null and void. Perpetual deacons, or "lay" deacons, may be married men since Vatican II, but not if they live with a second wife.

J.C.

**CELSUS.** A pagan philosopher of the second half of the second century who wrote a treatise, *The True Word,* against Christians and their teachings. His work is lost, but a vast portion of it has been preserved in extensive quotations in Origen's *Against Celsus.* This is the earliest detailed exposition of the objections of learned pagans to Christianity, to which many of the APOLOGISTS responded. Celsus himself was a follower of PLATONISM and a defender of the ancient religion and institutions of the Greco-Roman world. Thus his objections to Christianity have to do mostly with its logical inconsistency and with its negative consequences for civilization.

He had studied the Bible and Christian teaching and argued that the miracles and prophecies are either unbelievable or unclear, that the Christian God is a meddler whose constant interventions in the minutiae of human life are unworthy of the Supreme Being, and that Christian pacifism and lack of participation in civil ceremonies, if practiced by many, would render the empire vulnerable to the barbarians and would result in the end of civilization. Although his arguments were impressive, he does not seem to have made a great impact, for even the learned ORIGEN did not know of his work until asked by another Christian to refute it.

J.G.

**CENCHREAE.** The eastern naval station and harbor of Corinth located on the east side of the Isthmus (Acts 18:18; Rom. 16:1). Cenchreae provided sea communications to the Aegean Sea and the Orient. The seven-mile paved road (Cenchreae to Corinth) led to Corinth's east or Cenchreae gate. Paul passed through Cenchreae on his "painful" visit (II Cor. 2:10). Later, "at Cenchreae he cut his hair, for he had a vow" (Acts 18:18; see Num. 6:1-5). It is thought that Romans 16 is a letter from Paul to the church at Ephesus, and that Phoebe of the Cenchreae church (v. 1) was its bearer. At some earlier time and in some unspecified way, she had been a "helper" to Paul (v. 2).

P.L.G.

**CENNICK, JOHN** (1718–55). Author of the hymns "Children of the Heavenly King" and "Be Present at Our Table, Lord," Cennick was born on December

12 into a QUAKER family, although he was reared in the Church of England.

In 1739 he met JOHN WESLEY and soon became a lay preacher and a teacher at Kingswood School. Having parted with the Wesleys, Cennick joined the MORAVIANS in 1745 and was ordained by them.

N.H.

**CENSER.** A vessel used for burning incense during worship services in the Catholic, Orthodox, and Anglican churches. A censer is a bowl in which live coals are placed, covered with a rounded perforated top. Chains are attached to the bowl so it may be carried or suspended in the chancel.

J.C.

**CENTURION.** A non-commissioned Roman army officer, commander of "a century," or one hundred, foot-soldiers. The centurion was a key professional officer in war and peace. After twenty-five years of service, he could be rewarded with Roman citizenship, gifts, and other benefits (his pay was five times that of an ordinary soldier). The centurions in the NT are wealthy; they have slaves, large houses, and make lavish gifts. The centurion at the cross readily acclaimed Jesus "Son of God" (Matt. 27:54; Mark 15:39). Cornelius was also a centurion (Acts 10).

P.L.G.

**CEPHAS.** *See* PETER, APOSTLE.

**CERINTHUS.** One of the many teachers of GNOSTICISM, probably a Jew by birth, who taught in Asia Minor around the year A.D. 100. According to IRENAEUS, it was against Cerinthus that the Gospel of John was written. He taught that Creation was the work not of the Supreme God, but of a lesser being, and that Christ was the divine presence, which came to the human Jesus at baptism and left him before the passion.

J.G.

**CHALCEDON,** Council of; Definition of; Faith of. A council that gathered in A.D. 451 and condemned the teachings of Eutyches on CHRISTOLOGY, as well as the previously condemned views of the APOLLINARIANS and NESTORIANS. Two years earlier, at what Pope Leo called a Robbers' Synod, extreme ALEXANDRIAN THEOLOGY had been affirmed, and even the more moderate forms of Antiochene theology had been rejected. Leo's Tome, which reaffirmed the ancient Western Christology of "two natures in one person," had not even been read. At Chalcedon those actions were reversed, and the bishops rejected the extreme expressions of both Alexandrians and Antiochenes.

Since the COUNCIL OF EPHESUS in 431 had taken action against the proliferation of creeds, what was then decided was not to offer a new creed, but rather to compose a "Definition of Faith," which would clarify the christological implications of the faith affirmed at the councils of NICEA and CONSTANTINOPLE. This "definition," rather than explaining how the union of divinity and humanity takes place in the Savior, sets limits for future theological work by stating that it takes place: "without confusion, without change, without division, without separation."

Not all Christians agreed with the decisions of Chalcedon. Those who for various reasons rejected them were called Monophysites by the rest (*see* MONOPHYSITISM). Such was the stance of the Armenian church, the Jacobites of Syria, the Coptic church of Egypt, and the Ethiopian church. Thus resulted the first permanent break in Christian history.

J.G.

**CHALDEA.** A swampy, low-country region of South Mesopotamia that was inhabited by a fiercely independent people of a primitive culture, from the end of the second millennium B.C. Aramean tribes of like characteristics lived on higher ground between the Tigris and the Euphrates. The "language of the Chaldeans" (Dan. 1:4) is now understood as Aramaic. Nabopolassar (626–605 B.C.) founded the Chaldean dynasty, which under his son Nebuchadrezzar II extended its rule over former Assyrian territory and also Syria-Palestine. (The dynasty declined rapidly after Nebuchadrezzar's death in 562 B.C.) Such was the Chaldean's short-lived influence as a world power that, in OT passages, "Chaldean" generally designates any people from the entire country of Babylonia. "Ur of the Chaldeans" (Gen. 11:28, 31; 15:7; Neh. 9:7) explains the ancient city's location to the contemporary Bible reader. Chaldean magicians, astrologers, and diviners of all sorts migrated to and were immensely popular in Egypt, Greece, and Rome and were called magi.

P.L.G.

**CHALICE.** The cup used in celebration of Holy Communion. The chalice or cup is the only sacramental vessel directly referred to in the NT. All other sacramental vessels have developed out of church usage.

In the Catholic church, a chalice must be consecrated by a bishop. Most churches have several chalices, and priests generally have a chalice for their personal use. Chalices are generally made of gold or silver but may be of any metal if gold-plated on the inside of the cup. Some contemporary chalices are of earthenware or glass, while historically, chalices have been encrusted with jewels.

J.C.

**CHALMERS, THOMAS** (1780–1847). Scottish preacher, theologian, social reformer, and founder of the Free Church of Scotland. Born in Anstruther, educated at St. Andrews University, he rose from parish pastor, 1803, to professor at St. Andrews, 1823, and Edinburgh University, 1828, where he was acclaimed for his preaching, social work, and promoting education. He resisted the "moderate" trend to make Christianity largely ethical and established over two hundred new churches. In 1843 he led 470 Scottish ministers to form the Free Church of Scotland, which sought more freedom from civil domination. His works include *Political Economy*, 1832, and *Institutes of Theology*, 1843-47.

C.M.

Courtesy of the Metropolitan Museum of Art, The Cloisters Collection, 1950

*The Chalice of Antioch*

**CHANNING, WILLIAM ELLERY** (1780–1842). Known as the Father of Unitarianism (*see* UNITARIAN UNIVERSALIST ASSOCIATION), Channing was born April 7, 1780, to William and Lucy Ellery Channing of Newport, Rhode Island. After graduating from Harvard in 1798 and serving as a tutor there, he was ordained and installed June 1, 1803, as pastor of Federal Street Church, Boston, which he served until his death.

His 1819 ordination sermon for Jared Sparks in Baltimore titled "Unitarian Christianity" served as a manifesto for the growing movement among Boston CONGREGATIONALISTs. In 1820 he organized the Berry Street Conference for like-minded ministers and in 1821 began the *Christian Register*. His objections were directed more toward orthodox views of humankind than of God. In "The Moral Argument against Calvinism," he inveighed against depravity.

He greatly influenced many New England writers with his sermons and essays. His 1830 *Remarks on American Literature* called for American style, not English imitation. He died on October 2.

N.H.

**CH'AN SCHOOL.** *See* BUDDHISM.

**CHARACTER, INDELIBLE.** The inner seal, on the personality and spirit, communicated to a priest upon his ordination in the Roman Catholic church. According to church doctrine this character, or blend of moral and personal traits, cannot be removed. It sets a priest apart as always a priest.

J.C.

**CHARDIN, PIERRE TEILHARD DE.** *See* TEILHARD DE CHARDIN, PIERRE.

**CHARGE.** A pastoral responsibility, consisting of one or more congregations or preaching points, in The United Methodist church. The charge is equivalent to a PARISH in the Lutheran or Presbyterian churches. A charge is entrusted to an ordained minister by the superintendent of the district or the bishop of the conference.

J.C.

**CHARISMATICS.** This is a term referring to Christians who profess to have received the baptism or fullness of the HOLY SPIRIT. It usually is accompanied or followed by a conferring on the believer one of the gifts (charismata) of the Spirit described in the Pauline Epistles. This phenomenon, experienced in wide ranges of the church, is more precisely defined as the Charismatic Movement, the charismatic renewal, or neo-Pentecostalism.

The charismatic renewal has its roots in historic Pentecostalism, which embraces several denominations and had its inception at a three-day revival meeting held in 1906 in Los Angeles (*see* PENTECOSTAL CHURCHES). Most church historians date the rise of the Charismatic Movement to 1960, when distinctive teaching on the baptism of the Holy Spirit and emphasis on the gifts of the Spirit began to be accepted in traditional denominations. Up to that time non-Pentecostals showed little regard for those they sometimes called Holy Rollers. One of the earliest proponents of the movement was the Reverend Dennis Bennett, rector of an Episcopal parish in Van Nuys, California. From Episcopal churches the renewal spread to most of the major denominational groups—Lutherans, Baptists, Presbyterians, Methodists, and others. In its beginnings the renewal was regarded with deep suspicion, not only by those who retained their opposition to the older Pentecostalism, but by the historic Pentecostals themselves.

The Catholic pentecostal movement, or charismatic renewal, as many prefer to describe it, first emerged in prayer meetings convened at Duquesne University, Pittsburgh, in 1967. The original impetus came from Catholic lay people who had been in contact with old-line Protestant Pentecostals. From there the Catholic movement has spread rapidly around the world.

The word "charismatic" is derived from the Greek word *charisma,* which in NT usage means "a gift, freely and graciously given." The gifts of the Spirit are listed and described in Romans 12:6-8 and I Corinthians 12:8-10. (Ephesians 4:7-12 provides an additional listing.) The gifts, directly transmitted to individuals by the sovereign working of the Holy Spirit, always purpose the edification of believers in the Body of Christ. The gifts include those of healing, prophetic utterance, speaking in tongues (GLOSSOLALIA) and the interpretation of tongues, as well as less spectacular charismata such as "helps," "governments," or the lesser known but impressive "word of wisdom" and "word of knowledge."

Historic Pentecostals usually have taught that those who experience the baptism of (or in) the Spirit will speak in tongues as an outward evidence of the inward experience. Charismatics, whose theology has not yet been codified, generally are not as insistent that speaking in tongues is a universal experience of those who have received the baptism. Both charismatics and the older Pentecostals teach that the gifts of the Spirit persist in the church today.

R.H.

**CHARLEMAGNE.** King of the Franks and, after his coronation by Pope Leo III in A.D. 800, emperor of the HOLY ROMAN EMPIRE. He was both a military leader and an able organizer. Through a series of military campaigns, he forced the conversion of the Saxons. Against the Moslems in Spain, he undertook the unsuccessful campaign which resulted in the death of Roland, and in the ensuing legends about it. But later his armies succeeded in conquering a wide strip of land across the Pyrenees, and this became one of the starting points for the Spanish Reconquista. In Italy, he conquered the Lombards and took their crown. This was one of many steps that gained him the favor of the popes.

As an administrator, Charlemagne was responsible for the revival of learning that is often called the Carolingian Renaissance, and in which Alcuin of York played an important role. When ADOPTIONISM broke out in Spain, he took measures against it and encouraged his theologians to refute it. His coronation as emperor of the West, resented as it was in Byzantium, marked one more step in the growing breech between East and West.

J.G.

**CHARLES V.** King of Spain (as Charles I) from 1516 to 1555, and Holy Roman Emperor from 1519 to 1556. From his father, Philip of Burgundy, and his maternal grandparents, Ferdinand and Isabella, he inherited vast domains, which included Spain, Burgundy, the Netherlands, and southern Italy, as well as the Spanish territories in the New World. The very vastness of his domains forced him to deal with many enemies and rivals. These included Francis I of France, as well as the Turks, the Papacy, and the Protestant princes of Germany. He hoped for a reformation like that proposed by ERASMUS, and was convinced that LUTHER and his followers were heretics. At the DIET OF WORMS he put Luther under the ban of the empire. But political circumstances prevented him from crushing Protestantism, and after the Diet of Augsburg he had to tolerate it. This was one of the reasons for his abdication in 1556. He died in the monastery of St. Yuste, in Spain, two years later.

J.G.

**CHARTRES.** City in northern France, famous for its GOTHIC cathedral, completed in the thirteenth century. In the Middle Ages it was also noted for its

*Chartres Cathedral*

school. The cathedral is one of the most beautiful examples of Gothic architecture, and its stained glass windows are without equal.

J.G.

**CHASIDISM.** *See* HASIDISM.

**CHAUNCY, CHARLES** (1705–87). The leader of PURITAN rationalists was born in Boston on January 1 to Charles and Sarah Walley Chauncy. After attending Boston Latin School and Harvard University (B.A. 1721, M.A. 1724), he was ordained in First Church, Boston, on October 25, 1727, and served there for sixty years. He married Elizabeth Hirst on February 14, 1727; Elizabeth Townsend on January 8, 1738; and Mary Stoddard on January 15, 1760.

He was involved in three controversies—revivalism (*see* REVIVALs), the episcopacy, and God's benevolence. A person of intellect, he distrusted the emotions of revivals and replied to JONATHAN EDWARDS' *Religious Affections* with *Seasonable Thoughts on the State of Religion in New England* (1743) and two *Letters to Whitefield* (1744, 1745). His nine-year quarrel over the episcopacy stretched from the *Dudleian Lectures* (1762) to his *Complete View of Episcopacy* (1771). Wrestling with *The Benevolence of the Deity,* he published his universalist views anonymously in London in 1784. In 1785 he published *Five Dissertations on the Fall and Its Consequences.* He died on February 10.

N.H.

**CHEMNITZ, MARTIN** (1522–86). German Lutheran theologian, ranked next to LUTHER and MELANCHTHON. Chemnitz was a unifier of Lutherans under the *Formula of Concord,* 1577, which he helped write. Born in Brandenburg, he studied at Frankfurt-on-the-Oder and Wittenberg, and later at Königsberg and Rostock, where he received a doctorate in theology in 1568. An early disciple of Melanchthon, in 1553 he lectured at Wittenberg on Melanchthon's *Loci Communes* and began developing his own *Loci Theologici* to draw Luther and Melanchthon together (published posthumously, 1591). As a pastor and superintendent of churches in Brunswick, Chemnitz sought to unite Lutheran factions by reconciling Luther-Melanchthon differences. He defended Luther's view of Christ's real presence in the Lord's Supper, 1561, produced a four-volume standard Lutheran study of the Council of Trent, 1564–73, published extensive data on the divine-human nature of Christ, 1570, and fostered Lutheran orthodoxy in the *Formula of Concord,* adopted in 1580.

C.M.

**CHERUB/CHERUBIM.** Both the singular and plural are the Hebrew terms for the mythological figures common in Mesopotamian and Egyptian art and architecture—winged bulls or lions, usually with human faces, representing the spirit guardians at the portals of palaces, temples, tombs, and holy sites. In its numerous references to cherubim, the Bible has adopted a Near Eastern cultural motif with obvious religious connotations, though for the most part it is likely that it had now become little more than a symbol, literary or artistic.

The original mythological concept of the cherub is present in Genesis 3:24, where it is said to have been set to guard the entrance to the garden of Eden. Similarly in Ezekiel 28:13-14, which employs the same myth of "the garden of God." On the other hand, the cherub of Psalm 18:11 (Hebrew; RSV, v. 10), though it appears in a passage obviously modeled on the mythology of the Canaanite storm-god Baal, can hardly be more than a poetic figure of speech (paralleled with "the wings of the wind"). Ezekiel's vision of the strange "living creatues" surrounding or supporting the throne of God (Ezek. 1), who are identified with "the cherubim" in Ezekiel 8–10, is a prophetic interpretation of the significance of the embellishments of the Ark of the Covenant as it was the featured holy object in the preexilic Temple of Jerusalem. According to the Priestly source of the Pentateuch and the Deuteronomic history of Samuel and Kings, cherubim were omnipresent in the Mosaic tabernacle (Exod. 25:18-20), and in the Temple of Solomon, about the Ark of the Covenant, and in other decoration (I Kings 6:23-32). Ezekiel's vision of the temple of the future (Ezek. 41:18-20) shows a persistence in the recognition of the propriety of this sacred symbol. These cherubim were variously carved in wood, cast or overlaid in precious metal, or embroidered. In later Jewish and early Christian thought the cherubim—divorced from their earlier pictorial representation—were remythologized as real creatures and assigned to a place among "the angels." A further fusion with Roman mythology led to the Renaissance portrayal of a "cherub" as a winged infant hovering about heavenly scenes.

B.V.

**CHESHVAN.** *See* HEBREW CALENDAR.

**CHESTERTON, GILBERT KEITH** (1874–1936). An English writer, journalist, Christian apologist and illustrator, who converted to the Roman Catholic Church at age forty-eight. Chesterton was educated at St. Paul's School, the London Slade School of Art, and University College, London. Taking a love of English literature from their father, Edward, both Gilbert and his brother, Cecil (1879–1918), early became involved in writing and criticism. By 1900 Gilbert was well known and began a series of several thousand essays in the *Daily News* and the *Illustrated London News,* and later, *G. K. C.'s Weekly.* He also began writing his many books of poetry, literary criticism, social comment, and the defense of the Christian, and later, specifically, the Catholic faith. After 1922 he

192

seriously began commending Catholicism to the English as an antidote to the secularism, agnosticism, and materialism that were eroding traditional values. Chesterton's books *Heretics* (1905) and *Orthodoxy* (1908) are considered classics, which influenced C. S. LEWIS and Ronald Knox.

J.C.

**CHILDREN OF GOD.** In the OT Prophets, the concept of the sacred marriage between Yahweh, the husband, and Israel, the bride, was used, despite its analogy to Baalism, where the Lord Baal fertilized the land. Hosea especially made use of this, using the analogy of his own marriage to Gomer, who, like Israel, proved unfaithful. However, in the NT, only the CHURCH is spoken of in this way, that is, as the bride of Christ. Rather, the unique NT expression for the relationship of the believer to the Godhead is Paul's expression, "children of God," and its parallel, "heirs with Christ" (Rom. 8:16 ff.). This expression, then, is derived from Christology and soteriology, not from the doctrine of creation; it does not refer only to the fact that God created everything and everyone. To be a "child of God" is to be connected to Christ, saved by the grace of God given the sinner who is imbued with faith, and who has died and risen again with Christ in the waters of baptism. It is important to keep the christological meaning of the phrase in mind, since the expression "children of God" occurs in the Bible with various other meanings also.

In Job 1:6; 2:1; 38:7, it refers to angels or messengers of God. In Luke 3:38, it refers to human beings who have God for their Father whether they recognize God or not. In Exodus 4:22, the expression refers to all Israel. It can refer to specific Hebrews (Hos. 1:10) and even to the Gentiles (Isa. 19:25). Jesus is also spoken of as the Son of God (Matt. 3:17; 17:5; Luke 1:35). Finally, the redeemed are called the children of God in John 1:12.

The NT contains a great deal relating to the "sonship" of the redeemed Christian, especially under the metaphor of ADOPTION. Paul uses several key metaphors to discuss the meaning of the believer's salvation in Christ: redemption (bought with a price, that is, purchased from slavery to Satan by Christ's death); reconciliation (an enemy turned into a friend by the intercession of Christ); salvation (that is, cured from sickness); resurrection (raised up from death in the grave by baptism with the ever-living Lord); and adoption (turned from an outsider into a son by the Father's choice and legal action).

This last metaphor, adoption, is the basis for Paul's assertion that Christians are the children of God (Rom. 8 and throughout Romans). He was directly referring to Christ's adoption of those who have faith in him as his brothers and sisters—an adoption made possible by his defeat of Satan and his payment on the cross for humanity's sins. Christ has become our elder brother and sacrifices his own inheritance as the Father's "only begotten son" to share his relationship

to the Father and the joy of the Father's kingdom with all who have faith in Christ's death and resurrection. The faithful are, therefore, fellow heirs with Christ. God is now the Christian's patrimony. This is the unsearchable goodness and the unspeakable blessing that is the believer's in Christ.

J.C.

**CHILDREN OF GOD.** One of the most bizarre new religions or "CULTS" to arise in the late 1960s in the United States. It was founded by David Brandt Berg, a former Christian Missionary and Alliance minister, one-time Baptist minister, and the son of a woman radio evangelist. The group grew out of the "hippies" converted by itinerant ministers in southern California during the JESUS PEOPLE movement. Berg, who early changed to a cult name, Moses David, was successful in pulling together the newly converted, fundamentalistic young people into a communal movement. Ultimately, he drew almost all the "Jesus People" into his "revolutionary army for Jesus," which he at first named the Children of God and later, under the impact of Ted Patrick's deprogramming assault and adverse publicity, renamed "the Family of Love."

Berg built the Children of God on fundamentalistic lines and was befriended by an evangelist who allowed the group to stay at the "Texas soul winning ranch." Eventually, Berg's fanaticism caused the Children of God to be expelled and split up to establish communes in the United States and Europe. Berg wrote encyclicals to his followers called "Mo Letters." These letters have degenerated from their earlier sectarianism to later ones ordering female followers to become "flirty fish," that is, to use sex to attract followers. Later, Berg ordered male followers to use sex to raise money. Most active in Europe, the Children of God quickly became one of the Continent's largest organized vice rings. Such immorality brought public opposition and caused many members to defect.

J.C.

**CHINA INLAND MISSION.** A missionary organization founded by JAMES HUDSON TAYLOR in 1865, after he had been a missionary in China for more than ten years. This was an interdenominational and international body whose purpose was to make certain that the gospel was preached throughout China. Since missionaries to a particular area tended to come from a particular denomination in the sending countries, churches appeared in China that were very similar to those represented by the missionaries. Eventually, the China Inland Mission reached every province in China. During the Boxer rebellion it suffered heavy losses, but Taylor refused to accept indemnification, for fear that this would create even greater resentment among the Chinese. By the time of Taylor's death, in 1905, the work of the China Inland Mission was firmly established throughout China.      J.G.

**CHLOE.** A woman known and respected by Paul and the Corinthian church (I Cor. 1:11) whose "people," relatives or perhaps slaves, reported to Paul in Ephesus about the "quarreling" among Corinthian Christians.

P.L.G.

**CHRISM.** A mixture of oil and other substances used for anointing in various rites in the Roman Catholic and Orthodox churches. Chrism is consecrated by the bishop and administered to the dying or ill, at baptism, confirmation, ordination, and the consecration of altars and churches.

J.C.

**CHRIST.** *See* JESUS CHRIST.

**CHRIST, BODY OF.** *See* BODY OF CHRIST.

**CHRISTENDOM.** The name usually given to the area ruled by Christians or where Christianity has held cultural and social sway. Traditionally, this has meant Europe, the Russian territories in Asia, and the New World. Given the twentieth-century circumstances, it is doubtful whether one can still speak of "Christendom." J.G.

**CHRISTIAN.** The term is found only three times in the NT (Acts 11:26; 26:28; I Pet. 4:16), and interestingly it is there placed on the lips of persons outside the church as though to suggest that this particular title was given to Christ's followers rather than one they chose for themselves. But in the second century it became a current term preferred by those in the church, especially the Apologists (the anonymous author of *To Diognetus,* Justin, Athenagoras).

The origin of "Christian" is not certain. If its ancestry is in the Latin language, the ending *-ianus* suggests a member of a group owing allegiance to a historical personage (for example, Caesar, Herod). Then *Christianus* meant "one committed to Christ's cause" as his devotee or slave. If Acts 11:26 is correct in tracing the origin of the term to the people of Antioch in Syria, it may be that the Roman emperor's followers in that city (the *Augustiani*) coined the name to identify a rival group who professed allegiance to another emperor, Jesus. But there are dating problems with this suggestion. So it has been proposed that the counterpart is *Herodianoi,* that is, followers of Herod Agrippa I, who, according to Acts 12:1, was a persecutor of Jesus' followers in Palestine. The later Herod Agrippa II (in Acts 26:28) used the term ironically in response to Paul's fervent plea: "In a moment you will be persuading me to play the part of a *Christianus*"; this seems to be the cryptic meaning of Herod's reply.

The use of "Christian" in I Peter 4:16 depends on the dating of I Peter. If the letter was composed just prior to the persecution of the church at Rome by Nero (A.D. 65), the call to suffering matches the (later) description given by Tacitus. Of Nero, Tacitus wrote: he brought a charge against a sect "whom the common people were calling Christians." If, however, I Peter comes out of a subsequent decade, no firm link with Nero's pogrom is established, and the term "Christian" is regarded as an identity badge of believers in the Roman world generally (see I Pet. 5:9).

In later persecutions the standard question in the magistrates' interrogation was: "Are you a Christian?" This fact indicates that the title that seems to have begun as a nickname is now being accepted, by both the church and the Roman state authorities, as a well-known identification of the followers of Christ. The mention of *Christos* (Christ) as a title was turned to good effect by the Apologists who linked it with a similar sounding *chrestus,* "good, kind"; and some confusion over pronunciation (as in Suetonius' famous citation: "Claudius expelled the Jews at Rome because of a constant squabbling over *Chrestus*") was exploited by second-century Christian writers.

R.M.

**CHRISTIAN CHURCH (DISCIPLES OF CHRIST).** A Protestant Christian denomination that arose in the United States in the first quarter of the nineteenth century as a result of revivalism. The origins of the "Christians" or "Disciples" lie in several areas of the United States as evangelists called for a simple, primitive Christianity that would not demand adherence to creeds. On the basis of the Bible alone, these preachers proclaimed, Christians of every denomination should unite to promote the teachings of the apostles.

Thomas Campbell, a Presbyterian pastor in Washington County, Pennsylvania, founded the Christian Association of Washington in August, 1809. Almost immediately he published his "Declaration and Address," which sorrowed over the sharp party spirit among Christians. Campbell attributed this spirit of disunity to the stress on creeds, which he called human interpretations of the Word of God, among the various denominations. He called for Christian unity. An organization of those who agreed with him was formed in Brush Run, Pennsylvania, on May 4, 1811. The Christians were often called Campbellites because of the influence of Thomas and ALEXANDER CAMPBELL.

Christians are mainstream in most doctrinal positions, agreeing with the evangelical wing of Protestantism in belief while leaning toward the liberal position on social issues. The writings of the Christians stress the divine inspiration of the Bible, which is seen as God's revelation and a rule for the believer's faith and life; the Holy Trinity; the divine sonship of Jesus Christ; the alienation of humankind in sin from God and one another; the need of faith, repentance, and obedience for salvation; the final judgment, with rewards for the righteous and punishment for the unrepentant.

Christians and Disciples also have a very distinctive platform among Protestants, stressing the "restoration" of Christianity in the rejection of creeds; in a great emphasis on the divine sonship of Jesus; in insistence on NT names for the church and for Christians; special emphasis on the Holy Spirit's work in conversion; and their teachings on the Lord's Supper. The Lord's Supper, in the Christian's view, is to be celebrated every Lord's Day (Sunday); yet it is seen as a memorial feast and not as a sacrament. Christians also stress the Lord's Day as being not a Sabbath, but a unique NT institution.

J.C.

**CHRISTIAN AND MISSIONARY ALLIANCE.** A missionary alliance formed in 1897 from two preexisting bodies, the Christian Alliance and the Evangelical Missionary Alliance. Over the years, this alliance has become, in effect, a denomination of the Protestant conservative, holiness type. In 1985, the membership of the CMA was 215,857 in the United States and Canada, gathered in 1,532 congregations. The CMA is made up of some 2,094 pastors, evangelists, and licensed preachers in North America, and 900 foreign missionaries. The CMA is evangelical in the revivalist, holiness tradition and fundamentalist in doctrine. It stresses the four-square gospel; the need for conversion; the baptism of the Holy Spirit (speaking in tongues); an imminent Second Coming; and divine healing. In polity, each congregation is practically autonomous, yet confesses the faith of the CMA. The group has three Bible colleges in the United States and one in Canada, specializing in preparation for missions.

J.C.

**CHRISTIAN METHODIST EPISCOPAL CHURCH.** *See* METHODIST CHURCHES.

**CHRISTIAN REFORMED CHURCH IN NORTH AMERICA.** *See* REFORMED CHURCHES.

**CHRISTIAN SCIENCE.** *See* CHURCH OF CHRIST, SCIENTIST.

**CHRISTIAN YEAR.** The cycle of festivals, observances, and seasons celebrated liturgically by the Christian church. The Christian Year begins on the first Sunday of ADVENT and ends on the Saturday before Advent begins. Festivals or feast days (in Catholic terminology) are designated holy days with the purpose of focusing people on Christ. These festivals commemorate historical events in the life of Christ or in the experience of the early church. There are a few festivals dedicated to Christian doctrines such as Holy Trinity, Christ the King, and also in the Catholic calendar, the Sacred Heart, the Precious Blood, and the Holy Name of Jesus. Also included in the church's celebrations are memorials of apostles, saints, and martyrs. Saints' days have been completely revised in the Catholic church since Vatican II. The new liturgical calendar of the Lutheran church in America includes commemorations of such modern martyrs as Dietrich Bonhoeffer and modern humanitarians as Albert Schweitzer and Dag Hammarskjold.

The Christian Year moves around the person and work of Jesus Christ. Advent celebrates the coming of Christ in the Nativity and also points to the SECOND COMING. The Christmas season rejoices over the birth of Christ. EPIPHANY remembers the showing forth of God's glory in Christ. LENT leads people to consider their need of salvation and the sacrifice of Christ for human sin. EASTER celebrates Jesus' victory over death. PENTECOST and its lengthy season recalls the coming of the Holy Spirit and goes on to impart the activities of the early church and the teachings and actions of Jesus in the Gospels.

The Christian Year is highly symbolic and is marked by special colors for each season as well as for saints' days, martyrs' days, and festivals. The lectionary, or book of appointed scriptural readings, the Psalter, and the COLLECTS (prayers) used in liturgical churches and in many free churches, are guided by the festivals and seasons commemorated by the Christian Year. These "variables" change from Sunday to Sunday, as do offertories and other musical responses. The Christian Year holds the believer's attention on Christ and helps ministers present a balanced account of the faith.

J.C.

**CHRISTMAS.** The Christian church's celebration of the birth of Christ, the festival of the Nativity. In the Western churches (Roman Catholic and Protestant) this celebration occurs on December 25. In the Eastern churches, Christmas occurs on January 6. The actual date of Christ's birth is unknown but was probably in the spring.

The name Christmas is derived from "Christesmesse," Old English for the mass of Christ. In the Christian Year, observance of Christmas begins with the first Sunday in ADVENT (beginning the liturgical year) and runs through EPIPHANY (in the Protestant churches) and Candlemas (in the Roman Catholic church).

Celebration of Christmas on December 25 dates from A.D. 336, when the pagan festival of *natalis solis invicti* (the birthday of the invincible sun) established by the emperor Aurelian in the third century A.D. was converted to a Christian holy day, referring to "the Sun of Righteousness," Christ. The Eastern churches were already celebrating the birth of Jesus and his baptism on January 6 at that time.

J.C.

**CHRISTOLOGY.** The branch of theology that deals with the person and acts of Jesus Christ.

*Methods.* Any approach to Christology (that is, the teaching of Christ's person as both a figure of history and the object of Christian worship) must face the issue of methodology. Specifically, this means that a choice has to be made whether the interpreter will begin with creedal formulations that announce JESUS CHRIST as "true God" and "true man" and then work backward to the way this teaching arose as a beginning premise (Christology "from above"). The other approach is to begin with the empirical data of the historical and theological records (in the NT) and trace the way the church's understanding developed until the creeds were formulated (Christology "from below"). Another way to settling this issue before us is to ask whether NT Christology is ontological (that is, concerned with Christ's transcendent role in relation to God, the world, and the church) or primarily functional, (that is, relating God's person to divine achievement as savior and Lord and set in the context of Christ's earthly ministry). To put the matter in sharp focus, the two methods proceed from different starting points. The first asks, "Who is Christ and how is he related to God?" The second proposes the questions, "What did Jesus do in his human life, and how did it come about that the church accorded him titles of divinity because he did what only God could do?" At a practical level this choice is more than academic as we see when we pose the issue yet one more way. Is Jesus rightly called Son of God because he saves?—as functional Christology asserts? Or is it that Jesus saves because he is the Son of God—as ontological Christology states? Perhaps, however, the two approaches reach the same goal in the end; but as methods they are different, and a decision has to be reached. In what follows the "Christology from below" will be regarded as the better and more plausible model that can be described and deduced from NT and early Christian teaching, while not denying that there are ontological overtones, more implicit than explicit.

*The Course of New Testament Christology.* On our chosen approach it becomes possible to plot the path the NT writers took as we apply the tradition-historical method to their documents. This means that Christology developed in response to situational needs among the first congregations.

The early believers in Jerusalem were Jews who had come to faith in Jesus as MESSIAH and risen LORD. Their appreciation of who Jesus was took its point of departure from the conviction that, with his RESURRECTION and exaltation, the New Age of messianic triumph, described in the OT and intertestamental writings, had indeed dawned, and the OT scriptures had been fulfilled. But the cross had also to be explained, since Jesus' death at the hands of the Roman political powers stood in contradiction to all that pious Jews believed about the Messiah, God's expected deliverer of the chosen people (Deut. 21:23; cited in Gal. 3:13). A rationale was found in two ways: by asserting (1) that Jesus' rejection was already foreseen in OT scripture, notably Isaiah 53 and Psalm 118:22, and that his implicit claims to be the messenger and embodiment of God's kingdom showed only human unbelief; and (2) that at the Resurrection God had reversed this verdict, vindicated Christ, and installed him in the place of honor and power. The first christological statement therefore was based on two stages in Jesus' existence; he was son of David in his human descent, and since the Resurrection he is SON OF GOD (Rom. 1:3-4). The implicit messianic claims of his earthly life were made overt since his exaltation. The proof of the New Age he inaugurated is seen in the coming of the Holy Spirit (Acts 2:16-21 quoting Joel 2:28).

At a practical level this way of seeing Jesus' life and resurrection gave these believers a personal relationship with Jesus as a present reality and not simply a figure of the past, however recent. Hence the first prayer of which we have record is "marantha" ("our Lord, come") addressed to the risen Lord and placing him on a level with Yahweh, Israel's covenant to God (I Cor. 16:22; Rom. 10:9-13) as worthy of worship. This is the startling novelty of what the resurrection and elevation of Jesus meant.

Further meditation on OT scripture evidently gave a clue to Jesus' secret identity and explained his use of the mysterious title "Son of man." Drawn from Daniel 7:13-18, the SON OF MAN title is one of authority and dignity, two ideas that the resurrection of Jesus confirmed. The church preserved this teaching on the Son of man from Jesus' lips, and set it in the framework of his earthly life in order to accomplish several purposes: (1) to show how Jesus was misunderstood and rejected as messianic pretender, since "Son of man" spoke of God's kingdom and made him a sharer of the divine throne; (2) to show how Jesus brought in a New Age, wherein God's revelation was not tied to the Torah, Moses' law, but was universalized for all people. The "Son of man" in Daniel 7:22, 27 is the head of a supranational, worldwide kingdom; and (3) to find a missionary impulse, which led these believers, notably under the leadership of Stephen and his followers, to reach out to pagans (Acts 7:55-56; 11:19-21).

Such a mission brought the church into the world of Hellenistic religion in the setting of Greco-Roman society. The most relevant title in this religious milieu was "Lord," used of the gods and goddesses of the mystery cults, and in the prevailing EMPEROR WORSHIP directed, however obliquely, to the Roman Caesar. Both areas proved fertile ground for the application of the commonest christological title in the NT. "Lord" was already in use as the name of Yahweh applied to the exalted Christ; now it became useful in promoting the cultus of Jesus to those who were familiar with the deities of the Greco-Roman world (I Cor. 8:5-6), as later it was Christ's sole lordship that became the dividing line between Christian allegiance and the homage required to be paid to the deified state (the setting of the book of

Revelation in the A.D. 90s, when Domitian proclaimed himself as "lord and god"; compare Rev. 17:14).

The final step in NT Christology was taken in the church of the Letter to the Hebrews and of the fourth evangelist. The author of Hebrews sets out to prove the finality of Christ's revelation as Son (1:1-4) and High Priest (5:5; 7:1–9:28). John's writings are clearest in their ascription to Jesus of the name Logos (Word) and (only) God. (See John 1:1, 14, 18; 20:28.) John's indebtedness is evidently to the OT and intertestamental wisdom tradition where "wisdom" and "word" (often linked with the Mosaic law) are rated as mediators in creation (Proverbs 8) and the preexistent revelation of God (in the Wisdom of Solomon). John boldly claims both roles for Jesus of Nazareth (John 1:3; 18; 14:6, 9). He sets the earthly life of Jesus against the background of his eternal being as "one with the Father" and the visible glory of the unseen God, thus superseding the Torah of Moses (John 1:17) and the claims of the Roman emperor (John 20:28, "my Lord and my God").

Yet even those most explicit statements of Christ's divine nature (Phil. 2:6; Col. 1:15; Heb. 1:1-4; Tit. 2:13; and less certainly Rom. 9:5) never compromised the unity of God as a cardinal element in OT MONOTHEISM (belief in one God in a world of POLYTHEISM), nor did they lend countenance to the view that Jesus was a rival deity to the Father (see Phil. 2:9-11; I Cor. 11:3; John 14:28). God the Father is always regarded as the fount of deity; Jesus is God's Son in a unique sense but never confounded with him. Yet this uneasy correlation bequeathed a legacy that formed the substance of the christological debates leading to the COUNCIL OF CHALCEDON in A.D. 451.

*A Sketch of Later Christology.* The first aberration came as early as the problem the Johannine community had to face, namely a denial of Jesus' genuine and full humanity. Thus docetism (a denial of Jesus' true human existence) is roundly condemned in I John and by Ignatius. At the opposite extreme Jewish Christianity produced an Ebionite Christology, which thought of Jesus as only a good man adopted to be God's son. "ADOPTIONISM" continued into the second century, matched strangely by the opposite extreme of modalism, which asserted that the one God was shown in three successive modes or "masks." This was condemned by church fathers such as Tertullian and Origen.

The fourth century presented the conflict over our Lord's divine "nature"; was it "like" God (Arius)? or "identical with" God (Athanasius)? Apollinarius pressed Christ's deity to the exclusion of his human experience and left the church with a demigod. Nestorius exaggerated the two separate natures (human and divine), and so divided the unity of God's person. Eutyches went to the opposite extreme, and asserted only one nature in Christ (called monophysitism).

A turning point came at the Council of Chalcedon, where the teaching on two natures united in one person prevailed (the hypostatic union). This has remained the centralist position of the church ever since. Challenges have come in a theory of KENOSIS or self-emptying, whereby the divine Christ emptied himself of his deity at his birth and resumed it at the Resurrection, and in some speculation on Christ's assuming a representative human nature or in a teaching of an eternal modalism (Karl Barth). But in recent days Chalcedon has been ably defended, mainly by Eastern Orthodox theologians, and "Christology from above" passionately rehabilitated.

R.M.

**CHRISTOPHER.** A legendary figure, supposed to have lived in the third century, whose name means "he who bore Christ." The legend is that he helped travelers across a river, and that on one occasion he unknowingly carried the Christ child. For that reason he is the patron saint of travelers. The Roman Catholic church has deleted his name from the list of the saints.

J.G.

**CHRISTOTOKOS.** "Bearer of Christ," a title applied to Mary, particularly by the NESTORIANS, who rejected the use of THEOTOKOS or "bearer of God." The issue was one of CHRISTOLOGY rather than MARIOLOGY, for Nestorius' point was that the divinity and humanity in Christ ought not to be confused. He was condemned by the COUNCIL OF EPHESUS in A.D. 431.

J.G.

**I and II CHRONICLES.** In the present-day English Bibles two historical books of the OT, which were originally one book in the Hebrew canon, just as were I and II Samuel and I and II Kings. The original Hebrew title was probably "Events of the Past Times." In the Douay Version, these books are called paralipomenon (deutero-canonical). The name *Chronicles* derives from Jerome, who explained the books as a chronicle of the sacred history of the Jews. The material in I Chronicles is similar to II SAMUEL, and that in II Chronicles parallels I and II KINGS. Additionally, there is material derived from the Hebrew books of Genesis to I and II Kings, with the exception of Judges, plus non-canonical material excerpted from some twenty-one books mentioned in several places in I and II Chronicles (for example, I Chr. 29:29; II Chr. 9:29).

The two books of Chronicles were written by the same author as the OT books known as EZRA and NEHEMIAH. However, in the Hebrew text, Ezra and Nehemiah are presented first, and the Chronicles are placed at the end of the OT text. The author is unknown, although W. F. Albright thought Ezra might be the writer. Most other scholars would put the time of the Chronicles between 350 and 250 B.C., long after Ezra's time. The postexilic, strong law-centeredness of later Judaism is clear in the Chronicles, as is the writer's Priestly orientation and devotion to the Davidic royal line. David and Solomon are the Chronicles' heroes, and the kings of northern Israel are his villains. Devotion to the Temple and opposition to the Samaritans who continued the Israelite worship on Mount Gerizim is a strong theme in his work. Indeed, the aim of the book(s) seems to be to give a history not of Judah as a nation but of the Jewish "church" centered in Jerusalem.

A major theme of the Chronicles is similar to a sentiment expressed by Ezekiel, that people who eat sour grapes will have their teeth set on edge, that is, people get what they deserve. In the historical material the Chronicler has taken from I and II Samuel and I and II Kings, the author shows that good kings have long and successful reigns and those with short, unhappy reigns are sinners. Examples given include the sickness that afflicted Asa and Jehoram and the leprosy that Uzziah suffered. Manasseh's long rule, despite his wickedness, is explained by his repentance and reform (II Chr. 33). The good Josiah, who died at Megiddo, is explained by a failure to obey God (II Chr. 35) at the end of his life. The moralism of the Chronicler, like all moralism, was possible only by leaving out a good deal of history. This is especially true of his portraits of David and Solomon. These kings are presented as all good by the simple expedient of omitting the records of their many sins, which stand in II Samuel and I Kings. Solomon's building of the Temple is stressed; his many foreign wives and his idolatry are passed over in silence. The Chronicler seems to love large numbers, especially in giving the size of foreign and Jewish armies. Most historians dismiss these numbers as exaggerations. A strong hostility to the northern kingdom of Israel also skews the Chronicler's historical reports.

The Chronicler's major purpose in collecting new material and reworking the older material of the Hebrew Bible (the result of the Priestly editors' work during and after the Exile) is to show how the present reign of God (the theocracy) in Jerusalem came into being, by way of God's actions in history as well as by the good offices of the Persian Empire. All seems now for the best, since the faithful freely worship Yahweh in God's holy Temple.

J.C.

**CHRYSOSTOM, JOHN.** Patriarch of Constantinople from A.D. 397 whose eloquent preaching gained him the title of Chrysostom, the "golden-mouthed." A native of Antioch, he was already a famous lawyer and orator when he decided to leave the city and become a monk. Since his mother objected to his leaving her, he turned their house into a monastery, and after her death he withdrew to the nearby mountains in order to live in solitude. A few years of

monastic retreat convinced him that such was not his vocation, and he returned to Antioch, where he was ordained a deacon and then a presbyter. He then began preaching, and soon his fame was such that when the patriarchate of Constantinople fell vacant the emperor had him abducted from Antioch and made patriarch.

Chrysostom's preaching, although elegant and eloquent, was not well received by those who held power in Constantinople. He felt that excessive wealth and pomp were an affront to God, particularly in a city where many were living in squalor. In his sermons in the great cathedral of St. SOPHIA, he attacked those who "take over lands and houses, thus increasing poverty and hunger." Soon there was a conspiracy against the meddlesome preacher, which included both the empress and the patriarch of Alexandria. The result was that, after several other measures failed, Chrysostom was banished from the capital. While in exile, his pen continued to shame the powerful, and he was ordered to a more remote village. He never reached his new home, for he died on his way, in A.D. 407.

J.G.

**CHUANG TZU.** From the Chinese words for "Master Chuang." The second most important text in TAOISM, after the *Tao te ching* of Lao Tzu, and the name of its supposed author. Little apart from what is revealed in the book itself is known about Chuang Tzu, although his traditional dates, 369–286 B.C., are probably approximately correct. But significant portions of the book attributed to him are believed to be later. The commentary on the Chuang Tzu by Kuo Hsiang, in the fourth century A.D., is a Taoist classic in its own right.

Chuang Tzu comes through in the book as a charming eccentric who cares little for status, appearance, or convention. Upon the death of his wife, instead of mourning he sang and beat a drum, not, he said, out of callousness, but because he realized that her passing into nonexistence was as natural as her coming into existence, so nothing to lament. In another celebrated passage, after dreaming he was a butterfly, he asked himself whether he was Chaung Tzu dreaming he was a butterfly or a butterfly dreaming he was Chuang Tzu.

Indeed, the book opens with a series of brilliant illustrations to show that all our ideas, large and small, high and low, are but conventions, meaning nothing to infinite reality—the Great Tao—itself. Neither the human perspective nor any other is the absolute. Therefore the way to live in accordance with the Tao is not through conventional custom or morality but out of an inner "mindlessness" or "purposelessness," which is mystically attuned to the Tao and which is manifested in joyous spontaneity. In an image that may have roots in Shamanism, the freedom of this state is frequently compared with the flight of birds or gods through the sky. The Tao itself is a unity in all things, including, the philosopher pointedly and characteristically insisted, ants, weeds, rubble, excrement, and urine.

The book contains a valuable discussion, and repudiation, of rival schools. It was seminal for the Neo-Taoism of the period of Kuo Hsiang, with its emphasis on immediacy and living by impulsive spontaneity. Chuang Tzu was also important for the emergence of Ch'an (ZEN) BUDDHISM in China, which essentially synthesized the Indic religion with Taoism of the Chuang Tzu style.

R.E.

**CHU HSI** (1130–1200). Chinese philosopher; the most important thinker of the movement known as Neo-Confucianism, Chu Hsi exercised an immense influence not only in China but also in Korea and Japan, until the demise of traditional Confucian education. His interpretation of the tradition dominated both intellectual life and, as the reigning metaphysic, supplied the theoretical supports of state and society.

Chu Hsi viewed human and natural reality in terms of a dualism of *li* (principle) and *ch'i* (energy/matter); both derive from *T'ai Chi* (the Great Ultimate). In his view philosophy means "investigating the *li* that underlie both natural phenomena and human conduct"; thus, a good society would be one in which proper morality and right human relationships, as understood by Confucianism, had unhindered expression.

R.E.

**CHURCH.** The English word "church," like its counterparts in other modern languages (Scots *kirk*, German *kirche*, Dutch *kerk*) derives from the Greek *kuriakon*, meaning "belonging to the Lord" (*kurios*). As to what it is that belongs to the Lord (that is, God, or more likely the risen Jesus Christ) there is no certainty. Perhaps it is his people, the body of believers. In this case the term points us to the essential meaning of "church" in the biblical writings. The church is the people of God, created and called (the Greek *ekklesia* is from a verb "to call") by God, to be God's worshipers and witnesses, both in this world and in eternity. Less likely the term *kuriakon* could refer to God's day (the Lord's day, our Sunday—as in Rev. 1:10, when the first Christians met to worship the exalted Christ), or God's building dedicated for the corporate worship of God. The last reference is not appropriate for the NT period, since the early believers had no special church buildings, but met in their homes, as in Acts 2:46; 5:42; Colossians 4:15; and Philemon 2. Church buildings are not found before the third century.

*Old Testament Background.* The actual term "church" does not appear in the standard translations of the OT, but two Hebrew terms are prominent,

which suggest the idea of the congregation of Israel: these are the words *edah* and *qahal*. The English renderings vary between "assembly" and "congregation." *Edah* comes from a word meaning "to appoint," and the obvious sense of the noun as applied to Israel is that of a company that has come together by appointment, either at an appointed time for a festival (Exod. 9:5; I Sam. 13:8, 11) or more probably by divine appointment, notably as a result of God's deliverance at the Exodus (Exod. 12:3; note 12:6, "the assembled community of Israel" in NEB trans.). So Israel is viewed as God's assembled congregation, bound to God by covenant ties and obedient to the Lord's law (Num. 35:12, 24).

The other word *qahal* is closely linked with *edah*, with the overtone of "called by God" from a verb "to summon by voice" (*qol*). The best rendering is "mustering." It is interesting that the Greek OT renders *ekklesia* about one hundred times but never in translation of *edah* and only infrequently of *qahal*; instead the favorite Greek translation equivalent is *synagoge*, a gathering of the community in response to the divine summons and called to celebrate God's mercies both in the present and in the coming messianic age (Isa. 56:8; Ezek. 37:10). It is from the Greek OT term *synagoge* that the Jewish institution of the SYNAGOGUE took its name. And it may be that the first Christians sought a term to distinguish them from the Jews of their day (Jas. 2:2 is the one instance where their *synagoge* may mean a Christian assembly).

A third term was available for the NT writers to seize on; it is based on *kenishta*, "a gathering," in Aramaic paraphrases of the OT known as the Targums. The likelihood is that this word was a bridge from early Judaism to the NT use of *ekklesia* for the church as the gathered people of God under the terms of the new covenant in the eschatological era of messianic blessedness, which Jesus brought by his coming.

*New Testament Teaching.* The precise word *ekklesia* is found in the Gospels only at Matthew 16:18; 18:17, and both references have a specific allusion to the Jewish-Christian community, though it is possible that "I will build my church" is a promise of the new people of God, which Jesus' mission intended to create. So there are parallel terms such as "little flock" (Luke 12:32; see Matt. 26:31; Mark 14:27, 28), "my sheep" (John 10:26, 27), and "my brothers and sisters" (Mark 3:35) that may well support the idea of the church, at least in embryo. Certainly, at the Last Supper, there are covenant ideas linking Jesus and his disciples, especially in Luke's version (22:28-30) of the meal.

The record of Acts shows how the Christians who entered the realm of Messiah's salvation banded together as a body (Acts 5:11; 8:1, 3). These men and women had received the apostles' message as saving truth (Acts 2:36-37) and had acted upon it in professed repentance, faith, and (outwardly) in baptism (Acts 2:38-41). The result was that they remained in FELLOWSHIP (*koinónia*) and maintained a corporate life (Acts 2:42-47). This is what the author of Acts means by the church, namely, the eschatological community of Messiah's New Age that has received the OT promises and is living under Messiah's rule. Gradually Christians, under the impetus of Stephen and his followers (Acts 6:8–7:60; 11:19-21) came to see that the church had a wider meaning than a revamped Judaism or even a fulfilled Judaism, but that it took on a transnational, worldwide character. So while we find references to local churches at Jerusalem (Acts 5:11; 8:1), at Antioch (11:26; 13:1; 14:27; 15:3), Caesarea (18:22), and Ephesus (20:17), there are hints that a universal church is in view, especially at Acts 20:28. K. L. Schmidt is usually credited with the discovery that *ekklesia* means, in this extended context, the one people of God existing in several local communities which, in turn, form outcroppings of the great church.

Paul's contributions lay in his understanding of *the* church, of which his mission churches in Thessalonica (I Thess. 1:1), Asia (I Cor. 16:19; Philem. 2), and especially in Greece, both in Macedonia province (Phil. 4:15) and in southern Achaia (I Cor. 1:2; II Cor. 1:1), are local manifestations. So in his pastoral correspondence he can appeal to "all the churches" (I Cor. 7:17; 11:16; 14:33), and to the churches of his missionary work that have joined to send a collection for the Jerusalem church (II Cor. 8:18, 19, 23). But this is to speak the language of phenomena, that is, churches that were planted by his preaching and example. At a theological level Paul's teaching is more emphatic that there is only "one church," the church of God (Phil. 3:6), in which Christ or God has set offices and ministries (I Cor. 12:28) as gifts to the body of Christ (see too Eph. 4:7-11). The logical extension of this line of teaching comes in Colossians and Ephesians where "church" is indeed Christ's body because he is the sole head (Col. 1:18, 24); and the headship of Christ lends a transcendental flavor to the body (Eph. 1:22; 5:23). Other images of the church found in the Pauline literature are the building of God (I Cor. 3:10-17), and the bride of Christ (II Cor. 11:2; Eph. 5:23-32).

The remaining books of the NT add little to this appreciation of the church as God's chosen people, though other images fill out the picture. Hebrews is unusual in that it has one designation of the church "triumphant in heaven" (12:23) that is unique in the NT; otherwise Hebrews stays with the description of the church as a pilgrim people on the march to its eternal homeland (Heb. 4:1-10; 11:39, 40) a picture that runs through I Peter (2:4-11), which also stresses the church's social identity as a group of "exiles" and "strangers" (1:1) called to endure suffering (5:9-11). In the Pastoral Letters (I, II Timothy, Titus) we get a glimpse of the way the church is being organized with regular offices of ministry and formal structures.

*Later Developments.* The growth and broader understanding of what gives the Christian church its character was determined by several factors. We may single out the following as especially important. (a) The rise of the office of a single presiding minister (later called a BISHOP) led to a change in the church's nature. Coupled with the idea that one member of the clergy had supreme importance was an increased value given to the sacraments and to Christian worship in general. Hence, in Ignatius the bishop is the key figure, and this was developed at great length by Cyprian. (b) The onset of PERSECUTION in the second to the fourth centuries gradually gave way to the church's making peace with the empire under Constantine and his successors. It became fashionable and profitable to be a church member, and masses of people crowded into the visible church for social enhancement. (c) The rise of the PAPACY led also to a diminution of spiritual life among the laity, while conserving the infrastructure of the church and giving it cohesion and unity at a time when movements such as Islam tended to fragment the Christian cause. (d) At the REFORMATION a new lease on life made the appeal of the church to the proletarian elements of society, with emphasis on individual freedom and moral accountability, thus paving the way for democratic movements in the Western world. (e) In the nineteenth and twentieth centuries the image of the church has undergone some remaking with more flexibility and adaptation to modern ideas. In particular the boundaries of the church and the world are less rigidly drawn as the church has seen its mission as the permeation of all life with its saving mission.

R.M.

**CHURCH AND STATE.** *See* SEPARATION OF CHURCH AND STATE.

**CHURCHES OF CHRIST.** A Protestant denomination made up of autonomous local congregations that originated in the Restoration movement (the Christians, Disciples, or Campbellites) in the early nineteenth century. In 1974, the Churches of Christ had a membership of about 2,400,000 in the United States. The Churches of Christ are especially numerous in the South, particularly in Texas and Tennessee.

The early history of the Churches of Christ is the same as that of the CHRISTIAN CHURCHES or Disciples of Christ. A split between conservatives and liberals in the Disciples movement led to the founding of the (conservative) Churches of Christ. This body remained anti-creedal; congregational in polity; and kept the celebration of the Lord's Supper every Sunday, along with the baptism of adults by immersion.

The distinctive mark of the Churches of Christ is their prohibition of the use of instruments (organs, pianos, etc.) in worship. Later, some churches accepted musical instruments and styled themselves Churches of Christ (Instrumental).

The conservatives who founded the Churches of Christ objected to the Disciples' plan to establish a missionary society, the use of musical instruments in church, pastoral activities by some "preachers," and the practice of open communion. The conservatives said these activities had no basis in the NT, and accused the Disciples of innovations, whereas their churches remained true to the Restoration movement.

The Churches of Christ are fundamentalist in their approach to Christianity and orthodox in basic doctrines but opposed to any formal creed. The Bible alone is taken as the church's theological basis. Interestingly, the Churches of Christ stress the universality of sin but hold that it affects only those above the age of accountability.

The Churches of Christ do not belong to the National Council of Churches or the World Council of Churches, unlike the Disciples of Christ. They hold that ecumenicity is a departure from the principles of the Restoration movement, which stressed unity through return to the faith and practices of the NT Church. They refuse to be known as a denomination among other denominations, claiming this means the acceptance of post-NT ecclesiastical developments. The local congregations in the group maintain elementary and secondary schools, twenty-one colleges, and twenty homes for the elderly.     J.C.

CHURCHES OF GOD. A name taken from the NT by revivalists in America during the period 1823–1906 to designate their belief that the church is gathered and established by the direct work of God and to disclaim any continuity with the churches of the Protestant Reformation or the Roman Catholic Church. Essentially a sectarian label, the term has been used many times to cover splits within this tradition brought on by successive waves of revivalism, the influence of charismatic leaders, the holiness movement, adventist speculations about and announcements of the Second Coming of Christ, and even to claim that adherents were the true biblical Jews. The Church of God, with various qualifiers, including place names of sect headquarters, is now used to designate more than two hundred independent religious groups in America, most very small in numbers, as well as by other groups overseas.

Most Church of God groups stress that the church is an assembly of the regenerate, gathered from every nation by the Holy Spirit, including a gathering out of all other existing denominations. Members are added by revivalitic means, through the inducing of experiences of conversion, which leads to repentance, acceptance of Jesus Christ, and only then, to baptism by immersion. Interestingly, some of the original Church of God groups (the Winebrennerians) do not feel that baptism is necessary at all, laying all stress on conversion experiences.

Such views point up the basic importance of the revival service and the evangelist for the Church of God groups. These views also indicate why these groups are subject to disruption and splits by every wave of millennial speculation and conservative political reaction. A literal belief in the Bible as the only rule of faith is common to all the Churches of God groups, but each sect differs from the others in emphasizing particular biblical texts. Like the larger Restoration movement (the Campbellites), the Church of God groups stress that the NT contains all that is necessary to practice Christianity and reject supposed post-NT ecclesiastical developments. It is surprising, given this factor, to find various sects called the Church of God governed by bishops, others by Presbyterian-style polity, and others congregational, while most seem "connectional" in the Methodist sense.

Most, but not all, Churches of God practice the foot washing of the saints, especially in the Lenten season and in times of conferences or revival. Such foot washing is always connected to the observance of the Lord's Supper. The Eucharist is not considered a sacrament and is rarely observed otherwise. Baptism by immersion is generally, but not invariably, practiced at some time after a person is converted.

Some Churches of God stress several orders of ministers: apostles, bishops, deacons, evangelists, teachers, and exhorters. A large number of the groups emphasize glossolalia (speaking in tongues) that follows baptism by the Holy Spirit (as distinct from sacramental baptism). All these groups teach that salvation is freely given to those who accept it, and consequently they reject Calvinism and the Arminian strictures on double predestination. Most Church of God revivalistic rhetoric is synergistic, making people partners with God, who is indeed the deciding partner in salvation. In order for the saved person to join the church, signs of true conversion are required. These signs may be interpreted from group to group as speaking in tongues or as the claims to full holiness. This emphasis makes the entire movement generally legalistic, and, with a few exceptions, keeps these groups out of ecumenical cooperation with other churches. In all the sects, a converted ministry is valued above an educated one, so that majority of ministers are not well-educated despite the efforts of more progressive groups like the Church of God (Anderson, Indiana).

The Church of God bodies arose in three periods of time over more than eighty years. The first wave came in the Methodist revival among German-speaking Reformed Christians in Pennsylvania during the 1820s. While not the only leader, John Winebrenner, a German Reformed pastor at Harrisburg, Pennsylvania, became a figurehead in the separatistic struggles of 1823–25. Locked out of his church by the consistory, Winebrenner founded what he called the Churches of God (General Eldership). By 1830, Winebrenner's movement was organized as the

Churches of God in North America. This group, now the smallest of the Church of God sects, still exists under the name Churches of God (General Conference).

The second wave arose among German Brethren in Pennsylvania, led by P. J. Kaufman in 1886. This revival resulted in the Church of God as organized by Christ. The third wave of influence was the HOLINESS MOVEMENT, or the emphasis on the "second blessing," which was supposed to be a needed second work of grace by which the Holy Spirit cleansed the believer of sin. The Holiness movement largely took over the Winebrennerian group, when Daniel S. Warner caused the majority of congregations and ministers to separate from the General Eldership in 1881. This group became the Church of God (Anderson, Indiana). Richard J. Spurling, Sr. formed the Church of God, Cleveland, Tennessee, a holiness group, in 1906. This sect split into the Church of God of Prophecy, the Church of God (Queens Village, New York), and the original (Cleveland, Tennessee) Church of God. All these groups and most others called Church of God are part of the PENTECOSTAL movement.

Other bodies of this name include the Church of God and Saints in Christ, also called the black Jews, who claim to be the true Jews, whom, they claim, were originally black. The Adventist Church of God is a split, in 1866, from the Seventh-Day Adventist movement. There is also an Adventist Church of God in Christ (1851), and the Church of God in Christ (Mennonite), begun in 1859 by the revivalism of Elder John Holdeman.

All Churches of God share common characteristics, although all are not pentecostal. They are separatistic, Wesleyan in the revivalist and personal holiness sense, fundamentalist, legalistic in their stress on external conformity, and tend toward millenarian upheavals that lead to the creation of ever new small sects.                                                              J.C.

## CHURCH EXPECTANT/MILITANT/TRIUMPHANT.
Three terms used to refer to the body of Christians in different classes. Although not always used in the same sense, usually the term "church expectant" refers to those who are to believe, but have not yet believed. The "church militant" includes those who are currently living as Christians in this life. The "church triumphant" refers to those who have already completed their earthly course.
                                                              J.G.

## CHURCH FATHERS.
The collective name for all early Christian writers, both male and female—excluding those who were clearly heterodox, such as the Gnostics. The discipline that studies their lives, works, and theology is PATRISTICS—which however also includes the study of early heresies, without which the teachings of the "fathers" would often be incomprehensible. Although not all scholars agree as

to the limits of the patristic period, the general consensus is that the last of the Latin fathers was ISIDORE OF SEVILLE, who died in 636, and that the last Greek father was JOHN OF DAMASCUS, who died in 749.

The writings included under this category are extensive, amounting to hundreds of volumes. The earliest were all originally written in Greek. But Latin Christian literature began by A.D. 180, and soon rivaled its Greek counterpart. There are also a number of the fathers who wrote in other languages, particularly Syriac.
                                                              J.G.

## CHURCH GROWTH.
The question of how and why churches grow and flourish in varying numbers has always been of interest to Christians, especially those concerned with the planting of new chuches and mission. The subject has been treated in books; in the early years of the twentieth century by ROLAND ALLEN and in recent times by D. A. McGavran in his two books, *Bridges of God* and *How Churches Grow*. An institute for the study of church growth exists in Pasadena, California, in association with Fuller Theological Seminary.

Some of the principles accepted by most experts on the subject of church growth and mission developers have been listed as follows: (1) converts should live among their own people; (2) from the moment of baptism every convert should be a witness for Christ; (3) instruction should continue for a long period after baptism; (4) witness should follow the lines of kinship—tribe, family, clan, community; (5) ordinary people can be eloquent witnesses; (6) isolated converts should be regularly visited; (7) evangelism is the responsibility of every Christian but experts may be needed for some special purposes; (8) the habit of intercession for non-Christian friends and family should be encouraged; and (9) the most important witness is the life of the redeemed community.
                                                              W.G.

## CHURCH HISTORY.
*See* HISTORY OF CHRISTIAN DOCTRINE.

## CHURCH MISSIONARY SOCIETY.
The principal overseas missionary agency of the Church of England. Founded in 1799, the society initiated Christian witness in Africa, Iran, and other countries of the Middle East, India, Pakistan, Sri Lanka, China, Japan, and also to the Indians of Canada's northwest territories and the Maoris of New Zealand. At the peak of its operations, C.M.S. sponsored more than nine hundred missionaries. There are affiliated, but autonomous, societies operating from Australia, New Zealand, and South Africa.                          R.H.

## CHURCH OF CHRIST, SCIENTIST.
A religious organization or church, founded in the late nineteenth century, in Boston, based on the philosophy of

Mary Baker Eddy. Mrs. Eddy said she discovered "Christ Science" in 1866, and called it Christian Science in her book, *Science and Health, with Key to the Scriptures* (1875). The intellectual background of the movement includes New England TRANSCENDENTALISM, the works of EMANUEL SWENDENBORG, spiritualism, and mesmerism, as well as the faith healing and new thought of Phineas Quimby. Mrs. Eddy said Quimby healed her in 1862. She also believed she had rediscovered some lost emphases of early Christianity, especially Jesus' healing method. Healing through correct thinking or faith remains central to the Christian Science movement. Many people who receive such healing become church members.

Courtesy of Religious News Service

*Mary Baker Eddy*

In 1882, Mrs. Eddy institutionalized her teachings by founding the First Church of Christ, Scientist, of Boston. This is known as the Mother Church, and all other Christian Science churches and reading rooms throughout the world are regarded as branches. Mrs. Eddy wrote the constitution and bylaws of the First Church herself. At first opposed, Christian Science spread all over the world. The movement is centralized, directed by a self-perpetuating board of five directors, originally named by Mrs. Eddy. This board oversees the publication and distribution of literature, from Mrs. Eddy's writings to the *Christian Science Monitor;* healing through Christian Science practitioners; lectures; religious education; and the

orthodoxy of teaching throughout the movement.

Philosophically, Christian Science is a form of pure IDEALISM and is monistic in its denial of the reality of the material world. Their "all is mind" approach also denies the reality of evil and of sickness. Christian Science has won a great deal of respect in the twentieth century because of the purity of its members' life-styles, the serenity its disciplines encourage, and the objectivity of the *Christian Science Monitor.* The Bible, interpreted through Mrs. Eddy's teachings, plays a large role in Christian Science.

J.C.

**CHURCH OF ENGLAND.** *See* ANGLICAN CHURCHES.

**CHURCH OF JESUS CHRIST OF LATTER-DAY SAINTS (MORMONS).** A new religion, founded in the United States on April 6, 1830, by JOSEPH SMITH, a farmer in upstate New York, who reported receiving divine revelations through the angel Moroni. The popular and derogatory term "Mormons" was derived from Smith's published account of his claimed revelations.

Smith published the *Book of Mormon* in 1830. He claimed to have translated it from golden plates hidden in the area that were delivered to him by Moroni. This book alleges to be a record of God's activities among the ancestors of the native Americans, the Indians. The book declares that the ancestors of the Indians were actually the ten lost tribes of the Hebrews, who migrated to America in three waves.

From the beginning the Latter-day Saints had a stormy history, not unlike the experiences of the new religions in the 1970s and 1980s. A Mormon community was gathered and moved to Kirtland, Ohio, in 1831. Smith's area in New York state was one where considerable revivalistic religious frenzy had stirred up the population. In fact, it became known as "the burnt over district." In Kirtland, a community embodying Mormon ideals was begun, but it suffered a financial crisis. Smith moved on to Independence, Missouri, and later to Nauvoo, Illinois. Relative success there brought strong opposition, resulting in violence. The Mormons were driven away in the "Mormon War," which cost the church forty lives and $2 million. During the same period, Smith was killed and BRIGHAM YOUNG assumed leadership. Young organized the remnants of the community and led them on an amazing march to the far west on April 7, 1847. A group of 147 Mormons set out for Utah, settling finally by the Great Salt Lake. Thirty years later, at Young's death, there were 357 Mormon communities in Utah and the West.

The Mormon settlement of Utah made it a prime candidate for statehood, but the Latter-day Saint practice of plural marriage, polygamy, kept it out of the Union. In 1890, then church president Wilford

Woodruff declared polygamy no longer a church teaching. In 1896 Utah became a state. In the 1970s, popular resentment of Mormon teachings about the lower spiritual level of blacks also resulted in a pronouncement by the church president that black men could be admitted to the full order of Mormon priesthood. The strand of gradual accommodation to popular and political pressures toward social respectability seems characteristic of the Mormon movement.

There is a very simple but strong organization in the church, from the local ward, to the stake, up to the council of the seventy, to the twelve apostles, to the president of the church and his two counselors. The president is the supreme authority in the church. There are also patriarchs, high priests, elders, bishops, priests, teachers, and deacons.

Mormon theology is quite complex and eclectic. Formerly, they taught that polygamy was biblical, but do so no longer. They believe the Trinity is made up of three separate gods, that people do not inherit Adam's sin but earn their own punishments or rewards, that Christ atoned for original sin, that people are saved by faith, repentance, baptism by immersion, which gives remission of sins, and by the laying on of hands to receive the Holy Spirit. They believe in speaking in tongues, prophecy, revelations and visions, and divine healing. They also believe in continuing revelation; that God continues to reveal new truths and so believe the *Book of Mormon* is the Word of God as well as is the Bible.

The Mormons are very evangelistic and are presently one of the fastest growing religious groups in the United States. A new Mormon temple was opened in Washington, D.C. in the 1970s.

J.C.

**CHURCH OF SCOTLAND.** *See* PRESBYTERIAN CHURCHES.

**CHURCH OF THE BRETHREN.** The German Baptists, originating in 1708 at Schwarzenau, Germany, as a pietistic, ANABAPTIST protest against the Lutheran and Reformed established churches. The Brethren are also known as *Taufer, Tunkels, Dompelaars*, and *Dunkards*—all German terms referring to baptism. They were most popularly known historically as Tunkels (Baptists); the term derives from the German *tunken*, meaning "to dip or immerse." The Brethren's mode of baptism is unique. The candidate for baptism kneels and is pushed forward into the water three times.

As pietists, the Brethren seek less formal worship, less emphasis upon dogma, and more warmth in daily religious living. Historically, the Brethren are a "peace church," opposing participation in war, as well as the taking of oaths and membership in secret societies.

Doctrinally, the Brethren follow a common free church theology but officially reject all creeds and follow only the NT. Some portions of the OT are rejected because they are believed to uphold slavery, divorce, war, and revenge. The Brethren recognize four ordinances: baptism, the Lord's Supper, the anointing of the sick, and the laying on of hands.

In polity, voting delegates from each congregation meet for the annual conference. This conference elects twenty-five members to the General Brotherhood Board, which manages the daily life of the church. The Church of the Brethren belongs to both the National Council of Churches and the World Council of Churches.

J.C.

**CHURCH OF THE NAZARENE.** A denomination that arose from the "second work of grace" or complete SANCTIFICATION movement; a development of the HOLINESS and PENTECOSTAL movements in American FUNDAMENTALISM around the end of the nineteenth century.

The Church of the Nazarene was formed from a union of several associations of congregations that held strong beliefs about the doctrine of entire sanctification as a work of the Holy Spirit distinct from and following after justification. The Nazarene movement began on both coasts of the United States. In Los Angeles, an organization calling itself the Church of the Nazarene began in 1895. Meanwhile, a number of independent Holiness churches in New England formed the Association of Pentecostal Churches of America in 1897. Delegates from the eastern group attended the meetings of the California group in 1906 and proposed a union. This proposal was accepted and the union effected in Chicago in October 1907. In 1908, another union, with the Holiness Church of Christ, centered in the South and Southwest, took place. A manual of discipline was adopted by the church.

The manual details nine fundamental doctrines; belief in these is a basic requirement for church membership. They are: the Holy Trinity; the divine inspiration of the Bible; the fall of humanity; the eternal damnation of the ultimately impenitent; the atonement of Christ; the entire sanctification of believers by faith, subsequent to justification; the witness of the Holy Spirit to justification and sanctification; the return of Christ (Second Coming); and the resurrection of the dead and final judgment. Additionally, rules of conduct for members, like those in the early Wesleyan tradition, are set down in the manual. The use of alcohol and tobacco, and membership in secret societies are totally banned for members.

In polity, the Church of the Nazarene has district assemblies and a general assembly. The General Assembly elects general superintendents who hold executive authority between sessions of the assembly. These general superintendents preside at the general assembly and the district assemblies, ordain elders, appoint evangelists, and generally direct the work of the church. Licensed preachers can be elevated to elders (full ministerial) orders by the various district assemblies. The local church boards contact pastors directly to fill vacant pulpits.

J.C.

## CHURCH: VISIBLE AND INVISIBLE.

The church is the Lord's body; the term derived from the Greek *Kuriakou*. In the NT, the term *ekklesia* is used to mean the assembly of those called by God.

The distinction between the church visible and the church invisible goes back to Augustine. Luther used the distinction, and the concept plays a role in much Lutheran and other Protestant theology. There is only one church—the one, holy, Catholic, and Apostolic church, which is visible in the world wherever the word is rightly preached and the sacraments rightly administered. The invisible church is made up of those truly "saved."

J.C.

## CHURCH WORLD SERVICE.

The relief, rehabilitation, and resettlement agency of American Protestant and Orthodox churches, founded in 1946 by several national and international church groups. CWS became a department of the National Council of Churches when it was formed in 1950, and in 1965 was joined with the council's Division of Foreign Missions to form the Division of Overseas Ministries. Since its founding, CWS has shipped billions of pounds of clothing, food, medicines, and resettled more than 200,000 refugees in the U.S.A. CWS also helped to organize the Christian Rural Overseas Program (CROP) as a food collection agency of American farmers and maintains clothing centers in various parts of the country for the gathering and processing of clothing.

W.G.

## CILICIA.

A Roman province in Southeast Asia Minor. The name comes from *hilakku,* an Assyrian name for its population. The western part, Cilicia Trachea, is made up of the Taurus Mountains, along with the Cilician Gates and TARSUS. The eastern part, Cilicia Pedias, is a fertile, well-watered, subtropical, coastal plain.

The only OT references to Cilicia are I Kings 10:28 and II Chronicles 1:16, where Kue, from which Solomon's traders bought horses, is known to be east Cilicia. Cilician Jews shared the Synagogue of the Freedmen in Jerusalem (Acts 6:9). References to Cilicia in Acts and Galatians 1:21 relate to Paul's connections with Tarsus and his travels through the province.

P.L.G.

## CIRCUMCISION.

Requiring the removal of the foreskin, a ceremony performed on eight-day-old males symbolizing their participation as sons of the COVENANT binding Yahweh and Israel (Gen. 17:9-14). Circumcision was ordinarily implemented by fathers (21:4) who initially used flint knives (Josh. 5:2-3).

*Near Eastern Context.* The extent to which circumcision was practiced by Israel's neighbors is debated. Although the practice was attested in third-millennium B.C. Egyptian bas-reliefs, uncircumcised mummies are known. If Jeremiah 9:25-26 mentions circumcised Egyptians, Edomites, Ammonites, Moabites, and Arabians, Ezekiel 32:21-30 anticipates that the Egyptians will join the Assyrians, Elamites, Edomites, Phoenicians, and Syrians in an underworld region reserved for the uncircumcised. Circumcision was presumably widespread among Canaanite inhabitants, but a non-Semitic enclave at Shechem had to be circumcised before marrying eligible Israelite maidens (Gen. 34:13-24). For not embracing this practice, the Philistines were contemptuously called "the uncircumcised" (I Sam. 14:6; 31:4).

Generally circumcision was performed before marriage to facilitate sexual readiness. Narratives about the circumcision of the Shechemites (Gen. 34:13-24) and Moses ("a bridegroom of blood," Exod. 4:24-26) suggest that the Israelites behaved similarly. Indeed, the Arabic verb *hatan* ("to circumcise") spawned three Hebrew nouns—"bridegroom," "son-in-law," "father-in-law." Figurative uses, including uncircumcised hearts and lips to symbolize failure in perception and speaking (Jer. 9:26; Exod. 6:12), also hint that circumcision denoted readiness for adulthood.

*Israelite Significance.* The Bible reports that circumcision was first observed by the patriarchs, maintained during Egyptian captivity, ignored in the wilderness, and resumed after entry into Canaan (Gen. 34:13-24; Josh. 5:4-9). Circumcision was mandated of Israelite slaves and any resident aliens observing the Passover (Exod. 12:43-49). Prior to the early fifth century B.C., circumcision was made an infancy rite (Gen. 17;12; Lev. 12:3). With circumcision declining among Israel's neighbors, it superbly served as a distinguishing mark of covenantal communion with Yahweh. Israelite males joined Abraham's son, Isaac, in being circumcised on the eighth day (Gen. 21:4). Many Jews resisted Antiochus Epiphanes' second-century B.C. campaign to prohibit this Greek-scorned practice (I Macc. 1:60-61).

Jesus and Paul were circumcised (Luke 2:21; Phil. 3:5). Though some Jewish Christians demanded circumcision of Gentile converts, the Jerusalem Council (Acts 15) upheld the Gentile view that it was not binding on Christians. Here Paul was influential. He believed that "real circumcision is a matter of the heart"(Rom. 2:29).

J.K.K.

## CISTERCIANS.

One of the many orders resulting from movements of reformation within Benedictine MONASTICISM. The Cistercians, also known as "white monks," take this name from their mother house at

Citeaux, founded in 1098 by Robert of Molesme. But what gave the order its great impetus was the fame and influence of BERNARD OF CLAIRVAUX, who joined it in 1112 and is called its second founder. Since Bernard was one of the most famous preachers of the twelfth century, as well as one of the most influential leaders of the church, many followed his example. A hundred years after the founding of the first Cistercian house, there were more than five hundred Cistercian abbeys scattered throughout western Europe.

The Cistercians deplored the manner in which the rule of St. BENEDICT had been relaxed, particularly in that which had to do with manual labor and simplicity of life. For that reason they usually settled in barren lands, which they made fruitful through their efforts, and they thus contributed to the economic development of Europe. Eventually, however, the tilling of the land was left in the hands of lay brothers, and many felt the need for a new reformation of the order. The most notable outcome of these movements of reform among the Cistercians produced the TRAPPISTS, founded in the seventeenth century.

J.G.

**CITY OF REFUGE.** Six Levitical centers designed as asylum-towns to shelter those accidentally committing homicide (Num. 35:9-15).

Replacing the earlier custom of seeking refuge at the local sanctuary with its inviolable altar (Exod. 21:13-14), this procedure was probably established during the tenth century B.C. as a way of normalizing judicial practices within the burgeoning united monarchy. Thus personal vengeance was appreciably restrained and the land in which Yahweh "dwelt" was less often polluted by wanton bloodshed (Num. 35:34).

According to Numbers 35:13-14, three Levitical cities on each side of the Jordan were to be designated as asylums. Deuteronomy 4:41-43 discloses that Moses set apart Bezer in Reuben, Ramoth-gilead in Gad, and Golan in Bashan in the half-tribe of Manasseh as suitable Transjordanian locations. Joshua 20:7 reports that after the takeover of Canaan, Joshua and the tribal chiefs appointed Kadesh in Naphtali, Shechem in Ephraim, and Hebron in Judah to serve as asylum-towns to the west of the Jordan. Since all six are mentioned anew as Levitical cities in Joshua 21 (vv. 13, 21, 27, 32, 36, 38), each may have hosted an important sanctuary (Shechem and Hebron were known for such).

Although Deuteronomy 19:5 offers a legislative illustration involving an accidentally flung ax head, no biblical text poses as a historical illustration of how this institution actually functioned. The person guilty of accidental homicide presumably hastened to the nearest asylum-town. If not slain en route by the deceased's next-of-kin avenger, the guilty one was tried there by its elders (Josh. 20:4; surely an entire "congregation" was not involved as Num. 35:12 reports). The slayer was delivered to death if judged guilty of deliberate murder, or granted asylum if declared innocent. Such asylum necessitated residence in that city until the death of its high priest. Premature departure was risky because the roving avenger could kill the slayer with impunity. If the slayer accepted enforced detention until the high priest's death, the slayer was then permitted safe journey homeward (Josh. 20:6). Though murderers were expected to expiate the deed by their own deaths at the hands of the next of kin, in instances of unpremeditated homicide the high priest's death was deemed a worthy substitute.

J.K.K.

**CIVIL RELIGION.** A term denoting the melding of national and religious goals. Civil religion emerged in America with the Puritans, who thought of themselves as chosen by God to establish a New Israel where magistrate and minister would work hand in hand. William Bradford's *History of Plymouth Plantation* portrayed the Pilgrims as saints commissioned by God. Edward Johnson's *Wonder-Working Providence of Sions Saviour in New England* (1654) told of God's active assistance in colonial America.

Robert Bellah in "Civil Religion in America" (*Daedalus*, 1967) found strong civil religion in the inaugural speeches of United States presidents. As the nation expanded, chosenness developed into a national myth. American success represented God's blessings (Deut. 28). Liberal Christianity spoke of a kingdom of God being realized through social progress, and Fundamentalist Christianity stressed chosenness, individual piety, and a national mission to export Christian democracy. Sidney E. Mead in *The Lively Experiment* (1963) said the identification of American churches with nationalism was as complete as had ever been known in Christendom. However, the comfortable church-state consensus of religiosity and patriotism was denounced theologically in the Neo-orthodoxy of Karl Barth and Reinhold Niebuhr and was shaken by the defeat of the United States in Vietnam. Peter Berger's *Noise of Solemn Assemblies* (1961) called for the rejection of civil religion's reduction of religion to a corollary of national success.

Civil religion reaches back to ancient times when countries and even cities often had their own gods. Israel regarded itself as covenantally bound to God. Christian civil religion emerged when Constantine's Edict of Milan (313) established a partnership between church and state. Throughout the Middle Ages heresy and treason were virtually interchangeable capital crimes. Under Hitler the church in Germany became a govenmental bureau to justify Nazism, and in the U.S.S.R. the Russian Orthodox Church is directed by the state. Degrees of acculturation vary greatly, but if religion is confined to other worldly matters, religion is doomed to irrelevance. If religion is immersed in worldly affairs, compromise of religion looms. On the one hand, relevant Christian activity in the world is at stake, and, on the other, a compromising of divine sovereignty.

One of the first Christian writers to oppose civil religion was Tertullian (about 145–220). In *On Idolatry,* he called for Christians to break with the world, saying even ordinary activities of merchants compromise loyalty to God by contributing to idolatrous emperor worship. Augustine's *City of God* posited an earthly city based on love of self in its many forms and a heavenly city based on love of God to the relative exclusion of self-love. Only love of God can bring fulfillment, but in this world the two cities are commingled, human beings participate in both, and relative goods are to be found in both. Augustine knew that creation and the Incarnation bolster worldly involvement and that divine sovereignty and the cross negate human arrangements. Christians see the need to participate in politics; they also see the need to maintain divine sovereignty. Civil religion stands as a compromise of both.

C.M.

**CLASSIS.** A geographical ecclesiastical governing body in the REFORMED tradition; the same as a presbytery in the Prebyterian churches. The classis is made up of all the clergy and elected representative lay elders in the territory. It oversees congregations and the work of the clergy, and ordains and disciplines pastors.

J.C.

**CLAUDIUS** (10 B.C.–A.D. 54). Roman Emperor from A.D. 41 to 54, successor to his nephew Gaius (CALIGULA). According to Acts 18:2, Claudius "commanded all the Jews to leave Rome." Just as Paul came to Corinth (about A.D. 50), he met Aquila and Priscilla, who "lately" had come from Italy. Since neither Paul (Rom. 16:3) nor the author of Acts report that this couple were converts of the apostle, it is probable that they were already Christians when he met them. It is also probable that Christians in Rome were partly responsible for the action of Claudius.

Courtesy of the American Numismatic Society

*Claudius*

According to the Roman historian Suetonius, the emperor's edict was caused by Jews who were constantly rioting "at the instigation of a certain Chrestus" *(impulsore Chresto quodam).* Of course Christ *(Christus/ Chrestus)* was not in Rome in the time of Claudius, but Suetonius may have thought so. It is an almost certain inference that the rioting in Rome twenty years earlier was due to the introduction of Christianity into Rome's Jewish colony, and because of disputations among Christian and non-Christian Jews both were expelled. There is no evidence that the Edict of Claudius was formally rescinded to permit the return of Jews and Jewish-Christians to Rome. Just as a similar edict of Tiberias was nullified by this emperor's demise, so with Claudius' death the ban lapsed. With NERO's persecution a new chapter opened in the relations of church and empire.

J.L.P.

**CLEAN AND UNCLEAN.** Cleanness is the absence of physical, ceremonial, and ethical impurities that produce uncleanness.

*Introduction.* As a nation that took seriously the divine imperative, "You shall be holy; for I the Lord your God am holy" (Lev. 19:2), Israel developed elaborate legislation that addressed diverse situations marred by uncleanness. Detailed laws were mainly codified by priests active during the monarchy and early postexilic era. Theirs was the task "to distinguish between the holy and the common, and between the unclean and the clean" (Lev. 10:10; Ezek. 22:26). Issues involving ethical cleanness are often reflected in prophetic, wisdom, and psalm texts, but not at the expense of treating ceremonial cleanness with indifference. Above all, cleanness is perceived in the NT as an inner disposition. It receives apt expression in Jesus' teaching that "the things which come out of a man are what defile him" (Mark 7:15).

*Varieties of Uncleanness.* Because the spirits of the deceased might lurk nearby, human corpses defiled those touching them (Num. 19:11). With their disfigured skin, lepers were diagnosed as unclean (Lev. 13); once healed, they submitted to elaborate purifications (Lev. 14). Such bodily discharges as the menstrual flow (Lev. 15:19-24), semen (Lev. 15:18), and excretions accompanying childbirth (Lev. 12:2-5) induced uncleanness. Food could not be eaten from such unclean animals as those dying of natural causes (Deut. 14:21), those that failed both to divide the hoof and chew the cud (Lev. 11:3-7; Deut. 14:7-8), and flesh-eating birds (Lev. 11:13-19). Sometimes places sanctified by God's presence were declared unclean due to intrusive human pollution. Thus violence, sin, and idolatry respectively defiled the Israelite soil (Ezek. 22:24-29), Jerusalem (Lam. 1:8), and its Temple (II Chr. 29:12-19). Uncleanness was typically overcome by purification rituals involving a waiting period (Lev. 15:28), a cleansing element such as fire (Num. 31:23) or water (Ezek. 36:25), and sacrificial offering (Lev. 12:6).

*Moral Cleanness.* That concern for ethical purity resident in the prophetic admonition to be clean by ceasing to do evil (Isa. 1:16), and in the Psalms' references to clean hands (Ps. 18:20) and heart (Ps. 51:10), intensifies in the NT, where cleanness entails an affirmation of spiritual holiness (I Thess. 4:7). Paul and other Gentiles claiming that "nothing is unclean in itself" (Rom. 14:14) could ignore Jewish dietary regulations in the spirit of Jesus (Mark 7:15) without jeopardizing their quest for moral cleanness.

J.K.K.

**CLEMENT XI, POPE.** Giovanni Francesco Albani was made a cardinal in 1690 and was pope from 1700 to 1721. A scholar and a lover of the arts, when elected pope he was thrust in the midst of difficult political circumstances. The dominant event of his reign was the War of Spanish Succession, in which Clement at first supported the French. But when Austrian troops invaded Italy, the pope was forced to abandon his French ally. The result was that when the treaties of Utrecht and Rastatt put an end to the conflict the Papacy lost many of its territories.

Clement also had to deal with the continued controversy over JANSENISM, which he condemned in the bull "Vineam Domine Sabaoth." In China, and to a lesser degree in India, he intervened in the dispute between Jesuits and Dominicans over the question of accommodation. His decision against the Jesuits, who had gained great favor in China, dealt a severe blow to the church in that country.

J.G.

**CLEMENT XIV, POPE.** Pope from 1769 to 1774. The most notable event of his reign, which overshadowed his many accomplishments, was the suppression of the JESUITS. For several reasons, that order had won the enmity of the House of Bourbon, and in 1769 the courts of Spain, France, and Naples requested that they be suppressed. The pope's initial resistance was overcome, and the bull "Dominus ac Redemptor," of August 16, 1773, formally dissolved the order. The rulers of Russia and Prussia, who had reason to fear Bourbon power, refused to obey, and thus the Jesuits continued existing as a legal order in portions of Germany and Russia. Jesuit historians have depicted Clement as a weak pope who buckled under political pressure, while others have praised his courage in suppressing an order that was becoming too powerful. The truth probably lies between these extreme judgments.

J.G.

**CLEMENT OF ALEXANDRIA.** One of the greatest theologians of the second centry. A native of Athens, after his conversion to Christianity he traveled in search of "true wisdom," which he found in the Alexandrian teacher Pantaenus. He then settled in ALEXANDRIA, where he eventually succeeded Pantaenus as head of the catechetical school. In A.D. 202, the persecution of Septimius Severus forced him to leave Alexandria, and after that time little is known of his life. He probably died about A.D. 215. In Alexandria, he was succeeded by his disciple ORIGEN, who developed his theology along the lines set by Clement.

Five works of Clement are extant: *Exhortation to the Greeks, The Instructor, The Stromata, Who Is the Rich to Be Saved?* and *Excerpts from Theodotus.* The first three are the most important and form a trilogy: the first is an apologetic work, addressed to the pagans; the second seeks to instruct the believer in matters of the faith; and the third appears to be a series of notes for a more systematic work.

Clement was convinced that philosophy had been given to the Gentiles to lead them to Christ, just as the Law had been given to the Jews for the same purpose. Therefore, a great deal of his theology is in truth an interpretation of Christianity from the perspective of middle PLATONISM. This he did by means of allegorical interpretations of Scripture and on the basis of the doctrine of the LOGOS, which inspired both Scripture and philosophy, and which was incarnate in Jesus. Although his works were not widely read after his death, he was influential in the later course of theology through his disciple Origen and may be said to be the first great teacher of the Alexandrian school.

J.G.

**CLEMENT OF ROME.** Bishop of Rome toward the end of the first century, and author of an "Epistle to the Corinthians." His main concern there is the unity of Christians and the need for harmony. Most other information about him is of doubtful authority. Among other things, his place in the list of the early bishops of ROME varies, and for that reason some have suggested that in early times there was a "collegiate" episcopacy in that city. There is also a possibility that he may be the same as "Flavius Clemens," martyred in Rome during the reign of DOMITIAN. The "Second Epistle of Clement to the Corinthians" is not his, but is rather a second-century homily calling believers to repentance. Later, a number of adventures were ascribed to Clement in the Pseudo-Clementine literature, some of which seems to have originated in Gnostic circles.

J.G.

**CLEOPAS.** One of two disciples going to Emmaus on the first Easter when Jesus appeared to them (Luke 24:18). The name is Greek and is not to be confused with Clopas (John 19:25), a Semitic name.

P.L.G.

**CLEPHANE, ELIZABETH CECILIA DOUGLAS** (1830–69). Born June 18 in Edinburgh, Scotland, Elizabeth Clephane first published "The Ninety and

Nine" as a poem in *The Children's Hour* in 1868. Also well known is her hymn "Beneath the Cross of Jesus." She also wrote "Dim Eyes Forever Closed," "Into His Summer Garden," "The Day Is Drawing Nearly Done," and "Who Climbeth Up Too High." Her charitable work earned her the nickname Sunbeam among the poor and suffering of Melrose, where she lived.

In 1874, during D. L. MOODY's revivals in the British Isles, his music director IRA D. SANKEY picked up a paper to read on the train, noticed the above-mentioned poem, and clipped it. The next night in Edinburgh, Moody preached a sermon on "The Good Shepherd," and asked Sankey for a closing hymn. Suddenly Sankey remembered the poem and felt compelled by the Spirit to use it even though he had given no previous thought to music for it. He simply struck a chord in A flat and began. The music, which came note by note, remained unchanged from its now familiar tune. She died on February 19.

N.H.

**CLINICAL PASTORAL EDUCATION.** The system of education that began with the goal of bringing a professional dimension to pastoral ministry by placing theological students in supervised fieldwork settings. The need was early observed by Richard C. Cabot, M.D., of Harvard, who worked with a group of newly developing pastoral counselors to incorporate the Council for the Clinical Training of Theological Students in 1930. ANTON T. BOISEN, one of the founding group, disagreed with the insistence of some that general hospital settings were the most acceptable. He established programs in mental hospitals, first at Worcester, Massachusetts, and later at Elgin, Illinois. Eventually there were two organizations: the Institute of Pastoral Care and the Council for Clinical Training. A merger occurred in 1967 with the establishment of the Association for Clinical Pastoral Education.

The association is characterized by careful attention to the accreditation of hospital programs and of chaplain supervisors. The professionalism of the institutional setting encourages theological students to see their work professionally. Working with people in crisis situations challenges them to bring the resources of faith to meet such needs.

The term "education" rather than "training" suggests the added dimension of reflection on the experience. Students are required to become engaged in self-understanding. Working in small supervised groups enables students to have responses to and from patients, hospital personnel, and other students. A typical clinical pastoral education program requires a concentrated period of work/study—up to forty hours a week for several months. Seminaries look upon CPE as a valuable tool for professional ministerial preparation. They help develop programs, encourage use, and give academic credit for completion.

I.C.

**CLOUD OF UNKNOWING, THE.** An anonymous English mystical treatise, probably dating from the fourteenth century. It has been attributed to several English mystics, Richard Rolle among them. But the nature of its MYSTICISM is such that it probably should not be ascribed to any of the known English mystics. It is deeply influenced by the Platonism of DIONYSIUS the Areopagite, and its author was probably the equally anonymous translator of Dionysius' *Mystical Theology,* published under the English title of *Hid Divinite.* Its mysticism follows the "negative" way of the false Dionysius, based on the assumption that the intellect is incapable of knowing God. Contemplation is therefore an act not of the intellect, but rather of the affective faculty of the mind (*see* CONTEMPLATIVE LIFE). The ultimate is always hidden, even from the highest form of contemplative prayer, by a "cloud of unknowing"—hence the title of the work.

J.G.

**CLUNY.** A monastic house founded in 909 under the direction of Berno, which became the source for a vast reformation of MONASTICISM. Berno ruled at Cluny until 926, and then a series of able and long-lived abbots continued his work: Odo (926–44), Aymard (944–65), Mayeul (965–94), Odilo (994–1049), and Hugh (1049–1109). Thus, over a period of two centuries Cluny was ruled by six abbots. Although the seventh abbot was not of the caliber of his predecessors, the eighth, Peter the Venerable, regained much of what had been lost.

The influence of Cluny was far-reaching. Soon hundreds of "second Clunys" were founded and placed under the direction of the mother house. Although they did not form an order in the strict sense, their connection through their common abbot was such that it is customary to speak of the "order of Cluny." There were also Cluniac houses for women, of which the first was Marcigny.

The main occupation of the Cluniacs was the DIVINE OFFICE, to which they devoted so much time that at the apex of the movement 138 psalms were said every day. This led to the abandonment of manual labor, which was one of the pillars of Benedictine monasticism, and therefore other movements of monastic reformation arose. The ideals of Cluny made such an impact on the church at large that the reformation of GREGORY VII was largely patterned after them.

J.G.

**COCCEIUS, JOHANNES** (1603–69). The greatest representative of covenant or FEDERAL THEOLOGY was born in Bremen, Germany, and taught in Franeker and Leyden, where he died. As a biblical theologian and interpreter, Cocceius, through his hermeneutics, influenced the rise of the critical study of Scripture. His view of humanity as created in process toward consummation in God offers an alternative to

Augustinian views of creation, history, and Jesus Christ. This view has been important in modern theology and social thought.

C.M.

**CODEX.** There were two principal types of books in ancient times, the roll (or scroll) and the codex. The term codex means "leaf-book" and refers to books made from either parchment or papyrus leaves sewn together in the center, making the type of book with which we are familiar today. The roll, which was the older form, was made by simply sewing sheets together end to end up to a maximum average length of about thirty-five feet and then winding each end of the long sheet around a stick. It appears that the church adopted the more economical and convenient format of the codex for the production of its biblical books around the second century, while the Jewish synagogue continued to use the roll form as it does today for its most valuable copies of the Torah. As of 1976 the total number of NT manuscripts catalogued was 5,366, with 88 of these being papyri and 274 being uncial parchment.

The following are a few of the more important codices of the Bible. (1) Codex Alexandrinus—a fifth-century manuscript containing the OT, which is partly mutilated, and most of the NT. All of Matthew up to chapter 25 is lost, as well as the leaves that contained John 6:50–8:52 and II Corinthians 4:13–12:6. It was given to King Charles of England in 1627 by the Patriarch of Constantinople and now resides in the British Museum. (2) Codex Bezae—a fifth- or sixth-century manuscript written in Greek and Latin and containing most of the text of the four Gospels and Acts with a small fragment of III John. It was given to the library at Cambridge University in 1581 by Theodore Bezae. (3) Codex Ephraemi—a fifth-century manuscript that was erased during the twelfth century and much of it rewritten with a Greek translation of the sermons of St. Ephraem, a Syrian church leader of a century earlier. Scientific methods were used to bring out the underlying text containing portions of every book in the NT except II Thessalonians and II John. Only a small part of the OT remains. (4) Codex SINAITICUS—a fourth-century codex discovered by Constantine von Tischendorf in St. Catherine's Convent at the foot of Mt. Sinai in 1844. All of the NT was found intact and a considerable portion of the OT. In 1975 at least eight and perhaps as many as fourteen additional folios of this manuscript were found when workmen were repairing one of the walls of the convent. The codex was given to the Czar of Russia by the monastery, and in 1933, after the Russian revolution, it was sold to the British Museum, where it now resides. (5) Codex Vaticanus—one of the earliest and most valuable manuscripts of the Bible in Greek dates to the middle of the fourth century. It is missing almost forty-six chapters of Genesis, about thirty Psalms, and everything from Hebrews 9:14 onward. It resides in the Vatican Library in Rome and is thus called Codex Vaticanus. (*See also* WRITING AND WRITING MATERIALS.)

J.R.M.

**CODEX JURIS CANONICI.** The universal, systematic, ecclesiastical law of the Roman Catholic church, which deals with the constitution of the church, the relations between it and other bodies, and internal matters such as discipline, canonization, and beatification.

J.R.M.

**COGHILL, ANNIE LOUISA WALKER** (1836–1907). Author of the hymn "Work, for the Night Is Coming," Coghill was born near Staffordshire, England, the youngest of three daughters of Robert Walker, a civil engineer.

About 1857 the sisters moved to Canada, where they opened a private girls' school. During this period Anna wrote her hymn. In 1863 she returned to England, working as a governess and book reviewer. She married Harry Coghill, a wealthy merchant, in 1883.

N.H.

*COGITO ERGO SUM. See* DESCARTES, RENE.

**COKE, THOMAS.** An early companion of JOHN WESLEY, who, together with Wesley and a third Anglican priest, ordained the first two Methodist ministers and commissioned them to go to America. The next day, Coke was made a superintendent by Wesley and sent with the other two to the New World. The Christmas Conference of 1784 made him, jointly with FRANCIS ASBURY, one of the two superintendents or "bishops" of the newly founded Methodist Episcopal church.            J.G.

*Thomas Coke*

# COLERIDGE, SAMUEL TAYLOR (1772–1834).

Poet, philosopher, literary critic, and theologian, who was largely responsible for the rebirth of a vital English theology in the early decades of the nineteenth century. Coleridge represents the protest of English ROMANTICISM against the RATIONALISM and the decrepit orthodoxy of the eighteenth century. His writings had an important influence on J. H. NEWMAN, on F. D. MAURICE, and on many Broad Church and liberal Anglican theologians.

Coleridge's spiritual philosophy owed much to the poet WILLIAM WORDSWORTH and to his reading of KANT. Together they introduced Coleridge to the imaginative and active character of the mind, to what he called the power of reason, by which intellect, the senses, and the will together intuitively grasp spiritual truth. Coleridge contrasted reason with understanding, the empirical faculty which judges only according to the senses and which he saw as the source of materialism, atheism, and utilitarianism.

Coleridge abhorred the "proofs" of Christianity offered by NATURAL THEOLOGY and called for a moral and experiential test of religion. In *Aids to Reflection* he wrote "Evidences of Christianity! I am weary of the word. Make a man feel the want of it; rouse him to the self-knowledge of his need of it; and you may safely trust it to its own evidence." In his *Confessions of an Inquiring Spirit,* posthumously published (1840), Coleridge attacked "Bibliolatry," the belief in the literal inerrancy of Scripture, as well as the "negative dogmatism" of the skeptical rationalists. He insisted that the Bible's authority lies in its spiritual "fitness to our nature and our needs." Coleridge's *Constitution of Church and State* (1830) influenced Thomas Arnold (1795–1842) and others.

J.L.

# COLLECT.

A short prayer of gathering or "collection" that concludes the entrance ritual at Catholic mass, and the Confession, Kyrie, and the Gloria in Excelsis in the Lutheran, Anglican, and Methodist services. It gathers up the individual prayers of the worshiping community. It is called the opening prayer in the revised Roman missal.

J.C.

# COLLEGE OF CARDINALS.

The whole body of cardinals of the Roman Catholic church, which together make up the advisory body of the pope. CARDINALS are officers ranking just below the pope, and on the death of a pope they elect a new one. During the vacancy, the cardinals administer the Catholic church.

The sacred college is divided into three orders: cardinal bishops, cardinal priests, and cardinal deacons. The ranking cardinal bishop serves as the dean of the College of Cardinals.

The cardinals play a major role in the governance of the church, both by virtue of their advisory role to the pope and by their offices as heads of various bureaus and congregations. The principle of collegiality affirms that the pope shares power as *primus inter partes* with the whole body of bishops of the Roman Catholic church. This was defined by Vatican II under John XXIII and Paul VI.

J.C.

# COLOSSAE.

A great, ancient Phrygian city in Southwest Asia Minor, in the valley of the Lycus River near its joining with the Meander. Laodicea and Hieropolis developed as rival cities in Roman times. Colossae remained an active center of wool trade. Indications in the letters to the Colossians and Philemon suggest what life in Colossae was like in NT times. There was a house church in Colossae (Col. 1:2) that, despite its problems, survived under the name Saint Michael's through Byzantine times.

P.L.G.

# COLOSSIANS.

A letter of Paul to the church at Colossae.

*Background and Destination.* The city of Colossae lay in the valley of the Lycus River, in the southern part of ancient Phrygia, which would now be located in the west of modern Turkey.

When Paul wrote to the Christians living at Colossae, the city's population consisted of indigenous Phrygian and Greek settlers. Colossae was thus a cosmopolitan city in which diverse cultural and religious elements met and mingled—a fact which is important to remember when the origins of the Colossian "philosophy" (2:8) are sought.

The Christian gospel was introduced to Colossae during Paul's Ephesian ministry (Acts 19:10). The most likely person to have carried the message of Christ to Colossae was Epaphras, who was a native of the city (4:12).

*Occasion and Purpose.* During one of Paul's imprisonments (see below), news came to him of a threat to the Colossian church. The occasion of this letter may be traced to this impending danger and the need to rebut the error which lay at the heart of a strange doctrine.

Nowhere in the letter does Paul give a formal definition of the teaching, and its thrust only can be inferred. Yet it seems to have been a fusion of pagan and Judaic speculation, which resulted in a syncretism. The features of the religious amalgam were forms of ascetic practice and discipline, the cult of angelic worship (2:18), and a pride in superior wisdom and knowledge (Greek, *gnōsis,* or "knowledge").

Paul brands these notions as "self-abasement" (2:23) and as a species of human wisdom (2:8), essentially human devised just as the claim to "visions" (2:18) is a piece of self-deception. Positively he declares that all the fullness dwells in Christ, not in the angels (1:19; 2:9). Against the false claim to wisdom and knowledge, Paul protests that there is no higher mystery than Christ (2:2-3) who may be known not to a spiritual elite but to all people (1:26-28). The conclusion Paul enforces is irresistible: you died with Christ (at conversion-baptism) from the control of the elemental spirits (2:12, 20).

Another tenet of the Colossian errorists was DUALISM in which the high God was thought of as remote from matter, which, in turn, was considered to be alien to him. To attain to God one must be delivered from the evil influences of material things. This "liberation" was achieved along two quite diverse routes. One path to Gnostic salvation was ASCETICISM, which summoned the devotee to a life of abstinence and self-punishment (2:21, 23).

The other direction arising from GNOSTICISM was libertinism. If matter has no relation to God (the argument ran), then the material body has no relation to religion. Therefore one can indulge the body without restraint or conscience.

*Place of Origin.* Paul writes the letter as a prisoner (4:3, 10, 18). Acts tells of several places where Paul was detained for some length of time. The captivity at Jerusalem is hardly a viable possibility for the origin of this letter, as Paul had no opportunity for writing. The choice seems then to be a straightforward alternative: Caesarea or Rome. A third place name, however, is that of Ephesus or somewhere near the capital city of proconsular Asia, where according to Acts 19 and 20 Paul underwent a series of trials. Incidental allusions to this hypothetical Ephesian captivity are discovered in I Corinthians 15:32 and a graphic description in II Corinthians 1:8-10.

The traditional placing of the letter (a view which goes back to Chrysostom) during the time of Paul's custody at Rome (Acts 28) has many points to commend it. But the present writer argues for an Ephesian origin of Colossians.

*Authorship and Date.* The authorship of this letter is disputed in recent study. Those who deny the letter to Paul's hand do so on the ground of the letter's developed teaching on Christ's person, traces of a more formal attitude to Paul's apostleship, as well as a distinctive word usage that seems to put Colossians in a class apart from the undisputed Pauline letters. None of these points seems compelling, though E. Schweizer's proposal that a contemporary disciple of Paul used Paul's materials to edit the letter, thus explaining the unusual terms and phraseology, has tried to account for the marked features of Colossians.

The letter comes either from Paul's Ephesian (A.D. 55) or Roman (A.D. 60–62) imprisonment, or was published by his disciples after his death in A.D. 65.

*Theology.* The one section of the Epistle, which may be treated as non-Pauline in the sense that Paul has taken it over and embodied it in the letter, is the rich christological passage, 1:15-20. This hymn contains an unusual vocabulary and a number of unique stylistic traits. Its purpose is both polemical (in opposing the false teaching, see above) and positive (in setting forth the true doctrine of the person and

place of the cosmic Christ who is both Lord of creation and author of reconciliation). This is the important message of Colossians: "Christ is all, and in all" (3:11). CHRISTOLOGY for Paul is linked with Christian ethics, and the bridge is the call of 2:20 and 3:1-3. It is the ethical appeal of death to the old world of sin and self and resurrection to a new life in Christ. The ramifications of this new life are seen in the practical relationships of the home and family (3:19-21), masters and slaves (3:22–4:1), and the believers' conduct in the world (4:5, 6).

R.M.

**COMFORTER.** *See* HOLY SPIRIT.

**COMMANDMENTS.** *See* TEN COMMANDMENTS.

**COMMISSION, THE GREAT.** An expression uniquely associated with Matthew 28:16-20 but also related to Luke 24:36-49; John 20:19-23; Acts 1:6-11, and, for some to Mark 16:14-20 (the longer ending). The expression as such does not appear in the biblical text. It was, and is, widely popular with the relatively modern, evangelical Protestant world missionary movement. Creed-like, it affirms the multifaceted relationship between Jesus and the church. The Matthew passage, standing at the very end of the book and possessing such an awe-inspiring atmosphere, has impressed some students of literature as a kind of farewell address.

The main verb in Matthew 28:19 is not "Go," as the English translation suggests, but "make disciples" or literally "disciple." The Greek verb *matheteústhai* is Matthew's special term for becoming a follower of Christ (compare 13:22 and 27:57). The word's literal meaning is to "deepen the temporary and mainly intellectual relation of teacher-to-pupil." Following somewhat the relation between a Jewish rabbi and a DISCIPLE, the verb underscores the life-commitment of the disciple to be a loving and obedient emulator of one who is accepted not only as instructor, but, more importantly, as Lord and God (John 20:28). Jesus uttered other commands that could be and have been regarded as commissions. None historically has inspired a more wide-spread response in those who have gone to all nations, bearing the message of salvation through Christ. Matthew 28:18-20 still gives the vision of a worldwide church that motivates world missions and ecumenicity.

P.L.G.

**COMMUNION.** *Old Testament.* In the standard English translations of the OT the term "communion" is not found. The word "FELLOWSHIP" is there only twice in the KJV, but the Hebrew root *hbr* is frequent, and it is this Hebrew word-group that enters the Greek OT as *koinon,* an important NT idea, as we shall see.

The OT word carries the basic meaning "to bind together," sometimes in a physical way (Exod. 26:6), sometimes used of nations entering into agreement (Gen. 14:3), sometimes of persons who share a common trade (fishermen in Job 41:6) or a common task (II Chr. 20:35-36; Song of S. 1:7; 8:13) or a common bond, that is, marriage (Mal. 2:14). In the religious sense there are worshipers who are united (Ps. 119:63), or in the bad sense the word is used of those in evil complicity (Isa. 1:23; Prov. 28:24). Evildoers are said to have no "fellowship" with Yahweh, Israel's God (Ps. 94:20), just as idols have no part in Israel's religious life (Ps. 96:4, 5).

One interesting fact emerges from a lexical study of *hbr:* it is never employed of a human relationship with God. The probable explanation is that the Jewish mind could hardly conceive of such intimacy with the Divine, unlike the world of other contemporary religions that thought of humanity as sharing in the life of the Deity. The OT preserves a distinction between Israel and God, who is always sovereign Lord.

*New Testament.* In the NT the basic term, translated variously as "communion," "fellowship," "communicate," "partake," "contribution," and "common" (in the sense of "in common"), stems from the Greek root *koin-*. There are two adjectives, *koinōnos* (found ten times) and *synkoinōnos* (found four times), which are used as nouns also; and two verbs *koinōneō* (eight times) and *synkoinōneō* (three times); and the noun *koinōnia* (twenty times). The results of the recent linguistic research of scholars is: "the important thing is that these words (belonging to the *koin* family) refer primarily, though not invariably, to participation in something rather than to associations with others; and there is often a genitive to indicate that in which one participates or shares" (A. R. George). From this ground-plan of the word, the NT passages may be divided into three classes, according to whether the predominant idea is (a) having a share; (b) giving a share; or (c) sharing.

(a) *"Having a share."* Under this heading we may classify, first of all, the adjectives that are used to describe partners in some common enterprise, for example, Christian work (II Cor. 8:23), or secular business (Luke 5:10); also those who share in a common experience (for example, persecutions, Heb. 10:33; Rev. 1:9; suffering, II Cor. 1:7; worship, I Cor. 10:18; murder, Matt. 23:30; the compact with demons in pagan cult worship, I Cor. 10:20). The most important references are: I Corinthians 10:16; Philippians 2:1; and II Corinthians 13:14, because they describe the church's relationship to God.

(b) *"Giving a share."* The main text that supports the interpretation of *koinōnia* as "giving a share" is II Corinthians 9:13, "the generosity of your contribution for them and for all others." "Your contribution" represents the Greek *tēs koinōnias,* that is, in this context, "generosity." This same rendering may be suggested also for Philippians 1:5, in which case the object of Paul's gratitude to God is the generosity of the Philippian Christians in their support of the apostolic ministry for the progress of the gospel. Similarly, the same translation clarifies Philemon 6.

Another reference under this heading is Romans 15:26, which indicates that *koinōnia* can take on a concrete form as a generosity that clothes itself in practical action and is so applied to the collection for the saints of the Jerusalem church in their poverty-stricken condition (compare II Cor. 8:4). In this light we may consider, finally, Acts 2:42, meaning possibly "generosity."

(c) *"Sharing."* Under this heading there are only three possible occurrences where *koinōnia* is used absolutely or with the preposition *meta* (with). These are Acts 2:42; Galatians 2:9, and I John 1:3 ff.

R.M.

**COMMUNION, HOLY.** *See* LORD'S SUPPER.

**COMMUNITY CHURCHES, NATIONAL COUNCIL OF.** A fellowship of autonomous, ecumenically inclined, non-creedal churches of congregational polity. In 1950 two councils of Community churches merged. One was the Biennial Council of Community Churches, a black group, and the other, a white group named the National Council of Community Churches. The National Council meets for an annual conference. There are twenty state groups and three hundred local groups. It exists to promote the fellowship of community-type churches throughout the country and to provide an instrument through which community-minded and freedom-loving churches can cooperate in making a contribution toward a united church. It maintains a placement office for ministers, has commissions on church relations, clergy relations, ecumenical relations, faith and order, information services, laity relations, and social concerns. It publishes a community yearbook a pastor's journal, and the monthly *Christian Community News.*

J.C.

**COMPARATIVE RELIGION.** *See* WORLD RELIGIONS.

**COMPLINES.** *See* CANONICAL HOURS.

**COMTE, AUGUSTE** (1798–1857). French philosopher and founder of positivism, who has been called the father of sociology. Comte attended the École Polytechnique in Paris from 1814 to 1816. In 1818 he came under the influence of Saint-Simon, the most prominent French socialist of the time. Comte's *Positive Philosophy* appeared in six volumes between 1830 and 1842. During 1851–54 he published the four-volume *System of Positive Polity* and, in 1852, his *Positive Catechism.*

Comte meant by positivism "the knowledge derived from science and its extension to society," which he believed must be organized on a scientific basis. Comte viewed the human mind as evolving from a theological stage through a metaphysical stage—in which personal deities are transformed into metaphysical abstractions—to a third, scientific or positive, stage. In the positive stage, humanity takes the place of God as the object of devotion. Comte's religion included its secular saints, ritual, creed, and holidays. T. H. Huxley called it "Catholicism without Christianity." Positivist churches were established both in France and England. Comte had an important influence on the sociologist EMILE DURKHEIM (1858–1917) and on Frederic Harrison (1831–1923), the most prominent leader of English positivism.

J.L.

**CONCILIARISM.** A theory in Roman Catholicism that a council representing the entire church has supreme authority, even above the pope.

Pope Boniface VIII's claim to universal authority in 1302 suffered severely during the Babylonian Captivity (1305–77) when the papacy moved to Avignon and became a tool of France. The GREAT SCHISM (1378–1415) followed; rival popes in Rome and Avignon anathematized each other. The Council of Pisa (1409) then elected a third pope.

Calls for conciliar reform mounted. William Occam, an English scholastic philosopher, believed the church's will was a summary of the wills of individuals. He called for a council representative of the entire church. Marsilius of Padua (1275?–1342) argued that the emperor was superior to the pope, but said both were subject to the will of the people they represent; a council of the people can remove both. JOHN WYCLIFFE (1328–84) called for removal of bad stewards in church and state. Conrad of Gelnhausen, Heinrich of Langenstein, Pierre d'Ailly, John Gerson, and others agitated for a reforming council.

Emperor Sigismund and Pisan Pope John XXIII called the COUNCIL OF CONSTANCE (1414–18). It proclaimed all three popes deposed and issued its decree *Sacrosancta,* April 6, 1415, declaring it represented the people, derived power directly from Christ, and that everyone, even the pope, must obey its decrees. The pope was to be the church's executive. After Constance, conciliarism waned drastically. VATICAN COUNCIL II (1962–65) expressed a vestige of conciliarism in collegiality, stating all bishops as successors of the apostles share in the authority of the pope.

C.M.

**CONCLAVE.** A term both for the place where cardinals elect a pope and for the meeting itself. On the death of a pope, a conclave is called in fifteen days in a private place. Rules for the conclave were laid down by popes Pius XII, John XXIII, and Paul VI.

J.C.

**CONCORDANCE.** An alphabetically arranged index showing where in the text of a book or books each principal word is used. It is said that the format was devised by Bible students to demonstrate that the Bible's several parts are consistent with one another. Concordances have since been made for other writings, such as for Shakespeare's works.

P.L.G.

*CONCORD, BOOK AND FORMULA OF. See* BOOK AND FORMULA OF CONCORD.

**CONCUBINE.** The term means "one (female) who cohabits with another (male)," with the pejorative connotation that the cohabitation is irregular; that the relationship is one of man and mistress rather than husband and wife. It is, therefore, a term that presupposes as normative a society based on a monogamous family household. Obviously, it has no meaning—or at least no pejorative meaning—in a society that recognizes polygamy or polyandry; that otherwise departs from the one-man-one-woman nuclear family concept; or that has more than a single concept of what it is "to be married," for which there are different kinds of marriages that impose different kinds of obligations.

As far as the last mentioned is concerned, we have instances from the Bible to indicate that MARRIAGE concepts existed for which there are hardly any parallels to what we understand the institution to imply today. Samson was "married" to a Philistine woman whom he only visited on occasion and who eventually became the wife of someone else (Judg. 14). Was the woman his wife or concubine? In a polygamous society a fine distinction could hardly have been drawn. When Abraham's wife Sarah, who was sterile, gave her husband the handmaid Hagar, that she might bear children by surrogate, it was as "wife" not as "concubine" (Gen. 16:1–4). So also with Rachel and Leah, the two wives of Jacob: their maids Bilhah and Zilpah were also his "wives."

What, then, was the *pilegesh,* the concubine as distinguished from the wife or wives, even as the much-married Solomon is said to have had seven hundred wives—"princesses"—and three hundred concubines (I Kings 11:3)? If we can judge from Genesis 35:22 (where Bilhah is called a concubine), Genesis 22–24, Judges 19, II Samuel 5:13, and similar passages, the distinction had to do simply with fiscal legalities. The "wife" was—or her family was—the social equal of her husband. Not only would a dowry be provided on her part, there would also be a corresponding bridal gift (*mohar,* "purchase price") paid by the groom, which in some instances might entail an international alliance if not simply the alliance of two important families.

A "concubine," on the other hand, was simply one more wife in a polygamous marriage. She may, indeed, have been, among others, favored by her husband in a love-match that he did not reserve for his "official" wives. We have no information on the subject, and biblical law has nothing to say about the matter. We can only surmise what the situation must have been, on the presupposition that human nature has not radically changed over the past few centuries.

B.V.

**CONCUPISCENCE.** A traditional theological term to designate the desire for forbidden things. In popular language it is often equated with sexual LUST. Concupiscence itself is not sin, for it is a force, an impulse rooted in human nature as we know it ("fallen" humankind; what Paul calls "the flesh"). But it is closely related to sinfulness, for the desires of the flesh lead to the works of the flesh, which are sin (Rom. 5:16-24; James 1:14-15).

B.V.

**CONFESSION.** This term has many meanings in biblical and Judeo-Christian tradition. Etymologically it differs little from the idea of profess, that is, admit, acknowledge, own up to. Thus the summations of key doctrines professed by various churches have been termed "confessions" (the Westminster Confession, the Confession of Augsburg, etc.). The revelation or publication of personal experiences testifying to some spiritual development whether of faith or doubt often bear the title "confessions" (the *Confessions of Augustine,* the "confessions" of Jeremiah: the passages in which the prophet is seen quarreling with God, etc.). Thus the title "confessor" was accorded those who in popular estimation or by formal canonization were regarded as having witnessed by their lives to the truth of their religious convictions (Edward the Confessor, et al.). In this sense the Latin "confessor" is used in distinction to the Greek "martyr"—the two words mean essentially the same thing—since "martyr" came to be employed of one who had confessed his faith even to the point of laying down his life.

Here we are concerned with confession in the more restricted meaning that remains the one most familiar today, that is, the acknowledgment of one's sinfulness, a profession of guilt in petition of forgiveness. Confession of sins, whether of an individual or on behalf of the whole nation, was assumed to be the indispensable condition for forgiveness, whether the SIN in question was one of forgetfulness, human frailty, or outright malice (compare Lev. 5:5; Num. 5:7; II Sam. 12:13; etc.). Before there could be reconciliation between God and humans, it was necessary that acknowledgment be made that what separated the two had a moral dimension: then only could the gulf be bridged (compare Isa. 6:5-7). Thus the significance of the expression "knowledge of God," which was common to Hosea and Isaiah (Hos. 4:1; Isa. 1:3; etc.) and other prophets: to know God truly is to recognize this moral division and therefore need to confess it. Confession,

together with ritual, was sufficient to purge the sinner(s) of inadvertent sins, but for absolution from graver crimes confession could only be a means of appealing to the mercy of God (compare Ps. 51:15-17).

It is taken for granted also in the NT that there can be no forgiveness of sins unless the sin is frankly acknowledged (I John 1:9, for example). According to Acts 19:18-19 public confession was taken to be a routine measure to rectify a grave disorder in the Christian community. In James 5:16 there even seems to be the attempt to institutionalize confession. While the text says literally nothing more than that Christians should confess their sins to one another and pray for one another, still, the ecclesiastical context ("the elders of the church," "anointing with oil in the name of the lord," "the prayer of faith") indicates the beginning of a discipline.

That discipline was, of course, of much later development in the Christian church. Eventually "the elders of the church" of James 5:16, to whom confession should be made, were identified exclusively with the priesthood of the church. Furthermore, after some disastrous experiences with public confessions, it was thought best, at least in most of the mainline Christian communities, to make confessions auricular ("for the ears only"), that is, secret between the penitent and the minister of absolution, who at the same time bound himself to complete silence about what had been made known to him.

B.V.

**CONFESSION OF FAITH.** The creed, symbol, or statement of belief confessed by Christians during services. The confession of faith generally used in Roman Catholic and Protestant churches is the APOSTLES' CREED (in noncommunion services), while the NICENE CREED is used when there is Holy Communion. The confession of faith is the credo (meaning "I believe"), while being at the same time the "we believe," since all confess together as well as in harmony with the whole catholic church, scattered across all lands and found throughout Christian history in the communion of (all) the saints. The confession of faith includes belief in the Father, the Creator of heaven of earth and of all life; in the Son, who is the Redeemer, the Savior of all who have faith; and in the Holy Spirit, who calls us into the church and sanctifies us by grace.

J.C.

*CONFESSIONS OF AUGUSTINE.* AUGUSTINE's work, in thirteen books, written about A.D. 400, which includes his spiritual autobiography. The word "confession" does not refer primarily to a confession of sins, but rather to the confession of God's love and provident care. As a spiritual autobiography, the *Confessions* created a new genre, for, although precedents could be found in works by Cyprian and Gregory of Nazianzus, Augustine was the first to write in such depth and detail about his own spiritual pilgrimage. But, once again, to read this work as just a spiritual autobiography is incorrect, for the last four books deal with such themes as memory, the notion of time, and creation. What gives unity to such diverse subjects is the confession of the love and glory of God, which is seen in the details of Augustine's life as well as in the profundities of time and creation.

Scholars have debated the historicity of the *Confessions,* particularly in that which refers to Augustine's conversion. It is in the *Confessions* that he tells of the episode in the garden of Milan. But this was written many years later, and the books that Augustine wrote shortly after his conversion show that he was still to a great degree a Neoplatonist. It would seem that, while the conversion did take place as Augustine describes it, at that time his understanding of Christianity was very much colored by Neoplatonic influences, many of which he rejected later, when he became a leader of the church.

                                                                J.G.

**CONFESSOR.** A term used to describe a male saint, in the Roman Catholic cult of the saints, who did not die a martyr's death but whose life exemplified the Christian faith. The designation "confessor" is widely used to include monks, bishops, popes, priests, and religious (lay brothers) and lay persons. In the earliest church the only honorific title given deceased Christians considered saints was MARTYR. In the later second century, a new category of confessor was established. Confessors, for the early church, while not martyrs, were those who actually suffered persecution for their faith. Later, this characteristic of persecution was not insisted upon.

                                                                J.C.

**CONFIRMATION.** Part of the Christian rites of initiation. The word "confirmation" means "strengthening." It has two referents. Confirmation has been interpreted as bringing an added grace of the Holy Spirit beyond that received in baptism to strengthen the believer in living the Christian faith. The word may also refer to the fact that the person is confirming the promises made in his or her behalf by sponsors at the time of baptism.

By the fourth century, baptism was followed immediately by the anointing with oil, and the newly baptized then joined the congregation for the celebration of the Lord's Supper. After infant baptism became the custom in the Western church, the affirmation of faith with the anointing became separated as a later rite performed by bishops. It was not considered essential until about the eleventh century. The Orthodox churches continued to celebrate the tripartite rite for infants. Protestant groups emphasized the personal confession of faith more than incorporation into the community. Lutheran and Anglican traditions put more emphasis on the aspect of incorporation, although only the

Anglicans continued confirmation as an episcopal function. Anabaptist groups made the confession of faith a prerequisite to baptism. Protestant custom has been for first Communion to follow believer's baptism or confirmation. A recent trend is to follow the twentieth-century Roman Catholic custom of admitting baptized children to the Lord's Supper.

Current theological discussion tends to view baptism as the basic rite. The Book of Common Prayer (1979) contains one form that includes both rites. The Roman Catholic church is encouraging study of its Rite of Christian Initiation for Adults. Thus contemporary theological and liturgical studies try to find a balance between the Radical Reformation's emphasis on the personal response to the call of Christ and the traditional Catholic emphasis on incorporation into the community of faith.

Anthropological approaches to liturgy raise the question as to whether confirmation should be viewed as a rite of passage—thus asking questions about timing at the beginning of adolescence or of adulthood; or whether it is a rite of community to strengthen members for their roles. Psychological inquiries ask the type of commitment appropriate and possible at various ages.

                                                                I.C.

**CONFUCIANISM.** The system of social and personal morality that has been dominant in China and neighboring countries for almost twenty-five centuries. The term "Confucianism" is taken from its greatest teacher and example, CONFUCIUS (551–479 B.C.), but in the Far East it is known as the "Teaching of the Scholars (or Literati)."

Confucius stressed the importance of learning from the past, especially from the legendary emperors Yao and Shun, and his personal model, the Duke of Chou (eleventh century B.C.). Morality, he taught, is based on the will of heaven, and there are unchanging principles that must be followed in the family and in public life. He denied that he was an originator, insisting that he was only passing on the wisdom of the past.

Confucius chose "Five Classics" as expressing the beliefs he was teaching: *The Book of History,* a collection of documents from ancient times, some are authentic and some apocryphal; *The Book of Odes,* 305 poems collected around 600 B.C., though some are much older; *The Spring and Autumn Annals,* a record of events in Confucius' home state of Lu (now Shantung) from 722 to 481 B.C.; *The Book of Rites,* a collection of philosophical, narrative, and ritual writings; and *The Book of Changes (I CHING),* used largely for divination.

Over the next few centuries the teachings of Confucius (preserved in the ANALECTS) exerted greater and greater influence. Other ways of life competed for popular acceptance, but with the rise of the Han Dynasty (206 B.C. to A.D. 220) Confucianism became the ruling philosophy. With some ups and downs it maintained this position into the present century. The pressure to modernize Chinese life and the rise of Marxism have represented the most serious challenges to Confucianism. Today, however, even inside the People's Republic of China, Confucian ideals have remained alive.

*Classic Confucianism.* The movement arose in a time of great social disorder. From the eighth to the third centuries B.C. life was made bitter for many because of almost constant warfare among the small states of China. Old families fell on hard times and new ones rose to positions of influence. Confucius sought to train a select group of young men in the practical art of being moral and still being successful. After his death they continued to follow his teachings and handed them on to others.

At the heart of the moral life are the five basic relationships of mutual responsibility: father and son, husband and wife, ruler and subject, elder and younger brother or sister, and friend and friend. Everyone is capable of living up to the standard, but only a few have the love of learning that is necessary to become a teacher and a ruler. Noble birth is not significant, but ability and ambition are essential. The Confucian scholar must be involved in public life if at all possible, putting his learning to work for the good of all. It is a disgrace not to be part of a good government, or to be part of a corrupt one.

(a) *Mencius.* MENCIUS (371–289 B.C.) was Confucius' first great successor. Like Confucius he tried to influence governments for good. He believed that all humans are good by birth. Anyone seeing a child about to fall into a well will rescue the child as a matter of course. This sense of pity is one of Mencius' "Four Beginnings" of mature goodness. Properly developed, they become the basis of a truly good life. If they are neglected a person will become evil. Thus moral education and training are vital.

(b) *Hsün Tzu.* HSÜN TZU (298–238 B.C.), in direct opposition to Mencius, taught that everyone is by nature evil and must be controlled by laws and rules of proper conduct. Left to themselves, people become quarrelsome, lustful, violent, and greedy. They must be disciplined, just as blunt metal must be ground and whetted to make it sharp.

Hsün Tzu was also a rationalist. He believed that nature goes on its way regardless of whether people are good or evil. Rain falls whether or not people pray for rain. He felt that we should study the world of nature in order to use it wisely.

(c) *Other schools.* During this period there were several rival ways of understanding life, but only one, TAOISM, has endured. The Taoists criticized Confucians for being busybodies, for being too highly organized, and for forcing their concepts on others. Taoist writings teach a sense of wonder and excitement, an outlook that is willing to live and let live.

*Han Dynasty Confucianism.* Ancient China's period of turmoil was ended by Emperor Ch'in's ruthless unification of the country in 221 B.C. Violently anti-intellectual, he burned the Confucian classics and other "useless" books. After a brief period of splendor, his dynasty fell and was succeeded by the Han.

Under the Han emperors, Confucianism became the official state doctrine. It supported the imperial system by stressing that the people needed a king to rule them. At the same time, it emphasized the ancient concept of the Mandate of Heaven. Heaven, sometimes thought of as a personal being, sometimes as an impersonal force, withdraws its mandate from a wicked ruler and gives it to a righteous ruler who then becomes the new ruler. Would-be emperors appealed to this doctrine throughout China's history.

In this period Confucianism was supreme, but it was constantly in danger of degenerating into superstition. Wang Ch'ung (A.D. 27–97) fought that tendency and prepared the way for a rational attitude toward nature that continued long past the fall of the Han dynasty.

*The Rise of Neo-Confucianism.* During the Han dynasty BUDDHISM entered China, and it grew in power and influence until the ninth century A.D. After that it slowly declined but continued to be a major force. The confrontation with Buddhism forced Confucians to broaden their way of thinking. They began to take the entire universe as the background for their ideas. Buddhists taught that the world is an illusion. Confucians reaffirmed its reality and the importance of studying it. In opposition to Buddhist monasticism Confucians stressed the importance of family life and of involvement in government at every level.

This new stage of development, commonly known as Neo-Confucianism, began in the Sung Dynasty (A.D. 960–1279) and was dominant until the twentieth century. From 1313 to 1905 Confucian thought was the basis for national examinations for entry into government service. The greatest Neo-Confucian was CHU HSI (1130–1200), who declared Mencius was orthodox and Hsün Tzu was not. He established four books as the highest Confucian authority: The *Analects,* the writings of Mencius, and two shorter ancient texts, THE DOCTRINE OF THE MEAN and *The Great Learning.* From the last of these he took the statement, "The extension of knowledge consists in the investigation of things" and made it a major principle of his philosophy. He taught that we should investigate the ancient writings, the world of nature, and current affairs, and that we should do so while being involved in the day-to-day decisions of society.

*Confucianism as a Way of Life.* The highest virtues are family loyalty and social responsibility. Confucianism has coexisted with Buddhism and other religions under a division of responsibility by which Confucianism provided for successful living in this world, and the religions provided ways of dealing with the realm of supernatural beings.

# Chinese Religions:
## Confucianism and Taoism

⊙  Capitals of China (from the fourth
   century B.C) and contemporary
   centers of state (Confucian) religion

PA  Regions associated with the early
    development and spread of Taoism
    (third century B.C. to third century
    A.D.)

▲  Mountains having a strong, ancient Taoist presence

GREAT WALL

KOREA

Pei-ching (Peking) ⊙     YEN

Hêng Shan ▲     CHÜ-LU

CHAO         CH'I

CHIN         LANG-YEH

YELLOW SEA

T'ai Shan ▲

• Birthplace of Confucius, 551 B.C.
• Birthplace of Mencius, ca. 371 B.C.

Yellow River

• Lan-chou

Chung T'iao Shan ▲     CHIN     ⊙ K'ai-fêng

Lo-yang ⊙ ▲ Sung Shan

Ch'ang-an (Hsi-an) ⊙
▲ Hua Shan
▲ Chung Nan Shan

Nan-ching (Nanking)

Mao Shan ▲
WU
• Shang-hai

HAN-CHUNG
Wu Tang Shan ▲

▲ Huo Shan

SHU

CH'U
Wu-han •

Yangtze River

K'uai Chi Shan ▲
T'ien T'ai Shan ▲
K'uo Ts'ang Shan ▲

PA

▲ Lu Shan

Ch'ung-ch'ing (Chungking) •     ▲ Hsi Shan

▲ Hêng Shan

• K'un-ming

Lo Fu Shan ▲
Kuang-chou (Canton) •

TAIWAN (Formosa)

SOUTH CHINA SEA

Hainan

Miles    0          200        400
Kilometers 0     200     400

The two realms are most closely related in the veneration of ancestors. The eldest son in each family bears responsibility for preserving the wooden tablets that represent the ancestors, he conducts the worship that provides for the needs of the ancestors in the afterlife, and he secures their aid for their living descendants. Ancestral tablets are of wood, about a foot long, two or three inches wide, and half an inch thick. Each tablet is set in a low wooden base, and on the front the name of the ancestor is inscribed.

From the twelfth century to the twentieth, Confucian thought and practice were kept alive in academies located in major cities throughout China. Teaching stressed not only the elegant literary style required by the government examinations, but went beyond externals to emphasize building the character of each student. The goal was sagehood, or true wisdom. Students were to bring their minds under the control of good thoughts and to will only what was right. Only by doing so could they hope to attain wisdom. Even when they were alone their thoughts and actions were to be as upright as when others could observe them. Many Confucian scholars were exiled or persecuted for opposing public policies that they regarded as evil.

It was customary to provide tutors for the emperor in order to guide him in governing the people. The government itself was to be regulated at each level in a way proper to that level. Local affairs were guided by a *Rural Contract* that stressed mutual responsibility. Village elders were responsible for providing education that would induce people to do good, to aid one another in emergencies, and to avoid lawsuits.

In the twentieth century, Confucianism has slowly adapted to changing times, and many young people regard it as a barrier to progress. In 1931 Pa Chin wrote *The Family,* a novel depicting the tyrannical control exercised by many in the older generation. The book helped hasten the fall of the old order.

*Religious Aspects of Confucianism.* The veneration of Confucius was similar to that offered to ancestors. Although the educated elite resisted efforts to deify Confucius, temples were erected in his honor, and sacrifices were offered to him in midspring and midautumn. A rich variety of food was offered to the sage and to his closest followers. To the accompaniment of ceremonial music the worshipers would fall to their hands and knees and bend forward until their foreheads touched the ground. Other rites were observed in the temple compound to honor various folk deities and spirits. Such worship continues today at the great Confucian temple in Seoul, Korea, even though the ancient splendor was lost after the national examinations were abolished there in 1895. The seventy-seventh lineal descendant of Confucius is living in Taiwan, and there much of Confucian tradition remains vigorous.

*Confucianism and the People's Republic of China.* After the fall of the last imperial dynasty in 1911, many voices were raised against the Confucian tradition. The most thorough critics were the Communists. Mao Tse-tung was not entirely consistent in his attacks on Confucius, but the effect of it all was to confine Confucianism to the status of a dead system of thought. It became little more than a relic in a museum. Confucius was an important part of China's feudal past, but he has no role to play in the nation's present or future. His temples are no longer places of worship, and his teachings no longer serve to guide official policy.

*Confucianism and Christianity.* Jesuit missionaries to China in the sixteenth and seventeenth centuries discovered the writings of Confucius and his followers and became enthusiastic over the possibility of using them as a bridge to winning China to Christianity. They dressed like Confucian scholars and succeeded in convincing the papal office that Confucian rites were not pagan but could be practiced by Christians. In the eighteenth century the church reversed its ruling, and Christianity fell into disfavor.

Protestant attitudes have varied. James Legge (1815–97), a missionary who became the first professor of Chinese at Oxford, translated and commented on the Confucian classics. He held them in high esteem, but felt Confucianism was inferior to Christianity. Some Protestants have claimed that it is impossible to be a Confucian and a Christian at the same time. The Chinese scholar Lin Yutang (1895–  ) has replied that this is like saying it is impossible to be a gentleman and a Christian at the same time.                                                    K.C.

**CONFUCIUS.** Latinized name of K'ung Fu-tzu (literally "Great Master K'ung"), about 551–479 B.C. China's most revered teacher and philosopher. Though Confucius denied that he was an innovator, he reinterpreted the moral and social principles of China's ancient sage kings in order to make them applicable to the problems of his own age. He did this so successfully that subsequent generations have looked to him for norms and standards.

Confucius was born at Ch'ü-fou in the ancient Chinese state of Lu, now the province of Shantung. With the exception of about ten years of wandering (493–484 B.C.), Confucius spent all his life in Lu, in search of a ruler who would make him head of government. He won recognition for his scholarly ability, but never attained a responsible post that would enable him to put into practice his ideas for reforming society and putting an end to the wars that were devastating China. By the time of the first biography of Confucius in the second century B.C. he had come to be glorified as both a statesman and a sage.

The only reliable sources of our knowledge of Confucius are writings prior to the Han dynasty (206 B.C.–A.D. 220), especially the ANALECTS, a collection of sayings, many of which are attributed to Confucius, while others are ascribed to his disciples. The collection was probably compiled shortly after the great teacher's death, but other material seems to have been added later, some of which has a distinctly non-Confucian tone.

The Confucius we encounter in the *Analects* is an ambitious scholar, eager to reinterpret the lessons of the past and use them to solve the problems of the present. He believed that there is a morality inherent in the universe, and that those who flout it will be punished by the impersonal power he called "heaven" (*T'ien*). The family should be regulated by a clearly defined, mutual relationship of love and responsibility between father and son, husband and wife, and older and younger siblings. Government should be administered for the good of all the people by officials of high personal integrity, well trained in the wisdom of the past and loyal to their ruler.

Courtesy of the Philadelphia Museum of Art: Given by Horace H. F. Jayne

*Portrait of Confucius*

To achieve his goal he gathered about him ambitious young men—some nobly born, some from the lower classes. The only qualifications demanded were ability and a willingness to learn. They were attracted to him by his magnetic personality, his love of scholarship, and the prospect of a political career. Confucius challenged them to become examples of manhood at its best, possessing wisdom and the supreme moral quality of *jen,* variously translated as "human-heartedness," "Goodness," or "benevolent love." Of the twenty-two disciples mentioned by name in the *Analects,* nine are known to have held important positions. Later tradition increased the number of known names and the importance of their achievements.

Confucius himself was not an eloquent speaker and does not seem to have been cut out for a career in politics. He would praise a person behind his back but criticize him to his face. The *Analects* show him telling an occasional untruth and giving way to temper and tender grief. He saw music as an important subject for study and taught that some music builds up morality while other music leads to depravity. Creel has called him a "zealot with a sense of humor."

In his late sixties, after several years of wandering, Confucius returned to Lu. In the next few years death took from his circle his only son and his two favorite disciples. Shortly before his own death Confucius wrote, "To remain unsoured even though one's merits are unrecognized, is that not what after all is expected

of a Gentleman?" (*Analects* I, 1) and "At seventy, I could follow the dictates of my own heart, for what I desired no longer overstepped the boundaries of right" (II, 4).

K.C.

**CONGREGATION.** People assembled, especially for religious purposes, as in worship. Six Hebrew words, translated as congregation, (for example, Ps. 1:5) are used both for religious and for political assemblies (for example, "the mount of assembly in the far north," Isa. 14:13), a Ugaritic phrase for a plenary session of the gods.). In the Septuagint and NT, *ecclesia* (church) and *synagogé* (synagogue) are used interchangeably. Amid tensions of the NT period, Jews favored the term synagogue and Christians the term church (see Rev. 3:9 "synagogue of Satan").

P.L.G.

**CONGREGATIONAL CHURCHES.** A historic, free church tradition in Protestantism, once an American denomination; now merged with the Evangelical and Reformed Church to form the UNITED CHURCH OF CHRIST.

Congregationalism, as a preference in church polity, is sometimes traced to the early church, or to the sectarian movements of the high Middle Ages, or to JOHN WYCLIFFE and the Lollard movement in sixteenth-century England. What is certain is that Congregationalism developed after the rise of the Protestant Reformation in the British Isles.

Congregationalists are defined as Christians who hold that Jesus Christ is the only head of the church; that the Bible is the all-sufficient rule of faith and practice; that Christian character is the standard for church membership; and that sovereignty in church government lies in the local congregation, made up of God's people, covenanted together to walk in the ways of the Lord.

The English Separatists (called the Pilgrims) brought Congregationalism to America on the Mayflower in 1620. The Mayflower Compact, signed at Plymouth, Massachusetts, established a government for the colony based on the will of the majority. This played a signal role in the development of religion and politics in the colony, and in the nation later established.

The Pilgrims, or PURITANS, desired an educated ministry, and founded Harvard College in 1636 for that purpose. In 1701, the Congregationalists in Connecticut founded Yale and later Dartmouth, Williams, Bowdoin, Middlebury, and Amherst.

The Congregationalists did not believe in the separation of church and state, and so in the states where they were strong they founded a union of both to form a Christian commonwealth. This union was not broken until the nineteenth century. After this disestablishment, the denomination expanded across the continent, especially in the states of the Old Northwest.

Congregationalism is non-creedal, so it has little fixed dogma. In England, the church held to the Savoy Declaration. In America their theology was fluid and changing. In response to eighteenth-century RATIONALISM and in reaction to CALVINISM, the Congregationalists divided into Unitarians and Trinitarians. In the nineteenth century, Liberalism captured most Congregational Churches and this outlook continued into the twentieth century. At the same time, some congregations remained evangelical and conservative. In the twentieth century Congregationalists have embraced ecumenism and the search for church unity. Thus the Congregational church (or most of its congregations) entered the merger that resulted in the United Church of Christ in 1957.

J.C.

**CONSCIENCE.** In biblical writing "conscience" occurs only once in the OT and twenty-eight times in the NT. The Greek word is *syneidēsis,* meaning that aspect of the human psyche that "knows with itself," as an agent or faculty within the moral life that observes the self and witnesses to what it sees, whether approvingly (a *good* conscience) or not (a *bad* conscience).

There is a long history of the term in Greek thought, which usually understands the word as an accusing conscience. The most famous example is Orestes (in the play-cycle of Aeschylus), who killed his mother and looked on his conscience as his enemy that eventually destroyed him. The Stoic philosophers gave to conscience the role of a watchman who maintained a vigilant guard of an individual's inner life and encouraged the person to live "according to nature" or in response to the logos or reason that informed one as to moral decision making. This is clearly an important background to the NT picture of conscience, since it gave rise to the notion of a moral arbiter implanted within the human psyche (see Rom. 2:14-15).

The OT evidence is sparse, and the literature has no distinct word for conscience. The precise term occurs (in the RSV) in I Samuel 25:31, where it translates the Hebrew word for "heart" (see also I Sam. 24:5; II Sam. 24:10: David's heart "smote" him to remind him of his guilty actions). The Greek *syneidēsis* is found only in three late or intertestamental passages (Eccl. 10:20; Wisd. Sol. 17:11; Ecclus. 42:18). These verses reflect Greek ideas, especially Wisdom 17:11, where conscience plays the part of a court prosecutor. The Hebrew contribution to the development of conscience is thus limited, emphasizing the inwardness of moral decisions and human accountability before God.

The NT data are unusually distributed; the term is entirely absent from the Gospels (John 8:9 is a secondary text, printed only in the RSV margin). The bulk of the evidence comes from Paul, especially in his Corinthian correspondence. This fact has given rise to the suggestion that it was the freewheeling Corinthian Christians who appealed to conscience to justify their lax morality. They professed to be able to eat idol meats with a clear conscience, and so (they contended) their actions were permissible. Paul took up their word and argued against them by insisting that conscience alone is not a clear guide. A person cannot rely on such subjective responses (see I Cor. 4:4: "I have nothing on my conscience,"—an ironical statement, if it represents the Corinthians' position. Paul goes on immediately to qualify and correct it: "but that does not mean I stand acquitted" NEB).

Conscience needs to be educated and informed by some outside norm. It is interesting to see what Paul proposed as to these guidelines for human behavior. Weak Christians who are disturbed at the prospect of eating food offered to idols are afflicted with a bad conscience (v. 8:7, 10, 12). They need to learn how their consciences can be instructed, since "an idol has no real existence" (I Cor. 8:4). But equally the strong or enlightened Corinthians who claimed that freedom and ate with impunity have a responsibility not to wound the conscience of the sensitive brother (8:12); so love for one's fellow believer is a norm to keep conscience in place and subordinate it to higher imperatives (I Cor. 10:23-33). To appeal simply to conscience may be disastrous since, for Paul, it individualizes human action by being forgetful of one's social concerns. We need to respect not only our moral convictions but those of others.

In the later Pauline church, conscience became a debated topic. The Pastoral Letters echo this dispute with the sad reminder that some believers have so missed their way that they despise a good conscience (I Tim. 1:5, 6, 19), and have their conscience "seared" (that is, rendered insensitive) as with a hot iron (4:2). Deacons should aim to keep a clear conscience (3:9), but it is obvious that this is not an easy or an automatic process. Hence the call for allegiance to the apostolic "deposit" of the faith sounded in these Pastoral Letters.

The remaining NT documents emphasize the power of Christ to "cleanse the conscience" (Heb. 9:14; 10:22; compare 9:9, 10; 10:2; I Pet. 3:12; the verses are mostly drawn from OT ideas of forgiveness and moral renewal). Here conscience functions negatively in convicting people of their sins, and so it needs appeasing by the assurance of divine pardon. But as a guide to moral actions, conscience serves only with a limited scope. It needs to be measured against an objective norm, usually the will of God as revealed in Scripture, experience, and a concern for our lives in society.

R.M.

**CONSCIENTIOUS OBJECTOR.** *See* PACIFICISM.

**CONSECRATE.** To bless or set apart for God's service, as in the consecraton of the elements at Holy Communion or the consecration of a missionary. To consecrate means to invoke or call down upon a person, place, activities, or things, the power of God through the Holy Spirit. It also means to set apart certain believers for special offices or functions, as in the consecration of a bishop or a pope. Buildings and material objects are often consecrated, as in the consecration or blessing of a cathedral, a church or an altar, a cross or communion vessels. So seriously is this act of blessing taken that church buildings that are abandoned or sold are solemnly removed from God's service by use of a special service. The practice of consecration is as old as biblical religion. The Hebrews were set apart by CIRCUMCISION; Christians are set apart by BAPTISM.

J.C.

**CONSERVATIVE JUDAISM.** *See* JUDAISM, HISTORY OF.

**CONSISTORY.** A gathering of cardinals and sometimes of bishops, convened in the Roman Catholic church to transact business. Secret consistories are called to create cardinals and appoint bishops to vacant dioceses. In the Reformed church, it is the lowest court, made up of minister and elders in a congregation.

J.C.

**CONSTANCE, COUNCIL OF.** A general council of the church that met from 1414 to 1418 and marked the high point of CONCILIARISM. It was called by John XXIII, Pisan pope, at the insistence of Emperor Sigismund, mostly in order to put an end to the GREAT SCHISM. John XXIII hoped that the council would support his claims over those of Gregory XII and the Avignon Pope Benedict XIII, especially since he represented the line of the popes resulting from the earlier Council of Pisa. But the assembly, under the leadership of PIERRE D'AILLY, thought otherwise, and John deemed it best to flee and seek to have the council dissolved. Captured and returned to Constance as a prisoner, he was deposed by the assembly. Gregory XII resigned, as he had promised to do. Benedict continued calling himself Pope for the rest of his life, but his followers diminished constantly. Therefore, the Council of Constance effectively put an end to the Great Schism. After having promised to continue the work of reforming the church, Martin V was elected pope.

The council also dealt with the teachings of JOHN WYCLIFFE and JOHN HUSS. The former, who had died earlier, was declared a heretic, and his remains were ordered disintered from consecrated ground. Huss, who had gone to the council under Sigismund's safe conduct, was declared a heretic and burned at the stake. This caused a revolt in Bohemia.

The hope that the council would reform the church proved unfounded. Although decrees were passed against simony, pluralism, and other abuses, these were generally ignored once the council was dissolved. Finally, the council ordered that other such assemblies would be convened periodically, thus hoping to continue the work of reformation.

J.G.

Courtesy of the Metropolitan Museum of Art. Bequest of Mrs. F. F. Thompson, 1926

*Marble head of Constantine I*

**CONSTANTINE, EMPEROR.** Emperor from 306 to 337, who put an end to persecution and declared himself a Christian. He was the son of Constantius Chlorus, who ruled in Britain as one of four emperors who shared the empire under the leadership of DIOCLETIAN. On the death of Constantius Chlorus, Constantine was proclaimed his heir by the legions in Britain. After consolidating his power, he invaded the territories of Maxentius, who ruled in Italy, and defeated him in the battle of the Milvian Bridge. It was on the eve of that battle that he ordered his soldiers to fight under the *labarum,* which included a symbol that could be interpreted as a Christian Chi Rho-☧. He later told Eusebius of Caesarea and Lactantius slightly different stories as to how God had directed him to do this. Meanwhile, after defeating his brother-in-law Licinius, he became sole emperor.

During an earlier stay at the court of Diocletian, Constantine had become imbued with Eastern notions of the absolute power of monarchs. These clashed with the earlier Roman traditions, and particularly with the Roman Senate, which resisted such innovations. For this reason and others, Constantine decided to found a "new Rome," which was built at the site of the ancient city of Byzantium, and named Constantinople, that is, "City of Constantine." This gave him greater freedom from the Roman Senate (he created a new senate for the new Rome), and allowed him to grant ever-increasing favors to the church.

The Donatist controversy in North Africa forced Constantine to intervene in the life of the church. In agreement with a number of synods, he decided that the Donatists were at fault. When they refused to abide by his verdict, he had recourse to arms, with the blessing of most orthodox Christian leaders.

The Arian controversy proved even more difficult to solve. After the failure of his advisor in ecclesiastical matters, Hosius of Cordova, to settle the dispute, Constantine decided to convene a great council of bishops, which gathered at NICEA in 325. Although he was not even baptized, he presided at the sessions, thus giving an indication of the CAESAROPAPISM, which would become characteristic of Byzantine Christianity. The council condemned Arius, and to this Constantine added his sentence of banishment for Arius as well as for his main supporters. Three years later, however, he began to reverse his policies, partly through the influence of Arian bishop Eusebius of Nicomedia. It was then that he ordered Athanasius and other Nicene leaders into exile.

Constantine's support for Christianity, continued and increased by most of his successors, gave rise to the Constantinian Era, that is, to a period of over sixteen centuries in which Christianity could usually count on the support of the state. In the Eastern church, he is often called the thirteenth apostle and is counted among the saints.

J.G.

## CONSTANTINOPLE, COUNCILS AND CREED OF.

Three councils gathered at Constantinople are generally considered ecumenical by both Eastern and Western Christians: the First Council of Constantinople (Third Ecumenical), the Second Council of Constantinople (Fifth Ecumenical), and the Third Council of Constantinople (Sixth Ecumenical). Their respective dates are 381, 553, and 680.

The First Council of Constantinople was convened by Emperor Theodosius I in order to settle the ARIANISM dispute. Although Arianism had been condemned by the Council of NICEA in 325, it had gained new strength due to the vacillating policies of Emperor CONSTANTINE and to the outright support of many of his successors, particularly Constantius II. Theodosius, the most powerful emperor after Constantine, was a supporter of the Nicene faith and hoped that the council would put an end to the matter. In general, this was the case, although Arianism later reappeared within the borders of the empire as the result of the invasion of the empire by Goths and others who had become Arians when that was the faith of the emperors.

The so-called Creed of Constantinople, or Niceno-Constantinopolitan Creed, was probably not issued by this council, as has traditionally been held. Essentially, it is the creed that is currently recited in most churches as the Nicene Creed.

The Second Council of Constantinople (Fifth Ecumenical Council) dealt with the controversy of the Three Chapters. Ever since the Council of Chalcedon, Byzantine emperors had sought ways to reconcile their disaffected subjects, particularly in Egypt and Syria, who rejected the decisions of Chalcedon and who therefore were called MONOPHYSITES. Justinian sought to appease them by condemning, not the decisions of Chalcedon, but rather the work of three theologians of the Antiochene school whose views stood behind the condemnation of Eutyches, and whom the Monophysites suspected of Nestorianism. These three theologians were Theodore of Mopsuestia, Theodoret of Cyrrhus, and Ibas of Edessa. Justinian's policy was opposed by many who feared that it would lead to a wholesale condemnation of Antiochene positions, as well as by others, particularly Pope Vigilius, who felt that the emperor had no authority to intervene in matters of doctrine. But Justinian prevailed, and eventually Vigilius and the others had to agree to the condemnation of the "three chapters."

The Third Council of Constantinople (Sixth Ecumenical) was convened by Emperor Constantine IV in order to settle the MONOTHELITE controversy. Monothelitism, proposed at first by Patriarch Sergius of Constantinople, sought to appease the opponents of the "two natures" in Christ—the Monophysites—by declaring that, while there are two natures in Christ, there is only one will. For a time this had the support of Pope Honorius. But the Arab conquests had severed from the empire those areas where Monophysitism was strongest, and therefore the emperors were no longer interested in finding a theological compromise with those who rejected the Council of Chalcedon. Having lost its political value, Monothelitism was abandoned by the authorities and was therefore condemned by the Third Council of Constantinople. Throughout the Middle Ages, the Byzantine Church held several other councils at Constantinople. But these were generally of lesser importance.

J.G.

## CONSUBSTANTIATION.

A Eucharistic doctrine that holds that the substance of Christ's body and blood is conjoined with the substance of the bread and wine in the EUCHARIST. The doctrine dates to John

Wycliffe, who affirmed the identity of Christ's body and blood with the total sacramental use of bread and wine in the Mass. Perhaps because of their knowledge of Wycliffe and the British tradition, many British and American Protestants (Presbyterian, Methodist, and Baptist) have mistakenly identified the Lutheran doctrine of the REAL PRESENCE of Christ in the Eucharist with consubstantiation. Lutherans have never accepted the term or the description of consubstantiation. The chief reason for this is that consubstantiation is (like TRANSUBSTANTIATION) a philosophical explanation of what is a mystery of faith, which should be received in faith. Lutherans understand that Christ is really present in, with, and under the bread and the wine, while the bread and wine remain natural objects. They do not teach a union of Christ's body and blood with the bread and wine that would continue beyond the actual sacramental use of that bread and wine in the Eucharist. There is, therefore, no reservation or adoration of the host in Lutheran churches.

J.C.

## CONSULTATION ON CHURCH UNION
(COCU). Continuing formal conversations between several American Protestant denominations, held almost annually since 1960. COCU was proposed by Eugene Carson Blake of the United Presbyterian Church in the U.S.A. in a sermon at Grace Cathedral in San Francisco, in 1960. The plan became known as the Blake-Pike proposal. Enthusiasm was great for this ECUMENICAL venture in the 1960s, but waned in the 1970s. The 1980s have seen a return to interest in COCU since the merger of the northern and southern Presbyterian churches. Principles of church union were worked out, and in 1968 a plan of union was presented with the suggestion that it be considered by participating churches by 1970. The plan of union was not adopted because of the movement toward conservatism in America and the loss of interest in ecumenicity. The principles of church union declared: The church of Jesus Christ is one and that oneness ought to become visible; renewal is needed in the churches and an emphasis on mission and servanthood should be central to union; the laity should be fully involved in the ministry of the church; new forms of the church are needed in our complex society; and a church to be reconciling must first be reconciled.

J.C.

## CONTEMPLATIVE LIFE.
The name given to a life devoted mostly to prayer and devotional exercises—particularly the DIVINE OFFICE, meditation, silence, and fasting. Although every form of MONASTICISM, and indeed, all religious life, involves a measure of contemplation, certain orders, such as the Carthusians, Cistercians, and the Carmelite nuns, are known as the contemplative orders.

J.G.

## CONTRITION.
A theological term meaning "change of heart, inner sorrow, and regret for sin." Contrition is said to be imperfect if motivated by fear; perfect if motivated by the sincere love of God. Imperfect contrition is known as attrition. Perfect contrition brings the remission of one's sins. (*Compare also* PENANCE.)

J.C.

## CONVERSION.
To be changed inwardly, to turn to God, to be reborn; a shift from SIN to REPENTANCE and faith. Lutherans and Calvinists teach that such an experience of conversion is entirely the work of God through the Holy Spirit. Roman Catholics and Arminians (many Methodists, Baptists, and sectarians) declare that the person cooperates with God. The place, if any, of human cooperation (contrition; piety) in conversion has been hotly debated for centuries, and the controversy remains active among theologians, although it no longer is a barrier to cooperation between denominations. In the Bible, the word for conversion in Hebrew is *shub*, "to turn" or "to return," and in Greek, *metanoia*, "to turn around." To be converted means to have the direction of one's life shifted, so that it no longer points toward self, but points toward God. For example, Yahweh declares to the weary and complaining Jeremiah: "Therefore thus says the Lord: 'If you return, I will restore you, and you shall stand before me'" (Jer. 15:19).

This conditional "if" is in line with the basic theology of the Mosaic covenant, "*if* you do my will, *then* I will establish you." However, other references to turning to God, even in the same prophetic book, are less inclined toward the divine action and human response motif than they are to the predestinarian call of the sovereign God: "Before I formed you in the womb, I knew you, and before you were born I consecrated you; I appointed you a prophet to the nations" (Jer. 1:5).

Of course, the outlines of Jeremiah's call are in the mind of Paul, when he describes his own call in Galatians 1:13-17. Paul's call came into his consciousness only after a dramatic conversion experience (Acts 9:3-19; 22:4-16; 26:9-18; Gal. 1:13-17). Indeed, Paul's declaration in Galatians 1:15: "But when he who had set me apart before I was born, and had called me through his grace . . ." is clearly the same sentiment as Jeremiah expressed in Jeremiah 1:5. We may summarize by observing that God, in grace, always "converts" or "turns" the person, but there is also the opportunity for the person undergoing conversion to respond, even if it is only with a question like Paul's in Acts 9: "Who are you, Lord?"

Both Jeremiah's and Paul's experiences point out another aspect of conversion not usually understood in popular religion, and that is the possibility of several conversions (that is, Jeremiah's original call and his later need to convert or turn again; and Paul's belief that he was called from birth but became converted only on the road to Damascus). Conversions are not necessarily once for all. It seems human beings may be unaware of the depth of their dependence on God, or grow cold in their faith, or even fall away, and subsequently experience conversion again. This is what happened to Peter (Matt. 26:75; Mark 14:72; Luke 22:32—"when you have turned again"; Luke 22:62), although the Letter to the Hebrews declares such a second conversion is impossible. (Interestingly, the early Catholic church refused to accept this view in its struggle with the Montanists, over the readmission to fellowship of those who renounced Christ under persecution.) Conversion, as a turning to a more lively relationship with God through Christ, may be seen as any time of increased awareness of God's presence in one's life and of recommitment to God's service.

The term conversion is still used, although inappropriately, to mean a change of membership from one denomination to another. Before Vatican II, the Roman Catholic church followed this practice. Today, the Decree on Ecumenism speaks only of "becoming reconciled" with the Catholic church. Properly used, "conversion," in the sense of joining a church, should be used only for those coming to faith from atheism or from non-Christian religions. (*See also* BORN AGAIN.)

J.C.

**CONVOCATION.** From the Latin word *convocatio*, for "calling together." An ecclesiastical group called together to discuss church affairs. In the Roman Catholic tradition, convocations are usually of bishops only, but the Church of England uses the term in a special way. The provinces or dioceses of Canterbury and of York describe their diocesan conventions or assemblies as "convocations" and have done so for centuries. These convocations includes both the upper house of bishops and the lower house of ordinary priests. A convocation is prorogued or summoned by the archbishop. In York, this summons is given to each diocesan bishop; in Canterbury, to the bishop of London, who is dean of the province. Those attending the convocations, which traditionally are governed by the crown, are exempt from arrest while in session, in the same manner as members of Parliament. Convocations may pass acts of convocation, but they have no standing in British law.

J.C.

**COPTIC CHURCH.** The largest Christian church in Egypt, called Coptic because that is its liturgical language. After the COUNCIL OF CHALCEDON, most of the Egyptian population felt that Dioscorus had been wronged and that the council's decisions were heretical. This was coupled with resentment against the Greek-speaking authorities in Constantinople and against their representatives in Alexandria. In spite of many efforts to prevent the schism, eventually most Egyptian Christians left the communion of the imperial church. Since they rejected the doctrine of "two natures" of Chalcedon, they were dubbed MONOPHYSITES by the Orthodox, whom they in turn called Melchites—that is, imperial Christians.

After the Arab conquests, most Egyptian Christians left the Melchite communion and joined the dissident Monophysites. Since Coptic (a language derived from ancient Egyptian with many Greek accretions) was the language of this church, it came to be known as the Coptic church. In the eighteenth century a few thousand Copts joined the Roman Catholic communion, and to this day there is a small Coptic UNIATE body.

J.G.

**CORBAN.** An Aramaic word meaning "something set apart for or as a gift to God." According to the Mishnah, anything set apart as corban, even rashly, could not thereafter be used for any other purpose. Jesus' teaching in Mark 7:11-13 reflects the strictness with which this rule was then practiced.

P.L.G.

**CORINTH.** Located just south of the isthmus that joins the Peloponnesus to the mainland of Greece, Corinth served as a transshipping center for two ports: Cenchreae on the east, through which flowed trade to and from Egypt, Asia Minor, and Syria; Lechaeum on the west, with access to Italy, Rome, and the west. The southern end of the Peloponnesus was a notoriously dangerous place for ships because of storms and currents. Accordingly, shippers and sailors preferred the minor inconvenience of transporting their cargoes across the isthmus at Corinth in order to sail in the safety of the protected gulfs that led to the city in both directions. The city benefited enormously from the stream of commerce moving through it.

Corinth was almost completely destroyed in 146 B.C., following a war with the Romans, who were then a rising power in the West. Only vivid memory and ruins remained in the first century of the notorious Temple of Aphrodite, the goddess of love, whose shrine once had stood on the ridge of the massive rock, nearly two thousand feet high, which overlooks the site of the ancient city of Corinth.

The central marketplace, or Agora, was the location of the public rostrum (*bēma*) at which Paul's hearing before the Roman proconsul, Gallio, is described as taking place in Acts 18. An inscription from the time of Gallio's term in office was found in Delphi, a short distance north of Corinth, which enables us to determine the date of his consulship over the province of Achaia (which included Athens and Corinth). Its date is the equivalent of A.D. 52. Also surviving from the ruins of Corinth in this period are the remains of the Temple of Apollo and of a theater. These serve as vivid reminders of the vitality of Greek

and into the nature of the problems that arose in Christian communities where former pagans greatly outnumbered former Jews. The first letter takes up the issues point by point, which provides the modern reader with a primer on church problems. The second letter is not as organized, so that the argument is harder to follow. Indeed, some scholars have proposed that these letters as we know them are composites of fragments of several letters. But the practice of dictating letters that Paul followed (Rom. 16:22; I Cor. 16:21) probably accounts for the awkward transitions in these letters.

*Other Letters Between Paul and the Corinthians.* In I Corinthians 5:9 Paul refers to an earlier letter he had sent to Corinth, and he is responding to specific questions that they had asked in a letter to him (I Cor. 7:1). In II Corinthians 2:2 and 7:8 he mentions what is probably yet another letter of his in which he had sharply rebuked the Corinthians for their behavior and their attitude toward him. There is no doubt that the conditions within the churches at CORINTH and the vicinity were very much on Paul's mind and heart when he was at work in other churches in Macedonia and Asia Minor.

*Basic Issues.* Two broad questions that Paul addresses in the opening part of what we call I Corinthians are wisdom and apostolic authority. Some Corinthians were scornful of Paul because he did not use the style and substance of "wisdom"—that is, of intellectual speculation about how knowledge of God is granted to human beings. If Acts 18:24-28 gives us an accurate picture of Apollos, then the followers of Apollos in the internal struggle at Corinth (I Cor. 1:12; 3:5) may have admired his intellectual and rhetorical skills, comparing them with Paul's simple and more direct style to Paul's discredit. Paul's response was that the message of salvation through Jesus Christ was not expressed in the proud words of human wisdom, but was disclosed in what is—humanly speaking—foolishness and weakness: the cross. The Spirit of God communicates the message of true power to those who are attuned to hear. The upbuilding of the church requires people with a range of skills. Each must follow responsibly the assigned role, avoiding the prideful notion that one task is more important than another. To set up these false values within the church is to destroy it as the place where God dwells among human beings (I Cor. 3:16-17). All the leaders in the church are no more than administrators of power, which is derived solely from God. Paul has willingly accepted his life of obedience, even though it leads to persecution and humiliation rather than to prideful achievement in human eyes (I Cor. 4:1-13). Nevertheless, he has been commissioned by Christ and will exercise authority in Christ's name for settling disputes if the Corinthians have not straightened matters out by the time of his arrival (I Cor. 4:14-21).

At this point in the letter, Paul turns to a series of specific issues that were plaguing the churches at

religion and culture in this city, which was famous for its wealth and its immorality.

Leading west from the Agora was the Lechaeum road, which was lined with shops and residences. Among these would have been the house of Titius Justus, where Paul launched his work in Corinth (Acts 18:7). It adjoined a place where Jews met for study of the Scriptures. An inscription in a stone lintel that presumably read "Synagogue of the Hebrews" was found in this vicinity, but it likely dates from the second century A.D. These modest ruins represent well the informal settings in which both Jews and early Christians met for worship and instruction in this period. Beneath these buildings there ran a system of channels and wells, which provided not only water but also cooled the produce on sale and food for purchase. An inscription from the time of Augustus refers to a meat shop, using the same term as Paul does in I Corinthians 10:25 in warning against Christians eating meat that had been offered to idols.

From the personal references in Paul's letters to the leaders of the church in Corinth, one can infer that the officials there included women (Rom. 16:1), and that they were as prominent as the treasurer of the city (Rom. 16:23). Paul's initial contacts in Corinth were with a business couple, Priscilla and Aquila, who had come from Rome (Acts 18:2) and who later returned there (Rom. 16:3). In Corinth, one of the church groups met in their house (I Cor. 16:19). Thus Paul's work in Corinth demonstrates vividly the new kinds of human relationships that developed in response to the gospel.

H.K.

**I and II CORINTHIANS.** These two letters are nearly as long as all the other authentic letters of Paul combined. They provide us with unmatched insight into the role of Paul in relation to Gentile churches

Corinth and presumably Gentile churches elsewhere as well. The first of these was incest (I Cor. 5), which was considered a gross immorality by the Greeks (as in the story of Oedipus, who married his mother without knowing who she was) as well as by the Jews (Lev. 18). The Christians had condoned a man's marrying his stepmother (I Cor. 5:1), and Paul ordered his expulsion from the community. Rather than settling disputes from within the group, some were turning to the civil courts (I Cor. 6:1-6). The dominant factor in their common life was to share the mutual responsibility that they bore as a body (I Cor. 6:9-20). Corinth had a reputation in the ancient world for loose sexual behavior, and the Christians were living on a par with those low moral standards (I Cor. 7). In view of the imminent end of the age and the urgent need for evangelism, as Paul believed, it was better to be single than married. But he had no notion that to have sexual relationships was inherently evil. Some Christians were buying meat in the marketplace which had initially been presented to an idol. This was a common practice at the time, but some Christians who had converted from pagan religions felt that by eating such meat they were participating in idol worship. Paul declares against the practice (8:13) and then resumes discussion of the issue in I Corinthians 10.

Most of the other subjects Paul treats in I Corinthians concern the internal life of the church: the role of women, to whom he assigns a secondary place (I Cor. 11); the varieties of spiritual—literally, charismatic—gifts which are essential for the life of the church (I Cor. 12–14). In the midst of these discussions he inserts (1) instructions about the central rite by which the church celebrates its origins in the death and exaltation of Christ; the Lord's Supper (I Cor. 11:17-34); and (2) the beautiful words describing Christian love (I Cor. 13). The remaining subjects he covers are the resurrection of the faithful (I Cor. 15) and the financial contribution from the Gentile churches (like that at Corinth) to the Jerusalem Christians (I Cor. 16:1-4).

The final issue is related to one already discussed by Paul in I Corinthians 9—Paul's refusal to accept financial support from the Corinthians. This is in sharp contrast to the policy of those apostles and other leaders who follow the pattern set by Jesus for his followers—that they live from contributions provided by those among whom they minister (I Cor. 9:1-18; compare Mark 6:7-11). Paul knew he could claim such support, but refused to do so, and his refusal led his critics to question that he really was an APOSTLE.

It is this question of Paul's qualification to be an apostle that is the central concern in II Corinthians. The major criticisms of Paul on this score are that he is indecisive (II Cor. 1:15-22), that he lacks formal letters of recommendation from other Christian communities (3:1-3), and that he is not really qualified to be a minister of the New Covenant since

he was never associated with Jesus during the time of Jesus' earthly life. The letter of recommendation was a message sent by one congregation to another that was to be visited by the apostle. The sender seems to have paid for the apostle's transportation and expenses to reach the next place on his itinerary, as stated in Mark 6. The only money and food available was what the community provided. Paul had a fundamentally different view of financial responsibility. He made his own living at a trade and took up collections only for others: the Jerusalem church. He considered his having seen the Risen Lord (I Cor. 9:1; 15:8) and his subsequent visions of Christ (II Cor. 3:18; 4:6; 12:1-4) as of equal value with the original disciples' associations with Jesus. He makes the point directly that he is no longer concerned about Christ "from a human point of view" (II Cor. 5:16). That is, what is important for him and for all Christians is the living Lord, not the earthly Jesus, since in the living Lord everyone shares in the new creation. It is the encounter with the Risen Jesus that resulted in his being commissioned as an agent of God in the reconciliation of the world (II Cor. 5:17-20).

Paul addresses head on the issue of his apostleship by showing how he can match his opponents point for point. They are proud of their Jewish heritage, their descent from Abraham, their role as servants of Christ, their sufferings and revelations (II Cor. 10–12). On all of these Paul can match their qualifications. Where he diverges from them is his refusal to live by their donations. He insists that his financial independence gives him complete freedom in fulfilling his apostolic role (II Cor. 12:13-18). If his detractors want to observe his apostolic authority—in action, not merely in theory—they can wait until his much delayed return to Corinth.

Thus the two preserved letters bear testimony to a basic division among the apostles, in spite of their claim to mutual recognition. For most, their authorization derived from ongoing associations with Jesus during his public career. For Paul, it was the Risen Lord, whose continuing presence with him was confirmed by visions and by the power of the Spirit, who called and qualified Paul to be an apostle.

H.K.

**CORNELIUS.** A Roman centurion in Caesarea whose conversion (Acts 10:1-48) has been called the Gentile Christian Pentecost in parallel with the Jewish Christian Pentecost of Acts 2. The centurion may have been a descendant slave of Cornelius Sulla, who, about 80 B.C., at considerable expense, liberated many slaves. Numbers of these freedmen took the name Cornelius.

Cornelius was "a devout man who feared God with all his household" (Acts 10:2), which means that he followed some Jewish practices, but was not legally a Jewish proselyte. Acts 10:1–13:3 centers on the conversion of GENTILES. At the beginning, Peter is hesitant even to proclaim the gospel to god-fearing, devout Gentiles. But he is persuaded later by the conversion of Cornelius and his household, and by the gift of the Holy Spirit "even on Gentiles" (10:45). Peter had to defend his new insight before the Jerusalem church (11:1-18). The story ends with the gospel being preached to Gentiles who have no connection with Judaism (11:20), the conversion of "a great number," and is climaxed by the sending out of Barnabus and Saul by the Antioch church—the first Christian missionaries to Gentile lands.

P.L.G.

**CORPUS CHRISTI, FEAST OF.** A Roman Catholic feast and procession, which dates from the mid-thirteenth century, honoring the REAL PRESENCE of Christ in the Eucharist. This is a doctrinal festival, which aims to encourage frequent communion and the instruction of the faithful in the teachings of the church about Christ's real presence (that is, transubstantiation) in the Mass and to encourage devotion to it.

From the eleventh century to the thirteenth, reception of Communion declined, and several controversies over the belief that Christ was present in the Eucharist erupted. The Berengarian controversy in the mid-eleventh century and the practice of simply gazing on the consecrated host rather than personally communing were elements in this theological confusion. In the midst of this, Juliana of Liege (in A.D. 1209) reported a vision that called for a Eucharistic feast. This was not immediately accepted, but interest in such a new festival grew, and Corpus Christi (the Body of Christ) was celebrated for the first time in A.D. 1247. The practice was extended by the pope, Urban IV, to the universal church in A.D. 1264. The procession became the major part of the feast in the fourteenth century. This procession takes place after Mass, and the host displayed is one consecrated at the Mass celebrated earlier that day.

J.C.

**CORRELATION.** This theological method is especially associated with PAUL TILLICH, though a similar method has been used by many theologians both before and since his time. The method uses an anthropological approach, that is to say, it begins with an analysis of the present human and cultural situation and then tries to present the material of the Christian revelation as answers to the questions arising out of the culture. Such a method in theology certainly avoids the danger of irrelevance, which might affect a theology that simply expounds the KERYGMA without attention to the cultural context. Moreover, if the method is applied conscientiously, Tillich believes that it will genuinely evoke answers from the revelation, and not just spin them out of the questions themselves. But the objection is raised by kerygmatic theologians that by allowing the culture to specify the questions, one has already determined the kind of answers that the revelation is permitted to

give, and that one has also to consider the critical questions that the revelation raises for the culture.

J.M.

**CORRUPT TEXT.** A term used in the textual study (lower criticism) of the Bible to refer to a passage that has been modified in the transmission of the text to express a theological viewpoint or to harmonize it with a parallel passage. An example is I John 5:7 in the Authorized (King James) Version.

J.C.

**COSMOLOGICAL ARGUMENT.** See GOD'S EXISTENCE, ARGUMENTS FOR.

**COTTON, JOHN** (1584–1652). This Massachusetts Bay pastor was born in Derby, England, on December 4. Educated at Trinity College, Cambridge (A.B. 1603; A.M. 1606), he taught six years at Emmanuel College, a PURITAN stronghold. Ordained deacon and priest in 1610 at Lincoln, in 1612 he went to St. Botolph's at Boston in Lincolnshire, where he began to alter the liturgy to Puritan tastes. The bishop was tolerant, but Cotton resigned May 7, 1633. On July 3, 1613, he married Elizabeth Harrocks. After her death in 1630 he married Sarah Hawkridge Story on April 25, 1632.

Already interested in New England, and a friend of JOHN WINTHROP, he arrived in Boston, Massachusetts, on September 4, 1633. Serving as teacher to the Boston church until his death December 23, 1652, he became embroiled in controversies against ROGER WILLIAMS and ANNE HUTCHINSON.

Cotton published a number of books including *The Keyes of the Kingdom of Heaven* (1644), *The Way of the Churches of Christ in New England* (1645), and *Milk for Babes* (1646). He stressed the unconditional nature of ELECTION and the inner experience of the Spirit in regeneration.

N.H.

**COUNCILS OF CHURCHES.** See the place-names.

**COUNSELOR.** See HOLY SPIRIT.

**COUNSELS OF PERFECTION.** Stringent ethical commandments and ideals believed to be superior to and more suited to a life of perfection than the ordinary precepts required of all Christians to attain eternal life. They are based on certain NT passages: the Sermon on the Mount (Matt. 5–7) calls for love of enemies, Matthew 19:21 demands absolute poverty, I Corinthians 7 poses virginity as superior to marriage. Such commands seemed not for all but only for those voluntarily seeking perfection.

A higher-lower way of Christian living developed, mentioned by the Shepherd of Hermas, Tertullian, Cyprian, Ambrose, Pelagius, and Augustine. The traditional monastic vows of voluntary poverty, chastity, and obedience in Roman Catholicism came to symbolize the counsels of perfection. As a result salvation could be merited more quickly than in ordinary Christian living, and those honoring the counsels could even earn extra merits for others. Thomas Aquinas further developed the counsels of perfection as exalted expressions of love. However, the reformers led by Martin Luther rejected the notion of a higher-lower way as leading to false pride and devaluing ordinary Christian living. Luther declared we are justified by faith alone; the commandments convict us of sin; they do not establish less and more meritorious ways of life.

C.M.

**COUNTER REFORMATION.** *See* CATHOLIC REFORMATION.

**COVENANT.** *Definition.* The term "covenant" translates a Hebrew word in the OT whose primary meaning is "a binding pact" or "a compact." It is used of alliances between people, for example, Abraham and the Amorites (Gen. 14:13), Joshua and the Gibeonites (Josh. 9:6 ff), Israel and the Canaanites (Exod. 23:32), Solomon and Hiram (I Kings 5:2-6). But most often it refers to the agreement between God and humans, for example, Noah (Gen. 9:9-17), Abraham, Isaac, and Jacob (Gen. 15:18; 17:2-21, etc.), Israel at Sinai (Exod. 19:5; 24:7), Joshua and Israel (Josh. 24:25), and the prophetic covenant (Jer. 31:31). All such covenants are conditional, being predicated on stipulated terms at the time of ratification. In the cases of covenants between God and humans, the stipulations are made by God, and people have the choice of accepting or rejecting but not of offering alternative conditions. If people accept the conditions they will be blessed according to the terms of the agreement as long as they keep it or cursed if they violate it. The Israelites were promised the land of Canaan if they would keep the covenant; if not, the land would "vomit them out" (Lev. 18:24-30). The idea is clearly expressed in the Greek translations of the word, where the term *diatheke,* meaning "unilateral agreement," is chosen rather than the term *suntheke,* meaning "bilateral agreement." The latter term would suggest a treaty rather than a unilateral covenant in which all terms were dictated by God.

*Old and New Covenants.* Jesus spoke of the wine at the institution of the Lord's Supper as being a (new) covenant in his blood, which is poured out for the forgiveness of sins (Matt. 26:28). He was apparently thinking of the covenant spoken of by Jeremiah, which was to be a future blessing to Israel, associated in the minds of most with the coming of the Messiah (31:31 ff). The author of Hebrews quotes this passage in his eighth chapter and speaks of the "first covenant" (that is, the Mosaic) as one that is "becoming obsolete and growing old and is ready to vanish away" (8:13). He calls the Second Covenant (8:7) a "new covenant" (8:13), which is necessitated

by the imperfections of the old one. Since he speaks of the tabernacle ritual as a part of the first covenant (9:1-11), which clearly refers to the Mosaic covenant received on Sinai (Exod. 25-31), it is clear that his intention is to contrast the Mosaic covenant with the new one spoken of by Jeremiah (Heb. 8:8-9). However, the covenant that Moses received on Sinai was an addition to the original one God gave to Abraham (Gen. 12:1 ff; 15:1 ff.) according to the argument of Paul in Galatians, where he seems to divide the covenant into LAW and PROMISE. The Law given to Moses came 430 years after the promise made to Abraham and in no way disannulled it (Gal. 3:19). Both the promise and the Law are called covenants, as the above quotations show. The argument in both Galatians and Hebrews is that God through Christ fulfilled the pomise God made to Abraham (that is, God would bless all nations through Abraham's seed) and thereby made the Law obsolete because it was given to only one nation, Israel. The old covenant was national and therefore limited; the new one is international and therefore unlimited. Such is the inherent implication of the establishment of true monotheism (Rom. 3:29) by the death and resurrection of Christ (Rom. 3:21-26).

*Covenant and Testament.* The question of the relation between covenant and TESTAMENT arises by the fact that the new covenant is commonly called the New Testament, and thus designates the Christian part of the Bible in most translations, the Jewish part being called the Old Testament. The same Greek and Hebrew words lie behind the differing translations. Testament derives from the Latin term *testamentum,* which means "a will" and requires the death of the testator for the will to become effective.

This clearly creates a problem in Hebrews 9:15-18, because the one who made the first testament was God and God by definition cannot die. Thus the author argues that animal sacrifices provided the required death by substitutionary atonement. The Jerusalem Bible translates verse 18 as follows: "that explains why even the earlier covenant needed something to be killed in order to take effect." The handling of these difficult verses, in which the same Greek word occurs throughout, is not uniform in the modern translations. While the KJV renders the term consistently "testament," in verses 15, 16, and 18, the *Living Bible* and Phillips render it "agreement, will, testament." The NIV, TEV, RSV, and Jerusalem Bible translate it "covenant, will, covenant," while the NEB reads "covenant, or testament" in verse 15, "testament" in 16, and "covenant" in 18. Perhaps the meaning in the broadest context is that Christ put both covenants into effect by his death. When the author of Hebrews quotes Jeremiah, which has the same term throughout the passage in both Hebrew and Greek, he replaces the OT term meaning "put the covenant into effect" (8:9) with one meaning simply "make a covenant," when referring to the old covenant, but allows the term "put into effect" to stand in reference to the new covenant (8:8, 10). He seems to be arguing that God never actually ratified the old covenant but rather only temporarily made it, using the blood of animals to substitute for the required death until Christ came, who gave both covenants validity simultaneously but also at the same time replacing the former with the latter.

J.R.M.

**COVENANT THEOLOGY.** *See* FEDERAL THEOLOGY.

**COVERDALE, MILES** (1488–1569). A translator of the Bible and devotional works, a preacher, and bishop of Exeter. Born in Yorkshire, he studied theology at Cambridge, was ordained a priest (1514), and joined the Augustinian monastery. Influenced by Lutheran ideas, he left the monastery and preached against Roman Catholicism. He fled to the Continent in 1528 and in 1535 completed the first English Bible translation. Based on TYNDALE's NT and various German and Latin texts, it was printed in Geneva and dedicated to Henry VIII. Later English translations drew freely from it. In 1538 Thomas Cromwell commissioned Coverdale to make an official Bible translation for the Anglican Church. *The Great Bible, 1539,* for which he was a principal collaborator, was consigned to be placed in all English parishes. When Henry executed Cromwell, Coverdale left England for eight years, returning in 1548 to serve Edward VI. He became bishop of Exeter, 1551, but was jailed for two years by Queen Mary and later refused to honor Elizabeth's Act of Uniformity.

C.M.

**COWL.** A long, flowing robe with wide sleeves and a hood typically worn by monks. The cowl is presented to the monk upon his vows of profession. Most Benedictine cowls are black, and Cistercian and some Benedictine orders wear white. Sometimes the cowl is thought to be only the hood.

J.C.

**COWPER, WILLIAM** (1731–1800). Cowper wrote such hymns as "O! For a Closer Walk with God," "God Moves in a Mysterious Way," and "There Is a Fountain Filled with Blood."

Cowper was born on November 15 to a Church of England minister in Berkhampstead, whose wife died when William was six. Cowper was educated at Westminster and called to the bar in 1754. For nine years he practiced law and wrote satire and ballads for the press. Then, anxious over possible appointment as a clerk to the House of Lords, he attempted suicide three times. Fear that he was forever condemned by God haunted him for the remainder of his life.

To recover he spent two years at Huntingdon with his friend Mary Unwin, and the rest of his life at Olney under the influence of the equally despondent JOHN NEWTON. After another suicide attempt,

Unwin suggested he write poetry as a therapy. His first volume was published in 1782. He wrote productively until her death in 1796 plunged him again into a "fixed despair."

His famous *Olney Hymns* also include "Sometimes a Light Surprises," "Hark, My Soul! It Is the Lord," and "Jesus, Where'er Thy People Meet."

N.H.

**COX, HARVEY.** One of contemporary theology's most perceptive analysts of recent cultural and political currents as they bear upon religion and the church. An ordained Baptist minister, Cox was educated at the University of Pennsylvania (B.A., 1951), Yale Divinity School (B.D., 1955), and Harvard (Ph.D., 1963). Since 1965, he has been professor of church and society at Harvard Divinity School.

Cox is best known for his widely discussed book, *The Secular City* (1965). Building on themes found in F. Gogarten's analysis of the Bible's radical historicization of human life and D. Bonhoeffer's reflections on a "religionless" Christianity, Cox finds the life-style of the modern secular city to be consistent with biblical theology. The Israelite story of the Creation, Exodus, and the Covenant prohibition against idolatry all point to the desacralization of nature and the relativity of all political and cultural values. Cox sees the Bible as liberating humans to harness nature and to adopt entirely provisional and pragmatic attitudes toward politics and culture.

Four years later, in an apparent reversal of secular theology, Cox extolled the latest vogue: festivity, ritual, fantasy, and utopian thinking, in *Feast of Fools* (1969). Cox is also author of *Seduction of the Spirit* (1974) and *Turning East* (1979).

J.L.

**CRANMER, THOMAS** (1489–1556). English religious reformer, archbishop of Canterbury, chief author of the Forty-two Articles, which became the THIRTY-NINE ARTICLES of the Anglican church, liturgist, and Protestant martyr.

Educated at Cambridge University, he was ordained about 1520 and later achieved a doctorate in theology. In 1529 he suggested that HENRY VIII not wait for Rome to annul his marriage to Catherine but let the universities of Europe pass judgment. Henry rewarded Cranmer by making him royal chaplain, archdeacon of Taunton, and a diplomatic envoy. Having married in 1532, Cranmer hesitated to accept Henry's invitation to be archbishop of Canterbury, but Rome confirmed the nomination. Consecrated in 1533, less than two months later he declared Henry's marriage to Catherine invalid, and five days later he legalized Henry's earlier secret marriage to Anne Boleyn.

Cranmer promoted royal supremacy and along with Parliament pronounced Henry head of the Church of England. He encouraged Bible translations into English, tried to unite Lutherans and Anglicans under Henry's liberalized Ten Articles of 1536, and was ready to go further than Henry with REFORMATION practices. As religious adviser to EDWARD VI he started reforms that changed Anglicanism. He approved clerical marriages and the abolition of numerous papal ceremonies. He wrote the first two BOOKS OF COMMON PRAYER, 1549 and 1552, and authored the Forty-two Articles. Catholic Queen Mary imprisoned and tortured Cranmer in 1553. He made multiple recantations, then died at the stake, first burning the right hand that signed the recantations.

C.M.

**CREATION.** The divine action that calls the universe into existence and ensures its continuity.

*Angle of Vision.* The God biblical Israel worshiped was foremost the Lord of history who had powerfully rescued the covenant people from Egyptian slavery and facilitated their settlement in Canaan (Deut. 26:5-10). As Israel's savior, God was no less the creator of all. Israel perceived creation as the starting point of that continuing historical drama within which God's will became reality. Like its Near Eastern neighbors, Israel regarded the universe as a three-storied structure incorporating heaven, earth, and the underworld (Exod. 20:4). With them it entertained no direct notion of *creatio ex nihilo* (creation out of nothing, first explicit in II Macc. 7:28), but assumed the presence of preexistent matter. Also Israel understood that creation stories were more adept at answering the question, "What is the meaning of present creaturely existence?" than the question, "What really happened back then?" Unlike its neighbors, Israel denied that the created order owed its existence to a battle between divine beings that resulted in the destruction of chaos-monsters.

*Genesis Creation Accounts.* Perhaps dating to Solomon's reign, the earth-centered narrative of Genesis 2:4*b*-25 limits its creation concern to human origins. Using vivid verbs drawn from human handicraft and gardening, its author refers to Yahweh's creation of living space (the garden), the means of sustenance (fruit trees), work (garden cultivation), and communal existence (man and woman). Unlike the Babylonian Atrahasis epic, where the gods merely value humanity as the supplier of physical wants, the Yahwist's story abounds with God's concern for humanity. The opportunity to name the animals attests human authority over them (Gen. 2:19). Nevertheless, the garden is Yahweh's, and human acknowledgment of God's sovereignty is expected.

Ultimately achieving fixed written form in the sixth century B.C., the sophisticated Priestly narrative (Gen. 1:1–2:4*a*) depicts Israel's God as the transcendent cosmic organizer who creates through an efficacious word. Numerous categories are presented within a six-day span: time (1:3-5), space (1:6-10),

the creation of vegetation (1:11-13), celestial bodies (1:14-19), animals (1:20-25), and humanity (1:26-31). Thereupon the seventh day is portrayed as creation's goal, whereby the Creator rests from labor, and Sabbath observance is universalized in a cosmic framework (2:1-3). With its pronounced use of the verb "to create" *(bārā'),* which throughout the OT solely has God as its subject, this Priestly version celebrates an undeniably sovereign deity who stands over against creatures. Yet the earth putting forth vegetation (1:11-12), the celestial bodies controlling the calendar (1:18), and humanity exercising dominion over its environment (1:28) are accorded partial sovereignty. Made in God's "image" and "likeness" (respectively denoting concrete and abstract similarity, 1:26), blessed humanity is invited into a special relationship with God.

*Other Biblical Reflections.* Creation is also celebrated in the Psalms and in wisdom and prophetic texts. Creation via divine speech, so central in the Priestly account, is reaffirmed in Psalm 33:9 ("He spoke, and it came to be; he commanded, and it stood forth"). The idea of humanity's sovereignty within God's own sovereignty asserted in Genesis 1:26-28 finds superb expression in Psalm 8. Resembling Pharaoh Akhenaton's "Hymn to the Sun," Psalm 104 extols the sheer wonder of creation ("O Lord, how manifold are thy works!" v. 24). God's sovereignty over chaos attested at the head of Genesis 1 achieves much sharper restatement in Psalm 74:13-15, which personifies the restless waters as a chaos-monster.

Wisdom literature also reveres the Creator. The articulation of Proverbs 3:19, "The Lord by wisdom founded the earth; by understanding he established the heavens," is elaborately reinforced in the Deity's many questions to Job and "lecture" on the hippopotamus and crocodile (Job 38:4–39:30; 40:8–41:34). Then the mystery of creation is daringly highlighted in Proverbs 8:22-31 with its personification of wisdom as Yahweh's firstborn creature. Moreover, living in the late exilic era, Second Isaiah perceives creation as an all-encompassing category. More than being a cosmological event at the beginning of time, creation involves Israel's historical origins as well as its present, which gravitates toward a promising future. Israel's "Lord, who made all things" is identified as Israel's "Redeemer" (Isa. 44:24; 45:8). In a glorious new act of creation, Yahweh will secure Israel's rescue from Babylonian captivity.

Second Isaiah's new creation theme reappears within the NT message that in Christ, God's kingdom is already inaugurated. For Paul, "all things" exist through Christ (I Cor. 8:6). He declares, "If any one is in Christ, he is a new creation; the old has passed away" (II Cor. 5:17). Presently, a new humanity is emerging; ultimately, a new heaven and earth will be created (Rev. 21:1-4). In sum, early Christianity claimed that creation finds its unity and purpose in Christ (Eph. 1:9-10), and through him the sovereign design of the Creator-Redeemer Deity is fully realized.

J.K.K.

*CREDO UT INTELLIGAM.* A phrase used by ANSELM meaning, "I believe in order to understand." Once firmly established in FAITH, Anselm taught that one can understand by pure reason what one believes—for example, the necessity of the Incarnation. Augustine also taught that one must first believe in order to understand, but he placed greater emphasis on the essential role of the will in KNOWLEDGE.

J.L.

**CREEDS/CREDO.** A brief statement of faith, usually worded to be easily memorized. Though creeds are sometimes used as tests of orthodoxy, they are more typically liturgical in function. In the Christian church, the recital of creeds constitutes the "daily education and public self-definition of the community" (Jenson).

The most universal of the Christian creeds is the NICENE. It is used at the Eucharist in both Eastern and Western churches. It falls into three parts, the first affirming the Father as Creator, the second affirming the Son and reciting his saving works, the third affirming the Holy Spirit and the church as the community of the Spirit. This creed had its origin at the ecumenical Council of NICEA (325) but did not achieve its final form until the Council of CONSTANTINOPLE (381), so it is sometimes designated more correctly as the Niceno-Constantinopolitan Creed. In its original form, the creed spoke of the Holy Spirit as "proceeding from the Father," but from about the sixth century the words "and from the Son" (FILIOQUE) began to be added in Spain. By the eleventh century this addition was accepted in Rome, and it has remained a matter of contention between East and West—the Eastern churches affirming a single procession from the Father, the West claiming a double procession from the Father and the Son.

Both views can be defended theologically, but the Eastern churches are correct in maintaining that their version is the original one and has never been altered by an ecumenical council.

The APOSTLES' CREED is briefer than the Nicene but has the same threefold form. It is used only in the West, where it originated as a baptismal confession of faith. A legend relates that each of its several clauses was composed by one of the original apostles before they dispersed from Jerusalem on their missionary journeys. In fact, the creed did not reach its present form until the eighth century, but it may justly be called "apostolic" since its roots are much earlier than its final formulation, and it expresses the gist of the early apostolic teaching. In its recital of the events in the career of Christ, it includes the descent into hell, not mentioned in the Nicene Creed.

A third Christian creed is the Athanasian, also known as *Quicunque vult* from the opening words of the Latin version. In spite of the name, the creed has nothing to do with Athanasius and is a Western production. It does not share the threefold structure of the Apostles' and Nicene creeds, but expounds the doctrines of the Trinity and the Incarnation. Compared with the other creeds, it is lenghty, technical, and not easily memorized, and it is not much used in churches today. There have been many modern attempts to update creeds, but none of them have met with success. The ancient creeds, especially the Nicene, continue to be prized, for they give a sense of solidarity in faith with the whole church as extended in both space and time.

J.M.

**CRISIS THEOLOGY.** *See* BARTH, KARL.

**CRITICAL APPARATUS.** The lengthy series of footnotes, citations of other passages of scriptures, and references to ancient manuscripts and to early versions an editions of the NT that appear in scholarly editions of the Greek NT. By use of the critical apparatus, the student is able to discover the many variants in spelling and words of NT texts that occur in ancient witnesses.

J.C.

**CRITICISM.** *See* BIBLICAL CRITICISM.

*CRITIQUE OF PURE REASON. See* KANT, IMMANUEL.

**CROLY, GEORGE** (1780–1860). The hymn "Spirit of God, Descend upon My Heart" is attributed to him. Born August 17, 1780, in Dublin, Ireland, he received a B.A. in 1800 from Dublin University and an M.A. in 1804.

Ordained in Ireland by the Church of England, he moved to London in 1810, initially devoting himself to a literary career as the drama critic for *New Times.* From 1832 to 1835, however, he served the parish of Romford in Essex, and from 1835 until his death, November 24, 1860, he was rector of St. Benet Sherehog with St. Stephen's, Walbrook, in London. His hymns first appeared in *Psalms and Hymns for Public Worship* (1854).

N.H.

**CROMWELL, OLIVER** (1599–1658). English soldier, Lord Protector of England, and PURITAN leader. Born at Huntingdon, he received a strongly oriented Puritan education at the free school in Huntingdon and at Cambridge University. In 1628 he was elected to Parliament to represent Huntingdon and in 1640 to represent Cambridge County. He contended vigorously against opponents of Puritanism, attacked Charles I's handling of religious affairs, and openly called for abolition of bishops. He regarded Parliament's

Courtesy of the American Antiquarian Society

*Oliver Cromwell*

struggle against Charles I as basically religious, and in the First Civil War (1642–46) sided with Parliament. He commanded a cavalry troop at Edgehill in 1642, and his military prowess showed quickly. He later organized and superbly trained his Ironsides "men of religion" cavalry, many of whom were INDEPENDENTS. He won decisive victories for Parliament at Marston Moor (1644) and Naseby (1645), and empowered by Parliament he developed a disciplined New Model Army of religious men.

Cromwell felt called of God and considered the army his church. He disliked tyranny. When Scottish Presbyterians sought to disband the army, Cromwell occupied London. Charles, previously captured, escaped to Ireland. During the Second Civil War (1648–52) he crushed Royalist uprisings in Wales and defeated Scottish Presbyterians who had sided with King Charles at Preston (1648). He sat with the High Court of Justice that convicted Charles of treason and was the fourth signer of the death warrant (1649). Parliament then used Cromwell to quell insurrection. He ruthlessly crushed Irish opposition to Parliament in 1649 and defeated insurgent Presbyterian-Royalist Scots at Dunbar (1650) and Worcester (1651), ending armed resistance to Parliament.

In 1653 Cromwell ousted a troublesome Parliament, leaving himself and the army in control. A reassembled Barebones Parliament failed to create a satisfactory government, and on December 16, 1653, the army adopted an "Instrument of Government" and named Cromwell Lord Protector. He ruled with limited help from Parliament, favored religious tolerance generally, and refused the title of king. Puritanism decisively influenced his decisions. He was buried at Westminster Abbey. After the monarchy's restoration (1660), his body was hung at Tyburn, but in 1899 Parliament placed his statue in Westminster.

C.M.

## CROSBY, FRANCES JANE (FANNY) (1820–1915).

An incredibly prolific hymnwriter, Frances Jane Crosby was born on March 24 in southeast Putnam County, New York, the only child of John and Mercy Crosby Crosby. At six weeks old she permanently lost her sight due to improper treatment of an eye infection. Her father died shortly thereafter.

Her mother remarried and the family moved from North Salem, New York, to Ridgefield, Connecticut. With three younger siblings, Fanny had a happy childhood. Her early education consisted of listening to her mother reading and of memorizing long Bible passages. About 1835 she entered the New York Institution for the Blind in New York City. Convinced of the advantages of education, she was a diligent student and eventually a teacher of English grammar, rhetoric, and ancient history there from 1847 to 1858.

After visiting Scottish phrenologist George Combe pronounced her a poet, she became one of the school's star pupils, appearing before joint sessions of Congress in 1844 and 1847. In 1850 she departed her Calvinist Presbyterian upbringing to become a Methodist. In 1858 she married Alexander Van Alstyne, also a blind musician who taught at the school and served as a church organist. They made their home in Brooklyn and had one child who died in infancy.

Fanny Crosby, as she was always known, had her first poem published in 1841—a eulogy to President William Henry Harrison. She eventually published four volumes: *The Blind Girl and Other Poems* (1844), *Monterey, and Other Poems* (1851), *A Wreath of Columbia's Flowers* (1858), and *Bells at Evening and Other Poems* (1897). She first collaborated musically with George F. Root, who taught music at the institute. Together they wrote a popular cantata "The Flower Queen," and fifty to sixty songs such as "There's Music in the Air" and "Rosalie, the Prairie Flower."

She began writing hymns and gospel songs about 1864, allegedly at the urging of WILLIAM BRADBURY. Among her twenty other collaborators, undoubtedly the most famous was IRA D. SANKEY. In all she wrote probably between 5,500 and 9,000 hymns, using as many as 200 pseudonyms out of modesty. Although none of her hymns appears in current Presbyterian, Lutheran, or Episcopal hymnals, she is well represented in Methodist, Baptist, and more evangelical books.

Popular titles include "All the Way My Savior Leads Me," "Blessed Assurance," "The Bright Forever," "He Hideth My Soul," "I Am Thine, O Lord," "Jesus Is Tenderly Calling," "Jesus, Keep Me Near the Cross," "Jesus the Water of Life Will Give," "O the Friends That Now Are Waiting," "Pass Me Not, O Gentle Savior," "Redeemed, How I Love to Proclaim It," "Rescue the Perishing," "Revive Thy Work, O Lord," "Safe in the Arms of Jesus," "Savior, More Than Life to Me," "Some Day the Silver Cord Will Break," "To God Be the Glory," and "Thou My Everlasting Portion."

In 1900 she moved to Bridgeport, Connecticut, to live with her widowed sister. Her husband died in 1902. Yet she remained active, composing a two-volume autobiography: *Fanny Crosby's Life-Story* (1903) and *Memories of Eighty Years* (1906).

N.H.

**CROSS.** *See* ATONEMENT, THEORIES OF.

**CRUCIFIXION.** A form of execution by fastening the condemned to two crossed beams. Ezra 6:11 suggests that crucifixion was a practice of the Persians; the Greeks did not use it. Roman law ordered it for slaves, malefactors, religious and political agitators, murderers, pirates, and others who had no civil rights. Jesus, as a seditionist, might be crucified, but Paul, a Roman citizen, could not.

Crucifixion was intended to reduce crime by the public display of the shame and horror attached to the cross. Crucifixion was abolished in Europe when Constantine became a Christian (about A.D. 314). The Romans most often used a T or X-shaped cross. Christian tradition favors the Latin cross as the form of Jesus' cross.

Crucifixion, Roman style, as the gospels illustrate, began with a scourging of the prisoner followed by his carrying (at least the shorter part of) the cross to where he was to die. A public place was chosen, often where two or more heavily traveled streets or roads crossed and with a cememtery conveniently nearby. The upright piece was firmly fastened in the ground. The condemned man was then stripped of his clothing and either tied or nailed to the crossbeam, which was then hoisted in place by ropes until the feet were off the ground. Sometimes a ledge-like support projected from the upright piece. The feet were tied or nailed. A military guard took charge and remained until death came by exhaustion or heart failure. No vital organs were harmed. The victim was rigidly held in one position unable to deal with heat, cold, muscle cramps, natural body functions, hunger, or thirst. Often the crucified died in agony only after a number of days on the cross. After the body was removed, the cross was burned. Nails from crucifixion crosses were used by both Jews and Romans as means of healing. Pliny mentions this specifically in the treatment of epilepsy in his *Natural History*. During Jesus' youth, a massive Jewish riot, protesting the king's policies, heavily damaged Sepphoris, Herod Antipas' capitol, four miles from Nazareth. In the king's wrathful retaliation, thousands of Jews were crucified along roadways leading to the ruined city.

P.L.G.

**CRUSADES.** A series of military expeditions, beginning in 1096 and lasting several centuries, whereby Christians sought to retake the Holy Land from Moslem hands. After that time, the name has been used for other military campaigns under ecclesiastical leadership, or even more generally for any enterprise requiring extraordinary zeal, usually against a real or fictitious enemy.

The First Crusade (1096–99) was the only successful one, if one measures the crusades by their stated goals. In 1096, Pope Urban II called for a military enterprise to "free" the Holy Sepulcher from the Turks, who had taken it from the Arabs and whose growing power was threatening the Byzantine Empire. He promised plenary INDULGENCE to all who lost their lives in the campaign. Thus, the ideal of the crusades combined earlier notions of just war, the value of PILGRIMAGES to holy places, and the need to do PENANCE for sins.

The first wave of crusaders—who received this name because of the cross that they wore on their clothing—was a disorganized mob under the leadership of Peter the Hermit. On their way to Constantinople they massacred Jews, ravaged the land, and eventually had to fight with Christians, who defended their lands and crops. Their ragged remnant joined at Constantinople with the better organized military units under the leadership of a papal legate. Then the army crossed the Bosporus, took Nicea, and, after many hardships, conquered Antioch. By then the leadership was sharply divided, since the papal legate was dead. A contingent under Baldwin's leadership had abandoned the enterprise and accepted the Armenians' invitation to set up an independent county in Edessa. Finally, after much bickering, the crusaders marched on Jerusalem, which they took and put to the sword, after a long siege in 1099. Godfrey of Bouillon was then named Protector of the Holy Sepulcher. A year later, at his death, he was succeeded by his brother Baldwin, who took the title of king of Jerusalem. Under this kingdom, in imitation of the feudalism, which then prevailed in western Europe, several nobles were granted lands.

The Second Crusade was organized in response to the capture of Edessa by the Sultan of Aleppo, in 1144. Its great promoter was BERNARD OF CLAIRVAUX. Its leaders were Emperor Conrad III of Germany and King Louis VII of France. Their army of almost 200,000 men accomplished nothing, and after a half-hearted siege of Damascus the crusade was dissolved.

In 1187 Sultan Saladin took Jerusalem, and the news shook Christendom. The result was the Third Crusade, under the divided leadership of Emperor Frederick Barbarossa, Philip II Augustus of France, and Richard "the Lion-Hearted." Although this crusade has been the theme of much fiction, it too accomplished nothing but the conquests of Cyprus and Acre. It also obtained from Saladin the promise that Christian pilgrims would be respected and protected.

The Fourth Crusade, whose supposed purpose was to attack Egypt, was maneuvered into taking and sacking Constantinople, where the crusaders set up a Latin Empire of Constantinople. Pope Innocent III, who presided over the crusade, at first was dismayed, but eventually accepted the events as God's way of reuniting the Eastern and Western branches of the church.

The Fifth Crusade, under the leadership of the titular king of Jerusalem, attacked Egypt with little success. The Sixth Crusade was led by Emperor Frederick II, who had been excommunicated by Pope Gregory IX. Through negotiations, Frederick obtained Jerusalem, Bethlehem, and Nazareth, and safe-conduct for pilgrims to those cities, in exchange for a promise to halt further military campaigns from the West. The Seventh and Eighth crusades, led by Louis IX of France (St. Louis), were total disasters.

The crusading ideal was employed repeatedly in other contexts. Innocent III, for instance, called a crusade against the Albigensians of southern France. In Spain, the later stages of the Reconquista were seen as a vast crusade. And crusading principles were also employed in the conquest and colonization of the New World.

J.G.

## CUIUS REGIO, EIUS RELIGIO.

"Whose region, his religion," used during the REFORMATION to summarize the Peace of Augsburg, 1555. Lutherans and Roman Catholics agreed that the ruler's religion would be the territory's religion. Dissenters could emigrate, and free cities were to safeguard both faiths. It ended conflicts following Luther's death and lasted until 1648.

C.M.

## CULLMANN, OSCAR

(1902–). An active force to be reckoned with on the current theological scene. He has the distinction of being in the forefront, in his day, of an influential movement associated with the recovery of BIBLICAL THEOLOGY as a scholarly discipline. He was trained in liberal theology, which, in the 1920s, was in its heyday, and fell under its spell. He was appointed to Strassburg and later to Basel, while latterly combining with his Swiss professorship a post at the Sorbonne, Paris. His

influence lives on in many British and American students who came to do research under him.

Cullmann's name is linked with an interpretation of the Bible's chief theme called "salvation history." By this term he claims to be able to plot the course of divine revelation from creation to final redemption, with the cross and resurrection of Jesus holding the central place and forming the turning point. His most influential book is titled *The Center of Time* (Eng. trans. *Christ and Time*, 1950). He subsequently defended his notion of an ever-widening time line to allow for reversals and modulations in *Salvation in History* (1967). His interest in Christology and the sacraments has also been an enduring legacy. Many critics who find fault with salvation history as a key to the NT gladly pay tribute to his other works.

R.M.

## CULTS.

From the Latin word *cultus*, meaning "worship," cults may designate either forms of worship, such as the cult of Mary or one of the saints in the Roman Catholic and Eastern Orthodox churches, or a small, deviant religious group centered around a charismatic leader. A cult denotes an intensity of devotion and unusual life-style in its members. Such groups have arisen throughout history and have occasionally matured into SECTS with an ongoing historical existence, although the prominence of the dynamic personal leader often causes the cult to disappear after his or her death. This generally means the cult will not become a church or denomination.

While cults have always been part of the religious scene, they have come to public attention—or notoriety—since the mid-1960s in North America and western Europe. At first ignored, groups like the UNIFICATION CHURCH (originally the Unified Family, popularly called "the Moonies"); the INTERNATIONAL SOCIETY FOR KRISHNA CONSCIOUSNESS (ISKON, called the Hare Krishnas); the CHILDREN OF GOD (COG, now renamed the Family of Love); the Way International; and the Church of SCIENTOLOGY came to be feared by many Christian clergy, parents, and conservative Christians, as well as by rabbis and Jewish organizations. Beginning in the early 1970s parents, led by a Californian, Ted Patrick, author of the book *Let Our Children Go!* became upset over the estrangement of their children from them after their young people joined the Unification Church and the Children of God. Patrick, and other anti-cult leaders, declared that these young people were brainwashed, that is, mind-controlled by heavy psychological conditioning. Now organized as the Citizens' Freedom Foundation, these opponents of cults pointed to the isolation, continuous lecturing, lack of sleep, and poor diet of young people in cultic camps and communes, as well as the centrality of the religious leader, as evidences of brainwashing. Patrick and others therefore advocate forced extraction of their children from such cults and involuntary subjection to DEPROGRAMMING, a form of psycho-social confrontation designed to break the purported mind-control exercised by cult leaders.

Various marks of cults have been advanced by different students of this modern phenomenon. These marks or characteristics are of two types: one, theological; the other, phenomenological or behavioral. Theologically, conservative opponents point out that modern cults usually are heretical in their teachings on Jesus Christ, the Holy Trinity, salvation (most are works-righteous), and in their interpretation of Scripture. Behaviorally, cults (1) preach a literal apocalypticism—announcing the end of the age and great tribulations; (2) attack the churches and synagogues for false teachings or for not practicing what they preach; (3) are relentless in their proselytizing of new members, usually by the positive strokes of compliments rather than by fear of the apocalypse; (4) make a demand for a full and absolute commitment, including full-time service and donation of all personal possessions to the group; (5) an absolute leader whose word is law and gospel and who often claims to be a prophet and sometimes the Messiah or even God; (6) a continuous system of "mind-bending" or mind-control through lectures, prayers, chants, speaking in tongues, and meditation; (7) exploitation of the member's labor and—in truly destructive cults—even of prostituting young women; and (8) by a system of esotericism or secrecy, whereby the member does not know the real aims of the group, and in some groups members are led to deceive outsiders about the group in order to solicit funds.

Of course, any group that meets all these behavioral characteristics is a destructive cult. Certain groups, such as the Children of God (Family of Love), the Reverend Jim Jones' Peoples Temple, and the Manson family are obviously destructive cults. Many charges have been lodged against the Unification church, the Way International, and the Church of Scientology, and many of its leaders have been imprisoned for federal crimes.

Sociologists have estimated the number of modern cults in America from the hundreds to the thousands. There are undoubtedly many hundreds of these deviant religious groups, most of which have arisen since the 1960s, which come into and pass out of existence continuously. While the public is fascinated or frightened by the more exotic groups, like the Krishnas, the fact is that most contemporary cult groups are Western or Bible cults. These are splinters of the fundamentalist movement, which has expanded in the past two decades. Such cults include the Way International, the Church of Bible Understanding (COBU), the Walk, COG (Family of Love), Love Israel, the Glory Barn, and many other, purely local groups. Since the strong shepherd or dominant pastor is a key element in FUNDAMENTALISM, the ultra-conservative, independent congregation is subject to deformation if the strong leader becomes renegade.

The experience of Peoples Temple under the Reverend Jim Jones was precisely one of the subjections of a congregation to the ego-inflation of a dictatorial, messianic leader.

The Eastern-oriented cults, while quite visible, are not numerous nor are their memberships large. These groups range from the orthodox Hinduism of the Krishnas to the hippie-style celebration of sensuality and self-discovery of the Bhagwan Shree Rajneesh and his commune, until recently located in Antelope, Oregon. Some groups with Eastern elements in their makeup are actually eclectic, as is the Unification church, founded on Confucian and Christian teachings, or metaphysical ("mind-science") cults, such as Eckankar and Scientology. These mind-science groups mix positive thinking, the gnosticism of classical "religious science" (as in Mary Baker Eddy's Christian Science), and the Hindu doctrine of karma and reincarnation. A key feature of such groups is the graded nature of their teachings. Members are continually urged to pay fees to study for higher and higher rank, that is, for more and more illumination to escape the bonds of bad karma, to learn to astrally project or have out-of-the-body experiences and escape the limitations of finite existence. Techniques of meditation, autosuggestion, a form of counseling called "auditing" (in Scientology), and study of esoteric Eastern writings are used in this process.

Outside the ISKON group, where regular, elaborate temple services are held, group worship does not play a great part in the life of the modern cults. While the Unificationists hold worship services in their church in Washington, D.C., and at their headquarters in New York City, these are mainly for non-members. Beyond the huge public weddings that symbolize their theology, "Moonies" have only one regular service, the pledge (to the Reverend Moon) service held at 5:00 on Sunday mornings. Private study, small Bible study groups, and individual vows, prayers, and meditation are the norm in all cult groups, Eastern, Bible (or Western), and metaphysical (mind-science). Even the fundamentalistic groups, such as The Way International, hold yearly "Rock of Ages" (gospel singing concerts) and depend upon "twig" meetings (Bible study circles) rather than public worship services familiar to Christians and Jews.

While some cults have come to terrible ends, most groups have continued despite adverse publicity, court cases, civil suits, and the imprisonment of some leaders. Some high-ranking Krishnas have been arrested for drug smuggling, and charges have been made that Krishnas have stockpiled arms. However, the number of people involved in these groups has remained fairly constant over the past decade. There seems to be some thirty thousand core members of the Unification Church and about ten thousand Krishnas. One of the larger groups is Scientology. The Way International, despite defections, appears to be growing. Indeed, students of the new religious groups point out that it is precisely the Bible cults that will grow, and from whom continuing dangers (like the Peoples Temple tragedy) are likely to come.

Efforts have been made to identify the type of personality likely to be attracted to cults. Most of these studies, when scientifically done, tend to show little if any difference between those who join cults and those who do not. In general, young people, eighteen to twenty-five years old, who have not yet solidified a sense of personal identity, who are in transition from home to college, and who have recently lost a loved one by death, or the breakup of a romantic relationship or a divorce, seem most susceptible to cult recruitment. Cult recruiters frequent places where youth gather and look for the backpack that identifies the person "in transition." Yet not everyone who fits this category is recruited. Despite the stories of brainwashing and the counterclaims of the new religionists that they seek "conversions," the facts point to the exercise of free will by people who are highly idealistic, searching for meaning and purpose in their lives, and are alienated from home and cultural values, as reasons for cult membership. It is the adventurous who wish to throw off the usual and try something new, who not only join cults, but remain in them.

J.C.

## CUMBERLAND PRESBYTERIAN CHURCH.
*See* PRESBYTERIAN CHURCHES.

## CUNEIFORM.
From the Latin word *cuneus,* meaning "wedge." A writing system invented by the Sumerians employing wedgelike signs indented into clay. In about 3500 B.C., the Sumerians started drawing conventionalized pictograms (akin to Egyptian hieroglyphics) to denote specific physical objects (sun, donkey, orchard). Within three centuries, professional Sumerian scribes invented ideograms capable of expressing concepts (day, holy, kingship) and phonograms to represent syllabic phonetic values. Later the scribes eased their writing task by rotating the signs ninety degrees. Simplification and stylization greatly obscured the relation of the signs to their original pictographic values.

As Sumerian civilization spread, so did its writing system. Between 3000 and 2500 B.C. the Semitic Akkadians and their eastern Elamite neighbors adopted it. During the second millennium, the Hurrians of northern Mesopotamia and the Hittites of Anatolia appropriated cuneiform from the Akkadians. Alphabetic Ugaritic, reflecting fourteenth-century B.C. Syrian culture, and Old Persian (sixth-fourth centuries B.C.) are independent regional efforts whose only resemblance to Mesopotamian cuneiform consists in their wedgelike signs. Since Akkadian employed more than 450 signs and Ugaritic merely thirty, the latter was decidedly the easier writing system to master. (*See also* WRITING AND WRITING MATERIALS.)          J.K.K.

Courtesy of The University Museum, University of Pennsylvania

*A Sumerian "medical" tablet from Nippur (late third millennium* B.C.)

## CUR DEUS HOMO. *See* ANSELM.

## CURE OF SOULS.
The church's ministry whereby it seeks to heal, comfort, and direct the wounded souls of its members. It is also called the "care" of souls. In early times, this was done mostly through the LITURGY, in which there was opportunity for a public confession of sin and an announcement of forgiveness. This gave the entire community of faith a therapeutic function. In the early Middle Ages, probably at first in Ireland, the custom of private confession appeared, and this soon placed the main responsibility for the cure of souls on those who heard confession. To help priests perform this function, many PENITENTIAL BOOKS were written, analyzing the human soul and the motives for its actions.

The Reformation, while no longer counting PENANCE as a sacrament, encouraged pastors to continue hearing the confessions of their parishioners. Calvin, for instance, felt that the words of absolution were the private preaching of the gospel, and that for this reason it was those entrusted with preaching who should also hear the confessions of the faithful. The erosion of ministerial authority in much of later Protestantism also eroded the pastor's authority and responsibility for the cure of souls. In more recent times, the development of psychology as a science has given rise to the discipline of pastoral counseling, which performs some of the functions of the care of souls. In the late twentieth century, the therapeutic character of the church as a community, and particularly of its liturgy, is being rediscovered.

J.G.

**CURIA.** The *Curia Romana* or Court of Rome; the bureaus and agencies by which the pope administers the Roman Catholic church. The pope has several offices, each of which must be carried out through assistants. He is the bishop of Rome, the metropolitan of a province, and the primate of Western Catholic Christendom. The pope is also, in Catholic doctrine, the VICAR OF CHRIST, the successor to St. Peter, and thus exercises governing power over the universal Christian Church. The Curia's offices are in the VATICAN and in other church-owned properties scattered throughout Rome. These buildings enjoy extraterritorial status.

J.C.

**CUSH.** A Benjaminite personal name in the superscription to Psalm 7; otherwise a geographical reference to Nubian, Kassite, and Midianite territories. Ordinarily denoting the southern Nile valley, Hebrew *kûsh* is translated "Ethiopia" (Isa. 18:1; Ezek. 29:10; Esth. 1:1). The land and eponymous ancestor of the Kassites, who overran sixteenth-century B.C. Babylon, are also labeled "Cush" (Gen. 2:13; 10:8). Since Cushan's "tents" and Midian's "curtains" form a parallelism in Habakkuk 3:7, and Moses' wife, Zipporah, is called a "Cushite" woman in Numbers 12:1, a Midianite district south of Edom may also have been so named.

J.K.K.

**CYNICS.** A minor school of Greek ethics founded by Antisthenes (about 444 B.C.–after 371 B.C.), a pupil of Socrates and teacher of Diogenes of Sinope (400–325 B.C.). The good man, Cynics said, brings desires under control by strict rule of reason, and thus achieves independence from externals, such as family and wealth. The movement was known for efforts to provide schooling for children of mixed blood and for advocating universal abolition of slavery.

Later Cynics (after about 250 B.C.) were characterized by coarse protests against social customs, conventions, and laws. They earned a bad reputation by seeking to reduce possessions to bare necessities and avoid all social entanglements (family and wealth), so as to gain personal independence and serenity. Some thought extreme Cynics lived no better than dogs, hence the name Cynics—derived from the Greek word for dog or unclean scavenger. Others, especially the educated, appreciated the Cynics' ideals of freedom and humanitarianism. STOICISM, as taught by Epictetus (about A.D. 50-120), has been considered a less severe and more social outgrowth of Cynicism.

P.L.G.

**CYPRIAN OF CARTHAGE.** Bishop of Carthage from 248 to 258, and one of the most influential Christian writers of the third century. He had been converted to Christianity shortly before his election as a bishop, and until that point had followed a career in rhetoric. He then devoted himself to the study of Scripture and theology, particularly the writings of TERTULLIAN, whom he called the Master.

The persecution of Decius broke out before Cyprian had completed his first year as a bishop. He decided that his duty was to flee and hide and to continue shepherding his flock from exile through correspondence. Since many remained and suffered for their faith, he was accused of cowardice, and at the end of persecution his authority was challenged, particularly on the question of the restoration of the lapsed (see LAPSI). Some confessors, that is, people who had suffered for their faith but had survived until the end of persecution, took upon themselves the authority to restore the lapsed to the communion of the church. Cyprian insisted that this could only be done by the proper authorities, the bishops.

Two synods upheld his view, and established the need for a period of penance before restoration could take place. The schism of the Novatians (*see* NOVATIANISM) then caused him to clash with Bishop Stephen of Rome, who held that the baptism of schismatics and heretics was valid. Cyprian's view, that baptism could only be administered by those in communion with the church, was eventually rejected. When plague broke out in North Africa, and some pagans declared that this was a punishment of the gods for the unpiety of Christians, Cyprian wrote a refutation, which later influenced AUGUSTINE's *City of God*. Finally, when persecution broke out again, he proved his detractors wrong by offering up his life as a martyr.

J.G.

**CYPRUS.** The third largest Mediterranean island. It is located forty miles south of Asia Minor, sixty-five miles west of Syria, and is 140 miles long and sixty miles at its greatest width.

From about 1800 B.C. onward, Cyprus has been closely related by trade with Syria and Palestine, as well as to Mycenae and Ugarit. Its earliest name was Alashia, used as Elishah (Gen. 10:4; I Chr. 1:7; Ezek. 27:7). Later Kittim is used (Gen. 10:4; Num. 24:24; I Chr. 1:7; Dan. 11:30) for the whole island. This was when Kition (Larnaca) was the major city. Cyprus was famous throughout the ancient world for copper, which some thought originated in Cyprus. Copper and timber were exported from Cypress and cumin, wine, and dried figs were imported.

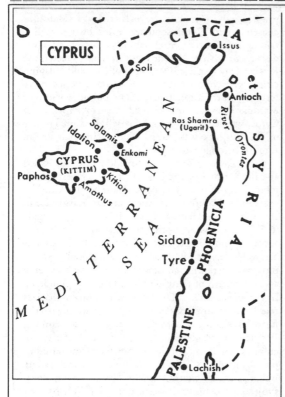

Cyprus was Greek first in the fifth century B.C. After a period of Phoenician colonization, it again became Greek under Alexander and his successors. There were Jews on Cyprus from the second century B.C. Herod the Great managed and profited from some of the copper mines. By the first century A.D., Cyprus had a large Jewish community. From it, Barnabus came as a student to Jerusalem, where he may have met Saul of Tarsus.

About A.D. 44, Barnabus and Saul, accompanied by John Mark, were sent by the Antioch church as Christian missionaries to Cyprus on what became the first Christian missionary journey outside Syria-Palestine. The routing followed the length of the island from Salamis to Paphos. During the preaching mission, the group encountered the magician Bar-Jesus and the proconsul Sergius Paulus. The proconsul's conversion (Acts 13:6-12) seems to have caused Saul to stop using his Jewish name in favor of his Roman name Paul (Acts 13:9). Barnabas later returned to Cyprus with Mark (Acts 15:39).

The Cyprus church had difficulties, but it flourished. At the Council of Nicea, A.D. 325, there were three bishops from Cyprus.

P.L.G.

**CYRENE.** A coastal city in North Africa, south of Crete, and the capital (ancient and modern) of Cyrenaica (Libya). A Greek colony from about 630 B.C., it became a Roman province in 74 B.C. The area

was fertile and well watered. Silphium (resembling prickly lettuce), the major crop, was in great demand for medicine and for use in Greek cooking. When Cyrene's production failed, the city declined.

Jews lived in Cyrene from the fourth century B.C. Cyrenians are mentioned several times in the NT. Pilgrims to Jerusalem from Cyrene shared in the synagogue of the Freedmen (Acts 6:9). Soldiers compelled Simon of Cyrene to carry Jesus' cross (Matt. 27:32; Mark 15:21; Luke 23:26). Cyrenians were also at Pentecost (Acts 2:10), disputed with Stephen (Acts 6:9), and evangelized Antioch (Acts 11:20).

P.L.G.

**CYRENIUS.** *See* QUIRINIUS.

**CYRIL OF ALEXANDRIA.** Patriarch of Alexandria, 414–444, and the champion of ALEXANDRIAN THEOLOGY, which was against the NESTORIANS. He combined theological ability with a pugnacious temperament, which soon manifested itself against pagans, Jews, and heretics. His zeal, if not his intention, was responsible for the lynching of the pagan philosopher Hypatia, as well as for several mob actions against Jews. It was in the Nestorian controversy, however, that he shone as a brilliant polemicist and an able politician. Cyril secured the condemnation of Nestorius by synods in Rome and Alexandria and wrote a dogmatic letter and twelve anathemas against Nestorius. He also presided at the COUNCIL OF EPHESUS, which condemned Nestorius.

At first he sought the outright condemnation of the Christology characteristic of ANTIOCHENE THEOLOGY; but in 433 he was forced to sign with John of Antioch a "Formula of Reunion," which condemned Nestorius but left room for more moderate forms of Antiochene CHRISTOLOGY. His own Christology was typically Alexandrine, and he may well have been the first to use the phrase HYPOSTATIC UNION, which became the hallmark of orthodoxy. What he held was that the humanity of Christ had no *hypostasis,* no subsistence of its own, but rather subsisted in his divinity. Since sometimes he used the term "nature"—*physis*—as equivalent to "hypostasis," later Monophysites claimed his authority in support of their views (*see* MONOPHYSITISM). Therefore, although variously interpreted, his writings still hold great authority both in Orthodox and in Monophysite churches.

J.G.

**CYRIL OF JERUSALEM.** Bishop of Jerusalem from A.D. 350 to 386, and a leader in the opposition to ARIANISM. Like many other opponents of Arianism, he was banished from his see for some time, but was eventually restored to it. On the other hand, he was not satisfied with the decisions of Nicea, for he objected to the HOMOOUSION clause as unbiblical and capable of erroneous interpretation. A discussion with

GREGORY OF NYSSA in 379 may have helped to allay his fears, for when the Council of CONSTANTINOPLE met two years later, he was ready to affirm the faith of Nicea. His main surviving work is a series of twenty-four lectures for the instruction of CATECHUMENS before their baptism on Easter Eve. These are valuable for their information on the liturgy of the time and on the process through which catechumens went before receiving baptism.

J.G.

**CYRUS.** Persian king (550–530 B.C.) who established the Achaemenian dynasty and the Persian Empire.

*Cyrus' Ascendancy.* As the vassal monarch of Anshan, a region northeast of Elam, Cyrus headed a successful revolt against his overlord, Astyages, king of Media (585-550 B.C.). Cyrus forthrightly stormed Media's capital, Ecbatana, ousted Astyages, and appropriated the far-ranging Median Empire. Thereupon he overtook Sardis, the capital of Lydia, and most of Asia Minor. Though his eastern territorial conquests are not precisely known, presumably by 539 Cyrus' huge empire spanned the Oxus River in the east and the Aegean Sea in the west.

Among those Jewish exiles in Babylon whose hopes were stirred by history's rapid change was the prophet-poet Second Isaiah (author of Isa. 40–55). While he does not mention the Persian takeover of Babylon as accomplished fact, he observes Cyrus' rapid ascent and anticipates Babylon's defeat. Indeed, he presents Cyrus as Yahweh's unknowing political instrument who would facilitate the Jewish return to Zion (Isa. 44:24–45:7). Cyrus is even referred to as Yahweh's "anointed" (45:1).

*Cyrus' Babylonian Takeover.* By summer 539 B.C., PERSIA's army reached the Babylonian frontier. Its king, Nabonidus (556–539), with whom much of the Babylonian citizenry had become dissatisfied, faced imminent defeat. It mattered little that he extended last-minute peacemaking overtures toward the worshipers of MARDUK, Babylon's patron god, whom he had offended, and mustered divine images from outlying sanctuaries into the capital to bolster Babylon's spiritual defense. At Opis on the Tigris River, Persian forces severely defeated the Babylonian army. Led by Gobryas, a Babylonian general who had deserted Nabonidus, the Persians infiltrated Babylon in October 539. Nabonidus fled but was promptly captured.

The Cyrus Cylinder, a clay barrel cuneiform inscription undoubtedly authored by Babylon's priestly establishment, reveals that as Marduk's chosen agent, Cyrus soon made his own peaceful, triumphant entry into Babylon. Many citizens, discontent with Nabonidus' government, greeted the Persian king as their liberator. Babylon and outlying cities were left intact. The divine images were returned to their sanctuaries. The public worship of Marduk resumed and evoked the participation of Cyrus, whose sensitivity for the religious preferences of his subjects was habit. The entire Babylonian Empire belonged to Cyrus.

*Cyrus' Decree of Restoration.* In 538 B.C. Cyrus issued an edict permitting the Jewish return to Palestine and rebuilding of the Jeusalem Temple. Lacking an extrabiblical counterpart, the decree appears twice in the Bible—in Hebrew (Ezra 1:2-4) and Aramaic (6:3-5). At base, both versions are historically accurate, though the Hebrew claim that Cyrus was Yahweh's devotee is dubious. The Aramaic version provides for temple construction at Persia's expense and the return of temple vessels formerly plundered by Nebuchadnezzar. The Hebrew version emphasizes that venturesome Jews may move homeward with the financial backing of comrades who prefer to maintain Babylonian residence. Cyrus' decree reflects an enlightened Persian rule unthreatened by religious pluralism. And since the empire did not incorporate Egypt, Cyrus would benefit from having loyal subjects along his southwestern frontier. When Cyrus was killed in a distant eastern campaign in 530, his son Cambyses (530–522) succeeded him.

J.K.K.

*Tomb of Cyrus the Great*

# Dd

**D DOCUMENT.** The name given to the OT book of DEUTERONOMY and to certain other passages in the PENTATEUCH that share the language and outlook of Deuteronomy. D seems to have been composed in something approaching its canonical form about the time of the fall of Samaria (722 B.C.) in circles native to the northern kingdom. (*Compare also* DOCUMENTARY HYPOTHESIS.)

J.N.

**DAGON.** The god of the Philistines (Judg. 16:23; I Sam. 5:1-5), adopted by them after their invasion of the coastland of Canaan. He was originally a Mesopotamian weather god, appearing in the cuneiform literature with the spelling Dagan, who was introduced into Canaan as a vegetation deity (Hebrew *dāgān* means "grain"). Several Canaanite sites have names that proclaim them to have been sanctuaries of Dagon (Josh. 15:41; 19:27). There was a sanctuary of Dagon at Ugarit, and in the Ugaritic myths Baal is called the son of Dagon. This originally minor Semitic deity apparently became the chief god of the PHILISTINES, who built for him a temple in their city of ASHDOD. This temple was destroyed by the Jews during the Maccabean wars (see I Macc. 10:84, where "Azotus" is the Hellenized form of "Ashdod").

B.V.

**DAILY OFFICE.** The daily worship service in liturgical churches that publicly praises God, prays for God's blessing, and hallows the day. The daily office includes prayers and liturgies and meditation. All religious, monks and nuns, and priests in Roman Catholicism are required to celebrate the daily office. The laity are encouraged to observe the daily office, also.

The daily office consists of CANONICAL HOURS, matins, lauds, vespers, prayers for the day, and compline, or prayers for the night. These services are held regularly in monasteries and convents. The secular or parish clergy read the daily office silently during free time during the day and evening.

J.C.

**DALAI LAMA.** From the Mongolian and Tibetan words meaning in effect "Monk (or incarnate BODHISATTVA) of Oceanic Wisdom." It is the title of the head of the Gelugpa order of Tibetan monks who, until the occupation of Tibet by the Chinese in 1959, was both the spiritual and political ruler of the nation.

The Gelugpa order, socially and intellectually the most prestigious of Tibet's four main orders of monks, was established as a reform movement by Tsong-kha-pa (1357–1419). A successor of his, dGe-Dun-Grub-Pa, founded a major monastery in 1438 and is considered the first Dalai Lama. But the term was not used until the time of the third Dalai

Lama, who received it in the sixteenth century from the Mongol Altan Khan when he and his people were converted to the Tibetan (VAJRAYANA) form of BUDDHISM. It was the great fifth Dalai Lama, Ngag-dBang bLo-bZang rGya-mTsho (1617–82), who extended the sovereignty of his office over all Tibet and established the imposing Potala palace in Lhasa as his seat. It was also from the time of this reign that the Dalai Lama was considered to be an earthly incarnation of the great bodhisattva of active compassion AVALOKITESVARA.

After the death of a Dalai Lama, his successor—the next incarnation—is selected by elaborate oracular means. The present Dalai Lama (b. 1935, consecrated 1940) has resided in Dharmsala, India, in exile since 1959. He is widely regarded as an effective leader of his people, especially in the Tibetan Diaspora. A living symbol of his nation and its unique spiritual and cultural heritage, he is an eloquent spokesman for Buddhism.

R.E.

**DAMASCUS**, Capital of the modern Republic of SYRIA; one of those cities that can lay claim to being the oldest continuously inhabited site in the world. The fact of its continuous habitation, in fact, has made it impossible to determine just how ancient Damascus is, since it has obliterated or rendered inaccessible the evidence obtainable through archaeological exploration.

Damascus is mentioned in Egyptian documents as early as the nineteenth century B.C., as a subject city of the Egyptian Empire. It enters into known historiography, however, only in the tenth century, in both Assyrian and biblical annals, which partly coincide and are partly complementary. Valued for its strategic location at the intersection of important trade routes, Damascus was conquered by David and incorporated into his little empire (II Sam. 8:3-8). In Solomon's time, however, it regained its independence (I Kings 11:23-25). Thereafter there was continual strife between the Aramean state headed by Damascus and Israel, with countless border wars and shifting boundaries, though at times they could be allies against the common threat of Assyrian expansionism. In the annals of Shalmaneser III, for example, a devastating victory is claimed to have taken place over Ben-hadad of Damascus and Aram and Ahab of Israel at the battle of Karkar (853 B.C., not mentioned in the Bible).

Damascus eventually fell prey to the Assyrians, even as the northern kingdom of Israel and the southern kingdom of Judah did in their separate ways. With the passing of the Assyrians in 612 B.C., it became subject to the Assyrians' successors: first to the short-lived new Babylonian Empire, shortly after to the Persians, and finally, after the victory of Alexander the Great in 333 B.C., to the Hellenistic and Seleucid empires.

In NT times Damascus was subject to the Nabatean kingdom: the Nabateans were a formerly nomadic Arabic people who had inherited this portion of the disintegrated Seleucid Empire. Rome had also entered to claim Syria as within its sphere of influence, but it had not yet taken Damascus under its direct rule. The city was prosperous and a center of international exchange and commerce. Though part of the nominally pagan Decapolis, it possessed a large Jewish colony with several synagogues, into which Jewish Christianity had already penetrated. Thus we understand the background to Paul's journey to Damascus and his sojourn there as described in Acts 9:1-25; 22:5-16; 26:12-20; Galatians 1:17; and II Corinthians 11:32. Damascus and Syria were early cradles of Christianity until the Muslim conquests began in the sixth century A.D.

B.V.

**DAMNATION.** The traditional Christian doctrine generally, although not universally, accepted by Christians from the first to the nineteenth centuries, which holds that SATAN, his fellow fallen angels, and those who persist in sin and refuse to repent will be eternally punished by God. HELL is the locus of this eternal punishment, although the literalistic language of the NT about a hell of fire has generally been understood as the pangs of guilt and a bad conscience compounded by the overwhelming sense of loss in being cut off from the divine fellowship. Damnation is, then, separation from the presence of God.

The King James Version uses the term "damnation" for three different Koine Greek words—*krisis, krima,* and *apoleia.* These words are more accurately rendered as (negative) "judgment," "condemnation," or even "destruction."

In the nineteenth century, theological liberals opposed the doctrine of damnation eternally as unfit for the character of a loving God. John F. D. Maurice lost his chair of theology at King's College, London, because of such a rejection (1853). Various cultic groups today such as the Jehovah's Witnesses reject the idea of hell and damnation as do liberal groups, such as the Unitarian-Universalists.

J.C.

**DAN** (city). Proverbially the northernmost reach of the land of ISRAEL ("from Dan to Beer-sheba"). Dan was, at the beginning of Israelite history, a satellite city of Sidon called Laish, which was conquered and resettled by Danite tribesmen (Judg. 18). Recent archaeology suggests that already in the time of David (tenth century B.C.) this frontier city had been strongly fortified as a bastion of the empire. That, together with other Israelite associations, which can only be surmised, doubtless accounts for the fact that after the separation of the two kingdoms of Israel and Judah on the death of Solomon, Dan and its sanctuary were declared a privileged royal shrine by Jeroboam I (I Kings 13:28-30), along with Bethel, probably the most venerated of all the holy places of early Israel.

B.V.

DAN (man). According to Genesis 30:4-6; 35:25; Exodus 1:4; and I Chronicles 2:2, Dan was the son of the patriarch JACOB (Israel) by Bilhah, the maid of his wife Rachel. No personality is assigned to Dan in the biblical narrative; he is simply a genealogical statistic.

Dan is the putative ancestor of the Israelite tribe of Dan, which is variously represented as very warlike (Gen. 49:16-17; Deut. 33:22) and as being slack in their enthusiasm for combat in favor of the Israelite federation (Judg. 5:17)—if we are to credit these poetic passages as evocative of the authentic Israelite past. Dan was, in any case, probably a minor component of what went to make up the eventual Israelite nation.

The Danites seem to have been originally a southern tribe like the Benjaminites and Judahites, with whom they were neighbors. In Judges 13–16 their folk hero Samson, a valiant champion against the Philistines, is pictured as active in this region. Hemmed in by hostile Amorites (Judg. 1:34) and the newly invading Philistines (the Samson stories), they were eventually forced to migrate northward. Judges 18 tells a story of this migration, first as an exploratory operation, then as a movement of the tribe in force, which ended in the conquest of the Sidonian city of Laish, which was renamed Dan, at the extreme north of Palestine. The story, despite its editing in favor of later interests, also appears to be the cult legend of the founding of the sanctuary of the city of Dan. Aside from geographical references, Dan has made no further or lasting imprint on Israelite history.

B.V.

DANCING. As in most societies ancient and modern, except where it has been artificially repressed, the dance was accepted and welcomed in biblical times as a natural and instinctive expression of feeling and enthusiasm, whether secular or religious. In those times, of course, the distinction between the secular and the religious was by no means as definable as it is today. The absence of dancing was equated with mourning and desolation in life (Lam. 5:15).

The earliest reference to dancing occurs in Exodus 15:20-21, when after the Israelites' successful passage through the Red Sea and the subsequent destruction of their Egyptian pursuers, Miriam and the other women of Israel danced to the sound of timbrels and sang "the song of the sea." A similar dance celebrating victory is recorded in Judges 11:34 (Jephthah's daughter) and in I Samuel 18:6-7 (the women of Israel greeting Saul and David). It is not clear what was the occasion of the dancing of the women of Shiloh mentioned in Judges 21:21; probably it was a festival celebrating and in thanksgiving for the grape harvest.

Dancing was far from being the prerogative of women. David, along with "all the house of Israel,"

danced, sang, and made merry before the Ark of the Covenant as it was brought by stages into Jerusalem (II Sam. 6:5, 14-16; this dance seems to have been conducted with some abandon). Dancing, probably more male than female, given the customs of the time, was the regular acampaniment of pilgrimages and liturgy (Pss. 87:7; 149:3; 150:4). It was also taken for granted as characteristic of Israel's restoration after exile (Jer. 31:13).

In the NT there are few references to dancing. Both in reaction to the often sybaritic dancing associated with some of the Gentile religions and cults, and because of the formalism that increasingly characterized Jewish Temple liturgy and synagogue instruction subsequent to the Exile, there was little scope for the spontaneity that had made the dance a natural religious expression. The little we know of the early Christian liturgy is that it emphasized credal hymns, baptismal and Eucharistic rites eschatologically oriented, and proclamation. There is no mention of dance, even though there could be ample room for spontaneity (compare I Cor. 14:26-36). Jesus is quoted once as citing a proverb about the piping and dancing of children (Matt. 11:17; Luke 7:32). The other reference to dancing is that of Salome, the daughter of Herodias, who so pleased Herod Antipas that the head of John the Baptist became forfeit (Matt. 14:6; Mark 6:22). This kind of sensual dance would have been highly repugnant to both Jews and Christians.

B.V.

DANIEL (book). A book that appears in Christian Bibles as the fourth book of the Prophets following Ezekiel but in Hebrew Bibles as the ninth book of the third division, the Writings, following Esther and preceding Ezra.

Contents. The book of Daniel falls rather naturally into two divisions of roughly equal length. The first part, Daniel 1–6, contains six stories about Daniel and his three companions at the royal court in Babylonia. These narratives, which speak of Daniel in the third person, depict him as a pious and loyal believer who possesses the power to interpret dreams. In the second part, chapters 7–12, Daniel has dreams, visions, and revelations, which are interpreted to him by angelic figures.

Part one contains the following six stories: (a) Daniel and his companions successfully avoid breaking their food restrictions and prove to be healthier and wiser than the other youths in training and also wiser than all the magicians and enchanters in the realm (1:1-21); (b) after all others fail, Daniel interprets King NEBUCHADNEZZAR's dream of a composite statue as foretelling a series of monarchical empires (2:1-49); (c) Daniel's companions remain faithful to the worship of their God and are rescued from the ordeal of the fiery furnace (3:1–4:3); (d) Nebuchadnezzar dreams of a great tree that is cut down, which Daniel interprets as foretelling the temporary madness of the monarch (4:4-37); (e) Daniel interprets the writing on the wall of Balshazzar's palace as a prediction of the fall of the CHALDEAN (Babylonian) empire to the Medes and Persians (5:1-31); and (f) Daniel is saved from the lion's den (6:1-28).

Part two contains four accounts of Daniel's dreams, visions, and revelations interpreted to him by angelic figures: (a) the dream of four great beasts is interpreted as about four kings who will arise with a horn of the fourth beast warring against "the saints of the Most High" until a final kingdom is established to be ruled over by "the people of the saints of the Most High" (7:1-28); (b) Daniel's vision of the ram and he-goat is interpreted by the angel GABRIEL as foretelling the struggle between Media-Persia and Greece, to be followed by the rule of a horn of the he-goat (8:1-27); (c) the angel Gabriel interprets the seventy years mentioned by the prophet Jeremiah (Jer. 25:11-12; 29:10) as the final seventy weeks of years (490 years), which will end with the destruction of Jerusalem's "desolator" (9:1-27); and (d) Daniel receives a "word," interpreted by an angel, concerning the future course of world history from the Persian period until the time when the "contemptible person," who will desecrate Jerusalem and the Temple, shall be destroyed and the resurrection will occur (10:1–12:13).

*History of Interpretation.* Throughout much of Jewish and Christian history, the book of Daniel has been understood as a work written by a historical person, Daniel, during the final years of Babylonian and the early years of Persian rule in the sixth century B.C. In this book, the future course of events before the end of time was believed to be predicted. In the ancient world, this view was challenged by some pagans such as the neoplatonist philosopher Porphyry (third century A.D.), who wrote: "[The book] was composed by someone who lived in Judea in the reign of ANTIOCHUS who was surnamed Epiphanes [175–164 B.C.], and he did not predict coming events but narrated past ones. Consequently, what he relates down to Antiochus embodies true history; but if he added any surmises about the future, he just invented them, for he did not know the future."

After many controversies and disputes, most scholars have adopted a view of the book similar to that of Porphyry. The book is now generally assumed to have been written during the MACCABEAN struggles with Antiochus Epiphanes after the king suppressed the practice of Jewish religion and halted Jewish sacrifices in the Temple. Some of the stories in Daniel 1–6 and even parts of Daniel 7–12 are sometimes thought to be older than this struggle since they depict the rulers in a reasonably favorable light or do not presuppose overt persecution of the Jews or the desecration of the Temple. The final form of the book is related to the Maccabean struggles before the death, in 164 B.C., of Antiochus

Epiphanes, who did not die as predicted in Daniel 11:40-45, the point at which true predictions begin in the book.

*Daniel and Apocalyptic.* Daniel is the only book of apocalyptic literature in the OT (*see* APOCALYPTICISM). It has many of the characteristics of apocalypticism: written in narrative form, containing revelations of the future mediated by otherworldly beings and through symbolic representations, exhorting and consoling a community in crisis and claiming divine authority.

*The Languages of the Book.* Daniel 1:1–2:4a and 8:1–12:13 are written in Hebrew. Daniel 2:4b–7:28 are written in Aramaic. In spite of various proposals, no satisfactory solution to the problem of this bilingual form is available.

*The Greek Version.* The Greek version of the book is much longer than the Hebrew-Aramaic text. This longer version, followed by the Vulgate and Catholic Bibles, contains the PRAYER OF AZARIAH and the SONG OF THE THREE YOUNG MEN (sixty-eight verses incorporated between 3:23 and 3:24) as well as the story of SUSANNA (sixty-four verses appearing as Dan. 13) and BEL AND THE DRAGON (forty-two verses appearing as Dan. 14).

*The Message of the Book.* Written to a community in crisis, the book of Daniel exhorted its readers to remain loyal to Jewish faith and practices in a time of trouble. While offering assurance of divine care and protection in a troubled present, it also encouraged its readers to understand the signs of the times and to look forward in hope to the soon-to-appear new age that would be ushered in by God's action, when they would see the establishment of God's final kingdom. For those who had died and to those who faced death and martyrdom, the author held out a hope of resurrection beyond death.

J.H.

**DANIEL** (man). The name Daniel, meaning "God *(El)* has judged" or perhaps "God *(El)* is my judge," appears in the Bible as the name of David's second son (I Chr. 3:1), a priest of postexilic times (Ezra 8:2; Neh. 10:6), and the hero of the book of Daniel.

According to the book of DANIEL, he was taken as a young lad into the Babylonian EXILE in the third year of the reign of King Jehoiakim (about 606–605 B.C.; Dan. 1:1). He continued to be active until after the capture of BABYLON by the Persians in 539 B.C. (Dan. 6:28). In exile, Daniel and his friends remained loyal to Jewish faith and practices and were persecuted; but they were always redeemed and vindicated. Daniel was not only an interpreter of dreams (Dan. 1–6) but also a visionary whose dreams were interpreted for him (Dan. 7–12). He is presented as a suffering and loyal martyr and as a man of great wisdom with the power to understand dreams.

Questions have been raised about whether Daniel was a historial person. Arguments for understanding him as a nonhistorical or purely legendary figure are fourfold. (1) The OT, outside the book of Daniel, speaks of a legendary figure, Daniel or Danel (Ezek. 14:14, 20; 28:3). (2) Nonbiblical texts mention a legendary Daniel. The fourteenth-century B.C. Ugaritic texts (see UGARIT) speak of a Daniel noted for his wisdom and judgment. In the book of Jubilees (in the PSEUDEPIGRAPHA), a Daniel is the great-great-grandfather of Noah. In some of the Aramaic QUMRAN or DEAD SEA SCROLLS a Daniel appears who offers summaries of world history. (3) The Greek version of Daniel has preserved additional legends about the man not found in the Hebrew text. (4) The nature of the book of Daniel suggests that he was a legendary figure of wisdom and piety rather than an actual historical person.

J.H.

**DANTE ALIGHIERI** (1265–1321). Italian poet, philosopher, and statesman, acclaimed for his *Divine Comedy* and *Concerning Monarchy*. Born in Florence, he grew up in middle-class surroundings, losing his parents at an early age, but little is known of his boyhood. Philosopher Brunetto Latini directed Dante's education toward philosophy and languages. He first met Beatrice (probably Beatrice Portinari) about 1274, but she married someone else and died at the age of twenty-four in 1290. Dante expressed his affection and pathos in *New Life*. Idealized, Beatrice inspired numerous works, especially the *Divine Comedy*. Dante married Gemma Donati of prominent Guelph lineage and fathered two sons and one daughter. His early works included a series of allegorical odes on Lady Philosophy, Liberality, Nobility, etc. After 1289 he became active in politics. For opposing Pope Boniface VIII, Florence exiled him, confiscated his property, and sentenced him to death in absentia. He wandered from town to town, finally dying in Ravenna, where he was buried.

His two greatest works were written in exile. Impressed by Emperor Henry VII, Dante wrote *Concerning Monarchy,* probably between 1311 and 1318. He believed humanity's temporal happiness could best be promoted by a universal earthly ruler independent of the papacy and equally empowered by God. Dante, an orthodox Catholic, drew heavily on Aquinas, but he marshaled historical-biblical data against papal supremacy and demanded that the church relinquish all temporal possessions and concentrate on spiritual matters. His strong anti-clericalism points to the future, and yet his thoughts reflect medieval tradition. *Concerning Monarchy* was declared heretical in 1329.

His greatest work, *Divine Comedy,* completed during his last years, pictures an imaginary trip through hell, purgatory, and paradise. Virgil, symbolizing reason, guides him through hell; Beatrice and St. Bernard, symbolizing faith, guide him to heaven, where he finds only one pope. Dante vividly portrays many contemporaries. A recurring theme insists that good works without faith will not

merit salvation. At the end, Dante stands before God in an ecstasy of mystic love. The *Divine Comedy* places him among the greatest poets of all time.

C.M.

**DARBY, JOHN NELSON** (1800–82). Founder of DISPENSATIONALISM and the PLYMOUTH BRETHREN, he was educated at Westminster and received a B.A. in law from Trinity College, Dublin, in 1819. Ordained in the Church of Ireland, he served a parish in County Wicklow before resigning in 1827.

Dispensationalism grew out of conferences hosted in the 1830s at the Wicklow estate of Theodosia Wingfield, Viscountess Powerscourt. In discussions of prophecy, Darby formulated a futurist interpretation of Revelation and invented the secret, any-moment RAPTURE. He saw the "church age" as a parenthesis between the sixty-ninth and seventieth weeks of Daniel. His *Collected Works* run thirty-four volumes.

He began to draw together small groups of dissatisfied believers, which eventually formed the Plymouth Brethren. After a schism at Plymouth (1845) and Bristol (1847), Darby led the stricter group known as Darbyites. He visited the United States and Canada seven times between 1862 and 1877. He also spent considerable time on the Continent and in Australia.

N.H.

**DARIUS.** The Greek (and Latin) spelling of the name under which three of the kings of ancient Persia (Iran) have entered into biblical and later Western literature.

*Darius I Hystaspis* (522–486 B.C.). Also called Darius the Great, he was the king of Persia who honored the decree of his predecessor CYRUS THE GREAT, to the extent that the liberated Jews of Babylon should not only be allowed to restore a homeland in Palestine but also be assisted in rebuilding there a temple to their God (Ezra 4:5; 5:3-17; 6:1-15). Darius was separated from the great Cyrus by Cyrus' son Cambyses, who had in 525 B.C. added Egypt to the Persian Empire. He was only distantly related to Cyrus, nevertheless he fulfilled perfectly the image of Achaemenid tolerance and ecumenicity that is drawn in the OT. The doctrinaire Zionists from Babylon, having repulsed offers of assistance from Yahwists indigenous to Judah and the surrounding areas whom they rejected as unfit to contribute to the new Israel, whose contours had been revealed in Babylon, were understandably opposed by their slighted suitors in their attempt to establish a new and exclusive Jewish polity in a land they called their own. Furthermore, these indigenous peoples were well established, part and parcel of the Persian bureaucracy Abar Nahara, "across the River (Euphrates)." It is significant, therefore, that Darius, having carefully ascertained the facts and searched out the relevant documents, found against the claims of

Courtesy of the Oriental Institute, University of Chicago

*King Darius I seated on his throne with his son Xerxes standing behind him*

his Palestinian agents and in favor of the privileges that Cyrus had decreed for the Babylonian exiles.

Darius I seems to have been a capable administrator and something of an idealist as a ruler. Having successfully quashed a rebellion that had accompanied the last days of Cambyses and restored order, he sought to codify a common law of justice and equity throughout the empire, due consideration being given to local cultures and traditions. He completed the political organization of the empire begun by his predecessors. He also instituted a system of roads and communications which was the envy and admiration of the contemporary world. Unfortunately, his last years were accompanied by failures, with the defeat of his armies in Greece and insurrection in Egypt.

*Darius II Nothus* (423–405 B.C.). Darius I was succeeded by his son Xerxes I (the Ahasuerus of the book of Esther). After the decisive defeat of the Persians by the Greeks, Xerxes was assassinated and was eventually succeeded by his son Artaxerxes I. After Artaxerxes's death there was a struggle for the throne from which, after much bloodshed, Darius II eventually emerged the victor. He was one of Artaxerxes's sons, by a secondary wife, by no means the first in line of succession. His rocky road to kingship led to equally perilous paths at home and abroad which he was forced to negotiate in order to maintain control in the face of domestic intrigues and foreign rebellions. In a measure he succeeded, but partly only by buying time against disasters that would follow him.

Darius II is mentioned only once in the OT (Neh. 12:22), as a temporal designation in connection with a census list. However, even this reference may apply to Darius III since some sources state that Jaddua was high priest when Palestine was taken by Alexander the Great. Far more important is the rolè assigned to Darius II in the history and circumstances of the Jewish colonists at Elephantine in Egypt. From the Aramaic correspondence preserved from this period it is evident that not only did Darius II protect and vindicate the religious rights of the Jews against the fanaticism of the indigenous population (always disposed to resist the Persians and their protégés), but the authority of the king was also involved to legalize, with some specificity, the details of the ritual and liturgy to be observed. This last mentioned is in

confirmation of the Achaemenid policy represented in Ezra 7.

*Darius III Codomannus* (336–330 B.C.). The successor of Artaxerxes III and the last King of Persia. He presided over the demise of the Persian Empire and its conquest by Alexander the Great, who was to build from it an even greater empire.

B.V.

**DARIUS THE MEDE.** According to biblical narrative, this Darius seems to be a composite created by the author of the book of Daniel. He is said to have "received" the kingdom of Babylon from the Chaldeans at the age of sixty-two and to have divided the kingdom into 120 satrapies (Dan. 5:31–6:1). In point of fact, CYRUS THE GREAT, the Persian king who actually wrested Babylon from the Chaldeans in a bloodless coup in 539 B.C., was about sixty-two years old at the time, and it was one of his later successors, DARIUS I of Persia, who perfected the satrap system throughout the empire. Darius the Mede is said to have been the son of Ahasuerus, that is, XERXES (Dan. 9:1). In point of fact, Xerxes was the son of Darius I, but Darius II was the grandson of Xerxes. Other recollections have doubtless entered into the composite. "Darius the Mede" can fairly be compared with "Nebuchadnezzar, who ruled over the Assyrians" who appears in the book of Judith.

Attempts to identify Darius the Mede as the disguise of a true historical character have failed to convince and are in all likelihood misguided. The book of Daniel deals not in history but in apocalyptic reinterpretation of prophecy. It was the Persian, not the Median, kingdom that succeeded the Chaldean: Cyrus had put an end to the Medes years before he turned his attention to Babylon. But texts like Isaiah 13:17; 21:2; and Jeremiah 51:11 had looked forward to a Median conquest of Babylon, and Daniel felt itself duty-bound to honor this prophecy as "fulfilled."

B.V.

**DARK NIGHT OF THE SOUL.** A phrase, made common in treatises on the CONTEMPLATIVE LIFE by St. JOHN OF THE CROSS. It refers to the common experience of mystics, that before attaining the blessings of a higher and more fulfilling form of prayer, they had to go through a long period of near despair, when they continued in their devotions without much reward. St. Teresa spoke of the same experience as the "drought" in the life of contemplation.

J.G.

**DARSANA.** From the Sanskrit word for "seeing." In HINDUISM, it refers to two concepts. One is the concept of seeing as a religious act. It is widely believed that simply to see a sacred object, such as the image of a deity in a temple or borne in procession, imparts a blessing in itself. Similarly, to see and thereby receive the grace of a holy or sublime person, a GURU or king, was and is a much-coveted privilege for which such persons would grant audience, quite apart from the exalted one's deeds or discourse.

The second concept is seeing as a "point of view," that is, a school, in Hindu philosophy. Traditionally, six philosophical systems have been considered orthodox. These are SAMKHYA, with its dualism of *prakriti* or matter/nature and *purusha* or spirit; YOGA, an ancient philosophical system but with the addition of a putative deity, Ishvara; the two schools of logical analysis, Nyaya and Vaishesika; and two schools emphasizing Vedic interpretation and tending toward non-dualism centered around the identification of BRAHMAN and ATMAN (though also producing modified non-dualist and even dualistic theism, Purva-mimamsa and VEDANTA).

However, it is widely agreed by historians of Indian philosophy that this classification is a poor guide to the actual contours of Indian thought. Not only does it overlook the distinctiveness of important systems associated with Saivism and Vaisnavism, it also omits the powerful and influential philosophical systems of the Buddhists and Jains. However, the Darsana approach, with its willingness to accept a diversity of philosophical systems within the same spiritual tradition, brings home an important feature of the Hindu world.

R.E.

## DARWIN, CHARLES/DARWINISM.
Charles Darwin (1809–1882) is one of the great revolutionary figures in modern thought and the scientist most closely identified with the theory of organic EVOLUTION. Darwinism is the theory of evolution advanced by Darwin with natural selection as the key to the mechanism of evolutionary change. Natural selection holds that organisms tend to vary, even if slightly; that these variations tend to be inherited; that since organisms multiply faster than nature's capacity to sustain them, there is a struggle for existence and the extinction of the less-adaptive organisms and the survival of the successfully adaptive or "fittest"— basically their ability to reproduce—in each generation of a species population. This variation leads to speciation, that is, the formation of new species. The extent and direction of adaptive change, speciation, and evolution depend on innumerable contingent variables operating in the interaction between organisms and their environment. Thus the slight variation of one species can have important consequences through the entire system. Darwin believed that species today are modifications of very different organisms living in the past, hence the possible common ancestry of all living things. Darwin's works, especially *The Origin of Species* (1859) and *The Descent of Man* (1871) threatened certain theological beliefs and provoked a struggle between Darwinian theory and theology which, on certain points, continues to this day.

Darwin was born in Shrewsbury, England, the son of a doctor and grandson of the distinguished evolutionist Erasmus Darwin. His mother was a daughter of Josiah Wedgwood, founder of the famous pottery. Darwin attended Edinburgh University as a medical student but abandoned medicine and entered Cambridge University with the intention of becoming an Anglican clergyman. At Cambridge he became seriously engaged in scientific studies under the tutelage of J. S. Henslow. Henslow was also instrumental in Darwin's appointment, at the age of twenty-two, as a naturalist on the voyage of HMS *Beagle.* The *Beagle's* circumnavigation of the world lasted five years (1831-36) and brought Darwin in contact with some of the earth's most remote, primitive, and exotic environments. It further trained Darwin's powers of observation and habits of scientific investigation and determined his career as a naturalist. His work on coral reefs, carried out during the voyage, established Darwin as a promising geologist and his friendship with the great geologist Charles Lyell, whose *Principles of Geology* profoundly influenced him. During 1837 to 1839, Darwin produced, gradually in a series of notebooks, the main ideas of his evolutionary theory. The theory was then sketched out in a thirty-five-page essay in 1842 and in a 230-page monograph in 1844, neither intended for publication.

In 1839 Darwin married his cousin Emma Wedgwood and they resided in London. Shortly thereafter his health began to decline, and the family moved to Down House in Kent, where he lived in virtual isolation for the rest of his life. He suffered from insomnia, intestinal ailments, and nausea, which allowed him to work only a few hours a day. The cause of Darwin's long illness has been much discussed but has not been clearly established.

By 1854 Darwin was prepared to make public the case for evolution and began to organize his vast collection of data in support of his theory. However, in 1858 he received an essay from Alfred Russell Wallace outlining the essentials of his own theory. Darwin's friends Lyell and Joseph Hooker urged him to allow some of his own work, with Wallace's essay, to be read before the Linnean Society. Darwin followed this with an "abstract" of his work, published in 1859 as *The Origin of Species by Means of Natural Selection.* The book produced an extraordinary response, both in the scientific community and among the general public. The most famous confrontation came in the exchange between Darwin's articulate defender T. H. Huxley and Bishop Samuel Wilberforce at Oxford in 1860. Darwin wrote a number of important works after 1860, including *The Descent of Man.* He died on April 19, 1882, and was buried in Westminster Abbey.

Darwin's theory disturbed his contemporaries, scientists as well as churchmen, because it appeared to challenge the foundations of Christian belief, especially the current interpretations of the biblical accounts of the Creation, the Fall, and redemption. Darwin's view of man as the *chance* result of natural selection over a long evolutionary process was at odds with the traditional interpretation of the biblical view of humanity's special CREATION in the image of God. In Darwin's view humans had risen from brute nature rather than fallen from a state of angelic perfection. Furthermore, evolution by natural selection, while not denying God, made God's creative and providential role ambiguous and seemingly unnecessary. What could be God's role and purpose in an evolutionary process of such endless duration, exhibiting such apparently fortuitous and chaotic development? These were the kinds of questions which inaugurated the controversy between Darwinism and theology.

Recent scholarship has demonstrated, however, that the idea of a "conflict" or "warfare" between Darwinian science and theology between 1860 and 1900 is too simplistic. There was no polarization between science on the one hand and theology on the other. Many eminent scientists were opposed to Darwin's theory, and there were orthodox theologians, such as Aubrey Moore in England and G. F. Wright in the United States, who accepted Darwin and can be called Christian Darwinists. The evolutionists of the period were, in the majority of cases, concerned to reconcile nature, man, and God. What confuses the history of the relation between Darwinism and theology is that many liberal theologians such as Frederick Temple, the archbishop of Canterbury, and Lyman Abbott, the popular American theologian, accommodated Christianity to a romantic, Hegelian vision of evolutionary development and progress, which did not touch the real implications of Darwin's theory of natural selection. Acceptance of various notions of evolution were often, mistakenly, equated with acceptance of Darwinism.

Darwin's own religious views developed, fluctuated, and remained ambiguous to the end of his life. He appears to have retained his orthodox beliefs during the *Beagle* voyage but to have given them up while remaining a theist or evolutionary Deist until the time of the publication of the *Origin* and beyond. The idea that Darwin became a materialist and atheist as early as 1839 has been refuted. It appears that Darwin's religious beliefs shifted constantly, and, while in later life he called himself an agnostic, he remained suspended between certain beliefs belonging to the older tradition of natural theology and the new scientific positivism. To the end, he found it difficult to view the universe as the product of blind chance and thus he sought forms of theistic accommodation from time to time. However, he would retreat from theistic expression whenever he felt the doctrine of special creation threatened to undermine the theory of natural selection. As Darwin himself remarked, whether a person is a theist depends on the definition of the term.

Darwin's nagging uncertainty about teleology or the idea of intelligent design in the world has continued to occupy the discussion of evolution to the present day. While strict Darwinians and Neo-Darwinians have rejected both vitalist and theological speculation, other scientific evolutionists have been responsive to a reconciliation between theology and evolution. This is due in large part to the influence of PROCESS PHILOSOPHY, the most enduring religious form of evolutionary thought in this century. However, the evolutionary metaphysics of BERGSON, WHITEHEAD, and TEILHARD DE CHARDIN are denounced by contemporary Neo-Darwinians as unscientific. Thus, while the "conflict" between Darwinism and theology needs to be qualified in important ways, it would be wrong to think that real differences do not continue to exist between Darwinian naturalism and Christian theism. To think otherwise would involve a failure to accept the full implications of evolution by natural selection or of the claims of Christian theism. For Darwin's influence on social theory, see SOCIAL DARWINISM.

J.L.

**DASEIN.** A term coined by the German philosopher MARTIN HEIDEGGER to describe the actual human situation. Literally meaning (in German) "being there," it refers to human life as we really find ourselves, in a world into which we are "thrown" and "abandoned for death," to use Heidegger's words. Knowing for sure that we are *there* in a world in which we shall sometime no longer exist, we are faced with the necessity for decisions.

I.C.

**DAVENPORT, JAMES** (1716–57). The eccentric revivalist of the GREAT AWAKENING was born in Stamford, Connecticut, to John and Elizabeth Morris Maltby Davenport. A graduate of Yale College in 1732, he studied theology there, and was licensed to preach October 8, 1735. He was ordained in 1738 to the Southold, Long Island, Congregational Church, which he served until ousted in 1743.

Under the influence of GEORGE WHITEFIELD and GILBERT TENNENT, he became an itinerant, holding REVIVALS in New York and New Jersey as well as Connecticut. Some of his meetings lasted twenty-four hours.

In response to such ENTHUSIASM, the Connecticut assembly in 1742 passed an "Act for Regulating Abuses and Correcting Disorders in Ecclesiastical Affairs." Davenport was judged mentally disturbed and deported back to Long Island. Now a martyr, he traveled to Boston and was similarly expelled. In March 1743 he led New London followers to burn their wigs, fine clothes, and books. After counseling by fellow pastors, he published his *Confessions and Retractions* (1744). In 1748 he took a pastorate among the Presbyterians of New Jersey, where he served until his death.

N.H.

# DAVID

**DAVID.** Son of JESSE and second king of Israel (about 1000–961 B.C.).

*Introduction.* The OT portrait of David is multifaceted. David stands at the center of a compelling royal theology that developed in monarchical Israel, one emphasizing Yahweh's choice of the Davidic house and his desire to reside permanently in Zion. This gave rise to royal Psalms celebrating Yahweh's affirmation of the Davidic monarchy (Pss. 18:50; 132:10-12, 17). Moreover, David is a key figure in exilic and postexilic Jewish messianism. The Chronicler offers a selective, idealized sketch of David (I Chr. 11–20). Significant omissions include David's days as an outlaw, affair with Bathsheba, orchestration of Uriah's death, and stormy latter years. Rather, David is cherished as chief patron of the Jerusalem Temple, who, nearing death, intently transmits plans for the cultus to SOLOMON, his son and successor (I Chr. 28). Thus I Samuel 16–I Kings 2 contains our main sources about David, including the superbly written succession narrative (II Sam. 9-20; I Kings 1–2), which presents public events in the guise of historical novel.

*Early Narratives.* Reared as the youngest of Jesse's sons in Bethlehem of Judah, David initially surfaces in the biblical narrative when the divinely dispatched Samuel visits Jesse's family to find Saul's successor. As David was anointed by Samuel, "the Spirit of Yahweh came mightily upon David" (I Sam. 16:13). Immediate word that SAUL was plagued by a divinely sent "evil spirit" (16:14) makes transparent the narrator's understanding that Saul's steady downfall and David's dramatic ascent harmonize with Yahweh's purpose. David entered Saul's court as an accomplished musician capable of calming the troubled king (16:15-23). Another tradition, however, claims that the initial meeting of Saul and David occurred when the courageous youth slew Goliath, the Philistine giant, with a skillfully discharged pebble. Second Samuel 21:19 attributes this deed to Elhanan, perhaps David's name before he mounted the throne. If not, the feat of a lesser warrior enhances David's reputation. By introducing another Philistine victim, I Chronicles 20:5 provides a lame harmonization.

Handsome (I Sam. 16:12), discerning in speech, blessed by divine presence (16:18), and befriended by Saul's son, Jonathan (18:1), young David was most favored. After the singing women demonstrated more enthusiasm for David's victories than Saul's (18:7), the anxious king made David a military commander to remove him from the court proper (18:13). Threatened by David's growing popularity, Saul thought he could dispense with David by requiring from him a hundred PHILISTINE foreskins as a dowry for his daughter Michal. David returned unharmed with twice that number to become the son-in-law of a further troubled Saul (18:20-29).

*Fugitive Status.* Saul's repeated attempts on David's life (I Sam. 19:9-17) forced him to flee. Presently David pursued the precarious existence of an outlaw and resourcefully interacted with the Philistines. After stopovers at Ramah (19:18) and Nob (21:1), David headed southwest for Gath. Feeling insecure before its suspicious Philistine king, Achish, David feigned madness and was permitted to depart (21:10-15). Arriving at Adullam in his native Judah, David attracted four hundred distressed, indebted, and discontented men to his side (22:1-2). As captain of this motley fighting force, which soon grew to six hundred (23:13), David rescued the nearby town of Keilah from Philistine raiders (23:5). The need to escape from Saul's clutches found David in the Ziph and Maon wilderness (23:14, 24), and at En-gedi on the western edge of the Dead Sea (23:29). In that vicinity, David forfeited a chance to kill Saul, whom he regarded as Yahweh's anointed (24:6). Further adventure took David to Carmel, some twenty miles west of En-gedi, which made possible his marriages to Abigail and to Ahinoam, from nearby Jezreel (25:40-43).

Weary of evading Saul, David sought asylum with Achish. Accepting David's signs of loyalty as genuine, the Philistine king gave him the frontier town of Ziklag, where David dwelt for sixteen months (27:1-7). From there David busily consolidated his position in southern Judah, concomitantly deceiving Achish into thinking that he had Philistia's well-being in mind (27:12). Since wary Philistine lords persuaded Achish to forbid David's participation in their battle against Saul's troops at Mount Gilboa, David was spared a potentially embarrassing moment (29:1-11). He returned to Ziklag, waged war against troublesome Amalekite villages, and thereby rebuilt his "kingdom" (30:1-31). Meanwhile, Israel suffered a stunning defeat at Gilboa that took the lives of Saul and three of his sons (31:1-7).

*King of Judah.* Informed of Saul's and Jonathan's deaths, the diplomatic David went into mourning and voiced a moving lament over Israel's tragic loss. Undoubtedly, this superb Hebrew lyric (II Sam. 1:19-27) influenced the tradition that made David the dominant author of the Psalter. David established himself at Hebron, where "men of Judah" declared him king (2:4). A seasoned politician, David sent a message of appreciation to the men of Jabesh-gilead who had, at considerable personal risk, given the bodies of Saul and his sons proper burial (2:5-6; see I Sam. 31:11-13). To this he appended a subtle, self-serving recommendation that they accept Judah's support of him as their model.

Meanwhile, with substantial help from his father's general, Abner, Ishbaal (Ish-bosheth) ruled Israel from Mahanaim in Transjordan, well beyond Philistine reach. Civil war raged between Ishbaal's supporters and David's. After two years, however, it ended with the assassination of both Abner (II Sam. 3:30) and Ishbaal (4:5-8), deeds in which David played no direct role. Given David's prudent responses to the deaths of Saul, Jonathan, Abner, and

Ishbaal, and the fact that Jonathan's lame son, Mephibosheth, was Saul's sole legitimate successor, Israelite elders followed the one sensible course available. Arriving at Hebron, they complimented David for past charismatic leadership and acclaimed him ruler over all Israel (5:1-3).

*King of All Israel.* Aware that a reunited Israel would count for little so long as the Philistines proved troublesome, David made triumph over these opponents his first goal (probably the two events of II Sam. 5 appear in reverse chronological order). Severely beaten by David in the Valley of Rephaim southwest of Jerusalem, the Philistines retreated twenty miles westward to Gezer (II Sam. 5:17-25). This and subsequent Davidic triumphs (21:15-22) ensured that the Philistines would no longer menace Israel.

After a 7½-year residence at Hebron, David seized the Jebusite city of JERUSALEM and moved his government there for the remainder of his thirty-seven years of rule (II Sam. 5:5). Jerusalem's central location, a strategically chosen area in the hills, and neutrality vis-à-vis Judean and Israelite religious history, made it an enviable choice. Assisted by personal troops (5:6), David took the city, though he refrained from slaughtering its Jebusite inhabitants.

Seeking to unite religious and political forces to his advantage, David transferred the Ark of the Covenant from Kiriath-jearim to Jerusalem (6:1-23). Though this involved both disaster and celebration, it was a masterful move. Yahweh's invisible presence in "the city of David" (6:12) was assured. Despite its later midrashic overtones, II Samuel 7, with its mention of Yahweh's eternal choice of the Jerusalem-based Davidic dynasty, further witnesses to the coalescence of religion and politics in Davidic government.

During his early Jerusalem years, David so thoroughly triumphed over the Moabites, Arameans, Ammonites, Edomites, and Amalekites that his kingdom reached the spacious perimeters assumed in Yahweh's ancient promise to Abraham (II Sam. 8:2-13; 10:6-19; 12:26-31; Gen. 15:18-21). The forthright succession narrative (II Sam. 9-20; I Kings 1-2), however, reveals that in personal and domestic affairs, David often came up short. David's affair with Bathsheba (II Sam. 11:2-5), his implementation of the death of her Hittite husband, Uriah (11:14-17), and Nathan's confrontive judgment, "You are the man" (12:7) attest David's abuse of regal power. That the penitent David was forgiven (12:13) did not exempt him from having to witness the disintegration of his household. His son AMNON raped his half-sister Tamar (13:1-20), and his son ABSALOM engineered the murder of Amnon (13:23-29). Absalom's rebellious lust for the throne returned David to precarious fugitive existence after his forced evacuation of Jerusalem (15:13-16). David reentered Jerusalem (20:3), but only after experiencing profound grief over Absalom's death at the hand of his assertive military commander, Joab (18:9-33). The succession narrative's final portrait of David is that of a weakened old man whose indecision concerning whether Adonijah or Solomon should follow him on the throne spawned extensive palace intrigue. Yielding to Nathan and Bathsheba, he decided in favor of Solomon (I Kings 1:30).

*Assessment.* The indulgent David was no model patriarch. He was not always the master of his emotions. Domestic sorrow even undercut his typically judicious rule over his people (II Sam. 19:5-7). On balance, however, David's accomplishments were impressive. The confidence he often engendered in his followers, his rigorous suppression of Philistine power, and his establishment of Jerusalem as the new capital speak well in his behalf. He is to be no less celebrated for his capacity to organize his Jerusalem court, cultivation of sound political relations with foreign powers, and respect for the ancient religious traditions of his people even as he sought new ways to address the future.

J.K.K.

**DAVID, CITY OF.** The city of JERUSALEM, from ancient to modern times, has had to acknowledge uncertain geographical boundaries and equally uncertain political and religious loyalties. Although Judges 1:8 might indicate that Jerusalem had been conquered by Judahites in the early days of the "conquest"—and may very well indeed point to an older tribal assault on the city—Joshua 15:63 confesses that Jerusalem remained Canaanite into the period of the monarchy. This accords with II Samuel 5:6-9, which recounts the conquest of the stronghold of ZION, the city of the Jebusites, to become the city of DAVID, his capital. It was not so much to distance himself from tribal loyalties that David chose a site for his capital that had no prior tribal history; the tribal system, as David, and Solomon after him recognized, was already an anachronism passing into history. What David did was to choose a neutral site to which neither North nor South could object—a site with no prior *Israelite* history—that could, therefore, serve for the new thing that had come into being, the United Kingdom of ISRAEL and JUDAH. Here he could establish the new nation with its own polity (partly traditional, partly adapted), bureaucracy (largely borrowed from Egypt), ritual (mostly taken over from the indigenous liturgy and priesthood), and so forth.

The original City of David, at the extreme east of the Tyropean valley that runs through Jerusalem, has left no vestiges of its Judahite conquest. There is a trace, however, of a wall that is claimed to be Jebusite. It was Solomon who first enlarged the site to the north, creating the city area that would later house the Temple. From then on, except in the east protected by the Kidron Valley, Jerusalem has otherwise extended itself in every direction and has become popularly known in its entirety as "Zion" or "City of David."

B.V.

# DAY OF ATONEMENT.

The holiest day in the Jewish calendar. In Hebrew it is called Yom Kippur. It is the climax of a forty-day period of self-examination and spiritual stocktaking, which includes the month of Elul, the two days of ROSH HASHANAH (the Jewish New Year), and the ten days of penitence.

Yom Kippur is marked by a total fast from sundown to sundown and by prayer and reflection. The commandment to observe it is in the Bible: "Howbeit on the tenth day of this seventh month is the day of atonement; there shall be a holy convocation unto you, and ye shall afflict your souls; and ye shall bring an offering . . ." (Lev. 23:27 JPS).

Rabbinic legend has it that, apart from the fact that the day is prescribed in the Bible as a day for atonement and forgiveness, on this very day Moses descended from Mount Sinai with the second tablets of the Ten Commandments and brought the good news to the Jewish people that they had been forgiven their sin of having worshiped the golden calf.

The keynote of Yom Kippur is repentance—self-scrutiny, confession of wrongdoing, pleas for divine forgiveness, and a determination for self-improvement. The evening service initiating Yom Kippur begins with the *Kol Nidre* prayer to wipe clean one's personal slate so that he or she may enter upon the Great Day with a clean conscience. Judaism teaches that Yom Kippur may atone only for the wrongs committed against God. The wrongs perpetrated against one's fellow human beings may be atoned for only by making amends and by securing the personal forgiveness of the injured person.

The confession of sins on Yom Kippur is expressed in the plural: "For the sins which we have committed. . . ." This reminds the worshiper that he or she is part of a community and also responsible for society's evils. The fasting and praying must result in a higher ethical standard. As the prophet Isaiah said, "Is such the fast that I have chosen? The day for a man to afflict his soul? Is it to bow down his head as a bulrush, And to spread sackcloth and ashes under him? Wilt thou call this a fast, And an acceptable day to the Lord? Is not this the fast that I have chosen? To loose the fetters of wickedness, To undo the bands of the yoke, And to let the oppressed go free, And that ye break every yoke? Is it not to deal thy bread to the hungry, And that thou bring the poor that are cast out to thy house? When thou seest the naked, that thou cover him, And that thou hide not thyself from thine own flesh? Then shall thy light break forth as the morning, And thy healing shall spring forth speedily; And thy righteousness shall go before thee, The glory of the Lord shall be thy reward. Then shalt thou call, and the Lord will answer; Thou shalt cry, and He will say: 'Here I am' " (Isa. 58:5-9 JPS).

L.K.

# DAY OF THE LORD/DAY OF JUDGMENT.

The "day of the Lord" was originally a promise of salvation-prophecy, an assurance that the Lord would eventually award God's client-people with victory over their enemies. In that day the Lord would settle accounts, obviously in favor of God's people. Amos 1:3–2:3 and the book of Nahum are typical of this kind of prophecy, which was in turn a legacy from the oracle of victory given by a court prophet to the king embarking upon a "holy war" (see I Kings 22). However, already with Amos it is evident that the "day of the Lord" was being demythologized in favor of moral issues. While Amos 5:18-20 refers to it as a well-known and accepted idea, the prophet hastens to disillusion the Israelites in their belief that it will be an unconditional intervention in their favor. Rather, he says, it will be for them a day of darkness and not of light. Since Israel by its conduct has shown itself to be the enemy of its moral God rather than God's faithful covenant partner, the day when the Lord intervenes to crush rebellion and destroy unrighteousness will signal Israel's downfall and exile, the loss of its distinctive national and religious institutions (compare Amos 7:1–8:3).

In Isaiah 2:12-19 the notion of the day of the Lord appears in a universalistic context, no longer restricted to Israel either as a time of vindication or of punishment. The theme is now that of a universal triumph of the Lord "against all that is proud and lofty," when "the pride of men shall be brought low; and the Lord alone will be exalted in that day."

With the Exile and postexilic prophets generally, this universalistic note continues and additional modifications also appear. First, with recognition of individual responsibility (Ezek. 18, for example) and the consequent distinction between good and bad persons even within the one people of God, the coming day of the Lord, which will affect all the nations (Joel 3:9 ff; Zeph. 2:8 ff.), is seen properly as a day of judgment. JUDGMENT in the OT, which corresponds with "justice," ultimately means to make prevail what is right. What is right is that Israel no less than the nations be punished for their sins, but the righteous, whether of Israel or of the nations, shall be saved (compare Isa. 66:15-21).

Second, the Day of Judgment becomes eschatological. That is to say, what was originally conceived as the Lord's settling of accounts in the foreseeable future toward which history was leading, now is seen as a once-for-all verdict to be passed on the wicked and the righteous at the end of time (compare Dan. 11:40–12:3).

The NT inherited the "day of the Lord" (Acts 2:20; etc.) from the OT in its eschatological interpretation: it is the final Day of Judgment (II Pet. 3:7) of the imminent coming of which the church lived in expectation (compare I Thess. 5:1-11). Christian adaptation includes the terms "day of our Lord Jesus Christ" (I Cor. 1:8) and "day of the Son of man" (Luke 17:24). The Day of the Lord or Final Judgment tended to be identified with the PAROUSIA or Second Coming of Christ to usher in the definitive establishment of the messianic kingdom of God. In

Matthew 25:31-46, the conclusion of Jesus' eschatological discourse, the Parousia is clearly identified with a final judgment pronounced by Christ himself over those whose worthiness of eternal punishment or eternal life will have been proved by their attention to the works of charity.

B.V.

**DEACON, DEACONESS.** Church officers involved in ministry to the congregation in the NT. The male officer, or deacon, (derived from the Greek *diakonos*, meaning "servant"), was probably an assistant to the elder (or pastor) in the congregation (Acts 6:3-4; I Tim. 3:8; Phil. 1:1), although he, too, had pastoral functions. It is not clear whether the seven men appointed by the apostles (Acts 6:3-4) were deacons or had some other assisting office. The text does not refer to them as deacons, and it appears from the preaching and stoning of Stephen (who is said to have worked miracles) recorded in Acts 6:8–7:60, that at least Stephen was primarily an evangelist. It is clear, however, from Acts 6:3-4 that the officers appointed there were to oversee the temporal administration of funds and charity, which are duties traditionally, since the era of Ignatius in the second century A.D., assigned to deacons.

The deaconess in the NT era was a female officer of the local congregation involved in pastoral and liturgical functions. Phoebe, of the congregation in Cenchreae, is called a deaconess, or female servant, by Paul in Romans 16:1. (The Greek term for "servant" is *diakonissa*.) The "widows" referred to by the author of I Timothy 5:3-10 were apparently also recognized officers of the congregation and may have been equal to deaconesses. These widows are said to have a special status and are enrolled at age sixty (I Tim. 5:9). They were actually widowed women who felt a call to serve the congregation. Widows of younger age were prohibited from enrollment since they were likely to want to marry again (I Tim. 5:11-15). The author of the Pastoral Epistle implies that the older widow, so enrolled, is symbolically married (or betrothed) to Christ (vv. 11-12). Widows, therefore, were expected to be celibate during their service. It is speculative to identify this order of enrolled widows with deaconesses, of course. Verse 13 mentions that widows go around "from house to house," so that visiting the homes of church members was one of the duties of widows. Pastoral visitation may, then, have been a function of female ministers in the period of the Pastoral Epistles.

The text in I Timothy 3:11 is unclear. The reference may be to the wives of deacons (so translated by the New English Bible) or may be to deaconesses, as a separate order. The RSV translates the term as "the women," yet goes on to translate verse 12 as saying, "Let deacons be the husband of one wife. . . ." This ambiguous reference probably is to a female order of ministry parallel to the male diaconate.

First Timothy is interesting in that it is the earliest Christian document to give evidence of the formal leadership of the early church. The offices mentioned are ELDER or BISHOP (translated "leader" or "bishop" by the NEB and "bishop" by the RSV; I Tim. 3:1-2) and deacon (I Tim. 3:8-13) and probably deaconesses ("wives," in the NEB; "women," in the RSV: I Tim. 3:11). This reference to deaconesses or widows is interesting, considering the admonitions of the author in I Timothy 2:9-15, which declare: "Let a woman learn in silence with all submissiveness. I permit no woman to teach or to have authority over men; she is to keep silent" (vv. 11-12 RSV). Note the Pauline basis for this advice (I Cor. 11:2-16; 7:1-16).

By the second century, the Christian ministry evolved into a threefold, hierarchical office of bishop, priest (or presbyter, elder), and deacon. The deacon served under the bishop, according to Hippolytus' *Apostolic Tradition*, from the third century. Deacons cared for financial and charitable matters. The Synod of Arles, A.D. 314, made it clear that deacons were under the authority of priests (elders) as well as bishops. Among the Greek (later Orthodox) churches, a man was ordained deacon for life, an office he held while holding a secular vocation as well. In the Latin churches of the West, the office of the deacon gradually became merely a hierarchical stage to the full priesthood.

After the Reformation the functions of the deacon in the Mass or public worship were largely discarded except in the Anglican Communion. In the various Lutheran churches the title of deacon was transferred to lay officers of the congregation in some instances (that is, in the Lutheran church—Missouri Synod) and abandoned altogether in others (that is, in the Lutheran Church in America), although the functions were carried out by "church council" men and women. Pastoral care, in the sense of home visitation, assistance at Holy Communion, and witnessing are Lutheran concepts of the diaconate.

The Lutheran churches of Europe and America have enjoyed a ministry of the deaconess since the modern deaconess movement was begun by Pastor Fliedner of Kaiserswerth, Germany, in 1836. By the end of the nineteenth century, the Lutheran practice was adopted by the Anglican Communion, the Methodist churches, and the Church of Scotland. Protestant deaconesses are generally single women (never married or widowed), who engage in pastoral care of congregational members. This type of service is close to the ministry of deaconesses between the fourth and eleventh centuries A.D. The *Apostolic Constitutions* of the late fourth century A.D., describe deaconesses as ministering to the women members of the church. The Catholic church of the Middle Ages feared the possible competition of deaconesses for priestly power and allowed the office to die before the eleventh century A.D.

Since the Vatican Council II begun by Pope John XXIII, the office of the deacon has undergone great study and considerable development in the Catholic church. The office of "permanent deacon" is now widely recognized and is used in more and more churchly activities by Catholic dioceses. This office, similar to the practice of the Eastern Orthodox church and the permanent deacon office of the Anglican and Episcopal churches, attracts many well-equipped laity. The deacon, today, does much to make up for the decline in vocations to the priesthood in the American Catholic church.

J.C.

## DEAD, ABODE OF THE.

The OT Israelites were practically unique in their contemporary society as evincing, for all practical purposes, virtually no interest in life beyond the present one. This lack of interest contrasts, particularly, with the Egyptian preoccupation with DEATH and the life beyond, which accounts for the great pyramids, the Valley of the Kings, and the mummification process that so enthralled ancient Israelite authors (Gen. 50:2-3, 26), among other phenomena. It is not that the OT was reluctant to accept ideas from without: Egypt, Edom, etc., were always recognized as sources of wisdom, and implicitly at least Canaanite and Mesopotamian sources were acknowledged as having provided models for prophecy, law, some theology, a great deal of liturgy, and the ritual of sacrifice.

As for the dead, however, Israel seems to have resisted all foreign suggestions in making up its own mind. This is rather strange in itself, for nothing had prepared Israel to be an innovative culture. Yet it remained an island of the here-and-now in a world much given over to what-will-be.

So the Hebrew SHEOL, also sometimes called *Abaddon* or "the pit," designations for the final destiny awaiting human existence, is often no more than a figure of speech for death itself, that is, extinction (I Kings 2:6). Usually, however, the terms do envisage a place, however vaguely, somewhere in the bowels of the earth ("the nether world," Ezek. 26:20), guarded by the waters that were thought to flow beneath the inhabited land (compare II Sam. 22:5-6). The assignment of an abode for the dead implied, however, no speculation about an afterlife nor any belief in a real survival of death, not even in the popular religion reflected in the story of I Samuel 28:8-19. Quite to the contrary, the dead ("the shades") have no meaningful existence in *Sheol*: theirs is the negation of life, where there is no communication between them and God (Ps. 88:10-12), where they neither remember nor are remembered (Eccl. 9:5), where they have really ceased to be (Ps. 39:13).

In later Judaism, perhaps anticipated by such passages as Ezekiel 32, and certainly in the NT, *Sheol* (the Greek *hadēs*, "hell"), now equated with "Gehenna," more and more tends to be conceived as a place of perdition and punishment of the wicked dead, while "life" or ETERNAL LIFE in some other dimension will be the gift of God as the lot of the just.

The variations on these themes were considerable and were much exploited by later theology.

B.V.

## DEAD, PRAYERS FOR THE.

A common practice throughout the religious world is intercession on behalf of the departed, particularly loved ones but also patrons and rulers, that they might receive repose and blessing in the next life. Yet such prayers often have had an ambivalent place in the great religions. Typically, a strict construction of doctrine precludes them as superfluous or presumptuous, since one's postmortem state ought to be determined solely by divine judgment, or KARMA, on the basis of one's piety and merit in a life now closed. Yet so natural is the impulse to plead special indulgence of the divine for the deceased of one's household, that prayer for the dead has a way of slipping into funeral and memorial services and indeed into public and private devotions generally. Rulers find that rites for dynastic ancestors help establish legitimacy. Examples of prayers for the dead include Hindu SRADDHA offerings; Buddhist practices to generate PUNNA on their behalf; and the prayers and requiem masses of Roman Catholic, Eastern Orthodox, and some Anglican Christians. Protestantism generally rejects the practice. Prayers *for* the dead should not be confused with ANCESTOR VENERATION or worship *of* departed forebears.

R.E.

## DEAD SEA.

This is a post-biblical designation of what the Bible variously calls the "Salt Sea," the "Sea of the Arabah," or the "Eastern Sea" (as far as the tiny geography of the OT was concerned, the Mediterranean was the "Western Sea"). It is the landlocked lake formed by the emptying of the JORDAN RIVER and its tributaries, over twelve hundred feet below sea level. It is roughly forty-five miles in length and ranges in depth from about twelve hundred feet in the north to thirty feet or less in the south. On both east and west it is bounded by high cliffs, affording it little shoreline. The extremely high saline content of the water, caused by evaporation, which is its only outlet, renders it incapable of supporting any marine life, while the oppressive heat of the region and the salt-laden soil of its surroundings combine to produce a wasteland bereft of vegetation. Both in ancient and modern times, however, it has been exploited for its mineral content: principally salt, bitumen (in Hellenistic times the Dead Sea was called "Lake Asphaltitis"), and potash. Though the blue water of the sea looks deceptively inviting when seen from an elevated distance afar, proximity reveals it for what it is, a desolation.

Exceptions to this rule are provided by the oases of the Dead Sea region supplied by independent water sources. The most famous of these is Jericho ("the city of the palms"), the oldest occupied site of the Near East and possibly of the entire world. Also En-gedi on the western shore was in biblical times fabled as a

Courtesy of the Israel Government Tourist Office, Houston, Texas

*The Dead Sea, with the Negeb mountains in the foreground*

place of lushness and beauty. Recent archaeology has likewise turned up evidence of a network of cities of some consequence that once dotted the southern shore. This fact is more readily explicable in view of the probability that the southernmost part of the Dead Sea was once dry land, that part south of el-Lisan ("the tongue"), the point of land that juts out from the eastern shore and narrows the width of the sea to only a couple of miles. As late as the mid-nineteenth century, there is attestation that here the sea was fordable from shore to shore. On the southwest shore Jebel Usdum, a salt mountain with grotesque formations, preserves reminiscences of the Sodom legend associated with this region (Gen. 19). By the Arabs the Dead Sea is known as the "Sea of Lot," as part of the same legend.

In Ezekiel's great eschatological vision (Ezek. 47:8-12; compare also Zech. 14:8), the Dead Sea is seen as becoming fresh water, supporting all kinds of fish life, its shores rife with vegetation (though, practically, provision will still be made for salt).

B.V

**DEAD SEA SCROLLS (DSS).** Beginning in 1947 with the chance find of some scrolls in a cave overlooking the Dead Sea, there have come to light portions of about six hundred manuscripts in addition to a few complete documents. They date from the end of the second century B.C. to the mid-first century A.D. Further exploration disclosed the sites of a residential settlement and some small industrial sites belonging to the group that produced the scrolls. The name QUMRAN, which is the local Arab name for the dry creek bed that drains the winters' rains from Jerusalem (about fifteen miles to the northwest), has become the popular designation for the site and the scrolls.

The herdsmen who found the first scrolls in clay jars brought their finds to an antiquities dealer in Bethlehem, who in turn took them to a religious leader and then to the American School of Oriental Research in Jerusalem. Initial publication of the scrolls began under Miller Burrows at the school, but the outbreak of the Arab-Israeli War in 1948

hindered the process. In the mid-1950s R. de Vaux and G. L. Harding excavated other caves in the area (of which eleven produced scroll finds), as well as the occupation sites nearby. One of these was the community center; the other was an installation where the agricultural and supply needs of the community were met. An international team of scholars began preparing the manuscripts for publication. Since the 1967 occupation of East Jerusalem by the Israelis and the purchase of several of the most important scrolls by Israel, Israeli scholarship has dominated the publication process. Searches in other caves along the western shore of the Dead Sea produced other scrolls at Murabaát and MASADA, including important copies of biblical texts—some of them known in modern times only in Greek translation. Many of the manuscripts from the caves south of Qumran, however, come from the later time and were related to the Jewish Revolt of the early second century.

Courtesy of Otto Betz

*View of a Qumran cave where many of the Dead Sea Scrolls were found*

The community center, which was built on the site of a fortress from the late eighth century B.C., included a large dining room—a meeting room with a kitchen and service area adjoining, a tower (for protection?), and storerooms. Equipment found in the ruins included benches and inkwells, which were part of the community's SCRIPTORIUM, where the scrolls were produced and copied. An elaborate system of conduits and pools provided the water supply, which seems to have included ceremonial baths. On the basis of coins and comparison of the pottery with other sites, it was determined that the site was in use in two periods from 135 to 31 B.C. and from A.D. 1 to 68. An earthquake, followed by a fire, seems to have caused the interruption of the occupation of the center. Three caves (1, 4, and 11) produced the most significant manuscript finds. At some distance from the center were the community burial sites, which included a special section where the remains of a relatively few bodies of women and children were found.

*Qumran as seen from a Dead Sea cave*

The manuscripts may be grouped under five categories: (1) biblical texts; (2) biblical commentaries; (3) foundation documents of the Dead Sea sect; (4) revelatory texts; and (5) liturgical texts.

Portions of more than one hundred copies of the Hebrew scriptures were found in a single cave (cave 4), though they survived in thousands of fragments. The writing styles of the manuscripts from all the caves indicate that some scrolls are as old as 250 B.C., whereas others date from the time of the destruction of the site. It has been suggested that adherents of the community brought copies of the scriptures with them on admission to membership. Both the alphabet used (whether the older style based on the Canaanite script, or the newer squarish letter derived from Aramaic) and the actual text copied vary widely. There are translations into Greek (the LXX, or SEPTUAGINT type) as well as paraphrases in Aramaic (the TARGUMS). Some manuscripts omit the so-called weak consonants (the rough equivalents of English w, h, y, and the glottal stop), while others include them. Difficult passages are occasionally provided with clarification by the insertion of a phrase from another scriptural text.

Courtesy of John C. Trever

*The complete Dead Sea Scroll commentary on Habakkuk found in a cave near Qumran*

Some manuscripts follow closely the traditional Masoretic Hebrew text (*see* BIBLE, TEXT OF), while others include distinctive features found in the LXX and apparently present in the original Hebrew text from which the Greek translation was made. In addition to copies of all the books of the Hebrew CANON (except Esther), complete or fragmentary copies of nearly all the so-called Apocrypha are represented. The exceptions are the Wisdom of Solomon, I and II Maccabees, Judith, and Baruch (except for a Greek version of an addition of that book). These were omitted because they were intellectually or ideologically incompatible with the outlook of the Qumran community. Especially important among the findings are portions of Sirach, which had otherwise been known only from the Greek translation until the discovery in the late nineteenth century in Cairo of some extensive fragments of the work in Hebrew.

Judging by sheer numbers of copies, the most treasured biblical writings at Qumran, apart from Deuteronomy, must have been Isaiah and the Psalms. For neither of these books, however, do the manuscripts provide what appears to be a more reliable or ancient edition of the Hebrew text than had previously been known. The Psalms scrolls include

Copyright © John C. Trever, 1970

*Scroll of Isaiah found at Qumran, opened to column 49 with Isaiah 59:17–61:4 showing. According to Luke 4:16-19 Jesus read Isaiah 61:1-3 in the synagogue of Nazareth. This scroll was copied with carbon ink about 100 B.C. and is the oldest complete biblical manuscript known to exist.*

materials, not found in the traditional Hebrew text, which have been given the designation of Psalms 151–155. The many copies of Deuteronomy, and Genesis and Exodus (with fewer of Leviticus and Numbers) underscore how the Qumran group saw itself as the climax of sacred history, as the faithful remnant to whom God had revealed, through the True Prophet (Deut. 18:18), the proper and final interpretation of the Law. Several of the biblical books are preserved in a form shorter than that found in the later standard Hebrew text—for example, Jeremiah and Job—which may mean that the briefer form is older. Above all it is clear that the Qumran community was more interested in transmitting a text of the scripture that was relevant to its purposes than it was in faithfully reproducing a traditional text.

Besides copies of the Hebrew scripture, the community produced paraphrases of the biblical writings in Aramaic (Targums), including one of Job, and interpretive expansions on biblical passages, such as one that recounts stories of characters in Genesis: Lamech, Noah, and Abraham, or the Prayer of Nabonidus which reads like an expansion of Daniel. Equally important are the extensive commentaries (called the PESHER) on biblical books (Habakkuk, Micah, Isaiah, Nahum, etc.), which are concerned to disclose the hidden meaning of the text for the community in the time of the commentators, not for the historical meaning in the time of the prophet. It was the Righteous Teacher who was given the keys to understand the scripture in the light of God's purpose for the new covenant, as the Habakkuk commentary states and as is confirmed in one of the Damascus documents. Other writings offer exposition of the Psalms and of historical reports of promise about the Davidic kingdom.

Most informative about the nature of the Qumran sect are the foundation documents discovered there in various editions. Foremost of these is the *Rule of the Community*, which probably goes back to 150 B.C. It depicts the sect as the true people of the new covenant foretold in Jeremiah 31–33 and gives detailed instructions how they are to live in the last days. Strongly dualistic in outlook, the Rule sees the world and its inhabitants as subject to Belial, the embodiment of evil, and humanity divided into children of darkness and children of light. The mode of entering the covenant community, instructions for those within, the structure of leadership within, the mode of expulsion of the unfit, the necessity to safeguard the truth within the community, and the pattern of communal worship are all specified. An appendix offers additional instruction and culminates in the depiction of a sacred meal of bread and wine at which the Messiah of Israel (a royal figure) yields priority to the Messiah of Aaron (a priestly figure).

The historical origins of the sect are sketched in the Damascus Document (CD), which has survived in multiple fragmentary copies at Qumran, as well as in a late (tenth century A.D.) copy found in 1896 in Cairo. The chief characters in CD are the Righteous Teacher and the Man of Lies. The latter is almost certainly Jonathan, son of Mattathias and brother of Judas the Maccabee. He is referred to in the Pesher on Habakkuk as the Wicked Priest, since it was he who replaced a high priest with the proper heritage (a descendant of Zadok) by one who lacked it. The Righteous Teacher led his followers out to their place of refuge in Damascus (Qumran) to maintain their purity there and to await God's deliverance.

The expectations of divine vindication are described in detail in other Qumran documents: *The War of the Children of Light and the Children of Darkness* describes the final battle; *The Temple Scroll* details how the sacrifices and other functions in the Temple are to be handled rightly in accord with God's expressed rules; *The Copper Scroll* tells where treasure lies hidden that is to be recovered. These revelatory writings are matched by liturgical documents, which help the community prepare for the end of the age, especially the *Hymns of Thanksgiving* (the *Hodayoth* and fragments from cave 4). The *Hodayoth* consist of a network of quotations, mostly the biblical Psalms and Isaiah. These hymns convey vividly the deep concerns and aspiration for the apparent triumph of evil, the need for courage in the face of persecution, and confidence in the future triumph of God over evil. All

Courtesy of the Israel Department of Antiquities and Museums

*First-century jar from Qumran inscribed with the name "John"*

this is set forth with a profound sense of gratitude for divine grace, which has enlightened and will sustain God's chosen few.

It is possible from this rich and diverse set of documents to infer something about the history of the sect for and by whom this material was produced. The dating of the origin of the movement at 390 years after Jerusalem fell to Nebuchadnezzar brings one down into the second century B.C. The other time span mentioned in the Nahum Commentary begins with Antiochus (175-163) and comes down to the coming of the "Kittim"—a reference to the Roman takeover of Jerusalem in 63 B.C. This marks the limits of the sect down to the time of the writer of the Nahum *Pesher*. The Righteous Teacher had apparently supported the Maccabees until Jonathan appointed an illegitimate priest, whereupon the withdrawal to the Qumran took place. The site by the Wadi Qumran may have been chosen in anticipation of the transformation of the river that is to flow from the Temple to the Dead Sea, as promised in Ezekiel 47. An earthquake apparently ruined the settlement in 31 B.C., but a rebuilding took place about the time of the birth of Jesus. The documents from this later period depict the Romans as allied with the children of darkness, and it was Roman troops that destroyed the settlement in A.D. 68. Some seem to have escaped southward to Masada, only to die in A.D. 73 in the futile last stages of the revolt of the Jews against Rome.

H.K.

**DEAN.** Ecclesiastical title, from the Latin *decanus,* or "ten." Originally a monk who supervised ten novices. Later, the superior of a cathedral who oversaw the clergy, their services, and the building. In the Anglican Church (and among some American Lutherans) deans assist the bishop in supervising clerical activities.

J.C.

**DEATH OF GOD THEOLOGY.** A movement that flourished in the United States between 1960 and 1970. *The Death of God* was the title of a book by Gabriel Vahanian drawing attention to the cultural fact that many people in the twentieth century get along very well without the "God hypothesis" and that all educated people today do not invoke God as an explanation of events once ascribed to God's agency (sickness and health, good harvests, natural disasters, etc.). The Death of God theology was an attempt to adjust to this cultural fact by restating Christian theology without a doctrine of God.

It was never a unified movement, and one can distinguish several varieties. Paul van Buren dispensed with God because he believed that theistic belief has been shown to be incoherent and incredible by modern philosophy. T. J. J. Altizer developed a Hegelian METAPHYSICS in which God is said to be completely finitized in the world of creatures. Both

Altizer and W. Hamilton believed further that the dignity and progress of humanity demand the abolition of God. Along with these Christian writers may be associated Richard Rubenstein, a Jewish rabbi who believed that the sufferings of his people had rendered incredible the God of the covenant. He also contrasted his own pessimistic atheism with what he considered to be the unjustified optimism of the Christian Death of God writers. The whole movement illustrates the crisis of theism, but to many it seemed that a theology founded on atheism is a contradiction. In S. Ogden's words, however absurd belief in God might be, it could hardly be as absurd as Christianity without God.

J.M.

**DEATH, THEOLOGY OF.** In the OT and NT, the end of physical life on earth, the separation of the SOUL from the BODY. Early Hebrew religion gave little thought to death, accepting it as a part of life, and it gave scant attention to life after death. Gradually, belief developed that the departed soul went to SHEOL or HADES (Ps. 88:12; 86:13; Prov. 15:24) where the soul barely existed as a shade or shadow. Death was considered the result of sin, as shown in Genesis 3:19, 22. Not until very late in Hebrew history (that is, the time of the writing of Daniel, about 350 B.C.) did belief in the resurrection of the dead, to be judged on their works, arise. Before Ezekiel and Daniel, there was little, if any, belief in personal IMMORTALITY. Rather, the nation, the people of Israel, was seen as immortal, as it continued from generation to generation. Many scholars believe such passages as Hosea 6:1-3, which sound personal, probably refer to the whole people of Israel. Such a reading rests on appreciation of the Hebrew belief that human beings are animated bodies, not incarnate souls, as in Greek thought.

In the NT, death is closely identified with sin (Rom. 5:12). Death, like sin, law, and the devil, is a hostile power; the very demonic powers that Christ struggles to overcome in his proclamation of the Kingdom and triumphs over in his death and resurrection. Paul puts it clearly: for those with faith in Jesus Christ, death no longer has any power to terrify or destroy (Rom. 6–9; I Cor. 15). People die physically; but spiritually believers have eternal life, so that alive or dead they cannot fall out of the hand of God.

J.C.

**DEBIR.** A royal Canaanite city-state in the hill country of Judah that figures prominently in the narrative of the Israelite conquest of the land of Palestine. In the oldest tradition (Judg. 1:12-15) this conquest was ascribed to Calebites and Kenizzites. Since these were later assimilated to the tribe of Judah, Debir eventually became a Judahite conquest (Judg. 1:10-11). And finally, in the Deuteronomic history with its picture of a single Israelite conquest under the leadership of Joshua, Debir becomes the prize of "all Israel," along with Lachish, Eglon, Hebron, and Libnah (Josh. 10:38). These sites, violently destroyed about 1200 B.C., remain for many an argument confirmatory of the historicity of the Israelite conquest.

Debir has long been identified with Tell Beit Mirsim, one of the most thoroughly explored sites of Palestinian archaeology, though the latter is not, strictly speaking, in the hill country. The identification was never undisputed, and recently the rival claims of the nearby Khirbet Rabud have commended themselves to scholars of the Near East. Khirbet Rabud displays the remains of several cities of the Late Bronze and Early Iron ages.

B.V.

**DEBORAH.** (1) Rebekah's nurse, who first appears anonymously (Gen. 24:59), is given this name in Genesis 35:8, where it is said that she was buried under an oak below Bethel. It is quite likely that this is a secondary accounting for the fact that there was a traditional "tree of Deborah" (Judg. 4:5; here, however, a palm rather than an oak) "between Ramah and Bethel in the hill country of Ephraim."

(2) The famous Deborah of the Bible is the heroine of Judges 4–5, who is variously termed a prophetess and a judge (Judg. 4:4), a mother in Israel (Judg. 5:7), and a songstress (Judg. 5:12). "Prophetess," in the sense of the nationalistic charismatics who handed down oracles promising victory over the people's enemies in the name of the covenant Deity (I Sam. 23:1-5; I Kings 20:13-15; etc.), seems to be the most applicable title as far as the prose story of Judges 4 is concerned. Perhaps the same is true of the poetry of Judges 5, though some have thought to find a closer parallel in a feature of Near Eastern nomadic tribal society verified only in later times: the "battle maiden" who with song and dance stimulated and goaded on the fighting men. In any case, "prophetess" is probably a flexible enough term to include this function as well. It should be noted, whatever the determination of Deborah's character and despite the attribution of Judges 5 to her as "the song of Deborah," it is Jael rather than Deborah whom the author of Judges regards as the "most blessed of women" in this episode (Judg. 5:24).

It has generally been assumed that the prose of Judges 4 is a more recent retelling of the story of the poetry of Judges 5, the latter being frequently described as one of the most ancient compositions preserved in the OT. This consensus has been challenged, however. While the prose envisages Deborah, the wife of Lappidoth, an Ephraimite, enlisting the services of a Naphtalite chieftain, Barak, to lead a coalition of Ephraimites, Naphtalites, and Zebulunites against Jabin of Hazor and his general Sisera—a limited engagement which, in any case, is finally resolved only by the action of the woman Jael—the poetry celebrates a much more heroic

exploit involving many more tribes, many more details, and much more drama, typical of later elaboration. There is, at all events, agreement enough between the two sources, once each is read without editorial embellishments, to conclude that together they testify to a crucial victory of Israelites over indigenous Canaanites in the time of the conquest/settlement of the Promised Land. A victory in the strategic Valley of Jezreel "at Taanach, by the waters of Megiddo" (Judg. 5:19) would have obliterated a Canaanite barrier to the union of northern and central Israelite tribal units and contributed measurably to the eventual Israelite domination.

B.V.

**DECALOGUE.** *See* TEN COMMANDMENTS.

**DECAPOLIS.** The name given in the Gospels (Matt. 4:25; Mark 5:20; 7:31) to a region, mostly east of the Jordan River in Palestine, consisting originally of ten Greek cities, which formed a league for defense and fostering trade. The earliest list of these cities is contained in Pliny's *Natural History,* written in the late first century A.D. It includes the following: Hippo, Gadara, Pella, Philadelphia, Galasa (Gerasa), Dion, Canatha, Damascus, Raphana, and Scythopolis, which Josephus calls the largest of the Decapolis. The cities were founded shortly after Alexander the Great's conquest and reflected the culture of Greece in the construction of temples, theaters, amphitheaters, hippodromes, aqueducts, fora, colonnaded streets, and baths. The presence of swine there so near to Jewish territory is understandable in such a Hellenistic environment. Ptolemy, a geographer of the second century A.D., includes eighteen cities in the Decapolis.

J.R.M.

**DECLENSION.** Second-generation New England PURITANS experienced a decline in piety, "experimental" religion, or experiential faith, which led to difficult questions of church order because only those members who had "owned the covenant," or had a full conversion experience, were qualified for full church membership and the right to have their children baptized. Pastors preached jeremiads against this declension, but eventually solved the baptism problem in 1662 with the HALF-WAY COVENANT.

N.H.

**DEDICATION, FEAST OF.** *See* HANUKKAH.

**DEDUCTION.** A reasoning process defined from mathematical theory, arising in Pythagoras and finding its basic formulation in Euclid. Beginning with a fundamental concept, postulates are proposed and a theory deduced. The person is thus led step by step to accept the completed formulation as true. Philosophically this is deductive logic, and it reached a high form under the Scholastics of the Middle Ages with the use of the syllogism and the formal disputation. Thomas AQUINAS, in the *Summa theologiae,* sets forth a proposition, deduces a number of objections, follows this with replies to each objection, then briefly states the conclusion.

HEGEL's dialectic, with its movement from thesis to antithesis to synthesis, is a form of deductive reasoning. This method of thinking goes from the general to the particular, in contrast with inductive reasoning, the method of scientific inquiry, which goes from the particular (the experimental) to the general, the principle being stated after the presentation of experimental proof. Deductive reasoning is also used in language theory.                I.C.

**DEEP, THE.** A semi-poetic term, used largely in the OT, with several applications, all connoting wet, unstable, unpleasant, even dangerous conditions, the positive contrast being the earth. The OT concept of the cosmos or world derives from its wider cultural environment. The Hebrews made use of their neighbors' mythology only in poetic ways. Otherwise they shared an overall, water-dominated picture of the world: (1) waters above the firmament; (2) heaven as the source of rain; (3) springs, rivers, lakes, and seas upon the earth; (4) the "fountain of the deep," that is, an ocean surrounding the earth; (5) waters under the earth; and (6) rivers of the underworld or Sheol.

Essential in any description of Hebrew thought of the deep is Genesis 1:2, where the chaotic matter God worked upon in creation was "the deep," "the waters." In Mesopotamian and Ugaritic thought, the sea, personified as Tiamat and Yam or Prince Sea, was rebellious to law and order, often hostile, even destructive. Hence the conclusion that human existence has been involved always in a cosmic struggle between order and chaos. In that struggle, terrifying watery things (the Deep, the Dragon) are hazardous and to be treated with awe and respect.                P.L.G.

**DEFENDER OF THE FAITH.** A title bestowed on King Henry VIII of England by Pope Leo X in 1521 for Henry's *Assertion of the Seven Sacraments* against Luther's *Babylonian Captivity* (1520) attacking the Roman views. Parliament confirmed the title in 1544, making it traditional for England's rulers.                C.M.

*DE FIDE.* In the Roman Catholic tradition a word that refers to the deposit of faith. Some truth is available to reason, for example, a knowledge that God exists. Other truth, such as the understanding of God as Trinity, is known only by faith. This comes from special revelation as a gift of God's grace. It is preserved and handed on through the teaching office of the church, the magisterium.                I.C.

**DEFROCK.** Literally, to "unfrock," to remove the frock or outer gown that monks and friars wear. Used more extensively to refer to the act of involuntarily depriving any minister of his or her authority and functions, usually for reasons of unethical behavior or theological deviation.                J.G.

**DEISM.** From the Latin word *deus* ("god"), the term is used both for a distinct belief about God and for a movement of the late seventeenth and the eighteenth centuries reflecting the religious views of the ENLIGHTENMENT. Deism teaches that God created the world but does not providentially guide or supernaturally intervene in nature or in human affairs. It is a belief of Deism that the world's intelligible order is demonstrable proof of an intelligent Creator and that reason alone is sufficient to deduce all that is necessary to know about God's nature and purpose. Deism rejects both ecclesiastical authority and special revelation. Worn out by the seventeenth-century Wars of Religion, European thinkers searched for a common religious foundation on which all rational people could agree. Since reasonable people could not agree on the interpretation of biblical revelation, the Deists sought to bring the truths of the Bible wholly within the sphere of natural reason. The "Father of Deism," Edward Herbert, the first baron of Cherbury (1583–1648), taught that everyone possesses five innate truths imprinted by God: (1) that God exists; (2) that God should be worshiped; (3) that the practice of virtue is the chief part of the worship of God; (4) that people have always abhorred evil and are under the obligation to repent of their sins; and (5) that there will be rewards and punishments after death.

Among the important Deist writers were JOHN TOLAND (1670–1722) and MATTHEW TINDAL (1655–1733) in England, VOLTAIRE (1694–1778) in France, H. S. Reimarus (1694–1768) and G. E. Lessing (1729–81) in Germany, and Thomas Paine (1737–1809) in America. In *Christianity Not Mysterious* (1696) Toland taught that, while religious truths may be made known to us by the testimony of others (revelation), they can never be mysterious or incomprehensible to reason once known. In *Christianity as Old as Creation* (1730), Tindal insisted that since God is perfect and all-wise, God's perfect religion cannot be altered or increased. It must then dispense its truth equally to everyone at all times. Some Deists, for example, Voltaire, Reimarus, and Paine, attacked orthodox Christianity, denouncing popular superstition, priestly intolerance, and biblical error. Deism in turn was criticized by DAVID HUME, JOSEPH BUTLER, and IMMANUEL KANT, but its legacy of reason, autonomy, toleration, and ethical seriousness lives on.                J.L.

**DEISSMANN, ADOLPH** (1866–1937). A German scholar who demonstrated, on the basis of the discovery of Greek papyri in Egypt, that the language of the NT was the common Greek of the marketplace.                J.R.M.

**DELILAH.** A Sorek Valley woman with a name meaning "flirt"—not a harlot (compare Judg. 16:1)—whom Samson loved. She enticed him and discovered "wherein his great strength lies," which was in his hair—it had never been cut. The Philistines seized and imprisoned Samson and paid Delilah with 5500 pieces of silver (about $1,200, Judg. 16:4-22).

P.L.G.

**DELPHI, ORACLE OF.** The most famous common sanctuary in ancient Greece, located on the slopes of Mount Parnassus. In classical times the *Oracle of Delphi* was a shrine to Apollo. This god was believed to give advice through an entranced priestess, the Pythia. The oracle had no small influence in political matters, although the ambiguity of many of its sayings was proverbial.

R.E.

**DELUGE.** *See* FLOOD.

**DEMAS.** A co-worker of Paul, mentioned only three times in the NT, unless the name be regarded as a shortened form of Demetrius and identified with the one in III John 12. An alternate spelling is Damas, a name worn by a bishop of Magnesia. He is mentioned favorably in Philemon 24 and Colossians 4:14 but later forsook Paul because of his love for worldly things (II Tim. 4:10).

J.R.M.

**DEMETRIUS.** (1) A silversmith of Ephesus. He was a maker of shrines of Artemis (Acts 19:24), the chief deity of the city, whose temple was considered one of the seven wonders of the ancient world. Paul's preaching against idolatry threatened Demetrius' business, so he led a protest against Paul in the theater. This theater still stands in a relatively good state of preservation.

(2) A man mentioned in III John 12. Perhaps he was a bearer of the letter to Gaius (v. 1), whom the author declares is one whose Christian life is witnessed to by all who knew him and by the truth itself. This is the only place he is mentioned in the NT, and there is no certain knowledge of him in early church history.

(3) Demetrius I Soter. He was the grandson of Antiochus the Great, and was king of Syria from 162 to 150 B.C. He was killed in battle by the forces of the Jewish Maccabean leader Jonathan in 150 B.C. The main sources of information for him are I Maccabees, Josephus, and some fragments of Polybius.

(4) Demetrius II Nicator. He was the elder son of Demetrius I and ruled Syria twice, from 145 to 139 B.C. and from 129 to 125 B.C. His exploits are recounted in I Maccabees and Josephus, including his conflicts with the Maccabeans Jonathan and Simon and his assassination while trying to escape after a defeat in battle.

J.R.M.

**DEMON.** Demons or evil spirits play a major role in the NT, especially in the Synoptic Gospels. In parallelism to the later Jewish belief (after the Babylonian exile) that God has a host of angels, or good spirits, to work the divine will, the belief arose that Satan, the accuser and tempter of humankind, also had his malignant (demonic) angels to pursue his assaults on people. That these demons were connected to the occurrence of disease, such as deafness, dumbness, blindness, and epilepsy, is shown in Jesus' healing of these conditions by way of exorcism of demons in Mark 9:25; Luke 11:14-16; Matthew 12:22; Luke 9:39; and Mark 1:26. Both demonology and angelology seem to be ultimately based on ANIMISM, a primitive belief that nature and human-kind are inhabited by many spirits, both good and evil.

Without doubt, the Synoptic Gospel account of Jesus' ministry is cast in the form of a confrontation between Jesus and the power of the kingdom of God, on one side, and SATAN and the kingdom of this world (the demons) on the other. The fact that the gospel is gospel, that is, good news, arises from Jesus' victory over Satan. This struggle and victory is illustrated by Jesus' parable about binding the strong man (Mark 3:27). Jesus pointed out to those who accused him of having supernatural powers because he was in league with Satan that Satan was not likely to give someone the power to overthrow his position of power in the world. Changing the metaphor, Jesus declared that no one could invade a strong man's house and despoil it unless he had first defeated and bound the strong man. Even so, since Jesus cast out demons and healed diseases, this activity proved that Jesus had defeated Satan. In Luke 10, upon the return of the seventy disciples from their preaching mission, the faithful rejoice because, "In your name, Lord . . . even the devils submit to us" (Luke 10:17 NEB). Jesus then tells them, "I watched how Satan fell, like lightning, out of the sky" (Luke 10:18 NEB). The very meaning of the gospel is that Jesus triumphed over Satan and the demons.

Cardinal Leon-Joseph Suenens recently addressed the question of demons and the presence of evil in the world in *Renewal and the Powers of Darkness* (Malines Document IV), speaking to a contemporary rise in belief in the devil and the resort to rites of exorcism among some charismatic groups. While Cardinal Suenens speaks to a Catholic context, his observations are applicable to Protestantism as well. He reflects:

If the Catholic Church clearly affirms the existence and influence of the Powers of Evil, her systematic theology nonetheless remains very guarded on this subject. If ever there was a domain that must be approached very soberly, as St. Paul advises, this is surely the one. We cannot even begin to describe the Devil except indirectly, by metaphors and the like. His strength lies in the very disguises he assumes; he is an illusionist by nature and the father of lies. Intrinsically and by definition, he is obscure. No one has ever seen the actual countenance of the Evil One, for he is a spiritual being, outside our reach, and known only as such through Revelation. . . . Therefore, it is all the more important to refrain from all exaggerations which could lead to obsessive psychosis. This would be the very negation of our Christian religion, which is Good News and the saving-grace of Christ's victory. (Ann Arbor; Servant Books, 1983 p. 77)

This is excellent advice for anyone interested in demons.

While the Hebrew conception of Satan developed rather late and is not fully developed in the canonical books of the OT, it does receive elaboration in the OT apocryphal books, especially the book of Enoch. Some of the apocryphal books suggested that the oppression of the Jews showed that the world was under the power of Satan. However, the kingdom of Satan will perish with the coming of the Messiah, who will inaugurate a new age of justice and peace. This development in late Judaism was limited to the apocalyptic writers; most respected rabbis paid little attention to demons or Satan. The apocalyptic writings were taken over, in the main, by the early Christians; hence demonology had far less development in Judaism than it did in Christianity.

In the book of Enoch, very influential on later Christian thought, Enoch is taken on a journey of inspection of the earth and Sheol (hell). Enoch sees the fallen state of people and concludes that evil was let loose in the world by the lust of the angels (sons of God) for the daughters of men (Gen. 6:4). Enoch makes it clear (which was not stated in Gen. 6:4), that these "sons of God" (in Hebrew, *bene ha-elohim*) are evil angels, or demons. Apocalyptic Judaism then went on to develop the hierarchy and names of the demonic hosts. At first, there were many different names for the devil: Belial, Mastema, Azazel, Satanail, Sammael, Semyaza, and Satan. Gradually all these names coalesced into one, Satan, the opposer, the accuser, or the obstructor. This was translated into the Greek, used in much apocalyptic literature, by the Greek word *diabolos*, or "adversary," and later into the Latin *diabolus* and the English DEVIL. Other apocalyptic books, such as the Book of Jubilees, the Testament of Reuben, and the Book of the Secrets of Enoch, develop the idea of evil angels or demons. The Secrets of Enoch specifically says the evil angels rebelled on account of pride.

The apocalyptic (non-canonical) development of demonology stands behind the generally accepted belief in demons of Jesus' day. All abnormalities and illnesses were credited to demonic influence. Mary Magdalene was said to have "seven demons" (Luke 8:2), and the poor wretch known as the Gadarene demoniac was reported to be infested with a legion (ten thousand) of demons (Luke 8:30). Jesus' powerful presence, stern words, and use of prayer (and sometimes fasting and a material element, as when he touched a man with his saliva) were effective in driving out the hold that belief in demons had upon the minds and bodies of the sufferers who came to him for help. The gospel was victorious over demons in his day and is still victorious over evil when men and women believe.

J.C.

**DEMYTHOLOGIZATION.** Demythologizing (German, *Entmythologisierung*) is a method of NT interpretation first expounded by RUDOLF BULTMANN in his essay "New Testament and Mythology" in 1941, and then developed in many subsequent writings. The presence of MYTH in the NT had, of course, long been recognized and was something of an embarrassment to liberal theology. Liberal theologians tended to ignore myth. Bultmann accuses HARNACK of reducing the NT proclamation to a few basic principles of religion and ethics. But the mythology, for example, the expectation of a speedy end to the age, enters so deeply into the NT that it cannot be simply ignored without serious mutilation.

On the other hand, Bultmann thinks that we live in a post-mythical age when talk of voices from heaven or an end of the world or an ascension into heaven have become meaningless in any literal way. Only by a kind of schizophrenia is it possible to believe reports of such happenings and yet at the same time make use of electric light, modern medicine, and all the other paraphernalia of scientific and technological society. So what is to be done? Bultmann's choice of the word "demythologizing" may have been unfortunate, for he is not proposing the elimination of myth, as the term might suggest. Rather, he is concerned to interpret it into a more meaningful language, for it is part of the proclamation. The first point then is to determine the true subject matter of myth. Because of its objectifying language and its narrative form, myth appears to be describing events that have happened or will happen "out there."

Bultmann believes that the primary function of mythology is to express a self-understanding. Myth comes from a period when abstract terms were little developed and human beings could reflect on their nature and destiny only by telling stories. A creation myth, for instance, is held by Bultmann to be an expression of human finitude and dependence. To interpret the mythology of the NT, it is necessary first to ask the right question—not "What happened?" but "With what possibility of existence does this present me?" or "Into what self-understanding does it bring me?"

In order that this question may be asked intelligently, it is necessary for the one who asks it to have some understanding of the structure of human existence and a language for discussing that structure. This is where EXISTENTIALISM comes in, especially the analysis of human existence given by MARTIN HEIDEGGER in *Being and Time*. Bultmann does not hesitate to call this the "right" philosophy for employment by the NT interpreter, but he acknowledges that there may be other descriptions of human existence that could serve the purpose as well as

Heidegger's. To give an example of Bultmann's method, he sees the NT teaching that life is to be lived in the face of the end of the age as a mythological equivalent of Heidegger's insistence that our human existence is a being toward death, that is to say, an eschatological existence.

Bultmann denied that this would mean the reduction of the Christian proclamation to a philosophy of existence, for he believed that Christianity brings the offer of a grace that is not found in any philosophy and that God has spoken a decisive word in Jesus Christ.

He gave fresh relevance to some obscure teachings of the NT but left many questions unanswered. While some felt that his demythologizing had gone too far in a reductionist direction, others wanted to carry it much further, even to the elimination of God.

J.M.

**DENARIUS.** A Roman silver coin with an impression of Tiberius Caesar's head, the most frequently used coin in the first century A.D., and the most frequently mentioned in the NT, equivalent to the Greek DRACHMA. The coin was used to pay soldiers, was the daily wage of a laborer (Matt. 20:9-10, 13), and was used to pay Roman taxes (Matt. 22:19; Mark 12:15; Luke 20:24). It took two denarii to make the half shekel of the Jewish head tax (Matt. 17:27). Twenty-five silver denarii was equal to one gold denarius in the Roman Empire.

P.L.G.

**DENOMINATIONALISM.** A largely American system in which Protestant Christianity has been divided into competing groups. The term applies to a religious situation in which there are many religious groups, none with privileged legal status and each receiving equal treatment before the law.

Historically Christendom was considered a unity with Eastern and Western expressions. Western Christianity was unified around the Roman pontiff until the Reformation. Thereafter churches tended to be geographic: the Church of England, the Church of Scotland (Presbyterian), the Russian Orthodox church. A corollary is the parish system, whereby all who live in a geographic area are considered members of one central church and are taxed by the state to support that church. Whereas many countries have religious unity and political diversity, the United States has religious PLURALISM and a rather homogeneous two-party political system.

In colonial America Congregationalism was established in Massachusetts Bay and Anglicanism in Virginia and South Carolina, until the first and second Great Awakenings witnessed the beginning of the disestablishment of American Protestantism. In early American history American denominations were often American expressions of European divisions. Many denominations reflected the cultural and language distinctives of their native roots. Denominationalism has encouraged Christians to resolve conflicts by division rather than political compromise. In this century many divisions created by ethnic or language groupings and by the Civil War have been healed, only to have new divisions created by such issues as the "inerrancy of the original documents" of Scripture and the question of women's ordination.

The mobility of American society tends to make denominations competitive yet interchangeable. Theology in mainline Protestant churches has become homogenized. Even in smaller Evangelical churches, often founded in sharp theological disputes, lay people, and even pastors, ignore or downplay theological distinctions.

H. Richard Niebuhr called denominationalism "an unacknowledged hypocrisy" in the church, a compromise between Christianity and the world, an accommodation to "the caste system of human society." Certainly many American denominations today still represent such distinctions as class, race, and sexual orientation. Denominationalism has even been exported to many Third World countries by competing missionary efforts. (See also VOLUNTARYISM.)

N.H.

**DEPRAVITY.** See ORIGINAL SIN.

**DE PROFUNDIS.** One of the seven penitential Psalms, named for its opening words in Latin, "Out of the depths" (Ps. 130:1). The Psalm probably dates from the Exile, and expresses the hopes of the exiled Jews to go up to Jerusalem. It is therefore called a GRADUAL or "going up" Psalm.

J.C.

**DEPROGRAMMING.** A process said to reverse the effects of "brainwashing" or mind control encountered in certain of the new religious CULTS. The theoretical basis of the process and its effect, if any, is controversial.

Deprogramming stems from a California layman, Ted Patrick, a state employee whose teenagers joined one of the new religions in the 1960s. Upset by this, Patrick determined to break the control he felt cult leaders exercised over his children. Pretending to join a group, Patrick's experience convinced him that rather than bringing about religious conversions, groups like the Unification Church actually "brainwashed" their recruits. Here Patrick pointed to the thought reform or brainwashing practiced on American prisoners of war during the Korean War by the Chinese Communists.

Assuming that cult members were brainwashed, Patrick set up a process of confrontation and challenge of the cultist's ideas, beliefs, and practices. He believed it was necessary to ask questions until the person ran out of "programmed ideas." Once that stage was reached, the mind would start thinking independently again; the cultist would see the contradictions inherent in cult belief and be psychologically free again.

Eventually, Patrick and others recommended to parents of cultists that they should kidnap (if necessary) their children and subject them to "deprogramming." The new religions, civil libertarians, and some clergy and professors of psychology, religion, and sociology, disputed the actuality of brainwashing and consequently the reality of deprogramming itself. This dispute continues. It appears that brainwashing and deprogramming are simplistic concepts that are said to work magically. But both processes may point to a reality in human experience, psychological conditioning. Camps in remote places, intensive study groups, and close personal attention—elements both of cult and church experience—do tend to condition (that is, to redirect consciousness) people into the likeness of the leaders doing the conditioning. Such a state decays over time unless it is reinforced. The discipline of cults and churches reinforces the original conditioning. It may also be possible to hasten the decay of conditioning and to recondition the person, directing the person to new ideas and values. Deprogramming may then be seen as reconditioning.

J.C.

**DEPTH PSYCHOLOGY.** *See* PSYCHOANALYSIS.

**DERVISH.** Persian term for a member of a Sufi (mystical) brotherhood; equivalent to the Arabic "fakir" (see SUFISM). In the early history of ISLAM, mysticism was limited to ascetic mendicants and small schools that had dispersed after their teachers died. Since the founding of the first permanent brotherhood in 1166, the number of brotherhoods has multiplied. Each claims that its secret teachings represent a special revelation, transmitted through a line of saints and teachers, so that its ritual is as orthodox as the ritual prayer *(ṣalāt)* that is one of the Five Pillars of Islam.

Dervish theology teaches that a person can have direct union or communion with God. Many brotherhoods have monasteries for study and retreat. Others, like the Kalanderis, wander constantly. Some Dervishes teach the concept, perhaps borrowed from Hinduism, that only God exists—that all is God.

The famous "whirling" of Dervishes is characteristic of the Mawlawi order, and is only one example of the use of ecstatic dance to cross the gulf between God and humans. A parallel could be drawn to Christian revival meetings, in which participants fall into trances or speak in tongues after hours of singing hymns and emotional tension.          K./M.C.

**DESCARTES, RENÉ** (1596–1650). French philosopher, mathematician, and scientist, often called the father of modern philosophy. Born into lesser nobility, at age eight he entered the Jesuits' La Flèche school in Anjou and later pursued law at Poitiers and higher studies at Paris. Descartes traveled widely and decided on a philosophical career in 1619. In 1629 he settled in Holland, soon achieving recognition for his mathematical prowess. He systematized and applied algebraic formulas to geometric figures and solids, thus founding analytic geometry. He believed all knowledge must have the certainty of mathematics and all less certain concepts must be strenuously doubted. This stance threatened accepted views of the church and state. In 1637 he published *Philosophical Essays,* containing his famous *Discourse on Method* and treatises on the principles of analytic geometry and the first statement of the laws of light refraction. *Meditations on First Philosophy,* 1641, and *Principles of Philosophy,* 1644, followed.

Descartes resolved to accept only demonstrably clear and distinct ideas as true. He began with *Cogito, ergo sum,* "I think, therefore I am." He could doubt everything, except the fact of his own thinking. From this he deduced his existence, and the existence of God and the physical universe as clearly necessary to a coherent whole. Descartes actually used variations of Anselm's and Aquinas' arguments for GOD'S EXISTENCE. God exists and is the cause of our idea of God. Mind and matter have their origin and unity in God. God gave matter its extension and motion. Descartes developed these ideas as clear and distinct truths. He depicted a mechanistic universe, started by God. The human mind, akin to God's, can then discover the laws that govern all substances by logically searching out everything step by step. The deepest mysteries of the universe can thus be unlocked. Humans live in an intelligible, mechanistic universe; God stands outside.

Descartes' philosophical method challenged scholasticism's methodology. His own self-consciousness—*Cogito, ergo sum*—heralded the primacy of consciousness and subjectivity in later philosophy. Leibniz, Locke, Berkeley, Hume, and Kant all felt his influence. Queen Christina invited him to Sweden in 1649, where he died in 1650.

C.M.

**DESCENT INTO HELL.** A number of early Christian authors taught that Jesus descended into hell (or perhaps only Hades) after his death and taught those who were imprisoned there. The purpose was to proclaim the gospel to them. Irenaeus, Justin Martyr, and Tertullian in the second century asserted that nothing happened in consequence. On the other hand, Clement of Alexandria, Origen, Athanasius, and Cyril of Jerusalem in the second to the fourth centuries argued that Jesus delivered some souls from this abode of the dead. Support for this was found in Matthew 27:52; Ephesians 4:9, and Acts 2:31 primarily, as well as in Ignatius' letter to the Magnesians (9:2). The earliest use of I Peter 4:6 and

3:18 (and following) in this connection seems to be in Cyprian's *Testimonia* in the mid-third century. The teaching is not in the earliest Western creeds preserved in Hippolytus' (about 215) and Marcellus' letters to Julius I (340) but appears for the first time about A.D. 400 in Rufinus' commentary on the Apostles' Creed used in Aquileia. He did not know the origin of the phrase himself, which suggests that it may have been introduced long before his time, perhaps the end of the second or beginning of the third century. The words were probably introduced to combat a Docetic heresy of the period that denied real humanity to Jesus. His descent into the abode of the dead would prove that he was human—possessing both a body and a soul. The phrase is not included in Eastern creeds or in many modern Reformed creeds such as the Westminster Confession of Faith.

J.R.M.

**DESERT FATHERS.** The collective name given to the founders of Egyptian MONASTICISM. In his *Life of Anthony*, Athanasius claims that ANTHONY was the first Egyptian monk; in a similar work Jerome claims that honor for Paul the Hermit. In truth, however, it is impossible to know who was the first of the thousands who left the cities in order to live in solitude and meditation in the Egyptian Desert. At first, these monks and nuns lived alone—in fact, the word "monk" means "solitary." Soon, however, they began gathering in loosely bound communities. Eventually this gave birth to "cenobitic" communities, meaning "life in common" monasticism. The great figure in this development was PACHOMIUS, who set the pattern of cenobitic monastic life for centuries.

The sayings, acts, and legends of the Desert Fathers were gathered in a number of collections, and these in turn were used both for the training of new monks and for the edification of other Christians. The common themes of such collections are humility, chastity, asceticism, and trust in God.

J.G.

**DESPAIR.** The absence of hope. Since it may be doubted whether any human being can go on living without some minimum of hope, it is questionable whether complete despair is ever found. Everything that we do is aimed at some future goal and therefore carries with it the expectation that, even if we are most likely to fail, there is at least a bare chance of achievement. Thomas Aquinas gave a very low-key description of hope when he wrote, "Hope's object is a good that lies in the future and that is difficult but possible to attain." Marcel has drawn attention to the universal prevalence of "low-order" hopes and takes it to be evidence of a virtually universal implicit faith in the worthwhileness of human existence. If this vague but widespread hopefulness were entirely lacking, then it is hard to see how anyone could be motivated to engage in any course of action whatever. An utter black despair would mean the end of the road and, perhaps, suicide.

One has therefore to be critical in reading the rhetoric of despair, especially philosophies that despair about the human condition. Bertrand Russell wrote that "only on the firm foundation of unyielding despair can the soul's habitation be safely built." This is romantic and self-contradictory. No positive achievement is possible on the basis of a genuine despair, and Russell could only write this because he hoped that in spite of the "alien and inhuman world," people can still achieve certain values. There is a similar romanticism in CAMUS, who counsels "metaphysical rebellion" against the scheme of things. Such rebellion is possible only if there is the hope of achieving something worthwhile. Russell was more realistic than Camus, for he advised against "impotent rebellion" and spoke rather of resignation. Perhaps the true wisdom here is to know what things cannot be changed and to accept them with resignation, and to know what can be changed and to approach these things with hope.

Perhaps SARTRE, in his early writings, is the philosopher who has most realistically grasped the consequence of a genuine despair. That consequence is indifference, so that, as he put it, it does not matter whether one leads the nations or gets drunk by oneself in a bar. But we find Sartre belying his own philosophy by engaging in political activity. He talks about the other side of despair, and this suggests that despair is never complete, but that we have to despair of some things in order to discover a reliable ground of hope. (*See also* ANXIETY.)

J.M.

**DETERMINISM.** The view that all human actions are the effects of earlier events that "caused" them, just as events in nature are causally linked together. In the case of human actions, many such causes may be at work, such as heredity, environment, psychological factors, or the chemistry of the body. Such a theory seems to contradict common sense, since most people believe that they have freely chosen their courses of action, perhaps after prolonged deliberation over alternatives. On the other hand, common sense also makes us look for causal connections in the world around us, so why should there be an exception in the case of human actions?

Arguments to prove the reality of either FREE WILL or determinism have always been inconclusive. Reflection on the human condition leads to the conclusion that there are in fact many factors in any human being that shape one's actions one way or another. These include genetic makeup, the level of intelligence, predispositions of emotion and desire; then all that arises from environment and upbringing, relations to parents, the values and pressures of the society in which one lives; then there are the many physical constraints arising from the body. There may in fact be very little scope left for free choice, and the extreme determinist would declare it to be an illusion.

However, the fact that universally people are praised or blamed, rewarded or punished, for their actions, indicates that in fact the great majority believe that there is an element of free choice in human behavior. As Kant showed, although there is no theoretical argument that could establish the freedom of the will, it is a postulate or presupposition of all morality. It would be senseless to say that one *ought* to do anything or that society *ought* to promote certain values if all human actions are determined by factors outside of our control. It should be noted that similar considerations hold for the exercise of thought. All scientific inquiry depends on our power to make rational judgments, and these are assumed to be based on the discrimination of truth and falsity, not on the operation of heredity, chemistry, etc. Without the freedom of rational judgment, argument becomes impossible. The determinist's own view is not something one has chosen to believe on rational grounds, but the effect of various hidden causes. Like many other forms of skepticism, it is finally self-destroying.

Like many other philosophical disputes, that between the rival views of free will and determinism has some truth on both sides. From the moment of birth or before, every human life is already largely determined by factors that the person in question has not chosen, which will predispose that person in one way or another. Yet, if we are talking about people, not just puppets or highly complex machines, we must also suppose that there is room for a measure of self-determination, in which the people concerned have a share in shaping the raw material of their personalities and of deciding between the alternatives open to them.

                                                        J.M.

**DEUS EX MACHINA.** Literally "God from a machine." The phrase is derived from classical dramas. When a difficult situation emerged, stage machinery brought in a god or goddess to resolve the problem. By implication the term is used whenever any falsely contrived apparatus of thinking or acting is introduced to resolve an argument or clarify a situation. It suggests a deliberate manipulation of the situation.

                                                        I.C.

**DEUTERO-.** A Greek prefix meaning "second," for example, "Deutero-nomy," the second law (the Law given on Mount Sinai regarded as the first). Scholars use the title Deutero-Isaiah to designate chapters 40–66 of Isaiah.

                                                        P.L.G.

**DEUTEROCANONICAL BOOKS.** *See* APOCRYPHA.

**DEUTERO-ISAIAH.** *See* ISAIAH.

**DEUTERONOMY.** A name derived from the Septuagint, the Greek translation of the OT, where the Hebrew phrase "a copy of this law" (Deut. 17:18) was mistranslated "second law" *(deuteronomion)*. This fifth book of the Bible, known in Hebrew as *'elleh haddebarim* ("these are the words") after its opening phrase, offers the farewell testament of Moses to the Israelites encamped in western Moab prior to his death and their crossing the Jordan River to claim the Land of Promise. With its sustained exhortation geared to engender in the Israelite faithful a fervent love for the Deity and strict adherence to covenant law, Deuteronomy issues a word of specific guidance for Israel's daily existence in the land that will imminently be its possession.

*Organization and Basic Content.* (a) Moses' first address (1:6–4:40). Deuteronomy actually contains three addresses by Moses. The first reviews main events between Israel's departure from Mount Horeb (the Deuteronomic name for SINAI) and its arrival in MOAB. Special mention is made of the spies' reconnaissance of the land, Israel's failure to overtake Canaan from the south, and its successful occupation of Transjordan. A shift from historical recapitulation to exhortation is evident in 4:1 as Moses urges the people to obey the benevolent Deity who is sovereign over history.

(b) Moses' second address (chaps. 5–28). This lengthy section opens with the TEN COMMANDMENTS (5:6-21, at some variance with Exod. 20:2-17) and continues with a meditation on the meaning of the First Commandment as fundamental to the rest. In chapters 12–26 specific ordinances are expounded in a less than orderly manner. Still, 12:1–16:17 deals mainly with correct worship and 16:18–18:22 with Israelite officials (judges, kings, priests, prophets). Issues dominating the legislation in chapters 19–26 include criminal law, the waging of holy war, and general humanitarian concerns. Chapter 27 is intrusive with its directives for a covenant ceremony at Shechem on the twin peaks of Mount Gerizim and Mount Ebal (implemented in Josh. 8:30-35). An emphatic termination is reached in chapter 28, with its ample listing of blessings for obedience and curses for disobedience.

(c) Moses' third address (29:2–30:20). Here Moses summons Israel to renew its covenant with Yahweh and admonishes that disobedience will thrust it into exile (29:22-29), though after repentance Yahweh will restore Israel (30:1-10). A climax is achieved in 30:15-20, where Israel's acceptance or rejection of the covenant is presented as a life or death matter.

(d) Appendixes (chaps. 31–34). Deuteronomy concludes with diverse material including Moses' final charge to the people and to Joshua (31:1-8), Moses' deliverance of the written law to the Levitical priests (31:9-13), Joshua's commissioning (31:14-23), the Song of Moses (32:1-43) contrasting Israel's infidelity with Yahweh's fidelity, the blessing of Moses pronounced on the Israelite tribes (33:2-29), and the narrative about Moses' death (chap. 34).

*Composition.* As now edited, Deuteronomy presents Moses' polished oratory to an attentive laity. Ordinance and persuasive argumentation intermingle as the law is "explained" (1:5) to listeners who hopefully will be moved to obedience. The nucleus of Deuteronomy lies in the ancient laws contained in the Deuteronomic Code (chaps. 12–26; 28), many of which are identifiable in the earlier Covenant Code of the Elohist (Exod. 20:22–23:19). Affinities with Hosea's oracles and the Elohistic sections of the Pentateuch, along with Shechem's prominence (11:26-32; 27:1-26), speak for a northern origin of this legislation. Long active in the town and country regions of northern Israel, the Levites are ordinarily regarded as the primary authors of Deuteronomy. These teachers were the custodians of wide-ranging legal, political, and cultic traditions originating within premonarchic Israel. With the Assyrian takeover of the northern kingdom in 722 B.C., the dispossessed Levites presumably brought the traditions to Judah, where they were modified.

Deuteronomy's multi-faceted legislation was undoubtedly gathered up on several occasions, with Hezekiah's reform program near 700 B.C. (II Kings 18:1-6) being perhaps the most crucial. Since Josiah's reform was significantly informed by the discovery in 622 B.C. of "the book of the law" (II Kings 22–23) a document roughly equivalent with the Deuteronomic Code, the legislation likely achieved its present shape not long before.

The full story about Deuteronomy's composition is necessarily complex. The manifestly late law prohibiting sacrificial worship except at one central sanctuary, which prominently heads the Deuteronomic Code (12:5-7), emanates from Judean circles. Deuteronomic affinities with biblical and extra-biblical wisdom literature reflect the impact of Judean court sages and scribes. Thus Deuteronomy's emphasis on the fear of Yahweh (synonymous with wisdom) and pervasive humanitarianism readily betray wisdom influence. Moreover, the two liturgical poems in chapters 32–33 enjoyed a long independent existence prior to their incorporation into the Deuteronomic corpus. As prologue material, 1:1–4:43 and 4:44–11:32 may function differently, with the latter introducing the Deuteronomic law itself, and the former prefacing the comprehensive, unified Deuteronomic history, which unfolds in Joshua, Judges, Samuel, and Kings. Finally, Deuteronomy manifests some post-Josian expansion and revision.

*Religious Message.* (a) The God who favors Israel. Deuteronomy celebrates a Deity who in incomparable majesty lovingly chose Israel for a special covenant purpose. Yahweh's uniqueness is best stated in the SHEMA, "Hear, O Israel: the Lord our God is one Lord" (6:4). Accordingly, idolatry is particularly odious, since "the Lord is God in heaven above and on the earth beneath; there is no other" (4:39). In an act of unlimited love, Yahweh delivered Israel from Egyptian bondage, claimed it as Yahweh's own in the law-giving moment at Horeb, and intends to give it the land of Canaan. The unmerited character of that love is persistently acknowledged, for when it comes to size (7:7), self-sufficiency (8:17), and righteous instincts (9:4-6), Israel has no advantage. Notwithstanding Israel's backsliding tendencies, Yahweh is determined to fulfill the earlier promise to the fathers (7:8; 10:15). Defying human comprehension (4:32), that election love is sufficient to meet the people's every need as they penetrate Canaan. Through the institution of holy war (20:1-4), which finds Yahweh leading the Israelite host, the land will slowly but steadily be conquered (7:22), thus permitting God's elect to pursue in Canaan that life to which they have been exclusively called.

(b) Israel's response. As a superb revision of the Mosaic faith into the idiom of the seventh century B.C., Deuteronomy lucidly expresses Yahweh's expectation of the elect. The results of past apostasy are readily apparent—a ruptured monarchy, the demise of northern Israel, and southern Judah given to compromise when the international climate threatens. Accordingly, Israel is challenged anew to turn fully to Yahweh with heart, soul, and might (6:5) and to take seriously the will of Yahweh, who has graciously caused the divine name to dwell among Israel (12:5). By resolutely resisting all enticements toward apostasy, ever favoring the needy (notably, the sojourner, fatherless, and widow) with compassion (24:19-21), and remembering the divine mandate that Israel actively pursue "justice, and only justice" (16:20), Israel will even yet realize its own uniqueness, which is anchored in the God who has chosen it.

J.K.K.

**DEVA.** From the Sanskrit word for "a shining being," that is, a god (compare Latin *Deus*). In Vedic HINDUISM particularly, this term refers collectively to the bright celestial gods to whom prayer and sacrifice are offered, and who are engaged in battle with the ASURAS. In later Hinduism, the term, taken to indicate a class of finite nature and weather deities, is contrasted with the saving or Ishvara gods of BHAKTI.

R.E.

**DEVIL.** The personal power of evil in the world, SATAN, or the accuser, the obstructor, or the tempter (from the Hebrew, Satan, and the Greek *diabolos* and *daimonion*). In a more general sense, a devil or DEMON, an evil spirit, believed, in Jesus' time, to fill the world, causing illness, physical and mental.

A devil is a parallel to an ANGEL. The belief that the world was full of helpers sent by God (angels) and enemies sent by Satan (devils) grew out of Israel's exposure first to Canaanite culture, and later to the experience of the exiles in the Babylonian captivity. It was easy for the Hebrews to understand the pagan gods (Baalim) as demons, as idolatry became tempting to many. Much later, in the sixth century B.C., upper-class Hebrews, including priests and prophets like Ezekiel, were exposed to the Persian religion that saw the universe as a battleground between a good God and an evil god (Ahura Mazda and Ahiriman). The divine power of EVIL, Ahiriman, may be the model for the later Jewish concept of Satan, whom Jesus refers to as "the prince of the power of the air."

The devil, or Satan, is found in the OT in Job 1–2 and Zechariah 3:1. In the NT, the devil is shown as always in opposition to God, and the prince of this world (John 12:31; 14:30; 16:11), who heads a demonic kingdom, which the kingdom of God defeats through the ministry and sacrifice of Jesus Christ, and which will be finally destroyed at the Last Judgment.

J.C.

*DEVOTIO MODERNA.* The Latin words for "Modern Devotion," a fourteenth-century spiritual revival in the Netherlands, southwestern Germany, Switzerland, France, and Italy. It stressed individual devotion, mystical meditation, and acts of charity. The revival developed during the century of the Babylonian Captivity (the removal of the papacy to Avignon, France) and the Great Schism (rival popes in Rome and Avignon vying for control of Christendom). Many ordinary people felt the need for reform and more dedicated living, and expressed this in the Modern Devotion. It fostered direct contact with God and often passed beyond righteous deeds to ecstatic visions and union with God. It had little to do with church sacraments and rituals. Gerhard Groot and Florentius Radewyn of the BROTHERS OF THE COMMON LIFE are linked with its beginnings. Others associated with the movement include John Tauler, Friends of God, Henry Suso, John Ruysbroeck, and Thomas à Kempis. Kempis' IMITATION OF CHRIST is acclaimed by some to be one of the most influential works of early Christian literature. His writings well represent the Modern Devotion movement of the fourteenth century. Loosely organized and having a practical, mystical turn, it drew strength from its wide acceptance among the common people and the secular clergy. Without intending to do so, the Modern Devotion spread a negative view of the institutional church.

C.M.

DEVOTION. *See* SPIRITUALITY.

*DEVOUT LIFE, INTRODUCTION TO THE.* One of the world's most popular books on religious devotion. Written by Bishop FRANCIS OF SALES (1567–1622), it figured prominently in the Catholic revival after the Council of Trent. Produced in 1609 as a small spiritual guide for Madame de Charmoisy, it received definitive form in 1619, went through hundreds of editions, and was translated into most of Europe's languages. Designed for people in every vocation and status in life, it contends that devotion (a true love of God) can be practiced amid worldly distractions, but not without ordered discipline. It starts with humanity, full of defects, but created in God's image, and calls for repentance, prayer, and trust in God's grace, for divine mercy will respond to our efforts. It also gives practical guidance for purging away evil inclinations and letting love reign supreme. Calvinists barred Francis from his Genevan bishopric, but his writings won thousands to Catholicism.

C.M.

DEWEY, JOHN (1859–1952). Philosopher, psychologist, and educator born in Burlington, Vermont, and graduated from the University of Vermont. He received the Ph.D. from Johns Hopkins University and taught at the universities of Minnesota (1888–89), Michigan (1889–94), Chicago (1894–1904), and at Columbia University (after 1904). At the University of Chicago, he was a professor of philosophy and psychology. There he established an experimental school and wrote *School and Society* (1899), developing his pragmatic approach, known in educational circles as instrumentalism.

His important philosophical works were written during the years at Columbia. His output was enormous. A few well-known titles are *Democracy and Education,* 1916; *How We Think,* 1909, and *A Common Faith,* 1934. He affirmed that theory and practice are interrelated, and that moral and social beliefs and actions can be changed for the better. The idea of "learning by doing," attributed to him, inspired a new flexibility in education and more space for individual student inquiry. Later this theory brought criticism from those who protested that he neglected "basics" and "discipline."

He was active in such social causes as the movement to outlaw war that eventuated in the Kellogg-Briand Pact; founder and first president of the American Association of University Professors; a charter member of the first teacher's union in New York City; held offices in the American Civil Liberties Union and the League for Industrial Democracy. He also frequently wrote and was a well-known spokesman for "progressive" education. He is recognized as one of the giants in American education and philosophy.

I.C.

DHAMMAPADA. From the Pali word for "Path of True Doctrine." A popular collection of sayings attributed to the BUDDHA. Being a part of the Pali canon of Buddhist scriptures, the Tripitika, assembled by the first century B.C., the Dhammapada is an anonymous collection of favorite aphorisms garnered from other parts of the scripture and popular Buddhist wisdom. Somewhat differing versions exist in Sanskrit, Chinese, and other languages.

The Dhammapada owes its great popularity to its presentation of BUDDHISM in cheerful and simple (though not shallow) lines, which make its profoundest insights accessible to laypeople and monks alike. It emphasizes that suffering is the result of a polluted mind, and the Buddhist path as a way of restraint of mind that leads to great happiness and an ethic of nonviolence, which conquers evil with love. "Hatred is never appeased by hatred in this world; by love alone is it appeased" (v. 5).

Buddhism, especially as presented in the Pali scriptures, can sometimes appear a rather austere path, but the Dhammapada makes it clear that on the other side of the great renunciations it inculcates lies great joy, the joy of all who have been able to learn the secret of having nothing yet possessing all things. "Let us live happily, hating none in the midst of men who hate. Let us live happily, free from disease. Let us live happily, free from care. Let us live happily, we who possess nothing. Let us dwell feeding on joy like the Radiant Gods" (vv. 197-200).

The Dhammapada has been immensely influential in the Buddhist world over more than twenty centuries. Monks and laypeople alike have memorized all or parts of it in great numbers, and it has often been used as a basic educational text. Its perusal is indispensable to understanding the attitudes and appeal of Buddhism as it really is.

R.E.

**DHARMA.** Dharma is among the most complex and significant of all concepts in the Indian intellectual vocabulary. Its patterns of meaning within Hindu, Buddhist, and Jain thought provide invaluable insights into fundamental connections made by the Indian world view.

The core meaning of dharma, [from the root *dhr,* "support, bear," and related to the English word *form*] is "structure or form." But that denotation is always closely aligned to another basic Sanskrit concept, *satya* or truth. Dharma always means the *true* structure or form of anything: the form which most truly reveals the underlying reality, the form as seen by one who sees truly, the forms of thought or behavior that best articulate truth or help one to be in rapport with it.

As far back as the RIG VEDA, dharma most commonly refers to that which upholds *rta,* the cosmic order. Rituals were believed to directly maintain dharma and express its nature. Codes of conduct were made to comply with its principles, and as a result the individual was brought into oneness with true reality. As Indian thought developed, dharma expanded in meaning to embrace cosmic, social, and moral principles in the broadest senses. It means "natural law," the patterns by which the universe operates. It means "social law," including

the division of human society into its basic classes or castes with their distinctive duties and rites, since to the Indian mind society was viewed as organic and continuous with nature. And it means "righteousness," personal ritual, and moral behavior, that is, the following of one's *svadharma* or individual dharma, which best accords with the social and cosmic dharma.

The classical literature of HINDUISM often refers to categorized ends or putative goals of human life. In earlier texts these are threefold, *kama* or pleasure, *artha* or gain, and dharma. Dharma, living righteously in harmony with ultimate reality through fulfilling one's social and ritual obligations, is the superior, indeed supreme, goal of life, giving an ultimate satisfaction pleasure and gain cannot. Here dharma means something very close to "religion." Later texts, however, add a fourth goal, MOKSHA, "liberation." In this context, dharma comes to mean the structures of this world that are good and the righteousness, with its spiritual fulfillment available to the householder, also good. But now both goods in the realm of dharma are to be contrasted to the supreme liberation, which the renunciant finds beyond all structures and forms whatsoever.

In BUDDHISM, dharma has three distinct meanings. First, it refers to the basic teachings of the religion, including morality, the Buddha's "gospel." Second, it indicates the Ultimate Reality of the universe beyond all known forms altogether, as in the MAHAYANA term *dharmakaya,* the most transcendent of the *trikaya,* the three "bodies" or forms of expression of the universal Buddha nature. *Dharmakaya* as ineffable cosmic Absolute is virtually equivalent to NIRVANA or the VOID. Third, dharma refers to the basic constituents of the universe—the irreducible, indefinable elements that arise to give it form.

These three meanings, however diverse, have something in common. They each point to a true, undistorted perception: the true teaching, the true inexpressible universe, the true elements of reality. To put it another way, a dharma is how any level of reality would be seen by a Buddha, a fully enlightened being.

In JAINISM, dharma refers, as elsewhere, to true teaching. But it also indicates the principle of activity that keeps the universe and the souls within it moving. It is contrasted, in that context, with *adharma,* the principle of rest to which souls strive and achieve upon liberation.

R.E.

**DIALECTICAL THEOLOGY.** Although this expression has been used chiefly of the theology of KARL BARTH and others who participated in the theological renascence of the 1920s, the theological employment of dialectic goes back to a much earlier time. Truth is rarely simple or one-sided, and dialectic consists in giving weight to opposing aspects of truth and attempting to reconcile them in a higher, more inclusive truth. Around the year A.D. 500, the mystical theologian Dionysius the Areopagite already was teaching that every assertion about God must be both affirmed and denied. For instance, if one says, "God exists," one must also say, "God does not exist," for his existence is of quite a different order from that of any finite entity. Dionysius then went on to assert that "God superexists," where "superexistence" denotes the incomprehensible mode of being that belongs to God and transcends the difference between existence and non-existence.

One finds similar teaching in later theologians in the mystical tradition, such as Nicholas of Cusa (fifteenth century), who taught that God is the "coincidence of opposites" *(coincidentis oppositorum)* and that this is not a destructive contradiction because the logic of the infinite is different from the logic of the finite, a point that he illustrated from mathematics. HEGEL's whole philosophy was built on a dialectical basis, and this is reflected in KIERKEGAARD, who, though he rejected Hegel's attempted reconciliation of opposites, continued to teach the clash of opposites, which he called "PARADOX" rather than dialectic. Kierkegaard was one of the influences at work on Barth in the new dialectical theology, which found perhaps its most powerful expression in his commentary on Romans. Nineteenth-century theology, Barth believed, had humanized and rationalized Christian faith. But the Word of God comes breaking in from outside our human culture. It cannot be reconciled with human ideas, but has a logic of its own in which God speaks both a yes and a no. Along with Barth may be mentioned Thurneysen, Brunner, Bultmann, Gogarten, and Tillich as theologians who, for at least part of their careers, were adherents of dialectical theology.

J.M.

**DIANA OF THE EPHESIANS.** The Latin name, not in the NT, of the Roman goddess identified with the Greek Artemis (Acts 19:27). Her temple in Ephesus was one of the seven wonders of the ancient world; her statues were found in excavations having multiple breasts (or dates), suggesting fertility.

J.R.M.

**DIASPORA.** The scattered members of a religious community separated from the main body of fellow believers either in the same country or in another country. The concept of a diaspora arose after 722 B.C., when Israel fell to Assyria, and 586 B.C., when Judah was conquered by Babylonia and many Jews were carried away into EXILE. Even with the restoration of Jerusalem to the Jews under Ezra and Nehemiah after 539 B.C., by edict of Cyrus the Great, a diaspora community continued. Not all of the Jews in Babylon returned to Judah, and even at the time of Christ many Jews remained in Mesopotamia, Egypt, Asia Minor, Syria, and had spread into Europe to

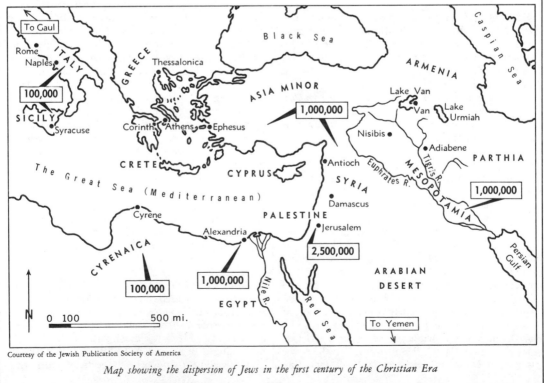

Courtesy of the Jewish Publication Society of America

*Map showing the dispersion of Jews in the first century of the Christian Era*

Rome. The great Greek city of Alexandria alone had one million Jewish residents.

The Roman-Jewish War of A.D. 66–70 ended in the destruction of the Jerusalem Temple and the Jewish state, and a new wave of Jews joined the diaspora community. Some Jews remained in Judah, now part of the Roman province of Syria, and, under the messianic preaching of BarKochba, these Jews revolted against Rome. At this time the Romans decimated the Jews, sowed the site of Jerusalem with salt, and built a Roman city on Mount Zion. From this point, until the creation of Israel in 1947, Judaism existed only as a diaspora.

While Judaism is the classic example and model for a diaspora, it is by no means the only diaspora in history. Various sects of Christianity, Islam, Hinduism, Buddhism, and Shintoism are now scattered over the face of the earth. While diaspora is a specifically religious concept, it is often concretely realized in historical, ethnic groups. The Scotch-Irish, for example, are a diaspora of Protestantism, settled in a Celtic, Roman Catholic land. The settlement of the New World in the sixteenth and following centuries made the Americas the location of many diasporas. In time, New York City came to have the world's greatest density of Jews.

The consciousness of being a diaspora is deep in many religious traditions at various times. The early Christians, as they spread from Jerusalem and Antioch to Asia Minor and Greece and on to Rome, saw themselves in terms of a scattered family of God dwelling in countries that were not really their homes. Paul spoke of Christians as living colonies of heaven. For him, the home country was the kingdom of God. During the period A.D. 33–312, while Christianity was spreading through the Roman Empire, this diaspora awareness was strong. After Constantine removed the legal disabilities Christianity suffered, the church gradually became established, and the diaspora feeling faded away. It was still present in Augustine, however, who contrasted the city of God (the catholic church) with the city of man (the empire) in his famous philosophy of history, *The City of God*.

A key notion included in the concept of diaspora is that the scattered believers remain in contact with the official leaders of the religious body. During the time after the return of the Jews to Jerusalem and the rebuilding of the second Temple under the preaching and leadership of Ezra and Nehemiah, the Jews in other countries came to Jerusalem at Passover and regularly paid a Temple tax. This custom is seen in the life of Paul as recounted in Acts. Of course, for Paul, as for Augustine, Christians remained in touch with their true King, Jesus Christ, through prayer and the sacraments, especially the Eucharist.

Almost every religion or sect exists as a minority in many lands, although it may form a majority in one country or other geographical region. While there are millions of Hindus in India, they form small minorities in North and South America, and larger minorities in many African countries. The same is true of Buddhists and Confucianists, especially among the millions of ethnic Chinese scattered all over Southeast Asia, Indonesia, the Philippines, Hawaii, Canada, and the United States. More recently, Koreans and Vietnamese have joined this diaspora.

After the outbreak of hostilities between Catholics and Protestants following the Reformation, the concept of diaspora was used for Catholic minorities living in Protestant territories and for Protestant minorities living in Catholic lands. Gradually, most German states and cities became predominantly Catholic or Protestant, and Dissenters were encouraged or forced to move away.

Although Christianity, as a whole, is no longer conscious of being a diaspora faith, and despite the era of warm ecumenical cooperation, Christianity, worldwide, is becoming more and more a minority. It would be realistic, as well as biblically sound, for the church to reclaim the Pauline insight that the followers of Christ form colonies of heaven. Those who follow Jesus are pilgrims and strangers on earth, a diaspora wherever they may reside.

J.C.

**DIATESSARON.** The first attempt to harmonize the four Gospels, composed by TATIAN in the second century. Although the original was probably in Greek, it was translated into Syriac at an early date and became the standard Gospel for the Syriac-speaking church. It held this position until the fifth century, when the Syrian church began using the four Gospels, which by then were used by the rest of the church. Although the actual text of the *Diatessaron* has been lost, it is possible to reconstruct it from a number of fragmentary sources, commentaries, and partial translations. The fact that Tatian chose precisely the four canonical Gospels as the basis for his *Diatessaron* indirectly testifies to the widespread acceptance of those four Gospels over any of their rivals that were beginning to circulate in Tatian's time. Thus, the *Diatessaron* itself provides an important link in the history of the CANON of the NT.

J.G.

**DIBELIUS, MARTIN** (1883–1947). The German biblical scholar was born in Dresden and studied at Neuchatel, Leipzig, Berlin, and Tübingen. He taught at Berlin (1910–15) and Heidelberg (1915–47). Building on the work of HARNACK and GUNKEL, he coined the term *formgeschichte* and developed NT FORM CRITICISM, though more conservatively than his followers. His writings include *From Tradition to Gospel* (Eng. ed. 1934) and *Gospel Criticism and Christology* (1935).

N.H.

**DIDACHE.** A document of uncertain date usually included among the APOSTOLIC FATHERS. Its fuller title is *Teaching* (or *Didache*) *of the Twelve Apostles*. It was discovered in Istanbul in 1875, and was probably written in Syria late in the first century or early in the second, although scholars are not in complete agreement on these matters. Its sixteen chapters can be divided into three sections. The first is similar to material found in the EPISTLE OF BARNABAS, and scholars usually refer to it as the "Document of the Two Ways." It is an admonition to follow the "way of life" rather than the "way of death."

The second section deals with worship and includes some of the earliest extant instructions for the celebration of baptism and Holy Communion. Baptism is to be done "in living water"—that is, running water. But if water is scarce, it can also be done by pouring water over the head three times in the name of the Father, the Son, and the Holy Spirit. The chapters on Communion are subject to various interpretations, for it is not clear whether the celebration is part of a "love feast" or not. There is also a reference to Communion as a "sacrifice," although this probably means that the act itself is a sacrifice that the believers present to God.

The last part of the *Didache* is a manual of Discipline, dealing with several practical issues in the life of the church. Foremost in the author's mind is the problem of distinguishing between true and false prophets. The moralism of this last section has led some critics to declare that the *Didache* falls far below the level of the NT or even some of the other Apostolic Fathers.

J.G.

**DIET OF WORMS.** From January 28 to May 26, 1521, an imperial German Diet summoned by Emperor Charles V. On April 18 LUTHER gave his "Here I Stand" speech, taking Scripture and right reason as his authorities and refusing to retract any writings. The Edict of Worms, May 26, placed Luther under the imperial ban (*see* REFORMATION).

C.M.

**DILTHEY, WILHELM** (1833–1911). The German philosopher of history and culture studied at Heidelberg and Berlin and taught at Basel (1866–68), Kiel (1868–71), Breslau (1871–82), and Berlin (1882–1911). The virtual creator of the philosophy of history, he saw all historical phenomena as expressions of human experience, inwardly understood before being scientifically analyzed. He stressed the differences in method between the physical sciences and the "human sciences" used to study culture, art, and religion. He opposed determinism and emphasized human creativity and dynamism. He was influenced by Schleiermacher, and in turn he influenced religion primarily through Troeltsch.

N.H.

*DING-AN-SICH.* A phrase from IMMANUEL KANT's philosophy. Literally, the "thing-in-itself" is the inner reality, the interior core of truth, which is recognized as real but incapable of being appropriated by the beholder. Thus in Kantian metaphysical philosophy we can "never transcend the limits of possible experience," yet all metaphysical thought seeks to reach the thing-in-itself.

I.C.

**DIOCESE.** A territorial division of the Roman Catholic, Episcopal (Anglican), and Old Catholic churches, presided over by a bishop ruling in his own right. It is called an eparchy in the Eastern Orthodox Church. It is "that portion of God's people entrusted to a bishop," according to Vatican II.

J.C.

**DIOCLETIAN** (245–313). A Dalmatian of humble origin, probably of slave parentage, he became Roman Emperor in A.D. 284 after a distinguished career in the army. He was made emperor by his fellow soldiers after the murder of the preceding emperor Numerian. He was an efficient civil administrator and effected a financial and administrative reorganization of the empire. In order to stop the frequent depositions of emperors by the military, he emphasized the divine sanctity of emperors and appointed three co-emperors to serve with him: Maximian, Galerius, and Constantius I Chlorus. They effectively divided the empire among them, Diocletian ruling Illyricum (his home country of Dalmatia), Egypt, and the east from his residence in the city of Nicomedia. Although he generally followed the example of his predecessor in granting religious toleration, he was swayed by the wishes of Galerius, a thoroughgoing pagan, and inaugurated an extremely severe persecution against Christians near the end of his reign. His first general edict was issued on February 23, 303, demanding that all copies of the Scriptures be surrendered and burned, churches closed, Christian meetings discontinued, and clergy imprisoned. In A.D. 304 a fourth edict required everyone to sacrifice to the Roman gods under pain of torture. This persecution ceased in the West after the forced abdication of Maximian in 305, due to the retirement of Diocletian on May 1 of that year. It continued in the East intermittently until the probable year of the death of Diocletian and the year in which CONSTANTINE, the new emperor, gave Christianity full legality.

J.R.M.

**DIOGNETUS, EPISTLE TO.** A document usually counted among the APOSTOLIC FATHERS, although in its nature and purpose it should be classified among the APOLOGISTS. Although some scholars disagree, it probably dates from the second century. Diognetus, to whom this writing is addressed, is completely unknown. The style is elegant, and the writer shows deep appreciation for Hellenistic culture and civilization. The central argument is that Christians surpass pagans in the quality of their behavior. "They obey the prescribed laws, and at the same time surpass the laws by their lives. They love all, and by all are persecuted." In conclusion, says our unknown author, Christians are to the world what the soul is to the body.

J.G.

**DIONYSIUS THE GREAT.** Bishop of Alexandria in the mid-third century. He was particularly noted for his theology, which he derived from his teacher ORIGEN. After fourteen years as head of the catechetical school of ALEXANDRIA, he became bishop of that city in A.D. 247. Although his writings have not been preserved, he was frequently quoted by other authors, particularly in connection with the Arian controversy. In those quotations, he appears as one of those "left-wing Origenists" who so stressed the distinction between Father and Son as to lay them open to the charge of ARIANISM. He was dead by the time this controversy broke out, and among those who supported the faith of Nicaea, there were those who felt that he was a proto-Arian. Athanasius, by then bishop of Alexandria, defended Dionysius against such charges.

J.G.

**DIONYSIUS THE PSEUDO-AREOPAGITE.** The unknown author of a series of mystical works, probably dating from late in the fourth century or early in the fifth. Since these writings were attributed to the Dionysius who heard Paul's preaching at the Areopagus (Acts 17), they were considered to have an authority almost equal to that of the apostles. Translated into Latin by JOHN SCOTUS ERIGENA, they made a significant impact on Western theology during the latter half of the Middle Ages. The mystical theology of Pseudo-Dionysius is an example of NEOPLATONISM in its inspiration, and therefore these writings were one of the main avenues of Neoplatonic influence on medieval theology. During the Reformation, most Protestants and some Catholics began to question their authenticity, pointing out the vast difference between them and the writings of Paul. Eventually all scholars came to the conclusion that they are indeed spurious.

J.G.

**DISCIPLE.** The word derives from a Greek term meaning "learner, pupil." In modern usage it has come to mean simply "a follower," without any connotation of schooling. In the Septuagint it is used only twice (Jer. 13:21; 20:11) but it becomes a common term in the NT referring to those who were taught by John the Baptist (Matt. 9:14), the Pharisees (Matt. 22:16), and Jesus (Matt. 20:17). Even after the death of Jesus, those who followed his teaching were called disciples of the Lord (Acts 9:1)

just as the Pharisees were called disciples of Moses (John 9:28). The twelve apostles, who were uniquely chosen by Jesus and assigned a special role in his preaching ministry, are referred to at times as the twelve disciples.

The two expressions are used interchangeably in places (Matt. 10:1-2; Luke 6:13). The word "apostle'" is necessarily more restrictive than the term "disciple." An APOSTLE is "one who is sent with a commission"; apostles are disciples, but disciples are apostles only if appointed (Luke 6:13). In Acts the term is used almost exclusively to refer to members of the newly established church. It is virtually synonymous with "Christian" (6:1; 9:19), a term that was given to disciples in Antioch (Acts 11:26) and which appears only three times in the NT (I Pet. 4:16; Acts 11:26; 26:28).

J.R.M.

**DISCIPLES OF CHRIST.** *See* CHRISTIAN CHURCH.

**DISCIPLINE.** Discipline is not a biblical term, but the concept is derived from the Hebrew law as found in the Decalogue, the Covenant Code (Exod. 20–23), and the Holiness Code in Leviticus, as well as from the practical or moral sections of Paul's epistles and the Pastoral Epistles in the NT. The Sermon on the Mount of Matthew and the sermon on the plain of Luke also contribute to the concept of a Christian discipline, in the sense of a rigorously pure life-style for believers. While all Christian communions teach and encourage growth in grace, or sanctification, the ideals of a strict Christian discipline are found in certain communions more than in others. The chief of these are (1) the disciplines of monastic orders in the Roman Catholic and Eastern Orthodox churches; (2) the disciplines of the priesthood in Roman Catholic and Eastern Orthodox churches (with parallels for the ministry in Protestant churches); (3) the various disciplines and ascetic practices of Protestant sectarians of the Holiness type (sometimes called Wesleyan); and, historically, the discipline laid on Geneva by the reformer John Calvin, with its parallels in early Scottish Presbyterianism. Until the contemporary period, the Reformed churches and the Methodist churches stressed discipline among their members more than the other Protestant communions.

Discipline may connote only the life-style prescribed by a church for either its ministers or its laypeople. Usually, as in the Roman Catholic Church, the discipline imposed on priests is stricter than that on the laity, and the ascetic practices of monks and nuns are more rigorous still. Indeed, "discipline" sometimes refers to the scourge or whip used in monastic acts of mortification.

J.C.

**DISESTABLISHMENT.** A state in which one religion is no longer established by law as the faith of the realm, and no specific church receives official status and favor.

In 1776 various churches were established in nine of thirteen American states. Because no church was large enough to claim national allegiance, the majority of Americans were Protestant, and most were indifferent to religion entirely, disestablishment came easily. The Church of England was disestablished in Virginia in 1785. Congregationalism was disestablished in Connecticut in 1818, New Hampshire in 1819, and finally in Massachusetts in 1831.

N.H.

**DISPENSATIONALISM.** A form of biblical interpretation derived from the teachings of JOHN NELSON DARBY (1800-82) of Dublin, Ireland, a leader of the Plymouth Brethren, and popularized by C. I. SCOFIELD (1843-1921) in his Scofield Reference Bible (1902-1909 and revised in 1917). This system is based on the belief that God deals with the human race in different ways at different times. Scofield said that there are seven dispensations, or epochs of time, and interpreted a dispensation (from the Greek *oikonomia*) as "a period of time during which man is tested in respect of obedience to some *specific* revelation of the will of God." The Darbyite term "dispensation" is taken from the Authorized Version (King James) translation of *oikonomia* as "dispensation." Darby, Scofield, and other Dispensationalists use this system to interpret the OT and NT.

While various Dispensationalists offer differing details, they generally accept C. I. Scofield's sevenfold series of dispensations. These are: (1) Innocence (Gen. 1:28) to the loss of Eden; (2) Conscience or moral responsibility (Gen. 3:7) up to the Great Flood; (3) Human government (Gen. 8:15) up to the call of Abraham; (4) Promise, the test of Israel's response to God (Gen. 12:1) down to the covenant at Sinai; (5) Law, to the death of Christ (Exod. 19:1); (6) the church, the dispensation of the Holy Spirit (Acts 2:1) to Christ's return (Second Coming); and (7) the millennial kingdom to eternity (Rev. 20:4).

Scofield held that while there is but one dispensation or overall plan of God in both the OT and NT, that is, redemption in Christ, nevertheless God progressively deals with humanity through the sevenfold series of dispensations. Specifically, Scofield thought that each of these epochs was a time of testing, in which God sets the human race to a particular test. He said "No particular portion of Scripture is to be intelligently comprehended apart from some concept of its place in the whole." Many scholars believe that this is an imposition or eisegesis since, according to them, there is no evidence of any dispensational thinking in the Scriptures, although the Greek term *oikonomia* (which means "economy" or "administration") does occur in I Corinthians 9:17; Ephesians 1:20; 3:2; and Colossians 1:25.

Dispensationalism is above all a system of biblical interpretation for the religious education of lay people. For the Bible reader, the Sunday school class, and for students in Bible schools who lacked knowledge of the ancient languages and ancient history, some simple, overall plan seemed needed so as to interpret the Bible as a whole. This need is both the reason for Darby's and Scofield's system and the cause of its early and continuing popularity. Although there are schools devoted to dispensationalism among fundamentalists in the U.S.A. and Britain, most of the system's influence flows from the steady popularity of Scofield's Reference Bible, which was revised again as recently as 1966.

J.C.

**DISPERSION.** *See* DIASPORA.

**DISSENTERS.** The word was first used of the five "Dissenting Brethren" at the WESTMINSTER ASSEMBLY of Divines, 1643-47. They were called NONCONFORMISTS in the penal acts following the RESTORATION (1660) and the Act of Uniformity (1662).

These terms generally apply to all English Protestants including Baptists, Congregationalists, Presbyterians, Methodists, Unitarians, Quakers, Plymouth Brethren, Moravians, Churches of Christ, the Salvation Army, and sects.

N.H.

**DISTRICT SUPERINTENDENT.** An elder in the Methodist churches who supervises ministers in the districts of a conference. Usually several district superintendents aid the bishop in charge of a conference. In the Christmas Conference of 1784, "district elder" denoted a district superintendent, and in 1797 the title was changed to "presiding elder." District superintendent now prevails.

C.M.

**DITTOGRAPHY.** A double writing in paleography. A scribe sometimes mistakenly copied twice what should only have been written once. It was a mechanical or unconscious repetition of a series of letters or words and is the opposite of haplography. For example, "Great is Artemis . . ." (Acts 19:34) is given twice in Codex Vaticanus.

J.R.M.

**DIVES.** From the Latin word for "rich." A name given in the Middle Ages to the rich man in the parable of Lazarus (Luke 16:19-31), arising from the mistaken notion that the Latin Vulgate translation of the phrase "there was a certain rich man" was naming the person rather than simply stating that the man was rich.

J.R.M.

**DIVINATION.** Magical practices by which men and women in ancient times sought to obtain information about the future. Such practices are now generally considered superstitious, but some (for example, astrology; dream interpretation) are practiced in Europe and America today. Although the covenant code condemns WITCHCRAFT, and the later prophets assailed reliance on ASTROLOGY and the dreams of false prophets, many acts of divination are recorded in the Bible, from the visit of Saul to the witch of Endor (I Sam. 28:3-25) to the casting of lots by the apostles to select a successor for Judas Iscariot (Acts 1:26).

Among the specific practices of the Hebrews (and presumably the early Christians) designed to disclose the future, we read of ORACLES (as at the terebinth of Moreh, Gen. 12:6); looking into a cup of water or wine (Gen. 44:5, 15); consultation of a witch or wizard, or woman or man with a "familiar spirit" or associated demon; necromancy, or communicating with the dead (generally by use of a witch); shaking arrows and casting them on the ground (similar to the I Ching today); dream interpretation (as in the case of Joseph in Egypt); and the casting of LOTS (probably stones of different sizes or colors).

Two of the most familiar characters in the OT were men of occult powers, respected for their ability in divination. They were Joseph in Egypt (Gen. 37:5 ff.; 40:8 ff.; 41:1-32) and Daniel in Babylon (Dan. 1:20; 2:2; 5:11). Joseph's rise to power, from prison to prime minister, is due to his occult power, by which he interprets future events disclosed in the dreams of the butler, the baker, and then of Pharaoh himself. Daniel is said to be given the power by God to discern the meaning of future events in Belshazzar's dreams. He supplants all the magicians and wise men in the Babylonian court and is made head of the magicians' guild (Dan. 5:11 ff.). Even though MAGIC was rejected early in Hebrew history, it kept coming back into popular religion and plays a major role all through the OT. A familiar spirit was thought to be the spirit of a dead person who had had a special relation with a witch, wizard, or medium. The witch could learn hidden secrets or future events by consulting such a spirit (I Sam. 28:7-25).

J.C.

## DIVINE COMEDY. See DANTE. ALIGHIERI

**DIVINE, FATHER** (1875–1965). Leader of an interracial religious movement in the United States that began in 1919. Its greatest influence and size were attained between 1935 and 1945. Father Divine was born George Baker on Hutchinson's Island, Georgia, near Savannah, around 1875. He lived there for the first part of his life, moving to East Baltimore around the turn of the century. Baker also used the name Major M. J. Divine. In 1907 he became a follower of Sam Morris, who called himself Father Jehovia. In 1909 he moved to the "Lift Ever, Die Never" movement of John Hickerson. In 1914 he began his own movement in Valdosta, Georgia. About 1915 he moved to Brooklyn and to Sayville, Long Island, where he founded his Peace Mission Movement and adopted the name Father Divine. He began a very popular—among urban blacks—ministry that involved housing and feeding his followers. He gave long meals at which he preached. This disturbed the residents of Sayville. Baker then moved to Harlem and named his meeting places "heavens," which then attracted blacks and whites in large numbers. Soon Father Divine's missions, hostels ("heavens"), restaurants, and stores spread across the nation.

Throughout the 1930s and 1940s, Baker's movement grew rapidly. A weekly magazine, *New Day*, spread Baker's message of personal morality, no alcohol, no tobacco, no gambling, no life insurance, and strict honesty. Interestingly, Baker taught that members should be celibate, even if married and living together. Those who lived in this manner were invited to live in one of those "heavens." The deep economic depression of the 1930s made this possibility very appealing.

Father Divine called for civil rights legislation at home and world peace abroad. However, he began to lose followers after 1946, when he married a white woman. Despite the beliefs of his followers that he was God, Father Divine died. The Peace Mission still exists, directed by Baker's widow.

J.C.

**DIVINE OFFICE.** The public prayers of the Roman Catholic church, including psalms, hymns, scriptural readings, prayers, and other readings. It is composed of various services for the hours of the day. The most recent revision of the office was issued under Pope Paul VI in 1970. This contains all the decisions of Vatican II. It contains the propers for the seasons, the ordinary text of the office, the psalter, the proper for the saints, and the office of the dead. The purpose of the office is to promote the worship of God and to increase the devotion of the faithful.

J.C.

**DIVINE RIGHT.** A theory asserting that authority comes directly from God, rendering one accountable only to God. Divine right was claimed by some ancient kings, popes, and especially seventeenth-century English and French rulers. For kings, the doctrine faded in England with William and Mary, 1689, and in France with the French Revolution, 1789–99.

C.M.

**DIVORCE.** In both the OT and the NT MARRIAGE is considered sacred, guaranteeing the stability of the family, the strength of the people (tribe or nation or church), and the creation of happiness for all concerned. However, from earliest times, the Hebrew law recognized that some situations could break a marriage, and provision was made for divorce, the dissolution of marital bonds (Deut. 24:1-4).

Hebrew marriage began with the engagement ceremony, hence even engagement could be broken only by a divorce (Hos. 2:19 ff.). This is the significance of Matthew 1:18-25, the desire of Joseph to break off his engagement to Mary privately, to spare her family embarrassment, once he discovered she was pregnant. Only a revelation in a dream (Matt. 1:20-25) convinced Joseph to go forward with the marriage.

While women, generally, did not have the same rights as men, the rabbinical law was just and extended the right of divorce to women as well as to men. Marriage was considered a contract, in which the man promised to provide food, clothing, shelter, and sexual relations. If any of these elements of marriage were withheld, then the wife could seek a divorce. The law of Moses (Lev. 21:14) forbade priests to marry divorced women, yet the divorced daughter of a priest could return to her father for protection (Lev. 22:13).

Adultery, on the part of the wife, was the only grounds for divorce (Exod. 20:14; Deut. 5:18), but there are echoes of other conditions that were apparently recognized as grounds for divorce. The prophets, in their criticisms of Israel and Judah, implied that men divorced their wives for small problems, flouting the sacredness of marriage. Adultery, too, was directed toward the woman, although when a married woman was caught in the act, the man with her (married or not) was also subject to death by stoning. However, the burden of this fell on women, as a wife could be stoned to death if it were later discovered that she had engaged in illicit sex before her marriage (Deut. 22:13-31). Divorce was formal, by the handing over of a written bill of divorcement.

J.C.

**DOANE, WILLIAM CROSWELL** (1832–1913). The first bishop of the Protestant Episcopal diocese of Albany who also wrote the hymn "Ancient of Days." He was born in Boston, Massachusetts, on March 2, to the rector of Trinity Church, George Washington Doane, later bishop of New Jersey, and Eliza Greene Callahan Perkins. An 1850 graduate of Burlington College, Doane was ordained deacon (1853), priest (1856), and consecrated bishop (1869), after serving parishes in Burlington, New Jersey; Hartford, Connecticut; and Albany, New York. He made All Saints' Cathedral into a model of social activity with the St. Agnes School, the Child's Hospital, St. Margaret's Home, and the Sisterhood of the Holy Child. Doane represented the American church at two Lambeth conferences. He was an activist for social and moral betterment and opposed any liberalization in divorce law.

N.H.

**DOCETISTS.** Those who held that Jesus did not have a real body, but simply appeared to have one.

The term "Docetist" derives from a Greek word meaning "to appear." Docetism was an important challenge to orthodoxy particularly during the second century, when GNOSTICISM was at the height of its popularity, for Docetism was especially appealing to those who, as most Gnostics, considered matter evil. Since matter is evil, the Savior—or, in some Gnostic systems, the Messenger from beyond—must not have taken a material body. MARCION was also accused of having Docetic tendencies, for he denied the birth of Jesus, claiming that he came into the world as a grown man during the reign of Tiberius. It was against such doctrines that the Apostles' Creed underscored the birth, suffering, and death of Jesus. In later times, all who in any way have denied the full humanity of Jesus have also been called Docetists.

J.G.

**DOCTORS OF THE CHURCH.** The great theologians whose authority is considered paramount. Traditionally, there have been four great doctors from the Latin-speaking West, and four from the Greek-speaking East. The great Latin doctors are AMBROSE, JEROME, AUGUSTINE, and GREGORY THE GREAT. Their Greek counterparts are ATHANASIUS, BASIL, GREGORY NAZIANZUS, and JOHN CHRYSOSTOM. Since the thirteenth century, the popes have occasionally added other names to the list of doctors. At present they number thirty-two. The last to receive such an honor are saints TERESA and CATHERINE OF SIENA, whom Paul VI declared doctors of the church in 1970. They are the only two women in the list, which also includes such prominent saints and theologians as THOMAS AQUINAS, BONAVENTURE, ANSELM, BERNARD OF CLAIRVAUX, and ALBERTUS MAGNUS. In total, the list includes two popes, three cardinals, fifteen bishops, nine priests, one deacon, and two nuns.

J.G.

**DOCTRINE.** See DOGMA/DOCTRINE.

**DOCTRINE OF THE MEAN** (Chung Yung). A basic Confucian text, traditionally ascribed to Confucius' grandson but now put as late as the second century B.C. by some scholars. The *Chung Yung* (literally, "Central and Normal") provides a brief yet profound summation of basic Confucian teachings. It instructs that to live genuinely one must cultivate one's own true nature, allowing it to manifest itself in outward behavior. Human nature requires right relations with others, in accordance with the five relationships, whether sovereign and subject, parent and child, husband and wife, older and younger brother, friend and friend. The ideal is a life that does not go to extremes, but which like an unwavering pivot holds to the center.

R.E.

**DOCUMENTARY HYPOTHESIS.** A theory developed in the eighteenth and nineteenth centuries that divided the material in the PENTATEUCH into four major blocks and sought to relate these to one another and to the course of Israelite history. The theory assumes that Moses did not compose the Pentateuch but that it was the product of various periods in Israelite history.

This horizontal division of the Pentateuch into sources involved three steps. (1) The material was divided among various sources according to what have been called the Five Pillars of documentary analysis: (a) the use of different names for God, (b) differences in language and style, (c) contradictions and divergencies among various texts, (d) duplication and repetition of material, and (e) the evidence of literary seams suggesting the combination of different sources. The results of such analysis suggested the existence of four sources in the Pentateuch: (a) a source with strong priestly interests and vocabulary (P or Priestly); (b) a source that throughout used the name YAHWEH (spelled *Jahweh* in German) for God (J or Yahwistic); (c) a source that, like P, used ELOHIM until the time of Moses (E or Elohistic); and (d) a source whose style and vocabulary are best seen in DEUTERONOMY (D or Deuteronomistic).

(2) The second step in the documentary hypothesis involved the establishment of a relative chronology for the sources. Scholars sought to establish such a relationship by analyzing the nature and development of various religious practices and institutions as these are reflected in the sources. Among the factors analyzed to establish the relationship of the documents were (a) the number and nature of sanctuaries, (b) the character and nature of various sacrifices, (c) the number and character of religious festivals, (d) the priesthood, and (e) the nature and regulation of priestly and clergy income. This analysis suggested that the relative chronological order of the documents was J, E, D, P.

(3) The last stage consisted of associating these sources with particular epochs in Israelite history as this could be constructed from the historical books (Judges–II Kings, I–II Chronicles, Ezra–Nehemiah). Scholars working with the documentary hypothesis associated J and E with the early monarchical period, D with the reform of Josiah, and P with postexilic Judaism.

Although many scholars contributed to the development of the documentary hypothesis, it is especially associated with the German scholars Karl Heinrich Graf and JULIUS WELLHAUSEN and the Dutch scholar Abraham Kuenen.

J.H.

## DODD, CHARLES H. (1884–1973).

British NT scholar and a leading influence in the field between 1920 and 1960. He is especially noted for his advocacy of "realized eschatology" in the teaching of Jesus, for his work on the Fourth Gospel, and for several popular and influential books on the study and interpretation of the Bible. Dodd took his B.A.

degree in classical studies at University College, Oxford, did research at the University of Berlin, and read divinity at Mansfield College, Oxford. Ordained in 1912, he served the Congregational church at Warwick (1912–15, 1918–19). He returned to Mansfield College as Yates Lecturer in NT before assuming the Rylands professorship at Manchester (1930–35) and the Norris-Hulse professorship at Cambridge (1935–49). He held many distinguished lectureships in Britain, Europe, and North America, and served as general director of the translation of the New English Bible (1950–65). Dodd was an honorary Fellow of Jesus College, Cambridge, and University College, Oxford, and a Fellow of the British Academy.

J.L.

## DODDRIDGE, PHILIP (1702–51).

The noted hymnwriter who refused university training rather than compromise his nonconformist principles. He attended instead the liberal theological academy at Kibworth, Leicestershire, and in 1723 became pastor there. He served several parishes before moving to Castle Hill Meeting, Northampton, in 1729, where he became principal of an academy and pastor to an Independent congregation. In all he wrote nearly four hundred hymns, all published posthumously, including "O Happy Day, That Fixed My Choice," "Awake, My Soul, Stretch Every Nerve,""Great God, We Sing That Mighty Hand," "Triumphant Zion, Lift Thy Head," "How Gentle God's Commands," "O God of Bethel, by Whose Hand," "Hark, the Glad Sound!" and "Let Zion's Watchmen All Awake." In 1751 he sailed for Lisbon, Portugal, where he died on October 26, shortly after his arrival.

N.H.

## DOGEN (1200–53).

An important Japanese Buddhist priest and philosopher, Dogen was the founder in Japan of the Soto school of ZEN BUDDHISM. Born of an aristocratic family, Dogen lost both his parents in childhood and entered a Tendai monastery. During study in China, however, he became engrossed in the study and practice of Zen. After his return to Japan in 1227, he established Japan's first separate Zen temple and monastery. In both his leadership of it and in his writings, he stressed a life of simplicity, labor, and the Soto practice of "quiet sitting" as the path to enlightenment. In his highly regarded philosophical treatises, Dogan pointed to the Buddha-nature as the essence of all things, the unity of the Absolute and the phenomenal world, and made observations on the relationship of time and existence, which have been compared to modern relativity theory.

R.E.

## DOGMA/DOCTRINE.

All religions involve their adherents in certain beliefs and these are called "doctrines," from the Latin *doctrina*, meaning "teaching." These beliefs may be more or less

precisely formulated and systematized. Where attempts are made at precise formulation, it is almost
inevitable that differences of opinion will arise, and
sometimes religious communities are sharply divided
even to the point of SCHISM over doctrinal differences.
The word "dogma," from the Greek verb *dokein*, "to
seem good," is a doctrine which has been given
authoritative status by the church. Dogmas have
usually been formulated after periods of doctrinal
controversy, for example, the definition of the person
of Christ by the COUNCIL OF CHALCEDON (451) came
at the end of a long period of Christological debate
and was meant to settle the issues in dispute. But it is
now generally recognized that all dogmatic formulations are infected by historical relativism and may
stand in need of revision.

J.M.

**DOME OF THE ROCK.** Located in Jerusalem on
the rise that is the traditional site of Solomon's
Temple, this mosque and pilgrimage center is the
third most venerated shrine in Islam, after Mecca and
Medina, and an important example of early Muslim
architecture. It commemorates the place where the
Prophet MUHAMMAD commenced his mystical ascent
into heaven, an event of immense importance to
Islamic devotion. Begun in A.D. 688, the Dome of the
Rock has linked Islam with the Holy City of Jews and
Christians for about thirteen centuries.

R.E.

*The Dome of the Rock*

**DOMINIC/DOMINICANS.** Dominic of Guzman
(1170–1221), better known as St. Dominic, was the
founder of the Order of Preachers, commonly called
Dominicans. He was born into an aristocratic Spanish
family and was a canon of the cathedral of Palencia
when he and his bishop traveled to southern France.
There he was profoundly disturbed by the popularity
of the ALBIGENSES and by the inability of the orthodox
leadership to refute them convincingly. He became
convinced that such refutation had to be based on
both sound scholarship and austerity of life. The
result was the Order of Preachers, who made vows of
poverty and devoted their lives to study and
preaching. In contrast to the FRANCISCANS, whose
vows of poverty they emulated, from the start the
Dominicans wished to establish themselves in
universities and other centers of learning. Also, since
poverty for them was a means to a mission, and not
the core of their self-understanding, they did not
undergo the divisions and controversies regarding
absolute poverty that rocked the Franciscan order
after the death of St. Francis. Also, they soon
amplified their mission and began dealing with not
only the Albigensian threat, but with all the various
intellectual challenges that resulted from the reintroduction of Aristotle into the West. In this regard, the
most noteworthy Dominican theologians were AL-
BERTUS MAGNUS and his disciple THOMAS AQUINAS.

The Dominicans also did remarkable missionary
work. Their most famous preacher among Jews in
Spain was Vincent Ferrer, and, among Muslims in the
Levant, William of Tripoli. Soon they had missionaries as far as India and China. With the discovery of
the New World, their field of action was greatly
increased. In the Spanish and Portuguese colonies,
they often took the side of the Indians against the
Spanish who oppressed them. Most famous for such
action and for strong advocacy for the Indians before
Spanish authorities was Bartolomé de Las Casas.

J.G.

**DOMITIAN** (A.D. 51–96). Roman Emperor from
A.D. 81 to 96; successor of TITUS, his brother.
According to Tertullian, a Latin Christian theologian, he was a persecutor of the church. Evidence for
this notoriety is slight. Clement of Rome, writing in
the A.D. 90s, refers to the "sudden and repeated
misfortunes and calamities" that had hindered him in
dealing with the strife in the Corinthian churches,
but it is not certain that Clement was referring to
state-instigated persecutions.

Some scholars associate two or three NT writings
with Domitian's reign: the Revelation to John, the
Letter to the Hebrews, and I Peter. Suetonius wrote
that Domitian desired that his subjects profess him as
"our Lord and God." The discovery of first-century
Roman coins in the province of Asia bearing symbols
of Domitian's deification has been taken as evidence
that the crisis facing the seven churches in this
province, described by John, occasioned the writing

Courtesy of the American Numismatic Society

*Roman coin showing head of Domitian*

of Revelation. Less certain is the assignment of Hebrews and I Peter to Domitian's reign.     J.P.

**DONATION OF CONSTANTINE.** A spurious document, probably dating from the eighth or ninth century, by which CONSTANTINE supposedly granted Pope Sylvester I authority over the entire church and the right to rule over the "Western lands." Believed to be authentic throughout the late Middle Ages, it was used to support both the primacy of the popes and their right to temporal rule. Scholars in the Renaissance, notably Lorenzo Valla, proved the "Donation" to be a forgery.

J.G.

**DONATISTS.** A schismatic group that appeared in North Africa in the fourth century, named for one of its leaders, Donatus of Casae Nigrae. With the advent of Constantine, persecution of the church had ceased. But the question still remained of what to do with those who had weakened during the persecution. A particularly difficult question was the status of those who had turned over the Scriptures to the authorities to be destroyed—the "traditores." If they were ordained, were their orders still valid?

The issue came to a head when a new bishop was elected and consecrated for Carthage, the most important city in North Africa. Some of his enemies declared that one of those who had consecrated him was a "traditor," and that therefore his consecration was not valid. Eventually the entire church in North Africa split over the issue of whether sacraments and ordinations performed by the unworthy were valid or not. In truth, the schism had ethnic and social overtones, for in general the Donatists were stronger in rural areas and among the lower classes and those of ancient Berber and Punic stock, while their opponents were particularly strong in Carthage itself, and among the Latin-speaking middle and upper classes. Both sides appealed to the rest of the church and to Constantine, and the decision went against the Donatists. Rejected both by other Christians and by the empire, some of the more extreme Donatists (the "Circumcellions") then formed an armed band that ravaged the country. Although the empire took stern action against both the Circumcellions and the more moderate Donatists, the schism persisted until the Arab invasions in the seventh century.

J.G.

**DONNE, JOHN** (1573–1631). English preacher, poet, prose writer, and eminent dean of St. Paul's Cathedral. Donne was born a Catholic in London. He received no degree but attended Oxford and Cambridge for six years, traveled, read law, and accompanied Essex and Raleigh against Spain, 1596-97. After careful reflection, he accepted Anglicanism. In 1598 he became private secretary to Sir Thomas Egerton (Lord Ellesmere), keeper of the Great Seal, but lost his position and was briefly imprisoned for secretly marrying Anne Moore (Egerton's niece) in 1601. For ten years he struggled in poverty and wrote *Biathanatos*, in defense of suicide (published 1744). His *Pseudo-Martyr* (1610), opposing Catholicism, pleased King James I, who later urged Anglican ordination (1615), made him royal chaplain, and in 1621 appointed him dean of St. Paul's Cathedral. Donne poured his genius into sermons, frequently dealing with death and God's mercy to sinners. *Devotions upon Emergent Occasions* (1624) masterfully probes illness, others, and God: "No man is an island . . . any man's death diminishes me . . . because I am involved in Mankind . . ." He preached "Death's Duel" just before his death. Most of his satire, love lyrics, and collections of sermons appeared posthumously. He directly influenced George Herbert, Henry Vaughan, William Yeats, T. S. Eliot, and W. H. Auden. There has been a revival of interest in Donne in the twentieth century.

C.M.

**DORCAS.** The Greek form of the Hebrew name Tabitha (Gazelle), which was worn by a woman in the NT who was well known in the city of Joppa (Tel Aviv) for her charity (Acts 9:36-42). When she died Simon Peter was summoned and raised her from the dead.

J.R.M.

**DORT, SYNOD OF.** From November 13, 1618, to May 9, 1619, a synod of the Reformed Dutch church to settle differences between Arminians (*see* ARMINIANISM) and strict Calvinists (*see* CALVIN, JOHN). Led by Johan van Oldenbarneveldt and Hugo Grotius, the Remonstrants in 1610 issued a statement rejecting absolute predestination, atonement of Christ only for the elect, irresistible grace, and the impossibility of losing grace. Dort reaffirmed rigid Calvinist doctrines: divine unconditional predestination, atonement for the elect only, human sinfulness, irresistible grace, and the perseverance of the saints. Disagreeing Arminians were banished. Oldenbarneveldt was beheaded on May 13, 1619, and Grotius was given life imprisonment but escaped in 1621.

C.M.

**DOSTOYEVSKY, FEODOR** (1821–81). Russian novelist, renowned for religious insights. Born in Moscow, Dostoyevsky attended the Military Engineers School in St. Petersburg (1838–43), was commissioned, and served until he resigned in 1844 to write. *Poor Folk* (1845) won acclaim, but he was arrested with other socialist thinkers in 1849 and sentenced to death. The sentence was later commuted, but not before he faced a firing squad. This tragic experience influenced his entire life. After four years of imprisonment in Siberia, he did compulsory army service, married unhappily in 1857, but could not return to St. Petersburg until 1859.

He was more religious than revolutionary, yet fared poorly. With his brother Mikhail, Dostoyevsky founded *Time,* a monthly journal, for which he wrote until its suppression in 1863, the year his wife and brother died. A second marriage (1867) brought happiness and financial improvement through his wife's management of his publications. However, Dostoyevsky was plagued by compulsive gambling, heavy debts, and epilepsy. He hastily produced masterful works embodying his prison experiences, religious probings, and profound character insights. His characters are complex, emotional, bound together by sin, and unable of themselves to find God. Committed to Russian nationalism and Christianity, Dostoyevsky agonized over suffering, revolution, crime, poverty, and faith. His world-renowned writings include *The Double* (1846), *The House of the Dead* (1862), and *Letters from the Underworld* (1864), studies of insanity and imprisonment; *Crime and Punishment (1866),* a psychology of murder; *The Idiot* (1869), reflections on Christlike perfection; *The Possessed* (1871), an attack on radicalism; and *The Brothers Karamazov* (1880), a search for God.

C.M.

**DOUAY-RHEIMS BIBLE.** Even older than the King James Version is this Roman Catholic Bible, which for more than three centuries has been the principal English-language, officially approved, Catholic Bible.

It was translated from the VULGATE by a band of British Roman Catholic exiles at the English College at Douay in northern France. The work was begun in 1578 at the prompting of the English cardinal, William Allen. The actual work of translation was conducted under the direction of Gregory Martin, who, like William Allen, had been trained and also taught at Oxford University.

The motive for this version was not so much to promote Bible reading but rather to counteract the "heresy" in Protestant versions of Scripture. When the English College was moved from Douay to Rheims in 1578, the translating team moved, too, thus giving this text the hyphenated name it has borne. The NT was published in 1582, but the OT, ready at that time, did not appear until 1609–10 because of a lack of funds. Martin did check with the extant Greek manuscripts and the Protestant version, especially Coverdale's Diglott version of 1538.

Ironically, not only did Coverdale's Protestant text influence the Douay-Rheims Bible, but this Catholic version, in turn, had impact on the KJV's rendition. Actually the KJV scholars using the Bishops' Bible as the principal base for their new translation also were instructed to consult all earlier English versions, including the Douay-Rheims NT and the Geneva Bible.

Throughout the centuries the Douay-Rheims Bible has been revised at least twice. Bishop Richard Challoner developed what came to be known as the Challoner-Rheims Version of 1749–50. This version was again revised by Catholic scholars in 1941 under the patronage of the Episcopal Committee of the Confraternity of Christian Doctrine. The publication of the New American Bible probably means the overshadowing of this hoary version.

R.H.

**DOUBLE PROCESSION OF THE HOLY SPIRIT.** The doctrine, common in the West, that the Holy Spirit proceeds from both the Father *and* the Son. Against this view, the Eastern churches hold that the Spirit proceeds from the Father, *through* the Son. The main source for the Western tradition is Augustine, for whom the Spirit is the bond of love between Father and Son, and thus proceeds from both. Eastern theologians, on the other hand, argue that there can be only one fountainhead of divinity, and this is the Father. Although these divergent views stem from different understandings of the TRINITY, they did not become a subject of heated controversy until the issue of the FILIOQUE came to the forefront in the ninth century.

J.G.

**DOVE.** A term denoting several smaller species of pigeons that were typically the subject of biblical metaphor. The dove symbolizes the gentle, affectionate attitude of the beloved (Song of S. 5:2) and human innocence amid hostile surroundings (Matt. 10:16).

The OT mentions the dove's moaning (Isa. 38:14), colors (Ps. 68:13), eyes (Song of S. 1:15), presence in valleys (Ezek. 7:16), nesting in rocks (Jer. 48:28), capacity for flight (Ps. 55:6), and even lack of sense (Hos. 7:11-12). After the Flood, Noah dispatched a dove from the ark to determine conditions outside (Gen. 8:8). As a victimized people, Israel is superbly symbolized as a dove within one communal lament (Ps. 74:19). All four Gospels portray the heavenly descent of God's Spirit as a dove alighting on Jesus at baptism (Matt. 3:16; Mark 1:10; Luke 3:22; John 1:32). Perhaps this reflcts the hovering aspect of the Spirit at the world's creation (Gen. 1:2).

J.K.K.

**DOXOLOGY.** A litany or liturgical response of praise said or sung at various points in divine worship, both Protestant and Catholic. The doxology that begins "Glory be to the Father, and to the Son and to the Holy Ghost" originated in Antioch, where it was derived from the primitive Christian baptism formula. It is clearly trinitarian and expresses the conviction of Latin or Western Christianity that God is triune and that there is complete equality among the three persons in the Godhead. The doxology holds that the Father is glorified by the Spirit through the Son.

The longer litany, the GLORIA IN EXCELSIS ("Glory to God in the highest") is called the greater doxology. It consists of the angels' song at Christ's birth, praise of the Father, and the praise of Christ and the Holy Spirit.

A simpler doxology, or short hymn of praise, has been used by Christians since apostolic times to conclude prayers. It declares glory to the Father and the Son and the Holy Ghost, world without end, Amen (or "glory throughout the ages"). A doxology is used after the recitation of a psalm in the Catholic and Lutheran liturgies.

J.C.

**DRACHMA.** A Greek silver coin equal to a Roman DENARIUS. Drachma appears in the NT only in Luke 15:8, 9, as the "lost coin." It took four drachmas to make one shekel. The "half-shekel" tax Jesus paid was a didrachma or two-drachma coin (Matt. 17:24). The "silver pieces" Judas received were probably tetradrachmas or "shekels" (Matt. 26:15; Mark 14:11; Luke 22:5).                                              P.L.G.

**DRUID.** A term applied to a caste of learned priests controlling religion among the Celts in Gaul, Ireland, and Britain as early as 200 B.C. Records of Julius Caesar (d. 44 B.C.) and Pliny's *Natural History*, A.D. 77, give our earliest written data on Druids. Well-organized, respected, feared, exempt from military service and taxation, the Druids controlled all religious functions, education, and justice. A supremely powerful Druid ruled over their bards, prophets, and priests. They believed in their descent from a Supreme Being, divinations, astrology, charms, magic, human sacrifice (probably criminals), and the immortality of the soul. Druids believed that at death the soul passed to a newborn child. They reverenced some plants and animals, particularly mistletoe growing on oak trees, and held their meetings in oak forests. They fiercely resisted Roman conquest, but Rome subdued them in Gaul, Wales, and England, and Christianity overcame the remnants. Some elements of the Druids, however, survive in the belief in local woodland fairies.

C.M.

**DRUZE (OR DRUZES).** An offshoot of the Ismailiyya sect of the SHI'ITE branch of Islam (Shi'ism). The movement began around A.D. 1000, during the reign of al-Hakin, caliph of the Fatimid dynasty in Egypt (A.D. 996–1021). The Ismaili sect considers al-Hakin as an infallible imam—almost as an incarnation of divinity. Al-Hakin's unusual claims caused much confusion, and a Persian, Hamza ibn Ali, founded the Druze movement in A.D. 1017. To the Druzes, al-Hakin is the incarnation of the Ultimate, the One, the Creator. The Druze worship al-Hakin and call themselves *muwahhidun* or "unitarians." They believe al-Hakin will return, and they teach the reincarnation of souls.

J.C.

**DUALISM.** The doctrine that there are two ultimate principles irreducible to a unity. A classic example is ancient Persian religion in its later phase, when Ahura Mazda, the spirit of light and goodness, had as his counterpart Ahriman, the spirit of darkness and evil. The still later MANICHAEISM (third century A.D.) combined Persian, Gnostic, Christian, and Jewish elements in its teaching, according to which the world is a mixture of light and darkness, or spirit and matter, and salvation consists in separating spirit from its entanglement with matter. Although traditional Christianity supposed that over against GOD there is a realm of demonic powers headed by SATAN or the devil, this was not a dualism, for Satan and his hosts were never considered to be of equal status with God but were fallen angels and therefore creaturely and destined for eventual defeat. In modern times, Descartes and his followers taught a dualism of mind and matter, but nowadays the tendency is to see the human being as a psychosomatic unity. (*See also* MONOTHEISM.)

J.M.

**DUFFIELD, GEORGE, JR.** (1818–88). The author of "Stand Up, Stand Up for Jesus" was the son and grandson of Presbyterian ministers named George Duffield. George Duffield, Jr., was the great grandson of Isabella Graham and grandson of Joanna and Divie Bethune. Born September 12 in Carlisle, Pennsylvania, he was educated at Yale College and Union Seminary in New York City. Ordained to the Presbyterian ministry, he served churches in Brooklyn (1840–47), Bloomfield, New Jersey (1847–52), Philadelphia (1852–61), Adrian, Michigan (1861–65), Galesburg, Illinois (1865–69), and Ann Arbor and Lansing, Michigan (1869–88). His famous hymn was inspired by the dying words of Dudley Atkins Tyng, rector of Epiphany Church, Philadelphia, who said, "Tell them to stand up for Jesus: now let us sing a hymn." It was first published in a Sunday school handbill in 1858.

N.H.

**DUKKHA.** From the Pali word for "unpleasant." (The Sanskrit rendering is "Duhkha.") In BUDDHISM it is the suffering, both mental and physical, which afflicts all conditioned existence, including human lives as they are ordinarily lived. The first of the Buddha's FOUR NOBLE TRUTHS is often translated, "All life is suffering {dukkha}." This may be taken to mean that, although every moment may not be filled with excruciating pain, we are seldom free of underlying currents of anxiety and frustration due to the conditions of existence itself. According to Buddhism, dukkha is a product of these features of life: it is unsatisfying (that is, it is full of pain and its hopes and desires are never wholly met), it is transitory, and it is an aggregate (that is, we are made of the several *skandhas* or psycho-physical elements, such as the senses, perceptions, and responses, which often miscue one another and with which we falsely identify). Desire or attachment on all levels is the basic cause of suffering. The Buddha's path, culminating in right meditation, is the way out of it.

R.E.

**DUNKARDS.** *See* CHURCH OF THE BRETHREN.

**DUNS SCOTUS, JOHN** (1265–1308). One of the foremost Franciscan theologians, known also as the Subtle Doctor and as the Doctor of the Immaculate Conception. Scotus marks one of the stages of the movement of late medieval theology away from the confidence in reason that had marked its high point at the time of BONAVENTURE and THOMAS AQUINAS. With Duns Scotus, the list of those items that reason cannot prove, but are known only by faith, grew much longer. He still believed in the harmony between reason and revelation, but disagreed with Thomas on the ability of reason to prove such things as the immortality of the soul. Furthermore, God is not subject to our human rationality and therefore may act in manners that to us seem capricious. Eventually, such views would undercut the basic assumptions of scholastic theology—although in Duns Scotus himself this is not the case. Duns Scotus is also known for his defense of the IMMACULATE CONCEPTION of Mary. This was a view that had been proposed earlier and rejected by many theologians— Thomas Aquinas among them. But through the influence of Duns Scotus and other Franciscan theologians it gained recognition and was finally declared to be official doctrine of the Roman Catholic Church in the nineteenth century.

J.G.

**DUNSTAN** (925?–88). English prelate, archbishop of Canterbury, monastic reformer, statesman, and educator. Legend surrounds much of his life, but he brought renewal to the church in his time, especially to MONASTICISM. Born into nobility near Glastonbury, he received an education in the abbey of Glastonbury, served in the court of King Athelstan, and at an early age became a monk at Glastonbury. He devoted himself to biblical and early church studies, lived ascetically, and undertook painting, music, and metal working, in which he excelled. He is said to have become an abbot at age twenty-one and to have made Glastonbury famous as an educational center. King Edgar appointed him bishop of Worcester (957), London (959), and archbishop of Canterbury (960). He advised Edgar on state affairs; and as abbot, bishop, and archbishop, he strove to restore monasticism, which had declined drastically. He is credited with establishing numerous new BENEDICTINE foundations.

C.M.

**DURA-EUROPOS.** An ancient city on the east bank of the Euphrates near the north edge of the Syrian Desert, 275 miles north of Baghdad, 160 miles east of Palmyra. Developed by the Seleucids (about 300 B.C.) as a military colony, river port, and trading center on the main east-west land route, the city was ruled by Seleucids until 140 B.C., and then by the Parthians (140 B.C.–A.D. 165), and the Romans (A.D. 165–256). Its destruction in A.D. 256 by the Persian Sasānians left the city in ruins until the twentieth century. Fortunately, the Roman defenders buried much of the city while buttressing the city walls.

Excavation of Dura-Europos began (1922–23) under Franz Cumont of Belgium and continued with French and American archaeologists (1928–1937). About a fourth of the city has been now excavated, enough to give an unusually detailed picture of a Roman fortress town guarding the empire's eastern border. The cultural climate shows international influences: the Seleucids used Greek city planning, the Roman soldiers were provided with a Mithraeum, and a major temple housed a colossal statue of the Babylonian god Bel/Baal-Marduk.

The Jewish community of Dura-Europos had built a house-synagogue with remarkable wall paintings, now exhibited at the national museum in Damascus. The Christian house-church had a baptistery and murals (now in the Yale University Art Museum) comparable, but in a different style, to those in the catacombs of Rome. A Greek papyrus of Tatian's *Diatesseron* found at Dura-Europos, suggests that Greek was the preferred church language for Christians in that city.

P.L.G.

**DURKHEIM, EMILE** (1858–1917). One of the founders of modern sociological theory. He was born in Epinal, France, and educated at the Ecole Normal Superiore, Paris, with an interest in political and social philosophy. He then became the first professor of sociology and education at Bordeaux, a post he held until 1902, when he was honored by an appointment to the Sorbonne.

Durkheim was interested in the application of sociology to education. He studied how societies were structured in order to satisfy the wants of people and the interrelationships between individual strivings and social cohesiveness. He also investigated the

*Fresco from Dura-Europos showing the consecration of the tabernacle*

extent to which individualism and social order could co-exist. In *The Elementary Forms of the Religious Life* (1912), based on a study of "primitive" societies, he posited the theory that religion is the matrix out of which culture develops. Deeply affected by the violence and upheaval of World War I, he died in 1917.

I.C.

**DWIGHT, TIMOTHY** (1752–1817). The Congregational minister and president of Yale (1795–1817) born May 14, 1752, in Northampton, Massachusetts, to Timothy Dwight and Mary Edwards, daughter of JONATHAN EDWARDS.

He entered Yale at thirteen, graduated in 1769, and received a master's degree in 1772. On March 3, 1777, he married Mary Woolsey. Licensed to preach the same year, he served as chaplain to the Continental Army. In 1783 he was called to the Congregational church at Greenfield Hill, where he was ordained November 5, and served for twelve years. His earnest preaching at Yale encouraged revivals there in 1801 and 1807–8.

Founder of New Haven Theology, he is the author of the five-volume *Theology, Explained and Defended* (1818-19); *The Conquest of Canaan* (1785), the first epic poem published in America; and the hymn "I Love Thy Kingdom, Lord." He helped to found Andover Theological Seminary, the Missionary Society of Connecticut, and the American Board of Commissioners for Foreign Missions. He died on January 11.

N.H.

# Ee

**E DOCUMENT.** One of the literary sources of the PENTATEUCH. The modern name for *E* derives from the repeated use of the Hebrew divine name Elohim. It is likely that *E* was composed in the northern kingdom (Samaria) during the ninth century B.C. (*Compare also* DOCUMENTARY HYPOTHESIS.)

J.N.

**EARLY CHURCH, HISTORY OF CHRISTIANITY IN THE.** The history of the early church covers the period from the end of the NT to the year A.D. 430. This date marks the death of AUGUSTINE of Hippo, usually considered the last of the ancient FATHERS OF THE CHURCH. Also, at that time the Vandals were besieging Hippo, thus marking the end of the Western Roman Empire.

The early centuries of the history of Christianity are divided into two very different periods by the momentous event of the conversion of CONSTANTINE. The period prior to that event was marked by PERSECUTION, and not many powerful or socially prestigious people were found in the ranks of the church. At the same time, the early church was clarifying the nature of its message and beliefs, partly in response to the challenge of what eventually were condemned as forms of heresy.

This double concern—persecution and heresy—can be seen in the earliest extant Christian writings outside the NT, the APOSTOLIC FATHERS. For instance, the seven letters of IGNATIUS OF ANTIOCH, written on his way to martyrdom in Rome, show that he was a victim of persecution in Antioch, that he was eager to prove worthy of the crown of martyrdom, and that he was greatly concerned over the deviant doctrines that were appearing both in Antioch and elsewhere.

The reasons for persecution varied through the years, as the nature of persecution itself also changed. In most of the NT the Roman Empire appears as the protector of Christians against attempts by some Jews to persecute them. But other sources make it clear that already in A.D. 64, during the reign of Nero, imperial authorities began persecuting Christians as such, at least in the city of Rome. At that time, they were accused of arson, being blamed for the great fire that destroyed a vast area of the city. This persecution, probably the most famous because it was the first, and because both Peter and Paul are said to have died under it, was far, however, from the worse, for it seems to have been limited to the city of Rome, and in any case abated after Nero's death.

Later in the century, Emperor Domitian unleashed another persecution that was particularly violent in Asia Minor. The book of Revelation in the NT reflects conditions at that time. The reasons for this persecution are not clear. It seems that Domitian resented the unwillingness of both Jews and Christians to grant him divine honors or at least to send to Rome the yearly contributions that Jews had usually sent to Jerusalem, which had been destroyed by Roman legions.

By the early second century, the empire was beginning to define its policy toward Christians, whose numbers now required such definition. Pliny, governor of Bithynia under Trajan, complained that the pagan temples were almost deserted due to the spread of Christianity. The policy that Trajan outlined in response was that Christians ought not to be sought, but that if accused and brought before the authorities they must worship the gods or be punished. But no anonymous accusations should be heeded. The net result of this policy was that Christians depended on the good will of their neighbors, who at any time could destroy them by a simple accusation. This in turn gave greater importance to the work of the APOLOGISTS, who sought to show that the various rumors about Christian practices were untrue, and that Christianity was more reasonable than its critics claimed. Foremost of these Apologists was JUSTIN MARTYR, who argued, on the basis of the doctrine of the LOGOS, that Christians could claim all the knowledge and virtue of the ancients.

By the time of Emperor Decius (A.D. 249–51), persecution took a new turn. The decline of Rome was evident, and Decius and many others were convinced that Rome was losing the favor of the gods because her subjects were abandoning their worship. Therefore he commanded that all must worship the gods, and have a certificate attesting that they had done so. Those who refused were not killed outright but rather tortured and promised release if they would only worship the gods. Those who stood firm through such trials, but did not become martyrs, the church called confessors, for they had confessed the faith in the most difficult circumstances. After the end of this persecution, the question of the restoration of the lapsed became a burning issue, particularly in North Africa, where Bishop CYPRIAN opposed the claim of some confessors that it was they who had the right to grant pardon to those who had fallen. For similar reasons, the church in Rome was also divided, for the followers of NOVATIAN insisted on greater rigor than Bishop Cornelius was willing to apply.

The greatest persecution, however, broke out early in the fourth century, under Emperor DIOCLETIAN (A.D. 284–305) and his associate GALERIUS (A.D. 293–311). At this point Christians were required to turn in their copies of Scripture. Those who did so were dubbed "traditores" by other Christians. Eventually the persecutors showed great cruelty, torturing and killing Christians in every conceivable way. Finally, in A.D. 311, Galerius put an end to persecution, which he had decided was futile. By that time, Constantine had begun his rise in the West. In 312, he defeated Maxentius in the battle at Milvian Bridge, in the outskirts of Rome. In that battle, his

soldiers fought under a sign that could be interpreted as a monogram containing the Greek letters chi (X) and rho (P), the first two letters of the name of Christ. The following year, in what is usually called the Edict of Milan, Constantine and Emperor Licinius put an end to persecution.

During all this time, the church also had to face the challenge of what it called "heresies." Drawing its converts from varied backgrounds, the church soon found itself flooded with divergent interpretations of its message, some of which seemed to threaten the very core of the gospel. The most important of these was GNOSTICISM, the name given to several schools of thought that held that salvation was attained through a secret knowledge ("gnosis"). Most Gnostics believed that matter was evil, and therefore denied the doctrine of the creation of the world by the Supreme God. For similar reasons, they held that the body was evil, and that therefore there would be no resurrection of the dead, for only the spiritual is worthy of continued existence. Also, most of them denied that Jesus had true human flesh—a doctrine called DOCETISM, from a Greek word meaning "to appear." MARCION, the son of a Christian bishop, was not a Gnostic, but he also denied creation by the Supreme God. According to him, the God of the OT is not the loving Father of Jesus, but a vindictive inferior being who made this world either out of folly or out of spite. Jesus was not born as a human being, but simply appeared as a grown man during the reign of Tiberius. For these reasons, Marcion rejected the OT and offered in its place a list of Christian books, consisting of the Gospel of Luke and the epistles of Paul, all cleansed from what he claimed were Judaizing interpolations.

Against these and other similar doctrines, the church responded by developing its own CANON of the NT, insisting on the apostolic succession and authority of its bishops, and composing creeds or "symbols" that could be used as tests of orthodoxy. The most important of these early creeds was the Old Roman Symbol, out of which our present APOSTLES' CREED developed. Its purpose was clearly to reject the docetic and dualist views of Marcion and others. Likewise, the insistence on several gospels (sometimes three, and eventually four), which did not agree on all their details, was a way of showing that the universal apostolic authority was on the side of the church, and against those heretics who claimed to derive their doctrines from the secret teachings of a single apostle or a single gospel—such as the Gospel of Thomas. At the same time, the church was challenged by the Montanists, who believed that in themselves a new "age of the Spirit" had begun. Against such a view, the church insisted both on the finality of Christ as the dawn of the last age and on the authority of bishops.

Christian theology during these early centuries centered mostly in ALEXANDRIA, Carthage, AN-TIOCH, and ASIA MINOR. In these various areas different theological types developed. In Alexandria,

Christianity was seen as the "true philosophy," in basic continuity with classical philosophy. In Carthage—and eventually in most of the West—it was understood basically in moral and legal terms, as a way of life leading to forgiveness and salvation. In Antioch and Asia Minor, it was seen as the keystone of history, the culmination of God's great creating and liberating acts, leading humankind to freedom and communion with the Divine. Eventually, these various views would cause conflicts among those who held them.

The worship of these first centuries was simple. For the most part, it took place in private homes or in burial places, such as the catacombs, although by the third century there were some buildings, or at least rooms, set aside for Christian worship. The center of such worship was Communion, which at first involved a full meal. By the second century, however, it consisted of bread and wine, and the meal was either separated from it or dropped altogether. Baptism, usually by descending into water and having it poured over one's head, was the act of Christian initiation. Scholars do not agree as to whether or not the early church baptized infants. But by the beginning of the third century, such was a clearly established practice. By then, baptism was usually administered on Easter—and sometimes on other great feast days—after a long period of preparation. The last few weeks of such preparation, in which the entire church made ready to renew its own baptismal vows, gave rise to the season of Lent.

Constantine's conversion, and the support he and his successors gave the church, brought about great changes. Of these the most obvious was the cessation of persecution. Eventually, it was paganism that was put at a disadvantage, although it lingered in rural areas at least until the sixth century. But there were also other significant changes. Church architecture developed into great basilicas, in imitation of the great buildings of the Roman Empire. In them, the liturgy became more elaborate, with the introduction of incense, choirs, processionals, vestments, and so forth. People flocked into the church, and among the newly converted were many of the most prestigious and powerful families of the empire. In the field of theology, doctrinal questions often became entangled with political issues, and there were those who sought to best their opponents, not by the force of their arguments, but by the force of imperial decree.

Probably, most Christians were delighted with these developments. After centuries under the constant threat of persecution, the new imperial favor seemed a boon from heaven. EUSEBIUS OF CAESAREA, the great church historian, was probably speaking for the majority of Christians when he sought to present the entire history of the church as culminating in the conversion of Constantine, and the persecutions of earlier times as the result of a grave misunderstanding on the part of the empire as to the true nature of Christianity.

Others, however, were not so thrilled by the events of their time. Many felt that Christianity must be akin to the hard struggle of an athlete, and that now Constantine and his successors were making it too easy. Thousands therefore took up MONASTICISM, which had earlier roots, but gained momentum after Constantine. By the late fourth century, some travelers commented, with slight exaggeration, that the Egyptian desert was as populated as some cities. Eventually, monasticism would develop into one of Christianity's main missionary instruments. But in its origins it was mostly preoccupied with one's salvation, particularly at a time when the outward success of the church made it so difficult to be a true Christian.

Others reacted even more strongly. In North Africa, DONATISM and its radical branch, the Circumcellions, broke away from the rest of the church, presumably over the question of the validity of rites performed by ministers who had lapsed during the persecution, but also over ethnic and socioeconomic issues. This division continued weakening the church in the area until Christianity was wiped out by the Muslim invasions in the seventh century.

But many of the greatest leaders of the church responded with neither total complaisance nor outright rejection. Most of the great leaders of the church during the fourth century—ATHANASIUS, BASIL THE GREAT, AMBROSE, JOHN CHRYSOSTOM, and others—clashed on occasion with the emperors or their officers. All of them rejected the worldly pomp that tempted so many of their contemporaries. In a way, all of them took up many of the monastic ideals. But instead of withdrawing to the desert they took up the task of leading the church as it sought its new place in society, and as it was rent by political and theological divisions.

In the field of theology, the great controversy immediately following the conversion of Constantine revolved around ARIANISM and the question of the divinity of the Son. Arius and his followers declared that the Son, although the first of all creatures, was nevertheless created. His opponents insisted that the Son was fully divine, and therefore eternal. In the Council of NICEA in A.D. 325, the bishops gathered at Constantine's invitation to settle this and other questions. There they decided that the Son was "of one substance" with the Father—homoousion—and therefore not a creature. But this did not end the controversy. Athanasius became the champion of the Nicene cause for over fifty years, and after his death his task was continued by the CAPPADOCIAN FATHERS. Finally, at the Council of CONSTANTINO-PLE in A.D. 381, Arianism was condemned once again. By then, the debate had been enlarged to include also the divinity of the Holy Spirit, and therefore this council actually promulgated the doctrine of the TRINITY. Arianism continued to exist, particularly among the Germanic tribes north of the Danube, and would become an issue once again after the invasion of western Europe and North Africa by those tribes.

The end of the fourth century and the beginning of the fifth was the time of JEROME (A.D. 348–420) and his younger contemporary AUGUSTINE of Hippo (A.D. 354–430). Jerome's greatest work was a direct translation of the Bible into Latin from its original languages. This translation, known as the VULGATE or popular Bible, became the standard text of Scripture for the Latin-speaking West throughout the Middle Ages, and for the Roman Catholic Church until recent times. Augustine was a native of North Africa, where he spent most of his life. After a long spiritual pilgrimage that took him to Manichaeism, Skepticism, and Neoplatonism, he finally returned to the faith of his mother, Monica. For a time he hoped to spend the rest of his life in monastic contemplation. But he was forced to become a priest and then a bishop, and as such he was involved in many of the controversies of his time. In his opposition to PELAGIANISM, he developed views on grace and predestination that would long influence and haunt the church. Against the Donatists, he argued for the validity of sacraments in spite of the possible unworthiness of the celebrant. His understanding of the nature of evil and of knowledge, which he drew mostly from Neoplatonic sources, would become standard for Western Christianity at least until the thirteenth century. For all these reasons, Augustine was the great teacher from whom the Middle Ages learned theology, and therefore all medieval theology bears his mark.

Augustine died in 430, when the Vandals were at the walls of Hippo. Twenty years earlier, Rome itself had fallen to the Goths. It was the end of an age, and the beginning of another in which the church would be called upon to play a substantially different role. (*Compare* MIDDLE AGES, HISTORY OF CHRISTIANITY IN THE.)

J.G.

**EASTER.** The festival celebrating the resurrection of Jesus Christ from the dead, the central focus of the Christian church's worship year.

While Easter, a spring festival, is paired in the average Christian's mind with Christmas, the winter festival of Christ's birth, the celebration of Easter with its message of Christ's victory over sin, death, and the devil is actually the foundation of the faith and the point around which the church's life turns. As Paul says in I Corinthians 15:17, "If Christ has not been raised, your faith is futile and you are still in your sins."

The early church worshiped on the first day of the week (Sunday) because it was "The Lord's Day," that is, the Day of Resurrection. Thus every Sunday is a celebration of Jesus' RESURRECTION. However, in the sub-Apostolic age, at the end of the first century, an annual commemoration of the Resurrection was established. It was simply called *Pascha;* the Greek

translation of the Hebrew festival of PASSOVER, the season at which Christ's death and resurrection took place. (The similarity of *Pascha* to *Paschein,* the Greek verb meaning "to suffer," caused many Christians at the time erroneously to think the festival meant "suffering." Similarly, it was formerly thought that the English term "Easter" was derived from the German *"Ostern,"* both words ultimately being based on the old Anglo-Saxon name *Eastre* or *Ostara,* for the goddess of spring. More recent studies seem to indicate that Easter may be derived from the Latin phrase *hebdomada alba,* the old term for Easter week based upon the wearing of white robes by the newly baptized. The octave of Easter, the following week, was known as *post albas,* the time when the white robes were put away.)

Easter may thus mean "white" and be named from early Christian baptismal practices. If this is the case, it is very appropriate, since Easter early became the favorite season for the instruction of converts, followed by their baptism, confirmation, and first Communion. Indeed, the period of preparation or catechesis of the new converts became the basis of the Lenten season, which was ultimately extended over a forty-day period, modeled on Jesus' forty-day fast in the wilderness *after* his baptism by John the Baptizer.

After the Christian Sunday (beginning on the very first Easter itself), the festival of Easter is the oldest festival (or holy day) celebrated by the Christian church. Because of the "every Sunday is Easter" feelings of the sub-Apostolic church, the annual celebration was early called "the Great Easter" (as it still is in the Orthodox churches). It is instructive that this festival is called *Pascha,* as Paul declares "Christ our passover is sacrificed for us" in I Corinthians 5:7 KJV. The earliest observance of *Pascha* was precisely the anniversary of the original event, the 14th of Nisan (March-April) as it is dated by the Synoptic Gospels, who hold that Jesus died the day after Passover (that is, the Last Supper, Mark 14; Luke 22; Matt. 16) was celebrated. This, of course, conflicts with the Fourth Gospel's account, which holds that Jesus died on the 15th of Nisan, the day before Passover was celebrated. Obviously, if the anniversary of the Resurrection is observed precisely on the 14th of Nisan every year, then the festival will usually not fall on a Sunday. This early led some churches to celebrate Easter on the Sunday nearest the 14th of Nisan. Already in the NT Paul speaks of the Christian worship day as "the first day of the week" (I Cor. 16:2), and the sub-Apostolic Ignatius simply speaks of "The Lord's Day" in his writings, because every Sunday is the Day of Resurrection.

Among the problems that arose was that *Pascha* on the 14th of Nisan was observed as a fast day, but this conflicted with the weekly observance of the Resurrection on Sunday. Those who insisted that the anniversary be kept as the chief observance were called QUARTODECIMANS, from the Latin for "fourteen." Polycarp of Asia Minor divided with Anicetus of

Rome over this issue, and the church in Asia Minor became quartodeciman. Rome considered Sunday as carrying more weight than the annual anniversary, so Sunday was always celebrated as Easter there. The conflict was resolved eventually by the Council of Nicaea in A.D. 325. The resolution of the proper day of celebration was quite complex. Nicaea held that Easter would be held on Sunday, the Sunday immediately following the fourteenth day of the Passover moon, that is, the moon that appears on or immediately after the vernal equinox (or March 21, in our modern calendars). Easter, therefore, must take place between March 22 and April 25, since, for the earliest date, the fourteenth day of the Passover moon would have to be the vernal equinox and for the latest date, the fifteenth day of the Passover moon would have to be on March 21, so that a full lunar month would have to pass before the fourteenth day of the moon after the vernal equinox could occur again. Because the fourteenth day could (and sometimes does) fall on a Sunday, Easter Day wouldn't be celebrated for another week—which is April 25.

This complicated decision was reaffirmed by the Council of Antioch in A.D. 341. However, changes in the calendar, especially the Gregorian reform in the sixteenth century and adjustments of the nineteen-year lunar cycle in the West, have caused a divergence between the date of Easter in the Latin West and the Orthodox East. Easter, only occasionally now, falls on the same date for these major wings of the Christian church.

From the beginning Easter has been observed with fasting, vigils, and the celebration of the Eucharist. The earliest observance was to keep the 14th of Nisan as a fast day. Early this vigil of fasting was instituted over Saturday night to Sunday (when Sunday was set as Easter). Baptism was sometimes performed during this night watch, which was ended with Holy Communion at dawn. Fasting was extended to Friday and later to Thursday. Gradually, the whole observance of HOLY WEEK was established, and, over a period of time, the forty days of LENT. After Easter arrived, it was celebrated with joy (no kneeling or fasting) for fifty days until Pentecost.

Easter is strongly bound up with the celebration of the Eucharist. According to the Lateran Council in Rome, A.D. 1215, those who were lax in church attendance were urged to commune on Easter, if at no other time, under pain of excommunication and refusal of Christian burial. Recent liturgical developments have strengthened the traditional, historical roots of Christian worship in the Western churches. Easter is now celebrated as the "Great Sunday" in the Roman Catholic Church and is more elaborately celebrated by all denominations of Protestants. Of course, Easter observance is opposed by certain world-denying sects, such as the Worldwide Church of God and other Sabbatarian groups. Controversies over the proper observance of Easter are quite traditional, as noted above. In part the growth of different observances and practices arose because of the conflicting accounts of the dates of Jesus' death and resurrection in the Gospels themselves. According to the Synoptic Gospels, Jesus rose on the 14th of Nisan, but according to John, it was the 15th of Nisan. Various scholars have held that either the Synoptics are correct (the majority) or that John is correct. Some have suggested that John was simply using powerful symbolism to show Jesus dying at the same time as the Passover lambs. One interesting harmonization holds that both traditions are correct. In John we have the reflection of the Sadducees' practice of Passover and in the Synoptics we have the Pharisees' practice, who celebrated the Passover early whenever it might fall on a Sabbath.

Easter is unusual, too, in that it is actually celebrated fifty-two times a year, every Sunday. Therefore, choosing one Sunday out of these fifty-two for a special celebration is a bit odd. Running against the whole concept of Christian holy days is the early Christian feeling that Paul expresses negatively concerning Jewish "new moons" and "fasts." We do not know how widespread the keeping of traditional Jewish practices and holy days was among the early Christians, but we do know that the Jewish Christians of Jerusalem continued to worship in the Temple until the Christians fled from the city during the Roman-Jewish war of A.D. 66–73. Certainly, Paul, despite his opposition to "new moons," kept the Jewish customs, for he was arrested at the Temple, where he had gone to fulfill a Jewish vow. (Contrast Gal. 3:1-5 with Acts 21:26ff. and 22:17.) Nonetheless, Paul stresses the observance of the first day of the week (I Cor. 16:2).

Justin Martyr mentions the celebration of the Resurrection annually. Tertullian's works reflect a controversy between Hebrew-Christians and Gentile-Christians about the nature of Easter observance. Tertullian implies that the Pascha was more like our Lent than our Easter, a time of sorrow for sin rather than joy in the Resurrection. It may be that the observance of the Father's day was actually like our GOOD FRIDAY, a recollection of the Lord's death, rather than of his victory over death. Then the following Sunday would have been celebrated as the day of resurrection, just as every Sunday was, but not necessarily in a special, annual way.

These controversies do nothing to diminish the sacredness and significance of Easter. Indeed, they demonstrate the overwhelming importance of the event that every Sunday—and every Easter—celebrates and commemorates. Christianity is the faith of those who participate in the resurrection faith of the apostles, martyrs, confessors, and simple believers of every land, in every time.

J.C.

**EASTERN ORTHODOX CHURCH.** See ORTHO-DOX CHURCHES.

**EBED-MELECH** ("servant of the king"). An Ethiopian eunuch who obtained King Zedekiah's permission to rescue Jeremiah from a miry cistern. The prophet was spared death by hunger when Ebed-melech, along with three assistants, lifted him out with ropes (Jer. 38:7-13). This deed was rewarded by Yahweh's promise that Ebed-melech would survive Jerusalem's imminent destruction (39:15-18).

J.K.K.

**EBENEZER** ("stone of help"). The scene near Aphek (possibly Majdel Yaba, northeast of Jaffa), where the Israelites were decisively defeated by the Philistines, who captured the ark (I Sam. 4:1-11; 5:1). Also the name that Samuel assigned a stone he erected near Mizpah to commemorate an Israelite triumph over the Philistines (7:10-12).

J.K.K.

**EBIONITES.** The name is derived from the Hebrew word for "poor." It refers to a sect of Jews, perhaps previously Essenes, who after the fall of Jerusalem in A.D. 70 turned to Jesus Christ as the greatest of the prophets but rejected him as the Son of God—a position resembling that of Muslims today. They can be considered as Christian only in the sense that they accepted Jesus as the Jewish Messiah. Epiphanius, our primary source of information about them, reveals that their theology included a denial of the virgin birth of Christ, a rejection of any implication of salvation in the religion of Jesus, an acceptance of Jesus as a prophet who came to lead Judaism back to its true purity, a continued observance of the Law including circumcision and the Sabbath, and a rejection of Temple worship and animal sacrifice. They are mentioned by Irenaeus in the second century, Origen in the third, and Epiphanius in the fourth. We have no certain information on them in the first century. What we do know is gleaned from these later authors. They are important because they testify to the various streams of heterodox Jewish Christian thought prevalent in the early Christian centuries.

J.R.M.

**EBLA.** A city known in antiquity, but only since 1964 has its true importance been revealed as a result of excavations carried out by the Italian Archaeological Mission of the University of Rome. The site of the excavations has been definitely identified with Tell Mardikh, a mound covering 138 acres about thirty-four miles southwest of Aleppo in Syria. The excavations have revealed in great detail the history, language, and culture of a powerful people who flourished in the third millennium B.C. and who influenced the history of that era in ways that had never been imagined prior to the discoveries that began in 1964.

*History.* The oldest known map in the world, a clay tablet found at the site of ancient NUZI in 1930, probably indicates Ebla at the far west of the world in the Mesopotamian perspective. It was a post on the trade route leading to UGARIT on the coast, and accordingly it was occasionally mentioned by Near Eastern historians as a city of some minor importance, one of what must have been many way stations in a land populated by a largely nomadic or semi-nomadic society.

This reasonable conjecture was completely shattered by the archaeological facts for which no tradition had prepared. Through archaeology Ebla has been revealed to have been not a nomadic caravan resting place but the chief city of a true empire, one that carried on trade on equal terms with the great Sargon of Akkad (2360-2310 B.C.) in Mesopotamia and which, as the occasion afforded, made war on Sargon's successors and subjected them to tribute. The kings of the Eblaite dynasty were Igriš-Halam, Ar-Ennum, Ebrum (probably equal to the biblical Eber of Gen. 10:21), Ibbi-Sipiš, Dubuhu-Ada, and Irkab-Damu. They were termed *mālik* (Hebrew *melek*, meaning "king"). Under Ebrum, Ebla seems to have achieved its greatest height, including the subjugation of Akkad. In his reign there were also relations with the Hittites to the north and the Palestinians to the south, and eastward as far as Elam. The capital city of Ebla at this time may have had a population of a quarter million or so.

The recent restitution of understanding about the significance of Ebla in the ancient Near East is almost, but not entirely, unprecedented in the historical reconstruction of antiquity. Almost, because (classical) Greece and Rome continue to be the "antiquity" of many Europeans and Americans, despite the fact that a two-century-old Egyptian and Mesopotamian archaeology should have separated them by several millennia from the age of Aeschylus and Horace. Ebla provides much opportunity for acquiring knowledge about a hardly known past and a cautionary example of what little we know about anything.

*Language.* This is one of the most controversial areas in Ebla research. On the one hand, what we have been able to say above about the history of Ebla derives first of all from the wealth of epigraphic material—about fifteen thousand clay tablets in cuneiform script—found in its ruins, most of them in a marvelous state of preservation. The tablets represent, for the most part, royal archives and commercial documents, which only indirectly bear on history, geography, politics, or culture. To the extent that they do have such a bearing, it is obviously in a quite neutral fashion. Most of the Ebla tablets are written in Sumerian—the *lingua franca* of the third millennium B.C., just as Akkadian would become the *lingua franca* of the second millennium, and Aramaic would be that of the first. The Sumerian syllabary (pending the invention of the alphabet a few centuries later) proved to be a serviceable, though imperfect, device for reproducing by sounds and ideograms the words and thoughts of other languages. The evidence shows that this syllabary was put to use to reproduce, rather clumsily, the native language of Ebla.

What precisely that language was continues to be the subject of some dispute. For some scholars it was a Proto-Hebrew, cognate with biblical Hebrew, down to some rather exact details. For others it was, indeed, a western Semitic language like Hebrew, but a different dialect entirely, simply another of the doubtless many languages that were used locally at that time in Syria/Canaan. The exact relation of the Eblaite to the Hebrew language, without doubt, has some connection with the historical relation of Ebla to the Bible, but at the present time the relation is more to be investigated than presumed. The ambiguity of the Sumerian ideograms continues to prevail in quite divergent conclusions and interpretations.

*Culture.* Have the Ebla discoveries cast any light on the Bible? Directly, probably not; but indirectly, probably so. (a) An Eblaite kingdom that flourished about 2300 B.C. can hardly have had any direct influence on Hebrew origins, which by even the earliest estimate of the "patriarchal age" could have occurred only centuries later. Names like the one we have noted above, Ebrum equals Eber, as well as many others verified or alleged to have been verified at Ebla (for example, Abraham, Israel, Ishmael, Michael, and others), are all common western Semitic, and no one would suggest that they imply a direct connection between Ebla and the Bible. Earlier thoughts that the five "cities of the plain" (Genesis 14) or the connection implied in Genesis 11:31 between Ur and Haran had been corroborated by the Ebla materials but now seem to have been abandoned as premature judgments.

(b) What Ebla has revealed is that there was in northern Syria prior to the "patriarchal age" a great center of civilization that could easily have served as one of the matrices of Hebrew origins, even as the Bible claims. The language of Ebla deserves, as it surely will get, the further examination that will determine its relation to biblical Hebrew and also, perhaps, the relation of the Eblaites to the biblical Hebrews. One of the common Hebrew and Eblaite cultural traits that seems to have been turned up is the prevalence of case law. Case law is one of the commonplaces of Semitic jurisprudence, first brought into conjunction with biblical law with the discovery in the past century of the law code of Hammurabi of Babylon (1728–1686 B.C.). The Ebla evidence advances the parallels by more than a half millennium.

The divine names inscribed in the Ebla tablets correspond strikingly with those that the Bible ascribes to its Near Eastern scene, though there are some significant differences. Thus Dagan, the god of grain and the fields, is the same at Ebla and in the Bible; the Eblaite Rasap (the god of disaster) is equal to the Hebrew Rešep; the sun-god(dess) Sipiš at Ebla is the Hebrew God Šemeš; the Eblaite Aštar, a masculine deity, is the Hebrew goddess Astarte; the

Babylonian Ishtar, patroness of fertility; and no one will have difficulty in recognizing in the Eblaite Kamiš the biblical Chemosh, the god of the Moabites.

Especially to be mentioned in this connection is the putative existence in the Eblaite pantheon of the god Ya. He was in any case certainly not the chief or even a chief deity in this pantheon (which numbered in its membership a minimum of five hundred gods). His very existence depends on the interpretation of Sumerian ideograms. If he did exist at Ebla, the fact could be significant in view of what happened with a later western Semitic people for whom the god Yahw(eh) became the primary and eventually the only God.

B.V.

*ECCE HOMO.* Latin words meaning "behold the man," derived from Luke 23:14, where Pilate turns Jesus over to the chief priests and rulers of the people. Traditionally, they have become the title for paintings depicting the sufferings of Jesus. In 1865, this phrase was used by John Seeley as the title for a book in which he offered a typically liberal portrayal of Jesus as a teacher of high moral values.

J.G.

**ECCLESIA.** *See* CHURCH.

**ECCLESIASTES.** An OT wisdom book whose title comes from the Greek Septuagint by way of Jerome's Latin Vulgate. The Greek translator chose the noun *ekklesiastes* to render the author's pen name, *Qoheleth,* a Hebrew participle denoting one who addresses an assembly. Since the time of Luther that name has often been translated "the Preacher," a misleading designation because the rambling, skeptical thoughts on the meaning of human existence here offered little resemble a sermon. No friend of Hebrew orthodoxy, this book won its way into the OT CANON, and as one of the five MEGILLOTH (festival scrolls) is read in the synagogue on the Feast of Tabernacles.

*Authorship and Date.* That Hebrew tradition that viewed Ecclesiastes as Solomon's handiwork is understandable from the book's superscription (1:1) where it is ascribed to "the Preacher, the son of David, king in Jerusalem." But whoever framed the superscription failed to perceive that when the author referred to himself as "king over Israel in Jerusalem" (1:12), he was engaging in a literary fiction intended to enhance the weight of his argument. That is similarly the case when he mentions "all who were over Jerusalem before me" (1:16), for Solomon was only the second Israelite monarch to rule from that city. Actually, fictitious royal authorship has no impact on content beyond chapter 2. Criticism leveled against the law court or Temple in 3:16, reference to unrelieved suffering of the oppressed in 4:1, and flaws of monarchy implied in 4:13 and 10:5 distill the sentiments of one who does not wield political authority. Moreover, the book's numerous Aramaisms (Aramaic being a late form of Hebrew anticipating that of the Mishnah), and general familiarity with Greek thought speak for an era that markedly postdates Solomon. Unfortunately, Ecclesiastes never mentions known historical events. The book could not be later than 200 B.C., since it influenced ben Sira (around 180 B.C.) and was found amid the manuscripts at Qumran. A third-century B.C. date therefore makes good sense.

Presumably the author was an older man of considerable experience (12:1) and perhaps also a person of means, for his renunciation of pleasure as the fruit of great wealth lacks the ring of a high-minded ascetic (2:1-11). While trained in conventional, pragmatic wisdom, this Hebrew existentialist advocated an unconventional, skeptical wisdom as he taught gatherings of students and disciples (12:9). His pursuit of wisdom, involving weighing, studying, and arranging the proverbs he gathered, was more than a private endeavor. Alexandria, Phoenicia, and Jerusalem have all been suggested as his home. The fiction of 1:12 with its mention of Jerusalem is not compelling, though Qoheleth's casual regard for religious observance (5:1-7) implies a Jerusalem residence in proximity to the Temple, whose existence he took for granted. Apart from the superscription (1:11), a composite epilogue (12:9-14), and a few interpolations programmed to salvage the traditional notion of retribution (for example, 3:17; 8:12-13; 11:9b), the entire book bears Qoheleth's own stamp as he sought to give his uncommon wisdom visibility.

*Literary Dimensions.* (a) Style and form. Qoheleth manifests a synthetic and cumulative style, which finds its inner unity in a uniformity of language. With the author's proclivity for repetition, a preferred vocabulary readily emerges including such favored expressions as "under the sun," "this also is vanity," "one fate," and "toil." The book's autobiographical form resembles the Egyptian genre of "royal testament" wherein the pharaohs or their viziers reflect about life for the benefit of young aspiring monarchs. Among the significant small units Qoheleth employs are the one-line sentence proverb (1:18), comparative saying (*A* is better than *B*, 4:13), and the negative exhortation (10:20). Some proverbs are cited for refutation purposes. Thus Qoheleth's approval of "a handful of quietness" (4:6) rebuts the traditional proverb, "the fool folds his hands, and eats his own flesh" (4:5). Moreover, the book contains many rhetorical questions ordinarily anticipating a negative answer (1:3; 2:22; 6:12). On occasion, large speech units derive from the fusion of various elements (1:12–2:26).

(b) Structure. Most contemporary scholarship denies that Qoheleth is merely a loose assemblage of independent aphoristic units lacking unified order or thought sequence. A basic structuring may underlie the polarities of Qoheleth's thinking (for example,

talk vs. silence, toil vs. joy). Helpful recent studies emphasizing patterns of verbal repetition in the text produce these observations: A prologue containing a poem on toil that is presumably Qoheleth's (1:2-11) and an epilogue that is not (12:9-14) frame the body of the book, which yields two large units (1:12–6:9; 6:10–11:6) and a concluding instruction about youth and old age (11:7–12:8). The phrase "(vanity and) a striving after wind" (1:17; 2:11, 17, 26; 4:6, 16; 6:9) serves as a structural divider terminating seven sections within the first unit. Ten sections within the second unit, concluding at 6:12; 7:14, 24, 29; 8:17; 9:6, 10, 12; 10:15; and 11:6, employ such phrases as "not find out," "who can find out," "no knowledge," "does not know." Clearly, the recognition of a structure based on the repetition of key phrases makes the author's driving concerns more accessible.

*Qoheleth's Message.* (a) Life's vanity. Ever pressing his famous phrase, "vanity of vanities" (1:2; 12:8), Qoheleth protests that life is absolutely empty (2:17, 22-23). Using the Hebrew noun *hebel* (normally rendered "vanity"), he underscores the tenuous aspect of mortal life. Human events pursue a wearisome and monotonous course (1:9). Knowledge (1:13-18), wealth (5:10-17), and pleasure (2:1-11) are illusory. History's ephemeral events are quickly forgotten (1:10-11). Justice is mocked in the real world where the wicked outlive the good (7:15). And if wisdom is better than folly (2:13), death, which ultimately overtakes humans and beasts (3:19), cancels any gain that wisdom might secure.

(b) God's inscrutability. Not at all agnostic, Qoheleth observes that God "has made everything beautiful in its time; also he has put eternity into man's mind, yet so that he cannot find out what God has done from the beginning to the end" (3:11). Though he recognizes God's transcendence and sovereignty, he complains that in God's action, God leaves insufficient traces for the divine presence to be recognized (11:5). Qoheleth cannot fathom the divine purpose, nor does he directly address God through prayer or lament. Indeed, any relation with this unknowable, all-powerful Deity had best be informed by prudence.

(c) Life's compensations. Qoheleth is not a nihilist given to recommending suicide. Rather, he soberly challenges humanity to embrace the God-given present as it is. He believes that individuals can derive satisfaction from daily work (3:22); experience restrained pleasure in social relationships (2:24; 3:12-13; 5:18; 9:7); and find joy in discreet worship (5:1-2), warm friendships (4:9-12), and marriage (9:9).

(d) Conclusion. Qoheleth's fondness for empiricism convinced him that the data of revealed religion should not be blindly affirmed. The glib solutions of orthodoxy that hovered about the doctrine of retribution irritated him. He chose to confront life's uncertainties with full honesty. Though the promise of his practical counsel bears a low profile, this existentialist insists that life should be lived fully (*Compare* EXISTENTIALISM).

J.K.K.

**ECCLESIASTICUS.** While the designation Ecclesiasticus first appeared in third-century A.D. Latin translations, as is evident from its alternative title, "The Wisdom of Jesus the Son of Sirach," here is a noteworthy example of Jewish WISDOM literature. The only book in the APOCRYPHA whose author is known by name (50:27), it contains a rich poetic collection of mainly practical precepts addressing quite diverse human activity.

*The Author.* Presumably residing in Jerusalem, Jesus ben ("son of") Sira published his distilled wisdom teaching between 190 and 180 B.C. This date assumes that the recently deceased high priest Simon, eulogized in 50:1-21, is Simon II mentioned in Josephus' *Antiquities,* who held office about 219-196. Several of ben Sira's professional activities are hinted in the text. Putting his leisure to good use (38:24), he diligently studied "the law of the Most High," yet examined non-Israelite wisdom traditions as well (39:1). A seasoned sage who traveled abroad and counseled rulers (39:4), he shared his empirical thinking with well-to-do young men who attended his academy (51:23). The prologue states that ben Sira's grandson translated the Hebrew text into Greek after he joined the Jewish Diaspora in Egypt in 132 B.C., during "the thirty-eighth year of the reign of Euergetes" (Ptolemy VII).

*Literary Aspects.* The book divides into two main sections (chaps. 1–23; 24–50), each beginning with a long poem celebrating wisdom (1:1-20; 24:1-31). An appendix yields a thanksgiving psalm for deliverance (51:1-12) and, in imitation of Proverbs 31:10-31, a concluding alphabetic acrostic (51:13-30) telling how ben Sira acquired and dispensed wisdom. He primarily drew his literary inspiration from Proverbs and Psalms. His book is full of short two-line proverbs normally gathered into larger topical units. Thus 2:1-18 contains exhortations to endure affliction patiently; 3:1-16 admonitions to obey parents; and 6:1-17 advice on cultivating friendships. Ben Sira likewise composed devotional lyrics taking the form of hymns (42:15–43:33), communal prayer for national deliverance (36:1-17), and thanksgiving (51:1-12). His well-known hymn praising God for Israel's past history and honoring the piety of its greatest heroes (44:1–50:24) assumes epic proportions.

*Message.* Ben Sira offers social advice and theological insight. The former covers such topics as family life, self-control, business partnerships, banquet behavior, giving alms, and the usefulness of physicians. Yet as a theologian, he deftly handles such matters as the coexistence of good and evil in the divine ordering of Creation (33:7-15); the reality of divine providence (16:24–17:24); the coalescence of wisdom and law, whereby personified, semi-divine

wisdom makes her dwelling in Israel (chap. 24); and the significance of Israel's Deity as a God of history who positively has much influence on its concrete existence (44:1–50:24, replete with phrases echoing the biblical narrative).

J.K.K.

**ECCLESIOLOGY.** That section of theology that deals systematically with the biblical and traditional teachings concerning the CHURCH. Ecclesiology developed from Paul's view of the BODY OF CHRIST to the medieval definition of the church as an institution to the Protestant view of an invisible fellowship with Christ the Head.

J.C.

**ECKHART, MEISTER JOHANNES** (1260-1327). German mystic, preacher, and theologian. Born in Hochheim, he joined the Dominicans and studied at Cologne and Paris, later teaching at both. Famed for preaching, he held numerous offices including Provincial of Saxony, vicar-general of Bohemia and Strasbourg, and regent-master at Cologne. His extensive, controversial writings—theses, sermons, commentaries, and treatises—aroused opposition. Accusations of heresy embittered his final years. Tried at Cologne for teaching heresy, he appealed but died before receiving a decision. Early in 1327 he publicly professed his faith at Cologne, revoking anything said or written not conforming to orthodoxy. Eckhart admitted rashness, not unorthodoxy, but Pope John XXII in 1329 condemned twenty-eight of his statements as heretical.

Eckhart believed in Neoplatonic MYSTICISM: God is beyond being and non-being, yet present in the world and the soul. Seeing God's spark within as our only reality, Eckhart strove for identification with God and a loss of self-identity. Preparation was accomplished by renouncing one's self and imitating Christ's good works and spontaneous love. Church rituals were secondary. Ecstatic, divine union came by God's grace, lifting one beyond consciousness of "I." Eckhart heavily influenced John Tauler, Henry Suso, and Thomas a Kempis.

C.M.

**ECSTASY.** *See* RELIGIOUS EXPERIENCE.

**ECUMENICAL COUNCILS.** Assemblies of bishops representing the entire church, usually convened in order to deal with pressing theological or practical issues. The Eastern churches, as well as several non-Roman Western churches, accept only the first seven such councils. These early councils were normally called by the emperor. At later times, particularly during the height of CONCILIARISM, there have been debates over who has the right to convene an ecumenical council. According to Roman Catholic canon law, that right belongs to the pope, and therefore all the more recent councils have been called by popes. The first seven ecumenical councils are as follows: (1) NICAEA (A.D. 325) rejected ARIANISM and issued a creed from which the modern NICENE CREED has evolved.

(2) CONSTANTINOPLE (381) confirmed the decisions of Nicaea and proclaimed the divinity of the Holy Spirit. Together, these two councils defined the doctrine of the TRINITY.

(3) EPHESUS (431) rejected the CHRISTOLOGY of the NESTORIANS, and declared that MARY is the "bearer of God."

(4) CHALCEDON (451) issued a *Definition of Faith,* which became the standard for christological orthodoxy. This spoke of "two natures" in the "one person" of Christ. Those who rejected the "two natures" were eventually dubbed Monophysites.

(5) II Constantinople (553) condemned the so-called "Three Chapters," which were the works of three theologians that supposedly supported Nestorianism.

(6) III Constantinople (680) condemned monothelitism—that is, the doctrine that there is only "one will" in Christ.

(7) II Nicaea (787) defined the veneration due images, rejecting the views of the iconoclasts.

The later councils, accepted only by the Roman Catholic Church, are: (8) IV Constantinople (869), which ended the schism of PHOTIUS; (9) LATERAN I (1123) confirmed the Concordat of Worms, thus ending the conflicts between papacy and empire over investitures; (10) Lateran II (1139); (11) Lateran III (1179); (12) Lateran IV (1215), which promulgated doctrine of transubstantiation and ordered yearly confession for all believers; (13) Lyons I (1245); (14) Lyons II (1274); (15) Vienne (1311–12); (16) CONSTANCE (1414–18), put an end to the GREAT SCHISM; (17) Basel and Ferrara-Florence (1431, 1438); (18) LATERAN V (1512–19); (19) TRENT (1545–63) responded to the Protestant Reformation both by rejecting its doctrines and by issuing decrees for the reformation of Roman Catholicism; (20) VATICAN I (1869–70) promulgated the infallibility of the POPE; (21) VATICAN II (1962–65), which sought to bridge the gap between the church and the modern world.                                         J.G.

**ECUMENICAL MOVEMENT.** The movement toward the goal of greater visible unity and ecumenical cooperation among all Christian churches. The ecumenical movement is almost coextensive with the twentieth century, growing out of the great missionary outreach of the various churches in the nineteenth century. More recently, the movement has sought to foster understanding and cooperation between the Christian churches and the other great religions of the world.

The contemporary ecumenical movement began at the 1910 Edinburgh World Missionary Conference. Even the turmoil of World Wars I and II did not shatter the desire of ecumenical leaders to transcend

*Symbol of the ship with the Greek word for ecumenical (oikoumene), meaning "the whole inhabited world." The ecumenical church is the whole church throughout the world.*

national divisions. Indeed, the WORLD COUNCIL OF CHURCHES was founded in Amsterdam shortly after the end of World War II, in 1947. The need for a worldwide missionary concern was stressed.

Other vital ecumenical growth factors included the interdenominational dimension of biblical and theological scholarship and the widespread Christian youth movements. The close cooperation of Christians of all communions in the struggle against Nazi brutality and to overcome the suffering of war victims and refugees also promoted the desire for more church unity.

The complex problems of the modern world made witnessing in home countries and on mission fields more difficult. A desire to inwardly renew all the churches and to learn from the "younger churches" of the mission fields, as well as a growing insight into the many beliefs and activities that already united the various churches, fueled the drive of the ecumenical spirit. The ecumenical movement still progresses, moving toward more unity with the Lord on the part of individual churches, which will one day result in more visible unity of the churches in the world. (*Compare* CONSULTATION ON CHURCH UNION.)
                                         J.C.

**EDDY, MARY BAKER.** *See* CHURCH OF CHRIST, SCIENTIST.

**EDEN, GARDEN OF.** The word Eden seems to have been derived from the Sumerian/Akkadian word *edin(u)* meaning "prairie, plain." As it figures in Israelite mythology, it is the name of no precise geographical determination (vaguely "in the east," Gen. 2:8), a land of a time before time with no connection with the real world of history.

The garden of Eden (Gen. 2:8 actually speaks of a garden *in* Eden), also called the garden of God (Ezek. 31:9), was the Israelite equivalent of the Greek Mount Olympus or the Canaanite "sources of the rivers and the two oceans," that is, the abode of God. Here were lush foliage and great trees, abundant water, and all the accompaniments of divinity: fiery and precious stones and metals, the mythical cherub, a locale in which primordial man could live idylically without pain or trouble (compare Ezek. 28:12-14).

It is easy to see how elements of this mythology have been adapted to the Yahwist's story of the FALL in Genesis 2:46–3:24. Neither Genesis nor the other biblical sources add up to a single myth, but all testify to the components of one. In Genesis the myth provides the framework for an etiological story of origins, retaining, among other themes, the notion of rejection from a previous ideal state. However, the details (for example, the functions of the cherub, the trees, many other particulars) vary so much in the sources, it may be there was no one myth on which they all depended, but rather they may have made use of what they would of a common fund of unrelated motifs.

B.V.

**EDICT OF MILAN.** The name usually given to the joint decision by CONSTANTINE and Licinius to put an end to persecution—although in truth it was not an edict, nor was it issued from Milan. The text announcing the emperors' decision is quoted, with significant variations, by Eusebius of Caesarea and Lactantius.

J.G.

**EDICT OF NANTES.** A proclamation issued by French King Henry IV, April 1598, guaranteeing freedom of conscience, places of worship, and full civil rights to French Protestants (HUGUENOTS). King Henry (Henry of Navarre) had been a Huguenot but turned Roman Catholic to clinch his kingship. The edict was revoked in 1685.

C.M.

**EDIFICATION.** The word is used figuratively to translate a Greek term whose literal meaning is "building." The derived meaning is, therefore, "to be built up spiritually or strengthened in faith." It is the privilege as well as obligation of mature Christians to "build one another up" (I Thess. 5:11), and this is done not through acquiring knowledge alone but through love (I Cor. 8:1). The early church used the full assemblies of its members especially for this purpose, during which they were to be especially careful to exercise their gifts in a way that would edify everyone because, according to I Corinthians, "he who speaks in a tongues edifies himself, but he who prophesies edifies the church" (14:4). They should "strive to excel in building up the church" (14:12). The rule, Paul asserted, was "let all things be done for edification" (14:26). When one edifies a neighbor one is following the example of Christ (Rom. 15:2-3). Paul insists that he received authority from Christ for the purpose of edifying, not tearing down, the Corinthians (II Cor. 10:8; 13:10). The spiritual gifts were, therefore, entrusted to all church leaders for the purpose of building up the Body of Christ (Eph. 4:12).

J.R.M.

**EDITOR.** *See* DOCUMENTARY HYPOTHESIS.

**EDOM/EDOMITES.** With this land and this people the Israelites maintained a love-hate relationship throughout the entirety of their historical existence. The relationship was fostered by a tradition that was dependent both on ethnological and historical fact and on mythical speculation.

Some of the western Semitic tribes who eventually made up the people of Israel were Edomite in origin. According to Deuteronomy 2:12-22 the Edomites were dispossessing the aborigines ("Horites" in this context) of the land of Seir about the same time the Israelites were invading the land further to the north of Palestine and dispossessing the Canaanites/Amorites. Furthermore, such elements of the Israelites (Judahites, in this case) as the Kenizzites, for example, or Calebites are clearly identified time and again as of Edomite ancestry (compare Gen. 36:11-15).

These data simply indicate that the Israelites retained the memory of an ethnic kinship with their Arab brothers to the south, even as they acknowledged kinship with various other Arab peoples. In the case of Edom, the kinship was memorialized in the legend of Jacob and Esau, twin brothers born of the patriarch Isaac, according to which Esau (continually in the story associated with Seir—by popular etymology, "hairy"—or Edom—by popular etymology, "red [land]") was presented as the foil to his more cultivated brother Jacob (Israel) who outmatched and outthought him at every juncture. Also, in Numbers 20:14-21, Israel is represented as having requested free passage through Edom in the name of brotherhood at the time of the conquest and, having been rebuffed, as having bypassed their territory. Amos 1:11-12 likewise obviously regards the Edomites as natural brothers of the Israelites.

The very origin of one of the most formative traditions of Israel, namely that of Sinai, may well have been Edomite. The location of Sinai/Horeb is notoriously impossible to pinpoint in any scientific way. According to Judges 5:4-5 (see also Deut. 33:2), in the most logical reading of the text, Mount Sinai is identical with Mount Seir-Edom. The biblical indications are ambiguous as to whether Mount Seir should be located on the east or the west of the Arabah gorge. The Edomites inhabited territory on both sides, in the Negeb of Palestine and south of the Dead Sea.

Edom was celebrated in Israelite tradition as one of the primary sources of "wisdom" (compare Jer. 49:7; Obad. 8). This tradition becomes very apparent, especially in the book of Job.

The Edomites organized a centralized monarchy long before the Israelites (compare Gen. 36:31-39). Under David they were subjected to Israel (II Sam. 8:13-14), and the Edomite port of EZION-GEBER provided Solomon with one of the sources of his fabulous wealth (I Kings 9:26). The mines of the

Arabah and control of crucial trade routes rendered Edom an imperialist prize. After the division of the kingdoms of Israel and Judah, Edom remained for a time subject to Judah, but it regained its independence definitively at least by the time of AHAZ (compare II Kings 16:6).

During the heyday of Assyrian domination the Edomites were faithful vassals of the great kings of the East: the annals of Adad-nirari III, Tiglath-pileser III, Sargon, Sennacherib, Esarhaddon, and Ashurbanipal provide us with the names of contemporary Edomite kings and also tell us the little we know about Edomite religion (the chief god was evidently named Qosh). Edom is not mentioned in the annals of the short-lived Chaldean empire, but there is no doubt it was included in the universal conquest of Nebuchadnezzar (compare Jer. 27:2-7). In fact, the Edomites seem to have joined with the Chaldeans in despoiling Judah (compare Ezek. 36:5; Ps. 137:7)—a fact which explains the bitterness of some of the anti-Edomite material in the OT.

Under John Hyrcanus (134–104 B.C.), founder of the Hasmonean dynasty, an Arabianized, Persianized, and Hellenized Edom (Idumea) was conquered by the Jews and forcibly converted to Judaism. Providence repaid them a century later by producing the Idumean tyrant Herod the Great, king of the Jews.

B.V.

**EDWARD VI.** King of England, 1547–53. The son of HENRY VIII by Jane Seymour, Edward VI promoted Protestantism and introduced the BOOK OF COMMON PRAYER. Tutored by Richard Cox, John Cheke, and Roger Ascham, Edward became king at the age of ten and even then leaned toward Protestantism. Henry had named a council to guide Edward, half favoring the old religion, half the new. However, Edward's uncle, Edward Seymour (Duke of Somerset, Earl of Hertford) was named Protector, and with Thomas Cranmer, Archbishop of Canterbury, dominated the council. The council repealed Henry's Six Articles: legalized both elements in the Communion, permitted clergy to marry, dissolved endowed Masses for the dead, reformed rules for fasting, promoted English in services, and affirmed justification by faith. During Edward's reign foreign reformers came to Cambridge and Oxford—Martin Bucer, Peter Martyr, Bernard Ochino. Edward's Prayer Book, 1549, the first Book of Common Prayer, changed little and was ambiguous on Holy Communion. The Second Prayer Book, 1552, was more Protestant and more popular.

Seymour's failure to secure the betrothal of Edward and Mary, later Queen of Scots, occasioned a short war, which saw the Scots suffering defeat at Pinkie in 1547. Seymour's agrarian policy backfired, and John Dudley (Earl of Warwick, Duke of Northumberland) displaced Seymour as Protector. Seymour was executed in 1552. Dudley then persuaded Edward to deprive Mary and Elizabeth, his half sisters, of succession rights, and to name Lady Jane Grey (Dudley's son's wife) successor. On Edward's death a show of force by Mary brought her the throne and death to Dudley and Lady Jane.

C.M.

**EDWARDS, JONATHAN** (1703–58). America's first theologian was born on October 5 in East Windsor, Connecticut, the fifth child and only son among ten daughters of Esther Stoddard and Timothy Edwards, a Harvard graduate and minister. Edwards entered Yale in 1716 and after his graduation in 1720, spent two years studying theology. Licensed to preach in 1722, he pastored a Presbyterian church in New York for two years before returning to Yale in May 1724 as a tutor for two years.

In 1727 he was ordained as a colleague to his grandfather SOLOMON STODDARD in Northampton, Massachusetts. When Stoddard died in 1729, Edwards inherited the parish. In July 1727 he married Sarah Pierpont of New Haven. During Stoddard's sixty-year ministry, the church experienced five revivals, and another came in 1734–35 as Edwards preached a series of sermons on justification by faith. He fanned the fire in 1737 with publication of *A Faithful Narrative of the Surprising Work of God,* and it blazed into the GREAT AWAKENING with the arrival of GEORGE WHITEFIELD in 1740. In 1741 Edwards followed up with a Yale commencement address "The Distinguishing Marks of a Work of the Spirit of God" and in 1742 with "Some Thoughts Concerning the Present Revival of Religion in New England." Edwards' monumental *Treatise on Religious Affections* was published in 1746. This defense of revivalism and classic in the psychology of religion is foundational to NEW ENGLAND THEOLOGY.

Edwards was dismissed from Northampton in 1750 in a controversy over the standards for admission

Courtesy of the Yale University Art Gallery. Bequest of Eugene Phelps Edwards

*Jonathan Edwards (1703-58)*

to Holy Communion. On August 8, 1751, he began a very productive ministry in Stockbridge, an Indian mission. The body of his theology was outlined in *Freedom of Will* (1754); *Original Sin Defended,* his 1758 reply to John Taylor; *The Nature of True Virtue* (1765); and *History of the Work of Redemption* (1737). He also edited David Brainerd's diary.

In 1757 Edwards was named president of Princeton. He died March 22, 1758, from an unsuccessful smallpox vaccination. Although he is most widely known for the frequently anthologized sermon "Sinners in the Hands of an Angry God" and his journal's scientific observations of spiders, he is the first original American theologian.

N.H.

**EGLON.** (1) A Moabite king who asserted his supremacy over western Jordan territory near Jericho for eighteen years. He was treacherously murdered in the outhouse by Ehud of Benjamin (Judg. 3:12-30). (2) A city situated southwest of Lachish that joined an Amorite coalition against Gibeon (Josh. 10:3-5) before succumbing to Joshua's troops (10:34-35). It is provisionally equated with Tell el-Hesi, which attests a late thirteenth-century B.C. destruction.

J.K.K.

**EGO.** *See* FREUD, SIGMUND.

**EGYPT.** An ancient home of civilization lying along the Nile River and occupying the northeastern corner of Africa plus the Sinai Peninsula, the extreme western edge of Asia. Egypt, from remotest times, has been bounded on the north by the Mediterranean, on the northeast by present-day Israel (ancient Canaan), on the east by the Red Sea and the Gulf of Aqaba, on the south by the Sudan, and on the west by Libya. Of Egypt's land area of 386,100 square miles, only 3.6 percent is usually inhabited. All the rest is desert. "Egypt is," as Herodotus remarked, "the gift of the Nile." Without the annual flooding of the NILE, bringing rich top soils from the interior of Africa, there would be no agriculture in the Nile Valley, and agriculture is the foundation of civilization.

An overview is given of Egypt's history in those periods in which its position and power exerted strong influence on Canaan, the Hebrew people, and the Hebrew states of Israel and Judah. Then, its own history and religion is examined. Egypt in ancient times always profoundly affected life in the Canaanite area, including Lebanon, since only the Wadi El Arish (or the river of Egypt) separated Egypt from its northeastern neighbors. Egypt also sailed its navy and trading ships to the Canaanite ports of Biblos (or Gebal) and Ras Shamrah (Ugarit). Egypt often invaded the Canaanite area in an attempt to maintain a forward base against Syria, Assyria, Babylonia, or whatever enemy threatened from the north. For example, Pharaoh Thutmose III recorded seventeen

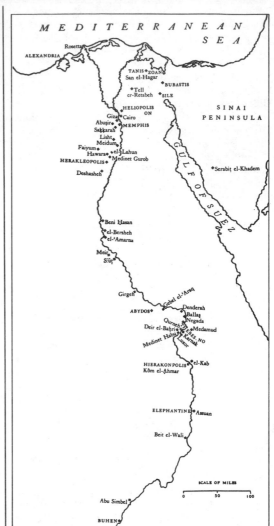

Adapted from James B. Pritchard, *The Ancient Near East in Pictures Relating to the Old Testament* (second edition with supplement). Copyright 1954, © 1969 by Princeton University Press. Map (p. 243) reprinted with permission of Princeton University Press.

*Egypt*

separate campaigns in Canaan and Syria, carrying off huge quantities of booty.

For all its wealth and military power, Egypt exerted little cultural influence on the lands of the Bible. Even with the period of 430 years said to be spent in Egypt by the Hebrew tribes, only a few Hebrews had Egyptian names. Moses was one and Aaron's grandson, Phineas, was another. Dress and architecture in Israel were modeled more on Mesopotamia and Asia Minor than on the powerful land to the southwest.

One development in religion among the Egyptians may have influenced the Hebrews, although the evidence is slim. This was the single-handed move toward monotheism of Pharaoh Ikhnaton (1370–1353

B.C.), who is sometimes called the first individual in history. A fanatically devoted worshiper of Aton, the sun-god Re-Horus, he worshiped at Heliopolis ("the house of the sun"). Ikhnaton (whose wife was Nefertiti) stopped the worship of AMON and the other old gods, infuriating the priesthood. He also built a new capital at Akhetaton (Tell el-Amarna) and abandoned THEBES, the traditional seat of power. All this reforming work caused Ikhnaton to neglect the political and military needs of his empire, and Egypt's Syrian holdings fell to the Hittites.

Throughout Hebrew history, the Israelites looked to Egypt as a source of food, and sometimes, generally mistakenly, for protection from Syria or the great Assyrian and Babylonian empires. Egypt saw Canaan only as a source of spoils and a buffer against Mesopotamia. But the smaller cities, nations, and especially the wandering tribes of the whole Middle East, looked to Egypt as a place of protection against the frequent droughts that brought famine to people and beasts.

On this basis, the Hebrews first came in contact with Egypt when Abraham journeyed there (Gen. 41:41-45). Later, Jacob's sons went into Egypt looking for food and found, to their terrified surprise, that the brother they sought to kill and sold into slavery, JOSEPH, was there before them. Joseph, now prime minister of Egypt with a special charge to provide supplies against famine, forgave his brothers and welcomed their clans into the sanctuary of the Nile Delta. Archaeology confirms that the construction work on the great store cities went on for the 430 years that the Bible says the Hebrews remained in Egypt. The date of around 1700 B.C. has been suggested by some scholars as Joseph's entry into Egypt, and the sojourn of the Hebrews placed during the fifteenth to seventeenth dynasties. This would make the pharaoh who trusted Joseph a HYKSOS, that is, a foreigner, probably a Semite like the Hebrews. These warlike horsemen conquered Egypt, during a weak period, almost without a battle and ruled about 1720–1550 B.C. They would feel sympathy for fellow Semites, so it is believable that Hyksos would permit the Hebrews to settle near their capital at Tanis (called Zoan in Ps. 78) in the delta. However, when the Hyksos were overthrown by the resurgent Egyptians, conditions changed drastically for the now large Hebrew community. The pharaohs that "knew not Joseph" (Acts 7:18 KJV) made life hard for the Hebrews, and one became the pharaoh of the oppression, forcing them into servitude to build the great store cities of Pithom and Rameses (or Tanis), mentioned in Exodus 1:11. According to most chronologies, the pharaoh of the Exodus was Ramses II (about 1290–1224 B.C.). The famous struggle between Moses, who was raised as an Egyptian and bore an Egyptian name, took place, with the Exodus occurring around 1290 B.C.

Later, Israel under Solomon enjoyed good relations with Egypt, as Solomon married one of Pharaoh's daughters. After the breakup of the kingdom, both northern Israel and southern Judah called upon Egypt for help from time to time. Egypt rarely was helpful, and several prophets, including Isaiah (Isa. 30, 31, 36), Jeremiah (Jer. 42, 43), and Hosea (Hos. 7:11), warned that Egypt was a broken reed that would pierce the hand that leaned on it.

After Jerusalem's fall in 586 B.C., many survivors fled to Egypt, even forcing Jeremiah to go with them (Jer. 42; 43:6). These Jews settled at Elephantine, where they even built a temple. But most Jews settled in ALEXANDRIA, where, by the time of the great Jewish philosopher, Philo (about 20 B.C.–A.D. 50), there may have been one million Jews. In this fruitful blending of Hebrew and Hellenistic cultural elements, Jewish scholars made the Septuagint translation of the Hebrew scriptures into Greek. In the NT period, the Gospel of Matthew tells us that Joseph and Mary fled into Egypt with the infant Jesus (Matt. 2:13-19). In Acts 2:10, we are told that Egyptians were present at Pentecost in Jerusalem, and Paul was taken for an Egyptian revolutionary in Acts 21:38. Of course, the sojourn in Egypt and the Exodus and wilderness wanderings are alluded to several times in the NT (Acts 7, and throughout the book of Hebrews). Early Christianity took deep root in Egypt, and many great church fathers were Egyptian, including Origen and Athanasius. The foundations of Christianity were so deep in Egypt that the church (called the Coptic church) survived the Muslim conquest of the seventh century A.D., and even today, some 25 percent of the Egyptian population is Christian.

*History.* Egypt is really two lands. Upper Egypt is almost all desert, with only a few miles of river valley in width and hundreds of miles in length. Lower Egypt, less hot and dry, has more flood plain and widens out into the rich delta. The traditional founder of the First Dynasty, Mena, is believed to have united Upper and Lower Egypt into one nation and to have founded Memphis as the capital. Lower Egypt comprised the delta; Upper Egypt the Nile Valley. The delta had twelve branches of the Nile in ancient times, and the land between them was divided into districts called nomes, centered on a city. These now lost cities (many under Nile water) included Heliopolis, Sais, Buto, Pelusium, Tanis, Mendes, Sebennytos, and Bubastis. The pharaohs after Mena remained "the lords of the two lands," wearing a double crown; white for Upper Egypt and red for Lower Egypt.

Egypt's history is incredibly long, dating from 4500 B.C. and stretching through thirty-one dynasties down to the coming of Alexander the Great in 332 B.C. A brief outline of ancient Egypt's dynasties begins with the earliest civilization some 4,500 years before Christ, in the New Stone Age when the first farming villages were founded. This was followed by a time of kings in Upper and Lower Egypt, some monuments of which still survive at Hierakonpolis.

The First Dynasty began with Mena and included eight or nine kings between 3100 and 2890 B.C. In this period, Upper and Lower Egypt were united and stone buildings constructed. Hieroglyphic writing began.

The Second Dynasty included ten kings, and saw rivalry between the priests of Horus and Set, from 2890 to 2686 B.C.

The Third Dynasty consisted of five kings between 2686 and 2613 B.C.

The "old kingdom" began with the Fourth Dynasty and ran through the Sixth Dynasty. Many pyramids were built during this period, including Zoser's Step Pyramid and those at Saqqarah.

The Fourth Dynasty (2613–2494 B.C.) was the age of the great pyramid builders and included eight kings, Cheops and Chephren (both of whom left pyramids), Sueferu, Dedefre, Baufre, Mycerinus, Shepseskof, and Dedefptah. Egypt spread out to Byblos and to Nubia, and the Giza Pyramids (near Cairo) were constructed.

Courtesy of Hirmer Verlag, Munich

*The Great Sphinx (about 2500 B.C.), Gizeh*

Courtesy of the Arab Information Center, New York

*The Sphinx and the pyramid of Khaf-Re at Gizeh, near Cairo*

Courtesy of Trans World Airlines

*Aerial view of the pyramids of Khufu, Khaf-Re, and Men-kau-Re at Gizeh*

Courtesy of Hirmer Verlag, Munich

*The pyramids of Mycerinus (about 2470 B.C.), Chefren (about 2500 B.C.), and Cheops (about 2530 B.C.), Gizeh*

The Fifth Dynasty (2494–2345 B.C.) consisted of nine kings, who battled the Libyans, sent expeditions to Punt and Nubia, and sponsored the rise of the worship of the sun god, Re, at Heliopolis.

The Sixth Dynasty (2345–2181 B.C.) included seven kings and a queen, Nitocris. The kings or pharaohs are not all known, but some were Teti, Userkare, Pep I, Meryre, Mereure, and Pepi II Neferkare. Pepi II was pharaoh for over ninety years, the longest reign of any king or state leader in history.

The Seventh, Eighth, Ninth, and Tenth dynasties form an intermediate period, 2181–2040 B.C., when there were weak kings. Upper Egypt went its own way, and Libyans and Asians took over the delta.

The "middle kingdom" represents the return of strong pharaohs and runs from the Eleventh to the Fourteenth dynasties (2133–1603 B.C.)

The Eleventh Dynasty had nine pharaohs. Mentuhotep II reunified Upper and Lower Egypt in 2040 B.C., and pushed the Asians out of the delta. He began to reconquer Nubia (2133–1991 B.C.)

The Twelfth Dynasty was of eight kings (1991–1786 B.C.) and included Queen Sobekneferu. This period represents the high point of ancient Egyptian art and craftsmanship. The capital was moved from Thebes to Al Fayyum. Nubia was conquered, and much trade was carried on with Canaan and Syria.

The "middle kingdom" ended with the Thirteenth and Fourteenth dynasties (1786–1603 B.C.), which had many kings. They were followed by a second intermediate period, made up of the Fifteenth to the Seventeenth dynasties (1720–1567 B.C.). During this period the Hyksos conquered Lower Egypt, and the Hebrews may have entered Egypt. Joseph's date is sometimes given as 1700 B.C.

The Fifteenth and Sixteenth dynasties (1720–1570 B.C.) consisted of some fourteen Hyksos pharaohs, who ruled from Avaris. The Seventeenth Dynasty (1645–1567 B.C.) had seventeen kings, including Seqeneure and Kamose. It was Kamose who drove out the Hyksos and reestablished Egyptian pharaohs.

"The new empire" included the Eighteenth to the Twentieth dynasties (1567–1085 B.C.). The Eighteenth Dynasty (1567–1320 B.C.) saw the final defeat of the Hyksos and the recovery of Nubia: the worship of Amon at Karnak. There were fourteen pharaohs, including Ahmose, Amenhotep I, II, and III; Thutmose I and II; Queen Hatshepsut; Thutmose III and IV; Ikhnaton (or Amenhotep IV, who became a monotheist, worshiping Aton, the sun-god); Smenkhkare; Tutankhamen (the famous King Tut); Ay; and Horemheb. During this period Canaan and Syria were conquered, the Tel el-Amarna correspondence was written, and Egypt became very wealthy. Tutankhamen restored the worship of Amon and dethroned Aton, who had been made the only god by Ikhnaton.

Courtesy of Hirmer Verlag, Munich

*Funerary temple of Hatshepsut, Deir-el-Bahari, Eighteenth Dynasty, about 1480* B.C.

Courtesy of Hirmer Verlag, Munich

*Court and pylon of Ramses II (about 1260 B.C.) and the colonnade and court of Amenhotep III (about 1390 B.C.). Temple of Amun-Mut-Khonsu, Luxor*

Courtesy of the Metropolitan Museum of Art, Rogerts Fund, 1915

*An Egyptian wall painting, from the tomb of Nakht at Thebes (fifteenth century B.C.). Upper section shows harvest scenes; middle section shows man chopping down tree and a laborer breaking soil; lower section shows a laborer plowing and a person watching laborers from a booth.*

The Nineteenth Dynasty included eight pharaohs (1320–1200 B.C.), among them Ramses I, Seti I, Ramses II, Merneptah, and Queen Tawosret. During this period Ramses II (1304–1237 B.C.) defeated the Hittites at Kadesh Barnea, thus ending their power in Canaan and their threat to Egypt.

The Twentieth Dynasty (1200–1085 B.C.) saw ten kings, Setnakht and Ramses III to XI. While the first two pharaohs stabilized Egypt, the Libyans and "sea peoples" (possibly from Crete) invaded it. Egypt declined, splitting into Upper and Lower Egypt.

The Twenty-first Dynasty (1085–945 B.C.) had seven kings, who ruled from Tanis.

The Twenty-second and Twenty-third dynasties (945–730 B.C.) were plagued with confusions in which rival kings, many with Libyan names, disputed rulership. There were capitals at Tanis, Bubastis, and (after 820 B.C.) at Thebes.

The Twenty-fourth Dynasty (730–715 B.C.) had its capital at Sais in the delta and consisted of two kings, Tefnakhte and Bocchoris.

The Twenty-fifth Dynasty (to 656 B.C.) was made up on kings from Cush and included five kings. Egypt prospered under them, but Egypt's operations in Canaan caused Assyria to attack and conquer Egypt. Necho was made pharaoh.

The Twenty-sixth Dynasty (664–525 B.C.) included seven kings, who drove out the Assyrians, with the help of Greek mercenaries. Necho invaded Canaan but was defeated by Babylonia.

The Persian Empire controlled Egypt during the final five dynasties, the Twenty-seventh through the Thirty-first (525–335 B.C.). The Twenty-seventh Dynasty was made up of Persian rulers, including Cambyses II and Darius the Great. These kings built a canal from the Nile River to the Red Sea (525–404 B.C.).

The Twenty-eighth Dynasty saw the liberation of Egypt, with the help of the Greeks. One king, Amyrtaeus, ruled (404–399 B.C.).

The Twenty-ninth and Thirtieth dynasties (399–343 B.C.) consisted of seven kings.

The Thirty-first Dynasty (recorded only by the church historian Eusebius) was one of a second Persian domination, 343–335 B.C. It included three rulers—Antaxerxes III, Arses, and Darius III.

ALEXANDER THE GREAT marched into Alexandria in 332 B.C. and was hailed as a god. His successor, PTOLEMY I, was crowned as Pharaoh in 304 B.C. Under the Ptolemies, many Syrians, Jews, ad Greeks settled in Egypt, but the Hellenistic rulers respected the Egyptian religion. The Romans conquered Egypt as part of the general struggle for power after the assassination of Julius Caesar. Augustus defeated Anthony and Cleopatra, whereupon Cleopatra committed suicide. Augustus exercised absolute control over Egypt, which became the bread basket of the Roman Empire. With some ups and downs in the third and seventh centuries, Rome controlled Egypt from 30 B.C. to A.D. 642, when the Arab general Amribu al-As conquered Alexandria for the new faith, Islam. The Egyptians, by now known as Copts, were Christian. The armistice of Babylon called for the Copts to pay a tribute that would exempt them from military service and allow them to practice Christianity and to administer their own community affairs. From A.D. 642 to 968, Egypt was ruled by governors sent by the Muslim caliph. There were 111 governors in these three centuries. By A.D. 706, Arabic was made the official language of the nation, and efforts were begun to convert the country to Islam.

In A.D. 969, an Egyptian caliphate was established, the Fatimids. They built Al Qahirah (or Cairo) as their capital and soon controlled all North Africa and Arabia itself. The Fatimids declined about the time of the Crusades. At first confused and weak, the Fatimids finally recaptured Jerusalem from the Franks. The Fatimids were followed by the Mameluke sultans, rulers drawn from the bodyguard of former rulers. In the early 1500s the Ottoman Turks occupied Egypt and ruled it for three centuries.

In the modern period, Napoleon Bonaparte invaded Egypt in July 1798, but the French were defeated by the Turks and the British in October 1801. A period of anarchy followed until Mohammed Ali took the throne, 1805–48. Later, Egypt went bankrupt, and in 1876 a joint Anglo-French condominium was established to administer the country. This dual control ended in 1883. Egypt entered the twentieth century under British control, and in 1914 was declared a British protectorate.

By the treaty of 1936, Egypt began to regain its independence and in May 1937, Egypt was elected to the League of Nations. During World War II, Egypt was a theater of war but did not declare war on Germany and Japan until February 24, 1945. In 1946 the British announced their withdrawal from Egypt. Many problems arose with the further withdrawal of the British from their Palestine mandate on May 14, 1948. Thereupon the Zionist settlers declared the establishment of Israel, and Egypt, along with several Arab states, invaded Palestine. Egypt fought two more wars with Israel before recovering the territories in the Sinai lost to the Israeli armies. In a surprising move, the hero of Egypt's last successful war with Israel signed a peace treaty with Israel at Camp David, Maryland, under the sponsorship of President Jimmy Carter. Despite the assassination of President Sadat, that peace treaty stll holds, and Egypt has been able to reestablish diplomatic relations with the Kingdom of Jordan.

*Egyptian Religion.* Egyptian religion was complex, fascinating, and of great antiquity. This is but a brief overview of its ancient pantheon. The primitive religion in Egypt was animistic nature worship, with each village having its own sacred tree, plant, or animal, in which dwelt its protective spirit.

The major gods were all represented as animals. Thoth was portrayed as having an ibis head. His sacred animal was the baboon. He was god of science, learning, and scribes.

Anubis was a god represented as a jackal, and was part of the cult of the dead, especially associated with mummification.

Photography by the Egyptian Exploration Society, Metropolitan Museum of Art

*The god Anubis as a jackal, lying on a funerary chest; from the tomb of Tut-ankh-Amon at Thebes*

Sebek was a crocodile god; Taweret was a hippopotamus god. Heqet was a frog goddess, who presided over birth. Bastet, the cat goddess, was the goddess of love. Sekhmet was a lion goddess. Buto was a cobra goddess, and sovereign over Lower Egypt. Nekhbet, the vulture goddess, was sovereign over Upper Egypt. Ernutet was another cobra goddess. Re

Courtesy of The University Museum, University of Pennsylvania

*An Egyptian painted wooden mummy case, used for burial*

(or Ra), the sun-god was represented as having the head of a hawk. Horus, the sky god, was also shown as a hawk. Re and Horus were often combined into one hawk and called Re-Horakhte, or the "Re-Horus of the horizon." Mentu, the war god, also was depicted as a hawk.

Mathor, a sky god, was shown as a cow goddess. Apis was shown as a bull and associated with Ptah, an older god. Khnum was a ram god. Amon and Min were two gods never shown as animals, but the ram was an emblem of Amon.

J.C.

**EGYPTIANS, GOSPEL ACCORDING TO THE.** An apocryphal gospel, known only in fragments, that apparently arose in Gnostic circles. This "gospel" may have been used by the author of II Clement. This

pseudo-Clementine work is a sermon that emphasizes a high Christology and the need to preserve the purity of the flesh.

J.C.

**EHUD.** According to Judges 3:15–4:1, Ehud was a judge of Israel in the early days of the Hebrew conquest of Canaan. He was a Benjaminite and left-handed (and therefore a difficult swordsman to fight). Ehud killed Eglon, king of Moab, and, it is claimed, ten thousand other Moabites.

J.C.

**EICHRODT, WALTHER** (1890–1978). German biblical scholar who taught at the universities of Erlangen and Basel. His far-ranging publications include a dissertation on the Priestly stratum in Genesis (1915), commentaries on Ezekiel (1959–66; Eng. trans. 1970), Isaiah (1960–67), and studies in eschatology (1920), anthropology (1943), and the history of Israelite religion (1953). Of greatest significance is his three-volume *Theology of the Old Testament,* appearing in 1933, 1935, and 1939 (two-volume Eng. trans. 1961, 1967). It is an impressive though controversial integration of historically diverse biblical ideas about God, humanity, and the world under the quasi-comprehensive category of the covenant relationship binding Yahweh and Israel.

J.K.K.

**EIGHTFOLD PATH.** In BUDDHISM, an outline of a disciplined way of life, leading to liberation from suffering, to NIRVANA. The Eightfold Path is the last of the FOUR NOBLE TRUTHS delivered by the BUDDHA in his first sermon after his enlightenment. After telling his hearers that life entails suffering, that suffering is caused by desire, and that there can be an end to desire, the Eightfold Path is the "How To Do It" clause that shows how a life can be made free from craving and hence from suffering.

While they are to be practiced simultaneously rather than as a series of steps, the eight aspects of the path do have an internal logic in their arrangement, culminating in right concentration or meditation, which is the true way to liberation, and fall into certain categories.

The first category embraces the first two parts of the eight, right understanding and right thought. Right understanding, or right views, refers to comprehending and accepting basic Buddhist insights as starting points for practice, especially the Four Noble Truths, and the meaning of KARMA in one's own life. Right thought means accordingly "to purify one's thought from desire, ill-will, and cruelty, directing it instead to kindness and compassion."

From this will follow a life-style centering on the next three of the Eightfold Path—right speech, right action, and right livelihood. Closely related, these prohibit any behavior that would harm others, whether human or animal; lying, stealing, killing, sexual misconduct, taking intoxicants, and the like. These are forbidden, as is any means of making a living that condones or depends on them.

The sixth part of the path, right effort, is transitional. It points back to the effort needed to sustain the foregoing; it points forward to the higher purification of the mind that follows. More technically, it refers to the generation of good karma to uphold one in the path and the avoidance of bad.

The last two of the Eightfold Path are right mindfulness and right SAMĀDHI, that is, right concentration or meditation. Mindfulness means that "inner-directed alertness" that makes one experientially aware of egolessness (ANATTA) and how the mind works. Right concentration means "unifying and stilling the mind, liberating it from attachment." It helps in following the other aspects of the path, just as they prepare one for the freedom of meditation.

R.E.

## EISENHOWER, DWIGHT (1890–1969). Thirty-fourth president of the United States (1952–60), supreme commander of the Allied invasion forces in Western Europe against Hitler's Nazi Germany. Born in Denison, Texas, he grew up in Abilene, Kansas, and was educated at West Point. His paternal roots were Bavarian and Mennonite; his maternal roots, Swiss; both families came to America before 1750. He pursued an army career with resounding success. As president, he made Health, Education, and Welfare a cabinet department; desegregated Washington, D.C., schools; and used federal troops to integrate Central High School, Little Rock, Arkansas. Pietistic and patriotic, he ignored Senator Joseph McCarthy's accusations of communism in government.

C.M.

## EISSFELDT, OTTO (1887–1973). German biblical scholar who taught at the universities of Berlin (1913–22) and Halle (1922–57). As J. WELLHAUSEN's student, Eissfeldt subjected biblical sources to rigorous critical analysis. In his Pentateuchal research, he posited a ninth-century B.C. "Lay Source" (L) reflecting a primitive nomadic ideal. As H. GUNKEL's student, he appreciated diverse OT literary forms and the role oral tradition played in their emergence. Assessing OT theology as a nonhistorical, subjective discipline reflecting the theologian's own faith, he preferred to investigate Israelite religion, which he regarded as a historical, objective enterprise. Often honoring comparative religions issues, his many essays are preserved in *Kleine Schriften* (6 vols.). Eissfeldt is best known for *The Old Testament: An Introduction, Including the Apocrypha and Pseudepigrapha,* an English translation (1965) of the third German edition (1964). Here he masterfully surveys the entire formation of the OT from oral inception to final crystallizaton as an authoritative literary canon.

J.K.K.

## EKRON. Identified as Khirbet el-Muqanna', Ekron was the northernmost of five major Philistine cities (Josh. 13:3). Though claimed by the tribe of Judah (Judg. 1:18), Ekron was a Philistine holding when Israel's ark was transported there (I Sam. 5:10-12). Elijah condemned King Ahaziah for conferring with Ekron's deity, Baal-zebub (II Kings 1:2-16). Also Amos (1:8), Zephaniah (2:4), and Zechariah (9:5, 7) denounced Ekron. Assyria's dominance over Ekron is attested in the eighth- through seventh-century B.C. annals of Sennacherib, Esarhaddon, and Ashurbanipal. Rewarding past loyalty, Syria's king, Alexander Balas (150-145 B.C.), gave Ekron to Jonathan Maccabeus (I Macc. 10:89).

J.K.K.

## EL. The common Semitic designation for "God" or "a god," sharing the same ambiguity of other languages, ancient and modern, to refer indifferently to a deity real or alleged or to the recognized Deity of national or personal veneration.

In the Ugaritic literature that testifies to a Canaanite religion of a time prior to the formation of the Israelite traditions, El is the supreme and still active deity in the pantheon, though there are some indications of its senescence. This picture lends truth probability to the Israelite patriarchal legends in Genesis that envisage pre-Israelite Canaan and in which the local deities are invariably designated by the name El, never by that of Baal. On the contrary, traditions relating to the Israelite conquest, the period of the Judges, and the subsequent mutualism of Israelite and Canaanite societies in Palestine, universally refer to the native Canaanite deity as BAAL. This, too, corresponds with history: Baal, the son (or nephew?) of El, later supplanted the latter as the "active" deity for Canaanites, Arameans, and others of the Near East, even as in Greek mythology Zeus supplanted his father Chronos. As a designation for "G(g)od," however, as distinct from that of *a* god separate from others, El remained in all the Semitic languages as a most used element of proper names.

In the patriarchal stories of Genesis, El of Canaan is freely identified with the God of Israel's ancestors, sometimes (as in Gen. 14:22 Jerusalem Bible) under the explicit Israelite name of YAHWEH. Usually El appears as part of a compound: El-Roi (Gen. 16:13), El-Shaddai (Gen. 17:1), etc. The second parts of these compounds were originally names of distinct deities in their own right (compare the syncretisms that would combine Amun-Re, Zeus-Ammon, Baal-Hadad, etc.). We are left to speculate whether the thought was that one El was venerated under various titles at various shrines, or that the El of one place was really a different deity from that of another—if, indeed, such questions were ever raised at the time.

El, along with the longer form Elohim (which can be singular or plural) and another variant Eloah, performed numerous roles in the theological vocabulary of the OT. It provided an "ecumenical" means of referring to Israel's God when there was some need to avoid the name Yahweh. It served, as an inherited mythological term, to describe the otherwise undefinable: the "sons of God" of Genesis 6:2 and Job 1:6; "sons of gods" in Psalm 29:1; the "god," which was Samuel's wraith in I Samuel 28:13; and even to designate an otherwise indescribable superlative (a "prince of god" equals "a mighty prince," in Gen. 23:10 and "a panic of god" equals "a very great panic" in I Sam. 14:15, etc.).

B.V.

**ELAM.** (1) A country to the east of Babylonia in southwest Iran whose non-Semitic inhabitants were often at war with Mesopotamian neighbors.

Early cuneiform texts attest interaction between Elam and western states. Thus Eannatum, the Sumerian king of Lagash (twenty-fifth century B.C.), and Sargon the Semitic founder of the Akkad Empie (twenty-fourth century B.C.), claimed triumph over Elam. Moreover, Sumerian resurgence under the Third Dynasty of Ur (about 2060–1950 B.C.) ended when Elam destroyed Ur and took captive its king, Ibbi-sin. Until Babylon's rise under Hammurabi (about 1728–1686 B.C.), Elam generally enjoyed mastery over the old Sumero-Akkadian Empire. Accordingly, within the Abraham narrative, mention of Chedorlaomer, king of Elam, as head of a coalition of Mesopotamian kings advancing westward (Gen. 14:1, 4-5), makes sense, though that episode is enigmatic.

The rising Assyrian Empire checkmated Elam. During the eighth and seventh centuries B.C., four Assyrian kings—Sargon II, Sennacherib, Esarhaddon, and Ashurbanipal—led successful campaigns against Elam. Indeed, Ashurbanipal's conquest of Elam and ravaging of Susa, its capital (about 640), decisively terminated Elam's lengthy conflict with Assyria. Around 625, a weakened Assyria allowed Elam to regain independence and participate in Persia's overthrow of Babylon in 539. Persia incorporated Elamite territory into its own vast empire, and Darius I located his palace at Susa.

Oracles by Jeremiah (49:35-39) and Ezekiel (32:24-25) refer to Elam's terrorism and demise. The NT mentions the Elamites only once, when they are listed among those present in Jerusalem at Pentecost (Acts 2:9).

(2) Shem's son, and the eponymous ancestor of the Elamites (Gen. 10:22; I Chr. 1:17).

(3) A Korahite who served as temple gatekeeper in David's time (I Chr. 26:3).

(4) A priest participating in the dedication of Jerusalem's walls in Nehemiah's time (Neh. 12:42).

(5) A descendant of Benjamin (I Chr. 8:24).

(6) The head of a family returning to Judah after Babylonian exile (presumably Ezra 2:7, 31; Neh. 7:12, 34 refer to the same family).

J.K.K.

**ELDAD.** One of seventy elders chosen by Moses to help in the administration of the wilderness camp. He failed to appear with them before the Tent of Meeting to receive some of Yahweh's spirit that had empowered Moses. Nevertheless he prophesied, and a nameless busybody informed Moses. Joshua's disdain of that irregularity is countered by Moses' desire that "all the Lord's people were prophets" (Num. 11:24-29).

J.K.K.

**ELDER.** From the Greek *presbuteros,* or "overseer"; the spiritual leader of a church in the NT, and a term retained by several branches of Protestants to this day.

According to Acts 20:28 and Titus 1:5-7, elder and BISHOP may have been the same. However, by the early second century, the bishop emerged as supreme. "Elder" is a term derived from Christianity's Jewish background. As in the synagogue, the early church in Jerusalem was ruled by elders (Acts 21:18). With the apostles, these early elders ruled over the entire Christian church.

"Elder" obviously refers to age, and elders were generally mature men respected for their sanctity and wisdom. In I Timothy 5:1-2, "elder" clearly refers to aged men (KJV). But the same letter (5:17-22) and other citations (Jas. 5:14; Acts 20:17) use the term to refer to a distinct office, regardless of the office-holder's age.

Both in the NT and in the post NT periods, the elder (as distinct from the bishop) seemed to function as the chief PASTOR of a local congregation. The PRESBYTER or elder, therefore, performed functions similar to those performed later by the priest or pastor. These presbyters directed worship, gave pastoral care, and helped to govern the congregation.

The title "elder" is still used in The United Methodist church, which recognizes two levels of ministry, the deacon and the elder. Only elders share the full pastoral power of the clergy. Among other Protestants, elders are lay people set aside for spiritual work, as in the Presbyterian and Disciples of Christ traditions.

J.C.

**ELEAZAR** (In Hebrew "God has helped"). A prominent name in the OT, that of eleven men. The most outstanding Eleazar is mentioned in Exodus 6:23 and Numbers 3:2; the third son of Aaron and father of Phinehas (Exod. 6:25). Chief of the Levites, overseer of the tent of the presence, he was Aaron's successor as high priest (Num. 20:25 ff.; Deut. 10:6), and served in that capacity for the rest of Moses' life and also under Joshua. Eleazar was instrumental in dividing up the territory in Canaan among the twelve tribes of Israel (Josh. 14:1). Another Eleazar was an ancestor of Joseph (Matt. 1:15).

J.C.

**ELECTION.** The belief that God chooses people and groups to be the special agents of God's saving purposes. Election (also called PREDESTINATION, in Christian theology, following Paul's doctrine in Rom. 8:29-30) is central to the OT, with its emphasis on Israel as the chosen people, and is basic to NT attempts to understand the unmerited grace of God, which freely saves us in Christ.

The election of one people to be God's own possession is the basis of Israel's faith in the OT. Abraham is called by God to come out of Ur and follow Yahweh as a wanderer until Yahweh gives Canaan to Abraham's descendants for a possession. Yet Israel's election is not because of any special worth on Israel's part but rather Abraham and his descendants are to be "a light to the Gentiles," an instrument of salvation for all other peoples (Isa. 49:3, 6 KJV). Israel, then, is chosen for a purpose, which is also the case in the NT, where faith is given to people as a gift of God, so that they accept Jesus Christ and become witnesses to others.

The NT basis for the doctrine of election is specifically the teaching of Paul, especially in Romans 8:29: "Those whom he foreknew he also predestined to be conformed to the image of his Son." Paul refers to "God's elect" in Romans 8, and the salutations of certain epistles speak of the elect who are in such and such a city. One of the epistles of John is addressed to "the elect lady." A first step in explaining the meaning of election (and the elect) in Paul is to bear in mind the early Christian claim that the CHURCH is the new Israel, that is, the newly elect people of God, the chosen people. Israel was chosen for a purpose and the church, the community of the elect, is the assembly of those called out of the world to faith in Christ.

There have been many controversies in the history of Christianity over the doctrine of election, called predestination since the time of Augustine's doctrinal disputes with Pelagius (a British monk living in Rome who taught "holiness" doctrines or perfectionism, and insisted that human beings, by their natural moral powers, and aided by God's grace, could avoid sin, do good, and so merit God's salvation). AUGUSTINE, following Paul and the logic of the whole salvation history of both OT and NT, stressed that believers realize that they depend on the free GRACE of God for salvation. As Luther so often pointed out, if we depend on our own efforts, even the efforts of a supposed FREE WILL, to respond to the good (as the semi-Pelagians and probably Pelagius himself held—a position later attributed, probably incorrectly, to Arminius in the seventeenth century), then, if we are honest about our inner state of egocentricity and self-concern, we must fall into despair. So Augustine held, against Pelagius (and semi-Pelagianism), that human MERIT (in the sense of

response to the good) is in no sense the ground of the believer's election, but that ground is purely the unmerited grace of God. As Luther later clearly stated, our faith by which we are alone justified, is the gift of God. Any goodness that may be in the Christian is the result of God's election, the result of the believer's incorporation into the Body of Christ, the church, done as in baptism, and is not the ground of election.

In Augustine's formulation, predestination (election) involves two elements: God's FOREKNOWLEDGE (God knows without doubt those who will be saved) and God's act of will in electing those who will be saved (the eternal decrees). This strong statement of election was ratified by the councils held at Carthage between A.D. 416 and 419, and was upheld by several later synods. Thus Augustinianism became the basic teaching and doctrinal position of the Catholic church. Despite this decision, the Catholic church has generally espoused a semi-Pelagian position—or one similar to it—and the full-blown Augustinian doctrine has been stressed chiefly in the Protestant churches (especially the Reformed churches) following Martin Luther, who taught the full Augustinian doctrine in his opposition to the humanist Erasmus of Rotterdam in his work, *De Servio Arbitrio (On the Bound Will)*.

Despite protests against the dogmatic hardening of Pauline predestination into double predestination by Augustine and John Calvin (in *The Institutes of the Christian Religion*), protests that have some real justification, an objective reading of the Bible shows God's election to be central to both OT and NT. The basic issue is assurance of salvation, especially the assurance of God's forgiveness ("justification") of those who are seriously honest with themselves. Anyone who plumbs the depth of one's self-centeredness (persons egocentricity or selfishness) is aware of the poisoned wells of human motivation—of the fact that sin is spiritual, it springs from the inner person. No amount of external good works can give the honest believer comfort. Martin Luther's struggles with his own sense of personal sin—not to mention original sin—provide a classic example of the believer's quest to "get me a merciful God." Interestingly, Jesus traced sin to the heart, saying in the Sermon on the Mount (Matt. 5:21-30) that anyone who is angry or lustful has already broken the commandments against murder and adultery. And it was deeply religious people, aware of their sin, such as Augustine (*Confessions*) and Luther (*On the Bound Will*), who found peace only in God's gracious initiative, God's election, not in the many outstanding religious things they both did in life.

Augustine and Luther were interpreters of human life, in the individual sense and in the world historical sense. They took their clues to God's plan of salvation from their common teacher, Paul, another believer who deeply felt his sin (he was a persecutor of the church of God, see Acts 26:9-18) and who came to see that God had predestined (elected) him to be a missionary to the Gentiles before he was born. All three, Paul, Augustine, and Luther, ultimately drew materials for their doctrine of election from the OT, which, throughout, asserts that the Lord chose Israel as an elect people out of pure, sovereign grace. Israel's election was not based on it's merits but was done in spite of it's shortcomings. And, although Israel sinned many times, and even suffered destruction as a nation, God's election and covenant was never taken away, only passed on to the believing remnant. For Paul, it might be said that the faithful remnant, "seven thousand men who have not bowed the knee to Baal," in Elijah's day (Rom. 11:4), was narrowed down to one: Jesus the Christ. And now, through incorporation into the Body of Christ, believers become the New Israel, because they are elect in Christ. This election to faith, regardless of merit, is seen in the very ministry of Jesus, in that he chose his apostles and called disciples to him without establishing qualifications. There were no special merits in Peter, James, or John. Both Peter (I Pet. 2:9) and Paul speak of the church as called (or chosen). In I Corinthians 1:27 and following, Paul says God purposefully chooses the humble so that no one would have a right to boast of being a church member. One of Paul's disciples, in Ephesians 1:4, speaks of the Christian's calling (or election) as being "in Christ," from before the foundation of the universe.

What is important to note in all this is Paul's stress on the humble attitude that should characterize believers and the prophet's insistence that God chose Israel in spite of it's flaw. Election in Christ is not a reward for good character or for good works either already done or that God foresees that one will do. We are not predestined to a status of privilege but chosen as instruments of God's will. Israel was to be a light to the nations. Christians are called to bear witness to the world and to love one another. Although believers may indeed "enjoy the testimony of a good conscience" and be aware of God's providential ordering of their lives, confident in God's love and the ever-present offer of forgiveness, most Christians who accept the doctrine of election have not pushed it to its logical limits, as John Calvin did in *The Institutes,* to "double predestination." Like Luther, most theologians and ordinary believers have seen election for what it is—a sign of God's love and grace—and not felt that God by a sovereign act of will, before the earth was made, condemned certain persons to hell. It is not that God does not have the power to do whatever God wishes; all believers recognize that God has that power. Rather, most believers recognize that God's essentially loving nature is predisposed to grace and forgiveness. As Ezekiel says, God takes no pleasure in the death of anyone (Ezek. 18:21-32). Election, finally, is God's plan of salvation, working its way out in human history, bringing people into conformity with God's loving will.

J.C.

**ELECT NATION.** PURITANS viewed the American colonies as a unique experiment established in the providence of God as a beacon on a hill, a lighthouse to the nations, a paradigm of Christian order. This Anglo-Protestant amalgam of land, people, and nation formed a mystical union for the world's salvation. Preacher Samuel Danforth saw America's mission as an "errand into the wilderness." Cotton Mather, an American Congregational clergyman, once said: "I write the *Wonders* of the Christian religion, flying from the Depravations of *Europe,* to the *American Strand.*"

Such thinking is still reflected in our national hymns: "America," "The Battle Hymn of the Republic," "America the Beautiful," and often appears in political rhetoric, particularly that of the religious right. (*Compare* CIVIL RELIGION.)

N.H.

**ELEPHANTINE PAPYRI.** In Upper Egypt, below the Aswan Dam, three groups of papyri were found at Elephantine Island (Aswan) dating to the fifth century B.C. They were published by A. H. Sayce and A. E. Cowley in 1906, Edward Sachau in 1911, and E. G. Kraeling in 1953. The documents were written in Aramaic and consisted primarily of legal texts and letters, which reveal that a colony of Jews, perhaps mercenary soldiers, lived on the island in a fortress called Yeb during the period of Persian rule. A temple

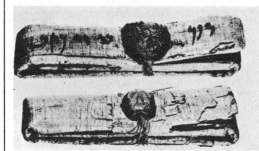

Courtesy of the Brooklyn Museum. Gift of Theodora Wilbour from the estate of her father, Charles Edwin Wilbour

*Papyrus from Elephantine, containing a marriage contract in Aramaic, tied, rolled, and sealed*

existed there, built before Cambyses' conquest of Egypt in 525 B.C., which was known as the Yau temple (Yahweh or Jehovah of the OT). It was destroyed by Egyptian priests but was rebuilt by permission of Persian authorities, who nevertheless refused to permit animal sacrifices. An order was issued by Darius II, the Persian king, in 419 B.C. instructing the Jews at Elephantine to observe the Feast of Unleavened Bread.

J.R.M.

**ELEUSINIAN MYSTERIES.** At Eleusis in Attica, the southern part of mainland Greece, rites and festivals of the holiest and most venerable of the ancient MYSTERY RELIGIONS were conducted since about the eighth century B.C. Their origin is unknown because of strict secrecy for over a thousand years of annual observance; it is still not known what went on in the festivals. The mysteries were ancient avenues to divine knowledge through participation with the gods in various rites, perhaps psychic trances, which seem to have been designed to enable the initiant to pass safely through the gates of death and enter the home of the soul without fear. The mysteries may have been introduced during the time when Attica was becoming a structured society based on the benefits of agriculture. The deity most closely associated with the origins of the mystery by ancient writers is Demeter, the goddess of agriculture.

J.R.M.

**ELI.** The priest in charge of the shrine at Shiloh in the latter period of the Judges, in the time when the Israelite confederation was in the greatest peril of extinction by the Philistines, immediately prior to the coming of monarchy and the beginning of Israelite nationhood. First Samuel 2:27-36 ascribes the origin of his priestly line to Mosaic times; so also I Chronicles 24:3, I Samuel 14:3, and I Kings 2:27 connect him with the Aaronic succession. In fact, as Israel emerged from its tribal status there were doubtless numerous unrelated priesthoods, of which Eli's was one, identified by no common Israelite tradition but rather by the separate sanctuaries that Israel had inherited, of which Shiloh was one.

The first chapters of I Samuel set forth some of the circumstances that led to the demise of Eli's priestly descent, due chiefly to the degeneracy of his immediate successors Hophni and Phinehas, and also, at least implicitly, the disappearance of the shrine of Shiloh, which certainly was proverbially destroyed (compare Jer. 7:12; Ps. 78:60ff., etc.), probably during the Philistine wars with which these chapters are concerned. The "temple of Yahweh" at Shiloh may have been nothing very elaborate (no evidence of anything elaborate has been turned up in the archaeology of Seilun, which is identified with Shiloh). Shiloh was simply the residence of the Ark of the Covenant and, naturally, a place of resort for consulting the Lord, as it is presented in I Samuel 1.

Eli is of interest to the biblical author chiefly as he introduces Samuel, with whom a new era begins, the era of Israel's nationhood, inaugurated by a new institution, or a renewed institution, which is of prophecy. In this acceptation, whatever his real historical significance, Eli has far greater meaning biblically as a "judge" than as a "priest."

B.V.

**ELIEZER.** In Hebrew the meaning is "my God is helper" or "God is my helper," Eliezer is the name of many men in the OT, beginning with the chief servant (or slave) of Abraham (Gen. 15:2), to whom Abraham at first thought he would have to leave his estate since he had no son. The youngest son of Moses was named Eliezer, as was one of the priests who escorted the ark of the covenant to Jerusalem (I Chr. 15:24). The prophet Eliezer declared that the ships of Jehoshaphat would be destroyed (II Chr. 20:37). One of Jesus' ancestors (Luke 3:29) was named Eliezer. The name also occurs in Ezra 10.

J.C.

**ELIJAH.** ("Yahweh is [my] God"). The most important of the preliterary prophets who flourished in Israel during the reigns of Ahab and Ahaziah (869–849 B.C.). He is first introduced to us, somewhat abruptly, in I Kings 17:1 as a native of Tishbe, in Transjordan Gilead, who was prophesying in his homeland about a drought and famine that would strike the kingdom of Israel. The Deuteronomic author of Kings thus begins a series of prophetic stories into which some believe that a biography of Elijah has been incorporated. If not a biography, at least it seems that the Deuteronomist was able to draw upon a cycle or cycles of biographical episodes concerning Elijah, and also ELISHA and others. These biographical episodes may very well have been composed by those who retained a living memory of the prophets in question.

The biographers of the Elijah and Elisha stories were much interested in their subjects as they were reputed to be workers of wonders; hence the sequel of Elijah's prophecy to Ahab of the drought is interrupted in I Kings 17:8-24 by narratives involving the widow of Zarephath (the first narrative tenuously connected with the main story). Even when the original narrative is resumed, much is made of Elijah's miraculous powers in the dialogue with Obadiah (I Kings 18:1-16). At the same time, the scene is prepared for the next episode, as the rivalry is revealed of the prophets of Yahweh, persecuted by Ahab's consort Jezebel, and the prophets of Baal, protected by her.

In I Kings 18:17–19:40 occurs the famous scene on Mount Carmel where Elijah destroys the 450 dervish prophets of Baal and 400 prophets of Asherah by his command of the power of Yahweh. As a consequence the drought is broken, but the slaughter of the Baalites has so enraged Jezebel that Elijah must flee for his life (I Kings 18:41–19:3). In turn, this development introduces what is probably intended by the biblical author to be his most significant affirmation about Elijah.

Elijah on Horeb (I Kings 19:4-18) is a story obviously modeled on that of Moses on Sinai and is intended to single out Elijah as the inaugurator of a new infusion of the spirit of Yahweh (the "still small voice") into the history of Israel: the kind of social prophecy that would later characterize the classical prophecy of Amos and his successors and which is anticipated by Elijah in the episode of Ahab and Naboth's vineyard (I Kings 21).

The rest of the Elijah story, nevertheless, portrays him quite consistently in the more primitive guise of one who preceded rather than participated in the great succession of Israel's prophets. Even the Horeb story involves Elijah in political meddling and nationalistic partisanship of a kind that would have been abhorrent to the classical prophets (compare I Kings 19:15-18). The story of Elijah's choice of Elisha as his disciple (I Kings 19:19-21) prepares for II Kings 9:1-13, the fulfillment of Elijah's commission to anoint Jehu to be king of Israel, just as the story of the anonymous prophets in I Kings 20 validates the other part of the commission, the substitution of Hazael for Benhadad as king of Aram.

The remainder of the story of Elijah, placed during the brief reign of Ahaziah (II Kings 1:1–2:12a), stresses the marvelous in his life, even sometimes grotesquely, and lays the foundation for the later legends that grew up about his figure. His miraculous translation into heaven naturally led to the popular belief that he would return, just as miraculously, to become part of the final accomplishment of all things. His precise role in this situation was variously interpreted (compare Mal. 3:23; Sir. 48:10; Matt. 1:14, etc.). By some he was thought to be the necessary forerunner of the Messiah, if not the Messiah himself. In the NT he is represented along with Moses at Jesus' transfiguration (Mark 9:4 and parallels). Consistent with this development is the fact that both Jewish and early Christian apocryphal literature include works ascribed to Elijah.

B.V.

**ELIOT, JOHN** (1604–90). Famed missionary to the Massachusetts Indians. Eliot first preached to the Indians at Dorchester Mills in 1646. His work was supported by The Society for the Propagation of the Gospel in New England. He published the NT and OT (1661, 1663) in the Massachusetts' language, the first Bible printed in North America; *A Primer or Catechism* (1654); and *The Indian Primer* (1669). In 1651 he organized Natick as a town for Christianized Indians. By 1674 fourteen such communities held eleven hundred people. The work was curtailed by King Philip's War (1675–76).

N.H.

**ELIPHAZ.** (1) The firstborn of Esau and his Hittite wife Adah from whom several Edomite clan leaders descended (Gen. 36:10, 15).
(2) As presumably the eldest and wisest of Job's three friends, Eliphaz staunchly defended God's just retribution for human behavior. Designated "the Temanite" (Job 2:11), he may have descended from Eliphaz (1), who had a son named Teman (Gen. 36:11).

J.K.K.

**ELISHA.** The disciple and successor of the prophet ELIJAH. He was evidently the son of the prominent farmer Shaphat of Abel-meholah, a town south of Beth-shean on the west bank of the Jordan, whom Elijah was instructed to anoint to the prophetic office (I Kings 19:16, 19-23). It may be worthy of note that only here in the OT do we read of the "anointing" of a prophet. The explanation of this fact doubtless lies in the attraction of context: Elisha is mentioned in the same breath with Hazael and Jehu, who were to be anointed kings respectively of Aram and Israel. Also it was to be Elisha, rather than Elijah to whom the commissions had been given in I Kings 19:15-16, who actually presided over these royal "anointings."

These associations point to the close connection of the cycle of Elisha stories (II Kings 2:19–8:15; possibly 9:1-3 and 13:14-21) with those concerning Elijah. In fact, it may plausibly be argued that the same circles were responsible for the preservation of both cycles of stories, namely the "sons of the prophets" who are mentioned not at all in the Elijah stories but frequently in the Elisha stories, and who appear prominently in the account of the transmission of the prophetic office from Elijah to Elisha (II Kings 2:1-18). Some of these "sons of the prophets" were undoubtedly prophets in their own right, but more importantly in this connection they are disciples of prominent prophets who formed their entourage and preserved the record of their words and deeds for posterity (compare the similar situation in Isa. 8:16).

The Elisha stories, like those about Elijah, are vignettes rather than a whole biography, and even more than the Elijah stories they reveal an interest in the prophet as a worker of marvelous deeds. Some of these, like the episode of the boys and the bears at Bethel (II Kings 2:23-25), may even repel the modern reader. But one may be sure that the contemporary Israelite for whom the story was told would have recognized in it a vindication of the prophetic dignity that was sometimes ridiculed as much as it was respected. Compare the characterization "mad fellow" used by Jehu's followers of the young prophet in II Kings 9:4-13, whose word they nevertheless follow, regardless of the prophet's often odd antics and habits. In any case, however, while several of the miracle stories concerning Elisha seem to have been inspired by a delight in the marvelous for its own sake, there is always some element in them of a divinely bestowed power working for the good of others and not simply vulgar display. This is true even of the famous episode of the floating axe head in II Kings 6:5-7. Also, the story told in II Kings 5:20-27 of Gehazi—who served his master hardly in the way that Elisha had served Elijah—brings out well the disinterestedness of Elisha's use of his powers.

Much more than Elijah, Elisha appears as a nationalistic prophet involved in both the internal and external politics of Israel of the ninth century B.C. Indeed, it may be that some of Elisha's political interventions, like those involving Hazael and Jehu, were credited only secondarily to Elijah in the mingling of the two prophetic legends, just as some of the other stories about Elisha seem to have been modeled on precedents original in the life of Elijah. Elisha, according to II Kings 6:8–7:20 especially (and also 13:14-19), was a prophet firmly on the side of Israel in its border wars and skirmishes with the Arameans. Contrary to the usual experience of prophets and certainly that of Elijah, he seems to have generally enjoyed the confidence of the kings of Israel and even of Judah as well, as is reflected in the story of II Kings 3 recording the joint venture of Jehoram and Jehoshaphat against Mesha of Moab, which Elisha prophesied would prevail.

All things considered, it is hard to avoid the impression that Elisha was remembered, first of all, largely because of his earlier association with Elijah. Afterward, for some questionable reasons, he became prominent because of his identification with the house of Jehu (compare the words of Joash in II Kings 13:14). Again in contrast with Elijah (Mal. 4:5-6, for example), Elisha made little imprint on the later tradition. In his "praise of the fathers" Ben Sira does, indeed, celebrate Elisha's wondrous deeds (though Sir. 48:13 is not certainly a reference to II Kings 13:21); but he is mentioned in the NT only in Luke 4:27 (compared to about thirty mentions of Elijah).

B.V.

**ELIZABETH.** The mother of JOHN THE BAPTIST was given this name, the same one worn by the wife of Aaron (Exod. 6:23), the priest from whose family Elizabeth descended (Luke 1:5). The name was erroneously transliterated in the Septuagint. Her husband ZECHARIAH was also of priestly descent (Luke 1:5). She is said to be a kinswoman of Mary, the mother of Jesus (Luke 1:36), but the exact relationship indicated by this Greek word is not clear. The original term refers only to one who is related to another. In the NT it refers to those who are simply members of the same nation (Rom. 9:3; 16:7, 11, 21). If the relationship is meant to be tribal then Elizabeth may have been related to Mary through Elizabeth's mother, who was not necessarily from the tribe of Levi, or through Mary's mother who was not necessarily from the tribe of Judah as was her husband Joseph (the lineage of David, Luke 2:4). Elizabeth, though barren, conceived John the Baptist by the power of God six months prior to Mary's divine

conception of Jesus (Luke 1:24-26, 36). When Mary visited her, she acknowledged Mary as the "mother of my Lord" and said that her own baby leaped for joy in her womb at Mary's greeting (Luke 1:43-44).

J.R.M.

**ELIZABETHAN SETTLEMENT.** The *via media* (middle way) accommodation instituted by England's Queen Elizabeth I (1558–1603). Elizabeth sought to favor neither extreme papalists nor extreme Protestants. A majority of her subjects were Roman Catholic, but Calvinism was rapidly advancing, and she aptly sensed a broadly based nationalism and desire for moderation. Against both religious parties she zealously guarded her royal prerogatives to make final decisions. She disliked the Calvinists' objections to bishops and the Catholics' objections to her legitimacy. The Act of Supremacy (1559), making her "supreme governor" of the Anglican Church, caused the resignation of all Catholic bishops, except one.

Courtesy of the National Portrait Gallery

*Queen Elizabeth I*

This action forced Elizabeth to turn to Protestant PURITANs to fill church vacancies. Marian exiles, mostly Calvinists, began returning to England. Elizabeth selected Matthew Parker as archbishop of Canterbury. His earlier marriage during Edward VI's reign had made Queen Mary remove him from office. Yet four bishops who held sees under Edward consecrated Parker. Catholics hotly rejected his legitimacy. (Because of this Pope Leo XIII in 1896 declared Anglican Orders invalid.) The controversy caused Elizabeth to appear more Protestant. In 1563 the Calvinistic Forty-two Articles (1553) were adopted as the Thirty-nine Articles of the Church of England. The Test Act (1563) condemned anyone upholding papal jurisdiction and barred Catholics from the House of Commons. Insurrection flared briefly in the north (1569), and persecution of Catholics mounted. Pope Pius V excommunicated Elizabeth (1570) as a heretic, causing fear that a zealous Catholic might assassinate her. Catholic plots to dethrone Elizabeth and enthrone Mary, Queen of Scots, multiplied. Mary had fled to England and was imprisoned by Elizabeth in 1568 and reluctantly executed in 1587.

In 1588 Spain's Philip II and Pope Sixtus V then sent the "invincible" Armada against England. Its defeat left England champion of Protestantism and the most powerful nation in Europe. In her last decades Elizabeth firmly maintained the *via media* against rebellious Puritans. Separatists Barrow, Greenwood, and Penry were executed, and many others imprisoned. Nationalism increased, economics improved, literature flourished (Shakespeare, Spenser, and Marlowe wrote under Elizabeth). Cecil and Walsingham gave her excellent counsel. Elizabeth ranks as one of England's greatest rulers.

C.M.

**ELLERTON, JOHN** (1826–93). Hymnwriter and English divine, Ellerton was born December 16 in London, England, and was educated at Trinity College, Cambridge, where he received the B.A. in 1849 and an M.A. in 1854. After being ordained, he served at Eastbourne in Sussex, Brighton, Crewe Green, Hinstock, Barnes, and White Roding. He wrote such hymns as "The Day Thou Gavest, Lord, Is Ended," "Savior, Again to Thy Dear Name We Raise," "God the Omnipotent! King, Who Ordainest," "God of the Living," "We Sing the Glorious Conquest," "Hail to the Lord Who Comes," and "Throned Upon the Awful Tree." He also translated ten Latin hymns, including "Welcome, Happy Morning." He edited *Hymns for Schools and Bible Classes* (1859) and *Church Hymns* (1871).

N.H.

**ELLIOTT, CHARLOTTE** (1789–1871). The author of "Just as I Am, Without One Plea," the daughter of Charles Elliott and granddaughter of Henry Venn of Huddersfield, was born March 18 in London, England. In 1823 the family moved to Brighton. Though in ill health most of her life, Elliott wrote about 150 hymns, characterized by deep devotion and perfect rhythm. They include "My God, My Father, While I Stray," "Jesus, My Saviour, Look on Me," and "O Holy Savior, Friend Unseen." For twenty-five years she edited the *Christian Remembrance Pocket-Book*. Her *Poems* were published with a *Memoir* by her sister in 1873.

N.H.

**ELLUL, JACQUES** (1912–   ). A professor at Bordeaux, Ellul is a jurist and student of human society and its institutions, and also a prominent lay theologian of the French Reformed Church. He is the author of many books dealing with the borderland between theology on the one side and ethics, politics, and sociology on the other. His views are often controversial, and he has been a sharp critic of the pronouncements on economics and politics of ecclesiastical bodies, such as the World Council of Churches. He does not deny that the churches must concern themselves with socio-political questions, but he claims that their views are usually simplistic and bring no specifically Christian wisdom to bear on the issues, but simply conform to the trends of the moment.

He has also been critical of the role of technology in modern society. We have become technology dependent and cannot survive without it, but technology has developed a life of its own and has become the fate of the human race, rather than its servant. It is naïve to think that technology is neutral and can be turned to good or evil according to our choice. Technology is motivated by the love of power and becomes a corrosive force in human life. Ellul is also strongly critical of those Christians who flirt with violence as a means to social justice. "Violence imprisons its practitioners in a circle which cannot be broken . . . it can never realize a noble aim, can never create liberty or justice." Among his books available in English are *Violence* (1970) and *The Ethics of Freedom* (1976).

J.M.

**ELOHIM.** *See* EL.

**ELUL.** *See* HEBREW CALENDAR.

**EMBALMING.** A method for preserving dead bodies from decay practiced by the Egyptians from the late third millennium B.C. until about A.D. 700. Since embalming is unattested in the archaeological discovery of thousands of Palestinian burials, it was not an Israelite custom.

Explicit biblical reference to embalming is limited to Genesis 50. In order that Jacob's body might be returned to Canaan for burial (50:13), his son, Joseph, ordered physician servants to embalm him (50:2). Joseph was likewise embalmed (50:26); yet only his bones are mentioned as transported by Moses (Exod. 13:19) so that they might be interred at Shechem (Josh. 24:32).

In pursuing their craft, Egyptian embalmers removed the internal organs, flushed out the body cavity with palm wine, and filled it with spices. Also the brain was replaced with spices after being removed with an iron hook through the nose. Once the corpse had soaked in natron for seventy days, it was rolled in linen bandages and placed in an anthropoidal mummy case. Made of wood or cartonnage (stucco-coated linen or papyrus glued together in many thicknesses), these cases were carved and painted to portray the person inside. Prayers and incantations also constituted a part of this manifestly religious undertaking, which sought to ensure the deceased a permanent residence where life might continue indefinitely.

J.K.K.

**EMBER DAYS.** The Wednesday, Friday, and Saturday of the weeks that mark four major seasons of the church year—Advent, Lent, Pentecost, and the week after the Triumph of the Cross. During Ember weeks, the church thanks the Lord and prays publicly for human needs. The Ember days have been favored for centuries as times for ordinations.

J.C.

**EMERSON, RALPH WALDO** (1803–82). A Boston Unitarian minister, Emerson is best known as a poet, essayist, and philosopher of TRANSCENDENTALISM.

He was born on May 25 to William and Ruth Haskins Emerson in Boston, where William pastored First Church until his death in 1811. In 1813 Ralph entered Boston Latin School, and in 1821 he graduated from Harvard. After teaching he returned to Harvard in 1825 to study theology. Licensed to preach on October 10, 1826, he married Ellen Louisa Tucker on September 30, 1829. She died February 8, 1831. In 1829 he became minister of Old North Church, Boston, but left the ministry in 1832 because of doctrinal conflicts.

In 1833 he toured Europe, meeting such notables as Coleridge, Wordsworth, Mill, and Carlyle. In 1835 he began his career as a lecturer. In September he married Lydia (Lidian) Jackson. The life of their son Waldo (1836–41) is celebrated in "Threnody." In 1836 he published *Nature,* the first expression of transcendentalism. In the same year he formed the Transcendental Club, including George Ripley, Bronson Alcott, Orestes Brownson, Margaret Fuller, and Nathaniel Hawthorne.

On August 31, 1837, he delivered his famous Phi Beta Kappa oration, "The American Scholar," which enunciated a declaration of intellectual independence from Europe. His address to Harvard Divinity School July 15, 1838, declared his own religious independence. His *Essays* were first published in 1841,

Courtesy of the Library of Congress

*Ralph Waldo Emerson*

followed by a second volume in 1844. His *Poems* appeared in 1846 and *Society and Solitude* in 1870.

N.H.

**EMMANUEL.** *See* IMMANUEL.

**EMMAUS.** A village mentioned only in Luke 24:13. Some manuscripts place it 60 stadia and some 160 stadia from Jerusalem (seven or eighteen miles). The most likely candidates for the site are El Qubeibeh, seven miles northwest of Jerusalem; 'Amwas (Imwas), twenty miles west northwest; and Abu Gosh, nine miles west.

J.R.M.

**EMPEROR WORSHIP.** As an issue in the political and religious background of the NT, the cult of the Roman emperor is not easily defined. In Egypt the ruling pharaoh had been worshiped since time immemorial, and Alexander the Great had set a precedent to his Roman successors as world rulers in accepting divine honors, both in Egypt and Asia Minor.

Temples were erected to AUGUSTUS (27 B.C.–A.D. 14) in Asia; at Smyrna there was a double devotion, to the emperor and to Rome (dea Roma). Augustus, however, was more interested in the political gains of receiving divine worth, and he permitted temples in his name mainly as a way of unifying the state, since in the eastern provinces emperor worship and king worship were traditional. Games honored the emperor, and the army took a religious oath of obedience to him as divine. So Augustus encouraged and developed a movement that began in JULIUS CAESAR's time of regarding the emperor as divine only after his death.

TIBERIUS (A.D. 14–37) allowed honors to be paid to his stepfather but restrained other acts of homage given to himself. NERO (A.D. 54–68) was alarmed at a proposal to erect a temple in his name, and he regarded the plan as an omen of his death.

DOMITIAN, who succeeded Titus in A.D. 81, made a bid to receive personal worship, with temples erected to him in Ephesus and Pergamum. According to Irenaeus, this claim to divinity provoked the crisis of faith that underlies the NT book of Revelation (2:13; 3:18; 17:7-14), and brought the church into direct conflict with the Roman state. Nero's persecution in A.D. 65 was a local affair confined to Rome. In Domitian's time the hostility was widespread, since the Christians could not accept the newly devised imperial claim to being dominus et deus ("lord and god") as Domitian professed. For them, only Jesus Christ was the rightful bearer of those titles (John 20:28).

R.M.

EMPIRICAL THEOLOGY (empiricism). An American development, arising out of an emphasis on experience. This comes partly from the expansiveness of the American scene and the pluralism that influences the acceptance of diversity. Validity is defined in terms of performance.

Empirical theology developed during the rise of the scientific method as a way of testing conclusions. Empiricism accepts the idea that religious statements should be verifiable. Basically, it is a method for dealing with experience. Individual experiences are not accepted as such (as in PIETISM) but are validated in relation to their being tested within the group experience.

Empirical theology asks questions and tests ideas. It remains open, even when stating conclusions. It expects tentative judgments and limited statements. Place is left for novelty, hence an emphasis on the relative rather than the absolute.

The roots of empirical theology are in PRAGMA-TISM, one of whose founding thinkers is ALFRED NORTH WHITEHEAD of Harvard. A basic book is Theology As an Empirical Science, written in 1919 by Douglas C. MacIntosh of Yale University. Empiricism became most deeply rooted at the University of Chicago, 1900–1940, with HENRY NELSON WIE-

MAN as its leading exponent. Empiricists have an operational concept of God in terms of how God is seen to work in the world. Hence there is a continuous process of redefining or describing God.

I.C.

ENCHIRIDION SYMBOLORUM. A handbook or manual detailing the doctrinal statements of the Roman Catholic magisterium. It particularly refers to Henry Denzinger's Enchiridion Symbolorum, first published in 1854, which appeared in a thirty-second edition in 1963. This manual is in general use by Roman Catholic priests and teachers.

J.C.

ENCYCLICAL. A literary form consisting of a very formal letter used by Roman Catholic popes to address the bishops and believing Catholics, or more recently, by popes John XXIII and Paul VI, all people of good will. It is named for the first few words of its text, as in Humanae Vitae.

J.C.

ENDOR. A town tentatively identified with modern Endor situated four miles south of Mount Tabor. Though initially unsuccessful in dislodging its inhabitants (Josh. 17:11), the tribe of Manasseh eventually acquired the town. Prior to the fateful battle of Gilboa, King Saul visited a medium there to consult with the dead Samuel (I Sam. 28:7-25). Endor's mention in Psalm 83:10 establishes in general terms the locus of Israel's victory over Sisera (see Judg. 4:1–5:31).

J.K.K.

END TIME. See ESCHATOLOGY.

ENGLISH REVISED VERSION. This version of the Scriptures, published in 1885, was the first revision of the KING JAMES VERSION (1611). Two companies of translators, including a few American scholars, were appointed—one for the OT and one for the NT. The original publication was known only as the Revised Version but because the American team of translators differed from their British colleagues on some minor issues, the Americans published the AMERICAN REVISED VERSION in 1901. To distinguish it from the ARV, the original Revised Version of 1885 is now often referred to as the English Revised Version (ERV).

R.H.

ENLIGHTENMENT. See NIRVANA; SAMADHI; SATORI.

ENLIGHTENMENT, CHRISTIANITY IN THE. The term used by historians for a cultural era, roughly the eighteenth century in Western history. Frequently Enlightenment and Age of Reason are used interchangeably, although the latter usually is meant to encompass a longer period of intellectual history, from Francis Bacon's *Novum Organum* (1620) to IMMANUEL KANT's *Critique of Pure Reason* (1781). The Enlightenment brought together the humanistic and optimistic spirit of the RENAISSANCE and the results of the scientific revolution from Copernicus to Isaac Newton, which together wrought a change in world view of the most profound significance.

The Enlightenment represents a sharp break with the medieval world and ushered in what we call the modern epoch. From the perspective of the history of religion, the Enlightenment hastened secularization, or the emancipation of Western society from theological dogma and ecclesiastical control. Since the Enlightenment the theories and sanctions of modern social and political life no longer are derived essentially from biblical revelation or church authority but are independently deduced from natural reason and social experience. For the improvement of human life, appeal to a world beyond this earth was no longer felt necessary, nor were the invoking of theological interventions or explanations required. The cure of disease, crime, and social disorder was to be looked for through the application of science and common sense. "Enlightenment," wrote Kant, "is man's release from his self-incurred tutelage. Tutelage is man's inability to make use of his understanding without direction from another. . . . *Sapere aude!* (Dare to know!). Have courage to use your own reason!—that is the motto of the enlightenment."

Reason, for the "enlightened" philosophers, or *philosophes* as they were called, was not the abstract speculative reason of the philosophers LEIBNITZ and DESCARTES. The model of reason was, rather, the empirical, experimental reason of JOHN LOCKE. That is, reason was not a set of innate ideas held in the mind. Rather, it was, like science, an experimental method by which fact was separated from opinion, truth from superstition. The *philosophes* saw orthodox Christianity, in its several forms, as the chief obstacle to enlightenment. The church was considered superstitious, corrupt, and intolerant. Voltaire's call, *Écrasez l'infâme* ("crush the infamous thing"), meaning orthodox religion, was widely shared. In the French *Encyclopédie* it was written: "Reason is to the *philosophe* what grace is to the Christian."

The *philosophes* believed that what was reasonable was also natural. This meant, first of all, that there was nothing *supernatural,* in the sense of contrary to nature (miracle) or beyond natural reason. While the "unnatural" exists, it represents what is artificial, parochial, and unreasonable. Like Newton's laws of nature, what is reasonable is what is common and universal—not what is imposed arbitrarily by authority, be it the throne or priest or Bible. Worn out and wary of the schisms brought on by the seventeenth-century Wars of Religion, the Enlightenment sought a common religious foundation that all rational persons could stand upon. All Christians could agree on the authority of the Bible, but they could not agree on its interpretation. It was necessary to bring the revealed truths of Scripture wholly within the sphere of reason itself. This effort was begun by John Locke in Book IV of *An Essay Concerning Human Understanding* (1690) and in *The Reasonableness of Christianity* (1695), but it was carried out more thoroughly and radically by the Deists. The Englishman John Toland (1670–1722) wrote: "I assert that *what is once revealed we must as well understand as any other matter in the world, Revelation being only of use to inform us while the evidence of its subject persuades us.*"

Revelation is never mysterious or incomprehensible once it is known. Matthew Tindal, in *Christianity as Old as the Creation* (1730), argued that while the word "Christianity" may be of more recent origin, the essentials of the Christian religion must have existed from the beginning, human beings possessing the natural reason required to know divine truths. These truths were thought to be few: belief that God exists and ought to be worshiped, that the practice of virtue is the chief part of worship, and that there will be rewards and punishments after death. Christianity is reduced essentially to a recognition of our moral duty as the divine commands of a Supreme Being, a conception Kant adopts in his *Religion Within the Limits of Reason Alone* (1793).

In seeking a common, rational foundation of religion, the *philosophes* attacked, often with a brutal relish, the incongruities, contradictions, and primitive morals they found in the Bible. Examples of this kind of polemic against the Bible and orthodox Christianity are found in VOLTAIRE's *Sermon of the Fifty* (1755) and in H. S. Reimarus' *Wolfenbüttel Fragments* (1774–78), and most popularly in Thomas Paine's *Age of Reason* (1794–95). It is important to note, however, that while most modern forms of secular faith have their origin in the Enlightenment, the eighteenth century was certainly not irreligious. Voltaire, ROUSSEAU, and Paine all believed in God. And were not JOHN WESLEY and the American theologian JONATHAN EDWARDS "enlightened" men? The term "Enlightenment," some historians now insist, must not be equated simply with what is infidel and unchristian. Room must be made for the likes of Jonathan Swift and Edwards and for the leaders of eighteenth-century dissent.

The Enlightenment often has been criticized for its faith in reason alone, its optimistic view of human nature, and its belief in historical progress. Despite its limitations, the Enlightenment bequeathed a rich legacy to modern religion: devotion to critical scholarship, skepticism regarding speculative dogma, and the insistence that religion be practical and fulfilled in a virtuous life. These remain central to liberal religion today. Perhaps the greatest religious contribution of the Enlightenment was its defense of religious TOLERATION. A series of treatises from Locke's *Letters on Toleration* (1689) to THOMAS JEFFERSON's *Bill for Establishing Religious Freedom*

(1786) helped to establish and secure modern religious toleration as we know it. As Locke argued, if you concede the right of government to enforce religious uniformity, you concede the right to all governments, but since various nations and states hold different religions to be the true one, it follows that you have conceded the right of forced uniformity to false religions as well as the true one. Religious toleration has proven to be a cornerstone of democratic society.

J.L.

**ENMITY.** A persistent feeling of hostility to another or others or hatred leading to a desire to injure or harm. In the Bible the relationship can be: person to person, as "Esau hated Jacob" (Gen. 27:41; Deut. 19:4, 6; Luke 23:12; I John 3:15); people to people (Esth. 9:1; Ezek. 25:15; 35:5); God at enmity with iniquity (Ps. 5:5; Prov. 12:22); the wicked at enmity with the righteous and God (Ps. 55:3; Amos 5:10; Luke 6:22; Rom. 8:7); or the world at enmity with the saints (John 15:19).

Basic in biblical ethics is the enmity SIN has toward the godly. For example, enmity is between the serpent and Eve (Gen. 3:1-15). "Sin is crouching [as a hungry, wild beast] at the door; its desire is for you, but you must master it" (Gen. 4:7). "The devil prowls around like a roaring lion, seeking some one to devour" (I Pet. 5:8).

P.L.G.

**ENOCH.** (1) Son of Cain, and father of Irad (Gen. 4:17*a*, 18*a*).

(2) The city Cain built and named after his son Enoch (4:17*b*).

(3) Son of Jared, and father of Methuselah (Gen. 5:18, 21). Owing to Enoch's close fellowship with the Deity, "he was not, for God took him" (5:24). Extensive legend developed around Enoch's translation (ascent to heaven without death). That Enoch "pleased God" is emphasized in Hebrews 11:5, and his prophecy about God's judgment of the ungodly is reported in Jude 14-15. Jewish intertestamental texts highlight Enoch's righteousness amid a wicked environment (Wisd. Sol. 4:10) and God's desire to favor him with esoteric revelation after his departure from earth (Book of Enoch).

J.K.K.

**ENOCH, BOOK OF.** A collection of originally independent writings composed during the third to first centuries B.C. under the names of Enoch and Noah. Most elaborate of the apocalypses within the PSEUDEPIGRAPHA, Enoch is fully extant only in an Ethiopic rendering of a Greek translation of the Aramaic original.

*Contents.* The book opens with Enoch's introductory discourse (chaps. 1–5) announcing God's imminent judgment of the world. Drawing on the mythology of Genesis 6:1-4, the Book of the Watchers (chaps. 6–36) reflects on the origin and judgment of sin; also Enoch's ascent to heaven and journey to the ends of the earth are depicted. In the Similitudes of Enoch (chaps. 37–71), several heavenly scenes portray the approaching judgment. Perceived as a unique figure elected to defend the righteous, the Son of man enjoys prominence here (see Daniel 7). In the Book of Heavenly Luminaries (chaps. 72–82), Enoch receives instruction concerning the heavenly bodies whose movements establish a 364-day calendar. The Dream Visions (chaps. 83–90) focus on the Flood and the history of humanity from Adam to the advent of messianic rule. A book of exhortations and woes (chaps. 91–105) encourages the righteous poor to remain faithful amid presently hostile circumstances. The conclusion of Enoch (chaps. 106–108) narrates Noah's miraculous birth as a foreshadowing of salvation and reiterates that reward and punishment respectively await the righteous and the wicked.

*Significance.* The Enoch corpus is noted for its diverse literary format, projection of both mythical and historical panoramas, preoccupation with eschatological and cosmological mysteries, stern morality motivated by sectarian concerns, and resolute belief in God's final judgment that will decisively overcome human and angelic rebellion and inaugurate a new and final age. Accordingly, it superbly testifies to the complex adventure involving mind and spirit in which intertestamental Judaism was engaged.

J.K.K.

**ENS.** *See* BEING AND NONBEING.

**ENTHUSIASM.** The word originally meant "being possessed by a god." In the seventeenth and eighteenth centuries it became a pejorative term for extravagant religious devotion. It is a charge frequently leveled against revivalists and CHARISMATICS.

The phenomena can be traced from the early Montanists, Donatists, and Circumcellions, through such medieval sects as the Albigenses, Waldenses, Cathars, Beghards, and Lollards, to the Anabaptists, Quakers, Pietists, Moravians, Camisards, French Prophets, Shakers, Methodists, Jansenists, and quietists. The term might also be applied to contemporary charismatics and Pentecostals.

Enthusiasm can be distinguished between mystical and evangelical (revivalist) strands. The former focuses on God, the Incarnation, the inner light, while the latter emphasizes the Fall, the Atonement, and the Bible.

Enthusiasts are often denounced as innovators, while they claim to be preserving or restoring the fervor and discipline of the primitive church. Their heightened spirituality is often manifested in prophecy, tongues-speaking (see GLOSSOLALIA), miracles (including HEALING), and other forms of ecstasy. They claim personal access to Deity apart from intellect or liturgy, appealing to inner light, conversion or mystical experiences, or the witness of the Holy Spirit. They often preach the simple life and tend toward perfectionism, sometimes falling into antinomianism (see ANTINOMIAN). Institutional churches have usually viewed their excesses as disorder and heresy, a critique of and threat to established order.

Because of their emphasis on experience and religious emotion, an avenue open to all, the history of enthusiasm can be viewed largely as a history of female emancipation. Indeed enthusiastic sects have frequently been denounced as heretical on the basis of the prominence and freedom given to women.

N.H.

**EPHESIANS, LETTER TO THE.** An epistle in the NT canon, written in the name of the apostle Paul. The destination of the letter is highly uncertain since a number of the better Greek manuscripts omit in the salutation the phrase "who are at Ephesus" (Eph. 1:1) and leave the document with an undesignated Christian audience (compare the RSV marginal reading).

*Authorship.* The letter claims to be written by Paul (1:1; 3:1) and was so accepted in the tradition of the church from the second century until the development of modern historical criticism. Within the last two centuries, however, an increasing number of interpreters have questioned Pauline authorship on a variety of grounds, cumulative in their force: literary style (excessively long and complex sentences, with a heavy use of synonyms to the point of redundancy); linguistic considerations (a fairly high number of otherwise non-Pauline words); structure (a letter form unlike the other Pauline letters in that half of the book is composed of liturgical patterns, 1:3–3:21); and contents (Pauline subjects such as the church, its organization, Jew-Gentile relations, and eschatology are dealt with somewhat differently from other Pauline letters, and many characteristic Pauline topics do not appear). Furthermore, according to Acts 20:31 Paul lived in Ephesus nearly three years, longer than any other place on his missionary travels. It would be surprising if he had written to the church there such a general and impersonal letter and had assumed that they had only "heard" of his ministry from others (3:2).

Since Ephesians closely resembles COLOSSIANS (which also has a disputed authorship), the argument is made that the author of Ephesians, a follower of Paul, was familiar with a collection of Paul's letters and had a copy of Colossians at hand at the time of writing to the Ephesians. For this argument the book is a mosaic constructed from the other letters of Paul reflecting both similarities and differences. The solution to the question of authorship continues to be debated in contemporary biblical scholarship and will not likely be settled for some time to come.

*Occasion and Date of the Letter.* If Paul in fact wrote the letter, then it was composed during a time of imprisonment (3:1; 4:1; 6:20) and was carried to its destination by Tychicus, who was to report on Paul's current situation (6:21-22). This traditional position usually assumed that Paul was also the author of Colossians and that Tychicus carried it as well. Onesimus, the runaway slave who was the subject of Paul's letter to Philemon, would have been a member of the travel entourage (compare Col. 4:7-9).

Since Ephesians is general in scope, not addressing specific pastoral problems, and since the readership is not designated in the salutation, some have suggested that the letter was a circular one intended for several Christian communities in Asia Minor. Marcion referred to it as the letter "to the Laodiceans" (compare Col. 4:16), not an unlikely judgment since Ephesus, Laodicea, and Colossae were in the same vicinity. The imprisonment from which Paul wrote would have been Rome and the date of Ephesians about A.D. 61–62.

If, however, Ephesians was composed by a follower of Paul, the date would be later and more difficult to pinpoint. One group of interpreters proposes that it was written as a covering letter for the collection of Paul's letters. The date then suggested is A.D. 90–95, to coincide with a renewed interest in Paul created by the appearance of the Acts of the Apostles. A more plausible setting is the period following A.D. 70, when the increasingly Gentile church was tempted to cut off its connections with the OT people of faith and disown its roots in Israel. The author, then following the lead of Paul, reminded the Christian community that it is built on the foundation of the prophets as well as the apostles and that it grows into "a holy temple in the Lord" (2:20-21).

*Structure and Contents of the Letter.* The epistle is cleanly divided into two major sections by a doxology that ends one section (3:20-21) and a change of tone that begins the other (4:1). The first half, just after the familiar epistolary introduction (1:1-2), is highly liturgical in form. An initial song of praise (1:3-14) is followed by a prayer of thanksgiving and intercession (1:15–2:10). A "reminder" intrudes momentarily (2:11-22) until the prayer is resumed (3:1, 14) and concluded with a doxology (3:20-21).

Throughout the first section the writer affirms the eternal purpose of God for people and for creation "to unite all things in Christ" (1:10). This purpose has its focus in the resurrection of Christ (2:5-7) with the result that God out of the old Jew-Gentile entities has created one new humanity where Gentiles can be "fellow citizens" and "members of the household of God" (2:11-22). Paul has a special place as the one to whom this mystery of unity has been revealed (3:1-6) and the one who expounds the church's mission to reveal God's wisdom even to "the principalities and powers in the heavenly places" (3:10).

The second half of the letter (4:1–6:20) becomes an exhortation to the readers to be faithful to God's call to unity and to a mutually supportive and growing church (4:1-16). Christians are urged to renounce their pagan ways (4:17–5:20), to demonstrate mutual submission within the structure of the household (5:21–6:9), and to be courageous in the warfare against the cosmic forces (6:10-20). A statement of purpose and double benediction conclude the letter (6:21-24).

C.B.C.

**EPHESUS.** A seaport city of Lydia on the Aegean Sea at the mouth of the Cayster River; the most prominent city of the Roman province of Asia, about equal distance from Smyrna on the north and Miletus on the south. Extensive excavations since the mid-nineteenth century have uncovered the ruins of a flourishing city with a large theater and baths, the library of Celsus, colonnade-lined streets, and the famous temple to Artemis.

In the NT the city is associated with the apostle Paul, who, according to Acts 18:19-21, spoke in the synagogue there and later returned for a two- to three-year visit (Acts 19:10; 20:31). His stay was marked both by success (Acts 19:20) and by conflict (Acts 19:23). From Ephesus he wrote some of his Corinthian correspondence (I Cor. 16:8-9). On his final journey to Jerusalem, Acts records Paul's farewell speech to the Ephesian leaders who gathered to meet him at Miletus (20:17-38).

The canonical Letter to the EPHESIANS may have been addressed to the church in Ephesus, though there is a textual problem in the salutation that makes this questionable (Eph. 1:1). The RSV is probably correct in relegating to the margin the phrase "who are at Ephesus," leaving the letter with an undesignated Christian audience.

Apollos of Alexandria also preached at Ephesus and was instructed there by Paul's companions Priscilla and Aquila (Acts 18:24-26). The book of Revelation lists Ephesus as first among the seven churches of Asia to whom letters were written. The Christians there were commended for their patient endurance, but chastised for having abandoned their initial love (Rev. 2:1-7). The church remained in Ephesus long past the NT era and was the host for the Third Ecumenical Council in A.D. 431.

C.B.C.

**EPHESUS, COUNCIL OF.** The third of the ECUMENICAL COUNCILS, gathered in A.D. 431, in order to deal with the debate caused by the teachings of the NESTORIANS. Nestorius, patriarch of Constantinople, declared that Mary should not be called "bearer of God" or THEOTOKOS, but rather "bearer of Christ." His concern, typical of Antiochian theology, was to preserve the full humanity of Jesus by distinguishing between it and his divinity. At the Council of Ephesus, those who supported ALEXANDRIAN THEOLOGY won the day. Nestorius was condemned, Mary was declared to be *theotokos,* and the

Herbert G. May

*The theater at Ephesus capable of seating about 24,000 spectators; it was here that silversmiths stirred up a riot against the disciples of Paul.*

typically Alexandrian doctrine of the *communicatio idiomatum,* that in Christ divinity and humanity are so joined that the attributes of one also belongs to the other, was affirmed.

J.G.

**EPHOD.** An OT noun ordinarily denoting a priestly vestment (I Sam. 2:18), though occasionally understood as an idolatrous cultic object (Judg. 8:27). As a garment reference, Hebrew *'ēphod* is corroborated by Ugaritic *'ipd* and Akkadian *ēpattu,* which respectively mean "robe" (worn by goddess Anath) and "costly vestment."

As priestly attire, the ephod, made of linen, girded eighty-five priests at Nob (I Sam. 22:18). David wore one while dancing before the ark (II Sam. 6:14). Probably it resembled a brief loincloth worn by minimally clad Egyptian priests—assuredly it poorly covered David (6:20)! Eventually, this simple loincloth evolved into the luxurious vestment of the high priest. Worn over his tunic and cloak (Lev. 8:7), it was a colorful, gold-threaded outer garment, with each of its two shoulder straps carrying an onyx stone bearing the engraved names of six tribes (Exod. 28:6-12). Fastened to it was a pouched "breastpiece of judgment" containing the sacred lots, URIM AND THUMMIM, used for obtaining oracles (28:15-30).

Some OT texts portray the ephod as a portable cultic image, possibly serving oracular purposes. Gideon fashioned one from gold seized from the Midianites. It "became a snare" in his hometown (Judg. 8:27). In Micah's domestic chapel stood an ephod presumably used as oracular consulting equipment (17:5). Perhaps the ephod was once a vestment adorning a divine image used in divination, with the noun later transferred to the image itself. Within imageless Yahweh worship, the vestment persisted as priestly attire. Absence of hard evidence invites such conjecture.

J.K.K.

**EPHRAIM.** As a geographical designation this name means "the fruitful land." It refers primarily to the central part of the hill country of Palestine, bordered on the north by the cis-Jordanian region of MANASSEH (inhabited by a related tribe, which it later absorbed) and the valley of Jezreel, and on the south by the territory of BENJAMIN. Sometimes it designates the whole of the northern kingdom of Israel during the period of the divided monarchy (see Isa. 7:2, 8), either because of its dominance among the northern tribes or (as in Hos. 5:9 ff.), after the Assyrian expansion to the west under Tiglath-pileser III, it was the only surviving remnant of that kingdom before its total dissolution in 721 B.C. Earlier, after the establishment of SAMARIA as the final capital of the kingdom of Israel, Ephraim was frequently called by that name, which proved to be the most enduring, both for the NT and subsequent times.

As a proper name, Ephraim is the eponymous ancestor of the Ephraimites, the more important of the "Joseph" tribes (compare Gen. 49:22-26; Deut. 33:13-17). According to Genesis 41:50-51; 48:1-20, Manasseh and Ephraim were born to Joseph in Egypt of an Egyptian wife as his first and second sons respectively. When his father, Jacob, on his deathbed adopted them as his own and blessed them prophetically, however, he accorded the precedence to Ephraim rather than Manasseh. This story both acknowledges the mixed ethnic origin of some of the Israelite tribes (though not necessarily the "right" ones) and also doubtless testifies to some otherwise unknown inner-tribal history and rivalry in consequence of which the Ephraimites were destined to prevail over their Manassehite cousins. The story also seeks to explain why there was no "Joseph" among the tribal names that emerged in Israelite Palestine. In fact, it appears from the Israelite traditions of the "conquest" in the book of Joshua as well as from various parts of the book of Judges that Ephraim probably represented one of the most powerful and decisive elements within the Israelite confederation(s) of the formative period of this people, an element whose leadership was virtually unchallenged.

There is an Ephraim mentioned in the NT associated with Jesus (John 11:54). It is generally identified with a site called et-Taiyebeh near BETHEL, but there are rival claimants in the lands traditionally called by the names of Ephraim and Manasseh.

B.V.

**EPICLESIS.** From the Greek word meaning "to call upon," "to invoke," meaning "to call upon the Holy Spirit," especially in the Roman Mass or the Greek Eucharistic liturgy. Any invocation of the Divine in an act of consecration is an epiclesis, but the term is usually reserved for the invocation at the act of consecrating the bread and wine of the EUCHARIST. At this point in the liturgy of the Mass, the priest prays, with the whole church, that the gifts of bread and wine may be set apart and consecrated so that they truly become the Body and Blood of Christ.

J.C.

**EPICTETUS.** A Greek Stoic philosopher of the first century A.D., who left nothing in writing but whose religious and ethical thoughts were transmitted by a pupil of his. He argued that apart from the human will there is nothing good or bad, and that one must not try to direct the course of life.

J.R.M.

**EPICUREANS.** The name was derived from the founder of the philosophy, Epicurus, who died in 270 B.C. He sought to find true happiness in life through freedom of the individual to do whatever brings ultimate contentment. This might take the form of unrestrained indulgence or of abject self-denial. It was not necessarily a mere sensual reaction to religion.

Although Epicureans denied a life after death, they nevertheless paved the way for Christianity in Greece by maintaining that the body was as essential a part of human nature as the soul. They argued against STOICISM'S idea of absolute fate controlling the destiny of people. True happiness can be found, Epicurus argued, only by rejecting superstition and the fear of death. When Paul came to Athens he immediately preached at Mars' Hill near the marketplace, addressing both Epicurean and Stoic philosophers. These two approaches to life had largely captivated Greek minds by the time of Paul's visit to the country. Their reaction to this Jew from Palestine was predictable in Acts 17: "What would this babbler say?" (v. 18). Paul's sermon to them seems to be directed against several Epicurean teachings, including the doctrines of creation (v. 24), providence (v. 26), inspiration (v. 28), and resurrection and judgment (v. 31).

J.R.M.

**EPIPHANY.** The feast celebrated on January 6, or on the Sunday between January 2 and 8. The Eastern church commemorates the baptism of Jesus at this festival, and the Western church celebrates the coming of the MAGI to adore Jesus. Of course, the baptism of Jesus is also remembered in the Western church, but the theme of the manifestation of the Christ, his "showing forth," which is the meaning of the Greek *Epipanos,* is taken to mean Christ's manifestation to the Gentiles. Epiphany may have been introduced by the church in Egypt to replace an Egyptian celebration of the birth of light at the winter solstice.

In the popular imagination, Epiphany is part of CHRISTMAS, hence so many Christmas cards with pictures of the Magi on them. Of course, the coming of the Magi is connected to the nativity, but if such a visit is historical it would have been long after the birth of Jesus. When the Magi came to Herod, his response to the news of the Messiah's birth was to order the slaughter of all male children two years old and under, showing the time that passed from the appearance of the star and the arrival of the Magi.

J.C.

**EPISCOPAL CHURCH.** *See* ANGLICAN CHURCHES.

**EPISTEMOLOGY.** Combining the Greek *episteme* (knowledge) and *logos* (discourse), epistemology refers to human thought dealing with the theory of knowing. It explores the methods of knowing, the presuppositions and grounds of what is affirmed as knowledge, and its reliability and limits.

PLATO (427–347 B.C.) originated epistemology in response to the Sophists' SKEPTICISM about uncritical pre-Socratic views that KNOWLEDGE was possible. He provides in his *Dialogues* one of its most comprehensive treatments, exploring the limits of sense experience for knowing, the relation of language and

knowledge, a theory of forms to explain the possibility and limitation of knowing, and a critical method for deriving what may be provisionally affirmed as knowledge by means of rigorous dialectical process within a community of interpretation.

The epistemology of ARISTOTLE (384–322 B.C.), far different from and less subtly conceived than Plato's, posits UNIVERSALS that inhere in and shape matter, impress themselves on the human soul or mind through sense experience, and become knowledge through the intellectual activities of imagination and judgment. This view led to the continuing problems of the relation of universals to matter, to particulars, to the mind, and the status of universals with reference to reality and God, illustrated in Neoplatonic thought, in the medieval debates over REALISM and NOMINALISM, and in the opposition between RATIONALISM and EMPIRICISM in early modern thought.

In the critical epistemology of KANT (1724–1804), knowledge is limited to the phenomenal realm, where sensation shaped by categories of understanding becomes experience. Judgments about the noumenal reality underlying the phenomenal are based on practical or teleological considerations and cannot be regarded as objectively valid knowledge.

The idealist epistemology stimulated by Kant led to a reaction of uncritical common sense represented by G. E. Moore (1873–1958), who held up his hands, saying, "Here is one hand, and here is another," as proving external reality. Logical atomism and LOGICAL POSITIVISM represent a similar lack of critical epistemology. Linguistic analysis and ordinary language thought limit their focus and avoid the uncritical naïveté of predecessor movements.

The most promising epistemological directions today, built upon the history of human thought and reaching toward a post-critical perspective, are represented by C. S. PEIRCE (1839–1914), who related knowing to human purposes within communities of interpretation; A. N. WHITEHEAD (1861–1947), with a relational epistemology akin to Plato's; Michael Polanyi (1891–1976), who showed the cultural and personal dimensions inherent in the entire range of human knowing, from scientific to historical; and by H. RICHARD NIEBUHR (1894–1962), whose epistemology integrates theology and ontology, history, and society, into what is affirmed as knowing and knowledge in human communities.

C.Mc.

**EPISTLE.** This term is a transliteration of the Greek word meaning "letter" (II Cor. 7:8; II Thess. 3:17; etc.). Efforts by ADOLPH DEISSMANN at the turn of the century to make a clear distinction between a letter written for private reading and an epistle written for public reading have not been entirely successful. He felt that the difference in the meaning one gives to the terms lies in the intent of the author.

He would write more formally if the document were to be read in public. Thus a letter would not be considered literature but an epistle would be. At issue is the question of whether the author of a "epistle" wrote with the consciousness that he was writing literature that would become Scripture. More recent study has shown that NT letters, both public and private, were written in the basic style of Greek letter writing in the early Christian centuries, consisting of a salutation, thanksgiving, body, paraenesis, and closing items. It is of interest that Paul's letters are known by their destinations (the churches and individuals to which they are addressed), whereas the General epistles are known by their authors (James, Peter, John, and Jude). This may be because there are so many more by Paul.

J.R.M.

**EPISTLES** (Apocryphal). Letters written in the third century A.D. and later, modeled after those in the NT. They were not widely used and did not become a part of the NT CANON. Best known are the Epistles of Christ and Abgar, the Epistles of Paul and Seneca, the Epistle to the Laodiceans, and the Epistle of the Apostles.

J.R.M.

**ERASMUS, DESIDERIUS** (1467–1536). Erasmus of Rotterdam, renowned Dutch humanist, scholar, and critic. Born illegitimate, Erasmus was educated at Gouda and the Deventer school of the BROTHERS OF THE COMMON LIFE. Poverty-stricken, he joined the Augustinians at Steyn (1486) and avidly read classics and the church fathers. Ordained in 1492, he became secretary to the bishop of Cambrai and in 1495 went to Paris for further study. By agreement he left his monastery, and in 1517 got all monastic duties waived. In Paris he tutored William Blount, later his patron, who invited him to England in 1499, where friendships began with humanists John Colet, Thomas More, and Thomas Linacre. He traveled repeatedly to Italy, France, England, and Switzerland. Writings, gifts, and teaching provided his support. He caustically satirized hypocrisy, ignorance, and corruption. The *Adages* (1500), collected ancient sayings with commentary, proved learned and witty. His *Handbook of a Christian Knight* (1503) advised soldiers to use weapons of knowledge and prayer— Erasmus' "Philosophy of Christ." *In Praise of Folly* (1511) poked fun at forms of self-love. *Julius Excluded from Heaven* (1513) highlighted papal crimes. *On the Education of a Christian Prince* (1516), for future Emperor Charles V, praised biblical-classical studies for encouraging peace. His *Colloquies* (1518) promoted good grammar and conduct while satirizing society's ills. Erasmus' Greek NT (1516), directly influencing Luther, corrected six hundred errors in Jerome's Vulgate Bible.

Erasmus believed purer knowledge could improve society and religion. In the same spirit he edited numerous church fathers and classical authors.

Erasmus' *On Free Will* (1524) attacked Luther's impotence of the will, saying ethical responsibility necessitates free will. Luther's *On the Bound Will* (1525) depicted the will enslaved to sin, rendering humans incapable of acting without sin. Erasmus retorted abusively in *Hyperaspites* (1526) but Luther did not reply. Erasmus was an interpreter, an intellectual. He died in Basel, a lonely man. Pope Paul IV (1558) and Sixtus V (1590) prohibited his writings, which were placed on the Index.

C.M.

**ERASTIAN.** A term denoting state control of the church, associated with Thomas Erastus (1524–93), a German-Swiss Zwinglian theologian, physician, and philosopher. He was a professor of medicine at Heidelberg and medicine and ethics at Basel. With Elector Frederick III's favor, Caspar Olevianus began introducing Calvinistic discipline in the Palatinate. Erastus liked Zurich's system of leaving discipline to the magistrate. He attacked Olevianus by saying that all coercive jurisdiction belongs to the magistrate (including excommunication carrying civil penalties), not to church elders. A restricted Presbyterian system was finally introduced in 1570. Erastus' theses on excommunication were published posthumously in London in 1589. He argued that the magistrate has the duty and authority in excommunication to punish sinners. Erastian thus came to signify the dominance of the church by the state. Thomas Hobbes developed a secular Erastianism in his *Leviathan* (1651). Hugo Grotius promoted Erastian notions in Holland's Arminian controversy. In Roman Catholic countries, GALLICANISM connotes national control of the church.

C.M.

**ERIGENA, JOHN SCOTUS** (about 810–880). A medieval philosopher and the translator of the writings of Dionysius the Aeropagite into Latin. (Charles the Bald called him to the palace school at Paris to do the translation.) His name connotes Irish origins. He opposed Gottschalk in *On Predestination* (about 851) and systematized his own views in his greatest work *On the Divisons of Nature* (about 870). Unwilling for Pope Nicholas I to censure his writing, he remained at court.

*On Predestination,* condemned by the Councils of Valence, (855) and Langres (859), held that people have some part in their salvation. All reality comes from and returns to God, and for God evil is nonexistent. Sin with its punishment is self-contained; there is no damnation. *On the Divisions of Nature* was clearly Neoplatonic and pantheistic. From God, the One All-encompassing Reality, everything emanates. First come universal ideas. From universal ideas unfold particular things. Everything returns to God in reverse—God being the nature that neither is created nor creates, motionless unity at rest. This logical reasoning, he said, needs no further authority.

On Charles' death (877) Erigena faded from history. Possibly, he went to England. Pope Honorius III condemned his works in 1225, yet his ideas greatly influenced SCHOLASTICISM and MYSTICISM.

C.M.

**ERIKSON, ERIK H.** (1902–    ). Psychiatrist and author. Erikson was born in Frankfurt, Germany, in 1902, and after graduation from gymnasium studied art and traveled throughout Europe. In 1920, through the invitation of Anna Freud, he began teaching at a private day school in Vienna and was concurrently in analysis with her. He later studied psychoanalysis and began therapy with children.

He came to the faculty of the Harvard Medical School in 1933, one of the first specialists in child psychiatry, and began the study of how the ego functions in a healthy individual. He joined the Institute of Human Relations at Yale in 1936, and two years later began the study of Sioux children at the Pine Ridge, South Dakota, reservation. His objective was to study Sioux children to find the correlation of personality growth with parental and community values.

He entered private practice at San Francisco in 1939 and three years later became professor of psychiatry at the University of California, Berkeley. He began writing the essays later edited by his wife Joan Serson Erikson under the title *Childhood and Society* (1950). When the University of California began to require a loyalty oath in the 1950s, he resigned and went to the Austin Riggs Center at Stockbridge, Massachusetts, to do clinical work. From 1960 to 1970 he was lecturer in psychiatry and professor of human development at Harvard. He is known for his delineation of the psycho-social stages of human development from infancy through old age. He also developed the genre of psycho-biography through his writings on the lives of Luther and Ghandi.

I.C.

**EROS.** One of the primordial gods, a son of Chaos, in ancient Greek religion. Later tradition made him the son of APHRODITE, goddess of sexual love and beauty, by ZEUS. In later poetry he was portrayed as a mischievous child; in art as a beautiful, winged youth.

In philosophy eros is identified with the element of desire and love in humans and the universe. FREUD adopted the concept with psychological meaning, designating eros as the libido, the creative energies flowing from love.

The term has been taken into twentieth-century Protestant theology in a view made popular by the Swedish theologian ANDERS NYRGREN, in *Agape and Eros* (Eng. trans. 1953). He made a distinction between divine LOVE (agape) and human love (eros), which even at its best is not equivalent to agape. Eros, however, transformed by agape, is capable of self-giving that makes possible Christian love among people and a self-giving that enhances all lives.

I.C.

**ESARHADDON**. King of Assyria (680–669 B.C.), Sennacherib's favorite son, and father of Ashurbanipal.

After Adrammelech and Sharezer had murdered their father, SENNACHERIB (II Kings 19:36-37), Esarhaddon moved swiftly to claim Assyria's throne. Though rebellious Babylon had suffered devastation under Sennacherib, the pro-Babylonian Esarhaddon sponsored the repair of the city and its Marduk temple and won the loyalty of Babylon's leaders. Esarhaddon's pillage of Sidon, colonizing of Samaria (Ezra 4:2), and demands for building material imposed on numerous monarchs in western Asia—including Manesseh of Judah—attest his vigorous kingship.

Aware of Egypt's habit of inciting Syro-Palestinian uprisings against Assyria, Esarhaddon made the suppression of Egypt his chief military goal. In 674 B.C., his army suffered initial defeat in Egypt, but by 671 it routed Pharaoh Tirhakah and conquered

*Baked clay prism containing the annals of Esarhaddon*

320

Memphis. Esarhaddon tried to govern Egypt through native princes made accountable to Assyrian governors. Mounting Egyptian revolt induced Esarhaddon to return in 669 on another campaign. He became ill and died en route, but his son and successor, ASHURBANIPAL, succeeded in further anti-Egyptian tactics.

J.K.K.

**ESAU.** According to Genesis 25:22-26, the twin brother of JACOB and a son of ISAAC and REBEKAH. The Bible stresses the opposition between the two brothers, even in their mother's womb (Gen. 25:19-26), extending through their youth when the clever Jacob deprives his dull-witted brother of his birthright (Gen. 25:27-34). Alternatively, with the connivance of his mother Rebekah, Jacob deceives his senile father Isaac into conferring upon him, in place of Esau, the blessings of the firstborn and heir (Gen. 27:1-45). The rivalry is implicit in the story of Genesis 27:48–28:9 and surfaces again and finally in Genesis 32:4-22 and 33:1-17, when Esau unaccountably becomes a mighty chieftain of the trans-Jordan and threatens to become the benign but certain suzerain of his younger brother were it not for the astute temporizing performed by Jacob.

What lies behind this story is the political and historical relationship of Jacob (ISRAEL) and Esau (EDOM, compare Gen. 25:30, etc.). Whatever may be the age of the Genesis traditions, the enmity between Israel and Edom was immemorial in Israelite thought, even though it was certainly enhanced in the aftermath of the Chaldean conquest of Judah in 587 B.C. when Edom played a jackal-like role to the Babylonian conquerors (compare Ps. 137:7), and despite the historical fact that many "certified" Israelites were in reality Edomite in origin, that is, Arabs of the Canaanite south (I Chr. 2, for example).

In keeping with the popular disposition of the Genesis history, Esau is represented as a boor, a lackwit, and as being easily cajoled by his clever brother, even when in a position of power. Nationalist prejudice has dictated the details of a well-told story.

B.V.

**ESCHATOLOGY.** That branch of theology that deals with the "last things"—death, judgment, heaven, hell, the final destinies of individuals and of the cosmos. Generally speaking, in archaic religions the worshipers looked to the past. In their myths and rituals, they recalled certain primeval happenings, which they took to be paradigms and which they repeated or imitated in their own experience. This type of religion induced a sense of timelessness as the cycle of events was repeated again and again.

At some point in time and in some places, there took place a shift in the focus of attention from the past to the future. This happened in Israel (as well as in some other cultures) and the change of perspective

obviously brought important consequences. As soon as people began to look forward to an end as well as back to an origin, they were expelled from the timeless realm of archetypes and thrust into time and history. Life came to be understood as not just the unending repetition of the past but the passage to the new. No doubt some writers have exaggerated the contrast between cyclical and linear conceptions of history, and even in Israel something of the cyclical element remained in the observance of annual festivals, including the Passover. Nevertheless, a fundamental shift had taken place, affecting even the consciousness of time.

There is much evidence to show that both in cultures and in individuals the early stages are relatively timeless. But as awareness of the future develops, consciousness of the passage of time increases and time seems to pass more quickly. The sense of urgency and of the shortness of the remaining time among the early Christians (I Cor. 7:29) who had a very acute eschatological awareness, is a good illustration.

*Eschatology in the Old Testament.* Looking back to the origins of their people, the writers of the OT believed that God had already promised to Abraham a land, a nation descended from him, and a great destiny (Gen. 12:1-3). Though these writers were reading their own beliefs into the past, it seems clear that from very early times the people of Israel had a future orientation, and this orientation remained throughout their history. Their expectations might seem to have been fulfilled when David established his kingdom, but this achievement turned out to be shortlived. Nevertheless, the eschatological expectation remained and took new forms. The prophet Amos (eighth century) speaks of a DAY OF THE LORD, and most commentators think that this was an idea not invented by the prophet but already current among the people. In popular expectation, there was coming a day when God, who had delivered Israel in the past, would decisively intervene to bring victory, peace, and prosperity. Amos, however, warns that because of the sins of the people, the day of the Lord will be a day of doom and judgment, rather than a happy festival (Amos 5:18 ff.).

In the following centuries, successive prophets kept alive the expectation of a decisive, divine intervention and alternated between promises and threats, depending on the faithfulness or lack of faithfulness of the people. Chief among these prophets was Isaiah, who was at work in Judah not long after the ministry of Amos in the north. In Isaiah we meet the idea of a coming wise and able ruler of the house of David, under whom the nation will prosper (Isa. 9:2-7; 11:1-9). Sometimes there is a mythological element, the promise of a "golden age" when wild animals will lie down with tame ones (Isa. 11:6-7) and the desert will blossom abundantly (35:1-2). But for the most part, Isaiah's expectation was this-worldly and realistic. The time of the ideal ruler would be one of justice, good government, freedom from oppression, plentiful harvests, and peace. But in Isaiah too this happy outcome depends on the faithfulness of the people. "He connects the happy assurance of Yahweh's intervention on behalf of his people inseparably with the profoundly serious reality of the judgment which must threaten the people so favored" (Eichrodt). The day on which the messianic kingdom would be established would be the same day on which all unrighteousness would be judged. "The Lord of hosts has a day against all that is proud and lofty, against all that is lifted up and high" (Isa. 2:12).

At a later time Jeremiah, though believing that the nation was doomed because it had broken the covenant, held out the prospect of a new covenant (Jer. 31:3-4). In all these preexilic prophets, the coming age is within history and continuous with what has gone before. Though this teaching looks for a decisive moment in the future, it is eschatological only in a very broad sense of the term. But in any case, the destruction of the Hebrew kingdoms and of the Temple itself put an end to such hopes.

*Postexilic Developments.* After the Exile, the immediate form of the eschatological expectation was that of a return to the Holy Land and a revived nation centered on a rebuilt Temple. When these hopes came to nothing, the eschatological expectation became increasingly otherworldly and supernaturalistic. We come to a new form of eschatology, called "apocalyptic," which appears in the OT in the late book of Daniel, and then in much of the intertestamental writings. In its lurid symbolism and its grandiose expectations APOCALYPTICISM is so far removed from the relatively sober eschatology of earlier times that one can hardly refrain from the suspicion that it represents an escapism from the harsh realities that had befallen the Jewish people. Of course, it might be replied to this that it is evidence for a continuing faith in the sovereignty and good purposes of God. What the apocalyptist looked for was not an ideal age or a restoration in the life of Israel, but a transformation of the entire cosmos and a new age of a different order from what had gone before. Such an age would be inaugurated not by a king naturally descended from David but by a preexistent supernatural figure from heaven who would judge the earth and set up the final rule of God. Another important development that belonged to the intertestamental period was the emergence of a definite belief in a life beyond death. This is generally supposed to have happened in connection with the Maccabean wars. Many young men were dying for the sake of the faith of Israel, and it seemed unjust that their early deaths should be the end of the story. If there is a just God, surely God would raise them from the dead and take them to a divine home.

*Eschatology in the New Testament.* Both the apocalyptic expectations and a belief in the RESURRECTION of the dead seem to have been widespread among many Jews at the time of Jesus, and he presumably shared them and was looking for the imminent inbreaking of the KINGDOM OF GOD. It is very unlikely that he identified himself with the apocalyptic figure of the Son of man, but the identification was made by his disciples, probably after his resurrection, and in the earliest days, we find them expecting his speedy return to judge the world and establish the New Age. It seems clear that Paul, in the early stages of his apostleship, believed that the end would come very soon, probably in his own lifetime. The end, of course, did not come, and this must have been a serious challenge to those who had been expecting it. Paul seems to take the view that it had been postponed until Israel too had been gathered into the Christian fold (Rom. 11:25-26). Nevertheless, the discomfort and even mild rebelliousness felt by Christians who were disappointed by the nonoccurrence of the SECOND COMING of Jesus is reflected in the complaint recorded in a late book of the NT: "Where is the promise of his coming? For ever since the fathers fell asleep, all things have continued as they were from the beginning of creation" (II Pet. 3:4). John's Gospel (end of first century) says virtually nothing about the Second Coming of Jesus or a future eschatological moment. Perhaps the coming of the Holy Spirit is considered to be the return of Christ, while it is also taught that the judgment of the world is going on now, and that the believer has already entered into eternal life (John 12:31; 5:24; 14:16).

*Eschatology in Christian Theology.* The general tendency in the history of Christian theology has been to postpone the last things to an indefinite and remote future. This, however, is to deprive them of that urgency which was the reason for their importance in the early days of the church. Only on rare occasions, in some enthusiastic individual or sect, has the expectation of an immediate end flared up. Joachim of Fiore is an example, also Thomas Münzer and the radical reformers. The situation has been constantly muddled because the Platonist idea of the IMMORTALITY of the soul has been inconsistently combined with the biblical expectation of a RESURRECTION OF THE DEAD, and the belief in an interim judgment of each individual at death has been brought in to supplement the expectation of a final judgment in the remote future.

During the present century, new attempts have been made by theologians to come to grips with the problems of eschatology. These attempts began with the findings of J. Weiss and A. Schweitzer, that the mentality and teaching of both Jesus and his immediate disciples were thoroughly saturated in eschatological and even apocalyptic expectations. The idea of the kingdom of God, as an ethical commonwealth gradually to be developed among human beings here on earth, was denounced by Weiss as a relic of the Enlightenment Christianity of Kant. The new emphasis on the all pervasiveness of eschatology in the NT was perhaps as much of a shock to modern liberal theologians as the failure of the *Parousia* had been to the first generation of Christians. For how can the twentieth-century mind come to terms with the manifestly mythological ideas of first-century eschatology?

One move, to be seen in different forms in R. Bultmann and C. H. Dodd, was to interpret these ideas as "realized eschatology," the last things have already happened. Christ has come and inaugurated the Kingdom; judgment, heaven, and hell are present realities. Basically, this is the solution that John's Gospel already offered in the first century. It may be felt, however, that it is a very reduced interpretation of the grandiose promise of a new heaven and a new earth. Thus, in conscious opposition to such rationalized and demythologized interpretations of the last things, another group of contemporary theologians, including J. Moltmann and W. Pannenberg, have insisted on a futuristic interpretation. They believe that it is of the essence of Christianity to look for a coming "resurrection of the dead," a radical transformation of human society. The problem about such teaching is that it seems to plunge us back into mythology, and neither Moltmann nor Pannenberg has been able to give a convincing refutation of this charge. Furthermore, by laying such overwhelming stress on the eschatological elements in Christianity, they are in serious danger of distorting the structure of theology as a whole.

Contemporary theologians who feel themselves unable to go back to a literal or mythological understanding of eschatology but who may not be content with the much reduced and, above all, highly individualistic interpretation offered by Bultmann and his allies, may find themselves somewhat perplexed. Perhaps the first point for them to notice is that it is unnecessary to give a detailed systematic exposition of such a speculative area of doctrine. Eschatology is not an independent theological inquiry, but simply a consequence of Christian teaching as a whole. If the world and the human race are the creations of a loving God, then this God must have a good purpose for them. It is, however, no more necessary to believe that this will come as a definite end to the whole movement of history than to believe that creation took place in a definite moment of beginning. God's creating and consummating (or bringing to perfection) are constantly going on. In this history, a sifting or judgment goes on, in the sense that there are certain constraints so that there are ways forward by which the human being fulfills potentialities for individual and communal development, and ways back by which humanity is diminished and brought nearer to dissolution. To the extent that human beings fulfill their potentiality as children of God, they enter into a relation with God that may be called ETERNAL LIFE and that by its very nature shares in the permanence and stability of God. This intimate sense of communion with God is the bliss called HEAVEN. On the other hand, HELL is

separation and exclusion from God. But whereas the older theologians thought of hell as the final and eternal destiny of some, perhaps most, human beings, few contemporary theologians would be willing to accept this.

The exclusion of some human beings from a saving relation to God would seem to be the defeat of God's loving purpose for creation and to be a permanent hindrance to "heaven" for any human beings at all. Thus there is a general tendency to accept a "universalist" solution to the problem of human destiny, that is to say, the belief that in the end, all will come to accept the proffered salvation of God. Such an interpretation of the eschatological images does not attempt to be too ambitious and confines itself to what may be reasonably expected if there is indeed a good and loving God. Even many Protestant theologians nowadays are attracted to the Roman Catholic belief in PURGATORY, and see this as an alternative to belief in eternal punishment in hell.

J.M.

**ESDRAS, BOOKS OF.** The first two books of the APOCRYPHA designated by the Greek form of the Hebrew name "Ezra."

*I Esdras.* This Greek translation of a Hebrew-Aramaic original, probably dating to 150-100 B.C., reproduces the substance of II Chronicles 35–36, the book of Ezra, and that portion of Nehemiah depicting Ezra's accomplishments (7:73–8:12). Manifesting considerable interest in Josiah, Zerubbabel, and Ezra, no other Apocryphal book is more closely linked with the OT. Yet some of the material is rearranged as well as revised, and the engaging story of the three guardsmen at Darius' court (3:1–5:6) lacks an OT counterpart. The product of an author who put Jewish piety ahead of historical accuracy, I Esdras richly extols Ezra, the Law, and proper temple worship.

*II Esdras.* Though known only from Latin and other translations, the core of II Esdras (chaps. 3–14) is an apocalypse written in Hebrew or Aramaic in about A.D. 100. Its four sections emphasize that the God who predetermines history will soon terminate Israel's oppression. The Salathiel Apocalypse (3:1–10:59) features four visions devoted to the problem of suffering and its alleviation in the life to come. The Eagle Vision (11:1–12:39) depicts the Roman Empire and its overthrow by the Messiah. The Vision of the Man from the Sea (13:1-58) further defines the Messiah's function, and a concluding vision-legend (14:1-48) portrays Ezra's rewriting of Israel's sacred literature. A Greek preface (chaps. 1–2), written by a Jewish Christian in about A.D. 150, argues that the church has displaced Israel in God's economy. A Greek appendix (chaps. 15–16), dating about A.D. 250, offers encouraging prophecies to Christians suffering persecution.

J.K.K.

**ESSENCE/EXISTENCE.** Two different ways of conceiving the being of anything. To speak of its essence is to consider *what* it is; to affirm its existence is to say *that* it is. Essences are abstract and universal; existences are concrete and particular. Essences remain identical in innumerable instantiations; each existent, on the contrary, is distinct and unique.

Some philosophies have been primarily those of essence. An obvious example is Platonism. To PLATO it seemed that the actual world of particular existents is a world of flux and impermanence, somewhere between BEING AND NONBEING. He contrasted it with the unchanging forms, or universal essences, and considered that a superior degree of reality belongs to them. ARISTOTLE, on the other hand, believed that reality belongs to the particular existing things and that the forms subsist only in thought. At a much later time, we find a similar contrast between HEGEL's exaltation of pure thought and KIERKEGAARD's insistence that thought is always the thought of an existent thinker, located among the actualities of the world. Any adequate philosophy, however, must account for both essence and existence and for the relation between them. WHITEHEAD is an example of a philosopher who tries to do this.

Another task is to distinguish different kinds of existence and the relation between essence and existence in each case. When we say that finite things exist, we mean that they can actually be found in the world of space and time. They "lie about," so to speak, so that their existence is passive. Such existent things have fixed, given essences. A piece of gold, for instance, exists if it occupies space and persists through time in some part of the world. Its essence is the sum of properties that distinguish gold from all other substances, and which are found universally in all golden objects. A human being, on the other hand, exists in an active way, as indeed EXISTENTIAL-ISM has emphasized by reserving the term "existence" specifically to human existence. The human being, unlike the piece of gold, is a center of freedom and creativity, and has no fixed essence. As SARTRE has expressed it, existence in the human case precedes essence. The human essence is not given, but is formed by the human existent through deeds and choices.

The existence of God would be of a different order still, for God's existence is certainly not passive like that of a thing—this is why TILLICH had doubts about the propriety of even saying "God exists"—and it has a fullness of creativity far exceeding even the existence of a human being. It has been claimed by THOMAS AQUINAS and others that God's essence is God's existence. Thus, as AUGUSTINE had already pointed out, to say that God *is* is already to say that he *is good, is just,* and so on. But although God, human beings, and things all exist in different ways, most theologians have held that there is an ANALOGY of being, which allows us to use the language of finite existence in a nonliteral way about divine existence.

J.M.

**ESSENES.** A Jewish sect that flourished from the second century B.C. until the later first century A.D., famed for its strict observance of the Law and its expectation of divine deliverance. Descriptions of the Essenes are preserved not only in Jewish writers (Josephus and Philo of Alexandria) but in the Roman historian Pliny's *Natural History.* Almost certainly, the Dead Sea sect, whose library and community center were found at QUMRAN overlooking the Dead Sea, was part of the Essene movement.

The name of the group probably comes from an Aramaic term, *Hasen,* which is the equivalent of Hasidim, the group that supported Mattathias and the Maccabees according to I Maccabees 2:42. Josephus, in his *Antiquities,* represents them as a philosophical school, distinguished by their unconditional belief in fate, but he was more interested in putting Judaism in a favorable light for Gentile readers than in accurate description of its teachings.

In his *Jewish War,* JOSEPHUS describes in detail the strong sense of community that characterized the Essenes, including the sharing of possessions and providing support for the needy. Except for a small group that permitted its members to marry, the Essenes were ascetic, and even those who married could have intercourse only for purpose of procreation. He details their prayers before sunrise, their ritual baths, their communal meals, their silence and freedom from conflict or dispute, their charity, their refusal to take oaths. The probationary period and stages of acceptance into membership are described. The solemn vow required of those admitted included commitment to practice piety toward God, justice toward other human beings, fidelity toward members of the community, and unrelenting resistance of evil. There was to be no opposition toward rulers, however, since they attain power by the will of God. Nothing was to be concealed from members of the group, and none of its secrets were to be revealed, even under torture. The sacred books and heavenly secrets of the community were to be disclosed to no outsiders. Any violation of the rules resulted in expulsion, which would likely lead to the death of the excluded member, whose convictions prohibited the eating of unclean food.

Josephus asserts that "after God they hold most in awe the name of their lawgiver," which probably refers to Moses, but could as well refer to their special interpreter of the Law, the Righteous Teacher, who was the central figure in their own literature. They were especially strict about abstinence from work on the Sabbath and were prohibited even from defecating on that day. A special mattock was given the novices to bury excretion. The members were ranked according to four grades, so strictly observed that for a member of a lower order to touch a member of a higher was to pollute him. Finally, Josephus notes their enormous courage in the face of persecution and their belief in the immortality of the soul, as well as in future rewards and punishments. Among their members were some who used the holy books (presumably their own, not merely the scriptures) to predict the future. Elsewhere (*Antiquities*) Josephus offers a loose comparison of the Essenes with the Greek philosophical school of the Pythagoreans, but he shifts to the ability of the Essene prophets to foretell the future.

In his treatise "Every Good Man Is Free," PHILO OF ALEXANDRIA describes how many different groups have found freedom through commitment to justice and goodness. One of his examples is the Essenes, whose name he derives from the Greek word for piety. He describes them as residing in villages, avoiding the acquisition of large holdings of land or money, living in frugality and contentment. They avoid weapons and strife. They have no slaves, but live in friendship and mutuality. Central to their life is the Sabbath and the public reading and exposition of their sacred writings when they gather in solemn assembly. Houses, wealth, and food are shared by the group and with visitors to their communities. Philo includes the Essenes among "the athletes of virtue."

When in 1947 the first of the scrolls of the Dead Sea community were found, to be followed by the discovery of the community center as well as other caves containing their writings, the connection was obvious with Pliny's account of Essenes living by the Dead Sea (see DEAD SEA SCROLLS). The discovery recalled the mention by Origen of Alexandria (A.D. 254) of the recovery of Greek and Hebrew manuscripts from a jar near Jericho. A similar report is preserved from the eighth century. Since Philo describes the Essenes as living in villages, rather than in a single place, and since Josephus reports that they lived in isolated groups within cities, it seems that the Dead Sea group was one distinctive branch of a larger Essene movement. Similarly, there were other baptizing sects in Judaism of this period, which did withdraw from society. John the Baptist would be an example of this type of prophetic summoner to repentance, announcing the end of the age. Furthermore, there is evidence that the Pharisees as we see them in the first century A.D. had developed out of the Hasidim. In the phrase of Jacob Neusner, the Pharisees shifted "from politics to piety"; that is, they moved away from direct support of the Maccabees to the fostering of ritual purity of their members as the covenant people. The Essenes shared this later goal, but believed it could be achieved only in isolation from secularized city life.

The Hasidim had been able to persuade Judas Maccabeus to appoint as high priest one Alcimus, who at least had the essential qualification of being descended from Aaron (I Macc. 7:9-16). For a time the group supported the Maccabees, though they later referred to that period as "twenty years of groping." In a commentary on the prophetic book of Nahum two crucial dates in the sect's history are pointed up: the reign of Antiochus (Epiphanes, 175–163 B.C.); the coming of the Kittim (Romans, under Pompey,

63 B.C.). The person who provided them direction after the disillusionment with the increasingly secularized Maccabees was one whom the Dead Sea documents refer to as the Righteous Teacher, or to paraphrase, "the One who teaches rightly." His title derives from a parabolic pun on a Hebrew word in Joel 2:23, which can mean either "rain" or "teacher." In the organizational books of this sect (*Covenanters of Damascus, Scroll of the Ruler*), in their prophetic documents (*Wars of the Children of Light and the Children of Darkness, The Temple Scroll*), as well as in their commentaries, their prophetic books, their pious paraphrases of scripture, and their collections of specially important texts, the Qumran library shows this Essene community in detail. The members lived withdrawn, viewing both the political and the priestly leadership of their land as hopelessly corrupt. There in the desert they maintained their purity, living in literal fulfillment of the words of Psalm 1 about meditating on the Law day and night. Above all they awaited the appearance of two messiahs: an anointed priest and an anointed king. Under these divinely appointed leaders, and with the aid of angelic armies, their enemies would be defeated, and they would then be vindicated and established in Jerusalem as the true people of the Second Covenant.

H.K.

**ESTABLISHED CHURCH.** The name given to the official church of a nation, usually supported by the state and given preferential treatment by the government. The term is often used in contrast with the FREE CHURCHES, meaning those that have no official relation with the state, and are supported by the voluntary gifts of their members.

J.G.

**ESTHER.** This OT book focuses on Esther and her cousin and former guardian, Mordecai, who braved a hostile environment to advance Judaism's cause. As one of the five MEGILLOTH (festival scrolls), it tells of dramatic Jewish deliverance under the Persians and accounts for the institution of PURIM, a popular festival not legislated by Mosaic law. Once designated by her Hebrew name Hadassah, meaning "myrtle" (2:7), the heroine is otherwise called Esther, presumably a Persian name derived from a noun meaning "star" (compare ISHTAR, the Babylonian star goddess).

*Organization and Basic Content.* Though the absorbing narrative involves more than a dozen successive scenes, a three-part division emerges—preliminary narrative setting (1:1–2:23); main action (3:1–9:19); conclusion (9:20–10:3). In the story that unfolds, the very lovely Jewish maiden, Esther, is chosen by King Ahasuerus to replace Queen Vashti, who has lost favor with the monarch and every other Persian "male chauvinist" for refusing to display her beauty during the lavish royal banquet.

Meanwhile, Haman "the Agagite," a descendant of the Amalekite king whom Saul conquered (I Sam. 15:7-9), is elevated to prime minister. As a Benjaminite and descendant of Saul, Mordecai finds loathsome the royal command that he should bow down to an Agagite. Before the king, Haman interprets Mordecai's unwillingness to comply as a symbol of Jewish refusal to assimilate. Haman thereby obtains royal support in sponsoring a pogrom (an organized massacre) of all Jews throughout the Persian empire, which by lot *(pur)* is scheduled for the thirteenth day of Adar. Pressed into action by Mordecai, Esther at great personal risk successfully entreats the king to reverse his decision and allow the Jews to mount a counterpogrom against their opponents on the very day that Haman had selected for Judaism's extinction. Ultimately Haman is suspended on the gallows he had prepared for Mordecai, the Jews slaughter their enemies, Mordecai is made prime minister, and the annual festival of Purim is officially instituted by Mordecai and Esther to commemorate the recent military victory.

*History or Fiction?* The book's many dates, enumerations of palace details, and the large cast of named characters parade as worthy historiography. A kernel of historical fact may undergird the narrative, but it cannot now be identified. Indeed, historical ineptitude abounds. The name AHASUERUS is the Hebrew counterpart for XERXES, king of Persia (486–465 B.C.), but the ages of Mordecai and Esther cannot be easily reconciled with his reign since Mordecai was exiled in 597 (2:6). It is unlikely that Xerxes had a Jewish queen and downright absurd that he would have allowed the Jews to annihilate seventy-five thousand of his subjects (9:16). The appointment of non-Persians to the crucial position of prime minister (3:1; 8:2; 10:3) taxes the imagination. Moreover, approximately seventy-five-foot high gallows sound implausible (7:9), as does the royal edict that "every man be lord in his own house" (1:22).

The book is cast in the fiction style by a master craftsman. He makes much of antitheses. Not only are Mordecai and Haman at odds, but the pogrom of the Jews becomes a massacre of their opponents. Concealment is central to the story. When Haman approaches Ahasuerus to arrange Mordecai's hanging (chap. 6), he is unaware that the king seeks to honor Mordecai. Nor is Ahasuerus cognizant of Haman's strategy. Also the author deliberately varies the tempo. Esther's postponement of the crucial dinner party involving the king and Haman (5:3-8) is an artful delay tactic designed to heighten suspense. Yet in chapters 6–7, which portray Haman's demise, the narrative proceeds swiftly. As fiction, the book was meant to be enjoyed, as indeed it was during its public reading at the Purim festival where, according to the Talmud, wine flowed in such abundance that the difference between "Blessed be Mordecai" and "Cursed be Haman" became blurred.

The exact antecedents of the Esther narrative elude us. If the individual stories of Vashti, Haman and Mordecai, and Esther claim a prehistory, they are merely distinct threads of plot in the present narrative. Babylonian and Elamite mythological influences have been suspected since the names Esther and Mordecai correspond with the Babylonian deities Ishtar and MARDUK, and the names Haman and Vashti with the Elamite deities Human and Mashti. Nevertheless, the Esther narrative confines itself to the doings of humans. Finally, we lack hard data about the origins of the Purim festival and the date of its introduction into Judaism. Such perplexity, however, cannot eclipse the compositional talents of Esther's unknown author.

*Date.* Although scholarly judgment is not unanimous, the book is often dated toward the end of the Persian period (539–332 B.C.). The following considerations are relevant: the narrative may reflect an actual mid-fourth-century B.C. threat to Jews of the Dispersion; the book contains Persian, but no Greek, vocabulary; Esther's Hebrew clearly predates second-century B.C. Hebrew texts from Qumran; and the Gentile king receives a sympathetic treatment before Jewish attitudes have hardened in the second-century B.C. Seleucid-sponsored Jewish persecutions. The omission of Esther and Mordecai in ben Sira's list of heroes (Ecclus. 44–50, around 180 B.C.) and the apparent absence of Esther in the Qumran library may encourage a second-century B.C. date, but are merely arguments from silence. Still, the text may have received minor Hellenistic revision.

*Religious Dimension.* The book of Esther is secular, militant, and narrowly patriotic. No allusion is made to the religious practices of Judaism, and God's name is never mentioned. Nevertheless, Mordecai's reference to Jewish deliverance "from another quarter" (4:14) betrays a belief in divine providence that is reaffirmed in 6:13. And the insidious threat against Jewish existence expressed in Haman's speech to Ahasuerus manifests an undeniably religious element: "There is a certain people scattered . . . in your kingdom; their laws are different from those of every other people, and they do not keep the king's laws, so that it is not for the king's profit to tolerate them" (3:8). This book realistically urges the covenant people to maintain guard against villain outsiders who would harm them. Later generations undergoing intense suffering would derive encouragement from Esther and Mordecai's stalwart example and be thankful that Esther had found a home in the OT Canon.

J.K.K.

**ESTHER, ADDITIONS TO THE BOOK OF.** Six extended passages lacking in the Hebrew text of Esther but found interspersed through its Greek (Septuagint) version. Questioning their canonical status, Jerome, the translator of the Latin Vulgate, appended them to his translation of the Hebrew. Appearing in the APOCRYPHA as a separate book, these supplementary units confer an explicitly religious aspect on the canonical text, augment its dramatic impact and appearance of authenticity, and intensify its anti-Gentile stance.

*Basic Content.* These additions, long designated by scholars as *A, B, C, D, E,* and *F,* present diverse material. Framing the book are Additions *A* (11:2–12:6) and *F* (10:4–11:1), which describe and interpret Mordecai's dream with mention of two dragons in combat (Mordecai and Haman) and the tiny spring that becomes a river of deliverance (Esther). Addition *B* (13:1-7) is a "copy" of Artaxerxes' decree mandating the annihilation of Jews who disturb the Persian peace. Addition *C* (13:8–14:19) yields two prayers, one by Mordecai with its pious explanation for his refusal to bow to Haman, the other by ESTHER wherein she expresses disdain for her Jewish-Gentile marriage and petitions the Deity to use her speech as a means of salvation. Addition *D* (15:1-16) portrays Esther's emotional audience with the king. Addition *E* (16:1-24) contains Artaxerxes' decree invalidating the original one against the Jews and providing for their self-defense. The additions link with the canonical text as follows: *A,* preceding 1:1; *B,* after 3:13; *C* and *D,* after 4:17; *E,* after 8:12; and *F,* after 10:3.

*Connection with Canonical Esther.* These additions subject the canonical text to a substantial theological transfusion. Unlike canonical Esther, God's name now surfaces (often!) and God is portrayed in traditional Jewish terms as omnipotent (13:9), righteous (14:7), the God of Abraham (14:18), and Israel's redeemer in the Exodus (13:16). The prayers in *C* are unmistakably rich expressions of Jewish piety. Occasionally the Greek text contradicts the Hebrew—Haman is labeled a Macedonian (16:10; compare Esth. 3:1), and the Jewish pogrom is scheduled for the fourteenth rather than thirteenth of Adar (13:6; compare Esth. 3:13). Above all, Jewish-Gentile hostility previously centering around Mordecai and Haman now escalates to cosmic proportions (10:10). This enlarged edition is likely the product of an Egyptian Jew dating near 100 B.C.

J.K.K.

**ESTRANGEMENT.** A term used by PAUL TILLICH to indicate the human state of sin due to the FALL, as portrayed in the symbolic story of Adam and Eve in Genesis. Tillich believes the word "estrangement" better conveys today, in the language of EXISTENTIAL-ISM, the meaning of sin. The human situation, due to the Fall, is one of sin or estrangement, the fact that "man as he exists is not what he essentially is and ought to be." The word "sin" cannot, however, be abandoned since it protects the fact that estrangement is personal and the result of human freedom and responsibility. Thus Tillich says that "man's predicament is estrangement, but his estrangement is sin." The word "estrangement" is preferable to sin in conveying the universal and inescapable fallen state of existence, since popular belief conceives of sin, not as a power that rules the human will, but as "sins," or mere deviations from particular moral law or conventions.

Tillich describes estrangement as "unbelief," as *hubris,* and as "concupiscence." Unbelief is the total turning away from God and toward the self. This disruption of human relations with God results in the turning in upon the self, or what the Greeks called *hubris.* It leads to the self-elevation of persons beyond their finite limits. They make themselves existentially the center of the world. The human unlimited desire to draw the whole of experience and the world into or around the self is concupiscence. This insatiable desire and acquisitiveness can be seen in all aspects of human life, for example, in the self's desire for wealth, power, sexual fulfillment, and knowledge. For Tillich the term ORIGINAL SIN points to the universal fact or destiny of human estrangement. Individual sin is simply the actualization of the universal act of estrangement. The destined or inevitable character of estrangement does not, however, nullify sin as a matter of personal freedom and responsibility.

J.L.

**ETERNAL LIFE.** *See* IMMORTALITY.

**ETHICAL CULTURE SOCIETY.** *See* AMERICAN ETHICAL UNION.

**ETHICS.** Ethics may be understood most comprehensively as reflection on the moral significance of human action. Ethics also includes the results of such reflection in rules of conduct or ways of life. The terms "ethics" and "morals" are derived from Greek and Latin words meaning "customs, conduct, and character." Ethics has come to mean "reflection on values and morality," and may also be called moral philosophy or moral theology. Morals has remained closer to the original denotations relating to the customary behavior of people and communities.

An understanding of the nature and scope of ethics can be derived from (1) major sectors of ethical reflection; (2) its history; (3) important types of ethics; and (4) contemporary tendencies.

*Major Sectors of Ethical Reflection.* (a) *Religious or theological ethics* is ethical reflection and formulation within the context of religious traditions. Jewish and Christian ethics are the dominant forms of religious ethics in the Western tradition. Hindu, Buddhist, Confucian, and Islamic ethics provide examples originating in other cultures. If one or another form of Western ethics is taken as the defining norm of all ethics, then the question may be raised whether there is any Hindu or Buddhist ethics. If, however, ethics is understood as reflection on the moral significance of action in all the varied forms this reflection appears, then ethics is clearly a part of non-Western traditions.

(b) *Philosophical ethics* is reflection on the moral significance of action in rational, philosophical perspective. A major pattern of ethics in ancient Greek and Roman cultures and in the Western tradition, philosophical ethics is often erroneously described by philosophers as the only form of ethics. Religious and philosophical ethics are frequently in close interaction with one another and may be combined in a single thinker.

(c) *Social ethics* is reflection on the moral significance of human action in communities and societies. The focus of social ethics may be on the overall social system, on particular sectors or issues in society, on organizations, or on individual action within social collectivities. Social ethics draws upon the resources of the social and natural sciences as well as upon theological and philosophical ethics.

(d) *Comparative ethics* is study and reflection on the moral significance of action in diverse cultures and social contexts. Comparative perspectives in ethics may be provided by different cultures, different historical periods, or different academic disciplines. Some methodological formulations in comparative ethics are too narrowly Western and rational to be useful for cross-cultural purposes. Cross-disciplinary approaches hold promise of more widely applicable methods.

*History of Ethics.* Reflection on the moral significance of action appears with the dawn of human history and pervades the religious literature of all cultures.

(a) *Hinduism* is the inclusive term designating the variety of religious and moral traditions indigenous to India. Within a monistic reality that is polytheistic, Hinduism teaches that humans are subject to KARMA, the moral law of sowing and reaping. People are bound to a round of rebirth in a social order of higher and lower castes until by goodness of life they enter a higher level of existence called MOKSHA.

(b) *Judaism* emerged among the Hebrew tribes of the Middle East around the twelfth century B.C. under the leadership of Moses. It teaches MONOTHEISM or belief in one God and is based on God's commands as given in the Hebrew Bible and interpreted in the Talmud. The TEN COMMANDMENTS and the proclamation of God's justice and love in the prophets provide the ethical core of the Jewish tradition.

(c) *Buddhism* was founded in India by Siddhartha Gautama (about 563–483 B.C.), the BUDDHA or Enlightened One, and has been a major cultural force in southern and eastern Asia. The DHARMA, as Buddhist theological and ethical teaching is called, holds that human existence is a continuing cycle of death and rebirth. People are born into higher or lower levels of life depending on their deeds in previous lives. Through moral discipline, people can rid themselves of all desire and escape life's pain and suffering into a condition of peace and happiness called NIRVANA.

(d) *Confucianism* derives from the teachings of CONFUCIUS (about 551–479 B.C.) and until recently was the strongest cultural force in China. Though not theistic, Confucianism affirms that the cosmos is a moral and social order to which persons and communities must conform to attain well-being. This order is learned through reason and developed by moral discipline that results in good character, respectful relations, and social harmony.

(e) *Greco-Roman culture* is the context within which ethics as reasoned discourse emerged. SOCRATES (469–399 B.C.), as depicted in the Dialogues of Plato, teaches that the unexamined life is not worth living. Ethical reflection, for Socrates, discloses that all the virtues are interdependent, require knowledge to understand and carry out, and are comprehensible only in terms of the Good. PLATO (427–347 B.C.), continuing the thought of Socrates, affirms that moral action requires insight into oneself, human nature, and the world around. Virtue means knowing the Good and also knowing how to accomplish what is good. The form of the Good comprehends what is true, represents the highest goal of human action, and provides the basis of happiness and fulfillment for humanity.

ARISTOTLE (384–322 B.C.) also teaches an ethics of human realization, with happiness resulting from life governed by reason and moderation. Intellectual virtue comes from learning. Moral virtue comes from practice and habit. Both Plato and Aristotle see humans as social beings and justice as the virtue informing political life. Their ethics is known as eudaemonism. STOICISM, another prominent form of ethics in the Greco-Roman world, teaches that the good is represented in a life of duty and of indifference to pain. Virtue alone brings happiness and results from living according to the law of nature and the divine will, which becomes known through human reason.

(f) *Christianity* emerged from Judaism in the first century A.D. based upon faith in Jesus of Nazareth as Messiah or Christ. Christian ethics derives from Hebrew/Christian Scriptures and deals with principles of human response to God's action in creation, revelation, and redemption. The emphasis is on the covenant of God as providing the context of nature and history into which law, justice, and love are woven as command of God and as condition of human liberation. Christian theology and ethics as they develop integrate elements from Greek and Roman thought into biblical faith.

AUGUSTINE (354–430) relies especially on NEO-PLATONISM. The thought of THOMAS AQUINAS (1225–1274) shows the influence of Aristotle and the Stoic teaching of natural law. MARTIN LUTHER (1483–1546) emphasizes the NT theme of justification by faith as the basis of ethics. In the Reformed tradition, the covenant becomes the foundation for federal theology and ethics that shapes the social and political life of Switzerland, Germany, the Netherlands, Britain, and the United States.

(g) *Islam* was founded by the Prophet MUHAMMAD in A.D. 622 and is based upon the KORAN as the revelation of Allah, the one God, through Muhammad. It exercises great cultural power in the Middle East, across southern Asia and Indonesia, and in Africa. Islam has both Judaism and Christianity as background and shares many traditions with them. The Koran contains stories from the OT and the NT, and the overall pattern of Islamic theology and ethics is similar. The one God, creator of the universe, is just and merciful and requires that humans repent of their wrongdoing and purify themselves in order to reach Paradise after they die. The morals taught in the Koran resemble those of the OT, including the virtues of faith in God, honesty, faithfulness, industry, courage, and generosity. All Muslims have the duty to pray, to give alms, to fast, and to go on pilgrimage to Mecca.

(h) *Modern philosophical ethics* contains diverse movements. Intuitionists like Cudworth, Shaftesbury, and Hutcheson maintain that there is an inborn moral sense in humans that leads them to act on values beyond immediate self-interest. Empiricists like LOCKE and Hobbes reject the notion of moral sense as inborn and view ethics as based upon the evaluation of experience. KANT, one of the most influential modern philosophers, is an idealist who bases ethics on ultimate principles derived rationally. Utilitarians like BENTHAM, James Mill, and John Stuart Mill ground ethics on the notion of the greatest good for the greatest number. An instrumentalist like JOHN DEWEY relates ethics to human capabilities for choosing among alternative courses of action by evaluating the results to be achieved. Contemporary philosophical ethics usually divides the field into descriptive ethics, normative ethics, and metaethics. The first is concerned with describing moral action; the second propounds moral norms to guide action; the third, metaethics, focuses on the analysis of moral concepts or language.

*Types of Ethics.* For purposes of classification, it may be helpful to delineate the most important types of ethical theory.

(a) *Teleological ethics* deals with purposes to be achieved, values to be fulfilled, and results to be attained. By this means, action is evaluated and directed. Teleological ethics is consequentialist in that it looks to the consequences of action as the primary basis of evaluation. Aristotle and Thomas Aquinas illustrate teleological ethics; both view action as having some good as its end and to be evaluated in terms of its goals. Hedonists in pursuing pleasure and utilitarians seeking the greatest good for the greatest number are also teleological or consequentialist in ethics, though they differ from each other and from Aristotelians in purposes, values, and criteria.

(b) *Deontological ethics* focuses on laws and rules to be obeyed, duties to be followed, and moral obligations to be fulfilled. Deontological ethics is concerned not with results but with obedience. Kant represents this type. "Let justice be done," he said, "though the

heavens fall." The rational will acts according to duty and obeys moral law without consideration of the consequences.

(c) *Ontological ethics* is based not on ends or laws but on the reality of the world to which human action responds. Confucian ethics, based upon a cosmic moral order guiding human behavior, illustrates this type. Buddhist ethics also begins with the moral reality of humans bound to a cycle of rebirth and the response required to achieve liberation. Stoic ethics starts with the moral law built into the natural order and into human nature and develops through rational perception of natural law and action in accord with it.

(d) *Kathekontological ethics* seeks the appropriate action as that which fits in with the actions that precede and follow. It is not goals or rules or cosmic reality but the context of action that controls ethical reflection. John Dewey's instrumentalism and Joseph Fletcher's SITUATION ETHICS illustrate this type, though it is H. RICHARD NIEBUHR who provides the most comprehensive account of it and puts it forward as a supplement to teleological and deontological forms of ethics.

(e) *Federal ethics,* building on Niebuhr's suggestion, combines the four types above rather than choosing one and rejecting the others. Purposes and consequences, principles and law, cosmic order, and the context into which actions fit are of equal importance for ethical reflection and responsible action. Though ethical traditions and individual thinkers seldom fit neatly into one type, most emphasize one of the first four types. In Greco-Roman culture, Plato illustrates best the comprehensive form of ethics. All the types appear in biblical ethics and may be viewed as integrally related in the covenant of God. Among contemporary moral thinkers, H. Richard Niebuhr combines the alternative methods most effectively into a federal pattern, though publication of his total vision was not accomplished before his death.

*Contemporary Trends.* Sweeping changes are occurring today within all traditions, primarily because of the global expansion and interpenetration of diverse cultures. These changes place ethical reflection in a wider, pluralistic context. Emerging configurations appear to be the following.

(a) *Attention to wholeness* increasingly characterizes ethical reflection. Dealing with experience by means of academic specialties is being questioned, and cross-disciplinary attempts to recover wholeness of perspective are becoming ordinary in ethics as well as in other areas. The preoccupation with theory and rational method in ethics is fading, and experience derived from practice in specific contexts is being integrated into ethical reflection.

Empirical and historical approaches are being combined in the search for comprehensive understanding of problems, contexts, and relations. Tendencies to reduce ethics to dilemmas, choices, and moral reasoning is less frequent, while the use of cases is on the increase. The recovery of tradition, faith, story, and character as central for ethical reflection is well under way. Indeed, ethics is participating in the general seeking for wholeness of vision that is moving beyond academic specialization and methodological dichotomies characteristic of the critical tradition and is leading toward a post-critical period in human thought.

(b) *Convergence and comparison of ethical traditions* is a second trend in contemporary ethical reflection. Cross-cultural contacts, intended and unintended; the meeting of religious traditions, in the ecumenical movement and elsewhere; and the coming together of diverse social groups are having impact in all sectors of society, especially in ethics and in areas concerned with values. These contacts are producing not ethical relativism, as some fear, so much as convergence and comparison of ethical traditions. The cooperation of Christian and Jewish leaders on scriptural, historical, doctrinal, and ethical concerns is leading toward reinterpretation of traditional positions.

Disagreement on basic ethical issues, such as natural law between Roman Catholics and Protestants, no longer appears impossible to resolve, though conflict over such actions as abortion remains intense. Convergence may be seen also in the "creative borrowing" among Eastern and Western traditions, and there are fewer attempts to put forward simplistic dichotomies as ethical answers, for example, East or West, Christianity or Communism, Aristotle or Nietzsche. Significant work is also developing in comparative ethics, and, though issues of method are stubbornly difficult, efforts bringing together different disciplinary, historical, and cultural perspectives are promising.

(c) *Greater consideration of the social context and the natural environment* is a third trend in ethics today. Focus on individual ethics and ethical theory has, over the past century, tended to isolate ethics from the developing natural and social sciences. The rise of social ethics in recent decades has done much to bring ethical reflection into closer relations with other disciplines. Social context and environment are receiving increased attention, in terms of relations with appropriate disciplines and also by including perspectives of people operating in particular social sectors, a trend illustrated in bioethics, in environmental ethics, and in organizational ethics. Drawing on wider resources in this manner contributes substantially to ethics, especially by affecting profoundly its scope and methods.

(d) *Recognition of the importance of liberation* is a fourth trend in ethics. Developments in every area of the globe emphasize ethical concerns as permeating all aspects of human life. Attempts to evade issues of value with a facade of academic objectivity or to escape the demands of justice by such theoretical distinctions as "descriptive" and "metaethical" have become increasingly difficult. LIBERATION looms as an unavoidable element of ethics and a challenge to

greater, rather than less, excellence of effort. Ethnic, Third World, and feminist perspectives have brought liberation to the forefront of attention. But liberation is perceived more and more as equally important for policy ethics, environmental concerns, issues of the political economy, ethics in the health fields, and the ethics of organizations. Liberation, in its varied dimension, has been a constant concern in the religious traditions of East and West and has become a major way that issues of justice are posed today.

These tendencies point to the changes taking place in ethics as it emerges from academic isolation and from its preoccupation with theory and rational method into fruitful relationships with other disciplines and with areas of social dynamism. As a consequence of these changes, ethics gives promise of recovering the breadth it had in earlier times and of making significant contributions to all sectors of society.                                                   C.Mc.

**ETHIOPIA.** The country south of Egypt and west of the Red Sea known in the biblical era as CUSH (Gen. 2:13; 10:6-8) or Nubia. Cush became independent of Egypt around 1000 B.C. and established its capital at Napata on the Nile River. In the eighth century B.C. the rulers of Napata conquered Egypt and exercised control over it during the Twenty-fifth Dynasty. Later, an Ethiopian army fought King Asa of Judah, but was defeated (II Chr. 14:9-15). One of the Nubian rulers, Tirhakah (Taharka) (690–664 B.C.), is mentioned in Isaiah 37:9 and II Kings 19:9 as one of Hezekiah's allies in his rebellion against Sennacherib.

Candace was the family name of a line of Ethiopian queens mentioned in conjunction with the ETHIOPIAN EUNUCH. The subsequent religious history of Ethiopia is represented by the ABYSSINIAN CHURCH.
                                                           W.G.

**ETHIOPIAN EUNUCH.** The single allusion to this person is found in Acts 8:26-40. Philip, one of the seven (evangelists? deacons?; see Acts 6:3; 21:8), is directed to a rendezvous on a desert road with the man described thus: "an Ethiopian, a EUNUCH, a minister of the Candace, queen of the Ethiopians, in charge of all her treasure."

The man in question was evidently an attendant in the royal harem, who had risen to a position of some responsibility. Eunuchs were literally "castrated" men. The Greek term *eunouchos* is, however, ambiguous. The origin of the term is from *eunēn echō,* "to keep the bed"; hence the sexual connotation. But the Hebrew *sārîs* may derive from a cognate Assyrian term, "he who is head," that is, in favor with the king and so a trusted official at court.

His place of origin is given as Ethiopia, the ancient kingdom of Nubia extending from Aswan in Egypt to the junction of the Nile River near the city of Khartoum. The Candace ruled this land centered in northern Nubia (modern Sudan) rather than present-day Abyssinia (Ethiopia). It was evidently part of the

Jewish Dispersion; the eunuch was reading Isaiah 53 in the Greek Bible. His physical defect placed him outside the life of Judaism (Deut. 23:1), but he may have been a "god-fearer," that is, one interested in and attracted to the Jewish faith but not a proselyte or convert.

His conversion to the Christian faith and baptism are described in some detail as he made a confession of Jesus as "Son of God" (Acts 8:37 KJV). Perhaps Luke saw in this story a fulfillment of Psalm 68:31: "let Ethiopia hasten to stretch out her hands to God."

R.M.

**EUCHARIST.** The chief sacrament of the Christian church, derived from the LAST SUPPER, which was either a Passover meal (the Synoptic Gospels) or a blessing meal (John), celebrated by Jesus the evening before his crucifixion. Believers are to eat the bread and drink of the cup in remembrance of him. (*See also* HOLY COMMUNION.)

J.C.

**EUCHARISTIC VESTMENTS.** The priestly garments worn at the celebration of the Eucharist, Mass, or Holy Communion. These ordinarily include the alb, chasuble, and stole, or the cassock, surplice, and stole, over which the chasuble is placed just before the consecration of the elements.

J.C.

**EUGENICS.** From the Greek *eugenes,* meaning "well-born," eugenics is the application of scientific knowledge and techniques to improve the hereditary qualities of a nation or other group of people. It has long been known that selective breeding of plants and animals can lead to the development of stronger and better strains, but whenever one considers the extension of such techniques to human beings, grave moral problems arise. When the Nazis advocated such selective breeding, there were howls of indignation from the free nations, on the grounds that sex and marriage were being reduced to the level of plant and animal breeding. Furthermore, the Nazi plan included the extermination of what were considered undesirable types and had strong racist overtones. Now, however, even countries with very different ideologies from the Nazi one have to face problems of population control. How would one decide on the types of human beings at whom to aim—strong, healthy bodies, acute minds, gentle dispositions, or what? What methods would be acceptable? The possibilities today are far wider than in Hitler's time, when the only solution would have been restriction of procreation to well-matched "superior" couples. Do we indiscriminately accept artificial insemination, sperm banks, womb renting, test tube conceptions, and whatever developments may come along in genetic engineering? Or, on the negative side, sterilization of those deemed unfit to be

parents and abortion of substandard children? Not only are the moral questions and the opportunities for abuse horrendous, this whole way of looking at human procreation threatens Christian and personal conceptions of sex, marriage, and family. (*Compare* BIOETHICS.)

J.M.

**EUNUCH.** From the Greek word *eunouchos,* meaning "guardian of the bed" or "chamberlain," which in turn is a translation of the Hebrew word *sārīs,* possibly meaning "the one in charge." The earliest sense of the term, therefore, obviously involves only a bureaucratic or official function, saying nothing about the physical character or quality of the person concerned.

In the sense of "castrated male," however, eunuch has a very ancient history. Castration was practiced not only in later times for obvious reasons with regard to the custodians of royal or noble harems, but also for less obvious reasons: docility, dedication, heightened professional concern among them. There were, of course, still other reasons that did not necessarily obtain in ancient time, such as *bel canto.*

As far as we know, officials were not castrated in Egypt, therefore the *sārīsim* (ones in charge) of Genesis 37:36; 39:1; 40:2, 7, may have been simply servitors. On the other hand, the biblical writer may have thought of these in terms of the Mesopotamian eunuchs with which he was more familiar. Castration was practiced by the Assyrians, Babylonians, and Persians; and doubtless eunuch, in the physical as well as political sense, is understood in such passages as Esther 2:14; II Kings 20:18; 9:32 (Jezebel's court). Possibly also Jeremiah 38:7 (Ebedmelech the Ethiopian). However, the numerous references to eunuchs in the OT and NT (such as Acts 8:27-39, the minister of the queen of Ethiopia) are ambiguous regarding the etymological or derived sense of "eunuch." References like I Kings 22:9; II Kings 8:6; etc.; referring to Israelite officials, almost certainly do not envisage eunuchs in the physical sense. The law of Deuteronomy 23:1-2 explicitly excludes eunuchs from the community of Israel. The later prophetic text Isaiah 56:3 nullifies this law in view of the eschatological future.

In Matthew 19:12 the "eunuchs for the sake of the kingdom of heaven" have been traditionally taken to be those who have forgone the state of marriage for the sake of a higher good.

B.V.

**EUPHRATES.** Known to us by its Greek name and to the OT writers by the Hebrew name *Prat* (Jer. 51:63) or as "The Great River" (Gen. 15:18; Josh. 1:4), this is the largest river of western Asia. From its sources in the district of Ararat in Armenia (now eastern Turkey), the Euphrates flows southwestward to a point less than one hundred miles east of the

Courtesy of William Sanford La Sor

*The Euphrates River near its source in the Armenian highlands*

Mediterranean coast of Syria. Near this point is the site of Carchemish, where Nebuchadnezzar achieved his decisive victory over Pharaoh Neco II in 605 B.C. (compare Jer. 46:2). A few miles further south the course of the river turns to the southeast, and it continues on its way to the Persian Gulf. Its entire length is about seventeen hundred miles, approximately three-fourths that of the Mississippi River. Along its banks were situated many of the great centers of ancient culture: Dura-Europas and the Amorite city of Mari in the middle of its course, Babylon and the Sumerian cities of Erech and Ur in the south.

As it enters its swampy delta area, the Euphrates joins the TIGRIS River and flows from thence into the sea through the often-disputed waterway known as the Shatt-el-Arab. The great alluvial flood plain that lies between the two great rivers (MESOPOTAMIA) supported three of the greatest civilizations of antiquity—the Sumerian, the Akkadian, and the Babylonian.

W.S.T.

EUSEBIUS OF CAESAREA (260–340). The great church historian of the fourth century, who to this day remains our most important source for the knowledge of Christian antiquity. Born about A.D. 260, he knew both the times of persecution and the period after Constantine. He was an admirer of Origen, to whose library in Caesarea he had access. With the help of that library, and of other books he gathered, he set out to narrate the history of Christianity up to his time. His view of that history was such that CONSTANTINE and his acceptance of Christianity appeared as the culmination of God's plans. Indeed, God had provided both the Roman Empire and the Christian faith, and in Constantine the two had finally come together. For this reason he portrayed the earlier persecutions as essentially a gross misunderstanding on the part of Roman authorities and was rather uncritical of Constantine himself. As a result of these views, and also of his Origenism, he tended to

spiritualize Christian eschatology and to disparage those earlier writers who had spoken in apocalyptic and chiliastic terms of a time when God would rule over the earth. Some modern historians, aware of the bases on which Eusebius selected and evaluated his sources, feel the need to correct some of his views on the early history of Christianity. Still, he remains the main source for the knowledge of that early history.

J.G.

EUTHANASIA. Euthanasia is an act through which, by request, a person in painful terminal illness may be eased into death. It is often referred to as "mercy killing." The meaning of the word, in Greek "an easy death," has been extended to encompass the action of accomplishing it. Medical opinion disagrees on a definition of clinical death and on whether there is irreversibility in the process of death.

The Judaic-Christian ethic rejects a utilitarian view of taking some lives in order to preserve others, affirming that life is the gift of the creator, God, who alone can release a person to death. The Christian tradition affirms some value in suffering, when it can be endured with grace and courage, but this is no reason for prolonging suffering. Steps may be taken to reduce suffering, even though this shortens life. Whether such steps extend to "benign neglect" is a controversial issue. Several situations brought about by modern medicine raise the question, such as the comatose patient who, as far as is presently known, will never recover, and the conscious patient kept alive by extraordinary means. Christian moral theory today tends to be situational more than legalistic, but subjective factors may obscure the issue for individual decision making. If death is a process, many factors bring about its completion. If it is an event, then the signs need to be clearly definable. (*Compare* BIOETHICS)

I.C.

EUTYCHUS. A young man of Troas, who fell asleep during a late night sermon by Paul, fell out of a third-story window, and was "taken up dead" (Acts 20:9). Paul declared him still alive. Whether he actually died is debated; Luke apparently thought so. Appropriately his name means "lucky."

J.R.M.

EVANGELICAL ALLIANCE. An international, interdenominational association founded in London in 1846 "to associate and concentrate the strength of an enlightened PROTESTANTISM against the encroachments of Popery and Puseyism, and to promote the interests of Scriptural Christianity." Essentially it was an organizational embodiment and extension of the EVANGELICAL UNITED FRONT.

In the United States the organization was an expression of anti-Roman Catholic nativism on the one hand and a demonstration of Protestant unity on the other. Full American participation was dampened, however, by a clause barring slaveholders from membership and by disintegration of the Congregational-Presbyterian Plan of Union. Leaders included Robert Baird, Edward Norris Kirk, LYMAN BEECHER, Abel Stevens, Samuel S. Schumucker, PHILIP SCHAFF, and JOSIAH STRONG (general secretary 1886–98).

The organization declined in the twentieth century and became more conservative, eventually being transformed into the World Evangelical Fellowship at a 1951 joint meeting of the British Evangelical Alliance and the American NATIONAL ASSOCIATION OF EVANGELICALS.

N.H.

## EVANGELICAL ALLIANCE OF GREAT BRITAIN.
A British alliance of generally conservative, free churches, founded in London in 1846, and still very active in evangelism and missionary work. Originally formed to combat Catholicism and movements in the Church of England that evangelicals thought unscriptural, the alliance promoted spiritual unity, helped persecuted Protestants, did prison evangelism, and overseas service. Although a British organization, fifty denominations represented by clergymen and laymen from different parts of the world were part of its founding, and the alliance is associated with the NATIONAL ASSOCIATION OF EVANGELICALS in the United States and similar groups in European countries and in Asian nations.

The doctrinal basis of the alliance include the divine inspiration and authority of the Bible; the right of private interpretation of the Scriptures; the doctrine of the Holy Trinity; the utter depravity of human nature (original sin); the Incarnation; Christ's atonement for sin; justification by faith alone; sanctification through the Holy Spirit; the immortality of the soul; the resurrection of the body; the final judgment by Jesus Christ; and the divine institution of the ministry. The universal week of prayer was begun by the alliance in 1846, observed during the first week of January. The week of prayer for Christian unity is now observed around the world.

J.C.

## EVANGELICAL AND REFORMED CHURCH.
See UNITED CHURCH OF CHRIST.

## EVANGELICAL COUNSELS.
In Roman Catholic tradition, superior guidelines in addition to the usual Ten Commandments for a more perfect way of life. Derived from Matthew 19:16-22, I Corinthians 7, and other NT passages, evangelical COUNSELS came to mean keeping vows of poverty, chastity, and obedience, usually taken by Roman Catholic clergy, monks, and nuns. The practice of these additional virtues was regarded as a means of earning greater spiritual perfection and merit on the way to salvation.

Hermas, Tertullian, Cyprian, Ambrose, Pelagius, Augustine, Aquinas, and other early and medieval church theologians wrote of higher and lower levels of

Christian living. Luther, in the sixteenth century, interpreted these biblical commandments not as opportunities for earning merit but as divine instruments to convict human beings of sinfulness. Thus, Luther rejected any division of divine commands into higher and lower. Human sinfulness, according to Luther, thus undercuts all efforts to win merit. In *The Freedom of the Christian Man* (1520), Luther maintained we are justified by faith, and that we are to keep the law not to elevate ourselves but to express love and gratitude toward God and others for what God has already done in justifying us.

C.M.

## EVANGELICALISM.
An ancient Christian term, derived from the Greek of the NT, *euangelion*, the good news, meaning the "gospel," or God's good news of the promise of salvation to all who have faith in Christ.

Evangelicalism is a broad term, based on the concept of the proclamation of the gospel, as recounted in the NT. Since the sixteenth-century Reformation, the term has generally been applied exclusively to Protestants, but since Vatican II and the rise of the Roman Catholic charismatic movement, there are those called Catholic Evangelicals as well.

From the time of Martin Luther (1483–1546), Evangelicalism has been a term used of Protestants, especially for those who adhere to the Augsburg Confession or the Heidelberg Catechism (Lutheran or Reformed or the Union churches). The reformers always called themselves Evangelical Christians, and the Lutheran churches (at least at the congregational level) refer to themselves as Evangelical Lutherans to this day. The term used in this way means adherence to Christ and the Bible as the only rule of faith and practice in the church.

Other than the Lutherans who settled in America, however, the term Evangelical has generally been used in a much different way. Evangelicalism became the name for the revivalism that characterized American Reformed and free-church Protestantism (especially Baptists and sectarians) from the time of Jonathan Edwards (eighteenth century) to Billy Sunday and Billy Graham in the twentieth century (see FREE CHURCHES). This movement differed widely from Lutheran and Reformed Christianity in that it stressed religious experience and demanded a conscious, decisive, individual conversion. American Evangelicalism, therefore, tended to de-emphasize confessions of faith, church order, liturgy, sacramental theology, systematic theology and biblical scholarship, and, after the last half of the nineteenth century, turned away from the application of Christian principles to social and political issues. This was not the case earlier in the century when many evangelicals had spoken out on slavery, temperance, and other social issues.

Sometimes the term Evangelicalism is used to contrast Protestant conservatives with Protestant liberals, called modernists in the 1920s and 1930s. Since the middle of the twentieth century some Protestant conservatives ("rational fundamentalists" as opposed to "cultic fundamentalists") have called for a reform of FUNDAMENTALISM. Men like CARL F. H. HENRY (of *Christianity Today*) have rightly criticized the lack of social concern, the absence of scholarship, and the lack of serious interest in systematic theology among Fundamentalists or "Evangelicals," as they are called in America. These critics became known by the 1970s as the New (or Neo-) Evangelicals. The New Evangelicals are not unified in outlook, ranging from moderate Fundamentalists to the more socially active Pietists of *Sojourners* magazine. Most Neo-Evangelicals stress the authority of the Bible although they disagree over the inerrancy of the Bible (a recent development, called the "Battle for the Bible" by Harold Linsell); stress evangelism; the need for personal conversion; and the need for more biblical and theological scholarship (although some Evangelicals do not accept much of the evidence of modern biblical and theological scholarship).

Evangelicalism has been characterized by a multitude of denominations in America (outside of the Southern Baptist Convention). Evangelicals have made many efforts, throughout the nineteenth and twentieth centuries, at interdenominational cooperation on the foundation of shared religious experience and doctrine. American Protestants joined together to found the AMERICAN BOARD OF COMMISSIONERS FOR FOREIGN MISSIONS in 1812, the AMERICAN BIBLE SOCIETY in 1815, and the EVANGELICAL UNITED FRONT. Although the Lutheran tradition was called Evangelical in contrast to the Calvinist churches, which were called Reformed, the books and speeches of Samuel Simon Schmucker of Gettysburg, Pennsylvania, and of Philip Schaff of Mercersburg, Pennsylvania (the "Mercersburg theology"), stressed the common heritage of Evangelical (that is, Reformation) Protestantism. After the deaths of Schmucker and Schaff, the new stress on the SOCIAL GOSPEL (following Walter Rauschenbusch) led to the founding of the Federal Council of Churches and later to the National Council of Churches. To many conservative Protestants, the councils were too liberal in theology, and they moved into the quiestistic, uninvolved world of American Fundamentalism. Although characterized by anti-intellectualism, ethnocentricism, nationalistic isolationism, biblical literalism, and revivalism, some of the major leaders of the Fundamentalist movement were scholars. Men like BENJAMIN WARFIELD and John Gresham Machen were learned but recoiled from the conclusions of modern biblical and theological scholarship. Ultimately, these theologians provided a transition to Carl F. H. Henry and others who developed the New Evangelicalism.

In 1941, several small Protestant churches that felt uncomfortable with the lack of social conscience among Fundamentalists formed the NATIONAL ASSOCIATION OF EVANGELICALS. In 1943, at Chicago, the N.A.E. adopted a statement of faith. This confession underscored the inspiration and authority of the Bible, the doctrine of the Holy Trinity, the Virgin Birth, divinity and bodily resurrection of Jesus Christ, and his atonement through his death for our salvation. The members of the N.A.E. do appreciate the need for Christian unity but generally have kept out of the ecumenical movement (including the National Council of Churches and the World Council of Churches) believing that ecumenicity means a downplaying of Christian doctrine for the sake of organizational cooperation. The N.A.E. members stand in the middle, between the liberalism and Neo-orthodoxy of the mainstream churches (and today, the liberation theology and social activism of the larger churches) and the Fundamentalists. The Neo-Evangelicals are thus in large measure drawn from the members of the N.A.E.

The Evangelicals are the heirs of continental PIETISM, transplanted to America through Lutheran, Reformed, Mennonite, and Moravian Christians from Germany and Switzerland, and by the Methodist REVIVALS of the eighteenth and nineteenth centuries. The Methodist movement itself was an outgrowth of Pietism. Evangelicals, like Pietists, have differed from the major churches—Anglican, Lutheran, Reformed, Roman Catholic, and Orthodox—in their insistence on a personal conversion experience, the interpretation of the gospel of salvation by faith in the atoning death of Christ alone, and in the de-emphasis on the need for or saving efficacy of the sacraments.

This emphasis on the sacraments as symbols rather than as a means of grace grows out of the stress put on personal religious experience. This stress divides Evangelicals from both the Catholic and Reformation churches and is also susceptible to a sectarian impulse. The Neo-Evangelical movement, particularly in its most liberal and open expressions, is a sign that this strand of American PROTESTANTISM may be making the transition from sect to church, described by H. Richard Niebuhr in *The Social Sources of Denominationalism.*                                                        J.C.

**EVANGELICAL UNITED FRONT.** The 1801 Congregational-Presbyterian Plan of Union and the Second GREAT AWAKENING created the climate for the Evangelical United Front, which swept antebellum America with a millennial crusade for missions, moral renewal, and humanitarian reform. Leaders included revivalists LYMAN BEECHER and CHARLES FINNEY, reformers Theodore Weld and the Grimké sisters, missionary organizers such as Sarah Platt Doremus, and financiers Arthur and Lewis Tappan.

The Front was apparent in such ecumenical efforts as the AMERICAN BOARD OF COMMISSIONERS FOR

FOREIGN MISSIONS (1810), which spawned the myriad denominational mission societies; the AMERICAN BIBLE SOCIETY(1816); AMERICAN TRACT SOCIETY (1823); American Sunday School Union (1824); American Home Missionary Society (1826); American Society for the Promotion of Temperance (1826), which became the American Temperance Union in 1836; the American Colonization Society (1827), which gave way to the American Anti-Slavery Society (1833). Most of these organizations held annual meetings each May in New York City.

They represent only the most visible of the cooperative efforts to revive the church and reform the world. Local efforts reached out to the poor, prostitutes, the blind, the deaf, and the insane. Protestants hoped to create a model Christian society in anticipation of Christ's coming.

N.H.

**EVANGELIST.** A person who brings or announces good news, and specifically "the gospel" of God or Jesus Christ. The etymology of the word relates it to "evangel," the good news, or in Greek *euangelion.*

There are only three occurrences of "evangelist" in the NT: Acts 21:8, used of Philip who still retained the title when he lived in Caesarea with his family, following his earlier work as a missionary preacher in Samaria and beyond (Acts 8:4-40); II Timothy 4:5 and Ephesians 4:11.

Second Timothy 4:5 can be easily interpreted since it appears to be a descriptive term applied to Timothy by the author. Timothy is exhorted to "do the work of an evangelist" in executing his duties as a MINISTER (I Tim. 4:6) in the congregation at Ephesus.

In Ephesians 4:11, in addition to "apostles" and "prophets" (drawn from I Cor. 12:28; Rom. 12:5 ff.) the writer includes "evangelists" along with "pastors" and "teachers" as the exercise of ministerial functions in the church. On the other hand, the context in Ephesians may be taken to denote the setting up of a distinctive office of evangelist alongside "apostle" and "prophet," terms that enjoy an exalted status in that letter (Eph. 2:20; 3:5) and in the *Didache,* an early Church Order.

Later, "apostle" and "evangelist" became analogous according to Eusebius' *Church History:* "there were even yet many evangelists of the word eager to use their divinely inspired zeal, after the example of the apostles." In the Church Fathers the term has another meaning, namely the Gospel writers, for example, Tertullian in *de Praescr.* and *de Corona* calls Luke both an apostle and an evangelist.

R.M.

**EVE.** See ADAM AND EVE.

**EVENSONG.** A traditional English name for VESPERS, the Anglican term for the office of evening prayer. The Book of Common Prayer of 1549 used the term evensong, but the 1552 edition used evening prayer. The 1662 edition once more used evensong for a service formed out of vespers and compline.

J.C.

**EVIDENCES OF CHRISTIANITY.** *See* APOLOGETICS.

**EVIL.** *The Philosophical Problem of Evil.* In principle, the concept of evil and its close relation, creaturely suffering, would not be problematical were there no concept of the good. However, since most philosophical systems posit a beneficent prime mover or ultimate being, the very existence of evil poses a severe challenge to the most fundamental premise. If God is both good and powerful, why would God permit evil and human suffering to spoil the beauty of the divine creation? One traditional approach, that of monism, denies the ultimate reality of evil in the name of a finally all-encompassing divine reality. Everything participates in the Godhead, and since God is good, evil is only illusory. Another traditional solution to the problem of evil is radical DUALISM, which pits goodness and the good God in a timeless struggle against evil and the anti-God, Satan. The predominant approach in Western thought has been to affirm the absolute sovereignty and transcendent goodness of God on the one hand, while acknowledging God's radical separateness from the creaturely world on the other. A world that is wholly other than God is both imperfect and free, capable of doing evil but also of seeking liberation from the grip of evil. This traditional outlook has been described as theologically monistic and anthropologically dualistic.

The philosophical and religious enterprise of reconciling the perfect goodness of God with the presence of evil in the world is called theodicy. Theodicy has traditionally dealt with evil under at least four headings, each of which requires its own precisely expressed explanation: sin or moral evil, suffering, bad luck or natural evil, and imperfection or finitude. Philosophers have addressed the problem of theodicy under one or more of these headings at least since Epicurus (about 341-270 B.C.), who taught "Is [God] willing to prevent evil, but not able? Then he is impotent. Is he able, but not willing? Then he is malevolent. Is he both able and willing? Whence then is evil?" Since that early time, other notable philosophers have addressed the problem of evil, particularly PLATO, John Stuart Mill, G. W. LEIBNITZ, and IMMANUEL KANT.

*Evil as a Theological Problem.* All of the world's great religions have found it necessary to address the problem of evil in their most fundamental writings. Hinduism, for example, treats all reality monistically. Evil only looks evil, but it participates in the good cosmic reality of the divine. Zoroastrianism, on the other hand, prefers the dualistic solution, and pits the good god Ahura Mazda in cosmic and eternal struggle against the evil god Ahriman. After the biblical writers themselves, one of the first theologians of the Judeo-Christian tradition to address the problem in a major way was AUGUSTINE (A.D. 354–430). Building upon the Neoplatonic philosopher PLOTINUS, Augustine taught that evil can be understood as privation, the corruption of originally good but changeable beings. In their freedom, humans chose to turn away from God and from their best nature. Out of that absurd but self-grounded choice has flowed all evil, even natural evil, such as death and disease. A second description of evil, also derived from Plotinus and fundamental to Augustine, is the aesthetic notion that from the point of view of God—who has, after all, the entire picture—there is no such thing as evil. Cockroaches and mosquitoes, earthquakes and tornadoes, all have their special purposes within the great chain of being. Even in our deaths we can and do glorify God by participating in the perfect rhythm of the created order. The Augustinian theodicy has dominated the thought of the Western religious tradition. It was accepted and reformulated by the thirteenth-century scholastic, Thomas Aquinas; the sixteenth-century reformers Luther and Calvin; and even the great eighteenth-century Jewish philosopher Leibnitz.

In his work *Theodicy* (1710), Leibnitz offered an updated version of the Augustinian position in his contention that this is the best of all possible worlds, not because it is free of evil, but because any other world imaginable would contain even more evil. No more dramatic expression of this aesthetic view ever emerged out of our Western tradition than that of the English poet Alexander Pope (1688–1744):

All nature is but art unknown to thee:
All chance, direction which thou canst not see;
All discord, harmony not understood:
All partial evil, universal good;
And spite of pride, in erring reason's spite,
One truth is clear. Whatever is, is right.

Criticism of this traditional theodicy has centered on two issues, the freedom of the human will and the ultimate outcome of the struggle between good and evil. In regard to the former, questions such as these have been raised: Why would an originally good and perfect human being ever have chosen to do evil? Does that not suggest an imperfection in the creature after all? However, FREE WILL must not be regarded as an imperfection, but as a jewel in the crown of God's beloved creature. As to the ultimate outcome, Augustine and, following him, Calvin, held that God finally overcomes all evil, and at the Judgment Day God demonstrates both goodness by redeeming sinners and justice by condemning evildoers. These choices are not dictated by human behavior, but by God in an eternal decree. Such a view, of course, suggests that God is less than perfectly good, because a perfectly good God would not sentence any beloved creature to eternal damnation.

At least since Irenaeus (about A.D. 120–202), Eastern Christianity has operated with a different type of theodicy. In this tradition, the effect of the FALL is reduced by the denial that humankind was ever perfect. In the garden, Adam was childlike in relation to God. A declaration of independence, expressed as rebellion, was a necessary step in the maturation of the race, just as it remains so in the maturation of individuals from childhood to adulthood. Only truly independent, self-sufficient beings can enter into full relationships with one another and with God. Moral evil is thus almost inevitable, but humanity can, with the help of God, exhibited and assured in the Christ-event, move toward perfection, since humanity has always been perfectable.

*The Biblical Address to the Problem of Evil and Suffering.* From the foregoing discussion, it is clear that the biblical motif of the Fall of humankind, identified above all with the story of Adam, Eve, and the serpent in Genesis 3, but transformed by Paul in Romans 5:12-21 and I Corinthians 15:21-23, 45-49 into the negative image of the Christ-event, has been a theme of utmost significance for all subsequent discussion of the matter. With the rise of historical criticism, it has come to be recognized that the account of the Fall, far from being a historical record, is actually an early narrative theological rendition of the basic notion that a willful human act of sin destroyed the right relationship between God and human beings and set in motion an agelong quest to recover the lost state of innocence. It follows, then, that the Bible never really purports to answer in any historical sense the questions: Where did evil come from? and How could a good God allow it? Discussion of the biblical treatment of the problem of evil has therefore shifted toward empirical and prescriptive addresses to the problem.

In the biblical response to the practical question, What can we do about evil? four components can be identified. (a) The world in which we live is a world of divinely established orders. Within this world of orders, human beings are given a sphere of competency within which they are charged by God to "be fruitful and multiply, and fill the earth and subdue it; and have dominion . . ." (Gen. 1:28). But that competency has to be exercised in relation to the divinely ordained orders. Laws of cause and effect operate in connection with events in this world. Indeed, human initiatives may be described as "destiny-producing deeds," for they unleash their own consequences for weal or woe. This outlook is especially deeply rooted in the wisdom tradition of the Bible. The writers of the Proverbs know that even though human preparations intersect with the divinely established orders ("the horse is made ready for the day of battle, but the victory belongs to the Lord," Prov. 21:31), at the same time, nothing is going to happen in the struggle against evil if people do not shoulder their responsibility and plan to act effectively within the elaborate network of cause and effect ("By wise guidance you can wage your war, and in abundance of counselors there is victory," Prov. 24:6). God established the world and the orders within it, and yet human beings can authentically exercise their free will within that world.

(b) God, however, does not withdraw from the human community as it goes about its exercise of responsibility. The book of Job is a primary witness to the continuing role of God within the sphere of human competence. Job suffers absurd evil, which to his friends has the outward appearance of punishment for sin. But Job rejects all connection between his suffering and punishment (and thus, well in advance, rejects the Augustinian principle that evil in the world consists of only two types, sin or the punishment for sin). In the end, Job's position is vindicated. The Lord speaks with him out of the whirlwind, acknowledging culpability neither on his part nor on Job's, but demonstrating that he who is the Creator of all the spheres is also Emmanuel, the one who is "present with us." This means that those who suffer the effects of evil in the world do so not alone, but in the company of God.

(c) Occasions of suffering become occasions to glorify God. This is not to say that moments of suffering are—as the Augustinian aesthetic understanding of evil would have it—simply tributes to the magnificent moral order of the universe, when they are seen in the context of God's big picture. On the contrary, it is to say that when confronted with evil and suffering, the human being has the opportunity to respond with good qualities such as realism, courage, trust, and jauntiness, which are inspired by the helping presence of God. The story of the man born blind in John 9 is a classic illustration of this third component of the biblical response to evil. When asked whether the man's blindness was a result of his own sin or that of his parents, Jesus denied both causalities, and taught that it simply provided an occasion in which "the works of God might be made manifest in him" (v. 3).

(d) Jesus' own life, death, and resurrection are an extended illustration of this principle. In his very crucifixion, Jesus sets forth an example of how evil can become an occasion for the glorification of God. He does so by accepting the cup given him to drink of, by remaining steadfast in his pain, and by praying for those who persecuted him. God vindicates his faithfulness in the Resurrection.

This analysis of the biblical address to the problem of evil makes most intelligible the famous Pauline teaching: "We know that in everything God works for good with those who love him . . ." (Rom. 8:28). This text is to be understood not as a denial of the reality of evil in some monistic sense, but rather as an expression of the deep conviction that in the rich interaction between free, responsible, and suffering humanity on the one hand and the good and trustworthy God on the other, victory over very real and powerful evil can, in fact, be obtained.     W.S.T.

**EVOLUTION.** The word means "unfolding," and it is usually understood that such an unfolding is both continuous and has a certain direction. Evolution can be considered as proceeding at several levels, and it is useful to distinguish at least three different levels. (1) Most commonly, evolution is taken to mean *biological* evolution. This is a scientific theory, based on empirical evidence and accepted by virtually all serious biologists. (2) Sometimes the term is used for a *cosmological* theory. In this case, the idea is extended to the whole universe, so that not only living things but planetary systems, stars, galaxies, and the wealth of chemical substances have their origins explained in terms of an evolutionary process that has gone on for billions of years. This too is, in the broad sense, a scientific theory, but the evidence is not so clear-cut as in the case of the biological theory, and some cosmologists uphold the theory of a "steady state" universe rather than an evolving one. (3) It is only a step to go on to a *metaphysical* theory of evolution, a speculative rather than a scientific theory, which seeks to account for the whole scheme of things, from subatomic particles to the human mind and even to God in terms of a unitary evolutionary process. We shall consider each of these levels in turn.

The idea of *biological evolution* may have occurred to some of the Greek philosophers, such as Anaximander, who held that living things originated in moisture and that the first humans were like fish in the beginning. Evolutionary ideas were again circulating in the eighteenth century, and early in the nineteenth century Lamarck constructed a full theory of evolution. These ideas, however, were still speculative, and it was only in 1859 that Charles DARWIN, in his famous book *The Origin of Species,* put the theory on a firm foundation, both supplying a vast amount of evidence and suggesting an explanation of the mechanism of evolution. Naturally, the theory has developed in many ways since his time, but the broad principles remain.

*The Theory of Biological Evolution Today.* There are millions of species of plants and animals on this earth. For a long time, it was believed that each species had been created just as we know it, by God in the beginning. If the theory of evolution is correct, there were only a few basic forms of life to begin with, and the multitude of species that we see today are all descended from these prototypal forms. This, of course, is true also of the human being.

*Evidences.* Perhaps the basic evidence is the *fossil record* of the rocks. The earth's crust gives testimony of the living things that have populated it over many millions of years. The human race itself reaches only a little way (comparatively speaking) into the past, and for most of the time the drama of life has been played without humans. Other familiar forms of life also disappear as we go back into time. On the other hand, we meet forms, such as the great reptiles, which once flourished but have for long been extinct. In the earliest layers, there are only animals that live in the waters—fish and still more primitive forms. So this record does suggest a continuous unfolding of life, with humans appearing only near the end. Another piece of evidence lies in *the basic similarities* of large numbers of living things. A human being, an elephant, a whale, an owl, a crocodile, and a frog all look very different at first glance. But in their basic structures, they are very similar—the same bones and other organs and tissues recur, though developed in different ways. Not only are the structures alike, so are the physiological processes. So we get the impression that they all constitute a family. This impression is reinforced by the further evidence of *embryology*. Although nowadays it is not considered so obvious as it was once supposed, that the life history of the individual organism recapitulates the evolution of the species, nevertheless the broad evidence remains. The embryo begins its life in a fluid environment, and in the early stages it may be impossible to determine to what species it belongs. Further evidence comes from the *geographical distribution* of species, which points to their interrelatedness. These matters all become intelligible on a theory of evolution.

Darwin accounted for the process by natural selection. All the individuals in a species are slightly different from one another. Some of these differences confer an advantage in coping with the hazards of life, and so the variations that enjoy such advantages will survive, while the weaker forms will die out.

*Consequences for Theology.* Bitter controversies arose between the exponents of biological evolution and church leaders who took the Genesis accounts of CREATION literally, and these controversies still go on. But clearly there is no genuine opposition between the scientific theory of evolution and the doctrine of creation. From the beginning of the controversy, enlightened Christians have seen that an evolutionary mode of working is entirely compatible with God's creative activity.

*Cosmic Evolution.* The astronomer's exploration of the universe takes us not only out into space but also far back in time. The evidence seems to show that at one time (perhaps fifteen billion years ago) the matter of the universe was packed tightly together. There was a vast primeval explosion, and since then the universe has been expanding, forming galaxies, stars, and solar systems. Some of these, in turn, go through the stages that we may suppose have happened on earth—the formation of heavy molecules, the emergence of the simplest living things, the advance from unicellular to multicellular plants and animals, then the whole panorama of biological evolution. It is an impressive and even awesome picture of the cosmos that is now presented to us, and this idea of a universe in evolution is, like the theory of biological evolution, entirely compatible with belief in a creator God—indeed, it might even seem to demand a theistic interpretation.

*Evolutionary Philosophies.* It was said at the beginning of this article that the term "evolution" suggests both continuity and direction. Something more can now be said about these points. While evolution does indeed proceed continuously, there would appear also to be "leaps" or "emergences" in the process, such as the appearance of living things out of the nonliving matrix, or of the rational human being out of merely animal ancestry. The direction of the process is (with some exceptions) from the simpler to the more complex and from the merely physical to the mental and autonomous. These general features of evolution have led several thinkers to put forward evolutionary metaphysics.

An excellent example is the rigorously argued philosophy of Samuel Alexander (1859–1938) in his work *Space, Time, and Deity.* He thinks of space-time as the original matrix out of which matter evolves. Out of that evolves life, which in turn gives birth to mind. By a process of extrapolation, Alexander looks forward to a further emergence, which he calls Deity. Here the idea of evolution has been extended to include God, who comes at the end rather than the beginning. Rather similar to Alexander's philosophy is that of Alfred North WHITEHEAD (1861–1947) as expounded in *Process and Reality* and other works. Whitehead avoids the difficult notion of an evolving God by supposing that God is dipolar. God has a primordial nature, which is ideal and eternal, but also a consequent nature through which God is immanent in the creative advance of the cosmos. The Jesuit Pierre TEILHARD DE CHARDIN (1881–1955) tried to combine evolutionary theory and Christian theology in *The Phenomenon of Man.* Although philosophically this book lacks the rigor of Alexander and Whitehead, its imaginative grasp of the potentialities of the cosmos has won for its author a wide following. He thinks of the whole evolutionary process as seeking to realize the purposes of God, as they found expression in Jesus Christ. Perhaps he does not sufficiently pay attention to the apparently tentative course of evolution or to versions of evolutionary theory that play down the notion of purpose. One may contrast with Teilhard's optimistic account of evolution the views expressed in *Chance and Necessity* by Jacques Monod (1910–76). As the title of this book suggests, Monod holds that evolution, so far from supporting theism, points to a view of the universe in which it is indifferent or even hostile to the spiritual aspirations of humanity.

J.M.

**EX CATHEDRA.** From the Latin phrase meaning "from the chair," for the chair of Peter. The term is used for any pronouncement by the Roman Catholic POPE in his capacity as the supreme teacher in matters of faith and morals. Such pronouncements are rare and, since Vatican Council I, are considered INFALLIBLE.

J.C.

# EXCOMMUNICATION

**EXCOMMUNICATION.** An act, by officially recognized authority in the church, barring a believer from participation in most services of worship, particularly Communion. It was practiced in the early church in cases where Christians had committed apostasy, adultery, or homicide. Such persons were usually allowed to participate in the early part of the worship service, but were dismissed when Communion was about to take place. At times, particularly during the third century in North Africa, there were disagreements as to who had the authority to impose excommunication and to lift it. While the bishops insisted that such authority belonged to their office, there were many among the "confessors"—those who had suffered for confessing the faith during a time of persecution—who argued that, since they had withstood and overcome temptations similar to those of the persons who were being judged, the power of excommunication and restoration ought to reside with them.

During the Middle Ages, the church used the power of excommunication to force believers, and rulers in particular, to conform to its moral teachings. But there were also many times when such power was used to force rulers to bend to the wishes of popes and archbishops. For that reason, as the Middle Ages advanced, excommunication lost its moral authority, and eventually many who were excommunicated paid little attention to such a decree.

Traditionally, there have been two levels of excommunication, and these have been continued until the twentieth century, although with some slight variation. The "greater excommunication" bans the believer from administering or receiving Communion or participating in any other rite of the church, except the last rites. Also, those under such excommunication are to be shunned by other believers. The "lesser excommunication," on the other hand, applies only to Communion itself. Usually, a decree of "greater excommunication" refers to the person by name, while that of "lesser excommunication" is applied more generally to any who disobey a particular directive from ecclesiastical authority.

Many Protestant churches include in their polity the possibility of excommunication. Among Anabaptists, excommunication takes the form of SHUNNING. But in most Protestant churches excommunication has become rare. (*Compare* DISCIPLINE.)

J.G.

**EXEGESIS.** From the Greek, *exegesis* is the word used for interpretation of a document or statement, the reporting or explaining of an incident, or the description of an event. The term was used especially for the revealing of divine secrets or the disclosure of meaning of sacred pronouncements. The Greek verb related to the noun *exegesis* is found in the NT where John asserts that Jesus, as the divine Word, makes God known to human beings (John 1:18), and when the disciples who had met the risen Jesus on the road to Emmaus report their experience to the others in Jerusalem (Luke 24:35).

*Modern Use of the Term.* Among biblical scholars, *exegesis* is used in a specific way to refer to the INTERPRETATION of ancient texts, and especially of biblical texts. In both Judaism and early Christianity, the text of Scripture was central in the self-understanding of the religious community. Its leaders and teachers, therefore, saw themselves as not only obligated to explain the meaning of Scripture for their adherents, but also as privileged through divine revelation to understand Scripture and thereby to interpret it to their followers.

*Ancient Exegesis.* Among the Jews of the centuries just before and just after the birth of Jesus, the interpretive task had several specific aims: to enable hearers to understand these ancient stories and laws and prophecies; to show how they were relevant for members of the Jewish community in spite of changed times and culture; to provide instruction and guidelines for the ongoing life of that community. In some cases, exegesis was little more than a paraphrase of the Scripture; in other cases, it sought to make a direct connection between the Scripture and the present situation of the interpreter and his reader, as the Dead Sea community did in applying the ancient prophecies to their own group.

In more sophisticated circles, such as in Alexandria, the Bible was interpreted allegorically. Building on Platonic philosophy and Stoic ethics, PHILO OF ALEXANDRIA sought to show that scriptural narratives and laws were symbolic statements of the same truths about God and the Creation that ancient philosophers had discerned. Early Christian interpreters of Scripture adopted these methods, especially that of applying prophetic oracles to their own time, as the common phrase in the NT shows, "This happened to fulfill what was spoken by the prophets. . . ." In the third century ORIGEN of Alexandria was allegorizing the NT, just as Philo had done to the OT three centuries earlier. Allegorical exegesis flourished through the Middle Ages.

*Modern Exegesis.* Under the combined influence of growing skepticism about the biblical account of the Creation and the rise of critical historical methods in the seventeenth and eighteenth centuries, scriptural scholarship began to concern itself with careful study of biblical language (philology), with the effort to reconstruct the original text of Scripture on the basis of differing manuscript tradition (TEXTUAL CRITICISM), and with reasoned analysis of the historical content of the writings (HISTORICAL CRITICISM).

In many cases philosophical concepts dominated exegetical work on the Bible, as did the theory of G. W. F. HEGEL (1770–1831)—that the course of history was shaped by force and counterforce (thesis and antithesis). Exegetes tried to explain differences within the NT by describing Paul's law-free gospel (thesis) in conflict with Jewish Christianity (antithesis), which produced catholic Christianity as a compromise (synthesis). Other philosophical systems have influenced exegesis in later years, such as ethical IDEALISM and EXISTENTIALISM. Yet exegesis continues to demand careful analytical work along textual, philological, and historical-critical lines down to the present day. Only when these tools are employed to try to determine what a text meant to its first readers can the interpreter move to the contemporary question of what it may mean today. (*Compare* HERMENUTICS.)                                          H.K.

**EXHORTATION.** One of the primary purposes of the early Christian assemblies was to provide the atmosphere, teaching, and sharing of faith that would result in the strengthening of disciples. Words like EDIFICATION, consolation, and exhortation (I Cor. 14:3) are used to describe the purpose and end result of such experiences. It seems that some individuals were especially endowed with gifts to provide the exhortation needed in the early church (Rom. 12:8). The author of Hebrews considers his entire epistle to be a "word of exhortation" (13:22), and throughout he uses the hortatory subjunctive "let us" in his exhortations (for example 4:1, 11; 6:1; 10:22-24; 12:1) or its equivalent (2:1; 3:1; 10:32; 13:1). Barnabas was probably given his name, which means "son of exhortation," because he was well known for this type of ministry (Acts 4:36). The Holy Spirit is referred to by a cognate term in Geek that means both exhortation and consolation. It is usually translated "counselor" in John 14:16, 26; 15:26; 16:7 but would probably be better understood as helper. It is used of Jesus in I John 2:1 with the sense of intercessor, a title that is also implied in John 14:16 when he spoke of the Holy Spirit as "another" intercessor. One of the primary duties of an EVANGELIST like Timothy was to provide exhortation by public reading of Scripture, preaching, and teaching (I Tim. 4:13).                                J.R.M.

**EXILE, THE.** That period between the years 597 and 538 B.C. in which a significant number of the citizens of Jerusalem and Judea were forced to live in BABYLON. The primary biblical sources for information about the beginning of the Exile are II Kings 24:18–25:30 and Jeremiah 52:1-34 (see also II Chr. 36). In 605 B.C., the triumphant Neo-Babylonians, under the leadership of NEBUCHADNEZZAR, defeated a coalition of Assyrians and Egyptians at the battle of Carchemish, an event alluded to in II Kings 24:7 and Jeremiah 46:2. JEHOIAKIM, king of Judah, became a vassal of Nebuchadnezzar by virtue of this victory. Second Kings 24 tells us that Jekoiakim revolted after three years, but died before Nebuchadnezzar could reassert his authority. His son, JEHOIACHIN, inherited the kingship and the rebellion, and, after a mere three months, was obliged to surrender Jerusalem to Nebuchadnezzar. Second Kings 24:12-

17 tells us that the royal house and the treasuries of the house of the Lord were carried into Babylonian captivity. The year 597 B.C. is confirmed in Babylonian records as the year of this first deportation.

More trauma was yet to come, however. Nebuchadnezzar replaced Jehoiachin with his uncle Zedekiah. After much political intrigue, this puppet king rebelled against the king of Babylon. The inevitable reconquest in 587 B.C. brought punitive action. This time Nebuchadnezzar burned the Temple and the city of Jerusalem, broke down its walls, and carried the rest of the leading citizens into Babylonian captivity. This was the second deportation. A third may have taken place in 582 B.C. Jeremiah 52:28-30 places the total number of persons exiled at forty-six hundred.

Concerning the end of the Exile forty-nine years later, the information that we have is largely indirect. The tale of Belshazzar's feast found in Daniel 5 recounts the events of the last day of the Neo-Babylonian empire before Babylon was conquered by Darius the Mede. Although the story is legendary in its present form, it is well established from extra-biblical sources that one Bel-shar-uṣar was regent during the reign of Nabonidus, the last king of Babylon, and that he may even have been in the city when it was taken by the army of CYRUS, king of Persia, on the night of October 11, 539 B.C. There is even a persistent legend in ancient sources that the people of Babylon were drinking copiously at a great feast when the Persian armies entered the gates!

The "Edict of Cyrus" preserved in Ezra 1:2-4 is more direct as historical evidence. Consistent with what we know from secular sources about his policy, Cyrus proclaims throughout his kingdom that the exiled Jews are free to go to Jerusalem and to rebuild the house of the Lord (Ezra 1:3). Ezra 2 then goes on to report that the rather extraordinary number of 42,360 Judeans, plus 7,337 servants and 200 male and female singers, together with numerous horses, mules, camels, and asses, and much wealth in gold and silver, were brought back from Babylon to Judea under the leadership of Sheshbazzar, prince of Judah. The priority of these returning exiles was the rebuilding of the Temple, and, although the work went slowly and required encouragement by the prophets Haggai and Zechariah, that task was completed in 515 B.C. The priestly group, which returned from Exile, consolidated the leadership position they had probably held in the Exile itself and ruled the Judean community as a theocratic state until the reappearance of a king in the second century B.C.

With these records of the beginning and end of the Exile, it becomes possible to evaluate what happened in the intervening years. Clearly the experience had a profound impact upon the life, literature, and religion of the Jews, none of which would ever be the same again. Some viewed it as an unmitigated disaster (LAMENTATIONS, OBADIAH); a psalmist cried, "By the waters of Babylon, there we sat down and wept, when we remembered Zion" (Ps. 137:1). But others took more positive views. The prophet JEREMIAH encouraged the first wave of exiles to settle down, marry, and acquire property with the promise that," "when seventy years are completed for Babylon, I will visit you, and I will fulfil to you my promise and bring you back to this place" (Jer. 29:10).

From secular sources we have evidence that the Babylonian Diaspora did exactly that, some individuals even becoming wealthy traders and artisans. The narratives of Daniel 1–6, though probably written long after the fact, picture Jews receiving great respect and high political rank in the Babylonian court. The prophet EZEKIEL receives his inaugural vision while dwelling by the banks of the river Chebar, among the exiles in Babylon (Ezek. 1:1). The fact that he saw the glory of God there, seated on the ark-throne, suggests that the exilic experience convinced the Jewish community that God's sovereignty extended also to Babylon, and that God could be manifested there as well as in Jerusalem.

Among the literary products of the exilic community, many include the so-called Priestly document (P), which provides a narrative framework for the entire Pentateuch and contains great blocks of cultic and ethical legislation such as the Holiness Code (Lev. 17–26). The P source reinforces the impression that the experience of exile awakened a high sense of their own identity in the Jews and led them to emphasize their distinctive practices of Sabbath, circumcision, and worship. The synagogue may have originated in this period as an alternative to the ruined Temple; however, Priestly groups also planned carefully for the restoration of Temple worship and the renewal of the holy commonwealth (compare Ezek. 40–48).

Finally, the greatest of all the literary figures of the Exile was the anonymous poet who composed Isaiah 40–55. Convinced that the Lord had anointed Cyrus to be the deliverer of Israel (45:1), this writer perceives the end of the Exile as a new exodus. The restored community, which lies beyond the Exile, is to be the fulfillment of all the prophetic hopes for a new age of peace and freedom.

During the exilic period, life also continued in Jerusalem and Judea. Although II Kings 25:12 reports that only "some of the poorest of the land" were left behind by Nebuchadnezzar, modern scholarship has suggested that the Former Prophets, Joshua–II Kings, may have been brought into their present shape as a single continuous document in Judea during the exilic period. Done by writers influenced by prophetic preaching and especially by DEUTERONOMY, this "deuteronomistic history" reflects the negative judgment on their royal house of a people who had experienced and lost a monarchy. However, by closing with the last king, Jehoiachin, still alive and seated at the table of the king of Babylon (II Kings 25:27-30), the implication is left open that further chapters in the story of the Davidic dynasty might yet be written. Obviously, one of the roots of messianic expectation is to be found just here.

W.S.T.

**EXISTENCE.** *See* ESSENCE.

**EXISTENTIALISM.** A style of philosophizing that has been influential in the twentieth century, though its roots go back to NIETZSCHE, KIERKEGAARD, PASCAL and even earlier. Philosophers who can be loosely included under the existentialist label are JASPERS, HEIDEGGER, SARTRE, MARCEL, and Unamuno.

The thinkers mentioned are so varied that it becomes clear at once that existentialism is not a body of doctrines. It is rather a way of doing philosophy that may lead to very different results. Its starting point is the questioning of human existence itself, understood as an open possibility to which individuals have to give shape and substance by their own decisions. This is what is meant by saying that existence precedes ESSENCE. The existentialists are agreed in making a more or less sharp distinction between humans and nature. In Sartre, this distinction is so sharp that it becomes virtually a dualism. But among all the existentialists, it is agreed that with the human phenomenon, something new has appeared on this planet, something which is not amenable to the methods of study employed in the investigation of nature.

There is further agreement that the most important characteristic of a human being is freedom. Some existentialists give the impression that it does not matter very much what one becomes so long as it is the result of one's free choice. To conform to patterns imposed by some external authority is to revert to the status of a thing or a manufactured object. Freedom thus becomes a value in itself. The free person is the authentic human being, while those who compromise their freedom are living inauthentically or in bad faith.

Another common characteristic of the existentialists is their stress on finitude. Human existence is free, but freedom is always limited by the factual conditions of existence. Thus there is a tragic element in existence. Some existentialists go so far as to suggest that there is a fundamental absurdity in the existence of a being who is both free and finite. It is at this point that we can see why some existentialists are atheists, others religious. The former see no sense in human existence and in any case believe that the existence of God would be incompatible with the full exercise of human freedom. The latter believe that only God (or transcendence in some form) can bring sense into the human situation, and they would see God as encouraging human freedom.

The existentialists are not, as is sometimes said, irrationalists, but they think that to define humans as rational animals is too narrow a view, and that we have to consider the whole person, including the will and emotions. It is perhaps not surprising that existentialism has made a strong appeal to theologians, for it allows more scope to the spiritual and creative aspects of human existence than does its chief philosophical rival in the contemporary world, empiricism. Among theologians who have been most influential are TILLICH, BULTMANN, and RAHNER.

J.M.

**EXODUS, BOOK OF.** A name derived from the Septuagint, the Greek translation of the OT, meaning "a going out." This second book of the Bible, known in Hebrew as *weelleh shemoth* ("and these are the names") after its two opening words, narrates the dramatic departure of the ancient Hebrews from Egyptian captivity and their journey to Mount Sinai, where they enter into a covenant relation with the Deity who favors them with divine presence.

*Organization and Basic Content.* A study of the oral transmission of ancient Israelite traditions suggests that Exodus contains three large blocks of material. The first, located in chapters 1–15, focuses on four major events—the summons of Moses, numerous plagues inflicted against Egypt, the celebration of PASSOVER, and the deliverance from the pursuing Egyptians at the Sea of Reeds (Red Sea). The second block spanning chapters 16–18 highlights harsh moments in Israel's wilderness journey when lack of food and water and pressure from hostile tribes severely tested its trust in Yahweh's providential care. The third block found in chapters 19–40 on Yahweh's theophany to Israel at SINAI when it formally became Yahweh's covenant people by receiving laws, including elaborate instructions ensuring an ongoing worshiping fellowship with the Deity.

*Composition and Historicity.* Like Genesis, Yahwistic (J), Elohistic (E), and Priestly (P) strata are all discernible in Exodus (*see* DOCUMENTARY HYPOTHESIS). The editors of the Deuteronomic school have also made their mark felt (minimally in 12:24-27; 13:3-16; 15:25*b*-26). The not always readily distinguishable JE strata dominate the first half of the book, whereas P prevails in the second half. Though the Ten Commandments (20:2-17) and Covenant Code (20:22–23:19) are ordinarily attributed to E and the so-called Ritual Decalogue (34:10-26) to J, this legal material may have been only secondarily linked with the literary strata. This is likewise true of such ancient poems as the Song of the Sea (15:1-18) and the Song of Miriam (15:21). In its final edited form, Exodus is a loosely unified composition of diverse elements, which have undergone a lengthy history of development.

The Exodus text should be understood form critically as confessional legend created and reshaped by the worshiping Israelite community. Exodus 1–15 is likely a cultic legend intimately associated with Israel's Passover festival. Also many cultic elements surface within the Sinai traditions in chapters 19–24;

32–34. Exodus is thus a sustained liturgical meditation on those moments in Israel's past that singularly equipped a band of enslaved Hebrews to become Yahweh's special people. Recurring occasions of Israelite worship provided for the effective reenactment of those remote historical events about which the text speaks. Israelite generations across the centuries could share the burden of Egyptian oppression and the joy of divine rescue.

The question of what really happened is not readily answered. Though the deliverance of the Hebrews from Egyptian servitude and their convenanting with Yahweh at Sinai may be anchored in historical fact, much is uncertain. The hasty exit of Hebrew slaves is nowhere mentioned in extant Egyptian literature. Nor can we confidently determine the actual role that Moses played. Reference to store-cities of Pithom (Tell er-Retabeh) and Raamses (Avaris) in Exodus 1:11, however, argue for a thirteenth-century B.C. date for the EXODUS. The Nineteenth Dynasty pharaohs, Seti I (around 1305–1290) and Ramses II (around 1290–1224), sponsored ambitious building programs at these sites as they moved Egypt to new levels of political and economic expansion. Presumably Seti I was the pharaoh of the oppression (whose death is reported in 2:23) and Ramses II, the pharaoh of the Exodus. Moreover, the actual locus of Israel's dramatic rescue is unknown, for the Hebrew in 15:4 merely attests "sea of reeds" (*yam suph*). A southern extension of Lake Menzaleh in the eastern Nile Delta with its papyrus marshes is often proposed. Nor is the exact location of Mount Sinai a settled issue. Notwithstanding the paucity of brute historical and geographical facts, the Exodus and Sinai events markedly affected Israel's subsequent religious history.

*Religious Message.* (a) Yahweh, the God of Israel. Above all, the Deity resolves to intervene in Israel's behalf. To Moses, God declared, "*I have seen* the affliction of my people who are in Egypt, and *have heard* their cry . . . *I know* their sufferings, and *I have come down* to deliver them" (3:7-8). Placing the mantle of leadership on Moses, he imparted the special name "Yahweh" (3:14 {E}, compare 6:2 {P}); yet God came as "the god of the fathers" (6:3) who pledged a constant presence. In the plague narrative, Pharaoh's chief opponent was not Moses but Yahweh, who sought to liberate the Hebrews and thereby be manifested as history's true sovereign. Through the human instruments, Moses and Aaron, Yahweh inflicted awful scourges on the Egyptians. As Lord over nature, Yahweh sent the pillars of cloud and fire to direct the people's way (13:21) and "drove the sea back by a strong east wind" (14:21) to ensure their escape. In the wilderness Yahweh benevolently provided for the people by sending manna and quail to satisfy their hunger, making desert springs available to assuage their thirst, and managing their triumph over hostile Amalekites (17:8-15).

Inviting the people into covenant fellowship at Sinai, Yahweh convincingly manifested a gracious *and* demanding nature. By instructing Moses to tell the people, "You have seen what I did to the Egyptians, and how I bore you on eagles' wings and brought you to myself" (19:4). Yahweh emphasized their miraculous deliverance as God's *gift*. By making God's law an intrinsic component in the covenant proceedings, however, Yahweh conveyed high expectations. If the people were to enter into a permanent association with this Deity, whose name was "Jealous" (34:14), they must know that Yahweh would lay upon them specific religious and ethical claims. Still, they will be magnificently supported by God's continuing presence—the glory of Yahweh that had settled on Sinai (24:16) transferred itself to the tabernacle (40:34) that would accompany Israel through the wilderness trek.

(b) Israel, the people of Yahweh. Exodus portrays Yahweh's chosen as those who profoundly understand that transformation is an essential dimension of religious pilgrimage. When the formerly benign Egyptian environment turned against them (1:8-16), they had no alternative but to cry for help. Though they accepted Moses as leader, they freely expressed their anger and fear when the situation worsened (5:21; 14:12; 17:3). In the threatening wilderness their posture was often rebellious. Even at Sinai, after they had learned firsthand Yahweh's saving deliverance and covenant purpose, they flaunted their infidelity by worshiping a golden calf that brought them and their leader to grief (chap. 32). Nevertheless, through those formative moments of exodus and covenant making, Israel recognized that it had been transformed from a "mixed multitude" of slaves (12:35) to a people chosen for Yahweh's own purpose, and that while God's grace was not cheap, God would not abandon Israel. Moreover, through regular moments of historical recollection that the festivals of Passover and unleavened bread would offer (12:1-28) through such tangible objects as the Ark of the Covenant (25:10-22) and the tent tabernacle (26:1-37) symbolizing Yahweh's real presence, and through the institution of priestly leadership (29:1-46), Israel found ample direction to aspire to become the people Yahweh intended them to be.

J.K.K.

**EXODUS, THE** ("a way out," from the Greek word *exodos*). The departure of the Israelites from the eastern Egyptian Delta, after they had been divinely emancipated from shameful servitude to Pharaoh.

*Religious Significance.* Tenaciously articulated by ancient biblical poetry (Exod. 15:1-18) and the prose of early Israelite cultic credos (Deut. 6:20-24; 26:5-9; Josh. 24:2-13), this formative moment became the cornerstone of Israel's faith. Perceiving that through the Exodus they had been marvelously borne "on eagles' wings" (Exod. 19:4), the Israelites recognized

Herbert G. May

*Rose granite statue of Ramses II, pharaoh of the oppression and the Exodus. Found at Memphis, the statue weighs seventy tons and stands about thirty-two feet high.*

that they had been uniquely summoned as Yahweh's people.

Historically, the Exodus was not experienced by all the ancestors of later Israel. Theologically, it did involve all of them as participants in a constitutive event that significantly defined Israelite existence. As cultic legend, the Exodus narrative (Exod. 1–15) was intimately linked with Israel's Passover festival. Consequently, subsequent Israelite generations could feel the pain of Egyptian oppression and exult in God's unlimited sovereignty that made deliverance possible.

*Historical Context.* Though biblical testimony to the Exodus is striking, it is nowhere attested in extant Egyptian literature. Pharaohs tended not to record defeat. Moreover, in Egyptian eyes, this was surely dismissed as a minor clash involving the border escape of a few foreign slaves. The role of MOSES is doubtlessly exaggerated in the book of Exodus, and no Egyptian pharaoh is ever named.

Dating evidence for the Exodus is tenuous. Mention in I Kings 6:1 that 480 years had passed between the Exodus and Solomon's fourth regnal year (about 958 B.C.) places the Israelite escape in the fifteenth century B.C., a date often discounted as too early. While archaeological data have not evoked uniform interpretation, arguments for a pre-thirteenth-century Exodus appear strained. Tentative correlation of the biblical account of the conquest with numerous city destructions marking Canaan's transition from the Late Bronze to the Iron Age (near 1200 B.C.) suggests that Ramses II (about 1290–1224 B.C.) was the pharaoh of the Exodus. His father, Seti I (about 1305–1290), is understood as the pharaoh whose emergence is reported in Exodus 1:8 and death in Exodus 2:23.

Mention of Israelite labor at the Egyptian store-cities, Pithom (Tell er-Retabeh) and Raamses (Avaris), in Exodus 1:11 coordinates with extrabiblical evidence that these strong Nineteenth Dynasty pharaohs sponsored rigorous building programs there. Formerly the Hyksos capital, Avaris, was reoccupied by the Egyptian court and redesignated the "House of Ramses." Many Semites were living in the vicinity. If the Israel that Pharaoh Marniptah (about 1224–1211 B.C.) claims to have conquered, in a stela commemorating his Palestinian campaign, was part of the "mixed multitude" (Exod. 12:38) that had fled under Moses, Ramses' identity as pharaoh of the Exodus would be compelling. But Marniptah might have battled another tribe by that name that had never left Canaan. Hence, the exit of a few thousand Semitic slaves well into the reign of Ramses II presents itself as reasonable conjecture, not dogma.

*The Exodus Route.* Since the biblical sites mentioned usually defy confident identification, the specific geography of Israel's Egyptian departure and wilderness wandering remains mostly unknown. That Israel's rescue from water lying ahead and advancing Egyptians behind did not transpire at the RED SEA is clear from the Hebrew text (Exod. 15:4), which reads *yam-sûph* ("sea of reeds"). The body of water at issue was presumably a southern extension of Lake Menzaleh in the eastern Nile Delta with its papyrus marshes (near modern El-Qantara on the Suez Canal). Having escaped by Yahweh's overpowering of the sea (14:21), the Israelites journeyed southeastward by way of Succoth to MOUNT SINAI (Jebel Mûsa) near the southern apex of the Sinai peninsula. Though other locations for this mountain (also called Horeb) have been proposed, this traditional locus accords with the notation (Deut. 1:2) that Sinai was an eleven-day journey from Kadesh-barnea, an impressive oasis some fifty miles south of Beer-sheba.

Leaving Mount Sinai (Num. 10:11-12), they advanced northward into the Wilderness of Paran and thence to the Kadesh oasis for a lengthy encampment. Failing to penetrate Canaan from the south (13:1–14:45), the Israelites departed from Kadesh (20:22) to experience a trying detour through Transjordan. Ultimately poised in the Moab plain, they were ready to infiltrate the Land of Promise from an easterly direction (36:13).

J.K.K.

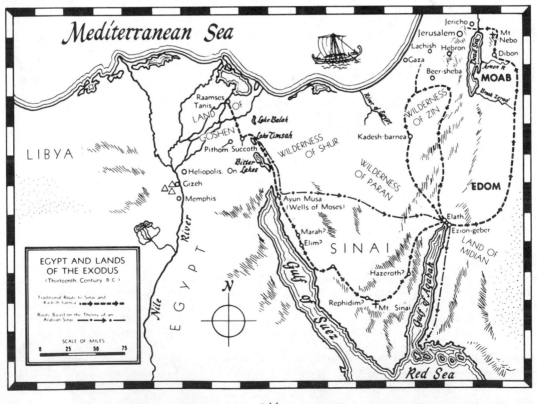

EGYPT AND LANDS
OF THE EXODUS
(Thirteenth Century B.C.)

Traditional Route to Sinai and Kadesh-barnea

Route Based on the Theory of an Arabian Sinai

SCALE OF MILES
0    25    50    75

These expressions are used to describe ways of
understanding how SACRAMENTS are efficacious. The
first expression may be translated "in virtue of the
action performed." On this view, the efficacy of a
sacrament is quite objective and does not depend on
the attitude of either the person who administers it or
the person who receives it. For instance, Augustine
maintained that baptism is valid even if administered
by a schismatic (Donatist) priest, while Roman
Catholics have held that the Eucharist does not
require (as Protestants had claimed) faith on the part
of the recipient. The second expression means "in
virtue of the performer of the action." In many
churches, it is held that only a properly ordained
minister can rightly perform a sacramental act.

J.M.

**EXORCISM.** The term comes from the Greek verb
*exorkizein,* "to charge solemnly," "to command," and
the object is an evil or demonic spirit which, it was
believed, had taken possession of an individual.

The origins of this practice are traced to ancient
Persian religion which, with a dualistic world view,
made much of evil powers and offered ways to
overcome them. There is only one instance of
exorcism in the OT literature, namely I Samuel
16:14-23, where David is able to pacify the troubled
Saul.

In early Judaism, however, perhaps under Persian
influence, interest in the demonic world became
morbidly excessive. There is some evidence of Jewish
exorcists in Luke 11:19; Mark 9:38ff. (equivalent to
Luke 9:49); as well as Acts 19:13. The later
Greco-Roman world produced its exorcists, sometimes using oriental or Semitic loanwords. This
suggests that exorcism entered Greco-Roman popular
religion from the East, perhaps not until the second or
third century A.D.

The Synoptic Gospels (but not the Fourth Gospel,
which is strangely silent about DEMONS) record Jesus
as performing such exorcisms. Jesus evidently
attached an importance to this side of his ministry as a
demonstration of the nearness of God's rule (Luke
11:20) and in fulfillment of OT prophetic expectation
(Matt. 11:4-6; Mark 7:31-37). Jewish witness to
Jesus' practice of "sorcery," a reference to his
reputation as an exorcist, is reported in the Talmud.

The early church, according to the Acts, emphasized miracle-working powers, with exorcism as part
of the same demonstration of divine power (Acts 5:16;
8:7; 19:12) at work over Jewish and pagan MAGIC.
One other case of Paul expelling an evil spirit is on
record (Acts 16:18), but the motive there seems more
one of compassion in the face of human need.

R.M.

**EXPIATION.** Of the several meanings of the OT
Hebrew verb *kpr* one is "expiate," which tends to
make minute variations according to its context. It is

normally associated with a ritual action for the
removal of SIN.

Expiation as covering is one meaning of *kpr.* There
was evidently an apotropaic or prophylactic power in
the Hebrew use of ritual, that is, the priestly acts
warded off evil and its consequences or protected the
sinner from divine wrath.

Sometimes the agent of expiation is concentrated in
an animal, such as the goat of Leviticus 16, with the
intent of diverting divine reaction away from the
community. The animal serves as a "ransom" (see
Exod. 21:30), a term that brings us the NT data.

The NT evidence centers on two much disputed
words: RANSOM (Mark 10:45; I Tim. 2:6) and
"expiation" (KJV, "propitiation") in Romans 3:25; I
John 2:2; 4:10. Various backgrounds to these texts
have been proposed: the servant of Isaiah 53:10 whose
soul is made a sin offering; the DAY OF ATONEMENT
ritual (Lev. 16), which is clearly in mind in the letter
to the Hebrews but remarkably absent from Paul
aside from a possible allusion in Romans 3:24-26; the
Maccabean martyrs who gave their lives as a "ransom"
for Israel. The debate turns on the issue of the effect of
Christ's death expressed in sacrificial terms: whether
that sacrifice simply removed sin's stain by purging
(Heb. 9:14) or cleansing (I John 1:7) or averted God's
wrath (as implied in "propitiation") by bearing divine
judgment as a proxy for sinners (II Cor. 5:18-21 is
often cited, but Paul stops short of saying that Christ
bore divine wrath against sin, as some Reformers
insisted). The points of general agreement are (1) in
Christ God dealt with human sin by removing its
penal consequences; and (2) sin is "expiated" as Christ
identified himself with our lot as sinners and died as
our representative and as sin's victim. (*See also*
FORGIVENESS.)

R.M.

**EXTRASENSORY PERCEPTION** (ESP). Sometimes called PARAPSYCHOLOGY, ESP began developing as an area of research from the time that a group
of Cambridge scholars established the Society for
Psychical Research in London in 1882. Subsequent
groups were started elsewhere in Europe and in the
United States. A milestone was reached when a
research center was established at Duke University by
J. B. Rhine and William McDougall in 1927.

Parapsychology includes a number of areas.
Telepathy is a knowledge of the thoughts of another
person. Clairvoyance is a supernormal awareness of
objects or events not known to others. Precognition is
the knowledge of future events, or of events not yet
reported. Psychokinesis is the ability to will the
movement of an object without touching it.
Intimations of survival after death come through
communication with people who have died.

These perceptions are seemingly experienced
independently of the five senses, hence the term
extrasensory. As validity is tested, the possibility
arises that there may be forces not yet explored within

the social and physical sciences. Critical and constructive work is being carried on today. Such research may point to human potential that has yet been little explored. This knowledge is being collected in two ways. One is through reports made by people of their experiences. Such narratives, subjective as they may be, are tested by carefully developed questions through which the elements of chance, coincidence, and personal memory are filtered. Another method of research is through controlled laboratory work. Tests are so arranged as to remove the element of coincidence when people seem to know hidden information. It has been found that subjects respond more accurately when they are relaxed and when the relationship with the researcher is good.

Recently dreams have been considered subjects for extrasensory perception, but not with the psychoanalytic goal of therapy. Research in this area is an inquiry into the possibility that people and events from the past or future may enter the dream life of some people. Faith healing is another parapsychological phenomenon, involving an interaction between seeker and healer by touch or voice, present to each other or absent.

Religious people have become interested in extrasensory perception because the Bible describes so many events in these categories: dreams, healings, moving from place to place, reports from those who have died, knowledge by one person of another's past, and premonitions of the future. There is an effort to recover these as religious phenomena for today.

I.C.

**EXTREME UNCTION.** *See* UNCTION OF THE SICK.

**EZEKIEL.** The name of one of the three Major Prophets and a book of the Hebrew OT. Both the prophet and the book are uniquely connected.

*The Prophet.* According to the canonical book, which is our only historical source for Ezekiel, he was one of those deported from Judah to Babylon in 597 B.C., part of the *golah* or Exile consequent on the conquest of Jerusalem by the Chaldean king Nebuchadnezzar II. Such a deportation would have involved only the more important citizens of the country, among whom Ezekiel, the son of Buzi, of a prominent priestly family, undoubtedly was to be numbered. The fifth year after the beginning of the EXILE, on July 31, 593, he received his call to prophecy (1:2-3), an office he fulfilled throughout more than the next twenty years. His last dated prophecy is of April 26, 571 (29:17).

Such precise dates, typical of the book of Ezekiel and calculated according to what would have been the reigning years of the exiled king Jehoiachin, point up one of the intimate connections between the prophet and the literary work that bears his name. At one time it was possible for scholars to postulate for not only Ezekiel but also EZRA and NEHEMIAH and other parts

of the biblical chronicle of the Exile a literary fiction created to account for a sequence of events otherwise hardly attested in history. Subsequent archaeological and epigraphical discoveries, especially of the Babylonian records of Jehoiachin's exilic household, have supplied this attestation at least in part, so that today no serious scholar would question Ezekiel's real existence on this score alone. The *golah*, which is the scene of the book, existed as described.

Difficulties remain in accepting the picture of Ezekiel exactly as he is portrayed. While he is said to have been a resident in Babylonia, where he received his call to prophecy (1:3; 3:15, 24), more than once (11:13, for example) he seems to have had firsthand knowledge of events that were transpiring in Jerusalem, toward which many of his prophecies were addressed. This fact has led many to posit a dual prophetic activity of Ezekiel, in Judea and also in Babylonia, a view which is hardly consonant with the book as we have it. Whatever is to be said in this regard, it must be borne in mind that the book, our only source for Ezekiel's life, is a work of intense revision and amplification, to the extent that it is often hard to determine what is original and what has been later added from knowledge of the events.

While Ezekiel, according to the record, obviously stood in the line of the classical prophets beginning with Amos, there is also much that makes him an exception to all the rules. One of the most obvious differences between Ezekiel and his predecessors is the attention he pays to purely ritual, alongside moral, concerns, putting them on an equal plane, with a concentration on individual devotion and morality. Ezekiel's prophetic discourses frequently sound very much like priestly catecheses (compare chap. 18). Ezekiel loves involved allegories, which are often expressed in rather turgid prose.

Ezekiel's often strange conduct—his dumbness (3:22-27), some of his symbolic acts (chap. 4, for example), his frequent transportation to "the plain" by the "hand" or "Spirit" of the Lord (3:22-23; 37:1-2), which has suggested to some a reference to ecstatic seizure, etc.—connect him in a certain fashion to earlier preclassical prophecy. On the other hand, the apocalyptic character of many of his visions (1:1–3:15, for example), betrays his kinship to postexilic prophecy and the apocalyptists. As already mentioned, he often sounds more like a priest than a prophet. The great vision of the Temple and the new Israel, beginning with chapter 40, not only manifests an uncharacteristically prophetic interest in the cult, it also gives it an uncritical emphasis that would be considered inordinate even in postexilic Judaism.

All in all, however, Ezekiel differs from his predecessors more in degree than in kind. This is true also of him in his character as "watchman" (3:16-21; 33), his commission to warn the people of coming disaster and to assume responsibility for them. This is only to develop the character of the prophet as mediator, a character that is as old as Amos.

*The Book.* The book of Ezekiel falls into four identifiable parts: (1) Chapters 1–7—Ezekiel's call and annexed events: 1:1–3:15 the call; 3:16-21 the watchman; 3:22-27 Ezekiel's dumbness and restraint; 4–5 symbolic acts against Jerusalem; 6–7 oracles against Israel. (b) Chapters 8–14—the Temple vision and its consequences: 8–11 the Temple vision; 12:1-20 symbolic acts of the Exile; 12:21-28 reflections on the above; 13:1–14:11 false prophets and others; 14:12-23 the irrevocability of judgment. (c) Chapters 15–24—mostly allegories: 15–19 the great allegory with commentaries; 20 prophecies of judgment; 21 the sword of the Lord; 22 the bloody city; 23 Oholah and Oholibah; 24 finale on Jerusalem. (d) Chapters 25–48—the salvation of Israel: 25–32 oracles against the nations; 33 the prophet as watchman; 34–37 salvation and vindication; 38–39 Gog and Magog; 40–48 the new Israel.

Built into the book is also a series of some fourteen precise dates, not in any perfect chronological order. The whole of this ordered material indicates that in the book of Ezekiel we have a work of redaction (revision, translation), which is the end result not of the prophet's efforts alone but principally of many disciples, who not only gathered together its various elements but are also responsible for the many amplifications and developments that make the book what it now is.

All of the prophetical books of the Bible are works of redaction. Ezekiel, however, is especially such. No other prophetic work has been submitted to such a logical and didactic structure. No other book of the prophets contains so many essays, extended sermons, discourses, treatises, along with involved allegorical developments, extended biographical details, etc., and wordy repetitions that hardly harmonize with the spontaneity generally associated with prophetic oracles. The conclusion must be drawn that in this work, as no other of the prophetic collections, we have a work of "scripture" (of canonical authors other than the prophet himself), which by the very nature of the case precludes what is authentically Ezekiel's from being distinguished as an entity separable from Ezekiel 1–48. As was said at the outset, the two—the prophet and the book—are uniquely connected.

The same may be said with regard to the language as well as the content of the book. Poetry was the rule, rather than the exception, in earlier prophetical works, since prophecy had its inception in gnomic, even cryptic, pronouncements characterized by brevity and devices of alliteration, assonance or the like, to make the message suitably impressive to the recipient. Ezekiel is largely prose. It is literature, but it cannot be called exciting literature. Efforts to discern a "primitive poetic core" behind Ezekiel's convoluted prose have generally proved futile. Ezekiel is, in its final form, what an earlier criticism thought was true of classical prophecy in general, a prime example of "literary prophecy."   B.V.

**EZION-GEBER.** A port city on the north shore of the Gulf of Aqaba (the eastern arm of the Red Sea) frequently mentioned in the OT. It was closely associated and sometimes identified with nearby Elath or Eloth (probably the biblical El-paran, the modern Aqabah), but the two seem to have been distinct (compare I Kings 9:26). Ezion-geber, the site now known as Tell el-Khalifa, has been thoroughly excavated archaeologically.

Ezion-geber is mentioned as one of the camping sites of the Israelites on their way to the conquest of the Promised Land (Num. 33:35; Deut. 2:8). However, it is generally thought that such an early reference is an anachronism, reflecting the geography of a later chronicler seeking to reconstruct the route of the book of Exodus as well as the event.

Ezion-geber was established by Solomon as the base for a commercial fleet manned by Phoenicians with which he carried on extensive trade with Arabia (I Kings 9:26–10:22). Archaeology has confirmed the importance of the base in Solomon's time. There was a very strong fort with large storerooms to serve commercial caravans and the maritime trade. By an earlier interpretation of the evidence, the excavations were thought to have uncovered the remains of smelters that had processed the copper ore of the mines of the Arabah. The interpretation has now been abandoned, though there can be no doubt that the mines played an important part in the trade that brought Solomon such vast wealth.

Solomonic Ezion-geber was destroyed by fire, probably in the time of Rehoboam as part of the invasion of Pharaoh Shishak. However, Judah resumed its domination of Edom, and under King Jehoshaphat (873–849 B.C.) an attempt was made to revive Solomon's fleet (I Kings 22:47-48). The fleet was wrecked and the site was again destroyed by fire. There was still a further rebuilding under Uzziah of Judah (783–742 B.C.). A seal has been found there with an inscription pertaining to Jotham, possibly Uzziah's son Jotham who ruled as regent during his father's illness (II Kings 15:5). Like the preceding level of the site, this one succumbed to a conflagration. We do not know the extent to which Judah was able to exploit the potential offered by the seaport during this period of its control.

In the time of Ahaz of Judah, Edom regained its independence (II Kings 16:6) and correspondingly Ezion-geber became Edomite once more. A seal bearing a name compounded with the element Qosh, the name of the chief Edomite deity, was found in the fourth and final habitation level. This phase of occupation extended down to Hellenistic times. During the period of Persian domination, especially at Ezion-geber, there seems to have been a bustling center of trade between the East and the West.   B.V.

**EZRA AND NEHEMIAH.** The protagonists who more than any others epitomize the "restoration" of

Judea after the BABYLONIAN CAPTIVITY of 597-535 B.C. These names are also attached to two biblical works that chronicle the events of this postexilic period.

*Ezra.* He was a priest (Ezra 7:11) but more importantly a "scribe" (7:6), that is, a teacher of the Law. Later, he would have been termed a rabbi. This teaching function makes Ezra typical of the new leadership that distinguishes postexilic Judaism from preexilic Israel: the postexilic experience being a doctrinaire monotheism, which had found its unity in a codified tradition, orthopraxis, and emphasis on identifying externals inculcated through the development of Jewish life that would be typified by the synagogue. The proclamation and interpretation of the Law, as described in Nehemiah 8–9, is a foreshadowing of the kind of synagogue service that would thereafter characterize Judaism.

Ezra was born in Babylonia, descendant of a priestly family that had been deported along with King Jehoiachin in 597 B.C., by the Chaldean Nebuchadnezzar II (II Kings 24:8-17). In all probability he was nurtured on prophetic assurances like those of Jeremiah 24, which assured these exiles that in them and them alone was the hope of a future renewed and Israel purified. Doubtless romantically attracted to a "homeland" he had never seen, Ezra headed one of the several migrations of Babylonian Zionists designed to reestablish a Judean state or sphere of influence in Palestine, in a territory now shrunk to a tiny vestige of what had once been and which now possessed only a shaky autonomy as a subprovince in the Persian Empire.

Ezra was far from being the earliest of the leaders of the Jewish return, which had been authorized by the Persian Cyrus II in 538 B.C., following his conquest of Babylonia (compare II Chr. 36:22-23; Ezra 1:1-4). In fact, we do not know precisely where to place Ezra in this chronology or how to relate him to Nehemiah, the other important figure in the common chronicle that concerns the two. One thing seems certain, that he was in a peculiar way an emissary of the Persian king, sent specifically in a religious capacity to serve in Judea as a kind of "minister for Jewish affairs" (Ezra 7). According to this account, the mission took place in the seventh year of the reign of King Artaxerxes. If Artaxerxes I is meant, we are in the year 458 B.C., therefore before the time of Nehemiah, who came to Palestine in the twentieth year of Artaxerxes I, or 445 B.C. There are considerable difficulties involved, however, in ascribing to Ezra a mission earlier by a dozen years than Nehemiah's, not the least of which is that Ezra's work as described would hardly have been conceivable without the reorganization and stability that Nehemiah was able to bring about in the community. But on the other hand, to think of Artaxerxes II in connection with Ezra (whose seventh year would have been 398 B.C.) is to suppose too great a span of time between two Jewish leaders whom our sources obviously understood to have worked in close

proximity. Though not accepted by all, the most plausible hypothesis is that in the manuscript tradition of Ezra 7:7-8, the numerical notation has been imperfectly preserved, that the text may have originally envisaged the thirty-seventh year of Artaxerxes I. This hypothesis would put Ezra in Jerusalem in 428 B.C. In this hypothesis it would be easy to understand, for example, how the priest Meremoth, a distinguished official at the time of Ezra's arrival (Ezra 8:33), could have worked as a young man fifteen or more years earlier on the rebuilding of Jerusalem's walls (Neh. 3:4-21).

Ezra has been frequently regarded as the effective promulgator of the PENTATEUCH, the Law of Moses, substantially as we know it today. However this may be, there is no doubt that he represented to a marked degree much that is typical of the Law as understood by postexilic Judaism: an emphasis on bloodlines as the touchstone of Jewish authenticity (note the genealogies of Chronicles for which these become an all-important factor), an intransigence in the face of the "foreign" Yahwism of "the people of the land" who had not become part of the Babylonian captivity (an attitude, however, manifested by the very first Zionist returnees and consistently thereafter), a total rejection of mixed marriages and assimilation with or of other related peoples (Ezra 9)—an attitude shared by Nehemiah and in conflict with other exilic and postexilic biblical witness, prophetic and other. Ezra may well have brought with him from Babylon the Law in virtually its finished form; but his (and Nehemiah's) interpretation of it as normative was doubtless of much later acceptance.

*Nehemiah.* As already noted, the chronological relation of Nehemiah to Ezra is to some extent uncertain. Much more certain is the differentiation in the function of the two men in the reconstitution of the Jewish state in Palestine and in their separate contributions to the eventual religion of Judaism.

Nehemiah, the son of Hacaliah, was also an ethnic Jew born in Babylon of a family which, like many others, had become assimilated to the local society, so that he had been in a position to rise high in the civil service of his adopted (and, for that matter, native) country. (Contrary to the Assyrian practice, the Chaldeans, and after them the Persians, encouraged their transplanted subject peoples to join with them in the common governmental enterprise.) Having heard of the less than ideal state of affairs in his Palestinian "homeland," however, Nehemiah, who had maintained close relations with relatives in Judea, took advantage of his favored position at the Persian court to get himself appointed governor of Judea as the emissary of the Persian king (Neh. 1:1–2:8). The Aramaic papyrus texts from Elephantine, a Jewish military colony established in Egypt during Persian times, contain numerous historical references that coincide with some of those of the book of Nehemiah and enable us to be sure that the twentieth year of King Artaxerxes (Neh. 2:1) refers to the reign of

Artaxerxes I, therefore to the year 445 B.C. Thus we have, as we do not have for Ezra, a firmly fixed date for at least part of the period of Nehemiah.

Nehemiah's work and function, as already indicated, were more political than religious, though of course the distinction between the two areas was far less clearly defined than it would be today. Furthermore, there is no indication that he would have tempered in any way the hard-line policies insisted upon by Ezra. Nehemiah's chief glory was his rebuilding of the walls of Jerusalem, reconstituting the Holy City as an autonomous city-state in the classic pattern of Canaan (Neh. 2:11–3:32; 6:15–7:3). He was instrumental in repeopling Jerusalem and other crucial cities of the province (Neh. 11), possibly to lay the foundations, in virtue of an official position which he used pragmatically, of a Jewish state that would outlive the Persian Empire, and the Hellenistic Empire that would succeed it. His memoirs are eloquent testimony to the tightrope that he had to walk in conflict with rival Persian appointees in surrounding provinces, where the limits of authority were poorly defined and bluff and bravado frequently had to take the place of a royal decree. He was in constant danger of his life by legal and illegal means, and his eventual success (to the extent that we know it) is an example of the triumph of will and statesmanship.

He was opposed as well by the religious leadership of the Jewish establishment. Though we know some of these details, we do not know to what extent his interests coincided with those of Ezra. The Chronicler has them working in tandem, but this may be a simplification of the case. Apparently in 432 B.C., Nehemiah was forced to return to Persia for renewed authority (Neh. 13:6). About the date of his resumption of jurisdiction in Palestine and its circumstances, and about much of which occurred thereafter, we have no knowledge. It is interesting, to say the least, that when the later Ben Sira decided to "praise famous men," the glories of his people, out of this epoch he celebrated Nehemiah (Ecclus. 49:13) but never mentioned Ezra.

*The Book of Ezra-Nehemiah.* (a) *The sources.* It is generally thought that Ezra-Nehemiah (originally one continuous work) is a work of REDACTION by the Chronicler, a continuation of the compilation of I, II Chronicles (in turn originally a continuous work), simply the completion of a theological reinterpretation of Israelite historiography. The sources for Ezra-Nehemiah seem to have been:

(1) Ezra 1:1–4:5, substantially a history of the early Jewish restoration complied from contemporary records. The Chronicler took this over and inserted into it 2:1-70, which he extracted from the Memoirs of Nehemiah (see below and compare Neh. 7:4–72a).

(2) Ezra 4:6–6:18, another such little history (written in Aramaic), probably from Temple archives, detailing the problems that had been incident to the rebuilding of the postexilic Temple.

(3) The Memoirs of Ezra (Ezra 7:27–9:15 and Neh. 7:72B–9:37), a report sent back to Babylon by Ezra.

(4) The Memoirs of Nehemiah (Neh. 1:1–7:72a; 12:27-43; 13:4-31): these look like Nehemiah's diaries.

(5) A few incidental sources and some redactional touches.

(b) *Composition.* The Chronicler did not try to organize these sources into a chronological history of the period; he rather systematized them into a theology. It took this form, divided into two parts, which have nothing to do with the later Jewish division of the material into the two books of Ezra and Nehemiah.

(1) The first part: the return from exile and the reorganization of the Temple worship. This includes Ezra 1:1–4:5, the Hebrew source that told of the return under Cyrus and the restoration of sacrifice. Then the Aramaic source Ezra 4:6–6:18, leading up through various vicissitudes to the final rebuilding of the Temple under Darius I in 515 B.C. The link between these two sections is ideological: Ezra 4:1-5 on the one hand and 4:6-23 on the other are both concerned with Samaritan (or what would later be construed as Samaritan) interference with the restoring work of the people of God, from the very beginning down to the time of Artaxerxes I, the age of Ezra and Nehemiah. Ezra 6:19-22 concludes this first part with a note on the celebration of the feast of Passover (in the year 515, as it happens), simply because what has been described immediately before is the dedication of the new Temple, which made the celebration possible.

(2) The second part describes, thematically, the reorganization of the postexilic Jewish community under Ezra and Nehemiah, again without undue concern for any relative chronology. The themes are, briefly: (1) Ezra's mission and the issue of mixed marriages (Ezra 7–10). (2) Nehemiah's mission and the rebuilding of Jerusalem's walls (Neh. 1–7). (3) The promulgation of the Law (Neh. 8–9). (4) The people's assent to the Law (Neh. 10). (5) The reorganization of the state (Neh. 11:1–12:43). And finally, (6) what might be called a summation of the *ethos* of the postexilic community (Neh. 12:44–13:31).

It is obvious that these divisions, which could easily be rarefied, respect source material only incidentally and chronological history not at all.

B.V.

# Ff

**FABER, FREDERICK W.** (1814–63). The author of "Faith of Our Fathers" and "There's a Wideness in God's Mercy" also founded the Wilfridians religious order. Educated at Balliol College, Oxford, (B.A. 1836), he served as a Fellow at University College. Taking holy orders in 1837, he was appointed rector at Elton, Huntingdonshire. But in 1846 he became a disciple of John Henry Newman and became a Roman Catholic. He founded the Wilfridians at Birmingham soon after, and in 1849 he moved to London to preside over the branch there, sometimes called Oratorians.

Emulating the *Olney Hymns* and those of the Wesleys, Faber wrote about 150 songs published in *Oratory Hymns* (1854) and *Hymns* (1862). They include "Hark! Hark, My Soul," "My God, How Wonderful Thou Art," "O Saviour, Bless Us Ere We Go" and "Jesus, Gentlest Saviour." "Faith of Our Fathers," a Protestant favorite, was written as a tribute to Roman Catholic martyrs during the English Reformation.

N.H.

**FAITH.** A basic concept of theology and religion, used to designate the attitude of the believer toward God. The word "attitude" is used here to mean an orientation of the whole person. Faith is not merely belief or intellectual assent; it includes also the will and the feelings.

*Faith in the Old Testament.* The Hebrew word *emuna,* usually translated "faith," is expressive of the idea of firmness or constancy and would be better translated "faithfulness." The famous text, "The just shall live by his faith" (Hab. 2:4 KJV), is used by Paul and many later Christian theologians in defense of the doctrine of justification by faith, but it is virtually certain that the verse does not mean this in its original context. In some modern English translations it appears as "The upright shall live by faithfulness," or something equivalent. But although there is no word in the OT exactly corresponding to what Christians were to call "faith," one might argue that the phenomenon of faith can be seen in the OT. Abraham has often been called the first man of faith. Although the word for faith is not used, the story of how Abraham, at the command of God, left his settled home and went out into the wilderness has been understood as an archetypal act of faith (compare Heb. 11:8). Again, at the command of God, he is willing to offer up his son Isaac, and although no word for "faith" is used in the OT account of the incident, the obedience and trust that Abraham showed came to be understood as a notable response of faith (compare Heb. 11:17). The whole story of the covenant relationship between God on the one side and his people Israel on the other can readily be interpreted as one in which the faithfulness of God awakens (or sometimes fails to awaken) a faithful response from the people.

*Faith in the New Testament.* In the Synoptic Gospels, faith is often mentioned in connection with those who are the beneficiaries of Jesus' healing miracles. Such faith is not, of course, an achievement on their part, but is their openness to receive the power of God into their lives. In Paul's epistles, faith is contrasted with works. Human beings are not saved through their good works, for no one is entirely obedient to the law of God, and no one can satisfy God's demands. But those who have faith in God are accepted and saved by God, their faith being counted in God's sight as righteousness. The Johannine teaching is similar, though instead of the noun *pistis,* "faith," John uses some form of the verb *pisteuein,* "to believe." The Epistle to the Hebrews gives a somewhat different view of faith. Here the contrast is not so much between faith and works as between faith and sight. "Now faith is the assurance of things hoped for, the conviction of things not seen" (Heb. 11:1). In the catalog of the heroes of faith given in the chapter from which this verse is taken, the general picture is that of men and women committing themselves to God in situations of suffering and uncertainty and finding that their faith in the unseen enables them to triumph over their adversities. The unseen reality, which is the object of faith, can be understood both as the ever-present reality of God and as the future realization of God's promises. In the latter case, faith is scarcely to be distinguished from HOPE.

*Faith as Understood in Theology.* As indicated above, faith is an attitude of the whole person and, on analysis, it is found to be a complex attitude, involving several factors. Perhaps the word "commitment" comes closest to expressing the full reality of faith. When one is committed to a person or a group of persons or a cause, one has attached oneself with passion, loyalty, and conviction; one holds certain beliefs about the object of one's faith; and one is prepared to let one's actions be guided by the person or cause in which one has faith. These three points call for further discussion.

(1) Faith is trust in or loyalty to the object of faith, and this trust is passionate, involving the whole person. Here we are thinking of the subjective element in faith, the faith that constitutes the state of mind of the person who has it, the *fides qua creditur* (faith by which one believes), in the traditional phrase. Some theologians, especially those of an existentialist outlook, have stressed this subjective side of faith and have claimed that the finite human being, because of finitude, needs to have faith in a larger reality. Bultmann, for instance, defines faith as a "new self-understanding." But while one can see that the attitude of faith brings with it a unifying and energizing focus for the self, critics of this view of faith argue that it is impossible to ignore the content of faith, the *fides qua creditur,* for otherwise faith may degenerate into mere fanaticism.

(2) That brings us then to faith as belief. Although faith cannot be simply equated with belief or exhausted by belief, it is bound to imply some beliefs. For instance, to have faith in God is certainly to imply that God exists. There have been periods in the history of the church when great stress has been laid on the content of faith and when the presence of faith in a person has been virtually identified with orthodoxy or right belief. One thinks, for instance, of the patristic, medieval, and Reformation periods as times when there were violent controversies over points of doctrine and sometimes harsh treatment for those whose faith did not conform to the accepted norms. Today, the broader concept of faith as an existential attitude of trust and commitment has tended to overshadow the importance once attached to orthodoxy. Yet it should not be forgotten that belief is an essential element in faith, and that wrong beliefs have their repercussions on the practical manifestations of faith. Nevertheless, as was already pointed out in NT times by the writer of the Epistle of James, a faith that is merely intellectual assent falls far short of Christian faith in its fullness.

(3) Faith is also obedience, the placing of the will at the service of the person or cause in whom one has reposed faith. To separate faith and works is a false disjunction. Faith indeed originates from God, no WORKS of our own can ultimately satisfy God, and faith itself is not another work. Yet if someone holds a faith with both passion and understanding, that person cannot help acting in accordance with it. In the words of one Reformation document, good works "do spring out necessarily of a true and lively faith; insomuch that by them a lively faith may be as evidently known as a tree discerned by the fruit." While, as has just been said, faith is not a work but a gift originating from God, this cannot mean that the recipient of faith is entirely passive. There is no compulsion in faith, but rather the reverse, because faith always lies beyond that which can be proved or manipulated. It requires a LEAP OF FAITH (Kierkegaard) or a decision (Bultmann). This does not turn faith into a human work, but it does mean that the gift of faith must be responsibly appropriated by those to whom it is offered.

J.M.

**FAITH AND KNOWLEDGE.** The relations of faith and knowledge constitute a long-standing problem for theology. The problem can be considered in both a narrower and a broader sense. In the narrower sense, the question is whether God is accessible to us only in FAITH, as the response to God's revelation in Jesus Christ and the whole history of salvation, or whether there is also a knowledge of God that is based on REASON and common human experience—the knowledge that is claimed by "NATURAL THEOLOGY." In the patristic and medieval periods, faith and knowledge went for the most part hand in hand. Theologians appealed to Scripture and to Christian tradition, but they also employed philosophical arguments for the reality of God and believed that these gave support to the truths of Christian faith. At the Reformation, the alliance between faith and knowledge was badly shaken, mainly on the grounds that human sinfulness had impaired the use of reason so that the human mind could not rise to the knowledge of God. At the Enlightenment, the gulf between faith and knowledge was widened. Kant held that our knowledge is confined to the phenomena of space and time, and he severely criticized the old natural theology. But he claimed that he was not promoting atheism, but abolishing an illusory knowledge in order to make room for faith.

The disjunction between faith and knowledge came to possibly its most extreme expression in KIERKEGAARD. Faith, in his teaching, is not an imperfect form of knowledge but belongs to a different sphere altogether, and the LEAP OF FAITH does not depend on probabilities derived from reason or empirical evidences. In recent times, the primacy and independence of faith has been maintained by Karl Barth. Nevertheless, natural theology in one form or another has continued, and every criticism of it has been met by new formulations designed to counter the criticisms. It continues to appeal to those who believe that human rationality cannot be satisfied by an unsupported faith, and that the mind must seek reasons that would at least lend probability to the claims of faith.

In a broader sense, there is a constant interaction between human knowledge and the content of Christian faith. As knowledge has increased, it has been found that at many points new knowledge has impinged upon various items of faith. Only obscurantists would try to keep secular knowledge and religious faith in separate compartments. Reasonable people feel the need to bring them into harmony. As examples, one may mention the rise of biblical criticism over the past two hundred years, or the theory of evolution in the nineteenth century. The former has given us a vast body of fairly well-assured knowledge about the dating, authorship, intellectual background, and so on of the Bible, and this has inevitably had its impact on doctrines of inspiration and revelation. The latter seemed to challenge the traditional understanding of creation. In both cases, however, Christian theology has found ways of adjusting to the new knowledge, and in the course of time it has become clear that this has resulted in gain rather than loss. In the two cases cited, there has come about a deeper and more intelligent grasp of biblical teaching, and a more impressive, even awe-inspiring, vision of the creative activity of God. The continuing expansion of secular knowledge is one of the major factors in what is called the "development of doctrine," that is to say, the continuous unfolding of the resources of Christian truth in new historical and cultural situations.      J.M.

**FAITH AND ORDER MOVEMENT.** This phrase commonly used for over three hundred years to characterize the doctrine, organization, polity, and character of the church was adopted as the name of a worldwide movement that began in 1910 at the WORLD MISSIONARY CONFERENCE at Edinburgh. The first world conference of the movement was held at Lausanne in 1927. Early leaders of the movement were Charles H. Brent of the Episcopal church in the U.S.A., bishops V. S. Azariah and E. J. Palmer of India, and three English churchmen: Archbishop WILLIAM TEMPLE, Professor A. E. Garvie, and Canon Leonard Hodgson. A second world conference was held in Edinburgh in 1937.

Faith and Order became an official part of the WORLD COUNCIL OF CHURCHES structure in 1948 as its chief instrument for exploring and promoting church unity. Ecumenical study projects on the nature of worship, the church, and intercommunion preceded the third world conference in Sweden in 1952. Staff secretaries were appointed by the WCC to head Faith and Order beginning in 1953. A fourth world conference was held in Montreal in 1963, and Roman Catholic members were appointed to the Commission on Faith and Order in 1968.

Through its history, Faith and Order has become recognized for its expanded range of studies on the church's unity, nature, and task and its influence on the negotiations for union between churches in many countries.

     W.G.

**FAITH HEALING.** Throughout the history of the church the practice of HEALING physical and emotional illness through nonmedical means has been well attested. The OT records the healing miracles of ELIJAH and ELISHA. Miraculous healings of physical and mental disease and the casting out of demons characterized much of the earthly ministry of our Lord. He empowered his disciples to heal "all manner of sickness and all manner of disease" and to cast out demons. The apostles, too, demonstrated similar powers after the Ascension and Pentecost.

Paul describes the special gift (charisma) of healing (I Cor. 12:9, 28, 30), which enables certain Christians empowered by the Holy Spirit to exercise this ministry in and for the benefit of the Body of Christ. Another means of healing is presented by James (5:14, 15), who describes the process by which the sick person calls for the elders of the church to "pray over him, anointing him with oil in the name of the Lord." In this instance it is declared that "the prayer of faith will save the sick man, and the Lord will raise him up." In the same context Christians are enjoined to confess their sins to one another and "pray for one another, that you may be healed" (James 5:16).

Some have viewed the use of oil by the elders and the good Samaritan's pouring of oil and wine into the wounds of the injured man as justification for the employment of medical treatment along with prayer. The Roman Catholic sacrament of EXTREME UNCTION is said to have developed from the earlier practice of anointing an individual for recovery but not for death.

Just as different expressions such as "spiritual healing," "divine healing," and "Christian healing" are employed as synonyms of "faith healing," there have been different emphases on the means of healing. Thus, sacramental uses of oil, the laying on of hands, and the celebration of the Eucharist were often involved in the healing ministry of the church in earlier centuries. During the Middle Ages the veneration of relics reportedly achieved dramatic results. The Reformation brought accounts of healing by prayer and the laying on of hands. This was common among Quakers, Baptists, and others.

The PENTECOSTAL movement and such associations as the CHRISTIAN AND MISSIONARY ALLIANCE, especially in the United States, have emphasized the importance of divine healing. This has been a central feature of the ministry of many evangelists of the electronic church, such as ORAL ROBERTS, Jim Bakker, Pat Robertson, Rex Humbard, Jimmy Swaggart, and the late KATHRYN KUHLMAN. Usually these television personalities declare that God has bestowed the gift of healing on them.

In recent years healing services have been held with greater frequency in the older churches, often communions that have not been historically associated with healing or miraculous phenomena. Episcopalians, Lutherans, and other major denominations have sponsored healing services conducted by those in the Order of St. Luke the Physician. Some of this activity has also been associated with the emergence of the CHARISMATIC MOVEMENT in both Protestant and Roman Catholic churches.

In addition to miracles of healings in orthodox churches, healings have been claimed by members of CHRISTIAN SCIENCE and by Spiritualists, MORMONS, and other nontraditional groups.

R.H.

**FALL.** *See* ORIGINAL SIN.

**FALSE** (Apostles, Christs, Prophets, Witnesses). The concept of duplicity or hypocrisy in speaking God's word or the truth is the subject of continual warning throughout both the OT and the NT. "You shall not bear false witness . . . ," one of the Ten Commandments, is interpreted to forbid lying and deceit in all human relations and especially in oaths taken in a court of law. Perjury and the slanderous destruction of another's reputation is expressly forbidden.

In a larger sense, the prohibition covers deceit in religious matters. The genuine prophets of the OT were often confronted with other "prophets" who gave different "messages" from God. Amos denied

being a prophet in the professional sense to dissociate himself from those who believed God would not punish Israel. Jeremiah declared that false prophets spoke words of comfort the people wanted to hear, while the genuine prophet spoke hard words from God.

In the NT, Paul makes reference to false apostles, referring to those who mingled the gospel with either Jewish legalism or Hellenistic speculation (II Cor. 11:13). False Christs are warned against by Jesus and are identified with the Antichrist and the end of the age in Revelation. Many false witnesses were willing to come forward and testify against Jesus that he might be put to death, according to Matthew 26:60.

J.C.

**FAMILIAR SPIRIT.** *See* DIVINATION.

**FAMILY.** The fundamental social unit in Bible times, a clan or household, claiming descent from one ancestor. The family (or clan) is absolutely basic to Hebrew social life and revealed religion. Adam and Eve constituted a family; and the second progenitor of the human race, after the great Flood, Noah, headed a family. The Hebrews began as a separate people with Abraham's family. The genealogies that fill the OT books (and which the Gospels give for Jesus) show the intense sense of family, clan, and tribe among the Hebrews. Marriage, children, and the sanctity of the home were sacred to OT peoples, and much of the Mosaic law consists in regulations to protect the family against actions that might threaten it: children were to honor their parents (Exod. 20:12); the safeguarding of inheritances (Deut. 18:8; 21:15-17); spiritual discipline; child welfare; and even protection of the unborn (Exod. 21:22).

The OT family was patriarchal, dominated by the FATHER, in the fullest sense. The father, in the earliest, "patriarchal" days, was priest as well as chief of the clan, leader in war (Abraham led his clan in battle), judge and jury, and the owner of all goods. The "patriarchal" families were actually nomadic clans or tribes, so the close relations of the contemporary nuclear family were not usual. The father was more like a political leader or an employer than a parent in many cases, although some fathers loved a son (as Jacob loved Joseph, and later Benjamin) in ways similar to contemporary expectations. Some scholars think Jesus and Paul were critical of the overly domineering father ("Provoke not your children to anger") in Luke 2:48-50 and Colossians 3:21. Nonetheless, the wife and MOTHER were deeply respected (especially the paramount or favorite wife in "patriarchal" days). The love of the father for his wife is well displayed in the case of Sarah, Rebekah, and Rachel. The wives of some kings became powers in their own right (I Kings 15:10 ff.; II Kings 11:1); Deborah became a judge (Judg. 4:5) and others prophetesses (II Kings 22). In the NT, the family received the greatest support and respect by Jesus, Paul, and the author of the Pastoral Epistles.

J.C.

**FAQIR.** From the Arabic word meaning literally "poor." Properly used of Islamic ascetics and mystics, the term is popularly used of Hindu "holy men" in India as well. The Islamic faqirs are usually followers of a SUFI path and associated, whether tightly or loosely, with a Sufi order and sheikh or spiritual master.

R.E.

**FASTING.** Pious, ceremonial, or penitential abstinence from food and drink, complete or partial to a greater or lesser degree. Fasting is a practice observed by believers in both OT and NT, as well as throughout the history of the Christian church up to today. Fasting generally is for a set span of time, often just before an important holy day or season like Lent, Good Friday, or Holy Communion.

In the OT, fasting is commanded or recommended in Judges 20:26; I Samuel 14:24; 31:13; II Samuel 1:12; 12:16-23; I Kings 21:27; and II Chronicles 20:3. The Day of Atonement was the occasion for a fast by the whole people, and many other special or penitential fasts were observed by the Jews.

Fasting is prominent in the NT. Both John the Baptist and Jesus fasted. Notably, Jesus fasted and was tempted by Satan for a long time following his baptism by John. Jesus encouraged fasting that was deeply expressive of true inner devotion rather than to give the appearance of piety in Matthew 6:16ff. and spoke of it approvingly in Matthew 9:14ff. The book of Acts mentions that the early Christians fasted in 13:2ff. and 14:23. With the rise of MONASTICISM, fasting was made even more popular in the early Catholic church.

Fasting is of ancient origin, based on the belief that purifying the body of internal digestive and excretory functions would also purify the soul. It is similar in this "sympathetic magic" basis to celibacy. Both practices are based on a general belief in a dualism, of the body (matter) and the spirit, often conceived in ancient times as a very refined form of matter.

Fasting also expresses the sense of sin, or alienation from God, as in the Hebrew fast on YOM KIPPUR. In the Catholic church, the forty days of LENT are days of penance during which fasting is appropriate as one contemplates the death of Christ, who paid the penalty for human sin. Although the restrictions on eating meat on Fridays have been reduced for Catholics by Vatican II, restraint from eating certain foods still is recognized as good spiritual DISCIPLINE.

While the contemporary Catholic church has relaxed much of its teachings on fasting, the practice has grown somewhat among Protestants in recent years. Luther retained a sense of the value of fasting. Fasting during Lent and before Holy Communion was recommended by Luther and has been practiced in Lutheran churches continuously since the sixteenth century. A similar approach to fasting has been observed in the Anglican communion. Nonetheless, fasting was not widely practiced in Reformed churches or among the Anabaptists. In the twentieth century, however, fasting as a sign of identification with the poor and hungry has become a common (though occasional) practice in Quaker and other liberal, and mainline, Protestant churches.

The other contemporary growth of fasting among Protestants has been among the neo-charismatics, many of whom have been influenced by Catholic charismatics (often priests and nuns), on the one side, and by old-line Pentecostals and "holiness" (perfectionistic) sectarian Protestants, on the other. Neo-charismatics, emphasizing the many "gifts of the spirit," often engage in faith healing and glossalalia. They also hold extended prayer services, some of which encourage fasting. The "New Religions," which have achieved prominence in the past several decades, such as the Unification church and the International Society for Krishna Consciousness (the Hare Krishnas), also stress fasting. During the civil rights movement and the widespread protests against the Vietnam War many days of fasting were observed both by religious and secular participants.

J.C.

**FATE.** The word is derived from the Latin word *fatum,* meaning "that which has been spoken." To believe in fate is to believe that important events in one's life, perhaps even all events, have been determined in advance, and they will happen no matter what one does. In classical mythology the Fates were three goddesses, daughters of Zeus, who spun human destinies. These figures symbolized an ultimate impersonal force, which controlled the destinies of the gods as well as of human beings. The Greek language was richly supplied with words for this supposed power of fate—*moira, tyche, anangke, heimarmene.*

Presumably the origins of the idea of fate lay in the experience most people have at one time or another of being swept along by powerful forces beyond one's control. So many things in human life are not chosen. They simply happen to the people concerned, and when they do happen, there is a sense of inevitability about them, so that these events seem to have been foreordained. The idea plays a major role in Greek tragedy, in which the heroes, however they may struggle against it, are irresistibly drawn by their fate to destruction. Although the idea of fate as an all-controlling impersonal power belongs to paganism, something very close to it may emerge in some forms of monotheistic religion, including Christianity. Where there is great stress on the absolute SOVEREIGNTY OF GOD, perhaps coupled with a belief in PREDESTINATION and explicit providential control of everything that happens, there may be a virtual fatalism. Extreme Calvinism came close to this, and there are parallels in Islam that likewise stress the sovereignty of God and have a doctrine of predestination. This kind of fatalism is often associated with the moment of death. It is supposed that for each individual there has been appointed a time to die. We still hear it said, "His time had come!" In a few cases, those who hold such views refuse medical assistance, believing that recovery or death has already been irrevocably fixed by the decree of fate. In time of war, a shallow fatalism tends to be widespread. Some people inexplicably survive, others just as inexplicably perish, so it is supposed that this is due to the working of some hidden agency. No doubt there are some things in life against which it is useless to strive and which one can only accept with resignation. But where fatalistic acceptance becomes a basic attitude, there is a weakening of human initiative and human responsibility and thus a diminution of the distinctively human quality of life. (*Compare also* ELECTION.)

J.M.

**FATHER.** The word is used in the Bible in essentially three ways: for a human parent; for the model or prototype of a group; as a designation for GOD.

*For a Human Parent.* In ancient Israel the father occupied the authoritative position, particularly in matters of property and inheritance, and together with the mother was to be honored and respected within the FAMILY (Exod. 20:12; Deut. 5:16; Prov. 19:26). The father in turn was to communicate to his children the story of God's grace to Israel (Exod. 10:2; 12:26; 13:8; Deut. 32:7, 46) and together with the mother to provide a general education (Prov. 1:8; 6:20). Likewise, in the households of the early church children were to obey their parents. Fathers were to avoid provoking their children and were to bring them up "in the discipline and instruction of the Lord" (Eph. 6:1-4; Col. 3:20-21).

*For the Model or Prototype of a Group.* Abraham, "the father of the circumcised," is described by Paul as "the father of all who believe" (Rom. 4:11-12, 16-17). The term is also used as a title of respect for honored persons.

*As a Designation for God.* Israel did not frequently address God as "Father," but when the phenomenon does appear in the OT it is clear that the relation of Father and child is the result of grace and not biological generation. It was because God chose Israel to be a special possession that Israelites had the right and privilege to call God "Father" and to acknowledge themselves as God's children (Exod. 4:22-23; Deut. 14:1-2; 32:6; Isa. 64:8). Hosea movingly describes the warm compassion of God—the caring parent who agonizes over disobedient and wayward Israel (11:1-7).

Undoubtedly because of his unique filial relation-

ship Jesus brings a new dimenson to the Father-child connection. In Mark 14:36 he uses the Aramaic "ABBA," an unprecedented address for God, indicating both a deepened intimacy and a total obedience. In any event, it was taken over by the early church and became an indication of the Spirit's presence in worship (Gal. 4:6; Rom. 8:15-16). The Gospel of John more than any other NT writing works out the close relation of Jesus as son to God as Father (5:17-29; 10:14-15; 14:28; 15:10; 17:11, 21).

It is important to note that the language of God as Father in the Bible is metaphorical. God in fact transcends gender and is neither male nor female. There are a number of images in the Bible that relate God's action and nature to a mother.

C.B.C.

**FATHERS OF THE CHURCH.** *See* CHURCH FATHERS.

**FATIMA, OUR LADY OF.** The Virgin Mary of Fatima, Portugal. She appeared to three children on May 13, 1917, telling them to return the thirteenth day of each month, and on October 13 she would reveal her message. Seventy thousand people came for the sixth and last appearance. The Virgin enjoined praying with the rosary and doing penance. Miracle cures were reported, and hospitals, retreat houses, and a shrine were built. Pope Pius IX in 1930 authorized devotion to Our Lady of Fatima. On May 13, 1967, a million people gathered to hear Pope Paul VI say mass at her shrine.

C.M.

**FAUST.** *See* GOETHE, JOHANN WOLGANG VON.

**FAWCETT, JOHN** (1740–1817). The author of "Blest Be the Tie That Binds" was born January 6 near Bradford, Yorkshire. Converted when he was 16, under the preaching of George Whitefield, Fawcett became first a Methodist and then a Baptist three years later. He began to preach and was ordained by the Baptists in 1765. In 1772 he was called to Carter's Lane in London, but after he had preached his farewell sermon, his congregation in Bradford convinced him to stay. They built a new chapel in 1777 at Hebden Bridge, and Fawcett opened a school in his home, Brearley Hall. He also wrote "Lord, Dismiss Us with Thy Blessing."

N.H.

**FEAR.** *Old Testament.* The Hebrew language is especially rich in verbs that have to do with a person's emotional attitude or sensibility that is subsumed under the general English term "fear." Human emotions of terror or dismay were occasioned by a variety of causes such as adversity or threats from an enemy. But the OT use of "fear" that makes it significant lies in another dimension.

In the phenomenology of Hebrew religion "fear" of God came to be used of the numinous dread (see NUMEN) felt by a human being in the presence of deity. Examples of this creaturely sense of finiteness and frailty, which R. Otto dubbed "numinous" (*The Idea of the Holy,* 1923), are seen in Jacob at Bethel (Gen. 28) and in the THEOPHANY on Horeb in the lives of Moses (Exod. 3) and Elijah (I Kings 19). Probably the often repeated "fear not" is associated with this reaction to the divine holy presence, though the use of the term in the Prophets (esp. Isa. 40–66) is matched more with Israel's sense of shame and bewilderment at the time of the Babylonian exile (see Isa. 41:10, 14; 43:1; 44:2; etc.).

*New Testament.* The limited usage of the term "fear" in the NT carries forward OT ideas, as Christians are exhorted to "fear God" (I Pet. 2:17; compare Luke 18:2, 4, for the opposite attitude, which is blameworthy). Yet Paul in particular uses "fear" as a religious term in a polemical way, by setting it in antithesis to "the spirit of sonship," which drives out fear (Rom. 8:15, 16; Gal. 4:6) caused by legalism in one's religious relationship to God. The same idea recurs in I John 4:17 ff. Fear, in the apostolic exhortations, is also a Christian disposition in the sense of respect shown to one's fellow believers (II Cor. 7:15) and the Roman state authorities (Rom. 13:1-7).

R.M.

**FEASTS.** The OT terms for "feast" or "feast for Yahweh" (Lev. 23:2, 4; Num. 15:3; Deut. 16:16) denote a time of national celebration and rejoicing. Those tied into the agricultural year functioned as seasons of thanksgiving for the ingathering of the harvest ("Booths," mentioned in Lev. 23:34-36; Deut. 16:13-15) at the fall of the year, just as the Feast of WEEKS commemorated the "day of the first fruits" (Exod. 23:16, 34:22; Num. 28:26), at the beginning of harvest season. The name "weeks" derives from the dating, namely by counting forward from Passover a week of weeks (forty-nine days plus one for inclusive reckoning; Exod. 34:22). Hence, weeks became known as Pentecost by reason of the fifty (the translation of "Pentecost" in Greek) days that separated the two festivals.

PASSOVER (otherwise called the Feast of Unleavened Bread, Exod. 23:15) came to occupy a central role. Originally an agricultural event in the spring equinox, it was given historical dimension by its link in the Hebrew tradition with the Exodus from Egypt, which it commemorated, just as later Weeks served to remind Israel of the giving of the law on Sinai.

These three events were spread over several days. "Unleavened bread" lasted for a full week, and later became marked by a call to Israel's distinctive destiny as a holy people (see I Cor. 5:7, 8 for a Christianized version of this). "BOOTHS" (or in later parlance "Tabernacles") also lasted seven days, and symbolically was an enactment of the wilderness wanderings,

as the people lived in coverings made of leafy branches (Lev. 23:39-43).

The remaining festivals are of a particular character related to historical events. Pride of place goes to the weekly SABBATH, memorializing the day of creation (Exod. 20:8-11; Deut. 5:12-15), but also a day of joy (Isa. 58:13), linked with the Exodus deliverance. It became a distinctive badge of postexilic Judaism, especially in days of persecution (the Maccabean revolt). The DAY OF ATONEMENT (Lev. 16), technically a fast not a festival, was a time of national stocktaking and religious confession, followed by forgiveness. The Day of the Blowing of Trumpets (Num. 29:1; Lev. 23:24) was a special version of Sabbath, and PURIM ("lots") recalled the deliverance of Israel as recorded in Esther. Again feasting and rejoicing marked the occasion.

Jesus (Luke 2:41; Mark 14:1, 12) and the apostles (according to Acts 20:16) observed these feasts, but there is an implied critique (Col. 2:16) of their externality. The Feast of Dedication in John 10:22 commemorated the Maccabean victory.

R.M.

**FEDERAL THEOLOGY.** The name derived from the Latin *foedus,* meaning "COVENANT." As a distinctive theology with God's covenant as its focal metaphor, federal theology originated with Heinrich Bullinger's *De testamento seu foedere Dei unico et aeterno* (1534). It was expanded by such Reformed thinkers as Ursinus and Olevianus, authors of the Heidelberg Catechism, and reached its greatest expression in the biblical theology of JOHANNES COCCEIUS. Emerging from the federal political context of Switzerland, federal theology influenced the development of federal political theory and practice in Germany, the Netherlands, Britain, and the United States.

Federal theology teaches that the inmost nature of God, the Faithful One, is a covenant among the Creator, Christ, and Holy Spirit; that God's covenant with the natural and historical order and with all humanity is a covenant both of nature and grace; that humanity is created incomplete and in process toward a consummation hidden in God; that human fallenness is resistance to this created hunger of the heart for completion; that God unfolds a faithful will through phases in the OT and decisively in the life, death, and resurrection of Jesus Christ. Federalism holds that humanity is symbiotically social by nature, that human social and political order rests upon God's covenant and the covenants humans make with one another before God, and that the world and human society are in process under the sovereignty of God toward increasing liberation and unfolding levels of justice and love.

C.M.

**FELIX, ANTONIUS.** The full name of this person is known from the references to him in works by the Roman historian Tacitus. He was appointed PROCURATOR of Judea in A.D. 52, and it should be noted that a recently discovered inscription, which records the name of a procurator in Judea named Claudius, looks as if it refers to this man, in which case his full name was Claudius Felix, as Josephus states in *Antiquities*. This nomenclature would make him a freedman of the emperor CLAUDIUS, who befriended Felix's brother Pallas. It was due to the good offices of Pallas that Felix received his procuratorial appointment.

His tenure of that office coincided with great social unrest in the province, and in turn was marked by fierce countermeasures. He was a "brutal and licentious" man, records Tacitus, "exercising the powers of a tyrant but showing the mentality of a slave." He ruthlessly quelled an outbreak of revolt led by an Egyptian messianic pretender, but the leader escaped according to Josephus' *Jewish War*. This may explain the mistaken reference to this man in Acts 21:38, where the tribune Claudius Lysias thought Paul might be that person.

Paul's arrest in Jerusalem led to his transfer to Caesarea, where he was brought before Felix. The two character traits mentioned by Tacitus were brought out: Felix's disregard of justice and his love of money, though Luke gives a kinder estimate (Acts 24:22, 23). Paul was detained for two years while Felix hoped for a bribe as ransom money to set Paul free (Acts 24:26). So Paul's case was passed over to please the Jews (24:27) or to gratify Felix's wife, Drusilla, according to one textual tradition. Felix was recalled by Nero in A.D. 59, and though he was saved from accusations brought by the Jews, he faded into oblivion.

R.M.

**FELLOWSHIP.** A term referring to the expression of Christian love among believers, expressed in worship, the reception of the sacraments (especially the Lord's Supper), and in simple social activities, such as meals taken together and recreation or physical work done for the church or for the larger community. Such fellowship or COMMUNION is called *koinonia* in the NT and is considered to be more than friendship or the morale of a close-knit group. Christian fellowship is based on the believer's primary relationship to Jesus Christ, the crucified and Risen Lord, who is spiritually present in the church, which is declared to be his body and all believers to be limbs of that body. Fellowship is then a sharing of the faithfuls' communion with Christ and with one another and, therefore, is a common participation spiritually that leads to close social interaction and mutual service. This spiritual participation is sometimes called life in the Spirit, life in Christ, life in love, sharing in God's grace, and participation in the Body and Blood of Christ. Contemporary Protestant theology and post-Vatican II Catholic theology emphasize the importance of Christian fellowship and speak of the church as a divine-human community.                    J.C.

**FEMININE DIMENSIONS OF THE SACRED.** An ancient tradition, known more through icons than writings, depicts the transcendent in female form, and, much later, with female characteristics. Magna Mater, the Great Mother in Mediterranean cultures, was queen over heaven and earth, under such names as ISHTAR, Asherah, or Demeter. She was the Primal Figure.

As agricultural societies developed, Ishtar's role became more identified with that of assuring the fertility of the soil. In myth, she produces a daughter, Persepone (Kore, Gaia), who represents earth. Persepone's abduction by the lord of the underworld brings about a recurring annual season of dormancy, infertility, and death. Daughters may also signify powerful deities: Artemis (Diana) presides over everything concerning the act of hunting; Athene, born not of woman but from the head of Jove, personifies wisdom; Artemis (Venus) is the deity of love. In another mythological strand, the mother produces a son, who becomes her lover and consort (ISIS and OSIRIS). There is a struggle for power, resulting in the death and resurrection of the son and the subsequent demotion of the mother.

Agricultural societies were settled ones, and the mother deity, such as Demeter, presided over an orderly cycle that assured life and continuity through both food and human fertility. She became part of a heavenly/earthly societal pattern in which the father deity became the ruler over heaven, earth, and the regions under the earth. Thunder and earthquake were symbols of an almighty power that subjugated all living creatures and all lesser deities. The queen became merely the consort of Jove/Jupiter, a less powerful figure, frequently characterized by jealousy and acts of petty vengeance. No longer was the mother a beneficent deity. Female deities had their votaries, festivals, and honors prescribed for them according to their position in the sacred pantheon.

The Hebrew people came into a land whose people looked to Ishtar as the queen, mother, earth/goddess figure because they were an agricultural rather than a nomadic community. Through all the centuries that the Hebrews struggled for and settled the land, Ishtar had her place in the life of the area and thus infiltrated the life of the Hebrews more than a cursory reading of the Scriptures might suggest. Almost every historical book from I Samuel through II Chronicles records the rulers who were faithless to YAHWEH. Almost every prophet exhorts the people to put away their sacred figures, alternately ridiculing and threatening the practice of idolatry. This seems to indicate that Yahweh was never worshiped as absolutely as had been commanded by the Law (Exod. 20:1-3) and promised in covenant.

On the surface, Yahweh would seem to have been the epitome of masculinity, patriarchy, and kingship. But a careful reading of the Scripture discloses the figure also to be one of compassion, mercy, pity, forgiveness, and yearning—traditionally feminine traits. Yahweh fed the people, led them with cords as a parent teaches a child to walk, desired them to show justice and love, which were also divine characteristics. The loyalty and faithfulness of Yahweh transcend the faithlessness of Israel. Using a feminine figure of speech, Numbers 11:12 implies that Yahweh conceived and brought forth Israel.

In Christian theology Jesus is the image of God as a human being. One expects to see earlier characteristics appear in the gospel writings. Jesus weeps at the tomb of Lazarus; he yearns over Jerusalem, "as a hen would gather her chickens together." He loves, feeds, and heals—descriptions of a person who nurtures, sustains, and keeps alive. Moreover, in the supreme moment of his passion, he is silent, accepting humiliation and injustice, bowing before the power of others over his life. Modern interpretations of Jesus in picture, song, and popular verse are frequently sentimentalizations of these images. The feminine aspect of God is one not of weakness but of strength. Only the strong can tolerate injustice, endure suffering, and continue to love when love is unrequited. Endurance has been characteristic of women.

As the figure of Jesus Christ became, in later Christian theology, that of lord and judge, "seated at the right hand of the Father," the feminine aspects of the divine, no longer to be perceived in either figure, were transferred to MARY, the mother of Jesus (in Orthodox language, THEOTOKOS, MOTHER OF GOD). Although not to be identified with Magna Mater of ancient Mediterranean and Canaanite religion, Mary has been the personification of gentleness, strength, faithfulness, and compassion. She intercedes for humans with the Father and the Son. She has been called QUEEN OF HEAVEN, symbolizing a transcendent dimension to the feminine for time and eternity. More particularly, the term VIRGIN gives her a special status.

In ancient Mediterranean religions, virgin figures such as Artemis (Diana) and Hesta (Vesta), protector of hearth and home, were characterized by their autonomy. They were not pubescent girls, awaiting a husband while still under the guardianship of fathers, nor were they wives under the rule of husbands. The virgin had an independent existence. As mother, she was related not only to her child but to all people to whom she was mother. She could act autonomously on behalf of her children without having to submit to the wishes of a husband. Only in the context of marriage law that made women dependent can one fully appreciate the authority of the virgin. In this also, she manifested characteristics of the transcendent, for she could act beneficently without fear or favor.

Feminine dimensions of the transcendent may be found also in other religions. Taoism provides the image of YIN/YANG, the masculine and feminine, which together make for wholeness. Tantric Hindu-

ism portrays SHIVA/Shakti, male and female working together. In Mahayana Buddhism Buddha has a wife/consort.

Early Christian thought indicated SOPHIA (a feminine word) as holy wisdom, whose most famous monument is the great church that Justinian built in Constantinople. SHEKINAH, the old Hebrew term for the presence of God, is also feminine. Although *spiritus* (spirit) is masculine in Latin, its Greek equivalent, *pneuma* (used for Holy Spirit in the NT), is feminine. The GNOSTICS, considered heretical in their time and whose writings were unknown until the recent discovery of the Nag Hammadi texts, gave a higher place to the feminine aspect of God than did orthodox Christianity. There are also biblical images of Israel as the consort of Yahweh, and the church as the bride of Christ. In such allusions the feminine was divinized by association.

In medieval Christianity, the mystics were aware of the feminine aspects of God. Dame JULIAN OF NORWICH addressed God as Mother. In the eighteenth century, Mother Ann and the people called SHAKERS, whom she founded, addressed God as Mother. MARY BAKER EDDY founded Christian Science in the nineteenth century, establishing the usage of Father-Mother God in *Science and Health with Key to the Scriptures*. Present-day interest in the feminine dimensions of the sacred is a continuation of a religious impulse that has been an aspect of religious understanding for millennia.

I.C.

## FEMINIST THEOLOGY.

**FEMINIST THEOLOGY.** Whether developed by women or men, a feminist theology is one rooted in the experience of women and seeks to promote equality and mutuality between the sexes, indeed among all people. It begins with the realization that sexism, the historic domination of men over women, is a fundamental expression of human sinfulness.

While women have long been aware of the distortions of the Bible used to support sexism (see Hardesty, *Women Called to Witness,* 1984), the contemporary movement began with a critique of patriarchalism, the male domination and emphasis on hierarchy evident in church history (see Mary Daly, *The Church and the Second Sex,* 1968). Daly's next effort was a scathing critique of classical Christian doctrines in *Beyond God the Father* (1973). She rejected andromorphic symbols for God and argued that the traditional identification of women with the Suffering Servant was self-destructive, while male identification with Jesus as Lord was a continuing rationalization of illegitimate power. Other early feminist theologies included Sheila Collins' *A Different Heaven and Earth* (1974) and Letty Russell's *Human Liberation in a Feminist Perspective* (1974).

The leading contemporary feminist theologian, Rosemary Radford Ruether, forged her theology in a series of articles, collected in *New Woman, New Earth*

(1975), before attempting a more systematic treatment in *Sexism and God-Talk: Toward a Feminist Theology* (1983). This work should be taken in conjunction with the biblical reinterpretation done by Letha Scanzoni and Nancy Hardesty in *All We're Meant to Be* (1974, 1986), Paul Jewett in *Man as Male and Female* (1975), Letty Russell, ed., in *The Liberating Word* (1976), Phyllis Trible in *God and the Rhetoric of Sexuality* (1978), and more recently Elisabeth Schüssler Fiorenza in *In Memory of Her: A Feminist Theological Reconstruction of Christian Origins* (1983), and *Bread Not Stone* (1984).

Feminist theology is more than a recovery of a usable past and a revision of some theological themes. Its implications touch every area of theology. As Elisabeth Schüssler Fiorenza notes, it begins with a "hermeneutics of suspicion" because of the androcentric bias of all sources—biblical, historical, psychological, even linguistic. Rosemary Radford Ruether particularly draws on prophetic and kingdom themes in Scripture, plus various strands of church history, some of which were labeled heretical by the builders of the patriarchal institutional church.

Discussions of hierarchy, inclusive language, and the meaning of symbols has led to a rethinking of the nature of God, the Trinity, and Jesus as God Incarnate. The insight that sexism is a root sin leads to a rethinking of all forms of domination and oppression—racism, nationalism, militarism, heterosexism. Indeed one of the goals of feminist theology is inclusivity; it rejects all forms of dualism. It has included also a recovery of a sense of oneness with the earth and stewardship for it.

In concrete social terms it has promoted a fresh look at Scripture's meaning for its original hearers and for today's culture, inclusive language in Scripture translation and worship, the full ordination of WOMEN, mutuality in marital relationships, an end to abuse in all forms between the sexes, and a rethinking of ethical issues originally rooted in sexism such as abortion and homosexuality. (*Compare also* FEMININE DIMENSIONS OF THE SACRED.)          N.H.

**FERTILITY CULTS AND RITES.** Fertility, the power by which life reproduces itself, has ever been a passionate concern of religion. For most premoderns, failure of the hunt or the harvest meant nothing less than starvation. The survival of the social unit, family, or tribe, was an imperative felt with virtually equal force. Small wonder, then, that when all power is believed ultimately to be of divine origin, and when sacred rites and symbols are thought to be able to petition or channel it, the fertility of plants, animals, and humans should become a major religious theme. In archaic and traditional religions especially, the enhancement of fertility is the primary object of a diversity of seasonal and quasi-magical practices and is intimately bound up with such other major themes as sacrifice and sacred kingship. Motifs common to fertility cults and rites include the principle of death

for life, sympathetic magic, and seasonal augmentation.

*Death for Life.* Just as the seed that seems to be dead, when buried, shoots forth new life, so the sacrifice of a life, whether vegetable, animal, or human, is often believed to generate fertility. Frequently the objective is reinforced by scattering the blood or dismembered body over the fields or exhibiting the skulls in those places believed to hold sacred power. The Jivaro of South America, for example, danced the shrunken heads they took through the fields in which they grew their crops to imbue them with the victims' life-force.

*Sympathetic Magic.* Though now somewhat old-fashioned, this term is as good as any to refer to those practices that endeavor to produce a given result through the making and manipulation of parallel acts and symbols. The sacred marriage of a divine king, and above all its consummation, may enhance the fertility of an entire kingdom. Figures such as the *lingam* or pillar that represent the Hindu god SHIVA undoubtedly had their origin in fertility religion.

*Seasonal Augmentation.* Religion very often seeks to "augment" and complement what nature is doing in the seasonal round. Spring, the time of planting and the birthing of animals, is therefore a critical time for fertility rites; remnants can be seen in the symbolism of Easter and the Maypole. The presentation of "firstfruits," characteristic of harvest festivals, also has fertility overtones; these offerings are like "seeds" to be returned by the gods many times over in the crops of next year.

Although fertility is less overtly a part of modern than of archaic religion, symbols, festivals, and language stemming ultimately from it, though sometimes with changed meaning, remain embedded in the world's faiths.

R.E.

**FESTIVALS.** See FEASTS.

**FESTUS, PORCIUS.** Festus succeeded to the office of Roman PROCURATOR in Caesarea, following FELIX, around A.D. 58. Virtually nothing is known about him except what Luke in Acts, and Josephus in *Antiquities* and the *Jewish War,* tell us about him.

Arnold Ehrhardt (*The Acts of the Apostles,* 1969) calls him "the one honourable governor Rome ever sent to Judaea," but Luke's assessment of his character is more negative (Acts 24:27–26:32). What comes through the narrative in Acts is Festus' decision to have Paul's case reach a conclusion, especially as Festus seems to have been convinced of his innocence (26:31).

In face of the possibility of a retrial in Jerusalem, Paul played a trump card and uttered words—"I appeal to Caesar"—which were his privilege as a Roman citizen (25:11). This statement at once nullified all local proceedings and automatically transferred his case to the imperial court at Rome

(25:12). In the interview of Paul with Herod Agrippa II, Festus was evidently out of his depth, though he saw the essence of the charge brought against the Apostle (25:19), even if he could not understand its implication (26:24). Festus was later involved in a dispute with Jewish leaders, and he died in office about A.D. 60.

R.M.

**FEUERBACH, LUDWIG** (1804–72). German philosopher, assailant of Christianity, and a predecessor of Marxism's rejection of God. Born at Landshut, Bavaria, he studied theology at Heidelberg and Berlin and in 1828 received a doctorate in philosophy at Erlangen. However, his teaching at Erlangen and Heidelberg brought little success, and from 1837 to 1860 he resided at Bruckberg, writing and managing his wife's interest in a declining porcelain factory. He moved to Nuremberg in 1860 and died in poverty.

HEGEL's IDEALISM heavily influenced Feuerbach's early years, but he rejected Hegelianism in two publications: *Toward the Critique of the Hegelian Philosophy* (1839) and *Principles of the Philosophy of the Future* (1843). He believed that reality resides not in abstract spirit but in nature, in the world of the senses, in "sense realism"; only sensuous being is true and real. Feuerbach's famous *Essence of Christianity* (1841) and *Lectures on the Essence of Religion* (1851) explained Christianity as a projection and false deification of human hopes. Feuerbach expounds transcendent theology as immanent anthropology— humanity in its fullness. His writings convey his belief that one should let human devotion be directed not to an unreal God and immortality, but to the realization of human aspirations now. Transcendent deity is illusion, only a knowledge of humanity is relevant, according to Feuerbach.

C.M.

**FICHTE, JOHANN GOTTLIEB** (1762–1814). German philosopher who helped found the University of Berlin. Born at Rammenau, Fichte studied at the "Prince's School" in Pforta and the universities of Jena and Leipzig. After tutoring privately (1784–87), he went to Zurich and settled at Leipzig in 1790. Drawn to Kantianism, he visited KANT and anonymously published *Critique of All Revelation* (1792). Kant praised the work, and the disclosure of Fichte's authorship brought immediate acclaim. Between 1793 and 1799 Fichte taught philosophy at Jena, but left for Berlin, accused of atheism.

In his philosophy he seemed to make the moral order absolute, leaving no place for God. Although interrupted by the Napoleonic wars, Fichte helped establish the University of Berlin, serving as its first rector and professor of philosophy (1810–14). Gradually Fichte modified his philosophy and departed from Kant. Fichte's *Vocation of Man* (1800) pictures humanity as related to the sensuous realm, where following one's conscience leads to harmonious

human unity. This book also related to the spiritual realm of eternal will, whose voice is conscience. Universal rational will, which finite beings apprehend incompletely, bonds everything, and heeding one's conscience brings immortality now. His other translated works include *The Science of Knowledge* and *The Science of Ethics*.

C.M.

**FIDEISM.** The doctrine that humanity is saved by faith alone. This is God's freely willed gift through the Atonement in Jesus Christ.

The doctrine took concrete form in the writings of AUGUSTINE, who insisted that the knowledge of God came only through the response of faith and that reason could not even assist in the process. It was not anti-intellectual, but it gave faith precedence over reason. LUTHER raised the doctrine as a rallying cry of the Reformation. The twentieth-century theologian of faith was KARL BARTH.

Others have disagreed, stating that the intellect is God-given and can be used to understand God. In reverse order, knowing about God could lead to faith in God. Fideism then becomes a disparaging word signifying viewpoints of those who are unwilling or unable to use reason for faith.

I.C.

**FILIAL PIETY.** The term commonly used to translate the Confucian virtue of *hsiao* (Chinese), refers to the obligation of children to serve their parents and to transmit their honor and lineage. Extended beyond the grave, it underlies the *ancestrism* of China and other lands, such as Korea and Japan, where the Confucian value system has spread.

R.E.

*FILIOQUE.* The Latin word meaning "and from the Son." Its addition in the West to the NICENE CREED caused friction with the East, which accused the West of both tampering with the creed and of heterodox views on the TRINITY. This interpolation, which probably originated in Spain, was in common usage in the Frankish kingdom by the ninth century, when the Eastern church discovered it, and bitter controversy ensued. What was at stake was the DOUBLE PROCESSION OF THE HOLY SPIRIT, a doctrine that the West affirmed and the East rejected. As the debate continued, each side accused the other of heresy, and therefore the *Filioque* became one of the stumbling blocks that eventually led to schism. A significant by-product of this controversy was the resurgence of the APOSTLES' CREED as the one most commonly used in the West. In order to avoid alienating either the Franks or the Byzantines, the popes began using that ancient Roman creed, which they attributed to the apostles. Eventually, that shorter creed gained widespread acceptance in the West, and the Nicene Creed fell into relative disuse.

J.G.

Courtesy of Oberlin College

*Charles G. Finney*

## FINNEY, CHARLES GRANDISON (1792–
1875). Revivalist and educator. Finney was born on August 29, in Warren, Connecticut, to Sylvester and Rebecca Rice Finney. In 1794 the family moved to Oneida County, New York. Educated in local schools and then for two years at Hamilton Oneida Academy in Clinton, Finney began the study of law in 1818 in Adams, New York. After a conversion experience on October 10, 1821, Finney studied for the ministry. Licensed to preach March 17, 1824, and ordained July 1, Finney married Lydia Andrews (1794–1847) of Whitestown that same year.

His ministry was soon marked by enthusiastic revivals, subsequently called the Second GREAT AWAKENING. His New Measures—anxious meetings, praying for people by name, protracted meetings, colloquial preaching, and, most controversial, women praying and testifying in public—provoked fellow revivalists Asahel Nettleton and Lyman Beecher to confront him in July 1827 at New Lebanon, New York.

The Second Free Presbyterian Church in New York City, meeting in the rented Chatham Street Theatre, became a home for Finney in 1832 and for the national conventions of the Benevolent Empire. Here in 1835 Finney gave his famed *Lectures on Revivals of Religion.*

In 1835 Finney became professor of theology at Oberlin Collegiate Institute in Ohio, serving as president from 1851 to 1866. In 1836 he withdrew from the Presbyterian Church and became pastor of New York's Broadway Tabernacle, a Congregational church, until 1837. He also pastored Oberlin's First Congregational Church, 1835–72.

Finney's New School theology was marked by an emphasis on human ability to repent and on the possibility of moral perfection. He was also noted for his encouragement of Christian participation in reform, particularly abolition, temperance, and woman's rights.

Finney also authored *Sermons on Important Subjects* (1836), *Lectures to Professing Christians* (1837), and two volumes of *Lectures on Systematic Theology* (1846–47). He served editorially with the "Oberlin Evangelist" and the "Oberlin Quarterly Review." He died in Oberlin on August 16.

N.H.

**FIQH.** From the Arabic word for "knowledge, understanding." In Islamic jurisprudence, *fiqh* refers to the application of the sources of law—the Qur'an, the Hadith or traditions of what the Prophet (Muhammad) said and did, and legal precedent—to specific cases. In its wider sense, then, *fiqh* refers to the entire body of Muslim law, which as a legal corpus is called the Shari'ah. In Islamic theory, orthodox law is derived from (1) the Qur'an, (2) tradition, (3) consensus of the faithful, and (4) analogical reasoning based on the foregoing. The law is held to be divine in origin; human reason or experience in themselves are not sufficient to create any part of it. In principle, this law is unchanging and covers every detail of human life. For this reason, however, some parts of it do not entail public or criminal retribution, but enjoin upon the offender such personal atonement as fasting or acts of charity. The application of *fiqh* or Islamic practical law to modern conditions is a matter of much concern in the Muslim world today.

R.E.

**FIRE.** Regarded as indispensable for human existence (Ecclus. 39:26), fire met diverse secular needs of ancient humanity and played a vital role in the Israelite cult. It was also perceived as a crucial element in divine appearance and action.

*Fire and Secular Life.* Though insatiable fire adversely affected human well-being (Prov. 30:16), a controlled fire served several well-defined human needs. Fire was used in cooking (Isa. 44:15; John 21:9), heating (Jer. 36:22; Acts 28:2), burning refuse (Lev. 8:17), as well as in refining metals and using them in manufacture (Exod. 32:24; Isa. 44:12). Moreover, during warfare, captured enemy cities were often destroyed by fire (Josh. 6:24 [Jericho]; 11:11 [Hazor]; I Kings 9:16 [Gezer]).

*Fire and Worship.* Fire was used to ignite sacrifices in the Israelite cult. Burnt offerings, involving victims "from the herd," were entirely burnt on the altar as sacrificial gifts to God (Lev. 1:1-17). The consumption of such gifts out of the worshiper's substance was interpreted as indicative of divine acceptance (I Kings 18:38). Since animal holocausts were a daily affair, the altar fire was ever-burning (Lev. 6:12-13). This also aptly symbolized God's presence in Israelite worship. Since they involved the sacrificing of humans to pagan gods, child holocausts were outlawed in Israel (Deut. 12:31; 18:10). Nevertheless, in the late monarchical period, that prohibition was sometimes violated (II Kings 16:3; 17:17; 21:6) and correspondingly evoked prophetic censure (Jer. 7:31; 19:5). Cultic fire was also used as a means for maintaining ritual cleanliness (Lev. 13:52; Num. 31:23; Isa. 6:6-7).

*Fire and Divine Appearance.* Fire imagery is conspicuous in many biblical depictions of God's self-revelation. In a ceremony establishing Yahweh's covenant with Abraham, mysterious divine presence is symbolized by fire passing between the pieces of the patriarch's offering (Gen. 15:17). Yahweh's initial theophany to Moses involves a BURNING BUSH (Exod. 3:2; Acts 7:30). A nocturnal pillar of fire denotes divine presence and leadership during Israel's wilderness wandering (Exod. 13:21-22; Num. 14:14; Deut. 1:33; Ps. 78:14). At Mount Sinai, the site of God's theophany *par excellence*, elements of fire and storm mediate compelling divine presence (Exod. 19:18; 24:17; Deut. 4:11-12, 33). Moreover, fire is central in poetic theophanies attesting divine intervention. In Psalm 18, a royal thanksgiving, Yahweh's arrival to rescue the elect is signaled by imagery involving devouring fire, glowing coals, and lightnings (vv. 8, 12, 14). And Psalm 50, a liturgy portraying Yahweh's dynamic appearance to summon the people to covenant accountability, declares, "Before him is a devouring fire, round about him a mighty tempest" (v. 3). Visions meditating on God's future self-revelation also depict divine arrival in fire (Isa. 66:15; Mal. 3:2). In sum, fire imagery deftly captures the terrifying aspect of God's nearness and resourcefully defends God's unapproachable holiness.

*Fire and Divine Action.* A God capable of dispatching lightning (heavenly fire) as arrows (Pss. 18:14; 144:6) sometimes subjects evildoers to fatal fiery punishment (Gen. 19:24 [Sodom and Gomorrah]; Lev. 10:2 [Nadab and Abihu]; Num. 16:35 [Korah and his Levitical colleagues]). Reports of actual judgment by fire are less common than figurative references to divine wrath that incorporate fire imagery. Amos admonishes his listeners to return to Yahweh lest he angrily "break out like fire in the house of Joseph" (5:6). The king asks Yahweh, "How long will thy wrath burn like fire?" (Ps. 89:46). Sinful Judah is threatened with exile since in Yahweh's anger "a fire is kindled" (Jer. 15:14). Indeed, jealous Yahweh's proscription of Israelite idolatry is buttressed by the stern observation that God is "a

devouring fire" (Deut. 4:24). In later OT writings and in the NT, fire dominates visions of inevitable eschatological judgment (Ezek. 39:6; Isa. 66:24; Dan. 7:11; Matt. 13:40-42; Mark 9:43-48; II Pet. 3:7; Rev. 14:9-10). Thus the Holy Deity, whose anger is kindled against human sinfulness, is destined to have the last word.

J.K.K.

**FIRSTBORN.** In its legal and cultic sense, the term refers to the eldest male child in a family; applied to animals it means the "eldest male offspring" ("firstling") of a beast. From beginning to end, the OT is clear that the firstborn was the preeminent offspring, eligible to receive a double share of the inheritance (Deut. 21:15-17) and blessed with extra emotional significance as well (compare Zech. 12:10). It is this sense of preeminence, and not the connection with atoning sacrifice, that is stressed in the only really significant NT use of the term (Col. 1:15-20). Here Christ is called both "the first-born of all creation" and "the first-born from the dead."

Moses tells Pharaoh that Israel is Yahweh's firstborn son, and that refusal to let this favored "son" go will result in punishment of Egypt's own firstborn (Exod. 4:22-23). Because Pharaoh persists in his refusal, when the angel of death passes over the houses of Israel, it is the firstborn of Egypt, even the firstborn of Pharaoh's own house, who pay with their lives (Exod. 12:29). Yahweh's mighty act of vengeance against the firstborn of Egypt is a theme repeatedly returned to in the Psalms (compare Pss. 78:51; 105:36; 135:8; 136:10).

At the end of the account of the Passover slaying of the firstborn in Egypt, "the Lord said to Moses, 'Consecrate to me all the first-born; whatever is the first to open the womb among the people of Israel, both of man and of beast, is mine'" (Exod. 13:1-2; compare Exod. 22:29-30; Lev. 27:26). On the face of it, this early legal injunction might be construed to suggest a practice of human sacrifice. Other texts hint at the possibility that this kind of sacrifice was actually made on occasion. I Kings 16:34 reports that "Hiel of Bethel built Jericho; he laid its foundation at the cost of Abiram his first-born" (compare Josh. 6:26). This obscure reference has been clarified by the discovery of human skeletons in foundation deposits, suggesting that a builder would sacrifice a human in order to guarantee good fortune for the structure. Even the prophet Micah protests against the possibility that a person might sacrifice the family's most precious possession in the hope of placating God: "Shall I give my first-born for my transgression, the fruit of my body for the sin of my soul?" (Mic. 6:7).

It is no surprise, then, to discover extensive legal provision for the "redemption" of the firstborn of the human family and of animals. After first announcing Yahweh's claim on "all that opens the womb," the Priestly text Exodus 34:19-20 continues, "The firstling of an ass you shall redeem with a lamb. . . . All the first-born of your sons you shall redeem." The meaning of this redemption is spelled out more precisely in Numbers 3:11-13, 40-51, which states that for every firstborn male in Israel, a male Levite is to be dedicated to the Lord, and any remainder of firstborn males is to be covered by redemption money to be paid to the Aaronic priests. According to Numbers 18:14-19, the firstborn of unclean animals and humankind shall be redeemed at the fixed price of five silver shekels, but the firstling of a cow or a sheep or a goat shall not be redeemed but sacrificed, its blood sprinkled on the altar, its fat burned in the fire, and its flesh given over to the Levites who attend the sacrifice to be their means of sustenance.

Although the firstborn son enjoys a privileged status, it is noteworthy that with minor exception here and there (compare I Chr. 26:10), primogeniture is not perceived as the essential guarantee to political or priestly succession. The special place of the firstborn begins with the preemptive claim of Yahweh upon that individual, and that claim is resolved through the cult.

W.S.T.

**FIRSTFRUITS.** In the OT, the FIRSTBORN son of a family, the firstborn lamb, calf, or kid of all the flocks and herds, and, in later times, the first cutting of the harvest and shearing of wool, which were offered to the Lord, in sacrificial worship. While the Canaanites sacrificed their own firstborn sons to gain the favor of their Baals and gods, the Hebrews ransomed their sons by offering animals instead (Exod. 22:29; 34:19 ff.). According to the Law of Moses, the firstborn of the flocks belonged to Yahweh (Exod. 13:2; 34:19, Lev. 27:26). Animals considered clean were sacrificed, and unclean ones were destroyed.

Human sacrifice was widely practiced in the ancient Near East, and the Hebrew faith early protested against it. Since this so often involved the firstborn son, such protests against rejection of human sacrifice plays a role in the continuing theology of the firstfruits throughout Hebrew history. The Hebrews gave special honor to the eldest son, giving him the father's place of honor as head of the family, plus a double portion of the father's estate (Gen. 43:33; Deut. 21:17). Some scholars have suggested that the story of Abraham and Isaac, which almost ended in tragedy (Gen. 22), may have been such a protest against sacrificing the firstborn son. Regardless of this, the law of Moses clearly recognized Yahweh's rightful claim on the firstborn (Exod. 13:2; 22:29; Gen. 4:4).

In the NT, Christ is viewed as the preeminent Firstfruits, the only begotten Son, whose death on the cross once for all put an end to the whole Hebrew sacrificial system. His death completely ended the need for blood sacrifices and burnt offerings. The book of Hebrews is essentially a long treatise on Christ as the one, perfect, and final SACRIFICE.

Indeed, the sacrifices of the firstfruits and all other rituals in the OT period were but shadows, foretellings, of the only real sacrifice, acceptable to God. In Christ, all of the Law, the Prophets, and the sacrifices, both ritual and ethical, have been fulfilled and forever rendered obsolete.

J.C.

**FISH.** See ACROSTIC.

**FISH.** The species figures prominently in the biblical literature since the Mediterranean Sea provided Israel with her coastline and the Sea of Galilee was rich in fish, providing a main trade for the Galilean population (Mark 1:16-20; Luke 5:6; John 21:3-11).

*The Old Testament.* Foreign nations such as Egypt and coastal towns such as Tyre were noted for their fish (Num. 11:5; Neh. 13:16). The Egyptians worshiped the fish, and a law in Deuteronomy 4:18 prohibits the making of fish images for this purpose. Fish were caught and used as part of Jewish diet in the maritime ports along the Mediterranean coast and especially in the Lake Gennesaret in Galilee. It is estimated that there are some twenty-four different types of fish found in this lake.

Sometimes fish are mentioned, in a symbolic way, in reference to Israel's captivity when she was "swallowed up" by a foreign power, likened to a sea monster (Jer. 51:34, 44; Ezek. 32:2, 3; Jonah 1:17). Tobias is described as in danger of being swallowed by a large fish in the Tigris (Tob. 6:2).

*The New Testament.* The chief concentration of references is in the Gospel accounts of Jesus' call to the fishermen who plied their trade on the coastline of the Sea of Galilee, notably at Capernaum and Bethsaida, "the house of fish." To them the call was addressed: "Follow me and I will make you become fishers of men" (Mark 1:17 and parallels; compare Jer. 16:16; see W. A. Wuellner, *Meaning of Fishers of Men,* 1967). It is not surprising that Jesus used the examples of fish and fishing in his parables (for example, Matt. 13:47-50) when he spoke to a Galilean audience (Mark 4:1; Luke 5:1), and the mode of operation— dragging the nets ashore to pick out the good fish from the bad—suggests the use of a large seine net to catch fish (John 21:8). Matthew records one incident (Matt. 17:27) of a coin found in a fish's mouth, implying a large fish now called *chromis simonis* after the episode involving Simon Peter. More likely the fish in question was the catfish, *clarias lazera,* a predator fish, and scaleless, therefore unclean and not sought by Galilean fishermen.

The fish in Lake Galilee were evidently best caught at night (Luke 5:5; John 21:3), and in the incident of John 21 were eaten at breakfast (John 21:12-13). From the latter story fish were given a eucharistic significance in the subsequent history of the church, and Christ is actually prayed to under the image of the fish in the Pectorius inscription (third century): "Divine offspring of the heavenly Fish . . . eat it with hunger, holding the Fish in thy hands. Fill me with the Fish, I pray thee, Lord Saviour."

R.M.

**FISKE, JOHN** (1842–1901). The famed apologist for CHARLES DARWIN and Herbert Spencer was born on March 30 to Edmund Brewster and Mary Fisk Bound Green of Hartford, Connecticut.

Fiske entered Harvard as a sophomore in 1860. There he discovered Spencer and began to openly advocate evolution. After obtaining his B.A. in 1863, he passed the bar exam in July 1864 but seldom practiced law, preferring to write and lecture on science, history, and philosophy. He married Abby Morgan Brooks of Petersham, Massachusetts, on September 6, 1864. They had six children.

Fluent in nearly twenty languages, Fiske authored more than thirty books including *The Origin of Evil* (1899), *The Destiny of Man* (1884), and his two-volume *Outlines of Cosmic Philosophy* (1874). He died July 4, 1901.

N.H.

**FLAGELLATION.** The practice of scourging oneself in order to expiate for sin, or to control the body and its passions. Several teachers of Christian asceticism have recommended it, and it has been practiced to various degrees throughout most of the history of MONASTICISM. In the late Middle Ages, however, flagellation became widespread and popular, giving rise to the movement of the Flagellants. These first appeared in 1260, but became most numerous in the fourteenth century. Such Flagellants joined the movement for thirty-three days, during which they followed a strict ritual of public self-flagellation twice daily, and again in private at night. At first, the leaders of the church did not disapprove. But when the Flagellants began speaking of their practices as a form of PENANCE and as a "second baptism," they were accused of usurping the "power of the keys," and their practices were banned. Still, the movement continued a clandestine existence for several generations. Similar practices have appeared at other times in places as far removed from each other as the Philippines and New Mexico.

J.G.

**FLESH.** *Old Testament.* Hebrew anthropology is based on a phenomenological approach, that is, people as members of the human family as distinct from the animal kingdom are seen as they appear to the eye of the observer. This is clearly borne out when we look at the term "flesh," which stands over against its opposite SPIRIT (*nephesh*, used of people as living persons, and *ruah*, applied to people in relation to God). *Nephesh* is used of the totality of those elements that constitute a human person ("souls" meaning people: Gen. 46:26, 27, KJV, compare RSV). So in Psalm 124:7 "our souls" means "we ourselves." Yet *nephesh* does not exist in its own right. The OT knows

next to nothing of a person as a disembodied "soul," a ghostly apparition. Every *nephesh* needs a BODY, for which the Hebrew term is "flesh" (*basar*), as completing one's total personhood and so making a human body different from the angels or God, who have no body (Isa. 31:3). In this sense "flesh" in the OT is a neutral term to denote the physical component of a person. It is the lifeless stuff of a person, the raw material out of which the real person emerges once *ruah*, "spirit," is breathed into it (Gen. 2:7) to make it a "living being" (Ps. 104:29). So the result is *nephesh*, which is what is produced once the flesh is animated by "spirit," usually thought of as a gift of God.

So OT anthropology is wonderfully self-consistent, and is the product of Hebrew observation: when a person stops breathing (there is no "spirit" left), the *nephesh* departs, and the "flesh" stops moving, and in due time starts to decompose. This is death. So "flesh" takes on the sense of dust, that is, that material from which a person emerged and to which one returns in death (Gen. 3:19; 6:3; Isa. 40:6; Jer. 17:5).

Yet, once animated by spirit, human flesh can have aspirations for God (Ps. 84:2), can rejoice in God (Ps. 16:9), or can reverence God (Ps. 119:120). But it is equally the seat of biological functions, for example, strength (II Chr. 32:8) and sex (Eccl. 11:10; Ezra 23:20). Yet the canonical OT does not link "flesh" with sin, as though to be human per se made a person a sinner. The flesh is weak, but not evil; it is other than God, but not alien to God since God made it (Gen. 2:7; Ps. 8:5; 139:13-15). Only in Hellenistic Judaism (for example, Wisd. Sol.) does flesh take on a negative connotation; and this is carried forward to one strand of NT teaching.

*New Testament.* The term for "flesh" is *sarx*, found ninety-one times in Paul, whose teaching is clearly the most emphatic in the NT. There are two distinct categories of meaning in Pauline thought: (1) There is a neutral sense where *sarx* carries the sense of "bodily existence" (Gal. 2:20; Phil. 1:22, 24) with a reminder that human beings are corporeal and weak (I Cor. 1:29; 15:50; Rom. 3:20; Gal. 1:16; Rom. 1:3). In this regard to live "in the flesh" means simply to exist as a person, and in one place (I Cor. 15:39) a person's life as *homo sapiens* is distinguished from life in other spheres (animal, reptile) because a person's "flesh" is different. (2) The second range of meanings is more characteristic of Paul. Some interpreters associate Paul's negative attitude to "flesh" with his Hellenistic world view, especially as it is seen in the later developments of GNOSTICISM.

According to this view, Paul thought of people as essentially evil because their "flesh" was part of material creation, utterly alien to God. But it is more likely that Paul took his cue from the OT tradition in which he was raised. For Paul as a former Pharisee, the meaning of "flesh" has a specific sense. It is derived from his Jewish-rabbinic background, where the

Hebrew equivalent of "flesh" meant the "evil influence" that goads people into sin. *Sarx* relates to a person's existence as a sinner in the eyes of the Creator. It seems that for Paul, this condition does not come about because a person has attachment to material things or a person has carnal desires ("sins of the flesh" in the popular phrase, though one passage may appear to point to this: Gal 5:16-24). Rather, for the NT generally, *sarx* is a person's weakness as a moral being that has been exploited and attacked by sin, which is often personified as a demonic force. People are frail in the ethical dimension of living, and fall easy prey to such an inroad (see Rom. 7:14-25). "Flesh" denotes a person's proclivity to selfishness (living for self; in fact "the self life" would be a good translation of *sarx*) and pride. The latter term is connected with boasting (I Cor. 1:29-31; Phil. 3:3, 4), which is the essence of a person's proud claim to be independent of God and to be self-confident on the ground of religious merit. In this respect "flesh" stands for a person's resistance to God's grace. And "flesh" with its downward pull can only be overcome by the HOLY SPIRIT, who, in Paul, is the power that leads men and women to God.

R.M.

**FLOOD.** In the poetry of the OT, a synonym for the ocean or sea. The term is also used for rivers, like the Euphrates or the Nile (Exod. 15:8; Ps. 93:3; Jonah 2:3; Amos 8:8), but is chiefly used for the Great Flood, which God sent upon the earth in the days of Noah (Gen. 6:5–8:22).

The story of the Flood is the longest of the prehistorical stories of the beginnings of humanity in the Hebrew Bible. One copy of a flood story is said by scholars to be a copy made in the seventeenth century B.C. from one written as much as two thousand years before. In Genesis there are two different legendary accounts of the Flood, one from the Yahwist (or J) and the other from the Priestly strand (or P). Scholars generally conclude that J dates from around 1000 B.C. and originated in southern Judah, while P originated among the Priestly class at the time of the Judean exile to Babylonia (586–539 B.C.). In the main outlines of the story the two traditions agree, but there are significant differences, due to the theological outlooks of the writers, which stand side by side in apparent contradiction in the text. At some later date than the return from exile, perhaps 450–400 B.C., a redactor (editor) joined the J and P stories together and gave the Jews and the world the Flood story as we now know it.

The study of ancient history, comparative literature, and archaeology adds immeasurably to our appreciation of the Flood story. The Flood story (at least in its Mesopotamian expression) originated in Babylonia, a country often ravaged by huge floods. Flood deposits of clay five feet deep and others eight feet deep, overlying wreckage twenty-five feet deep, have been found in Ur and Uhaimir. As Genesis 8:4

says, the Great Flood struck the valley of the Tigris and Euphrates rivers. Just because the Mesopotamian area suffered unusually severe floods some six thousand years ago does not mean that the entire globe was covered with water. Nor does the occurrence of flood stories in the myths and legends of peoples from all over the world prove that there was a universal flood. It is the case that flood stories are found among almost all peoples, even among the American Indians, one of whose myths says the first man rode to safety on the back of a huge turtle. Interestingly, ancient Egypt, which depended on the yearly flooding of the Nile, had no story of a punishing flood.

The Flood story, in texts from Mari, name NOAH as a god. Texts from Nineveh, the GILGAMESH EPIC, call the hero of the Flood Ut-Naphishtun, who built a boat to exact specifications, put his family and the needs of all life aboard and escaped the Flood, which destroyed humankind. Ut–Naphishtun sent out birds—a dove, a swallow, and a raven—to check the water's depth. The gods (plural) in this story are not dignified but quarrel, fear, and swarm like flies around Ut-Naphishtun's sacrifice. A flood text from Nippur calls the hero Ziusudra and declares him a very religious person.

The Genesis story is religiously elevated over all the more ancient accounts. God sends the Flood only after long-suffering with human sin. Because God does not want to destroy the human race, God instructs Noah to build an ark (or houseboat) and stock it with provisions, load his family (including his sons and daughters-in-law of child-producing years) and (the J and P accounts differ) one pair (or seven pairs, Gen. 7:2, 9) of every kind of animal, including reptiles and birds, that exists on the earth. Noah remains faithful to God despite the mockery of his neighbors, becoming a model of obedient faith. Like Abraham later, Noah obeys and trusts God, believing in the things not seen (as the writer of Hebrews puts it). By the Flood, God punishes sin and saves the faithful remnant that is righteous. Thus the Petrine letters later refer to Noah and the Flood as exemplars of salvation, the power of baptism to save (I Pet. 3:20), and of God's ultimate righteousness (II Pet. 2:5). The early Christians were the heirs of this thousand-year-old tradition. Peter, Matthew (24:36-41), and Luke (17:26 ff.) naturally used Noah as a symbol of the judgment of God to come and of the urgency to win people for Christ's kingdom before Judgment Day.

Of course, the NT refers to Noah as a hero of faith and never questions whether it is a true story or not. The NT writers were not comparative religion scholars or textual critics. The story of Noah became part of Hebrew religion with its adoption by the Yahwist (J) one thousand years before Christ. According to the Yahwist, Noah was the first man to offer Yahweh sacrifices (although God did not reveal the sacred name until the time of Moses and the burning bush). Five hundred years later, the Priestly writer (P) tells us Noah was given a covenant by God, with the rainbow as the sign of God's promise to providentially preserve the world. Throughout the centuries, the story of the Flood illustrated the ethical character and just but loving nature of God.

The story of the "Great Flood" (or "Deluge") is the product of the religious imagination of the early Hebrews who borrowed it from their pagan neighbors and recast it (perhaps three thousand years after it was first written on clay tablets) in the terms of their developing monotheistic, ethical faith.

J.C.

**FLORENCE, COUNCIL OF.** A church council noted for achieving union with the Greek Orthodox Church. It was actually part of the conciliar struggle with the papacy for power in the aftermath of the COUNCIL OF CONSTANCE. A council to guide the church in keeping with the *Frequens* decree of Constance was long delayed. It finally met at Basel (1431–37). Sharp rivalries between pope and council created a split. Pope Eugene IV translated a minority to Ferrara, 1437–38; to Florence, 1439–42; and then to Rome, 1442–48. Meanwhile Basel elected a rival pope, Felix V (1439). Basel lost international interest and support, and Felix stepped down in 1449. The papacy had won over conciliar reform. Excitement soared at Ferrara. Seven hundred Greeks arrived, and the emperor and the patriarch of Constantinople met. The Greeks needed help against the Turks. Reluctantly, the Greeks acknowledged FILIOQUE (the Spirit proceeds from the Father *and* the Son) but refused to make it their symbol, and they insisted on keeping their own rites and the marriage of priests. Papal primacy remained ambiguous, each side interpreting "primacy" in its own way. One hundred and fifteen Latins and thirty-three Greeks signed the union document. The reunion was triumphantly celebrated in Florence on July 6, 1439. Union was also achieved with the Armenians in 1439 and the Jacobites in 1442. However, several Greek leaders retained objections, including Greek Bishop Mark of Ephesus. A real union was not actually achieved. Constantinople fell in 1453, and a synod in Constantinople (1472) revoked action at Florence.

C.M.

**FONT.** A basin, of stone or metal, generally resting on a pedestal, in which baptismal water is kept. The minister holds the child above the font and sprinkles or pours water on the child's head. Adults kneel for baptism. Although developed for infant baptisms, some early fonts could hold an adult.

J.C.

**FOOTWASHING.** A pious ritual, practiced since ancient times in the Eastern Orthodox and Roman Catholic churches, of washing the feet of worshipers at the Holy Communion service on Maundy Thursday. In recent years the pope has revived the custom of personally washing the feet of communicants at Maundy Thursday Mass, and the practice has been adopted by many Lutheran and other Protestant congregations.

The ritual is based on Jesus' washing the disciples' feet before the Last Supper, recorded in John 13:4-20, and referred to in I Timothy 5:10. The early Lutheran church rejected the ritual as a Roman Catholic attempt at righteousness by ceremonial works. It was elected as a preferred practice by Protestant sectarians after the Reformation, especially by Anabaptists and Mennonites, who saw in it a sign of brotherhood and humility. Among these groups, footwashing became a rite equal in sacredness to the Lord's Supper. The Anabaptists felt that the ritual was part of their desired return to the practices of the primitive church. They also felt that Jesus' command that the disciples ought to wash one another's feet should make the act obligatory for all Christians. Because of their understanding of the Lord's Supper as only a symbol of Christian fellowship, and not a sacrament, the acted parable of brotherly love seen in washing one another's feet seemed to have the same value as the communion itself. Later sectarians, "The Footwashing Baptists" and the Winebrennarians in the Church of God (after A.D. 1825), also adopted the practice.

J.C.

**FORBEARANCE.** In the RSV the noun "forbearance" and the verb "forbear" are used to translate a variety of Hebrew and Greek words. In several instances the word designates simply the act of refraining from a particular type of conduct (for example, I Kings 22:6, 15; II Chr. 18;5, 14; Job 16:6; Eph. 6:9). More often, however, it describes the tolerance and restraint demonstrated in the face of provocation and becomes nearly synonymous with PATIENCE and long-sufferance. God shows restraint toward persistently sinful humanity in hopes that such forbearance will lead to repentance (Rom. 2:4; II Pet. 3:9, 15; Jer. 15:15). God suspends judgment for a time and does not immediately respond with punishment (Rom. 3:25). The same quality of patience is expected of Christians in their relationships. They are to forbear "one another in love" (Eph. 4:2; Col. 3:13; II Cor. 6:6; Phil. 4:5; II Tim. 2:24).

C.B.C.

**FORBIDDEN BOOKS.** *See* INDEX OF PROHIBITED BOOKS.

**FOREIGNER.** To the ancient Hebrews, a Gentile, someone of another nation, ethnic group, or race. In the OT, this meant a worshiper of a false god or gods; an idolator (Exod. 20:10; in contrast to Israel, who is God's people, holy, "set apart," Deut. 14:2). All foreigners were seen as a threat, religiously and politically. The ancient Hebrews were called upon to be exclusivistic during the era of the conquest of

Canaan (or at least the later historians claimed this, including the ban or war of extermination against the Canaanites), and much later, after the return of the Jews from Babylonian exile in 539 B.C. There were strict rules against mixed or foreign marriages (Exod. 34:15 and especially Ezra) and the worship of other, false, gods.

The occasional foreigner or stranger who settled among the Hebrews was to be treated fairly and justly, however. Such a settler was called a stranger or SOJOURNER (Exod. 20:10). Such strangers had definite rights according to the Law of Moses (Exod. 22:21; 12:19). They were to be treated respectfully, with kindness (Lev. 19:33 ff.; Deut. 10:18 ff.). The word "foreigner" occurs only in four places in the Bible: Exodus 12:45; Deuteronomy 15:3; Obadiah 11; and in the NT in Ephesians 2:19 KJV.

J.C.

**FOREKNOWLEDGE.** A person who has foreknowledge knows in advance what is going to happen, even while the events are still in the future. Usually, too, it is implied that this is a quite specific and detailed knowledge of what will happen, not just a general hunch. Obviously human beings do not possess foreknowledge; it is part of the finite human condition that the future is unknown, though indeed people can make intelligent guesses. But theologians and philosophers have commonly ascribed foreknowledge to God, and have believed that the future lies open to God. Sometimes this is part of the wider teaching that past, present, and future are all equally present to God.

The difficulty in such a view is that it seems to entail a strict DETERMINISM. If God already knows that *A* will murder *B* on such and such a date in such and such a year, then is not that event irrevocably fixed, and presumably all the intervening events that will lead up to it? What then becomes of human responsibility and FREE WILL? Where foreknowledge is identified with foreordaining (as in Calvin's theology), it does seem to be the case that one has opted for a rigid determinism and that the human experience of freely choosing one course of action rather than another is only an illusion.

There is a different interpretation of foreknowledge that avoids such unacceptable conclusions. Leibniz taught that God indeed foresees the entire future course of events, but that God's foreknowledge includes not only what will in fact happen but every other possible course of events. Thus, at any given moment, God has foreknowledge of all *possible* future events. Exactly what possibilities will be realized, even God does not know, but God's PROVIDENCE is able to cope with whatever is actualized within the total range of possibilities. On this view, room is left for the exercise of human freedom, and there is a measure of plasticity and openness in the cosmic process. It acknowledges the reality of divine foreknowledge but interprets the concept in a way that is compatible with the world we know in everyday experience.

A further question is raised by the foreknowledge ascribed to Jesus in the Gospels. In particular, he foretold to his disciples the coming events of his passion, death, and resurrection (Mark 9:31; etc.). It seems clear that what he foretold was a fairly specific account of the events, not just a premonition that Jerusalem would remain constant to its reputation for killing the prophets. Perhaps there was a time when this foreknowledge might have been taken as proper to the divinity of Christ and even as evidence for it, but it creates serious problems for modern scholarship. It suggests a kind of Docetism, as if Jesus only appeared to be a man and was really a divine figure in disguise. If there was indeed a true incarnation, then we cannot ascribe to the earthly Jesus the kind of foreknowledge that belongs only to God. As was said above, the finite human condition has no detailed knowledge of future events. So if Jesus was truly human, he too would have no detailed knowledge of the future, even if he could make intelligent guesses about the future course of events. So the tendency among scholars at present is to believe that the predictions of his death, put into the mouth of Jesus by the evangelists, were not actually spoken by him but reflect the evangelists' understanding of events as they recalled them many years after they had happened. It is claimed that this way of looking at the matter not only guards against Docetism, but increases our admiration for Jesus as one who had to face the future as we do, without any foreknowledge that things would turn out in one way rather than another. (*Compare* ELECTION, PREDESTINATION.)

J.M.

**FOREORDINATION.** *See* ELECTION.

**FORESKIN.** *See* CIRCUMCISION.

**FORGIVENESS.** There are three OT terms that enshrine its teaching on forgiveness, defined by the verbs *kpr*, "to expiate sin"; *ns'*, "to lift, bear" the weight of guilt from the conscience; *slh*, a verb whose root meaning is unclear but which is normally rendered "to forgive," "to remit" sin's penalty.

The consistent teaching is that God alone may grant pardon to sinners (Ps. 130:3-4; compare Ps. 49:7-8) since SIN is, at its deepest level, thought of as directed against God (Ps. 51:4). God's nature is expressed in that God forgives sinners (Neh. 9:17; Dan. 9:9) as in the eloquent confession of Exodus 34:6-7. So forgiveness is an expression of God's GRACE. The sacrificial ritual that came to be thought of as a precondition of God's forgiveness in the postexilic period was itself a gift of God's (Lev. 17:11).

Graphic word pictures describe the divine action in forgiveness: God removes human guilt from one end of the world to the other (Ps. 103:12). God casts our sins behind his back (Isa. 38:17), and drowns them in the depths of the sea (Mic. 7:19). God remembers human transgressions no longer (Jer. 31:34) and blots them out forever (Isa. 43:25).

The NT writers stand in the Hebraic tradition in regarding God as the author of forgiveness, a prerogative that Jesus claimed in his ministry (Mark 2:1-12). God's grace is displayed in setting captives free (where sin is likened to a bond or chain; John 8:34; Rev. 1:5), and in cleansing the springs of human inner life—the conscience, the affections, the disposition—in an act that removes the polluting influence and thereby purifies (I Cor. 6:9-11; I John 1:7; Heb. 9:14; compare Jesus' teaching in Mark 7:14-23).

This teaching on God's gracious pardon is often set in contrast to the OT counterpart (in Heb., chaps. 8–10) where sin's forgiveness is described as limited and temporary, needing a repeated application. For the writer to the Hebrews, the new covenant offered a final and lasting relationship with God based on Christ's once-for-all SACRIFICE.

Forgiveness is tied in with Jesus' death and resurrection (Matt. 26:28) in apostolic preaching (Luke 24:47; Acts 5:31; 13:38) and instruction (Eph. 1:7-9), and is conditional on the exercise of faith (Acts 10:43) as a response of gratitude and obedience to the offer of divine grace.

Forgiveness too is a human attitude to be shown to those who do us wrong (as in the Lord's Prayer, Matt. 6:12; Luke 11:4; and Jesus' parables, such as Matt. 18:23-35). Paul's teaching picks up this requirement (Col. 3:12-13).

R.M.

**FORM CRITICISM.** *See* BIBLICAL CRITICISM.

**FORNICATION.** *See* ADULTERY.

**FORSYTH, PETER TAYLOR** (1848–1921). The Congregational minister whose writings anticipated the theology of Barth was born in Aberdeen, Scotland. After studying at the University of Aberdeen and at Göttingen, where he was deeply influenced by Albrecht Ritschl, he served Congregational churches in England, including Emmanuel Church, Cambridge, before becoming principal of Hackney Theological College, London. His works include *The Person and Place of Jesus Christ* (1909); *Christ on Parnassus* (1911), *The Justification of God* (1916), and *Lectures on the Church and the Sacraments* (1917).

N.H.

**FOSDICK, HARRY EMERSON** (1878–1969). The liberal minister, author, and teacher was born in Buffalo, New York, on May 24. Ordained a Baptist in 1903, he served in Montclair, New Jersey (1904–15), and then became associate at First Presbyterian

Courtesy of Union Theological Seminary Library Archives, New York City

*Harry Emerson Fosdick*

Church, New York City. There he drew crowds and the ire of Fundamentalists. His sermon "Shall the Fundamentalists Win?" on May 21, 1922, led eventually to his resignation (1925).

Called to Park Avenue Baptist Church, he requested construction of a larger, nondenominational church, so John D. Rockefeller, Jr., built Riverside Church, which Fosdick pastored from 1926 to 1946. He also preached on the nationwide radio show "National Vespers" (1926–46) and taught at Union Theological Seminary (1908–46). Fosdick authored *The Manhood of the Master* (1913), *The Secret of Victorious Living* (1934), *On Being a Real Person* (1943), *A Faith for Tough Times* (1952), and *The Living of These Days, an Autobiography* (1956). He also wrote the hymn "God of Grace and God of Glory."

N.H.

**FOUR NOBLE TRUTHS.** In BUDDHISM, these are a succinct summary of the basic message of the religion, attributed to the Buddha in his first sermon after his Enlightenment. They are presented in a form that has often been compared to a physician's assessment of a patient: symptom, diagnosis of the cause, prognosis, and lastly, a prescription designed to cure the ailment. This comparison not only affords a convenient outline of the Four Noble Truths, but also points to the essential nature of the Buddha's teaching as he saw it: not an overall metaphysical world view that would answer all possible questions, but a focused treatment designed to cure human suffering, more akin to modern psychotherapy than philosophy.

First is the truth of suffering (DUKKHA), often rendered "All life is suffering." This does not mean that all of human life is excruciating pain, which would be manifestly untrue, but that in all life as it is ordinarily lived there lie causes of suffering, whether in birth, aging, sickness, or death, or in that which seems to be good but brings suffering because it is transitory.

The second truth is that the cause of suffering is craving or attachment (tanha). This refers to craving for and attachment to specific objects of desire in this world of transitory phenomena. Attachment need not be toward gross sensual pleasures; the subtlest, most deeply rooted attachments are for such goals as fame, knowledge, immortality, and being itself—or for nonbeing, the "death wish." Most fundamentally, attachment is toward the ego, toward being a separate individual self, which according to Buddhism is a delusion contrary to the truth of anatman, "no self," and hence a snare leading to suffering. Because attachment is toward partial and passing-away objects, it can only result in pain.

The third truth, the "prognosis," is that there can be an end to craving or attachment. Craving arises through the senses, which the Enlightened One compared to a fire, burning on the fuel of objects perceived and imaged by them. The solution, then, is to cut the fuel supply and extinguish the fire; in other words, to give craving nothing on which to subsist, so that it will cease, and with it suffering.

The way to do this is through the fourth truth, the EIGHTFOLD PATH, which reorients life away from egocentric reaction to sensory stimuli, toward detached but compassionate freedom and finally NIRVANA. Significantly, the path culminates in right concentration or meditation, which in Buddhism is the sovereign practice for freeing oneself from bondage to sufferng and desire because it cuts off sensory input and stills the restless mind.

R.E.

**FOURSQUARE GOSPEL.** The fundamentalist, charismatic summary of the Christian faith, taught by Holiness and PENTECOSTAL churches and sometimes espoused by neo-charismatics in recent years. According to Pentecostalism, the complete gospel message has four themes: justification by faith (upon an adult conversion experience, generally in a revivalistic setting); the experience of entire sanctification (complete holiness) through the baptism of the Holy Spirit (the "second blessing," which involves speaking in tongues); divine healing (faith healing); and premillenarianism (Jesus will return in the Second Coming before the one thousand-year reign of the saints). In the Pentecostal view Jesus is Savior, Sanctifier, Healer, and coming Lord.

The evangelist AIMEE SEMPLE MCPHERSON became famous as pastor of the Church of the Four Square Gospel in Los Angeles. Her flamboyant style brought her fame and fortune, although she flirted with scandal at one point in her career. After her death, the movement she headed continued in a pentecostal, fundamentalist denomination called The Church of the Four Square Gospel. The rise of the contemporary neo-Pentecostal movement has contributed to its growth. It has also benefited from the turn toward fundamentalism symbolized by the Moral Majority.

J.C.

**FOX, GEORGE** (1624–91). The founder of the QUAKERS was born in July 1624, the son of a weaver in Leicestershire. Apparently of Puritan background, Fox left home at eighteen and began preaching in the Midlands and the northern counties among the SEEKERS. He was most successful in the Lake District, gathering followers and fellow preachers, male and female, called Publishers of Truth. The loose groups gathered between 1649 and 1680 were called the

Courtesy of Religious News Service

*George Fox*

Society of Friends. Fox's radical reliance on the inner light and his denunciation of all creeds and ecclesiastical customs, as well as political and economic conventions, resulted in eight imprisonments between 1650 and 1674.

Upon his return from a missionary visit to Ireland in 1669, Fox married Margaret Fell, of Ulverston, Lancashire. Though they were a devoted and well-matched couple, they spent much time apart due to his missionary trips to the Caribbean and North America, 1671–73 and 1677, and to Holland and northern Europe in 1684.

About 1675 Fox began dictating a running summary of his life, which was published posthumously as his *Journal*. During his lifetime he published a number of tracts on social and theological matters. His *Works* were published in eight volumes in 1831. He died January 13, 1691, and was buried in the Quaker cemetery near Bunhill Fields, London.

N.H.

**FOX, MARGARET** (1833–93). With her younger sister Kate, she alleged communication with spirits through table rappings. Born on October 7 to John D. and Margaret Fox in Hydesville, New York, Margaret and Kate, promoted by an elder sister Leah Fox Fish, first appeared publicly in 1849.

Their "communications" sparked great interest in SPIRITUALISM. On October 21, 1888, Margaret exposed their work as a hoax in a speech at the New York Academy of Music, but she later recanted. She died on March 8 in Brooklyn.

N.H.

**FOX, MARGARET FELL** (1614–1702). The Quaker leader and wife of GEORGE FOX was born to John Askew of Lancashire. Tradition says she was the great-granddaughter of martyr Anne Askew. At seventeen she married Judge Thomas Fell and bore him eight children before his death in 1658. She met Fox in 1652 and became his ardent follower, suffering imprisonment three times. They married in 1669. She became leader of the Quaker women—preaching, teaching, writing, organizing. Margaret died on April 23 and was buried on her estate at Swarthmore Hall, Lancashire.

N.H.

**FOXE, JOHN** (1516–87). The author of *Book of Martyrs*, Foxe was born in Boston, Lincolnshire, and studied at Oxford, where he held a fellowship for seven years. Ordained deacon in 1547, and priest in 1560, Foxe refused all church offices though he preached frequently.

Queen Mary's rise to power in 1553 forced him to flee to Strasbourg, France, where he completed and published the first draft of his book in 1554 in Latin. He visited Protestant leaders in Frankfurt and Basel. Returning to England at the beginning of Elizabeth I's reign in 1559, he published a full account of

Protestant suffering from the fourteenth century to the present under the English title *Actes and Monuments of These Latter and Perilous Dayes* (1563). Subsequent editions were published in 1570, 1576, and 1583. It became a PURITAN classic and shaped British views of Roman Catholicism for at least a century. Foxe died April 18, 1587.

N.H.

**FRACTION.** The breaking of the host in the eucharistic liturgy. "The breaking of the bread" was synonymous with the Lord's Supper in the early church. In the Eastern Orthodox liturgy, the host is broken into four parts and arranged in the shape of a cross, then put in the chalice.

J.C.

**FRANCIS OF ASSISI/FRANCISCANS.** Giovanni di Bernardone (1182–1226), founder of the Franciscan Order. Son of a rich merchant of Assisi, he was a carefree, indulgent youth. Captured in a war with Perugia, he spent a year in prison, seriously ill. Returning to Assisi in 1202, he vowed to follow a life of poverty—begging, restoring churches, and helping lepers. Following a trip to Rome, a voice told him to repair God's house, but undue liberality with his father's goods landed him in jail. In court he stripped naked to symbolize a complete family break. Unstintingly he repaired chapels and attended lepers—the first to call him saint. On hearing Matthew 10:7-10, he began preaching the nearness of the Kingdom. Others joined him, particularly Bernard of Quintavalle, a rich merchant, and Peter Catani, a lawyer. In the freedom of renunciation they distributed their goods to the poor. Having dreamed a beggar was upholding the church, Pope Innocent III in 1210 reluctantly granted Francis' group informal approval. Using a few biblical injunctions for guidance, they continued helping others and denying themselves.

Returning in 1220 from an unsuccessful trip to Egypt to convert Muslims, Francis found discord about owning property. He feared ownership would lead to attachment to things; he feared rules would prompt pride in keeping them. Francis wanted neither, but the Franciscans' growing numbers necessitated both. An unhappy Francis consented to the Rule of 1221 enjoining poverty, chastity, obedience, standards of prayer, habits for novitiates, and general regulations. Spontaneity waned. The Third Rule, 1223, confirmed by Pope Honorius III, officially sanctioned the Franciscan Order and established papal supervision through appointment of a cardinal as corrector and protector. Learning was not encouraged, but by 1234 the Franciscans had a flourishing seminary at St. German des Pres. In 1212 St. Clare organized the Poor Clares for women. Francis organized the Tertiaries in 1221, for those still living normally in society. In 1224 while on

Mount Alverno, Francis received the stigmata—the wounds of Christ. After forty days of fasting, he wrote the *Hymn of the Sun,* an Italian hymn of joy and praise for everything in God's world. Pope Gregory IX canonized Francis in 1228.

> Most High Omnipotent, good Lord, to Thee
> The praises and the honor and the glory be!
> All blessings, O most High, befit Thee only,
> And no man is worthy to speak of Thee!
> Be praised, O My Lord, by all Thy creatures!
> And chiefly by Monsignor Brother Sun,
> Whom in the day Thou lightenest for us;
> For fair is he and radiant with resplendence;
> And of Thee, Most High, beareth he the semblance.
>
> Be praised by Sister Moon and Stars of Night:
> In Heaven Thou hast made them, precious, fair and
>     bright.
>
> Be praised, O My Lord, by Brother Wind,
> By Air and Cloud and Sky and every Clime,
> By whom Thou givest sustenance unto all kind!
>
> By Sister Water, O My Lord, be praised!
> Useful is she and lowly, precious and chaste.
>
> Be praised, O My Lord, by Brother Fire,
> By whom Thou lightenest our steps at night,
> And fair is he and merry, masterful and of might!
>
> Be praised, O My Lord, by our Mother, Sister Earth,
> Who governeth and sustaineth us and giveth birth
> To divers fruits and colored flowers and to herbs!
>
> O bless and praise my Lord and thankful be
> And serve My Lord with great humility!

Francis of Assisi's *Hymn of the Sun*

The Franciscans' insistence on total poverty silently criticized much church life and proved unworkable. The SPIRITUALS wanted to live strictly like Francis; the majority wanted accommodations. After prolonged disputes Pope John XXII in 1318 decided against the Spirituals and permitted ownership by the order. Many Spirituals became schismatics, known as Fraticelli, and suffered persecution. The order declined. Eventually reform-minded Observants challenged the lax group called Conventualists and gained recognition and a separate vicar-general in 1443. By 1517 the Obervants were declared the true Order of St. Francis. Matteo da Bascio's reform in the sixteenth century led to formation of the Capuchins. Political upheavals in the eighteen and nineteenth centuries spawned other reform groups. The order was finally reunited and revitalized by Pope Leo XIII in 1897. Bonaventure, Duns Scotus, and William of Occam are among its greatest scholars. Mission and social service have marked its history.     C.M.

**FRANCIS OF SALES** (1567–1622). French Roman Catholic prelate, preacher, writer, and leader in the CATHOLIC REFORMATION. Born a noble in Savoy, he pursued studies in philosophy, classics, law, and theology at Paris and Padua, and despite family objections became a priest in 1593. Sent to win Chablais back to Roman Catholicism, he tried persuasion, then resorted to conversion by force. Pope Clement VIII in 1597 directed him to recover Geneva. Officially, he was bishop of Geneva, which he viewed as a den of heretics by 1602, but Beza, the aged successor of Calvin, kept him from functioning there. In 1610 he helped found the Visitation of Our Lady for handicapped people barred from other orders. Famed for *An Introduction to the Devout Life* (1608) and *Treatise on the Love of God* (1616), he converted thousands to Catholicism. Canonized in 1665 and made a doctor in 1877, he ranks as one of Catholicism's greatest leaders.

C.M.

**FRANCIS XAVIER** (1506–52). Early Spanish Jesuit missionary to the Orient. An aristocrat by birth, he was born in Pamplona, and studied for a religious career at the University of Paris. He practiced IGNATIUS OF LOYOLA's spiritual exercises and was one of six chosen by him to form the SOCIETY OF JESUS. They took vows in the church of St. Mary on Montmartre in 1534, and received papal approval in 1540. Ordained a priest in 1537, Xavier began his missionary activities in 1541 when he left Lisbon and traveled to India. Skilled in languages, he preached and established missions around Goa, extending his work into South India and Ceylon. In 1545 he reached Malacca and traveled the Malay Archipelago for two years. After returning to Goa, he sailed for Japan, landing at Kagoshima in 1549. During two years in Japan, he spent one year studying the language and one year preaching. By 1551 he had established several Christian missions. He died on the island of Sancion trying to get into China. His baptisms were hasty, without much instruction, and he depended heavily on children memorizing prayers, songs, and ceremonies. But he sowed the seeds of Catholicism and was canonized in 1622.

C.M.

**FRANCKE, AUGUST H.** (1663–1727). Renowned German Pietist, educator, and pastor. Born at Lübeck, he studied philosophy at Erfurt and Kiel and in 1685 became a lecturer at Leipzig University. Influenced by PHILIP J. SPENER, Francke started devotional biblical studies at Leipzig, and his interest in PIETISM deepened. By 1689 his lectures were attracting crowds. However, opponents forced him to leave Leipzig (1690) and Erfurt (1692). He then joined the new Halle University and preached at nearby Glaucha. In 1698 he became a full member of Halle's theological faculty, making it a pietistic center that strongly influenced Lutheranism. His many enterprises won wide acclaim: a pauper's school, an orphanage, Bible institute, Latin school, dispensary, publishing plant, and related facilities—all, he claimed, in answer to prayer for relieving human need. His *Marvellous Footsteps of Divine Providence* (London, 1707) prompted many foreigners to support his work. Francke's most valuable accomplishment was the founding of Francke Institutes at Halle, which is still active.

C.M.

**FRANKINCENSE.** The aromatic gum resin of trees grown in Africa and Arabia of the genus *boswellia*. Since it gives off a fragrant odor when burned, frankincense was widely used as a part of the cult, especially in the OFFERING of SACRIFICES (for example, Lev. 2:1-2, 15-16). Levitical rules declared that it be used only for sacred purposes (Exod. 30:37-38). Together with gold and myrrh, frankincense was one of the expensive gifts brought by the magi in Matthew's account of the infant Jesus (2:11).

C.B.C.

**FRANKL, VICTOR E.** (1905– ). Psychiatrist and author. Born in Vienna in 1905, Frankl received an M.D. from the University of Vienna in 1930 and a Ph.D. in 1949. He founded and was head of a youth advocacy center in Vienna (1928–38) and was on the staff of the Neuro-psychiatric Clinic (1930–38). He headed the Neurological Poliklinik Institute at Vienna (1946–70) and was a professor at the University of Vienna during the 1950s and 1960s.

The break in his professional life came from 1942 to 1945, when he was imprisoned in a concentration camp. This experience greatly influenced him. According to Frankl, only those who have an indestructible sense of the personal self can survive such brutal attempts to erase selfhood. His aim since then has been to build self-affirmation in people. He founded the school of logotherapy, or existential analysis, and has been professor of logotherapy at the United States International University, San Diego, since 1970. He also chairs the board of the Logotherapy Institute.

Frankl does not believe that uncovering the past, as in classical PSYCHOANALYSIS, can be helpful in therapy. Rather, he focuses on the future. His basic book, *Man's Search for Meaning—An Introduction to Logotherapy* (1963), interprets logos as "meaning" and is designed to instill in people a sense of meaning for their lives. One of his more recent interests has been in personal journal keeping as a way of developing the self.

I.C.

**FRAZER, SIR JAMES GEORGE** (1854–1941). Scottish-born anthropologist and folklorist. He spent most of his career at Cambridge, and through his immense work of collecting and synthesizing data,

largely on archaic religion from around the world, he did much to shape modern comparative religious studies. His multi-volumed major work, *The Golden Bough: A Study in Magic and Religion,* was first published in 1890. While Frazer's belief that magic preceded religion is no longer accepted, his basic definition of magic as the attempt to manipulate supernatural entities and forces, and religion as the supplication of them, remains influential. His work also served to isolate important areas of religious typology and define problems for future study; in particular this was the case with the sacred king. At the same time, Frazer was perhaps the last of the great armchair anthropologists. He traveled little, depending on the reports of missionaries, explorers, and colonial officials, as well as wide reading, for the material that went into his encyclopedic project.

R.E.

**FREE CHURCHES.** Free churches are churches free of government or external ecclesiastical control and are self-supporting. The term is usually applied to such churches as the Baptists in Scotland, the Presbyterians in England, the Waldensians in Italy, and the Mission Covenant Church in Sweden. Two-fifths of the churches represented at the 1948 meeting of the World Council of Churches in Amsterdam were free churches.

The term was first appropriated by the four nonepiscopal evangelical communions in England that convened the Free Church Congress in 1892 and in 1896 formed the National Council of the Evangelical Free Churches. They were the Baptists, Congregationalists, Methodists, and Presbyterians. Known as PURITANS before 1662, then NONCONFORMISTS, then DISSENTERS, such denominations came to prefer the term "free churches" in the late nineteenth century.

The "free church tradition" stems from the ANABAPTISTS of the left-wing Protestant Reformation, with their emphasis on NT church order, believer's baptism, the leading of the Holy Spirit rather than human authority, Communion as a memorial, the priesthood of all believers, and the separation of church and state. The tradition is opposed to the parochial patterns of medieval Christianity and the territorial churches of the magisterial Reformation. They insisted on the fellowship of visible, regenerate saints and tend toward local church autonomy.

In worship they favor free or spontaneous prayers, hymns and gospel songs, and an emphasis on preaching over liturgy. Their pietistic fervor led to the missionary movement. Some argue that their emphasis on the local church fostered grass roots democracy. They denied the state the right to compel belief, and some refused to take civil oaths or to bear arms. They also attempted to mold public life around the imperatives of the gospel.

N.H.

**FREEDOM.** A key NT term that is one of the benefits accruing to Christians from the redemption wrought by Christ. But there is a clear OT anticipation which, on balance, is the more likely source of the NT terminology than other parallels (for example, drawn from the setting free of slaves by act of manumission in Greco-Roman society).

The OT consistently harks back to the Exodus as a time recalled in Israel's national consciousness when Yahweh intervened to set free the tribes from Egyptian overlordship (for example, Deut. 26:5-11). The purpose of God's deliverance was to constitute those tribes, under Moses and Joshua, as covenant people and install them in Canaan, the Land of Promise. Their continued freedom would be contingent on their remaining in the covenant relationship, an obedience that was the pledge of life (Deut. 30:15-20).

The NT exploits this background, specifically by calling the death and resurrection of Jesus a new Exodus (Luke 9:31) with covenant overtones (Luke 22:28-30; I Cor. 5:7, 8; I Pet. 1:18, 19) and regarding the church's freedom as one of being set free from bondage to sin (Gal. 4:4-6; Rom. 8:15-25); and summoned to a life of freedom in worship as the new Israel of God (Rom. 12:1, 2; I Pet. 2:4-10). The call is one of obedience (Rom. 6:17; I Pet. 1:14) to new standards of ethical endeavor, both personal (Rom. 6:5-23; Gal. 5:1, 13, 15) and in society (Rom. 12:4-21; I Cor. 7:17-24), that are grounded in freedom from all manner of evil bondage.      R.M.

**FREE MASONRY.** The teachings and practices of the secret fraternal order of Free and Accepted Masons, one of the largest worldwide secret societies. Though begun in England, 4 million out of an estimated 5.9 million members live in the United States. Originally evolving from guilds of stonemasons and cathedral builders of the Middle Ages, they began to accept honorary members. In the seventeenth and eighteenth centuries they adopted rites and trappings of more ancient religious orders and chivalric brotherhoods and thus developed free-masonry's modern symbolic or speculative aspects. The first Grand Lodge, an association of lodges, was formed in England in 1717.

The Masons are not a religious institution though they are sometimes mistaken for one. They have been opposed by organized religion, particularly Roman Catholicism, and are banned in Communist countries. In turn Masons have been charged with bigotry against Jews, Catholics, and nonwhites. The group has basically three levels—apprentice, fellow of the craft, master mason—but numerous "degrees," which vary from country to country. Female relatives of master masons can join the Order of Eastern Star. Youth organizations include the Order of De Molay and the Order of Builders for boys and the Order of Job's Daughters and the Order of Rainbow for girls.
                                                                        N.H.

**FREE WILL.** The concept of human freedom to choose between good and evil; the opposite of DETERMINISM. Human responsibility for actions is implicit in most biblical writings, and the majority of Christian thinkers have assumed human free will in moral matters. The concept of CONSCIENCE, so basic to later Greek thought and to Paul's arguments for universal sinfulness in Romans 1, also assumes moral free will. The problems that have plagued theology in the questions about human free will have had to do not with human guilt and responsibility, but with the reconcilation of the assumed human capacity to choose, and with the confusion of moral free will with a supposed ability (granted by God) on people's part to accept or reject God's salvation. This brought human free will into conflict with God's SOVEREIGNTY, omnipotence, and omniscience. In another area, Christian theologians have had to defend human free will against materialistic determinisms, like the atomism of Democritus, dialectical materialism (classical Marxism), and logical positivism; the last entailing the denial of all inner states of mind, including both determinism and freedom of the will.

The usual outlines of the debates over human free will versus God's determinism (that is, PREDESTINATION, PROVIDENCE, FOREKNOWLEDGE, foreordination) would include the struggle of Augustine (who died in A.D. 430) in *De libero arbitrio,* and Pelagius (a British monk living in Rome in the late fifth century A.D.) over the absolute necessity of God's grace to be operational in a person before his or her will could be so moved as to choose the genuine good. It would also include the work of Beothius on God's foreknowledge (he declared that God does know all that will happen, but God's knowledge is outside of time, in eternity, so that God's previous knowledge of what people will choose does not cause them to choose as they do). Another example is the conflict documented in Luther's *De Servo Abitrio (On the Bound Will)* between Erasmus of Rotterdam, the humanist, and Martin Luther (1491–1546), the Protestant reformer, whose theology was based on Paul and Augustine, both of whom were predestinarians. And, finally, the later (second generation of the Reformation) work of John Calvin, who opted for strict predestination, indeed, for so-called "double predestination," in which people are elected by God for heaven or hell from before the foundation of the earth. Other reformed theologians, following Calvin, like Jonathan Edwards (eighteenth century) denied human free will altogether. More liberal theologians resisted this "hard shell" position and, like John Wesley, sought to find a place for human free will without denying God's grace. Most such theologians, like Wesley, followed the lead of JACOB ARMINIUS of the Lowlands, who denied the double predestination and limited Atonement (Christ died only for the elect) doctrines of the Synod of Dort.

Much later, Immanuel Kant sought to make a place for human moral freedom in his *Critique of the Practical* (that is, moral) *Reason*. Kant said we are free because we feel free. We are not conscious of being determined in our choices. He argued that a moral code demands freedom, indeed, establishes the fact of human freedom, since ought implies can. Kant, by recourse to his famous dichotomy of the universe into phenomena (that is, the outer, material world) and noumena (the inner, mental world), resolved this by saying that people are determined phenomenally but free noumenally (that is, our thoughts are free).

In a general sense Protestantism has emphasized a person's lack of, or severe defects in, freedom of the will. This is the case despite the decisions of the councils held at Carthage from 416 to 419, which made Augustine's teaching on predestination the official position of the Catholic Church.

J.C.

**FREE WILL BAPTIST CHURCH.** *See* BAPTIST CHURCHES.

**FREUD, SIGMUND** (1856–1939). Austrian physician and neurologist and founder of psychoanalysis. Freud was born in Freiberg, Moravia (now Czechoslovakia), moved with his family to Leipzig three years later, and then to Vienna, where he lived until a year before his death.

Educated at the University of Vienna in the field of medicine, he began work on the staff of a psychiatric clinic, engaged in research, and was appointed a lecturer at the university in neuropsychology.

Freud's first work with Josef Breuer (with some attention to Charcot's work at Paris) convinced him that symptoms with no physiological basis could be alleviated by hypnosis and therefore had a psychogenic basis. In 1895 he published, with Breuer, *Studies in Hysteria*. Their conclusions were not well accepted by the medical profession, but the book probably marked the beginning of the PSYCHOANALYSIS movement.

In 1897, Freud began a self-analysis, something which most psychiatrists would not attempt, but which gave him new insights for his theories, including that of childhood sexuality and the "oedipal complex." Freud viewed sexuality as one of the bases for adult behavior. During 1895–99 he did the research that resulted in *Interpretation of Dreams,* one of his most important works.

The Vienna Psychoanalytical Circle began at Freud's house in 1902, where a distinguished gathering grew but was later torn apart by differences. In 1909 he was pleased by the invitation to lecture in the United States under the auspices of E. Stanley Hall, president of Clark University. In 1912, he developed his theory of the unconscious in a lecture to the London Society for Psychical Research. *The Ego and the Id,* written in 1923, developed his tripartite understanding of the person as Id-Ego-Superego. The

*Future of an Illusion* (1927) and *Moses and Monotheism* (1939) are two of his philosophical discussions of religion. Freud, who was Jewish, stayed in Vienna until the Nazi soldiers came to his door. Only then was he persuaded to move to London, where he died a year later. Freud was an original thinker whose ideas changed human thinking. He ignored the socioeconomic factors in psychological development and minimized the nature-nurture elements. He opened the understanding of the depths of the person as no one before him had.

I.C.

**FRIAR.** A title first used by MENDICANT orders in the Middle Ages, signifying "brother." It stresses the brotherhood of humility and Christian witness. Friars wandered throughout the cities and countryside begging, preaching, and aiding the poor and sick. The title is widely used in the reformed orders since Vatican II.

J.C.

**FRIENDS OF GOD.** A loosely organized mystical group, laity and clergy, in southwestern Germany and Switzerland in the fourteenth century. They wrote letters and distributed books signed "a Friend of God." They stressed personal piety and oneness with God over ordinary church life. Luther published their *German Theology* twice.

C.M.

**FRIENDS, SOCIETY OF** (Quakers). A mystical reform movement in English Protestantism that grew out of the "Inner Light" experiences and preaching of GEORGE FOX and other itinerant preachers in the mid-seventeenth century. Persecuted from their origins around 1650, the Quakers spread their unique message throughout Britain, Ireland, North Europe, the British colonies in America, and the West Indies within a few years. These early missionaries were called "First Publishers of Truth."

The first half century of Quaker activity was stormy, since their principles made them offensive to most classes of society. Strong disapproval by the public was punctuated by occasional mob violence. By the end of the seventeenth century, restrictive legislation was passed against the Friends. Against all this persecution, the Quakers responded with public non-resistance, refusing to go "underground" and meet in secret.

The Quaker tenets that raised such opposition were: rejection of compulsory church attendance; rejection of military service; disregard of social conventions, such as the use of "my Lord" and other such titles for the aristocracy; rejection of judicial oaths; a strong anti-papal outlook; anti-clericalism; and rejection of formality in worship and belief in creeds.

The Quakers claimed that only beliefs and practices recorded in the NT should be permitted. They pointed out that there is no use of the term "saint" for persons or churches (as in St. John's) in the NT, and no precedence for observing Christmas and other Christian holidays. There was also no basis for tithes, or for weddings in churches, by a priest with a ring, which they condemned as relics of medieval superstition. The Quakers even rejected the Bible as the basis for church authority; for although they studied it, they did not accept it as the only rule of faith and practice. The Quakers preferred a divine, immediate revelation within to the authority of church, creed, or Bible. Because of their lack of a creed, the Quakers permitted a wide variety of beliefs to develop, and this condition exists to this day.

Because of their opposition to ritual in worship, even to the informal services of the Protestant sects, the Quakers adopted the practice of spontaneous, unprogrammed, cooperative group worship. They had no formal leadership or ordained ministry. They did not consecrate buildings or altars, had no music, readings, or liturgy. They did not even recognize the sacraments of baptism in water or the Lord's Supper in bread and wine. Early proponents of equality of the sexes, both men and women spoke and prayed whenever they felt the Spirit move them. The most striking feature of Quaker worship was—and is—silence.

A polity evolved consisting of a union called the local meeting, which was formed into ever larger units called monthly, quarterly, and yearly meetings. On an international level, Quakers unite in fellowship in the World Committee on Consultation. Within the society, leadership is recognized as existing without human appointment. No distinction is made between laity and clergy or men and women.

The Society in America has participated in all the social, political, and theological movements that gave rise to so many revivals, sects, and social reforms. The Quakers have been affected, experiencing schism in 1827 and after. A sensitivity to social needs, especially to the suffering of black slavery and the injustices done to the native Americans, characterizes American Quakerism. Throughout their history, to the present day, Quakers have worked for prison reform, better treatment for the mentally ill, opposition to war, and for international relief for refugees and others. This social leadership won for the Quakers the Nobel Peace Prize in 1947, and makes them influential beyond their actual numbers.

J.C.

**FROMM, ERICH** (1900–80). Psychoanalyst and social philosopher born in Frankfurt, Germany. He believed that many emotional problems arise from the stresses of modern society and that only by building a society responsive to human needs can there be harmonious social interactions that promote mental health. He envisioned an improved human nature developed through love and based on ethical living.

Fromm graduated from the University of Munich in 1924, and the Psychoanalytic Institute in Berlin (1925), where he was educated in Freudian principles, which he applied to social, economic, and cultural questions, an unorthodox approach. He left Germany in 1934, and lectured at Columbia University until 1941. His book *Escape from Freedom* (1941) was an influential intellectual and political philosophy, which posited that some people prefer not to be free. He taught at Bennington College (Vermont), 1941-50, and wrote *Man for Himself* in 1947. It is his thesis in this book that individuals must take personal responsibility for their decisions and actions. From 1957 to 1961, Fromm taught at Michigan State University and became professor of psychiatry at New York University in 1962.

Although he used insights from FREUD and JUNG, he affirmed that psychiatric therapy tended to encourage people toward conformity (adjustment) rather than autonomy. He wrote several books in the area of religion, such as, *The Dogma of Christ and Other Essays on Religion, Psychology, and Culture* (1963). His views were, understandably, unorthodox.

I.C.

**FUJI, MOUNT.** Virtually the trademark of Japan, Mount Fuji, also known as Fujiyama, is a dormant volcano some seventy-five miles southwest of Tokyo. Of exceptional beauty, it is a place of pilgrimage now visited by more than 100,000 people every summer. Fuji is given scattered notice in early poetry and other literature and was a haunt of *yamabushi*, mountain ascetics whose esoteric Buddhist practice owed much to shamanism, at least since the early Middle Ages. But it was not until around the beginning of the Tokugawa period in 1600, when the relatively nearby city of Edo (modern Tokyo) became the capital and metropolis of Japan, that its cultus took on exceptional popularity. Takematsu Hasegawa (known as Kakugyo, sixteenth century) taught that the mountain was the earthly abode of the supreme god. From his doctrine came two Fuji-centered Shinto sects, Jikkō-kyō and Fusō-kyō, still active. But for most pilgrims the mountain's spiritual importance is no doubt conceptualized more vaguely, yet related to a general deep-seated Japanese belief that mountains are places for inner transformation and access to the Other World of gods and Buddhas.

R.E.

**FULL GOSPEL BUSINESSMEN'S FELLOWSHIP INTERNATIONAL.** A Pentecostal layman's association founded in Los Angeles in 1951 by Demos Chakarian, a businessman, and Oral Roberts, the evangelistic faith healer. The association exists for fellowship of charismatics and to promote the spread of the experience of baptism by the Holy Spirit. Membership has grown steadily, and witnessing by members has contributed to the interest in the

*Mount Fuji, Japanese silk hanging scroll*

reception of the Holy Spirit and speaking in tongues, as well as in divine healing, which helped bring about the neo-Pentecostal movement in mainstream Protestant churches and among Roman Catholics. The movement has spread to many countries, especially to other English-speaking nations and throughout Latin America. Its theology is fundamentalistic, in its PENTECOSTAL form, and members are actively evangelistic in spreading the message of the need to receive the Holy Spirit and speak in tongues.

J.C.

**FULLNESS OF TIME.** The sole occurrence of this phrase is found in Galatians 4:4 KJV; the text runs in RSV, "But when the time had fully come, God sent forth his Son, born of woman. . . ." The point of the Pauline phrase is to assert, in the context of his discussion with his readers, that the appointed time of

their emancipation from servitude to alien powers had come (4:3). The time phrase relates back to verse 2 where, in Roman law, the heir attained legal and civic rights when he became of age (at fourteen years).

In theology the phrase has taken on a different meaning. It refers to the outworking of divine providence in the course of history, leading up to the coming of Christ. Irenaeus and Augustine saw that God's age-old plan culminated when "the time" was ready, politically and culturally, and above all in the desire humankind had for a new beginning to world history. The most noble anticipation lies in Virgil's *Fourth Eclogue,* where the poet yearns for the arrival of "the last age" *(ultima aetas),* which will be "the golden age" of world peace, following the birth of a boy who will lead a "new breed of men sent down from heaven." John Milton borrowed these ideas in his poem "Ode on the Morning of Christ's Nativity" and set them in a Christian context, finding in Virgil a prophet of Christmas and a true *praeparatio evangelica,* or anticipation, of what God would do "in the fullness of time."

R.M.

**FUNDAMENTALISM.** A term derived from a series of twelve booklets on conservative Protestant Christian theology published and mailed to three million people over the years 1910-15 by two wealthy Los Angeles laymen, Lyman and Milton Stewart. These booklets attacked naturalism, which conservatives believed to be the basis of contemporary liberal theology in various American Protestant denominations. Entitled simply *The Fundamentals,* these works expounded "the five fundamentals"adopted by the General Assembly of the Presbyterian Church in the U.S.A. in 1910, and ratified again in 1916 and 1923.

These included: the INERRANCY of the Scriptures in the original documents, the deity of Jesus Christ and his VIRGIN BIRTH, the substitutionary theory of the ATONEMENT, the physical resurrection of Christ, and Christ's miracles. To these original "five fundamentals," conservatives also added ORIGINAL SIN (human natural depravity), justification by faith, the personal, physical return of Jesus Christ (the Second Coming), and a literal heaven and hell. Many Fundamentalists are also premillennialists, who believe in the physical return of Christ at the end of the "age," whereupon he and his saints will literally reign on earth for one thousand years. (PREMILLENNIALISM declares Christ's Second Coming will be just before the millennium, and holds that human history will degenerate more and more until Christ's return.)

As a movement within conservative Protestantism, Fundamentalism exists in most English-speaking countries but especially in the United States, Canada, and Great Britain. The major characteristics of those generally identified as Fundamentalists include a strong emphasis on the total inerrancy of the Bible, which is believed to be free of any error, even in matters of science, chronology, and geography; a strong dislike of modern theology and particularly of modern biblical criticism; and a belief that people who don't share Fundamentalist beliefs are not Christian.

Fundamentalism, in its struggle with LIBER-ALISM—or today more generally with more moderate conservative Protestants—split several denominations and caused loss of membership. No major denominations became Fundamentalist, but a number of smaller ones in the United States did. In Great Britain, no denomination became Fundamentalist, although wings of various communions became dominated by conservative believers.

Fundamentalism began and continues as an ecumenical or interdenominational phenomenon. People from various backgrounds—Presbyterian, Methodist, Baptist, and Disciples—joined together in prophetic conferences, revivals, Bible conferences, Bible schools, federations, ministers' groups, and through religious literature and later radio and, more recently, television programs, to promote their conservative beliefs.

For most Fundamentalists the legitimate translation of the Bible is the Authorized Version, the King James Version. However, Fundamentalists often prefer to use the Scofield Reference Bible, an Authorized Version text to which the Reverend CYRUS I. SCOFIELD added his own interpretive notes and annotations. Scofield, a Congregational minister, interpreted the Bible's salvation history in dispensational and premillennial terms, publishing his work in 1909. A new edition was issued in 1919 and another as recently as 1966.

The number of Fundamentalists in America has never been determined. John Warwick Montgomery, conservative Lutheran Church—Missouri Synod clergyman, estimates their number at seventeen million. The difficulty of distinguishing Fundamentalism from EVANGELICALISM makes an exact census impossible, especially so since some Fundamentalists call themselves Evangelicals.

Fundamentalism, like the revivalism out of which it grew, has had a colorful history. BILLY SUNDAY, the famous evangelist, was identified with Fundamentalism, as was William Jennings Bryan, politician, temperance advocate, populist leader, and attorney at the famous SCOPES MONKEY TRIAL in Tennessee. John Gresham Machen, a Presbyterian seminary professor who split the theological faculty at Princeton and founded a Fundamentalist seminary of his own, became the scholarly authority for the movement. The Presbyterian Church in the U.S.A. expelled Machen from its ministry in 1935, and he thereupon founded the Presbyterian Church of America (1936). The name was changed in 1939 to the Orthodox Presbyterian church. Out of this group the very conservative Carl McIntyre of Collinswood, New Jersey, led a small band who founded the Bible Presbyterian Synod in 1937. McIntyre became a

strong anti-Communist and a promoter of Taiwan, South Korea, South Africa, and other repressive governments during the McCarthy Era and continued in this activity through the Vietnam War.

Fundamentalist leaders tend to be authoritarian, single leader personalities, who often fail to develop lay leadership and are unwilling to cooperate with non-Fundamentalist leaders. Historically, Fundamentalism remains a diverse, uncentered movement, an expression of the divisive, sectarian spirit.

In the 1970s, Fundamentalism had a strong resurgence, due to the social turmoil of the Vietnam War, the accumulated culture shock of new scientific and social developments, and the growing strength of Communism in the world. Today the MORAL MAJORITY, under leaders like the Reverend Jerry Falwell, who clearly states himself to be a separatistic Fundamentalist, continues the attacks on Liberals in the churches, on evolution, on contemporary lifestyles (especially sexual mores), and on the threat of Communism that have marked Fundamentalist rhetoric since World War I. The National Council of Churches is a target of contemporary Fundamentalists, just as its predecessor, the Federal Council of Churches, was attacked by earlier Fundamentalists like J. Frank Norris, John Roach Straton, and William Bell Riley.

J.C.

**FUNDAMENTAL THEOLOGY.** In Catholic theology, the basic teaching that God is revealed and that this revelation is totally presented in Jesus Christ, who founded the Christian church on St. Peter, and that the church continues to bear witness to that revelation throughout human history. Fundamental theology has been presented in various ways throughout Catholic history, in historical, philosophical, and theological ways. Today it is chiefly presented in a theological manner, as (in Anselm's words) faith seeking understanding.

This faith, the innate desire of people to know God, is directed toward the Word of God—Scripture—preserved, explained, and transmitted through the people of God—the universal church. Fundamental theology thus combines both faith and reason, theology and philosophy, revealed truth and human intellectual development. Basically, Catholic theologians have proceeded on an ontological basis, seeing humankind as open to the revelation of God, which shines through all being. The most basic elements of fundamental theology are, then, the fact of God's revelation and the certain preservation and transmission of this supernatural knowledge through the Catholic church. Among modern Catholic theologians, KARL RAHNER has distinguished himself by dealing extensively with questions of fundamental theology.

J.C.

**FUTURE LIFE.** *Compare* IMMORTALITY.

# Gg

**GABRIEL.** A messenger of God sent to interpret visions and to announce good news. In Hebrew the word means "warrior of God" or "God has shown himself mighty." Gabriel appears to Daniel to explain to him his dreams and to give him wisdom and understanding (Dan. 8:15-27; 9:21-27). In the NT he is the one who announces to Zechariah as he prays in the Temple that his wife Elizabeth will have a son to be named John (Luke 1:8-20) and announces to Mary that she will bear a son to be named Jesus (Luke 1:26-35). In the pseudepigraphal books of I and II Enoch, Gabriel's functions are more precisely defined.

C.B.C.

**GAD.** The name of one of the twelve tribes of ancient Israel, named for the oldest son of Jacob, by his wife Zilpah (Gen. 30:10 ff.; 35:26). The territory allotted to Gad in the Promised Land was northeast of the Dead Sea between the Jordan River on the west and ancient Ammon on the east and ran north to approximately the valley of the Jabbok River. Gad is referred to as the land of GILEAD in the book of Judges (chap. 11). Fierce, continual warfare between the tribe of Gad and the Ammonites called forth the judge, Jephthah, who delivered Gad from its foes (Judg. 11). The tribe of Gad supported David in the struggle with Saul, but at the death of Solomon revolted along with Jeroboam, helping to create the northern kingdom of Israel. At the fall of Samaria to

Assyria, the tribe was taken into captivity by Tiglath-pileser III (733 B.C.).

Another Gad was a prophet in the days of David (I Chr. 21:9 ff.). He condemned the counting of the people of Israel, served in the worship of Yahweh, and left a history of David's administration (I Sam. 22:5; II Sam. 24:11 ff.; I Chr. 29:29; II Chr. 29:25).

After the Exile, a spirit or god of good luck named Gad had a cult following in Judah (Isa. 65:11).

J.C.

**GAIUS.** There seems to be four different people in the NT who bear the name Gaius.

(1) A believer at Corinth, baptized by Paul and recognized for his hospitality (I Cor. 1:14; Rom. 16:23).

(2) A traveling companion of Paul from Macedonia, involved in the riot at Ephesus (Acts 19:29).

(3) A person from Derbe who is listed among those accompanying Paul on his last trip to Asia (Acts 20:4). He could possibly be the same person mentioned in Acts 19:29.

(4) An influential Christian to whom III John (v. 1) is written. (See CALIGULA.)

C.B.C.

**GALATIA.** The name Galatia (given in Gal. 1:2) covers a wide region of Asia Minor, modern Turkey. The Greek term for these inhabitants was Celts, and strictly in the context of Paul's Letter to the Galatians it refers to those who lived in the area around Ancyra (modern Ankara) who left Gaul (France) in the fourth century B.C. and settled there soon after 280 B.C. In the first century B.C., the Roman Emperor Augustus reorganized the kingdom as a province of the empire under a legate. In Luke's (Acts 16:6; 18:23) and Paul's day, Galatia reached from the northern region of Pontus around the Black Sea (see I Pet. 1:1) to the Mediterranean. Debate has continued on the thorny issue: Did the recipients of Paul's letter live in the northern part of the region (Provincia Galatia) or in the south, around the Phrygian and Lycaonian cities of Pisidian Antioch and others (Acts 13, 14)? Currently the weight of research is on the side of the former view, but that Paul wrote to churches on the south side of the Anatolian plateau is still defensible.

R.M.

**GALATIANS, LETTER TO THE.** A letter from Paul addressed to Christian congregations scattered throughout an extensive area of GALATIA, a province in Asia Minor (modern Turkey).

*Identity.* The name "Galatia" (Gal. 1:2, see 3:1 for the inhabitants) covered a wide region in Paul's day reaching from the northern district of Pontus around the Black Sea (see I Pet. 1:1) to the Mediterranean. The precise location of the churches to which this letter was sent is debated. One view sees the recipients as living in *Provincia Galatia* in the north of the region (the references in Acts 16:6 and 18:23 are apparently to this district). The alternate theory views the letter as sent to churches established on Paul's so-called first missionary journey, that is, churches in south Galatia with centers in Antioch, Iconium, Lystra, and Derbe (Acts 13, 14). This position has been advocated on the basis of detailed historical and geographical research based on nineteenth-century travelers' personal survey of the terrain in Asia Minor and its archaeological significance coupled with a study of epigraphy and classical literature. If we take the evidence of Paul's travels in Acts at face value as historically accurate and detailed, the latter view has much to commend it.

Interpreters who argue for a sending of the letter to south Galatian congregations tend generally to link this view with a dating prior to the Jerusalem Council of A.D. 50, thus making the letter the earliest Pauline document to survive. On the other hand, a placing of the recipients in the north of the Roman province means that they cannot have been evangelized before the time of Acts 16 (after the council—Acts 15), and thus the letter belongs to Paul's later ministry, while he was at Ephesus (A.D. 54–55).

*The Nature of the Trouble.* The question relates to the situation in Galatia referred to in 1:6-9 and 5:10, 12, where Paul remarked that a grave crisis had broken out in the churches in Galatia. False teachers had appeared on the scene, and their aim was evidently to unsettle Paul's converts. We have to ask what precisely this new teaching was.

The traditional view is that these men were Judaizing Christians aiming to promote the necessity of CIRCUMCISION as needful to Gentile Christians who would be assured of complete salvation and full membership of the new Israel, the church (5:2; 6:12ff.).

But if they were Jewish teachers, akin to those in Acts 15:1, it is difficult to explain pagan elements in the message that threatened the Galatians (4:3, 8, 9: "elemental spirits" are almost certainly star gods, as in current astrological religion). It is also unclear how Paul can regard their teaching as a threat to morality since the Galatians were guilty of gross sins (5:13-26) and a selfish attitude (6:1-10). These items have led to the conclusion that it was a type of gnostic Christianity that had invaded the congregation. Paul had to defend his gospel on two fronts: on the one side, against a Pharisaic legalism, which had been infected, on pagan territory, by GNOSTICISM; and on the other, against antinomian tendencies that led to ethical laxity in the church.

A third option has most to commend it. In 5:11 Paul regarded himself as being persecuted for his preaching of a message that dismissed the need for circumcision, a point he returns to in 6:11-17. The occasion of this controversy is found in renewed Zealot activity in Judea at the time of the letter, subjecting Jewish Christians to pressure to declare themselves loyal Jews at a time of nationalistic upsurge. One way they could do this was to insist on circumcision, and they carried this argument to its logical extreme in requiring baptized pagans to receive the rite as a token of belonging to the Israel of the Abrahamic covenant (Gen. 17:9-14). The Galatian Gentiles listened to this promise of membership in a new community and interpreted it as giving them license to live as they pleased. Hence they slid into a lax morality.

*Paul's Response.* Paul repelled the Jewish Christian arguments by appealing to Genesis 12 and 15, where the promise to Abraham said nothing about circumcision when it offered a worldwide family, but rather made acceptance with God conditional on the sole requirement of faith (Gal. 3:10-14). Yet "faith" for Paul has ethical implications, chiefly the act of love (5:6) and the call to act out a person's new relationship to God in socially responsible ways (5:13–6:10).

R.M.

**GALILEE (GALILEAN).** A region as part of northern Israel in biblical and modern times. Allusion to Galilee occurs in the OT a few times (Josh. 20:7, identifying Kedesh in Galilee; I Kings 9:11, twenty cities in Galilee ceded to Hiram of Tyre; and in particular Isa. 9:1, "Galilee of the nations," that is, the forested regions of Galilee). The Isaiah 9 reference probably points to Galilee's exposure to non-Jewish influence, and this made Galilee isolated from the mainstream of Jewish life and open to paganizing pressures, especially in upper Galilee.

The NT references to the region are to lower Galilee, about one thousand feet lower in elevation than the northern part of Galilee and falling dramatically to more than six hundred feet below sea level at the SEA OF GALILEE. The lower Galilee area, less wooded, was marked by greater fertility on account of several streams, and it drew to itself a large, mixed population engaged in raising olives and cereal crops and in fishing in Lake Galilee.

The region passed under the political jurisdiction of Herod Antipas at the death of his father Herod the Great in 4 B.C. In the area Antipas built a large city on the banks of the Lake Tiberias, named after the reigning emperor, in A.D. 22. Herod Agrippa succeeded to the rulership of Galilee in NT times.

The separation of Galilee from Judea in the south by the intervening land of Samaria is the reason for Galilee's isolation, culturally and religiously, from rabbinic influence centered in Jerusalem. Hence there was a distrust of the Galileans, bordering on a demeaning attitude (John 7:52).

In lower Galilee Jesus' boyhood was spent; and here was the locale of his ministry before his journey south to Judea for his passion, according to Mark's account. Roman roads passed through Galilee, and Roman influence was felt in the northern province. A cosmopolitan aura was present in Galilee, though it is remarkable that the Gospels do not mention the leading large cities, such as Sepphoris, which Jesus apparently never visited. The accent of the people was the Galilean dialect of Aramaic, the spoken language, and Peter was detected as a Galilean in Jerusalem by his speech (Matt. 26:73).

R.M.

Courtesy of the Israel Government Tourist Office, Houston, Texas

*The Sea of Galilee, with modern Tiberias in the foreground*

**GALILEE, SEA OF.** A lake set in the region of GALILEE, a province in northern Israel in biblical and modern times. There are various spellings such as "Chinnereth" (Num. 34:11) or "Chinneroth" (Josh. 12:3) or, in NT references, "Gennesaret" (Luke 5:1) or the "Sea of Tiberias" (John 21:1), an allusion to a large town built on its water's edge.

The Jordan Valley, a geological rift that runs down the land of Israel north to south, places a considerable area under sea level, and the Lake of Galilee is six hundred to seven hundred feet below sea level. The configuration of the lake is pear-shaped—thirteen miles in length by seven miles broad at its widest extremity.

The mountain region that encompsses the sea means that the lake lies in a basin. It is therefore subject to storms caused by a shift in atmospheric pressure which, in turn, is created by the neighboring mountains. There are sudden squalls, which make treacherous the crossing of the lake in open boats such as Galilean fishermen used because of their shallow draft. This feature is seen in the story of Mark 4:35-41 and parallels.

The fishing industry was prosperous in NT times since the water is sweet, and there are considerable

Courtesy of the Israel Government Tourist Office, Houston, Texas

*Hills surrounding the Sea of Galilee*

numbers of fish in their different species to be found there. On the banks of the lake several towns grew up, such as Capernaum, Bethsaida, and Tiberias.

R.M.

**GALILEI, GALILEO** (1564–1642). Famed Italian scientist and mathematician. Son of a Pisan merchant and musicologist, he studied medicine and mathematics in Pisa at Vallombrosa monastery and the university. Keen observation and experimentation yielded him numerous discoveries: the isochronic law of pendulums, a measure for specific gravity of solids, parabolic paths of projectiles, rate of falling bodies, and so on. His treatise on gravity (1588) won him a university post at Pisa, 1589–91. From 1592 to 1610 he was professor of mathematics at anticlerical Padua, lecturing to large crowds. Improving on the telescope in 1609, he discovered moon configurations, Jupiter's satellites, and sunspots. In 1610 he went to Florence to teach. His support of "heretical" Copernican views brought warnings from Rome.

Then in 1632 Galileo's *Dialogue on the Two Chief Systems of the World* boldly defended Copernicus' views, even suggesting some scientific truth was equal to scriptural truth. The Inquisition in 1633 forced Galileo to say that the sun moves around the earth—a major setback for Italian science. Galileo's *Dialogues on the New Science* (1638) forcefully restated his earlier discoveries. Besides influencing Newton and Torricelli, he contributed greatly to the rise of science. His writings were removed from the Index in 1835.

C.M.

GALL (BITTER HERB). The term "gall" refers to a digestive fluid secreted by the liver also known as bile. Because of its extreme bitterness, "gale" is either literally or figuratively used for anything extremely bitter. In the Bible, gall is the name for any bitter substance, such as a poison (Job 20:14; Acts 8:23); hemlock (Hosea 10:4 KJV); or the herb "wormwood" (Jer. 9:15). The phrase "wormwood and gall" refers to anything too bitter to bear and hence means extreme suffering, like the trials of Job or the passion of Christ.

Gall is used loosely in the English translation for a number of actual herbs, as well as metaphorically for extreme suffering. Jesus was offered vinegar and gall while he suffered on the cross (Matt. 27:34 KJV). This must have been a pain-killer provided for the crucified (see also Ps. 69:21 KJV). Jesus refused the opiate, choosing to face his death with a clear mind.

J.C.

GALLICANISM. A theory that denotes the nationalistically fueled struggle of the French church and state against absolute papal power. Rooted in Gaul's ancient tribalism, where prince prevailed over priest, Gallicanism has continually manifested itself in French life, sometimes as episcopal attempts to gain independence or equality with the pope, sometimes as political struggles for temporal autonomy. Often the struggles coalesced. Gallicanism can be seen in Charlemagne's theocratic rule, and in King Philip IV's struggle against Pope Boniface VIII, a conflict precipitating the Babylonian Captivity (1307–77) and removal of the papacy to Avignon. The Council of Constance, 1414–18, elevated councils above popes. The Pragmatic Sanctions of Bourges (1438) placed ultimate authority in bishops in council with the pope. In 1682 King Louis XIV forced clerical acceptance of Gallicanism's four principles, prepared by Bishop Bossuet. They asserted the king's independence of the pope in temporal matters and the superiority of councils. They demanded respect for French church customs, mores, and political laws,

and denied papal infallible authority without episcopal consent. These were ordered taught in all French higher schools. The French Revolution secularized religion, but at Vatican I (1870) French bishops repudiated Gallicanism. Church and state formally separated in France in 1905, yet resistance to the papacy continues.

C.M.

GAMALIEL. According to Acts 5:34 the first apostles were saved from their fate by the intervention of Rabbi Gamaliel I in the Jewish council. He represented the liberal tradition of the school of HILLEL, and was highly regarded as a venerable "teacher of the law" (Luke's term—*nomodidaskalos*—in Acts 5:34).

His speech argued that the Jewish hierarchy should take no decisive action regarding the Christian leaders, but should leave the issue to divine providence, a typically Pharisaic sentiment. Appeal is made to historical precedents: first, Theudas, a Jewish magician, according to Josephus in *Antiquities,* who raised a revolt against Rome and was crushed; then, Judas of Galilee, also referred to in *Antiquities,* who led a Zealot uprising that was similarly put down in A.D. 6, the time of the census. There is a confusion here, since Theudas' rebellion occurred later than that of Judas and at a time subsequent to Gamaliel's speech. It may be that Luke's report was not intended to be chronologically exact.

At all events, Gamaliel's advice was forthright: "Do not molest Christians," since God will bring the movement to nothing, if it is spurious. His counsels prevailed (Acts 5:40), and the apostles were dismissed with a cautionary beating.

R.M.

GANDHI, MOHANDAS K. (1869–1948). Leader of the Indian independence movement, advocate of nonviolence on both the practical and philosophical planes, exemplar of the use of "soul-force" to achieve righteous this-worldly ends. Gandhi demonstrated, as have few others in world history, the thorough combination of the spiritual and the political in one person.

Born in west India and educated for a legal career in England, Gandhi lived in South Africa (1893–1914), where he fought vigorously against the racial discrimination under which Indians there suffered and perfected his nonviolent techniques of demonstrations, selective civil disobedience, strikes, and fasting. After his return to India in 1915, he began using these methods in the struggle against British rule and on behalf of the underclasses of Indian society.

Gandhi firmly believed in the unique power of nonviolent resistance to attain righteous political ends. It can be wielded equally by strong and weak, rich and poor, and it ultimately can turn the foe through its moral power. But to be effective it must be based in a life of utter nonattachment, spiritual

Courtesy of the Israel Government Tourist Office, Houston, Texas

*Mahatma Gandhi*

purity, and dedication, and must exemplify a courage at least as great as that of the soldier. Gandhi also excoriated the West for its materialism and urban industrialism. He urged India, not entirely successfully, to embrace a simple economy based on the village and handcrafts.

After independence and the division of the British Raj into India and Pakistan in 1947, Gandhi was saddened by the bloody communal riots between Hindus and Muslims and worked mightily for reconciliation. But he was shot by a Hindu extremist while on his way to a prayer meeting in 1948.

R.E.

**GANESHA** (Ganesa). From the Sanskrit word literally meaning "lord of a group (of Shiva's attendants)." An elephant-headed god of HINDUISM who is the son of SHIVA and Parvati, Ganesha is widely worshiped as a "remover of obstacles" and a bestower of prosperity.

Ganesha came into prominence in the PURANAS with the rise of BHAKTI. According to myth, he acquired his elephant head in this way: Shiva was gone, and his consort, Parvati, desired to have a son. So she fashioned and brought to life one made from material scrubbed from the surface of her body. When Shiva returned, he was angered at seeing the strange youth in the house and cut off his head. Then Parvati, in tears, explained to her lord that he had killed her own son. Shiva vowed to provide him with the first available head, which turned out to be that of an elephant.

Images of Ganesha are frequently found at the entryways of temples and in places of business, and his

festival, Ganesha Caturthi, is popular in north India. As an auxiliary remover-of-obstacles god, he is worshiped by Hindus of all schools. One small sect, the Ganapatyas, make him central, regarding him as the manifested form of BRAHMAN. The largeness of the elephant head in relation to the body is said to represent the greatness of Brahman in relation to the world. The mouse, the vehicle or animal associated with the god, shows the relative smallness of the human, unless the oneness of its ATMAN with Brahman is realized. The curved trunk tells us that the path to enlightenment is difficult, but the way of access is present.

The worship of Ganesha has flourished in modern India. This is partly because the militant nationalist B. G. Tilak used his festival as an occasion for fervent affirmation for Hindu tradition and protesting British rule, and partly because in a time of rapid social and economic change his role of removing obstacles has seemed of special significance.     R.E.

**GANGES RIVER.** Major river flowing out of the Himalayas across most of north India. In HINDUISM this river, personified as the lovely goddess Ganga, is very sacred and a magnet for pilgrimage. Two of the "Seven Sacred Cities" of India—Hardwar to the north, and above all Varanasi (Benares), holiest of all—are on its banks. To bathe in its waters cleanses one spiritually. The devout also come to die near its shores. Bodies of the deceased are brought from far and near to the edge of the holy river to be burned and the ashes thrown into its waters.     R.E.

**GARRISON, WILLIAM LLOYD** (1805–79). The militant abolitionist was born on December 10 to Abijah and Frances Maria Lloyd Garrison. He served as editor of the *National Philanthropist,* a Baptist temperance journal, and then helped Quaker abolitionist Benjamin Lundy edit *The Genius of Universal Emancipation.* The first issue of Garrison's own *Liberator* appeared January 1, 1831. A militant pacifist, radically anticlerical, Garrison formed the New England Anti-Slavery Society in 1832, and helped to found the American Anti-Slavery Society in 1833, serving twenty-two years as its president. The organization split in 1840, however, over Garrison's repudiation of political action and his support for women's rights.     N.H.

**GATH.** Of the five cities of the Philistines on Israel's coastal strip, Gath is the furthest from the Mediterranean Sea. The corresponding adjective is Gittite (for example, II Sam. 15:18; 21:19, 20). Gath played a prominent part in the Philistine campaign to subdue the Israelite tribes. After the ark had been taken in battle, it was removed to Gath (I Sam. 5:6-10; 6:17). Goliath the giant is named as living there (I Sam. 17:4). Achish, king of Gath, was David's enemy who later enlisted him in service (I Sam. 21:10-15; 27:2-12). Eventually the city was ceded to David, and Rehoboam fortified it (II Chr. 11:5-8). But in Amos's time (mid-eighth century), it was retaken as a Philistine city (Amos 6:2). Its present site is uncertain.                                    R.M.

**GATHA.** *See* AVESTA.

**GAZA.** One of the five main Philistine cities, Gaza stood on the coast; in fact it has given its name to the Gaza Strip, the coastal area of Israel's mainland, though classified as the "west bank" by Palestinians. Its original settlers evidently emigrated from Crete (Deut. 2:23). But they were dispossessed by Joshua (Josh. 10:41). Yet this occupation was only temporary, and we read (Josh. 13:3) of the king of Gaza as a thorn in Israel's side. The tribe of Judah retook it (Judg. 1:18), but it was lost later, since the captured Samson was taken there by his enemy (Judg. 16:21-31). As it stood on the main caravan route, Assyria in her campaigns against Egypt frequently laid it waste. In Jeremiah's day it was Egyptian territory (Jer. 47:1), finally to be besieged by Alexander the Great in the fourth century. Its role in the NT is seen in Acts 8:26-40.            R.M.

**GEBAL.** An ancient Canaanite and Phoenician seaport known to the Greeks as Byblos or "book," since papyrus used for books was shipped from there. Gebal simply means "mountain" and was located in Lebanon twenty-five miles north of Beirut. Men of Gebal served as stonecutters in the construction of Solomon's Temple.                            J.C.

**GEDALIAH.** The name of five men in the OT, among them the grandson of Hezekiah and grandfather of the prophet Zephaniah (Zeph. 1:1); the Jewish governor appointed in Judah after the destruction of Jerusalem in 587 B.C. (Jer. 40:11, II Kings 25:24-25; Jer. 40, 41); and a musician consecrated to service in the Temple (I Chr. 25:3).                        J.C.

**GEHAZI.** The companion (either servant of, or associate of) the prophet ELISHA. Elisha did not give the status to Gehazi that Elijah gave to him when he was Elijah's associate (II Kings 4:12; 8:4). Gehazi proved less than trustworthy, as he was unable to help the Shunanmite woman who requested Elisha's aid, and even lost his temper (II Kings 4:8 ff.; 4:27). Later he misrepresented Elisha to Naaman, the Syrian army commander who sought, successfully, for a cure of his leprosy at Elisha's hands. Gehazi sought to extort a talent of silver and new clothes from Naaman, as a price for the miraculous cure. Because of this, Gehazi was struck with leprosy himself (II Kings 5:20-27). J.C.

**GEHENNA.** The word is composite, meaning "the valley of Hinnom," and it has two distinct usages. As a geographical place-name it forms the west-south boundary of Jerusalem, known as the gorge of Hinnom or of the sons of Hinnom (from Josh. 15:8; see II Kings 23:10). The Greek Bible renders the name in Joshua 18:16 as *Gaienna*, and this gave the later name "Gehenna" in NT times. The association of the valley of Hinnom with pagan cult practices, especially the fearful rite of child sacrifice (Jer. 7:30-33), gave it an unsavory reputation. The apostate kings Ahaz and Manasseh offered human sacrifices here (II Chr. 28:3; 33:6). From the way the land became desecrated it was a convenient place for Jerusalem's garbage to be disposed of by burning. These two elements gave Gehenna a meaning synonymous with destruction by FIRE.

The religious significance of Gehenna may be traced to the second century B.C., when this valley was thought of as the place of the final destruction of the enemies of God and God's people (perhaps based on Isa. 66:24). In rabbinic eschatology (that is, the final separation of the righteous and sinners), Gehenna is referred to as a place of torment, though no longer confined to Jerusalem's site. The NT data are confined to the Synoptic Gospels and James 3:6. The language of Jesus, obviously metaphorical but nonetheless serious, warns of a penalty for flagrant disobedience to the moral claims of God (Matt. 5:21, 22, 29, 30, RSV marg.) and injury to other people who are defenseless (Mark 9:42-47; Matt. 18:9) in terms of "being thrown into the hell of fire." One verse (Matt. 10:28; see Luke 12:5) attributes such judgment to God; and "child of Gehenna" (Matt. 23:15) means—in the figurative idiom—one deserving of severest condemnation. Note that such judgment, in Jesus' reported teaching, is reserved for professed followers and religious leaders, not incorrigible sinners.                                         R.M.

**GEIST.** The German word for spirit, mind, intellect, or wit has even wider meaning through usage. *Der Heilige Geist* is "Holy Ghost" in English. In Hegelian philosophy *Geist* means "mind," but in an ontological, historical sense *Geist* has come to mean culture in such usages as *der Geist der Zeit* (the spirit of the time) and *Geisteswissenschaften* (human or cultural studies).                                        C.Mc.

**GEMARA.** A Jewish term, of Aramaic origin, to denote commentary material added—the word means "completion"—to the MISHNAH, itself an explication of the books of Moses in the Hebrew Bible. The Mishnah was assembled in literary form in the third century A.D. and attracted the rabbis' comments. When these rabbinic interpretations were appended to the Mishnah the result was the TALMUD, the final repository of Jewish authoritative teaching.   R.M.

**GEMARIAH.** The name of two men in the book of Jeremiah. One was the son of Hilkiah, sent as a messenger to Nebuchadnezzar by King Zedekiah. He also carried Jeremiah's letter to the Babylonian exiles.

The other was the son of Shaphan who asked the king not to harm Jeremiah's scroll (Jer. 36).        J.C.

**GENEALOGY.** This subject may be said to be of much greater importance in the OT than in the NT. The term "genealogy" is defined as a roll call of names that trace the ancestry of descendants of an individual, tribe, or nation. There is an obvious social and anthropological significance in this list; but the biblical interest is not merely antiquarian, rather it is religious. The purpose is to trace the providential ordering of family and group life in such a way that God's overruling purpose may be detected. Hence the lists are far from complete as ancestral records. In key instances (notably Matt. 1:1-17; Luke 3:23-38) the choice is highly selective and theologically motivated. Specifically, the evangelists or their sources have endeavored to pick out those ancestors (women, in Matthew's case) or names (Abraham, David) who presaged the coming of Messiah, or else by a use of numerical values to demonstrate how the Messiah as great David's greater son was already foreshadowed in David's lineage.

The word "genealogy" occurs in the OT according to the RSV only at Nehemiah 7:5, referring to returning exiles under Sheshbazzar. But this is untypical, for the reason given above. The longer lists are seen in Genesis 5; I Chronicles 1:1-42, cast in the form of A lived X number of years and gave birth to B; thereafter lived Y number of years, and all A's years were Z, and he died. Genealogies begin with Adam, but other patriarchal figures are listed with their descendants (Cain, Noah, Shem to Abraham, Gen. 11:10-26; Ishmael, Esau, and with special importance given in Gen. 46, to Jacob and his sons, whom the nation regarded as founders of the later twelve tribes). Of special interest in postexilic Israel was the assemblage of Levite names (I Chr. 6:1-53). By direct contrast Jesus' ancestry is traced back (in Heb. 7:6-14) to Melchizedek, whose priestly office was non-Levite.

A peculiar use of genealogies is reported in I Timothy 1:4; Titus 3:9, where the Christian writer opposes a Jewish interest in family connections, or a tracing of pairs of "eons" or emanations from Deity, cherished by Gnostic systems to explain the universe.        R.M.

**GENERAL ASSEMBLY.** The highest governing body in churches with a PRESBYTERIAN form of government. Its members are ministers and elders elected by lower governing bodies, usually presbyteries. Most Presbyterian denominations hold an annual General Assembly.        J.G.

**GENERAL ASSOCIATION OF REGULAR BAPTIST CHURCHES.** *See* BAPTIST CHURCHES.

**GENERAL CONFERENCE.** The highest legislative body in most Methodist bodies. In The United Methodist Church, the General Conference meets every four years. It is made up of elected representatives, clergy and laity in equal numbers, from the ANNUAL CONFERENCES. It has the power to revise the *Book of Discipline*.        J.C.

**GENESIS.** A name derived from the Septuagint, the Greek translation of the OT, meaning "origin," "beginning," or "creation." This first book of the Bible, known in Hebrew as *bereshith* ("in the beginning") after its opening word, constitutes the prologue to Israel's unique faith history. It distills the belief of the Israelite community in a God whose deeds of creation, blessing, judgment, and redemption operate foremost for Israel's welfare, but also for the welfare of the world.

*Organization and Basic Content.* Numerous early Israelite traditions have been woven into a continuous narrative spanning from the Creation of the universe to Joseph's death in Egypt. Genesis readily falls into two parts, with chapter 12 being the pivotal element that confers new meaning on chapters 1-11 and advances the theme of Israel's election, which integrates the different components in chapters 12-50. The activities of Hebrew history from Adam to Abraham are presented in chapters 1-11. Of primary concern are the CREATION of the universe, the origin of evil, the emergence of civilization, the great Flood, and the Dispersion of humanity. In chapters 12-50 the history of the patriarchs is organized in such a manner that chapters 12-25 focus on Abraham; 26-36 on Isaac and his sons, Jacob and Esau; and 37-50 on Joseph.

*Composition.* (a) Genesis 1-11. Most biblical scholars maintain that two separate strata, the Yahwistic (J) and Priestly (P), are represented within this so-called primeval history. In turn, J and P are respectively regarded as the tenth and sixth-century B.C. authors, who recast what they inherited in the way of independent and largely oral traditions. Though J establishes the narrative framework here, P provides a subsequent chronological backbone as well as two substantial narrative segments—the Creation (1:1-2:4a) and the Flood (portions of chaps. 6-9).

Since its major intention is not to account for specific happenings in remote antiquity, but to meditate on present reality, Genesis 1-11 is often classified as MYTH. Accordingly, the traditions are valued for their timeless appeal and capacity to engage the reader personally. Thus in 1:1-2:4a, the Priestly writer was less absorbed by the question, How did the universe actually come into being? than he was by the question, What does it mean for one to belong to creation and to exist as God's creature among the other creatures? As the mythology of chapters 1-11 was written and edited into its present shape, answers were sought for a variety of questions, some of which probed the meaning of life itself. Thus in his account of the couple's eviction from the garden (chap. 3), the Yahwist wrestles with a query that has haunted every age—why are people mortal? Truth, not entertainment, is the fundamental agenda item in these chapters whose universalism celebrates not so much what was, as what is.

(b) Genesis 12–50. Several differences set these chapters apart from the preceding. First, the Yahwistic (J) and Priestly (P) strata are joined by still another, the Elohistic (E), the creation of a ninth/eighth-century B.C. Israelite. Preserved in the now edited patriarchal history in a shortened format, and first detected in chapter 15, E mainly presents itself as the supplement of J. Second, the narratives in chapters 12–50 exhibit a more sustained quality than do those in chapters 1–11. Entire cycles of stories develop around such figures as Abraham and Jacob. Third, the engaging mythology of chapters 1–11 now yields to the colorful legend of chapters 12–50. This latter literary classification is not to be confused with solid historiographic writing, which Israel was also capable of producing. The patriarchal legends center on a small number of people who experience only fleeting contact with outsiders. Segments of remote time are portrayed in quite general terms. Typically the doings of the Israelite fathers are telescoped, refracted, and chronologically rearranged. Nevertheless, the Genesis legends relate the patriarchs to such specific geographical settings as Shechem, Hebron, and Beer-sheba, and impart both the feelings and actions of real individuals. They are not wanting in historical significance.

The stories that clustered around Abraham, Jacob and Esau, and Joseph are diverse in format and theme. The Abraham cycle (chaps. 12–25) consists of many independent stories that highlight the heartfelt concern of parents for offspring and Yahweh's determination to come near in the promise. Within the Jacob and Esau cycle (chaps. 26–36), larger groups of narratives reflect on the relationship of two brothers and the power of coveted patriarchal blessing. The uniqueness of the Joseph story (chaps. 37–50) resides in the fact that it is a single narrative that opens with family conflict and, thanks to divine providence, ends with reconciliation.

*Religious Message. (a) God as creator.* Though Genesis manifests a multiplicity of sources and literary forms, a well-integrated religious message is projected. The two different creation accounts (1:1–3:24) jointly acknowledge the Deity as the author of the cosmos, life, and humankind. Rather than offering a scientific explanation of the world's origins, these chapters celebrate the God whom biblical Israel knew to be the universal sovereign. Yet the God who organizes the cosmos lavishes a special interest in humanity. In both accounts, the creative process is climaxed by the making of man and woman. According to P, the couple is given dominion over nature (1:28). Created in God's "image," man and woman are equipped to rule over the animals. Yet made in God's "likeness," denoting abstract similarity, humans and God are assuredly

distinct (1:26). Moreover, in J, man *(adam)* derives from dust *(adamah)*, not from some divine component as is evident in earlier Babylonian cosmogony (2:7). Still, Genesis 1–3 affirms that God and humanity are linked in a unique relationship that sets man and woman apart from the plant and animal kingdom.

*(b) Humanity as rebels.* With its talent for meditating on historical actuality, Genesis 1–11 regularly underscores human rebellion. In the garden, the couple shuns its servant status and quests for divine omniscience (3:5-6). God discovers that "every imagination of the thoughts" of the human heart is "only evil continually" (6:5). Human presumption reaches its zenith in the Tower of Babel incident when humanity would "make a name" for itself by storming the very heavens (11:4). A psychological realism admits to humanity's innate drive toward autonomy. Above all, Genesis 1–11 testifies that this rebellion of creature against Creator is inveterate within the human family and that a gain in self-awareness is outdistanced by a strong sense of alienation from God. In the stories of the garden (chap. 3), the brothers (chap. 4), the Flood (chaps. 6–9), and the tower (chap. 11), the sinful condition of humankind is deftly portrayed. No less impressive is the depiction of divine judgment that steadfastly refuses to tolerate such rebellion.

*(c) God as Savior.* From beginning to end, Genesis highlights God's determination to deliver humanity from its sinful, lost condition to a new relationship with the Deity. According to J, the God who renders judgment also says, "Nevertheless!" By clothing the couple with animal skins prior to their expulsion from the garden (3:21), placing a protective mark on Cain before sending him away (4:15), and promising Noah that the pattern of "seedtime and harvest" will persist so long as "the earth remains" (8:22), Yahweh laces judgment with mercy. By contrast, after dispersing the peoples and confusing their languages in the Babel incident (11:9), no divine "Nevertheless" is spoken.

Yet when all seems hopeless, Yahweh discloses in the next narrative episode (12:1-9) the intention to deliver humankind through the divinely chosen human instrument—the people of Israel. Humanity's prospects for salvation are rekindled through Yahweh's gratuitous choice of Abraham and his seed. Wherever issued in the Genesis patriarchal stories (12:2-3; 17:5-8; 18:18; 28:13-14; 35:11-12), God's promise never depends on patriarchal virtue or accomplishment. Indeed, the Israelite fathers are realistically sketched as men of faith *and* flesh (see 12:10-20; 28:20-21). Such honesty, however, does not detract from the tenacious position of the patriarchal narratives that through God's saving design, "all families of the earth shall bless themselves" (12:3).                              J.K.K.

**GENTILE.** Anyone who is not of the Jewish faith or who is of a non-Jewish nation. The biblical text presents a complicated problem in translation since the various Hebrew words and the primary Greek word for "Gentile" can also be rendered (in the plural) as "nations," sometimes including the Jews (for example, Matt. 24:9; Mark 11:17), and sometimes excluding the Jews (for example, Gen. 27:29: Lam. 1:3). The immediate context is the determinative factor.

In the OT, Israel, God's chosen people, had a mission to non-Jewish nations. Five times in Genesis the promise to Abraham is repeated that "by you all the families of the earth shall bless themselves" (12:3; 18:18; 22:18; 26:4; 28:14). Though at times Israel anticipated crushing her enemies and ruling over other nations (for example, Gen. 27:29; Ps. 18:43), she knew that God's sovereignty was universal and the king was to be an agent to fulfill God's purpose among the nations (for example, Ps. 72).

The early Christian community saw in Jesus the fulfillment of the Abrahamic promise (Gal. 3:6-14). Though Matthew's Gospel reserves the mission to the Gentiles until after Jesus' resurrection (Matt. 10:5; 28:20), Luke from the beginning depicts Jesus (in the words of Isaiah) as "a light for revelation to the Gentiles and a glory to thy people Israel" (Luke 2:32; compare Isa. 42:6; 49:6). Jesus' initial sermon at Nazareth documents God's concern for two non-Jewish figures in the OT narrative (Luke 4:26-27), and the disciples are commissioned by the risen Christ to preach "to all nations" (Luke 24:47; Acts 1:8).

Paul, himself a Jew, was called to declare the gospel specifically to the Gentiles (Gal. 1:16; Acts 9:15; 26:16-17) in hope that as Jews had been the occasion for the inclusion of Gentiles, so would the Gentiles' response lead to the final salvation of Israel (Rom. 11:13-15, 25-26). A meeting between Paul and the Jewish Christian leaders at Jerusalem confirmed that Gentile believers would be accepted into the church without the rite of CIRCUMCISION (Gal. 2:1-10; Acts 15:1-21), though social relations between Jews and Gentiles remained unsettled for some time (Gal. 2:11-14).       C.B.C.

**GERAR.** A town of the Middle Bronze Age, the period of the patriarchs, located on the border of Israel and Egypt, southeast of Gaza. According to Genesis 20:1 and following and 26:1 and following, both Abraham and Isaac had adventures revolving around their wives and the king of Gerar, Abimelech. King Asa defeated the Ethopians near Gerar (II Chr. 14).       J.C.

**GERASA.** The location of Jesus' healing of the Gadarene demoniac (Mark 5:1; Matt. 8:28; Luke 8:26). While the exact location of Gerasa is disputed, it was probably on the eastern side of the Sea of Galilee opposite Magdala. There was a city of considerable size and population, still under construction by the Romans in Jesus' day, named Gerasa by Greek speakers and called Jerash by the Jews. Unfortunately, this city was across the Jordan, forty miles southeast of the Sea of Galilee. The details in Mark 5 make it unlikely that Jesus crossed the lake and walked forty miles before meeting the demon-possessed sufferer.       J.C.

**GERHARD, JOHANN** (1582–1637). German Lutheran theologian and churchman, author of Lutheranism's classic exposition of strict orthodoxy, *Loci Theologici* (1622). Born at Quedlinburg, on becoming seriously ill at fifteen, he vowed to become a minister. Two years later he began studying theology, philosophy, and medicine at Wittenberg University. At Jena University he studied Bible, receiving the M.A. in 1603. He studied further at Marburg but returned to Jena to avoid living under a Reformed Church regime. At twenty-four he was granted a doctorate and made superintendent of Heidelberg and later at Coburg. In 1616 he became professor at Jena. An earnest churchman and author of

Herbert G. May

*General view of Gerasa (Jerash), the street of the columns leading to the forum, and Hadrian's arch, the temple of Zeus, and the theater beyond*

numerous works, he influenced Lutheranism toward strict orthodoxy, causing many Melanchthonians to turn to Calvinism. His systematically arranged *Loci,* a detailed explanation of Lutheran doctrine, stressed the infallibility of Scripture and literal biblical inspiration, including Hebrew vowel points.

C.M.

**GERIZIM, MOUNT.** A mountain, located in Samaria, near Shechem and adjacent to Mount Ebal. Its nearest inhabited dwelling today is Nablus. Its biblical history centers first in the story of Moses' calling the tribes to possess the land (Deut. 27:11-14). Gerizim stands over against Ebal as good is opposed to evil. Joshua is said to have read the Law to the assembly here (Josh. 8:30-35), and later to have recalled the people to the covenant promises under the shadow of Gerizim (Josh. 24:26). Thus Gerizim became a sacred shrine, and these stories offer the reason for Israel's holy regard for it. The sympathy of the writer of I Kings is tilted against Jeroboam, who established a breakaway kingdom in Shechem "in the hill country of Ephraim" (I Kings 12:25). Assyria's invasion and conquest of the northern kingdom is held to be suitable punishment for this. Into the vacuum created by Israel's exile, the Samaritans came to center their cult of feasts, especially Passover, on Mount Gerizim, a tradition in evidence in John 4:20-23. This in turn is based on the fact that a Samaritan temple was built in the fourth century B.C., only to be taken and destroyed by John Hyrcanus when he took Shechem in 128 B.C.    R.M.

**GERSHON.** The oldest son of LEVI, whose family camped west of the tabernacle during the wandering of the Hebrews under Moses (Num. 3:23). This family had sacred tasks to perform for the tent of the presence of God. Even after the return from exile, Gershon's descendants were prominent in the service of the second Temple.    J.C.

**GERSON, JEAN DE** (1363–1429). French theologian, nominalist, mystic, and conciliarist, a leader at the COUNCIL OF CONSTANCE in ending the GREAT SCHISM. At fourteen he went to Paris and studied under Pierre d'Ailly. Upon becoming a doctor of theology in 1394, he succeeded d'Ailly as chancellor of Notre Dame and the University of Paris. With controversies raging over the Great Schism (1378–1417), Gerson worked for reform and renewal. He left Paris to become a pastor in Bruges in 1397. There he wrote *On the Manner of Conducting Oneself in Time of Schism,* counseling charity and recognition of the validity of the doctrine and use of the sacraments under both popes. He approved the Council of Pisa's efforts in 1409 to heal the schism, and actively participated in the Council of Constance (1414–18), called by Emperor Sigismund and the cardinals of both popes. He asserted conciliar superiority over the pope and argued for doctors of theology, cardinals,

and bishops to participate in any future general council. He spent the last years of his life in seclusion at Lyons writing *The Consolation of Theology.* Among his mystical writings, the *Mountain of Contemplation* (1397) stands out as an example of his influence on the Brothers of the Common Life and Ignatius Loyola.

C.M.

**GESENIUS, WILHELM** (1786–1842). German Semitic scholar and biblical critic who from 1810 until his death taught at the University of Halle. Resolutely separating Hebrew linguistics from dogmatic theology, this popular lecturer and exacting investigator approached biblical Hebrew in a solely rational, comparative manner that took serious account of cognate Semitic languages. As his major lexicographical effort, his Hebrew and Chaldean Dictionary first appeared in 1810–12, underwent numerous revisions, and laid the groundwork for the Hebrew Lexicon (1906) of Francis Brown, Samuel R. Driver, and Charles A. Briggs. Subsequently, the first edition of his definitive *Hebrew Grammar* was published in 1813 and his only exegetical study, an Isaiah commentary, in 1820–21.    J.K.K.

**GESHEM.** Arab leader who harassed the Jews as they were rebuilding the walls of Jerusalem under Nehemiah's direction (Neh. 2:19; 6:1 ff.). Geshem spread rumors that Nehemiah was arming the city with a view to revolting against the Persian Empire in order to become king of the Jews.    J.C.

**GESTALT PSYCHOLOGY.** A twentieth-century form of psychology. In contrast to atomism, or connectionalism, which concentrated on parts or affirmed that the whole is a linkage of parts, Gestalt stressed a basic unity of the whole. The term "gestalt" means "form" or "structure," and it is with whole structures that these psychologists did their research. Max Wertheimer, Wolfgang Köhler, and Kurt Koffka worked in Germany in the 1920s, but a decade later were forced by events to leave. The attempt to transfer their research into a different culture may have limited its development. Undoubtedly it has opened areas still to be fully explored.

One basic emphasis of gestalt psychology is on perception. For example, it is known that motion is not a series of sensations following one on another. The technology of motion pictures is based on a running together of images. The sensation of motion is a whole. There is a grouping within a visual field. The principle of *pragnanz* states that grouping tends toward simplicity and balance, which makes "good form." Gestalt principles of perception may be seen on a practical level in camouflage, during which an object may be hidden and only with difficulty be perceived within the whole. In a deliberately planned illusion *(trompe l'oeil)* something may seem to be what it is not; that is, figures drawn on a plane may seem to be three-dimensional.

Köhler carried the explanation of this principle into physiology, theorizing that specific brain functions enabled parts to be perceived as wholes. Memory and experience are related. Memory is not a connected chain of events but part of a total structure reaching backward from present experience. Memory can be developed because it forms a gestalt.

Thinking is a process that also fits the gestalt. Insight does not result as the end product of a chain of ideas. Insight comes as ideas draw together into a whole. It is not an evolutionary process so much as a new pattern, a sudden awareness, resulting from a restructuring of relationships among previously known facts. Hence thinking is more than recall because it is the result of reconstruction into new configurations of previously known facts and insights.

Gestalt psychology has had an effect on social psychology particularly through the work of Kurt Lewin, who also came from Germany to the United States in the 1930s. The movement known as group dynamics theory and its methods arose from his studies of how groups function with relation to members and authority figures. I.C.

**GETHSEMANE, GARDEN OF.** The place to which Jesus led the disciples, following the Last Supper (Mark 14:32; Matt. 26:36). John reports that they withdrew to a garden, without naming the site (John 18:1). Since Jesus and his followers left Jerusalem for the MOUNT OF OLIVES and crossed the brook Kidron, which lies just to the east of the temple mount, the traditional location on the western slope of that mountain is probably correct. Gethsemane is probably from the Hebrew *gat shemanim,* which means "oil press," although it could derive from *ge shemanim* ("valley of drunkards," as in Isa. 28:1) and thus refer to a wine press. On the side of the hill is a large cave that may have been the site of a press among the olive trees, which then and now cover parts of the slopes.

From the fourth century on, various spots in the area were identified as the location of Gethsemane, and especially of the place where Jesus struggled in prayer in the face of his impending death (Mark 14:34-36). Remains of earlier churches, dating back to the fourth century and commemorating these events, have been covered over by more recent structures: the Russian Orthodox Church of Mary Magdalene and the modern Franciscan Church of Gethsemane. H.K.

**GEZER.** An ancient city in Canaan, settled as early as 3300 B.C. Located eighteen miles northwest of Jerusalem on the road to the port of Jaffa, in recent times the ruins have been identified as the Tell-ej-Jazar, usually called the Tell Gezer. Gezer was often controlled by the Egyptians, especially during the fourteenth and thirteenth centuries B.C. The city had a large water tunnel running through solid rock, probably cut by the Egyptians.

During the Hebrew conquest, Gezer's king was slain by Joshua but the city was never occupied by the tribe of Ephraim, which settled that part of Canaan (Josh. 10:33; 12:12; 16:10; Judg. 1:29). It was probably occupied by David (I Chr. 6:67). Captured by Egypt once more, the destroyed city was given by the pharaoh back to Solomon, who rebuilt it, as part of the dowry when Solomon married a princess of Egypt.

An inscribed tablet, called the Gezer Calendar, dating from the late tenth century B.C., has been discovered in the ongoing excavations of this site. Earlier excavations in 1902–1909 were badly carried out, and the records of discoveries are practically useless. Since 1964, scientific excavations under the direction of Hebrew Union College's Biblical and Archaeological School have discovered many things, including a casement wall and a buttressed gate. During the war for Judah's independence, Simon Maccabeus captured Gezer (142 B.C.) and fortified it. J.C.

**Al-GHAZZĀLĪ, ABŪ HĀMID** (1058–1111). Muslim scholar and mystic whose erudition, acute intellect, and prodigious literary output did much to synthesize ISLAM's diverse legal, doctrinal, philosophical, and mystical aspects. Born in Persia, he crowned his academic career as a professor in Baghdad, but in 1096 caused much comment by resigning to adopt the life of a SUFI contemplative.

Widely learned but orthodox, al-Ghazzali rejected the views of those extreme fundamentalists who said that faith should have nothing to do with rational philosophy; he studied Greek thought and viewed its logic as a preparation for theology. Yet he insisted that the divine revelation itself is beyond human rational comprehension; it can only be received in faith and trust. Such attitudes were only enhanced after his mystical "conversion," when he fervently affirmed that direct experience of God is far greater than any other kind of knowledge. Nonetheless, just as he countered the claims of fanatic fundamentalists and rationalists, so did his teaching also check the antinominian tendency of some mystics. Al-Ghazzali's contention that inward mysticism must deepen but not supplant normative Muslim religious and moral practice helped keep Sufism within the circle of orthodox Islam. R.E.

**GIBBON, EDWARD** (1737–94). English historian, renowned for his *History of the Decline and Fall of the Roman Empire.* Born at Putney, he went to Magdalene College, Oxford, was expelled for joining Roman Catholicism, and returned a short time later to Anglicanism. As part of an intellectual ENLIGHTENMENT set, he corresponded with international scholars, traveled widely on the Continent, and served in Parliament from 1774 to 1783. Poor in health, he lived off of scanty earnings and an inherited annuity. He never married.

Started in 1772, the first volume of his monumental history appeared in 1776, the fifth and last in 1788. Detailed and precise in research, it covered thirteen centuries and demonstrated the unity of Western civilization. Gibbon's work was antichristianity and anti-revelation. He assumed the self-sufficient rational order of all human knowledge, and selectively excluded religious faith and other non-supportive data. Chapters fifteen and sixteen treated Christianity, whose spread in the Roman Empire Gibbon felt was due to Christianity's non-supernatural zeal derived from Judaism, its views on immortality, reputed miracles, rigid morality, and good organization. Christian claims per se were ignored or denigrated. Gibbon's exclusion of divine elements in early Christianity prompted criticism which Gibbon responded to in *A Vindication,* 1779. Miscellaneous writings, including his *Memoirs,* were published posthumously. *The Decline and Fall,* scientific in method and critical of traditional truths, ranks as a great historical work, marking for some the beginning of modern historical literature.    C.M.

Courtesy of the Library of Congress

*James Cardinal Gibbons*

**GIBBONS, JAMES** (1834–1921). Roman Catholic archbishop of Baltimore for forty-three years, Gibbons advocated the church's accommodation to and full participation in American society.

Born on July 23 in Baltimore to Thomas and Bridget Walsh Gibbons, he traveled to Ireland with his family in 1837. He and his widowed mother settled in New Orleans in 1852. He entered Baltimore's St. Charles College in 1855 to study for the priesthood. He was ordained June 30, 1861, in the Baltimore Cathedral.

In 1865 Gibbons became secretary to Archbishop John L. Spalding. He was assistant chancellor at the Second Plenary Council in 1866 at Baltimore. At thirty-two he was named to head the Vicarate Apostolic of North Carolina and on August 16, 1868, became the youngest of America's twelve hundred bishops.

In 1872 Gibbons became bishop of Richmond, and in May 1877 he became bishop co-adjutor of Baltimore, succeeding James R. Bayley upon his death in October. Gibbons organized and presided as Apostolic Delegate over the Third Plenary Council in Baltimore in 1884. Its decrees have guided the church ever since. It also established Catholic University, Washington, D.C.

While accepting a cardinal's biretta from his friend Leo XIII in Rome, June 30, 1886, he lobbied for acceptance of the Knights of Labor and an understanding of American democracy. Gibbons' publications included *The Faith of Our Fathers* (1876), and *Our Christian Heritage* (1889). He died on March 24.

N.H.

**GIBEON.** The name means "hill." Scholars believe Gibeon was situated six miles north of Jerusalem. A tell (an ancient hill or mound) called El-Jib, is all that remains.

The Gibeonites, the inhabitants of the Horite (or Hivite) city of Gibeon, were assimilated into the tribes of Israel and played a leading role in OT events. Joshua (chap. 9) was tricked into establishing a covenantal relationship with the Gibeonites. This brought on a war between Jerusalem and Joshua's forces. Joshua defeated five kings of the Amorites, and Gibeon was made part of Benjamin's territory (Josh.

Courtesy of The University Museum, University of Pennsylvania

*The pool at Gibeon, showing part of the seventy-nine rock-cut steps*

10 and 18). Later, the city was handed over to the Levites (Josh. 21). The general Abner was conquered at Gibeon by David's forces. Joab slew Amasa in the same place (II Sam. 2 and 20). A shrine to Yahweh was established there under Solomon (I Kings 3; II Chr. 1). Jeremiah 28 says Hananiah the prophet was a Gibeonite. After the Babylonian captivity, Gibeonites returned to Jerusalem (Neh. 7; Ezra 2).

Archaeology has established that Gibeon was not occupied during Joshua's conquest but was rebuilt only in 1200 B.C. Nonetheless, the importance to Hebrew history of Gibeonites is underscored by the place name given it by the ancient historians.

J.C.

GIDEON. The fifth of the twelve "judges" listed in the book of JUDGES, and along with Samson, one of the most significant. All that can be said about him is based on Judges 6–9, there being no other reference to him in all of Scripture except for a passing mention, under his other name, Jerubbaal, in I Samuel 12:11.

The period of the judges is usually dated around 1200–1000 B.C., that is, between the conquest under Joshua and the emergence of Saul as the first anointed king of Israel. It is a time variously pictured as an age of primitive democracy, as a mutual defense league of twelve tribes, or as a howling anarchy. The book of Judges itself seems to lean toward the latter understanding, for it describes the era rather unfavorably as a time when "there was no king in Israel; every man did what was right in his own eyes" (21:25). Such leadership as there was consisted of charismatically endowed military leaders who arose in response to threats from common foes.

Gideon was one such figure. The account of his call to deliver Israel from the hand of Midian, the common oppressor, is contained in Judges 6:11-24. The call is in standard form, consisting of a salutation by an angel, two objections by Gideon coupled with two assurances from Yahweh, and finally a "sign" that the call is authentic (compare 6:19-24). The pattern is the same as that found in the call to Moses in Exodus 3, and is strikingly similar to the Annunciation to Mary in Luke 1:26-38. (One can hear an echo of the angel's salutation to Gideon—"The Lord is with you, you mighty man of valor"—in Gabriel's salutation to Mary—"Hail, O favored one, the Lord is with you"!) One of Gideon's initial tasks is to break down an altar and an asherah of Baal in his hometown (6:25-32). His success in this bold attack on the popular religion

of his day gives him his adopted name, Jerubbaal, which the people interpret to mean "Let Baal contend against him." However, Gideon's primary function is to free Israel from the oppressive hand of Midian. This he accomplishes in the well-known manner described in Judges 7. First, he reduces the number of men in his army from thirty-two thousand to a mere three hundred. After receiving assurance through the medium of a dream report, which he overhears while spying out the Midianite camp, that the Lord would deliver the enemy into his hand, he then has his men ring the camp in the dark. At the appointed signal, each man smashes the jug that concealed his flaming torch, blows on a trumpet, and shrieks, "The sword of the Lord and of Gideon!" The strategy has its desired effect; Midian flees from Israel.

In the aftermath of this victory chapter 8 pictures a punitive Gideon, who requites fellow Israelites who had refused to take part in the campaigns against Midian. But the story also tells of a wise Gideon who, when the men of Israel seek to make him king, says, "I will not rule over you, and my son will not rule over you; the Lord will rule over you" (8:23). Eventually Israel tended to agree with Gideon's rejection of monarchy in favor of direct rule by God, although, of course, Israel knew no polity but monarchy through much of OT history. Although Gideon makes a golden ephod (some kind of statuette?) with which Israel "played the harlot . . . and it became a snare to Gideon and to his family" (8:27), on the whole the tradition treats him kindly. He gave the land rest forty years, and he had seventy sons. His seventy first, by a Canaanite concubine, Abimelech, attempted to succeed Gideon as a king and was destroyed in the process. In spite of his flaws of initial timidity and ultimate idolatry, the tradition judges Gideon to be one to whom thanks were due "for all the good that he had done to Israel" (8:35).

W.S.T.

GIDEONS. An organization of Christian laymen committed to evangelism through the medium of Bible distribution. Originally, the group was called the Christian Commercial Men's Association of America. It was founded by two commercial travelers who met each other in a hotel in Janesville, Wisconsin, in 1898. These men organized the association in 1899 and began placing Bibles in hotel rooms, hospital rooms, prisons, and schools. The present headquarters is in Chicago.

The name "Gideons" is taken from the book of Judges in the OT (chaps. 6–8). Gideon was a judge or leader of ancient Israel. Each year, Gideons request the opportunity of addressing Protestant congregations. They describe their work and seek help in their ministry. Gideon Bibles are found in almost every hotel and motel room in the United States and Canada. Many travelers with personal and spiritual problems have found help in the Scriptures because of the Gideons' work.

J.C.

**GIFFORD LECTURES.** A lecture series founded by Lord Adam Gifford and given at four Scottish universities since 1888. These lectures were established to promote, advance, teach, and diffuse the study of natural theology, that is, the knowledge of God. These lectures are some of the most respected in the world.            J.C.

**GIFT OF TONGUES.** *See* GLOSSOLALIA.

**GIFTS, SPIRITUAL.** Two Greek words refer to the topic of "spiritual gifts." In introducing the theme, which evidently was much discussed at Corinth and about which the Corinthians had apparently consulted Paul, he writes: "Concerning spiritual gifts . . . I do not want you to be uninformed" (I Cor. 12:1). The reference could be to persons but more likely it is to gifts of Spirit, as in 14:1 and 14:12. The point of I Corinthians 12 is that Paul takes up the Corinthians' questions about *pneumatika* (what is spiritual), which relate to the gifts exercised in public worship and sets them within a larger framework of God's *charismata,* a broader term referring to all manifestations of God's favor, finding particular and concrete expresson in service of whatever kind (I Cor. 7:7). Both are traced to the HOLY SPIRIT's activity, but a distinction seems clear to most modern scholars.

"Spiritual gifts" in the wider application relates to the service of the church and is inherent in people who are thus endowed. In I Corinthians 12:4-6 Paul states this clearly, and in 12:7-11 he lists nine such gifts relevant to the Corinthian church. Paul elaborates this list in I Corinthians 14, with great stress placed on (a) the need for love (*agapē*) to accompany whatever gift is exercised; (b) the concern for all gifts to lead to the unbuilding of the entire church (I Cor. 14:12, 26); (c) the requirement that no gift, especially GLOSSOLALIA, should lead to disorder or excess (I Cor. 14:32-33, 39-40).

The list in Romans 12:6-8 is associated more with service to the church in a practical way and relates to the social function of the *charismata.* Other lists are in I Corinthians 12:28-30, as well as in the deutero-Pauline (Eph. 4:7-13) and Petrine (I Pet. 4:10-11) Epistles. These are confined to gifts of ministry.

A controversial issue is whether spiritual gifts of the more exotic and spectacular kind (glossolalia, healings, miracle working, EXORCISMS) were intended for the Apostolic Age only as a means of accrediting the message, or to have a permanent and universal place in the church in every age, especially our own. All are agreed, however, that the NT lists are specimens, and the contemporary Spirit fashions new gifts for the church in our present situation.      R.M.

**GIHON.** "The virgin's spring" (in Arabic, "Mary's spring"), which formed the main water supply of ancient Jerusalem, along with the Enrogel Spring, located somewhat to the south. Both springs are located in the Kidron Valley close to the walls of the ancient Jebusite city that became Jerusalem (after 2000 B.C.). These ancient people cut a forty-foot-deep well through the rock, the shaft of which ended in a cave that served as a reservoir. This shaft, now called Warren's Cave, was inclined so that women could walk down to the spring and back up again into the walled area of the city. It is likely that David's men, under Joab, stole undetected into Jerusalem through this shaft, leading to its capture (II Sam. 5:8; I Chr. 11:6). Later, Hezekiah walled up an "upper spring" and dug a tunnel, 1,777 feet long, through the rock in order to bring Gihon's water safely inside the city (II Kings 20:20). This created the pool of SILOAM and made the city better prepared to resist the invasion of Sennacherib in 701 B.C.      J.C.

**GILEAD.** A mountainous area in ancient Palestine, east of the Jordan River. The name can refer also to a person, the great grandson of Jacob's son Joseph. It sometimes refers to a tribe or to the territory the tribe lived in, or possibly to a city in that region.

In the song of Deborah (Judg. 5:17), Gilead seems to be a tribe, along with Reuben and Dan. The name seems to be used occasionally for the tribe of Gad. Gilead is called a "city of evildoers" in Hosea 6:8. But the writer may have meant the city of Jabesh-gilead or of Ramoth-gilead. Biblical writers sometimes shortened names for the sake of rhythm.

Gilead is mostly a highland region. It rises from the valley of the Jordan, at least 700 feet below sea level, and ascends to heights of more than 3,300 feet. The hills and valleys were well forested and grew grapes and olives in biblical times. It was also known for the "balm of Gilead," an aromatic resin used in medicine.

Gilead was contested property in OT times, belonging at various times to the Amorites, Moabites, Israelites, Midianites, Amalekites, Ammonites, Syrians, and Assyrians.      B.J.

**GILGAL.** The name of a number of towns and cities mentioned in the OT, especially during the early Hebrew conquest under Joshua. The name probably means "circle of stones," referring to religious monuments, similar to the Druid Stonehenge. Each town so named most likely had such a stone circle.

There was a Gilgal to the southeast of Jericho, by the Jordan. Here twelve symbolic stones were set up to symbolize the twelve tribes of Israel. Joshua made camp in this place upon reaching the west bank of the Jordan River (Josh. 4:1-9, 20; 5:10). Later, at Gilgal, the kingship of Saul was confirmed by the people (I Sam. 11:15). Still later, because he ran afoul of Samuel, Saul lost the throne at the same place. Hosea, Amos, and Micah all denounced corrupt religious practices at Gilgal, although it was originally a shrine to Yahweh (Hos. 4:15; 9:15; 12:11; Amos 4:4; 5:5; Mic. 6:5).      J.C.

*Fragment of the Babylonian account of the Flood, from Nineveh. Tablet XI of the Gilgamesh Epic.*

**GILGAMESH EPIC.** This epic, like Homer's *Odyssey,* is one of the principal heroic stories of ancient times, dating to at least 2000 B.C. It exists in a number of ancient editions including Babylonian, Sumerian, and Assyrian. Gilgamesh, according to the Sumerian King List, was the fifth king of the First Dynasty, which reigned in Uruk after the FLOOD (*see also* CREATION). The epic, which tells the story of his dangerous journey seeking the immortality of the gods, was found written on twelve clay tablets, in the middle of the last century by archaeologists working in the ruins of seventh-century B.C. Nineveh. Other portions of it were found in Boghazkoi, Nippur, Kish, Asshur, Sippar, and Ur. The twelfth tablet contained the Babylonian account of the Flood and is remarkably parallel to the later Hebrew account recorded in Genesis 6–9. The hero is Utnapishtim, corresponding to the biblical NOAH. The ark is called both a boat and a great house, built as an exact cube about two hundred feet in dimension. It had seven stories and was divided into nine sections, having a total of sixty-three compartments. It had a door and at least one window. Utnapishtim put on board "the seed of all living creatures," but it appears from the account that these only included herbivorous animals. The Flood lasted seven days, and then a dove, a swallow, and a raven were successively sent out to look for dry land. Utnapishtim, like Noah, was finally blessed by the gods after he offered a sacrifice.

J.R.M.

**GILMORE, JOSEPH HENRY** (1843–1918). Author of the hymn "He Leadeth Me, O Blessed Thought," Gilmore was born April 29 in Boston, to Joseph Albree and Ann Whipple Gilmore. The family moved to New Hampshire, where his father served as a state senator and then governor (1863–65). Joseph Gilmore graduated from Phillips Andover Academy (1854), Brown University (1858), and Newton Theological Institute (1861), where he taught Hebrew. After serving as a Baptist minister in Fisherville, New Hampshire, and Rochester, New York, he became professor of rhetoric, logic, and English literature at the University of Rochester from 1868 to 1908. He authored a number of college texts. His famous hymn was written during a course of lectures he gave at First Baptist Church in Philadelphia in 1862. It came out of the depression he was experiencing over the Civil War.      N.H.

**GILSON, ETIENNE** (1884–1978). Noted French philosopher and teacher of medieval Christian philosophy. Born and educated in Paris, Gilson received a doctorate from the Sorbonne (1906) and held philosophy professorships in Paris, Lisle, Strasbourg, Toronto, and Cambridge. An expert on Thomas Aquinas, he enabled many to understand THOMISM. He labored to relate reason and faith meaningfully, believing that both are necessary for science, philosophy, and Christianity. Among his principal works are *The Philosophy of Descartes* (1912), *Studies in Medieval Philosophy* (1922), *The Philosophy of St. Bonaventura* (1924), *The Unity of Philosophical Experience* (1937), *God and Philosophy* (1941), and *The Philosophy of the Middle Ages* (1955).      C.M.

**GIVING.** *See* TITHE.

**GLADDEN, WASHINGTON** (1836–1918). Congregational minister, crusading journalist, advocate of the SOCIAL GOSPEL, Gladden grew up on a farm in Pennsylvania and worked for a small-town newspaper. After graduating from Williams College in Williamstown, Massachusetts, he became religion editor of the *New York Independent* (1871–75), and helped to expose the Tweed Ring. He held pastorates in Springfield, Massachusetts (1875–82) and Columbus, Ohio (1882–1918). He opposed both socialism and classical economic theories. He applied "Christian law" to social problems. A charter member of the American Economics Association, he was one of the first clergy to support labor unions. He also served for two years on the Columbus City Council. He wrote forty books, including *Applied Christianity*

Courtesy of the Library of Congress

*Washington Gladden*

(1887), *Social Salvation* (1902), and *Recollections,* an autobiography (1909). Perhaps more familiar, however, is his hymn "O Master, Let Me Walk with Thee."      N.H.

**GLADSTONE, WILLIAM EWART** (1809–98). Leader of the Liberal Party and four-time prime minister of Great Britain. Gladstone was born on December 29, in Liverpool to Anne and John Gladstone. His father, a prosperous merchant prince of the slaving port, served in Parliament, 1818–27.

Educated at Eton and Christ Church College, Oxford, Gladstone graduated in 1831. Originally planning to take Anglican orders, Gladstone was persuaded by his father to enter politics. He began as a Tory, elected in December 1832. In 1838 he published the narrowly Anglican *State in Relation to the Church.* In July 1839 he married Catherine Glynne, who bore him eight children. Though having an evangelical mother and strongly influenced by friends in the OXFORD MOVEMENT, Gladstone remained High Anglican, noted for his moral stands on issues and his concerns for prostitutes and prisoners.

After years in Parliament and service in several cabinet posts, Gladstone served as prime minister 1868–74, 1880–85, 1886, and 1892–94. He was noted for his sound economic policies, his conciliatory foreign policy, and his advocacy of Irish Home Rule. His writings included *A Chapter of Autobiography* (1868), and a two-volume edition of the *Works of Joseph Butler* (1896). He died on May 19.

N.H.

**GLORIA IN EXCELSIS.** From the Latin wording of Luke 2:14, "Glory (to God) in the highest," and used in Christian liturgy as an acclamation of praise in celebration of God's gift of Christ.

The setting of the Lukan canticle—one of several Jewish-Christian hymnlike passages the evangelist has incorporated into his birth stories—has been much discussed. The most likely view is stated by R. E. Brown (*The Birth of the Messiah*, 1977, pp. 346-55) to the effect that these tributes of praise, such as the MAGNIFICAT and including the *Gloria,* emanated from a section of Jewish Christianity and had been turned into Greek before Luke came upon them and placed them in his Gospel.

At Luke 2:13-14 the angelic host breaks out into praise at the announcement of the Messiah's birth (2:10-12). There are some textual issues at stake in the song, but the better evidence reads "of good will" (genitive), and the sense of the passage supports this reading.

Modern editors and translators are virtually unanimous in connecting "good will" with God, not humankind, and interpreting the term as God's "good pleasure." The witness of a parallel phrase in the Dead Sea Scrolls makes the sense of divine election and grace even stronger: peace is given to those "on whom God's favor now rests" (compare RSV: "among men with whom he is pleased," as in Luke 2:14. Incidentally, the same verse in the *Living Bible* perpetuates an inferior reading and is in serious error with its translation: "peace on earth for all those pleasing him," which suggests that the Incarnation is good news only for an elite).

The final question is whether the text falls into three lines or is a couplet. The latter arrangement is strongly suggested by the newer translations:

Glory in the highest to God,
And on earth peace among those favored (by him).

R.M.

*GLORIA PATRI.* The ascription of praise to the Holy TRINITY used in Christian worship as a conclusion to recital or chanting of the Psalms. The "Gloria" is also known as the lesser doxology. It consists of the phrases "Glory be to the Father, and to the Son, and to the Holy Spirit [Ghost]." The Gloria Patri serves as a constant reminder of the doctrine of the equality of the divine persons in the Holy Trinity. The Gloria is also recited after each decade of the rosary in that Catholic devotion. It is probably one of the most frequently used forms of Christian devotion in history. Many Christian congregations, of whatever background or theological outlook, make use of the Gloria Patri in their worship.          J.C.

**GLORIFY.** In many instances in the Bible the verb "glorify" can mean simply "to extol, worship, bestow praise and honor" upon another. Both humans and God can be the objects of such glorification (for example, Matt. 5:16; 6:2; I Cor. 12:26). More characteristic, however, are those occasions when the verb draws its significance from the distinctive history of the noun "glory" and means "to have or give a share in the divine glory, the lofty majesty of God." Paul

says that those whom God justified "he also glorified" (Rom. 8:30; compare 8:17). The Gospel of John develops this dimension more extensively than any other book in the Bible in describing the entire life of Jesus as a Glorifying of the Son by the Father (for example, 8:54; 17:1, 5) and a glorifying of the Father by the Son (for example, 13:31-32; 14:13). The divine glory in which both share is also given to the believing community (17:22).          C.B.C.

**GLORY.** As a theological term used of God, glory is best defined as the outward shining of God's inner being. But there is a long history behind the word.

The Hebrew word had originally the idea of weight or heaviness (compare II Cor. 4:17 for a play on this). The usage in classical Greek was neutral, that is, meaning opinion, reputation. But to the Hebrew mind when something has weight it also has importance and value. Hence a rich person is taken to be successful (Gen. 45:13; I Kings 3:13), and so to have "glory."

The majority of the OT references refer to God whose revelation to Israel is in terms of a making known of God's "glory." Natural phenomena (storm, wind, earthquake, volcano) are associated with God's glory. Yahweh is often pictured as a storm god, especially at the Sinai theophany (Exod. 19:16-20; 24:15-18) when God's fire and lightning were vehicles of the divine presence (see too Pss. 29; 68:8; 17; 97:3-6). This is the OT way of ascribing worthiness or uniqueness to Israel's God, whose glory calls out human awe and worship. It is a reminder—deepened by the prophets (Ezek. 1:4-28; Isa. 6:1-7; 42:8)—of the mystery surrounding Yahweh's person and the sense of numinous fear, combining both dread and fascination, that it evoked. Yet God's glory was communicable (Exod. 33:17-23) and localized in the Temple (I Kings 8:10, 11). In postexilic times the divine glory, which made God unapproachable, was centered in the cult, notably the Priestly service and festivals, and as the historical books were edited this feature was read back to the wilderness (Exod. 40:34) and monarchy (Ps. 24:7-10) periods.

Building on an OT foundation, the NT writers see the glory of God in the person of Jesus Christ (II Cor. 4:6; Phil. 2:6; Col. 1:15; John 1:14) in whom the new era of God's dealings with humankind is actualized. The church is called to share that new age by its worship of God in Christ and so recover the "glory" of the new Adam as the ravages of sin are reversed (Rom. 3:23; II Cor. 3:18). The hope has cosmic dimensions (Rom. 8:17-30) in fulfillment of the prophetic yearning that the whole earth will one day reflect the divine presence (Hab. 2:14). Paul connects this hope with the "resurrection of the body," patterned in Christ's body of glory (I Cor. 15:43, 49; Phil. 3:21), but John sees the glory already realized in the presence of Christ by the Holy Spirit (John 16:14).          R.M.

**GLOSS, TEXTUAL.** The term is used in the discipline of textual criticism. It takes note of the few instances where the scribal copyist or final editor of the text has inserted a word or phrase into the text either from the margin (where a previous copyist had added it, for clarity's sake) or by his own hand, with the same purpose, namely to elucidate a puzzling verse or make a theological point. Examples are Genesis 10:14, where the mention of Philistines has been added, and John 5:4 (KJV; compare RSV marg.). R.M.

*GLOSSA ORDINARIA.* The work of Accursius (1182–1260), in which he compiled all the glosses or commentaries that earlier scholars had made on ancient Roman law—specifically, on the code of Justinian. This became the main text for the study of law for generations and had a profound influence on the development of CANON LAW. J.G.

**GLOSSOLALIA.** The word "glossolalia," though not found in the Bible, refers to the phenomenon of speaking in other tongues, or languages, under the influence of the Holy Spirit. It is a nineteenth-century word, made up of the Greek noun *glossa* ("tongue") and the verb *laleo* ("to speak").

No examples of tongues-speaking are found in the OT. The first NT reference occurs in the passage dealing with the events at PENTECOST. The disciples "were all filled with the Holy Spirit and began to speak in other tongues, as the Spirit gave them utterance" (Acts 2:4). From the context it can be deduced that "other tongues" in this instance means "foreign languages," not ecstatic religious utterances, as some have conjectured. The Aramaic-speaking disciples are described as miraculously uttering languages they had not previously known or been taught. The Jews of the Dispersion who were present in Jerusalem at the time heard the message of Pentecost in their own languages and dialects. These included most of the languages of the known world of that day. Some theologians have argued that the unifying experience of Pentecost symbolized in a dramatic way a reversal of the events of BABEL when the tongues of people were confused. Alienated from God and one another, the impious men of Shinar were scattered abroad.

In two subsequent portions of the book of Acts there are additional accounts of tongues-speaking—both dealing with Gentile converts (Acts 10:46; 19:6). The reception of the Holy Spirit, accompanied by speaking in tongues, may be designed to reveal that the blessings of salvation are no longer possessed by a single covenant nation but extend to all who acknowledge the lordship of Jesus Christ.

PENTECOSTALS and most charismatic believers today interpret the references in Acts as a basis for teaching that the Pentecostal baptism with (or in) the Holy Spirit is not just a historic event but should be the normative experience of all believers. This is the teaching that separates Pentecostals from non-Pentecostals.

The second biblical portion dealing with glossolalia is found in three chapters of I Corinthians (12–14). Commentators are quite divided in their interpretation of these passages. While there is general agreement that actual languages were uttered by the disciples at Pentecost, there are various explanations of the tongues of I Corinthians 12–14. Were they ecstatic utterances incomprehensible to those voicing them and to others in the assembled church unless they were explained by those having the gift of interpretation? All this is treated by the Apostle Paul in I Corinthians 14.

Pentecostals testify to instances of both those who speak heavenly or unknown tongues (see I Cor. 13:1) and of the instantaneous ability of Christians to speak recognizable specific foreign languages. Stephen B. Clark, Roman Catholic lay theologian of the Word of God Community in Ann Arbor, Michigan, describes a man speaking Hebrew without any previous training in the language.

Contemporary linguists have analyzed taped examples of glossolalia. They report that the portions they have examined are vocal utterances that lack the full characteristics of any type of known, human language. Proponents of tongues-speaking, however, feel that whether the utterances fit the specifications of human speech patterns or not, the divine message may be heard.

The gifts of the Spirit, including that of speaking in tongues, are imparted to individual believers for the edification of the church. Yet I Corinthians 14:4 declares: "He who speaks in a tongue edifies himself." On the basis of this verse many Christians today feel they have authority for speaking in tongues in their private devotions. In this same chapter in Corinthians the Apostle Paul takes considerable pains to emphasize the superiority of prophesying over tongues-speaking. The Apostle stresses the importance of proper order in public worship; while he expressly prohibits a ban on tongues-speaking, he diplomatically sets down regulations for the use of the gift in public services.

Some schools of Christian thought argue that the gifts of the Spirit were temporary, limited to the Apostolic Era. With the completion of the NT canon, it is said that Christians today have a means of obtaining the revelation God has given in the Scriptures. Some base their teaching on I Corinthians 13:8, which expressly declares "as for tongues, they will cease." Those who believe the gifts are a part of a continuing manifestation point out that the charismata are needed in the church until Christ ushers in the perfect age of the Kingdom.

Tongues-speaking today is no longer confined to those in the historic Pentecostal denominations. CHARISMATIC believers in the major Protestant communions and sects and Roman Catholics are involved in the same practice. R.H.

GNOSTICISM. A modern designation for a religious and philosophical view of the world that understands knowledge (*gnosis*) of reality to be attainable only by divine disclosure and which sees the goal of human existence as the liberation of the soul from its present captive state in the material world. This understanding of reality and of human destiny reached a climax of popularity in the second to the fourth centuries, when it came to be regarded as a threat to Christianity. The violent reaction of the church to Gnosticism during that period has been known chiefly through the writings of leading Christian thinkers of the early church who attacked the Gnostics. Fortunately, the discovery in 1945 of a Gnostic library in Egypt at a place called NAG HAMMADI has provided direct information and scores of texts preserved by devotees of the movement.

These Gnostic writings, as well as others found in ancient manuscripts or preserved in ancient writers, are of several types: (1) collections of proverbial wisdom sayings, lacking any distinctively Christian feature but akin to Jewish wisdom; (2) accounts of the creation of the universe, which describe the struggle between the Ultimate God and the intermediary divine forces, which seek to thwart the purpose of the high God, or to seize power for themselves; (3) descriptions of a redeemer figure who willingly comes down into the material world from the highest realm of being, and who reveals the secret knowledge by which imprisoned human souls may escape and return to the highest heaven; (4) gospels and revelations that report the teachings of Jesus and his disclosures to his followers, but that lack any narratives of his birth or activities, his death, or his resurrection. Running through all four types of Gnostic material is the theme of WISDOM as the means of restoration of the human soul to God.

Scholars have debated whether (1) Gnosticism was a widespread scheme that flourished before the birth of Christ and influenced Christianity from the outset, or (2) whether it was a movement that developed concurrently with Christianity and came to affect it significantly only in the second and subsequent centuries, or (3) it was a basic alteration of Christianity that arose after the disappointment of the earliest Christians' expectation of the end of the age. The discovery of the Gnostic library does not give a clear-cut answer to the question of the origins of Gnosticism, but it does offer some important clues.

The two most common themes in this literature as a whole are the creation of the world as a perversion of the divine plan, and the role of wisdom and/or Jesus as the bearer of the divine message of deliverance from the world of matter. Not all documents contain these features, and some offer only one or the other. A plausible hypothesis for the development of Gnosticism at the stage at which it can be documented—in the second to fourth centuries—is that it began in Jewish speculation about the role of wisdom in creation, under the influence of Platonic philosophy.

In Proverbs 8 and Sirach 24, wisdom is portrayed as God's consort and aide in the creation of the world. In the Wisdom of Solomon 7, "she" is pictured as the light that radiates from the Divine, and in technical Platonic terminology as the visible counterpart of the invisible God (Wisd. Sol. 7:24-26). During the time of Israel's exile in Babylon, the nation had come under the influence of Persian dualism, which pictured God and an adversary, Satan, as in eternal conflict, with the world divided into a realm of darkness and a realm of light. Under this influence, actions which had earlier been attributed to God were assigned to Satan. Thus David's sin in conducting a census after the Exile (II Sam. 24:1) is said to have been the work of Satan (I Chr. 21:1). Thus the idea developed within Judaism that sorrow and evil in the world are the result of actions by arrogant superhuman powers, rather than being the work of God. In the Hellenistic period, Greek philosophy profoundly affected Jewish thinking, so that ultimate reality was regarded by many Jews as in the realm of the spirit, while the physical universe was only a passing shadow of reality.

This outlook is fully documented in the writings of the Jewish philosopher and interpreter of scripture, PHILO OF ALEXANDRIA (27 B.C.–A.D. 45). For example, he understood Exodus 25:40 to mean that what was shown to Moses on Mount Sinai were the eternal patterns of reality, as described in the philosophy of Plato. Moses was instructed to build the earthly counterparts of these heavenly forms. Aiding this effort to escape from involvement in the material world were the Jewish failures to achieve political independence in the days of the Maccabean revolt against the Hellenistic rulers and twice against the Romans (A.D. 66–70 and 130–35). The destruction of the Temple in Jerusalem in A.D. 70 led the Pharisees to decide that true worship could be carried on in the home or in private, since God met the people there.

The resulting disillusionments gave rise to the idea that the material world was merely transitory and basically evil. The Creation, therefore, was not to be attributed to the God of Israel, but to wicked usurpers of power. Yet, it was believed, the ultimate God did make provision for the elect to come to knowledge by which they could escape the world and return to the heavenly place of their origin.

These interests and themes are evident in the documents from the Gnostic library. Details of the process by which the material world was formed are offered in the *Hypostasis of the Archons* and in *On the Origin of the World*. Descriptions of the agents of revealed wisdom are presented in *Zostrianos* and in *Thunder, the Perfect Mind*. OT figures serve this revelatory role in the *Apocalypse of Adam*, the *Paraphrase of Shem*, and the *Second Treatise of the Great Seth*. Many of the Gnostic writings picture the Risen Christ as the instrument of revelation, either directly or through one of his disciples: *Dialogue of the Savior, Gospel of Philip, Gospel of Mary, Sophia of Jesus Christ*.

Other revelations come through one of the apostles: *Apocalypse of Paul, Apocalypse of James, Apocryphon of James, Apocalypse of Peter, Apocryphon of John.* In the *Gospel of Truth,* knowledge of the true self is the key to salvation. In the Gospel of Thomas, the sayings of Jesus have been altered and supplemented to show that salvation involves loss of sexual differentiation of male and female that took place in biblical creation (Gen. 1:27; 2:21-25).

In the NT, the expectation is that on earth Jesus will accomplish God's purpose for the Creation (Matt. 6:10; I Cor. 15:24-28; Rev. 21:10). But in the Gnostic writings, the Creation is fundamentally evil and beyond remedy. Salvation lies in escape. And that is possible only for those who attain the knowledge that enables them to recognize the incurable evil of the material world and to ascend to the god who is above and beyond the Creation. The systematized forms of Gnosticism known from ancient sources, which differed from each other in detail, are linked with the names of Simon Magus, Valentinus, and the mythological figure Hermes Trismegistus in Egypt, and with Mani in Iran. As can be inferred from these and from the newfound sources, these Gnostic ideas were regarded as wholly incompatible with the biblical doctrine of God as the one who both creates and redeems and with Jesus' message of the renewal of God's creation. Accordingly, the mainstream of the church forcefully rejected Gnosticism. H.K.

**GOBIND SINGH** (1666–1708). The tenth and last of the gurus or spiritual and social leaders of SIKHISM, Gobind Singh succeeded his father to that post at the age of nine. He is chiefly noted for strengthening the Sikh military tradition, and above all for his founding of the Khalsa, the Sikh military order, in 1699. He loved the soldierly life, and power at arms was also seen as important for Sikh survival as conditions deteriorated in India with the decline of the Mogul empire and the rule of the fanatically Muslim emperor Aurangzib (1618–1707).

Gobind Singh founded the Khalsa at a Sikh festival. Holding up his sword, he called for Sikhs who would willingly give their lives for the faith. Eventually five men came forward. The guru took them into a tent, the thud of a falling blade was heard—then he brought them out, unharmed. They, the "five beloved ones," were the first of the Khalsa, devoted to the cause to death, wearers of five emblems—sword, uncut hair under turban, comb, steel bracelet, and shorts—and takers of the name Singh ("lion"). Gobind Singh wrote poetry, much of it extolling martial virtues and celebrating the sword as a "sacrament of steel." He proclaimed that after him there would be no personal guru, only the authority of the *Adi Granth,* the Sikh scripture. R.E.

**GOD.** *Introduction.* God is the object of religious worship for most of the earth's population and is taken to be the supreme reality on which all else depends. In modern secular society, where many of the happenings once attributed to divine activity are now given natural explanations, and where the reference of the word "God" has become questionable, serious talk of God has become difficult for many people. But it should be remembered that even devout believers in God have always had difficulty in talking about God. The important mystical tradition in all religions has declared God to be ineffable. MYSTICISM has been associated with negative theology, according to which we can only say what God is not. Since God is so utterly different from all finite beings, it is hard to see how we could say anything significant about God at all. Yet if God were WHOLLY OTHER, we could have no idea of or relation to God or a name for God.

The religious have always believed that there is some kinship between God and what is deepest in human nature itself—perhaps spirit, or even personality. The difference between a religious believer and an atheist is precisely that the former believes that there is some affinity, however remote, between our human being and the being of that ultimate reality that sustains the world, while the latter denies this. So if the otherness of God (TRANSCENDENCE) makes us reticent about God and points toward negative theology or even silence, the sense of an affinity to God allows the believer to talk of God by way of analogies, while realizing that all such talk falls short of the transcendent reality and can only point toward it.

The opposition between the otherness and the affinity of God is only one of many, and the consequence is that all talk of God must be dialectical or even paradoxical, that is to say, whatever we affirm about God has to be corrected by a counter-affirmation of apparently opposite tendency. If we say that God is distant, we have also to say that God is near; if we say that God is unknown, we have also to say that God is known. God has been called the "coincidence of opposites" (Nicholas of Cusa). Such language would be illogical if we were talking about finite entities within the world, but language about that unique and infinite reality that we call "God" is bound to have a logic of its own.

*God in the Old Testament.* It is an interesting fact that the common Hebrew word for "God," *elohim,* is a plural form, though grammatically it is treated as a singular and used with singular verbs and adjectives. The plural form may point back to a time when the Hebrews believed in many gods, but their retention of the plural form may imply, whether consciously or unconsciously, that all the gods are included in the God of the Hebrews, that all deity is comprehended in this God. Certainly MONOTHEISM, belief in one God, is a distinctive mark of the OT. "Hear, O Israel: The Lord our God is one Lord" (Deut. 6:4). This was a central tenet of OT religion, and, indeed, as soon as a people emerge from POLYTHEISM, it is apparent that logically there can be only one God. God is one both in the sense that God is unique and in the sense that God is a unity—"faithful," in the language of the OT, that is to say, consistent in actions, not capricious. All through the Hebrew scriptures, the one God of Israel is contrasted with the many gods of the pagans. Israel's God alone acts, the idols are only pretended gods, unreal and ineffective. The OT makes no attempt to prove the existence of God. The reality of God is presupposed.

At the beginning of Genesis, God is represented as creating, that is to say, God is not so much one who exists as one who confers existence, not so much "He who is" as later theologians were to call God, as "He who lets be," which implies that God is a reality of a different order from all existing things. God is not an existent, but the presupposition of all existence. God transcends the world and may not be included among the beings that make up the world.

As creator in the sense just mentioned, God remains mysterious. God is the transcendent reality, sharply contrasted with human beings and with the things of the world. One of the prophets represents God as saying: "My thoughts are not your thoughts, neither are your ways my ways . . . . For as the heavens are higher than the earth, so are my ways higher than your ways and my thoughts than your thoughts" (Isa. 55:8-9). God is the "Holy One" of Israel, a numinous reality inspiring awe. (The Hebrew word for "holy" had the meaning of "separate.") OT writers can speak too of the "hiddenness" of God. This God had a name, YAHWEH, which God had made known to the people. Whatever its origin may have been, it sounded like the Hebrew "I am," though it was only in much later times that it gave rise to ontological speculation. This name was regarded as so holy that the faithful would not pronounce it, but used instead the expression, "The Lord." All these points then kept in view the transcendence, mystery, and otherness of the God of the Hebrews.

But the other side of the dialectic also finds expression in the OT. A whole series of attributes are ascribed to God, and these are attributes derived from personal human existence, so that there is assumed an analogy between God's mode of being and the human mode. God is above all righteous, but God is also merciful, gracious, patient, and it is even said that God shares in the afflictions of God's (chosen) people. God's personal being is expressed sometimes in almost cruelly anthropomorphic ways. God speaks to patriarchs and prophets and very occasionally is even seen. God makes covenants and utters both promises and threats. God experiences emotions and is frequently angered or displeased. In spite of what was said above about God's faithfulness, God's mind is sometimes repentant or changed. Though transcendent over the Creation, God is very much involved in its affairs and exercises control over the history of Israel and its neighbors. God is represented by various metaphors and images. Most of these are taken from

human society, again stressing the affinity between God and the personal being of humanity. God is represented as king, judge, shepherd, warrior, father. Sometimes material objects are used as metaphors— God is a rock or a tower, for instance.

It is a noble picture of God that inspires the OT, though there are occasional lapses. God is a God of justice and mercy, exercising moral governance over the world and demanding righteousness from people. The moral character of God is closely bound up with the belief that there is only one God. It is true that the oneness or unicity of God seems to be occasionally qualified—for instance, in some of the early stories the "angel of the Lord" seems hardly distinguishable from the Lord, and likewise one meets the Spirit of the Lord and, in the wisdom literature, the divine Wisdom, described in the Apocrypha as a "pure emanation of the glory of the Almighty" (Wisd. Sol. 7:25). But the language is probably metaphorical and does not imply actual divine hypostases. It is mentioned here, however, because it helps us understand how it came about that Christian theology, beginning from the God of OT monotheism, was able to move to the conception of a triune God.

*God in the New Testament.* Obviously there is a sense in which the God of the NT is the same as the God of the OT. Jesus was a Jew; the Christian movement began within Judaism, and its members were to begin with Jewish monotheists. Yet, as the new movement gained self-consciousness and began to define itself more closely, questions were bound to arise about the precise nature of its agreements and disagreements with mainstream Judaism. How far did the differences and innovations go? Did they perhaps touch even on the doctrine of God? After all, if Jesus had brought a new revelation of God, if he was, as Christians soon came to believe, the promised Messiah, then perhaps even the doctrine of God needed to be rethought in the light of the new revelation.

The word "God" and its equivalent in other languages is not a specifically Christian word. Did the Christian understanding of God conform in all respects to the Jewish understanding? And what about the many GODS or so-called gods of the pagan world? As early as the letters of Paul we see the first stirrings of such questions. Around A.D. 55 we find him writing: "Although there may be so-called gods in heaven or on earth—as indeed there are many 'gods' and many 'lords'—yet for us there is one God, the Father, from whom are all things and for whom we exist, and one Lord, Jesus Christ, through whom are all things and through whom we exist" (I Cor. 8:5-6). This is one of the earliest attempts to specify and distinguish the Christian God from the many "gods" and "lords" worshiped in other cults, and even to distinguish the Christian God from the God of the Jews. The Christian God is distinguished from the latter because God is brought into the closest relation with Jesus Christ, the Lord who stands alongside God the Father. Christians no longer speak of God without reference to Christ, nor do they speak of Christ without reference to God. Nothing is yet said about the Holy Spirit, who was destined to become the third person of the TRINITY. But soon afterward, in a further letter to the Corinthians, we find the familiar threefold formula: "The grace of the Lord Jesus Christ and the love of God and the fellowship of the Holy Spirit be with you all" (II Cor. 13:14; see also I Cor. 12:4-6). Of course, all this is still far from the doctrine of the triune God as developed in later Christian theology, but it is the beginning of a move away from the strict monotheism of the OT to a more differentiated conception of God, reflecting the specific Christian belief that God was "in Christ" (II Cor. 5:19).

From then on, the doctrine of the triune God develops in parallel with Christology. As Christians came to believe that Jesus Christ is divine as well as human, living from God, for God, and in God, then the need to recognize distinguishable "persons," as they came to be called within the Godhead, became pressing. One gets the impression, however, that it was only slowly and reluctantly that the church came to apply God-language to Jesus. Christians were unwilling to infringe the Jewish monotheism that they had inherited. The NT writers are very reticent about the divinity of Christ (there are only two or three instances where he is definitely called "God") and the later trinitarian theology tried hard to reconcile trinity with unity in God.

*God in Philosophy.* This article began by noting that God is the object of religious worship, but can also be described in more philosophical terms as the supreme reality on which all else depends. This second, philosophical significance of the word "God" cannot be ignored, though so far we have concentrated attention on the religious usage, as found in the Bible. A philosophical interest in God had developed in Greece, and it eventually made its influence felt in both Jewish and Christian thinking about God. The Jewish scholar Philo of Alexandria led the way in developing a new philosophical theism, and the task was continued by early Christian writers. The God who had been represented by such naïve images as "king" or "shepherd" became conceptualized as the principle of being—"He who is" or "The Being," which was justified by an appeal to the "I am" of the OT (Exod. 3:14). In course of time, names even more distant from the biblical tradition were used, for example "necessary being." This meant that God was thought of in terms much less personal than we find in the Bible. Philo introduced the idea of the LOGOS (or hypostatized Word) as an intermediary between the distant metaphysical God and the creatures. So, for instance, it was not God as ultimate Being but the Logos that had spoken to Moses at the bush. Anthropomorphisms were removed or explained away by allegorical interpretation of the Bible. Again,

whereas the Bible begins with the living creative God, the new philosophical theism began to look for arguments that would prove GOD'S EXISTENCE.

There has always been some tension between the biblical teaching about God and philosophical speculation. Tertullian in the early centuries and, in more recent times, such acute thinkers as Calvin, Pascal, Kierkegaard, and Barth, have regarded philosophical theism with profound suspicion. The philosophical concept of God, whether we call him "Unmoved Mover" or "Ground of Being" or "Supreme Intelligence" or something else seems, as Pascal held, a pale unreal abstraction alongside the God of Abraham, Isaac, and Jacob, or the Father of Jesus Christ. Attempts to prove the divine existence, as Kierkegaard believed, are as likely to sow new doubts as to provide assurance. The whole enterprise of philosophical theology may seem to be a theoretical matter, divorced from the actual life of religion.

Yet at this point too we have to recognize the dialectical claim of the other side. There are minds that cannot rest until they have inquired into the very foundations of religious belief—and if there were no such critical minds, religious belief might soon become a luxuriant jungle of superstition. Philosophical reflection on God is needed for the criticism and elucidation of the Christian doctrine of God. A philosophical concept of God is no substitute for the concrete reality who encounters us in biblical faith, but the God of faith must include everything that philosophical reflection shows to be necessary to a viable concept of God.

*God in Christian Theology.* The trinitarian concept of God, of which the beginnings are already visible in the NT, continued to develop through many controversies in the patristic period, though it was not until the fourth century that something like a satisfactory formula was achieved. God is said to be of one "substance" or "being" in three "persons" or "hypostases." The danger of such a formula is that the three persons are so sharply distinguished that they become three gods (tritheism) or so weakly distinguished that they disappear in the undifferentiated essence of Godhood. Probably the greatest statement of the Christian belief in God is that of Thomas Aquinas in the opening sections of his *Summa Theologiae* (thirteenth century). This has been called "classical theism" and represents the orthodox Christian teaching about God. Its foundations are biblical, but philosophical ideas have been skillfully incorporated and subordinated to the biblical emphases.

In modern times, however, many Christian theologians have expressed uneasiness about some features of the classical theism they have inherited. It is felt by some that God has been represented in the Christian tradition in terms that are too starkly transcendent, perhaps because of a tendency to revert to the strictly monotheistic and therefore "monarchical" concept of God. Does God, for instance, share in the suffering of the world? It would be hard for a Christian to deny that God does, if God is indeed love and is made known in the crucified Lord. Yet the formulations of classical theism seem to make God so transcendent that God is placed beyond suffering. Others have problems over the question of God's action in the world. Can God intervene in the world's affairs? If we say yes, we seem to be contradicting a basic assumption of modern science. But if we say no, we seem to be denying a fundamental power of the biblical God.

In the face of such problems, theologians have again turned to current philosophies in search of answers. Some have found WHITEHEAD's concept of the dipolar God, at once transcendent yet deeply engaged in the affairs of the Creation, a possible way of overcoming the weaknesses of classical theism. Others, such as Tillich, have revived the mystics' idea of a "God beyond God," a reality of a different order from any being and of whom one cannot even say that it exists—not because it lacks existence, but because, as we noted in connection with the biblical story of the Creation, this reality is prior to existence or "superexistent," as some mystics have expressed it. It would seem that we are still seeking a concept of God that will be loyal to the biblical tradition and yet coherent and tenable in the contemporary world.

J.M.

**GODDESS.** Deities or personifications of the divine of female gender, goddesses have had an ambiguous role in religion. Widespread in archaic, classical, and some Eastern religions, goddesses have received from the great monotheistic and monistic faiths attitudes ranging from vehement hostility to condescending acceptance in a subordinate role.

Perhaps the most basic goddess roles are those connected with FERTILITY CULTS AND RITES, in which she is the earth-mother, giver of harvest, and the "corn-maiden," like Persephone or Ishtar, whose descent to the Underworld has been seen as an allegory of the life cycle of plants, but which may also acquire soteriological overtones. This was particularly the case when the goddess was associated with a dying and rising son or lover, as Isis and Osiris, or Ishtar and Tammuz.

Goddesses appear in other guises as well. Like Athena or the Japanese goddess Amaterasu, they may possess a warlike aspect and personify sovereignty. Like the Hindu Kali, they may depict the "terrible mother," embodying the destructive nature of the temporal world. Or the goddess may be simply the merciful mother, like the Blessed Virgin Mary, who virtually approaches goddess status in much popular Catholic piety. It is also not uncommon for Wisdom, Sophia, to take personification as a goddess, like the Mahayana Buddhist Prajnaparamita, "Wisdom Gone Beyond,"known religiously as the goddess Tara.

R.E.

**GODHEAD.** See TRINITY.

**GODLINESS.** The qualify of reverence and piety evidenced by devout adherents of the religion of Israel and of early Christianity. In the Psalms the common Hebrew term is translated "pious worshippers, godly persons, saints." In the NT the quality of godliness is urged predominantly in those books with an orientation toward Hellenism: I and II Timothy, Titus, and II Peter. Christians are to strive for godliness "as it holds promise for the present life and also for the life to come" (I Tim. 4:8). Together with "holiness" it marks the lives of those who wait for the coming of the day of God (II Pet. 3:11-12). It is contrasted with the love of money, which is "the root of all evil" (I Tim. 6:6-10).

C.B.C.

**GODS.** A translation of the Hebrew word *'elîm* less frequent of two renderings of *'elōhîm*. Both Hebrew nouns bear witness to biblical Israel's predominantly polytheistic environment. Ordinarily translated in the singular to refer to Israel's deity, Yahweh, *'elōhîm* in many cases means "gods."

*Divine Pluralism: An Overview.* Truly awed by nature's manifold powers that directly impinged upon day-to-day existence, Israel's neighbors understandably believed in many gods. The nature religions of the great Near Eastern powers affirmed that the high gods commanded cosmic domain, though lesser gods had significant functions to fulfill as well. On occasion, the Bible collectively refers to the gods according to their nationality: thus "the gods of Egypt" (Exod. 12:12; Jer. 43:12), or "the gods of Syria" (Judg. 10:6). Since the gods were typically represented by manufactured idols, their composition is also noted: "gods of gold" (Exod. 20:23); "wood and stone" (Deut. 4:28); or "silver, bronze, iron" (Dan. 5:4). Among the nature deities specifically named are the Philistine Dagon (I Sam. 5:2), Moabite Chemosh and Ammonite Milcom (I Kings 11:33), Canaanite Baal (II Kings 10:21), and Sumerian Tammuz (Ezek. 8:14).

Since biblical faith tenaciously held that Israel shall worship only Yahweh, a deity sovereign over history rather than locked in by nature, a polemic against foreign gods readily developed. Yet the existence of other deities sometimes receives matter-of-fact mention. Thus Jotham's fable claims that wine "cheers gods and men" (Judg. 9:13). Naomi reminds Ruth that her sister-in-law, Orpah, has returned "to her people and to her gods" (Ruth 1:15). And the Philistine giant, Goliath, "cursed David by his gods" (I Sam. 17:43; see I Kings 19:2; 20:10). Israel could not help recognizing the POLYTHEISM of its neighbors as fact.

*A Snare to Israelite Faith.* The first commandment, "You shall have no other gods before me" (Exod. 20:3; Deut. 5:7), evoked Israel's uncompromising obedience to Yahweh, the one God who had graciously rescued her from Egyptian servitude. A "jealous" God (Exod. 20:5; Deut. 5:9; 6:15), Yahweh demanded Israel's total allegiance. Lacking pantheon and consort (Hebrew has no noun for "goddess"), this incomparable deity (Exod. 15:11) regularly warned the covenant people that to "go after other gods and serve them" would spell their undoing (Deut. 8:19; see 11:16). As Yahweh's vassal, Israel would have but one overlord. In his farewell address, Joshua interprets the worship of other gods as blatant covenant transgression (Josh. 23:16; see Jer. 22:9). Though Israel was not expected to assume that other gods did not exist among its neighbors, *for it* there was but one God (eloquently reaffirmed by Paul in I Cor. 8:5-6). Not given to abstraction, Israel entertained a practical MONOTHEISM that often struggled for its life. In settling into Canaan, Israel "played the harlot after other gods and bowed down to them" (Judg. 2:17). In his autumn years, Solomon's foreign wives "turned away his heart after other gods" (I Kings 11:4). When Jeroboam provided northern Israelites with two golden calves at the inception of the divided monarchy he said, "Behold your gods, O Israel, who brought you up out of the land of Egypt" (I Kings 12:28; see Exod. 32:4). That the service of other gods became a "snare" for Israel, as the Covenant Code predicted it would (Exod. 23:33), was painfully clear when Samaria fell to the Assyrian army. Israel's "fear" of other gods was viewed as directly responsible for the catastrophe (II Kings 17:7). Strange gods appeared capable of undermining Israel's covenant loyalty toward Yahweh, and when it "stirred him to jealousy with strange gods" (Deut. 32:16), judgment was unavoidable.

*The Gods as Nothing.* The Shema—"Hear, O Israel: The Lord our God is one Lord" (Deut. 6:4)—Judaism's famous confession, likely dating to Josiah's reform (about 622 B.C.), conveys an intensification of monotheistic perspective that finds deft expression in Jeremiah and Second Isaiah. Speaking just prior to the Babylonian takeover of Jerusalem (587 B.C.), Jeremiah emphasizes the impotence of gods that are mere idols. "The instruction of idols is but wood!" he says sarcastically (Jer. 10:8). "False gods" cannot bring rain (14:22). As the product of human craft, these gods "who did not make the heavens and the earth shall perish" (10:11). Jerusalem's destruction cannot be averted by "the gods to whom they burn incense" (11:12). Such gods, whom the people "have not known" (7:9; 19:4), are unreal (16:20). Their nothingness is further asserted by Second Isaiah speaking on the eve of the exiles' release from Babylonian captivity (538 B.C.). As mere fragments of wood and metal (Isa. 40:19-20; 46:6-7), these pagan deities are no match whatever for Yahweh, the Creator and Sovereign of the universe, who is "the first" and "the last" (44:6). Capable of denouncing idolatry with biting satire (44:9-20), Second Isaiah would surely endorse these words of the psalmist, "There is none like thee among the gods, O Lord" (Ps. 86:8), as would Paul, who was reported to have said, "gods made with hands are not gods" (Acts 19:26).

J.K.K.

**GOD'S EXISTENCE, ARGUMENTS FOR.** There are several basic types of arguments: (1) common consent, (2) ontological, (3) cosmological, (4) moral, (5) teleological, and (6) psychological. It is important to emphasize that these are arguments, the validity and persuasiveness of which are open to wide-ranging disagreement, rather than proofs.

Arguments based on *common consent* hold that belief in Deity is universal among human groups and that this universality demonstrates God's existence. The Roman Stoic philosopher Seneca writes: "That there are gods we infer from the sentiment engrafted in the human mind; nor has any nation ever been found so far beyond the pale of law and civilization as to deny their existence" (*Moral Letters*). A variation appearing in Augustine (A.D. 354–430) affirms that humans yearn for God whether or not this emerges into overt belief. Though the argument can be found from ancient times to the present, it is difficult, if not impossible, to demonstrate that humans and human societies in all times and places believe in or yearn for God. Even so, universal belief or yearning would prove no more than that humans agree, not that God exists.

The *ontological argument,* so named by Kant, holds that the nature of human thought requires affirmation of the existence of Deity. Though the gist of the argument appears in the thought of Plato (427–347 B.C.) and Augustine, the earliest extensive formulation appears in the *Proslogion* of Anselm of Canterbury (1033–1109). Like Augustine, Anselm holds that FAITH precedes and provides the context for reasoning. Thus, Anselm writes in the form of a prayer asking for a rational demonstration of the existence of God, in whom Anselm already believes. The argument he receives begins with the concept of God as "that, than which nothing greater can be conceived." The notion of God as existing is greater than the same notion minus existence. Therefore, Anselm affirms, God cannot be conceived not to exist. Gaunilo, a contemporary of Anselm, responds that this argument could be applied, for example, to the idea of the Islands of the Blessed, as islands of which none more excellent can be conceived. Anselm replies that his argument would not apply to ideas of particular things; only of the most comprehensive concept, of God alone, of that than which nothing greater can be conceived, can it be said that conceiving its nonexistence is impossible.

Thomas Aquinas (1225–74) rejects Anselm's argument in favor of the cosmological arguments (see below). Descartes (1596–1650) reaffirms Anselm's view, reiterating the point that the inclusion of existence in the essence of the idea of God applies only to this highest being, as also do Spinoza (1632–77) and Leibniz (1646–1716). Kant (1724–1804), calling an ontological *proof* of God's existence impossible, argues that our consciousness of existence belongs exclusively to experience (*Critique of Pure Reason,* trans. by N. K. Smith). He agrees with Anselm, however, that thinking requires the assumption of comprehensively real being, though the circumstance that we cannot avoid assuming it does not prove it. Hegel (1770–1831) affirms the ontological argument in holding Being as the presupposition of all thought and existence. Josiah Royce (1855–1916) develops a variation based on Augustine and argues that the existence of God can be derived from the possibility of error. Charles Hartshorne (1897–   ), in *Man's Vision of God* and *The Logic of Perfection,* provides the most extensive contemporary version of the ontological argument. Bertrand Russell (1872–1970) rejects the ontological argument, based on the dubious assumption of a dichotomy between thought and things, and on the naïve epistemology of logical atomism. The pattern of the argument from Plato, through Anselm and Kant, to Royce and Hartshorne, based on implications of intelligibility, shows that it is actually an epistemological argument with ontological meaning.

The *cosmological arguments* appear in ancient philosophy but are given most explicit formulation by AQUINAS. In the *Summa Theologica* (Isa. 2, 3), he offers five arguments for the existence of God, the first three of which are cosmological: from motion, from efficient cause, and from the contingency of things. In each case, he begins with human experience (of motion or change, of a chain of efficient causes, of everything we experience as contingent). Because an infinite regress is in his view impossible, motion must be traced to a prime mover, causation to a first cause, and contingency to necessary being, each of which, he concludes, "we call God."

The *moral argument* holds that the moral experience of humanity confirms the existence of God. Implied in Plato's discussion of the Good, it receives explicit formulation in Thomas Aquinas' fourth argument, from the gradation of goodness, which necessarily implies the existence of the Good as the standard of better and worse. In his *Critique of Practical Reason,* Kant holds that God is a necessary postulate of moral reason. Alfred E. Taylor (1869–1945) combines insights from Plato, Aquinas, and Bergson in *The Faith of a Moralist* (1930), where he holds that moral experience points beyond itself to theism. C. E. M. Joad (1891–1953) turns the moral argument around and holds that the experience of evil demonstrates the existence of God.

*Teleological arguments,* also found among Greek and Roman thinkers, rely on the notion that the presence of purpose in the world demonstrates the existence of Deity. The fifth argument of Aquinas is teleological: from the governance of things. The existence of God is demonstrated by the order and purpose of the world. Teleological arguments may draw on historical or scientific materials to show developmental patterns in human affairs and nature, patterns to be attributed to divine power and intention. Based on the notion of emergent evolution, C. Lloyd Morgan (1852–1936) affirmed God as purposively directing activity in world events, and Samuel Alexander (1859–1938) posited a notion of immanently creative Deity. On similar grounds, the thought of Alfred North Whitehead (1861–1947) requires God as the Principle of Concretion. Drawing on evolutionary science, Pierre Lecomte du Nouy asserts that "our entire organized, living universe becomes incomprehensible without the hypothesis of God" (*Human Destiny,* 1947).

The *psychological argument* rests on the clinical evidence that human activity and welfare require the integration that belief in and worship of God provide. Viktor Frankl (1904–   ) represents this perspective in emphasizing the necessity of meaning for human health and survival. Here, as with the other arguments, it is a matter of demonstration rather than proof.

The arguments for the existence of God, taken individually or collectively, offer impressive evidence that faith in God can be given rational justification, but they are persuasive in relation to what people already believe. If Kant is correct that all the arguments rest on the ontological, then they become most clear in Anselm's perspective as "faith seeking understanding." (*See* FAITH AND KNOWLEDGE.)

C.Mc.

## GOETHE, JOHANN WOLFGANG VON (1749–1832).

German novelist, poet, dramatist, and scientist. Born in Frankfort on the Main, he studied

Courtesy of the German Information Center
*Goethe*

law at Leipzig and Strasbourg, and began practice in Frankfort (1772). However, his consuming drive was to find life's meaning. Influenced by Johann Gottfried von Herder, he studied art, literature, music, anatomy, and chemistry. In a dramatic tragedy, *Götz von Berlichingen* (1773), he used a Robin Hood character to rebel against injustice, and in *The Sorrows of Young Werther* (1774), he probed suicide as a solution to life's seeming meaninglessness. These successful works launched the romantic "storm and stress" movement in German literature.

In 1775 Goethe became secretary to Prince Karl August of Saxe-Weimar. He moved to Weimar, Germany's intellectual center, where he lived until his death. For ten years he wrote little, immersing himself in practical science, official public duties, wider literary interests, and illicit love affairs. Yet in his restless quest for meaning, he perceptibly moved beyond his "storm and stress" period of rebellion against everything, including God. A trip to Rome (1786–88) brought classical influences and balance to his writings, and saw the beginning of Germany's classic literary period. He wrote *Egmont* (1788), *Torquato Tasso* (1790), *Contributions to Optics* (1791–92), and encouraged by Friedrich von Schiller worked on *Faust,* the first part published in 1808, the second in 1832. Faust strikes a bargain with Satan, but finally discovers that real pleasure is in striving and helping others—the key to the meaning of life. Among his many works, *Faust* stands preeminent.
C.M.

**GOG AND MAGOG.** Originally the name of a legendary ancestor of the tribe of Reuben (I Chr. 5:4), Gog was later used by the prophet of the Exile, Ezekiel, to symbolize kings in opposition to Israel (Ezek. 38:1 ff., 14, 16, 18; 39:1, 11). Apparently, Gog stands for northern nations or tribes, such as the Scythians, who periodically swept down on Israel and its neighbors. Efforts to identify Gog with actual rulers seem fruitless. Centuries later, the author of the Revelation to John (Rev. 20:8) also spoke of enemies of the kingdom of God as "Gog and Magog," also used symbolically. Revelation may draw its symbolism from the son of Japheth, Magog, in Genesis 10:2. Sectarians since the eighteenth century and modern Fundamentalists often literalistically associate Gog and Magog with certain nations and political leaders such as Stalin and the Soviet Union or Hitler and the Nazi state. Contemporary Fundamentalists lean toward the precise identification of God and Magog with Soviet Russia and predict that Russia will invade Israel and precipitate the battle of Armageddon and the end of the world.
J.C.

**GOGARTEN, FRIEDRICH** (1887–1967). German Lutheran theologian, educated at Berlin, Jena, and Heidelberg. After a period of years as a pastor, he taught theology at Breslau (1931–35) and Göttingen (1935–55). After World War I, Gogarten was allied with KARL BARTH and others in the movement known as the "theology of crisis" or DIALECTICAL THEOLOGY. He joined in the attack on the assumptions of liberal culture and theology in the journal *Between the Times.* Later he broke with Barth, and with Rudolf Bultmann championed an existentialist theology.

The key to Gogarten's theology lies in his interpretation of Luther's "existential" understanding of faith. According to Gogarten, Christian theology was, until Luther, bound to a static Greek metaphysics, which reasserted itself again in seventeenth-century Protestant orthodoxy. However, for Luther faith is a radically existential reality, in that it involves risk and the awareness that humans are responsible for their own history. Gogarten contends that modern theologians, while rejecting an outmoded Greek metaphysics, still attempt to establish Christian belief on the scientific objectivity of certain historical events recorded in the Bible. Gogarten considers this both scientifically hazardous and, more importantly, contrary to the very nature of faith.

The Bible as God's Word cannot be established by philosophy or by scientific demonstration; it can be appropriated only existentially, that is, by faith that God's Word is spoken in and through the Bible. Gogarten had, with Bultmann, an important influence on American theology in the 1950s and 1960s. J.L.

**GOLDEN CALF.** *See* CALF, GOLDEN.

**GOLDEN MEAN.** A translation from Horace of the Latin phrase *aurea mediocritas,* it refers to a moderate position between extremes, to a happy medium between polar alternatives, and to a prudent, safe course of action. The notion that the way of moderation represents what is good in human life appears in such Socratic dialogues of Plato (427–347 B.C.) as the *Laches* (on courage) and the *Charmides* (on temperance and self-control). Aristotle (384–322 B.C.) formulated the notion into an ethical principle in the *Nicomachean Ethics.* "Virtue," he writes, "is a state of character concerned with choice of a mean relative to us . . . between two vices. . . . Virtue finds and chooses what is intermediate." Roman writers turned this Hellenic notion into the Golden Mean, an ideal of moderate behavior recommended by moralists in all ages, yet an ideal that appears pedestrian and dull when compared with the possibilities of heroic sacrifices on behalf of a great cause.
C.Mc.

**GOLDEN RULE.** Basically this phrase sums up the ethical maxim or moral imperative—live so as to treat others as you wish they would treat you. It is found as early as in the Greek historian Herodotus, who showed the influence of the Sophists, a group of Greek moralists who delighted in expressing moral ideals in an aphoristic form, and in Isocrates in the fourth century B.C.

In Jewish literature the rule appears in a negative way: "Do to no one what you would not want done to you" (Tob. 4:15, as well as in Philo and rabbinic literature).

In the Gospels the statement appears in its positive form in the common sayings source that embodies the teaching of Jesus in Matthew and Luke, with a more affirmative thrust. It is not so much, Do not injure others lest they retaliate, but treat others irrespective of how they choose to treat you. So Luke has put the saying in a context of love to one's enemies, which seems its logical place (Luke 6:27-36). In Matthew the words are used to form the conclusion of the main part of the Sermon on the Mount (7:12). Typically Matthew sees in the rule the epitome of the "law and the prophets" of the OT.

The Golden Rule appears in Acts 15:20, 29 (according to some texts), in the *Didache* (an early compendium of moral instruction) as well as later in Confucius' *Analects*.                                    R.M.

GOLGOTHA. There are three references to Golgotha in the NT: Matthew 27:33; Mark 15:22; John 19:17, each mentioning the place where Jesus was crucified. The Greek translation is "the place of a skull"; the last word in Latin is *calva,* whence the term Calvary in Luke 23:33 (KJV). The site is described as outside the city of Jerusalem (Heb. 13:12, but this allusion may be only symbolic), yet near to it (John 19:20). Tradition locates it on a hill, either because it was on a high elevation to be seen from a distance (Mark 15:40), or because the ground was shaped like a human skull or, with the church father Origen, because of the idea that Adam's skull was supposedly found there.

The exact location of Golgotha is uncertain. There are two rival views, now hardened into ecclesiastical and doctrinal persuasions. (1) The place of the Crucifixion, connected with the burial site (John 19:41) lay within the area now occupied by the Church of Holy Sepulchre. This tradition is traced back to the fourth century, but the fall of Jerusalem in A.D. 70 and again in A.D. 135 means that no one can trust tradition as late as Eusebius (A.D. 337), who makes the identification, and Constantine, who had a church built at the original site just before A.D. 340. Recent excavation of Jerusalem's walls have revealed that in Jesus' day the line of the second city wall ran south of the proposed site. This would endorse the witness of Jesus' death "outside the gate," marked by the present Russian Alexander Hospice.

(2) The other proposal begins with the shape of a raised prominence, thought to be skull-shaped. It is near the Damascus Gate, and close to "The Garden Tomb" (John 19:41). Two British army officers, Conder and Gordon, proposed this chiefly on the ground of the natural setting and the popular idea of "There is a green hill" hymn. This identification is less convincing, and we have to remain in uncertainty as to the precise site.                                    R.M.

GOLIATH. The Philistine giant from Gath, said to have been slain by the boy David (I Sam. 17). Goliath was declared to be nine feet tall. His defeat was seen as a religious victory for Israel, and Goliath's sword was placed in the Yahweh shrine at Nob (I Sam. 17:43, 45). While the association of Goliath's death with David gave impetus to his popularity and eventual ascent to power, the OT honestly records a parallel and different account of the defeat of Goliath. Second Samuel 21:19 declares that Elhanan, also from Bethlehem, killed Goliath (compare I Chr. 20:5). Excavations of Canaanite graves tend to support the belief that people of great height lived in Canaan at the time of the Hebrew conquest. Historical probability would hold that the unknown Elhanan defeated Goliath, and later the victory of the man from Bethlehem was associated with the most famous son of Bethlehem, David.                                    J.C.

GOMER. The name of two people in the OT, one a man and one a woman.

Gomer, son of Japheth and grandson of Noah, founded a people, probably the Cimmerians (Gen. 10:2; I Chr. 1:5; Ezek. 38:6).

Gomer, a woman of Samaria in the eighth century B.C., became the wife of HOSEA, the prophet of God's mercy and love. Hosea believed that Yahweh directed him to marry Gomer, who later proved unfaithful to him to such an extent that he doubted the paternity of his children. The Lord told Hosea to name these children "Not pitied" and "Not my people" (Hos. 1:6-8). However, even after Gomer ran away and fell to the depths of degradation, Hosea still cared for her and ultimately purchased her from slavery and restored her to his house on the condition that she not stray again. Hosea then saw (had a revelation) that Gomer was a symbol of faithless Israel, who committed adultery (idolatry) with the Baals over and over, forsaking the true worship of Yahweh. However, God would forgive Israel and restore her to favor if she gave up the Baals.                                    J.C.

GOMORRAH. A legendary city at the western border of Canaan (Gen. 10:19), which has become synonymous with corruption and wickedness. Gomorrah is never mentioned apart from the name of its sister city in sin, SODOM. In Genesis 14, Birsha, king of Gomorrah, was one of five kings of the Vale of Siddom or Dead Sea region who was defeated by a coalition of four eastern kings, only to be rescued by Abram. The only other memory of Gomorrah is the story of its destruction (Gen. 18:16-19:29). Because of their notorious lasciviousness, Yahweh destroys the twin cities with fire and brimstone rained from heaven (Gen. 19:24).

All other references to Gomorrah are simply reflections of the Genesis 19 account of its destruction and, with one exception, add no new information. The exception is Jude 7, which adds the idea that the fire that punished Gomorrah was "eternal."                                    W.S.T.

**GOOD FRIDAY.** The day commemorating Jesus Christ's death on the cross, which is probably to be dated April 3, A.D. 33. In the liturgical calendar of the Western church, the Friday before EASTER. "Good," as an adjective applied to the day, is an Old English expression for "holy." Good Friday services lasting from noon to three in the afternoon are traditional, commemorating the hours Christ spent on the cross. In recent decades, these services have been ecumenical. An evening rite, stressing the Passion of Christ, adoring the cross, and celebrating mass, has long been observed in the Roman Catholic church. Reception of Communion is encouraged.

J.C.

**GOOD NEWS.** *See* GOSPEL.

**GOOD NEWS BIBLE** (TODAY'S ENGLISH VERSION or TEV). The American Bible Society, with a goal of reaching a wider span of literates, was the sponsor of a translation of the Scriptures in "common English." This level of literacy is a step above the earlier concept of "basic English."

The TEV, as it was known at first, was largely the work of one man—Robert E. Bratcher, a one-time missionary to South America. *The New Testament in Today's English Version* was first published in 1966. The entire Bible was released in 1976 as the *Good News Bible—The Bible in Today's English Version.* In a very short time many millions of the new version had been distributed. Now similar Bibles, based on the same philosophy of translation, have appeared in a number of modern languages.

R.H.

**GOOD SAMARITAN.** The figure in Jesus' familiar parable in Luke 10:29-37, who helps a man lying wounded in the ditch. Traditionally he has become the symbol for hearers of the parable, who are called to replicate his acts of kindness for needy people: "Go and do likewise" (10:37).

Another interpretation of the passage, however, reverses the point of contact by noting the hostility between Jews and Samaritans during the time of Jesus. The lawyer whose question evoked the parable could hardly identify with a despised outsider like a Samaritan, but rather must see himself in the wounded man needing help. "And who is my neighbor?" he asks (10:29). "The one who showed mercy," he later answers (10:37). From the vantage of the ditch he learns that the neighbor is the one who helps. Having discovered this, he can then "go and do likewise."

C.B.C.

**GOODSPEED, EDGAR J.** (1871–1962). American Greek scholar. Born in Quincy, Illinois, he was graduated from Denison University and received a B.D. and Ph.D. from the University of Chicago in 1897 and 1898. He taught at the University of Chicago from 1898 to 1937, pioneering in the collation of NT manuscripts and studying Greek

papyri. He is principally known for his translation of the Bible in contemporary language. *The New Testament—An American Translation* appeared in 1923 and *The Complete Bible—An American Translation* (with J. M. Powis Smith) appeared in 1939. He taught history at the University of California, Los Angeles, from 1938 to 1951.

R.H.

**GORE, CHARLES** (1853–1932). Controversial Anglo-Catholic English theologian and bishop and an advocate of social reform based on traditional orthodoxy. Educated at Oxford, he became a Fellow in 1875; priest, 1878; and bishop, 1902. He resigned his bishopric in 1919 to write and teach, serving as dean of theology, London University (1924–28). *Lux Mundi* (1889) and other works sought to interrelate Christian thought, science, history, and social reform without compromising historic orthodox creeds or rational thought. *Christ and Society* (1928) espoused a Christian social order through associations of dedicated Christians. The three-volume *Reconstruction of Belief* (1921–24) most fully stated his views.

C.M.

**GOSHEN.** (1) This is the name by which the Bible designates that part of Egypt in which the Israelites were supposed to have been settled in the time of Joseph (Gen. 45:10; 46:28-34), "the best of the land" (Gen. 47:6). What is meant, apparently, is the fertile pastureland in the northeastern Nile Delta, north of the Wadi Tumilat, which runs eastward from the delta to Lake Timsah, which is now part of the Suez Canal. These and the other sites associated with the Israelites' sojourn in Egypt and their subsequent exodus (Zoan, Rameses, Succoth, Pithom, etc.) all seem to have belonged to the same region. "Goshen" is not an Egyptian name, nor does any such name occur in Egyptian records of any time.

(2) Goshen was probably a Canaanite name that got transferred into the Israelite epic of eisodus/exodus by the natural process of anachronism and association (similarly with Rameses, Succoth, etc.). "The land of Goshen" is the designation of a territory in the southland of Judah that fell prey to the Israelites in their conquest (Josh. 10:41; 11:16), apparently getting its title from a city of the same name in the hill country (Josh. 15:51).

B.V.

**GOSPEL.** The English word derives from an Anglo-Saxon term meaning "God's story" (*godspel*). But the word enters the language of the Bible as a translation of the Greek *euangelion,* "good news." The verb behind the noun means to announce or publish news as a herald (Greek *keryx,* from which we get *kerygma,* public preaching; there is no distinction in meaning between this latter word and *euangelion*: both mean "good tidings"). It is very important to observe that in the NT period the verb "to evangelize" or "preach the gospel" was an activity of public or private speaking. The gospel was the content of what was uttered, not what was written down or read. The use of "gospel" in the sense of written documents (for example, the Four Gospels) came much later, first found in Justin's description of Sunday worship at Rome, A.D. 150. The plural "gospels" is not a NT usage (see Gal. 1:6-9 for opposition to more than "one gospel").

*Background.* *Euangelion* in Greek meant originally a reward offered for good news brought by a messenger. Then it came to be linked with the content or substance of the message that was brought. Thus news became "good news," for example, victory in battle.

The Roman emperors, especially Augustus, used a form of the term "gospel" to announce a new age of prosperity and world peace, which their reign promised. Some scholars trace the NT use to this setting (especially in Luke 2:1-14; Acts 17:7). More likely, the first preachers got the term from the OT, especially second Isaiah's announcement that a new age would come when God is acknowledged as King (Isa. 40:9; 52:7-10). Thus "gospel" is linked with the reign of God, and this connection prepares the way for the terms as used in Jesus' proclamation of God's kingdom (Mark 1:14-15).

*New Testament Use.* Several books have a special interest in attaching "gospel" to a different aspect of the Christian message. Luke and John studiously avoid the term (except in one special instance, Rev. 14:6ff.). The main users of the word are Mark and Matthew, with Paul appropriating the term "gospel" as a central idea in his vocabulary (sixty times in his letters, excluding the Pastorals, which have four instances). Mark chooses "gospel" to sum up Jesus' proclamation of the imminent rule of God (1:14 ff.). Indeed the term is the title of his entire Gospel book (1:1) and summarizes all that the church preaches (13:10; 14:9). Matthew editorializes the verses he borrows from Mark and gives an instructional flavor to the term in keeping with his idea of the church as a "school of Christ." The gospel is to be learned and obeyed (Matt. 11:28-30; 13:52; 28:18-20).

Paul's witness is the clearest of all. For him "gospel" means "the death and resurrection of Jesus as saving events," to be proclaimed (vv. 1-5) and believed (I Cor. 15:11). His apostolic task can be summed up in this one word: to preach the *gospel* (Gal. 1:15-17; I Cor. 1:17; 9:16). And he can lay claim to "my gospel" (Rom. 2:16), set over rival versions of the Christian message, which he repudiated (II Cor. 2:17; Phil. 1:12-18; Gal. 1:6-9). The gospel became for Paul the touchstone of his ministry as "apostle to the Gentiles," a designation picked up in later tributes (Eph. 3:1-9; I Tim. 2:7). There is also an ethical standard implied in "living according to the gospel" as Christians are thereby summoned to live out their faith (Phil. 1:27; Gal. 2:14).

*Summary.* "Jesus Christ, risen from the dead, descended from David, as preached in my gospel" (II

Tim. 2:8), may well stand for an epitome of what the NT writers, mainly in the Pauline tradition, meant by "gospel." Both the person and saving achievement of Christ are involved as he fulfilled OT prophecy and brought messianic salvation to the church. This news is to be published to all peoples (Rom. 10:5-15), since God in Christ has reconciled the world (II Cor. 5:18-21) and brought in a new age.          R.M.

**GOSPEL OF TRUTH.** An Apocryphal work used, according to the church father Irenaeus (second century A.D.) by Valentinian GNOSTICISM. It is a mystical-homilectical writing that claimed to be based on secret traditions of Jesus' teachings, but it actually was a mixture of Christian doctrine and Gnostic speculations of Jewish origins. It is believed that one of the fragmentary Coptic Gnostic manuscripts discovered at NAG-HAMMADI in Egypt is the Gospel of Truth.

The authors of apocryphal gospels tried to convince their readers that they, and not the canonical Gospels, were giving the true history and teachings of Jesus. They did this by professing to teach secret doctrines that Jesus had taught only to a few, select disciples. They then mingled together portions of the canonical Gospels and their own teachings. The church fathers recognized the hidden purposes of the authors of such works and rejected them. (*Compare* APOCRYPHA, NT.)          J.C.

**GOSPELS, THE FOUR.** The historical problem of "the four Gospels" is sharply posed by the fact that Paul, in his lifetime, had more than once opposed the idea of there being more than one GOSPEL (Gal. 1:7-9; II Cor. 11:4) (*see* SYNOPTIC GOSPELS). Yet by the time of Justin (A.D. 150) Christian worship at Rome is described as including a public reading of "the memoirs of the apostles . . . called gospels." About the same time the church was driven to do two things, paradoxically interconnected: it had to delimit the number of "gospels" to the canonical four we know in the face of apocryphal and gnostic gospels gaining currency; and it had especially to oppose MARCION's attempt to appeal to an abbreviated Gospel of Luke as solely authoritative in his CANON. And it had to resist the temptation, in a third course of action inspired by TATIAN's *Diatessaron* or *Harmony* (A.D. 170), which ran together the four Gospels into a single account, to ignore or deny the plurality of four Gospels, each with its own distinctive way of telling the story of Jesus.

In the end the view that prevailed was that which attributed each Gospel to an apostolic source, whether direct (as in the case of Matthew and John, believed to be disciples-apostles who wrote down their eyewitness reports) or indirect (Mark, a follower of Peter according to PAPIAS, A.D. 130, and Luke, a companion of Paul the apostle). This is Tertullian's ground for affirming that the church's appeal to the four Gospels rests on apostolic authority.

*Traditional Symbols for the Four Gospels*

Yet, from earliest times, Christians recognized that each Gospel had a distinctive pattern and emphasis.

MARK is traditionally believed to be the first of the Gospels to appear. The novelty of this Gospel lies in its appropriation of the title "gospel" (1:1), which before the evangelist's time meant the public preaching, to apply to a written composition.

MATTHEW is clearly constructed with a view to its use in a pedagogical (educational) situation. The evangelist's church is like a school in which the occupation of study is led by Christian teachers (13:52).

LUKE, drawing on a source of Jesus' words common to Matthew and other written compositions in his day, presumably Mark, has written what may rightly be called a "life of Jesus" (Luke 1:1-4). His purpose is chiefly pastoral.

JOHN is the most distinctive of the four Gospels, ostensibly published as an apostolic document (21:24) and intended to awaken or confirm the faith of its readers in Jesus as Messiah and Son of God (20:30-31). The transcendental dimension is explained by Clement of Alexandria: John, seeing that the outward facts had been set down by the other evangelists composed a "spiritual Gospel" (cited in Eusebius, *Church History*).

R.M.

**GOTHIC.** A style of art, particularly distinct in architecture, that evolved from the Romanesque style in the twelfth century and became dominant in western Europe in the thirteenth century. The name "Gothic" was originally pejorative, given to it by Renaissance enthusiasts of classical art for whom the centuries immediately preceding were the Middle Ages and their highest artistic expression "Gothic" —that is, derived from the barbaric Goths. One of the main characteristics of Gothic architecture is its vertical lines, achieved through the repetitive use of pointed arches, ribbed vaults, and buttressing systems (usually flying buttresses) that allow great height without massive walls. The large windows that were made possible by the buttressing system gave opportunity for the extensive use of stained glass, which in turn made the interiors much lighter than the earlier Romanesque churches. Among the

greatest examples of Gothic architecture are the cathedrals of CHARTRES, Cologne, and Paris (Notre Dame).

J.G.

**GOTTSCHALK (805–868).** A ninth-century monk noted for his theories on PREDESTINATION, which led to an extended controversy. Gottschalk had carefully studied the teachings of AUGUSTINE and on that basis declared that God has predestined some to salvation and others to damnation, and that in our present fallen state there is nothing we can do to please God. Upon learning of these teachings, several contemporary theologians were convinced that Gottschalk was a heretic. Foremost among these were Rabanus Maurus and Hincmar of Rheims, two of the most respected leaders of the church in the ninth century. Hincmar, in particular, sought the support of a number of theologians. But most of these had to agree that what Gottschalk taught was very close to the teachings of Augustine, and Hincmar found himself in a difficult position. Defeated in the field of theological debate, Hincmar made use of his personal influence with Charles the Bald. At the king's command, a council declared that Hincmar's position was in full agreement with Augustine's, which was historically false. Gottschalk, who had earlier been condemned as heretical, deposed from the priesthood, and imprisoned by his superiors, died in captivity, where he went mad shortly before his death. The entire controversy was one more example of the ambivalent attitude of medieval theology toward Augustine, whose authority all affirmed, but whose teachings few followed. A work by Gottschalk, *Predestination*, was discovered in Switzerland in 1930.          J.G.

**GRACE.** The language and literature of the Bible are especially rich in words for grace, just as there are several other terms, such as FORGIVENESS, SALVATION, LOVE, which convey the idea behind grace. Basically grace is God's free and loving regard for humankind expressed in all God has done and continues to do for men and women as sinners and as God's people.

*Old Testament.* Two Hebrew words are significant. *Hesed* (in the RSV, "steadfast love," but best translated by incorporating the idea of covenant favor, that is, God freely chose Israel to make them a special people) can refer both to God's favor shown to Israel and to Israel's response in loyalty and obedience to the covenant relationship (Hos. 6:6). The idea of praising God for free favor runs through the Psalms (5:7; 57:3; 89:1, 2, 33), especially when the writers have been in trouble and have known deliverance. *Hen* is a more general term, but is used unilaterally, that is, a superior's condescending attitude to a subordinate (Gen. 33:8ff. of Esau's attitude to the servile Jacob). In that sense *hen* describes God's loving decision to select and claim Israel as chosen of God (Deut. 7:7, 8; Jer. 31:2).

*New Testament.* The Greek word used in the Septuagint to translate *hen* is *charis.* The corresponding verb *charizesthai* means "to show favor" in the sense of "forgive" (Col. 2:13; 3:13). A second NT translation word is *eleos,* meaning "mercy," often used to render *hesed* in the OT Greek Bible. But *charis* is the dominant NT term. In classical times it meant "beauty," "charm," a meaning that may survive in Luke 4:22 and Colossians 4:6.

Ordinarily "grace" for the NT writers carries the specialized meaning of God's kindly attitude to men and women, bestowing on them pardon and receiving them into God's family as unworthy but beloved children. It is thus part of the vocabulary of salvation, and may be said to be a Pauline term par excellence (see Rom. 3:21-26). Hence the phrase "saved by grace" is a faithful summary of Paul's teaching (Eph. 2:5, 8). Grace thus stands in antithesis to LAW, when the latter term denotes a human effort intended to gain acceptance with God, usually by placing confidence in one's unaided strength (Phil. 3:4), or through the Torah religion thought of as a merit-conferring system (Rom. 10:3-4; Phil. 3:9). Paul vehemently opposed both ways of achieving salvation, since it can only be received from God as a gift in grace (Rom. 5:2; 6:23). Attempts to gain favor with God in other ways imply that we have fallen from grace (Gal. 5:4).

Several derivative senses of this primary meaning of grace are also important for Paul: grace means strength (II Cor. 12:9) for him to fulfill his apostolic tasks; it is used of the SPIRITUAL GIFTS, that is, gifts of God by the Holy Spirit to equip the Christian congregation for practical service both in the church's ministry of worship and in the world (Rom. 12:3-8; I Cor. 12:4-11); and in one special way Paul expected the Corinthians to excel in the *charis* (that is, "virtue") of a generous contribution to the collection for the poor in Jerusalem (II Cor. 8:7). The "grace" of the incarnate Lord is held out as a model for such sacrificial giving (II Cor. 8:9).

Later writers, both in the Pauline school (Tit. 2:11-14; I Tim. 1:12-17; II Tim. 2:1) and elsewhere (I Pet. 3:7; 4:10; 5:12; Heb. 2:9; 12:14, 15; John 1:17), echo these lines of teaching whose capstone is placed by yet one further variation of *charis,* namely thanksgiving for God's gracious action in Jesus Christ, both past and present (Rom. 7:25; II Cor. 9:15) as well as "grace over food" referred to in a few places (I Tim. 4:3; compare Mark 14:22, 23 and parallels; Acts 27:35).                                                    R.M.

**GRACE, CHARLES E.** (1881–1960). Known as "Sweet Daddy Grace," he was the charismatic founder of a Pentecostal holiness group, the United House of Prayer for All People. Born in the Cape Verde Islands, of Portuguese and African descent, he did not claim divinity as did FATHER DIVINE, but he emphasized his personal mediation of the Divine. Services were often enthusiastic and included faith healing and

speaking in tongues. In addition to worship centers, his organization ran church cafeterias, low-income housing, and retirement homes. He published *Grace* magazine, which could be applied to one's body for healing. He also sold toothpaste, soap, and cold cream with alleged medicinal value. Grace died January 12 and was buried in New Bedford, Massachusetts. His mantle passed to Elder Walter McCollough, who then became known as Sweet Daddy Grace McCollough. The group, headquartered in Washington, D.C., but strongest in the Southeast, has more than 130 congregations coast to coast and some 27,000 members.                    N.H.

**GRADUAL.** In the liturgy of the eucharist, a psalm or sentence from a psalm read or sung between the first lesson and the gospel lesson for the day. The term comes from the Latin *gradus* or "step," since this reading was originally given from a raised portion of the chancel.                                                         J.C.

**GRAHAM, BILLY** (1918– ). American evangelist and one of the best-known religious figures of his day. He was born November 7 in Charlotte, North Carolina, and named William Franklin Graham; his parents were William Franklin and Morrow Coffey Graham. Educated at Florida Bible Institute, and Wheaton College, Graham received no seminary training. Although he had been reared in a Presbyterian home, Graham dates his conversion at

Courtesy of the Billy Graham Evangelistic Association

*William F. (Billy) Graham*

age sixteen to a tent revival meeting in his home city conducted by Baptist evangelist Mordecai Ham. After serving as a lay preacher while attending the Florida Bible Institute, Graham was ordained as a Southern Baptist in 1939. Married on August 13, 1943, to Ruth McCue Bell, daughter of a medical missionary to China, Graham served for a time as the pastor of the Western Springs (Ill.) Baptist Church, which he called the Village Church.

In 1943 he became the first evangelist of the newly founded Youth for Christ movement. He was elected president of Northwestern College, Minneapolis, in 1948, and conducted an evangelistic crusade in Los Angeles in 1949, springing instantly into national prominence.

He founded the Billy Graham Evangelistic Association with headquarters in Minneapolis. His first London Crusade in 1954 catapulted him to world fame. Thereafter he conducted meetings in major United States cities and in Europe, Africa, South America, Asia, New Zealand, and Australia.

The weekly "Hour of Decision" radio broadcast was launched in 1950. Later he began to produce evangelistic films and appeared on television specials. Graham has a weekly syndicated column, "My Answer." In 1956 he was one of the founders of the biweekly magazine *Christianity Today,* and in 1960 he started the monthly magazine *Decision.* Graham has authored a number of books, many of which have reached the best-seller list.

He was the major force behind several international gatherings: the World Congress on Evangelism at Berlin in 1966, the International Conference on World Evangelization at Lausanne in 1975, and a conference for itinerant evangelists at Amsterdam in 1983. He has appeared on the platform of general assemblies of the World Council of Churches.

Graham was invited to the White House by all the presidents of the United States from Truman on, but he was particularly close to Eisenhower, Johnson, and Nixon. The Grahams have three daughters, Virginia (Gigi), Anne Morrow, and Ruth (Bunny), and two sons, William Franklin and Nelson Edman.

R.H.

**GRAIL, HOLY.** A legendary cup supposed to have great powers, whose quest inspired several romantic tales beginning late in the twelfth century. In some cases, it was identified with the cup that Jesus used at the Last Supper. In general, however, the legend of the holy grail, while having a profound influence in literature, made little impact in theology or even in the popular religious views of the time.       J.G.

**GRANT, ROBERT** (1779–1838). The British hymnwriter was born in Bengal, where his father, Charles, was a well-known philanthropist. Robert was sent home to England in 1790. He graduated from Magdalene College, Cambridge (B.A. 1801; M.A. 1804) and was admitted to the bar at Lincoln's

Inn in 1807. He was elected to Parliament, representing Elgin in 1818, Inverness in 1826, and Norwich in 1830, and became a privy councilor in 1831. Noted for his attempts to repeal all civil disabilities for Jews, he initiated a bill to remove civil restrictions imposed against them in 1833. Knighted and appointed governor of Bombay in 1834, he assumed the post in March 1835. Grant died at Dalpoorie, India, on July 9. His hymns, published posthumously by his brother Charles in the volume *Sacred Poems* (1939), include "Saviour, When in Dust to Thee," "O Worship the King," "By Thy Birth and by Thy Tears," and "When Gathering Clouds Around I View."       N.H.

**GRATIAN.** The twelfth-century author of the *Decretum Gratiani,* a compilation of texts from popes, councils, and ancient Christian writers, arranged according to various issues in canon law. Although very little is known of Gratian's life, his work has been credited with having founded the discipline of CANON LAW, and was eventually incorporated into the *Corpus Juris Canonici.* During the late Middle Ages, it was widely used in debates on the authority of popes, councils, bishops, and others.       J.G.

**GRATITUDE.** The basic human response corresponding to God's GRACE is gratitude. It permeates the life and worship of the community of faith in both the OT and NT. "It is good to give thanks to the Lord" is a prominent theme (Ps. 92:1; compare Pss. 42:4; 95:2; 100:4; Col. 2:7; Eph. 5:20). Ingratitude is the essence of sin (Rom. 1:21; compare Luke 17:11-19).

*Gratitude Is Offered to God.* In the Bible the predominant number of references to thanksgiving specify or imply that it is God to whom words of appreciation are spoken. God is the source of "every good endowment and every perfect gift" (Jas. 1:17). The prayers of thanksgiving in most of the NT epistles are directed to God, even as they celebrate the faithfulness and love of the epistles' recipients (for example, II Thess. 1:3-4).

*Gratitude Is Offered for God.* Thanksgiving is not quantified to correspond to specific material or even spiritual blessings, as if God were a capricious deity and gratitude were only appropriate when one became sufficiently prosperous. Instead, God is faithful to promises made and is reliable. God's goodness and trustworthiness become occasions for thanksgiving; all other reasons for thanksgiving are derivative. It is not surprising that a repeated refrain in Israel's liturgy ran, "O give thanks to the Lord, for he is good; for his steadfast love endures for ever!" (Pss. 106:1; 107:1; 118:1, 29; 136:1-3).

*Gratitude Is Offered "in All Circumstances."* It is not merely in response to desired benefits that thanks are given, nor only when one's lot in life appears blessed, at least more blessed than that of others (compare the prayer of the Pharisee in Jesus' parable: "God, I thank thee that I am not like other men," Luke 18:11). The gracious character of God shapes the human response; therefore, praise can be the mark of every situation (I Thess. 5:18). Paul even spoke of rejoicing in sufferings, not in a masochistic mood but because the presence of God led to hope (Rom. 5:3-5).

Gratitude is the context out of which the life of obedience is lived. "And whatever you do, in word or deed, do everything in the name of the Lord Jesus, giving thanks to God the Father through him" (Col. 3:17). The Heidelberg Catechism appropriately considers "good works" and the demands of the Ten Commandments under the rubric of "thankfulness." Gratitude to God expresses itself in the responsible ways neighbors and needy people are treated.

C.B.C.

**GRAVEN IMAGE.** An IDOL or likeness of a human being or animal used as an object of worship; the use of which is expressly forbidden by the Second Commandment of the Mosaic Decalogue (Exod. 20:4). Specifically, graven images are three-dimensional, cultic idols made of poured molten metal (Exod. 34:17). Throughout the OT, idols are opposed, condemned, and ridiculed, as the purely spiritual nature of Yahweh is stressed. Perhaps at first, in their wilderness wanderings, the Israelites were not seriously threatened by the widespread idolatry of Egypt, Canaan, Assyria, and Babylonia, but after settling in Canaan and feeling the attraction of and pressure from their neighbors, idolatry became a severe threat that had to be fought constantly. Additionally, intermarriages with idolators, the need to show respect to powerful neighbors like Egypt, Assyria, and Babylonia, and the popular belief that local GODS controlled their territories and had to be respected and appeased, contributed to widespread attempts to serve Yahweh and other gods. The great prophets rose up again and again to denounce this idolatry, which they termed spiritual adultery. As the OT books were written, opposition to idols was seen as a prime mission of the Hebrew people. According to Joshua 24:2, Abraham left Ur because he wished to escape from the idolatry of his fathers. J.C.

**GREAT AWAKENING** (First and Second). As defined by William McLoughlin in *Revivals, Awakenings, and Reform,* awakenings are occasioned by crises in beliefs and values that lead to cultural revitalization and reorientation, often marked by religious REVIVALS. Puritanism was one such revival. There have been four awakenings in American history: the First (1730–60), Second (1800–30), Third (1890–1920), and Fourth (1960–  ).

The First and Second Great Awakenings were seen as spontaneous works of the Holy Spirit, visitations of God's grace for the renewal of America's sacred mission. Socially the First contributed to the founding of the American republic; the Second to the bonding of the Union and the rise of Jacksonian

participatory democracy. The revivals were integrated into the awakenings. The Third and Fourth were more secular, with the revivals more often being attempts to stabilize the status quo rather than formulating creative solutions to society's new challenges.

The First Great Awakening is usually dated from the 1734 revivals at JONATHAN EDWARDS' Northampton, Massachusetts, church. His account, *A Faithful Narrative of the Surprising Work of God* (1737), influenced John Wesley and his colleague George Whitefield, whose 1739 and 1740 tours of the eastern seaboard gathered many conversions. Local itinerants Gilbert Tennent and James Davenport continued the work.

The awakening was characterized by highly emotional preaching, such bodily effects as weeping and fainting, and an emphasis on conversion as a single soul-shaking experience. Church membership increased by about fifty thousand members. It also divided Old Lights from New Lights among Congregationalists, Old Side from New Side among Presbyterians, and created the Separate Baptists. Revivalists formed such coalitions as the 1801 Plan of Union and the Benevolent Empire.

The Second Great Awakening had two phases. It began with the 1800 camp meeting revivals of Gaspar River and CANE RIDGE, Kentucky. Marked by extreme enthusiasm and bodily "exercises," it spread to the Carolinas and south into Georgia, spawning such churches as the Disciples of Christ. The second wave began in 1826 with CHARLES FINNEY's work in upstate New York. His New Measure—protracted meetings, the anxious bench, praying for people by name, colloquial preaching, and allowing women to pray and testify—set new standards for revivalism, routinized by his *Lectures on Revivals* (1835).

The Second Great Awakening was based on an "arminianizing" of Calvinism, a shift away from original sin to moral responsibility, a renewed emphasis on conversion as an act of the will rather than God's gift to the elect. An emphasis on "usefulness" led to attacks on such social ills as slavery, sexism, poverty, prostitution, alcoholism, and war. Presbyterians split between Old School and New School, which led to an actual schism in 1837. A corollary emphasis on perfection led to the formation of the Wesleyan and Free Methodist churches, from the Methodist Episcopal church, which benefited most from the revival. N.H.

**GREAT COMMISSION.** *See* COMMISSION, GREAT.

**GREAT SCHISM.** The period from 1378 to 1423, when there were two rival popes—and three at times—claiming the allegiance of a divided Europe. Gregory XI had brought the Papacy back to Rome after the long period of its residence at AVIGNON. At his death, the cardinals elected Urban VI to succeed him. But Urban soon alienated most of the cardinals, who then left Rome, declared that Urban's election had taken place under coercion and was therefore invalid, and elected a rival pope, who took the name of Clement VII. After an unsuccessful attempt to take Rome by force of arms, Clement settled his residence in Avignon. Urban named a new group of cardinals, and thus there now were two rival popes with two rival colleges of cardinals. After the death of each of the two claimants, others were elected to succeed them, thus perpetuating the schism. This state of affairs, as well as the prevalence of such evils as simony, absenteeism, and pluralism, gave added impetus to CONCILIARISM, which aimed to reform the church and end the schism by means of a universal council. In 1409 the Council of Pisa declared the two rival popes deposed and elected a third in their stead. But since the other two claimants refused to accept the conciliar decision, there were now three popes. The Council of Constance finally forced the abdication of the Roman Pope Gregory XII and the the Pisan Pope John XXIII. Although the pope of the Avignon line, Benedict XIII, refused to abdicate, he lost most of his followers, and for all practical purposes the schism came to an end. With his death in 1423, the last remnant of the Great Schism was healed. By then, however, the Papacy had lost much of its prestige and power.

J.G.

**GREAT SEA.** *See* MEDITERRANEAN SEA.

**GREAT TRIBULATION.** *See* TRIBULATION, GREAT.

**GREECE** (Biblical). The point of contact between Greek history and biblical narrative and chronology is the fourth century B.C. The war between the city states of Athens and Sparta, lasting twenty-seven years, left both important centers impoverished and exhausted. The immediate result was the rise of Macedonia under the leadership of Philip II, who had

energy and access to natural resources along with numerical strength—all factors denied the Greeks in the south. The upshot was that Greek hegemony passed to Macedonia in a war against Persia, and in particular threw into prominence Philip's brilliant son, ALEXANDER THE GREAT.

Alexander's meteoric campaign from Greece to India and China brought HELLENISM onto the scene, but also led to a confrontation between Judaism and Greek polytheistic and naturalistic culture (seen in Dan. 7–12, where Alexander is referred to, for example in 8:21).

On Alexander's death in 323 B.C. Greek influence became expressed in the rising Seleucid power, which later led to Syrian expansionism and the Maccabean revolt (168 B.C.), which marked its virtual decline. World power passed over to the Romans, but Greek legacy lived on in the concept of "one world" (*oikoumenē:* Luke's word in Luke 2:1, rendered "all *the world*" in RSV) and a common language (*koinē* or spoken Greek as a hallmark of civilization: see Acts 21:37-39)—both important factors in the spread of the Christian mission in Greco-Roman society, as well as in the memory of classical civilization, which later Christians exploited in their insistence that the best aspirations of Greece in its golden period were met in a "natural theology" (seen in the second century A.D. Apologists, but also in Acts 17: the speech given to the Areopagus with its allusion to Aratus and Cleanthes, Greek poets who celebrated human kinship with the Divine).

R.M.

**GREEK ORTHODOX CHURCH.** *See* ORTHODOX CHURCHES.

**GREEK RELIGION, PHILOSOPHY, LANGUAGE.** Greek language and culture served as the prime media through which Judaism and Christianity spread throughout the Mediterranean world in the three centuries before and after the birth of Jesus.

Courtesy of the Metropolitan Museum of Art. Purchase 1890. Levi Hale Willard Bequest

*Model of the Parthenon in Athens, Greece*

The Letter of Aristeas (first century B.C.) claims that there was so great an interest in Judaism among Greeks in the reign of Ptolemy II Philadelphus (255–246 B.C.) that the monarch ordered a translation of the Jewish Torah into Greek for the royal library in Alexandria. The legend goes on that six men were chosen from each of the twelve tribes to journey to Egypt, where they completed the project in seventy-two days. The work was probably done by Alexandrine Jews in the early third century. The number of translators was rounded off to seventy, for which the later Latin designation was SEPTUAGINTA (LXX). The existence of this translation stimulated study of the Bible in Alexandria in correlation with Greek literature and philosophy. Books were written that claimed to be by earlier writers—such as Ezra or Solomon or the sons of Jacob—which clearly show the influence of Greek philosophy. The use of the LXX and the process of adaptation to Greek literature and philosophy were carried further by the early Christians, including the NT writers. Indeed the existence of the LXX is one of the most important factors that made possible the rapid spread of Christianity and the grounding of its adherents in biblical tradition.

The language level used by Jewish and Christian writers varied from the awkward, yet vivid style of common speech (*koinē*) in the Gospel of Mark (where traces of Semitic linguistic features are apparent) to the more sophisticated narrative and discourse style of Acts, Hebrews, and the Wisdom of Solomon (in the Apocrypha). The author of Acts was obviously familiar with the literary strategies of contemporary historians and writers of romances, just as the writers of documents like Hebrews and the Wisdom of Solomon knew technical Greek philosophical language.

The dominant philosophical systems that most directly influenced Jewish and Christian writers in this period were Stoicism, Platonism, and Cynicism. The method of spreading the faith by itinerant preachers-teachers was similar to that of the CYNICS, whose propagandists wandered from town to town, addressing crowds gathered in the marketplaces, living from whatever food or lodging was offered them. But instead of the Cynic appeal to free oneself from any personal or social obligation, the Christian itinerants announced the end of the age and called for commitment to the inbreaking rule of God.

The Stoic influence on Jewish and early Christian ethics was pervasive. STOICISM regarded the universe as operating by the inherent law of nature. Conscience was what made one conscious of this universal law. Courage and wisdom led one to overcome lower urges and live according to nature. The story of the Maccabean triumph over the Seleucids is retold in IV Maccabees as though it were chiefly a matter of victory of self-control over unworthy motivations. In the Testaments of the Twelve Patriarchs, a document which purports to have been written by Jacob's sons,

## New Testament Greek Alphabet

| Capital letter | Small letter | Name | Latin |
|---|---|---|---|
| A | α | alpha | a |
| B | β | beta | b |
| Γ | γ | gamma | g, n |
| Δ | δ | delta | d |
| E | ε | epsilon | e |
| Z | ζ | zeta | z |
| H | η | eta | ē |
| Θ | θ | theta | th |
| I | ι | iota | i |
| K | κ | kappa | k |
| Λ | λ | lambda | l |
| M | μ | mu | m |
| N | ν | nu | n |
| Ξ | ξ | xi | x |
| O | ο | omicron | o |
| Π | π | pi | p |
| P | ρ | rho | r, rh |
| Σ | σ,ς | sigma | s |
| T | τ | tau | t |
| Υ | υ | upsilon | y, u |
| Φ | φ | phi | ph |
| X | χ | chi | ch |
| Ψ | ψ | psi | ps |
| Ω | ω | omega | ō |
|  |  |  | h |

*New Testament Greek Alphabet*

the sin of one of the sons in committing incest is denounced, not by reference to a legal precept from the law of Moses, but because it is contrary to the law of nature. Paul in Galatians enumerates the "fruit of the Spirit," that is, the good works that the Spirit enables the faithful to perform. Among them are "gentleness and self-control" (Gal. 5:23). When he asks how non-Jews, who lack the revealed law of Moses, can know what God demands of them, his answer is "conscience" (Rom. 2:14-15).

The basic claim of PLATO—that the world of the senses was comprised of imperfect, impermanent copies of the forms of reality—directly influenced both Judaism and Christianity as they sought to gain credibility in the Greco-Roman world. In the Wisdom of Solomon, for example, a writer near the turn of the Christian Era depicts Wisdom as the mediating agent through whom ultimate reality is disclosed in the material world: "She is a reflection of eternal light, a spotless mirror of the working of God" (Wisd. of Sol. 7:26). As an emanation of the transcendent God, she reveals God's power, purpose, and ultimate reality to a transitory world, subject to corruption and decay.

Philo of Alexandria (30 B.C.–45 A.D.) so stressed the transcendent and otherness of God in his allegorical interpretations of the five books of Moses (the PENTATEUCH) that he had to posit the existence of the Divine Word (LOGOS) through which God created the physical world and by which natural order was maintained within it. Exodus 25:40 reports God as instructing Moses to make the Ark of the Covenant and the equipment of Israel's central sanctuary "after the pattern for them, which is being shown you on the mountain." Philo interpreted this to mean that Moses had been privileged to glimpse the eternal forms in the divine presence, and that the tabernacle built for Israel was the earthly copy of the heavenly reality. The Letter to the Hebrews quotes this passage from Exodus 25 to make precisely the same point (Heb. 8:15), but adds the distinctive Christian claim—basically Platonic in its point of view—that Christ's sacrificial offering of himself has been present in the true ideal heavenly sanctuary so that his offering is the ideal sacrifice. The whole Jewish sacrificial system consists of transitory copies of the eternal reality, which is embodied in Christ's offering.

Greek popular religion also deeply affected both Judaism and Christianity. Most pervasive was the role of ISIS. She became identified by Hellenistic times with Wisdom (Maát, the Egyptian goddess). But her role was more personal than intellectual. Although she was venerated as the divine agent by which the stars were kept in their courses and the cycle of seasons and fertility were maintained, she was also the personal beneficiary of those who turned to her in need. She was therefore the object of deep personal devotion, so that many dedicated their lives to her service. Inscriptions have been found telling of benefits her faithful followers received. By the late first and early second century, in the writings of Plutarch and Apuleius respectively, Isis is portrayed as the symbolic figure by which one may find meaning in life, and as the mistress of the universe in whose service are freedom, fulfillment, and renewal of life. Biblical portraits of Wisdom include one in Proverbs 8, where she is God's companion, and in Sirach 24, where she is the instrument through whom beauty of nature and harmony in human relations are brought about. The three roles of Isis—agent of creation, beneficiary of the needy, central figure around whom are gathered those with faith and true insight—are assigned in the Gospel of John to Jesus as the Logos made flesh.

Similarly, Asclepius, the god of healing, was regarded in Hellenistic times as the one to whom the blind, the crippled, or those who had lost children should turn in order to regain health or to find the loved one who had disappeared. He was thought to dwell in a shrine at Epidauros in Greece. Visitors spent the night in his sanctuary and were visited during the night by sacred dogs or sacred snakes whose touch might restore them. If they were especially blessed, the god himself might appear. Testimonies to the effectiveness of his cures survive on carved slabs found in the ruins of the Asclepion. By the second century, however, Asclepius was turned to, not merely to heal the body, but to give encouragement to the frustrated, direction to the perplexed, and a sense of kinship with the divine to those who felt alienated or aimless. Aelius Aristides, who lived for ten years adjacent to Asclepius' shrine in Pergamum on the Aegean coast of Asia Minor, described in detail in his *Sacred Discourses* how the god enriched his native gifts as orator and gave him a sense of importance in his world.

The religion of Dionysus, which probably originated in Asia Minor, but soon gained a popular following in Greece and Rome was a dynamic cult that promised direct participation in the life of the god. Incited by wine and rhythmic music, the devotees of Dionysus entered a trance-like state in which they shared a sacred cup and food with the god. Our knowledge of the Dionysiac movement derives largely from those who scorned it (Livy, the Latin historian; Euripides, the Greek dramatist), but enough has survived to show that the cult promised a renewal of life through participation in the sacred ceremonies. Over a period of centuries throngs flocked to his shrine at Eleusis, near Athens, to share in the divine life. That kind of longing finds expression in the Gospel of John, where the writer builds on the OT story of the bread from heaven (John 6; Exod. 16; Num. 11) that fed Israel in the wilderness. The sacred bread and wine of the Christian Eucharist (John 6:11) recall that experience, but John described its effects as bringing transformation of life (John 6:41, 50-51). Instead of an invisible divine figure who offers the transforming cup, John sees it as presented by "Jesus of Nazareth, the son of Joseph" (John 1:45), a thoroughly historical figure whose earthly parentage, suffering, and death are recounted by John.

Thus, the traces of Greek religion that have survived enable us to see what human aspirations were in the culture of the Roman world as the claims made in behalf of various divine agents—including

Jesus—competed for the loyalty and devotion of seeking men and women. Greek language, philosophy, and religion have provided basic questions; the religious answers to these were offered by Jews and Christians, who addressed their contemporaries as they set forth their own distinctive claims.

H.K.

**GREGORIAN CHANT.** The traditional musical form of Roman Catholic liturgical texts, deriving its name from collections made by Pope GREGORY I (590–604). Of very early origins in Antioch and Jerusalem, the Gregorian chant (also known as plainsong) was standardized and enhanced by Gregory's *Schola Cantorum* (school of singers). This chant was introduced into England by Augustine of Canterbury at the end of the sixth century. English missionary monks carried it back to the Continent, and it dominated medieval musical forms by the eleventh century. With the development of contrapuntal music, madrigals, and polyphony, the Gregorian chant rapidly declined to virtual non-use by the sixteenth century.

Revivals fared poorly until popes Pius IX, Leo XIII, and Pius X showed interest during the nineteenth and twentieth centuries. Efforts of the Benedictine Abbey of St. Pierre de Solesmes, France, to recover the true Gregorian chant form received papal approval in 1903. Pius X ordered use of the Gregorian chant in 1904. The chant's modal melody, sung by one or more voices in unison, is traditionally unaccompanied and elaborates the Latin biblical text with pauses, flourishes, and a flow appropriate to its meaning.

C.M.

**GREGORY I, THE GREAT** (540–604). Pope from 590 to 604, and one of the four great Latin DOCTORS OF THE CHURCH. He belonged to an aristocratic Roman family and had a high position in the government of the city when he decided to become a monk. By then, he had disposed of most of his wealth by giving it to the poor and to various monastic foundations. A period as the pope's representative in Constantinople convinced him that the Byzantine Empire was weak and corrupt, and that the West should expect no hope from it as it sought to rebuild after the Germanic invasions. In Italy, the Lombards were ravaging the land, and Gregory decided that the West, and the papacy is particular, would have to respond to that challenge on the basis of its own resources.

Back in Rome, he was elected pope, a post he accepted only after great hesitation and soul searching. As pope, he followed the policies that his stay in Constantinople had led him to espouse. Instead of awaiting support from the East against the Lombards, he simply moved ahead in negotiations with them and eventually reached an agreement on his own authority. Since this agreement involved the disposition of several territories in Italy, it was a major step in the development of the temporal power of the popes.

As a result of the Lombard wars, Italy was in chaos. The neglect of aqueducts and drainage systems and the disruption of trade had led to widespread disease and famine. It was Gregory's task to organize the public works and the trade necessary to restore a measure of health and well-being, and this also contributed to the growing power and prestige of the Papacy.

Gregory had always been an ardent supporter of MONASTICISM. Shortly before he became pope, the Lombards destroyed the monastery of Monte Cassino, the result being that many Benedictine monks fled to Rome. Through contacts with them, Gregory became a staunch advocate of the RULE OF ST. BENEDICT, which he helped spread throughout western Europe. A significant episode in this process was his sending of Augustine, later to become archbishop of Canterbury, on a mission to England. Gregory's biographers tell us that he had wished to go on such a mission himself, but was prevented from doing so by his admirers in Rome. Also, through extensive correspondence, and with the support of monks in various areas, Gregory sought to improve the life of the church in Gaul and Spain—thus adding to the prestige of the papacy.

As a theologian, Gregory was not original. His own goal was to be no more than the mouthpiece for earlier teachings, particularly those of Augustine of Hippo. But in truth his theology differed from that of Augustine on two major points: first, it reflected the age in which Gregory lived, with its superstitious fascination for miracles and legends; second, what for Augustine had been no more than possibilities, Gregory took as facts, mostly on the grounds that Augustine had spoken of them. A case in point is purgatory, of which Augustine spoke with hesitation, and which for Gregory was an established fact. Also, Gregory laid great stress on penance, which he discussed and systematized in a way that would be influential throughout the Middle Ages.

J.G.

**GREGORY VII, POPE** (1020–85). Pope from 1073 to 1085, but a highly influential person in the life of the church for years before his election as pope. A man of humble origins named Hildebrand, he was serving as chaplain for Gregory VI, who died in exile. He then retired to monastic life, until the newly elected Leo IX asked him to accompany him in his pilgrimage to Rome. Once there, first under Leo and then under his successors, Hildebrand became the leading force behind a vast program of reformation. Although historians have at times described him as hungry for power and a tyrant, more recent opinion is that he was a sincere reformer, and that his seemingly harsh measures were the result, not of a thirst for power, but rather of a zeal for reformation. Finally, in 1073, he was unanimously elected pope.

Gregory's program of reformation was directed against simony, the practice of lay investiture, and clerical marriage. It was he who most promoted the ideal of clerical CELIBACY, which eventually became the practice of the entire Western church. In his struggle against lay investiture, he clashed with a number of sovereigns, notably those of France, England, and Germany. In France, he was able to push through his reforms in spite of the opposition of Philip I. In England, he was willing to compromise with William the Conqueror, who refused to obey his decrees on lay investiture, but was actively reforming the church and even using his powers of investiture to that end. It was in Germany that his policies were most openly rejected. Henry IV refused to yield to the pope's entreaties and threats, and had two German synods declare Gregory deposed. The latter responded by excommunicating Henry, declaring him deposed, and freeing all his subjects from their vows of allegiance to him. Threatened with the loss of his throne, Henry submitted to the pope at Canossa. But this did not bring peace, and eventually Henry marched on Rome and forced Gregory into exile, where he died.                                          J.G.

**GREGORY OF NAZIANZUS** (329–389). Also known, particularly in the Eastern church, as Gregory the Theologian. With BASIL THE GREAT and GREGORY OF NYSSA, he is also one of the great Cappadocians who led the battle against ARIANISM in the second half of the fourth century. He befriended Basil the Great at Athens, where they were fellow students, and some time later decided to withdraw from the world and become a monk. But the church demanded his leadership, and he was made a priest against his will. After an unsuccessful attempt at flight, he returned to his priestly duties and on that occasion delivered his famous sermon "On the duties of a priest," which has become a classic. When the struggle against Arianism required it, Basil made him bishop of the hamlet of Sasima, which he never visited. He resented this action by Basil, and for this reason their friendship was strained until Basil died. He continued serving as a priest in Nazianzus, where his father (also named Gregory) was bishop, and after his father's death he again retired to the monastic life.

Once again Gregory was required to fight against Arianism and in 379 went to Constantinople, where all churches were in Arian hands, and began celebrating orthodox worship. Pressured by the authorities and mocked and pelted by the mobs, he persisted in this ministry. Finally, when the faith of Nicaea triumphed, he was made bishop of Constantinople, and as such presided over the Council of Constantinople in 381. But his enemies said that he could not be bishop of Constantinople, since he was already bishop of Sasima, and Gregory took the opportunity to resign and return to the monastic life.

Among his works are the *Five Theological Orations*, in which he developed his doctrine of the Trinity, and particularly of the PROCESSION OF THE HOLY SPIRIT; several other theological treatises, including some against Apollinarians; and hundreds of poems, some of which have become classics of Christian hymnody.
J.G.

**GREGORY OF NYSSA** (331?–?396). One of the Great Cappadocians, and a younger brother of BASIL THE GREAT. His was a profoundly religious family, of which several members are officially listed as saints, notably his brothers Basil and Peter, and his sister Macrina. Although for a time he pursued a career in rhetoric, he was a mystic and a man deeply devoted to his monastic vocation. The Arian controversy, however, came to trouble his rest, for his brother Basil and others required him to employ his great intellectual gifts in the struggle against ARIANISM. For the same reason, much against his will, he was made bishop of Nyssa. His works and his sanctity eventually gained him great fame, and by the time of the COUNCIL OF CONSTANTINOPLE he was generally considered one of the great champions of the Nicene faith. At that council he played an important role, and Emperor Theodosius, profoundly impressed by his wisdom, made him one of his advisers in theological matters. In that capacity he traveled to various areas of the empire, and even as far as Arabia. But he still longed for the contemplative life and finally was allowed to fade once again into obscurity. In this he succeeded to such a degree that the manner and time of his death are not known. His extant works fill several volumes; but the most valued and influential throughout the history of the church are those on MYSTICISM. Since his piety and theology were profoundly shaped by NEOPLATONISM, these works were instrumental in the growing Neoplatonic influence on Christian faith and theology.     J.G.

**GROUND OF BEING.** A phrase referring symbolically to God made prominent in current theological discussion by PAUL TILLICH (1886–1965). Drawing on the mystical tradition represented in Jakob Boehme (1575–1624) and Friedrich Schelling (1775–1854) to overcome the limitations of critical rationality, Tillich affirmed God as beyond theistic concepts, subject-object categories, and symbolic utterance. The one nonsymbolic statement about God is that God is BEING itself. As being itself, God is the ground of being, a phrase already symbolic in character. "Ground," says Tillich, "oscillates between cause and substance and transcends both of them" (*Systematic Theology*).

Ground of being means for Tillich the creative source of all that has being. God is the religious term for this depth of being, the ABYSS into which all tracing of the finite by reason disappears; God is at once power of being and burning fire. All human concern, or FAITH, has its ultimate ground in this depth of our own being. Reason is extended by Tillich beyond "technical" reason to "ontological" reason and at last to "ecstatic" reason that participates in and reflects the depth of being, which is its source. God as being itself is the ground of REVELATION, both its origin in the divine life and its manifestation in human faith and action.

In the phrase "ground of being," Tillich is attempting to relate theology and philosophy, the "abyss" of inexhaustibility and ineffability to the "logos" of meaning and structure, the depth of the Divine to the form of human experience in a mysterious and dynamic unity called "Spirit."

C.Mc.

**GUARDIAN ANGELS.** In ancient thought every nation, people, and religious group had its guiding and guarding spirits. Paul speaks of principalities and powers, meaning the angels, or from the Christian view, demons, who stood behind the Roman Empire or the pagan religions (Rom. 8:38; Eph. 3:10; 6:12; Col. 1:16; 2:15). The archangel Michael was thought to be the protector of God's chosen people. Acts 12:15 implies that one's personal angel was a spiritual double, reflecting a popular belief. Guardian angels protect people and facilitate their prayers to God. Such beliefs show the need for a mediator between humanity and God and are consequently criticized by Hebrews 1:4-14.

J.C.

**GUILT.** See SIN.

**GUNKEL, HERMANN** (1862–1932). German biblical scholar who taught at the universities of Halle (1889–94, 1920–27), Berlin (1894–1907), and Giessen (1907–20). A pioneer investigator of biblical literary genres, Gunkel defined the form-critical and history-of-religions task in which much twentieth-century OT scholarship has engaged. Not discounting the gains of J. Wellhausen's source criticism, Gunkel concentrated on the preliterary history of the OT. He listened carefully to the distinctive rhythms of biblical texts in which the ongoing life of individuals and communities was reflected. Thus he posited the *Sitz im Leben* (life setting) that triggered specific oral formulations. Collecting specimens of a given *Gattung* (literary type), Gunkel often drew from available ancient Near Eastern literature. Convincing illustrations of his methodological insights appear in two monumental commentaries on Genesis (1901) and Psalms (1926). His introduction to the former is available in English under the title *The Legends of Genesis: The Biblical Saga and History* (1964).

J.K.K.

**GURDJIEFF, GEORGES IVANOVITCH** (1872–1949). Colorful leader of a religious movement that sought to bring its members to "higher planes of consciousness." He based his beliefs on the teachings of a "hidden brotherhood" in central Asia. The movement had its center in the Institute for the Harmonious Development of Man, located in Fontainbleau, France. The Gudjieff Foundation of New York continues his work.

K.C.

**GURU.** In Hinduism, the term "guru" (from the Sanskrit word meaning literally "weighty") is today usually used to refer to a spiritual teacher, especially one believed to be "God-realized," or in special communication with the Deity. The guru thus has more than an intellectual relationship with disciples, initiating and otherwise transmitting spiritual power to them according to their ability to receive it, and imparting to them techniques for reaching the same state as the guru's. Gurus are often credited with supranormal insight regarding the spiritual needs of others, as well as other psychic powers. The worship of one's guru as a vessel of God, whether in person, or at a distance in the form of a picture, or the imprint of the guru's footprints, is a standard practice in Hinduism.

R.E.

**GUTENBERG, JOHANN** (about 1397–1468). German printer and inventor of movable type. Born in Mainz, he moved early with his family to Strassburg. In Strassburg in 1438, he joined three others to experiment with printing. In 1450, in Mainz, he formed another partnership with lawyer Johann Fust to print a large Latin Bible. Fust loaned venture money, and in 1455 he sued for repayment. Gutenberg lost his press. Peter Schöffer, Fust's partner, then printed the famed forty-two-line Gutenberg Bible, the first book known to be printed with movable type. Only forty-eight copies still exist, one of the finest being in the Library of Congress. Gutenberg died blind and destitute.

C.M.

**GUTMANN, BRUNO** (1876–1966). One of history's most outstanding missionaries to the African continent, distinguished in ethnology and the scientific study of missions. Gutmann served as a missionary of the Leipzig mission from 1902 to 1938. He did extensive research on ideas of tribal and racial psychology and operated on the basic principle that a person is to be understood as a member of an organic whole, not just as an individual. Many of his ideas were opposed by Christian and mission leaders, but he made many significant contributions to the nature of the meeting between the gospel and African societies.

W.G.

**GÜTZLAFF, KARL FRIEDRICH AUGUSTUS** (1803–51). The first Lutheran missionary to China. Trained at the Jänicke Mission School in Berlin and in the Netherlands, Gützlaff was influenced by the Moravians and by a meeting in London with Robert Morrison, an early missionary to China. Gützlaff first went to Indonesia as a missionary and there learned the language of the Chinese to work among members of the dispersion there. He later worked in Thailand, where he translated the Bible into Siamese, took a

Chinese name, wore Chinese clothing, and traveled along the coast of China. He later traveled into the interior of China and made several contacts, which later developed into mission fields. He trained evangelists and was an early pioneer in the indigenization of the church in China. Although most of his projects might be termed failures, Gützlaff was a pioneer of great influence who has sometimes been called the "grandfather of the CHINA INLAND MISSION."                                    W.G.

**GUYON, MADAM** (1648–1717). The mystic writer and exponent of QUIETISM was born Jeanne Marie Bouvier de la Motte on April 13 in Montargis, France. She was educated in convent schools. At age sixteen she married Jacques Guyon, a man of wealth and nobility twenty-two years her senior, yet sickly and still dominated by his mother. Jeanne Marie bore him five children. At age twenty she gave up all worldly amusements. When she was twenty-eight, her husband died. She devoted her life to God and her fortune to good works. At thirty-four she began an apostolic mission of travel and teaching. Church authorities harassed her, accused her of heresy, cast aspersions on her character, and finally had her imprisoned. She spent most of seven years in prison, the last four in the Bastille. She was released in 1703 under house arrest. Fenelon, archbishop of Cambray, defended her views in his writings and at a trial in 1695 at which quietism was officially condemned. Guyon published a number of books on prayer and the inner life. John Wesley called her "a pattern of true holiness."

N.H.

# Hh

**HABAKKUK.** A cultic prophet of Judah whose career likely dates from a period immediately following the battle of Carchemish in 605 B.C., which elevated the Babylonians to political supremacy throughout the Near East. Although the legend of Bel and the Dragon in the Apocrypha mentions a certain Habakkuk being miraculously transported to Babylon to feed Daniel in the lion's den, details about the ancestry and life of this OT prophet are unavailable. His name, however, may derive from an Akkadian plant name—*hambakukū*— and his thinking is partially revealed in the OT book that bears his name.

*The Book of Habakkuk.* Employing the style of an individual lament, which often raised the anguished question "How long?" the book opens with a twofold sequence of prophetic complaint and divine oracle. In 1:2-4 Habakkuk poignantly voices an objection to Yahweh that the ruthless (domestic?) behavior of the wicked goes unchecked. Indeed, "the law is slacked and justice never goes forth" (v. 4). Is God indifferent toward social violence? In 1:5-11 Yahweh answers that a virtually unbelievable deed is being planned. God is raising up the powerful Chaldeans (Babylonians), "that bitter and hasty nation" (1:6), to punish the oppressor.

But the emergence of this new world power, "whose own might is their god" (1:11), was for this Judean prophet an outrageous extension of the evil already perpetrated by the hated Assyrians. Renewed complaint was his only option. Thus in 1:12-17 Habakkuk puts this question before the "everlasting" and "holy" Deity: "Why . . . art [thou] silent when the wicked swallows up the man more righteous than he?" (1:13). Both the enemy without (the Chaldeans) and within (wicked Judeans and their recalcitrant king, Jehoiakim) weigh heavily on the prophet's mind. Again Habakkuk challenges Yahweh to abolish human tyranny.

Stationing himself at a site propitious for a revelation (2:1), Habakkuk awaits the divine reply. It unfolds in 2:2-4. He is granted an assurance, which he is commanded to write succinctly and in large letters on tablets "so he may run who reads it" (2:2). The prophet and his contemporaries are met with instruction and challenge. Though the vision be protracted, "it will surely come" (2:3), and in the face of history's enigmas, "the righteous shall live by his faith" (2:4).

Five rather cryptic woes now issue against the enemy (both outside and within Judah), who engages in oppressive greed (2:6-8), unprincipled gain (2:9-11), policies of violence (2:12-14), needless cruelty (2:15-17), and idolatry (2:18-20). The third chapter offers a sublime hymn portraying God's majestic coming to avenge the people (3:2-16) and a bold assertion of faith defending God's goodness in the face of a manifestly imperfect environment

(3:17-19). Though lacking in the Dead Sea Scroll of the Habakkuk Commentary, chapter 3 confers a thematic unity on the entire biblical book.

*Religious Significance.* Partly due to its autobiographical style, this book compellingly raises the issue of theodicy—how can a just God condone rampant EVIL in the world? The human-divine dialogue is intense. The answering oracle in 2:3-4 clarifies that the world's governance does reside in God's hands, and that righteousness does not depend on human mental capacity to understand divine intentions within the historical arena. Rather, it depends on a sure posture of obedience that believes in Yahweh's promise. This dramatic theology of expectation insists that ultimately, treachery rebounds upon the doer. Divine justice *is* inexorable. Thus the righteous need only rely on Yahweh's ability and integrity. The personal trust here manifested reappears in bold relief in the writings of Paul (Rom. 1:17; Gal. 3:11).                          J.K.K.

**HABDALAH.** A home ceremony of prayer among Jews signifying the end of the SABBATH or of other festivals. It concludes the time of rest of the Sabbath or festival and marks the distinction between the sacred character of the Sabbath or festival and the work days of the week.                          J.C.

**HABIRU.** A rootless people of mixed race and language attested all over the Near East throughout the second millennium B.C. They appear to have been less an ethnic entity than a stratum in society. Some texts portray them as vagrants who disrupted settled town populations, especially in Palestine in the Amarna period (fourteenth century B.C.) Other texts from ancient sources present them as indigents who improved their social position by hiring themselves out as mercenaries, or who, in times of dire need, became voluntary slaves. Though no easy equation between "Habiru" and "Hebrew" is possible, the roving Hebrew patriarchs may have been members of the wide-ranging Habiru social stratum.     J.K.K.

**HABIT.** The robe, head covering, or other distinctive clothing worn by members of religious groups, which often identifies the religious order to which the person belongs. Special dress for the religious was provided by the rules of St. Basil, as a way of reminding religious of their monastic obligations.
J.C.

**HACHIMAN.** A Japanese deity worshiped in both BUDDHISM and SHINTO. He has been honored as the god of war, and represented as riding on horseback and wearing a war helmet. He was also the friend of children, to whom he appeared as a simple, honest monk. Buddhists identify him with Jizo, a popular BODHISATTVA.                          K.C.

**HADES.** *See* GEHENNA.

**HADITH.** A tradition concerning something that MUHAMMAD said or did, or concerning his appearance or character. The term may refer to an individual item of tradition or to the entire collection of such traditions. Each Hadith contains a text (the content of the tradition) and a record of the chain of those who transmitted the text from the time of the prophet to the time of the latest transmitter. Much effort was devoted to investigating the chain of transmission in order to make certain it was genuine. This was necessary in order to weed out false Hadith that had been circulated in the first two centuries of Islam.

Especially in Sunnite Islam the Hadith have been used as a major source of religious authority. The QUR'AN is the most important authority, but it is often hard to interpret, and on many issues it is silent. In those cases, answers are sought first of all in the Hadith.

SUNNIS have nine collections of Hadith, and SHI'ITES have three. Many Shi'ite traditions concern various IMAMS, especially ALI, whom Shi'ites honor as the first iman.

The contents of the Hadith provide much historical information, especially details of the life of Muhammad. What Muhammad did or did not do often became a legal precedent. Hadith also contain stories about God, angels, prophets, and the last judgment. Some give rules about personal hygiene and ritual practices.

The Hadith are believed to be divinely inspired, but only in content, not word for word, as is the Qur'an. They have influenced the major genres of Islamic writing and have always been of the highest importance for Islamic faith.                          K.C.

**HADRIAN I.** Pope from 772 to 795. The most important feature of his pontificate was his continued alliance with CHARLEMAGNE against the Lombards, whose King Desiderius was eventually deposed by Charlemagne. He also appealed to Charlemagne for help against the adoptionism of several Spanish bishops. In the iconoclastic controversy, however, he and Charlemagne disagreed, for Hadrian accepted the decisions of the Second Council of Nicea, and the Frankish king rejected them.                          J.G.

**HAGAR.** An Egyptian maid of Sarah. The P stratum in the PENTATEUCH refers to Hagar for chronological purposes (Gen. 16:3, 15-16), but J and E offer moving accounts of Hagar's expulsion from Abraham's household.

*The J Tradition.* In Genesis 16:1b-2, 4-14, the Yahwist reports that in an effort to realize Yahweh's promise to Abram (12:1-3), Sarai gave Hagar to him so that he might secure a son (a practice attested in fifteenth-century B.C. Nuzi texts). Once pregnant, this concubine of Abram forgot that she was still Sarai's slave. When she acted arrogantly, Sarai obtained Abram's consent to treat her harshly. Hagar fled to the Wilderness of Shur in northern Sinai. The angel of Yahweh appeared to her at a well. He urged her to return to Sarai and promised her a long generation of descendants through her unborn child, the fierce Ishmael ("a wild ass of a man," 16:12).

*The E Tradition.* In Genesis 21:8-21 the Elohist likewise mentions Sarah's jealousy, the expulsion, and divine concern. The crisis, however, occurs after the births of Ishmael and Isaac. The disturbed Sarah, unable to tolerate the two boys playing together as equals, demanded that ABRAHAM expel Hagar and Ishmael, who threatened her own son's inheritance. Upon learning that God approved of this tactic, Abraham acceded. In their flight to the wilderness of Beer-sheba, the two were spared an untimely end by virtue of an appearance of the angel of God who showed Hagar a well. Moreover, Hagar was assured that from Ishmael "a great nation" would emerge (21:18).

*Significance.* Through these traditions, the Israelites acknowledged that the wild Bedouins inhabiting the southern wilderness were in fact their relatives. Moreover, in Galatians 4:21-31, Paul interprets the Hagar narrative allegorically. Ishmael, a slave's son, and Isaac, a free woman's son, respectively symbolize the old and new covenants.

J.K.K.

**HAGGADAH.** The book that occupies the attention of the participants in the Jewish PASSOVER SEDER. Interwoven with the ritual for the Seder service are readings from the Bible, selections and legends from the TALMUD and MIDRASH, prayers and blessings, hymns and songs.

The spirit pervading the Haggadah is one of longing for redemption and freedom, a belief in the survival and continuity of the Jewish people, and an unyielding confidence in divine salvation. According to Maimonides, the reading of the Haggadah is reckoned as one of the positive commandments that are incumbent upon all Jews: "It is a positive commandment of the Law to narrate the miracles and wonders that happened to our ancestors in Egypt on the night of the fifteenth of Nisan, as it is said: 'Remember this day, in which you came out from Egypt'" (Exod. 13:3).

The pivotal passage of the Haggadah—"Every person in every generation must regard himself as having been personally freed from Egypt"—is based on the MISHNAH. The prologue to the Haggadah, an invitation to the needy and a prayer for redemption, reads:

> Behold the bread of poverty which our forebears ate in the land of Egypt. Let all who are hungry come and eat with us; let all who are needy come and celebrate Passover. This year we are here; next year may we be in the land of Israel. This year we are slaves; next year may we be free.

Endeared to Jews, the Haggadah has appeared in thousands of editions—printed, illuminated, illus-

trated. Many translations have been made, and it has been adapted to meet different needs and interests.

L.K.

**HAGGAI, BOOK OF.** A prophetic book consisting of only thirty-eight verses, which offers a narrative account of Haggai's five prose oracles and the response they evoked within the postexilic Jewish community. With his prophetic colleague, ZECHARIAH, Haggai successfully motivated the Jews, who had returned from Babylonian exile to finish rebuilding the Jerusalem Temple, and predicted a brilliant future for Yahweh's people.

*Historical Context.* Abundant date formulae (1:1, 15; 2:1, 10, 18, 20) indicate that Haggai spoke his oracles in 520 B.C., during the second year of the reign of Darius I Hystaspis, king of Persia. Everyday existence within the Jewish community was grim. Poverty resulting from drought and meager harvests called into serious question the stirring vision about Jewish restoration that Second Isaiah had articulated two decades earlier (Isa. 40–55). Overwhelmed by economic hardship, many of the returned exiles projected an indifference toward things religious. Though the Temple foundations had been laid (Ezra 3:8-13), building efforts had ceased for fifteen years. Clearly, the morale of the Jewish community, and its two leaders, ZERUBBABEL (governor) and JOSHUA (high priest), had plummeted. Informed by both political and theological insights, the spirited Haggai advanced a positive message, which called forth an immediate, energetic response. Mindful that the Persian Empire was rife with revolt during these opening months of Darius' rule, Haggai believed that Persia's future was far from certain. Moreover, he regarded Yahweh's decisive intervention as imminent. Accordingly, God's people must be prepared.

*Oracles.* In his first oracle (1:1-14), Haggai castigates those who preferred working on their own paneled houses instead of rebuilding Yahweh's Temple. Perceiving the present drought as a manifestation of divine punishment, Haggai promised that prosperity would return once first things were put first. Zerubbabel, Joshua, and "the remnant of the people" (1:14) responded positively to the challenge and resumed work on the Temple. Seven weeks later, Haggai spoke an encouraging oracle (1:15*b*–2:9) to those who lamented that the new Temple could not possibly measure up to Solomon's Temple. He predicted imminent political convulsions that would usher in a new world order, and tribute from all nations would pour into the Temple. The new edifice would eclipse the old in splendor, and poverty would be lifted from Judah. In a third oracle (2:10-14), Haggai instructs that evil is more contagious than good. In referring to "this people" (2:14), he may have leveled a criticism against Samaritans, who opposed the endeavors of the postexilic Judean community. Or Haggai may simply be insisting that for the sake of their religious well-being, the Jews should not waver in their resolve to rebuild the Temple. A fourth oracle (2:15-19) highlights the economic blessings that will accrue once Yahweh's house is rebuilt. (This is probably a misplaced component, since it appears to have been introduced by the suspended date formula in 1:15a.) In his last oracle (2:20-23), Haggai again anticipates the arrival of the new age by speaking anew about the overthrow of the nations. By referring to Zerubbabel as Yahweh's "signet ring" (2:23), Haggai was promising a special divine power to the governor, who represented the royal line of David.

On balance, this book usefully reflects some of the historical configurations within the restored Jewish community as well as the political and theological optimism of one of its prophets, who insisted that Yahweh's people need not despair about their future.

J.K.K.

**HAGIA SOPHIA.** The largest surviving church of ancient times, sponsored by the Eastern Roman Emperor Justinian and built between A.D. 532–537. Designed by Anthemius of Tralles and Isidorus of Miletus, Hagia Sophia was damaged by an earthquake in A.D. 558. The building was rebuilt in 563. After the Turks conquered Constantinople in 1453, they converted the church into a mosque, adding four minarets (towers) to the building. In February, 1935, Hagie Sophia was converted again, this time to a museum.

The church was originally named Hagia Sophia meaning "Holy Wisdom" in Greek and was sometimed called Sancta Sophia (Latin) or St. Sophia. The original building is a rectangle 79 by 73 meters (260 by 240 feet), divided longitudinally into the nave proper and side aisles. There is a dome over the nave, 30 by 32 meters (100 by 106 feet), rising fifty-six meters (184 feet) high. There are also half domes to the east and west that abut the main dome.

J.C.

**HAGIOGRAPHA.** *See* CANON.

**HAGIOGRAPHY.** The writing of lives of saints. In the Middle Ages, such lives followed standard patterns, and edification was more important than historical accuracy. In more recent times, a critical hagiography has developed, which seeks to discover the historical facts behind traditional hagiographic materials.

J.G.

**HAGRITE, HAGARENE.** A Bedouin tribe residing east of Gilead, whose ethnological association with HAGAR, Ishmael's mother (Gen. 16), is uncertain. These pastoralists were conquered by the tribe of Reuben during Saul's reign (I Chr. 5:10, 19-22). Among David's officers was "Jaziz the Hagrite," who oversaw the flocks (I Chr. 27:30). In a national lament, the Hagrites are mentioned as one of Israel's Transjordanian enemies (Ps. 83:6).

J.K.K.

**HAIKU.** A Japanese poetical form, generally in seventeen "sound units," or syllables, arranged in groups of 5, 7, 5 lines. Each haiku stands by itself, although haiki on the same theme are sometimes grouped together. The subject matter varies widely, but a haiku should reflect an immediate experience of nature, seeing beauty or truth in everyday sights.

While many followers of ZEN have written haiku, few of their poems are narrowly religious. Instead

Courtesy of G. E. Kidder Smith

*Hagia Sophia, Istanbul*

they express a fusion of nature and spirit, reflecting loneliness and mystery. In many of the best haiku there is a surprise, often a sudden awareness of the presence of ultimate reality.

> Buddha    Is the cherry blossoms
> On a moon-lit night.
> Hōitsu (1760–1828)

It has often been said that in Zen the doer and the deed are undivided, the perceiver and the perceived are one. Bashō (1644-94) wrote:

> This autumn— Old age I feel,
> In the birds, the clouds.

Bashō was also sensitive to the fusion of Buddhism and SHINTO, in which Shinto gods were identified with manifestations of the Buddha. At Isé, the holiest of Shinto shrines, he saw

> On the fence around the shrine,   Unforeseen,
> The Buddha entering Nirvana.

K.C.

## HAIL MARY. *See* AVE MARIA.

## HAJJ.
The pilgrimage to MECCA, one of the five PILLARS, or basic requirements, of ISLAM. Every Muslim must perform the pilgrimage at least once, unless prevented by poverty, poor health, or some other problem that cannot be overcome. A person who has made the pilgrimage is known as a Hajji, a title of honor.

The pilgrimage must be made during the twelfth month of the Muslim calendar. This is a lunar calendar that is not coordinated with the solar calendar, so the month of the Hajj comes at different times of the solar year.

There are specific qualifications for pilgrims. A pilgrim must be an adult; must ask permission of his or her parents, especially if they are old or sick; and must make a will concerning property and other important matters. All debts must be paid before setting out, enough money must be left behind for the family, and enough taken along to meet all expenses.

The city of Mecca and the surrounding area is holy. Only Muslims may enter the area, and they must observe strict rules. Pilgrims must not comb their hair, use perfume, or wear fine clothing. Hunting is prohibited, vain and vulgar talk must be avoided, and sexual intercourse is forbidden. There is a prayer to be said during every rite that is performed. Since no pilgrim can be expected to know all the things to do and not to do, local guides make a profession of conducting groups on the pilgrimage.

During the Hajj huge crowds gather in the courtyard surrounding the KA'BA, with its sacred black stone that fell from heaven. Pilgrims kiss the stone if they can get close enough to do so. They move counterclockwise seven times around the Ka'ba, offering prayers during each circuit.

Other rites include visits to various holy places, offering animal sacrifices, and casting stones at a column that represents Satan. Pilgrims drink water from the sacred well of Zamzam, which refreshed Ishmael, ancestor of the Arabs, and Hagar, his mother, after Abraham sent them away from home.

Since pilgrims come in increasing numbers from all parts of the world, communicable diseases have always been a threat. In recent years, the government of Saudi Arabia has provided sanitary facilities and health care for the pilgrims. Lodging ranges from modern hotels to tents or to sleeping in the open.

K.C.

## HALAKAH.
The legal side of JUDAISM. It embraces not only the practices and observances of the Jewish religion but personal, social, national, and international relationships as well. The word comes from the Hebrew for "to go." In the Bible the good life is frequently spoken of as a way in which persons are "to go." Deuteronomy 1:32-33 (JPS) reads in part: ". . . the Lord your God, who went before you in the way . . . to show you by what way ye should go. . . ." (See also Exod 18:20.)

Halakhah is the distinctive feature of Judaism as a religion of obedience to the word of God. It includes jurisprudence, worship, ethical injunctions, and ceremonial observances.

The chief differences between Orthodox and Reform Judaism depend on their different attitudes to the halakhah. Orthodox Judaism considers the halakhah to be absolutely binding since it emanates from God. Reform Judaism, while guided by the legal decisions of the past in some areas, rejects the absolute binding force of the traditional halakhah. Conservative Judaism has a midway position. It treats the traditional halakhah as binding, but it feels somewhat free to interpret it. It attempts to preserve the dynamic principle of legal development which, it claims, is typical of the talmudic period.     L.K.

## HALDANE, JAMES ALEXANDER (1768–1851) AND ROBERT (1764–1841).
Scottish evangelists. James was born in Dundee, Scotland, and Robert in London, of a distinguished Scottish family. Both were educated in Dundee schools and at Edinburgh University. The brothers both served in the British navy, James becoming an officer. Robert left the navy to return to his Stirlingshire home, where he became a widely known landscape gardener. Both brothers were converted about 1794. Robert sold his estate and sought to serve as a missionary to India but was thwarted in this ambition by the East India Company. He was also blocked from a missionary career by the Church of Scotland, at that time opposed to overseas witness. Robert employed his fortune in building preaching tabernacles and theological seminaries. James began preaching all over Scotland

and in 1797 founded the Society for Propagating the Gospel at Home. Disenchanted by the Church of Scotland's lack of interest in both evangelism and overseas work, James became the first Congregational minister in Scotland in 1799. Two years later he was installed as pastor in a new three-thousand-seat tabernacle in Edinburgh, where he served for nearly half a century.

Both of the Haldanes sought to restore the spirit and form of the apostolic church. In this they wielded wide influence on other Christian leaders of the day, including ALEXANDER CAMPBELL, one of the founders of the Disciples of Christ and the Churches of Christ. Campbell embraced the restorationist views of the Haldanes during the year he studied theology in Scotland. Robert Haldane wrote a number of books including *Evidences and Authority of Divine Revelation* and a commentary on the Epistle to the Romans. Both brothers penned the lyrics of several hymns.

R.H.

## HALF-WAY COVENANT.
The Cambridge Synod of 1662 declared that baptized parents could have their children baptized, even though the parents themselves had not experienced saving grace. Such parents were banned from Holy Communion, and they were allowed only some of the privileges of church membership. This controversial decision was denounced by many as a serious sign of DECLENSION.

N.H.

## HALLELUJAH
("praise Yah," meaning "praise the Lord"). A doxology summoning the entire congregation to praise the Deity. The OT attests both secular and religious uses of the intensive stem of the Hebrew root (*hll*) for praise. Pharaoh's servants praise Sarah's beauty (Gen. 12:15). The newly acclaimed king is the object of the people's praise (II Chr. 23:12), as are the works of the good wife (Prov. 31:31). As the Philistines celebrate their god Dagon (Judg. 16:24), so the Israelites celebrate Yahweh (I Chr. 23:5), Yahweh's name (Ps. 135:1), or Yahweh's word (Ps. 56:4).

Eleven Psalms open with a "Hallelujah" exhortation (106, 111–113, 117, 135, 146-150), and thirteen conclude with it (104–106, 113, 115–117, 135, 146–150). The presence of "Hallelujah" at both extremities of Psalms 146–150 ensures that the Psalter appropriately terminates on an emphatic liturgical note. These five so-called "Hallelujah Psalms" comprehensively praise divine activity, be it past, present, or future. Moreover, as the Hallel ("praise"), Psalms 113–118 were recited in synagogue worship on such joyous holy days as Passover, the Feast of Tabernacles, and Pentecost, when Yahweh's sovereignty over both nature and the nations was celebrated. Ordinarily in the Jerusalem cult, the "Hallelujah" was given antiphonal expression by the several choirs and the congregation there assembled (Ps. 135:19-21).                    J.K.K.

## HAM.
Noah's second son (Gen. 5:32). Along with his parents, wife, two brothers (Shem and Japheth), and their wives, Ham survived the Flood and partook in divine blessing (Gen. 9:1-17). A prose text then reports that Ham saw his father's nakedness during the latter's drunken sleep (Gen. 9:20-22). Yet on awakening, NOAH pronounces a poetic curse against Canaan (9:25). Presumably an ancient poem attested Canaan, not Ham, as the subordinate brother of Shem and Japheth. By identifying Canaan as Ham's son (9:18, 22), an editor harmonized the prose and poetic traditions.                    J.K.K.

## HAMATH.
A prominent city located on the Orontes in Syria, some 120 miles north of Damascus. During much of its history, Hamath was the nucleus of an independent kingdom whose southern border constituted Israel's northern border (Num. 13:21; Josh. 13:5; Judg. 3:3). Numerous Hittite hieroglyphic inscriptions found there reveal that for a time Hamath was a significant Hittite center.

During the tenth century B.C., Hamath's king, Toi, and David were allies. The former sent the latter handsome gifts after his triumph over King Hadadezer of Zobah, their mutual enemy (II Sam. 8:3-10). Though Damascus and Hamath claimed territory at Israel's expense during the early decades of the divided monarchy, in the mid-eighth century, Jeroboam II presumably extended Israel's border northward to Hamath's southern frontier (II Kings 14:25).

At the battle of Qarqar (853 B.C.), Hamath supported the successful Ben-hadad II of Damascus and Ahab of Israel against Shalmaneser III of Assyria. A century later, Hamath was subjugated by Assyria (II Kings 19:13). In 720 B.C., following Assyria's capture of Samaria, Hamath joined Samaria's remaining inhabitants in revolt. King Sargon of Assyria soon mastered the situation. He mandated a population shift that moved some of Hamath's colonists into Samaria (II Kings 17:24) and some of the Israelite exiles into Hamath (Isa. 11:11). Still an important city during the Hellenistic Age, Hamath became known as Epiphania.

J.K.K.

## HAMMURABI.
The sixth king (about 1728–1686 B.C.) of the First Dynasty of BABYLON (about 1830–1530 B.C.), when it reached the zenith of its power. He is never mentioned in the Bible ("Amraphel," in Gen. 14:1, 9, cannot be equated with Hammurabi), yet the impact of his famous law code is felt in OT legislation.

*Sources.* Though our knowledge about Hammurabi's reign is sketchy, the following sources are useful: royal inscriptions such as stelae and foundation tablets, administrative correspondence, and official names assigned to the forty-two years of Hammurabi's Babylonian rule. Of considerable interest is the poetic, yet historically oriented section of the preamble to the Code of Hammurabi, which celebrates the king's social accomplishments and lists the major cities over which he held sway. Moreover, various inscriptions reflect Hammurabi's concern for Babylon's canals, walls, temples, and divine statues.

*Early Conquests.* The five Babylonian monarchs who preceded Hammurabi were largely unimpressive. If their efforts sometimes assured Babylon's independence, Babylon was repeatedly forced to recognize the sovereignty of Isin or Larsa. Yet during the reign of Sin-muballit, Hammurabi's father, Babylon's strength increased. Still, a strong Assyria kept Babylon from pressing northward. Mari to the northwest and Larsa to the south were likewise worthy opponents. Assyria's waning strength, however, enabled Hammurabi to engage in military expansion between his seventh and eleventh regnal years. He overtook Uruk, and, with the help of Rim-Sin of Larsa, conquered Isin.

*Peacetime Achievements.* Since the period from the twelfth through the twenty-ninth years of Hammurabi's reign mentions no wars, Hammurabi was presumably active in consolidating and organizing his empire. Babylon enjoyed governmental efficiency, economic stability, and intellectual attainment. Numerous texts dealing with magic, astrology, grammar, and mathematics were written. In the religious sphere, Babylon's patron deity, Marduk,

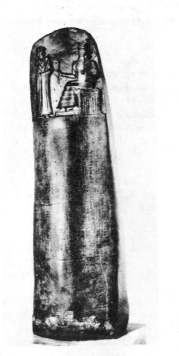

*Stele containing the Code of Hammurabi. At the top the sun-god Shamash extends the ring and rod to Hammurabi, who stands as a worshiper before him. The original of the stele is in the Louvre, Paris.*

was promoted to the summit of the Mesopotamian pantheon. The king's most outstanding achievement was the Code of Hammurabi, which normalized the diverse legal traditions current within various regions of the kingdom.

*Renewed Warfare.* During the last dozen years of his rule, Hammurabi was regularly required to return to the battlefield, often to confront entire coalitions of enemies. Hammurabi's territorial holdings sometimes suffered reduction, though in his thirty-second year he seized Mari from his former ally, Zimri-Lim. If the extent of Hammurabi's military influence at his death is unclear, the overall effectiveness of his rule is symbolized by the fact that all successive Babylonian kings chose Babylon as their capital. This dynasty endured for another 130 years, but often tasted defeat.                                                                                     J.K.K.

**HANDS, LAYING ON OF.** The belief that the power resident in certain people can be transmitted through touch or the laying on of hands is widespread in ancient and modern cultures. It figures importantly in the NT and carries a range of meanings. The most common significance of this act in the Gospels and Acts is the touch that effects healing. In Mark's Gospel, Jesus' touch cures a man of leprosy (1:40-42) and restores the sight of another (8:22-26). The synagogue ruler, Jairus, asks Jesus to come touch his daughter in order to heal her, and the hemorrhaging woman touches him and is healed (Mark 6:5; Luke 4:40). But he also places his hands on those whom he wishes to bless, as in the cases of the little children (Mark 10:13-16; Matt. 19:13-15).

In Acts, there are similar healings by the laying on of hands: Paul has his sight restored (9:17) and heals a man who is sick (28:8). But the imposition of hands also conveys the Holy Spirit, in the case of Paul (9:17). And God is implored to stretch out the divine hand in order to perform miracles through Jesus (4:30). Those who have received only water baptism are granted the Spirit through the laying on of hands, in Samaria (8:16-17) and in Ephesus (19:1-5). Paul never mentions the practice in his own letters, however.

In Acts and the later books of the NT, laying on of hands has an important function: as the instrument of commissioning people for specific forms of ministry or service. The seven who are chosen at Jerusalem for a ministry of service, probably linked with the diaconate ("serve" in Acts 6:2), are designated for their new roles by the laying on of the apostles' hands (6:6). Barnabas and Paul are sent out on their mission after performance of a similar rite by the hands of the leadership of the church in Antioch (13:1-3). The rite accomplishes the communication of the Spirit and the gift (*charisma*) of ministry for the work of the church in the Pastorals (I Tim. 4:14; II Tim. 1:6). At the same time, the younger generation of church leaders is forewarned against hasty ordination of potential workers (I Tim. 5:22). In the opening part of

Revelation, John's vision is of "one like a son of man," who commissions him to carry the message of doom and deliverance to the seven churches of Asia Minor by laying his hand upon the messenger (Rev. 1:17). With such importance attached to this rite in the later NT writings as a whole, it is surprising that the "laying on of hands" is listed by the writer of Hebrews among the "elementary" features of Christian instruction (Heb. 6:2). H.K.

## HANIFITES.

One of the four traditional schools of Islamic law. It is named after Abu Hanifa, founder of the school, who died in A.D. 767.

His starting point for legal practices was the teachings of the QUR'AN, and he paid little attention to the HADITH. Since the situation in Iran, where he lived, was different in many ways from that in Arabia in Muhummad's time, he sought to find ways to apply the teachings of the Qur'an in ways appropriate to Iran. He did this by drawing analogies. If the analogy proved to be contrary to the public good or to justice, he considered the opinion of the time and made a legal ruling on that basis. This school has followers today in many parts of Asia. K.C.

## HANKEY, A. CATHERINE

(1834–1911). Hymn writer. Daughter of a wealthy English banker, during an illness she wrote a long poem on the life of Christ. Later she adapted the words from the first section of her poem for the children's hymn, "Tell Me the Old, Old Story." Subsequently she adapted the second section of her poem for the text of the even more famous hymn, "I Love to Tell the Story." The Hankey family were members of the celebrated Clapham Sect, made up of wealthy Anglicans who were influenced by the evangelical movement that swept over nineteenth-century Britain. Miss Hankey organized Sunday school classes for rich and poor throughout London. From these classes many of those trained became zealous Christian workers. Catherine, or Kate as she was affectionately called by many, being musically inclined, set many of her hymns to music. However, the best known tune to "I Love to Tell the Story" was written by William G. Fischer, of Philadelphia, a musician and piano dealer. R.H.

## HANNAH

("grace"). Favorite wife of Elkanah the Ephraimite and mother of the prophet Samuel (I Sam. 1:2-20). Hannah endured years of barrenness, which triggered taunts from Peninnah, the rival wife. Hannah directly faced her problem during one of the family's annual visits at the Israelite sanctuary of Shiloh. She vowed that if she gave birth to a son, she would consecrate him as a Nazirite to God (1:11). Hannah returned home to Ramah, and with Samuel's birth, her wish was fulfilled.

As soon as possible, Hannah delivered the boy to Yahweh's service at the Shiloh sanctuary (1:24-28). Since it poorly reflects Hannah's personal circumstance, the highly lyric thanksgiving psalm spoken by Hannah at the moment of Samuel's dedication (2:1-10) is surely of secondary origin. Emphasizing the triumph of the lowly, the poem theologically foreshadows the Magnificat of Mary (Luke 1:46-55). Subsequently, Hannah had three other sons and two daughters (I Sam. 2:21). J.K.K.

## HANUKKAH.

The eight-day Jewish festival of "dedication" that recalls the first fight for religious freedom in recorded history.

The Syrian king Antiochus IV, who reigned 175–163 B.C., was especially bitter toward the Jews since they had rejected his claims to divinity. He instituted a violent anti-Jewish policy. Circumcision, the keeping of the Sabbath, teaching the Torah, and observance of the commandments were all punishable by death. Books of the Law were burned, the altar of the Temple in Jerusalem was desecrated by idol-worship, and orders were issued to erect altars to Zeus and other Greek gods throughout the country. Jews who resisted were mercilessly slaughtered, and many were sold into slavery.

In the village of Modin, the Hasmonean priest Mattathias raised the standard of revolt in 168 B.C. against Antiochus and the Hellenists, as those who were attempting to spread Greek culture and religion were called. Upon Mattathias' death in 166 B.C., his son Judah the Maccabee succeeded him as leader of the revolt. Judah succeeded in recapturing Jerusalem and purifying the Temple, which was rededicated on the twenty-fifth day of the Hebrew month *Kislev* in 165 B.C. (*see* MACCABEAN REVOLT).

"Then Judas and his brothers and all the assembly of Israel determined that every year at that season the days of the dedication of the altar should be observed with gladness and joy for eight days, beginning with the twenty-fifth day of the month of Chislev" (I Macc. 4:59). In a poetic embellishment of the historical reason for the length of Hanukkah, the Talmud states that the festival was instituted for eight days because the pure oil found in the Temple, though sufficient for only one day, miraculously burned for eight days.

Hanukkah is celebrated by kindling lights in an eight-branched Hanukkah MENORAH from a "servant" light on each of the eight nights, generally followed by singing the *Maoz Tzur* ("Rock of Ages") hymn and other Hanukkah songs. Beginning with one candle on the first night and ending with eight candles, the light of freedom is said to overpower the darkness of idolatry. The Hanukkah menorah is supposed to be placed in a prominently visible place "to advertise the miracle." Blessings accompany the lighting of the candles.

Hanukkah is the only non-biblical Jewish festival in which Psalms 113–118 are recited. The special scriptural reading consists of the passage that describes the gifts brought by the princes for the dedication of the sanctuary in the wilderness (Num. 7).

Work is not prohibited on Hanukkah. The prophetical portion read on the first Sabbath of Hanukkah is from Zechariah, including the verse, "Not by might, nor by power, but by my Spirit, says the Lord of hosts" (Zech. 4:6).

Hanukkah customs include gift-giving, spinning a *dreidel,* a four-sided top with Hebrew initials of the phrase "A great miracle occurred there," eating potato pancakes *(latkes)* and other foods dipped in oil, putting on Hanukkah plays, and singing.

L.K.

**HARAN.** A northern Mesopotamian city located within a region called Paddan-aram in the OT. Haran was famous for its aggressive role in caravan trade (Ezek. 27:23) and religious devotion to the Mesopotamian moon god, Sin.

*Haran in Patriarchal History.* Though the tradition that Terah, his son ABRAHAM, and other relatives migrated northward from Ur of the Chaldeans to Haran (Gen. 11:31) may be historically suspect, their sojourn in Haran and Terah's death there (Gen. 11:32) are widely accepted. Haran was the starting point of Abraham's southwestern journey of faith into Canaan (Gen. 12:4-5). Long after his arrival, and Isaac's birth, Abraham kept in touch with Haran. Rebekah, Isaac's wife, was secured from Haran's neighbor city Nahor (Gen. 24). Later, their son Jacob fled to Paddan-aram to obtain asylum with his uncle Laban, whose daughters, Leah and Rachel, he married (27:43; 28:10; 29:21-29).

*Haran in Assyro-Babylonian History.* When Assyria's capital, Nineveh, fell to the Babylonians and Medes in 612 B.C., Assyria's last king, Ashur-uballit II (612–609), retreated with a reduced army to Haran and established a refugee government. It expired in 610 B.C. when the enemy overtook the city. Assyria's attempt to reclaim Haran a year later was abortive. Babylon's last king, Nabonidus (556–539), hailed from Haran. His rebuilding the lunar temple there incurred the wrath of Babylon's priesthood and laity alike.

J.K.K.

**HARDNESS OF HEART.** A phrase denoting human defiance, callousness, or lack of understanding. Though some texts emphasize that God hardens the heart (Exod. 4:21; Josh. 11:20; Isa. 63:17), others claim that it is of a person's own doing (Exod. 9:34-35; Deut. 15:7; Prov. 28:14). If in the Exodus story God hardens Pharaoh's heart (Exod. 7:3), Pharaoh is also presented as hardening his own heart (8:32). Less interested than we in distinguishing between cause and effect, the biblical authors did not think that attributing such behavior both to God and humanity was inconsistent. Indeed, God's will was unwittingly honored in the enterprises of self-willed humanity. In Mark 6:52, the imperceptiveness of Jesus' disciples is explained as hardness of heart.

J.K.K.

**HARE KRISHNA.** See KRISHNA CONSCIOUSNESS, INTERNATIONAL SOCIETY FOR.

**HARIJAN.** See UNTOUCHABLE.

**HARLOT.** See PROSTITUTION.

**HARMONIALISM.** This describes those forms of religion in which spiritual well-being, physical health, and even economic prosperity are seen to depend on a person's harmony with the universe.

Of ancient lineage, its modern examples include New Church, CHRISTIAN SCIENCE, NEW THOUGHT, POSITIVE THINKING, Unity, and the Emmanuel Movement. Charismatic leaders include EMANUEL SWEDENBORG, MARY BAKER EDDY, Ralph Waldo Trine, Emmet Fox, Charles and Myrtle Fillmore, Charles Poyen, and NORMAN VINCENT PEALE.

N.H.

**HARMONY OF THE GOSPELS.** See SYNOPTIC GOSPELS.

**HARNACK, ADOLF VON** (1851–1930). Protestant German theologian, dogmatician, and patristic historian, who sought to uncover and discard Hellenistic influences on early Christianity. Born in Dorpat, Estonia, and educated at the universities of Dorpat and Leipzig, Harnack distinguished himself in successive professorships at Leipzig, Giessen, Marburg, and Berlin, in addition to directing the Prussian National Library (1905–21) and the Evangelical Congress (1902–12). His reputation was worldwide, and in 1914 he was made a noble. Outstanding as a patristic scholar, Harnack published his *Lehrbuch der Dogmengeschichte* (3 vols.; 1886–89), translated as *History of Dogma* (7 vols.; 1894–99). He regarded Greek thought as an alien intrusion on Christianity. Heavily influenced by both Kantian and Ritschlian idealism, Harnack stressed human possibilities, brotherhood, and the moral side of Christianity in his famous *Das Wesen des Christentums* (1900), translated as *What Is Christianity?* (1901), which won global attention. In his NT studies he argued early dates for the Gospels, Acts, and the enigmatic Q source. Other works included *Luke the Physician* (1907), *The Sayings of Jesus* (1908), and *The Acts of the Apostles* (1909), all translated from *Beiträge zur Einleitung in das Neue Testament* (1906–11).

C.M.

**HARRIS, WILLIAM WADE** (Waddy) (1865–1929). A native Liberian Christian who later worked as a charismatic evangelist among the people of the Ivory Coast. Raised as a Methodist but later a member of the Anglican church, Harris was a leader of a revolt in Liberia. After release from prison, where he claimed a mystical vision that he was to be the "prophet" to convert West Africa, he spent his time preaching and converting in French territory, the

Ivory Coast. Later Methodist missionaries built their work on his foundations. Many Christians today in Liberia, the Ivory Coast, and Ghana claim to be his true followers, emphasizing spiritual healing and suspicious of European influence.                W.G.

**HARTSHORNE, CHARLES** (1897– ). American philosophical theologian and the most important influence, after A. N. Whitehead, on PROCESS THEOLOGY and on the conception of God referred to as panentheism. Hartshorne completed his doctorate in philosophy at Harvard and served as an assistant to Whitehead, appropriating important aspects of Whitehead's process philosophy at this time. Hartshorne taught at the University of Chicago from 1928 to 1955, where he had great influence on the faculty and students of the university's divinity school. He later taught at Emory University and the University of Texas. In *Man's Vision of God and the Logic of Theism* (1941) and in *Divine Relativity: A Social Conception of God* (1948), he criticizes traditional supernaturalism and defends PANENTHEISM, which declares that no being, including God, is in all respects absolutely perfect. Hartshorne argues that God is absolutely perfect in some respects but relatively perfect in others, for example, in power. Hence in certain respects God is capable of changing and surpassing the divine nature in the future. God's power is maximal, the greatest possible, but it is not the only power. There is nothing illogical about a God who cannot be surpassed but who can grow in experience. Hartshorne argues that panentheism preserves human freedom and spares God responsibility for evil. He also argues that only panentheism makes genuine sense of the Christian doctrine of divine love, since love is meaningless apart from free relationships of giving and receiving. Hartshorne's works include *Philosophers Speak of God* (1953), *Reality as Social Process* (1953), *The Logic of Perfection and Other Essays in Neoclassical Metaphysics* (1962), and *Creative Synthesis and Philosophic Method* (1970).                J.L.

**HASIDEANS.** Mentioned in I Maccabees 2:42 as a group that joined the Maccabees (that is, the sons of Mattathias), led by Judah (I Macc. 3:1) in the revolt against the Seleucid ruler, Antiochus IV Epiphanes. This king, in keeping with his empire-wide policy, converted local cities into models of Greek culture, complete with theaters, gymnasia, and temples to the gods worshiped by the Greeks. For centuries before this, some Jews had adopted a policy of quiet resistance to the imposition of pagan culture, whether Persian or Greek, and strove to maintain their separate identity as the covenant people by preserving the purity of the Temple, observing the Sabbath and feasts decreed in the Law of Moses, as stated in II Maccabees 6:6. Their attitude toward the foreign corrupters of the Temple and the land is powerfully expressed in Psalm 79, as well as their longing for God to intervene in their behalf. Psalm 149:1 calls for

a new song to be sung "in the assembly of the *hasidim*" (pious, devout, faithful).

As the MACCABEAN rulers became increasingly secular, to the point of dependence on foreign powers for their appointment as high priest and their assumption of the title of king, though they were not from the Davidic line, the Hasidim became disillusioned and withdrew completely from society. They then took up life in the Judean desert, where they could live in ritual purity, in devotion to God and the Scriptures, and where they waited until God intervened and purified the temple. These were the Dead Sea sect. Another group remained in the towns and cities of Israel, but shifted their concerns for purity to the family. Groups of the pious met for prayer and Bible study. These were the Pharisees.
H.K.

**HASIDISM.** A mystical revivalist movement. Its followers are known as Hasidim—the "pious ones." Hasidism originated in Poland in the eighteenth century as a reaction to physical persecution, disillusionment with the false messiah Shabbethai Tzvi and the spiritual bewilderment and moral chaos that followed, extreme poverty, and religious ignorance. Its founder, Israel ben Eliezer, was known as the Baal Shem Tov ("Master of the Good Name"). His message was "serve God with joy." He taught that sincere devotion, zeal, and heartfelt prayers are more acceptable to God than great learning. Known widely as a healer and a miracle worker, the Baal Shem Tov taught by parables and sayings. He wrote no books.

The Hasidic doctrines of joy, enthusiasm, and communion with God all come from Jewish sources. But in Hasidism these were not only interpreted more radically, but they were also expressed in song, dance, feasting, and rejoicing, to a degree that seemed inappropriate to other Jews.

Hasidism emphasized inwardness both in life and in learning. Underlying all Hasidic thought was the kabbalistic concept of the world as an emanation and reflection of "higher worlds" (see KABBALAH). The Hasidim held that meditation on the doctrine, "There is no place empty of God," would dispel all fear and sadness. How can there be fear or sadness if God is with you wherever you go? How can evil exist if there is no place empty of God?

More important than the outer act of work or prayer was *kavanah*, the inner devotion with which it was carried out. God will accept even the prayers of an ignorant person so long as they are accompanied by inner sincerity.

Hasidism has no articles of faith. It does not demand adherence to a formal code. Hasidim are known not by the beliefs they hold but by the lives that they lead. In the Bible, the Hasid connotes a person of piety. "Let the faithful [Hasidim] exult in glory: let them sing for joy on their couches. Let the high praises of God be in their throats . . ." (Ps. 149:5, 6).

Hasidism produced a type of leader unique in the Jewish religious hierarchy—the *tzaddik* ("rebbe"). Acting as teacher, counselor, and confessor, the *tzaddik* is perceived as a friend in this world and as an advocate in the world to come. Viewed as heretics by the Mitnagdim led by the scholar Elijah ben Solomon of Vilna, the Hasidim were subjected to a bitter campaign that included a ban on marriage between members of the two groups. But the threat of a common enemy, "modern Enlightenment," made them close their ranks.

The great centers of Hasidism were destroyed by the Nazi HOLOCAUST. A number of dynasties have reestablished themselves in Israel and the United States. Among the largest of these are the Satmarer and the Lubavicher. Hasidim still wear the clothes favored by their ancestors. These include the *kapote,* a long, black overcoat; the *shtreimel,* a fur hat; and the *gartel* (girdle). They button their coats from right to left. They do not countenance trimming their beards and sidelocks. Many rituals distinguish Hasidim from their fellow Jews.

L.K.

**HASMONEANS.** The name given to John Hyrcanus and his successors as priestly and political leaders of the Jews in Palestine. The Hasmonean dynasty lasted from 134 to 63 B.C., when the Romans under Pompey assumed direct control of the land.

Since both kingship and the high priesthood in Israel were hereditary (the kings, from David; the high priests, from Aaron), the move by the Maccabean family to claim both titles was a source of conflict among Jews. Finally in the reign of Simon (143–134), the last surviving son of Mattathias, the dual role was recognized by the Jews. They were so impressed by Simon's diplomatic negotiations with

the Romans and with the relative security this relationship brought that they acclaimed him as "leader and high priest for ever, until a trustworthy prophet should arise" (I Macc. 14:41). The dynasty was later given the name of "the Hasmoneans," apparently derived from the name of Mattathias' great-grandfather, Asamonaeus (in Hebrew, Hasmonah) as Josephus attests in *Antiquities.*

The preoccupation of the Seleucid ruler Antiochus VII with the Parthians, who were pressing him on the northeastern border of Syria, enabled John Hyrcanus to capture extensive territory and flourishing cities east of the Jordan and down into the southern desert (Negev). He destroyed the temple of the Samaritans as well as their capital city.

An important new factor was the rise of two sharply divided religious-political parties in this period: the SADDUCEES and the PHARISEES. The former, as wealthy traditionalists, exercised considerable power, while the latter with their emphasis on the contemporary relevance of the Law had a wider popular appeal and influence with the masses. The Hasmonean rulers had to reckon with these forces in shaping internal and external policies. The requirement that some of the subject peoples, such as the Idumeans in the east Jordan territory, submit to circumcision and other Jewish requirements was to have profound significance for the future of Palestine, when the Idumeans moved into position of power. The Pharisees' demand that John Hyrcanus abandon the priesthood, because of some doubts about the purity of his ancestry, was rejected by him, and led him to side with the Sadducees. At his death he was succeeded for a brief period (104-103) by his son, Aristobulus I, who was the first in the Maccabean line to take the title of king, in addition to his role as high priest.

Out of the fratricidal struggle for power under Aristobulus, Alexander Jannaeus emerged as king

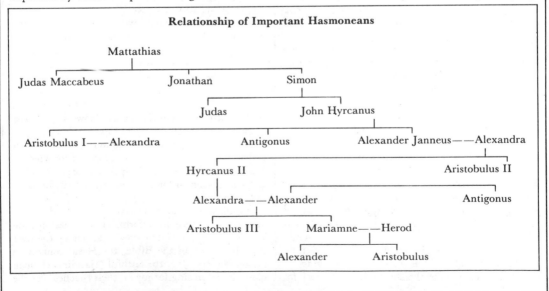

**Relationship of Important Hasmoneans**

and high priest. His long reign (103–76) was marked by conflict with the Ptolemaic, Seleucid, and Nabatean (Arabian) monarchs. The series of defeats wrought by Ptolemy Lathyrus in the coastal cities and in the Jordan Valley nearly deprived Alexander of much of his domain. By flattering Cleopatra, Ptolemy's mother, and showering her with gifts, he was able not only to regain control, but also to capture additional cities and lands on the Mediterranean and east of the Jordan. Many of the Jews were opposed to him, however, charging that he was unfit for office by reason of the impurity of his ancestors. When he appeared at a feast in the Temple, he was pelted with citrons. In retaliation, he slaughtered six thousand of them. So unpopular was he that he had to hire foreigners as soldiers in order to maintain order. On another occasion, while feasting with his concubines, he had eight hundred Jews crucified, and then had their wives and children killed as the fathers watched from the crosses. Before he died from alcoholism, he counseled his wife, Salome Alexandra, to ingratiate herself with the Pharisees.

After Jannaeus' death, Alexandra reigned as queen (76–69) and her son, Hyrcanus II, became high priest. Josephus *(Antiquities of the Jews)* remarks that "she had the title of sovereign, but the Pharisees had the power." Internal conflict and decadence in the Seleucid dynasty enabled Armenians to move into Syria—a development that led the Romans under Pompey to interfere directly, eventually converting Syria into a province of Rome. In order to put down unrest on the eastern border, Pompey subdued Asia Minor all the way to the Caucasus. Alexandra had fallen ill, and her son, Aristobulus II, began to plot and fight to assume royal power—a goal that he achieved at his mother's death in 69. His struggle with his brother Hyrcanus II for the throne gave Pompey the occasion to invade Palestine. Both sides tried to bribe the Roman leaders, but Pompey marched on Jerusalem. Partisans of Hyrcanus opened the city gates to him; Aristobulus, backed by the Sadducees, retreated to the Temple mount, which fell to Pompey in 63 B.C. Pompey horrified the Jews by entering the Holy of Holies, where only priests were permitted. Hyrcanus' son married Aristobulus' daughter; their daughter Mariamme married Herod, son of the Idumean (Arab) opportunist Antipater, who had been adviser to Hyrcanus and who helped the Romans consolidate power over Palestine and the east Jordan territories. By reason of his descent from the Hasmoneans, Herod claimed a right to the royal title, which the Romans bestowed on him, 37–34 B.C. (*See* MACCABEAN REVOLT.)                              H.K.

## HAVERGAL, FRANCES RIDLEY (1836–79).
Hymn writer. Born in a Worcestershire rectory, she was the daughter of the Reverend Henry Havergal (1793–1870), who had written many hymns. Frances began writing poetry when she was seven. Her first accepted poem was "I Gave My Life for Thee," but the best known of all her hymns was "Take My Life and Let It Be." Endowed with both musical and literary ability Miss Havergal published several volumes of hymns. In Victorian England, few young women pursued higher education, but Frances had a good working knowledge of Latin, Greek, and Hebrew and could speak French, German, and Italian. She knew whole books of the Bible by memory and could play through Handel and much of Beethoven and Mendelssohn without the score. Most of her life was plagued by ill health, but she was engaged in a very active life—mostly in Christian service. Some of her other hymns are "Who Is on the Lord's Side?," "O Savior, Precious Savior," "I Am Trusting Thee, Lord Jesus," and the English Keswick Convention favorite. "Like a River Glorious."                              R.H.

## HAWKS, ANNIE SHERWOOD (1872–1918).
Hymn writer. Unlike other writers of sacred verse, Annie Hawks had no great claims to fame. She was a contented Brooklyn housewife. She was born in Hoosick, New York, and in 1857 moved to Brooklyn, where she joined the Hanson Place Baptist Church. Her pastor was the Reverend Robert Lowry, author-composer of many notable hymns. He encouraged Mrs. Hawks in the writing of Christian poetry. Thus it was that she showed her poem "I Need Thee Every Hour" to her pastor, who wrote a chorus and set the hymn to music. Then Lowry published it in his songbook, *Royal Diadem*. The hymn caught on and soon became very popular. Then Ira Sankey sang it at the revivals held by Dwight L. Moody in England and America. This increased the popularity of the hymn. She wrote over four hundred hymns, but only this one remains in common use. When her husband died in 1888, the woman who previously had known only "hours of sweet security and peace" suffered great loss.                              R.H.

## HAZAEL ("God sees").
King of Damascus (about 842–806 B.C.). When Hazael, an officer under Ben-hadad II of Damascus, was told by the prophet Elisha that he was king-elect of Damascus, he promptly assassinated Ben-hadad and mounted the throne (II Kings 8:7-15; compare I Kings 19:15). Immediately this usurper reclaimed Ramoth-gilead from Israel and amid the battle severely wounded Jehoram, king of Israel (849–842 B.C.; II Kings 8:28-29).

In 841 B.C. Hazael sustained Assyrian aggression under Shalmaneser III (859–825), who attacked Damascus and devastated its environs. Nevertheless, Hazael was not forced to capitulate. Assyria's army was soon required elsewhere, which gave Hazael ample occasion to harass Israel and Judah.

Unable to resist Hazael, Israel's king, Jehu (842–815 B.C.), lost all Israelite holdings in Transjordan (II Kings 10:32-33; Amos 1:3). Jehu's son, Jehoahaz (815–802), likewise fell victim to Hazael and suffered a radical reduction of his army (II Kings

13:1-3, 7, 22). Subsequently, Hazael penetrated southward into Philistia and conquered Gath (12:17). By awarding Hazael extensive Temple and palace treasure, Joash, king of Judah (837–800 B.C.), spared Jerusalem a similar fate (12:18). At death Hazael was succeeded by his son, Ben-hadad III.

J.K.K.

**HAZOR.** (1) Tell el-Qedah, located in the Jordan Valley ten miles north of the Sea of Galilee. Hazor's occupation began in the early Bronze era. To the north of the tell (the 26-acre Upper City) its Middle Bronze residents constructed an extensive 175-acre plateau, called the Lower City, which was defended by a massive bank. Though this installation may have served as a Hyksos compound for horses and chariots, various buildings erected within the plateau attest its function as a suburb when Hazor's population outgrew the walled Upper City.

Excavations in the Lower City have uncovered six late Bronze Era temples in use until the thirteenth century. One contained a row of small stelae and a seated figure on whose breast was an inverted crescent, presumably representing the moon god Sin. Another temple was tripartite in plan. Its inner room, the Holy of Holies, housed altars, libation tables, and offering vessels. The well-attested destruction of Hazor's Upper and Lower cities in the latter part of the thirteenth century recalls the biblical claim that Joshua destroyed Hazor, "the head of all those kingdoms," as he triumphed against a northern Canaanite coalition headed by Jabin, king of Hazor (Josh. 11:10-11). Though the Lower City was permanently abandoned, an insignificant settlement emerged in the Upper City.

In the tenth century, Solomon fortified Hazor as one of his military centers along the nation's perimeter to repel enemy attacks (I Kings 9:15-19). He equipped Hazor with a defensive casemate wall (a double wall joined by cross walls) and a four-entryway gate system, which are also in evidence in Solomonic levels at Megiddo and Gezer. An imposing public building (royal storehouse?), whose roof was supported by two rows of pillars, witnesses to Hazor's significance as a provincial administrative center during the ninth century under Ahab's rule. In 732 B.C. the city suffered full-scale destruction by the Assyrians under Tiglath-pileser III during his campaign against Pekah, king of Israel (II Kings 15:29). The Israelite city never recovered, yet above its ruins a citadel was erected, which served as a military and administrative center until about 400 B.C.

(2) A Judean city in the Negeb (Josh. 15:23) identified with el-Jebariyeh.

(3) Kerioth-hezron, a Judean village in the Negeb (Josh. 15:25) identified with Khirbet el-Karyathein.

(4) A village of the Benjaminites located north of Jerusalem (Neh. 11:33).

(5). A region in the Arabian Desert plundered by Nebuchadnezzar in 598 B.C. and the focus of Jeremiah's oracle (Jer. 49:28-33).          J.K.K.

**HEALING/HEALTH.** The Hebrew *shālôm,* meaning "peace," and *shālēm,* meaning "healthy," "whole," are cognate terms. From this one may infer a belief that peace (a consequence of right relations with God) was an essential condition of good health and physical vigor. Throughout the history of the people of the Bible a popular notion prevailed that sickness and an early death were concrete signs of God's judgments. A corollary was the belief that only God can forgive sins and deal with the causes of illness (Ps. 103:1-5). It is often noted that the dominance of these beliefs inhibited the development of medical science in ancient Israel. The professionals nearest to physicians were the priests, but their functions were limited to instruction in health care and the certification of the existence or nonexistence of certain social diseases. The book of Job is a protest against a crude expression of the old dogma that all sickness and misfortune are God's punishment for, and an exposé of, sin. It is twice reported in the Gospels that Jesus also rejected this notion, still current in his time (Luke 14:1-5; John 9:1-3). The corrections are not to be understood, however, as a denial of all connection between health and salvation or between illness and sin. The metaphorical reference to disease as characterizing a culture's spiritual malaise, expresses a belief in an inner relationship between sin and sickness, that God willed the physical as well as the spiritual renewal and well-being of his people (Isa. 1:4-6, 16-20).

*The Mosaic Law and Health.* Israel's Torah (especially the book of Leviticus) contains principles and legislation concerning health care that were a great advance over those of other Near Eastern cultures. Emphasis is placed upon the prevention of disease rather than its cure. For example, the institution of the Sabbath prevented the overexertion of labor as well as provided occasions for spiritual growth. It also extended the idea of Sabbath rest to the land, so that its mineral resources were preserved. Laws regarding edible foods and their preparation were safeguards against food poisoning and parasite infestation. Laws governing sexual relationships prevented the deleterious effects of incest and served to curb promiscuity and bestial behavior. Sexual hygiene, like other rules pertaining to cleanliness and public sanitation, prevented the spread of common communicable diseases.

*Healing and Health in the NT.* All of the Gospels, especially Luke, use "to heal" with reference to Jesus' mission (Luke 5:17; 6:19; 13:32). Jesus is reported to have called himself a physician (Luke 4:23). As noted above, Jesus rejected the dogma of retribution in its non-exceptional form, but he perceived that in some cases illness was attributable to sin, that his power over disease was evidence of his power to forgive sin (Mark 2:1-12 and parallels; John 5:14), and overcome evil (Mark 3:27 and parallels). Casting out demons and performing cures were essentially a part of his divine commission (Luke 13:32).

The accounts of Jesus' healing ministry stress the importance of faith, of belief that the hoped-for kingdom of God was being manifested in "signs and wonders" (Matt. 12:25-29; Luke 11:17-23: also Matt. 11:20-24; Luke 10:13-15). While there is no explicit demand that the persons healed acclaim Jesus' messiahship, his citation of Isaiah 35:5-6 implies that an essential connection existed between his healing ministry and his messianic mission (Matt. 11:2-6; Luke 7:18-25). Whether John the Baptist and/or the disciples saw this connection during Jesus' lifetime is uncertain, but after his passion, death, and resurrection, this faith was an essential part of the Christian gospel (Acts 20:38; also 3:1-10; etc).

Historians of religion have held that although Jesus' cures are not an isolated phenomenon in late antiquity, the miracle stories of the Gospels may be distinguished from their "parallels" with respect to the form and content of the narratives and to the motives attributed to their healer. No magical formulas are employed by Jesus, the common means of healing is Jesus' word of power (Mark 1: Luke 4:36; Mark 2:10 and parallels; Matt. 8:8-10; Luke 7:6-9).

This power Jesus gave to his apostles as part of their mission heralding the imminent coming of the Kingdom, a mission they began before Jesus' death but continued afterward with great effectiveness (Mark 3:14-15: Matt. 10:1; Acts 3:1-10; 8:4-8). The apostles declared that the cures they wrought were operations of the exalted Christ or evidence of the power of the Holy Spirit (Acts 3:16; 9:34; Rom. 15:18-19). In Paul's letters one reads that members of the Gentile churches exhibited "gifts of healing" that, along with other charismatic powers, were to be employed not for self-glorification but for the common good (I Cor. 12:4-11). The apostle Paul was plagued with a persisting, debilitating illness. He earnestly prayed to be delivered from it, but Paul's own gift of healing was not to benefit him: God's power was to be manifested in the apostle's weakness (II Cor. 12:7-10.)                                          J.P.

**HEART.** *Physical.* The heart is referred to more than seven hundred times in the Bible but almost never as a physical organ. The clearest such use is in II Kings 9:24, where Jenu shot an arrow through the heart of Joram. Only one or two other such references may be found in the entire Bible (for example, I Sam. 4:13ff., which may refer to a heart attack, and Ezek. 11:19; 36:26). Almost all other occurrences to the heart are metaphorical.

*Religious.* One of the most important uses of the term is to express the Israelite's total devotion to monotheism. This is stated as serving God "with all one's heart and soul" (Deut. 13:3; 26:16; 30:2, 6, 10; Josh. 22:5; II Kings 23:3; II Chr. 15:12; Jer. 32:41).

When Jesus emphasized this point to a scribe on one occasion, he gave a standard Jewish reply to the question of what the greatest commandment was by quoting the Shema (Deut. 6:4-5), which is an expansion of the formula "heart and soul" to include also mind and strength (Mark 12:30). King Solomon's idolatrous wives are described as having turned his heart away from the Lord (I Kings 11:2-13). That this is an intellectual activity is indicated in verse eleven. The expression "heart and mind" is frequent in the Scripture (I Sam. 2:35; Pss. 26:2; 64:6; Jer. 17:10; 20:12). From the Jewish perspective, to be lacking in monotheistic religious conviction is to be "uncircumcised in heart and flesh" (Ezek. 44:7-9; Acts 7:51). They who are spiritually dull are descibed as being slow of heart to believe (Luke 24:25).

*Intellect.* In general, it may be observed that the range of meanings given to the term in Scriptures is essentially the same as that found in modern society. At times the word "heart" refers to the intellect, as in the following passages: "The fool says in his heart, 'There is no God,' " (Ps. 14:1); "Let the words of my mouth, and the meditation of my heart, be acceptable in thy sight" (Ps. 19:14); "A heart that devises wicked plans" (Prov. 6:18); "you shall indeed hear but never understand . . . for this people's heart has grown dull" (Matt. 13:14ff); "And his mother kept all these things in her heart" (Luke 2:51). The heart is the source of wicked thoughts as well (Matt. 15:19).

*Emotion.* Another use of the term is to refer to human emotion. First Peter speaks of a "tender heart" (3:8) and Paul asks "what are you doing, weeping and breaking my heart?" (Acts 21:13). Jesus spoke to his doubting disciples on the Sea of Galilee: "Take heart, it is I; have no fear" (Matt. 14:27). The idea is more fully expressed in Proverbs where one of the authors says, "A glad heart makes a cheerful countenance, but by sorrow of heart the spirit is broken" (15:13). Similarly Jeremiah says, "My heart is broken within me" (23:9).

*Volition.* At times the human will is intended by the term. A vivid example is the response of Simon Peter to Simon the Sorcerer: "Repent therefore of this wickedness of yours, and pray to the Lord that, if possible, the intent of your heart may be forgiven you" (Acts 8:22). The author of Hebrews writes that the word of God discerns "the thoughts and intentions of the heart" (4:12). Other instances may be found in Psalm 24:4; Proverbs 3:1; and Galatians 6:9.

*Conscience.* Occasionally the conscience is referred to by the term "heart" as when David writes: "Create in me a clean heart, O God, and put a new and right spirit within me" (Ps. 51:10). The anonymous author of Psalm 94:15 speaks of the "upright in heart," while David insists on "integrity of heart" (Ps. 101:2). Paul exhorts Timothy to "call upon the Lord from a pure heart" (II Tim. 2:22).                                        J.R.M.

**HEAVEN.** In the ancient world, among peoples of the Bible and their neighbors, "heaven," or "the heavens," had a double reference. Basically heaven denoted the visible sky. Nearest to sight was "the firmament," perceived to be a bell-shaped covering, enclosing the earth, and supported by pillars, dividing the upper waters from the flat earth and from the watery depths below the earth (II Sam. 22:10-13; Job 38:4-11; 26:11-13; Isa. 40:22). Affixed to this (metallic?) firmament were the moon and starry hosts; rain fell through the gates of heaven, snow and hail, and through this lower heaven clouds formed and birds flew (Gen. 1:20; Ps. 8:3-4). Stretching beyond the firmament lay the vastness of space, "the highest heaven," or "the heaven of heavens" (Deut. 10:14; I Kings 8:27).

Closely allied to this common view concerning the near and distant heavens was the other belief that in a space or spaces above the earth the gods and other superterrestrial beings dwelt. For Jews and Christians there was but one God, the creator of heaven and earth and all that in them is (for example, Isa. 45:18, 22-23; Exod. 20:1-6; I Cor. 8:3-6; Ps. 102:25-27). As the High and Holy One, God is depicted as enthroned in heaven or above the heavens (Pss. 11:4; 57:5; 108:5; Isa. 57:15). Yet, God is not a solitary being, in splendid isolation from creation, unchanging and impassive. In several OT passages God's throne-room is the setting for a council of living creatures who serve God in the governance of the world (I Kings 22:19-23; Pss. 82:1; 91:11-13; compare Luke 12:8; Rev. 3:5). In Jewish and early Christian apocalypses this "angelology" receives a remarkable development. Jewish apocryphal and pseudepigraphical texts, which lie behind Christian tradition, are replete with angels and archangels, lords, authorities, guardian angels, and princes of nations. The Christian book of Revelation is a fine example of this rich profusion of "living creatures" populating heaven. Besides the good angels who sing praises to God and the Lamb (Jesus Christ), there is in heaven a host of evil spirits, arch-rebels under the command of Satan, who are able to war in heaven and wreak havoc on earth (Rev. 1:4; 20:4; 12:1-12; compare I Cor. 5:3-5; 7:5; I Pet. 5:8-11; II Cor. 11:13-15). These evil "principalities and powers in the heavenly places" (Eph. 3:1-10) remain the enemies of Christ and his church, even after he had triumphed over them (Col. 2:11-15; Luke 10:17-20) and exposed their true nature. Thus a new heaven must appear as well as a new earth. Before this cosmic re-creation, Satan and his minions will be destroyed by God (Rev. 20:1-3, 7-10; I Cor. 15:23-28).

In both the OT and the NT the God of heaven is concealed from human sight. Yet references to the opening of (the door of) heaven manifest God's purpose to be revealed, God's plan of salvation and judgments, to the Lord's earth-bound creatures. In such passages the biblical doctrine of God's transcendence stands in tension with that of God's immanence (for example, Deut. 4:32-40; 10:14-22; 30:12-14; Isa. 57:15). A poignant aspect of the ESCHATOLOGY of the Bible is the yearning for a full disclosure of God's power and glory, among those who have received God's former revelations through the agency of Israel's prophets and visionaries, and, for Christians, in and through Jesus the Christ (Isa. 64:1; Ps. 11:4-7; Dan. 2:19-23; John 1:18, 51; 3:13; 6:30-33; Heb. 1:1-14; 12:25-29; Rev. 4:1-2; 21:1-4). The apostle Paul writes that Christians "wait for [God's] Son from heaven, whom he raised from the dead, Jesus who delivers us from the wrath to come" (I Thess. 1:10). Belief in Christ's RESURRECTION was the basis for belief in his present and future lordship. For the present, Christ's authority is concealed by his heavenly session; it is, however, nonetheless real (Acts 3:21; Matt. 28:18-20). The opening of heaven is directly related to the Messiah's revelation, from its beginning to its consummation.

The diversity of the word-pictures in our sources concerning the life of the blessed after their deaths prevents the formulation of logically consistent views. It is, however, clear from the NT that not only Jesus and the first Christians, but also the Pharisees believed that by God's power the elect would be raised from death. This miracle is often associated with the Last JUDGMENT, after which the redeemed will enjoy everlasting life (Dan. 12:1-3; Isa. 35:3-10; Matt. 25:31-46). Sayings of Jesus and of Paul exclude the notion that the human physical organism survives; the resurrection of the believer's "spiritual body" takes place with the final Coming of Christ to judge and save his own (I Thess. 5:2-11; I Cor. 15:47-57; Phil. 3:20-21). But alongside this hope is the expectation that after death Christ's own are "at home with the Lord" (II Cor. 5:8). The meaning of these statements of the apostle Paul have been variously interpreted, but it is certain that he believed that the ultimate destiny of the redeemed is that they have "a house not made with hands, eternal in the heavens" (II Cor. 5:1; see also I Cor. 2:9; Rom. 8:34-39; I John 3:1-3).                                              J.L.P.

**HEAVE OFFERING.** Translation of Hebrew *terumah* signifying diverse sacrificial portions and offerings that were set apart (dedicated) from a larger mass and taken up ("heaved") initially for Yahweh and later for the priesthood. Among these sacred gifts were thank offering cakes (Lev. 7:12-14), the first yield of baked bread (Num. 15:19-20), the flesh of redeemed fatlings (Num. 18:15-18), and the tithe (Num. 18:24-29).                                              J.K.K.

**HEBER, REGINALD** (1783–1826). Anglican clergyman and prolific hymn writer. Heber, who was born in Cheshire, England, and educated at Brasenose College, Oxford, became one of the foremost nineteenth-century hymn writers. He wrote fifty-seven hymns, most of which are still in use. Throughout his ministry, Heber was particularly interested in overseas missions. Thus it can be understood that he would pen the popular missionary hymn, "From Greenland's Icy Mountains." In 1822, because of his involvement in world missions, he was made bishop of Calcutta. After three years in India, his health failed and he died at the age of forty-three. Some of his other widely known hymns are "Holy, Holy, Holy," "Brightest and Best of the Sons of the Morning," "God, That Madest Earth and Heaven," "Hosanna to the Living Lord," "The Son of God Goes Forth to War" "By Cool Siloam's Shady Rill," and "Bread of the World in Mercy Broken."        R.H.

**HEBREW.** Meaning "one from beyond, passing through." Biblical tradition presents the Hebrews as people from the other side of the Euphrates (Gen. 12:5; 14:13; Josh. 24:2-3). The name either indicates that the Hebrews were not indigenous Canaanite inhabitants or denotes their descent from Eber, who is introduced in the Table of Nations (Gen. 10) as their ancestor (vv. 21-24). Popularly derived from the name "Eber," the noun "Hebrew" closely resembles the noun "HABIRU," which denotes a rootless social stratum of mixed race and language widely known in the Near East throughout the second millennium B.C. Though some connection between the two nouns is probable, a precise etymological equation is unwarranted.

With few exceptions, the noun "Hebrew" is confined to OT narratives depicting the earliest phases of Israelite history. It is mainly found in the speech of foreigners, notably Egyptians and Philistines, who refer to the Israelites (Gen. 39:14, 17; 41:12; Exod. 2:6; I Sam. 4:6, 9; 14:11), or in the speech of Israelites concerned to identify themselves as foreigners (Gen. 40:15; Exod. 3:18; 5:3; 7:16). By the time of David (tenth century B.C.), the noun no longer enjoyed general use. In the NT, Paul uses it to emphasize the authenticity of his Jewish heritage (II Cor. 11:22; Phil. 3:5), and Luke refers to early Aramaic-speaking Christians as Hebrews (Acts 6:1).
J.K.K.

**HEBREW BIBLE.** The basic and most sacred collection of books of the Jewish people. In Hebrew the Bible is most commonly called TaNaKh—an acronym made up of the first letters of *Torah* ("Instruction," "Law"), *Nevi'im* ("Prophets"), and *Ketuvim* ("Writings"). According to Jewish tradition, the Bible contains twenty-four books. The Torah is made up of the five books of Moses, the Hebrew designations of which are based on the first significant word of each book: *Bereshis* ("In the beginning"); *Shemos* ("Names"); *Vayikra* ("And he [the Lord] called"); *B'Midbar* ("In the wilderness"); and *Devarim* ("Words"). *Nevi'im* is divided into two parts: (1) *Nevi'im Rishonim* ("Former Prophets"): Joshua, Judges, I, II Samuel, I, II Kings; and (2) *Nevi'im Aharonim* ("Later Prophets"): Isaiah, Jeremiah, Ezekiel, and the twelve (minor) Prophets. *Ketuvim*

contains Psalms, Proverbs, Job, the five *Megillot* ("Scrolls"), Daniel, Ezra (including Nehemiah), and I, II Chronicles. If each volume is counted separately, the total number is thirty-nine. While Christians refer to the Hebrew Bible as the OT, Jewish believers feel that there are no interpolations in the Hebrew Bible that point the way toward Jesus.

Some Jewish scholars maintain that the differences between Christianity and Judaism may be contingent on the translations of the Bible into Greek. The original Hebrew words took on, in the Greek translation, connotations that were not intended by the Hebrew authors, with the result that they suggested views and ideas entirely alien to the Jewish spirit. One of the many examples is the origin of the virgin-birth dogma in Christianity, a concept that is associated with the mistranslation of the word *almah* (Isa. 7:14). In Hebrew, *almah* merely means "young woman." The Greeks mistakenly rendered it *parthenos*, which means "virgin." Another example is the Hebrew word *ruah*, which, in the Greek translation, connoted the non-Jewish concept of spirit versus body.

The Hebrew Bible occupies a central place in Jewish life and tradition. Its original texts were guarded zealously and scrupulously. The rabbis admonished against tampering with the original text of the Bible. They were opposed to translations, but within the Hebrew displayed considerable latitude with regard to interpretation. The Torah was likened by them to "a hammer that breaketh the rock in pieces" (Jer. 23:29), that is, just as the rock is split into many pebbles, so also may one biblical verse convey many meanings.

The traditional faith in the unlimited meaningfulness of the Hebrew Bible is expressed in the rabbinic exhortation: "Turn it over again and again, for everything is in it." (*See* HEBREW LANGUAGE.)
L.K.

**HEBREW CALENDAR.** The Hebrew calendar is largely linked to the cycle of the moon. Since Jewish festivals must be kept in their proper season, however, the calendar is adjusted every few years to the cycle of the sun.

According to the Bible, the first month is the spring month of Abib, or Nisan, as it is now known. The Jewish year, however, begins with the first day of the seventh month, Tishri. Apparently at one time there were two calendars, now reconciled in one.

The Jewish year is dated from what is believed to be the year of Creation. The time span between this and the year of the Christian Era is 3,760 years. The first of Tishri in A.D. 1985 will begin the Jewish year 5746.

Each month begins with the new moon. Generally, the Jewish year has twelve months of twenty-nine or thirty days each. This totals approximately 354 days. To keep the festivals from "wandering" through the seasons, an extra month is inserted in every Jewish leap year. This occurs seven times in every moon cycle of nineteen years.

The Bible records only four original Hebrew names of the months. The Hebrew names were dropped, however, and all twelve months now have names of Babylonian origin established after the Babylonian Exile.

Following are the months of the Hebrew calendar, their equivalents, and major holy days:

Tishri (September–October)
ROSH HASHANAH (New Year) Tishri 1 and 2
". . . in the seventh month, on the first day of the month, ye shall have a holy convocation: ye shall do no manner of servile work; it is a day of blowing the horn unto you" (Num. 29:1, JPS).
YOM KIPPUR (DAY OF ATONEMENT) Tishri 10
"And on the tenth day of this seventh month ye shall have a holy convocation; and ye shall afflict your souls; ye shall do no manner of work" (Num. 29:7).
SUKKOT (Feast of Tabernacles) Tishri 15-21
One of three Jewish pilgrim festivals (Exod. 23:16; Lev. 23:34, 39; Deut. 16).
Heshvan (October–November)
Kislev (November–December)
HANUKKAH (Feast of Dedication) Kislev 25–Tevet 2 or 3
Hanukkah celebrates the rededication of the holy Temple by the MACCABEES. The Temple had been defiled by the forces of the Syrian king Antiochus Epiphanes, who had tried to suppress the Jewish religion.
Tevet (December–January)
Shevat (January–February)
Adar (February–March)
PURIM (Feast of Lots) Adar 14
Purim celebrates the narrow escape of the Jews of Persia from being destroyed according to the plot and plan of Haman. God intervened through MORDECAI and Queen Esther.
Nisan (March–April)
Pesach (Feast of the Passover) Nisan 15-22
PASSOVER is a pilgrimage festival that celebrates the Jewish people's deliverance from Egyptian slavery through the intervention of God.
"In the first month, on the fourteenth day of the month at dusk, is the Lord's passover. And on the fifteenth day of the same month is the feast of unleavened bread unto the Lord; seven days ye shall eat unleavened bread" (Lev. 23:5, 6 JPS).
The "feast of unleavened bread" is called a SEDER. The Last Supper was a Seder.
Iyar (April–May)
Sivan (May–June)

SHAVUOT (Pentecost) Sivan 6 and 7
Shavuot is a pilgrim festival that comes seven weeks after Passover. One of its names is the Feast of Weeks. It celebrates God's giving of the TORAH (which includes the Ten Commandments) on MOUNT SINAI.
Tammuz (June–July)
Av (July–August)
Elul (August–September)
(See also JEWISH HOLIDAYS.)                L.K.

**HEBREW LANGUAGE.** The language of the religion, culture, and civilization of the Jewish people since ancient times. In the Bible, Hebrew is called *sefat Canaan*, the "language of Canaan" (Isa. 19:18). A member of the northwest Semitic family of languages, Hebrew is the only one of the ancient tongues spoken in the Near Eastern cradle of civilization that has survived to the present day.

The earliest literary records of the Hebrews, such as the Song of Moses, after passing through the Sea of Reeds (popularly known as the Red Sea), as well as the Song of Deborah, dating back probably to the thirteenth and eleventh centuries B.C., respectively, are written in pure Hebrew, as are the later Prophets. The first use of the term in Hebrew in referring to the Hebrew language is in the *Book of Jubilees*, which probably dates back to about the third century B.C.

Hebrew, as the language of the Scriptures, is known as "the holy tongue." The term is used because even when Aramaic displaced Hebrew as the spoken language of the people during the time of the Second Temple, Hebrew remained the language used for sacred purposes such as the liturgy in the Temple and later in the synagogue.

The Hebrew language, the literature of which covers a period of more than three thousand years, has gone through many changes in grammatical form and vocabulary content. During the first thousand years of Jewish history, Hebrew was a spoken language. During the next two thousand years Hebrew was mainly used for literary purposes and as the language of worship. In modern times, Hebrew has once again become a living language, and is the official language of the State of Israel.

The language may be classified according to the following categories: Biblical Hebrew, Haskalah Hebrew, Medieval Hebrew, Mishnaic Hebrew, and Modern Hebrew. The tongue continually absorbed outside influences such as Babylonian, Egyptian, Aramaic, Greek, Ugaritic, and Arabic.

The classical Hebrew of biblical literature has a unique stylistic and grammatical pattern. It is succinct, but rich in imagery and picturesqueness. For example: When a house is built by evil and sin, "the stone shall cry out of the wall, and the beam out of the timber shall answer it" (Hab. 2:11 KJV); "The heavens declare the glory of God" (Ps. 19:2 KJV); "The floods clap their hands; let the hills sing for joy

## Biblical Hebrew Alphabet

| Hebrew | Name | Latin |
|---|---|---|
| א | aleph | ' |
| ב | beth | b, bh |
| ג | gimel | g, gh |
| ד | daleth | d, dh |
| ה | he | h |
| ו | waw | w |
| ז | zayin | z |
| ח | heth | ḥ |
| ט | teth | ṭ |
| י | yod | y |
| כ,ך | kaph | k, kh |
| ל | lamed | l |
| מ,ם | mem | m |
| נ,ן | nun | n |
| ס | samekh | s |
| ע | ayin | ' |
| פ,ף | pe | p, ph |
| צ,ץ | sadhe | ṣ |
| ק | qoph | q |
| ר | resh | r |
| שׂ | sin | ś |
| שׁ | shin | sh |
| ת | taw | t, th |

*Biblical Hebrew Alphabet*

together" (Ps. 98:8). When God was angry, "smoke went up from his nostrils" (Ps. 18:8). When the sun rises, it is "like a bridegroom leaving his chamber, and like a strong man runs its course with joy" (Ps. 19:5).

The ancient Hebrew texts of the Bible were transmitted in a consonantal form of writing. There were no signs, or very scanty and inadequate signs, to indicate vowel sounds. When the MASORETES of the seventh and eighth centuries A.D. undertook to fix the Hebrew vocalization, they treated the texts all alike, regardless of how old the texts were, in accordance with the traditional pronunciation prevalent in Palestine during the age of the Talmud. The system was adopted as the norm for Hebrew texts and has remained the basis for Hebrew grammar down to modern times.

The Hebrew alphabet consists of twenty-two letters. Transliterated, they are: aleph, bet, gimel, dalet, he, vav, zayin, het, tet, yod, kaph, lamed, mem, nun, samekh, ayin, pe, zade, koph, resh, shin, and tav. (See chart.)

According to Hebrew tradition, the text of the Torah that was given to Moses at Mount Sinai had no vowel signs. The Torah Scrolls to this day are unvocalized so that the commandment in the Bible, ". . . thou shall not add thereunto" (Deut. 13:1), is not violated.

A number of vowel systems developed. Three systems are not extant: the Babylonian, the Palestinian, and the Tiberian. The first two are preserved only in a few ancient manuscripts. The Tiberian system is the one now in use. The basic unit is the dot. The varying position, as well as the change in the arrangement and the number of the dots, determines the sound values of the vowels in their variations. The system also includes one short line. With two exceptions, the vowel signs are below the consonants.

Hebrew is read from right to left. The source of the original Hebrew script is shrouded in obscurity. The square script now used in printed Hebrew has been in vogue only since the time of Ezra and Nehemiah (about 430 B.C.).

The one person who must be given credit for the modern revival of Hebrew as a spoken tongue and for enriching its vocabulary is Eliezer ben Yehudah (1858–1922). Born in Lithuania, he settled in Jerusalem in 1881, where he began his fanatic fight to introduce Hebrew as the language of instruction in the schools. A journalist and editor of several Hebrew journals, he strongly urged that Hebrew be used as the spoken language by young and old alike. In this he never compromised, and in his private life he would refuse to speak any other language to members of his family or to his friends. He organized and built the *Vaad Ha-Lashon* (Council for the Development of Hebrew) and devoted himself stubbornly and heroically to his life work, the *Dictionary of the Hebrew Language*.

Because of the unique experiences of the Jewish people, Hebrew has incorporated a great many religious ideas and concepts that have been adopted by other people. Hebrew has influenced English, largely through the process of translating the Bible into the King James Version and through Shakespeare. Many of the early American settlers were good Hebraists and were deeply rooted in the original biblical literature. Samuel Johnson, the first president of King's College, now known as Columbia University, declared in 1759 that "Hebrew was a gentleman's accomplishment." He further asserted that "as soon as a lad had learned to speak and to read

English well, it is much the best to begin a learned education with Hebrew . . . the mother of all languages." A number of Hebrew words and expressions are interspersed in the writings of Cotton Mather. Ezra Stiles, president of Yale University, assigned to Hebrew a predominant place in the college curriculum. Hebrew likewise ranked high in the curriculum of Harvard. The lower schools also attempted to provide instruction in Hebrew. Governor William Bradford, second governor of Plymouth Colony, was said to have studied Hebrew most of all languages so that "he would see with his own eyes the ancient Oracles of God in their native beauty." (See also LANGUAGES OF THE ANCIENT NEAR EAST AND OF THE BIBLE.)                                    L.K.

**HEBREWS, LETTER TO THE.** One of the most obscure letters in the NT Canon, posing still unresolved questions about its author, its first recipients, its date, and even its genre as a letter, Hebrews still claims the attention of Bible readers. Two factors make this so. One is that this lengthy document stands out as a unique specimen in the NT collection; it reads like a sermon, or at least a spoken utterance (see 2:5; 8:1; 9:25; and 13:22 for marks of an oral style), employing rhetorical (11:32) and elegant features (1:1-4, which is a remarkable opening to any document). (We can well imagine how the author framed his words to catch and hold the hearers' attention.) The second distinctive lies in its contents. Passages from the OT are often used in full quotation, with twenty-nine actual citations and about seventy allusions, and the author's purpose is clear: to use the ceremonies and rites of the Jewish religion as a foil to proclaim the excellence of the Christian gospel. In his estimation, Judaism existed to prepare for and point to the religion of the new COVENANT, so that with the dawn of the New Age of Christ's coming Jewish practices no longer have validity or meaning (8:1-13; 10:1-18; 11:39, 40; 13:10). We may infer that there was a historical circumstance for this position, and most scholars find it in the threat facing the letter's readers as they were in danger of lapsing into the Jewish faith, which they had left on becoming believers in Jesus the Messiah of Israel.

*The Recipients.* The traditional view is that this document was intended as a warning to Hebrew Christians who were on the point of apostatizing and slipping back into their ancestral faith. They had been disowned by their fellow Jews (10:32-34) and were wistfully looking back in a time of persecution to their former life. The letter, in this view, is essentially a call to go forward, not back (6:1), and the appeals that punctuate the letter's theoretical argument (for example, 4:1, 14: 10:22; 12:28) are intended to awaken and alert the recipients to their present duty.

The problem with this older interpretation lies with the nature of the Judaism from which the readers had turned. There are signs that it cannot have been Palestinian Judaism as we normally understand that term, admittedly vaguely defined. The links with Alexandrian Judaism, that is, the Hellenistic features that are found in the Judaism of the Dispersion, notably in Egypt as represented by Philo, are too numerous to ignore, and they suggest a readership in the Greek-speaking, Hellenistic culture where Jews lived in the first century A.D. The ties between the Jewish ceremonials and those of the Dead Sea Scrolls are tenuous; and the most we can say is that the first addressees were a body of people who were threatened to abandon their Christian faith and embrace a type of Christianity, partly Jewish, partly pagan (3:12; 10:26: both texts suggest a lapse into irreligion, even atheism), which the author sees as totally inferior to the Christian message.

One or two other matters need to be mentioned in an attempt to pinpoint the clear and present danger overhanging the readers. The letter places strong emphasis on the full humanity of Jesus (whose human name is especially noteworthy in the document, occurring by itself ten times, and placed at the close of the sentence for emphasis). His real incarnation (2:14), his genuine temptation (2:17, 18; 4:15), his fidelity to death (2:9; 13:12), and his being obedient through suffering (5:7-9)—these are all telltale signs that the readers were neglecting the human side of Christ's person, probably on the mistaken idea that he was a semidivine character. The presence of Docetism (that is, denying Christ's real humanity) may be suspected as in the background of the recipients' embrace of a heterodox faith.

The other side is the stress this letter places on the promise of Christ's parousia or return in glory (9:28). The readers were evidently puzzled over the nonappearance of their Lord and the windup of the age; hence the author has to reassure them, on the basis of the OT (Hab. 2:3-4), that the Lord will soon come and that they should not abandon their hope (10:35-39; see 10:25 for the practice effect of what the jettisoning of this hope entailed).

*Reasons for Writing.* We have already touched on some of the reasons why this composition was sent out, on the basis, it may be, of a homily the author had given (13:22). In essence, the point of the letter is to call the congregation—possibly a set of house fellowships—to recognize their identity as the pilgrim people of God and to live accordingly. Their overlooking of the true marks of the church brought on two disfiguring features, which the author warns against. First, the ethical laxity that had afflicted the community is obvious from 12:16; 13:4; coupled with a reluctance to face the rigors of Christian discipleship (12:3-11). Hence, the writer's stern call to holiness of living. Second, the author's severest words are directed against the slide into apostasy on the part of the readers (6:4-9; 10:26-31). These sections have given rise to serious questions about whether Christians may be readmitted to the church's fellowship.

The insistence of our epistle is to be persevering (12:1) and not to allow its readers to quit the race (2:1; 4:1). The author's great fear is that his friends will fail to reach the heavenly city (13:14) which, to the vision of faith (11:1), already exists (12:12-18). He summons the people to obey their leaders (13:7, 17, 24) and to remain true to their baptismal pledge (3:1; 4:14; 10:23) as they fix their minds on the example of Jesus, who endured suffering and won through to find victory because he was obedient and faithful (4:14-16; 5:7-10; 12:2).

*Dating.* The critical issue is whether the fall of the Jerusalem Temple in A.D. 70 is already a thing of the past for the author. If it is, it is surprising he never refers to it as a proof of God's judgment on Israel. On the other hand, his preoccupation is rather with the tabernacle in the wilderness in Moses' time than with the actual Temple, whether past or present. References to suffering in "former days" (10:32) may look back to Nero's persecution in A.D. 65—if the church in question is at Rome. More decisively, in one place (2:3) the author puts some distance between himself and the apostles whose memory is invoked (13:7). It seems that several decades separate the letter's composition from the age of Paul and Peter; and we place the date around A.D. 80. But nothing is certain in this inquiry, and the message of Hebrews does not depend on a precise setting.

R.M.

**HEBRON.** An OT city, located near Mamre and probably identical to the contemporary city of El Kahlil (Arabic), which lies eighteen miles southwest of Jerusalem. Hebron was a royal city, built seven years before Zoan in Egypt (Num. 13:22). The ruler of Hebron in the fourteenth century B.C., Shuwardata, is mentioned in the letters found at Tel-el-

From *Atlas of the Bible* (Thomas Nelson & Sons Limited)

*Aerial view of the setting for the ancient city of Hebron*

From *Atlas of the Bible* (Thomas Nelson & Sons Limited)

*The town of Hebron*

Amarna. Abraham bought a field near Hebron, Machpelah, and buried his wife Sarah in a cave there. During the Hebrew conquest, Joshua destroyed Hebron. The site was given to Caleb and later to the Levites, for a city of refuge.

Hebron is closely connected with David, as he was anointed king of Judah there, and six of his sons were born there during his seven-year reign. Later, during his rebellion, David's son Absalom used Hebron as his headquarters. At the time of the Exile (586 B.C.), the Idumeans (Arabs) occupied Hebron. Judas Maccabeus destroyed it in 164 B.C., after which time it was rebuilt. Herod the Great constructed elaborate memorial buildings over the cave of Machpelah in honor of Abraham. The city was destroyed again during the Roman-Jewish war in A.D. 68.

J.C.

**HECKER, ISAAC THOMAS** (1819–88). The founder of the PAULIST FATHERS was born December 18, in New York City, the youngest son of John and Caroline Freund Hecker. Baptized a Lutheran and associated for a while with the Methodists, he met Orestes Brownson in 1841, and became active in the Workingmen's Party. Toying with transcendentalism, he visited Brook Farm in 1843, Bronson Alcott's Fruitlands, and lived for a time with the Henry David Thoreau family.

He was baptized a Roman Catholic August 1, 1844, and was confirmed in 1845. He began a novitiate in the Redemptorist order in St. Trond, Belgium, in 1845. Ordained a priest on October 23, 1849, in London, he returned to the United States in 1851, and wrote *Questions of the Soul* (1852) and *Aspirations of Nature* (1857).

With four other converts, he felt the need for an English-speaking order to evangelize American Protestants. Applying to Rome in 1857 they were encouraged by Pius IX to form the Missionary Priests of St. Paul the Apostle in July 1858 in New York City. Keen on communications, Hecker founded the *Catholic World* in 1865, organized the Catholic Publication Society in 1866, and founded the *Young Catholic* in 1870. He died on December 22.

N.H.

**HEDONISM.** From the Greek word for pleasure, (1) an ethical theory holding that pleasure alone is desirable and the highest criterion for human action, and (2) a psychological theory affirming that pleasure and pain—past, present, or anticipated—determine human behavior.

*Ethical hedonism* teaches that only pleasure is desirable in itself, and that only pain is undesirable. Achieving the highest degree of pleasure and avoiding as much pain as possible provide the norms for action that can be called right and good. In various forms, hedonism has been taught by thinkers from the Hellenic period to the present. The teaching that pleasure is the highest good was already strong in the time of Socrates (469–399 B.C.). Plato (427–347 B.C.), in the *Philebus,* raises questions about hedonism that remain basic: What is meant by "pleasure"? Are there pleasures that are better than others? Does this not require criteria beyond pleasure alone? and Does this not lead beyond hedonism toward a wider conception of happiness and fulfillment?

UTILITARIANISM as formulated by Jeremy Bentham (1748–1832) teaches that the highest good is the greatest happiness for the greatest number, calculated according to what produces the most pleasure and the least pain. John Stuart Mill (1806–73), influential philosopher and social reformer of the nineteenth century, expanded the utilitarian criteria of happiness to include self-realization and general societal welfare.

*Psychological hedonism* affirms that the goal of pleasure actually determines human behavior. Though difficult to verify or falsify, psychological hedonism tends to use the circular argument that people seek pleasure, and that what people seek gives them pleasure.

Ethical hedonism and psychological hedonism do not entail each other; nor does either provide support for the other. Hedonism will persist in variant forms, especially popular ones, but persuasive arguments questioning its adequacy have existed since the earliest periods of human thought.

C. Mc.

**HEGEL, GEORG W. F.** (1770–1831). The greatest of the German idealist philosophers and one of the most fertile minds in the history of European thought. Hegel had a profound influence on Christian theology in the nineteenth century. Born in Stuttgart, he studied theology at Tübingen and served as a private tutor in Berne and in Frankfurt. Hegel joined the faculty at Jena in 1801 and was appointed professor in 1805. From 1808 to 1816 he served as rector of a gymnasium at Nuremberg in Bavaria. He returned to professorships in philosophy at Heidelberg (1816–18) and Berlin (1818–31), by which time he had gained unrivaled prominence in Germany. Chief among his books are *The Phenomenology of Mind* (1807), *The Science of Logic* (1812–16), *The Encyclopedia of the Philosophical Sciences* (1817), *The*

Courtesy of the Library of Congress

*Georg Wilhelm Friedrich Hegel*

*Philosophy of Right* (1821), and *Lectures on the Philosophy of Religion* (1832).

Hegel brought the insights of Enlightenment RATIONALISM and nineteenth-century ROMANTICISM together into a grand synthesis. During the early years as a private tutor he came under the influence of Kant and wrote a "Life of Jesus" (1795) under his inspiration. However, in *The Spirit of Christianity and Its Fate,* Hegel broke with Kant and depicted Jesus as departing from the estrangement inherent in Hebrew religion—what he called "the contrite consciousness"—and restoring humankind's original unity through love, a love that heals the division between duty and inclination. Here the beginnings of Hegel's concern to reconcile dialectically the opposites of experience are apparent.

Between 1800 and 1807 Hegel developed a philosophy capable of accounting for a synthesis of intellect and emotion and of thought and life. He also came to a greater appreciation of the positive and historical nature of Christianity whose truth, he now believed, needed to be grasped and justified on a higher philosophical level. "The universal," he wrote, "must pass into actuality through the particular" or the historical, so that it might be seen in its rational necessity. Hegel thereafter sought to demonstrate that Christianity was the actualization of the unity of the divine and the human in the historical coming into being of Absolute Spirit. Hegel sees humanity's contrite or unhappy consciousness depicted in mythopoetic form in the biblical story of the

Fall of Adam. However, for Hegel the Fall is a necessary movement from innocence to self-consciousness, that is, to the knowledge of good and evil and freedom. It is also the necessary step toward reconciliation.

In God's Incarnation in Jesus Christ, the movement of reconciliation is begun. The *implicit* unity of God and humanity is made *explicit* in a concrete historical event. God passes from transcendent abstract idea into the historically immanent and finite. But the death of Christ actually symbolizes the destruction of finitude, that God's finitude is only a transitional moment in the emergence of Absolute Spirit. God dies as a being standing over us, the transcendent God of traditional theism. The coming of the Holy Spirit and the spiritual community or church represents the universal reconciliation of the Divine and the human implicit from the beginning. It is the goal of history, the advent of the Absolute Religion.

For Hegel the Holy Trinity is the symbolic representation of the entire dialectical process of the coming of Absolute Spirit. God becomes fully actualized only in the kingdom of the Spirit. God comes to full consciousness in and through the world, through the spiritual community. Hegel concludes that "the spirit of man which is to know God is only the spirit of God Himself." For Hegel it is the very "translation" of Christianity into philosophy that justifies and preserves it. The right-wing disciples of Hegel agreed and found in his philosophical translation a means of reconstructing Christian theology in the face of scientific criticism. Left-wing Hegelians, such as D. F. STRAUSS, Bruno Bauer, and L. FEUERBACH, discerned in Hegel the process of rationalizing and ultimately overcoming the Christian religion. Hegel's ambiguous relation to Christianity is a matter of dispute even today.

J.L.

**HEGIRA.** *See* HIJRA.

**HEIDEGGER, MARTIN** (1889–1976). A German philosopher, considered one of the leading exponents of EXISTENTIALISM, although his philosophy went far beyond what is commonly called existentialism. He believed that the central philosophical question is, What is the meaning of being? In his major work, *Being and Time* (1927), he sought to answer this question by inquiring into the being of the one who asks the question, that is to say, the human being. The question of being can be asked only because the DASEIN (or human being) already has some preconceptual understanding of being, given in its very existence.

Heidegger's account of Dasein given in the work cited has been a major contribution to philosophical anthropology and has influenced theologians, psychiatrists, educationists, and others. But this first approach to the question of being broke off, and in later writings Heidegger sought a more direct confrontation with being, which he could describe as "wholly other" to beings. His later style is obscure and verges on the mystical. He taught for most of his life at Freiburg and caused controversy by serving for a year as rector under the Nazi regime. He was the major philosophical influence behind BULTMANN's demythologizing.

J.M.

**HEIDELBERG CATECHISM** (1563). A German Reformed confession combining Calvinistic, Lutheran, and Zwinglian elements. PHILIP MELANCHTON helped reorganize Heidelberg University and introduced Lutheranism in the Palatinate. However, violent disputes erupted over the Lord's Supper. Desiring a conciliatory reformation, Frederick III, Elector of the Palatinate (1559–76), commissioned Zacharias Ursinus, a disciple of Melanchton, and Caspar Olevianus to write a harmonious catechism. Adopted in January 1563, the Heidelberg Catechism weathered stormy criticism to become one of the Reformation's most widely accepted statements of faith. Its 129 questions systematically treat misery, human redemption, and new life under thankfulness. It modifies predestination and stresses the Ten Commandments and devotional prayer.

C.M.

**HEILSGESCHICHTE.** A German expression, meaning "salvation history." Although it was already used in the nineteenth century, it is more commonly associated with the movement known as "biblical theology," which flourished in the middle decades of the twentieth century. BIBLICAL THEOLOGY was an attempt to expound Christian faith in concepts and even language drawn from the Bible itself, and salvation history was held to be one of the key concepts. On this view, the Bible is primarily the record of the "mighty acts" of God—the calling of Israel and its subsequent history, the sending of Jesus Christ in the "fullness of time," the founding and mission of the church, leading to the final consummation. One of the clearest expositions of salvation history was given by Oscar Cullmann in his book *Christ and Time*. He claims that at the heart of the biblical revelation is its understanding of time and history, and that theologians must put aside any other conceptions of time. In Cullmann's view, salvation history is coterminous with general history, but it is much narrower—it is like a scarlet thread running through the fabric of universal history. Unlike the cyclic understanding of time characteristic of paganism, biblical time is linear, with a beginning and an end and a mid-point (Jesus Christ). This conception of salvation history and its accompanying biblical theology has been severely criticized (see, for example, James Barr, *Semantics of Biblical Language*, 1961) and is no longer influential.

J.M.

**HELIOPOLIS.** One of the great cities of ancient Egypt, located in the Nile Delta, northeast of modern Cairo. It was a religious center rather than a political center, although it was a capital of lower Egypt. Heliopolis means "City of the Sun" in Greek, which is translated Beth-shemesh, "House of the Sun," in Hebrew. It was the center of Heliopolitan theology, which originated in the Third Dynasty. Its god, Atum, was identified with Re as Atum-Re, the god of the sun. Other deities included Isis, Osiris, Seth, and Nephthys, the gods of birth, death, hades, and rebirth. It was destroyed by Cambyses, the Persian emperor, according to the historian Strabo. The ruins contain the originl Obelisk, which symbolizes the hill on which Atum-Re stood after emergence from chaos. Jeremiah declared that the sacred pillars of Beth-shemesh would be smashed, thus pronouncing Yahweh's judgment on Egyptian religion.                J.C.

**HELL.** *See* GEHENNA.

**HELLENISM/HELLENISTIC.** The term "Hellenism" is difficult to define. It is best regarded as the goal and fulfillment of Alexander's dream of "one world," embracing a single culture—chiefly urban—and speaking a common language, *koine,* a form of GREEK.

The Maccabean revolt of 168–165 B.C. can be seen best as the conflict between adherents of Torah Judaism and those who professed to be Jews but had imbibed the spirit of Hellenism. The actual term "hellenization" or adopting "the Greek way of life" is met in the literature of this period (II Macc. 4:10, 13). From this history we can itemize what Hellenism meant: a freedom in regard to the human body expressed in athletics and concern for physical prowess; social life centered on the stadium and theater, borrowed respectively from the Greek games at Olympia and Corinth, and the Athenian love of dramatic and pictorial art; and above all, a city-oriented type of living, with a love of learning in the fields of philosophy, science, and culture, for which the symbol was the library, the debating hall, and the covered walkways in which the philosophers conversed and from which the Stoics got their name.

All this posed a threat to traditional Judaism, which saw God's revelation to Moses (in Torah) as the essence of all wisdom and knowledge (a thought expressed in Sirach's writings) and its final embodiment.

Hellenists in the NT (see Acts 6:1) were evidently bilingual Jews or, better, Jews who spoke only Greek, but even more, Jews who were open to Greek influences from the world of the DISPERSION and were represented by the liberal outlook of Stephen (Acts 7) and his followers (Acts 11:19-20), leading to Saul of Tarsus, a Hellenistic Jew who became a missionary to the Greco-Roman cosmopolitan world (Rom. 1:14-16).                R.M.

**HELVETIC CONFESSIONS.** Two ecumenical Swiss Reformed confessions. The First Helvetic Confession (1536) compiled by Heinrich Bullinger and others, united Switzerland's Protestant cantons. The Second Helvetic Confession (1566), written by Bullinger and published by Palatinate Elector Frederick III, skillfully combined Calvinistic and Zwinglian theology. It united Reform churches in Switzerland and beyond.

C.M.

**HENRY, CARL F. H.** (1913– ). Evangelical theologian and journalist. He was born in New York City on January 22 to Karl F. and Johanna Vaethroeder Henry. Carl Henry received a B.A. from Wheaton College (Ill.) in 1938 and an M.A. in 1940. His B.D. from Northern Baptist Theological Seminary came in 1941 and a Th.D. in 1942. Boston University conferred the Ph.D. degree in 1949. He was married to Helga Bender on August 17, 1940, and ordained to the Baptist ministry in 1941.

Henry was an assistant professor, then professor, at Northern Baptist Theological Seminary from 1942 to 1947. In 1947 he became acting dean of Fuller Theological Seminary, Pasadena, and professor from 1947 to 1956. He gained worldwide fame through his career as founding editor in 1956 of the the newly launched *Christianity Today,* which was a major

Courtesy of the National Association of Evangelicals

*Carl F. H. Henry*

factor in acquainting the Christian world with a resurgence of evangelical theology. He continued with the magazine until 1977.

His book *The Uneasy Conscience of Modern Fundamentalism* (1948) revealed that EVANGELICALISM was concerned with social as well as personal ethics. Thereafter, a number of books have come from his prolific pen including his magnum opus, the six-volume *God, Revelation and Authority*.

Recognized as author, lecturer, educator, and theologian, Henry has spoken to gatherings on America's most prestigious campuses and in countries of every continent. For a number of years he has served as lecturer-at-large with WORLD VISION INTERNATIONAL.                                   R.M

**HENRY, MATTHEW** (1662–1714). English nonconformist, famed for the devotional commentary *Exposition of the Old and New Testaments* (1708–10), which was left unfinished but was completed by thirteen of his colleagues. His father, Philip Henry, was deprived by the Act of Uniformity (1662). Educated at Islington Academy and Gray's Inn, Henry chose theology over law and pastored Presbyterian congregations at Chester and Hackney.
C.M.

**HENRY VIII** (1491–1547). King of England from 1509 who broke papal authority in England, made himself head of the church, and tentatively approached Protestantism. Henry was Henry VII's second son. Arthur, the first son, died shortly after marrying Catherine of Spain. In 1503 a papal dispensation set aside the restrictions of Leviticus 21:14, allowing Henry's betrothal to Arthur's widow. After becoming king, Henry married Catherine. Henry supported papal supremacy; his children's succession depended on the legitimacy of the pope's dispensation. In 1521 he eagerly published *Assertion of the Seven Sacraments* against Martin Luther. For this Pope Leo X rewarded him with a new title, "Defender of the Faith." By 1527 Henry sought papal invalidation of his marriage to Catherine "for reasons of state," but Pope Clement VII refused. Emperor Charles V's army controlled Rome, and Catherine was Charles's aunt. At THOMAS CRANMER's suggestion, Henry sought a decision "out of God's Word" from Europe's universities. The answers favored Henry's plans. Cranmer immediately became a court favorite.

Henry then moved to break all papal ties. In 1530 he accused chancellor Cardinal WOLSEY of treason for breaking a 1353 statute of *Praemunire*, forbidding papal appointments in England. In 1532 he used the same statute to force the clergy to name him supreme head of the Church of England and give him a huge "gift" as well. The clergy also agreed to withhold from the pope the annates (first year's income) of each English benefice. By threatening to take those annates (which he later did), Henry got the pope to name Cranmer archbishop of Canterbury. Cranmer then nullified Henry's marriage to Catherine. Henry had already secretly married Anne Boleyn, mother of Elizabeth, born that same year, 1533. Parliament supported Henry in a series of new laws—made appeals to Rome illegal (1533), forbade papal dispensations and payment of Peter's pence (1534), passed the SUPREMACY ACT making Henry "supreme head" of the Church of England (1534), declared Princess Mary illegitimate, and named Elizabeth heir to the throne (1534). For refusing to affirm Henry's supremacy, THOMAS MORE and John Fisher were both executed (1535). In 1536 and 1539 Henry seized and dissolved England's 645 monasteries, using their assets for his own royal purposes.

Henry was by no means Protestant. Except for royal supremacy, his views were Catholic. Henry made political overtures to the Germans in 1536 and issued his partially Protestant Ten Articles. But Henry could not accept the Augsburg Confession. The Six Articles (1539) clearly reaffirmed his Catholicism.

Henry's marriages were hardly satisfying. Anne Boleyn was beheaded for adultery in 1536. That same year Henry married Jane Seymour; she died in giving birth to Edward in 1537. Thomas Cromwell attempted an alliance with Germany through the marriage of Henry to Anne of Cleves in 1540, but Anne was ugly; Henry had not previously seen her. The marriage was quickly nullified, and Cromwell was beheaded for favoring the Protestants. That same year Henry married Catherine Howard; she was beheaded for adultery in 1542. He married Catherine Parr in 1543; she survived him.

Henry allowed some religious changes. For instance, Cranmer brought out several Bibles. Henry read much of Tyndale's translations. Coverdale's Bible (1535), the first complete Bible in English, received tacit sanction. Matthew's Bible (1537) also bore the king's authorization. However, in 1543 and 1546 Henry proscribed lay Bible reading, fearing such would produce radicalism. Before his death Henry appointed a committee, half Protestant, half Catholic, to guide his son EDWARD VI. Under Edward, with Cranmer leading, Protestantism flourished.                                   C.M.

**HERDER, JOHANN GOTTFRIED VON** (1744–1803). German philosopher, clergyman, and man of letters, Herder was a pioneer of the romantic revolt against Enlightenment rationalism. He studied at Königsberg, where he got to know both Kant and Hamann. He was unattracted by the prevailing emphasis on reason and stressed instead feeling and spontaneity. Because of this, he found Hamann congenial and was influenced also by the pantheistic tendencies in Bruno and Spinoza. Herder's own thinking ranged over such wide fields that it is impossible to summarize it. His main work was on the philosophy of history, but almost equally important were his researches into the origins and nature of language. These researches led him in turn to the study of Slavonic philology, on which he became an authority. Among his latest writings were severe criticisms of Kant's critical philosophy.

J.M.

**HERESY.** A Greek term for a peculiar philosophical position, which is used in a pejorative rather than a neutral way in the later books of the NT. In face of the Judaizing controvesy and the Gnostic systems of DOCTRINE, the apostles denounced "other gospels" as divisions and threats to the truth of the gospel and the unity of the church. By the second century, several heresies were identified by the church fathers. Augustine declared later that heretics violate the faith by thinking falsely about God.

Not every error in doctrine was considered heresy, for human beings are subject to misunderstanding and most people do not oppose the church's true teachings, even when they also hold some erroneous views. A heretic is one who thinks falsely about the faith and who also opposes the church's teaching, and moreover seeks to overthrow the church's position and replace it with his or her own. Many church fathers wrote extensively against various heresies, and lists of heresies were drawn up by Justin Martyr, Irenaeus, Hippolytus, Epiphanius, Augustine, and John Chrysostom. In the contemporary ecumenical era, most mainstream Protestants and Roman Catholics refrain from speaking of other denominations' beliefs in terms of heresy.

J.C.

**HERRMANN, WILHELM** (1846–1922). Professor of theology at Marburg, Herrmann had both Barth and Bultmann among his students. A follower of Ritschl, he tried to exclude metaphysics from theology, holding that theology is "only to be understood as the expression of new personal life." The "inner life" of Jesus, as attested in the NT, impresses modern readers in the same way as it did the first disciples, bringing them into communion with God. The witness of the NT is confirmed by the moral consciousness belonging to every human being. These teachings are expressed in Herrmann's book *The Communion of the Christian with God.*

J.M.

**HERMAS, SHEPHERD OF.** *See* SHEPHERD OF HERMAS.

**HERMENEUTICS.** Derived from the Greek term *hermeneutikos* (of or for interpreting), it means "the science of INTERPRETATION" or "the principles utilized for discovering the meaning of a text." Applied before the nineteenth century mainly to interpreting Jewish and Christian Scriptures, hermeneutics now includes methods for interpreting any text or situation.

*Early Centuries A.D.* Jewish interpretation of Scripture took the text in its plain meaning, with a continuing reinterpretation informed by (a) prominent events in Hebrew history, (b) stories called the "haddada," (c) applications of the Law called the "halakah," and (d) apocalyptic writings of postexilic Judaism. Hellenic interpretation of Homer and Hesiod developed the allegorical method in order to make these classics meaningful to later generations. Drawing on both these traditions, early Christian hermeneutics emphasized allegory (ALEXANDRIAN school) and a plain reading of Scripture (ANTIOCHENE school), with Jerome favoring the latter and Augustine the former.

*Middle Ages.* In the early Middle Ages, the allegorical method for interpreting Scripture was more prominent, though it was controlled by doctrine and patristic authority. Renewed influence from rabbinical sources led to modification of this tradition and the emergence of a fourfold hermeneutic combining historical, allegorical, moral, and spiritual principles.

*Renaissance and Reformation.* Humanist scholars emphasizing classical studies brought knowledge of Greek and Hebrew back to scriptural interpretation. Martin Luther (1483–1546) attacked ecclesiastical control of the Bible by the papacy and affirmed the competence of all Christians to interpret Scripture within the community of faith. In the wake of these influences, biblical studies developed and flourished. Johannes Cocceius (1603–69) utilized philology, history, Oriental studies and archaeology, and rabbinical sources for interpreting Scripture in a hermeneutic that foreshadowed the development of the modern study of the Bible.

*Modern Hermeneutics.* As critical methods became dominant in biblical studies following the Enlightenment, much creative work was done in the literary and historical study of the Bible. But the principles of interpretation tended to become restricted to the narrow horizons of positivistic objectivism. Hermeneutics in historical and philosophical studies has increasingly emphasized the presuppositions of the interpreter, the audience to whom interpretation is addressed, and the location of both interpreter and audience within particular communities of interpretation and sociocultural contexts. Hermeneutics in the post-critical era gives promise of combining the strengths of critical scholarship with the comprehensive horizons of pre-critical wholeness. (*See also* BIBLICAL CRITICISM.)

C.Mc.

**HERMES.** A god worshiped by the ancient Greeks as a giver of fertility and as the messenger of the gods. He was often identified with the Roman god Mercury. The people of Lystra in Asia Minor wanted to worship the apostle Paul as Hermes, because he was the chief speaker of the group (Acts 14:12).

K.C.

**HERMETISM.** An outlook or school of mystical religious thought related to the *Hermetica,* a series of religious and philosophical treatises attributed to Hermes Trismegistus, or Thoth-Hermes, scribe of the gods and god of wisdom. Containing material written by various authors between the second and fourth centuries A.D., the tracts include astrological elements from the Egyptian tradition, interest in secret rites and lore from Persia, and concern with regenerative experience and religious ecstasy from Hellenistic sources. Affinities with Judaism appear in some of the earlier treatises and with Gnosticism in the later ones. Though it was not a movement with cultus and organization, Hermetism had continuing influence in the Middle Ages and during the Renaissance.

C.Mc.

**HERMIT.** One who retires to a solitary life of asceticism and contemplation. Etymologically, hermit refers to one who lives in the desert, for in the early years of monasticism the Egyptian desert was a favorite place of retreat. In the East, eremitical monasticism still exists, while in the West it disappeared after the sixteenth century.

J.G.

**HERMON, MOUNT.** The great snow-covered mountain that forms the southern spur of the Anti-Lebanon range and is visible in Galilee and throughout northern Israel. Today it is called Jebel esh-Sheikh. Mount Hermon has three peaks, rising 9,232 feet above sea level. It is the highest mountain in the area of Syria and Israel. Historically, it formed the northern boundary of Hebrew conquest east of the Jordan River. In Judges 3:3, Mount Hermon is called Baal-hermon, showing its use as a center of Baal worship. References to majestic mountains in the Psalms and the Prophets of the OT probably reflect the awe the Israelites felt for Mount Hermon. Since it lies close to Caesarea Philippi, many commentators hold that it is the location of Jesus' transfiguration.

J.C.

**HEROD.** Readers of the NT may expect to meet no fewer than five people belonging to the generic family name of Herod, a powerful dynasty in Palestinian politics and religion from the middle of the first century B.C. to the end of the first century A.D.

Herod the Great is surnamed "king of the Jews" from 40 B.C. to A.D. 4, though he was only half Jewish. During the Roman occupation of Judea he played a significant role, aided the Romans, and was awarded an honorary title, "king." Never popular, he became obsessed with fear at losing his position and conducted a reign of terror against even his family, whom he regarded as rivals. He contributed much, however, to consolidating Israel through friendship with the Romans and magnificent building programs and expansion of his territory. He is the Herod

referred to in Matthew 1 and 2, where the slaughter of the Bethlehem babies is at least "in character" with his morbid fears.

At his death in 4 B.C. the kingdom was divided. One son, Archelaus, known as the ethnarch (Matt. 2:22), but not king, controlled Judea and Samaria (4 B.C.–A.D. 6). His repression of his people led to a revolt that was only averted by his being deposed and exiled, leaving Judea under direct Roman rule.

Herod the tetrarch (Luke 3:1, 19) is known as Antipas. Another son of Herod the Great, he was given Galilee as his domain in 4 B.C. This is the ruler whose role is seen in the imprisonment and death of John the Baptist (Matt. 14:1-12 and pars.), and in his encounter with Jesus, according to Luke 23:7-12. His character may be judged from the description "that fox" (Luke 13:32); yet he was the most capable of all Herod's sons, and built several important cities, for example, Tiberias on Lake Galilee. In A.D. 39 he was denounced to the emperor and banished from his realm.

Herod "the king" (Acts 12:1) carries the subtitle Agrippa; he was a grandson of Herod the Great. Already having been appointed the lands of northeast Palestine, he was awarded Antipas' kingdom in A.D. 39, when the latter was exiled. To these Judea and

Courtesy of the Museum of Fine Arts, Boston. Edwin L. Jack Fund

*Herod*

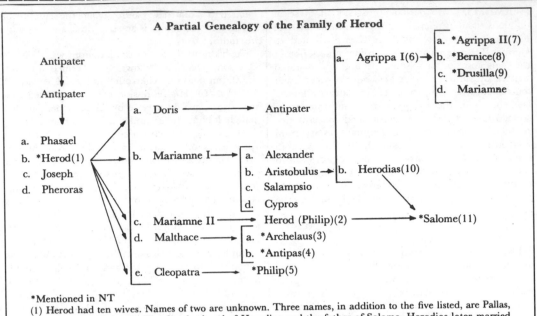

**A Partial Genealogy of the Family of Herod**

Antipater
↓
Antipater
↓

a. Phasael
b. *Herod(1)
c. Joseph
d. Pheroras

a. Doris → Antipater

b. Mariamne I → 
 a. Alexander
 b. Aristobulus → b. Herodias(10)
 c. Salampsio
 d. Cypros

c. Mariamne II → Herod (Philip)(2) → *Salome(11)
d. Malthace → 
 a. *Archelaus(3)
 b. *Antipas(4)

e. Cleopatra → *Philip(5)

a. Agrippa I(6) → 
 a. *Agrippa II(7)
 b. *Bernice(8)
 c. *Drusilla(9)
 d. Mariamne

*Mentioned in NT
(1) Herod had ten wives. Names of two are unknown. Three names, in addition to the five listed, are Pallas, Phaedra, and Elpis. (2) The first husband of Herodias and the father of Salome. Herodias later married Antipas. Salome married her uncle Philip, the son of Herod the Great and Cleopatra. (3) King of Judea. (4) Tetrarch of Galilee. (5) Tetrarch of Ituraea. (6) King of Judea. (7) King of Judea. (8) Mistress of Titus. (9) Wife of Felix. (10) First the wife of (2), then of (4); the mother of (11)

Samaria were added in A.D. 41. Thus he ruled over a wide realm. Acts 12:19-23 dramatically records his horrible death, an account to be supplemented by Josephus. This was in A.D. 44.

His only son, also known as Agrippa, was born in A.D. 27 and succeeded to his father's position in later life, receiving more territorial power at the bequest of Nero in A.D. 56. He was king in Israel during the tempestuous years of A.D. 66 onward, when the Great Jewish rebellion against Rome occurred. He tried to prevent this, and was later rewarded by the Romans, surviving until A.D. 100. His meeting and dialogue with Paul is in Acts 25:13–26:32.
R.M.

**HERODIANS.** The Herodians are mentioned three times in the Gospels: Mark 3:6; 12:13; Matthew 22:16. There are two separate incidents: (1) toward the beginning of Jesus' ministry, when his powers of healing so alarmed the Pharisees and the Herodians that they joined in laying a plan to destroy him; (2) a joint attempt between these groups to force Jesus to take a public stand on the touchy issue of paying taxes to the Romans. If he recommended paying it, he would be considered a traitor to the cause of Jewish nationalism. If he refused to pay it, he could be reported to the civil authorities as a subversive. Instead he forced his interrogators to determine what is to be rendered to Caesar and what rendered to God (Mark 12:17). The Herodians were not a religious group; they were the supporters of the Herodian rulers, especially of Herod Antipas, who was tetrarch

of Galilee from 4 B.C. to A.D. 34. They were presumably secularized people whose jobs or whose personal welfare depended on the continuance of the Herods in power.
H.K.

**HERODIAS.** The wife of Herod Antipas, tetrarch of Galilee from B.C. to A.D. 39, she was in part responsible for the death of JOHN THE BAPTIST (Mark 6:17; Luke 3:19). She was the daughter of Aristobulus, the son of Herod the Great and Mariamne. Her first husband was her uncle, Herod Philip, son of Herod the Great by another Mariamne. They had a daughter, Salome, though she is not necessarily the daughter mentioned in Mark 6:22. Herodias also urged Herod Antipas to move against her own brother Herod Agrippa I, tetrarch of Batanaea and Trachonitis (Acts 12:1). This effort brought down the wrath of Emperor Caligula, who banished them in A.D. 39.
N.H.

**HERODIUM.** A conical hill crowned by a palace, about nine miles southeast of Jerusalem. It was fortified by Herod the Great and designated by him as his place of burial. The architectural style was Hellenistic, with colonnades, baths, pools, and porticoes. This grand structure served as administrative center for this section of Judea. Herod apparently designed this enormous artificial cone in conscious imitation of the monumental mausoleum that Augustus had recently built for himself in Rome. Its facilities included pleasure rooms. It not only offered grand vistas across the Judean desert and the Jordan valley to the mountains eastward, but it also included a synagogue. Herod was careful to avoid any pictorial representations of humans or animals, since these would have offended pious Jews, whose laws forbade any "graven images."　　　　　　　　　　H.K.

**HERODOTUS.** Greek historian of the fifth century B.C. whose wide travels and keen observation can be seen in his nine books on *History.* Although his main theme is the war between Greece and Persia, he had also traveled to Egypt, to the east as far as Babylonia, and to other regions, and his narrative includes data from all those areas. His observations in the field of religion have long been a source for those who seek to reconstruct the beliefs of antiquity.　　　J.G.

**HERRNHUT.** Meaning "Watch of the Lord," this is a village on Count Nicolaus Ludwig von ZINZENDORF's Saxon estate near Dresden, East Germany, established by refugee Moravian United Brethren in 1722. Zinzendorf, a Lutheran Pietist, became the Moravians' leader in 1727. A. G. Spangenberg in Georgia and Peter Böhler in London greatly influenced the Wesleys. John Wesley visited Herrnhut in 1738.　　　　　　　　　C.M.

**HERZL, THEODOR** (1860–1904). The Austrian Jewish writer who was the founder of political ZIONISM. Born in Budapest, Herzl studied for the bar in Vienna but practiced journalism as his profession and was successful both as journalist and as playwright. The famous "Dreyfus affair" in Paris, involving a Jewish captain in the French army who was falsely accused of selling military secrets to Germany, created such an anti-Jewish agitation that Herzl was aroused to seek a solution to the plight of the Jewish people. In 1896, he published *The Jewish State: An Attempt at a Modern Solution to the Jewish Question.* The following year he called into being the first Zionist Congress in Basel, Switzerland. The result of the deliberations was a platform calling for a Jewish national home in Palestine recognized by international law. His campaign to influence European statesmen in behalf of the Zionist cause was unsuccessful, but Herzl persisted. As a result of his visit to Palestine, he wrote *Altneuland,* a novel depicting a modern Jewish state in the ancient land of Israel. It ended with the words, "If you will it, it is no dream," which became the slogan of political Zionism. Herzl's dream came true posthumously when the State of Israel was proclaimed in 1948.　　　　　　　　　　　　　　　L.K.

**HESCHEL, ABRAHAM JOSHUA** (1907–72). Jewish scholar and theologian. Born in Warsaw, Heschel received a thorough Jewish education in Poland. In 1934 he received his doctorate from the University of Berlin for a study on the biblical prophets. Deported by the Nazis in 1938, Heschel came to the United States in 1940 to teach at Hebrew

Courtesy of Lotte Jacobi

*Abraham J. Heschel*

Union College. He later became professor of ethics and mysticism at the Jewish Theological Seminary in New York. His published works range from studies on the piety of East European Jewry and the inward character of Jewish observance to religious symbolism, Jewish views of humanity, and contemporary moral and political issues. A descendant of two Hasidic dynasties, Heschel drew on both Hasidic tradition and modern existentialism. He described his teaching as "depth theology." Among his published works are *Man Is Not Alone* (1951), *Man's Quest for God* (1954), and *God in Search of Man* (1956). He was respected among American religionists of various faiths not only for his writings but also for his active role in the civil rights and peace movements of the 1960s and in the Judeo-Christian dialogue.

　　　　　　　　　　　　　　　L.K.

**HESYCHASM.** A form of MYSTICISM prevalent on Mount Athos in the fourteenth century. The term "hesychasm" is derived from the Greek word for "silence," since the hesychasts practiced sitting in silence for long periods. One of the earlier hesychasts, Gregory of Sinai, recommended sitting with the chin resting on the chest, looking at one's navel, and holding one's breath as long as possible, while repeating "Lord Jesus Christ, have mercy on me." This drew the ridicule of some who also supported closer ties with the Western church, and therefore the controversy over hesychasm soon became also a controversy over relations with the West. Gregory Palamas, one of the foremost Byzantine theologians of the time, came to the support of hesychasm—although not of its more extreme practices—and in 1351 a council declared itself in favor of hesychasm as an approved method of contemplation and condemned those who had ridiculed it.    J.G.

**HETERONOMY.** From the Greek words *hetero* (other or different) and *nomos* (law), meaning "subjection to external authority or law." Heteronomy is opposed to AUTONOMY, the condition of being self-governing. In the thought of Immanuel Kant (1724–1804), heteronomy refers to the limitations imposed on humanity by nature in the form of passions and desires as opposed to the autonomy of humans governed by reason. Paul Tillich (1886–1965) contrasts heteronomy as the imposition of alien laws on the human mind with THEONOMY, which provides a solution to the problems presented by human autonomy and fulfills human life with religious substance and ultimate meaning.    C.Mc.

**HEXAPLA.** A compilation made by Origen (A.D. 185–253) of the Hebrew text of the OT and five Greek translations in order to promote the study of the Bible. It is in six columns. Composed about A.D. 240, it contains a transliteration in Greek and the translatins of Aquila, Symmachus, the Septuagint (LXX), and Theodotion.    J.C.

**HEZEKIAH.** The Hebrew name meaning "Yahweh [is] my strength."

(1) King of Judah (about 715–687 B.C.), who succeeded his father, AHAZ, to the throne (II Kings 18:2; II Chr. 29:1). In II Kings 18, the Deuteronomic editor lavishly praises this able monarch for his nationalistic bent in foreign policy and impressive religious reform, which advocated the centralized worship of Yahweh in Jerusalem (vv. 3, 5-6). He was the antithesis of his anxious father, Ahaz, who was a submissive, tribute-paying vassal of Assyria.

*Hezekiah's Religious Reform.* Judah's loyal Yahwists found Ahaz's syncretic policies intolerable. If heavy taxation designed to raise ample Assyrian tribute struck them as odious, so did Ahaz's willingness to install an Assyrian altar in the Jerusalem Temple (II Kings 16:10-18). Early in Hezekiah's reign, Judah's response to the Assyrian yoke became more restive. Perhaps under Hezekiah's lead, ancient covenant traditions, once maintained at the northern sanctuaries, were transferred to Jerusalem and became the basis of the king's reform program.

In any event, Hezekiah instituted a thorough cultic reform (II Kings 18:3-6; II Chr. 29–31). Presumably spanning many years, the reform likely began circumspectly and gained momentum after it appeared that Assyria was in no position to interfere. Hezekiah destroyed the paganizing high places,

which hitherto had enjoyed Ahaz's patronage. Moreover, Hezekiah shattered the bronze snake image (Nehushtan), a popular cult object allegedly fashioned by Moses, which rested in the Jerusalem Temple (II Kings 18:4). Given Hezekiah's resolve to purge Judah's worship of any foreign dross, his reform ultimately must have involved a repudiation of the Assyrian gods, which implied outright rejection of his vassal status.

According to the Chronicler, Hezekiah cleansed the Temple of its idolatrous cult paraphernalia (II Chr. 29:3-17), rededicated the venerable edifice with requisite offerings (29:18-30), and sponsored a Passover observance to which he invited pilgrims from the defunct northern state of Israel (30:1-27). Apparently, Hezekiah's hopes included the reunification of northern and southern Israel, which again would find in the Davidic throne and Jerusalem Temple its religio-political nucleus. Though Hezekiah evoked a favorable response from some inhabitants of the Galilean region and Manasseh, he was rebuffed by Ephraim. This reaction undoubtedly reflected sectional jealousies and a lack of nerve to abandon the sanctuary of Bethel, which had been reestablished by the Assyrians to rival Jerusalem (II Kings 17:27-28). Hezekiah's dream of a united Israel went unrealized, and the local shrines were only temporarily closed. Nevertheless, Hezekiah's reform made a difference. Indeed, with its defense of the ancestral Israelite faith, it must have improved the health of Judean society by appreciably reducing the economic exploitation against which Hezekiah's prophetic contemporary, Micah, railed (Jer. 26:16-19; Mic. 3:12).

*Hezekiah's Political Activity.* Signs of Assyrian weakness and Egyptian resurgence significantly shaped international relations during Hezekiah's tenure. Early in his Assyrian reign, SARGON II (721–705) failed to suppress a Babylonian rebellion headed by the Chaldean prince, Marduk-apaliddina ("Merodach-baladan" of II Kings 20:12). Campaigns that kept Sargon busy for a decade there and elsewhere offered Palestine needful respite from Assyrian intrusion. Also, under an emerging Twenty-fifth (Ethiopian) Dynasty, Egypt consolidated its power and sought anew to influence affairs in western Asia. When the Philistine city of Ashdod rebelled against Assyria in about 714, help was sought from Egypt and Judah. Though Egyptian envoys visited Hezekiah to enlist his cooperation in this rapidly expanding conspiracy, he apparently took seriously Isaiah's stern warning to remain aloof (Isa. 20). It was an astute move, for Egyptian assistance disintegrated, and by 712 Sargon crushed the rebellion and transformed Ashdod into an Assyrian province. Judah, however, was left undisturbed.

Sargon's death in 705 and the accession of his son, SENNACHERIB (704–681), afforded Assyria's enemies fresh opportunities to conspire. Marduk-apaliddina reestablished himself as king over Babylonia and for several years resisted Assyria's efforts to overthrow him. When he sent envoys to enlist Judah's participation, they were graciously received by Hezekiah, who showed them his Jerusalem armory (II Kings 20:12-19). Moreover, Hezekiah joined rulers of several Phoenician and Philistine cities in withholding tribute (18:7). Then, impressed with the vigorous Ethiopian king, Shabako, Hezekiah negotiated a treaty with Egypt, which evoked Isaiah's censure (Isa. 30:1-7; 31:1-3). That Hezekiah was a leader in the anti-Assyrian rebellion is clear from Sennacherib's own record that Hezekiah consented to the Jerusalem imprisonment of King Padi of Ekron, one of Assyria's few remaining western friends. Realizing that a showdown with Assyria was inevitable, Hezekiah soon repaired Jerusalem's walls and enlisted his engineers in cutting the impressive 1750-foot Siloam tunnel underneath the hill of Jerusalem so that water from the Gihon spring might flow directly into the city (II Kings 20:20; II Chr. 32:30).

Having regained control over Babylonia in 701, Sennacherib advanced westward. Though some historians argue that Sennacherib conducted two separate invasions of Judah (the second in about 688), a second invasion is neither readily discernible in the relevant, but confusing, biblical text (II Kings 18:13–19:37) nor attested in Assyrian records. Therefore the following reconstruction is plausible.

Sennacherib met little resistance as he strode through Syria and Phoenicia. He took the Philistine cities of Ashkelon and Ekron, defeated a large Egyptian army allied with Ekron, and overran Judah. According to his annals, Sennacherib seized forty-six of Hezekiah's fortified cities, and by cutting off Jerusalem from all outside assistance, he confined Hezekiah inside his royal city "like a caged bird." While Sennacherib was still leveling Lachish, Hezekiah dispatched a message of surrender (II Kings 18:14a). Sennacherib's demands were high. He ordered Hezekiah to render such enormous tribute that he had to relieve the Temple of its gold and silver, and surrender his royal treasuries (18:14b-16). Jerusalem, however, was spared. Sennacherib's sudden withdrawal from Judah may be understood as his response either to a devastating epidemic that crippled his army (II Kings 19:35), or, more likely, to a "rumor" that reached him and required his attention elsewhere—undoubtedly renewed rebellion in Babylonia (19:7). Hezekiah's bid for Judah's independence had failed, and his son, Manasseh, who succeeded him in 687, did not challenge Assyria on the matter of Judah's vassalage.

(2) An ancestor of the prophet Zephaniah (Zeph. 1:1).

(3) A member of the royal family of Judah (I Chr. 3:23).

(4) A man who, together with his descendants, returned with Nehemiah from the Babylonian exile and later subscribed to the covenant (Ezra 2:16; Neh. 7:21; 10:17). J.K.K.

**HIERAPOLIS.** A city in Phrygia, near Colossae and Laodicea, on the Lycus River. It is mentioned in Colossians 4:13, but is not said to have been visited by Paul. Hierapolis was early converted to Christianity and by the fourth century had four churches and was recognized as a Christian center. J.C.

**HIGH CHURCH.** The party within the Anglican Church that emphasizes the Catholicity of the Church of England, and so sometimes is referred to as the ANGLO-CATHOLIC party. The name originated in the seventeenth century to designate those people who stressed the continuity of the Church of England with the undivided Catholic church, before the Reformation, and interpreted the sacraments in a way conformable to Catholicism.

The High Church movement represents a theological school of thought and never became a separate church. Typically, it means elaborate ceremonies. The tendency to exhibit LOW CHURCH, BROAD CHURCH, and High Church opinions within one communion is characteristic of the worldwide Anglican Communion, including The Episcopal Church in the United States. Among Episcopalians, High Church people are sometimes called "Spikes" as opposed to Low Church people or "Prots" (Protestants). Historically, the High Church movement often took political positions, especially promoting the concept of the divine right of kings. J.C.

**HIGHER CRITICISM.** See BIBLICAL CRITICISM.

**HIGH MASS.** The pre-Vatican II tridentine mass of the Roman rite, known in Latin as the *Missa Cantata*, "the chanted mass." It is sung by one priest accompanied by a chanter and choir along with the congregation. Since it is more elaborate than some other ("low") masses it became known as "High Mass." It is celebrated on Sundays, holy days, and on other occasions. The Low Mass is recited, and the solemn mass is assisted by a deacon and subdeacon, thus distinguishing them from High Mass. Since solemn masses are celebrated on festivals, the High Mass became the usual form of service for the parish priest. Originally, High Mass was derived from the pontifical mass, which bishops celebrated with the lower clergy and parishioners. Since Vatican Council II's revisions of the Roman liturgy and the offering of the Mass in the vernacular, distinctions between masses no longer apply. J.C.

**HIGH PLACES.** Open-aired and roofed sanctuaries established by the Canaanites, which the Israelites regarded as both abhorrent and attractive after their settlement in Palestine.

Herbert G. May

*Canaanite high place at Gezer with cult pillars (Micah 5:13)*

Though a high place (Hebrew *bāmă*) might well consist of a hilltop shrine, it could also be situated in a valley (Jer. 7:31), within a town (I Kings 13:32), or at a city gate (II Kings 23:8). "High place" basically denotes a natural or artificially constructed elevation for cultic use. Equipped with round rock altars, unhewn stone pillars, and wooden poles, high places invited worshipers to engage in diverse activity. Here they ate (I Sam. 9:13), wept (Isa. 15:2), prayed (Isa. 16:12), burnt incense, and offered sacrifice (I Kings 11:8).

The biblical portrayal of high places is often pejorative. Yahweh commands their destruction as the Israelites overtake Canaan (Num. 33:52). Faithless Israelites who frequent Canaanite high places and erect some of their own incur God's wrath (Ps. 78:58). Because Deuteronomic legislation advocated the pure worship of Yahweh at a centralized sanctuary (Deut. 12), the attitude of specific Israelite and Judean kings toward high places determines their final assessment. Solomon is criticized for installing high places to support the worship practices of his foreign wives (I Kings 11:6-8). Conversely, the war that Asa (II Chr. 14:3, 5), Hezekiah (II Kings 18:4), and Josiah (II Kings 23:8) waged against high places is favorably viewed. Manasseh is condemned for rebuilding previously destroyed high places (II Kings 21:3), and a complaint is lodged against six Judean kings for failing to remove them—Asa (I Kings 15:14), Jehoshaphat (I Kings 22:43), Jehoash (II Kings 12:3), Amaziah (II Kings 14:4), Azariah/ Uzziah (II Kings 15:4), and Jotham (II Kings 15:35).

Nevertheless, some prophets (I Sam. 10:5-13) and priests (II Kings 17:32) function at high places without censure. Moreover, the priestly tabernacle (I Chr. 16:39) and tent of meeting (II Chr. 1:3) are positively associated with Gibeon's high place, as is Solomon, who goes there to petition Yahweh for regal wisdom (I Kings 3:4-15). Since such public and private devotion transpired prior to the establishment of the Jerusalem Temple on Mount Zion, its legitimacy was unquestioned. As Zion-centered worship of Yahweh intensified, idolatrous practices at high places received a crescendo of criticism (Ezek. 6:3, 6). Cultic installations at Megiddo, Gezer, and Dan, dating respectively to about 2700, 1600, and 920 B.C., are the most outstanding high places thus far excavated in Palestine.          J.K.K.

**HIGH PRIEST.** The head of the priestly hierarchy whose origins trace from Eleasar, the son of Aaron (Num. 3:32; 25:11-13). As Israel's supreme spiritual leader, he is aptly described in the Holiness Code as "chief among his brethren" (Lev. 21:10). Since the designation "great priest" (that is, high priest) is used sparingly in both preexilic and postexilic biblical texts, the development of the office cannot be readily traced. That the investiture and duties of the high priest are only clearly delineated within postexilic texts constitutes no denial that the high priesthood was a well-established institution several centuries earlier.

*Centrality in Postexilic Israel.* Following the sixth-century B.C. return of the exiles from Babylon, the reconstituted Judean community was no longer a monarchy. Rather, it became a hierocracy, with much of the king's dignity transferred to the high priest. According to the early postexilic writings of Haggai and Zechariah, the rule of the restored Jewish community was shared equally by Zerubbabel, the governor, and Joshua, the high priest (Hag. 1:1, 12, 14; 2:2, 4). The rebuilding of the Temple progressed under their joint leadership (Ezra 3:1-13), and these "two anointed" (Zech. 4:14) were expected to cultivate a relationship of "peaceful understanding" (Zech. 6:13). Concerning Temple affairs, however, authority resided in the high priest (Zech. 3:6-7).

With the disappearance of the office of governor, the high priest assumed civic as well as religious responsibilities. The dignity of the expanded office is evident in the eulogy on Simon II (about 218–192 B.C.) offered in Ecclesiasticus 50:1-24. During the second century B.C., the high priest presided over the "senate" (I Macc. 12:6; II Macc. 4:44) from which the Sanhedrin evolved (Mark 14:55). Two unprincipled individuals greatly discredited the high priesthood. In 175 B.C., Jason bribed the Seleucid ruler, Antiochus Epiphanes, into deposing Onias so that he might grab the office (II Macc. 4:7-10). Three years later, Jason was supplanted by Menelaus, who resorted to both bribery and murder (4:23-26, 33-35). The Maccabees returned the high priesthood to its former dignity, and the Hasmonean dynasty of high priests (142–63 B.C.) procured for Judea a brief interval of independence.

*Investiture and Vestments.* Priestly legislation presents the consecration into the high priesthood as a three-stage ritual (Exod. 29:4-7; Lev. 8:6-12). It involved ceremonial washing, putting on official vestments, and anointing with oil. The instructive account of the consecration of the first postexilic high priest, Joshua, mentions no anointing (Zech. 3:1-9). Perhaps this practice was introduced into the investiture ceremony shortly thereafter.

In Joshua's office, the high priest wore distinctive vestments (Exod. 28:4-39; 39:1-31; Lev. 8:7-9). These included (a) a long blue robe with alternating pomegranates and golden bells affixed to its hem; (b) a colorful, gold-threaded EPHOD, with each of its two shoulder straps carrying an onyx stone bearing the engraved names of six tribes; (c) a pouched breastpiece, made of material identical with the ephod, which was set with four rows of three precious stones each, with the names of the twelve tribes inscribed thereon, and serving as a receptacle for the sacred dice URIM AND THUMMIM; and (d) a linen turban to which was fastened a golden plate bearing the inscription "Holy to Yahweh." These ceremonial vestments highlighted the mediatory function of the high priesthood. Their luxurious quality denoted God's glory, and the twofold inscription of tribal names ensured that all Israel would be represented by the high priest in the sanctuary. On the DAY OF ATONEMENT, however, the high priest set aside these vestments and entered the Holy of Holies wearing simple linen garments (Lev. 16:4, 23).

*Duties.* The high priest was the chief administrator of the sanctuary, its cultic service and treasure (II Kings 12:7-8; 22:4-6). He consulted the Deity by manipulating the Urim and Thummim (Num. 27:21). He presided over the Sanhedrin as it addressed religious issues (Matt. 26:57; Acts 5:21). The most crucial function of the high priest was to enter the Holy of Holies on the annual Day of Atonement to expiate the people's sin by sprinkling blood on the mercy seat (Lev. 16:14-15). (*Compare also* LEVITES.) J.K.K.

**HIJRA.** Also spelled Hegira, this is the term used for the migration of MUHAMMAD from MECCA to MEDINA in A.D. 622, the first year of the Muslim era. In European languages the years of that era are identified by the initials A.H. (*anno hegirae*).

By 620 the Prophet had met with considerable opposition in Mecca. That year a group of six pilgrims from Medina came to Mecca and became convinced that Muhammad could help them solve the problems they faced in their home city. Muhammad saw Medina as a haven for his followers and a secure base for the expansion of Islam. Two years later arrangements had been completed and Muhammad quietly sent most of his followers ahead. He and his close friend Abu Bakr slipped out of the city and remained hidden nearby until they had thrown their Meccan enemies off their track.

Medina lay 250 miles to the north. Traveling on camel back by devious and unfrequented routes, Muhammad and Abu Bakr arrived safely at the oasis town of Medina on September 24. A new period in the prophet's career had begun. K.C.

**HILARY OF POITIERS.** A convert to Christianity from Neoplatonism who became bishop of Poitiers in the mid-fourth century. During the Arian controversy he was the foremost Western theologian in the defense of the faith of Nicaea. Like many others, he was exiled by Emperor Constantius, who sought to impose Arianism. His main work is *On the Trinity,* in twelve books. He was also influential as the teacher of Martin of Tours. J.G.

**HILDEGARD.** A German abbess of the twelfth century, noted for her mysticism, and admired by many of her contemporaries, including several crowned heads. Her main work is *Scivia,* in which she recorded twenty-six mystical experiences and spoke of great evils to come. But she also wrote on theology, commenting on the Gospels, the Athanasian Creed, and the Rule of St. Benedict. To a degree unusual in her time, she was a keen observer of nature and wrote on medicine, zoology, and other similar subjects.

J.G.

**HILLEL.** Jewish spiritual leader and scholar of the latter part of the first century B.C. and the beginning of the first century A.D. Born in Babylonia, Hillel went to Palestine when he was forty and enrolled in an academy of learning. Because of his brilliant scholarship, he was appointed president of the SANHEDRIN (high court). He established his own academy, the House of Hillel, which became known for its liberal interpretation of the laws of the Torah. One of the legal reforms he introduced kept private debts alive, even though the Torah canceled them at the end of each six-year period. Hillel's reform allowed the poor to borrow money since the lender was guaranteed full payment even after the sabbatical year.

Hillel was known for his extreme patience. When a skeptic asked him to teach him the Torah while he stood on one foot, Hillel replied: "What is hateful to you, do not unto others. That is the whole Torah. All the rest is commentary. Go and learn."

L.K.

**HILTNER, SEWARD** (1909–84). An early leader in pastoral psychology, Hiltner was born November 26, 1909. He received his A.B. from Lafayette College (1931), his Ph.D. from the University of Chicago (1952), and was ordained by the United Presbyterian Church in 1935.

After serving as executive secretary of the Council for Clinical Training in New York City (1935–38) and the Federal Council of Churches' department of pastoral services (1938–50), he began to lecture at Union and Yale (1945–50). From 1950 to 1961 he was professor of pastoral psychology at the University of Chicago. From 1961 to 1980 he was professor of theology and personality at Princeton Theological Seminary. Hiltner is the author of many books, including *Religion and Health* (1943), *Pastoral Counseling* (1949), *Sex and the Christian Life* (1957), *Preface to Pastoral Theology* (1958), *The Christian Shepherd* (1959), *Ferment in the Ministry* (1970), *Theological Dynamics* (1972), and *Toward a Theology of Aging* (1976).

N.H.

**HINAYANA BUDDHISM.** *See* BUDDHISM.

**HINDUISM.** *General Features.* The word Hindu is a variant of "India"; hence, Hinduism simply means "India-ism"—the religion and culture of India. It is thus a very broad term, embracing all those beliefs and practices of various peoples of the Indian subcontinent who are not self-assigned to religious traditions other than the mainstream: ISLAM, BUDDHISM, JAINISM, SIKHISM, PARSISM, Christianity, or

JUDAISM. Hinduism thus includes an immense gamut of religiosity, from the folkways of simple villagers to highly sophisticated metaphysical systems, from the lavish festivals of popular temples to the yogic meditations of ascetic recluses.

However, Hinduism is not merely a catch-all concept; despite its diversity, some common features run through it. First, all Hindus would accept, at least implicitly, the authority of the VEDIC scriptures and of the priestly caste known as Brahmins. Second, most Hindus would see themselves as part of a social order in which the caste system has had a major structural role and would know what their caste background is, even though many would now reject its conventions as binding. Third, most Hindus would acknowledge that the worship and the mythology of such great deities as VISHNU, KRISHNA, SHIVA, and KALI are part of their spiritual world; however, they interpret the meanings of these deities themselves. Finally, most thoughtful Hindus would see religion as presenting two paths: a way of life in this world and a way to liberation from this world through realization of union with the divine.

These last two levels can be thought of as DHARMA, the form or order of this world, including the social order and one's obligations within it; and MOKSHA, liberation, the ultimate goal of life. Philosophical Hindus tend to see God or the Absolute, often called BRAHMAN but also identifiable with one of the great gods, as the sole Reality underlying all other things, and so actually found in dharma as much as in moksha. But moksha is its full internalization, the goal of true spiritual seekers. It is reached in several ways. Modern sources talk particularly of three, drawn from the ancient BHAGAVAD GITA: *jnana-yoga,* intellectual and meditative insight into the true nature of reality; *karma-yoga,* selfless service and doing of duty within the dharma of the social order; and BHAKTI, love and devotion toward the gods as manifestations of the universal divine Reality.

*History.* The roots of the Hindu tree reach back to two disparate cultural strata: the indigenous civilization that found its climax in the ancient territories of the Indus Valley, and the culture of the Aryans or Indo-Europeans who invaded India between 2,000 and 1,000 B.C. The Indus Valley civilization, an agricultural people who built great urban centers, is thought by many scholars to have stressed fertility cults, yoga, mother goddesses, and water. These are all features that have found their way into developed Hinduism. The Indo-Europeans, on the other hand, brought in such formal structural features as the brahmin priesthood and its fire sacrifices, and above all the Vedic scriptures. The Vedas (not actually committed to writing until fairly recently, but transmitted orally and memorized) contain hymns, often of considerable poetic power, chanted by brahmins in their rituals; ritual instructions; and in the last and most philosophic portion, the UPANISHADS, a metaphysical discourse culminating in the

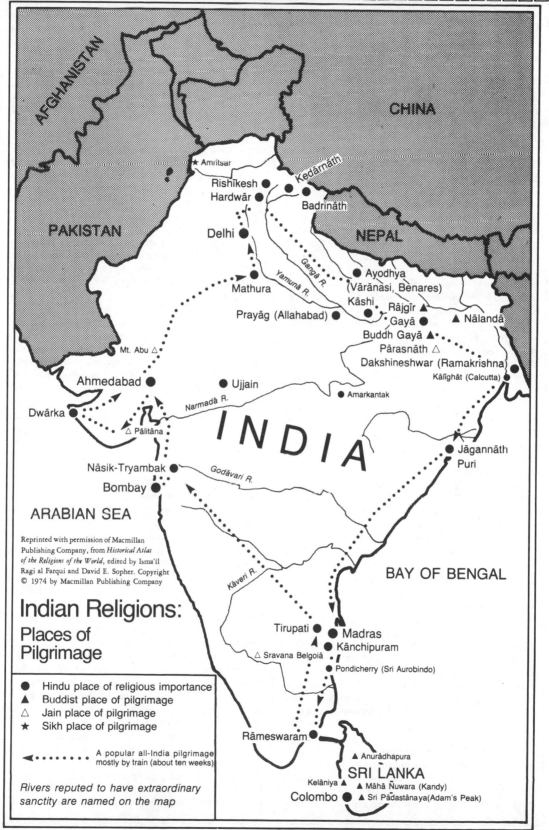

AFGHANISTAN

CHINA

PAKISTAN

★ Amritsar

Rishīkesh ●
Hardwār ●

Kedārnāth

Badrināth ●

Delhi ●

NEPAL

Yamunā R.

Ganga R.

Ayodhya ●
(Vārānasi, Benares)

Mathura ●

Kāshi ●

Rājgīr ▲

Prayāg (Allahabad) ●

Gayā ●

Nālandā ▲

Buddh Gayā ▲

Mt. Abu △

Pārasnāth △

Dakshineshwar (Ramakrishna) ●

Ahmedabad ●

Ujjain ●

Amarkantak ●

Kālīghāt (Calcutta) ●

Dwārka ●

Narmadā R.

INDIA

△ Pālitāna

Jāgannāth ●
Puri

Nāsik-Tryambak ●

Godāvari R.

Bombay ●

ARABIAN SEA

BAY OF BENGAL

Reprinted with permission of Macmillan
Publishing Company, from *Historical Atlas
of the Religions of the World*, edited by Isma'il
Ragi al Farqui and David E. Sopher. Copyright
© 1974 by Macmillan Publishing Company

Kāveri R.

# Indian Religions:
## Places of Pilgrimage

Tirupati ●

Madras ●

Kānchipuram ●

△ Sravana Belgoiā

Pondicherry (Sri Aurobindo) ●

● Hindu place of religious importance
▲ Buddist place of pilgrimage
△ Jain place of pilgrimage
★ Sikh place of pilgrimage

Rāmeswaram ●

◄····· A popular all-India pilgrimage
mostly by train (about ten weeks)

▲ Anurādhapura

*Rivers reputed to have extraordinary
sanctity are named on the map*

SRI LANKA

Kelāniya ▲

▲ Māhā Ñuwara (Kandy)

Colombo ●

● Sri Pādastānaya (Adam's Peak)

realization that the ATMAN, one's innermost nature, is one with Brahman, the universal Reality.

The rise of Buddhism and Jainism after the fifth century B.C. spurred development within the Vedic tradition as it became what is now known as Hinduism. The new spiritual paths taught by the Buddha and MAHAVIRA emphasized wisdom and meditation over Vedic or Brahminical authority. These teachings undermined the caste system and soon embraced temple devotion to enlightened beings. Hinduism responded in such texts, usually dated between 200 B.C. and A.D. 200, as the Bhagavad Gita, inculcating devotion to God and the ideal of *karma-yoga;* the LAWS OF MANU, which offers a rationale of the caste system, and a life devoted first to the ideal of dharma or righteousness as a householder, then to moksha as a renunciant seeker; and the Yoga SUTRA of Patanjali (dated later than A.D. 200 in their final form by some), providing a philosophy and guide for the practice of yoga leading to liberation. Yoga combines physical and mental techniques for stilling movements of the mind to allow the true self, *purusha* or *atman,* to shine through. Yoga has been associated with Hinduism in some form for millennia.

The early centuries A.D. saw the rise of bhakti or devotionalism. Texts called PURANAS extolled the lives and merits of deities introduced, or considerably modified, from non-Vedic sources, just as Hinduism incorporated more and more of spiritual India into a broad synthesis. Bhakti theoreticians advocated devotion as not only a means to divine boons, but also as a way to salvation through the selfless love of unstinting faith and fervent, uncalculating piety. Bhakti movements, colorful and easily accessible to the simple as well as the learned, quickly won mass support as well as brahminical endorsement and aristocratic patronage, overshadowing Buddhism, Jainism, and more conservative forms of Hinduism. They did much to preserve India for that faith.

Other movements were also influential. Advaita (nondualist) VEDANTA philosophy, founded by the great Shankara (about A.D. 788–820) emphasized the late Vedic (that is, Vedanta) Upanishadic teaching that Brahman is the sole Reality. It sees the gods benignly but relativistically as manifestations or accommodations of the ineffable one, in whom the world of Maya or phenomena rises and falls like waves on an infinite sea. The movement known as TANTRISM, which also has a Buddhist wing, originated in more or less "underground" spiritual circles to practice a "short path" to power and liberation through radical initiations, use of mantras, visualization, and sexual yogas. It was often antinomian.

After the twelfth century, Islamic religious influence, following Muslim invaders, was potent in north India. Over the subsequent centuries some 20 percent of the subcontinent's population became Muslim, a segment now largely concentrated in Pakistan and Bangladesh, though also represented by a minority of about 10 percent in the Republic of India. Hinduism itself was affected by the Islamic presence in two basic ways. First, the rigorous conservatism on social and religious matters, which characterized the Hindu world until quite recently, was really an understandable counterpoint to rule by non-Hindu conquerors, first Muslim and then British. As elsewhere in the world, people of one faith subjugated by overlords of another clung to their religion all the more tenaciously, as one remaining realm of separate dignity and identity. Second, other people have been challenged by the presence of two faiths to go beyond them both, seeking a truth transcendent to all institutional forms of expression. This was the burden of the poet Kabir (1440–1518), who sang of a God neither in the mosque nor the Hindu image, but rather found within the heart and breath of all. That vision of a God greater than in the existing faiths was also proclaimed by NANAK (1470–1540), founder of the Sikh religion.

UNIVERSALISM, combined paradoxically but creatively with Indian nationalism, has been a dominant theme of modern Hinduism. As India in the nineteenth and twentieth centuries has had to deal with full-scale encounters with the West, it has, as in the earlier encounter with Islam, taken many turns. Ram Mohun Roy (1772–1833), perhaps the first modern Hindu intellectual, founded the Brahmo Samaj as a reform movement based on a universal ethical monotheism uniting all religions. Swami Dayananda (1824–83), on the other hand, through his Arya Samaj, urged his countrymen to go back to the Vedas and in the process to reform numerous abuses and corruptions he perceived in later Hinduism. The Theosophical Society, brought to India a few years after its founding in New York in 1875, encouraged the confidence of Hindus in the worth and world value of their own tradition.

But the most influential strand of modern Hinduism has been Neo-Vedanta, associated with the Hindu Renaissance of the late nineteenth century and especially with the teachings of the mystic RAMAKRISHNA (1834–86) and the Ramakrishna Mission, an educational and service monastic order, founded by his disciple Swami Vivekananda (1863–1902). Its basic premise has been Shankara's Advaita Vedanta, augmented by a modern emphasis on viewing all religions as alternative paths to the mountaintop of seeing Brahma/God as the Sole Reality. The Ramakrishna Mission's centers in Europe and America, often called Vedanta Societies, have been quite influential in disseminating the Hindu classics and this philosophical perspective. Numerous other modern Hindu spiritual leaders, from the yogin Swami Sivananda (1887–1963) to the advaitin mystic Ramana Maharshi (1879–1951), and the academic philosopher and president of India SARVEPALLI RADHAKRISHNAN (1888–1975), have taught essentially the same message.

The Hindu Renaissance went hand in hand with rising Indian nationalism. While it affirmed a generous spiritual universalism, it also projected India and Hinduism as a particularly clear reservoir of the timeless wisdom underlying it, and so promoted pride on the part of Indians in their heritage.

It was the work of the great MOHANDAS K. GANDHI (1869–1948), leader of the independence movement and apostle of nonviolence, to draw from that heritage both ideals and a practical program for achieving independence. Combining the yogic and Jain ideal of *ahimsa,* harmlessness, with the *Bhagavad Gita*'s karma yoga, and inspired also by such Western writers as THOREAU, Ruskin, and TOLSTOY, Gandhi made nonviolent resistance and principled civil disobedience highly effective tools for political change.

*Intellectual Expression of Hinduism.* Hinduism, like all religions, is expressed conceptually through both philosophy and myth. We have already spoken of Shankara's Advaita Vedanta, considered the best-known school of Hindu philosophy. But just as important in Hindu religious life is the modified non-dualism (Visista Advaita) of Ramanuja (about 1017–60), which endeavored to bring together Advaita and the bhakti experience. According to Ramanuja, the universe is not simply Maya, as "God in disguise," but bears a relation to God like that of the body to the head. While the universe is sustained by divine energy, and selves possess divinely derived immortality, God is a loving, personal deity distinguishable from universe and having the ability to receive the ardent devotional love bhakti loves to bestow.

Another kind of Hindu intellectual expression is through its deities and their mythology. Although at first glance a baffling array, the great gods of devotionalism can be comprehended through understanding their relationships. They each belong to one of two great families, the Vishnu (or Vaishnava) and the Shiva (or Saiva). Vishnu, the chief deity of his family, can be thought of as something like the God of Christianity, a personal, loving deity who, when righteousness declines, takes AVATAR or "incarnate" (literally, "descent") form in the world to defeat the forces of evil. His wife is Lakshmi, or Sri, goddess of fortune, wealth, and prosperity; he often has a second consort also, Bhudevi, the earth. The creator-god Brahma is associated with Vishnu; according to myth he appears on a lotus growing from Vishnu's navel when the world is to be constructed anew. His consort is Sarasvati, the popular goddess of culture and wisdom. Vishnu's most popular avatar forms are Rama, the hero of the great epic the RAMAYANA, whose consort is Sita; and Krishna, accompanied by Radha. Krishna is beloved in his various forms as divine infant, young lover of Radha and other of the gopis—his milkmaid-devotees; as hero; and as sage of the *Bhagavad Gita.* Some Krishnaites make Krishna himself the supreme lord, and Krishna is the most

popular of all objects of bhakti. Another favorite Vaishanva figure is the monkey-god Hanuman, prominent in the Ramayana.

Shiva, more than Vishnu, simply represents the totality of all things, the oneness and power that lies beyond all dualities. Shiva's representations include the lingam, the quasi-phallic pillar suggesting the life-force; the *nataraja* or "Lord of the Dance," whose movements dance out the universe; the Mahayogin, or great yogi, whose meditations sustain the world, and who is also the great teacher of ineffable wisdom, youthful but surrounded by disciples. Shiva is the universal Absolute. His consort is the Great Goddess who represents the phenomenal world, also eternal but eternally changing. She is his shakti or power, and has many forms ranging from the beautiful to the horrible: as Parvati, the lovely maiden; Durga, the dragon-slaying woman warrior; and Kali, the dark, blood-drinking terrible mother, receiving sacrifices of male goats, but in an ultimate sense benign, embodying the universe's awesome cycle of birth and destruction. Also associated with Saivism are two sons of Siva known, among variant names, as Ganesha, the elephant-headed god of fortune and remover of obstacles; and Skanda, a warrior seen also as personification of Siva as teacher.

*Hindu Worship.* For most traditionally devout Hindus, the most significant place of worship is not the temple but the home. In such homes, the family priest or head of household arises early and, opening the small family shrine, honors the image of its deity with chants, bathing, and simple offerings, including food which will be consumed by the family during the day. A very pious worshiper will also put the marks of the deity on the forehead.

Temple worship, though popular, has a more optional character. The sanctuary of a temple is essentially seen as the throne room of a deity, and its procedures are like those of a royal court, the priests being servants and the worshipers petitioners. Although festivals and major ceremonies are held, a worshiper generally approaches the temple as an individual, buying and presenting an offering such as flowers, or a coconut, with the help of a priest. Yet the great temples are also splendid repositories of Hindu art and symbols and centers of community identity and celebration.

Pilgrimage is very important in Hinduism. Certain temples and sites draw millions from all over India, above all the holy city of Varanasi (Benares) on the banks of the sacred Ganges River, in whose waters believers purify themselves.

Yoga exercises combining physical posture, breath control, and meditation, are practiced by numerous Hindus (as well as non-Hindus), religious specialists, and lay people alike. The use of MANTRAs, sacred words of power repeated less for meaning than for the spiritual effect they impart, is widespread in both ritual and meditational settings. Emerging from Vedic and SANSKRIT origin, the store of mantra has come to include phrases from sectarian, Tantric, and other sources.

*Hindu Sociology.* Hinduism as actually experienced in India is bound up with the sociology of the Hindu community. The way it is known and practiced by any individual is heavily influenced by that person's sex, family, and caste background, as well as by geographical region.

In traditional India, and to no small extent today, family and caste go together. The traditional caste system is basically a matter not of occupation but of purity and is expressed most definitively in who can eat with or prepare food for whom, though it also involves marriage and occupation, since marriages have to be at proper levels of purity and some occupations are much purer than others. Higher castes are vegetarian and avoid work involving products of human or animal bodies. The highest are BRAHMINS, ideally priests, scholars, and religious specialists (though most are not such professionally), who alone perform the most sacred Vedic rites. The caste system has been justified on the basis of classic Hinduism's organic, dharma view of society, but today is weakening, and is under political attack in modern India, while only the most ultraconservative religious spokespersons defend its traditional form.

A significant class within Hinduism is the sadhus, or "holy men." These are persons who, renouncing worldly goods and the privileges and responsibilities of family and caste, seek to realize and exemplify moksha. A sadhu may live as a hermit, a wanderer, or follow a semi-monastic life in an ashram or spiritual community, whether as master or disciple. A sadhu is usually recognizable by distinctive garb and symbols, though these may vary. Generally beginning his religious career as the disciple of an established sadhu who serves as his GURU or teacher and initiator, he may in time be authorized by the latter to become a *guru* himself, and receive both religious and lay disciples. Sadhus manifest an immensely important dimension of the Hindu religion, for they keep continually alive its vision of the divine within all and the possibility of now realizing it, through renunciation of all that is less than God.                    R.E.

**HIPPOLYTUS.** Third-century theologian and priest in Rome. He clashed with Bishop Zephyrinus and his successors over the doctrine of the Trinity and over the tendency of the bishops of Rome to be more lenient toward those who had sinned than Hippolytus thought proper. His view of the Logos, developed against the Patripassian doctrines of Noetus, tended toward subordinationism. He also refused to call the Holy Spirit a person. Eventually he broke with Bishop Callistus and took the title of bishop. Some ancient authorities assert that he and Pontianus—his rival bishop at the time—were reconciled while both were exiled in Sardinia. Later the bodies of the two rivals were returned to Rome, and Hippolytus was considered a martyr. His most important works are

*Refutation of All Heresies, Against Noetus,* and the *Apostolic Tradition.* The latter is particularly significant as a source for our knowledge of early Christian worship.                    J.G.

**HIRAM.** The king of Tyre, a city-state in Phoenicia, the coastal settlements made by the "sea peoples," who probably originated in Cyprus. Hiram ruled Tyre from approximately 970 to 935 B.C. He was famed for his magnificent buildings in Tyre and for his great merchant navy and overseas commerce. Hiram was a faithful friend to both David and Solomon. Indeed, he literally built Solomon's Temple of Yahweh in Jerusalem, since he furnished the craftsmen and the cedar wood ("the cedars of Lebanon") essential to its construction. In payment, Solomon furnished Hiram with wheat and oil and also ceded a small district of Israel to him. Hiram assisted Solomon in building a merchant marine for Israel, and Solomon's sailors sailed with Hiram's on their journeys to the Middle East and Africa (to "Ophir"). The Jewish Midrash declares that Hiram began as a pious man, but his many successful ventures caused him to become filled with pride. He then built an artificial "heaven," and for this presumptuousness he was given defeat and death by God.                    J.C.

**HISTORICAL CRITICISM.** *See* BIBLICAL CRITICISM.

**HISTORICISM.** In its variety of usages, historicism represents the conviction that human experience cannot be understood or evaluated apart from the particular social, historical context of development and change in which it appears.

In the nineteenth century, the term historicism was used to depreciate theories of society dependent upon historical knowledge. Wilhelm Dilthey, Heinrich Rickert, and others, developed the distinction between natural sciences and historical sciences, the latter appropriate for human, societal phenomena, the former for the study of nature. Ernst Troeltsch (1865–1923), convinced that skepticism resulted from viewing knowledge and experience as subject to change, spoke of the crisis of historicism, which can be overcome only through historical involvement, not by resort to transhistorical perspectives. Josiah Royce (1855–1916), as he modified his early idealism, developed a social theory of reality with a changing community of interpretation moving toward universal community, a view contributing much to historicist perspectives. Karl Mannheim (1893–1947), asserting that static epistemologies are outdated, founded the sociology of knowledge, which viewed all knowledge as inescapably related to particular socio-historical contexts.

Michael Polanyi (1891–1976) and H. Richard Niebuhr (1894–1962) give historicism its most significant contemporary statements. Polanyi, moving toward a post-critical philosophy, demonstrates that the natural sciences, no less than the humanities, have tacit, fiduciary dimensions rooted in social and cultural contexts. Niebuhr affirms that humans must conceive all things as temporal and historical, not in terms of abstract time, but rather in terms of time that is "particular and concrete . . . the time of a definite society with distinct language, economic and political relations, religious faith and social organization" (*The Meaning of Revelation*).      C.Mc.

**HISTORICITY OF THE BIBLE.** This title raises questions of wide-ranging concern and ongoing debate among biblical scholars, both Jewish and Christian. Indeed, students of the ancient Near East and Greco-Roman society have contributed to the discussion. Moreover, there are philosophical issues that are involved, raised in BULTMANN'S probe that, following KIERKEGAARD and Lutheran theologians, led to a detachment of the Christian faith from empirical history in the interest of an existential appeal of the NT message. Bultmann did not deny a foundation of historical facts to the ministry of Jesus and his death on the cross. But he did not attach much theological value to these events because, in his view, faith can never be at the mercy of HISTORICAL CRITICISM and suspend its activity while the historians debate the problematic question surrounding the events recorded in the Gospels: "Did they happen exactly as reported?"Christian faith for Bultmann and his followers can find no resting place in historical uncertainties since "history" for us, looking back over two thousand years to the recorded happenings of the Gospels, can offer no more than approximations to "what really took place." We must seek, it is said, faith's point of reference in a life-changing encounter with the living Christ of the church's proclamation. Later followers of Bultmann have been more positive in their assessment of historical data in the Gospels, but their philosophical position remains much the same.

On the other side, classical scholars and conservative writers have been more confident in appealing to the witness of external corroboration of NT events, such as the findings of archaeology, the supportive evidence of ancient Greek and Latin authors, and the internal consistency they find in the NT documents. Often this approach has led to a degree of forced harmonization and special pleading. But also many of the arguments brought forth have probative appeal. Thus the historical accuracy of the record in the Acts of the Apostles is often argued for by scholars (for example, Martin Hengel) who theologically are by no means traditionalists. But it is now generally conceded that the author of Acts is more a theologian than an impartial historian. Indeed, he uses history for his own purposes, which are theological.

The debate over OT history is more straightforward, since it is now widely held that the Hebrew mind was less interested in detailed factual reports than was earlier believed to be the case. The presence of oral tradition in Israel and the community's recall of the past in its festivals and ceremonies have indicated how Israel's "history" came to be written down much later than the events reported. The era of Israel's history writing may not have begun until David's reign. Distinctive ways of reading history are seen in Deuteronomy and the books of Chronicles as well as the Priestly editor of the Pentateuch. Nonetheless, Israel's faith rests on certain dramatic events that form the nodal points of the OT history: the Exodus, the entry into Canaan, the prophetic movements of the eighth and seventh centuries in particular; some would also include a tradition centered on the call of Abraham.

Both OT and NT serve as libraries of historical data that bear witness to Israel's faith preserved in liturgical dramas of Israel's celebrations and the church's sacraments and the church's assurance that God works in history and personal life as a divine arena and workshop. In all cases, however, it is history as seen through the eyes of belief and interpreted to display what God did in the lives of people.      R.M.

**HISTORY OF CHRISTIAN DOCTRINE.** By the time EUSEBIUS OF CAESAREA wrote his *Church History,* it was generally believed that Christian doctrine did not (or at least should not) change or evolve. This was in part due to the acceptance within the Christian church of a static view of truth, derived mostly from the Greek philosophical tradition. Therefore, Eusebius took pains to show that what the church believed at his time was what it had always believed. Such was also the view of the opponents of Augustine's innovations, particularly of Vincent of Lerins, who argued that one should hold fast to what has been believed "always, by all, and in every place." Therefore, during the Middle Ages there was little interest in the history of doctrine, except in the sense of claiming ancient authorities in support for one's position, or against one's opponents.

The Protestant REFORMATION, and the studies of the Humanists at the same time, challenged this view. Protestants held that doctrine had indeed developed, and had done so in a way that contradicted the original faith. At Magdeburg, under the leadership of Matthias Flacius, a group of Protestant scholars began publishing a history of the church and its doctrine, devoting one volume to each century, and which therefore became known as the *Centuries of Magdeburg.* This in turn prompted Cardinal Cesar Baronius to refute the Protestant view in twelve volumes of *Ecclesiastical Annals,* which he published between 1588 and his death in 1607—at which point he had brought his history to the end of the twelfth century. From that point on, Catholic historians usually stressed continuity in the development of dogma, while Protestants took the opposite tack.

This tendency was aggravated by the contrasting attitudes of ROMAN CATHOLICISM and of many

Protestant scholars in relation to the developments of the modern world. Catholicism condemned many of those developments and became increasingly rigid—a process that culminated in the time of PIUS IX with his *Syllabus of Errors*. Many Protestants, on the other hand, welcomed such developments, often to such a point that they were accused of abandoning the essentials of the traditional faith. In that setting, Catholics insisted on the uniform development of dogma, and even such moderate works as Cardinal John Henry Newman's *Essay on the Development of Christian Doctrine* (1845) were regarded askance. Therefore, Protestants took the lead in the exploration of the development of doctrine, and their work culminated in ADOLF HARNACK's seven volumes on the *History of Dogma* (1886–90), where he sought to show that Christian dogmatic development was the history of the progressive Hellenization of the faith, and of the abandoning of a living faith for the sake of fixed DOGMAS.

In more recent times, both Protestants and Catholics have moderated their positions, thus reapproaching each other in their understanding of doctrinal development. This is particularly true of the contemporary efforts to see such development in the light, not only of its intellectual setting, but also of its socio-political setting, and of the sociopolitical agendas involved. Although a number of monographs on this subject have been published in recent times, these inquiries have not yet resulted in a work reviewing the entire development of doctrine from this perspective.

J.G.

## HISTORY OF RELIGIONS. *See* WORLD RELIGIONS.

## HITTITES.

An Indo-European people, who in about 1600 B.C. formed a state in east-central Anatolia (present-day Turkey), which expanded into a vigorous empire and fell around 1200 B.C.; also, their descendants (Neo-Hittites) in southeastern peripheral regions from about 1200 to 700 B.C.

*Hittites in the Bronze Age.* Originally the name "Hatti" denoted the indigenous non-Indo-European inhabitants of central Anatolia, whose language resembles no known linguistic family. Before 2000 B.C., newcomers speaking closely related Indo-European languages, such as Luvian, Nesian, and Palaic, settled there among the older inhabitants. Displacing Hattian, Nesian became recognized as the Hittite language, and its speakers as Hittites. Though (cuneiform) Hittite, patterned after Mesopotamian prototypes, became the official language of the Hittite Empire and of its capital, Hattusas (Boghazköy), hieroglyphic Hittite and Akkadian are also well attested.

Tradition credits Labarnas with founding the Old Kingdom in the late seventeenth century B.C. Under his son and successor, Hattusilis I (about 1570–

Courtesy of Stattliche Museen, Berlin

*Hittite prisoners, probably from the time of Ramses III (about 1195–1164* B.C.*)*

1540), the Hittites mounted a concerted campaign to annex northern SYRIA. By 1530 B.C., Hattusilis' impressive son and successor, Mursilis I, had overtaken Aleppo and sacked Babylon, thereby terminating the three hundred years of rule that the First Dynasty of Babylon had enjoyed. For a full century thereafter, external pressure from the expanding Hurrian kingdom of Mitanni and frequent anarchy over throne succession forced the steadily weakening Hittite power to retreat into Asia Minor.

In about 1400 B.C., the founding of the new kingdom led to Hittite resurgence. Mindful of Egypt's weakness under Akhenaton, Shuppiluliuma (about 1370–1335) wrested northern and central Syria from Egyptian control and established a protectorate over Mitanni. Inevitably, his successors became involved in wars with the Egyptians, who were trying to reclaim Syria. In about 1286 B.C. this culminated in an encounter near Kadesh in which the Hittite king, Muwattalis (about 1306–1282), secured an indecisive victory over Pharaoh Ramses II (about 1290–1224). Due to the escalating Assyrian menace, Hattusilis III (about 1275–1250), brother of Muwattalis, concluded a peace treaty with Ramses II. Though the Hittites continued as masters in Syria, they could not stop Assyria from annexing Mitanni.

Late in the thirteenth century B.C., the Hittite Empire collapsed under the impact of invading Sea Peoples consisting of coalitions of displaced Aegeans. With this telling defeat, Anatolia entered a dark age.

*Neo-Hittites and the Old Testament.* From about 1200 to 700 B.C., Hittite culture and traditions were kept alive within the independent states that emerged in the mountainous Taurus area and northern Syria. With an influx of Anatolian refugees, the Hittite population intensified. Though cuneiform Hittite disappeared, hieroglyphic Hittite became widespread. As the Arameans gradually gained control over the Syrian states, they transmitted the Neo-Hittite tradition. By the end of the eighth century B.C., Assyria had annexed numerous Neo-Hittite territories. And with the advance of Assyria's militia, the name "Hatti" spread to southern Syria and all of Palestine. The annals of Shalmaneser III (859–825) and Esarhaddon (680–669) aptly disclose that the kings of Hatti, over whom the Assyrian monarchs triumphed, ranged over a vast stretch of western Asia.

Accordingly, the tendency for the OT to refer to the early inhabitants of Palestine as Hittites directly derives from ninth-century B.C. Assyrian practice. In six lists enumerating Palestine's ancient settlers, the Hittites appear first (thus Deut. 7:1) and in nine cases they occupy second place (thus Josh. 3:10). Unfortunately, the lists offer no specifics about the localization of the Hittites in Palestine. As occupants of Syria, the Hittites are counted as Canaan's offspring in the Table of Nations (Gen. 10:15, with the mention of Heth). In Abraham's day, Hebron's inhabitants are presented as Hittites (Gen. 23). Esau and Solomon married Hittite women (Gen. 26:34; I Kings 11:1). The Palestinian hill country is described as hosting both Hittite and Amorite occupants (Num. 13:29). Moreover, Ahimelech (I Sam. 26:6) and Uriah, Bathsheba's first husband (II Sam. 11), are introduced as Hittite contemporaries of David.

Clearly, Palestine's Hittite population was never large, and Hittite conquests failed to extend southward into Palestine. In the OT, "Hittites" consistently denotes the Neo-Hittites of northern Syria, and individual Hittites bear Semitic names betraying a thorough assimilation into Semitic culture. The Hittite label for Ahimelech and Uriah may merely indicate that northern Syria was their homeland. Certain princes in that region undoubtedly figure behind the references to Hittite kings in the monarchical narratives about Solomon (I Kings 10:29) and Joram (II Kings 7:6). Moreover, the transaction between Abraham and Ephron the Hittite in Genesis 23 reflects Neo-Babylonian rather than Hittite business custom. Finally, Ezekiel's metaphorical statement that Jerusalem's mother was a Hittite (Ezek. 16:3, 45) simply mirrors contemporary geographical terminology that locates Jerusalem in the land of Hatti.

If it be remembered that by "Hittites" the OT means "Neo-Hittites deriving from northern Syria," and that the biblical writers appropriated the Assyrian practice of including all of Palestine under the "Hatti" appellation, the biblical portrayal of Hittite presence in Palestine ceases to be a disconcerting enigma.                               J.K.K.

**HIVITES.** A Canaanite tribe that inhabited the northern section of Palestine in the Lebanon and anti-Lebanon ranges, around Mount Hermon and at Hamath, but who also were located at Shechem and Gibeon, to the south (see Josh. 11:3; Judg. 3:3; II Sam. 24:7; Gen. 34:2 and Josh. 9:7). There were seven traditional tribes in Canaan, and the Hivites were traditionally said to descend from Eve. Other theorists hold that the Hivites were actually the HORITES, or that they were kinsmen to the ancient Achaeans of Greece. The Hivites were supposed to have migrated to western Asia and the Achaeans to have gone into Greece. After the Hebrew conquest the Hivites were friendly to the Israelites. Solomon made them servants in the Jerusalem Temple.

Many other scholars believe that the Hivites (and Horites) are the same people as the HURRIANS, who entered Palestine from the Indo-Iranian area of Asia. We know the Hurrians were settled over the whole Middle Eastern area by the second millennium B.C. Recently many clay tablets writen by the Hurrians that date from 1500 B.C. were discovered. These tablets, chiefly from Ras Shamrah in northern Syria, give much information about religion, magic, and ancient society. While still in process of translation, many parallels to ancient Israelite customs have already been found.                               J.C.

**HOCKING, WILLIAM ERNEST** (1873–1966). American philosopher and professor at Harvard. In the idealist tradition, he opposed both the idea of an evolving God and that of an impersonal Absolute, holding that there is no higher category for the understanding of God than that of personality. Nature is to be known not only through the sciences but also in a more mystical fashion, as God's self-communication to us. Hocking was a pioneer in promoting dialogue among the great religions. His writings include *The Meaning of God in Human Experience* (1912) and *Living Religions and a World Faith* (1940).                               J.M.

**HODGE, CHARLES** (1797–1878). American theologian, born December 27, in Philadelphia, the son of a Princeton physician. He was a protégé of ARCHIBALD ALEXANDER, who was the first president of Princeton Theological Seminary, which he helped found. Hodge graduated from the College of New Jersey (1815) and Princeton Theological Seminary (1819), and was licensed to preach in October, 1819. In 1822 he married Sarah Bache, great-granddaughter of Benjamin Franklin.

Hodge was a developer and defender of theology at Princeton. In May 1820, he was appointed instructor in the original languages of Scripture at Princeton Seminary, and in 1822 he was named professor of Oriental and biblical literature. He later (1840) became professor of exegetic and didactic theology with polemic theology added in 1851. Hodge taught Bible and theology at the seminary for fifty-eight years.

For forty years he edited the *Biblical Repertory and Princeton Review,* founded in 1825. His books include a *Commentary on the Epistle to the Romans* (1835), *The Constitutional History of the Presbyterian Church in the U.S.* (1839–40), and his classic defense of Old School Calvinism, his three-volume *Systematic Theology* (1871–73).

N.H.

## HOLINESS CHURCHES/HOLINESS MOVEMENT. *See* PENTECOSTAL CHURCHES.

**HOLL, KARL** (1866–1926). German Protestant historian who helped spark a Luther renaissance by exploring justification by faith. He is known widely in America for *The Cultural Significance of the Reformation,* translated by Wilhelm Pauck (1959). Born and educated in Tübingen, Holl held professorships there and at Berlin, distinguishing himself in early church and Reformation studies.

C.M.

**HOLMES, OLIVER WENDELL (SR.)** (1809–94). American poet, essayist, novelist, and physician. Son of Abdiel Holmes, a noted divine, Oliver Wendell Holmes was born August 29 in Cambridge, Massachusetts. Holmes, who throughout his life represented the most urbane and polished aspects of New England culture, was educated at Phillips Academy, Andover, and Harvard College. He spent a year reading law before studying medicine in Cambridge, in Paris, and at Harvard Medical School. He began his career as a general practitioner but shifted later to the academic field. He served as professor of anatomy and physiology at Dartmouth College from 1838 to 1840, dean of Harvard Medical School from 1847 to 1853, and Parker Professor of Anatomy and Physiology at Harvard from 1847 to 1882. His first important poem, "Old Ironsides," was written in 1830. A collection of his witty poems was published in 1836. In 1857 he began to contribute to the *Atlantic Monthly,* in which his famous "Breakfast-table" sketches appeared before they later were incorporated into *The Autocrat of the Breakfast Table* (1858). He also wrote several novels and biographies. He was father of the famed jurist who bore his name.

Reared in a Calvinist household, Holmes became a Unitarian. His hymn "Our Father! While Our Hearts Unlearn," records his change in belief. His hymns that have become accepted in the wider church are "Lord of All Being, Throned Afar," and "O Love Divine, That Stooped to Share."

R.H.

**HOLOCAUST.** The term generally applied to the methodical murder of approximately six million Jews in Europe by the Nazis under Adolf Hitler.

Between 1933 and 1939, Nazis set the ground work for what was to happen later, in several stages, to the Jews. At first, they passed measures eliminating Jews and other non-Aryans from the civil service, the legal and medical professions, and schools and other public institutions. Then came the Nuremberg Laws of 1935, which deprived the Jews of Germany of the rights of citizenship, wiping out a century and a half of "emancipation." Germans were forbidden "illegal intercourse" with Jews. Anyone with a Jewish grandparent was considered Jewish. In 1938, the third stage began when Jews were ordered to register their property, and Jewish communal organizations were put under the control of the Gestapo (German secret police). The assassination of a German diplomat by a Jewish youth in Paris was used as the excuse for a government-organized program and *Kristallnacht*—"night of glass"—during which Jewish shop windows were smashed, their synagogues burned, and Jews themselves were tortured and murdered. Jewish buildings and holdings were expropriated. Of Germany's little more than 500,000 Jews, 300,000 had fled by 1939, and most of them had no place to go. The Nazis discovered that except for verbal protests by the Western democracies, nothing would be done to oppose their anti-Jewish policies. The stage was set for the Holocaust.

Complete control of communications and transportation provided the cover of secrecy. Total mobilization of resources, including ruthless exploitation of what was called "human material," provided the general economic framework. The expansion of the SS (German guard troops) into a state within a state provided the instrument. The SS received the cooperation of other branches of the German bureaucracy, the German army, and the Nazi puppet governments in the satellite countries. Under Heinrich Himmler, the administrative apparatus for the elimination of "undesirable" populations was constructed. An impersonal bureaucratic jargon freed the Nazis from any residual moral inhibitions and at the same time hid their real intentions from their victims. "Evacuation," "resettlement," "transport," "actions," "special treatment," "final solution"—all were euphemisms for the torture and murder of two-thirds of the Jewish people in Europe.

Beginning with the lightning conquest of Poland in 1939, the Nazis occupied one country after another. The Jewish leaders were interned or shot. Other Jews were ordered into walled ghettos. A large network of transit, concentration, and forced labor camps were set up. During the summer of 1941 orders were given for the construction of death camps. The largest of the camps was at Auschwitz, where one to two million Jews were killed by hydrogen cyanide gas (Zyklon B) between January 1942 and November 1944. The gas chambers—the chief instrument of death—were called "shower rooms" to deceive the victims.

When it was over in 1945, approximately three million Jews in Europe out of a total population of nine million remained alive. One million of those slain were children. Millions of non-Jews were also killed by the Nazis.          L.K.

**HOLY/HOLINESS.** The Hebrew scriptures contain several words formed from the root q-d-sh: the verb, "to be holy" or "make holy," "to sanctify"; the adjective, "holy" (for example, holy temple); and the substantive, "holiness." The primary meaning of this group of words (which have near parallels in other Semitic cultures) is uncertain, but most scholars agree that the terms convey the notion of separation. Holy is that person or thing that is separated from all that is profane, common, or defiling. Israel's conceptions of holiness are most clearly presented in the book of Leviticus, especially chapters 17–26, the so-called "code of holiness," and the books of the prophets Isaiah and Ezekiel.

One may say first of all that holiness is ascribed to Yahweh, the God of Israel; Yahweh alone is "the Holy One" (Ps. 71:22; Jer. 50:29; Isa. 1:4; 5:19; also 40:25; 41:14-16; Ezek. 39:7). Second, those persons, places, or things that belong to God are holy—they are sanctified by God for divine use or they manifest God's presence or activity (Exod. 29:42-46; Lev. 21:1; II Kings 4:9; Exod. 3:1-5; 19:3-6; Ps. 15:1; Isa. 11:9).

The testimony of ancient Israelites is that various people or groups have from time to time been confronted by an incalculable energy or power—wholly Other than human—a Presence perceived to be at once terrible and deadly and beneficent and life-giving. Those who experience this overwhelming force are often painfully aware of their creatureliness and are moved to worship. An example of the destructive effect of q-d-sh is the narrative concerning the fate of Uzzah (II Sam. 6:6-7). Uzzah's sudden death was a result of his steadying the ark to prevent harm to it when the oxen bearing it began to stumble; however, the same ark that brought death to Uzzah, brought a blessing to the household of Obed-edom (II Sam. 6:11-12). It would be a mistake to regard these stories concerning the ark as an example merely of Israel's primitive conception of holiness as an impersonal, quasi-materialistic phenomenon. Holiness was not inherent in the ark; its holiness consisted in the presence of the invisible Redeemer-King enthroned above it, who was revealed to Moses and the children of Israel (compare I Sam. 6; II Chr. 26:19; also Lev. 10:1-3; Num. 4:17-20).

Stories from the OT, such as those above, teach that one does not treat a holy object as one would treat a common one, since in some way or other it is a manifestation of God's holy Name (or Person), or an expression of God's holy will. The whole of the Priestly legislation in the Hebrew bible is based on these premises: the faithful Israelite must know what is holy and what is profane, what makes holy and what defiles or renders one unclean (Lev. 10; 16; 22:17-33). Much of this "code of holiness' presupposes the teaching of the major prophets of Israel-Judah who lived in the eighth century B.C. Their proclamation "Yahweh our god is holy" was accompanied by the demand that Israel's conduct be consistent with the divine nature. The moral content of q-d-sh is summarily stated by Isaiah of Jerusalem: "the Lord of hosts is exalted in justice, and the Holy God shows himself holy in righteousness" (Isa. 5:16). The account of Isaiah's call reflects earlier accounts of the external effects of an encounter with holiness, but the significance of the narrative in Isaiah 6:1-5 lies less in the awesome setting of Isaiah's call than in the prophet's conviction of his own and of his people's sinfulness deriving directly from his vision of the thrice HOLY ONE. The prophets' legacy is also found in some of the cultic Psalms that reflect a spiritual world in which the moral and personal quality of holiness, as conceived by the prophets, is expressed. Those who are saints (sanctified) praise the person of the Holy One of Israel (Pss. 71:22; 22:3; 89:5, 18).

Because of the prophets' teaching, the ritual and external manifestations of holiness were given a secondary status, but this did not diminish the growth and importance of the purity laws. The expansion of the oral law had the effect of ensuring the cultic purity of priests and people. Distinctions between the clean and the unclean were carefully drawn; holy days and seasons were carefully observed. Visions of the holiness of the Temple, of the Temple mountain, and of the holy city, Jerusalem, figure prominently in Jewish eschatology. Ezekiel's prophecies are especially noteworthy (Ezek. 36:16-36; see also Isa. 27:13; 52:7-12; 65:25; Joel 3:17; Jer. 31:23-25).

Early Christians reaffirmed Israel's confession: The Lord our God is holy (Ps. 99:1-3; Rev. 15:3-4; 16:5). The Christian prophet of the Apocalypse combines Isaiah 6 and Ezekiel 1 as he describes the heavenly throne room: living creatures sing unceasingly, "Holy, holy, holy, is the Lord God Almighty, who was and is and is to come!" (Rev. 4:8). As often in the OT, so in the NT, the reality of God's holiness confronts worshipers with moral demands (compare Isa. 5:16; I Pet. 1:15-16; Lev. 11:44-45). Again as in the OT, the hallowing of the "Name" is associated with the end-time, with the coming of the Kingdom of God (Matt. 6:9-10). In the Gospel of John, Jesus affirms the personal holiness of his Father (John 17:11).

When in the Gospels Jesus is declared to be "the Holy One," a messianic ascription is intended (Mark 1:14; Luke 1:35; 4:34; compare Mark 8:27-29; John 6:69; I John 2:20). Possibly other messianic appellations are more frequently employed in the Gospel tradition because the revelation of holiness is almost universally associated with the Spirit's activity, Jesus' gift to his disciples, thus fulfilling the proclamation of John the Baptist (Mark 1:8).

Paul was a major contributor to the spiritualization of the cultic character of holiness, espoused especially by the Pharisees. To the Roman Christians he writes: "I appeal to you therefore, brethren, . . .present your bodies as a living sacrifice, holy and acceptable to God, which is your spiritual worship" (Rom. 12:1). Those who are "sanctified in Christ Jesus" are able to do this (I Cor. 1–2; 6:11; II Thess. 2:13; Rom. 15:16). Or as the writer of I John declares, believers in Jesus the Christ "have been anointed by the Holy One" (v. 20); or as the writer of the book to the Hebrews proclaims: "Jesus . . . suffered outside the gate in order to sanctify the people through his own blood" (13:12). "For by a single offering he has perfected for all time those who are sanctified" (I John 2:20; Heb. 13:12; 10:14). For this reason alone Christians are addressed in the NT as "the saints." J.P.

**HOLY CITY.** A designation for JERUSALEM, a city sacred to three world faiths—Judaism, Christianity, and Islam. In Revelation, Jerusalem is specifically called the Holy City (Rev. 10; 11:2; 21:2; 22:19). The Holy City referred to is the heavenly or new Jerusalem (Rev. 21:2), in distinction from the historical city, however. J.C.

**HOLY CLUB.** A group of Oxford students, originally gathered by CHARLES WESLEY and soon headed by JOHN WESLEY, who came together in 1729 to study the Greek NT, pray, and engage in good works. They were also called Bible Moths, the Godly Club, Enthusiasts, and Methodists. They fasted on Wednesdays and Fridays, kept regular hours of prayer and Bible reading, took Communion weekly, and ministered to those in a local prison. N.H.

**HOLY GHOST.** See HOLY SPIRIT.

**HOLY KISS.** The greeting of the faithful during the Eucharistic liturgy. It is a sign of love and unity in Christ. Greeting one another with a holy kiss is of apostolic origin, as it is mentioned in Romans 16:16; I Corinthians 16:20; II Corinthians 13:12; I Thessalonians 5:26, and I Peter 5:14 (where it is called "the kiss of love"). J.C.

**HOLY OF HOLIES.** See TABERNACLE.

**HOLY ONE, THE.** One of the names attributed to YAHWEH, Israel's GOD. The title is often extended by the addition of the phrase "of Israel," especially in Isaiah, who uses the title twenty-nine times (1:4, etc.). The term "Holy One" denotes God's transcendence above the earth that God has made and over which God rules (Isa. 6:1-5). The notion of "apartness" is basic; but the prophets also remind the people that God is righteous (Isa. 5:16) and requires a

"holy people," that is, a people both separated from evil practices and dedicated to God. R.M.

**HOLY ORDERS.** Ordination to the priesthood in the Roman Catholic, Old Catholic, and Eastern Orthodox churches, said to confer special spiritual powers and graces on the person. In the Roman Catholic view, an INDELIBLE CHARACTER of priesthood is obtained through holy orders. Orders comes from the Latin *ordo,* meaning "rank." J.C.

**HOLY ROMAN EMPIRE.** The name usually given to the institution that claimed to be the heir of the Roman Empire in the West and that existed from the crowning of CHARLEMAGNE in A.D. 800 to the abdication of Francis II in 1806. During that time, it took many different shapes, for under Charlemagne, and later under the Ottos, it was the greatest power in Western Europe, while at other times it was little more than an empty title. Its relationship to the papacy was never clear, for Popes tended to see it as the secular arm of the church, on the grounds that Charlemagne and his successors, up to CHARLES V, were crowned by Popes. But the stronger emperors resisted attempts on the part of the papacy to intervene in their affairs. This led to repeated clashes, of which the most notable was the INVESTITURE CONTROVERSY. After the Reformation, the empire became an increasingly empty title. J.G.

**HOLY SEPULCHRE, CHURCH OF THE.** A large basilica in Jerusalem, portions of which date to A.D.

Courtesy of the Philosophical Library

*Court and facade of the Church of the Holy Sepulchre*

335, built on the traditional site of Christ's crucifixion, burial, and resurrection. The Romans built a Temple of Venus on the hill of Calvary or Golgotha ("the place of a skull") in A.D. 135, after the second Roman-Jewish war or Bar-Kochba revolt. The emperor Constantine destroyed this temple and excavated down to the rock. A cave tomb and its stone covering were discovered. Constantine built a basilica with three aisles over this tomb and, supposedly, the site of Christ's crucifixion. The surrounding rock was hewn away and the sites incorporated into the building. In A.D. 624, the Persians destroyed this basilica, and later another church was raised by Modestus. Within the rotunda of this building the two sites can now be seen in two chapels. This is one of the most sacred sites in the Christian world.

J.C.

**HOLY SHROUD.** *See* SHROUD OF TURIN.

**HOLY SPIRIT.** In Christian theology the Holy Spirit is ranked within the Godhead as divine and, since the early creeds, worshiped as a member of the Holy TRINITY. The stages of evolution of this belief are complex and belong to the history of Christian doctrine. What follows surveys the biblical data to do with "spirit," and here again a long line of development is traceable.

*The Old Testament.* The Hebrew term *rûah* occurs nearly four hundred times in the OT and is rendered generally by "spirit" or "wind," from a verb meaning "to blow or breathe." It is thus associated with the principle of life or "center of activity" (see Gen. 2:7; 6:17; 7:15; etc. when used of a person as a human being). Creation itself is the product of divine activity described as God's breath (Gen. 1:2; Ps. 33:6), but an earlier understanding of Spirit as applied to God thought of it as an invading or violent power that came upon people and took possession of them. If the Spirit was diminished or lost, they faded away and died (Josh. 5:1; Ps. 143:7; Isa. 19:3). When God's Spirit came forcefully upon the leaders of Israel, they were "persons of spirit" and did exploits, such as the Judges (Judg. 3:10; 6:34; 11:29; 13:25; 14:6; the classic example is of Samson in 15:14-17) or the early ecstatic prophets in I Samuel (10:6, 10; 19:20, 23, 24) who, possessed by the divine Spirit, did strange things as a sign of their being considered "holy persons." The basic meaning of divine Spirit in this period is something like a driving force that gave to special persons a supernormal dynamic for what they did, usually eccentric, in the service of God. Spirit was thus a manifestation of divine power, put forth in a visible, tangible, and experiential way. The hallmarks were ecstasy, often induced by music (I Sam. 10:5ff.; II Kings 3:15), and a superhuman ability of leadership, whether of the crassly physical (Samson) or overtly moral (Samuel) kind. Divine and human "spirit" tended to merge in this literature, with no clear distinction drawn.

In the period of the early monarchy (such as the reigns of David and of Solomon) the Spirit was brought into association with the anointing of kings and elaborated in a later time (I Sam. 16:13ff. God's Spirit left Saul, and David was later idealized as a man of the Spirit, Ps. 89:20, 21, who set the pattern for the coming perfect king on whom the Spirit would rest, Isa. 11:2; 61:1; Pss. of Sol. 17:37; 18:7, and the Dead Sea Scrolls). The preexilic prophets showed a remarkable reluctance to claim divine inspiration through the Spirit (only Mic. 3:8), and this fact may be explained by their disdain of ecstatic experiences associated with either popular or cult prophets (Isa. 28:7; Jer. 5:13; 6:13; Mic. 2:11).

In the exilic and postexilic periods attributing claims of prophetic authority returned, especially in Ezekiel and Isaiah (Ezek. 2:2; 3:22-24; Isa. 42:1; 44:3), and two important developments took place. First, the divine Spirit became more openly related to creation (Gen. 1:2) and to a moral sense of personal responsibility of people to God (Ps. 51:13; Isa. 63:1ff.). The Spirit was consciously dignified with the title "holy," that is, God's power set men and women apart from evil and enlisted them in a crusade to make Israel a holy nation. The second development arose out of a sense of frustration and failure in the postexilic era. Already in the exilic prophets (for example, Jer. 31:31-34; Ezek. 36:26-27, 37) there was the promise of a new beginning, called a "new age," when the Spirit would be in evidence in human experience (Isa. 59:21; 61:1-4; 63:11) and create a new people (Ezek. 39:29; Joel 2:28ff.; Zech. 12:10), sometimes offering the promise of a new world order (Isa. 66:18, 22). This eschatological expectation brings us to the threshold of the NT with a further reminder that in the period between the Testaments, the Holy Spirit was believed to have forsaken apostate Israel until the new age should arrive.

*The New Testament.* The clearest sign Jesus reportedly gave of what he came to do was a claim to usher in God's kingdom (Mark 1:14-15), whose presence and power were certified by his "mighty works," that is, healings, exorcisms, and concern for the religiously and socially outcast. His ministry was attributed to the Spirit at work in him (Luke 4:18-19; Matt. 12:28; Acts 10:38). Jesus came to fulfill the expectations of a new age of the Spirit, seen and felt to be present in Jesus' person as divine Son (Mark 1:10-12) and in ministry as one who would also grant that Spirit to his followers (Mark 1:8 and pars.). While Jesus spoke only reservedly about the Spirit, the later church came to see that the signs of this messianic presence could only have been the work of the Spirit in him.

At Pentecost Jesus' promise was made good (Acts 1:4-5). The Spirit came on the apostles in consequence of Jesus' exaltation (Acts 2:33), and ancient prophecies (Joel 2:28ff.; Ps. 110:1) were realized. The new society that gathered around the name of the Risen Lord was full of the Spirit's tokens—in mighty deeds, convincing proclamation, and in a community spirit *(koinōnia)* of mutual regard and sharing (Acts 2:44-45; 4:32-37). Preachers and leaders, such as Stephen (Acts 6:10), Philip (Acts 8:26-40), and Saul (Acts 9:17), are described as "full of the Spirit" who led the Christian mission ever onward and outward, from Jerusalem to Rome (Acts 1:8), according to sixty-two times in Acts, a tribute to the narrator's belief in the church's life setting in the eschatological age.

Paul is the great NT exponent of the Christian life as "living in the Spirit" (Rom. 8:14-17; Gal. 4:6). For Paul Christian experience originated in a receiving of the Spirit (I Cor. 12:3; Gal. 3:2ff.), who initiated men and women into the fellowship of the church (I Cor. 12:13; this is the "baptism of the Spirit" associated with baptism in water, Rom. 6:3; Gal. 3:27; and following the usual pattern in Acts 8:12-17; 10:44-48; 18:25—19:6).

For Paul the gift of—and subsequent life in—the Spirit had strong ethical dimensions, empowering believers to live no longer under the power of sin ("the flesh"), but rather in the energy of the Spirit (Gal. 5:16-26). But there is no separate experience different from living "in Christ" (Rom. 8:9-17; II Cor. 5:17; 12:1). The reason for this equation lies in Paul's apparent linking of the Spirit with the Risen Christ (II Cor. 3:17-18), so that having the "fruit of the Spirit" is identical with living "in accord with Christ" (Rom. 15:5-6), and the SPIRITUAL GIFTS (I Cor. 12:4-11; Rom. 12:3-8) are practiced under the lordship and inspiration of Christ (I Cor. 12:3; 13:1-13).

The other NT writers, with varying terminology, agree with these main Pauline emphases. The Spirit is the author of new life for the believer and the community (John 3:3, 5-6; 20:22; Heb. 2:4; I Pet. 1:12; I John 4:13; 5:6-7), usually connected with the exaltation of the Risen Lord and an initiatory rite of baptism. The Johannine literature stresses the inner meaning of such sacramental action, making the Spirit the presence of God or Christ in the individual (John 6:53-63: the Spirit gives life to the eucharistic elements and makes possible a "spiritual" communion). The Spirit is given distinct personality as Jesus' gift of the PARACLETE (or helper, in John 14—16); and the way is thereby prepared for ascribing to the Holy Spirit an independent "center of consciousness" *(persona)*, which was later incorporated into the creeds of the church, with their formula of "three persons, one God."                                                    R.M.

**HOLY WATER.** A sacramental in the Roman Catholic Church; water blessed for religious use. It is used to bless people (when entering the church) and things (by sprinkling). Its use dates from the second century A.D. Water is a natural symbol for purification of the profane and consecration to God.
                                                                    J.C.

**HOLY WEEK.** The most sacred portion of the Christian liturgical year; the week preceding EASTER. Consecrated to the central mysteries of the Christian faith, Christ's sufferings, death, and resurrection, Holy Week began in the third century A.D., as a three-day celebration of the Passover season and the institution of the Lord's Supper. By the fourth century, the commemoration was expanded to a full week and Holy (or MAUNDY) THURSDAY was especially honored. Holy Week developed naturally out of the practice of Christian pilgrimages to Jerusalem yearly, where they could celebrate the Lord's Supper and reenact the events of Jesus' last week in liturgical drama and solemn processions. Holy Week eventually came to embrace the whole period from Palm Sunday (or the Sunday of the Passion) to Easter. Later, the commemoration was expanded to forty days, with the designation of Ash Wednesday, and the Lenten season was complete.

In the liturgical revival of the twentieth century, the observance of Lent, and especially of Holy Week, spread to embrace the free churches of Protestantism as well as the liturgical churches. Today it is almost universally celebrated in America.                          J.C.

**HOLY YEAR.** A special period of piety proclaimed by the pope, in which he grants plenary indulgence to Catholics who visit Rome to venerate the tombs of Peter and Paul. The most recent Holy Year was proclaimed by Pope Paul VI on Christmas, 1974, to pray for reconciliation among peoples.          J.C.

**HOMER.** A measure of capacity in OT times. Most measurements were informal, such as a "handful" (I Kings 20:10); however, there were formal designations. The homer was a pile of grain, often one donkey-load. After the Exile such measures were standardized. The homer was about six and one-fourth United States bushels.                          J.C.

**HOMOOUSION/HOMOIOUSION.** Two words that held center stage during the controversy over ARIANISM. The first means "of the same substance (or essence)," and the latter "of a similar substance (or essence)." The NICENE CREED had declared that the Son was *homoousios* with the Father. There were many, however, who were afraid that this could be interpreted as meaning that there is no distinction between the Father and the Son, thus leaving the way open for Sabellianism. As an alternative, they proposed the term "homoiousios," which they felt would do justice to both the unity and the distinction between Father and Son. These theologians have been mistakenly called semi-Arians, when in fact they were anti-Arians who were also concerned with the danger of Sabellianism. After long negotiations, in which ATHANASIUS as well as the CAPPADOCIAN FATHERS played an important role, most of the homoiousian leaders agreed to the Nicene formula, *"homoousios."*
                                                                    J.G.

**HOMOSEXUALITY**. Having a sexual orientation toward those of the same sex. The word has been used in many different ways, but here it will be used to refer to adult sexual preference for those of the same sex.

*Background.* It is not known with certainty whether sexual orientation is determined by genetic inheritance or by the chemistry of the mother during pregnancy. Or whether psychological, sociological, and other factors play the predominant role in shaping sexual orientation. Adolescents go through a stage in which they prefer to associate with those of their own sex. Do some people remain in this stage into adulthood? Is homosexuality a psychiatric issue? Or a moral issue? Or does it have a physical origin that is not yet understood?

*Social Acceptance.* There are those who argue that all conduct, even when the motivations are unconscious, is the result of choice. They say, therefore, that people are ultimately responsible for whatever they do. Such people would try to help those with a homosexual orientation understand that they are not victims of something beyond themselves. Rather, choices they have made in the past, however unconsciously, have brought them to this position. To them, these choices can be reviewed and new decisions can be made. Others see homosexuality as an orientation that one is born with or that develops in the first two or three years of life. They would urge society to look on homosexuals in the same way that it does all other people—that they are individuals created by the same God. Some draw a distinction between practicing homosexuals and those who are inclined toward homosexuality but do not practice it. Still others would distinguish those who are loyal to one other person in a homosexual relationship from those who are homosexually promiscuous. Estimates are that 10 percent of the population has a homosexual orientation. Thus most families can be expected to have at least one person with this orientation somewhere in the relationship.

*Old Testament.* In the OT, the men of SODOM demanded that Lot bring out his two male guests to them, apparently for sexual purposes. Not realizing that the guests were messengers from God, the men called out, "Bring them out to us that we may *know* them" (Gen. 19:5). Here the word "know" probably has the meaning of having sexual relations with. Two other OT passages speak against a man lying with another man as he would with a woman (Lev. 18:22 and 20:13).

*New Testament.* There are no clear references in the Gospels to homosexuality. Either Jesus offered no teachings on the subject or the Gospel writers did not consider them of enough importance to preserve them.

*Summary.* There is much confusion in our society today among Christians regarding homosexuality. Some denounce only promiscuous practice; others are judgmental toward anyone with a homosexual orientation.

The biblical call is toward responsible use of one's whole life, including one's sexuality. Our bodies are to be the temple of the Holy Spirit. And underlying all, needs to be the awareness that all people are sinners in need of God's gracious forgiveness.

B.J.

**HOOKER, RICHARD** (1553?–1600). Exponent of Anglican theology and author of *The Laws of Ecclesiastical Polity*; born in late 1553 or early 1554 near Exeter. John Jewel, bishop of Salisbury, became his patron and sent him in 1568 to Corpus Christi College, Oxford, where he received his M.A. in 1577.

In 1585 he was elected master of the Temple Church. On February 13, 1588, he married Joan Churchman, and her dowry enabled him after 1591 to devote himself to writing. His *Polity* was the last salvo in the "admonition controversy," in response to the June 1572 publication by certain Puritans of *An Admonition to the Parliament.*

Hooker's magnum opus was to be eight volumes, though only five appeared in his lifetime. He defended the ELIZABETHAN SETTLEMENT against both Roman Catholics and Puritans. He argued that the English tradition has a threefold base—the Bible, the church, and reason. A proponent of sound constitutional government, he believed in the unity of church and state.

N.H.

**HOOKER, THOMAS** (1586–1647). Puritan cleric born on July 7 in Marfield, England. At Emmanuel College, Cambridge, he received the B.A. (1608), the M.A. (1611), and served as a fellow (1611–18). After serving two parishes, his PURITAN views brought him into conflict with the government, and he fled to Holland in 1630.

From Holland he sailed for New England in 1633. A powerful preacher and a sensitive pastor of souls, he was chosen in 1635 to argue against Roger Williams and in 1637 to be co-moderator of the trial of Anne Hutchinson. He also presided at the Cambridge Synod. After serving the Newtown (Cambridge), Massachusetts, congregation for three years, he helped found Hartford, Connecticut, and served there until his death July 7.

His writings include *The Soules Preparation for Christ* (1632), *Four Godly and Learned Treatises* (1638), *A Survey of the Summe of Church Discipline* (1648), *The Saints Dignitie and Dutie* (1651), and the two-volume *Application of Redemption* (1656-57).

N.H.

**HOPE**. In Christianity faith, love, and hope are the three theological virtues. In the biblical religions, hope is understood in terms of hope in God and in God's covenant promises and is associated with ESCHATOLOGY. Hope would appear to be a natural, human, as well as a theological, exigence or need.

Immanuel Kant maintained that human reason concerns itself with three questions: (1) What can I know? (2) What ought I to do? and (3) What may I hope? Emil Brunner points to the universal significance of human hope when he writes that "what oxygen is for the lungs, such is hope for the meaning of human life . . . the fate of humanity is dependent on its supply of hope." Hope means the presence of a future. Without hope there can be no openness to a future, only a fatedness that brings a sense of purposelessness and paralysis. Here, however, we are concerned with hope in its biblical and theological context.

A recurring question in the OT is: on whom should one's hope and confidence rest? If one's hope rests on what is not secure, it is doomed to futility and disappointment (Ps. 49:6-12; Isa. 36:4-9; 44:9-20). For the OT writers, God alone is the firm ground, the rock and fortress, of the "hope of Israel." Israel's trust in and fidelity to its God, Yahweh, is grounded in the covenant established between God and the people at Sinai. While the covenant promises are partially fulfilled in the promised land of Canaan and in the Davidic kingdom, events such as the Babylonian Exile leave Israel's hope for the kingdom of God unfulfilled and future-oriented. Delays in the fulfillment of God's promise teach Israel patience, courage, and a confident expectation in God's salvation, undiminished by historical disappointments and disasters.

In the NT the ground of hope is also "the God of hope" (Rom. 15:13); it, too, rests on God's promise (Rom. 4:17-21), and is expressed in faith, patience, and endurance. However, in the NT hope is centered on the indwelling Christ who, Paul says, is "in you, the hope of glory" (Col. 1:27). For the NT writers, hope is grounded in Christ's resurrection and victory over death, perceived as the fulfillment of God's PROMISE to the fathers (Acts 26:6-7). Paul's hope, for example, stands or falls with the trustworthiness of God's resurrection of Jesus from the dead (Acts 26:8). Paul associates human hope in God's promise in Christ with confidence (Rom. 4:18), rejoicing (Rom. 5:2), endurance (Rom. 5:4), freedom (Rom. 8:21; Gal. 5:5), and with love (I Cor. 13:7). The NT hope is both personal and corporate and is perceived as both a present reality and a hope that will consummate in the future eschaton. Eschatological hope in the NT is already present in Christ—what the NT scholar C. H. DODD calls "realized eschatology." Jesus announces, for example, that the "time is fulfilled" and that the kingdom of God is "at hand" and in our midst (Mark 1:15). John speaks of the Christian as having "passed out of death into life" (I John 3:2). Yet it is also true that hope in the NT is, as Albert Schweitzer demonstrated, a forward-looking expectation of a future consummation in the parousia, the general resurrection, the final judgment, and the new creation, "a new heaven and a new earth" (Rev. 21:1).

One of the formative contributions of theology in this century is the rediscovery of the radically eschatological, and even apocalyptical, character of much of the Bible. This was brought to light by NT scholars such as Johannes Weiss and SCHWEITZER, as well as by more recent scholars who have shown the importance of the themes of PROMISE and fulfillment and apocalypticism in the OT. After World War I, KARL BARTH and other Neo-orthodox theologians appropriated the rediscovery of biblical eschatology and made it central to their theology, especially to their sense of cultural crisis, their rejection of all liberal ideas of historical progress, and their appeal to an entirely transcendental hope. In returning eschatology to the center of theological reflection, the Neo-orthodox theologians focused attention once again on the theme of hope. In 1954 the World Council of Churches, in its Second Assembly in Evanston, made hope the central theme of its deliberations. This theme an the council's report, *The Christian Hope and the Task of the Churches* (1954), stimulated an unprecedented discussion of and numerous books and studies on Christian hope.

Concurrent with this new attention on Christian hope, there appeared philosophical studies on the theme, for example, Ernst Bloch's *Das Prinzip Hoffnung* (1959), and Gabriel Marcel's *Homo Viator: Introduction to a Metaphysic of Hope* (1951). Bloch's work has been an especially important influence on post-Neo-orthodox theologians such as Jürgen MOLTMANN and Johannes Metz, both of whom have made eschatology, and especially the theme of Christian hope, central to their theological work. Bloch sees the principle of hope as the driving force of all human activity, since it is the future, not the past, that is decisive in determining both the present and the coming of any new creative initiative in history. Bloch's this-worldly, historical focus on hope has turned theologians such as Metz and Moltmann away from "other-worldly" and purely transcendental ideas of Christian hope to embrace a radically horizontal and historical one, without endorsing earlier liberal ideas of inevitable historical progress. According to these theologians, God must be viewed not statically but eschatologically, as the power of the future. So conceived, God does not rob humans of their freedom or their historical responsibility, and yet, God alone possesses power to liberate lives and to release forces that can overcome and save the present.

The new theology of hope claims to overcome the traditional opposition between religion and revolution or between reliance on salvation and responsibility for the world. This has made possible a new dialogue and rapport between the theology of hope and Marxist and humanist concerns for liberation from oppression and for socioeconomic change and progress. Such a Christian hope refutes the notion of hope as bad faith (Sartre) or an opiate (Marx), that is, the idea that "he who lives by hope dies of hunger." A theology of hope rejects all Promethean "attempts at self-redemption or self-production" and, at the same time, the quietist's refusal to accept responsibility for the world, in the belief that all will be resolved or redeemed in the end without human effort. For a theologically grounded hope, day-to-day self-sacrifice "becomes possible and becomes human within that horizon of expectation which transcends this world" (Moltmann). Hope is a virtue, for it is what gives life its sense of the holy, what keeps life open to new possibilities, to the transcendent or what Marcel calls "the absolute recourse."                                J.L.

**HOPE, THEOLOGY OF.** See MOLTMANN, JÜRGEN.

**HOPKINS, JOHN HENRY, JR.** (1820–91). Designer, musician, and hymn writer. Hopkins was born in Pittsburgh, Pennsylvania, and graduated from the University of Vermont. He moved to New York City, where for a time he worked as a newspaper reporter and at the same time prepared himself for a law career. Later however, he received a master of arts degree from the University of Vermont (1845), then studied for the ministry at General Theological Seminary, New York. He remained at the seminary after graduation and became its first teacher of music. He also was founder and editor of the *Church Journal*. He expressed his abilities in art by designing stained glass and other art objects. He later was ordained priest and served as rector of churches in Plattsburg, New York, and Williamsport, Pennsylvania. In 1863 his *Carols, Hymns and Songs,* in which he demonstrated his gifts as poet and musician, was published. His carol, "We Three Kings of Orient Are," became very popular. His hymns included"Alleluia! Christ Is Risen Today," "God of Our Fathers, Bless This Our Land," and "Like Noah's Weary Dove."
R.H.

**HOPKINS, SAMUEL** (1721–1803). Disciple of JONATHAN EDWARDS and exponent of Hopkinsian theology, Hopkins was born September 17, in Waterbury, Connecticut, to Timothy and Mary Judd Hopkins. After earning his degree at Yale in 1741, he studied theology with Edwards in Northampton, an association that continued during Hopkins' tenure as a minister at Housatonic (Great Barrington), Massachusetts, from 1743 to 1769. From 1769 until his death on December 20, 1803, he served First Congregational Church, Newport, Rhode Island.

Inheritor of Edwards' library and his principal systematizer, Hopkins propounded the New Divinity, emphasizing the sovereignty of God, a governmental theory of the Atonement, love as the greatest human virtue, obligation that involves ability, and sin and holiness as matters of the will. His works include *Sin . . . an Advantage to the Universe* (1759), *The True State and Character of the Unregenerate* (1769), *An Inquiry into the Nature of True Holiness* (1773), and *System of Doctrines Contained in Divine Revelation,*

*Explained and Defended* (1793). In *A Dialogue Concerning the Slavery of Africans* (1776), he became one of the first Congregationalists to oppose it.
N.H.

**HOPPER, EDWARD** (1818–88). Presbyterian minister and hymn writer. Born in New York City, Hopper attended New York University and Union Theological Seminary. He held pastorates in Greenville, New York, and Sag Harbor, then a whaling port on Long Island, before serving the Church of the Sea and Land, New York City. This accounts for the nautical themes of some of his hymn texts, best known of which was "Jesus, Savior, Pilot Me," published anonymously. He also was the author of "They Pray the Best Who Pray and Watch," and "Wrecked and Struggling in Mid-ocean."
R.H.

**HOR, MOUNT.** In Hebrew, *"hor"* means "mountain." The name first appears in Numbers 20:22-28, where it is said to be the place where Aaron was buried. Hor was on the route of the Israelites' wilderness wandering, but its exact location is unknown. Perhaps it was north of Kadesh-barnea. Some scholars have identified Hor with the highest mountain in the ancient kingdom of Edom, now called Jebel Harun. Others dispute this identification. It has also been said to be one of the mountains on the northern border of Israel, near Hamath. This would make it a part of either the Lebanon or anti-Lebanon range. Some indications in Numbers 34 could lead to such an identification, but it is far from certain.

Very clearly, Mount Hor is said to be near the frontier of Edom in Numbers 20:23; then, in the description of the frontiers of the Promised Land, we read: "This shall be your northern frontier: you shall draw a line from the Great Sea to Mount Hor and from Mount Hor to Lebo-hamath . . ." (Num. 34:7-8 NEB). It seems probable that two different mountains are involved here. Since "Hor" means mountain, it probably was used to designate the highest, largest peak in any mountain range. It meant something like "the mountain" (or a "real" mountain) in the popular speech of the day.                                J.C.

**HOREB.** See SINAI, MOUNT.

**HORITES.** The ancient inhabitants of Syria and Mesopotamia in the second millennium B.C. The Horites may be the same people as the HURRIANS. They lived at Seir at the time of Abraham and later were driven away by the Edomites. The name may mean "cave-dwellers," but this is doubtful.
J.C.

**HORNEY, KAREN** (1885–1952). Trained under Karl Abraham, a close associate of FREUD, Horney criticized Freud's reliance on sexual libido and refused to accept Freud's view that female psychology was just a corollary of male psychology. She theorized that social and environmental factors largely determine individual personality and cause neurosis. She authored *The Neurotic Personality of Our Time* (1937), *Our Inner Conflicts* (1945), and *Neurosis and Human Growth* (1950). A native of Hamburg, West Germany, she moved to New York City in 1934 to enter private practice and teach at the New School for Social Research. She founded the Association for the Advancement of Psychoanalysis.                N.H.

**HORNS OF THE ALTAR.** Extensions from the four corners of the altars on which the sacrifices and incense were burned. These were the altars of holocaust and of incense. The horns were considered their most sacred parts. The blood was smeared on them. Fugitives who grasped them were protected from harm.                J.C.

**HORUS.** Egyptian sky god, whose cult arose in the Nile Delta and spread throughout the country in prehistoric times, taking many forms. He has the head of a falcon and his eyes are the sun and moon. The kings of upper Egypt, who unified the country, were considered his incarnations. When the cult of OSIRIS spread over Egypt around 2425 B.C., Horus became identified as his son. The Greeks identified him with the god APOLLO.                K./M.C.

Courtesy of the Brooklyn Museum, Charles Edwin Wilbour Fund

*A hawk, wearing a crown, represents the Egyptian god Horus*

From Minoru Ooka, *Temples of Nara and Their Art* (John Weatherhill, Inc.)

*Aerial view of the West Precinct, Horyu-Ji*

**HORYU-JI.** A Buddhist temple at the city of Nara, Japan, dating from the seventh century A.D. It is the oldest surviving temple in Japan. Its buildings are prized as the finest example of the combination of Chinese and Korean traditional architecture with native Japanese elements. They contain unique art treasures, including paintings, sculpture, and textiles.

Horyu-ji, like other temples in the Far East, is a complex of buildings of varying sizes and functions. The West Precinct is a rectangle surrounded by a cloister three hundred by two hundred feet. It is built of wooden columns covered by a tile roof. In the south side of the cloister there is a large two-story gateway of similar construction. Inside the compound on the right is the main hall, and on the left a five-storied PAGODA, twice as high as the main hall. Beyond them is the main lecture hall.

The temple was founded by Prince Shotoku (A.D. 573–621) near his own palace. He was probably the person most responsible for the establishment of BUDDHISM in Japan. From A.D. 710 to 784 Nara was the capital of Japan, and during this time Buddhism flourished. A new compound and temple buildings were erected on the former site of Prince Shotoku's palace. It is known as the East Precinct.

Because the main structural material is wood, fires have been a constant threat, and several of the buildings have burned and been rebuilt. Even so, many works of art from the earliest period have survived.

K.C.

**HOSANNA.** Consisting of two Hebrew words, the imperative of the verb *yasha'*, "save!" followed by the particle of entreaty, *na'*, "please!" this expletive seems to belong to the realm of worship in ancient Israel. This is confirmed by its appearance in Psalm 118:25, "Save us, we beseech thee, O Lord! O Lord, we beseech thee, give us success!" and many other places in the psalter (for example, Pss. 12:1; 20:9; 28:9; 60:5; 108:6). However, few of these and other OT contexts of the phrase resemble each other, and by no means are all laments and entreaties for help. In fact, some are occasions of the glad announcement of divine help and salvation.

In the NT the term is used exclusively as a cry of triumph almost perfectly synonymous with the term HALLELUJAH. The only six occurrences of the term all occur in the context of the triumphant entry of Jesus into Jerusalem on Palm Sunday (Matt. 21:9, 15; Mark 11:9-10; John 12:13). It is significant that in these texts, the term is never translated but only transliterated, indicating that it had become meaningful in its own right. No longer did the people intend to shout, "Please save us!" Now they intended to praise and bless "the Son of David," the very one to whom they believed Psalm 118:26 was referring when it continued, "Blessed is he who enters in the name of the Lord." W.S.T.

**HOSEA.** According to the superscription of the book of Hosea (1:1), the prophet who gave us the first in the order of the twelve so-called minor prophetic books lived and worked during the days of JEROBOAM II (786–746 B.C.), ruler of the northern kingdom of Israel, where Hosea worked. More is known about him as a person than is the case with most of the prophets of the OT because of the account contained in chapters 1–3 of the prophet's symbolic marriage to a "wife of harlotry." From this marriage with Gomer, three children were conceived who were given the symbolic names Jezreel ("for yet a little while, and I will punish the house of Jehu for the blood of Jezreel," 1:4), Not Pitied ("for I will no more have pity on the house of Israel," 1:6), and Not My People ("for you are not my people and I am not your God," 1:9). The first three chapters understand this strange marriage as a metaphor for Yahweh's relationship with Israel.

Assuming that the same woman is spoken of in all three chapters, the married life of Hosea consisted of five stages: (1) Hosea made a covenant with a woman; (2) the covenant was broken; (3) she is to be punished; (4) he cannot let her go; and (5) she will finally return, and their covenant will be renewed. Clearly these are the very things that Hosea wishes to say about the relationship between Israel and God: God made a covenant with Israel at Sinai and there God chose Israel to be his bride, but Israel was faithless and whored after other gods. So God is going to punish the faithless Israel by returning Israel to the wilderness. There God will start afresh with Israel with a new salvation history.

More than date and symbolic marriage, we can say little else about the prophet Hosea except that the word of God in his mouth glows with an intensity and intimacy matched in the OT only by the later prophet Jeremiah. This passion was no accident but sprang directly up from the context in which the prophet worked. The kingdom of Israel was deeply infused by the practices of Canaanite religion, which may even have been mistaken for authentic Yahwism at local sanctuaries. Part of the practice of the fertility cult of Canaan was cult prostitution through which men and women alike sought to achieve union with God and to activate the growth of the crops through sexual union with the god Baal. When Hosea accused Israel of leaving God to play the harlot, he meant it literally (see, for example, 4:11-14). But precisely against such a background, Hosea was willing to draw upon the language of human intimacy; he was the first to speak of the covenant relationship between Yahweh and Israel as one of love (11:1) and to refer to Israel as a wife (Hosea 1–3) or an infant son (11:1-4) of God.

*The Book of Hosea.* This OT book can be divided into two major sections. Chapters 1–3 contain both the biographical account of Hosea's marriage to GOMER (chaps. 1–2) and a first-person autobiographical account of that marriage (chap. 3). The remainder of the book (chaps. 4–13) consists of an extended collection of oracles describing Israel's unfaithfulness to Yahweh, not any longer under the metaphor of marriage, but nonetheless highly charged with the imagery of "whoring" after Baal. This collection of oracles culminates in chapter 14 with a call to repentance and a promise of forgiveness.

*A Theological Summary of the Book of Hosea.* The burden of the message of Hosea is contained in his indictments. These fall into four categories. (a) *Ethics.* Hosea says with passion that Israel has transgressed the covenant (4:1-4; 12:7-8). Unlike his contemporary Amos, who viewed the ethical failure of Israel as a legal transgression, Hosea sees it as a failure of a right relationship with Yahweh. God's people have turned their backs upon the gracious one who gave them the covenant. What God in Amos took as a justification for a death sentence on Israel, in Hosea God takes as a personal affront and the occasion for the most intense divine suffering (9:10-14; 11:1-5). (b) *Politics.* Hosea also condemns the political machinations of the Israel of his day (7:3-7). He is against political intrigue which, during his lifetime, led to the rise and fall of six kings, most of whom came into power by *coup d'etat.* (c) *Cult.* Hosea does not simply indict Israel for the transgression of particular cultic laws but calls the whole practice of religion into question. Against the Canaanized religion that in fact existed, Hosea calls Israel back to the religion that it ought to have observed. The Decalogue, which he knew and proclaimed, laid heavy stress against idolatry; "you shall not make for yourself a graven image, or any likeness of anything . . . you shall not bow down to them or serve them" (Exod. 20:4-5). But in the Israel of Hosea's day, graven images were everywhere, depicting not only Baal but even Yahweh in the golden calves that Jeroboam I had placed in Dan and Bethel (II Kings 16:2-4). Every place had its local BAAL, and in the OT alone we hear of Baals of Samaria, Carmel, Ekron, Herman, Peor, Tabor. The name of Baal's game was fertility, fertilizing the land on an annual cyclical basis and fertilizing people through sacred prostiution. Hosea thunders against such practice as an abomination and calls religion like that, even if intended to strengthen the economy of the land, "harlotry" (see 4:12-14; 9:1-3).

(d) *The priesthood.* The final topic of indictment in Hosea centers on the priests of the land. The attack is not upon priesthood as such but upon priests who are responsible to convey to people the knowledge of God but who do not do so (4:6). Such a failure means that the people perish because they no longer know the sacred traditions of the past, the account of God's saving activity and the covenant with Israel. The life of the people of God stands or falls as they are successfully related to the objective facts of the faith. Hosea teaches that the recitation of the saving acts of God toward Israel results in the people's inner acknowledgment and their personal bonding with God. Only the people who can acknowledge Yahweh's self-description through Hosea, "I am the Lord your God from the land of Egypt; you know no God but me, and besides me there is no savior" (Hos. 13:4) can understand their past and trust their future.

W.S.T.

**HOST.** The bread used in Holy Communion, to become Christ's Body; usually a wafer of very thin, unleavened flour. Often, unconsecrated wafers are referred to as hosts, although the consecrated remnant of the Mass kept on the altar of a Roman Catholic church is also called a reserved host.     J.C.

**HOSTS OF HEAVEN.** The "twelve legions of angels" referred to by Jesus in Matthew 26:53; God's heavenly army. The "heavenly hosts" are mentioned in I Kings 22:19 and Luke 2:15, where the angelic host praises the newborn Christ child. Yahweh is known as "the Lord of Hosts" (or armies) in the OT (I Sam. 17:45).

According to Psalm 46:7 and Amos 4:13, as well as Judges 5:20, the hosts of heaven included the stars, heavenly bodies, and all the powers of nature. The song of Deborah (Judges 5) declares: "The stars in their courses fought against Sisera." In popular Christian piety and religious art the angels (or messengers of God) are often represented as armed with swords and viewed as protectors of the weak and the faithful. In Jesus' teaching about the judgment, angels are said to divide the righteous from the wicked, and in Revelation 12:7-9, Michael, the archangel (or general of God's armies), is said to fight the devil and his fallen angels and to defeat them. Revelation 19:11-16 shows the triumphant Christ riding as a warrior at the head of the heavenly host during the final battle of good and evil, decisively and finally winning victory over Satan.     J.C.

**HOURS, CANONICAL.** The set prayers in the DAILY OFFICE of the Roman Catholic church and the Eastern Orthodox church. These include the eight services of prime, lauds, terce, sext, none, vespers, compline, and matins. (The hours have been extensively revised by the canons of Vatican II.) Recitation of the daily office (the Breviary) is a duty of every priest, as part of his spiritual growth. Monasteries regularly observe the full rituals of each of the canonical hours.     J.C.

**HOWE, JULIA WARD** (1819–1910). The author of the "Battle Hymn of the Republic" was born on May 27 in New York City. Howe studied languages, religion, and philosophy, wrote poetry and drama with autobiographical themes—violent love, betrayal, and suicide. Her poem, written during a visit to Washington, D.C., and published in the *Atlantic Monthly* (February 1862), was unnoticed until it was set to the tune "John Brown's Body."

Later Howe became very active in public life as director of the American Peace Society, founder of the

Woman's Peace Association, founder and officer of the New England Women's Club, the New England Woman Suffrage Association, the American Suffrage Association, the Association for the Advancement of Women, and the General Federation of Women's Clubs. She often preached in Unitarian and Universalist pulpits. For twenty years she edited the *Woman's Journal*.                                              N.H.

**HSÜAN TSANG** (596?–664). Chinese Buddhist monk and scholar, famous for his pilgrimage to India (A.D. 629–645) in search of Buddhist scriptures, images, and relics. Unable to get permission of the reigning Chinese emperor, Hsüan Tsang slipped away secretly and traveled through central Asia, across the Hindu Kush mountains into India. On the journey he faced many perils and on several occasions almost lost his life.

In India, Tsang traveled widely, studying with famous scholars, visiting places sacred to the memory of the Buddha, and receiving honors from monarchs. Indian monks tried to persuade him not to return to China. At Bodhgaya he saw the bodhi tree, under which the Buddha was enlightened, and a famous statue of Avalokitesvara. According to legend, by the time that this statue had sunken completely into the ground, Buddhism would have disappeared from India. It had then sunk as far as the chest.

On his return to Ch'ang-an, the capital of China, he received a tumultuous welcome. He wrote an account of his travels and spent the remaining years of his life translating into Chinese the scriptures he had brought back with him. He also translated Indian Mahayana texts and founded the "consciousness only" school of BUDDHISM.

In the sixteenth century Wu Ch'eng-en wrote an account of Hsüan Tsang's travels, combined with satire and allegory into a rollicking folk tale known in English as *Monkey*.                                    K.C.

**HSUN TZU.** From the Chinese word for "Master Hsun." A Chinese philosopher of the third century B.C., Hsun is the leading spokesman of the extreme rationalistic and naturalistic wing of CONFUCIANISM. Little is known about him apart from the book that bears his name. Rejecting the importance of both supernatural entities and the authority of the past, Hsun Tzu contended that all that is worthwhile to humans is made by humans and transmitted through human culture, which must be continually adapted to changing conditions. Directly countering the assertion of Mencius that human nature is essentially good, Hsun Tzu said that it is evil in the sense of being self-centered originally, but can be made good through education and a good social environment. He thus affirmed in his own way the high value Confucianism places on those factors. He also affirmed the great importance the tradition gave to rites, but taught that for the wise their worth was not really connected to gods or heaven but lay in their

power to embellish or release human feeling, channel it into socially valuable forms of expression, and so help hold human society together. Hsun Tzu is of general interest for his early and brilliantly argued attempt to find meaning within a naturalistic world view for traditionally religious values and practices.
                                                          R.E.

**HUBMAIER, BALTHASAR** (1485–1528). German ANABAPTIST martyr who wrote the Reformation's first plea for complete religious toleration. A protégé of John Eck at Freiburg and Ingolstadt, he received a doctorate in theology and became cathedral chaplain at Regensburg in 1516. Although anti-Semitic, he thought abuse of Regensburg's Jews was excessive. In 1521 he accepted a parish at Waldshut. He supported Zwingli, and began reforms. Yet in 1524 he defended believers' baptism and published *Concerning Heretics and Those Who Burn Them*, advocating full toleration. In 1525 he repudiated infant baptism, was rebaptized, and published *On the Baptism of Believers*, in which he called infant baptism idolatry. Siding with the peasants in 1525, he helped write the Twelve Articles. In December 1525 Austrian troops occupied Waldshut. Hubmaier fled to Zurich, where Zwingli arrested and forced him to recant Anabaptism. In 1526 he renounced the recantation and successfully preached around Nikolsburg, Moravia. Austrian authorities burned him at the stake in Vienna in 1528.                        C.M.

**HÜGEL, BARON FRIEDRICH VON** (1852–1925). British Roman Catholic modernist theologian and biblicist. Born in Italy, son of an Austrian diplomat, he received a broad education and developed interests in mysticism, geology, history, and biblical criticism, which he tried to reconcile with his Catholicism. From age fifteen, he lived in England, married, and became naturalized. Modernism racked Catholicism despite Pius IX's *Syllabus of Errors* (1864), Leo XIII's *Providentissimus Deus* (1893) upholding biblical inerrancy, and Pius X's *Oath Against Modernism* (1910). In 1897 Hügel openly propounded multiple sources for the Hexateuch, thus questioning established doctrine on the inspiration, inerrancy, and Mosaic authorship of the Pentateuch. He was a close friend of Alfred Loisy and George Tyrrell, both condemned for their modernism; but Hügel, whose influence extended far beyond Roman Catholicism, escaped official condemnation. Among his books are *The Mystical Element of Religion* (1908), *Eternal Life* (1912), and *Essays and Addresses on the Philosophy of Religion* (1921).              C.M.

**HUGH OF ST. VICTOR.** The main figure of the theological school of St. Victor, which flourished in the outskirts of Paris in the twelfth century. His principal work, *The Sacraments of the Christian Faith*, is also known as *De sacramentis Christianae fidei*. His main thesis there is that all knowledge, even that which is not directly theological, is valuable inasmuch as it relates to creation and restoration. To this, Hugh added a mysticism of the type espoused by DIONYSIUS the pseudo-Areopagite. By thus combining theology with general science and with piety, he became one of the main forerunners of SCHOLASTICISM.     J.G.

**HUGUENOTS.** A name given French Protestants after 1560. Before JOHN CALVIN, Protestantism made limited progress in France and enjoyed some royal favor. But in 1533 Francis I began persecuting Protestants, prompting Calvin to dedicate the *Institutes* to him. Calvin's doctrines spread rapidly, and in 1559 French Protestants meeting in Paris organized along Calvinistic lines. By 1561 Calvinists were a significant political minority. Violent Catholic resistance ensued. War raged between Catholics and Huguenots from 1562 to 1594, almost continuously. On St. Bartholomew's Day (1572) an infamous massacre of Protestants occurred. Following bitter fighting, Huguenot Henry of Navarre became King Henry IV, 1589, and accepted Catholicism in 1593 to secure his kingship. He issued the Edict of Nantes (1598) granting Huguenots toleration. Louis XIV revoked this edict in 1685, causing over 300,000 Huguenots to flee, many to America. Huguenots again won legal standing under Napoleon's concordat with Pope Pius VII (1801).     C.M.

**HUMANAE VITAE.** An encyclical issued by Pope Paul VI, July 29, 1968, that condemned all forms of artificial contraception, leaving abstinence and the rhythm method, approved by Pius XI's encyclical *Casti connubi* (1930), as the only sanctioned means of birth control for Roman Catholics. The encyclical cited no scriptural texts, went against the study committee's recommendations, and evoked angry protests from Roman Catholics throughout the world. This pronouncement, seen by many as a deliberate show of papal authority, asked world governments to ban all birth control means contrary to divine and natural law and jeopardized Vatican Council II's principle of collegiality.     C.M.

**HUMANISM.** A cultural movement usually identified with the Renaissance and Reformation (1350–1600) revival of Greco-Roman-Hebraic antiquities. It represents a gradual shift from other-worldly to this-worldly concerns, symbolized in Protagoras' statement that "man is the measure of all things." With the rise of modern rationalism and science, the transcendent element in humanism greatly weakened. "The Humanist Manifesto" (1933), issued by John Dewey and other social leaders, discarded belief in God as a helpful ingredient for living.

Originating in fourteenth-century Italy when papal credibility was low, humanism revived the classical sources of Western culture and exalted literature and art as ends in themselves. Early proponents include Francesco Petrarch (1304–74), who promoted classical literature and philosophy for personal, human enrichment; Poggio Bracciolini (1380–1459), who reveled in the paganism of old; and Coluccio Salutati (1330–1404), who saw in humanism a means of social betterment. Humanism was called the New Learning in sharp contrast to scholasticism's Old Learning. Before the fall of Constantinople to the Muslims (1453), hundreds of classical manuscripts were collected and translated. The printing press made wide circulation possible. Florence, a leading humanistic center, soon boasted a full translation of Plato's works into Latin. Nobility an clergy alike became patrons. Many humanists worked within the church, but a subtle denigration of ecclesiasticism emerged, particularly in the celebration of paganism and materialism as laudable goals, in Lorenzo Valla's forgery exposure in 1440 of *The Donation of Constantine* (a self-serving papal document), and in Machiavelli's *The Prince,* which glorified self-interest.

Northern humanism exemplified in Johann Reuchlin, Philip Melanchthon, and Jacques LeFèvre greatly extended Hebraic studies and education. The acknowledged prince of northern humanism was Desiderius ERASMUS, who sought to advance piety and culture with his Greek NT (1516), "philosophy of Christ," and humorous satires of cultural inadequacies. William Grocyn and Thomas Linacre introduced humanism into Oxford University, and Erasmus and John Fisher influenced the humanistic blossoming of Cambridge University. Humanism in its many facets is especially known for stressing human reason, education, freedom, optimism, anticlericalism, and belief in progress.     C.M.

**HUMAN NATURE.** Human beings have long been aware that they occupy a peculiar place in the world. Obviously they are, in some degree, a part of nature, and the theory of evolution has made it clear that we are descended from animal ancestors and share many characteristics with the animals. Yet we differ from even those animals that stand nearest to us on the evolutionary scale in ways that are not merely quantitative but qualitative. A leap into a new manner of existence has taken place, even in matters like sexuality and death, which on the surface seem to be very similar in human and animal life. For human beings, sex has become a personal, not a merely biological relation, while the fact that we know we are going to die makes possible a relation to time that an animal cannot have.

In addition, human beings have developed a whole range of activities that are simply unknown at the lower animal level or, at the most, are only very dimly foreshadowed. Such activities are language, art, science, religion, politics, and dozens of others. This special place of the human being finds expression in the theological statement that we are made in the image of God (Gen. 1:26). Admittedly, there has been much debate over the meaning of this affirmation. Some have seen the image in dominion, in human responsibility for the Creation, so that humans are in some sense God's steward or vice-regent; others have seen the image in rationality, but this may be too narrow a reading of the relation. Perhaps the most satisfactory interpretation is that the image of God in the human being is the capacity for a limited measure of freedom and creativity.

It is this in human existence that makes a difference from the animals and suggests a similarity, however distant, to God as the Creator of all that exists. Some of the early Christian writers, including Irenaeus, noted that in the Genesis story God had made the man and woman "in our image, after our likeness," and they supposed that the image was the potentiality for growth toward God, while the likeness would be the completion of the process, a relation so close to God that they spoke of "deification." Although their reading of Genesis was exegetically improbable, it nevertheless afforded a genuine insight into biblical anthropology. The Bible sees our human nature as unfinished and embarked upon a pilgrimage, the end of which will be a full communion with God.

This insight accords very well with modern conceptions of human transcendence, a continual crossing of new horizons without any end in sight. Many other principles of Christian and Jewish anthropology can be derived from the early creation stories. The fact that we are dealing with the couple, man and woman, points to the fundamentally social nature of the human being, often expressed in modern times by the statement that there is no "I" without a "thou." (See I-THOU AND I-IT.)

Again, the human being is from the beginning embodied. The body is prior to any mention of a fall, so that in opposition to GNOSTICISM and its modern equivalents, the Judeo-Christian tradition has had respect for the body and has been concerned about the material conditions of life, and has never represented SALVATION as an escape from entanglement in the material world. The story of the Creation is succeeded by that of the Fall. Though humanity may have been created in the image of God, the humanity that we know is disordered. It is important to note, however, that although SIN enters the human story very near the beginning, the story makes it quite clear that there is a goodness and righteousness that is more original than the most original sin. So sin is not itself a part of human nature, but rather its perversion. However, the Fall into sin is an inescapable element in the human condition, and the NT even more strongly than the OT insists on its universality (Rom. 3:23). Some theologians have held that the spiritual sin of pride is fundamental, for although humanity is called to the closest union with God, it wishes rather to usurp God's place—so the original temptation was, "You shall be like God" (Gen. 3:5). Others, in view of the unmistakable sexual overtones of the story of the Fall, have stressed the sins of sloth and sensuality.

Actually, both types of sin can be seen as following from the biblical understanding of the human being as compounded of freedom and finitude. Humans are tempted to deny their finitude and seek to be God, and on the other hand to reject their freedom and descend to being creatures of the appetites.

The OT anthropology is taken over by the NT, and there are still many allusions to it, but it is transformed by the central place given to Jesus Christ. He is the one in whom the image of God has been fulfilled and who has overcome sin, so that he is the archetype of the new humanity. The distinctively Christian anthropology is worked out most fully by Paul. He introduced new concepts, such as conscience, and stresses the place of faith and grace. Love is set forth as the highest of the Christian virtues. Paul also develops teaching about the resurrection life and human destiny beyond death, far beyond anything in the earlier tradition.

Much of the Christian and biblical anthropology was expressed in a terminology that has now become outmoded and that was in any case pictorial and inexact. Modern writers on the subject have made use of new terminologies offered by psychology, sociology, existentialism, and other philosophies of human nature. The Christian teaching accords very closely with many modern insights. We have seen that the basic notion of pilgrimage corresponds to the modern idea of transcendence, and parallels have been drawn also between sin and alienation, between faith and commitment, between salvation and integration, and so on.                                                           J.M.

## HUME, DAVID

HUME, DAVID (1711–76). Scottish philosopher, skeptic, and historian. Born in Edinburgh and educated at Edinburgh University, Hume failed to secure a professorship, yet distinguished himself through writing. He lived most of his life in Edinburgh, but held several government posts and became a popular British embassy secretary in Paris. Jean Jacques Rousseau was a close friend. Hume's outstanding works include *Treatise of Human Nature* (3 vols.; 1739–40), *Essays Moral and Political* (2 vols.; 1741–42), *Philosophical Essays,* containing "Essay on Miracles" (1748), *An Enquiry Concerning Human Understanding* (1751), *Political Discourses* (1752), *History of England* (5 vols.; 1754–61), and *Dialogues on Natural Religion* (posthumous, 1779).

Hume maintained that human knowledge comes from experience, from impressions. We can relate ideas logically, but cannot know actual reality. Cause-and-effect is the product of customary association, not logic. The existence of material things, God, and an experiencing "I" cannot be proved. This incisive skepticism shook metaphysics and science. Concerning miracles, Hume argued it is more likely that reporters of miracles are deceived or deceivers than that nature's regularity, which we experience, has been interrupted. Hume's skepticism left human knowledge in shambles and directly inspired IMMANUEL KANT'S famous critiques of reason. C.M.

**HUMILITY.** Judaism and Christianity teach that humility characterizes the proper attitude of human creatures toward God and one's fellows. Greek literature exposes the folly of *hubris* (PRIDE, arrogance), and the triumph of the gods is sometimes consequent upon their humiliation; but the concept of humility in Westen civilization has its primary roots in the OT.

*Humility in the Old Testament.* The remembrance of Israel's humble origin provided a restraint upon the creation of social structures based on military might and wealth. Israel's God was revealed as one who delivers the humble, the poor, and the afflicted, and brings down the haughty (I Sam. 2:6-8; Deut. 7:7-8). In much of Israel's history humility or humiliation, a condition of material poverty and oppression, becomes a spiritual trait of "the righteous" or devout (Pss. 22:22-26; 25:6-9; Prov. 16:5-9, 18; 22:4, 22-23).

*Humility in the New Testament.* The OT background of the Gospels' teaching concerning humility is given prominence in the Beatitudes of Jesus ("blessed are you poor," Luke 6:20; "poor in spirit," Matt. 5:3-6), and in Mary's *Magnificat* (compare Luke 1:52 and I Sam. 2:7). The old expectation is affirmed, but most references to humility in the NT relate not to a spiritual self-abnegation but to objective states of poverty and affliction (Jas. 4:6; I Pet. 5:6). Above all else, the divine condescension of Jesus exemplified humility (John 3:1-17; Phil. 2:3-8; II Cor. 10:1; I Cor. 13:4-5; Rom. 12:3).                    J.P.

**HURRIANS.** An ancient, powerful nation, originating in Armenia, and moving into the Near Eastern area around 2500 B.C. These people, also known in the OT as the HORITES and HIVITES, flourished in the middle Euphrates Valley from about 2500 to 1000 B.C. The Hurrians were the overlords of the Assyrians, and Assyria was not able to develop until the Hurrians' Mitanni Empire declined. The Hurrians were so widespread that they were present in Canaan when the Israelites arrived at the time of the conquest. They are mentioned in Genesis 14:6; 36:30; Deuteronomy 2:12, 22; and Joshua 9:1.

Significant literary remains of the Hurrians have been discovered at Ugarit, Nui, and Mari. These writings show that many myths and legends of the Assyrians, Babylonians, and the Israelites originated among the Hurrians. The Hurrians fell under the rule of the Hittites from Asia Minor in the fourteenth century B.C. and became part of the Assyrian Empire in the thirteenth century B.C.                    J.C.

**HUSS, JOHN** (1373?–1415). Bohemian Czech reformer, martyred at the Council of CONSTANCE for Wyclifite views. Born a peasant at Husinec, he earned an M.A. at Prague University (1396), lectured in theology, was ordained (1400), and became rector at Prague (1402). Despite the condemnation of WYCLIFFE's views, Huss continued translating and preaching them in his Czech sermons at Prague's Bethlehem Chapel. Huss insisted on scriptural guidance, God's sovereign ownership, responsible stewardship, Christlike poverty, abolition of priestly immoralities, and a predestinated church of the elect. His popularity combined with growing Czech nationalism to make him a hero.

The GREAT SCHISM (1378) had left Christendom with popes at Avignon and Rome. To remedy this situation the Council of Pisa (1409) elected Alexander V pope, but the other two popes did not quit. Christendom now had three popes, each of whom had significant political backing. Alexander V and John XXIII (his successor) both condemned and excommunicated Huss. Bohemia's ruling authorities went along, but the followers of Huss, called Hussites, supported him. Two conferences during 1412–13 failed to achieve peace. Huss's *On Simony* and *On the Church* (largely dependent on Wycliffe) declared the pope was Antichrist and appealed to a general council. Emperor Sigismund granted Huss safe-conduct for the Council of Constance (1414–18), but once there Huss was betrayed, imprisoned, and burned at the stake—a victim of political-religious intrigue. His death sparked over fifty years of Czech revolution and directly influenced the REFORMATION.                    C.M.

**HUSSERL, EDMUND** (1859–1938). Successively professor at Hälle, Göttingen, and Freiburg, and celebrated as the principal exponent of PHENOMENOLOGY. His aim was to make philosophy a strict science. That would mean that it must differ from the empirical sciences, whose results can be only approximate, and from any form of philosophy depending on chains of argument, which are always liable to error.

Phenomenology is intended to be a purely descriptive science. It describes what shows itself in consciousness as it shows itself and seeks to exclude both distorting presuppositions and dubious deductions. If this program is to be carried out, it demands a rigorous discipline on the part of the investigator. The investigator has to concentrate on universal essences, and to do this must "bracket" or exclude from consideration elements that belong to the particular instance and likewise exclude from the mind influences that come from earlier philosophical theories. Husserl himself moved toward an idealist metaphysics, recognizing consciousness as the fundamental reality. However, his descriptive method can be employed apart from his own philosophical conclusion, and it has in fact been widely used in investigating various areas of conscious experience, including religious experience.                    J.M.

**HUTCHINSON, ANNE MARBURY** (1591–1643). The woman who first questioned NEW ENGLAND THEOLOGY. Her mother was Bridget Dryden, her father Francis Marbury, an outspoken

Church of England cleric repeatedly censured for his views.

The family moved to London in 1605, where on August 9, 1612, Anne married William Hutchinson. Influenced by JOHN COTTON, the Hutchinsons emigrated to Massachusetts Bay in 1634. They soon became leaders: William as a merchant and landowner; Anne as nurse and midwife.

Anne, as she had in England, conducted semiweekly classes for women to discuss Scripture and sermons. Elaborating on Cotton's "Covenant of Grace," Hutchinson taught the indwelling witness of the Spirit, which made external evidence of sanctification superfluous. She was labeled ANTINOMIAN.

Soon the colony was divided between the Hutchinsons and Governor John Winthrop. Condemned by a church synod in September 1637, the General Court in November 1637, and a church trial in March 1638, she was excommunicated and banished to Rhode Island. After William's death in 1642, she and six children fled Puritan harassment and went to Dutch territory on Long Island, where they were murdered by Indians in 1643.    N.H.

**HUTTERIAN BRETHREN.** Oldest surviving Anabaptist group, originating in Moravia (1529). Swiss refugees led by Jacob Wiedemann pooled their resources (Acts 4:32-37) and settled at Nikolsburg, Austerlitz, and Auspitz. The Hutterites' name derives from Jacob Hutter, a Swiss minister who joined them (1529), became their charismatic leader and reorganizer (1533), and was martyred (1536). Despite severe persecution, the Hutterites survived. The communities, called Bruderhofs, resembled disciplined monasteries: they allowed marriage, held property in common, stressed crafts, and practiced pacifism. At their height, 1556–1620, they had one hundred communities and numbered twenty thousand. (During the Thirty Years' War, persecution reduced this number to two thousand.) Many, known as Habaner, were forced into Catholicism: others fled east. In 1802 many settled in Russia. The first Russian Bruderhof was established in 1857. Fearing military conscription, in company with Russian Mennonites, the brethren emigrated to South Dakota (1874–79). Abuse during World War I caused them to flee to Canada, Paraguay, and England. Many have since returned. They preach old sermons, use modern machinery, and speak English and German (*compare* RADICAL REFORMATION).    C.M.

**HUXLEY, THOMAS** (1825–95). English biologist and advocate of evolution. Born in Ealing, Middlesex, he studied medicine and was admitted to the Royal College of Surgeons in 1845. Becoming an assistant surgeon on HMS *Rattlesnake* (1846–50), he studied tropical life-forms while touring Australasian waters, and was made a Fellow of the Royal Society on returning to England. In 1854, after publishing several scientific papers, he became professor of natural history and paleontology at the Royal School of Mines. For him scientific study was a way to solve human needs. He enthusiastically endorsed DARWIN'S *Origin of Species* (1859) and lectured widely in support of evolution. His *Zoological Evidences as to Man's Place in Nature* (1863) defended humanity's descent from lower animals. He published a favorable study of Hume in 1879 and subsequently abandoned belief in a personal God in favor of an abstract unknowable impersonality. He heightened his attacks on Christian orthodoxy and extended his agnosticism to knowing little about Christ with certainty. The lucidity of his writings helped make evolution palatable to both scientists and commoners. His writings also include *Lay Sermons* (1870), *Science and Culture* (1881), and *Evolution and Ethics* (1893). Aldous and Julian Huxley were his grandsons.

C.M.

**HYKSOS.** Invaders from Asia who ruled Egypt during the Fifteenth and Sixteenth Dynasties (1720–1550 B.C.). The term "Hyksos" was given this vigorous people by the Egyptian historian of the Ptolemaic period, Manetho. The name is derived from Kikau-Khoswet, Old Egyptian for "rulers of foreign countries," and actually was used before Manetho to apply to chiefs of Nubian tribes and nomadic leaders. Some have seen the meaning "shepherd kings" (or nomadic tribal chiefs) behind the name. We have Manetho's assessment of the Hyksos only through Flavius Josephus' *Contra Apionem*. Actually, Josephus misconstrued history, identifying the Hyksos with the Hebrews (from Joseph to Moses). Josephus wanted to show that the Jews had a longer history than the Greeks and declared that the Hyksos were Hebrews who subjugated Egypt until driven out at the time of the Exodus.

What is sure is that the Hyksos, who ruled Egypt from Avaris-Tanis rather than the capital at Thebes, controlled Egypt during the time of Joseph. The stories in Genesis fit in well with a Hyksos (foreign) domination of the country. The Hyksos introduced the use of horses and armored chariots and the powerful compound bow to Egypt, and the use of these weapons spread throughout the Middle East. This warlike people worshiped Baal and the mother goddess, Anat.

J.C.

**HYMENAUS.** A teacher in the early church, mentioned in the Pastorals (I Tim. 1:20; II Tim. 2:17). In both instances he is associated with doctrines and practices adjudged false by the Pauline writer, namely a denial of the future resurrection and consequent relaxing of morality. Both features were attributed to later Gnostic teachings.

R.M.

**HYMNS.** *See* the individual authors.

**HYMNS, ANCIENT AND MODERN.** This volume, first published in 1861 and last revised in 1950, represents the beginning of modern English hymnody. Characterized by an austerity of style and conformity to the Book of Common Prayer, this book sets each hymn to a proper tune. Its publication represented a milestone because the Church of England, spurred by the Wesleyan revival, only accepted hymn singing as part of its services in the 1820s. Prior to hymns, metric and chanted psalms were used. The book was influenced by the OXFORD MOVEMENT.

N.H.

**HYPOCRISY.** The terms "hypocisy" and "hypocrite" are derivatives of Greek words for acting, actor. Metaphorically, in Greek literature they refer to a person's appearing to be what one is not. The predominant usage is moralistic; thus the hypocrite is one who pretends to be good or upright when one really is not so. It is often noted that there were no comparable Hebrew or Aramaic words. The RSV correctly registers this fact by eliminating from earlier English versions of the OT the words hypocrisy, hypocrite.

Since Jesus spoke in Aramaic, it is improbable that he rebuked the Pharisees of feigning piety. Several passages in the Synoptic Gospels provide alternative readings. For example, "their hypocrisy" in Mark 12:15 is corrected by Matthew by using a Greek term that is translated "their malice" (Matt. 22:18). In Luke 20:23 another Greek synonym is used, which is translated "their craftiness."

In Galatians 2:13 the verb and noun translated "acted insincerely" and "insincerity" refer to the refusal of Peter and Barnabas, under pressure from Judaizers, to continue to have table fellowship with Gentile Christians. Paul accuses them, not of playing a false part but for exhibiting a "lack of principle" (NEB), a breach of faith!

In view of the above it may be concluded that Jesus accused certain scribes of being outwardly religious while inwardly profane (Mark 7:6). In this context Jesus quoted Isaiah 29:13: "this people . . . honor me with their lips, while their hearts are far from me. . . ."

J.P.

**HYPOSTATIC UNION/HYPOSTASIS.** The term *hypostasis,* which can be translated literally as "substance," played an important role in the controversies having to do with the TRINITY and with CHRISTOLOGY. In the trinitarian context, it was used by the Greeks to distinguish between Father, Son, and Holy Spirit, and therefore they spoke of "one ousia (or essence) and three hypostases." This in turn led to confusion, for the Latin-speaking West, which preferred the formula "one substance and three persons," feared that the Greeks were speaking of what would be three "substances" to the Latins. It was only after these matters of terminology were clarified that the Greek and Latin branches of the church could agree on the final trinitarian formulas, "one substance [or ousia] in three persons [or hypostases]."

In the christological controversies, the term "hypostasis" was used to refer to the person in which the divine and the human natures are united. The phrase "hypostatic union," first used by CYRIL OF ALEXANDRIA in the NESTORIAN controversy, meant that in Christ the divine and human natures subsist in the one divine "hypostasis." In other words, that Christ is fully human, but that Christ's humanity subsists in Christ's divine hypostasis, or person. Cyril's views on this matter, variously interpreted and adapted, became standard christological orthodoxy.

J.G.

**HYSSOP.** *Origanum maru* or marjoram, a member of the mint family; a small shrub grown in Palestine. It has hairlike leaves and stiff branches, which made it suitable for sprinkling water or blood in ceremonies and sacrifices. Hyssop is mentioned as being used to convey water to Jesus on the cross in John 19:29, but Matthew 27:48 and Mark 15:36 refer to this as a reed. John may be using symbolism here, as hyssop is connected with sacrifices.

J.C.

# Ii

**I AM.** As soon as Moses had received his call from God while standing in awe before the burning bush on Horeb, the mountain of God (Exod. 3:1-12), he urgently asked the Holy One for his name (v. 13). Although God did very shortly disclose to Moses the sacred personal name YAHWEH, God elected first to propound to Moses a riddle: "I am who I am" (v. 14). Through all the ensuing ages the faithful have struggled to grasp the meaning of this cryptic utterance. At one level it seems to propose an etymological connection between the name YHWH and the verb HYH, "to be"—as though God's personal name were "being" itself. This is what the Septuagint translators of Exodus 3:14 understood the puzzle to mean: "I am Being." Most interpreters have understood verse 14 as a commentary upon Yahweh's name, but even then questions remain. Is Yahweh's answer to Moses an affirmation of his immutability and eternality: I AM WHAT I AM (RSV margin)? Is it an assurance of his utter steadfastness: I AM WHO I AM (RSV text)? Or is God teaching Moses that the profile of the divine character will be disclosed in the history of salvation, which lies ahead; I WILL BE WHAT I WILL BE (RSV margin)? Any of these three meanings is possible grammatically, and each of them conveys an important theological truth. **W.S.T.**

**IBN 'ARABĪ** (1165–1240). A Muslim mystic. He wrote a total of 270 works, most of which dealt with SUFISM. In *The Wisdom of the Prophets,* he describes the way each of the twenty-seven major prophets approached the question of the unity of God. The contents of this book were revealed to him in a single night when he was sixty-five years old.

**K.C.**

**IBN HANBAL** (780–855). A scholar of Islamic law and founder of one of the four legal schools accepted by SUNNI Muslims. Since Islam was from the beginning a total way of life, legal decisions in every area were based on the principles of the religion. The Hanbalite school is conservative, basing its teachings on the QUR'AN and the Sunna (traditions) that had been handed down from the time of the Prophet Muhammad. Ibn Hanbal rejected the two other bases for Islamic legal decision: (1) reasoning by analogy, and (2) opinions given by qualified jurists and accepted by the believing community as expressing a general consensus.

The Hanbalite school had been declining in influence until the rise of the WAHABI movement in Saudi Arabia in the nineteenth century, when it began to gain new importance.

**K.C.**

**IBN TAYMĪYYA** (1263–1328). A scholar of Islamic law in the Hanbalite school (*see* IBN HANBAL). He was often involved in controversy and as a result spent much of his adult life in prison. He interpreted the QUR'AN literally, including the descriptions of God in anthropomorphic terms, and rejected any customs lacking a basis in the Qur'an or the SUNNA (tradition). One such custom was the veneration of saints.                                          K.C.

**ICHABOD.** The son of Phinehas and grandson of Eli, priest of the shrine at Shiloh. He was born on the day that the Philistines defeated Israel and captured the ark, the news of which caused Eli's death (I Sam. 4:17-22). In Hebrew, Ichabod means "no glory."
                                                        J.C.

**I CHING.** The ancient Chinese *Book of Changes,* one of the five Confucian classics and a book of divination. It assumes a cosmic order of growth, degeneration, and renewal that can be tapped into through the religious or magical rite of divination. Confucian scholars study the I Ching to obtain a fuller understanding of the underlying processes of the world and of how to take advantage of them.

The text describes the eight trigrams, each composed of three broken or solid lines, and the sixty-four hexagrams formed by all possible combinations of two trigrams. The broken lines represent *yin,* the feminine principle, and the solid lines *yang,* the male principle. The trigrams and hexagrams are symbolic of the various states of nature, society, and the individual. The circular arrangement of the trigrams represents the cycle of time.

The creation of the trigrams and their first circular arrangement is attributed to Fu Hsi, a figure of ancient Chinese legend. The sixty-four hexagrams are attributed to King Wen (reigned 1191–1122 B.C.), who also made the second circular arrangement of the trigrams. Fu Hsi's arrangement is easily grasped, as opposite trigrams are also opposite in the arrangement of broken and solid lines: broken, solid, broken is across from solid, broken, solid, etc. However, the King Wen arrangement of the trigrams has puzzled scholars. Furthermore, the only order apparent in the arrangement of the hexagrams is that each even-numbered one is either the preceding hexagram upside down, or its opposite (exchanging solid and broken lines).

To consult the I Ching the inquirer should phrase a question such as, What will the consequences be if I take the action I have in mind? The diviner then constructs a hexagram line by line from the bottom up. The traditional method uses stalks of yarrow *(achillea millefolium)* in a complicated ceremony to arrive at a number from six to nine: six is a *yin* line, seven is an "old" *yang,* eight is an "old" *yin,* and nine is a yang line. The faster method, popular with diviners who work at fairs and on the street, uses three coins to produce each line. Interestingly enough, the two methods result in different probabilities of producing "old" lines, a fact that has not affected the accuracy of the prophecies. After the hexagram is complete, "old" yang lines are changed to yin and "old" yin lines are changed to yang to produce a new hexagram. The commentaries on both hexagrams are then consulted to find an answer to the question. Because the meaning is expressed in vague and symbolic language, it requires considerable interpretation. (*See* YIN/YANG.)

King Wen wrote the first commentaries: the "Judgments," expressing the good or bad consequences of the action recommended, and the "Images," describing the meaning of the hexagrams in archetypical terms. King Wen's son, the Duke of Chou (died 1094 B.C.), wrote the "Appended Judgments," the last addition to the book before the time of CONFUCIUS (551–479 B.C.). There is a tradition that Confucius said, "If some years were added to my life, I would give fifty to the study of the Yi [I Ching], and might then escape falling into great errors." Confucian scholars added commentaries to the I Ching down to the first century A.D., when the present edition took final form.            K./M.C.

**ICHTHUS.** *See* ACROSTIC.

Courtesy of the National Gallery of Art, Washington, D.C. Andrew W. Mellon Collection
*Madonna and Child on a curved throne, an example of a Byzantine icon*

**ICON/ICONOGRAPHY.** The word "icon" means "image," but since the ICONOCLASTIC CONTROVERSY icon has been used to refer specifically to the Eastern images, which are flat, and usually paintings or mosaics. Iconography, on the other hand, studies not only icons in this narrow sense, but all representation of Christian ideas, events, and legends. The iconography of the early church was both symbolic—the fish and the shepherd, for instance, represented Jesus—and pictorial, in paintings of the Last Supper, Noah in the ark, and others. After Constantine I, Christian art took on a triumphant character, often representing Christ enthroned in glory, and decorating crosses with precious stones. It also became didactic, particularly in the West, where it was seen as a way to teach Christian doctrines and stories to the illiterate masses. Romanesque and Gothic architecture made ample use of iconography, both as a didactic and as an ornamental device. At the time of the Reformation, many rejected the use of images altogether, although other Protestants saw value in them as long as superstition was avoided. The Council of Trent reaffirmed the use of images, but also sought to avoid superstitious abuses.                J.G.

**ICONIUM.** A town in Asia Minor visited by Paul and Barnabas on their first missionary journey (Acts 13; 14). Its place in the later tradition of Paul's mission cities is seen in II Timothy 3:11. Timothy is said to be recommended by the leader of the church at Iconium (Acts 16:1-2), and it became the scene, in the apocryphal literature, for the encounter between Paul and Thecla, a female convert from Iconium.                R.M.

**ICONOCLASTIC CONTROVERSY.** A controversy regarding the use of images, or ICONS, in worship, which raged in the Eastern church during the eighth century, and also involved the West. It began in A.D. 725, when Byzantine Emperor Leo III ordered the destruction of a much venerated image of Christ. This was followed by other decrees against images. The inconoclasts (destroyers of images) based their actions on the biblical injunctions against images and also on the criticism of their Moslem neighbors. Political and economic interests were added, which the iconoclastic emperors sought to further by curtailing the power of the monks, who were the main defenders of images.

The controversy eventually led to persecution of defenders of images in the East, and to the excommunication of the emperor by Pope Gregory II. In 787, the seventh ecumenical council gathered at Nicaea under the auspices of Pope Adrian I and regent Empress Irene. This council upheld the use of images, although distinguishing between the "respect and veneration" due them and the "true worship" (latria) to be reserved for God. Even after the council, there was a revival of iconoclasm in the East, until the images were finally restored by regent Empress

Theodora on March 11, 842—still celebrated in the Eastern churches as the Feast of Orthodoxy. In the West Charlemagne refused to accept the decrees of the council, terming them "idolatry," but the decline of Carolingian power finally brought the Frankish church to agreement with the use of images.

                                        J.G.

**ID.** See FREUD, SIGMUND.

**IDEALISM.** One of the basic philosophical streams in Western thought, affirming that what is not seen is more real than what is seen. Idealism is the theory that affirms that ideas are more real than concrete observable phenomena. It gives a central role to the ideal or the spiritual. Abstractions and principles are considered more fundamental than sensory experiences.

Ethical idealism puts emphasis on moral principles and frequently universalizes and accents moral freedom. Metaphysical idealism, in opposition to MATERIALISM, affirms that the idea is the real. Epistemological idealism asserts that the mind grasps only what can be perceived—in opposition to REALISM.

PLATO is credited with being the originator of idealistic thought in the Western world. He believed, as did his teacher Socrates, that truth could be found through the development of the mind. Greek thought early influenced Christianity, and NT ideas are sometimes couched in Greek terms, although perhaps not with Greek meanings: Logos (Word), truth, light. The struggle with Neoplatonic thought occupied the early centuries, and heresy was often synonymous with GNOSTICISM. The soul or spirit was viewed as superior to the flesh and the Hebrew concept of body/soul synthesis was obscured. AUGUSTINE, a seminal theologian writing during the period of the fall of Rome, combined Greek and Christian thought in ways that became basic to the medieval philosophical tradition.

Modern idealism takes its rise from RENÉ DESCARTES (1596-1650), whose famous dictum "I think therefore I am" reaffirmed the mind as the primary force in human existence. The process of thinking and the intellectual life took on a transcendent quality. In IMMANUAL KANT idealism was interpreted as moral philosophy, going beyond "pure reason" to postulate the "categorical imperative" with the thesis that moral law is written into the universe. In Kant the search for truth takes on a moral dimension.

Still working in the realm of ideas, HEGEL developed his theory of dialectical thinking: thesis, antithesis, and synthesis, through which opposites become reconciled to achieve wholeness and rationality. Paradox and ambiguity do not exist in the idealistic realm.

The American form of idealism is PERSONALISM, as developed by E. S. BRIGHTMAN. His thesis states that the person, or human personality, is the true reality; not the physical being, but the inner person who thinks, purposes, and holds ideals.

Idealism has always been a strong note within Eastern philosophy, particularly in India. Idealistic schools were earlier found in China. Idealism strongly influenced nineteenth-century Protestant theology in England, Germany, and the United States, particularly through the transcendentalist movement in New England.                                              I.C.

**IDOLATRY.** Both in the Bible and in modern usage, this term ranges in meaning from the narrow sense of offering sacrifice and prayer to a material representation of deity (an "idol") to the broad sense of treating as of ultimate importance some person, thing, or concept other than God. The actual term "idolatry" *(eidōlolatreia)* is used most frequently in the NT, where it is listed among the "works of the flesh" (see Gal. 5:20; I Pet. 4:3). In Colossians 3:5, the figurative sense appears in the phrase "covetousness, which is idolatry." The same equation (though with the term "idolator") is also offered in Ephesians 5:5 and indirectly in Philippians 3:19, "their god is the belly." The more literal sense, worship of idols, is treated at some length by Paul in I Corinthians 8:1-13 and 10:14-33. In these passages the apostle makes light of idols as such ("we know that 'an idol has no real existence,' and that 'there is no god but one,' " 8:4). The issue is whether or not a Christian believer is wrong to be present at the festival table of a non-Christian friend at which food blessed in the name of pagan deities is eaten. While acknowledging that the idolatrous practice is of no effect, being based upon no reality whatever, Paul cautions against letting "this liberty of yours somehow become a stumbling block to the weak" (8:9).

The term "idolatry" as such occurs only three times in the RSV of the OT. In I Samuel 15:23, it is a translation of the Hebrew term *teraphim*, elsewhere taken to mean a household god image (see Gen. 31:19-35; Judg. 17:5–18:20; II Sam. 19:13-16; II Kings 23:24; Ezek. 21:21; Hos. 3:4; Zech. 10:2). In Ezekiel 23:49 the very common term *gillulim*, "idols," is translated abstractly as "idolatry." Ezekiel 43:9 reads "now let them put away their idolatry" (*zenuth*, KJV, "whoredom"). However, the concept, if not the actual term, is richly pervasive. In addition to those already mentioned, a whole repertoire of synonymous terms and euphemisms is employed to indicate the presence of misplaced allegiance in worship. Hebrew and Aramaic terms sometimes translated "idol" can also mean iniquity, terror, horror, grief, abomination, form, graven image, pillar.

Now it is not in the least surprising that Israel should have had to contend with the lure of idolatry. The ancient Near Eastern context out of which Israel emerged at the end of the thirteenth century B.C. was replete with cults and state religions that stressed the presence of deity in all aspects of nature. Egyptian religion identified the sun as AMON-RE, the king of the GODS; other deities were shown in animal forms, including the jackal-headed god of the dead, Anubis, and Hathor, the cow goddess. Mesopotamian religion, with which Israel had contact in its formative periods but again during the period of Assyrian domination and the Babylonian exile, represented the greater and lesser gods in both animal and human forms and permitted worship in local sanctuaries with the use of crude images and amulets.

Above all, Israel had to contend with the religion of Canaan that preceded and surrounded Israel throughout its ancient tenure in the land of Palestine. The chief god in the Canaanite pantheon, El, was entitled "the bull," and the rain god, the cloud-rider Baal, was seen as a warrior who wore a bull-horned helmet. The fertility goddess ASTARTE (alluded to in the OT by the terms *ashtaroth*, Judg. 2:13, and sometimes *asherah*, Judg. 6:25-32; I Kings 18–19; II Kings 21:7) was widely and crudely pictured in statuettes and amulets throughout the Near East, even in Israel. In fact, it is clear that the popular religion of Israel, in contrast to the pure Yahwism described by the pentateuchal writers and proclaimed by the prophets, was deeply affected by the idolatrous practices of Canaan. This is explicit in the account of the establishment at Samaria by King Ahab of Israel of the BAAL cult of his wife, the Sidonian princess Jezebel (I Kings 16:31-32). It is equally explicit in the much later account of the reforms of Hezekiah (II Kings 18:3-4) and Josiah (II Kings 23). The latter text speaks specifically of idolatrous priests "who burned incense to Baal, to the sun, and the moon, and the constellations, and all the host of the heavens" (23:5). It speaks of the ASHERAH that was in the house of the Lord, the male cult prostitutes, the high places all over the country, and the place called Topheth in the vale of Hinnom near Jerusalem where people burned their children as offerings to Molech. It speaks of the chariots of the sun and the altars on the roof, and even of the high places that "Solomon the king of Israel had built for Ashtoreth the abomination of the Sidonians, and for Chemosh the abomination of Moab, and for Milcom the abomination of the Ammonites" (v. 13).

If popular religion in Israel was so deeply penetrated by the practices of Canaan, it is no wonder that the first commandment—like the rest of the Decalogue probably incorporated into the Sinai account by the Elohistic writer who is believed to have worked in the northern kingdom of Israel in the ninth cenury B.C.—makes a fundamental distinction: "You shall have no other gods before me" (Exod. 20:3; compare Deut. 5:7). "Other gods" may exist; the commandment does not deny that possibility. But they must not interfere in the complete bonding that is to take place between Yahweh and the chosen people, Israel. This commandment is a demand for total allegiance and bears a direct relationship to

Israel's most fundamental confession, "Hear, O Israel; the Lord our God is one Lord" (or perhaps even better, "the Lord is our God, the Lord alone," Deut. 6:4).

The account of the reform of Josiah (about 621 B.C.) already alluded to concludes with the remark that Josiah pulled down "the altar at Bethel, the high place erected by Jeroboam the son of Nebat, who made Israel to sin" (II Kings 23:15). This is a reference to the cult established as a rival to that of Jerusalem by the first king of the northern kingdom of Israel after its secession from the united monarchy of Solomon (I Kings 12:25-33). Many now suggest that the two golden calves that Jeroboam placed, one in Dan and one in Bethel, were actually either footstools or representations of Yahweh. If so, the king may have been speaking of Yahweh when he dedicated them with the words, "Behold your gods, O Israel, who brought you up out of the land of Egypt" (v. 28). However, the establishment of an image, even an image of Yahweh, was regarded by the deuteronomistic writers as a sin that affected the entire history of Israel (see I Kings 14:7-16). In forbidding graven images, the second commandment (Exod. 20:4-6; Deut. 5:8-10) probably intends to forbid exactly the kind of thing represented by Jeroboam's golden calves, or for that matter the original golden calf (Exod. 32:4). To localize and concretize God, creator of all that is, in an object is not only absurd, but it is also a self-serving act because it suggests that God can be manipulated to the advantage of those who own the shrine. Yahweh will not permit this, because God discloses truth and direction not through the ministrations of priests before an idol but to those faithful servants to whom God freely chooses to speak.

Iconoclasm (the abhorrence of graven images and likenesses of deity) and opposition to idolatry in general survived the strife with Baal that permeated the period of Elijah and Elisha, Hosea, and Jeremiah. In and after the Babylonian exile, it became a hallmark of Judaism. The latest OT testimony to the revulsion of Israel against the practice of idolatry is found in Daniel 3, the story of the three young Jews who refuse to fall down before the golden image that Nebuchadnezzar, king of Babylon, placed upon the plain of Dura. Just before they are to be cast into the fiery furnace, Shadrach, Meshach, and Abednego make this memorable assertion of their liberty from the bondage of idolatry: "If it be so, our God whom we serve is able to deliver us from the burning fiery furnace; and he will deliver us out of your hand, O king. But if not, be it known to you, O king, that we will not serve your gods or worship the golden image which you have set up" (Dan. 3:17-18).

This utter refusal to acknowledge any legitimacy whatever to the representation of Deity in an idol points directly toward the tendency of both the Pharisaic rabbis and the writers of the NT to regard idolatry as a silly, vacuous sin based upon no reality whatever. In a sense, the demise of idolatry and the triumph of the living and imageless religion of the Judeo-Christian tradition was summed up by Paul on the Areopagus hill. As he stood there among the fading splendor of pagan worship, he proclaimed that the unknown god whom the Athenians acknowledged and who "made the world and everything in it, being Lord of heaven and earth, does not live in shrines made by man, nor is he served by human hands, as though he needed anything, since he himself gives to all men life and breath and everything" (Acts 17:24-25).                                              W.S.T.

**IDUMEA.** This is a Greek word, used to render EDOM, but in regard to a geographical region in western Palestine. The strife between the Israelites and the Edomites became acute at the time of Jerusalem's fall in 587 B.C., and this explains the condemnation in such places as Jeremiah 49:7-22, Obadiah, and Psalm 137:7. Later the area was occupied by Nabateans and conquered by the Maccabeans, thereby explaining how Herod the Great came from Idumea. It is referred to once in the NT (Mark 3:8).                                              R.M.

**IGNATIUS OF ANTIOCH, EPISTLES OF.** Seven letters written by Bishop Ignatius of Antioch on his way to martyrdom early in the second century and now included among the writings of the APOSTOLIC FATHERS. Five of them were addressed to churches in Asia Minor, one to Bishop Polycarp of Smyrna, and a seventh to Rome. They are one of the most important sources for our knowledge of early Christian theology. In them, Ignatius shows that one of the great dangers of the time was the DOCETISTS, against whom he stresses the doctrine of Incarnation, the Eucharist, and the authority of Bishops. He is also the earliest Christian writer to employ the terms "Christianity" and "Catholic church."                                              J.G.

**IGNATIUS OF LOYOLA** (1491–1556). Founder of the JESUITS (Society of Jesus), author of the *Spiritual Exercises,* and a powerful figure in the CATHOLIC REFORMATION. Born into Spanish nobility, he planned on a military career, but at Pampeluna (1521) a cannonball fractured his right leg. During recovery he read books on Christ and the saints and resolved to be a soldier for Christ. In 1522 at Montserrat's Benedictine abbey, he confessed and vowed chastity, poverty, and service to Christ. During further recovery at Manresa, he sketched *Spiritual Exercises* (completed 1548), a manual for dedicating oneself to Christ. After an abortive trip to Jerusalem, he vowed to fight Protestant heretics. Within four years he advanced from a boys' school to the University of Paris. His charisma attracted others, and the Inquisition investigated him three times. In Paris he and six followers vowed lives of poverty, chastity, and service. They did hospital work in Venice, were ordained (1537), and placed themselves at the pope's disposal. Paul III hesitantly approved the Jesuits (1540), with a note about special obedience to the pope. Initially limited to sixty, the Jesuits grew phenomenally and soon dominated Catholic education, missions, and the Catholic Reformation.                                                C.M.

**I.H.S.** An abbreviation or monogram for Jesus. ("IHS" stands, in Latin and English, for the letters iota, eta, sigma in Greek.) This monogram often occurs in ecclesiastical art, as in stained-glass windows. It also is used as an emblem by the Society of Jesus. IHS may also serve as a symbol for the sign Constantine supposedly saw before he attacked the Roman army in his bid for the throne of Caesar. Constantine is said to have adopted the Christian cross as his insignia after seeing a cross and the legend *"In Hoc Signo Vinces,"* meaning "In this sign conquer" in the sky. Christianity was made a legal religion by Constantine after his victory in A.D. 312.      J.C.

**IJMA.** From the Arabic word for "settling, resolving." In ISLAM, the "consensus" of the Islamic community that, together with the KORAN and the SUNNA or tradition, especially of the Prophet MUHAMMAD, is one of the three major sources of authority in SUNNI law. In practice *ijma* is determined by legal scholars, with early precedent given definitive weight by conservatives.      R.E.

**ILLUMINISM.** The doctrine or practice of people or groups who believe themselves to possess special spiritual, moral, or intellectual enlightenment. The term has been associated with various groups of "illuminati" in history, for example, people related to the Enlightenment of the eighteenth century and religious sects claiming knowledge of truth.      C.Mc.

**ILLYRICUM.** A land mass extending from modern Yugoslavia, across Albania, and into northeast Italy. It took its name from one of the tribes that settled in the area. The Romans made it part of the empire in the first century. It is referred to in Romans 15:19 as the outer limit of Paul's mission in the eastern Mediterranean.      R.M.

**IMAGE OF GOD.** The doctrine of an image of God (*imago dei*) in humanity seems to imply that in the human creature there is some finite reflection of the divine nature. The point is made several times in the opening chapters of Genesis. "Then God said, 'Let us make man in our image, after our likeness; and let them have dominion over the fish of the sea, and over the birds of the air, and over the cattle, and over all the earth, and over every creeping thing that creeps upon the earth.' So God created man in his own image, in the image of God he created him; male and female he created them" (Gen. 1:26-27). A second passage repeats the substance of the one just quoted: "When God created man, he made him in the likeness of God. Male and female he created them" (Gen. 5:1-2). A third passage is of interest, because it appears to assert clearly that the divine image was not lost by the FALL: "Whoever sheds the blood of man, by man shall his blood be shed; for God made man in his own image" (Gen. 9:6).

It is perhaps somewhat surprising to find this teaching in the OT. Does the idea that in some way the likeness of God is reflected in the finite creature not infringe the transcendence of the creator God and blur the line, so clearly marked, between Creator and the creature? At least, it seems to qualify the distinction. We have also to remember that in the alternative Creation story, when God makes Adam of the dust of the ground, God also breathes into his nostrils the breath of life, and this "breathing" is a very different activity from "making" and implies that in some way God imparts to Adam something of God's own being. If the Hebrew scriptures insist on the difference between God and the Creation, they also insist on the difference between the human creature and all other creatures, and it is this difference that finds expression in the doctrine of an image of God.

What is the content of the image? A variety of answers have been given. In the first two passages of Genesis quoted above, the creation of the human pair is joined to the granting to them of dominion over the other creatures, and some theologians have claimed that the image of God is dominion or rule. The human race exercises rule over the earth, in the place of God. But many theologians would question whether power is the basic attribute of God, and whether it is in exercising dominion that human beings are most like God. In more rationalistic times, it has been claimed that it is in possessing reason and the powers of mind that human beings resemble God. But again it may be felt that this is inadequate. There is more plausibility in a third view, that creativity is the essential attribute of God, and that this is mirrored in the limited creativity of the human race, whereby they are able to "co-operate" with God in the continuing work of creation. Karl Barth, drawing attention to the fact that the image is represented by the human couple together, not by either of them individually, sees the image in sociality and fellowship. Human beings are made for one another, and their loving relations reflect the inner life of God.

There is a fundamental disagreement among theologians about the extent to which the divine image has been damaged or even destroyed through human SIN. The Reformers and, more recently, Barth, have maintained that the image of God has been completely obliterated by the Fall. Such a view is hard to defend. As we have seen, it contradicts the biblical teaching, and it also makes it difficult to see how there could be any human response to the grace of God. The human being would be reduced to the level of those other creatures that do not share in the image of God.

A much better interpretation was given by Irenaeus. He distinguished between the *image* of God and the *likeness,* though it is improbable that any such distinction was intended in the Hebrew. In Irenaeus' view, the image is the potentiality in the human person for spiritual growth and development; the likeness is the goal of this process, when the full spiritual potentialities of humanity have come to fruition and mirror the divine nature on the finite level. This visualizes the creation of humankind in two stages: the first stage endows them with the possibility for growth, the second is the process by which this growth comes to its goal. This makes a great deal of sense, for a human being cannot be created fully mature, but can only come to maturity through a process of many-sided experience, including testing and suffering.

When we turn to the NT, we find that something very close to the Irenaean understanding of the image is presupposed in its teaching. In several passages, we find what may be called an "image Christology," that is to say, an elucidaton of the person of Christ in terms of the man in whom the divine image has been fully manifested. He is called "the likeness of God" (II Cor. 4:4), "the image of the invisible God" (Col. 1:15), and it is declared that "he reflects the glory of God and bears the very stamp of his nature" (Heb. 1:3). Christ is in a unique and original way the bearer of the image of God brought to maturity as likeness to God, but the goal of the Christian life is that every Christian is also to be brought to this fullness: "And we all . . . beholding [or reflecting] the glory of the Lord, are being changed into his likeness from one degree of glory to another; for this comes from the Lord who is the Spirit" (II Cor. 3:18). (*Compare* HUMAN NATURE.)                                     J.M.

**IMAM.** (1) In SHI'ITE Islam, a religious leader in the line of succession from MUHAMMAD, starting with ALI. In his lifetime only he can pass authoritative judgment on law and theology. He is considered infallible. A dispute over the number of imams (seven or twelve) has split the Shi'ites into two major groups, the SAB'IYYA and the IMAMIYYA. Both groups expect the return of the last imam as the MAHDI, who will restore justice and Islamic purity. Sunni Islam rejects the Shi'ite concept of imam, but honors Ali.

(2) In Sunni Islam, the leader of worship in the MOSQUE.                                     K./M.C.

**IMAMIYYA.** In ISLAM those SHI'ITES who accept twelve IMAMS as successors to MUHAMMAD the Prophet, and thus differ from Shi'ites who are followers of seven imams (*see* ISMA'ILIYYA). Shi'ites believe that God revealed a testament to Muhammad, which announced the names of those who were to succeed him. The testament also gave instructions for each imam to follow.

The first imam was ALI, and the others followed him in a line of succession in which each imam

designated his successor. There is agreement on the first six, but differences arose over who was the seventh. This caused a division between the two groups.

The Imamiyya are often known as "Twelvers" in contrast to the "Seveners." The twelfth imam, Muhammad al-Muntazar, went into a state of "complete concealment" in A.D. 940. It is believed that he will continue in this state as long as God wills. Then he will reappear as the MAHDI take control of the world and restore justice. Twelvers are the dominant religious group in Iran today.

The imam is regarded as infallible, and because of his prophetic heritage true religion will survive through him. While he is in concealment he works through the learned jurists who are his spokesmen. They can guide the Shi'ites in matters of religion and in social and practical issues.

Devotion to the imams finds expression in the annual commemoration of the wrongs committed against the household of the Prophet Muhammad, especially his grandson, al-Husayn, who fell as a martyr in battle at Karbala, Iraq, in A.D. 680. Special visits are regularly paid to his tomb and to the tomb (MASHHAD) of each imam.                                     K.C.

*IMITATION OF CHRIST, THE.* A classic Christian devotional book, one of the most widely read writings of the Middle Ages, and a guidebook for achieving spiritual piety. Its acknowledged author was Thomas á Kempis (1380–1471), a student of the BROTHERS OF THE COMMON LIFE at Deventer, who spent most of his life at the Augustinian monastery of Mount St. Agnes, near Zwolle, in the Netherlands. Many others, especially Gerhard Groote (1340–84), have also been suggested as the author of this book, which appeared in Latin early in the fifteenth century. It quotes Scripture frequently and was part of the DEVOTIO MODERNA reform movement. It counsels true Christians to imitate Christ as their model by turning away from worldly matters and truly seeking to live inwardly and spiritually. This means humility, contemplation of things invisible, and conquest of the self's desires and passions. It means rooting out one's faults, resisting temptations, enduring hardships, and disciplining both body and mind. It means surrender to and dependence on God. The author exhorts, admonishes, and directs the reader to cultivate the inner life, converse with Christ, commune devoutly, and finally to place all hope and trust in God.                                     C.M.

**IMMACULATE CONCEPTION.** The belief that the Virgin Mary, the mother of Jesus Christ, was free from ORIGINAL SIN from her conception. The Immaculate Conception was defined as a dogma of the Roman Catholic church by Pope Pius IX in 1854. Orthodox Christianity teaches that *all* humans inherit a nature infected with sin as a result of the Fall of Adam. The Roman Catholic church, however, teaches that the BLESSED VIRGIN MARY, by a unique grace, was preserved from original sin and, therefore, is said to have been conceived immaculate. While holding that the Immaculate Conception is a doctrine entrusted to the original apostles, Catholic scholars acknowledge that the doctrine is not referred to *explicitly* in Scripture nor, perhaps, was it even a part of the early oral tradition. Rather, it is taught implicitly in Scripture and was made explicit in the church as an inference drawn from Mary's special holiness.

The early Church Fathers considered Mary to be holy but not sinless. Nevertheless, the doctrine was given impetus in the East as early as the third ecumenical council, held at Ephesus (A.D. 431), which gave to Mary the title MOTHER OF GOD. The doctrine was greatly disputed in the high Middle Ages. Thomas Aquinas opposed it on grounds that it detracted from Christ's dignity as Savior of *all* people. John Duns Scotus favored the teaching, and his support appears to have turned the tide in its favor. During the seventeenth century and again in the early decades of the nineteenth century, there were expressions of popular support in favor of a definition. The dogma, as it was defined by Pius IX, was published and explained in the bull *Ineffabilis Deus*. J.L.

**IMMANENCE.** The term "immanence" derives from the Latin *in manere,* meaning "to dwell within." It denotes an indwelling that is either inherent or that has an abiding quality. Immanence may be contrasted with TRANSCENDENCE, understood as being above and apart from.

Though it may be used to characterize any presence within, immanence has been most often applied by theologians and philosophers to Deity as permeating and sustaining the world. The immanence of God in the universe is distinguished from the concept of a creator or ruler external to and transcendent of the universe.

In Plato, both the Form of the Good and the Best Soul are understood as within the world. In Aristotle, God becomes a transcendent Unmoved Mover unaware of the world. In Stoicism, God is the immanent, indwelling Logos. Neoplatonism affirms the One as pervading Being, yet transcending it.

Though transcendence has had its representatives in Christian thought, the immanence of God has been emphasized by mystics, who verge on pantheism; by evangelicals and pietists, who focus on God's effective presence in human hearts; by the romantics and idealists, who understand God as the inner meaning of the universe; and by process thinkers, who view God as the vital force within the world as an organism. C.Mc.

**IMMANUEL.** A Hebrew phrase, used as a personal name in Isaiah 7:14; 8:8, meaning "God (is) with us,"

so rendered in Isaiah 8:10 and in the Gospel fulfillment of Matthew 1:22, 23.

The historical setting gives the key to the naming of this child. At its simplest level the announcement was a prophetic assurance that God's presence was a "sign" (Isa. 7:11-14) of the abiding protection of God's people at a time when Judah was threatened by the Syro-Ephraim coalition and tempted to turn to Assyria for help. Ahaz of Judah was invited to trust God in a time of crisis, and Isaiah's promise to the wavering king was an assurance, seen in the birth of a child, that God was the nation's hope. Such is the strictly historical context. In a Christian reinterpretation of the OT text, Matthew seized on this name as pointing to Jesus the Messiah born of Mary a virgin (Greek *parthenos,* which is more precise than Isaiah's Hebrew term *'almā*; RSV states "a young woman"), he sees the pledge of God's presence in Jesus with his people—a characteristic Matthean idea (18:20; 28:20). R.M.

**IMMERSION.** *See* BAPTISM.

**IMMORALITY.** That which does not conform to the moral expectations or requirements of a particular society or of a social or religious group with moral rules. Immorality is the opposite of or sharply at variance with morality. Though morality and legality are related in societies, immorality is distinguished from illegality in that it is defined in relation to moral directives rather than in relation to laws. Amorality refers to a condition of being without moral awareness, as exemplified in sociopaths or in animals in relation to human morality. Nonmorality is that which is without moral significance. In ordinary usage, immorality often refers specifically to violation of sexual mores. C.Mc.

**IMMORTALITY.** The concept of immortality, of not dying, of RESURRECTION, especially in the OT, was not yet nearly so developed in the age of the patriarchs as at the time of the Babylonian exile. Immortality was directly related to the concept of a living Jehovah, the Lord of LIFE, who did not die like pagan gods or pagan idols, and who also would not allow the people of Israel to die (Ps. 18:46; Jer. 23:36; II Kings 19:16).

There is no doubt that at least in the popular imagination many ideas about life after DEATH were borrowed from the Semitic cultures in which the people of Israel lived. In Egypt, for example, the cult of the dead was highly developed, with elaborate preparation of embalmed bodies, and for the pharaohs, pyramids, food, and servants to accompany them in the afterlife. Similar expectations existed in the Aramaea and Canaan of Abraham's day, of a heaven and hell, an upper world and a lower world, of reward and punishment.

Both in Hebrew and in Greek thought there was considerable speculation whether a human being consisted of three elements, body, soul, and spirit, or only two, body and soul. Dichotomists point to the story of Adam and Eve, with bodies formed by God and souls breathed alive by the breath of God. Trichotomists use such passages as Mark 12:30, "You shall love the Lord your God with all your heart, and with all your soul, and with all your mind, and with all you strength" (compare I Thess. 5:23).

The body was of course the material and the physical element of a human being. The soul, in Hebrew *nephesh*, in Greek *psyche*, was the animal principle of life, heartbeat and breath. The spirit, in Hebrew *ruach*, in Greek *pneuma*, was the thoughtful or rational element that controls reason, will, and conscience. Exactly which of these elements continued to exist after death, or at the time of resurrection, and in what form, and when resurrection would occur, is not as clear in either the OT or the NT as many believers would like.

In the OT there are several examples of people who never died. Elijah (II Kings 2:11), who still has a popular role in the Passover and in Jewish tradition, especially for children, moved into the presence of Jehovah alive and riding a chariot of fire. Enoch (Gen. 5:24) walked alive into eternity with God. Though the biblical evidence is scant, popular tradition also made of Moses a prophet who joined God without first dying.

Even people who came in contact with a living Jehovah through one of the prophets sometimes came back to life, like the Moabite marauder whose body was thrown into the grave of Elisha, or the son of the widow of Zarephath and Elijah, whose prayer brought back the boy's "soul" (I Kings 17:17-23). Though these five stories do not speak directly to the immortality of everyone, they do provide at least some insight into the popular understanding of the times.

References to an afterlife or to being raised from the dead appear more frequently in the prophets of the Exile, as contact with the more sophisticated and urban Babylonian-Assyrian culture intensified. The most famous story is probably Ezekiel's vision of the dry bones (chap. 37), where "the whole house of Israel" has been cut off and Jehovah promises to "open your graves, and raise you from your graves, O my people; and I will bring you home into the land of Israel" (v. 12).

The prophet Hosea (6:2) says God will raise up the dead on the third day so that they "may live before him." The famous passage from Job (19:26), "And though after my skin worms destroy this body, yet in my flesh shall I see God" appears a stronger proof text in the KJV translation of the Bible than in the Hebrew original. The authors of Psalms 16, 17, 49, and 73 identify with Jehovah as a living God who will not allow death to be a force that forever wipes them from the face of the earth or separates them from God.

The NT expresses somewhat more firmly developed concepts about immortality and resurrection than the OT. In Christ's day the Pharisees actively taught immortality, but the Sadducees rejected it. The Talmud was careful to separate resurrection of the body from that of the soul. In the Apocrypha, the underworld, Hades, lay somewhere in the west, and heaven, paradise, somewhere in the east.

Paul, Jesus, and John often use phrases like "eternal life" or "everlasting life" (Matt. 19:29; Mark 10:30; John 6:47). The resurrection of Christ was a popular testimony to the resurrection of all believers, though Paul's view that Christ's Second Coming was likely to occur in the lifetimes of those to whom he was writing tended to emphasize an eternal life in which many people would continue living without first dying. Paul does, however, also allow for a new glorified body based on the frame of the old physical body (II Cor. 4:16; Phil. 1:23; I Cor. 15:51).

In Paul's celebrated chapter on death (I Cor. 15) and how human beings relate Christ's death to their own, he takes to task those who deny the resurrection of the dead. "If there is no resurrection of the dead, then Christ has not been raised. . . . If Christ has not been raised, your faith is futile and you are still in your sins. Then those also who have fallen asleep in Christ have perished . . . . For as in Adam all die, so also in Christ shall all be made alive."

In the book of Revelation John pictures a peaceful repose for the blessed who die in the Lord, an end of suffering, an early awakening from the dead for some and a later one for others. In his figurative language depicting the times of the Christian martyrs under Roman persecution, his words express pious understanding and trust, as much as strongly formulated dogma.

Those hopes and that trust of wanting to be near the Lord at the time of resurrection probably explain why tens of thousands of Christians, Arabs, and Jews have chosen to be buried on the slopes of the Kidron outside Jerusalem's Golden Gate, where the Lord is by ancient tradition expected to return on Judgment Day, just as he did on the first Palm Sunday.

T.J.K.

**IMPRIMATUR.** Certification, by Roman Catholic ecclesiastical authority, that a book bearing on religion or morals contains nothing damaging to the faith or morals of believers. A NIHIL OBSTAT ("nothing poses impediments to faith") from the church censor is required first. Notice of this decision is printed in the book.                J.C.

*IMPRIMI POTEST.* A pre-permission from a bishop or other religious superior in the Roman Catholic church for a subject's seeking an *imprimatur* for a book bearing on faith or morals. The *imprimi postent* may or may not be printed in the book. It is not required.                J.C.

**INCARNATION.** The most central, but perhaps also the most complex, of all Christian doctrines. It teaches that in Jesus Christ the divine LOGOS or second person of the TRINITY assumed humanity, that he was and is truly and fully human and truly and fully God, and that this HYPOSTATIC UNION (as it is called) will never cease.

This doctrine, of course, took time to formulate. When the disciples first began to follow Jesus, they presumably thought of him as no more than a charismatic prophet. Perhaps at some point they began to think of him as the promised prophet who would be like a new Moses (Deut. 18:15), then as the Messiah (Mark 8:29), though still as a human Messiah. But after the cross and the Resurrection, new dimensions are added to the understanding of Christ's person. The earliest belief was probably adoptionist, to use a later terminology: Jesus had been "designated Son of God in power according to the Spirit" (Rom. 1:4) or "God has made him both Lord and Christ" (Acts 2:36). Moves toward a more definite view of the Incarnation may be noted in Paul's words that "God was in Christ" (II Cor. 5:19) and in the Epistle to the Hebrews: "God spoke of old to our fathers by the prophets; but in these last days he has spoken to us by a Son" (1:1-2).

However, the full Incarnation position is reached only in the late writings of the NT, especially in the famous words of the prologue to John's Gospel: "The Word became flesh and dwelt among us" (1:14). This already presupposes an understanding of God that permits the distinction between the Father and the Word or Logos. Notice the subtle language of the prologue, which asserts both distinction and identity: "The Word was with God, and the Word was God" (1:1).

Actually, the NT is very cautious of directly saying that Christ is God. But already in the early second century Christian writers like Ignatius were frankly calling Christ God, and this does not seem to have caused them any discomfort or to have offended their MONOTHEISM. The belief that a man was also God was so extraordinary (Kierkegaard was later to call it the "absolute paradox") that it was almost impossible not to stress one side at the expense of the other or to slide into sheer contradictions. It is impossible here to give more than the barest outline of the confused controversies that went on over the meaning of incarnation.

Some reduced the divinity to the point where Jesus was simply a specially inspired human being (Ebionitism); others declared him a divine being whose humanity was only appearance (Docetism). Many of the early Christian writers thought of Christ as a kind of second God, subordinate to the Father, and it was only after the Arian controversy that the Council of Nicea declared Christ to be "one in being" or "of one substance" (HOMOOUSIOS) with the Father. Christ's oneness with the Father having been established, the next phase of the controversy concerned the relation of the humanity and the divinity within the person of Christ. Apollinarius

(condemned in 381) thought of Christ as a hybrid being, partly human and partly divine, but not fully either; Nestorius (condemned in 431) was alleged, perhaps wrongly, to have separated the divine and the human in Christ to the point of a double personality; Eutyches (condemned in 451) was so opposed to Nestorius that he let the humanity of Christ be swallowed up in the single nature of his divinity, a view called MONOPHYSITISM and still held in the Coptic and other churches. The COUNCIL OF CHALCEDON (451) tried to sort out the confusion. It was stated that in Jesus Christ there are two natures, the human and the divine, each complete and entire; they are unmixed, yet they are not separated and concur together in one person.

Though there were still some sterile disputes over the question of whether Christ had one will or two wills, the Chalcedonian definition became the classic statement of the doctrine of incarnation and the touchstone of Christological orthodoxy. With various refinements, it persisted through the Middle Ages and was adopted by the major Protestant churches at the time of the Reformation.

Of course, it should be remembered that the Chalcedonian definition was not intended to be a final statement, but some explanation of the question of incarnation. It was meant to exclude certain ways that had been found misleading and to establish a terminology drawn from the philosophical language prevailing at that time. In the past two hundred years, however, the Chalcedonian formula has been called in question. Even those who believe in the Incarnation, in the sense of a genuine union of the human and divine in Jesus Christ, have in many cases come to ask whether we must look for new ways of expressing the matter.

Schleiermacher in *The Christian Faith* (1821) sharply criticized the Chalcedonian formula on logical grounds, holding that its key terms, "person" and "nature," were ambiguous and had been used in an inconsistent way. He himself proposed a radically new approach, which would begin from the humanity of Jesus. He believed that in Jesus alone do we see a perfect or mature humanity, and that this includes a full God-consciousness, which he also declares to be a veritable indwelling of God in that person. So although he rejected the traditional formula, he believed himself to be restating a full doctrine of incarnation.

Later in the century, Ritschl attacked Chalcedon because of its scholastic or academic character. (Actually, Luther and Melanchthon had raised similar objections in the sixteenth century, but they did not press them.) Ritschl sought to replace the traditional doctrine with a theory based on the idea of value. In calling Christ God, we are asserting that for us the mysterious word "God" has been given a definite value and is to be understood in terms of Christ. This is an eminently practical solution, but it betrays Ritschl's positivist tendencies and hardly delivers us from the task of inquiring what is the ontological relation of Christ to God that would justify our value judgment.

Later still, Harnack criticized incarnational Christology as a Hellenizing of the gospel, which had the unfortunate result of putting the person of Christ at the center of the proclamation, rather than the kingdom of God as in Jesus' original gospel. So Harnack would have reverted to a preincarnational understanding of Jesus. Meanwhile, a somewhat different and more conservative attempt was being made to restate the meaning of incarnation. A number of scholars, first in Germany and then in England, put forward "kenotic" theories. Appealing to the NT passage, which says of Christ that he "emptied himself, taking the form of a servant, being born in the likeness of men" (Phil. 2:7), they claimed that incarnation of the divine in the human, the infinite in the finite, was made possible by a voluntary self-emptying *(kenosis)* in which the divine Logos laid aside those attributes that are incompatible with a truly human existence (for example, omniscience) while retaining others that are essential to a truly divine being (for example, perfect love). The theory had its attractions, such as explaining the limitations of Christ's knowledge. But critics felt that it was too speculative, and some saw in it a revival of the rejected views of Apollinarius.

The main thrust of contemporary thinking about the Incarnation seems to have gone back to the way pioneered at the beginning of the modern period by Schleiermacher. That is to say, it begins from anthropology and in particular from the human reality of Christ. Humanity has an openness toward God, so that the unfolding of humanity is a progressive realization of the image of God in which, according to the Bible, human beings were created.

Christ himself is the fulfilled image of God on the human level, bearing "the very stamp of his nature" (Heb. 1:3). This is reminiscent of patristic teaching about the deification of man and also harmonizes well with many modern views of human nature. If it is objected that this approach is a reversion to ADOPTIONISM, it may be replied that the original Christology of the earlier parts of the NT should not simply have been swallowed up by full-blown incarnationalism, since this has probably led to an unconscious Docetism in the church and an undervaluing of the true humanity of Christ.

There is a determination among theologians of many schools that no doctrine of incarnation can be satisfactory if it obscures the full humanity of Jesus Christ, hence the tendency to begin from an unambiguous assertion of the human reality. But it is also conceded that adoptionism tends to complete itself in some form of incarnationalism, for there could be no ascent of the human to the divine without a descent of the divine into the human.

J.M.

Courtesy of The University Museum, University of Pennsylvania

*Cylindrical incense stand from Beth-shan (about eleventh century* B.C.*)*

**INCENSE.** The Hebrew word *qetoret,* commonly translated with the English term "incense," in its earliest OT occurrences has to do with the smoke rising from an animal being sacrificed upon the altar (Deut. 33:10). However, in time this general term and others referring to more specialized forms of incense came to refer specifically to the aromatic compound of gums, herbs, and oils used in the Temple worship. (For the recipe, see Exod. 30:34-38.) According to Exodus 30:1-10, the priest (Aaron) was to burn fragrant incense on the altar of incense every morning and every evening (compare Luke 1:8-11); and upon the horns of the altar of incense he was to make atonement with blood once a year. According to Leviticus 16:12-13, this latter act on the Day of Atonement could be accomplished only after a cloud of incense had been raised adequate to cover the mercy seat, for to stand unprotected in the divine presence meant death even for the high priest. (The warning is underscored by the report in Lev. 10:1-2 of the death of Nadab and Abihu, the sons of Aaron, whose incense was laid upon unholy fire and who were consumed by divine fire.)

Most of the pentateuchal legislation regarding the use of incense is found in materials emanating from the latest stratum, the Priestly source. But this should not be taken to suggest that the introduction of incense into the cultus of Israel was only a late development. Ancient Near Eastern sources show that incense had long been associated with holy and numinous occasions. Its sensuous odor and the purity of its smoke had functioned since time immemorial to ward off evil spirits (and perhaps noxious fumes) and to invoke divinity. Its great value made it an ideal gift with which to honor God, or a lover (Song of S. 3:6), or a personage of great importance (Dan. 2:46). Such a treasured substance could obviously be abused, and the historians and prophets alike accused their fellow countrymen of offending God by burning incense to foreign deities (compare II Kings 22:17; Ezek. 6:13). But it was obviously also a valued adjunct to the experience of Israel with God, an accompaniment to visions of the Holy One (Luke 1:8-12), and one of the three gifts most suitable to lay before the baby whom the magi from the East perceived to be the Anointed One of Israel (Matt. 2:11).                W.S.T.

**INCEST.** Sexual intercourse between close relatives or those considered related within degrees wherein marriage is prohibited by law or custom. The OT prohibitions against incest are outlined in Leviticus 18 and 20, though they frequently occur elsewhere as individual stories. The Lord instructs Moses that the people should not follow the marriage practices they had experienced in Egypt and Canaan. For example, one was forbidden to have intercourse with one's mother, another wife of one's father, a sister, the daughter of one's father or mother, a granddaughter, an aunt, a niece, a daughter-in-law, a mother-in-law, or a sister-in-law. One penalty for incest was barrenness (Lev. 20:21) or sometimes death by fire to all involved if a man slept with both a woman and her mother.

Genesis 19:31-35 tells how the daughters of Lot got their father drunk and after sleeping with him bore sons who founded the tribes of the Moabites and the Ammonites. Genesis 20:12 records that Abraham said that his wife Sarah was a half sister. Amnon raped his beautiful half sister Tamar (II Sam. 12:7-14) even though she argued that their mutual father, King David, would give her to Amnon if asked. In the OT period a king often inherited his father's harem.

In the NT Paul advises that a man who married his father's wife (I Cor. 5:2) be cast out of the congregation so that both parties would not lose their souls. In the early Middle Ages the taboo against incest forbade marriage between people related to the seventh degree (seventh cousins, for example) or even those in the seventh degree of relationship as godparents or godchildren.                T.J.K.

**INDELIBLE CHARACTER.** In Roman Catholicism, indelible character refers to a belief that divine grace confers a permanent spiritual mark on a person when the sacrament of baptism, ordination, or confirmation is duly administered, even though the administrant might be immoral. This imprint makes repetition of the sacrament a sacrilege. Many Protestants so regard baptism.                C.M.

**INDEPENDENTS.** This is the name given British Congregationalists, also called Separatists. These were people who in the sixteenth and seventeenth centuries wanted to separate from the Church of England and found local independent congregations of professing believers. One group left for Holland in 1608 and came to New England in 1620 as the Pilgrims. Oliver Cromwell was an Independent; thus they were most influential during the Commonwealth in 1649–60.                N.H.

**INDEX OF PROHIBITED BOOKS.** In Roman Catholicism, a list of books containing views on faith and morals that Catholics are forbidden to read except in special cases where permission to do so is granted for purposes of refutation and so forth. In 1557 the Congregation of the Inquisition under Pope Paul IV published the first list of prohibited books. The Council of Trent (1545–63) anathematized anyone who printed, sold, or possessed books without episcopal approval, and in 1571 Pope Pius V created a special Congregation of the Index to oversee censorship. In 1917 Pope Benedict XV placed supervision of the Index in the holy office. Prohibition of heretical or unfit books was not uncommon in the early and medieval church, so that the Index represents the formalizing of a old practice. In the twentieth century, bishops have assumed much responsibility for censorship of books, and in 1966 the Index was discontinued.                C.M.

**INDRA.** In HINDUISM, a god very important in the VEDAS, though much diminishing in importance after the end of the Vedic period and the rise of the ISVARA or salvation-giving deities. Indra is supremely a god of the Indo-European mythology of the Vedas. He is patron of the Aryan warrior class and dwells in the atmosphere between heaven and earth. Accompanied by the Maruts, his band of warrior companions, he defeats demons and powers of darkness. His weapon is the *vajra* or thunderbolt. He is gigantic, boisterous, and prodigious in his capacity for food and drink, consuming countless cattle and lakefuls of the sacred drink SOMA.

But he is friendly to humankind. He stole the soma plant from heaven—himself often experiencing the sacred hallucinations the plant's liquor affords—and destroyed the drought-giving demon Vrtra. But late mythology, in a time of changing gods and spiritual tension between warrior and brahmin castes, portrayed Indra in a less favorable light.                R.E.

**INDUCTION.** A process of reasoning from particulars to the general, the reverse of DEDUCTION, which is a process of reasoning from the general to particulars. Aristotle described the inductive process but did not develop it. Francis Bacon extended induction by ampliative inference, which uses analogy to draw general conclusions about a group from observing a single specimen. David Hume doubted "necessary connections" in inductive cause and effect, and John Stuart Mill further refined rules for using induction. While science employs induction to build hypotheses and theories, the difficulty (or perhaps impossibility) of strictly observing and controlling all or even limited particulars results in a high degree of verifiable probability rather than certainty. Variant forms of induction are widely used in scientific experimentation and especially in social statistics, which allow for margins of error. Darwin's use of induction to arrive at evolution illustrates both the possibilities and inadequacies of the process.

C.M.

**INDULGENCE.** The remission by the church of the penalty for sin. This developed from earlier practices of PENANCE for post-baptismal sins, which required that sinners atone for their sins in various ways. In principle, an indulgence was the commuting of one form of penance for another, although there was little theological reflection as to the bases for such practices. By the eleventh century, Pope Urban II, in promoting the First Crusade, made use of the term "plenary indulgence," which applied to post-baptismal sins in general, without specifying the sin in question. In the thirteenth century, two new ideas appeared: that in granting indulgences the church was using its treasury of merit, and that this could be done, not only for the living, but also for the dead who were in PURGATORY. These ideas, combined with the possibility of commuting penalties, led to the sale of indulgences, which was then employed to raise funds. By the late Middle Ages, such sales had become scandalous, and several reform-minded Christians—Luther among them—protested against them. The Council of Trent reaffirmed the doctrinal grounds for indulgences and their sale, but the practice fell into general disuse. J.G.

**INERRANCY.** "Freedom from error" as applied especially to the Holy Scriptures. Obviously, God does not make mistakes, so if the Bible is the Word of God, must it not be free from error? But when one actually turns to the Bible, the doctrine of verbal inerrancy is very hard to maintain. In both the OT and the NT, there are inconsistencies, especially when more than one account is given of the same incident, and these are found to differ on points of detail.

Examples from the OT would be the accounts of the Flood and of the crossing of the Red Sea. An example from the NT would be the all-important story of the resurrection of Jesus. The points of detail may not be in themselves very important, but since such divergences destroy the theory of inerrancy, those who hold that theory have gone to great (and quite unconvincing) lengths in trying to "harmonize" the different accounts. Sometimes the Bible is in contradiction with views derived from secular sources, but widely held in the modern world. Here one recalls the controversies, still going on, between upholders of inerrancy and those who accept the theory of evolution.

In this case, inerrancy can be maintained only by rejecting a well-established scientific theory and sometimes in addition by the suggestion that God "planted" the evidence for evolution! Other discrepancies in the Bible, such as the wrong attribution of a quotation, are less easy to explain, yet even one such contradiction is fatal to the theory. But the main objection to a doctrine of inerrancy lies in its inadequate understanding of revelation and INSPIRATION. These are not mechanical processes that result in a set of propositions directly derived from God. They are in the first instance personal encounters between God and people, and when these people report them in words, they do so as human beings who may be faithful witnesses but are not exempt from error. The faithfulness of these witnesses is not enhanced by claiming for them the negative character of inerrancy. J.M.

**INFALLIBILITY.** The inability to err in teaching divine truth or, put positively, fidelity to revealed truth. Infallibility is one of the most misunderstood doctrines. It does not imply the sinlessness of the church or the pope, nor should it be confused with INSPIRATION. The latter is uniquely attributed to the revelation attested to in the canonical books of the OT and the NT. Through the centuries many Christians have held the church to be infallible. It is argued that it is a necessary teaching of any doctrinal religion, for such a religion must hold that some truths are "guaranteed." The simple declaration "Jesus Christ is Lord and Savior" is a case in point. It is a proposition essential to Christian identity. The Christian churches are agreed that the church is infallible or indefectible, in the sense that the church cannot, in the long run, teach error—and with the guidance of the Holy Spirit persists in the truth. Numerous NT passages point to Christ's promise that the Spirit will lead his disciples into all truth and that the church is "the pillar and ground of the truth" (I Tim. 3:15 KJV).

The churches have, however, differed as to where the seat of infallibility resides. Some would argue that it lies exclusively in an inerrant Bible, others that it rests in the teaching authority of the MAGISTERIUM or the episcopate. Conciliarism insisted that infallibility resides in the decisions and definitions of the great ECUMENICAL COUNCILS, such as Nicaea (A.D. 325). At the First Vatican Council (1869–70) the Roman Catholic church declared the pope infallible when, under certain conditions, he defines doctrines concerning faith and morals. The infallibility of the pope has remained the focal point of the discussion of infallibility during the past century, especially since VATICAN II (1962–65).

Defenders of papal infallibility traditionally have produced biblical and patristic proof texts, as well as practical arguments, in favor of the 1870 dogmatic declaration. They argue that, while not formulated in the early church, the doctrine unfolded organically in the post-apostolic age. Opponents of papal infallibility, both within and outside the Roman Church, argue on historical grounds that papal infallibility did not form any part of the church's theological or canonical tradition before the thirteenth century. While the infallibility of the church was universally taught in the Roman church through the mid-nineteenth century, the infallibility of the pope remained an open question. Supported by the modern popes because it suited their interests, the doctrine had long been opposed, for example by the strong Gallican tradition during the early modern period. The growing movement of Ultramontanism in the early decades of the nineteenth century and the distinctive authority of Pope Pius IX (1846–78) seen, for example, in his definition of the Immaculate Conception of the Blessed Virgin Mary (1854), strengthened both popular and episcopal support for the 1870 definition.

The First Vatican Council opened on December 8, 1869, and the majority of bishops, led by Archbishop Edward Manning of Westminster, favored a declaration of papal infallibility. A minority party, led by bishops Dupanloup and Hefele, was assisted by the eminent Catholic historians J. J. I. von Döllinger and John (Lord) Acton. The minority party argued that as GALLICANISM had separated the church from the pope, so would papal infallibility separate the pope from the church. They also argued that the doctrine had no foundation in Scripture, tradition, or in the ecumenical councils. Furthermore, they insisted that a definition could not be written that avoided ambiguity. They feared that extreme infallibilism would mean that infallibility would attach to any and every utterance of the pope. A number of bishops, known as "inopportunists," favored papal infallibility but felt that the historical circumstances did not favor a definition at the time. Some America bishops argued that a definition would forever alienate Protestants and would be a permanent setback for Catholicism in the United States. On July 13, 1870, a vote was taken on a conditional draft and 451 bishops voted in favor; 88 against; 62 were in favor conditionally; and 91 abstained. When the final outcome was seen as inevitable, many minority bishops left Rome rather than oppose the wishes of the pope or possibly risk anathema for rejecting a dogmatic teaching of the church. On July 18, 533 fathers voted in favor of papal infallibility; only two opposed. Pius IX then confirmed the First Dogmatic Constitution on the Church, entitled *Pastor aeternus*. Those, like Döllinger, who continued to oppose the dogma were excommunicated; many among the opposition established a separate Old Catholic church.

*Pastor aeternus* affirms that the pope possesses infallibility when he speaks *ex cathedra*, that is, in his office as pope, when he defines a doctrine regarding faith and morals to be held by the universal church. Such definitions "are irreformable of themselves and not from the consent of the Church." Extreme infallibilists considered most papal teachings to be infallible, including, for example, Pius IX's *Syllabus of Errors* (1864). However, moderate infallibilism has prevailed in the Roman church during the past century. According to the moderate interpretation of the Dogmatic Constitution, certain conditions must be met by any infallible teaching: (1) the pope must speak in his office as pope, *ex cathedra,* not simply as a theologian; (2) the utterance must be a doctrine of faith and morals, a divinely revealed truth; (3) the utterance must not be merely advice or warning; it must terminate controversy by pronouncing a dogmatic definition; (4) it must be a truth necessary to salvation; and (5) while it need not be addressed to all believers, it must be intended for the universal church.

The difficulty that the dogma has raised for the Roman church is posed by the question: what particular papal decrees are infallible, since no pope has said, "This is an infallible declaration." There is no infallible list of infallible decrees. This uncertainty and lack of guidance led to a severe crisis of authority in the church with the issuance of Pope Paul VI's encyclical *Humanae vitae* (1968) concerning birth control. The encyclical's teaching was widely opposed by both clerical and lay Catholics and sparked an extended debate on papal authority and the meaning of infallibility. In *Lumen Gentium,* Vatican II reaffirmed the doctrine of Vatican I; nevertheless, it integrated papal infallibility into the doctrine of the collegial magisterium (teaching office) of the bishops united with the pope. It affirmed that the Roman pontiff can exercise his power freely, but *together* with the consent of the pope, the bishops are the subject of supreme and full power over the church. It is now understood that the church always acts in the *union of the bishops with their head, the pope.*

How is this to be reconciled with the Vatican I declaration that infallible decisions of the pope are "irreformable of themselves, not from the consent of the Church"? The present view of most Catholic theologians is that infallibility implies the agreement of a dogmatic definition with the Word of God in Scripture and tradition. Infallibility is always exercised in the service of the Word. Furthermore, its binding character assumes a consensus in the church. This view is stated by Joseph Cardinal Ratzinger, head of the Congregation of the Faith: "Where there is neither consensus on the part of the universal Church nor clear testimony in the sources, no binding decision is possible." Finally, it must be recognized that while Vatican II underscored the need for a "religious submission of will and of mind" to the pope's authentic teaching authority, absolute infallibility belongs to God alone. The Roman church teaches that the conscience of the Christian before God remains the final resort for the individual's decision.                                                  J.L.

**INFANT BAPTISM.** *See* BAPTISM.

**INFERENCE.** A process whereby one passes from one statement regarded as true to another statement whose truth is derived from and dependent on the truth of the first. Aristotle inferred universals from many particulars. Francis Bacon related inference to INDUCTION by describing analogy that draws general conclusions about a group from observing a single specimen as ampliative inference. Modern logic allows inference as a kind of independent source of inductive hypothesis, its reliability being dependent on the recurrence of particular characteristics. This was a great help to science, for example, in reconstructing animals from a few fossil remains. This assumes a uniformity of nature or correspondence of cause and effect in identical circumstances, but changing circumstances make final conclusions untenable. Kant justified analogical inference with the maxim that many characteristics do not unite in one thing without a reason. He speaks of inference as a function of thinking in the interplay of sensibility and understanding by which one judgment or conclusion is derived from another. John Stuart Mill and modern thinkers modify inference by isolating agreements and differences that become important for refinements of inference. God's existence may be inferred from various "proofs," but not with finality.

C.M.

**INHERITANCE.** In its most basic sense, in the Bible as elsewhere, this term refers to that portion of property assigned to an heir. Naturally this can be thought of as a transaction between an *individual* and the next generation in the family:

> A good man leaves an inheritance
>   to his children's children,
> but the sinner's wealth is laid up
>   for the righteous (Prov. 13:22).

Not only sons but also daughters could receive inheritances as individuals (Num. 27:1-11). But even more frequently the OT thinks of inheritance in a *collective* vein. A large section of the book of Joshua, for example, is devoted to the allotment (the word is well chosen, because the divisions were made by the casting of divinely guided lots; see Num. 36:2; Ezek. 45:1; 47:22) of the land of Canaan into the "inheritances" of the tribes that descended from the twelve sons of Jacob (Josh. 13–19). These tribal allotments were considered inalienable, and marriage between the tribes is discouraged in Numbers 36:1-13, lest transfers of tribal lands take place through individual bequests. Only Levi received no share of the land; his people were to serve the Lord in priestly functions and find in the Lord their inheritance (Deut. 10:9; Ezek. 44:28). In fact, the entire land promised by God to Abraham and his descendants and conveyed to Israel in the conquest is often described by the metaphor of "the inheritance" (see Deut. 4:21; I Kings 8:36; I Chr. 28:8; Ezra 9:10-12). From this sense it is only one additional metaphorical step to refer to the people as Yahweh's inheritance (Deut. 4:20; Isa. 19:25), a usage frequently found in the Psalms (28:9; 33:12; 78:62-71; 106:5).

The same variety of meanings of the term "inheritance" can be discerned in the NT, all derived from the Greek word *klēros,* "a lot, possession." (Our English terms "cleric" and "clergy" are derived from this root: *klērikos,* a lot-caster or an allotter.) Family property is of course an inheritance (Mark 12:7) and so is the land promised to Abraham (Heb. 11:8). However, in the NT the term acquires a rich new significance. Often it is the eternal kingdom of God, "the inheritance of the saints in light" (Col. 1:12; see also Eph. 1:15; Heb. 9:15; I Pet. 1:4), and even that portion of the world to come that is given to a righteous individual (Eph. 5:5).

W.S.T.

**INIQUITY.** *See* SIN.

**INITIATION.** *See* BAPTISM.

**INNATE IDEAS.** Certain concepts and ideas that various philosophers have insisted are inborn, being implanted in the mind at birth or derived from the constitution of the mind, in contrast with ideas and perceptions derived from experience through the senses. Such intuitive rather than empirical ideas might be of a circle (a Platonic form as distinguished from perceptible particulars), or of right and wrong in the sense of Aquinas' infallible *synteresis,* which indicates a difference between right and wrong but does not specify particulars. In modern philosophy, Descartes argued for the innateness of God, mind, and matter (extension). These are not copies of sense experience; they are pre-reflective, pure ideas used to comprehend experience. Leibnitz further developed Cartesian views into principles of innateness, which are unlearned from experience, while both Locke and Hume argued against innate ideas in favor of empirical, sensory experiences. Kant set forth *a priori* intuited concepts of space and time and twelve categories that the mind uses in transforming empirical sensations into knowledge. The argument over innate versus empirical ideas continues into the present despite the overwhelming impact of the empirical sciences. The controversy is religiously important especially if one assumes God cannot be derived from sense data.

C.M.

**INNER LIGHT.** The term used by GEORGE FOX to denote the Spirit of God that exists in every person. The Light functions in two ways. It illumines the darkness (that is sin) indicating to a person the existence of evil so that the person might turn toward goodness. This understanding is basic to the morality and life-style of members of the Society of FRIENDS. The Light is also power. God and Christ are the Light and are in the Light. Salvation lies in turning to the Light. To have faith is to accept the Light into one's life. The Light gives inspiration beyond that of

Scripture and church and is the true and ultimate source of authority. The inner Light is also the transcendent Light. It is not a part of God but a gift from God and the source of revelation. The inner Light unites people to one another. Although Fox includes scriptural references in his teaching, he lays less emphasis on the Gospel story of Jesus and more on the living presence of Christ in the believer. This presence convicts people of sin, enables them to live righteously, and empowers them for unity within the Society of Friends. I.C.

**INNOCENT III.** Pope from 1198–1216, in whom the PAPACY reached the apex of its political power. Claiming that the pope ruled over souls and the emperor over bodies, as the sun rules over days and the moon over nights, and that this made him superior to the emperor, he intervened in the internal affairs of the HOLY ROMAN EMPIRE, deposing an emperor and placing another in his stead. England's John Lackland and the young king of Sicily made their kingdoms fiefdoms of the papacy. The pope's political power was felt also in France, Spain, Portugal, Bohemia, Hungary, Denmark, Iceland, and as far as Bulgaria and Armenia.

Although this was done without the pope's consent, the Fourth CRUSADE took Constantinople in 1204 and established the Latin Empire of Constantinople, thus temporarily and forcefully reuniting the Greek East and the Latin West under the pope's authority.

The Fourth LATERAN COUNCIL gathered in 1215 under Innocent's direction. In three days it approved a long series of measures dictated by the pope, who was in truth the power behind the council. These included the promulgation of the doctrine of TRANSUBSTANTIATION, decrees against the WALDENSES, ALBIGENSES, the followers of JOACHIM OF FIORE, Muslims, and Jews, the order that all the faithful must make confession at least once a year, and a number of administrative matters. This was part of Innocent's program to clarify and codify the law of the church and to promote uniformity throughout Europe.

It was also under Innocent's rule that the orders of the FRANCISCANS and the DOMINICANS were founded. Although Innocent did not wish to see a proliferation of new orders, he saw the potential in these movements and approved them somewhat reluctantly. J.G.

**INQUISITION.** A name given Roman Catholic tribunals established to deal with heresy and related offenses. As far back as 313 church-state partnership had virtually equated heresy and treason, and formal tribunals to ensure religious unity materialized about 1150. French Cathari and Italian Waldensians threatened social stability, and, consequently, popes, councils, and civil rulers used severe penalties to exterminate them. In 1184 Pope Lucius III required bishops to examine all their subjects under oath for heresy. In 1199 Pope Innocent III declared heresy a capital crime. The Fourth Lateran Council (1215) provided secular punishment for heretics, which included the confiscation of property and excommunication for non-cooperation. In 1220 the Dominicans took charge of the Inquisition. In 1229 the Synod of Toulouse systematized inquisitorial rules, leaving alleged heretics virtually no rights. In 1252 Innocent IV authorized the torture of witnesses and the accused. Inquisitors were often ruthless; they were not subject to the law, only to the papacy. They accused, prosecuted, and judged. Victims had to prove their innocence and could have no counsel.

The marriage of Ferdinand and Isabella in 1469 inaugurated the infamous Spanish Inquisition, aimed especially at Marranos (converted Jews), Moriscos (converted Muslims), illuminists, and witches. This inquisition also included Spain's New World colonies. Each nation's sovereign controlled its inquisitions, for Pope Sixtus IV in 1478 gave rulers the power to name Inquisitors—with little accountability to the church. Spain's first Grand Inquisitor was Dominican Tomás de Torquemada (1483–98); the second, Cardinal Ximenes (1498–1517). Thousands were executed and a hundred thousand imprisoned. It was medieval in procedure with the accused practically helpless. Church and state seized the victim's properties. Sentences were announced in public worship celebrations. In 1492 Spain's Jews were given the choice of conversion or exile. In 1502 the Moriscos were victimized.

In 1542 Pope Paul III created the Holy Office of Inquisition to combat Protestantism. Its domain extended throughout Catholicism, and its directing committee of cardinals was independent of episcopal control. It became excessive under popes Paul IV (1555–59) and Pius V (1566–72), was suppressed in 1834, revived in 1908, and renamed the Congregation for the Doctrine of the Faith by Pope Paul VI (1965). It now deals mostly with heretical writings. C.M.

**I.N.R.I.** The first letters of the inscription Pilate had written and nailed to Jesus' cross; in Latin: *Iesus Nazarenus Rex Iudaeorum,* meaning, "Jesus of Nazareth, the King of the Jews" (John 19:19; Matt. 27:37; Mark 15:26; Luke 23:38). This abbreviation is generally used in Christian art, appearing on a plaque above Jesus' head. J.C.

**INSPIRATION AND REVELATION.** When it is claimed that the knowledge of God is revealed, it is meant that this knowledge is not gained by unaided human effort but is a gift from God. God has taken the initiative in establishing the divine-human relation and has communicated the knowledge of himeself to human beings. Clearly, there is an analogy between the way in which anyone receives a revelation of God and the way in which anyone comes to know another person. No doubt one may learn quite a lot about fellow human beings just by observing them and inquiring about them. But we come to know people as people only when they are willing to know us and open up to us in conversation and social intercourse. Only if people open themselves and show themselves can we truly know them, and such opening and showing are like a gift. Some theologians have spoken as if God's revelation is exactly like the I-thou relation between two people, but in fact the analogy should not be pressed quite so far. Knowing God is much more like knowing a human being than it is like knowing some impersonal fact that we have investigated, but it is not quite the same. In the case of knowing another human being , we meet that person on a level of equality, and the process of getting to know each other is mutual and reciprocal. In the case of knowing God, the weight of the relation is overwhelmingly on God's side and God's gift to the human recipient completely surpasses any contribution from the human side. Furthermore, when human beings get to know one another, the relation is mediated by their bodies— they see and hear one another, they use audible language, they may even touch one another. But God is not manifested in these ways.

Can we say then how God is revealed or manifested? The religions testify that there are many ways in which human beings have claimed that a revelation of God has come to them.

Some people have claimed that God is revealed to them in the depths of their own souls. This is the mystical awareness of God, and it is the most direct. It would seem that only a small minority of the human race have known the mystical experience, but that minority is found among all races and all religions and has included many of the most spiritually sensitive of men and women. The form of this experience in which God is made known in the innermost depth of a person is very similar in all cultures, and there is certainly a *prima facie* case for the validity of the mystical experience. There have been many Christian mystics, but also Jewish ones and Greek ones, together with representatives in Islam and in the religions of Asia. When mystics retire into their own souls, they are not getting lost in narcissism, but find that the depth or ground of their own being is continuous with the depth or ground of all being—the reality called "God." However, it is typical of mystics to say that this experience is really inexpressible in words, and thus they may even find the word "God" too restrictive for the mysterious being that has touched their lives. This kind of experience is at the furthest distance from that popular misunderstanding of revelation, which infers that it consists of propositions that have fallen ready-made from heaven.

A second type of revelation comes through nature. The revelation is mediated through some inner-worldly reality that is seen as not just a natural phenomenon but as a manifestation of God. Much primitive religion arose from a sense of the divine in nature and so did the more sophisticated religion of nature found in poets like Wordsworth. For them, the things of nature are a vehicle in and through which a divine Presence manifests itself. In such cases, God is not an inference from nature, but rather is intuited as a spiritual reality interfused with nature. This is properly called a revelatory experience and is quite different from any human attempt to argue from the phenomenon of nature to the reality of God (the argument from design).

A third type of revelation is the THEOPHANY, the self-communication of a god in a vision or verbally or both together. No doubt accounts of theophanies are elaborated by the imagination, but some genuine revelation may underlie the stories. Usually theo-phanies occur after long periods of meditation, when some incident, perhaps trivial in itself, is experienced as an encounter with God. A famous case was the theophany granted to Moses at the burning bush. This incident focalized his thoughts about his people and their God, and he believed that God was in the bush, addressing him and calling him.

More typical of the OT is a fourth type of revelation, seen in the large-scale events of history. In the course of the world's history, it is claimed that one can read the character of the God who governs the world. The classic case is the event or series of events connected with the deliverance of Israel from slavery in Egypt, the formation of a new nation under God, and their pilgrimage toward the Promised Land. This event was taken as the manifestation of what God is doing in the world—casting down tyranny, deliv-ering the oppressed, and building up a genuinely human community. This historical revelation im-pressed itself so deeply on the minds of the Israelites that their successors celebrate it to this day, and it has also inspired other groups and been taken as a revelation of God.

In the NT, we find still another type of revelation. Here a human person, Jesus of Nazareth, who is also the center and inspirer of a new human community, is taken as the revelation of God. Soon those who had received this revelation began to speak of an incarnation, an actual personal embodiment of God in the midst of creation. If indeed humanity is made in the image of God, then it would seem natural that the fullest revelation of God that can be given would be revelation in and through a human person or community of persons. It is worth noting that although the idea of incarnation is most fully worked out in Christian theology, related ideas are found in Hinduism and in Buddhism.

In all the cases mentioned, revelation was given first of all not in verbal formulations, but in a total experience, much more inclusive than the hearing and understanding of words. But since human beings are fundamentally linguistic, attempts are inevitably made to put revelation into words. Still, the revelation itself will always be more than the words can express. This point is important when we consider the role of scriptures and dogmas. Though we sometimes speak of the "revealed" word of the Bible, this is not the primary revelation. The propositions of scriptures, dogmas, creeds, and the like, are witnesses or testimonies to revelatory encounters that elude complete verbalization.

This brings us from revelation to the closely related subject of inspiration. The Bible is said to be inspired, and so it is, but this does not mean that every word and sentence comes directly from God, still less that they are inerrant—that would be far too mechanical a way of understanding inspiration. Inspiration occurs first in people, and only in a secondary sense can one speak of "inspired" writings. Men and women have been inspired in the sense that they have been illuminated by the divine Spirit and made recipients of revelation. But we have seen that revelation does not come first in the form of words and sentences. Even in the case of the OT prophets, when we read that "The word of the Lord came to . . ." we need not suppose that the encounter was in the first instance verbal, though the prophet has to put it into words in order to communicate it. (An interesting sidelight comes from Islam at this point. Muhammad is reported as saying that when he was receiving a revelation, it began like the sound of a bell, and this sound gradually resolved itself into words. The words are important, but they are derivative from a more original experience.)

When we speak of the inspiration of the Bible or some other writing, we mean that when its words are read or preached today, they have the possibility of awakening in the hearer the same kind of revelatory experience that was known to the inspired writer who first set down these words as an attestation of his experience. There are many stories of men and women from Anthony of Egypt to Albert Schweitzer for whom, in the course of reading or preaching, the words of the Bible came alive and spoke with revelatory force. It was not a mere repetition, but a reenactment in new circumstances of the original revelation, summoning to a new self-understanding and a course of action appropriate to the situation. Great religious writings are inspired in the sense that they can still speak to the human condition and be the instrument for divine revelation.                J.M.

## INSTITUTION, WORDS OF.

The NT texts of Jesus' institution (or consecration) of the Last Supper (I Cor. 11:23-26 and parallels in Matt., Mark, and Luke) later called the Lord's Supper, the Eucharist, the Holy Communion, or the Mass.

The Pauline words of institution in I Corinthians 11, "This is my body which is for you"; "This cup is the new covenant (or testament) in my blood"; along with the Lord's injunction to "Do this . . . in remembrance of me," are solemnly recited in both the Catholic and Protestant Eucharist services. Luther believed in the absolute necessity of announcing these words over the elements.                J.C.

## INTERCESSION. See INTERMEDIARY.

## INTERDICT.

In the Roman Catholic church, an ecclesiastical penalty imposed by the pope or a bishop over his diocese, barring those interdicted from religious rites, such as Holy Communion. However, persons under interdict may receive the sacraments if in danger of death, and interdicts on places (such as a city or nation) are suspended on Christmas, Easter, Pentecost, and the Assumption of Mary.

Interdicts may be personal—on one person—or on a locale or group, for example, on a city or an organization. A personal interdict excludes that person from the sacraments, church services, and from burial as a Christian (that is, in consecrated ground). The interdict is almost never used in modern times, and it has been suggested that it should be abandoned entirely in the post–Vatican II church.                J.C.

## INTERMEDIARY.

One who acts as a mediator or peacemaker between people or groups. Paul writes, "There is one God, and there is one mediator between God and men, the man Christ Jesus, who gave himself as a ransom for all" (I Tim. 2:5-6).

Jesus Christ is the one who, through his death on the cross and his resurrection, has opened the way to his Father's kingdom. Paul underscores the need for such an intermediary. He sees humankind's sin and need for deliverance and writes, "None is righteous, no, not one" (Rom. 3:10).

In the OT Moses served as a mediator, bringing God's law to the people. As such he was allowed to see more of God than any person had ever seen. The Law itself also was regarded as a mediator. In the OT the word "law," *torah*, usually refers to all of God's teachings. Psalm 1 stresses that the person who delights in the Law (the teachings) of the Lord will be known by God.

The prophets also served as mediators, delivering God's newly revealed Word to their people. The priests on the other hand, interpreted God's Word that had previously been revealed. Kings were to represent the people before the Lord.

OT prophets spoke the Word of God, but Jesus embodied it. OT priests offered sacrifices on behalf of the people to God, but Jesus offered his own life. OT kings were expected to rule the people well on God's behalf, but selfishly did not always do so; Jesus, the king of all creation, gave his life as a ransom for all.

The reference to an intermediary by Paul in Galatians 3:19-20 is difficult to interpret. He writes, "The law . . . was ordained by angels through an intermediary." He goes on, "Now an intermediary implies more than one; but God is one." He may be speaking of Moses as the intermediary between humankind and the angels, who in turn were intermediaries for the Lord. Or he may be speaking of the "offspring" mentioned in preceding verses, Jesus Christ, the great intermediary.                B.J.

## INTERNATIONAL MISSIONARY COUNCIL.

This worldwide missionary body had its beginnings in the World Missionary Conference in Edinburgh in 1910 and had a continuous evolution until its formal constitution in 1921. In principle the IMC was the first worldwide ecumenical council of churches. Among its accomplishments were the creation of a network of councils of churches in many nations, the convening of major world missionary conferences, and the formulation of major policies for mission, support of orphaned missions during World War I and II, and a major contribution to the emergence of the WORLD COUNCIL OF CHURCHES. In 1961 the IMC merged with that larger body and continued to function as the WCC's Commission on World Mission and Evangelism.                W.G.

## INTERPRETATION, HISTORY AND PRINCIPLES OF.

Understanding the Bible and biblical texts, like all other texts, requires interpretation that is based on certain principles and methods for reading texts. Generally such principles and methods, or what might be called hermeneutical guides, are derived, not directly from the texts themselves, but from the contexts in which the texts are interpreted and the reasons for their interpretation. As a rule, the Bible and biblical texts have been interpreted within the context of Jewish and Christian communities, although in recent centuries, nonreligious and academic settings have become contexts for biblical interpretation and thus have introduced new emphases into the picture.

*Pre-biblical Interpretation of "Biblical" Materials.* During much of what might be called "the biblical period," there was no such thing as the Bible, either in its Jewish or Christian form. During this period certain traditions and collections of material, which eventually came to be part of the Bible, were employed and interpreted in the life of the religious communities that used them. Although such material was treated as authoritative or "scriptural," it was subject to interpretation and reinterpretation in contexts different from the situations in which the materials originated or were first utilized. This earliest type of interpretation may be spoken of, with some license, as inner-biblical or pre-canonical interpretation.

Numerous examples of this inner-biblical interpretation may be seen in both the OT and NT. Such interpretation of earlier material could be the result of desires to extend its frame of reference, to clarify or modify its content or meaning, to reapply the material to new contexts, to read some hidden meaning out of the material being interpreted, to supply what was felt to be missing in the earlier form,

and so on. Such interpretation might be made by supplementing the initial text in the form of editorial additions or glosses or by completely recasting. Additions were made to prophetical texts to make them apply to new contexts (see the reference to Judah in Hos. 5:5) or to modify the original material (see the appendix in Amos 9:11-15). The law of the Hebrew slave (Exod. 21:2-6) was reinterpreted in two other texts (Deut. 15:12-18; Lev. 25:39-46). The story of why David did not build the Temple in II Samuel 7:1-13, has been supplemented in I Chronicles 22:8 and 28:3 to explain the reason for his failure. Jeremiah's reference to seventy years for Jerusalem's desolation (Jer. 25:11-12; 29:10) is reinterpreted in Daniel 9:24-27 to mean seventy weeks of years or 490 years and so forth. In the sayings of Jesus, his statements about divorce in Mark 10:1-12 have been reformulated in Matthew 19:1-9 to provide an interpretation with an "exception clause." The emphasis on the immediacy of the Second Coming found in numerous Synoptic texts has been reinterpreted in II Peter 3:8 to extend the time frame considerably.

*Early Jewish Interpretation.* Within the early Jewish communities, it was generally assumed that the OT was divine in origin and that the words and contents of the texts had some form of immediate relationship to their own life and faith. Since they tended to assume that God's truth was a unity, what was taught in scripture and what was believed and practiced in the community had to be in agreement. Interpretation, or MIDRASH (from *darash* meaning "to seek, investigate"), of texts occurred in various contexts in the communities: synagogue preaching, translation activity, law courts, and scholarly academies. In all of these, an effort was made to uncover the timeless truth and significance of scripture in response to and under the guidance of contemporary issues, opinions, and beliefs.

Most all branches of early Judaism interpreted the scriptures to determine, or to produce support for, their systems of beliefs and legal practices. Some of the earliest forms of this interpretation can be seen in the Qumran scrolls dating primarily from the last century B.C. and first century A.D. Like rabbinic Judaism, the Qumran community interpreted the Torah and other texts to establish its HALAKAH ("legal rules") and developed paraphrases and commentaries on texts. A special emphasis in the interpretation of scripture at Qumran was its reading of texts, especially those in the prophetical books, as predictions about the community's own life and history and the coming end of the present world orders. They developed a special genre of literature to give exegetical expression to this perspective. This is the so-called PESHER (from a word meaning "to interpret"), in which a biblical book is quoted continuously, a section or verse at a time, and then its "pesher" or interpretation given.

Classical rabbinic interpretation, coming from a

later historical period, was far less oriented to the predictive and eschatological reading of the materials than the Qumran community, being more concerned with establishing legal rulings such as one finds in the MISHNAH and TALMUD and in producing *midrashim* on the scripture, which might be either legal (*halakah*) or nonlegal, homiletical, or story-like (*haggadah*) in character. In all cases, however, the desire was twofold: (1) to make the contents of the Bible, even those most obscure, which had come from another age, provide directives and supports for practices and beliefs in a new situation, and (2) to stress the unity of the biblical world and text with the contemporary world of the community and its beliefs and practices.

In establishing halakic and haggadic interpretations, rabbinic scribes, believing everything in the text to be important, frequently sought to read significance into any unusual features: linguistic peculiarities, the formation of letters, modes of expression, and so forth. One rabbi declared: "Search it [Torah] and search it, for everything is in it." In order to preserve some regularity in interpretation, however, rabbis drew up rules or guidelines. Seven such hermeneutical rules are attributed to Hillel, thirteen to Ishmael, and thirty-two to Eliezer.

Translations have always been a form of interpretation. This was certainly the case when the Hebrew text was translated into Aramaic to produce the Targums, and various forms of Greek translations came into being. Some of the Targums and Greek translations are more literal than others. In places, the Targums are more paraphrase than translation and contain major additions not found in the Hebrew. Throughout they try to harmonize contradictions in the text, clarify and modernize obscure points and terminology, emphasize messianic predictions, and reduce the amount of language that speaks of God in human terminology.

Finally, it should be noted that quite early in places like Alexandria, in allegorical reading of texts the plain sense was bypassed or modified, so that a more modern or philosophical or less embarrassing interpretation might be read into the text. The most famous Jewish allegorical interpreter in antiquity was PHILO OF ALEXANDRIA, who died about A.D. 50.

*Old Testament Interpretation in the New Testament.* In the early church of the first century, the Bible of the Christians, if it is possible to speak of one at this stage, was the scriptures that came to make up the OT. The church's interpretation of the OT, in its emphasis on predictive and eschatological reading of the material, tended to parallel that of Qumran. Paul, for example, could declare that "whatever was written in former days was written for our instruction" (Rom. 15:4). This perspective assumes a basic principle of interpretation, namely, the OT was written for the benefit of the church, not merely or even primarily for the original contexts in which it was composed. Thus early Christians were willing to appropriate the OT in

a rather free and charismatic fashion. They believed themselves to be endowed with insight by being Spirit-filled. They used Jesus as the key for understanding many OT passages; they used the OT to understand the NT proclaimed in Jesus. Since Christianity was offering something that went beyond Judaism and the OT, this NT was often read into OT texts through schemes based on prophecy-fulfillment (see Matt. 1:22-23, etc.), typology (for example, Christ as the second Adam; Rom. 5:12-21), or even allegory (see Gal. 4:21-31). On at least one occasion, Paul denies the straightforward meaning of a text about oxen (Deut. 25:4), relating it instead to the question of payment for Christian preachers (I Cor. 9:3-12).

The NT shows Jesus taking a rather critical attitude toward the OT and the secondary traditions or oral laws built on OT texts. He ascribed the permission of divorce to Moses not God (Mark 10:4-5) and contrasted his teaching with that of the OT: "You have heard that it was said . . . but I say to you" (Matt. 5:21-48).

*Interpretation in Late Antiquity and Medieval Times.* Throughout this period, most interpreters, but especially Christian ones, operated with the assumption that biblical texts could have more than one meaning. Paul's statement that "the written code kills, but the Spirit gives life" (II Cor. 3:6) was taken to mean, among other things, that the literal or plain meaning of a text was not all there was in a text. Exegetes thus searched behind the literal, surface meaning to discover deeper spiritual meanings. The Alexandrian ORIGEN, influenced by Greek and Hebrew allegorical treatment of texts, argued that many passages were never intended to be taken at face value, for example, much of the material in Genesis 1–2. For him, the contents of many narrative texts were figurative expressions that indicated certain mysteries through a resemblance to history but without referring to actual events. For him, what was unbelievable or unedifying was to be understood allegorically.

AUGUSTINE (354–430) applied a more theological argumentation about how to handle the literal meaning of texts. Since the message of the Bible was primarily about love (but also hope and faith) "whatever appears in the divine Word that does not literally pertain to virtuous behavior or to the truth of faith you must take to be figurative," that is, one must search for a secondary or hidden meaning behind the actual statements of many parts of Scripture. Thus Augustine allegorizes literal texts and in the Psalms, for example, has Jesus, the church, or Christians as the speaker.

The search for hidden or secret meanings in the texts was not unopposed in the early church. The so-called school of Antioch—whose most famous theologian was Theodor of Mopsuestia (about 350-428)—argued against excessive allegorical interpretation. In the debates and discussions between the Alexandrians (the allegorists) and the Antiochenes (the more literalists), JEROME (331–420) occupied a middle position.

Eventually, with the triumph of Origen's and Augustine's method, Christian exegetes sought for at least four meanings in a text—literal or historical, allegorical, tropological, and anagogic. In offering the example of Jerusalem, John Cassian (360–425) wrote that historically or literally the name refers to the city of the Jews, allegorically it denotes the church of Christ, tropologically it indicates the human soul, and anagogically it signifies heaven or the eschatological Jerusalem. Thus any text about Jerusalem could be interpreted with all four significations. As a rule, Christian figurative or nonliteral interpretation of biblical texts to discover their spiritual meaning was applied more to the OT than the NT. Exegetical conclusions based on the fourfold meaning of texts practically always remained within the accepted faith of the church.

Within medieval Judaism, a similar fourfold scheme was employed to discover various senses in a text. The four meanings of a text were called *peshat* (the plain meaning), *remez* (allusion or allegory), *derash* (the homiletical), and *sod* (the mystical or secret).

During the eleventh and twelfth centuries, a great renaissance of Jewish learning took place. Among the scholars of the time were Ibn Ezra (1092–1167) and Rashi (1040–1105). A renewed emphasis on the plain meaning of the text (the *peshat*) was stressed in most of their work. Many Christians were influenced by this focus on the literal meaning and stressed this as of primary importance. Among these were scholars at the Abbey of St. Victor in Paris (founded in 1110) and the later Nicholas of Lyra (1270–1349).

*The Renaissance and Reformation Periods.* During the Renaissance, interest in classical antiquity and ancient texts blossomed and gave rise to a number of concerns that influenced biblical interpretation. (a) The roots of a true historical perspective began to develop. Whereas medieval art, literature, and thought tended to see the past and the present as homogeneous, Renaissance scholars emphasized the past as truly different from the present. When applied to the Bible, this meant that one could not assume that contemporary issues and viewpoints were identical with those of the biblical writers. (b) The analysis of ancient sources and documents became a primary concern so that the later documentary analysis of biblical materials has its antecedents here. (c) Renaissance scholars argued for an understanding of texts based on grammatical analysis, textual criticism, and other methods that would allow the texts to speak on their own rather than be primarily a sounding board for later tradition and beliefs. Such a perspective challenged the idea of a fourfold meaning in every biblical text.

New approaches and principles of interpretation came out of the Reformation. The Reformers stressed the importance of Scripture, arguing that Scripture alone *(sola scriptura)* was to be the final judge of the faith of the church and believer. In addition to this central emphasis on the Bible, the Reformers also stressed the plain sense of the text and that Scripture should be compared with Scripture to determine its meaning rather than appealing to church tradition. The Reformers used the Bible to criticize the traditions of the Catholic church as well as its teaching. This meant that the Reformers viewed the contents and the teachings of the Bible as different from what the church had come to claim. What this did was to put a historical and theological gap between the Bible and the church of their day. Such a separation between the Bible and contemporary faith and practice had built into it the need for a critical and historical approach to Scripture, since the "biblical" had to be established in order to use it to critique post-biblical developments.

Although many of the principles of modern approaches to the Bible had their roots in the Renaissance and Reformation, it was not until later, and then partially influenced by people and movements outside the church, that critical and historical methods came to be clearly articulated. Protestant scholasticism, which developed in the late sixteenth century and dominated most of the seventeenth and eighteenth centuries, argued for the inspired infallibility of the Bible and treated it as a source book of doctrines, thus ruling out most critical-historical analysis.

*The Modern Period.* Developments in various nonreligious fields, as well as developments within the church and synagogue—a shift to more scientific world views and liberal outlooks—challenged the authority of the Bible and its orthodox interpretation in the seventeenth and eighteenth centuries. Questions were raised about the world view of the Bible; its presentation of world history; the claims about its inspiration; contradictions, repetitions, and conflicts in its content. The consequence of these developments was a number of methodologies that have come to be called the historical-critical interpretation of the Bible.

Several principles underlie this approach. First of all, historical criticism argues that the books of the Bible should be interpreted, as far as possible, like any other documents from antiquity. The same sort of questions should be asked about the Bible or the biblical books as about any other document. Who wrote it? When? For what purpose? In what context? How reliable is the material? What special interests did the author have? Second, critical research, not religious beliefs or tradition, must be relied upon to engage and answer these questions. Third, biblical texts have one meaning and that was the meaning intended by the author, which must be arrived at through grammatical, philological, and critical analysis. Fourth, interpretation must seek to understand what the author wrote in terms of the ancient historical context within which it was written. All of these principles assume that the books of the Bible were humanly written, intended for particular audiences in the ancient world, and composed to serve particular purposes.

In recent years, the historical-critical approach and the principles on which it rests have been challenged by other methods such as structuralism and new literary criticism. The basic position of this challenge is the assumption that all literary texts may be read and appreciated in a number of legitimate ways. A portion of the Bible, like a play by Shakespeare, may be read, interpreted, and appreciated merely as an independent text without reference to its original historical context and without the employment of special critical tools.

In the present situation, we appear to be moving toward multi-faceted approaches in biblical interpretation. Such approaches certainly include the historical-critical but also include interpretations based on aesthetic and literary appreciation of the material.

(*Compare* HERMENUETICS, CANON, BIBLICAL CRITICISM.)                                                    J.H.

**INTERTESTAMENTAL.** Strictly speaking, between the OT and NT. The term is used to speak both of a period of time and of literature. Chronologically speaking, it is the time extending from the conclusion of the OT to the beginning of the NT. When used of literature, the term has a wider reference denoting many works, some written even earlier than the last books of the OT.                                                    J.H.

**INTERVARSITY CHRISTIAN FELLOWSHIP.** An interdenominational ministry among students in secular colleges and universities. The movement had its beginnings in 1939 under the leadership of C. Stacey Woods, one of its major goals being the recruitment of foreign missionaries. In 1945 Intervarsity was united with the Student Foreign Missions Fellowship, which had its beginnings among students in American Christian colleges and Bible institutes. Chapters of the united group have been formed in approximately 750 colleges, including nursing schools. Area missionary conferences are held under the sponsorship of the SFMF. Its headquarters is in Madison, Wisconsin, and a publishing operation, Intervarsity Press, is maintained in Downers Grove, Illinois.                                                    W.G.

**INTROIT.** The opening chants or responses at the beginning of the Roman Catholic mass or the Lutheran service. It takes place at (or symbolizes) the entrance of the ministers for the service. It is to give a feeling of community to the worshipers. The introit was made part of the Mass by Pope Celestine I (mid-fifth century), as a psalm. Later it was reduced to several psalm verses and a refrain. In services without music, the refrain alone is recited by the priest. The Latin text of the introit often supplies the name for the

Sunday (for example, *"quasi modo geniti,"* "as newborn babes"). This usage was retained by the Lutheran and Anglican churches after the Reformation.                                                    J.C.

**INTUITION.** An immediate insight into reality or truth that transcends ordinary cognitive and experiential means of gaining knowledge. Although controversial, intuition is often said to be more valid than other methods of discovering truth. René Descartes observed that reason is based on intuitively known presuppositional beliefs, and Blaise Pascal spoke of such fundamental truths as "intuitions of the heart," first principles that reason cannot attain. Benedict Spinoza considered intuition one of the highest forms of knowledge, more reliable finally than knowledge gained from experience and science. Immanuel Kant regarded his own apprehension of the mind's forms of space and time as pure intuitions. Henri Bergson maintained intuition has revealed that relations can never be absolutely constant because reality itself is not constant, thus making intuition essential for completing the knowledge gained by scientific observation. Edmund Husserl likewise insisted that intuitive metaphysical truth is necessary to complete science.
                                                    C.M.

**INVESTITURE CONTROVERSY.** The dispute between the civil and the ecclesiastical powers regarding who had the right to name and invest the occupants of high ecclesiastical office, who also wielded great political power. Although the debate continued over a long time, it turned into heated controversy in the clash between Pope GREGORY VII and Emperor Henry IV, who eventually was humiliated by the pope at Canossa. But the dispute continued for years, until a compromise was reached in the Concordat of Worms (1122).                                                    J.G.

**INVISIBLE CHURCH.** *See* CHURCH: Visible and Invisible.

**IOTA.** The smallest letter of the Greek alphabet. Iota corresponds to the Hebrew letter *yodh* and to the English letter *i,* also the smallest letters. Thus iota has come to mean "a very small quantity." The RSV translates Matthew 5:18, "Not an iota . . . will pass from the law" (KJV, "jot").                                                    B.J.

**IRENAEUS OF LYON.** Bishop of Lyon in the last quarter of the second century, and one of the most significant theologians of his time. He was born in Asia Minor (probably in Smyrna) about A.D. 135. There he knew Bishop POLYCARP, whom he always held in high regard. Around the year 170, and for unknown reasons, he migrated to Gaul and settled in Lyon, where there was already a Christian community. In A.D. 177, persecution broke out in Gaul, and Irenaeus was elected to succeed Bishop Pothinus, who suffered martyrdom. In A.D. 202, persecution broke out again, and we are told that Irenaeus suffered martyrdom at that time.

Irenaeus was above all a pastor, and as such he wrote several works whose purpose was to guide his flock to a deeper understanding of the Christian faith, and away from error, particularly GNOSTICISM. Two of his works survive: the *Denunciation and Refutation of the So-called Gnosis*—best known as *Against Heresies*—and the *Demonstration of Apostolic Preaching*.

Irenaeus' theology is pastoral in the deepest sense, for he conceives of God as a shepherd leading humanity through history toward the divine goals. Thus, history, and God's action in it, are his main interests. The divine goal for humanity is for us to have close communion with God. The highest point of this communion is God's incarnation in Jesus Christ, who is both the model after which humans were created (the "divine image" of Genesis) and the goal of our creation. Thus, the Incarnation is not the contingent result of sin, but rather something that God had always intended and which now, because of sin, has the added dimension of redemption. Christ was made human so that we may be made divine, that is, so that we may grow in communion with God. From the very beginning, humans were intended to "grow in justice" under the guidance of the Word, and even though sin has intervened, God is still working to that end.

Irenaeus' theology, which has enjoyed a revival in the twentieth century, represents a very early tradition, and it is likely that the study of it will lead to a better understanding of the NT.                J.G.

**IRRESISTIBLE GRACE.** A doctrine developed from the writings of JOHN CALVIN and stabilized by the Synod of Dort in 1619 as a rebuttal to the Remonstrant, or Arminian viewpoint, that human beings have a part in their salvation.

Calvinists hold a high doctrine of God's sovereignty that leaves no room for free will. All things are ordered by God, and God's saving purpose will be fulfilled in spite of anything humans might do to prevent it (*see* PREDESTINATION). Since all humanity is born in TOTAL DEPRAVITY, the ELECTION of some to salvation by God's sovereign grace is an act of unmerited love.

Only God knows who have been elected, but those who love God and are seeking to do God's will should assume their election. There is no way that they can fall from grace, because if this could happen, God's sovereign power would have been successfully challenged by a human being. The Synod of Dort quotes Romans 8:29-30 to defend its position.
I.C.

**ISAAC.** The second of the three founding fathers or patriarchs of Israel; the son born to ABRAHAM and SARAH in their old age. The name Isaac is interpreted by the pentateuchal writers as having to do with the phrase "to laugh." In Genesis 18:9-15 Sarah laughs when the heavenly visitors announce that God's promise of progeny to Abraham will be fulfilled through the hitherto barren and now aged Sarah. In

that passage the laughter is subject to the Lord's criticism: "Is anything too hard for the Lord?" (Gen. 18:14.) In Genesis 21:6 the laughter is interpreted as the joy of the community at the miraculous birth to the aged Sarah of a son: "And Sarah said, 'God has made laughter for me; every one who hears will laugh over me . . . who would have said to Abraham that Sarah would suckle children? Yet I have borne him a son in his old age.'"

The birth of Isaac occasioned the casting out of the slave woman HAGAR and her son ISHMAEL, fathered by Abraham at the suggestion of Sarah (Gen. 21:8-21). During the childhood of Isaac, the severe testing of Abraham on Mt. Moriah recounted in Genesis 22 takes place. Abraham is ordered to sacrifice his only son as a burnt offering and evidences his faithfulness in his willingness to do so. But God spares Isaac by providing a ram as a substitute sacrifice and so guarantees the continuance of the progeny promised to Abraham in Genesis 12:1-3. (Many modern commentators take this story to be not so much a historical account as an explanation for why Israel rejected the practice of human sacrifice.)

Genesis 24 recounts the father's effort to find a wife for Isaac among Abraham's kinspeople in the Mesopotamian land of his origin. In answer to the prayer of Abraham's servant, the Lord guides REBEKAH, Abraham's great niece, into his line of sight, while his caravan was drawn up outside the city walls. The servant takes it as a sign that this fair maiden alone draws water for him and his camels to drink. At last, Rebekah leads Abraham's servant to her brother Laban, and after suitable negotiations, Laban grants Rebekah permission to return to Canaan to become Isaac's wife.

As compared to the much longer accounts of Abraham and Jacob, the Isaac saga is relatively brief and fragmentary. We learn in Genesis 25:19-34 of the twin brothers Esau and Jacob, who were born to Rebekah when Isaac was sixty years old. In Genesis 26 Isaac is located in Gerar in the lands of Abimelech, king of the Philistines. It is there that he repeats the deception already recounted twice about his father and mother (see Gen. 12:10-20 and chap. 20); that is, he attempts to pass off Rebekah as his sister rather than his wife in the hope of saving his life. In the end, Isaac takes up his residence in Beersheba (Gen. 26:23-35), where he pronounces his final blessing upon his sons. Tricked by his wife and son Jacob into imparting the irrevocable fatherly blessing upon the younger son rather than the elder, he can give Esau only the bitter legacy, "By your sword you shall live, and you shall serve your brother" (Gen. 27:40). He is said to have died at Hebron at the age of one hundred eighty years and to have been buried there by his sons Esau and Jacob in the tomb of his father and mother, Abraham and Sarah (Gen. 35:28-29; compare 49:31).

Many modern scholars believe that the stories of Isaac belonged to the sanctuary at Beersheba, and that he was the founding father venerated at that place before Israel ever appeared in the land of Canaan. The Isaac stories came to be part of the patriarchal tradition preserved in the Genesis 12–50 saga, when the indigenous legends of the land coalesced into a unified account of the origins of Israel during the formative period between the conquest and the beginnings of kingship under David and Solomon.

W.S.T.

**ISAIAH.** *The Prophet.* Isaiah, the son of an otherwise unknown Amoz (Isa. 1:1), received a call to prophesy to his people in the final year of King UZZIAH (Azariah) of Judah (Isa. 6:1-8), that is, about 742 B.C. It is conceivable, though the matter must remain conjectural, that he had a previous career in another prophetic capacity, as a "professional" prophet of cult or court. Such a conjecture rises from the circumstances of his call in the Jerusalem Temple, the evident ready access that he had to the king (Isa. 7:1-9; II Kings 20), the nationalistic tenor of some of his prophecy (compare II Kings 19:21-28), the fact that he apparently had a consort who was also a "prophetess" (Isa. 8:3), and his occasionally eccentric behavior (Isa. 20), among other things that imply that he must have had a former prophetic career.

This guess about Isaiah's possible origin is typical of what can only be surmised about him from inferences derived from his own words and other scanty biographical details. What can be said with fair certainty is that he was born and raised in Jerusalem. Of all the canonical prophets of Israel and Judah, Isaiah is virtually alone in paying no attention to the Mosaic traditions of the Sinaitic law and covenant to provide the bases of moral and social imperatives. Rather, he reverts to an ancient ethos, even a pre-Israelite ethos, of the city Jerusalem, once known (Isa. 1:21) as the dwelling place of righteousness and justice. In basing his prophecy on such premises, Isaiah might be compared with more recent religious thinkers who have forgone the "standard" paradigms in the search for a more indigenous and ethnically identifiable version of the common faith.

One aspect of this distinctive interpretation of Yahwistic religion, however, Isaiah certainly shares with other streams of Israelite tradition, even though the connections may be casual. Jerusalem, after all, as far as Israel was concerned, was the creation of David. Isaiah is the one prophet above all who in his authentic words looked to the Davidic dynasty as embodying the hope of an eventual king who would be the chief political and judicial officer of Israel, fulfilling the Canaanite ideal of kingship (Isa. 7:10-17; 9:1-6; so also in "royal" Psalms, such as Pss. 2, 21, 45, 72, 110). It is Isaiah, virtually alone of the traditional prophets of Israel and Judah, to whom an original "messianic" teaching can be ascribed. Later prophetic messianism is largely secondary, derivative, and imitative.

It has been mentioned that Isaiah was married. He had children, though it may be questioned whether their highly symbolic names (Isa. 7:3; 8:3) have been designed for the purposes of prophecy or if they were actually born of an unusual father. It would appear that he did not long outlive the devastation of Judah by the Assyrian king SENNACHERIB in 701 (the background, probably, presupposed by Isa. 1). All else that is said of Isaiah's further life is legend.

His value as a prophet, which must be garnered from his own words, is both quantitative and qualitative. Quantitative, to the extent that he adds to the account of social abuses that were chronicled by earlier prophets for his documentation of such antisocial activities as land-grabbing (Isa. 5:8-10). Qualitative to the extent that Isaiah, who is presumably an urbane and cultivated citizen of the eighth-century capital city of Jerusalem, agrees fundamentally with the presumably rural MICAH of Moresheth, that the evils perceived by prophecy extended throughout Judah without distinction of class, and that divine judgment was eminently deserved by city and country alike.

*The Book.* The book of Isaiah is possibly the most complicated of all the OT literature. The first thing to be recognized is that only Isaiah 1–39 can be considered the work of the eighth-century prophet whom we have been discussing above. But the question is not that simple. Isaiah 1–39 is a composite of diverse works.

*Proto-Isaiah.* This consists, in large part, of the prophecies of Isaiah, from various periods. (1) Chapter 1. Aside from 1:1, which is a standard postexilic chronological indexing of the prophet according to what was to be derived from his own words and the tradition that had grown about him, this chapter is a collection of mostly Isaianic oracles. They probably date from the last period of his ministry, the devastation of Judah (compare vv. 7-9) that accompanied the invasion of Judah by Sennacherib in 701 B.C. This collection of prophecies was doubtless prefaced to the rest of the book by an editor who wished thereby to sum up the prophet's most important themes: observance of social justice rather than verbal honor of God in the cult, retribution of crimes through foreign invasion, the centrality of the Jerusalem ideal, and repentance as the price of restoration.

(2) Chapters 2–5. The introductory verse 2:1 indicates that what follows was originally an independent collection of Isaianic oracles that probably preceded that of chapter 1. It, too, is a summary collection of Isaianic preaching from indeterminate times in the prophet's career, treasured up, like chapter 1, by his disciples, doubtless not without occasional commentary and amplification.

(3) The so-called book of Immanuel: 6:1–9:6. This may have been the first nucleus about which the Book of Isaiah eventually grew. It begins with the prophet's own account of his call to prophecy (though in an edited form that envisages its results as well as its beginnings), continues with the circumstances of the

Syro-Ephraimite war, embodies some Isaianic "signs" and exposes Isaiah's acceptance of the "messianic" character of the scion of the Davidic dynasty. Noteworthy is 8:16-23, a passage by which we are informed how the prophetic "literature" of the OT was preserved for us through the memory and literary activity of prophetic disciples.

(4) From 9:7 to 12:6 appear oracles against the northern kingdom of Israel (from the time of the Syro-Ephraimite war?), against the social sins of Judah itself, against ASSYRIA—the scourge of the Lord, interspersed with messianic promises. This complex seems to be another parallel Isaianic collection that has been thoroughly edited and expanded by some of the prophet's disciples.

(5) Chapters 13–23: The oracles against the (foreign) nations. Most of the prophetic books contain such oracles. In the postexilic editing of these works such oracles usually have been collected at midpoint between prophecies of doom and of salvation to signify that although it was by means of the nations that Israel had been chastised, still the Lord held these instruments of his wrath equally accountable for their own sins. The postexilic editors also tended to build on these oracles and extend them down into their own times, envisaging the contemporary enemies of Israel. There is no doubt that the preexilic prophets, though their primary mission was to Israel or Judah and that alone, did also on occasion prophesy against foreign nations (so Isaiah against Assyria, so Amos 1:3–2:3, so Nahum, etc.). Thus there is no problem about acknowledging an Isaianic nucleus to this collection, which concerns traditional enemies like Egypt, Moab, Assyria, and others. But it is also obvious that later amplifiers are responsible for texts like chapter 13, against Babylon (read "Chaldea"), which was not to exist as a threat to Israel till more than a century after the prophet's death.

(6) Chapters 24–27: the Apocalypse of Isaiah. This is a highly complicated mass of material of various stages of development and authorship, which for the first time regarding the Isaianic passages we have been considering probably has nothing whatsoever to do with the eighth-century prophet Isaiah. It is of postexilic composition, doubtless the very last segment to be inserted into this book, and probably for no better reason than that Isaiah had been chosen to be one of the repositories of miscellaneous prophetic and para-prophetic material of late origin that was being distributed over the existing body of literary prophecy.

(7) In chapters 28–33 we rejoin the prophet Isaiah. Here we have a collection of "woe" oracles, which date from the latter part of his career, the years prior to 701. Interspersed is non-Isaianic material, some of it imitative of Isaiah, some of it salvation prophecy of a later time.

(8) The two chapters 34–35 are also late and of different, though related, character. The first is prophecy of doom for Edom, in the spirit of exilic detestation of this predatory enemy of Israel (compare Ps. 137). The second is salvation prophecy reminiscent and probably imitative of Deutero-Isaiah.

(9) Chapters 36–39 form a historical supplement taken, with some modifications, from II Kings 18:13–20:19.

*Deutero-Isaiah.* There is no longer any critical doubt that Isaiah 40–55 is the work of a prophet or prophets from exilic times composed long after the eighth-century Isaiah for whom the book is named. For lack of a better designation, the anonymous prophet or prophets is conveniently titled Second Isaiah. It is not impossible, of course, that the fairly routine name Isaiah ("Yahweh is salvation") was borne by more than one person within the prophetic tradition of Israel and Judah. The argument that Deutero-Isaiah's place in the prophetic collections is to be accounted for as the work of Isaianic "disciple(s)" is not as easy to maintain. While there are inevitably some traits that were shared in common by all these Judahite and Yahwistic prophets, still the circumstances of the exile and exilic theology have separated Deutero-Isaiah from the career and thought of Isaiah ben Amoz in quite essential ways.

It may be debated whether one or several hands are responsible for Isaiah 40–55. Probably the prevailing scholarly consensus today would favor single authorship. The composition is a unity, not developed on logical lines but rather through the reiteration of certain key ideas. Its leitmotiv is expressed in 40:1-2: it is the Book of Consolation of Israel, preaching the good news of pardon and salvation (52:7) after the days of punishment and travail during the Exile. It celebrates the power of Yahweh not only as superior to the gods of the Gentiles but as the only God. A theoretical monotheism is professed, along with a sustained polemic against the idols of the nations.

Correspondingly, the destruction of Babylon the oppressor is cheerfully prophesied, at the hands of the up-and-coming CYRUS of Persia, whom the prophet does not hesitate to call the Lord's anointed, his Messiah (45:1). Cyrus did, of course, in 539 B.C. conquer Babylon, and in the following year he proclaimed the freedom of the Jews exiled there to return to Judah and rebuild the city and the temple (II Chr. 36:22-23). Deutero-Isaiah's openness to the pagan Cyrus as Israel's savior is matched by his universalism in relation to the extent of the salvific design of the God of Israel (55:1-14). It is true, this is a universalism of proselytism and triumphatism (45:14; 54:1-3), a glorification of Judaism and of Jerusalem. Similarly, though the Lord's mercy is extended to all freely, for his own sake (43:25), Deutero-Isaiah continually refers to Israel's ancient traditions (see 43:3 and note the patriarchal traditions, for example, 41:8, little invoked by earlier prophets) as precedent for his here-and-now dispensation.

Deutero-Isaiah's prophecy is of a new dispensation of God, which amounts to a new creation (43:1). This connection of redemption with the notion of creation has influenced the doctrine of the Priestly story of Creation in Genesis 1:1–2:4*a*.

The so-called Servant Songs of Deutero-Isaiah, usually designated as Isaiah 42:1-4; 49:1-6; 50:4-6; and 52:13–53:12, are from a body of material whose relation to Deutero-Isaiah continues to be disputed. For some critics the Servant Songs, with their doctrine of a prophetic "messianism" of vicarious atonement, are an addition to Deutero-Isaiah by a later author; for others they were a prior complex adapted by the exilic prophet. In part, the dispute is further complicated by the lack of agreement concerning the identity of the Servant (an individual? of what character? historical, symbolic, eschatological? a collectivity? etc.) and therefore the compatibility of the doctrine of the Songs with the rest of Deutero-Isaiah's convictions. As far as the adapted position of the Songs is concerned, it would appear that Isaiah 41:8-10 (not one of the putatively independent Servant Songs) has deliberately incorporated them into the concept of "Israel, my servant," and for still other critics, therefore, that is the figure that they originally had in mind as part of Deutero-Isaiah's own work. The Israel that is redeemed is also the Israel in which has been made manifest an undeserved suffering that is an atonement for others (compare Isa. 40:2, where it is said that Israel has received from the Lord's hand "double for all her sins").

*Trito-Isaiah.* Isaiah 56–66 is another segment of prophetic literature that is judged today to be separate, not only from Proto-Isaiah, but also from Deutero-Isaiah as well. Internal considerations would make it fairly evident that we are no longer in contact with a prophet who was preaching on the eve of an anticipated glorious restoration of Judah after its exile, but rather with the situation of far less romantic reality of resettlement and reorganization, which is documented by the chronicles of Ezra-Nehemiah and such postexilic works as Zechariah, Haggai, and Malachi.

Trito-Isaiah is not the work of a single author. Rather, like Deutero and Trito-Zechariah, as well as the Book of Malachi, it is anonymous, postexilic prophecy produced by various sources, sometimes at cross purposes, which in the final editing of the Hebrew Bible was used to supplement the prophetic literature and to adjust it to prevailing theological positions.

Trito-Isaiah occasionally agrees with Deutero-Isaiah and frequently goes beyond it. Its universalism is more generous (56:3-8) though it is no less triumphalistic (60:1-22) and can be fiercely vengeful, especially in relation to Edom (63:1-6). Like Deutero-Isaiah it is a book of consolation and glad tidings (61:1-4) proclaiming an entirely new order (65:17-19), a new creation. Frequently it is evocative of the language and the particulars of preexilic social prophecy, but it threatens as sanction not foreign devastation but rather delay in restoration of the land

and of the city (58:8-12). Also, it appeals very specifically to the legalistic imperatives of postexilic religion (65:1-7) just as readily as it asks the reader to reflect on the spiritual and internal religion that alone gives significance to external observances (58:1-9*a*).

The attentive reader finds in Trito-Isaiah a continuity not only with Deutero-Isaiah but also with Isaiah, Ezekiel, other preexilic prophets, and the concerns of the postexilic prophets in the restored Judah of Ezra and Nehemiah. It is not, in the main, an unworthy conclusion to the more than half a millennium of the flowering of Israelite prophecy.

B.V.

## ISAIAH, ASCENSION OF. *See* PSEUDEPIGRAPHA.

*The main sanctuary of the Isé Shrine from the northwest*

**ISÉ SHRINE.** In Japanese, the Ise Daijingu, the "Grand Shrine of Ise." Ise is the most important SHINTO shrine, being the principal place of worship of Amaterasu, the sovereign solar goddess and ancestress of the imperial house. Located on the Eastern seaboard of Japan some two hundred miles southwest of Tokyo, Ise is actually comprised of two shrines about five miles apart, the Naiku of "Inner Shrine" dedicated to Amaterasu, and the Geku or "Outer Shrine" of Toyouke, goddess of food. Dating back to prehistoric times, the shrines are constructed of unpainted wood and celebrated for their austere, archaic architecture. They are ritually rebuilt every twenty years. Associated with the main Ise shrines are a number of auxiliary shrines. Ise is a popular magnet for pilgrimage, and during the Tokugawa period (1600–1868) visits to its holy places sometimes became mass enthusiasms.

R.E.

**ISHBOSHETH.** The Hebrew word for "man of shame." Son of King SAUL, who reigned for a period over the northern tribes of Israel after the death of his father (about 1000 B.C.). In I Chronicles 8:33 and 9:39 Ishbosheth's name is given as Eshbaal, Hebrew for "Baal exists." Many scholars have concluded that this is the original form of the name and that someone associated with the authors of I and II Samuel, a party sympathetic to the Davidic dynasty, altered the form of the name, thus slandering its owner.

Ishbosheth/Eshbaal was apparently placed on the throne by the commander of Saul's army, Abner, after the Hebrew defeat at Mt. Gilboa at the hands of the Philistines. The fact that Ishbosheth/Eshbaal reigned from Mahanaim, a site east of the Jordan, suggests that the central hill country (the location of Saul's former stronghold) was now in the hands of the Philistines. There was protracted warfare between forces loyal to Ishbosheth/Eshbaal and those loyal to DAVID, whose center of power was Hebron, in the south (II Sam. 2:1). The effort to perpetuate the Saulite dynasty collapsed when Abner defected to David (II Sam. 3:17-21), and Ishbosheth/Eshbaal was murdered by two Benjaminites (that is, members of Saul's own tribe) named Rechab and Baanah (II Sam. 4). In a bloody climax to this series of events, Abner was killed by Joab, while the Benjaminites were condemned to death by David.                        J.D.N.

**ISHMAEL.** The name of Isaac's half brother, which means "God hears" or possibly "May God hear!" As is true of so many biblical names, the name is intimately related to the story about the man who bears it. The barrenness and advanced age of Sarah, Abraham's wife, threatened the fulfillment of Yahweh's promise to make of Abram a great nation (Gen. 12:2); furthermore, it deprived Sarah of the joy of child-rearing. Therefore, according to Genesis 16:1-2, Sarah invited her husband to impregnate her Egyptian handmaid HAGAR, saying, "It may be that I shall obtain children by her." In fact Hagar did conceive and then "she looked with contempt on her mistress" (v. 4). Driven out of the household by an angry Sarah, Hagar experienced the first of her saving encounters with the "angel of Yahweh." At a wilderness oasis he assured her of the greatness of the child's destiny—through him her progeny would be innumerable. At his instruction she named the infant Ishmael, because, as the story explains the name, "the Lord has given heed to your affliction" (v. 11).

Yahweh's continued gracious favor toward Ishmael, whom later tradition understood to be the progenitor of the Arabian peoples, is exhibited again and again in the cycle of stories in Genesis 16–28. He participates in the original covenant act of circumcision (Gen. 17:22-27); he is saved from death once again in the wilderness by the angel of God after Sarah, jealous of his friendship for her own child of the promise, Isaac, casts him and his mother out for the final time (Gen. 21:8-21); he becomes the father of twelve sons in his own right (Gen. 25:12-18), thus enfleshing the promise made to his mother that God would "greatly multiply your descendants so that

they cannot be numbered for multitude" (Gen. 16:10).

Of the other five Ishmaels mentioned in the OT, only Ishmael son of Nethaniah, a member of the royal family (II Kings 25:25), needs mention here. According to Jeremiah 40:7–41:15, he led an uprising against the provincial administration left behind in Jerusalem by the Babylonians after the conquest and deportation of 587 B.C.        W.S.T.

**ISHMAELITES.** The name of those neighboring tribes whom the Israelites regarded as having descended from ISHMAEL, the half brother of Isaac. In Genesis 37:25-28 they are pictured as camel caravaneers, plying a trade in gum, balm, myrrh, and slaves between the east bank of Jordan and Egypt. The Ishmaelite band to whom Joseph was sold by his brothers ultimately retailed him to the Egyptian officer Potiphar (Gen. 39:1). Genesis 37:28 and 37:36 appear to identify the Ishmaelites with Midianites (another nomadic people centered in southern Palestine), but some critics contend that the Elohistic writer simply favored the latter term over the term "Ishmaelites" employed by the Yahwistic writer.

Elsewhere in the OT the (con)fusion of the Ishmaelites and Midianites continues. The spoil of the armies of Midian destroyed by Gideon included golden earrings, a fact that a glossator explains cryptically as follows: "They had golden earrings, because they were Ishmaelites" (Judg. 8:24*b*).

Individual Ishmaelites who receive passing notice in the OT include Jether (I Chr. 2:17), the husband of David's sister Abigail and father of David's nephew Amasa, who became one of his trusted military commanders. Another Ishmaelite who served David was Obil, the steward of the king's camels (I Chr. 27:30). These brief notices suggest that relations between Israel and the Ishmaelites were amicable enough; only once, in Psalm 83:6, are they listed among the enemies of Israel alongside a southern border people, the Edomites.        W.S.T.

**ISHTAR.** In the ancient world of Babylon and Assyria, Ishtar was the goddess of love, fertility, motherhood, and war. In Canaan, Arabia, Phoenicia, Aramaea, and Egypt her name was usually spelled Astarte, and she sometimes also appears in the OT as ASHTORETH. King Solomon built an altar to her, perhaps because of the foreign wives in his harem, and King Josiah destroyed it. In Greece she was known as Aphrodite, and in Rome as Venus.        T.J.K.

**ISIDORE OF SEVILLE.** Archbishop of Seville from about A.D. 600 to 636. The leading figure of the Spanish church at the time, and a scholar whose writings were widely read in later centuries.

Isidore succeeded his brother Leander as archbishop of Seville shortly after King Recared had abandoned ARIANISM in favor of orthodox Christianity. Then came a period of political chaos in which the church sought to restore order. The Fourth Council of Toledo (A.D. 633), under Isidore's leadership, declared who was the rightful king, ordered clerical celibacy (with minor penalties for offending clerics and harsh punishment for their wives), and put Jews under severe handicaps.

His main work, the *Etymologies,* summarizes the knowledge of his time on all subjects, including not only theology, but also astronomy, agriculture, zoology, and medicine, to name a few. Many of the etymologies Isidore suggests are quite fanciful, as is also some of the information he offers. In another work, he sought to bring up to date the chronicles *On Illustrious Men* by JEROME and Gennadius. His *History of the Kings of the Goth, Vandals, and Suevi* is still an important source. Through these writings Isidore, who was not an original thinker, left his mark on the course of science and theology throughout the Middle Ages.    J.G.

**ISIS AND OSIRIS.** Gods in the religion of ancient Egypt. Isis was the wife of Osiris and the mother of Horus. From the earliest period of prehistoric Egypt, Isis was worshiped as the supreme mother god, symbol of the fertility of the soil. In the course of time she became identified with various Semitic, Greek, and Roman gods. Osiris was identified with the waters of the Nile and the sun.

According to one form of the myth, Osiris was killed by his brother Set, who stole Osiris' "third eye," a symbol of kingship. Isis found the corpse, embraced it, and when Osiris revived he impregnated her. She bore their son Horus, who later set out to avenge his father's murder. Horus found his father's corpse and defeated Set, regaining the "third eye."

Osiris came to be regarded as the lord of the realm of the dead and the judge before whom the dead must appear. Thus the myth reflects the "death" and "rebirth" of vegetation and the hope for new life for the dead. Osiris was often identified with the bull god Apis and known as Osiris-Apis. This became the name Serapis, by which he was known in the Roman world. The cult of Isis and Osiris flourished there around the beginning of the Christian Era as one of the so-called MYSTERY RELIGIONS.    K.C.

**ISLAM.** The monotheistic religion that had its beginnings with the prophet MUHAMMAD (A.D. 570–632), but lays claim to the whole history of the people of the One God. The prophets of the OT—Adam, Abraham, Moses, David, Solomon, Jonah, and the rest—are honored as forerunners of the last and greatest prophet of all, Muhammad. So too is Jesus, son of the Virgin Mary, who, according to Islamic belief, foretold the coming of Muhammad.

The word "Islam" means "submission (to God)," and a person who professes Islam is a Muslim. From its origins in Arabia, Islam spread west across North Africa into Spain and east through Syria, Iraq, and Iran to India, and later to Indonesia and the Philippines. Large Muslim populations are found in the Soviet Union and in China. Under the Turks, Islam ruled large areas in southeast Europe for centuries. By the eleventh and twelfth centuries Islam was strong in many parts of Africa south of the Sahara, and it continues strong there today.

As a major cultural force, as the inspiration of rich traditions in literature, philosophy, and art, and as the power behind the splendor of some of the world's great empires, Islam has shaped the civilization of large areas of the world.

*Origins.* At the beginning of the seventh century A.D., the old pagan religion of Arabia was still strong. Various gods and goddesses were worshiped, and their images were honored. The city of MECCA was a center of this religion. Pilgrims came long distances to worship at the Ka'ba, a shrine filled with idols. At the same time, there were large and flourishing Jewish communities in Arabia, and contacts with Christians were common. Thus there was knowledge of the other two monotheistic faiths from the start.

Muhammad was born in Mecca. Orphaned at an early age, he grew up under the care of an uncle. He entered the employ of a wealthy widow, Khadijah, and although he was fifteen years younger than she was, they were married. She bore him several children, all but three of whom died in infancy. Only one, his daughter FATIMA, outlived Muhammad. Khadijah was a loving wife, loyal to Muhammad, and an encouragement during the early years of his career as a prophet.

Around 610 Muhammad began to receive revelations, which he was certain came from the one true God. Over the next twelve years they continued to come, but his efforts to establish the worship of God in Mecca bore little fruit. Finally, in 622, accompanied only by his closest friend, Abu Bakr, Muhammad left Mecca to escape the threats of his enemies. He took refuge in the city of MEDINA, 280 miles to the north, and there his movement steadily gained strength. Other revelations came to him there. Before his death in 632 he was able to enter Mecca in triumph and put an end to the worship of idols. The migration to Medina is known as the HIJRA, or Hegira, and marks the first year of the Islamic calendar.

*Major Beliefs.* (a) The first half of the Muslim creed, "There is no god but God," affirms the oneness of God, without equal, without partners. He stands alone and supreme. He is the Creator of all that exists, and on the last day he will be the sole judge of the living and the dead. The QUR'AN was created by God and given to Muhammad by direct revelation. All of its chapters except one begin by affirming that God is "merciful and compassionate." He is known by "ninety-nine beautiful names." These names include the Knower, the Seer, the Truth, the Sustainer, and the Wise. It has been customary in English to use the name Allah to designate God as he is worshiped by Muslims. The Arabic name is used, however, of God as he is known and worshiped by other monotheists as well. Thus to use it only in speaking of Muslim beliefs is misleading. The similarity of Jewish, Muslim, and Christian concepts of God is striking, but the differences are significant and should not be overlooked.

(b) "And Muhammad is the apostle (prophet) of God." This completes the basic creed and affirms the supreme role of Muhammad. The word translated "apostle" is *rasul*. It expresses Muhammad's role as God's messenger and as the head of the community of God's people. In general, *rasul* refers to a special task given to a prophet, and prophet is the broader term. Muhammad is the greatest of the prophets and the "seal" of the prophets. That is, he authenticated the message of the earlier prophets and brought to completion their mission. After him there can be no successor to the office of prophet. While God has highly favored him above all other humans, Muhammad is not more than human.

*Major Practices.* Muslims are required to perform five duties, known as the Five Pillars of Islam.

(a) The first Pillar is the affirmation of the creed "There is no god but God, and Muhammad is the prophet of God." It is recited each time the call to prayer is given and also on many other occasions. To sincerely affirm this makes a person a Muslim, and he or she is then obligated to observe the other Pillars.

(b) Second is ritual prayer, which must be performed five times each day (at dawn, noon, midafternoon, sunset, and evening). There are strict prerequisites. Purification must be performed with water, or, lacking water, with clean sand or a stone. Specific parts of the body are cleansed in a specified order. The body must be properly covered; males must be covered from the navel to the knees, and females must cover the entire body, except for face, hands, and feet. The place of prayer is also important. Any clean and tranquil place will do, but most community prayers are performed at a MOSQUE. Finally, wherever they are, worshipers must face Mecca. In a mosque the direction of prayer *(qiblah)* is indicated by a special prayer niche in one wall.

(c) Third, alms must be given to the poor and certain other classes of recipients. Often these alms have been collected as a tax on property and distributed by the government.

(d) Fourth, every Muslim is required to fast from dawn until sunset each day during the month of RAMADAN. Since the Muslim world follows a lunar calendar, this month moves through the solar year, occurring a little earlier each year in relation to the seasons.

(e) The fifth Pillar is the only one not absolutely required. It is the HAJJ, or pilgrimage to Mecca, which must be made once in a lifetime if the individual's health and resources permit.

*The Struggles to Succeed Muhammad.* (a) *The first caliphs.* When Muhammad died unexpectedly at the age of 63, there were no procedures for choosing a successor as leader of the community of faith. Should the successor be a member of the prophet's family, a close associate, or a person of strict orthodoxy? ALI, Muhammad's cousin and son-in-law, had a good claim, but he was passed over for Abu Bakr, who lived only two more years. He was the first caliph (successor) in a line that continued until the office of caliph was abolished in Turkey in 1923.

Again Ali was passed over, this time for Umar, a brilliant leader, who was caliph from A.D. 634 to 644. During these years the Muslim armies won overwhelming victories in Syria and later in Egypt. Jerusalem and Damascus were conquered, and the Byzantine Empire was pushed out of territories that had been under Greek rule since Alexander the Great, nearly a thousand years earlier. Egypt was conquered in A.D. 639–41, and the victorious armies pushed on across North Africa. To the east, Iraq was conquered and the ancient Persian Empire crushed. Many of the people of these lands welcomed the change in government, even though not all of them embraced the new religion.

Umar began the transition to empire by establishing controls over the military and over provincial administrators. Assassinated by a disgruntled slave, he was the first of three successive caliphs to meet a violent death. His successor was Uthman (in office A.D. 644–56), another close associate of Muhammad. His greatest achievement was the establishment of the standard text of the Qur'an. Until then there had been disagreement over its precise contents. Uthman aroused hostility by appointing too many of his relatives to office. He was mortally wounded by Egyptian army rebels who had grievances against him.

Finally Ali became caliph in 656, but he was already about sixty years old, and events were beyond his control. The governor of Syria, Mu'awiya, was a member of the Umayyad clan, a clan that had resisted Muhammad almost to the end. Ali dealt weakly with Mu'awiya and lost the chance to assert his authority. Some of Ali's supporters deserted him in disgust, and soon afterward one of them struck him with a sword, mortally wounding him. This left Mu'awiya the unchallenged ruler of the Muslim world.

(b) *The rise of the Shi'ites.* Those loyal to Ali felt that terrible injustice had been done and refused to recognize either the legitimacy of the first three caliphs or the authority of the new Umayyad dynasty. They formed the *shi'a,* or party of Ali, causing the most serious division ever to arise in Islam. The SHI'ITES have developed distinctive practices and beliefs over the centuries, and they are often at odds with Sunnites, followers of the Sunna (tradition), who comprise the vast majority of Muslims today.

Shi'ites honor Ali as the first IMAM and trace his successors through a line of infallible imams. The IMAMIYYA is the largest group of Shi'ites. They recognize twelve imams, the last of whom is in "concealment." He will return as the MAHDI, when

God so wills, and set up the perfect reign of justice. They are the dominant force in Iran today.

The ISMA'ILIYYA recognize only seven imams, the seventh of whom is to return as the Mahdi. They have split into a number of smaller sects and are scattered throughout the Muslim world.

*The Umayyad Dynasty* (A.D. 661–750). From their capital city of Damascus, the caliphs of this dynasty ruled the vast new Muslim Empire. They extended its boundaries to Spain in the West and to India in the East. Their rule was efficient, and they encouraged the development of literature and of translations from Greek into Arabic. This preserved much of Greek culture and enabled Muslims to transmit this culture to Europe in later centuries. Many great buildings stand today as evidence of their skill in architecture.

Two problems plagued the Umayyads. First, they were unable to deal effectively with the non-Arab peoples who had been added to the empire. Second, they could not reconcile those who regarded them as having betrayed Ali and his family and as being unfaithful to the purity of early Islam. Their dynasty collapsed, but in Spain Umayyad rulers continued in power until 1031.

*The Middle Period.* (a) *The political scene.* The ABBASID dynasty ruled from A.D. 750 to 1258. All the Abbasid caliphs claimed authority as descendants of al-Abbas, the prophet Muhammad's uncle. They moved the capital from Damascus to the new city of Baghdad in Iraq. From there they presided over an age of great splendor. The powerful invasions of the Mongol armies from central Asia put an end to this dynasty.

In the meantime a Fatimid dynasty had ruled Egypt (A.D. 909–1171). In the East, the Seljuk Turks, invaders from central Asia, overran Persia, Iraq, and Syria, and were converted to Islam. The Mongol invaders were also converted.

(b) *Schools of law.* Islam has always been a total way of life, and religious leaders sought to show the way to serve God in everything that a person or a community did. An elaborate system was developed for deciding disputed questions. There came to be four different schools of thought as to how to interpret the law (SHARIA).

The first of these was the HANIFITE school, which uses speculation liberally. It began with the teachings of the Qur'an and then tried to see how those teachings apply in different circumstances. Legal scholars of this school are also careful to consider the public good and general principles of justice.

Next, the Malikite school uses the traditions about Muhammad's teachings and practice (HADITH) along with the Qur'an. They lean heavily on the consensus of public opinion, and finally they consider issues of what would be to the general advantage of the community.

The third school is known as Shafi'ite, after AL-SHAFI'I (A.D. 767–820), the first person to study previous legal rulings and to develop a scholarly,

systematic method of interpreting the law. Because of his vast knowledge he was able to analyze the practices of his time in terms of the Qur'an, the SUNNA, or practice of Muhammad as seen in the Hadith, the consensus of the community, and reasoning by drawing analogies.

The fourth school, the Hanbalite, is the most conservative. Everything is to be decided by reference to the letter of the Qur'an and to the Hadith. This school was a reaction to the loose standards that prevailed under some of the Abbasid caliphs.

(c) *The mystics.* In the early centuries of Islam there were great individuals who emphasized the inward life of religious devotion. They stressed love for God and proclaimed the goal of oneness with God. Some of them seemed to stray too far from the standard faith, but they kept alive a warm, personal experience in religion. They came to be known as Sufis, a name derived from the simple wool garments many of them wore.

SUFISM's contribution to Islam was made permanent by the work of AL-GHAZALI (1058–1111), a mystic, but also a theologian. He felt driven to investigate all the schools of thought and to understand their strengths and weaknesses. The fruit of this mature reflection was a book of over a thousand pages, *The Restoration of the Sciences of Religion.* It surveyed the whole range of Muslim thought in the Middle Ages and imparted a mystical fervor.

Among the mystics were some of the greatest poets of the Islamic world. Jalal ad-Din Rumi (A.D. 1207–73) wrote not in Arabic but in Persian. His most famous poem, the *Mathnavi,* has been called the "Qur'an of the Persian language." In one of his songs he compares the voice of a reed flute, sorrowing over separation from the place where it grew, to the mystic's voice longing to be united with God.

Many Sufis belonged to groups or religious orders, headed by a gifted master. Rumi founded an order popularly known as Whirling Dervishes, because of the physical activities they used to bring on a religious state. Other Sufis were eccentrics who flouted the normal rules of behavior. Europeans called them fakirs.

*The Modern Period.* The expansion of European power in Asia and the Middle East brought much of the Muslim world under non-Muslim dominance. This was a theological problem as well as a political problem. How could God permit this to happen to those who were submissive to him? One response was extreme conservatism, as seen in the WAHHABI movement in Saudi Arabia from the eighteenth century to the present. Wahhabis have sought to return to the pure Islam of Muhammad's lifetime. They attacked such unorthodox practices as the veneration offered at the graves and shrines of people regarded as saints.

In the twentieth century the Ahmadiyya movement in India sought to evangelize non-Muslims and has sent missionaries to Europe and Africa. Its own orthodoxy has been suspect, however, and in Pakistan one branch has been declared a non-Muslim minority, and its members are barred from holding public office.

The Iranian revolution of the late 1970s marked the rise to power of militant Shi'ites, and the prolonged war between Iran and Iraq was made more bitter by hostility between Shi'ites and Sunnis.

*Muslims, Jews, and Christians.* In spite of their common origins in the Bible and their monotheistic faith, these three religions have often misunderstood and failed to appreciate each other. The Qur'an speaks of Jews and Christians as "People of the Book" and expresses respect for them. At the same time it condemns their failure to accept Islam. The belief that Jesus is the "Son of God" is particularly offensive, since it places a partner beside God and appears to violate monotheism.

Christians have regarded Muhammad as a heretic, charging him with departing from the true faith. They have also condemned Muhammad for having more than one wife and have accused him of lechery. During the CRUSADES (eleventh to fifteenth centuries), feelings were high on both sides as European armies sought to establish Christian kingdoms in the Holy Land. In 1453 Ottoman Turks conquered Constantinople, destroying the ancient Christian Empire of Byzantium and bringing the Crusades to an end. The Turks advanced as far as the gates of Vienna during the Protestant Reformation in the next century, and Protestants and Catholics alike feared the continuing expansion of Islam. It was only after Ferdinand and Isabella drove the last Muslim armies out of Spain in 1492 that they could turn their attention to expeditions across the Atlantic.

Ironically, at the end of World War I, when France and Britain were dividing up the Muslim Middle East between them, Turkey, the defeated Muslim power, was massacring Christian Armenians. The hostility between Druses (a Muslim sect) and Christians in Lebanon has perpetuated ongoing blood feuds. Because Iranians view America as a Christian nation, it was easier to denounce America as the "great Satan" in the 1970s and 1980s.

Jews have generally fared better at the hands of Muslims through the centuries. When they were expelled from Spain after 1492, along with the Muslims, they took refuge in Muslim lands. Large Jewish communities lived for centuries in Muslim societies. Only with the rise of modern ZIONISM did relations turn bitter. The basis for understanding is there. It is usually the will that is lacking on all sides.

K.C.

## ISMĀ'ĪLIYYA.

ISMĀ'ĪLIYYA. In Islam, the group of SHI'ITE sects that are loyal to the seventh IMAM, Muhammad, son of Isma'il (late eighth century A.D.). They are therefore also known as "Seveners." They believe that the seventh imam is in concealment and will return as the MAHDI, a messianic figure who will be the culmination of the mission of all the prophets. They emphasize that the secret meaning of all religious statements is known only to Ali and those descended from him.

In the tenth century A.D. a Sevener named 'Ubaydullah claimed to be the Mahdi and the legitimate ruler of all Muslims. He based his claim on being a descendant of Fatima, the daughter of MUHAMMAD the prophet. He founded the Fatimid caliphate, which ruled Egypt A.D. 909–1171, a period of great cultural achievement.

Several of the Isma'iliyya sects were quite radical. The Qarmatians flourished in the ninth century A.D., and at one point raided the holy city of MECCA and stole the sacred Black Stone from the KA'BA. The Assassins (Hashishiyya) were so called because of their use of hashish to gain a taste of paradise. The crusaders made the name "Assassins" well known in Europe, and it came to be used in various European languages. Marco Polo wrote of the "Old Man of the Mountains," the leader of the sect's mountain fortress at Alamut, south of the Caspian Sea. They survive in the Nizārīs, whose present leader is Agha Khan IV. They are scattered in Syria, Iran, India, and East Africa. Another sect has continued to be dominant in Yemen, and others exist in India.

K.C.

## ISRAEL.

ISRAEL. The name given to Jacob at the brook Jabbok just prior to his inevitable confrontation with Esau (Gen. 32:28; compare 35:10). Also the name for the entire body of Jacob's descendants (34:7), and subsequently, for the ten northern tribes which, after the schism of the Hebrew people in 922 B.C., functioned independently of Judah (I Kings 12:16).

*Overview.* Our main task involves summarizing the history of biblical Israel in a manner that takes account of crucial social and economic developments. Israel's self-awareness, however, constitutes a prior issue demanding our attention. Historical honesty invites the assertion that the collective corporate Israel did not emerge until various related Hebrew tribes had firmly established themselves in the land of Canaan, otherwise known as Palestine. Yet theologically, Israel traced her origins to Yahweh's call of Abraham (Gen. 12:1-3), which required his migration from Haran in upper Mesopotamia to a new homeland in Canaan. That land would be the heritage of his many descendants.

The gift of land and progeny was viewed as a special manifestation of divine love that eluded rational explanation. Though Israel was "the fewest of all peoples" (Deut. 7:7) and lacking in moral worth (9:4-6), she knew that she was the people of God in a special sense. Her God said, "You only have I known of all the families of the earth" (Amos 3:2a). Yet if Israel were Yahweh's "own possession" (Exod. 19:5) chosen for God's unique purpose, she was given no license to live capriciously (Amos 3:2b). While merciful, Yahweh expected uncompromising fidelity from her. As a "light to the nations" (Isa. 49:6), Israel was charged to welcome outsiders who would join her. Yahweh's plan for universal salvation necessarily involved Israel. Even so, this chosen nation must resolutely shun all idolatry. Any compromise would spell disaster as the people fell victim to their enemies. Thus Israel saw herself as the descendants of Abraham, Isaac, and Jacob-Israel, who were charged to serve Yahweh faithfully in the land that God had awarded them (Josh. 24:14). And regularly the OT presents Israel thinking of herself as a worshiping community meaningfully linked with the deity in ongoing covenant fellowship.

In the NT, "the Israel of God" label is attached to Christianity with its unmistakable Jewish roots (Gal. 6:16). Gospel genealogies (Matt. 1:1-17; Luke 3:23-38) affirm the early church's OT ancestry. In the preaching of John the Baptist (Matt. 3:7-9), spiritual lineage surpasses physical lineage. In God's economy, Jews are therefore regarded as having been supplanted by Christians as "God's own people" (I Pet. 2:9-10). In defense of this position, Paul resorts to a Sarah-Hagar allegory wherein Christians are regarded as free and Jews as slaves (Gal. 4:21-31). Nevertheless, Paul also holds that at some future moment, the Jews will be restored to the divine favor they hitherto have known (Rom. 11:25-27).

*Pre-monarchic Israel.* (a) *Patriarchal era.* In biblical tradition, the Genesis patriarchs are regarded as Israel's earliest ancestors. Though Hebrew origins are sufficiently complex to have incorporated both Semitic and non-Semitic elements, the patriarchs appear to be well linked with Syria and northwest Mesopotamia, the locus of the Semitic Arameans. One of Israel's confessional liturgies properly recalls, "A wandering Aramean was my father" (Deut. 26:5).

Regrettably, not even one individual or event narrated in Genesis can be confidently equated with its counterpart in the numerous ancient extra-biblical texts now available. Even so, the patriarchal traditions are ordinarily set against the broad cultural horizon of the Middle Bronze II Era (about 2000–1550 B.C.), though sometimes the Late Bronze Era (about 1550–1200 B.C.) is preferred. Patriarchal names, customs, life-styles, and religion make sense in such a context. The patriarchal groups, including those large families (clans?) led by Abraham, Isaac, and Jacob, seem to have originated in upper Mesopotamia as part of the Amorite and Aramean migrations respectively attested in the Middle and Late Bronze eras.

If Israel's founding fathers roamed about Canaan's hill country with relative ease, they were not simply self-sufficient pastoralists as once supposed. Rather they were members of a mixed society in which urban and agricultural-pastoral components coexisted. As persons who farmed (Gen. 26:12), owned land (23:17-18; 33:19), and possessed heavy livestock (including oxen, 12:16; 21:27), the patriarchs kept company with Canaan's settled farmers and villagers. With its patriarch as authority figure, the family was the sole identifiable unit in patriarchal society. Canaanite drought sometimes necessitated Semitic migrations to the Egyptian Delta. Undoubtedly the Joseph narrative, which witnesses to the relocation of Jacob's family in Egypt (46:1– 47:12), telescopes several such movements.

(b) *Moses and the Exodus.* During the Nineteenth Dynasty, a confident Egypt existed under Seti I (about 1305–1290 B.C.) and Ramses II (about 1290–1224 B.C.). Though their archives mention neither Moses nor the flight of Hebrew slaves, the report that Jacob's descendants substantially fell out of favor with the Egyptian court is likely authentic (Exod. 1:8 ff.). Significant confessional liturgies (Deut. 6:20-24; 26:5-9; Josh. 24:2-13) and the ancient Song of Miriam (Exod. 15:21) speak for the historicity of Israel's formative exodus event. The embellished biblical saga in Exodus 1–15, however, reflects the life experience of but one ancestral strain of later Israel.

The Exodus 1:11 allusion to Hebrew slave labor at the store-cities of Pithom and Raamses suggests a thirteenth-century B.C. date for the EXODUS. Indeed, Seti I and Rameses II are remembered in Egyptian history as ambitious builders in the Nile Delta. Moreover, the stela of Marniptah (about 1224–1211 B.C.), son of Rameses II, attests Israel's presence in Canaan in about 1220 B.C.

Israel's deliverance at the "Sea of Reeds" (*yam suph* in the Hebrew of Exod. 15:4) cannot be pinpointed, but the southern extension of Lake Menzaleh in the eastern part of the Nile Delta is likely. Since the linking of the Exodus and Sinai traditions need not be secondary, Moses presumably led his marvelously delivered people to Sinai, located by tradition at the southern apex of the Sinai Peninsula. Having received Yahweh's law and entered into covenant relation with Yahweh (Exod. 19–24), the people trekked through the wilderness to the Kadesh Oasis (Num. 10:12– 20:22). Failing to penetrate Canaan from the south (Num. 13–14), they advanced eastward to a Transjordanian position in the Moab plain to await the proper moment to ford the Jordan into the Land of Promise.

(c) *Rise to power in Canaan.* Diverse biblical, sociological, and archaeological data have elicited conflicting answers to the question, How did the Hebrews successfully come to occupy Canaan? Three differing models have been posited involving conquest, immigration, and revolt. The conquest model, accepting the fundamental integrity of Joshua 1–11, argues that various Hebrew tribes, united under Joshua's leadership, often tasted victory as they waged war on Canaan's citizens. The military conflicts are dated to the last decades of the Late Bronze Era (late thirteenth century B.C.), when Canaan experienced sweeping cultural shifts. Such geographically distant cities as Hazor, Bethel, Lachish, and Debir sustained extensive destruction before being rebuilt by a people—presumably hailing from the desert—whose material culture was inferior to what was previously there. The archaeological evidence, however, does not specifically confirm that Israelite energies were here involved.

Assuming that Joshua played a more circumscribed role than Joshua 1–11 projects, and that combined tribal effort was more the exception than the rule, the immigration model holds that for many decades Canaan hosted numerous migrations of seminomadic herdsmen who peaceably quested pasture. As they occupied sparsely inhabited areas in the hill country, they cleared the forests and moved toward an agrarian life-style. Intermittent warfare only erupted toward the end of the era of the Israelite Judges (mid-eleventh century B.C.), when these immigrants, pressing for more space, met Canaanite city-states head on. Recent perceptions about the interrelatedness of pastoral, rural, and village life in the ancient Near East, however, have partially rendered this model inoperative.

The revolt model posits a sociopolitical upheaval wrought by disgruntled Canaanite peasants who fought against the injustices of a feudalism that the city-state overlords had imposed on them. Among the varied lower-class people this revolution attracted were restive free farmers and belligerent serfs. When newly arrived Israelites joined their egalitarian cause and recounted their own rescue from Egyptian servitude and Yahweh's promise of salvation, new advances were realized. The imperialistic yoke of the Canaanite overlords was overthrown in favor of more democratic tribal rule (Judg. 21:25). The emphasis on social process rather than on exact historical reconstruction makes this model attractive. But it entertains egalitarian goals nowhere implied by the biblical record, and in the Canaanite urban oppressor it assumes a shadowy villain. In any event, Israel's rise to power in Canaan, which ultimately involved an intertribal confederacy to answer both religious and defense needs, was assuredly a multi-faceted phenomenon.

*Israel as United Monarchy.* (a) SAUL. Eventually the intertribal Israelite confederacy proved incapable of dealing effectively with increasing enemy pressure. The eastward advance of Philistine power was particularly menacing. After the Philistines' triumph over Israel at Aphek, a monarchy was established. As one who decisively overwhelmed the Ammonites who were besieging Jabesh-gilead, Saul was installed by the prophet Samuel as Israel's first monarch (about 1020–1000 B.C.). A rustic king who ruled from his Benjaminite hometown of Gibeah, Saul was constantly required to address the Philistine problem. Even lacking the services of a standing army, he died fighting the enemy at Mount Gilboa.

(b) DAVID. Unmistakably talented, popular, and calculating, David (about 1000–961 B.C.) became king over his native Judah. Then following the murder of Saul's ineffectual son, Ish-baal, David was soon acclaimed monarch over all Israel. Unlike Saul,

David reduced the Philistines to vassalage. He then took the hitherto impregnable Jebusite city of Jerusalem and made it his capital. By transferring Israel's sacred ark of the covenant there, David made certain that politics and religion would coalesce to his own advantage. Without neighboring nations strong enough to thwart him, David soon headed a kingdom greater than that ruled by any subsequent Israelite monarch. Nevertheless, David did not always evoke tribal support. Judah backed Absalom's rebellion against him and Benjamin, through such trouble-makers as Shimei and Sheba, rejected him as a throne usurper.

(c) SOLOMON. In David's son, Solomon (about 961–922 B.C.), the United Monarchy had its last king. If Solomon enjoyed the blessing of international peace, his subjects suffered from the curse of oppressive court policy. Under Davidic instigation and ready Solomonic endorsement, Israelite society moved speedily from a pattern of decentralization and social egalitarianism characteristic of the Judges Era to one of urban centralization and social stratification. By founding the Jerusalem Temple to serve as royal dynastic chapel as a well as national sanctuary, sponsoring courtly wisdom in imitation of imperialistic Egypt, maintaining a standing army and court harem, establishing an ambitious taxation program that consciously violated earlier tribal boundaries, using forced labor to implement his many building enterprises, and engaging enthusiastically in both overland and sea trade, Solomon ruled Israel with a heavy hand.

With expenses regularly exceeding income, Israel's economy was sick and Solomon's splendor hollow. Moreover, international alliances with an unnamed Egyptian pharaoh and with Hiram, king of Tyre, sealed by marriages with foreign princesses, introduced alien cultural and religious influences that offended many Israelites of village and rural orientation. Nor were they enamored with the emergence of an urban aristocracy of governmental bureaucrats, military dignitaries, and well-to-do merchants. Clearly, the liberating aspects of the earlier Mosaic tradition fell under serious threat.

*Israel as Divided Monarchy.* (a) *The independent kingdoms of Israel and Judah.* When Solomon's son and successor, Rehoboam (922–915 B.C.), refused to loosen the reigns of government (I Kings 12:14), the United Monarchy split into the two rival kingdoms of Israel/Ephraim (north) and Judah (south). Beginning with JEROBOAM I (922–901 B.C.), who enjoyed Ahijah's prophetic support, Israel was governed for exactly two centuries by a succession of nine different dynasties until Assyria leveled its capital, Samaria, in 722 B.C. Apart from Athaliah's intrusive presence (842–837 B.C.), Judah knew only the dynasty of David.

With the collapse of the United Monarchy, the state's imperialistic ambitions were frustrated. Yet this was no return to Israel's tribal past. Indeed, under such self-serving monarchs as AHAB (869–850 B.C.)

and Jeroboam II (786–746 B.C.), urban centralization and social stratification revived. Lower-class individuals were ruthlessly exploited. From both central and peripheral positions within their society, however, several prophets attempted to redress monarchy. Ahab and Jeroboam were respectively challenged by ELIJAH and AMOS, who deftly advanced the liberating consciousness of the Mosaic tradition. And in his confrontation with AHAZ (735–715), king of Judah, ISAIAH behaved similarly.

(b) *Judah after Israel's demise.* Though regularly incapable of steering an independent course, the southern kingdom survived for 135 years following Assyria's conquest of northern Israel. Notably under Ahaz and MANASSEH (687–642 B.C.), Judah was essentially an Assyrian satellite. The religion of Yahweh was necessarily compromised by Assyrian influence. Traces of extremes of wealth or poverty were relatively rare in Judah, though corrupt judges and selfish landlords manifested social and moral indifference. This triggered stern rebuke from such prophets as Isaiah, MICAH, and JEREMIAH, who sought to restore their people to a social and religious unity.

Favorable international circumstances allowed HEZEKIAH (715–687 B.C.) and JOSIAH (640–609 B.C.) to launch reform programs that reversed earlier syncretic policies and centralized Judah's religion in Jerusalem (II Kings 18:3-7; 22:1–23:25). In Josiah's case, the claims of the socially liberating Mosaic Torah were advanced ahead of the imperialistic claims of the Davidic state. But Judah soon succumbed to Babylon, which had wrested world dominion from Assyria. After Jerusalem's fall to the Babylonians in 587, many Judeans were ushered into BABYLONIAN CAPTIVITY.

*Post-monarchic Israel.* (a) *Israel in exile.* While some Jews resumed agrarian life as best they could in a ravished Judah, and others, having fled to northern Egypt, established there an ongoing colony, Judaism's nucleus endured a dark interval of Babylonian exile (587–538 B.C.). Obviously shaken by abrupt relocation, many Jews, under the prophetic leadership of Ezekiel and Second Isaiah, embraced their ancestral faith with new zeal and looked forward to restoration in Judah. Indeed, this was a theologically creative moment for Yahweh's people. After Persia's takeover of Babylon under CYRUS (550–530 B.C.), the exiles were allowed to return to their homeland. Some of the exiles who were not encumbered by successful business ventures courageously accepted the invitation.

(b) *Restoration and beyond.* Amid physical hardship, the Jews rebuilt Jerusalem and its Temple. Thanks to such able governors as NEHEMIAH and dedicated priestly leaders as EZRA (about 450–400 B.C.), a viable restoration community was established. The peasant masses, however, sustained new economic hardship (Neh. 5:1-13) when the Samaritan elite, recently descended into Judah, competed for positions of power with the Jewish elite, who saw themselves as the true Israel now returned from Babylon.

New challenges came when the conquests of Alexander the Great in 332 B.C. subjected Palestine to Greek rule. After Syrian-based Seleucid monarchs annexed Palestine and reactivated Alexander's policy of imposing Hellenic culture on non-Greek subjects, Jewish revolt under the Maccabees broke out in 167 B.C. Though an interval of Jewish independence ensued, Rome overtook Palestine in 63 B.C. Thereupon Jewish-Roman relations generally deteriorated until the Jewish Revolt erupted in A.D. 66. Four years later, Jerusalem and its Temple were destroyed. Yet thanks to its indomitable spirit, Judaism, the Israel of God, assuredly did not expire.

J.K.K.

**ISSACHAR.** One of the twelve sons of JACOB, whose name appears to mean "May God show mercy." According to the earliest tradition, he was one of the sons of Leah born in her later years, and so he is nearly always mentioned together with Zebulun, Leah's sixth and final son. The shady circumstances of Issachar's conception, involving Leah's purchase from Rachel of Jacob's affections for one night for the price of some sought-after mandrakes, gave rise to the popular interpretation of the meaning of his name, "God has given me my hire" (Gen. 30:18)—assuming that the name contains the two Hebrew words *ish,* "man," and *sakar,* "price."

The tribe of Issachar was assigned territory between Mt. Tabor and the Jordan River just south of the Sea of Galilee according to the division of Joshua 19:17-23. Perhaps this reflects an identity at best only semi-differentiated from the Canaanite tribes whose cities stood in that area. The Canaanite connection may be reflected in the judgment against the tribe preserved in the Blessing of Jacob (Gen. 49:1-28). Mentioned after his younger brother Zebulun (as is also the case in Joshua 19 and Judges 5), Issachar is described as "a strong ass" who "became a slave at forced labor" (Gen. 49:14-15). And yet the assessment of Issachar's role in the battle celebrated by Deborah (Judg. 5:15) is altogether positive. The tribe of Issachar is ultimately assigned one of the twelve full provincial administrations during the reign of Solomon (I Kings 4:17). In the only NT reference to the tribe (Rev. 7:7), Issachar has recovered his rightful place in the order of Leah's sons, for his twelve thousand are sealed unto salvation before those belonging to Zebulun.

W.S.T.

**ISVARA.** From the Sanskrit word for "Master" or "Lord." In religion Isvara is a common term in HINDUISM for a supreme personal god, usually one which, in one way or another, facilitates his worshiper's salvation or liberation. The Isvara deity therefore contrasts on one hand with the DEVAS or finite cosmic gods of Vedic religion, and on the other with the impersonal spirit of SAMKHYA or VEDANTA philosophy. In the YOGA sutras of Patanjali, the student is admonished to worship Isvara at early stages of the path, apparently as an ideal or symbol of his purusha, or true spiritual nature. It is in BHAKTI, however, that Isvara deities, such as Vishnu or Shiva, come into great prominence. Many bhaktas think of them as genuinely supreme personal gods. But in philosophical Vedanta, a personal god is ultimately of Maya, an accommodation of BRAHMAN shaped by the mind of a worshiper still unfree of Avidya, or ignorance.            R.E.

**ITALY**. A long, boot-shaped peninsula in the Mediterranean Sea.

*Biblical*. Paul lived in ROME, the capital of Italy, the last two years of his life as recorded in the book of Acts. He may have written the "prison letters"—Philippians, Philemon, Colossians, and Ephesians—while imprisoned there. He had been brought to Italy when Roman soldiers rescued him from an angry temple mob. Paul, asserting his Roman citizenship, asked to be tried before Caesar. Acts 28 indicates that Paul stopped at two Italian cities, Rhegium and Puteoli, on his journey from Jerusalem to Rome. It also notes that Christians came from the Italian cities known as Forum of Appius and Three Taverns when they learned that Paul was in Rome. Two Jewish Christians who worked closely with Paul, Priscilla and Aquila, had earlier fled Rome when the emperor Claudius had commanded all Jews to leave the city.

Italy is also mentioned in the NT book of Hebrews. In the closing words the writer says, "Those who come from Italy send you greetings."

*Historical*. The ROMAN EMPIRE controlled the Mediterranean world and Western Europe from about 30 B.C. to the fifth century A.D. It was within the Roman Empire that Christianity arose and developed. The book of Acts shows Roman officials as either protecting or ignoring Christians. But later Roman emperors ordered many Christians to be put to death. Then the Roman Emperor Constantine, after his conversion in 312, declared Christianity the state religion. Rome remains today a principal city of the Christian faith.        B.J.

**I-THOU/I-IT**. Phrases that came into currency through the title of MARTIN BUBER's seminal book, *I and Thou* (1924; Eng. trans. 1937; new trans. 1970). Steeped in the biblical tradition, he explored forms of address as indicative of relationships. I-I represents the person who knows only the self. I-it represents the person who knows people or things objectively. Some have little "I" and cannot relate to another. Others live in an undivided world of only "we." Still others divide the world into "us" and "them."

I-Thou is the language of relationship. In the original German, "thou" is the familiar form used between friends, lovers, and family. To see the other

as you (thou) is to live in relationship. It is an act of grace, a personal encounter, where neither is looking for something from the other. Buber writes that "all actual life is encounter." This is also the relationship to God. Yahweh is the One who is always present. To study about God is to see God as "it." To know God is to be encountered by God as "thou."

Buber's epigrammatic style gives the book a unique quality, and it must be read slowly in order to be understood. It is deeply expressive of the Hasidic tradition, which richly recognizes the warmth of the divine-human relationship.        I.C.

**ITURAEA**. A geographical region in present-day Lebanon, north of the land of Israel. It is uncertain whether the term comes from Jetur, a son of Ishmael (Gen. 25:15, 16: I Chr. 1:31), or the tribe named after him when it migrated to northeast Galilee from an area to the east of Jordan (I Chr. 5:19). In the early Roman period the descendants of the Ituareans had extended south to Upper Galilee. Their leader, Ptolemy (85–40 B.C.), had control of a vast area of territory around Damascus, according to the geographer Strabo. He paid a tribute to the Roman general Pompey in 64 B.C. and passed on his rule to his son Lysanias (40–36 B.C.), who was murdered by Antony, who gave the lands to Cleopatra. These domains of Lysanias augmented by regions of Trachonitis and parts of Galilee passed eventually to Herod the Great. After Herod's death (in 4 B.C.) his kingdom was divided and the region of Ituraea passed to Philip his son. At this juncture Ituraea enters the NT story, according to Luke 3:1. The kingdom remained in the family of Herod in the person of Herod Agrippa I, who was confirmed as ruler of the region by the emperor Gaius (A.D. 38). On the death of Agrippa the land of Ituraea came, by annexation, into the Roman province of Syria and was controlled by procurators.        R.M.

**IYAR**. *See* HEBREW CALENDAR.

**IZANAGI AND IZANAMI**. The primal parents in the Japanese creation myth, as recorded in the *Kojiki* and *Nihonshoki* (eighth century A.D.). Descending from the high plain of heaven on a floating bridge, they made the first land by churning the primordial ocean with a spear, then proceeded to procreate the many KAMI and islands of Japan. Izanami, the female figure, eventually died giving birth to the fire god, and went to the underworld. Izanagi pursued her there, but could not retrieve her because she had already eaten of its food. Although widely known as mythological figures, Izanagi and Izanami are worshiped in only a few SHINTO shrines.        R.E.

# Jj

**J DOCUMENT.** One (and probably the earliest) of the literary sources of the PENTATEUCH, so called because of the author's frequent use of the Hebrew personal name of God (Jahveh or Yahweh). J was probably written in or near Jerusalem in the tenth century B.C., perhaps during the reign of David or Solomon. (*See also* DOCUMENTARY HYPOTHESIS.)

J.D.N.

**JABBOK.** A river flowing through a deep gorge of the same name in a rough semicircle for fifty to sixty miles, east from the mountains near Amman, Jordan. It converges with the Jordan River twenty miles north of the Dead Sea. Its modern name is Nahr ez-Zerqa (zerqa meaning blue). Once the Israelites had defeated the Ammonite king Sihon (Num. 21:21-24), it formed the boundary between the Ammonites and Gadites (Deut. 3:16; Josh. 12:2). Jacob forded it with his family just before he wrestled with the angel (Gen. 32:22). Its name may be a play on the word for "wrestle." It is sometimes spelled "Jaboc." N.H.

**JABESH-GILEAD.** An Israelite town in Gilead, east of the Jordan River. Its citizens were not among the Israelites who swore at Mizpah not to give their daughters as wives to the Benjaminites, so the other Israelites killed all its inhabitants except four hundred virgins whom they gave as wives to the tribe of Benjamin (Judges 21). Here King Saul routed the Ammonites (I Sam. 11). The grateful citizens later rescued his body (I Sam. 31:11-13; I Chr. 10:11-12) and gave it a decent burial.

Eusebius says it is a town on high ground six miles from Pella in the Jabesh Valley (modern Yabis). Glueck identifies it with Tell Abu-Kharaz on the north side of Wadi Yabis, two miles inside the Jordanian border, nine miles from Bethshan.

N.H.

**JABNEEL** ("God [El] causes to be built"). A city near Mt. Baalah, close to the Mediterranean Sea, thirteen miles south of Joppa (Josh. 15:11). It is probably the same as Jabneh, a Philistine city captured by Uzziah (II Chr. 26:6). In the Greco-Roman period it was called Jamnia (see I Macc. 4:15, 5:58; and Josephus). Here, after the fall of Jerusalem in A.D. 70, the Sanhedrin reconvened. While they discussed whether or not certain books were acceptable, there is little historical evidence that a specific council about A.D. 100 established definitive parameters to the Jewish canon. Today the village is called Yebna. The name is also applied to a town in Naphtali (Josh. 19:33), to be identified with the modern Khirbet Yamma. N.H.

**JACHIN AND BOAZ.** Twin bronze ornamental pillars that stood at the entrance to Solomon's temple (I Kings 7:21; II Chrn. 3:15-17). When Jerusalem was destroyed in 587 B.C., they were broken up and their metal was taken to Babylon (II Kings 25:13).

Cast by Hiram of Tyre, they were hollow cylinders about one meter in diameter, topped with solid capitals for a total height of about twelve meters. The spherical bowl or knob at the top was decorated with "lily work" or four open, downward "petals," and with chains adorned with pomegranates. Similar columns have been found in tenth-century Palestinian shrine models and in an eighth-century B.C. ruin.

The names may have commemorated David's ancestry, Boaz being a member of his paternal line (Ruth 4:21-22). Jachin was a Simeonite name (Num. 26:12), perhaps David's maternal line. Others conjecture that the names are derived from an oracle assuring the throne to the Davidic line.

N.H.

**JACOB.** The third of the founding fathers or patriarchs of Israel whose family saga is recorded in Genesis 12–50. The Jacob cycle begins as a grace note in the story of ISAAC and REBEKAH, his parents, with the account of the birth of Jacob and his twin brother ESAU in Genesis 25:19-34. From the very beginning of the sibling rivalry between the two sons, Jacob had the edge: Not only did his mother prefer him to his brother (25:28), but even in their youth Jacob was able to deprive Esau of his primacy ("birthright") by purchasing it for some bread and lentil soup on a day when Esau was famished (25:29-34). The younger brother practiced deceit upon the older one once again when their dying father was ready to make his last will and testament. Jacob disguised his hands with hair so as to resemble Esau (who was "a hairy man," Gen. 27:11) and claimed the blessing that Isaac intended for the other. Even though the deceit was soon revealed, the last blessing could not be reversed, and the name Jacob (which the writer understands to mean "he supplants") is actualized once again: "Esau said, 'Is he not rightly named Jacob? For he has supplanted me these two times. He took away my birthright; and behold, now he has taken away my blessing' " (Gen. 27:36).

Duplicity and sharp dealing continue to characterize the life of Jacob, whose story dominates Genesis 28–35. Yet it is through exactly such a very human and ambiguous figure that Yahweh's promise to the grandfather Abraham is carried out. Just as that promise was threatened in the case of Abraham and Sarah by barrenness and in the case of Isaac by the possibility that the young lad might be sacrificed (Gen. 22), so also in the case of Jacob the promise is threatened. The dangers are of his own making, and it is his own kindred who are outraged at his deceit and seek revenge (for example, Laban in Gen. 31). But alongside these unattractive qualities in Jacob are also displayed a willingness to follow the divine call (the story of the vision of the ladder in Bethel, Gen. 28), persistence in winning the hand of Rachel, the daughter of Rebekah's brother Laban (Gen. 29), and

courage in wrestling with the "man" beside the river Jabbok in order that he obtain divine blessing (Gen. 32:22-32). When that blessing is given, God also changes Jacob's name to Israel, "he who strives with God."

Jacob/Israel was the father of the twelve tribes that bear his name. The story of Jacob's several marriages and other sexual relationships explain how this came about. From the very beginning Jacob loved RACHEL, the younger daughter of Laban, and served his future father-in-law seven years for her. At the completion of this period of indentured servitude, Laban tricked Jacob by bringing to him in the darkness of the wedding night his older daughter, the weak-eyed Leah. Though the deception was discovered in the morning (Gen. 29:25), Jacob found himself compelled to serve yet another seven years for Rachel. Leah was fertile and bore Jacob a total of six of his twelve sons. In her later years Leah gave Jacob her handmaid Zilpah, who bore him two more (Gen. 30:9-13). Rachel could only present Jacob her handmaid Bilhah, who bore Jacob yet two more sons (Gen. 30:1-8). At long last Rachel bore to Jacob his eleventh son, JOSEPH (whose name means "he adds"). In giving to Jacob his twelfth son, Benjamin, Rachel died in childbirth and was buried in a tomb on the way to Bethlehem, "which is there to this day" (Gen. 35:20). Leah also bore to Jacob a daughter, Dinah, who was seduced by Shechem, the son of the prince of the land, Hamor. Shechem also fell in love with the girl and proposed a formal marriage agreement to the brothers of Dinah. They were offended by this proposal, but through deceit appeared to agree to it on the condition that these native dwellers of the land of Canaan be circumcised and thus made part of Israel. When this was accomplished on the third day, "when they were sore" (34:25), Simeon and Levi, Dinah's brothers, killed all the males in the city of Shechem and plundered their possessions.

Jacob is particularly associated with BETHEL. He is presented as founding this cult center by erecting there a pillar in response to his dream of angels ascending and descending and by naming it Bethel, "the house of God" (Gen. 28:10-22). He is also commanded to return there near the end of his life (Gen. 35). According to that account, at that time those who followed Jacob put away all the amulets and likenesses of foreign gods and affiliated themselves exclusively with the God of Israel, Yahweh. Many scholars now believe that the Jacob cycle was preserved and repeated at Bethel and that it legitimated the sanctuary at that place. Jacob became linked in a familial way with Isaac before him and Joseph and the eleven brothers after him only when a unified Israelite tradition emerged out of the stories that individual tribes contributed to the whole nation as that nation coalesced during the period of the judges.

The Jacob cycle really ends with the account of the death and burial of Isaac in Genesis 35:29. Following the Priestly genealogies in chapter 36, attention turns to the proudest of Jacob's sons, Joseph. At the end of his life, however, Jacob returns briefly to the center of the stage (Gen. 48–49). In Egypt with his family now, the dying Jacob settles questions of status and announces the destiny of each of the twelve sons (tribes), which were his issue. After this blessing, he asks that he be buried with his grandparents Abraham and Sarah, his parents Isaac and Rebekah, and his first wife Leah in the cave of Machpelah near Mamre (Hebron; Gen. 49:28-33). Genesis 50:1-14 records the elaborate funeral ceremonies: forty days of embalming and seventy days of mourning followed by a ceremonial procession back to Canaan, which had been personally authorized by Pharaoh.

W.S.T.

**JACOBITE CHURCH.** The old Syrian church born in reaction to the Council of Chalcedon's declaration that Christ is One Person, truly divine and truly human in nature. Large factions of Syrian and Egyptian Monophysites who exalted Christ's divine nature threatened the Roman Empire's unity. When Emperor Zeno in 482 issued his *Henotikon* to reconcile the various factions, Pope Felix III anathematized him for presuming that the state could settle religious questions. Jacob Baradaeus organized the Jacobite Monophysites in the sixth century. During the Muslim conquests in the mid-seventh century, the Jacobites suffered great losses but have survived into the twentieth century.

C.M.

**JACOB'S WELL.** About half a mile east of Tell Balatah, near Sychar, on the south edge of the plain at the foot of Mt. Gerizim. Here Jesus met the Samaritan woman (John 4:5-42). There is no evidence that Jacob actually dug the well, but he did purchase the land (Gen. 33:19; Josh. 24:32). The well is now in an underground crypt that was part of a crusader church destroyed in the twelfth century. On the surface stands an unfinished Greek Orthodox church.

N.H.

**JAHANNAM.** In Islam the place where the wicked are punished after death. The Arabic word is derived from the Greek *gehenna*, the place of punishment mentioned in the NT (Matt. 5:22, 29-30, etc.).

According to the Qur'an, it is like a huge pit, a place of fire and intense heat, into which the wicked are thrown. It has seven gates through which those who are condemned enter to suffer there. An angel named Malik is the keeper of jahannam. Passages in the Qur'an indicate that punishment in jahannam is eternal.

K.C.

**JAHWEH.** *See* YAHWEH.

**JAINISM.** A religious minority in India numbering some four million in the 1980s. Emphasizing asceticism and harmlessness, Jainism is a spiritual tradition which, all in all, has remained remarkably unchanged over twenty-five centuries.

*History.* Jainism began as a movement with the teaching of Vardhamana Jnatrputra (sixth century B.C.), called MAHAVIRA, "the great hero." Jains view him as the last in a series of twenty-four great teachers or Tirthankaras ("bridge-builders"); next to the last was the quasi-historical Parsva (around 850 B.C.), but the earlier names on the list are legendary. Mahavira, a contemporary of the BUDDHA, shared with him a milieu conducive to the founding of new religions. It was a time of spiritual ferment, philosophical questing, and ascetic experimentation. Mahavira taught a path of rigorous self-denial designed to liberate the spirit from the flesh. He often wore nothing, fasted for long periods, and lived the life of a wandering mendicant.

Mahavira attracted many disciples, both monastic and lay, and the movement continued after his death. Like BUDDHISM, it was patronized by the Mauryan dynasty (321–185 B.C.). Around the first century A.D., the monks were divided into two orders, chiefly on the issues of nudity and admission of women. The more rigorous order, the Digambaras, asserted that monks should be free of clothing, that women cannot enter orders and, in fact, cannot attain liberation until reborn as males. The Svetambara order, conversely, is clothed, admits women to an order of nuns, and makes no spiritual distinction between the sexes. These two divisions, with their respective lay followers, have persisted to the present. Despite their asceticism, Jains have maintained a long tradition of learning. Jain monks have been among India's most influential grammarians, philosophers, and men of letters.

*Doctrine.* Jains believe that the universe is infinite and eternal, though passing through immense cycles. Within it an infinite number of *jivas,* or souls, are trapped in material bodies and held in bondage by KARMA. In Jainism, Karma is a subtle kind of matter engendered by action, especially action based on attachment, including mental agitation. The way to liberation of the *jiva* lies in reducing negative activity and doing mortifications, which counter attachment and wear down karma. This results in the great asceticism of monastic Jainism, which can even culminate, in rare cases, in self-starvation. At the time of liberation, or *kaivalya,* the *jiva* is separated from matter, attains perfect knowledge and bliss, and moves to the top of the universe.

According to Jainism, souls are in everything, even the stones and air particles most others would consider inanimate matter. Sensitive to the suffering of all entrapped beings, the ethics of Jainism emphasize *ahimsa,* or harmlessness. Jains accept and pray to a number of gods, mostly borrowed from Hinduism, but see them as subordinate to the Tirthankaras and Siddhas who are liberated souls.

*Practices.* Jainism puts more emphasis on asceticism than meditation to liberate the *jiva,* and together

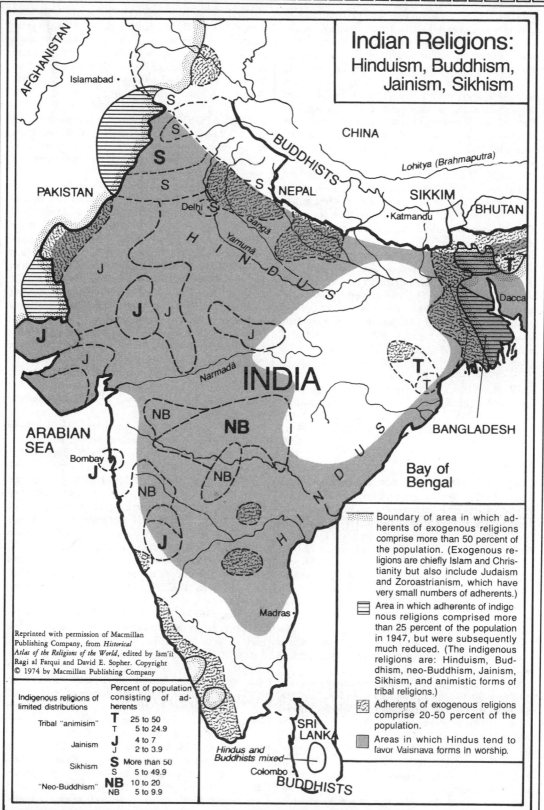

Indian Religions:
Hinduism, Buddhism,
Jainism, Sikhism

AFGHANISTAN

Islamabad •

CHINA

BUDDHISTS

Lohitya (Brahmaputra)

PAKISTAN

NEPAL

SIKKIM

BHUTAN

• Katmandu

Delhi

Ganga

Yamuna

HINDUS

Dacca

Narmadá

INDIA

ARABIAN
SEA

BANGLADESH

Bombay

Bay of
Bengal

HINDUS

Madras

Reprinted with permission of Macmillan
Publishing Company, from *Historical
Atlas of the Religions of the World*, edited by Ism'il
Ragi al Farqui and David E. Sopher. Copyright
© 1974 by Macmillan Publishing Company

Boundary of area in which adherents of exogenous religions
comprise more than 50 percent of
the population. (Exogenous religions are chiefly Islam and Christianity but also include Judaism
and Zoroastrianism, which have
very small numbers of adherents.)

Area in which adherents of indigenous religions comprised more
than 25 percent of the population
in 1947, but were subsequently
much reduced. (The indigenous
religions are: Hinduism, Buddhism, neo-Buddhism, Jainism,
Sikhism, and animistic forms of
tribal religions.)

Adherents of exogenous religions
comprise 20-50 percent of the
population.

Areas in which Hindus tend to
favor Vaisnava forms in worship.

| Indigenous religions of limited distributions | Percent of population consisting of adherents |
|---|---|
| Tribal "animisim" | **T** 25 to 50 |
| | T 5 to 24.9 |
| Jainism | **J** 4 to 7 |
| | J 2 to 3.9 |
| Sikhism | **S** More than 50 |
| | S 5 to 49.9 |
| "Neo-Buddhism" | **NB** 10 to 20 |
| | NB 5 to 9.9 |

Hindus and
Buddhists mixed

SRI
LANKA

Colombo

BUDDHISTS

with stilling the mind through concentration, monks daily vow and undertake acts of mortification, such as fasts or exposure. Laypeople are supposed to live as closely as possible to the ideal of the monk. They are strict vegetarians and may undertake fasts or other ascetic practices for periods of time. PUJA, or worship through prayer, hymns, washing of images, and simple offerings is also presented to images of Tirthankaras or deities at home altars and in the clean, richly ornamented Jain temples. Jainism has several annual festivals, and pilgrimage to major sacred sites is popular.

*Sociology.* While the Jain world is clearly divided into monks and laity, the two are closely interlinked. Rather than living in cloisters, the monks frequently travel from one Jain community to another, teaching. But rites such as weddings are usually performed by Hindu clerks and officials, since the monks do not undertake priestly functions. The Jain community in India is generally prosperous and close-knit. Its charities, especially humanitarian work on behalf of animals, are famous. The Jain concept of *ahimsa*— harmlessness to all beings—was an important influence on the thought of MOHANDAS K. GANDHI, and also indirectly on such Western advocates of nonviolence as Martin Luther King, Jr.

R.E.

**JAIRUS.** A ruler of a synagogue whose daughter Jesus healed (Mark 5:21-43; Luke 8:41-56; compare Matt. 9:18-26). Jairus may be derived from the Hebrew name meaning "Yahweh enlightens."

N.H.

**JAMES I** (1566–1625). King of England as James I (1603–25) and King of Scotland as James VI (1567–1625). Son of Mary, Queen of Scots, and Henry Stuart (Lord Darnley), James became king of Scotland on his mother's abdication in 1567. JOHN KNOX preached the coronation sermon. Groups of Protestant and Catholic nobles sought to control the young James, who gradually asserted royal independence by pitting religious factions against each other and establishing a strong central government. In 1598 he published *The Trew Law of Free Monarchies* in which he stressed the DIVINE RIGHT of kings over all laws and Parliaments, accountable only to God. His motto, "No bishop, no king," developed from a conviction that objections to episcopacy were attacks on his right to appoint bishops.

On Queen ELIZABETH's death he became James I of England. On his way to London he rejected PURITAN demands for ridding Anglicanism of Roman vestiges in the Millenary Petition (1603). However, he authorized a new translation of Scriptures—the King James Bible of 1611. It included the Apocrypha, which Puritans eliminated from their editions by 1629. In 1610 James persuaded the Scottish church to accept episcopacy, but English Puritans in large numbers resisted. Many Separatists left England for

Holland and in 1620 sailed to Plymouth, Massachusetts; they were the vanguard of thousands a few years later. James married Portestant Anne of Denmark (1589), but his treaty with France in 1624 caused many to suspect him of Roman Catholic tendencies. James was a scholar, writing especially on poetry, demonology, and politics.

C.M.

**JAMES, APOSTLE.** The Greek name translated as James is *Iakobos,* from the Hebrew JACOB, the father of the twelve sons of ISRAEL. All our information about the apostle James comes from the Gospels and Acts.

James first appears (Mark 1:19) among the group from Galilee, whom Jesus is calling to be his disciples. The others first mentioned are Simon Peter and Andrew, and James' brother John. All four are fishermen, and all leave their families and means of livelihood in order to follow Jesus. According to Mark 1:16-20 and Luke 5:10, the four had a partnership in the fishing business. Here and elsewhere in the Gospels, James and John are designated as "sons of Zebedee." This may imply that their father was also a well-known figure in the early church. The departing brothers leave the prospering business to their father and "the hired servants." Later (Mark 3:17) James is named among the Twelve whom Jesus chose to be with him and to be sent out with his message and with his power over the demons. James' priority over his brother is suggested by John's identification as "the brother of James."

In the course of Jesus' ministry, James—along with Peter and John—is granted special information and insight, such as witnessing the raising to life of Jairus' daughter (Mark 5:37-43); at the transfiguration of Jesus (Mark 9:2); at his predictions about the end of the age (Mark 13:3). On the other hand, they boldly ask Jesus for special places in the kingdom of God (Mark 10:35-45) and foolishly propose calling down fire from heaven on an unrepentant village (Luke 9:54). James is listed among the disciples who gather in the upper room after the Resurrection (Acts 1:12-14). He was put to death by Herod Agrippa I in A.D. 44 (Acts 12:2).

H.K.

**JAMES, BROTHER OF JESUS.** This James (in Hebrew, Jacob) is to be distinguished from other NT figures who bear this familiar name: JAMES THE APOSTLE, James the Younger (Mark 15:40), and the father of Judas (Luke 6:16; Acts 1:13). Our information about Jesus' brother James derives from four sources: the Gospels, the letters of Paul, Acts, and from Josephus, the Jewish historian. Each portrays James in a different light.

James is first identified in the Gospels as Jesus' brother in Mark 6:3 (also in Matt. 13:55). The incident is the rejection of Jesus as an offensive person by his fellow townspeople of Nazareth. His humble family, with a carpenter at its head, and several sisters and brothers included in it, are well-known to them.

But the local people are not prepared to accept the words and works of Jesus. Luke omits this passage in his story of Jesus' rejection at Nazareth, possibly to safeguard the reputation of James, who was to figure so importantly in Luke's later account of James as leader of the Jerusalem church.

The mother, sisters, and brothers of Jesus—presumably including James—appear in the story of the coming of his family (mistakenly translated as "friends" in KJV, Mark 3:21) to take him away because they think he is crazy. The story shifts to the discussion of Jesus' exorcisms (Mark 3:22-30), but he asserts that he has a new definition of family: those who do the will of God (3:31-35). Evidence of a misunderstanding with his brothers appears in John 7:3-8, where we read that they try to persuade him to go and perform miracles in Jerusalem in order to increase the circle of his followers. He is going to Jerusalem, but not for that kind of display.

Paul (I Cor. 9:5) contrasts his own bachelorhood, his refusal to accept support from others, and his insistence on working for a living with the life-style of "the other apostles and the brothers of the Lord and Cephas [Peter]." In I Corinthians 15:3-8, where Paul is listing the appearances of the risen Christ to his followers, he includes James among the apostles, but differentiates him from "the twelve." Presumably these were those who followed Jesus from the beginning of his ministry, while James became a follower somewhat later, though before Paul. James and Paul were numbered among the apostles, however. Indeed, James had moved into the prime position among the apostles based in Jerusalem since Paul felt it necessary to consult with him about requirements for Gentile admission to the church. In Acts, that leadership role is heightened. Peter's escape from prison is reported to James (Acts 12:17). Paul reports to him on the occasion of both visits to Jerusalem (Acts 15:13-19; 21:17-18), and agrees to accept his formulation of the requirements for accepting Gentiles in the church (15:28-29; 21:25).

H.K.

**JAMES, LETTER OF.** One of the NT general Epistles. Only the opening lines of this "letter" are written in the style one would expect in an actual letter from around A.D. 100. The rest of the writing consists of a string of ethical exhortations in the style of a philosophical diatribe of the period. The diatribe was a philosophical tract, written to challenge and provoke the reader to moral responsibility. By means of vivid illustration, based on everyday life, the author scoffs at those who take pride in their moral achievements. The specifics of some of James's illustrations would be appropriate for people with some knowledge of the Jewish Bible, since Job, Abraham, Elijah, and Rahab are set forth as examples. Jesus is mentioned by name only in the opening greeting (1:1) and in 2:1. He is referred to as "the Lord" in 5:7-8, where his coming at the end of

the age is predicted, and in 5:10, 14, 15, where the power of his name is mentioned. Unmentioned are the cross, Resurrection, or the redemptive role of Jesus.

*Origins of the Letter.* Some scholars have suggested that the book is basically a Jewish document, with a few Christian additions. But its moral appeals show clear kinship with the SERMON ON THE MOUNT at several points: compare 1:22 with Matthew 7:24; 4:12 with Matthew 7:1, for example. These similarities suggest the writer is drawing on a common Jesus tradition. The references to the coming of the Lord confirm that conclusion.

The clearest evidence that the book comes from a Christian group is the direct attack in 2:14-26 on Paul's teaching of justification by faith (Rom. 3:28). One can argue that James has misunderstood Paul, but that Paul's doctrine is the target of James is unmistakable. James understands Paul to be promoting moral irresponsibility, which a careful reading of Romans and Galatians shows not to be the case. See, for example, Romans 3:31, where Paul claims to "uphold the law."

*Authorship.* Which of the persons named James in the NT is responsible for this book? Although the writer apparently wants to present himself as the brother of Jesus, who came from Galilee to head the Jerusalem church, his excellent Greek style makes this most unlikely (*see* JAMES, BROTHER OF JESUS). His extensive vocabulary, including technical, philosophical, and even astronomical terms (1:17), seems impossible for an uneducated, Aramaic-speaking son of a village craftsman. Furthermore, the presumed audience for this book must have been relatively sophisticated and accustomed to rhetorical style that would be unfamiliar to the impoverished Christian circles of which James became the leader.

*Aims.* James's concept of the Law, as evident in this letter, is a mixture of Stoic natural law, Jewish morality, and Jesus tradition. At its center is the "royal law": love of neighbor (based on Lev. 19:18; quoted in 2:8). Similar blending of pagan and Christian features is evident in the image of the new birth (1:18), which resembles that theme in John 3 ("you must be born anew"), and which uses the Christian term for Word (Logos), but employs an entirely different word for birth—one that is found only here in the NT. This writing is evidently produced in a segment of the early church and is concerned chiefly with steadfastness and wisdom (1:2-5). Its members live as aliens in the world ("tribes in the Dispersion" 1:1), but have primary concern for mutual responsibility within the community (2:1-17; 4:11; 5:9).

H.K.

**JAMES, PROTEVANGELIUM OF.** *See* APOCRYPHA.

**JAMES, WILLIAM** (1842-1910). American philosopher and psychologist. James was born in New York

Courtesy of Harvard University News Office

*William James*

City into a cultivated family who educated him in schools or by tutors abroad: England, France, Switzerland, Germany. At the age of eighteen he decided to study painting but soon realized that while he had aesthetic perceptions he was not vitally interested in art as a career.

He graduated from Harvard (M.D., 1869) but because of ill health did not practice. He began to teach at Harvard in the fields of anatomy and physiology in 1872, but his real interest was in the developing field of psychology. It was at Harvard that he started the first psychological laboratory in the United States. His marriage in 1878 to Alice H. Gibbins was a turning point in his physical and psychic life. Imbued with new energy, he turned to the writing of the *Principles of Psychology* (1890).

James affirmed that consciousness includes the whole person—psycho/physical—and that choice (free will) is part of consciousness. Habits are developed within the structure of people and not through memorization. In his book *Talks to Teachers on Psychology* (1899), he demolished the theory of transfer of training.

His interests turned from psychology to philosophy, where he is best known for the theory of PRAGMATISM: truth is important only as it is in coherence with life and is worthwhile insofar as it is effective for living. James was aware of the evils in society but affirmed that human effort could improve social conditions.

His famous work on religion, *The Varieties of Religious Experience,* given as the Gifford Lectures in 1902, places the healthy-minded and sick-souled person side by side. He affirms that each expresses a valid dimension of life. The healthy-minded may have an illusory notion of the goodness of the world, which is corrected by the sick-minded person's realization of the power of evil. The latter is made whole through the process of regeneration.

James was interested in psychical research and for two years was president of the Society for Psychical Research of which he was a member from 1884 until his death. His openness, tolerance, and appreciation of other viewpoints were unusual in his time.

I.C.

**JAMNIA.** *See* JABNEEL.

**JANNA.** In ISLAM the place where the righteous are rewarded after death. It is a paradise full of delights. The images of pleasure would be particularly attractive to a desert people. There will be trees and gardens yielding their fruits. Refreshing rivers flow through paradise, with places for repose and rest.

The heavenly books in which human deeds are recorded are kept there. There also is the heavenly archetype of the QUR'AN, the original of the revelations that were dictated to MUHAMMAD. Later traditions teach that the original KA'BA is in heaven, directly above the earthly Ka'ba in MECCA.

Particular interest has been aroused by the houris, perpetual virgins of great beauty, who are there for the pleasure of righteous men. According to some commentators, they are the wives of the righteous, restored to their original youth and beauty. The most important of all rewards is being in the presence of God himself and being able to behold him.

Janna is also the abode of angels, of whom Michael and Gabriel are mentioned in the Bible. Israfel, celebrated by Edgar Allan Poe in his poem of that name, has a trumpet always at his lips, ready to blow it and announce the day of judgment. K.C.

**JANNES AND JAMBRES.** Names of two Egyptian magicians who opposed MOSES, according to II Timothy 3:6-9 (some mss. read "Jannes and Mambres"). Although the OT does not name them, the Talmud, Targums, and various Rabbinic writings had made these names traditional and familiar. Origen knew a written work about them. By the fifth century A.D. their alleged tombs were tourist sites. N.H.

**JANNEUS.** Jonathan, the king of Judea from about 103 to 76 B.C., also called Alexander. According to Josephus, he was the son of John Hyrcanus and half brother of Aristobulus I, who on becoming king imprisoned him. But when Aristobulus died within a year, Janneus married his widow and became high priest. Backed by the Sadducees, he feuded with the Pharisees and massacred thousands of them. The Pharisees opposed his military attempts to increase the boundaries of Judea. His wife Salome ran the civil government during his final three-year illness, and she succeeded him.                                            N.H.

**JANSENISM.** A seventeenth-century revival, primarily among French and Dutch Roman Catholics, of the ancient AUGUSTINE-PELAGIUS controversy over grace and free will. In 1640 Cornelius Jansen's *Augustinus* appeared posthumously. It countered Jesuit views that effective grace requires the recipient's assent and cooperation. Jansen argued that efficacious grace does not require such cooperation, and that human beings cannot alter God's predestination. The convent of Port-Royal, France, emerged as a popular symbol of the controversy when Antoine Arnold became its leader in 1643 and vigorously defended Jansenism. The Sorbonne (1649) and Pope Innocent X (1653) declared five summary propositions culled from Jansen's book heretical. Jansenists maintained the propositions were distortions, but Pope Alexander VII in 1656 ruled otherwise and demanded that Jansenists submit.

Blaise Pascal, whose sister was at Port-Royal, excoriated the Jesuits in his famous *Provincial Letters* (1656–57). In 1679 King Louis XIV exiled Arnold and forced Port-Royal to close. A shaky peace prevailed until Pasquier Quesnel's *Moral Reflections* (1692) revived the controversy. It climaxed in 1713 when Pope Clement XI's *Unigenitus* condemned 101 propositions drawn from Quesnel's work. Jansenism virtually died out in France but gained wide support in Holland and marked the beginning of the Old Catholic church.                                            C.M.

**JAPANESE RELIGION.** Although modern industrialized Japan is a fairly secularized society, its present religious heritage is complex, ranging from practices going back to archaic agricultural society to recently born "new religions." SHINTO, the "Way of the KAMI" or gods, is the perpetuation of the ancient deities of Japan; it is practiced in innumerable shrines where offerings of food and prayer are presented. BUDDHISM, introduced into Japan in the sixth century A.D., has taken many denominational forms, of which the best known in the West is probably ZEN, and has deeply intertwined itself with Japanese culture. CONFUCIANISM, while it has seldom taken explicitly religious form in Japan, has had a pervasive influence as an articulation of moral values. "New religions" founded in the nineteenth and twentieth centuries have helped many Japanese interpret spiritually the crises associated with modernization by, typically, combining teachings about the dawn of a new age with such familiar themes as Shintoistic worship, reincarnation, and Confucian morality.

Amid its diversity, Japanese religion enjoys several common themes that partly explain how Japanese live comfortably with the diversity and partly unify the culture spiritually despite it. Some common attitudes are these.

*Relativism and Pluralism.* Supported by much of Buddhist philosophy and the particularism of Shinto, as well as the tendency of Japanese language and manners to be highly "situational," Japanese tend to look at actual religious pespectives and practices as offering only partial truth. Appropriate as each may be to a particular need, it can be supplemented by others. Most Japanese have a relation to more than one spiritual tradition.

*Traditionalism.* Japanese religion tends to be very conservative in organization, ritual, and links to families and communities. Thus, in a rapidly changing society, it provides an access to stability and "roots."

*Charismatic Leadership.* Traditionalism is countered, however, by another trait: the tendency of Japanese religion to produce dynamic, charismatic leaders. This tradition goes back to ancient shamanism, which was most often feminine, and has engendered a succession of god-possessed or enlightened men and women, from medieval Buddhists like Kobo Daishi or Shinran, down to founders of modern "new religions," who have drawn enthusiastic disciples and started mass spiritual movements.

*Practice and Experience.* A final general characteristic of Japanese religion is an orientation toward practice, experience, and sociology rather than ideology. Propositional belief, for most Japanese, is less significant than what religion communicates wordlessly through its practices and sociological role.

Japan has been called a living laboratory of religion. Certainly its rich blend of old and new, in which the old never seems to quite disappear while new religions keep spawning, presents a remarkable panorama. The wide religious pluralism, however, is in large part a result of the fact that the real center of values lies elsewhere, in Confucian morality and the family relationships it exalts. (*See map on following page.*)                                            R.E.

**JAPHETH.** The son of NOAH usually named last (Gen. 5:32; 6:10; 7:13; 9:18; etc.), though his descendants are listed first in Genesis 10 and I Chronicles 1:5-7. He, along with Shem, covered their father's nakedness (Gen. 9:20-23). Noah prayed that God might enlarge him and that Canaan might be his slave (Gen. 9:27). His descendants are associated with regions north and west of the Mediterranean, especially Anatolia and the Aegean.                                            N.H.

**JAPJI.** In SIKHISM, a prayer composed by the religion's founder, Guru NANAK, which is believed to sum up the essence of Sikh teaching and which also comprises the opening passage of the Sikh scripture, the *Adi Granth*. The prayer is recited daily by the

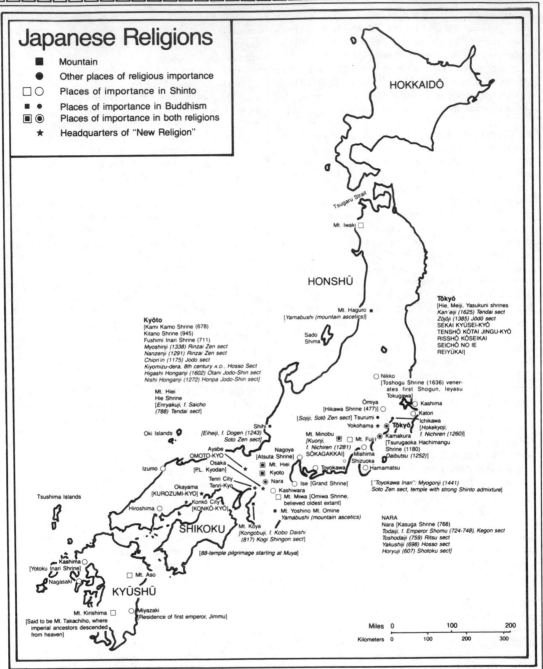

# Japanese Religions

- ■ Mountain
- ● Other places of religious importance
- □ ○ Places of importance in Shinto
- ■ • Places of importance in Buddhism
- ▣ ◉ Places of importance in both religions
- ★ Headquarters of "New Religion"

HOKKAIDŌ

Tsugaru Strait

Mt. Iwaki □

HONSHŪ

**Tōkyō**
[Hie, Meiji, Yasukuni shrines
*Kan eiji (1625) Tendai sect
Zōjōji (1385) Jōdō sect*
SEKAI KYŪSEI-KYŌ
TENSHŌ KŌTAI JINGU-KYŌ
RISSHŌ KŌSEIKAI
SEICHŌ NO IE
REIYŪKAI]

Mt. Haguro ●
[*Yamabushi (mountain ascetics)*]

Sado Shima

○ Nikko
[Toshogu Shrine (1636) vener-
ates first Shogun, Ieyasu
Tokugawa]

**Kyōto**
[Kami Kamo Shrine (678)
Kitano Shrine (945)
Fushimi Inari Shrine (711)
*Myoshinji (1338) Rinzai Zen sect
Nanzenji (1291) Rinzai Zen sect
Chion'in (1175) Jodo sect
Kiyomizu-dera, 8th century A.D., Hosso Sect
Higashi Honganji (1602) Ōtani Jodo-Shin sect
Nishi Honganji (1272) Honpa Jodo-Shin sect*]

Mt. Hiei
Hie Shrine
[*Enryakuji, f. Saicho
(788) Tendai sect*]

Ōmiya
[Hikawa Shrine (477)] ○
[*Sojiji, Sotō Zen sect*] Tsurumi ●
Yokohama ★

● Kashima
Katori
Ichikawa
◉ **Tōkyō** ★ [Hokekyoji,
f. Nichiren (1260)]

Shihi
[*Eiheiji, f. Dogen (1243)
Soto Zen sect*]

Oki Islands ●○

Mt. Minobu
[*Kuonji,
f. Nichiren (1281)*]
Nagoya
[Atsuta Shrine]
SŌKAGAKKAI] ▣ ● Mt. Fuji □
Mishima
Shizuoka
○ Toyokawa
● Hamamatsu

Kamakura ●
[Tsurugaoka Hachimangu
Shrine (1180)
Daibutsu (1252)]

Ayabe ★
OMOTO-KYO
Osaka
[PL. Kyodan]
Izumo ○
Okayama
[KUROZUMI-KYO] ★
Hiroshima ○

Tenri City
Tenri-Kyo
◉ Nara
● Kashiwara
□ Mt. Miwa [Omiwa Shrine,
believed oldest extant]
■ Mt. Yoshino Mt. Omine
Yamabushi (mountain ascetics)

★ Konkō City
[KONKŌ-KYO]

● Ise [Grand Shrine]

["Toyokawa Inari": Myogonji (1441)
Soto Zen sect, temple with strong Shinto admixture]

**NARA**
Nara [Kasuga Shrine (768)
*Todaiji, f. Emperor Shomu (724-748), Kegon sect
Toshodaiji (759) Ritsu sect
Yakushiji (698) Hosso sect
Horyuji (607) Shotoku sect*]

Tsushima Islands

SHIKOKU

■ Mt. Kōya
[*Kongobuji, f. Kobo Daishi
(817) Kogi Shingon sect*]

[88-temple pilgrimage starting at Muya]

Kashima ○
[Yotoku Inari Shrine]
Nagasaki ●
KYŪSHŪ
□ Mt. Aso

Mt. Kirishima □
[Said to be Mt. Takachiho, where
imperial ancestors descended
from heaven]

○ Miyazaki
[Residence of first emperor, Jimmu]

| Miles | 0 | | 100 | | 200 |
|---|---|---|---|---|---|
| Kilometers | 0 | 100 | 200 | 300 | |

Reprinted with permission of Macmillan Publishing Company, from *Historical Atlas of the Religions of the World*, edited by Isma'il Ragi al Farqui and David E. Sopher. Copyright © 1974 by Macmillan Publishing Company.

faithful as their morning devotion. Its first lines, called the *Mul Mantra,* are the most important of all. According to Sikh tradition, they were first recited by Nanak when, in his thirtieth year, he was called by God to his work of religious reconstruction. He then sang:

There is one God
He is the Supreme Truth
He, the Creator, is without fear and without hate . . .
He, the Omnipotent,
Pervades the Universe.
He is not born,
Nor does He die to be born again.
By His Grace shalt thou worship.

The remaining thirty-four stanzas emphasize that God is unapproachable except through a good life and with the help of divine grace, and they praise both God's greatness and the joy of God's faithful worshipers.                                        R.E.

**JASHOBEAM.** David's leading warrior, whose real name may have been Ishbosheth or Eshbaal, "man of Baal." According to II Samuel 23:8, he slew eight hundred people at one time, though the number three hundred in I Chronicles 11:11 is considered more likely. A Hachmonite or Tachemonite, he was chief of the three captains.                                     N.H.

**JASON.** A Greek name adopted by many as the equivalent of the Hebrew name JOSHUA and preferred by some Greek-speaking Jews to the more identifiably Jewish name Jesus. (1) The name of Paul's host in Thessalonica (Acts 17:5-9). He was probably a Jew and a Christian. (2) A Christian at Corinth (Rom. 16:21) described as "kin," probably a fellow Jew. Could be the same person as (1) if Sosipatros is the same as Sopater of Acts 20:4. (3) The name of the leader of the Greek Argonauts.                        N.H.

**JASPERS, KARL** (1883–1969). One of the great philosophers of the twentieth century, born in Oldenberg, Germany. He studied medicine at Heidelberg, Berlin, and Göttingen. After receiving his degree, he carried out volunteer research at the Heidelberg Psychiatric Clinic in order that he might work without restraints imposed by a paid position. In this role he brought phenomenological methods into the field of clinical psychiatry; heretofore observations had been less systematic. In 1911 he published a basic book, *General Psychopathology* (Eng. trans. 1965).

Jaspers joined the faculty of philosophy (which included psychology) at Heidelberg in 1913 and soon became interested in philosophical issues. For purposes of comparison, he defined science as the knowledge of facts and philosophy as a subjective interpretation of being. Philosophy illuminates human existence.

This viewpoint was developed in *Philosophy*, 1932 (Eng. trans. 1969) as EXISTENTIALISM. Jasper's thesis is that personal existence in the world is more important than the state of "being" there. People are the center of reality. They need to know their freedom to exist and to think. This is subjectivity, not philosophical objectivity. Jaspers, with MARTIN HEIDEGGER, was a founder of the philosophy of existence.

When the Nazis came to power, Jaspers remained in Germany with his wife, who was Jewish. They were saved from deportation by the arrival of American troops on April 13, 1945. For several years he dedicated himself to helping rebuild the university, intellectually and morally, but in 1948 accepted a professorship at the University of Basel. His later interests were in world philosophy and world federation.                                       I.C.

**JATAKA.** From the Sanskrit and Pali words meaning literally, "having to do with birth." In BUDDHISM, the Jataka Tales, found in several collections of varying length, are stories of the BUDDHA as a BODHISATTVA, or Buddha-to-be, in previous lifetimes. As many as 547 of these tales are found in the largest collection. They are very popular, especially in the THERAVADA Buddhist countries of southeast Asia.

In these stories, the future Buddha appears sometimes as an animal, sometimes as a human. Some stories are obvious adaptations of animal fables comparable to those of Aesop. Others show greater length and depth. But in any case, the Bodhisattva emerges as the wisest, most generous, and most courageous figure who saves a desperate situation or exemplifies great virtue, commonly displaying such distinctive Buddhist attributes as nonattachment, self-control, and compassion. These stories have done much to popularize Buddhism by putting such ideas as rebirth, and such values as the preceding, into an idiom accessible to ordinary men and women.
                                                      R.E.

**JEALOUSY.** The biblical usage of the word covers two contrasting ideas. On the one hand, it is a moral term used pejoratively to denote an emotion combining PRIDE and envy when one's rights are infringed or when our neighbor seems to be favorably treated at our expense. In this sense the reaction is universally condemned in both OT and NT as a sinful attitude based on human pride. So the sons of Jacob are envious of their brother Joseph on account of his dreams (Gen. 37:11; Acts 7:9). Dathan and Abiram are jealous of Moses' authority (Ps. 106:16-18; Num. 16:12-40). The book of Proverbs condemns jealousy as the antithesis of wisdom and contentment (Prov. 6:34; 27:4). The same condemnation passes over into the NT, especially in catechetical sections of the Epistles (Rom. 13:8-14; Gal. 5:20). The Corinthian church was beset by this problem (I Cor. 3:3; compare 1:12). Love is the Christian antidote to the jealous spirit (I Cor. 13:4) also evident in II Corinthians 12:20. The wisdom tradition of the OT is picked up by James (3:14; 4:5).

The other side of jealousy is seen in those places where both Hebrew and Greek use the word in the sense of "zeal." In the OT God is often called a "jealous God" (Exod. 20:5; 34:14; compare Deut. 4:24; 5:9; 6:15; Josh. 24:19; Ps. 79:5). The meaning must be that God is devoted to honor and will not compromise it by sharing worship with idols. No emotional content is assumed, and "jealousy" in this sense is part of the covenantal relationship by which God and Israel are bound together (Exod. 20:3). Failure on Israel's part to rise to their loyalty evoked

God's judgment on the part of divine "jealousy" to preserve the integrity of the covenant (see Ezek. 36).
R.M.

**JEALOUSY, ORDEAL OF.** One special case of a use of "jealousy" as a moral term is based on Numbers 5:11-31, where, at verse 25 (RSV) the words run, "the cereal offering of jealousy." But it is likely that the Hebrew word ought to be translated "cereal offering of suspicion."

The issue at stake is the case of a woman in Israel suspected of adulterous relationships, which she seeks to hide from her husband. She is to be brought to the sanctuary and to undergo certain rites designed to prove her innocence or guilt. She is "under suspicion"; hence it is the "ordeal of suspicion." The chief rite is the taking of a mixture of water and dust, coupled with a solemn oath. If abortion or stillbirth of a child follows, she is plainly held to be guilty. If her drinking "the waters of testing" (Num. 5:24) brings no curse and has no ill effect, she is cleared. The ceremonial with a cereal offering runs parallel and is not easily disentangled from the earlier account of the water and dust concoction, which the woman has to drink. The story, evidently from the Priestly source, has one point: the author regards marital infidelity as

*Jefferson's "Wall of Separation" letter, 1802*

a serious business and seeks to elicit a response, determined by a good or bad conscience.

R.M.

**JEBUSITES.** One of six pre-Israelite ethnic groups of Canaanites living in the Palestinian hills around Jerusalem (Num. 13:29; Josh. 15:63). They were descended from the third son of Canaan (Gen. 10:15-16; I Chr. 1:13-14). Jebus was the name given to Jerusalem, the principal city of their territory (Judg. 19:10, 11; I Chr. 11:4, 5). Jebusites sometimes refers simply to the inhabitants of the city (Gen. 15:21). Unless Melchizedek as king of "Salem" was its ruler (Gen. 14:18), its earliest ruler named is Adoni-zedek (Josh. 10:1), who rallied Amorite allies to defend the city (Josh. 10:5). The Israelites burned the city (Judg. 1:8), but its former inhabitants regained it until David permanently captured it (II Sam. 5:6). The Jebusites were then absorbed into the Israelite population.

N.H.

**JEFFERSON, THOMAS** (1743–1826). Third president of the United States (1801–1809) and defender of religious freedom, Jefferson was born April 13, at "Old Shadwell" in Albemarle County, Virginia, to Peter and Jane Randolph Jefferson. He graduated from the College of William and Mary in 1762 and was admitted to the bar in 1767. On January 1, 1772, he married Martha Wayles Skelton, who bore him six children before her death in 1782.

In May 1769 he was elected to the Virginia house of burgesses and served until 1774. Serving in the Continental Congresses of 1775 and 1776, he drafted the Declaration of Independence. After serving as minister to France (1785–89), secretary of state (1790–93), and vice-president (1796–1800), he was elected president (1800–1808).

After 1764 he began applying historical tests to the Bible and lost faith in conventional religion, though not in conventional morality. He became a Deist. While governor of Virginia (1779–81), he proposed a bill for establishing religious freedom, which was adopted in 1785 and completed in 1799. He opposed all forms of "tyranny over the mind."

About 1803 Jefferson began selecting passages he believed to be authentically part of Jesus' message; these he published as parallel texts in four languages in *The Life and Morals of Jesus of Nazareth*. He loathed Calvinism and leaned toward Unitarianism. Distinctly anticlerical, he favored strict separation of church and state. Jefferson supported education and helped found the University of Virginia. He served as president of the American Philosophical Society (1797–1815) and contributed to the development of paleontology, geography, botany, and architecture. His library became the basis of the Library of Congress.

N.H.

**JEHOAHAZ** ("God has grasped"). (1) The king of Israel (about 815–800 B.C.), son of and successor to Jehu. His religious policies brought his people impoverishment. Thus the military invasions of Hazael and Ben-hadad of Syria, which took a heavy toll in life and property (II Kings 13:2-7), were seen as evidence of God's wrath. He reigned for seventeen years (II Kings 13:1). Deliverance came under his son Joash.

(2) The king of Judah (608 B.C.), anointed on the death of his father, Josiah (II Kings 23:30). He reigned for three months. Jeremiah calls him Shallum (Jer. 22:11-12). Perhaps his name was changed when he became king. Pharaoh Neco deposed him. He was taken to Riblah, then to Egypt, where he died (II Kings 23:33-34; II Chr. 36:4).

(3) A variant form of Ahaziah, son of Jehoram, king of Judah (II Chr. 21:17; 25:23).

(4) Ahaz's full name according to an inscription of Tiglath-pileser III.

N.H.

**JEHOIACHIN.** A king of Judah, whose name (meaning "Let God establish") also appears as Jeconiah, Coniah, Jechonias, or Yaukin. In 598 B.C., at the age of eighteen, he succeeded to the throne of his father, JEHOIAKIM, who had apparently been put to death and left to rot after a palace revolt by advance agents of Nebuchadnezzar.

Jehoiachin ruled only three months before the full invading army arrived, sacked the temple and the palace, and carried away all treasures. This time the Babylonians took not just hostages but the whole ruling party. Jeremiah 52:28 reports the number of captives sent to Babylon at 3,023. Second Kings 24:14 reports 10,000. Jeremiah predicted correctly that Jehoiachin would never return to his throne, nor would his offspring—he might just as well have been childless. In Babylon the royal family appears for many years to have lived under house arrest (I Chr. 3:17). A Babylonian tablet dating from 592 B.C. talks about Yaukin, the king of Judah, and his five sons, listing their rations of olive oil and grain. Under Nebuchadnezzar's son, Evil-merodach, Jehoiachin's status improved. He was now about fifty years old. From then on he was treated as a king, above other kings, and dined at Evil-merodach's table. Under these improved conditions the Jewish exiles in Babylon dreamed of a messianic return to Jerusalem, which had lain in ruins for a long time.

In his first listing of OT genealogy, Matthew skips the evil Jehoiakim, Jehoiachin's father, and makes Jehoiachin the son of Josiah, not the grandson. First Chronicles 3:17 lists seven sons of Jehoiachin. One of them, Shenazzar, was probably the first governor of Jerusalem after the return from Babylon. The second governor, Zerubbabel, was a grandson of Jehoiachin.

T.J.K.

**JEHOIADA.** (Meaning "God knows, God discerns"). There are five Jehoiadas in the OT, or four if one regards as a scribal error a confusion over one who is once described as the father, once as the son, of Benaiah. Of the two best-known Jehoiadas, one recruited 3,700 troops for King David at Ziklag and served as the captain of the royal bodyguard (I Chr. 12:27). As a respected advisor to the king, he is also known as "prince Jehoiada of the clan of Aaron."

The better-known Jehoiada was probably the high priest at the Temple in Jerusalem who established the boy king JOASH on the throne. After the death of Ahaziah, king of Judah, in 842 B.C., the queen mother, Athaliah, killed off Ahaziah's children and took over the throne. Jehoiada hid one princeling, Joash, and thus preserved the line of David from extinction. Seven years later he organized a coup d'etat (II Kings 11:4-20), assassinated the queen mother, and crowned young Joash. As chief priest he served a leading role in counseling the young king, in restoring services at the Temple, and in limiting the worship of Baal. Because of his high regard in court and with the people, on his death Jehoiada was buried as if he were a king, in the tombs beside the kings of Judah. T.J.K.

**JEHOIAKIM.** The Hebrew word for "Yahweh raises up." Son and successor (after his brother Jehoahaz) of JOSIAH upon the throne of Judah. His reign lasted from about 609 to 598 B.C. The fact that Jehoiakim was initially passed over in favor of his younger brother may reflect popular suspicion that, unlike the independent-minded Josiah, Jehoiakim was disposed to strengthen Judah's ties with Egypt. It is clear that he was placed on the throne by Pharaoh Necho as an Egyptian puppet (II Kings 23:24). Close ties between Judah and Egypt continued for some time, as the story of the prophet Uriah indicates (Jer. 26:20-23).

Following an Egyptian defeat by the Babylonians in 605 B.C., Jehoiakim's allegiance was claimed by the latter nation. However, a Babylonian military setback in 601 inspired Jehoiakim to revolt, probably in expectation of Egyptian aid. King Nebuchadnezzar of Babylon did not act to suppress this insurrection until 598, but before Jerusalem fell, Jehoiakim died, leaving his eighteen-year-old son JEHOIACHIN to be carried into captivity in Babylon. Jehoiakim's policies, and the king himself, were bitterly denounced by the prophet Jeremiah. The latter's indictments of the king portray Jehoiakim as greedy and oppressive (Jer. 22:13-19), and there may have been lingering popular resentment against him throughout his reign. However, there is no evidence that Jehoiakim, as some have speculated, was murdered by nationalists or by pro-Babylonian elements within his court. J.D.N.

**JEHOSHAPHAT.** Hebrew for "Yahweh judges." Son and successor of ASA upon the throne of Judah, Jehoshaphat's reign embraced the period about 873-849 B.C. He is depicted in a favorable light by two primary OT sources: I Kings 22 and II Chronicles 17-20. Jehoshaphat was a contemporary of the powerful AHAB of Israel (northern kingdom) and sealed an alliance with the latter monarch by permitting his son to marry Ahab's daughter. This alliance brought an end to hostilities between Judah and Israel that had marred their relations since the breakup of the old Davidic Empire (about 920 B.C.). It also led to a disastrous joint military campaign against Ramoth-Gilead that resulted in Ahab's death. Relationships with Ahab's successor, AHAZIAH, were less cordial, and the proposal of a cooperative effort to establish maritime trade routes for the benefit of both nations was rejected by Jehoshaphat (I Kings 22:48 ff.).

The account of Jehoshaphat's reign in II Chronicles provides additional details not found in I Kings. The monarch's concern for the teaching of the Law by itinerant Levites resulted in spiritual renewal throughout Judah, and, Chronicles seems to imply, in peace from Judah's traditional enemies, including the Philistines (II Chr. 17:7-11). The peace doubtless also was enhanced by Jehoshaphat's extensive measures to increase Judah's fortifications and the nation's standing army (II Chr. 17:12-19). Chronicles also reports, in an extended narrative, a victory won by Jehoshaphat over an army of Moabites, Ammonites, and Meunites. This account is interesting not only for its description of military matters, but perhaps more so because of the portrait it contains of Jehoshaphat as a pious ruler. Second Chronicles 20:5-12 contains a long prayer by the king. A campaign by Jehoshaphat and Jehoram of Israel against Moab is related in II Kings 3. Jehoshaphat apparently died in peace, passing a strong and united Judah to his son Jehoram (not to be confused with the Jehoram above). J.D.N.

**JEHOVAH.** An assumed pronunciation of the personal name of the Hebrew God *YHWH*. This form, which made its appearance in late medieval times was widely used from then until modern times. Jehovah is actually a composite of the consonants for one word and the vowels for another. When only consonants were written in ancient Hebrew texts, the divine name was written *YHWH* (or *YHVH*, depending on the transliteration). Later, vowels were added to texts by a series of dots and dashes written below, within, or above the consonants. By this time, the name of the deity had become so sacrosanct it was no longer pronounced in reading the text. Instead, the word ADONAI was generally read. Thus the scribes wrote the vowels for Adonai with the consonants *YHVH*. When the vowels of Adonai are combined with the consonants *YHVH*, the form "Yehovah" results. Since many languages, such as German, seldom use the letter *y* but use *j* instead, the form "Jehovah" resulted. There is no evidence that the personal name of the Israelite deity was ever pronounced Jehovah in antiquity. J.H.

**JEHOVAH'S WITNESSES.** An indigenous American religious movement launched in 1872 by "Pastor" CHARLES TAZE RUSSELL (1852–1916), a Pittsburgh Congregationist haberdasher. Russell found it difficult to accept the doctrine of everlasting punishment. He was also troubled about the reliability of Holy Scripture. He reported that the Seventh-Day Adventists restored his faith, particularly pertaining to the Bible. The ADVENTIST teaching on the imminence of Christ's Second Coming and the total annihilation of the wicked appealed to Russell. Soon his International Bible Readers Association, as the enterprise was first known, began to grow, under Russell's dynamic leadership, and he became a popular lecturer who dealt primarily with what he said the Bible taught about future events. Soon the movement was referred to as Millenial Dawn, for Russell declared that the MILLENIUM had begun and Christ would return again and usher in his kingdom in 1914. His followers were colloquially known as Russellites.

In 1879 Russell founded a publication he called *Zion's Watch Tower,* which is known today as *The Watchtower Announcing Jehovah's Kingdom* and has a multimillion copy circulation in the United States and overseas. To publish the growing number of pamphlets that have been used extensively by the group in its prosyletizing efforts, the Watchtower Bible and Tract Society was founded.

Theologically, Jehovah's Witnesses are often described as Arians because they believe that Christ was the first and highest created being on the same level essentially as Michael the Archangel. When he became man, he became only man, and although at his resurrection he was exalted above the angels as a spirit being, his body remained dead, although it was removed from sight by Jehovah, the Supreme Being. Witnesses believe that Satan is the invisible ruler of the world.

The sect has continually expected Armageddon, the final battle when Christ will defeat Satan. Only 144,000 faithful Witnesses will go to heaven to rule with Christ over the earth. Their refusal to submit to government authority, including refusal to do military service, has brought Jehovah's Witnesses much persecution. They have also received adverse publicity for refusing blood transfusions for ill members of their families.

"Pastor" Russell was succeeded as president of the organization by his attorney, Judge Joseph Franklin Rutherford (1869–1942), who gave the movement its current name. Rutherford, a prolific author of books and pamphlets and a popular radio speaker, had as much influence on the growth of the work as its founder. He was succeeded by Nathan K. Knorr (1942), who was followed by the current (1983) president, Frederick W. Franz. During the Franz administraton there have been reports of a huge loss in membership, which was reported to be 588,503 in 1982. One of the principal causes for these losses was the more recent prediction by leaders that the world would end in 1975.                        R.H.

**JEHU.** Probably Hebrew meaning "Yahweh is he." King of Israel (northern kingdom) from about 842 to 815 B.C. Jehu was the son of an otherwise unknown Jehoshaphat (not to be confused with the Judean king of that name) and is also remembered as the descendant of his grandfather Nimshi, also otherwise unknown (II Kings 9:2, 20).

Jehu, who was a commander in the Israelite army, came to the throne as a result of a bloody *coup d'etat* described in II Kings 9, the background of which was both economic and religious. Large numbers of people in the northern kingdom had become alienated from the ruling dynasty of Omri because of the royal house's close identification with the moneyed mercantile class and their frequent exploitation of the peasant farmers and because of their close identification with the worship of the Canaanite deity Baal. This conflict had grown especially sharp during the lifetime of the prophet Elijah, who often clashed with his contemporary, the Omride king of Israel, Ahab.

One aspect of this struggle is illustrated by the story of Naboth in I Kings 21. AHAB coveted the vineyard of the peasant farmer Naboth, but the king's offer to buy the land was rejected by Naboth on the grounds that it was an inheritance from his ancestors. Ahab's wife, Queen JEZEBEL, who was the daughter of the Canaanite king of Tyre, upon learning of her husband's frustration arranged to have Naboth murdered and his land seized, an arrangement that Ahab gladly accepted. ELIJAH responded to the news of the atrocity with a fierce denunciation of Ahab and a promise of the king's death. This story also highlights the connection between the Israelite royal court and Canaanite (Phoenician) maritime centers along the Mediterranean coast. The marriage of Ahab and Jezebel cemented political and economic ties between the two groups, which allowed the Israelite entrepreneurs to profit greatly from trade with Phoenicia and, through the use of Phoenician ships, with the larger world beyond. This economic activity led to the polarization of society between merchants and farmers.

The other aspect of the crisis of which Jehu's revolt was an important expression, the religious, is also to be seen in Elijah's conflict with Ahab. The worship of the Canaanite-Phoenician deity BAAL was widespread in Israel and, among other things, led to the famous contest on Mt. Carmel between Elijah and the prophets of Baal (I Kings 18). As a result of Elijah's slaughter of the latter, he was persecuted by Ahab and forced to flee to Mt. Horeb (the term current in the northern kingdom for Mt. Sinai). There, in a theophany, Elijah was directed by God to intervene in the political affairs of both Syria and Israel, in the latter instance by anointing Jehu king (I Kings 19:16). However, it remained for Elijah's disciple and successor, ELISHA, to carry out the divine command.

Photo by H. T. Frank

*The Black Obelisk of Shalmaneser III, showing
King Jehu of Israel prostrating himself before the
Assyrian king and bringing tribute*

At some time subsequent to the death of King Ahab, Elisha arranged the anointing of Jehu as king, an act that inaugurated a bloody revolt against Ahab's son and successor, Joram (II Kings 9). Not only was Joram killed, along with the members of his family (including the Queen Mother, Jezebel), but Judean King Ahaziah, who was visiting in the north at the time, was also assassinated. In addition, there was a widespread slaughter of Baal worshipers and destruction of shrines where Baal was worshiped. Jehu's reference to the memory of Naboth (II Kings 9:26) reveals the spirit in which these bloody purges were carried out.

Jehu's revolt was effective, but it left the northern kingdom politically and militarily isolated. Thus, there was little to prevent the subjugation of Jehu's kingdom by the mighty Assyrian army of Shalmaneser III (about 840 B.C.), and the duration of Jehu's reign seems to have been carried out in the capacity of an Assyrian vassal. He is portrayed on an Assyrian victory monument, the so-called Black Obelisk of Shalmaneser, groveling before the Assyrian monarch, the only contemporary artistic representation of a personality from the Bible known to exist. Jehu is denounced by the authors of the books of Kings because "he did not turn from the sins of Jeroboam, which he made Israel to sin" (II Kings 10:31). Jehu's violence is also vigorously condemned a century later by the prophet Hosea (Hosea 1:4-5).          J.D.N.

**JEPHTHAH.** Transjordanian warrior who rescued Gilead from Ammonite oppression, sacrificed his daughter to fulfill a needless vow, and defeated troublesome Ephraimites.

*Jephthah's Origins.* Born of a harlot, Jephthah suffered banishment from his home and denial of any share in his father's inheritance. He lived as a fugitive near Tob, a site thought to be about forty miles east of the Jordan on Ammon's northern border. There Jephthah became the leader of an outlaw gang and subsequently was visited by the elders of Gilead, who had earlier condoned his eviction (Judg. 11:7). Through a canny bargain, Jephthah moved swiftly from bandit to ruler status.

*Ammon's Challenge.* Westward pressure from the Ammonites in possibly the early eleventh century B.C. produced crisis conditions in Gilead. Discerning divinely empowered leadership in Jephthah, the elders pleaded with him to return home as "head over all the inhabitants of Gilead" (Judg. 11:8). Jephthah agreed. Through messengers Jephthah spoke at length with the Ammonite king. This passage (11:12-28) constitutes a perplexing interpolation whose main body (11:16-26) reviews former Israelite relations with Moab, not Ammon. Perhaps it dates to the seventh century B.C., when Ammon was absorbing Moabite territory. Thus Judges 11:24 mentions Chemosh, Moab's national deity, rather than Milcom, his Ammonite counterpart. When the conversation between leaders proved unproductive, warfare erupted. Visited by Yahweh's Spirit (11:29), Jephthah led his men in a decisive triumph over the Ammonites, who bothered Israel no more until Saul's lifetime (I Sam. 11).

*Jephthah's Daughter.* Jephthah doubted the sufficiency of Yahweh's abiding Spirit. Preferring manipulation by oath, he rashly bargained that if Yahweh would ensure his victory, he would, on his return, offer as a human holocaust whoever came out of his house to meet him (Judg. 11:30-31). His only child, a nameless daughter, greeted him in the manner that the Israelite women later received their triumphant warriors, Saul and David (I Sam. 18:6-7). Jephthah's intense grief was outdistanced by his daughter's self-denial. Holding her father to his vow, she merely asked permission to leave with her companions for a two-month vigil of lamentation over her virginity (Judg. 11:37). While her death was tragically premature, she was annually remembered in a four-day lamentation ceremony (11:39-40).

*Jephthah and Ephraim.* Quarrelsome Ephraimites falsely protested that Jephthah had slighted them in the call to arms for the Ammonite campaign (Judg. 12:1-3). Not at all a diplomat like Gideon (8:2-3), Jephthah waged war against them. Though the number of slain Ephraimites (42,000) is surely exaggerated, this episode attests to dialectical variations among the Israelites. Ephraimite fugitives were detected by their inability to pronounce the "sh" sound in "Shibboleth" (12:5-6). Jephthah remained Gilead's leader until his death six years later.

J.K.K.

**JEREMIAH, BOOK OF.** The second book in the order of the so-called Major Prophets of most

English-language Bibles, the book of Jeremiah occupies a similar place in the Latter Prophets of the Hebrew Bible (Isaiah, Jeremiah, Ezekiel, The Book of the Twelve). Modern literary scholarship has demonstrated that the final form of Jeremiah is the result of a long and complex history of which the details are only imperfectly understood. Even the casual reader will sense anomalies in the structure of the book as, for example, in the fact that the prophet's important "Temple Sermon" of about 609 B.C. is reported twice (Jer. 7 and 26) and in very different fashions. There is no doubt that the book contains genuine words of the PROPHET and accurate records of his deeds, but it is also beyond question that a number of editorial hands have been at work on this material. The task of distinguishing the words of the prophet from the reflection of later editors is often quite difficult. At the same time, however, it should be noted that the book of Jeremiah is the most autobiographical of the prophetic books in the sense that the inner struggles of the prophet are verbalized in passages of great pathos (see the Confessions of Jeremiah below).

The literary material in Jeremiah contains both prose and poetry. Much of the prose is biographical narrative, but there are also sermons (7:1–8:3), visions (24:1-10), and a letter (29:4-28). The poetry is largely in the nature of prophetic oracle, although within this broad category are many different types of material reflecting a wide variety of moods: pleading (3:11-14), lament (4:13-22), introspection (11:18-20), judgment (46:3-12), and others.

The structure of the book is as follows:

1. Visions and oracles, perhaps from Jeremiah's early ministry (627–622 B.C.): chapters 1–6.

2. Other declarations reflecting primarily the years 605 B.C. and after: chapters 7–25.

3. The Memoirs of Baruch: chapters 26-29.

4. Further oracles and biographical references: chapters 30–45.

5. Oracles directed against foreign nations: chapters 46–51.

6. A historical appendix: chapter 52.

While it is not possible to establish with absolute certainty that the material in the first sections (chaps. 1–6) is limited to the early years of Jeremiah's active life, there is much to suggest that this may be the case. The account of the prophet's call (1:4-10), the influence of an older generation of prophets, and the lack of precision in identifying the "foe from the north" (1:14; 4:5-8; 5:15-17 [compare the prophet's later identification of Nebuchadnezzar of Babylon, 32:28]), suggest the activity of the years before the reforms of King JOSIAH in 622 B.C. (II Kings 22–25). The material in this section contains an emphasis on the sin of the people of God, often described in terms of idolatry (2:20-25) and an absence of justice and truth (5:1-3), and upon the judgment that God will send, if there is no repentance (6:1-8).

The second section (chaps. 7–25) is composed of sermonic and oracular literature, which seems to come from a number of different moments in time, but which probably all reflect the period after the death of Josiah in 609. The passage with which this section begins, 7:1-15, is the earliest in point of time (the so-called Temple Sermon delivered in 605), but other materials are to be dated well into the reign of King Zedekiah (21:1). The reader finds here a variety of material: oracles, parables, prayers, poems, and narrative prose.

The third section (chaps. 26–29) is entirely prose and, in terms of chronology, reaches back again to the prophet's "Temple Sermon" of 605 (26:1-9), although most of the material reflects the period of ZEDEKIAH's reign (597–587 B.C.). A number of scholars have concluded that these narratives are from some person close to the prophet, probably his friend and scribe BARUCH. Primary attention is given here to the conflict between Jeremiah and the contemporary religious and political establishment.

The fourth section (chaps. 30–45) is also made up of biographical information (again, the likely source is Baruch) punctuated by summaries of Jeremiah's sermons. There is no consistent chronological pattern to this material, and references are found to both Jehoiakim and Zedekiah, as well as to the period following the second fall of Jerusalem in 587 B.C. Jeremiah's messages here reflect his growing pessimism that God's judgment can be avoided, but there are also important passages dealing with hope for the future (Jer. 31, 32).

The fifth section (chaps. 46–51) consists of oracles against foreign nations, a feature also found in other prophetic books (Isa. 13–23; Ezek. 25–32). Some of this material may come from Jeremiah, but much of it is by later hands. The historical appendix (chap. 52) is reproduced with very little change from II Kings 24:18 to 25:30.

Although they do not constitute a separate section as such, the so-called Confessions of Jeremiah deserve comment, for they constitute a distinctive element within this literature. These texts are usually identified as 10:23-24; 11:18–12:6; 15:10-21; 17:9-10, 14-18; 18:18-23; and 20:7-12. The appellation is something of a misnomer, for the prophet's confession of sin is only one of several autobiographical elements to be found here. There is also anger at God over Jeremiah's call to bear the prophetic word, sorrow over God's word of judgment to the nation, and joy over the presence of God in Jeremiah's and the nation's life. Because of the Confessions, the complex personality of the prophet is expressed with unparalleled vividness.

The history of the composition of this book has been of interest to scholars, both because of the structural complexity of the book and also because in 36:1-32 we seem to have an account of the circumstances under which the nucleus of the book was composed. Many scholars feel that the second scroll mentioned here (the first having been burned by King Jehoiakim) formed a kind of "first edition" of the book. To this first edition were later added (again, likely by Baruch) other sermons, prayers, poems, and the like composed by the prophet after the incidents recorded in chapter 36. Subsequent to this, the book came into the hands of a group of editors who were, in some fashion, associated with the editors of the Deuteronomic History (the biblical books of Joshua-Kings). These people probably contributed to the present arrangement of the book and introduced material of their own that continued their own particular theological understanding (for example, Jer. 9:12-16).                                    J.D.N.

**JEREMIAH, LETTER OF.** An anonymous composition originally composed in Hebrew, Aramaic, or Greek of which the oldest extant copies are in Greek. Inspired by Jeremiah 29:1-23, the document presents itself as a letter from the prophet to the Jews in Babylonian exile. It contains an attack upon pagan idolatry, and it has been variously dated from the late fourth to the early first centuries B.C. Modern scholarship has demonstrated that Jeremiah could not have been the document's author.                          J.D.N.

**JEREMIAH, PROPHET.** One of the most important of the OT prophets, Jeremiah was active from about 627 B.C. to sometime after 587 B.C. He lived through the turbulent years surrounding the fall of the kingdom of JUDAH, and his words and deeds provided a theological perspective to the events of this time and also provided insights of an enduring nature into the divine-human relationship. Because the book that bears his name is, in many respects, the most autobiographical of the OT prophetic books, we know a great deal about the experience and personality of Jeremiah, even if there is some disagreement among scholars concerning details.

Jeremiah was the son of a priestly family from the Benjaminite village of Anathoth, a few miles from Jerusalem (Jer. 1:1). Of his father, Hilkiah, nothing is known, for it is beyond doubt that he was not the same Hilkiah who served as high priest during Jeremiah's lifetime (II Kings 22:4). We cannot be sure if Jeremiah ever actively filled the priestly office himself.

*Early Ministry* (627–622). Jeremiah's call to the prophetic office came in 627 or 626 and the prophet's later reflection on this experience reveals his conviction that it was part of a divine plan laid before his birth. This experience occurred at about the same time as the death of the last great Assyrian emperor Ashurbanipal, an event that seems to have signaled the imminent decline of this most powerful of the Near Eastern states and the increasing independence of the Assyrian's former colonies, including Judah.

The Judean king, JOSIAH, took advantage of the new political situation by extending his nation's influence into areas of the old northern kingdom (Samaria), territories that had not been controlled by a Davidic king since the death of Solomon in about 920

B.C. (II Chr. 34:6-7). More importantly, Josiah inaugurated a program of religious reforms according to which idolatrous practices, many of which had been encouraged by his grandfather Manasseh, were suppressed. During this time the prophetic activity of Jeremiah bore close similarities to that of earlier prophets such as Amos, Hosea, and Micah, his reliance upon Hosea being especially apparent (compare Jer. 2:2 with Hos. 2:15; 9:10; 11:1-2). Idolatry, greed, and injustice are denounced, and the destruction of the nation by a "foe from the north" (1:13-15; 4:5-8) is promised, if the people do not repent.

*Period of Withdrawal* (622–609). Jeremiah's reaction to the reform movement led by King Josiah at the time of the finding of the "book of the law" (II Kings 22:1–23:23) is unclear. Some scholars are of the opinion that the prophet supported the reforms because its ideals were very close to Jeremiah's own. Others believe that he was less sympathetic, seeing the reforms as superficial and temporary. In any event, it is likely that Jeremiah was silent during the later years of Josiah's reign, a judgment based on the absence of oracles or sermons in the book of Jeremiah that can be dated specifically to this period.

*Ministry under Jehoiakim* (609–597). The death of Josiah at the hands of the Egyptians in 609 resulted in a profound theological crisis, since the principles of Josiah's reformation appeared to die with the monarch. The new king installed by the Egyptians, JEHOIAKIM, was a son of Josiah, but the circumstances of his enthronement make it clear that he was little more than an Egyptian vassal (II Kings 23:31-35). Typical of Jeremiah's response to the changed religious and political fortunes of the nation is his so-called Temple Sermon, preached at or near the time of Jehoiakim's coronation (Jer. 7:1-15; 26:1-19). The prophet denounces a series of personal and corporate sins and warns of the destruction of the nation, if the people do not repent. In a violent reaction to this sermon, the people threaten the prophet with death, and Jeremiah is saved only by the timely intervention of a group of officials at Jehoiakim's court (Jer. 26:16-19).

In 605, four years into Jehoiakim's reign, Judah's Egyptian masters are soundly defeated by the Babylonian army under Nebuchadnezzar at Carchemish, and Jehoiakim is forced to acknowledge a new overlord. In the meantime, Jeremiah has continued to denounce the people, and especially the king, for their sins, a confrontation that places the prophet's well-being in ever greater jeopardy. When he is banned from the grounds of the Temple and the royal palace, Jeremiah dictates a message to his scribe Baruch, who carries the scroll to the Temple where he reads it aloud (Jer. 36). Royal officials, alarmed at this denunciation of the king and people, force Baruch into the presence of Jehoiakim. There, as the scroll is read, the king cuts it up bit by bit and feeds it to a fire burning nearby.

Undaunted, Jeremiah simply dictates another message, which Baruch places on a new scroll, a document that may have formed the nucleus of our present book of Jeremiah. It is clear that by this time Jeremiah, who in the days of Josiah had spoken of a "foe from the north," identifies Babylon as the agent of God's judgment, a declaration that only increases the hostility of Jehoiakim (Jer. 36:27-31). It may have been about this time that many of Jeremiah's so-called Confessions were written. These are not confessions in a literal sense, but are passages in which the prophet opens his soul to the reader, displaying both his joy over the presence of God in his life and his anguish that God has called him to bear such pain and speak such terrible words (Jer. 10:23-24; 11:18– 12:6; 15:10-21; 17:9-18; 18:18-23; 20:7-12). When Jehoiakim revolts in 597 and the Babylonian army enters Jerusalem a few months later, Jeremiah's promises achieve a frightful realization.

*Ministry Under Zedekiah and Beyond* (597-587). The new king whom the Babylonians placed on the throne is a brother of Josiah. Jehoiakim is now dead, but other members of the royal family and many of Jerusalem's leading citizens are exiles in Babylon. In order to dispel any false sense of security on the part of the new administration Jeremiah reports his vision of the figs (Jer. 24:1-10), the point of which is that those left in Jerusalem will meet the same fate as the Jews now in exile. Jeremiah warns ZEDEKIAH against the folly of rebellion against Babylon, and he reaffirms his view of Nebuchadnezzar as the agent of God (Jer. 27:1-11). Jeremiah also writes to the exiles in BABYLON, advising against their expectation of an early release (Jer. 29).

These and other statements earn the prophet the continuing enmity of Judah's officials, and Jeremiah is beaten and placed in the stocks (Jer. 20:1-6), while on another occasion he is cast into a dungeon to die (Jer. 38). Zedekiah's revolt against the Babylonians in 598 results in a siege of Jerusalem that was to last for a year and a half. In spite of bad relations between the prophet and the king, Zedekiah seems to have harbored a quiet respect for Jeremiah and, on at least one occasion, has the prophet secretly brought to him from his prison cell in order that he may benefit from the prophet's sense of God's will. In a dramatic confrontation, Jeremiah reveals his own faithfulness to his vision of God's future for Judah, and he reveals his own sufferings as well (Jer. 37:16-21). When Jerusalem falls, the Babylonians torture Zedekiah and carry him to Babylon, placing a governor over the country, while Jeremiah is released from prison (Jer. 39). Shortly thereafter, the governor is murdered by a group of Jewish zealots who take Jeremiah hostage and flee to Egypt for safety. Jeremiah's last recorded words are a denunciation of the sin of his captors (Jer. 44).

An evaluation of the life and work of Jeremiah will recognize the fact that, although his prophetic message was often gloomy, thus earning him the later reputation as the "weeping prophet," Jeremiah also held out hope for a new and brighter day for the people of God (Jer. 31, 32). When the tragedy that he foresaw and feared finally took place, Jews of his and succeeding generations were able to see a divine logic in their suffering and, therefore, were able to survive it. Because of Jeremiah's own suffering, brought about by his faithfulness to God, the prophet is frequently identified as the most Christlike figure in the OT.                                                                J.D.N.

**JERICHO.** A city prominent in events related in both the OT and the NT, Jericho is located in the southern JORDAN Valley. The area has been the subject of important archaeological excavations, some of the more valuable work including that done in the 1930s by John Gatstang and in the 1950s by Kathleen Kenyon.

The earliest settlement at Jericho has been dated to about 7000 B.C. It was located at modern Tell es-Sultan, where an abundant spring still flows and

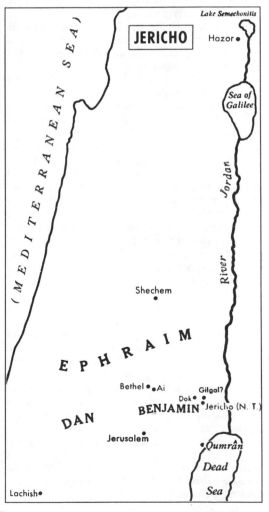

provides water for the region. This astonishingly early date for Neolithic Jericho (which has been confirmed by, among other things, Carbon 14 tests) means that it was one of the first settlements in the region and a thriving center for the development of early civilization. Architectural remains of a variety of types have been discovered, including houses and a fortified stone tower. The artistic skills of the inhabitants of neolithic Jericho are reflected in pottery, decorated bricks, and, curiously, human skulls covered with plaster in which facial features were sometimes reproduced.

During the Early and Middle Bronze Age (about 3000–1500 B.C.) Jericho became a thriving center, but its size and importance seem to have weakened considerably by the Late Bronze (1500–1200 B.C.) and Early Iron (1200–1000 B.C.) Ages. This has presented biblical historians with a complex problem because the Late Bronze Age is generally considered to be the time of the Israelite conquest under JOSHUA. The story of the Hebrews marching around Jericho, blowing their rams' horns, and of the subsequent collapse of the city walls (Josh. 6:1-21) is one of the more dramatic narratives in the Bible. This inability of scholars to reconcile the biblical account with the available archaeological data has given rise to a number of proposals, including the suggestion that the Hebrew conquest may have taken place in several stages over a considerable span of time. To further compound the problem, the archaeological evidence also suggests that the city that would have been built atop "Joshua's" Jericho is missing. Jericho was repopulated at least as early as the time of David (II Sam. 10:5) and probably earlier (the "city of palms" in Judg. 3:13 is probably a reference to Jericho). Yet no trace of this later city can be found at Tell es-Sultan. (See also II Chr. 28:8-15, which may have inspired Jesus' parable of the good Samaritan.)

The Jericho of the NT period was founded by Herod the Great, one of a number of examples of the energy of this ruler as a builder. The NT city was located at modern Talul Abu el-'Alayiq, approximately one mile south of the older city. Because of its lower elevation, Jericho experienced a warmer climate than Jerusalem, a fact that caused Herod to use the city as his winter capital. It thus enjoyed a prestige and a quality of architectural beauty that would not otherwise have been the case. Jericho was the destination of the traveler in the parable of the good Samaritan (Luke 10:30-35), an individual who presumably would have been traveling down to the city through the steep-sided Wadi Qelt, a terrain well suited for ambush. Jericho was also a stopping place for Jesus on his final journey to Jerusalem, the occasion for his remarkable conversation with Zacchaeus (Luke 19:1-10). The economic strength of NT Jericho suggests that this tax collector would have been a very wealthy person. As Jesus left the city for Jerusalem, his route would have been along the same road suggested in the parable of the good Samaritan.

With the Roman destruction of Jerusalem (A.D. 70) Jericho declined in importance. The city enjoyed new prosperity during the Byzantine (A.D. 324–640) and Umayyad (A.D. 661–750) periods.     J.D.N.

**JEROBOAM (I and II).** Hebrew for "the people will increase" (or "may the people increase"). The name of two of the kings of Israel.

Jeroboam I (who ruled from about 922 to 901 B.C.) was a member of the tribe of Ephraim, his father being a certain Nebat and his mother Zeruah (I Kings 11:26). According to the account in I Kings, Jeroboam was the master of a corvee, a group of forced laborers, during the time of SOLOMON. Such labor seems to have been used on many of Solomon's extensive building projects, and in his position, Jeroboam would have had an opportunity to witness the cruelty inflicted upon the laborers, many of whom were probably native Hebrews. It is reported that a prophet named AHIJAH approached Jeroboam and predicted that, because of Solomon's worship of false gods, the kingdom would be divided after his death and that he, Jeroboam, would rule over the ten tribes of Israel (I Kings 11:29-39). It is not recorded what seditious acts Jeroboam then committed, if any; nevertheless "Solomon sought therefore to kill Jeroboam" (v. 40), but the Ephraimite fled to Egypt for safety.

Following Solomon's death Jeroboam was among the leaders of the northern tribes who approached the new king, Rehoboam, and asked for a more lenient treatment from the Jerusalem monarchy (I Kings 12:2-4; II Chr. 10:2-4). When the answer was returned in the negative, the northerners repudiated their allegiance to the Davidic family and chose Jeroboam as their new king. The mettle of Jeroboam was soon to be severely tested. First, there was fighting with Judah, which, quite naturally, was reluctant to see the northern tribes go their own way. First Kings 12:21-24 and II Chronicles 11:1-4 seem to suggest peaceful relations between the two Hebrew kingdoms at this time, but I Kings 15:6 and II Chronicles 12:15 are probably nearer the mark: "There was war between Rehoboam and Jeroboam all the days of his life." Also, both Hebrew kingdoms suffered the severe devastation inflicted by the invading Egyptian armies of Pharaoh Shishak about 918 B.C. The reference in I Kings 14:25 refers to an invasion of Judah only, but the northern kingdom was doubtless also subjected to the Egyptian attack. In spite of these and other, unrecorded, perils, Jeroboam and his kingdom survived.

In order further to assert the political independence of the north and to overcome the traditional importance of Jerusalem as a place of worship and seat of government, Jeroboam took measures that were to have lasting effects. He made the city of Shechem his capital (I Kings 12:25), but later he appears to have moved the seat of his government to Tirzah (I Kings 14:17), perhaps because the latter was a more defensible location. Jeroboam also established cultic centers at Bethel and at Dan, sites that perhaps had been places of Canaanite worship long before the Hebrews entered the land (I Kings 12:26-33). In each of these centers Jeroboam erected a golden calf, probably as a representation of Israel's God, Yahweh (compare Exodus 32). He also appointed a non-Levitical priesthood to preside over these centers of worship and, on occasion, he functioned in the priestly role (I Kings 33).

Jeroboam I was a strong and capable leader, yet one who was viewed as evil in the eyes of the southern writers from whose hands we have received Kings and Chronicles. The story of the denunciation of Jeroboam by the same prophet, Ahijah, who had appointed him to his task in the beginning (I Kings 14:1-16) undoubtedly reflects the viewpoint of devout individuals in the Jerusalem community. The evil deeds of Jeroboam I were often used as a standard by which the evil of subsequent Israelite rulers was measured (I Kings 15:34).

Jeroboam II (who ruled Israel from about 786 to 746 B.C.) was not related to Jeroboam I, but was a descendant of King Jehu, who had overthrown the ruling Omride dynasty in a bloody coup (II Kings 9-10). It was Jeroboam's good fortune to preside over the northern kingdom during a period of relative strength and prosperity, the last such period the nation was to experience before its collapse in 722.

What little information the OT gives us about Jeroboam II is found in II Kings 14:23-29, from which we infer that he was a vigorous monarch who expanded the borders of Israel toward the north (at the expense of the Aramean power centers of Damascus and Hamath) and toward the south as far as the Dead Sea (the "Sea of the Arabah"). This military expansion is confirmed by the book of Amos (6:13), which refers to the capture of the cities of Lo-debar and Karnaim, both to the east of the Jordan. These successes were due, in part, to the fact that both Egypt and Assyria were momentarily occupied elsewhere.

Israel's military and political power under Jeroboam II resulted in increased commerce and wealth. Yet it was not a wealth that was shared equally by all classes in society. The prophet AMOS, who was a contemporary of Jeroboam II (as was the prophet Hosea), portrays an economic polarization that produced a very wealthy class of merchants and rulers who "feel secure on the mountain of Samaria" (the capital of Jeroboam II, Amos 6:1), but who "oppress the poor" and "crush the needy" (4:1). This state of affairs undoubtedly contributed to the following judgment concerning Jeroboam II on the part of those responsible for II Kings: "And he did what was evil in the sight of the Lord; he did not depart from all the sins of Jeroboam the son of Nebat, which he made Israel to sin" (II Kings 14:24).          J.D.N.

**JEROME** (about 340–420). Christian scholar and monk, translator of the official Roman Catholic Latin VULGATE Bible, and promoter of scholarship and service in MONASTICISM. Born in Stridon, Dalmatia, he studied in Rome, and then traveled in Gaul, Greece, and Asia Minor. While visiting Antioch in 373, he became ill and had a vision that turned him to "God's books." He spent six years as a hermit in the Syrian desert, returned to Antioch, and was ordained a priest in 379. After studying in Constantinople under Gregory of Nazianzus, he became secretary to Pope Damasus who commissioned the Vulgate. Jerome completed the NT and Psalms by 384, the year Damasus died.

Many people in Rome sought Jerome's spiritual guidance, including rich women who turned their homes into monasteries. Among these were Saint Paula, her daughter Eustochium, and Melania the Elder. Paula followed Jerome to Bethlehem in 385, founding three convents for nuns and one for monks. Jerome presided over the latter, laboring there for thirty-five years. In Egypt and Palestine Jerome collected biblical materials that helped him in translating the OT from Greek and again from Hebrew, finally completing the Vulgate by 405. Despite controversy, Jerome's Vulgate became accepted. He also wrote commentaries and letters, and ecclesiastical defenses against PELAGIUS and others. His asceticism, interest in relics, and studies influenced monasticism and the Middle Ages.

C.M.

**JERUSALEM.** A city of unique significance in world history, occasioned partly by its geographical locale in Israel and its central place in three major world religions—Judaism, Christianity, and Islam—all faiths that believe in one God and are related. Jerusalem stands on an elevation (Ps. 122:3-4) that slopes toward the southeast. It is thus easy to fortify and defend, since access to the city is limited, and the entrances are difficult to approach except on the north side. As a drawback there has always been a problem with Jerusalem's water supply; hence the importance of rainfall and manmade aqueducts in addition to springs inside the city area (for example, Bethesda, referred to in John 5).

*History.* The name "Jerusalem" antedates Israelite occupation, and it appears in Egyptian texts of the nineteenth-eighteenth centuries B.C. and the Amarna tablets. An even earlier reference is found according to the discovery of the name for "peace" (*shalom* or *shalem,* a Canaanite god) in the Ebla tablets, to be dated around 2500 B.C. (See Gen. 14:17-24 for Melchizedek, king of Salem, a name that is often linked with Jerusalem; Heb. 7:2.) There is a tradition both Jewish and Muslim that Moriah (Gen. 22:2) is the site of the future Temple.

When the Israelites came to the land of Canaan, Jerusalem was occupied by Semitic nomads called Jebusites, under their king Adoni-zedek. He was defeated by Joshua, according to Joshua 10:1-28. The city later fell to the tribe of Judah (Judg. 1:8; see also

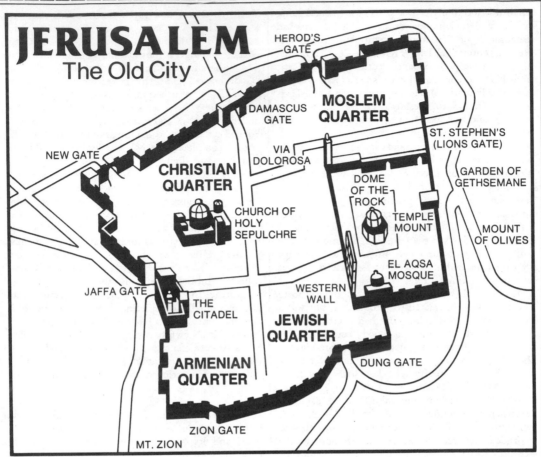

# JERUSALEM
## The Old City

HEROD'S GATE

DAMASCUS GATE

MOSLEM QUARTER

ST. STEPHEN'S (LIONS GATE)

NEW GATE

VIA DOLOROSA

CHRISTIAN QUARTER

GARDEN OF GETHSEMANE

DOME OF THE ROCK

CHURCH OF HOLY SEPULCHRE

TEMPLE MOUNT

MOUNT OF OLIVES

EL AQSA MOSQUE

JAFFA GATE

WESTERN WALL

THE CITADEL

JEWISH QUARTER

ARMENIAN QUARTER

DUNG GATE

ZION GATE

MT. ZION

Courtesy of the Trustees of the British Museum

KENITES), though it appears from Judges 1:21 that the allied tribe of Benjamin occupied Jerusalem, at least in part, in association with the Jebusites.

DAVID became king first in Hebron, but he quickly realized the strategic importance of Jerusalem as a neutral city set midway between Hebron in the south and the northern tribal center of Shechem. He therefore launched an attack on Jerusalem and overwhelmed the occupants by surprise (II Sam. 5:6-10). He made the city his national capital as a focus of unity and gave it its distinctive title "the CITY OF DAVID"; it was also called Zion at this time, a term that seems to relate to the fortress of the city. Here David planned to erect the Temple as a counterpart to his royal palace. It was left to his son SOLOMON, however, to undertake both major building projects, with the palace becoming more extensive and costly than the Temple of Yahweh to which the Ark of the Covenant—a symbol of the divine presence—was eventually brought.

As a center of national wealth and prestige, Jerusalem was naturally open to prey. Egyptian invaders looted the area in Solomon's son's time (I Kings 14:25-28). Two large-scale invasions occurred later, the first in the reign of Hezekiah when the city

resisted the siege and was spared (II Kings 18, 19). A century later, Jerusalem was twice invaded, first in 597 B.C. and then in 587-586 B.C. by the Babylonians. It was taken and sacked, with the main population either scattered or deported into exile. Nearly a century later, with the Persians becoming world masters, some Jews were permitted to return and rebuild the Temple. NEHEMIAH, in the middle of the fifth century, was the chief agent for the rebuilding of the city walls, and he set the city on a new course of civic life and eventual prosperity.

The next serious threat to Jerusalem came in 168 B.C., when the Syrian leader ANTIOCHUS IV, having been defeated in Egypt, turned aside on his homeward route to plunder the Temple and defile it. He set up a Syrian garrison, but this combined endeavor only provoked armed resistance by the Maccabean family, a revolt that led to the recapture of the city in 165 B.C. The Maccabeans were given a taste of freedom, and under the later Hasmonean dynasty they strove for territorial expansion. Jerusalem became a metropolis at the center of an empire that rivaled the kingdom of David for size and importance.

The Romans came on the scene in 63 B.C., when Pompey entered the Temple area; then after a

Parthian invasion in 40 B.C., HEROD the Great regained its control. He goes down in history as the one who made Jerusalem an architectural and aesthetic center, with his massive building programs and a refurbishing of the Temple. Henceforth the latter is known as Herod's Temple, exceeding the splendor of Solomon's edifice.

The Jewish War of A.D. 66–70 led to a Roman siege in Jerusalem which, in turn, was followed by the city's utter ruin by Titus, the Roman general. He left only a few towers erect, and the population was again dispersed. It regathered in the following years, only to suffer a final crushing blow in A.D. 132–35 when, at the close of another rebellion against Rome, Jerusalem was leveled and its place as a sacred shrine destroyed. An altar to Jupiter, the Roman deity, was put up on the Temple site.

The Jews were banished, and not until Constantine's reign in the fourth century A.D. were they permitted to return. The city was now a Christian venue, filled with churches and monasteries. Subsequent centuries witnessed invasions by Persian, Arab, Turkish, Crusader, and British armies, until the mandate after World War I. The creation of the State of Israel after World War II led to an Israeli longing to repossess Jerusalem, and after the Six-Day War in 1967, they eventually gained access to their most treasured locale, the western wall. The Temple area still remains under the shadow of Islam with the Dome of the Rock mosque dominating the landscape.

*Significance.* It is difficult to overestimate the role of Jerusalem in Hebrew narrative and poetry, Christian history and hymnody, and Muslim aspiration where it remains with Mecca and Medina a "holy city," as its Arab name implies.

In the OT Jerusalem stands for the guarantee of God's presence with the people and was often thought

*Jerusalem. At the center is the Dome of the Rock, where tradition says Abraham bound Isaac for sacrifice. The rock sheltered by the dome is in the center of Mount Moriah, upon which the Bible says the Temple of Solomon was built. The Garden of Gethsemane, with its onion-domed Russian church, is just to the left beyond the Dome of the Rock.*

to be inviolate—a notion that the prophets had to oppose (Jer. 7:4-15; Mic. 3:9-12). They preached that Jerusalem needed to be a holy city (Isa. 1:21-26), filled with social righteousness and faithful religion.

Jesus' attitude follows this pattern, since he revered the city and its Temple as his Father's house (Matt. 5:35) but cried against Jerusalem's follies and rejection of his message (Luke 19:41-48). His prophecy against the Temple (Mark 13) was fulfilled in A.D. 70. Yet Christian theology has seen in Jerusalem a picture of the heavenly city, a new Jerusalem, which epitomizes the reign of God and the claims of righteousness and peace (Gal. 4:25-28; Heb. 12:22; Rev. 21:1–22:5).

          R.M.

**JERUSALEM BIBLE** (JB). This Bible is the English version (1966) of *La Bible de Jerusalem,* which was produced by French scholars at the Dominican Biblical School in Jerusalem. Under the general editorship of Pére Roland de Vaux, this verion was published first in 1961. While the Jerusalem Bible is an approved Roman Catholic version, it has been accepted widely by non-Catholics both in Britain and the United States.

          R.H.

*Bronze coin of the period of the Jewish revolt led by Simon Bar-Kokhba (A.D. 132-135)*

*Silver tetradrachma of the period of the Jewish revolt against Rome (A.D. 132-135). The portal of the Temple is shown.*

## JERUSALEM, SYNOD OF

**JERUSALEM, SYNOD OF** (1672). The ecclesiastical council of 1672 that clarified Greek Eastern Orthodox Church beliefs in an attempt to combat Cyril Lucar's accommodating tendency toward Calvinism early in the seventeenth century. Synods at Constantinople (1638) and Jassy (1643) condemned Cyril Lucar's Calvinistic tendencies, but European Calvinists continued to quote Eastern church writers in support of Calvinistic views. Jerusalem Patriarch Dositheus promoted the Jerusalem Synod, which rejected subtle false claims made by Calvinists who appealed to Greek theologians and gave a declaration of orthodox faith in eighteen decrees and four questions. It declared that predestination and foreknowledge do not exclude works, justification is by faith and works, the church and Scripture are equally infallible, God is not the cause of evil, people who fall from grace can be purified after death, and sacraments do not depend on the receiver's faith. It treated other topics and accepted the Apocrypha, images, and veneration of saints. Wide acceptance made the synod's statements virtually definitive.

C.M.

## JESHUA

**JESHUA** ("Yahweh is salvation"). A later form of the name JOSHUA, used frequently by Ezra and Nehemiah. Haggai and Zechariah call some of the same people Joshua. It is also used for a place name in Judah (Neh. 11:26), which may have been the Shema of Joshua 15:26 or the Sheba of Joshua 19:2

Those bearing the name include the head of a division of priests (I Chr. 24:11); a Levite mentioned in Hezekiah's reorganization (II Chr. 31:15); a high priest (Ezra 2:2); a man of Pahath-moab who returned from the Exile with Zerubbabel (Ezra 2:6); the head of a house of priests associated with the "children of Jedaiah" (Ezra 2:36); the father of Ezer, ruler of Mizpah (Neh. 3:19); and the son of Nun (Neh. 8:17); a Levite, the son of Azaniah (Neh. 10:9); a chief of the Levites, the son of Kadmiel (Neh. 12:24). Some of these, of course, may be the same people.

N.H.

## JESSE

**JESSE.** The grandson of Boaz and the father of King David (I Sam. 16:10-11). An Ephrathite from Bethlehem in Judah, he had eight sons (I Chr. 2:13-15). Nahash was at least the mother of his daughters (II Sam. 17:25). He is last mentioned at the cave of Adullam in Moab, where David sent his parents for safety (I Sam. 22:3-4).

N.H.

## JESUITS

**JESUITS.** Members of the Society of Jesus (SJ), Roman Catholicism's strongest order in the twentieth century, organized in 1534 by IGNATIUS OF LOYOLA, confirmed in 1540 by Pope Paul III. They were mainstays of papal power at the Council of Trent (1545–63), led in the Roman Catholic Reformation, and became renowned worldwide for education and missions. Thwarted by war in their desire to convert Muslims, Loyola and his original group committed themselves to be missionaries under absolute obedience to the pope, to go wherever sent.

Originally the order was limited to sixty members, but it proved so effective in the Catholic Reformation, education, and missions that this limitation was lifted. By 1626 the Jesuits had 15,000 members and 803 houses; their missions had spread all over the world, and they dominated Roman Catholic education with 476 colleges, 36 seminaries, and thousands of lower schools.

Their very success aroused formidable reactions. They attacked the Augustinian theology at PORT-ROYAL, France, which stressed divine grace over human works in salvation, saying it affronted their achievements. Blaise Pascal mercilessly exposed the Jesuits' casuistry, and Port-Royalists argued that the Jesuit doctrine of free will denied God's omnipotence and that their good works denied the efficacy of grace. Nevertheless, the papacy condemned the writings of Port-Royal leaders Cornelius Jansen (1653) and Pasquier Quesnel (1713). Port-Royal was destroyed. Refugees established the Jansenist Old Catholic Church in Holland.

This episode was not an isolated one. Many Catholics feared the enormous wealth and political power of the Jesuits. Catholic princes expelled them from Portugal, Spain, and France for subversion, and in 1773 pressured Pope Clement XIV to dissolve the order. However, it survived in Prussia and Russia, where the pope's power was limited. Forty-one years later, in 1814, Pope Pius VII reconstituted the Jesuits. They continued their phenomenal growth and spearheaded Roman Catholic reforms at Vatican Council II (1962–65). In 1980 they numbered about 35,000.

To promote the church, all Jesuits swear absolute obedience to the pope, all go through Loyola's *Spiritual Exercises* to deepen their religious dedication and resolve, and all must have extensive educational training. Novices normally spend two years in seclusion and prayer before taking their usual monastic vows of poverty, chastity, and obedience. As scholastics the candidates study classical subjects, mathematics, physical sciences, and philosophy for five years. Candidates then teach five years in Jesuit schools, study theology four additional years, and devote a year to prayer and introspection before ordination and final vows. Their special vow is absolute obedience to the pope. They have no special habit and are not ascetic. The order, with substructures in various countries and provinces, is administered by a general. Ignatius Loyola was the first; other early generals included ROBERT BELLARMINE, Peter Canisius, Claudio Aquaviva, and Matteo Ricci.

The early Jesuit schools were tightly structured to promote church views. Studies centered on grammar, philology, poetry, and rhetoric; texts were expurgated, and extra readings had to be approved in advance. History and mathematics received little attention. Latin was the official language; no modern languages were officially taught until 1832. Despite shortcomings, the Jesuit schools proved highly successful, especially through the gifted leadership of Bellarmine, Canisius, and Aquaviva.

The Jesuits scored spectacularly in missions. Led by FRANCIS XAVIER and Matteo Ricci in the Orient, the Jesuits have established missions in India, Japan, China, the Philippines, Indochina, the Congo, Morocco, Ethiopia, Brazil, Peru, Paraguay, the United States, and Canada. Many suffered martyrdom. In Paraguay, the Jesuits established their Reductions of Paraguay, a communal Christian nation of native Indians that lasted two hundred years.                                                         C.M.

## JESUS CHRIST, LIFE AND TEACHINGS OF.

The basic sources for the life and teachings of Jesus are the four Gospels of the NT. Since these were written by Christians for the purpose of informing members of the church about the beginnings of Jesus and the movement he launched, they have been challenged as biased and therefore historically suspect. Careful search for information about Jesus in Jewish and Roman sources from the first and second centuries of our era has provided a basic confirmation of, but no significant supplement to, the Gospels. In Josephus, the Jewish historian, and in the rabbinic traditions that probably go back to the first century, we learn only that Jesus was put to death under the Roman governor of Palestine during the reign of Tiberius (probably in A.D. 29), and that his message was being propagated and followers were rallying to the movement from the villages and towns of Galilee to the capital of the empire. Attempts have been made to link Jesus with the ESSENE movement at QUMRAN that produced the Dead Sea Scrolls, but if he ever had connections with that group, he must have repudiated its views completely in later life, since his message of inviting the ritually impure and the religious outcasts to join his group stands in sharpest contrast to the intense ritual exclusivism of the Qumran community. More probably, he never had any associations with this group of ritual purists.

From other writings of the NT and the early centuries of the church, we learn nothing substantive to supplement what is presented in the Gospels. Paul has only oblique references to Jesus' teachings, as in the command to love one's neighbor (Rom. 13:9-10). He does quote in a form close to that of the Gospel tradition the report of Jesus' actions and statements on the occasion of the Last Supper (I Cor. 11:23-25). Of the details of the life and teachings of Jesus, we learn from Paul nothing new or in conflict with the Gospels. From later writers, in the body of material now known as the Apocryphal NT—coming from a wide range of settings and written in the second and subsequent centuries—we have only gross speculation and crass propaganda about Jesus' childhood and career. In the Infancy Gospel of Thomas, for example,

Jesus is reported to have responded to those who charged him with breaking the Sabbath law when he made some clay pigeons by clapping his hands, whereupon the pigeons flew away. Or again, when his father cut a board too short, Jesus stretched it to the proper size. These late, fantastic narratives offer no reliable additions to the canonical Gospels, which are indeed our basic sources of information about Jesus' life and teachings.

Perhaps the oldest Jesus tradition that has been preserved is embodied in the source that was used by MATTHEW and LUKE to supplement the first complete Gospel, MARK, as they were writing their respective Gospels. Known to scholars as Q (from the German word for source, *quelle*), this non-Markan—and probably pre-Markan—material presents a vivid picture of Jesus as the messenger of the rule of God, which is already breaking into the present age through Jesus' acts and words. The three major themes of the Q material (given here in the form that Luke preserves) are: (1) Jesus as the prophetic revealer and agent of God's Rule; (2) the call to discipleship; (3) the warning of repentance or judgment. In the Q source there seems to have been no report of either Jesus' birth or death.

It is in association with JOHN THE BAPTIST that Jesus launches his activity. John is linked with the prophets as messengers of God whose word of judgment the covenant people as a whole have rejected (Luke 3:16-17; 11:49-50). A major factor in this rejection is that John announced a new basis on which God would constitute the covenant people, abandoning the notion that a genetic link with Abraham was a sufficient qualification (Luke 3:8-9). Even so, Jesus mourned over Jerusalem's rejection of God's messenger (Luke 13:34-35). Important as John is in his role of the one who prepares the way for Jesus (Luke 3), his work marks the end of the old era, while Jesus' work is pictured as the beginning of a new age in which God's rule is already visible and active (Luke 16:16-17) through the successful conflict with evil in which Jesus and his followers are engaged.

From the outset of his public career, Jesus is described as accomplishing the defeat of the attempts by the devil to lure him into using his extraordinary powers for the purpose of mere publicity or in the service of the devil (Luke 4:2-12). Although John is reported to be puzzled about what Jesus has undertaken, Jesus is quoted as sending to the imprisoned John the explanation that his acts of liberation and his extension of benefits to the economically and religiously deprived are signs that God's rule is coming, and that it is in fulfillment of what was promised through the prophets of Israel (Luke 7:18-35; compare Isa. 29:18-19; 35:5-6; 61:1). Just as ancient Israel was delivered from slavery in Egypt by God's hand (Exod. 8:19), it is by God's "finger" that Jesus has performed his exorcisms, as a sign of the inbreaking of God's kingdom in the present (Luke 11:20).

To become a follower of Jesus, according to the *Q* tradition, requires a break with the ordinary human ties of family (Luke 9:57-62) as well as the creation of conflicts within families (Luke 12:51-53; 14:26-27). It is not the religiously and socially respectable, but those who are in need and know it who are invited to share in the kingdom of God, as the *Q* parable of the messianic banquet describes the situation (Luke 14:16-24). His followers are to carry forward the work for which Jesus called them (Luke 10:2-20). To them has been granted special insight into God's purpose in the world (Luke 10:21-23) and a promise of participation in God's rule in the New Age (Luke 22:28-30).

The first narrative account of Jesus' career to have been written was the Gospel of Mark, which begins its story with the baptism of Jesus, including his divine acclaim as God's son (Mark 1:11), and continues through the account of his seizure by the authorities, his death, and the discovery of the empty tomb (16:1-8). Mark describes Jesus' call of his followers as having begun with the summons of two pairs of brothers to leave the family fishing business behind in order to become his followers (1:16-20). Later, when the number of the immediate circle of his followers reached twelve (3:13-14), he commissioned them to carry forward the work that he had begun, including preaching and healing of the sick (6:7-13). For this work they were to have neither funds nor organized support, but rather were to go out in dependence on the hospitality and response of the hearers as they moved from village to village. He had set the pattern for them by traveling throughout all Galilee, preaching in their synagogues and casting out demons (1:39). The exorcisms are seen as manifestations of his power over the work of Satan (2:19-27), whose hold on human beings is already being broken by the control that Jesus exercises over the demons.

The work to which he called the disciples is not to be seen as immediately producing spectacular results. Rather, its effects will be unobtrusive, like a mustard seed growing or like the sowing of grain on the ground (4:1-32): modest beginnings but spectacular results. Only those privileged by God will be able to discern the meaning and the outcome of what Jesus began and what is being continued by his chosen followers (4:10-12). The disciples are also granted insight into the special relationship to God that Jesus enjoys and his unique place in the purpose of God. These insights are disclosed through the incidents told by Mark, such as Jesus' walking on the water, stilling the storm, and feeding the hungry five thousand (4:35-41; 6:30-52). All the public sees is that they received a free meal and that they might benefit from his healing powers (6:53-56). Only the inner circle of his followers recognized him as God's Messiah (8:27-30), and even they did not yet understand what his messianic office involved, as Peter's rebuke of him on his mention of suffering and

death reveals (8:31-33). The disciples continue to think of the Messiah as a figure of power, rather than of obedience and suffering in behalf of others (9:33-37; 10:35-45).

In the first century, the PHARISEES were chiefly concerned with defining the covenant community in terms of ritual purity, Sabbath observance, and obedience to those laws that preserved the separate identity of Jews as the people of God. In Mark it is clear that Jesus disagreed with the Pharisees on these points and sought instead to define the community on non-ritual, inclusive lines. What Jesus declared essential for purity was moral, rather than ritual, since what defiles is not what comes from without but what arises within the individual (Mark 7:1-23). This attitude is apparent in the fact that he befriended and healed those who were non-Jewish, like the demoniac from Gerasa (Mark 5), the child of the woman from the region of Tyre and Sidon (7:24-30), which lay outside Jewish territory, and the blind beggar in Jericho (10:46-52). His challenge to the religious authorities and the movement on the part of the crowds to acclaim him as king (11:1-10), as well as his actions in cleansing the Temple (11:15-19) and his predictions of the destruction of the Temple (13:2) and the turning over of the "vineyard" to others (non-Jews) in the parable of 12:1-12, led those leaders to accuse Jesus before the civil authorities as a subversive. It was on the ground of seeking to be king (15:2, 18, 21-32) that he was arrested and executed by the Roman governor's order. In the final hours of his life, he gathered his followers to share a meal of bread and wine, which he told them symbolized both his own impending death in their behalf and the vindication of him and them by God, which would take place when the kingdom of God fully came (14:22-25). They forsook him in the hour of his agony, and in spite of having had a vision of his ultimate glorification by God on the Mount of Transfiguration (9:2-8), they are portrayed by Mark as perplexed when the messenger at the empty tomb tells them to return to Galilee. There the risen Jesus will meet them, and from there they are to resume the work for which he called and commissioned them (16:1-8).

Matthew adds important elements to Mark's basic story. The account of his birth in Bethelehem is pictured as accompanied by cosmic events, such as the unusual course of a star (2:1-3). His lineage is traced back through David, and his birth is depicted as in fulfillment of scripture, including his having been born of a virgin (1–2). Matthew has arranged the teachings of Jesus in several large blocks: the SERMON ON THE MOUNT (5–7), the instructions to the Twelve (chaps. 10), the PARABLES of Jesus (13), advice to his followers about regulating their common life (chap. 18), judgments on the Pharisees (chap. 23), and the combination of predictions of the destruction of the Temple and the violent events that will precede the coming of the end of the age (chaps. 24–25). The tensions between Israel and the church are heightened, as in the sad outcry of Israel's leaders accepting responsibility for the death of Jesus (27:25), as well as in the sharp contrast between Jewish understanding of God's law through Moses and Jesus' understanding of divine will for his people (5:21, 27, 31, 33, 38, 43). There is a heavy emphasis on both the authority of Jesus and on his assignment of authority to the disciples (16:15-19; 18:15-20), which reaches a climax in the post-Resurrection commissioning of the disciples by Jesus in 28:18-19, "All authority in heaven and on earth has been given to me. Go therefore . . ."

By contrast, Luke stresses throughout his Gospel the open, inclusive attitude of Jesus toward those who are ritual, ethnic, or social outsiders to the Jewish covenant standards. Luke's genealogy is universal in implication, since it traces Jesus' lineage back to Adam, the progenitor of the human race (3:23-38). His first public statement in his hometown announces his aim to reach with the good news of redemption "the poor"—that is, those who are deprived on whatever grounds of sharing in the riches of God's grace (4:16-21). And he defends this policy by appeal to the precedents of the benefits bestowed on non-Israelites by the prophets of Israel, Elijah and Elisha (4:25-30). There is in Luke a second story of Jesus sending out his followers on a mission. This time they are seventy in number—which the Jews believed to be the number of the nations of the world (Luke 10:1-12). His teachings praise the humane concerns of a Samaritan (10:29-37) and the right priorities of a woman who seeks to learn from him, in defiance of then-current norms, which excluded women from full participation in the religious communities (10:38-42). His parables in Luke 15 depict God as the shepherd who seeks the wanderer, as the woman who looks for what has been lost, and as the father who is concerned only for reconciliation with the estranged son. Repeatedly in Luke, it is the tax collectors—regarded by Jews as unscrupulous collaborators with the Romans—who are welcomed into the fellowship of Jesus' followers (5:27-30; 7:29-34; 15:1; 18:10-13). In this final instance, Jesus defies social and ritual norms of first-century Judaism by inviting himself to eat a meal with Zacchaeus the tax collector (19:5). Women figure prominently among his followers in Luke (7:36-50; 8:1-3; 21:1-4), especially in the scenes depicting his death, burial, and Resurrection (23:27-31; 23:55-56; 24:1-11). As a foreshadowing of the church's subsequent celebration of the presence of the living Christ in its midst, Luke alone reports that Jesus was known by his followers after the Resurrection through the interpretation of the scriptures (24:32) and in the breaking of the bread (24:35). These inclusive features of Luke serve to prepare the reader for the launching of the world mission of the church that he will recount in the second volume of his work, the book of Acts.

Although in broad outline JOHN's Gospel tells the same basic story of Jesus as do the other three Gospels, there are fundamental differences in detail as well as in overall style of John. His prologue begins, not with the birth or baptism of Jesus, but with the realm of eternity, in which the divine Word (Logos) is always with God, sharing the divine nature, and in time coming down into the human sphere—"the Word made flesh" (1:14). Jesus' purely human birth is assumed, however, since he is spoken of as the "son of Joseph" without mention of Mary (1:45; 6:42). The background influencing the book seems to lie in the Hellenistic religions, such as the cult of Isis, whose devotees saw in her the divine agent through whom the creation was kept in order, as well as the personal benefactor through whom individual needs were met (as by healings) and direct knowledge of the divine was possible, especially through her pronouncements in the first person singular: "I am Isis. . . ." What John has done is to adapt and transform this pattern of pagan piety by showing that the miracles, or "signs" that Jesus performs, attest to his role as revealer of the glory of God (2:11; 20:30-31). He was in past eternity the instrument through whom God created the world (1:3), just as he is the one through whom the light and life that come from God are revealed to the faithful (8:12; 14:6) and the central figure around whom the new people of God is gathered, under the OT images of shepherd (10:11) and vine (15:1). John's account of Jesus' activities and his teachings are filled with rich symbolism, so that they are intended to be understood at both the literal level of human event and the spiritual level of divine redemptive disclosure. The oneness of Jesus with God that is implied in the other Gospels is made explicit in John: "I and the Father are one" (10:30).

The community that is represented by John's Gospel seems not to have been concerned for questions of structure or discipline, as in Matthew. Rather, the recurrent emphasis in Jesus' teaching according to John is on the mutuality of relationships within the community. The members' love for one another is the chief sign of their identity as disciples of Jesus (13:34-35). It is remarkable that in John, love for neighbor has been supplanted by love for one's fellow disciple. The outward expression of that love is given in the ceremony of washing of feet, symbolizing mutual forgiveness and humility (13:1-20). Both the details of Jesus' public career and his style of teaching and action are depicted differently in John from the other Gospels, but it is clear that John is more interested to convey his theological understanding of the significance of Jesus for faith as the creative-redemptive agent of God than in passing on historical tradition. Yet his conviction is that, unlike the pagan deities that promised communion with the Divine, Jesus' role as revealer of God was in genuinely human form, in the midst of the social, political, and cultural factors that condition all human existence.

H.K.

**JESUS PEOPLE.** A counter-cultural religious movement made up chiefly of young people who embraced Jesus Christ but maintained many of their anti-establishment mores. Known also as Jesus Freaks or Street Christians, the revivalistic phenomenon had its origin in 1967 and 1968, chiefly on the West Coast and particularly in California. Later some groups moved to other parts of the country to set up communes to engage in various forms of unconventional Christian witness. Various clusterings of young people, often led by strong leaders, sprang up, seemingly spontaneously, which has caused some self-appointed chroniclers to regard the Jesus Movement as a part of the American revivalistic tradition that dates back to the Great Awakening of the colonial period.

It is true that some of the converts had been drug users and had adopted the transient life-style of dropouts from straight society, but some were young people influenced more or less by the cultural norms of the turbulent 1960s. Lonnie Frisbee, who left the San Francisco Academy of Art to conduct a witness to street people, had a novel explanation for the movement. He suggested that the Six-Day War between Israel and adjoining Arab nations had set the stage for the last days before Christ's Second Coming. Ted Wise, a Sausalito sailmaker, became a Christian and soon began talking to people on the streets of Haight-Asbury about Jesus Christ. This brought him into contact with Jim Heefner, a disc jockey, and Jim Doop, a cigarette salesman, who became Christian converts. They were joined by Danny Sands, an old friend of Wise and his wife, Elizabeth. This quartet of men and their wives established a coffeehouse called the Living Room in Haight-Ashbury. There they rapped with thousands of street people about the claims of Christ and the authoritative place of the Bible. Later they were joined by Frisbee and his wife and established a communal family of five couples in a farmhouse, at Novato, California, some miles north of San Francisco. The Frisbees later moved to southern California and with a new acquaintance, John Higgins, rented the House of Acts. Later they moved to Santa Ana and opened a home they called the House of Miracles. Heefner and Doop, after a time, left Novato and joined up with Victor Wierwille of The Way, an ultra-dispensationalist ministry, headquartered in New Knoxville, Ohio. Similar movements developed in Oregon and Washington, and some of their converts moved to Midwest and East Coast locations.

The theology of the Jesus People generally was fundamentalistic and, more often than not, charismatic. Yet sociologically they did not align themselves with the straight churches of FUNDAMENTALISM until later years. Most of the Jesus People, with their strong reliance on the King James Version of the Bible, were anti-intellectual and anti-cultural. By the 1980s the Jesus People movement had been either formed into house churches or absorbed into more conventional churches such as Calvary Chapel of Costa Mesa or the Peninsula Bible Church of Palo Alto.

R.H.

**JESUS PRAYER.** "Lord Jesus Christ, Son of God, have mercy on me!"; the traditional prayer accompanying meditation in the Greek Orthodox church and orthodoxy generally, especially among monastics. This prayer is said to be from the heart, a motion to be "hid with God through Christ," drawn from the Christ mysticism of Paul. In orthodoxy, such mystical prayer is known as HESYCHASM.

The Greek monks devoted themselves to the remembrance of the name of Jesus. From repetition of the name "Jesus," the prayer developed to its present form by the twelfth century. It also became part of various meditation exercises and positions that are supposed to focus the mind on the Divine. Hesychasm has a long history in orthodoxy, from Origen, Athanasius, Gregory of Nyssa, the Hermits such as Simeon Stylites, and a multitude of practitioners in the thirteenth and fourteenth centuries.

J.C.

**JETHRO.** Moses' father-in-law, sometimes called Reuel and Hobab (Exod. 3:1; 4:18; Judg. 4:11). He was a priest of Midian of the Kenite clan (Exod. 18:1). He brought Moses' wife Zipporah and their sons to meet MOSES at Mt. Horeb and held a sacrifice of thanksgiving for the Israelites' safe exodus from Egypt. He also advised Moses to delegate the administration of justice, which became the institution of judges (Exod. 18). His son Hobab joined the Israelites. Descendants of the family settled in Negeb and were friendly with David. Some have suggested that Yahweh was the name of the Kenites' god.

N.H.

**JEW.** A member of the Hebrew people; particularly, of the tribe of Judah. The term "Jew" is used for members of Judea who were taken to Babylon in captivity (586–539 B.C.) and their descendants who returned to restore Jerusalem, and to all those through history who descended from them. The reforms of Ezra and Nehemiah set the standards as to who is a Jew, emphasizing birth from a Jewish mother.

Historically, Jews are part of the Hebrew family, an Aramaean (Syrian) branch of the northwest Semitic group, which originated in Arabia. The closest living racial relatives of the Jews are the Arabs, which is reflected in the Genesis stories of Ishmael and Isaac (Gen. 15–26) and Jacob and Esau (Gen. 27–36). Originally, the Hebrews were known as *'Apiru* or "outsiders" (river crossers) because of their wandering nomadic ways of life.

Although "Hebrew," "Jew," and "Israelite" are generally used interchangeably, Israel was only one branch of the larger Hebrew movement in history, and Judah ("the Jews") was only one of twelve Israelite tribes.

The history of the Jews is one of God's initiative in dealing with humankind. Yahweh ("I Am") appeared to Moses and brought the Israelites out of Egypt to freedom, gave them the covenant at Mt. Sinai (Exod. 19–23), and helped them conquer Canaan. Much of Jewish history was conflict, defeat, occupation, and suffering. But Jews came to see that there is only one God, and even the defeats of history are God's attempt to redeem them and all humankind.                    J.C.

## JEWISH HISTORY AND THOUGHT. See JUDAISM, MODERN THOUGHT OF.

## JEWISH HOLIDAYS.
The Jewish holidays are of several kinds. The Bible commands the observance of the following: The Sabbath and the New Moon; the "day of blowing the trumpets," which today is ROSH HASHANAH or the Jewish New Year; the DAY OF ATONEMENT (Yom Kippur); and the three pilgrimage festivals—PASSOVER, the Feast of Weeks (SHAVUOT), and the Feast of Tabernacles (SUKKOT).

Rosh Hashanah and Yom Kippur are celebrated solely as religious occasions of judgment, atonement, and reconciliation with God, while historical and agricultural motifs combine in each of the pilgrimage festivals. Thus Passover, which commemorates the Exodus from Egypt and slavery, is the spring festival, Shavuot, which is a reminder of the revelation at Mount Sinai and the receiving of the Ten Commandments, is the festival of the firstfruits. Sukkot, a reminder of the Israelites wandering in the wilderness, is the fall harvest festival. The seventh day of Sukkot is distinguished as the "great Hosha'na" (the Gospel accounts of Jesus' entry on Palm Sunday seem to have confused this with Passover). The eighth day, Shemini Atzeret (Eighth Day of Assembly), is treated as an independent holiday from the point of certain rabbinical prescriptions, such as mourning. The ninth day is Simhat Torah (joy of the Torah). It marks the conclusion of the annual cycle of Torah readings and the beginning of a new cycle.

Holidays of later origin than the Torah (and which therefore do not have the force or prohibitions of the biblically ordained holidays) include HANUKKAH and PURIM. Hanukkah, the Festival of Dedication (25th of Kislev to 3d of Tevet, corresponding to December), celebrates the victory over those who try to destroy the Jewish religion such as the Syrian King Antiochus. It marks the rededication of the Temple. Purim celebrates the deliverance of the Jewish people from the threat of extinction in Persia because of the slanders of Haman.

Fast days besides the Day of Atonement include Tisha b'Av (9th of Av), which marks the destruction of the first Temple in Jerusalem by the Babylonians in 586 B.C. and the destruction of the second Temple by the Romans in A.D. 70; the Fast of Gedaliah (8th of Tishri), which commemorates the climax of the disasters that befell the first Jewish commonwealth in 586 B.C.; Asarah b'Tevet (10th of Tevet), which marks the day when the Babylonians began their siege of Jerusalem in 586 B.C.; the Fast of Esther, which commemorates the time when the Jews of Persia fasted and prayed that they be spared the massacre planned by Haman; and Shiva Asar b'Tammuz (17th of Tammuz), which marks the day when the Babylonian army made the first breach in the wall of Jerusalem in 586 B.C.

Tu b' Shvat (15th of Shvat) is the Jewish Arbor Day, also called the New Year of Trees. Lag b' Omer (33d day in the counting of the Omer between Passover and Shavuot) is called the scholars festival.

Yom HaShoa (27th of Nisan) is Holocaust Day. Yom HaAtzmaut (5th of Iyar) is Israel Independence Day. Yom Yerushalayim (28th of Iyar) marks the anniversary of the unification of Jerusalem during the Six-Day War on June 7, 1967 (see also HEBREW CALENDAR).                    L.K.

## JEWISH THEOLOGY (MODERN). See JUDAISM, MODERN THOUGHT OF.

## JEZEBEL.
(1) Queen of Israel. The daughter of Ethbaal, priest-king of Tyre and Sidon. She married AHAB about 880 B.C. to cement the alliance which Omni, Ahab's father, proposed to offset the hostility of Damascus. Her prenuptial agreement allowed her to continue to worship Baal (I Kings 16:31). She was a particular devotee of Melqart, the Tyrian Baal. During the time she and Ahab were full rulers (about 874–853 B.C.), her retinue included 450 of his prophets and 400 prophets of the goddess Asherah (I Kings 18:19). This led to the confrontation at Mt. Carmel with the prophet Elijah in which her priests were slaughtered (I Kings 18:17-40). This did nothing to diminish her religious zeal (I Kings 19:2).

It was her concept of the monachy that alienated the people, since it was at variance with the Hebrew concept of a religious covenant between God, the king, and the people. Her part in the seizing of Naboth's vineyard led to the downfall of Ahab and his house (I Kings 21), though she continued in power for ten years as queen mother of Ahaziah and Joram. When Jehu killed Joram, she attired herself regally and awaited her death with dignity (II Kings 9:30-37).

(2) The name given to the prophet of Thyratira (Rev. 2:20), who was advocating idolatry. Though the name has become an epithet for sexual laxity, it is doubtful if either woman was sexually immoral since biblical writers often used the metaphor of "adultery" for idolatry. Both women were simply adherents of a religion different from that of the men writing about them.                    N.H.

## JEZREEL.
A city in Issachar and the valley or plain where it stood (Josh. 19:18; Hos. 1:5). The east end of what is also called the Plain of Esdraelon, it formed an ancient trade route between the Jordan valley and the coastal plain. Mt. Carmel and Mt. Gilboa were to

Courtesy of the Israel Government Tourist Office, Houston, Texas

*The valley of Jezreel, with Mount Gilboa in the background*

the south and Mt. Tabor to the north. The Israelites assembled at the fountain in the city of Jezreel before facing the Philistines at Gilboa (I Sam. 29:1). It was the location of Naboth's vineyard (I Kings 21:1). The city is identified with the modern Zer'in, about fifty-five miles north of Jerusalem. N.H.

**JIHAD.** In ISLAM, the struggle for righteousness and the spread of the faith. The struggle can be against personal ungodliness or against the enemies of Islam. In the latter case jihad can mean a "holy war," waged with the military means available in order to defeat and subjugate the enemies of the faith. Those who are slain in a holy war are martyrs, assured of salvation in heaven (JANNA).

While it was always advantageous for defeated peoples to become Muslims, conversions were not forced, and significant minorities of Jews, Christians, and others have always existed in the Islamic world. K.C.

**JIMÉNEZ DE CISNEROS, FRANCISCO, CARDINAL** (1436–1517). Roman Catholic Spanish cardinal, humanist scholar, grand inquisitor, defender of orthodoxy. A Castilian native, Jiménez studied at Alcalá, Salamanca, and Rome. Returning to Spain in 1465, he encountered opposition and was briefly imprisoned. After serving in Siguenza as vicar general under Cardinal Mendoza, he retreated to a Franciscan convent in Toledo. His extreme asceticism attracted notice, and he withdrew to a remote monastery to be a hermit. In 1492 he reluctantly became confessor to Queen Isabella, who maneuvered his appointment as Provincial of the Franciscans in 1494. Despite opposition he drastically reformed the Franciscan Conventuals, using force and moral severity. He became archbishop of Toledo and high chancellor of Castile (1495), and in 1507 was made a cardinal and appointed grand inquisitor (1507–17). Subsequently he was heavily involved in politics and religion. As grand inquisitor he executed over 2,500 victims in efforts to purify the church and promote orthodoxy. During his last two years he ruled Castile as regent for Charles V. A humanist scholar, Jiménez promoted education, established the University of Alcalá (1500), and issued his Complutesian Polyglot Bible (1522) in original languages. His repressive measures helped prevent a full Renaissance and Reformation in Spain. C.M.

**JIVA.** From the Sanskrit word meaning literally "life, life-principle." In philosophical HINDUISM and JAINISM, Jiva refers to the mental/spiritual nature of the separate individual self. Hindu VEDANTA thought speaks of the Jiva or "ego self" as what a person regards himself to be when in a state of AVIDYA, ignorance, concerning the ATMAN or true self, which is one with BRAHMAN, unqualified Reality. In actuality the Jiva is atman, but regards itself as something finite and separate, and experiences several states of consciousness. In Jainism, Jivas are the souls that animate the universe; ordinarily, they are trapped in matter by KARMA, but upon liberation as *mukta-jiva* they enjoy their full potential for consciousness and bliss. R.E.

**JNANA MARGA.** *See* VIDYA.

**JOAB.** A Hebrew name meaning "Yahweh is father." (1) Son of Zeruiah, DAVID's sister, brother to Abishai and Asahel (II Sam. 2:18), and commander of David's army (8:16). Joab strengthened David's position following Saul's death. In a war game staged beside the pool of Gibeon (2:12-17), Joab's forces triumphed over Abner's, who were serving Ish-baal, Saul's son, whom Abner had installed as monarch over a refugee government in TransJordan. The fleeing Abner was pursued by Asahel, who ignored Abner's warning to desist. Suddenly Abner speared him to death. Though Joab and Abishai continued the pursuit, Abner's pleading and the reassembly of his soldiers influenced them to withdraw. Joab buried his brother and returned to Hebron.

After Abner's rift with Ish-baal, he made overtures with David. When the absent Joab learned how well Abner had been received at Hebron, he arranged a private audience with Abner. Joab avenged his brother's death by killing Abner, which ensured that Abner would never supplant him as commander of Judah's army (II Sam. 3:27).

Joab contributed significantly to David's conquests. He starred in David's capture of Jerusalem and was entrusted with its repair (I Chr. 11:5-8). Manifesting excessive cruelty, Joab was active in David's campaign against Edom (II Sam. 8:13-14; I Kings 11:15). He triumphed against Syrian (Aramean) forces who assisted the Ammonites in their campaign against Israel (II Sam. 10:6-14). After capturing Rabbah, the Ammonite capital, he magnanimously invited David to leave Jerusalem and wield the final blow so that credit for the triumph would be his (12:26-28).

In David's dealing with his obstinate son, Absalom, Joab acted decisively. Employing a wise woman from Tekoa, Joab orchestrated Absalom's return to Jerusalem and uneasy reconciliation with his father (II Sam. 14:1-3, 23, 31-33). During Absalom's rebellion, Joab supervised a third of David's troops (18:2). Defying David's orders, Joab slew Absalom and left him hanging by his hair from an oak

(18:5, 9-15). When he judged that David had grieved long enough, Joab forcefully jolted the king back to the realities of statecraft (19:4-8). His rash behavior, however, was not ignored. David appointed Amasa, leader of Absalom's rebel forces, to replace Joab as army commander. When Amasa proved ineffective in dealing with Sheba's rebellion against David, Joab slew Amasa, reclaimed his position, and quelled the rebellion (20:1-22).

Joab also served David by conducting a census of which he did not approve (II Sam. 24:1-9) and cooperating with the king's stratagem, which wrought the murder of Uriah, Bathsheba's first husband (11:14-24). For having supported Adonijah in the dispute over throne succession during David's last days, Joab incurred Solomon's wrath. The new king readily complied with David's deathbed orders to avenge Joab's murder of Abner and Amasa. Though Joab sought sanctuary at the altar, he was slain there by Benaiah, who inherited his position (I Kings 2:5-6, 28-35).

(2) Son of Seraiah and descendant of Kenaz, within the tribe of Judah (I Chr. 4:13-14).

(3) The founder of a family, some of whose children joined Zerubbabel in the return from Babylonian exile (Ezra 2:6; 8:9; Neh. 7:11).          J.K.K.

**JOACHIM OF FIORE** (about 1132–1202). Italian mystic, monastic biblical scholar, famed for his apocalyptic Age of the Spirit to begin in 1260. Born in Cosenz, Italy, he became a Cistercian monk after visiting Palestine and was elected abbot in 1177. After about eleven years, he withdrew to Fiore, founded his own monastery of San Giovanni, and provided direction for about thirty more. Intensely ascetic and loyal to the church, he devoted himself to biblical studies. He divided history into three ages: that of the Father governed by OT laws, the Son governed by NT grace, and the Spirit governed by the "eternal gospel," with humanity living in spiritual freedom. Ushered in by monastics, the Age of the Spirit would bring the conversion of Jews and Gentiles, union of the Greek and Roman churches, overthrow of Antichrist, and inauguration of the Sabbath of God. Many in the Middle Ages, especially Franciscans, welcomed his biblically based ideas. His writings were submitted posthumously to the papacy for approval and condemned by the Lateran Council (1215) and the Council of Arles (1263). The papacy could not accept Joachim's implied censure and displacemnt of the OT and NT by the "eternal gospel."          C.M.

**JOAN OF ARC** (about 1412–31). Soldier, martyr, and saint, Joan of Arc was born in Domremy-la-Pucelle near Lorraine. From age thirteen she heard voices and saw visions, particularly of MICHAEL the archangel and saints CATHERINE OF SIENA and Margaret. The French crown was in dispute between the dauphin Charles, alleged son of Charles VI, and

the English King Henry VI, whose armies occupied most of northern France. In 1428 the British put Orleans, key city of the Loire Valley, under siege. Joan met Charles at Chinon and convinced him he was the rightful heir. She told him of her voices' instructions to attack Orleans and to help him be crowned officially at Rheims, the sacred seat of French kings now under British rule.

Armed and dressed as a knight, she led a force into Orleans, attacked the besiegers, and liberated the city in May 1429. It was the turning point of the Hundred Years' War. She then urged Charles to Rheims and prophesied his victory at Patay on June 17, 1429. When her mission was accomplished, Joan had wished to return home, but Charles urged her to stay. His inertia involved her in petty warfare, and she was captured at Compiègne on May 23, 1430. Though she answered her interrogators with skill and sincerity, she was condemned for heresy and burned at the stake May 30, 1431. Her remains were thrown in the Seine River. After Charles VII's ultimate victory, a French court annulled the verdict in 1456. She was canonized by Pope Benedict XV on May 16, 1920. Her feast day is May 30.          N.H.

**JOASH.** In Hebrew, Jo'ash, a shortened form of Jehoash, meaning "Yahweh has given" or "Yahweh has come to help." Joash is the name of eight people in the OT, from Judges to II Chronicles.

The first Joash was Gideon's father (Judg. 6:11). who put up an altar to Baal (vv. 24-25). The second Joash was one of King Ahab's sons in Samaria, to whom his father sent the prophet Micaiah for imprisonment (I Kings 22:26; II Chr. 18:25 ff.)

The third was a Judean of the Shelah family (I Chr. 4:22). The fourth was a supporter of David in Ziklag (I Chr. 12:3). The fifth and sixth men named Joash were kings, one of Israel and one of Judah, who actually ruled at the same time. Number seven was one of the sons of Becher (I Chr. 7:8), and number eight was a steward in David's service (I Chr. 27:28).

Joash, son of Ahaziah, was the eighth king of Judah, ruling in the ninth century B.C., for about forty years (II Kings 11; 12; II Chr. 22:11; 24:1). Joash was saved from murder by his aunt, the wife of the high priest Jehoiada. He was hidden in the Temple for six years and at the age of seven was presented to Jerusalem's leaders by Jehoiada. A covenant of loyalty was made, and the usurper, Athaliah, was slain. The priest guided the king's career (II Chr. 24), and until Jehoiada's death, Joash was declared a good king, although he did not fully root out Baal worship (II Kings 12). Once the priest died, Joash turned for the worst (II Chr. 24). He was finally murdered and denied burial in the royal tombs.

Joash, the twelfth king of Israel, followed Jehoahaz (II Kings 13). While an apostate, because of his encouragement of the worship of the golden bull in Samaria, he was spoken of favorably because he recovered lands lost to Syria. He also showed respect for Elisha (II Kings 13:14) and told the fable of the cedar and the thistle (II Kings 14:9-10; II Chr. 25:18-19), as an attempt to discourage King Amaziah of Jerusalem from attacking Israel. When that didn't work, he attacked Amaziah, captured him, pushed on to Jerusalem and broke down 540 feet of its wall. He looted the Temple and took treasure and hostages home to Samaria. He was succeeded by Jeroboam II (II Kings 14:16).　　　　　J.C.

JOB, BOOK OF. One of the OT "The Writings" (books of wisdom), that addresses the perennial problem of absurd and excessive human suffering (see EVIL). The narrative medium employed is an old folktale about an extraordinarily righteous foreigner named Job, who enters into dialogue with four friends regarding his fate. The book ends without a clear-cut solution; however, following a confession of repentance and renewal Job experiences restoration of his fortunes.

*The Composition of the Book.* It is quite easy to analyze the structure of the book of Job into four distinct parts.

(a) *Prologue and epilogue (chaps. 1–2; 42:7-17).* In a folktale that can be paralleled in various ways by similar tales of righteous sufferers both in ancient Egypt and in Mesopotamia, the original tale of Job presents the hero of the story as so selfless that he would "rise early in the morning and offer burnt offerings" for his sons in case they had sinned in their hearts (1:5). According to the tale, Satan (who is not yet the devil, but simply that member of the heavenly court whose task it is to probe and test those humans whose hearts might conspire to do evil), suggests that no one serve God disinterestedly, not even righteous Job. God permits Satan to put Job to the test by means of a series of incredible torments, culminating in the loss of his family and fortune, and including personal suffering in the form of disease and rejection by the community, including his wife. This is the story of the patient Job (James 5:11), whose teaching has become proverbial: "The Lord gave, and the Lord has taken away; blessed be the name of the Lord" (1:21). In the epilogue Job receives double indemnity for all of his losses, and vindication before the eyes of the community because of his steadfast faithfulness.

(b) *The dialogues (chaps. 3–31).* At some point in the evolution of the story of Job, an Israelite theologian split the ancient folktale in two and inserted three lengthy cycles of dialogues between Job and his friends Eliphaz the Temanite, Bildad the Shuhite, and Zophar the Naamathite. Included in this section as well is the lovely soliloquy on wisdom, the subject of chapter 28, which culminates in a teaching that in many ways is the slogan of the wisdom writers of Israel: "Behold, the fear of the Lord, that is wisdom; and to depart from evil is understanding" (28:28). In the dialogues, the friends confront Job relentlessly with what may have been the typical religious

position of the day regarding suffering. Suffering must be regarded as a punishment for some hidden sins, for to regard it in any other way would be to make God unjust. Certainly Job's suffering does have the outer and public appearance of punishment, for he had experienced many of the very elements of the curse pronounced in Deuteronomy 28:15-32 against those who disobey the covenant of God. However, Job staunchly resists the suggestion that his suffering is a punishment and protests his innocence time and again (compare 31:16-23). Eliphaz is, of course, correct in saying, "Can a man be pure before his Maker? Even in his servants he puts no trust, and his angels he charges with error; how much more those who dwell in houses of clay, whose foundation is in the dust, who are crushed before the moth" (4:17-19). Nevertheless, it is a universal premise that the punishment should fit the crime, and Job has committed no crime warranting such treatment.

Throughout the dialogues, Job presses a legal claim against God and seeks to bring him into court: "Behold, I have prepared my case; I know that I shall be vindicated. Who is there that will contend with me? For then I would be silent and die . . . how many are my iniquities and my sins? Make me know my transgression and my sin" (13:18-23). In this connection Job calls for a "witness" (9:33-35), also termed a "redeemer." The most famous of these calls is that which in older translations appeared to suggest the possibility of immortal life: "For I know that my Redeemer lives, and at last he will stand upon the earth; and after my skin has been thus destroyed, then from my flesh I shall see God, whom I shall see on my side, and my eyes shall behold, and not another" (19:25-27).

In the long series of dialogues, the friends also raise the idea that God inflicts suffering for pedagogical purposes: "Behold, happy is the man whom God reproves; therefore despise not the chastening of the Almighty. For he wounds, but he binds up; he smites, but his hands heal" (5:17-18). Like all of the other proposals for making sense of absurd evil, however, this one too is rejected by the writer, speaking through Job.

(c) *The Elihu speeches (chaps. 32–37).* A fourth friend, mentioned nowhere else in the book, appears in this section to reiterate much of the discussion of the previous speakers. Considered by some scholars to be of little theological and literary worth, and late in date, the Elihu cycle nonetheless concludes with the important observation that one cannot know the transcendent God, but only as God turns toward humans with the relational qualities of justice, power, and righteousness (37:22-24). Even if it is a later insertion, this teaching wonderfully prepares the way for God's own speeches, which follow immediately.

(d) *The Yahweh speeches (38:1–42:6).* At last Yahweh answers Job out of the whirlwind. In spite of Elihu's strictures against trying to understand the transcendent Deity, God speaks to Job about the role of Creator. God dazzles Job with visions of the great cosmic order and suggests that every aspect of the world is beloved to Yahweh. God even dares to touch upon the ostrich (39:13-18), Behemoth, the hippopotamus (40:15-24), and Leviathan, the crocodile (41:1-34) —ungainly creatures, positive aberrations in the created order, and yet beloved of God. In the aftermath of this speech, Job makes his famous confession: "I had heard of thee by the hearing of the ear, but now my eye sees thee; therefore I despise myself, and repent in dust and ashes" (42:5-6).

*A Theological Summary of the Book of Job.* Although the book ends without offering a clear account of why Job suffered and what role God had in that suffering, at least the answers of the traditional religion are confounded. God can affect events, and yet profound evil does exist in the world. Such evil is not punishment sent from God, in spite of its appearance. Suffering is neither meaningless, nor is it a chastening unto perfection, nor is it an avenue to heavenly reward. Although God's ways are unfathomable, God also speaks out of the whirlwind. In the midst of such paradoxes, the meaning of the book of Job emerges in three parts. (a) Job is forced by a process of radicalization through sharp painful outer pressure and hard inner intellectual activity to recognize his own creaturehood and mortality. (b) He is also forced to recognize the ultimate inaccessibility of the transcendent God whose perfect attributes of justice, power, and omnipresence must be affirmed, but cannot be used to explain the suffering that Job has experienced. In no way can God's absolute justice ever be made to account for Job's situation on the dunghill. (c) Job also comes to see that God's presence with people is real: God is accessible, God is immanent. When people confess God's power and trust in God as one who will be alongside them in their struggle to overcome the suffering they face, then a victory can be obtained. That surely is the key to the words with which the book of Job culminates: "I had heard of thee by the hearing of the ear"—I had my doctrine in order, and could say the right things about God's absolute attributes. "But now my eye sees thee"—and I know that you are with me and I am yours. Thus is the concept of God in the OT enriched with the motifs of presence, intimacy, and the shared experience of suffering, which are so richly dramatized by the book of Job.                     W.S.T.

**JOCHEBED** ("Yahweh is glory"). Although her name is not in the account of Moses' birth (Exodus 2), she was the mother of Moses, Aaron, and Miriam (Exod. 6:20; Num. 26:59). Their father was Amram. Jochebed was sister to his father Kohath (Exod. 6:18, 20), and thus a daughter of Levi (Num. 26:59).
                                              N.H.

**JOEL**. Hebrew for "Yahweh is God." A prophet who was active in Jerusalem about 400 B.C. Joel's message consisted in the affirmation that God will punish those who commit evil and will vindicate Israel. Apocalyptic elements within the book of Joel in the OT profoundly affected both Jewish and Christian authors, including some writers of the NT.

Nothing is known about Joel, the son of Petheul, who is mentioned in 1:1. The name was somewhat common among Hebrews of the OT period, but it is not possible to connect the prophet with any other person of the same name who is mentioned in the OT. Joel worked in Jerusalem in the period following the Exile (3:2). The Temple (1:14) and the walls of the city (2:9) had been rebuilt, and the priests were a prominent group within the community (1:13).

The prophet was a very literate person, not only in the sense that he knew and used previous prophetic writings, but also in that his powers of language were especially keen. With respect to his references to previous prophetic literature, (1) his concept of the DAY OF THE LORD (2:1) draws upon a prophetic tradition that goes as far back as the time of Amos (Amos 5:18); (2) at one point (2:32) Joel acknowledges that he is quoting from another prophet (Obadiah 17); (3) the statement that is found in both Isaiah 2:4 and Micah 4:3 is reproduced by Joel (3:10), but its meaning is inverted so that what was a cry for peace has become a promise of war.

Joel's literary skills may also be seen in the graphic manner in which he describes the locust plague (2:3-11) and the drought (1:15-20). Swarms of hungry insects darken the sky and lay waste to the countryside, while the drought has caused the fields to burn and watering places to become dry so that both human being and beast are in anguish. Just as remarkable is the manner in which the prophet uses this natural disaster as a conceptual springboard by which he moves into his various images of the coming Day of Yahweh.

Two divisions may be identified within the book of Joel: oracles concerning the locust plague and the drought (1:1–2:27) and oracles concerning the Day of Yahweh (2:28–3:21).

Some scholars have suggested that the locust plague and the drought may be only symbolic in nature, but the vividness of their description makes that unlikely. The prophet and his compatriots probably experienced genuine disasters of this type, and Joel understood these as signs of the Lord's displeasure. His initial response is to call the people to repentance for the sin that has roused God's anger (1:14). He promises that, when the people have repented, the Lord will respond graciously. The locusts will be driven away (2:20), and there will be rain to restore the health of the land. Joel's concern, however, is not limited to these natural disasters, for he sees them as symbols of a deeper significance, the coming of the Day of the Lord. It may be that the hordes of locusts that covered the sky and blotted out the sun, moon, and stars (2:10) caused the prophet to reflect upon the "day of darkness" when the Lord would judge the earth (2:1-2).

In the second section of the book, 2:28–3:21 (in the Hebrew text this constitutes chaps. 3 and 4), the prophet's interest in the Day of the Lord is paramount. The day is described in frightening terms: blood, fire, smoke, and darkness (2:30-31). But there will be two aspects to this day, the first of which is that it will be a time for an unprecedented outpouring of God's grace. The prophetic spirit will be rekindled, as in days of old (2:28-29), and those Jews who call upon the Lord will be saved in Jerusalem (2:32–3:1). The Lord will reign there (3:16), while foreigners who have inflicted great suffering upon God's people will be excluded from the Holy City (3:17). The other aspect of the Day of the Lord will be that of terrible judgment. The nations that have oppressed God's people will be gathered into the valley of Jehoshaphat (3:2), and there will be a final conflict in which the Lord confronts those nations and their evil (3:9-15). They will be destroyed, while faithful Jews will be gathered into a Jerusalem where the Lord reigns (3:19-21).

In addition to its anticipation of a final Judgment Day, the book of Joel influenced in other ways the writers of the NT, some of whom saw the Pentecost experience (Acts 2, see especially vv. 17-21) as the fulfillment of Joel's prophecy concerning the outpouring of God's spirit.                                        J.D.N.

**JOHN, APOSTLE.** One of the Twelve whom Jesus called to follow him and who became a central figure in the later apostolic church. His call is recorded in all the Gospels, with the Fourth Gospel (John 1:35-42) adding the detail that he was a disciple of John the Baptist at the first. This information is known only by inference, as John does not name himself. He is elsewhere identified as Zebedee, and brother of James, with his mother's name, Salome, known again by inference (Mark 16:1; Matt. 27:56). He may even have been related to Jesus as cousin, if Salome was a sister of Mary, Jesus' mother (John 19:25).

His trade was fishing (Mark 1:19-20), which he shared along with his brother. The family home was at Capernaum on the banks of Lake Galilee (Matt. 4:21, 22; Mark 1:19, 20; Luke 5:10), and the fishing trade was evidently prosperous, since the family took on hired help (Mark 1:20). At this point in the Gospel story they became disciples of Jesus. It may be gauged from the nickname "Boanerges" ("sons of thunder" or "wrath," Mark 3:17) that their temperament was energetic, and Luke 9:51-56 (RSV marg.) suggests that they were quick-tempered and aggressive. They were certainly ambitious (Mark 10:35, 41). John was one of the favored three companions of Jesus (Mark 5:37; 9:2; 14:33). He was also one of those disciples who questioned Jesus about the fall of Jerusalem (Mark 13:3, 4). Although he is not mentioned as such in the Fourth Gospel, his family name is referred to in

21:2, which may be an appendix to the GOSPEL OF JOHN.

In the Acts of the Apostles, John lives in the shadow of Peter (4:13; 5:33, 40; 8:14), and Paul mentions him only incidentally (Gal. 2:9). Later tradition links him with an exile on Patmos (Rev. 1:9) and with the Ephesian church where the Fourth Gospel was published. There is a well-attested notion (found in Eusebius, the church historian) that at the beginning of the Jewish war in Palestine in A.D. 66, John migrated to Asia Minor and took up residence with Mary, the Lord's mother, at Ephesus (John 19:26, 27). He became a leader of the church in that city, and there he died in ripe old age, having composed the Fourth Gospel. He may well be referred to obliquely in that Gospel (21:20-24) as the disciple whom Jesus loved. But the "elder," also called John, is the person spoken of in the Epistles of JOHN (II John 1; III John 1), and he was evidently a different person from John the apostle, though some scholars dispute this.

A separate source of tradition outside the NT and the orthodox Christian writers of the first few centuries offers another portrait of John. A Gnostic document bears the title the *Acts of John,* dated in the mid-second century. It is full of miracles and speeches linked with John. Its understanding of Jesus' person is docetic, that is, it denies his full humanity. It is interesting that the Gnostic writers of the second century, such as Ptolemaus and Heracleon, were drawn to John and found in his Gospel much material that served their purpose. These items have to do with the teaching on Jesus' divine origin, his earthly glory, and his apparent indifference to suffering. The Nag Hammadi library contains books *(Apocryphon* [Secret Book] *of John,* the *Gospel of Philip),* which also hold John in high esteem.

The Orthodox writers tried to counter this tendency by associating John with the beloved disciple who "leaned close to Jesus' breast" at the supper (John 3:23; 21:20). Polycarp, bishop of Smyrna, is said to have heard the gospel from John's own lips, according to Irenaeus. The Orthodox tradition then started to grow with the claim of Polycrates, bishop of Ephesus (A.D. 189–98), that John was both a priest and a martyr, a double distinction that history does not endorse. Eusebius reports, and apparently accepts, this embellishment, probably because he is opposing heretical endeavors that wanted to turn John into a proto-Gnostic.
                                                                                            R.M.

**JOHN, EPISTLES OF.** The three Epistles of John range in size from about six pages to less than a page. The first is not a letter but a tract on doctrinal and moral issues. The other two are apparently actual letters, offering advice, encouragement, and warning. All three are anonymous, but resemble each other—and the GOSPEL OF JOHN—in style and vocabulary. For example, the term "Paraclete" ("counselor" or "helper") is found in the NT only in John 14:16; 15:26; 16:7, and in I John 2:1. The emphasis on love and the centrality of the love command are shared by the Gospel and the Epistles of John. One can speak of a Johannine community, or group of communities, as that segment of Christianity through and for whom these writings were produced.

At least two major shifts are evident from the time of the Gospel to that of the letters, however. The Gospel's portrayal of Jesus as one who is preexistent and one with the Father (John 1:1, 14; 10:30), but who also hungers, thirsts, and suffers, has created a problem. Now members of the group affirm his unity with God, but see no need for his earthly life and death. Against this position, I John affirms the tangible reality of the Jesus whom his followers saw, heard, and handled (I John 1:1). And he denounces as a "deceiver" and an "antichrist" (II John 7; I John 4:1-2) anyone who refuses to acknowledge his full humanity and the benefits of his death. The second new factor in the letters is the insistence on excluding from the fellowship of the group anyone whose standards of faith and morality do not measure up to those laid down by "the elder." Rather than primary conflict with the Jews about Jesus' messiahship, as in the Gospel (John 9:22), former members are now separated from the group because of their faulty views of Jesus as the Christ (I John 2:18-23; II John 7). Nevertheless Christians are to be bound together in mutual love and support (I John 3:11-24; II John 5), and are to offer hospitality to those of similar persuasion (III John 5-8).                                    H.K.

## JOHN, GOSPEL OF. 

*Introduction.* This account of the ministry of Jesus stands as one of the Four Gospels accepted as canonical, but it is clear, even from a cursory glance, that this Gospel is in a class by itself and unlike the Synoptic Gospels. To be sure, both sets of Gospels describe in general outline the course of Jesus' earthly life, but they diverge also in a remarkable way. John has consciously prefaced his Gospel with a lengthy prologue (1:1-18) tracing back the heritage of Jesus Christ not to David, Abraham, or Adam, but to his life in God in eternity. His title of Jesus as LOGOS (the Word) is unique, though it is later picked up in the EPISTLES OF JOHN. Also remarkable is the clear ascription of Deity to the incarnate Christ in titles such as "I am" (8:58) and "my Lord and my God" (20:28).

At a lower level, John's narrative stands apart from the other Gospels: he remarks that Jesus visited Jerusalem five times (2:13; 5:1; 7:10; 10:22-23; 12:12) over against a single visit in Mark (11:1 ff.). The Temple is cleansed at the outset of Jesus' ministry (2:13 ff.), not at the close as in Mark 11:15-19. There is no Last Supper with teaching on "This is my body and blood" in John; instead he has a Eucharistic discourse set in the synagogue at Capernaum (6:25-59). Then, the date of the Crucifixion is different. In the Synoptics, Jesus died after Passover had commenced (Mark 14:12); in John his death coincided in time with the sacrifice of the Passover lambs in the Temple (John 18:28; 19:30 ff.). The last piece of evidence puts us on the track of John's purpose. He is less interested in strict historical detail than in drawing out the theological significance of the historical events, for it is part of his plan to depict Jesus as the lamb of God (1:29). Events that have created historical difficulties (for example, the changing of water into wine, 2:1-10, and the raising of Lazarus, 11:1-53, which are both absent from the Synoptics) may well be seen as symbolic in the evangelist's intention, even if they do rest on some historical reminiscence. Clearly John is looking back on the life of Jesus through the prism of the Resurrection and exaltation of his Lord and casting back his heavenly glory onto the canvas of what the evangelist sees and describes. (See 2:21-22; 7:39; 11:51, 52; 12:16 for data to support this conclusion, which is really the key to an understanding of this "spiritual Gospel," as Clement of Alexandria rightly called it).

*Purpose.* No one is absolutely sure why John wrote this Gospel—except for the one clue he has left us in 20:31: "These are written that you may believe that Jesus is the Christ, the Son of God, and that believing you may have life in his name." Strictly speaking, the verse as quoted refers to the witness of selected "signs" that Jesus performed throughout his ministry, beginning with 2:10. C. H. Dodd and R. T. Fortna have helpfully postulated a "Book of Signs" as the first draft of the Gospel that the evangelist had enriched, and we may infer from 20:30 that he had other data on which he might have drawn. The simplest view is to see John as writing to convince his fellow Jews that Jesus was the true Messiah of Israel and so to encourage them to accept him as such; he therefore appealed to OT prophecy as fulfilled in Jesus. At the same time, John passed a negative judgment on Abraham (8:48-59) and Moses (1:17), whose time as religious authorities had now been superseded (5:45-47). By his "signs" (John's word for Jesus' miracles), he is shown to be the rightful Messiah and the true hope of Israel's expectation.

At the opposite end of the spectrum others, such as Bultmann, have argued that John's Gospel has to be read on its contemporary background, which is said to be the Hellenistic world of GNOSTICISM, that is, an amalgam of various religious and philosophical movements in the Greco-Roman world of the first century, all seeking to meet the human quest for unity with the Divine and to explain life's mysteries. Hence Jesus is seen as universal "reason" *(logos)*, a Stoic term, enlightening the world (1:9), and as "the truth" (14:6), replacing all that is shadowy and unreal. The contrast between the two worlds—one above (heaven), the other below (earth)—is basic to the Gnostic world view and plays a significant role in the Fourth Gospel (8:23). One other suggestion that

Jesus in this Gospel moves through history as a Greek hero without real contact with earthly realities—a tenet in docetism (a belief that denied Christ's full humanity)—has been made, but not convincingly. See, on the contrary, the evidence in 1:14; 11:25; 12:20-36, as well as the fact that Jesus died a true death, a point John wants to establish (19:31-37).

A mediating view that has much to recommend it sees John as using the material he has drawn from a Palestinian tradition of Jesus' conflict with the Jewish leaders of his day in order to defend the gospel in a Jewish-Hellenistic society in Asia Minor. We should therefore see the Johannine Gospel as having two editions: an earlier statement of Jesus' life in Galilee and Jerusalem, in debate with the Jewish hierarchy, his rejection in Jerusalem, his teaching to the Twelve, leading to his death and resurrection; and a final redaction as the material is edited and employed to assist the church in Ephesus in its dialogue with the Jewish-Hellenistic synagogues of the Roman province of Asia. In this view we can explain why the form of the Gospel is cast as a trial narrative, with witnesses (John the Baptist, Moses, Jesus' works, the disciples, the various men and women on the scene in chaps. 3, 4, 5, 11) for the defense called to bear witness. The final version was written as a Gospel and so made avalable to John's church in Asia.

*Author and Date.* If there is plausibility in the third option (above), we can also explain the ambiguous church tradition that (a) associated this Gospel with John the apostle and located his final residence at Ephesus; (b) knew of another person called "John the elder," who was also linked with the apostles but was not one of them. He too was located at Ephesus. So it becomes feasible to see the first draft of the Gospel as emanating from an eyewitness source—JOHN THE APOSTLE—but subsequently taken over, edited, and published by a church leader named "the elder," whose similar influence in the community at Ephesus is seen in 21:24-25 as well as in those key places where Jesus or the narrator speaks in the first person plural (1:14, 16; 3:11; 4:22; 9:4). The date for the final work is around A.D. 90-100, and the place of publication is almost certainly Ephesus.

*Theology.* This Gospel has always had a treasured place in Christian thought, devotion, and esteem. Its main contribution is Christological, since we are reading in John the distillation of NT teaching on the person and achievement of Jesus Christ after some decades have elapsed since the Incarnation, death, and glorification of the church's Lord. Two key terms are *Logos* (word) and *parakletos* (helper, advocate, comforter). *Logos* means that the revelation of God is expressed in the coming to this world of one who was with God and existed as God in eternity (1:1-18). "Paraclete" (14:15-17, 26; 15:26-27; 16:7-11, 13-14) is used of the Holy Spirit who, sent by the Father, is Jesus' *alter ego* after his leaving the disciples. The paraclete abides with the church to ensure Christ's unseen, yet real, presence, and to evoke

Christ's reality through his words (6:63; 14:26) and works, notably in the sacraments (6:48-51, 53-58; 13:10).        R.M.

**JOHN OF DAMASCUS** (about 675–749). Authoritative Greek Orthodox theologian, defender of images, early advocate of the Virgin Mary's sinlessness and assumption into heaven. Born in Damascus, he lived under Moslem rule and succeeded his father in financial services for the caliph of Damascus. Sometime between 715 and 730 he joined the Monastery of St. Sabas near Jerusalem. He was ordained and under Moslem protection wrote against Byzantine Emperor Leo III's edict in 725 condemning icons and images in worship and against the subsequent destruction of images by Leo III and his son Constantine V.

His greatest theological work, *Source of Knowledge,* comprehensively synthesized six hundred years of Greek theology. Part I dealt with Aristotle's philosophical terms, in preparation for theology. Part II identified over one hundred heresies and touched on iconoclasts. Part III presented GREEK ORTHODOX faith—Trinity, Christology, hypostatic union of God and man in Jesus, Mariology, images, Resurrection, etc. He disclaimed originality and subordinated reason to faith, the state to the church, and human learning to Scripture. He praised images, saying God used the visible incarnation to reveal the invisible Divine, but declared images of saints must not be worshiped. This work became standard for the Greek Church. His *Sacred Parallels* was a collection of patristic passages on vices and virtues. In his final years John preached throughout Syria against iconoclasts. His poetry influenced Greek liturgy, and two hymns survive: "Come, ye faithful, raise the strain," and "Day of Resurrection." Both Rome and Constantinople canonized him.

       C.M.

**JOHN OF THE CROSS** (1542–91). Spanish mystic, and founder of Discalced Carmelites, part of the CATHOLIC REFORMATION. Of poor parentage, he was schooled by the Jesuits, became a Carmelite monk in 1563, and studied at Salamanca from 1564 to 1568. Ordained in 1567, he grew increasingly dissatisfied with lax monastic discipline and soon joined in TERESA OF AVILA's monastic reforms. He assisted Teresa in establishing fourteen Discalced Carmelite branches for men, who stressed ascetic exercises, self-mortification, and mystical ecstasies. John was master of the Discalced Carmelite College at Alcala (1571–72). He aroused enmity there and was imprisoned by unreformed Carmelites in 1577. Nine months later he escaped. Amid bitterness, the Discalced Carmelites and the unreformed separated. Later John established a college at Breza and was rector from 1579 to 1582. He was prior at Granada and later at Segovia, but rival factions of Discalced Carmelites forced him from office. Finally he was banished to remote Andalusia in 1591, where he died.

His devotional, mystical masterpiece, *Dark Night of the Soul,* appeared about 1587. It sought to guide seekers through purging stages of darkness to union with God. Sensual darkness comes from relinquishing all desires for earthly goods, spiritual darkness from relinquishing all spiritual desires, even the desire to be with God. Both stages are painful preludes to complete surrender in faith to God's love and grace. This brings triumph over the dark nights of the soul and union with the Divine. His commentaries on his poetry provide a rare record of the mystical process.

C.M.

**JOHN PAUL I, POPE.** Albino Luciani (1912–78), pope, September 3-28, 1978. The son of an Italian socialist bricklayer, he was ordained in 1935, earned a doctorate in theology, taught briefly, and rapidly rose from bishop (1958) to archibishop (1969) to cardinal (1973). He opposed Marxism and in doctrine and discipline was a traditionalist.

C.M.

**JOHN PAUL II, POPE.** Karol Wojtyla (1920–   ), chosen pope in 1978, is the first Polish pope and the first non-Italian pope in 455 years. He is known for his journeys abroad, traditional doctrines, friendly

Courtesy of Religious News Service

*Pope John Paul II*

personality, and concern for human rights and justice. Born in Wadowice, Poland, to working-class parents, Wojtyla attended the University of Krakow, which the Nazis closed in 1939. While working in a quarry and factories, he studied at an underground seminary. Ordained in 1946, he received a doctorate in philosophy at Rome's Angelicum University in 1948. Returning to Poland, he taught at Lublin, published several books, and became auxiliary bishop of Kraków (1958), archbishop (1964), and cardinal (1967). Popular with Polish workers, he demonstrated practical negotiating skills with Communists. By taking the name John Paul as pope, he signaled admiration for three predecessors, but has acted independently. Proficient in six languages, John Paul has demonstrated concern for people and traditional views on doctrine and discipline.

During his first year as pope, John Paul visited the Dominican Republic and Mexico, speaking out against Marxist influences and warning against identifying the church with one political system; in Poland, he said the Mass in Warsaw and Kraków, conferred with Communist leader Edward Gierek, and stopped briefly at Auschwitz. Huge crowds greeted him everywhere. In the fall of that same year, John Paul visited Ireland and the United States, speaking before the United Nations General Assembly in New York, talking with President Jimmy Carter and journeying to Boston, Philadelphia, Des Moines, and Chicago. Also during his first year John Paul issued his first encyclical, *Redemptor Hominis,* in which he criticized both capitalist and Communist materialism and excoriated governments that stifle human freedom and dignity.

In 1980 John Paul journeyed to six African nations, France, thirteen cities in Brazil, and West Germany. In 1981 he was seriously wounded by an assassin's bullets on May 25, in St. Peter's Square. That same year he visited Pakistan, the Philippines, Guam, Japan, and Alaska en route, speaking for fundamental human rights and against nuclear arms. Another encyclical, on God's mercy, said that divine favor already received should motivate social justice; and another, aimed at Poland, said labor unions are indispensable.

In 1982 John Paul again visited West Africa, Portugal, Great Britain, Scotland, Wales, and Argentina. He also received Ronald Reagan and the PLO's Yasir Arafat in Rome.

John Paul marked Luther's five-hundredth anniversary by preaching in a Lutheran church in Rome in December. He also journeyed to Central America and Haiti and returned to Poland for eight days, where he conferred with General Wojciech Jaruzelski and labor's Solidarity leader Lech Walesa. In January 1983 he approved a new canon law code that granted more authority to bishops but curbed the authority of councils.

John Paul stands opposed to a married priesthood, abortion, birth control, polygamy, ordination of women, secular dress for nuns, and clerical involvement in politics, and has censured Swiss theologian Hans Küng and cautioned Dutch theologian Edward Schillebeeckx. The full impact of his pontificate remains yet to be assessed.

C.M.

From *Atlas of the Bible* (Thomas Nelson & Sons Limited)

*Remains of the fortress of Machaerus, where tradition says John the Baptist was imprisoned and suffered death*

**JOHN THE BAPTIST.** The ministry of Jesus began with the mission of John the Baptist for, in the preaching and baptism of John, Jesus received his first impulse to public action. No man exerted a greater influence over Jesus; for him, John was the greatest of the prophets. Yet he was more than a prophet. John's career marked the boundary between the Old Age and the New Age (Matt. 11:7-15; Luke 7:24-30; 16:16; Acts 1:21; 10:36-37).

John was a wonder-child, born to a priestly couple in their old age. For some years before his "manifestation to Israel," John lived "in the wilderness of Judea" (Luke 1:5-25; 2:57-80). Since the discovery of the Dead Sea Scrolls, it has been thought probable that John's wilderness sojourn was not solitary; perhaps he lived for a time in a community of the ESSENES. Josephus, first-century Jewish historian, writes that the Essenes "adopted other men's children" and "molded them according to their principles." All speculation aside, the locale of John's ministry and the residence of these dissident priests were inspired by the same summons of Isaiah: "in the wilderness prepare the way of the Lord" (Isa. 40:3; Mark 1:3). John's eschatological message of imminent judgment closely resembles that held by the Dead Sea sect, but John's rite of baptism differs in meaning from the "purifying waters" of the Essenes.

John's public proclamation demanded "a baptism of repentance for the forgiveness of sins" (Mark 1:4; Luke 3:3). He also "preached, saying, 'After me comes he who is mightier than I, the thong of whose sandals I am not worthy to stoop down and untie. I have baptized you with water; but he will baptize you with the Holy Spirit [and with fire]' " (Mark 1:7-8; compare Matt. 3:11 and Luke 3:16). In the Synoptic Gospels there is a tendency to identify John with (in Jewish eschatology) the Elijah who is to come (Matt. 11:14; 17:10-12; also Mal. 4:5-6). In the Fourth Gospel, John is merely the "voice" of Isaiah 40:3, and John's identity with Elijah or the Messiah is sharply denied (John 1:6-8, 19-22; 3:25-36).

John's preaching was intensely eschatological. He heralded the imminent day of judgment; God's retributive punishment would soon fall upon the apostate within Israel. The merits of the patriarchs would provide no escape and descent from Abraham would afford no advantage. Only sincere repentance would avert "the wrath to come," and this must lead to baptism. Moreover, those who confessed their sins and received John's baptism as a sign of this repentance were commanded to "bear good fruit," following in "the way of righteousness" taught by John. Luke reports that John's preaching aroused the conscience of special groups, tax collectors and soldiers, who were especially susceptible to expropriating goods belonging to others (Luke 3:10-14). All of his disciples were taught the disciplines of prayer and fasting (Luke 5:33; 11:1; Mark 2:19-20).

First-century Jewish sources provide no exact antecedents for or parallels to John's baptism. Cleansing ceremonies, using the waters of purification, are prescribed in the Torah, and the priest-prophet Ezekiel declared that God, at the endtime, will purify the people from their defilement with clean water and give them a new heart and a new spirit (Ezek. 36:22-36). At the time of John, conditions in the land promoted an elaboration of the purity laws. The Pharisees who did not retreat into the wilderness, but lived among the corrupt, attached great importance to ceremonial bathing. The custom of baptizing Gentile converts to Judaism is closer to John's rite, although it cannot be proved that proselyte baptism antedates John. If the practice was current it is possible that John deliberately applied to the "children of Abraham" a rite devised by them to benefit pagans, thus evidencing his conviction that the whole Jewish nation needed to be reconstituted as the people of God. It seems that the form of John's baptism was determined by the nature of his proclamation. Whatever partial parallels existed in Jewish practice, John's imagery was drawn from Jewish apocalyptic eschatology, which represented divine judgment as a stream of fire, sometimes issuing from the throne of God or as the fiery breath of the Messiah (Dan. 7:10-11; II Esd. 13:10-11; II Thess. 2:8; Rev. 8:5; 20:9-15). Repentant individuals were called to enact in advance their acceptance of the eschatological judgment of God. The uniqueness of John's baptism consists in the fact that it dramatized the substance of his eschatological proclamation.

From the perspective of the Gospels, the climax of John's mission was his baptism of Jesus. Given the significance of the rite as a confession of sin, it is not surprising that some early Christians were puzzled by this event. Only Matthew, among the three early Gospels, offers an explanation. In defense of his baptism, Jesus' response to John's hesitation is: "we do well to conform in this way with all that God requires" (Matt. 3:15 NEB). The Son's perfect obedience, and the Father's choice of his "beloved

Son" foretell the significance of Jesus' work (compare John 5:20, 30).

Following Jesus' baptism, John carried his campaign to Samaria. Jesus remained in Judea and conducted a brief baptismal ministry of his own. Some of John's disciples attached themselves to Jesus: was Jesus' withdrawal to Galilee prompted by a wish to avoid potential rivalries? (John 3:22-24; 1:35-37.) Upon his return to the original locale of his ministry, John was arrested by Herod Antipas, whose territory included Perea as well as Galilee. Antipas may have feared the rapid expansion of the Baptist movement, as Josephus says. The Synoptic evangelists report that John had denounced Antipas's marriage to his sister-in-law, a denunciation that also had political fallout (Mark 6:7-29; Luke 3:19). While in prison (at the remote Perean fortress, Machaerus), John sent a message to Jesus: "Are you he who is to come, or shall we look for another?" (Matt. 11:2-6; Luke 7:18-23). John's reaction to Jesus' reply is not recorded.

John's influence extended beyond his martyrdom. Six years later Herod Antipas was defeated by a Nabatean army, an event regarded by some as a divine punishment for Herod's murder of the Baptist. From Acts 19:1-7 we learn of a group in Ephesus who claimed to have been baptized with John's baptism. The fourth evangelist's treatment of the Baptist suggests the presence of persons ascribing to John a messianic status. The historical connection between John's followers and the Mandaeans, surviving today in Iraq, is uncertain. In spite of the existence of these later rivalries, it is clear that from earliest times Christians have believed that John was the divinely appointed "forerunner" of Jesus the Christ, that in his life and death he prepared the way of the Lord.

J.L.P.

JOHN XXIII, POPE (1881–1963). Born Angelo Giuseppe Roncalli, John XXIII was one of Catholicism's most active and independent popes (1958–63). He convoked the twenty-first Ecumenical Council, VATICAN II (1962–65), which brought a new spirit of openness, cooperation, and collegiality to Roman Catholicism, but no major doctrinal changes. Born in a small village near Bergamo, Italy, into a tenant farm family of thirteen children, Roncalli began training for the priesthood at an early age. He studied at Bergamo seminary and the Pontifical Seminary in Rome, receiving ordination and a doctorate of theology in 1904. Until World War I he worked in his home diocese as secretary to the bishop. During the war he served in the Italian medical corps and as a military chaplain. Afterward he taught religious history at the Bergamo seminary and published several works. For sixty-seven years he kept a spiritual diary, published in English in 1965 as the *Journal of a Soul.*

Recalled to Rome in 1921 to help reorganize the Congregation for the Propagation of the Faith, Roncalli soon began serving as a Vatican diplomat

Courtesy of Religious News Service

*Pope John XXIII*

when Pope Pius XI in 1925 made him an archbishop in Greece and appointed him apostolic visitor to Bulgaria. He rose rapidly in the diplomatic service, was elevated to apostolic delegate in Bulgaria (1930), went to Istanbul as apostolic delegate to Turkey and Greece (1934), and became papal nuncio to Paris, France (1944). Roncalli's diplomatic service prepared him for papal leadership. The approach of World War II while he was in Turkey forced him to deal with different warring factions without losing their respect. In France he had to deal with difficult post-war problems.

In 1953 Archbishop Roncalli was made a cardinal and patriarch of Venice. There he became widely known for his accessibility, his concern for ordinary people, and his staunch stand against Communism in Italy.

On October 28, 1958, he became Pope John XXIII on the eleventh ballot of the College of Cardinals. Almost seventy-seven years old when elected, Pope John XXIII was expected to be an interim caretaker of the papacy. Yet during his four and a half years as pope, he revitalized Roman Catholicism. Without departing from traditional doctrine, Pope John encouraged liberal trends. He explored ways to improve relations with other churches, and in 1961 he sent official observers to the World Council of Churches at New Delhi. A major encyclical, *Mater et Magistra* (1961), dealt with post-war colonialism and problems of labor. Fifty million Catholics in a changing world had been caught in the orbit of Communism in Russia and China. An outstanding encyclical, *Pacem in Terris* (1963), pleaded with the nations of the world to promote peace and better living conditions. John created twenty-three new cardinals and increased the College of Cardinals from seventy to seventy-five. He also revived the custom of papal visits to prisons and hospitals in Rome. Widely beloved as a pastor, he convoked Vatican II to prepare the church for its complex role in society. Many Protestant theologians were invited as official observers and consultants.     C.M.

**JOHNSON, PAUL E.** (1898–1974). Psychologist and author, born at Niantic, Connecticut. He graduated from Cornell University in 1920, received an A.M. from the University of Chicago (1921), a S.T.B. (1923), and a Ph.D (1928) from Boston University School of Theology.

Johnson taught at Brown University, West China Union University, Hamline University, and was dean and professor of philosophy and religion at the Boston University School of Theology (1941–57). He then became professor of psychology and pastoral counseling (1957–63) and director of pastoral counseling services. He had a long association with the American Association of Pastoral Counselors and was influential in its work. His basic books are *Psychology of Religion,* 1945 (rev. 1959), *Psychology and Pastoral Care,* 1953; *Personality and Religion,* 1957.     I.C.

**JOHNSON, SAMUEL** (1709–84). Poet, essayist, and critic. He was born in Lichfield, Staffordshire, the son of Michael Johnson, a bookseller and sheriff, and Sarah Ford, a devout woman with Calvinist leanings. Educated at Pembroke College, Oxford, he married Elizabeth Porter in 1735. In 1737, with his pupil David Garrick, Johnson went to London, where he wrote criticism of Shakespeare. His eight-volume edition of the bard was published in 1765.

After eight years of work Johnson published his *Dictionary of the English Language* in 1755. From 1750 to 1752 he edited the *Rambler* and thereafter the *Idler.* His other major work was the *Lives of the English Poets* (1781). His *Prayers and Meditations* (1785) included such hymns as "Life of Ages, Richly Poured," "City of God, How Broad and Far," "Father, in Your Mysterious Presence Kneeling." Johnson met his biographer James Boswell, then twenty-two, in 1763. A champion of the poor and oppressed, debtors, prostitutes, and blacks, Johnson in his religious life was given to melancholy and heart-searching.     N.H.

**JONAH.** The name of a prophetic figure whose story is told in an OT book that bears his name. The book of Jonah is different from other prophetic literature in that it is not a collection of the oracles, visions, or sermons of a prophetic figure, but rather is a narrative about an episode in the life of such a figure. In fact, the only prophetic oracle in the book of Jonah is the eight-word message of 3:4*b*.

Jonah, the son of Amittai, is otherwise known to us only from a reference in II Kings 14:25, in which we are told that he was a native of the northern community of Gath-hepher. We also learn there that he was a contemporary of King Jeroboam II of Israel (about 786–746 B.C., which means that he was also a contemporary of AMOS and HOSEA), and that he predicted a favorable outcome for Jeroboam's military adventures.

In the book of Jonah the Lord commands the prophet to preach repentance to NINEVEH, the capital of the great Assyrian Empire. Instead, however, Jonah refuses and flees on a ship bound for Tarshish. Once on the high seas, the ship encounters a storm and the members of the crew conclude that some deity has been offended. By means of the casting of lots it is determined that the guilty party is Jonah. Jonah admits that he is fleeing from the Lord, and he suggests that the sailors cast him overboard in order to appease the Lord's wrath. When this is done the storm dies away. In the meantime, Jonah has been swallowed by a great fish and, after he cries for mercy from the belly of the fish, he is vomited upon the shore.

Once more the Lord commands Jonah to proceed to Nineveh to preach to the people. This time the prophet obeys and discovers that, when he preaches, his words result in the repentance of the Ninevites. Yet Jonah is bitter because he had hoped that these despised people would be destroyed. In anger Jonah retreats to the countryside, where the Lord causes a plant to grow up so that the prophet is shaded from the sun. Later the Lord sends a worm to destroy the plant, and Jonah's anger is intensified. When Jonah expresses his feelings, the Lord responds by pointing out that the welfare of a city is of far more importance than a plant to whose growth Jonah had contributed nothing.

There are several important reasons for concluding that the tale of Jonah is not based on historical record. For example, in 3:3 the statement is made that Nineveh is so large that it takes the traveler three days to cross through it. On the other hand, archaeologists have determined that the diameter of the city walls was about two miles. Another problem is related to the "great fish." The difficulty here is not so much that of the ability of the fish to swallow a man, but whether a person could survive three days and nights in the stomach of a fish (1:17) and compose there a psalm in the style of classical Hebrew poetry (2:2-9).

For these reasons and others (some of which have to do with matters of literary style and vocabulary), many scholars have concluded that the story of Jonah is either a parable or an allegory that borrowed the figure of Jonah from II Kings 14:25. Whichever literary genre the story fits, however, its central message is clear: the love of the God of Israel extends to all peoples upon the earth, even those who are as different and as hated as the citizens of Nineveh. Moreover, God's people Israel are under special responsibility to be the means by which God's love is made known.

It is not possible to establish with precision the date or location of the writing of the book of Jonah. Nor do we know its author. It is likely, however, that it was written well into the postexilic period by someone in the Jerusalem community who wished to counteract the prevailing mood of exclusivism (see Ezra 10; Neh. 13) with a reminder of Israel's international missionary obligation expressed so eloquently by the Second Isaiah in the period before the restoration (see Isa. 42:5-9).

One other word is in order about the nature of this literature. A great deal of heat has been expended in the argument over whether the story of Jonah "really happened," and in the midst of that controversy reference has been frequently made to Jesus' statement in Matthew 12:39-41. It should be remembered that literary authorship was viewed by ancient men and women (including those to whom Jesus spoke) in a manner different from that in which it is viewed today. One should not stumble over whether the book of Jonah is "historical" any more than over whether Jesus' parable of the good Samaritan or the prodigal son are "historical." The truth to which the narratives point lies within the narratives themselves.                          J.D.N.

**JONATHAN** ("Yahweh has given"). The oldest son of King SAUL and Ahinoam (I Sam. 14:49-50), whose relationship with David became an ideal of what friendship can be. The fact that Jonathan was heir to the throne and yet supported David for it, and even agreed to be his advisor (I Sam. 23:16-18), makes it even more unusual.

Jonathan first appears as victor at Geba, a Philistine fortress (I Sam. 13:3). He and his armor-bearer then successfully attacked another garrison alone (I Sam. 14; note in v. 14 the devotion of the armor-bearer). His pact of love and loyalty with David (I Sam. 20:12-23) led him to defiance and deception of his father at risk to his own life.

Jonathan died with his father Saul in battle with the Philistines at Mt. Gilboa (1 Sam. 31:1-13). His body, rescued by the citizens of Jabesh-gilead, was buried at Jabesh, but David later reburied the remains in the land of Benjamin (II Sam. 21:12-14). When David learned of his death, he uttered a moving elegy (II Sam. 1:17-27).                          N.H.

**JONES, E. STANLEY** (1884–1973). Renowned Methodist missionary and educator in India. Born in Clarksville, Maryland, Jones was educated at City College, Baltimore, and Asbury College, Wilmore, Kentucky. In 1907 he became a missionary of the Methodist Episcopal Church in India, serving as pastor, superintendent, teacher, and evangelist in the Lucknow area, especially among the low castes of India. Convinced that Christianity had a valid message that complemented Indian culture and in turn gained enrichment, Jones became a missionary to virtually all of India, educated and uneducated

alike. His first book, *The Christ of the Indian Road* (1925), received world acclaim and was translated into twelve languages. In 1926 Jones, a keen observer and scholar of Indian life, studied at the Bengal school of Rabindranath Tagore (1861–1941), Indian poet and winner of the Nobel Prize in 1913. Jones was elected Methodist bishop in 1928 but chose instead to continue his missionary work. Among his many publications are *Christ and Human Suffering* (1933), *Christ's Alternative to Communism* (1935), *Christ and Present World Issues* (1937), *The Christ of the American Road* (1944), *Mahatma Gandhi—an Interpretation* (1948), *How to Be a Transformed Person* (1951), and *Mastery* (1955).                          C.M.

**JONES, RUFUS M.** (1863–1948). Noted American Quaker, author of fifty-seven books on Quaker spiritualism, history, mysticism, and practical Christianity. He was educated at Haverford College; traveled widely; served as principal of Oak Grove Seminary, 1889–93; professor of philosophy at Haverford College, 1904–34; editor of *The American Friend*, 1893–1912; and chairman of the American Friends Service Committee for European Reconstruction, 1917–28 and 1933–44. Jones took a strong interest in education and served on several college boards of trustees, including Yenching University in China. Theologically, he was a critical liberal who believed the vitality of religion was not in ritualism or doctrine but in an immediate inward experience of God expressed outwardly in holy living and active love. He remained open to new truths in philosophy and science, convinced that new discoveries could not undermine a genuine direct experience of God's love. Among his many publications were *Practical Christianity: Essays on the Practice of Religion*, 1902; *A Dynamic Faith*, 1900; *Studies in Mystical Religion*, 1909; *Spiritual Reformers in the Sixteenth and Seventeenth Centuries*, 1914; *The Faith and Practice of the Quakers*, 1927; *Rethinking Religious Liberalism*, 1935; *The Eternal Gospel*, 1938; *The Flowering of Mysticism in the Fourteenth Century*, 1939.                          C.M.

**JOPPA.** A port city in Israel, south of Tyre and Sidon and thirty-five miles northwest of Jersualem. Joppa is ancient, having been inhabited from prehistoric times. It is mentioned in ancient Assyrian and Egyptian writings, and in the OT (Josh. 19:46) it is connected to the tribe of Dan, although the Philistines controlled it until the time of David.

Joppa is from the Hebrew *YAFO*, meaning "beauty." It is now a suburb of Tel Aviv. Excavations begun in 1955 have uncovered a fortress dating to the eighteenth century B.C. Captured by the Egyptians in the sixteenth century B.C., Joppa served as a military outpost until the Philistines conquered it after the twelfth century B.C.

The prophet Jonah left on his journey to Tarshish from Joppa (Jonah 1:3). According to Acts 9:36-42, Peter raised Tabitha from the dead in Joppa, and he stayed at the house of Simon the tanner (Acts 9:43). It was in Joppa that Peter received the vision of clean and unclean foods, which revealed that all foods are clean for the Christian, and Peter also was directed to visit the centurion Cornelius in Caesarea.          J.C.

**JORAM.** An abbreviated form of Jehoram, which means "Yahweh is exalted"; the name of both a king of Israel (Ephraim) and a king of Judah, whose reigns overlapped (about 849–842 B.C.).

(1) Jehoram (Joram) of Judah is mentioned in I Kings 22: 50; II Kings 1:17; and II Chronicles 21:1, 3. He was the oldest son of King Jehoshaphat and shared power with his father for five years before becoming king himself. He ruled eight years and was a bad king; he permitted Baalism to be practiced. Elijah predicted he would die miserably and he did, according to II Chronicles 21:18 ff. Before that, Jehoram lost all his wives and sons, except Ahaziah, in war against the Philistines (II Chr. 21–22).

(2) Jehoram (Joram) of Israel was the son of Ahab and is mentioned in II Kings 3:1. His reign overlapped that of three kings of Judah—Jehoshaphat, Jehoram, and Ahaziah (II Chr. 22:1). The prophet Elisha preached during this period and helped with Jehoram's war against Moab. Jehoram was wounded at Ramoth-gilead and was later murdered at Gezreel by Jehu, who then took the throne (II Kings 8:29). The siege of Samaria by the Syrians (II Kings 6) under Benhadad may have taken place during Jehoram's reign.          J.C.

**JORDAN RIVER AND VALLEY.** The Jordan is the most important river of Palestine, flowing southward from its headwaters in the region of Mount Hermon to its mouth at the northern end of the Dead Sea. This is a distance by air of little more than one hundred miles, yet the course followed by the river is much more than this due to its frequent bends and twists. As its headwaters lie more than a thousand feet

From *Atlas of the Bible* (Thomas Nelson & Sons Limited)

*The Jordan Valley, near the Dead Sea, south of Jericho, looking west*

above sea level and its mouth at nearly thirteen hundred feet below sea level, the river passes through a variety of climatic zones, as well as types of terrain. The Jordan lies in the bed of an extended geological rift that may be traced into East Africa.

The stages of the river may be described as follows: (1) From its headwaters to the area of former Lake Huleh. This is a distance of less than ten miles, and the course of the river here makes its way through areas of marsh where reeds and grasses grow in abundance. Lake Huleh, a body of water of some two or three miles in diameter has been drained in recent years for agricultural purposes.

(2) From the area of former Lake Huleh to the Sea of Galilee. Over this ten-mile course the river level falls nearly a thousand feet, thus much of its course is characterized by precipitous descent through rocky gorges. Just north of its entrance to the Sea of Galilee the river slows in order to traverse a plain near the village of Bet Zayda (Bethsaida).

(3) From the Sea of Galilee to the Dead Sea. For about twenty-five miles after the river leaves the Sea of Galilee it passes through an especially fertile region, one that has supported a variety of agricultural enterprises in both ancient and modern times. In this stretch of the Jordan, the river is joined by the Yarmuk, one of the important tributaries that feed the Jordan from the Transjordanian Plateau. During the rainy season the volume of water can be doubled at this confluence. Further along, the river enters successive geographical areas that grow increasingly hot and arid until it finally passes through the salty wasteland that embraces the northern approaches to the Dead Sea.

Because of its conspicuous nature the Jordan River and valley played a role in a number of memorable events from both OT and NT. Lot, upon his separation from Abraham, "chose for himself all the Jordan valley" (Gen. 13:11). Jacob wrestled with his adversary at the ford of the Jabbok, the Jordan's chief tributary in its final run to the Dead Sea (Gen. 32:22). Moses prayed in vain that the Lord would permit him to cross the river "and see the good land beyond [that

Courtesy of the Israel Government Tourist Office, Houston, Texas

*The Jordan River in Upper Galilee, showing Mount Hermon in the background*

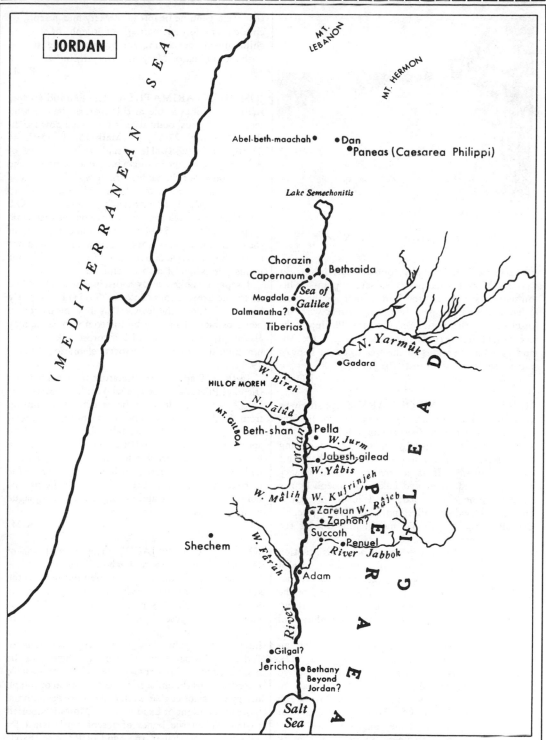

**JORDAN**

(MEDITERRANEAN SEA)

MT. LEBANON

MT. HERMON

Abel-beth-maachah •    • Dan
• Paneas (Caesarea Philippi)

*Lake Semechonitis*

Chorazin
Capernaum • • • Bethsaida
*Sea of*
Magdala • *Galilee*
Dalmanatha? •
Tiberias •

*N. Yarmûk*

• Gadara

*W. Bîreh*

HILL OF MOREH

*N. Jâlûd*

MT. GILBOA

Beth-shan •    Pella •
• *W. Jurm*

*Jordan*

• Jabesh-gilead
*W. Yâbis*

*W. Mâlih*    *W. Kufrinjeh*

*W. Râjeb*
• Zarelan *W.*
• Zaphon?
Succoth •
• Penuel
*River Jabbok*

Shechem •

*W. Fârâh*

G I L E A D

P E R A E A

River

• Adam

• Gilgal?
Jericho •
• Bethany
Beyond
Jordan?

*Salt*
*Sea*

is, to the west of] the Jordan" (Deut. 3:25). When Israel, under the leadership of Joshua, arrived to cross the river, the flow of water stopped so that the people crossed over on "dry ground" (Josh. 3:17). When David and those loyal to him fled from his son Absalom, the crossing was accomplished at night in order to avoid detection and "by daybreak not one was left who had not crossed the Jordan" (II Sam. 17:22). The most important NT event relating to the Jordan is the baptism of Jesus, which was performed by John

Courtesy of the Israel Government Tourist Office, Houston, Texas

*The southern part of the Jordan River*

the Baptizer, traditionally, but not certainly, near Jericho (Mark 1:5 and pars.). At several points in his ministry Jesus crossed the Jordan, perhaps the most celebrated such incident being his retreat with the disciples to the region of Caesarea Philippi, the occasion of Peter's confession of faith (Matt. 16:13 ff and pars.) The springs in the area (modern Banyas) form one of the sources of the Jordan.

J.D.N.

**JOSEPH, HUSBAND OF MARY.** Surprisingly he is not named in Mark's Gospel, and the two allusions to him in the Fourth Gospel (John 1:45; 6:42) are indirect. This fact is usually explained by suggesting that Joseph was already deceased when Jesus began his public ministry. It is in the birth and infancy narratives of Matthew and Luke that Joseph figures most prominently. In Matthew 1:20 his ancestry is traced to David's family, and Luke recites Joseph's genealogy (Luke 3:23-37) mentioning him as the putative father of Jesus.

Both evangelists incorporate stories of a conception of Jesus by the Holy Spirit, without the agency of Joseph, who is said to be betrothed to MARY at that time (Matt. 1:18; Luke 1:27). The mystery of the birth of Jesus is communicated to Joseph in Matthew, whereas Luke records a visitation of God to Mary, and Joseph is passed over.

Joseph, however, fulfilled a parental role in taking Jesus to Jerusalem for purification rites (Luke 2:22), and led the family into Egypt, according to Matthew's version (Matt. 2:13-15), and back to Nazareth where they settled (Matt. 2:19-23). Joseph took Jesus to the holy city for Passover (Luke 2:41); at this point he fades from the Gospel picture.

The other family members, referred to in Mark 3:31, with parallels in Matthew 12:46 and Luke 8:19, may show how Joseph and Mary lived together as man and wife and produced children, both sons and daughters (Mark 6:3). But Christian conviction is divided on the status of these siblings as to whether they were genuine offspring of Mary and Joseph, or children of a former marriage of Joseph, or adopted children—all depending on one's attitude to the Catholic dogma of Mary as "ever virgin."

R.M.

**JOSEPH OF ARIMATHEA.** The fourfold Gospel tradition ascribes a role to this man as the one who took care of Jesus' body after it was lifted down from the cross (Matt. 27:57, 59; Mark 15:43, 45; Luke 23:50; John 19:38). He is said to be a native of Arimathea, a village in Judah but, as a member of the Jewish council or the Sanhedrin, he would be resident in Jerusalem at the time. He is called a rich man (Matt. 27:57, but Matthew's interests in OT fulfillment may reflect a dependence on the messianic prophecy of Isaiah 53:9) and a prominent citizen of the community (Mark 15:43). His wealth is seen not only in his provision of burial rites for Jesus' body but in his possession of a rock tomb in Jerusalem.

Joseph is spoken of as a disciple who cherished messianic expectations (Luke 23:50-51) but secretly because of "fear of the Jews." This may mean a fear of being ostracized socially by his compatriots; it may also imply that contact with a corpse would render him unfit to share in the Passover celebrations (Num. 19:11).

In the NT apocryphal literature he is named as a friend of Pilate, and the one who cared for Mary, the Lord's mother, a role that other traditions, stemming from John 19:26-27, associate with John. Legend that dates from William of Malmesbury tells how the apostle Philip sent him to Britain in A.D. 63, where he founded the first Christian settlement in England, to be known as Glastonbury. A later tale, dated in the thirteenth century, describes him as bringing the holy grail to England and ridding Ireland of a plague of snakes.

R.M.

**JOSEPH, SON OF JACOB.** The eleventh son of JACOB by his favorite wife, Rachel. The account of the birth of Joseph to his hitherto barren mother and the significance of his name (which is derived from the Hebrew "he adds") is given in Genesis 30:22-24. However, the Joseph cycle itself begins only in Genesis 37. It then continues with the single interruption by the story of the levirate marriage of Judah and Tamar (Gen. 38) through the end of the book of Genesis. The very last verse of Genesis (50:26) records the death, embalmment, and burial of Joseph in Egypt—a notice that is alluded to once again in the haste of the night of Exodus, when Moses is reported to have taken the bones of Joseph with Israel for subsequent reburial in the Land of Promise (Exod. 13:19).

The Joseph story differs from those of his forebears, the patriarchs, Abraham, Isaac, and Jacob, in many respects. Unlike them, Joseph has no real setting in the land of Palestine, but belongs above all to Egypt.

His story is one of the longest continuous, coherent narratives in the OT. With setting, plot, and character development, it has all the marks of a literary piece that did not undergo the same kind of oral transmission as was the case with most of the earlier material in Genesis. Furthermore, Joseph is presented in the narrative as a kind of ideal wise man, a dream interpreter, counselor to Pharaoh, as judicious as Solomon was in his day. For all these reasons, some recent scholarship has tended to see Joseph as a portrait of the ideal courtier and wise man in the court of the united monarchy, perhaps during the reign of Solomon. That Joseph did effectively serve as a role model can be proved very simply by comparing him to Daniel, and particularly the account of Daniel's interpretation of Nebuchadnezzar's dream in Daniel 2. Daniel is a new Joseph in that chapter. Just as Joseph did in Genesis 41, Daniel succeeds in making sense of the king's dream when all the indigenous wise men and dream interpreters failed. He offers wise counsel to the king and helps him come to terms with the prophecy contained in the dream, and he does all this on the basis of empowerment by God, which grew out of his own life of faithfulness.

Perhaps, therefore, the Joseph cycle of Genesis 37–50 should be understood as a kind of romance, emanating from those courtly wisdom circles that first set down Israel's religious tradition in writing, which was designed to depict the best of all possible governors at a time when kingship had reached its fullest flower in Israel itself.

Of course, it is also the task of the Joseph story to transport Jacob's sons to Egypt, from which they would reappear centuries later as refugees and heirs of a promise. That part of the story begins with a dream. It was a dream guaranteed to get Joseph into trouble with his eleven brothers, who were already jealous of him because his father Jacob preferred him to all the others and had given him "a long robe with sleeves" (Gen. 37:3). He dreamed that the sheaves that they were binding in the field all stood up and that the eleven sheaves of the brothers bowed down to his sheaf. He dreamed that the sun and the moon and eleven stars bowed down to him. Dreams like these are the fuel of family feuds; even his father rebuked him for the implication that he and Rachel would bow down to this second youngest of all the sons (Gen. 37:10).

Not long afterward the brothers had an opportunity to punish this upstart. As they were tending the flocks near Dothan, they saw him coming from his father's house and plotted to kill him. Only the intervention of Reuben spared his life, but the compromise resulted in Joseph's being cast into a pit and ultimately sold to a passing caravan of ISHMAELITES who in turn sold him to the Egyptian captain of the guard, Potiphar. The brothers returned to Jacob with the torn and bloody robe of Joseph and told him that a wild beast had killed his beloved son (37:35).

Because he was wise and witty, Joseph rose quickly in Potiphar's household to become his chief overseer. Because Joseph was "handsome and good-looking" (39:6), he became the object of the lust of Potiphar's wife and the victim of a blackmail scam. But even in the prison in which he was cast he stood out, and the Lord gave him favor in the sight of the keeper of the prison (39:21). It was here that he earned his initial reputation as a dream interpreter as well, correctly understanding the dreams of Pharaoh's chief butler and chief baker. The same butler later told Pharaoh himself of the existence of a Hebrew who could interpret dreams, and because Joseph wisely understood that Pharaoh's dream of seven fat cattle and seven lean cattle represented years of plenty and years of famine respectively, he came to be the vizier in charge of all of Pharaoh's lands. Joseph rode in a chariot second only to Pharaoh and before him they cried, "Bow the knee!" (Gen. 41:43). Pharaoh even gave Joseph a wife, Asenath, the daughter of an Egyptian priest (Gen. 41:45). She bore him his sons Manasseh and Ephraim (41:50-52).

The grain that was laid aside from the seven years of plenty ultimately brought Joseph back into contact with his father and his brothers. The seven lean years affected not only Egypt but Canaan as well, and when Jacob heard that there was grain in Egypt, he sent ten of the brothers to buy some (42:1-3). Only Benjamin stayed at home. In the chapters that follow, the Joseph saga spins out the theme of the gradual disclosure of hidden identity of the ex-slave to his brothers. When the latter came before the governor to apply for grain purchases, they could not recognize him, but he immediately knew who they were and knew that his youngest brother Benjamin was not with them. They were then imprisoned for three days on suspicion of spying. Joseph released them with their grain purchases but kept back his brother Simeon as a hostage. As proof of their credibility, he ordered them to come back again with their youngest brother. On the way home, they were horrified to discover their purchase money in the mouths of their sacks of grain, and of course could not imagine returning to Joseph for fear of being charged with theft. But the food supplies could not suffice for seven years of famine, so in time, in spite of the great reservations of their father Jacob, they returned to Joseph in Egypt with their youngest brother Benjamin. Joseph was secretly overjoyed to see his youngest brother and reassured his brothers that the money that was found in their sacks was a gift of God (43:23). A great feast was mounted, and Joseph could not control himself for weeping and had to excuse himself lest his joy be discovered (43:30).

The story concludes with another case of deception. Joseph orders his silver divining cup to be embedded in Benjamin's sack of grain. Not long after the brothers leave the city, they are pursued by a servant of Joseph and accused of stealing the silver cup. Judah offers to take the place of Benjamin for whatever punishment awaits him, because, he says, "When I come to your servant my father, and the lad is not with us . . . he will die; and your servants will bring down the gray hairs of your servant our father with sorrow to Sheol" (44:30-31). At that Joseph can bear the deception no longer; he sends everyone out and makes himself known to his brothers (45:1-3). In spite of their terror, they are forced to recognize that he is alive and that his life has meant life for all of the family in Canaan, and that all was according to the will of God (45:7-8). In the end Jacob is sent for and enriched with the material goods that constitute "blessing" in the OT—the choicest land in Egypt, flocks and cattle. In time he dies there, but only after blessing his descendants and watching them grow into a mighty people (Gen. 49-50).

The last chapter of the Joseph story (Gen. 50) recounts the return of the family to Canaan to bury their dead father Jacob in the cave of Machpelah near Hebron alongside his parents and grandparents. Following the period of mourning the brothers express fear that Joseph would now at last take revenge upon them for their evil deeds. But Joseph reassures them with the famous slogan that many regard as the theological key to the entire Joseph cycle: "Fear not, for am I in the place of God? As for you, you meant evil against me; but God meant it for good, to bring it about that many people should be kept alive, as they are today" (Gen. 50:19-20). This richly suggestive theological assessment appears to be saying that in the events of Joseph's life a kind of double causality was at work. That the brothers' intention in selling him into slavery was evil cannot be denied, and they are fully responsible for it. But in that very same evil act commissioned by human beings, God could commission good. God's intention could override the evil intention of the brothers and transform the story of the treacherous elimination of a troublesome younger brother into the story of the salvation of a whole people. By God's mysterious working in the words and deeds of Joseph, the stage was set for the emergence from Egypt of the Israel of a subsequent generation, a people ready to receive the land of their inheritance and capable of changing the course of human history.

W.S.T.

## JOSEPHUS, FLAVIUS.
A Jewish history writer, born about A.D. 37 and died around the turn of the century. He was born of noble and priestly ancestry in spite of his acquired Roman name. His personal history is recounted in his *Life*, which includes the information that he became pro-Roman in his outlook and remained so to the end of his life. For services to the empire he was rewarded with citizen rights as a client of the emperor, whose family name Flavius he took on.

Josephus' firm attachment to the Roman power explains the bias that runs through his writings. He opposed the Jewish uprising against Rome in A.D. 66, which led to an all-out war, though he was drawn in on the side of his nation and given a military command in Galilee. After being taken prisoner by the Roman army, he agreed to go over to the invaders' side and sought to win the favor of the commander VESPASIAN by foretelling that the latter would soon be emperor. At the siege of Jerusalem he acted as interpreter for the Roman leader TITUS, who was in charge of the operation. Following the fall of the city Josephus went to Rome, where he later died.

His writings are voluminous, including the account of *The Jewish War* of A.D. 66-73/74, whose outbreak he attributed to Zealot or nationalist pressure, which he dismissed as no better than gangsterism. In twenty books he published a vast history of the Jewish people, *The Antiquities*, in A.D. 93, and wrote this as a propaganda piece to commend the Jews to their pagan neighbors. An even stronger apologetic work is *Against Apion.*.

Allowing for the partisan nature of Josephus' historic writings, he still remains an indispensable source of information, chiefly on the Herodian and Roman background to the politics of the centuries just prior to and extending into the NT period.

R.M.

## JOSHUA.
The successor to Moses (Num. 27:18-23; Deut. 31:7-29), whose leadership of Israel in the conquest of Canaan is recounted in the BOOK OF JOSHUA. His name, sometimes spelled Hoshea (compare Num. 13:8, 16), means "Yahweh is salvation." A Greek equivalent is "Jesus" (compare Acts 7:45; Heb. 4:8 KJV). In many ways, the OT writers present Joshua as a new Moses—prophet, priest, and king. As prophet, Joshua had a "spirit of wisdom" like Moses (Deut. 34:9; see Ecclus. 46:1 of the Apocrypha, where he is called "successor of Moses in prophesying"). As priest, like Moses, he called upon the people to sanctify themselves and commanded the priests in the movements of the Ark of the Covenant (Josh. 3:5-6). As king, like Moses, he led Israel in the definitive covenant ceremony at Shechem (Josh. 24:1-28). From beginning to end, however, Joshua is preeminently a military figure. He first appears as the leader of Israel's war against Amalek (Exod. 17:8-16). With Caleb, he spied out the land of Canaan (Num. 13:16-29) and correctly argued, though failed to convince, that it should be taken (14:6-10). After Moses' death at the border of the Promised Land, Joshua led the attack on Canaan, beginning with the crossing of the Jordan (Josh. 3:7-4:24) and the destruction of Jericho (Josh. 6). The main thrust of his conquest, and that best supported by archaeological evidence, must have been toward the southern foothills and the Negev (10:28-43), with one major incursion into the north against Hazor (11:1-15). Joshua is reported to have died at the age of 110, and to have been buried at Timnath-serah in central Palestine (Josh. 24:29-30).

W.S.T.

## JOSHUA, BOOK OF.

**JOSHUA, BOOK OF.** The sixth book of the OT, which recounts the story of how, under the leadership of JOSHUA, son of Nun, Israel came into possession of the Promised Land. From one point of view the book may be seen as the necessary completion of the account of Israel's beginnings contained in the Pentateuch. Since the promise of the land to the fathers is fulfilled in the conquest, it may be most correct to think of the Hexateuch, or the first six books of the Bible, as the opening unit of the OT. On the other hand, Joshua can also be regarded as the first part of the great historical account, Joshua–II Kings, which describes the rise of Israel into a nation-state within the borders of the land of Canaan. Clearly its concern with both the fulfillment of ancient promise and the continuation of the Mosaic leadership tradition, and with the details of the history and geography of Canaan, make it a unique and transitional work.

*Contents.* The structure of the book of Joshua may be analyzed as follows: (a) Israel crosses the Jordan River and sacks Jericho, chapters 1–6; (b) the capture of Ai, chapters 7–8; (c) the alliance with Gibeon, chapter 9; (d) the conquest of the south, chapter 10; (e) the triumph in the north, chapter 11; (f) a summary of Joshua's victories, chapter 12; (g) division of the land, chapters 13–22; (h) Joshua's farewell address, chapter 23; (i) the covenant ceremony at Shechem, chapter 24.

As this analysis immediately shows, a major change in the contents of the book occurs at chapter 13. Whereas the first half of the book presents a highly schematized picture of total conquest under Joshua, part two (chaps. 13–19) begins with long lists of borders and towns belonging to the twelve tribes, followed by a list of the cities of refuge, chapter 20, and another of the Levitical cities, chapter 21. Conquest is no longer really the issue in these chapters, though 21:43-45 records the completion of the conquest of Canaan and sets the stage for the dismissal of the tribes of Reuben and Gad and the half-tribe of Manasseh to return to their inheritances on the east side of the Jordan (compare Josh. 22). The boundary lists given for Judah and Benjamin (15:21-62; 18:21-28) are relatively precise and are thought to represent the actual administrative lines of the period of the Judean monarchy. The lists given for the northern tribes, on the other hand, are vague and sketchy and may thus be the work of writers who worked long after the conquest and perhaps even after the northern kingdom of Israel had ceased to exist.

*Authorship and Redaction.* The foregoing evidence supports the contention that the book of Joshua as we now have it emanates from circles of writers living after the composition of the book of DEUTERONOMY (about 621 B.C.). It is seen to reflect the holy war concept and the reward-and-punishment theology so typical of Deuteronomy and the rest of the Deuteronomic history. This theory of authorship might put the date of the composition of the book as

we now have it as late as the time of the Babylonian exile (597–538 B.C.). It would explain the following phenomena: (a) the idealized picture of total conquest presented in chapters 1–12 contrasts sharply with the so-called "negative conquest list" of Judges 1:21, 27-35, which specifically excludes from the area captured by Joshua a number of the places here alleged to have been taken by him; (b) the relative obscurity of the tribal boundary lists given in chapters 13–22, especially touching those groups associated with the north; (c) the centrality assumed by Shechem and the covenant-making ceremony reported in chapter 24 and anticipated in 8:30-35 (a passage that may once have been the conclusion of the ceremony in chap. 24).

The account of recitation and sacrifice contained in Joshua 24 has great affinities with the combination of "little historical credo" and its affiliated religious rites preserved both in Deuteronomy 6:20-23 and in 26:1-11. The combination of these three passages may reflect an idealized picture of an annual "covenant renewal ceremony" in premonarchal times which was cherished in Deuteronomic circles. Such a ceremony would have been the glue that held together the covenant federation of twelve tribes led by charismatic leaders like Joshua, the twelve "judges," and Samuel, whose federation was a conception about the distant past favored by later OT writers.

Unfortunately, Shechem figures not at all in Joshua outside these two texts; the principal sanctuaries in view seem to have been Gilgal (5:9) and Shiloh (18:1ff.). Coming as it does rather anticlimactically after Joshua's farewell speech, Joshua 24 may for all these reasons have to be understood not as a record of the polity actually established by Joshua, but as an expression of later idealism about how Israel's community life was organized in the golden age of pristine Yahwism.

*Historical Reliability.* Given the relatively late redaction of the book of Joshua and even acknowledging the presence in it of older sources, it would appear quite unlikely on the face of it that the book would provide a reliable guide to the actual history of the conquest of Canaan by the Israelites. G. Mendenhall doubts that a sweeping military victory of Israel over the Canaanite city states ever took place, but prefers to describe the conquest as a series of uprisings of oppressed and landless elements under the impetus of a small band of Hebrew outlaws coming across the Jordan. The German biblical scholar Martin Noth envisions a gradual infiltration of Israelite tribes from various directions and their slow rise to dominance in the land. The only extra-biblical testimony to the events reported in the book of Joshua has been brought up out of the soil by archaeologists, and that evidence is mixed. Just as Joshua would suggest, extensive destruction layers of the late Bronze Age (about 1300–1200 B.C.) have been found at Lachish (10:3ff.) and Hazor (11:1ff.). On the other hand, no evidence of any occupation whatever from the time of Joshua has come to light at the sites of Jericho, Ai, and Gibeon—all cities that figure prominently in the narratives of conquest in chapters 1–9. The conclusion must be drawn, then, that the book is best viewed not as a contemporary historical record, but as a theological work written in narrative form, which comes to provide a normative interpretation of the historical fact that Israel did emerge from utter marginality into a people who possessed a land of their own.

*Theology of the Book of Joshua.* The conquest of the land is understood by the Deuteronomic writers to be the final act of a great history of salvation, which sweeps from promise to fulfillment. The book of Joshua announces that in the conquest God completed the work of liberation and enfranchisement that was first promised to the patriarchs (for example, Gen. 28:13-15), and that was always recounted in the brief statement of Israel's faith recited in cultic occasions (Josh. 24:11-13). All this was God's work; the victory of the conquest was God's, not Joshua's or Israel's. Only a perspective such as this can cope with the difficult theme of "holy war," which portrays Yahweh as ordering the absolute destruction of cities like Jericho and Ai, together with their men, women, children, oxen, sheep, and asses (compare Josh. 6:21). Although we cannot express it in their way, the narratives of Joshua can support our deep conviction that God is absolutely sovereign. The drama of God's sovereign work in human history is brilliantly played out in God's selection of a weak and scattered people bent under the servitude of Pharaoh to receive an inheritance in Canaan and from thence to become the mediators of God's saving purpose throughout the world.

W.S.T.

**JOSIAH.** "Good King Josiah" of Judah, whose name means "healed by God," ruled from 640–609 B.C. He succeeded his father AMON when he was only eight years old. At that time Zephaniah was prophesying the collapse of the kingdom. In the eighteenth year of his reign, as he was consolidating his territory and rebuilding the temple, his high priest Hilkiah discovered in the temple a book of the law, probably the Deuteronomy code. The king celebrated with public readings, conducted the first countrywide Passover "since the time of the judges," and carried out drastic religious reforms. The altars of Baal and Asherah in the temple were hammered to pieces, as were the Assyrian ones dedicated to the sun, moon, and stars. The rubble was dumped into the Kidron Valley. Live sacrifices of children to Molech in the Hinnom Valley just outside Jerusalem were ordered stopped. Wizards and sorcerers were put out of business, as were the sacred prostitutes.

Josiah had sufficient power to carry out these reforms even in the Baalistic high places of the north, which was under the dominance of Assyria. But

Zephaniah and his prophecies foretelling serious troubles for Israel proved correct. Though Assyria had only recently attacked Egypt, the newest common enemy was now Babylon, and an Egyptian army marched north up the Via Maris, the way of the sea, to assist the Assyrians. Josiah attempted to resist the Egyptians at the fortress of Megiddo, where the highway swings inland. His army was sorely defeated and he was sorely wounded. Rushed back home in his chariot, he died in Jerusalem, much loved and long mourned for his wisdom, uprightness, and justice.

T.J.K.

**JOTHAM.** King of Judah, who began to rule as co-regent about 750 B.C. when his father, Uzziah (Azariah), contracted leprosy (II Kings 15:5). His mother was Jerushah, the daughter of Zadok (II Chr.

Courtesy of Nelson Glueck

*Impression of the seal of Jotham from Ezion-geber*

27:1). He ruled as sole monarch from about 740 to 732 B.C. A godly man, he built and ornamented the high gate of the Temple, subdued the Ammorites, and fortified and extended the land of Judah (II Chr. 27).

N.H.

**JOY.** As a human emotion joy runs through the biblical literature corresponding to the various occasions and circumstances in which the writers found themselves. There is a flexibility and mobility about this term for this reason, yet one fact remains a settled conviction: human joy is not dependent on fluctuating feelings or changing conditions of prosperity and adversity. Rather it is grounded in God, who is the giver of joy. The term also has both an individual and societal aspect. It is not easy to separate the two because the speaker who rejoices is often reflecting the sentiments of the community, whether of Israel or the church.

*Old Testament.* At times of national feasts and festivals joy is a characteristic feature, the obvious exception being the Day of Atonement (Yom Kippur), when Israel confessed its sins with fasting and contrition. Yet, even today, the week (based on Lev. 23:34: "for seven days is the feast of booths") in the fall of the year (when the Atonement comes) is known as the Feast of Booths and is linked with the glad "rejoicing in the law" celebration that occurs on its final day. Worship at the Temple in Solomon's day was a joyful affair (Ps. 42:4; 81:1-3) according to I Kings 8. The disasters that befell the Temple in the sixth century B.C. only made the task of rebuilding and restoring more gladsome (Neh. 8:13-18; compare Ps. 126). The prophet of Isaiah 56–66 looks ahead to a new Temple in a city of cosmic size with a new dimension of joy to herald in an age of God's triumphant Kingdom (Isa. 65:17-25).

*New Testament.* The NT writers invariably connect their joy with the onset of the messianic era heralded by the coming of Jesus Christ—his birth (Luke 2:10), his entry into Jerusalem on Palm Sunday (Mark 11:1-11), and his post-resurrection appearances (Matt. 28:8-9). The descent of the Holy Spirit at Pentecost likewise is an occasion of joy; in fact, in the Acts of the Apostles, joy is one of the visible and sentient effects of the Spirit's presence (2:28, 46; 8:39; 13:52). This "exultation" (Greek *agalliasis*) has overtones of joy at living in the days of eschatological renewal, when God's kingly presence is known and experienced, with an awareness that looks back to Christ's resurrection and enthronement as Lord. This belief gave the early church an ability to rejoice even when they were called to suffer persecution and loss (Heb. 10:32-34; Jas. 1:2-4).

Paul associates joy with the fruit of the Spirit (Gal. 5:22) and traces its source to God's gift of Christ (Rom. 5:2-11) and the achievement of human salvation. This is the primary reason for rejoicing in the Pauline churches. But also Paul as mission preacher and pastor can call on his converts to rejoice over their standing in the church (I Thess. 2:19-20; Phil. 2:2). Even when his congregations are called on to endure hardship, they are summoned to be glad (Phil. 2:17-18) as Paul sets the example. The same holds true for I Peter (4:13-14), and even the dramatic scenario of the Revelation includes the call to joy in time of testing, though the writer evidently expected some direct intervention of God to defeat hostile evil powers (Rev. 18:20). The anticipation in the final reign of God is yet another cause for joy in the NT, whether death supervenes (Phil. 1:19-26) or the Kingdom comes in power (I Thess. 2:19).

R.M.

**JUBILATE DEO.** The third Sunday after Easter, in the Roman Catholic, Anglican, and Lutheran church year. The name is from the opening words in Latin of the Sixty-sixth Psalm, sung as the introit on that day. It means "Shout for joy unto God" or "Make a joyful noise unto God."

J.C.

**JUBILEE, YEAR OF.** A sacred year, ordained in the Bible, in which the land was to be returned to its original owners or to their descendants.

"And thou shalt number seven sabbaths of years unto thee, seven times seven years; and the space of the seven sabbaths of years shall be unto thee forty and nine years . . . And ye shall hallow the fiftieth year, and proclaim liberty throughout all the land unto all the inhabitants thereof; it shall be a jubilee unto you; and ye shall return every man unto his possession, and ye shall return every man unto his family" (Lev. 25:8, 10).

The Jubilee was a safeguard against continued slavery and against poverty. The Hebrew slaves and their families were to be freed. Property, with the exception of houses in walled cities, was to revert to its original owner. Houses and lands were thus kept from accumulating in the hands of the few, pauperism was prevented, and a race of independent freeholders assured. The land was to lie fallow during the Year of Jubilee; nothing was to be sown or reaped; not even grapes were to be gathered.

According to the Talmud, the law of the Jubilee, which represented a rare and striking introduction of morals into economics, was observed as long as the entire territory of the Holy Land was inhabited by Israelites. When a portion of the tribes went into exile, the law lapsed.

L.K.

**JUBILEES, BOOK OF.** *See* PSEUDEPIGRAPHA.

**JUDAH.** (1) The fourth son of JACOB and Leah, whose name is interpreted by Leah's words, "I will praise Yahweh" (Gen. 29:35), and eponymous ancestor of the tribe of Judah. In Jacob's deathbed testimony, Judah is generously blessed through highly eulogistic poetry (49:8-12). Said to be a "lion's whelp," his strength is celebrated. Also the possessor of scepter and staff, he will be the object of his brother's praise. Paternal favoritism is not the main issue here. Rather, the Judah oracle likely reflects an era when Judah enjoyed preeminence over the other Israelite tribes. This blessing probably received its present shape during the tenth-century B.C. Davidic monarchy.

Twice in the JOSEPH story, with its heightened interest in family conflict and reconciliation, Judah expresses authentic concern for another's welfare. First, Judah persuades his brothers that selling Joseph, whom they do not love, to a passing Ishmaelite caravan is preferable to causing him physical harm (Gen. 37:26-27). Second, knowing how shattering it would be on his father if his youngest son, Benjamin, should not return home from Egypt, Judah offers to take Benjamin's place, to remain as a slave in Egypt, while his brothers return to Jacob (43:8-10; 44:18-34).

In complete isolation from his brothers, Judah is portrayed to his disadvantage in Genesis 38 as an uncooperative father-in-law who defied the custom of levirate marriage. That custom ensured the continuity of the name and family of a man dying without a male descendant. Reflecting Judahite-Canaanite clan interaction, this story turns upon Judah's refusal to give his youngest son to Tamar in marriage and upon

Tamar's vindication when, disguised as a harlot, she attracts Judah and bears twins by him.

(2) A Levite who took part in the Jewish return from Babylon to Jerusalem (Neh. 12:8).

(3) A Levite who helped oversee the rebuilding of the Jerusalem Temple during Zerubbabel's governorship (Ezra 3:9).

(4) A Benjaminite, second in command over Jerusalem during Nehemiah's governorship (Neh. 11:9).

(5) A participant in Nehemiah's dedication of Jerusalem's walls (Neh. 12:34).

(6) A Levite who, following Ezra's mandate, divorced his Gentile wife (Ezra 10:23).

J.K.K.

**JUDAH, KINGDOM OF.** The southern kingdom of the dual monarchy, consisting of the tribes of Judah and most of Benjamin, which remained loyal to the Davidic house when the ten northern tribes defected in 922 B.C.

*Judah Prior to the Schism.* This tribe, which claimed JUDAH, the fourth son of Jacob and Leah (Gen. 29:35), as its ancestor, steadily took possession of southern Palestine (Judg. 1:1-21). Consigned to historical obscurity until the time of David, Judah was a manifestly diverse tribe that encompassed Simeonite, Calebite, Othnielite, and Kenizzite elements. The rocky, barren territory occupied by most of Judah's residents incorporated a north-south geographical stretch of about fifty miles, and an east-west distance of about forty-five miles, bounded by the Philistine plain and the Jordan rift.

Judah often confronted pressure from hostile neighbors. Othniel, of the Kenizzite clan situated at Debir, presumably delivered his people from Edomite threat (in Judg. 3:8-11 "Mesopotamia" as the enemy is likely a textual corruption). Increasingly, the tribes of Judah and Benjamin felt the brunt of Philistine pressure. This led to the appointment of a Benjaminite named SAUL (about 1020–1000 B.C.) as Israel's first king, whose realm embraced Judean as well as Benjaminite territory. Following Saul's death, Judah successfully campaigned to place its own son, DAVID (about 1000–961 B.C.), on the throne. Establishing his capital at Jerusalem, a city near the Judah-Benjamin border, David excelled in the ways of statecraft. At his death, a substantial kingdom passed over to his son SOLOMON (about 961–922 B.C.) The concept of "big government" that he implemented evoked opposition when his son, Rehoboam, succeeded him on the throne. When Rehoboam refused to curb the ambitions of monarchy, the ten northern tribes seceded (I Kings 12:1-20). Israel's united monarchy suddenly terminated.

*Judah after the Schism.* Consisting of Judah and most of Benjamin, the southern kingdom persisted as an entity unto itself from 922 to 587 B.C., when Jerusalem fell to the Babylonians. During this interval, the people were governed by nineteen kings

boasting Davidic ancestry and one outsider, Queen Athaliah (842–837 B.C.), from Samaria. The first half of the century of dual monarchy witnessed intermittent civil war with its attendant depletion of life and goods. When Jehoshaphat of Judah allied himself with Ahab of Israel, the political and social climate became more tranquil and prosperous. But the marriage of Ahab's sister (daughter?), Athaliah, to Jehoram, son of Jehoshaphat, did more than formally seal that alliance. It led to the installation of the Baal cult in Jerusalem and the consequent dissipation of Judah's Yahwistic religion. While such kings as Hezekiah and Josiah were worthy defenders of the ancestral faith, others such as Ahaz and Manasseh, who ruled during politically tense periods, manifested syncretistic tendencies that favored the worship of Baal and other deities.

If religious deviation and social abuse were generally less extreme in Judah than in the northern kingdom, they nevertheless evoked sustained attention from such prophets as Isaiah, Micah, Zephaniah, and Jeremiah, who labored, often unsuccessfully, to correct them. Judah's internal difficulties, however, were balanced by oft-related external difficulties occasioned by far stronger nations locked in struggle for dominion of the ancient Near Eastern world. Egypt, Assyria, and Babylon all affected Judean existence. In 918 B.C. Pharaoh Shishak's armies seized numerous Judean cities, and in 609 B.C. Pharaoh Necho killed Josiah in battle at Megiddo. On occasion, Egypt joined Judah's cause in countering eastern aggressors, but the support actually rendered was often so negligible as to be unworthy of the trust given to it by the pro-Egyptian party in Jerusalem.

Though the southern kingdom outlived the northern by 135 years, during much of that interval Judah was condemned to Assyrian vassalage. Judah's religion was much diluted with Assyrian accretions, and its land was noticeably scarred by the invasion of Sennacherib's army in 701 B.C. If Assyria's gradual demise during the second half of the seventh century afforded Judah some respite, with Babylon's ascendancy under Nebuchadnezzar, Judah's political ruin was imminent. A final deportation of Judah's citizens to BABYLON was realized in 597 B.C., only to be followed by a second, and Jerusalem's full-scale destruction, in 587 B.C. (II Kings 25:1-21). Thus the nation of Judah expired. J.K.K.

**JUDAISM, HISTORY OF.** The history of the Jewish people begins with the covenant the Lord made with Abraham:

> And I will make of thee a great nation, and I will bless thee, and make thy name great; and thou shalt be a blessing: And I will bless them that bless thee, and curse him that curseth thee: and in thee shall all families of the earth be blessed (Gen. 12:2-3 KJV).

It was in the time of Moses that monotheism became the faith of the entire nation of Israel. It was an entirely new religious idea, an original creation, and one that had no roots in polytheistic civilization. The people of Israel conceived a different world view from paganism. The pagan idea was that everyone, gods included, was subjected to a supernatural, primordial realm. Paganism did not accord ultimate freedom to its gods, nor were they, in the final analysis, sovereign; they emerged out of a preexistent realm. Judaism's idea, on the other hand, is that the will of God is transcendent and sovereign over all. There is only one God, Judaism believes, and God created the universe, guides history, commands justice and mercy, and has chosen the Jews to be God's people.

The institution of the Judges was succeeded by the monarchy, a prophetic creation. Samuel was the last representative of the old order of prophet-judges. The people turned to him with the plea to give them a king, an idea he opposed for its lack of faith in God; ultimately, he yielded and anointed Saul as king. The books of Kings fix the beginning of Israel's decline and fall after the close of Solomon's reign. For two hundred years (from 922 to 722 B.C.) there were two kingdoms—ISRAEL in the north, JUDAH in the south. The northern kingdom was destroyed by the Assyrians. With the last rays of the northern kingdom's setting sun, classical prophecy emerged. Its first representatives were the Judean Amos and the northerner Hosea. Its last spokesman was Malachi. Classical prophecy lifted the Jewish religion to new heights. The prophets taught that what God requires of the human being is morality rather than ritual. The revolutionary idea of classical prophecy is that Israel's history is determined by two factors, the moral as well as the religious, and that both are equally decisive.

The southern kingdom fell in 586 B.C., and the people were exiled to Babylonia. Since the first Temple had been destroyed, what was to become of Israel's religion? Until the EXILE, it had been a national religion, rooted in the Holy Land. By the end of the Babylonian Exile it had become clear that the people and the religion had stood the test. Judaism began to reveal its universal significance. The Exile in no way weakened the loyalty of the people to YHWH (God). Their worship consisted of prayer, confession, fasting, honoring the Sabbath, and the study of sacred texts.

In 538 B.C., Cyrus gave the exiles permission to return to Jerusalem and reconstruct the Temple. ". . . And all the people shouted with a great shout, when they praised the Lord, because the foundation of the house of the Lord was laid" (Ezra 3:11).

The TEMPLE was completed around 516 B.C. About a century after the return under Zerubbabel, in the time of Ezra and Nehemiah, an event of enormous significance took place: the TORAH was fixed and canonized. On New Year's Day in 444 B.C. the completed Torah was publicly read before the assembled throng in Jerusalem. In this solemn act, the Torah was given anew to Israel. Now, however, it was no longer the special possession of the priests, but was the property of the entire people, who participated in its study.

*Confrontation with Hellenism.* During the very period in which the edifice of Judaism was being consolidated, the culture of Greece was reaching its climax. Jewish and Greek culture were destined to conflict with each other and to influence each other, but they forever remained two worlds. Judaism embodied the idea of divine revelation, of prophecy, and the Holy Spirit. It aspired to mold life in accordance with the inspired utterances of its ancient prophets. Greek culture was distinguished by its idea of scientific reason. It aspired to perfect a system of thought, a world view based on rational awareness.

ALEXANDER THE GREAT's victorious campaign in Palestine, Egypt, and Syria had an immediate impact upon Judea. As part of his plan to merge the conquered peoples into one cultural unity, he left garrisons in Samaria and other cities. The Macedonian kings who followed him built a network of Hellenistic cities on the very borders of Judea. Hellenistic influences made themselves felt soon after the Ptolemies began their hundred-year rule of Palestine in 300 B.C. There was a considerable amount of Helenization among the ruling classes of Jews. While many of the masses learned the Greek language and adopted Greek customs and ideas, they insisted on remaining Jews, so well had the scribes, successors to the prophets in the religious life of the Jews, done their work. While almost all the ancient peoples whose names are mentioned in the Bible disappeared completely, swept away by the flood of Greek influence, the Jews remained steadfast in their own faith.

The Seleucid king Antiochus III conquered Palestine about 200 B.C. When Antiochus IV came to power, Judaism was declared illegal, and the Maccabees began their fight for survival and religious freedom—the MACCABEAN REVOLT. A permanent result of the conflict was the unfading memory of Jewish heroism. The conflict strengthened loyalty to the Jewish faith and widened the breach between Jewish and Greek thought.

HELLENISM had a decided impact on Jewish life, however. The language of Judaism in the Hellenistic-Roman diaspora—including the language of prayer—was predominantly Greek. The Bible was translated into Greek—the Septuagint. Even the burial inscriptions of the Roman Jews and their personal names were mainly Greek. And some of the books of the Bible, such as Ecclesiastes, with its pessimistic outlook, have a markedly Greek influence.

In his famous essay "Hebraism and Hellenism," Matthew Arnold noted that to the Jews virtue meant righteous life, while to the Greeks it meant physical excellence. Jews sought the knowledge of God, while Hellenists sought the knowledge of nature. For Hebraism, virtue is beauty; for Hellenism, beauty is virtue. The Jews welcomed the ideals of the Greeks but refused to be assimilated into the Greek ideal.

It was not long before Rome became the ruling power and became directly involved in Judea's political affairs. Pompey reduced the size of Judea and demanded an annual tax. Judea had become a vassal state of Rome. Procurators were overtly hostile to the Jews. Open rebellion broke out in A.D. 66. It took five years before the Romans could lay siege to Jerusalem. The siege lasted from April to September, every section of the city being taken with great effort and loss of life. During the fighting on August 28 in A.D. 70 (the ninth day of the Hebrew month of Av), the second Temple went up in flames.

Once again the Jews were faced with the problem of preserving Judaism. They still had the Torah. Yohanan ben Zakkai was given permission to develop an academy of higher learning at Yavneh, which became the center of Jewish religious life. The SYNAGOGUE replaced the Temple, prayer replaced sacrifice, and Jewish study became more important than it had ever been before. The aristocrats were replaced by the spiritual nobility, who came to be known as RABBIS.

*Rabbinic Judaism.* Rabbinic Judaism undertook the further development of the Torah and its laws. It was also the fulfillment of an essential implication of classical prophecy: that the religious life does not depend on a functioning sacrificial system but on ethical and penitent action in the here and now.

The sages at Yavneh summarized the teachings of the earlier schools of HILLEL and Shammai. They completed the canonization of the Scriptures, gave a more precise form to the daily prayers, and transferred to the synagogue and the Sanhedrin (rabbinical assembly) some of the observances associated with the Temple in Jerusalem. The Yavneh Sanhedrin was high court, supreme legislature, and an assembly of peers. The rabbis collectively constituted a new religious leadership class. They attracted students who came to learn their oral traditions and scriptural interpretations and to see them actualize the Torah in their daily lives. The new sages settled throughout Judea and Galilee with their circles of disciples. During the first decades of the second century, the most prominent figure was Rabbi AKIBA, the pioneer of an extremely flexible method of biblical interpretation based on the assumption that no word in Scripture is redundant. Akiba's system made it possible to extract infinite levels of meaning from the texts of the Bible.

The orally transmitted teachings of the Scribes and sages were crystallized into the Mishnah. Law code, textbook, and repository of traditions deemed most authoritative, the Mishnah assumed a status in rabbinic Judaism not unlike the NT in Christianity, although their contents are vastly different. The Hebrew Bible and Mishnah together constitute the matrix of the developing rabbinic Judaism. The scholars interpreted and applied the Mishnah and other rabbinic teachings to everyday situations. These oral teachings and opinions were eventually written down and compiled into the TALMUD, one in Babylonia, the other in Palestine. The Talmud is made up of the MISHNAH and its exposition, the GEMARA.

Rabbinic thought can be divided into two types: alakhah and haggadah. HALAKHAH refers to the required action, the practical rule of ritual or civil law, the way that a Jew guides his or her life. HAGGADAH is theological speculation, general ethical teachings, parables, maxims, legends, and folklore. Aggadah seeks to inspire and enlighten; halakhah seeks to apply God's will to specific situations.

In its Talmudic stage, Judaism became a universalist religion, which welcomed into its fold—and what is more astonishing, into the community of Jews—all who would accept its discipline. For the first time in recorded history a closed society opened its doors to all with an invitation to *equal* membership. The change from the religion-of-one-people to the people-of-one-religion enabled Jews and Judaism to transcend the limitations of land, language, and even conflicting economic-political interests.

A method of rabbinic teaching was *midrash*—getting meanings from biblical verses beyond the literal. MIDRASH interprets a biblical text or group of texts according to their contemporary relevance. Talmudic civilization was to become the basis of Jewish—and to a large extent Christian and Muslim—communal life in the Middle Ages.

*Judaism in the Middle Ages.* Jews were deeply affected by the Muslim conquests of the seventh century. The extension of internal autonomy to the Jewish communities under Islam made possible the continuance of a Jewish way of life, the cultivation of Jewish learning, and patterns of behavior that remained rooted in Talmudic literature, though they underwent an evolution and modification. The gradual shift from Aramaic to Arabic as the language of the Jews was a change of radical importance. By the tenth century most of them used Arabic as their vernacular. Great works written in Arabic by Saadiah Gaon, Judah ha-Levi, Moses ibn Ezra, MAIMONIDES, and others, had a profound influence on Jewish life. The greatest Jewish legal authority of his time, Saadiah Gaon played a decisive role in two major controversies in Jewish life. He fought the disrupting influence of the Karaites, who rejected the authority of the Talmud. He also prevented the acceptance of revisions of the Jewish calendar advocated by Ben Meir, the head of an academy in Palestine. Judah ha-Levi, a poet and philosopher, wrote the *Kuzari* as a philosophic dialogue in defense of Judaism. Moses ibn Ezra wrote a number of penitential poems, which became part of the Jewish liturgy. Maimonides' greatest philosophic work, the *Moreh Nevukhim* (Guide for the Perplexed), was written in Arabic and tried to harmonize the teachings of Judaism with the philosophy of Aristotle.

The great codes of Jewish law were compiled during the Middle Ages. The KABBALA, which teaches about the hidden nature of God, was produced. The emphasis in medieval Jewish thinking among the philosophers was on the impersonal aspects of the Deity. In reaction, the kabalists developed the doctrine of the *sefirot,* the ten divine emanations by which the world is governed. The kabalists also developed, however, the doctrine of the *Ein Sof* ("The Limitless"), God as God is in God's self.

In Europe, Jews and Judaism did not fare well. Jewish rights were restricted, Jews were threatened with death or expulsion if they did not convert to Christianity, false accusations were leveled against them, and they were persecuted in many ways. Many Jews believed that the Messiah would come to rescue them. They were bitterly disillusioned when Shabtai Zvi was proven to be a false messiah. A fear of new tendencies in Judaism became pronounced. At the same time, the revivalist trends in other religions led to the rise of HASIDISM and the worship of God through joy and fervor.

Through outer pressures and inner fears, the Jews had grown inward. It took the philosopher Moses Mendelssohn to bring the Jews face to face with the modern world.

*The Modern Period.* Under the impact of philosophies and ideologies critical of revealed truth, the concept of Judaism underwent striking modifications. MENDELSSOHN, the first eminent Jewish figure to make the transition from the ghetto to modernity without breaking away from the Jewish people, inspired generations of young Jews looking for new moorings. His greatest impact was to foster a Jewish Enlightenment, the *Haskalah.* The rationality of Jewish belief, the uniqueness of Israel, the impact of a historical perspective, the need for rejuvenation and reformulation—all were issues in the ideological controversies that surfaced in mid nineteenth-century German Jewry, producing the three modern forms of Judaism that came to be known as Reform, the Positive-Historical School, and Neo-orthodoxy.

The early phase of the Reform movement sought to bring the externals of Judaism into closer harmony with contemporary European standards of decorum. The sermon and many of the prayers were in German; choral singing was accompanied by an organ. References to a national restoration were deleted in prayer books. By the beginning of the nineteenth century the term Orthodox had come into general use for those who maintained, contrary to the Reformers, that the entire written and oral Torah was divinely revealed and immutable. For the Orthodox, the *Shulhan Arukh*—the sixteenth-century code of law compiled by Joseph Caro—together with commentaries and later decisions, constituted a fixed and binding standard for proper Jewish practice. The great divide between Orthodoxy and Reform was on the question of Jewish law. Reform Judaism rejects the idea of a permanently binding religious law. A middle-of-the-road position was advocated by the followers of the Positive-Historical School and later by Conservative Judaism in the United States. This school believes that Reform Judaism is in error in rejecting Jewish law, but it also believes that Orthodox Judaism is mistaken in wedding adherence to Jewish law to a fundamentalism that rejects changes or development in Judaism.

Judaism's main influence on civilization has been in the realm of religion. The church and mosque are direct descendants of the synagogue. Words such as "amen" and "Hallelujah" have become part of the religious vocabulary of a large portion of humanity. The Sabbath, the Psalms, the prophetic readings, the weekly sermon are, through Judaism, the common heritage of the Christian world. (*See also* HANUKKAH; JUDAISM, MODERN THOUGHT OF; SABBATH; WISE, ISAAC MAYER; and ZIONISM.)

L.K.

**JUDAISM, MODERN THOUGHT OF.** Modern Jewish philosophy begins with MOSES MENDELSSOHN (1729–86). Mendelssohn tried to reconcile traditional Judaism with the ideas of the eighteenth-century ENLIGHTENMENT in Europe. He was the first eminent Jewish figure to make the transition from the ghetto to modernity. His view was that because God is the most perfect Being, the divine will must be directed toward producing the highest moral perfection. Judaism, Mendelssohn said, possesses a divine legislation—commandments, statutes, rules of conduct, instruction in God's will, and ways to attain temporal and eternal salvation. The doctrines and ethical teachings of Judaism are those of reason and hence universal. Israel's unique heritage is a specially revealed ceremonial law. Mendelssohn insisted that Jews must be integrated into civil society in such a way that their right to observe the ceremonial law is not infringed. His greatest impact was to foster a Jewish Enlightenment, the *Haskalah.*

A modern thinker who dealt with Jewish peoplehood was Nachman Krochmal (1785–1840). His main thesis was that Israel (the people) is devoted to what he called the Absolute Spirit—God, who is the source of all spiritual ideas. Israel must be dedicated to the furtherance of the spiritual in its most absolute and eternal form. Therefore, Israel's work is never done. Israel may have its ups and downs, but it will never disappear completely because it is wedded to the God-idea, which is eternal. Krochmal's concept of the Jewish mission influenced Reform Jewish thinkers.

Hermann Cohen (1842–1918) was particularly taken with Judaism as an ethical religion. The Messiah, he believed, cannot come and the world cannot be redeemed unless human beings know all the miseries of existence and learn to fight against them. Cohen taught that the prophets interpreted suffering as a stage in the evolution of the human condition. The separation of suffering from guilt and punishment is one of the most significant consequences of the belief in One God. Cohen also believed that the pauper is the symbol of the human race. Far from being outcasts, poor people are the favorites of God—living witnesses to the truth that compassion matters.

Franz Rosenzweig (1886–1929) and MARTIN BUBER (1878–1965) are considered religious existentialists. Rosenzweig emphasized the religious, trans-historic quality of Jewish existence. Of the three dimensions of existence—creation, revelation, and redemption—the most crucial to Rosenzweig is revelation. God gives the individual the Divine Presence, and the experience of divine love takes the form of a command to love God in return. Redemption is the turning toward others of one who has experienced revelation. Rosenzweig saw Judaism and Christianity as mutually exclusive yet complementary. Both traditions are authentic communities of love through which eternity enters the stream of time.

To Buber, relationship is everything. Every relationship is either an I-THOU relationship or an I-It relationship. In the I-It relationship, there is no real personal involvement—one studies, one observes, one uses. The I-Thou relationship goes beyond experience and feeling. It is an encounter, a basic dimension of human existence and the key to what Buber calls the realm of relation. The "absolute relation" is the human being's relationship with God. The only way we can know God is through the I-Thou relationship. God is "the eternal Thou." If you hallow this life, you meet the living God. Whenever we attain an I-Thou relationship with other human beings, God speaks to us too. A balance between the I-Thou and the I-It is essential for the recovery of meaning and fulfillment in private and social life.

THEODOR HERZL (1860–1904) is considered the father of modern political ZIONISM. He saw ANTI-SEMITISM as a constantly growing menace. If they wanted to preserve themselves it was necessary for Jews to have a homeland. At first his idea was for a Jewish state anywhere in the world, but eventually he saw that this dream could only be realized in Palestine, the home of the Jewish people.

Ahad Ha-Am (1856–1927) developed the idea of Palestine as a spiritual center for Jews everywhere. He opposed Herzl, who he felt had a too political and uncultural view of Zionism. Jews should be concerned with more than physical survival. Zionism cannot confine itself to the work of rebuilding Palestine. Jews must do what is necessary to make Palestine a permanent and freely developing center of their national culture, their science and scholarship, art, and literature. He advocated the establishment of a single great school of learning in Palestine, which would be a source of inspiration and generate a revival of Jewish culture.

Can Jews believe in God in the face of the HOLOCAUST? Richard Rubenstein says that we live in the time of the DEATH OF GOD. By this he means that the thread uniting God and the human being has been broken. Despite this, he thinks that Judaism still has meaning and power, that it is the way Jews share the decisive times and crises of life through the traditions of their inherited community. Emil Fackenheim asserts that Jews must cope with the contradiction of confronting the Holocaust and yet not despair. If they do not have faith enough to live in the Jewish tradition, they hand Hitler a posthumous victory, and that they are forbidden to do. Buber talked about "the eclipse of God," which occurred in certain dark, historical hours like the Holocaust. He foresaw the possibility of a renewed divine-human encounter.

The most striking difference between modern thought of Judaism and that which was before is the shift in emphasis from an otherworldly to a this-worldly approach to the religious life. The ancient rabbis taught that this life is a preparation for the afterlife, for the *Olam Haba* (world to come). Louis Jacobs argues that it is indeed possible for a religion to be both this-worldly and otherworldly, for viewed from the aspect of eternity this world and the world to come are one.                                                    L.K.

**JUDAIZING** (Judaizers). A term, used pejoratively, to refer to Christians in the early church, mentioned in Acts and Galatians (and perhaps in I Corinthians 1), who observed the Jewish law, especially dietary customs and circumcision. The first apostolic council, recorded in Acts, decided that the Jewish law (especially circumcision and food prohibitions) was not binding upon Christians. One did not have to become a Jew before becoming a Christian, for by this time (about A.D. 50) the majority of converts to Christianity were Gentiles. Paul, too, in Galatians, shows the theological groundlessness of holding people saved by Christ to the need for circumcision and dietary rules. However, Judaizers remained part of the Christian scene until after the fall of Jerusalem in A.D. 70, and the gradual decline of Palestinian Christianity, which moved across the Jordan River to Pella.

The term was also used in a negative sense during the Middle Ages, especially at the time of the Spanish Inquisition, to refer to the "Moriscos" or Spanish Jews who were forcefully converted to Christianity, having accepted baptism to avoid persecution or being driven from their homes in Spain. These outwardly Catholic, but inwardly still Jewish, people were called Judaizers as they either practiced Jewish ceremonies in secret or were suspected of doing so.

J.C.

**JUDAS ISCARIOT.** Probably the original form of this name was Judah Ish-Keriot, meaning Judah from Kerioth in southern Judea. Some scholars have tried to trace Iscariot to the term *sikarios,* meaning "dagger," which is used by Josephus to refer to the fanatical nationalists who vowed to murder any who stood in the way of achieving political independence for the Jews. Some interpreters have supposed that Judas was disillusioned when Jesus announced the coming of God's Rule but refused to take any action to bring it about.

The Gospels all attest that Judas was one of the original twelve followers of Jesus (Matt. 10:4; Mark 3:19; Luke 6:16; John 6:71). But he plays no part in the activities of Jesus until the final days, except that in John 12:4-5 he complains because the costly ointment poured out on Jesus might have been sold and the money realized thereby given to the poor. The Gospels agree that Judas is the one foreseen as the betrayer of Jesus and describe that process of betrayal as set in motion at the Last Supper (Matt. 26:14; Mark 14:10; Luke 22:3; John 13:2).

What Judas actually betrayed was, apparently, where Jesus might be seized outside the city and therefore away from crowds that might have rallied to his support. The guards seize him in Gethsemane, and Jesus offers no resistance (Matt. 26:47, 57; Luke 22:47-50; John 18:12). Only in Luke (22:48) does Jesus address Judas. Matthew reports that guilt-ridden Judas hanged himself (27:3-5), while Acts describes a divine judgment that results in Judas' bursting apart in a ghastly death, to be replaced by Matthias through drawing lots (Acts 1:16-26).

H.K.

## JUDAS MACCABEUS. *See* MACCABEAN REVOLT.

## JUDE, LETTER OF. This brief letter claims to have been written by one Judah (Jude), a brother of James. In Mark 6:3, James and Jude are listed as brothers of Jesus. There are several indications, however, that the work is from a considerably later period in NT times, perhaps as late as A.D. 100. The apostles are referred to as a venerated group of authorities, rather than as contemporary co-workers (v. 17). Faith is used to refer to a body of fixed doctrines rather than in the sense of trust or reliance on God, as in Paul and the Jesus tradition. There are references to the passage of time since the promise of Jesus' return (vv. 17-22). And Jesus is directly identified as God (v. 25), which Paul never does. The letter is almost certainly late and by someone writing in the name of "Jude."

All the illustrations used by the writer to warn of divine judgment on those who depart from the truth are drawn from the OT or related documents. This does not require us to suppose that its first readers were from a Jewish background, since the Jewish scriptures had from the outset been the Bible of all the Christians. But Jude also quotes or refers to Jewish apocalyptic writings, which did not make it into either the Jewish or Christian canon: the Ascension of Moses and the Book of Enoch (Jude 9, 14-15). These writings were treasured by Christians, who regarded them as providing special information about God's plan for the end of the age. Most remarkable about

Jude is that a later writer expanded this book to form what we know as II Peter.

H.K.

## JUDEA. A geographical name, initially attested in Greek in Ezra, Nehemiah, and Maccabees, which denotes the postexilic Jewish state. During Nehemiah's governorship, Judea was a small province claiming limited territory around Jerusalem. After Persian rule had given way to Greek, Judea strove for independence. Maccabean rulers won extensive territorial holdings, including Samaria and Galilee to the north, Idumea to the south, much of the coastal plain to the west, and Perea to the east.

These rulers did not claim that they had dramatically enlarged Judea. Rather, they saw themselves as holding sway over extensive subject lands. Nevertheless, under Roman rule, Herod the Great was called king of Judea when he controlled roughly the same area. The rule of his son, Archelaus, who became ethnarch of Judea, however, embraced Idumea and Samaria, but no longer Galilee and Perea. Subsequently, various Roman procurators of Judea dominated Idumea and Samaria, though the seat of their government moved northward from Jerusalem to Caesarea.

As a geographical division of Palestine, Judea contained about two thousand square miles, most of which lay south of Jerusalem and half of which was desert. It included the rugged Judah plateau (Luke 1:39), the lowland or Shephelah (Josh. 15:33-43), and the coastal plain. Well-populated JERUSALEM was Judea's nucleus. The economy, however, was mainly pastoral with shepherds traversing a rocky terrain and being sustained by its vineyards and olive groves. Understandably, the most frequent biblical mention of Judea occurs in the NT Gospels, which locate the birth, baptism, temptation, crucifixion, and resurrection of Jesus there.

J.K.K.

## JUDGES. Although many civil and religious leaders of the Bible are called judges, it is preeminently the twelve military leaders of the book of JUDGES who are known by the title. These heroes arose to meet specific threats from enemy peoples during the approximately two centuries of the tribal confederation that preceded the monarchy in Israel (about 1200–1000 B.C.). They achieved their fleeting prominence because of their courage and charisma. As soon as a judge's task was completed, the judge receded into obscurity and Israel languished until a new "judge" arose.

Six of the judges are minor figures of whom only very brief accounts are given: Shamgar (Judg. 3:31; 5:6); Tola and Jair (10:1-5); Ibzan, Elon, and Abdon (12:8-15). Many interpreters regard these figures as local in origin and folkloristic in literary record, and some even suggest that they were invented in order to fill up the number twelve. On the other hand, the six major judges become heroes to be cherished in memory and even emulated. The least significant of these is Othniel, known only for his victory over Cushanrishathaim of Mesopotamia (3:7-11). After him came EHUD, a left-handed Benjaminite lad who assassinated Eglon, the king of the Moabites, while the latter was sitting in his private roof chamber (3:12-30). DEBORAH, the prophetess-judge, whose call for strong measures against the Canaanites is celebrated in marvelous poetry as well as prose (Judg. 4–5), conducted her business from her seat under a palm tree halfway between Ramah and Bethel. GIDEON exhibited legendary courage and faithfulness in his victory over the Midianites (Judg. 6–8). JEPHTHAH delivered Israel from the Ammonites, but only at the tragic cost of his virgin daughter's life. Because of his ill-advised vow to offer to Yahweh the first thing that greeted him following his victory, his daughter became one of the rare cases of human sacrifice in Israel (Judg. 11). The last judge, SAMSON, is described more fully than any other (Judg. 13–16). His life was haunted with tragedy, mostly centering on his love for the treacherous Delilah.

A thirteenth figure, ABIMELECH (Judg. 9), the son of Gideon, is not described as a judge even though he ruled over Israel for at least three years. Undoubtedly this is because he is regarded as a murderer and usurper. On the other hand, Samuel, who "judged Israel all the days of his life" (I Sam. 7:15), matches all the qualities of charismatic military leadership possessed by the greatest figures of the book of Judges. However, he is a man for all seasons, because he is also described as priest (I Sam. 2:35; 3:1ff.) and prophet (I Sam. 3:20). Through him the transition from the episodic leadership of judges to the permanent rule of kings is made, first with Saul (I Sam. 10:1) and then with David (I Sam. 16:1-13).

W.S.T.

**JUDGES, BOOK OF.** This seventh book of the OT preserves tales and traditions coming down from that period in the life of Israel before the rise of kingship when it maintained a somewhat tenuous existence in the land of Canaan as a tribal confederation. Most of the book chronicles the story of twelve charismatic JUDGES who rose up for brief careers of leadership against the military threats of neighboring peoples during the two centuries after the conquest under Joshua (about 1200–1000 B.C.).

*Composition of the Book.* The book of Judges falls into three principal parts: (a) a résumé of the conquest of Canaan, which deviates in some respects from the picture presented by the book of JOSHUA (1:1–3:6); (b) the stories of the twelve individual judges (3:7–16:31); (c) an appendix that details the migration of the tribe of Dan from the southwestern part of Palestine to the extreme north, to which account are also appended miscellaneous narratives about primitive Yahwistic idolatry and civil war with the tribe of Benjamin (chaps. 17–21).

(a) *The résumé (1:1–3:6).* Modern commentators generally assume that the structure of the book was given it by editors working in the theological tradition of the book of DEUTERONOMY, between the late seventh and middle sixth centuries B.C. Although they utilized many ancient traditions, they also inserted interpretive material, such as Judges 2:11–3:6, which contains their typical apostasy-punishment-supplication-deliverance scheme. The traditions with which they worked were not always pliant, so they were left with discrepancies such as that between the so-called "negative conquest list" of Judges 1:27-36 and the idealized picture of total victory, which they had already presented in Joshua 1–12. Yet the editors do not hesitate to comment theologically on the historical record that they had received. In 2:1-5 the angel of the Lord attaches a negative theological evaluation to the failure of Israel to complete absolutely the task of holy war with the root-and-branch extermination of Canaanite civilization. He threatens, "they shall become adversaries to you, and their gods shall be a snare to you" (2:3).

(b) *The lives of the judges (3:7–16:31).* Six of the judges are known by little more than their names, while the lives of six others are described at varying lengths. One of the two most extensive cycles of stories gathers around the figure of GIDEON (chaps. 6–8, supplemented in chap. 9 with an account of the abortive attempt of a non-judge, ABIMELECH, Gideon's son, to establish a royal dynasty in Israel). In a scene reminiscent both of Moses at the burning bush and Mary at the annunciation, Gideon, the weak and lowly son of the least important clan in Manasseh, is called by an angel to deliver his people Israel from Midianite oppression (6:11). By following Yahweh's directions, Gideon accomplishes the incredible rout of 135,000 Midianite warriors through a strategy that ultimately involved only 300 of his own men (7:19-23). His combination of military prowess and refusal to usurp the ultimate authority of God (8:23) causes the author(s) of the book to regard Gideon as the best of all the judges.

The other extensive cycle of stories concerns the last of the twelve judges, SAMSON, of the tribe of Dan (Judg. 13–16). Samson was a Nazarite, pledged from the moment of his miraculous birth never to cut his hair or to touch strong drink. Devoid of any great theological significance, but rich in folkloristic details, the stories of Samson present him as the Paul Bunyan of the OT. His magnificent wit and strength are manifested when he tears a live lion apart with his bare hands (14:6), and when he takes revenge upon the Philistines by setting fire to their crops, using the tails of live foxes as torches (15:4-5). He slays one thousand men with the jawbone of an ass (vv. 14-16), and interrupts a quiet night with a harlot to tear the gates off the wall of the city of Gaza (16:1-3). His lustiness is finally his undoing, when his tragic love affair with the Philistine woman Delilah leads him to allow her to cut the hair protected by his sacred vow (16:15-22). Even so, Samson redeems his life through his final act of heroism, when he pulls the temple of

Dagon down upon the heads of the Philistine lords and himself.

The accounts of tribal affairs with which the book concludes (chaps. 17–21) betray the growing need for strong leadership. The abominable household shrine of Micah (chap. 17), its seizure by the tribe of Dan, and the death and dismemberment of the Levite's concubine with the resulting slaughter of the tribe of Benjamin, all lead to the expressive conclusion of the book of Judges. Its final sentence is not to be understood as a positive statement, but rather as a sad acknowledgment of the failure of the primitive polity: "In those days there was no king in Israel; every man did what was right in his own eyes" (21:25).

*Historical Reliability.* During the two centuries in which the people of Israel lived in Canaan as a loose confederation of tribes, it would seem likely that some kind of charismatic judge figures did in fact provide leadership from time to time. On the other hand, no secular or extra-biblical sources are available that would throw light on the nature of the Israelite community during that period, much less confirm the biblical account of the life or work of any of the individual judges. It does seem quite unlikely that the present "all Israel" perspective of the book of Judges would actually have prevailed in that early period, for the tribes were only then discovering one another, and cementing their allegiance to one another around the common traditions of Yahwism preserved and reenacted at the sanctuaries. But editorial perspective and older source material are two different matters. The older stories of the book reflect real cultural conditions and institutions, such as weddings and human sacrifice, pagan festivals and giants, blood revenge, and the telling of riddles. They ring with the authentic voice of ancient people speaking in their coarse but very human tongue.

*The Theology of the Book of Judges.* Because of its coarse and human spirit, the book of Judges confronts us in a special way with the incarnate nature of the Bible as the Word of God. God took the great risk of disclosing a purpose in human history through the words of people, and nowhere is this fact felt more keenly than here. Although Israel is still in its formative stages, the cult of Yahweh is well established. In fact, Yahweh is depicted in a silver statuette, the object of worship in the household shrine of Micah (17:1-5)! The battle with Baal is being joined in full force for the first time during this period. Jephthah's sacrifice of his daughter suggests

that Israel had not yet fully differentiated itself from the rituals and sympathetic magic of Canaan; however, Gideon's fierce attack upon the altar of Baal at Ophrah suggests that a clear judgment had already been made about things that do not pertain to Yahweh. Faith in Yahweh's leadership in holy war is evidenced in the song of Deborah, where even the stars, the visible manifestation of the Lord's "hosts," fight against the enemies of Israel (5:20). The capacities of the judges to win victories in the face of overwhelming odds (7:7; 16:28-31), to elicit miraculous signs from Yahweh (6:36-40), and to outwit all opposition (14:10-20) bespeak a deep confidence in Yahweh's sovereignty in human history. But human history is also the history of disobedience and apostasy. Israel's repeated lapses into slavery and suffering represent, in the theology of the Deuteronomic editors of the book of Judges, Yahweh's constant retributional response to Israel's faithlessness. Far from a golden age, then, the period of the judges is presented as a history constantly oscillating between the two poles of human treachery and divine trustworthiness.          W.S.T.

**JUDGMENT.** A characteristic part of the Bible's teaching is that all people are accountable for their moral actions, and that they will be summoned to a time of reckoning. This is the basis for the Jewish and Christian teaching under the heading of judgment.

It is an axiom for OT writers that God is "judge" (Gen. 18:25), and that God's dealings both now and in the future are on the basis of fairness and truth (Isa. 5:16). So God may be appealed to vindicate the righteous cause of people, especially when they are oppressed. The negative side of such vindication and deliverance is divine judgment passed on Israel's enemies (Amos 1:3–2:3; Hab. 1:5–2:5, and prophetic oracles against the nations in Jer. 47–51).

The eighth-century prophets, however, introduced a novel idea centered on their interpretation of the "day of Yahweh." In popular religion, it was evidently a day for national SALVATION of Israel and the doom of Israel's foes. Amos (5:18-20) reverses this to announce that Israel will be judged for its infidelities to the covenant and its neglect of social justice in the land (4:1-5; 5:12-13). He calls the nation to REPENTANCE; otherwise it will be judgment for Israel. This then is renewed in Isaiah, Jeremiah, and Ezekiel in later times.

*Part of an early Christian sarcophagus, symbolizing the theme of the Last Judgment: Christ separating the sheep from the goats*

The NT writers stand in the OT Jewish tradition. God is impartial and will punish all wickedness (Rom. 1:18; Heb. 12:23; I Pet. 1:17; Rev. 16:5-7). The moral basis for such judgment is laid in God's character, but with the extra dimension that the "light" of the coming of his Son Jesus Christ has shown up all "darkness" as evil. This theme is particularly clear in the Fourth Gospel (John 3:19-21), which sees the Judgment as a present reality (5:24).

The Judgment is associated elsewhere in the NT with the PAROUSIA of Christ, or his coming in power (Matt. 25:31-46; I Cor. 4:3-5; Heb. 10:36-39). The scenario differs, but the essential fact of a future day of reckoning is clear in the different parts of the NT (plainly described in Acts 17:31). Judgment is thus part of NT eschatology, and in Christian theology it took its place as one of the four "last things"; the other parts are death, heaven, and hell.          R.M.

**JUDITH, BOOK OF.** The Apocryphal book of Judith is a highly inventive and patriotic appeal to the people of Israel to rise up and defend their country. The heroine is a young widow, Judith, which means "a woman from Judah." General Holofernes of the Assyrian army has put under siege the imaginary city of Bethulia in the Esdraelon Valley, trying to starve it out. The high priests plan to surrender as soon as the water gives out. But Judith takes off her widow's weeds, puts on her best finery and perfume, and at nightfall visits the tent of Holofernes. She persuades him she will show him an unguarded entrance to the city and in fact guide him all the way to Jerusalem. Instead, as he lies in half-drunken sleep, she uses his own scimitar to cut off his head and carries this in secret to the high priests of Bethulia. The next morning the enemy army flees in terror as it discovers the headless body of its leader.

In many ways the story reminds one of Jael's murder of Sisera (Judges 4:17-22). The book probably dates from the Maccabean times when Israel was being encouraged to throw off an oppressor. It is filled with anachronistic inconsistencies and badly spelled or nonexistent place-names. Nebuchadnezzar is wrongly cited as king of Nineveh, not Babylon. The oldest manuscript of the book is in Greek, but there probably was also an older Hebrew or Aramaic version. Judith has proved to be a popular subject for classical painting, for example, Caravaggio's *Judith with the Head of Holofernes*.          T.J.K.

**JUDSON, ADONIRAM** (1788-1850). American Baptist, one of the pioneers of the modern missionary movement. Born the son of a Congregational minister in Massachusetts, Judson was stimulated to consider foreign missons at Andover Seminary. He sailed for India in 1812 under the sponsorship of the American Board of Commissioners for Foreign Missions, but while aboard ship he was convinced of the Baptist position and was baptized in Calcutta. He later received the support of American Baptists and went to Burma in 1813. A brilliant linguist, Judson did much translation work into the Burmese language, and traveled extensively in the cause of the unification of Baptist missionary work in Asia.          W.G.

**JULIAN OF NORWICH** (about 1342-1423). English mystic, author of *Revelations of Divine Love*. At age thirty, during grave illness, she received sixteen revelations. *Revelations* taught that God sees all things as good, sin is part of God's purpose, our sufferings preface bliss, and we are to rejoice now in Christ's great love.          C.M.

**JULIAN THE APOSTATE** (331-63). Roman emperor (361-63) who attempted to turn the Roman Empire from Christianity to paganism. CONSTANTINE the Great died in 337, and his son Constantius became ruler in the East. He murdered possible rivals, including Julian's father, a half brother of Constantine, but spared young Julian. Born in Constantinople, Julian grew up in a remote part of Asia Minor. At twenty he received permission to study in Greece, where he turned toward Greek philosophy and pagan traditions and immersed himself in ancient Greek culture. Made Caesar in 355, Julian was sent to govern Gaul, Britain, and Spain. His troops successfully resisted barbarian incursions, defeated the Alamanni, and stopped the Franks. To check Julian's rising popularity, Constantius ordered Julian's troops to the East. Instead, the army proclaimed Julian emperor in 360. Civil war loomed, but Constantius died in 361 before Julian reached Constantinople. Julian renounced Christianity, discontinued the church's special privileges, placed pagans in high offices, and wrote pamphlets against Christianity. He also allowed Athanasius and other exiles to return, hoping to weaken the church, but Athanasius' frequent conversions of pagans caused Julian to banish him again. On a campaign against Persia, Julian died. He was Rome's last openly heathen emperor.          C.M.

**JULIUS CAESAR.** *See* CAESAR, GAIUS JULIUS.

**JUNG, CARL GUSTAV** (1875-1961). Son of a Swiss Reformed pastor, Jung was early interested in religion, but adolescent experiences left him uncomfortable with the prospect of studying theology. He turned to psychiatry, graduating from the University of Basel (1895-1900) and receiving the M.D. from the University of Zürich in 1902. He first worked at the university psychiatric clinic, then at the Bergholze Asylum in Zürich, where he had the unique experience of working under the direction of Eugen Blueler, who was engaged in foundational research into mental illness.

While working with small groups probing associational memories, Jung became conscious of clusters of words that seemed to trigger hesitant responses from patients because of "forbidden" content. Out of this experience he coined the word "complex" to suggest the kinds of responses made.

He collaborated with SIGMUND FREUD from 1907–12, after which they parted over differences concerning the role of sexual bases in neuroses. Jung established a school at Zurich and named his approach to the field "analytic psychology." One of Jung's important contributions was the identification of two personality types: the extrovert, who is warm, outgoing, and most at ease in the company of other persons; and the introvert, who is quiet, inward-looking, preferring to work alone or be in the company of a few people. He identified also four functions of the mind: thinking, feeling, sensation, and intuition, affirming that one or more might predominate in a person.

As a child Jung had a rich fantasy and dream life. In developing his approach to psychiatry he permitted this side of his personality to function freely and began to keep notes on his dreams. From this research developed another area in which he made significant contributions. He affirmed that dreams arise from the collective unconscious, that reservoir of memories in each person that precedes historical memory.

His theory of archetypes is important for the study of the psychology of religion. An archetype is an instinctive pattern, a basic universal image that appears in the dream life of people in many unrelated cultures. He saw these images expressed in heretical traditions from Gnosticism to alchemy and believed that the Christian tradition limited its own self-expression by eliminating these insights from its collected experience. Jung's theories about archetypes and the collective unconscious point to the importance he attached to history. Individuation (another of his technical terms) referred to discovering one's own myth and dream as a way of most fully knowing the self.

Jung affirmed that religion can help the process of individuation by bringing archetypal images into consciousness. He had an appreciation for religious symbolism, noting that dream symbols were indications of intuition and revelation. He found among many religious traditions the symbols of quaternity, trinity, and duality. The animus-anima, or male-female components of existence, together expressed the interaction and wholeness that belong to being human. Jungian theories have become influential in the area of religious studies.                              I.C.

JUSTICE. The term justice is rarely used in modern English translations of the Bible. There are no OT terms that convey the usual meaning of "justice" (from the Latin *justitia*): all members of society receiving from the gods or other persons their just deserts—retributive justice. The Hebrew term sometimes translated "justice" should read "righteousness," which is not to be equated with "strict justice," for it includes mercy, reflecting God's

dealings with people according to covenant love or faithfulness. Where the English word "justice" is retained in modern versions it should convey this meaning (see, for example, Amos 5:24).

The Greek term for "justice" (*dikē*) appears only three times in the NT (for example, Acts 28:4). Paul is chiefly responsible for establishing the theological importance of the OT concept, in the light of the person and work of Jesus Christ. Whether "justice" should ever be preferred to the term "righteousness"—God's, and one's own—is an open question. Compare the following passages in the RSV and the NEB: Matthew 6:33; Romans 3:21-26; 5:17-18; 10:1-4; Philippians 3:8-11. Roman Catholic English translations reflect the influence of the Vulgate: *justitia* is translated "justice," *justus*, "just."

J.L.P.

JUSTIFICATION. Justification is the free acceptance of sinners into God's favor and the forgiveness of their sins, on account of the sacrifice of Christ, appropriated by faith.

*Overview.* Traditionally, in Protestantism, this doctrine is stated as "justification by faith," or better, as "justification by grace through faith," or even more comprehensively, as "justification by grace through faith on account of Christ."

"Justification" or "to be justified" is from the Greek verb *Dikaioo.* Generally, in both the OT and the NT the verb is translated "to be made righteous" and other forms of the word are translated "righteousness" or "righteous." Paul, for example, uses the verb *Dikaioo* twenty-five times and other forms of the word seventy-three times, of which "righteousness" is used fifty-two times. In the OT the Hebrew words *tseded* and *tsedaqah* are translated "righteousness" or "justice." The basic Hebrew meaning is "conformity to the character of God" who is wholly righteous.

Justification is the act of becoming a Christian. It is not earned by any merit or works on the person's part, but is a gracious gift of God. One cannot justify oneself. Only God can do it, and God does it as a gift to us (Rom. 3:24).

It is erroneously held by many that Roman Catholics and Protestants differ widely on justification. For centuries Protestants believed that Catholics felt they could justify themselves by good works. While there are different emphases in the two traditions, both have always held that a sinner is justified by the grace of God that comes through the Lord Jesus Christ. For Catholics, Christ's work for us has made the Holy Spirit available to people. First, people must receive an infusion of righteousness by the HOLY SPIRIT. Once repentance occurs, God then pronounces the believer justified because of the Holy Spirit's work. Here Protestantism in general, following MARTIN LUTHER's lead, developed by JOHN CALVIN and later by JOHN WESLEY, diverges from the Catholic position. Although Luther was close to the Catholic doctrine at first, he later developed the concept of imputed righteousness, that is, people are justified by the righteousness of Jesus Christ—won on the cross—when they are in faith, a relationship of trust, in Christ. For Luther, this faith, or trust, is itself the gift of God (as it is for Paul, Rom. 3:24; 5:15-17). This faith, then, justifies without any good works, as Paul declares in Romans 4:6, "God reckons righteousness apart from works" and Romans 3:28, "For we hold that a man is justified by faith apart from works of law."

Justification is a term taken from law courts and means "to be declared righteous or blameless." This is the forensic (or declared) meaning of the term. We are said to be blameless by God even though we are actually sinners. This God does for us out of love and grace, basing the divine action on (that is, by imputation) the atoning work of Christ. To be justified is tied directly to trust in the sacrificial death of Christ, as the objective reason for our being declared righteous. Christ's death shows the integrity of God. God does not simply ignore our sin; Christ paid the penalty for our sin. Therefore, by believing in him we share in the righteousness that belongs only to him. "While we were still weak, at the right time Christ died for the ungodly. . . . But God shows his love for us in that while we were yet sinners Christ died for us" (Rom. 5:6-8).

*Biblical.* Justification is clearly related, as a biblical concept, to the other major biblical ideas of RECONCILIATION, FORGIVENESS, GRACE, FAITH, ATONEMENT, and SALVATION. All of these concepts have to do with the relationship of the human person to God—and in both the OT and the NT they are cast in terms of the activity of a loving God who acts decisively to restore persons to full enjoyment of love and trust, and to active participation in God's plans for humanity.

To be justified means to be righteous or clothed in righteousness in both the OT and the NT, carrying the connotation of being brought into right relationship with God or humans. The OT clearly states (Ps. 143:2; Job 25:4) that human beings can do nothing to become justified or righteous in relation to God. Isaiah 57:12 and 64:6 state that one is not justified by works as clearly as Paul says in Acts 13:39; Galatians 2:16; Romans 3:28, and Romans 4:1-25. People may, of course, justify or make themselves righteous in their dealings with other people.

To be reconciled means "to have removed barriers that prevent a close relationship from developing between people." Forgiveness means "the setting aside of the actions that constitute those barriers." Grace is unmerited divine favor that forgives and reconciles people, so that they are justified. Such a condition of justification is the equivalent of salvation, the moment of being saved from the wrath of God. In the NT, such justification, chiefly developed by Paul in Romans and Galatians, is based upon the atonement of Christ, the saving act of his death, which pays the penalties that humans rightly incur by their sinfulness. The objective results of this atonement (also called propitiation, from the analogy to OT sacrifices) are subjectively appropriated by faith. Yet this faith is not the human will to believe but is a trust and confidence given to persons by God. This saving faith is the power to hold on to Christ firmly, with full conviction and confidence. As Paul declares in Romans 9:16: ". . . it depends not upon man's will or exertion, but upon God's mercy."

*Theological.* In selecting a few of the more important studies of justification and related concepts throughout the eighteen or more centuries of serious Christian theology, one naturally thinks of Martin Luther, since the REFORMATION of the sixteenth century grew out of Luther's experience of justification by faith. Yet the great reformer never wrote a specific work on the subject. John Calvin covers justification in *The Institutes of the Christian Religion* but is everywhere dependent upon Luther's later views, as elaborated and systematized by PHILIP MELANCHTHON. The infusion theory is rejected and the imputation of Christ's merits to the sinner is stressed by both Melanchthon and Calvin.

Most interesting is the 1957 study of HANS KÜNG, *Justification: The Doctrine of Karl Barth and a Catholic Reflection.* This warmly accepting study goes far to demonstrate the genuine Catholic teachings on justification and to reconcile them to the theology of the Reformed thinker KARL BARTH. Indeed, Barth, in a letter to Küng (Jan. 31, 1957) says that what he holds about justification objectively concurs on all points with the correctly understood teaching of the Roman Catholic church. Barth goes on to say that while Protestants and Catholics are divided in faith, they are divided within the same faith.

According to Barth, the most comprehensive Protestant theologian of this century, Luther was right in holding that justification is "the article [of faith] by which the church stands or falls." Nevertheless, both Protestant Barth and Catholic Küng see that justification is only one aspect of the message of Christ's salvation. In the NT, only the Fourth Gospel is easy to harmonize with Paul's teaching. The early church and the Eastern Orthodox churches never developed a full-blown doctrine of justification. Even in the post-Reformation period Calvin made the predestination of the Sovereign God more central than justification by faith. Along with justification, theologians have always, even in the Lutheran churches—following Luther—developed a doctrine of sanctification, or of the progressive growth in holiness of the Christian.

Additionally, in all theologians, including Luther and Calvin, and especially in the Roman Catholic and Eastern churches, there is the development of the doctrine of Christian calling or vocation. Because of this insight both Barth and Küng agree that the article by which the church stands or falls is not justification but the confession of faith in Jesus Christ.

This attempt at irenicism, or peacemaking, between Christian communions on justification is not new. The basic document of the Lutheran churches, the AUGSBURG CONFESSION, was written by Melanchthon in such a cordial spirit: "Our churches also teach that men cannot be justified before God by their own strength, merits or works but are freely justified for Christ's sake through faith when they believe that they are received into favor and that their sins are forgiven on account of Christ, who by his death made satisfaction for our sins. This faith God imputes for righteousness in his sight" (A.C., 4).

Throughout the Confession, Melanchthon seeks to create the impression that the controversy between Wittenberg and Rome was not over doctrine but only over certain abuses. While this may have been too optimistic a position for the sixteenth century, it may be a genuine reflection of the growing appreciation of Catholics and Protestants for each other in the late twentieth century. (See SANCTIFICATION.)          J.C.

**JUSTIN MARTYR** (about 100–165). Early Christian apologist and martyr who united Christian thought with philosophy and helped preserve the OT for Christians. Little is known about his life. Greek in culture and education, he was born in Flavia Neapolis in Palestine and was drawn to Platonism, but finally found true philosophy in the wisdom of the prophets. He became a Christian teacher and was martyred in Rome for his faith. Justin regarded Christianity as a superior philosophy—the LOGOS of the OT was prophesied of and made incarnate in Christ. His *First* and *Second Apology* were briefs for Christianity, the first written about 155, the second shortly before his death. In both apologies Justin asked a fair hearing for Christians. Justin explained traditional Christian truths as handed down from the apostles, who taught that God cares and loves humanity. This is shown in the OT and in the dying and rising Savior. Christians live in gratitude for all of God's gifts and show this in their actions. *Dialogue,* with Trypho the Jew, was written after the *First Apology* and concentrates on Jesus as the promised Messiah. Justin was orthodox in belief but wrote little about Jesus' life. He opposed Gnosticism, regarded Christianity as a philosophy, and continued to wear the philosopher's gown.

C.M.

**JUST WAR.** *See* WAR.

# Kk

**KA'BA.** A cube-like building, the house of ALLAH (God) in ISLAM, and the goal of the HAJJ (pilgrimage). Five times daily Muslims turn toward it in prayer. It is about forty feet long, thirty-three feet wide, and fifty feet high, and is made of Meccan granite. It is empty except for gold and silver lamps hanging from the ceiling and is cleaned every year. A thick black covering (*Kiswa,* or "robe") embroidered with verses from the Qur'an covers the entire building; it is remade every year. Around the Ka'ba stands the MOSQUE of MECCA, separated from the Ka'ba by a wide courtyard. Fire, flood, and war have damaged the Ka'ba many times throughout its history, and the current structure dates from the seventeenth century. The oldest part of the Ka'ba is the black stone, referred to as "the right hand of God on earth." It was part of the Ka'ba long before Islam arose; myths claim that it fell from heaven and is the only extant part of the original structure built by Abraham. Today it is encased in silver and is a focus of attention during the pilgrimage. MUHAMMAD cleansed the Ka'ba in A.D. 630, casting out the idols and consecrating the building to the worship of the one God.

K./M.C.

**KABBALA.** Traditional name for MYSTICISM in JUDAISM. Although esoteric doctrines have a long history in Jewish thought, the Kabbala proper only arose around the twelfth century A.D.

The first four hundred years of the Kabbala, through the expulsion of Jews from Spain and Portugal in 1492, followed three traditions: rabbinic Judaism, Jewish Gnosticism, and Neoplatonic philosophy. One of the earliest Kabbalist books, the *Sefer Bahir,* was written in southern France in the late twelfth century, before NEOPLATONISM began to influence the Kabbala. The *Zohar,* written in Spain around 1285, used Gnostic and Neoplatonic language to describe cosmic unity. It linked much of orthodox theology in a complex net of symbols, particularly the *sefirot.* These were ten revealed aspects of God (such as Wisdom, Beauty, etc.), which pointed toward the One, who is *"en sof,"* or "without end." After 1492 the Kabbala took on a more apocalyptic and messianic tone. Isaac Luria, who wrote in Safad, Galilee, embraced theism and a dualism of God and the universe. He taught that the actions of the mystic could lead to the reunification of God with himself, away from the illusory world of things. His theory fit well with the experience of the Diaspora—the scattering of Jews throughout Europe, Africa, and Asia—and influenced the pietistic revivalism of the eighteenth-century Hasidic movement.

K./M.C.

**KABIR.** An Indian holy man (A.D. 1440–1518?) who brought together elements of Islam and Hinduism in order to overcome sectarian disputes and divisions.

His teachings influenced Guru NANAK, founder of the SIKH religion. Some of his hymns are included in the Granth, the Sikh scriptures. Born of working class Muslim parents, he held firmly to the concept of the one true God and rejected such outward forms of religion as worship of images, elaborate rituals, scriptures, and the Hindu caste system. He declared that anyone, of any caste or race, who loved God freely could escape the power of KARMA and the cycle of rebirth. He also taught the importance of following a spiritual master, or guru, as the only way of developing right attitudes toward life.

K./M.C.

**KADDISH.** A special Jewish prayer of praise to God, recited with congregational responses at the close of individual sections of the public service and at the conclusion of the service itself. Although there is no reference to the dead in the kaddish, it is also used as a mourner's prayer. It is recited by the mourner at the graveside of parents or close relatives, and during the three daily prayers in the synagogue for the first eleven months following the death of a parent or relative and on each anniversary of the death. Written in Aramaic, the kaddish is characterized by an abundance of praise and glorification of God and an expression of hope in the speedy establishment of God's kingdom on earth. "May He establish His kingdom" in the Ashkenazi version is broadened by Sephardic Jews with the additional "May He make His salvation closer and bring the Messiah near." The congregational response, "May His great name be blessed forever and to all eternity," is the kernel of the kaddish. The opening phrase, "Magnified and sanctified be His great name in the world . . ." has some resemblance to the opening phrases of Ezekiel 38:23 and the Lord's Prayer (Matt. 6:9).

L.K.

**KADESH-BARNEA.** An oasis important to certain OT narratives, located between the Wilderness of Zin and the Wilderness of Paran. Several sites have been suggested as the location of the biblical settlement, with perhaps that of 'Ain el-Qudeirat having the best claim. The springs there are among the most abundant in the Sinai Desert.

The Kadesh mentioned in Genesis 14:7 is probably the same as Kadesh-barnea (also here called En-mishpat or Spring of Judgment). The rebellious kings (whom Abram was soon to fight) conquered the settlement and the surrounding territory.

Kadesh-barnea was the location in which the Hebrew tribes under Moses settled for a period (Num. 13) during the WILDERNESS WANDERINGS. From there twelve spies were sent into the land of whom only Joshua and Caleb returned to advise the people to proceed, the other ten discouraging any attempted invasion. This caused many of the people to grumble that they wished to return to Egypt, a timidity that so angered the Lord that the older generation was

sentenced to die in the desert without ever entering the Land of Promise (Num. 14). In desperation, the Israelites, against the advice of Moses, launched an assault against the Canaanites but were thrown back to Kadesh, where they remained for some undetermined period.

It was at Kadesh-barnea that Miriam, the sister of Moses, died and was buried (Num. 20:1). It was here also that the people complained for lack of water, leading Moses to strike the rock in order to cause the water to gush forth. The narrative of this incident connects the name Meribah or Meribath ("contention") to Kadesh (see below). For his act Moses was condemned by the Lord and not permitted to lead the people into the Land of Promise (Num. 20:2-13).

At a later period Kadesh-barnea was considered to mark the extent of Judah's southern territory. It is referred to in this manner in Joshua 15:3 and Ezekiel 47:19 and 48:28. (In these latter two references it is termed Meribath-kadesh.)

J.D.N.

**KAFKA, FRANZ** (1883-1924). Writer of philosophical novels and stories, Kafka was born at Prague, then within the Austro-Hungarian Empire. More than one interpretation of his writings is possible, but he is most commonly taken to express the sense that human beings are thrown into a world that they do not comprehend and in which there is no obvious purpose for their lives. His best-known novels, *The Trial* (Eng. trans. 1956) and *The Castle* (Eng. trans. 1965), were both published posthumously. In the former, the hero's life is suddenly interrupted by his arrest. He experiences great frustration trying to discover what the charges are, and who are his accusers. The theme of *The Castle* is similar. A land surveyor arrives in a village and tries to contact the people at the castle for his instructions. But he cannot discover who is in charge up there—the telephone rings unanswered, or he gets a cryptic message, which breaks off. Appropriately, the novel is unfinished. While Kafka's writings can be read as a literary expression of what EXISTENTIALISM calls the "facticity" or even "absurdity" of human existence, he was deeply concerned with his Jewish inheritance, the Bible, and Hasidic mysticism. It has been claimed that there is a profoundly religious significance in his thought.

J.M.

**KAGAWA, TOYOHIKO** (1888-1960). One of the outstanding modern Christian witnesses in Asia. The son of a wealthy Japanese businessman and his *geisha* wife, Kagawa was baptized in 1903 and promptly disowned by his family. He went to live in the slums of Kobe and experienced the desolation of the poor in the age of Japan's change from a medieval state to a modern industrial economy. He strongly believed that the Christian witness must find expression in social service. His views on social and political matters expressed in his writings made him an object of suspicion, and he was arrested and jailed during the early 1940s. After World War II he was invited to enter politics and rebuild Japan. He refused but continued to preach and work for social justice among the people. His influence was probably greater in the West than in Japan, but he is rivaled by few in the art of making the authentic voice of Asian Christianity heard outside of that continent.

W.G.

KÄHLER, MARTIN (1835–1912). German theologian who taught for many years at the University of Halle. He is remembered chiefly for his book *The So-Called Historical Jesus and the Historic Biblical Christ* (1892). This was an attempt to liberate theology from dependence on historical research, and it had a profound influence on a whole generation of theologians, including Paul Tillich. Kähler argued (as many others were to do after him) that the many biographies of Jesus produced by the nineteenth-century "quest for the historical Jesus" had no claim to be scientifically objective studies but simply reflected the subjective interests of the biographers. They were, he claimed, just as much products of the human imagination as had been "the notorious dogmatic Christ of Byzantine christology." The Gospels are misinterpreted if they are taken as either history or dogma. They are *kerygma* or proclamation. Hence the real Christ is the preached Christ, Christ as apprehended and proclaimed by Christian faith. One cannot get behind or beyond the kerygmatic Christ. Kähler's work not only dealt a blow to the quest for the historical Jesus but led scholars to reconsider what kind of writings the Gospels are and what we may reasonably expect to learn from them.

J.M.

KAIROS. One of two words in Greek to designate time. The other word is *chronos*, which refers to clock or calendar time, which is quantitative, measurable, and repetitive. *Kairos* is "fulfilled time" or "the right time." It points to unique temporal moments that are related to but are qualitatively different from other time and are filled with special meaning. The word *kairos* appears frequently in the NT and refers most specifically to the unique appearance of Christ who came "in the fulness of time." PAUL TILLICH has made special use of the concept of *kairos* in his theological reflections on history, particularly concerning his early involvement in and writings on the movement of Religious Socialism in Germany. Throughout Christian history, prophets and Reformers have interpreted their time as a special *kairos*, dependent however on the central *kairos*, the appearance of Christ. Tillich saw Religious Socialism after the First World War as such a special *kairos*. It rejected both the historical pessimism of traditional Lutheranism and the optimism of secular socialism. It was a special time (*kairos*) for creating a new social order, but one continuously judged by the criterion of the central *kairos*, Jesus Christ.

J.L.

KAIVALYA. From the Sanskrit word meaning "isolation, detachment." In JAINISM, and the Samkhya and YOGA schools of HINDUISM, the term "Kaivalya" is used for the ultimate liberation of the soul or self, termed in this connection *jiva* in Jainism and *purusha* in the Hindu schools. In both, the soul is seen as entrapped in KARMA (Jainism) or matter (Samkhya and Yoga), from which it can be released by asceticism and spiritual experience.

R.E.

KALAM. In ISLAM, theological doctrine and the means by which it was developed. Kalam has never been the dominant concern of Muslim scholars. They have accorded much more attention to legal and ritual issues, because Islam is more a religion of doing what is right than of solving speculative issues.

Even so, doctrinal issues arose early. One was the question of human free will in relation to God's sovereign will, by which he controls everything. Another was the question of who should hold political power in the Muslim world, and what his qualifications should be. A third was the question of the status of a Muslim who has committed a grave sin. All these questions had political as well as purely religious aspects.

Greek philosophy influenced much of Islamic theological thought. For instance, does God do good because it is good, or is everything he does good because he is the one doing it? The solution arrived at was that God is absolutely one, he is sovereign, and humans cannot comprehend him by rational means. The QUR'AN is eternal, and everything that it contains is literally true, even the anthropomorphic statements that speak of God sitting on a throne and having human attributes and features.

Theologians objected to painting, especially paintings that show the human form. In spite of this, Muslim rulers in many ages commissioned great works of art. Theological issues continue to challenge Muslim thinkers, and there have been new developments in the present century.

K.C.

KALI. From the Sanskrit word for "The Black One." An important goddess of HINDUISM, Kali represents the terrifying aspect of the earth mother. Often identified with the consort of SHIVA, in this capacity she is the phenomenal world, both productive and destructive, over against the god as the Absolute. Kali is frequently portrayed as black with eyes bulging and tongue hanging out, wearing a necklace of skulls. Her worship includes animal sacrifice. But while fearsome, Kali is ultimately good, for what she represents must be confronted by those who would seek liberation, and she has received the devotion of such noted saints as Ramakrishna. Kali is particularly popular in Bengal, the Kalighat temple in Calcutta, after which that city is named, being her best known place of worship.

R.E.

**KALLEY, ROBERT REID** (1809–88). Medical doctor, ordained clergyman, and hymnwriter, Kalley, born in Scotland, was a "missionary to the Portuguese of three continents." Unable to go to an assigned mission in China because of his wife's health the couple began an independent medical mission in the Madeira Islands in 1838. The mission, which included a program of literacy and Bible study, flourished. Persecution of Protestants beginning in 1842 forced Kalley to flee the islands. He served brief terms in the British West Indies, Malta, and Palestine, and then went to Brazil, where he made a notable contribution to the cultural and religious life of the nation. He composed a Portuguese hymnbook that became a standard for church singing. Authorities have termed the work done by Kalley "the greatest achievement of modern missions."

W.G.

**KAMA SUTRAS.** From the Sanskrit phrase meaning "Aphorisms on Erotic Love." The Kama Sutras are a class of textbooks on the arts of love, of which the best known is that attributed to Vatsyayana, who lived in north India around the beginning of the fourth century A.D. According to such texts as the Laws of Manu, *kama,* pleasure, especially erotic, is one of the four human goals, along with material gain, righteousness (DHARMA), and liberation (MOKSHA). Its cultivation is appropriate as part of the role of the householder who has not yet turned to the renunciant quest for liberation, but who is committed to the dharma of perpetuating human life and maintaining the social order. Thus *kama* and its skills have religious significance. R.E.

**KAMI.** From the Japanese word for "god or deity." The objects of worship in SHINTO —the polytheistic religion that embraces a vast number of kami, ranging from the solar goddess Amaterasu and the primal parents IZANAGI and IZANAMI to tiny spirits worshiped at wayside shrines. Kami are conceived of as finite, particularized spirits within a pluralistic universe who have traditional associations with places, occupations, or families. Some are connected with natural phenomena such as mountains or waterfalls; others are figures from the ancient mythology of the *Kojiki* and *Nihonshoki*; still others are deified historical figures, including the Meiji emperor (1868-1912), whose shrine is a prominent Tokyo landmark. Most Shinto shrines contain, usually behind the closed doors of the *honden* or inner sanctuary, an object such as an ancient mirror or sword called the *shintai,* which is said to manifest the presence of the kami. Kami are worshiped by priests with offerings of food and prayer and are celebrated in periodical *matsuri* or festivals. R.E.

**KANT, IMMANUEL** (1724–1804). German philosopher whose influence on theology is greater than that of any other philosopher in the modern period.

*Immanuel Kant*

Born in Königsberg in East Prussia, Kant was nurtured in the tradition of devout PIETISM. Later he came to abhor Pietism's emotional fervor, but its strict morality was enduring and is reflected in his thought. Kant attended the University of Königsberg, became a tutor to a private family, and in 1755 joined the faculty of the university, where he became a professor in 1770 and where he remained for the rest of his life. Kant's works include: *Critique of Pure Reason* (1781), *Prolegomena to Any Future Metaphysics* (1783), *Principles of the Metaphysics of Ethics* (1785), *Critique of Practical Reason* (1788), *Critique of Judgment* (1790), and *Religion Within the Limits of Reason Alone* (1794).

*Critique of Pure Reason* is one of the great works in the history of thought. It ushered in the Kantian "Copernican Revolution" in philosophy and theology. The empiricist tradition had conceived of the mind as passive, receiving sense impressions from the external world. From these impressions the mind "collects" ideas based on these impressions. With Hume empiricism led to skepticism regarding our knowledge of the external world. Kant began with a new hypothesis: the external objects that we perceive are already in some respects constituted by *a priori* forms of cognition imposed upon those objects by the mind itself. The raw material of experience is molded and shaped by such cognitive forms as space, time, substance, and causality, which are not themselves observable. These *a priori* categories of human understanding ensure our scientific knowledge of phenomena, the world of sense experience. However, we cannot know *noumena,* supersensible objects that transcend space, time, and perception. Kant's revolution was thus twofold. He established the possibility of a science of nature but also denied that such metaphysical concepts as God and the immortality of the soul are matters of empirical experience. Such beliefs, if rational, must be established by some other means.

In the next section of the *Critique,* Kant extends Hume's criticism of the ontological, cosmological, and physicotheological (design) proofs for the existence of God. While some aspects of Kant's critique of these proofs are disputed today, generally they remain compelling. While metaphysical beliefs are not objects of scientific *knowledge,* they do, according to Kant, have a *regulative* use. For example, the idea of God as a supreme intelligence and cause of the world assists us in conceiving of nature as a systematic whole, under the guidance of intelligible, causal laws. Kant's defense of a rational theism did not, however, rest primarily on the regulative use of metaphysical concepts. In *Critique of Practical Reason* (1788), he sought to establish theistic belief as a postulate of practical reason. Kant denied that morality is founded on theology. On the contrary, freedom, God, and immortality are all postulates, that is, logically required by our moral reasoning. Moral responsibility, for example, must assume freedom. Since the perfect good, the distribution of happiness in exact proportion to morality, is not achieved in this life, we can reasonably postulate the immortality of the soul and God as cause adequate to effect perfect justice. Religion, then, is founded on moral faith, on the rational requirements of our practical reason.

Kant believed that Christianity came closest to approaching a pure, rational, moral faith. *Religion Within the Limits of Reason Alone* sets out to demonstrate how human free will, though radically evil, can regenerate itself and how Christianity, rationally conceived, exemplifies this process. Worshiping God is synonymous with obeying the moral law. Christ is the archetype of humanity, the ideal of a Son well-pleasing to God. Yet the *historical* example of Christ is not required as our pattern. Since we *ought* to conform to this moral ideal, we must *be able* to do so. In all of this, Kant shows his kinship with Enlightenment DEISM. Kant's contribution to modern theology lies in the suggestivenes of the first two *Critiques,* rather than in his own theological doctrine. Kant's *Critique of Pure Reason* contributed to the demise of natural theology, and liberal theology has followed the lead of the *Critique of Practical Reason* in constructing an ethical theism.               J.L.

**KAPLAN, MORDECAI M.** (1881–1983). Rabbi, scholar, founder of the Jewish Reconstructionist movement in America. Kaplan called for a rational and democratic reformulation of Jewish religious identity in harmony with a modern scientific world view. Born in Lithuania in 1881, Kaplan came to the United States at the age of eight. He attended New

Courtesy of Religious News Service

*Mordecai M. Kaplan*

York public schools and Columbia University, where he absorbed a modern critical approach to religion and to the Bible. Ordained by the Jewish Theological Seminary of America in 1902, Kaplan served as rabbi of an Orthodox synagogue in New York. In 1909, he was appointed dean of the newly established Teachers Institute of the seminary. Soon after he became professor of homiletics, Midrash, and philosophies of religion. During more than fifty years on the seminary faculty, he attracted a devoted following of students.

In 1917, Kaplan became the leader of the first synagogue to incorporate a broad range of cultural and recreational activities into its program. After a split developed in the congregation over his innovative views, he and his supporters left to organize the Society for the Advancement of Judaism, a synagogue and Jewish center based on Kaplan's position that worship is only one of the functions that a congregation should foster. His first major book, *Judaism as a Civilization* (1934), criticized existing Jewish movements and called for a "reconstruction" of Jewish life. *The Reconstructionist,* a journal of Jewish affairs, which first appeared in 1935, has had a considerable impact on the leadership of non-Orthodox American Jewry.

Originally, Reconstructionism was an ecumenical position cutting across Jewish denominatinal lines; later it was transformed into a small, separate movement.

Kaplan agreed with Conservative Judaism's commitment to the scientific study of the Jewish past, its sympathy for Zionism, and its concern for the unity of the Jewish people. Later he came to feel that the Conservative movement remained too closely bound by the traditional methods and contents of Halakhah and was not adequately responding to new conditions and needs. The solution, he felt, was to redefine JUDAISM as "an evolving religious civilization." Kaplan called for the reestablishment of a network of all-embracing, "organic" Jewish communities around the world. Membership would be strictly voluntary, its leadership would be democratically elected, and private religious beliefs would not be infringed upon. Kaplan, a strong advocate of cultural and religious pluralism, maintained that American Jews should participate fully and creatively in both Jewish and American civilization. He was against authoritarianism in religious life, dogmatic claims of infallibility, and recourse to supernatural revelation. He defined God as "the Power that makes for salvation." He insisted that the traditional notion of the Jews as a chosen people be eliminated from Jewish theology and from the liturgy.                     L.K.

**KARMA.** From the Sanskrit word meaning "action." Karma is an important concept in HINDUISM, BUDDHISM, and JAINISM. It asserts that a universal law of cause and effect, or action and reaction, called karma, operates in the moral and personal sphere just as such laws operate in the physical universe. Karma is closely associated with belief in REINCARNATION. One's state in life, whether high or low, rich or poor, happy or trouble-plagued, is said to be determined by one's behavior in previous lives. According to many sources, karma may even determine whether one is born human, animal, or insect. However, the concept of karma embraces more than just personal rebirth. Karmic consequences can also be received in the same life and in intermediate states between earthly births. We also share in the collective karmas of the larger communities to which we belong.

Karma is usually seen as inexorable, impersonal law. Every thought, word, and deed bears its necessary fruit. But in BHAKTI Hinduism, God's grace, given in response to fervent devotion, can burn away bad karma. In some Hindu circles it is also said that a person of great spiritual development can vicariously assume the karmic debt of another, as a GURU might take on the karma of a disciple, fostering the latter's growth by releasing the disciple from it.

In any case, one can always prepare now for a better karmic fate in a later life while working off the karma of past sins in this life, through good works, spiritual practice, and the patient acceptance of one's present DHARMA, or duty and station. For whatever fate karma sends one, at least in the case of human births, it does not destroy free will, so the opportunity to do better is always there. So is the opportunity to obtain release from the realm of *samsara,* or rounds of rebirths caused by karma, altogether through MOKSHA, or ultimate liberation.

Buddhist views of karma differ somewhat from the Hindu in theory, though the impact of the concept is much the same in the end. Since Buddhism holds there is no separate individual self (ANATTA), no actual entity is reborn. The notion is instead kinetic; the karmic "waves" created by the life of one composite "self" make another composite which, as it were, takes up where the first left off after its dissolution, and so can roughly be spoken of as its reincarnation. Buddhism, with its characteristic psychological emphasis, stresses that one's thoughts and mental attachments are as potent as deeds in weaving one's karmic net. Final release from karmic *samsara* is through becoming a BUDDHA or arhat, that is, realizing NIRVANA.

In Jainism, karma is a subtle material substance, attracted by ignorance and attachment and removed by asceticism, which coats the JIVA, or soul, and holds it to this material world of suffering, clearing oneself of it is KAIVALYA, or liberation.          R.E.

**KARMA MARGA.** From the Sanskrit word for "the path of action." In HINDUISM, marga means the path to ultimate salvation or liberation, and karma is here used in a very broad sense. As presented in its classic source, the BHAGAVAD GITA, Karma Marga or Karma Yoga entails doing one's work in the world—that is, accepting one's given station and clear duty in life—without attachment to the fruits of the work. One is then simply an instrument of God (BRAHMAN) or moral law (DHARMA) working through one impersonally. In this way, the same detachment and inner freedom may be found in the midst of worldly life as the reclusive yogi finds in the cave, and so the same MOKSHA, or ultimate liberation. Traditionally, the Karma Marga concept was commonly seen as a support of the established Hindu social order, including the caste system, since it offered a way of liberation within its structures. However, many modern leaders such as MOHANDAS K. GANDHI, have made it instead the spiritual foundation for the life of the activist reformer or even revolutionary, since it frees one to wage the struggle one knows must be engaged in, without debilitating anxiety over immediate success or failure, or whether one will receive praise or persecution. Either way, one is inwardly free.          R.E.

**KEBLE, JOHN** (1792–1866). A leader of the OXFORD MOVEMENT, he was born April 25, in Gloucestershire. He entered Corpus Christi College, Oxford, at the age of fourteen and graduated with high honors. He became a fellow at Oriel in 1811 and a tutor from 1818 to 1823. Keble was ordained priest in 1816. From 1831 to 1841 he was professor of poetry at Oxford.

Keble initiated the Oxford movement with his sermon "National Apostasy," delivered in July 1833. Of the ninety "Tracts for the Times," Keble wrote nine. He edited the works of Richard Hooker and in 1838 translated the works of Irenaeus to inaugurate the Library of the Fathers. His poetry published in *The Christian Year* (1827), *The Oxford Psalter* (1839), and *Lyra Innocentium* (1846) includes the hymns "New Every Morning Is the Love," "Blest Are the Pure in Heart," "Sun of My Soul, Thou Savior Dear," and "God, the Lord, a King Remaineth."

Keble College, Oxford, was named in his honor in 1869.                                                          N.H.

**KEDAR.** The word means "black" or "swarthy" and usually refers to a nomadic tribe living in the Syro-Arabian desert east of Palestine named for a son of Ishmael (Gen. 25:13; I Chr. 1:29). Sometimes in Scripture and rabbinic literature the word is applied to Bedouins in general. They were skilled archers (Isa. 21:16-17) who bred sheep (Isa. 60:7), traded with Tyre (Ezek. 27:21), and lived in beautiful tents (Song of S. 1:5). Jeremiah's comment (49:28-29) refers to an attack by Nebuchadnezzar, king of Babylon, on the Arabs southeast of Damascus in 599 B.C.
                                                              N.H.

**KEN, THOMAS** (1637–1711). English bishop, hymnologist, and the author of the DOXOLOGY. Ken was educated at Winchester and New College, Oxford (B.A. 1661), and was ordained and held several positions before joining the staff of Winchester Cathedral in 1669. In 1680 he became chaplain to Charles II and in 1684 bishop of Bath and Wells. In 1688 he was imprisoned for refusal to publish James II's Declaration of Indulgences and accused of sedition but was acquitted. Still loyal to James, he was deprived of his office in 1691 by William of Orange. He spent his last twenty years in retirement.

In 1674 he published *A Manual of Prayers for the Use of the Scholars of Winchester College.* It mentions three hymns for morning, evening, and midnight, the texts of which were appended to the 1695 edition. Best known is the evening hymn, set to the Tallis Canon, "Glory to Thee, My God, This Night." The morning hymn is "Awake, My Soul, and with the Sun." For midnight he wrote "My God, Now I from Sleep Awake."                                                         N.H.

**KENITES.** An ancient nomadic tribe, originating near the Gulf of Aqaba, that moved into southern Judah. Numbers 24:21-22 implies that the term derives from Cain. The name means "coppersmiths," as the Kenites worked in metal. Israel probably got its use of metal and knowledge of making tools from this wandering band of artisans.

The Kenites were related to Moses by marriage and were part of the larger group called the MIDIANITES. The clans of Kenites who joined the people of Israel during their wilderness wandering moved into Canaan with the early "conquest" tribes (Judg. 1:16), but later moved back to the wilderness south of Judah. Kenites lived with the Amalekites during Saul's reign. This was also true at the time Balaam's prediction and forced blessing was given. One family, that of Heber the Kenite, lived in Ephraim, or the north of Palestine (Judg. 4:11). Apparently, the

Kenites always resisted urbanization or becoming farmers and remained nomadic shepherds throughout Israel's history. This attachment to the old ways was a symbol of their devotion to the Mosaic covenant and their resistance to Balaam. Indeed, the Kenites are identified as the Rechabites, fanatical devotees of Yahweh, in I Chronicles 2:55.                              J.C.

**KENNEDY, JOHN F.** (1917–63). First Roman Catholic and youngest person elected president of the United States. Born on May 29, at Brookline, Massachusetts, John was the second of nine children. He descended from Irish forebears who immigrated to Boston. Kennedy was graduated *cum laude* from Harvard University (1940). His thesis, *Why England Slept,* became a best-selling book (1940). He served in the U.S. Navy (1941–45), was elected to the U.S. House of Representatives (1946), and to the Senate (1952). His book *Profiles in Courage* (1957) won the Pulitzer Prize. He shattered anti-Catholicism in politics by defeating Richard Nixon for the presidency in 1960.

As president he promoted civil rights for blacks and women, created the U.S. Peace Corps (1961), and ordered an end to discrimination in federal housing (1962), but failed to get medical aid for the aged. When Freedom Riders tested Alabama segregation laws in 1961, he used troops to restore order. In 1962 he again used troops to have James Meredith, a Negro, enter the University of Alabama. The Bay of Pigs invasion to wrest Cuba from Fidel Castro in 1961 failed, but later that year he forced Russia to withdraw nuclear missiles from Cuba. In 1963 he helped bring one hundred nations to outlaw atomic testing. He was assassinated in Dallas, Texas, November 22, 1963, having served only two years and ten months.                                                      C.M.

**KENOSIS.** This Greek term is formed from the verb *heauton ekenōsen,* "he emptied himself" (Phil. 2:7). As a substantive it is used of the christological theory that sets out to show how Christ could enter human life and live there in a genuinely human experience. In its classic form this CHRISTOLOGY goes back no farther than the middle of the last century to the time of the German philosopher Thomasius, about the beginning of the eighteenth century.

The essence of the original kenotic view is that "the Divine LOGOS by His Incarnation divested Himself of His divine attributes of omniscience and omnipotence, so that in His incarnate life the Divine Person is revealed and solely revealed through a human consciousness," according to J. M. Creed. This christological statement is open to exegetical and theological objections.

The use of *kenoun,* "to empty," in Philippians 2:7 in the active voice is unique in the NT, and the whole phrase with the reflexive is not only non-Pauline but non-Greek too. This fact supports the suggestion that the phrase is a rendering into Greek of a Semitic original. Recent scholars have found this original in Isaiah 53:12: "He poured out his soul to death." Thus, the *kenosis* is not that of his incarnation but the final surrender of his life on the cross. Even if this novel interpretation is regarded as somewhat forced, it puts us on the right track. The words "he emptied himself" in the Pauline context say nothing about the abandonment of the divine attributes. Linguistically the self-emptying is to be interpreted in reference to the preincarnate renunciation, which took place at the same time as the act of taking the form of a servant. His taking of the servant's form involved the necessary limitation of the glory, which he laid aside that he might be born "in the likeness of men." It led inevitably to the final obedience of the cross when he did, to the fullest extent, pour out his soul unto death (see Rom. 8:3; II Cor. 8:9; Gal. 4:4-5; Heb. 2:14-16; 10:5 ff.).                                                R.M.

**KERYGMA.** The Greek word transliterated into English, which in the NT means "preaching." It sometimes designates the event of preaching (I Cor. 2:4); at other times the content of preaching (I Cor. 1:21).

The term became a prominent topic in biblical discussions partly due to the work of C. H. Dodd, an English scholar (*The Apostolic Preaching and Its Development*, 1936). Dodd isolated various statements of the kerygma in the early speeches in Acts and in the letters of Paul (for example, Acts 2:14-39; 3:13-26; I Cor. 15:1-7) and detected common themes running throughout: the fulfillment of OT prophecies and the inauguration of the New Age by the coming of Christ; Jesus' descent from David, his crucifixion, burial, resurrection, exaltation to the right hand of God, and his future return as Judge and Savior; and an appeal for repentance and an offer of forgiveness. Dodd also sharply distinguished kerygma, which was an announcement of good news, from teaching (*didache*), which described the instruction given to converts in the NT churches.

More recent scholarship has challenged the narrowness of Dodd's definitions and is prone to employ the term kerygma to mean God's word as it confronts human beings or to mean simply "saving message."                                                C.B.C.

**KETHE, WILLIAM.** Sixteenth-century Scottish minister and writer of twenty-five metrical versions of the Psalms in the Anglo-Genevan Psalter of 1561, which later became the Scottish Psalter. The dates of Kethe's birth and death are not known, but he was among those who fled from England when Queen Mary ("Bloody Mary") ascended the throne in 1553. In 1558 he worked with English refugees in Basel and Strasbourg. After Mary's death he became the rector of Childe Okeford, near Blanford, in 1561. He retained that post until about 1593. Kethe's paraphrases of the Psalms in the psalter of 1561 were made at Geneva. This edition produced such celebrated numbers as "All People That on Earth Do

Dwell" (Psalm 100—Tune: Old Hundredth), "Such As in God the Lord Do Trust" (Psalm 125), "Thy Mercies Lord, to Heaven Reach" (Psalm 36).
                                                          R.H.

**KETHUBIM.** Variously spelled *ketubim, ketuvim,* and *chetubim,* the word is used for the Jewish sacred Writings (*hagiophaphia* in Greek) beyond the Pentateuch and the Prophets. As the third division of the OT canon, it includes Psalms, Proverbs, Song of Solomon, Job, Ruth, Lamentations, Ecclesiastes, Esther, Daniel, Ezra, Nehemiah, and I and II Chronicles.                                            N.H.

**KETURAH** ("The perfumed one"). Abraham's wife after the death of Sarah (Gen. 25:1-4), she was the mother of Zimran, Jokshan, Medan, Midian, Ishbak, and Shuah, ancestors of various northern Arabian peoples (I Chr. 1:32-33).                        N.H.

**KEYS OF THE KINGDOM.** The expression is used only in Matthew 16:19, in connection with Matthew's much more elaborate version of the confession by Peter that Jesus is the Messiah, or Christ (compare Mark 8:29). Following the declaration by Jesus that Peter's perception of who Jesus is has come to him as a revelation of God (Matt. 16:17) and that Peter—or his confession—is the foundation on which the new community will be built and prevail against opposition (16:18), Jesus goes on to assign the keys to Peter. As symbols of authority, they represent the responsibility to determine who may become participants in the life of the community. Further, the obligations of membership are to be determined by the Apostolic leaders (compare Eph. 2:20 and Rev. 21:14, where all the twelve apostles have a foundational role in the church).

These details are appropriate to Matthew's Gospel, since he is concerned throughout to define the differences between the Christian and the Jewish communities. In the late first century, Judaism's leaders are reported to have gathered at Yavneh to draw up the guidelines for covenant participation—a program that developed into what we know as rabbinic Judaism. Matthew portrays Jesus as doing the same through his apostles, although the law of Moses (Matt. 5:17-48) is radically reinterpreted by Jesus, and all nations are invited to share in the new covenant (Matt. 28:18-20). The apostles are given responsibility to control this new undertaking, as symbolized by the "keys of the kingdom."

                                                          H.K.

**KEYSSER, CHRISTIAN** (1877–1961). Lutheran missionary to New Guinea and teacher of missions. Born in Bavaria, Keysser came under the influence of the YMCA as a young man and received misssionary training at the Institute at Neuendettelsau. He was sent to New Guinea in 1899, where he distinguished himself as a missionary and in several fields of endeavor, including studies of botany and zoology, and as an ethnographer and geographer. He began a new approach of tribal conversions in his missionary endeavors, which met with much success. He also contributed to the worship life and hymnody of the church of New Guinea. In 1920 he returned to Germany, where he spent the rest of his active life as a teacher of missions at Neuendettelsau and he had a profound influence on the preparation of missionaries. He also wrote books about his work that were influential in mission approach.                    W.G.

**KHAJURAHO.** A village in the state of Madhya Pradesh, India, where there is a cluster of eighty-five temples that were built around A.D. 850–1150. They are dedicated to SHIVA, VISHNU, and other beings that are sacred in HINDUISM or JAINISM. Twenty temples survive today.

The most unusual of the sculptured figures at Khajuraho are those that show couples in a great variety of sexual embraces. Several explanations have been offered as to why these images were created. They may have been designed to give sexual instruction, or as a spiritual test to see if a person can look at them and not feel lust.

It is more likely that they express religious ideas. Since the faces express contentment rather than lust, they may teach that one can find the transcendent world even in the midst of this world. Or they may express the unity of opposites, such as matter and spirit, male and female, human and divine. In any case they are a popular tourist attraction.     K.C.

**KHIDR.** From the Arabic word for "The Green One." A popular figure in Islamic folklore, Khidr is a miracle-performing, immortal saint associated with spring and vegetation, and regarded by some mystics as an initiator into divine mysteries. Commentators have identified him with a servant of Moses mentioned in the KORAN (Sura 18:60-82). Scholars have also seen possible origins of the figure in GILGAMESH and Jewish legends concerning ELIJAH.     R.E.

**KIDDUSH.** A Jewish ceremony and prayer proclaiming the holiness of the Sabbath or festival. It is recited, standing up, over a cup of wine on the eve of the Sabbath or festival. The person chanting the kiddush takes the kiddush cup in the palm of his right hand, chants the kiddush, and drinks, after which others at the table also sip the wine. If no wine is available, the kiddush may be recited over bread.     L.K.

**KIDRON, BROOK OF.** Kidron means "a torrent valley or roiled valley." The Kidron, now almost completely dry except after a heavy downpour, runs for about three miles along the eastern wall of the Old City of Jerusalem. It begins northwest of the city on Mt. Scopus, runs between the Mt. of Olives and the temple mount, intersects the village of Silwan (Siloam) and the City of David, continues past the spring of Gihon (Pool of Siloam), merges into the Tyropean Valley and the Valley of Hinnom and eventually flows into the Dead Sea.

The valley played a prominent part in the history of the people of Israel and in the life of Christ. The upper part of the valley opposite the temple mount is often called the Wady Sitti Miriam, the Valley of the Lady Mary, from a church and monastery built there to honor her in the fifth century. Another name for the whole area is the Valley of Jehoshaphat.

The valley has always been the traditional burial ground for Jerusalem. Archaeological explorations indicate that the level of the valley floor is thirty-five to fifty feet higher now than in biblical times, which may explain why water seldom flows in the stream bed now. The area contains tens of thousands of tombs, including elaborate Hasmonean ones by legend connected with Absalom, Jehoshaphat, James, and Zechariah.

King David crossed the Kidron with the ark of the covenant during his troubles with his son Absalom. Christ crossed the Kidron often—for example, when he wept over the city, when he visited the home of Lazarus in Bethany, when he entered Jerusalem on a donkey, and when he prayed at Gethsemane on Maundy Thursday.

Jews and Muslims alike believe that the Valley of the Kidron, especially near the Golden Gate, will be the site for Judgment Day and prefer to be buried there so that they will not have to be transported there again for judgment. Orthodox Jews resist any road repairs on the main highway from Jerusalem to the Jordan Valley or any archaeological research near the Kidron because they fear it will disturb those who are awaiting Judgment Day.     T.J.K.

**KIERKEGAARD, SØREN** (1813–55). Danish philosopher and man of letters, generally regarded as the founder of EXISTENTIALISM. Kierkegaard was in violent reaction against the RATIONALISM that had dominated Europe since the ENLIGHTENMENT, and in particular he abhorred the philosophical system of HEGEL, who had tried to embrace all reality within a rationally structured world view. Kierkegaard believed that only someone standing outside of the world could see it in that way. But even philosophers are themselves part of the world and part of history. So over against the speculative philosopher Kierkegaard set what he called the "existing thinker." For such a thinker, everything is much less tidy. There is no coincidence of thought and reality, nothing is finished and complete, for we are always on our way from one thing to another, truth is not spread out objectively for our contemplation but has to be appropriated inwardly in passionate subjectivity. This does not mean that truth is an arbitrary matter, but that the deepest truths cannot be reached by argument or learned from textbooks. For instance,

Courtesy of the Danish Ministry of Foreign Affairs

*Søren Kierkegaard*

like PASCAL, Kierkegaard thought poorly of attempts to prove God's existence. That is something that can be known only in the inward appropriation of faith.

Another way in which Kierkegaard expounded his philosophy was in terms of the stages of life—not so much chronological stages as stages of deepening. In the aesthetic stage (typified by Mozart's Don Juan) a human being lives for the immediate satisfaction of each situation of his life. Such a life is a series of episodes. The ethical stage introduces the seriousness of resolve and helps to unify life. But even the ethical is not the last word. Sometimes the ethical is suspended in the face of the higher demand of faith, as when Abraham resolved to sacrifice Isaac at the command (as he believed) of God. As already mentioned, faith cannot be proved. In the last resort, it demands what Kierkegaard calls a "leap." In that leap, the believer embraces the paradox, the unresolved contradiction that is nevertheless the truth of God. Hegel and the rationalists tried to resolve the contradiction and make it all acceptable to reasonable people. Kierkegaard teaches that "reason makes a collision," at which point one either takes offense and turns away or else makes the LEAP OF FAITH. The absolute paradox is the teaching that in Jesus Christ God has become human. There is no way that human reason can make sense of this. Yet, for Kierkegaard, this is the central truth of Christianity—that God has come among us as a servant.

Even critics of Kierkegaard who are put off by what they consider to be his irrationalism do not deny the perceptiveness and subtlety of many of his analyses of human existence, including such elusive phenomena as anxiety and sin. Though his works were neglected for many decades, Kierkegaard has turned out to be one of the most influential figures in the making of twentieth-century theology. Karl Barth, the Niebuhr brothers, Bultmann and the existentialist theologians, and Marcel and other Roman Catholics, have all been deeply indebted to him.                   J.M.

KIMBANGUISM. The Church of Jesus Christ on Earth by the Prophet Simon Kimbangu, to give this religion its full name, is the most successful of the numerous African nativist forms of Christianity that have appeared since the beginning of modern missionary endeavor on that continent, and was, in 1969, the first admitted to the World Council of Churches. Founded in the former Belgian Congo, it is now an influential though non-partisan force in Zaire.

The founder, Simon Kimbangu (1889–1951), was first converted by Baptist missionaries, but after an increasingly independent work as evangelist and healer established his own movement in 1921. Fearing the sect's anti-European overtones, the Belgian colonial authorities arrested Kimbangu and sentenced him to death, though the sentence was commuted to life imprisonment. His followers compared his life and alleged miraculous healings to those of Jesus, and the imprisoned prophet was regarded as a living martyr until his end thirty years later.

Headed by sons of the founder, the church combines a Baptist form of worship with some ecstatic phenomena and extensive social service work. Its membership was over three million in several countries by the 1980s.                   R.E.

KING. Supreme, male ruler or sovereign over an independent nation or territory, often centered on a state or city, a permanent head of state, at times acclaimed as a sacred or divine person.

*Kingship in the Ancient Near East.* The styles of kingship, worldwide and throughout history, have developed differently. In Egypt, the pharaoh or king was believed to be a god or son of a god. His will was accepted absolutely as identical with the divine will. In Mesopotamia, only rarely was this pattern followed. Usually, the Mesopotamian king, while human, was accepted as uniquely the earthly agent of the nation's chief deity, possessing the god's unqualified authority and power. In both Egyptian and Mesopotamian culture, the king was thought to be solely responsible for the people's welfare in war and peace, and in the administration of justice. He also was considered to be in charge of the regularity of the seasons, fertility of the soil, rainfall, and freedom from epidemics and pestilences. At his inauguration, the divine king was required to be a model human being but, should he be judged by the people later to be out of touch with the god by age or sickness, he could be removed from office by assassination, suicide, or retirement. The petty monarchs of Syria-Palestine, as seen at Ebla, Ugarit, and among the Philistines, imitated the divine king pattern as closely as possible. They were often of foreign origin and ruled absolutely and independently with the support of a military aristocracy.

*Kingship Among the Hebrew People.* From their beginnings as a people, Israel had a tradition of THEOCRACY. Whatever their leaders might be called, supremacy belonged to Yahweh. Theocracy was the ideal, however far from it certain leaders and "kings" might deviate. The Ten Commandments begin with this acknowledgment. Recent studies find striking parallels between biblical covenants and extra-biblical "suzerainty treaty" forms, as that of vassal to lord, which are theological as well as political in character.

The most extensive early experience Israel had with kings was with the Egyptian god-king, the pharaoh. The Joseph and Exodus accounts highlight Pharaoh's arbitrary, irrational abuse of his absolute authority. In the settlement of Canaan, Israel knew well what Canaanite kings were like (I Sam. 8:11-18; the disaster of Abimelech, Judg. 9:6; Jotham's fable, Judg. 9:7-15; Samson's and David's experiences with the Philistine kings).

In early OT writings, YAHWEH is referred to as King only occasionally (Deut. 33:5; I Sam. 12:12; Exod. 15:18). With the connotation the term "king" had, it is understandable that Israel hesitated to call Yahweh King. The regular designation of Yahweh as King appears in Isaiah 6:5; Micah 2:13; and repeatedly in Jeremiah and the Psalms, long after the monarchy was well established.

The PATRIARCH was the earliest kind of leader Israel knew. The patriarch had power through inheritance and popular support, and was accorded respect almost to the point of absolutism. The role model of the patriarch was the shepherd. The ideal shepherd projected theologically, as in Psalm 23; Micah 5:12; and Ezekiel 34:12-23, was a self-sacrificing man whose primary concern was for the well-being of his sheep. The shepherd ideal was the hallmark of Israel's expectations of a leader, whether he was called patriarch, judge, prince, prophet, priest, messiah, or king. Whenever Israel's kings adopted absolutism (as Ahab, Athaliah, Ahaz, and Manasseh), the traditional ideal sparked strong revolutions that attempted the reinstitution of theocratic principles. Thus, throughout the monarchy, the king-as-shepherd theology came to serve as the nation's "constitutional" safeguard against tyranny.

Moses and Joshua functioned as patriarchs. During the early settlement in Canaan, the tribes were ruled by village chieftains or elders who, in times of war, chose a person to lead the militia against the enemy, as Jephthah (Judg. 11:9), Deborah (Judg. 4-5),

Gideon (Judg. 8:2), and Abimelech (Judg. 9:6). The writer of Judges attributes the social chaos of the time to the lack of a king (19:1; 21:25).

Samuel ruled as a trusted PROPHET-JUDGE. Saul, first in Israel to bear the title of king, arose as a charismatic leader and was mainly, though only partially successfully, a military commander.

David, the first widely accepted king, was so successful in fulfilling the ideal that, even long afterward, he was regarded as the model Hebrew king. He instituted succession by inheritance, beginning a dynasty that remained virtually unbroken for four hundred years, to the destruction of the nation. The theocratic character of David's reign was symbolized by his bringing the ark and the tabernacle into Jerusalem in order to reinstitute sacrificial worhip and by his making plans for the Temple. The "covenant with David" (II Sam. 7:11-16) describes David's adherence to Israel's ideal of kingship as theocracy.

In sum, there seem to be in the OT two opposing answers to the question, Should Israel have kings? There are warnings against absolutism, as in I Samuel 8:5-18; there are directives for the king Yahwah directs Israel to have (Deut. 17:14-20; Ezek. 45:7-9). Basically, these are a negative and a positive descripton of Israel's traditional ideal for its leaders, essentially theocractic and characteristically patriarchal and paternalistic. Israel's ideal provided a hope for better kings and kingdoms yet to come (see KINGDOM OF GOD and MESSIAH). In the Maccabean period (165-37 B.C.) certain high priests assumed the title of king and were acclaimed Messiah, such as John Hyracanus (135-105 B.C.).

*Kingship in the New Testament.* The message of the NT is that the Messianic hope is fulfilled in Jesus Christ. Although, during his ministry, Jesus declined to be made king (John 6:15) and refused the title "King of the Jews" (Matt. 27:11; Mark 15:2 and pars. Luke 23:3; compare Matt. 27:37 and pars.), he chose to enter Jerusalem as a king (Matt. 21:5; Isa. 62:11; Zech. 9:9) and claimed allegiance above all earthly kings (Matt. 6:33). His kingdom is an everlasting kingdom (Rom. 14:10-11; compare Isa. 45:23; II Pet. 1:11), yet to be consummated (Luke 22:16; I Cor. 15:24-28). He is "Lord of lords and King of kings" (Rev. 17:14) to whom every knee must bow on the Day of the Lord (Phil. 2:9-11).

P.L.G.

**KINGDOM OF GOD/KINGDOM OF HEAVEN.** This is a typically Jewish phrase to denote the new order of human life in society set up by God's saving activity as King. A background in the OT and intertestamental literature is indispensable for an appreciation of this term in Jesus' ministry and the early church.

*The Old Testament.* The phrase "kingdom of God" or "of heaven" (which is synonymous with it) is, contrary to appearance, a tribute to God's role as King rather than a statement of human affairs under divine rule. It is thus a dynamic, not a static, concept, and could well be translated as "God ruling." The rule of God is celebrated in many ways by the OT writers at all periods of the nation's history and pilgrimage, but especially in the Psalms. God is hailed as "eternal king" (125:13) since God is Creator from the beginning (95:3-5). God rules the nations (22:28; Jer. 46:18; 48:15; 51:57), and controls both all nature (33:13ff.) and the heavenly world (I Kings 22:19), where God sits on a royal throne (29:10; 93:1-4). As such the Creator is worthy of praise by all creation (97:1; 98:6ff.), and especially by Israel, the chosen nation, who are called to live under kingly authority and to obey God and God's word (48:2; 99:1; Jer. 8:19).

Israel's kings, notably David and Solomon, were to reflect the nation's dependence on its God, Yahweh, since they ruled in God's name (II Chron. 9:8). But the story of the OT is one of national disobedience and rebellion against their rightful Lord. Hence the two periods of exile (in the ninth and sixth centuries B.C.) simply confirmed the sad verdict that Israel had thrown off the pledge of submission to Yahweh. Their later kings had sought worldly power and political status in the face of various imperial forces that surrounded them, the Assyrians and the Babylonians. This bitter experience of exile and the collapse of Israelite theocracy gave rise to a new dimension in understanding the kingdom of God.

In the Babylonian exilic period, the hope became articulate that Israel's secure future would be found in a coming of God to establish a new age, often called the Messianic Era, but better described as God's reign exerted over all peoples by a supernatural intervention into mundane affairs. The precise terms of this hope vary, and it was refined in the second century B.C. with the rise of the apocalyptic seers who set world history on a cosmic canvas, looked beyond political changes, and greeted the arrival of a new world, wholly divine and miraculous in its coming, destined to come at a time when God would appear and break upon earth with catastrophic force. Daniel's chapters 2 and 7 are the best example of this literature, which spawned a new genre of writing, seen also in I Enoch, the Assumption of Moses, and Jubilees. There is a clear distinction drawn between "this age" and "the age to come." The advent of God's kingdom marks the boundary (Dan. 2:44).

*The New Testament.* Central to Jesus' proclamation was the announcement of the kingdom of God ("of heaven" is found chiefly in Matthew, where it occurs thirty-two times, whereas he has "of God" only four times, but with no appreciable change of meaning). It is found about eighty times in Jesus' reported teaching in the four Gospels.

More than these statistics, the Synoptic Gospels show how Jesus' whole ministry was modeled on the assumption that he both proclaimed the nearness of the rule of God (Mark 1:15; Matt. 4:17; Luke 4:43)

and acted in such a way as to bring the power of the new age into human experience (Luke 11:20). The "sign" of the kingdom's power, which Jesus regarded as a force at work, was his confrontation with Satan by which the latter's "kingdom" was being invaded and his power neutralized (Matt. 12:22-32) as Jesus drove out demons and healed the sick. To that extent the kingdom of God was already present in Jesus' ministry, and he both announced its imminence and embodied its reality. As Origen's phrase put it, "He is himself the kingdom" *(autobasileia).* The parables Jesus told all illustrate the nature of the kingdom's scope and significance (Mark 4; Matt. 13) and warn against false notions, such as the Zealot determination to bring in the kingdom of God by a holy war against Rome (see Mark 12:17-17). Jesus moreover invited men and women to enter the kingdom here and now (Mark 10:17-27).

Yet there is equally another strand to Jesus' teaching. He promised that the kingdom would come in power beyond his death and resurrection (Mark 9:1), and associated this promise with the coming of the Son of man in glory (Mark 8:38; 14:62 as well as the apocalyptic chapter, Mark 13; Matt. 24). The parables of the kingdom, notably in Matthew (for example, chap. 25), all point forward to a future climax at which the kingdom will come as a cataclysmic intervention in world history and lead to both resurrection and judgment (see Luke 14:14). It is not easy to relate these two parts of Jesus' teaching and expectation, but the most satisfactory view sees them both as true to Jesus' announcement with the special sense given to the kingdom's present reality, namely that the signs are anticipatory of a future and fuller disclosure of the kingdom's presence beyond the cross. This is to be linked with the coming of the Spirit at Pentecost, but may also include future events, such as the fall of Jerusalem in A.D. 70 (Mark 13:14-23) and, some maintain, point to the coming of Christ as Judge at the end of the age (13:26) when the kingdom will be consummated.

The apostles' teachings continued these two strains, though with new terminology. For Paul, the kingdom is a present reality (Rom. 14:17; I Cor. 4:20), and Christ is now reigning in the church (I Cor. 15:25). Yet Paul anticipates a future kingdom of God (15:24; 27, 28), when the present reign of Christ merges into the ultimate rule of God and the kingdom is universally acknowledged. The latter aspect is fleshed out in the dramatic scenario of the book of Revelation (1:8; 4:8; 11:17; 15:3; 17:14; 19:6, 15).                                              R.M.

**KINGDOMTIDE.** The portion of the Protestant church year after PENTECOST and before ADVENT (the Sundays after Pentecost or the Sundays after Trinity in other liturgical calendars) in which no major festivals of the life of Christ occur, and which centers on the teachings of Jesus, especially on the Kingdom of God.
                                                          J.C.

Photo by H. T. Frank

*The title page of the original King James Bible (1611)*

**KING JAMES VERSION** (KJV). This is the principle English translation of the Holy Scriptures, which for more than three centuries has had impact on the spiritual life of the church and has influenced the literature of many generations. It was preceded by several earlier translations, particularly the heavily annotated Geneva Bible, beloved by the Calvinists, and the Bishops' Bible, authorized by the ecclesiastical authorities for use in church, but never widely accepted by the people.

At the Hampton Court Conference, which was convened in 1604 by James I "for the hearing, and for the determining of things pretended to be amiss in the church," Puritan John Reynolds, president of Corpus Christi College, Oxford, made a motion that a new translation of Scriptures be made. The king seized upon the suggestion and the project was approved immediately.

The work of translation was entrusted to three panels of scholars, a total of forty-seven. Instructions were given that the Bishops' Bible was to be followed, and that no marginal notes were to be employed. The regulation pertaining to the Bishops' Bible was not scrupulously observed, for the translators worked with the original texts before them and checked the previous versions in English and other languages.

Although the KJV has been long called the Authorized Version, the records do not confirm this. The Privy Council Records from 1600 to 1613 were destroyed by fire. Yet it became the Authorized Version because of its general acceptance in Great Britain and throughout the English speaking world. No other Bible has quite captured the cadence of the KJV, and even those unmoved by its spiritual message are strong in their praise of its literary merit. Even in the 1980s, with the plethora of contemporary translations, sales of the KJV have held up better than any single version.                                    R.H.

## KING, MARTIN LUTHER, JR. (1929–68).
Martin Luther King, Jr., American clergyman and civil rights leader, was born January 15, in Atlanta, Georgia, the second of three children. Named at birth Michael Luther King, his father decided to change his own and his son's first name when Martin was six years old to honor the great reformer. King received a bachelor's degree in sociology from Morehouse College (1948), a bachelor of divinity degree from Crozer Theological Seminary (1951), and a doctor of philosophy degree from Boston University (1955). While studying in Boston, he married Coretta Scott, a fellow student, in 1953. During his first pastorate at the Dexter Avenue Baptist Church in Montgomery, Alabama, he inaugurated the year-long bus boycott, which had been launched by Mrs. Rosa Parks when she defied the municipal ordinance requiring segregated seating on buses. This action thrust the young black pastor into national prominence in the civil rights movement.

King had been greatly influenced by the writings of Mahatma Gandhi, especially his espousal of passive resistance and nonviolent civil disobedience. King formed the Southern Christian Leadership Conference (SCLC) with a program to promote desegration. In 1960 he became the associate pastor, with his father, at Ebenezer Baptist Church in Atlanta. From that point he became an even more active campaigner and demonstrator in the cause of racial equality. He organized the March on Washington, August 28, 1963, when he gave his famed speech, "I Have a Dream." In January, 1964, he was *Time* magazine's "Man of the Year," the first black to receive this honor. Later the same year he was the recipient of the Nobel Peace Prize. In behalf of black voter registration, he was involved in the march from Selma to Montgomery, Alabama. Because he felt economics and poverty had a deep relationship with racism, on April 4, 1967, he declared: "The Great Society [President Lyndon Johnson's anti-poverty program] has been shot down on the battlefields of Vietnam."

Early in 1968 he was planning for a multiracial poor people's march on Washington. After flying to Memphis to support the cause of striking sanitation workers, he was killed on April 4, 1968, by an assassin's bullet. James Earl Ray, an escaped convict, pleaded guilty to the slaying and was sentenced to ninety-nine years in prison. Late in 1983 Congress passed legislation, subsequently signed by President Ronald Reagan, marking the third Monday in January as a national holiday in memory of King. (*See also* BLACK THEOLOGY.)                     R.H.

## I AND II KINGS.
The books of Kings may be viewed as part of a major story that begins with the account of the creation of the world (Gen. 1) and extends to the report of the release from prison of the exiled Judean king Jehoiachin (II Kings 25:27-30). In the divisions of the Hebrew Bible, I, II Kings are classified as part of the "former prophets," that is, they conclude the section containing the books of Joshua, Judges, I, II Samuel, and I, II Kings.

*Unity and Title.* The two books were originally considered as one work in the Hebrew tradition. That they form a single unit can be seen from the fact that stories about the prophet Elijah are found both at the end of I Kings and the beginning of II Kings. The division into two books goes back to the Greek tradition. The title for the work is based, of course, on the contents of the books—material about the Israelite and Judean kings.

*Contents.* The material in the books covers three main periods: (a) the end of DAVID's reign, which continues the story line of II Samuel 20, and the rule of SOLOMON (I Kings 1–11); (b) the separation of Solomon's kingdom into ISRAEL and JUDAH, and the history of the two kingdoms (I Kings 12–II Kings 17); and (c) the history of the state of Judah after the destruction of the state of Israel by the Assyrians (II Kings 18–25).

Much of the books is concerned with the reigns of the various kings. For each Judean king, after the division of the kingdom, we are told the following: (a) the year of rule of the Israelite king when the Judean ruler became king, (b) facts about his age, length of reign, and the name of the queen mother, (c) evaluation of his rule in comparison with David, (d) events during his reign, (e) reference to where further information may be found in the book of Chronicles of the kings of Judah, and (f) concluding statements about his death and successor. For Israelite kings, we are told: (a) the year of the rule of the Judean king when the Israelite king began to rule, (b) statements about the length and place of his reign, (c) a condemnation of the ruler for his doing evil and walking in the way of the first Israelite king, Jeroboam, (d) events during his reign, (e) reference to further material related to his reign in the book of Chronicles of the kings of Israel, and (f) concluding statements about his death and successor. These two schemes are expanded when the author wished to report special material and events, particularly that associated with religious life and especially matters concerning the Temple in Jerusalem.

In addition to the material about the kings, the books contain special material about certain prophets, especially Elijah and Elisha (I Kings 17–II Kings 13), Isaiah (II Kings 19–20), Micaiah (I Kings 22), but also less significant prophetic figures. In many ways, the material has been edited to give prominence to the prophets, perhaps to suggest that the prophets as divine spokesmen possessed a special importance over against the political monarchs. In Solomon's reign, for example, the prophet Nathan plays a role in its beginning (I Kings 1) and the prophet Ahijah at its end (I Kings 11).

*Composition.* One thing seems clear about the composition of the two books. They were composed by editors whose sympathies lay with Judah and Jerusalem. All the kings of Israel are condemned for failure to remain loyal to the Judean family of David and to the Jerusalem Temple. Only two Judean kings, other than David and Solomon, are praised, namely Hezekiah (II Kings 18:5) and Josiah (II Kings 23:25), both of whom emphasized and purified worship in the Jerusalem Temple.

Various sources seem to have been available to those who produced the books. References are made to the "book of the acts of Solomon" (I Kings 11:41) as well as to the chronicles of the kings of the two states. Since the book concludes after the fall of Jerusalem in 587 B.C., undoubtedly the books were given their final editing after this event. Perhaps some form of the chronicles of both Israel and Judah survived the fall of Jerusalem and served as source material. Difficulties in the various versions, and even in the Hebrew text about the chronology of the kings and their reigns, suggest that the two state chronicles were probably kept without much cross reference to events in the other state. This means that the synchronisms between Israelite and Judean reigns were the work of the editors and not part of the original archives. In addition, the editors seem to have possessed collections and cycles of stories about various prophets, most Israelite, which they incorporated into their history. Much of the material at the end of II Kings has parallels in the book of Jeremiah (compare especially Jer. 52 with II Kings 25).

*The Purpose of the Books.* In addition to continuing the narrative story of history begun in Genesis, several specific interests can be noted in I, II Kings. (a) The reign of Solomon and the building of the Temple are presented as a major highpoint in the people's history. (b) History is shown to happen according to the will and word of God proclaimed through the prophets. (c) The books offer explanations for the tragic fall of both Judah and Israel. (d) The books were no doubt written for the benefit of those who survived the end of the state of Judah. Thus they could be read as lessons from the past, both as warnings and as promises for the people in thinking about and planning their future.                                    J.H.

**KIPLING, RUDYARD** (1865–1936). The celebrated British novelist, short story writer, and poet is also the author of several hymns including "Non nobis, Domine!" "Father in Heav'n, Who Lovest All," and "God of Our Fathers, Known of Old." Born December 30, in Bombay, India, Kipling was sent home to England for schooling at Westward Ho in Devon, which he immortalized in *Stalky and Company* (1899). He returned to India in 1882 to work as a journalist but went back to England in 1889. Kipling received the Nobel prize for literature in 1907. Most famous of his works are *The Light That Failed* (1890), *The Jungle Book* (1894), *The Second Jungle Book* (1895), *Captains Courageous* (1897), and *Kim* (1901).

N.H.

**KIRIATH-JEARIM.** This town, identified with a site near the modern Arab village of Abu Ghosh, 8½ miles northwest of Jerusalem, was the Baalah of Joshua 15:9-10 and I Chronicles 13:6. It was also known as Baale-Judah (II Sam. 6:2), Kiriath (Josh. 18:28), Kiriath-baal (Josh. 15:60; 18:14), and Kiriatharim (Ezra 2:25). As these names suggest, the place must have had a strong identification with indigenous religion before it submitted to the conquering Israelites under Joshua (Josh. 10:17). It is assigned to Benjamin in Joshua 15:60 and 18:28, but in Judges 18:12 (see I Chr. 2:50-53) it belongs to Judah. From biblical times to the present day it has been known as the place in which the ARK OF THE COVENANT resided after it was returned first to Beth-shemesh by its harassed Philistine captors and then hurried on from there by an awed Judean populace (I Sam. 5:1-7:2). Only David dared to remove the holy object from the house of Obed-edom the Gittite in Kiriath-jearim, forever setting the village free from its burden and its glory (II Sam. 6; I Chr. 13; 15).                                    W.S.T.

**KIRTANA.** From the Sanskrit word meaning "praise." In HINDUISM, a BHAKTI devotional activity especially practiced by Vaisnavas of Bengal. It consists of ecstatic singing, and sometimes dancing, in praise of KRISHNA, usually regarded by its practitioners as the supreme God. Accompanied by drum and cymbals, *kirtana* is most frequently performed in homes or temples, but on occasion devotees may process with *kirtana* singing and dancing through the streets of towns and cities. The practice has been brought to the West by the International Society for KRISHNA CONSCIOUSNESS.

R.E.

**KISHON.** A river that drains the western part of the valley of Jezreel (Esdraelon) in central Galilee. Several water sources converge in the center of the valley at a point about four miles northeast of Megiddo to form

Herbert G. May

*The Kishon River*

the Kishon. The course of the river follows the Carmel ridge all the way to the Mediterranean just east of present-day Haifa. For all but the last four of its approximately twenty-three-mile length, the Kishon is an intermittent stream, sometimes in flood after the winter rains but dry by mid-summer.

The most important event connected with the Kishon in the OT was the defeat of a force of nine hundred Canaanite chariots commanded by Sisera. According to Judges 4, the prophetess Deborah ordered Barak to summon ten thousand men from the northern tribes of Zebulun and Naphtali to challenge Sisera by the Kishon (vv. 7, 13). Whether because of divine intervention or because the spring flood had made the Kishon impassible to chariots (both possibilities seem to be raised in Judg. 5:19-21), the Canaanites were routed. Later Israel came to regard this as a classical example of God's saving intervention on Israel's behalf (Ps. 83:9).

The only other reference to the Kishon is also a bloody one. After his decisive victory in his contest with the prophets of Baal on top of Carmel, Elijah brought the losers down to the river and executed them there (I Kings 18:40).     W.S.T.

**KISLEV.** *See* HEBREW CALENDAR.

**KISS OF PEACE.** The kiss of peace, or Christian greeting, a part of the Roman Catholic Mass, the Orthodox Eucharist, and the Lutheran Communion. It is often observed as a kiss or handshake in Protestant services. Of apostolic origin, the holy kiss is mentioned in Romans 16:16; I Corinthians 16:20; II Corinthians 13:12; I Thessalonians 5:26; and I Peter 5:14 (called "the kiss of love"). Other references to kissing in the NT include Luke 15:20 and Acts 20:37. The action symbolizes the unity of Christ and love that binds Christians together. The precise manner in which the action is performed varies, from a kiss on the mouth, to a kiss on the cheek, to an embrace or a handshake. It is usually called the *pax* or the peace, and the activity is known as "passing the peace" or "greeting one another in the name of the Lord." The sentence, "Peace be with you," often accompanies the kiss of peace.     J.C.

**KITTEL, GERHARD** (1888–1948). A NT scholar, son of the famous OT scholar Rudolf Kittel, who edited the *Biblia Hebraica,* a standard edition of the Hebrew Bible. After studies at various German universities, including Leipzig, where he received his doctorate, Gerhard Kittel was appointed to Tübingen, where he spent most of his academic life (1926–1948).

His fame links him with the *Theological Dictionary of the New Testament,* whose German original version began to appear in sections from 1933 on (Eng. trans. 1964-76). He was its first and formative editor. His labor as editor is stamped on the early volumes (there are ten in all) and is recognized by the various contributors, one of whom paid tribute to him as "a genius of an editor." His views, like those of his father, on the Jewish people, the so-called *Judenfrage* ("question of the Jews") in Hitler's Germany, provoked much controversy and gave support to the racist "German Christian" movement in the 1930s.     R.M.

**KITTIM.** *See* CYPRUS.

**KNIGHTS** (Templar and Hospitaler). Medieval religious orders to aid crusaders and pilgrims in the Middle East. The Order of the Poor Knights of Christ and of the Temple of Solomon, called Knights Templar for their site at Solomon's Temple, were a military order formed in Jerusalem in 1119 by French knight Hugues de Payens and companions to protect Holy Land pilgrims. Granted papal approval in 1128, the Templars lived austerely under modified Cistercian rules and spread throughout Christendom. Headed by a Grand Master, their ranks included knights, sergeants, squires, and chaplains. Only knights wore their distinctive white mantle with a red Latin cross on the back. Faced with increasing Muslim victories, they moved from Jerusalem in 1187 to Acre, Caesarea, and finally to Cyprus. The Templar's depots between Europe and Palestine served as conduits for supplies and funds, and gradually became banks for Europe's trade, bringing the Templars great wealth. In 1307 when Pope Clement V was transferring the papacy to Avignon, he and Philip IV of France charged the Templars with Satanism, immorality, and heresy. Grand Master Jacques de Molay and many others confessed under torture and were burned. Clement suppressed the order in 1312. The Knights Hospitaler received some of their property, but Philip IV seized most. England's Edward II also appropriated some. The Templars' innocence is now generally conceded.

The origin of the Knights Hospitaler or Knights of the Order of the Hospital of St. John of Jerusalem (also called Knights of Rhodes and Knights of Malta) is uncertain. Beginning with hospital work in Jerusalem, the Hospitalers were organized about 1100 under Master Gerard and approved in 1153 by Pope Eugenius III. Members took vows of poverty, obedience, and chastity, some caring for the sick, others safeguarding pilgrims. In the eleventh century the Hospitalers established houses throughout Europe. On the Moslem capture of Acre (1291), they transferred to Cypress and in 1309 to Rhodes. Defeated by the Turks in 1522, they moved to Malta, later helping defeat the Turks at Lepanto (1571). Internal laxity prompted their decline and surrender to Napoleon in 1798. Although the order still has knights, its work today is largely hospital related.

C.M.

**KNIGHTS OF COLUMBUS.** A fraternal benefit society of Roman Catholic men founded by the Reverend Michael J. McGivney, curate of St. Mary's Church, New Haven, Connecticut. The organization was chartered by the state of Connecticut on March 29, 1882. Since then the society has spread to every state in the Union, as well as to Canada, Mexico, the Philippines, and several Latin American countries. More than 1,300,000 members had been listed by 1980, with more than 60 state councils and more than 5,000 subordinate councils serving under the supreme council, with headquarters in New Haven, Connecticut. The chief officer is the supreme knight.

The organization seeks to further charity, unity, brotherly love, and patriotism. It has promoted social welfare, war and disaster relief, parochial education, veterans' benefits, historical studies, and a number of other projects. The society operates an extensive insurance program for its membership.

Since 1947 the Knights of Columbus has sponsored an advertising program employing the major media that encourages listeners and readers to become involved in religious instruction. During recent wars in which the United States has been involved, the society has engaged in war relief, including setting up clubhouses for servicemen, and afterward has provided for veterans' training in a variety of fields. Scholarships have been supplied for children of knights killed in battle.

As an advocate of Catholic parochial education, the Knights of Columbus have been active in lobbying efforts seeking to influence Congressional legislation. The organization has fought for the revision of textbooks that it feels have misrepresented historical facts, particularly pertaining to the Catholic faith.

Other projects and programs undertaken by the society include the promotion of the priesthood as a vocation and underwriting the costs for telecasting papal ceremonies throughout the world by satellite. One churchman described the Knights of Columbus as "the American expression of Catholic Action."

R.H.

**KNOWLEDGE.** When we say that we know something, we are claiming to have a well-grounded understanding of it. In the history of philosophy, there have been many theories of knowledge, and in modern times, philosophy has been very much occupied with the theory of knowledge. One type of knowledge has come to be esteemed above all others, or has even come to be considered as the only genuine knowledge. This is the kind of knowledge exemplified in the natural sciences and is sometimes called empirical knowledge, because it is based on experience interpreted by reason. It is expressed in propositions, often of a high degree of generality. Of course, if one accepts that only empirical knowledge deserves the name of knowledge, then one has gone far along the road toward POSITIVISM. There is no way by which the knowledge of God or any other supersensible reality could be brought within a strictly empiricist EPISTEMOLOGY.

But many theologians and philosophers would challenge the present exaltation of empiricism. It would be pointed out that as well as knowledge of facts, which for empiricism is the paradigmatic case of knowledge, there is also knowledge of people, and in some ways this is more fundamental. In the experience of every individual, knowledge of people is earlier than knowledge of things, and, more than this, while we can know things only from the outside, our knowledge of people is more direct and intimate, for it is based on our immediate experience of living as human beings. Again, while knowledge is usually put into words or propositions, there is a vast penumbra of unspoken or tacit knowledge that provides the context for the propositions. Still another point is that there is a personal dimension in all knowledge, which reflects to some degree the interests and values of the knower. When knowledge is understood in this wider sense (and it would be arbitrary to restrict it in the way that the positivist does) then the way lies open to those types of knowledge that enter into religion and theology. (*Compare* FAITH AND KNOWLEDGE.)

J.M.

**KNOX, JOHN** (about 1515–72). Scottish religious reformer and architect of Scotland's Presbyterianism. Born in Haddington and educated at the University of Glasgow and St. Andrews, Knox was influenced by George Wishart, an early evangelical preacher in Scotland. About 1545 Knox converted to REFORMATION principles. In 1546, Wishart was burned by Cardinal David Beaton. A small group of men then invaded St. Andrews Castle, killed the cardinal, and for fifteen months resisted civil and church authorities. Knox's role is unclear, but he joined these resisters in 1547, serving as their pastor and preaching powerful evangelical sermons at St. Andrews Castle. That same year, French Catholic forces captured St. Andrews, and Knox was a prisoner for nineteen months, serving much of the time as a galley slave chained to an oar.

Released in 1549, he went to England to become a pastor at Berwick and in 1551 became a royal chaplain under Edward VI, whose *Second Prayer Book* he helped revise. On Mary's accession in 1553 to the English throne he fled to the Continent, met JOHN CALVIN, and briefly served an English refugee church at Frankfurt. A dispute over worship—he believed kneeling at Communion was idolatrous worship of the elements—resulted in his dismissal. In 1555 he briefly served an English congregation in Geneva. Late that year he was again in Scotland, successfully preaching forbidden Reformation views. In 1556 he married Marjorie Bowes; they had two sons. Hounded by Catholic authorities, he returned to Geneva in 1556 to pastor an English congregation. He published *The First Blast of the Trumpet against the Monstrous Regiment of Women* (1558) against Scotland's Mary of Guise. According to Knox, feminine rule was against both natural and divine law. Queen Elizabeth resented this and would not allow Knox to return to Scotland via England in 1559.

As head of Scotland's reforming party, Knox helped incite an uprising against Mary of Guise and her French allies. Knox asked the English for help, but Mary of Guise on her deathbed requested the withdrawal of foreign troops. After Mary of Guise died in 1560, Scotland's Parliament adopted Knox's "Scots Confession," the *First Book of Discipline,* and forbade performing or attending mass on pain of death. Mary, Queen of Scots, returned to Scotland in 1561 as a widow of nineteen. Knox denounced her immorality and practice of Catholicism and resisted her attempts to reinstate Roman Catholicism. She abdicated in 1567 and fled to England in 1568, leaving Protestant forces in control. Knox preached the coronation sermon of her infant son, James VI, and worked closely with the regent earl of Moray to entrench Protestantism. However, Moray was murdered in 1570 and Knox's influence diminished. He died in Edinburgh without living to see his work triumph. After Knox's death, however, Presbyterianism prevailed in Scotland. *History of the Reformation of Religion within the Realm of Scotland,* posthumously published, and a *Treatise on Predestination* (1560) stressing strict predestination, are Knox's two best writings.　　　　　　　　　　　　　　　　　　　　C.M.

**KOAN.** Japanese term derived from the Chinese word *kung-an,* meaning literally "public record," in the sense of a precedent in law that serves as a test case or standard example. In ZEN Buddhism, koans are exercises in the form of puzzles or enigmatic statements used as a focus for meditation and for dialogue between a Zen master and a disciple, to bring the student up against the limitations of the rational mind and facilitate a breakthrough to *satori* or enlightenment. The use of koans originated in the "golden age" of Chinese Zen during the T'ang Dynasty (A.D. 618–906). They were recorded most importantly in the Blue Cliff Records by Setchō (980–1052) and the book called the "Gateless Barrier" of Mumon Ekai (compiled 1228). In Japan, to which Zen was transmitted in the thirteenth century, koans were systematized into a course by the priest Hakuin (1685–1768). They are now used primarily in the Rinzai school of Zen to which he belonged.

Koans are formally assigned one at a time by a Zen master to a student. In subsequent interviews, the teacher will ask the student to demonstrate its meaning, perhaps wordlessly, until he is satisfied. Famous koans include "What is the sound of one hand?" "What was your face before you were born?" and anecdotal questions and answers such as, "What is the Buddha? Three pounds of flax," said by a monk who was weighing flax when asked.　　　　R.E.

**KOHELETH.** *See* ECCLESIASTES.

**KOINE GREEK.** *See* LANGUAGES OF THE ANCIENT NEAR EAST; GREEK RELIGION, PHILOSOPHY, AND LANGUAGE.

**KOINONIA.** *See* FELLOWSHIP.

**KOL NIDRE.** The Hebrew phrase meaning "all vows." The opening words of the evening service that begins the Jewish DAY OF ATONEMENT, also called Yom Kippur. The declaration states that all rash and unfulfilled vows made during the year be counted as null and void. It refers only to vows made between the individual and God, not between person and person; these can only be canceled by mutual agreement.
　　　　　　　　　　　　　　　　　　　　　　　L.K.

**KONARAK.** A famous temple of the sun god of HINDUISM, Surya, located in Orissa state, India. Constructed in the thirteenth century A.D., this temple is in the form of a gigantic chariot, the sun's vehicle as he rides across the sky. It is celebrated also for its beautiful, and often erotic, sculpture. The explicit nature of some of this work is probably related to the Tantric notion of the ultimate oneness of the material and the spiritual, with its implication that the one can be found experientially through the other.
　　　　　　　　　　　　　　　　　　　　　　　R.E.

**KONKO KYO.** A Japanese term meaning "religion of golden light." One of the "new religions" of Japan, Konko Kyo was founded by the peasant Kawate Bunjiro (1814–83), known by his followers as Konko Daijin, in 1859. After a series of misfortunes ascribed to the demonic god Konjin, Kawate believed himself directed by a benevolent high god, Tenchi Kane no Kami, to mediate between heaven and earth. He devoted the remainder of his life to this ministry, which after his death eventuated in the Konko Kyo church.

The most distinctive practice of Konko Kyo is *toritsugi,* "mediation," an occasion for individual spiritual guidance by a clergyman of the church, which has been compared with confession in the Roman Catholic Church. Liturgical worship, offered daily in most churches, is SHINTO in character although presented to the monotheistic Konko Kyo deity rather than to Shinto Kami.

For practical reasons the religion was registered as a Shinto sect until 1945. It is headed by two chief officials, a spiritual leader, the *Kyoshu*, who is a descendant of the founder, and a *Kyokan* or chief administrator. Konko Kyo has churches in Japan and abroad, educational and welfare work, and some 500,000 adherents. Many of its priests are women.

R.E.

**KORAH.** There are at least six individuals in the OT with this name, sometimes also spelled Kore or Core. One was a son of Esau and Oholibamah, who founded a tribe or clan in Edom. Another was the grandson of Esau, also an Edomite sheik. Probably the best-known Korah, together with Dathan and Abiram, was the leader of a rebellion against Moses and Aaron in the desert over the spiritual and political leadership of the people of Israel. Though several different rebellions seem to be woven together in the OT account, Numbers 16 tells how this Korah argued that the whole people of God were holy, not just the spiritual leaders appointed from the tribe of Levi. When Moses invited Korah to a trial by ordeal, Yahweh ordered Moses and Aaron to separate themselves from the Korathites and then burned them up with fire. Apparently the story was included to emphasize the spiritual authority of the priestly party and to silence opposition to their leadership. Other biblical Korahs include a son of Hebron, a grandson of Kohath, and a son of Imnah. At a later period, men known as Korathites from a Levitical family served the temple as gatekeepers, bakers of sacred bread, and under King David, as cited in several psalms, as sacred singers and musicians.

T.J.K.

**KORAN.** *See* QUR'AN.

**KOREAN RELIGION.** Through the centuries the ancient and enduring Korean folk religion has coexisted with Confucian, Taoist, and Buddhist beliefs and practices introduced from China. Roman Catholicism entered Korea in the late eighteenth century as an underground movement that produced many martyrs. Protestants, at first chiefly Methodists and Presbyterians, began work in 1884. Under Japanese rule, 1910–45, Shinto was propagated, only to disappear when Korea regained independence at the end or World War II. In addition, various new religions have flourished during the last hundred years.

Folk religion has honored and feared a wide variety of supernatural beings, including the spirits of mountains and rivers, ghosts of the dead, werewolves, and the legendary founder of Korean society, Tangun. Tangun was the descendant of a high god and a she-bear, and he taught the people to worship Hanunim (or Hananim), the one supreme God, whose name the early Protestants adopted as the name of the Christian God.

The practitioners of folk religion included exorcists, geomancers, and fortune tellers. Various rites guard against evil, hostile forces, and invoke the favor of forces that can be persuaded to give blessing. Even after Korea was liberated from Japanese rule, "Spirit Posts," large logs carved and painted with grotesque features, were placed upright at the entrance to villages and were honored with traditional rites.

From as early as 1100 B.C. Korea was influenced by Chinese culture. CONFUCIANISM was introduced during the Han dynasty (206 B.C.–A.D. 220) and has remained the dominant intellectual and moral force down to the present. Early in the fifth century A.D., BUDDHISM was introduced and produced a rich heritage of art and architecture. It became the main source of beliefs about life after death and the standard for burial customs. Buddhist monks and nuns, however, were seen as a threat to ancestor veneration. Tensions between Confucian emphasis on the family and the Buddhist quest for individual salvation often spilled over into the political realm. The Koryo dynasty (A.D. 936–1392) was dominated by Buddhist ideology, and in reaction to this the succeeding Yi dynasty (1392–1910) was strongly Confucian and anti-Buddhist.

In the 1890s a movement called Tong-hak (Eastern Learning) arose in protest against Western influences and Japanese encroachment. It is officially known as Ch'undo-ky (Religion of the Heavenly Way). Other new movements have appeared from time to time. Only one, the UNIFICATION CHURCH of Sun-Myung Moon, has spread beyond Korea. It emphasizes the evil of Communism and foretells the coming perfect era of peace and material prosperity, under the "Lord of the Second Coming," usually thought to be Moon himself.

Catholicism is a strong force with a well-trained Korean clergy and sophisticated lay leadership. The church leaders have often protested against authoritarian government practices. Presbyterians constitute the largest Protestant group, though they are divided into separate denominational organizations. Together with the Methodists they have stressed higher education, health care, and participation in worldwide Christian activities. Many have been active in politics.

K.C.

**KOSHER.** The state of being fit to eat or drink, according to the Jewish dietary laws. The laws appear in Leviticus and again in Deuteronomy. Clean and unclean four-legged creatures are characterized in Leviticus 11:1-8; clean and unclean fishes are described in Leviticus 11:9-12; unclean birds are listed in Leviticus 11:13-19; forbidden and permitted winged insects are dealt with in Leviticus 11:20-23; and other unclean creatures are enumerated in Leviticus 11:29-43. The characteristics of clean and unclean beasts, fishes, and birds are repeated in Deuteronomy 14:3-20.

To be kosher, four-legged animals must chew their cud, have parted hooves, and be cloven-footed. Thus pigs (and their products—pork, ham, bacon, lard, etc.), hares, camels, donkeys, horses are not kosher. Cows are kosher, and sheep, goats, and oxen are also kosher, with the exception of part of their abdominal fat and hip sinew. Animals that are defective, diseased, crippled, mauled, shot dead, or die of natural causes are forbidden. So are creatures that have paws or travel on their bellies.

Fishes that have fins and scales while in the water are kosher. Thus catfish and other scaleless fish and all shellfish (lobsters, clams, crabs, oysters, shrimp, scallops) are not kosher. Neither are seals or whales. All birds of prey and those that live in dark places or marshy land are not kosher. Only those insects with jointed legs (for example, crickets, grasshoppers) are permitted.

Animals and poultry permitted by the Bible must be killed according to Jewish law. Moreover, since the blood of beasts and birds is forbidden (Lev. 17:12-14), their meat must be made kosher for eating by soaking (for half an hour) and covering with salt (leaving it for one hour) before cooking.

Any mixture of meat and dairy products is strictly forbidden. This is based on the threefold repetition of the biblical prohibition against seething a kid in its mother's milk (Exod. 23:19; 34:26; Deut. 14:21). Separate dishes and utensils are required for preparing and serving meat and dairy meals.

According to the Bible, God differentiated the clean from the unclean creatures to set the Jews apart as a holy people. God concludes the commandments: "For I am the Lord who brought you up out of the land of Egypt, to be your God; you shall therefore be holy, for I am holy" (Lev. 11:45). Attempts have been made to explain the dietary laws on the basis of hygiene. This explanation, however, has been criticized as missing the basic intent of the laws, which is to instill holiness in a people. Not all Jews keep kosher. In 1885, a conference of United States Reform rabbis in Pittsburgh affirmed that "all laws regulating diet are apt to obstruct modern spiritual elevation." L.K.

## KRAEMER, HENDRIK (1888–1965).

For three decades in the middle of the twentieth century, Kraemer, a Dutch layman, probably exercised as great an influence on missionary thinking as any other single person in the Protestant world. He served the Netherlands Bible Society from 1922 to 1936 in Indonesia, where he acquired an expert knowledge of the relation of Christianity to other faiths and cultures. He was asked to write a book in preparation for the third World Missionary Conference in 1936 and produced the influential volume *The Christian Message in a non-Christian World*. He served for a while as professor at Leiden but was interned by the Germans in a concentration camp toward the end of World War II. In 1947 he became the first director of the Ecumenical Institute at the Chateau de Bossey, where his extensive knowledge of theology and his genuinely ecumenical outlook, contributed greatly to the reputation of the institute.

W.G.

## KRISHNA.

In HINDUISM, Krishna is the BHAKTI god par excellence. Regarded by some schools as an AVATAR of VISHNU and by others as the supreme God in his own right, Krishna's combination of incomparable charm and omnipotent divine might makes him a peerless ideal and object of devotional love for millions. The Krishna mythology, as collated from several sources such as the MAHABHARATA (including the BHAGAVAD GITA) and the Srimad Bhagavatam, tells us that the god was born in human form into a royal house, but when the wicked king, Kamsa, tried to slay him, he was smuggled into the country to be brought up by a cowherd, Nanda, and his wife Yasoda. Many stories are told of him as a mischievous infant who nonetheless contained within him the eternal godhead. Once, for example, he put some clay in his mouth, and when his exasperated mother tried to take it out, she saw within the entire universe. As a child he also destroyed demons and humbled the Vedic god INDRA.

On becoming a youth of irresistible appeal, Krishna engaged in much amorous play with the *gopis,* or milkmaids, of his community, who on hearing his flute of an evening would leave their legitimate husbands to dance and entertain the young god. Sometimes he would hide, and they would search for him in tears; at other times, he might multiply himself so that each would think she was dancing with him alone. His favorite was Radha, often worshiped as his consort. The *gopis,* in the utter abandonment of their love for the Lord, are seen as the ideal of the Krishna devotee.

In time Krishna, with his brother Balarama, left this paradisal life at Vrindavan (where he lived as a youth and a major place of pilgrimage today), killed King Kamsa, and set up court as a ruler in Dvaraka. He then took part in the great war recounted in the Mahabharata as King Arjuna's charioteer, in which capacity he delivered the mighty discourse of the Bhagavad-Gita. But upon his return to Dvaraka, his men fell to quarreling. Saddened and unable to stop them, Krishna wandered into a forest, where he was accidentally shot by a hunter, the only Hindu god to die a tragic death before returning to his eternal home.

Though undoubtedly drawn from several sources, this composite Krishna myth explains his appeal. He fills at once several major divine archetypes. He is marvelous child, divine lover, actor in history, mature sage, and tragic hero. His worship is characterized by PUJA and by such ecstatic singing and dancing as in KIRTANA.

R.E.

**KRISHNA CONSCIOUSNESS, INTERNATIONAL SOCIETY FOR.** Commonly called the Hare Krishna movement, this organization promoting devotion of the BHAKTI type to Krishna as the "supreme personality of Godhead" was founded in America by A. C. Bhaktivedanta Swami (Abhay Charan De, 1896–1977) in 1965. In the tradition of the medieval Bengali saint Caitanya, it emphasizes KIRTANA, devotion through singing, dancing, and chanting the Hare Krishna MANTRA. Colorful and sometimes controversial, this movement has made bhakti visible throughout the world.

R.E.

**KRISHNAMURTI** (1895–  ). Jiddu Krishnamurti has been a leading spiritual figure of the twentieth century. Born of a BRAHMIN family near Madras, India, he was raised by theosophists who expected that he would fulfill the role of world teacher. When he was a young adult, however, a series of mysterious inner experiences changed his view of his vocation. In 1929 he left the Theosophical Society, rejecting any formalized role or religion for himself. He has since traveled about the earth as a lecturer and teacher, presenting a path of "choiceless awareness" beyond ordinary thought. Many of his talks have been published, and he has attracted a devoted following.

R.E.

**KSHITIGARBHA.** From the Sanskrit word meaning literally "earth-womb." A BODHISATTVA of MAHAYANA BUDDHISM whose worship became especially popular in China and Japan, where he is known respectively as Ti-ts'ang and Jizō. He is considered protector of souls of the departed. In Japan he is especially regarded as guardian and guide of dead children in the other world and is often invoked on their behalf. He is also perceived as one who watches women in childbirth, travelers, and all in need. Wayside shrines to Jizō are very common in Japan, as are images in temple courtyards. He is usually portrayed as a shaven-headed monk of benign countenance.

R.E.

**KUBERA.** In HINDUISM, the mythological king of the *yakshas,* or nature spirits. He is also god of the North and of wealth. In Sanskrit his name means literally "ugly body," and is is portrayed as a paunchy, misshapen dwarf holding a moneybag or a pomegranate. He is said to live in great luxury in a palace near Himalayan Mount Kailas, where SHIVA dwells. A popular figure in the Hindu epics and PURANAS with very deep roots in Indo-European folklore, his image is frequently carved on temples as a guardian, though he has no extensive devotional cultus today. In the literature of BUDDHISM he sometimes appears as an attendant of the BUDDHA.

R.E.

Courtesy of Religious News Service

*Kathryn Kuhlman*

**KUHLMAN, KATHRYN** (1910?–76). A charismatic evangelist and faith healer who through her preaching services, television and radio programs, and books became widely known in the United States, Canada, and in many parts of the world. She was an ordained Baptist minister (American Baptist churches).

Miss Kuhlman did not discuss her age. She was born in Concordia, Missouri, presumably in 1910. Her father, Joe, was mayor of Concordia and was greatly admired by his daughter, although he despised members of the clergy so heartily that he would cross the street to avoid meeting them. Her mother, Emma Walkenhorst, was a devout Methodist.

The young Kathryn was only thirteen when she underwent an intense religious experience, followed by a feeling she had been called to the ministry. Dropping out of high school at the end of her sophomore year, she began preaching at the age of seventeen. She was first ordained by the Evangelical Church Alliance, starting her itinerant preaching career in Idaho.

For twenty years she worked among poor farming congregations in the Midwest. In that period, she recounted, she attended a number of healing services and became very disillusioned by the practices of many faith healers. She felt their healing lines were manipulative and impersonal.

In 1946, while minister of a congregation in Franklin, Pennsylvania, she received what she called "the baptism in the Holy Spirit." In one of her services in the Franklin church, unbeknownst to her, a woman in the congregation was cured of a tumor. Pittsburgh became the center of her ministry in 1947. For many years she refused to travel. But in the 1960s and 1970s she accepted invitations to other parts of the country and soon was drawing large crowds in the major cities on the East and West coasts.

In conducting a healing service, she would designate who were the ones in the audience who would be healed and these individuals would be escorted to the platform by ushers. When she laid her hands on the head of an individual, that person would (literally) fall to the floor. Miss Kuhlman attributed this reaction to the "power of the Holy Spirit."

While professing believers were healed in the services conducted by other faith healers, it was just as likely that atheists and unbelievers would be healed in Miss Kuhlman's meetings. Allen Spraggett, psychic researcher and former religious editor of the *Toronto Star,* once said that Kathryn Kuhlman was the "greatest faith healer since biblical times." Miss Kuhlman died February 27, 1976 from complications following open heart surgery in a Tulsa, Oklahoma, hospital.                                                        R.H.

KU KLUX KLAN (KKK). Several secret organizations advocating white supremacy, starting just after the Civil War. The name is fashioned from the Greek word *kyklos,* circle, and the English word "clan" and spelled phonetically.

The first Klan was a secret society established in the South during the Reconstruction Period. The organization was launched in the fall of 1865 in Pulaski, Tennessee. Wearing white robes and hoods with white sheets covering their horses, the Klan members set out to keep blacks from voting, a privilege granted by the Reconstruction Acts of 1867, and the Fourteenth Amendment of the Constitution. Many blacks and their white sympathizers were beaten by members of the Klan.

The first organized meeting was in Nashville in 1867. It resulted in the election of the KKK'S first leader, or Grand Cyclops, Nathan Bedford Forrest, a former Confederate general. The Klan spread into the Carolinas, Georgia, Alabama, and Mississippi. In Louisiana a similar organization was known as the Knights of the White Camelia. Other groups were called the White League or the Invisible Circle. Congress passed "Force Laws" in 1871 and 1872, which gave President Grant the authority to use federal troops against the Klan and related groups. The societies soon disappeared.

In 1915 William J. Simmons, a former Methodist clergyman, organized a new Klan at a meeting on Stone Mountain, near Atlanta. In general, it followed the principles of the earlier Klan although it operated ostensibly as a patriotic, Protestant fraternal society. It directed its activities not only against blacks, but against immigrants, Jews, and Roman Catholics. Its appeal reached beyond the South to other parts of the country. By the 1920s the revived Klan had enlisted more than two million members. But public criticism of the movement and internecine quarrels weakened the organization. By World War II this phase of Klan history came to an end.

Samuel Green, an Atlanta physician, revived the Klan again in 1945. Green died in 1949, and the Klan split into several conflicting groups, although all opposed racial integration. Increased civil rights activities during the 1960s started a new wave of Klan violence. Klansmen were involved in a string of terroristic attacks, including the bombing of a Birmingham church in which four little black girls were killed. President Lyndon B. Johnson used the F.B.I. to investigate the Klan; as a result several Klan members received prison terms.

Membership fell to about six thousand in the 1970s. In 1979 five persons were killed in a shootout between Klan members and anti-Klan forces at Greensboro, North Carolina. Later in the same decade and into the 1980s middle class whites became alarmed about job competition and special programs for blacks and other minority groups. This fueled new interest in the Klan, which reportedly had attracted some ten thousand members.

R.H.

KUMARAJIVA. Buddhist monk and scholar of Indo-Iranian background who lived A.D. 350–413, whose extensive translations of the literature of MAHAYANA BUDDHISM played a key role in the development of that religion in China. Born in central Asia, Kumarajiva became a monk at age twenty, and in 383 he was taken to China by a conquering Chinese army. Detained there but lavishly patronized by Chinese rulers, Kumarajiva and a large staff of Chinese scholars working under his direction translated from Sanskrit to Chinese and edited such important texts as the Lotus, Heart, Diamond, and Vimalakirtinirdesa Sutras, and the works of the great Mahayana philosopher Nagarjuna. In addition, his correspondence vividly portrays the life of the Chinese Buddhism of his time.                                   R.E.

KÜNG, HANS (1928–  ). Born in Switzerland, after Vatican II he speedily emerged as one of the leaders of the new breed of Catholic theologians. His pronouncements have often been controversial and have led to conflicts with the ecclesiastical authorities. Although he is a professor at the University of Tübingen (West Germany), he has been deprived of the status of a Catholic teacher. His work has followed three main directions: (1) ecumenics, in which he has reached out especially to the churches of the

Courtesy of The Westminster Press

*Hans Küng*

Reformation; (2) fundamental theology or apologetics, in which he has tried to state basic Christian beliefs in conversation with the thinking of a secular age; and (3) a critique of some of the authoritarian structures within the Roman Catholic church.

His ecumenical interest became apparent in the early work *Justification* (Eng. trans. 1964), based on his doctoral thesis done under the supervision of the distinguished Catholic theologian Louis Bouyer. In this book Küng addressed himself to the doctrine that had been at the heart of the differences between Catholics and Protestants at the time of the Reformation. Küng's method is to compare the teaching on justification by the Council of Trent with the restatement of the Protestant position by Karl Barth. The book is clear proof of Küng's power as a theologian—indeed, judged from a strictly theological point of view, it contains some of his best work. His conclusion is that the differences between the Catholic and Protestant understandings of justification are not so fundamental as to justify the separation of the two groups into different churches. In his later book *The Church* (Eng. trans. 1967), Küng continued to seek common ground within a broadly based concept of the church. The book was dedicated to the archbishop of Canterbury, but the dialogue partners in the argument seem rather to be the Protestants of northern and central Europe. Like *Justification*, *The Church* contains much fresh and perceptive theology.

But critics have claimed that in both books there are oversimplifications and even superficialities that allow Küng to leap to conclusions beyond what his argument can support. Lutherans have been upset by a passage in *Justification* that implies that their differences with Catholics have been "imaginary," while in the discussion of apostolic succession in *The Church*, it is said that "we are all successors of the apostles"—a remark that is true in a very general sense but contributes nothing to the ecumenical problem of apostolic succession and merely blurs the issues.

Küng is at his best as a Christian apologist. It is ironical that he has been disciplined by the church, for his writings in which he sets forth the Christian faith as a live and credible option for men and women living in a secular time have been very influential and of great service to the church. They have probably brought many people into the church and have certainly kept within the church many who were thinking of leaving. We may notice two books commending the Christian faith, both of them quite long and demanding on the general reader, yet both of them read by hundreds of thousands of people. One is *On Being a Christian* (Eng. trans. 1976). It begins with the challenge of modern humanism, leads into the question of transcendence, and surveys virtually every aspect of Christian doctrine and practice. His aim is to present Christianity as a radical humanism, as indeed the truly human fulfillment. He has to acknowledge, of course, that this has often been obscured in Christian history. His treatment of the relation of Christianity to other religions is particularly well done, being more penetrating and more dialectical on this particular topic than Rahner's. While the book is a model of free inquiry, its conclusions are, in the main, orthodox. On such fundamental questions as the doctrines of the Trinity and the person of Christ, Küng tells us that we must neither thoughtlessly accept nor thoughtlessly reject the traditional teachings, but seek to interpret them discriminatingly for our own time.

Küng's other major work of apologetics followed soon afterward—*Does God Exist?* (Eng. trans. 1980). This massive volume discusses the central problems of theism and atheism in a depth of detail that was not possible in the earlier volume. The treatment is basically historical, beginning with the radical doubt of Descartes and his attempt to found certainty on the conscious human subject. Küng continues with an eminently fair account of the rise of atheism, with detailed discussions of such leading representatives as Fuerbach and Marx. He dwells particularly on the significance of Nietzsche. Admittedly, this philosopher can be interpreted in more than one way, but Küng sees him as the one who brought atheism to its most extreme expression in nihilism. He speculates whether Nietzsche may not represent the turning point in the controversy with atheism. On the affirmative side, Küng points to the deep human confidence in the worthwhileness of existence, and this is at least an important element of belief in God. Inevitably this book does not reach any indubitable conclusion, but it is one of the most sustained attempts in recent years to show the credibility of theism and at the same time to expose the weaknesses and incoherences of atheism.

Finally, we turn to those writings in which Küng has criticized some of the structures and concepts in his own church. *Infallible?* (Eng. trans. 1971) is a short book that deals with the thorny problem of papal infallibility. Küng states bluntly that "in every century the errors of the church's teaching office have been numerous and indisputable." He also points to the fact that at certain periods of history there seems to have been a craving for precise dogmatic formulations, and the nineteenth century was such a period in the Roman Catholic church. It was against that background that the Vatican Council of 1870 proclaimed the dogma of papal infallibility, thereby turning into a formal article of faith the profound authority that had for many centuries attached to the teaching of the pope. Küng, as might be expected, is unhappy with this concentration of authority in the pope, and he has been something of a gadfly under successive popes. But he still wants to retain a watered down infallibility for the whole church and identifies it with the "indefectibility" of the church. But this identification is not convincing, for indefectibility is an eschatological idea and means that in the end, in spite of all its lapses, the church will be true to its destiny, whereas infallibility, whether of the pope or of the whole church, implies that even now, in the course of history, certainty is attainable on specific questions of faith and practice.

Another small book, *Why Priests?* (Eng. trans. 1972), discusses the role of the priesthood in the modern church. While recognizing the abiding place of an ordained priesthood in the church, Küng is opposed to clerical dominance. He makes the valuable distinction between "constants" and "variables" in the ministry. The former are theologially grounded, the latter are sociological accidents and have to be challenged when they have outlived their usefulness.

J.M.

**KYRIE ELEISON.** Meaning "Lord, have mercy," this is one of the oldest forms of Christian litany, representing profound penitential supplication, used traditionally in offices of the Greek Orthodox and Roman Catholic church, and also in other Christian churches. Originating in the OT and often considered the germ of all litanies, *Kyrie Eleison* appeared very early in the liturgies of St. James, St. Mark, and the Greek Fathers, as well as in Armenian, Syrian, and other rites. *The Apostolic Constitutions* record its use in fourth-century worship, and the Benedictine Rule used it in the fifth century. Pope Gregory I (590–604) supplemented it with *Christe Eleison* and placed it at the beginning of the Mass. Although varied, the historic ninefold form (three *Kyrie Eleison,* three *Christe Eleison,* three *Kyrie Eleison*) prevailed until modern times. Now Roman Catholics often use the vernacular sixfold form of "Lord, have mercy" and "Christ, have mercy," each repeated three times.

C.M.

**LABAN.** The word means "white," probably a common name of the moon-god. Laban appears in the patriarchal narratives (Gen. 24:29-61; 28:2–32:1) in a dual capacity. First as a person bound up in the complicated family relationships of the Terahites, the larger clan of which ABRAHAM and his descendants represent the segment that had migrated to Palestine; then as a personification of the Arameans in their various conflicts and agreements with the Israelites, particularly regarding border disputes.

As a person Laban is represented as grandson of Nahor, Abraham's brother, and proximately as both uncle and father-in-law of the patriarch JACOB. All of Nahor's descendants had elected to remain in the Terahite ancestral homeland (Gen. 12:1) of Paddan-Aram or Aram-Naharaim, that is, that part of northern Mesopotamia surrounding the ancient city of Haran. There is no doubt that Laban was regarded by the author(s) of Genesis as a genuine person involved in the patriarchal history, following and enforcing laws and customs that were at home in Mesopotamia rather than in later Israel. However, given the longevity of these customs in the Near East through the centuries, scholars are no longer as disposed as they once were to argue from their presence to an early (second millennium B.C.) historical memory in these stories.

The fact that Laban also personifies the Arameans (in Gen. 28:5; 31:24 he is called "the Aramean") no doubt accounts for the traits of wiliness and untrustworthiness that are ascribed to him in these stories. The account in Genesis 31:45-54 doubtless reflects an ancient agreement recognizing Gilead as a border between Israel and Aram at the beginning of the first millennium B.C.                    B.V.

**LACHISH OSTRACA.** During the 1932–38 archaeological excavations of biblical Lachish, one of the most significant finds consisted in the discovery of a number of ostraca, sherds of pottery that were commonly used for casual correspondence in lieu of expensive papyrus or parchment. The exact number of the Lachish ostraca is not known, since some sherds found in the same place that are now blank may have lost their ink through weathering. Those that can definitely be identified as incribed ostraca number twenty-one, but of these only the first six yield satisfactorily to decipherment; the rest are fragmentarily preserved and problematical. From internal evidence the legible ostraca can be dated between 597 and 587 B.C., the period of the Judean resistance of the final Babylonian conquest and destruction of Jerusalem under Nebuchadnezzar II.

These ostraca hold considerable value for the specialist in historical linguistics. and comparative Semitics, but for specialist and layman alike their chief value lies in their content. More precisely, they are to be prized for the light they shed on the events

*Sennacherib (705–681 B.C.) receives booty as he sits on his throne, at Lachish; from the Lachish Relief*

that were being experienced in the Judah of the prophet JEREMIAH and for their Jeremian flavoring that helps to illustrate the prophetic book. For the most part, if not all, they appear to be reports from one or more military commanders addressed to the governor of Lachish from nearby fortresses (possibly Azekah or Debir).

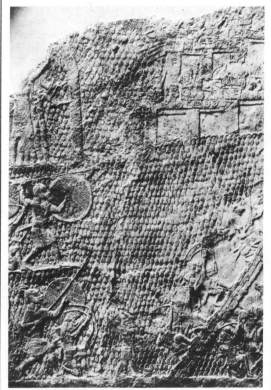

*Lachish attacked by Sennacherib (704–681 B.C.) and siege engines, which are protected by warriors who shoot from behind shields*

About twenty proper names of persons occur in the correspondence, most of them compounded with the name of Yahweh and almost all of them found in the book of Jeremiah or contemporary writings. Ostracon number three mentions a certain anonymous prophet whose word is commended to the governor by his correspondent, who we may be confident was one of those nationalistic prophets with whom Jeremiah found himself so often in conflict (compare Jeremiah 28). On the contrary, the letter of ostracon number six possibly speaks of another anonymous prophet who is "weakening the hands" of the defenders of Judah against the Babylonians. (The exact expression is used as a reproach against Jeremiah in Jer. 38:4.) There is no possible identification of this passage with Jeremiah, of course. But the prophet in question—if it was a prophet, for the text is not entirely clear—would have been one doing Jeremiah's work. Finally, the writer of the letter of ostracon number four is hauntingly evocative of Jeremiah 34:7—"Lachish and Azekah . . . were the only fortified cities of Judah that remained"—when he reports that he has seen the fire signals of Lachish, "but Azekah we do not see."

B.V.

**LAITY.** From the greek word *laos,* meaning "people."The term is first used in the Epistle of Clement, the early church father. It refers to Christians, members of the church, who are not clergy. The view of the laity as the PEOPLE OF GOD in mission to the world is scriptural and has long been the Protestant understanding of church membership. This is expressed in Luther's doctrine of the PRIESTHOOD OF ALL BELIEVERS, which is accepted by most Protestants. The idea of the people of God is now central to the post-Vatican II Roman Catholic church, but traditionally and doctrinally Catholicism understands the laity to be those who have membership in the church without authority. The belief expressed in this is that the distinction between laity and clergy is of divine institution. Only the clergy of the highest orders—deacons, priests (or presbyters), and bishops—have governing power in the church. The laity in the Catholic church have been incorporated into ruling bodies and given wider ecclesiastical functions since Vatican II, but the clergy-laity distinction is still maintained. The three types of religious associations for laity in the Catholic church are Third Orders, Confraternities, and Pious Unions.

In Protestantism, laity and clergy share governing power, and lay people play larger roles in ecclesiastical affairs. There is no insistence on the divine institution of holy orders in most Protestant churches. The ministry is seen as an office, a function, for the good order of the church and as a means of carrying out the mission of the church.

J.C.

**LAMA.** From the Tibetan word meaning literally "superior one." A monk in Tibetan BUDDHISM. Originally employed as the Tibetan equivalent of the Sanskrit GURU or spiritual preceptor, the word has come to be used as a title of respect for any worthy monk. But the term "Lamaism," sometimes used by Westerners to designate Tibetan or VAJRAYANA Buddhism, is incorrect.                    R.E.

**LAMB.** Biblically, the chief symbol of innocence and sacrifice, applied by the evangelists to Jesus Christ, "the Lamb of God who takes away the sin of the world."

In the OT, the lamb is the major sacrificial victim, offered up at major feasts, daily offerings at the temple, and at the Passover. The figure of the lamb taken to slaughter awoke feelings of sympathy in those who watched. God, too, was called the Shepherd of Israel (Ps. 23), and the pious comforted themselves that Yahweh would care for them as the shepherd protected his lambs. In the NT, Jesus appears as the great Shepherd of the sheep in the Gospel of John as well as the letters of Peter. The images of care, innocence, and sacrifice remain intertwined, as in the case of Jeremiah, who, threatened with death, spoke of himself as a lamb led to slaughter. In the Suffering Servant Songs of Isaiah 42–53, the same metaphor is used for the Servant of the Lord. The church applied this metaphor to Jesus Christ.

The Suffering Servant texts and the Passover tradition were utilized by the church to make the lamb the major symbol of Jesus' passion: his suffering, innocence, and obedience unto death. John, especially, uses this motif, from John the Baptist's declaration, "Behold, the Lamb of God who takes away the sin of the world" to the hour of Jesus' death on the cross, the very hour when the Passover lambs were sacrificed.

The Revelation, too, uses the image of the lamb to expound the office and ministry of the now risen and glorified Christ. In John's visions he is the exalted Lamb, both victim and priest, who carries out God's judgments on the wicked. The lamb is the commander of God's army, which wars at the end of the age against Satan. He is also the shepherd who leads God's saints into the heavenly kingdom. This identification of Christ and the lamb is shown to be Jesus' own conception, since, at his last Passover he reinterpreted the lamb and bread and wine, saying, "This is my body."                    J.C.

**LAMBETH CONFERENCES.** Gatherings of worldwide ANGLICAN bishops about every ten years at Lambeth Palace, under the direction of the archbishop of Canterbury, to consider pressing religious concerns. Suggested officially by the Anglican Church in Canada in 1865, the first Lambeth Conference of seventy-six bishops met in 1867 and dealt with the controversy over the liberalism of Bishop John Colenso and Essays and Reviews (1860). It issued a non-binding "Address to the Faithful." Successive conferences in 1878, 1888, 1897, and 1908, grew in episcopal attendance and influence in Anglicanism. The 1888 conference recommended a basis for Christian unity: Scripture, Apostles' and Nicene creeds, Baptism and the Lord's Supper, and episcopal continuity in history. The 1920 conference of 252 bishops issued its significant "Appeal to All Christian People" for reunion, which was sent to all Christian communities. Conferences in 1930, 1948, 1958, and 1968, discussed ecumenism, marriage, ministry, peace, Bible, churchmanship, and other matters. In 1968, observers from other churches were officially present. The conference of 1978 dealt largely with the ordination of women. Women were being ordained in the breakaway Anglican Church in North America, organized in 1978. The conference advised "mutual respect" among all Anglican provinces, but did not legislate any binding stance.                    C.M.

**LAMECH.** The identity of Lamech is confused. In Genesis 4:17-24, the Yahwistic writer presents Lamech as a direct descendant of Cain and the son of Methushael. Through his wife Adah he was the father of Jabel, the progenitor of nomads, and Jubal, the father of all musicians (vv. 20-21). Through his other wife, Zillah, he fathered Tubal-cain, the original metalworker. Besides being remembered for originating these well-known communal functions, Lamech sang a strange song, a fragment of which is preserved. In it he praises vengeance by bragging about having slain a young man who had hurt him (Gen. 4:23-24), and says, "If Cain is avenged sevenfold, truly Lamech seventy-sevenfold" (Gen. 4:24).

In Genesis 5:25-31, the Priestly writers make Lamech the son of Methuselah and the father of Noah. In this tradition, Lamech shared with his father the quality of extreme vigor and longevity; at the age of 182 he became Noah's father, then went on to have other children until his death at the ripe old age of 777.

Lamech's parentage is recalled in the genealogies of I Chronicles 1:3 and Luke 3:36, following the order of Genesis 4:25-31. That ancient Israel had more to say about Lamech than is acknowledged by the OT is demonstrated by additional information about him contained in the Book of Jubilees (4:28) and in the Genesis Apocryphon from Qumran (II:1-26).
                    W.S.T.

**LAMENTATIONS, BOOK OF.** The traditional attribution of this collection of five poems to the prophet JEREMIAH is underscored not only by its location immediately after the book of Jeremiah in the Greek, Latin, and modern versions, but by the subheading in the English versions, "the lamentaions of Jeremiah." This deeply rooted tradition of authorship is reflected in Michelangelo's treatment of Jeremiah on the ceiling of the Sistine Chapel in Rome as a brooding, sorrowful figure. The connection makes sense when one considers that only Jeremiah, among all the classical prophets, gives voice to his personal grief at the terrible misfortune of Judah and Jerusalem, using his characteristic poetic genre of "prophetic lament" (see Jer. 11:18–12:6; 15:10-21; 17:14-18; 18:18-23; 20:7-18). Furthermore, Jeremiah personally witnessed the greater disaster in response to which the book of Lamentations was written, namely, the downfall of Jerusalem and the destruction of the Temple by the Babylonians in 587 B.C.

However, in spite of the statement in II Chronicles 35:25 that Jeremiah composed a "lament" on the death of Josiah, other considerations lead most interpreters to conclude that these five poems were written by persons other than the prophet, possibly on separate occasions, and were collected into the present book to serve as a text suitable for recitation on a day of remembrance for all the tragedies that ever befell Jerusalem and the Jews. Indeed, *Ikah* ("How?" —the first word of the book, which became its name in the Jewish tradition) is the scroll (*megillah*) read even today on the ninth of Ab, when Jews remember the tragedies of their history. In Christian lectionaries, passages from Lamentations are designated for Holy Week and are affiliated with the Passion of Christ.

Authorship is given to others than Jeremiah both on grounds of style and date. The style is much too literary and contrived to have emanated from the mouth of an impassioned preacher. Chapters 1–4 are acrostic poems, each of the twenty-two stanzas of each chapter being introduced by a succeeding letter of the Hebrew alphabet. Chapter 5, while not acrostic, also contains twenty-two stanzas. In the central chapter 3, the only one of the poems spoken entirely by a single individual, each line of each stanza begins with the appropriate Hebrew letter. Except for the last chapter, which is essentially a communal psalm of lament (compare Pss. 74; 79), the limping meter of the dirge (*qinah*) predominates: a line of three beats is followed by a line of two beats.

Besides these evidences that the book was carefully composed, perhaps even written rather than preached, the point of view is that of people living in the neighborhood of the ruined Temple and in a desolated and starving city after years of oppressive occupation. Jeremiah, it will be remembered, is supposed to have been taken by Judean fugitives to Egypt about 582 B.C. and to have concluded his work there (see Jer. 43:1-7).

If chapters 1 and 5 are seen as general descriptions of the plight of fallen Jerusalem, and chapters 2 and 4 are nested within them as more specific descriptions of the pitiable situation of the people (the end of worship, 2:6; famine, 2:12; 4:8, leading to cannibalism, 2:20; 4:10), then chapter 3 becomes the climactic utterance of the book. In 3:1-21, the poet, like the writer of Job, confesses the belief that the violence which he has experienced is divine retribution. But in verses 22-51, he looks at God's other side and cries, "great is thy faithfulness" (v. 23); suffering is seen as remedial in its effect. The psalm closes with the cry of a man who, though like Jonah is drowning in affliction (v.54), expresses confidence in God's ultimate self-vindication through the redemption of the righteous and the destruction of the destroyer.

W.S.T.

**LANDMARKISM.** A movement, originating in the 1850s in Nashville, Tennessee, which claimed that since the kingdom has always prevailed, and since Baptist churches are the only true churches, Baptist churches have existed throughout all Christian history. Based on James M. Pendleton's work, *An Old Landmark Reset* (1854), which declared there is no universal church in the NT, local churches are independent and a succession of properly baptized Christians is essential for the ministry.     J.C.

**LANFRANC** (about 1010–89). Archbishop of Canterbury, theologian, defender of TRANSUBSTANTIATION. Born and educated in Pavia, Italy, Lanfranc went to northern France to teach, and about 1040 became a monk at the abbey of Bec, where he established a celebrated school. Anselm of Canterbury and Pope Alexander II studied under him there. Prior of Bec by 1045, he counseled Duke William of Normandy (William the Conqueror). Among the first to counter BERENGER OF TOURS' opposition to transubstantiation, in *On the Body and Blood of Christ,* Lanfranc argued that the bread and wine in the Mass contain the invisible human body of Christ. Lanfranc won over Berenger at Tours (1054) and the Lateran Council (1059).

About 1063 he became the first abbot of St. Stephens, and in 1070, archbishop of Canterbury. With William the Conqueror he reorganized the English Church, removed civil cases from clerical courts, curtailed appeals from England to Rome, and won lands and privileges for the church. He held several English synods, regulated monasteries, brought in Norman bishops, and bent the bishop of York to his control.     C.M.

**LANGUAGES OF THE ANCIENT NEAR EAST AND OF THE BIBLE.** The major languages of the Near East and the Bible may be classified broadly in two types: Semitic and Indo-European. The Semitic languages are subdivided into three groups: Northwest Semitic—HEBREW, Aramaic, Ugaritic, Canaanite, Phoenician, and Moabite; East Semitic—primarily Akkadian (in Babylonia and Assyria); South Semitic—Arabic and Ethiopic. Of the many languages of the Indo-European family, those of chief interest for biblical history (which include those spoken from India to western Europe) are Old Persian and GREEK. Nearly all the OT was written in Hebrew, though parts were written in Aramaic, and some of the later so-called apocryphal or deutero-ca-nonical OT writings were written in Greek.

One of the distinctive features of the Semitic languages is that the verbs, and many nouns derived from them, consist of three basic consonants. Both conjugated forms of these verbs and other words of associated meaning retain in their spelling the three basic consonants, but there are various vowels placed within the consonants, and other letters added at the beginning or the end of the words. The consonants alone remain constant. For example, the Hebrew root, M-L-K, means "rule" or "reign." With one set of vowels inserted, *melek,* it means, "king." With another set, *malkah,* it means "queen." As *mahlak,* it means "he rules," but as *himlik,* it means, "he makes someone king." Since the title *melek* had been given to a Canaanite god, the Israelites would not honor him by pronouncing his name correctly. Instead they used the vowels from the Semitic word for "shame," *bosheth,* and referred to this pagan deity as Molek (or Molech).

The name "Hebrew" was probably given to the speech of the ancient Israelite in a derogatory sense, since the term seems to be based on a Semitic word meaning "nomad" or "wandering brigand." Thus they must have been regarded by the Canaanites, whose land they invaded and occupied. Their language may earlier have been closer to South Semitic dialects, but the literature we have from ancient Israel is closely akin to the other Northwest Semitic languages.

An important development was the emergence of alphabetic writing, as distinguished from other more cumbersome modes of writing, such as the wedge-shaped impressions in clay or stone tablets known as CUNEIFORM used by Semites farther to the north and east. An ancient inscription, written in what has been called Proto-Sinaitic (since it was found in the Sinai desert), appears to be the oldest known form of alphabetic writing, dating from the fifteenth century B.C. Whoever invented this style of writing matched each sound made by one speaking the language with a tiny stylized pictorial representation of a common object, the name of which began with the sound that the symbol was to represent. Thus, a small box stood for the sound "b," because it suggested a house, which in Hebrew is *beth.* An ox-goad, *aleph,* was represented by a line with a small hook at the end, and served as the first letter, "a," of what we still know as the alphabet—a term derived directly from these ancient Semitic roots. Similarly, a few wavy lines represented water, which in Hebrew is *mayim,* and which served as the equivalent of "m." The development of the alphabet was a major contribution of the Semites to world culture and to communication down to the present day.

In the sixth and fifth centuries B.C., when the Jews were taken into captivity in Babylon, which was soon dominated by the Persians, the common language of commerce and international exchange in the Middle East was Aramaic. Aramaic words show up in the OT writings, and parts of Ezra and Daniel are written in Aramaic. This became the common language of the Jews when they returned to Palestine and continued to be widely used down into NT times. From the late fourth century on, however, following the spectacular military and political successes of Alexander the Great, Greek became the dominant international language throughout the eastern Mediterranean and the Near East. Loanwords from Persian, Aramaic, and Greek appear in the later Hebrew OT writings.

By the third century B.C. most Jews lived outside Palestine. For them, Hebrew was a little-understood liturgical language, so that it became necessary to translate the Bible into Greek. The early version of the Bible in Greek is known as the SEPTUAGINT, meaning "seventy," on the basis of an old legend about the miracle of its origin (in the *Letter of Aristeas*). The Greek of this edition shows the strong influence of the Semitic original, but is written on the whole in the common language of the era, known by scholars as *koinē* Greek (meaning "common").

Although some of the Jesus tradition may have been preserved orally in Aramaic, the oldest NT writings—including the letters of Paul and the Gospel of Mark—were written in Greek. Most literate people in Palestine would have understood Greek, and it was the only possible means of communicating the Christian message to Jews and Gentiles living in the wider Mediterranean world. The literary level of these writings ranges from the extreme simplicity and awkwardness of John and Mark to the more sophisticated later books, such as Hebrews.                                      H.K.

**LAODICEA.** A city in southeastern Asia Minor, mentioned in the NT as the recipient of a letter from Paul (Col. 4:16) and of one of the seven letters to the "seven churches" in Revelation 1–3 (Rev. 3:14-22). The location of the city in the Lycus Valley, the fine quality of the wool produced nearby, and the generosity and political connections of some of its citizens made it a place of considerable wealth and considerable distinction at the turn of our era. It produced a famous line of rhetoricist-politicians, who were helpful to the Romans as they were taking charge of this part of the world, and who were accordingly rewarded by Rome.

It is perhaps that attitude of wealth and complacency that is the basis of the angel's denunciation of the church there for its vanity and self-satisfaction. No evidence has survived of the circumstances of the founding of the church there or of its leadership. There were evidently close links, however, between the church at Laodicea and the Christians at nearby Colossae, to which Paul (or someone writing in his name) addressed the Letter to the Colossians. In Colossians 1:7 we read that Paul had sent Epaphras there to evangelize and instruct the converts. The Laodicean Christians are the subjects of concern of Paul and his emissary (Col. 2:1-3; 4:15). In Colossians 1:16 the writer refers to a letter to the Laodiceans, which some scholars have suggested is what we know as the Letter to the Ephesians, but which is more likely simply a letter of Paul that did not survive.       H.K.

**LAODICEANS, EPISTLE OF THE.** *See* APOCRYPHA.

**LAO TZU.** Semi-legendary sage of TAOISM, author of *Tao Te Ching* (dou dajīng; literally, "The Classic of the Way and Its Power"), also called simply *The Lao Tzu.* Tradition holds that Lao Tzu was an older contemporary of Confucius, which would place him in the sixth century B.C. Many modern scholars hold that the *Tao Te Ching* was written between 350 and 275 B.C., although parts of it may be much older. These scholars regard Lao Tzu as completely legendary and the *Tao Te Ching* as an anthology of wise sayings. Some traditionalists also reject the authorship of Lao Tzu, while accepting the dating of the *Tao Te Ching* to the sixth century. So much legend and apocryphal tradition surround his life (if he existed) that we can only guess whether anything said about him is true.

The *Tao Te Ching* is a small book of only 5,227 to 5,722 words, depending on the edition. The present standard edition is dated A.D. 708 and has two parts: part one called the "Classic of Tao (the Way)," with thirty-seven chapters, and part two called the "Classic of Te (the Power)," with forty-four chapters. The number of chapters varies with different editions, depending on how the material is divided. The two earliest extant editions (discovered in 1973) have no chapter divisions and, moreover, reverse the order of the sections on Tao and Te. This and other textual problems create difficulties in interpretation. By far the greatest problems are the cryptic nature of its poetic language and the use of archaic words. Translation is so difficult, yet so enticing, that over forty translations have been made into English.

Chinese scholars have long been entranced by the *Tao Te Ching.* Over 350 commentaries and annotated editions exist in Chinese, and there are many in Korean and Japanese. The most popular are interpretations in terms of religious Taoism—the Taoism of the common people, closely related to the traditional Chinese world view and to SHAMANISM. These commentaries emphasize internal alchemy and physical immortality through the use of elixirs. Other commentaries emphasize breath control (*T'ai Ch'i*) and the importance of a moral life for longevity. Finally, there is philosophical commentary. Most modern translations follow this line, although they differ from one another in the way they translate cryptic passages.

Some scholars see Tao as a being who created the world, a view derived from a more or less literal interpretation. Most interpreters, however, choose a more symbolic understanding of Tao as natural law or the way of all things.

A more concrete application of the symbolic understanding of Tao is seen in the concept of time. Some scholars interpret the *Tao Te Ching* as advocating coordination with the cycles of life: taking action or remaining quiet as the situation indicates. Others disagree and see the Tao as advocating holding to the negative, soft, YIN pole and not striving for greatness—the YANG pole. The great always decline, but the weak do not always rise. Thus to succeed whatever the situation, one seeks an unassuming place. This idea was brought out explicitly by Chuang Tzu, another important sage of Taoism.

Finally there are two views of Lao Tzu's conclusions on the proper way to act. Many emphasize the idea of nonpurposiveness in the *Tao Te Ching.* Actions should be taken without deliberate thought, through "non-action" *(wu-wei).* Attention must be paid to the gaps, the spaces between things; it is the door and windows that make a room useful. Those are the principles behind Oriental art, music, military strategy, and martial arts. However, the *Tao Te Ching* also indicates that the Tao can be used to bring things about. "He who is to be made to dwindle (in power) / Must first be caused to expand. / He who is to be weakened / Must first be made strong, / He who is to be laid low / Must first be exalted to power. / He who is to be taken away from / Must first be given—This is the Subtle Light" (chap. 36). Other translations of this passage are less Machiavellian.

The influence of the *Tao Te Ching* has been enormous. It has touched all parts of Chinese thought. In religion it exercised considerable influence not only on Taoism but also on CONFUCIANISM and BUDDHISM. *Ch'an* Buddhism, which became Zen in Japan, was in large part a synthesis of Buddhism and Taoism. The inexpressible nature of the Tao was identified with the Buddhist idea of Shunyata, or "nothingness," and Chinese Buddhism adopted the Taoist ideal of non-action, passive resistance, and retreat from the world.       K./M.C.

**LAPSI.** Lapsed Christians who denied their faith during persecution, especially under Decius (249–51) and Diocletian (303–305). CYPRIAN, who was martyred in 258, inclined toward readmission of the lapsed in *On the Lapsed* and his letters. NOVATIAN left the church at Rome, refusing to readmit the lapsed. This problem occasioned the Donatist schism in 311.       C.M.

**LAST SUPPER.** The LORD'S SUPPER or Holy Communion; the central feature of Christian worship instituted by Christ the night before his death (I Cor. 11:23-26; Matt. 26:26-28; Mark 14:22-24; Luke 22:17-19; I Cor. 10:16).

Christian worship from the beginning (Acts 2:46) centered in the presence of the Risen Christ. This living presence was experienced especially at mealtime. In the breaking of bread, the Resurrection was made real to Christians (Mark 16:14; Luke 24:35, 42; John 21:12-13; Acts 10:41).

The earliest account of the supper (in time) is in I Corinthians 11:23-26. Paul gives his account in a reproof of the Corinthians for unruly common meals (I Cor. 11:17-22, 27-34) that deny Christ and love for one another. The supper was first celebrated on the night of the Lord's betrayal. Christ broke bread and said, "This is my body which is given for you. Do this in remembrance of me" (Luke 22:19). Christ then took the cup after supper and called it "the new covenant in my blood." Paul connects celebration of the supper with proclaiming the Lord's death until he returns.

Mark 14:22-24 gives the earliest account of the supper in the Gospels. Mark calls it a Passover meal (Mark 14:14). John reports that it took place "before the feast of the Passover" (John 13:1) and omits the words of institution. Some scholars think the "Bread of Life" sermon in John 6 refers to the words of the Last Supper—that the bread is his body, and the wine is his blood (John 6:53-56). Mark's account is similar to Paul's, but adds the promise that Jesus will drink wine again in the kingdom of God (Mark 14:25).

J.C.

**LAST THINGS.** See ESCHATOLOGY.

**LATERAN COUNCIL.** The name given five Roman Catholic ecumenical gatherings held in a group of Rome's historic buildings known as the Lateran. The First Lateran Council (1123), under Pope Calixtus II, forbade simony and clerical marriages, and ended the church-state investiture conflict by confirming the Concordat of Worms (1122). The Second (1139), under Innocent II, healed the schism of antipope Anacletus II by excommunicating his followers. The Third (1179), under Alexander III, condemned the Cathari, forbade Waldensian preaching, and established papal election rules, requiring a two-thirds vote of the college of cardinals. The Fourth (1215) and most important, under Innocent III, condemned the Cathari and Waldensians, made transubstantiation official, forbade new monastic orders, required yearly Communion, and sanctioned another crusade against Moslems to rescue the Holy Land. Over twelve hundred church leaders, secular representatives, and two Eastern church patriarchs attended. The Fifth (1512–17), under Julius II and Leo X, regulated and abrogated many Gallican Church privileges by approving a concordat between Leo X and French King Francis I, and decreed printed books had to have ecclesiastical approval. Other Lateran councils, such as in 649 on monothelitism, 769 on icnonoclasm, and 1059 to form the college of cardinals, were not ecumenical.

C.M.

**LATHBURY, MARY ARTEMISIA** (1841–1913). Hymn writer. Mary Lathbury was born August 10 at a Methodist parsonage in Manchester, New York. Her father and two brothers were Methodist ministers. She began early in life to compose verses and illustrate them. For a time she taught art in the schools of New York and Vermont and contributed material to children's periodicals. Increasingly involved with religious journalism, in 1874 she became an editor of Methodist Sunday school lessons, serving under Dr. John H. Vincent, secretary of the Methodist Sunday School Union. Through her work with Bishop Vincent she became active with him in the Chautauqua movement. The Chautauqua Assembly was located on the old Methodist camp meeting grounds at Lake Chautauqua, New York. Soon Miss Lathbury was known as the Poet Laureate and Saint of Chautauqua. When the leaders of the assembly expressed the need for an evening vesper hymn in 1877, she was asked to write the text. That was when she wrote "Day Is Dying in the West." She was also the author of "Break Thou the Bread of Life."

R.H.

**LATIMER, HUGH** (about 1485–1555). English preacher, bishop of Worcester, reformer, and Protestant martyr. Born in Thurcaston, Leicestershire, and educated at Cambridge, he embraced humanistic ideals, was ordained, and in 1522 was commissioned to preach throughout England against social injustices. Converted to Lutheran views by Thomas Bilney about 1524, he had to stop preaching. He supported Henry VIII's bid for divorce from Catherine of Aragon, and was made a royal chaplain in 1530. In 1531 he was appointed to West Kington, Wiltshire, but was excommunicated in 1532 for opposing ecclesiastical authority. Thomas Cranmer's appointment to Canterbury in 1533 improved Latimer's status. He subsequently became an adviser to Henry VIII and in 1535 was made bishop of Worcester. He also promoted Henry's dissolution of the monasteries and approved Henry's Ten Articles (1536).

However, the political situation changed. Henry moved toward Catholicism in his Six Articles (1539). For not approving these, Latimer lost his bishopric, was imprisoned briefly, and forbidden to preach. Jailed again in 1546, he gained freedom when Edward VI became king. Latimer's famous sermon "On the Plough," attacking social immorality, was preached at St. Paul's Cross (1548). However, Queen Mary (1553–58) had him arrested along with other Protestants. Refusing to recant, he was burned to death.

C.M.

**LATIN RITE.** The ritual of worship, especially for the MASS, associated with the Roman Catholic church. It is distinct from but shares common features with the Antiochene, Alexandrian, and Gallican liturgies that emerged by the fourth century. Under

Pope Pius V (1566–72) the Latin Rite was standardized but has been periodically revised.

C.M.

**LATITUDINARIANS.** Term applied in the seventeenth century to Church of England clerics favorable to the "liberal" or Arminian views of Dutch theologian JACOBUS ARMINIUS. In the Church of England and in America it led to an openness to Enlightenment rationalism and eventually Unitarianism. Adherents continued as members of the church but attached little importance to doctrinal distinctions, ecclesiastical organization, or liturgical practices. The Latitudinarians were precursors of the Broad Church party in nineteenth-century England.

N.H.

**LATOURETTE, KENNETH SCOTT** (1884–1968). American historian of missions. Latourette was born in Oregon and educated at McMinnville College, where he came under the influence of the STUDENT VOLUNTEER MOVEMENT, and Yale University. An ordained Baptist minister, he went to China in 1910 as a teacher, but illness forced his return in two years. He taught at Reed College and Denison University before assuming a teaching position at Yale in 1921, where he taught until his retirement. His major contributions were the education of several generations of students in world missions and his writings on East Asia history and the history of the Christian mission. His major books are *A History of the Expansion of Christianity, History of Christianity,* and *Christianity in a Revolutionary Age: A History of Christianity in the Nineteenth and Twentieth Centuries.* He was an active participant in international and ecumenical affairs and organizations as well as the mission activities of the American Baptist Convention. He also served as president of the American Society of Church History and the American Historical Association. W.G.

**LATTER-DAY SAINTS.** See CHURCH OF JESUS CHRIST OF LATTER-DAY SAINTS.

**LAUD, ARCHBISHOP** (William Laud, 1573–1645). Anglican archbishop of Canterbury and an opponent of Puritanism. Laud's "popish" rules on ritual, clerical dress, and worship caused thousands of PURITANS to migrate to Massachusetts. Born in Reading and educated at St. John's College, Oxford, Laud was ordained (1601) and chosen president of St. John's (1611). He resigned from St. John's to become bishop of St. David's in Wales (1621). Against Fisher the Jesuit (J. Percy), he argued that Rome and Canterbury were equally parts of the universal (catholic) church.

As a supporter of King James I's divine-right-of-kings views and an adviser to Charles I, Laud rose rapidly to become bishop of London (1628), chancellor of Oxford University (1629), and arch-bishop of Canterbury (1633). As chancellor he promoted manuscript collection and scholarship. As archbishop he advised Charles, helped administer the nation, and strove to enforce liturgical uniformity in part to support Charles' royal absolutism. Laud abolished the popular Puritan lectureships, emphasized Communion over preaching, and enforced compliance. Hostility mounted.

Charles had dismissed Parliament in 1629, saying he alone would rule, but his arbitrary taxes aroused resentment, and Laud's attempt in 1637 to Anglicize Scottish Presbyterianism prompted Scottish riots and rebellion. To raise money to suppress the rebellion, Charles reconvened the Long Parliament (1640). Dominated by Puritans, Parliament did not comply. It maneuvered to imprison and behead Laud, a prelude to beheading Charles himself (1649). Laud was an early controversial Anglo-Catholic who secured some political-economic gains for Anglicanism, and before his execution repudiated charges of "popery."

C.M.

**LAUDS.** The morning hour of worship in the Catholic divine office. The name means "praise," drawn from the three psalms of praise that formerly were invariably part of the office. Lauds includes five psalms, scripture, a hymn, the Benedictus, a homily, as well as opening and concluding versicles.

J.C.

**LAVER.** A basin used in both ancient Jewish and continuing Roman Catholic worship for the ritual cleansing of the hands (and in ancient times, the Hebrew priests' feet) before prayer and sacrifice. Lavers are still in use in Orthodox Jewish synagogues for washing the hands, as far up as the wrists, before prayer. A laver is used for ritual ablutions. In the ancient Hebrew tabernacle (tent), the laver was in two parts—a basin and a stand. Aaron and his sons washed their hands and feet before entering the tabernacle.

In Solomon's temple, there were five bronze lavers on the right and five on the left sides and a huge laver, "the brazen (or bronze) sea," in which the priest washed before sacrifices were offered. The smaller lavers were used to wash the parts of the sacrificed animals. These lavers were basins resting on wheeled bases and were ornamented with engravings of lions, oxen, and cherubim.

The second temple had only one laver, in which the priests washed before sacrificing animals. Since the destruction of the temple in A.D. 70, prayer has replaced sacrifice in Judaism, and all the people share in the holiness of the priests and Levites. For this reason, Orthodox Jews wash before prayers.

For the Catholic church, the laver or lavabo is an ancient part of the Mass. The priest uses water, from a laver, usually set on a stand to the left of the altar (facing the altar) to symbolically wash his hands before the Mass. J.C.

LAW. A collection of moral, ethical, civic, and religious rules or precepts, regarded among the early Hebrews as having originated with God, or at least from priestly interpreters of God's laws.

*Law in the Old Testament.* The basic word for Law in the OT is TORAH, a term that may also refer to the five books of MOSES (the Pentateuch) or even to the collective religious teaching and instruction of the whole people of Israel. Torah really means "instruction" or "guidance" and is still used in that sense in the synagogue. When the writers of the Septuagint translated the Torah in Egypt, the word in Greek came out as *nomos*, which is somewhat narrower in meaning than Torah.

In Hebrew tradition all law originates with God, not with human beings. Apparently Abraham and his clan brought with them at least some concept of law when they migrated from the Tigris-Euphrates Valley to Canaan, but the vast bulk of their ethical code did not develop until after the sojourn in Egypt. In Babylon the most famous and highly developed code of laws had been the Code of Hammurabi, probably dating from the eighteenth century B.C. The Babylonians had had much greater need for a complex code of laws in their urban society than did the Hebrews, who even at the time of immigration to Egypt were still a wandering band of herdsmen numbering less than a hundred souls.

Even before the giving of the TEN COMMANDMENTS on Mount Sinai, there are already indications that the people were coming to Moses for a determination of what was wrong and what was right (Exod. 18:15). This apparently had also been the case in the age of the patriarchs, when the head of the clan was also by tradition the lawgiver and the interpreter of the Law. Moses writes that he served as judge and arbiter in disputes, though also applying the teachings of God at his hearings. More difficult cases were brought to a sanctuary for judgment, where the name of God was first invoked and where specially trained priests would be available (compare I Sam. 2:25). From these early and rather primitive kinds of law and courts developed the more sophisticated systems of law found in the five books of Moses.

The dramatic delivery of the Ten Commandments on Mount Sinai highlights the covenant relationship between the people of Israel and their God. The lightning, the thunder, the sound of the trumpets, and the theophany of God all accent the importance of this relationship and the importance of the laws that God was promulgating.

The collection of detailed laws that follows the giving of the Ten Commandments as cited in Exodus 20:22–23:33 is often called the Book of the Covenant, a term found in Exodus 24:7. Many of these laws are not unlike those found elsewhere in the ancient Near East, but they focus on a life that is still largely agricultural and nomadic. These laws deal with worship, slavery, bodily harm, the owning of property, relationships to God, and support for travelers and widows. They have much in common with the Code of Hammurabi, especially in relationship to servants, slavery, marriage, property, personal injury, and the care of animals.

The book of Deuteronomy (which means the second Law or set of laws) is by rabbinic tradition the code of laws delivered by Moses to the people at the end of their forty years of wandering in the desert, probably given on the plains of Moab as they were about to cross the Jordan. In its present form, at least, DEUTERONOMY more likely dates from the eighth century B.C., with at least a few additions that come from a still later period. Likely this is the book of the Law discovered in the temple, which caused the great religious reforms in the reign of Josiah (II Kings 22–23), even though the text as we have it now was not yet so developed at that time. During the period of the prophets there was a major attempt to codify and write down the teachings, precepts, and interpretations of the prophets as a living addition to already existing law.

The Deuteronomic Code deals with a broad and detailed variety of needs: kings, priests, sacrifices, war, cultic practices; the interests of citizens and town dwellers and members of the family; concern for the poor, the widowed, the parentless, and the stranger; the use and care of animals.

What is remarkable about the Deuteronomic legislation in an age when the reigning philosophy was an eye for an eye and a tooth for a tooth was its kindly and humanitarian outlook. To mistreat slaves, for example, was to repeat the evils the people of Israel had suffered in Egypt. To cut down fruit trees or burn crops after a successful battle was forbidden. To bring in foreign idols was to corrupt the people and destroy their relationship with Jehovah. All worship was to be focused in a central place, most often Jerusalem but earlier also at Dan or Bethel, a settled place where God could cause the sacred name to dwell. After the fall of the northern kingdom the focus of worship at the holy of holies in the Temple at Jerusalem came to be a central tenet of the Deuteronomic Code.

The Priestly Code appears largely in Exodus, Numbers, and Leviticus (which means "of Levi," relating to the priestly tribe of Levi). The oldest part of this code is probably the Law of Holiness in Deuteronomy 17–26. Other parts may come from the time of the Babylonian Captivity (587–538 B.C.) or perhaps even later. Once King Josiah had taken a stand against the Egyptians at Megiddo, dying in battle, the hopes for new laws and the development of old religious laws ground to a halt. Up till this time the Temple of Solomon had been a strong and enduring symbol of religious and COVENANT law. Now it lay destroyed. As one prophet put it, "The law is no more" (Lam. 2:9).

Priestly or levitical law had been developing ever since the first legal system was put together, when the tribes were still in the desert. Some of the place-names in the semi-arid grazing land near Kadesh-barnea indicate that even during the sojourn in the wilderness the priests had actively begun formulating and administering courts of law. Though God was perceived as the original lawgiver, the interpretation of those concepts and precepts often fell to the LEVITES. These levitical courts dealt with a broad variety of human and religious experience: murder, circumcision, Passover, the tabernacle, sacrifices of every sort, holy days, consecration of priests, clean and unclean animals, keeping of vows, marriage relationships, personal injury, inheritance, holy wars, and refuges for those who were fleeing their enemies.

The hundreds and hundreds of times in which the concept of Law keeps recurring in almost every book of the OT stresses again how firmly the people of Israel were the people of the Law and the people of the book. In the Prophets (Amos 5:18; Isa. 2:12) the phrase "the day of the Lord" emphasizes again and again how divine wrath will consume those who do not heed the Law. Jeremiah, Isaiah, Ezekiel, and Hosea all speak of a NEW COVENANT of law God will make with the people in the latter days. These prophecies come largely from the time of the Exile, but they nonetheless look forward to a time not merely of the rebuilding of the Temple in Jerusalem but even to a golden age far beyond, when the people of God will once again be God's chosen people.

This idealized vision is summed up in the words of Psalm 19:7-9:

> The law of the Lord is perfect,
> reviving the soul;
> the testimony of the Lord is sure,
> making wise the simple;
> the precepts of the Lord are right,
> rejoicing the heart;
> the commandment of the Lord is pure,
> enlightening the eyes;
> the ordinances of the Lord are true,
> and righteous altogether.

Though the period of the Exile cut off for a time the formal religious practices of the Jews at the Temple, it did establish a more informal kind of worship and of gathering together in private homes to celebrate the Sabbath. The old laws of the Sabbath and of circumcision helped the people of Israel retain their distinctiveness as children of Jehovah. Such study of the Law in small groups in the Diaspora may well have been the reason for the development of the synagogue system (Ezek. 33:30-33).

In summary, the Law of the OT originated with God, helped people understand how they were to live and worship, and helped them understand what hopes they could one day have of a messiah and of an eschatological "day of the Lord."

*Law in First-Century Judaism.* The ceremonial laws of the OT tended to stamp into the awareness of the people the conviction that Jehovah was the true God and that they were Jehovah's people. At the time of the Exile the ceremonial law went largely by the boards, and when the people once more returned to the Promised Land, their loyalties were in some ways less worship-related and ceremonial, and perhaps more focused on the local synagogue and less on the national Temple.

As seen from the viewpoint of the writers of the NT Gospels, the more important functions of religious law—stressing sin, forgiveness, faith, trust—were overlooked in favor of more mundane subtleties and refinements. The strenuousness with which Christ denounced the scribes, Pharisees, Sadducees, and Essenes for their focus on religious trivialities and their total disregard for important truths reflects at least some of the developments that were occurring in first-century Judaism. His concern for real worship and a real understanding of the Sabbath, not mere keeping of the ceremonial law, is a good example, as is his anger at those who viewed the Temple as a place to make money, not a place to deepen one's spiritual relationships to God.

The vast number of writings and traditions that came out of the rabbinic schools in this period reflect an activist and intellectual approach to OT law, such as one finds in the Mishna, Midrash, Talmud, and Halakah. There was a broad range of religious views in the period, and there is some danger in focusing too closely on any one interpreter, no matter how well known and revered, such as Rabbi Johanan ben Zakkai at Jamnia and his many Pharisaical colleagues. The apocryphal scriptures of the time, plus the writings of Josephus, Philo, and the Qumran community, shed further light on first-century attitudes toward Mosaic law.

Sacred writings read in the synagogues included most of the canon of the OT. The sections known as the Law and the Prophets were especially honored and revered, although the Writings (for example, Ruth or Jonah) were in some quarters questioned and were not normally read as a part of public worship. Luke 16:16 and Matthew 11:13 confirm the reading of the Law and the Prophets at the synagogue. As proof texts, made to prove a point in a debate, a quotation from the Torah was beyond reproach, often bolstered by a quotation from the Prophets or from the Writings, to assure that Jehovah had not changed the Law since first giving it on Mount Sinai. At Jamnia such books as Ecclesiastes and the Song of Songs were not accepted as scripture, because they were written late, at a time when the Holy Spirit was deemed to have departed the land of Israel.

Another major development of the period was the rise of ORAL TRADITION as law, a concept that goes back to the learned rabbinical schools of Hillel and Shammai. Through such learned interpretations, new answers could be found to questions that would never have been raised in Mosaic or Deuteronomic times. Cultural conditions changed materially as the Babylonian rulers were superseded by the Persians, then the Greeks, then the Romans. In fact, the whole concept of SCRIBES, the *sopherim* or teachers, developed to interpret changing cultures and changing ways, though the scribes were often disliked and belittled.

In brief, in the various views of parties like the scribes, Pharisees, Sadducees, and Essenes, in the rabbinical schools of Hillel, Shammai, or Zakkai, the believer was forced to look at the Law and measure oneself against it as God might do the measuring, even if there was a good deal of misgiving and ignorance about the precise outcome.

*Law in the New Testament.* The use of the word "law" more than one hundred times in the NT usually refers to the Mosaic code or to the books of the Pentateuch, not to contemporary or civic laws of the Greeks or Romans. Usually Christ refers to "the law" or to "the law and the prophets" (Matt. 5:18; 11:13; Luke 16:16) or simply to the "scriptures." He distinguishes clearly between OT law and "the traditions of the elders," the "tradition of men," or "oral law," and in fact often downgrades such interpretations when he adds, "But I say to you" (Matt. 5:22).

The concept of religious law and of Christ as the living fulfillment of that law occurs much more frequently in the epistles than in the Gospels. Yet Christ makes his case very plain in his own words in Matthew 5:17-18 when he says, "Think not that I have come to abolish them but to fulfill them. For truly, I say to you, till heaven and earth pass away, not an iota, not a dot, will pass from the law until all is accomplished." Christ's coming has become a new revelation of the Law, a law incarnate. As Mark (2:22) explains it, one can't put new wine in old wineskins, because they will burst from the fermenting.

One reason that Christ appears at times to resist OT law is his personal contact with hordes of sinners, of tax collectors, of the lame and the blind. One of the continuing refrains of the miracle stories is, "Son, your sins are forgiven you; take up your bed and walk." His authority as "Son of man" and "Son of God" allowed for the forgiveness of sin, even though that status to alter OT law was not accepted by most of the scribes and Pharisees. Although for the most part he did uphold OT law, he actively resisted codes of oral law and interpretation that he regarded as out of harmony with the basic concepts of the law of Moses.

In dealing with what was "clean and unclean," he insisted that the intent of the heart and the conscience was primary (Mark 2:13-17), not outward appearances. And if he associated with unsavory tax collectors, it was because "Those who are well have no need of a physician, but those who are sick." The Pharisaical interpretations of the laws of the Sabbath were a special target of his attack. Mark (2:23-27) explains how he and his disciples picked ears of grain on the Sabbath and ate them, and when they were confronted by the Pharisees, he uses a starving David for his model. He concludes, "The sabbath was made for man, not man for the sabbath."

In another confrontation with the Pharisees over his right to cure a man with a withered hand in a synagogue on the Sabbath, he asks rhetorically, "It is lawful on the sabbath to do good or to do harm, to save life or to kill?" (Mark 3:1-6). As a boy in synagogue school he had memorized huge portions of "the law and the prophets" in preparation for his bar mitzvah. It is clear that Jesus' treatment of OT law flowed not out of ignorance but out of deep understanding.

In Christ's role as the fulfiller of the Law, both Matthew (10:32-40) and Mark (8:38) make it clear that what now counts is the believer's relationship to him as the Son of God, not a relationship to an older covenant with Jehovah under OT law. A similar reinterpretation of OT law appears in Christ's stance toward divorce or the ceremonial cleanliness of various foods, which later came to be a cornerstone of missionary teaching in the Greek and Roman worlds.

Even the method and timing of Christ's death appear to have replaced the OT Passover laws for a new order in which Christ himself became the lamb and the sacrifice. Caiaphas as high priest may not have realized the full implications of his pronouncement when he declared, "You know nothing at all; you do not understand that it is expedient for you that one man should die for the people, and that the whole nation should not perish" (John 11:49-50).

The writings of Paul, who was trained as a Pharisaical LAWYER, are loaded with more than one hundred references to the Law. He emphasized especially how Christ's death in obedience to the will of the Father was the fulfillment of the Law. In a special sense Christ's death was a return to the final jurisdiction and judgment of his Father. The course law took in which the crucifixion of Christ established a new covenant and disestablished a considerable portion of Deuteronomic law troubled Jewish-Greek Christians more than a little in the early church, as the detailed account of the conflicts in the synagogues in Jerusalem (Acts 2-3) points out, at the time when Stephen was stoned.

Practicing Judaism and the Deuteronomic Code was no longer the path of salvation. In the decades following the death and resurrection of Christ there early seems to have been agreement that salvation came by faith in Christ, not through fulfillment of the ceremonial law. Paul stresses this as a recurring theme throughout the letters to the Ephesians, Romans, and Corinthians. In this sense Christ put an end to the Law, even though he sometimes also demanded loyalty to certain elements of the old Law. But the system of priests and of sacrifices came forever to its end.

In summary, the NT showed how Christ was the fulfillment of the old Law and how the old Law had passed away. Yet in the figure of Moses, Christ still proclaimed God's will and God's law, made alive again for a New Age, fine tuned for a new culture, still the best summary of God's will and God's love for all people whether on earth or in heaven.

T.J.K.

**LAW OF MOSES.** See LAW.

**LAW, WILLIAM** (1686–1761). English devotional and controversial writer. Born at Kingscliffe, Northamptonshire, he was educated at Cambridge, becoming a Fellow in 1711. Refusing allegiance to King George I, because, he regarded the exiled Stuarts as England's rightful rulers, Law lost his Fellowship. Between 1727 and 1737 Law tutored the father of Edward Gibbon, the historian, and counseled the family. In 1740 he returned to Kingscliffe, and with two prosperous women, he established and supervised schools and almshouses and lived a devout life of regular prayer and strict rules.

*Three Letters to the Bishop of Bangor* (1717–19) displayed his sharp wit; he satirically criticized making sincerity the only Christian standard. *The Case of Reason* (1732) debunked finite reason as a final guide in religion. *A Practical Treatise upon Christian Perfection* (1726) exhorted Christians to practice Christian virtues—marks of true repentance and renewal. The *Serious Call to a Devout and Holy Life* (1729), his best-known work, summoned Christians to serious devout living in every aspect of life. Law urged internal spiritual guidance through disciplined daily prayer and meditation, and in external affairs he urged disciplined service to God and others—as preparation for life eternal and joy and satisfaction now. Law directly influenced John Wesley.

C.M.

**LAWYER.** A term used in the NT in two distinct ways. According to Titus 3:13, Zenas, a friend of Paul, is commended on his journey, and he is described as a "lawyer," presumably an expert trained in Roman legal procedures. The second meaning of the same noun refers exclusively to those trained in Jewish and rabbinical laws, and the Greek term *nomikos* is a synonym for "scribe" (*grammateus*). Matthew (2:4; 13:52; 16:21; 23:2) uses the title "scribe," where Luke prefers *nomikos*, with apparently the same meaning intended (see Luke 10:25 in comparison with Mark 12:28; Matt. 22:35). The word thus designates a person proficient in deciding the intricate meaning of the Jewish law.

R.M.

**LAY BROTHERS, LAY SISTERS.** An unordained religious or permanent member of an order, such as a monk or a nun. Lay brothers and sisters are not clerics but are regular or true religious and rank higher than lay people. Lay sisters generally did the domestic work of convents and did not recite the divine office daily. In the Cistercian reform a distinction was made between the *conversi*, or lay brothers, and choir religious. The lay brothers were inferior to the choir religious, doing mostly manual work. The same distinction held true for lay sisters and choir sisters.

J.C.

**LAYING ON OF HANDS.** See HANDS, LAYING ON OF.

**LAYMEN'S FOREIGN MISSIONS INQUIRY.** An investigation of the status and methods of foreign missions on behalf of seven denominations in the 1930s. The impetus for the investigation came from a committee called together by John D. Rockefeller, Jr., and John R. Mott, who had become aware of the difficulties of missionaries around the world. The inquiry was carried out by a fifteen-member commission of which WILLIAM HOCKING was chairman. Their report "Re-thinking Missions" was presented to representatives of foreign mission boards at a meeting in 1932. The report, which recommended the continued coexistence of other religions along with Christianity, met with much criticism because it suggested a rethinking of the approach of foreign missions. The controversy diverted attention from the great wealth of information that the committee had gathered, which was subsequently published in seven volumes in 1933.

W.G.

**LAYMEN'S NATIONAL BIBLE COMMITTEE.** An organization of Christian and Jewish laity formed in 1940 to "encourage belief and faith in God, daily reading of the Bible, and to strengthen religious life in America." Since 1941 the major activity of the organization has been the promotion of National Bible Week at Thanksgiving time. A governing board of thirty-four directors and one hundred national associate chairmen supervise the distribution of thousands of packets of materials about the Bible, radio and TV ads, billboard advertising, and other means through which the country is alerted to the importance of the Bible and its message. The work of the committee, headquartered in New York City, has regularly been endorsed and promoted by the presidents of the United States, several congressmen, governors, and mayors throughout the country.

W.G.

**LAY READER, LECTOR.** In the early church a lector was a clergyman in minor orders, appointed to read the Scriptures and inspirational works during public worship. This was an important post due to the great stress placed on oral reading of Scripture. In early days, the lector may have preached also, but by the fourth century, reading the gospel was restricted to priests and deacons. In modern times, the lay reader is an honored post for lay men and women in the Anglican and Episcopal churches. With the adoption of lectionaries in other Protestant churches, lay readers or lectors are now becoming quite common in many denominations. "Lay ministers of the word" are recent ministries promoted by the Roman Catholic church since Vatican II.

J.C.

**LAZARUS** (of Bethany.) Lazarus of Bethany is mentioned in the Gospels only in John 11–12 as the brother of Mary and Martha (the sisters also appear in Luke 10:38-42). In the account Lazarus dies and has been entombed for four days when Jesus arrives. Jesus raises Lazarus from the dead as a demonstration of his statement, "I am the resurrection and the life" (John 11:25). In John's presentation of the event it is clear that the raising of Lazarus is meant to confirm belief in Jesus as the revealer of God's glory (see John 1:14; 11:4, 15, 40-42). In the Johannine account the raising of Lazarus from the dead occasions the belief of many Jews in Jesus (11:45; 12:11). The event also is the point at which the chief priests and Pharisees determine to put to death both Jesus (11:47-53) and Lazarus (12:10). Since this dramatic event is not mentioned in the Synoptic Gospels and since the Synoptic Gospels note other events as the turning point against Jesus, some scholars have argued that the story of the raising of Lazarus is a Johanine "parable."                                                      D.S.

**LAZARUS** (the beggar). Lazarus, a common Jewish name that means "one whom God helps," is the poor man in the parable of the rich man and Lazarus (Luke 16:19-31). He is not to be identified with Lazarus of Bethany. Lazarus' fate is reversed in the afterlife. The parable illustrates Luke's concern for the rich and the poor (for example, Luke 1:53; 4:18; 6:20, 24; 7:22; 12:13-34; 14:13, 21, 33; 16:1-13).

D.S.

**LEAH.** The story of Leah, the elder daughter of LABAN, begins in Genesis 29. When Jacob followed the orders of his father Isaac to return to the ancestral seat in Mesopotamia to obtain a wife from the family of his mother's brother, he first encountered Laban's younger daughter, the lovely Rachel. He willingly served Laban seven years in exchange for the promise of her hand in marriage, but on the night of the wedding feast Laban substituted his "weak eyed" daughter Leah for Rachel. Unable to recognize her, perhaps because of her nuptial veils, Jacob acted in good faith in having intercourse with Leah. When by morning light the deception was discovered, Jacob had no choice but to keep Leah as his wife—though after the week of wedding feasting was completed, he also was promised Rachel in return for another seven years of service. Though Jacob loved Rachel more than her sister, Leah was the more prolific, and bore to Jacob six sons and a daughter, Dinah (Gen. 30:1-21).

W.S.T.

**LEAP OF FAITH.** An idea especially associated with KIERKEGAARD. The truth of Christianity, he believed, is above reason and is a paradox. Reason cannot arrive at the paradox and comes into collision with an unknown, which surpasses it. Then two courses are possible. Reason may take offense and turn away from the paradox, or there may occur the leap of faith. Faith is said to be the happy passion that unites reason and the paradox.

One may agree with Kierkegaard that reason can never establish the truth of Christianity and that a leap beyond what is demonstrable is necessary. One might also agree with him that the multiplication of historical knowledge about Jesus could never bring one to the point of believing that he is the God-man—that is a belief of a different order—and to arrive at this point would still require a leap of faith even if we had a perfect historical knowledge about Jesus. But what is less easy to accept is Kierkegaard's apparent dismissal of all evidential claims in the matter. Suppose, for instance, evidence came to light that Jesus had been a fraud or a hypocrite; would that not prevent the leap? And if negative evidence can have that effect, then must not affirmative evidence be allowed to have some relevance also? Does it not provide a basis of probability for the leap?

At this point, one might compare Kierkegaard's view with the related view of NEWMAN. The latter also believed that in matters of religion one has finally to make a leap beyond what the evidence warrants, and he even thought that there comes a point where one is justified in claiming certitude. But in this progression to the leap of faith, Newman allowed an important role to probability. He suggested that it is like inscribing a polygon in a circle. As one keeps adding sides, the polygon approaches ever more closely to the circle. It will never turn into a circle, yet there comes a point when one sees with certitude that this is the end of the progression. Here, however, a definite role is given to probability which Kierkegaard denies to it. Theologians remain divided between those who approve the decisive leap of Kierkegaard and those who favor the more cautious approach of Newman.                                      J.M.

**LEAVEN.** Popularly considered in the ancient world to be a form of corruption (as indeed it is). It is this concept that prevails mainly in constituting it as taboo for religious purposes. The taboo did not extend into secular life. Leavened bread was always preferred to unleavened because of its superior taste and texture, and the same yeasting process was widely employed in the brewing of beer and wine (though the process was probably not recognized to be the same).

In the OT the instances are rare in which leavened bread is brought into conjunction with religious ritual. It forms a part of the so-called "peace offering" (Lev. 7:11-18), which is to ask a blessing on what is destined for human consumption. Otherwise, liturgical bread had to be unleavened, on the "corruption" principle.

Sometimes, as in the Passover ritual (Exod. 12:15-20), a rationalization is given out of salvation history for the insistence on unleavened bread: it is to commemorate the Israelites' hasty departure from Egypt when there was no time to wait for the bread to leaven (Deut. 16:3). Even here, however, the provision that houses must be thoroughly purged of leaven prior to the feast (Exod. 12:17-20) shows that its original import involved the ritual impurity of leaven.

In the NT the notion of leaven as corruption also prevails, no longer in a ritual but still in a religious sense. Only a couple of times (Matt. 13:33; Luke 13:21) does it appear as a positive ferment: the dynamism of the proclamation of the kingdom of God. Otherwise it is a pejorative metaphor: symbolizing the deleterious influence of the Sadducees and Pharisees (Matt. 16:6, etc.), of the "Judaizers" opposing Paul (Gal. 5:9). In I Corinthians 5:2-8 Paul also characterizes the "incestuous man" of Corinth as a corruption and evokes the Passover ritual in calling on the Corinthians to purge themselves.

Though the Synoptic Gospels (but not John) have described the Last Supper of Jesus and his disciples as a Passover meal, the technical term for unleavened bread *(azymos)*, which was and is the essential component of that feast, never appears in their texts. Instead, the word for ordinary or leavened bread *(artos)* invariably is featured in the "Eucharistic" texts of the NT. This might indicate that an earlier stage of the Last Supper story had not yet identified it with the Passover, despite the Synoptic redaction. Partly as a result of the Gospel ambiguity, the liturgical traditions of the Eastern and Western churches have long divided over the propriety of leavened or unleavened Eucharistic bread.

B.V.

**LEBANON.** From the Hebrew word meaning "white," Lebanon was probably thus named because of the snow-capped Mount Hermon, also known as Sirion (Ps. 29:6), visible throughout the year and dominating the horizon of northern Palestine. Actually, Mount Hermon forms a part of the anti-Lebanese range, a higher sierra that parallels the

Herbert G. May

*Cedars of Lebanon with summer snow on hill in background*

coastal mountain chain of Lebanon, separated from it by the Biqa' ("Valley"), which constitutes much of the modern Republic of Lebanon. The Biqa' is a rift or geological fault that continues southward in the Jordan Valley and the Ghor south of the Dead Sea to the Gulf of Aqabah, whence it travels beneath the gulf and the Red Sea to terminate in the Great Rift of Africa.

Lebanon is featured frequently in the OT (Deut. 11:24; Josh. 1:4; etc.) as in a general way the northern boundary of Palestine, dividing it from Phoenicia and Syria. More precisely, the border was defined by Mount Hor on the west, a peak in the Lebanese range, to Lebo Hamath in the east (Num. 34:7; Ezek. 47:15). These designations are rather vague and can only uncertainly be identified today. The gorge of the Nahr el-Litani forms a more enduring and defined separation of Phoenicia and Lebanon from Galilee.

In the Bible Lebanon is celebrated in various capacities. Its imposing range was emblematic of natural strength and solidarity, therefore a perfect poetic foil to the majesty of God revealed in a thunderstorm so powerful that it "makes Lebanon to skip like a calf" (Ps. 29:6). It was a proverbially lush land, noted for its fragrance and the abundance of its vineyards (Hos. 14:6-8). Above all, however, "the glory of Lebanon" consisted in its magnificent forests (Isa. 60:13), especially "the cedars of Lebanon" (Judg. 9:15; Isa. 2:13), which for the tree-poor Palestinians symbolized the ultimate in natural wealth and beauty. In Psalm 104:16 the psalmist calls these ancient and beautiful cedars "the trees of the Lord . . . which he planted." Cedars as well as other woods of Lebanon were used in great abundance in the construction of Solomon's Temple and palace buildings (I Kings 5:13-18; 7:2), and Ezra 3:7 says that Lebanese cedar was obtained also for the building of the second Temple or Temple of Zerubbabel.

The forests of Lebanon had been exploited by Egypt and Mesopotamia long before biblical times, and they continued to supply precious timber well into the Roman Era. Only in the comparatively modern period of Lebanon, under the Ottoman Empire, did they disappear almost entirely, victims of human greed and irresponsibility.

B.V.

**LECTION.** One of a systematic series of readings from the Scriptures, arranged according to the church year. A lection is one individual reading, while a lectionary is a list or group of readings from the OT, the Epistles, and the Gospels. The practice of reading systematically through the Scriptures throughout the year was taken from the Jewish synagogue by the early church. From ancient times the books of Moses were read every Sabbath. By Jesus' time, the prophetic books were divided into lections, as is shown by Jesus' reading from Isaiah in Luke 4:16-21. The church began reading the OT and added the Epistles and Gospels. Fixed lessons were used by the third century. The Third Council of

Carthage (A.D. 397) forbade the reading of anything but the Bible in church services. Traditionally, the liturgical churches (Catholic, Lutheran, Episcopalian) have used lectionaries and the free churches have not. Recently many non-liturgical churches have begun to use the lectionary.                    J.C.

**LECTOR.** *See* LAY READER.

**LEE, MOTHER ANN.** *See* SHAKERS.

**LEGALISM.** A technical term referring to law. Canon law is the legal system of the church, specifically used among Roman Catholics and Anglicans. It defines and describes the ecclesial structures, the responsibilities of lay and clerical officers, and the conditions under which a person might be admitted to or barred from receiving the sacraments.

Orthodox Jews pattern their lives by a system of law that gives them a sense of identity under the covenant. The rigid interpretation of Torah by the Pharisees as reflected in the NT has become a prototype of legalism, used pejoratively by many Protestants. Some Protestant traditions have careful prescriptions mandating the life-style of a Christian, and members are expected to conform or leave the church. The juridical nature of canon law is mitigated by the exemptions possible under extenuating circumstances. Legalism leaves no such loopholes. Legalism frequently implies a power of judgment on the part of humans that ignores motives and looks only at acts. For this reason the word has come to have a negative meaning. By contrast, a flexible attitude toward religious rules would seem to exemplify the grace of God and to suggest that mercy befits fallible humans better than judgment does.             I.C.

**LEGGE, JAMES** (1815–97). A native Scotsman, missionary, and teacher, best known for his research into and translation of the texts of Taoism and of the Confusian classics. He first went to Malacca in 1839 for the London Missionary Society. After Hong Kong became a British possession in 1842 he was moved with other missionaries to Hong Kong and the Treaty Ports in China. He served as minister of the First Union Church in Hong Kong and was head of the Anglo-Chinese College, a theological college and boy's school, which he developed. His translation work opened up a new field of study of the Chinese classics. He retired from Hong Kong and was subsequently made the first professor of Chinese at Oxford, a position that he held until his death.
                                                        W.G.

**LEGION.** A Latin loanword that first appeared in Greek in the first century B.C. It refers to the basic unit of the Roman army. In Imperial Rome a legion, the symbol of Roman power, comprised about 6,000 foot soldiers and 120 cavalry. This term does not appear in Josephus and is not used in the NT to refer to the Roman army. The NT borrows this term to refer to powers in the spiritual world, both demons (Mark 5:9, 15; Luke 8:30) and angels (Matt. 26:53). In the Matthew text Jesus claims that God could send more than twelve legions of angels to help him, a powerful symbol in the Roman context.
                                                        D.S.

**LEIBNITZ, GOTTFRIED WILHELM** (1646–1716), German philosopher, mathematician, ecumenist, and statesman. Born in Leipzig, he studied law, philosophy, and mathematics at Leipzig, Jena, and Altdorf. In 1666 Leipzig said Leibnitz was too young for a doctorate in law, but Altdorf granted it. By age twenty-one Leibnitz had written several philosophical works on individuation, symbolic logic, and philosophical method. Regarded as a genius, Leibnitz entered the employ of the Elector of Mainz in 1667 and during the last forty years of his life resided in Hanover, serving the Duke of Brunswick-Lüneburg. Diplomatic missions took him to Paris, London, Berlin, and Amsterdam, enabling him to meet Malebranche, Huygens, Spinoza, Newton, and Boyle. In 1672 he invented a calculator that could multiply, divide, and extract square roots, and in 1673 was made a Fellow of London's Royal Society. In 1675 he discovered the basic principles of differential and integral calculus, and in 1700 was elected to the French Academy and helped found Prussia's Academy of the Sciences. He tried unsuccessfully to unite Protestant and Roman Catholic churches.

His *Essais de Théodicée* (1710) partially developed a philosophy of a universe of infinite monads in preestablished harmony and argued this was the best of all possible worlds, a view Voltaire satirized in *Candide*. His *Monadology* (published 1720) postulated a universe of monadic centers of force, each an individual mirror of the whole universe, arranged in ascending order with God as the highest monad. Leibnitz defended traditional proofs for God, but his monadology did not harmonize well with traditional Christian doctrine.                 C.M.

**LENT.** "Lent" is derived from the old Anglo-Saxon word "Lencten," for spring. In the Christian year, Lent is the forty-day period of prayer and spiritual self-examination that prepares for the festival of the Resurrection, EASTER. Lent is thus identified with the passion or suffering of Christ, who died for our sins. Forty days is reflective of the forty days Jesus fasted in the wilderness, tempted by the devil.

Lent is not merely concerned with remembering the suffering of Christ, but is designed to prepare the Christian to celebrate the death and resurrection of Christ. The object of such Lenten observance is a participation, a reliving of the events of our historical atonement, the life, suffering, rejection, death, and triumph over death of Jesus Christ. Lent does not include the Sundays in Lent. These "Lord's Days" are themselves weekly celebrations of the Resurrection. Lent, therefore, is made up of forty week days and Saturdays. These forty days point to Jesus' forty days of testing, immediately after his baptism by John the Baptizer. Lent is a time when Christians renew their baptism, deepen their conviction, and complete their conversion to Christ. In liturgical churches this period of renewal may be marked by fasting as well as attendance at special worship services. Such special services include Ash Wednesday, services on Wednesdays throughout Lent, Holy Week services (from Palm Sunday to Easter), and especially the celebration of Holy Communion on Maundy Thursday and commemorative services on Good Friday. Communal worship is particularly appropriate since Lent is the worship of the church, the universal Body of Christ, and not simply a matter of individualistic piety, sentimentalism, or emotionalism.

Lenten observance began very early, as both Irenaeus and Tertullian refer to it, but it was originally very brief, only gradually growing to forty days. At first, a fast of forty hours was observed, then a week. But by A.D. 325, the Council of Nicaea recognized forty days of Lent. These forty days included Sundays, but by the seventh century Lent was extended to forty days, excluding Sundays, and Ash Wednesday was established.

J.C.

**LEO I** (390?–461). Pope (440–461) Leo the Great, the most important of Rome's early bishops. Born probably in Rome, he was early involved in church affairs and was on a mission in Gaul, France, when chosen pope. He asserted the primacy of the Roman bishop over all other ecclesiastics and secular rulers, and he had annual sermons preached on Peter's confession of Christ as God's Son (Matt. 16:13 ff.). Leo believed Christ delegated authority specifically to Peter and only generally to the other disciples. He resisted Manichaeism and Pelagianism, and in 451 insisted that the Council of Chalcedon accept without debate his *Tome* on the fully divine and fully human Christ, with each nature fully preserved in the historical Christ. He personally confronted Attila the Hun (452) and Genseric the Vandal (455), saving Rome from destruction. With administrative skill Leo fed thousands, ransomed prisoners, promoted celibacy, and initiated issuing papal encyclicals.

C.M.

**LEO XIII** (1810–1903). Pope (1878–1903) who sought to reconcile Roman Catholic ULTRAMON-TANISM to a modern world dominated by LIBERALISM, democratic trends, and science. He left a legacy of eighty-six encyclicals. Born Vincenzo Gioacchino Pecci in Carpineto, Italy, he studied in Jesuit schools, and gained a doctorate in canon law and practical experience as a police chief and governor. Ordained in

Rome in 1837, he rose rapidly from nuncio to bishop to cardinal in 1853.

His first significant encyclical, *Aeterni Patris* (1879), required the teaching of Thomas Aquinas in all Catholic schools. *On Marriage* (1880) warned against marriages between Catholics and non-Catholics and asserted the church's control of marriage. *On Civil Government* (1881) said political power must be guided by Catholic doctrine. *The Christian Constitution of States* (1885) asserted states should profess Roman Catholicism as the only true religion, but that Catholics could tolerate religious error in a state for the sake of securing some good or avoiding a greater evil. *On Human Liberty* (1888) rejected liberty of speech, press, teaching, conscience, and tolerance, except as determined by the pope, because truth and error should not have equal privileges. *Rights and Duties of Capital and Labor (Rerum novarum,* 1891) urged better treatment of laborers and sanctioned unions of workers.

Leo achieved better relations in Belgium and Germany, established an Apostolic Delegation in Washington, and made contacts with Japan and Russia. However, relations with England foundered when Anglican ordinations were declared invalid in 1896. His censure of "Americanism" in 1899 hampered American Catholic developments. He never accepted the Italian Republic, and forbade Catholics to participate in Italian politics.

C.M.

**LEONARDO DA VINCI** (1452–1519). Italian artist, sculptor, engineer, architect, scientist, mathematician, and inventor—a genius among RENAISSANCE geniuses. Born in the Tuscan town of Vinci, the illegitimate son of Ser Piero da Vinci, a noted Florentine notary, and Catarina, a peasant woman, he was raised in the paternal home in Vinci. The family settled in Florence about 1469, and da Vinci was apprenticed to Andrea del Verrocchio to study painting and sculpturing. By 1472 he was a guild master, by 1478 had his own studio, and by 1482 completed his first masterpiece, *Adoration of the Magi,* followed in 1483 by *St. Jerome,* both considered unfinished.

Lacking formal philosophy, he pursued practical projects, mathematics, natural sciences, and anatomy. He valued personal experience and observation above accepted authority, experimented with color, and brought new insights to nature and life through his artistry. He was a leader in the Renaissance emphasis on life now. From about 1482 to 1499, he worked in Milan as the chief military engineer of Duke Lodovico Sforza, helped build the cathedral of Milan, gathered a group of aspiring artists, wrote his *Treatise on Painting,* and labored for years on a colossal, unfinished bronze monument to the father of Lodovico.

Four masterful paintings date from this period:

*Virgin of the Rocks, Lady with an Ermine, A Musician,* and *The Last Supper.* When France invaded Milan, he returned to Florence. In 1502 he served as military engineer to Caesare Borgia, mapped central Italy, and studied mechanics. From 1503 to 1506, he was again working in Florence. He painted portraits, but only one, that of the wife of Francesco del Giocondo, survives—the famous *Mona Lisa* at the Louvre. Da Vinci considered it unfinished.

Invited to Milan by French King Louis XII and later to France by Francis I, da Vinci spent most of his last years in Milan and France, but maintained a studio in Florence. His virtually illegible notebooks on numerous subjects contributed later to biology, optics, and mechanics. Famous at his death, he influenced his own time and generations of artists following.                                                C.M.

**LEPROSY.** An infectious disease that by an extraordinary paradox, though pervasively mentioned in both the OT and NT (over fifty instances of the term in the OT, a round dozen in the NT), probably never existed in the Near East during biblical times. The affliction, which is now commonly called Hansen's disease, was known to the Greeks as *elephantiasis.* It is a bacterial disease that takes various forms, all degenerative, and slowly eats away the body's tissue or nervous sytem. It was one of the plagues of medieval Europe, whence it was doubtless introduced into the Near East (not endemically). It occurs today especially in hot, humid climates, is arrestable but fatal, and is not contagious; the leper has no cause to be shunned.

Biblical and modern confusion over leprosy stems from the accidence of translation, together with subsequent misconceptions. The Septuagint Greek translators of the Hebrew Bible, confronted by the more than fifty instances there of the Hebrew *sara'at* did not—could not—translate it by *elephantiasis,* a disease that they knew very well and that they knew would not fit the Hebrew. So they used the word *lepra,* which in Hellenistic medicine referred to just about any unpleasant or unaesthetic skin disease. From the Greek OT via the NT and into the Latin came *lepra* and "leprosy" and eventually its identification with a disease wholly unknown to the Bible.

It is not hard to see why it is that the "lepers" of the OT could suffer from temporary rather than degenerative disease (Exod. 4:6; Num. 12:10). Furthermore, as the Priestly laws of Leviticus 13–14 make quite plain, "leprosy" is an ailment that can encompass all kinds of skin eruptions and disfigurements (eczema, warts, and the like) all the way to "leprosy" of garments (mildew) and houses (mold, dry rot).

The Greek translators did not choose *lepra* without thought to translate the Hebrew word, however. They chose a word that expressed that which was aesthetically unpleasant to make the equivalent of what in the Hebrew was ritually unacceptable. For that is the ultimate sense of "leprosy" in the OT: it is not so much a physical evil to be endured as it is a ritual defilement to be expiated under the sometimes rather arbitrary rules of ritual rectitude.

In the NT leprosy has almost precisely the same contours as it possesses in the OT: in this respect, at least, the transition from OT to NT has been imperceptible. Leprosy is an affliction frequently cured, and its curability is part of the Apostolic mission (Matt. 10:8). This is to remember, among other precedents, the story of Elisha, Naaman, and Gehazi in II Kings 5. Lepers are kept at a distance according to the ritual laws (Luke 17:12; probably Mark 1:40-41). When Jesus appears as a guest in the house of Simon the leper (Matt. 26:6), he is obviously being entertained by a host whose leprosy is of the past. Though there is, for obvious reasons, no perpetuation in the practice of early Christianity of the ritual law surrounding leprosy, it is evident that the same concepts governed the physical phenomena and that the same rudimentary medicinal judgments were derived.

B.V.

**LESSING, GOTTHOLD EPHRAIM** (1729–81). German Lutheran dramatist, critic, biblical scholar, and advocate of religious toleration. Born into a Lutheran minister's family in Kamenz, Saxony, he studied theology, medicine, and philosophy at Wittenberg and Leipzig, and chose drama as a vocation. In 1748 he published his first play, *Der Junge Gelehrte,* followed by other plays and numerous essays published in Berlin's *Vossische Zeitung.* By extolling William Shakespeare he helped stem the influence of French writers Corneille, Racine, and Voltaire on German literature. During his final eleven years, he was ducal librarian at Wolfenbüttel. A blank-verse drama, *Nathan der Weise* (1779), portraying a wise Jew, pleaded for enlightened tolerance, as did his theological polemic, *Erziehung des Menschengeschlechts* (1780), which helped pave the way for German liberalism. Lessing was a leader in the German Enlightenment; his perceptive, critical essays set standards for painting, drama, theology, poetry, and sculpture. The *Wolfenbüttel Fragments,* from H. S. Reimarus, edited by Lessing, appeared in seven parts (1774–78) and widened the Enlightenment's understanding of NT origins. Lessing believed Matthew was based on an earlier Aramaic writing. An interest in archaeology led to his discovery of a Berengar manuscript on the Eucharist in 1770.
C.M.

**LESSON.** A selection from Scripture chosen to be read during worship services. These passages are taken from a lectionary. Lessons may be from the OT, the Epistles, or the Gospels. Occasionally, other portions of Scripture such as Acts or the Revelation are used as lessons.
J.C.

## LEVELLERS

**LEVELLERS.** This party arose about 1645 during the English Civil War among radical Parliamentarians who wished to "level men's estates." Their progressive social and economic reforms included manhood suffrage and regular sessions of Parliament. Their 1647 manifesto, *Agreement of the People,* was debated until their leader John Lilburne was imprisoned in 1649 and his followers suppressed. They appealed to reason rather than arguing from tradition and the Bible. Some of their ideas were later adopted by the Quakers.                          N.H.

**LEVI.** The third son of JACOB and LEAH (Gen. 29:34) and the ancestor of the priestly clan that bore his name. As an individual, he is presented as a violent avenger of his sister's honor (Gen. 34:25-31). This violence earned Levi the deathbed "blessing" of his father, Jacob, to be scattered in Israel (Gen. 49:7). This "scattering" occurred when, after standing with Moses at the crisis of the golden calf, the LEVITES were ordained to the service of the Lord (Exod. 32:25-29). Their tribe received no allotment of the Promised Land (Josh. 13:14). They were to be substitutes for the firstborn sons of all of Israel, dedicated to serve the Lord at the sanctuary as a lower order of priests (Num. 3:5-51; 8:5-22).                          W.S.T.

**LEVIATHAN.** Although mentioned only five times in the Bible, this sea monster is well known in Canaanite texts. Its many heads are alluded to in Psalm 74:14, where, representing both God's primordial cosmic enemies and the human adversary Egypt, it is subdued at the sea (see Isa. 47:1). In Psalm 104:26 it is a friendly monster, possibly a whale, and in Job 41 it is more like a crocodile. The curious reference in Job 3:8 suggests that Leviathan caused eclipses.                          W.S.T.

**LEVITES.** The meaning of the word Levite is unknown. Many ingenious explanations have been offered, and each has its probability. As for the real and historical meaning, it may be best to begin with the final and most certain knowledge that we have of the Levites and thence to work back to earlier and more problematical indications.

In the postexilic Jewish community, those designated "Levites" were appointed to be the minor ministers overseeing the upkeep of the sacred fabric of the restored Temple and serving as acolytes to the priesthood (Ezek. 44:9-14). They replaced in this function the Canaanite serfs ("Solomon's servants," Ezra 2:43-58), who had fulfilled this hereditary office in the days of the monarchy. The reference in Ezekiel makes it quite clear that this assignment of the Levites represented a downgrading, a new development in the Torah elaborated in Babylon that was to govern the community, which "returned" to Judah. This reduced status of the Levites doubtless explains in part the difficulty that Ezra experienced in persuading "the sons of Levi" to accompany him to Jerusalem,

necessitating compromise in a man not lightly given to compromise (compare Ezra 8:15-20).

The postexilic demotion of the simple Levites was accompanied by a restriction of Priestly status in the Jewish community to only one group within the Levites, those who were putatively descended from AARON, the brother of Moses. In the Priestly law and narrative (Exodus 28–29 for example), this late development is portrayed as though it had been the rule from the beginning, but other biblical sources reveal the much more complicated history. In Deuteronomy and the Deuteronomic history, "priest" and "Levite" are interchangeable terms (compare Deut. 18:1), pointing to a time when all Levites made up the professional and hereditary Priestly class in Israel.

Ezekiel (44:15) refers to the Levitical PRIESTS as "the sons of Zadok." This reference doubtless signals a final development that had also taken place in Babylon, whereby the Zadokite priesthood of Jerusalem, favored by David (II Sam. 8:17) and Solomon (I Kings 2:35), was now regarded as the only legitimate one of the restored Israel. Whatever their actual origins, by the Chronicler (I Chr. 24:1-3) the Zadokites are accorded a Levitical and Aaronite ancestry. They were without doubt the priesthood most represented among the influential families deported from Judah and brought to Babylonia by Nebuchadnezzar II in 597 and again in 586 B.C. This Zadokite monopoly of the priesthood was anticipated, surely, by the Deuteronomic reform of King Josiah about 621 B.C. (II Kings 22–23), in which the old shrines and sanctuaries outside Jerusalem were shut down, thus leaving their local priesthoods largely without employment. This situation explains why the lawcode of Deuteronomy so frequently commends the Levite, along with resident aliens, orphans, and widows, to the charity of the Israelites (Deut. 14:29, among numerous other examples). Landless in a society in which possession of the land was all, and now deprived of the priestly tithes and perquisites that had provided their living, those Levites who could not find a place within the newly reorganized religious establishment—and these were probably most of the Levites—were reduced to the status of dependents subject to public mercy.

The Levitical character of Israel's traditional priesthood is doubtless very ancient. One would expect something of this kind initially in any case, for in the Near East of which Israel was only a minor part most callings and occupations were hereditary, restricted to designated classes and families. Thus the stories in Judges 17–18 make a great deal of sense. According to these stories an Ephraimite named Micah first installed one of his own sons to be priest in his household, following the ancient patriarchal practice (or even that of David in II Sam. 8:18) on whose terms the head of the family was in charge of all matters of religion. However, as soon as Micah encounters a wandering Levite looking for "a place" for a living, he quickly seizes the opportunity to engage him for his priest, replacing his son. Micah expresses his confidence in the Lord's blessing, "because I have a Levite as a priest."

Thus it is evident that while other priesthoods existed—well into the time of David—the Levitical was preferred. Micah's Levite, according to Judges 18, went on to found the priesthood of the sanctuary of Dan, one of the two royal shrines that were refurbished by Jeroboam I of Israel at the time of the division of the United Kingdom after Solomon's death (I Kings 12:29). Non-Levitical priests, however, continued to exist into the days of the early monarchy, and not always for lack of Levites. Not to mention David's sons and the Zadokites and others who may have been inherited from pre-Israelite Canaan, there were Eli (I Sam. 1:3) and his sons at Shiloh, ancestor of David's priest Abiathar, who was deposed by Solomon, and the great Samuel (I Sam. 3:18; 7:9-10; etc.), an Ephraimite. First Chronicles 24:3 and 6:18-28 supply Eli and Samuel, respectively, with Levitical genealogies to accommodate to the later theology. Other non-Levitical priests as well can be discerned in the sources.

What is the historical origin of the Priestly caste of the Levites in Israel? One theory has it that they were originally a secular tribe or clan that formed part of the Israelite tribal confederation, which either failed to secure a territory for itself in the Promied Land or later lost the one that it had initially secured, and thus was destined to reside in no fixed geographical region but to have its members scattered throughout the land, finding a way of living where they could. Some credence might be given to this theory by Genesis 49:5-7, part of a poetic collection generally considered to be quite old, which indicates that both the tribes of Simeon and Levi, for undisclosed reasons but probably alluding to the story of Genesis 34, were doomed to disappear as distinct geographical entities in Israel. It is true, the ethnic name Simeon did disappear quite early in Israelite history; it was absorbed into the orbit of Judah. And LEVI, as far as we know, was never a geographical entity. But this fact does not explain why the Levites should precisely have become priests, unless on the premises of medieval Europe, which dedicated the last, unprovided son to the church. Furthermore, Deuteronomy 33:8-11, in a poem that has equal claim to antiquity with Genesis 49, celebrates the Levites' priesthood rather as its glory than as its last resort, and has nothing pejorative to say about Levi.

Our information about the origins of the Israelite tribes is far too scanty for us to say a great deal concerning the tribe of Levi and its relationship to the Levites. Traditionally, the Levites are the descendants of Levi, one of the "Leah" tribes (along with Reuben, Simeon, Judah, Issachar, and Zebulun) generated by the patriarch Jacob (Gen. 35:23). These tribal names are sometimes geographical, sometimes ethnic, and as already was stated, we do not know in which

category, or some other perhaps, "Levi" belongs. Some scholars have professed to find in the early genealogies attached to Levi a preponderance of Egyptian names. If this is true, it possibly has something to say with regard to the tradition that has persistently connected Moses with the Levites and the priesthood, and all of these in turn with the Exodus from Egypt at the beginning of Israel.

B.V.

**LEVITICAL CITIES.** According to the standard history of Israel's election by Yahweh in its liberation from the bondage of Egypt and its taking possession of the Canaanite Land of Promise, the LEVITES, destined to be the priestly caste of the Israelite people, were assigned no territory of their own but were rather distributed throughout the other tribal areas into various cities, where their separate clans would dwell with sufficient pastureland to support their families. Numbers 35:1-8 ascribes this determination to Moses, and Joshua 21 details the specific assignments of the cities, not all of which are named. The cities add up to forty-eight in all, of which six (Kedesh in Galilee, Shechem, Hebron, Bezer, Ramoth-Gilead, and Golan-in-Bashan; compare Josh. 20:7-9) are also designated "cities of refuge," that is, sanctuaries where people who had inadvertently incurred the peril of blood-vengeance might plead their case before an impartial court.

The question rises whether the Levitical cities are a figment of theology or point to some historical reality. And, if historical, to what period do they properly belong? The "cities of refuge," which probably pertain to a tradition older than that of the Levitical cities, make good historical sense. The distribution of the Levitical cities, at least in the eventual form in which we read them, is romantic rather than real. Some of them are the major cities of Israel, and they have been mechanically assigned to the various tribal areas. Yet there were in later Israel certain priestly cities (for example, Anathoth, Josh. 21:18; Jer. 32:7-9). It is a good guess that in the Deuteronomic reform of King Josiah (640–609 B.C.) certain cities were set aside for Levitical priests who exceeded the number of priests needed after the centralization of the cult in Jerusalem under the Zadokite priesthood, and that the tradition of "Levitical Cities" is the result.                    B.V.

**LEVITICUS.** A name first given to the third book of the Bible in its Latin (Vulgate) version. This in turn derives from the title of the Greek (Septuagint) version, *Leuitike Biblos,* meaning "the Levitical book," a writing primarily concerned with the responsibilities of Levitical priests. Known in Hebrew as *wayyiqra'* ("and he called") after its opening word, this book schooled Israel's priests in the proper techniques of official public worship and informed the laity about their religious and civil duties as Yahweh's holy covenant people.

*Organization and Basic Content.* Though Leviticus is a separate book in the PENTATEUCH, it belongs to a larger body of priestly legislation (Exod. 25:1–Num. 10:28, minus Exod. 32-34). The contents of this relatively uncomplicated book divide into six parts: the sacrificial system (chaps. 1–7); consecration of the priesthood (chaps. 8–10, a logical extension of Exod. 35–40); laws enjoining ritual purity (chaps. 11–15); the Day of Atonement (Yom Kippur) ceremony (chap. 16); precepts directing Israel's existence as a holy people (chaps. 17–26); and an appendix on religious vows (chap. 27).

*Composition.* The process whereby Leviticus achieved its present form is lengthy and complex, for its full legislation originated across several centuries. As a literary product, however, Leviticus fully belongs to the Priestly (P) stratum of the Pentateuch and presumably was completed during the sixth-century B.C. Babylonian exile (*see* DOCUMENTARY HYPOTHESIS). In content, style, and outlook, chapters 17–26 are distinguishable from chapters 1–16 and 27. For more than a century, this special unit in P has been labeled the Holiness Code (H). Its ethical and ritual precepts, alternately addressed to PRIESTS and laity, are continuously punctuated with an appeal for holiness. Unlike chapters 1–16 and 27, the intentionality of the legislation is frequently articulated, and the phrase, "I am Yahweh," appears nearly fifty times as a fitting means for motivating Israel's fidelity to the Torah. Nevertheless, the Holiness Code has been well accommodated to the overall legislative perspective of the finally edited book.

*Legislative Centers of Gravity.* There are five "centers." First, the opening legislation distinguishes between (a) spontaneously motivated sacrifices (the burnt offering {*'olah*}, the cereal offering of grain or cakes {*minhah*}, and peace offerings {*shelem*}, enumerated in chapters 1–3) and (b) mandatory sacrifices for the expiation of sin that ruptures the individual's relation with deity and threatens communal well-being (the sin offering {*ḥaṭṭa'th*} and guilt offering {*'asham*} mentioned in chapters 4–5). Second, in the legislation on priestly consecration in chapters 8–10, the spotlight falls more on Moses than Aaron. As the unique mediator of Yahweh's law, Moses conducts the consecration service and assigns the priests their duties. Third, the differentiation between clean and unclean in chapters 11–15 is considered a vital priestly task. Ritual impurities involving animals (chap. 11), childbirth (chap. 12), various skin diseases (chaps. 13–14), and genital discharges (chap. 15) assume a rationale now lost in oblivion; yet originally this legislation undoubtedly fostered in Israel a proper appreciation of the divinely ordered natural world. Fourth, with its use of the scapegoat that symbolically receives the nation's transgressions and is driven into the wilderness for Azazel (a desert demon?), the Day of Atonement legislation in chapter 16 provides Yahweh's people a solemn occasion for

returning to spiritual wholeness. Finally, with its heterogeneous stipulations on such matters as animal sacrifice, unlawful marriage, sexual offenses, necromancy, blasphemy, and the sabbatical and jubilee years designed to curb economic exploitation, the precepts in chapters 17–26 assist Israel in honoring the divine mandate, "You shall be holy; for I [Yahweh] your God am holy" (19:2).

*Religious Significance.* Notwithstanding its proclivity for legislative detail, Leviticus espouses a theological position most congenial to Israel's fundamental covenant faith. It freely recognizes that in Yahweh's ineffable purity and glory, Yahweh chose Israel as a special people. God separated and sanctified them by securing their liberation from Egypt (22:32-33). Presently Israel's incomparable Deity challenges the chosen to pursue a life-style that will reflect Yahweh's own holiness. Everything profane must be shunned. Only so can Israel shoulder its covenant duty to be like Yahweh. Having received its final editing after Jerusalem's destruction and Israel's loss of nationhood, Leviticus challenges Yahweh's people to learn from past tragedy and embrace the future, armed with full knowledge of the covenant claims of the God of Sinai, which are ever normative. These claims include ethical as well as cultic obligations. Most celebrated among the former is 19:18, "You shall love your neighbor as yourself," which reappears in Mark 12:31 within Jesus' teaching about the Great Commandment.                    J.K.K.

**LEWIS, CLIVE STAPLES** (1898–1963). Noted literary critic and urbane Christian apologist whose writings have attracted a wide following. Born on November 29, in Belfast, Ireland, C. S. Lewis spent most of his life in the rarified atmosphere of Oxford and Cambridge. Following his youth and early education, which was poignantly described in *Surprised by Joy* (1955), Lewis entered Oxford University in 1917. He soon left to serve as a second lieutenant with the Somerset Light Infantry. He was wounded in the fighting near Lillers, France, hospitalized, and ultimately discharged in December 1918. Back at Oxford in 1919, he received a bachelor's degree in 1923 and later a master's degree.

He became a lecturer at University College, Oxford, in 1924, and the following year he became a Fellow and tutor of Magdalen College, Oxford. There he remained until 1954. In that year he was given the chair of Medieval and Renaissance Literature at Cambridge.

Lewis began his writing career with a two-volume book of verse, *Spirits in Bondage,* published under the pen name of Clive Hamilton. In 1936 he made a name in scholarly circles with *The Allegory of Love: A Study in Medieval Tradition.* He also wrote *A Preface to Paradise Lost* (1942) and *English Literature in the Sixteenth Century* (1955). The latter volume is a part of the *Oxford History of English Literature.*

But Lewis is known to the Christian world for his witty, sophisticated apologetics, starting in 1941

Courtesy of Wheaton College, Marion E. Wade Collection

*C. S. Lewis*

when *Screwtape Letters,* consisting of correspondence from Screwtape, a senior devil, to his nephew, struck the Christian world. The letters were instructions on tripping up a Christian convert. He had written *The Problem of Pain* in 1940.

Then followed *The Abolition of Man* (1944), dealing with the basic philosophy of education, *The Great Divorce* (1945), and *Miracles* (1947). Later works include *Mere Christianity* (1952), *Till We Have Faces* (1956), *Reflections on the Psalms* (1958), *The World's Last Night* (1959), *The Four Loves* (1960), and *Christian Reflections* (1967), which was published posthumously. His trilogy of novels include *Out of the Silent Planet* (1938), *Perelandra* (1943), and *That Hideous Strength* (1945).

Many of his followers, who have become a sort of cult, hold in highest esteem his seven "Narnia" books for children. They include *The Lion, the Witch, and the Wardrobe; The Magician's Nephew;* and *The Last Battle.*

Lewis had remained a bachelor most of his life but in 1956—at the age of fifty-eight—he married Joy Davidman Gresham, an American Jew who had been converted to Christ. She was already suffering from cancer when they were married. She lived only four years but she brought great joy to the distinguished author. His tribute to her, *A Grief Observed,* was published in 1963, the year of Lewis' own death.

On both sides of the Atlantic, C. S. Lewis is esteemed as one of the greatest writers of this generation.                                                                R.H.

**LEX TALIONIS.** Drawn from the common law of the ancient Near East, the law of retaliation, "eye for eye, tooth for tooth," which receives its earliest OT formulation in Exodus 21:23*b*-25 (see Lev. 24:19-20; Deut. 19:21). Harsh as it seems, it embodies the principles of proportionality and equal treatment before the law. In Matthew 5:38-42, Jesus approaches the law from the point of view of the victim, substituting for an exact retaliation a principle of confrontative nonviolence, which responds to a slap on the cheek with an offer of the other cheek (see Luke 6:29-30; Rom. 12:17-21; I Pet. 3:9).                W.S.T.

**LI.** Two different terms in CONFUCIANISM spelled *li* in English. The first means "proper conduct," or "good form," in keeping with rules and traditional standards; it is the outward expression of true goodness. The second term has two related meanings: (1) the individual principles that bring order to matter and energy and produce all the variety in the world, and (2) that supreme principle, which unites all individual principles in itself.                K.C.

**LIBERALISM.** Liberalism as a theological movement—distinct from a general spirit of religious liberality and tolerance—is the creation of the nineteenth century. It reached its zenith early in the twentieth century. Liberal Catholicism must be distinguished from Protestant Liberalism, although they share a commitment to critical inquiry.

The beginning of political Liberal Catholicism is identified with Félicité Robert de Lamennais (1782–1854). He and his associates called upon the pope to "baptize" the liberal ideals of the French Revolution. In his newspaper, *L'Avenir,* Lamennais called for separation of church and state, freedom of religion, press, and association. Political Liberal Catholicism was condemned by Pope Gregory XVI in the encyclical *Mirari vos* (1832). In Germany two centers of theological Liberal Catholicism were especially important. The earliest is associated with the Catholic theological faculty at Tübingen, led by J. S. Drey (1777–1853) and J. A. Mohler (1796–1838). They were influenced by German ROMANTICISM and IDEALISM and, contrary to SCHOLASTICISM, sought to interpret dogma in more experiential and historical terms. After 1840 the center of Liberal Catholicism shifted to the University of Munich and to the leadership of the learned ecclesiastical historian Johann Ignaz Döllinger (1799–1890). Döllinger denounced Scholasticism and the dogma of papal INFALLIBILITY and upheld the use of the sciences in the study of church history and doctrine. Liberal Catholicism in England is identified with the historian John (later Lord) Acton (1834–1902), a disciple of Döllinger's. While sharing certain common aims, Liberal Catholicism is a movement distinct from Catholic MODERNISM.

Protestant Liberalism is a rather general term for several theological movements of the past two centuries which, while distinguishable, share a temper of mind and certain tenets. The fathers of Protestant Liberalism are F. SCHLEIERMACHER and A. RITSCHL. Liberals hold in common a suspicion of natural or speculative theology; consider dogma an illegitimate mixture of religion and metaphysics, therefore secondary or dispensable; cherish human freedom and reason; endorse the application of critical scholarship to the Bible and ecclesiastical tradition; and emphasize the practical side of religion, especially the ethical imperatives of the Hebrew prophets and of Jesus. A classic expression of Liberalism is found in ADOLF VON HARNACK's (1851–1930) popular *What Is Christianity?* (1900), where he summarizes Jesus' gospel as "the kingdom of God and its coming; God the Father and the infinite value of the human soul; and the higher righteousness and the commandment of love."

The most characteristic expression of Protestant Liberalism in America was the SOCIAL GOSPEL movement associated with WALTER RAUSCHEN-BUSCH, which rejected individualistic and pietistic forms of Christianity. An important distinction can be made between Protestant Evangelical Liberalism and a more radical form of American Protestantism appropriately called Liberal Modernism. The former stood squarely within historic Christianity; the latter was concerned less with preserving the historic doctrines and traditions of the faith. Liberalism's conception of the historical Jesus was shaken by ALBERT SCHWEITZER's *Quest of the Historical Jesus* (1907). Its optimistic view of human reason and freedom and its progressive vision of history were profoundly challenged by KARL BARTH and REINHOLD NIEBUHR. While certain tenets of earlier Liberalism are obsolete, its legacy endures. Many of its principles and commitments inform theological work today.                                      J.L.

## LIBERATION THEOLOGY.

Liberation theology designates various Christian theologies emphasizing social justice, freedom from oppression, and God's liberating action in history, and calling for empowerment of the oppressed rather than charity from oppressors. In different forms, liberation theology has become a point of ecumenical convergence, relating diverse groups seeking economic and political justice. The movement can be understood through its background, major manifestations, and appraisal.

*Background.* Liberation and salvation, with theological/ethical dimensions, are central in most world religious traditions. Hinduism and Buddhism seek liberation from the round of rebirth. The Judeo-Christian-Muslim tradition promises liberation from sin, oppression, and the fear of death. Greco-Roman thought speaks of liberation from life's ills and limitations, for example, Plato's myth of the cave. Biblical traditions have been the primary historical source for Western movements of liberation.

As Western society emerged from the Middle Ages seeking liberation from ecclesiastical, political, and economic oppression, power shifted from autocratic rulers to the rising middle class. Revolutions usually took a federal form, with governments not overthrown but changed from centralized to republican control. Federalism (from the Latin *foedus,* meaning "covenant") developed from federal theology and ethics and must be distinguished from liberalism, which is individualistic, optimistic about human nature, and dedicated to ideal democracy.

In the nineteenth century, federal revolution as transformation of power structures was eclipsed by the Marxist conception of revolution as the overthrow of government. Whereas federalism sought liberation of oppressed middle classes, Marxism intended liberation of oppressed lower classes. Marxist revolutions have immediate liberating impact but tend to become static around gains achieved, whereas federal revolutions provide for continuing social change.

Federalism and related biblical traditions produced many social reforms: abolition of slavery, protection of labor, assistance to farmers, conservation of the natural environment, rights of women and children, improved treatment of racial and ethnic minorities, etc. In Protestant Christianity, these concerns merged into the SOCIAL GOSPEL and informed the ecumenical movement as it developed into the World Council of Churches. Roman Catholicism, allied with remnants of feudal autocracy until the late nineteenth century, began with Leo XIII (*Rerum novarum,* 1891) to develop social teachings that since 1960 have emphasized liberation.

A major milestone on the way to recent liberation theology is the civil rights movement in the United States. Based on concern for unjust treatment of blacks, this movement forged tactics of protest against racial discrimination in the 1930s and 1940s, gained national attention in the 1950s as MARTIN LUTHER KING, JR. applied those tactics in the Montgomery bus boycott, won political success in the sweeping civil rights legislation of the early 1960s, and achieved international recognition when he received the 1964 Nobel Peace Prize.

*Major Manifestations.* Liberation theologies build on traditions of social justice and experiences of oppression. Forms considered here are: (a) black, (b) third world, (c) feminist, and (d) white. More extensive treatment might include political theology and the theology of hope, for example, JÜRGEN MOLTMANN, Johann-Baptist Metz, and Dorothee Soelle.

(a) *Black liberation theology* emerged from the shift in the 1960s from civil rights to black power. Civil rights goals were political and economic equality in an integrated society. Limited success brought increased power to blacks and also disillusionment.

Black power advocates rejected integration and affirmed "black is beautiful." For black theologian James Cone (*A Black Theology of Liberation*, 1970), theology explicates "the meaning of God's liberating activity so that those who labor under enslaving powers will see that the forces of liberation are the activity of God" and takes "the oppression of black people as a point of departure for analyzing God's activity in contemporary America." For Gayraud Wilmore oppression and blackness exemplify a "singular religiosity" present in many religions and point beyond Christian theology (*Black Religion and Black Radicalism*, 1972). Liberation theology comes also from other ethnic perspectives, for example, Vine Deloria in *God Is Red*, 1973.

(b) *Third world liberation theology* emerged from situations of oppression and exploitation in Latin America, Africa, and Asia. In the writings of Gustavo Gutierrez, Jose Miguez-Bonino, Juan Luis Segundo, Allen Aubrey Boesak, and Kim Yong Bock, an understanding of biblical Christianity appears unlike that in most Western theology. First, theology must start with the poor and the oppressed because the God of biblical faith is on their side. Second, Marxist social analysis aids Christian theology and ethics by disclosing social conflict, systemic evil, and the necessity of commitment to societal change. Third, human liberation defines eschatological hope and historical reality as given in Christian faith.

(c) *Feminist liberation theology* developed in interaction with black and third world movements, emerging from women's experience of oppression, "the oldest form of oppression in human history" (Rosemary Radford Ruether, *Liberation Theology: Human Hope Confronts Christian History and American Power*, 1972). Some feminist theologians reject biblical faith as hopelessly patriarchal and turn to goddess symbols and traditions, for example, Mary Daly. Other feminist theologians seek to recover the prophetic, messianic power of the Bible as the basis of critique and theology, for example, Rosemary Ruether, Letty M. Russell, and Elisabeth Moltmann-Wendel.

(d) *White liberation theology* responds to and interprets black, third world, and feminist liberation theologies. White liberationists emphasize that North Atlantic white theologies are not normative for Christian theology and that the experience of oppression must be central. Frederick Herzog (*Liberation Theology: Liberation in the Light of the Fourth Gospel*, 1972) writes: "Theology today must begin with an identification with the wretched of the earth, . . . the marginal figures of life who are still struggling for personhood and dignity." Benjamin Reist asserts that whites must learn to be white with a sense of particularity and ethnic consciousness, knowing that all human groups are "equally present in the historical space that is human liberation" (*Theology in Red, White and Black*, 1975). For Charles S. McCoy (*When Gods Change: Hope for Theology*,

1980), liberation has plural meanings related to different experiences of oppression, and pluralism is viewed as having liberating power within the faithful action of the covenant God.

*Appraisal.* Liberation theology is making many contributions to Christian thought and action. First, it emphasizes anew salvation as deliverance, with God leading humanity out of bondage. God's faithful action incarnate in Jesus Christ reveals a future filled with divine justice and love. Second, liberation theology affirms that solidarity with the poor, the perspective of the oppressed, and empowerment of the powerless are required to achieve social justice. Third, liberation theology relates Christian faith and Marxism so that both are useful for critique of feudal, capitalist, and socialist forms of oppression.

Liberation theologies have difficulties. First, the theology of revolution, by opposing military power with eschatological dreaming, often has aided oppressive regimes. Second, some liberation theologies have used Marxism not only for social analysis but have permitted it to displace biblical faith as an encompassing world view. Third, some view one liberation theology as the only one (for example, black, Latin American, feminist, or some other), ignoring the oppression of other groups and the long history and diverse stories of human liberation throughout the world and among all peoples. Liberation theology was not invented by this generation, nor does it come from only one situation of oppression. Its differing manifestations in the past and around the globe today add richness to the liberation theme and power to the liberation movement.

The significance of liberation theology lies in its protests against injustice, its articulation of the pain and hopes of oppressed peoples, and its continuing rediscovery of the eschatological anticipations of newness, change, and liberation as the shared experience of all humanity. Martin Luther King, Jr., informed by GANDHI as well as the prophets and Jesus, articulated clearly that liberation of the oppressed means liberation of the oppressor; that black liberation will accomplish white liberation; that the liberation of women will also free men; and that only as liberation is the cause of God can it be the hope of humanity.                                           C.Mc.

**LIBER PONTIFICALIS.** Latin for "The Papal Book," a collection of papal biographies from the early church through the fifteenth century. The first compiler drew heavily from the *Catalogus Liberianus*, containing a list of popes that ended with Liberius (352–366) and apparently continued the biographies to Stephen V (885–891). Subsequent writers under papal sponsorship continued the *Liber pontificalis* through Sixtus IV (1471–84). Some popes received little attention, others a great deal. Generally the style is formalized and stereotyped. Pope Damasus is often credited with originating the *Liber pontificalis*, but such is not entirely clear. It was not printed until early in the seventeenth century.                    C.M.

**LIBERTY, RELIGIOUS.** Unrestricted freedom to practice religious beliefs; often called toleration, meaning "an established authority allows such practices," limited by the liberty of others. The Edict of Milan (A.D. 313) granted freedom to Christians and all others to follow their religious convictions. However, after 385, when Theodosius I made Christianity the only legal religion in the Roman Empire, religious liberty and toleration ceased. The partnership of church and state made unfavored religions heretical and intolerable. During the Reformation Luther seemingly advocated toleration but soon perceived social anarchy in individual religious liberty and opted for territorialism. Territorialism allowed limited toleration for Lutherans and Catholics following the Peace of Augsburg (1555), with neither side conceding truth or full privileges to the other. Both persecuted the Anabaptists, believing that individual liberty would lead to social anarchy. Anabaptist Balthasar Hubmaier in 1524 issued *Concerning Heretics and Those Who Burn Them*, the Reformation's first plea for full religious toleration. Anabaptists passively resisted civil government saying that Christians did not need magistrates. Calvin staunchly opposed toleration.

Separatist Robert Browne took a large step toward religious liberty in *Reformation without Tarrying for Any* (1582). He argued that magistrates should not interfere with religious practices. John Smyth, a Separatist exiled in Holland, advocated the SEPARATION OF CHURCH AND STATE, as did his Baptist associate, Thomas Helwys, whose *Mystery of Iniquity* (1612) openly called for full religious freedom. English Baptists pressed for liberty and gained relative religious equality under Oliver Cromwell, for all except Unitarians, Anglicans, and Catholics.

In America neither New England's Calvinistic Puritans nor Virginia's Anglican establishment allowed religious freedom. However, Roger Williams established Rhode Island (1636), permitting freedom of conscience; and other Baptists, and freethinkers like Jefferson and Madison, eventually secured freedom of religion in Virginia and adoption of the church-state separation amendment to the U.S. Constitution. The United States experiment with VOLUNTARYISM influenced most of western Europe's countries eventually to adopt toleration. Roman Catholicism, claiming to be the true church, has traditionally maintained that untruth should not have equal privileges with truth. It has accommodated itself to modified religious toleration without officially repudiating its traditional stance. Totalitarian regimes that subordinate the individual to the state by their nature cannot allow religious liberty (*Compare* DENOMINATIONALISM.)                    C.M.

**LIBIDO.** *See* FREUD, SIGMUND.

**LIBNAH.** (1) A wilderness site mentioned in Numbers 33:20-21.
(2) A Canaanite town sacked by Joshua (Josh. 10:29-39), later described in Joshua 15:42 as a Judean community on the border of Philistia and one of the cities given to the Levites (Josh. 21:13). Though it revolted against Jehoram (II Kings 8:22), it supported Hezekiah in his struggle against Assyria (19:8). It is the modern Tell es-Safi, twenty air miles west southwest of Jerusalem.                    W.S.T.

**LIBYA.** The well-known central North African nation of modern times encompasses only part of what the biblical and ancient Near Eastern records meant by the geographical term "Libya." Called *Cub* in Ezekiel 30:5, Libya is listed among other peoples in league with Egypt who are destined to be destroyed by Yahweh. One of those peoples is *Put*, itself translated "Libya" in Ezekiel 38:5, where it is a hostile power in league with the eschatological enemy Gog of the land of Magog. The ancestor of Put is described in Genesis 10:6 as a son of Ham and brother of Ethiopia, Egypt, and Canaan. In II Chronicles 12:3; 16:8; Daniel 11:43; and Nahum 3:9, we hear of *Lubim*, "Libyans," always in association with Egyptians and Ethiopians. The Chronicles texts (and I Kings 14:25-26) report the conquest of Judah by the Egyptian Pharaoh Shishak, about 917 B.C., during the reign of Rehoboam. This pharaoh was a Libyan and founder of the two-hundred-year Libyan dynasty in Egypt. In Acts 2:10, Libyans were among those who witnessed the miracle of Pentecost.
                    W.S.T.

**LIFE.** The quality of animation, of living; the opposite of DEATH and loss of being. The Bible clearly states that God creates life, and that the life of each person is God's gift. In the OT (Gen. 2:7) God is said to breathe life into people, and the Psalms praise God as the preserver of life (Ps. 66). The ancient Hebrews thought of a long life as a reward for a godly life and saw Yahweh's blessing in the attainment of old age. However, the Wisdom literature was more pessimistic and spoke of the shortness of life (Job. 7:6; 9:25).

Above all, the Hebrews, along with the rest of the ancient world, identified the animating principle of life with BLOOD. Life is in the blood according to Deuteronomy 12:23 and Leviticus 17:11. Because of this belief, blood was splashed upon the altar during sacrifices and also sprinkled on the worshipers. Blood was shed in making (or "cutting") a covenant by sacrificing animals and also in ritual circumcision. The need to drain all blood from meat slaughtered for food (the dietary laws) also derived from this ancient belief.

In the NT, life is used both in the physical and the spiritual sense, with the major use (in the writings of John) referring to life in communion with God (John

1:4; 14:6; 20:31). Jesus is said to be "life"; physical existence apart from faith in Jesus as the Christ is called "death" or "darkness." Regularly, the term "life" in John might be translated "eternal life." This ETERNAL LIFE is not something the believer enters into only at death, rather it begins now, in this world, when one is born anew through faith in Jesus Christ. Jesus declares, "I am . . . the truth, and the life" (John 14:6), and John proclaims that the faithful move from death into life (John 5:24). Life, then, for John, and also for Paul (Rom. 8:6), is more than animation, movement, consciousness. It is to be filled with the power of God's endless life, which flows into the redeemed from the risen, living Savior.

J.C.

**LIFE CYCLE RITES.** The rituals performed at the time of a person's transition from one stage of life to another; also called "rites of passage." The rituals and the life stages they mark vary between cultures, but certain similarities can be found nearly everywhere in the world.

The stages in the life cycle define each individual. In America, the eighteenth and twenty-first birthdays mark the individual's progression into adulthood, bringing with them increasing rights and responsibilities. Many non-European cultures have elaborate ceremonies to mark the transition to another status. These rites redefine the individual socially, putting him or her in the next-older category. Many cultures define the lifespan with three or four familiar-sounding stages: childhood, adolescence, adulthood, and sometimes elder. All cultures, but especially those that practice ANCESTOR VENERATION, add the stage of ancestorhood, for which the transition is death. Some cultures subdivide the stages, and some, especially in eastern and southern African tribes, practice age grouping. That is, all individuals born in a seven-year or ten-year interval undergo the rituals of transition together. Thus ten and twenty-year-olds may undergo the puberty ritual at the same time.

The rites of transition protect the individual and the people around him or her from the danger involved. Anthropologists have pointed out that things that are between categories are considered uncanny and dangerous. Individuals between age categories are dangerous to themselves and to others, vulnerable to sorcery, and create bad luck around themselves. Accordingly people perform life cycle rites carefully to remove individuals from their previous status, to protect them during the transition period, and then to bind them into their new roles and identities. These rites are rarely so clear-cut, but those elements can be found universally.

Life cycle rites take many forms. Scholars have argued whether confirmation and baptism are life cycle rites. Circumcision is a common ritual performed when an infant has lived the first few days and can be considered a "real" child, destined to stay. Some cultures perform circumcision at adulthood.

Other adulthood rituals include symbolic death and rebirth. Naming or renaming can occur at any stage. Filing of the canine teeth is performed on all Balinese at puberty. Other symbols of transition include cutting or tying up the hair, knocking out of teeth, new clothes, and new residence.

Death rituals—not only funerals but later commemorations such as death-day offerings, All Souls' Day, and reburial—separate the individual from this world. This transition may be to rebirth (REINCARNATION), an eternal afterlife, or the spirit world. Frequently these rituals separate the survivors from the dead person, allowing them to go on. In China, a red string is tied to the corpse, and all the survivors line up, holding a part of the string. A priest then cuts the string between each person. In many cultures, casting handfuls of dirt onto the casket signifies the separation of the deceased from the living.

Some cultures practice reburial of the deceased's bones after a period of years. Tibetans observe a forty-nine day period after death, during which the soul may achieve release from rebirth, or at least birth into the Pure Land paradise.

K./M.C.

**LIGHT.** The symbol for God's presence in both the OT and the NT. According to Psalm 4, Yahweh is the light of the believer's face, that is, God gives life and also that discernment by which the human being can "see" what is real and true.

Psalm 119 says that God's word spoken through the prophet Moses and the other prophetic witnesses, is a light to enlighten the path of the believer. Genesis 1 affirms that God created the light and the universe by separating light from the darkness of chaos. God's presence in the tent of meeting (tabernacle) and later in the temple was marked by the eternal light and the menorah (seven-branched candlestands; I Sam. 3:3; II Chr. 4:7).

In the NT, John the Baptist spoke of the coming messiah as the light that would enlighten everyone (John 1:4) and Jesus spoke of himself as the light of the world (John 3:19-21; 8:12). In the Synoptic Gospels, Matthew records that Jesus called his followers the light of the world and warned them not to hide their light (Matt. 5:14-16). Both Paul (Eph. 5:8) and John (I John 1:5-7; 2:11) use "light" as their term for the salvation brought into the world by Jesus Christ.

The common practice of lighting candles on the altar during Christian worship services preserves the biblical symbolism of God's presence. Traditional candlelighting ceremonies on Christmas Eve affirm the faith that in Jesus, God became incarnate and brought divine light into a world darkened by sin and unbelief. The Jewish Festival of Lights (Hanukkah) also symbolizes God's presence, in particular, the return of the desecrated temple to the worship of Yahweh by Judas Maccabeus (I Macc. 4:52).

J.C.

**LIGHTFOOT, JOSEPH BARBER** (1828–89). An important leader within the Anglican church in England and a significant scholar in the fields of NT, especially Pauline studies and patristics, specifically the Apostolic Fathers. Lightfoot was ordained deacon in 1854 and priest in 1858. He became Hulsean professor of divinity in 1861, Canon of St. Paul's in 1871, Lady Margaret professor of divinity, Cambridge, in 1875, and Bishop of Durham in 1879.

Lightfoot was an outstanding NT and patristics scholar whose influence and value still remain in the late twentieth century. Among his many scholarly achievements, the three most important and lasting are these: (1) membership from 1870–80 in the Company of Revisers, which produced the English Revised Version of the NT (1881); (2) his major commentaries on various letters of Paul, especially Galatians, Philippians, Colossians, and Philemon (1865–75); and (3) his massive text, translation, and commentary on the Apostolic Fathers (2nd ed. 1889–90 in 5 vols.).                          D.S.

**LILA.** From the Sanskrit word for "sport" or "play." Key term in the teaching, emphasized by the Vaisnava school of HINDUISM, that God's creation of the universe is like sport or play. Because God, being infinite, could need nothing outside of God, it cannot be said that God's eternal acts of creation stem from any necessity or are a form of divine "work." Rather, we are told, God's creativity is analogous to those forms of self-expression in which humans engage out of sheer delight: games, artistry, the playtime acting out of imaginative fantasies. The term "lila" is also used of particular acts of gods and AVATARS, such as the charming activities of KRISHNA as an infant or youth engaging in dalliance with his *gopis,* or milkmaid companions. These are major focuses of BHAKTI and well express the theme of divine playfulness encapsulated in the word "lila."

R.E.

**LILY.** A flower mentioned often in the Bible, in both the OT and the NT, as in Jesus' reference to the "lilies of the field" in his Sermon on the Mount (Matt. 6:28 ff.; Luke 12:27). The "lilies" to which Jesus referred may, however, be a general term for a variety of flowers that bloom in springtime in Israel, Egypt, and the Middle East. In the OT, the lily is mentioned in the Song of Solomon (5:13; 6:2), as well as in Hosea 14:5. The lily family includes the lotus, perhaps the most commonly seen flower in the Nile Valley of Egypt. The lotus became the model for numerous artistic and architectural designs, including the capitals, or tops, of columns. Solomon's famous Temple, designed and built by the craftsmen of Hiram, king of Tyre, had many decorations based on the lily motif. These lily-shaped column capitals and embellishments on the huge ceremonial wash basin ("the molten sea") are mentioned in I Kings 7 and II Chronicles 4:5. During the period of Jewish independence under the Maccabees, the coins issued by several kings pictured the lily.          J.C.

**LIMBO.** The place and spiritual state of departed souls who do not deserve hell, or yet merit heaven, according to traditional Roman Catholic theology. Limbo includes the place just before the atonement of Christ as well as the state of unbaptized children, who suffer from original sin alone.

J.C.

**LINCOLN, ABRAHAM** (1809–65). The "Great Emancipator" was born February 12, 1809, to Thomas and Nancy Hanks Lincoln. Though his father was a hard-shell Baptist, the couple was married by a Methodist. In his youth Lincoln shunned the frontier camp meetings and avoided church membership.

He served in the Illinois state legislature from 1834 to 1841 and was licensed as an attorney September 9, 1836. He married Mary Todd on November 4, 1842. In 1847 he was elected to the United States House of Representatives over Methodist Peter Cartwright. He opposed the Mexican-American War and proposed abolition of slavery in the District of Columbia.

Returning to Illinois, he was a successful lawyer. His "House Divided" speech on June 17, 1858, denouncing the Dred Scott decision, and his debates with Stephen Douglas in 1858 won him national attention. He became president of the United States in 1860, precipitating the secession of the South and the Civil War. On January 1, 1863, he issued the Emancipation Proclamation and on November 19,

Courtesy of the Library of Congress

*Lincoln's letter to the Methodists*

1863, he gave the Gettysburg Address. He was assassinated by John Wilkes Booth on April 15, 1865.

A man of deep piety who regularly attended Presbyterian services, he kept a very private faith.

N.H.

**LINGA.** From the Sanskrit word meaning literally "sign." An upright pillar, frequently rounded on top, which serves as the main object of worship representing SHIVA in the temples and shrines of HINDUISM. Clearly phallic in origin, the *linga* often has an elliptical base that stands for the *yoni,* or female organ. However, modern Saivas do not ordinarily describe the *linga* as phallic, and it can also be compared to a flame or the axle of a wheel. Sometimes a human form of Shiva is carved on the side of the stone column. Worship of the *linga* is done in PUJA manner, with offerings of flowers, grass, fruit, leaves, and rice. Water is poured over it, or allowed to drip on it, as a devotional act of cooling.

R.E.

**LINGAYAT.** A sect of HINDUISM that has some four million followers in south India. The name comes from the practice of its adherents always wearing a small LINGA, symbol of SHIVA, on a cord around their necks. The movement originated in the twelfth century A.D. in the teaching of a GURU called Basava. It regards Shiva as the only god. He is worshiped in BHAKTI manner. Worship is offered primarily in the home, temples being not highly regarded. Each member is expected to have a personal *guru,* who generally comes from a special class of Lingayats. These *gurus* are held in great regard, and their visits to a home are the occasion of major ceremonies, including the ritual washing of the teacher's feet.

The Lingayats, also called Virasaivas, are in an anomolous relation to Hinduism, rejecting many of its normative tenets. They are antipathetic to the BRAHMIN priesthood, accept the authority of their own scriptures rather than that of the VEDAS, and do not believe in reincarnation. Typically liberal in their attitudes toward caste and family, the Lingayats anticipated many modern reforms in Hindu society and have made significant contributions toward education and social welfare.

R.E.

**LINGUISTIC ANALYSIS.** Known also as ANALYTICAL PHILOSOPHY, this movement focuses on the function and uses of language as central for philosophy. Originating in England as a reaction to absolute idealism, linguistic analysis in varied forms has exercised wide influence in twentieth-century philosophy.

*Language in Traditional Philosophy.* A pervasive theme in Plato's dialogues, language receives sustained analysis in the *Cratylus.* Aristotle, in the *Metaphysics,* distinguishes subject from predicate and,

on this basis, assigns fundamental ontological position to substances. After the medieval debate between realists and nominalists, critical philosophy distinguished analytic from synthetic statements, limiting the latter to the phenomenally verifiable. Language as symbol has, in the twentieth century, received attention in its cultural (Cassirer, Langer) and logical (Whitehead and Russell) significance.

*Reaction to Idealism.* Linguistic analysis began as a common sense attack by G. E. Moore (1873–1958) on absolute IDEALISM, which denigrated ordinary thinking as representing appearance rather than reality. Moore held that philosophy should clarify the obvious meaning of what we say. As proof that things exist external to us, he said, "Here is one hand, and here is another." Moore influenced English philosophy to turn from ideal abstractions to the analysis of ordinary truisms.

*From Logical Atomism to Ordinary Language.* Pushing further, Bertrand Russell (1872–1970) seeks simple, atomic propositions that state atomic facts, a basic language yielding complx propositions corresponding to reality. For Russell, linguistic analysis becomes the path to truth.

Ludwig Wittgenstein (1889–1951), a Russell disciple, at first locates meaning in atomic propositions depicting atomic facts (*Tractatus logico-philosophicus,* 1919). He later rejected this narrow view of language. Ordinary language is as varied as tools in a toolbox (*Philosophical Investigations,* 1953). "Don't think, but look!" he insisted.

Released from the confines of atomism and positivism, linguistic analysis developed in directions represented by Gilbert Ryle (1900–76), J. L. Austin (1911–60), P. F. Strawson (1919– ), and others whose work shows renewed attention to history and traditional philosophical concerns.

Continuing issues and problems for linguistic analysis include: Whose ordinary language is the norm for analysis? Can meaning be separated from particular contexts? Can precision emerge from the ambiguity of ordinary language apart from the analyst's presuppositions? Can clarification of relations of language to thought, meaning, or reality go beyond making explicit meanings implicit in the analyst's own community of interpretation?

C.Mc.

**LITANY.** An ancient prayer form consisting of the presiding minister's invocation or petition and the worshipers' responses. The congregational responses are fixed, such as "Lord, have mercy," "Pray for us," or "Hear our prayer." Examples of traditional litanies include the AGNUS DEI (Lamb of God), the KYRIE ELEISON (Lord Have Mercy) and the Litany of the Saints. The Kyrie Eleison forms a portion of the worship preceding the actual Mass itself in the Roman Catholic liturgy. The Agnus Dei immediately precedes the Holy Communion, in both the Roman and Lutheran Mass.

Approved litanies are those appointed for public worship services. Such litanies are liturgical litanies. The term litany may also designate a religious procession, such as the Greater or Lesser Litany. The Litany of the Saints, in two parts, then is used.

In free church Protestant services, litanies written by the worship leader for special occasions such as Christmas, Easter, or Pentecost are often used. These litanies often use parts of the traditional ones. Often such litanies are so clearly designated for a specific occasion, such as the desire for peace, or the need to work for civil rights, that they have little future usefulness.                     J.C.

**LITERARY CRITICISM.** *See* BIBLICAL CRITICISM.

**LITURGY.** From the Greek word for "the work of the people," meaning "the public worship of the church" in the Orthodox, Roman Catholic, Anglican, and Lutheran traditions. By extension, liturgy refers to the public worship of Protestant congregations and the worship of the Jewish synagogue.

"Liturgy" derives from the ancient Greek term for community service done for the common good without pay. The Greek translation of the OT, the Septuagint (LXX) used the term for worship. At first, Christians used "liturgy" for any form of prayer, but the word soon came to designate public rather than private worship. By the time of the Reformation "liturgy" was used as a title for mass or service books.

Liturgy is worship, specifically the worship of the gathered Christian community. It is active, not passive. In worship believers recognize the sovereignty of God and submit themselves to God's rule. Liturgy consists of prayer, praise, and thanksgiving, including the bringing of tithes and offerings, all of which come from the human side; and of the reception of the sacraments, which communicate gifts and graces from the divine side. In Christian worship both God and humankind are active. Praise most often takes the form of hymns. Congregational singing, in fact, may combine prayer, praise, and thanksgiving in one supreme, beautiful act of human devotion. In Roman Catholic liturgies there are also the elements of sacrifice, in the sense of the sacrifice of the Mass, and, occasionally, the making of vows or oaths. All such actions are counted as liturgy if done publicly with the approval of the church. In the Catholic tradition, followed also by Anglicans and Lutherans, the liturgy is held only when a community of believers gathers under the leadership of a regularly called (ordained) minister of the church.

In the Catholic tradition, all liturgical actions are considered sacramental. This means every symbol expresses the life given the church by Christ, and the offering of the people of worship to the Father through Christ. Indeed, all true Christian worship is based in the Incarnation of Christ and in Christ's sacramental, spiritual presence in the community of faith. The congregation worships as the Body of Christ, praying through its glorified head to the Father. As it is called, gathered, and enlightened it is animated in its prayer, praise, and thanksgiving by the Holy Spirit.

The liturgy of the church is chiefly seen in the great Sunday service, the Mass, and the Eucharist or Holy Communion. However, among most American Lutherans and Protestants, other than Episcopalians, the Sunday service does not always include the Holy Communion. Other forms of liturgy include matins, vespers, and special offices such as the baptismal rite, confirmation, ordination, marriage, and the burial of the dead. In the Eastern Orthodox churches there is a rich liturgical tradition, parallel to but more elaborate than the rituals of the West. In the twentieth century there has been a growing richness of liturgy in America, first among the Episcopalians and Lutherans, and now extending to the free churches also.                   J.C.

**LIVING BIBLE.** (LB) This paraphrase of the Bible in colloquial American English, which has made publishing history, started out humbly. While commuting between his home in Wheaton, Illinois, and his office in Chicago, Kenneth Taylor, a seminary-trained publisher, began translating the Scriptures in order to make them more comprehensible to his large family of children, who were having trouble with the King James Version.

Taylor's first segment covering the NT Epistles was a slim self-published volume called *Living Letters* (1962). Because his translation effort failed to find acceptance with publishers, Taylor, with very little capital, launched his own publishing firm in Wheaton called Tyndale House Publishers. This was followed by other biblical portions until *The Living Bible* was released in 1971. Within short order *The Living Bible* became a best seller.

Later Taylor devoted himself to the creation of adaptations of *The Living Bible* in the major languages of the world. To achieve this goal, he created a separate corporation, Living Bibles International. Meanwhile Tyndale Publishing House has become a major force in the evangelical publishing field, releasing books on a wide spectrum of subjects.                   R.H.

**LIVINGSTONE, DAVID** (1813–73). One of the world's best-known missionaries to the African continent. His accomplishments as a missionary, explorer, geographer, and ethnographer displayed a heretofore unseen Africa. He first left his native Scotland in 1841 as a missionary of the London Mission Society. He is best known for his travels throughout Africa to open up the heart of the continent to mission work. After sixteen years in Africa, he returned to Britain a popular hero. For the next several years he led expeditions to Africa. Much of his effort was spent in trying to wipe out the slave trade. He died in Africa, where his heart was buried, and his emaciated body was buried in Westminster Abbey. His life work directed the attention of the world to Africa. After his death the great missionary expansion of the late nineteenth century began.

W.G.

**LOCKE, JOHN** (1632–1704). English philosopher, political theorist, advocate of toleration, and defender of Christianity's reasonableness. Born in Wrington, Somerset, educated at Christ Church, Oxford, Locke studied for the ministry, then turned to philosophy, science, and politics, and devoted his final years to religious writings. His first book was his *Essay Concerning Toleration* (1666). The following year he went to London as secretary to the Earl of Shaftesbury, upon whose political downfall he fled to Holland (1683–89) and returned a celebrity on the accession of William and Mary. From 1691 he lived with the Cudworths at Oates Manor, Essex.

Locke eschewed promoting Christianity by force and vigorously defended toleration. *Letters Concerning Toleration* (1689–92) advocated a broadly tolerant national church that excluded atheists for nonbelief in God, and Roman Catholics for subversive political activities. Locke's influential *Two Treatises of Government* (1690) rejected inherited divine right rule and argued that individuals have inalienable rights to life, liberty, and property and that governments that do not safeguard such rights may be overthrown. Locke's *Essay Concerning Human Understanding* (1690) depicted the mind as a *tabula rasa* or blank slate where sensations leave impressions that the mind reflects on. He rejected innate ideas and maintained that knowledge of empirical reality via the senses is

*John Locke*

probable rather than absolute. *The Reasonableness of Christianity* (1695) depicted the NT as inherently credible, probable, and in full harmony with reason. However, he declared that miracles and dogmas could not be proved.

C.M.

**LOCUSTS.** Various species of winged insects of the family of *Acrididae* are indicated by a number of Hebrew and Greek terms in the Bible, some of which are usually rendered "locusts" in the RSV. Modern readers may not share John the Baptist's predilection toward these insects as food (Matt. 3:4; Mark 1:6), though even today they are prepared in various ways to be eaten by Bedouins and certain Oriental Jews. (Lev. 11:22 excepts various species of locusts from the general ban on eating winged insects.) But many of us, particularly people who live in arid lands such as Nebraska and Wyoming, can share the ancient dread of a plague of locusts. Joel 1:4 pictures the desolation left by such an infestation: "What the cutting locusts left,/ the swarming locust has eaten./ What the swarming locust left,/ the hopping locust has eaten,/ and what the hopping locust left,/ the destroying locust has eaten." Indeed, the entire first part of the book of Joel (1:1–2:27) is a description of a locust disaster, interpreted as the very day of the Lord's judgment upon the people (2:1). The locusts are pictured as a powerful, relentless army (2:5-9), and like crackling flame devouring the stubble (2:5). For the book of Deuteronomy, a plague of locusts is one of the curses with which God threatens a disobedient people (Deut. 28:38, 42). In Revelation 9:1-12, a plague of horrible humanoid locusts is one of the tribulations of end-times.

The earliest plague of locusts to be mentioned in the OT was not directed against Israel at all, but against Egypt (Exod. 10:3-20). The infestation of this eighth plague brought by God against Pharaoh and his people "covered the face of the whole land, so that the land was darkened" (v. 15). The affiliation of this memory with North Africa is not inappropriate, for the desert locust begins its life cycle in the Sudan. After reaching its gregarious phase, it can migrate in three days of unbroken flight as far as 1240 miles from its place of origin. When rain and temperature conditions are favorable, huge swarms can develop, such as took place in 1927–30, when much of the fresh vegetation of the Near East was destroyed.

W.S.T.

**LOGIA.** The Greek term for "sayings" or "words." According to Papias, there was a document containing the Logia of Jesus circulating in the early church. This is generally considered to be the Gospel of Mark, or an earlier version of Mark (Proto-Mark or Ur-Mark). The hypothetical "second source" used by Matthew and Luke (in addition to Mark) has been called the Logia or Q (from the German *quelle*, or "source"). "Logia" is also used to refer to possible sayings of Jesus not recorded in the four canonical

Gospels, such as quotations in Paul's letters or other parts of the NT, as well as in noncanonical "gospels," such as the Gospel of Thomas. Primarily, however, "logia" is used to refer to the hypothetical Q, since it is chiefly a collection of "sayings" or discourses of Jesus recorded in a similar manner by Matthew and Luke, but not found in Mark.                                        J.C.

**LOGICAL POSITIVISM.** A type of philosophy that combines language analysis with an extreme form of empiricism. The classic statement was given by A. J. Ayer in *Language, Truth and Logic* (1936).

On this view, there are two types of meaningful propositions. There are the A PRIORI propositions of logic and mathematics. These yield no information about the real world, but simply draw out the implications of the definitions constituting the foundation of a logical or mathematical system. Their truth or falsity is determined by rules of logical inference. The second class of propositions are A POSTERIORI and do yield information about the world. If they are to be meaningful, there must be some empirical state of affairs that is relevant to their truth or falsehood. "Verification by sense experience" became, therefore, the central plank in the edifice of logical positivism.

It is obvious that this philosophy greatly reduced the area of meaningful discourse. Metaphysics, ethics, and theology were all dismissed as strictly meaningless, for they are incapable of verification by sense experience and can, therefore, be neither true nor false. Ayer pointed out that the logical positivist cannot be rightly described as either an atheist or an agnostic, for, since the assertion of God's existence is meaningless, it cannot be denied, nor can we suspend belief about it.

The most serious weakness of this philosophy was the fact that its own central tenet, the verification principle, does not itself fall within either of the two categories of meaningful propositions. It is in itself a metaphysical principle and is therefore condemned by the very theory based upon it. Not for the first time in the history of philosophy has an extreme skepticism been found to be self-destroying. We are indeed forced to ask the questions: What is the scope of human experience? Is it confined, as the positivists allege, to sense experience, or is it much richer than that so that we are not confined to the narrow world of the positivist? These, however, are questions that logical positivism has, by its own principles, rendered incapable of discussion.

J.M.

**LOGOS.** A Greek word with various meanings, which in its religious context is associated especially with the divine Word, reason, or wisdom. In the Greek Septuagint translation of the OT, the Hebrew term "Word" of God is translated as Logos or reason. It is this use of Logos as "Word of God" that plays such a formative role in Jewish and especially in Christian theology, where it refers to the second Person of the Trinity— Christ. In the OT, God's word is both the medium of communication, especially of God's will or law, and the agent of creative power (Gen. 1:3, 6, 9) by which God calls all things into being. By the time of the Hebrew prophets (ninth-eighth centuries B.C.), the "Word of the Lord" had almost achieved the status of an independently divine hypostasis or substantial reality.

The Stoic philosophers (fourth-third centuries B.C.) taught that the universe is governed by a divine Logos, "reason," or "law." When Hellenistic Judaism came under the influence of Stoic ideas, the "Word of the Lord" was assimilated to the Stoic Logos and also associated with the originally distinct Hebrew concept of WISDOM (Wisd. Sol. 9:1-2). The Hellenistic emphasis on the absolute transcendence of God resulted in the interposing of divine intermediaries between God and creation. Thus in Judaism the divine "Word" and "Wisdom" were further personified and conceived of as God's divine agents in creation. In PHILO of ALEXANDRIA the OT Word and the Stoic Logos are identified. The Logos is both the divine "pattern" from which the creation is copied and the divine power in the creation, the intermediary between the transcendent God and humanity. Philo uses a variety of titles to describe the Logos as mediator. The Logos is God's "first-born son," the "image" and "ambassador," and humanity's "advocate" and "high priest." In identifying the preexistent Logos with Christ, it is clear that the NT Pauline and Johannine writings are influenced by the same background of ideas as is Philo. In the concept of the preexistent Christ, Paul joins the Jewish ideas of the preexistent Messiah and the preexistent Wisdom and Law. In the prologue to the Johannine Gospel, the Logos is identified with the eternal God as God's creative Word, by whom all things are made, and who becomes incarnate in the man Jesus of Nazareth.

The theologians of the early church found in the Logos the perfect concept for expressing the relationship of Christ to God, as well as an apologetic point of contact with Hellenistic philosophy. The orthodox Christian teaching held that the preexistent Logos (Christ) is eternally begotten or generated of the Father, not made, and thus is of the same substance of God and coeternal. Before this orthodox position was worked out explicitly in the Christian creeds, two divergent heretical views were supported by church theologians. One tendency, that of the school of Alexandria, was to view the Logos as subordinate to the Father. The extreme form of this view was ARIANISM, which said that "there was a time when the Son was not." It held that the Logos was created by God out of nothing, and thus was not God. This view was condemned at the Council of Nicaea (A.D. 325).

The other tendency identified the Father and the Logos (Son) so closely as to deny any distinctions in the being of God. The Logos was considered only a power of God. This view had many exponents in the third century and is known as MONARCHIANISM or Sabellianism, after Sabellius who taught that Father, Son, and Holy Spirit are only names applied to the modes of God's action. This latter view was condemned at the Council of Constantinople in A.D. 381. The contest between these two heretical tendencies led to the orthodox formulation of the TRINITY.                                                              J.L.

**LOHAN.** In MAHAYANA BUDDHISM a disciple of the BUDDHA. The word is the Chinese form of the Sanskrit term *arhant*.

In early Buddhism the lohans were the ideal followers of Buddha, but in Mahayana they lost this position to the BODHISATTVAS. A bodhisattva is a being who has vowed to work for the salvation of every living being, and thus could be seen as the model of mercy and compassion. A lohan, on the other hand, worked only for his own salvation and was therefore considered selfish.

As a result, Mahayana paintings and images show bodhisattvas as serene, beautiful beings, beyond human ills, but show lohans as merely human and at times even grotesque. Their features are distorted by loneliness and old age. At the end of their quest they have not reached NIRVANA but are caught in a lesser realm from which there is no escape.

On the positive side, lohans came to be honored as protectors of the Buddhist DHARMA, or teaching. Many holy persons have been regarded as living lohans in disguise.                                                    K.C.

**LOINS.** As an anatomical term referring to that section of an animal torso below the rib cage and above the hips, this word still enjoys current English usage and is employed in current Bible translations in this sense to render several Hebrew terms and one Greek term. In Leviticus 3:4-15; 4:9; 7:4, the fat attached to the kidneys at the loins of beasts is specified for use in burnt offerings. In Genesis 37:34, Jacob puts sackcloth on his loins in mourning for Joseph; a "girdle" or belt of leather (II Kings 1:8) could be fastened around the same part of the lower torso, and a soldier would keep his sword there (II Sam. 20:8). In preparation for a journey (II Kings 4:29; 9:1), a foot race (I Kings 18:46), or a meeting with God (Job 38:3; 40:7), one prepared by "girding up one's loins."

The loins could be girded metaphorically as well. In Proverbs 31:17, the good wife girds her loins with strength; in Isaiah 11:5 the coming messiah's loins are girded with faithfulness; and in Ephesians 6:14, the loins of the spiritually armored believer are girded with truth.

The proximity of the loins to the sexual organs extended some of the Hebrew terms to mean the source of progeny. Because this sense is archaic in modern English, the RSV usually declines to make the literal translation, but it is still employed to render the Greek term *osphus* in Hebrews 7:10.
                                                                                          W.S.T.

**LOIS.** The name, evidently uncommon in antiquity, of Timothy's grandmother who is commended for her sincere faith as an example to Timothy (II Tim. 1:5). Presumably, Lois was the mother of Eunice, Timothy's mother, and a Jew, since Acts 16:1 states that Timothy's mother was a Jewish believer.
                                                                                          D.S.

**LOISY, ALFRED** (1857–1940). French Roman Catholic biblical scholar, excommunicated for modernist views. Born a commoner at Ambrières, educated at the Catholic seminary at Châlons-sur-Marne and the Institut Catholique in Paris, Loisy was ordained in 1879 and briefly served a country parish. Historical criticism of the Bible prompted him and others (Louis Duchesne, Maurice D'Hulst, George Tyrrell, Herman Schell, and Baron von Hügel) to advocate modernizing the church's traditional biblical views. In 1890 he became the controversial professor of Sacred Scripture at the Institut Catholique, a post he lost in 1893 when Pope Leo XIII condemned modernism in his *Providentissimus Deus*. Leo upheld biblical inerrancy, saying the Bible was dictated by the Holy Spirit. In 1903 Pius X, who succeeded Leo, placed two of Loisy's books on the Index. Loisy formally submitted to papal authority in 1904, but in 1907 Pius X's *Lamentabili sane* condemned sixty-five modernist propositions (fifty drawn from Loisy's writings) and *Pascendi gregis* condemned misguided reformers as instigators of schism. In 1908 following the publication of volume two of his *Les Evangiles Synoptiques,* Loisy was excommunicated. He later taught at the College de France (1909–30), but his writings lacked much of their reforming power.                                                 C.M.

**LOLLARDS.** Followers of JOHN WYCLIFFE, who helped prepare England for Lutheran Reformation ideas. Wycliffe, appealing directly to Scripture, advocated a theology of good stewardship and sharply criticized English prelates, the Avignon papacy, and the Great Schism's two popes. Using personal faith and Scripture as authorities, Wycliffe and his Lollards condemned transubstantiation, celibacy, exoricism, greed, clerical immortality, prayers for the dead, pilgrimages, relic veneration, auricular confession, indulgences, premature vows of continence, and religious endowments. Pope Gregory XI in 1377 condemned Wycliffe's writings, and in 1382 the Blackfriars London Council and Archbishop Courtenay condemned ten Wycliffe beliefs, causing Lollards to lose their academic base at Oxford even before the Council of Constance condemned Wycliffe's views in 1415. In 1401 Parliament's *De Haeretico Comburendo* authorized burning Lollards as heretics. Sir John Oldcastle in 1414 led a Lollard uprising and was hanged and burned three years later. Driven underground, but still preaching two by two from English biblical translations made by Wycliffe and Purvey, the Lollards suffered suppression and persecution, especially under Kings Henry V, VI, and VII, who wanted papal support for their dynastic claims. However, Lollardy remain potent and eventually merged with the English Reformation in the sixteenth century.       C.M.

## LONDON MISSIONARY SOCIETY.

The LMS, founded in 1795 by evangelical churchmen from several denominations in England, was established to "spread the knowledge of Christ among the heathen and not to propagate Episcopacy, Presbyterianism, or Independency" or any particular form of church government about which the founders and their churches had serious differences of opinion. This fundamental principle was carried out and made it possible for the society to send many missionaries, among whom are a distinguished list of pioneers: Ellis and Williams in the Pacific; Moffat and Livingstone in Africa; Morrison in China; and Lawes and Chalmers in New Guinea. The main support for the LMS churches has come through the years from Congregational churches. In 1966 the society's constitution was revised and it became the Congregational Council for World Missions, the members of which are seven Congregational Unions of the British Isles and Commonwealth countries.       W.G.

**LOOSING.** *See* BINDING AND LOOSING.

**LORD.** With roots in feudal class structure, this English title acknowledges the nobility and authority of the addressee. Several Hebrew, Aramaic, and Greek biblical terms are rendered by this single word.

*Old Testament Usage.* The term *ba'al* has the generic sense of "lord, master," and is used of secular nobility in Numbers 21:28 and Isaiah 16:8. However, it was also the personal name of the most important Canaanite deity, and because of this association this term was specifically rejected as a title for the God of Israel (Hos. 2:16).

The term *'adon*, "Lord," while doubtless originating in the secular sphere (for example, Sarah calls her husband "lord" in Gen. 18:12; Aaron refers to his brother and superior Moses as "my lord," Num. 12:11), becomes the most important single title by which YAHWEH is addressed or described. Yahweh's throne is the "ark of the covenant of the Lord" (Josh. 3:11-13), the Lord's name is excellent in all the earth (Ps. 8:1, 9); indeed, the Lord can be called "God of gods and Lord of lords" (Deut. 10:17). In Psalm 110:1, God's lordship is juxtaposed with the human authority of the king in such a way as to suggest that the latter is derived solely from the former: "The Lord says to my lord: 'Sit at my right hand, till I make your enemies your footstool.' "

The process of exaltation of God by title and of precluding any untoward familiarity or misuse of the name of God (see Exod. 20:7) is visible in the use of the term *'adon*, "Lord." When referring to God, the word is typically used in its plural form with a possessive pronoun attached, *'adonai* ("[my] Lord[s]"). Though never rendered this way in English, this form of the title occurs in the dialogue between Abram and God in Genesis 15:2, 8; in the calls of Gideon (Judg. 6:15-22), and Jeremiah (Jer. 1:6); in the standard formula of Ezekiel; and countless times elsewhere in the Prophets and in the Psalter. The process of distancing the individual Israelite from the powerful name of God reaches yet a third stage when the title *'adonai* altogether supplants Yahweh, the proper name of God. This development must have occurred after the biblical period itself, because the consonants YHWH continue to be used even in the latest OT writings. But the Masoretes routinely supplied these four consonants (the Tetragrammaton) with the vowels for 'ADONAI, indicating that the sacred name itself was never to be pronounced, and that the title "Lord" was to be read in every instance. The term "JEHOVAH" is the hybrid result of the consonants of Yahweh and the vowels of *'adonai*; it is not and never was a Hebrew word or the name of God.

*New Testament.* The Septuagint routinely translated both the name Yahweh and the terms *'adon/adonai* with the single term *kyrios*, "lord." Like the Hebrew term, this word had its use in secular communication among human beings: the slave owner was *kyrios* to the slave (Acts 16:16, 19), and Jesus taught that no one can serve two "masters" (Matt. 6:24; Luke 16:13). But the NT radicalized this term, which was, of course, the primary title for God in the Greek OT, by applying it as a title to Jesus of Nazareth. The most original Christian message contained in the church's first sermon is "God has made him both Lord and Christ" (Acts 2:36). Paul ceaselessly repeats the formula, "The Lord Jesus [Christ]," and asserts that no one can say, "Jesus is Lord," except by the Holy Spirit (I Cor. 12:3). For doubting Thomas, the essence of his newfound faith was summed up in the phrase, "My Lord and my God" (John 20:28).

An Aramaic term of address to a person of nobility, *mara'*, which occurs in that sense in Daniel 4:19, 24 (and as a title of God in Dan. 2:47; 5:23), reappears as a title of the Christ who is to come in the prayer *"maranatha"* ("Our Lord, come!") in I Corinthians 16:22 (*compare* Rev. 22:20).       W.S.T.

**LORD OF HOSTS.** The title, "Lord of Sabaoth" (KJV) used for God in Romans 9:29 and James 5:4 accurately reflects the Greek transliteration of the OT epithet for God, *Yahweh ṣebha'oth*, "Lord of [angelic] hosts." The title is not used in the Pentateuch but is favored by the Prophets—Malachi uses it twenty-three times in four chapters! Although Israel itself can be described as "the hosts of the Lord" in Exodus 12:41, the more normative sense is that preserved in the account of Joshua's confrontation with the angelic "commander of the army [host] of the Lord" on the eve of God's great victory over Jericho (Josh. 5:13-15). Like a king of flesh and blood, the king of heaven had an army, too! The heavenly host created by God in the beginning (Gen. 2:1) is not that army. The sun and moon and stars were not divine beings, and certainly were not to be worshiped in their own right (Deut. 4:19; 17:3; II Kings 23:4-5). No, the hosts were the myriads of heavenly beings who served God in the divine court (Dan. 7:10), and who accompanied God in battle and at the great event in Bethlehem (Luke 2:13).                                 W.S.T.

**LORD'S DAY.** Sunday, the first day of the week, upon which Jesus Christ rose from the dead. It is the special day of Christian worship from NT times to the present, sanctified by the Resurrection. The early church gathered to proclaim the announcement of Christ's coming to deliver humanity from sin, to celebrate the Lord's Supper, and to make offerings. Every Lord's Day is a celebration of the first EASTER, of the Resurrection, although once a year there is also the celebration of the "Great Easter," fixed as closely to the date of the original Easter as the peculiarities of the lunar calendar allow.

The Lord's Day is one of victory and joy. Even during Lent, Sundays are referred to as "in" not "of" Lent. The suspension of the celebration of the victory of Christ over death is not allowed even for Lent. For this reason, the early Christians did not fast or kneel when praying on SUNDAY. The connection of Sunday and the Resurrection is demonstrated in the early liturgies of Ireland, Gaul, and Spain.

The Lord's Day is explicitly mentioned only in Revelation 1:10, where John the Prophet is caught up in a vision on the Lord's Day. There is much evidence in the NT that, taken together, shows the early church observed Sunday as its official day of worship. Since there is dispute over the "proper" day of Christian worship, we summarize this evidence here:

All the Gospels stress that the Resurrection took place on the first day of the week. Luke connects the breaking of bread with the Resurrection day in 24:13-35. In Acts 20:7 (often said to be by Luke), the breaking of bread is connected with the first day of the week. This is further buttressed by Acts 2:42 and I Corinthians 10:16. Paul (I Cor. 16:2) shows that alms for the poor are to be collected at the Corinthians' church services on the first day of the week. The writings of the early church fathers confirm that the Sabbath was almost immediately replaced by Sunday as the Christian day of worship.                        J.C.

**LORD'S PRAYER.** The prayer of Jesus known among English-speaking Christians as the Lord's Prayer is found in the Gospels in two different versions: Luke 11:2-4 and Matthew 6:9-13. Both have probably derived it from a body of Jesus tradition that Matthew and Luke used, in addition to Mark, and which seems to have contained mostly sayings of Jesus rather than narratives about him. In general, this Q source, as it is called by scholars, is more faithfully preserved in Luke than in Matthew, who tends to expand the tradition. This observation applies to their respective versions of the Lord's Prayer as well.

In Luke the prayer begins with a direct address to God as "Father." That sense of intimacy (which is also reflected in Paul's use of the affectionate term, *Abba,* in Rom. 8:15 and Gal. 4:6) is further evident in Mark 14:36, where Jesus uses this endearing term for God (equal to the Aramaic equivalent of Papa, or Daddy) at the hour of his seizure by the authorities on the eve of the Crucifixion. Jewish piety would have used "my Father" or "our Father," as Matthew does (6:9). The strong likelihood, however, is that Jesus used this term of immediacy of relationship to God, which would have offended his Jewish contemporaries. Throughout his teaching in all the Gospel tradition, "Father" is Jesus' favorite designation for and address to God.

To hallow God's name means to ascribe to God the honor that is appropriate to God's very nature. In Semitic culture, the name is the essence of power as well as the basis for personal identity, so that to honor God's name is to attribute to God the majesty, power, and saving purpose, which are the essence of the divine being. Linked with this, therefore, is the prayer that God's rule will become effective in the world. As Creator, it is God's design that all the created order should be obedient to the divine will. Jesus' hope for and dedication to that goal is focused in his announcement that the kingdom of God is about to be established, and that its powers are already evident in the present through his defeat of the evil powers, his pronouncement of divine forgiveness, and his founding of the obedient covenant community.

Before that promise is fulfilled, however, the community must survive, and he instructs his followers to pray for "bread"—the basic item of survival. The word used to define this bread, *epiousion,* may have several meanings: (1) what is necessary for existence; (2) day-by-day necessity; (3) for the day following—that is, enough to make it until tomorrow; (4) future—that is, the bread or food that will be eaten when the new age comes. The Dead Sea community had a ceremony in which the sharing of bread and wine was an anticipation of the day when the kingly and priestly messiahs would be in the midst of the community, and there would be elements of this future reference of the Communion in the Eucharistic tradition of the Gospels (Mark 14:25; Luke 22:30).

The petition for forgiveness of sins is a challenge to God to be as forgiving of the sins committed by people as they are to forgive those who are indebted to them. The word usually translated as "debts" refers to unfulfilled obligations, or what are sometimes described as "sins of omission," rather than financial debts. The final prayer to be spared being led into temptation or testing may refer to God's protective care in general terms, or it may be pointing to the final ordeal, which would try the fidelity of the people of God in the last days before the New Age came. In that view of the future, Matthew's addition (6:13), the deliverance from "evil" may refer to the last violent effort of Satan and the evil powers before God triumphs and the hosts of evil are defeated. The prayer would then ask for special divine protection in this future time of testing.

In Matthew's version of the prayer there are liturgical expansions throughout. It is *Our Father* who is addressed, and God is identified as a resident "in heaven." The coming of the kingdom is explained as accomplishing the fulfillment of God's will on earth, just as it is already effective in heaven. The result of this change is to generalize the petition, so that the emphasis on the future coming of God's rule is replaced by the petition for an on-going actualization of God's rule. Reference to sins is replaced by the double use of "obligation," with a slight shift in meaning: instead of God's being asked to match human forgiveness (as in Luke), there is the simple statement that there is a match between human and divine forgiveness (Matt. 6:12).

Although in Matthew's version of the prayer, the best ancient manuscripts conclude with the prayer for deliverance from (the) evil (one), it is clear that as early as about A.D. 100, a liturgical conclusion was added, beginning with the words, "For thine is the kingdom. . . ." Probably these lines are adapted from the conclusion of a prayer attributed to David in I Chronicles 29:11, reportedly uttered on the occasion when he announced that Solomon would build the Temple in Jerusalem. Since these lines were not appended to the Greek manuscripts of Matthew used by Jerome when he made the standard Latin translation of the Bible (known as the Vulgate), they did not find their way into Roman Catholic tradition. Later Greek manuscripts did include them, however, and so they found their way into Protestant translations based on the Greek, as in the King James Version.        H.K.

**LORD'S SUPPER/LORD'S TABLE.** The celebration of Jesus' last meal with his disciples before his betrayal, arrest, trial, and death on the cross. Early evolved from an actual meal (called "the Agape" or "Love Feast") into a symbolic meal (by the time of the *Didache* or *Teaching of the Twelve Apostles*), the LAST SUPPER, called the Lord's Supper or Eucharist ("the Thanksgiving") or Holy Communion (COMMUNION with God through Christ and with fellow Christians), from the beginning became the central act of Christian worship. In the Roman Catholic tradition, the celebration is called the MASS, from the final words spoken by the priest, *"ite missa est,"* "go, it is finished." Since the sixteenth century, Protestants have differed from Catholics and often from one another in their understanding of the Lord's Supper.

In contemporary theological and churchly circles, the Lord's Supper has become more and more prominent for three interrelated reasons: the liturgical movement, the advances of biblical research, and the theological maturity of the ecumenical movement in its several manifestations.

*Theological Developments—New Testament.* In the NT there are four reports of the institution of the Lord's Supper (I Cor. 11:23-26; Mark 14:17-26; Luke 22:14-23; Matt. 26:20-30). Additionally, the presence of the risen Christ is connected with breaking bread (meals) in Mark 16:14; Luke 24:35, 42; John 2:12-13; and Acts 10:41. There is a split witness as to the original significance of the meal in which the Lord's Supper was instituted. The Synoptic Gospels present it as a PASSOVER seder (especially the longer text in Luke 22), while John declares it to be held on the night before Passover. In all events, the texts stress the presence of Christ with the followers who continue to observe this meal; the sacrifice of Christ for human sin; the participation of the believer in the forgiveness so accomplished; the memorial aspect of the meal and the proclamation of Jesus' death to the world, until such time as Jesus returns and gathers believers together for an eschatological meal in the kingdom of God. Overall, it is clear that Christian celebration of this meal testifies to faith in Christ and to thanksgiving for what Christ has done.

*Ancient Church.* Several kinds of sacred meals were celebrated in the early church, including full meals or agapes. Gradually, the meal was reduced to bread and wine, taken at the conclusion of worship services, probably every morning. The connection to the Jewish Passover and to looking for the soon coming of the kingdom of God was also developed.

*Middle Ages.* During the Middle Ages, by the thirteenth century, an increasing realism in theology resulted in the concept of TRANSUBSTANTIATION. Based on Aristotelian categories, this doctrine held that the bread and wine became the actual Body and Blood of Christ, except for the surface appearance (or "accidents"). Also, the ancient idea of sacrifice was stressed, seeing the priest's consecration of the elements as an actual reenacting of Christ's sacrifice on the cross—an offering of God to God.

*Reformation.* The Reformers reacted against the idea of sacrifice and the concept of transubstantiation in various ways. Luther, Zwingli, and Calvin all rejected—in different terms—transubstantiation and the belief that the Eucharist is a sacrifice. Basically, Zwingli saw the Eucharist as simply a memorial of the death of Christ and a testimony before people of the faith of the Christian who participates. It is thus not a sacrament or means of grace. Luther rejected sacrifice but saw the meal as a SACRAMENT. In it the believer actually receives Christ, and therefore the forgiveness of sins. While denying transubstantiation Luther held to the REAL PRESENCE of Christ in the bread and wine—a mystery of faith that likens Christ's presence in the elements to the presence of fire in red hot iron (*see* CONSUBSTANTIATION). Calvin later tended more to the sacramental ideas of Luther but attempted to phrase his ideas of "spiritual presence" in terms agreeable to the remaining influence of Zwingli's thought on the Reformed church. There were many disputes between the Lutherans and the Reformed churches over the Eucharist, beginning with Luther's and Zwingli's confrontation at Marburg in 1529.

*From the Sixteenth Century to Today.* The Reformation was followed by a period of rigid orthodoxy in both Catholic and Protestant churches. Numerous disputes between churches took place. A period of rationalism and pietism caused the loss of traditional ritual and a sentimental interpretation of Christian doctrine in Lutheran and Reformed churches. While the Catholic church stressed sacrifice and transubstantiation, the meaning of the Lord's Supper—and its frequent practice—was lost in Protestantism. The rise of the liturgical movement, in Catholicism, Anglicanism, and Lutheranism, stimulated by new developments in biblical research, slowly reversed this trend. Increasingly, the results of this renaissance informed all communions, so that the Eucharist is more frequently observed today than it has been for centuries in Protestantism. Many Protestant communions have agreed on common statements on the meaning of the Lord's Supper and there is an increasing tendency among Catholic theologians to speak of transfiguration instead of transubstantiation. The recent declaration that Anglicans may commune at Lutheran altars and vice versa (New Orleans Episcopal Convention and Louisville American Lutheran Church and Lutheran Church in America Conventions, 1982) symbolizes the growing unity of Christians on the Lord's Supper.

Since the early decisions of Vatican Council II, the traditional Latin Mass has been translated into the vernacular languages of countries around the world. The Mass in English is very similar in structure, content, and even wording to the Eucharistic liturgy of the Episcopal and Anglican communions and to the Holy Communion service of the American Lutheran churches. The free churches have also enriched their Eucharistic liturgies and moved toward more frequent communion than the standard Lenten observance of four-times-a-year usage, which was widespread several decades ago.

Of particular interest in contemporary eucharistic celebration is the presence of "lay ministers," or lay men and women, who assist the priest by distributing the wine at Catholic masses in many parishes. The old controversy over giving the laity only the bread and reserving the cup to the priest alone is completely over. Along the same line, the very recent view by some free church Protestants that only grape juice should be used at Communion instead of wine, seems to be correcting itself. This view, which has no historical basis (grape juice is a modern product; the Jews drank wine in the first century), arose during the prohibition era, when abstinence from alcohol assumed the proportions of an article of faith for some Protestants. Fortunately, the growing influence of the liturgical revival, the publicized results of scientific biblical studies, and the growing ecumenical closeness of the Protestant denominations to one another and to the Roman Catholic church, have given most Christians today a better historical and theological grasp of the meaning and practice of the Lord's Supper.                                      J.C.

**LOT.** A son of Haran and nephew of ABRAHAM, with whom he migrated from the Sumerian city of Ur to Haran in upper Mesopotamia and then to Canaan. Lot's story in Genesis 11:27–14:16 and 19:1-38 associates him with the magnanimous Abraham, the perverse citizens of Sodom, and his two nameless daughters.

*Lot and Abraham.* Lot accompanied Abraham as he initially entered Canaan (Gen. 12:5) and made camp at Shechem. According to Genesis 13:1, Lot joined Abraham and Sarah in their journey to Egypt (Gen. 12:10-20). Later they settled in Benjaminite hill country, but its pastures proved inadequate for their increased livestock (13:6-7). When Abraham offered Lot the fertile Jordan basin, Lot accepted without qualm. Then Lot settled in Sodom (13:12). Subsequently, Lot was captured by an alliance of four eastern kings, headed by Chedorlaomer, who subdued five rebellious Canaanite kings from the Sodom-Gomorrah vicinity (14:12). But Abraham with 318 retainers pursued the alliance and rescued Lot (14:16).

*Lot, Sodom, and his daughters.* In Genesis 19 Lot is visited by two angels who announce Sodom's imminent destruction and urge his family to flee. Lot and his daughters reach the city of Zoar. For having glanced back toward their lost property, Lot's wife is changed to a pillar of salt (conspicuous salt masses in the region account for this legend). Genesis 19 concludes with an ethnic etymology explaining in unflattering terms the origins of the Moabites and Ammonites. Now dwelling in the Moab plateau (v. 30), Lot's daughters orchestrate incestuous relations with their father, leading to the births of Moab and Ben-Ammi.                                      J.K.K.

**LOTS, CASTING OF.** A method of DIVINATION of appeal to God (or the gods) used to decide matters or choose someone for a job or position. In the time of both the OT and the NT, the casting of lots (that is, drawing out a ball or pottery shard or slip of paper placed in a container) enjoyed wide respect as a means of learning God's will. Apparently, the Jews never considered casting lots as magical, so it escaped the condemnation of the occult made so forcefully in Deuteronomy 18:10-12. According to the Wisdom writer (in Prov. 16:33), "the lot is cast into the lap, but the decision is wholly from the Lord." Lots were resorted to in many important religious matters. The early disciples used them to elect a replacement for Judas (Acts 1:23-26), and the high priests seemed to have consulted God's will by way of lots with some regularity. The high priest drew the lots (probably smooth stones, perhaps of different colors or marked with symbols) out of his ephod or priestly apron. Such an event was done in the context of prayer, with the decision left to God's will. Thus, lots were cast "before the Lord."                                                                    J.C.

**LOTUS POSTURE.** In HINDUISM and BUDDHISM, the *padmasana*, as it is called in Sanskrit, is the most popular pose for meditation. The back is straight, and the knees are bent with the feet placed on the thigh of the opposite leg. The Buddha and the Hindu god Shiva are often portrayed in this posture.          R.E.

**LOTUS SUTRA.** A major scripture of MAHAYANA BUDDHISM. The oldest of the twenty-seven chapters of this work were probably composed in Sanskrit in the first century of the Christian Era; a version of it was translated into Chinese as early as the third century. The book has been immensely influential in China and Japan, where it was the textual basis for important Buddhist movements.

The Saddharma-Pundarika Sutra, to give it its Sanskrit title, stakes out the spiritual terrain of Mahayana Buddhism in visions of awesome cosmic grandeur combined with vivid parables reminiscent of the NT. It presents itself as the teaching of the Buddha in his ultimate nature as the infinite, eternal being of the universe itself, a reality beyond all words and concepts, from out of which he calls into visibility innumerable worlds, each with its own Buddha. His grace falls like rain on all beings in all realms. But out of compassion for human finitude he comes over and over again in conditioned form, as in the historical Buddha, to teach and, as an example, to appear to become enlightened and enter NIRVANA.

Thus the Theravada teaching that one can seek no higher goal than becoming an arhat, or the idea of becoming a *pratyeka-buddha* ("private buddha," one who becomes a Buddha for one's own sake without regard for others), are shown to be only accommodations for the benefit of those not ready for the fullness of truth. In reality there is but one path, that to Buddhahood; all beings are potentially Buddhas. The theory of accommodation is presented in a parable of a father who, coming home to the house containing his children and seeing it on fire, calls out that he has toy carts for them to play with; rushing delightedly from the house they are saved from the flames. Once out, we can realize our eternal Buddha nature; it is like a jewel sewn into the coat of a desperate man unaware of it. This enlightenment does not depend on following an ascetic path but is simply letting go of egocentricity by whatever means avail. Justifying the growing practice of devotionalism in Mahayana, the Sutra tells that a child presenting a handful of flowers

to a Buddha-image may be closer to enlightenment than a proud supposed arhat or *pratyeka-buddha*.

In China and Japan the Lotus Sutra was the cornerstone of the highly influential T'ien-T'ai (Japanese: Tendai) school, which viewed it as the supreme expression of Buddhist doctrine, all other sutras being more or less partial accommodations. In medieval Japan, NICHIREN preached that the Lotus is the sole scripture for the present age, founding a denomination based on it alone, in which chanting *Nam Myoho Renge Kyo*, "Hail the Marvelous Teaching of the Lotus Sutra," is a central practice. The important SOKA GAKKAI movement, which grew rapidly in mid-twentieth-century Japan, is a product of Nichirenism that demonstrates that the Lotus Sutra retains its vitality as a religious force.          R.E.

**LOURDES.** A town in southwest France, where, in 1858, the BLESSED VIRGIN MARY is said to have appeared to Bernadette Soubirous. Located in the foothills of the Pyrenees Mountains, Lourdes was unknown to the world before the fourteen-year-old Bernadette reported that the Virgin appeared to her eighteen times between February 11 and July 6, 1858. Since that time Lourdes has grown into one of the largest shrines to Mary on earth. Bernadette visited the grotto of Massabulle with a crowd of twenty thousand on March 4, 1858. However, only Bernadette received the visions. On March 25, Bernadette reported that the Virgin declared "I am the Immaculate Conception"—a dogma proclaimed only by Pope Pius IX in 1854. The last appearance was on the Feast of Our Lady of Mount Carmel. Today two million pilgrims visit Lourdes. There have been five thousand healings, of which eight are declared miraculous. Bernadette was canonized by Pope Pius XI in 1933; her feast day is February 18 in France and April 16 (the day she died) elsewhere.          J.C.

**LOVE.** In the Christian understanding of God's nature, love ranks as the superlative quality. This fact is seen not only in that the only formal definition of who God is has love as its content (I John 4:8, 16), but also that in Jesus Christ, Christians have always recognized the sign of the divine regard for our human race (John 3:16; Rom. 5:8). To that extent love takes on a unique quality since it draws its meaning from the Christian claim that God's action in Christ—supremely his cross and resurrection—is one of a kind (I John 4:9-10). Yet this statement does not imply that the character of God as love is without precedent. The evidence of the OT prepares the ground for the coming of Christ, even if his life and teaching imparted a new meaning to the term, and his death and victory crowned the revelation. But it remains true that the NT terminology (especially AGAPE, "love") marks out love as in a class by itself. Other terms are found, to be sure, but their meanings stand on a lower level than *agapē*. Thus PHILIA, while used only once in the NT (James 4:4), expresses a social relationship based on affection and affinity uniting friends or family. The Greek *storgē* has a similar sense in Romans 12:10, but the two remaining instances of NT use are negative (Rom. 1:31; II Tim. 3:3). Eros, implying sexual attraction, is remarkably absent from biblical literature; even in the Song of Solomon and Hosea, where the term *erōs* for sexual passion may well have been expected, the term is not found, and the Greek translators have used *agapaō* as a verb meaning "to love." It is also remarkable that the noun *agapē* is almost entirely missing from pre-biblical Greek. So we conclude that the verb *agapaō* takes pride of place as the outstanding word used by Christians to express all that they meant and had experienced by fellowship with a God whose name and nature are best described by love.

*Love in the Old Testament.* The OT verb equivalent *agapaō,* "to love," is used by the Greek Bible to translate the Hebrew *ahēb,* with its noun *ahābāh.* In English these terms are uniformly expressed as love. Some other words are important, however. We should note the Hebrew *rāham,* "to have pity" or "compassion" (Exod. 33:19, there are thirty-four occurrences in all), and *hesed,* "loving-kindness, mercy," which is often linked with the verb. *Hesed* is such an important OT word—it is found 245 times there—that we should note its wide range of meaning and translation (RSV gives "steadfast love" in 178 places, but NEB has 33 different ways of rendering *hesed,* using 85 times the noun "love" and adjectives such as "true," "unfailing," "constant," "faithful"). The last named, "faithful love," is the most suggestive, since researchers show how basic to *hesed* is God's choice of Israel in love and God's resolve to maintain a covenant relationship with God's people (Lam. 3:22, 31ff.). The Jewish people, on their side, are called to pledge "loyalty" *(hesed)* to their God, Yahweh (Exod. 19:4-6; 24:1-8; Hos. 4:1; 6:6; 10:12; 12:6).

The verb *rāsāh,* "to be pleased with," "to accept with favor," should also be included here, since God's choice of Israel in love is linked with the thought of God's acceptance of the nation as the divinely chosen people. The noun *rāson* means "good-will" and is significant as a background to the NT teaching of Jesus as the Father's Son whom God loves (Mark 1:11; Col. 1:13; Eph. 1:6) and the church as God's new Israel (I Pet. 2:1-10).

OT writers invariably trace back God's concern for Israel to the Exodus from Egypt (see Deut. 26:5-9, an Israelite creed, confessing its faith in all that Yahweh did in calling the nation into existence. See also Amos 3:2; 7:15). Interestingly, there is no reference to God's love in this connection in the Exodus narrative, but Deuteronomy (notably at 7:6-11) makes the point: God chose you because God loved you. And there was no attraction in Israel to cause God's love to flow. God loved Israel because God would love this people. The prophet Hosea picks up this same theme, mirrored in his own experience with Gomer, an unfaithful wife whom he rescued from shame and restored to dignity and honor (Hos. 3:1-5). The lesson of Gomer is applied to Israel's case, and the argument for Israel's return from apostasy is based on God's unchanging *hesed,* which calls for a corresponding love on the nation's part.

After Hosea, the celebration of divine love for Israel as a husband for life is repeated (Jer. 2:2, 32ff.; 3:1, 14; 31:32; Ezek. 16:8; 23:1-49; Isa. 50:1-3; 54:5; 62:4). In all this corpus of teaching we can detect certain salient motifs: (a) God's love is an expression of the divine self-giving nature (Hos. 11:8, 9; Jer. 31:20; Isa. 63:15); (b) God's calling of Israel is one of free choice when there was no merit or goodness on Israel's part to warrant it (the book of Deuteronomy echoes this sentiment repeatedly, as it links divine love wih God's election); (c) yet the action of God lays a claim on Israel, as divine love evokes a response of gratitude and obedience—both expressed by the nation's *hesed* and central to Deuteronomy, for example, 5:10; 26:18—and such love is expressed in a moral union between Yahweh and Israel. Unlike the Canaanite baals (see Hosea), Yahweh was a moral agent who could and would judge and punish Israel as an expression of love (Amos 3:2). Yahweh's love is unwearying (Isa. 7:13) and never gives Israel up. But it will chastise and correct the nation in the bitter experiences of exile and dispersion until Israel regains her sense of destiny as God's "light to the nations" (Isa. 49:6). (d) There is not much said in the OT about God's love for either individuals (one such exceptional reference is the case of Solomon whom "the Lord loved," II Sam. 12:24; in the Psalms the speaker who is loved by God, for example, Ps. 91:14, may well represent the nation or the remnant within the larger group) or for all nations (the books of Ruth and Jonah are universalistic in their teaching, and God's love for the Moabite woman or the Ninevites may be inferred but it is not explicitly stated). This limitation is typical of OT religion, which in the postexilic period became increasingly moralistic and exclusivist. "Love your neighbor" in Leviticus 19:18 relates to one's fellow Jew. Divine love in the covenant became a ground on which Israel forgot that the nation had no claim on God. God's gift of his law (Torah) was understood—at least by some sections of Judaism—as a mark of God's favor to be boasted in and to be kept exclusively for Israel as though the nation were bounded by a fence. The NT shows how with the coming of Jesus as the world's Savior such boundaries were broken (Eph. 2:11-22), and God's love became truly worldwide (John 3:16; I John 4:14).

*Love in the New Testament.* The chief features that distinguish the NT picture of love from that of the OT are three in number. First, a religious outlook that is essentially incarnational is drawn to express love in terms of God's presence in Jesus Christ, the beloved Son and the image of God's person (Col. 1:13-15; Heb. 1:1-3; II Cor. 4:4-6). The NT writings resonate with this theme in several ways, sometimes polemically, as when the love of God in Christ is seen to offset the Jewish claim that the fullness of God's gift is in the law of Moses (John 1:17; Gal. 3:2–4:7), or as when Paul and John and their disciples oppose Gnostic limitation of love to a group of elite believers. Then a truly universalist tendency making God's love freely and widely known and available to all people is clear (II Cor. 5:14–6:2; I John 4:1-16). Second, it is in the NT that God's truest nature is expressed simply in terms of love in such a way that love reveals the divine being without remainder (I John 4:8, 16). That statement, "God is love," implies, as C. E. B. Cranfield observes, that the equation is true independently of our being able to be loved. Yahweh's love in the OT is bound up with Israel as the chosen people. God's love in the NT is shown similarly in what has been done for the church, but such love existed prior to, and apart from, the expression of God's love to humanity. God is eternally love, with the object of that love being Christ (John 17:5, 24); or more properly, God's nature is love from all eternity, and even if there were no object, God would be self-existing love. This metaphysical statement is perhaps one of the most philosophical in the NT and marks a clear advance on the highest OT teaching.

Third, it is a corollary of what was said above that God's love will be all-embracing and is in no way confined to a favored nation or chosen people. The church, to be sure, inherited the promises made to ancient Israel (see Gal. 3:26-29; 6:16; I Cor. 10:32), but it is set apart as a supra-nationalistic, multi-ethnic society, since God's redeeming action embraces all races (Rev. 5:9) and its borders are as wide as the world itself (I John 2:2). At the heart of this assertion is the conviction that the love of God is a universal reality, not bounded by national or tribal religion or limited to cultic observance (this argument for universality and finality of God's self-revelation in the Messiah of Israel, who is universal Lord, runs through the Epistle to the Hebrews).

So long as these three caveats are borne in mind, much of the OT teaching is reproduced in the NT writers. God's love is seen in the choice of people, though it is found in the mission of Jesus who came to restore them to God. So God's love and Christ's love merge (Eph. 5:25).

In the Gospels, Jesus embodies the divine initiative in seeking a wayward people. Modern NT study has isolated this feature as one of the obviously unique elements in Jesus' ministry: he actively reached out to those whom official Judaism rejected, in particular, the tax collectors and "sinners" (Luke 15:1-2, and the three parables of Luke 15; 19:1-10). The tribute of Luke 7:34 is typical. Moreover, Jesus' distinctive name for God as Father (Abba) is on the same order, since the Father shows no discriminating regard for all his creatures (Matt. 5:45). In so acting and teaching, Jesus was claiming to be making known the true nature of God and bringing Jewish exclusiveness to an end, a point that Paul was later to theologize as "Christ is the end of the law, for every one who has faith may be justified" (Rom. 10:4).

The cross is the historical focus of God's loving nature (Rom. 5:8). The chief NT writers see the death of Christ as revelatory of divine love, however they interpret the effect of that event and no matter what diverse categories (sacrificial, cultic, legal, dramatic, personal) they use to explain what the cross achieved. Nor is the personal element missing (Gal. 2:20) alongside the cosmic reality that, according to Paul especially, Christ's death brought an end to the regime of malevolent spirit-forces (demons) that held in bondage the first-century world (I Cor. 2:8; 15:24; Col. 2:8, 15, 20; Heb. 2:14, 15; Rev. 1:18).

The proclamation of a new age that came with Christ's advent is linked with the announcement that God's love is manifested in setting prisoners free (Luke 4:18-19) and delivering men and women from servitude to evil. The goal is the restoration of humanity to God's family in freedom (Gal. 4:1-7), with the image of God renewed (II Cor. 3:17-18). But that image is nothing less than Christ himself (Col. 1:15), so we are drawn back to the relationship between God and Jesus—one of filial love—as the prototype of the union into which believers are invited and expected to enter as their share in the new age (Rom. 8:14-23), along with the promise of new creation. The fact is set out in the phrase that we may "be conformed to the image of his Son" (Rom. 8:29), as Christ is himself the image of the Father, who has loved him from all eternity.

Human response to God's offer is strangely, for NT writers, not expressed in a reciprocating love. To be sure, the twin OT commandments to "love God/love one's neighbor" (Deut. 6:4 ff.; Lev. 19:18) are taken up in Mark 12:29 ff., and echoed in Paul (Rom. 13:9-10). So love becomes the ethical norm of Christian behavior, and I Corinthians 13—the hymn to love—has always been regarded as the high peak of the Christian's calling. Paul placed great emphasis on agapē as the spirit that should motivate believers in their personal and social relations (Gal. 5:14). The fruits of the Spirit are, for him, the essential qualities of Christian living, and love stands at the head of the list (Gal. 5:22). The Holy Spirit's gift is indeed agapē (Rom. 5:5), reminding us that this love is no native virtue or ethical ideal to be achieved in our own strength.

Yet it remains the case that the believer's response to God's love is more adequately called "faith," and the exhortation to "love God" is found only peripherally in Paul (Rom. 8:28; I Cor. 2:9; 8:3). Perhaps this is intentional. If so, it highlights the uniqueness of agapē as a divine quality and God's gracious gift to be received; for such a response "faith" would be the normal term. Or maybe Paul did not draw a hard-and-fast line between love and faith, as we can see from Galatians 5:6.

Love is to be the badge of all Christians in the

Johannine community (John 13:35), and it is the mark that they belong to God (I John 4:7), having passed from life to death (I John 3:14). Such love is more than lip service; it is essentially practical and sacrificial (I John 3:17 ff.; James 1:27; 2:14-26). The call is "Love one another, as I have loved you"; and that may be said to be the hallmark of biblical teaching on love.                                          R.M.

**LOVE FEAST.** Meals shared by the early apostles and disciples with one another, beginning in the Upper Room immediately after the Resurrection. These common meals became known as agape, from the Greek term for love preferred by Paul and other early Christians, and so are designated "love feasts." The agape either preceded or included the more sacred and formal celebration of the LORD'S SUPPER, as is clear from Paul's discussion of certain excesses of the agape in connection with Holy Communion (I Cor. 11). Love feasts are also mentioned in Jude 12 and II Peter 2:13 (marg.), where the authors also stress the warnings of Paul that agapes must be shared in sobriety and with unselfishness and a lack of social and class distinctions. It is likely that the practice of these congregational meals died out because of the actions of the wealthier members who egotistically displayed their wine and luxurious foods before the poorer members of the church. Paul strongly attacked this in I Corinthians 11, and James also denounced the humiliation of the poor by church people who were overly impressed by rich men.

The practice of sacred meals, or meals taken in the temple in the presence of a god, was common in both Judaism and the pagan cults that flourished in the Mediterranean area in the first century. The PASSOVER meal was a full meal and not just a symbolic one like the bread and wine of the Lord's Supper. Pagan worshipers dined together in their temples and ate meat that had been sacrificed to their idols. It was natural that Christianity incorporate congregational meals in its practices. However, the high moral demands of Christianity seemed to be more than recently converted pagans could live up to. Paul made it clear that the church was no place to display one's social status (I Cor. 11).                             J.C.

**LOW CHURCH.** A term originating among pietistic members of the Church of England who objected to churchly ritual and denied that bishops were essential to the nature of the church and so rejected apostolic succession. The Low Church party held strictly to a literal interpretation of the THIRTY-NINE ARTICLES of religion. This party continued within the Anglican communion but more and more people migrated to non-conforming congregations, that is, toward Presbyterian, Congregational (Independent), and Baptist churches. Their "meetinghouses" were usually called "chapels," in distinction from the Anglican cathedrals or churches. Low Church services, which are characteristic of many

fellowships in Great Britain, Canada, and the United States, as well as across the modern world, generally emphasize preaching more than Holy Communion. These "low" or less formal services are the mark of free-church Protestantism (See FREE CHURCHES). The priesthood of all believers, a less sacramental worship, and congregational singing are elements of this form of worship.

J.C.

**LOWELL, JAMES RUSSELL** (1819–91). American poet, essayist, and diplomat. A product of New England's golden age, Lowell was a contemporary of Longfellow, Emerson, and Holmes. Born on February 22 at Cambridge, Massachusetts, Lowell was graduated from both Harvard College and Harvard Law School before starting his career as poet and editor. He succeeded Longfellow as professor of modern languages at Harvard. He also became editor of *Atlantic Monthly* and later of the *North American Review*. He served as United States minister to Spain from 1877 to 1880. Like other American poets such as Longfellow and Whittier, Lowell turned his hand to writing hymns. These were contained in *A Book of Hymns for Public and Private Devotion,* edited by Longfellow's brother Samuel and Samuel Johnson while they were students at Harvard Divinity School. This work became a landmark in Unitarian hymnody. One of Lowell's best-known hymns, written in 1845, is "Once to Every Man and Nation." The hymnbook in which it first appeared gave new prominence to the humanitarian aspect of religion.           R.H.

**LOWER CRITICISM.** *See* BIBLICAL CRITICISM.

**LOW MASS.** A simple form of celebrating Holy Communion in the Roman Catholic Church. MASS was offered only to a congregation in the early church, but with the requirement that a priest offer mass every day, it became necessary for some priests to say mass for a few people or by themselves.           J.C.

**LOWRY, ROBERT** (1826–99). Baptist minister and gospel hymn writer and composer. Lowry was born in Plainfield (N.J.), joined a Baptist church at an early age, and soon became an active Christian worker, serving in the Sunday school and in the choir. At age twenty-one he decided to enter the ministry and subsequently obtained bachelor of arts (1854) and master's degrees (1857) at Bucknell University. He then served pastorates in West Chester (Pa.), New York City and Brooklyn (N.Y.), and Lewisburg (Pa.). During the Lewisburg pastorate he was professor of belles-lettres at Bucknell. His last pastorate was at Plainfield. He traveled extensively from 1880 to 1885 in Europe, Mexico, and the southwestern United States. Upon the death of William Bradbury, Lowry became the music editor of Bigelow and Main publishing company, where he produced a series of songbooks. He wrote both words and music for "Shall We Gather at the River?" and the tunes for "I Need Thee Every Hour," "One More Day's Work for Jesus," "Savior, Thy Dying Love," and "Five Were Foolish."                                    R.H.

## LOYOLA, IGNATIUS DE. *See* IGNATIUS LOYOLA.

**LSD.** Lysergic acid diethylamide, a hallucinogenic drug derived from ergot alkaloids that, when ingested, produces psychological states similar to the functional psychoses such as schizophrenia and mania. It was discovered in 1938 by Dr. Albert Hofmann in Basel, Switzerland.

Of course, various psychologists differ on the evaluation of the "high" or drug-induced state produced by LSD (or "acid," as it is commonly called). Some see these states (or "trips," as they are popularly referred to) as being of a different order than schizophrenic trances, while others see the drug as mimicking stages of insanity. Among those who see LSD as non-pathological is Dr. Timothy Leary, who declared "acid trips" are a religious experience in which one "sees God." He was dismissed from Harvard University and eventually imprisoned for his evangelistic use and spread of LSD to others. The Reverend Walter Clark has advocated controlled research on LSD.                                    J.C.

## LUCIFER. *See* SATAN.

**LUKE, EVANGELIST.** Our knowledge of this NT person is limited to what Paul says of him and what we may learn by inference from the two sets of writing (the GOSPEL OF LUKE, the ACTS OF THE APOSTLES) traditionally ascribed to him. The prologue (Luke 1:1-4) is written in the first person, and the opening verse of Acts refers to the "first treatise," presumably the Gospel, thus binding the two books together in a common authorship.

Luke's part in Paul's Apostolic career is seen in Colossians 4:10-14 (compare Philem. 24). From this evidence we may conclude that Luke shared Paul's imprisonment (perhaps the same as in II Tim. 4:10-11, where his name reappears), and that he was a physician. The idea he attended to Paul's medical needs is fanciful, even if it is proposed by E. Lohmeyer. His role as a doctor became part of church tradition. The anti-Marcionite prologue to Luke's Gospel (about A.D. 170) calls him "a physician by profession" and places his native city in Antioch. The medical language that some scholars have found in his writings is hardly a confirmation of this fact, as it can be paralleled with the writing of other non-medical authors in his day.

It is also doubtful if we should conclude from these verses that he was a Gentile Christian, as is popularly thought mainly on the basis of the way Paul separates him (in Col. 4:14) from Jewish Christians referred to in earlier verses. There is considerable evidence to argue the case that Luke was a Hellenistic Jew. If so, it

becomes feasible that he is to be identified with Lucius (Rom. 16:21).                                    R.M.

**LUKE, GOSPEL OF.** This Gospel, though anonymous like the other Gospels, is traditionally ascribed to LUKE and has the unusual distinction of carrying a full preface (1:1-4) in which the author states several things.

*Luke's Prologue.* First, he acknowledges that he had other writers before him, on whose work he drew. This reference is customarily taken to include Mark and the hypothetical "sayings-source" comprising two hundred or so verses found in both Matthew and Luke. Second, Luke pays tribute to his fellow Christians ("eyewitnesses and servants of the word"), who were yet another source on which he has drawn, though in an undefined way. Possibly Luke had access to catechetical material of Jesus' teaching, used in training new converts. Third, Luke professes to have researched his subject with care and in detail in order to produce "an orderly account" (perhaps in contrast to—as some church fathers say—Mark's Gospel, which was written "not in order," according to Eusebius' *Church History*). Finally, the purpose of the Gospel is seen in the use of Theophilus' name as its prime addressee, though it is quite impossible to say who Theophilus may have been. That he was a high-ranking Roman official in a position to influence state policy regarding the church of Luke's day has been proposed. Perhaps he was regarded by the evangelist more in a representative sense as a symbol of the great Gentile world to which Luke would send his Gospel. If the latter, the Gospel is best described as evangelistic, that is, intended to awaken faith. The designation of Theophilus as one who "had been taught" the Christian message suggests rather that he was a catechumen, and so the Gospel was intended more to confirm his already held faith. How this may happen may be understood from the phrase "the things that have been fulfilled among us" and refers to the feature of Luke's appeal to the "proof-from-prophecy," which characterizes his Gospel. He wanted to point to the theme of "promise-and-fulfillment" as confirming to his initial readership that God's age-old plan of salvation in the OT has surely come to fruition in the ministry, life, teaching, death, resurrection, and ascension of Jesus of Nazareth.

*Luke's Emphases.* So far we have taken Luke's prologue at its face value. Not all scholars are willing or able to do this. They argue that we should treat the entire Gospel as revealing Luke's purpose, along with his "second volume," the ACTS OF THE APOSTLES. Such an attempt to encompass the comprehensive range of Luke's writing, in recognizing that "the writings of no other single author in the NT occupies (*sic*) the amount of space that Luke-Acts does" (J. A. Fitzmyer, *The Gospel According to Luke I–IX*, Anchor Bible, 28 [p. 3]; this commentary is by far the most complete repository of pertinent information on Luke's Gospel) has produced a bewildering crop of theories. They fall into two main areas.

(a) Understanding Luke as an early Christian "apologist." Under this head the major influence has been H. Conzelmann's *Theology of St. Luke,* and the leading motif in Luke's books has been identified as a revising of ESCHATOLOGY. According to Conzelmann and others Luke achieved a rewriting of theology appropriate to a new situation in which he found himself. The earliest decades of the church were filled with a fervent hope that history would soon end with the return of Christ. When this expectation failed to materialize, the church was faced with several problems, namely what to make of a protracted interval before the end and how to relate the gospel it proclaimed to the ongoing flow of human history.

Luke's effort matched those needs as he proposed a philosophy of history in which God's plan embraced three stages, the time of the OT climaxing in John the Baptist (Luke 16:16); the time of Jesus, so called the "middle period," the reason for Conzelmann's original title being *The Middle of Time;* and the time of the church. Luke made the church part of world history and gave the believers of his day an agenda in terms of witness (Luke 24:45-49; Acts 1:8) and suffering. He therefore contributed significantly to the church's self-identity as a social community with a future in this world and an institution with history to make as well as to look back upon.

One of the weaknesses of Conzelmann's influential theory has been his virtual overlooking of Luke's use of the OT. An alternative way of viewing Luke (taken by C. H. Talbert, *Luke and the Gnostics*) stresses how Luke wrote to defend the Gospel against Gnostic tendencies. The latter are seen in Luke's defense of historical detail, particularly to do with Jesus' birth, baptism, death, burial, and resurrection events, which are all described in a literal fashion (see 2:7; 3:32; 24:37-43). His appeal to the OT (1:5-80; 24:44-45) is part of this anti-Docetic thrust, since Gnostic teachers both denied Jesus' full humanity and disdained the OT revelation. While there may be some basis in Luke's apology for historical reality, it is difficult to see this as the sole category of his purpose.

Yet another apologetic purpose in Luke's Gospel is more widely approved. It is clear from the data that Luke wanted to stress how the early church was not a politically dangerous movement, and in particular it was not to be confused with Judaism. Since the war with Rome in A.D. 66–73, the Jews were in bad repute throughout the empire, and Luke wanted to show the distance between ethnic Jewry and the fulfillment and completion of the Jewish hope in a now ecumenical church. There is much truth here, especially when the Acts data are brought into the discussion. But even from the Gospel alone we can see how Jesus' story and teaching highlight interest in Gentile races, particularly the Romans (Luke 7:1-10). In the Passion narrative the innocence of Jesus and the impartiality of the Roman authorities are repeatedly attested.

(b) The universal scope of Luke's Gospel is well known, and this feature has been taken to mean that Luke wrote simply to proclaim the gospel of salvation to his readers. The worldwide character of the Gospel is sometimes explicit (2:1; 2:32; 3:1-2). Sometimes it is cryptic (as in 10:1, where the number seventy or seventy-two disciples reflects and parallels the number of nations listed in Gen. 10:1-32). Sometimes the emphasis is made by what is said on the surface of the narrative (Jesus' appeal to women, to sinners, and social outcasts, like lepers and tax collectors, to Samaritans, a race despised by the Jews, to the economically poor). Yet in other places the emphasis lies just beneath the text itself (4:16-30; 5:1-11).

Searching for some sort of umbrella term or terms to label Luke's purpose, S. G. Wilson describes Luke's aim as "a combination of historical and practical elements." Luke wanted to write history, but history with a special slant (often called salvation history) "that had a message for his contemporaries." Wilson wisely chooses the title "pastor" for Luke's role as a Gospel writer. His chief interest was to aid the church in his lifetime by proclaiming the substance of Jesus' preaching and by offering pastoral counsel and encouragement to his fellow believers who, to be sure, may well have needed some corrective teaching and have required a fresh retelling of the earthly life of their Lord. Luke has played the part of a pastor-teacher seen in the way he assembled the traditions at his disposal (the sayings-source and some special matter he alone uses. They were joined to form a "mini-Gospel" called Proto-Luke *before* Luke saw Mark and slotted into his framework the Markan additions).

Other examples of Luke's editorial work are the use he made of liturgical and catechetical elements (in chaps. 1, 2: the hymns of Jewish Christianity are traced back to such sources as Mary's *Magnificat* and Simeon's *Nunc Dimittis,* and chap. 7—the Sermon on the Plain), the prominence he ascribed to the character of the truly human Jesus as man among people, and especially his emphasis in the tradition about Jesus on those elements that figured so prominently in Paul's kerygmatic message, for example, the kindness and compassion of God in Christ, the call of salvation (a key Lukan word), and Jesus' offer of free grace to the undeserving. This closely paralleled series of teachings, even if the idiom is different (though occasionally it is strikingly identical—Luke 18:13 and Rom. 3:24-26), is best viewed in a special part of this Gospel: the central section (9:51–18:14), which plays another important part in Luke's overall composition.

*Luke's Gospel and Christian Living.* In Luke's central section we meet several special motifs that run like a core through his entire Gospel book but are chiefly accentuated here. Jesus' purpose is clear (9:51): it is to go to Jerusalem, where salvation has to be accomplished (13:31-35). On the road to the Holy City Jesus teaches the true nature of the kingdom of God, whose coming is soon but not "to appear immediately" (19:11). He reaches out to touch and bless the lives of non-Jews and the socially disadvantaged

(9:52-56; 16:19-31; 18:1-14, 35-43). But one aspect should not be forgotten: here Jesus' teaching is oriented to the cost of Christian discipleship, whose motto is summed up in the word "Take up [the] cross *daily*" (9:23). The price to be paid in terms of sacrifice for God's kingdom is renewed (9:57-62); the disciple is summoned to a life of prayer (11:1-12) and trust (12:13-34); the road is hard, and there is much suffering to be endured (12:49-53) if a person is to be saved (13:22-30); and the follower of Jesus must show the same forgiving spirit as has been offered to him (17:1-10). These are particular emphases found in Luke, and they constitute the church's first efforts to build up a pastoral theology out of the tradition of Jesus' teachings. Yet again our designation of Luke's Gospel as the work of a pastor-theologian is reinforced.                                          R.M.

**LULL, RAYMOND** (about 1235–1315). Medieval mystic, poet, missionary to Muslims, advocate of local languages for Christian missionaries. Born in Majorca, trained as a knight, he served Majorcan King Don Jamie II from 1246 until his conversion vision about 1263. For nine years he studied Arabic and Christian thought preparing for Arabic missions. In 1276 he established Miramar College in Majorca to train Franciscans and others in Oriental studies. He lectured and traveled widely, promoting language studies for missionaries and finally persuading the Council of Vienne (1311–12) to sanction Oriental languages in five universities. His missionary enterprises took him to Asia, Armenia, and four times to Africa. On his last African mission he was stoned in Tunisia and died four years later.

Lull was prolific as a writer. His *Grand Art* uses rational arguments to convince Muslims that Christian truth is irrefutable. *The Great Book of Contemplation* discusses stages in the ascent to God—the sensible, intellectual, and final mystic stage of union. *The Blanquerna* is reminiscent of St. Francis' joy in things of nature created by God. The *Book of the Lover and the Beloved* presents Lull's mysticism in brief form. Lull influenced St. Teresa of Avila, St. John of the Cross, and Nicholas of Cusa.                                 C.M.

**LUNDENSIAN THEOLOGY.** A name applied to a school of Swedish theologians centered on the University of Lund and active in the middle decades of the twentieth century. Among its representatives were G. AULÉN and A. NYGREN. Its adherents practiced the method of MOTIF RESEARCH. They believed that one must penetrate beneath the outward form of a doctrine to its fundamental motif, understood as a distinctive and dynamic idea. Thus Aulén claimed that the conflict/victory motif underlies the Christian doctrine of atonement and is essential to a right understanding of it, while Nygren found the central Christian motif in *agape* or disinterested love, to be distinguished both from *eros* as the motif characteristic of Greek philosophy and

from *nomos,* which has a corresponding role in Judaism.                                          J.M.

**LUST.** One of the traditional SEVEN DEADLY SINS. Lust is an unhealthy sexual appetite that desires not love or spiritual union but only physical satisfaction. Lust goes beyond the normal desire for relief from sexual tension in that it is an inordinate, all-consuming desire for sexual activity. Lust is not related either to the Platonic EROS, which is the drive for union with the beloved person or object, or to AGAPE, the NT love that seeks the good of the loved one even at the expense of one's own needs. It is not related to PHILIA, the brotherly love that binds the citizen to his or her fellow citizens, or to *storge*, which is patriotism or love of country. Lust is a distortion of the good sexual drive in an utterly selfish manner. Lust may be, in the modern world view, a psychological addiction, similar to alcoholism or drug abuse. In the traditional view, derived from Aristotle's ethics, lust is a sin of excess, of exceeding the mean or measure of moderation that alone can lead one to true happiness. Lust, in the Platonic view, is the allowance of the base, animal, or instinctual nature to dominate the intellectual nature and so to lead the soul away from the highest good.                                 J.C.

**LUTHER, MARTIN** (1483–1546). German church reformer who began PROTESTANTISM. Born November 10 at Eisleben into a peasant family

Courtesy of the Museum of Fine Arts, Boston, Henry D. Parker Collection
*Martin Luther. A portrait by Heinrich Aldegraver*

experiencing an economic incline, Luther attended lower schools at Magdeburg and Eisenach, and received B.A. and M.A. degrees from the University of Erfurt in 1501 and 1505. He was ready to enter law school when a bolt of lightning made him so fearfully conscious of death that he vowed to become a monk. On July 17, 1505, Luther entered the Augustinian cloister at Erfurt in order to save his soul. He scrupulously fulfilled all requirements for monkhood, and on May 2, 1507, he said his first mass. Luther underwent a long religious crisis, doing everything the church prescribed to acquire divine favor. He performed religious works, chastised his body, made lengthy confessions, and even tried mystical contemplation but found no spiritual peace. He taught one semester at Wittenberg University in 1508 and went to Rome (November 1510–April 1511) to represent the Augustinians in a dispute. On returning he transferred to Wittenberg, studied theology, and received a Th.D. on October 19, 1512.

Later, saying he had not yet seen the light, Luther began lectures on Psalms, Romans, and Galatians. Luther's experience of justification by faith alone, traditionally dated 1513, forced him to disavow all attempts to merit favor from God. God freely forgives our sins; sinful human beings do not earn forgiveness by their works. Christ's atonement is based on God's love, not on our merits. This was the insight, though not fully formulated, out of which Luther wrote and posted his ninety-five theses, October 31, 1517, regarded as the inauguration of the REFORMATION. Luther's theses questioned Johann Tetzel's selling of papal indulgences, which the church said wiped out sins but which Luther said were sold so that St. Peter's Church in Rome could be rebuilt. He desired not schism but a truer understanding of Christian living and repentance more in keeping with Scripture. Others saw his theses as an attack on the authority of the pope and the church's treasury of merits. Within weeks Luther became the center of a European controversy.

The papacy ordered Luther to Rome, but Elector John Frederick of Saxony circumvented that. Various attempts through Cardinal Cajetan and others to silence Luther culminated in the Leipzig debate with Johann Eck, July 4-14, 1519. At Leipzig Luther acknowledged agreement with JOHN HUSS, a condemned heretic, and on June 15, 1520, Pope Leo X issued his *Exsurge Domine* bull branding Luther a wild boar in the Lord's vineyard and giving him sixty days to recant.

While awaiting the bull, Luther published three influential essays. *The Appeal to the German Nobility* attacked church abuses, developed the sacredness of all vocations and the priesthood of all believers, and urged secular rulers to reform the church. *The Babylonian Captivity* argued from Scripture for only two sacraments—baptism and the Lord's Supper—though Luther wondered about penance. *The Freedom of the Christian* elaborated justification by faith alone

acting in love. On December 10, 1520, Luther publicly burned the pope's bull, and on January 3, 1521, was formally excommunicated in the bull *Decet.*

At the imperial Diet of Worms (1521) Luther, with his life at stake, made his "Here I Stand" speech, saying he would not recant unless proved wrong by Scripture and right reason. Emperor Charles V placed him under the imperial ban, but friends of Luther hid him at the Wartburg Castle for ten months. He returned to Wittenberg in March of 1522 and quelled rising disturbances by preaching eight sermons on faith and love. That same year he published the New Testament in German, and the entire Bible, including the Apocrypha, by 1534. He quietly began implementing his views in ritual. In 1523 he produced *On the Order of Worship,* in 1524 an evangelical hymnbook, and in 1525 a *German Mass.* In 1524 he also urged civil authorities to establish public schools, a task carried out by PHILIPP MELANCHTHON.

In 1524–25 Luther and ERASMUS clashed over free will. Erasmus, prodded by Catholic leaders, wrote *On the Freedom of the Will* (1524), saying human beings are moral agents who can make righteous choices. Having a deep sense of human sinfulness, Luther replied with *On the Bound Will* (1525), saying human choices originate in a disoriented sinful center and cannot be meritorious before God. Justification is therefore by faith, not works. Luther lost the support of many humanists who believed in human goodness.

Luther's belief in social order prompted him to write against the rebellious peasants in 1525. In his first essay he chided the princes for being unjust, even though he believed the peasants had misconstrued faith. In a second essay, *Against the Robbing and Murdering Horde,* Luther urged the princes to stab and kill as if among mad dogs. He believed the rampant peasants had usurped the political prerogatives given by God to the established authorities. At Frankenhausen, May 15, 1525, some fifty thousand peasants were slain.

In 1525 Luther married Catherine von Bora, a nun who had left her convent. Five children were born of the marriage, which set a precedent of non-celibacy in Protestantism. In 1529 Lutherans protested the limiting of evangelical freedom at the Second Diet of Spires, thus inaugurating the term "Protestant." Despite Luther's influence, the Protestants found little unity. In 1529 Luther and Ulrich Zwingli failed to agree on the Lord's Supper, and in 1536 the agreement with Martin Bucer and the South Germans on the "real presence" of Christ in the Lord's Supper proved abortive. Luther did not frame Protestantism's basic creed, the Augsburg Confession (1530). He later composed a less conciliatory doctrinal statement in his Schmalkald Articles (1536).

During his final years Luther had poor health and was irascible. He wrote a bitter essay on the Jews (1543), which Hitler later used, and a sharp tirade against the papacy. He died at Eisleben trying to settle a dispute between two counts of Mansfeld. Through his life and writings he founded Protestantism.                                                    C.M.

**LUTHERAN CHURCHES.** Lutherans form the oldest and third largest branch of Protestant Christianity in the United States, part of a worldwide communion numbering more than seventy million. The name derives from the great figure of the Protestant REFORMATION, MARTIN LUTHER. The major tenet of Luther's theological position was justification by grace alone through faith in Jesus Christ. It is significant that in 1983, the five-hundredth anniversary of Luther's birth, a panel of United States Roman Catholic and Lutheran scholars announced their agreement on the teaching of justification. "Only by God's grace do we have justification," they unitedly declared.

Luther and his followers have always insisted that their movement was a continuation of Christianity, not a new church. Except for the strong emphasis Luther placed on justification by faith and his denial of the primacy of papal authority, Lutherans are in many ways closer to Catholicism than they are to the FREE CHURCHES of Protestantism. One theologian has said that Roman Catholics are their first cousins. The Lutheran liturgy was shaped largely by that of the medieval church, to which Luther added great hymns and solid expository preaching. The Lutheran doctrine of the Eucharist is closer to that of Rome than to the "memorial" concept of many Protestant groups.

Lutheranism's confessional position is contained in the BOOK OF CONCORD, which contains the three ecumenical creeds—Apostles', Nicene, and Athanasian—plus the AUGSBURG CONFESSION and its Apology, Luther's Small and Large Catechisms, the Smalcald Articles, and the Formula of Concord.

Luther reasoned that because of original sin, people need to be reconciled to God. Reconciliation and forgiveness of sins are the essence of justification, and the righteousness of God in Christ is imputed to the believer by the action of the Holy Spirit. It is not by one's works or merit but solely the grace of God that justifies one before God. Luther often used the expression, *simul justus et peccator* ("justified but still a sinner") to emphasize the progressive aspect of sanctification. The redeemed sinner needs the means of grace—baptism, the Word, and the Lord's Supper.

Lutheran theology is always Christocentric: Christ's redemptive work is the central teaching of the Scriptures. Baptism is regarded as the water of regeneration. The Eucharist permits the believer to partake of the Body and Blood of Christ, who is there as a Real Presence. Lutheranism also emphasizes the difference between law and gospel—the law condemns; the gospel saves.

In polity there is a wide divergence in various parts of the Lutheran ecclesiastical world. Some churches, such as those in Sweden and Denmark, and more recently some of the major churches in the United States, give the title of bishop to the person occupying the highest ministerial office. Other Lutheran communions emphasize the congregational or presbyterial form of organization.

Lutheran churches have been established in all fifty states of the U.S.A., but their membership is now concentrated in the contiguous states of the upper Midwest—the Dakotas, Minnesota, Wisconsin, Iowa, and Nebraska. North Dakota is heavily Lutheran; 35 percent of the population is of this faith. Pennsylvania, once the matrix of Lutheranism, has now yielded first place to Minnesota.

Despite the numerical prominence of Lutherans, other Christian groups in the United States know relatively little about them. Restricted by edicts from abroad, the first Lutheran settlers were prohibited from having their own clergy until 1664. Due in large measure to unique customs and practices that Germans and Scandinavians developed in the nearly two hundred years between the time of the Reformation and major migrations to the New World, Lutherans became a somewhat excluded and exclusive denomination. Their common languages and cultural bonds served to unite them and provide them with a distinct identity when they came to America. Like their ancestors before them, a large share of the Lutheran population settled in rural communities. This, together with the language barrier, often resulted in enclaves of Lutherans living as religious foreigners in their adopted land.

More than evangelistic outreach, it was the tide of immigration—especially in the latter half of the nineteenth century—that served to enlarge the ranks of the Lutheran church. Before long the Lutherans debated over maintaining their parental tongues and traditions. Some felt it was important to become Americanized as citizens of the new land, while others felt maintaining their ethnic identity would preserve their theological and spiritual conformity.

There are perhaps three or four streams of varying emphasis discernible in United States' Lutheranism: (1) the nominalistic type that follows the tradition of the European state churches; (2) the scholastic conservatives who are rigid in their doctrinal orthodoxy; (3) the pietistic emphasis found in both Scandinavian and German streams; and perhaps (4) Lutheranism that has been influenced by contemporary theological liberalism. Lutheran scholars have been heavy contributors to textual criticism and higher criticism, as well as form and redaction criticism.

In the last decade or so there is a sizable charismatic renewal movement that has had an impact on many churches, particularly in the American Lutheran church. To the astonishment of staunch Lutherans, who are not noted for demonstrative religion, the charismatic movement has gained headway in many congregations. Like the historic Pentecostals, charismatics stress the gifts of the Spirit (charismata), which enable those so endowed to speak in tongues or to exercise various ministries within the church.

It was inevitable that each of the Lutheran groups would develop its own congregations and synods. As a result, as many as one hundred separate and autonomous bodies have appeared at one time or another in this country. In the last two decades continuing mergers have reduced the ecclesiastical diversity to two major groupings and at least nine smaller ones. The largest of these smaller groups is the Wisconsin Evangelical Lutheran Synod, with more than 400,000 members. In 1983 the American Lutheran church, the Lutheran church in America, and the Association of Evangelical Lutheran Churches (a recent breakoff from the Lutheran church—Missouri Synod) voted to merge into one synod. The only other large segment of Lutheranism—the Lutheran church—Missouri Synod—did not join the merger.

Throughout their history in America, Lutherans have placed a strong emphasis on education and intellectual achievement. All synods have maintained denominational colleges and universities, as well as seminaries for the training of their clergy and theologians. In addition, the Missouri Synod has a tradition of providing high quality parochial schools for primary and secondary education.

Because of their strong emphasis on parochial life, Lutherans in the past tended to be slow to engage in the cause of social justice and misson. In recent years, however, they have made up for lost time. Vast sums have been raised to extend their ministry and mission. Millions of dollars have been contributed annually, for example, to the cause of world hunger. Lutheran thinkers envision "a church of catholic comprehensiveness, confessional integrity . . . with structures flexible enough to embrace ethnic distinctives, regional differences, variety of piety." To this they add, "and movements of the Spirit . . . resulting in a more diverse and dynamic Lutheranism. . . ."

Lutheranism, concentrated in Germany and Scandinavia, now can claim to be a worldwide communion with vital autonomous churches in Africa, South and Central America, Japan, India, Korea, the U.S.S.R., and mainland China.

The international voice of the church is the Lutheran World Federation, which is an association of Lutheran churches in about one hundred countries. The federation does not exercise church functions on its own authority, nor does it have authority over member churches. The LWF is successor to the Lutheran World Convention organized in Eisenach, Germany, in 1923. World War II inflicted such damage on the Lutheran churches in western Europe and elsewhere, that it was felt necessary to establish a more functional organization. Thus, the LWF was organized July 1, 1947, at Lund, Sweden, and plunged immediately into programs of emergency relief, interchurch aid, and studies. Currently it functions through major departments of studies, church cooperation, and world service. It maintains its headquarters in Geneva, Switzerland.

In 1983 the five-hundredth anniversary of Luther's birth was celebrated around the world not only by Lutherans but by Protestants, Roman Catholics, and even the authorities of Marxist East Germany. During the Advent season, Pope John Paul II participated in a Lutheran church service in Rome. It was the first time such an event had occurred in almost five centuries, since the Reformation.     R.H.

**LXX.** *See* SEPTUAGINT.

**LYCAONIA.** A high tableland north of the Taurus Mountains in ancient Asia Minor. It became part of the kingdom of Galatia in 35 B.C., and, along with Galatia, part of the Roman Empire in 25 B.C. Derbe and Lystra, two cities visited by Paul (Acts 14:6, 11) were in Lycaonia.     J.C.

**LYDIA.** A woman from Thyatira (Asia Minor), whom Paul met at Philippi (Acts 16:11-15). Possibly her name was taken from the adjective phrase "a woman of Lydia," for Thyatira was a Lydian city. Paul does not refer to Lydia in his Letter to the Philippians, but the munificence of this church, so dear to Paul, must have owed much to this generous woman. After Lydia's conversion, and the baptism of her household, Paul and his companions were prevailed upon to stay at her place. Paul was therefore relieved of the necessity of earning his living in Philippi as he needed to do elsewhere (compare II Cor. 11:8-9; I Thess. 2:9-12; Phil. 4:15-16).

Luke's incidental reference to Lydia as "a seller of purple goods" comports with inscriptions that record that the region of Lydia was famous for its dyeing. Some capital was needed to maintain this trade, which leads one to surmise that Lydia was a woman of considerable means.     J.L.P.

**LYDIA.** In the seventh century B.C., Lydia developed into a significant geopolitical entity in west central Asia Minor, centered around its capital city of SARDIS. The architect of Lydian nationhood, Gyges (about 680–652 B.C.), sought the aid of the Assyrian king ASHURBANIPAL to ward off raids by the Cimmerians (marauders known in Ezek. 38:6 as "Gomer and all his hordes"). A record of this negotiation was made in the annals of the Assyrian king, where Gyges is known as Guggu of Luddu (that is, Gog of Ezek. 38:2). Gyges was killed fighting the Cimmerians, but his son Ardys (about 652–615 B.C.) inaugurated a policy that culminated in their defeat and in Lydian control of all of Asia Minor from the Greek coastal cities (except Miletus) to Phrygia as far as the Halys River. The most renowned king of the independent Lydia was also its last, Croesus (560–546 B.C.). A man of wealth and Hellenized sophistication, he made splendid gifts to the sanctuary at Delphi and to the temple of Artemis at Ephesus. His defeat and imprisonment by Cyrus in 546 B.C. reduced Lydia to a satrapy of the Persian Empire, and it remained a mere province in Greek and Roman times. Little is known about the culture, language, or religion of Lydia, although ancient tradition held that the Etruscan nobility of Italy were Lydians in their origin. Tradition also credits Lydians with the invention of coinage, the fables of Aesop, and the enhancement of music, textiles, and perfume.                    W.S.T.

**LYING.** In both the OT and the NT, telling lies is equated with the devil and telling the truth with God. God's holy people were not to suppress or pervert the truth (Lev. 19:11). When Cain lied about killing his brother, or Abraham said that Sarah was his sister, not his wife, the tone of the OT writer is one of total disapproval. Perjury was condemned outright (Exod. 23:1). Jehovah was considered to be the fountain of all truth, and his followers were expected to demonstrate continuing truthfulness. On the other hand, for proper cause, Rehab is not condemned for lying to protect the spies who were sent into Jericho.

In the NT, Christ says that Satan is "the father of lies" (John 8:4). Ananias and Sapphira are put to death because of their selfishness and their lies (Acts 5:1-10). Paul points out that what is worst about the mystery cults of his world is that they are based not on truth but on lies (Rom. 1:22-25). And John says that what is worst about those who lie is that it permanently cuts them off from the One whose word is truth (John 17:17).                    T.J.K.

**LYON, COUNCILS OF.** Roman Catholicism's thirteenth and fourteenth ecumenical councils (1245 and 1274). Pope Innocent IV called the first council of Lyon to curb Holy Roman Emperor Frederick II, who had driven him from Rome, and also to deal with clerical immorality, the Saracens, the Greek schism, and the Tartars' invasion of Hungary. The council formally deposed the already excommunicated Frederick II. Frederick's envoy accused the council of irregularity for allowing the pope to both accuse and judge. The recently approved Dominicans and Franciscans were charged with publicizing the council's decrees, but politically and ecclesiastically the council was ineffective.

The second council of Lyon, called by Pope Gregory X, effected reunion with the Greek church, which lasted until 1289. Many medieval leaders attended, including Albert the Great and Bonaventure. Aquinas died while journeying to the council. The Greeks agreed to accept Roman Catholic doctrines, especially agreeing that the Holy Spirit proceeds from the Father and the Son, and reunion

was temporarily achieved. The council also deposed several undesirable ecclesiastics and suppressed some mendicant orders, while reapproving the Dominicans and Franciscans. In addition the council confirmed Gregory's previous acknowledgment of Rudolf I as Holy Roman Emperor, thus ending a twenty-year hiatus.                    C.M.

**LYSANIAS.** The governor of Abilene, a region of ancient Palestine north of Mount Hermon, lying between Damascus and Baalbek (or Heliopolis). The title given the governor in that period was tetrarch. According to Luke 3:1, Lysanias was tetrarch during the time of John the Baptist. Many modern scholars believe that this was not the case, since John's period was not the same as Lysanias'.                    J.C.

**LYSTRA.** A city in Lycaonia, a section of the Roman providence of Galatia in Asia Minor. Lystra lay twenty-five miles southwest of Iconium on the Roman imperial road that ran to Pisidian Antioch. Lystra was the scene of Paul and Barnabas' tremendous reception by citizens who were so impressed by Paul's miraculous healings that the two disciples were declared to be gods (Acts 14:6-19). When the people called them "Jupiter and Mercury" (in the Latin fashion; "Zeus and Hermes" in the Greek manner), Paul declared that he and Barnabas were only men like themselves. Paul sometimes visited Lystra (Acts 14:6, 21; 16:1; 18:23).                    J.C.

**LYTE, HENRY FRANCIS.** (1793–1847) Poet, musician, and minister. Born in Scotland on June 1, Lyte was educated at Trinity College, Dublin. Throughout most of his life, Lyte suffered from poor health, but he persisted in serving Christ faithfully. Indeed he is said to have coined the expression, "It is better to wear out than to rust out." For the final twenty-three years of his short life, Lyte served as curate of an Anglican parish at Lower Brixham in Devonshire. When his health became progressively worse, he decided to go to Italy where the weather would be milder. However, he never reached Italy. He died at Nice, France, and was buried there on November 20. Lyte was said to have written the text for his most famous hymn, "Abide with Me," shortly before his last Sunday in the Lower Brixham Church. The text for his great hymn was taken from the account of Christ's appearance to the two disciples on the way to Emmaus, who said "Abide with us, for it is toward evening and the day is now far spent" (Luke 24:29). Lyte also wrote "Praise, My Soul, the King of Heaven," and "Jesus, I My Cross Have Taken."                    R.H.

# Mm

**MACCABEAN REVOLT.** In 167 B.C., a Jewish priest, Mattathias, launched an uprising against the efforts of the ruler of Syria, Antiochus IV, to force the Jews in Palestine to abandon their distinctive worship and purity laws, and to adopt instead a Greek style of life. Antiochus IV, who called himself Epiphanes ("manifestation of the Divine"), was eager to unify his kingdom culturally, economically, and religiously. By claiming a kinship with Zeus, the supreme god of the Greek pantheon, he hoped to add both prestige and legitimacy to his rule. By insisting that all his subjects honor Zeus, he was claiming their loyalty and devotion to himself.

Ever since the Persians permitted the Jews to return from the EXILE in Babylon in the sixth century, the acknowledged head of the Jewish people was the high priest. After the death of ALEXANDER THE GREAT in 323 B.C., his generals and those he had placed in charge of the conquered regions began to carve up his vast empire, which stretched from mainland Greece to India, and from Egypt to the Black Sea. Palestine was first claimed by the Egyptian rulers, the Ptolemies, but in 198 B.C., the Syrian king (of the Seleucid dynasty) had added Palestine to his territory, and such it continued down into the reign of Antiochus IV.

On assuming control over the land of the Jews, Antiochus III decided to allow them to live by their traditional law, with Torah as the law of the land and the high priest as head of state. Antiochus and his son were so pressed by the Romans, militarily and financially, as they extended their power into the eastern Mediterranean, that in desperation they seized the silver and gold that had been placed for safekeeping in the treasury of the Temple at Jerusalem. Understandably, the Jews were horror-struck at this desecration of their shrine (II Macc. 3:1-21).

From the time of Alexander onward, the Ptolemaic and Seleucid rulers of Syria and Palestine had founded or rebuilt cities according to the Greek model, with theaters, baths, schools, and geometrical layout. Greek-type citizenship was offered to those Jews who welcomed and conformed to this way of life. The rulers saw in these strategies a means of welding alien peoples into a unified citizenry, whose culture and personal allegiances would serve to unify the kingdom. In an effort to persuade Jews to conform to the pattern of Greek life, including honoring the Greek gods, Antiochus IV accepted a bribe from Jason of Cyrene and removed from the post of high priest Onias III, who had been faithful in obeying the Jewish sacred law. Unlike Onias, who had favored the Ptolemies, Jason ingratiated himself with the Syrian ruler by building a gymnasium in the city. These institutions were for the instruction of male youths and placed the major emphasis on participation in Greek-style sports. As the word gymnasium (from

Greek, *gymnos,* "naked"), implies, those engaged in these athletic activities did so in the nude, in violation of Jewish custom. And further, they even sought to have operations performed that would cover up their circumcision. Both priests and populace lost interest in the sacrifices and worship ceremonies that had traditionally been carried on in the Temple at Jerusalem.

Antiochus was not content to have the process of "Hellenization" (conforming people to Greek or Hellenic ways; compare II Macc. 4:13) move ahead at its own pace. In 169 B.C., on his return from a plundering expedition in Egypt (I Macc. 1:16-20), Antiochus entered the Temple at Jerusalem and stripped it of its sacred vessels and its gold and silver decorations, motivated in part by financial pressures and in part by resentment of the Jews who resisted Hellenization. Two years later his agents attacked the city, destroying houses, slaughtering many of its inhabitants, and carrying off women and children into slavery (I Macc. 1:30-32). At the same time Antiochus established a garrison in a tower overlooking the Temple, and in a final act of scorn, erected a shrine—probably to Olympian Zeus—within the Temple itself (I Macc. 1:54; Dan. 11:31). Further, he decreed that all the Jewish subjects must join in divine honors to him, and that the sacrificial program at the Jerusalem Temple must be stopped under penalty of death (I Macc. 1:41-50). Many Jews conformed to the royal orders, but in the town of Modein, northwest of Jerusalem, a priest named Mattathias could not bear to see his fellow Jews taking part in sacrifices to the pagan king. When a man stepped forward to do so, Mattathias ran and killed not only the one about to make sacrifice, but also the Syrian officer who had been set to enforce the decree (I Macc. 2:23-25). Calling for all who were zealous for the Law and the covenant to follow him, he and his sons fled to the desert. Others went out into the desert from cities in order to destroy them, and so he and his followers resolved to take up arms if attacked on the Sabbath (I Macc. 2:29-41).

Mattathias and his supporters were joined by the HASIDEANS (I Macc. 2:42), or HASIDIM, who sought to maintain loyalty to Torah, the traditional law of Moses, at the cost of their lives if necessary. Their policy initially was one not of passive resistance, but of active warfare against those, like Antiochus and his agents, who were trying to force them to abandon the Law, and thereby to lose their covenant identity as the pure and true people of God. Together with Mattathias's guerrilla fighters, they attacked not only the Syrians but their fellow Jews who were submitting to the Hellenizing pressures. They went so far as to circumcise forcibly all the uncircumcised Jewish boys they found in their land (I Macc. 2:46).

In 166 B.C., Mattathias died, after designating his son Simon as the one to provide counsel for the people and another son, Judah, to lead the armies of the insurrectionist movement. Judah (or Judas) had been given the nickname of "Maccabee," which probably means "hammerhead," as an indication of his drive and toughness. The Syrians were joined in suppression of the Jews by the Samaritans, a Semitic people living in north-central Palestine, who claimed descent from the northern tribes of Israel, and whose central shrine was located on Mount Gerizim, overlooking their major city, Shechem. Later their capital was relocated at the foot of Gerizim, and called the New City, which in Greek is Neapolis (modern, Nablus). The shrine was originally dedicated to the God of Israel, but later was the seat of worship of Olympian Zeus, perhaps in conformity with the decree of Antiochus IV. Against overwhelmingly superior numbers, Judah and his followers met and defeated the Syrians and their allies, who fled down the slopes of the Judean hills to the safety of the Philistine cities on the Mediterranean coast (I Macc. 3:1-24). The reputation of Judah and his army was made in the first engagement under his leadership.

Antiochus poured additional funds and troops into the effort to defeat the Maccabean hosts, but Judah's courage and strategic skills defeated the Syrian forces repeatedly. By 164 the Jews were in effective control of their lands and were able to purify the Temple in Jerusalem, restoring the proper worship of Israel's God in the rededicated Temple—an event still remembered in the Feast of Hanukkah (I Macc. 4:36-59). Judah was able to extend his power over adjacent territories, including Ammon and Gilead east of the Jordan, Idumea to the south, Galilee to the north, and the coastal regions to the west. After the death of Antiochus IV and the brief reign of Antiochus V, Demetrius became king of Syria. In his reign, Alcimus, an advocate of Hellenization, sought to be appointed to the high priesthood, even though he was not a member of the family for whom this office was hereditary (I Macc. 7:21-23). He tried to ingratiate himself with the king by reporting on Judah's nationalistic actions. But Demetrius' attempt to destroy Judah through yet another attack on Jerusalem met with disaster for the Syrians (I Macc. 7).

With the aim of gaining support from a powerful third party, Judah entered into an alliance with the rising power to the west: Rome (I Macc. 8). But continuing pressure from Syria weakened Judah's forces, with the result that his supporters were routed and he fell in battle (I Macc. 9). Another brother, Jonathan, assumed command of the nationalist troops and defeated the Syrians. A dynastic struggle in Syria led to the offer of support for Jonathan, and even his appointment as high priest, by a new claimant of the Syrian throne: Alexander Balas. He and Demetrius vied with each other to gain the support of the Jews. Alexander, who was favored by the Romans, became king in 150, and honored Jonathan by appointing him as general and governor of the province of Judea. As the dynastic struggles among the Seleucids in Syria and with the Ptolemies in Egypt continued, the descendants of the Maccabees relied increasingly on their alliances with the Romans to maintain themselves in power. With the death of Jonathan and Simon, the last sons of Mattathias, power passed to Simon's son, John Hyrcanus, who served as high priest from 134 to 104 B.C. Increasingly, the leaders of the HASMONEAN family, while maintaining the title of high priest, assumed a royal role and life-style, with the result that the champions of the original goal of the Maccabean revolt—the purity of the covenant people—became disillusioned with the nationalistic leaders and turned their hopes and energies instead to the promotion of personal piety. Chief among those fostering this development were the PHARISEES.

H.K.

MACCABEES, BOOKS OF. Esteemed as fully authoritative writings in the Catholic tradition, I and II Maccabees are considered apocryphal by Protestants and Jews. Two other books of Maccabees are reckoned among the pseudepigraphical writings. Third Maccabees deals with the problems of the Alexandrian Jewish community around the turn of the second century B.C., and IV Maccabees presents Judaism as a religion of reason in the Hellenistic mode.

*First Maccabees.* This book is our most important source for the history of the rise of the HASMONEAN house, which dominated Israelite life from 164 B.C. to A.D. 70. Led by Mattathias, the father of Judas, surnamed the Maccabee (the "Hammerer"), and his brothers, this family of rebels arose in opposition to the first pogrom ever launched against Judaism, namely, that of Antiochus IV Epiphanes (175–163 B.C.), the Greco-Syrian ruler of the Seleucid kingdom descended from the empire of Alexander the Great. The book begins with an account of the excesses of Antiochus' program of Hellenization, which culminated in the desecration of the Temple in 167 B.C. This terrible event, accompanied by violent suppression of Jewish customs, is also reported in Daniel 11:31 and 12:11. In fact, the books of Maccabees provide indispensable information about the environment in which the book of Daniel was written.

After describing the onset of an armed revolt against imperial oppression in chapter 2, I Maccabees offers a detailed record of the military achievements of Judas (3:1–9:22). The greatest of these accomplishments was, of course, the recapture of Mount Zion and the liberation of the Temple from the profanation to which it had been subjected by the Syrian garrison. The rededication of the Temple was celebrated in 164 B.C., and is the basis of the Jewish feast of Hanukkah, "The Feast of Dedication" (I Macc. 4:52-58). The book concludes with narratives of the military and political careers of Judas' brothers Jonathan (9:23–12:53) and Simon (chaps. 13–16). Most scholars believe that it was originally written in Hebrew (though it is now known only in the Greek text), and

date it about 110 B.C., shortly after the death of Simon.

The book stands in the tradition of OT historiography and tells the story of the insurrection of faithful Jews against the Seleucids and their Hellenizing Jewish allies as a history of salvation. So pleased were the writers of the book with the success of the powerless, observant Jews against a powerful empire that they endorsed expansionism and wars of conquest (15:33) and spoke of the later leaders almost in the language of messianism (see the poetic exaltation of Simon in 14:4-15).

*Second Maccabees.* Though it deals with the same dramatic history, this book surveys only the fifteen years from the accession of Antiochus IV Epiphanes in 175 B.C. to the death of Nicanor, the general of Antiochus, at the hands of Judas in 160 B.C. For various reasons its composition is assigned to about the year 120 B.C.

Second Maccabees is a theological work as much as it is a historical one, and it is believed to reflect the piety of early Pharisaism. It acknowledges the role of angels in history and believes in the resurrection of the dead. Its firm confidence in the efficacy of martyrdom reaches its height in chapter 7, the morally edifying story of the martyrdom of seven brothers and their mother. As King Antiochus personally oversees the frying of these martyrs in a giant frying pan, he hears one brother cry out the words that have inspired generation of readers ever since, "You dismiss us from this present life, but the King of the universe will raise us up to an everlasting renewal of life, because we have died for his laws" (7:9). Hebrews 11:35 may have this account in mind when it says of faithful people, "Some were tortured, refusing to accept release, that they might rise again to a better life."

W.S.T.

MACCABEUS, JUDAS. *See* MACCABEAN REVOLT.

MACEDONIA. A country that stretched across the peninsula from the Adriatic to the Aegean Sea on the northern limits of what is now GREECE. Its population was probably not Hellenic, but its royal family was. It rose to world prominence under Philip II, who in 338 B.C. defeated the combined forces of Athens and Thebes, and launched his aggressive plan by which he came to dominate the Greek mainland and islands, as well as Asia Minor. In 336 B.C. he was succeeded by his son, Alexander, who went on to conquer the Middle East, Egypt, Mesopotamia, Persia, and took his armies as far as India—all in the name of Macedonia.

Both the letters of Paul and Acts attest to the effectiveness of Paul's mission to the people of Macedonia. In Acts 16:9, it is a vision of a man from there that moves Paul to extend his evangelism to the mainland of Europe. He and his companions passed through this area frequently, visiting the cities of Philippi (Phil. 4:15), which had been named in honor of Philip of Macedon, and Thessalonica (I Thess. 1:7; 4:10; Rom. 15:26), where the Christians were exemplary as to their faith and their generosity. Paul's movements through Macedonia are reported in the Corinthian letters (I Cor. 16:5; II Cor. 1:16; 7:5; 8:1) and in Acts (16:10, 12; 18:5; 19:21; 20:1, 3).

H.K.

**McGIFFERT, ARTHUR CUSHMAN**, (1861–1933). American liberal theologian, prominent professor of church history at Union Theological Seminary (1893–1927), where he was also the president (1917–26). Conservatives forced him to leave the Presbyterian ministry in 1900, during the biblical inerrancy controversy. His many books include *The Apostles' Creed* (1902) and *A History of Christian Thought* (1932).

C.M.

**MACINTOSH, DOUGLAS CLYDE** (1877–1948). Liberal theologian, who studied at Chicago and taught at Yale. He was impressed by the success that had attended the application of empirical methods to the sciences of human behavior and with the empirical spirit of the Chicago Divinity School. The character of his theology is expressed in the title of his best-known book, *Theology as an Empirical Science* (1919). He had himself undergone significant religious experiences in his youth, and believed that in such experiences there is a perceptual element that is amenable to empirical investigation. Critics, however, have maintained that, like many other "empirical" theologians, Macintosh stretched the meaning of "empirical" to such an extent that it loses definition and comes to cover virtually any kind of inquiry. In addition, he took over many presuppositions and valuations from traditional theology without obviously giving to them an empirical grounding.

J.M.

**MACHPELAH, CAVE OF.** The cave at Hebron where the three patriarchs—Abraham, Isaac, and Jacob—and three of the four matriarchs—Sarah, Rebekah, and Leah—are buried, according to tradition. The Bible states that Abraham, wanting to bury Sarah, bought Machpelah from Ephron the Hittite for four hundred silver shekels. Genesis 23:17 describes Machpelah as "the field of Ephron." Following the Six-day War in 1967, the cave became a popular point of pilgrimage; and Jews, after a period of seven hundred years, were once more able to visit the tombs of the patriarchs and matriarchs and pray there.

L.K.

**McPHERSON, AIMEE SEMPLE** (1896–1944). Founder of the International Church of the FOURSQUARE GOSPEL. Born October 9, near Ingersoll, Ontario, Canada, Aimee Elizabeth was the only child of James Morgan Kennedy, farmer and Methodist church choir member, and Mildred Pearce Kennedy, a member of the Salvation Army.

At the age of seventeen she experienced conversion in a Pentecostal revival meeting and proceeded on August 12, 1908, to marry the Irish evangelist Robert James Semple. In 1909 she was ordained as a preacher by the Full Gospel Assembly in Chicago. Semple felt called to China, but he died within three months of their arival in Hong Kong. A month later their daughter Roberta Starr Semple was born. Aimee and her daughter returned to the United States. On February 28, 1912, she married Harold Stewart McPherson, a bookkeeper from Providence, Rhode Island. Rolf Kennedy McPherson was born in 1913. The stormy marriage ended in divorce in 1921.

After a long illness, which she felt was God's punishment for leaving evangelism, McPherson felt called again to preach in 1915. She emphasized crisis conversion, speaking in tongues as evidence of baptism by the Holy Spirit, faith healing, and the premillennial return of Christ—the "foursquare gospel." In 1917 she began publishing *Bridal Call.*

Arriving in Los Angeles about 1918, she began construction of Angelus Temple in 1921. It was dedicated in 1923, and the church became a denomination in 1927. Scandal arose in May 1926 when she said she had been kidnapped while swimming. Some said she simply vacationed with Kenneth Ormiston, a former employee. In 1931 she married David Hutton, though that marriage also ended in divorce four years later. Her later years were marred by estrangements from her mother and daughter. She died on September 17, after an overdose of sleeping pills, which was ruled accidental. She is buied in Forest Lawn, Glendale, Califonia.

N.H.

**MĀDHYAMIKA.** A Buddhist meditational exercise, later a school of thought, meaning "the middle way." The school of thought was founded by the monk Nagarjuna (about A.D. 150–250) in India, and spread to China in the fifth century, where it was called *San-lun* ("Three Treatise School," in reference to its three most important scriptures). It also spread to Korea, Japan, and finally to Tibet. The Indian school divided into two factions in the late fifth century. Later, the school as a whole died out but continued to influence Buddhist thought through its texts.

The Mādhyamika school taught that it is dangerous to become entangled in concepts, opinions, and emotions. The way to enlightenment begins with realizing that there is no eternal reality either in the self or in any ultimate reality. All things are empty of any reality. "Nothing becomes real, nothing becomes non-real; nothing is eternal, nothing is extinct; nothing is identical, nothing is different; nothing comes, nothing goes." Critics charged that Nagarjuna was a nihilist, a charge that he denied.

K./M.C.

**MADISON, JAMES** (1751–1836). The fourth president of the United States was born March 16, 1751, to Eleanor "Nelly" Rose and James Madison of Orange County, Virginia. He graduated from the College of New Jersey at Princeton in 1771, and spent a year studying for the Church of England ministry.

A member of the Virginia convention in 1776, he helped frame its constitution and declaration of rights. He tried unsuccessfully to make the free exercise of religion a right rather than a matter of toleration and to disestablish the Anglican Church. He later completed those tasks as a member of the Virginia House of Delegates 1786–89.

As a member of the Continental Congress, Madison helped frame the Constitution and the Bill of Rights and defended them in *The Federalist Papers*. He served Thomas Jefferson as secretary of state and succeeded him as president of the United States in 1808, serving two terms. He later succeeded Jefferson as rector of the University of Virginia in 1826.

Madison married Dolly Payne Todd on September 15, 1794; they had no children. A slaveholder who abhorred slavery, he proposed the three-fifths rule of representation and supported the American Colonization Society.

N.H.

**MADONNA.** A sculptured figure of wood, stone, or other material of the VIRGIN MARY. A Madonna may also be an icon or painting of the Virgin. The Virgin is usually depicted with the Christ child or in a scene from Jesus' ministry. In Italian, madonna means "my lady."

J.C.

**MADRASA.** A school, college, or university in Islam, sometimes associated with a mosque. Although some madrasas provided primary education in the Qur'an and in grammar and poetry, madrasas were most important in the Middle Ages as centers of studies in jurisprudence. Professors and students also studied Qur'anic interpretation (*tafsir*), theology (*kalam*), and other fields: logic, linguistics, mathematics, music, and medicine. The madrasas contended with the followers of philosophy who studied the Greek classics. European universities borrowed from the madrasas the long robes of the professor and the practice of endowing a "chair" in each subject. In modern times, madrasas have westernized.

K./M.C.

**MAGDALA.** An ancient Jewish fishing town (from the Hebrew *migdal* meaning "tower"), probably the medieval and modern Mejdel, on the western shore of the Sea of Galilee just a little northwest of Tiberias. The Greek name in Josephus was Tarichea. It is referred to in the Gospels as Magadan (Matt. 15:39; some manuscripts read Magdala) or Dalmanutha (Mark 8:10; some mss. read Magadan or Magdala). One of Jesus' prominent women disciples was Mary

Magdalene (that is, the one from Magdala; Matt. 27:56, 61; 28:1; Mark 15:40, 47; 16:1; Luke 8:2; 24:10; John 19:25; 20:1, 10-18). Limited archaeological work reveals that there was a harbor, possibly a few first-century A.D. Roman structures, and perhaps a very small synagogue.

D.S.

*Star of David*

**MAGEN DAVID.** From the Hebrew phrase for "Shield of David." The term applied to a six-pointed star, or two interlaced equilateral triangles, which has come to be an accepted symbol of Judaism. It has neither biblical nor Talmudic authority, and its origin as a Jewish symbol is obscure. The Magen David is a part of the blue and white flag of the State of Israel. The Red Magen David in Israel corresponds to the Red Cross in other countries.

L.K.

**MAGI.** From inscriptions, literary evidence, and ancient art, it is known that a magus was a member of the Persian priestly caste, which had responsibility for daily fire worship and other sacrificial and liturgical duties in Persia from at least as early as the sixth century B.C. Later, the term came to be used in two distinctly different ways: (1) a diviner, who by studying the movement of the stars was able to predict the course of events in the future; (2) a magician, especially if regarded as a quack or one who exploited the gullible. Careful study of the movement of the stars, combined with the belief in the determinative effects of the heavenly bodies on earthly affairs lay at the basis of the pronouncements of the magi in the former sense. People claiming to possess this knowledge and the insight to divine the future were called magi, whether they were actually from the eastern lands or not. On the other hand, those who claimed to be able to shape the lives and destinies of others through secret formulae and magical processes were called magi in the second sense of the term. This is the signification of the terms used in Acts to describe SIMON, who wanted to buy the secret of the apostles' power (8:9-24), as well as Elymas (or Bar-Jesus), who tried to dissuade the proconsul in Cyprus from believing Paul's message (13:4-12). Simon Magus figures importantly in the apocryphal writings, such as the Acts of Peter, which describe elaborate public contests of power between Simon and the apostles in Rome. The single positive presentation of magi is in Matthew 2:1-16 where, on the basis of the movement of a star (planet?), these interpreters of the stars predict when and where the one destined to rule Israel would be born. Belief in the interpretation of the stars and their motions was widespread among various ethnic groups, including the Jews, among the cultured and the simple. From the basic order of the stars was deduced the divine ordering of events in human history.    H.K.

MAGIC. In primitive society, magic can be described as an attempt to set aside the normal laws of the universe. In biblical terms, magic, and the superhuman powers that go with it, can be thought of as good when it originates with God or furthers God's purpose but evil when it does not. Thus Moses casting down a staff before Pharaoh and turning it into a serpent has accomplished something God-pleasing and miraculous. But Saul talking to the Baalitic witch of Endor is misusing her to call up the ghost of Samuel and speak to the dead.

Magic appears in such forms as sorcery, DIVINATION, soothsaying, wizardry, conjuring, incantation, casting of LOTS, curses, blessings, spells, numerology, dreams, visions, augury, ASTROLOGY, OMENS, necromancy, EXORCISM, charms, amulets, potions, ordeals, and SIGNS. Both the NT and the OT are filled with references to such kinds of magic, both among the people of God and the pagans among whom these people lived. Yet Gerhard von Rad makes a valid case that the children of Israel, in their worship of Jehovah, were unique, compared with other peoples of the Near East, for how little they used magic, invocations, incantations, charms, images, and other magical forms of worship. God's name also sufficed, without physical intervention.

The word "magic" originates in Persia, with the *magi* or *magoi*, as cited in the story of the wise men who visited the infant Jesus. Their ability to divine, to prophesy, to interpret the stars, to tell dreams, to advise royalty, and to perform sorcery to some degree defined our concept of magic. Similar professional diviners and sorcerers are cited in biblical passages like Micah 5:3-11; Genesis 41:8; Daniel 2:2. The Hebrew word for priest, *cohen*, and even more its cognates in other Semitic languages, carried the meaning not just of an individual who tends the altar and offers sacrifice but also one who foretells the future, a function in Israel that was usually reserved for major prophets, and even then, often only as a result of a special vision. Such prophets or soothsayers generally were set apart by the special clothing they wore, the special food they ate, and the special oaths they swore (II Kings 1:8).

In the days before the Exile the people of Israel carried on a continuous religious struggle to ward off the worship practices of the other Semitic peoples among whom they lived. Jacob's wife Rachel stole the teraphim or household gods when she left her family home (Gen. 31:19), in the hope that these would bring continued blessing to the family and flocks. In the wilderness, the people of Israel did not think Jehovah alone adequate to solve their problems and wanted to improve their chances by adding local gods, like the golden calf (Exod. 32). Not much later Moses, on Jehovah's instructions, cast a brazen serpent, perhaps a brazen mockery of the Canaanitic serpent god, as a response to the people's complaints. Later, as the Assyrians gradually dominated the north of Israel, their religious practices more and more swamped the true worship of Jehovah, with household gods, sacred groves, high places, divination, and witchcraft. In one attempt to wipe out false religion, Saul put to death "the mediums and the wizards" (I Sam. 28:3).

The giving and interpreting of dreams and visions is another form of God's intervention with people, as recorded in biblical accounts. Sometimes these involved mystical words and images, as was the case with Joseph in Egypt or Daniel in Babylon, almost as if the biblical pattern was to be a later encouragement for Jewish Cabalism and Muslim Sufism. Usually the dreams were more straightforward, like Joseph's in Bethlehem or Peter's in Joppa. Casting lots or picking marked arrows was an accepted practice, and the Scriptures generally speak positively of such actions. The mystical urim and thummim that most scholars think were small stones or bones carried in the priest's breastplate are frequently cited as a means of seeking a God-pleasing outcome, for example, in dividing up the land of Canaan among the tribes or in choosing out soldiers for a given assignment (Judg. 20:9; Num. 26:55).

Generally, amulets and incantations are condemned in Scripture. At Ephesus, Paul considered magical books, statuary, and amulets as worthy only of the fire and as misleading true believers in their search for God. In the same way, those who practiced magical or occult sciences, common throughout the Egyptian world, were strongly condemned, like Simon Magus and Elymas (Acts 8:9; 13:8).

Foretelling the future by omens was also generally condemned. Some of the commoner methods were to observe water in a dish or glass, to watch the formation of clouds, to determine the confluence of stars and planets, or to examine the flight of birds or the entrails of animals (Dan. 2:48; Gen. 30:27; Isa. 2:6). Scriptures for the most part approved of ordeals. Numbers 5:12-31 describes how a suspected wife proves her fidelity to her husband by bringing a sacrifice and mingling it with water and dust from the floor of the tabernacle. In fact, trials of one sort of another were so popular in the Scriptures that they persisted in Christian practice right through the Middle Ages. Even in our present culture, separating that which is religious, magical, superstitious, or merely cultural is an almost impossible task.

T.J.K.

**MAGISTERIUM.** A term used in the Roman Catholic Church referring to the teaching authority of the church. The pope and the bishops are regarded as direct successors of the apostles (see APOSTOLIC SUCCESSION), hence as continuing witnesses to and interpreters of the apostolic faith. This authority is deemed to have been conferred on the apostles and their successors by Jesus (Luke 22:31; Matt. 16:19; John 21:15-17). "Extraordinary magisterium" is exercised by the pope and ecumenical councils, whose pronouncements are regarded as infallible. "Ordinary magisterium" refers to doctrinal interpretations capable of revision as the bishops exercise their teaching role.                                          I.C.

**MAGNIFICAT.** Mary's hymn of thanksgiving and praise for the mighty acts of God and the revelation of God's salvation to Israel, in Luke 1:46-55. It is called the Magnificat because of its first word in Latin, "magnifies": "My soul magnifies the Lord." The song of Mary identifies Israel and Mary and stresses the love of God for the poor and humble. Its theme is the great reversal, the special favor of God shown to the weak of the earth. God's salvation comes to the wretched of the earth; rulers and the wealthy are cast down from their thrones and power. The Christ who is to come turns the world upside down.

The first two chapters of Luke are full of elevated poetry, songs, and hymns of spiritual power, beloved by the church in every generation. In these hymns Luke reconciles the majesty of the Christ-event with the lowly origins of Jesus among the poor. The Magnificat is Luke's synthesis of these two themes. Liturgically, the Magnificat is used as a canticle in the vespers service of the Catholic, Lutheran, and Episcopal churches. It is generally sung. Many musicians have elaborated on the Magnificat for church use.                                              J.C.

**MAGOG.** See GOG AND MAGOG.

**MAHABHARATA.** With the RAMAYANA, one of the two principal epics in the literature of HINDUISM. The Mahabharata is of great importance to students of religion for the light it casts on such ancient Hindu concepts as DHARMA, for the rich mythological material found in it, and for the immensely influential BHAGAVAD GITA, incorporated into the epic as its sixth book. Ascribed to Vyasa, the Mahabharata was probably composed in large part between 200 B.C. and A.D. 200.

The epic's nearly 100,000 verses center around rivalry between two branches of the royal house of Kuruksetra (the area of modern Delhi) for the throne. The great god KRISHNA, in AVATAR form, is an ally of the Pandava house against their cousins, the Kauravas. The Pandavas win after many vicissitudes to reign over an era of peace and justice before setting out toward the Himalayas to enter Indra's heaven.

Sections of the Mahabharata gave impetus to the exaltation of Krishna and VISHNU, and so to the rise of BHAKTI. But its supreme message is of the power of dharma, the eternal ordering of the world and the righteousness that accords with it.

R.E.

**MAHANAIM.** Said in Genesis 32:1-2 to have been named by Jacob, this village became the provincial capital of Gilead in Transjordan in later times (Josh. 13:26-30). Saul's son Ishbosheth was proclaimed king in exile there (II Sam. 2:8). Years later, when Absalom led a coup against him, David also fled across the Jordan to safety in Mahanaim (II Sam. 17:21-29).                                          W.S.T.

**MAHARISHI MAHESH YOGA.** See TRANSCENDENTAL MEDITATION.

**MAHĀSATIPATTHĀNA SUTTA.** A SUTRA that appears twice in the canon of scriptures in the Pali language. It gives a meditation technique for the production of an awareness of DUKKHA (human suffering), one of the FOUR NOBLE TRUTHS OF BUDDHISM. Through constant analysis of the motions of his body, the monk following this sutra becomes aware of, but detached from, his material form. For example, when breathing, the monk thinks to himself, "Breathing occurs." Meditation may concentrate on the body of the monk, or on the various stages in the processes of a corpse's decay. When this is mastered, the monk focuses his attention on his own emotions and perceptions. Gradually, craving can be eliminated, and the Buddha's Eightfold Path is followed to enlightenment.

K./M.C.

**MAHAVIRA.** The common title, meaning "Great Hero," of Vardhamana, founder of JAINISM. A contemporary of the BUDDHA, and like him of Kshatriya or warrior caste, Mahavira was born about 550 B.C. or 599 B.C. by traditional accounts. At age thirty he left the householder life to become a wandering religious mendicant. He practiced great asceticism, including nudity and prolonged fasting. After thirteen years he is said to have attained KAIVALYA, or full liberation, as understood in the teaching of Parsva (about the ninth century B.C.), whose successor Jains consider Mahavira to be. He became a *jina*, "conqueror," and TIRTHANKARA, or great teacher. Thereafter he occupied himself instructing and organizing disciples to lay the foundations of the Jain movement. He died at the age of seventy-two of the advanced Jain ascetic practice of self-starvation.                                          R.E.

**MAHAYANA BUDDHISM.** See BUDDHISM.

**MAHDI.** The messiah in ISLAM; especially important for SHI'ITES, who have always felt persecuted. Consequently, the coming of the Mahdi has long been a focus of their desire for justice. The Shi'ites believe that God commanded the last IMAM (a descendant of MUHAMMAD) to go into hiding until the proper time comes. He will return as Muhammad al-Mahdi and establish a just society under the guidance of God. However, various sects disagree as to who it is that will return (see IMAMIYYA; SAB'IYYA). From time to time various people have been acclaimed as the Mahdi. Two of them led revolts against British colonialism. In late SUNNI tradition, the Mahdi is Jesus, who will return to earth to slay the ANTICHRIST.

K./M.C.

**MAIMONIDES, MOSES.** Considered the greatest Jewish philosopher and codifier of the Middle Ages. He was popularly known as RaM.BaM, from the initials of his Hebrew title and name, Rabbi Moses ben Maimon. Born in Cordoba, Spain, in 1135, Maimonides lived most of his life in Egypt, where he became the personal physician of Saladin, the sultan of Egypt. He became known for his great scholarship and as the greatest Talmudic authority of his time. His principal religious writings are a commentary to the Mishnah, a code of Jewish law, and *The Guide for the Perplexed.* His Mishnah commentary is a religious code of fourteen books, designed as a systematic summary of the legal formulations of the Talmud and other rabbinic writings. It was accepted as an authoritative code by most Jewish communities in Europe, Africa, and the Near East, and later was used by all codifiers and other scholars as the basis for their own works.

*The Guide for the Perplexed* attempted to harmonize the teachings of Judaism with the philosophy of Aristotle. The guide has exercised considerable influence on both Jewish and Christian thinkers. Maimonides' theology is summed up in his thirteen principles of faith. These affirm that (1) God is Creator and Guide; (2) he is uniquely One; (3) he is incorporeal (does not have a physical existence); (4) he is eternal; (5) God and God alone is to be worshiped; (6) God revealed his will through the prophets; (7) Moses was the greatest of all the prophets; (8) the Torah was revealed to Moses; (9) the Torah is eternal and unchangeable; (10) God is all-knowing; (11) he rewards and punishes; (12) the Messiah will surely come; and (13) the dead will be resurrected. L.K.

**MAJOR ORDERS.** See ORDERS AND ORDINATION.

**MAJOR PROPHETS.** See PROPHETS (MAJOR AND MINOR).

**MALACHI.** The Hebrew term for "my messenger," a title extracted from Malachi 3:1. Also the last of the so-called Minor PROPHETS of the Hebrew Bible.

Along with the so-called Deutero-Zechariah (Zechariah 9–11) and Trito-Zechariah (Zechariah 12–14), Malachi forms a work of anonymous prophecy that owes its present form to careful editorial work, which has made of them the final retouches of the book of the twelve minor prophets. Each of these three units is roughly the equal of the others, and each has the editorial introduction "an oracle" (compare Zech. 9:1; 12:1; Mal. 1:1). Regardless of the editorial work, it appears that the book of Malachi records, in substance, the voice of a single prophetic figure who was active in the postexilic Judea of restoration sometime during the Persian period after the rebuilding of the Temple in 516 B.C. and probably before the era of Ezra and Nehemiah, which began in 432 B.C. This prophetic collection has been divided into six dialogues between Yahweh (or the prophet speaking for Yahweh) and people, in which there is an intermingling of charges, responses, counter-responses, and threats. The six dialogues are: (1) Yahweh's love of Israel and rejection of Edom, which had proved to be the jackal to the lion of Babylon in the conquest of Judea (1:2-5); (2) Yahweh's condemnation of the Jerusalemite priesthood for its unworthy conduct of the cult and dereliction of its other duties (1:6–2:9); (3) Yahweh's condemnation of the people for the repudiation of the ancient covenant concerning alien marriages (2:10-17); (4) Yahweh's announcement of a coming purification of Temple and priesthood (2:1-5); (5) Yahweh's rebuke of the people's niggardly response to the cult, corresponding with the slovenliness of the priests (3:6-12); and (6) Yahweh's decree of a coming day of judgment, when the just will be vindicated and the wicked punished (3:13-21; 3:13–4:3 in the AV/RSV enumeration). A final 3:22-24 in the Hebrew Bible (Eng. Bible, 4:1-6), in which the messenger of the covenant of 3:1 is identified with a returning Elijah, is generally thought to be a later addition.

The prophetic level of Malachi is hardly that of the great figures who had appeared in the Israel and Judah before the Exile. It tends to repeat old formulas and to dwell on paltry shortcomings without much seeking of the underlying evils of which they were merely symptoms. It is as equally concerned with external proprieties as with the internal dispositions and moral conduct that defined true religion for the preexilic prophets. It is not certain whether 2:13-16, which on the surface seems to adopt an attitude toward monogamous marriage and an abhorrence of divorce rather superior to that of the rest of the OT and of subsequent Judaism, is not rather an idealized figure of speech referring to cultic purity. Even 1:11, which speaks of pure offerings made to Yahweh by the Gentiles, is less a prediction or affirmation of any such thing than it is a rhetorical device to underscore the inadequacies of the Jerusalem cult. It must be admitted, nevertheless, that in even entertaining the possibility of such offerings it shares something of the openness to universalism that was manifested by some elements of postexilic Judaism and rejected by others.

B.V.

**MALCHUS.** The name, given only in John (18:10), of the Jewish high priest's slave whose ear was cut off by a follower of Jesus at the time of Jesus' arrest (see Matt. 26:51; Mark 14:47; Luke 22:50-51—only Luke notes that Jesus healed him; Luke and John note it was the right ear; only John names Peter as the one who cut it). Noting the specific name in John may indicate either an early tradition or a tendency to name people as tradition develops. Malchus is a Syrian or Nabatean name, datum which may be relevant for social identification of slaves in ancient Judaism.

D.S.

**MALTA.** According to Acts 27:39–28:11 Malta, an island sixty miles south of Sicily, was the place Paul and his friends beached after their shipwreck. Here Paul did miracles and stayed three months (through the winter; compare 28:2, 11). Publius, the chief official (*prōtos*), a title attested by Greek and Latin inscriptions from Malta, entertained Paul. Ancient sources (for example, Scylax' *Periplus*, Diodorus of Sicily, and Cicero) attest the importance and excellence of Malta's harbors.

D.S.

**MAMMON.** An Aramaic Jewish term meaning "wealth" or "property," which occurs in the NT only in the words of Jesus (Matt. 6:24; Luke 16:9, 11, 13). Although in Jewish texts the term can be used neutrally, mammon (used frequently in the Targums) often connotes a sense of dishonesty or censure. Thus, it is not surprising that the two passages in the Gospels in which mammon occurs (Matt. 6 and Luke 16) imply a materialistic, anti-godly sense. In fact in the first two occurrences in Luke (16:9, 11) the expression used is "unrighteous mammon." The Gospel sayings concerning mammon stress the priority of one's devotion to God over money and one's responsibility to use one's money for others, especially the poor (Luke 16:9, 11; compare 12:33; 14:33; 16:19-31; 18:22).

D.S.

**MAMRE.** We first hear of this sacred grove in Genesis 13:18, when Abram camped by the "oaks" (or terebinths) of Mamre and built an altar to Yahweh there. The name is briefly understood to be that of an Amorite who owned the "oaks" (Gen. 14:13, 24), but subsequently it is always the name of the place of the altar and the oaks. Abraham and Sarah were camped there when the Lord's messengers brought the news of Sarah's impending conception (Gen. 18:1). The place, traditionally located just under two miles north of Hebron, achieved its lasting importance from its association with the tomb of the patriarchs, for the cave of Machpelah purchased by Abraham as a burying place for Sarah was "east of Mamre" (Gen. 23:17, 19). In Genesis 25:9, Abraham is buried there by his sons Isaac and Ishmael, and in due course, Isaac and Rebekah, their son Jacob, and his wife Leah are all interred there (Gen. 35:27-29; 49:30; 50:13).

W.S.T.

**MAN.** *See* HUMAN NATURE.

**MANA.** In many traditional religious cultures, an impersonal force believed to adhere to certain sacred places, objects, and persons. Mana gives power to those who possess it or are qualified to manipulate it, such as kings or priests, but can curse or destroy the incautious.

R.E.

**MANASSEH.** Originally, Manasseh seems to have been a most vital element in the formation of the Yahwistic Israelite federation in Palestine. It was composed of a people who inhabited both the east and the west banks of the Jordan (the two "half-tribes" who received their double share of the Promised Land according to the Deuteronomic scheme of Josh. 13:29-31; 17:1-12). Whatever their origin and pre-Israelite history, the Manassehites were destined to recede in the accession of their cousins of EPHRAIM, at least on the west bank. The indications are that prior to the more warlike gestures inaugurated by the Ephraimites, Manasseh as a Yahwistic group sought a *modus vivendi* with the Canaanites (compare the story of Shechem in Judg. 9ff., etc.). As far as the east bank (Gilead) was concerned, something similar took place. In Judges 5:14 it is Machir rather than Manasseh who is a tribe in Israel: the Machir who according to Joshua 17:1-2 was the firstborn (that is, successor) to Manasseh and "father" of Gilead. Manasseh, in these acceptations, seems to have been a people doomed to a secondary memory in Israel's annals, despite nostalgic recollections to the contrary.

Manasseh was also the elder son of JOSEPH, according to the traditions of the Pentateuch, and thus the eponymous ancestor of one of the "Joseph" tribes (compare Gen. 49:22-26; Deut. 33:13-17).

Manasseh was also the longest-lived of all the kings of Judah (887–642 B.C.), the twelfth of the line of David, a source of embarrassment to the Deuteronomic author of Kings for whom only good men should prosper while evildoers should perish quickly. There is no doubt about Manasseh's evildoing. He set out systematically to undo the reforming work in Judah initially achieved by his predecessor Hezekiah. The ease with which he was able to accomplish this was probably due to the disillusionment felt over Hezekiah's policy of resistance to Assyria, which had brought on invasion and devastation of the land under the Assyrian king Sennacherib. Under Manasseh, Judah became even more subservient to Assyria than it had been in the earlier days of Ahaz. Political alliance carried with it much else: erecting pagan altars in the house of the Lord in Jerusalem, worshiping the "host of heaven" (the astral deities of Assyria), resuming the Canaanite practice of the sacrifice of infants, and the fostering of other practices abominated by Yahwistic tradition (II Kings 21:1-9). Along with such alien ways of religion, alien morality went hand in hand (compare Jer. 7:9; Zeph. 1:8-9). The annals of the contemporary Assyrian kings Esarhaddon and his son Ashurbanipal confirm the fact of Manasseh's total subjection to their rule, and the pagan name given to his son and successor Amon speaks eloquently of the father's disposition. Second Kings 21:16 also claims that Manasseh was responsible for much bloodshed, without giving details.

It must be noted, however, that from the material standpoint, Manasseh's reign seems to have been a prosperous one for Judah. Assyrian domination guaranteed the peace, and Palestinian archaeology (of such sites as Mizpah and Debir) suggest economic and commercial well-being. It is difficult to evaluate the historical reliability of the story of II Chronicles 33:11-17, which tells of an exile and later conversion of Manasseh. Modern scholars no longer dismiss the Chronicler's deviations from Samuel-Kings as necessarily the product of a revisionist imagination, but this account can hardly be credited precisely as it stands; it probably has noted some events that were susceptible to other interpretations.     B.V.

**MANASSEH, PRAYER OF.** This beautiful example of penitential prayer stands in the RSV Apocrypha just before I Maccabees. It was not part of the original Septuagint of the OT, so there is no reason to assume that this work enshrines any authentic memory of the life of the wicked Judean king MANASSEH (687–642 B.C.). The abominations and idolatries of Manasseh's long reign in Jerusalem are recounted in II Kings 21:1-18; indeed, the Deuteronomic historian blames the subsequent destruction of Jerusalem squarely on him (vv. 10-15). Oddly, however, Manasseh's image is refurbished somewhat in the later parallel account given in II Chronicles 33:1-20. There we learn that in Assyrian captivity Manasseh "humbled himself greatly before the God of his fathers" (v. 12). We are also told that the acts of Manasseh "and his prayer to his God" (v. 18) were recorded in the chronicles of the kings of Israel and in the chronicles of the seers. It seems evident that a devout Jew of some later generation provided the text of that missing prayer so that his people could see what kind of contrition would induce God to forgive so great a sinner. The prayer begins with an ascription to God the creator and motivator of repentance (vv. 1-8). The petitioner then acknowledges his sin (vv. 9-10), and beginning with the striking sentence, "And now I bend the knee of my heart," he earnestly asks forgiveness (vv. 11-13). He concludes with an expression of trust "that thou wilt save me in thy great mercy" (vv. 14-15).     W.S.T.

**MANDEANS.** Early sect of GNOSTICISM of uncertain origin of which a small community survives in Iraq. Mandeans could be pre-Christian but probably originated in the first or second century A.D. Sometimes called St. John's Christians, because their literature exalts John the Baptist, they are also called Sabeans, from their repeated baptizings and the Aramaic word *saba* "to baptize," and Nasoraeans, based on an esoteric commentary about generation, purification, and rebirth containing the name. Although hostile to Christians and Jews, they could be an early Christian sect. Mandeans believe in a dualism of soul (light) and body (darkness), respectively good and evil. Salvation is freeing the imprisoned soul. They believe their redeemer, Manda da Hayyé, the personified "Knowledge of Life," was victorious over earthly darkness and can guide souls through the heavenly realms. Frequent baptisms prepare one for ascension after death. They practice polygamy and allow female priests. Their sacred writings include the *Ginza*, which gives several conflicting creation accounts; *Sidra de Yahya* or *John's Book*, which claims John the Baptist was a Mandean and Jesus a false messiah; the *Qolasta*, a collection of liturgies; and *Sfar Malwašia*, a collection of horoscopes and magical remedies. Mandeans differ markedly from Gnostics in making marriage and procreation sacred duties.     C.M.

**MANDALA.** Mandalas are Hindu or Buddhist paintings in which deities or Buddhas and other sacred figures are arranged in geometric patterns, most commonly circular, to indicate their interrelationships, and to serve as focuses of meditation. (*Mandala* means "circle" in Sanskrit.) They are fundamental to the ritual and thought of the Tantric traditions (see TANTRISM) of both HINDUISM and BUDDHISM. Usually a mandala will center on a particular major deity or Buddha, then surround it with concentric circles or ranks of other divinities emanating from it, all with their appropriate symbols. Some mandalas, particularly Hindu, are abstract, like the well-known Sriyantra displaying the relation of SHIVA and his consort, who represents Shiva's energies and the phenomenal world, in the form of interlocking triangles.

Meditators use mandalas to aid concentration, to clear and steady the mind through the orderly vision of the transcendent world they impart, and above all to prepare one for the Tantric practice of evoking and visualizing deities in meditation. More broadly, mandalas can be thought of as gradated passageways from this world to the supernal realms represented by divine or enlightened beings, as avenues from the particular to the universal, for the god-packed diagrams portray the intermediate, blissful level of reality between this world and Nirvana.

Temples are often constructed in mandala form, with the sacred images positioned to form what might be called a three-dimensional mandala. In the West, C. G. JUNG and his followers have shown considerable interest in the mandala as a symbol of psychological wholeness.     R.E.

**MANI.** *See* MANICHAEISM.

**MANICHAEISM.** A syncretism of Gnosticism, Zoroastrianism, Buddhism, and Hinduism, originating in Persia through the teachings of Mani (about 216-276). Mani, a Persian scholar, received a divine call to preach his religious views when about thirty years old. He journeyed to China and India, and his views spread in the Roman Empire in the fourth and fifth centuries. Augustine of Hippo was a Manichaean for nine years. Mani, whose writings are now lost, was crucified by Persian rival religious factions. Manichaeism posed a universe of good light (spirit) and evil darkness (created world), ruled respectively by God and Satan locked in conflict. It represented human beings as bits of spirit imprisoned in bodies made by Satan. Liberation of the spirit meant salvation. Manichaeism considered sex an evil activity of the body, not of the real person. The Manichaean perfecti, expecting imminent liberation, took vows of vegetarianism and abstinence from sex and flesh. The hearers lived normal lives, expecting to be reincarnated eventually as perfecti and finally liberated with all spirit. They taught that since the body is evil, Christ was never really incarnated. After his Christian conversion Augustine wrote fourteen major works and other pieces against Manichaeism.    C.M.

**MAÑJUŚRĪ.** A BODHISATTVA who embodies insight and wisdom; the object of popular veneration in MAHAYANA BUDDHISM. He is apparently an invention of later Buddhist thought and became popular in writing and art only after the third century A.D. He is depicted as a young man with a five-pointed headdress or tiara. In his right hand he holds a sword for slaying ignorance and in his left hand a copy of the Prajñāpāramita SUTRAS. He has been associated with the mountain Wu-t'ai-shan in Shansi province, northeast China. In Japan he is important only in the TENDAI school. Sometimes Mañjuśrī appears in dreams and meditative visions to help those who seek enlightenment.    K./M.C.

**MANNA.** Of uncertain origin, in Exodus 16.14 it is given a popular etymology *man hu,* meaning, "what is it?" Manna was the miraculous food on which the Israelites were fed during their journey from Egypt into Canaan according to the biblical history of the EXODUS and conquest.

Those who seek a historical reason for the biblical story of the Exodus point to the fact that a desert plant known as the *tamarix mannifera* (named, of course, from the biblical story of the manna) produces, under certain conditions, an edible discharge, which with a certain tolerance could be termed "bread from heaven" (the expression customarily used for the manna in the OT). Whatever may be the "natural" accounting for the manna, it is certain that the vagrant droppings of the tamarisk could never have sustained a sizable population in the desert.

In any case, the later strata of the Pentateuchal history have so enlarged upon the original fact, if fact there was, that there is no possibility of retrieving it for history. The manna, in these acceptations, fell every day except on the Sabbath: on the day before, a double amount would fall, and the manna would rot if it were preserved contrary to ritual prescriptions (Exod. 16:4-8, 22-30). It was a food of infinite taste (Exod. 16:31), a prelude to Wisdom 16:20-21: "providing every pleasure and suited to every taste . . . ministering to the desire of the one who took it . . . changed to suit every one's liking." Here and elsewhere there is no purpose in trying to separate fact from interpretation. "Manna," whatever may have been its beginnings in historical experience, has become a wholly theological note.

In the NT the "bread from heaven" of the OT is contrasted principally in John 6 with the "heavenly bread," which Jesus alone can give. This is Johannine irony, part and parcel of a subtlety that runs throughout the Fourth Gospel. While the manna only (apparently) fell from heaven and sustained natural life only, the bread that Jesus gives is truly heavenly, for it is to heavenly life that it leads.    B.V.

**MANOAH.** This Israelite of the tribe of Dan figures only in connection with the miraculous birth and tragic death of his son Samson. Except for the report in Judges 16:31 that Samson was buried with his father in a tomb somewhere between "Zorah and Eshtaol," Manoah is mentioned only in Judges 13. There we learn that his barren wife received word from a "man of God" that she would conceive and that the son would become a man of destiny (compare Gen. 18:1-15; 21:1-7; I Sam. 1–3; Luke 1–2). In due course Manoah also met "the man of God" who had spoken to his wife (Judg. 13:8-10). After questioning the "man" about the Nazirite discipline into which the son was to be raised, he asked the stranger for his name. When the "man" said, "Why do you ask my name, seeing it is wonderful?" (v. 18), and then ascended on a flame, Manoah knew that it was "an angel of the Lord" (v. 21).    W.S.T.

**MAN OF SIN.** *See* ANTICHRIST.

**MANTRA.** The word mantra, meaning literally "instrument of thought," is used in both HINDUISM and BUDDHISM to indicate verbal formulas—chants, hymns, or words—recited primarily because of the power of the sound itself to evoke spiritual force or to align oneself with a particular deity. In the VEDIC world view, sound was the fundamental constituent of the universe. Sounds that harmonized, as it were, with major lines of force—the great gods and reality itself—could unite one's sacrifice and mind to that same reality. The hymns of the RIG VEDA were such mantras. According to the UPANISHADS, the supreme syllable is *Om,* the sound that evokes BRAHMAN, the universal Sole Reality.

In later devotional Hinduism, mantras with specific references to the great bhaktic gods emerged. In Tantric Hinduism and Buddhism alike, mantras are of immense importance (*see* TANTRISM). Their recitation is usually an essential feature, combined with visualization techniques of evocational meditation—a prominent aspect of the path of Tantric YOGA. Non-Tantric yoga has also found mantra recitation to be of great value in its exercises. On the other hand, the ease with which the simple, nontechnical use of mantras can be pursued has made them prevalent in popular religion as well.

The Tantric Buddhist mantra *Om mani padme hum,* "Hail the jewel in the lotus," is chanted and found on countless prayer flags and prayer wheels wherever Tibetan Buddhism has spread. Characteristically, it has several levels of meaning. The Pure Land Buddhist chant, *Namu Amida Butsu* (Japanese; "Hail Amida Buddha"), is essentially a mantra, and the saving Amida Buddha it invokes is ultimately to be identified with Reality itself.

Apart from its Judeo-Christian parallels, such as the Eastern Orthodox JESUS PRAYER, mantra recitation has found some modern following in the West, especially among practitioners of YOGA and TRANSCENDENTAL MEDITATION.

R.E.

**MANUAL OF DISCIPLINE.** *See* DEAD SEA SCROLLS.

**MANU, LAWS OF.** This work, the *Manavadharmasastra* or *Manu Smrti* in its original Sanskrit, is a very important Hindu legal manual dating from between 200 B.C. and A.D. 100. It is ascribed to Manu, the Hindu primal man. Its twelve chapters span a very wide range of political, ethical, and ritual topics, offering an invaluable insight into classical Hindu society and mentality, as well as delving into such philosophical matters as KARMA and MOKSHA.

In particular, the book establishes clear links between Hindu religious views and society. In part, the Laws of Manu may be a Hindu response to the challenge of BUDDHISM and JAINISM, which tended to undercut belief in such social expressions of HINDUISM as CASTE and sacred kingship by emphasizing liberation as the only significant goal of life. But the Laws of Manu stress observing caste as necessary to the smooth ordering of the world and the gaining of merit for this world and the next rebirth. The problem of reconciling one's obligation to the social order with the quest for individual liberation is dealt with by the doctrine of the four *ashramas,* or stages of life: student, householder, forest-dweller, wandering ascetic. The influence of the Laws of Manu on subsequent Hindu thought and life has been immense. R.E.

**MANUSCRIPTS OF THE BIBLE.** *See* BIBLE, TEXT OF.

**MĀRA.** A demon who represents death in BUDDHISM and HINDUISM; also known as Namuci, the Tempter. In Hinduism, he is a common figure in the VEDAS and the later epic poems. In Buddhist scriptures, he represents the temptations of pleasure and attachment to the world, which lead to death (and endless rebirth). Māra is depicted as tempting Gautama the BUDDHA, trying to lead him away from enlightenment. Mara tried to lead the Buddha into the sensual life of health and comfort involved in Hinduism. The Buddha responded by steadfast dedication to truth and goodness. The Buddha triumphed and achieved enlightenment, but later Māra tempted him again. This time Māra presented the way of asceticism and self-denial. The Buddha rejected this path as ineffective and unworthy and as encouraging attachment to the world. He followed instead the middle way between asceticism and indulgence.

K./M.C.

**MARANATHA.** An Aramaic expression meaning "Our Lord, come!" used by Paul in I Corinthians 16:22. From the *Didache* (or Teaching of the Twelve Apostles) we gather that maranatha was a liturgical expression like the Hebrew "Hosanna" or "Amen." It is probably an invocation or prayer for the Second Coming of Christ.

J.C.

**MARCEL, GABRIEL** (1889–1973). French Catholic philosopher with affinities to EXISTENTIALISM. He was not, however, content with any narrow restriction of philosophy to human existence alone, and his views stand in sharp contrast to those of SARTRE. Human existence, Marcel believed, merges into mystery, a term he used for a reality that can never be grasped objectively or exhaustively, because we ourselves are involved in that reality. The sciences deal with manageable problems, which can be grasped and analyzed, but philosophy treats the mystery of human existence and its place in the scheme of things.

Parallel to the distinction between mystery and problem is that between being and having. The fulfillment of the human being is to be, but we are sidetracked by our concern with having, though in fact the increase of possessions leads to increasing anxiety and is finally enslaving. Marcel differs from Sartre also in his rejection of individualism. Human existence takes place not in the isolated "I" but in the "we," and Marcel stresses the role of engagement and fidelity in encouraging the transcendence and enhancement of human beings. Also, he does not believe that God puts a block in the way of human transcendence but is rather its goal.

He has summarized the connection of his thought in the words "person—engagement—community—reality." We must transcend the limits of a narrowly egocentric existence to join with others, and this

*Assyrian relief of Marduk fighting Tiamat, from Kalakh*

transcendence does not stop short until it arrives at the wider being of God. Marcel's method is to engage in detailed and subtle phenomenological analyses of aspects of human existence, such as hope or fidelity, and to show that these carry ontological implications pointing us in the direction of theism (*see* PHENO-MENOLOGY and ONTOLOGY).                          J.M.

**MARCION** (about A.D. 85–160). Founder of the Marcionite church and compiler of an early NT canon. Born in Sinope, Asia Minor, probably of Christian parentage, Marcion became a rich ship-owner and gave the congregation at Rome a large gift when he joined. Controversy arose when he rejected the OT and preached against Rome's moral laxity. Excommunicated about A.D. 144, he started his own church in Asia Minor. Marcion was Gnostic in outlook, regarding this world and human affairs as evil. According to Marcion a demiurge created this earth, not God. Jesus was not incarnate; he merely seemed to be human. There was no resurrection; the body is evil. Salvation is spiritual liberation from this world. Marcion's followers rejected earthly things, festivities, marriage, meat, wine, and adornment. Only celibates were baptized. Marcion compiled a NT canon consisting of his own *Antitheses* (contrasting the OT to the NT on love, justice, and so forth), an expurgated Gospel of Luke, and ten expurgated letters of Paul. He omitted what did not promote

love. Marcionism flourished, rivaled Rome, but faded in the fifth century when Manichaeism was popular. Marcion forced Christianity to declare a canon and to compose the Apostles' Creed over against GNOSTI-CISM.                                             C.M.

**MARDUK.** The chief god of the Babylonian pantheon. Marduk was the son of the creator god, En-lil, but he rose to the status of king of the gods by leading them to victory over the ocean dragon, Tiamat. Marduk was known to OT writers as Bel and Merodach (Jer. 50:2; see also the Apocryphal addition to Daniel, "Bel and the Dragon").      W.S.T.

**MARI.** An ancient crossroads city on the Euphrates, halfway between Babylon, Harran, and Damascus. It is now known as Tell Hariri. Abraham doubtless passed this way with his flocks en route from Ur to Harran, though the city is not mentioned in the Bible. It flourished between about 3000 and 1700 B.C., and in its heyday was more important than Babylon.

W. F. Albright surveyed the tell for excavation in 1932, and M. A. Parrot began excavating it for the Louvre in 1935. The site sheds significant light on the culture of the patriarchal period. Some of the more significant finds include a huge temple or ziggurat dedicated to ISHTAR, a royal palace of more than three hundred rooms, and a library of twenty thousand

Courtesy of The University Museum, University of Pennsylvania

*Ishtup-ilum, of Mari*

tablets in Sumero-Akkadian. These tablets describe the trade, religion, and customs of Sumeria and remarkably parallel accounts in the OT.

Genesis 11:2 may refer to the culture of Mari when it speaks of men who came from the east and "found a plain in the land of Shinar and settled there," making their buildings of burned brick. Marians were skilled at carpentry, stone carving, masonry, and pottery. They grew grain and fruit. They fished and tended flocks. They brought new techniques of building dams, dikes, and canals, both for irrigation and navigation. They developed high levels of mathematics, astronomy, literature, law, and religion. Mari was a central melting pot between the Indo-European cultures of Persia and India, like those of the Hurrians and Hittites, and their west Semitic neighbors farther up the Fertile Crescent, and Akkadians and Arameans.

Once ruled by the kings of Ur, Mari became independent about 2020 B.C. Hammurabi conquered it in 1765 B.C., but when it tried to regain independence, it was totally leveled.          T.J.K.

**MARIJUANA.** *Cannabis sativa* (Linnaeus, 1753), a weed-like plant, also known as Indian hemp, which grows widely and has psychoactive properties. The first use of hemp as an euphoriant (that is, a drug giving psychological pleasure) is recorded in the *Herbal,* (fourth century B.C.).

Marijuana has been widely used and abused in North America and the West generally since the 1960s, when its use spread from criminals and musicians' circles to college students. Severe legal penalties for its sale have been the rule, although more recent legislation has reduced the punishment for simply using it. A vast literature on the plant exists. In 1971, the Commission on Narcotic Drugs produced a bibliography of two thousand titles and the list still grows. Known popularly as "weed" or "grass," marijuana is connected with hedonism today. Some historical data seem to show the plant was used in mystical religious practices in ancient India.          J.C.

**MARIOLOGY.** *See* BLESSED VIRGIN MARY.

**MARITAIN, JACQUES** (1882–1973). Roman Catholic philosopher, who led the neo-scholastic revival of THOMISM and became one of the foremost contemporary interpreters of Thomas Aquinas. Born in Paris of Protestant parents, he was influenced by Henri Bergson while at the Sorbonne and, with his Jewish wife, Raissa, his close intellectual and spiritual collaborator, was converted to Roman Catholicism by Léon Bloy. Maritain became professor of philosophy at the Institut Catholique de Paris in 1914 and taught also at Toronto, Columbia, Chicago, Notre Dame, and Princeton. His books in English include: *True Humanism* (1938), *A Preface to Metaphysics* (1939), *Existence and the Existent* (1948), *Approaches to God* (1954), *St. Thomas Aquinas* (1958), and *The Degrees of Knowledge* (1959).

Maritain bases his thought on ARISTOTLE and AQUINAS but draws also on the social and physical sciences. The object of human thought is being itself, but metaphysics must not eclipse sense experience in knowing, nor should preoccupation with human existence obscure our relation to the existent, to being, and to God. In moral and social philosophy, Maritain maintains that Christian faith discloses a true humanism fulfilling that which is perceived by natural reason. He strongly affirms democracy as the best political order but believes the inspiration of the gospel is needed. Art for Maritain continues the divine work of creation and will become sterile if, in seeking "pure art," it cuts itself off from experience, nature, and God. Though profoundly intellectual, Maritain remained a very spiritual person who was, like his mentor Bloy, "a pilgrim of the absolute."
          C.Mc.

**MARK, GOSPEL OF.** The earliest of the four Gospels to be written, according to the most generally accepted understanding of the SYNOPTIC GOSPELS and their interrelationships.

*The Traditional View* sees this Gospel as the product of John Mark acting as Peter's interpreter and associate when the Apostle was in Rome, A.D. 65, at the time of Nero's persecution. The simplest way of looking at the Gospel's life setting is to regard it as a deposit of Peter's teaching. Jerome, for example, so regarded it in his celebrated phrase, "Peter spoke, he [Mark] wrote it down"; and more than one commentator has followed C. H. Dodd's lead in viewing the Gospel as an elaboration of the historical details given in Peter's speech in Acts 10:36-43.

In this view the Gospel was put together after Peter's martyrdom, and it stresses, above all, the cost of discipleship, as that price had been paid by the martyrs of the Roman church. Irenaeus, bishop in Gaul (around A.D. 200), wrote, "After their deaths [Peter's, Paul's], Mark, the disciple and interpreter of Peter, himself also handed down to us in writing the things which Peter had proclaimed." The appeal of the Gospel, according to this proposed life setting, is essentially that of a historical narrative, traced back to an eyewitness and intended to convey through this narrative an encouragement to a persecuted church at a time of trial.

*The New Look at Mark's Gospel.* Three sets of inquiry in the present century have combined virtually to demolish this simplistic understanding of Mark's Gospel. They are: (a) the literary analysis of Mark associated with form criticism, which had its avowed object in placing each section (or pericope) of Mark in a suitable life setting in the early church. This analysis suggested that the stories and sayings of Jesus first circulated as small independent units before being brought together into the final edition of the Gospel. Coupled with this approach was the contention that the connecting links or seams that joined the isolated units of Mark's Gospel do not rest on historical reminiscence or geographical or temporal fact, but are editorial additions supplied by the evangelist who often gathered his material on the topical basis of common subject matter, like the collections of "controversy stories" (chaps. 2, 3) or "miracle stories" (chaps. 4, 5).

(b) A second consequence directly followed. The earlier view of Mark's Gospel as a transcript of uninterpreted history gained its support from the use made of the Gospel in the so-called "Life of Jesus" research. The liberal "quest of the historical Jesus," as ALBERT SCHWEITZER chronicled it, set its aim as the recovery of a life of Jesus in history, largely free from miraculous happenings and with a sequence of one event in Gospel history following another in a cause-and-effect pattern. In the hands of some of our modern writers this somewhat naïve understanding of Jesus as a simple Galilean peasant-preacher was shattered, and his image was remade as an apocalyptic herald of a cataclysmic kingdom. Mark's Gospel, with its MESSIANIC SECRET, became a book of profound (Markan) theology in which history was made subservient to a dogmatic theory, namely that only after the Resurrection was the messiahship of Jesus revealed. The liberal portrait of Jesus was shown

to be a piece of idealistic speculation. BULTMANN was to reject all use of Mark as a way of access to the inner life of the historical Jesus.

(c) W. Marxsen brought the form critic's skepticism to a more positive position with an epoch-making theory, which introduced redaction criticism in 1956 with a book on *Mark the Evangelist.* This newer approach to Markan studies had the effect of assessing the role of the evangelist as a theologian in his own right. It saw him less as a faithful scribe and reporter of Petrine memoirs and much more as a theological teacher in the church. To be sure, Mark is thought to have used traditions about Jesus but to have stamped them with his own theological and pastoral imprint, whether by selective emphasis or by editorial adaptation (hence the name redaction or compositional criticism marking a distinct advance on form criticism, which was content to think of John Mark as a faceless, "anonymous" scribe). (*Compare* BIBLICAL CRITICISM.)

These three influences, particularly the advent of redaction criticism, have been generally applauded. There would be scholarly agreement that henceforth Mark must be read as a theological book addressing a set of serious problems in the church of his day. Much less consensus is evident when we press the inquiry about the nature of the catalyst that provoked this Gospel's publication and give a reason for its leading themes.

The agreements are first worth rehearsing. They include the following items: (a) Mark collected a body of isolated paragraphs, and he was the first person we know to have published them in connected sequence to form a narrative of Jesus' life. Mark is usually taken to be the first Gospel to be written. Recent challenges to Mark's priority still lack full persuasive power to overthrow this conviction. (b) The title of "Gospel" (1:1) for his book is also his own creation; he innovated this, since before his time "gospel" meant the oral proclamation of the apostles. (c) The story of Jesus' passion occupies a disproportionate amount of space for a special reason. Evidently Mark wanted to emphasize the "theology of the cross," partly to encourage the martyr church of his own day but chiefly to show how central Jesus' death was in the church's ministry, liturgy, and service, possibly in the face of false ideas current in his time. Marxsen's theory has focused on this unusual but undeniable feature of Mark's storyline: he composed his Gospel "backwards," that is, with the end in view right from the beginning, seen in 1:14; 2:20; 3:6. (d) Mark the evangelist is much more than a historian offering a biography of Jesus (though this term has recently been reclaimed in the light of Hellenistic society's interest in the "lives" of famous persons). Mark stands out preeminently as a theologian whose use of traditional materials to do with Jesus' earthly career served a pointed intention, namely to proclaim the good news—the gospel—in written form. His literary activity raises the fascinating question, What was it that compelled Mark to set down this report of Jesus' ministry as a basis for his preaching of the gospel?

In some new studies the question has been considerably broadened. What kind of person in what kind of primitive Christian group would have been motivated to produce this kind of writing? Answers fall under three main headings.

(a) *Apologetic interest.* Mark is believed to have a concern for his fellow Christians in Syria or Rome who were puzzled over the political events preceding the Jewish war of A.D. 66-73. The apologetic thrust of this Gospel has taken the shape of a philosophy of history offered to sustain the faith of bewildered Christians, upset by the threat of persecution or confused by the claims of nationalist Jews, the Zealots who urged armed rebellion against Rome. Mark's chief retort is to assert Jesus' teaching on the divine kingdom, which is peaceable and yet will soon be established by Jesus' return in power. There is also a revival of interest in Jesus' role as apocalyptic Son of man in this theory.

(b) *Pastoral motives.* The inner life of Mark's church was, in this view, split by faction and strife and was faced by a variety of pressing pastoral needs. These were caused mainly by the tension of Jewish Christian believers in Jerusalem who clung to their association with the earthly family of Jesus and his first disciples. Some have studied Mark to find therein echoes of pastoral disputes centered on missionary preaching and living, family ties and earthly possessions, and above all the claims of a Davidic messianism (10:46-52; 11:10; 12:35-37) and a veneration of the Jerusalem Temple. Peter's role as spokesperson of a "theology of glory," which Mark strongly opposes, has been accentuated and rightly calls our attention to the theological issues that are debated in the various dialogues of this Gospel, especially in 8:27-33.

(c) *Christological disputes.* More promising is the appreciation of Mark's Gospel as a proclamation of the person of Jesus Christ in narrative form. We are to think of his Gospel as refuting false notions of a Davidic messiah or, more adequately, as stressing Jesus' person as truly human, set over against the idea that he was a "divine man" or a Hellenistic magician. His full share in our human life even to death repels the idea of a phantom-like figure cherished by some Christian groups called Gnostics or Docetists (I John 4:2-3). Above all, the picture of Jesus as obedient Son of God and Suffering Servant provided a model for authentic Christian living in terms of self-denial and sacrifice (8:34-37). The last mentioned emphasis brings us to the heart of this Gospel. We are encouraged to read the "good news according to Mark" as a transcript in story form of Paul's teaching of "dying to live" with Christ, whose earthly career is cast by Mark in the pattern of rejection-vindication, a two-beat rhythm also used by Paul in his statements of Christian existence (for example, II Cor. 4:7-12).

R.M.

**MARK, JOHN.** The traditional author of the Second Gospel, based on the earliest known allusion to the Gospel.

*Mark's Association with Peter.* Early church testimony says three things that have formed the substance of much modern debate on the relation of Mark to the Gospel that bears his name. First, it traces back to Peter's teaching one of the sources that Mark used. Then, it remarks that Mark himself had no firsthand knowledge of the sayings or deeds of Jesus but was dependent on eyewitnesses. Third, the information Mark picked up was gleaned in the course of his work as Peter's *hermeneutēs,* "translator" or "interpreter."

Modern discussion has generally been skeptical about PAPIAS' testimony, regarding it as either a fiction or highly biased; but it still has its supporters.

*Mark's Identity in the Early Church.* On a traditional understanding of the evidence, John Mark is the person known to us from the record of Acts (12:12, 25; 13:5, 13; 15:37, 39) and the writings ascribed to Paul (Col. 4:10; Philem. 24; II Tim. 4:11) and Peter (I Pet. 5:13).

On leaving Jerusalem, Mark spent some time with Paul as a member of his team (Acts 13:5). Relations with Paul were later broken off, with some bitterness (Acts 15:39). The result was that BARNABAS, out of loyalty to his cousin Mark, separated from Paul and went off with Mark to Cyprus.

Later Mark was restored to Paul's favor, according to Colossians 4:10, and the tradition reflected in II Timothy 4:11 speaks similarly of a reinstatement to Apostolic service. If this occurred at the time Paul was in Rome, the datum of I Peter 5:13 attests Mark's link with Peter, if that verse is correctly understood as referring to the imperial city.

Later church tradition brought Mark to Alexandria, where he died. At a much later period his memorial was taken to Venice, where he became the patron saint under the figure of a winged lion.

R.M.

**MARK OF CAIN.** According to the primeval legend of Genesis 4, when Yahweh condemned Cain for slaying his brother Abel, Cain cried out, "My punishment is greater than I can bear. . . . I shall be a fugitive and a wanderer on the earth, and whoever finds me will slay me" (Gen. 4:13-14). The Lord then made provision for Cain's safe passage by putting a mark on him and by threatening sevenfold vengeance upon anyone who would slay the marked Cain (v. 15). Since time immemorial, those who study the Bible have speculated on what the protective mark might have been. Extrapolating backward from the customs of modern Bedouins, many scholars now argue that the narrator had a tattoo in mind. If Cain was connected in the popular mind with the Kenites, those original Yahwists who dwelt along the southern borders of Judah (Judg. 1:16), perhaps his mark provided an explanation or etiology for body adornment practiced by that tribe. Be that as it may, like other biblical "marks" (the blood of the Passover lamb on the doorpost of Israel in Egypt, Exod. 12:13; the mark that the Lord commanded Ezekiel to make on the foreheads of the righteous, Ezek. 9:4, 6), this one was designed to ward off evil.                    W.S.T.

## MARKS OF THE CHURCH.
Understood traditionally as unity, holiness, catholicity, and apostolicity, the marks of the church derive from the Nicene Creed, adopted at Nicea (325) and modified at Constantinople (381). The Roman Catholic church claims to be the one true Church of Christ because it possesses these four attributes: unity as a single society professing one faith and in communion with the pope; holiness as imparted by Christ through the Roman Catholic church; catholicity as universality through time and around the world belonging to those in communion with Rome; and apostolicity through the uninterrupted succession of popes from Christ and Peter.

The Lutheran, Reformed, and Anglican traditions affirm the same marks of the church, emphasizing the presence of Jesus Christ in the church as his body that gives unity, holiness, catholicity, and apostolicity. The Anglican interpretation is closer to that of Rome, while Lutheran and Reformed teachings underscore the preaching of God's Word, the right administration of the sacraments, the presence of the Holy Spirit, and the response of faith in the covenant community of Christ. In varying ways, these latter characteristics manifest the marks of the church in free-church and sectarian sectors of Protestantism. (For recent expositions of the marks of the church, see Karl Barth, *Church Dogmatics* and Hans Küng, *The Church*.)                    C.Mc.

## MARRANOS.
A term applied to "new Christians," Jews who were forced to convert by persecutions in Spain and Portugal. Suspected of practicing Judaism in private and Christianity in public, they were targets of the Spanish INQUISITION, a religious court established in 1480 by Ferdinand and Isabella to root out heresy. The property of heretics was confiscated, and they were condemned to various penances. Those who refused to repent were burnt at the stake. In the late 1480s, inquisitors using threats of torture extracted confessions concerning a blood libel (the case of the "infant of La Guardia"—although no corpse was ever discovered), which set the stage for the expulsion of Jews from Spain in 1492.

But not all Marranos were secret Jews. Many were devout Catholics and had no intention of changing their faith; others were religiously ambiguous or apathetic; still others were passive Jews. Eventually they escaped to more tolerant countries, and the secret Jews publicly embraced Judaism. The SEPHARDIM communities of the West were founded mainly by escaping Marranos.                    L.K.

## MARRIAGE.
The union of a man and a woman. In the Bible, marriage also symbolizes the relationship of God and people.

*The Marriage Covenant.* In the Bible, marriage is a COVENANT, a relationship of a special type, entered into by two people. In the ancient Near East there were no hospitals, doctors, police, or paramedics. Each FAMILY, therefore, had to take care of all the needs of each of its members. It was understood that all the members of a family would share whatever they had with any other family member who was in need. All family members would risk their own lives to protect the life of another family member. Thus those who were members of a family knew that they could count on their family to help them whenever necessary. They in return would help family members when necessary. This sort of relationship made life possible in a geographic area where just surviving could be difficult.

But what about the traveler, the person too far from family to be helped by them? Or the young man or woman who married someone in a different family? This is where the covenant came in. The biblical covenant is an agreement between those who have not previously been members of the same family. They agree that they will, from now on, be to each other as family and do for each other as they would for any other family member. The making of such a covenant usually involved the shedding of the blood of an animal, as when Abraham covenanted with God (Gen. 15). This cutting in two of an animal could have the meaning, "May the Lord so do to me if I am not as faithful to you as a brother or sister, parent or child, husband or wife."

The marriage covenant between a man and a woman was that they, who had not been of the same family, would now be family to each other. They would love each other and care for each other, even to the giving of their lives. The families of the bride and groom also covenanted that they would be as family to the newcomer. Thus the lives of the young couple and their children could have stability and permanence.

Faithfulness is also part of the marriage covenant. The prophet Malachi speaks to his people who are complaining that the Lord does not seem to be looking on them favorably. Malachi (2:14) explains to them why this is: "Because the Lord was witness to the covenant between you and the wife of your youth, to whom you have been faithless, though she is your companion and your wife by covenant."

*The Marriage Arrangements.* Planning for the Marriage. When Isaac reached the age to be married, his father, Abraham, was afraid he might marry a Canaanite woman who did not follow the living God. So he asked a servant to go back to their home country to find a wife for Isaac from among their own people (Gen. 24:1-67). This servant was afraid that the young woman would not choose to come with him. "Perhaps the woman may not be willing to follow me to this land," he said. But Abraham assured him that the God who had spoken to him and made promises to him would send an angel to prepare the way. So the servant went to the city of Nahor in Mesopotamia and asked the Lord to give him a sign by having the young woman of the Lord's choosing come to the well and draw water for him. Rebekah came to the well, drew water for him, and invited him to spend the night with her family. When the servant reached her home and explained his mission, Rebekah's family believed this to be the work of the Lord. They were willing that she should go, but they wanted to make sure that she was also willing. They said, "We will call the maiden, and ask her." And they called Rebekah and said to her, "Will you go with this man?" She said, "I will go."

*The Betrothal.* In the NT, Mary is spoken of as a virgin who is betrothed to Joseph: "Now the birth of Jesus Christ took place in this way. When his mother Mary had been betrothed to Joseph, before they came together she was found to be with child of the Holy Spirit" (Matt. 1:18). Luke speaks of her as "a virgin betrothed to a man whose name was Joseph" (1:27). To be betrothed meant to have made an agreement that a marriage would take place in the future. Betrothal was a time of preparation for the marriage.

*The Marriage Ceremony.* A procession often started the festivities. The groom and his family and friends left his home to meet the bride, who was approaching with her family and friends (I Macc. 9:39). Musical instruments and singing may have added to the gaiety (Ps. 78:63). The marriage ceremony might be held in the house of the bride (Gen. 29:22) or of the groom (Matt. 22). The wedding feast often went on for days. Judges 14:12 mentions a wedding feast that lasted seven days. Tobit 8:20 mentions one that lasted two weeks.

*Marriage Customs. Monogamy.* The marriage of one man to one woman seems to be basic in the Bible. The Creation story in Genesis tells of the first marriage in clearly monogamous terms (2:24): "a man leaves his father and his mother and cleaves to his wife." The love of one man for one woman is also celebrated in the Song of Solomon. The Ten Commandments warn against looking beyond one's own marriage toward others (Exod. 20:17): "You shall not covet your neighbor's wife." Leviticus states (20:10) that if a man commits ADULTERY with the wife of his neighbor, both the adulterer and adulteress shall be put to death. The man who serves as a priest must be married to only one woman, a woman who is a virgin at the time of her marriage (Lev. 21:13). Psalm 128 speaks of the happiness of the person who fears the Lord and walks in his ways: "Your wife will be like a fruitful vine within your house. . . . Thus shall the man be blessed who fears the Lord." Proverbs 31:10-31 speaks of the good wife who manages her household well: "She is far more precious than jewels; the heart of her husband trusts in her; . . . strength and dignity are her clothing, and she laughs at the time to come."

All the marriages in the NT seem to be of one man and one woman: Mary and Joseph, Elizabeth and Zechariah, Priscilla and Aquila. A bishop is to be above reproach, the husband of one wife (I Tim. 3:2). Deacons also must be the husband of only one wife (3:12). The writer of I Timothy goes on to warn against those "who forbid marriage . . . which God created to be received with thanksgiving. . . . For everything created by God is good" (4:3-4). The apostle Paul apparently felt that it was best for him to remain unmarried in order that he might devote his time to the furtherance of the gospel. He even expresses a wish that others might do the same (I Cor. 7:7). He apparently spoke in this way because he felt that the Lord might return any day, that there was much to be done to prepare, and that there were many difficult times to get through before that day. He writes (I Cor. 7:26-27): "I think that in view of the impending distress it is well for a person to remain as he is. Are you bound to a wife? Do not seek to be free. Are you free from a wife? Do not seek marriage." But he does encourage those who feel that they should marry to do so (7:9). Paul urges each husband to love his wife as he loves his own body (Eph. 5:28) and each wife to respect her husband (5:33). The writer of Hebrews (13:4) urges, "Let marriage be held in honor among all, and let the marriage bed be undefiled; for God will judge the immoral and adulterous."

*Polygamy.* The Bible also speaks of situations in which a man had more than one wife or had a wife plus CONCUBINES. The dangers of the seminomadic way of life in Israel's early days often resulted in there not being enough men for each woman to have a husband. The wealthier men might therefore take additional wives. This gave them the chance to have more children to love and to be loved by. The children could by their labors further increase the family's well-being. Children were considered a gift of the Lord (Ps. 127:3).

The writer of Genesis (29:9-28) recounts how Jacob worked seven years to gain Rachel as his wife because he loved her, only to find that he had been tricked into marrying her older sister Leah. He then worked another seven years to win his beloved Rachel, and thus had two wives. David, after he had reigned over Judah for seven years, captured the city of Jerusalem from the Jebusites and began to reign over all Israel. At that time, according to the writer of II Samuel (5:13), David added to his household more concubines and wives from the city of Jerusalem. The writer of I Kings (11:3) states that Solomon had seven hundred wives and three hundred concubines. Rehoboam had, according to II Chronicles 11:21, eighteen wives and sixty concubines.

But the practice of having more than one wife was never advocated by biblical writers. Through the prophet Malachi (2:15) the Lord says: "let none be faithless to the wife of his youth." Provisions were made, however, so that when a man did take more than one wife his property might be divided rightfully. Deuteronomy 22:15-17 states that if a man has two wives, one liked and the other disliked, he cannot favor the son of the favored wife to the detriment of the son of the other wife.

*Intermarriage.* Intermarrying with persons who worshiped idols would pose a threat to the covenant relationship of God's faithful people. Abraham was very concerned to secure a wife for his son Isaac from among his faithful kinfolk (Gen. 24:4, 10). Similarly Isaac charged his son Jacob not to marry one of the Canaanite women but to go back to the same kinfolk to find a wife (Gen. 28:1-2). Moses warned the people of Israel that when they entered the Promised Land they must not marry the people there who worshiped false gods (Exod. 34:11-16). When Samson asked his parents to arrange a marriage for him with a Philistine woman, they urged him rather to marry an Israelite woman (Judg. 14:1-4).

Solomon's wives included many foreign women: Moabites, Ammonites, Edomites, Sidonians, Hittites. The Lord had said to his people concerning these nations, "You shall not enter into marriage with them . . . for surely they will turn away your heart after their gods (I Kings 11:1-2). Later, when the people of Israel returned from captivity in Babylon, many men brought with them foreign wives and children. After much deliberation it was agreed that the men must separate themselves from these women and children (Ezra 10:1-44).

In the NT Paul speaks against marrying outside the faith: "Do not be mismated with unbelievers. . . . What has a believer in common with an unbeliever? . . . For we are the temple of the living God; as God said . . . I will be their God, and they shall be my people" (II Cor. 6:14-16). But some people come to faith after their marriage to an unbeliever. In such an instance, Peter advises them, in this case women, to be patient, reverent, and chaste so that their husbands, seeing the work of the Lord in their lives, may also come to faith (I Pet. 3:1-2).

*Levirate Marriage.* If a man died without leaving a child to continue his name, the law of Israel provided that the man's brother should help his widow to gain an heir for him. If the brother refused to do this, he could be called to account by the elders gathered at the gate. The woman so spurned could pull the sandal off his foot and spit in his face (Deut. 25:5-10).

The term "levirate" comes from the Latin word "levir" meaning "husband's brother." An example of the levirate marriage is found in Genesis 38, the story of Tamar and Judah. When Tamar's husband died without leaving any children, her father-in-law Judah ordered another son, Onan, to perform the duty of a brother-in-law. Onan refused, and when she was not given the other brother when he came of age, Tamar tricked Judah into having intercourse with her, and she gave birth to twins, Zerah and Perez.

In the book of Ruth, Naomi seeks to secure a new husband for her widowed daughter-in-law. In this case there are no remaining brothers, so Naomi has her approach a close male relative, Boaz. Boaz, realizing that there is a man even more closely related, speaks to him about making Ruth his wife. When this relative announces that he cannot enter into such a contract with Ruth, Boaz declares that he will marry her. Later they are blessed with a son, Obed, who becomes the father of Jesse, the father of David. It is interesting to note that it is through Perez, the child of the levirate marriage mentioned above, that Boaz himself was born. The line of descendants was: Perez, Hezron, Ram, Amminadab, Nahshon, Salmon, Boaz. It is also interesting to note that through Obed, Boaz's child of a levirate marriage, Jesse, David, and later Jesus the Christ were born. Jesus' life depended on two levirate marriages.

*Marriage as a Symbol of the Lord and People.* Marriage is one of the best ways of describing the relationship that the Lord seeks to have with people. God covenants with us, making us who were no people God's people. God makes us family through the blood of the covenant, through Jesus' gift of himself to us. God promises to do for us all that we need, and calls us to pledge ourselves to the same type of relationship with each other and with God.

Isaiah writes, "your Maker is your husband" (54:5) and adds, "as the bridegroom rejoices over the bride, so shall your God rejoice over you" (62:5). Jeremiah contrasts the desolation of the people that have forsaken the Lord and the Lord's ways with the joy of those related to God who are attending a wedding feast (7:30-34). The Song of Solomon likens the Lord's love for people to that of a newly married young man and young woman: "He brought me to the banqueting house, and his banner over me was love" (2:4).

Jesus tells a parable about marriage (Matt. 22:1-14) in which he says, "The kingdom of heaven may be compared to a king who gave a marriage feast for his son." The dinner is made ready, but when those who are invited do not appear, the king sends out his servants into the streets to compel others to come in. Jesus also compares the kingdom of God to ten young women who were to provide light for the wedding procession (Matt. 25:1-12). Five were prepared but five were not. Like some of the guests in the previous parable, those who were unprepared were excluded from the great marriage feast.

*Conclusion.* In the OT the prophet Hosea is called by God to marry a woman who proceeds to be unfaithful to him. He entreats her to return to their marriage covenant, but she prefers to go her own way. The Lord says that Israel is like an adulterous marriage partner. Though God has loved them tenderly, they have strayed far away. As they continue to wander, God continues to call them back. Because of their wickedness God withdraws from them, waiting for them to acknowledge their guilt and seek God's face, waiting for them to say, "Come, let us return to the Lord" (Hos. 6:1). Then the Lord says, "I will heal their faithlessness; I will love them freely" (14:4).

In the NT, Paul says to the people of the church in Corinth, "I betrothed you to Christ to present you as a pure bride to her one husband. But I am afraid that as the serpent deceived Eve by his cunning, your thoughts will be led astray from a sincere and pure devotion to Christ" (II Cor. 11:2-3). In the book of Revelation, John likens the coming of Christ to be united with his people, the church, to a great wedding feast: "Let us rejoice and exult and give him the glory, for the marriage of the Lamb has come, and his Bride has made herself ready" (19:7). The angel said, "Blessed are those who are invited to the marriage supper of the Lamb" (19:9). Thus, in his kingdom, the marriage of Christ and his people takes place, his new and joyous creation.

B.J.

**MARS.** Ancient Roman god, protector of the city. By historical times he was considered the god of war and identified with the Greek god Ares. The cult of Mars flourished under the emperors, who made him their personal guardian. The festivals of Mars fell in the months of March (named for him) and October.

K./M.C.

**MARS HILL.** *See* AREOPAGUS.

**MARTHA.** A woman who, along with her sister Mary, had a brief encounter with Jesus, according to Luke's Gospel (10:38-42). The sisters lived in Bethany and were dear friends of Jesus. They witnessed Jesus' raising of their brother Lazarus from death, narrated in the Gospel of John (11:1–12:8).

According to both accounts, Martha was a no-nonsense, domestic type, a responsible hostess who busied herself to meet the physical needs of her remarkable guest (Luke 10:40; John 12:2). Her sister Mary, a contemplative type, subordinated all other interests to give rapt attention to Jesus' teaching. Consistent with her nature, Martha leaves the scene of the sisters' bereavement to welcome Jesus and to explain events surrounding the death of their brother. In visiting his tomb she warns that the decomposing body will add unpleasantness to sorrow (John 11:39).

The Fourth Gospel notes that Jesus loved Martha as he loved Mary and Lazarus (John 11:5). He didn't disparage Martha's practical interests, nor slight her hospitality; but neither should Martha disparage Mary's choice. Jesus would not rebuke her for not helping in the kitchen (Luke 10:41-42). A question deserving discussion: does John represent Martha's confession as being fully adequate, or is her faith, like that of his disciples, incomplete until the event and proclamation of Jesus' resurrection? (John 11:21-27 and 16:26-33; also 20:30-31).

J.L.P.

**MARTIN, CIVILLA DURFEE** (1867–1948). Gospel hymn writer. Civilla Martin, wife of Dr. W. Stillman Martin, a Baptist evangelist, usually accompanied her husband on his preaching tours. When they were visiting an invalid couple in Elmira (N.Y.), by the name of Doolittle, Dr. Martin asked them how they endured twenty years of illness. Mrs. Doolittle answered: "His eye is on the sparrow, and I know He watches me." Soon after, Mrs. Martin wrote the words of "His Eye Is on the Sparrow." A native of Nova Scotia, Mrs. Martin had collaborated with Dr. Martin to write the hymn "God Will Take Care of You." She wrote the words, and her husband composed the music.

R.H.

**MARTIN OF TOURS** (about A.D. 317–397). Patron saint of France; he was born at what is now Szombathely, Hungary. A member of the Roman army as his father had been, he gave half his cloak to a naked beggar, whom he then recognized as Christ. He was baptized, and about A.D. 339, he petitioned Julian the Apostate to be released from army service.

He settled in Poïtiers under the guidance of Hilary. He was a missionary to the Balkan Peninsula, he opposed the Arians who forced his retreat. In 360 he rejoined Hilary and founded a community of hermits at Liguge, the first monastery in Gaul.

In about 371 he was made bishop of Tours, but he lived in a monastery he founded at Marmoutier outside the city. He opposed the execution of Bishop Priscillian of Avila, Spain, by the imperial court about 385, raising important questions of church and state. His feast day is November 11. He was one of the first non-martyrs venerated as a saint. His biographer was Sulpicius Severus.

N.H.

**MARTYR.** The English word is a transliteration of the Greek word meaning "witness." The word is used in Acts 1:8 of the apostles as witnesses to Christ's life and resurrection. But as PERSECUTION spread, the term became reserved for those whose witness for their faith had cost them their lives. Those who were persecuted and survived were called confessors.

The first martyr was the deacon Stephen (Acts 7:54-60). Then James the Apostle was executed by Herod Agrippa, who ruled A.D. 41–44. The age of the martyrs as classically understood closed with Constantine's adoption of Christianity in 324, though the classic *Foxe's Book of Martyrs* centers on the English Reformation.

Early Christians embraced martyrdom, believing that it would aid the Christian cause and that they would be spared the agonies of death (see the letters of Ignatius). Martyrs soon became venerated as powerful intercessors before God. Their bones and other relics were used to sanctify places of worship. Accounts of their lives, often embellished with legend, were popular forms of devotional literature. The formal origins of the cult of martyrs can be traced to a custom begun in Smyrna about A.D. 156, commemorating the death of Polycarp with a celebration at his tomb.

N.H.

**MARX, KARL** (1818–83) **AND MARXISM.** In all its varieties, Marxism derives in differing degrees from the teachings of Karl Marx, German philosopher, economic theorist, socialist, and professed revolutionary. Through political movements influenced by his thought, Marx and Marxism rank among the most powerful forces in the twentieth century. Communist movements represent both a continuation and an extension of Marx's ideas, and most socialist movements of the contemporary period bear the imprint of his views.

*Life of Marx.* Karl Heinrich Marx was born in Trier, in the German Rhineland, on May 5, the second child and oldest son of Heinrich and Henrietta Marx. After the defeat of Napoleon, the Rhineland had been given by the Congress of Vienna to Prussia. Marx's family had been Jewish, and his father had been born Herschel Levi, son of Rabbi Marx Levi. Under the influence of the Enlightenment and a rationalist education, Herschel Levi, a lawyer, left that heritage behind and changed his name to Marx. In the wake of the Prussian anti-Jewish statutes of 1816, to avoid being denied the right to practice law, he joined the Lutheran Church in 1817, the year before Karl was born, and changed his first name to Heinrich.

A neighbor, Freiherr Ludwig von Westphalen, befriended Karl in his teen years, contributed to his rapid intellectual development, and eventaully gave the hand of his daughter Jenny to Karl in marriage. In 1835, Marx became a law student at the University of Bonn, and the following year transferred to the University of Berlin. There he came under the spell of HEGEL's philosophy, the most important intellectual influence of his life. In 1841, he received a doctorate from the Univesity of Jena, with a thesis on Epicurus and Democritus dedicated to von Westphalen. After his marriage to Jenny von Westphalen in 1843 and the suppression of the *Rheinische Zeitung,* which he edited, Marx went into exile in Paris, where he began a lifelong friendship with Friedrich Engels, became a dedicated social radical, and embarked upon a career as a revolutionary publicist.

His *Economic and Philosophic Manuscripts of 1844* provide a sketch of the historical materialism that he would elaborate in later writings. Expelled from France in 1845, Marx moved to Brussels. There he made his first contacts with actual movements of working people, and, at the request of a laborers' league, Marx and Engels wrote the *Communist Manifesto* (1848) as a critical analysis of capitalism and false socialisms and as a call to revolutionary action. Expelled from Brussels, Marx returned to Paris and then to Cologne. Arrested for sedition, Marx was expelled from Germany and went to London, where he spent the remainder of his life. Throughout the London years, his only regular work was for a brief period when he wrote articles for the New York *Tribune.* For the most part, he and his family lived in poverty, supported by gifts from Engels with funds from family textile interests and made bearable by the courageous sacrifices of Jenny Marx.

Karl Marx spent most of his time in the British Museum writing political pamphlets and doing research for his analysis of capitalism, *Das Kapital.* He was able to complete and publish (in 1867) only the first volume of this massive undertaking before his death. Engels completed the work, publishing the second volume in 1885 and the third volume in 1894.

Jenny died of cancer in 1881. Karl Marx died in London on March 14, 1883. In the eulogy at his funeral, Engels said: "His mission in life was to contribute in one way or another to the overthrow of capitalist society . . . to contribute to the liberation of the present-day proletariat. . . . Fighting was his element. And he fought with a passion, a tenacity which few could rival . . . and consequently was the best-hated and most calumniated man of his time. . . . He died beloved, revered and mourned by millions of revolutionary fellow workers from the mines of Siberia to the coasts of California, in all points of Europe and America. . . . His name and his work will endure through the ages."

*The Marxism of Karl Marx.* At the core of Marx's teaching is the theory of dialectical or historical materialism. The material conditions of human life and the basic modes of production provide the context shaping decisively other aspects of consciousness and society. The struggle between oppressors and oppressed occurs in every era. The dialectic appears today as the class conflict between capitalism and the proletariat, a conflict that of necessity produces revolution and change. The conflict is rooted in economic realities. Goods are priced on the basis of the labor going into their production, a view called the labor theory of value. Workers, however, are paid on a subsistence level, and the additional value created by the workers' labor is kept by the capitalists. This exploitation of workers by the ruling class will be overcome through revolution and the establishment of a socialist state.

*Marxism Today.* The continuing influence of Marxism is exhibited in the Communist parties around the world, in nations where the Communist party controls the government, in socialist parties and governments, and in the impact of Marxist teaching on such movements as Christian LIBERATION THEOLOGY.

As one of the most dynamic and powerful currents of the twentieth century, Marxism provides the central teaching for political parties in many nations of the world. Whether legal or underground, these Communist parties are a major force in shaping the political alternatives for contemporary societies in the industrialized world and in the Third World.

As represented in the Communist parties of the

Soviet Union and the People's Republic of China, Marxism informs the rulers of two of the most populous and important nations of the world today, as well as the governments in their spheres of influence. In the Soviet Union, the form of Marxism providing the basis of the Communist party is the extension and revision of Marxian teaching known as Leninism. In the People's Republic of China, Marxism rose to power in the version known as Maoism and continues in pragmatic revisions of Maoist doctrine.

Through a great variety of thinkers and political leaders, Marxism has had decisive though differing influences on socialist movements around the globe. Socialism existed before Marx, and many socialist movements and political parties arose with little or no relation to Marxian teaching. Even where the overall historical and philosophical views of Marx are not accepted, his economic analysis and social goals have influenced socialist thought and programs.

More recently Marxism has emerged as an important influence on Christian liberation theologies. It is particularly surprising and noteworthy that Marxist economic and social analysis has found a receptive hearing among theologians of the Roman Catholic Church, which in the past had a strong aversion to most forms of socialism and has regarded Communism as a dangerous enemy of Christian faith. The influence of Marxism on Protestant Christian liberation theologians is less surprising in the light of Christian socialist movements related to Protestant groups in many countries of Europe and America and the use made of Marxist thought by SOCIAL GOSPEL leaders and by such neo-orthodox thinkers as Karl Barth and Reinhold Niebuhr. The crucial issue in the relation of Marxism to Christian liberation theologies—Catholic or Protestant, black or feminist, first world or Third World—is whether Marxist analysis is used within biblical Christian faith for prophetic critique of social injustice or whether Marxist historical and philosophical views have displaced the overall Christian perspective.      C.M.

**MARY.** Since the name Mary is derived from Miriam, the sister of Moses and Aaron (Exod. 15:20), it was widely used among Jews throughout history. At least four women of that name appear in the NT, in addition to the mother of Jesus (Mark 6:3; Luke 1:27). All four Gospels picture women by the name of Mary among the faithful followers of Jesus, who witness his Crucifixion and then go to the tomb to prepare his body for proper burial after the Sabbath has passed, since only then was such labor of love permitted by Jewish law. It is they who go to anoint him (Mark 16:1; Luke 24:10), and who in one or more of the Gospels meet the Lord, risen from the dead (Matt. 28:9; John 20:1-18). In addition, women by this name are described as followers of Jesus (Luke 8:2), as cordial hostesses to Jesus on his journeys (Luke 10:38-42), as special beneficiaries of his miraculous powers (John 11), and as the mother

of Mark, one of Paul's associates (Acts 12:12-25).

The Mary of whom we hear the most is Mary Magdalene. This designation derives from her place of origin, Magdala, a city on the western shore of the Sea of Galilee. She is linked in the Gospel accounts with Mary, the mother of "James the Younger" (Mark 15:40, meaning that he was younger or of lesser rank than another James). These women, together with another named Salome, had been followers and supporters of Jesus from the days of his activity in Galilee (Mark 15:41). In Luke 8:2-3 Mary Magdalene is listed along with women having connections with the Herodian administration who provide from their financial means to support Jesus' itinerant ministry of preaching and healing. The other Mary's son is named Joses, or in some ancient manuscripts, Joseph. Since the list of Jesus' brothers in Mark 6:3 includes both these names, some scholars have inferred that this Mary was actually Jesus' mother. The evidence is complicated by the fact that in John 19:25, the witnesses at the cross include Jesus' mother and her sister, who is called "Mary the wife of Clopas." It is not very likely that the mother of Jesus would have a sister by the same name, athough curiously John never mentions the name of Jesus' mother. On the other hand, only John describes her as present at the Crucifixion and the empty tomb. The common element in the Gospel tradition is that Mary Magdalene and another Mary had been his supporters in Galilee and continued to serve in this way until his death and burial (Mark 15:40, 47; 16:1; Matt. 27:56, 61; 28:1, 9; Luke 24:10; John 19:25; as elsewhere and especially John 20:1-18). Only Luke (8:2, followed by the late unauthentic ending of Mark 16:9) adds the detail that Mary Magdalene had demons expelled from her by Jesus.

Almost certainly the village where Mary and Martha make their home (according to Luke 10:38-42) is Bethany (John 11:1-45). There the sisters wait in vain for Jesus to come across the Jordan and heal their desperately ill brother, Lazarus. His delay becomes the occasion for raising Lazarus from the dead. In Luke's narrative, Mary takes her place in Christian history as the one who has her priorities straight: she values more highly learning from Jesus than providing him the hospitality demanded by Middle Eastern custom.

     H.K.

**MARY, MOTHER OF JESUS.** Mary, the young maiden or VIRGIN chosen by God to be the mother of Jesus Christ (Luke 1:26-38; 2:7-14; Matt. 1:18-25). She may equally be descended from David with Joseph, although the genealogies in Matthew and Luke trace Jesus' descent from David only through Joseph. After Jesus' birth, in the Protestant view, Mary and Joseph led a normal married life in which they produced a number of children (Acts 1:14). Jesus is, after all, referred to as Mary's firstborn son in Luke 2:7. Between the angelic announcement of Jesus' coming miraculous birth and the nativity, the scripture is clear that Joseph and Mary were married in name only.

Mary is mentioned throughout the Gospel story: at Jesus' circumcision; his visit to the Temple at the age of twelve; at the wedding at Cana; during his preaching ministry (where she and Jesus' brothers and sisters are rebuked for not believing in Jesus' mission); and at the Crucifixion, where she is given into the care of John by the dying Lord (John 19:25-27). In Acts, Mary is part of the apostolic group gathered in the upper room (Acts 1:14).

Gradually, the early church developed a devotion to Mary as the virgin mother of Christ that tended to increase in depth and scope over time. She was venerated because of the worshipful awe in which the God-man, the Christ, was held by believers. Much of this religious awe came to attach itself to the BLESSED VIRGIN MARY, who was the earthly means by which Christ entered the world. In the fourth century A.D., the Western church declared it a heresy to teach that Mary had other children by Joseph, after Jesus' birth. Numerous legendary stories arose glorifying Mary, and several apocryphal "gospels" concerning her were composed and circulated. By the end of the fourth century, a cult of devotion to Mary arose, quite probably due to the large accessions of pagans to the now-established Catholic church. These former pagans were familiar with mother-goddesses, and there is some similarity in the devotion of women to Mary to the ancient worship of the goddess.

J.C.

**MARY, QUEEN OF SCOTS** (1542–87). Mary Stewart, daughter of James V and Mary of Guise, became queen when she was one week old. Her life was lived amidst warring factions, English and French, Protestant and Catholic.

At HENRY VIII's death, Somerset, hoping to unite England and Scotland by marrying young Edward VI to Mary, invaded Scotland. This angered the Scots, who sent Mary at age six to France and eventually married her to the dauphin, Francis II, who became king of France in 1559. In 1554 her mother became regent, surrounding herself with French advisors. John Knox returned from exile in 1559 and strengthened Protestant positions. Since Mary laid legitimate claim to the English throne, ELIZABETH I invaded Scotland, expelled Mary of Guise, and encouraged Parliament to repudiate the authority of the pope, abolish the Mass, and adopt a confession of faith written by Knox.

By the time Mary returned to Scotland in 1561, following the deaths of her mother and her husband, the country was firmly in the control of Protestants allied with England. Although she agreed to tolerate the new religious state of affairs, she alienated her subjects by attending a private Mass. Then despite English pressure to marry Robert Dudley, Earl of Leicester, in 1565 she suddenly married her cousin

Henry Stuart, Lord Darnley, also in line for the English throne since both were great-grandchildren of Henry VII. Their son James VI of Scotland became JAMES I of England. In 1567 Darnley was assassinated, some thought by the Earl of Bothwell, whom Mary then married. An uprising of the Protestant lords followed.

Mary was imprisoned, and in late 1567 she was forced to abdicate. She escaped and fled to England. Elizabeth I, fearing for the security of her throne, kept Mary in captivity. After Mary was implicated in the Babington Plot against Elizabeth, she was executed on February 8, 1587.

N.H.

**MARYKNOLL FATHERS.** The more popular name of the Catholic Foreign Mission Society of America, Inc., a society of brothers and secular priests established by the archbishops of the United States and approved by Pope Pius X in 1911. The Congregation of Maryknoll Sisters is an order whose work and aims are similar to those of the Maryknoll Fathers. The first four missionaries left for China in 1918. The work grew rapidly, spreading to Korea, Japan, Manchuria, and the Philippines. Work began after the Second World War in Latin America and Africa. A heavy emphasis in the work of the Maryknoll Fathers and Sisters is placed on social service work, educational institutions, and the operation of cooperatives and credit unions designed to bring up the level of life in the communities in which they work. The society accepts members from the United States and attempts to build up an indigenous clergy to whom the work of the Maryknoll Fathers can be transferred.

W.G.

**MARY TUDOR** (1516–58; "Bloody Mary"). Queen of England from 1553 to 1558. The daughter of HENRY VIII and his first wife, Catherine of Aragon, Mary was declared illegitimate in 1534, after Henry divorced her mother. She was excluded from succession on the birth of Elizabeth, but in 1544 she was given second place in line after Edward VI.

She succeeded to the throne on July 19, 1553, after the death of Edward and only after the failure of an abortive attempt to put Lady Jane Grey on the throne. Her 1554 marriage to Philip II of Spain was opposed by her subjects and precipitated Wyatt's Rebellion. Until then she had been tolerant of her Protestant subjects, though proscribing their religion. But in 1555, Cardinal Reginald Pole reconciled England to the papacy, and heresy trials began. Four bishops were eventually burned, and about 270 others executed. Philip, never a devoted husband, left her after his campaign against France failed in 1557. They had no children. A swelling, which she thought to be a pregnancy, turned out to be a fatal malignancy.

N.H.

**MASADA.** A historically famous fortress on the top of a mountain in the Judean desert overlooking the Dead Sea. It was on Masada that Jewish patriots made their last heroic stand in the Roman-Jewish War, which began in A.D. 66. The immediate cause of the hostilities was a conflict over the respective rights of Jews and the pagans in Caesarea, the headquarters of

Courtesy of Paul Gross

*Masada, Herod's rock fortress close to the Dead Sea*

Courtesy of the Israel Exploration Society (*Masada* by Yigael Yadin)

*One of the large cisterns, excavated from solid rock, which supplied water to Masada. Sunbeam is coming through a hole through which water filled the cistern; staircase is on the right*

Courtesy of the Israel Government Tourist Office, Houston, Texas

*Masada, where Jewish Zealots in A.D. 73 chose suicide rather than surrender to Roman troops*

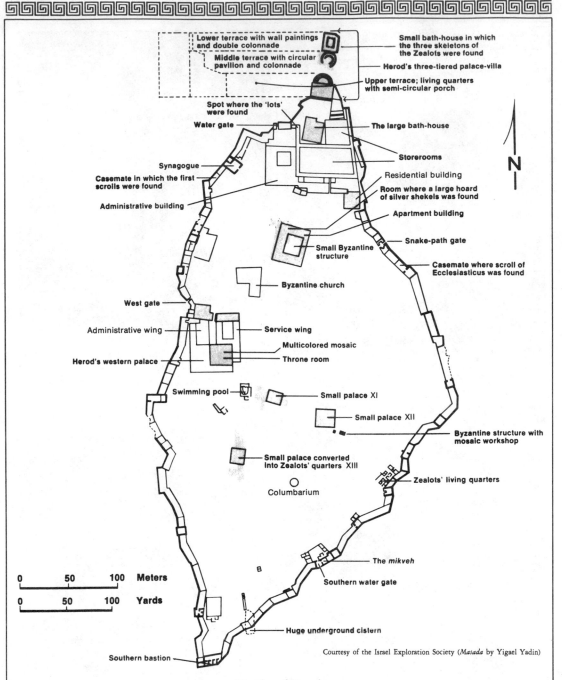

*Site plan of Masada*

Courtesy of the Israel Exploration Society (*Masada* by Yigael Yadin)

the Roman administration in Judea. Provoked by the Roman administrator Florus, who permitted his troops to pillage Jerusalem and crucify a number of prominent Jews, the Jewish patriots killed pro-Roman Jews and members of the Roman garrison in Jerusalem. In August of A.D. 66 the patriots halted sacrifices in behalf of the emperor, an act tantamount to a declaration of war. In October, the governor of Syria marched to Jerusalem and laid siege to the Second Temple. Meeting fierce resistance, he retreated. In the same mountain passes where the MACCABEAN REVOLT had won its first victories, the Jews mauled the Roman forces, and Judea was left free of Roman soldiers.

But the Romans had might on their side. By the end of A.D. 67, Jewish resistance in Galilee and northern Transjordan was crushed. The Roman general VESPASIAN subjugated southern Transjordan, western Judea, and Idumea, as well as Samaria and Jericho. All that was left in Jewish hands were Jerusalem, its environs, and several Herodian fortresses. Vespasian, one of three generals elevated to the throne, appointed his son TITUS as head of the Judean campaign. In April of A.D. 70, Titus set up camp outside the walls of Jerusalem. Jerusalem was in the hands of the Jewish Zealots, who had overthrown the moderate government during the winter of A.D. 67–68. The siege by the Romans lasted from April to September. During the fighting on August 28, the Temple went up in flames. After all resistance ceased, Titus ordered Jerusalem razed, except for the towers of Herod's palace. He arranged celebrations in various cities, highlighted by throwing Jewish prisoners to wild animals and forcing them to fight in gladiator shows. In A.D. 71 Titus and Vespasian crowned their victory with a triumphal procession in Rome. But it took the Romans several more years to capture the remaining fortresses. Masada, the last to hold out, fell in April of A.D. 74. When the Romans breached the wall on top of the mountain, they found that the defenders had committed suicide rather than be taken captive.

Masada has become a symbol of Jewish heroism.

L.K.

**MASHHAD.** (1) The shrine at the grave of an IMAM who SHI'ITES believed died a martyr *(shahid)*. Since all of the imams were persecuted or killed by the CALIPHS of SUNNI Islam, there are many such shrines. The first and most important is that of the second imam Husayn, the son of Ali, who was murdered by the forces of the Umayyad Caliph Yazid I at Karbala (Iraq) in A.D. 680. The shrines are the objects of annual pilgrimages, during which ritual salutations *(ziyara)* are performed. The pilgrimage to Karbala is of such importance that, in years of strife with the Sunnis, it has been a substitute for the pilgrimage (HAJJ) to Mecca.

(2) A city in northern Iran; burial place and shrine of Harun al-Rashid (died in A.D. 809) and his son-in-law, the imam Ali al-Rida. (*See also* ABBASSID CALIPHS.) K./M.C.

**MASLOW, ABRAHAM** (1908–70). An American psychologist best known for his studies in motivation. His doctoral dissertation at the University of Wisconsin, a study of simians, affirmed that dominance is usually established by visual contact without any need to fight. This research was so carefully done that no further work was begun on the subject for thirty years.

Maslow's work on motivation was first enunciated in *A Theory of Human Motivation* (1943). He established a hierarchy of motives, based on needs. He distinguished these in order as: physical (food), safety (security, freedom from anxiety), belonging (being accepted), and esteem (achievement). He later (1950)

added "self-actualization." The self-actualized person has cognitive and aesthetic goals. Such people have "a more efficient perception of reality and a more comfortable relation to it." Maslow also affirmed that, for most people, some satisfaction of "lower" needs (physical, safety, and belonging) needed to be met before they could work toward the needs for esteem and self-actualization. He coined the phrase "peak experiences" to describe high moments in life that came to self-actualized persons. They feel less need to conform to expected norms and to have more identity with humanity. He linked this kind of life experience to religion in the book *Religions, Values, and Peak Experiences* (1964). I.C.

**MASON, LOWELL** (1792–1872). American hymn composer and musical editor; regarded by many as the greatest single influence upon Protestant church music in the nineteenth century. Born on January 8 in Medfield, Massachusetts, as a young man (1812) he served as a bank clerk in Savannah, Georgia. He played the organ, led the choir in the Independent Presbyterian Church, and helped develop the Sunday school in that city. He also found time to study under a capable German musician, Frederick L. Abel. He collected a number of psalm and hymn tunes, which were published in 1832 by the Boston Handel and Haydn Society Collection of Church Music. The book was a success, and Mason moved to Boston, where he became a leader there in both public school and church music. In 1838 he introduced music in the curriculum of Boston public schools. He also led the choir in Bowdoin Street Church, where Lyman Beecher was the minister. Mason, active in the Handel and Hadyn Society, founded the Boston Academy of Music. Some of the best known of Mason's hymn tunes were "Nearer, My God, to Thee," "My Faith Looks Up to Thee," "From Greenland's Icy Mountains," "When I Survey the Wondrous Cross," and one of the tunes to "More Love to Thee, O Christ." R.H.

**MASORETES.** Without the work of these "transmitters" (from the Aramaic term *mesorah*, "to hand down, transmit") the ancient books of the HEBREW BIBLE would never have reached us in the full and comprehensible form in which we have them. Beginning about A.D. 500, the Masoretes carried on the scribal tradition of scrupulous reproduction of the sacred texts accompanied by supporting grammatical and critical notes. But the Masoretes did not merely continue to copy texts, for they were innovators as well. In their centers in Tiberias in Palestine and in Sura and Nehardea in Babylon, they began to write down the textual notations that they had received from the past in oral form and to enlarge upon them. Their notes were inserted in the margins and at the top and bottom of the columns on a scroll, and at the end of a book. Although the Masoretes were disinclined to emend the received form of the consonantal text, they indicated known corruptions by raising letters, writing one letter smaller than the rest, putting dots over words, or simply by putting the correct reading in the margin. In at least twenty places, the so-called *tiqqune-soferim*, "the corrections of the scribes," they actually changed a text, usually on dogmatic grounds. In Genesis 18:22, for example, the text originally read, "But Yahweh still stood before Abraham"; the Masoretes found that picture theologically objectionable and changed the text to read, "But Abraham still stood before Yahweh."

Perhaps the most significant single contribution of the Masoretes to the textual preservation of the Hebrew Bible was their development of a system of vowels that could be superimposed upon the hitherto strictly consonantal Hebrew text. This system of vocalization enabled a reader to reproduce accurately all types of vowel sounds, even murmured ones, in a language that was no longer anyone's vernacular. Different types of notations were developed in Babylon and in Tiberias, but ultimately the Tiberian system of the Masoretic family of ben Asher prevailed. The last member of the ben Asher family, Aaron ben Moshe ben Asher, was the copyist of the oldest full manuscript of the Hebrew Bible still extant. Dating from the first half of the tenth century A.D., this Aleppo Codex is now at the Hebrew University of Jerusalem, and is the basis of a new critical edition of the Masoretic text of the Hebrew Bible, which is now being issued.                                          W.S.T.

**MASS.** This term is derived from the Latin word *missa* for the celebration of the Lord's Supper or Holy Communion in the Roman Catholic church. The EUCHARIST or Communion is the main focus of all Christian worship and is especially characteristic of the Roman Catholic church. According to the Council of Trent (sixteenth century), the bread and wine used in the Mass are miraculously transfigured into the actual Body and Blood of Jesus Christ, except for the surface appearance of the elements. This is known as TRANSUBSTANTIATION. In recent decades some Catholic theologians have moved to other terms to explain this central mystery of faith.

The Mass includes the Eucharist, which is a SACRAMENT by which God's GRACE is conveyed to human beings. It is also a sacred meal, although the Communion has been only a symbolic meal since the end of the first century A.D. The whole action of public worship in the Mass is called the sacrifice of the Mass.

The Mass is divided into the Liturgy of the Word, which involves OT and NT readings, the Gospel, and the Creed. Then follows the Liturgy of the Eucharist. Here the offertory, the canon, and the Communion itself take place. In the canon, the priest recites the rite of consecration, and in the Communion the priest (and lay ministers of the Eucharist) distributes the elements.                                          J.C.

**MASSA.** The seventh of Ishmael's twelve sons (Gen. 25:14; I Chr. 1:30). Because Israel believed that Ishmael was the father of the Arab tribes (see Ezek. 27:21), we can assume that the Priestly authors of this genealogy knew Massa as a North Arabian clan. So did the Assyrian king Tiglath-pileser III, who lists it in his annals as one of his tributary nations.
W.S.T.

**MASSACHUSETTS BAY COLONY.** During the 1620s, groups of English people founded several small communities in Massachusetts, north of Plymouth and independent of the Pilgrims, most notably SALEM, which was founded in 1626. The sizable influx of landowners and merchants arriving during the next decade wanted to purify the Church of England, not to separate from it.

In 1629 Charles I chartered the Massachusetts Bay Colony with authority to trade and colonize between the Charles and Merrimack rivers. Members of the company organized about a thousand emigrants to found a PURITAN commonwealth. A group arriving in 1630 joined with earlier settlers to found Boston. The charter and administration was transferred to America with Governor JOHN WINTHROP and his court of assistants responsible to a general court of stockholders. By 1640 there were fifteen thousand settlers.

A strict theocracy designed to be a "light on a hill," the colony was riddled with theological disputes in the 1630s, with ROGER WILLIAMS leaving for Rhode Island, THOMAS HOOKER for Connecticut, and ANNE HUTCHINSON for Long Island.

The original charter was revoked in 1684. From 1686 to 1689 Massachusetts and Plymouth became part of the Dominion of New England. A new charter in 1691 joined it to the Maine territory and ended the theocracy, though the Congregational Church was not formally separated from state government until 1833.                                          N.H.

**MATERIALISM.** A philosophy that holds that matter is the primary or only reality, mind and will being dependent upon and reducible to physical causes and processes. Materialism opposes philosophies that assert that there are spiritual beings, gods, or powers at work in the world. It also opposes idealism, which reduces matter to mind. Since materialism teaches that everything can, in principle, be explained by physical causes and conditions, materialists have usually been determinists, insisting that there is a physical cause for every event.

Materialism was taught by some of the early Greek philosophers, including the atomists Leucippus and Democritus (fifth century B.C.), who sought to explain all things through the movement of material atoms. Epicurus (342–270 B.C.) taught that nothing comes from nothing and that composed bodies are the result of the collision of simple atoms in motion. Lucretius developed Epicurean materialism in his poem *De rerum natura (On the Nature of Things)*, which argued against the immortality of the soul and thereby sought to assuage the religious fear of the gods and of death. In the seventeenth and eighteenth centuries, philosophers such as Thomas Hobbes and the Frenchmen La Mettrie, Diderot, and d'Holbach championed materialism and applied it to human psychology. Materialist ideas were given further impetus with the rise in popularity of DARWINISM in the nineteenth century, and of materialist biology, biochemistry, and cybernetics in this century. The dialectical materialism of MARX and Engels shares with classical materialism its belief in one reality, matter, and its claim that all true knowledge derives from the natural sciences. However, Marxism rejects extreme forms of mechanistic materialism and allows for genuine dialectical or historical openness and progress.

J.L.

**MATHER, COTTON** (1663–1728). Puritan cleric and historian. He was born February 12, 1663, to Increase and Maria Cotton Mather, grandson to Richard Mather and John Cotton. He enrolled in Harvard at age twelve, the youngest student ever admitted, and graduated in 1678. He became assistant to his father at Second Church, Boston, which he served until his death February 13, 1728. He received an M.A. from Harvard in 1681 and was ordained in 1685. In 1686 he married Abigail Phillips.

In all he wrote about 450 books. Against royal Governor Edmund Andros he wrote *The Declaration of Gentlemen . . .* (1689). *Memorable Providences Relating to Witchcraft and Possessions* (1685) warned judges against reliance on "spectral evidence" and counseled mild sentences. *Wonders of the Invisible World* (1693) was his account of the Salem trials. His master works

Courtesy of the American Antiquarian Society
*Cotton Mather*

were the *Magnalia Christi Americana*, "Christ's Deeds in America" (1702), and *Christian Philosopher* (1721), which tended toward Deism and revealed his lifelong interest in science. He defended inoculation for smallpox.

Identification with unpopular government policies and arrogance in his arguments made Mather unpopular, but he supported schools for slaves, the building of churches in needy communities, missions to the Indians, and work with children.     N.H.

**MATHESON, GEORGE** (1842–1906). Hymn writer and Church of Scotland minister. Born March 27 in Glasgow, George Matheson even as a small child suffered from poor vision. Nevertheless he entered Glasgow University where he was a brilliant student. At age eighteen he became totally blind, but was aided in his university work by a sister who learned Latin, Greek, and Hebrew to help him in his studies. Despite his handicap he was able to complete undergraduate work and also studies at the theological college of the Church of Scotland. He subsequently became one of Scotland's most eloquent preachers, serving for twelve years at the parish church in the seaport of Inellan and later at St. Bernard's Church in Edinburgh. He wrote the words to the hymn "O Love That Wilt Not Let Me Go" on the day of a sister's wedding. There seems to be no documented basis for the story that the hymn was written after his fiancée refused to marry him because of his blindness. He was the author of several devotional books and other hymns including "Make Me a Captive, Lord, and Then I Shall Be Free."

R.H.

**MATHEWS, SHAILER** (1863–1941). The American Baptist educator and champion of the SOCIAL GOSPEL was educated at Colby College and Newton Theological Institute. He taught at Colby (1887–94), interrupted by a year's study at the University of Berlin (1890–91). In 1894 he joined the faculty of the University of Chicago Divinity School, serving as dean from 1908 until he became professor emeritus in 1933.

An advocate of theological liberalism, his *Social Teaching of Jesus* (1897) was followed by twenty more influential volumes. Active in ecumenical affairs, he was president of the Northern Baptist Convention in 1915 and of the Federal Council of Churches from 1912 to 1916.     N.H.

**MATINS.** From the Latin word for "the morning hours." Originally an early morning worship service, which is now called LAUDS. In modern usage matins celebrates the end of the night and thus precedes the prayers at dawn, lauds. Prayers during the night are of ancient usage, going back to the third century.

The form of matins on festivals is extremely long, since the Roman liturgy has nine psalms and nine scripture readings and the monastic liturgy, twelve psalms, and twelve readings from scripture. Matins is divided into three parts, or nocturns, of three psalms and three readings each. The length of the service has caused a steady shortening of it by several popes, and Vatican II completely revised it. This shorter version will make the use of matins for spiritual growth more possible for parish priests. Matins is known as morning prayer in the Anglican and Episcopal churches. The Lutheran matins, or early morning service, has recently been revised in *The Lutheran Book of Worship.*                                    J.C.

**MATTHEW.** Mentioned in the various lists of the disciples (Matt. 10:3; Mark 3:18; Luke 6:15) and apostles (Acts 1:13) Matthew also appears in a story of Jesus calling a tax collector to become one of his followers (Matt. 9:9). Mark and Luke both tell the same story, but give his name as Levi (Mark 2:14; Luke 5:27). In some ancient manuscripts of Mark, he is called James. Only the Gospel of Matthew links the converted tax collector with Matthew. Besides this puzzling information, we learn from the NT nothing further about Matthew.

The fourth-century church historian Eusebius of Caesarea reported in his *Ecclesiastical History* a claim made by Papias (a church leader in Asia Minor in the early second century) that our First Gospel originated as a collection of sayings of Jesus, which Matthew interpreted from the Hebrew. But since what we know as the Gospel of Matthew gives no hint as to its authorship, and since it depends upon a Greek document, the Gospel of Mark, Papias' claim must be dismissed as an uninformed guess. Later tradition assigned to each of the supposed writers of the Gospels a symbol. Matthew's was an angel.

                                                H.K.

**MATTHEW, GOSPEL OF.** The first of the four canonical Gospels in the received order of the NT.

Most modern biblical scholarship has concluded that Matthew was written after MARK, as also was LUKE, since all of Mark's contents, in the order Mark gives them, are included in both Matthew and Luke. A considerable conservative scholarship insists that Matthew is the earliest Gospel to be written; a position recently defended by the scholar William Farmer. However, the demonstrated dependence of Matthew and Luke on Mark, plus another large body of material (called Q, from the German *quelle* or "source") common to both Matthew and Luke, gives strong credence to "the Markan hypothesis" or "the two document hypothesis" of Gospel construction. Matthew also contains materials peculiar to this Gospel alone, known as "M," just as Luke contains unique materials known as "L."

Matthew's special material (besides Mark and Q) include a collection of OT passages specifically developed to show that Jesus fulfilled all the promises and predictions of the Messiah, which was used by early Christians in controversies with other Jews who

rejected Jesus' messiahship. Scholars have hypothesized that this collection of "sayings" was written in Hebrew but was translated into Greek before Matthew used it. This could be the *Logia* or "sayings" that may refer to the words of Jesus, originally written in Aramaic.

Matthew early received first place in the lists of Gospels, that is, the SYNOPTICS—Matthew, Mark and Luke—plus the Fourth Gospel, JOHN, since it makes such a close connection of early Christian origins with the Hebrew scriptures. The early church saw Matthew as the most comprehensive, and thus, the most authoritative, of the accounts of Jesus' life and ministry. For early Christians, Matthew shows how the life of Jesus is the fulfillment of Hebrew prophecy and the Law.

Indeed, Matthew treats the entire OT as prophecy and pays particular attention to the Law (Torah), to Jesus' many miracles ("mighty acts of God"), and explicitly mentions the church (Matt. 16), all of which were key interests of the developing church after A.D. 70, when the Gospels were written. Matthew shows a detailed knowledge of the fall of Jerusalem to the Romans (as does Luke), and his quotations of the OT come, in many instances, direct from the Septuagint or Greek translation that was popular among Jews, and Christians, of the Diaspora. Matthew thus originated around A.D. 80, among Greek-speaking Jews.

None of the authors of the Gospels is named in the manuscripts, but ancient tradition ascribed the First Gospel to an apostle, the tax collector called Levi in Mark 2:14 and Luke 5:27, and called MATTHEW in 9:9. Papias, bishop of Hierapolis in Asia Minor around A.D. 130, tells us that "Matthew collected the words (*Logia,* that is, the sayings of Jesus) in the Hebrew language and each one interpreted them as he was able." Most modern scholars agree that Matthew was originally written in Greek, and so Papias cannot be referring to Matthew as we have it. At most, due to the writer's dependence on Mark and other written sources, we can say Matthew was written by a Jewish Christian who was not an early disciple. The Christian-Jewish nature of Matthew is revealed in the intense interest in prophecy, the genealogy of Jesus, which is traced to David and Abraham, the prominence of the Law in Matthew's rendition of Jesus' teaching, and the high regard for the blessings given the Jews by the covenant God. The Sermon on the Mount is presented, in fact, as a parallel to Moses at Sinai, and Jesus is shown to give a new law. Yet, at the same time, Matthew is extremely negative toward "the Jews" who did not accept Jesus as the Messiah. Only in Matthew do the priests say, at Jesus' condemnation, "His blood be on us and on our children." Scholars have thus called Matthew the most anti-Semitic of the Gospels.

While the place of origin is unknown, internal evidence, such as the Jewish interests, on the one hand, and interests in Gentiles like the Roman centurion (8:5-13), suggests a place like Antioch of Syria, where Jewish and Gentile influences were both present.

Most commentators point out Matthew's fondness for structure. The genealogy is arranged in sets of fourteen generations, and the main portion of the book is divided into five sections (perhaps corresponding to the five books of Moses), each of which ends with a formula phrase such as "when Jesus had finished these sayings . . ." (7:28; 11:1; 13:53; 19:1; 26:1). Each of these five sections begins with a narrative of Jesus' activities and ends in a long discourse or sermon. The Gospel opens with the birth narratives and ends with the passion and resurrection of Jesus.

A possible outline of Matthew is:

I. The Coming of the Messiah (chaps. 1–2)
II. The Ministry of the Messiah (chaps. 3–25)
   A. Preparation for the Ministry (chaps. 3–7)
     Narrative: Baptism, Temptation, and Call of Disciples
     Discourse: The Sermon on the Mount
   B. Jesus' Authority (chaps. 8–10)
     Narrative: Healings and Forgiveness
     Discourse: The Mission of the Apostles
   C. The Coming Kingdom (chaps. 11–13)
     Narrative: Failure to Discern the Kingdom's Coming
     Discourse: Parables of the Kingdom
   D. Life in the Community of the New Covenant (chaps. 14–18)
     Narrative: Warnings of Hostility to the New Community
     Discourse: Rules for Life in the New Community
   E. The Consummation of the Present Age (chaps. 19–25)
     Narrative: Conflict with "the Jews"
     Discourse: The Synoptic Apocalypse—The End of the Age
III. The Passion and Resurrection of the Messiah (chaps. 26–28)
   A. Jesus' Betrayal, Trial, Death, and Resurrection
   B. The Commissioning of the Disciples for a World Mission

While Matthew does not completely follow such an orderly scheme (section B of Division 2 is quite undifferentiated), in the main it is clear that Matthew intends such a presentation because of his summary sentences, such as: "And Jesus went about all the cities and villages, teaching in their synagogues and preaching the gospel of the kingdom, and healing every disease and every infirmity" (9:35).

The peculiarly Jewish viewpoint of Matthew makes it likely that his intended audience was made up not of Gentiles but of Jewish Christians. His purpose must be considered to be a demonstration of Jesus'

credentials as the Messiah, promised by God and predicted both by the Torah and the great Prophets of Israel and Judah. In Jesus all the great promises have been fulfilled, so that the Christian church must be seen as the New Israel, the successor to the people of the old covenant who have forfeited their place in God's kingdom because of their refusal (symbolized by the priests, scribes, and Pharisees) to receive Jesus as the Messiah. Indeed, Matthew carries his theme, "that the Scripture might be fulfilled," so far that he combines bits of various verses in unique ways and even quotes one source that is unknown to scholarship (Matt. 2:23). Matthew proceeds to show that Jesus is the fulfillment of the Torah, the fulfillment of prophecy, and the eschatological basis for true righteousness. He then shows the need for believers to be watchful, for the delayed but coming Kingdom that will usher in the end of the age. Matthew shows this need for constant preparation for the Kingdom's breaking into history in the three apocalyptic parables of the wise and faithful servant (24:45-51), the wise and foolish maidens (25:1-13), and the parable of the talents (25:14-30).

For Matthew, the church, which in his time probably was consciously separated from the rest of Judaism and was subjected to hostility by the synagogue and the possibility of persecution by the Roman government, was nonetheless the community of the New Covenant, the new and true Israel. As such a people in struggle dwelling in the expectation of Christ's return to judge the earth, the church has a strong responsibility to preach the gospel to the whole world. There is a catholic, universal dimension to Matthew's thought, then, that lifts it far above any narrowly Jewish-Christian interest despite Matthew's setting in such a situation in life.

Matthew, standing as it does at the head of the NT, is probably the most widely read book in Christendom. Its lovely birth story and inspiring resurrection narratives make it the favorite of millions at Christmas and Easter. The very size and detailed structure of the book make it authoritative in tone and keep alive and convincing to many the tradition that it is the First Gospel to be written, despite two centuries of critical biblical scholarship.

The appeal of Matthew can be gleaned from the fact that the Church of the Nativity in Bethlehem, alone of Constantine's basilicas, escaped destruction at the hands of the Muslims because it contained a painting showing the three (Persian) magi following the star to worship Jesus. Such is the universal appeal of the only Gospel to recount that wondrous journey.

J.C.

**MATTHIAS.** The apostle chosen by casting lots to fill the office vacated by JUDAS ISCARIOT. Along with the other apostles, he helped to manage the first business of the church in Jerusalem following the ascension of Jesus, according to Acts 1:15-26. Peter declared that the Scriptures, which had prophesied

Judas' betrayal, provided that his place be filled by another (Ps. 109:8; Acts 1:20, 22). A qualified candidate must have "accompanied" Jesus and his disciples "beginning from the baptism of John until the day when he [Jesus] was taken up." (This profile marks off the Twelve as the only apostles. This alone explains Luke's denial of this office to Paul, who so vehemently claimed it for himself. Acts 14:14 is the exception that proves the rule.) When places among the Twelve were later vacated, no successor was needed; the martyred James would sit on one of the "thrones judging the twelve tribes of Israel" for, unlike Judas, James had continued with Jesus in his trials (Acts 12:1-2; Luke 22:28-30).          J.L.P.

**MATZAH.** Unleavened bread eaten by Jews during the festival of PASSOVER. The ingredients are specially prepared flour and cooled water. After the first two nights, matzah prepared with other ingredients may be eaten, but it must not have any leaven. The dough must not be allowed to ferment, a symbol of the haste with which the Jews left Egypt. The Bible calls matzah "the bread of affliction." Spiritually and allegorically, leaven is regarded as the symbol of impurity.                                             L.K.

**MAUNDY THURSDAY.** Thursday in HOLY WEEK, commemorating the institution of the LORD'S SUPPER or Holy Communion. "Maundy" is a corruption of the Latin *mandatum*, meaning "command." This is derived from John 13:34, where Jesus declared, "A new commandment I give to you."

Holy Week is one of the earlier developments of the CHRISTIAN YEAR, stressing preparation for remembrance of the crucifixion of Christ and the Lord's resurrection. Maundy Thursday was instituted early in the so-called Great Week of the Eastern Orthodox churches. It not only commemorates the Last Supper, but also includes the reenactment of the foot washing done by Jesus on that evening. From the Middle Ages until today many churches, including the Roman Catholic, washed feet as part of the humility proper for Lent. Recently, Protestant churches have revived the rite, and the Catholic church has stressed it by the participation of the pope in its observance.     J.C.

**MAURICE, FREDERICK DENISON** (1805–72). The Anglican divine's given name was John Frederick Denison Maurice. Under the influence of Samuel Taylor COLERIDGE's theological and philosophical thought, he went to Trinity College, Cambridge, in 1823. Leaving the Unitarian faith of his parents, he was baptized into the Church of England in 1831 and was ordained January 26, 1834, after a preparatory course at Exeter College, Oxford.

In 1846 he became professor of theology at the newly created theological school of King's College, London. His leadership among Christian socialists led to questions about his orthodoxy, and publication of *Theological Essays* (1853), in which he questioned the

endlessness of future punishment among other things, led to his dismissal from King's College.

He was closely associated with Charles Kingsley, and they together published a series of *Tracts for Priests and People,* beginning in 1854, concerned with the problems of society in the throes of industrialization. They also founded a Working Men's College. In 1866 he became Knightsbridge Professor of Moral Theology at Cambridge. His other works included *The Kingdom of Religion* (1842) and *The Claims of the Bible and of Science* (1863).                              N.H.

**MAXIMUS THE CONFESSOR** (about 580–662). Greek ascetical writer and chief theologian of the seventh century. Formerly an imperial secretary under Emperor Heraclius, about 614 he became a monk at Chrysopolis (Scutari), near Constantinople. With the Persian invasion of 626 he fled to Carthage.

From 640 on he opposed Monothelitism and defended the doctrine of the two wills of Christ. Taken to Constantinople in 653, he refused adherence to the "Typos" of Constans II and so was banished to Thrace. In 661 he was tried for treason. One tradition says his tongue and right hand were cut off before he was banished to the Caucasus Mountains.

His mystical works include *The Ascetic Life, Four Centuries on Charity,* and the *Mystagogia,* a mystical interpretation of the liturgy. A Christian Platonist, he believed that sin entered the world because of human desire for pleasure, which destroyed the dominion of reason over the senses. Redemption is through return to our true nature, which the perfect exercise of human will by Christ illustrates. His feast day is August 13.                                    N.H.

**MAY, ROLLO** (1909–   ). Born April 21 in Ada, Ohio, May attended Michigan State University and graduated from Oberlin College. He taught literature for three years at Anatolia College, Thessaloniki, Greece, and attended summer institutes with Alfred Adler in Vienna. After a brief stint in student counseling, he entered Union Theological Seminary (New York). Upon the completion of two years in a Congregational parish, he enrolled at Columbia University, where he received the Ph.D. in 1949.

His dissertation formed the basis for *The Meaning of Anxiety.* Influenced by PAUL TILLICH, about whom he wrote in *Paulus* (1973), and by existentialists KIERKEGAARD, NEITZSCHE, and CAMUS, he has become known for his existentialist psychotherapy outlined in *Existence: A New Dimension in Psychiatry and Psychology.* (See EXISTENTIALISM.)

Adler's emphasis on individual responsibility was another factor in his thought. Acknowledging potential benefits from free-floating ANXIETY, brought on by the normal uncertainties of societal living, he counseled that people should develop self-responsibility and self-affirmation through personal motivation instead of looking for outside approval. During a bout with tuberculosis in his early thirties, he found that life depended on his own struggle against death. In 1948 he joined the faculty of the William Alanson White Institute of Psychiatry, Psychoanalysis, and Psychology (New York) and later became a training and supervisory analyst. He has taught at Yale, Princeton, and Harvard universities and is the author of *Love and Will* and *Man's Search for Himself.*  I.C.

**MAYA.** Sanskrit, related to "magic," often translated "illusion." In HINDUISM, this important term has two distinct but related meanings. In the VEDAS, maya refers to the wizard-like power of the gods to create bodies for themselves and otherwise work miracles. In Vedanta thought, especially the Svetasvatara UPANISHAD and its interpretation by the great philosopher of Advaita VEDANTA (non-dualist Vedanta) SAMKARA, maya is the power by which BRAHMAN or God creates the world, and it is that phenomenal world seen in its misleading manyness rather than its unity.

Maya is frequently rendered "illusion," but that term easily leads to misconceptions. To say that the world is maya does not mean that all is illusion in the sense of being a hallucination, but that it is not perceived correctly owing to *ajñana* or avidya, ignorance. We see it as separate and transitory things, as we see ourselves, rather than as the power and being of Brahman. With full enlightenment, according to Advaita, the false realities of maya dissipate, and Brahman alone is seen to be real.  R.E.

**MAYFLOWER COMPACT.** Dated November 11, 1620, the Mayflower Compact is an instrument of government drawn up by the Separatist majority of pilgrims before disembarkation from the *Mayflower,* hailed as the first step of the American colonists toward framing a constitution. The *Mayflower* sailed from Plymouth, England, in September 1620. Its 101 passengers were led spiritually and politically by their ruling elder, William Brewster. Not all the passengers were Separatists, however, and the grumbling of non-Separatists occasioned the writing of the compact. On the day the *Mayflower* dropped anchor off Cape Cod, forty-one adult male Separatists, including John Alden, William Bradford, William Brewster, John Carver, Myles Standish, and Edward Winslow, composed and signed the Mayflower Compact. Beginning with "In the name of God, Amen," the signers of the compact affirmed loyalty to King James and covenanted before one another and before God to form a political body to promote the glory of God, advance the Christian faith, and establish a colony. The signers further committed themselves to enact just and equal laws and promised all due submission and obedience. This compact, America's first written constitution, formed the basis of government for Plymouth Colony until it merged with Massachusetts in 1691.  C.M.

**MEAD, GEORGE HERBERT** (1863–1931). A social psychologist whose theories have become basic to many research areas. He studied physiological psychology in Germany and later at Harvard with William James, Josiah Royce, and Charles Sanders Peirce. Philosophically a pragmatist, he, with John Dewey and Charles H. Cooley, developed a psychological system called symbolic interactionism. He believed that human personality is not innate, but is formed by interaction with other people, primarily through gestures and word symbols. The mind evolves and self-consciousness emerges through social processes. This is how a child becomes differentiated from others in the environment and develops a sense of self. Throughout life, this self is tested by reference to the regard of other people and in this way the self-image is maintained.

People work out their own purposes and modify one another's behavior through social activities. Such interaction can change environments. Mead believed that progress could take place and an improved society evolve when people use their minds to solve problems by intelligent planning and action. For him social acts were determinative of the development of culture. Feedback was given through interaction and this enabled an individual to develop a sense of self.

Mead's teaching career was at the University of Chicago, where his ideas were disseminated through extemporaneous lectures and articles in the fields of education, psychology, and sociology.  I.C.

**MECCA.** The holiest city of ISLAM and birthplace of MUHAMMAD. Mecca is located in western Arabia near the Red Sea, and lies midway between the Indian Ocean and the Mediterranean, on an important caravan route. Its present importance is due to its religious significance and the presence there of the KA'BA, the center of the Muslim world. Five times daily all Muslims face the *kiblah,* the direction of the Ka'ba, for prayer. At least once in their lives, all Muslims who are able to do so must make the pilgrimage (HAJJ) to Mecca and the area around it. Mecca is so holy that non-Muslims cannot enter it.

Despite the hostile climate and infertile soil, Mecca had been important for a long time before the birth of Muhammad. The Ka'ba was the most important religious center of Arabia. Tribes from many areas made seasonal pilgrimages to it. The Quraish tribe, inhabitants of Mecca, grew rich both from trade and from the pilgrimage. Muhammad was born into the Quraish, but into a poor clan, the Hashimites. The most powerful of the dozen clans was the Omayyad, which later became the first ruling dynasty of CALIPHS. However, during Muhammad's ministry, the Omayyad and other important clans ridiculed him. After the HEGIRA, they organized economic and military opposition to him. In A.D. 630, Muhammad's forces from MEDINA conquered Mecca. Muhammad destroyed all the idols in the city, and established Mecca as the religious center of Islam, but

Courtesy of the Royal Embassy of Saudi Arabia

*The Holy Mosque at Mecca*

returned to Medina, his temporal capital. Muhammad made one last pilgrimage to Mecca in 632, just before he died. Later Muslim rulers improved the city and expanded the MOSQUE around the Ka'ba. The Karmathians, a Ishi'ite sect, sacked Mecca in 930, carrying away the sacred black stone of the Ka'ba. Twenty years passed before it was returned. In 1925, 'Abd-al-'Aziz Ibn-Saud', founder of modern Saudi Arabia, took control of Mecca and Medina.

K./M.C.

**MEDIA.** The Priestly genealogists (Gen. 10:2; I Chr. 1:5) associate the "Madai" with other Indo-Europeans, including "Javan," the Greeks. That the Medes were subject to the Assyrians in the eighth century B.C. is confirmed by the notices in II Kings 17:6; 18:11 that Sargon II exiled the Israelites captured in 721 B.C. to the cities of the Medes. Isaiah regarded the Medes as a ferocious nation (Isa. 13:17; 21:2). Their empire reached its zenith during the time of Jeremiah's ministry (see Jer. 25:25; 51:11, 28), and under Cyaxares (about 625–585 B.C.) they controlled an area reaching from central Asia Minor to central PERSIA, centered on the capital city of Ecbatana (Ezra 6:2). However, Cyrus defeated Astyages, the last independent Median king, in 539 B.C., and incorporated Media as a province into the Persian Empire. Late OT writers tended to view the

Courtesy of the Oriental Institute, University of Chicago

*Head of a Mede, with his high rounded hat and his beard and mustache; from the stairway of the Apadana, Persepolis (521–465 B.C.)*

two kingdoms as a pair, as is evident in the phrase "the law of the Medes and the Persians" (Dan. 6:8, 12, 15). Daniel's "Darius the Mede" (Dan. 5:31; 9:1; 11:1), never existed; he must be confused with some later Persian king. Jewish "Parthians and Medes and Elamites" (Acts 2:9) were among those present in Jerusalem on the day of Pentecost.

W.S.T.

**MEDIATOR.** This term is used in the NT, as well as in Greek legal and literary documents in the centuries before and after the birth of Jesus, to designate one who arbitrates between two parties in order to resolve a dispute or to achieve a common purpose. It is found in technical legal usage in secular material arising from legal controversy and from the attempt to settle competing claims. But it also appears in both pagan and Jewish writings with reference to those divine or divinely ordained figures who adjudicate disputes between the gods, or God, and human beings.

In Plutarch's treatise on Isis and Osiris, for example, the Iranian god, Mithra, mediates between the divine and the human. In Jewish apocalyptic writings the term is found as well. For example, in the Testaments of the Twelve Patriarchs (Test. Dan. 6:2; Test. Levi 5:7) there is an angel who intercedes in behalf of suffering Israel in the presence of God. In I Enoch 89:76, the seer himself takes up to God the record of the difficulties through which God's people have passed, in an effort to move God to intervene in Israel's behalf.

The term "mediator" is used in three of the NT writings. Paul describes Moses as the mediator through whom the Law was given to Israel (Gal. 3:19). In keeping with the heightened notion of the remoteness and transcendence of God within first-century Judaism, Paul notes that it was angels (rather than God alone) who transmitted the Law to Moses, but Moses is clearly the mediator in the transaction. Then follows an enigmatic remark that "a mediator implies more than one, but God is one" (Gal. 3:20), which probably means that the covenant of law is inferior to the covenant of promise, since the former was made indirectly through multiple agents, while the latter was made directly between God and Abraham (Gen. 18:1-10).

In I Timothy 2:5 and Hebrews 8:6; 9:15; and 12:24, Jesus is the mediator of the new covenant, the one who bridges the gulf between the seeking, saving God and disobedient, estranged people. First Timothy stresses that Jesus is the sole mediator between God and human beings, while Hebrews in all the passages where the term occurs makes a sharp distinction between the old covenant and the new. The old is merely transitional, and has already become obsolete (Heb. 8:13). It could only cover human sin; Jesus, as mediator of the new covenant, removes sin (9:6-15). The community of faith has been brought by this new and final mediator into the presence of God (Heb. 12:23-24).

H.K.

**MEDINA.** A city in western Arabia, about 280 miles north of MECCA. MUHAMMAD's journey there in A.D. 622, known as the HEGIRA, marks the beginning of the Islamic calendar. In Medina, Muhammad built the first MOSQUE and established the UMMA, or community of believers. He lived the last ten years of his life there and is buried there.

Unlike Mecca, Medina was a city with a large and fertile oasis and a favorable climate. The population consisted of several Jewish tribes that had come from the north and several Arab tribes that had come from the south. Because of conflict among the tribes, an arbiter was needed. Muhammad was invited, and he settled many of the conflicts within the city. He wrote the "Constitution of Medina," which set forth the basic ideas of the Islamic state. However, most of the Jews did not accept his claims to be a prophet, so Muhammad had them expelled. Meanwhile, Muhammad's forces fought the Meccans. Medina was besieged in 627; Muhammad ordered a trench dug across the only safe access to the city, and the Meccan force, mostly cavalry, could not cross it. Eventually, the siege was lifted.

Although Muhammad captured Mecca in 630, he returned to Medina shortly afterwards, making it his capital as he spread Islam throughout Arabia. After his death, Medina continued to be the capital of Islam until Ali, the fourth caliph, moved the capital to Kūfa in Iraq. Medina declined in importance, but remained the second holiest city in Islam.

K./M.C.

**MEDITATION.** Methodical reflection, deep thought on eternal truths, which becomes a religious exercise because of its spiritual goals and reverent approach. Meditation plays a role in all religions, ancient and modern, major and minor, from the contemplative exercises of Tibetan Buddhist monks to the vigils before the consecrated Eucharistic hosts of certain orders of Roman Catholic nuns.

Meditation is called discursive prayer or mental prayer. Among Eastern Orthodox, Roman Catholic, and some Protestant circles (Anglican monks, as well as a small number of Reformed and Lutheran monks), meditation is engaged in for seeking deeper insight into the will of God. Among Buddhists, meditation may be followed to achieve the state of "non-self" or Nirvana, the nothingness that is considered the real under the appearances of the material world. Meditation, by whomever practiced, is an attempt to still the ordinary thoughts of the human mind, to explore the depths and, if possible, to break through the bounds of the finite into the infinite. In the spiritual formation of priests and religious in the Roman Catholic church, meditation is urged by canon law and manuals used by spiritual directors. *The Practice of the Presence of God* by Brother Lawrence and Ignatius' *Spiritual Exercises* both see meditation as necessary for the development of faith and a deep prayer life.

Meditation is subject to several meanings and has changed in meaning over the centuries. Aids to meditation are prominent in some traditions (icons, crucifixes, mandalas, mantras [sounds], bodily poses [yoga], celibacy, and fasting) and absent in others.

J.C.

**MEDITERRANEAN SEA.** "The Sea at the Middle of the Earth" to the Romans, who called it *Mare Nostrum* ("our sea"). Most of the important nations of ancient times were either on the Mediterranean's shores or else operated in its 2,300 miles of water: Israel, Syria, Greece, Rome, Egypt, Philistia, and Phoenicia. The Israelites called it "the sea of the Philistines" and feared it. Indeed, when Solomon built a navy and merchant marine, he furnished it with ships and seafarers from Tyre in Phoenicia. When the author of Jonah wished to show utter terror, he wrote of Jonah's being cast overboard and swallowed by a great fish.

The Mediterranean plays a large role in the NT, especially in the ministry of Paul. Paul made three missionary journeys plus a final voyage under Roman arrest to Rome across the Mediterranean. He was particularly active at the northeastern edge of the Mediterranean, in the Aegean Sea, working for years in Ephesus and Corinth. Paul's work involved Mediterranean cities: Caesarea, Antioch, Troas, Corinth (and its port of Cenchreae), Ptolemais, Tyre, Sidon, Syracuse, Rome (and its port of Puteoli), as well as Ephesus. He was involved in at least one unrecorded ship sinking as well as the foundering of the Roman galley on Malta on his final voyage to Rome.

J.C.

**MEDIUM.** *See* DIVINATION; SPIRITUALISM.

**MEDLEY, SAMUEL** (1738–1806). Baptist minister and prolific hymn writer. Medley was born June 23 in Hertfordshire, England. As a rebellious youth, he joined the Royal Navy, where, while serving aboard a naval vessel engaged in a sea battle off the coast of West Africa, he was severely wounded in one leg. The surgeon aboard expressed fear that the leg would have to be amputated. Young Medley, who had been reared in a devout home, prayed for many hours that the Lord would forgive his sins. The next morning the doctor said his leg was healing, and he would not have to remove it. On his release from the navy, Medley studied for the ministry and was ordained as a Baptist. His first church was at Watford. During the early period of his ministry there, he wrote his famous hymn, "O Could I Sing the Matchless Worth." Subsequently he wrote a number of hymns, which first appeared in leaflets or were published in religious periodicals. The last twenty-seven years of his fruitful life were spent serving a Liverpool church.

R.H.

**MEGIDDO.** Usually identified with modern Tell el-Mutesellim in central Palestine, Megiddo has been a traditional battle site throughout known history, the result of its strategic location at a crossroads of international traffic, involving it inevitably and deeply in the politics of the ancient Near East. It was a fortress city in control of the Wadi Ara, the pass through the Carmel range separating the plain of Esdraelon from the Palestinian coastal plain, thus the entrance to the "way of the sea," which was the all-important trade route connecting Egypt with Syria and then with Mesopotamia.

In pre-Israelite Palestine, Megiddo was alternatively a center of resistance to the Egyptian domination of CANAAN and, at other times, a faithful vassal of the Egyptian pharaoh. It is mentioned among the conquests of Thutmose III (1468 B.C.) and Seti I (about 1300 B.C.), at which time Canaan was a province of Egyptian rule. During the Amarna period of Amenophis IV (1377–1358 B.C.) it is clear from correspondence from the "king" of Megiddo directed to the pharaoh that it was a city crucial to Egypt in its recurring warfare against the nomadic tribes that continually threatened its domination of the Canaanite city-states. Such written sources corroborate the archaeological evidence, which testifies to a very ancient history of settlement at the strategic site of Tell el-Mutesellim. Remains both from the Neolithic (8300–4000 B.C.) and the Calcholithic (fourth millennium B.C.) periods abound, prelude to the many levels of habitation that belong to several phases of the Canaanite period (third and second millennia), which display massive walls and fortifications, sophisticated dwellings, and temples. Megiddo is, in fact, a parade example of urban opulence during the late Canaanite period. Here the archaeologists found gold implements, ivory plaques, jewelry, and art objects of various precious materials—the richest collection of such luxury items ever unearthed in Palestinian archaeology.

Though Megiddo is named in Joshua 12:21 as one of the cities taken in the initial phase of the Israelite conquest of Canaan (contrast Josh. 17:11-12), it is likely that it did not become Israelite until a somewhat later period. "Taanach by the waters of Megiddo" is mentioned in Judges 5:19 as the site of the battle waged under Deborah and Barak against a coalition of Canaanites, the success of which presumably made possible the union of northern and central Israelite tribes to form a confederation. The

Herbert G. May

*Stalls with mangers, from Megiddo stables*

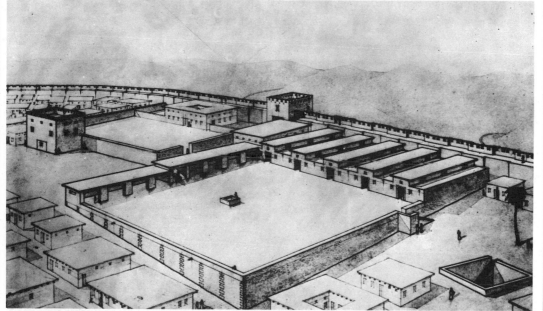

Courtesy of the Oriental Institute, University of Chicago

*Reconstruction of stables at Megiddo, probably from the time of Ahab. A walkway about eight feet wide ran down the center of each unit; rows of pillars on each side of the passage supported the roof and served for hitching; between the pillars were mangers and stalls. Compare Solomon's cities for his chariots and horses (horsemen) in I Kings 9:19 and 10:26*

battle may have taken place between 1150–1050 B.C., a time during which the habitation of Tell el-Mutesellim was suspended. Who occupied the site immediately after 1050 B.C. is the subject of debate, but there is no doubt that from about 950 B.C. on Megiddo was an important Israelite stronghold.

Here Solomon established one of his administrative centers (I Kings 4:12; 9:15) of his highly consolidated and bureaucratic kingdom. The Bible evidently regards Solomon's building at Megiddo as one of the marvels of his flamboyant reign, and the archaeology of the place would tend to confirm this judgment. The massive city gate, wall, storehouses, and the expert masonry represent some of the best efforts achieved by Israelite architecture.

Megiddo's Israelite history seemed to have ceased in 732 B.C., when it was destroyed by the Assyrian conqueror Tiglath-pileser III, only to be made by him into a center for Assyrian administration. Its strategic importance continued: in 609 B.C. King Josiah perished there in a futile attempt to stop Pharaoh Neco in his march to aid the foundering Assyrian Empire in its final days (II Kings 23:29). (Josiah's effort, in fact, may not have been in vain. He may have delayed Neco sufficiently to render his aid ineffective.) As a strategic stronghold, Megiddo seems to have been definitively abandoned only in Roman times. Revelation 16:16 reflects the legendary character of Megiddo as the "valley of decision" by making Armageddon (Hebrew, *har megiddon*) "the

mount of Megiddo," the scene of God's final judgment.                                    B.V.

**MEGILLOTH.** Plural of megillah, Hebrew for "scroll." In Judaism, five scrolls are read in the synagogue on special occasions. They are the biblical books Song of Songs, Ruth, Ecclesiastes, Esther, and Lamentations. The Song of Songs is read during Passover week (on the Sabbath); the Book of Ruth is read on Shavuot (Feast of Weeks), when God gave the Commandments on Mount Sinai; Ecclesiastes is read on Sukkot (Feast of Tabernacles); Esther is read on Purim, and Lamentations is read on the ninth day of the Hebrew month Av (Tisha b'Av), when both the First Temple and the Second Temple were destroyed.
                                                        L.K.

**MEHER BABA** (1894–1969). Indian guru, born Merwan Sheriar Irani in Poona, India, to Persian parents. Reared in Zoroastrianism, exposed to Hinduism and Christianity, Merwan converted to Sufi Muhammadism in 1913, influenced by Hazat Babajan of that mystical sect. He adopted the name "Meher Baba," which means "compassionate father," when he decided he was God. He said "There is no doubt of my being God personified . . . " In 1921, he founded a colony, Meherabad, and decided to stop speaking, communicating by spelling out words. In 1931 he traveled to England and the United States and made disciples that continue to worship him. He died in a car accident in Oklahoma.        J.C.

## MELANCHTHON, PHILIPP

**MELANCHTHON, PHILIPP** (1497-1560). Lay colleague and friend of MARTIN LUTHER for twenty-eight years, author of the AUGSBURG CONFESSION and its *Apology,* founder of Germany's Protestant public school system, and leader of Lutheranism after Luther's death. Born in Bretten and orphaned at age ten, Melanchthon nevertheless became a distinguished linguist, teacher, and theologian. Educated at Heidelberg University (B.A., 1511) and Tübingen (M.A., 1514) he joined the faculty at Wittenberg University in 1518 to teach Greek. Influenced by Luther, he studied theology and received a Bachelor of Theology in 1519. Thereafter, he taught both classics and theology. In 1521 Melanchthon published his *Loci Communes,* Protestantism's first systematic theology. His published writings were enormous—textbooks, translations, classical treatises, theological works, commentaries. He authored Lutheranism's basic creedal statement, the Augsburg Confession (1530), and defended it in his *Apology to the Augsburg Confession* (1531). Basically Melanchthon agreed with Luther, but his humanism, irenic attitude, and desire for peace led many to believe that he compromised Luther's views on justification by faith alone. After Luther's death (1546) and the Lutheran military defeat at Mühlberg (1547), Melanchthon yielded to Roman Catholicism on "non-essentials" in the Augsburg-Leipzig Interims (1548) and was accused of betraying Luther. His final years were embittered by controversy.      C.M.

## MELCHIZEDEK

**MELCHIZEDEK.** This name first appears in Genesis 14:18-20 as the priest-king of Salem (Jerusalem) who blessed Abraham on his successful return after pursuing the kings of the East and whose God (*El elyon,* "God Most High") Abraham recognized as his own (Gen. 14:22). At the very least, the purpose of this story is to bring into close conjunction one of Israel's remote ancestors with the city, the royalty, and the priesthood of that place that historically, only in the time of David, became Israelite. At the most, there may be an effort to evoke the circumstances of the relationship established between David and the Jebusite priesthood of Zadok after his conquest of the holy city (II Sam. 5:8-10; 8:17; I Sam. 2:35).

In Psalm 110:4 the same traditional figure of Genesis 14 appears, this time as the name for a Judahite king, who in a prophetic oracle is pronounced "a priest for ever, in the manner of Melchizedek." While we cannot be sure of the precise circumstances that dictated the wording of the oracle, it is clear that the priestly character of the kingship is being affirmed (II Sam. 8:18), even as the king's predecessor in ancient Jerusalem had been a priest-king. This sacral dimension of the monarchy (compare Pss. 45 and 72, for example) was obviously of great theological significance to important elements in Israelite society.

Hebrews 5–7 in the NT introduces Melchizedek as a type of Christ, utilizing the texts of both Genesis and the Psalms in a purely midrashic and arbitrary fashion. The author exploits the popular etymology of the name ("king of justice," "king of peace"), the fact that he is introduced without ancestry or progeny and therefore "continues for ever," that he blessed Abraham, in whom was the seed of Levi, the Jewish priesthood, and was therefore its superior. This was done in order to establish from scriptural precedent a priestly character of Jesus independent of and greater than that of the Jewish tradition from which Jesus had admittedly sprung.

This NT treatment of Melchizedek is independent of but also correlative with parallel developments in Jewish speculation (Philo of Alexandria, the Qumran literature), which delighted in seizing on the "mysterious" figures of Scripture (Enoch is another prime example) and making of them objects of unbridled imagination. In Hebrews, Melchizedek remains a type, significant only as a foreshadowing, real or contrived. In the Jewish speculation he easily becomes an eschatological figure, the personification of good versus evil, or the embodiment of a heavenly priesthood in which allegorism has taken the place of reality.      B.V.

## MELITO OF SARDIS

**MELITO OF SARDIS.** Late-second-century bishop and vigorous defender of orthodox Christianity who directly addressed Emperor Marcus Aurelius. Data about him are few, and only fragments of his numerous writings were known before Campbell Bonner in 1940 published a liturgical work preserved on papyrus. He scorned gnosticism and upheld Christ's true humanity.      C.M.

From *Atlas of the Bible* (Thomas Nelson & Sons Limited)

*Palm trees at Memphis, where once stood the palaces of the pharaohs of the Old Empire*

## MEMPHIS

**MEMPHIS.** This ancient metropolis of lower Egypt was located on the banks of the Nile about fourteen miles south of present-day Cairo. Known in the OT as Moph (Hos. 9:6) and Noph, it figures largely in the oracles of the prophets against Egypt. Isaiah taunts "the princes of Memphis" as deluded (19:13). Jeremiah announces Yahweh's threat: "Memphis shall become a waste, a ruin, without inhabitant" (46:19; compare Jer. 2:16; 44:1-10; Ezek. 30:13).

Memphis did come to ruin, of course, but not before it enjoyed a long and brilliant career. It was the capital of all of Egypt during the Old Kingdom, from the Third through the Fifth Dynasties (about 2686 to about 2160 B.C.). It never regained its central position after the reunification of Egypt by the pharaohs of the Eleventh Dynasty because the capital shifted to THEBES, but the presence of the major pyramids of Egypt near the site of Memphis gives evidence of its long importance. Fortunately, the founder of the so-called Ethiopian (XXV) dynasty, Shabaka (about 716 B.C.), ordered a record of the theology of the Memphitic cult inscribed upon a black granite stele. From this text we know that Ptah was revered there as the oldest god and as the creator of humankind. The sacred name of Memphis, "the house of the Ka of Ptah," was transliterated from the Egyptian into Greek as *aiguptos*; from thence it reached our Western languages as the word "Egypt."

W.S.T.

**MENAHEM.** The entire account of the reign of this sixteenth ruler of the northern kingdom of Israel is found in II Kings 15:14-23. Menahem became king by assassinating Shallum, who had attained the throne only one month earlier by killing Zechariah. According to verse 17, Menahem ruled ten years, but secular sources suggest that eight years (about 745–738 B.C.) is a more accurate time span. He came from Tirzah, the original capital of the northern kingdom (I Kings 16:23-24), about nine miles east of Samaria. In connection with his coup against Shallum, Menahem sacked the neighboring town of Tappuah and disemboweled the pregnant women whom he found there. Menahem was also remembered for paying a thousand talents of silver to the Assyrian king Pul (that is, Tiglath-pileser III), which he raised by taxing all the wealthy men of Israel fifty shekels each (II Kings 15:19-20; it has been estimated that about sixty thousand men would have had to contribute in order to raise the full sum). This report squares with Tiglath-pileser's own annals, which report receipt of tribute from Menahem of Samaria in about 738 B.C.

W.S.T.

**MENCIUS.** The Latinized form of the name Meng Tzu (372–289? B.C.), a Confucian scholar second only to CONFUCIUS himself in importance. Mencius was born in the state of Ch'i and studied with a disciple of Confucius' grandson. Like Confucius, he wandered the country, searching for a just ruler who would put into practice his ideas of government. His ideas met with scorn, and he retired to teach his philosophy to a group of disciples.

The compilation of his works (called the *Book of Mencius*) was probably accomplished by his disciples after his death, although tradition credits Mencius with that work. Like the *Analects* of Confucius, it is a collection of statements, dialogues, and anecdotes.

Mencius insisted that human nature is basically good. Anyone seeing a child about to fall into a well will rescue the child without thinking. Evil is merely the result of a misdirection of original goodness.

Mencius counseled rulers to be virtuous and benevolent, because "the benevolent man has no enemies." He saw four beginnings that lead to virtue: the feeling of distress at the suffering of others is the beginning of humanity; the feeling of shame and dislike is the beginning of righteousness; the feeling of deference to others is the beginning of propriety; and the feeling of right and wrong is the beginning of wisdom.

K./M.C.

**MENDELSSOHN, MOSES** (1729–86). Jewish philosopher who tried to reconcile the teachings of traditional Judaism with the ideas of the eighteenth century ENLIGHTENMENT in Europe. Born in Dessau, Germany, he received a traditional Jewish education and later studied European languages, literature, and philosophy along with further studies of Jewish classical literature, especially the works of MAIMONIDES. He argued for the belief in the immortality of the soul and asserted that there is no conflict in JUDAISM between belief and reason. Faith in God's wisdom, righteousness, mercy, and, above all, faith in God's goodness are Mendelssohn's most fundamental religious convictions. For the celebrated dramatist Gotthold Ephraim Lessing and other liberal Germans, Mendelssohn was the realization of the Enlightenment ideal that non-Christian peoples could also produce people of innate refinement, profound knowledge, and cosmopolitan rationality. At the height of his literary fame, Mendelssohn was called the "Jewish Socrates."

L.K.

**MENDICANT FRIARS.** Members of Roman Catholic religious orders who vow poverty, live by begging, and are forbidden as individuals to own property. The mobile medieval begging friars contrasted sharply with MONASTICISM'S stable counterparts who were bound to monastic houses. The friars' poverty was a serious criticism of monastic institutional wealth. Exempt from episcopal control, active chiefly in towns, friars preached, heard confessions, and aroused the enmity of more stationary monks and clergy. The principal early mendicant friars included the Franciscans (1210), Dominicans (1215), Carmelites (1245), Augustinians (1256), Servites (fifteenth century), and others. As feudalism disintegrated, the mendicant friars greatly influenced the growing urban centers. Many became renowned teachers, for example, Aquinas. When various bishops and princes restricted begging, friars were forced into corporate ownership of property, living chiefly by accepting group gifts and bequests. Some friars, particularly Franciscans, attempted to adhere to the original individual begging.

C.M.

**MENE, MENE, TEKEL, PARSIN.** These words, found in Daniel 5:24-28, are the Aramaic equivalents of the *mina* (fifty shekels), the *shekel,* and the *peres* (a half-mina). These were units of weights and measurements which, according to the story of Daniel 5:1-6, were inscribed on the wall of the royal palace by a mysterious hand in the midst of a feast given by Belshazzar of Babylon, when blasphemous use was being made of the sacred vessels that had been pillaged from the Jerusalem Temple. When the king's wise men proved to be incapable of interpreting the writing, the Jewish hero was called in. Daniel's reading of the inscription was a prediction of the downfall of Belshazzar's kingdom, fulfilled that very night in the accession of Darius the Mede (Dan. 5:7-30).

Daniel's interpretation depends on some elaborate wordplays. *Mene* equals *menah,* meaning "numbered": "God has numbered the days of your kingdom." *Tekel* equals *tekiltah,* meaning "weighed": "You have been weighed and found wanting." *Peres/Parsin,* "division," "Persians": "Your kingdom is divided and given to the Medes and Persians."                    B.V.

**MENNINGER, KARL AUGUSTUS** (1893–   ). Founder of the Menninger Foundation, headed its School of Psychiatry as dean from 1946 to 1969, and is chairman of the board. Born in Topeka, Kansas, Menninger attended Washburn College, the University of Wisconsin (M.S., 1915), and Harvard (M.D., 1917).

He has been active in the Association for Clinical Pastoral Education. The Menninger School has long had a training program designed for clergy. Among his books are *Man Against Himself* (1938), *Love Against Hate* (1942), *The Crime of Punishment* (1968), and *Whatever Became of Sin?* (1973).                    I.C.

**MENNONITES.** The name given to a number of denominations that descended from the radical Anabaptist movement of the Protestant Reformation. The first Anabaptist congregation was established in Zurich, Switzerland, in 1525 by Conrad Grebel (1489–1526) and others influenced by the Swiss Reformer Ulrich Zwingli. They called themselves "Brethren" (Swiss Brethren) but were known popularly as *Taufer* (the term applied to a candidate for baptism). The appellation Anabaptist (meaning rebaptizer) came from their rejection of the practice of infant baptism and their insistence on the baptism of believers. Since Zwingli was willing to settle for reforms in the Roman Catholic church and maintenance of a church-state relationship, Grebel and his friends withdrew from Zwingli's leadership. In 1534 the first Anabaptist congregations were organized in Holland by Obbe Philips. Two years later Obbe baptized Menno Simons (1496–1561), a converted Roman Catholic priest. Soon Simons became the most prominent leader of the "Obbenites," and by 1550 the name Mennonite began to be used. (Actually the name was not used much in Holland, where the terms employed were *Doopgezinden* or *Doopers,* the Dutch equivalents of "Baptists").

Persecution of the dissenting sect in the countries

Courtesy of Paul M. Schrock

*Menno Simons*

of continental Europe with their established churches drove Mennonites from their homelands. The roll of Mennonite martyrs was great. After the founder of the Dutch Republic, William of Orange, had embraced the Reformed faith, he ordered the cessation of the persecution in 1577. In Switzerland the persecution continued well into the seventeenth century. After the Thirty Years' War, Mennonites were permitted to settle in the Palatinate in south Germany.

When William Penn acquired Pennsylvania from the English crown, he offered a home to all who were persecuted for their faith. The Mennonite pioneers in America were thirteen families from Crefeld, Germany, who came on the ship *Concord,* in 1683, and settled at Germantown, now a part of Philadelphia. During the seventeenth century many Swiss Mennonites emigrated to Pennsylvania. As their numbers increased early in the eighteenth century, the Mennonites spread northward and westward from Germantown into the surrounding counties of southeast Pennsylvania, and southward into Virginia. Later settlers moved westward into Ohio, Indiana, and Illinois, and also to Canada. Except in Holland, where they have been urban and upper class, Mennonites generally have settled in rural communities.

The beliefs of Mennonites include a strong conviction that church and state should be separated, freedom of conscience, voluntary membership in a "brotherhood" church, a discipleship that stresses the literal following of Christ and his teachings, rejection of war and violence, the practice of love and nonresistance, and practical holiness in life. Mennonites are one of the three historic peace churches, the others being the Quakers and the Church of the Brethren.

In the United States and Canada, Mennonites have established a number of colleges and secondary schools and have been involved in a variety of charitable enterprises and missionary work. While Mennonites are now concentrated in North America, particularly the United States, there are enclaves of Mennonites in Holland, Switzerland, Germany, and the U.S.S.R. (including Siberia), as well as India, Japan, Africa, and South America.

The Mennonite Central Committee is the relief and service agency of North American Mennonite and Brethren in Christ churches. All of the major Mennonite church bodies of the world participate in the program of the Mennonite World Conference. (*See also* AMISH and RADICAL REFORMATION.)

R.H.

Courtesy of the Israel Government Tourist Office, Houston, Texas

*This giant menorah, the symbol of the State of Israel, stands in the plaza facing the Knesset*

**MENORAH.** The Hebrew name for the seven-branched candlestick originally made by the biblical artisan Bezalel and placed in the sanctuary of the tabernacle. In the first Temple, built by Solomon, there were ten golden menorahs; in the second Temple, there was one. The menorah has since become an important symbol of Judaism and is the official symbol of the State of Israel. The one used at Hanukkah is eight-branched, with an additional socket for the "servant" light used to kindle the Hanukkah candles. L.K.

**MEPHIBOSHETH.** The deliberate corruption in the text of the books of Samuel of the name Meribbaal (compare I Chr. 8:34), done because for later readers the element Baal ("Lord"), originally applied to the Israelite God Yahweh, now was referred only to the chief deity of Canaanite mythology. (Bosheth means "shame.") The name was borne by two of the descendants of King Saul.

(1) So named was one of the sons of Saul by his wife RIZPAH. David delivered this son over to the Gibeonites demanding blood vengeance and human sacrifice in recompense for the wrongs that Saul had committed against them (II Sam. 21:7-9).

(2) A nephew of the same name, a son of JONATHAN, David's friend, was spared in this slaughter, but the biblical record of his subsequent relationship to David is somewhat ambiguous. This Mephibosheth, a cripple, was taken into David's household, and his estates were protected by royal decree (II Sam. 9). This solicitude was probably also dictated by political prudence, that the last survivor of a supplanted dynasty be kept under close observation. During the insurrection of Absalom, Mephibosheth was charged with abetting the revolution in the hope of regaining Saul's throne (II Sam. 16:1-4). The charge was later refuted by Mephibosheth, who laid it to an act of treachery on the part of his sevant Ziba (II Sam. 19:24-30). David's response on this occasion may indicate his inability to decide where the truth lay. B.V.

**MERCERSBURG THEOLOGY.** This movement toward historic catholic traditionalism flourished from 1840 to 1860 at the German Reformed seminary at Mercersburg, Pennsylvania. Theologians JOHN W. NEVIN and PHILIP SCHAFF rejected American revivalism in favor of Reformed-Lutheran vitality, medieval piety, sacramental theology, and liturgy. They stressed Christology and the historical development of the church in their *Mercersburg Review* and numerous books. N.H.

**MERCURY.** Ancient Roman god, patron of merchants. His worship became important only after Greek influence became widespread, when he was identified with the Greek god Hermes. However, the two gods seem to have little in common except a penchant for acquiring money. His major festival fell on May 15—the ides of May. K./M.C.

**MERCY.** Jesus, quoting Hosea 6:6, declared, "Go and learn what this means, 'I desire mercy, and not sacrifice,'" (Matt. 9:13). Mercy, in the sense of compassion, not only on the old, the weak, the sick, and the poor, but also in forgiving sinners and withholding punishment for sins, is the chief characteristic of God in much of the OT and the NT. While God will surely finally allow sinners who fail to repent to find their own place outside God's fellowship with the fallen angels, nonetheless, God does not desire the death of the sinner and goes to extreme lengths to call the wicked to repentance. Yahweh, above all, is merciful. This quality of the biblical God is evoked in the great Western religions to this day.

To show mercy, an empathy for other people, despite what they may have done to us, is a cardinal virtue for Jew, Christian, and Muslim, and is equally recommended by Hinduism and Buddhism. "Love your enemies" is Jesus' extension of the practice of mercy to the furthest limits.

In the OT, Hosea is the great spokesman for God's mercy. His figure of Yahweh as the husband who cannot leave his wife (Israel), despite her sins, shows the mercy of God. Micah tells us that since we have received mercy, we must pass it on to others (Mic. 6:8). Not ceremonies and religious works, but mercy shown to others by those he has redeemed is the true wish of God (Hos. 6:6).

J.C.

**MERIT.** In Roman Catholic theology, the concept of a work or action that rightly deserves reward from God. While even traditional Catholic teaching on merit recognized that good works (or merits) are possible only because of God's grace, Protestantism, from Luther's 95 Theses to today, criticized the concept of merit on the basis of the Pauline doctrine of JUSTIFICATION by grace through faith on account of Christ's merits, not our own.

The idea of merit for good WORKS, especially for prayer, virginity, charity, and martyrdom, goes back to the Apostolic Fathers and is based on implications in Scripture. The classical passages cited include statements in the NT as well as the OT: Proverbs 19:17; Exodus 23:20-22; Deuteronomy 5:28-33; Matthew 5:3-12; 3:26; 6:1, 18; 7:21; 11:29; 25:34; Luke 12:8; John 4:36; Romans 2:2, 6; I Corinthians 3:8; II Timothy 4:8; Revelation 2:10; 14:3.

In this case, as in the question of good works, much of the conflict in the past grew out of a failure to recognize the development of doctrine within Scripture itself, written as it was over many centuries. The idea that good works merit a reward is an ancient one. Its major critique was in the OT, in the book of Job, which demolished the bookkeeping idea that righteous conduct automatically brings reward.

J.C.

**MERKABA MYSTICISM.** The earliest phase of Jewish mysticism in post-biblical times. The name is derived from the golden chariot (*merkabah*) of the cheubim (I Chr. 28:18). This movement emphasized God's grandeur and majesty, far removed from ordinary human affairs. To bridge this gap and reach the throne of God, humans need special methods, such as ascetic practices and special hymns. The journey toward God took the believer through a series of seven heavens and various angelic realms. On the way, there were hostile angels and other perils, but at last the mystic would achieve an ecstatic vision of God.

K./M.C.

**MERODACH-BALADAN.** The Hebrew distortion of an Akkadian name that means "Marduk [the god of Babylon] has given a son." The bearer of the name was a Chaldean prince who was often a thorn in the side of the Assyrian kings in the heyday of their empire and is frequently mentioned in their annals. He first appears as a vassal of Tiglath-pileser III (745–728 B.C.), but shortly after was a rebel king of Bablyon resisting Sargon II of Assyria until about 710 B.C., when he was forced to flee into exile in Elam. Again under Sennacherib (704–681), he returned from exile, reassumed briefly the throne of Babylon, and reigned there until 689, when Sennacherib destroyed the city. After that he disappears from history.

In the OT Merodach-baladan appears in II Kings 20:12-19 (Isa. 39:1-8) as the king of Babylon who sent an embassy to HEZEKIAH, the king of Judah, apparently to compare resources for a possible joint resistance to the Assyrian domination of the Near East. This embassy must have taken place before 701 B.C., when Sennacherib devastated Judah (though he was unable to conquer the capital city of Jerusalem). The embassy evidently came to nothing; Assyria was not yet ready to be successfully toppled. The biblical authors who have transmitted the historical recollection of this embassy have put it into prophetical refraction and seen it as a foreshadowing of the Chaldean conquest of Jerusalem that occurred nearly a century and a quarter later.

B.V.

**MEROM, WATERS OF.** Merom was the site of JOSHUA'S great conquest over Jabin of Hazor and the other kings of northern Galilee. Traditionally, the site of Merom was thought to be Lake Huleh, a broad marshy plain in the Jordan Valley north of the Sea of Galilee. Nineteenth-century Zionists drained this area so that Lake Huleh is now mainly farmland. Unfortunately, this site does not match the description of the battle scene in Joshua 11, nor is it reasonably close to Hazor, King Jabin's fortress city.

The more likely location of Merom is on a lesser trade route a few miles northwest of Safed. In this once-wooded area Joshua's foot soldiers would have had a much better chance to outmaneuver the chariots of the Canaanites, and to entangle them in the trees, or, as Joshua reports, to hamstring the horses and burn up the chariots. Wadi Meiron at this place carries off a considerable amount of water from a year-round spring, where the wadis eventually pass Safed heading toward the Sea of Galilee. There are in fact significant archaeological ruins at Meiron, including an ancient synagogue. Perhaps because of its fame as a shrine in Jewish history, Meiron played host to such famous first- and second-century rabbis as Hillel and Shammai, both of whom are buried there. Meiron is also twice cited in lists of cities conquered by the Egyptian kings.

T.J.K.

**MERTON, THOMAS** (1915–68). A French-born, American TRAPPIST monk, famous as a poet and

Courtesy of Religious News Service

*Thomas Merton*

spiritual writer. Born January 31, in Prades, France, of a New Zealand father and American mother, Merton studied literature in Europe (Cambridge) and America (Columbia University), especially concentrating on poetry. He was early recognized for his free verse and blank verse creations. Strong social concerns and religious feelings moved Merton to become a Roman Catholic in 1938 and to enter the Trappist Abbey of Our Lady of Gethsemani in Kentucky, in 1941. This abbey was operated by the Reformed Cistercians of the Strict Observance (Trappists). He served as master of students, 1951–55, and as master of novices, 1955–65.

Merton became internationally famous with the publication of his autobiography, *The Seven Story Mountain,* in 1948. He continued writing, emphasizing the contemplative life, social concerns, and scholarship. Although he lived as a hermit, he was constantly sought out for advice by people of all social stations. During his twenty-seven years as a monk, Merton wrote three hundred articles and almost fifty books. Besides contemplation, Merton's major topics were pacifism and social justice. He particularly supported civil rights during the struggle of blacks in the 1960s. Above all, he championed nonviolence at home and peace among nations. Merton also investigated ways of developing the inner life, studying Eastern mysticism for clues. He became interested especially in Zen Buddhism and was given permission to attend a conference of Buddhist and Catholic monks in Bangkok, Thailand, in 1968. This conference delighted him, but was the cause of his death. He accidentally touched an electric fan with a faulty wire and was electrocuted on December 10.

                                    J.C.

**MESCALINE.** A substance made from the peyote plant that grows in Mexico and the southwestern United States. Discovered by Native Americans, it has been used in religious rituals to induce hallucinations. It usually requires two to three hours before taking effect and the results may last beyond twelve hours. Results include mystical visions, an experience of total unity, a sense of eternity, or an experience of the holy. Among groups using it in religious ceremonies, no evidence has been found that it is addictive.                   I.C.

**MESHA.** King of Moab. According to II Kings 3:4-27 (see also 1:1), Mesha successfully revolted against Israel after the death of Ahab, ending a subjugation that had begun a century earlier as part of the conquests of David (II Sam. 8:2). The king of Israel enlisted the aid of the kings of Judah and Edom in an attempt to bring Moab back under Israelite control. They are said to have been victorious in their attacks from the south and to have conducted an effective siege of the capital city, but they withdrew, for some reason not fully explained, after the king of Moab sacrificed his son and heir on the city wall. Extrabiblical information about Mesha is found on the MOABITE STONE.                 B.V.

**MESHECH.** A geographical/ethnic name that occurs several times in the Bible. It first appears in Genesis 10:2 (see also I Chr. 1:5) in the "table of nations" after the Flood, where Meshech is listed as one of "the sons of Japheth," along with Gomer, Magog, Madai (the Medes), Javan (the Greeks), Tubal, and Tiras. Other certain occurrences are in Ezekiel 27:13 (again with Tubal and Javan); 32:26 (with Tubal); 38:2 (with Magog and Tubal); 38:3 and 39:1 (paired with Tubal). These associations make doubtful the textual tradition of I Chronicles 1:17 and Psalm 120:5, where Meshech is otherwise related. Meshech is generally identified with the Mushku of Assyrian sources, a people associated with the Tabali (Tubal). Tiglath-pileser I (1112–1074 B.C.) claims to have conquered them, but they appear again in the time of Sargon (722–705 B.C.). They may have been the people known as Phrygians by classical authors.

                                  B.V.

**MESOPOTAMIA.** "(The land) between the rivers" was the name given in Hellenistic times to this great plain bounded by the Tigris and Euphrates rivers, a region that now lies mainly in Iraq, partly in Syria. In the Bible it is called, or at least the northern portion of it is called, Aram-naharaim, "Aram (Syria) of the two

THE FERTILE CRESCENT

rivers" (compare the title to Psalm 60), or Paddan-aram (Gen. 25:20). This was regarded as the ancestral homeland of the patriarchs.

Directly and indirectly Mesopotamia exercised enormous influence on the course of biblical history.

Palestine, the land of the Bible, lay at the crossroads of the two great centers of ancient Near Eastern civilization, Mesopotamia and Egypt, and inevitably partook of the culture of both. Whether from the time of Sumero-Akkadian Ur (around 2000 B.C.), with which biblical tradition associates the ancestry of Abraham (Gen. 11:28), or the Old Babylonian period (nineteenth to sixteenth century), with its famous law code of Hammurabi, archaeological and epigraphical evidence confirms the many cultural affinities of Palestine and Mesopotamia.

Political interference in the affairs of Syria, Canaan, and Israel did not take place from Mesopotamia until the time of the New Assyrian Empire. Under Shalmaneser III (858–824 B.C.) the Assyrians began a series of westward conquests that culminated in the destruction of the northern kingdom of Israel in 721 B.C. The successors of the Assyrians were the Chaldeans, or New Babylonian Empire, who sacked Jerusalem in 586 and carried off its chief citizens into exile. The Babylonian captivity (597–537 B.C.) was the matrix of postexilic Judaism.                         B.V.

**MESSIAH.** The English transliteration of a Semitic term meaning "anointed." It was used in the religion of ancient Israel and in other religions, ancient and modern, in connection with a rite by which a person was formally and publicly designated as having been divinely chosen and commissioned for a task or role. In early Israelite tradition, the anointed one could be a priest, a prophet, or a king. In later Jewish thinking, these roles are combined, as they were by early Christians who identified Jesus as Messiah, or God's Anointed One. In addition to using the term of those functioning in these various ways in situations contemporary with the biblical writers, hopes for renewal of Israel and defeat of its enemies were often expressed in terms of messianic expectations, or divinely commissioned agents who were yet to come. There was no single, uniform pattern for these figures, either historically or as their roles were projected into the future.

In the older biblical writings, the rite of anointing Aaron and his sons as high priests reaches its climax in the pouring of oil on the head of the one commissioned for the priesthood (Exod. 29:7; Lev. 16:32). The scene is vividly pictured in Psalm 133:2, where the precious oil runs down on Aaron's beard and the collar of his robe. Similarly, Israel's first king, Saul, is described as "the Lord's anointed" (I Sam. 24:6). Samuel had been instructed to anoint Saul (I Sam. 9:16), and soon did so (10:1), explaining to him "the word of the Lord," that he was chosen by God to reign over Israel and to deliver them from their enemies. When Saul was divinely disqualified, David was chosen to succeed him, and was anointed to replace Saul (16:6-13). In Psalm 2 the king (v. 2:6), who is described as the Lord's anointed (v. 2:2) is acclaimed as God's son (v. 2:7). This matches precisely with the divine promise to David that God has chosen him and his posterity as a "kingdom forever," and that the kings are sons of God (II Sam. 7:8-14). In Psalm 110:4, however, the one who rules over the earth in God's behalf is also described as a "priest forever." Thus even in the historical situation

of Israel, the anointed agents of God are depicted as having their authority extend without limit into the future.

That implication is made explicit in the words of the prophets of Israel, especially those writing at times when the future survival of the nation seems humanly impossible. These prophetic hopes are expressed with reference to the future kings and prophets of Israel, though frequently without direct use of the term "messiah." The first stage in this development of messianic hope is to be seen in the prophecies of Isaiah of Jerusalem, who was living at a time when the northern tribes of Israel had already been carried off into captivity, and when it seemed that Judah was soon to experience the same disaster. Isaiah's visions disclose that a woman is already pregnant with the child who will grow up to see the nation's enemies defeated and the Davidic dynasty still in power (Isa. 7). Indeed, the Davidic kingdom will survive forever, as symbolized by the one whose counsel is wonderful, whose might is divine, whose paternal care endures throughout all time, and whose rule is characterized by peace (Isa. 9:6). Although this prophecy may originally have spoken of the next occupant of the throne of David, it soon came to be understood of an ideal, future king, or coming Messiah. At about the same time (eighth century B.C.), Micah was predicting that Judah's deliverance from its assailants would come through someone of lowly shepherd origins from the insignificant town of Bethelehem, which had been the birthplace of David (I Sam. 17:12). In the prophecies of Haggai and Zechariah, however, the deliverance and renewal of Israel are seen as taking place through the agency of two anointed figures: Joshua the high priest and Zerubbabel the king (Hag. 2:1-9; Zech. 3:1-10).

The messianic expectations developed to yet another stage in the sixth century B.C. after the fall of Babylon to the Persians, which resulted in the Jews being permitted to return from captivity to their own land. The Persian king who allowed them to go back to the land of Israel is called the Lord's anointed in Isaiah 45:1, since through him the restoration of God's covenant people and the transformation of their land is in process of occurring (Isa. 40:1-11). It is God who will renew the covenant people, beginning with the act of this pagan ruler, and who will bring about the triumph of God's purpose throughout the whole of creation. The instrument through whom the renewal will be consummated is not Cyrus, however, but an anonymous servant (Isa. 42:1-4), who will achieve God's purpose not by force, but by compassion and justice. Echoing the language of the servant prophecies of Isaiah 42–53, Isaiah 61 records the divine anointing of one who is the instrument of God to meet the needs of the afflicted, the imprisoned, the oppressed. In the power of God's Spirit, he effects the restoration and renewal of the land and its people, and brings to share in this new time of blessing people from alien lands and cultures

(61:5-7), with the result that non-Israelites share in the worship of its God. It is this passage that Jesus is reported in Luke 4:16-21 as having first quoted and then declared to be in process of fulfillment through him.

Another term used in the OT to announce the coming of God's rule over his people and the whole of creation is the SON OF MAN (Ps. 8:4). But then the psalmist goes on to declare that God has given to this one a place of honor next to God's own and has assigned "dominion over the works of thy hands" (8:6). In Daniel 7 the term appears once more. After a vivid description of a succession of horrible beasts, which symbolize the successive pagan empires that have dominated the Middle East in the centuries down to the time of the writer (early second century B.C.), Daniel describes the throne of God and God's assignment of a universal and everlasting rule over the creation (7:14) to a mere human being ("one like a son of man," 7:13). Although Daniel goes on to identify the "one like a son of man" as the faithful remnant of God's people, or "the saints of the Most High" (7:18, 22, 27), subsequent Jewish understanding identified the Son of man as a single individual: God's agent to defeat the powers of evil and to establish God's rule on the earth.

Another anointed figure of ancient Israel's tradition was the prophet. In I Kings 19:16 Elijah is instructed to anoint, not only the kings of Syria and Israel, but Elisha, who was to be his successor. The promise of God in Deuteronomy 18:15-18 that he would raise up a prophet for Israel came to be understood as a kind of messianic expectation of a prophet, whose coming would prepare his people for the final judgment. Thus in Malachi 3:1 and 4:5, a messenger, or even Elijah, is awaited to call the faithful to repentance, "before the great and terrible day of the Lord" comes on all the earth.

Out of this range of hopes and promises, Judaism, by the time of Jesus, had formulated several messianic ideas. One of them was that God would send a nationalistic leader, who would organize Jewish armies to drive out the Romans, as Joshua had defeated the Canaanites and Judah the Maccabee had freed Jews from pagan domination in the second-century revolt. Those claiming to be messiah appeared in the A.D. 60s and again in the A.D. 130s, when two unsuccessful attempts were made to establish an independent Jewish state. Clearly, this was the "messianic" charge that the Romans brought against Jesus, since he was crucified as a pretender to the Jewish throne (15:16). Even Jesus' disciples are pictured in the Gospels as expecting him to stage a power play in establishing the kingdom of God, rather than submitting to crucifixion (8:33; 9:34; 10:37). Though the disciples are represented as acknowledging him to be the Messiah (for which the Greek equivalent is *Christos,* also from a word for anointing), they cannot understand a messiah who suffers and dies (10:45).

At Qumran, the Dead Sea community expected two messiahs: messiah of Aaron was a priestly figure; messiah of Israel was a lay figure, whose role was one of royal authority. Their central act of corporate worship was a meal eaten in anticipation of the banquet to be celebrated in the end time, when the two messiahs would be among them, and God's purpose for and through them would be fulfilled.

In the NT, different writers draw on different messianic titles or images to portray Jesus as Messiah or CHRIST. For Mark, Jesus is the suffering, soon to be vindicated Son of man (15:16). For Luke, Jesus is the one anointed by the Spirit to bring the good news of God's grace to the poor (4:16-21). For John, Jesus is both Lamb of God and Messiah (1:41). For Paul, Jesus is both SON OF GOD and Son of David (Rom. 1:1-4). In Hebrews, Jesus is eternal priest (5:5-6). And in Revelation he is King of kings and Lord of lords (19:11-16). That he is the Messiah, all agree. The nature of his messianic role is variously described, as the writers and the Christian communities they represent draw on and transform the rich range of messianic images in the tradition of Israel.

H.K.

**MESSIANIC SECRET.** It is difficult to explain the fact that in Mark, Jesus is reported as frequently forbidding both the demons (1:23-25, 34; 3:12) and the people whom he helped (1:43-45; 5:43; 7:36; 8:26) to disclose his identity as MESSIAH or agent of God. His purpose in speaking in parables is said to be in order to keep his teachings secret (4:11-12, 33-34). Near the end of his earthly career, even the disciples are forbidden to tell anyone of his identity as Son of God, "until the Son of man should have risen from the dead" (Mark 9:9).

In 1901 William Wrede, professor of NT at Breslau, published his *Das Messiasgeheimnis in den Evangelien* (Eng. trans. *The Messianic Secret,* 1881), which Albert Schweitzer in his *Quest of the Historical Jesus* (Eng. trans. 1910) declared to have brought that quest to a dead end, since Wrede regarded all the appeals to secrecy in Mark as contrived by him as a means of concealing the fact that Jesus had never actually claimed to be Messiah. Subsequent study has pointed out: (1) that the evidence about secrecy in Mark is far more complex than Wrede's theory assumed; (2) that in the apocalyptic world view from which Mark writes, and which was that of Jesus, it is assumed that however public the message and acts of God's prophet may be, only the elect community will grasp the truth; and (3) that Jesus' strategy as Mark portrays it is to prevent the crowd—or even his disciples—from drawing false conclusions about his messiahship until they have witnessed the central factors in that role: the cross and the Resurrection.

H.K.

**METAPHOR.** A metaphor is a comparison that is implied by using a word or phrase that is ordinarily linked with one thing, but is now applied to something else. For example, in Isaiah 64:8, the prophet describes Israel's relationship to God in the words, "We are the clay, and thou art our potter." In the NT Jesus tells his followers, "You are the salt of the earth" (Matt. 5:13).

In the Bible, the subject matter and the aims of metaphorical language vary widely. Some metaphors are in the realm of human relations, as in the extended portrayal of Israel as a disobedient child (Hos. 11:1-4), or the nation as an unfaithful wife (Hos. 2; Ezek. 16). Other metaphors are based on natural phenomena, such as Jude 12-13, where the faithless Christians are called "waterless clouds," "fruitless trees," and "wild waves of the sea." Elsewhere the metaphors are architectural, as in Ephesians 2:19-20, where the church is pictured as a building, although the metaphor is mixed, since it is also said to grow. Paul's favorite metaphor for the church is the body, of which Christ is the Head (I Cor. 12).        H.K.

**METAPHYSICS.** Metaphysics refers to the analysis of the necessary and universal causes and structures of being. The word originally referred to the fourteen books of Aristotle "after the writings on physics," that is, to those works that went beyond the investigation of the several aspects of the natural world to those permanent "first causes and principles" of being, such as God, the world, and the human soul.

Inquiry into the first causes of being linked metaphysics with NATURAL THEOLOGY and, until the ENLIGHTENMENT, metaphysics was considered the natural ally of Christian theology. The philosophers DAVID HUME (1711–76) and IMMANUEL KANT (1724–1804) challenged the scientific claims of metaphysics and sought to demonstrate that it went beyond our analysis of existence, thus beyond experience, and therefore was unverifiable. For many philosophers today, metaphysics represents mere speculation or ideology. Also, since Kant, many Protestant theologians, for example, KIERKEGAARD, RITSCHL, and BARTH, have dissociated themselves from metaphysics and have appealed to biblical revelation as the only source of a true knowledge of God and man. Most Roman Catholic theologians and exponents of PROCESS THEOLOGY argue that the Kantian critique is not compelling and that metaphysics remains an important, even essential, foundation of Christian theology.        J.L.

**METHODIST CHURCHES.** The denomination of churches that adhere to the beliefs and practices of Methodism—a revival movement sparked by the PIETISM and EVANGELICALISM of the European continent in the early eighteenth-century CHURCH OF ENGLAND. Its greatest leaders were JOHN WESLEY, CHARLES WESLEY, GEORGE WHITEFIELD, and Countess Selina Hastings, of Huntingdon.

The term "Methodist" was originally a derogatory nickname for the extremely pious Oxford students who formed the Holy Club in 1729. The leaders of the Holy Club were John and Charles Wesley, who led the group in worship and acts of charity. The club broke up in 1735, but the name continued to be applied to the Wesleys' followers. John Wesley made use of the term himself, saying that a Methodist lived according to the method of life given in the Bible.

Anglicanism was heavily infiltrated with RATIONALISM, DEISM and religious indifference during Wesley's time. The House of Bishops had been subject to the Royal House since the split from Rome under Henry VIII. The church was highly ritualistic, but the piety the laypeople saw in the Separatists and in Moravians and other German Pietists was not characteristic of the Church of England. An evangelical wing developed in the church, and many of these Anglican evangelicals became Methodists, adopting Wesley's piety.

The Wesleys hoped to remain within the established church and sought to direct their followers to evangelical Anglican priests. This hope was crushed by the opposition of the bishops and much of the clergy. All pulpits were denied to Methodist "preachers." John Wesley then embarked upon itinerant preaching, in fields and on commons, and even in work areas near factories and mines. The dimension and depth of church life in England and Wales in Wesley's time was narrow and shallow. There was little active religious observance among the poor, and among the upper classes an empty ritualism. The fervent emotionalism of the new Methodist converts and Wesley's denunciation of loose living did nothing to make the Methodist revival popular among the ruling classes. Methodism was forced, then, against Wesley's will, into an independent stance over against the Anglican church. The outbreak of revolution in the American colonies, which meant the cutting of communications with the Wesleys on the part of American Methodists, propelled John Wesley into a formal break with the established church. He ordained bishops and elders to work in America, although only a priest in the Anglican communion himself. Wesley was concerned for the mission in America, although, as a devout conservative, he supported the crown.

The Church of England had an evangelical wing before John and Charles Wesley; indeed, their father, Samuel, was part of it. There had been a system of "societies" for various pious works since 1678. These societies were, in fact, divided into "classes" of twelve people; both Anglicans and dissenters belonged, the class leader visited the class members weekly, and the group met every week for prayer. The Methodists simply adopted this system and built on it. A new tier of the organization was the circuit. Wesley and others constantly traveled to visit the societies in the circuits. After Wesley died, the next tier of the system was developed, the district. Ultimately, the districts were organized into the conference, the highest level of authority. This system of society—circuit, district, conference—became the famed Methodist "connectionalism." Methodist polity to this day is very similar to the original organization. Contemporary Methodism is governed by a series of conferences, from the quarterly meetings of the circuit, to the district assembly, to the annual meeting of the conference. At conference meetings, three hundred lay people and three hundred ministers represent the whole conference and deal with the budget and expenditures of money. In a pastoral session, pastoral and disciplinary matters are discussed. The United Methodist church (formed 1968) has a Council of Bishops as well as a general conference.

In doctrine, the Methodist movement stood in the Protestant tradition. Wesley accepted the THIRTY-NINE ARTICLES of Anglicanism, with certain omissions and modifications. Ultimately, the Methodists embraced about twenty-four of the Thirty-nine Articles of Religion. Wesley, and his followers, modified the Protestant Reformation and the Anglican position due to Wesley's emphasis on some particular NT passages and on his own religious experience—an experience of inspiring power communicated to Wesley by the Moravian Pietists who met in London. Interestingly, Wesley's deep-felt assurance of salvation came not in an emotional revival but in a Bible study—while the German Pietists were reading Martin Luther's preface to his commentary on Paul's Epistle to the Romans. Wesley remained a pious intellectual throughout his life.

Wesley's doctrine caused him serious problems with the Anglican clergy, and these controversies disturbed him personally and deeply. It was his stress on the necessity of cooperation with God's grace in order to achieve salvation and especially his conviction (later surrendered, to some degree) that it was possible for the Christian to achieve the state of perfection in this life, that made Wesley the target of ecclesiastical criticism. Add to these theological positions Wesley's urging of rigorous behavioral norms on a rather loose-living age, and one can see that Wesley's road was a difficult one to follow.

But Wesley's theology was heavily indebted to the Protestant Reformation. From it he took his reliance on the Bible as the Word of God and as the chief rule of faith and practice, along with rejection of the cult of the saints, relics, and purgatory. From Pietism he took his puritanical ideas on personal behavior, his emphasis on preaching, and his stand on the sacraments. He did not see regeneration as taking place in baptism, as the Catholics and Lutherans did, but saw it as a sign of a regeneration that had already occurred. He did not, however, like the sectarians, deny baptism to infants, feeling that it would strengthen their faith. Wesley emphasized the memorial aspect of the Eucharist, stressing the passion and death of Jesus rather than the real Presence.

Fundamental Methodist doctrines include: universal redemption as a possibility, since Christ died for all, not just a portion (or the elect) as held by Calvinism; justification by faith, which brings the new birth ("born again"). In this justification, Wesley thought human free will played a large role, as did good works. In justification, Wesley believed, there is freedom from outward sin, but the victory over inward sin comes only in the new birth, which renews the fallen nature of humanity. Throughout this process the Holy Spirit bears witness to the human spirit that we are adopted children of God. Ultimately, the Christian may attain to PERFECTIONISM, a state of complete holiness or sanctification, which means the believer will not voluntarily commit sin. This emphasis on holiness caused so much scandal (and was theologically problematic) that Wesley backed down somewhat and the later Methodist church considerably modified Wesley's claims. It is said to be the inherent righteousness of the justified that gives the power to resist sin in contemporary Methodism. The holiness sects split away from the Methodists as the SANCTIFICATION doctrine was de-emphasized.

Wesley did not so much stress doctrine as he did the love of God and the living of a religious life through the observance of worship, festivals, and personal codes of conduct. To the traditional holy days of Anglicanism, Wesley added love feasts (the Agape) and the Moravian Watch Nights. From the beginnings of the Methodist revivals, the singing of hymns was emphasized. Charles Wesley wrote many beautiful hymns, which sparked the revival and are sung by most Christians to this day.

There was no designated creed for the early Methodists, but Wesley told American converts to adapt the Thirty-nine Articles for their use and the British preachers to use his four volumes of sermons and his notes on the NT as standards.

The Methodist movement was never unified, since the Arminian Wesleys and the Calvinistic George Whitefield did not really agree on doctrine; this division persisted after Whitefield's death. The Calvinistic Methodists divided into three sects: Lady Huntingdon's connection; the tabernacle connection (or Whitefield's Methodists); and the Welsh Calvinistic Methodists, organized in 1743. The first two groups mingled with the congregational groups, and the third persisted and grew.

Among the various early Methodist bodies formed was the Methodist New Connection of Alexander Kilham in 1796, which gave the laity an equal voice with the clergy in conference affairs. Another was the primitive Methodists, who arose from the camp meeting revivals of Lorenzo Dow in 1810. This was a Presbyterian-style church. The Protestant Methodists split off in 1828 in a conflict over the installation of an organ in a chapel at Leeds. This body no longer exists.

In 1857, in Great Britain, the United Free church was formed by the merger of the Protestant Methodists, the Wesleyan Methodist Association, and the Arminian Methodists with Welsh Independent Methodists. In 1907, a union of the United Methodist Free church, the Methodist New Connection, and the Bible Christians resulted in the United Methodist church. This was accomplished by an act of Parliament. Thus three Methodist bodies emerged in Great Britain and northern Ireland in the twentieth century: the Wesleyan Methodists, the Primitive Methodist church, and the United Methodists in Great Britain.

In America the Methodist Episcopal church originated in the work of Philip Embury, who migrated to the colonies in 1766. Methodist revivalism spread along the eastern seaboard. In 1779 a controversy broke out among Methodist preachers in the South over their inability to give Communion or even administer baptism under Wesley's Anglican restrictions. These preachers proceeded to ordain themselves and set up a church organization. North of Virginia, such measures were opposed and the conference of 1780 declared the Southerners out of fellowship. The difficulties of administration by Wesley, in Britain, of colonies in revolt against the crown, caused Wesley to instruct FRANCIS ASBURY not to receive any preachers from Britain not recommended by him, and not to retain any ministers who would not agree to the disciplines of the conference. In 1784, Wesley took it upon himself to ordain THOMAS COKE and sent him to America to ordain others and set up a church organization. In December 1784, at the Baltimore Conference, preachers were elected and ordained, thus establishing the Methodist Episcopal church.

In 1844, the Methodist Episcopal church split over slavery, years before the nation divided over the same issue. Bishop James O. Andrew of Georgia became a slave owner, through marriage. The conference discipline forbade ownership of slaves, but Georgia state law prohibited setting the slaves free. The southern districts protested the conference law, but were turned down. They then signed a separation agreement, and in May 1845, the Methodist Episcopal church, South, was organized. Both northern and southern churches grew until 1861, when the Civil War devastated the Methodist Episcopal church, South. However, the southern group recovered, and in 1866 almost half the Protestants in the United States were Methodists.

A number of black Methodist churches were founded, beginning with the earliest days of mission work. The African Methodist Episcopal church dates to 1787. It grew out of Bethel Church, an all-black congregation in Philadelphia, under the leadership of Richard Allen. This establishment was due to the blacks' experience of discrimination in white churches. In 1816, the A.M.E. church became an independent church, severing ties with the Methodist Episcopal church.

The African Methodist Episcopal Zion church was begun in 1796 after friction developed between whites and blacks at John Street Church in New York City. Other black congregations joined with "Zion Church" to form an independent body in 1822.

The Christian Methodist Episcopal church was founded in 1870 as the Colored Methodist Episcopal church. The black Methodist churches quadrupled their membership in the South between 1860 and 1870.

The Methodist Protestant church was organized in 1830 in Baltimore after protests against the autocratic authority of bishops. It entered the merger in 1939 that founded the Methodist church.

The Wesleyan Methodist church was formed in 1843 over objections to compromises over slavery. It was a church "free from episcopacy and free from slavery."

The Free Methodist church was formed in 1843 over objections to compromises over slavery. It was a church "free from episcopacy and free from slavery."

The Free Methodist church was organized in 1860 by preachers and laypeople disfellowshiped by conferences in western New York. These people loudly condemned pew rents, liquor, tobacco, the use of musical instruments in church services, and what they called neglect of the preaching of entire sanctification. The name "free" was adopted to stand for free seats, freedom from clerical domination, freedom from sin, and freedom in worship.

In 1939, after long negotiations, the Methodist Episcopal church, the Methodist Episcopal church, South, and the Methodist Protestant church merged to form the Methodist church. The Methodist church had six jurisdictions: five geographical and one racial. Each had the power to elect and assign its own bishops.

The Primitive Methodist church is a transplant from England. It is divided into three annual conferences. Congregations in Maryland, Tennessee, and the District of Columbia make up the Independent Methodist churches. Among blacks, there is the Evangelist Missionary church (1886), formed in Ohio by dissidents from the A.M.E. Zion church. The New Congregational Methodists were formed in 1881 in Georgia. Also in Georgia, the Congregational Methodists were established in 1852. In 1816, the African Union Methodist Protestant church was formed by members of the A.M.E. church who disagreed on paid ministers, itinerant evangelists, and bishops. The A.M.E. Zion church was organized in 1801 in New York. The Zion Union Apostolic church was founded in Virginia in 1869.

The Evangelical United Brethren church and the Methodist church merged in 1968 to form the present United Methodist church. The U.M.C. is very large, with over nine million members, the second largest

Protestant body in the United States. It is a complex mix of rural and small-town conservatism and urban and intellectual liberalism. It is, in fact, the middle of mainstream Protestanism. In recent years the U.M.C. has suffered a decline in membership due to the inroads of resurgent fundamentalism ("the Moral Majority") and the secularism that has affected most mainline churches for decades. The U.M.C., a member of both the National Council of Churches and the World Council of Churches, is ecumenical and is very active in refugee and relief work around the world.

J.C.

**METHUSELAH.** In the genealogy of Genesis 5, Methuselah appears as the longest-lived of the pre-Flood patriarchs, having attained an age of 969 years (Gen. 5:27). The precise rationale of the numbers in this genealogy eludes present-day interpretation; its general purpose is to indicate the passing of considerable time between the Creation and the Flood. Methuselah is probably the same as the Methushael of Genesis 4:18, who appears in a parallel genealogy employing ancient traditional names.

B.V.

**METROPOLITAN.** The bishop of the provincial capital, exercising jurisdiction over a whole church province and not merely a diocese. The metropolitan presides over a see approved by the pope, and exercises authority over suffragan bishops in the province. Diocese and province are church structures derived from the Roman Empire.

J.C.

**METROPOLITAN COMMUNITY CHURCHES.** An association of liberal Protestant churches that are either wholly homosexual in membership or else consist of both homosexual and heterosexual members. Many of their clergy are homosexual and believe this life-style is Christian. The group was denied membership by the National Council of Churches in 1984.

J.C.

**MICAH.** The abbreviated form of Micaiah, meaning "who is like Yahweh," the name of a quite different PROPHET of northern Israel (the son of Imlah; see 1 Kings 22:8-9; Mic, 1:1). Micah, a native of Moresheth in Judah of the south, for whom the title of the sixth book of the twelve Minor PROPHETS of the Hebrew OT is named, prophesied during the reigns of the Judahite kings Jotham, Ahaz, and Hezekiah (742–687 B.C.), partly overlapping the prophetic career of Isaiah. Micaiah ben Imlah was active in Israel to foresee the death of its king Ahab in 850 B.C.

Micah has the rare distinction of being recalled in another prophetic book: in Jeremiah 26:18 he is named as a prophet of the time of Hezekiah, and a citation is made of Micah 3:12. As is usually the case with Israel's prophets, however, few or no biographical data are supplied, and we are forced to rely on what

can be conjectured from his prophetic oracles for details of his personality and career. Unlike some other prophets, he has recorded nothing about the circumstances of his call to prophecy. The Moresheth with which both Jeremiah 26:18 and Micah 1:1 identify him, also called Moresheth-gath in 1:14, was one of the towns of the hill country of southwest Judah, which along with the others mentioned in 1:10-15 undoubtedly define the neighborhood in which he lived and where he exercised his ministry.

Though he sometimes alludes to Samaria in his condemnations, a fact that dates at least part of his words prior to the demise of the northern kingdom in 721 B.C., the burden of his message is denunciation of the Judean leadership centered in Jerusalem whom he holds responsible for the exploitation and social injustice that have happened to his familiar countryside. The degree of Micah's involvement with the sufferings of the peasants and urban proletariat, whose rights he defends, has raised the question of the prophet's situation within the society for which he became a spokesman. It was frequently assumed in the past that he was one of the oppressed whose cries for redress we hear in his oracles. On the other hand, the proprietary interest that he shows in his appeal for justice enraged (3:8; compare 1:9; etc.; "my people"), together with the lofty style of so much of the prophecy, exhibit a man who was of some standing in his community, one who could confront the civil and religious establishment of Jerusalem as a social equal.

The exact significance of Micah's prophecy as well as its exact duration are questions that cannot be answered adequately, as long as it cannot be determined how much of the seven chapters of the canonical book is really, in substance at least, the utterances of the eighth-century prophet that bears his name. Hardly anyone will question that chapters 1–3 (with the exception of 2:12-13, an obvious postexilic supplement) belong to Micah. About chapters 4–5 and 6–7, respectively, however, a more censorious verdict must be rendered. In both cases, it can be argued plausibly that there is a Mican nucleus that has been progressively augmented and supplemented by later prophetic authors who kept alive in the faith community a message whose continuing relevance they recognized. Whether successive strata can be isolated and identified with precise redactional eras in later Jewish history is another question.

In its present form, whatever its redactional history, the book of Micah consists of four parts: (1) the condemnation of (Samaria and) Judah for violation of the ancient traditional laws of equality and brotherly solidarity (chaps. 1–3); (2) the future glory of a restored Zion, heir to the promises made to the Davidic dynasty (a concept shared by Isaiah, chaps. 4–5); (3) a further condemnation of Jerusalem's injustice and social anarchy, including the magnificent "prophetic lawsuit" encapsulating the essence of prophetic religion in 6:1-8 (6:1–7:6); and (4) a prophetic liturgy of future glory (7:7-20), probably mostly of a later date.

B.V.

**MICAIAH.** The son of Imlah who appears in I Kings 22:8-28 as a prophet of the ninth century B.C. According to this story, he was summoned to reveal the word of the Lord concerning what was to be expected from the military campaign contemplated by AHAB the king of Israel and Jehoshaphat the king of Judah against the Arameans of Ramoth-gilead. Already Ahab's court prophets, "about four hundred men," had been consulted, and predictably they had assured the king of certain victory. Micaiah (also spelled MICAH), whom the king consulted only reluctantly, because "he never prophesies good concerning me," at first mocked the king's prophets by reiterating their words, but eventually prophesied the evil that the king had anticipated: Israel would be defeated. He accounted for the contrary predictions of the court prophets not by denying their prophetic credentials, which consisted of symbolic gestures and probably ecstatic speech, but by attributing their prophecy to a lying spirit sent deliberately to deceive and destroy the king.

Micaiah may be thought of as a kind of bridge or link between the "spirit" prophecy of the older period and the classical prophecy of word and vision characteristic of Amos and his successors in the prophetic tradition. Unfortunately we have no further information concerning him, save that he was imprisoned pending the return of the king of Israel in triumph, something that never occurred.

B.V.

**MICHAEL** (the archangel). In Daniel 10:13 and 10:21, in an apocalyptic vision Michael is described as "one of the chief princes" and "your prince" who struggled with "the prince of Persia," who was trying to prevent the messenger of the Lord from reaching Daniel. In Daniel 12:1 he is again characterized as "the great prince who has charge of your people." Taken together these texts reflect the late Jewish belief that every nation had its own guardian protector in the spirit world that lay behind the world of the visible. Angelology was slow in developing in OT thought, and even slower was the practice of endowing ANGELS with personality and names. The apocryphal literature was to carry the development much further.

Jude 9, which calls Michael an archangel, speaks of him as contending with the devil over the body of Moses, which is probably an allusion to the apocryphal *Assumption of Moses,* a midrash inspired by Deuteronomy 34:5 referring to the unknown burial place of Moses. In Revelation 12:7-8 Michael and his angels appear, again in apocalyptic vision, in combat with the dragon (Satan) and his angels, who are defeated and cast out of heaven. This passage is doubtless responsible for the later Christian theology of Michael as angelic protector of the church.

B.V.

**MICHAL.** A daughter of king Saul; the first wife of David, given to him after SAUL had reneged on his promise to marry David to her elder sister Merab (I Sam. 18:17-27). This was at first a love match, at least on Michal's part. She was loyal to David rather than to her father. Having learned of Saul's plan to have David killed, she arranged for his escape and concealed his absence until he was safe (I Sam. 19:11-17). However, after David's flight and during the period when he lived as the head of an outlaw band, he took other wives and Michal was given by Saul to a certain Palti or Paltiel (I Sam. 25:39-43). David's demand that Michal be returned to him as the condition of his contending for the throne after Saul's death (II Sam. 3:12-16) was doubtless motivated by his desire to legitimate his succession as heir to Saul. Michal may have had for her new husband the same devotion Paltiel so touchingly showed for her according to II Samuel 3:16. At any rate, the episode of II Samuel 6:20-23 indicates that she now despised David as a vulgar upstart, which led to the end of their marriage in all but name.

B.V

**MICHELANGELO** (1475–1564). Italian Renaissance artist, renowned as a sculptor, painter, architect, and poet. Few people have reached the pinnacle achievements of Michelangelo Buonarroti. He set standards for his day and the future. Born in Caprese, Tuscany, he was raised in Florence in a stonemason's family and was apprenticed to painter Domenico Ghirlandaio at thirteen. Noticing his ability, Lorenzo de' Medici took Michelangelo into his house, allowing him to study classical sculpture and meet leading humanists. These influences and SAVONAROLA's preaching inspired the harmonizing of classical humanism and Christian austerity in his works: *Bacchus,* 1497; *Pietà,* 1499; *David,* 1502–1504; and many others.

Summoned to Rome by Pope Julius II, Michelangelo planned a grand sculpture of Law, Grace, and Nature for the pontiff's tomb, but Julius changed his mind. The tomb was completed on a much smaller scale after Julius' death. The famous statue of Moses, majestically angry, is part of this tomb. Although Michelangelo preferred sculpture, Julius II had engaged him to paint the SISTINE CHAPEL ceiling, 1508–12, resulting in the magnificent *Creation of Light* and *Creation of Man* frescoes. Leo X and Paul III engaged him for architecture. Under popes Clement VII and Paul III he painted *The Last Judgment,* 1534–41, on the altar wall of the Sistine Chapel. It displays the tragedy and gloom of much of his later work. His painted and carved nudes later created moral controversy. In the final period of his life he wrote impassioned poetry. In each artistic field Michelangelo excelled.

C.M.

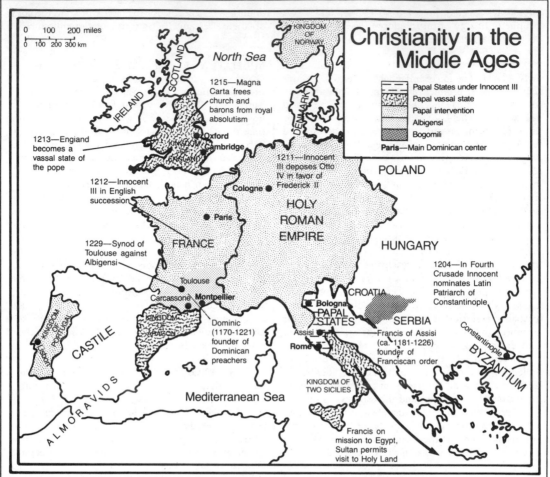

*Christendom in 1215*

**MICHMASH.** Today known by the Arabic name Mukhmas, Michmash was a town about seven miles northeast of Jerusalem. In the territory of Benjamin, it was probably founded early in the Israelite occupation of Canaan. It was militarily a strategic site and figures frequently in this capacity in the OT. Perhaps it is best known as the scene of the battle of Saul and Jonathan with the Philistines and their eventual victory, even though it was temporary (I Sam. 13–14).

B.V.

**MIDDLE AGES, CHRISTIANITY IN THE.** The Middle Ages are usually considered to have begun with a series of momentous events that took place in the fourth and fifth centuries A.D., the most dramatic of which was the series of Germanic invasions, culminating with the fall of Rome in 410. In 476, the last Western Roman emperor was deposed. Thereafter, the West would be divided among a series of Germanic states, which would be the forerunners of

modern states: the Visigoths in Spain, the Franks and Burgundians in France, the Angles and Saxons in Great Britain, and the Ostrogoths and Lombards in Italy. Meanwhile, the Eastern Roman Empire, with its capital in Constantinople, would continue existing for another thousand years.

The power vacuum left in the West by the demise of the empire was partially filled by the church; particularly by the bishop of Rome, who gradually gained dominance over the entire Western church, and a measure of political authority over most of Western Europe. When, in 800, the Western Empire was revived in the person of CHARLEMAGNE, the new emperor was crowned by the pope. This in itself was a sign of the growing power of the papacy, which would repeatedly clash with secular rulers.

The early centuries of the Middle Ages were marked by chaos and a loss of many of the achievements of classical civilization. In that situation, monasteries played an important role as the main guardians and transmitters of the wisdom of antiquity, both Christian and classical. In that process, increasing authority was given to the ancient Christian writers, to the point that eventually they came to be seen as practically infallible and possessing an authority similar to that of Scripture.

The eleventh and twelfth centuries saw the offensive against Islam in the form of the CRUSADES in the East, and the Spanish reconquista in the West. They were also a time of sharp conflict between the emperors and the popes, leading to the Concordat of Worms in 1122.

The thirteenth century was the high point of the Middle Ages. It was then that the two great mendicant orders of FRANCISCANS and DOMINICANS were founded, that GOTHIC art reached its peak, and the papacy attained its greatest power, during the reign of INNOCENT III. The thirteenth century was also the time of SCHOLASTICISM's theologians BONA-VENTURE and THOMAS AQUINAS.

The fourteenth century saw the beginning of changes that some would consider a decline, and others the birth of modernity. In 1303 Pope BONIFACE VIII, who had made unprecedented claims for the papacy, was humiliated by his enemies. From that point on, with some minor exceptions, the papacy continued a decline that would only be interrupted after the Reformation of the sixteenth century. From 1309 to 1377 the popes resided at Avignon, under the shadow of France. Since this was the time of the Thirty Years' War, which involved most of Western Europe, and in that conflict the popes generally served the interests of France, their prestige throughout Europe suffered. Then, in 1378, the GREAT SCHISM began, in which there were two parallel claimants to the papal throne, and two colleges of cardinals—and at times three—until 1423. That was the heyday of CONCILIARISM, a movement claiming that a general council of the church had more authority than the pope. Eventually, conciliarism itself was divided, with two rival councils, each claiming to be the legitimate one. When the papacy finally came out of the Great Schism, most of the popes were so imbued with the spirit of the RENAISSANCE that they spent more time waging war and supervising great works of art than at their proper functions.

Meanwhile, Scholasticism had become so subtle in its distinctions that it had lost its initial power; a new sense of nationality had emerged, eclipsing the former unity of Western Christendom; Gothic art had fallen from its heights; and many of the ancient documents considered authoritative until recent times had been shown to be spurious. The Middle Ages were coming to an end.

The end of the Middle Ages is usually set at a time toward the end of the fifteenth century and the beginning of the sixteenth, when a series of events took place that would change the face of Christendom: the fall of Constantinople in 1453; the invention of the movable type printing press at about

the same time; the discovery of the New World in 1492; the end of Muslim power in Western Europe in the same year; and the Protestant Reformation, early in the sixteenth century. Eventually, overenthusiastic admirers of classical times and of the Renaissance would dub the intervening thousand years the "Middle Ages," as if they had been of no significance. The truth, however, is that modern Europe was shaped during the Middle Ages, which blended the contributions of antiquity with those of the Germanic invaders.                                                           J.G.

**MIDDLE WAY.** *See* EIGHTFOLD PATH.

**MIDIANITES.** The biblical name of a nomadic tribe or tribes with whom the Israelites acknowledged kinship through Abraham (Gen. 25:1-2). They are represented, as one might expect of nomads, inhabiting various rather widely separated areas, each of which could be designated "the land of Midian" (see Gen. 37:28; Exod. 3:1; Num. 22:4-7; etc.).

As with other related peoples who figured in Israel's early history, a love-hate connection was part of the tradition, according to which Midian was alternatively at the origins of Israel's religion and genius or the source of some of its most disastrous downfalls. Thus Moses is represented as having fled to Midian out of Egypt, where he wed a Midianite woman, and where he also received from her father, a Midianite priest, vital instruction in statecraft and lawgiving (Exod. 2:15-19; 18:15-27).

On the other hand, the Israelites remembered that the Midianites had harassed them in the desert (Num. 25), in the time of conquest of the Promised Land (Judg. 6–8), that they had been allied with their Moabite enemies (Josh. 13:21), and that they had sold their ancestor Joseph into slavery (Gen. 37:28).

There are no extra-biblical sources that testify to the existence of any group called "Midianites" or to any territory designated "Midian." However, the late Israeli archaeologist Yohanan Aharoni has denominated "Midianite" a distinct type of pottery from the late Canaanite period that was found in an area that at least one biblical tradition (Gen. 36:35) identifies as Midianite prior to an Edomite conquest. This ware, of geometric patterns and decorations unparalleled elsewhere in Palestine, is reminiscent of the Hurrian pottery of Nuzi in Mesopotamia. What makes this fact especially intriguing is the biblical datum that the Hurrians (in biblical language the HORITES) were aboriginal in Edom (Gen. 36:20-30). The Hurrians were, in some of their manifestations, a venerable powerful, cultivated, major non-Semitic people of the ancient Near East.                                                       B.V.

**MIDRASH.** A literary creation used by rabbis to interpret passages of the Bible. The use of the midrash is a special technique or method of learning through rigorous study and painstaking inquiry into biblical verses. One type of midrash aims to define the full meaning of biblical laws; the second type seeks to derive a moral principle or lesson from the biblical text.

A midrash can take the form of a parable, saying, legend, story, or the like. For example, Genesis 12:5 reads: "And Abram took Sarai his wife, and Lot his brother's son, and all their possessions which they had gathered, and the persons that they had gotten in Haran . . ." (the Hebrew refers to "the souls they made").

How does one "make souls"?

A midrash answers that someone who brings a person near to God is as though that "someone" had created that person.

Soon after Terah and his family settled in Haran, the Haranites heard of Abram and his good works. Because he was hospitable, gave freely to the needy, and executed righteousness, Abram's name was blessed.

"Everything that you do prospers," the Haranites said to Abram. "Teach us, that we may do that which is right before God and our fellow human being."

Thus Abram "made souls."

This is a midrash.

L.K.

**MILETUS.** An important commercial city of Ionia on the west coast of Turkey, which reached its height in the Hellenistic period just before Christ. Like Ephesus, it had two marketplaces and a theater, which was rebuilt at the end of the first century A.D. Paul spoke to the elders of the church of Ephesus here on his third journey (Acts 20:15-35).

J.R.M.

**MILLENNIUM/MILLENARIANISM.** A period of one thousand years; and the teaching regarding the thousand-year period mentioned in Revelation 20:2-7. There are many forms of millenarianism or millennialism, which in earlier years was known as chiliasm. Both orthodox and heterdox segments of the church have adhered to some form of millenarianism throughout the centuries—and this is still true today. Some forms of the doctrine were taught by the Gnostics and Montanists, and many of the early church fathers were promulgators of some form of millennial teaching. Justin Martyr, Irenaeus, and Hippolytus are said to have been premillennialists.

There are three major views of the thousand-year period of blessedness—postmillennialism, premillennialism, and amillennialism. Within each of these positions there are variants.

*Postmillennialism.* The proponents of this view, once widely held, declare that the Second Advent of Christ, the PAROUSIA, will occur after the millennium. Those holding to this position have taught that as a result of the preaching of the gospel by the church, a period of peace and righteousness would ensue for the thousand-year period. World War II disillusionment seemed to dampen the concept that society was making moral progress. The day when the knowledge of the Lord would fill the whole earth seemed to be a wistful ideal.

*Premillennialism.* This is a major view held by many evangelicals, especially in the United States and Great Britain, who hold that the millennium is the time when Christ will literally reign over the earth. This, of course, means that the Second Advent must occur before Christ supernaturally sets up his millennial rule.

Premillennialists, as opposed to both postmillennialists and amillennialists, interpret the Revelation passage quite literally. Opponents of the view state that since the book of Revelation falls into the genre of apocalyptic literature, this is an indefensible approach to its interpretation. Detailed descriptions of the millennial state are provided by citations from the OT prophets who predict the restoration of a divinely ordained kingdom, when the Messiah will rule with peace and righteousness (*see* APOCALYPTICISM).

One of the major schools of premillennialism is called DISPENSATIONALISM, because the advocates of this viewpoint believe God has been revealed in a series of seven, more or less, dispensations. They teach that "the Kingdom" will be Jewish in orientation and will be the reestablishment of David's kingdom. In the plan of God, Christ will establish this Kingdom, postponed at his First Advent because it was spurned by the Jews.

In recent years, the variants of this position date the return of Christ as pre-tribulation, mid-tribulation, or post-tribulation. They agree that there is a period of approximately seven years called the Great Tribulation, which occurs just before the millennial reign of Christ. The pre-tribulation position, espoused by JOHN NELSON DARBY and C. I. SCOFIELD, declares that Christ will come for his church before the TRIBULATION period and thus believers will be delivered from a time of great persecution and sorrow. The alternate views place Christ's return in the middle or after the Tribulation. Dispensationalist premillennialism received a major boost through the widely distributed best seller by Hal Lindsey entitled *The Late Great Planet Earth*.

An increasing number of British and American evangelicals hold to what is called historic premillennialism. In so describing themselves they disavow much of the minutiae of Dispensationalism and particularly the concept that Christ's kingdom is not initiated until his Second Advent.

*Amillennialism.* This view is based on a symbolical interpretation of Revelation 20. Thus the figure one thousand is symbolic of fullness and completeness. Some of this school date the beginning of the millennium at Christ's First Advent. They do not accept an earthly thousand-year reign of righteousness but believe that the next eschatological event will be the return of Christ to inaugurate his reign after the present earth is destroyed in judgment and a new heaven and a new earth are revealed. The chief argument against the amillennial position is that it interprets Revelation 20 symbolically.

Many of the major communions of the church ignore or spurn all millenarian teaching. (See also ESCHATOLOGY.) R.H.

**MILLER, WILLIAM** (1782–1849). An early American leader of the ADVENTIST movement, Miller was born in Pittsfield, Massachusetts, to Captain William and Paulina Phelps Miller. A radical Jeffersonian and Deist, Miller was converted in 1816 as a "Calvinist" Baptist.

In order to answer his former Deist friends, he began to study the Bible. After fifteen years of study, particularly of Daniel and Revelation, he concluded that if Nehemiah 2:1 refers to 457 B.C. in Bishop USSHER's chronology, then "seventy weeks" comes out to A.D. 33, Christ's crucifixion. Thus 2,300 "days" (years) later would be 1843—Christ's SECOND COMING.

Ordained a Baptist minister in 1833, Miller began to preach his discoveries two years later. He published his lectures in 1836 as *Evidence from Scripture and History of the Second Coming,* dating the Second

Coming of Christ between March 1843 and March 1844. The final date he set was October 22, 1844. When this date passed, Miller, sick, discouraged, and rejected by the Baptists, returned to a small Adventist church in Vermont. In 1845 he and others formed the Adventist Association. N.H.

**MILTON, JOHN** (1608–74). English poet, independent religious thinker, controversial defender of freedom of the press, divorce, and separation of church and state. Born in London, educated at St. Paul's School and Christ's College, Cambridge, Milton prepared for Anglican orders, but Archbishop Laud's stringent rules turned him instead to literature.

During his early literary years (1625–40), he published "Ode on the Morning of Christ's Nativity" (1629), "L'Allegro" and "Il Penseroso" (1632), and the elegy "Lycidas" (1637) on a friend's death. Turning to politics and Presbyterianism about 1641, Milton for nineteen years wrote mostly political-social tracts, plus twenty-one sonnets, one being "On His Blindness." In 1641 he wrote *Reformation of Church Discipline in England* and *The Reason of Church Government Urged Against Prelaty,* extolling individual liberty over ecclesiastical control. *The Doctrine and Discipline of Divorce* (1643) argued that incompatibility was a sufficient ground for divorce, despite priestly

*The blind John Milton dictating* Paradise Lost *to his daughters*

inventions about marital sanctity. In 1644 Milton's pamphlet *Areopagitica* defended freedom of the press. When Parliament executed Charles I (1649), Milton repeatedly defended the action in *The Tenure of Kings and Magistrates* (1649), *Eikonoklastes* (1649), *Pro Populo Anglicano Defensio* (1651), and *Defensio Secunda* (1654). He argued for separation of church and state in *A Treatise of Civil Power in Ecclesiastical Causes* (1659).

Imprisoned briefly on the restoration of Charles II, Milton returned to poetry, and during his third literary period (1660–74) produced acknowledged great pieces. *Paradise Lost* (1667) dealt with cosmic themes: God, humanity, creation, evil, justice. *Paradise Regained* (1671) dealt with Christ's wilderness temptations and reconciliation for humanity. *Samson Agonistes* (1671) depicted the blind biblical Samson and Milton's own struggle with blindness.

In 1643 Milton married Mary Powell, who soon left him. They were reconciled in 1645, and she died in 1652, the year Milton became totally blind. His second wife (1656) died in 1658. His third wife (1660) survived him. From 1649 to 1660 Milton was foreign secretary under CROMWELL, corresponding with foreign governments in Latin. Milton is best known for his poetry, independent views, and advocacy of intellectual freedom. He was a Puritan, but highly individualistic. *De Doctrina Christiana*, published posthumously, rejected the orthodox Trinity and creation *ex nihilo*.                C.M.

*The Qutb minaret at Delhi (thirteenth century)*

**MINARET.** A tower attached to a MOSQUE, from which the muezzin delivers the call to prayer *(adhan)* in ISLAM.

The earliest mosques did not have minarets, and the call to prayer was delivered from the roof of the mosque or of a house. Everywhere that Islam spread, it adopted the native architectural style for the construction of minarets. In formerly Christian areas in the Middle East, North Africa, and Europe, square bell towers became minarets, and new minarets were built in similar shapes. In Iraq, spiral minarets were built. In Persia (Iran), cylindrical minarets with balconies became the style. Some minarets, such as the beautiful and imposing Qutb minaret in Delhi, are symbols of political power.            K./M.C.

**MINISTER.** A minister is ordinarily understood, in both the OT and NT, as a person set apart and authorized to conduct or assist in conducting public worship. The term is from the Latin, meaning "servant." In a broader sense, the term is used for anyone in public life who oversees some business for society, as in a prime minister or minister to the king.

*Old Testament.* In the OT Joseph was a minister at Pharaoh's court (Gen. 39:4). In I Kings 1 and 10, ministers at the courts of David and Solomon are mentioned. In the religious sphere, Joshua was a minister to Moses (Exod. 24; 33; Josh. 1), as was Elisha to Elijah (I Kings 19; II Kings 3). The PRIESTS and LEVITES (often called Levitical priests) who served first in the tabernacle (or tent of meeting) and in the First and Second Temples were called ministers (that is, servants) of God (Exod. 28; I Kings 8; Ezra 8). It is clear that the term minister, while still used for secular governmental positions (as it is used to this day in parliamentary systems), soon came to denote a religious official of settled, recognized authority. From the time of the building of the Temple a hierarchy of high priest, priests, and Levites was established (although Moses' supposed sermons in Leviticus and Deuteronomy place the development as early as the wilderness wandering).

*New Testament.* In the incident when Jesus read scripture and spoke in the synagogue at Nazareth, a "minister" of the synagogue is mentioned (Luke 4:20 KJV). This was the attendant who assists the teacher or RABBI by carrying the Torah scroll from its case to the lectern. Here, the servant or assistant theme is established. John Mark (Acts 13:5) was a minister to the older Paul and Barnabas, in this sense.

Perhaps most place-names in the NT that we translate "minister" actually read *diakonos* in Greek, that is, slave or servant. The humble nature of serving God by serving others is the major characteristic of Christian ministry in the NT. "Whoever would be great among you must be your servant" (Matt. 20:26). This characteristic is due to the humble, selfless example of Jesus Christ, to be sure, but it may also be a rejection of the pride and officiousness of the Temple priesthood. Mary and Martha, interestingly enough, are said to minister to Jesus, and so are other women. *Diakonia* is the term used (Luke 10:40; Matt. 27:55; John 12:2). Paul was ministered (*diakonia*) to by the slave Onesimus, showing that ministry meant physical assistance as well as spiritual encouragement.

Undoubtedly, the various names applied to people clearly carrying out the functions of leading public worship, instructing others in the faith, and administering the affairs of the congregation in NT churches developed in different locales and originally meant the same thing. The terms "minister," ELDER, DEACON, BISHOP, probably pointed to the president of the congregation, the one who officiated at the daily celebration of the Eucharist. But before even this development, there was a recognized ministry of the church: the APOSTLES. These original fellow servants of Jesus came to be called "those sent" because they were empowered and "sent" by Jesus to proclaim the Kingdom of God. Whether these were only the Twelve mentioned by name or included the seventy (or even larger number) is unclear, but the limitation of the apostolate to only twelve seems a later development in the Gospel tradition. What was absolutely required (according to the church, only a few years after the Resurrection, when Paul was converted) was that the person had followed Jesus during his earthly ministry. This apostolate was to preach the gospel of the Kingdom, to cast out demonic spirits, and to bear witness to the reality of the resurrection of Christ.

By the subapostolic age (mid-first century), bishops and elders (that is, presbyters or priests) were found in most churches. In the second century, the office of bishop was elevated above presbyters, and over the next century, the monarchical bishop (or single ruling bishop) developed in most cities. From this development, the office of PATRIARCH grew, and the patriarch of the West became the POPE in Rome.

By the subapostolic age, ordination to the ministry by the laying on of hands became a fixed rite. As early as the missionary ministry of Paul and Barnabas, believers were set apart for the Lord's work by a public rite of the laying on of hands (Acts 13:3). The Pastoral Epistles mention Timothy's ordination by the laying on of the elders' hands (I Tim. 4:14). The early church's ideal portrait of the minister is given in I Timothy 4, and Paul's concept is given in II Corinthians 6.

Over the centuries the minister became a more formal, even legal, official, as canon law in the Catholic Church developed. By the late third century the ministry was hierarchically divided into bishops, priests (presbyters), and deacons. The originally equal bishops (overseers) and elders (presbyters, priests) now had quite different functions, although both bishops and priests proclaimed the gospel, officiated at the Holy Communion and baptism, led public worship, ministered to the poor and ill, and buried the dead. However, later, the right to govern the church, to ordain other ministers, and to confirm members was reserved to the bishop alone. This was one of the factors that led to the rise of the papacy and its ultimate dominance of the Western church. Eventually, the demand for reformation of the church arose in Europe in the late fifteenth and early sixteenth centuries as a direct consequence of the concentration of authority in the church in episcopal hands—especially in the bishop of Rome—alone.

After the Protestant Reformation, the power of bishops was severely curtailed and the Lutheran and Reformed churches reorganized the churches in their territories with a one-level ministry. The powers of the bishops were given to the Lutheran and Reformed synods, consistories, and presbyteries. The Church of England alone retained episcopal polity and was followed in this, in modified form, by the Methodist movement in the late eighteenth century. Although some Lutheran churches (as in Sweden) retained bishops—and several in America have recently restored the title to use—the Catholic-type episcopal power was removed from the offices.          J.C.

**MINOR ORDER.** The lower orders of the Roman Catholic clergy, below the major orders of priest (presbyter) and bishop. The contemporary Roman Catholic Church does not believe minor orders to be sacramental since they were not instituted by Christ or the apostles. Clergy in minor orders have all the ecclesiastical privileges but are not bound by celibacy and may marry. However, with the exception of the contemporary permanent diaconate since Vatican II, if someone in minor orders marries he gives up his privileges. Minor orders are conferred by presenting the candidate with the instruments of the task to be performed.          J.C.

**MINOR PROPHETS.** *See* PROPHETS (MAJOR AND MINOR).

**MIRACLE.** Reports of miracles appear in ancient sources—biblical (Jewish and Christian) as well as non-Israelite, Greek and Roman. Even the contents are frequently the same: healing the sick, restoring the dead to life, movements of heavenly bodies in conjunction with important earthly events. The question to be raised is not, "Do miracles happen?" but "What do they signify?" The ancients, with very few exceptions, were not troubled by the notion that a miracle was a violation of the laws of nature. Rather, miracle was a special manifestation of divine power or purpose. What that purpose was would have been understood in a variety of ways, given the changing cultural and religious context of the one reporting the miraculous occurrence.

In the OT, for example, the older layers of tradition depict miracles as signs of divine confirmation of a leader of the nation, especially in a time of crisis. In Exodus 4, Moses has been commissioned by God to lead the people out of slavery in Egypt and into the land of the Canaanites, which God has promised to give them. When Moses asks how he can persuade the people that he has indeed been called of God for this task, God provides him a series of signs intended to persuade any doubters: his rod turns into a snake and then back into a rod; his hand is stricken with, and then loses, leprosy; when he pours out the water of the Nile it becomes blood (Exod. 4:1-10). In I Kings 18, where Elijah is engaged in a contest with the priests of Baal, "the fire of the Lord" (18:38) fell and consumed the burnt offering, the wood, the stones of the altar, the dust, and the water in the trench around it. All the onlookers proclaim that Yahweh is God. Other miracles are signs of divine judgment, as when the prophet warns the wicked king Jeroboam that the pagan priests and their altar will be consumed, as indeed they quickly are. Still other miracles are signs of divine compassion, as when God, through the prophet Elisha, feeds the poor widow and her guest (II Kings 4:1-7).

In the later OT tradition, miracles are promised as signs of God's coming deliverance of the people from their oppressors and of God's special care for the faithful during their times of difficulties before the promise is fulfilled. Thus in Isaiah 35:1-7, the restoration of the nation will be accompanied by the renewal of the whole created order, with the result that the desert blossoms, new streams of water appear in it and transform it, the blind see, the deaf hear, the lame leap about, the dumb sing. In Daniel 1–3, the assurance of the divine protection of the faithful few is symbolized in the stories of God's nurturing those who refuse to eat impure food, God's preservation in the fiery furnace of those who refuse to worship the pagan king as a god, and God's protection from the lions of those who defy the royal prohibition against prayer to the God of Israel. The point is clear: God will act directly in behalf of those who stand firm against the forces of evil and their schemes to corrupt or destroy God's faithful people.

In the Gospel tradition, there is a further development of this motif, which sees miracle as a sign of God's intention to restore the creation and vindicate the divinely chosen people. In the story of Jesus' controversy with both the scribes and his own family over his ability to expel demons from those possessed of these evil powers (Mark 3:19-35; Matt. 12:22-50; Luke 11:14-16; 8:19-21), there is no question that Jesus does indeed possess this power. The issue is, What is the source of his power? Is he in league with Satan (Beelzebul)? The clear answer (Luke 11:20) is that his exorcisms are manifestations of God's power, preparing for and already bringing into reality the divine rule over the creation: "If it is by the finger of God that I cast out demons, then the kingdom of God has come upon you." Elsewhere in the Gospels, Jesus' miracles are seen as signs of divine forgiveness, as in the story of the paralytic who is both cured and pronounced forgiven (Mark 2:1-12). In Mark 5:21-43, the raising to life of Jairus' daughter is clearly a sign of triumph over death. In Acts 10:38-43

and in Paul's Letter to the Romans 1:1-4, it is the resurrection of Jesus that is presented as the sign of God's vindication of Jesus as the Son and the ground of human hope for the resurrection (I Cor. 15:20-24).

Elsewhere in Acts, miracles are represented as fulfilling a range of functions. In Acts 1:18, Judas is destroyed by an act of divine judgment, as a consequence of his having betrayed Jesus to the authorities. In Acts 5:1-11, a theme is sounded that will figure importantly in the post-NT writings, such as the so-called apocryphal Acts: failure to fulfill one's obligation to the Christian community on the part of its members may result in their sudden death. Here in Acts 5, Ananias and his wife, Sapphira, withhold part of their possessions when the Christians are to share all things in common, and accordingly they both are struck dead. In the popular romances of the period, people making a religious pilgrimage are guided on their way by visions. Just so, in Acts 10 Peter has a vision that leads him to go to the household of the Roman centurion Cornelius, and the Roman officer in turn has a vision that Peter is to visit him. This theme, which is paralleled in religious propaganda of the Roman world, is used by the author of Acts to show that God is behind the spread of Christianity from its initial center in Jerusalem to the center of the pagan world, Rome itself (Acts 28).

Similarly, the Gospel writers have accounts of divinely granted portents, through which discerning eyes can see the hand of God shaping history. Thus, the magi are led by a strange star to visit the birthplace of Jesus. Earthquakes occur (only in Matthew) at the moment of Jesus' death and of the opening of his tomb on the morning of the Resurrection (Matt. 27:51-54; 28:1-6). The Synoptic Gospels agree that the sun was darkened as the hour of Jesus' death approached (Mark 15:33; Matt. 27:45; Luke 23:44). These and similar reported occurrences are narrated by the Gospel writers as a way of pointing out that the hand of God is at work in the events that are being portrayed.

In the Gospel of John, the miracles are told in such a way as to point beyond the incidents themselves to some higher significance (20:30-31). Thus, the story of the feeding of the five thousand (6:1-14) is told in a way not dissimilar to the accounts in the other Gospels (Mark 6:30-44; Matt. 14:13-21; Luke 9:10-17), but it is followed by a lengthy discourse on Jesus as the Bread of Life (John 6:25-59). In this section, Jesus makes explicit the contrast between the benefits and limitations of God's having fed Israel through Moses in the desert of Sinai on the one hand, and God's sustaining the people through the life and ministry of Jesus on the other: "If anyone eats of this bread, he shall live forever" (6:51). Spiritual communion under the image of eating the flesh of Jesus and drinking his blood brings the promise of eternal life (6:52-59). Similarly, the story of Jesus' raising Lazarus from the dead is more than another anticipation of a resurrection: it is a guarantee of the resurrection of all the faithful to share in eternal life (11:25-26). Important as the miracles are as events in themselves, they are more significant as symbols of the new resources and rewards that are available to the community of faith.

In the eighteenth and nineteenth centuries, in both Britain and on the Continent, rationalistic thinkers began to question the possibility of miracles, on the ground that they were contrary to or violations of natural law. Some well-meaning apologists sought to show that, rightly understood, the miracles were no more than natural occurrences. For example, the explanation of the feeding of the five thousand was that everyone had brought food, but they kept it up their sleeves until the little boy shamed them by sharing his lunch with Jesus (John 6:9). The seeming miracle of Jesus' walking on the water was only a matter of his tramping through the shallows of the lake, but the misty surface led the credulous disciples into thinking Jesus was walking on the deep. Such explanations miss the point in at least two ways: the ancient world had no problem with the notion of divine intervention in human affairs; and the rationalistic explanations ignore the clear significance that these miracles were seen to have had for those who first reported them, or who passed on the older tradition. Miracle was understood to be a sign of God at work.                                                H.K.

**MIRIAM.** The sister of MOSES and AARON, the daughter of Amram and Jochabed (Num. 26:59). If she is to be identified with the sister who figures in the story of Exodus 2:4-9, then she was older than Moses. However, the details of Moses' life, his family, his wife and children, and so forth, have been drawn from various strands of tradition that have not always been harmonized, and the same holds true for the figures of Miriam and Aaron.

In Exodus 15:20-21 she is called a prophetess and pictured as leading the women of Israel in dance and song, rejoicing over the destruction of Israel's Egyptian pursuers with "the Song of the Sea," thought to be one of the oldest pieces of poetry in the Bible. In Numbers 12 the story is told that she and Aaron, using Moses' marriage to a Cushite woman as a pretext, challenged the authority of Moses, putting their prophetic character on a level with his. For this presumption Miriam was temporarily afflicted with what the Bible calls leprosy. The story reflects the tendency to portray Moses as the unique person responsible for Israel's formation and may conceal the larger role that was played historically by Miriam and Aaron. In Micah 6:4 they are mentioned equally with Moses as leaders of the Exodus. According to Numbers 20:1, Miriam died during the Israelites' wandering and was buried at Kadesh.               B.V.

**MISHNAH.** The oldest post-biblical collection of Jewish laws. The Mishnah, arranged and edited by Rabbi Judah the Prince, includes the vast mass of oral interpretation and application of the biblical laws and the decisions based thereon that had accumulated from the days of Ezra (about 450 B.C.) until about A.D. 200. Originally handed down by word of mouth through the generations, the laws became too numerous to remember unless they were organized in some logical way, and so it was necessary to compile the Mishnah. The Mishnah both lays down decisions and gives contrary legal opinions of various scholars. It is arranged in six major sections, called Orders. They are:

1. *Zera'im* ("Seeds"), which deals primarily with the laws of agriculture.

2. *Mo'ed* ("Appointed Time"), which deals with the laws of the Sabbath and the festivals.

3. *Nashim* ("Women"), which deals with the laws of marriage and divorce and with problems of family life.

4. *Nezikin* ("Damages"), which includes civil and criminal statues and court procedures.

5. *Kodashim* ("Sacred Matters"), which deals with laws of sacrifice and Temple rituals.

6. *Tohorot* ("Purities"), which deals with laws of ritual uncleanliness.

Once the Mishnah was published, it in turn became the basis for further study in the academies of learning in Palestine and Babylonia. After many centuries, these discussions were compiled to form the GEMARA. Both the Mishnah and Gemara make up the TALMUD.                                       L.K.

**MISSAL, ROMAN.** The office (or worship service) book of the Roman Catholic church. The Mass is included in this book, which was called the "sacramentary" until the eighth century. The missal, as a standardized text of the various rituals of the Mass, dates from the sixteenth century. The first printed missal was issued July 14, 1570. It was revised in 1604, 1634, and 1884. Since Vatican II (1962–65), the Missal has been extensively revised because of the decision to offer the Mass in the vernacular of each country.                            J.C.

**MISSA SOLEMNIS.** A sung mass held in parish churches on Sundays and in cathedrals on a daily schedule. It is marked by the presence of a priest, a deacon, a subdeacon, and other assistants. A large number of candles are lit and incense is used.   J.C.

**MISSIOLOGY.** This is a comparatively recent term dealing with the science of the Christian church's cross-cultural ministry. This discipline, elevated to a more scholarly level than the approach of nineteenth-century missionary philosophy, explores the nature, the purpose, and the methods of MISSION in the contemporary world. Missiology employs the discoveries of anthropology, linguistics, comparative religions, and sociology. The journal *Missiology* serves the interest of experts in various aspects of this field.
                                                    R.H.

# MISSION, HISTORY OF.

Carrying the Christian message to others has been an important part of Christianity since its origin. Mission was implicit in the message of Christianity and practiced by Paul in his journeys before the appearance of specific injunctions (Matt. 28:19; Luke 24:47-49; Acts 1:4-6). By A.D. 313, despite persecutions, Christianity had penetrated the entire Roman Empire and beyond. Legends persist that some early Christians went to Arabia, Persia, and India. Ulfilas (about 311-383) invented the Gothic alphabet and translated the Bible into Gothic, and Frumentius (about A.D. 330) went to Abyssinia in Africa. Roman church missions predominated in the West; Greek Orthodox church missions in the East. The Nestorian church, begun by Nestorius, sent missionaries to India and China. Christian missions to the East and in Africa virtually ceased with the rapid expansion of the Muslims in the seventh century. The Muslims were stopped by Charles Martel at Tours in 732 and did not take Constantinople until 1453. Greek Orthodox missions expanded among the Slavs and Russians in the ninth and tenth centuries, particularly through the work of Cyril and Methodius. The Benedictine monks, founded by BENEDICT of Nursia (about 480-542), spearheaded missions in the West. Benedictine rural self-sufficiency and stability proved remarkably effective in the Middle Ages.

In the fifth century, St. PATRICK carried the gospel to Ireland, and his successors expanded to Iona, Lindisfarne, Scotland, England, and the Continent, through the work of Columba, Aidan, and Columbanus. This Irish monasticism melded with Benedictine monasticism in the eighth century, exemplified in Boniface, the greatest missionary in this period. Europe's barbarian tribes did not convert easily and often only after military conquest. In the thirteenth century the Dominicans and Franciscans arose to further Roman Catholic missions in Europe and afield. Franciscan John de Monte Corvino worked for thirty years in China, translating the Bible and winning thousands of converts.

Franciscans, Dominicans, Recollects, and Jesuits had missions in the Americas. Bartholomé de las Casas, Eusebio Kino, Jacques Marquette, Junipero Serra, and others did heroic work, converting millions to Catholicism in the Southwest, Mexico, South America, and Canada. Soon after the highly mobile and adaptable Jesuits were officially approved (1540), they began dominating Catholic education and missions. They won back much of the territory lost during the Reformation, and through Francis Xavier and Matteo Ricci extended Catholicism in India, Japan, China, and Africa. In 1622 Gregory XV formed the Congregation for the Propagation of the Faith to direct all missionary work, and Roman Catholic missions, greatly aided by the use of women religious, were very active worldwide in the eighteenth and nineteenth centuries. In 1919 Pope Benedict XV directed Roman Catholics to develop native, self-sufficient congregations, a stance that gained further recognition in Vatican II (1962-65).

Protestantism struggled for survival against the Catholic Reformation in the sixteenth and seventeenth centuries, and Protestant missions were largely to nearby localities. Calvinistic Reformed churches vigorously evangelized along the Rhine, as far east as Poland, in the British Isles, and in New England. Puritans in America began missions among the Indians with the work of John Eliot (1604-90), who translated the Bible into the Mohican language, and David Brainerd (1718-47), whose brief career inspired many later missionaries. A Protestant mission in India was established as early as 1706 by Bartholomaus Ziegenbalg (1683-1719), who was sent out by the Pietists at Halle University, Germany. Christian Friedrich Schwartz (1726-98) continued this mission with great success. Heavily influenced by Pietism, the Moravians of Germany dedicated themselves to missions, and under Count Zinzendorf, despite persecution and hardship, established self-sustaining missions throughout the world.

The Wesleyan-Whitefield evangelical revivals in England and America in the eighteenth century were springboards for numerous missionary societies that blossomed in the nineteenth century. The Methodist Missionary Society was organized in 1786, and the Baptist Missionary Society was organized in 1792 to support William Carey (1761-1834), who sailed with his large family for India in 1793. The London Missionary Society (1795), Netherlands Missionary Society (1797), Church Missionary Society (1799), British and Foreign Bible Society (1804), and the American Board of Commissioners for Foreign Mission (1810) were forerunners of scores of missionary societies in Europe and America. They sent missionaries to almost every country in the world. David Livingstone (1813-73) made African explorations that prompted the forming of the Universities' Mission to Central Africa (1859). Robert Morrison (1782-1834) distinguished himself as a translator and spearheaded Protestant work in China, and J. Hudson Taylor (1832-1905) of England founded the CHINA INLAND MISSION (1865). William Martin (1827-1916), Timothy Richard (1845-1919), and many others did significant work in China.

The powerful London Missionary Society began missionizing the South Pacific (Tahiti) in 1797 and had notable success in the work of John William (1796-1839), who was killed in New Hebrides. The Methodists won the Tonga Islands and Fiji. American Congregationalists concentrated on Hawaii. American Baptists backed the work of Adoniram Judson (1788-1850) in Burma, and the Rhenish Missionary Society supported Ludwig Nommensen (1839-1918) in Sumatra. Alexander Duff (1806-78) of Scotland pioneered educational missions in India, and education gradually became a major thrust of missions. Henry Martyn (1781-1812) became widely known for his evangelism among the Muslims in India. These early missions were almost always fraught with great danger.

The diminishing returns of competitive missions led to cooperation and division of territory among Protestants. Missionary conferences beginning in New York in 1854 resulted in forming the World Missionary Conference for ecumenical evangelism at Edinburgh in 1910 and eventually the forming of the International Missionary Council in 1921. These groups inspired twentieth-century ecumenical movements, and in 1961 the International Missionary Council united with the World Council of Churches. Missions focused on evangelization in the eighteenth and nineteenth centuries, but this focus slowly shifted to social assistance in education, medicine, agriculture, housing, etc. Outside direction has largely been displaced by the development of self-directed, indigenous leadership and sustenance.          C.M.

Courtesy of the General Direction of the Vatican Museums

*Mithras sacrificing a bull*

**MITHRAISM.** The worship of Mithra, an Iranian deity, was prevalent at various periods from 1400 B.C. to 400 B.C. In Persia, from the eighth to the sixth centuries B.C. and in the Roman Empire in the second and third centuries A.D., the cult was especially prominent. Mithra was the only Iranian deity to be assimilated in the West, brought there in all probability by the Roman legions. The religion was especially appealing to the military because of its strict discipline, hierarchic series of grades, and the central motif of Mithra killing the primordial bull, which was the first act of creation. In 1973 a medallion was found in the excavation of a Mithraeum in Caesarea Maritima, Israel, depicting the bull scene. In the West the cult became a MYSTERY RELIGION and a strong rival of Christianity because of its emphasis on blood atonement, fellowship, a strong moral code, strict discipline, and a distinctive emphasis on dualism. Like many religions of the time, Mithraism taught that the soul ascended through seven realms (heavens; compare Eph. 4:9-10;

Heb. 4:14), a personal salvation after death for the faithful, and punishment for the wicked. Mithra was sometimes identified with Sol Invictus, the sun god worshiped by the Romans on December 25.

J.R.M.

**MITRE** (Miter). A headdress of satin worn by bishops and abbots in the Roman Catholic church, while Greek Orthodox bishops wear crowns. Originally mitre meant turban. These badges of office are also worn by Anglican bishops. There are three kinds—the precious mitre, the golden mitre, and the simple mitre.

J.C.

**MITZVAH.** From the Hebrew term that is usually translated into English as "commandment." The religious experiences of the Jewish people and their feeling of exultation in the performance of religious responsibilities have invested the word with a cluster of associations and connotations not inherent in it. Technically, a mitzvah is an injunction in the Bible. In addition to the biblical mitzvot, there are many mitzvot of rabbinic origin. In a general sense, the word "mitzvah" is also used for any good deed or act of piety or kindness.

L.K.

**MIZPAH/MIZPEH.** A fairly commonplace name in the OT, referring to at least five different sites. (1) The best-known Mizpah, probably the excavated site known as Tell en-Nasbeh, in the territory of Benjamin about eight miles north of Jerusalem, played a significant part in Israel's history from the very beginning. It was probably also built by Israelites, after the area had remained unoccupied for some time by the Canaanites. It was a place of tribal and religious assembly, where important decisions were made. Here Samuel had Saul proclaimed king (I Sam. 10:17-24), and it was one of the holy places in the circuit of Samuel's judgeship. It was spared in the devastation wrought by the Chaldeans and became the seat of government under Babylonian control (II Kings 25:23). It remained a religious center after the exile and well into Maccabean times.

(2) Another Mizpah, in southern Judah, is listed in Joshua 15:38. Its location is unknown, but the biblical context suggests that it was near Lachish.

(3) There was a Mizpah of Gilead on the Israelite-Aramean border (Gen. 31:49). This is the Ramath-mizpeh of Joshua 13:26, also the Mizpah of Judges 10:17 and, probably, the headquarters of Jephthah (Judg. 11:11).

(4) Still another Mizpah, a scene of Israelite conquest, lay south of Mount Hermon in northern Galilee (Josh. 11:3).

(5) Finally, there was a Mizpeh in the land of Moab (I Sam. 22:3), where David deposited his father and mother for safekeeping during the time of his struggle with Saul.

B.V.

**MOAB/MOABITES.** *Geography.* The land of Moab encompassed in biblical times the fertile tableland that extends eastward from the Dead Sea about thirty miles to the western edge of the Arabian desert. On the south it was bordered by Edom, divided from it by the Wadi el-Hesa (probably "the brook Zered" of Deut. 2:13). Its northern boundary was always in dispute, but nominally the Arnon gorge (the modern Wadi el-Mojib) separated it first from the Amorite kingdom of Sihon and later from the Transjordanian Israel. The distance between the two wadies north and south is about sixty miles. The Moabite plateau, rising all the way from two thousand to four thousand feet, was largely a pastureland, since climatic conditions and the proximity of the desert render agriculture difficult.

*History.* Surface archaeology has indicated that at the end of the Early Bronze and beginning of the Middle Bronze periods (2400–2100 B.C.), the Moabite region enjoyed a sizable sedentary population, presumably the result of incursions of the nomads out of the desert who settled the surrounding inhabitable land east and west, which makes up the so-called Fertile Cresent. It is also likely that Moab as referred to is included in the tribal name of Shutu in the Egyptian execration texts of the twentieth-nineteenth centuries B.C. (compare Num. 24:17, which parallels Moab with "the sons of Sheth"). (The execration texts, semi-magical incantations by which the pharaohs of the Twelfth Egyptian Dynasty consigned to perdition their enemies in Phoenicia, Canaan, and the Transjordan, contain numerous contemporary geographical and ethnic names and also help to document in those regions the transition from nomadic to sedentary society.) On the contrary, the Amarna correspondence (letters written to the pharaohs Amenophis III and IV in the fifteenth and fourteenth centuries B.C. from Egyptian vassals in these same regions), which in more than 350 communications thoroughly accounts for many sites in Phoenicia, Lebanon, Syria, Gilead, and all parts of Palestine, is totally silent with regard to Moab. This fact may confirm some archaeological opinion that maintains that this land was virtually uninhabited during this period.

In the time of the pharaohs Ramses II and Merneptah, Moab once again shows up on Egyptian inscriptions. Correspondingly, in the biblical story of the Exodus, which is conventionally dated to this period (1200s B.C.), the Israelites coming into Palestine from the Transjordan side after the desert wandering found there a flourishing and well-developed society with a complex history of recent development (Num. 21–24). According to this story, Moab possessed a well-established monarchy, even though its borders were insecure, like those of many other local kingdoms, in this case because of the incursions of "Amorites" and "Midianites," that is to say, some of their aggressive Semitic neighbors.

At the beginning of the Israelite monarchy, Moab seems to have been a well-stabilized kingdom enjoying good relations with the Israelite confederation on its frontiers and probably acknowledging some kind of ethnic relationship. According to I Samuel 22:3-5, David in his flight from Saul was able to take refuge there and to leave there his parents for safekeeping. A tradition transmitted by the late book of Ruth even ascribes to David a Moabite ancestry (Ruth 4:17-22). The relationship, however, did not prevent David from incorporating Moab into his little empire when he came into full power (II Sam. 8:2; Pss. 60:8; 108:9). This subjugation of the neighboring little kingdom could hardly survive the dissolution of the united kingdom after the death of Solomon.

As far as we can judge from the Moabite stela of Mesha, Moab took advantage of the breakup of the united kingdom to regain its independence only to be subjugated again under the powerful rule of Omri, king of northern Israel. But under Ahab, Omri's successor, who was otherwise occupied with other wars, and in his aftermath, Moab again successfully shook off the Israelite yoke and regained its independence (II Kings 1:1; 3:4-27). Not only did it attain autonomy, however, it also extended itself to some of its ancient frontiers, incorporating into its territory some sites that had long been considered Israelite. The neighboring land of Edom, long subject to Judah, also took the occasion of this period of weakness to become independent. Independence of Israel and Judah, however, probably counted for little in these times of rival hegemonies in Syria/Palestine.

The Arameans (centered first at Damascus, then at Hamath) were perennial marauders, but they were succeeded by the Assyrians, who subjugated the entire region in a far more businesslike fashion and submitted it to tribute. In the lists of the kingdoms subject to the Assyrian king Tiglath-pileser III (745–727 B.C.), Moab features as one. It seems to have been sufficiently pacified by the Assyrians to have escaped the devastation that Sennacherib visited upon the countryside in the 700s, and it is credited with having been a dutiful vassal to Esar-haddon (681–669) and Ashurbanipal (668–633).

The final fate of Moab is somewhat obscure. The Chaldeans, who succeeded the Assyrians as overlords of the Near East, probably put an end to Moabite polity and nationalism once and for all. The Moabites were, at all events, engulfed along with the Edomites in the Nebatean incursions of the fourth century B.C., forming part of that "Arabia" that bordered the Roman Empire in this area of the world after 63 B.C.

*The People.* The Moabites were a people with whom the Israelites acknowledged an ethnic relationship but whom they also rejected for historical reasons. The ethnic relationship appears, for example, in Genesis 19:30-38, an etiological story that purports to account for the origins of both Ammonites and Moabites, peoples who were forever excluded from acceptance into the communion of Israel (Deut.

23:3-4). The Genesis story is scurrilous, surely, admitting kinship only reluctantly and pejoratively. The historical circumstances that distanced Moab from Israel are stated or alluded to in numerous OT passages, beginning with the story of Numbers 21–24, which represents the Moabites as attempting to interfere with the Israelites in the initial stages of their conquest of the Promised Land. Persistent prophetic oracles against Moab (Amos 2:1-3; Isaiah 15–16; Jeremiah 48; etc.) testify to a continuous anti-Moabite animus, for reasons not clearly defined. Ezekiel 25:8-11, also an oracle against Moab, indicates that the animosity was reciprocated, and that the Moabites had taken pleasure in Judah's defeat and devastation by the Chaldeans.

Unfortunately, our knowledge of the Moabite people is virtually limited to the data supplied by the Bible. Archaeology, however, does tend to confirm the cultural affinity of Israelites and Moabites by revealing no significant differences between the two, while the stela of Mesha shows that the Moabite language was practically identical with biblical Hebrew. B.V.

**MOABITE STONE.** In 1868 nomadic Arabs in the Transjordan unearthed a basalt stela, over a meter in height, which proved to be a record of the exploits of MESHA, king of Moab, written in the first person. Unfortunately the nomads shattered the stone, thinking that an object that attracted so much interest from the scholars to whom it had been shown must contain treasure, but not before a squeeze had been made of the inscription. Though imperfect, the squeeze has permitted restoration of the major part of the stela, which now stands in the Louvre museum.

The inscription appears in the Phoenician or old Hebrew script and is beautifully incised. The language differs very little from the biblical Hebrew of the period and contains some of the same idioms. Linguistically the stela confirms what the archaeology of ancient sites has suggested, that Israelites and Moabites shared much the same culture.

In the text Mesha boasts of having liberated MOAB from "the son of Omri," an evident reference to the revolt under Jehoram, Omri's grandson, described in II Kings 3:4-27. He also claims to have regained for Moab various cities occupied by Israel. Among these was Dibon, claimed by the tribe of Gad (Num. 32:34; Mesha also mentions Gad), but indeed later on proverbially Moabite (see Isa. 15:2). Dibon is doubtless to be identified with the site called Dhiban, where the stela was found, and it is likely that this city, rebuilt and renamed by Mesha, was constituted his capital. The circumstances of the geographical details and developments chronicled in the inscription lead to the conclusion that it dates from a later period in Mesha's reign than that described in the book of Kings.

The text of the Moabite Stone speaks of "devoting" conquered peoples and cities, that is, consecrating

From *Atlas of the Bible* (Thomas Nelson & Sons Limited)

*The Moabite Stone, stele of Mesha, king of Moab*

them to the national deity by total destruction even as the Israelites are represented as doing on occasion (see Josh. 6:17). It also confirms that Yahweh, mentioned by name, was and remained the God of northern Israel's worship, although the text of I Kings 13:25-33, written from a later Judahite standpoint, insinuates that the actions of the first Jeroboam resulted in wholesale apostasy from Yahwism. B.V.

**MODEIN.** A town, identified with Khirbet el-Midya, about fifteen miles southeast of Tel Aviv, Israel, where the Maccabees began their desperate revolt against the Syrian monarch Antiochus IV in the second century B.C. Here the Maccabean family was born and buried (I Macc. 2:1, 70; 9:19; 13:25). Josephus saw the tomb (*Antiquities*), and Eusebius says it was still present in his time (*Onomasticon*). J.R.M.

**MODERATOR.** The presiding officer of any of several Protestant denominations or Christian organizations. The term is employed particularly by chuches of the Reformed or Presbyterian family. Thus, the moderator of the Presbyterian Church (U.S.A.) presides over the denomination's General Assembly for a one-year term. The nomenclature is used also for the presiding officers of the lower courts of Presbyterian churches, synods, presbyteries, and sessions. Reformed doctrine has always opposed the concept of permanent moderators or any ecclesiastical office corresponding to that of a bishop.          R.H.

**MODERNISM.** This term is used for a variety of religious and theological movements, all of which have been critical of traditional ideas and have consciously sought to adapt Christianity to the modern world.

In the context of American Protestantism, modernism, also called scientific modernism, flourished in the early decades of the twentieth century. It stood opposed, not only to conservative biblicism, but also to middle-of-the-road LIBERALISM and advocated a more radical acceptance of modern scientific ways of thinking. SHAILER MATHEWS, author of *The Faith of Modernism,* defined the movement as "the use of the methods of modern science to find, state, and use the permanent and central values of inherited orthodoxy in meeting the needs of a modern world." An empirical philosophy of religion, drawing on the natural, social, and historical sciences, was to be the basis of modernist theology. The movement had its center in Chicago, but its influence was felt throughout the United States.

In the Roman Catholic church, modernism was the center of much controversy in the closing years of the nineteenth century and the opening decade of the twentieth. It included many strands: radical biblical criticism, evolutionary philosophy, and a strongly pragmatic approach to the interpretation of dogma. Among its leaders were Alfred Loisy, Lucien Laberthonniere, and GEORGE TYRRELL, who defined a modernist as "a churchman of any sort who believes in the possibility of a synthesis between the essential truth of religion and the essential truth of modernity." The modernists were condemned by the pope in 1908 and their leaders excommunicated or silenced.

In the Church of England, the word "modernism" would often be taken to mean the Modern Churchmen's Union, founded in 1898 to promote liberal ideas and maintain the comprehensiveness of the Anglican churches. In its great days it included the biblical scholar H. D. A. Major, who founded its journal, *The Modern Churchman,* and is often regarded as the arch-modernist of Anglicanism, and also such distinguished philosophical theologians as Hastings Rashdall and W. R. Inge. The history of the movement has been marred by its hostility to Catholicism, and though it still exists, it no longer has much influence.          J.M.

**MOFFATT, JAMES** (1870–1944). Born in Scotland and educated at Glasgow University, James Moffatt served as a minister in the United Free Church of Scotland (1896–1912) before assuming academic posts at Mansfield College, Oxford, where he was professor of Greek (1912–15) and then at United Free College in Glasgow as professor of church history (1915–27). In 1927 he came to Union Theological Seminary in New York as Washburn Professor of Church History, and remained at Union until his death. In addition to filling distinguished lectureships (Jowett, Cunningham, Hibbert), he produced many books on a wide range of subjects, including *Primer to the Novels of George Meredith* (1909), *Introduction to the Literature of the New Testament* (1911), the International Critical Commentary on the Epistle to the Hebrews (1924), *Presbyterianism* (1928), *Love in the New Testament* (1929), *Day Before Yesterday* (1930), *Grace in the New Testament* (1931), *First Five Centuries of the Church* (1938), *The Books of the Prophets* (1939). He is perhaps best remembered today, however, for his translation of the Bible (the New Testament in 1913; the whole Bible in 1925) and for the Moffatt Commentary Series, which was based on his translation.          H.K.

**MOHR, JOSEPH** (1792–1848). Austrian Roman Catholic priest and author of the famed Christmas carol "Silent Night! Holy Night!" Mohr was born in Salzburg, Austria, where as a youth he was a chorister in the Cathedral of Salzburg. In 1815 he was ordained a priest. While serving as the vicar of the Church of St. Nicholas in the Tyrolean village of Obendorf, high in the Austrian Alps, he was preparing for the Christmas Eve mass in 1818. To his consternation the church pipe organ broke down just before the festive occasion. That evening the young pastor wrote the poem "Stille Nacht, Heilige Nacht." He prevailed on the local schoolmaster and church organist, Franz Grüber, to write music for guitar accompaniment. On Christmas Eve, the young priest and organist sang the song for the first time. It met with quick success in the surrounding villages. When Kare Maurachen of Zillerthal, a widely known organ builder, came to repair the Obendorf organ, he heard the song played by Grüber. Through Maurachen's influence, the Strasser Children's Quartet sang "Stille Nacht" throughout Austria and Germany and even in a concert performed in the Royal Saxon Court Chapel in Pleissenburg Castle. Before long the song ws being sung in many languages and versions around the world.          R.H.

**MOKSHA.** In terms of the Hindu world view, moksha means "release, freedom, liberation," in the sense of leaping free of all constraints into unlimited being; release from bondage to the endless rebirth wrought by KARMA, and so from the toils of MAYA.

Although the particular path to liberation varies from school to school, most Hindus would regard moksha as the supreme goal of human life and would hold that it is obtained by desisting from activity that generates Karmic retribution, and above all by wisdom that sees into the true nature of reality.

Moksha's ultimate nature is one with BRAHMAN, the timeless Sole Reality, and so is unconditioned by birth, death, or grasping. Meditation is the royal road to this realization, though it can also be attained by devotional love and, according to the BHAGAVAD GITA, selfless pursuance of duty in the world. A *jivan-mukta,* a person believed to have attained moksha in this life, is afforded great veneration in HINDUISM and sought as a spiritual teacher. R.E.

**MOLECH.** It is generally thought that this word is a contemptuous deformation (using the vowels of *bosheth,* "shame") of the Semitic *malk, melek,* "king," a title sometimes bestowed on various deities (in Isa. 6:5 Yahweh is called "the King"). This explanation is preferable to that of a few scholars who point to the fact that in some languages cognate with Hebrew *molk* has the meaning "sacrifice," and therefore propose that the frequent expression "to Molech" (II Kings 23:10; Jer. 32:35) merely means "to offer sacrifice." Passages like Leviticus 20:1-5 seem to indicate clearly that Molech was a deity to whom human sacrifice was offered, specifically the sacrifice of infants and, even more specifically, the sacrifice of the firstborn. It is possible that the cult of Molech was a perversion of Yahwism: though human sacrifice was forbidden by the Mosaic law and attacked by the prophets, passages like Genesis 22 and Judges 11:30 show that in earlier times it was conceived as acceptable to the Lord. Much more likely, however, is that it was the resurrection of a Canaanite practice, encouraged by Judah's subjection to foreign domination. Human sacrifice was a commonplace of Israel's Semitic neighbors (see II Kings 3:27). King Ahaz, who became the vassal of Assyria, imported a foreign cult into the Jerusalem Temple (II Kings 16:10-18) and offered his own son as a burnt offering (II Kings 16:3). In the final days of the Assyrian Empire, the cult of Molech seems to have been particularly prevalent in Jerusalem, carried out at Topheth ("fiery place"), in the valley of Hinnom alongside the city (Jer. 7:31; 19:6; II Kings 21:6). B.V.

**MOLTMANN, JÜRGEN,** (1926– ). A leading German Protestant theologian in the period following that of KARL BARTH and RUDOLF BULTMANN. Educated at Göttingen University, Moltmann taught there and at Wuppertal, Bonn, and Hamburg, and presently serves as professor of systematic theology at Tübingen. He has focused attention on ESCHATO-LOGY as the central principle in theological reconstruction. Moltmann was thrust into prominence with the publication of his *Theology of Hope* (1964; Eng. trans. 1967), a book that concentrated on such themes as God's promise and fulfillment, the coming of God's kingdom, and the calling of Christians to historical responsibility as the starting point for thinking about God, Christ, salvation, and the church.

Like Wolfhart Pannenberg's theme of revelation as

Courtesy of Religious News Service

*Jürgen Moltmann*

history, Moltmann's concentration on eschatology reasserts theology's fundamental connection with history and a rejection of all supra-historical conceptions of knowledge of God, faith, and hope. Revelation is given in and through historical existence—especially in the record of God's promise and covenant faithfulness and in the eschatological hope that quickens human openness and responsibility for history. Human obedience in facing the risks of history "between the times" is the other side of God's promise. Moltmann's "theology of hope" is profoundly influenced by and a response to the philosopher Ernst Bloch, who, in *Das Prinzip Hoffnung,* speaks of a "God who has the future as the mode of his being."

Moltmann's "theology of hope" leads to his second theme: political theology. The arena of Christian obedience is politics. Moltmann sees the beginning of political theology in the criticism of theology's cultural and ideological commitments. Here he is dependent on the critical theory of the Frankfort school of social criticism, especially that of Theodor W. Adorno and Max Horkheimer. Theology must disavow subjectivism and individualism and ask what effect it has in the fields of politics, economics, and social life. Here the Calvinist tradition, with its emphasis on Christ's transformation of culture, is dominant in Moltmann's thought, in contrast to the Lutheran teaching regarding the "two realms" of church and state. Much of his writing is directed to the struggles for liberation from racism, sexism, war, and to defending human rights. Identification with the captive, the dispossessed, and the suffering focuses on Moltmann's third theme: a theology of the cross.

Hope for a politics of human liberation is, paradoxically, grounded in the cross, the sign of God's own abandonment and suffering. According to Moltmann, there is no hope for humanity in the hands of the "apathetic man of action" and the suffering that he causes. Only "Christian pathos," leading to genuine sympathy, sensitivity, and sacrificial love—and rooted in the vivifying memory of the suffering God on the cross—can be truly liberating. Pathos is the pattern of empathetic suffering, both the suffering of God for the people Israel and the church, and God's people's suffering love in solidarity with humankind. Through suffering one lives in God. For Moltmann there is no true theology of hope that is not first of all a theology of the cross.

Moltmann has lectured widely throughout Europe and North America and regularly engages in dialogue with Jewish and Roman Catholic thinkers, as well as with Marxists and secular humanists. Among his writings, in English, are *Religion, Revolution, and the Future* (1969), *Hope and Planning* (1971), *The Crucified God* (1974), *The Experiment Hope (1975), The Church in the Power of the Spirit* (1977), *The Future of Creation* (1979), and *The Trinity and the Kingdom* (1981).

J.L.

**MONARCHIANISM.** A term designating a theological movement in the early church (second-third centuries) that sought to safeguard the unity of the Godhead over against charges of tritheism on the one hand and on the other against Gnostic emanations of the one Deity which separated God from the world. Adoptionist or Dynamic Monarchians maintained the man Jesus was God only in the sense that the power of God the Father resided in him, thus detracting from the Incarnation. Theodotus of Byzantium and Paul of Samosata fall into this category. The Modalist Monarchians believed that Father, Son, and Holy Spirit were different modes of the one God. Noetus, Praxeas, and Sabellius fall into this typology. Tertullian modified Monarchianism by saying God is One and that Father, Son, and Holy Spirit are roles or functions of the one Godhead. His view helped shape the orthodox view expressed at Nicaea (325) and CHALCEDON (451) (*See* NICENE CREED/COUNCILS OF NICAEA.).

C.M.

**MONASTICISM.** A movement within the ancient and medieval Catholic church, developed out of early Christian asceticism, some elements of GNOSTICISM (dualism), and late Greek philosophy (Neoplatonism). The monastic movement stressed separation from the world, celibacy, strict observance of worship, and a moral, ascetic life. Gradually, earlier Anchorites (hermits) who lived alone in the desert drew together into communities, where a development of communal rules of living and an emphasis on work, study, and contemplation developed. The high point of this communal development, which became dominant in the West, was under BENEDICT of Nursia in the sixth century, whose rule remains the foundation for later monastic life in the Roman Catholic Church. In the East, hermits continued to flourish, although gradually, monks in the Orthodox churches drew together in monasteries also.

Monasticism is thus an institution formalizing the ascetic life of celibacy, poverty, and obedience (to the abbot or ruler of the order, and to the pope), which regulates the conditions of work, prayer, study, and contemplation of those committed to a life of religious devotion.

Monasticism drew on early Christian roots; the sense of being a small, saving minority in a pagan world of the NT era, the high honor given virginity and celibacy that derived from Paul and the early veneration of Mary, and the sharing of goods in the apostolic community in Acts. Early asceticism was drawn from the intense belief in the Second Coming of Christ and the soon end of the age that animated the early church. It does not derive from Manichaeism (absolute dualism), but is influenced by the philosophy of Neoplatonism current in the first five Christian centuries. Upon the elevation of Christianity to the chief religion of the Roman Empire, after Constantine, and the influx of pagans into the church, a reaction against worldliness set in. Monasticism began to grow as a moral reform movement. Augustine (fifth century) was drawn to it, also, because of his struggle to control his sexuality. After Benedict's reform, monasticism stabilized and spread throughout the West.

J.C.

**MONEY CHANGERS.** Two different Greek words in John 2:14-15 are used to refer to those who exchanged foreign currency and currency of different denominations. Since the time of Moses the people, rich or poor, had been required to pay a half-shekel as atonement money for the service of the tabernacle (Exod. 30:15-16). This was continued until the time of Jesus, who along with Peter is recorded as having paid the tax (Matt. 17:24-27). It was required of every male Israelite who was at least twenty years old (Exod. 30:14). According to the Mishnah, tables of money changers were set up in the provinces a month before Passover and then ten days later they were moved to the Temple in Jerusalem. Money taken up in a city was gathered together and sent on to Jerusalem as a unit. Although Roman currency prevailed at the time, the tax was to be paid in Syrian drachmae or Hebrew half-shekels (Matt. 17:27). In the last week of his life Jesus cleansed the Temple's outer court, the Court of the Gentiles, and drove out the money changers, who were also selling doves and animals (John 2:15-16). This outer Court of Gentiles was supposed to be a house of prayer for "all peoples"

(Isa. 56:6-8), not just Jews. It had been made a den of thieves (Jer. 7:11; Matt. 21:13).               J.R.M.

**MONICA** (331–387). Mother of AUGUSTINE of Hippo. Determined and ambitious for her gifted son to be both educated and Christian, Monica was a dominant influence in Augustine's life. He regarded her as "the voice of God" in his development and wrote a moving tribute on her death (*Confessions*, IX).
                                                                       C.M.

**MONOPHYSITISM.** A term denoting that Christ had only a divine nature after the Incarnation—*mono* meaning "one," and *physite* meaning "nature." This controversial view about the relation of Christ's divine-human nature agitated the Eastern chuches from the fourth through sixth centuries and prompted formation of the Coptic, Abyssinian, Jacobite, and Armenian churches.

The long theological-political contention in the fourth century over Christ's humanity-divinity in relation to the Father was seemingly settled at the Council of CONSTANTINOPLE in 381. However, the mode of the union of the divine-human natures in Christ soon inflamed the East. Leaders who stressed Christ's divinity at the expense of his humanity became stereotyped as Monophysites. Apollinarius, Gregory of Nazianzus, Eutyches, Jacobus Barbadeus, and Julian of Halicarnassus were so vilified. The orthodox view of the two natures in Christ reflected Cyril of Alexandria's thought and was championed by Pope Leo I, who sent his famous *Tome* to the Council of Chalcedon in 451. Dominated by Leo, Chalcedon declared that Christ was truly human and truly divine without any confusion, division, separation, or loss of the two natures in the single person of Christ. Many Eastern church leaders who desired to exalt the divinity of Christ rejected this declaration and formed Monophysite churches. (*See also* MONOTHELITISM.)
                                                                       C.M.

**MONOTHEISM.** Literally, a belief in one god. The idea is more complicated, however, because the statement has many variants. It may be asserted that there is but one God who created and continues to sustain the world. History continues to reveal this creative will, and the ethical viewpoint of human beings arises from God who is holy. Judaism, Christianity, and Islam view God as personal.

Judaism and Islam strictly affirm that God is One. This is spelled out in the Shema (Deut. 6:4). The Qur'an emphatically voices the theme as contradicting the Christian assertion about God as TRINITY. Christianity has viewed God as being One, but having three persons or aspects. During the first few centuries of the Christian Era, theologians wrote voluminously in explication of this basic affirmation. The Nicene Creed (325) was the church's official statement to explain the relationship between the first two Persons of the Godhead.

PANTHEISM affirms that God is in all creation, in contradistinction to the idea that God created but is a Being separate from creation. Panentheism, usually connected with the thought of TEILHARD DE CHARDIN, combines pantheism with classical monotheism in saying that God is completely present in the world but has individual being apart from the world.

Some religions, including Hinduism, have affirmed that God is One but has many names. Henotheism is the belief that there are many gods, but that a particular people worship and give allegiance to one God while recognizing that other peoples act similarly in worshiping another deity. This is also referred to as monolatry. Pluriform monotheism may be described by saying that God has many forms, not simply many names or several aspects. An early form of monotheism may be found in the belief of preliterate peoples in one high God who is beyond the lesser gods in power.

Monotheism must deal with the problem of theodicy whenever it recognizes the existence of evil. Zoroastrianism solved this problem with a dualistic approach that personified evil as a force constantly at war with the good. This theme entered Christianity through Manichaeism with the assertion that the God who created the world was evil, but was superseded by the God and Father of Jesus Christ. This view was rejected by the church. (*See also* POLYTHEISM.)
                                                                       I.C.

**MONOTHELITISM.** A term designating the belief that Christ had only one will. The CHALCEDON (451) statement that Christ had divine and human natures did not settle the controversy over Christ's nature. MONOPHYSITISM, a belief that Christ had only one nature (divine), embroiled the East in schisms. To unite the empire against possible Persian and Muslim invasions, Emperor Heraclius issued a statement about 624 intended to reconcile Chalcedon and Monophysite adherents. The statement declared that Christ had two natures but only one will or activity. Patriarch Sergius of Constantinople approved, after finding a similar view in Cyril of Alexandria. Some Monophysites returned to the church. When consulted, Pope Honorius loosely used the term "one will," saying the human and divine wills were indistinguishable. Honorius then approved Heraclius' *Ecthesis* (638), which not only used "one will" but forbade other expressions. Two councils in Constantinople (638 and 639) accepted the *Ecthesis*. However, popes after Honorius condemned Monothelitism as a form of Monophysitism. Emperor Constans II withdrew the *Ecthesis* in 648 and prohibited further discussion. The Roman Lateran Council of 649 condemned this action, causing an East-West rift. After the Muslims conquered Syria and Egypt, the Council of Constantinople in 680 condemned the Monothelites, including Honorius, and declared that Christ had two wills, divine and human.                                       C.M.

**MONSIGNOR.** A clerical member of the papal household, but also a title of honor used (in French) for cardinals and vicars—generals of dioceses, who are honorary Prothonotaries Apostolic. The title is French, derived from the exile of the papacy in Avignon and means "my lord."     J.C.

**MONTANISM.** A Christian lay movement in Asia Minor in the second and third centuries that proclaimed the age of the Holy Spirit had come as promised in John 15:26 and that all Christians should prepare for the eschaton and the establishment of the New Jerusalem at Pepuza. According to Epiphanius, Montanus began preaching about 156, saying the Spirit had seized him. He often spoke as if he were the Holy Spirit, thus giving his pronouncements a divine sanction greater than that of established church authorities, many of whom were morally lax. Two women, Prisca and Maxmilla, joined Montanus and prophesied ecstatically. Montanism stressed ascetic living, celibacy, fasting, vegetarianism, and plain dress, and denounced art, ornaments, pleasures, second marriages, and flight to avoid persecution. TERTULLIAN, its greatest convert, joined the movement shortly after A.D. 200. With its universal priesthood, moral strictness, and direct spiritual inspiration, Montanism troubled the clerical establishment and caused schismatic rifts.     C.M.

**MOODY, DWIGHT L.** (1837–99). Evangelist D. L. Moody was born February 5 in Northfield, Massachusetts, to Edwin and Betsey Holton Moody. His father died when Dwight was four, leaving his mother to rear nine children. He was baptized a Unitarian. At seventeen Moody went to Boston

Courtesy of the Moody Museum, Northfield, Massachusetts

*Dwight L. Moody*

to clerk in his uncle's shoe store. Through a Sunday school teacher, he was converted and joined Mount Vernon Congregational Church on May 3, 1856.

That fall he migrated to Chicago, where he joined Plymouth Church, organized a Sunday school, evangelized among Civil War soldiers, and became president in 1866 of the YMCA. About 1860 he began to preach full time. With organist and singer IRA D. SANKEY, he conducted revivals in the British Isles in 1860, 1870, 1873–75, 1881–84, and 1891. His literal interpretation of the Bible and simple, sincere offers of salvation brought immediate response. His messages in American cities were often filled with anecdotes stressing themes of children, home, and mother's love.

Moody used funds from his and Sankey's popular hymnal to build Northfield Seminary for girls (1879), Mount Hermon School for boys (1881), Chicago (now Moody) Bible Institute (1889). His Northfield conferences for college students (1886) led to formation of the Student Volunteer movement. On August 28, 1862, he married Emma C. Revell, sister to Fleming H. Revell, who built a religious publishing empire. She gave Moody social graces and three children.     N.H.

**MOON, SUN MYUNG.** *See* UNIFICATION CHURCH.

**MOONIE.** *See* UNIFICATION CHURCH.

**MORALITY PLAY.** An allegorical, medieval religious play very popular in the fifteen-sixteenth centuries in which characters were personifications of abstract moral qualities such as gluttony, hope, envy, love, and so forth. The anonymous *Everyman*, deserted by all but Good Deeds as Death looms, and Christopher Marlowe's *Dr. Faustus* are classic examples of morality plays.

     C.M.

**MORAL MAJORITY.** A political coalition of conservative Protestants, Roman Catholics, Jews, and Mormons banded together to exert influence on the United States government on behalf of various social, political, and economic issues. The movment was founded by the fundamentalist pastor and television evangelist Jerry Falwell, of Lynchburg, Virginia. Moral Majority, organized in 1979, along with a number of other conservative groups, was credited with aiding the election of Ronald Reagan to the presidency in 1980.

However, Moral Majority leaders claim that the organization is not a political party itself nor identified with any particular party. Moral Majority insists that it favors the separation of church and state and is committed to the principle of a pluralistic political and religious society. Its leaders declare that they do not endorse political candidates and do not attempt to elect "born again" candidates, although they have been charged by their opponents with this activity.

Moral Majority supports a number of issues, such as anti-abortion. It favors the traditional family and is opposed to homosexual practices and "special rights for homosexuals." It is opposed to the illegal drug traffic and pornography, yet insists it does not favor censorship. Moral Majority supports the State of Israel and a strong national defense. It supports equal rights for women; but has been opposed to passage of the Equal Rights Amendment. The movement boasts of a following "made up of millions of Americans, including 72,000 ministers, priests, and rabbis."

R.H.

**MORAL REARMAMENT.** The name given to an international moral and religious movement that developed in 1938 from the OXFORD GROUP MOVEMENT, founded by Frank Nathan Daniel Buchman (1878–1961). Buchman was born at Pennsburg, Pennsylvania, and after being educated at Muhlenberg College and Philadelphia's Lutheran Theological Seminary was ordained as a Lutheran clergyman. He was involved for a time in youth work and for three years served a Lutheran parish in Philadelphia. Somewhat disillusioned by what he felt was a lack of success in his work, he left and went to England. There, while attending the Keswick convention, he reported that he had been converted. He returned to the United States to engage in work among college students at Pennsylvania State University. Subsequently he visited India and the Far East.

Then in 1920 he met some undergraduates at Cambridge University who accompanied him on a visit to Oxford University. This was the beginning of the movement known as the Oxford Group. Employing house parties as a means of recruiting followers, Buchman promoted "conversions" through confession, surrender, guidance, and sharing. Then he stressed a life of four absolutes in purity, unselfishness, honesty, and love. Critics objected to the subjective character of his teaching with little emphasis on biblical teaching or orthodox theology. Yet the Oxford Group grew rapidly during the 1930s. The Group metamorphosed into Moral Rearmament in 1938, on the basis that Group principles could change societies as well as individuals. It soon became international in its influence, especially in Switzerland, Germany, and Africa, as well as in England and the United States.

On Buchman's death Peter Howard became his successor. Howard died in 1965 but the work has continued under a board of directors. The world headquarters is based in New York.            R.H.

**MORAL THEOLOGY.** A more restrictive term than Christian ethics. While both expressions refer to the study of the significance of Christian faith for the moral life, moral theology refers particularly to the practically oriented work of Catholic theologians in working out a kind of basic or minimal Christian morality for the faithful. This traditional moral theology also had a definite method. It began from the study of human nature and the question about the end of humanity, and from this it deduced a basic NATURAL LAW. It then went on to discuss the virtues and vices. An important part of moral theology was casuistry, the application of general laws to particular cases. This, in turn, was closely connected with the penitential system.

In recent years, there has been a major rethinking of moral theology. While it is still agreed that the study of human nature provides the obvious starting point, it is now seen that human nature is not, as it was long conceived, an unchanging nature set in the midst of an unchanging hierarchically ordered universe, but is a changing nature in a dynamic process of transcendence. This in turn affects the concept of natural law, which is to be understood not as an unchanging universal absolute, but as itself changing in line with developments in the human being. Also, it has been thought that the place given to natural law in the traditional scheme had a minimizing effect in the presentation of Christian morals and that a larger role has to be found for love and other distinctively Christian values and virtues.

There are questions too about CASUISTRY. Traditional casuistry often seemed excessively moralistic and legalistic, and even more it seemed to be concerned with the laxest position one could take and get by as "Christian," rather than with the radical demands of the full Christian ethic. On the other hand, the sentimentalism and generalization of so-called SITUATION ETHICS has demonstrated the need for some form of casuistry, in the sense of a detailed study of concrete moral problems. This need is reinforced when we consider how technological advance keeps raising problems that are unprecedented.            J.M.

**MORAVIAN BRETHREN.** An evangelical church that came into being in Bohemia and Moravia among the followers of JOHN HUSS, the Reformer, who was martyred in 1415. Huss' disciples formed an organization that came to be known as Unitas Fratrum (Unity of Brethren), which remains today as the official name of the Moravian church.

The Catholic Reformation virtually destroyed Protestantism in Bohemia and Moravia. Yet some of the believers managed to survive clandestinely until well into the eighteenth century. In 1722 Christian David gathered a few of the "hidden seed" and escorted them to the Saxony estate of Count NIKOLAUS LUDWIG VON ZINZENDORF, a German Pietist.

In combination with German Pietists the stragglers from Moravia and Bohemia worshiped at the Bertholsdorf Lutheran Church. They called their settlement Herrnhut (literally, "the Lord's keeping"). Zinzendorf became deeply interested in the Moravians and was consecrated in 1737 as their "bishop." Under Zinzendorf's leadership the Herrnhutes experienced a great spiritual awakening. Zinzendorf broke away from the strict legalism of AUGUST HERMANN FRANCKE, the German Pietist who had taught him at the University of Halle. He was also opposed by orthodox Lutherans and unbelieving rationalists who were suspicious of Zinzendorf's "religion of the heart," based on intimate fellowship with the Savior.

Evangelism was a dominant note in the Moravian movement. They were missionaries from the start. In 1732 two of their number were sent as missionaries to the West Indies, and in the following year a mission was begun in Greenland.

Then a group of Moravians was sent to America under the leadership of Augustus Gottlieb Spangenburg. The objects of their mission were the Creek and Cherokee Indians of Georgia. It was on a second voyage to America in 1735 that Spangenberg met a High Church Anglican, John Wesley, who was also bound for Georgia to preach to the colonists and convert the Indians. In 1738 Peter Bohler, another Moravian, established a "religious society" at Fetter Lane, London, and exercised a deep religious influence on Wesley when he returned to London. Subsequently on May 24, 1738, Wesley testified to a conversion experience as he listened to the reading of Martin Luther's *Preface to the Epistle to the Romans* at a meeting in Aldersgate Street.

Spangenberg's party was escorted from Georgia to Philadelphia by George Whitefield. The great Calvinistic Anglican evangelist employed the Moravians to build a school at Nazareth, Pennsylvania. Later the Moravians clashed with Whitefield over doctrine and moved to another site. Zinzendorf, newly arrived in the colonies, named the new Moravian settlement Bethlehem on Christmas Eve in 1741. Soon the Moravian missionaries moved into various parts of the world—Lapland, South America, South Africa, among the Australian aborigines, and even to the Tibetan border. They established their mission to the Miskito Indians of Nicaragua in 1849.

Theologically, the Moravians have refused the confinement of a formal creed. They are broadly evangelical, insisting upon a principle of "in essentials unity, in nonessentials liberty, and in all things charity." Their main doctrinal emphasis may be said to be upon the love of God manifested in the redemptive life and death of Jesus, the inner testimony of the Spirit, and Christian conduct in everyday affairs. The Moravian Church in America is divided into two provinces—the northern headquarters in Bethlehem and the southern in Winston-Salem, North Carolina. Membership in the United States was 54,710 in 1983. Moravians compiled the first Protestant hymnbook.                    R.H.

**MORDECAI.** A hero in the book of ESTHER who helped save Persian Jewry from destruction. According to the story (Esth. 2:5–10:3), Haman, the prime minister, conceived a plan to kill the Jews because they would not bow down to him. Mordecai, an older cousin of Esther, the Jewish queen of Persia, found out about the plot and persuaded Queen Esther to intervene with King Ahasuerus. The king permitted the Jews to defend themselves and they were saved. According to the book of Esther, Mordecai became prominent in the court of King Ahasuerus, whose life he had saved by discovering a plot against the throne. Jews celebrate the festival of PURIM to mark the saving of the Jews.                    L.K.

**MORE, SIR THOMAS** (1478–1535). More has been both canonized as a saint and listed among the heroes of the Russian Revolution in Red Square. Born February 7, 1478, son of Sir John More, he attended Oxford University and studied law at Lincoln's Inn. About 1504 he married Jane Colt, and after her death in 1511 he married Alice Middleton.

Truly a Renaissance man, More was friend and host to ERASMUS, wrote a history of Richard III (1518), edited HENRY VIII's *Defense of the Seven Sacraments,* and responded to LUTHER's criticism with seven books against heresy (1529–33). In *Utopia* (1516), which continues to inspire readers, More outlined an ideal society. Henry VIII named him Lord Chancellor in 1529 to succeed THOMAS WOLSEY. After the Submission of the Clergy (1532) More resigned, hoping to keep silent and avoid trouble despite Henry's break with Rome. But after the Act of Supremacy, which appointed Henry, a layman, head of the church, and the Act of Succession (1534) designated Anne Boleyn's offspring as heirs to the throne, More refused to sign the oath of supremacy and thus was beheaded July 1, 1535. His last words were, "I die the king's good servant, but God's first." He was beatified in 1886 and canonized in 1935.

More was the subject of Robert Bolt's 1960 play *A Man for All Seasons* and a 1966 movie version.

N.H.

**MORIAH, MOUNT.** In his paraphrase of I Kings 6, the author of Chronicles gives this name to the area formerly used by one Ornan (Araunah in II Sam. 24) the Jebusite as a threshing floor (II Chr. 3:1), the level crest of one of the hills of Jerusalem. It was on this site that David had had a vision of the Lord, and he had built an altar and offered sacrifice that plague might be averted from Jerusalem. This site, which had become part of the royal patrimony by David's purchase, was in turn chosen by Solomon as the place where he was to build his Temple. It is to be identified with the hilltop site in the Old City of present-day Jerusalem, bounded by the Western Wall of Herodian masonry, all that remains of the Temple that replaced Solomon's after the destruction of the latter in 586 B.C.

In Genesis 22:2 "the land of Moriah" is given as the locale of Abraham's intended sacrifice of his son Isaac. Some scholars have thought that the author of

Chronicles borrowed the name from Genesis to suggest a continuity of Israelite sacrifical cult with that of the patriarchs. It is much more likely that the word is original in Chronicles and that its presence in Genesis is due to a later Jerusalemite redaction, replacing another place-name previously there, perhaps "Amorites." B.V.

## MORMON. See CHURCH OF JESUS CHRIST OF LATTER-DAY SAINTS.

## MORMON, BOOK OF. See BOOK OF MORMON.

## MORTAL SIN. According to Roman Catholic moral theology, a mortal sin is one of such magnitude that it separates the sinner from God. While forgiveness for a mortal sin is possible through the sacraments of the church, a person dying unforgiven is condemned to hell. Such sins are contrasted with VENIAL SINS, which are not as serious in nature or else have been committed out of ignorance or in the heat of passion. PENANCE is the remedy for such sins, and at death, purgatory is available for the purging of venial sins.

In Protestantism, no such distinctions between sins are made. Sin, for Lutherans, Reformed and Anabaptists, is pride, a state of revolt against God and God's will. One is under either the power of sin or the power of God. Forgiveness cannot be obtained by acts of penance but only through the acceptance of God's freely forgiving love. J.C.

## MOSES. One of the most dominant figures in the religious and historical traditions of ISRAEL, popularly regarded as the founder of its religion and chief institutions and mediator of its formative revelation of God.

*His Life.* The only source material for the life of Moses is the traditions preserved in the Bible, of varying age and intrinsic reliability but all remote in time from the Mosaic era and all partaking of the quality of legend. They present a composite picture of an idealized Moses that must be critically examined for its elements of internal plausibility.

The birth and origins of Moses are a case in point. In Exodus 2:10 his name (Hebrew, *Mosheh*) is ascribed to his having been drawn out (*mashah*) from the water, an obvious folk etymology. It is generally agreed nowadays that the name is actually the residue of an Egyptian proper name containing an element meaning "born of," represented in such common Egyptian names as ThutMOSE ("born of Thoth"), RaMSES ("born of Ra"), etc. At the very least, then, Moses bore an Egyptian name, which probably identified him as under the protection of a deity such as Thoth or Ra. For obvious reasons, Israelite tradition later abbreviated the name.

If he was Egyptian by name, was he also Egyptian by birth? This is not an extraordinary question. Exodus 12:38 acknowledges that the Israelites who fled Egypt in the EXODUS were a "mixed multitude,"

that is, combined with "foreign" elements (compare Neh. 13:3, where the same word is used). Also Genesis. 48 records the "naturalization" into Israel of the two sons of Joseph, Ephraim and Manasseh, ancestors of two of the most important tribes at the time of the Israelite confederation, born in Egypt of an Egyptian mother (Gen. 41:50-52). Moses' Israelite genealogy in Exodus 6:20 may represent another such "naturalization." In other traditions he is said to have had a foreign wife and in consequence to have been heavily influenced by his priestly father-in-law, variously called Jethro or Reuel or Hobab, a Midianite (Exod. 3:1; 2:18-21; Num. 10:29), or a Kenite (Judg. 4:11), or, perhaps, a Kushite (Num. 12:1). The story in Exodus 2:1-22 has been designed to account for Moses' Egyptian and other foreign background in later Israelite terms.

Whatever his origins, there can be little doubt that Moses became the leader of a mixed but largely Semitic population of oppressed slave-laborers engaged in the massive building projects of the Egyptian pharaohs around their capital, at that time in the Nile Delta. The message that Moses brought to this people was one of liberation in the name of a desert God whom they were able to identify with the worship of their nomadic past (Exod. 3:2-18). To what extent, if any, the Mosaic revelation was influenced by the "monotheistic" experiment of the pharaoh Amenophis IV over a century before cannot be determined. More likely, the primary influence came from Moses' Midianite/Kenite connections, which indeed the Bible suggests. Midianites and Kenites appear indifferently throughout the OT as Semitic allies, adversaries, but always close relatives of the Israelites. How many of the tribal components of what would later become in Palestine the Israelite confederation and eventually a nation formed of that mixed populace of which Moses became the leader is also uncertain. Probably there were at least the "Joseph" tribes of Ephraim and Machir (later Manasseh).

Having polarized the "Hebrews" (Exod. 1:15-20) in Egypt with the message of God's liberation and election, Moses is credited with having effected their exodus from Egypt, despite official opposition, by the working of prodigies in which the power of the Lord was made manifest (Exod. 7–12). According to Exodus 13:17 the route of the Exodus was not by way of the seacoast, which was fortified by Egyptian garrisons, but circuitously to the south. From then on, however, the biblical chronology and geography become confused and confusing. The "traditional" route of the Exodus (at its most complete in Num. 33) most certainly depends on the very latest stage of development of the composite history. On the one hand, it is quite easy to credit the stories that ascribe to this or that faction various challenges to Moses' leadership, various crises of survival, and the like. Similarly, abortive attempts to escape the desert and invade the settled land like that described in

Numbers 13–14 are not hard to believe of a wandering, land-hungry people. But the stories are multiple, reduplicative, and conflicting.

The narrative of Numbers 13–14, for example, when analyzed closely, involves the Calebites, a Judahite clan that probably pertains to a quite different tradition from that of Exodus. So also, the great story of Sinai, the enactment of the covenant, and the delivery of the Law (Exod. 19 ff.), may, like the tradition of Kadesh of which the story of the Calebite incursion is a part, originally have been the property of some other component of what was eventually to become the people Israel. This is not to deny, as we shall see, the assured place that Moses has in Israelite tradition as standing at the beginning of its legal tradition.

The Moses tradition of the Exodus, which in the biblical history has been joined with that of the promise of the land to the patriarchs, leaves off before the story of the conquest, which is ascribed to Joshua, leader of the tribe of Ephraim. A connection has been made by the device of constituting Joshua as Moses' lieutenant and successor. However, it is acknowledged that Moses never had any part in Palestine but rather died before the conquest and was buried in Moab where "no man knows the place of his burial to this day" (Deut. 34:6).

As is evident, the Bible has provided less a life of Moses than it has the impression of a profound influence. Moses is credited with a typically fabulous age of 120 years (Deut. 34:7), artificially compartmentalized into three forty-year spans: in Egypt, in Midian, and in the Exodus wilderness. Little effort has been made to ascribe to him any defined personal traits. Even the note in Exodus 4:10-17, which marks him slow of speech and in need of an interpreter in the person of his brother Aaron, is not followed up. Moses acts in his own right in all that follows, and we are left to imagine that this note is an isolated Aaronite strand in the tradition.

*The Figure of Moses.* Like other figures of history known to us only by the legends they have inspired and the imprint they have left upon consequent events and movements, Moses is of less interest to us as a person than as the personality that lies behind and is presupposed by enduring institutions that hardly could be conceived in its absence. The existence of Israel and later of Judaism is testimony to the historicity of Moses, since neither the one nor the other has ever been ascribed to any other author, and had there been no Moses it would be impossible to account for either. In Israelite and Jewish tradition Moses has been celebrated primarily as founder, lawgiver, prophet, and priest—in a word, as giving these living entities their essential identity as people, religion, and elected community with a transcendent vision and vocation.

Though the Exodus experience was doubtless proper to only some elements that made up the incipient Israel and was appropriated by others, there is no doubt that it, together with its identification as the saving act of the God Yahweh, formed the single most essential constitutive of this people, to which every other was explicative or supplementary. The subsequent history of Israel gives almost unanimous voice to this fact. There is no rival to Moses in the subsequent tradition to whom the responsibility for the fact was ever ascribed.

That the whole of Israel's legal tradition, encompassing the codes and collections now found principally in the books of Exodus through Deuteronomy, should be described simply as the Law of Moses, speaks to the recognition of his dominance in the formation of this tradition. Much of Israelite law, it is true, can be closely paralleled in the legislation of the rest of the ancient Near East of which Israel was a part, due allowances made for the disparities between the specific societies to which the laws were tailored. But while a comparative study of Israel's law over against the parallels can yield both pluses and minuses, there is litle doubt that it yields also the impression of a distinct and exclusive inspiration that guided the application of common legal principles. Also, though it is not entirely true that Israel was in sole possession of apodictic law in ancient times (the imperative "thou shalts" and the "shalt nots" of laws such as those of the Decalogue), still, quantitatively, it is overwhelmingly true, a fact pointing once more to a distinct and magisterial influence standing at the origin of Israel's legislation. Again, biblical tradition allows no claimant other than Moses to have exercised such influence. Typical of the global attribution of Israel's legal tradition to Moses is Numbers 18:13-27, according to which even the organization of court procedure was of his devising—at the instigation of his Kenite/Midianite father-in-law.

The prophecy that Moses is credited with having begun in Israel is that of the ecstatic type (Num. 11:24-30), which is characteristic certainly of Israel's early days (I Sam. 10:10-13; 19:20-21; etc.), and not only of its early days, but also of most other religions, contemporary and afterward, ancient and modern. This affirmation surely must be put down to the tendency of the later tradition to make Moses the author of literally everything Israelite. Nowhere is it suggested (as it is suggested, for example, of lesser figures such as Samuel or Elijah) that Moses stood at the head of the really distinctively Israelite classical prophecy represented in the prophetical literature of the OT. On the other hand, Israelite tradition represented in the OT habitually makes no distinction between one kind of PROPHET and another. Furthermore, as Deuteronomy 34:10-12 points out, Moses was remembered not so much as being one, even the chief one, of the prophetic succession as he was the one superior to all prophets, as having had an immediacy to the mind of God that was not possessed by a mere prophet.

The priestly character of Moses is similarly ambiguous in the tradition in view of conflicting concerns. In the final form of the tradition, Moses is given instructions from the Lord for the ordination of his brother AARON and his descendants to be the sole priesthood of Israel (throughout the book of Leviticus). This represents some successive developments. For one thing, it reflects an Aaronite tendency in some of the traditions at the expense of Moses (similarly in Exod. 4:10-17 Aaron is appointed spokesman for an "inarticulate" Moses—a theme that is followed up not at all in the rest of the succeeding narrative). Also involved was the legitimation of the Zadokite priesthood, which David found in Jerusalem and which was given an Israelite genealogy through Aaron (I Chr. 6:35-38). The phrase "Levitical priests," customary in the Deuteronomic literature, reflects an older, less restrictive concept of the hereditary priesthood according to which all LEVITES pertained to the priestly order. In turn, this represents only one stage in a complicated development, but there is no doubt that at one time the priestly character in Israel was calculated on the criterion of descent from Moses (see Judg. 18:30).

*Moses and Judaism.* The late tendency of Israelite tradition to maximize the figure of Moses could only result in the even later Judaism that so exalted the Law of Moses as the essence of the religion derived from the OT into a concept of Moses that quite surpassed the historical and made of him a mythical personage. Both in Hellenistic Judaism (Philo of Alexandria) and in that of Palestine, Moses becomes a figure of legend, the subject and also the putative author of various Apocryphal works, the source of revealed knowledge that has enlightened humankind and not Jews only, and even a messianic figure (based on a reading of Deut. 18:15-18): a "prophet like Moses" would return (from Egypt? compare Acts 21:38) to restore Israel—a theme that some NT scholars have found lying at the background of John's Gospel. This latter idea, indeed, might have found a home in the speculation of northern Palestine (Galilee and Samaria), where the Pentateuch reveals that Moses tended to be regarded as the whole of the revelation God had given through Israel, in distinction to the Pharisaical Judaism of Judea, which featured the Prophets (in an apocalyptic and Midrashic interpretation). Never, however, in Judaism did Moses ever assume the centrality of attention that the NT has accorded to Jesus. Moses is always a mediator between God and humanity, never a divine person. It is conceivable that Jewish tradition could, if necessary, dispense with Moses in a way that Christianity could never dispense with Jesus.

*Moses and the New Testament.* In the NT Moses is, predictably, the most predominant of all OT figures. He is perceived as mediator of a revelation of God of whom Jesus is the fulfillment, a predecessor of Jesus typologically, who, along with the rest of the OT, foreshadowed Jesus both symbolically and by defect: the beginning of which Jesus is to be the end. To this

extent, aside from the christological orientation, the NT appreciation of Moses hardly differs from that of Judaism.

There is also, however, a depreciation of Moses made inevitable by the early separation of church and synagogue, to which the NT also bears witness. For Paul, Moses represents the Law, which can come into conflict with the gospel (Rom. 10:5-17). John notes that while the Law was given by Moses, grace and truth (heavenly life) came only through Jesus Christ, and no one (in the OT) ever saw God as God has been revealed in Christ (John 1:17-18). Throughout the Fourth Gospel, there is a systematic denigration of the deeds of Moses (and others of the OT) in favor of those of Christ. But again, these are only alternate ways, more negative ways perhaps, of exploiting the typology of Moses.                                                    B.V.

**MOSES, ASSUMPTION OF.** *See* PSEUDEPIGRAPHA.

**MOSES BEN MAIMON.** *See* MAIMONIDES.

**MOSLEM.** *See* MUSLIM.

**MOSQUE.** The house of prayer in ISLAM. In MUHAMMAD's time, it was only an open courtyard for the performance, five times daily, of the ritual prayer (*ṣalā*). With the passage of time, it acquired additional features and functions.

Muhammad built the first mosque in MEDINA. The *kibla,* or direction of prayer, was to the north, the direction of JERUSALEM. A roof was built over that end, and it remained there when the *kibla* was shifted to the south, toward the KA'BA in MECCA. The Medinan community also also met in the mosque for sermons on Friday and for important discussions.

Since the beginning of Islam, the call to prayer (*adhan*) has been delivered by a designated worshiper known as a muezzin. Originally, the call was made from the roof of the house or mosque; later it was delivered from a MINARET. As worshipers enter the mosque, they remove their shoes and perform ritual ablutions. The prayer is led by an IMAM, who stands in the pulpit (*minbar*), just to the right of the *mihrab* (a decorated niche in the *kibla* wall).

Each city has one main mosque, where the sovereign or his representative sits in an enclosed booth (*maqsura*) beside the *mihrab*. However, most cities and towns have other mosques—some built for universities (*madrasas*), some for individual tribal groups, and some for individual sects. Sometimes the building of a mosque is an act of piety.

Many mosques were originally churches, synagogues, or ZOROASTRIAN fire temples. Those constructed for Muslim worship usually have low roofs supported by pillars, a style that allows expansion simply by adding more roof. Although architectural styles vary, one popular configuration

*Mosque of Ahmed I, Istanbul*

has naves running parallel to the *kibla* wall, with one large central nave running perpendicular to it. Mosques as far apart as Damascus, Syria, and Cordoba, Spain, use this form. Many mosques, including the one around the Ka'ba in Mecca, retain the open courtyard of Muhammad's time. The special lamps and rugs used in the mosque, as well as the walls and pillars, are often decorated. Because images of animals and people are forbidden, decoration is limited to calligraphy and geometric designs.

K./M.C.

**MOST HIGH.** The conventional translation of the Hebrew divine appellative Elyon. Elyon was originally a distinct deity, known from Aramaic and Phoenician documents, among others (see Deut. 32:8). In pre-Israelite Canaan, Elyon had been identified with the Canaanite high god El, under the form of El Elyon (Gen. 14:18). The Israelites eventually applied both of these names to their God, Yahweh (Gen. 14:22). B.V.

**MOST HOLY PLACE.** Also called Holy of Holies, this is the name given the innermost recess (on the western side), first of the sacred TABERNACLE in the wilderness (Exod. 36; 40) and later of the successive temples of Solomon, Zerubbabel, and Herod. The pattern of these sacred structures in the Bible seems to have been more or less the same tripartite one that was conventional for the sanctuaries of other contemporay Near Eastern religions. The Most Holy Place would have corresponded, then, with the inner shrine where the statue of the god of a pagan sanctuary was displayed. Since the Israelite religion forbade pictorial representation of the deity, the Most Holy Place contained instead of a statue the ARK OF THE COVENANT, which was conceived as the throne or footstool of the invisible presence of God. In postexilic times, when the Ark was no more, the Most Holy Place was simply empty except for this invisible presence. It was entered by no one except, once a year, the high priest on the solemn Day of Atonement, to make expiation for the sins of the people. B.V.

**MOTHER.** A woman who has successfully born a child. Among early artistic representations of human figures are those of mothers with children or of a pregnant woman. Typical is a terra cotta figurine from Muhata, Syria, dated about 4500 B.C. It was with awe and wonder that throughout history people observed the birth of a child. Eve, after bearing Cain, exclaimed, "I have gotten a man with the help of the Lord" (Gen. 4:1). Adam called her Eve ("living"), "because she was the mother of all living" (3:20).

It has been thought that, in early societies, matriarchy preceded patriarchy. Mothers knew their own offspring! "Can a woman forget her sucking child?" (Isa. 49:15). FATHERS, on the other hand, were unknown or considered not responsible. Thus, mothers came to direct the affairs of the tribe or clan as well as of the family.

Since mothers multiplied the family, motherhood came to be thought of in connection with growing things and with fertility in general. In many languages, the land is called "mother earth." From this, the transition was easy to represent by a mother figure a goddess of fertility who was considered responsible both for child-bearing and for success in multiplying crops and domesticated animals. An example would be the nude, female, Astarte figurines used by Canaanites. Mother-goddesses appear in nearly every polytheistic religious system. The term "mother" also has been used figuratively, by Plato of matter as "mother of all things," by Philo of wisdom, mother of the world, and, similarly, by the Gnostics. In the pictorial script developed by the Chinese (about 1500 B.C.), the symbol for "good" is the symbol for "woman" plus the symbol for "child."

In Hebrew there is a distinctively different word for mother from that for woman, wife, or female. Motherhood, especially being the mother of a son, put a woman in a highly honored social position. Conversely, the barren wife was frowned upon; Rachel cried to Jacob, "Give me children, or I shall die" (Gen. 30:1; compare Isa. 54:1).

In the Ten Commandments, a wife may be spoken of as a possession, but a mother is to be "honored" equally with the father (Exod. 20:12, 17; Deut. 5:16, 21). Proverbs 31:10-31 is an acrostic, praise for a good wife, but, as verse 28 indicates, the author assumed that the good wife was also a good mother, praised and blessed by her children. Deborah, "a mother in Israel" (Judg. 5:7), was a figure of strength and wisdom in her tribe. The commander of the army would not go into battle without her (Judg. 4:9).

A mother's womb was freely mentioned in the OT (Pss. 22:9 with "breasts"; 71:6; 139:13). Motherhood out of wedlock (Judg. 11:2) was a disgrace. Motherhood through adultery "displeased the Lord" and is "what is evil in his sight" (II Sam. 11:27; 12:9). Jezebel was a negative example of a mother's powerful example and precept. She influenced her son, Ahaziah, and her daughter, Athaliah, to become ardent supporters of Baal Melcarth (I Kings 22:52, 53). Mother is also used metaphorically for the Hebrew people (Isa. 50:1-2; 49:1-4; Hos. 4:5; Mic. 4:9-10; 5:3).

In the NT, respect for one's mother is enjoined (Matt. 19:19; Mark 10:19; Luke 18:20; II Tim. 1:5). Among Arabs today, the mother of a son is given the honorific title "mother of _____," so addressed instead of by her maiden name or her husband's name. This Oriental custom is observed in the Gospels. In the Synoptic Gospels we hear, without any other name, of "the mother of the sons of Zebedee" (Matt. 20:20; 27:56) and "the mother of James the younger and of Joses" (Mark 15:40). In the Gospel of John, Mary is often mentioned as "the mother of Jesus" (2:1; 3; 19:25, 26, 27), never with her given name.

Figuratively, mother is used in the NT of Paul himself as mother (Gal. 4:19), of "the Jerusalem above" (Gal. 4:25, 26) and of "Babylon the great," who is "mother of harlots and of earth's abominations" (Rev. 17:5, 7).

When Mary visited Elizabeth before either gave birth, Elizabeth addressed her as "the mother of my Lord," whereupon Mary sang, "Henceforth all generations will call me blessed" (Luke 1:48). Although a special veneration for Mary began only after the NT (Acts 1:14), for NT Christians and others scarcely any higher honor could be given mothers than that "God sent forth his Son, born of woman . . . to redeem" (Gal. 4:5).          P.L.G.

**MOTHER OF GOD.** From the Greek term *Theotokos,* a title of reverence for MARY, MOTHER OF JESUS, adopted by the Council of Ephesus in A.D. 431. The growth of Christology, reflecting the worship of the God-man, also caused increased veneration of his mother. Mary was seen as the vehicle by which the Incarnation was made possible.          J.C.

**MOTIF RESEARCH.** *See* BIBLICAL CRITICISM.

**MOTT, JOHN RALEIGH** (1865–1955). Missionary statesman, YMCA official, and pioneer ecumenist. Mott was born in Livingston Manor, New York, and converted through the ministry of J. E. K. Studd while a student at Cornell University. Upon graduation in 1888, he joined the YMCA organization and became successively student secretary, foreign secretary, and general secretary of the American international committee (1915–31). Mott attended a Bible conference called by Dwight L. Moody in 1886 at Mount Hermon, Massachusetts. Before the conference ended, one hundred students had offered themselves for missionary service. In 1888 the movement was formally organized as the STUDENT VOLUNTEER MOVEMENT with Mott, one of the one hundred, as chairman, a post that he held for thirty years. While Mott was traveling about the world promoting the cause of missions, he developed a sense of the need for church unity. He was involved in convening the 1910 Edinburgh Missionary Conference. Out of this gathering an interdenominational committee was formed. This is now regarded as the beginning of the ecumenical movement.

Mott became chairman of the new INTERNATIONAL MISSIONARY COUNCIL, which was formed in 1921, later to become an integral part of the World Council of Churches. He was chairman of the second Life and Work Conference at Oxford in 1937 and vice-chairman of the provisional committee of the World Council of Churches in 1938. In 1948 he was made a co-president of the newly formed council. In 1946 Mott was a co-winner of the Nobel Peace Prize for years of service in missionary and ecumenical endeavors. He was also the author of many books and articles.                                                    R.H.

**MOUNT.** See the individual name.

**MOWINCKEL, SIGMUND** (1884–1965). This Norwegian scholar was one of the most distinguished of a distinguished line of Scandinavians who dominated OT studies, particularly in the 1920s and 1930s. Mowinckel is best remembered for his *Psalmenstudien II* (1922; *The Psalms in Israel's Worship,* 1962), in which he elaborated from his analysis of the Psalms the theory of an annual feast of covenant renewal modeled on the Babylonian New Year's festival. Features of this celebration would have included the symbolic enthronement of Yahweh as King and processions with the Ark of the Covenant as his throne. While few have accepted this reconstruction in its entirety, it has been generally agreed that Mowinckel's cultic interpretation of the Psalms was both basically sound and a seminal contribution to OT critical study. Mowinckel is also well known for a thorough reexamination of OT messianic doctrine, whose title in English is *He That Cometh.*
                                                              B.V.

**MOWRER, O. HOBART** (1907–82). Mowrer, an educational psychologist who has significantly influenced pastoral psychology, was born on January 23 to John Andrew and Sallie Ann Todd Mowrer. He graduated from the University of Missouri in 1929. During his doctoral work at Johns Hopkins University (Ph.D. 1932), he married child psychologist Willie Mae Cook in 1931. They have two daughters. After teaching at Harvard University (1940–48), Mowrer taught at the University of Illinois, Champaign-Urbana. In 1975 he was named professor emeritus. His books include *Learning Theory and Personality Dynamics* (1950), *Psychotheraphy: Theory and Research* (1953), *Learning Theory and Behavior* (1960), *The New Group Therapy* (1964), and *Psychology of Language and Learning.* (1980). Particularly of interest to theologians are his *Crisis in Psychiatry and Religion* (1961), *Morality and Mental Health* (1967), and *Conscience, Contract and Social Reality* (1972). An autobiography, *Leaves from Many Seasons,* was published in 1983. He died June 20, 1982.
                                                              N.H.

**MUFTI.** A professional jurist who interprets SHARIA, the Muslim law, in SUNNI Islam. Judges base their decisions on his formal opinions, and individuals may follow his opinions in their private lives. The grand mufti is similar in authority to the supreme AYATOLLAH of the SHI'ITES.
                                                              K./M.C.

**MUHAMMAD** (A.D. 570?–632). Founder of ISLAM. He is regarded by Islam as the "seal of the prophets," that is, the last and greatest of the line of prophets from Adam through Abraham, the prophets of the OT, John the Baptist, and Jesus, to Muhammad himself. Most of our information about him comes from the QUR'AN and the HADITH (traditions).

He was born in the city of MECCA in west-central Arabia at a time when Mecca was a prosperous center of the caravan trade from South Arabia to the Mediterranean. Orphaned at an early age, he was raised by his uncle Abu Talib. Although Muhammad was a member of the Quraish tribe that ruled the city, his clan, the Hashimite, was weak. As a result, he had trouble establishing himself in business. At the age of about twenty-five he married a wealthy widow, Khadijah, who owned a flourishing business. She was about fifteen years older than he was. She bore him two sons, who died in infancy, and four daughters, only one of whom outlived him, FATIMA.

*The Call to Be a Prophet.* Until about the age of forty Muhammad led the normal life of a businessman of that time. Then he had a series of experiences that terrified him. A giant being, whom he later identified as the angel Gabriel, appeared to him and commanded him to "recite" the messages he would receive. Uncertain whether the messenger was good or evil, he hesitated. With his wife's encouragement he came to believe that his visions were sent by God. The messages he received were in rhythmic, beautifully phrased language, suitable for reciting and memorizing. They came to constitute the earliest portions of the Qur'an.

The doctrine of God (*Allah* in Arabic) was at the center of Muhammad's religious experience. God is one, with no partners and no equals. God is powerful and good, and has set a time when he will judge the world. Muhammad was to warn the people to give up their evil ways, especially their "presumption," or insolent pride, and their reliance on material wealth. They should show gratitude to God for his goodness, should worship him, and should be generous to the poor and needy.

*Early Responses to His Message.* From about A.D. 610 to 622 Muhammad met with little success. The Meccans ridiculed him, and he won only a few converts. Still he remained faithful to the revelations that continued to come to him. Most of them were aural rather than visual. At one point he sent his followers across the Red Sea to the Christian nation of Ethiopia to escape persecution, but they soon returned to Mecca.

His uncle and protector, Abu Talib, died about this time and so did his wife Khadijah. These were severe blows. Together with his nephew and son-in-law ALI, and his close friend Abu Bakr, Muhammad began to make plans to leave Mecca. In 622, pilgrims from the city of Medina persuaded him to make their city his headquarters. Some of the hostile Quraish had plotted to kill him, but he

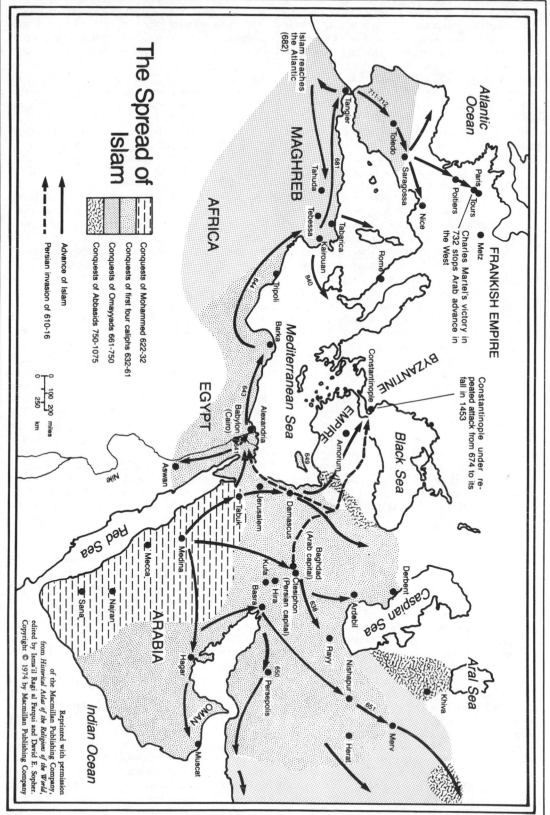

# The Spread of Islam

Conquests of Mohammed 622-32

Conquests of first four caliphs 632-61

Conquests of Omayyads 661-750

Conquests of Abbasids 750-1075

Advance of Islam

Persian invasion of 610-16

0    100   200  miles
0         250   km

Islam reaches
the Atlantic
(682)

Atlantic
Ocean

FRANKISH EMPIRE

Charles Martel's victory in
732 stops Arab advance in
the West

Constantinople under re-
peated attack from 674 to its
fall in 1453

MAGHREB

AFRICA

Tangier

711-712

Oviedo

Paris
Metz

Tours
Poitiers

Saragossa

Nice

Rome

681

Tahuda

Tebessa

Tabarca

Kairouan

840

Tripoli

644

Barka

Mediterranean Sea

BYZANTINE

Constantinople

Black Sea

EMPIRE

Amorium

649

EGYPT

643

Babylon
(Cairo)

Alexandria

641

Aswan

Nile

Red Sea

Tabuk

Jerusalem

Damascus

Baghdad
(Arab capital)

Ctesiphon
(Persian capital)

638

Derbent

Caspian Sea

Aral Sea

Khiva

Mecca

Medina

Kufa

Hira

Basra

Ardebil

Rayy

Nishapur

650

651

Merv

ARABIA

Sana

Najran

Hagar

OMAN

Persepolis

Herat

Muscat

Indian Ocean

Reprinted with permission
of the Macmillan Publishing Company,
from *Historical Atlas of the Religions of the World*,
edited by Isma'il Ragi al Faruqi and David E. Sopher.
Copyright © 1974 by Macmillan Publishing Company

escaped in time. Accompanied by Abu Bakr, he hid out not far from Mecca until his enemies were thrown off his trail. Then they headed for Medina on camel back. This was the HEGIRA, the migration that marked the great turning point in his career, and is the occasion from which the Islamic calendar is dated.

*The Years at Medina.* Revelations continued to come to Muhammad, but now they were less poetic and more concerned with the details of administering a political community. Islam had become more than a group of adherents to a new set of beliefs. He married the ten-year-old daughter of Abu Bakr, 'A'isha, who played a significant role after the Prophet's death. To challenge the power of Mecca, he sent his followers out to raid Meccan caravans. The clashes grew in seriousness until the Battle of Badr in 624, when he inflicted a serious defeat on a large Meccan force. Over the next few years the military advantage lay first with one side and then with the other. Gradually, however, various tribes in western Arabia converted to Islam, and Muhammad's strength grew.

During these years the Jewish clans in Medina became hostile to Muhammad's claim to be the Prophet of God. These clans were wealthy and militarily strong, but Muhammad exiled some of them and defeated others. The Jews who remained in Medina and did not convert to Islam lost all power and political influence.

*The Years of Triumph.* In March 628, Muhammad set out for Mecca with a force of fourteen hundred to sixteen hundred men. The Meccans threatened to resist by force any Muslim attempt to perform the pilgrimage (HAJJ). A treaty was drawn up, under which Muhammad agreed to withdraw that year, and the Meccans agreed to evacuate the city for three days the following year so the Muslims could carry out the various pilgrimage rites. The power of the Meccans had declined to the point that they had to treat Muhammad as an equal.

In January 630, a large Muslim force invaded Mecca, meeting with only slight resistance. Muhammad remained in the city fifteen or twenty days. He destroyed shrines to pagan goddesses and cleansed the KA'BA and all private homes of idols. His tact, diplomacy, and skill as an administrator won over both the leaders and the common people. During the remaining two years of his life the movement grew in strength, and the groundwork was laid for it to expand beyond the borders of Arabia.

Abu Bakr made the pilgrimage in 631, and in 632 Muhammad led the pilgrimage in person. When he returned to Medina toward the end of March it was clear that he was in poor health. He stayed in 'A'isha's living quarters, and there on June 8, 632, with his head in 'A'isha's lap, he died.

Abu Bakr had been commissioned to lead the prayers, but no other arrangements had been made for the succession. To the confused and sorrowing community Abu Bakr proclaimed, "O ye people, if anyone worship Muhammad, Muhammad is dead, but if anyone worships God, He is alive and dies not."

Many stories were handed down by those who had known the Prophet during his lifetime. One of these tells of a journey he made from Mecca to Jerusalem just before the hegira. From the site in Jerusalem where the Dome of the Rock now stands, Muhammad soared up into the seventh heaven on the back of the steed Burak. He was admitted to the presence of God and then returned to earth.

No claims were made that Muhammad was divine. He remained man, for Muslims the greatest man of all.

K.C.

**MUHAMMAD, ELIJAH** (1897–1975). Born Elijah Poole on October 7, on a farm near Sanderville, Georgia, this son of parents who had been slaves became the charismatic founding leader of the BLACK MUSLIMS. Poole, after working at various jobs, moved to Detroit, where he worked on an auto assembly line. In 1931 Poole met Wali Farad, the former Wallace D. Fard, who had established what he called the Temple of Islam the previous year. When Farad disappeared mysteriously in 1934, Poole changed his name to Elijah Muhammad and assumed the leadership of Farad's followers, claiming he was a "messenger of Allah." He taught that the only salvation for blacks in the United States was to withdraw and form an autonomous state. Difficulties arose that forced Muhammad to move his headquarters to Chicago, where he proclaimed himself the divinely appointed head of the Nation of Islam, the formal name of the first Black Muslim movement. The work grew, and at one point his followers could be numbered in the tens of thousands. He headed a network of business enterprises, schools, and other institutions that were valued at millions of dollars. His most notable convert was Muhammad Ali, the noted heavyweight boxer. He died on February 25.

R.H.

**MUHLENBERG, HENRY MELCHIOR** (1711–87). The founder of the German Lutheran Church in the United States, Muhlenberg was born September 6, 1711, in Einbeck, Hanover, to Nicolaus Melchior and Anna Maria Kleinschmid Muhlenberg. Educated at the University of Göttingen, he was ordained August 24, 1739.

Answering the call of congregations in Philadelphia, New Providence, and New Hanover, Pennsylvania, Muhlenberg arrived in November of 1742. He built churches in Tulpehocken (1743), Providence (1745), Germantown (1746), New Hanover (1747), and Philadelphia (1748). On April 22, 1745, he married Anna Maria Weiser.

Muhlenberg organized the Evangelical Lutheran Ministerium in 1748 with six Swedish and German pastors and twenty-four lay delegates. It outlined synodical organization and prepared a book of common worship. Serving as "overseer," Muhlenberg helped write its constitution in 1762. Speaking pure German and graceful Latin, he learned to preach ably in English and Dutch. His three-volume *Journal* reveals a dedicated pastor and gifted administrator with broad knowledge of medicine and law as well.

N.H.

## MUHLENBERG, WILLIAM AUGUSTUS
(1796–1877). The leader of the Anglican Memorial movement was born September 16, 1796, to William Henry and Mary Sheaff Muhlenberg. The great-grandson of HENRY MELCHOIR MUHLENBERG, William was baptized a Lutheran and confirmed and reared Episcopalian. After his ordination in 1820, he served churches in Philadelphia and Lancaster, Pennsylvania, and Flushing, Long Island. In 1828 he became headmaster of the Flushing Institute, a preparatory school for boys, which he ran for eighteen years.

In 1846 he became rector of the Church of the Holy Communion, New York City, the first Episcopal church to eliminate rented pews. During his tenure (1846–58) he introduced weekly Eucharist, daily morning and evening prayers, antiphonal chanting, and lighted candles. In 1853 he wrote a "Memorial" to the House of Bishops suggesting reforms of the liturgy along the lines of the Oxford movement, and asking for extension of Episcopal ordination to clergy of other churches.

Muhlenberg founded the Sisterhood of the Holy Communion, St. Luke's Hospital, and the community of St. Johnsland. He also authored such hymns as "Shout the Glad Tidings, Exultingly Sing," "I Would Not Live Alway," and "Savior, Who Thy Flock Art Feeding."

N.H.

## MUKYOKAI.
From the Japanese words for "no church." A Japanese Christian movement founded by Kanzo Uchimura (1861–1930), which endeavors to present Christianity independent of ecclesiastical institutionalism. Uchimura first came in contact with Christianity at Sapporo Agricultural College in the 1870s. From then on he devoted himself to establishing independent, "non-church" prayer groups and Bible study groups. The movement has tended to draw Japanese of liberal and humanitarian disposition, among them prominent writers, educators, and statesmen; it has thus, despite its lack of institutional structure, had substantial influence on modern Japan. Many members shared Uchimura's strong opposition to growing authoritarianism and militarism in the Japan of his day.

R.E.

## MULLA.
A scholar of religious law (SHARIA) in SHI'ITE Islam. He performs such minor tasks as leading prayer in small mosques, reciting the stories of the IMAMS, and teaching the QUR'AN.

K./M.C.

## MÜLLER, GEORGE
(1805–98). Eminent Plymouth Brethren leader who relied on faith and prayer to sustain his orphanages near Bristol, England. German-born Müller was led to devote himself to religious work by Pietists at Halle. He journeyed to London in 1829, worked with the Society for Promoting Christianity among the Jews, and left London in 1830 to join the Plymouth Brethren founded that year by JOHN NELSON DARBY, a former Anglican clergyman, near Plymouth. Darby rejected creeds, insisted all Christians are priests, and relied on the Holy Spirit for guidance. Müller became a devoted leader in this expanding group. He refused a salary, depended on contributions for support, and about 1832 began concentrating on caring for orphans at Bristol. When he published his *Narrative of the Lord's Dealings with George Müller* (1837, 1841), funds increased enough to provide for over two thousand children. He died in Bristol after a seventeen-year worldwide preaching tour.

C.M.

## MÜNZER, THOMAS
(about 1489–1525). Radical German Reformer, leader in the Peasants' Revolt (1525), an early Anabaptist, and Marxist precursor. Born in Stolberg in the Harz Mountains, Münzer studied at Leipzig and Frankfurt and became a priest. In 1519 he allied himself with Martin Luther, but soon felt Luther's justification by faith alone and political conservatism did not sufficiently promote reform and justice for the poor. Münzer instituted radical liturgical changes during his stormy pastorate at Zwickau (1520–23), but his reliance on direct inspiration from the Holy Spirit over Scripture brought him into dispute with Luther. Expelled from Zwickau, Münzer went to Allstedt, where he preached open rebellion. Luther helped drive him from Allstedt in 1524. He then went to Mühlhausen, was again expelled, but returned to inspire and lead a peasant army against the princes. Philip of Hesse overwhelmingly defeated the peasants at Frankenhausen, May 25, 1525. Münzer and other leaders were beheaded.

C.M.

## MURATORIAN CANON.
Probably the oldest extant listing of NT writings, reflecting a canon of twenty-two books to be read in worship services and accepted as authoritative in doctrinal disputes. Lodovico A. Muratori (1672–1750), an Italian antiquary and historian who collected and published old Italian scriptural writings and chronicles from the fifth to the sixteenth century, discovered the listing in an eighth-century manuscript. The listing, which mentions Pope Pius I, Hermas, Basilides, Marcion, and Montanus, dates from the late second century. The fragment of eighty-five lines, which Muratori discovered in 1740, has missing narrative portions at the beginning and end, but contains references to the Four Gospels, Acts, the Pauline letters, Apocalypse of

John, Epistles of John and Jude, and the Apocalypse of Peter and Wisdom of Solomon, which are no longer included. Hebrews, James, and I-II Peter are not mentioned. It specifically rejects the Shepherd of Hermas, Paul's letters to Laodicea and Alexandria, and several Gnostic and Montanist works. The original writer of the fragment is believed to be Hippolytus.                                                       C.M.

**MUSLIM.** Also spelled "Moslem"; a believer in ISLAM. Islam means "submission," and a Muslim is therefore one who submits in obedience to God. A Muslim acknowledges the oneness of God, accepts Muhammad as God's prophet, and lives his or her life in accordance with the norms of the religion.
                                                                        K.C.

**MUSLIMS** (U.S.A.). ISLAM, the youngest of the world's three monotheistic faiths, had its origins in Arabia, but today its faithful disciples may be found all over the world. The Islamic Center in Washington, D.C., estimates that there are a billion Muslims in the world, but other authorities reduce that figure by one half. The Center states that there are three hundred mosques in North America and possibly six million Muslims—half of whom are native born in the United States or Canada and another half made up of arrivals from other lands. There are two groups of BLACK MUSLIMS—the Nation of Islam led by Louis Farrakhan, formerly Eugene Walcott, and the American Muslim Mission (formely called the World Community of Al-Islam in the West), which is headed by Warith (Wallace) Muhammad, Elijah's son. Both groups are based in Chicago, with followers in other parts of the country. Muslims from other backgrounds accept the Black Muslims as true followers of the Prophet.                                    R.H.

**MU'TAZILA.** The "standing aloof" school of early Islamic theology (KALĀM), so called because they took a neutral position concerning the status of a Muslim who commits a grave sin. It flourished under the ABBASSID CALIPHS between the ninth and tenth centuries A.D., and used much of Greek rationalism. Orthodox SUNNI Islam condemned it, but the SHITITES still follow it.                            K./M.C.

**MYSTERIUM TREMENDUM.** A term referring to the unique feeling associated with experience of the holy or divine, made current by the theologian Rudolf Otto in *The Idea of the Holy* (1923). For Otto, the elementary datum of religion is the non-rational, non-moral experience of the holy or numinous, which cannot strictly be defined. This unique religious feeling includes a sense of the uncanny, a sense of creature-feeling or total dependence and impotence, as well as feelings of awe, rapture, and exaltation. Otto analyzed the holy in terms of three distinctive qualities: the *mysterium tremendumet fascinans*. The *mysterium* is the experience of the HOLY as "wholly

other," as unfathomable mystery. The *tremendum* evokes the emotion of fear or demonic dread. However, the holy is also *fascinans*, the fascinating, begetting the emotions of love, bliss, and beatitude. Otto's analysis of the holy has had wide influence on both the comparative study of religion and on theology.                                                        J.L.

**MYSTERY RELIGIONS.** In the Greek and Roman periods of history, the mystery religions offered adherents hope of sharing in the life of immortals in the present and of life beyond the grave. Although evidence for these religions is as early as the fifth century B.C., they seem to have been particularly popular in the second and third centuries A.D. Their myth and ritual connected with the mysteries concentrated on symbols of fertility and of the renewal of life. The mythical characters included male and female, heavenly and human figures.

The fact that many of the myths are concerned with crops or fertility suggests that the religions may have originated as a means of assisting or guaranteeing the annual cycle of agricultural produce. In the OSIRIS and ISIS myth, for example, Osiris is the symbol of the Nile, the annual flooding of which (and the resultant irrigation of the crops) made possible the growth of food and the sustaining of life in the otherwise arid central valley of Egypt. In the myth, he is put to death by his enemies, but Isis enables him to be restored to life. In Greek mythology, the loss by Demeter of her daughter, Kore, and the latter's stay in the underworld, are linked with the sowing of grain, just as the recovery of the daughter represents its growth and harvest. The death of Dionysus, the god of wine and ecstasy, and his recovery, are symbolic of the crushing and fermentation of the grapes in order to produce the wine. In the cult on the Greek island of Samothrace, the slaughter of the sacred bull and his return to life is clearly a symbolic cycle of fertility. A major symbol in the mysteries (especially of Dionysus) was the human phallus.

By the Roman period, the major interest in the mysteries had become personal renewal and participation in the life of the gods. Characteristic are the roles of Hermes and Orpheus, both of whom were seen in their respective mythical traditions as messengers of the gods, who brought divine secrets of life to the initiates. Under various names (Cybele, Artemis, Isis) the figure of the divine mother was enormously popular. Seeking a lost child or spouse, she wandered about in sorrow until with joy her mission was achieved. Her followers saw their own sorrows and exaltation mirrored in her experience. Similarly, the figures of dying and rising heroes or gods—whether Kore, Dionysus, or Osiris—offered hope of the escape from darkness and death and the attainment of eternal life.

The mysteries had wide appeal geographically and socially. Those initiated into the mysteries ranged from the simplest Roman subjects to the emperors.

Shrines of the mystery cults have been found from eastern Syria to the British midlands. The remains of the cults include crude inscriptions on graves as well as sophisticated murals painted on the walls of a villa in Pompei. Public reaction to the mysteries was often hostile, as in the official Roman prohibition of the worship of Dionysus (Bacchus, in Latin) in the early second century B.C. The Greek dramatist Euripides (fifth century B.C.), by his vivid portrayal of the gruesome features of the Dionysiac cult—including dismembering and devouring human beings—brought the religion into popular disrepute. Yet in the second century A.D. as sophisticated a writer as Plutarch was representing the Isis cult as an allegory of participation in eternal life, and Lucius Apuleius (also second century A.D.) attracted a wide popular interest in the Isis myth by portraying her devotees as those who found renewal of life, meaning, and purpose in a world filled with strife and frustration.

H.K.

**MYSTICISM.** A form of religious experience that emphasizes immediate awareness of God. It is an expression of the innate tendency of human beings toward complete harmony with God.

*Definition.* The goal of mysticism is communion or "mystical union" with the Divine. While the ultimate attainment of this is a gift of grace, mysticism implies commitment to a life process ordered in that direction. It is not intellectual speculation, a theological system, or a philosophy.

Mystical elements are found in all religions. Although it is stronger in Hinduism and Buddhism, it exists as a major element even in the historical religions: Judaism, Christianity, and Islam. As Saint Martin observed: "All mystics speak the same language and come from the same country."

Mysticism is often loosely applied to any personal religious experience, especially to higher degrees of PIETY. However, CONVERSION or CHARISMATIC phenomena are not properly termed "mystical." Mysticism does not apply to the occult, to peak experiences, or to moments of transcendent clarity induced by drugs, sexual orgasm, or one's car going into a skid. While some mystics have exhibited parapsychological gifts, such as visions and voices (JULIAN OF NORWICH), trances (CATHERINE OF SIENA), automatic writing, clairvoyance, and telepathy (MADAME GUYON), these are merely infrequent incidents given by God to encourage the soul, not to be sought or treasured in themselves. Mysticism is not simply a catch-all term for "close encounters" or "warm fuzzies" in the spiritual realm.

Practically all religious people might well adopt a more disciplined life-style, but in the lives of true mystics prayer, devotion, and centering in the Divine also become ordering principles. While most people can take piano lessons and learn to play a few songs for their own enjoyment, mystics are akin to the musical geniuses who take lessons, practice, and have the gift of interpreting the very soul of the music in their performance.

Mysticism is sometimes called the interior life, and the mystical way does involve withdrawal from and renunciation of the world and its attachments. However, those who achieve mystical union are usually directed back into a life of intense and productive service. Catherine of Siena mediated between city-states and brought the pope back to Rome. Catherine of Genoa built hospitals. TERESA OF AVILA reformed the Carmelites.

*The Mystical Way.* Mysticism is usually outlined in three stages—purgation, illumination, union. EVELYN UNDERHILL in her classic treatment, *Mysticism,* lists five.

*a) Awakening.* This experience is similar to conversion in its most intense form, more comparable perhaps to sanctification in the Wesleyan tradition. Preceded by restlessness and uncertainty, this commitment to seeking the unitive life, to loving God with one's whole being, is marked by joy and exaltation.

*b) Purgation.* Purification of the self may run concurrently with later stages. It may contain several phases: contrition and repentance; detachment, including the EVANGELICAL COUNSELS of poverty, chastity, and obedience; and mortification, or dying to one's self. While this period may include various ascetic practices, the mystics are not to be confused or identified with monastics, for whom such practices are the end (*see* ASCETICISM and MONASTICISM). For mystics they are only means and cease after a definite period.

*c) Illumination.* This refers to those pleasurable and exalted states in which the mystic glimpses the goal and has fleeting moments of contact with God's essence, even though "selfhood" remains. This is the stage in which some people may have psychic experiences. Symbolically it is often referred to as "betrothal" in contrast to the "marriage" of union. It includes a joyous apprehension of the Absolute, a heightened perception of the world, and sometimes automatic activity such as special smells, tastes, sounds, and so on.

*d) Dark night of the soul.* Here all "consolations" of illumination are withdrawn. One loses a sense of God's presence; has an acute sense of imperfection; and experiences aridity, a loss of intellectual power, and assaults of evil. This may have been Jesus' temptation in the wilderness. A state of psychic fatigue, a final purification, it is often referred to as the "desert." The soul, through sheer commitment of will, must blindly continue to seek God.

*e) Union.* The soul is "one'd to God" says THE CLOUD OF UNKNOWING. Union comes to those who persevere, those to whom it is given. Teresa says this unity is "two distinct things becoming one." While some Christians, like Georgia Harkness, insist on the term "communion" to avoid a more Eastern sense of the negation and annihilation of the self, Christian mystics have made clear distinctions within the mystery. NICHOLAS OF CUSA called it a union of opposites. JAN VAN RUYSBROECK spoke of union but insisted, "Each of these keeps its own nature." It is the consciousness of one's "selfhood" that is subsumed in the experience of oneness with the HOLY ONE.

*History.* The OT contains little evidence of mysticism, though the SONG OF SOLOMON, interpreted as an allegory of the soul's love for God, is a favorite of mystics. In the NT the Gospel and Epistles of John speak mystically. In church history three periods—the third, fourteenth, and seventeenth centuries—stand out as eras of much mysticism.

Major authors includes PLOTINUS, AUGUSTINE, and DIONYSIUS THE AREOPAGITE in the early period; MEISTER ECKHART, Jan van Ruysbroeck, THOMAS À KEMPIS, Catherine of Seina, and Julian of Norwich in the middle and most glorious period; FRANCIS OF SALES, Brother Lawrence, and Madame Guyon in the last period.

In our day a resurgence of interest can be seen in the work of WILLIAM JAMES, Evelyn Underhill, Georgia Harkness, THOMAS MERTON, and Henri Nouwen, as well as the interest in Eastern religion and the emphasis on such spiritual disciplines as fasting, prayer, and meditation.

N.H.

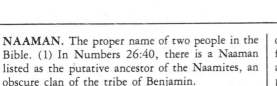

# Nn

**NAAMAN.** The proper name of two people in the Bible. (1) In Numbers 26:40, there is a Naaman listed as the putative ancestor of the Naamites, an obscure clan of the tribe of Benjamin.

(2) The far more important occurrence of the name is a feature of the lengthy story of II Kings 5. Here Naaman is identified as commander of the army of the king of Syria who was cured of LEPROSY by intercession of the prophet Elisha. The story is part of the cycle concerning Elijah and Elisha, a highly popular series of narratives that glorify the two prophets primarily as miracle workers. Naaman's affliction, since it obviously did not interfere with his daily activities and freedom of movement, could hardly have been the degenerative disease of leprosy as known to medical science. What was meant, as so often when the Bible speaks of leprosy, was some kind of skin disease, probably only cosmetically disturbing.

The story has other historical values besides its literary qualities. It testifies to the border raiding that went on between the Israelites and the Arameans (Syria), as well as Israel's subservience, at least temporarily, to Syria. Interesting, too, is Naaman's resolve to worship only Yahweh, even though he must accompany his master the king to the temple of the Syrian god Rimmon, a progressive idea that he nevertheless joins to the ancient belief that every deity is bound to one particular land. The end of the story, Elisha's rebuke of the venal Gehazi with its talk of

orchards, vineyards, sheep and oxen, servants, and so forth, is probably intended as commentary on the abuses committed by contemporary professional prophets. B.V.

**NABAL.** A wealthy sheep owner in the story of I Samuel 25. His name, which means "fool," is deemed appropriate by his wife ABIGAIL. (Probably the name has been tailored to the story, however, since it is hard to imagine parents giving a son such an unlucky name.) His foolishness consisted in refusing to pay tribute out of his considerable wealth to the followers of David, who at that time was little better than the head of a band of outlaws who preyed on the countryside exacting "protection money" from the landowners. Not only did Nabal refuse, he did it in such insulting terms that David was roused to come against him in force and destroy him. Abigail's intercession dissuaded David from these measures, but when Nabal, in drunken condition, heard of this he suffered a stroke and died soon after. David took Nabal's widow as one of his wives. B.V.

**NABATEANS.** These were an Arab people who made their first certain appearance in history about 312 B.C., when the Seleucid king Antigonus, one of the successors to the empire of Alexander the Great, made two unsuccessful attempts to subjugate them and dislodge them from their capital city of Petra. It

Herbert G. May

Herbert G. May

*Scenes at the ruins of Petra, famous capital of the Nabateans. At the top is a tomb facade in a cliff; below is the Roman period forum area.*

would appear that at this time they had only recently become a sedentary people, having occupied a part of Edom and Moab, which had previously been the resort of nomadic tribes, of which, presumably, the Nabateans were then one. (The Nabateans may be the Nebaioth mentioned along with the nomadic Kedarites by Isa. 60:7, a text that dates from Persian times.) At the height of their expansion the Nabateans held sway over a kingdom that extended southward halfway down the Arabian peninsula and, off and on, as far north as Damascus.

By Maccabean times the Nabateans had adopted kingship (in II Macc. 5:8 Aretas I is called *tyrannos,* a royal title). They seem to have made a great success of it, administering their extensive territory excellently well, capitalizing on their strategic location at the juncture of profitable trade routes and respecting and conserving the scanty natural resouces available to them. As a result they supported a more numerous and more prosperous population than any that has subsequently inhabited the region. They attained a high cultural level, including the arts. The magnificence of "the red rose city" of Petra, whose massive structures (largely Hellenistic in inspiration) were carved from the livng stone, is proverbial, constituting it one of the wonders of the world. The Nabateans preserved their economy and their independence for four centuries: not until A.D. 106 were they absorbed into the Roman Empire as the Province of Arabia.

Though they originally spoke a north Arabic dialect and eventually developed their own script, in most of the many inscriptions and records that they left behind they employed Imperial Aramaic, the standard language of the region since Persian times. Their religion was polytheistic and eclectic, with an extensive pantheon of deities drawn from both Arabic and local traditions. In cultic practice they shared the procedures and institutions that were basically common to the Semitic Near East.                B.V.

**NABI.** In the Semitic languages in general, the word "nabi" refers to a PROPHET, in the sense of one through whom God (or a god or spirit) speaks a message. In ancient Mesopotamia, and also among the earlier Hebrews, nabis were little more than mediumistic soothsayers who, often accompanied by ecstatic phenomena, would go into trances and utter divination. But among the later Hebrew prophets, especially the great writing prophets, deliverances ascribed to the Lord became a powerful literary and religious vehicle.

In Islam, nabis or prophets play a crucial role. They are people specially chosen by God in diverse times and places to deliver a message from God. The message is always essentially that of calling humankind back to pure monotheism, the worship of the one God instead of idols. Among those cited in the Qur'an as the greatest are Abraham, Noah, Moses, and Jesus. A few prophets are in addition *rasul,* often translated "apostle"; more than "ordinary" prophets, they also deliver a divine Law and Book to a community of people. In Islamic eyes, the greatest and last of the prophets and apostles is "the seal of the prophets," the deliverer of the consummate final message, MUHAMMAD.                R.E.

**NABONIDUS.** The last emperor, along with his son and co-regent BELSHAZZAR, of the Neo-Babylonian Empire. He fell from power when Cyrus the Great conquered Babylon in 539 B.C. Nabonidus was a cultured man, interested in Babylonia's ancient past and its traditional worship of Sin, the moon god. He rebuilt the great ziggurat (or "tower of Babel") in Ur and appointed his daughter, Belshaltinannar, as priestess in the temple of Sin. He practiced achaeology, supported scholars, and even had a museum. Unfortunately, in pursuing these interests, Nabonidus absented himself from Babylon and neglected the needs of its citizens. He also neglected, the Babylonians believed, Merodoch (or Marduk or Bel), the chief god of the Babylonian pantheon. CYRUS of Persia capitalized on this belief and declared, on the Cyrus cylinder, that Marduk had appointed him to rule the world as a righteous prince. The people of the city believed Cyrus and surrendered the city without a struggle. Nabonidus and Belshazzar both were out of touch, not only with their people's needs but with the realities of political and military events. Living many miles from the capital, indulging their intellectual interests, they forfeited the respect of their people.                              J.C.

**NABOPOLASSAR.** A Chaldaean or Babylonian adventurer who established the Neo-Babylonian Empire and rebelled against Assyrian overlordship in 616 B.C. He was victorious and completely rebuilt BABYLON. Nabopolassar's revolt enabled Josiah to reconquer the lost territories of Israel and reform Jewish worship. He captured Nineveh in 612 B.C.
                                                                       J.C.

**NABOTH.** A landowner of Jezreel, an agricultural center on the plain of Jezreel during the kingship of AHAB of Israel (I Kings 21; II Kings 9). Naboth owned a vineyard (part of his ancestral inheritance) that lay beside fields owned by King Ahab. A terrible drought afflicted Israel for years but apparently Naboth's vineyard survived it well. Ahab coveted the property and offered to buy it for silver, or to exchange a larger vineyard for it (I Kings 21:2). Naboth refused, however, as it was not proper to dispose of family property (I Kings 21:3). Queen Jezebel thereupon trumped up charges of blasphemy and treason against Naboth and had him stoned to death (I Kings 21:7-14). Ahab took possession of the property, but Elijah met Ahab at the field and pronounced doom on his whole family for this crime. Ahab repented, however, and the Lord delayed punishment for a generation (I Kings 21:17-29).
                                                                       J.C.

**NADAB.** The name of four men in the OT, meaning "generous" in Hebrew.

(1) Aaron's oldest son (Exod. 6:23; Num. 3:2; 26:60). He went up to Mount Sinai with Moses and his father, but later died (Exod. 28; Num. 3: I Chr. 24) because he profaned the sacrificial fire.

(2) A descendant of Caleb (I Chr. 2).

(3) A son of Gibeon, of Benjamin's tribe (I Chr. 8).

(4) A king of Israel, son of Jeroboam (I Kings 14).

He ruled only one year (about 901-900 B.C.); he was killed by Baasha, who took over the throne.
                                                                       J.C.

**NAGA.** Serpentine semidivine beings popular in Hindu and Buddhist mythology and folk religion. The Nagas may appear either as half human and half cobra, or as entirely snake. They are sometimes represented as living in an underground paradise. The Nagas, whose cult has very deep roots in India, are regarded as dangerous and in need of propitiation, yet also capable of great blessings. Their ambivalent race ranges from Kaliya, a demon defeated by Krishna, to the numerous serpents of modest shrines, near temples or under trees, to whom women pray for health or fertility. The queen of the Nagas, Manasa, is widely worshiped in Bengal.
                                                                       R.E.

**NAGARJUNA.** Foundational philosopher of MAHAYANA BUDDHISM who flourished in India about A.D. 200. He taught that all separate existing things are "empty," that is, have no being of their own; one should therefore have no attachments to them. All SAMSARA, existence, is really NIRVANA, unconditioned reality, and all beings are really Buddhas.
                                                                       R.E.

**NAG HAMMADI.** In December of 1945 a cache of thirteen ancient books (codices) was discovered by two peasants in a cemetery just across the Nile east of Nag Hammadi, Egypt, about sixty miles south of Luxor. The books are a collection of fifty-two tractates translated from Greek into Coptic, the language of early Egyptian Christians. The authors of the documents were Christians; so were those who collected and translated them. However, the kind of Christianity they practiced, which we know now as GNOSTICISM, was ardently attacked by some of the best-known, early mainline Christians such as Irenaeus, who wrote in the second century. Some of these documents were probably composed at that time, though the copies found in the Nag Hammadi "library" were made in the fourth century (in the opinion of James Robinson, who published the first full translation of the documents in any language, English). There is evidence that the collection derives from at least three smaller collections, since some books like the Apocryphon of John and the Gospel of the Egyptians appear more than once and in variant texts. No one book is copied by the same scribe twice. The hands of several scribes have been noted in the thirteen documents, but exact dates have not yet been determined for them.

The story of the documents subsequent to their discovery is high drama and is filled with all the elements of a mystery novel, including murder, blood revenge, deception, and intrigue. Eventually twelve of the books were brought back to the Coptic Museum in Cairo, although part of the library had been burned

Courtesy of the Institute of Antiquity and Christianity, Claremont Graduate School

*Nag Hammadi Codex VI, page 65*

before getting into responsible hands. Codex I (the thirteenth) was taken out of the country by a Belgian antiquities dealer in Cairo and was eventually purchased by the Jung Institute in Zurich (1952) and named the Jung Codex. It is now back with the other twelve in Cairo.

These documents reveal a great deal of information about an aberrant form of early Christianity that became a formidable rival to the orthodox faith for many centuries, primarily because of its denial of the reality of Christ's humanity.      J.R.M.

**NAHASH.** A name meaning "serpent," borne by two people in I and II Samuel. The first was a king of Ammon (I Sam. 11; II Sam. 10) who oppressed Jabesh-Gilead and caused Saul to rescue them. The second was an obscure relative of David, mentioned in II Samuel 17:25.      J.C.

**NAHUM.** The seventh book of the Minor Prophets of the Hebrew Bible, ascribed according to the title of the opening verse to an otherwise unknown prophet from an otherwise unknown Elkosh.

The book consists of several related poems of high dramatic quality and probably the work of a single author. They contain some of the most eloquent words of the OT uttered in the name of the God of Israel against the pretensions of human arrogance, in this case the mighty Assyrian Empire, which had long tyrannized the other countries of the ancient Near East and whose demise the poet contemplated with the utmost satisfaction.

Nahum is unique among the prophetic works of the OT, however, in that it has no reproaches to offer Israel or Judah for their crimes against their God that had brought about the Assyrian oppression as the instrument of God's punishment. This failure to reflect what is otherwise a commonplace of prophetic religion and proclamation has prompted some authors to regard Nahum as the work of one of those wholly nationalistic prophets with which various OT passages have made us familiar (see I Kings 22:5-28; Jer. 23:16-17; etc.), who stood in contradiction to everything that constituted the classical prophetic tradition of Israel, one of the chief glories of OT religion. However, the three chapters of the book of Nahum, while they are certainly nationalistic, do not necessarily tell us all there is to know about their author. The prophet Isaiah was also capable of nationalistic prophecy (see II Kings 19:20-34; Isa. 7:1-9; etc.), but we have enough of his other work to make no mistake about his right to the title of one of Israel's truly great prophets.

The poetry of Nahum is fairly easy to date. The most natural interpretation of the numerous references to Nineveh, the Assyrian capital (3:1, "the bloody city"), is that it was on the brink of destruction, not yet destroyed. It was in 612 B.C. that Nineveh was overrun and sacked by the Medes and the Neo-Babylonians, preparatory to the definitive fall of ASSYRIA around 609 B.C. At the same time, 3:8 rather mockingly speaks of the sack of Thebes in Egypt by the Assyrians, which had taken place in 663 B.C. Thus we are within the enviable position of reading a biblical text that is virtually contemporaneous with what it describes.

Chapter 1 of Nahum (1:1–2:1) is a poem of Yahweh's vengeance against enemies. The condemnation is generic, which has allowed the question that this chapter may have been adventitiously added to the Nahum text as a kind of standard introduction. The poem is an acrostic—each successive line beginning with a-b-c, etc.—and an incomplete one, an added factor that suggests the possibility of subsequent redactional activity.

About chapters 2–3 there can be hardly any question. Chapter 2 in loving detail pictures the siege of "the bloody city," so soon to be brought down into degradation. Chapter 3, nevertheless, contains theological reflections on the destruction of Nineveh, not simply a taunt sung over the defeat of an enemy. The final word is: "Upon whom has not come your unceasing evil?"                                    B.V.

**NAIN.** A village in southwest Galilee mentioned in the NT only in the story of Jesus' raising of a widow's son (Luke 7:11-17). The location of Nain is almost certain, for the name survives in the Arab village of Nein, about five miles southeast of Nazareth, and about twenty-five miles from Capernaum. An unlikely alternative is the place called Nain near the region of Idumea. According to Luke it was near Nain that Jesus met a procession of mourners bearing the body of the only son of a widow. Luke notes Jesus' compassion in several instances in which he restored the lives of children of parents with no other children (Luke 8:42; 9:38).                          J.L.P.

**NANAK.** The founder of SIKHISM, Nanak (1469–1539) sought to reconcile the rival religions of ISLAM and HINDUISM through the name of the true God above them both. He was born in the Punjab, a region where both faiths meet, of an official family. His own background was Hindu, but he had a Muslim teacher who taught him something of his faith, and as a youth he enjoyed conversing with holy men of both Hindu and SUFI persuasion. He married, had two children, and worked in a granary. However, as a gifted poet and musician, Nanak was drawn to hymnody and religion as well.

At the age of thirty, according to tradition, he experienced a mystical vision. He disappeared for three days, then at length appeared to his distraught friends to say he was beside himself in the Satnam, the divine name, which God had called him to teach to humankind, and that "There is no Hindu, there is no Muslim."

Tradition has it that he then undertook four long pilgrimage journeys about India and neighboring lands, venturing as far as Mecca. Scholars question many of these accounts, however. In any case, it appears that by 1520 Nanak was settled at Kartarpur in the Punjab, where he spent his remaining years as GURU of his burgeoning faith.

Nanak taught the existence of one supreme personal God and salvation from rebirth through inward devotional meditation upon him. He rejected all external aids to worship, such as images, temples, mosques, or places of pilgrimage, and held that God may be honored by any name so long as the worshiper does not make it exclusive. His many hymns and religious poems are of a rare coherence and beauty.                                                         R.E.

**NAOMI.** The mother-in-law of RUTH. The book of Ruth tells the story of Elimelech and Naomi of Bethlehem and their two sons moving to Moab during a famine. There the sons married, and later Elimelech and both sons died. Naomi encouraged her daughters-in-law to return to their family homes. One, Orpah, did, but Ruth chose to go back to

Bethlehem with Naomi. Naomi urged Ruth to contact Boaz and ask his protection as next of kin. Boaz married Ruth, and their child Obed became the father of Jesse, the father of David, the ancestor of Jesus.                                                        B.J.

**NAPHTALI.** The name of a region in northern Palestine at the time of the Israelite settlement there, also of the tribal element that inhabited this region, and finally the name of one of the sons of Jacob (Israel), from which this tribe was thought to have descended.

(1) Probably Naphtali, like the other northern tribal names, was originally geographical (Deut. 34:2). The extent of the territory is described in Joshua 19:32-39 and Deuteronomy 33:23.

(2) That Naphtali and DAN are listed as full brothers in Jacob's polygamous household (Gen. 30:4-8) indicates some special historical relationship between the two. That their territories were contiguous only after Dan's migration northward could mean that Naphtali, too, was remembered as having inhabited its present area only after resettlement. (Gen. 49:21 seems to ascribe a restless character to Naphtali.) Also, that Naphtali and Dan were children by a concubine probably points to their mixed ancestry (like Ephraim and Manasseh), perhaps that they were indigenous to Canaan.

(3) Naphtali played an important role in the early years of the Israelite federation, but it is seldom heard of later. Barak, leader in the crucial battle at Taanach, was a man of Naphtali (Judg. 4:6), and Naphtali acquitted itself bravely in this war of liberation (Judg. 5:18). Naphtali became the eighth of the twelve administrative districts in which Solomon organized his kingdom (I Kings 4:15). Because of its strategic position and its rich land, Naphtali was subject to frequent border incursions (I Kings 15:20). It was also among the first of Israel's cities and territories to be subjugated by the Assyrians and see its people go into exile.                                                    B.V.

**NARA BUDDHISM.** In Japan, the Nara period (710–784) was a time of great importance for the development of Buddhism. Nara, Japan's first permanent capital, was a center of Buddhist art and architecture lavishly patronized by the state; it has left an undying cultural legacy. For the imperial house and the government, the imported religion was a vehicle for displaying its wealth and taste, centralizing spiritual and temporal authority and gaining quasi-magical protection. These ends were only furthered by an ongoing process of combining Buddhism and SHINTO. Official Buddhism in Nara comprised six schools. Three of them survive; though small, they have exercised considerable influence and hold important temples, such as Kegon's Tōdaiji, the temple of the "Great Buddha" of Nara. At the same time, popular Buddhism in the countryside, often in tacit opposition to the elite, moved in shamanistic directions. R.E.

**NARRATIVE THEOLOGY.** The concept of theology as "story" is a prominent and fruitful one in the contemporary church. The idea of the church as the people of God, living out the story of God's love and salvation, stretching from the Creation, throughout the history of Israel and the Incarnation of Christ, and on through the Christian centuries, is a strong one today. Certain theologians have developed the idea that evangelization is simply to tell the story of God's dealings with humanity. John Gregory Dunn of Notre Dame University has deepened and broadened the area of story or narrative theology to include the examination of one's inner life and one's psychological reactions to the experiences of one's own life. Just as Augustine saw the working of God's gracious providence in his own life experiences (recorded in The *Confessions*), even so every Christian can see God's loving care in his or her own life if one's memory is examined in faith (J. G. Dunn, *A Search for God in Time and Memory*, 1977).

Narrative theology seeks to learn from the insights into human nature found in all classical literature, from the Bible to the writings of other religions to the great literature of the world, including the modern novel. It seeks to point out these insights and to give guidelines for deciding if these insights are true or false. This approach sees the biblical narrative as a story, as "history like," and is not caught up in efforts to prove the Bible historical. The Scripture is seen as awakening the response of the reader to a deepened appreciation of what it means to be human. This approach is also used on secular literature and the writings of other faiths.

Narrative theology seeks to understand myths, symbols, rites, and images that, as David Tracy observes, disclose a reality we must recognize as true.

Narrative theology is exciting but controversial. It is exciting, for it brings a wealth of new material into theological discussion. It can be the question asked by the secular world to which the Christian tradition gives the answer of faith (based on the Bible), as Paul Tillich believed modern philosophy could be the source of such questions (the method of correlation). On the other hand, narrative theology can be a massive use of the materials of culture as the content of theology, and thus so relativize theology that it is no longer the historic Christian faith.          J.C.

**NATARAJA.** From the Sanskrit words for "lord of the dance," Nataraja is the Hindu god SHIVA, represented as a dancer. This form is popular as a work of art and as an object of devotion in temples, particularly in South India. The deity is characteristically shown with four arms, holding a drum, hair flowing outward, his symbols of a skull and crescent moon over his head, and trampling on the demon of ignorance and delusion. He is surrounded by a circle of flames signifying the cosmos. Originally a portrayal of Shiva's wild and destructive aspect, the nataraja is now commonly said to show his creative "dancing out the universe," his place as source of animation within the cosmos and the human heart, and his triumph over falsity.          R.E.

**NATHAN.** The name of several men in the OT, the chief of whom were the son of David and the prophet who condemned David for his sin with Bathsheba.

(1) David's son (II Sam. 5:14) was born in Jerusalem.

(2) Nathan, the prophet, served as an adviser to both David and Solomon. His famous parable of the poor man's ewe lamb made David condemn himself for stealing Bathsheba from Uriah. David repented, and Nathan named Solomon "the Beloved of Yahweh" (II Sam. 12:25). However, Nathan felt moved to deny David's wish to build a temple to Yahweh, because of David's sin. Nathan and the priest Zadok anointed Solomon king (I Kings 1). Nathan helped save the throne by uncovering the plot of Adonijah (I Kings 1). The Chronicles author tells us that Nathan wrote a book, "The Book of Nathan the Prophet," which recorded the events of the reigns of David and Solomon (II Chr. 9). He was the father of Zabud and of Azariah, who were both prominent in royal service (I Kings 4).          J.C.

**NATHANAEL.** In Hebrew, a man's name meaning "God has given." The name of one of the disciples called by Jesus in John 1:45. This name does not appear in the Synoptic Gospels, and commentators for centuries have attempted to equate Nathanael with BARTHOLOMEW, who is included in all four lists of the twelve apostles (Matt. 10:3; Mark 3:18; Luke 6:14; Acts 1:13). It is true that Bartholomew is always connected with Philip, who was the disciple who brought Nathanael to Jesus.

In John's Gospel, Nathanael plays a large role, being shown as a thoughtful, meditative man, skeptical but open, who immediately confessed faith in Jesus upon meeting him. He declared that Jesus was Rabbi, King of Israel, the Son of God. He was one of those visited by Jesus after the Resurrection, when Peter and the apostles were fishing in the Sea of Galilee (John 21:1-14).          J.C.

**NATIONAL ASSOCIATION OF EVANGELICALS.** Thwarted by the liberal trends in the major Protestant denominations and excluded from any real voice in the existing ecumenical movement, a group of evangelical leaders met at Moody Bible Institute, Chicago, in 1941 to discuss the advisability of forming a creedally guaranteed Christian organization. The following year the NAE was officially, formed in St. Louis, Missouri. Unlike the Federal (later the National) Council of Churches, the NAE did not limit membership to denominations. It was possible for individual Christians, individual congregations, segments of small and large denominations to become members of the new association. Many observers regard the EVANGELICAL ALLIANCE, formed in London in 1846, as the NAE's progenitor. The alliance stated it was formed to "associate and concentrate against the encroachments of Popery and Puseyism and to promote the interests of a Scriptural Christianity." Perhaps the reason for the existence of the NAE could be traced more directly to the deep divisions in United States Protestantism as aftermath of the Fundamentalist-Modernist controversy of the 1920s.

While the NAE from its beginning welcomed evangelicals belonging to mainline denominations, in the years that followed its principal adherents were drawn from smaller Pentecostal and Holiness denominations as well as such groups as the Evangelical Free Church, the Baptist General Conference, and Conservative Baptists. Large evangelical communions such as Southern Baptists and Missouri Synod Lutherans never were attracted to the main body of the NAE.

However, much of the association's impact has been effected through its commissions, some of which are larger than the parent body. The National Religious Broadcasters, affiliated with the NAE, have welded together most of the conservative religious radio and television broadcasters, as well as religious television and radio station managers. The Evangelical Foreign Missions Association, an NAE-sponsored effort, has banded together a sizeable segment of evangelical independent and denominational foreign missionary societies. The World Relief Corporation (formerly the World Relief Commission), an arm of NAE, is an interdenominational service agency engaged in relief, rehabilitation, refugee resettlement, and self-help development. For some years the National Sunday School Association was an active force in evangelical Christian education.

One of the significant contributions of the NAE is the work of its Washington office, which serves evangelical interests in various church-state situations. The office now serves as a watchdog on legislation affecting EVANGELICALISM and as an aid to evangelicals dealing with various agencies of the federal government.      R.H.

## NATIONAL CONFERENCE OF CATHOLIC BISHOPS.

The episcopal conference of Roman Catholic bishops in the U.S.A. It was established in 1966 in response to Vatican II's decree on the bishop's pastoral office. The NCCB is made up of local bishops and associate bishops and is active in the campaign for human development; pro-life movements; the promotion of human rights in Latin America; and issues concerning nuclear weapons, war, and peace. The conference is active in promoting the liturgical reforms of Vatican II, upgrading religious education and the education of priests. The United States Catholic Conference is closely associated with the NCCB.      J.C.

## NATIONAL CONFERENCE OF CHRISTIANS AND JEWS.

A non-profit human relations organization that aims to create greater understanding between Christians and Jews and to eliminate intergroup prejudice. Its headquarters in New York City is called the Building for Brotherhood. The NCCJ sponsors Brotherhood Week, programs in interreligious relations and education, youth programming, police-community relations, and other community-oriented programs. The NCCJ was founded in 1928 as the reaction to the virulent anti-Catholic campaign against the presidential aspirations of Alfred E. Smith, a Catholic. The NCCJ has conducted national institutes of human relations, college workshops for teachers, youth conferences, seminars, labor-management activities, institutes on police and community relations, interracial colloquies, intercultural seminar tours on Christian-Jewish-Muslim relations in the Holy Land, an annual scholars' conference on the church struggle and the Holocaust, and other goodwill-building activities. It publishes a variety of materials to aid intergroup education.      L.K.

## NATIONAL COUNCIL OF THE CHURCHES OF CHRIST IN THE UNITED STATES OF AMERICA.

This cooperative federation of thirty Protestant and Eastern Orthodox denominations is the main representative of the ECUMENICAL MOVEMENT in the United States. Its present membership includes most of the major Protestant communions, except the Southern Baptist Convention, the American Lutheran Church, and the Lutheran Church—Missouri Synod. Other denominations share in some of the other programs of the NCC. The NCC describes itself as "a cooperative agency of Christian communions seeking to fulfill the unity and mission to which God calls them. The member communions, responding to the gospel revealed in the Scriptures, confess Jesus, the incarnate Son of God, as Savior and Lord. Relying on the transforming power of the Holy Spirit, the council works to bring churches into a life-giving fellowship and into common witness, study, and action to the glory of God and in service to all creation."

Some of the specific areas in which the council has been involved are those of civil rights, racial conflict, and world peace. It has also been active in facilitating the work of its member denominations in both home and overseas mission, Christian education, family life, broadcasting, and films. Through the Church World Service, the council has contributed to a worldwide program of relief for famines and other disasters.

The NCC was organized in 1950, combining its predecessor, the Federal Council of the Churches of Christ in America, with the Foreign Missions Conference and the International Council of Religious Education. The FCC was formed in 1908 as an official recognition of the need of the churches to implement the SOCIAL GOSPEL. After years of struggle, the FCC became a prominent force in the American scene. The NCC has continued to provide an effective framework for cooperative Protestant social action.

As sponsor and copyright owner, the council has been active in promoting the distribution of the Revised Standard Version of the Bible. The detailed operations of the NCC are conducted through its constituted divisions and departments, with a specialized staff functioning under a general secretariat. It is governed by a General Assembly that meets

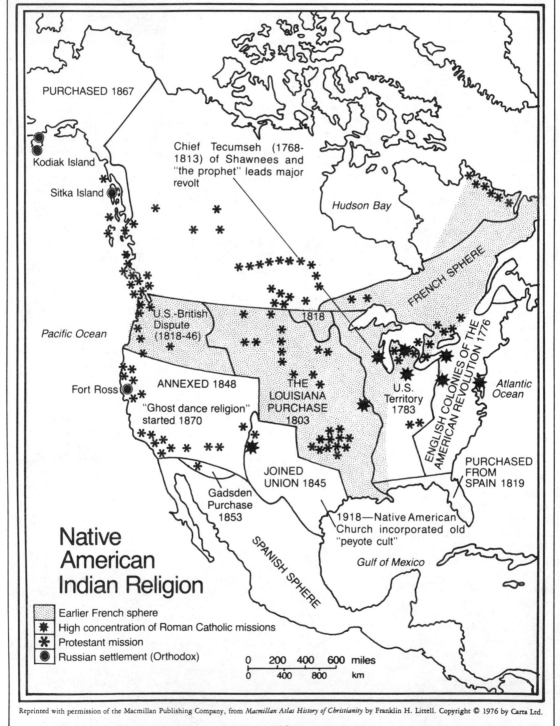

PURCHASED 1867

Kodiak Island

Sitka Island

Chief Tecumseh (1768-1813) of Shawnees and "the prophet" leads major revolt

Hudson Bay

FRENCH SPHERE

Pacific Ocean

U.S.-British Dispute (1818-46)

1818

Fort Ross

ANNEXED 1848

"Ghost dance religion" started 1870

THE LOUISIANA PURCHASE 1803

U.S. Territory 1783

ENGLISH COLONIES OF THE AMERICAN REVOLUTION 1776

Atlantic Ocean

PURCHASED FROM SPAIN 1819

Gadsden Purchase 1853

JOINED UNION 1845

1918—Native American Church incorporated old "peyote cult"

SPANISH SPHERE

Gulf of Mexico

## Native American Indian Religion

- Earlier French sphere
- ✳ High concentration of Roman Catholic missions
- ✴ Protestant mission
- ⦿ Russian settlement (Orthodox)

| 0 | 200 | 400 | 600 | miles |
| 0 | 400 | 800 | | km |

biennially and a General Board that meets bimonthly.

In recent years the council has been under attack especially by conservative elements of the churches and by some of the major media. The N.C.C. is financed by its member churches and has its headquarters in New York City.          R.H.

## NATIVE AMERICAN RELIGION.

The religion of the native inhabitants of North America, including Mesoamerica (Central America and Mexico) and that of the Eskimos in Alaska and northern Canada. Since the time of Columbus' colossal mistake in thinking he had discovered India, and his consequent naming of the inhabitants of the Bahamas and Caribbean Islands "Indians," Europeans (including Americans of European descent) have spoken of "Indian religion." With wild swings of repulsion or attraction, Americans, who virtually destroyed the Indians of the East Coast, the Middle West, the South, and California, have considered Native American religion "heathen superstition" or have venerated the vanquished Indian as far more spiritual and wise than other people. Neither assessment is true.

Native Americans were not one people but consisted of hundreds of different groups speaking very different languages. Their lifestyles and even religious outlooks also varied. Nonetheless, certain common themes and practices run through the religions of these widely dispersed and culturally diverse peoples. There was, and is, in the continuing traditional religions of the pueblo dwellers, the Navajo, the Hopi, and the Zuni, and the recovered religious rites and beliefs of the Oglala, Lakota (Sioux), the Iroquois, and other northern peoples, a belief in a single, overarching deity, the Great Spirit or Wakan-Tanka (to use the Lakota term). This is the creator of the world and the preserver of nature; the one who guides the destiny of all living things. Humanity is seen not as separate from nature, but as part of nature, so that people are related to the animals on which they are dependent for their livelihood. All life is sacred, human and non-human. The earth and its creatures are to be used, preserved, and respected. Many different cult practices are followed, from the sacrifice of self in the sun dance to the prayers for crops in the corn dance. The use of the sacred pipe (the Indians discovered tobacco), and the experience of sacred dreams and visions was—and is—widespread.          J.C.

## NATURAL LAW.

An idea that originated among the Greeks. Heraclitus seems to have been the first to talk of a cosmic law that is normative also for human beings. The idea was further developed by Aristotle and is recognized by Paul when he says that Gentiles have a law in their hearts corresponding to the Law of Moses (Rom. 2:14-15). The idea passed into Catholic moral theology, though many Protestant writers have criticized it. The advantage of a concept of natural law is that it recognizes that all human beings have a moral sense and that there is therefore a large area of morality that is shared by Christians and non-Christians alike. This probably outweighs the disadvantage, that if natural law is given too much prominence, it tends to overshadow distinctively Christian contributions to the moral life.

Obviously, natural law can be expressed only in the most general terms, otherwise it becomes positive law and shares in all the relativity and specificity of the latter. That good should be done and evil avoided is a general principle of natural law, but is so vacuous as to have little value. One might add recommendations that are more concrete and that derive from human nature, for example, that cooperation is better than competition, or that one should reverence life. But natural law is more a criterion for judging positive laws than a law in itself. Originally conceived as unchanging, natural law has more recently been considered to be developing and dynamic, in accord with more dynamic ideas of human nature.   J.M.

## NATURAL RELIGION AND THEOLOGY.

Natural religion flourished among intellectuals in the seventeenth and eighteenth centuries. Contrasted with revealed or positive religions, with their specific doctrines, ceremonies, scriptures, etc., natural religion distills the essence of these, which it vindicates by reason and the evidences of nature. It was already criticized as abstract by Schleiermacher.

Natural theology is the intellectual basis for natural religion and also has been used as both a defense and an introduction for revealed religion. The claim of natural theology is that by the powers of reason and observation, the human mind can rise to an elementary knowledge of God, of the freedom and immortality of the human soul, and of the basic demands of morality. The mind can reach these truths, it is claimed, unaided by revelation. This last phrase is ambiguous. It may mean "unaided by a *specific* or historical revelation," such as Christianity. But this would not exclude the possibility of a *general* revelation in nature, and some advocates of natural theology would certainly wish to posit such a general revelation as a genuine self-communication of God, who could scarcely be known in any religious sense simply through observation and speculation.

It is sometimes held that Paul recognized the possibility of natural theology (Rom. 1:19-20), and it has regularly formed part of Catholic theology. Aquinas' "five ways" of proving the existence of God provide a classic example, and Vatican I reaffirmed the capacity to know God without a specific revelation. Protestant theologians have been much more skeptical about natural theology. While Calvin acknowledged that God is manifested in divine works, he held that the human mind as well as the human will has been impaired by sin, so that we are unable to discern God through divine works and instead set up idols—the products of our own minds. More recently, Karl Barth has waged a polemic against natural theology, holding that there is no way from our finite human minds to God, and that God can be known only through specific revelation in Jesus Christ. Natural theology is the theme of the many series of Gifford Lectures, given at the Scottish universities since 1888.     J.M.

**NATURE AND GRACE.** The classic discussion of this theme is found in AUGUSTINE's controversy with the Pelagians. Long before that controversy arose, Augustine had already been stressing the sinfulness of human beings and their impotence in the face of the demands of God. Salvation can come only from God. The initiative must be God's and must come to us even in our sinfulness—the doctrine of PREVENIENT GRACE. Even the faith with which we respond to God must be itself a gift of God, for our nature is so infected by sin that of ourselves we cannot even receive the divine gift.

Augustine believed that such teachings are compatible with the acknowledgment of a measure of free will in humanity, but as time went on and he got into controversy, his teaching became more extreme. The doctrine of the divine initiative in salvation was developed into a full-blown theory of PREDESTINA-TION and any human part in the process seemed to be eliminated. Freedom of the human will and the significance of the church's preaching and its sacramental system are abolished if everything depends finally on the inscrutable decrees of God.

PELAGIUS, on the other side, thought that the stress upon grace weakened the human sense of responsibility and led to an antinomian attitude to the moral life. Was it not an encouragement to sin, that grace might abound? Humans had been created with the capacity for doing the good, and whether in fact they do the good depends on their own free will. But if Augustine had exaggerated the impotence of the human will, Pelagius went to the opposite extreme of error and did not adequately allow for the disabling effects of sin in human life.

In the subsequent stages of the dispute between Augustinians and Pelagians, something like a compromise was eventually reached. The Council of Orange (529) gave general support to the Augustin-ian position, but did not sanction its extreme view of predestination. The controversy is not yet over. It was revived at the Reformation, and persists today in the rival claims of Christian and secular humanism. But the general tendency in Christian theology has been to move toward some form of synergism or co-working of God and humans, with the emphasis on the priority of the divine grace. Nature and grace are not opposed, for human nature is itself the creation of God and was originally disposed toward the good. In Aquinas' words, grace does not abolish nature but perfects it.     J.M.

**NAUVOO.** A city in Illinois founded by the Latter-day Saints or Mormons, followers of JOSEPH SMITH, in the first half of the nineteenth century. The Mormons moved there from Kirtland, Ohio. Next they went to Missouri, where they had been forced to leave, and then on to Illinois. Severe opposition to their beliefs arose, Joseph Smith was killed, and most of the Mormons went to Utah, following BRIGHAM YOUNG.     J.C.

**NAZARENE.** The English word translates two different Greek words (one of which may be Semitic [Aramaic] in origin) having no discernible difference in meaning. The distinctly Greek term occurs in Matthew (2:23), Mark (14:67), and Acts (24:5). Matthew (26:71), John (18:5, 7; 19:19), and especially Luke (18:37; Acts 2:22; 3:6; 4:10; 6:14; 22:8; 26:9) use the Semitic form.

It is clear that the NT writers considered Jesus to be a Nazarene because he was from Nazareth (Matt. 21:11; John 1:45; Acts 10:38). However, Matthew adds the additional note that the title was given in fulfillment of the word of the prophets, "he shall be called a Nazarene" (2:23). But this statement does not occur in the OT, and Matthew may have been referring to the general teaching of the prophets or perhaps he understood the Semitic form of the term to derive from a Hebrew form meaning NAZIRITE, which appears in the Former Prophets (Judg. 13:7), referring to Samson: "the boy shall be a Nazirite to God."     J.R.M.

**NAZARENE, CHURCH OF THE.** *See* CHURCH OF THE NAZARENE.

**NAZARETH.** A modern city, which was an ancient village, lying on the northern ridge of the Jezreel

From *Atlas of the Bible* (Thomas Nelson & Sons Limited)

*A street in Nazareth*

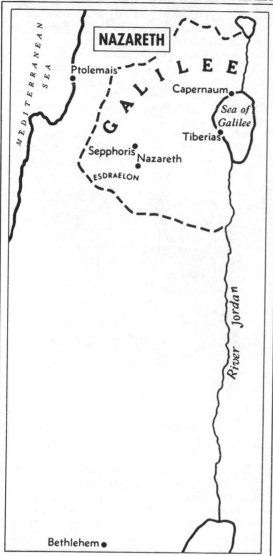

Courtesy of the Israel Government Tourist Office, Houston, Texas

*Nazareth set within the hills of Galilee*

Tiberius, was brought to Paris purportedly from Nazareth in 1878, which prescribes capital punishment for disturbance of graves. This may be an imperial response to the resurrection of Christ, which occasioned a tumult in Rome resulting in Claudius' expulsion of Jews in A.D. 49 (Acts 18:2).          J.R.M.

**NAZIRITE.** The term refers to those who have been dedicated or consecrated to religious service. They refuse to eat unclean food, cut their hair, drink intoxicating beverages, and they avoid contact with the dead. Laws governing Nazirites are laid out in Numbers 6. Samson was a typical example of such a person who, in spite of his moral lapses, remained a Nazirite until his death (Judg. 13–16). Whether John the Baptist was a Nazirite is not clear, though he was consecrated from his birth (Luke 1:15), as was Samuel (I Sam. 1:11), who did not become a Nazirite. Paul's vow, taken in the Temple in Jerusalem, may have been a temporary Nazirite vow (Acts 21:23-26), which some think may have begun at Cenchrea, where he shaved his head (Acts 18:18). This latter point is unlikely, however, since the Nazirite vow forbade the cutting of one's hair. It seems rather that Paul had been under a vow while in Corinth and brought it to an end in Cenchrea by cutting his hair, as prescribed in Numbers 6:18. By Paul's time, accommodation had to be made for the Jews in the Diaspora who could not comply with the requirement of ending the vow at the tent of meeting (or the tabernacle/temple). Details of Nazirite vows in the NT period are set out in the Mishnah, tractate "Nazir," where special rules apply to those who complete a vow and then go to the Holy Land (chap. 6).          J.R.M.

**NEALE, JOHN MASON** (1818–66). Anglican priest, scholar, and noted translator of Greek and Latin hymns. Born on January 24 in London, England, Neale was educated at Trinity College, Cambridge. Although he came from a family of Evangelicals, Neale espoused the High Church emphasis of the Oxford Movement. An able scholar, Neale dug deeply into the trove of ancient Greek

Valley in Lower Galilee. Jesus Christ lived here during his early life. The major trade routes ran through the Jezreel Valley to the south and the Beit Netofa Valley to the north, leaving Nazareth largely isolated. It is not mentioned in the OT, the Talmud, or Josephus. No prophet, priest, or king ever came from the city, thus provoking the astonished Nathanael's response: "Can anything good come out of Nazareth?" (John 1:46). The village is identified as the home of Joseph and Mary before Jesus was born, and his birth was announced there (Luke 1:26). He left Nazareth after his rejection in the synagogue and the attempt upon his life (Luke 4:29).

There is no reliable evidence of the first-century village in the few archaeological remains extant in Nazareth, but a first-century inscription from Caesarea Martima names it among towns where the twenty-four priestly courses were located. A lengthy inscription attributed to Claudius, or perhaps hymns of the Orthodox liturgy and Latin hymns of the medieval church, rendering them into English. One of these was the great Advent hymn, "O Come, O Come, Emmanuel," which had been a part of the twelfth-century Latin liturgy. Another great number was "The Day of Resurrection," adapted from an original eighth-century Greek hymn by John of Damascus. Other similar translations that have become popular English hymns are "All Glory, Laud, and Honor," "Of the Father's Love Begotten," "Good King Wenceslas," and "O Happy Band of Pilgrims." Although Neale was weak in body most of his life, he was a prodigious and scholarly author. He died at East Grinstead, England, where he served as warden of Sackville College. R.H.

**NEANDER, JOACHIM** (1650–80). German hymn writer, school teacher, and pastor. Neander was born in Bremen, on May 3, and is regarded as the greatest hymn writer of the German Reformed Church. The author of sixty hymns and composer of many tunes, while an assistant pastor and teacher in a church-sponsored school at Dusseldorf, Neander wrote "Praise Ye (to) the Lord, the Almighty." He also wrote "Praise to the Earth, and Sea, and Air," based on the Nineteenth Psalm. In a dispute with the elders of the church at Dusseldorf, he was forced to flee to a cave. While there he wrote a number of hymns, all marked by a note of triumphant praise. Neander died in Bremen, the city of his birth. R.H.

**NEBO, MOUNT.** The mountain in the land of MOAB from which MOSES was permitted to view the Promised Land, which he was destined never to enter (Deut. 32:49; 34:1-5). It is with all probability to be identified with Jebel Neba, an elevation from which on a clear day most of Palestine from Galilee to the Negeb and from the Dead Sea to the Mediterranean can be seen. Here are the remains of a Byzantine church and monastery that once commemorated the biblical events. According to Numbers 33:47, Mount Nebo is part of the Abarim chain, and according to Deuteronomy 34:1 it is a peak of the Pisgah, a term taken to mean the mountain slope, on another of whose heights Balaam offered sacrifice and prophesied over Israel (Num. 23:14-24). It was in a cave on Mount Nebo, according to II Maccabees 2:4-5, that the prophet Jeremiah hid the tent, the ark, and the altar of incense after the destruction of the Temple by the Babylonians. B.V.

**NEBUCHADNEZZAR.** More exactly Nebuchadrezzar. The name of several Babylonian kings, the most famous of whom is Nebuchadnezzar II (605–562 B.C.); also the most famous of the kings of the Neo-Babylonian Empire, who figures prominently in the final history of the kingdom of JUDAH. Nebuchadnezzar was the son of Nabopolassar, founder of the Chaldean or Neo-Babylonian Empire, formerly a governor under the Assyrians in the days of

their declining empire. In 625 B.C. he formed an alliance with the Medes, and in a series of campaigns he succeeded in completely demolishing ASSYRIA; destroying Nineveh, their capital, in 612; obliterating their last redoubt at Haran in 609; and ending their final hope for survival by defeating the Egyptians under Pharaoh Neco at the battle of Carchemish in 605. Neco, who had gone to the aid of the Assyrians in the face of the Chaldean threat, had been delayed en route at Megiddo by Josiah of Judah (II Kings 23:29). Though Josiah was slain in the encounter, his intervention may also have contributed to the downfall of the hated Assyrians.

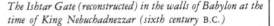

*The Ishtar Gate (reconstructed) in the walls of Babylon at the time of King Nebuchadnezzar (sixth century B.C.)*

Between 607 and 605 B.C., Nebuchadnezzar served with his father in the western campaigns and was, in fact, the commanding general in the battle of Carchemish. In that same year, however, he was recalled to Babylon to assume the throne on Nabopolassar's death. During the next several years he was back in the west, consolidating this part of his empire and expanding on it. The Egyptians, who had briefly dominated Palestine after Josiah's death, deposing and deporting his successor Jehoahaz and placing Jehoiakim on the throne in his place (II Kings 23:30-35), were in turn expelled from the land and driven back to Egypt. Jehoiakim became Nebuchadnezzar's vassal.

In 601 Jehoiakim attempted to throw off the Babylonian yoke (II Kings 24:1), doubtless emboldened by Nebuchadnezzar's having been bogged down temporarily in an unsuccessful attempt to invade Egypt. The result was the beginning of the end for Judah. Second Chronicles 36:6-7 and Daniel 1:1-2 testify to a tradition that already in Jehoiakim's reign Nebuchadnezzar successfully besieged and pillaged Jerusalem. What is certain is that in 597 B.C. the "Babylonian captivity" began. Jehoiakim, under whatever circumstances, was succeeded briefly by Jehoiachin, who with the removal of Egyptian

Courtesy of The University Museum, University of Pennsylvania

*Cylinder of Nebuchadnezzar inscribed with three columns of text about 586 B.C., found buried in the foundation of a temple in Babylon*

protection became the prey to Babylonian conquest and was carried off captive to the east, along with all the influential leadership of the Judean state, leaving behind only those who were regarded as inconsequential by the Babylonians (II Kings 24:7-16). Jehoiachin never returned from this exile, though he and his fellow Judeans eventually, after initial deprivations, settled down in their involuntary new homeland and frequently prospered there as an earlier Jewish Diaspora (II Kings 25:27-30).

Nebuchadnezzar had set up in place of Jehoiachin his uncle Mattaniah as a Babylonian puppet king, to whom the name Zedekiah was given (II Kings 24:17). Zedekiah was counseled by the prophets Jeremiah, who had remained in Judah, and Ezekiel, who was among the exiles in Babylonia, to submit to Babylonian rule as an inevitability, and to wait on the pleasure of the Lord for a restoration of Israel. However, Zedekiah was finally persuaded by his nationalist advisers to rebel, with totally disastrous results. In 586 Jerusalem was devastated by Nebuchadnezzar's army, the king and his family were taken into ignominious EXILE, and Judah disappeared as an independent political entity (II Kings 24:20–25:21).

Because Nebuchadnezzar had become, in Jewish tradition and folklore, the legendary enemy *par*

*excellence* of the people of God (just as Nineveh or Sodom, later on Babylon or Rome, would figure as "the sinful city" *par excellence*), he appears in such works as Daniel 1–4 and Judith 1:1, 7 etc. (where he is called "king of the Assyrians!") simply as a symbol of malevolence. This is a mythical Nebuchadnezzar *redivivus*, a character of fiction.          B.V.

**NEBUZARADAN.** The captain of the guard in King Nebuchadnezzar's household (II Kings 25:8). He was given power to destroy the Temple, palaces, and walls at Jerusalem after its capture in 587 B.C. He looted the Temple and carried the chief priests and other officials to exile at Riblah in Syria. He showed favor to Jeremiah (Jer. 39).          J.C.

**NEGEB.** The desert region south of Judah, running down to the Gulf of Aqabah and into the Sinai Peninsula and Edom (modern Jordan). Negeb means "the dry" in Hebrew, as there is little rain and little water there.

The natural barriers of the ridges and ravines that go across this area, from east to west, made it an effective defense for Judah and Israel. Very few attempts were made to attack Israel through the Negeb. Indeed, the Israelites under Moses at the time of the Exodus tried to enter Canaan this way and gave up the attempt (Deut. 1).

When David was forced to flee Saul's wrath he went into hiding in the Negeb (I Sam. 27). For most of its history the Negeb was the home of wandering nomads who grazed their flocks in the ravines that sprouted grass after the winter rain. The Amalekites lived here and also the Edomites. Edom became a primary enemy of Israel. After the rise of monasticism (third century A.D.), many Christian monks lived in the Negeb and the many monastic communities irrigated and farmed land there. This enterprise was destroyed by the Islamic invasion in the seventh century A.D.          J.C.

**NEHEMIAH.** *See* EZRA AND NEHEMIAH.

**NEO-CONFUCIANISM.** *See* CONFUCIANISM.

**NEO-ORTHODOXY.** A movement in Protestant theology that began in Switzerland after the outbreak of the First World War and spread rapidly through Europe and North America. It was the most influential and, in some respects, the most creative theological movement of the first half of this century. Neo-orthodoxy is also referred to as "dialectical theology," "the theology of crisis," or the "theology of the Word of God." It was in large part a protest against nineteenth-century liberal theology, which appeared wedded to a bourgeois, optimistic culture unable to respond to the crisis of Western civilization occasioned by the war and the loss of confidence in liberal programs for "Christianizing the social order."

The movement of prophetic protest was initiated by KARL BARTH with his commentary on the Epistle to the Romans (1919) and his discovery of what he called "the strange new world within the Bible." The book sought to direct attention to the infinite qualitative difference between the holy and transcendent God and finite, sinful persons; to the fact of human helplessness and the crisis of faith; and to the stark revelation of the righteousness of God and the fact that the gulf between God and humanity can be bridged by grace alone through faith. A number of younger pastors and theologians rallied around Barth, including EMIL BRUNNER, EDUARD THURNEYSEN, Georg Merz, FRIEDRICH GOGARTEN, and RUDOLF BULTMANN. The movement voiced its concerns in the journal *Zwischen den Zeiten (Between the Times),* published between 1922 and 1933. While members of the group soon found that they disagreed and controversy divided them, they all concurred in protesting against theological liberalism.

In the writings of PAUL the Apostle, AUGUSTINE, LUTHER, CALVIN, and in the recently discovered works of KIERKEGAARD and DOSTOEVSKY, the Neo-orthodox theologians rediscovered the power of doubt, evil, and human sin, but also the boundless grace and mercy of God's love. Above all, Neo-orthodoxy grew out of a passionate engagement with the Bible itself in the expectation that the Word of God, free of a culture in crisis, would disclose itself in new and unexpected ways.

With Kierkegaard, Neo-orthodox theologians recognized that divine truth is never direct and transparent but always indirect and dialectical, that is, always found in a tension between one truth and another. This tension is never fully resolved because revelation is a union of eternity and time, which can only be expressed paradoxically, as in the claim that Jesus Christ is both human and God. For Barth, God is "Wholly Other"; the finite cannot contain or even mirror the infinite. There is no natural theology—no analogy between humans and God. God is known only through the divine self-revelation in the Bible. But even here the revealed God is also the hidden God, the *Deus absconditus.* God's unveiling is also a veiling. For seeing God in Christ requires the eyes of faith, which is a gift of grace.

Neo-orthodoxy does not represent a return to the Protestant ORTHODOXY of an earlier time. The Neo-orthodox theologians accept the results of modern science and apply the most radical historico-critical methods to the study of the Bible and the Christian tradition. The Neo-orthodox theologians often interpret doctrines symbolically rather than literally, pointing to the religious meaning of biblical events. This approach to the Bible has remained one of the most disputed and unresolved aspects of Neo-orthodoxy.                                    J.L.

**NEOPLATONISM.** The philosophy originating in Alexandria, developed by Plotinus (205–270), and continued by such figures as ORIGEN (about 182–251), a Christian theologian; Porphyry (233–304), an anti-Christian thinker; and Proclus (about 409–487), an Athenian associated with the later stages of Plato's Academy. Drawing on Pythagorean, Aristotelian, and Stoic sources more than on Plato, Neoplatonism formed a significant school of thought until the conquest of Egypt by the Muslims in 629 and continued as a major influence in Western thought mainly through its impact on AUGUSTINE (354–430) and through him on subsequent Christian theology and philosophy.

In Neoplatonic thought, being emanates from the One or the Good. From the One comes the realms of *Nous,* of Soul, and then of Matter, which represents a falling away toward nonbeing or nothingness. Some souls remain unembodied and are not contaminated by incarnation; human souls exist as embodied and are called to turn away from Matter as evil and ascend toward knowledge of and ecstatic union with the One.                                    C.Mc.

**NEO-THOMISM.** A movement of the late nineteenth to the mid-twentieth century associated with the rebirth of a vital Roman Catholic theology based on a renewal of the theological synthesis of THOMAS AQUINAS. Neo-Thomism received impetus from Pope Leo XIII's encyclical *Aeterni patris* (1879). The pope called upon the church "to restore the golden wisdom of Thomas and to spread it far and wide for the defense and beauty of the Catholic faith." Special institutes were established for the study of Thomism, a critical text of Thomas' writings was prepared, and St. Thomas was made the patron of all Roman Catholic colleges and schools.

Neo-Thomism attempts to demonstrate that the teachings of Thomas Aquinas are perennial and capable of adaptation to the problems of modernity. Neo-Thomists are Aristotelian, they insist on an empirical or sensory basis of knowledge and thus begin with an analysis of the natural world and its contingency. From this inquiry they move to the question of that Being which is its own existence, whose essence is to exist, that is, God. Neo-Thomists remain almost unique in this century in their efforts to restore Aquinas' traditional proofs for the existence of God, especially by attempting to show that KANT's critique of those proofs is not decisive, and that the proofs are compatible with developments in contemporary science. Among the most important Neo-Thomists are ETIENNE GILSON, JACQUES MARITAIN, and the Anglican theologian E. L. Mascall. Since Pope John XXIII (1958), the rigid adherence to Neo-Thomism was relaxed, and a new openness to other philosophical approaches is possible in Roman Catholicism.                                    J.L.

**NEPHILIM.** Giants or semidivine beings produced by intercourse between human females ("the daughters of men") and divine or angelic beings ("the sons of God"), according to ancient Canaanite mythology.

The Nephilim resemble, in concept, the mythical heroes, half-man, half-God, found in ancient Greek mythology. Such mythical figures appear in the OT, but only briefly. Genesis 6:4 speaks of the giants in the earth, or Nephilim, and refers to their mixed parentage. Later, in Numbers 13:33, the Israelite spies sent into Canaan reported the strength of the Canaanites by saying they looked like the Nephilim or giants.

There is no way to reconcile the concept of Nephilim, and of intercourse between angels and human beings, with the beliefs about God in the rest of Genesis. Genesis 6:4 must represent a fragment of a longer account of an ancient myth that escaped removal from the text by the Priestly redactors (or editors) at the time of the Exile and after (586 B.C.). The concept of heavenly beings engaging human beings sexually belongs to ancient non-Hebrew mythology and, throughout history, to the occult, that is, the incubi (demons), who, superstition holds, visit men and women by night.                    J.C.

**NERO.** Successor of CLAUDIUS as Roman Emperor (A.D. 54–68). Nero's mother, Agrippina, was largely responsible for Nero's rise to power, persuading Claudius, who later became her husband, to adopt Nero as guardian of his son and heir (by a previous wife), Brittanicus. She was also instrumental in obtaining the senate's confirmation of Nero as emperor upon the death of Claudius. The following year Brittanicus was murdered, and in A.D. 59 Nero had his mother put to death. Another woman, Nero's mistress, Poppea, became a power behind the throne.

Profligate and a spendthrift, Nero confiscated large estates and devalued the currency to support his fun and games and the cost of his military adventures. In July A.D. 64, a third of the city of Rome was destroyed by fire. The Roman historian Tacitus records in his *Annals* that in order to escape suspicion of having started the fires to further his rebuilding projects, Nero found scapegoats among a people "hated for their crimes," the mob called "Christians." The first to be arrested confessed, under duress, to arson or Christianity, and accused others. Nero exposed his victims to savage attacks by wild dogs, and others were crucified or immolated in Nero's gardens. According to Clement of Rome, Peter and Paul were put to death during Nero's reign of terror. Subsequently, in A.D. 68, revolts erupted in Gaul, Spain, and Africa, and the emperor committed suicide.

A rumor spread abroad that Nero had not died but that he would return from a hiding place in the East to reclaim his throne and wreak vengeance upon the opposition. Several pretenders attempted to give credence to this myth, but they were caught and put to death. Dio Chrysostom, a second-century historian, wrote that "most men believe that Nero is still alive." Some interpreters of the Christian apocalypse, the book of Revelation to John, see a reference to this

Courtesy of the Trustees of the British Museum

*Bust of Nero*

myth in 13:3, 12, 14. It is uncertain whether or not Nero's persecution of Christians spread beyond the capital, or became a legal basis for later persecutions.

A combination of Nero's persecutions and of the flight of others from Jerusalem, before its destruction in A.D. 70, may have led to a consolidation of the movement: to the composition of some writings (later canonized), notably the Gospel of Mark, and, possibly, I Peter; to a rethinking of the apocalyptic eschatology of the early church; and to a provision for the church's order and offices of ministry, which were principal concerns in the last third of the first century.
                                                                                J.L.P.

**NESTORIANS.** Followers of Nestorius, a fifth-century monk from Antioch, patriarch of Constantinople (428–431), father of the Nestorian churches. Nestorius objected to calling Mary the MOTHER OF GOD, which he felt did not do justice to the human Christ. Mary bore the human Jesus, not the divine. Nestorius claimed Christ's two natures were conjoined and acted as one but were not a unified, single person. CYRIL, patriarch of rival Alexandria (412–444), opposed Nestorius by emphasizing the divine in a unified Being. Ambiguous terms confused the issue. Cyril secured Nestorius' condemnation at a Roman synod (430) and again at the Council of Ephesus (431), which exiled Nestorius and his followers and denounced Nestorian beliefs. Pope Leo I's *Tome* settled the question temporarily when the Council of CHALCEDON (451) recognized in Christ two natures without confusion, change, division, or separation in one person and subsistence. Further attempts to reconcile variant views caused prolonged dissensions. The Council of Constantinople (681) reaffirmed Chalcedon and finally closed the controversy. Exiled Nestorians dispersed into Persia, where Barsumas led a strong group at Edessa, India, China, and Mongolia, and have continued with diminishing strength until current times. In 1625 a monument was excavated in Changan, China, showing Nestorians were there in 781.                   C.M.

**NETHINIM.** The term, which is Aramaized Hebrew, means "those dedicated" or "those given." It is found only in the books of Ezra-Nehemiah and I Chronicles, where it is usually translated "temple servants" and designates an inferior class of ministers apparently charged with the menial works associated with the care of the Temple and its paraphernalia. Sometimes, as in Ezra 8:17, the Nethinim seem to be part of the Levitical class, and in Numbers 3:9 the proper Hebrew word for "dedicated," "given," is used of the Levites. However, the Nethinim are usually, as in Ezra 8:20, categorized apart from the Levites and said to be in attendance on them. In Ezra 2:58 they are associated with yet another group called "the sons of Solomon's servants." In view of the genealogies provided the Nethinim, there can be no doubt that they were regarded as Israelites in the time of Ezra-Nehemiah. Some of their names appear to be foreign, however, which leads to the suspicion that they, like various others of the postexilic community, were Israelites by virtue of "naturalization." They probably replaced a category of state slaves, who were usually prisoners of war otherwise subject to death, who had performed the servile functions in the preexilic Temple. In Ezekiel 44:7-9 Israel is rebuked for having introduced foreigners into the Temple to assist in its sacred functions.                       B.V.

**NEVIN, JOHN WILLIAMSON** (1803–86). The Mercersburg theologian was a graduate of Union College (1821) and Princeton Seminary (1826). He became professor of biblical literature at Western Theological Seminary near Pittsburgh in 1828. Called to Mercersburg Seminary in 1840, he changed from Presbyterianism to the Reformed Church. His writings include *The Anxious Bench* (1843), opposing revivalism; *The Mystical Presence* (1846); and *The*

*History and Genius of the Heidelberg Catechism* (1847). From 1841 to 1853 he was president of Marshall College and from 1866 to 1876 president of Franklin and Marshall.                       N.H.

**NEW AMERICAN BIBLE.** (NAB). The biblical movement within the Roman Catholic church, given greater impetus by the Second Vatican Council, was responsible for this new version of Scripture. It has become the official approved version of the Roman Catholic church in the United States and is recommended for use in the liturgy. The NAB was produced in 1970 by members of the Catholic Biblical Association of America under the patronage of the Bishops' Committee of the Confraternity of Christian Doctrine. In its foreword by Pope Paul VI, the decree *(Dei Verbum)* is quoted in part, prescribing that "up-to-date and appropriate translations be made in the various languages, by preference from the original texts of the sacred books."
                       R.H.

**NEW AMERICAN STANDARD VERSION** (NASV). A group of unidentified evangelical scholars, working under the direction of the Lockman Foundation of LaHabra, California, were the translators of the New American Standard Bible. As the name implies, this is another revision of the AMERICAN STANDARD VERSION of 1901. Like the Revised Stardard Version, it is another continuation of the Bible in the tradition of Tyndale's King James Version. The translators attempted to follow faithful rendering of the original text into contemporary English, seeking a version acceptable for pulpit reading and memorization. Despite competition from the LIVING BIBLE and the NEW INTERNATIONAL VERSION, the NASV has gained a wide and enthusiastic number of users, particularly among conservative Christian groups.           R.H.

**NEW BEING.** A term used especially by PAUL TILLICH to refer both to Jesus as the Christ and to those who, in faith, are in union with Christ. Tillich regards the term as both authentic to the Pauline witness that "if any one is in Christ, he is a new creation" (II Cor. 5:17) and relevant to modern humanity's existential quest for the healing of estrangement and the regaining of essential personhood, or a new being. In the West this spiritual quest is expressed in the expectation of a messiah who will actualize what each person is essentially meant to be under the conditions of existential estrangement and who will overcome the forces that threaten existence. Christianity is founded on the claim that Christ is the medium of this final revelation, or the New Being.
                       J.L.

**NEW BIRTH.** The concept of the Christian as a new creature is taught in II Corinthians 5:17, where

CONVERSION is regarded as a death to the unregenerate way of life and a rebirth into a new and better way. This is typified in the act of baptism, in which one is symbolically buried with Christ in the likeness of his death and raised in the likeness of his resurrection to walk in "newness of life" (Rom. 6:1-14). This death is considered to be a putting off of the old nature and the putting on of a new nature (Col. 2:20—3:17). This transformation of nature is made possible by the same miraculous power that raised Christ from the dead (Col. 2:12).                                   J.R.M.

**NEW COVENANT.** The author of Hebrews (8:6-13) affirms that a new (that is, fresh) COVENANT has replaced the former one. The author states in 9:15-17 that a new covenant necessitates the death of the one who made it, thus becoming a "will" or "testament." The reference is to the words of Christ at the Last Supper (Matt. 26:28; Mark 14:24; Luke 22:20).                                              J.R.M.

**NEW EARTH/NEW HEAVEN.** The whole creation has been awaiting its rebirth in new creation, Paul writes (Rom. 8:18-25). The book of Revelation climaxes in a vision of "a new heaven and a new earth" replacing the former ones (Rev. 21:1; compare II Pet. 3:13). Similar teaching may be found in pre-Christian centuries (I Enoch 45:4-5) and in the OT (Isa. 65:17; 66:22).                                              J.R.M.

**NEW ENGLAND THEOLOGY.** Originally rooted in Puritanism, the Westminster Confession, William Ames' *Marrow of Sacred Theology,* and Petrus Ramus' logic, the New England theology culminated in the work of America's first, and some would say greatest, theologian, JONATHAN EDWARDS. In his train followed the New Divinity men: Joseph Bellamy, SAMUEL HOPKINS, Jonathan Edwards, Jr., Nathanael Emmons, and TIMOTHY DWIGHT. When Harvard drifted toward Unitarianism, Yale became their citadel. Based on "experimental" or experiential religion (as Edwards said, "True religion, in great part, consists in holy affections"), the New England divines wrestled with the questions of God's sovereignty, the nature and extent of original sin, and the nature of the Atonement.                    N.H.

**NEW ENGLISH BIBLE** (NEB). A Joint Committee of the non-Roman Catholic churches of the British Isles was formed to sponsor a new translation of the Scriptures in contemporary English. A prestigious group of scholars working under the direction of Charles H. Dodd, noted theologian, produced the New English Bible. The NT appeared in 1961 on the 350th anniversary of the publication of the King James Version. The complete Bible, including the Apocrypha, was published in 1970. The Oxford University Press and Cambridge University Press served as joint publishers.

Even though its sponsors declared the New English Bible was to be rendered in "timeless English," it has met with limited general acceptance even in Great Britain, where the Revised Standard Version and later translations in current idiom are preferred.

R.H.

**NEW INTERNATIONAL VERSION** (NIV). The concept of a contemporary language version of the Scriptures that is both scholarly and free of liberal bias had its beginnings in 1965, after several years of exploratory study by committees from the Christian Reformed Church and the National Association of Evangelicals. In 1967 the New York Bible Society, later renamed the International Bible Society, provided the initial funding of the project. Starting out with the Gospel of John in 1970, other books of the Bible were translated until the NT made its appearance in 1973 and the complete Bible in 1978. From the start the NIV met with success, and already millions of the new version have been sold.

R.H.

**NEW JERUSALEM.** Jerusalem was the holy city, the center of God's direction of Israel and the focal point of the return of the MESSIAH, according to Jewish theology. Periodically, Jerusalem was destroyed and its future glory anticipated. Isaiah spoke of it (54; 60) as did Ezekiel (40; 48). It was a common theme in the period between the OT and the NT (II Esd. 10:27; II Bar. 4:3; Test. Dan. 5:12) and is discussed in various NT passages (Gal. 4:26; Heb. 12:22), the most vivid of which is Revelation 21:2, in the context of John's revelation of the new creation. The New Jerusalem is the bride, the wife of the Lamb, that is, the church (Rev. 21:2, 10; compare Eph. 5:25 ff.).                                      J.R.M.

**NEW JERUSALEM, CHURCH OF THE.** *See* SWEDENBORG, EMMANUEL.

**NEW JEWISH VERSION.** Jews, like Protestants and Roman Catholics, have sought to keep abreast of changing language patterns and to render their versions of the Bible into contemporary English. The Jewish Publication Society of America issued the first volume of the Scriptures, the Torah, in contemporary English in 1962. The overall name of the new Bible is *The Holy Scriptures According to the Massoretic Text.* Dr. Harry M. Orlinsky, professor of Bible at Hebrew Union College, Jewish Institute of Religion, served as editor in chief. Two eminent Jewish scholars were his fellow editors: Dr. H. L. Ginsberg, professor of Bible at the Jewish Theological Seminary, and Dr. Ephraim A. Speiser, head of the Department of Semitic and Oriental Languages at the University of Pennsylvania.

The Hebrew Scriptures are divided into three sections—the Torah (the five books of Moses), the Prophets (historical and prophetic books), and the

Writings (consisting of the Psalms and other books). The Torah appeared first, and those scriptures containing the Prophets and the Writings appeared later in separate volumes. The translators declare that this work is not a revision but is a new translation.                                                R.H.

**NEW LIGHTS.** The pro-revivalist party among Congregationalists and Presbyterians that emerged from the First GREAT AWAKENING. In opposition to the Old Lights, the New Lights lauded the effects of the REVIVALS, accepting emotional preaching, a renewed emphasis on conversion as the basis for church membership, a tolerance for "excitement" in services, and more of an openness to lay participation. Theologically they were Edwardsean or New Divinity. They tended to be postmillennial, optimistic, progressive, individualistic, and believers in the special destiny of America.                      N.H.

**NEW MAN.** The Letter to the Colossians speaks of putting off the old man and putting on the new man (3:9-10) using *neon anthropos* and thus referring to a totally new kind of nature, a Christian one embracing a new attitude toward life. This new life is the same for a Jew or a Greek, circumcized or uncircumcized, barbarian, Sythian, slave or free (Col. 3:11). In Ephesians (2:15) these divergent aspects of society are described as formerly being separate entities but now through Christ have become one new man (*kainon anthropon*). The old man (nature) belongs to their former manner of life and is characterized by deceitful lusts whereas the new man is created after the righteousness and holiness of God (Eph. 4:22-24). Envisioned here is the church, the body of Christ, which has broken down the walls of division between its diverse elements (Eph. 2:14-15) and maintaining a unity of the spirit (Eph. 4:1-6) proclaims the mysterious plan of God in bringing about this oneness to the principalities and powers in the heavenly places (Eph. 3:10).(*Compare* NEW BIRTH.)         J.R.M.

**NEWMAN, JOHN HENRY CARDINAL** (1801–90). British Anglican church leader of the OXFORD MOVEMENT, who converted to Roman Catholicism and became a cardinal. Born in London and educated at Oxford, Newman received the Oriel College fellowship at Oxford in 1822, and was ordained an Anglican deacon in 1824. He tutored at Oriel, and in 1828 became vicar at St. Mary's, Oxford, where his learned sermons attracted wide attention. While touring Europe (1832–33), he composed his famous hymn "Lead, Kindly Light." On returning he heard John Keble's controversial sermon at St. Mary's on national apostasy accusing England of straying from true apostolic Christianity. Deeply impressed, Newman joined the new Oxford movement and was soon its acknowledged leader. His sermons at St. Mary's, *Parochial and Plain Sermons* (1834–42), drew national attention and affected England's religious outlook.

He contributed twenty-four or more pieces to *Tracts for the Times* (1833–41), writings that gave a Catholic interpretation to Anglicanism, Newman authored the highly controversial *Tract 90* (1841), arguing that Anglicanism's Thirty-nine Articles were Roman Catholic in substance. Newman, more and more doubting Anglicanism's *via media* between Protestantism and Catholicism, left Oxford to live at Littlemore (a chapelry at St. Mary's) in seclusion with a few friends. In 1843 he resigned his post at St. Mary's and in 1845 joined the Roman Catholic church. His *Essay on the Development of Christian Doctrine* (1845) clearly showed his turn toward Catholicism. In 1846 he was ordained a priest in Rome.

Returning to England, Newman joined the Congregation of the Oratory, priests living in community without monastic vows, and from 1854 to 1858 he administered the Catholic University in Dublin, Ireland. This experience led to *The Idea of a University Defined* (1873) in which he emphasized mental cultivation over practical information in education. *Apologia pro vita sua*, a classic account of his spiritual development, appeared in 1864. *A Grammar of Assent* (1870) carefully analyzed how human beings arrive at religious certitude. In 1877 he was elected an honorary Fellow of Trinity College, Oxford, and two years later Pope Leo XIII made him a cardinal. A man of integrity and a superb writer, Newman led thousands back to Catholicism.                C.M.

**NEW MOON.** The religious calendar of ancient Israel was based on lunar calculations. The new month corresponded to the new moon. Trumpets were blown to herald the new moon while sacrifices were being offered (Num. 10:10). It appears that no work was done on the day of the new moon (Amos 8:5). Detailed instructions for additional offerings on that day are given in Numbers 28:11-15, with special musical services indicated in Psalm 81:3. The holiest day of the year, the Day of Atonement, occurred in the seventh month, whose new moon (first day) seems to have been regarded as especially important (Lev. 23:24ff.). Many of Ezekiel's visions were received on the first day of the month (26:1; 29:17; 31:1; 32:1; see Hag. 1:1). On the first day of the month in which Atonement occurred, Ezra read the Law to the assembly of Israel from early morning till midday (Neh. 8:2). Eventually the practice of observing every new moon in order to determine the date of the new month gave away to calendars, which set the months and gave them predictability. A Jewish type of heresy confronting the early church in Asia Minor prompted the warning in Colossians against the imposition of the observance of new moons, Sabbaths, and certain festivals upon Christians (2:16-17; compare Gal. 4:10-11).

J.R.M.

**NEW MORALITY.** *See* SITUATION ETHICS.

**NEW ROME.** A designation Emperor Constantine I gave Constantinople, according to Sozomen's *Ecclesiastical History.* Constantine enlarged Byzantium and renamed it Constantinople in 330. The Council of Constantinople (381), called by Theodosius I, who declared Christianity alone legal in the empire, proclaimed Constantinople's bishop second only to the bishop of Rome.                                    C.M.

**NEW TESTAMENT.** The name commonly given to the portion of the Bible considered by Christians to contain the NEW COVENANT, which Christ made with his disciples. Comprising twenty-seven documents of several literary types (Gospels, historical theology, letters, and apocalypse), the NT conceives itself to be a continuing chapter in the history of God's dealing with Israel. It tells of the work of Jesus Christ, the teaching, and future anticipations. The books were written in Greek, though some may have been written in Aramaic and translated into Greek. They are generally acknowledged to have been written largely in the first century. The name derives from the Latin word *testamentum* and refers to a "will" that Christ bequeathed to his church at his death (Matt. 26:26; Heb. 9:15-17). The terms COVENANT, "testament," and "will" are all used to translate the same Greek word (*diatheke*).                          J.R.M.

**NEW TESTAMENT IN MODERN ENGLISH.** J. B. Phillips, an Anglican clergyman seeking to make the Bible comprehensible to the young people in his London parish, issued *Letters to Young Churches* in 1947. This name for the Epistles of the NT had been supplied by C. S. Lewis, who also wrote a foreword to the slim little book and launched Phillips into fame. This volume was followed by *The Gospels* in 1952, *The Young Church in Action* in 1955, and *The Book of Revelation* in 1957. His complete NT translation, an appealing paraphrase, was published in 1959.

R.H.

**NEW THOUGHT.** Similar to CHRISTIAN SCIENCE, New Thought took shape in the 1880s among those opposed to or alienated from Mary Baker Eddy. A periodical of that name appeared after 1890, the Metaphysical Club of Boston was founded in 1895, the International Metaphysical League in 1899, and the International New Thought Alliance in 1915. Their ideas were publicized by Warren Felt Evans, a New Church minister healed by Phineas P. Quimby in 1863. He championed Emmanuel Swedenborg in *The New Age and Its Messenger* (1864), *The Mental Cure* (1869), and *Mental Medicine* (1872).

Leaders of the movement included Quimby; Charles Poyen, the French mesmerist; Andrew Jackson Davis, seer and healer; Augusta Stetson; Annie C. Bill, founder of the Church of the Universal Design; Emma Curtiss Hopkins, of the Christian Science Theological Institute in Chicago; Nona Brooks, of Divine Science in Denver; Ernest Holmes, of the Religious Science Movement in Los Angeles; and Charles and Myrtle Fillmore, founders of Unity School of Christianity in Kansas City. A form of mind cure, New Thought offered "to teach the infinitude of the Supreme One; the Divinity of Man and his Infinite possibilities through the creative power and constructive thinking in obedience to the voice of the Indwelling Presence, which is our source in Inspiration, Power, Health and Prosperity."                   N.H.

**NEWTON, JOHN** (1727-1807). Evangelical Anglican clergyman and hymn writer. John Newton was born July 24 in London, to a devout mother who sought to rear her son in the Christian faith. But when he was seven, she died; and when he was eleven, he went to sea with his father, a sailor. In a few years young Newton drifted into a profligate life, and he was arrested by the Royal Navy and flogged publicly for desertion. Newton returned to the sea and became involved with the slave trade. For a time he lived on one of the islands off West Africa and sank even deeper into degradation.

While aboard a ship caught in a violent storm, Newton cried out to God for mercy. Saved from the fury of the storm, he began to read Thomas à Kempis' *Imitation of Christ,* which turned his heart back to the memories of his childhood. He took a step of faith but did not immediately give up his discreditable livelihood. For a time he was commander of his own slave ship. He was married to Mary Catlett when he was twenty-three and at twenty-seven left the slave trade and took a shore job in Liverpool.

Newton met John and Charles Wesley and George Whitefield, and they encouraged him to prepare for the Christian ministry. After years of hard study, he was ordained when he was thirty-nine and was appointed curate of the Anglican church in Olney, not far from Cambridge. The Evangelical Revival was in progress, and John Newton was swept along by it to become one of the movement's most effective leaders. The poet WILLIAM COWPER, a member of his congregation, collaborated with Newton to compose a number of hymns, which had great impact on the hymnody of the revival. Included in *Olney Hymns* were many numbers that are still sung in the church. After serving the Olney parish for sixteen years, Newton was called to serve as rector of St. Mary Woolnoth in London. There he came in contact with William Wilberforce and others involved in the abolition of the slave trade. Newton died on December 21, the same year the British Parliament outlawed slavery. Some of Newton's most famous hymns were "Amazing Grace," "How Sweet the Name of Jesus Sounds," and "Glorious Things of Thee Are Spoken."

R.H.

**NICENE CREED/COUNCIL OF NICAEA.** The Nicene Creed is the confession or doctrinal formulation adopted by the first Council of Nicaea (Nicea), which met in A.D. 325 at Nicaea, the modern city of Iznik, Turkey, near Constantinople or New Rome.

The Council was convened by the emperor Constantine to deal with the theological dispute over ARIANISM, which was troubling the Eastern churches. Some three hundred bishops attended, of whom all but five were Christians from the East, although Hosius of Cordova, a Western bishop and adviser to the emperor, presided. No minutes of the discussion, which took place between June 19 and July 25, were preserved, but Eusebius of Caesarea and Athanasius of Alexandria (the great defender of orthodoxy against Arius) report the general movement of the debate.

The Creed adopted decisively rejects Arianism, which held that the Son of God was created, and that there was a time (therefore) when he was not. To affirm the essential unity of the Father and the Son, the Council used a non-biblical term in a creed for the first time, the compound word *Homoousion*, meaning, in Greek, that the Son is "of the same substance" with the Father. This creed was held out to be a touchstone of orthodoxy, which it eventually became and continues to be to this day. It concluded with a list of anathemas, or condemnations, of Arianism.

The Council may have used a baptismal formula from the church of Eusebius of Caesarea as the basis for the Nicene Creed, but it more likely that the creeds of Syrian and Palestinian Christianity (Antioch and Jerusalem) were used. Nicaea also settled the dispute over the date of Easter, made provisions for the readmission to the church of lapsed believers, and established canons for the ordination and practices of clergymen.

The text of the Creed is divided into three parts, dealing with the Father as Creator; the Son as consubstantial deity, the Savior of the world; and the Holy Spirit, who leads the church into all truth. The Nicene Creed reads thus:

I believe in one God the Father Almighty, Maker of heaven and earth, And of all things visible and invisible:

And in one Lord Jesus Christ, the only-begotten Son of God; Begotten of his Father before all worlds, God of God, Light of Light, Very God of very God; Begotten, not made; Being of one substance with the Father; By whom all things were made: Who for us men and for our salvation came down from heaven, And was incarnate by the Holy Ghost of the Virgin Mary, And was made man: And was crucified also for us under Pontius Pilate; He suffered and was buried: And the third day he rose again according to the Scriptures: And ascended into heaven. And sitteth on the right hand of the Father: And he shall come again, with glory, to judge both the quick and the dead; Whose kingdom shall have no end.

And I believe in the Holy Ghost, The Lord, and Giver of Life, Who proceedeth from the Father and the Son; Who with the Father and the Son together is worshipped and glorified; Who spake by the Prophets: And I believe one Catholic and Apostolic Church: I acknowledge one Baptism for the remission of sins: And I look for the Resurrection of the dead: And the Life of the world to come. Amen. (Book of Common Prayer, 1928)

J.C.

**NICHIREN.** The Japenese Buddhist prophet Nichiren (1222–82) remains among the most important and controversial religious figures of his country. He was founder of the Nichiren group of Buddhist denominations. They have generally seen Nichiren's own ministry as the commencement of a new Buddhist age, in which a simple but militant faith in the LOTUS SUTRA alone was to be the norm.

Nichiren was the son of a simple fisherman. He began his monastic career at the age of eleven, studying in several temples and monasteries, both Tendai and Shingon. It was a time when the samurai class with its plain soldierly values had recently come to power, when war and calamity had circulated widespread belief that a new and degenerate age had arrived, and movements like PURE LAND BUDDHISM were popularizing radically simplified Buddhisms of salvation by faith. In this context Nichiren came to affirm, and then to proclaim fearlessly, that everyone could be enlightened by a simple act of faith in the truth of the Lotus Sutra, expressed by chanting *Nam Myōhō Renge Kyō* ("Hail the marvellous teaching of the Lotus Sutra"). If the entire nation were to adopt the Lotus faith, banishing all other sects, Nichiren said with typical assurance and intolerance, then Japan's troubles would cease and the country would eventually become a spiritual light to the world. Nichiren suffered persecution, but his movement took hold. It has experienced a twentieth-century revival to become Japan's largest single form of Buddhism. R.E.

**NICHOLAS OF CUSA** (1401–64). A German cardinal, mystic, and philosopher of religion who stood in the Neoplatonist tradition. His most famous writing was his *Docta Ignorantia* ("Learned Ignorance"), a version of negative theology in which the highest wisdom is to recognize the incomprehensibility of God. Whatever we may say about God, we have also to say the opposite. If we say, "God exists," we have also to say, "God does not exist," and so with all God's attributes. In a way beyond our comprehension, God is the "coincidence of opposites" *(coincidentia oppositorum)*. But this does not mean that the idea of God is nonsensical. Nicholas calls to his aid the logic of infinite quantities as developed in mathematics, and claims that it affords an analogy to the logic of God. His book contains many illustrations of the way in which propositions about infinite lines or surfaces have a logic of their own and make sense, though they break the laws of the logic that applies to finite entities. This austere negative theology is somewhat mitigated by Nicholas in his spiritual writings, such as *Visio Dei (The Vision of God)* in which he seeks to express the concreteness and the universality of the divine being. J.M.

**NICODEMUS.** A Pharisaic teacher who came to Jesus secretly to inquire about his teaching (John 3:1 ff.) and was so impressed that he later argued that

Jesus should not be judged until he had been heard (John 7:45-52). He was a "ruler of the Jews" (John 3:1; 7:50; probably a member of the Sanhedrin) and very wealthy (John 19:39). It is possible that he is the same person as the Nicodemon ben Gorion (or Bunai) mentioned in the Babylonian Talmud (Taanith 19b, 20a) as one of the wealthiest Jews in Jerusalem before its fall to Rome in A.D. 70. And this may be the same Bunai whom the Talmud names as one of five disciples of Jesus (Sanhedrin 43a). The family of Nicodemon ben Gorion became poverty stricken, and it is not difficult to conceive of this unfortunate change in welfare as a result of conversion to Christianity (or was it just the consequence of the Roman War?). Nicodemus' secret meeting with Jesus (John 3), subsequent defense of him (John 7), and eventual lavish open expenditure on his burial (John 19) suggest his likely conversion. He shared Jesus' burial expenses with another wealthy, secret disciple, JOSEPH OF ARIMATHEA (John 19:38-42). Stories about Nicodemus circulated into the fourth century, the probable date of the compilation of the Gospel of Nicodemus, an apocryphal book that gained great popularity in the Middle Ages under the title Acts of Pilate.          J.R.M.

## NICOLAITANS.

**NICOLAITANS.** The letters to the SEVEN CHURCHES that begin the REVELATION of John castigate the immoral teachings of the Nicolaitans, whose influence was being felt both at Ephesus (2:6) and Pergamum (2:12, 15), and possibly at Thyatira (2:20-23). Although nothing is known for certain about this heresy from contemporary records, it is a reasonable guess that it is the same group referred to by Irenaeus, who was a student of Polycarp, who studied with John, according to early tradition. Irenaeus derives the group from heretical followers of Nicolaus, one of the seven Hellenistic evangelists mentioned in Acts (6:5) in the Jerusalem turmoil following the establishment of the church there (Acts 2:1 ff.). An apostasy from apostolic teaching is assumed, but it is not clear whether it was by Nicolaus or his followers. Clement of Alexandria lays it upon the latter. Hippolytus suggested that Nicolaus had become heretical himself. Eusebius supports Clement's view that the immoral sect was a later, short-lived heresy whose name came to be a designation for heretics.          J.R.M.

## NICOPOLIS.

**NICOPOLIS.** A city referred to by Paul in his letter to TITUS exhorting him to join Paul there (3:12). The name in Greek means "city of victory" and was given to many cities built after a battle was fought and won in the vicinity. Pompey built one by this name in Lesser Armenia, as did Augustus in northern Egypt, and Trajan in northern Macedonia. Paul planned to spend the winter in Nicopolis and would not likely choose the one in Bithynia or the one in Cilicia, since either Tarsus or Antioch would be nearby and preferable. More likely Paul was referring to

Nicopolis in Epirus, on the west coast of modern Greece, built by Augustus (Octavian) near Actium, where he defeated Mark Antony in 31 B.C. Herod the Great built many of the public buildings there, and philosopher Epictetus lived there after A.D. 89.          J.R.M.

## NIEBUHR, HELMUT RICHARD

**NIEBUHR, HELMUT RICHARD** (1894–1962). Influential twentieth-century Protestant theologian, born in Wright City, Missouri, the younger brother of Reinhold Niebuhr. Niebuhr graduated from Elmhurst College (1912), Eden Theological Seminary (1915), Washington University (1917), Yale Divinity School (1923), and received a Ph.D. from Yale (1924) with a dissertation on Ernst Troeltsch. Niebuhr was ordained a minister of the Evangelical and Reformed Church in 1916 and served as a pastor in St. Louis, 1916–18. He was professor at Eden Seminary (1919–22, 1927–31) and served as president of Elmhurst College (1924–27). In 1931 he joined the faculty of Yale Divinity School, where he served, at the time of his death, as Sterling Professor of Theology and Christian Ethics.

Like many dialectical theologians, Niebuhr sought to remain true to the best insights of both liberal theology *and* the classical Christian tradition. This is reflected in the fact that the two greatest influences on

Courtesy of Yale Divinity School Library, Memorabilia Record Group 53

*H. Richard Niebuhr*

his theology were Troeltsch and Karl Barth. The former influence is reflected in Niebuhr's interest in the sociology of religion and his appreciation of the conditionedness or relativity of all historical religions. This is evident in such books as *The Social Sources of Denominationalism* (1929), *Christ and Culture* (1951), and his major theological work, *The Meaning of Revelation* (1941). The influence of Barth is seen in Niebuhr's emphasis on the sovereignty of God and on the primacy of revelation.

Since our knowledge always is conditioned by the point of view that we occupy, Niebuhr insists that Christian faith begins with revelation, which is mediated through a historical community, the church. Revelation is that *inner history* of events that gives meaning and shape to *outer*, or impersonal, history. Niebuhr contends that Christian revelation enables people to avoid a narrow tribal perspective on events as well as the impersonalism of much modern scientific positivism, since it offers a personalistic vision that is at the same time universal and stands in judgment on all egocentric interpretations of experience. For Niebuhr sin is both *disloyalty*, the failure to worship the true God, and *idolatry*, the giving of one's ultimate loyalty to something less than God. Since every person trusts in something and has some object of commitment, Niebuhr insists that to have such a faith is to have a god. However, a true faith is trust in that reality (God) which is the absolute and eternal ground of Being, that which abides when all else passes. Such a faith frees people from ultimate reliance on merely finite values and hopes. Faith, or our apprehension and response to Being, always begins, however, with revelation, with the way Being reveals itself to us. Such a revelation lies, finally, beyond scientific proof and therefore calls for personal, existential decision, trust, and loyalty.

Niebuhr is often spoken of as "a theologian's theologian." This does not imply that his work is remote and esoteric. Rather, it refers to the fact that all of Niebuhr's writings deal with the most sophisticated and fundamental issues facing theology and the church, and to the fact of his profound influence on an entire generation of younger theologians and clergy. J.L.

**NIEBUHR, REINHOLD** (1892–1971). The foremost American-born Protestant theologian and ethicist of this century. Niebuhr was born in Wright City, Missouri, on June 21, the son of a minister of the Evangelical Synod of the Lutheran Church. He attended Elmhurst College (1910), Eden Theological Seminary (1913), and Yale University (B.D., 1914; M.A. 1915). Ordained in 1915, Niebuhr served as pastor of the Bethel Evangelical Church in industrial Detroit until 1928. He then joined the faculty of Union Theological Seminary in New York City, where he taught until his retirement in 1960. During the 1930s and 1940s, Niebuhr was involved in an extraordinary variety of activities in addition to his

Courtesy of Union Theological Seminary Library Archives, New York City

*Reinhold Niebuhr*

teaching. These included a leading role in founding the Liberal Party and Americans for Democratic Action; establishing publications such as *Radical Religion, The World Tomorrow*, and *Christianity and Crisis*, serving as editor of the later. Niebuhr also served on the editorial board of several journals and wrote hundreds of editorials and articles. In 1939 he gave the prestigious Gifford Lectures at Edinburgh, published as *The Nature and Destiny of Man* (2 vols.; 1941–43), his major work. During these decades, Niebuhr was one of America's most influential social critics and the leading Christian apologist in the English-speaking world.

Early in his career Niebuhr espoused the religious liberalism and social idealism that was then current. His turn to a more realistic diagnosis of man and society is reflected in *Moral Man and Immoral Society* (1932). This book, and a dozen subsequent ones, reveal the special influence of Augustine, the Protestant Reformers Luther and Calvin, Kierkegaard and other existentialist writers, as well as Barth and Brunner. Certain themes run like threads through all of Niebuhr's writings, although they are applied to a vast range of intellectual questions and social issues.

These themes include the unique self-transcendence and freedom of the human person; the paradoxes and ambiguities of finite, creaturely existence; the anxiety and sinful egoism that leads to prideful efforts to secure power, as well as to guarantee one's moral virtue and intellectual certainty. Human sin, for Niebuhr, is *original* in that no person can claim to be free of the taint of destructive egoism. We are, therefore, saved only by God's free grace through faith. The fruit of grace is repentance, humility, or absence of pretension, and love. According to Niebuhr, the Christian norm of perfect, heedless love is revealed in the cross of Christ, which stands in judgment on all human moral effort. Nevertheless, for the Christian, perfect love is often expressed through justice, the relative embodiment of love in a sinful world. Since Christian love must often be expressed through justice and therefore through the coercive use of power, the Christian's action is always tainted. Therefore, one must be saved by faith and by forgiveness.

Niebuhr's Christian realism had wide influence between 1930 and 1960, not only within the church but also among secular intellectuals, politicians, and pundits.                                    J.L.

**NIETZSCHE, FRIEDRICH** (1844–1900). One of the most influential philosophers of modern times. By combining the Dionysian (will and emotion) with the Apollonian (intellect) he diverted philosophy from strict RATIONALISM and may be seen along with KIERKEGAARD as one of the pioneers of EXISTENTIAL-ISM. He stood opposed to all ready-made conventional values in morals, religion, and art.

Nietzsche's philosophy takes its departure from the death of God. According to Nietzsche, we must recognize the universe to be a collection of purely contingent facts. There is no providence, no goal, no center, no fixed values. It is as if the earth has been set adrift and wanders through endless space. Given sufficient time, everything will return to where it began and repeat the process. This is the doctrine of eternal recurrence. These teachings earned Nietzsche the reputation of being an advocate of NIHILISM.

But against this was his affirmation of life. Only the death of God and the abolition of the divine rule can liberate us for our true destiny. Nietzsche's hatred of Christianity arose from his belief that it glorifies weakness and inhibits the stronger virtues. Humanity itself is only a transitional phase, between animality and the superman *(Uebermensch)* of the future. The superman will create new values and, taking over control from the defunct God, will build a new world. In 1889 this passionate thinker suffered a mental breakdown, which ended his writing. His greatest work is *Thus Spake Zarathustra,* esteemed for its literary as well as its philosophical merits.
                                               J.M.

**NIHILISM.** Nihilism is the doctrine of negation, or the assertion that there are no rational grounds for belief in moral or religious truth or traditional values. Nihilism is often accompanied by radical, even anarchistic or absurd, expressions of personal freedom.

The origins of modern Nihilism are associated with Russian political and literary movements of the latter decades of the nineteenth century. Bazarov, the chief character in Ivan Turgenev's novel *Fathers and Sons* (1861), is a Nihilist, a man "who does not bow down before any authority, who does not take any principle on faith." The prototypical Nihilist is Ivan in DOSTOEVSKI's novel *The Brothers Karamazov* (1880). Ivan declares: "If God does not exist, everything is permitted."

In this century Nihilism is characterized by two rather distinct images. The first is found in the philosopher NIETZSCHE's depiction of the *Übermensch,* or superior man. It is he who recognizes the "death of God," that is, the death of the ultimate ground and support of all traditional values and is thrown back upon himself where "there is no one to command, no one to obey, no one to transgress." The *Übermensch* accepts the fact of cultural nihilism and yet heroically transcends it through the affirmation of radical freedom. Another image of nihilism is portrayed in the novels of FRANZ KAFKA and ALBERT CAMUS, whose heroes express the nihilism of impotence and indifference, the mood of despair and emptiness that attends a sense of life's triviality and meaninglessness. Nihilism is prominent in atheist EXISTENTIALISM from Nietzsche to SARTRE's *Being and Nothingness* (1943).                                  J.L.

**NIHIL OBSTAT.** The Latin term for "nothing hinders," meaning that the book or article on which it is printed contains nothing objectionable to the faithful. Also called the IMPRIMATUR, it is authorized by the official censor of the Roman Catholic church. The phrase appears on the title page along with the name of the censor.                           J.C.

**NILE RIVER.** The second longest river in the world (after the Amazon), running more than four thousand miles from the great freshwater lakes of central Africa and the mountains of East Africa (Ethiopia). The Nile is the physical reason for the existence of EGYPT as a country, inhabited as early as one million years ago.

The name "The Nile" is Greek. In Latin, it is Nilus; in Arabic En-Nil. In Coptic (or Egyptian), it is El-Bahr or simply "the sea." The ancient Egyptians called it Hapi. Throughout history, and in the OT scriptures, the Nile is regularly referred to as "the river." Herodotus, the Greek historian, quoted an earlier scholar, who said, "Egypt is the gift of the Nile." This observation is true. Without the annual flooding of the Nile, which both waters and fertilizes the arid soil of the valley of Egypt, no civilization would be possible there.

Herbert G. May

*Nile River at flood tide*

The Nile has two branches, the White Nile and the Blue Nile; the White running down from equatorial Africa with its great Victoria Lake and the Blue running down from the East African high mountains. In the south (near the Sudan), one-thousand-foot-high cliffs border the river. For much of its length the desert extends to the banks of the river. Four thousand miles from its sources, the Nile divides into several mouths, which flow into the Mediterranean Sea. In the OT period, there were seven mouths, of which the Pelusiac and the Canopic were the most important for commerce.

The stories of the OT patriarchs involve the Nile River many times, from Abraham's sojourn in Egypt to Jacob's family seeking shelter in Goshen (the northeast portion of the Nile Delta nearest to Canaan) to escape famine. The epic story of Joseph, who rose from slavery to the prime ministry of Egypt, probably reflects the period when the Hyksos, or "shepherd kings," fellow Semites with the Hebrews, ruled Eygpt.

The Nile played a major role in the story of Moses, who caused plagues of frogs and insects, followed by turning the river's water the color of blood in his struggle with Pharaoh. Of course, rivers have frogs and insects, and the Nile's waters can be darkened by the red mud washed down from central Africa.

The Nile as symbol occurs in all the myths and religions of the eastern Mediterranean. It was worshiped by the ancient Egyptians as a god. The Romans identified the Nile as the origin of "Rome's grainery," the rich fields of the delta area. The Nile stood for plenty in a world where drought and famine often plagued one region or another every year. It is no wonder that the expanding Roman Empire was drawn to Egypt in the same way the nomadic Hebrews were centuries earlier. Today, the Nile River still supports a huge population in a quarter of the world covered with desert and near-desert. It is also dotted, along its length, with majestic monuments from many periods of the past.

J.C.

**NIMROD.** According to Genesis 10, a hunter. There are many sites in Mesopotamia that bear his name, leading scholars to consider "nimrod" the Babylonian god Merodach or the hero, Gilgamesh. Nimrod was the great-grandson of Noah, grandson of Ham, and son of Cush, according to Genesis 10:8-12.

J.C.

**NINETY-FIVE THESES.** *See* LUTHER, MARTIN.

**NINEVEH.** The final and greatest capital of the ASSYRIAN Empire, founded as early as 5500 B.C. It was located on the banks of the Tigris River and now exists only as two tells (or mounds of rubble), named Kuyunjik and Nebiyunus. These tells, along with smaller mounds, are encircled with the ruins of a brick wall more than seven miles in circumference. Nebiyunus is the site of a contemporary village, and according to Islamic legend, it is the place of Jonah's tomb.

Genesis 10:11 and following says Nineveh was founded by Nimrod. It is one of the oldest cities in the world and was rebuilt many times, especially by the famous Tiglath-pileser I (1115–1077 B.C.). The book of Jonah tells us Nineveh was very large, around 120,000 in population. Sennacherib (704–681 B.C.) made Nineveh the center of his empire. Sennacherib besieged Jerusalem, and King Hezekiah sent tribute to him at Nineveh, whereupon the siege was lifted (II Kings 18–19; Isa. 37).

Nineveh was beautified by Ashurbanipal (668–633 B.C.). The library of his palace has been uncovered and many famous texts recovered, including the story of

Courtesy of Scala

*Bronze head from Nineveh, about 2415-2290* B.C.

Adapa (called the Mesopotamian Adam), the epic of Gilgamesh, and the Creation Epic, which has parallels to Genesis.                                                   J.C.

**NIPPUR.** A Sumerian city, the ruins of which lie south of Babylon on a now abandoned channel of the Euphrates River. It also lies close to ancient UR. Nippur was an important religious site, for Enlil, the most widely worshiped of the Sumerian deities, was the earth god, and his consort was Ninlil, the goddess of war. Because of Enlil's national significance, the priests of Nippur exerted great political power in Sumer. The temple of Enlil was called Ekur, and it was so sacred that the Sumerians attributed the fall of an imperial dynasty (that of Agade) to some affront to the temple by the king.

*Clay-tablet map of Nippur, showing plan for temple, walls, canals, and gates*

The universities of Pennsylvania and Chicago have intensively excavated Nippur. Fifteen hundred years of Sumerian history, literature, economy, and law have been discovered in the forty thousand tablets or clay bricks unearthed by the American archaeologists. Variations of the Flood myth, stories of paradise, and epics of Gilgamesh are among these numerous ancient writings. Many tales of the goddess Inauna, as well as a temple built for her 5,400 years ago, have been found. A temple devoted to Enlil's consort, Ninlil, also adorned this sacred city.                         J.C.

**NIRVANA.** From the Sanskrit word meaning literally "blowing out." The Pali equivalent is *nibbana*. Though the term is occasionally used in HINDUISM and JAINISM, it is most characteristic of BUDDHISM. There it refers to the ultimate, unconditioned reality whose inward realization is the supreme goal of the Buddhist spiritual quest.

Nirvana is not to be confused with an afterlife or a heaven (of which Buddhism has many), for they still presuppose the separate and individual, though blissful, existence of the "self." Nirvana, on the other hand, is absolute unconditioned reality, unlimited by time, space, psychological moods or traits, or the sense of selfhood, which stems (in Buddhist theory) from the attachments of the mind based on input from the senses. The "blowing out" of Nirvana is not annihilation, but the extinction of attachments and desires and of the separate individual selfhood, which is constructed by them. Buddhist literature also speaks of it as the cessation of DUKKHA, suffering; this is a closely related insight, for according to the FOUR NOBLE TRUTHS suffering is caused by the desire of which Nirvana is the absence. Nirvana may be realized in this life and is by an arhat; it is then Nirvana with the supports of phenomenal existence. After death a person who realizes Nirvana does not reincarnate in the usual manner, and, the Nirvana, though not qualitatively different than before, is without such supports or even the remnants of a separate existence.

The language of Nirvana is necessarily negative, for language itself is a product of life in separated, conditioned reality. From the vantage point of those in conditioned reality, Nirvana can only be thought of as its opposite—the opposite of the wheel of samsaric existence with all its transitoriness, suffering, and unreality. But it is, in words attributed to the Buddha, "an unborn, a not-become, a not-made, a not-compounded . . . where there is no wavering . . . no coming and going, . . . no falling from one state to another, no 'here,' no 'beyond,' no 'here-and-yonder.' That is the end of woe. The ceasing of becoming is Nirvana."

Later Buddhists, less restrained than their master, have been willing to use such mild metaphors as "light" and "calm" in describing the nirvanic state—a state clearly rooted in meditational experience. But for the most part, despite the florid descriptions Buddhism gives its heavenly realms, Nirvana remains indescribable, beyond all words and concepts. Yet the appeal of a state so utterly opposite to all we can know and think in ordinary existence has been a potent force within Buddhism for about twenty-five centuries.                         R.E.

**NISAN.** *See* HEBREW CALENDAR.

**NOAH.** OT patriarch, to whom is attributed the construction of the ark, in which the survivors of the primal FLOOD rode to safety, as well as the origins of vinegrowing. "Noah" means "rest," referring to the ark he built as a place where the survivors of mankind "rested" while the world was scoured by floods and destruction.

Noah, according to the Genesis chronology, was of the tenth generation after Adam (Gen. 5:3 ff.). The story of his faithfulness to the divine command to build the ark (Gen. 6:5–9:17) seems to be set in the midst of another story about Noah as the first cultivator of the grape (Gen. 5:29; 9:18-27), which ends with a rather disgraceful drunken bout on Noah's part.

Noah, however, is best known in Judaism, Islam, and Christianity as the faithful one at the time of great wickedness that caused God to lose patience and send the Flood. God, wishing to preserve the future of humankind and the beasts, told Noah to build an ark and move his wife, his three sons, Shem, Ham, and Japheth, along with their wives, and a pair of every kind of creature, into it. This Noah did, to the great merriment of his neighbors. The rains came and all the rest of earth's inhabitants drowned. As the waters subsided, the ark grounded on top of Mount Ararat. Noah set free a raven, which returned, and doves, some of which did not return, showing that the earth was uncovered in spots. Noah's family disembarked, set up an altar, and offered sacrifices of thanksgiving to God. God responded with the rainbow sign, marking the covenant that promised God would never destroy the world by water again.

The story of Noah in Genesis is similar to the Babylonian flood account recorded in the GILGAMESH EPIC. The Babylonian hero is like Noah, and there are similar details about the building of the ark, the cargo, the use of birds, and the sacrifice. However, the Hebrew story is rewritten from a monotheistic viewpoint. In the Babylonian account, there are many gods; in the Hebrew, only one.                 J.C.

**NOB.** A town, or possibly several towns with the same name, mentioned in I Samuel 21; 22; Nehemiah 11:32 and Isaiah 10:32. Nob (I Sam. 21; 22) was "the city of the priests" or the place where Yahweh's priests resided during the dark period when the ark was captured and held by the Philistines. Later, Saul massacred the people of Nob because Ahimelech, who ruled the town, aided David. Ahimelech fed David's soldiers and gave him the sword of Goliath.

Isaiah predicted that the Syrians would advance to Nob and threaten Jerusalem. Nehemiah speaks of Nob as one of the towns reoccupied by the tribe of Benjamin after the Exile. Nob, in these two cases, certainly was located north of Jerusalem. Some scholars believe Nob was on Mount Scopus, near Bethphage.                 J.C.

**NOBILI, ROBERT DE** (1577–1656). Born in Italy, Nobili spent his life as a Jesuit missionary in India. He has been called one of the ablest and most original missionaries of his time. After a short period of missionary work among the Indian peoples of the coastlands, Nobili discovered that few converts were being made because the Indians thought of Christianity as a Portuguese religion. He changed his methods and approach, studying Indian philosophy and religious literature and dressing in Indian style. He devoted much of his time to finding points of agreement between Christianity and Hinduism, for which he was criticized by many as diluting Christianity. He was an active writer and was successful in winning many high-caste Indians to Christianity.                 W.G.

**NOMADISM.** A term, originally Latin, meaning "to graze," applied to a life-style that goes back many thousands of years before Christ. The OT patriarchs Abraham, Isaac, and Jacob were nomads, as was Moses, who lived with his shepherd father-in-law, Jethro, who was also a priest. Nomads still exist, although in small numbers, throughout the Middle East and North Africa. The life-style of moving herds of sheep and goats from one oasis to another across the desert is the same in 3500 B.C. or the 1980s.

Four great waves of nomads spread from the Arabian peninsula into what is now Israel, in 3500 B.C., 2500 B.C., 1500 B.C. and 500 B.C. Most of the great empires of the Middle East were founded by nomads who "settled down"—the Akkadians, the Hittites, and the Hyksos of Egypt in the eighteenth century B.C. (when Joseph may have risen to power). Moses, in the Exodus, gave the motley collection of former slaves in Egypt the Decalogue, which was a reflection of the stern morality of the nomad and of the high spirituality of deeply religious people. Gradually, other tribes who had not been in Egypt became part of Israel.                 J.C.

**NOMINALISM.** A medieval philosophy that evolved from ARISTOTLE, which held that UNIVERSALS (Plato's forms) are not existing entities; only individuals exist, univerals are simply names (*nomina*). Individual men exist, not Man. This undermined the ecclesiastical claims of reality for the Trinity, God, Goodness, and so forth. Roscellinus, sometimes called the father of nominalism, maintained the Aristotelian position that universals are derived from our observation of individuals; many cows give rise to the concept Cow, which does not exist. Because he held that God is a concept while the three trinitarian persons are the divine reality, he was accused of tritheism and condemned for heresy at Soissons in 1092.

REALISM, the opposite of nominalism, held, in the tradition of PLATO, that universals (or forms) exist prior to and are independent of individual objects. Universals are real, not individual things. William of Champeaux maintained this Platonic position, saying universals come before individuals, that individuals have reality by participating in the universal. Humanity precedes individual men; God precedes the Father, Son, and Holy Spirit who share in God.

In the fourteenth century WILLIAM OF OCCAM denied universals, saying they could not be found in objective reality, only in the mind. We experience individuals, and then draw universals from them. The controversy greatly weakened medieval SCHOLASTICISM.                                                     C.M.

**NOMMENSEN, LUDWIG INGWER** (1834–1918). One of the pioneer missionaries to Indonesia, known as the Apostle of the Bataks. He was born in Schleswig, at that time under the Danish crown. He went out to do missionary work under the sponsorship of the Rhenish missionary society. He did pioneer work among the Batak people and wrote a worship order that was used long after his death. He lived and worked in several areas of Sumatra, commissioning and instructing elders who could carry on the indigenous work of the church in the villages of the country. The Batak church flourished under his influence, and his name lives on in Nommensen University, established in 1954.                    W.G.

**NONBEING.** *See* BEING AND NONBEING.

**NONCONFORMIST.** An individual who does not conform to an ESTABLISHED CHURCH, or its doctrine, discipline, or polity. It was first used to describe two thousand clergymen in England who refused to submit to the Act of Uniformity (1662), which restored the Anglican establishment. The term does not apply in England to Roman Catholics but is used of such Protestant groups as Methodists, Congregationalists, Baptists, Presbyterians, and Quakers.                                                     R.H.

**NORTH, FRANK MASON** (1850–1935). Methodist minister, hymn writer, and religious organization executive. Frank North was born in New York City on December 3. After a private school education, he received a bachelor of arts degree from Wesleyan University. Thereafter he returned to take further work at the university and was ordained to the Methodist ministry. He served pastorates in Florida, New York, and Connecticut, then was appointed corresponding secretary of the New York Church Extension and Missionary Society and corresponding secretary of the Methodist Episcopal Church. In 1916 he was elected president of the Federal Council of Churches of Christ in America, an organization he had been active in forming. He was the author of several hymns, best known of which is "Where Cross the Crowded Ways of Life."                    R.H.

**NOTH, MARTIN** (1902–68). Noth's influence on twentieth-century OT research has been profound and in the best tradition of German scholarship. The range of his interests was broad, and in every area that engaged his attention he both furthered the state of research and left the way open for further developments that would otherwise hardly have taken place. He is perhaps best remembered for his pioneering work on the tradition criticism of the Pentateuch and more particularly the Deuteronomic tradition his-

tory. After Noth, the earlier attempt to extend the four Pentateuchal sources or "documents" into a Hexateuch or Heptateuch, and so forth, was definitively abandoned, and the Deuteronomic history (the books of Joshua through Kings) was recognized as the continuation of a Tetrateuch. Noth's historical reconstruction of the pre-monarchical Israel as a cultic amphictyony in the fashion of early Greek society, once widely accepted, has now been challenged by subsequent research, but elements of the theory continue to be considered valid.                    B.V.

**NOVALIS.** Latin for "fallow land," a pseudonym of Baron Fredrich von Hardenberg (1772–1801), a German poet and novelist who helped found the German Romantic movement, known especially for the mystical, religious quality of his works. Born in Prussian Saxony, of Moravian parents, he studied at Jena, Leipzig, and Wittenberg. *Hymnen an die Nacht* (1800), his best-known writing, expresses in poetic prose a deep sense of grief on the early death of Sophie von Kühn, his fiancée. Other works include *Heinrich von Ofterdingen*, a spiritual allegory, and *Die Lehrlinge zu Sais*, a prose romance, both left unfinished.                    C.M.

**NOVATIANISM.** A term designating the rigorist stance of Novatian and his followers, who denied restoration to Christians who faltered during PERSECUTION. Novatian was a Roman presbyter and prominent theologian in Rome in 250. He expected to succeed Roman Bishop Fabian, martyred in 250 during the persecution of Decius (249–251), but the majority chose the not well-known Cornelius, who took a lenient stance toward the lapsed (LAPSI). Disputes ensued, leading to a schism in 251, headed by Novatian, often called the first anti-pope. Known later as Donatism (*see* DONATISTS), Novatianism lasted until the Muslim conquests of North Africa in the seventh century. A Roman synod (251) and a synod in Carthage (252) undercut Novatianism by allowing the lapsed to be restored after severe penance. This was a view rooted in Bishop Cyprian of Carthage. It finally prevailed, despite the rise of Donatism following Diocletian's persecution (303–305). Novatian died a martyr under Valerian's persecution (257–258).                    C.M.

**NOVITIATE.** The period of time when a person serves as a novice, or period of probation, to test a person's fitness for profession in a religious order. Before entering a novitiate, the person serves as a postulant. After the novitiate, the novice professes temporary vows. "Novitiate" also refers to the quarters appointed for the housing of novices. These living quarters are required to be entirely separate from those of the professed religious. During the novitiate, a female must undergo special episcopal examination about her free choice of profession before she is allowed to profess.                    J.C.

## NOYES, JOHN HUMPHREY

NOYES, JOHN HUMPHREY (1811–86). Social reformer, perfectionist, and founder of the ONEIDA COMMUNITY, Noyes was born September 3, in Brattleboro, Vermont, to John and Polly Hayes Noyes. A graduate of Dartmouth (1830), Noyes studied law for a year. In 1831 he experienced a conversion and so enrolled in Andover Theological Seminary. After a year he transferred to Yale. There his abolitionist fervor and his February 1834 announcement that he had attained sinless perfection led to his expulsion and the revocation of his preaching license.

Despite his affirmation of free love in his 1837 "Battleaxe Letter" proposing to her, Harriet A. Holton married Noyes in 1838. He then drew around himself a community of family and friends in Putney, Vermont, which began in 1846 to practice "complex marriage." When uproar followed, the community moved to Oneida, western New York, in 1848. Noyes published his views in *The Perfectionist* (1834–36), *Bible Communism* (1848), *Male Continence* (1848), *History of American Socialism* (1870), and *Scientific Propagation* (1873). He guided his community to self-sufficiency until its reorganization as a silver-plated flatware company in 1881.   N.H.

## NUMBERS

NUMBERS. The name of the fourth book of the Bible, informed by the titles *Arithmoi* and *Numeri,* which respectively appear in its Greek (Septuagint) and Latin (Vulgate) versions. Such nomenclature is inspired by two censuses of the Israelites reported in chapters 1–4 and 26. The Hebrew name *bemidbar* ("in the desert"), lifted from a phrase in Numbers 1:1, however, more accurately denotes the main theme of Numbers. The beginning and end of Israel's forty-year wilderness sojourn receive chronological emphasis, while the themes of divine leadership and human rebellion evoke the greatest theological attention.

*Organization and Basic Content.* Linking the epic of Israel's liberation from Egypt with the epic of its conquest of the Land of Promise, Numbers yields to a three-part division.

(a) *Numbers 1:1–10:10.* This opening unit is concerned with necessary preparations for Israel's departure from Mount Sinai. These include the census and assignment of camp location of each tribe, along with special directives for the Levites (chaps. 1–4); Mosaic instructions concerning the treatment of lepers and of wives charged with adultery, the Nazirite vow, and Aaronic benediction (chaps. 5–6); an enumeration of gifts for the service of the tabernacle (chap. 7); guidelines for the consecration of the Levites (chap. 8); and supplementary Passover legislation (chap. 9).

(b) *Numbers 10:11–22:1.* The focus falls on specific happenings in Israel's desert trek, though cultic legislation in chapters 15, 18–19 interrupts the narrative flow. The people head northward into "the wilderness of Paran" (10:12) and thence to the Kadesh oasis (13:26), their primary site of encampment. Themes prominent in Exodus 15–18 resurface in the several episodes anchored here—new murmuring and rebellion by the "rabble" (11:4); Moses' regular intercession in their behalf; and Yahweh's providential care in providing manna, quail, and water. The narrative excels in its portrayal of tension-filled moments involving Miriam's leprosy (chap. 12), Israel's abortive attempt to penetrate Canaan from the south (chaps. 13–14), the uprising of Korah against Moses' authority (chap. 16), and the faithlessness of Moses and Aaron at Meribah, evoking the divine prohibition that they will never set foot in Canaan (20:2-13). Leaving Kadesh (20:22), the Israelites move into Transjordan and triumph over Sihon, the Amorite king of Heshbon, and Og, the king of Bashan (21:21-35).

(c) *Numbers 22:2–36:13.* This section portrays the Israelites encamped in the Moab plain and poised to attack Canaan from the east. Most engaging within its narrative segments are those episodes involving Balaam, a Babylonian diviner who must yield to Yahweh's will rather than to Balak's who hired him (chaps. 22–24), and Israel's defection to the Moabite gods (chap. 25). Diverse legislation in this section covers such matters as the rights of women to inherit property (27:1-11); the sacrificial calendar (chaps. 28–29); the laws concerning women's vows (chap. 30); and the establishment of Levitical cities and cities of refuge (chap. 35).

*Composition.* Source-critical analysis has uncovered a dominant postexilic priestly (P) stratum and an earlier, thoroughly edited JE stratum, which defies further differentiation (*see* DOCUMENTARY HYPOTHESIS). Form-critical studies have pointed to the probable origins of the separate Numbers traditions. Various narrative episodes may have originated at local cult centers at Kadesh and in Transjordan. Stories about the outpouring of Yahweh's spirit upon the seventy elders (11:16-30), the challenge of Moses' authority by Miriam and Aaron (chap. 12), and Korah's rebellion (chap. 16) likely betray the presence of rival claimants in the later Israelite priesthood. Ancient poetic fragments (10:35-36; 21:14-15, 17-18, 27-30) along with the somewhat later (tenth century B.C.?) Balaam oracles (23:7-10, 18-24; 24:3-9, 15-24) are well integrated into the narrative and confer a note of authenticity. Though all of the Numbers legislation is mediated through Moses, little of it seems to predate significantly the book's final editing.

*Religious Message.* If Israel's wilderness existence receives an incomplete recounting in Numbers, it does attract lucid theological interpretation under the heading of divine testing and guidance. A wandering mob given to fear, petulance, and faithlessness, along with its manifestly human leaders, is deemed worthy of God's concern. Within a harsh environment, Yahweh trains the people for the challenge ahead when they will conquer Canaan. Rebellion and apostasy cannot induce Yahweh to renounce the promise to the fathers. The population that perishes in the desert is replaced by one of like size (1:46; 26:51), and Eleazar is divinely appointed to replace the deceased Aaron (20:26). Indeed, through the "curse" of a foreign diviner (24:17), the ascendancy of David is legitimated! Numbers celebrates a God whose sovereign purpose, which assuredly involves a developing people, cannot be thwarted.          J.K.K.

## NUMBERS, RELIGIOUS SIGNIFICANCE OF.

Numbers, for example, one, three, seven, etc., play a role in the OT and NT, just as they do in many ancient and modern religions. There is an ancient, still practiced, form of divination called numerology. Various numbers are assigned to different letters, or else certain numbers stand for concepts or doctrines, for example, "three in one" for the trinitarian Godhead.

The fourth book of the OT is called "Numbers," and it begins with the counting of the Hebrew tribes. However, the religious significance of numbers is wider than that in the Bible. The number *four* generally stands for the earth, as in the four corners of the earth. The number *three* usually represents heaven. SEVEN, the sum of four and three, represents completion, fullness, the infinite. Multiples of seven occur, as in Jesus' words "seventy times seven."

Numbers in the Bible are chiefly found in the book of Revelation. The book is organized around a series of enumerations: the SEVEN CHURCHES, seven lampstands, seven stars, seven plagues, seven angels, one thousand years and, above all, the number of the beast, 666 (Rev. 13:18). The hidden meaning of 666 appears to be that it refers to Nero Caesar, which in Hebrew letters (which double as numbers) equals 666.

The concept of the spiritual power of numbers is very old, arising along with astrology. The philosopher-mystic Pythagoras believed that all things were made of numbers. He discovered the mathematical sequence of the musical scale and assigned numbers to the planets and stars. Numerology is part of the occult rather than of religion. Superstition, which thrives even today, sees certain numbers as lucky and others as unlucky. The number thirteen has been considered unlucky for centuries.

The doctrine of the Holy Trinity, with its emphasis on the reality of the three persons (hypostases or personae or "faces") of God in the oneness of the Godhead, made the numbers one and three religiously significant. The parallel development of the doctrine of two natures (the human and divine) in the one person of Christ added to this significance.
                                                                J.C.

**NUMEN.** The Latin word for authority, divine will, or deity, taken over into English to mean the "mysterious power" within reality calling forth religious faith and awe.

"*Numen*" and the "numinous" are associated especially with the thought of the German theologian RUDOLF OTTO (1869–1937) as set forth in his book *Das Heilige* (1917), translated into English as *The Idea of the Holy* (1923). In contrast to Schleiermacher, who viewed religion as based on the feeling of absolute dependence, Otto understood religion as rooted in a reality objective and external to the self, known in the encounter with the HOLY. The object of numinous awareness is the "mysterium tremendum et fascinans." The distinctive experience of the holy gives rise to the concept of the *numen,* so that Otto's numinous is the a priori of the religious parallel to Kant's a priori of the theoretic reason.

Experience of the *numen* is characterized by awe and majesty, by a sense of being in the presence of great power and urgency. There is also awareness of a wholly otherness that evokes a feeling of uncanniness and dread, yet is tremendously attractive and fascinating. The numinous involves reverence and wonder that make one feel unworthy and at the same time are uplifting and entrancing. The numinous transcends and envelops reason, provides the basis of religious and moral knowledge, and points to the origins of religion in the mysterious depth of the spirit. The result of Otto's thought is the affirmation of the *numen* as the reality at the core of all logic, ethics, and religion, a reality beyond sense experience and feeling. (*see also* RELIGIOUS EXPERIENCE.)
                                                                C.Mc.

**NUN.** A woman in professed religious orders. In the Roman Catholic church, the term nun is reserved to a female religious professed in vows, temporary or perpetual, in a convent. A nun's life is one of contemplation and mortification. Distinctions are made between choir sisters and lay sisters. Choir sisters are sworn to sing the divine office every day, as well as to private recitation of the office. In a general way the term nun is used for all women in the religious life, including sisters who serve in teaching or nursing orders. The term is also used for sisters in the Anglican Communion and in the Eastern Orthodox churches. There has been a severe decrease in the number of professions among Catholic women in recent years. This has caused a need for many lay teachers in Catholic parochial schools.          J.C.

**NUNC DIMITTIS.** The song of Simeon sung at the presentation of Jesus in the Temple, recorded in Luke 2:29-32. This hymn of praise is entitled "Now Let Us Depart," from the first verse of the hymn in Latin, which says: "Lord, now let your servant depart in peace." Simeon was moved by the Holy Spirit to see in the infant Jesus the Messiah, long expected by the pious in Israel. In this Jesus, God's salvation is fully realized for all people, Jews and Gentiles. The Nunc Dimittis is regularly used in liturgical worship in the Roman Catholic, Lutheran, Anglican, and Episcopal churches. It is used at Compline, the prayer for the night of the Catholic church. It is used in the vesper service of the Lutheran church. The words, "Let your servant depart in peace, for my eyes have seen your salvation," are appropriate as one lies down to sleep.

J.C.

**NUNCIO, PAPAL.** A representative of the pope who, according to the order of precedence of the Congress of Vienna, is ranked as an ambassador. This rank is operable only when a government accepts a nuncio in the diplomatic sense. A nuncio is a heirarchical authority to the church he visits.

J.C.

Courtesy of the American Schools of Oriental Research

*Cuneiform tablets found at Nuzi*

**NUZI.** Ancient city in northern Mesopotamia, east of Ashur, near the site of modern Kirkuk in Iraq. Excavations begun by the University of Pennsylvania in 1925 found the site to be inhabited from 4000 B.C. Many clay tablets written in old Babylonian cuneiform, dating from the fifteenth century B.C., were found.

J.C.

**NYGREN, ANDERS** (1890–1978). Lutheran minister, theologian, bishop, and ecumenical leader. Nygren was born at Goteborg, Sweden. Educated at the University of Lund, he served as a minister of the Lutheran church from 1912 to 1920, was appointed professor of systematic theology at Lund in 1924, and became bishop of Lund in 1949. He served as president of the Lutheran World Federation (1947–52) and participated in ecumenical conferences at Lausanne (1927), Oxford (1937), Edinburgh (1937), Amsterdam (1948), Lund (1952), and Evanston (1954). He was a leader in the founding of the World Council of Churches and served as a member of its Central Committee. His books in English include: *Agape and Eros* (vol. I, 1932; vol. II, 1938), *Commentary on Romans* (1949), *The Gospel of God* (1951), *Christ and His Church* (1956), and *Meaning and Method* (1972).

A representative of the LUNDENSIAN school of theology, Nygren's irenic Christian faith contributed much to ecumenicity among Protestants and between Protestants and Catholics. In *Agape and Eros,* Nygren contrasts the self-giving love (agape) of God with the self-serving love (eros) that characterizes humanity. God loves because it is God's nature to love. Nygren, following Luther, views humans as completely just and completely sinners. They are sinners insofar as their righteousness depends upon their own works. But in Christ, they receive through faith complete righteousness, as God forgives sin and receives humanity into divine community. Peace and blessedness come into human life as God's love supplies them, providing assurance of God's grace and enabling humans to serve one another in love.

C.Mc.

# Oo

**OATES, WAYNE E.** (1917– ). Educated at Wake Forest College, he received the Ph.M. and Th.D. degrees from Southern Baptist Theological Seminary, Louisville, Kentucky. He is married and has two children. Oates was professor of psychology and pastoral care at Southern Baptist Seminary. He was later a chaplain at the Kentucky State Hospital and a theological consultant at the Norton Psychiatric Clinic. He is now professor of psychiatry and behavioral sciences at the Louisville University School of Medicine, and director of the program in ethics and pastoral counseling at the Louisville General Hospital. His books include *Religious Dimensions of Personality* (1957), *Pastoral Counseling* (1974), *New Dimensions in Pastoral Counseling* (1970), and *The Christian Pastor* (3rd ed. 1981). I.C.

**OATH.** The Hebrew word is used in regard to both God and Israelite society. In both cases it refers to a solemn statement of intention or PROMISE that is held to be binding and irrevocable. The natural association is in the various ceremonies of covenant-making, beginning with God's pledge to Abraham (Gen. 24:8). This is evidently a landmark case, since God's oath to the patriarch is picked up in Luke 1:13-20 and Hebrews 6:13-20. The Mosaic covenant too is confirmed by a divine oath (Deut. 29:12, 14; compare Deut. 7:8). This practice of confirming a treaty by an oath is well attested in Near Eastern texts that describe covenant-making among ancient tribes and nations.

Paul draws out the significance of God's oath, ascribing to Jesus Christ the power to ratify such divine promises (II Cor. 1:19-20; Rom. 15:8). The reliability of God in covenant faithfulness lies at the heart of such picturesque descriptions of God whose "oath" is an assurance to believers that God will not break or alter a declared intention to bless the people (Heb. 6:13-20; Ps. 110:4; Num. 23:19; Rom. 11:29; Luke 1:73).

On the level of human relationships, oaths and VOWS go together. People would invoke the divine name as a witness to their own credibility or resolution to make good a promise (I Sam. 14:39, 44; 20:23). The negative side of this is a CURSE formula (I Sam. 14:24), by which a judgment is invoked on an unnamed person who offends. Such a curse enforces a command. Perjury was held to be a serious offence in Israel (Zech. 5:3ff.; Num. 5:21ff.), and one was punished by death (Ezek. 17:15ff.), even if the oath was taken in ignorance (Josh. 9; II Sam. 21:1ff.). But oaths could be taken lightly; hence the warnings of Matthew 5:33-37 and James 5:12 against easygoing oath-taking. See too Matthew 12:36-37 on the high value placed by Jesus on human words used in pledges. Paul often uses a mild form of oath-taking (II Cor. 1:23; 11:11, 31; Phil. 1:8; Gal. 1:20) as if to guarantee that what he says can stand scrutiny by God that it is truthful or well-intentioned.          R.M.

## OATMAN, JOHNSON, JR. (1856–1922).

Business executive and hymn writer. Oatman was born on April 21, near Medford, New Jersey. He joined the Methodist church when he was nineteen and later was licensed as a local preacher. Although he was active in a merchantile organization most of his life and an executive of a New Jersey insurance company, Oatman found time to write five thousand hymns, including the popular "Count Your Blessings." Music for this hymn, which was as accepted in Great Britain as America, was the work of composer-publisher Edwin O. Excell.          R.H.

## OBADIAH.

The prophetic work that bears the name of Obadiah, "the servant of Yahweh," is, at twenty-one verses, the shortest book in the OT and the third shortest in the Bible. It is entirely given over to a diatribe against Judah's southern neighbor, EDOM. The book divides naturally into three parts: (a) verses 1-4, a threat of divine destruction against proud Edom living in its impregnable fastness "in the clefts of the rock" (often taken to be a reference to Petra, the rock-hewn city whose remains in the southwestern part of the Hashemite Kingdom of Jordan are still accessible only through a long, narrow defile between high cliffs); (b) verses 5-14, an insistence that the present and future pillaging of Edom are divine retribution for its refusal to come to the aid of its beleaguered neighbor state of Judah; (c) verses 15-21, a futuristic oracle that juxtaposes the extermination of Edom on the coming DAY OF THE LORD with the return of the house of Jacob to its own inheritance. This section can be compared with Isaiah 63:1-6, in which the eschatological holy warrior begins his retributive work in Edom. The book culminates with a vision of the universal rule of God within which Israel totally displaces Edom in order to play its own central role: "Saviors shall go up to Mount Zion to rule Mount Esau; and the kingdom shall be the Lord's" (Obad. 21).

Although the close verbal correspondence of Obadiah 1-9 with the preexilic oracle of Jeremiah 49:7-22 suggests that the writer of Obadiah drew upon some older tradition, the book as it stands appears to be a unity, and to have been addressed to a specific generation in Judah. The tones of nationalistic pride and vengeance that pervade the work suggest that that generation must have been one in which Israelites felt keen personal disappointment at the perfidy of Edom. Such a setting is not hard to find in the events following the conquest of Jerusalem by the Babylonians in 587 B.C. Other OT texts tell us that Edom rejoiced in Judah's pitiable plight (Lam. 4:21), took part in razing the Temple to the ground (Ps. 137:7), and occupied part of the country (Ezek. 35:10). The ancient enmity felt by Israel toward Edom, which is enshrined in the early memories of

tension between the twin brothers Jacob and Esau (who were the founding fathers of the two peoples respectively—see Gen. 25:23; 27:39-40) and which is reiterated in such prophetic threats as Amos 1:11-12 and Isaiah 34:5-17, must have reached its zenith in the years immediately following 587. It is reasonable, therefore, to assume that the book emanates from this period.

If, however, verse 7 is specifically referring to the expulsion of the Edomites from their ancestral home, we might assume a slightly later date. Malachi 1:3-4, thought to be mid-fifth century, also knows of this expulsion, and secular records show Arab names at Ezion-geber, on the southern coast of Edom, by the fifth century B.C. When driven from their homeland, it appears that the Edomites moved west into the Negeb, which came to be known in post-OT literature as Idumea. Their descendants were forcibly converted to Judaism after 120 B.C., and one of them, Herod the Great, founded the last dynasty of native rulers in Judea in 37 B.C. That the last great king of Judah should have been of Edomite extraction and should have built his fame upon magnificent public works and horrific despotic rule provides an ironic counterpoint to the triumphal expectation of divine vengeance against Edom preserved in the strange little prophetic book of Obadiah.

W.S.T.

## OBEDIENCE.

The biblical term rendered "obedience" covers a wide-ranging field of human response to the divine will. By their etymology both the Hebrew and Greek words suggest a listening to the voice of another person, specially as that person, whether a fellow human being or God, claims our attention and responsiveness. Israel is condemned for failing to hear God's commands and so living for itself (Jer. 7:24; Ps. 81:12-14), and disobedience is judged to be a cardinal sin in the NT (Eph. 2:2; 5:6, disobedience to God; compare Rom. 1:30, disobedience to one's parents).

In Jewish and Christian theology humanity's Fall is traced back to Adam's disobedience (Gen. 3:17, Adam listened to another voice and doubted God's goodness). But it is only in Paul that there is worked out an elaborate scheme of Christ's obedience reversing the Fall and restoring humanity's original state (see Rom. 5:12-21). Jesus Christ is the preeminently obedient one (John 6:38), even to the point of death (Phil. 2:8; Heb. 5:8). Such a signal obedience is the ground on which God clears sinners from their disobedience and views them as "in Christ." Not surprisingly, therefore, Paul can describe faith as obedience (Rom. 1:5), that is, our response to God's offer of grace in Christ. The Christian life, in the NT, is consistently one of living in obedience to God (I Pet. 1:14) and by extension, to political (Rom. 13:1-7) and ecclesial (Heb. 13:7) authorities.

R.M.

**OBLATION.** An OFFERING to God, especially in the sense of the offering of a sacrificial victim to God in the OT and of the offering of the sacrifice of the Mass in Roman Catholic theology. SACRIFICES, and consequently oblations, play a major role in the OT. The concept of the sacrifice (oblation) of Christ on the cross and the concomitant ending of the need for temple sacrifices form a large part of the NT, especially in the epistles of Paul and the Epistle to the Hebrews.

In the OT, the sacrifice of animals, especially lambs, calves, goats, and pigeons, is early shown to have displaced the older, pagan practice of human oblations. The story of Abraham and Isaac on Mount Moriah symbolizes this. A great concern for the purity of the oblation (sacrificial victim) is seen in Leviticus. Proposed victims must be free of any deformity and in perfect health. The precise way in which the victim was to be dispatched and its blood splashed on the altar is spelled out.

Oblations may also be prayers or offerings of gifts in kind (bread, wine, the produce of the fields) to God.                                                    J.C.

**OCCAM, WILLIAM OF.** See WILLIAM OF OCCAM.

**OFFERING.** See SACRIFICIAL OFFERINGS.

**OFFERTORY.** A sentence, or, in free Protestant churches (and others today), a choral work, sung at the collection of the offering in Christian worship. The custom of singing a psalm at this time is of ancient origin. It is known to go back to Augustine's time.

The sentences, psalms, or musical works vary with the liturgical season of the church year. Such responses are chosen to reflect praise and prayer, especially the sentiment that the congregation's offerings will be acceptable to God. In some services the sentence is said by the presiding minister or priest. In the Mass, the oblation over the bread and wine given by the priest is known as the offertory.

The offertory symbolizes the total surrender of human beings to God. In the presentation of material gifts, the faithful acknowledge that all life is a gift from God. Worshipers only give back to God a small portion of the bounty given them, so that God can bless and use these offerings to advance the kingdom. These gifts include both the sacramental elements, the bread and wine, and the offerings of money to be used to support the church's work and to assist the needy.     J.C.

**OG.** According to Numbers 21:31-35, Og was the king of Bashan in northern Transjordan Palestine who was defeated by the Israelites on their way to the Promised Land. He was a character of folklore, thought to be a remnant of an ancient race of giants (Rephaim, Josh. 12:4), probably because of an "iron bedstead" (a basalt dolmen?) of enormous size that was popularly regarded as his tomb at Rabbath Ammon (Deut. 3:11). This legendary character also accounts for Og's defeat becoming proverbial of the way the Lord gives victory to people despite all odds (Deut. 31:4).     B.V.

**OIL, HOLY.** Oil, which invariably was olive oil, was used extensively for sacred purposes in the OT liturgy and ritual anointings. It fueled the lamps that burned in the sanctuary of the Lord (Num. 4:9); it was, along with blood, credited with a purificatory function in various ceremonies (Lev. 14:10-20); it was used in the preparation and execution of cereal offerings (Lev. 2:1-10); and it was the medium for the consecration of sacred objects (Exod. 30:25-29), of kings (I Sam. 10:1; 16:13, and others), and of priests (Exod. 3:30). Oil for these ritual uses had to be "pure" (Exod. 27:20; Lev. 24:2).

There is no instance of a sacred anointing in the NT, unless it occurs in the visitation of the sick as described by James 5:14. Here the technical term for anointing (chriō) is not used, but rather a purely secular word. Oil was credited with having medicinal qualities (Mark 6:13; Luke 10:34). It is true, this anointing is done "in the name of the Lord"; still it is "the prayer of faith" that saves the sick person.

Holy oils are featured in the liturgies of various Eastern and Latin churches. In the Roman liturgy three oils are used for distinct purposes: chrism, a mixture of olive oil and balsam; and the oil of the sick and the oil of catechumens, both of which are pure olive oil.     B.V.

**OLD TESTAMENT.** A term of Christian provenance used to designate the Scriptures inherited by the church from Judaism. For most Protestants this OT means only the books of the Hebrew Bible. For Eastern and Latin Christians it is these books together with a number of others that were habitually included in the Greek version of the Bible used by the Jews of the Diaspora. The term rises out of the ambiguity of the word *diatheke* as used in the Greek Bible. The word did mean "last will and testament," but as simply expressing God's will it had been used to translate the Hebrew *berith,* "covenant." The Lucan-Pauline version of the Last Supper (Luke 22:20, I Cor. 11:25) has Jesus speak of the new *diatheke* in his blood. The Epistle to the Hebrews picks up this terminology and refers to Judaism as the first or old *diatheke.* In Hebrews 9:15-22 *diatheke* appears as covenant, as will, and as written record of the covenant/will. It is in this final sense that we speak of the OT.     B.V.

**OLIVER, HENRY KEMBLE** (1800–85). Musician, hymn composer, teacher, and public official. Henry Kemble Oliver was born on November 24 in Beverly, Massachusetts. He learned many religious tunes from his musical mother and at ten years old was a boy soprano in Boston's Park Street Church, where he later served as organist. After training at Boston Latin

*The Church of All Nations in the Garden of Gethsemane. Behind it is the Mount of Olives and the Russian Church of St. Mary Magdalene*

School and Phillips Andover, Oliver attended Harvard College for two years and completed his work at Dartmouth. He taught school for many years in Salem and on Sundays played the organ at St. Peter's Church and later at North Church. He was superintendent of the Atlantic Cotton Mills in Lawrence (Mass.), and served as organist at the Unitarian church. As a public servant, he was adjutant general of Massachusetts, and subsequently director of the commonwealth's Bureau of Statistics of Labor. During the Civil War he served as state treasurer. Returning to Salem, he became mayor of that historic city for four years. He died in Salem on August 12. Oliver composed many hymn tunes, including those for hymn texts by William Cullen Bryant and Oliver Wendell Holmes.     R.H.

**OLIVES, MOUNT OF.** A mile-long ridge of raised ground, nearly three thousand feet in elevation, that overlooks Jerusalem on its east side. It is thus the most conspicuous marker on the Jerusalem landscape, especially as the terrain drops to the Kidron Valley (II Sam. 15:14, 23, 30). An accurate description is the "mountain which is on the east side of the city" (Ezek. 11:23), and it was reached by covering a walking distance on a Sabbath (which equals 960 yards, according to Acts 1:12). This hillside was covered with olive trees in NT times. Hence the name Mount of Olives was applied.

The most prominent references to this locale in the OT are in connection with David's escape from Jerusalem during Absalom's revolt (II Sam. 15:30), Ezekiel's vision of a theophany on its summit (Ezek. 11:23), and Zechariah's apocalyptic scenario (14:4), which entailed an earthquake whose epicenter at Olivet would produce a new valley.

In the Gospels, Jesus, John reports (7:53–8:1), used the Mount of Olives as a retreat. On entering the city on Palm Sunday (Luke 19:29, 37, 41-44), he grieved over it and foretold its destruction. In Gethsemane on one of the lower slopes he prayed (Luke 22:39), and here he was arrested. In Luke's artistry the same location is made the scene of the Ascension (Acts 1:9, 12), a tradition marked today by the Russian Orthodox Church of the Ascension and an Islamic mosque. Both buildings are intended to mark the scene of the Ascension.

By historical irony the strategic elevation of the Mount of Olives was capitalized by the Roman general Titus at the time of the Jewish war (A.D. 66-70), and from the commanding position of this area the Roman army was poised to lay siege to Jerusalem.     R.M.

**OM (AUM).** From the Sanskrit word meaning literally "yes" or "so be it." A syllable used in HINDUISM especially as a mantra or sacred sound to evoke the realization of BRAHMAN itself. It is treated as, and occasionally virtually used as, a name for Brahman, since as early as the UPANISHADS.     R.E.

**OMEN.** Part of the apparatus of DIVINATION and ASTROLOGY in antiquity was the widespread practice of seeking and giving portents of the future called omens. The most popular forms of divining the future were the inspection of the entrails of animals, especially their liver (considered the seat of life), and the observation of migratory habits of birds (see Jer. 8:7). Other well-attested means were the predicting of natural phenomena such as earthquakes (for example, Amos 1:1; Mark 13:8), and cosmic irregularities like eclipses (Amos 8:9; Joel 2:30-31), and the appearance of stars and comets (Matt. 2:1-10 is the best-known example). In Hellenistic religion there is a deep strain of belief in superstition, and omens were a way to avert one's fate. Theophrastus' entertaining description, "The Superstitious Man" in his *Characters* (written in 319 B.C.) is one of the best known. This account describes how a nervous man will act when, as a believer in the power of omens, he will run to the diviner and soothsayer to inquire what god to pray to, will constantly purify his house with water, and will avoid animals, like the cat or weasel, which were thought to bring a bad spell. To see an epileptic or mentally disturbed person is an omen, and he must shudder and spit into his chest to avert the danger.     R.M.

**OMNIPOTENCE.** From the Latin word meaning "all-powerful," and in classical Christian theology is applied to God. Power can be demonic or beneficent. Because humans are limited by their own perceptions, they necessarily apply to God their own definitions and feelings about power. The Bible describes a God who is good and who loves all creation. It is unthinkable that such a God would use power arbitrarily to create or destroy. The God of the Bible is also a moral Being, insisting on righteousness. A corollary of this is that evil will be punished, hence the power of God will be used in judgment. However, one who has power is not required to use it, and God can be merciful and forgiving, thus mitigating the effects of justice. The Bible says that those who repent and return will be saved.

The idea of God's omnipotence raises the question of EVIL. Some answer this question by denying that God is all-powerful. Others say that God's power has been self-limited by giving free will to human beings. Only at the final judgment will justice ultimately be done.     I.C.

**OMNIPRESENCE.** An attribute of God in classical Christian theology, omnipresence comes from the Latin word meaning "present everywhere." If this is so, God must know all that is going on in the world. God's presence is the creative force that maintains life. This presence, however, does not guarantee God's action, although it could imply that God is concerned with what happens. God's intervention is a corollary not so much of presence as of power.

To say that God is everywhere does not mean that

God is *in* everything, the position of PANTHEISM. It denotes that God is the Other and therefore able to be present. If God is omnipresent, there is no way to hide from God. This could evoke fear (of judgment and punishment) or confidence (that God loves).

The omnipresence of God raises the question as to why God is in the world. If God is good, why is there evil? If God is indifferent, why be present? Recently philosophers have speculated on the "absence" of God, not in the sense that God has withdrawn, but that humans are unable to perceive God's presence. The omnipresence of God implies a Being of a different order from humans, yet related to the world.      I.C.

**OMNISCIENCE.** A description of an attribute of God, coming from the Latin word meaning "all-knowing." In Christian theology this was a statement about the cognitive qualities of God. However, in biblical terms, to "know" means to be closely related to, to have an inner knowledge of. The omniscience of God would have both subjective and objective elements.

To think about God as all-knowing could bring fear, because nothing is hidden, or comfort, because God could act wisely on this knowledge for the benefit of creation. It assumes that God is good and implies that evil cannot be hidden from God who can punish evildoers. The purpose of setting up a descriptive category called omniscience is a human effort to say that God is qualitatively different in ways that human beings can neither imitate nor fully comprehend.

Omniscience also suggests foreknowledge, but not necessarily foreordination. As a parent knows that the toddler learning to walk will fall (but the toddler does not know), so God knows when human beings will fail. Omniscience raises the question as to why EVIL exists without intervention from God. The equation of omniscience and goodness were profoundly called into question by the HOLOCAUST.      I.C.

**OMRI.** King of Israel (876–869 B.C.), who succeeded to the throne as the army's choice after the murder of his predecessor, Elah. He restored order, overcame rival claimants, and stabilized the kingdom for years to come. Though the single-minded author of I Kings 16:21-28 pays scant attention to Omri, the archaeology of Samaria, where he established his capital, Assyrian records, and a few scriptural details have convinced historians that he was one of the most effective and far-seeing of Israel's kings. He negotiated advantageous military and commercial alliances and subjugated enemy states such as Moab (attested by the Moabite Stone). Long after his dynasty had disappeared, Israel was still called "the land of Omri" by the Assyrians.      B.V.

**ONAN.** Son of Judah by a Canaanite woman (Gen. 38:4-10), who serves chiefly as a detail in the scene setting of the story of Judah and Tamar. He is reprobated by the biblical author for having failed in this familial obligation under the Levirate law by the practice of *coitus interruptus.* Hence he has the distinction of having the vice of onanism named after him.

     B.V.

**ONEIDA COMMUNITY.** A religious communitarian experiment in western New York state founded in 1848 by JOHN HUMPHREY NOYES, after his experiments in "complex marriage" had offended the community's neighbors in Putney, Vermont. By 1851 it had 205 members. In 1854 Oneida began to manufacture steel traps in addition to its profitable farming and logging operations. An allied community at Wallingford, Connecticut, manufactured sewing silk and silver-plated flatware. One of the few such experiments to survive, Oneida depended more on industry than farming and was a model of efficiency. Noyes eventually proposed it forsake "complex marriage" and become a joint stock company in 1881. The community was controversial because as an outgrowth of PERFECTIONISM, Noyes discouraged "special love" between couples and instead regulated sexual activity and procreation according to his theories of male continence, and "stirpiculture" or eugenics.      N.H.

**ONESIMUS.** A Christian slave residing at Colossae, who on his flight from servitude went to Paul (Col. 4:9). The conversion and subsequent service of Onesimus are to be inferred from that text. In the letter addressed to Philemon, Paul uses the slave's name (Onesimus means "useful") as part of his appeal for the man's pardon by his Christian master as the former is sent back (Philem. 11-12). Paul regards Onesimus' conversion to new life as genuine (v. 10). Onesimus had evidently done wrong by stealing or more simply by running away (v. 18); in the latter case a runaway slave was liable, under contemporary law, for the loss of work incurred by his absence. Paul therefore is promising to make good the loss incurred (vv. 18-19) with a promissory note. An unresolved question is whether Paul is in fact asking for Onesimus' discharge from slavery and his being set free (see v. 16).

Onesimus is the name also of a second-century bishop of Ephesus, according to Ignatius, and this reference with the same example of punning on the man's name has led to the theory that the slave became a later church leader. But this is uncertain, since the name was by no means uncommon, and a later bishop might well have adopted it simply because of its appropriate meaning, that is, "useful" in Christian service.      R.M.

**ONESIPHORUS.** Greetings are sent (II Tim. 4:19) to the "household of Onesiphorus," and the writer prays that divine mercy rest upon it and that Onesiphorus find favor from God in the Day of Judgment. The man is commended for his courage and kindness in seeking out Paul in prison and assisting him. He evidently lived up to his name, meaning "profit-bringing." The question whether Onesiphorus was deceased when II Timothy 1:18 was written has played a significant part in the larger issue of "prayers for the dead." No decision on the basis of this verse is possible.                                                        R.M.

**ONIAS** (II & III). The family name of Onias goes back to Onias I, a Jewish high priest who held office from 320 to 290 B.C., mentioned in I Maccabees 12:7, 19, 20. His grandson Onias II held the post in the time of Ptolemy III, Euergetes (246-221 B.C.). A much more significant character is Onias III, a grandson of Onias II, since he represented the conservative wing of Judaism. He was absent from Jerusalem at a time when Hellenizing practices were introduced, a turn of events that led to the Maccabean revolt in 168 B.C. When Onias III protested these Greek customs, such as sports and dress, he was summarily assassinated by Menelaus (Dan. 9:25-27 is taken to refer to this event).                        R.M.

**ONLY BEGOTTEN.** This is the traditional way of rendering the Greek word *monogenés* in John 1:18 (KJV). The composite word unpacks its meaning as "of a single [*mono*] kind [*genos*]," but modern scholars are suspicious of connecting *genos* with the verb *gennaó*, "to beget," a procedure that yields "only begotten." The translation "only begotten" gained importance when Jerome tried to answer the claims of Arius that Jesus was not begotten but a creature made by God like the angels. So Jerome puts the Greek into the Latin *unigenitus* at John 1:18; 3:16, 18, with the result that the Vulgate influenced the makers of the KJV. But of itself *monogenés* cannot mean uniqueness (see Heb. 11:17, where Isaac is *monogenés*); rather the idea is that of "precious," based on Genesis 22:2, 12, 16.

The text of John 1:18 (see RSV and margin) is difficult, with the manuscripts varying between the "only begotten Son" and "the only begotten God." The latter reading, *monogenes theos*, has a stronger claim, but "only begotten Son" is found elsewhere in John's Gospel and in I John 4:9. The rule of the "more difficult reading" preferred to explain a simpler one applies, and recent scholars prefer the RSV marginal be read as a series of nouns in apposition: "No one has ever seen God; the only begotten God, the one in the bosom of the Father, that one has explained him" (Paul R. McReynolds' translation).          R.M.

**ONTOLOGICAL ARGUMENT.** *See* GOD'S EXISTENCE, ARGUMENTS FOR.

**ONTOLOGY.** Literally, the study of BEING. Although it is a perennial subject within philosophy, the word was coined in the seventeenth century. "Being" is of the essence of personhood, but it is also attributed to God. Being is not acquired, one has it.

Being is grasped as an intellectual idea. The various attributes of humanness are grafted upon it. No one can "prove" being inductively. One of those deductive truths discussed by philosophers, "being" as such is not in the realm of the psychological.

Ontology has been put into new focus through the twentieth-century philosophy called EXISTENTIALISM. HEIDEGGER and JASPERS discuss both being and existence but give priority to the latter. Being is a state, inert and inactive. One accepts being and has no responsibility toward it.

Existence is what a person makes of being. There is a personal responsibility for existence implied in the act of living itself. Being can be an abstraction made up by philosophers. Nevertheless, being points to life, and ontology is a study of both the divine being and the human being.                                     I.C.

**OPHIR.** A region probably on the southwest coast of the Arabian peninsula, possibly on the opposite eastern coast of Africa across the Red Sea, at any rate reached by ship from Ezion-geber (I Kings 9:28). It was proverbial as a source of gold (compare Isa. 13:12). Solomon joined the Phoenician king Hiram to equip a fleet berthed at Ezion-geber to bring out the gold of Ophir.                                     B.V.

**OPUS OPERATUM.** *See* EX OPERE OPERATO.

**ORACLE.** A term used to denote a divine revelation conveyed in various ways and then recorded for posterity. Among the media of revelation used in Israel we note: by dreams (I Sam. 28:6), by a method of casting lots (Lev. 16:8), and by prophetic utterance (see the various prefaces to the eighth- and seventh-century prophetic books in the OT as well as the prophecies uttered against foreign powers in Isaiah 13–19 and Jeremiah 46–51). In the NT the term stands for the OT as written down (Rom. 3:2) as well as distinctively Christian compositions, whether oral (I Pet. 4:11) or written (Heb. 5:12).

Oracles were commonplace in the ancient world, being associated with shrines of the Hellenistic deities, notably Apollo at Delphi. Hence the Delphic oracle to which people came with puzzling questions and were given an answer via the priestess. Similarly at Cumae, near Naples, the famous oracle of Sibyl was consulted. At Corinth and Pergamum oracles were communicated along an underground tunnel—thus heightening the sense of expectation—and the sick were healed by autosuggestive means.          R.M.

**ORAL TRADITION.** By its definition the term speaks of the transmission of stories, teachings, and illustrations of the Bible that were passed on in the community by word of mouth before becoming fixed in written form. It is natural to assume that these traditions were adapted and changed across the generations before their written shape led to their fixation. Yet it is only from the final written text that we may infer the existence of oral tradition and try to trace the stages of its passage with the reasons for its adaptation.

The theory behind oral TRADITION rests on the cultural setting of the biblical material, for we know that Israel, as a primitive Semitic people of the ancient Near East, cherished the accounts of its early history more in the context of tribal storytelling than in producing documents. It is the same with early Norse and Greek sagas, which had their birth in community recitation and cultic drama. Added to this milieu are the amazingly retentive memory of the Jewish people and the stress that the later rabbis placed on learning by memorization with a consequent distrust of book lore. The setting down of the early traditions of Israel's origins in the patriarchal period, the Egyptian hardship and the nation's deliverance under Moses and Joshua, and the settlement of the tribes in Canaan, was not codified until centuries later, though we may recall two safeguards to ensure the integrity of the oral tradition. One is that the Hebrews attached a great deal of significance to a rehearsal of their origins in the liturgy of the sanctuaries at Shechem and Gilgal and later at the Temple in Jerusalem. They believed that these liturgical dramatizations not only reviewed the past but recalled it from memory into living experience in the present. Second, a focal point of such re-presentation was the annual Passover, when Israel relived its humble origins in slavery. No nation would have tolerated this picture and kept it alive unless it was founded on substantial fact in history.

The apostolic church similarly, stemming from its Jewish origins, cherished the life and teachings of Jesus for several decades before having them written down in the canonical Gospels. Preachers, catechists like John Mark (Acts 13:5), researchers like Luke (Luke 1:1-4), and then evangelists (for example, John 20:30; 21:25) were all active in the oral period prior to the composition of our Four Gospels. This type of understanding has led, especially among Scandinavian scholars, to the view that the "oral tradition" represents a first edition of the Gospel later expanded into our canonical four. The oral tradition in time died out, but it left a dubious legacy in the Gnostic notion that Jesus, between his resurrection and ascension, had entrusted "a secret gospel" to selected leaders whom the Gnostics appealed to in their writings. Sundry verses, such as Luke 24:44, 45, John 16:12, were claimed to be part of that oral tradition on which the Gnostics based their religion as an improvement on the catholic, orthodox faith in the second and third centuries.                          R.M.

**ORATIONS.** Prayers, from the Latin word *orationes.* In the Latin Mass, the priest addresses the congregation with *Orate Fratres,* "Let us pray, brothers." This emphasizes the unity of the priest, people, and church in offering the sacrifice of the Mass. An *oratio* is a short liturgical prayer or COLLECT. An *oratio imperata* or "ordered prayer" is a collect added to the Mass for a specific purpose by order of a bishop or the pope. The *oratio super oblata* is the prayer said over the oblation or offering in the Mass. The *oratio super populum* is the prayer over the people, which occurs post-Communion.

Orations or prayers are of various kinds. There are prayers of praise for God's greatness and goodness; prayers of thanksgiving for divine favors received; prayers of confession, in which sorrow for sin is expressed; and prayers of intercession, in which believers ask God to bless others, for example, the fellowship of believers, the nation, specific people in need, or for all sorts and conditions of people. In orations, believers reach out from their hearts to God.
                                                                       J.C.

**ORATORY.** From the Latin word *orare,* meaning "to pray." The precise designation in Catholic canon law of a church; that is, a building set apart for divine services, consecrated for the use of a monastic community, religious school, or private family. Mortuary chapels in cemeteries are private oratories. There is no general right for the public to use such churches or chapels, although they may do so in semi-public oratories, such as hospital or prison chapels. Public oratories are open to all the faithful during such times as mass is celebrated. There are two Catholic orders referred to as oratories: the congregation of the oratory of St. Philip Neri, instituted to save souls through the pastoral activities of priests supported by private finances, and the French oratory, founded in 1611 and reinstituted in 1852 under the name of the Oratory of Jesus and Mary.        J.C.

**ORDER OF PREACHERS.** *See* DOMINIC/DOMINICANS.

**ORDERS AND ORDINATION.** "Orders," in Roman Catholic theology, implies ordination, or the state of being consecrated and set apart for the Christian ministry. There are several different orders, divided into major and minor orders in the Roman Catholic church, but the phrase "to be in orders" or "holy orders" is generally reserved for the ranks of DEACON, PRIEST (PRESBYTER), and BISHOP. These major orders may be conferred only by a bishop, although, in theory, the pope could delegate any priest to confer the minor orders and the diaconate.

"Ordination" refers to the SACRAMENT (in Roman Catholic theology) of conferring such holy orders, and, in Protestantism generally, to the ritual by which persons are set apart for the ministry of word and sacrament (or ordinances, in the Free churches). The Protestant conception of ordination differs widely from the Catholic view, except among a few groups such as the Anglo-Catholics or High Church party of the Church of England, which may consider ordination as a sacrament also. Generally, Protestants do not consider the rite of ordination as a sacrament, nor do they accept the traditional Catholic teaching that such a rite, with the laying on of the bishop's hands, confers an indelible character as a priest. No special status, aside from commissioning for an office, a function, in the church is ascribed to ordination by most Protestants. Catholics do not (even before Vatican II) deny the priesthood of all believers, for they teach that the sacraments of baptism and confirmation confer on every Christian a real participation in the priesthood exercised eternally by Jesus Christ. Nevertheless, the holy order of the priesthood is different precisely because of the INDELIBLE CHARACTER imparted, which gives the priest the power to administer divine grace both by the sacraments and the proclamation of the gospel.

In Protestantism ordination is generally to one rank of ministry, that is, to the office of presbyter or PASTOR, sometimes called ELDER. For example, in the Lutheran churches, ministers are all of one rank, although some may be elected to the office of bishop in certain churches. In the Reformed and Presbyterian churches, the clergy are all ministers or teaching elders (presbyters). However, in the Anglican and Episcopal churches the clergy are ordained, in ascending order, to the rank of deacon, priest, and bishop. In the Roman Catholic church there are seven degrees of holy orders. These include the minor orders of doorkeeper or porter, lector or reader, exorcist, and acolyte. The major or sacred orders are subdeacon, deacon, and priest. Bishops are priests who have all the priestly powers and rule over other priests. ARCHBISHOPS, PATRIARCHS, and the POPE are degrees within the episcopate. CARDINALS do not form an order but fill an office. The same is true of abbots, canons, and other prelates. The Council of Trent declared that once a man has been made a priest he cannot again become a layman. This is not accepted by Protestants.

The rite of ordination for the minor orders of the Catholic church is accomplished by handing the symbols of office to the man, with the appropriate ritual and words. Ordination to the ranks of deacons, priests, and bishops is done by the laying on of hands of the bishop and all priests who are present. The deacons, being made priests, have their hands anointed with oil and are given a chalice and paten with these words: "Receive the power to offer sacrifice to God and to celebrate Mass both for the living and the dead, in the name of the Lord." After communing with both bread and wine, the bishop lays his hands on the new priests and says, "Receive the Holy Spirit, whose sins you forgive on earth shall be forgiven in heaven." Then after a promise of obedience, the bishop blesses the new priests together.

Protestant ordination services are not quite so elaborate, but involve many of the same elements. The candidates for ordination are set apart by the laying on of hands of the bishop or presiding minister and all the other ordained persons present. The right to administer the Lord's Supper and baptism is conferred on the new ministers, and vows and blessings are mutually exchanged.     J.C.

**ORDINAL.** The service of ordination in the Roman Catholic Church, consisting of prayers, vows, and blessings. Holy ORDERS, which set a man apart as a presbyter or priest, convey, according to Catholic theology, an INDELIBLE CHARACTER. This stamp of priesthood cannot be lost. It gives the priest the ability to consecrate the host and to reenact the sacrifice of Calvary in the sacrament of the Mass. The ordination of a deacon does not confer this ability. The ordinal can be done only by a bishop.     J.C.

**ORDINARY.** A Roman Catholic clergyman with ordinary jurisdiction over a specific territory. The pope is ordinary universally, bishops are ordinaries over their dioceses, abbots over their orders. "The ordinary" means the "regular bishop of a diocese." The Ordinary of the Mass is the unchangeable part of the liturgy of the Mass.     J.C.

**ORDINATION.** See ORDERS AND ORDINATION.

*ORDO SALUTIS.* "The order of salvation" or the stages through which a person passes as one moves from the state of SIN to SALVATION. In Roman Catholic thought, the order begins with grace, leading to baptism and, through the sacramental system, the infusion of habitual grace and the development of the virtues. The end is the vision of God. The Protestant dogmaticians of the seventeenth century divided over the order of salvation. Lutherans saw the pattern as God's call, illumination, conversion, assurance of justification, regeneration, mystical union with Christ, the new obedience (sanctification), and finally, glorification. Reformed theologians disagreed and placed predestination at the head of the list.     J.C.

**ORIGEN** (about A.D. 185–254). Outstanding theologian, biblical exegete, writer, and teacher in the early Christian church. Controversial in his own lifetime, at NICAEA in 325 he voiced views that fed both sides of the debate about Christ's nature. The Council of CONSTANTINOPLE in 553 condemned him as a heretic; yet his influence on the history of Christianity has been monumental.

Origen was born of Christian parents in Alexandria, Egypt. His father, Leonides, was beheaded during the persecution under Roman emperor Lucius Septimus Severus (193–211) when Origen was about twelve. The gifted young Origen studied under Clement of Alexandria, who was headmaster of the Christian catechetical school at Alexandria. Clement fled during the persecutions of 202, and Origen at about eighteen was appointed to fill his place, thus beginning a brilliant teaching career. He attracted

Christians and non-Christians to his classes. Dedicated, disciplined, and extremely ascetic, Origen produced some six thousand works of which only a few have survived. An admiring patron provided him with funds for copyists. Recognized as a profound Christian thinker, Origen occasionally visited Antioch, Palestine, Greece, and Italy. Invited by the bishops of Caesarea and Jerusalem to Palestine, Origen preached in the area in 216, while still a layman. This angered his bishop, Demetrius of Alexandria, who was struggling to consolidate his power in Egypt. He recalled Origen from Palestine. About 230 these same bishops, without consulting Demetrius, ordained Origen to the office of presbyter. Demetrius then influenced an Alexandrian synod to rescind Origen's teaching privileges, and a subsequent synod with the compliance of the bishop of Rome deposed Origen from the priesthood and sent him into exile. Origen's statement just after his ordination, that even the devil could be saved, counted heavily against him. Origen then established a school at Caesarea in Palestine, about 232, where he continued his prodigious writings while teaching philosophy, theology, literature, and Bible. About 250, during the persecution under Roman Emperor Decius (249–251), Origen was imprisoned and tortured. When Decius died in 251, Origen was released, but the ordeal had weakened him physically and he died shortly thereafter.

To interpret Scripture and answer Jewish and Gnostic attacks on Christianity, Origen published his famous *Hexapla*, composed of six texts of the OT: the Hebrew, a transliteration of the Hebrew into Greek, followed by four current Greek versions—the Septuagint, Theodotion, Aquila, and Symmachus translations. Drawing on these texts, Origen wrote extensive commentaries explaining biblical passages in three senses—the literal, moral, and allegorical. The literal sense and the historical context interested him only secondarily. He primarily emphasized the inner meaning or soul of a passage and gave a moral-mystical tone to his interpretations.

Origen's principal work, *De Principiis (On Principles)*, systematized his views on God, humanity, and the world. *On Prayer* examined prayer as a communion of the soul with God, and *Exhortation to Martyrdom* portrayed ascetic austerity and the benefits of dying a martyr. His *Commentary on Romans* was badly translated into Latin and altered in his own day. *Contra Celsus (Against Celsus)* quoted extensively from Celsus' writings and helped preserve the work of Celsus, an early critic of Christianity.

Origen presupposed that nothing unworthy should be said about God, and allegory enabled him to explain scriptural incongruities and maintain biblical unity. He believed that God was Perfect Being, a perfect balance of all virtues, and that God is expressed in three coequal hypostases known as Father, Son, and Holy Spirit. In explaining this Trinity Origen tended to make the Son subordinate to the Father, and the Holy Spirit subordinate to the Son, through whom the Holy Spirit came into being. At other times he made Father and Son equal. Origen pictured the Holy Spirit as active only in the souls of saints, whose superior gnosis enabled them to contact the Spirit. To the Father, Origen assigned existence, to the Son rationality, and to the Spirit sanctity.

According to Origen, God first created a realm of intelligences with ethereal bodies endowed with reason and free will. Some of these intelligences fell away from God by allowing their love to lapse. A hierarchical order of celestial realms resulted. Some intelligences fell further than others and became demons or souls imprisoned in human bodies. God created this world as a place where through temporal trial, judgment, and pain souls might be redirected back toward God. Virtuous living would enable one to begin ascending to God at death. Immoral living would cause further descent. This ascent and descent could last a long time, but Origen believed God would not finally be defeated. Suffering and pain are part of God's redemptive plan to retrieve fallen souls through education and training. So also are order and beauty. They help point fallen souls back to the higher realms from which they originally came. Origen thus pictured evil as distance from God, privation of good, brought about by misuse of free will. He maintained that in the end all moral creatures would be rescued, even the devil, but that the whole process could begin anew through misuse of free will.

In Jesus, Origen said, human flesh and divine Logos were united in one person. However, the humanity in Jesus suffered on the cross, not the divinity. Following the Ascension, the humanity was absorbed into the divinity. Christ was a physician to sinners and a teacher to those made pure. Christ broke the hold of Satan who would drag souls further from God, and the Holy Spirit helps believers achieve sanctity. True knowledge brings salvation and expresses itself in good works, making virtuous works essential to salvation. In the reascent to God the body is left behind.

Origen's philosophical assumptions about the preexistence of souls, eternality of worlds, spiritual resurrection, universalism, and recurrence of the Fall caused extensive controversies that have not been resolved fully to this day. Origen's "errors" were declared heretical at Constantinople in 543 and 553.

C.M.

**ORIGINAL RIGHTEOUSNESS.** An important idea in Christian anthropology as a counterbalance to the idea of ORIGINAL SIN. Where this latter idea is stressed in a one-sided way, it leads to an exaggeratedly pessimistic view of human nature, and it is important to remember that original righteousness is more original than original sin. But what is original righteousness? Only if one understood the Genesis myth of the FALL in a crudely literal way could one suppose that the first human beings were morally perfect or completely righteous. Such a literal understanding seems to be held by those who maintain that through the Fall, original righteousness has been totally lost. A more plausible interpretation of the doctrine holds that this original righteousness was given to the human race as a potentiality toward which it was directed. If that is the case, then the Fall was not a *falling away* from an actual righteousness but a *falling short* of a potential righteousness that actually has never been realized. On this second view, original righteousness remains as the goal of human life. SIN hinders its attainment but has not obliterated it, though GRACE is needed to overcome the counter influence of sin.    J.M.

**ORIGINAL SIN.** The doctrine that throughout the history of the human race, human nature has been flawed and disordered in every human group and every human individual. The flaw has several dimensions, and we most naturally think of it as a moral flaw. But in calling it sin, we are recognizing that fundamentally it is a separation from God, the Creator and Sustainer of life. The gravity of original sin lies in the fact that it means that human life is cut off at the very roots, and that all the particular sins and wrongdoings of the race arise from this deep disablement.

The adjective "original" can be understood in more than one way. When the Genesis story of the disobedience of the first human couple was taken literally as describing an event that took place in the dawn of human history, then original sin might be taken to mean this supposed first sin that took place in the beginning. But it could also be taken to mean the whole history of sin that had flowed from it, and nowadays when it is more common to think of the Genesis story as myth rather than as history, this second meaning of "original" remains. The doctrine of original sin has become the doctrine of the universality of sin, and perhaps the word "original" is not very apposite.

Even if one believed in a historical fall at the beginning of human history, one might still think that the expression "original sin" is unfortunate, for sin was not the original state of the first couple. However "early" sin may be in human history, there was a still earlier righteousness. If one talks about "original sin," one has to acknowledge that sin was never as original as righteousness. Any Christian theologian who develops a doctrine of original sin ought to devote at least as much attention to the meaning of original righteousness. Theologians have often failed to maintain this balance, with the result that their teaching about sin has become distorted, and they have presented overly gloomy and pessimistic views of the human condition. The notion of original righteousness does not cease to be meaningful for those who reject a literal historical interpretation of the Fall. For them, "original" is not understood in a temporal sense. They do not believe that there was a Golden Age when human beings were without a flaw and that they subsequently fell away into sin. By the "original" condition of humanity, they would understand an ideal or archetypal humanity, or a "true" humanity, as we often say. Human beings were created with the potentiality for achieving such an authentic humanity, but they have from the beginning consistently fallen short of it. On this view, the Fall is a falling short of the full human potentiality, not a falling away from a righteousness that was once actually enjoyed.

The principal biblical basis for the doctrine of original sin is the story of Creation and the Fall in the early chapters of Genesis, but not all the ramifications of the doctrine can be clearly established from Genesis. Thus, while death and other grievous consequences of the sin of Adam and Eve will pass to the whole human race, it is not stated that sin itself will be passed on. Indeed, in some later Hebrew writers, the tendency was to consider sin a matter of individual responsibility, each generation making a fresh start (Ezek. 18). On the other hand, Paul taught something like a solidarity in sin when he claimed that "sin came into the world through one man" (Adam) and contrasts the case of the righteousness that came "through the one man Jesus Christ" (Rom. 5:12-21).

Even if we read the biblical teaching to mean that sin is transmitted from generation to generation, it is still a question about how the sin is transmitted. The sin of the first parents could hardly be simply imputed to their descendants, for this would seem to rule out any conception of individual responsibility and would be difficult to reconcile with the doctrine of a just and righteous God. Is the transmission of sin then hereditary—passed along in the genes, so to speak, like the color of one's eyes? Something like this has been the view of many theologians. It would seem, however, to be a very fatalistic view, quite subversive again of any belief in individual responsibility. If it is correct that original righteousness is more original than original sin, sin is not of the essence of human nature but is a secondary deterioration and therefore not part of the original human inheritance.

It was AUGUSTINE who firmly established the doctrine of a hereditary original sin. He associated its transmission with the sexual act that is necessary for the conception of each new individual. This act involves concupiscence, understood as excessive and sinful desire. Augustine could find support for his teaching in some isolated biblical passages, for example, "in sin did my mother conceive me" (Ps. 51:5). While in the centuries before Augustine the doctrine of original sin was not too closely defined and was not part of the nucleus of faith as defined in the creeds, the hereditary interpretation gained strength from Augustine onward.

The British monk PELAGIUS opposed the teaching of Augustine, holding that God has endowed human beings with the capacity for choosing good, and that each one is responsible for either choosing the good or failing to do so. The church authorities sided with Augustinianism in this controversy, though not without some modifications. Eventually, however, a hereditary view of original sin prevailed as official Catholic teaching. The Council of Trent stated that it is by propagation, not imitation, that the sin of Adam is transfused into all his descendants, in such a way that it becomes each one's own.

The contrast here between "propagation" and "imitation" suggests still another way in which the transmission of sin could be visualized. "Imitation" is not perhaps the best word, but the idea is of a more external relation of the generations than is suggested by inheritance. The sinful influence of each generation corrupts the one that comes after it. Though orthodox theologians have tended to be critical of such an understanding of original sin, it is such a view that is most likely to be found among modern liberal theologians, provided they are willing to countenance a doctrine of original sin at all. This way of looking at the matter has been given more plausibility by increasing recognition that no individual exists in isolation, and that the corporate nature of human life calls for a conception of corporate sin. In the social, political, and economic structures of human life, there are endemic "sins" that persist from generation to generation, which inevitably distort individual lives.

Schleiermacher, for instance, spoke of original sin as a "sinfulness which is prior to all action" and described it as "not something that pertains severally to each individual and exists in relation to him by himself, but in each the work of all, and in all the work of each." Such a view would seem to allow for whatever truth there is in a doctrine of original sin, while getting rid of the objectionable ideas associated with the notion of "hereditary" sin.

There would seem to be still another possibility, perhaps more individualistic than those so far considered. This is the view that the fall into sin is repeated in the existence of every human individual. The story of Adam and Eve represents an experience repeated in the history of every human being. KIERKEGAARD is the best-known exemplar of this view. In his thought, sin is closely associated with the paradoxical condition of humanity as beings who are at once finite and free. From the beginning, such beings experience a kind of instability—this is what Kierkegaard calls ANXIETY (Angst). It is a kind of malaise or premonition that already disturbs the tranquillity of innocence. Kierkegaard associates anxiety also with freedom. In the face of freedom and the openness of possibilities that it sets before us, we feel anxiety. It would be going too far to say that anxiety is a predisposition to sin, but it does, so to speak, show us the individual teetering on the brink, so that the fall into sin is virtually inevitable. Kierkegaard uses the illustration of the passage from

innocence to the sensuality of sexual experience, but one may not conclude from this that the sins of sensuality are primary.

A different view of original sin is found in the writings of William Temple, but it may be set alongside Kierkegaard's because the finitude of the individual existence is seen as the condition of the fall into sin. It is the simple fact that people look out on the world from their own unique point of view that Temple equates with original sin. This fact means that each one begins with an egoistic tendency, and this has to be overcome if a truly human existence is to be attained.

The biblical story of the Fall does not make it quite clear what the nature is of the sin called "original." Certainly, one could say that the sin is disobedience, though the mere taking of a forbidden fruit might seem to be in itself a trivial matter. There are undoubtedly sexual overtones in the story, and these were probably more pronounced in pre-biblical versions. But the emphasis seems to have moved from the sins of sense to those of the spirit, from sensuality to pride. The basic temptation is "to be as God." It is the same sin that recurs a little later in Genesis in the story of the Tower of Babel. Many theologians have in fact seen PRIDE as the fundamental sin, especially the pride that drives people to usurp the place of God. This is important, because it sharply differentiates the Christian and Jewish understandings of sin from those found in Gnosticism, Manichaeism, and various Eastern religions, where sin is associated with the material and the "original sin" was the mixing of the spiritual and the material. In the biblical tradition, spirit is not immune from sin; indeed, the sins of the spirit are the worst of all.

Neither does the biblical tradition make clear the extent of the fall into sin. Certainly, it is taken to be universal; in Paul's words, "all have sinned and fall short of the glory of God" (Rom. 3:23). But what is not clear is the extent to which sin has gained its hold on human nature, and this has been a matter for controversy among theologians. THOMAS AQUINAS believed that human reason is exempt from the effects of sin and can attain to a natural knowledge of God and of the good, and that people have a natural tendency to seek the good. The great Reformers, on the other hand, believed that sin had been much more disabling than the medieval theologians had allowed. CALVIN taught a doctrine of "total depravity." The ravages of sin had affected the human intellect as much as the will. So he denied the possibility of natural theology, not because there are no evidences of God in the Creation, but because the human mind is too depraved to read them aright. For both Calvin and Luther, the human will was corrupt and in bondage to sin. It could achieve no good by its unaided efforts, only by the grace of God.

The subsequent centuries saw great changes in the status of the doctrine of original sin. The age of the ENLIGHTENMENT came to believe in the perfectibility of humanity. People are by nature inclined to the good. Only inadequate and unjust social structures pervert them from the way toward goodness. LESSING is a good example of a thinker from that period who fervently believed that with the spread of knowledge and of enlightened principles of government, people would attain to a kind of heaven on earth. This whole tendency received a new boost in the nineteenth century with the rise of evolutionary theories. It now came to be widely believed that the doctrine of original sin was a precise reversal of the facts of the case. The human race had not fallen into sin; on the contrary, one should speak of the rise or ascent of humanity, from animality to ever higher levels of culture and civilization. Sin was taken to be the surviving impulses of animality and irrationality in humanity, or, in some cases, artificial taboos restricting free human activity. Not only secular thinkers but many theologians turned away from any doctrine of original sin. It looked as if Pelagianism had finally triumphed, in a form going far beyond anything Pelagius himself had maintained.

However, not all philosophers and theologians were swept away by the fashionable new optimism. The greatest philosopher of the eighteenth century, IMMANUEL KANT, began his book *Religion Within the Limits of Reason Alone* with a lengthy discussion of the "radical evil" in human nature. He rejected the common belief in progress (at least, progress in moral matters), as hopelessly contradicted by the evidence of history. Of course, Kant's belief in a radical principle of EVIL is not the same as a doctrine of original sin. Nevertheless, the persistence of evil in spite of all human progress in knowledge does raise a problem, and the doctrine of original sin would be one possible answer to that problem. Kant was swimming against the stream in the eighteenth and nineteenth centuries, but the view that there is a radical principle of evil in human nature has to be taken much more seriously in the twentieth century. Two world wars and a great many lesser wars have brought unprecedented death and destruction; oppressive regimes in many parts of the world engage daily in plunder, murder, and torture; crime, unemployment, poverty, and inflation show no signs of being eliminated. We are told that in the case of some of these evils the techniques are available for overcoming them, but the will is lacking. The acknowledgment that there is a question of will here brings us right back to such questions as the bondage or impotence of the will, to original sin, radical evil, and more or less equivalent ideas. Thus the twentieth century has witnessed a revival of interest in these topics, and this has received an impetus of urgency from the almost apocalyptic anxieties roused by fears of nuclear war and environmental deterioration.

The twentieth-century revival of the concept of original sin found its ablest advocate, ironically enough, in the supposedly optimistic and Pelagian United States. This was REINHOLD NIEBUHR. He criticized as "Pelagian" the writings on sin of such liberal predecessors as F. R. Tennant. His own major work, *The Nature and Destiny of Man* (vol. I, 1941; vol. II, 1943), contains a detailed and brilliant critique of that whole optimistic view of humanity that had developed since the Enlightenment. For Niebuhr, the root sin is pride. "The human ego assumes its self-sufficiency and self-mastery and imagines itself secure against all vicissitudes. It does not recognize the contingent and dependent character of its life and believes itself to be the author of its own existence, the judge of its own values, and the master of its own destiny." The Tower of Babel was a favorite image used by Niebuhr to symbolize this fallen state of the human race. We have to remember, of course, that he was writing against the background of the power politics and absolute dictatorships of the early twentieth century. This proud and egoistical self-assertiveness, so evident in the dictators but present in some degree in every human being, constitutes a predisposition toward sin. But Niebuhr rejected any doctrine of total depravity that might turn sin into a fate or deprive the human will of its freedom. So he maintained paradoxically that sin is inevitable but not necessary.

The heavy emphasis on sin was characteristic of other theologians of Niebuhr's generation. BARTH came near to a doctrine of total depravity, and, like Calvin, he rejected natural theology and even "religion" (as he understood the word) as attempts by fallen humanity to grasp God. Such attempts could only end in the construction of distorted idols. Niebuhr flatly rejected such teaching as exaggerated and dangerous. He claimed that it really blamed human beings for being human and not divine.

Some of these theologians found allies among existentialist philosophers, who had likewise revolted against the optimistic anthropology of previous generations. They too were claiming that human nature is flawed. HEIDEGGER, for instance, was talking about the "falling" or "deterioration" of the human existent, who resigns freedom and responsibility to become an unthinking unit in mass existence; or who, in preoccupation with the world of things, becomes just another item in that world. The Russian existentialist BERDYAEV made a similar claim, though in a different language. He held that the original sin is objectification. Human beings have put the objectifying relation to things before intersubjective relations, and in doing so have gone far to becoming manipulable objects themselves.

Writers both theological and philosophical have been less obviously concerned with original sin in the later decades of the twentieth century. Why this should be so is not obvious, since the conditions that provoked Niebuhr and the others have not gone away. Perhaps this simply means that original sin continues to be a fact of human life.                        J.M.

**ORTHODOX CHURCHES.** The worldwide communion of a number of self-governing or autocephalous (independent of external, especially patriarchal, authority) churches, situated originally in eastern Europe and the Middle East. The term "Orthodox" means "right doctrine."

The churches of Eastern Orthodoxy are generally independent of one another, but they share the same faith, are in communion with one another, and acknowledge the primacy of the patriarch of Constantinople. There are four highly honored ancient patriarchates: Constantinople, Alexandria, Antioch, and Jerusalem. Then come the more recent patriarchates of Russia, Serbia, Romania, Bulgaria, and Georgia, as well as the Orthodox churches of Cyprus, Greece, Czechoslovakia, Poland, and Albania. There are independent churches also in Finland, China, and Japan, as well as three administrations among Russians living outside the Soviet Union.

The family of Eastern Orthodoxy claims to be a segment of the continuing Christian church established by Christ and the apostles. The first fracture in the church of Christ occurred in the fifth and sixth centuries, when the Nestorian church of Persia and the five Monophysite churches of Armenia, Syria, Egypt, Ethiopia, and India broke away. But the GREAT SCHISM between the Eastern and Western branches of Christendom occurred in 1054, resulting in the Roman Catholic church of the West and the Orthodox church of the East. The Orthodox church often describes itself as the Church of the Seven Councils (held between 325 and 787): Nicaea (325), Constantinople (381), Ephesus (431), Chalcedon (451), Constantinople (680–81), and Nicaea (787).

Orthodoxy recognizes the pope of Rome as the chief bishop in Christendom but he is looked upon merely as "the first among equals" and is not granted the universal supremacy he holds over ROMAN CATHOLICISM. The Eastern church respects the place of the episcopate and priestly office, but gives a much larger place to the laity, who sometimes become theologians and preachers.

Orthodoxy recognizes the seven sacraments, or mysteries, as they call them. Baptism is performed by immersion. Chrismation (confirmation) is administered by the priest immediately after baptism, and from infancy onward children are permitted to participate in Communion. The bread and wine in the Eucharist are considered to be the true Body and Blood of Christ. Communion is taken four or five times each year after confession.

The veneration of icons (pictures of saints and sacred scenes) is a standard feature of Orthodox worship, private and public. The liturgy often includes prayers to the Mother of God and saints. However, the Eastern churches do not acept the Roman Catholic doctrines of purgatory or the Assumption of Mary. Monasticism has always been a part of the religious life in Eastern Orthodoxy. Actually bishops are normally chosen from the ranks of the celibate monastic clergy, whereas parish priests are permitted to marry.

Long separate from the churches of western Europe and North America, the adherents of Eastern Orthodoxy have difficulty in accepting the ways of both Protestants and Roman Catholics. Since 85 percent of the Orthodox believers live in Communist countries, their isolation from Christians in the West has been accentuated. Best known to Western Christians are members of the Greek and Russian Orthodox churches because of large-scale emigration. There are more than three million Orthodox believers in the United States, belonging largely to the Greek Orthodox church and the Orthodox Church in America.                                                R.H.

**ORTHODOX JUDAISM.** *See* JUDAISM, HISTORY OF.

**ORTHODOXY.** From the Greek words *orthos* (correct) and *doxa* (opinion) and meaning the holding or practice of right belief, in contrast to heresy or heterodoxy, or the departing from correct or established belief or doctrine. Orthodoxy can refer to the normative teachings of any group but is usually associated with the holding of correct religious belief.

In the history of Christianity, the term "orthodoxy" has been used in at least three distinct ways: (1) Originally the term denoted those parties or churches that conformed to Christian belief as taught in the established canonical books of Scripture as interpreted and formulated in the early confessions and creeds, such as that issued by the Council of NICAEA. (2) Eastern Orthodoxy is the term applied to those churches that include the ancient Byzantine patriarchates (highest ranking bishops) of Constantinople, Alexandria, Antioch, Jerusalem, and the later national Orthodox churches of Greece, Russia, Bulgaria, Romania, and others. These churches are autocephalous, that is, are independent, national, or territorial churches with their own hierarchy of bishops, priests, and deacons. They do not recognize the primacy and authority of the Roman pontiff. While they afford the patriarch of Constantinople a primacy of honor, the highest authority in the Eastern Orthodox Church is vested in the episcopacy. It is of interest that, while these churches are called "Orthodox," they have not been required to define belief by means of finely drawn dogmatic statements. Rather, Eastern Orthodoxy stands for the passing on of a sacred tradition, which includes the Scriptures as interpreted by the church, the doctrinal teachings of the earliest ecumenical councils, the testimony of the Church Fathers and, most importantly, the Byzantine tradition of liturgical worship. (3) Protestant orthodoxy is a movement of the late sixteenth through the early eighteenth centuries within the Lutheran and Reformed churches. The theological insights of Luther and Calvin were systematized into precise, logical propositions in a manner reminiscent of the medieval Schoolmen. Religious certainty was equated with intellectual assent to these propositions. The Bible was viewed as a verbally inspired and inerrant deposit of objective information, historical and scientific as well as religious and moral. This contributed to the conflict between science and theology in the eighteenth and nineteenth centuries. (*See* RATIONALISM.)

J.L.

**OSIRIS.** *See* ISIS AND OSIRIS.

**OTHNIEL.** In Joshua 15:16-17 a Kenizzite chieftain who wrested the city of Kiriath-sepher (Debir) from the Canaanites, for which he was rewarded by receiving from the clan leader Caleb the hand of his daughter Achsah in marriage. The same story is told in Judges 1:12-13. Then in Judges 3:9-11 he is listed as the first of the Judges, credited with the defeat of Cushan-rishathaim, king of Aram Naharaim (translated "Mesopotamia" by the RSV). Probably Aram is a misreading of Edom (in Hebrew spelling the two words are easily confused): Cushan is an Edomite name (compare Hab. 3:7), and the Kenizzites were originally a Midianite (Edomite) tribe, later assimilated into Judah. What is described is internecine Edomite warfare, which the author of Judges has made conformable to the pattern he set for his narrative in 2:11-19.

B.V.

**OTTO, RUDOLF** (1869-1937). German theologian and philosopher of religion, best known for his influential study *The Idea of the Holy* (1917; Eng. trans. 1923). Educated at Erlangen and Göttingen, he taught at the latter university, at Breslau, and at Marburg. He began as a disciple of Ritschl but turned to a broader study of the religious consciousness and to inquiry into the religious a priori, or what distinguishes religion from other human forms of experience, for example, morality or reason.

The uniquely religious, for Otto, is found in the category of "the holy." The HOLY, or what he calls the numinous (*see* NUMEN), is the suprarational, mysterious, inconceivable core of religion. While inconceivable, the holy can, nevertheless, be grasped in certain feelings that comprise the numinous experience. In the presence of the holy, one is, first of all, acutely conscious of what Otto calls creature-feeling—a profound sense of one's own finitude and nothingness. The object of the creature-feeling is experienced as the *mysterium tremendum et fascinans*. The *mysterium* is apprehended as a transcendent "Wholly Other," a reality felt but beyond conceptual expression. The *tremendum* indicates the quality of awe, majesty, and dread in the presence of the holy, while the *fascinans* points to the simultaneous experience of religious rapture, joy, beatitude, or grace. According to Otto, religion inevitably develops ethical and conceptual dimensions, but the *sensus numinis* is the unique, a priori essence of religion. Otto has had a profound

influence on the historical and phenomenological study of religion in this century.

J.L.

**OUR FATHER.** *See* LORD'S PRAYER.

**OUR LADY.** The English equivalent of the Italian term "Madonna" and the Latin "Domina," meaning the BLESSED VIRGIN MARY. This title is the most popular one given the Virgin in common Catholic piety. Its use in English dates back to the eighth century.

J.C.

**OUSIA.** A Greek term meaning "that which makes a thing what it is," often translated into English, with varying connotations, as "substance, essence, and character." It figured prominently in the early theological controversies over the divine-human nature of Christ, frequently because when translated into Latin, subtle differences in meaning resulted.

C.M.

**OXENHAM, JOHN** (1852-1941). Wholesale grocer, novelist, poet, and hymn writer. John Oxenham was the pseudonym used by William Arthur Dunkerley, who was born on November 12 in Manchester, England. Dunkerle was the proprietor of a large wholesale grocery business that operated in England, France, and the United States. A devout Congregationalist layman, he wrote sixty-two books, including more than forty novels and twenty volumes of verse and prose. In 1908 his nephew, the Reverend Dugald Macfadyen, was in charge of a huge missionary exhibition held in London called The Orient in London. Macfadyen prevailed upon his noted uncle to help with the scenario of the pageant. Included in it was the hymn "In Christ There Is No East or West."

R.H.

**OXFORD GROUP.** The name given to a religious movement initiated by Frank N. D. Buchman, an American Lutheran minister. Later it became known as MORAL REARMAMENT. Buchman stressed four spiritual principles: confession, surrender, guidance, and sharing. These were aimed toward four "absolute" goals: absolute purity, absolute unselfishness, absolute honesty, and absolute love.

Buchman concentrated his efforts on reaching university students who met at house parties where there was an emphasis on meditation, public confessions, quiet times, and recreation. In 1928 Buchman conducted a team of Rhodes scholars to South Africa. The group was referred to then as "the Oxford group," and the name stuck until 1938, when the movement, which now had become international, was designated as Moral Rearmament.

It spread from Great Britain and the United States to Switzerland, Germany, and parts of Africa. In addition, Buchman emphasized that the principles of the movement could transform societies as well as individuals. He was highly praised and received honors and decorations from France, Germany, Greece, Japan, China, the Philippines, Thailand, New Zealand, and Iran.

Buchman employed drama, films, and musicals to promote his cause. Training centers were established at Caux, Switzerland, and Odawara, Japan. After Buchman's death in 1961, Moral Rearmament continued to function with a central office in New York City.                              R.H.

**OXFORD MOVEMENT.** An effort within the Church of England that sought to restore HIGH CHURCH standards and practices. Also known as Tractarianism it was so named because a number of *Tracts for the Times* were issued by its proponents, a group of clergymen at Oxford.

There were several elements that contributed to the thinking behind the movement—the decline in church life, theological liberalism, growing nonconformity, and the fear that the Catholic Emancipation Act (1829) might lead Anglicans into the Roman Catholic church. The proponents of Tractarianism promoted the Church of England as a divine institution. This included emphasis on apostolic succession and the Book of Common Prayer as a rule of faith. A return to pre-Reformation beliefs and practices was urged. This emphasis resulted in the movement's advocates being called Anglo-Catholics.

Leaders in the original movement were the poet and hymn writer JOHN KEBLE, R. Hurrell Froude, EDWARD BOUVERIE PUSEY (whence the name Puseyites), Charles Marriott, Richard William Church, Robert Isaac Wilberforce, Isaac Williams, and JOHN HENRY NEWMAN. Newman, like most of his colleagues in the movement, was a learned man. It was Newman's tracts that developed the thesis of the *via media*, the teaching that the Church of England held an intermediary position between Roman Catholicism and Protestantism. In time, however, he moved more to the Roman Catholic position and in 1845 was received into that church. Ultimately he was made a cardinal by Pope Leo XIII. Newman, Pusey, and others in the movement wielded immense influence on the High Church trend within worldwide Anglicanism.                    R.H.

**OXYRHYNCHUS SAYINGS OF JESUS.** A corpus of sayings attributed to Jesus written in Greek on papyrus in four small fragments and discovered in the late nineteenth century at Oxyrhynchus, about 120 miles south of Cairo, Egypt.

There were many literary finds unearthed at this site when it was explored. The documents were published by B. P. Grenfell and A. S. Hunt and are available today in translation (1898–1977 in forty-five volumes). The sayings of Jesus were recorded on separate fragments. These fragments in part reproduce the material in the Gnostic Gospel of Thomas. This material is found in *Papyrus 1*, a sheet that

Courtesy of the Committee of the Egypt Exploration Society

*Oxyrhynchus papyrus with new "sayings of Jesus," belonging to the third century* A.D.

contains seven "words of Jesus." The best-known is "Raise the stone and you shall find me; split the wood and I am there." But at least one saying ("Jesus says, I stood in the center of the world . . . and I found all men drunk, but I found none thirsty among them") has a Gnostic flavor, with its pessimistic outlook on fallen humanity from which the Gnostic believer was delivered.

Other caches of papyrus writing contain sayings of Jesus that are similar to the canonical Gospels (for example, Matt. 7:7, 10:26; Luke 17:20, 21). Yet another document (*Papyrus 655*) has a freely worded rendering of Matthew 6:25-30, about the lilies of the field. A fourth fragment *(Papyrus 840)*, found in 1905, has provoked some discussion. It records a discussion between Jesus and a Pharisee.

The date of the papyri is the middle of the third century A.D., but *Papyrus 840* is considerably earlier (about A.D. 150). Estimates as to whether any of the sayings are authentic or derive from a deviant form of early Christianity vary.

R.M.

**P DOCUMENT.** One of the literary components of the PENTATEUCH, P is also referred to as the Priestly History. It was written (likely in Babylon) during the period of the Exile (597–538 B.C.), but utilized much older literary material, both legal and non-legal in nature. P surveys the history of Israel from the creation, and, at a time near the end of or just subsequent to the Exile, the document was used to form the framework of the Pentateuch. (*See also* DOCUMENTARY HYPOTHESIS.) J.N.

**PACHOMIUS.** A founder of communal or cenobitic MONASTICISM in Egyptian Christianity in the fourth century A.D. After conversion during army service, Pachomius founded a monastic community at Tabennisi in A.D. 320. Before his death in A.D. 346, eleven monasteries, including two for women, encompassing thousands of monks and nuns, followed his supervision. J.C.

**PACIFISM.** A view that may mean (1) opposition to WAR and armed violence as ways to settle disputes and conflicts between nations; (2) convictions, usually based on religious faith, opposing all use of force and violence in human relations, even in self-defense; or (3) the pragmatic belief that nonviolent resistance and action are more effective than violence for accomplishing social goals such as greater justice, freedom, and equality.

Though the term has emerged into general usage over the past century, the hope for peace and the rejection of violence have ancient origins. The teachings of Taoism include the idea of *wu-wei* (non-action) as a way to inner balance and peace. Jainism, which emerged from Hinduism in the fifth century B.C., emphasizes *ahimsa* (nonviolence toward living creatures), a doctrine stressed also in Buddhism and some sectors of Hinduism. Among the ancient Greeks, exhaustion from war produced ideas of benevolence and escape from violence. In the Hellenistic period, the practice of amnesty and the notion of universal humanity emerged.

The teachings of Jesus in the NT, with his emphasis on turning the other cheek and loving even one's enemies, provide a firm basis for nonviolence and pacifism in the Christian tradition, though many Christians were soldiers even in the early church. In the Middle Ages, nonviolence was taught by certain groups, for example, the Franciscans. The Protestant Reformation included movements that rejected violence on the basis of the NT and produced denominations known today as "peace churches," with pacifism as a central conviction, for example, the Friends or Quakers, Mennonites, and Church of the Brethren. Most contemporary Christian churches affirm pacifism as one valid Christian view and provide moral support for individual members who, on religious grounds, take a pacifist position and become conscientious objectors to participation in war.

In the twentieth century, the development of highly destructive weaponry and the rising pressure for human liberation have resulted in the growth of peace movements and the refinement of techniques of nonviolent action. Since the slaughter of World War I and the advent of atomic weapons at the end of World War II, there has been a rising tide of efforts aimed at disarmament, the limitation of types and numbers of armaments, and international organization designed to decrease war and violence by means of negotiation, treaty, and law. In a related development, pacifism has been articulated in methods of civil disobedience and nonviolent protest and linked closely to action for human liberation from oppression and injustice.

The establishment of the League of Nations after World War I, the series of disarmament conferences and pacts between the wars, and the attempts to limit the buildup of arms by the major powers represent efforts for peace related to the pacifist movement, though by no means identical with it. The formation of the United Nations after World War II, the extensive negotiations over strategic arms limitation and nuclear testing, and the protests against nuclear weapons illustrate similar endeavors in recent decades. The danger of global destruction by nuclear missiles has led to the emergence of "nuclear pacifism," a movement of those opposed to the production and use of nuclear weapons but not necessarily opposed to all forms of violence or war.

Equally important for an understanding of pacifism today is its relation to nonviolent action and liberation. HENRY THOREAU (1817–62) formulated and practiced the notion of "civil disobedience" and taught that people ought to refuse to obey laws they believe unjust. Developed further by the women's suffrage movement, the most significant strides in nonviolent techniques were made by MOHANDAS K. GANDHI (1869–1948) and MARTIN LUTHER KING, JR. (1929–68).

Gandhi, called Mahatma (Great Soul), shaped a method of direct action founded on the notion of *ahimsa* (avoidance of injury to living creatures), on the belief in *satyagraha* (the power of truth), and on the example and teachings of Jesus. In South Africa, from 1893 to 1915, he worked for the rights of oppressed Indians and developed the techniques of nonviolent resistance. In 1915, he returned to India, became leader of the Indian nationalist movement, and, in a brilliant and sustained campaign of protests, fasts, and social programs, compelled Britain to grant India independence in 1947. His last great act was a personal fast in January 1948 that brought an end to the fighting between Hindus and Muslims. But twelve days after this success, he was assassinated by a conservative Hindu opposed to Gandhi's teaching of religious toleration.

Martin Luther King, Jr., Baptist minister, combined the example and teaching of Jesus with the methods and beliefs of Gandhi to guide and empower the movement for civil rights for blacks in the United States. Building on the experience of groups like the Fellowship of Reconciliation and the Fellowship of Southern Churchmen, King forged a strong movement, first, in Montgomery, Alabama, to protest segregation on city buses, and then across the South and the nation to win equal rights for blacks. The method of nonviolent protest, King stressed, is mandated by religious faith and is the most effective form of social action because in the end it wins a double victory: it overcomes oppression and injustice and also changes the opponent. For his civil rights leadership, King was awarded the Nobel Prize for Peace in 1964. He was assassinated in April, 1968, while in Memphis to lead a protest movement.

The beliefs, commitments, and methods of pacifism have been given decisive shape as the movement has broadened and deepened over the past century. Peace has been linked indissoluably to justice and liberation. The techniques of nonviolent action have been tested and refined. The most significant developments now under way are: (1) the recognition that peace is more than the absence of conflict and needs careful research to discover the varied elements uniting humans in covenants of peace (for example, the emergence of peace studies programs); and (2) the insight that it is of crucial importance to train people in conflict resolution by nonviolent methods and to work in specific situations of tension to develop a world of peace with justice (for example, programs like the National Peace Academy, the Peace Brigades International, and Peaceworkers).

C.Mc.

**PADMA-SAMBHAVA.** Buddhist teacher of the eighth century who was invited in 747 by the king of Tibet to visit his land on behalf of BUDDHISM. According to traditional accounts, which are packed with legendary material, he bettered the shamans of the indigenous Bon religion in both argumentation and magic, and defeated and then converted to Buddhism the native gods and demons of Tibet. Padma-Sambhava is credited with establishing TANTRIC or VAJRAYANA Buddhism in Tibet and with founding the Nyingmapa tradition of TIBETAN BUDDHISM, by which he is highly venerated.

R.E.

**PAGODA.** A multi-storied tower frequently associated with Buddhist temples, the pagoda derives from the ancient Indian *stupa* or shrine containing relics, as of the Buddha. The pagoda is usually seen as having symbolic meaning, though interpretations vary. If threefold, it may represent the three worlds or the three forms of expression of the Buddha-nature; if multiple, it may represent the many heavens layered

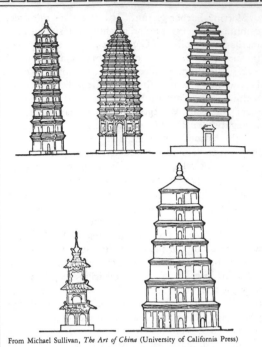

From Michael Sullivan, *The Art of China* (University of California Press)

*Types of pagodas*

above earth or the stages of the bodhisattva path. In China, pagodas in a landscape are considered auspicious for reasons largely connected with *feng-shui* or geomancy.                                                        R.E.

**PALESTINE.** One of the names, found four times in the OT, to denote the land of Israel (Exod. 15:14; Isa. 14:29, 31; Joel 3:4). These texts, however, more properly speak of Philistia, which reflects the name of the land as the original home of the Philistine people in the coastal region from Gaza in the south to Joppa in the north. The title "land of Israel" (I Sam. 13:19) came on the scene with the invasion of the Israelite tribes who eventually, in the reign of David and the later Hasmonean kingdom, took as possession the land from Dan in the north to the Negeb, with Beersheba as the principal town in the south. Palestine is now an archaic name for Israel, but is still adhered to by non-Israeli dwellers, for example, Palestinian inhabitants in Judea-Samaria.

*Topography and Trade Routes.* Palestine occupies a strategic position on the map of the Syrian Levant or Fertile Crescent, which spans the two great ancient civilizations of EGYPT and MESOPOTAMIA. The coastal corridor was a much traversed region, affording commerce and armies an easy passage in both directions. The coastal road, traditionally known as *via maris*, ran "by the way of the sea," the Mediterranean or Great Sea. The route ran from Egypt across the coastal plain to the west side of the SEA OF GALILEE, thence to Damascus in Syria and on to Mesopotamia. Other routes of lesser importance

follow the rim of the Transjordan plateau from the Gulf of Aqabah in the south, and go north to Damascus. The occupation of this area can be observed from the towns listed in Numbers 21:27-30. The third route offers the shortest distance between Sinai and the land of Israel, connecting towns such as Kadesh—barnea and Beersheba in the south via Hebron, Jerusalem to Shechem in Samaria, and linking the important meeting place of Megiddo at the point where several other caravan routes converge. We observe, with geographers and the flow of OT historical narrative, that all these routes follow a north-south axis, with mountainous regions forbidding much easy passage along an east-west alignment.

*Regions.* Palestine is divided into several distinct areas, each with its own geology, climate, agriculture, and distinctive contact with other cultures. (a) The Central Highlands, called in the OT the "hill country," rises to about three thousand feet, with a gentle slope to the west toward the Mediterranean Sea and a more abrupt descent to the Jordan Valley. The upland areas, largely infertile, are seen around JERUSALEM (see Pss. 121:1; 122:4; 125:2 for allusions to "going up" to the hills surrounding the city), and the mountainous region around Samaria that extends to the Carmel Range (about two thousand feet but dips to the Plain of Esdraelon). (b) The Plain of Esdraelon lies in the path of the elevated backbone of the Palestinian geological ridge that runs north-south. Its alluvial soil made it a prized agricultural center and much sought after in Israel's history, especially as the main trade routes passed through this basin around Megiddo. (c) GALILEE denotes a hilly area to the east, with two sections, upper and lower. The rainfall and the condition of the soil made Galilee a thriving agricultural locale, with other trades, such as fishing and commerce in the Sea of Galilee adding to prosperity and attracting a large population. The northern aspect of Galilee made it more open to outside influence, culturally and religiously, than the more sheltered south. (d) The Coastal Plain, as its

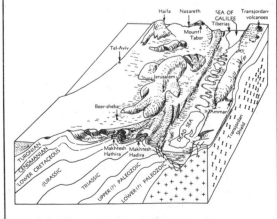

*Structural block diagram of Palestine*

namc implies, denotes the cities bordering the Mediterranean, originally Philistia, extending from Gaza to the Plain of Sharon in the north. The Kishon Valley links this northerly region with the Plain of Esdraelon. (e) The Shephelah, literally "valley," describes an undulating belt of land connecting the coastal area to the mountains of Judea. It is the setting of much of the history in the time of the Judges and the early monarchy (I Sam.), and at one end of the Shephelah lies the Valley of Aijalon, another main route for conquering armies to pass. (f) The Jordan Rift Valley is set on the east of the backbone of the chain of mountains that run north-south. This depression in the earth's crust forms not so much a valley as a hole in the surface of Palestine's terrain. The Jordan River follows its course through a geological fault, and there are levels that are among the lowest anywhere in the world. There is a dense jungle of wild animal life and vegetation (see Jer. 49:19; 50:44: "the jungle of the Jordan"), until the river empties itself into the Dead Sea, with a network of caves and mountainous areas containing the citadel of Masada on the western shore. (g) Transjordan, as the name betokens, denotes the region on the east bank of the river settled by the two and a half tribes (Num. 31:1-27) after the wilderness wanderings. The region is fertile—a factor in the tribes' choice to remain on the east of the Jordan and bordering on Moab, which was noted for its sheep-rearing (II Kings 3:4).

*Settlement.* Place-names have posed a problem since Josephus' writings were critically examined, with their plentiful references to Jewish historical geography, and Eusebius produced his *Onomasticon* in the fourth century. Edward Robinson in 1838 took a major step forward in identifying 177 place-names, which expeditions by the early twentieth century have increased to 434. It has been estimated that there are 622 places mentioned by name in the area west of the Jordan in the Bible. Some discoveries have attracted worldwide attention, notably at Jericho and the various sections in Jerusalem, both in the Old City and more recently the ancient city of David at Ophel, thanks to both Israeli and Christian archaeological work. Ancient Canaanite cities, that is, predating the Israelite occupation, have been unearthed at Gezer, Megiddo, Hazor, and Bethel. In Transjordan ancient fortress towns such as Petra and Bozrah have been revealed. Tells at Lachish and Shechem have indicated how civilizations existed long before the Israelites came on the scene. But some identifications remain uncertain because several sites (for example, Emmaus in Luke 24:13) had the same or similar names, and names did change even in the framework of the biblical narrative, for example, Luz became known as Bethel (Gen. 28:19; 35:6). But Joshua 16:2 makes a distinction between the two towns; compare Judges 1:23-26, which shows how the ancient Canaanite nomenclature persisted, in spite of Joshua 18:13, which makes the names synonymous.                R.M.

**PALESTRINA, GIOVANNI** (about 1525–94). Sixteenth-century Italian composer, famous for his works during the Catholic Reformation. Giovanni Pierluigi da Palestrina was born in Palestrina and went to Rome as a boy, returning home to serve as an organist. He later returned to Rome and held prominent positions in church music. He lost his first wife and several older sons in an epidemic, but later remarried. Palestrina's church compositions became the ideal for Roman Catholic church music, as he wrote some 250 motets, many based on the Song of Solomon. He personally wrote the music for over one hundred masses. His *Missa Brevis* (short mass) and *Missa Papae Marcelli* are well known. Palestrina is considered to be the musical master of the Roman Catholic Reformation.                J.C.

**PALEY, WILLIAM** (1743–1805). Anglican archdeacon of Carlisle from 1780 until his death. He authored a number of influential books used as texts at Cambridge and elsewhere during the eighteenth and nineteenth centuries. Paley's *Natural Theology* (1802), *Evidences of Christianity* (1794), and *Principles of Moral and Political Philosophy* (1785) were said by him to form a system reflecting the elements of British eighteenth-century theology, not in sophisticated fashion, but in plain arguments. Paley especially founded his apologetic approach on the argument for God's existence from design, that is, that the logical working of the universe, from the movements of the planets to the form and function of the human eye, proves the reality of a divine creator. *Natural Theology* goes on to show that the God who exists is good. *Evidences of Christianity* is an attempt to show that Christianity is the one genuine religion based on God's revelation.                J.C.

**PALI CANON.** Buddhist scriptures written in the Pali language, an ancient Indian tongue closely related to Vedic SANSKRIT. The Buddha is said to have favored transmission of his teachings in this vernacular language rather than in the sacred Sanskrit associated with the VEDAS and the BRAHMIN priestly caste, whose authority he opposed. The Pali scriptures, known as the Tripitaka or "Three Baskets," alone are accepted as canonical by THERAVADA BUDDHISM; MAHAYANA Buddhists acknowledge both the Tripitaka (of which they know several variants) and the Sanskrit SUTRAS.

The Pali Canon as now received by Theravadins was, according to traditional accounts of which some aspects are questioned by scholars, standardized as oral tradition by monks in a series of three councils held during the two centuries following the Buddha's death in 483 B.C. It appears to have been first put down in writing in Sri Lanka in the first century B.C. While the Tripitaka is largely teachings put into the mouth of the Buddha, it is impossible to say, after this canonization process, what part of it may be in his exact words. However, it is generally believed that it is true to the style and essential content of the Enlightened One's discourse.

The three "baskets" into which the Tripitaka is divided are these. The Vinaya Pitaka is a book of monastic discipline, presenting detailed rules governing the lives of monks and nuns. The Sutta Pitaka is composed largely of discourses of varying length by the Buddha presenting his basic teachings. The Abhidhamma Pitaka, clearly later than the Sutta Pitaka, presents treatments in technical philosophical language of basic themes of the latter.          R.E.

**PALMER, RAY** (1808–87). Congregational minister and hymn writer. Palmer was born on November 12, in Little Compton, Rhode Island. After receiving training at Phillips Academy in Andover (Mass.), he attended Yale University, graduating in 1830 with a bachelor of arts degree. He was ordained as a Congregational minister and served churches in Bath (Maine) and Albany (N.Y.). He was chosen as secretary of the American Congregational Union, serving in that office in New York City for many years. One of the best-known hymn writers of his day, Palmer is probably best known for "My Faith Looks Up to Thee." Besides his many original hymn texts, Palmer rendered a number of early Latin hymns into English. He died on March 29 in Newark, New Jersey.          R.H.

**PALM SUNDAY.** The Sunday before EASTER, celebrating the entry of Jesus into Jerusalem before his arrest, trial, and CRUCIFIXION. Palm branches were waved and placed on the road before his donkey by the cheering crowd. This event gives the Sunday its name. In liturgical and many free churches today, there is a service outside the church—or even in another place—in which the palms to be used in the day's service are consecrated, then carried in a procession to the church, where Holy Communion is celebrated.

The palms symbolize victory—the final victory over death by Jesus' sacrifice and RESURRECTION. The mood of the day is a mixture of triumphant joy in the procession, followed by a growing realization that the crowds that cheered on Sunday would shout "crucify him" on Friday. Palm Sunday sets the tone of HOLY WEEK with its emphasis on the redeeming death of Christ.          J.C.

**PAMPHYLIA.** A term to describe the coastal area of Asia Minor in its southern area. It is the region referred to in Acts 13:13; 14:24; 15:38 as territory covered by Paul in his first mission. When he sailed from Cyprus, he evidently landed at the port of Attalia, a town founded by Attalus II of Pergamum in the second century B.C. His next stopping place was Perga, an inland town; thence he moved to Pisidian Antioch and left the region of Pamphylia. But his return trip brought him again to these centers, according to Acts 14:24, 25. Evidently the earlier

decision to venture beyond the Taurus Mountains into Pisidia occasioned the defection of John Mark, who, it is said (Acts 15:38), "had withdrawn from them in Pamphylia, and had not gone with them to the work" of Paul's missionary outreach.          R.M.

**PANENTHEISM.** A form of THEISM or belief in the existence (or being) of God held by the philosophical theologian PAUL TILLICH and the philosophers and theologians of the Whiteheadian or process school. Tillich seems to have developed (independent of Whitehead) his conception of panentheism, which means that everything exists in God, yet God is not the unity of the all, since God transcends even the totality of the world. Tillich's notion of God as Being Itself may be contrasted with the theism of Whitehead's theological follower CHARLES HARTSHORNE. Hartshorne calls his position "di-polar theism," and claims it fully recognizes the perfection of God more than traditional theism, which he calls "mono-polar theism." Di-polar theism recognizes that God includes the world, and thus God is affected by, changed by, the experiences God has with the world. God is, at least on one pole, involved in time and dependent upon the events of the world. However, in essence, God remains (as traditional theism holds) immutable, absolute, eternal, and independent of the world. Hartshorne calls these two poles the primordial and the consequent natures of God. Tillich spoke of the deity as the Ground of All Being, as Being Itself, but he did not identify God with the world. Rather, the structures of Being are grounded in God, while God transcends them in divine depths or abysmal nature.          J.C.

**PANNENBERG, WOLFHART** (1928– ). A distinguished German theologian of the generation following the era dominated by Barth, Bultmann, and Tillich. Pannenberg's theology represents, in part, a response to and a corrective of NEO-ORTHODOXY and EXISTENTIALISM. He studied under the philosopher Nicolai Hartmann at Göttingen and Karl Barth and Karl Jaspers at Basel. His most important years as a student were spent at Heidelberg, where he worked with, among others, Gerhard von Rad, Hans von Campanhausen, Edmund Schlink, and the philosopher Karl Löwith.

At Heidelberg he joined with other graduate students in what is called the Pannenberg group, to work on problems left unresolved by theologians such as Barth and Bultmann. The critical issue was the relation of REVELATION and theology to critical history. Both Barth and Bultmann saw the latter as a problem for theology. They sought to make revelation, understood as God's self-disclosure in history, immune to the results of historical-critical research. Barth spoke of events such as the Resurrection as "primordial history" (*Urgeschichte*), and Bultmann sundered *Geschichte*, history understood in terms of its existential significance, from

Courtesy of The Westminster Press

*Wolfhart Pannenberg*

*Historie,* or scientific history. In both cases the historic Christ of faith was freed from the judgments of critical history regarding the events of Jesus' life and activity. Pannenberg and his circle reject this dualism. Revelation *is* historical event, and the two cannot be disjoined. This key to Pannenberg's theology is the theme of the book *Revelation as History* (1961; Eng. ed. 1968), which he published with members of the group.

Pannenberg served as lecturer in theology at Heidelberg upon completion of his dissertation on Dun Scotus' doctrine of predestination in 1954. Subsequently, he has served as professor of theology at Wuppertal (1958–61) and has held the chair of systematic theology at Mainz (1961–68) and Munich (1968– ). He has lectured extensively throughout Europe and North America. Pannenberg has taken a positive view not only of critical historical research but also of philosophy and the natural sciences. In *What Is Man?* (1962; Eng. ed. 1970), he develops the question of God out of a searching philosophical analysis of anthropology. It is through an "openness to the world," a sense of limitlessness and restlessness, that humankind is drawn to the question of God. And it is radical historicity, not nature, that distinguishes the human from other forms of life. According to Pannenberg, it is in the history of Israel that history in this true sense is first experienced. Historical life entails the search for the meaning of the temporal process and thus raises the question of God.

For Pannenberg revelation is not esoteric knowledge conveyed from on high. It is the self-disclosure of God *in* history. Revelation is historical event interpreted as "act of God." Since all history is interpreted history, the biblical interpretation of the revelatory meaning of history is not distinct from any other history in this respect. Revelatory history, too, must be open to the judgment of critical history. Christianity must defend its historical claims on historical grounds. Reversing a trend in modern Protestant theology, Pannenberg defends the resurrection of Jesus Christ as an objective historical event. Historiography must not rule out any possibility a priori, and Pannenberg argues that the evidence of the appearances of Christ and the empty tomb give sufficient reason to accept the Resurrection as the most probable explanation of the facts.

Pannenberg sees the Resurrection as the fulfillment of the apocalyptic expectation of Israel and the vindication of Jesus' claim that the fate of individuals in the coming eschatological judgment and kingdom would be determined by their relation to him and his message. The Resurrection, then, is a "foretaste" of the end of history and focal point of God's self-revelation. God's final disclosure of glory, justice, and constancy are already anticipated in Jesus Christ. The Resurrection also is a sign of the openness of history and the future of God. God's eternity does not imply a timelessness and impassability. One can conceive of a genuine openness and futurity in God's relation to the world, as in Hegel, without sacrificing God's constancy and sovereignty. Pannenberg's theology is radically future-oriented and eschatological. For Pannenberg, however, the credibility of Christianity is predicated finally on what we know about Jesus. Therefore he advocates a "Christology from below," one arising from the historical Jesus, his message and fate, to a recognition of his divinity, seen in his perfect communion with and openness toward God the Father and vindicated in the Resurrection.

Pannenberg's principal contribution is his re-engagement of theology with critical history, philosophy, natural science, and culture generally. While his prolific writings have moved theological discussion ahead on many fronts, his work leaves questions requiring further elucidation. His objective historical claims for revelation and his claims regarding Jesus' message and life provoke dissent from some theologians and NT scholars, as does his ambiguity regarding the status of theological discourse. Some consider the epistemological and metaphysical grounding of his theology as needing a greater systematic elaboration. Among Pannenberg's other writings, available in English, are *Jesus: God and Man* (1968), *Basic Questions in Theology,* vols. I–III (1970–73), *Theology and the Kingdom of God* (1969), *The Idea of God and Human Freedom* (1973), *Theology and the Philosophy of Science* (1976), *Faith and Reality* (1977), *Ethics* (1981), and *Anthropology in Theological Perspective* (1985).

J.L.

**PANTHEISM.** Religious, philosophical doctrine that identifies the world with God and God with the world. As a result the IMMANENCE of God is stressed and the idea of TRANSCENDENCE negated.

Platonic thought, with its emphasis on the idea as the real, has a tendency toward pantheism. It is a monistic system within which evil becomes no more than the other face of good or is viewed as illusory. Spinoza enunciated this philosophy in the West in the eighteenth century, affirming that God is not only the cause of the world but is also to be identified with the world. Idealistic thought has affinities with pantheism, as has transcendentalism, the New England nineteenth-century form of German idealism. Although "immanentism" is not strictly pantheistic (it could allow for the transcendence of God), the stress is on the subjective existence of God in the world. Pantheism takes away the distinctiveness of God, the "otherness" that has been characteristic of the understanding of God in Western religions. Bergson's idea of creative evolution is not completely pantheistic. Teilhard de Chardin coined the word PANENTHEISM to indicate his understanding that although God has objective reality, God is also completely existent within the created world.

I.C.

**PANTOKRATOR.** A Greek term meaning "The Almighty," applied to Jesus Christ in Byzantine times. Many paintings show Jesus as lifted up high above the earth, moon, and stars as Lord of all. The term shows Christ as universal ruler and source of the authority of the church and the state.          J.C.

**PAPACY.** *See* POPE.

**PAPIAS** (about A.D. 60–130). Bishop of Hierapolis in Asia Minor, whose chief literary credit is his *Exposition of the Lord's Oracles* in five books, but only fragments remain, mainly in Eusebius' *Church History*. His testimony to the apostolic authorship of the Gospels is the subject of much dispute, and his worth as a historical source has been in contention since Eusebius' day. The latter had a low view of Papias' intelligence on account of his millenarian beliefs, which Eusebius discredited. More recently Papias is believed to be reacting to MARCION, a teacher who championed the Gospel of Luke. Papias evidently wanted to assert the authority of the other three Gospels as emanating from the apostles or their close followers.          R.M.

**PAPYRUS.** A species of reed, grown particularly in the Nile Delta marshes but also in parts of Palestine.

Courtesy of the Department of Rare Books and Special Collections, The University of Michigan Library

*Papyrus leaves of the Pauline Epistles dating from about* A.D. 300. *On the left is Hebrews 9:10-16, and on the right is Hebrews 9:18-26.*

As a plant it grows ten to fifteen feet high. When cut the stem is divided into sections and two layers are formed running crosswise to form a surface that is polished smooth. The sheets are stuck together to make a roll or scroll. The two sides are usable for writing purposes; the smoother side called recto, the obverse side verso.

Papyrus became the original writing material for Christian purposes, though it lacked convenience and made quick reference to selected passages a difficulty, since one had to unwind the scroll to find a chosen place. It was, however, relatively inexpensive, as we see from wide margins left and large unwritten areas of surviving documents. The ink used for writing lacked an acid base, and so the script could be erased by a sponge and a papyrus used afresh. Indentations made by the stylus, itself formed from a papyrus reed sharpened to a point, remained. In that case, the papyrus was discarded, or if there was urgent need, reused. Thus we have extant specimens of a palimpsest (writing material on which the earlier writing, now erased, is just visible, underneath a second set of letters).

From the Hellenistic period thousands of papyri have survived in the sands of Egypt, and have been collected, edited, and published in translation, notably by G. Milligan. (*See* WRITING AND WRITING MATERIALS.)                                                    R.M.

**PARABLE.** A variety of types of literature are designated *mashal* in the Hebrew Bible. Proverbs or aphorisms translate *meshalim* (Ezek. 12:21-23; riddles or dark sayings, Ps. 78:2); bywords (terms of derision or contempt, Jer. 24:9); taunt songs (Mic. 2:4; Isa. 14:3-6). Job's complaint is refered to as a *mashal:* the English rendering "discourse" shows how far removed is the common view concerning the identification of "a parable" (Job 27:1; 29:1).

Biblical Hebrew lacked the linguistic nuances available to the Greek OT translators so that *parabolē* could distinguish with greater precision a particular literary type. The English language provides the same advantage. However, the writers of the Synoptic Gospels do not adhere to such niceties of speech. Twenty-two sayings of Jesus are called parables. Four of these are in words attributed to Jesus—Mark 4:11; 4:30; 13:28; Luke 4:23. Of these four parables, two are not of the same type: Mark 13:28, "lesson"; Luke 4:23, "proverb."

Modern scholars distinguish the typical parable from (a) a metaphor, (b) a simile, (c) a parabolic saying or similitude, and (d) an example story. For a greater appreciation of the parable as a teaching instrument, particularly as used by Jesus, one may focus on the parables in the narrower sense, but in order to perceive the characteristic manner of Jesus' thought, the full range of Jesus' figurative speech needs to be examined. An example of a simple metaphor found in the Gospels is Luke 13:32, where Jesus said "go tell that fox" (Herod Antipas); also Mark 11:17, Jesus likens the Temple to "a den of robbers." An example of a simile is found in Luke 22:31. Jesus warns Peter that Satan would have him to sift him *like* wheat. A few of the many parabolic sayings or similitudes in the Gospels may be cited: Luke 4:23, "physician, heal yourself!"; Matthew 5:14, "a city set on a hill"; Matthew 7:17-19, "a tree and its fruits." Features of the "example story" come closest to those of the parable (in the narrow sense), but the former lack the indirect reference typical of the parable type. For example, in the story of the Pharisee and the publican in Luke 18:9-14, the attitudes of the two men are directly portrayed, one is not led by the story to imagine a situation analogous to, but outside of, its world of thought.

With these distinctions in mind, we may define a parable as an extended metaphor (drawn from nature; common, human experience; or the Scriptures) that may or may not be a free invention, but that in any case describes a situation analogous to "real life" (it *might* have happened). The story line of the parable arrests the hearer with the aptness or strangeness of the analogy, and leaves the mind in sufficient doubt as to its application, thus actively directing the person or group addressed to the storyteller's intended meaning. The Synoptic Gospels contain many parables of Jesus that evidence his masterful use of this form of teaching.

From earliest times the aptness of Jesus' parables was perceived by his followers, and they were appropriated to meet the needs of particular Christian communities. These developments are evidenced in the forms and settings of the parables in Mark, Matthew, and Luke. (The Gospel of John does not contain "parables" so defined.) In some of the synoptic parables, three levels of meaning may be discerned. There is, first of all, the parables' original setting-in-life, reporting the situation occasioning the parable as spoken by Jesus to specific groups: his disciples, opponents, or a crowd of listeners. Second, the texts of some of Jesus' parables may reflect their application to various situations facing his followers after Easter and before the composition of the Gospels. And, finally, one may locate in some of the parables the particular concerns of each of the evangelists by observing their selection, placement, and interpretation of the parables of Jesus. Thus one may speak of the parables of the Gospels as "thrice-told tales."

Brief notice may be taken of certain modifications of Jesus' parables during the period of their oral transmission and/or when they were given their canonical shape by the evangelists. A change of audience may be seen to alter the meaning of a parable (compare Matt. 18:12-14 and Luke 15:1-7). Allegorical interpretations of a whole or detail may be secondary (compare Mark 4:13-20 and parallels; Matt. 13:36-43; also Matt. 22:1-14. [note 22:7, a post A.D. 70 gloss?]; see Luke 14:16-24 [v. 21-23, the second invitation, a Lukan addition?]). While it is a doubtful principle to attribute every evidence of allegory to early Christian exegesis, the eschatological parables of Jesus were especially susceptible to reinterpretation: some having a reference to the crisis precipitated by his ministry were applied to the imminent crisis of his return in glory (Matt. 28:14-30; compare Luke 19:12-27).

While signs of the transformation of the parabolic tradition of the Gospels are demonstrable, it may be concluded that the main "parables," as defined above, are distinctive, and as creations of Jesus are revelatory of his mind and message. They are of incomparable importance for knowledge of the historical Jesus.

Perhaps one may say that the parables of the Gospels, both for Jesus and his followers, are intended to clarify the nature of the coming Kingdom of God, to impress upon all who reflect upon them the original thoughts of Jesus concerning this kingdom, and to stir them to make the appropriate resolves and responses.                                                            J.L.P.

**PARACLETE.** The Greek word *parakletos* belongs to the world of the law court, and is variously rendered as "counsel for the defense, advocate, intercessor." It belongs primarily to the vocabulary of the Fourth Gospel (John 14:16, 26; 15:26; 16:7), with the only remaining reference being found in I John 2:1. There are two specific uses of the term. (1) In I John 2:1 Jesus Christ is given this title as the one who represents the church in the heavenly court as its advocate, a theme elaborated in the intercessory prayer of John 17. The same title is known by inference in John 14:16, where Jesus is clearly both claiming to be the disciples' helper and promising to give them "another Counselor" (NIV), the HOLY SPIRIT. (2) The balance of the NT texts that use the term *parakletos* refer to the ministry of the Spirit, who fulfills a manifold function as Christ's agent in the church and the world. Specifically the Spirit leads into truth, exposing human folly and need, and the Spirit strengthens believers in time of testing. More centrally to Johannine thought, the paraclete acts as Christ's *alter ego*, making up for the absence of the exalted Lord by becoming to the church after the Ascension all that the historical Jesus had been to the disciples while he was on earth.

R.M.

**PARADISE.** Literally implying a park, the Persian loanword "paradise" is linked in both Jewish and Christian thought with the seat of God's presence, where there is bliss and untroubled serenity such as the ancients conceived in a garden (EDEN) of delight (see Gen. 2:8-17 for the classic description, as well as Song of S. 4:13 and Ezek. 31:1-9, 16-18; Ezek. 28:11-14 is sometimes related to this scene).

The parkland thus takes on the meaning of the home of the blessed dead in Jewish apocalyptic writings in contrast to GEHENNA, a place of torment for the evildoer, based on a refuse area in the Hinnom Valley in Jerusalem.

"Paradise" occurs three times in the NT. (1) Luke 23:43, which is Jesus' promise to the penitent thief on the cross: "Today you will be with me in Paradise." Jewish cosmology divided the heavenly world into two sections: the lower region of paradise was a temporary resting place prior to the Resurrection; the upper part was to be peopled after the Resurrection as an eternal home. So Jesus' promise relates to the lower compartment. (2) In II Corinthians 12:3, "caught up into Paradise" refers to Paul's out-of-the-body rapture, when in ecstasy he visited the heavenly regions. The background here is the Jewish mystical tradition that thought of Israel's great people as ascending to God's presence. (3) Revelation 2:7 contains descriptions modeled on Genesis 2, since the "tree of life" is evidently the same in both cases (see Rev. 22:2). In Christian expectation and hymnody the yearning for paradise is tantamount to the soul's desire to be at rest in the city of God. This is likened to paradise restored, as Revelation 21–22 are full of echoes in Jewish apocalyptic for a blissful existence in the divine presence.

R.M.

**PARADOX.** That state of affairs in which mutually contradictory predicates are ascribed to the same subject, yet it is felt that in spite of the contradiction, both predicates must be so ascribed. Paradox is therefore often defined as an apparent contradiction. Paradoxes occur in many fields, and philosophers have long been aware of them. The logical enigmas known as the paradoxes of Zeno were much discussed in ancient times, and only in recent decades have they been solved (if indeed they have been solved). Another paradox often mentioned is the fact that in modern physics light can be considered as wave-motion or as a stream of particles. Here, however, we are concerned with paradox in theology and philosophy of religion. God is said to be transcendent and immanent, the most distant and the nearest, and so on. Jesus Christ is claimed to be truly and fully God, and truly and fully human. Can such paradoxes be justified, or do they point to a fundamental contradiction and incoherence in the whole enterprise of God-talk?

The notion of paradox is associated especially with KIERKEGAARD. He developed it in opposition to the panlogism of HEGEL. Hegel was as much aware as Kierkegaard of the dialectical clash of opposites in human experience, but he believed that reason has the capacity for reconciling such opposites in a higher synthesis. This conviction underlies the triadic structure of the whole Hegelian system. Kierkegaard did not share this confidence in the omnicompetence of reason. There are situations where, as he expresses it, reason "makes a collision," that is to say, it strikes against something that it cannot penetrate or analyze. When that happens, there are two possibilities. Either one takes offense, and turns away from the irrational absurd; or one takes the LEAP OF FAITH, leaping ahead of reason to embrace the irresoluble paradox. The "absolute paradox" for Kierkegaard was the doctrine of the God-man, Christ. There is no way reason can explain it. So either there is offense, or faith is a paradox. Many critics have thought that Kierkegaard's advocacy of paradox is too arbitrary and his attitude too much one of "take it or leave it!"

Long before Kierkegaard, Nicholas of Cusa had taught that God is the coincidence of opposites (*coincidentia oppositorum*), but he had defended this teaching by elaborate arguments that appealed to the logic of infinity in mathematics. In his treatment of infinite quantities, the mathematician employs a logic that contradicts the logic of everyday discourse. May it not be that a similar contradiction must arise when one speaks of the infinite being of God?

More recently, Donald Baillie has given an interesting defense of paradox. He points out that there is no way in which the curved surface of the earth can be projected upon a flat piece of paper without distortion—in other words, there can be no map that accurately shows the earth's surface, just as, presumably, there is no language that accurately describes God. Some map projections distort areas, while preserving shapes; others distort shapes, but correctly represent relative areas. It is impossible to combine these maps in one; they can only lie side by side, but then each can correct the other and lead to a better understanding than a merely one-sided representation. J.M.

**PARAN.** The name given to the region surrounding Kadesh (Num. 13:26), frequently called the Wilderness of Paran, encompassing the land of the southern Negeb of Palestine and the northern reaches of the Sinaitic peninsula. Kadesh (Kadesh-barnea in Deuteronomy), a cult center for some elements of the later Israelite tribal federation, has been worked into the standardized history of the Exodus as a way station (of forty years' duration, see Deut. 1:1-3) of all Israel in its journey from Egypt to Canaan. Paran, in this outline, was the scene of a nomadic existence after the events that had taken place at Mount Sinai, and from it the land of Canaan was spied out (Num. 13:1-3). The El-paran of Genesis 14:6 is probably Elath, on the border of Paran; this same verse indicates that Mount Seir of Edom is included in the area of Paran. In Deuteronomy 33:2 Sinai, Seir, and Mount Paran appear as three names for the same place, probably reflecting the tradition of a more northern location of Mount Sinai. B.V.

**PARAPSYCHOLOGY.** See EXTRASENSORY PERCEPTION.

**PARCHMENT.** The name is taken from the Latin *pergamena*, itself derived from the city of Pergamum, where, tradition has it, the WRITING material was invented by King Eumenes II (197–158 B.C.). The material used is that of animal skin, which is shaved, tanned, and scraped to make a smooth surface. The two sides are available for use, with the hair side preferred by the rabbis who copied the sacred books of Judaism onto this substance. It is the chief material on which the Dead Sea Scrolls were recorded. R.M.

**PARDON.** See FORGIVENESS.

**PARISH.** A definite territorial district served by a Roman Catholic church, the pastor of which is in charge of all spiritual work with the faithful. In Protestant usage it refers to the people within a territory who attend a specific church. Most people belong to parishes near their homes. J.C.

**PARK, JOHN EDGAR** (1879–1956). Pastor, hymn writer, educator. John Edgar Park was born on March 7 in Belfast, Ireland. He was educated at New College, Edinburgh, the Royal University of Dublin, and later in the United States at Princeton Theological Seminary. He pastored churches in New York and Massachusetts and in 1926 was made president of Wheaton College, Norton, Massachusetts. He wrote the text of the hymns "We Would See Jesus" and "Lo, His Star Is Shining." Park died in Chicago, Illinois, on March 4. R.H.

**PARKER, THEODORE** (1810–60). Unitarian theologian and leader of TRANSCENDENTALISM. He was born on August 24 in Lexington, Massachusetts, the son of John and Hannah Stearns Parker. Largely self-educated, he entered Harvard Divinity School and graduated in 1836. On April 20, 1837, he married Lydia Cabot and on June 21, was ordained to the West Roxbury Congregational Church, which he served until 1845.

His May 19, 1841, ordination sermon, "The Transient and Permanent in Christianity," reflecting acceptance of German critical studies, scandalized Christians of every stripe, including conservative Unitarians. Parker asserted that Christianity did not depend on the actual existence of Christ at all. His beliefs were further elaborated in a series of lectures (1841–42) published as *A Discourse of Matters Pertaining to Religion*. Parker was a regular member of the Transcendental Club. In 1845 Parker became pastor of the new Twenty-eighth Congregational Society of Boston, where he could freely expound his views on abolition, war, divorce, temperance, prisons, and human rights. N.H.

**PAROUSIA.** The Greek term *parousia*, literally "presence" or "arrival," used in first-century literature of the visit of an important dignitary to a city or land, and is usually translated as "coming." A religious meaning in Greco-Roman religion has to be noted, as when *parousia* speaks of an occasion when a god was revealed in glory or a blaze of light to devotees. The NT usage combines these two nuances with descriptions of the future event at which Jesus Christ will come from the Father's presence to set up God's kingdom, judge the world in righteousness, and show himself in glory (see Matt. 24:3, 27; I Cor. 15:23-25).

The exact time of this "coming of Christ"—Hebrews 9:28 is the only place to mention a "second" coming—is not known (Matt. 24:36), and NT Christians are warned to be ready for it whenever it may occur (Matt. 24:36-44) and to wait with vigilance (Mark 13:35-37) and patience (James 5:7-8) for its arrival. Evidently many Christians in NT times looked for Christ's *Parousia* in their lifetime (I Thess. 5:1-11; compare II Thess. 2:1-12, which corrects this impression), but in later experience Paul reckons with the possibility of having to die before the *Parousia* (II Cor. 5:1-10; Phil. 1:21-23). The "delay of the *parousia*"—in that Christ did not return in glory before the death of the Christians in the first and second generations—posed a threat to Christian hope, and the later NT documents show how the church sought to reply to denials that Jesus would ever return (II Pet. 3:3-5). The Johannine literature offers a more thought-out response in the teaching that the Paraclete, the Holy Spirit, has already come to make Jesus' presence real to believers. The hope of a glorious *Parousia* was still retained and found a place in the early creeds, for example, "from thence he shall come to judge the living and the dead" (the Apostles' Creed, dated about A.D. 150). (*See also* ESCHATOLOGY.)                                            R.M.

**PARSIS.** Members of the ZOROASTRIAN community in India, also commonly written Parsees, literally "Persians." This community, centered in Bombay, numbers no more than 100,000 but has had considerable influence in modern India, owing to the comparative wealth, high educational standards, and public activity of its constituents.          R.E.

**PARTHENOS.** A Greek noun rendered "maiden" or "virgin," according to context. The original sense of *parthenos* seems to be a young woman of marriageable age, and as virginity was celebrated in the Greek pantheon it is only to be expected that Artemis (also called Diana by the Romans) should be known as Parthenos, a virgin goddess.

The OT background of the word is found in *bethulah,* meaning a maiden, often unmarried, and also applied figuratively to Israel (Amos 5:2; Jer. 18:13; 31:4, 21) or Jerusalem (Lam. 1:15; 2:13). The other Hebrew term, *almah,* also meaning "a young woman" before her marriage and childbearing, is rendered by *parthenos* in two key places (Gen. 24:13; Isa. 7:14). Here the word enters the NT vocabulary in reference to Mary, a virgin at the time Jesus was conceived, according to Matthew 1:20-24. Other NT references are in I Corinthians 7, used of wives who retained a celibate relationship to their spouses; and in II Corinthians 11:2 and Revelation 14:4 "virgin" is used of the church. (*See also* VIRGIN BIRTH.)
                                                           R.M.

**PARTHIANS.** The sole reference to the inhabitants of Parthia is in Acts 2:9, but there are possible allusions in Revelation 6:2; 9:14ff.; and 16:12, because of the cultural and geographical significance of these verses. The Parthians were an Iranian tribe dwelling in a region southeast of the Caspian Sea, corresponding to the modern province of Khorasan in Iran. The tribes revolted against the Persians in 521 B.C., but fell under the sway of Alexander the Great and his Seleucid successors. Under the energetic ruler Arsaces I (250–248 B.C.), they achieved some independence, and with a later ruler, Mithridates I (171–138 B.C.), a Parthian empire came into existence, extending from the Caspian Sea to the Persian Gulf, with its western boundary the river Euphrates. Hence the allusions in Revelation given above.

Strife with the Romans followed in their history, and in 40–37 B.C. the Parthians overran Asia Minor and Syria and took Jerusalem, installing Antigonus, the last of the Hasmonean rulers, on the throne. The Parthian tribes were a continual thorn in the side of the Romans, and Nero's rumored suicide gave rise to the belief that he was not in fact dead but had escaped to Parthia, from where he would return at the head of Parthian armies.                                             R.M.

**PARTITION, MIDDLE WALL OF.** According to Josephus in both *Antiquities* (5) and *The Jewish War* (5) a barrier separated the Court of Women from the Court of the Gentiles in the first-century Jerusalem Temple. An inscription, unearthed in 1871 by M. Clermont-Ganneau, was posted on this balustrade. It read: "No man of another race [other than Jewish] is to enter within the fence and enclosure around the Temple. Whoever is caught will have only himself to thank for the death which follows." This fence is called by a term that shows the seriousness of any contemplated trespass, a fear illustrated by Acts 21:27-29. The precise phrase "middle wall of partition" is taken from Ephesians 2:14 (KJV), which is taken by some scholars to refer to this Temple fence. The text in Ephesians will then be using the fall of Jerusalem in A.D. 70 and the ruin of the Temple as a sign, whether anticipated or fulfilled, of the end of Jewish restrictions on access to God and the opening of the door to the Gentiles, who may now gain entrée into the divine presence (Eph. 2:11-13).      R.M.

**PASCAL, BLAISE** (1623–62). French mathematician, physicist, and philosopher of religion, with associations with JANSENISM. His religious philosophy is contained mainly in the collection of fragments known as the *Pensées,* put together at the time of his death. He upheld the autonomy of faith and the importance of the will and the emotions in religion, in opposition to the strict intellectualism of DESCARTES. His position can be summarized in the famous fragment that he carried around close to his heart: "God of Abraham, God of Isaac, God of Jacob, not the God of the philosophers and wise men." The philosopher might indeed prove the existence of God, but this brought no relation to the reality of God. Indeed, such proofs might even weaken faith, for even if they were persuasive at one moment, an hour later one might begin to doubt whether one had been deceived. Faith is altogether a more inward and passionate matter than believing an intellectual demonstration. In an often quoted passage, he compares it to a wager. He advises his readers to wager that God exists—if they win, they win everything, and if they lose, they lose nothing.

It would be wrong, however, to think that a man with Pascal's interest in logic and science became anti-intellectual when he discussed religion. Rather, he was pleading for a broader epistemology than was offered by a narrow RATIONALISM: We should be guided not just by logic but by spiritual intuition. We know the truth not only by the reason but also by the heart. The heart has its reasons, which are unknown to reason. This religious faith, which turned away from the abstract and the rational, found its concrete center in an immediate apprehension of Jesus Christ. He becomes the clue to all truth. "Jesus Christ is the object of all and the center to which everything tends. Whoever knows him knows the reason for everything." This is not just empty rhetoric, but depends on a view of humanity as placed midway between nothing and infinity, and so able to grasp both intuitively. Though an important philosopher of religion in his own right, Pascal can also be seen as a forerunner of KIERKEGAARD and Christian EXISTENTIALISM.                                J.M.

**PASCHAL.** Pertaining to the festival of the Resurrection—EASTER. The term is derived from *Pesakh,* the Hebrew for the feast of Passover. In the Roman church, Paschal time extends for fifty-six days, from Holy Saturday to the Sunday after Whitsunday. It is the period of rejoicing with the risen Christ.                                J.C.

**PASCHASIUS RADBERTUS** (about 790–865). Abbot of the French Benedictine monastery at Corbie, who gave the earliest known formulation of TRANSUBSTANTIATION. Although he was chosen abbot in 843, he preferred to study and soon resigned. In 831 he published *De corpore et sanguine Domini* (*The Body and Blood of the Lord*), maintaining that when the priest celebrates mass and consecrates the bread and wine, they are changed into the Body and Blood of Christ—for believers. He regarded this as a creative act of God through the priest. While the change was invisible (because the bread and wine retained their appearances), substantially and metaphysically

change took place. Although the term "transubstantiation" was not used, Radbertus wrote about the bread changing into a lamb and spoke of the REAL PRESENCE as the flesh born of Mary.

Long theological controversies followed. Rabanus Maurus, abbot at Fulda, supported Radbertus' view but said there was no absolute identity between the sacramental and historical Christ. A fellow monk at Corbie, Ratramnus, opposed Radbertus, saying no real change occurs in the elements, as the sacraments are symbols and occasions for God to act spiritually in believers. The controversies were not settled until the Fourth Lateran Council (1215) dogmatized transubstantiation.                                C.M.

**PASSION.** *See* CRUCIFIXION.

**PASSIONISTS.** Name given the congregation of Barefoot Clerks of the Most Holy Cross and Passion of Our Lord Jesus Christ, an order founded in 1720 by St. Paul of the Cross. It aims to keep the memory of Christ's sufferings and death on the cross alive in human memory.                                J.C.

**PASSION SUNDAY.** Traditionally the Sunday in LENT before Palm Sunday, marking the beginning of the two-week season of Passiontide. In the *Lutheran Book of Worship* (1978), Palm Sunday is called the Sunday of the Passion. The theme of Passion Sunday is the suffering of Christ on our behalf.                                J.C.

**PASSIONTIDE.** The last two weeks of LENT. The Sunday before Palm Sunday traditionally is called Passion Sunday. Passiontide would include Passion Sunday and the week following, plus Palm Sunday and Holy Week, with the observance of Maundy Thursday, Good Friday, and Holy Saturday, and ending at dawn on Easter Sunday.                                J.C.

**PASSION WEEK.** The final week of LENT, from Palm Sunday through Holy Saturday. The Holy Communion on Palm Sunday begins the reading of the Passion of Christ. Throughout Holy Week the Passion narratives are read, and thoughts are turned to the sufferings of Christ, who died for the sins of the world.                                J.C.

**PASSOVER.** *In the Old Testament.* The spring festival of freedom, celebrated by Jews in Israel and Reform Jews for seven days and by Orthodox and Reform Jews outside Israel for eight days. It commemorates the Exodus of the Israelites from Egypt. The first and last days are considered a full festival on which work is prohibited, while on the intermediate days work is permitted.

One biblical name of the holy day is "the feast of the passover" (Exod. 34:25). God said, ". . . I will pass over you, and no plague shall fall upon you to destroy you, while I smite the land of Egypt" (Exod. 12:13). Another name is "the feast of unleavened bread" (Exod. 23:15; Lev. 23:6; Deut. 16:16). *Pesakh,* the Hebrew name of the festival, refers to the paschal lamb, offered as a sacrifice on the eve of the feast (the 14th day of the Hebrew month of Nisan) in Temple times. It was eaten in family groups after having been roasted whole (Exod. 12:1-28, 43-49; Deut. 16:1-8). (Samaritan families to this day roast and eat lambs on Mount Gerizim.)

The Passover rites were divinely ordained as a permanent reminder of God's deliverance of the people from Egyptian slavery. The deliverance from Egypt, however, is more than physical freedom for the Jewish people; more important, it is spiritual freedom. God's act was designed to free the Jews from all heathen influences and to consecrate them to the service of God. That is why seven weeks after Passover, the holy day that commemorates the receiving of the Ten Commandments is celebrated (Shavuot).

Numerous biblical passages set out the observance and laws of Passover. It is described as a festival to be observed "throughout your generations" (Exod. 12:14). All leaven—a substance that causes food to ferment—is prohibited, and only unleavened bread is eaten during the entire festival, in accordance with God's command in the Bible; "Seven days shall ye eat unleavened bread; . . . the first day ye shall put away leaven out of your houses" (Exod. 12:15 KJV). The prohibition against leaven applies to the fermented products of wheat, barley, oats, and rye, and to the use of any foods containing these or which are likely to become fermented. Some scholars say that leaven is the symbol of corruption, passion, and sin. Current practice among ASHKENAZIM Jews is to prohibit the eating of rice, peas, and all kinds of beans; SEPHARDIM Jews permit these. The duty to eat *matzah* (the unleavened bread) is binding on the first night of Passover, although the partaking of leaven is forbidden throughout the festival.

As a reminder that the Lord passed over the houses of the children of Israel (Exod. 12:27) and spared their eldest sons on the eve of Passover, when the firstborn of the Egyptians were slain, the fourteenth day of Nisan is observed as a fast day for the firstborn sons of Jewish families.

The SEDER, an elaborate ritual feast, takes place on the first two nights of Passover (the first night, for Reform Jews). Its purpose is to awaken hope for the final redemption. The ceremony is based on the injunction in the Bible to parents to inform their children of the deliverance from Egypt: "And thou shalt tell thy children in that day, saying, It is because of that which the Lord did for me when I came forth out of Egypt" (Exod. 13:8).

The Seder dramatizes the only event in recorded history in which the Lord freed an entire people. Through rituals, questions, prayers, discussions, special foods, wine, and song, the Exodus is reenacted and its meaning probed. On the table a platter includes: (1) a roasted egg, symbolizing the festival

offering; (2) a roasted bone, commemorating the paschal lamb; (3) bitter herbs, as a reminder of the suffering of the slaves in Egypt; (4) a green vegetable, symbolizing renewal; (5) a mixture of nuts, wine, cinnamon, and the like, as a reminder of the bricks and mortar the slaves were compelled to make; and (6) salt water, signifying tears. Three matzoth (unleavened bread) are on another dish. Those around the table sit in a reclining position, as a sign of freedom.

The HAGGADAH is the script that sets forth the order and narrative of the Seder service. The youngest child asks four questions, and the story unfolds through the answers and the dramatization. Four cups of wine are drunk, corresponding to the four expressions of redemption in the book of Exodus. Elijah, the herald of the Messiah, is welcomed with his cup of wine (Mal. 3:23, the Hebrew Bible).

All Jews in every generation are commanded to regard themselves as having been personally freed from Egypt. They count as the first of the Ten Commandments, "I am the Lord thy God who brought thee out of the land of Egypt, out of the house of bondage." Passover is also a harvest festival and one of the three pilgrimage festivals, the other two being SHAVUOT (Feast of Weeks) and SUKKOT (Feast of Booths).                                                          L.K.

*In the New Testament.* In the first Christian century, during the life of Jesus and the period of the apostolic church in Jerusalem (to the period A.D. 66–70), so many pilgrims from the Jewish DIASPORA came to Jerusalem that only the ritual slaughter of lambs took place in the Temple courts. Then blood was sprinkled on the altar, and the meal was celebrated in each devout Jew's home or hired lodging. Jesus observed three Passovers in Jerusalem according to John's Gospel, but only one (the occasion of his passion and death) according to Matthew, Mark, and Luke, the Synoptic Gospels. Much messianic speculation surrounded Passover at the time, and many believed the Messiah would come during Passover night. Those who became Christians shared in this eschatological hope and saw the celebration of the Last Supper, Jesus' death on the cross, and the Resurrection as God's promised deliverance—a new exodus producing a new Israel. As the angel of death "passed over" the Israelites marked by the blood of the lamb, even so Christians, the new Israel, are freed from sin, death, and hell by the blood of Jesus Christ, the Lamb of God.

Passover language, ritual, and tradition surround the passion story in the Gospels. The Synoptic Gospels clearly state that the LAST SUPPER was a Passover (Mark 14:1 ff; Matt. 26:2 ff. Luke 22:1 ff.), while the Fourth Gospel portrays Jesus' death on the cross as taking place while the Passover lambs were being slaughtered (John 13:1; 19:31), so the Last Supper could not have been a Passover according to John. Rather, Jesus' death on "the day of preparation," in John, implies that in that year, the Passover fell on a Sabbath (John 19:31). Nonetheless, all the Gospel accounts strongly suggest that the Lord's Supper is a reinterpretation of the Passover meal and tradition. As the original Hebrew meal is a celebration of liberation from physical and spiritual bondage, so too, the Christian Lord's Supper is a celebration of the freedom—and a reception of the grace that gives that freedom—that Christ died to make available to everyone who has faith.     J.C.

**PASTOR.** The English term is borrowed directly from the Latin, where it denotes "shepherd," and it comes over into Christian usage chiefly to describe one of the traditional roles performed by a minister or the clergy. The OT has a limited number of references to pastor(s), confined to the book of Jeremiah and used mainly of the rulers of Israel who are charged with shepherding God's people (Jer. 23).

The word is found only once in the NT (Eph. 4:11), where it is used in conjunction with Christian leaders in their capacity as teachers of the congregation. The same role, however, is implied in the verb "to feed" sheep (as in John 21:15) and to act as a shepherd (I Pet. 5:2). Both verses look back to the model of Christ as the Good Shepherd (John 10:1-18) and pastor of his church, a motif that found its way into early Christian literature and epigraphy. No image in Christian art is more appealing than the depiction of Christ as one who tends his flock, a role that the early Christians found to be anticipated in the OT (Isa. 40:11).     R.M.

**PASTORAL EPISTLES.** This name designates the letters attributed to PAUL and addressed to TIMOTHY and TITUS. The term was first used by P. Anton of Halle, Germany, in 1726 on the supposition that they appeared to him to be written by a pastor for fellow pastors. This assessment is too narrow, however, since there is much in these three letters applicable to congregational life, polity, and worship. The body of letters under this title may be rightly claimed as "pastoral" in another, more satisfactory, way. They provide the reader with insight into Paul's role—whether direct or as understood by his followers—as a pastor to pastors, a leader who provided for continuing leadership in the churches. It is this feature that makes these short letters of special value.

*Authorship and Setting.* These two matters are interwoven. On face value the letters are addressed to Paul's faithful travel-companions Timothy and Titus, according to the Acts of the Apostles, who have been allotted special spheres of labor: Timothy in the Macedonian churches and Titus in the church at Corinth. It is not surprising that both men received, according to these letters, positions of pastoral leadership in the Pauline churches, at Ephesus and Crete respectively, and that Paul would wish to write to them in a way that fitted their needs as church

"officials," offering directives for the congregations on such matters as controlling, guiding, and instructing new members. False ideas had entered on the scene and are menacing, so the two pastors are called to be alert and active in repelling them.

Though these letters speak of Pauline themes such as justification, baptism, the Holy Spirit, and the call to newness of living, and they contain a number of personal names known to us from Acts and other Pauline letters (LUKE, MARK, AQUILA, PRISCILLA), doubts have been raised about two matters. One is the setting of these letters, traditionally placed at the close of Paul's ministry in Acts during his time in Rome. The other relates to whether Paul actually wrote these letters or whether a later writer employed Paul's name to give credibility and authority to what he put down by ascribing it to Paul, presumably believing that he was representing the apostle's mind for a later generation. An intermediate position, much ventilated in recent decades, is that a member of Paul's school used Paul's fragmentary materials, especially to do with travel plans and personalia (II Tim. 3:10-11; 4:9-18), around which he wove these letters to relate Paul's teaching as he understood it, to a fresh set of circumstances that arose after Paul's martyrdom in A.D. 65.

The reasons offered to deny these letters to Paul himself may now be given. (a) There is the presence of language, both in style and content, that stands at odds with what we find in the accepted letters of Paul. The Pastoral Epistles have about 360 words not found in the other Pauline letters. Some of these terms are well-known words, yet in these letters they carry a special meaning: "sober," "religious," "appearing." On the other side, key terms in letters such as I and II Corinthians and Galatians, such as "covenant," "righteousness by faith," "boast," are singularly missing. But this argument must not be overpressed, since the genre of these Pastorals, matching a special clientele and addressed to a particular situation, may explain the unusual vocabulary. Nonetheless it is a strange word list, and there are links with Jewish-Hellenistic moral philosophy.

The assessment of style is more problematic. Grammatical connectives (like the ever-present "and" {*kai*}), are used in a remarkable way in these letters, and there is a flatness to the writing when contrasted to Paul's earlier letters, which came out of the intense pastoral confrontations at Galatia, Philippi, or Corinth. And those local scenes may well explain the distinctiveness of the type of composition. On the other side, we still have to account for the heavy style, the insertion of hymnic and confessional passages (for example, I Tim. 3:16; II Tim. 2:11-13), and the recital of ethical lists of virtues and vices (I Tim. 1:9-10; 3:2-3; 6:11; Tit. 1:7-8) along with the lengthy regulations given to control the selection and appointment of church leaders.

Conscious of these objections, some scholars have submitted that the differences in style and content, including the variations of titles ascribed to Christ and the heavy emphasis on ethical seriousness, can all be put down to the use of a secretary whom Paul employed. Paul dictated the main themes to be inserted, but left it to his amanuensis-secretary to fill out the letter in the way he saw fit; hence the exceptional style and addition of non-Pauline language.

(b) The type of ministry outlined in these letters, notably at I Timothy 3, has been seen as pointing to a development of the Pauline model in a later decade. The role of presbyter-bishops, deacons, deaconesses, and others, along with teaching on ordination and credentials (I Tim. 4:14; II Tim. 1:6), and disciplinary measures taken against wayward elders (I Tim. 5:19), suggests a time when the church is moving to the rule of a single leader (monepiscopacy). On the other side, it has been argued that the model of ministry in these letters is based on the OT-Judaic pattern rather than the situation of an institutionalized church, which we see in I Clement (A.D. 95) and Ignatius (about A.D. 110).

(c) The false teaching opposed by the writer has similarly been interpreted in different ways. Some think of a Jewish GNOSTICISM that showed interest in myths and genealogies (I Tim. 1:4; compare 4:7; Tit. 3:9; II Tim. 4:4). Others recall how the Greek Corinthians denied the future resurrection (I Cor. 15:12) and find a parallel in II Timothy 2:18 as in the asceticism advocated in I Timothy 4:1-4 and suggest this points to Hellenistic influence. The Tübingen school confidently appealed to I Timothy 6:20 as a sign that the Pastorals were written to counteract the influence of MARCION (about A.D. 140), a teacher deemed heretical and who wrote a book titled *Antitheses*—"Contradictions"—the very term used in this text (I Tim. 6:20).

But it is extremely unlikely that the Pastorals are so late, since the false ideas are not those of the second century and share a more Jewish character. Decisively the persecutions envisioned in these letters predate the imperial policy of hostility that came on the scene first with the emperor DOMITIAN (about A.D. 90).

*Message.* The uncertainty of being able to locate these short letters in any given period makes interpretation hazardous. But certain broad conclusions are possible. These letters reflect the beginnings of the "institutional church," with a growing organizational fixity and accommodation to this world's life. Hence the ethical admonitions are slanted, and orders of ministry, with rudimentary creeds and confessions, are part of the church's essence. The writer sends a clear signal via Timothy and Titus to the churches to remain faithful to the Pauline gospel in the face of gnosticizing threats, and this call is one of holding fast to the "deposit" of apostolic teaching. Yet there is also a sensed danger of formalism and a dead orthodoxy. So the writer recalls Paul's teaching and warns against mere creedalism (II Tim. 3:5).                                                      R.M.

**PASTORAL THEOLOGY.** One of the classical divisions of theology, the others being biblical, historical, systematic, and ethical. It is the study of the practical work of the clergy and is frequently called practical theology, practice of ministry, or pastoral care, although there are distinctions among these terms. In small, traditional denominational or diocesan seminaries, one professor would instruct students in the various aspects of the ministerial role, such as counseling, catechetics, administration, liturgy, and preaching.

Advice about the pastoral office can be found in the writings of the rabbis, the apostle Paul, and such early Christian writers as Clement. The French term *curé* refers to the pastor as the one devoted to the cure or healing of souls. Pastoral concern in the first Christian generations was to help people prepare for the apocalypse. Later it was to enable them to face persecution and then to live in a Christian culture. During the Middle Ages the sacramental system functioned for pastoral care. The Renaissance and Reformation brought an emphasis on the individual in contrast to earlier generations who knew their identity through identification with a family or community. This perspective brought new emphases in pastoral care. With the eighteenth century came a dependence on rational approaches to meeting life questions, and in the twentieth century, being a Christian has become, almost everywhere, a voluntary commitment.

As the term suggests, pastoral care is based on theological understandings. The basic proclamation of the gospel comes to believers through the liturgy. Here they find themselves strengthened for the perplexities of life through the affirmations that God creates, redeems, and judges. Without this foundation, pastoral care would simply be personal comfort. An understanding of the connections among sin, repentance, forgiveness, and reconciliation, as the process of redemption, is the basis for the Christian effort to help people deal with guilt and broken relationships. The passion and resurrection of Christ form the basis for answering questions about suffering and death. Scripture and preaching, as well as hymnody that accurately reflects Scripture, are avenues for pastoral care. The sacraments of baptism and the Lord's Supper strengthen people with the assurance of the continuing presence of Christ. The minister presiding at these liturgies is functioning in pastoral care. The pastoral offices are opportunities for helping people bring Christian understandings to life situations, such as preparing for marriage and facing bereavement.

From here it is a short step to the counseling process itself. The minister is called upon to help people deal with sin and guilt, understanding these terms in psychological, sociological, and theological perspective. Whatever the techniques of counseling, there is need for people to feel the relief of confession before God, the assurance of forgiveness, and a beginning of the process of reconciliation. In some Christian groups this is a community action, as among the Society of the Brethren. The Roman Catholic Church frequently uses an office of reconciliation to deal positively with confession and penance. People need to feel assured that the pastor speaks a word from God that cleanses and restores. Healing of mind and body are interrelated.

The preparation for these liturgical actions is a teaching function. In reflecting on the marriage service with the pastor, the people become aware of the biblical references and the theological intentions. Talking with families about scriptural materials and hymns for a funeral helps them understand the biblical meanings of eternal life. Reconciliation requires reflection on the meaning of redemption. Healing is reflected in Gospel stories. Those who are being prepared for baptism (or parents and sponsors of infants) and those being prepared for confirmation, the adult confession of faith, will be reflecting on the renunciations to be made, the promises to be accepted, and the confession of faith to which they will give themselves. As pastor and confirmands talk together, a whole dimension of pastoral care is established. New relationships are formed with families, young people, and adults entering upon church membership. The biblical and theological understandings of baptism and confession of faith in Christ are the foundation on which such catechetical pastoral care takes place.

Pastor means "shepherd," and if the pastor is leader of all the people, then the nature of Christian community is an element in pastoral theology. Church administration is different from business administration. It is a stewardship process through which people live their commitment. At its best, it leads them to know that the church is called to witness to the gospel. It involves interrelationships among people on boards and committees. Evangelism and service are aspects of pastoral theology, involving lay and clerical members.

For this reason, pastoral theology must address the meaning of laity in the church as well as the meaning of clergy. The functions described here have seemed to be clerical. It is also clear that they could not be accomplished without cooperation from laity who also function pastorally. Pastoral theology is also concerned with the role of lay ministers, whether or not they have been "set apart" by ordination.

In the past theology rested on philosophical bases regarding the nature of human beings. Today it also includes insights from psychology, sociology, history, and the natural sciences. Important as these are in giving basic theory and useful methods, they must be evaluated in terms of the basic Christian understandings about God and human beings on which pastoral theology is based. Pastoral psychology is a tool for pastoral care, which is an expression of pastoral theology.                                    I.C.

**PATER NOSTER.** The LORD'S PRAYER, taken from the first two words in Latin ("Our Father"). The Latin term was once used to refer to a rosary or other aid to prayer, whether the prayer was the Lord's Prayer or some other prayer.

J.C.

*PATICCASAMUPPADA.* From the Pali words meaning "chain of causation," or, more literally, "dependent origination." In the philosophy of Buddhism, an important concept that interprets the continual arising *(samudaya)* and passing-away *(nirodha)* of all phenomena of the world, including separate human existence. The chain of causation is a never-ending process within "conditioned reality," for every cause has itself a prior cause. *Paticcasamuppada* was first applied in Buddhist texts to the understanding of human existence through a series of "links" in the chain of causation, which perceived the deep interrelationship of mental and physical existence. In the most common versions these *nidanas* or links are twelve in number, beginning with ignorance. Ignorance begets volition, volition consciousness, consciousness dependence on the physical sense, which leads to birth in this world and the production of further KARMA, which after the end of the chain in old age and death starts it all over again. In Mahayana philosophy "dependent origination" has developed further cosmic and metaphysical meaning.

R.E.

*PATIMOKKHA.* From the Pali language, meaning literally "that which binds." A part of the VINAYA PITAKA, the Buddhist book of monastic discipline, which give some 227 rules by which monks are expected to abide. These range from the citation of serious offences, such as theft and murder, for which a monk would be expelled from the order, to rules of etiquette and methods for handling disputes. These rules are formally read to monks at services held every new and full moon.                                    R.E.

**PATMOS.** An island in the present-day Sporades chain in the Greek Archipelago of the Mediterranean Sea, southwest off the coast of Turkey, west of Miletus. It is ten miles long by six miles wide, and notable for its rocky terrain. Here, according to Revelation 1:9, John, the author of the Apocalypse, was exiled for his faith. According to tradition he saw the visions of the book of REVELATION in a cave at Patmos, and the present monastery of St. John was built over the site in A.D. 1088. Originally a temple dedicated to the Greek goddess Artemis, the location of the St. John monastery became a center of learning and the home of an important library. Patmos became an island bastion of the Greek Orthodox faith. In the sixteenth century it passed to Turkish rule but enjoyed a measure of self-determination. In 1947 it was made part of the Greek Dodecanese (see photo on next page).                                    R.M.

Herbert G. May

*View of the island of Patmos showing the harbor. The island was one of several in the Aegean Sea used by the Romans to banish political prisoners.*

**PATON, JOHN GIBSON** (1824–1907). A missionary from Scotland to the New Hebrides, Paton left school early to devote his spare time to studying. While working as a city missionary in Glasgow he studied theology and medicine at the university there and volunteered for the Presbyterian missionary work in the New Hebrides, where he was sent in 1859. His early work met with little success and he was forced to flee in 1862. He traveled widely in Australia and Scotland in the following years raising funds for the New Hebrides mission. He later returned to mission work there from 1866 to 1881, when he worked on the island of Aniwa. In later years he personally raised funds for the mission, and when his biography, written by his brother, was published, a John G. Paton mission fund was established.

W.G.

**PATRIARCH.** A bishop who holds the highest rank in the Roman Catholic Church, after the pope. There are several patriarchates, other than Roman Catholic: the Coptic Patriarch of Alexandria, the Melkite, Syrian and Maronite Patriarchs of Antioch, the Armenian Patriarch of Cilicia, and the Chaldean Patriarch of Babylon.

J.C.

**PATRIARCHS.** Derived from the Greek *pater,* "father," and *archos,* "ruler," the term "patriarch" refers to the male head of a tribe or a religious community, or even simply a venerable elder. In looking back upon Israel of old, the NT writers used the term of David (Acts 2:29), the twelve progenitors of the tribes of Israel (Acts 7:8-9), and specifically of Abraham (Heb. 7:4). The term is sometimes applied generally to the progenitors of the various human races and tribes mentioned in the primeval history (Gen. 1–11). In the tradition of modern biblical interpretation, however, the term has come to refer above all to the three great figures who stand at the beginning of Israel's history, ABRAHAM, ISAAC, and JACOB, whose saga is recounted in Genesis 11:26–35:29; 49:28-33.

Many scholars assume that the stories of the three patriarchs (and the matriarchs as well) were told in Canaan long before Israel ever stepped out onto the stage of history. Abraham was the founder and hero buried at Hebron, and his story was preserved at the sanctuary there. Isaac belonged to Beersheba, Jacob to Bethel. But as local traditions coalesced around the fundamental traditions of the Israelite group after its appearance from across the Jordan, the patriarchal legends coalesced as well. In time they became a single family saga through which was woven the scarlet thread of Yahweh's continuing covenant promise of land, progeny, and blessing.     W.S.T.

**PATRICK** (about 389–461). Early British missionary and bishop in Ireland, called the patron saint of Ireland. Many legends but few facts are known about Patrick. He was born in Britain, but exactly where is uncertain. His father was connected with the church, possibly a deacon, and owned property, but whether Patrick received Christian training is conjecture. Captured by Irish pirates at sixteen, Patrick was a slave herdsman for six years, probably near Antrim or in Connaught. Turning to religion, he received a vision to escape and made his way to South Ireland, where some sailors agreed to transport him. He landed either in Gaul or Britain, and some pigs appeared when he prayed for his starving companions. Ordained fourteen years later, Patrick resolved to return to Ireland. The extent of his education remains vague, but he thoroughly studied the Latin Bible and some religious rules, perhaps in Britain, perhaps at St. Lerins. Known contact with Rome is uncertain.

His work probably centered at Armagh. The withdrawal of Roman legions from England isolated Ireland, but that Patrick successfully converted Ireland is attested by its many monasteries and missionaries who in the next century evangelized Great Britain, Burgundy, Switzerland, and northern Italy.                                                    C.M.

**PATRIPASSIANISM.** *See* MONARCHIANISM.

**PATRISTICS.** Pertaining to the study of the writings of the early Christian Fathers, proceedings of councils, ecclesiastical pronouncements, and related matters to about A.D. 600. A few of the patristic authors of the EARLY CHURCH, who wrote on virtually every significant topic in early Christendom, were Irenaeus, Tertullian, Basil, Origen, Athanasius, Gregory of Nazianzus, Augustine, and Pope Gregory I.                                                               C.M.

**PATRON SAINT.** In the Roman Catholic church, a saint venerated as a special protector of a specific city, profession, group, or nation, and even of individuals. An individual patron saint is one for whom a person is named at baptism, or whose name is taken by a religious person at one's profession.

J.C.

**PAUL, ACTS OF.** An Apocryphal work, probably from the later second century (about A.D. 160), said by the church father Tertullian to have been written in honor of the apostle Paul by a presbyter (priest) in Asia Minor. The original work was about 3,600 lines long, of which about 1,800 lines remain, in Coptic, Armenian, Latin, and Greek manuscripts. Professor Carl Schmidt reconstructed the text now generally used, which appears in *The Apocryphal New Testament*, translated by M. R. James (Oxford: The Clarendon Press, 1955).

The most interesting aspects of the legendary romance, constructed from some details of Paul's life, include a supposed romantic relationship between Paul and a woman called Thecla, and a highly imaginative account of Paul's martyrdom outside Rome. There is also a charming description of Paul's personal appearance. The unknown author says Paul was "a man little of stature, thin-haired upon his head, crooked in the legs, a good state of body, with eyebrows joining, and nose somewhat hooked, full of grace; for sometimes he appeared like a man, and sometimes he had the face of an angel" (James, p. 273). Paul is said, at one point, to have been condemned to slavery in the mines. He was reported to be miraculously spared by lions in the arena at Ephesus and to have confronted Caesar Nero as a spirit after his execution.

J.C.

**PAUL, APOCALYPSE OF.** A Gnostic work probably by the Cainites sect, mentioned by Epiphanius and Augustine. Augustine viewed the work as mockery, saying it was full of fables. It was said to have been found in Paul's house in Tarsus of Cilicia—a story denied by the priests of Tarsus. The book was disapproved of by all church officials and condemned by the Gelasian Decree. Nonetheless, the book was widely popular among Western Christians. There are many versions, in Latin, Syriac, Coptic, and Ethiopic, as well as in almost every European language. The outline of the book includes the discovery of the book by way of a revelation, an appeal of the Creation against man, a report of the angels against men, a vision of paradise, and a vision of hell. The vision of hell is terrible, and Paul is said to have interceded and obtained a Sunday of rest for the damned.                                             J.C.

**PAUL, APOSTLE.** *Sources.* Our knowledge of the historical Paul is determined by what we read in his authentic letters (that is, those letters traditionally ascribed to him minus the Pastoral Letters which may, however, contain some fragments of Paul's personal notes, and Ephesians, which is best understood as the work of a disciple of Paul who published a refurbished collection of his master's teachings after his death; some scholars also doubt that II Thessalonians and Colossians are genuine). To a lesser extent we may draw on the data in Acts that give an outline of the Apostle's travels, but are self-confessedly incomplete and enunciate Paul's teaching in the style of its author. The Apocryphal ACTS are fanciful, with their description of Paul as short in physical build, bald, and bow-legged, and they are replete with romantic elements, for instance, the case of the "baptized lion" at Ephesus which, preached to by Paul, did not attack him in the arena.

*Background.* Paul was born and raised as a Jew, with his birth name Saul (he is so called in Acts until the first mission to Asia Minor in chap. 13). He belonged to the PHARISEE party (Phil. 3:5), and was evidently trained in a rabbinic school (Acts 22:3; Gal. 1:13-14). This heritage gave him an inestimable advantage, which may be summarized thus: he was brought up to accept the OT books as a source of divine revelation, and he inherited his father's faith in one God of Israel (Deut. 6:4) whose will was made known in the law, the Torah which was God's chief gift to Israel, the chosen people. Paul never lost the sense of Israel's privilege and destiny (Rom. 9:1-5; 10:1), no matter how much he came to dissociate himself from his compatriots' obstinacy and "blindness" in failing to respond to his preaching of the Messiah (Rom. 9:31-32; 10:2-3, 21; 11:25, 28; compare I Thess. 2:14-16).

Then Paul's career as a Christian missionary brought him into direct touch with the contemporary world of Greco-Roman civilization. He was no stranger to that society. Even if we grant that his

The Church at the Close
of Paul's Ministry

formative years were spent as a youth in Jerusalem (Acts 22:3; 26:5), it is still true that Judaism was then no protective cocoon shielding Jews from outside influences. Moreover he had family connections with TARSUS, a Greek university city in Cilicia (Acts 21:39; 22:3), which gave him exposure to the Greek language (Acts 21:37) and culture. So he spoke to the wide audience of the civilized world around him. Recent social studies on Paul's milieu and that of his chief converts have shown that they belonged to an upper- or middle-class bourgeois stratum of Hellenistic society. In particular, Paul's Roman citizenship gave him entré to many situations that were otherwise closed (Acts 13:7; 25:10-14; compare Acts 16:37-39; 19:31; 28:7; Phil. 4:22; Rom. 13:1-7).

The most powerful influence of Paul's life,

however, came as a result of his "conversion" in the Damascus road encounter. If conversion is defined as an exchange of one religion for another, there is a sense in which it is a misnomer in Paul's case, for he never ceased being a Jew. What occurred, however, was a change in the "center" of his life's motivation and purpose as a direct consequence of his seeing the risen Christ, hearing a call to his service, and responding with a life-changing obedience (see Gal. 1:15-16; I Cor. 9:1, 16; 15:8; Phil. 3:12; and Gal. 2:20: these verses are the vital autobiographical descriptions he provided later in life, even if he did not refer explictly to the Damascus meeting). The turning point is not to be understood psychologically as release from past guilt and frustration (Phil. 3:5 denies that; Rom. 7:7-25 does not refer to Paul's life before he became a Christian). Rather, Paul came to see that Christ's resurrection from the dead was the apocalyptic inauguration of a new era in world history (II Cor. 5:17), and that he was privileged to live in that new age of the Messiah's exaltation (II Cor. 3:18) in which Torah religion was effectively displaced by Christ's authority as "Lord" (Rom. 10:4; 14:7-9), his favorite title for Jesus as the head of the church and of the universe (II Cor. 4:5; Col. 1:15-20; Phil. 2:6-11). Being a Christian was being "in Christ" for Paul (a phrase found 164 times in Paul's corpus of writings), and that meant being "inserted" into a new age of God's dealings with humankind, with a fresh allegiance to Christ the Lord and a transforming motive for living, namely to please God with a worthy ambition (see Rom. 12:2; I Thess. 4:1; II Cor. 5:9; Col. 1:10; Eph. 5:10).

*Life.* Paul's conversion may be dated around A.D. 35. For the next decade, until A.D. 45 when he came to Antioch for what proved to be a second turning point in his career, namely a call to missionary service in Asia Minor (Acts 13:1-3), we are left with only sporadic details. In this time period may be placed his trip to Arabia (Gal. 1:17), his return to Damascus and his subsequent escape, a visit to Jerusalem and a stay in Tarsus (Acts 9:23-25; II Cor. 11:32-33). Possibly also to be included are such events as his experience of II Corinthians 12:1-12 as well as exposure to the many dangers referred to in II Corinthians 11:23-29. His time at Tarsus (Acts 9:30; Gal. 1:21) brought him into touch again with Barnabas (Acts 11:25), who came to seek him and to escort him to the busy seaport of Antioch.

The first mission was launched from Antioch and took the apostolic band to cities in Roman Asia. The success that attended their preaching labors provoked discussion on a topic of central significance: Was the Jewish rite of CIRCUMCISION necessary for male Gentile converts when they sought to be members of Messiah's people? This was a question destined to haunt Paul's mission where, after a disagreement, he broke free from Barnabas (representing Jewish Christianity) and teamed up with Silas, a Gentile, to launch a full-scale assault on the urbanized provincial centers of Philippi, Thessalonica, Berea—with an abortive witness at Athens—and notably Corinth (Acts 16–18).

Paul's church-planting at Corinth was fraught with great consequences (Acts 18:1-17). It gave Paul a base of operations in southern Greece and provided him with a settled ministry for some time (Acts 18:18). As events turned out the Corinthian church became a major pastoral problem, requiring Paul's continuing attention especially during his lengthy stay at Ephesus (A.D. 52–54, Acts 19:10). His work in the Roman provinces seems to have driven him further from the support of the church at Antioch and given him a new independence as a Gentile-oriented missionary in his own right. He sensed the danger of alienation and the prospect of there developing two distinct wings of the Christian movement, one centered in Jerusalem, the other in the Greco-Roman world. This led to his plan to raise a fund to relieve the material needs of "the poor" (that is, Jewish Christians) in the holy city as a way of cementing relations between Jewish Christians and Gentile believers. It was his concern with this fund raising (detailed in Rom. 15; II Cor. 8–9), which brought him on his visit to Jerusalem in A.D. 57-58 where he was arrested in the Temple area; and as far as our certain knowledge extends he was never again a free man (Acts 21.27-33).

After two years in Caesarea as a detainee, Paul uttered the fateful words, "I appeal to Caesar" (Acts 25:11). The effect of this privilege exercised as a Roman citizen was the right to go to Rome to be tried in the emperor's court. Following a hair-raising sea voyage he eventually came to Rome, where in due time he was either set free (so Eusebius the church historian) or exiled and returned later to Rome or—many consider likely—executed in Nero's outburst.

*Teaching.* It is not easy to reduce Paul's teaching to a system, since he was a missionary pastor and teacher, not a theologian. His teaching was given on a situational basis, as the need arose. He also built on the tradition he had received from his predecessors, so elements of novelty are not easily discerned.

We take our starting point from (a) what he learned from those "in Christ" before him (Rom. 16:7; I Cor. 15:3-5), mainly confessional or hymnic materials he quotes, and (b) the change that came following his encounter with the risen Lord in whom Paul saw the dawning of a new age in God's dealings with humankind, setting divine-human relations on a new basis, that is, not of nomistic obedience but freely motivated love and gratitude (see Gal. 5:6 for a typical Pauline sentiment).

A third component shaping his thought was the kinds of pastoral and theological problems that engaged his converts. In the main these issues were three: (1) A Judaizing faction made much of the continuity between the old Israel and the new. Their platform may be read in Galatians 2:14, and the test case was circumcision as the required badge of belonging to the Messiah's people. Paul sternly opposed this imposition on Gentile believers on the ground that, with the new age of the Messiah's coming, God's covenant with Abraham was opened to embrace all nations (Gal. 3:28-29; Rom. 4:16). So religious restrictions are a denial of what Christ's cross has achieved, namely a freedom to share in God's family as God's children, open to all. (2) At the other end of the spectrum, Paul's preaching of this message—that God's free love is available to all in Christ—was misunderstood. Gentile Christians turned liberty into license (Rom. 6:1, 15; Gal. 5:13) and needed to be reminded forcefully that freedom from legalistic religion did not spell antinomian self-indulgence but called them to a new lordship under Christ's authority, which believers gladly accept and live under (Rom. 6:6–8:39) by the power of the Holy Spirit (Gal. 5:13-26), who is the token of living in the new age. (3) At Corinth and Colossae Paul, or his disciples, met head on an attempt to reduce his message about Christ to a system of philosophy (Col. 2:8) and to turn the church into a Gnostic assembly of the elite. Paul resisted this tendency to indulgence in esoteric wisdom and to split the Christian community into groups (I Cor. 12:12-13; Col. 1:27-28).

From the single premise that in Christ a new chapter in world history has opened, Paul can deduce several other corollaries as diverse as social equality (Gal. 3:28, 29; Col. 3:11); the joy and intimacy of living under the fatherly care of God (Rom. 8:15-17; Gal. 4:1-7); the sense of corporate identity in the church as Christ's body, where each person is valued and the well-being of the whole is of paramount concern (I Cor. 12:12-27); and above all, the primacy of love (I Cor. 13) as the hallmark of Christian existence, in this life and the world to come (I Cor. 15:35-58).                                              R.M.

**PAUL VI** (1897–1978). Giovanni Battista Montini, pontiff of the Roman Catholic church, 1963–78, born at Brescia, Italy. His father was editor of *Il Cittadino di Brescia* (1881–1912). Suffering from poor health in his youth, he was ordained in 1920. Later he studied at the Gregorian University and the University of Rome and entered Vatican service in 1924, joining the secretariat of state. He later served as university chaplain and as head of the Catholic University Federation of Italy.

He joined the staff of Cardinal Pacelli, the future Pope Pius XII, in 1937. Upon becoming pope in 1944, Pius XII gave Montini the duties of the secretary of state. He refused a cardinal's hat in 1952 and in 1954 became archbishop of Milan. In Milan, Montini sided with labor, arguing for social justice in his book, *The Christian in the Material World*. The reforming Pope JOHN XXIII made Montini a cardinal in 1958. The winds of change and accommodation to the modern world brought on by John XXIII's VATICAN COUNCIL II were not resisted by Cardinal Montini, but his outlook was more moderate than John XXIII's. Upon the death of the much loved John XXIII, a curia that wished to accommodate some of the protests from conservatives and give time to assimilate the council's changes elected Montini pope (June 30, 1963). While more oriented toward the hierarchy and tradition than John XXIII, Pope Paul VI nonetheless was faithful to the widespread call for further reform and reconvened Vatican II on September 29, 1963. His plea was for both renewal and unity. In the same way that the more conservative Lyndon Johnson actually put more of the liberal John F. Kennedy's programs into legislative effect than Kennedy did, Paul VI put many of John XXIII's

Courtesy of Religious News Service

*Pope Paul VI*

dreams into practice. He produced the Constitution on the Liturgy, the Constitution on the Church, and the Decree on Ecumenism, and reorganized and modernized the curia.

Pope Paul VI was active in liturgical reforms, approving three new canons and eight prefaces to the Mass. Regulations concerning church music, rites, and the Eucharist were adopted under his direction. This was the most extensive liturgical reform in Catholic history. The Decree on Ecumenism literally changed the relationships between Catholics and Protestants, and Catholics and Eastern Orthodox, from one of passive coexistence to one of active interfaith dialogue and actions. Relations with non-Christians were improved by the establishment of the Secretariat for Non-Christians in 1964.

Paul VI produced many significant encyclicals or official papers on Catholic teachings. These included *Ecclesiam Suam* (Aug. 6, 1964), on the aims of Vatican II; *Mense Malo* (Apr. 29, 1965), promoting prayer through the Virgin Mary for Vatican II; *Mysterium Fidei* (Sept. 3, 1965), restating traditional positions on the Eucharist; *Christi Matri Rosarii* (Sept. 15, 1966), urging prayers for peace through the rosary; "The Development of Peoples" (Mar. 26, 1967), directed to the Third World and applying the council's "Pastoral Constitution on the Church in the Modern World"; "Priestly Celibacy" (June 24, 1967) restated the traditional view of the church; "Of Human Life" (July 25, 1968) reaffirmed traditional Catholic opposition to birth control and caused much public criticism of Paul VI as pope. Paul VI was open to dialogue with Communism but adamant that Christians not compromise Christian beliefs and social positions. He stood for world peace and especially for bans on nuclear bomb testing. Above all, Paul VI carried the papacy beyond the confines of Italy, visiting Jerusalem; Bombay, India; the World Council of Churches in Geneva, and the Orthodox Patriarch at Istanbul.                                   J.C.

## PAUL AND SENECA, EPISTLES OF. *See* APOCRYPHA.

## PAUL AND THECLA, ACTS OF. *See* APOCRYPHA.

## PAULICIANS.
An obscure Gnostic-Manichaean Christian sect, which held PAUL OF SAMOSATA and Paul the Apostle in high regard, founded by Constantine of Mananalis about 650. Believing matter was evil and spirit good, they maintained Christ was docetic, an angel sent by God, not a physical person. Only Christ's teachings were important. Like Marcion, they exalted Paul's letters and Luke's Gospel and ordained women. They rejected the OT, the cross, relics, images, the sacraments, and Roman Catholicism. They grew strong in Armenia, but were repeatedly persecuted by other Christians and eventually gave military aid to the Saracens. They are vaguely linked with Bulgaria's Bogomiles and the Albigenses in France.    C.M.

## PAULIST FATHERS.
The Missionary Society of St. Paul the Apostle, which was founded by Father I. HECKER in 1858 in New York, to work for the conversion of non-Catholics. The Paulist Fathers do not take monastic vows but give a "solemn undertaking." The regulations of the society are based on the Redemptorist Fathers, to which order the founder belonged. In their work of conversion, the Paulists send missionaries, write books, and hold seminars and retreats. Most of the Paulists' work is in the United States. A house of studies is maintained in Rome, and the mother house is in New York.
                                                                                          J.C.

## PAUL OF SAMOSATA.
A third-century heretical bishop of Antioch. A wealthy native of Samosata, Paul was appointed bishop of Antioch in about 260. His doctrine of the person of Christ was condemned by at least two synods of Antioch, which resulted in his being deposed in 268. He taught a trinitarian MONARCHIANISM of Father, Wisdom, and Word. His Christology held that in the Incarnation, the Word rested upon Jesus as one person upon another, making the Incarnate Christ different only in degree from the prophets. His followers were called PAULICIANS.    W.G.

## PAX.
The Latin term for "peace." In Catholic, Lutheran, and Episcopal (Anglican) services, the versicle "Peace be with you" and the response, "And also with you," occurs before the collect or prayer for the day. The term is drawn from the Roman goddess of peace, Pax. In the Roman Catholic Church, a plate engraved with scenes from the Scriptures is kissed by the priest during the Agnus Dei of the Mass, then passed by the acolyte to each concelebrating priest. Each celebrant kisses the plate in turn saying, "*Pax tecum*" or "Peace be with you."

In contemporary services, both Lutheran and Catholic, there is the ritual of "passing the peace," derived from the kiss of peace observed in ancient liturgies and still observed in Eastern Orthodox Communion liturgies. This consists, in modern Western services, of a handshake and the words, "Peace be with you."    J.C.

## PEABODY, G. FRANCIS
(1847–1936). Clergyman, author, and Unitarian professor of theology and social ethics at Harvard University (1880–1913). Peabody was a founder of the study of Christian social ethics in America, developing a systematic course on that topic in the 1880s that was a favorite of both the divinity school and undergraduate Harvard students for many years.

Peabody was born in Boston, Massachusetts, the son of a Unitarian minister. He attended Harvard (A.B. 1869), Harvard Divinity School (S.T.B. and A.M., 1872), and studied in Germany at the University of Halle in 1872-73, where he was strongly impressed by the work of Otto Pfeiderer. Thereafter, a strong strain of historical study and theology derived from religious experience ran through his work. Peabody's works include: *The Approach to the Social Question* (1909); *Jesus Christ and the Social Question* (1900); *The Apostle Paul and the Modern World* (1923); *The Church of the Spirit* (1925); *Jesus Christ and the Christian Character* (1905); and *The Christian Life in the Modern World* (1914).    J.C.

## PEACE.
One of the key words of biblical theology. The essential meaning of peace is "harmony, wholeness, integrity," with an emphasis on completeness (Hebrew *shalom*) and order rather than a negative connotation of the absence of strife or hostility.

In the OT the stress falls on peace as a divine gift (Num. 6:26) and a sign of God's favor to people (Gen. 41:16 uses "favorable" to connote "peace"). The basis of such an offer is the reestablishing of the COVENANT (Isa. 54:10; Ezek. 34:25; 37:26), which has been broken by Israel's sin or infidelity. Political harmony or the absence of war is associated with Israel's destiny as living within the covenant relationship. Solomon is the archetype of a "man of peace" (II Sam. 7:11-16; I Kings 2:1-46), whose reign was marked by making Jerusalem "a place of peace," "a quiet habitation" (Isa. 33:20). Disillusion with the later monarchy led to several important developments. For the eighth- and seventh-century prophets of Israel peace was linked with righteousness as a precondition (Amos 5:24; Isa. 32:17), and so there was opposition to the false prophets who proclaimed "peace" on easygoing terms (Jer. 6:14; 8:11, 15; Ezek. 13:10; Mic. 3:5). The failure and collapse of the Hebrew monarchy gave impetus to the prospect of a new king, called "prince of peace" (Isa. 9:6), whose age of justice and integrity is often celebrated in the prophetic literature (Isa. 2:2-4; Mic. 4:1-3; Isa. 11:1-9; 32:15-20; Jer.

Courtesy of Abby Aldrich Rockefeller Folk Art Center, Williamsburg, Virginia

*The Peaceable Kingdom* by Edward Hicks (1830-40)

23:5-6). The signs of the new age of peace are given as the peace of Jerusalem, whose name means "city of peace," the reconciliation of the two factious kingdoms of Judah and Israel, and the submission of all nations to Israel and Israel's God (Isa. 49:8-12; 60:17, 18; Zech. 9:9, 10; Mic. 5:4). Several psalms look forward to a similar hope being realized (Pss. 2; 72; 110).

According to the NT, the fulfillment of the expectation of peace is found in the coming and kingdom of Jesus, Israel's Messiah and the Lord of the world. But the immediate effect of Jesus' mission is division and conflict, not peace (Luke 12:51; Matt. 10:34). To be sure, in later reflection, Jesus is credited with announcing the offer of peace (John 12:27; 16:33), but that assurance can only be meaningful in the light of his destiny to die and rise again. His work is that of peacemaking, even if it is costly. So he is the author of "peace," between humankind and God (Rom. 5:1; Col. 1:20) as between the contentious elements in first-century society, typified by the animosity between Jews and Gentiles (Col. 3:11, 14; Eph. 2:14-17: see PARTITION, MIDDLE WALL OF). The effect of God's reconciling work in Christ is that we have "peace with

God," leading to an awareness of God's peace in our experience when life's trials surround us (Phil. 4:7, 9; Col. 3:15; II Thess. 3:16).

The future hope of the NT authors is for a reign of peace, linked with Christ's role as universal Lord (I Cor. 15:24-28). Whether this is to be interpreted as a millennial kingdom of global peace (based on Rev. 20) or as a symbolic pledge of a new age of world harmony between races is much debated; but both sides of the discussion agree that Christians should act now as "peacemakers" (Matt. 5:9), relieving domestic, national, and worldwide tensions.        R.M.

**PEALE, NORMAN VINCENT** (1898–   ). Protestant clergyman and popular author, internationally known as the preacher of POSITIVE THINKING. Peale was born in Bowersville, Ohio, on May 31, the oldest son of a physician who was also a Methodist minister. Peale's brother Robert became a physician and his brother Leonard a minister. He attended Ohio Wesleyan University, graduating in liberal arts in 1920. After college, he became a newspaper reporter in Findlay, Ohio, and later, Detroit. After a year, he entered Boston University to study for the Methodist ministry. He was ordained in 1922 and in 1924 received both the S.T.B. and A.M. degree from Boston University. Over the years, he was awarded thirteen honorary doctoral degrees from such schools as Duke, Syracuse, Brigham Young, and Iowa Wesleyan.

Peale married Ruth Stafford on June 20, 1930, and they have three children, Margaret, John, and Elizabeth. He served pastorates in Berkeley, Rhode Island (1922–24); Kings Highway Church, Brooklyn (1924–27); University Church, Syracuse, New York, (1927–32); and Marble Collegiate Church, New York City, (1932–84). Peale has been featured on a nationwide weekly Sunday radio program, a ninety-second daily program called "American Character," and served as co-publisher and editor of *Guideposts*, an inspirational magazine (the fourteenth largest of all magazines published in the United States).

Peale has served on many distinguished commissions, including the Mid-century White House Conference on Children and Youth, and the President's Commission for Observance of the Twenty-fifth Anniversary of the United Nations. The recipient of numerous awards, he received several Freedom Foundation Awards, the Horatio Alger Award in 1952, the Presidential Medal of Freedom Award from President Reagan in 1984, and others. He is a Rotarian and a Shriner.

A prolific author, generally on the upbeat and inspirational theme of repressing negative feelings and thinking optimistically ("positively"), Peale has written many books: *The Art of Living, You Can Win, A Guide to Confident Living, The Power of Positive Thinking, Stay Alive All Your Life, The Healing of Sorrow, Enthusiasm Makes the Difference, You Can If You Think You Can, The Positive Principle Today, The Positive Power of Jesus Christ, Treasury of Joy and Enthusiasm, Dynamic Imaging* and *The True Joy of Positive Living*, an autobiography.     J.C.

***PEARL OF GREAT PRICE. See* CHURCH OF JESUS CHRIST OF LATTER-DAY SAINTS.**

**PEIRCE, CHARLES SANDERS** (1839–1914). American philosopher, physicist, and mathematician, best known as the founder of PRAGMATISM. Born in Cambridge, Massachusetts, and educated at Harvard, Peirce spent his early career as an astronomer and physicist. He worked privately as a philosopher, publishing papers from 1867 on. He never achieved a permanent university position but served as a lecturer at Johns Hopkins University (1879–84). Peirce's papers cover a broad range of philosophical topics, including epistemology, philosophy of science, metaphysics, ontology, and mathematics, but his outstanding contribution was in the field of logic. He wrote less extensively on ethics and religion. After 1887 Peirce lived in relative isolation and poverty until his death. He published many papers, but no books, during his lifetime. Much of his best work remained unpublished until the appearance of the eight-volume *Collected Papers of C. S. Peirce* (1931–58).

Peirce had little influence on philosophy during his life, although his contemporaries, WILLIAM JAMES and JOSIAH ROYCE, drew upon aspects of his work. Peirce propounded a pragmatic theory of meaning by which the meaning (not the truth) of a concept is associated with its experiential or practical results or effects. Peirce accepted the existence of a personal, omnipotent God as a philosophical hypothesis and offered several arguments in favor of such a reality. He believed that the evolutionary process supports theism, as does our instinctive inclination to natural piety, awe, and prayer.     J.L.

**PEKAH.** A king of the northern kingdom of Israel, Pekah came to the throne by the assassination of his predecessor, whom he had served as leader of the army (II Kings 15:25). Pekah is said to have reigned for twenty years, but II Kings 15:29-31 describes an ignominious end to his reign in the invasion and conquest of the northern part of the kingdom by the Assyrian king Tiglath-pileser III and Pekah's consequent deposition and execution. Isaiah 7:1-8 and II Kings 16 provide considerable background to this story. Pekah and REZIN, the kings of Syria and northern Israel, had formed an alliance to invade Judah with the purpose of deposing the king and replacing him with a puppet of their own, a venture that resulted only in driving Ahaz into the arms of Assyria and bringing down the Assyrian wrath. But for the complete picture we have to look to

Courtesy of the Foundation for Christian Living

*Norman Vincent Peale*

Tiglath-pileser's own annals. From these combined sources it becomes evident that Pekah's seizure of power was part of an anti-Assyrian movement to which not only Israel and Aram were committed but also Phoenicia, Philistia, and other of the small neighboring states. The invasion of Judah took place in the vain effort to force it to join this coalition. During the period between 734 and 732 Tiglath-pileser crushed the members of the coalition one by one, ending by absorbing Galilee and the Transjordan into his empire, subjecting the rest of Israel (and Judah) to vassalage, and replacing Pekah on the throne of Israel with its last king, Hoshea.                          B.V.

**PELAGIUS/PELAGIANISM.** Pelagius was a fourth-century British ascetic and theologian who claimed that humans have the natural capacity to take the first step toward salvation. The controversy regarding his teaching lasted several centuries, and therefore not all the tenets that were eventually called Pelagianism were held by Pelagius himself.

Pelagius attacked the Manichaean notion that some are by nature evil and some are good (see MANICHAEISM). He claimed that all have the power to turn to God, and that this is part of human nature. This doctrine became popular among the aristocracy in Italy, and later in North Africa and even the Eastern Mediterranean, for Pelagius and his disciples traveled to all these areas.

Two elements in Pelagianism drew opposition. First, it seemed to deny the need of divine grace for salvation. If humans have by nature the ability to take the first step, and then to continue on the right road, does this not imply that we are able to save ourselves? Second, as the controversy developed, many accused Pelagius and his followers of ignoring the consequences of Adam's sin. Pelagius was not particularly interested in this point. But some of his followers declared that the sin of Adam was not transmitted to his descendants, and thus the Pelagian controversy turned increasingly toward the question of ORIGINAL SIN and its transmission.

It seems that Pelagius himself was overwhelmed by the controversies his teachings provoked and therefore withdrew from the debate. But some of his disciples were more belligerent, and thus the controversy dragged on.

The chief opponent of Pelagianism was AUGUSTINE, bishop of Hippo in North Africa. Although he agreed with Pelagius on the need to affirm FREE WILL against the Manichaeans, he felt that this should not be done in such a way as to deny the initiative of grace in salvation. According to Augustine, before salvation, grace "operates" in us the will to turn to God, and then "cooperates" with our will to serve God. This led him to the doctrines of irresistible GRACE and of PREDESTINATION. Also as a result of this controversy, original sin came to be understood in the West almost exclusively in terms of inheritance—this had not been the case in earlier theology.

Pelagianism was condemned by the Third Ecumenical Council, which gathered at Ephesus in 431, and repeatedly by other ecclesiastical bodies (see EPHESUS, COUNCIL OF). But the extreme views of Augustine also aroused the opposition of some theologians, inexactly called SEMI-PELAGIANS. For another century the controversy continued, until it was settled by a synod gathered in Orange in 529. What this assembly did was to proclaim itself in favor of Augustine's views, but at the same time to interpret them in such a way that they approached semi-Pelagianism. Thus the Middle Ages interpreted Augustine in a very mitigated form, particularly on the issues of predestination and irresistible grace.

For this reason LUTHER declared that almost all medieval theologians were Pelagians. Both he and CALVIN sought to return to Augustine's views on grace and predestination and argued that the Roman doctrine of salvation was Pelagian. Since that time, particularly among Protestant theologians of the Reformed tradition, the term "Pelagian" has been applied to any doctrine that seems to exaggerate human participation in salvation. Within Roman Catholicism, the controversy over JANSENISM resurfaced some of the issues debated by Augustine and the Pelagians. (See also ARMINIANISM.)          J.G.

**PELLA.** A city in Transjordan on the east bank of the river at or close to Khirbet Fahil. Its ancient place-name was Pahel, which is found in the Amarna Letters and the letter of the Pharaohs Thutmose III and Seti I. The Greek name Pella derives from Macedonian colonists who came there after Alexander the Great had invaded Syria. It was colonized by Romans after Pompey restored it following its ruin by Alexander Jannaeus. To this city Christians fled from Jerusalem at the outbreak of the Jewish war in A.D. 66, according to early tradition, sometimes thought to stem from Mark 13:14.          R.M.

**PENANCE.** From the Latin word *poenitentia*, meaning "to regret"; implying REPENTANCE for sins. Penance may be understood as personal, public, and, in the Roman Catholic church, as canonical and sacramental.

Personal penance is the movement of sinners' hearts so that they hate their own sin so much that they resolve to abandon it. Such rejection of sin is necessary before one can be forgiven.

Public penance was practiced in the ancient church but was abandoned by A.D 1000. Extreme sinners, such as murderers and idolators, were required to repent publicly, before the congregation. Sometimes penance, as an activity of continually showing sorrow for sin, was laid on such people for life. Today, some Protestant sects may require a form of public penance and censure.

Canonical penance involves prayers, pilgrimages, good WORKS, retreats, or any other activity imposed on a sinner in the Catholic church by a priest or bishop. Such penances are required to reconcile a heretic to the church.

Sacramental penance involves the imposition of a good work or the saying of a number of prayers on the sinner by the confessor (priest) before absolution is given. Most penances involve praying aloud with the aid of the rosary or some other symbolic gesture. The penance usually bears little relation to the gravity of the sin committed. (*See also* FORGIVENESS.)

J.C.

**PENITENTIAL BOOKS.** Books of rules and directions for dealing with penances to be laid on communicants during confession in the early Roman Catholic Church. These rules were collected together as penitential canons from the many decisions of bishops and councils. The kind of penance and its duration along with modifying factors are discussed in these books.                                          J.C.

**PENITENTIAL PSALMS.** The seven psalms that express deep repentance of sin and desire for divine pardon (6, 31, 37, 50, 101, 124, and 142). They are widely used in both Catholic and Protestant services to express the sense of sin and need of forgiveness. They are appropriate for LENT.                      J.C.

**PENN, WILLIAM** (1644–1718). The QUAKER founder of Pennsylvania was born on October 14, the son of Margaret Jasper Penn and Admiral Sir William Penn, the conqueror of Jamaica. Reared an Anglican, he was expelled after two years at Christ Church College, Oxford, for nonconformist views. He studied law at Lincoln's Inn.

Converted to Quaker ideas, he was imprisoned in

*William Penn*

1669 for publishing *The Sandy Foundation Shaken*. While in the Tower he drafted the devotional classic *No Cross, No Crown*. His first interest in America was as a trustee of land in west New Jersey. With the colonists who settled there in 1677, he sent Concessions and Agreements guaranteeing the right of petition, trial by jury, protection from arbitrary imprisonment, religious freedom, and an elected assembly.

Charles II granted Penn land north of Maryland in 1681, with more land in Delaware in 1683 (see map on next page). Penn visited there in 1682–83 and 1699–1701. It became a haven for many religious groups and a model of relations with the Indians. A friend of kings and philosophers, Penn was a complex figure, both practical and spiritual.          N.H.

**PENTATEUCH.** Derived from the Greek words *pente*, "five," and *teuchos*, "book, tool," this term refers to the first five books of the OT, the so-called "five books of Moses." Known in Judaism simply as TORAH, this earliest stratum of the Israelite tradition, which is preserved in the HEBREW BIBLE, achieved the status of scripture (if not of immutably fixed canon) long before many other parts of the OT did. The reference to "the book of the law of Moses," which Ezra the scribe read before the assembly of the people on the first day of the seventh month in about 458 B.C. (Neh. 8:1-2), is thought by some to be the first intra-biblical allusion to the entire Pentateuch as such, even though the citations from "the book" that follow in Nehemiah 8:14-15 (as well as in Ezra 9:11-12) are not actually found in our Pentateuch. Certainly by the middle of the third century B.C. the translation of the book of the law of Moses into Greek (allegedly at the command of the Egyptian king and inveterate collector of sacred books, Ptolemy II Philadelphus) gives us a firm date by which the Pentateuch must have been regarded as sacred scripture by all Jews in and out of Palestine. After the definitive schism between the Samaritans and the Jews in the second century B.C., a separate Pentateuchal textual tradition began to emerge in the Samaritan community. That community recognized as authoritative scripture only the five books of Moses.

*Authorship.* The Mosaic authorship of the Pentateuch implied in Nehemiah 8:1-2 continued to be affirmed in both Jewish and Christian communities down to modern times. As recently as 1893, the denial of this traditional notion on historical-critical grounds by Professor Charles A. Briggs of Union Theological Seminary in New York was one of the charges that led to his suspension from the ministry of the Presbyterian church. Today, however, most interpreters in the mainline regard the attribution of the Pentateuch to the hand of Moses as a tradition of later Jewish piety and so no longer feel constrained to account for such technical difficulties confronting the theory as the fact that Moses would have had to report his own death in the last verses of the Pentateuch

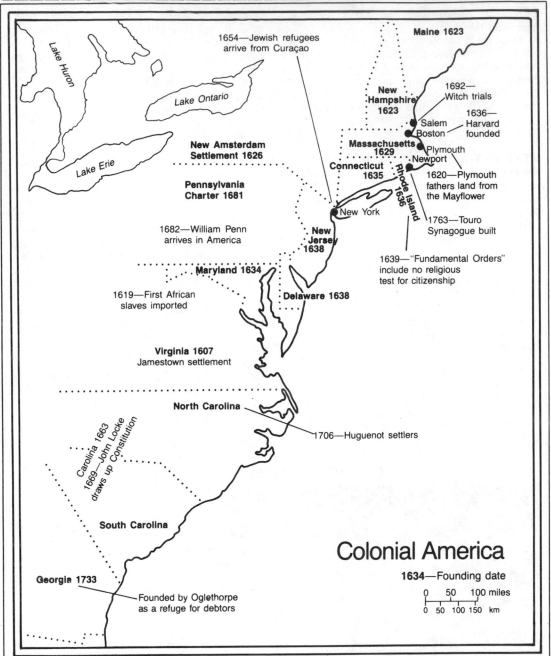

1654—Jewish refugees
arrive from Curaçao

Maine 1623

New
Hampshire
1623

1692—
Witch trials

1636—
Harvard
founded

Salem
Boston

Plymouth
Newport

Massachusetts
1629

1620—Plymouth
fathers land from
the Mayflower

Connecticut
1635

Rhode Island
1636

1763—Touro
Synagogue built

New Amsterdam
Settlement 1626

Pennsylvania
Charter 1681

1682—William Penn
arrives in America

New York

New
Jersey
1638

1639—"Fundamental Orders"
include no religious
test for citizenship

Maryland 1634

1619—First African
slaves imported

Delaware 1638

Virginia 1607
Jamestown settlement

North Carolina

1706—Huguenot settlers

Carolina 1663
1669—John Locke
draws up Constitution

South Carolina

Georgia 1733

Founded by Oglethorpe
as a refuge for debtors

Lake Huron

Lake Ontario

Lake Erie

Colonial America

1634—Founding date

0      50      100 miles

0   50  100 150  km

Reprinted with permission of the Macmillan Publishing Company, from *Macmillan Atlas History of Christianity* by Franklin H. Littell. Copyright © 1976 by Carta Ltd.

(Deut. 34:5-8). It is in fact quite possible to discover in the Pentateuch evidences of compositeness and growth over many generations of devout reflection upon the received tradition.

*Structure and Content.* The Pentateuch opens with an account of world origins (Gen. 1–9). Beginning with a single pair of persons and following their offspring through a history of human tragedy and divine grace, the primeval history culminates in the rescue of the human race from the deluge. After an interlude that traces the descent of tribes known to ancient Israel from the survivors of the Flood (Gen. 10), and an account of the dispersion of humanity into alienated and warring factions spread over the face of the earth in the story of the Tower of Babel (Gen. 11:1-9), the Pentateuchal account focuses in upon a single man, Abram, to whom it is promised, "by you all the families of the earth shall bless themselves" (Gen.

12:3). In GENESIS 12–50, the great saga of Abram's family, the patriarchs and matriarchs of Israel, is spun out in a way that begins to show how the accursed and alienated human community will one day be able to find that promised blessing in the descendants of this Abram and his wife Sarai. Woven into the story of the movement from that promise to its fulfillment are the lives of Isaac and Rebekah, Jacob and Rachel, and the twelve sons of Jacob, who, through the instrumentality of Joseph, emigrate to Egypt and grow there to be a mighty people.

EXODUS 1–15 is the account of the oppression of the Israelites in Egypt and the subsequent "root" experience with the liberator God who acts through the towering figure of the Pentateuchal story, Moses. This Moses, who learned to know the name of God, YHWH, at the burning bush on the mountain of God (Exod. 3:1-15), has to contend with murmuring and backsliding on the part of the Israelites, free but frightened in the wilderness after their wonderful escape from Egypt. But with the arrival of the Israelites at Sinai, the second decisive "root" experience takes place. Exodus 19 is the account of the theophany in which the entire community of Israel personally encounter the single God whom they are to worship; in 20:1-17 the Ten Commandments set forth in most basic terms the stipulations of the covenant, which will henceforth link the two.

Following this legal epitome or creed is the largest single block of the Pentateuch, Exodus 20:18–Numbers 10:9. With a few narrative interludes, such as the conclusion of the covenant ceremony in Exodus 24, this block is a vast collection of cultic law intermingled with civil and criminal legislation, much of which reflects the later practices of the Temple period, but all of which is attributed to the revelation of God to Moses at Sinai. Embedded in this material is the "Book of the Covenant" (Exod. 20:22–22:33), which reflects conditions in a settled agricultural community and is thought to contain indigenous Canaanite law adopted by Israel at a later time. Also embedded is the so-called Holiness Code, Leviticus 17–26, which spells out in detail the ways in which Israel can achieve the ritual and moral holiness appropriate to a people holy unto God.

The latter part of the book of NUMBERS (10:11–36:13) picks up the account of the wandering of the Israelites in the wilderness and reports conflicts within Israel itself, such as the rebellion of Korah (Num. 16), as well as conflicts with other peoples. The Pentateuch concludes with a single unified block, the book of DEUTERONOMY, the great last will and testament given by Moses before his death on the east bank of the Jordan and before the entry of the tribes into the Promised Land. As its name suggests, Deuteronomy is a sermonic repetition. It opens with a summary of the history of God's saving acts with the people (chaps. 1–3), followed by exhortations to obedience and loyalty (chaps. 4–11), and another great block of legal material known as the Deuteronomic Code (chaps. 12–25). It concludes with a ceremony of covenant recommitment, curses and blessings, Moses' final song and blessing, and an account of his death (chaps. 26–34).

*Sources of the Pentateuch.* By the middle of the eighteenth century, students of the OT had begun to realize that a vast collection of materials of such widely divergent character as those which make up the Pentateuch undoubtedly represented the work of many hands over many generations. A source-critical approach began to detect specific strands in the material, and by 1878, when JULIUS WELLHAUSEN published the first edition of *History of Israel*, a four-source hypothesis had reached the shape that it retains to this day. SOURCE CRITICISM identifies as the oldest continuous stratum of the Pentateuch a "Yahwistic" source (known as J after the first letter of "Jahweh," the German spelling of the divine name). This source was set down in writing in the tenth to ninth century B.C., probably during the united monarchy of David and Solomon. It is distinguished by the use of the divine name YHWH as well as by other linguistic tags, such as the name "Sinai" for the mountain of God and "Canaanite" for the indigenous peoples of the land. The style is earthy and direct; God is often spoken of in anthropomorphic terms. It is animated by that scheme of promise leading to fulfillment under the guidance of God that is first predicted in Genesis 12:1-3. The J source begins with an account of the Creation and the Fall (Gen. 2:4b–4:26), runs on throughout Genesis to Exodus 24, reappears again in parts of Numbers, and makes a final appearance in Deuteronomy 34.

Woven together with the J source is an "Elohistic" or E source, written in the northern kingdom of Israel in the century following the division of the two kingdoms (ninth to eighth century B.C.). It knows God by the generic name "Elohim" until the revelation of the divine name to Moses on the mountain of God in Exodus 3:14-15. It typically refers to the mountain of God as "Horeb" and to the indigenous people of the land as "Amorites." Though it is much more fragmentary in character than the J source, it seems to supplement it, beginning with Genesis 15, making a major contribution in the story of the "binding" of Isaac in Genesis 22, and running on through Exodus, parts of Numbers, and concluding in Deuteronomy 31:14-34. Scholars have detected a heightened role for Moses in the Elohistic source, a tendency toward a more spiritual conception of religion and a more delicate and ambiguous understanding of human nature.

The key for dating the entire scheme is the Deuteronomistic or D source, which consists of the book of Deuteronomy and of editorial touches in the other four books of the Pentateuch. By identifying Deuteronomy with the book that was found in the Temple during its renovation in the days of King Josiah, and which led that king to centralize worship in Jerusalem and to suppress local cults as demanded by the book of Deuteronomy (II Kings 22–23), source critics were also able to locate in prior times the two sources that had first recorded the history of Israel's formative experience and would thus have provided the basis for the great recapitulation of that experience undertaken by D.

The final Priestly or P source, deemed to be the work of learned priestly circles in the exilic or early postexilic period, provided the editorial framework for the entire Pentateuch. But the P "writer" was no mere copy editor, for this source brings its own perspective on Creation (Gen. 1:1–2:4a), the Flood, and the Exodus; furthermore, it incorporates vast blocks of cultic and legal tradition in Exodus 25–31; 35–40, all of LEVITICUS, and Numbers 1–10. Themes of the Priestly source center around a view of the world as a great organism in which the Sabbath, the Temple, and the people of Israel are the heartbeat, the regulator, and life-giving element. In Israel's cult God had provided the means necessary to make human life possible, and in so doing had elevated Jerusalem and its sanctuary to the very pinnacle of the world.

*The Prehistory of the Pentateuch.* Building upon the work of nineteenth-century source critics, twentieth-century scholarship has devoted much of its effort to reconstructing the evolution of the Pentateuchal tradition prior to its reduction to writing at the hands of the great theologians J, E, D, and P. Scholars such as HERMANN GUNKEL, Albrecht Alt, and GERHARD VON RAD, using the methods of form criticism, which can trace small orally transmitted units back to their original forms and points of origin, have shown that the stories of Creation, the patriarchs and matriarchs, and the Egyptian sojourn of Israel were originally independent traditions that coalesced during the slow process of unification of the tribes of Israel in Canaan. In the process they were attached as preface and prologue to the memory of the root experiences of those tribes.

In his famous 1938 article, "The Form-Critical Problem of the Hexateuch," von Rad argued that in the cultic, preserved "little historical credo" of Deuteronomy 6:21-23 (see also 26:5-9; Josh. 24:2-13), the confession that "we were Pharaoh's slaves in Egypt; and the Lord brought us out of Egypt with a mighty hand . . . and he brought us out from there, that he might bring us in and give us the land which he swore to give to our fathers," one could see not simply an epitome of the history of salvation, but the very source and kernel out of which the entire Pentateuch grew. Around this early testimony of a group of escaped slaves around whom had gathered other tribes who accepted allegiance to the same Yahweh who had brought liberation were woven the rest of the traditions and memories coming from disparate sources that constituted the collective religious memory of Israel. The memory of the other great root experience of the past, the covenant given

at Sinai, was also woven into this primitive confession, yielding the great tapestry of Pentateuchal history that now lies before us. From von Rad's perspective, the book of Joshua, which tells of the conquest of the land and thus brings to fulfillment the promise of blessing that animated the entire story, ought to be included in the earliest stratum of Israel's tradition. Therefore, he prefers to speak of a Hexateuch, a six-book Torah rather than a Pentateuch. Others, such as MARTIN NOTH, prefer to link the book of Deuteronomy to the historical writings that follow it from Joshua through II Kings in a single unified work of ancient Israelite historiography called the Deuteronomistic history. For Noth, then, the earliest stratum of the OT is a four-book block, a Tetrateuch.

While these modern judgments regarding the proper scope of the original confession of Israel are worth considering, the historic identification of the five books of Moses as the foundation upon which all the rest stands still has the weight of tradition behind it, and a great deal of merit in its own right. It leaves the reader poised on the eastern bank of Jordan, looking across at the Promised Land, and faced with the burning questions that confront the covenant community in every age: What are we going to do? Will we be obedient to the one who has blessed us and led us all this way? Have we the courage to decide against death and curse and for life and blessing, with all the loyalty and the love that the latter require (Deut. 30:19)?                                                    W.S.T.

**PENTECOST.** Biblically, the Feast of Weeks, in both the OT and the NT; the second of three festivals on which every male Jew was required to worship at the Temple (Exod. 34:22-23; II Chr. 8:12-13). It means "fifty days," because the feast falls seven weeks after the opening of the harvest season (Lev. 23:15-16). The Sadducees considered Pentecost to be the Sabbath that falls during the festival of unleavened bread; others held that Pentecost is the first day of the festival of unleavened bread. Sometimes the day is called the Day of Firstfruits, celebrating the harvest. Later Christian tradition held that Pentecost is the day on which Moses received the Law, but there is no historical evidence for this.

For Christians the most important Pentecost festival was the one that took place after Jesus' resurrection. On that day the Holy Spirit fell upon the believers and gave them the power of xenoglossy, or the ability to speak and be understood in foreign languages. This was not the glossolalia or tongues-speaking of modern Pentecostals, which is the expression of syllables without content, but the ability to address Parthians, Medes, and others and be understood (Acts 2:7-8). This event is sometimes called the birthday of the church.

Pentecost in the Christian Year is the fiftieth day after Easter. From early times this became an important festival in worship. Believers fasted in preparation, and many baptisms were performed on that day. Today it is the longest portion of the church year for those who follow the interdenominational lectionary.                                        J.C.

## PENTECOSTAL CHURCHES.
A conservative evangelical grouping of several denominations that stresses the necessity of believers receiving the BAPTISM OF THE HOLY SPIRIT, an experience that occurs subsequent to conversion. This inward experience is attested to by external evidence of the individual speaking in tongues (GLOSSOLALIA), a duplication of the event at Pentecost. Pentecostals, besides confessing faith in the major tenets of orthodox Christianity, have emphasized the ministry of the HOLY SPIRIT in the life of believers, especially SPIRITUAL GIFTS that, besides speaking in tongues and their interpretation, include such gifts (*charismata*) as prophetic utterance, HEALING, etc. Whether the tongues spoken are recognizable foreign languages or some form of ecstatic utterance or unknown or unidentified speech varies in individual experience.

While the conduct of worship services in Pentecostal churches is quite similar to that of other evangelical groups, there are times when individuals in the congregation may utter "a message from the Lord" that may be delivered in vernacular speech or in a "tongue." If in the latter, most Pentecostal assemblies insist that an interpretation be given in the language understood by the congregation.

In earlier years Pentecostals, especially those in rural or mountain areas, were referred to as Holy Rollers. This appellation was given because Pentecostal services were marked by convulsive bodily movements and highly emotional scenes of weeping, shouting, singing, and ecstatic cries. Because of what non-Pentecostals regarded as bizarre behavior, Pentecostals were often ostracized and persecuted by other believers. What Pentecostals described as evidences of the Holy Spirit's activity, other Christians felt was excessive emotionalism. Some even ascribed the activity and teaching to Satanic influence.

Actually similar CHARISMATIC conduct has occurred in various segments of the church throughout the centuries of its history. But the Pentecostal movement is essentially a modern phenomenon that can be traced to the early part of the twentieth century in the United States.

While there are reports of earlier Pentecostal signs in American religious history, most scholars regard Pentecostalism as emerging from the Holiness movement of the latter half of the nineteenth century. Advocates of that revivalist movement followed the Methodist teaching of crisis sanctification and Christian perfection as taught by John Wesley. Thus entire SANCTIFICATION takes place instantly in an emotional experience similar to conversion. Some of its earlier proponents spoke of it as "a second work of grace." However, HOLINESS people never advocated a baptism in the Holy Spirit that was evidenced by speaking in tongues. In fact, Holiness teaching historically has been completely opposed to this central teaching of Pentecostalism.

Yet at the turn of the century certain American Holiness ministers became interested in manifestations of spiritual enthusiasm such as glossolalia, or tongues-speaking. Charles Fox Parham, a Methodist minister in the Holiness movement, had established the Bethel Bible College in Topeka, Kansas. While Parham was away from the school on January 1, 1901, Agnes N. Ozman, one of the Bethel students, testified to experiencing the baptism of the Spirit, and she spoke in tongues. Parham and other students had similar experiences, and with a new zeal they began to evangelize in Missouri and Texas. Houston became the new center of Parham's activities. With W. F. Carothers, a local minister, he opened a school. One of their converts was William J. Seymour, a humble black man with one eye. Parham urged Seymour to conduct a mission in Los Angeles. In 1906 in the Apostolic Faith Gospel Mission on Azusa Street, Seymour was used to launch the real beginnings of modern Pentecostalism. Despite his unimpressive appearance, Seymour was the instrument in a revival effort that soon drew nationwide attention, and ultimately took Pentecostalism to the four corners of the earth. Soon there were virile Pentecostal movements in Britain, the Scandinavian countries, Germany, India, and South America, especially in Chile and Brazil.

Most of the major Pentecostal denominations of the United States can trace their beginnings to the Azusa Street revival. Out of it came movements that later developed into the Assemblies of God, the Church of God (Cleveland, Tennessee), the black Church of God in Christ, and the International Church of the Four-Square Gospel, 10-51. Representatives of these so-called historic Pentecostal churches were agents in the 1960s in introducing their distinctives, which are now called the Charismatic movement, or renewal, to leaders in mainline denominations and the Roman Catholic church.                                        R.H.

## PENUEL.
A sanctuary and fortified town in central Transjordan Palestine. Alternately called "Peniel," the town played a strategic role at various times in Israelite history. It is listed among the cities conquered by Pharaoh Shishak in 918 B.C. In Genesis 32:30 a folk etymology "face of God" is applied to it, since it was made the site of Jacob's mysterious struggle with a supernatural being, after which he said that he had "seen God face to face." Its exact historical location is disputed.                                        B.V.

## PEOPLE OF GOD.
This term belongs to both the OT and the NT; indeed it is one of the several links that connect the Jewish religion and the Christian faith as sharing in a common ancestry.

The root idea of people of God is twofold,

suggesting the interrelation of PROMISE and COVENANT community. God's promise to Abraham (Gen. 12:1-3) centered in the rise of a people to whom the promise of both nationhood and special relationship to Yahweh were promised. Yahweh calls them "my people" (Isa. 51:4; Zeph. 2:9), as a nation chosen out of all the tribes of the earth to be God's special "treasure" (Exod. 19:6 KJV). The self-designation of Israel as "God's people" (II Sam. 14:13) implies that they belong to God (Deut. 14:2; 26:18) and are God's "possession" (Deut. 4:20). The classic passage in which this is described is Deuteronomy 7:6-8, with its notes of election, calling, and God's free love for Israel. All these terms underlie the covenant that God initiated and Israel accepted, under Moses' direction. But unhappily there was infidelity on Israel's part (Jer. 31:31-34), leading to the inauguration of a "new covenant" (II Cor. 3; Heb. 8), and a fresh focus placed on the concept of the people of God (I Pet. 2:1-10).

Both John the Baptist and Jesus are set in the context of Israel's religious life and hope for a New Age (Luke 1:16, 17, 68-79). They come on the stage of history to create a new people of God which, while having roots in the past and maintaining direct continuity with historic Israel, will have a new definition, that is, this people will be transnational and multiracial, harking back to Genesis 12:1-3. The inclusion of non-Jews within the covenant people is seen as anticipated in the OT (Rom. 9:25; II Cor. 6:16; Tit. 2:14; I Pet. 2:9, 10), but largely lost in a time of Israel's nationalism and exclusiveness. The membership of the people of God is now a wider term than ethnic status but embraces all who believe in Jesus as God's Messiah (Rom. 10:4-13). Israel as a believing remnant is included (Rom. 9:6-13) along with Paul's mission churches; together they form one united people as a promise of universal reconciliation (Rom. 11:25-32).

R.M.

### PERDITION, SON OF.

The single allusion to this term in the NT is in II Thessalonians 2:3, where the writer, traditionally taken to be Paul, is answering some pressing pastoral needs at Thessalonica. Evidently the church was of a mind to suppose that the final day of world history had already dawned. Paul writes to assure them that this is not so (II Thess. 2:1-3), since the final "day will not come" until "the man of lawlessness is revealed, [he is] the son of perdition." This eschatological figure is described in a well-known Semitic manner, meaning a person who transgresses God's law (2:8) and so is destined for destruction—a fate that will, in Jewish-Christian apocalyptic, overtake the embodiment of evil in the last days. Opinions are greatly divided over who this person may have been, but it seems clear, from the descriptions in 2:4-10, that some political force in the Roman Empire, hostile to the church, was in view. (See ANTICHRIST.)

R.M.

### PEREA.

The Transjordan region inherited by Herod Antipas after the death of his father, Herod the Great, in 4 B.C. Paralleling Samaria and Judea, Perea extended north and south between Pella and Machaerus. Its eastern edge flanked Nabatea. A non-biblical designation, Perea corresponds to the NT expression "beyond the Jordan" (Mark 3:8, John 10:40). Jesus traversed Perea on his final journey to Jerusalem (Matt. 19:1).

J.K.K.

### PERFECTIONISM.

The belief, held at different times and places among Christians, that a person is able to achieve perfect union with God in this world. Perfectionism has been held in the ancient church, the medieval church, and notably in Protestantism was taught by John Wesley and held by much of the Methodist movement, being modified and/or given up around the end of the nineteenth century. Once Methodism stopped emphasizing perfectionism, sectarian groups promoted the idea, producing the HOLINESS movement. Several contemporary churches and sects have a background in the Holiness revivals, including the Church of the Nazarene and the various Free and Wesleyan Methodist churches.

Roman Catholicism teaches the possibility of attaining a relatively perfect union with God in the world, based on the degree of charity or Christian love one possesses and exercises. Thomas Aquinas defined perfection in the believer's life as charity. However, one in such a state still commits venial sins. Wesley was so criticized for his early beliefs in perfectionism, that he more and more qualified his teachings. The Methodist ideal became one of "going on to perfection" rather than a claim to possess it.

The "councils of perfection" in Catholicism (voluntary poverty, perpetual chastity, complete obedience) are not necessary for salvation but are taken up by those who aim at the greatest degree of moral perfection. (See also SANCTIFICATION.)

J.C.

### PERGA.

The three allusions to Perga all occur in regard to Paul's mission to Asia Minor in Acts 13:14. Perga was the capital town of the province of PAMPYLIA and was visited by Paul and Barnabas both on the outward and return visits to the Asian hinterland (Acts 13:13-14; 14:25). The locality was famed for the shrine of the goddess Artemis (Roman, Diana), who was known as the queen of Perga.

R.M.

### PERGAMUM.

An ancient town in Mysia, now Turkey, where the site is known as Bergama, a small township. Referred to in Revelation 2:12-17 it is one of the places to receive letters from John in the name of the risen Christ (KJV, Pergamos). In the first century it had many temples, including the famed altar of Zeus, which may be referred to in Revelation 2:13 as "Satan's throne." The altar is now reconstructed in a museum in East Berlin.

Courtesy of Ahmet Dönmez, archaeologist, Izmir, Turkey

*The Asclepieum theater at Pergamum*

Pergamum was the center of Caesar worship because of its place as the capital of the Roman province of Asia Minor. Equally it had a famous shrine of Asklepios, the god of healing, and it was the center of a therapeutic cult. It also boasted a large library, established by Eumenes II, which later was moved to Alexandria in Egypt. Parchment as writing material was said to have been used first at Pergamum; the city's name is derived from the Latin word for parchment (*pergamena*).          R.M.

**PERIZZITES.** A Palestinian people linked with the Canaanites to denote the two major populations preceding Israelite penetration into the land (Gen. 13:7; 34:30; Judg. 1:4-5). If "Canaanite" and "Perizzite" respectively designate occupants of fortified cities and unwalled villages, "Perizzite" may reflect class as well as ethnic condition. Typically the Perizzites are associated with five population groups —Canaanites, Hittites, Amorites, Hivites, and Jebusites (Exod. 3:8; Deut. 20:17; Judg. 3:5). Later, Perizzite remnants were drafted into Solomon's assemblage of forced laborers (I Kings 9:20).

J.K.K.

**PERPETUA AND FELICITAS.** North African Christian martyrs of the early third century A.D. Perpetua was a noblewoman of Carthage, and Felicitas was most likely a slave woman in her household. Perpetua had a son and Felicitas a daughter, born in prison. They all died in the Circus at Carthage, along with their teacher, Saturus.

J.C.

**PERRONET, EDWARD** (1726–92). Clergyman and hymn writer. Edward Perronet was born in the village of Sundridge, England, the son of Vincent Perronet, a devout Anglican clergyman. The Perronets were descendants of a Huguenot family that fled from France to Switzerland and then to England. Both Perronets were sympathetic to the evangelical movement and its leaders, John and Charles Wesley, and George Whitefield. The younger Perronet once wrote: "I was born and am likely to die in the tottering communion of the Church of England, but I despise her nonsense." However, he later broke from the Anglican church and worked with the Wesleys for several years. For this Perronet suffered persecution and opposition from the opponents of Methodism. Eventually, he separated from the Wesleys and became the pastor of an independent church in Canterbury. Perronet's greatest contribution to hymnody was the text of "All Hail the Power of Jesus' Name." Dr. John Rippon, a Baptist minister, rewrote some stanzas and dropped others. Today various versions of this triumphant song of worship are sung to the accompaniment of at least three tunes.

R.H.

**PERSECUTION.** The harassment within a society of individuals or groups who have different opinions or are of a different background from the dominant group in the society. The harassment may range from the infliction of physical violence and even death, through imprisonment, fines, civil disabilities, to discrimination in employment, housing, and so forth. The differences that give rise to persecution may be racial or ethnic, political or religious. Here, we are considering religious persecution, which seems to be almost as old as religion itself and is still common in the present day. The existential character of religious beliefs means that they are held passionately, so that alternative beliefs may seem like a serious threat to someone's deepest convictions. But often this religious fanaticism is combined with political or racial motives where the dominant group feels its power to be threatened. The decline of religious beliefs in modern times and the rise of indifference may have reduced the incidence of purely religious persecutions in many parts of the world, but political and racial or ethnic motivations still keep alive some of the old religious rivalries.

*The Church and Persecution.* The Christian church had its origins as a movement within Judaism, but when the differences reached a certain degree, Christianity was experienced as a threat to the Jewish traditions, and in its very earliest days the church was subjected to persecution by Jews. This is attested in the NT, which tells how Stephen became the first Christian to die for his faith (Acts 7). At that time, Christians may have thought of the Roman authorities as affording some protection, but soon it was the Roman Empire that became the most persistent and dangerous persecutor of the new religion. Traditionally, there were ten great persecutions of the church by the empire, but this figure is only conventional, and the true picture is of sporadic hostility for a period of about two hundred and fifty years, sometimes becoming very severe in particular areas.

The most famous of these persecutions under the empire were the following: (1) NERO subjected the church to severe persecution in Rome in A.D. 64 and 65, and at that time both Peter and Paul perished. (2) The writer of Revelation claims to have been an exile for the faith on the island of Patmos near the end of the first century, and this was probably the result of a persecution under the emperor DOMITIAN. (3) IGNATIUS, bishop of Antioch, was martyred in A.D. 107 in the reign of TRAJAN, and correspondence between Pliny and Trajan in 112 makes it clear that there were persecutions of Christians in Asia Minor at that time, though it also suggests that Christians were not being actively sought out. (4) There was a bad outbreak of persecution at Lyons in 177, under Marcus Aurelius. (5) The beginning of the third century saw an attempt to end conversions to Christianity, and it is to this time that the sad story of the martyrdom of PERPETUA and her companions at Carthage belongs. There followed a time of relative quiet, broken about the middle of the century by (6) the persecution of Decius, who required all citizens to sacrifice to the emperor, leading to many apostasies. (7) The last persecution, under DIOCLETIAN, was the most systematic and severe of all, leading to the destruction of many churches and sacred books. It began in 303, and was terminated by the emperor Constantine in 313, when the Edict of Milan granted toleration to the church.

As we continue the story, the ironies of persecution begin to emerge. As the Christian church became increasingly entrenched in the empire, it took itself to persecuting the remaining pockets of paganism. In the Middle Ages, Jews, Muslims, and heretics were sought out and punished with great severity by the Inquisition. The Reformation brought little improvement. Calvin caused the unfortunate Servetus to be burned at the stake in Geneva for his anti-trinitarian views. In England Roman Catholics burned Anglicans under Mary, while the roles were reversed under Elizabeth I. Even in the American colonies, where many people had fled to escape persecution in Europe, new intolerances and persecutions came about. The situation began to improve in the seventeenth century. A major figure in bringing about change was Roger Williams, author of *The Bloody Tenent of Persecution* (1644) and founder of the state of Rhode Island, where religious freedom was written into the charter. Meanwhile in England the Toleration Act (1689) and subsequent legislation gradually established full religious liberty.

*Modern Persecutions.* In the world at large, persecutions continue. Throughout the nineteenth century, Jews were persecuted in various European countries, and this culminated in the twentieth century in the attempted mass extermination of European Jewry under Hitler. For sheer magnitude and malevolence, nothing like this had ever been known before in the history of the human race. Death camps for the mass destruction of human beings were set up, and it is estimated that six million people perished in them. In this case, of course, racial and religious motives were mingled, and the Nazi creed was itself a quasi-religion (*see* HOLOCAUST). Much the same can be said about Soviet Communism in Russia and, since 1945, other countries of Eastern Europe. In these countries the Christian faith has been seen as a rival to Marxist ideology. In some cases, the persecution has been severe; in others, while it may not be overt, it is subtly maintained, and Christians are debarred from certain forms of employment and from positions of influence. The human race, including, it would seem, those who count themselves Christians, has still much to learn about the basic human right to freedom of religion. (*See* LIBERTY, RELIGIOUS.)                                    J.M.

**PERSEVERANCE.** The capacity to maintain a belief or an allegiance in the face of discouragement or even persecution. In the early church, those who persevered in the faith even to the point of martyrdom were highly esteemed, while nothing was blamed more severely than the behavior of those who lapsed and became apostates. But perseverance is not considered primarily as a human virtue, but rather as a gift of God. As doctrines of ELECTION and PREDESTINATION arose in the church, it came to be believed that in electing the faithful or making a covenant with people God gave with it the gift of perseverance. God would not let go of those who were chosen. God's grace would make up for their weakness, and even if they temporarily lapsed, God would bring them back. Paul gives eloquent expression to these ideas in Romans 9–11, which speak of the election, apostasy, and final restoration of the chosen people of Israel.
                                                          J.M.

**PERSIA.** The name refers to the country in ancient times that today is called Iran, although Iran is sometimes used to include a wider range of territory including Afghanistan, Baluchistan, and West Turkistan. Persia was bounded on the west by Elam or Susiana, on the north by Media, on the south by the Persian Gulf, and on the east by Carminia. The term "Persia" (Dan. 11:2; Neh. 12:22) derives from a geographical region of southern Iran known as Persis (Pars, Parsa; modern Fars). It was apparently extended to the whole of the country during the Achaemenid dynasty, which was founded in the middle of the sixth century B.C., and was used until the Pahlavi dynasty (Reza Shah) initiated the change to Iran ("the Land of the Aryans"). The government of Iran officially requested on March 21, 1935, that other governments adopt and use that name. However, the tradition had been too long standing and too well imbedded in Western minds, and in October of 1949 the government of Iran officially announced that the name Persia would also be acceptable.

The change in name to Iran was intended by the Shah to emphasize the Indo-European nature of the people who had migrated there in the second millennium B.C. from central Asia to the north and who were now living among largely Semitic and Oriental people. The people of Iran, however, are of mixed ancestry, and the country is composed of many diverse elements including Arab, Turkish, Armenian, Assyrian, Kurdish, and others. The language of ancient Persis was Indo-European. It is called Old Persian and is known primarily through the cuneiform inscriptions of the Achaemenian kings from the sixth to the fourth centuries B.C. The best-known example is the Behistun Rock. Imperial inscriptions, as on this rock, were usually trilingual in the Achaemenid period—Old Persian, Elamite, and Akkadian. Avestan, the language of the ZOROASTRIAN scriptures, is equally old; it and Old Persian constitute two of the oldest attested languages of Iran. In order to facilitate the administration of a linguistically diverse country, the Achaemenids introduced ARAMAIC (Ezra 4:7), which became the *lingua franca* of the empire until it was replaced by Greek under the impact of Alexander the Great's conquest. People spoke Aramaic, however, in remote stretches of the empire until the time of Christ. It is thought by many that Christ probably conversed normally in this language. Many Aramaisms appear in the NT. Modern Hebrew is written in this Aramaic block script. In Persia itself, during the period from 300 B.C. to A.D. 700, five different major forms of Persian are known to have been used. From A.D. 700 onward modern Persian appears as the standard language of Persia written in the Arabic script. Other languages include Kurdish, Ossetic, Baluchi, Pashto, Wakhi, and Azerbaijani.

The religion of Persia before Zoroaster (traditional date of birth 660 B.C. but may be older) was polytheistically associated with nature—sun, moon, stars, earth, fire, water, and winds, which were in the control of supernatural powers. In the hierarchic organization of the gods, Mithra (Vedic, Mitra) was very popular among Aryans everywhere. His presence is recorded in a Hittite document of the fourteenth century B.C. found in Asia Minor. The Roman Mithras was modeled after this god. The gods were worshiped and sacrificed to openly by priests using fire worship and the psychdelic potion made from the *haoma* plant. Zoroaster instituted reforms that tended toward ethical monotheism, that is, he taught that his system of morality came from a supreme good God, who was already well known as AHURA MAZDA ("Wise Lord"). He seems to have held to the existence of lesser divine beings who were subordinate to the one supreme being. He taught a kind of dualism with an Evil Spirit opposing the Good Spirit. Each human soul is the seat of a war between good and evil. He found the support of an influential priestly group called the magi, concerning whose identity there is still much confusion. They were known as far away as

Courtesy of the Oriental Institute, University of Chicago

*Ahura-Mazda, the Persians' winged god, on the east doorway of the main room of the Council Hall at Persepolis*

Athens for their adeptness in the practice of magic. In the Achaemenid period they seem to have been at odds with the Zoroastrian rulers of Persia, and it is not certain that they were of Aryan stock. Perhaps they were Semitic. Some of their group may later have visited Jesus as a babe in Bethlehem (Matt. 2:1; "wise men" in Greek is magi).

The AVESTAS, the sacred scriptures of the Zoroastrian religion, were assembled in the Sasanian period (A.D. 226–651). The oldest Zoroastrian traditions indicate that their founder did not write any books, but that his disciples later wrote them out of their remembrance. During this long period a number of changes were made in Zoroastrian religion: a highly worshipful reverence of Zoroaster; a change in Zoroaster's "monotheism" that brought back the old Aryan nature gods; a greater emphasis on the place of Mithra among the common people; the development of a fuller doctrine of ethical dualism; a shift from moral regeneration to considerations of ceremonial purity; an elaborate doctrine of the future life involving a multiple layered hell and heaven; a day of resurrection and judgment based on one's moral consciousness; and a new heaven and new earth. Three great deliverers would be born of a virgin, one each thousand years before the Day of Judgment. Although much of this is to be found also in Judaism, Christianity, and Islam, there is no demonstrably formative influence of Zoroastrianism on the theology of these religions. It is of interest, however, that Cyrus the Great, king of Persia, who in 538 B.C. allowed the Jews to return from captivity and rebuild their Temple in Jerusalem as a part of his general policy regarding captured nations, is regarded favorably by the prophet Isaiah, who calls him "the Lord's anointed" (45:1). He was, nominally at least, a Zoroastrian.

The period of Persian history that is of most importance for readers of the Bible is that of the Achaemenid kings whose reigns are as follows: CYRUS II (559–530), Cambyses II (530–522), Smerdis or Gaumata (552), DARIUS I (522–486), XERXES I (486–465), Artaxerxes I (465–424), Xerxes II and Sogdianus or Secydianus (424–423), Darius II (423–404), Artaxerxes II (404–359/358), Artaxerxes III (359/358–338/337), Arses (338/337–336/335), and Darius III (336/335–330). These span the period covered during the BABYLONIAN CAPTIVITY of the Jews and their subsequent servitude to the Persians down to the time of Alexander the Great. Perhaps Cyrus II was especially favorable to the Jews (II Chr. 36:22; Isa. 45:1; Ezra 1:1-8; 3:7; 6:4-5) because when he conquered the Babylonians he found the exiled Jews to be a subjugated race that abhorred idols, whose basic views of religion were somewhat like his own. The Bible states that "the Lord stirred up the spirit of Cyrus king of Persia," who said "the Lord, the God of heaven, has given me all the kingdoms of the earth" (II Chr. 36:22-23). Cyrus gave the Jews considerable assistance in returning to their homeland to rebuild their Temple (Ezra 1:1-11), a practice we now know from the discovery of the Cyrus Cylinder to be a matter of policy with Cyrus for all conquered peoples such as Armenians, Lydians, Greeks, and others. That the Jews fared well under Persian rule is evident from the OT book of Esther. The books of the Jewish Apocrypha do not speak harshly of Persian rule. After the death of Cyrus, work lagged in Jerusalem on the Temple; but when Darius I, his successor, located the edict of Cyrus commissioning the building project he financed its completion (Ezra 6). The prophets Haggai and Zechariah participated in the effort (Ezra 5:1).

Another Persian king who was prominent in Jewish history was AHASUERUS, unknown by that name in Persian history but probably to be identified with Xerxes I since he is mentioned in Ezra 4:5-7 between Darius and Artaxerxes. He was the king who made Hadassah, a Jew whose Persian name was Esther, his queen (Esth. 4:7, 17). His successor, Artaxerxes I, permitted two other groups to return to Judah. One was led by Nehemiah, who rebuilt the walls around the city of Jerusalem (Neh. 1). The other was led by Ezra, who restored the spiritual life of the people (Ezra 7–10).

Persians are not referred to by name in the NT, but they are the Parthians mentioned in Acts 2:8 along with the Medes and Elamites. Jewish pilgrims came from these countries to the feast of Pentecost in Jerusalem. The Parthians (or Arsacids) ruled eastern Persia from the third century B.C. till the third century A.D. The Romans were never successful in subjugating Parthia, both Crassus (53 B.C.) and Mark Antony (36 B.C.) having been defeated in their attempts.                                                              J.R.M.

**PERSONALISM.** Any type of philosophy that takes personal existence as its primary clue to an understanding of reality. The personalist believes that more is to be learned about the universe from the higher levels of being (and personality is the highest known to us) than from the lower levels (hydrogen atoms and such). Thus personalism tends to be a philosophy of spirit and stands opposed to materialism and other reductionist theories. It also tends toward some form of THEISM.

The expression "personalism" was applied especially to a school of philosophy centered at Boston University. Its leading advocate was Borden Parker Bowne (1847–1910), and it still has eminent representatives, for example, Peter Bertocci (b. 1910). The school had affinities with Lotze and Eucken in Germany, Boutroux in France, and Ward in England. The very fact that the universe has brought forth personal beings is claimed to be evidence of a personal creative source. It is argued too that the categories that we employ in our understanding of the world, for example, causation, are ultimately derived from personal experience.

As well as this narrower use of the word "personalism," it is applied also to such thinkers as MARTIN BUBER and GABRIEL MARCEL. With Buber, it is the knowing of other persons rather than the knowing of facts that is the paradigm of knowing. The "between" of interpersonal relations is the environment of human existence, rather than the impersonal physical universe. Though he uses a different philosophical idiom, Marcel also stresses the ontological ultimacy of the personal, especially as it transcends the merely individual existence into the realm of the intersubjective and of human community. It is at this point that one may make a distinction between personalism and EXISTENTIALISM. While both types of philosophy stress the uniqueness and irreducibility of personal existence, known to us primarily in human existence, the personalists insist that personal being fulfills itself only in community, while existentialists (SARTRE is the obvious example) are concerned with individual existence and even tend to regard interpersonal relations as essentially frustrating.                J.M.

**PESHER.** In ancient Judaism an application of biblical prophecies to the events of the end times. Such peshers are especially common in the texts found at Qumran, called the Dead Sea Scrolls. The term "pesher" is found in Ecclesiastes 8:1: "Who knows the interpretation of a thing?" The Aramaic word *peshar* occurs thirty-one times in the section of Daniel written in Aramaic. It is used for the interpretation of Nebuchadnezzar's dreams and the handwriting on the wall at Belshazzar's feast by Daniel. The angel's interpretation of Daniel's night vision (Dan. 7) is also called a *peshar*. This shows that peshers are the result of divine revelation, rather than of human wisdom. The Aramaic section of Daniel uses a Pesian noun, *raz,* to designate mysteries, such as Nebuchadnezzar's dream. The idea is that both the mystery, or *raz,* and the interpretation of it, the pesher, come from God.

                                     J.C.

**PESHITTA.** A version of the Bible in Syriac, so called after its designation "peshitta" meaning "the simple [version]" and intended to be used in a popular way as easily readable by Syrian Christians. The OT parts are extant in an ancient codex in the British Library, London, and cover Genesis, Exodus, Numbers, and Deuteronomy. The NT Peshitta was in circulation before A.D. 431 and is ascribed to Rabbula, bishop of Edessa. But this attribution is uncertain. Discoveries of a Peshitta text that Rabbula used cast doubt on the tradition.      R.M.

**PETER, ACTS OF.** An Apocryphal work probably written in Greek by a resident of Asia Minor around A.D. 200. The author seems to have modeled his work on another Apocryphal work, the Acts of John. While not completely so, the Acts of Peter is generally orthodox. It is some 2,750 lines long, about the length of the Acts of the Apostles. The text is preserved in Coptic, Latin, Greek, Slavonic, Syriac, Armenian, Arabic, and Ethiopic. The manuscript contains supposed speeches or sermons of Peter, as well as a legendary account of Peter's martyrdom in Rome. The canonical Acts of the Apostles is obviously the pattern for this book. For example, Peter is said to have caused the deaths of Ananias and Sapphira in Acts 5:1-6. Augustine (*Against Adimantus* XVII, 5) criticizes the Manichaeans for retelling this story from the Apocryphal Acts.            J.C.

**PETER, APOCALYPSE OF.** An early pseudonymous work, attributed to Peter but probably from the second century A.D. In the early church the Apocalypse of Peter was almost as popular as the canonical Apocalypse (or Revelation) of John. Indeed, it is mentioned in the late second-century list of biblical books prepared in Rome, the Muratorian Canon, although the Canon adds, "some will not have it read in the church." The work is about three hundred lines, but a full text has not survived. The text is reconstructed from a Greek fragment (the Akhmim fragment), an Ethiopic version, and quotations from the book found in ancient writings.            J.C.

**PETER, APOSTLE.** The NT literature gives prominent place to Peter, whose life and ministry fall conveniently into the three categories.

*Early Days.* Occasional references to Peter's original name Symeon show that he belonged to the Jewish community (Acts 15:14 Modern Language Bible). His home was in Galilee, at Bethsaida (John 1:44), and it is known that, while this locality was Jewish, it was also of a cosmopolitan nature. Both Andrew, Peter's brother, and Philip, who also hailed from Bethsaida, bear Greek names. The bilingual setting arising from Greek culture explains why Simon became his adopted name.

His father's name was Jonah, which is the same as John (Matt. 16:17; John 1:42). At some point in his life not specified he had married (Mark 1:30), and in later days his wife accompanied him on his missionary tours, evidently to Corinth, where she was known (I Cor. 9:5).

His trade, both at Bethsaida on the east bank of the Jordan River and at Capernaum, another port on Lake Gennesaret, was fishing (Mark 1:16-21). Luke 5:1-11 is a passage that indicates something of his trade, which he resumed for a while in the later part of the Gospel story (John 21:1-3).

As to his cultural attainments, Acts 4:13 should not be pressed unduly. It is probably to be seen as a description of Peter and John as "uneducated, common men," which implies no more than that they were ignorant of the finer points of the rabbinical interpretation of the Jewish law. Exposure to Hellenistic culture in Bethsaida is a counterbalancing argument in favor of Peter's general education. He spoke his native language with a special, recognizable accent (Mark 14:70; Matt. 26:73). Both he and his brother ANDREW were followers of John the Baptist (John 1:35-42), as indeed were a considerable number of the original disciples (Acts 1:22) before their call to service by Jesus.

*Call to Discipleship.* John preserves an authentic tradition of Jesus' Judean ministry, part of which included the summons of John 1:40-42. In this context we first meet the nomenclature by which "Simon" is replaced by "Peter." The middle link-term is the Aramaic *Kepha* meaning "stone" or "rock." This is to be his new name, symbolizing a change of character. Hereafter he will be a new man, consolidated by his relationship to Christ his Lord. The name-giving is probably postulatory, anticipating the time when Peter will take his place as a pillar apostle (Gal. 2:9) and the foundation-stone, which he and the other apostles were to be as original witnesses to the gospel (Eph. 2:20; Rev. 21:14). "Cephas" is Paul's normal appelation of him, except for Galatians 2:7 ff.

This first introduction to Jesus in Judea makes more intelligible the subsequent response Peter made when Jesus called him to abandon his trade and become his disciple in a full-time capacity (Mark 1:16ff.; 10:28; Luke 5:1-11 gives an expanded version of this call). A further invitation to belong to the inner group of the Twelve is given in Mark 3:13ff., and the new name is mentioned at that time. Mark calls him Simon up to 3:16; thereafter he refers to him as Peter.

*Peter's Role in the Ministry of Jesus.* Still another honor was his as Jesus permitted a group of three disciples to accompany him on special occasions. Peter is included in the trio along with James and John (see Mark 5:37; 9:2; 14:33). In the lists of the Twelve, Peter stands out at the head (Mark 3:16; Acts 1:13). In Matthew's Gospel special incidents are told in which Peter plays a unique role, both in action (Matt. 14:23-33) and word (Matt. 16:13-17).

The confession at Caesarea Philippi is problematical. The authenticity of the passage (Matt. 16:17-19) has been challenged on textual grounds. Harnack tried to show that the passage is an interpolation into the original text, made at Rome in the time of Hadrian, A.D. 117-138. But this is a vain plea, without any external support. Moreover, the Semitic coloring of the passage testifies to its primitive character.

On a second argument, it is objected that linguistically the term for "church" (Greek *ekklesia*) is an anachronism. But linguistic researches show that the true equivalent of *ekklesia* is the Hebrew word for "assembly" or the Aramaic term for "gathering." Thus it is more appropriate to translate the Greek word as "people of God" than "church." In this way we remove the idea that Jesus could not have envisioned an institutional body at Matthew 16:18 and 18:17. No such concept is required since he more reasonably had in view the eschatological people of God, which he had come to gather in his earthly ministry and beyond.

A third objection raises the issue of the subsequent history of the church. It is said that Peter did not occupy the authoritative position, which would inevitably have been secured for him by this saying of Jesus in Matthew 16:19. The argument hinges on the meaning of the power of "the keys." Evidently what is meant here is the spiritual perception that will enable Peter to lead others in through the door of revelation through which he has passed himself. This "key" was not the exclusive possession of Peter, though on the day of Pentecost by common consent he was the first to use it. In Acts 10 he opened the door of faith to Cornelius as the firstfruits of the Gentile mission (see Acts 11:18).

Peter's confession was the turning point in Jesus' ministry. To him was accorded, by divine revelation, the insight into the mystery of Jesus' person, whom he acknowledged as Israel's Messiah and the divine Son. The subsequent rebuke (Matt. 16:21-33) is directly related to Peter's misunderstanding of what Messiahship involved and his attempt to dissuade Jesus from the path to the cross. Mark preserves the vivid narration (Mark 8:32-33), which exposes Peter's frail humanity.

An integral part of the confession at Caesarea Philippi is the subsequent experience of the TRANS-FIGURATION. Peter is again spokesperson for the three, and again misguided and fallible (Mark 9:5). Later reflection showed the reality of this vision, and Peter benefited from hindsight (I Pet. 5:1; II Pet. 1:16ff.). His proud claims to loyalty are shown up as

hollow mockery by the events in Gethsemane, and his threefold denial (Mark 14:66ff.) is painfully told. The end is not without hope as the promise of "good-bye" (Mark 14:28) is confirmed by a personal message to Peter (Mark 16:7) and is followed by a personal appearance of the living Christ (Luke 24:34; I Cor. 15:5).

*Peter's Apostleship.* After Pentecost Peter became the leading figure in the apostolic church. The first twelve chapters of Acts show that he was clearly the dominant influence, both in decision-making and public preaching (see Acts 1:15ff.; 2:14ff.; 3:12ff.).

Before the Jewish authorities (4:5ff.) Peter was spokesperson. His many-sided role included that of forceful leader (5:1-11) and miracle-worker (5:15). Peter is presented as a church leader in his handling of the situation at Samaria (8:14ff.) and his encounter with Simon the sorcerer. Luke evidently decided to give prominence to the conversion of Cornelius by the way the narrative is written, with great fullness of detail and repetition for emphasis (Acts 10–11). Peter's Jewish susceptibilities were overcome and his convictions redirected as he came to learn that "God shows no partiality" (10:34), and that Gentiles such as Cornelius were suitable recipients of the gospel message, offered and received on the basis of trust in Christ, without any ceremonial requirement. Peter's sermon announced the good news, which was accepted gratefully and movingly. Peter's association with this embryonic Gentile mission is clear.

But his sympathies lay more with a mission to his Jewish compatriots, if we place the concordat with Paul (Gal. 2:7-10) in the period prior to the Jerusalem Council. His native weakness peeps through in the vacillations he practiced at Antioch (Gal. 2:14ff.), and he needed the stern reproof of Paul.

His arrest in Jerusalem at an earlier date (Acts 12:1ff.) led to imprisonment and release, the apparent hopelessness of his plight as a prisoner of Herod being described to highlight the need for him to leave Jerusalem. This he did, and "departed and went to another place" (Acts 12:17).

Aside from a brief reappearance at the Jerusalem Council (Acts 15:7ff.), Peter now vanishes from the NT story of the church. Attempts have been made to argue that he left Jerusalem for Rome, to become the first bishop there. But this is countered by the fact that when Paul wrote his Letter to the Romans, he had no knowledge of Peter's presence in the imperial city, and recent Roman Catholic writers are more flexible than heretofore in leaving this identification of "another place" with Rome as an open question. No certain answer is possible. The rise of James in his absence, however, requires that he soon moved away from the Holy City and engaged in missionary work elsewhere (Gal. 2:9), possibly Corinth (I Cor. 1:12) and the regions of Pontus-Bithynia (I Pet. 1:1).

*Peter the Martyr.* The apostolic authorship of I PETER requires that Peter wrote his epistle from Rome, if (as is very likely) 5:13 in that document conceals the name of the imperial city. If, on the other hand, I Peter originated as a group document, composed by a Petrine school—as is more likely— that group associated with Peter's name is best located at Rome.

Christian tradition speaks with a divided voice over Peter's stay in Rome. Irenaeus makes the two apostles, Peter and Paul, the founders of the church there; but this cannot be so, in view of Paul's letter in A.D. 58 to the Roman church, which he had not then visited (Rom. 1:13). More reliably, Eusebius, in citing Dionysius, witnesses to the cooperative work of the two men in Italy at a time when Paul was a prisoner there, presumably at the close of Acts.

The Neronian persecution in A.D. 64 marks the turning point, though our sources of information about the apostles are not clear. First Clement 5, 6 speaks of Christian martyrs at Rome in such a way as to fit the description of Tacitus, that it was during Nero's persecution that Paul and Peter perished. This would preclude any release of Paul and further ministry after Acts 28, unless the date of the two-year confinement in "free custody" is brought forward to make possible a release and further missionary work in the West. Many scholars accept the direct evidence of I Clement 5, 6 and insist that the two apostles were martyred in Nero's outburst (see CLEMENT, EPISTLES OF). The tradition that Peter was crucified head downward (found in the Apocryphal Acts of Peter) looks as if it is an embroidered version of John 21:18ff.

The burial sites of the apostles were evidently well known, according to Eusebius, who quotes Gaius, at the time of Bishop Zephyrinus, A.D. 198217: "You will find the trophies (Greek *tropaia*) of those who founded this church." The maximum conclusion to be drawn from the recent Vatican excavations is that Peter's memorial was cherished near the spot where he died. His body was never recovered—therefore all talk of Peter's bones is unrealistic—but with the later concern for relics for apologetical reasons Christians piously believed that his exact grave could be located.
R.M.

**PETER, EPISTLES OF.** The letters, designated "Catholic Epistles," ascribed to Peter and written to churches in northeast Asia Minor in the case of I Peter and to churches of unspecified destination (II Peter).

*I Peter—Authorship.* The evidence of the letter itself attributes this document to the apostle Peter (1:1), and tradition supported by a number of scholars endorses this claim. Verbal links between the letter and Peter's recorded teaching in Acts are often appealed to. But other interpreters have cast doubt on these arguments and regard the letter as a document emanating from the late first century, notably on the grounds that the classical language is hardly that of a Galilean fisherman, and that the nature of the persecutions facing the church suggests a confrontation with the Roman state that came about in the early second century. Again there are counter-

challenges to both these positions. Some scholars argue that there is no hint of state persecution in I Peter. Rather it is the local population in Pontus that is finding Christian social conduct a source of irritation and a reason for hostility. The first objection is answered by the supposition, for which there is some evidence in the letter itself (5:12), that the author employed a scribe-secretary, namely Silvanus, to "ghost-write" the letter, thereby accounting for the elevated style and rich language.

The letter, if Petrine, may be dated in the final year of the apostle's life, around A.D. 64–65, reflecting conditions that led to Nero's persecution of Christians in Rome. If the letter is not genuinely Peter's, its date is usually set in the eighties or nineties or in the first decades of the second century.

*Purpose.* The purpose of the letter is decided by our choice of its setting. If it is addressed to Christians about to face Nero's persecution, we can identify the contours of Peter's teaching: (1) to encourage harassed believers in their trials (1:3-9; 4:12-19); (2) to counsel them to remain patient and blameless in spite of unprovoked attacks on them (3:8-22); (3) to remind them to act in a socially responsible way (2:11-17); and (4) to admonish their church leaders to accept patterns of lowly service (5:1-5). All this pastoral advice is set against the backdrop of a church faced with impending—if not actual—hostility from the civil authorities (2:13-14).

If the letter comes from a later decade, we can only guess who its readers may have been and their chief need. Recent studies have drawn attention to the social significance of Peter's constituency, namely as members of a disadvantaged and alienated social group in the Roman world and needing reassurance that in the church they can find their true identity as the people of God (2:1-10).

*II Peter—Authorship.* The problem of knowing the setting of II Peter is notoriously complex. The document professes to be written by "Simeon Peter, a servant and apostle of Jesus Christ" (1:1), who also claims to have been an eyewitness of the Lord's transfiguration (1:16-18), though the verb used is plural—"we were eyewitnesses"—as if to emphasize the corporate nature of apostolic testimony. The writer also speaks of a close relationship with Paul, his "beloved brother" (3:15). These two pieces of evidence lead some scholars to argue for Peter the disciple and apostle of the Lord as the author, and the epistle is then dated in Peter's closing years.

On the contrary there are other data that point more in the direction of a much later dating and imply that the author may have been someone other than Peter. There is the Hellenistic coloring of the language used, the presence of a developed Gnostic teaching (2:1ff.; see GNOSTICISM) that emerged later than Peter's lifetime, the postponement of the hope of Christ's imminent return (3:3-13), and the way in which Paul's letters have already been assembled to form a collection (3:15-16) that has the authority of sacred scripture. These items have indicated to most modern interpreters that this letter is best seen as a "testament of Peter" or a putting together of his teaching by faithful disciples or colleagues who in a later decade published this book in his name in response to pressing needs in the church of their day. The intention behind this type of publication is not to deceive the readers but to serve as a mark of respect for the teacher believed to be still speaking through his followers—a common idea in antiquity. The letter therefore was claimed as Peter's, though its passage into the church's canon was slow and cautious. Jerome speaks of it as being "rejected by the majority," but by A.D. 367 the church in the West had accepted it.

*Teaching.* If the setting of the epistle is in the closing years of the first century, and if the letter carries its authority as "the testament of Peter" as understood in the church at Rome, we can see some of the problems it addresses. There is the influence of "false teachers" who propagate a type of esoteric doctrine that advocates antinomian license, makes proud claims, and reviles the angels (II Pet. 2). Irenaeus matches these traits with a teaching traced back to Simon Magus in Acts. The author builds his opposition on the deposit of apostolic teaching current in Rome and calls on his readers to resist both Gnostic tendencies and antinomian libertinism.

R.M.

**PETER, GOSPEL OF.** An Apocryphal, pseudonymous work written before A.D. 190, of which all is lost but two fragments. An unorthodox, even heretical writing, according to Serapion, bishop of Antioch, the Gospel of Peter, because of its Gnostic doctrines, was said to have been written by the Docetists. However, Theodoret credited the work to the Nazarenes, that is, Jews who accepted Christ only as a righteous man. The contents (as much as we know of them) of the Gospel of Peter do not make Theodoret's claim very likely. Eusebius (fourth century) declares that this Gospel (as well as the Acts, Apocalypse, and Preaching of Peter) was a writing not handed down among the catholic (that is, orthodox) Scriptures, and thus is not used as a testimony to the faith by orthodox church teachers either before his time or during his era. Most scholars today would date the book around A.D. 150.                      J.C.

**PETER, PREACHING OF.** A lost Apocrphal book of the NT, known principally from the quotations from it made by Clement of Alexandria and Origen. Gregory of Nazianzus and John of Damascus also briefly refer to the work. Gregory referred to it in Epistle 16, " 'A soul in trouble is near unto God,' saith Peter somewhere—a marvelous utterance." Origen declared that the Preaching of Peter "is not reckoned among the books of the church" and observed that the writing was not by Peter nor by anyone else who was inspired by the Spirit of God.

The fragments we have of the work give a supposed critique of pagan worship among the Greeks.

J.C.

**PETER DAMIAN** (1007–72). Catholic monk, prior, cardinal bishop of Ostia, and church reformer. Damian was born in Ravenna and entered the Benedictines in 1035. He rose to prior and founded several monasteries before being made cardinal bishop against his will. He wrote many letters, sermons, monographs, and essays, as well as poetry, all stressing the need for asceticism and devotion to the church. He sharply criticized clerical laxity, defended Pope Alexander II against the antipope Honorius II, and supported the monastery at Cluny. Damian was involved in church polity and the relationship of the church to the Holy Roman Empire at the highest levels. He was never made a saint, but Pope Leo XII made him Doctor of the Church in 1828.     J.C.

**PETER LOMBARD** (1095–1169). French theologian famous as "the master of the Sentences" because of his brief history of doctrine created out of citations of works of the church fathers and from medieval theologians. This popular work was entitled *Libri Quatuor Sententiarum* or the Four Books of SENTENCES. The work is an amazing achievement and became the standard text in theology by A.D. 1222. Eventually, all students in theology were required to study it for their doctoral degrees. Hundreds of commentaries were written on the Sentences from the thirteenth to the seventeenth centuries—some 180 commentaries in the English language alone. Lombard was constantly defended by the church as orthodox, although some of his material was held to be heretical by Pope Alexander III in A.D. 1177. Lombard was eventually displaced by the system of Thomas Aquinas.

Lombard was born in Lombardy, educated in Bologna, and was elected bishop of Paris in A.D. 1159. He wrote on scriptural topics, including Paul and the Psalms. Lombard's great work was the first to posit seven sacraments and to hold to sacramental efficacy, that is, that the Sacrament is the cause of the grace of God of which the Sacrament is also the sign. His work is divided into four books: On the Mystery of the Trinity; Concerning Creation and the Formation of Physical and Spiritual Things; Concerning the Incarnation of the Word; and Concerning the Sacraments and Sacramental Signs.     J.C.

**PETER'S PENCE.** A tithe or tax sent by the English church to the pope, originally to assist English pilgrims in Rome, and later paid directly to the pope. The tax was ended after Henry VIII assumed leadership of the church and rejected papal supremacy in 1534. It lasted from A.D. 787 until that time.

J.C.

**PETRARCH, FRANCESCO** (1304–74). Italian scholar of the High Middle Ages and a devoted recoverer of the ancient classics, whose work paved the way for the RENAISSANCE. Called "the father of humanism," Petrarch spent his life searching for ancient manuscripts in both Latin and Greek, editing the Latin ones and preserving the Greek ones, which he could not read. It is to Petrarch that we owe the phrase "The Dark Ages," as he felt an age of light, a golden age, was about to dawn through the recovery of the learning of the classical past. Petrarch had that mixture of love for God and for the world together that later fueled the Renaissance scholars. His lady love, one Laura, was already married, so he sublimated his feelings in the courtly Romantic style by writing sonnets praising her. These sonnets helped form Italian literature. His religious beliefs were expressed in a book called *Secretum*.             J.C.

**PFISTER, OSKAR** (1873–1956). A Swiss pastor interested in counseling, who observed that theological training alone is inadequate for interpreting the human side of redemption, regeneration, and sanctification. He then turned to the study of psychology. In 1908 he was offered a chair of systematic and practical theology, but he declined, believing that he would be dealing with theory instead of practice.

He became acquainted with the writings of SIGMUND FREUD, and this led to a long correspondence in which they shared experiences and discussed philosophy. Pfister disagreed with Freud's philosophical base, yet the two had a mutual respect for each other's positions. Pfister was helped by Freud's findings that neuroses were caused by repressed conflicts in conscience. This explained to him why religious people seemed unable to live a life of love and instead retreated into dogmatism and legalism. Neuroses, he found, destroyed faith. His book, *Christianity and Fear,* was translated into English in 1948, and his correspondence with Freud appeared later.             I.C.

**PHARAOH.** The Hebrew form of the Egyptian title "the Great House." Initially a designation of the palace, from the reign of Thutmose III (about 1490–1436 B.C.) on, it became the official title of the king himself. By about 950 B.C. the title was prefixed to regal names (thus, Pharaoh Shishak). Shortly after 700 B.C. it was written beside the regal name within the sovereign's cartouche (name ring).

*Pharaoh and Egypt.* At history's dawn, widely separated territories were fused into a single Egyptian monarchy. Though basic geographical isolation from the world and dependence on the Nile conferred a sense of unity on most ancient Egyptians, the separation of Upper and Lower Egypt was thoroughly perceived. To reverse Upper Egypt's attachment to the African desert and Lower Egypt's link with western Asia would have been impossible. Yet with the establishment of the First Dynasty near 3000 B.C., a single, effective nation emerged, and with it, the dogma that the pharaoh was divine. EGYPT and its absolute sovereign came to be

Courtesy of the Museum of Fine Arts, Boston

*Pair Statue of Mycerinus and his Queen Kha-Merer-Nebty II from Gizeh*

respectively regarded as the daughter and son of the sun-god Re, the supreme deity.

Moreover, as the embodiment of Horus, a god of distant spheres, the pharaoh possessed a fullness of divinity that went unchallenged for centuries. Indeed, by the Fifth Dynasty (mid-third millennium B.C.), Egyptian dogma held that at death, this god-king became Osiris, who enjoyed the same resuscitation and prospects for eternal life as had the god with whom he was identified.

Civilized Egyptian existence gravitated around the divine monarch, who exercised extensive ownership, authority, and responsibility over the "Two Lands" entrusted to him. Written Mesopotamian law codes found no counterpart near the Nile, for the pharaoh's word *was* law. Egypt's sovereign was the earthly interpreter of "justice" (*ma'at*, that which conforms with predestined cosmic order). Yet the pharaoh was no tyrant. Rather, in lonely seclusion, he worked for state consolidation and the stabilization of life.

As the Egyptian government grew in complexity, the pharaoh was required to delegate his regal functions. The bureaucracy was headed by a vizier, who occasionally enjoyed widespread authority. Similarly, the priests who served Egypt's more important deities and the commander of Egypt's militia asserted their leadership. In about 935 B.C., one such commander, Shishak, founded Egypt's Twenty-second Dynasty. Moreover, the high priest of Amon-Re was a sturdy national figure. If the pharaoh's power became increasingly shared, the dogma regarding his claim to rule as Egypt's authoritative divine sovereign persisted. Though the pharaoh became a more remote palace figure, the Egyptian state remained centralized in his person.

*Pharaoh and the Bible.* In the OT, the Egyptian sovereign is ordinarily called "Pharaoh" (Gen. 12:15) or "Pharaoh king of Egypt" (Ezek. 32:2), though his own name may be added (thus, "Pharaoh Neco" [II Kings 23:29]; "Pharaoh Hophra" [Jer. 44:30]). Other biblically named pharaohs include Shishak (I Kings 14:25), Zerah the Ethiopian (II Chr. 14:9), and Tirhakah (II Kings 19:9).

The pharaohs who confronted Abraham (Gen. 12:18), promoted Joseph (41:39-40), and oppressed the Israelites prior to their exodus cannot be confidently identified. Still, it is often suggested that Seti I (about 1305–1290 B.C.) was the pharaoh of the oppression (whose death is reported in Exod. 2:23) and Ramses II (about 1290–1224) the pharaoh of the Exodus.

The composite biblical portrayal of Egyptian monarchy combines legendary and historical elements. Extra-biblical evidence warrants our accepting the following OT allusions as historically credible: Pharaoh's preoccupation with dream interpretation (Gen. 41:1-15), appointment of foreign servants to supervise his herds (47:6), subjection of Hebrew slaves on public works projects (Exod. 1:11), consultation with courtly "wise men" and "magicians" (7:11), and consent to an international marriage of royalty in order to strengthen ties with an ally nation (I Kings 3:1 reporting Solomon's marriage to Pharaoh's daughter).                                                J.K.K.

**PHARISEES.** The origin of the Pharisees is not entirely clear. Their name means "separated" in Hebrew and probably reflects an early tendency toward separatism in a syncretistic world. They were a Jewish sect that arose sometime in the period between the time of Ezra (fifth century B.C.) and the first century A.D. They may have arisen as a result of the separatist tendencies in the teaching of Ezra after the return from Babylonian and Persian exile. The name does not seem to be earlier than the time of the Maccabean revolt in the second century B.C.

The Pharisees were not a political party, but they did exercise considerable power due to their orthodox teaching, educational activities in the synagogues, and their considerable number. Josephus writes that they were the most influential of the three major Jewish sects in the first century A.D.: "the Pharisees have the multitudes on their side." "They are able

greatly to persuade the body of the people"; "they have so great a power over the multitude." He speaks in one place of about 6,000 Pharisees and later of about 4,000 SADDUCEES, who evidently were the second largest sect. Josephus explains the difference in the two at the time of his writing: "the Pharisees have delivered to the people a great many observances by succession from their fathers, which are not written in the laws of Moses; and for that reason it is that the Sadducees reject them, and say that we are to esteem those observances to be obligatory which are in the written word but are not to observe what are derived from the tradition of our forefathers" (*Antiquities*).

The traditions referred to are oral traditions that have been handed down for centuries in what we today know as the TALMUD, consisting of the older MISHNAH (about 200 B.C. to A.D. 200, when it was codified by Judah the Prince of Sepphon's in Galilee) and the GEMARA (about A.D. 200 to 500). These earlier "traditions of the elders" are referred to by Jesus as "your traditions," the "precepts of men" (Matt. 15:3, 9) and "traditions of men" (Mark 7:8). These were interpretations of the Torah by rabbis of the intertestamental period who felt they were in reality preserving the understanding of the Torah itself given to Moses at the time he received the Torah. One section of the Mishnah declares: "Moses received the Law from Sinai and committed it to Joshua, and Joshua to the elders, and the elders to the Prophets, and the Prophets committed it to the men of the Great Synagogue." The Great Synagogue was a body of 120 elders, including many prophets who came up out of exile with Ezra. Herbert Danby comments, "The Mishnah . . . maintains that the authority of those rules, customs, and interpretatons which had accumulated around the Jewish system of life and religion was equal to the authority of the written Law itself, even though they found no place in the written Law." The sect that perpetuated these traditions was the Pharisees. Josephus speaks of the "exact skill they had in the law of their fathers" (*Antiquities*) and says they are "supposed to excel others in the accurate knowledge of the laws of their country" (*Life* 38). They "seem to interpret the laws more accurately" than other sects (*War*).

Other important teachings of the Pharisees include, according to Josephus, following the conduct of reason, high regard for the elderly, the immortality of the soul, the resurrection of the body (compare Acts 23:8), divine reward and punishment in the afterlife for human conduct, frugal living, diets that exclude delicacies, and a perception of fate that allowed for the freedom of human will. They were normally pacifists although they participated in the revolts against Rome. The Pharisees were the only sect to survive the destruction of the Temple, and their thinking about law and religion thus became the core of rabbinic Judaism represented in the Mishnah and in much of subsequent Judaism. Whether they were strictly a sect or represented basically the theology of the masses is not clear.

Several prominent people in the NT were of the Pharisaic party. Nicodemus, the rabbi who was a member of the Sanhedrin, who came to Jesus secretly at first (John 3:1) and later publicly defended him (John 7:50) and buried him (John 19:39), was a "man of the Pharisees . . . a ruler of the Jews" (John 3:1). Paul was a Pharisee (Phil. 3:6) who describes himself as "extremely zealous for the traditions of my fathers" (Gal. 1:14). He seems to have maintained this association even after his conversion, declaring before the SANHEDRIN: "Brethren, I am a Pharisee, a son of Pharisees" (Acts 23:6). Paul was trained in Jerusalem by Gamaliel, "educated according to the strict manner of the law of our fathers" (Acts 22:3). Gamaliel was the grandson of the noted Pharisaic teacher Hillel, a contemporary of Christ who represented the most liberal wing of Pharisaism. He was a member of the Sanhedrin (Acts 5:34). The kind of teaching to which Jesus responded in the Sermon on the Mount in Matthew's account (5–7) is best understood as Pharisaic, and one might say that he was correcting a Pharaisic distortion of Mosaic Judaism in that sermon. The attitudes expressed toward the Law are characteristically Pharisaic in Matthew's account. Luke has none of the peculiarly Jewish elements in his record of the occasion (6:20-49). The Pharisees were involved in the successful attempt to have Jesus put to death (Mark 3:6; John 11:47-57).      J.R.M.

**PHELPS, SYLVANUS DRYDEN** (1816–85). Baptist minister, author, and hymn writer. Born May 15, in Suffield, Connecticut, Phelps was educated at the Connecticut Literary Institute, Brown University, and Yale Divinity School. Ordained as a Baptist minister, he served the First Baptist Church, New Haven, Connecticut, for twenty-eight years. While still a college student, Phelps authored several hymns and children's songs. Some of his poetry and prose works were published, including a book on the Holy Land that went through nine editions. Probably his best-known hymn was "Savior, Thy Dying Love," published in Ira D. Sankey's *Gospel Hymns*. He was the father of William Lyon Phelps, who served for many years as professor of English literature at Yale and attained fame as a literary critic. Sylvanus D. Phelps died at New Haven on November 23.     R.H.

**PHENOMENOLOGY.** A method of philosophical investigation associated chiefly with the name of EDMUND HUSSERL (1859–1938). Husserl's aim was to transform philosophy into an exact science, and he believed that he could do this by concentrating on pure description, avoiding interpretation and deduction, which are always fallible. In order to arrive at the pure phenomenon (that which shows itself), the investigator's mind has to be emptied of all

presuppositions, even, for instance, the presupposition that the phenomenon investigated exists within some objective natural order. The mind has to be emptied of all traditional philosophical interpretations and theories. This phenomenological "reduction," as it is called, should bring one to confront the pure essence, the thing in itself as it presents itself to consciousness.

The phenomenological method was taken up by HEIDEGGER, and is basic to his analysis of human existence. That analysis consists of careful, even minute, descriptions of the various aspects of a human life. But Heidegger did not agree that such descriptions can be without presuppositions. On the contrary, the investigator always brings a preunderstanding to a task. Even to ask a question is to have some idea, however vague, of what would constitute a possible answer.

In one form or another, phenomenology has come to be widely used in theology, philosophy of religion, and religious studies generally. Tillich gives a good statement of the use of phenomenology in theology: "The test of a phenomenological description is that the picture given by it is convincing, that it can be seen by anyone who is willing to look in the same direction, that the description illuminates other related ideas, and that it makes the reality these ideas are meant to reflect intelligible." In philosophy of religion, OTTO's classic work *The Idea of the Holy* is a masterly exercise in the phenomenology of religious experience and was highly praised by Husserl. Finally, the methods of phenomenology have been widely employed in the comparative study of religions by Gerardus van der Leeuw and many others.     J.M.

**PHILEMON.** The name refers to the man who received Paul's letter that bears his name. He is called Paul's "beloved fellow worker" as well as his "dear friend." A recent suggestion is that the first term was Paul's own coinage to denote those who worked with him in the task of missionary preaching, especially to the Gentiles. If this is so, we should recognize in Philemon a person, presumably a non-Jew by race, who was committed along with Paul to the evangelization of the Lycus Valley, where his home was.

Philemon's family associations are given in the opening verses of the letter. Apphia, whom Paul calls "our sister," is usually taken to be Philemon's wife, a tradition that goes back to the church fathers. Archippus, whose name follows directly, is often believed to be Philemon's son, a suggestion that cannot however be proved (see Col. 4:17 for a mention of the same person). The home of Philemon was a gathering place of Christians who met there for worship, thus forming "the church in your house," a common feature of early Christian societies in days before church buildings were erected.

Philemon's remaining characteristic explains the

reason why Paul wrote to him. He was the owner of the slave Onesimus, who had wronged his master when both men were living at Colossae (Col. 4:9). Onesimus had absconded with some money. He met Paul, perhaps in the same place where Paul was detained, and was subsequently converted to the Christian faith (Philem. 10). Paul was greatly drawn to this man and found him useful (vv. 11-13). But he responded to the prompting of duty and felt he must let Onesimus return to his master.

The accompanying letter is to plead for leniency on several grounds, namely that Philemon should receive the runaway slave as he would receive Paul (v. 17) and with the reminder that the slave is now a Christian brother (v. 16). The final appeal is that Philemon owes a debt to Paul for his Christian standing (vv. 9, 19). And we have reason to be confident that Philemon heeded the Apostle's gentle but firm admonition to treat Onesimus kindly—otherwise the letter would not have survived. R.M.

*PHILIA.* Among the several Greek words for LOVE, *philia* is the most frequent, with the basic meaning of being attracted to a person or object. A natural expression is love for one's family, friends, country (patriotic attachment). Hence *philadelphia,* "love of a brother," carries the general sense of friendship and devotion. In Greek *philos* is a friend, and *philēma* is a kiss, both terms used in the NT.

There is no religious flavor to the word in classical Greek, but in the Bible *philia* and AGAPE share a commonality of meaning, and can be used interchangeably of God's love for humans, where *eros* is singularly absent. They are also used of a person's response to the divine love (see John 21:15 ff., which has the verbs *phileō* and *agapaō* with no distinction of meaning). R.M.

**PHILIP, APOSTLE.** One of the Twelve whom Jesus called as his followers and who became a founder-member of the apostolic church. He originated in Bethsaida (John 1:43-44). His attachment to Jesus is told in some detail in John 1:45-51, where Philip's messianic faith leads to Nathanael's becoming a disciple. Later in the Johannine story of the ministry of Jesus, Philip is tested by his reaction to Jesus' promise to feed five thousand hungry people (John 6:5-6). A third incident involved Philip and Andrew, who negotiated the coming of certain non-Jews to see Jesus (John 12:20-22). In these three episodes Philip is depicted as an ideal follower of Jesus who wishes to bring others to him. The slow emergence of his faith in Jesus as Divine Son is seen in John 14:8-9, but he has an undoubted place in the ranks of the Twelve (Matt. 10:3; Mark 3:18; Luke 6:14), both in the days of the ministry and after the Ascension of Jesus (Acts 1:13). His name does not feature in the later NT, but he has given his name to Gnostic writings claimed to emanate from him.

Philip's name is attached to the Gospel of Philip, which is a medley of Gnostic writings dealing chiefly with how the sacraments of baptism and the Eucharist were perceived and practiced among the Valentinian Gnostics. The one place where the apostle does feature in this body of catechetical instruction is interesting. He names Jesus' father, Joseph, as the carpenter who made the cross from the wood of his workshop. In another Gnostic book, *Pistis Sophia,* Philip is one of the three disciples commissioned to write down the oral teaching on the risen Christ. R.M.

**PHILIP OF HESSE** (1504–67). Early defender of Lutheranism, signer of the Augsburg Confession, organizer of the Schmalkaldic League, and one known for tolerance. Because of his bigamous marriage in 1540, Philip lost status. After Charles V defeated the Lutherans at Mühlberg (1547), he imprisoned Philip. Released in 1552, Philip never regained power. C.M.

**PHILIPPI.** A city in Macedonia, northeast of Thessalonica, and approximately ten miles from the Aegean Sea. The city was once called Krenides, but in 356 B.C. it was enlarged by Philip II, father of Alexander the Great, and given his name. In 42 B.C. Antony and Octavian defeated Brutus and Cassius just west of the city, and shortly thereafter it became a Roman colony.

Acts 16:12-40 records the visit of Paul and Silas to Philippi. Lydia of Thyatira heard Paul preach and was baptized; a slave girl exploited for her powers of soothsaying was healed; Paul and Silas were beaten and imprisoned; and following an earthquake the jailer and his family believed and were baptized. Paul maintained a close relationship with the Christians there, as evidenced by their repeated gifts sent to him and his canonical letter addressed to them. (See PHILIPPIANS, LETTER TO THE.) C.B.C.

**PHILIPPIANS, LETTER TO THE.** A letter written by the apostle Paul from imprisonment to the Christian community at PHILIPPI in Macedonia. It serves as an expression of thanksgiving for a gift given to him by the Philippians, as a warning against false teachers whose influence he fears, and as an appeal to unity within the church. With its repeated mention of mutuality and joy, the letter is Paul's most intimate communication to a congregation. He had established the community himself (Acts 16:12-40), and the Philippians had provided him with monetary help on at least two previous occasions (Phil. 4:15-16; II Cor. 11:8-9).

*The Occasion of the Letter.* There were three reasons why Paul wrote to the Philippians. (a) *Thanksgiving.* Epaphroditus had brought a gift from the Philippians to Paul during his current imprisonment and had perhaps intended to stay longer and share the ministry. He became critically ill, however, and Paul, knowing the anxiety of his friend, sent him

Courtesy of Stella G. Miller

*General view of the ruins of Philippi*

back home. The letter, which Epaphroditus carried with him, contained a word of thanksgiving for the Philippians' support (4:10-20) and a word of commendation for Epaphroditus' service (2:25-30).

(b) *Warnings.* Paul is also concerned about the vulnerability of the Philippians to sectarian teachers. He issues a sharp warning against such teachers who might make inroads in the Christian community. Opponents are mentioned in three places in the letter (1:27-28; 3:2-11, 18-19), but the references are such as to make it difficult to piece together a clear portrait of who they were. One plausible suggestion is that they were Jewish-Christian sectarians who offered perfection through circumcision and who represented the Christian life as one of spiritual exaltation immune to suffering. Paul calls them "dogs, evil-workers, mutilators of the flesh" (3:2), and "enemies of the cross" (3:18).

(c) *Call to unity.* Finally, though the Philippians merit high commendations (1:3-11), Paul takes the occasion of the letter to urge the congregation to maintain a unified front against the opposition (1:27-28) and specifically to settle the local squabble betwen two active members, Euodia and Syntyche (4:2-3).

*The Structure of the Letter.* Paul follows the typical form of Hellenistic letters including: salutation (1:1-2), prayer of thanksgiving (1:3-11), body of the letter (1:12–4:20), closing greetings, and benediction (4:21-23).

The body of the letter, though orderly, does not evidence a sustained rational argument. (a) *1:12-26* describes Paul's situation in imprisonment and his

confidence that his confinement and anticipated release will turn out for the advancement of the gospel.

(b) *1:27–2:18* contains a series of exhortations to unity and to faithfulness in the face of persecution. The early Christian hymn cited in 2:5-11 serves to anchor the appeals in the story of the crucified and exalted Christ.

(c) *2:19-30* details Paul's immediate plans for Timothy, Epaphroditus, and himself.

(d) *3:1-21* relates Paul's warnings against the sectarian teachers and offers his personal experience as an answer to their insistence on circumcision for Gentile Christians. Christian life in the present entails sharing Christ's sufferings, becoming conformed to his death. Perfection comes only with the resurrection of the dead, when lowly bodies are transformed to be like Christ's glorious body.

(e) *4:1-9* deals with the pastoral problems and more general admonitions.

(f) *4:10-20* brings the body of the letter to a close by expressing gratitude for the concern and the gift of the Philippians.

*Place and Date of the Letter.* Paul writes as a prisoner, but it is not exactly clear from the letter where he is imprisoned, whether in one of the places mentioned in Acts or some other. Three locations are possible: Rome (see the mention in the letter of "the whole praetorian guard" and "Caesar's household"), an imprisonment recorded in Acts 28:14-31; Caesarea, noted in Acts 23:33-26:32; and Ephesus, not mentioned in Acts but possibly alluded to in I Corinthians 15:30-32 and II Corinthians 1:8-10. The location of the writing cannot be determined with any certainty. If Rome is the choice, the date would be A.D. 58–60; if Caesarea, A.D. 56–58; if Ephesus, A.D. 54–55.

C.B.C.

**PHILISTINES.** The people who lived along the Mediterranean Sea in the southern part of Palestine. The whole country apparently took its name from them.

*Geography.* The land of the Philistines began at the seacoast city of Joppa, which is a few miles south of modern Tel Aviv. From there it extended south past the city of Gaza, with the Negeb desert forming the southern boundary. The Philistines occupied the coastal plain toward the mountains to the east, a distance of about twenty miles. The major cities of the Philistines were Gaza, Ashkelon, and Ashdod on the coast and Gath and Ekron inland. The Philistine plain is fertile, but in constant danger of sand dunes encroaching from the south.

*Language.* For many years it was believed that the Philistines, known as the "People of the Sea," had come from the island of Crete. But there is no archaeological indication of a Philistine occupation of Crete. Wherever they came from, when they arrived along the southeast Mediterranean coast they began to speak a Canaanite dialect. Gradually this in turn gave away to Aramaic.

*Religion.* All of the Philistine gods known to us have Semitic names. The Philistines had temples dedicated to DAGON, a senior god associated with grain and fish, in Gaza and Ashdod. It was in their Dagon temple in Ashdod that they deposited the Ark of the Covenant after capturing it from the Israelites. They also had temples dedicated to the goddess ASHTORETH in Ashkelon and the god BAALZEBUB in Ekron.

*Political and Military Organization.* Before they were defeated by David, the Philistines lived mainly in their five major cities, which were ruled by lords, who also acted as a council that ruled the whole nation. The council as a whole could overrule the decision of any of its five members. At that time they were able to muster a large army of foot soldiers, archers, and charioteers. The Philistines had a monopoly on iron working. Goliath's weapons were most likely made by Philistine ironsmiths. After their defeat by David, the title "lord" was replaced by "king," and they thereafter lived mainly along the coast.

*History.* The Philistines began settling the coast of Palestine after being driven out of Egypt by Ramses II. They apparently captured the cities of Ashkelon, Ashdod, Gath, and Gaza from their Canaanite inhabitants. They perhaps did this with the permission of the Egyptians, who controlled the area. They may later have founded Ekron since there is no earlier mention of the city. They then proceeded to expand into surrounding areas. The pressure they put upon the people of Dan and Judah is portrayed in the story of Samson (Judg. 13–15). When the Israelites tried, unsuccessfully, to force them back at Ebenezer (I Sam. 4:1-10), the Philistines destroyed Shiloh and captured the Ark of the Covenant. Samuel and Saul each were able to push back the Philistines to some extent. After Saul's death, however, the Philistines were able to make deep inroads into Israelite territory. After David became king over all Israel they attacked him in the Valley of Rephaim near Jerusalem. David, with his well-trained troops, was able to drive them back and reduce them to a non-threatening status. They did, however, continue to participate in the Phoenician slave trade, as Joel records (3:1-8).

Nebuchadnezzar later ended Philistine independence by deporting their rulers and many of their people. The cities in succeeding centuries became Phoenician and then Greek, with increasingly diverse citizenship.

B.J.

**PHILLIPS, PHILIP** (1834–95). Singing evangelist, composer, hymn writer. Philip Phillips, also known as "the Singing Pilgrim," was a farm boy who became a forceful influence in introducing gospel hymns to the Christian public. Born in Chautauqua County, near Jamestown, New York, Phillips was reared on a farm. His natural aptitude for music gave him the ability to sing when he was a boy of five. When he was nineteen, he became a singing master. At twenty-one he began his ministry as a singing evangelist, using a melodeon for accompaniment. His singing was said to increase the appetite for popular religious songs. As he traveled from church to church, he sold the songs he had published.

During the period after the Civil War, Phillips was one of several Americans who gave impetus to the acceptance of gospel songs. His *Hallowed Songs* was one of the hymnbooks used by Moody and Sankey in their evangelistic campaigns. Phillips published several hymnals, including *The Singing Pilgrim,* based on Bunyan's *Pilgrim's Progress; New Hymn and Tune Book (1867); Hallowed Songs,* and *The American Sacred Songster.* He wrote the words for "I Have Heard the Savior's Love," which was included in Sankey's *Songs and Solos.* Phillips also composed the music for "The Lord Will Provide" and "One Sweetly Solemn Thought." He wrote the book *Song Pilgrim Around and Throughout the World* (1880). Phillips died June 2, 1895, in Delaware, Ohio.

R.H.

**PHILO OF ALEXANDRIA** (about 30 B.C.–A.D. 45). A Jewish philosopher of Alexandria in Egypt, often called Philo Judaeus, or Philo the Jew. An outstanding intellectual, Philo's influence on the early Christian church, specifically on the church fathers Clement of Alexandria, Origen, and Ambrose, was immense. These Church Fathers adopted many of Philo's Stoic and Neoplatonic concepts and especially made use of his allegorical interpretations of Scripture. ALEXANDRIA was an outstanding intellectual center at the beginning of the Christian

Era and also was home to a very large, flourishing Jewish community. Philo was the supreme example of HELLENISM's influence on the cosmopolitan intellectual life of the Jews in the Egyptian Diaspora.

Only one date for Philo's life can be set with precision, the year A.D. 39-40, when Philo was sent to Rome by the Jewish community to protest the persecution of Jews by Flaccus, Prefect of Egypt, and to explain why the Jewish religion prevented Jews from participating in the cult of emperor worship.

Philo was a prolific writer, and thanks to the value put on his works by the Christian church, most of his writings have survived. He seems not to have known Hebrew but wrote Greek in a rich, distinguished style. Some of Philo's surviving work is known, however, only in Latin or Armenian translation. The Jewish historian Josephus discusses Philo, but no other ancient Jewish writing mentions him. Scholars have identified the influence of Philo on Midrashim, such as the saying of *Genesis Rabbah* 1:1.

Philo was of a rich and powerful family that was connected to Herod's dynasty and even to the court of the Roman Emperor. Nonetheless, little is recorded of Philo's life. His writings demonstrate that he was highly educated in classical Greek philosophy, rhetoric, and the natural sciences. Those same writings, covering as they do the Pentateuch, show that Philo was reared in a devout Jewish family. Philo's usual manner of dealing with the five books of Moses was to disregard the narrative per se and to turn the characters and events into abstract philosophical concepts. Philo, a very sophisticated but devoted Jew, mentions that he questioned the Jewish elders about Jewish traditions, and that he journeyed to Jerusalem to visit the Temple.       J.C.

**PHILOSOPHICAL THEOLOGY.** A branch of theology that employs philosophical concepts and arguments. Its aim may be simply intelligibility, for the philosophy current at any given time is an expression of the mentality of that time. If Christian theology is to be intelligible and relevant, then it will be useful to express it as far as possible in the prevailing philosophical idiom, thus exposing both its agreements and its disagreements with current secular thinking. Beyond that, philosophical theology may have (and usually does have) an apologetic aim, in showing the reasonableness of Christian faith and that it is no mere arbitrary set of beliefs but is philosophically defensible. The old natural theology, for instance, performed this function and could be considered as a type of philosophical theology.

THOMAS AQUINAS is a good example of a philosophical theologian. This statement is made not only because in the early part of his theological exposition he uses natural theology to establish the reality of his principal subject matter, God, but because throughout his work he employs philosophical concepts for the explication and articulation of his theology. In recent times, PAUL TILLICH is an obvious example of a philosophical theologian.

Because philosophical theology serves the needs of theology and may even have an apologetic function, it must be distinguished from the PHILOSOPHY OF RELIGION. The latter also employs philosophical concepts for the explication and even sometimes the justification of religion, but it relates to religion in general and does not share the theological concern with a particular tradition of faith and the vindication of that faith. It sometimes happens, however, that the philosophical theologian becomes so enamored of the philosophy that is used that it dominates the philosopher's position and may lead to the distortion or misrepresentation of the Christian doctrines that are the true theme of theology. Tillich, for instance, has been accused of setting up a "religious philosophy" that uses Christian symbols "in an alien and dechristianized meaning."

This is no doubt an exaggeration, but it points to a real danger and explains why KARL BARTH and others have been so reluctant to allow any philosophical influences to enter the structure of Christian theology. Even Barth is compelled to admit that at least in matters of terminology, theologians are bound to use some philosophically derived language. He insists, however, that it must be kept subordinate to the theological interests. It might be replied that as soon as theologians begin to speak of, let us say, "history" or "human nature" (and one can scarcely avoid such topics) then, whether they like it or not, they get into areas of philosophical controversy. It would surely be arrogant if they were to deny that anything can be learned from the philosopher in the handling of such topics. The attempt to restrict theology to biblical concepts hardly allows for intelligibility. (*See also* SYSTEMATIC THEOLOGY.)
      J.M.

**PHILOSOPHY.** From the Greek words *philos* ("love of") and *sophia* ("wisdom"). Tradition claims that Pythagoras was the first to describe himself as a philosopher or lover of wisdom. He held that people can be divided into three types: those who love activity, those who love pleasure, and those lovers of contemplation who seek wisdom. Pythagoras distinguished philosophy from both native shrewdness and trained skill. For Pythagoras wisdom leads to salvation, conceived in religious terms. For Plato philosophy is the search for eternal, unchanging truth or Reality, that is, for the causes and principles of things. The truth can be obtained only by a dialectical process of testing received opinions. By questioning and cross-examination, assumptions can be brought out in the open, critically examined, and the true nature of reality thus distinguished from the changing appearance of things.

In some cultural traditions, for example, in China and India, there is little, if any, distinction between the work of the philosopher and that of the wise man or sage. An appropriate distinction might be that the truth of the sage is, or can be, arrived at by direct intuition, while the truth of the philosopher is critical, that is, the result of rational or logical analysis. This is not to claim that one or the other offers greater insight into the human situation. Furthermore, to say that philosophy involves critical inquiry does not isolate what is unique to philosophy, since science, for example, engages in the critical testing of assumptions or hypotheses. Some modern philosophers have attempted to identify philosophical activity with a particular methodology. DAVID HUME essentially equated it with the procedures of experimental science; EDMUND HUSSERL with a phenomenological description of essences; Gilbert Ryle with the uncovering of fundamental category mistakes; and LUDWIG WITTGENSTEIN with the exposing of what literally is nonsense.

Modern philosophy has been characterized not only by a variety of methodologies but also by an increase in the fields of philosophical investigation. Aristotle had listed the areas of philosophy to include logic, physics, metaphysics, ethics, aesthetics, psychology, and political philosophy. Today physics and psychology are separate sciences, but there is important work being done in both the philosophy of science and in the philosophy of the social sciences. The PHILOSOPHY OF RELIGION began in the eighteenth century as a discipline independent of sectarian theology. Currently, philosophical analysis is applied and important journals published in such fields as the philosophy of law, history, biology, and education. The most important schools of twentieth-century philosophy include PRAGMATISM, EXISTENTIALISM, LOGICAL POSITIVISM (or empiricism), and LINGUISTIC ANALYSIS.                                       J.L.

## PHILOSOPHY OF RELIGION.

That branch of philosophy that seeks to describe and evaluate the concepts and beliefs, experiences and practices, of "religion." Since this term "religion" has been defined in so many ways and must be taken in a very broad sense, the scope of philosophy of religion is quite extensive and its precise boundaries not easily defined. It can, however, be clearly distinguished from SYSTEMATIC THEOLOGY. The latter expounds the content of some particular tradition of faith, whereas philosophy of religion is concerned with the whole panorama of religion, past and present. The philosopher of religion may not have any such affirmative attitude to religion as a theologian will normally have to the faith that is expounded.

Does this mean that a philosopher of religion may be an atheist or a non-religious person? The question is not easy to answer. Insofar as philosophy of religion is concerned with the coherence of concepts and the criticism of arguments, what is needed in the philosopher of religion is rationality and a grounding in the principles of logic. One's own religious opinions might be considered irrelevant.

On the other hand, if the philosopher of religion has also to explore and evaluate religious experiences, it might be thought that that person could hardly do this effectively if one had never known any such experiences. The philosopher might seem to be in the position of one who, having no appreciation of art or beauty, attempted to write a book on aesthetics. Even here, however, the atheistic philosopher of religion might be defended on the ground that one could study the many written descriptions of religious experiences undergone by others, and that nothing prevents a person from assessing the validity of these experiences, especially the interpretations and claims put upon them by those who have them. Nevertheless, religion is such an inward affair that any assessment from outside is suspect.

Philosophy of religion has also to be distinguished from NATURAL THEOLOGY. The traditional natural theology was indeed a philosophical exercise, and modern philosophy of religion may have developed out of it. But philosophy of religion is a broader study than the old natural theology, and before turning to arguments for or against the existence of God would be likely to raise the more radical question about the meaning of "God-talk" and the question of what is meant by the "existence" of God.

A contemporary philosophy of religion then is likely to begin with questions of language and logic. What do we mean when we use the word "God"? What is the "holy" or the "sacred"? Is any God-talk literal or descriptive in the way that our talk about entities within the world is? Or is all such talk symbolic and indirect? Then the question arises about its cognitive status. Is symbolic language only a language that evokes feeling, or is it (as is claimed for analogy) an indirect way of describing a reality that cannot be directly described? It is important here also to investigate and compare different types of related language—myth, poetry, metaphor, and so on. Again, one may ask about the nature of symbols and their cognitive functions. Is there any parallel between the non-picturing symbols employed by the physicist and those used by the philosopher of religion or the theologian or the ordinary believer? All these questions come "before" the traditional natural theology, just as that natural theology was often supposed to come "before" revealed theology.

Assuming that one had worked through the questions of language and meaning (and some modern textbooks of philosophy of religion might deal only with these questions), one might then go on to ask the question Does God exist? though almost certainly this question would be rephrased in the light of the analysis of the concepts of "God" and "existence." At this point, the traditional theistic arguments would be proposed for discussion, though expressed in new forms. It is interesting to note that each time the traditional "proofs" of GOD'S EXISTENCE are "refuted," they are soon refined and restated in a form that meets the objections. Probably few philosophers of religion today would claim that any one of the traditional arguments constitutes a "proof," but many would say that the traditional arguments, restated to take account both of objections and of new knowledge, constitute a cumulative case for theism in some form.

The philosophy of religion has also to turn its attention to the human pole of the religious relation. Who or what are human beings? Many religions have attributed to the human being an immortal SOUL. Here again one would have to begin by asking about the meaning of such a belief. Can we form a concept of "soul"? What about the problems of personal "identity"? Can the soul exist apart from the body, and, if not, is it possible to make sense of the concept of "resurrection"? These questions cannot be separated from more general questions about the nature of a human being. Is a naturalistic account of humanity adequate, or is the human being in some sense a breach in the texture of nature? At this point, the philosophy of EXISTENTIALISM, even in its atheistic forms, has drawn attention to the uniqueness of the human being and its transcendence of the merely natural mode of existence.

In studying the human being, philosophy of religion pays special attention to RELIGIOUS EXPERIENCE. It is important to distinguish the treatment that this subject receives from philosophy of religion and from the treatment in PSYCHOLOGY OF RELIGION. The latter is content to describe religious experience as a phenomenon of the psyche, but philosophy of religion goes more deeply into the matter and raises the difficult question whether it is some objective reality that confronts the religious consciousness or whether it is all explicable in terms of subjective factors in the believer's own mind. The question has been particularly discussed in relation to MYSTICISM. Here we have a form of religious experience which, although it seems to be restricted to a relatively few individuals, nevertheless seems to have a universal core that reappears among mystics in many cultures and in all the great religious traditions. This universality is itself an evidence in favor of the validity of the mystical experience. When one adds the strongly intentional character of such an experience, namely, that the experiencing mind refers it to some objective reality with just as much force as it does in sense-experience, then there might seem to be objective grounds for the mystical experience.

On the other hand, virtually all mystics tell us that their experience is ineffable, and this may be held to count against the claim that there is a mystical way of knowing the ultimate reality. Problems are caused too by the fact that there are drug-induced states of mind that appear to share many of the characteristics of the mystical vision. In any evaluation of religious experience, it is difficult to say how much is experience and how much is interpretation. Two people may have closely resembling experiences, but may interpret them very differently, according to the

tradition of ideas each has inherited. For instance, a Christian mystic and a Hindu mystic may have similar experiences, but each will interpret the experience in terms of one's own religion. A more serious problem arises when a non-religious person has an experience similar to the mystical one, but interprets it without reference to any objective agency, such as God or the Absolute. Of course, there is never a merely raw experience. Some interpretation is always at work. But the philosopher of religion must, as far as possible, distinguish the experiential and interpretative elements, and, where there is a conflict of interpretations, try to decide which is the more convincing.

Philosophies of religion vary with changing philosophical fashions. The first great treatments of the subject appeared in the nineteenth century and were influenced by IDEALISM in either its Kantian or Hegelian form. Over against these were naturalistic interpretations of religion, often associated with the rising subjects of anthropology, psychology, psychoanalysis, and sociology. In the twentieth century there has been a wider range of influences at work. The so-called "process" philosophy of WHITEHEAD and HARTSHORNE has given birth to a philosophy of religion that finds a place for God and religious experience in a world view that is consonant with the findings of modern physics. PHENOMENOLOGY has furnished a technique for the careful investigation of religious experience. Existentialism has shown the inadequacy of naturalistic views of humanity and has exposed the tendencies in human nature that are inclined to a religious interpretation of the human being. Finally, ANALYTICAL PHILOSOPHY, as has been shown, has raised important questions about the fundamental concepts and language of religion.

J.M.

PHINEHAS. (1) The son of Eleazar and grandson of Aaron (Num. 25:7), whose priestly deeds are reported in postexilic OT narrative.

In Moses' time, a contrite Israelite assembly endured a divinely sent plague as punishment for having succumbed to Midianite idolatry at Peor. When a defiant Israelite entered the camp with a Midianite woman, Phinehas speedily killed them both. Now appeased, Yahweh terminated the plague and delivered to Phinehas and his descendants "the covenant of a perpetual priesthood" (Num. 25:6-18). Subsequently, as Israel fought against Midian, Moses dispatched Phinehas with sanctuary vessels and trumpets (31:6).

In Joshua's time, Phinehas headed a delegation of ten chiefs from nervous western tribes to investigate the rumor that their eastern counterparts had erected an altar out of a desire for schismatic worship. Phinehas accepted the explanation that the Transjordan tribes were giving visible expression to their determination to have "a portion of Yahweh" and in Israel. Needless intertribal warfare was averted (Josh. 22:9-34). Finally, at Bethel, Phinehas rendered an oracle favoring Israelite retaliation against those Benjaminites who condoned the rape of the Levite's concubine (Judg. 19:22-26; 20:27-28).

(2) One of Eli's sons, who, with his brother Hophni, abused the priestly office by acting contemptuously toward Yahweh's offering and lustfully toward women serving in the Shiloh sanctuary (I Sam. 2:17, 22). After bearing the Ark of the Covenant into battle against the Philistines near Aphek, Eli's incorrigible sons met untimely death, and Israel sustained bitter defeat (4:11).

(3) The father of a priest, Eleazar (Ezra 8:33).

J.K.K.

**PHOEBE.** A Christian woman who had been a helper of the apostle Paul. She is called a deaconess in Romans 16:1-2, the only mention of her in the NT. It is not certain whether the term is to be taken generically as "servant" or technically as "deaconess."

J.R.M.

**PHOENICIA.** A small country lying north of Palestine along the Mediterranean coast and roughly comparable to modern Lebanon and adjacent parts of Israel and Syria. It was narrow, consisting essentially of the seacoast and adjacent mountains running about 130 miles north-south. The name is Greek, probably a translation of the Semitic word "Canaanite," which reflected the Canaanites' background and was used by them to refer to themselves. The Greek name comes from a root word meaning either "palm" or "purple," the latter being also the meaning of the term "Canaan." It had its origin as a state about the thirteenth century B.C. and was a great maritime power from about 1000 B.C. until its culture was absorbed by the Greeks around 600 B.C. However, important cities of Phoenicia are much older. Excavations have dated structures at Byblos (Gebal) to about 2500 B.C., but the city was probably founded around 3000 by the Egyptians for commercial purposes. Written records from Egypt speak of Phoenicia about 1600 B.C. Sidon was of such importance that Phoenicians were known as Sidonians in the time of Homer. Tyre was equally important and, even after its destruction by Alexander the Great, moved its location slightly and became again an important city until Roman times. Berytos (Beirut) was an important industrial center in the ancient world.

J.R.M.

**PHOENICIANS.** A nation of people who in ancient times occupied the area along the northern coast of the eastern Mediterranean. Their origins are hidden in obscurity, but excavations in PHOENICIA indicate they were there in 3000 B.C., SIDON being their oldest city. Herodotus thought they came from around the Persian Gulf. Their country, roughly modern-day Lebanon, was predominantely mountainous and not especially productive of commercial agriculture, but they were blessed with several important natural harbors on the coast and consequently became a great maritime nation, trading and colonizing as far west as Africa and Spain, perhaps even reaching the Atlantic. Carthage was among their better-known colonies.

The Phoenicians became famous through commerce, exporting enormous quantities of cedar trees, papyrus leaves for scrolls and books, glass (which they may have invented), purple dye (from the plentiful murex seashell), and boats for navies all over the known world (for example, Sennacherib, Pharaoh Neco II, and Xerxes). With no known mineral resources except iron, Phoenicia developed into one of the greatest trading nations in ancient history. The nearby island of Cyprus became a virtual Phoenician colony. Trade was fostered by the fact that the Phoenicians lived at a crossroads of both land and sea trade routes, and enjoyed the protection of Egypt. The invention of the alphabet appears to have been a product of the Phoenician need for effective commercial bookkeeping, just as was their production and use of numbers, weights, and measures. Their exports included cedar and pine, fine linen, dyed cloth (especially purple), Phoenician glass, metalwork, salt, wine, and dried fish. In turn they imported papyrus, ivory, spices, horses, gold, silver, copper, silk, ostrich eggs, and precious jewels. Phoenicians, under Hiram, king of Tyre, imported many of these things for King Solomon (I Kings 10:11, 22; II Chr. 9:10, 21), including apes and peacocks. Phoenician workers who built the Temple of Solomon may have designed it on Phoenician models, some of which are known to us now (I Kings 5:1-12; II Chr. 2:3-16).

A number of people in the OT were associated with Phoenicia in one way or the other. Ethbaal is mentioned as the king of the Sidonians (I Kings 16:31). His daughter, the infamous Jezebel, married the Israelite king Ahab, who allowed her to introduce the worship of Baal into Israel (I Kings 16:29-34; 18:19). There were two HIRAMs from Tyre who had part in the building of the Temple in Jerusalem. The first was the king who was a friend of David (II Sam. 5:11), who after his death befriended Solomon by sending cedar and cypress trees from Phoenicia down the Mediterranean made into rafts, for use in the building of the Temple (I Kings 5:1-12). The second Hiram, whose father was a Tyrian, was of partial Jewish extraction. His mother, a Danite by birth (II Chr. 2:14), was the widow of a man from the tribe of Naphthali (I Kings 7:14). He was a skilled craftsman who was sent by Hiram the king (II Chr. 2:11-14) to do the bronze work in the Temple (I Kings 7:13-47). The city of Zarephath, where the widow lived to whom Elijah was sent, was located near Sidon (I Kings 17:9).

In the NT, Jesus went to Phoenicia on a preaching tour to Jews and encountered a Syrophoenician woman (Mark 7:26; called a Canaanite in Matt. 15:22), whose daughter he healed. Paul and Barnabas passed through Phoenicia on the way to Jerusalem from Antioch, reporting on the conversion of Gentiles (Acts 15:3). Phoenicia had received the word earlier through the missionary efforts of those who had been scattered by the persecution of Stephen (Acts 11:19). At the end of his third journey Paul met with Phoenician Christians for a week, after which he bade them good-bye in a prayer meeting on the beach near Tyre and went on to Jerusalem (Acts 21:3-6).

The Ras Shamra tablets, discovered at UGARIT, were written in Ugaritic, a Semitic language closely akin to biblical Hebrew. They reveal a culture of religious depravity known in the OT as Canaanite. Carthaginian settlers from Phoenicia called themselves Canaanites until the fifth century A.D. Ugaritic is written in a twenty-nine-letter cuneiform alphabetic script, which reads from left to right like Akkadian. Numerous tablets, written in a variety of languages including Ugaritic, were discovered at Ugarit by C. F. A. Schaeffer, who directed thirty campaigns there during the period from 1929 to 1968. When deciphered the texts revealed the cultural life, social institutions, and religious beliefs and practices of the Phoenicians. Their religion was polytheistic, with El, Asherah, Baal, and Anath occupying the most important positions in the pantheon. It was largely a fertility cult, apparently, with many cultic practices centering in various temples. Human sacrifices were offered to Baal Ammon in Carthage and to Malqart in Tyre.

J.R.M.

**PHOTIUS** (about 810–895). Highly honored Greek Orthodox churchman, twice patriarch of Constantinople, a key figure in East-West struggles for supremacy. Born into nobility, the scholarly Photius chose a career in politics. He advanced rapidly to first imperial secretary and ambassador to Assyria. When Emperor Michael III in 858 deposed Patriarch Ignatius of Constantinople, he named Photius his successor. Photius received the necessary sacred orders in five days and was consecrated patriarch on Christmas Day by Archbishop Gregory Asbestas of Syracuse, whom Ignatius had previously dethroned. Ignatius refused to vacate. Photius vainly sought help from Pope Nicholas I, even though some Roman delegates participated in dethroning Ignatius. A Roman synod (863) annulled all earlier actions, said Ignatius was still patriarch, and deposed Photius, Asbestas, and all appointed by them. However, Photius, supported by the emperor, retained the patriarchate.

Further disputes between Constantinople and Rome erupted over control of missionaries in Bulgaria. In 867 Photius excoriated Rome's missionaries and questioned Rome's saying the Holy Spirit proceeds from the Father *and the Son* (*Filioque*), and a council at Constantinople excommunicated the pope. When Basil murdered and succeeded Michael as emperor in 867, Ignatius was reinstated, and councils at Rome and Constantinople in 869 anathematized Photius. After Ignatius' death in 877, the emperor reinstated Photius as patriarch. However, Emperor

Leo VI in 886 again deposed Photius, who faded from history. Photius' most important writing was *Myriobilion* (*Bibliotheca*), reviews and excerpts from nearly three hundred books, many now lost.

C.M.

**PHRYGIA.** A large area, difficult to define, in southwest Turkey through which Paul passed on his journeys (Acts 13:14–14:24; 16:6; 18:23) establishing and revisiting churches. In Roman times part of it, including the cities of Antioch and Iconium, lay in the province of Galatia, and the other part including the cities of Colossae and Laodicea, lay in the province of Asia.

J.M.

**PHYLACTERIES.** In Hebrew, *tefillin*. Two small black leather cases containing scriptural passages and fastened with long black leather straps to the arm and forehead of the Jewish male during the weekday morning prayers. They are put on in response to God's command to wear them as a "sign upon thine hand, and they shall be as frontlets between thine eyes" (Deut. 6:8 KJV), as well as used in the prayers themselves. The scriptural passages in the black cases are on parchment made from the skins of ritually clean animals, preferably calves. The passages are written in square (Assyrian) script and refer to the words of the TORAH.

One cube is placed on the left arm facing the heart (unless the person is left-handed, in which case it is put on the right arm). The other cube is placed in the center of the forehead. This one should be particularly prominent, so that all can see it, in order to fulfill God's command: "And all people of the earth shall see that thou art called by the name of the Lord; and they shall be afraid of thee (Deut. 28:10 KJV). The leather thong of the second cube is wound seven times around the arm between the elbow and the wrist, and, after the cube for the forehead is donned, the hand strap is wound three times around the middle finger. With each action, blessings are recited. Some scholars do not like the word "phylacteries" because in the Greek this word means "amulet" or "safeguard," and this is not the purpose of *tefillin*. They are worn in obedience to a biblical commandment and as a reminder that the Torah must be studied and obeyed every day. They are not worn on the Sabbath and other biblical holy days, since these days are already reminders of God's Law.

L.K.

**PIA DESIDERIA.** PHILIP JACOB SPENER's book in 1675 that launched PIETISM in German Lutheranism. Spener called for intense, devotional Bible study, lay fulfillment of Luther's priesthood of all believers, love as well as intellectualism in religion, higher morality among professors and students, and revival of evangelical preaching.

C.M.

## PIERPOINT, FOLLIOTT SANDFORD. (1835–1917).

Classical scholar and hymn writer. Pierpoint was born in Bath, England, and educated at the local grammar school and Cambridge University. Somewhat of a Victorian dilettante with strong High Church convictions, Pierpoint wrote considerable poetry and many hymns. However, the one hymn for which he is remembered is "For the Beauty of the Earth," which was published in 1864 in an anthology entitled *Lyra Eucharistica*. Pierpoint, a young man of twenty-nine years, wrote this beautiful hymn late in the spring as he sat on a Bath hillside, overlooking the Avon River.            R.H.

## PIETÀ.

A representation, generally in sculpture, of an individual holding the dead body of Christ following the descent from the cross. The most famous perhaps is that of the sorrowing Virgin Mary holding Christ's body on her knees. The statue, now located in St. Peter's, Rome, was one of several by MICHELANGELO dealing with the same theme. The Florentine Pietà, now in Florence Cathedral, shows a compassionate Nicodemus holding the Lord's body. Found in Michelangelo's studio at his death was the Rondanini Pietà, which is displayed in the Castello Sforzesco, Milan. The Pietà concept is found in Christian art of thirteenth-century Germany and even back to the Byzantine era.            R.H.

## PIETISM.

A reaction, mostly within German Lutheranism, against the cold RATIONALISM of the philosophers and the rigid orthodoxy of Protestant Scholasticism. Against both rationalism and Scholasticism, Pietism proposed a life of deeper personal piety, supported by groups or "colleges of piety" formed by those within the church who wished to attain a deeper religious life. Its founder was PHILIPP JACOB SPENER, whose book *Pia Desideria*, published in 1675, set the tone and basic methodology of the movement.

While Spener did not disagree with any of the doctrines being taught by Lutheran orthodoxy, he felt that such orthodoxy was not enough, and that at times it tended to obscure the need for personal commitment. For that reason he suggested that candidates for the ministry should be examined in order to ascertain that they were "true Christians." Naturally, such a suggestion brought criticism and opposition from many of the leading theologians, who felt that their endeavors were being attacked. This, coupled with his insistence on giving the laity more participation in the life of the church, led Spener to repeated clashes with ecclesiastical authorities. But in spite of this, his suggestions were well received by many, particularly in Saxony, where he gained the adherence of AUGUST HERMANN FRANCKE.

The work of Spener, Francke, and others eventually led to the founding of the University of Halle, where Francke was a professor, and which soon became a center of Pietism. Under Francke's inspiration, the movement then took an interest in missions, which most Protestants had neglected since the time of the Reformation, and Halle became a center for the training and sending of missionaries. As a result, many churches throughout the world bear the mark of the Pietist movement.

One of those who was deeply impressed by Pietism was Count NIKOLAUS LUDWIG VON ZINZENDORF, who allowed a group of Moravian refugees to settle on his lands, and eventually so imbued them with his vision that the MORAVIANS spread throughout the world as missonaries.

JOHN WESLEY, the founder of the Methodist movement, was also profoundly influenced by the Moravians. It was they who led him through the difficult times when he doubted his salvation, and for that he was always grateful. From them, and from Pietism in general, Wesley also learned of the need for a personal commitment and life of faith. But he could never bring himself to become a Moravian or a Pietist in the strict sense, for the evangelical tradition in which he had been brought up, and which he always cherished, impelled him to be more concerned than the Moravians or the Lutheran Pietists with sanctification and with the application of the Christian faith to the life of society.            J.G.

## PILATE, ACTS OF.

Variously known as the Acts of Pilate and the Gospel of Nicodemus, the work in the NT APOCRYPHA dates from the fourth century, and is in two main parts: (1) the story of the passion, burial, and resurrection of Jesus; (2) the narrative of his DESCENT into the abode of the dead, and the ensuing delivery of the faithful dead, as well as his final triumph over Satan. References by Justin Martyr (about 100–165) to Acts of Pilate have led some scholars to assume that this document was known to him, but he is apparently merely assuming that there were official Roman records of the crucifixion of Jesus. Far more likely is the view that the first part of this work is an apologetic expansion of the Gospel of Matthew in its report of these events. The writer of these Acts is trying to expand and strengthen the Christians' claims about the empty tomb and the post-Resurrection appearances, as well as the commissioning of the disciples. To this end the author heightens the sense of injustice that was done to Jesus, by both Jewish and Roman legal standards, and uses the testimony of his opponents to reinforce that evaluation of Jesus' death and execution.

The second part of the work is concerned not only to demonstrate the facticity of Jesus' resurrection, but also to show how his descent into the realm of the dead makes it possible for him to give life to the saints of former times, reaching back to Adam himself. The final defeat of Satan is depicted here as well, for which the vivid symbol is that Jesus leaves his cross behind in hell as a perpetual evidence of his victory through seeming defeat. Among those who share in his triumph are not only such biblical figures as Enoch and Elijah, but also the penitent thief who was crucified with Jesus.

In several versions, the work is considerably expanded. One Latin version has the high priests testify to the reality of the Resurrection and to Jesus' divine sonship, which leads Pilate to write a letter to the emperor Claudius, explaining the Christian claims for Jesus and the Jewish opposition to him. Other additions describe how Pilate determined that Jesus' body had not been stolen from the tomb; how he provided accounts of these events to Roman authorities as well as Herod; how Veronica, who was supposed to be the woman cured of a bloody flux by Jesus and had wiped his face at the cross, was brought to Rome and honored by the emperor.    H.K.

**PILATE, PONTIUS.** The discovery of an inscription at Caesarea on the coast of Palestine in 1961 has yielded evidence of the historical figure otherwise known from the Gospels as Pontius Pilate, although his career is briefly mentioned by Tacitus, Josephus, and Philo. The four Gospels all agree on making him the decisive Roman figure at the trial of Jesus, and there are occasional allusions to him in other NT books (Acts 3:13; 4:27; 13:28; I Tim. 6:13).

He came to his office as prefect of Judea in A.D. 26, and assumed large-scale military and judicial powers as well as wielding authority over the Jewish leaders and the Temple treasury. His relations with the Jews were not happy, and he constantly aggravated the situation, first by trying to introduce Roman military standards into the city, then by seeking to dedicate some golden shields in his Jerusalem residence. On both counts he was defeated and forced to back down. When he tried to use Temple money to finance an aqueduct to bring water to Jerusalem, his action led to resistance and bloodshed (see Luke 13:1).

At the trial of Jesus he was confronted with a political allegation, which he took seriously, but he vacillated because his position at Rome was tenuous, following the loss of his patron Sejanus in October A.D. 31. The emperor Tiberius was pro-Jewish, and Pilate had no wish to offend him. His final year saw his disgrace in Judea and recall to Rome, where he died, leaving a memory in the Apostles' Creed of the church ("suffered under Pontius Pilate").    R.M.

**PILGRIMAGE.** An important ritual practice in the majority of the world's religions is pilgrimage —travel for religious reasons, generally to a sacred shrine or center. The pilgrimage goal is usually a place of mythological or historical significance. Those completing the trek to it may receive special boons of healing, answered prayers, or inner grace. Additional benefits to the pilgrim are likely to be enhanced fidelity to the religion, strengthened bonds of fellowship with one's coreligionists and particularly those with whom one traveled in pilgrimage, and greater prestige within the faith-community after return. In some cases, of which the most important is undoubtedly the Muslim HAJJ to Mecca, pilgrimage fulfills a definite religious obligation. More often, however, the grace of pilgrimage lies precisely in the fact that it is a supererogatory work that goes beyond minimal spiritual duties, and hence exemplifies extra devotion or zeal. At the same time, the truth that, especially in premodern times, pilgrimage often combined spiritual enthusiasm with recreation and diverting, if strenuous, travel cannot be overlooked; pilgrimage also indirectly has done much to spread cultural features and knowledge of the world.

Besides the Muslim hajj, important pilgrimage practices have included Roman Catholic journeys to Rome, Lourdes, or Fatima; Japanese to the grand shrine of ISE or various sacred mountains including FUJI; Hindu to the sacred Ganges River and a number of famous temples; Buddhist to sacred relics and footprints of the Buddha; and Islamic to the shrines of numerous saints. Almost alone among major religious traditions, Protestant Christianity has no important role for pilgrimage in the traditional sense. Pilgrimage is also frequently used by spiritual writers as a metaphor for inward growth toward God.
   R.E.

*PILGRIM'S PROGRESS. See* BUNYAN, JOHN.

**PILLAR OF FIRE AND OF CLOUD.** A crucial means of God's self-revelation to the Israelites as they trekked through the wilderness and advanced toward the Land of Promise (Num. 14:14; Deut. 31:15; Neh. 9:12, 19; Ps. 99:7). The pillar of cloud and fire provides Yahweh's transient people needful guidance and protection. When designed solely as a pillar of cloud, it becomes the locus of divine revelation.

The pillar of cloud and fire is introduced early in the narrative of Israel's departure from Egypt as indication that active divine presence would accompany Yahweh's people throughout their wilderness wandering (Exod. 13:21). As the Egyptian force gained ground on the fugitives, the pillar moved between the two hosts to prevent the Egyptians from immediately overtaking the Israelites (14:19).

The pillar of cloud is deftly portrayed in its revelatory aspect in two passages. First, Exodus 33:9-10 reports that whenever Moses entered the tent of meeting to converse with Yahweh, "the pillar of cloud would descend and stand at the door of the tent." Accordingly, God's presence was manifested to the people who responded reverently. Second, Numbers 12:5 records identical divine descent prior to the disclosure of Yahweh's word defending the incomparability of Moses to Aaron and Miriam, who had defied their brother's authority.

The origin of such imagery is conjectural. Some suggestions include: (1) the use of burning braziers to indicate an army's line of nocturnal march; (2) the notion entertained by desert inhabitants that active volcanoes emitting fire and smoke betokened divine presence; (3) the ascent of sacrifical smoke at ancient sanctuaries, if not the smoke and flame discharged by two bronze pillars fronting Solomon's temple (I Kings 7:15-22). Since cloud and fire often denote presence and guidance in the OT (Gen. 15:17; Exod. 3:2; 19:9; 24:17; 40:34-38; I Kings 8:10-11), this wilderness symbol is singularly apt.          J.K.K.

**PILLARS OF ISLAM.** Five fundamental religious obligations of Muslims are commonly referred to as the "Five Pillars of Islam." They are: the profession of faith in the form of the simple Muslim creed, "There is no god but God (*Allah,* the one God), and Muhammad is his prophet"; the formal prayer or worship *(salat),* done in a prescribed manner five times a day, facing in the direction of Mecca; giving alms, which for fulfillment of this obligation is in prescribed amounts, often collected as taxes from the faithful only in traditional Islamic states; fasting in the form of abstention from food and drink between sunrise and sunset during the month of Ramadan in the Muslim lunar calendar; and the hajj or pilgrimage to Mecca incumbent upon those believers able to undertake it. The Five Pillars, ideally performed in the same way throughout the Muslim world and focused on the holy city of Mecca, have done much to enhance a sense of unity among Muslims.     R.E.

*PIRKE ABOTH.* Popularly known in English as "Ethics of the Fathers." It is the part of the MISHNAH that comprises the selected wisdom, sayings, ethical and religious principles, and rules of conduct. The "fathers," scholars believe, are the early rabbis (from 300 B.C. to A.D. 200) who composed the various aphorisms and moral sayings. *Aboth* (or *Avot*) teaches good human relationships, the value of studying the Torah, how to serve God, love of peace, and the importance of charity, modesty, and humility to all humankind.          L.K.

**PISGAH, MOUNT.** A mountain in the Abarim Mountains, opposite Jericho, from which Moses viewed vast stretches of Canaan west of the Jordan (Deut. 34:1-4). On its slopes Balak built seven sacrificial altars when he hired Balaam to curse Israel (Num. 23:14). If ancient Pisgah corresponds to Ras es-Siyaghah, it lies immediately west of Mount Nebo.          J.K.K.

**PISIDIA.** An area located in southwest Asia Minor, now in Turkey. In NT times it formed part of the Roman province of Galatia. To the churches in this region Paul wrote the LETTER TO THE GALATIANS, according to one theory. The two references to Pisidia are in Acts 13:14 and 14:24. According to the first, ANTIOCH is called a Pisidian city to distinguish it from the more important Antioch on the Orontes (Acts 11:22-26; 13:1). Pisidia is known to have been a place where Jews settled in large numbers, though it is also attested that in this mountainous region the tribes were illiterate (that is, did not understand Greek) and both superstitious and savage (see Gal. 3:1).          R.M.

**PISTIS SOPHIA.** A religious tract, written originally in Greek by Egyptian Gnostics and translated into the dialect of Sahidic. It is the latter translation that is extant. The theme of the document is the revelation made by the risen Lord to the chosen disciples, including PHILIP, who are bidden to write it down. This message of GNOSTICISM offers a way of escape from the material world to a spirit-filled existence in the realm of light. The title is taken from the name of the heroine, who in turn personified philosophy. She is set free from bondage to chaos by Jesus who ascends to the presence of God on high after defeating evil powers. Much is made of this engagement, and the work aids our understanding of how Egyptian believers in esoteric mysteries came to attach the story of Jesus and his disciples to contemporary mysticism.          R.M.

**PIUS II** (1405–64). Pope (1458–64) and Renaissance humanist named Enea Silvio de Piccolomini, known in literature as Aeneas Silvius, who reasserted papal supremacy over councils. A native Italian from Tuscany, he was educated in humanism at Sienna's university and became secretary to Bishop Capranica at the Council of Basel, living in Switzerland from 1431 to 1435, and distinguishing himself at the council. His history of the council in 1440 defended conciliar supremacy. In 1442 he began working for Holy Roman Emperor Frederick III as poet laureate and wrote irreverent, romantic works. On being ordained in 1446, he renounced his conciliarism and romantic writings, and in 1447 became bishop of Trieste. He then wrote new treatises on Basel, education, and other things, from a papal perspective. In 1456 he was made a cardinal and two years later elected pope. He took the name Pius from Virgil's "pius Aeneas." He served ably as pope, sought unsuccessfully to mount a crusade against the Turks, and in 1460 issued the bull *Execrabilis* against anyone appealing to a council.          C.M.

**PIUS IX** (1792–1878). Pope (1846–78) with the longest papal reign in history, who opposed modern liberalism, proclaimed the Immaculate Conception of Mary, and pushed papal infallibility through VATICAN Council I. Born in Senigallia, Italy, and named Giovanni Maria Mastai-Ferretti, Pius was inclined to constitutional reforms and liberalism when elected pope, but in 1848 revolutionists under Giuseppe Mazzini established a republic of Rome and briefly imprisoned Pius, who escaped. Restored to his throne in 1850 by French troops, Pius bitterly opposed liberalism and branded Catholic liberals as traitors. In 1861 Victor Emmanuel unified Italy, with most papal states included. Pius opposed the new state, and in 1864 issued his sweeping SYLLABUS OF ERRORS, which condemned eighty modernist errors including separation of church and state, civil control of education, and civil recognition of other religions. The Immaculate Conception of Mary (1854), removing Mary from original sin, proved popular in Catholicism; however, when Vatican Council I in 1870 voted for papal infallibility, reactions created the Old Catholic church under Jansenist auspices. On the withdrawal of French troops in 1870, Victor Emmanuel captured Rome, and the remaining papal states joined the new Italy. Pius retained Vatican City and received special privileges, but considered himself a prisoner. This "Italian question" was not settled until 1929, when Mussolini and the pope made a concordat.                              C.M.

PIUS XI (1857–1939). Pope (1922–39) known for stressing liturgy, missions, and concordats with Mussolini and Hitler. Born near Milan, Italy, and named Achille Ambrogio Damiano Ratti, educated in Milan and Rome, Ratti taught dogmatic theology at Milan (1882–88), and from 1888 to 1918 rose to prefect at Milan's Ambrosian Library and later at Rome's Vatican Library. He became apostolic visitor to Poland (1918) and archbishop of Milan (1921). Elected pope (1922), he produced several encyclicals on social issues and concluded a concordat with Mexico (1929) allowing the church to function. But he is chiefly remembered for accommodating concordats with Mussolini (1929) and Hitler (1933), neither of whom kept the agreements. Fearing Communism, Pius supported Francisco Franco in Spain's civil war (1937). Disillusioned by the bad faith of totalitarian governments, Pius lashed out with *Non abbiamo bisogno* (1931), saying Catholics could not be Fascists, *Mit brennender Sorge* (1937), saying Nazism was utterly anti-Christian, and *Divini Redemptoris* (1937), saying Communism was false and deceptive.                              C.M.

PIUS XII (1876–1958). Pope (1939–58), diplomat, humanitarian, and canon law expert, who decreed excommunication for Catholics who became Communists, and dogmatized the Assumption of Mary. Born into a family of lawyers and named Eugenio Pacelli, Pius XII became a priest in 1899 and that same year received doctorates in theology and law. A pastor for two years, in 1901 he began serving in various high papal offices including chamberlain, consultor, nuncio, secretary of state, and legate. His diplomatic missions carried him throughout the Catholic world. Elected pope in 1939, he sought peace and succored refugees, but vacillated on denouncing Hitler's genocide of Jews and later encountered severe criticism for not taking a strong stance against Hitler. As pope he visited France, the United States, Hungary, and Argentina. His encyclical *Mystici Corporis* (1943) pictured the church as Christ's mystical body. In 1946 he named thirty-two new cardinals, including five from the United States,

raising the number of cardinals to seventy. In 1949 he declared excommunication for Catholics who became Communists, and in 1950 dogmatized Mary's bodily ascension into heaven. He opposed non-Catholic ecumenism, saying all should return to Rome.                              C.M.

PLAGUES OF EGYPT. A sequence of natural disasters victimizing Egypt prior to Israel's release from Egyptian servitude (Exod. 7:8–11:10). Variously labeled "plagues" (9:14), "signs" (10:1-2), and "wonders" (7:3), they jointly constitute God's "great acts of judgment" (7:4) against Egypt.

The ten plague episodes are as follows: (1) Nile to blood (7:14-25, following 7:8-13, a preface); (2) frogs (8:1-15); (3) gnats (8:16-19); (4) flies (8:20-32); (5) diseased cattle (9:1-7); (6) boils (9:8-12); (7) hail (9:13-35); (8) locusts (10:1-20); (9) darkness (10:21-23); (10) death of the "firstborn" (11:1-10).

These stylized plague episodes claim a historical nucleus. Interpreters have often introduced various natural Egyptian phenomena into the discussion, and sometimes argued for a causal relationship whereby one scourge triggers another. Tiny organisms tend to give the Nile a dull reddish hew when it crests in August. Scourges of frogs have been attested in September. An abundance of dead frogs might readily attract gnats and flies, subsequently inflicting disease upon cattle and humanity. Egyptian hailstorms, while infrequent, are known, as are locusts and severe sandstorms capable of darkening the skies. All plagues, save the death of the firstborn, can be said to make sense within an Egyptian setting.

Such rationalizations, however, ignore the wonder surging through these episodes. Natural law held no fascination for biblical Israel. Rather, with eyes of faith, Yahweh's people emphasized the reality of *unnatural* happenings providentially executed in their behalf. Their immunity from those plagues that devastated their Egyptian neighbors was not perceived as fortuitous. Nor was the hardening of Pharaoh's heart understood as anything but the outcome of Yahweh's own determination to manifest impressive "wonders" for Yahweh's own glory.

In sum, the plague episodes of Exodus 7:8–11:10 fit comfortably within the entirety of Exodus 1–15, chapters perceptively grasped by Johannes Pedersén as cultically shaped PASSOVER legend celebrating Yahweh's special intervention for the rescue of Yahweh's people. Nature was thus subjected to divine purpose as Yahweh claimed Israel in a most memorable manner.                              J.K.K.

PLAINSONG. Vocal music or chanting, rhythmic but not metrical, also called plainchant. It is the usual music of the Roman Catholic Mass. Plainsong is an extension of speech, and its scales are limited to the intervals of the human voice. Individual notes are usually of the same time length. Many times plainsong is performed by two choirs singing the same melody alternatively. It is a pure, beautiful music well suited to its sacred use in divine services.

Since the far-reaching revisions of the Catholic liturgy by Vatican Council II, the Mass is now sung or said in the vernacular, the language of the people. The Mass now is also accompanied by various kinds of instruments and several forms of music.          J.C.

PLATO/PLATONISM. Probably the most influential philosopher who has ever lived (428–348 B.C.), Plato was a member of a distinguished Athenian family. As a young man, he was deeply influenced by the teaching and example of SOCRATES, who was put to death by the Athenian authorities in 399. About twelve years after this event, Plato founded his famous academy at Athens for the discussion and study of philosophical, scientific, and mathematical questions. The Academy claimed his energies for the rest of his life, except for two periods in 367 and 361–60, when he was persuaded to take part, without much success, in the political affairs of the Greek colony at Syracuse in Sicily. He is said to have been buried within the Academy. His philosophical work survives in the form of about thirty dialogues, distinguished not only for their contributions to epistemology, ethics, metaphysics, aesthetics, politics, and the philosophy of religion but also, in many cases, for their dramatic and literary power.

*The Early Works.* Plato's earlier dialogues are still strongly under the influence of Socrates, who appears as the principal spokesman. Three of these dialogues present us with a portrait of Socrates, and though that portrait may be to some extent idealized, we may well believe that its outlines are reliable. The *Apology* contains Socrates' defense, made before the magistrates of Athens, concluding with the dramatic words: "The hour of departure has arrived and we go our ways—I to die, and you to live. Which is better is known to God, and *only to him.*" *Phaedo* claims to be a record of the conversation that Socrates had with his friends on the last day of his life in the prison. The theme of the conversation is the immortality of the soul, and the dialogue ends with Socrates drinking the cup of hemlock (the mode of execution in Athens at that time). The relatively brief *Crito* shows that although Socrates had come into collision with the state, he was the true patriot who respected the laws, for when he was offered the opportunity of escaping to another city-state, he declined, preferring to depart "in innocence, a sufferer and not a doer of evil, a victim, not of the laws, but of men."

Of the other early dialogues in which Socrates has a leading role, many follow a definite pattern. A question is asked, for example, "What is courage?" or "What is piety?" A number of answers are given by participants in the dialogue, but Socrates proceeds to show that these answers are inadequate. So these dialogues do not so much expand our knowledge as make us aware that much of what passes for

knowledge has no right to the name. It is likely enough that this exposure of the pretentiousness of those who claimed to know does accurately portray the activities of Socrates in Athens, and it may well have been a factor in making him unpopular with those in high places. It fits very well with the incident mentioned in the *Apology,* according to which Socrates was declared by the Delphic Oracle to be the wisest of men, and the explanation is given that he alone was protected from illusion by his knowledge of his own ignorance.

A number of philosophical doctrines already find expression in the early dialogues, though it is not clear whether they represent Socrates' own views or are put into his mouth by Plato. We have already noted that *Phaedo* makes a case for the immortality of the soul, and it seems highly probable that this belief was held by Socrates; but certainly the belief in the reality, importance, and immortality of the soul, together with the duty of tending and cultivating the soul, becomes a major tenet in the philosophy of Plato himself and in subsequent Platonism.

The important doctrine of recollection appears in the *Meno.* A slave boy, who has never learned geometry, is skillfully questioned by Socrates so that he gives correct answers to mathematical questions. "Do you observe," asks Socrates, "that I am not teaching the boy anything, but only asking him questions?" Though his ability to answer is mythologically explained in terms of the immortal soul's remembering from former existences, the important point is that significant truths are present a priori in the mind and do not arise from sense experience. The theory of Ideas or Forms is also early, and is closely connected with belief in the immortality of the soul. The world of sense is in constant flux, but as the soul withdraws itself from the life of the senses, it becomes aware of the forms, ideas, or universal essences that are eternal and unchanging and that alone yield knowledge that is permanent and reliable.

*Middle and Later Works.* Of all Plato's dialogues, *The Republic* is the most famous. This writing raises the question, "What is justice?" and it brings together themes from ethics, politics, anthropology, and metaphysics. Justice is a theme ideally suited to raise a most difficult question, which is still being debated in ethics today—what is the relation between individual virtue and what might be called social virtue? Plato's way of answering this question is to claim that there are parallel structures in the individual and in society. Both are tripartite. On the one hand, the human soul has three parts or levels. The highest of these is reason, the faculty by which we can know the eternal Ideas; below that is the "spirited" part, characterized by courage and enterprise; below that again lies a multitude of passions and desires, clamoring for gratification. In the soul of the just person, these three parts are in harmony. The ideal life is that in which rational judgment prevails. It is therefore a life of intellectual contemplation, directed upon the Forms or Ideas, and especially on the Form of the Good, which stands at the apex of the hierarchy of Forms. The active life, dominated by the "spirited" element in the soul, is inferior to the contemplative life, but both of these are far superior to the life of the senses. In his well-known allegory of the cave, Plato suggests that the mass of human beings are the victims of illusion, and only a few penetrate to truth. The state shows a structure corresponding to that of the individual human person. The guardians are those devoted to wisdom, the philosopher-politicians; the soldiers and administrators rank next, and correspond to the spirited part of the soul. Below them are the ordinary people who need to be guided. Plato, it will be observed, had little use for democracy. Justice in the state, parallel to justice in the individual, depends on the harmonious relationship of the three classes.

Other important dialogues include the *Symposium*, which reports speeches in praise of love (*eros*) made at a banquet. This too praises the contemplative life, for the highest *eros* is that of the philosopher, who aims at a mystical union with the Good and the Beautiful. The *Theaetetus* and the *Sophist* both deal with the question of knowledge. Even if no very clear theory of knowledge emerges at the end, the point is again driven home that knowledge cannot be founded on sensation or sense-perception. The *Timaeus* is an essay in cosmology. A subordinate deity, the *Demiourgos*, is said to have formed the objects in this world of space and time, using the eternal Forms as his model. So there is a kind of imperfection about this empirical world. Full reality belongs only to the eternal world of ideas, and the physical world is but a copy of it. In an often quoted phrase, Plato describes time as "the moving image of eternity." While the *Demiourgos* gives form to the world, he does not actually create it but makes use of a preexistent matter (*hyle*). It has often been said that this makes a difference between Plato's teaching about creation and the Judeo-Christian doctrine of creation out of nothing. But the matter used by the *Demiourgos* is said to be completely without properties or determinations, and therefore it might be hard to say what is the difference between this indeterminate matter and nothing.

Plato's last and longest dialogue, *Laws*, contains his last reflections on ethics and jurisprudence. But it is also important as containing his last thoughts on theology or the philosophy of religion. He offers arguments for the existence of God and claims that God is wise and righteous. Here we seem to have reached a fully theistic position. But some matters remain obscure. How is this God related to the Form of the Good, which appears to be the (impersonal) ultimate being of the earlier dialogues? Or how is he related to the *Demiourgos*? Or how is he related to the many gods and goddesses of Greek religion, for, although Plato criticizes the unworthy and sometimes immoral myths that were told about the gods, it does not seem that he denied their existences.

*Platonism*. After Plato's death, the Academy continued to develop his philosophy, and in fact continued until A.D. 529, when it was closed by Justinian. As early as the first and second centuries A.D., Platonism was combining with Jewish and Christian theology (Philo, Justin Martyr, Clement of Alexandria, Origen, and many others). From the third century onwards, Platonism was being superseded by the related NEOPLATONISM, which strongly influenced Christian theology from Augustine until the Middle Ages. Platonism returned as a powerful influence in German IDEALISM. It is an exaggeration to say with Whitehead that Western philosophy is a series of footnotes to Plato, but no other thinker has been more formative.                          J.M.

**PLENARY COUNCIL.** According to part II of the Code of Canon Law of the Roman Catholic church, "Particular Councils," a plenary council (that is, a council of the whole) of all the churches in an Episcopal Conference is to be held as often as the Episcopal Conference considers it necessary and has the permission of the pope. "Plenary" refers to the whole, to all Catholic parishes in a given territory.
J.C.

**PLENARY INDULGENCES.** An INDULGENCE, granted by the pope, that remits the entire temporal punishment that the sinner deserves according to divine justice. Such indulgences generally are said to be applicable to all the souls in PURGATORY. The degree to which it is accepted is up to God.
J.C.

**PLENARY INSPIRATION.** *See* INSPIRATION AND REVELATION.

**PLEROMA.** *See* FULLNESS OF TIME.

**PL KYODAN.** A Japanese "new religion," whose name means "Perfect Liberty Church." This religious movement was founded by Miki Tokuchika in 1946 on the basis of two prewar movements. By 1970 it claimed over a million adherents, both in Japan, and largely among persons of Japanese descent, around the world. Its headquarters community at Tondabayashi, near Osaka, is imposing, including a temple, hospital, and golf course.

A basic tenet and the motto of PL is: "Life is Art." Like a masterly painting, one's life should be a carefully planned and balanced composition, with proportionate attention to work, family, culture, and recreation. To this end PL churches are noted for their cultural and sports activities.

PL's worship is liturgical, its rites of singing, chanting, and offering being of unusual grace and beauty. PL has a special prayer, the *oyashikiri,* which combines words and gestures and is said to be particularly powerful in healing. PL provides its members with guidance in spiritual and personal matters from designated elders through a formalized procedure for exchange of correspondence. In this way, like other of the new religions of Japan, it gives particular attention to the needs of the individual.

                R.E.

**PLOTINUS** (207–270). Philosopher and mystic, Plotinus was born in Egypt and studied at the school of Alexandria under Ammonius Saccus. After travels in the East, he opened a school in Rome in A.D. 44, and while there he wrote fifty-four tractates expounding the philosophico-religious system known as NEOPLATONISM. These writings were arranged in six groups of nine each, and so were called the *Enneads* (from Greek, *ennea*, "nine"). At the head of his metaphysical system stands The One, the Source of everything but so utterly transcendent that it is beyond personality and all human comprehension. We cannot even call it "God" or say that it "is," though the mystic may in rare moments attain to communion with The One in an ecstatic experience that Plotinus calls a "leap." But The One does not remain shut up and hidden in itself. It has come forth in a series of emanations. The first of these is *Nous* (Greek, "reason" comparable to the *Logos* of Christian thought). The *Nous* generates (or perhaps is constituted by) an intelligible world of ideas, in Plato's sense. From the *Nous* there emanates the *Psyche* or world Soul, compared by some early Christian writers to the Holy Spirit. The Soul extends through the world, and in and through this universal Soul our finite human souls are united. Strictly speaking, it is the Triad of The One, the *Nous*, and the *Psyche* that constitutes the Plotinian Godhead, not The One by itself. Plotinus' philosophy profoundly influenced patristic and medieval Christian thinkers, and its traces are to be found in such modern philosophers as Hegel and Heidegger.     J.M.

**PLUMTRE, EDWARD HAYES** (1821–91). Anglical clergyman, theologian, author, and hymn writer. Plumtre, born in London, England, was a widely respected Victorian clergyman and man of letters. During his distinguished career, he was a writer of history, biography, and poetry and held high university positions. As a loyal churchman, influenced by the Oxford Movement, he held many high posts in the Church of England, including dean of Wells Cathedral. Plumptre was the author of several works of theology and composed verse translations of Sophocles and Aeschylus. He also wrote the *Life of Thomas Ken*, a seventeenth-century bishop of the Anglican Church, and served on the Revision Commitee of the Revised Version of the Bible (1881). He is remembered best for the hymn "Rejoice Ye Pure in Heart," which he was commissioned to write for the annual choir festival at Peterborough Cathedral in 1865. Another beloved hymn he left to the church was "O Light, Whose Beams Illumine All."     R.H.

**PLURALISM.** The de facto social system in the United States and other Western democracies, in religions, life-styles, and philosophical beliefs. Pluralism recognizes the legitimacy of many religious systems and tolerates many different philosophies and life-styles. Although traditionally pluralism stood for belief in more than one ultimate principle and opposed monism, the belief in one ultimate principle, the modern use of the term does not necessarily imply a denial of one ultimate reality: God. Rather, pluralism is the practical and necessary outgrowth of a democratic social order that recognizes the religious LIBERTY of every person. In order to allow people to follow the dictates of their own consciences, equal respect must be paid to every religious expression. This is not a denial of the unity of the Divine or of the objectivity of truth but is the recognition of the dignity and sanctity of each human personality. Such a social order, affirming religious pluralism, with corresponding freedom for various life-styles and world views, is a natural outgrowth of the American concept of the SEPARATION OF CHURCH AND STATE and the principles of religious TOLERATION worked out in England by John Locke.

Pluralism is a fundamental part of any free society but is fragile, as is democracy itself. The recognition of the inalienable rights of the minority by the majority, which is always changing, must constantly be promoted and protected. From time to time religious pluralism is challenged by zealots who feel they constitute a majority of the electorate and consequently should be able to enforce their religious practices by law. This religious imperialism is the antithesis of democracy and, in the case of Christianity, is a devolution from faith to a cultural religion, a CIVIL RELIGION that makes an idol out of one form of religion. In the contemporary world such threats to democratic pluralism and to the purity of faith have come from the religious right in America and from the political left in some Communist countries. Both attempts to suppress individual liberties are equally wrong. Only where people can worship or not worship as they decide is there genuine freedom.

        J.C.

**PLYMOUTH BRETHREN.** Also known as simply "Christian Brethren," this group developed among the followers of JOHN NELSON DARBY, former cleric of the Church of Ireland. Its name came from a large group that assembled in Plymouth, England, about 1830. Members had met for some time in small groups in Ireland and England for prayer and fellowship. They were particularly concerned about biblical prophecy and the Second Coming.

The group split after 1845 over doctrine and church discipline. Darby's followers, termed "Exclusive Brethren," subdivided a number of times and now comprise about five separate groups, whose United States congregations number 250, with an approximate membership of 19,000. The "Open" group, under the leadership of George Müller, adopted less rigorous membership standards and a congregational polity. They have 850 United States "assemblies" with about 79,000 members and 400 designated leaders.

Plymouth Brethren stress the priesthood of all male believers and make little distinction between clergy and laymen. They have Communion every Sunday and usually practice believers' baptism. They have been quite active in missions, particularly in central Africa, India, and Latin America.          N.H.

**POETRY** (Biblical). Given its innate simplicity, imaginative character, and emotional appeal, Hebrew poetry provided a superb means for biblical Israel to express itself about God, nation, and world. Approximately one-third of the OT is cast in poetry. Diverse poetic genres convey the judgment oracles of the prophet, the aphorisms of the sage, and the hymns, thanksgivings, and laments of the psalmist.

*Basic Features of Hebrew Poetry.* (a) *Parallelism.* Clearly, parallelism is the most significant structural feature of Hebrew verse. The poetical line (bicolon) consists of two members, the second echoing or extending the thought of the first. This often involves *synonymous* parallelism, whereby the first colon is creatively restated in the second:

The heávens are télling the glóry of God;
   and the fírmament proclaíms his hándiwork (Ps. 19:1).

Sometimes the parallelism is *antithetic* with the second member set against the first in contrasting manner:

The líght of the ríghteous rejóices,
   but the lámp of the wícked will be put óut (Prov. 13:9).

The parallelism is termed *emblematic* when the message of one colon is echoed in the other through metaphor or simile:

The Lórd has becóme like an énemy,
   he has destróyed Ísrael (Lam. 2:5).

*Synthetic* or *formal* parallelism is evidenced when the thought of the first colon spills over into the second. No repetition is involved; yet the two cola are quantitatively balanced:

Í have sét my kíng
   on Zíon, my hóly híll (Ps. 2:6).

(b) *Meter.* In Hebrew poetry, meter is defined in terms of accented syllables. Since parallelism and meter are closely linked, the most typical metric pattern (3 + 3) involves three accented syllables in each colon (see Ps. 19:1 above). An early 2 + 2 meter operates in the Song of Miriam (Exod. 15:21), and a Qinah (lament) meter of 3 + 2, incorporating cola of unequal length, prevails in Lamentations 1–4 (see Lam. 2:5 above). Nor are tricola with 3 + 3 + 3 meter

unusual (see Ps. 111:9-10). Since metrical irregularities are admissible in Hebrew rhythmic patterns, one poem may utilize several different meters.

(c) *Strophic structure.* The larger verse units into which Hebrew poetic lines group themselves are designated as strophes. Ordinarily they are not of equal length in a given poem. Though the strophic structure of many OT poems is elusive, several clues are trustworthy. These include use of a recurring refrain (Pss. 42–43), changes of person, the use of key words ("behold," "therefore"), and recourse to the acrostic whereby successive consonants of the Hebrew alphabet initiate the respective strophes (Ps. 119; Lam. 1–4).

*New Testament Poetry.* Though poetry is less prominent in the NT than in the OT, it surfaces at crucial junctures. Many NT texts draw upon OT poetry—Joel 2:28-29 is cited in the Pentecost narrative (Acts 2:17-18); and in its meditation on Jesus, Hebrews 2:6-8 quotes Psalm 8:4-6. Reporting the births of John and Jesus, Luke includes three expressive hymns—Mary's "Magnificat" (1:46-55), Zechariah's "Benedictus" (1:68-79), and Simeon's "Nunc Dimittis" (2:29-32). In Philippians 2:6-11 Paul presumably cites a known christological hymn (see also Col. 1:15-20). As teacher, Jesus apparently honored the canons of Semitic (Aramaic) poetry. In Matthew 7:7, "Ask, and it will be given you; seek, and you will find; knock, and it will be opened to you," synonymous parallelism is evident. Luke 13:30, "Some are last who will be first, and some are first who will be last," exhibits antithetic parallelism, and the Beatitudes (Matt. 5:3-10) employ synthetic parallelism.

*Significant Poetic Techniques.* Studies in Ugaritic poetry emphasize the importance of parallel word pairs. Though the correspondence in thought of parallel poetic lines remains a concern, focus has recently fallen on the correspondence of those specific terms that comprise these lines. The "cup" / "bowl" word pair appears in Isaiah 51:17, and the "strange" / "foreign" pair in Psalm 81:9. The isolation of almost a thousand fixed pairs in the Ugaritic language has highlighted the oral dimension of poetic composition in ancient Israel, when poets often fashioned their craft in on-the-spot situations with frequent reliance upon established poetic diction.

The omission of one or more words is called *ellipsis.* Proverbs 19:22 presumably contrasts a poor, honest man with a wealthy liar, though what is literally stated is "a poor man is better than a liar." Perhaps Psalm 113:4 is elliptical since Yahweh's glory is praised for reaching above "the heavens," rather than above "the hosts of heaven," a phrase more explicit and familiar.

*Inclusion* involves an exact or approximate repetition of an opening phrase at the conclusion of a literary unit. The final verse of Psalm 8 faithfully repeats the psalm's opening bicolon, and Psalm 70 opens and closes with synonymous imperatives addressed to the Deity—"make haste to help" and "do not tarry." This device appreciably unifies the composition in question.

J.K.K.

**POINT OF CONTACT.** A term used in Christian theology and associated with the doctrine of REVELATION. At issue is whether God's saving revelation is present exclusively in Jesus Christ or whether God is also truly revealed in nature and in the events of history. Is the IMAGE OF GOD in humans so effaced by sin as to leave no natural point of contact with God? Or are people, despite sin, capable of knowing God, if imperfectly, through nature and history? The issue was especially joined in a dispute between KARL BARTH and EMIL BRUNNER. Barth maintained that saving revelation is found only in Christ and accused Brunner of yielding to a dangerous NATURAL THEOLOGY. The dispute initiated an important debate on the nature of humanity and divine revelation.

J.L.

**POLITICAL THEOLOGY.** A term derived from the works of JURGEN MOLTMANN and J. Metz in Europe. Alistair Kee has been a leading spokesman for this overall view of theology that calls for religion to engage in political life, not to dominate it—or be used by it—but to criticize it with biblical insight.

Political theology is peculiarly conscious of the destructive unions of religion and political powers in the past, and, increasingly today in the conservative capture of mass Fundamentalist support in the American New Religious Right. From the cult of the emperor in ancient Rome to Constantine's use of the Catholic Church to unite the Roman Empire, to the involvement of the medieval popes in European political affairs, to the Nazis' abuse of the church, political theologians point out that, despite many pious protests by both conservatives and liberals in America, religion has always been "political." (*See* CIVIL RELIGION.) To make the believer conscious of these false ways of relating religion and politics is the necessary first step, according to political theologians, before the church can relate positively to the political order.

It is not possible for the church to withdraw from politics for that way (formerly used by Fundamentalists) is to legitimize the status quo simply by default. Another erroneous attitude toward religion is the conservative Protestant belief that religion is a matter of personal decision and hence a private matter. Religion then is quietistic, a devotion to the inner life, with an abandonment of the social and political realm. This effectively removes Christian witness from all the affairs that affect the lives of human beings. The powerful then control society, and the weak and poor have no one to stand up for them. This position, as political theologians from the

various camps of BLACK THEOLOGY, FEMINIST THEOLOGY and LIBERATION THEOLOGY point out, is the way of selfishness, not the way of love.

The past two decades have produced many variants of political theology in response to major social and political upheavals such as the Montgomery bus boycott that led to the civil rights drive; the response of many Christians and Jews to the ten-year conflict in Vietnam with a vast peace movement; the Watergate break-in that led to President Nixon's resignation; the drive for the ERA by feminists; the nuclear freeze movement; the Catholic bishops' statements on nuclear war and on America's economy and society.

J.C.

**POLYCARP, EPISTLE OF.** Polycarp, bishop of Smyrna in the first half of the second century, was the author of several letters, according to Irenaeus, but only one letter has survived. This is his letter to the Philippian church. The purpose of this writing is twofold: to warn his readers against creating disorder in the church and falling into false teaching, and to encourage the Philippians to collect the letters of IGNATIUS into a corpus. To that end Polycarp is sending to the Philippian church the copies of Ignatius' letters in his possession. The date of this "covering letter" of Polycarp (K. Lake's phrase) is somewhere between A.D. 110 and 117, but it is possible, following P. N. Harrison, that the letter has two separate parts, with chapters 13–14 written first and chapters 1–12 much later, about 135–137, just before the arrival of MARCION, the heretical figure in Rome. The allusion (in 7:1) to a false leader as the "first-born of Satan" has suggested an identification with Marcion, since Irenaeus at a later time associates this designation with Polycarp's criticism.

Throughout the letter are encouragements to virtue, especially in a warning against covetousness, and a call to perseverance in the Christian life, with a special section of admonition addressed to deacons and elders at Philippi.

R.M.

**POLYGAMY.** *See* MARRIAGE.

**POLYGLOT BIBLE.** A Bible containing several versions of the same text in parallel columns. The first OT of this sort was probably the *Hexapla,* compiled by Origen in the third century A.D. When the invention of printing permitted their production, a number of such Bibles were published, including the six-volume *Complutensian Polyglot* of 1522, produced under the patronage of Cardinal Jiménez of Spain. In 1952 *The Genesis Octapla,* compiled by Luther A. Weigle, chairman of the National Council of Churches' committee that sponsored the Revised Standard Version of the Bible, included eight English translations in one folio volume. In the 1960s several volumes were published that included the King James Version alongside other contemporary BIBLE TRANSLATIONS.

R.H.

Courtesy of the Beinecke Rare Book and Manuscript Library, Yale University

*The first page of the book of Genesis in Jimenez's* Complutensian Polyglot Bible (1514-17). *In the upper left is the Greek Septuagint. In the middle is the Latin Vulgate, and at the right is the Hebrew. In the lower left is an Aramaic version and in the lower right a Latin translation of the Aramaic.*

**POLYTHEISM.** Belief in and worship of many gods. As the theologian Paul Tillich once remarked, polytheism is really a matter of quality rather than quantity; the polytheist not only has more deities than the monotheist, but experiences the sacred in a profoundly different way. Instead of seeing all that is ultimately under a single divine being or will, one sees divinity as finite but richly diversified, linked to innumerable particular places, functions or moods. While polytheisms frequently tend toward unity, either under an impersonal, universal force or a potentially monotheistic "king of the gods," particularism is its most salient characteristic.

Despite its much-discussed "high gods," primitive religion had many polytheistic elements: personifications of nature, masters of animals, ancestral spirits, and mythological figures. It was in the ancient agricultural societies such as those of Egypt, Mesopotamia, Greece, Rome, or northern Europe, however, that polytheistic pantheons become most highly developed. The unification of many peoples into empires typically meant that their various patronal gods had to be incorporated into a single system, and the increasing complexification of human society called for a heavenly counterpart with extensive division of labor.

Today, the great historical religions of MONOTHEISM and monism have overwhelmed traditional forms of polytheism in most of the world. SHINTO is perhaps the only thoroughgoing polytheistic religion remaining in a major advanced society. But HINDUISM and TAOISM retain polytheistic pantheons set against a monistic background. Even in BUDDHISM and the Western monotheisms, devotion to various buddhas, bodhisattvas, saints, angels, and spirits, especially on a popular level, often displays polytheistic characteristics, revealing a persistent human desire to find the sacred in finite, particularized forms as well as in the One.                                                                    R.E.

**PONTIFEX MAXIMUS.** A title in Roman Catholicism designating the chief priest of the Pontifical College, the POPE. However, like the title "pope," which was not formally restricted to the bishop of Rome until the Council of Rome in 1073, "pontifex maximus" often designated other leading bishops until the eleventh century.                                    C.M.

**PONTIFICAL.** A synonym for "papal," referring to the POPE, the bishop of Rome, and the head of the Roman Catholic Church. "Pontiff" is derived from the Latin word *pontifex,* or high priest. Its root meaning seems to be derived from the Latin words *facere,* to make, and *ponteus,* bridge, meaning to create a bridge between God and humans. Pontifical is used in many connections, as in the pontifical family (the pope's household), the pontifical gendarmerie (or police in the Vatican), the pontifical chapel, the pontifical Mass, and pontifical services.

"Pontificals" per se refer to the ceremonial robes and paraphernalia worn by a Catholic bishop, especially the pectoral cross, bishop's ring, the miter, and pastoral staff. It also includes the bishop's sandals, gloves, tunic, and dalmatic, as well as the episcopal throne. At one time, pontificals were also worn by Anglican bishops in cathedral services. Cardinals and abbots in the Catholic church use pontificals.                                                            J.C.

**PONTIFICAL MASS.** A high MASS sung by a cardinal, a bishop in his own diocese, or an abbot in his own abbey, and elsewhere only by permission. There are assistant priests, two assistant deacons, and at least nine acolytes. During the opening the bishop is vested at the altar.                                            J.C.

**POPE.** In Roman Catholic theology, the pope is the VICAR of Christ on earth, and the head of the universal Christian church, as well as the bishop of Rome and the patriarch of the West. According to the ecclesiology (doctrine of the church) of the Catholic church, the apostle Peter was the first pope, appointed to that office by Jesus Christ at the encounter in Caesarea Philippi recorded in Matthew 16. Jesus asked the disciples who people said he was. John the Baptist, Elijah, and Jeremiah were mentioned, but Jesus asked them who they thought he was. Simon Peter, the son of Jonah, answered: "You are the Christ, the Son of the Living God." Jesus then told Peter: "Blessed are you, Simon Bar-Jona! For flesh and blood has not revealed this to you, but my Father who is in heaven. And I tell you, you are Peter, and on this rock I will build my church, and the powers of death shall not prevail against it. I will give you the keys of the kingdom of heaven, and whatever you bind on earth shall be bound in heaven, and whatever you loose on earth shall be loosed in heaven."

From Peter's time to the present, some 263 other men have occupied Peter's place as Christ's vicar, according to ROMAN CATHOLICISM. A strong tradition tells us that Peter was martyred in A.D. 64, under Nero. Tradition also says that the Roman congregation elected Linus of Tuscany as bishop, establishing the concept of the transferability of the powers of Peter from one bishop of Rome to another down through the generations. This tradition was affirmed by the Council of Nicaea (A.D. 325), which declared "The Church in Rome always holds primacy."

In the early second century A.D., Ignatius of Antioch was martyred in Rome and acknowledged in a letter to the then reigning bishop of Rome the preeminence and special authority of the Roman church. Toward the end of the second century, Irenaeus, bishop of Lyons, wrote, "All churches everywhere must agree with this church [Rome] because of its more effective leadership, since in it Christians everywhere have preserved intact the apostolic tradition."

Tradition records that the first thirty-three bishops of Rome (or popes) were martyred. Terrible persecutions broke out throughout the second and third centuries and into the fourth, culminating in the fiercest oppression ever, under the emperor Diocletian, from A.D. 300 to 305. Persecutions ceased when Constantine defeated Maxentius and became emperor in A.D. 312. In A.D. 313 full freedom of worship was granted Christians throughout the empire. Eventually Christianity became the state religion. Constantine moved the government east, to Constantinople, and the pope, by default, acquired many of the civil powers exercised formerly by the emperor. The prestige of the papacy increased dramatically because of this, and even more because of the ecumenical (universal) council called by Constantine at Nicaea. In the fifth century, Rome fell to the barbarians who spared the churches, increasing the pope's authority even more. Throughout the Middle Ages the popes grew more powerful because of the chaotic conditions in the Mediterranean area, after Odoacer overthrew the last Western emperor in A.D. 476.

The Council of Chalcedon recognized the Roman church as preeminent in A.D. 451, after the demands of Pope Leo I (440–461), who saw the bishop of Constantinople gaining in governmental prestige.

Gregory the Great, in the sixth century, was a strong pope but died in A.D. 604. The king of the Franks, Pepin, gave political authority over some seventeen thousand square miles of Italy to Pope Stephen III in the eighth century. This territory became the papal states, and the pope became a king for eleven centuries, until 1870 when the papal states were absorbed into the newly united kingdom of Italy. (In the thirteenth century, the city of Avignon and its environs in southern France were added to the papal states.) Later, Charlemagne confirmed this grant of territory and Pope Leo IV built high walls about the Vatican because of the frequent warfare in Italy. Upon the collapse of the empire of Charlemagne, the popes became pawns in the many struggles of feudalism. The state of the church degenerated, and at times, several men claimed to be pope (the anti-popes). This period, around A.D. 1000, was the low point of the papacy. Several popes abdicated in this difficult period. Pope Leo IX instituted reforms, but during his reign a split developed between Rome and the Eastern churches. In 1059, East and West mutually excommunicated each other. This schism has been largely healed since Vatican II, after nine hundred years. One of the most notable popes was Hildebrand, the reforming monk, who became bishop of Rome in A.D. 1075. Under Urban II, the first crusade was called, and Jerusalem and the sites of Christ's ministry were retaken from the Muslims. Innocent III (1198–1216) was a constructive pope who endorsed both the Franciscan and Dominican orders.

In the fourteenth century a conflict arose between Pope Boniface VIII and King Philip IV of France over control of church affairs. Under Clement V the seat of the papacy was moved from Rome to Avignon in France and remained there through the next six papacies. Pope Gregory XI returned the papacy to Rome in 1377, because of the reforming work of the dynamic Dominican nun, St. Catherine of Siena. She had a three-point program for church reform: (1) The pope should reside in Rome, (2) the church should be morally cleansed, and (3) political and social peace should be achieved for Italy.

The Renaissance was a glorious period for art and learning in Rome, sponsored by the papacy, but the worldliness and luxury of the papal court contributed to the greatest schism in Christian history—the Protestant Reformation. Half of Europe repudiated papal church leadership because of Rome's decadence and refusal to reform the church. Pope Leo X precipitated this break and excommunicated Martin Luther. The fifth Lateran Council, under Pope Julius, and the Council of Trent reformed the papacy somewhat, but it remained for the Vatican Council of 1870 and the Second Vatican Council under Pope John XXIII to institute far-reaching reforms. Angelo Giuseppe Roncalli (born 1881), as John XXIII, did more to reform and modernize the Catholic church than any of his predecessors. He also raised the world's respect for the papacy to its highest point since the Middle Ages. J.C.

**PORT ROYAL.** A Benedictine foundation near Paris, France, that became a Cistercian convent. Port Royal became the center of bitter seventeenth-century controversies over free will. Antoine Arnauld, head of the convent, and Blaise Pascal, whose sister was a nun at Port Royal, upheld the extreme Augustinian views of Cornelius Jansen, against the Jesuits. Port Royal was destroyed. C.M.

**POSITIVE THINKING.** A concept that takes it name from a book by NORMAN VINCENT PEALE, popular radio preacher and pastor of the Marble Collegiate Church in New York City. In 1952 he outlined the technique, giving examples from the lives of people to illustrate how anyone can develop "peace of mind, improved health, and a never-ceasing flow of energy." He assures his readers that they can have a life full of joy.

The basic principles of positive thinking are that, while accepting the fact that obstacles will arise, one must not permit these to dominate but must overcome or cast them out. People must *will* not to be defeated. Then they can become channels for spiritual power. Anyone can modify or change circumstances. With God's help they can build up the self. This is a system of creative living based on spiritual techniques, through which people can improve relationships with other people, maintain good health, and increase pleasure in living.

Prayer power is described as a spiritual technique based upon opening the mind humbly to God in order to stimulate the power of God to flow into the person. In praying, one should hold a mental image of what is needed, and in time this will become actualized in life. Create your own happiness, Peale affirms. Expect the best and receive it. Break wrong habits. Give up your worries to God. Emotions and health are interrelated. Relaxation is an affirmative way to a positive attitude. Peale's book is included in compilations of long-time best sellers of inspirational and self-help books. I.C.

**POSITIVISM.** See LOGICAL POSITIVISM.

**POSTMILLENNIALISM.** See MILLENNIUM.

**POTENTIALITY.** A philosophical term first used comprehensively by ARISTOTLE, referring to a capacity in a being to achieve some action or perfection. The term was later used by THOMAS AQUINAS and more recently by philosophers and theologians of NEO-THOMISM. Aristotle held that all things are made up of matter and form. However, prime matter is mere potentiality, whereas substantial form is what Aristotle and the Thomists call act, that is, what determines a material being's specific class or essence. A person's potential essence is

rationality. Only God has no potency or aptitude for change. God's essence is pure act or existence. J.L.

**POTIPHAR.** Meaning "the one Re [the Egyptian sun-god] has given". Potiphar is identified as "an officer of Pharaoh, the captain of the guard." Potiphar bought JOSEPH from Ishmaelite (or Midianite) caravan traders just after he had been taken to Egypt as a slave (Gen. 37:36; 39:1).

We know neither the precise meaning of Potiphar's title nor whether any exact Egyptian equivalent exists. Yet he appears to be the chief steward within the court of an unnamed pharaoh. Potiphar's name is virtually identical with that of Joseph's priestly father-in-law, Potiphera (Gen. 41:45; 46:20). Presumably it was abbreviated so that the two names could be distinguished. Favorably impressed by Joseph's abilities, Potiphar placed his household in Joseph's charge (39:4). Then duped by the false accusation of his lusty, nameless wife that this "handsome and good-looking" slave had attempted to seduce her, Potiphar angrily consigned Joseph to prison (39:20). J.K.K.

**POTTER'S FIELD.** A piece of ground in Jerusalem, traditionally located on the southern slope of the valley of Hinnom, which was purchased by the chief priests (Matt. 27:6ff.) with the money that belonged to Judas Iscariot and thus in a sense was his purchase (Acts 1:18). The thirty pieces of silver he received for the betrayal of Jesus was subsequently considered "blood money" (Matt. 27:6) and the "reward of his wickedness" (Acts 1:18). When he returned it, the money was used to purchase the field where potters dug their clay as a burial place for strangers (Matt. 27:7). It was appropriately designated by an Aramaic term Akeldama (Field of Blood, Acts 1:19). J.R.M.

**POWER OF THE KEYS.** See KEYS OF THE KINGDOM.

**PRACTICE OF THE PRESENCE OF GOD, THE.** The spiritual effort to become increasingly aware of the presence of God dwelling in the heart or soul. This practice aims at finding God at the center of our being as our friend. In order to come to this realization, contemplative practices throughout Christian history have stressed silence and solitude. A life of constant prayer (as Paul recommended, "prayer without ceasing") is cultivated, in which God is praised often and God's presence held constantly in mind. The practice of a sacramental life, frequent reception of the Lord's Supper, humility, gentleness, and compasson for others, will lead one to an ever-lasting realization of the Divine Presence. Some spiritual writers hold that Christian perfection is the constant practice of God's presence.

A layman, Brother Lawrence, produced a spiritual classic entitled *The Practice of the Presence of God*. In it, Lawrence declared that he felt as closely in the Divine Presence while he was in the kitchen washing the monastery's pots as he did when he was on his knees at the Eucharist. It is just such a perpetual awareness of God as friend that the practice of the presence of God is designed to produce.                                          J.C.

## PRAETORIAN GUARD/PRAETORIUM.

The elite household guard drawn from the Roman legions to protect the emperor, and also to protect the governors of Roman provinces. A praetor was an army officer ranking only behind a consul in the Roman army, and thus was equal to a four-star general in modern American terms. His headquarters was named a praetorium, and such a headquarters, including barracks for the troops, a parade ground, offices and a military prison, was located in the emperor's palace in Rome and, in the provinces, provided safe quarters for the governor (procurator) and other officials.

In the NT, the Praetorian Guard is mentioned in Philippians 4:22, as is Caesar's household. This is usually understood to refer to Rome, and specifically to Christians who were part of Caesar's personal staff. More recent research suggests that the Praetorian Guard was present in the Roman province of Asia, and so Ephesus might be the location referred to. In Jerusalem, during the time of Jesus, Pilate had his residence in the praetorium, which today is known as the Castle of Antonia. Jesus was taken to the praetorium for trial by Pilate and on its parade ground was mocked as a kingly pretender, draped in purple, crowned with thorns, and beaten, before being led away for crucifixion (Mark 15:16-20; Matt. 27:27-31). Paul was imprisoned in the praetorium in Caesarea (Acts 23:35).                                          J.C.

## PRAGMATISM.

An early twentieth-century American contribution to philosophy, resting on the assertion of the priority of experience over principle, of action over doctrine. The test of the validity of an idea lies in its usefulness and practicality. Hence pragmatists are critical of theories such as IDEALISM that give priority to mind. By contrast they assert the relative and contingent character of reason. In the pragmatic approach, ideas take their meaning from the consequences, and truth from its verification. Ideas are instruments for obtaining results.

Pragmatism is a philosophy of relativity, not of absolutes. Taken into business ethics it seems to support the idea that the rightness of a policy is to be seen in successful results. It has been used in educational theory to base learning on reflection from experience. Pragmatism has been influential in the United States but has not been accepted to any extent as a philosophical system in Europe.

Pragmatism began with a gathering in Cambridge, Massachusetts, called the Metaphysical Club, during the 1880s. Key people were CHARLES SANDERS PIERCE and WILLIAM JAMES, philosophers on the Harvard faculty. Later JOHN DEWEY at Columbia became an exponent of the movement. Pragmatism was a revolt against idealism and took its first cues from British empiricists such as John Stuart Mill. William James was concerned about values and worth, but saw these within the framework of life rather than as abstract principles. John Dewey's thought has been called "instrumentalism." He wrote that the ends should lead to a constant reevaluation of the means in order to refine and reconstruct the goals to higher ends. Far from seeing pragmatism as without ethical norms, he believed that a pragmatic philosophy could lead to the achievement of higher ethical norms, goals, and achievements. Ethics would be relative, but in a positive way. Ideas are the instruments through which change is achieved, but are not ends in themselves.

Pragmatism in combination with logical positivism led into logical empiricism. While people may not be writing in the field of pragmatism today, its basic ideas permeate education, business, and government.                                          I.C.

## PRAJAPATI.

In the VEDAS of HINDUISM, Prajapati, identified with Agni and PURUSA and later with BRAHMA, is the creator god. He made the universe after generating mystical heat *(tapas)* through a sacrifice with which he himself is one; creation is his dismembered being. In the BRAHMANAS, he is acknowledged as the chief deity and father of the gods.                                          R.E.

## *PRAJNA.*

From the Sanskrit word meaning "intelligence, wisdom." In Hinduism and Buddhism, *prajna* is not mere factual knowledge, but that direct intuitive insight that sees things as they really are, distinguishing between reality and illusion. It accompanies enlightenment or God-realization, for only when one has overcome all ego can one perceive the true nature of the universe and divine Reality.                                          R.E.

## PRAYER. *Kinds of Praying.*

Two types of prayer are known in the teaching and example of the NT church. There is private prayer, whether we think of the instructions of the Sermon on the Mount (Matt. 6:5-8), or Jesus' parables on prayer (Luke 11:5-13 and 18:1-14, which are perhaps the best-known examples), or the many requests that Paul makes that his friends should pray for him (for example, II Cor. 1:11).

There are also the "private" prayers of Jesus himself. He prayed at the critical moments of his life—at his baptism (Luke 3:21); at the choosing of the Twelve (5:12); at his transfiguration (9:28); and at his agony in the garden (22:39-45; Heb. 5:7 also describes this scene). Indeed, he died—as he lived—praying (Luke 23:46). From these episodes we gather that he sought the face of his Father at special times of crisis and need. But it is clear that communion with God was the daily inspiration of his life. And the Lord's prayers were far richer in content than a mere list of requests and preferences. Deep fellowship with God (9:29), the exultation of thanksgiving (10:21ff.), and an all-embracing intercession (Luke 23:34; 22:31ff.; John 17:9)—these are the features of his life of prayer, which set a standard for his disciples of all ages.

But, in addition to the account of private prayer, there is the record of the church's corporate prayer as the united assembly of believers expressed its praise and supplication. The Acts of the Apostles describes the prayer fellowship of the earliest believers. Acts 2:42 refers to the practice of their corporate assembly, whether at home (Acts 2:46; 4:23ff.; 5:42) or in the Temple (3:1, 11; 5:12, 42). It is interesting to observe the circumstances that drew Christians together. They needed and sought guidance (1:14, 24). They came together under the duress of persecution and hostility (4:23-31), and requested grace to continue their witness. They took the arrest and imprisonment of Peter (12:5) as a challenge to earnest intercession. They gathered at Antioch to worship the Lord, seeking the guidance that came in the Spirit's summons, "Set apart Barnabas and Saul." With further united prayer, these men who later hazarded their lives for the name of the Lord Jesus (15:26) were sent forth to the work of the gospel in Asia Minor, and the Christian mission was launched on its epoch-making way (13:1-3). Other allusions to the united praying of the people of God are in Acts 20:36 and 21:5—both touching scenes of tender pathos.

*The Contents of Prayer.* From the biblical records there is little to guide us when we try to discover the contents of the prayers in the early church. The prayers of the church in Acts are ad hoc utterances, called forth by the demands of the hour. Yet there are some principles to be noted, chiefly in the use of the Psalms, which is important, as Christians instinctively, like their Lord (Luke 23:46), turned to the Psalms of David for language in which to give vent to their deepest emotions (Acts 4:24-30). Acts 13:1 and following is important because we learn from it that the church at Antioch offered worship to the Lord. It is possible to relate this to the worship of Jesus, a calling upon him in devotion and supplication, as Stephen did (Acts 7:59), and Paul too (II Cor. 12:8). Many scholars find Christ-hymns (as in Phil. 2:6-11; I Tim. 3:16), in which Jesus is praised with a worship that belongs properly to God. The phrase, "calling upon the name of the Lord" (Acts 2:21; 9:14; 22:16; Rom. 10:13), points in the same direction, for it seems to show that Jesus was hailed in worship as one worthy of adoration. It is likely that the phrase is borrowed from the OT scripture, where it denoted that men, even then, would call upon the name of the Lord (Gen. 4:26; 21:33, etc.). If this is so, it is

evidence that right at the beginning of the church ag Jesus Christ was hailed with divine honors and placed at the center of a cultus that drew its inspiration from his living presence in the midst of his own.

There is one datum that is interesting: It is the strange-sounding Aramaic term MARANATHA (I Cor. 16:22), which our English translations render as either "our Lord is coming" or "our Lord, come!" It seems fairly certain that the second alternative is to be preferred, and that this phrase is a prayer of invocation addressed to Jesus. Similar language is found in Revelation 22:20; and the Teaching of the Twelve Apostles (or the *Didache*) uses the exact formula for a service preparatory to the Lord's table (10:6). The use of an Aramaic phrase can only be satisfactorily explained on the assumption that *Maranatha* is an ancient watchword that takes us back to the earliest days of the church in Palestine, where Aramaic was the spoken language.

Now the evidence of this ancient Christian invocation to Christ throws a flood of light on the way in which the Jewish-Christians worshiped their Lord. For not only is *Maranatha* the oldest Christian prayer of which we have record; it can only mean that those who lately had invoked the name of their covenant God as "Lord" in the synagogue liturgy came to apply the same divine title to Jesus the Messiah.

*Some Special Words for Prayer.* We turn to consider some unusual expressions that found a place in the prayer-speech of the early believers.

(a) ABBA suggests our Lord's Gethsemane prayer, recorded in Mark 14:32-39: "Abba, Father, all things are possible unto thee." As was the case with *Maranatha* in I Corinthians 16:22, this Aramaic word recurs in its original form in Paul's Greek letters (Rom. 8:15; Gal. 4:6) and is translated for the benefit of the first readers. It seems certain therefore that *Abba* was current coinage as a title of special significance and depth of meaning for God in the early churches.

*Abba* is our Lord's favorite designation for God. *Abba* was avoided by Jews because it was thought to be too daring and familiar an expression to be used to the King of the Universe. Now, God's son uses exactly this expression, which perhaps is not surprising if from his early boyhood he was conscious of a unique filial relationship with God (Luke 2:49). The staggering thing is that he teaches his disciples to do the same. The leads us to the so-called LORD'S PRAYER, recorded in Matthew 6:9-13 and Luke 11:2-4. We should notice at once that it is more the disciples' prayer than the Lord's, but the title is now part of our speech and may be justified on the ground that it was the Lord who gave this prayer to his people in response to the request, "Lord, teach us to pray." There is evidence to show that very early in the church's history this prayer became accepted as a pattern prayer and was backed by dominical authority. As early as the time when the *Didache* was compiled as a manual of church order and practice about A.D. 80–100), this prayer had become an integral part of Christian worship.

The range of the Lord's Prayer should be noticed, extending from the highest aspirations of which the human emotion and will are capable. The prayer reveals God as concerned with all things in life. It is the sum of Jesus' teaching on the fatherhood of God; and if we desire to learn what this means, it is the Lord's Prayer that will show us.

While the Lord's Prayer is not referred to as such in the NT Epistles, it cannot be accidental that Paul frequently begins his prayers for the churches by invoking the name of God as Father. He prays to the Father of Jesus Christ—and so by implication, the Father of all who are bound to Christ in the one family of his grace (see Rom. 8:15-17). And it is surely significant that in this paragraph Paul uses the Aramaic term *Abba* (as in Gal. 4:6) to highlight the spirit of filial adoption, which becomes ours as the Holy Spirit witnesses to our membership of the family of God. It may even be that *Abba* in these texts (as in I Pet. 1:17) is a veiled allusion to the Lord's Prayer. This would then explain the following reference to "newborn babes" (I Pet. 2:2).

(b) "Amen" is a familiar Christian term. In the synagogue worship, as in the OT, it was the people's full-hearted and full-throated response to and endorsement of the words of another (for example, Neh. 8:6). The word means literally "to be firm, true," and is connected with the verb "to believe." It occurs most obviously at the close of the NT doxologies, which ascribe praise to God and Christ. (See Rom. 1:25; 9:5; 11:36; 16:27; Gal. 1:5; Eph. 3:21; Phil. 4:20; I Tim. 1:17; 6:16; II Tim. 4:18; Heb. 13:21; I Pet. 4:11; 5:11; Jude 25.) Revelation 5 portrays a dramatic scene and probably reflects the worship of the church on earth as well as the church triumphant in heaven.

Two other passages are full of interest. Second Corinthians 1:20 and following pictures a scene that most likely takes us back to early worship. Christ confirms to us the promises of God, and our fitting response to God's faithfulness is the Amen, which accepts and endorses all that God has promised in the gospel. In I Corinthians 14:16 Paul rebukes the church for their unbridled indulgence in the more exotic gifts of the Spirit in public assembly. He is concerned lest an uninstructed person, an "outsider," should come into the church meeting and be embarrassed by a display of strange speech. "How can any one . . . say the 'Amen' to your thanksgiving when he does not know what you are saying?" asks the Apostle, thus making it clear that Amen was in common use as the worshiper's assent to what was heard from the lips of fellow-believers.

(c) The same verse quoted above (I Cor. 14:16) also contains a reference to the prayer of *thanksgiving*. The presence of the definite article "the thanksgiving" seems to suggest that a particular type of praying is envisaged, as distinct from the general use of the term "to give thanks" (as in II Cor. 1:11; 9:12; I Thess. 5:18). Little is said about the content of such a thanksgiving prayer. It is possible that the prayer at the Lord's table is in mind; and it is the verb (Greek, *eucharistein*—"to give thanks") that has given the name Eucharist to the Lord's Supper. Nevertheless, in the Pastoral Epistles, we read of such thanksgiving prayers that are not connected with the Lord's table—in I Timothy 2:1 and 4:4-5. The last-mentioned is particularly significant for it hints at a thanksgiving over food.

Further prayers of gratitude to God and Christ are scattered throughout the book of Revelation. The seer, caught up in the Spirit on the Lord's day (Rev. 1:10), records the visions he saw of the heavenly hosts who worship God unceasingly (4:8). But the language he uses is that of the church upon earth, and in 11:16-18 we may overhear something of the hymns of worship and thanksgiving that are offered.

R.M.

**PRAYER BOOK.** *See* BOOK OF COMMON PRAYER.

**PRAYER OF AZARIAH AND THE SONG OF THE THREE YOUNG MEN.** The Prayer and the Song, two literary pieces, form one book of the OT APOCRYPHA. Together with SUSANNA and BEL AND THE DRAGON it comprises the Additions to the book of DANIEL. The Song of the Three Young Men (or the Song of the Three Holy Children) occurs in Greek and Latin Bibles following Daniel 3:23. The book is composed of the Prayer of Azariah (vss. 1-22), the heating of the furnace (vss. 23-28), and the song of praise of the three young men (vss. 29-68). Verses 35-65 form the Benedicite of the Anglican Prayer Book.

J.C.

**PRAYERS FOR THE DEAD.** In Roman Catholic theology, prayers for those who are presumed to be in PURGATORY. Because of the belief that extraordinary actions (such as a life of self-denial or especially martyrdom) earn even more merit than is needed for salvation, some of this surplus merit (the treasury of merits of the saints) is transferable within the communion of saints, the church, from the saintly to those less saintly. Prayers for the dead, then, underline pre-Vatican II Catholic theology, if undestood in that way. Yet even some Protestants pray for the dead, in the sense of commemoration, as in the prayers included in the *Lutheran Service Book and Hymnal*. The Christian belief in eternal life and the communion of saints, both living and dead, makes prayers for the dead possible without reference to works of merit considered transferable to others.

The veneration of the dead forms a major part of the development of religion. The elaborate rituals of the ancient Egyptians, the ancestor cults of China and Japan, and even among the Hebrews in ancient Canaan, all point to the human continuing concern for respected ones who have departed from this life.

J.C.

**PRAYER WHEEL.** In TIBETAN BUDDHISM, the *mani chos akhor* or "prayer wheel" is a hollow cylinder attached to a stick. The cylinder, inscribed with MANTRAS and containing a scroll printed with more mantras, can be spun by hand action; this is believed to release the efficacy of these mantras. Large permanently installed prayer wheels, as high as twenty feet, can be found at shrines and around the walls of temples. They are rotated by worshipers who ritualistically circumambulate the temple.    R.E.

**PREACHING.** The OT picture of the prophets of Israel who were charged with "the word of the Lord" is the starting point for preaching in the Bible. In early Judaism, after the Exile, the synagogue was born; and with that mode of worship, readings from the Law and exposition of a sacred text became prominent. This kind of setting for worship provided both Jesus (Luke 4:16-31) and the first preachers (Acts 13:16-41) with a platform for their ministry.

The Acts of the Apostles has several examples of early Christian PROCLAMATION, called KERYGMA, that is, a declaration of God's offer to all who hear, calling for acceptance and obedience. Sometimes the audience is Jewish (Acts 2:14-40), sometimes pagan (Acts 14:14-18; 17:19-31), and sometimes mixed, representing the Jewish Dispersion in the Greco-Roman world (Acts 13:15-41). There is also one example of preaching to a Christian group: Paul's address to the Ephesian elders at Miletus (Acts 20:17-35), and one additional allusion to Paul's preaching to a church audience (Acts 20:7-12).

Paul is the chief exponent of the NT kerygma, since he believed that God had called him to this service (Gal. 1:15-16; I Cor. 9:16). He maintained that in his message God was making an appeal (II Cor. 5:20). But Paul shared with the other NT writers a second type of preaching called teaching (Gal. 6:6; I Cor. 12:28; compare Eph. 4:11; I Tim. 4:6-16; II Tim. 2:2) or exhortation (I Cor. 14:3 KJV; *see* Acts 11:27-28; 21:10, for Agabus as a prophet; Rev. 1:1-13; 22:9 for John the prophet). Above all, NT preachers were witnesses to what they had seen (Acts 2:32), had received by tradition from others (I Cor. 15:1-11), and had experienced themselves (II Tim. 1:11-12; I Pet. 1:12). They invariably linked their preaching task to the gift of the Spirit (II Cor. 2:3-15; Heb. 2:4; I Pet. 1:12). This suggests that while there are formal patterns of similarity between the NT writers as they report their spoken utterances and contemporary teachers and philosophers (notably the Cynic-Stoic popular preachers), the NT preachers are claiming certain distinctives. They were messengers of the risen Lord whose Spirit has charged them to declare his "mind" (I Cor. 2:16). This distinguishes NT preachers from their current non-Christian rivals and from some persons in the apostolic churches whom Paul regarded as no better than purveyors of an alien gospel (Gal. 1:6-9; II Cor. 11:4).

Contemporary preaching is based on models wrought out in the course of church history. As early as Justin Martyr (A.D. 150) we have one type of preaching, the exposition of the Scriptures, for which there are many twentieth-century counterparts (for example, G. Campbell Morgan, James S. Stewart, John Stott). The explaining of Christian doctrine by the fathers of the fourth century has left its legacy for such preachers today whose theme is a rational defense of the faith (Paul Tillich, Helmut Thielicke, Reinhold Niebuhr, with varying emphasis). The evangelist or herald of the gospel, mentioned in II Timothy 4:5, is seen today in such people as Billy Graham. Those who stand in the tradition of the Hebrew prophets who called for social justice and economic reform on behalf of the poor and oppressed are seen in Savonarola in sixteenth-century Florence and today in Latin American preachers, both Catholic and Protestant, who expound and apply liberation theology. Finally, the pastor-preacher of the pre-Nicene church (mentioned by Polycarp) is represented in our day by such people as David Read, Peter Marshall, and TV personalities like Fulton Sheen and Robert Schuller.    R.M.

**PREDESTINATION.** The doctrine that God, from the beginning, has determined the ultimate destiny of every human person: some are destined for salvation and eternal life, others are not. Those who are predestined to salvation are said to be "elected" by God, that is to say, "chosen." Most theologians have preferred to be reticent about those who are not predestined to salvation, the non-elect, and so the words "predestination" and "election" are often synonymous. But a few theologians have taught a doctrine of "double" predestination, holding that God not only predestines some (the elect) to salvation but actively predestines others to damnation or perdition (the reprobate). Here a third term has been introduced—"reprobation," the act of rejecting some persons from the possibility of salvation and of assigning them to eternal damnation. On this reading of the doctrine, "predestination" and "election" are not synonymous. "Predestination" is then understood as a generic term, the fixing of human destinies by God, and within this generic term are the two possibilities, the affirmative possibility of ELECTION and the negative one of reprobation.

The motivation behind the doctrine is a desire to uphold the glory and sovereignty of God. Sinful human beings are unable to achieve their own salvation. All depends on the initiative of God. God's grace alone can save human beings from their sins, and that GRACE is freely given. So salvation does not depend on human efforts or human merits, but entirely on whether God has elected a person to be the recipient of saving grace. This teaching can be seen as an extension of the doctrine of PROVIDENCE. God has set certain goals for the Creation and exercises over the course of events the controls that will bring these goals to fruition.

The doctrine of predestination emerges in the OT. Abraham is called or elected to a special destiny and to be the father of a people. In the subsequent generations, we see one person elected and another, if not positively rejected, at least set aside: Isaac is preferred before Ishmael, Jacob before Esau. The nation of Israel becomes God's elect or chosen people, over against the Gentile races. Within Israel, particular individuals are elected to special vocations—David is chosen and anointed to be king, Jeremiah is conscious of having been chosen by God before his birth for a prophetic career. Already in the OT the elect are represented as a minority, and this may be the origin of the belief among later theologians that the elect comprise only a tiny minority among the mass of humanity. The majority of human beings are not of the elect, so that the elect are, in the modern sense of the cognate French word, very much an *elite*.

When we turn to the NT, a doctrine of predestination is generally accepted. The Christian church is the new Israel or chosen people, and its members are the new elect. The author of Acts uses the language of predestination for the action of Jesus' contemporaries in rejecting him: "both Herod and Pontius Pilate, with the Gentiles and the peoples of Israel" did "whatever thy hand and thy plan had predestined to take place" (4:27-28); it was all done "according to the definite plan and foreknowledge of God" (2:23). But the language of predestination is specifically used not of events but of persons. It expresses the consciousness of these early Christians that they had not chosen Christ but he had chosen them, or God had chosen them in Christ. While this belief is common to the NT writers, it receives a definite formulation from Paul: "We know that in everything God works for good with those who love him, who are called according to his purpose. For those whom he foreknew he also predestined to be conformed to the image of his Son, in order that he might be the first-born among many brethren. And those whom he predestined he also called; and those whom he called he also justified; and those whom he justified, he also glorified" (Rom. 8:28-30). With this may be compared: "Blessed be the God and Father of our Lord Jesus Christ, who has blessed us in Christ with every spiritual blessing in the heavenly places, even as he chose us in him before the foundation of the world, that we should be holy and blameless before him. He destined us in love to be his sons through Jesus Christ, according to the purpose of his will, to the praise of his glorious grace which he freely bestowed on us in the Beloved" (Eph. 1:3-6). The gratuitousness of election and the idea of being elected "in Christ" are clearly expressed in these passages. But the main passage in which Paul discusses predestination is Romans 9-11. Paul, like other Christian preachers, had to ask himself: "Why do some respond to the preaching, while others reject it?" Especially difficult was the fact that Israel, the elect people, had rejected Christ. It is in considering the destiny of Israel that Paul touches on questions of predestination that were to provide fuel for later controversies.

The exegesis of these three chapters is difficult and disputed. When Paul talks of "vessels of wrath made for destruction" (Rom. 9:22), he seems close to a doctrine of double predestination and has sometimes been interpreted in that sense. But he also seems to be saying that God will not desert the elect people, Israel, but that although God has temporarily hardened their hearts, God will eventually bring salvation to them when the mission to the Gentiles has been completed. "The gifts and the call of God are irrevocable" (Rom. 11:29). What is not entirely clear is whether only a remnant of Israel is predestined to salvation or whether election still extends to the whole people. If the former of these alternatives is the case, then already predestination is being understood in a mainly individualistic way.

*History of the Doctrine.* The post-biblical development of the doctrine may be conveniently studied in four major theological figures, each of whom has made an important contribution. AUGUSTINE firmly believed (not least on the basis of his own experience) that salvation is the gift of God and that God's grace may be experienced as irresistible. The church itself is a mixed body that does indeed contain the elect but also a large number of people who, though baptized and members of the church, do not really belong to it. Only the elect, predestined by God from the beginning, truly belong to Christ, and their number is relatively small. Augustine believed that this number was also definite *(certus numerus)* and when that number had been made up, then God's purpose would be complete and his kingdom would have come. The certain number was supposed to correspond to the number of rebel angels who had fallen away from God in a premundane rebellion. Their defection had upset the harmony of the universe, and it was necessary to replace them by precisely the same number of souls—though these souls would be human rather than angelic. One may not question God's justice in what seems to be his arbitrary choice of men and women for salvation. Those who are rejected simply receive the due reward of their sin, while the elect owe their salvation solely to the divine mercy. But Augustine admits that we confront a mystery at this point. Furthermore, he stops short of a thoroughgoing double predestination, if that means an active reprobation of the non-elect. It is simply that they are left out and therefore left to suffer the just punishment for their sin. God cannot be accused of injustice. Rather, we have to acknowledge God's grace in being merciful to a few.

Augustine's views were sharpened in controversy with PELAGIUS, who held that a human being is free to choose between good and evil. The controversy between Augustinians and Pelagians continued after Augustine's death, and although Augustinianism

triumphed, it was a chastened and modified Augustinianism that fell just short of double predestination. Nevertheless, one has to ask whether the doctrine does not constitute a fundamental incoherence in Augustine's theology as a whole. For what is the point of preaching, faith, the church, and the sacramental system if everything has been decided by God in advance? Again, in spite of what Augustine may say, does he allow any real freedom to human beings on these vital matters of faith and salvation, or are not people reduced to little more than puppets?

The main points of Augustine's teaching about predestination reappear in the philosophy of THOMAS AQUINAS. The question of predestination is treated immediately after his discussion of providence. The business of providence is to ensure that the ends of God are attained. Now, the end for humanity is eternal life, but this is not an end that can be reached by natural human power. People must be lifted up and sent there by another, and "the planned sending of a rational creature to the end, which is eternal life, is termed 'predestination,' for to predestine is to send." This predestining is entirely a work of God, in which the human person is passive. In reply to the question whether anyone is reprobated by God, Thomas gives a qualified assent. God does reject some people, in the sense that God permits them to fall into sin, but, strictly speaking, they destroy themselves. In their cases there is not that active planned sending to an end that is the essence of predestination to eternal life. "The causality of reprobation differs from that of predestination" for the reason that we have already noted. When Thomas uses the word "predestination," he uses it in the affirmative sense of election. There is no positive activity of reprobation parallel to the work of predestination. Thus Thomas also stops short of a strict doctrine of double predestination. Like Augustine, he teaches that human merit plays no part in these matters. We are saved not by good works but purely by God's mercy. Predestination is said by Thomas to be certain. He maintains too, with Augustine, that the number predestined to eternal life is fixed, but though he knows the view that the number of the elect is equal to the number of fallen angels, he says this matter is best left undecided, and that God alone knows the number of the elect.

We pass on to the Reformation, and especially to the teaching of CALVIN, in whose system the doctrine of predestination has an important place. In general, Calvin follows Augustine, but he introduces an extra rigor into the doctrine, and some of his followers become more rigorous still. The essence of Calvin's teaching on the subject is contained in four chapters of the *Institutes* (Book III, chaps. 21–23), and is prefaced by a warning that we must not be too curious in searching into the secrets of God. He chooses some and rejects others by his good pleasure, and we cannot inquire into the reasons for this. Calvin uses the word "pleasant" for the doctrine of predestination—and no

doubt it is a pleasant doctrine for those who are assured that they belong to the elect. For God has done everything for their salvation, and his election is irreversible, no matter how sinful they are. As for the criticisms of "profane men," Calvin is unperturbed, for he says they will likewise criticize any Christian doctrine.

The tendency to individualize predestination, already evident in Augustine, is prominent in Calvin's teaching. The true church, according to Calvin, is the invisible church, and its membership is known to God alone. The visible church contains not only the elect but others whose membership is in outward things only and who do not belong to the elect. So not only the human race as a whole but even the church is divided into two exclusive classes of individuals, the elect and the reprobate. Obviously such a view would not make for a strong feeling of solidarity or community in the church, and indeed there is plenty of evidence that many people suffered lifelong anxieties, wondering whether or not they truly belonged to the elect. As in the case of Augustine, one has again to ask whether the doctrine of predestination, in this strong form, does not entirely undermine baptism, preaching, mission, and most of the other acts of the church.

Calvin is at great pains to insist that election has nothing to do with human merit or with God's foreknowledge of such merit. God does not elect those who will prove worthy of grace—the election is purely gratuitous and the only reason, if it be a reason, is to say that it depends on God's good pleasure. At this point he comes into conflict with Aquinas, whom he suspects of allowing some weight to the foreknowledge of merit. He differs also from Thomas in upholding a very strong interpretation of reprobation. Calvin teaches that reprobation is not just due to the permissive will of God but is something that God positively ordains. This in turn is linked with his doctrine of providence, which sees God as the ultimate author of every event that happens, even the sins of the wicked. Why God should ordain that people should sin we do not know. "It is certain, however, that it was just, because he saw that his own glory would thereby be displayed." Such teaching is bound to strike us as inhuman, and even Calvin's supporters find it hard to defend him. We seem to be dealing with a God of sheer power, not the God of Jesus Christ. The reprobate "were raised up by the just but inscrutable judgment of God, to show forth his glory by their condemnation."

In the high Calvinism that followed Calvin's own teaching, the doctrine of predestination was made, if possible, even more rigorous. The WESTMINSTER CONFESSION of faith, which became the doctrinal standard for English-speaking Reformed churches, made God's eternal decree foundational. Before there is any mention of the saving work of Christ, it is taught that "by the decree of God, for the manifestation of his glory, some men and angels are predestinated into everlasting life, and others foreordained to everlasting death." In spite of Calvin's own warning against curious speculation, there was soon a controversy between those who held that the eternal decree was made without regard to the question whether people would fall into sin or not (supralapsarianism) and those who held that it was made only in the light of God's foreknowledge of the Fall (infralapsarianism). It is not surprising that just as there had been a reaction against strict Augustinianism, so there was one against high Calvinism. ARMINIANISM toned down the doctrine of predestination, and although it was condemned, it steadily gained ground. By the nineteenth century, the rigor of the traditional doctrine was being modified in the Calvinist churches. In Scotland, for instance, John McLeod Campbell taught that Christ's atoning death was for all humanity, not just for the elect, and though he was himself deposed from the ministry, his teaching has come to be generally accepted.

We move on to KARL BARTH, the greatest representative of the Reformed tradition in the twentieth century. He treats at length of predestination in *Church Dogmatics*. He tells us that in this matter he is not able to follow in the tradition of Calvin's teaching. Indeed, he is severe in his criticism. Calvin's electing God is a hidden God, and "all the dubious features of his doctrine result from the basic failing that in the last analysis he separates God and Jesus Christ." Barth, on the contrary, claims that "if we would know who God is and what is the meaning and purpose of his election, we must look only to the name of Jesus Christ and the existence and history of the people of God enclosed in him." So Barth intends to take seriously a point hitherto neglected, though it already appears in Paul—that the election of individual Christians is an election *in* Christ. Or, to put it in another way, Christ is himself the original elect one, and all further election is in and through him. In a recurring phrase, Barth speaks of Jesus Christ as "the beginning of all God's works and ways." Since Christ is the God-man, this also means that from the beginning there is a humanity in God, and God has elected people to be God's covenant partners. Further, since Jesus Christ is the God-man, we can think of him as both the electing God and the elected man. He has, so to speak, elected himself, and elected humankind in himself. Insofar as Barth still speaks of reprobation, he teaches that this is taken by Christ upon himself, and so he moves toward a universalism. "If the teachers of predestination were right when they spoke always of a duality of election and reprobation" (we should note the hypothetical character of Barth's language here) "then we may say already that in the election of Jesus Christ, God has ascribed to man election and to himself he has ascribed reprobation."

This teaching is not altogether clear. What is the relation of God the Father to Jesus Christ? Or of Jesus Christ as God to Jesus Christ as incarnate? Is there still lingering here some thought of the Father rejecting and punishing the Son? In spite of these obscurities, what clearly emerges is a doctrine of predestination in which we get away from individualism to the teaching that the whole human race is elected in Jesus Christ. It is interesting to note that even Judas, the "son of perdition," retains the indelible character of his election and vocation. "His election excels and outshines and controls his rejection." In spite of some doubtful points, Barth's reconstruction of the doctrine of predestination must be accounted one of the greatest achievements of his theology. He has insisted on Christianizing a doctrine which, in the past, was too often developed in relation to a hypothetical God, very different from the God of the Christian revelation.

*The Contemporary Situation.* At the present day, the doctrine of predestination does not excite the interest and passion that attached to it in the past. Since the Enlightenment, we have thought of the human being in terms of autonomy, freedom, and responsibility, and if some people today still think of themselves as pawns at the disposal of a destiny that they cannot control, they are more likely to think of this in terms of mechanical DETERMINISM than as due to the secret decrees of an all-disposing God. Nevertheless, those who believe in God have still the problem of reconciling human freedom with the divine government of the world. Furthermore, contemporary religious experience still reports the feeling of having been chosen or called by God, and confesses that the experience of grace is that of a divine initiative, which impinges on our lives before we have ourselves looked for God. Some doctrine of predestination is still needed to account for these matters, but it would be a doctrine that made room for the contribution of human FREEDOM, not one that turned human beings into puppets. It would also be a doctrine that interpreted predestination positively as election, with reprobation understood as the (unrealized) possibility that it might have been otherwise.      J.M.

## PREEXISTENCE OF SOULS

**PREEXISTENCE OF SOULS.** A religious doctrine, also known as REINCARNATION, transmigration of souls, or rebirth. It is often assumed that preexistence implies the IMMORTALITY of the soul, which undergoes a series of rebirths. However, preexistence does not mean the eternity of the soul. Buddhism, for example, teaches reincarnation but denies that the soul is immortal.

The origin of the belief in the soul's preexistence is obscure. It is not present in early Greek or Indian religion, but later the belief is widespread in these cultures. Preexistence teaches that the present self has lived before in another physical body and that it will live again in a future existence. It is not the empirical self or body, however, that preexists and is reborn but, rather, what the Hindus call the "subtle body." It is this "subtle body" that bears the individual karma or deeds of its previous existence, and it is this that determines the character of the next rebirth. Good karma will ensure rebirth in a higher state of existence, perhaps as a spiritual being or god. Evil karma will likely ensure rebirth in a lower order, as an animal or plant.

While the preexistence of souls was taught in ancient Greece (by Pythagoras, Orphism, Plato, and Plotinus), the doctrine has not prevailed in the Western religions. It remains a prevalent belief in those Eastern cultures deeply influenced by Hinduism and Buddhism. Associated as it is with the doctrine of KARMA, the preexistence and rebirth of souls has provided these religions with a highly rational theodicy or explanation of the existence and amelioration of EVIL. The question of whether preexistence of souls is at all compatible with the doctrine of the RESURRECTION OF THE DEAD has been a topic of recent discussion.                    J.L.

**PREFECT APOSTOLIC.** The head of a prefecture apostolic, or the first ecclesiastical organization of a mission field, in the Roman Catholic church. This means the mission territory is directly supervised by the pope and the Congregation for the Propagation of the Faith. A prefect apostolic is not usually a bishop.
                                                        J.C.

**PRELATE.** An official of the Roman Catholic church, from the Latin *praelatus,* meaning "one set before." Actual prelates include bishops, vicars and prefects apostolic, abbots, and curia members. Honorary prelates are those honored by the pope for their service in the church. All prelates are called monsignor and wear special dress.          J.C.

**PREMILLENNIALISM.** *See* MILLENNIUM.

**PRESBYTER/PRESBYTERY.** The term "presbyter" is a transliteration of the Greek word for ELDER. The early Christian churches were administered by a body of elders, the collegiate system referred to in Acts 11:30 and Acts 15:22. This followed the practice of "the elders of Israel" who directed both civil and ecclesiastical rule. The presbyters functioned as BISHOPS (*episkopoi*) or overseers. Gradually one elder assumed the presidency of the governing group. Thus he became the bishop or chief presbyter, although the terms seem to have been interchangeable in the earliest days of the church.

During the Middle Ages the term "presbyter" was shortened to priest, but the identification of a priest as Christian minister did not occur until the second century. Calvin and his followers in the Reformed and Presbyterian tradition felt that biblical principles dictated the concept of church government by the elders or presbyters. Thus elders in a particular Presbyterian or Reformed church are responsible for the admission of new members and the supervision of the local church body. The minister is a teaching elder, whose office is on a parity with the ruling lay elders.

Presbyterian or Reformed polity consists of a series of courts, starting with the session or consistory that governs the particular congregation. The presbytery or classis is made up of ministers and elders who represent churches in a prescribed geographical area and has the oversight over the congregations and ministers of that region. The SYNOD consists of members of several presbyteries within a larger area. The GENERAL ASSEMBLY is the highest court, with final authority over the entire ecclesiastical organization.          R.H.

**PRESBYTERIAN CHURCHES.** A major Protestant communion, part of the Reformed wing of the sixteenth-century REFORMATION, owing its distinctive polity, doctrine, worship, piety, and discipline more to JOHN CALVIN than to ULRICH ZWINGLI. Presbyterianism, as a term, refers to a form of church government, that is, ruling by ELDERS or PRESBYTERS. According to Calvin's *Institutes of the Christian Religion,* the form of government of the church is revealed in the NT, since the church possesses divine authority. In doctrine, Presbyterians are similar to the other Reformed churches of Switzerland, Germany, France, and Holland. The term "Presbyterian" then is generally used to refer to the Reformed churches as they developed in Britain (especially in Scotland) and North America.

John Calvin was a French lawyer who experienced a deep but quiet conversion to Luther's Reformation teaching of justification by faith. After a stormy life he eventually settled in Geneva and directed the continuation of the Reformation there after Zwingli's death in battle. Calvin's adherence to the basic doctrines of the Lutheran Reformation can be seen in his long friendship with Philip Melanchthon and in his signing of the altered Augsburg Confession. Over many years, Calvin developed a systematic, tightly reasoned body of doctrine, *The Institutes of the Christian Religion,* which probably has exerted more influence on the development of Reformed Protestantism than any other work. Calvin, and thus the Presbyterianism derived from him, tended toward controversy and dogmatism, and, due to a necessary emphasis upon discipline, also to legalism. Nonetheless, Calvin and Presbyterianism reflect a deep loyalty to the SOVEREIGNTY OF GOD, making life and theology theocentric. Calvinism tends to be all-embracing, desiring to regulate all of life by the divine will, which it believes to be given in the Bible.

The doctrinal basis of the Presbyterian church is the conviction that the Bible is the Word of God, and is the only rule for faith and practice. Whatever the Bible affirms, Presbyterianism affirms. Whatever the Bible condemns, Presbyterianism condemns. While *The Institutes of the Christian Religion* form the historical and theological basis for Presbyterianism, the WESTMINSTER CONFESSION of Faith and the Westminster Shorter Catechism—along with the Heidelberg Confession and HEIDELBERG CATECHISM—form the traditional basis of the church.

Over the years Presbyterian doctrine, particularly in America, has undergone considerable change. The historic divisions between ARMINIANISM and high Calvinism over predestination have largely disappeared. Indeed, part of the reason for the long division between the northern and southern churches was the increasing liberalism of much of the northern church. The United Presbyterian Church in the U.S.A. confession of 1967, a result of modern biblical and theological studies, is accepted as the basic doctrinal position of the church. It is an impressive restatement of Reformed doctrine in contemporary terms.

The Reformation moved from the Continent to Britain by way of the low countries, where Lutheran and Reformed views were widespread. Lutheran doctrine was spread in Scotland before 1528 by traveling merchants, one of whom was martyred. JOHN KNOX, who had gone to Geneva, brought Reformed teachings to Scotland in 1559. By the end of 1560 the Scots church was in process of reform. By 1564, the General Assembly affirmed the *Book of Common Order*. Presbyterianism became the church of the great mass of Scots people, although the Church of Scotland underwent controversy and divisions between 1680 and 1843. Most of these divisions were resolved in church union by 1929. Presbyterian churches were also formed in England, and, after 1610, in northern Ireland. Presbyterians early came to America, although Presbyterianism in the U.S.A. has many origins. Until recently, there were at least ten important denominations called either Presbyterian or Reformed in America. All these churches are similar in polity or government—the distinguishing feature of Presbyterianism. The principles of the system of polity are derived either from the canons of the SYNOD OF DORT, the Westminster Confession, or the Heidelberg Catechism.

Presbyterians were generally united across the United States before the Civil War. However, with the coming of secession, Presbyterians in Virginia, North Carolina, upper South Carolina, and elsewhere in the South, met in Augusta, Georgia, and organized the Southern Presbyterian church. The churches in states holding to the union continued as the Presbyterian Church in the U.S.A. After several years of merger negotiations and votes by presbyteries north and south, the northern and southern branches merged into the Presbyterian Church in the U.S.A. in 1983.

Other Presbyterian bodies in America include the Presbyterian Church in America, more conservative than either the northern or southern churches, and the Bible Presbyterian church, an ultra-Fundamentalist body founded by the Reverend Carl McIntyre.

The Church of Scotland moved toward reunion of the divisions occasioned between 1680 and 1843 in the last part of the nineteenth century. This unity was accomplished in spite of the intellectual controversies of the era and the heresy trial of William R. Smith. In 1929, the United Free church and the established church reunited. The Scottish National church is free of state control and self-governing.

Before the mergers, there were several other bodies besides the United Free church, such as the Free Church of Scotland, the Free Presbyterian Church of Scotland, the Reformed Presbyterian Church, and the Original Secession Church. The Free Presbyterian church dates to 1893 and essentially represented Fundamentalist beliefs in the Scriptures and a stand against the use of instrumental music in church. The Original Secession church dates to 1733, when Ebenezer Erskine and three other ministers withdrew from the established church as they felt it had departed from evangelical teaching. Erskine also felt the state should stay out of church affairs.

Interestingly, the Reformed Presbyterian church took root in America, resulting in the Associate Reformed Presbyterian church, chiefly found in the South. This small body maintains a college and seminary (Erskine) at Due West, South Carolina. The ARP group does not use hymns in its church services, but only the Psalms, as did the Reformed Presbyterian Church in Scotland. The ARP holds to the Westminister Confession of Faith and objects to secret oaths and secret societies.

In England, the Presbyterian Church of England was formed in 1876 from the English Synod of the United Presbyterian Church of Scotland. In Ireland, Presbyterian settlers began to arrive after 1610 and the beginning of the Ulster Plantation under James I. The established Anglican church persecuted Presbyterian ministers, and in 1661 ejected sixty-four pastors from their congregations. Many Presbyterians then migrated to America. Nonetheless, the church grew in Ireland and in 1741 a split occurred between the Secession Synod and the Synod of Ulster. Arian (Unitarian) beliefs developed in the Ulster Synod, and the cause of Trinitarianism was championed by the Reverend Henry Cooke, who prevailed in 1825. A Remonstrant Synod (of liberals) was formed in 1829 (only seventeen ministers), and the two orthodox synods united in 1840 to form the General Assembly of the Presbyterian Church in Ireland.

There are several smaller Irish bodies—the Reformed Presbyterians or the Covenanting Church of Ireland and the Secession Church in Ireland. Some congregations did not enter the union of 1840 and formed the Associate Synod of Ireland, also known as "the Presbyterian Synod of Ireland Distinguished by the Name Seceder."

In the United States, until recently, there were major Presbyterian churches in the North and the South. The merger of 1983 formed the Presbyterian Church in the U.S.A. from the United Presbyterian Church in the U.S.A. (North) and the Presbyterian Church in the U.S. (South). The northern church has diverse origins, embracing Scottish, English, German, and other national backgrounds; people who came from the Reformed churches in Europe.

Francis Makemie originally worked with Presbyterians coming from northern Ireland through the port of Philadelphia. Many of these "Scots-Irish" moved southward to Virginia, North Carolina, and the piedmont of upper South Carolina. A flourishing growth took place until the coming of secession in 1861. At that time, the presbyteries in the South renounced their connection with the general assembly (called the Old School Presbyterians). Forty-seven presbyteries met in Augusta, Georgia, December 4, 1861, and organized a new general assembly.

The Synod of the Reformed Presbyterian Church of North America, the "Covenanter Church," is descended from the Church of Scotland. It was constituted in 1774 in Pennsylvania and reorganized in 1809.

The Associate Reformed Synod of the South was formed in 1782. There were four synods in the Associate Reformed church, but the Associate Reformed Synod withdrew from the church in 1822. The differences were due to the distance from other synods in New York and Pennsylvania, and questions about psalm use and closed Communion.

The Reformed Presbyterian Church in North America began in 1774. The Cumberland Presbyterian Church was formed on February 10, 1810, and merged with the Presbyterian Church in the U.S.A. in 1906. The Cumberland church was the result of the revivals in southwest Kentucky and Tennessee in 1797 and following under the leadership of the Reverend James McGready. The Cumberland church grew to constitute three presbyteries. It differed from the Westminster Confession, in holding that Christ died for all and in saying "There are no eternal reprobates." There was also a Cumberland Presbyterian Church, Colored.

In 1982, two conservative Presbyterian churches merged in Grand Rapids, Michigan. The Presbyterian Church in America and the Reformed Presbyterian Church in America, Evangelical Synod, joined to form the Reformed Presbyterian Church in America.

J.C.

**PRESBYTERIAN CHURCH, U.S.A.** *See* PRESBYTERIAN CHURCHES.

**PRESBYTERY.** *See* PRESBYTER.

**PREVENIENT GRACE.** Not some special kind of GRACE, but a general description of all grace, as this is understood in Christian theology. The word "prevenient" means "coming before," and all grace is prevenient in the sense that God's gracious action precedes any turning toward God on the part of the recipient of grace. To speak of "prevenient" grace is simply to acknowledge the Christian testimony that God has loved us before we loved God. Such grace may be at work without the recipient's being explicitly aware of it. It may, for instance, be mediated through the Christian community. Paul's

sudden conversion may well have been unconsciously prepared by experiences of grace through his contacts with Stephen and other Christians. In INFANT BAPTISM the child receives grace through the incorporation into the Christian community, though only later does the child recognize what has taken place. There are many other ways in which grace is at work before there is any turning to God.

J.M.

**PRIDE.** Considered by moral theologians to be one of the SEVEN DEADLY SINS, and is said by some to be the worst of all and the root of all the rest. The first sin of Adam and Eve is in response to the temptation, "You will be like God" (Gen. 2:5). This is the temptation to go beyond their creaturely status and usurp the place of God. The theme of human pride is continued in the story of the Tower of Babel, which the people built in order to reach to heaven and make a name for themselves (Gen. 11:1-9). Augustine declared that "pride is the origin and head of all evils," and he points out that it was pride that led the devil to rebel against God. The devil had no body, and this was interpreted to mean that sins of the spirit (including pride) are worse than sins of the flesh. These views have been restated in modern times by Reinhold Niebuhr, who held that the sins of the flesh flow from the evil will of the spirit that has ceased to trust in God and has set itself up as its own ultimate. Pride takes many forms. Pride of power is perhaps the most dangerous and produces patterns of domination and even dictatorship. But pride of knowledge and pride of righteousness are particularly repulsive. Not all pride is sinful, for there is the proper pride of self-respect and the satisfaction of doing something well. Aristotle saw this proper pride as a virtuous mean between the vices of arrogance and self-depreciation.

J.M.

**PRIESTHOOD OF BELIEVERS.** The concept that all Christians participate in the priesthood of Christ as mediator by virtue of their baptism. The vocation of the ordained, as well as the lay priesthood, is derived from the priesthood of Christ as described in the Epistle to the Hebrews. They are intended to be a mutually supportive priesthood.

Luther made a distinction between the priesthood of word and sacrament (ordained) and the priesthood of the laity. Some groups recognize no distinction between the people of God (the *laos,* or laity) and the clergy. The Society of Friends, for example, has no ordained ministers.

The Reformation emphasis on the priesthood of believers countered the strong role that the priest earlier had as mediator through receiving confessions and assuring absolution of sins. It removed the priest as mediator between God and the believer. The Catholic Reformation, in reaction, made the laity distinctly subordinate to the ordained ministry so that the idea of the priesthood of believers almost disappeared. The Constitutions on the Church from Vatican II tried to rectify this by recognizing the mediatorial role of the laity. The laity mediate God's redemptive purpose, specifically in the prayers of the people in the liturgy as well as in their daily work. The priesthood of believers is also connected with vocation because they are called out by their baptism. The key verse is I Peter 2:9, "But you are a chosen race, a royal priesthood."            I.C.

PRIESTLY, JOSEPH (1733–1804). English clergyman and scientist, prominently associated with instituting English and American Unitarianism, who helped found modern chemistry, advanced the knowledge of electricity, discovered oxygen, and isolated several gases. Born in Fieldhead, Yorkshire, he studied for the ministry at Daventry Academy. Ordained a Presbyterian minister in 1755, Priestly served three-year pastorates at Needham and Nantwich and in 1761 began teaching science at Warrington Academy. He shared the eighteenth century's confidence in rationalism and soon questioned "orthodox" beliefs. Appointed minister in Leeds (1767), he continued experiments with electricity and helped Theophilus Lindsey establish Unitarianism despite laws against rejecting the Trinity. Priestly advocated congregational polity and authority and reliance on Scripture rather than human creeds. While a librarian to Lord Shelburne (1772–80), Priestly had more time to write and experiment. His controversial books included *Institutes of Natural and Revealed Religion* (1772–74) and *Disquisitions relating to Matter and Spirit* (1777). On leaving Lord Shelburne, he actively promoted Unitarianism in Birmingham, writing *History of the Corruptions of Christianity* (1782) and *History of Early Opinions concerning Jesus Christ* (1786). He supported the French and American revolutions and in 1794 moved to Northumberland, Pennsylvania, where until his death he helped emerging Unitarianism in New England. *Theological and Miscellaneous Works* appeared posthumously (26 vols., 1817–32).        C.M.

PRIESTS AND LEVITES. In ancient Mesopotamian and Egyptian civilizations the role of the priest grew up under the shadow of the king. The priests evolved as a hierarchical caste who were thought to support the monarchy. By contrast the biblical pattern is different, as we shall see.

*Old Testament.* The traditions of Abraham and the later patriarchs in Genesis show these figures as priests in their family groups. They build altars and offer sacrifices (Gen. 12:7ff.; 13:18; 22:13; 26:25; 46:1). The only royal priestly persons who enter the scene in the patriarchal narratives are figures outside Israel (Melchizedek in Gen. 14:18ff.) and the priests of Pharaoh in Genesis 41:45; 47:22. The tribe of LEVI (in Gen. 34 and 49:5ff.) has still to be given priestly functions.

Moses is called a Levite, and with him the Levitical

office begins. Exodus 22:25-29 describes the real character of Israelite priesthood: the tribe of Levi is chosen to serve God and to act in the name of the entire people. The early days of the nation's self-consciousness witnessed the rise of priests as guardians of the ark (I Sam. 1–4) and as functionaries at the sacred shrines. The essential role of the priest was the offering of sacrifice, as Moses is said to have done (Exod. 24:4-8) as well as Levi (Deut. 33:10). AARON's family retained a distinctive role, but Levites were priests in a wider context, connected with various sanctuaries (Judg. 17:7-13; 18, 19). Families too had their local priests (Judg. 6:18-29; 13:19; 17:5; I Sam. 7:1).

With the advent of David as undisputed king over Israel, priesthood received a royal patronage, and two families were set apart for this purpose: ABIATHAR and ZADOK. Later genealogies in I Chronicles 6:49-53 connect both names with the family of Aaron. The rise of the office of HIGH PRIEST in Jerusalem gave impetus to the entire priestly role, and in 621 B.C. importance in a central and exclusive sanctuary in Jeusalem was emphasized (Deut. 18:16ff.). The effect of this revolution was to curtail the activities of local sanctuaries and their personnel and centralize worship at the Jerusalem Temple. Another vital result was to restrict priestly activity to Zadok alone (II Kings 23:5, 9) and so pave the way for the postexilic distinction between priests and Levites (Ezek. 44:1-31).

The fall of Jerusalem and the fate of the Temple in 597 and 586 B.C. also led to the collapse of the monarchy in Israel with the consequence that priesthood was set free from its sacrificial and royal connections and able to lead the nation as its "conscience" and mentor. The eclipse of the prophetic movement after the Exile also contributed to the importance given to Israel's priests. Both Ezekiel and Third Isaiah (Isa. 56–66) give prominence to the Levites as the only true priests, and the assembling of a final version of the Pentateuch and the work of the Chronicler (third century B.C.) also gave opportunity for the sacerdotal rites of the priesthood to be highlighted. It is from this redactional work that we derive the traditional picture of the Aaronic priesthood according to a pyramid configuration with Aaron on top, his sons next in succession, and then the Levites as tribal clergy below. The Zadokite line simply perpetuated this arrangement.

In Maccabean times the role of high priest came into prominence, and the Hasmonean family combined the office of priest and king—but not without protest, whether from the "pious ones," who later became the Pharisees, or the sectarians of the Dead Sea Scrolls who regarded their enclave at Qumran as the priestly offshoot.

*New Testament.* Jesus never claimed a priestly function, a fact exploited by Hebrews 7 in two ways: it asserts that Jesus was descended from Judah, not Levi, and yet it claims that Jesus does fulfill the role of

Melchizedek (Gen. 14:18ff.), who was both king and priest. The oath of Psalm 110:4 is cited as supporting Jesus' office as messianic high priest, but in a superior way to the Aaronic-Levitical priesthood. The argument is then made that Jesus' ministry led to the offering of a perfect sacrifice on the cross and the opening of a new age of restored relationship between humanity and God that has the note of finality and completeness about it. Jesus is still, however, a priest (Heb. 7:26ff.) with a service of intercession as mediator of the Second Covenant (Heb. 8:6-13; 10:12-18).

If the task of priesthood is essentially one of sacrificial representation, then it may be said that other parts of the NT endorse the teaching of the Epistle to the Hebrews, even if they do not use the priestly language that it employs. The presentation of Jesus as suffering servant of God (Mark 10:45; 14:24) has links with Isaiah 53, and the setting of both the Last Supper meal and his death on the cross at Passover time recall the sacrificial rites of the OT (I Cor. 5:7-8). Mention of Christ's blood in several NT locations (for example, I Cor. 10:16-22; Rom. 3:24-25;5:9; Col. 1:20; Eph. 1:7; 2:13; I Pet. 1:18-19) echoes an indebtedness to the idea that he died as both a priest and a victim, with the emphasis more on the latter term than the former.

An interesting development is to see the way the priestly language of the NT indicates a spiritualizing of the OT cult. Paul can utilize the terms of the Levitical ministry but in a new way and in reference to the church itself (Phil. 2:17; 4:18). Paul's notion of worship is one of a "spiritual worship" (Rom. 12:1; see Phil. 3:3; compare Heb. 9:14; 12:28) in contrast to what he regards as external and ceremonial (Rom. 2:27-29) under the OT rubric. The same application is seen in I Peter 2:5, 9 and in the Apocalypse (Rev. 1:6; 5:10; 2:6; compare Exod. 19:6).

The final element of the way "priests and Levites" are taken over by the NT writers is seen in their teaching on the ministry of the church. Again, the teaching is more by contrast than by direct correspondence. The apostles of Jesus were laypersons, not priests. Their colleagues are known as elders or presbyters (Acts 14:23; 20:17; Tit. 1:5), not successors in a priestly line. Yet priestly language can be used as in I Corinthians 4:1; II Corinthians 3:4-6; Romans 1:9; 15:15ff., however much it is qualified by the overriding considerations that apostolic ministry is not hierarchical or sacral but is dependent on the will of God in Christ (Rom. 1:1), and also that such apostolate is shared by the entire people of God.
                                                                    R.M.

**PRIMACY OF THE POPE.** The recognition of the authority of the pope (or bishop of Rome; the patriarch of the West) over the universal church. This primacy is jurisdictional and legal in the Catholic church, that is, the pope is the administrative head of the church, but a primacy of honor to the pope is also recognized by some Orthodox churches and High Church Anglicans.

The primacy of the pope in Catholic thought is based on the belief that Peter founded the Church of Rome, and further, that he was chief of the apostles. This is based on Matthew 16:15-19; Mark 3:16; 17:7; Luke 22:31-32; John 1:42; 21:15-17; Acts 2:14; 3:12; 4:8; 15:7-11; and I Corinthians 15:15; Galatians 1:18-19; 2:7.Christ said, "You are Peter, and on this rock I will build my church" (Matt. 16:18). Catholics see this promise as based on Peter, the man; Protestants believe the promise is based on the faith that Peter confessed.                    J.C.

**PRIMATE.** A bishop of the Roman Catholic church, not a patriarch, who has jurisdiction over all metropolitans and bishops in a country or specific territory. The primate is himself supervised only by the pope. This title is no longer recognized in canon law, although it is used by some archbishops.
                                                                    J.C.

**PRIME MOVER.** A philosophical expression applied to God. Everywhere in the world one can observe motion—and the word "motion" here is being used in a very broad sense; in modern language, we might rather say "evolution" or "ordered development." It is argued that if one begins from inert formless matter, then it is impossible to account for the evolution or ordered movement of the universe. There must be an active source for this, a prime mover that is itself unmoved. These views were put forward by ARISTOTLE, who claimed further that this prime mover works through being an object of desire, that is to say, it is a final rather than an efficient cause. The argument reappears in THOMAS AQUINAS, as the first of his five ways of proving GOD'S EXISTENCE. We plainly see processes of change going on in the world. But anything that is changing must be changed by something else. As we trace this process back, we arrive eventually at "a first cause of change, not itself being changed by anything" (*aliquod primum movens quod a nullo movetur*). This, says Thomas, is what everyone understands by God. A similar idea appears in ALFRED WHITEHEAD, who argues that an organic universe could not arise from formless matter and who thinks of God as drawing the world in a certain direction through a "lure," which is like a final cause.                    J.M.

**PRINCIPALITY.** The KJV uses this term to translate a Greek word for "rule" or "dominion" (*archē*). It is one of the names given to angelic or demonic forces in Hellenistic cosmology, thought to control human destiny. In Paul's letters, confidence is expressed that these powers cannot separate believers from God (Rom. 8:38) since Christ is both their creator (Col. 1:16) and ruler (Eph. 1:21, 22). In Titus 3:1 the term is used of earthly authorities in the Roman Empire.                    R.M.

**PRIOR/PRIORESS/PRIORY.** *Prior:* A superior of a monastic order. Generally priors hold office for a set term of years rather than for life. The word is from the Latin meaning "superior" or "elder." *Prioress:* A superior of a convent of nuns, or an assistant to an abbess, in ruling such a convent. Not all convents are ruled by prioresses; in some, the superior is called mother superior. *Priory:* A monastery or convent ruled by a prior or prioress. A priory may be self-governing (conventual) or dependent upon an abbey or mother house.                     J.C.

**PRISCILLA.** *See* AQUILA AND PRISCILLA.

**PROBABILISM.** In Roman Catholicism a theory that people involved in cases of moral doubt may follow a sound, probable opinion about acting morally. In the seventeenth-century controversies over JANSENISM, Blaise Pascal ridiculed and scorned the Jesuits for twisting the theory into a justification for practically anything, by using probabilism to vindicate probable opinions in favor of liberty even though opinions favoring law were more probably moral. In his *Provincial Letters* (1656) PASCAL depicted the Jesuits using probabilism in their confessionals to declare any act to be perfectly acceptable to Christ if there was any probability that it might be all right, thus approving murder, adultery, and so forth. The Jesuits were defending their use of free will against extreme Augustinianism at Port Royal, France, voiced by Cornelius Jansen, Antoine Arnauld, and Pasquier Quesnel. Pope Clement XI's bull *Unigenitus* (1713) formally condemned Jansenism.         C.M.

**PROCESSIONAL.** The hymn or musical composition, vocal or instrumental only, which is played near the beginning of a worship service. In liturgical churches, the processional will cover the entrance of the choir, the crucifer, the presiding minister, and assisting ministers. It occurs immediately after the public confession in Lutheran churches and as the first element of the service in Reformed churches.
                                                              J.C.

**PROCESSION OF THE HOLY SPIRIT.** A doctrine characterizing the relationship of the Holy Spirit to the Father and Son in the TRINITY, the manner of procession creating sharp controversy in early Roman and Greek Christianity. After prolonged acrimonious debate, Father, Son, and Holy Spirit received orthodox definition at Nicaea (325), Constantinople (381), and Chalcedon (451)—one Godhead in three persons, equal in glory and majesty, the Holy Spirit being different from the Father as the Son is different from the Father. The Father expresses paternity; the Son, filiation; the Holy Spirit, spiration. Controversy arose over whether the Holy Spirit proceeds *from the Father and the Son* or *from the Father through the Son.* Cyril of Alexandria used both phrases. However, Eastern theologians tended to

support the latter. Western theologians Jerome, Ambrose, and Augustine supported the former (double procession, also called FILIOQUE—meaning "and the Son"). Opponents gave different interpretations of John 14:15-17; 14:15-17, 26; 16:5-15; Acts 5:32; 16:6-7; Romans 8:9-11, 16; Galatians 4:6; Philippians 1:19; and related passages. In 864 Eastern Patriarch Photius assailed Rome's double procession as invalid. The doctrine continues to mark a theological difference between Roman and Eastern Orthodox Christianity.                     C.M.

**PROCESS PHILOSOPHY/PROCESS THEOLOGY.** The name given to the METAPHYSICS of modern philosophers such as HENRI BERGSON and ALFRED NORTH WHITEHEAD and to the thought of those contemporary philosophers of religion and theologians influenced by them. As the name implies, process philosophy begins with the conviction that time, process, and becoming are constitutive of all reality, rather than being or unchanging substance. The beginnings of process philosophy and theology can be traced to two important movements of the nineteenth century: German romantic idealism, especially GEORGE W. F. HEGEL, and Darwinian evolution. These movements perceived evolutionary development as the key to both nature and history. The writings of Bergson and Whitehead had, in turn, a profound influence on two important, but very different, mid-twentieth-century process theologians: PIERRE TEILHARD DE CHARDIN and CHARLES HARTSHORNE.

According to these process thinkers, the world is not made up of static, discrete entities—what Whitehead called the "fallacy of simple location"— but is, rather, dynamic, organic, and social. The world is a creative, interdependent process of entities that give and receive from one another. It is a society of societies, growing together into an ever more complex unity.

According to Whitehead, whose metaphysical scheme has been most influential, the actual temporal world reveals the presence of four factors. The first is *creativity,* whereby the world advances toward novel modes of being. Creativity is not an entity but is real only through the *actual entities* that exemplify it. Actual entities are the final real things of which the world is made. Actual entities are, however, interdependent. They appropriate the past, realize their own subjective form, and eventually perish and become a datum for another entity or entities. To account for the orderly process of the world, Whitehead posits a third factor: *eternal objects* or pure potentials. An example is a color that comes and goes but does not perish. Eternal objects are the patterns, structures, qualities, and grades of relevance and value that are revealed in the world. Actual entities incorporate creativity and these eternal potentials in complex ways in realizing their own subjective form or aim. The fourth component of all process is *God,* an everlasting actual entity. God does not perish. It is God who accounts for the actual course of becoming, since neither creativity alone nor eternal objects (being potentialities) possess the necessary causal efficacy. God makes possible the entrance of the potential patterns and qualities into the process of becoming and supplies each entity with its initial aim and relevance. While God is unique in this respect, God is the chief exemplification of the metaphysical scheme—not its foremost exception. God is *not* independent, immutable, impassible, but, like other entities, is in some respects dependent, changing, and in process. Whitehead holds that God is *di-polar*. God's *primordial nature*—like the mind of finite entities—orders, grades, and adjusts the eternal objects as they enter the temporal process. However, God's primordial nature is lacking or deficient in actuality. The other pole of God's being, God's *consequent nature,* corresponds to the body of other entities and takes in and is affected by the other entities of the world. God is enriched by the world—God and the world being interdependent—a position known as panentheism.

Classical theism differs most profoundly with process theology at this point, since the former conceives of God as independent of the world, unchanging, and impassible. The God of process theology is best conceived as Savior of the world rather than its Creator. God's relation to the world is one of persuasive love, not coercive power. While finite creatures perish, they furnish God with new experience to incorporate into God's consequent nature. What God receives never fades away—hence all perishing entities achieve a kind of objective immortality in God. God in turn pours back into the world new ideal visions of the possibilities of creative advance. However, finite creatures are free to reject God's will and persuasion. There is, then, real loss and tragedy in the world and in God. Thinkers such as Hartshorne have made much of God's persuasive agency and human response as alone making sense both of God's love and human freedom. Among contemporary theologians most influenced by process thought are Norman Pittenger, John B. Cobb, Jr., and Schubert M. Ogden.                                  J.L.

**PROCLAMATION.** The word group in Greek of terms for "proclaim," "tell," "announce" is made up of variants of the Greek root *angell-*. *Angelos* is a messenger, giving us the English "angel." The basic meaning is the carrying of a message, usually with good news and involving a quasi-religious setting, to do with the offering of sacrifice to the gods for the news received.

In the NT the eighty-eight or so allusions to "proclaim" and "proclamation" are divided into two categories: in the Lukan writings there are forty-eight references, and the remaining forty are split between John and Paul. It can be seen that this Greek root *angell-* is thus a favorite expression for LUKE, who

loves to tell the GOOD NEWS as a message from God through "angels," human (Acts 10, 11) as well as otherworldly (Luke 1, 2), conveyed to men and women in this world and centering in Jesus as God's gift to humankind, especially the disadvantaged and the weak.

For Paul the proclamation centers on the KERYGMA of Jesus' death for sinners and resurrection. He regards this task of proclaiming the gospel as his life's work (I Cor. 1:23; 9:15-18; Gal. 1:16). But while this proclamation is verbal, it also has a sacramental nuance (I Cor. 11:26), the latter text using the same verb as in I Corinthians 2:1. The upshot of both types of proclamation is to awaken in those who hear or share in the Eucharist a lively sense of the divine presence, leading to an acknowledgment that God is present in human experience (I Cor. 14:25).

For the writer of the Fourth Gospel the proclamation is also to be lived out in human lives (I John 1:2-5), with a concern for the needy and the despised (see I John 3:15-17). The life of Christ is thus proclaimed not in word only but also in deed and truth (I John 3:18) and expressed to the church as brotherly love (I John 2:10).                              R.M.

**PROCONSUL.** As the name implies, it refers to a Roman official who acted for a consul. In specific terms the proconsul was the highest Roman authority in a province of the empire and was appointed to maintain law and order, to collect revenues and taxes, and to supervise the lower officials called quaestors. Various proconsuls are referred to in the Acts of the Apostles (13:7; 18:12; 19:38), such as Sergius Paulus in Cyprus, and Gallio, proconsul of Achaia.

R.M.

**PROCURATOR.** The Latin term translates as "administrator." He, unlike the proconsul, was a direct appointee of the emperor, and the revenues and monies he received in the imperial provinces were paid directly into the emperor's personal fund. Though the procurator was strictly under the authority of the governor, he represented the emperor as the province's military and legal governor, a role played by various procurators in NT times, especially in Judea.

Judea, along with Samaria and Idumea, passed into Roman control in A.D. 6, when Archelaus was deposed by Augustus. PONTIUS PILATE was sent to be procurator (or better, prefect, a term that procurator later replaced) in Caesarea in A.D. 26, at the appointment of Emperor Tiberius. FELIX was appointed by the emperor Claudius in A.D. 52, to be followed by FESTUS in A.D. 60 on the nomination of Nero (Acts 24–27).                                        R.M.

**PROFANE.** A verb or adjective, meaning literally "before the temple" and connoting that which is outside the holy place. By extension, to profane is to violate, debase, or defile the sacred; to have contempt for something holy or to be irreverent. Profane can also mean not devoted to the sacred or unconcerned about religion. Secular, meaning "worldly" or "nonreligious," is a possible synonym. The profane is also something that is unconsecrated and therefore not fit for religious purposes.

Although the technical meaning of the word relates to the sense of taboo in a consecrated environment, it is used more broadly today to refer to that which is not religious, by contrast, and without negative meaning. Hence, reference to the sacred and profane might mean no more than a description of religious art and general art, or between religious drama and plays for the theater.                                                  I.C.

**PROMISE.** The obvious division into which promises in the Bible fall is (1) human pledges of agreement, as when Jacob extracted a promise from Joseph that he would not inter his remains in Egypt (Gen. 47:29-31), or when Moses warned the tribes that wished to settle on the east bank of the Jordan that such an act would break a promise (Num. 32:24); and (2) divine assurances of favor to an obedient people or trusting individuals. The second category is more significant.

Promises, then, are words spoken with a future reference. A person agrees to keep a contract or to perform a deed, sometimes in exchange for a reward (for example, Esth. 4:7; Mark 14:11). Biblical writers attach importance to such vows as binding pledges, and those who treat "promises" lightly are held up to blame and guilt (for example, Acts 5:1-11).

When the author of the promise is God, certain new factors enter in. The relationship between God and Israel is unequal since God is their Lord. Hence, God's promises have a covenantal character, and are based on the divine nature as trustworthy (Ps. 12:6); they are not empty words (Isa. 55:11). That God fulfills promises is a basic element in Hebrew religion (I Kings 8:15), seen in God's redemption of Israel from slavery and all later enemies (see Luke 1:46-55). The building of Solomon's Temple is often referred to as a sign of God's faithfulness in making good God's promises (II Sam. 3:18; 7:13; I Kings 8:20, 56), chiefly because it confirmed the initial promise of God to create a people who would be installed in a land, "the land of promise" (Gen. 17:8). God is thus praised for bringing Israel to its destiny in Canaan, with Jerusalem and its Temple as the focal point.

The NT takes over this characterization of God, but shifts the emphasis from a temporal sphere to blessings in the coming of Jesus as Israel's Messiah and the church's Lord. All God's promises are realized "in Christ" (II Cor. 1:20), and the pledges to Abraham of a people and a land are transformed to apply to a multinational community of faith (Gal. 3:16-29) and to a spiritual possession that is the gift of the Holy Spirit, "the promise of the Father" (Luke 24:49; Acts 1:4) to all believers of all races. The promise that God will dwell with people is seen to be fulfilled in the presence of the Spirit with the church (Gal. 3:22; 4:4-7; Eph. 1:13).                        R.M.

**PROOF TEXT.** The term, in modern biblical studies, usually carries a pejorative sense. It stands for an illegitimate use of scripture when texts are isolated from their context and arranged to form a network of probative evidence without regard to the historical or situational meaning of the original authors.

A secondary application of the term is to the use of the OT in the writings of the NT. In this sense NT authors appeal, in different ways, to OT prophecies as the ground of their claim that the coming of Jesus as Messiah was an event foretold long ago. Matthew's Gospel is particularly rich in this use of the OT, while Paul and the writer to the Hebrews quote the OT to buttress their conviction that the messianic ministry and work of Jesus as the Christ were "prefigured" in the Law and the Prophets (Rom. 1:2; 15:4; I Cor. 10:1-11; Heb. 1:1-2; see Acts 26:22, 27).                    R.M.

**PROPAGANDA, THE.** From the Latin *de Propaganda Fide,* that is, for the spread of the faith. A congregation, or institution, of the Roman Catholic church established in 1622 by Pope Gregory XV to oversee the worldwide missionary work of the church. Its official name is the Sacred Congregation of the Propaganda. The Propaganda has oversight of all mission countries and mission districts. These undertakings are organized as prefectures and vicariates apostolic. The Propaganda uses the urban college for the education of missionaries from all over the world.                                                    J.C.

**PROPERS.** The "propers" refers to those portions of the Catholic Mass, or Lutheran or Anglican liturgies, that vary according to the season, day, or festival being celebrated. These include the Introit, Collect, OT lesson, Epistle lesson, Gospel lesson, the Gradual, Offertory, prefaces to Communion, and post-Communion prayers. In the Roman Catholic church, there are also propers for the saints, which include the feast days of the Lord, the Virgin Mary, and the saints. The propers of the season turn on the church year, with variable features that observe Advent, Christmas, Epiphany, Lent, Easter, Pentecost, and the Pentecost season. These propers are recorded in the Catholic missal, the breviary, and the *Book of Common Prayer,* as well as the *Lutheran Service Book and Hymnal* and the *Lutheran Book of Worship.*                                                  J.C.

**PROPHET/PROPHECY.** The word means "one who speaks for [another]." In the Judeo-Christian tradition the "another" is assumed to be God, so that the prophet is regarded as God's spokesperson, mouthpiece, messenger. The origin of the term in Western language is somewhat more complicated. The Greek *prophētēs* was actually an "interpreter" of what some would consider to be the *real* prophet, that is, the one who claimed to be in actual contact with some deity or other source of esoteric knowledge, whose revelations had to be interpreted or translated for general understanding. The *real* prophet in the Greek sense was the *mantis,* one who in a trance or some extraordinary spiritual seizure (compare the word *mania*), like the Pythonic prophetess of Delphi, delivered utterances in ecstatic frenzy that were then "interpreted" (and put into suitably ambiguous "oracular" responses) for the benefit of the paying devotees.

Biblical language has been extremely careful in its choice of words in order to distinguish biblical prophecy from some of its less acceptable antecedents. The Greek Septuagint, the first translation of the Hebrew Bible into a Western language, used the word *prophētēs* exclusively to translate the Hebrew *nābî'* (see below) and reserved the common term *mantis* only in a few instances (Josh. 13:22; I Sam. 6:2; Mic. 3:7; Zech. 10:2; etc.) for one who was obviously considered to be a *false* prophet (for which the Septuagint also invented the word *pseudo-prophētēs,* a distinction that does not exist in the Hebrew Bible). Similarly, in the Latin biblical tradition and derived ecclesiastical tradition, *propheta* has been the operative word, in deliberate rejection of the Latin *vates,* which is the equivalent of the Greek *mantis.*

*In the Old Testament.* In Exodus 7:1 Aaron is designated as Moses' prophet, in the sense that he is his interpreter and spokesman (Exod. 4:14-16). But this is to grossly oversimplify the development of the concept of "prophet" in the OT.

(a) *Early and pre-Israelite prophetism.* As with everything else in its early history and cultural formation, Israel was a borrower of its institutions—cult and priesthood, liturgy, law, wisdom, and the rest. Prophecy is no exception, and therefore it is necessary to inquire into the origins of the common Near Eastern phenomenon, which also accounts for the Greek institution and its vocabulary as we have seen above. In Mesopotamia, both *mahhu* and *bārū* priests were institutionalized in society; the former uttered oracles under an ecstatic experience, the latter depended upon divination of various kinds. "Priest" and "prophet," it should be noted, were fairly interchangeable terms (as they are in some of the Israelite evidence): the Arabic *kāhin,* "prophet," is cognate with the Hebrew *kōhēn,* "priest." The Mesopotamian pattern seems to have succeeded, to the best that we can judge the situation, in all the surrounding nations and cultures of the Near East that affected ancient Israel: In Egypt, Phoenicia, Canaan, Moab, Aram, etc. The burden of the prophecy was ordinarily official, that is, provided by court or cult prophets for the direction of the king or his officers. But there are also instances of private oracles (as at Delphi, later on) and even of prophecies, which could hardly have been viewed as expressly welcomed by their recipients.

In early Israelite history all these traits of nascent prophecy can be verified. Divination is practiced by David and Abiathar according to I Samuel 30:7-8, ecstaticism is taken as a matter of course (I Sam. 10:9-13; II Kings 3:15, etc.), and I Samuel 9:5-9 testifies that in earlier times the one who was later known as a "prophet" had been designated simply a "man of God," a "seer." The seer was a clairvoyant who literally "saw" what was otherwise undisclosed to the non-prophetical eye. This "seeing," in turn, might be aided by divination, ecstaticism, oneiromancy (revelation through dreams, frequent in both the OT and the NT), or necromancy (consultation of the dead, as in the tragic story of I Sam. 28:3-19).

In the later theology that could afford to forget these ambiguous origins, words like "diviner," "seer," "charmer," "dreamer," and their synonyms tend to become equated with unacceptable prophetic forms and are eschewed in favor of the single term *nābî'.* It is this word that the Septuagint and all subsequent translations have rendered as "prophet."

(b) *Pre-classical prophecy.* It is apparent that the common Near Eastern phenomenon of prophecy assumes new forms in Israel (I Sam. 9:5-9; in the story of Samuel's emergence in I Sam. 3:1-7; in the revelation to Elijah in I Kings 19:4-12, and elsewhere). Though court and cult prophecy continued as a matter of course, though odd and exotic conduct was anticipated and tolerated in these "men of God" (see I Kings 13:1-32), and though the prophet whose word was heeded and respected might at the same time be regarded as a "mad fellow" (II Kings 9:11-13), there was nevertheless by repute and in fact a novel kind of prophetism that began to make its appearance with the beginning of the Israelite monarchy, that is, Israel's taking on nationhood.

The Pentateuchal tradition, which ascribed to Moses the beginning of Israelite prophecy as it did of all the rest of Israel's institutions, obviously had ecstatic prophecy in mind (Num. 11:24-30). It is the same kind of frenetic spirit that possessed the "sons of the prophets" who are associated with Samuel, Elijah, and Elisha, and among whom Saul fell according to I Samuel 10:9-13. Saul's "prophetic" character, in this sense, is also noted in I Samuel 19:22-24. The "raving" of Saul provoked by "an evil spirit from God" in which he sought David's life (I Sam. 18:10) is, in the Hebrew, his "prophesying." This ambiguity of the prophetic spirit visible in the ecstatic state doubtless accounts for Jehu's followers' speaking of their "mad fellow." In I Kings 22:19-28 Micaiah ben Imlah ascribes the favorable word of the prophets, four hundred strong, offered to the kings of Israel and Judah to a "lying spirit" sent by the Lord. The "false" prophet Zedekiah obviously appeals to his ecstatic credentials as countering the word of Micaiah who possessed none.

Thus it is plain that ecstatic prophecy continued late in Israelite history to play a decisive role in the popular imagination. It cannot be denied that the Elijah and Elisha cycles in the books of Kings celebrate more the mystery and wondrous aura surrounding these men of God than they do their character as prophets. In much later times (see Jer. 27–28) Jeremiah had to warn against "prophets, diviners, dreamers, soothsayers, and sorcerers," who could produce impressive credentials to captivate the popular imagination. The canonical book of Nahum, among others (like the book of Esther in another genre), witnesses to the fact that an almost purely chauvinistic interpretation of prophecy could be treasured up and preserved for posterity as well as any other kind. In other words, even in its evolution and transformation in Isaiah, prophecy never entirely escaped its moorings. But still it must be insisted that something new had taken place, according to the record.

That something new may, as some believe, be due to the influence of the later prophetic tradition upon the stories about the older prophets. Against this view, however, are other important considerations. These older prophets have not been simply reinterpreted in later terms; too much of the bygone has remained to persuade us that a revision of the history has been written. Even more important, it is hard to believe that the "classical" prophecy, which begins with Amos, broke upon the world completely unheralded in the eighth century B.C. A much more natural assumption is that which the OT itself makes, namely that it had been prepared for by a development that had been taking place since the Israelite religion had first begun to assimilate to itself the institution of prophetism.

So, for example, there is no reason to doubt the authenticity of the substance of the oracle of Nathan in II Samuel 12:1-15 uttered against the king in condemnation of David's machinations detailed in II Samuel 11. That this oracle should have rebuked the arbitrary power of kings in favor of traditional Israelite values is just as much to be expected as is Nathan's participation as a court prophet in the palace cabal that guaranteed Solomon's accession to the throne in place of his presumptuous half brother Adonijah (I Kings 1:32-40). The oracles of Nathan guaranteeing an eternal destiny to the Davidic house in its present Deuteronomistic form evidently has Solomon in its purview (II Sam. 7:1-17). Psalm 89:19-37 (probably a much older text) doubtless testifies to an early court-prophetic testimony to a royal mystique (the Royal Psalms 2, 110, etc.), which nevertheless could be judged prophetically since the kings of the Gentiles ordinarily were not. Similarly, in I Kings 21 Elijah, whose title thus far had been "troubler of Israel" (I Kings 18:17) because he had decreed (prophesied) famine and drought for Israel's cultic crimes, in this further censure rejects the king for his desertion of Israelite justice and adoption of the ruthlessness of Gentile kingship. It is the same Elijah, nevertheless, who served as nationalistic prophet in respect to Israel's foreign and domestic politics (I Kings 19:15-18), as did his disciple Elisha (II Kings 8:7-15; 9:1-3).

(c) *Classical prophecy*. This term is applied to the prophecy that flourished in the separated kingdoms of Israel and Judah from the time of Amos, about the middle of the eighth century, and, after the dissolution of the northern kingdom in 721 B.C., in Judah alone down to and including the Exile and Babylonian captivity about 597–535 B.C. It can be called classical to Israel because it is this prophecy that is distinctive to that religion with few and insignificant parallels elsewhere. It presents the God of Israel as a deity concerned with morality, preeminently social morality, rather than with the formalities of national religion, a God who has covenanted with Israel not for its political success or aggrandizement but to prepare a holy and exemplary people. This God was a God of reward and punishment, in proportion as the people would abide by the terms of divine election.

The term "literary prophecy" was often used in the past, under the assumption that what distinguished earlier prophets like Nathan and Elijah from Amos and Hosea, for example, was that the latter had written down their prophecies whereas the former had not. It has now long been recognized that this was a false distinction, since probably none of the prophets of Israel was a literary author in his own right, except perhaps on rare occasions and only incidentally (see Ezekiel 4:1-3). We owe the prophetic works to disciples of the prophets who, first of all, remembered their masters' works and handed them on to subsequent collectors and editors who became the actual literary authors of the prophetic "Books."

"Literary prophecy" retains some validity as a designation for classical prophecy, however, when we consider that during this period there must have been an untold number of prophets active in the two kingdoms whose names we know but who have not been remembered because of neglect or because of deliberate obliteration (see II Kings 21:10-15). As with the other types of Israel's literature that have found their way into the canonical scripture of the Bible, the prophetical is the result of a highly selective process that has resulted in a collection that is representative and at the same time has preserved, with some reservations, those which were most worthy of preservation.

In more or less chronological order, the preexilic prophets who are also "literary" prophets are these: Amos (a Judahite who prophesied in Israel), Hosea (roughly contemporary, but an Israelite), Isaiah and Micah (both Judahites), and a succession of other Judahites: Zephaniah, Nahum, and Habakkuk. Their relative value as prophetic witnesses must obviously be determined on their own merits.

From the period immediately before and during the Exile come two of the most important of the major prophets, Jeremiah and Ezekiel. Also, from the Exile itself, came that anonymous prophet to whom we must give the name of Deutero-Isaiah (Isa. 40–55). In view of the influence that prophetism had on the development of Israelite religion, it is remarkable that such a few names can be attributed to the roll of those who are responsible. Again we must mention the uncounted prophetic influence, especially as represented by the Deuteronomistic theologians who have put their imprint on practically all of Israelite history.

(d) *Postexilic prophecy.* This includes, from "classical" prophecy, the works of Joel (an apocalyptic work from about 400 B.C.), Obadiah (a judgment on Edom for its crimes against Judah), and Haggai, Zechariah, and Malachi. The last three, like Trito-Isaiah (Isa. 56–66), envisage the postexilic community restored on the soil of Palestine after the liberation under Cyrus (II Chr. 36:22-23; Ezra 1:1-4). This prophecy tends to imitate preexilic prophecy in its thought forms, adding apocalyptic motifs and imagery borrowed from native Israelite and foreign resources (chiefly Persian), and attempts to recapture the immediacy of ancient prophecy by calling into actual being what were destined to remain forever prophetic ideals (for example, the restoration of the Davidic dynasty). It is no wonder that prophecy, reduced to these extremes, soon became only a memory in Israel and was recalled only as a former institution that might, magically, be restored to solve all problems (see I Macc. 4:46).

It must not be denied, however, that during this period the prophetic literature took on the character it now possesses, not through the infusion of a new prophetic spirit but through the editing of the prophetic books, which is itself a form of prophecy in the traditional sense of biblical inspiration. The prophetical literature, during this period, was subjected to the editing of the Deuteronomistic school of historiography and theology, which has affected every part of the OT, and it was subject also to other influences that have often changed the meaning of original prophecies. Ideas such as the eventual reunion of Israel and Judah under a common Davidic ruler, for example (Amos 9:11-15), were never to come to be. The messianic hope, nurtured by Haggai and Zechariah (and furthered by Deutero- and Trito-Zechariah in this period) had already been abandoned by Deutero-Isaiah and Ezekiel.

In short, postexilic prophecy, whether canonical or otherwise, must be characterized as derivative. It is not unfair to say that the "Spirit" had departed from the religion of Israel during the late Persian and early Hellenistic periods to the extent that Israel would now enter into a new period of self-examination independent of prophecy that could eventually be called the age of "wisdom."

*In the New Testament.* First of all, of course, the NT accepts what was then the conventional wisdom with regard to the OT prophets: they had predicted, down to the last detail, the most meticulous items of statistics that were now being verified. Such details are used as "proof texts" particularly in the Gospel of Matthew. Unfortunately, the spirit in which

Matthew (and others) entered into this Midrashic interpretation was not always understood by his successors, and artistry was reinterpreted as historical fact.

In the NT there are persons designated as prophets. Apparently these prophets were of the ecstatic kind, given to "revelations" (Acts 11:27-28). Some of them had traits that remind us of ancient Israelite prophecy (Acts 21:10-11). They played a prominent part in the assemblies of the early Christian communities (I Cor. 13–14), but also had to be regulated by "hierarchical" direction. Yet at the same time, they also sometimes functioned on an administrative level (Acts 12:1-3). The prophetic office was as likely to be held by women as by men (Acts 21:9).

Primitive Christianity seems, in this respect, to have shared the experience of most eschatological groups from earlier and later periods. There was a prevalence of free spirits charismatically called to make known the mind of God, often in unintelligible babblings that required interpretation (I Cor. 14:26-33). In describing the "birth of the church" in Acts 2:1-13, the biblical author has adapted in Midrashic fashion a portrayal of the kind of ecstatic prophetism that was undoubtedly routine in early Christian assemblies. As the Pauline injunctions in I Corinthians already make clear, it was an exuberance that had to be brought under institutional control for the sake of order and continuity. Order and continuity prevailed, as the subsequent history of Christianity demonstrates, but the church was ultimately no more successful in institutionalizing prophecy than had been the OT (Deut. 13:1-5, for example). Prophecy, true or false, authentic or deluded, was and is a highly personal experience of direct access to an agreed source of truth, by definition incapable of being subjected to predictable norms.                                                    B.V.

**PROPHETS** (Major and Minor). The biblical works of Joshua through II Kings, in modern critical terminology the Deuteronomic History, are in Jewish tradition classified as Early Prophets. (Traditionally, the authorship of these works was ascribed to one or another person who was regarded as a prophet.)

Both Jewish and Christian tradition designate as "prophetic" certain other OT works (these are, in the Jewish canon, the Latter Prophets), which are in turn distinguished as "Major" and "Minor." Major and Minor do not, of themselves, reflect qualitative judgments on the relative importance of the prophetic figures to whom these works are ascribed; they rather are quantitative indexes to the amount of material so ascribed.

In the Jewish CANON Isaiah, Jeremiah, and Ezekiel are the Major Prophets. The Christian canon adds to this list after Jeremiah the book of Lamentations (Roman Catholics also the book of Baruch) and after Ezekiel the Book of Daniel: such works in the Jewish tradition are classified as non-prophetical "writings."

In both the Jewish and Christian canons the Minor Prophets are Hosea, Joel, Amos, Obadiah, Jonah, Micah, Nahum, Habakkuk, Zephaniah, Haggai, Zechariah, and Malachi. Together, this "Book of the Twelve" is roughly equivalent in length (71 chapters) as a four-volume complement to the works of Isaiah (66 chapters), Jeremiah (52), and Ezekiel (48). However, all these prophetic collections, whether of Major or Minor Prophets, contain supplementary material from later times, while the book of Jonah is not the work of a prophet but rather a story about a prophet.                                                          B.V.

**PROPITIATION.** *See* EXPIATION.

**PROSELYTE.** A convert from one faith to another. In the NT, all those who became Christians were proselytes, either from Judaism or paganism. Proselytes were known among the Hebrews in OT times, when non-Jews were allowed to offer sacrifices, be circumcised and, after ritual washing, became full members of the congregation. This growth of Judaism by the accession of proselytes continued through the centuries, as the presence of Gentile proselytes in Jerusalem on the day of Pentecost (Acts 2) demonstrates. These proselytes came from all over the Roman world.

After the explosive growth of the early church began at Pentecost, many people who were formerly Jewish proselytes became Christian proselytes. This process is specifically recorded in Acts 13, where Jewish proselytes in Antioch of Pisidia embraced the new faith preached by Paul and Barnabas. Paul continued to attract proselytes to the synagogue, which undoubtedly explains the hostility of Jewish synagogue leaders to Paul's mission. In Acts 6:5, a Gentile proselyte to Judaism, Nicolaus of Antioch, was made a deacon at the same time as Stephen and Philip.                                                          J.C.

**PROSOPON.** In classical Greek, *prosopon* meant the "face" of a person, and it came also to be used for the mask worn by an actor; in Latin, this was called *persona*. The word *prosopon* came into theology to denote the "persons" of the Trinity, as the closest equivalent to the Latin *persona*. It is also used for the person of Jesus Christ. Though many Eastern theologians preferred the word *hypostasis, prosopon* and *hypostasis* stand side by side as alternatives in the Chalcedonian definition of 451.                          J.M.

**PROSTITUTION.** OT writers speak of prostitution in a twofold way. There are those who engage in prostitution for commercial gain (Rahab in Josh. 2 and the two women in Solomon's court, I Kings 3:16, are obvious examples), and those who practice "sacred prostitution" as part of the cultic worship of Canaanite religion whose deities (Asherah, Astarte, Anath) encouraged this practice. At Ugarit there were prostitutes of both sexes, regarded as "holy" people

devoted to the worship of Baal. The influence of cultic prostitution affected Jewish life, as the OT narrative makes clear (I Kings 14:24), and reforming kings such as Josiah (II Kings 23:7; compare I Kings 15:12; 22:46), and prophets like Amos (2:7, 8) and Jeremiah (13:27) sought to eradicate the presence of these ideas, which they or the editors of the texts regarded as morally offensive to Israel as a "holy people" of Yahweh. In popular Israelite religion, however, it seems that no clear distinction was made between various "religious" acts, and the common people in Israel tended to associate sexual acts performed in Canaanite holy places as appropriate, since, in their view, Canaanite religion lacked a moral basis. Hence the word of the eighth- to seventh-century B.C. prophets was timely (see Isa. 1:4-31; 5:16).

In the Greek world the cult of Aphrodite (called Venus by the Romans) was widespread. If Strabo is to be trusted, the temple at Corinth was serviced by a thousand prostitutes; and it cannot be accidental that Paul's letter (I Cor. 6:9, 15-20) shows how Christians there were being exposed to this influence. The NT writers uniformly warn of immoral living involving prostitution (Eph. 5:3, 5; Rev. 21:8; 22:15) and picture the church as a "pure bride" (II Cor. 11:2). Harlotry, in both OT and NT, is used figuratively of the evils of apostasy and idolatry (Isa. 57:3-5; Hos. 1:2; 2:2-8; Ezek. 16; Rev. 17:1-6, 15).            R.M.

**PROTESTANT EPISCOPAL CHURCH.** *See* ANGLICAN CHURCHES.

**PROTESTANT ETHIC.** The Protestant ethic, or, more fully, the Protestant work ethic, means an attitude to work and economic activity that has been widespread in the West in the past few centuries, and that some scholars have traced to certain theological ideas that were promoted by the Protestant Reformation. In this ethic, hard work and thrift have been esteemed important virtues, while idleness has been counted a serious vice; and there is often a tendency to regard poverty as blameworthy and the consequence of idleness. The accumulation of wealth, which might once have been considered a vice, becomes rather the outward evidence for one's industriousness and even a sign of divine favor.

It was the German sociologist of religion, MAX WEBER, who drew attention to these connections in his celebrated but controversial book *The Protestant Ethic and the Spirit of Capitalism*, written in 1904–1905. In this book and in a series of other writings, Weber set out to counter the Marxist claim that religion belongs only to the superstructure of society and that its character is determined by economic factors. Weber sought to show that, on the contrary, religious and theological ideas have a profound influence on economic attitudes and institutions. His investigations had shown him that in Germany the leaders of industry came overwhelmingly from Protestant backgrounds, and, looking at

Europe as a whole, he noted that it was in the predominantly Protestant northern countries that industrial development had taken place, while southern Catholic Europe retained the features of a rural economy. This suggests that there may be some deep-seated connections between Protestant theology and the rise of modern capitalism with its industrial empires and commercial enterprises.

Weber reminds us of some of the changes that took place at the Reformation. The contemplative life of the monasteries came to an end and the active life was commended. The otherworldly asceticism of the monks was replaced by a this-worldly asceticism of the Puritans, who did not lavish their money on sensual indulgences but set it aside as capital. This was connected too with the Calvinist doctrine of election. One proved that one belonged to the elect by self-discipline that took the practical form of thrift. A further important idea was that of vocation. God calls each one to a place in society, and to perform the duties of one's station well is to fulfill this vocation. This is the life well-pleasing to God, but it is inevitably also the life in which wealth will accumulate. Weber's thesis has found both supporters and critics, and in such complex matters it is always hard to know whether all the factors have been taken into account. Weber himself never claimed that Protestant theology was the *sole* factor in the rise of capitalism. Even so, one can recognize that praise of hard work and thrift have been features of Protestant communities.

The rise of affluence in the West, together with the fact that automation and computerization are diminishing the amount of work that human beings have to do, is nowadays calling the Protestant ethic into question. On the other hand, some politicians urge the revival of the old virtues of industriousness and thrift. Certainly these values have so impressed themselves on the Western mind that it would need a radical and probably painful readjustment to replace them with new values.                                    J.M.

PROTESTANTISM. The movement that developed out of the religious and political events that attended attempts to reform certain abuses in the Roman Catholic Church. Protestantism became an important segment of the historic church that embraced the teachings of the sixteenth-century REFORMATION.

The nomenclature can be traced to the use of the term *Protestatio,* the document signed by certain German princes and representatives, generally supporters of MARTIN LUTHER, and presented at the second Diet of Speyer in 1529. The protesters objected to the repeal of the more tolerantly worded edict passed by the first Diet of Speyer in 1521. Both Diets had been called by Emperor Charles V, who wanted to squelch the politico-religious revolt of the German princes allied with Luther.

Dean Inge has pointed out that the employment of the word *Protestatio* has less of a sense of protest in modern usage and rather stresses the idea of positive witness. Roland H. Bainton, author of Luther's popular biography, *Here I Stand,* held a similar position. The distinguishing mark of Protestantism was its testimony to the supreme authority of the Word of God. This, of course, inevitably meant a disavowal of the supremacy of ecclesiastical authority as embodied in the traditional papal system. The Protestants of the sixteenth century, and later, held that they were seeking to recover the faith of the early church that had eroded through the centuries. Today, of course, the term Protestantism designates that segment of CHRISTENDOM that is not allied with the churches of Eastern Orthodoxy or the Roman Catholic Church.

The early Protestants—Lutherans, Calvinists, and the disciples of Zwingli—insisted that there was a single source of divine revelation, namely, the Holy Scriptures, not a combination of SCRIPTURE and TRADITION. It was not that they denied a place to tradition, but they refused to accept it as an equal source of divine disclosure.

Both Roman Catholics and Protestants were aware that the grace of God conferred righteousness upon needy men and women, but Protestants ruled out the sole efficacy of human meritorious acts and sacramental grace. According to them, God declares a person righteous, based on the righteousness of Christ and thus received through the response of faith. Certitude of salvation for Protestants is based on the objective authority of the Word of God alone.

While Protestants hold to varied views on the role of the sacraments they generally agree on the idea that the LORD'S SUPPER is not a sacrifice. There is also some consensus in opposition to the teaching of TRANSUBSTANTIATION, confirmed by the Council of Trent, that Christ is "truly, really and substantially contained in the sacrament under appearance of sensible things. . . . By the consecration of the bread and wine a change is brought about of the whole substance of the body of Christ our Lord and of the whole substance of the wine into the body of his blood." Protestants also declare that faith on the part of the believer is required when the Lord's Supper is received. They would all agree that the observance of the Lord's Supper is a visible declaration of the gospel.

Protestants have turned away from the hierarchical structure and the clerical authority of the Roman Catholic church. They generally declare that the church as the living Body of Christ has come into being through God's initiating grace, calling people to God as they respond in faith to the proclamation of the gospel. Most communions teach that the church is recognized by the preaching of the Word and by the proper administration of the rites of baptism and the Lord's Supper. Finally, Protestants stress the idea of the PRIESTHOOD OF BELIEVERS.

The branches of proliferating Protestantism first emerged through the influence of Luther, Calvin, and others. What came to be known as Lutheranism spread over Germany and central Europe and to all the countries of northern Europe. The disciples of ULRICH ZWINGLI were to be found largely in Switzerland. JOHN CALVIN, the French lawyer-turned-theologian, was the human instrument in launching the Presbyterian or Reformed churches in Switzerland, France, Holland, and Great Britain, and especially Scotland. The English Reformation developed partly through the exigencies of political history and through the less visible influence of the Continental Protestant teachings of the Lutherans, the Calvinists, and ANABAPTISTS. The Anglican Church was rent by various controversies and movements. The PURITANS, who set out only to achieve certain reforms in the Church of England, actually produced several major denominational groupings—the Independents, who later became Congregationalists, and from them came the BAPTISTS, who also may have been influenced by the Anabaptists, especially on the teaching of believers' baptism. QUAKERS were regarded as a radical segment of the Puritan Reformation. It was well over one hundred years later that METHODISTS left their Anglican roots to become a separate communion.

In America, where FREE CHURCHES thrived, the proliferation of Protestantism continued at a stepped-up pace. But in the early part of the twentieth century the practice of spawning new sects and segments of the church was challenged by a historical tenet of biblical faith: the unity of the church. One of the major forces in interdenominational cooperative witness was the Sunday school movement. The concept of conducting Bible schools or church schools in the churches was followed by interdenominational Sunday school rallies and conventions. In time, most of the churches were following the curriculum of uniform lessons, which became a major function of the International Council of Christian Education. Thus the Sunday school movement was an early and important factor in the dawning of the ECUMENICAL MOVEMENT.

Likewise United States Protestants who had learned to work together in Christian education also found similar compatability in planning and directing overseas missionary work. This led to the formation of the INTERNATIONAL MISSIONARY COUNCIL, which in turn became a major factor in promoting the ecumenical movement and the launching of the WORLD COUNCIL OF CHURCHES in 1948.                                              R.H.

**PROVERB.** A colorful saying, usually short, offering wisdom or keen observation, such as those collected in the biblical book of PROVERBS and elsewhere in the Bible and Apocrypha, but particularly in the biblical WISDOM literature.

Some proverbs are brief, such as:

My son, if sinners entice you,
  do not consent. (Prov. 1:10)

Do not boast about tomorrow,
  for you do not know what a day
    may bring forth. (Prov. 27:1)

The fear of the Lord is the beginning of knowledge. (Prov. 1:7)

Others offer lengthier observations:

Trust in the Lord with all your heart,
  and do not rely on your own insight.
In all your ways acknowledge him,
  and he will make straight your paths. (Prov. 3:5-6)

Still others offer rather full discussions, as in the case of the description of a good wife in Proverbs 31:10-31. Or in the meditation on the transience of life and wealth in Psalm 49:1-20. Or in the meditation on the justice of God in Psalm 73:1-28. Such sayings encapsulate the experience of a people, imparting gathered wisdom to future generations. Their freshness, simplicity, and directness make them a delight and a wise companion. Their brevity makes them memorable.                              B.J.

**PROVERBS, BOOK OF.** Epigrams or PROVERBS can be found scattered throughout the OT. Jeremiah 31:29 (compare Ezek. 18:2), "the fathers have eaten sour grapes, and the children's teeth are set on edge" is an example; so are the rhetorical question of Jeremiah 13:23, "Can the Ethiopian change his skin or the leopard his spots?" and the famous remark of Ezekiel 16:44, "like mother, like daughter." But the single greatest collection of pithy maxims touching on all of nature and human experience is, of course, the book of Proverbs. Tradition has attributed it to no less a sage than King SOLOMON, who "spoke of trees, from the cedar that is in Lebanon to the hyssop that grows out of the wall; he spoke also of beasts, and of birds, and of reptiles, and of fish" (I Kings 4:32-33).

The book of Proverbs discloses its own four-part structure by means of internal headings and thematic changes: (a) chapter 1–9, a rather well-integrated section of instruction to "my son" under the general heading "the fear of the Lord is the beginning of knowledge" (1:7); (b) 10:1–22:16, entitled "Proverbs of Solomon," a miscellaneous collection of maxims and epigrams, many of which deal with the theme of retribution; (c) 22:17–24:22, untitled but apparently the words of a teacher to a student; (d) and chapter 25–29, entitled "proverbs of Solomon which the men of Hezekiah king of Judah copied" (25:1). In addition to these principal parts, the book contains five shorter appendices which, except for 24:23-24, are gathered into the concluding chapters 30–31.

The rich variety of materials that it contains, topics that it treats, and literary styles (beside the epigram) that it employs all immediately suggest that the book of Proverbs came into its present form over many years and drew upon many sources for its materials. This hypothesis is readily borne out when it is discovered that the third section, 22:17–24:22, is very similar to an Egyptian wisdom text entitled "The Instruction of Amen-em-Ope," which is thought to predate 1000 B.C. As the texts recovered from Egypt and Mesopotamia show, the ancient Near East had a rich sapiential tradition, and Israel's wisdom tradition had roots in that soil. Parts (b) and (d) have much more of the character of indigenous folk wisdom. The popular theology of reward and punishment and the stress upon common sense derived from experience that appear here give us the flavor of popular etiquette and mores in Israel, particularly in postexilic times. In contrast, the opening section of the book, chapters 1–9, is often felt to reflect the rather more sophisticated thinking of courtly WISDOM. It holds up for emulation the virtues of prudence, knowledge, and discretion, and in its very opening verses sets forth as a model the wise man who, like Joseph or Daniel, courtiers to kings, can understand proverbs, the words of the wise, and their riddles. These chapters of "theological wisdom" also introduce us to Dame Wisdom.

In 1:20-33 and 8:1-36, wisdom is personified as a woman, the "first of [God's] acts of old," God's cohort in creation (8:22). She is God's daily delight, "rejoicing before him always, rejoicing in his inhabited world and delighting in the sons of men" (8:30-31). In 9:1-6, 13-18 it is Dame Wisdom and not the harlot, Dame Folly, through whom one can get sense and walk in the way of insight. This full-fledged personification of wisdom in Proverbs 8–9 continues to develop through later Jewish literature in texts such as Ecclesiasticus 14:20-27; 24:1-12; and the Wisdom of Solomon 7:22–8:18, until Dame Wisdom becomes almost an emanation of God and a mediator between the Creator and the creation. It seems quite possible that the writer of the prologue of the Gospel of John had personified wisdom in mind as he described the preexistent Word who was with God from the beginning and without whom was not anything made that was made (John 1:3).                                                              W.S.T.

**PROVIDENCE.** Derived from the Latin *providere*, "to foresee," the word "providence" originally meant much the same as the word FOREKNOWLEDGE. However, when one speaks of the providence of God, it is meant not only that God foresees future events but that God actually brings them about. God's providence, in Calvin's words, "extends to the hand as well as to the eye." All Christian theologians are agreed that God did not simply create the world and then leave it to its own devices (the view usually called DEISM). They believe that God has continued to govern the world and to direct it toward the ends that God has set for it. A very rigorous doctrine of providence (like the one taught by Calvin) seems to lead to a DETERMINISM in which the divine will has laid down in advance the detailed course of history and which would therefore allow no space for free human decisions. Calvin states bluntly that "men and angels do nothing, except at the secret instigation of God," though he also wishes to maintain (inconsistently, it would seem) that these agents are responsible for their actions.

But whereas Calvin seems to think that even the most trivial events are directly decreed by God, many theologians would be content with a much less strict doctrine of providence. They hold that although God maintains a general government over the affairs of the Creation and will bring to realization divine purposes for it, God can reach this goal by more routes than one, so there is considerable flexibility, including scope for free human action. William James was one of several philosophers who used the analogy of the chess master to illustrate the point. The master can play a less skilled opponent or even a dozen such opponents simultaneously, and although the master does not know in advance what these opponents will do, the master's skill at the game is so much greater than theirs that the master can always bring it round to the desired position and is assured of victory in the end. This is rather like the view of foreknowledge advanced by Leibnitz, who taught that what God foreknows (or foresees) is every possible course of events, and that God can take care within the overall plans of any contingency that arises. Leibnitz also taught a somewhat different doctrine of a "pre-established harmony" set up by God at the Creation and forming a kind of "program" for the universe. But if this were interpreted in a rigorous way, it might seem once again to rule out human FREEDOM.

Hegel, who believed that reason is the ultimate principle of the universe, held that the real is the rational and the rational is the real. If we could see the total course of universal history, we would understand that every event in it is a necessary moment in the unfolding of the absolute Spirit. At work in this process is what he called the "cunning of reason" and claimed that although God permits human beings to do what they please and to follow their passions, God so orders things that these human actions end up by serving not the purposes of their authors but the purposes of God. This philosophical doctrine of Hegel is obviously a sophisticated version of the view underlying the OT versions of the history of Israel and its neighbors, a history in which even God's enemies unwittingly serve God's purposes. (*See also* ELECTION; PREDESTINATION.)                                          J.M.

**PROVINCE.** The area governed by an archbishop of the Roman Catholic Church as a metropolitan, which includes his own archdiocese and at least one suffragan diocese. The term is also used for a division of a religious order including all houses and members of the order in a territory.                                    J.C.

**PRUYSER, PAUL W.** (1916 – ). Psychologist, born in Amsterdam, Netherlands, who studied at the University of Amsterdam. In 1948 he married Jansze Marthe Fontijn and they have three children. He came to the United States in 1948 and received the Ph.D. in clinical psychology from Boston University in 1953. He became a lecturer in the psychology of religion at McCormick Theological Seminary, Chicago, in 1959, and has also been professor at the Menninger Foundation since 1954. He has also been active on committees of the United Presbyterian Church and the National Council of Churches, and is involved in programs for clinical pastoral education. His books include *A Dynamic Psychology of Religion* (1968) and *Between Belief and Unbelief* (1974).

                                      I.C.

**PSALMS, BOOK OF.** In the Hebrew biblical manuscript tradition, Psalms appears as either the first or one of the first books in the third part of the canon, the Writings. In the ancient Greek biblical tradition, which had a different order for many of the books, Psalms was placed along with other poetical works preceding the prophetical books. Such a difference in location shows something of the fluid quality of the CANON in its early days. English versions follow the Greek tradition, which reflects the canon of the early church.

*Title of the Book.* The name "psalms" comes from the Greek by way of the Old Latin translation of the Bible. The Greek term *psalmos* originally referred to the plucking of a stringed instrument and then was applied to songs sung to the accompaniment of such instruments. Thus a "psalm" was a "song." The Hebrew title for the book is *tehillim*, "praises." As we shall see, neither of these designations is adequate to describe the contents of the book.

*Number of Psalms.* Just as there are two titles for the book, so there are two traditions (Greek and Hebrew) for the numbering of the psalms. The Hebrew Bible contains 150 psalms, but the Greek Bible followed by the Catholic Vulgate (Latin) tradition has 151. Psalm 151 is said to stand "outside the number." In addition, some psalms are combined and others divided into two in the two different traditions. Thus in reading Protestant and Catholic translations one has to be aware of minor differences in how they are numbered.

*Structure of the Book.* The final form of the material, as noted in the RSV, suggests that the larger book is made up of five smaller books. This is indicated by the concluding doxologies at Psalms 42:13; 72:18-19; 89:52; 106:48; with Psalm 150 serving as a final doxology. This division into five books was probably intended to parallel the five books of the Pentateuch. Early Jewish tradition spoke of the five books of Moses and the five books of David. In addition, there is evidence that all of the five books are made up of several smaller collections. This is indicated by the headings to the psalms, which refer to Psalms of David (Pss. 3–41, for example), Psalms of Asaph (Pss. 50; 73–83), Korah Psalms (42–49; 84–85; 87–88), songs of ascent (120–34), and so on. Thus the book probably grew over the years by the addition and combination of smaller collections.

*Headings of the Psalms.* Most of the psalms have some type of heading giving such information as personal names, musical instruments, occasional directions for usage, the ancient name of the psalm type, and technical terms. Most of the technical terms, like *selah,* used in many psalms, were no longer understood by ancient commentators. Modern interpreters are still baffled about the meaning of most of the information supplied in those headings. The NEB translation, for example, simply omits these. In all probability, these headings functioned like the notations found at the top of modern hymns and thus would have offered significant directions to those using the psalms.

*History of Interpretation.* In early Jewish tradition, the personal names noted in the headings were assumed to indicate authorship, so David was considered the author of most of the psalms and ten or eleven other persons were seen as authors as well. (Adam was considered the author of Ps. 92, since it was thought to have been composed for use on the first Sabbath!) Historical type information was added to the headings of some psalms, supposedly written by David during particular times in his life (see Pss. 3; 7; 18; 34; 51; 52; 54; 56–60; 63; 142). Gradually, tradition came to consider David as the author of all the entire book.

More modern scholarship has concluded that David probably did not write many or any of the psalms, and that "of David" in the headings to many of them is a late addition or denotes that the psalms came from a "Davidic collection" of psalms.

*Interpreting the Psalms.* Many modern scholars are agreed that the vast majority of the psalms were written for use in worship services and thus must be understood as part of the liturgies used in the Temple. The great diversity in the psalms suggests, however, that the psalms were not just songs or praises. The content of the psalms is as diverse as the various components and interests that went to make up the services of worship. Thus some psalms are prayers to God in time of need, others are thanksgiving, some are hymns sung about God, some contain words of God addressed to the worshipers, others have words spoken by the priests to the worshiper or by the worshiper to a congregation, and so on. Thus in reading the psalms one should constantly ask the following questions: Who is speaking? Who is being addressed? What is being talked about? What is the mood of the psalm? What conditions of life are reflected in the psalm? Frequently changes in speaker, addressee, and mood take place within the same psalm indicating that the psalm was related to various aspects of the liturgy.

Worship services in ancient Israel served many

different functions, focused on different concerns, and centered on both congregational and personal matters. In some services, the general community and its needs were the primary concern, in others the king, and still in others some individual or small group. The purposes of worship services were also varied. Some services were festive and celebrative, others were held to request divine help in time of trouble, others to offer thanksgiving. If psalms were used under these various conditions, then we would expect them to reflect such diverse interests, and they ought to be capable of being placed in categories according to their content, mood, and other factors.

*Psalm Types.* Most of the psalms can be divided into types or genres depending on whether they are hymns of praise, laments with petitions for help, thanksgiving after some disaster, and so forth. Further classifications can be made depending on whether the main participants in the worship were the community, the king, or some individual.

*Laments* were psalms used, along with sacrifices, during times of distress, petitioning God for help. Individuals offered laments during times of illness (Pss. 6; 13; 31; 38; 39), when they felt falsely accused of a wrong (Pss. 7; 17; 26; etc.), when they were oppressed and persecuted (Pss. 3; 35; 109), when they were penitent over sin (Pss. 25; 51), and so forth. The king could offer similar laments but also petitions when the country and his rule were threatened (Pss. 20; 22; 89). The community offered laments when the nation suffered defeat in battle or experienced other major calamities (Pss. 44; 60; 74; 79). Generally, laments contain the following elements: an address to the Deity, a description of the trouble or distress, a plea for redemption, a statement of confidence in God, confession of sin or statement of innocence, a pledge or vow to do certain things if God provides a rescue, and a conclusion.

*Thanksgivings* were offered, along with sacrifices, after the worshiper or community had been saved from distress, whether sickness (Pss. 30; 103), sin (Ps. 32), loss of faith (Ps. 73), or danger in battle (Pss. 18; 118). Of course, thanksgiving could be offered for normal blessing when no prior distress existed. For this purpose, hymns were probably used. Most thanksgiving psalms contain a call or statement about giving thanks, a description of the distress from which one was saved, thanksgiving, and references to fulfilling one's pledge or vow.

*Hymns* were sung on routine festival occasions and when the community wished to praise God. Examples of hymns are Psalms 8; 29; 47; 93; and 95–100. Most of the hymns were sung about rather than to God. Hymns generally contain the following features: a call to praise, the body of the hymn, which praises God for deeds and/or attributes, and a conclusion. Some hymns focus on very specific subjects, such as those that extol God and the city of Zion or Jerusalem (Pss. 46; 48; 76). Special *royal psalms* were used at the king's coronation (Pss. 2; 72; 110), when he took the

oath of office (Ps. 101), went forth to battle (Pss. 20–21), or married (Ps. 45).

Although most of the psalms can be seen as belonging to one of the above types, many psalms are too general to be classified specifically. Such psalms may have been used or recited on various occasions and therefore preserved and used because of the value of their contents.

J.H.

**PSALMS OF SOLOMON.** *See* PSEUDEPIGRAPHA.

**PSALTER.** *See* PSALMS, BOOK OF.

**PSEUDEPIGRAPHA.** Jewish writings from a few centuries before and after Christ that are not included in the Bible, APOCRYPHA, or rabbinic literature.

Among the most well-known are:

(1) *The Apocalypse of Abraham*, which tells of Abraham's discovery of God and his vision of the heavens, the divine throne, and human history.

(2) *Apocryphal Psalms*, a collection of psalms and poems.

(3) *Aristeas*, which relates the events connected with the preparation of the first Greek version of the Torah.

(4) *The Book of Enoch*, which deals with the origin and judgment of sin, including the rebellion of the angel Semihazah.

(5) *The Book of Jubilees*, which divides the history of the world into Jubilee periods. Also known as *Jubilees*, *Little Genesis*, *Apocalypse of Moses*, *Testament of Moses*, *Book of Adam's Daughters*, and *Life of Adam*.

(6) *The Greek Apocaylpse of Baruch*, which tells of Baruch's vision of the capture of Jerusalem and of the coming of the Messiah. It is also known as *the Syriac Apocalypse of Baruch* or *Apocalypse of Baruch*.

(7) *The Greek Apocalypses of Esdras and Sedrach*, which relate to the OT books of Ezra, Nehemiah, and II Chronicles.

(8) *The History of Zosimus*, the story of the Rechabites.

(9) *The Ladder of Jacob*, which narrates Jacob's vision.

(10) *Liber Antiquitatum Biblicarum*, which paraphrases biblical history from the Creation to the time of II Kings.

(11) *The Life of Adam and Eve*, which expands the biblical story.

(12) *The Lives of the Prophets*, which deals briefly with each of the main prophets of the Bible.

(13) *The Martyrdom of Isaiah*, which amplifies the statement in II Kings 21:16 that King Manasseh shed much innocent blood, focusing on his martyring of the prophet Isaiah.

(14) *The Odes of Solomon*, which presents forty-two joyful poems.

(15) *The Paralipomena of Jeremiah*, which tells of Jeremiah's life from the destruction of Jerusalem

onward. It is also known as the *Rest of the Words of Baruch*.

(16) *The Psalms of Solomon*, composed of eighteen psalms emphasizing the covenant.

(17) *Pseudo-Phocylides*, which presents pithy sayings in verse form.

(18) *The Questions Addressed by the Queen and the Answers Given by Solomon*, which supplements the biblical stories of Solomon and the Queen of Sheba.

(19) *Quotations from Lost Works*. This book can be found in patristic and other ancient medieval sources.

(20) *The Sibylline Oracles*, which affirms the sovereignty of God over all nations.

(21) *The Slavonic Apocalypse of Enoch*. Also known as *Secrets of Enoch* or the *Slavonic Book of Enoch*, this book reflects sacrificial practices.

(22) *The Story of Joseph and Asenath*, which tells of the conversion and marriage of Asenath to Joseph.

(23) *The Testament of Abraham*, which relates Abraham's heavenly travels before his death and his struggle with death to retain his soul.

(24) *The Testament of Job*, which expands on the biblical book.

(25) *The Testament of Moses*. Also known as *The Assumption of Moses*, this book depicts Moses' instructions to Joshua.

(26) *The Testament of Solomon*, which urges hearers to consider last things.

(27) *The Testaments of the Twelve Patriarchs*, which consists of the teachings of Joseph's twelve sons.

B.J.

**PSEUDO-CLEMENTINE.** *See* CLEMENT, EPISTLES OF.

**PSEUDO-MATTHEW, GOSPEL OF.** Although it is attributed to MATTHEW, this gospel of the NT APOCRYPHA dates from the eighth or ninth century and is based on the Infancy Gospel of Thomas and the Protoevangelium of James. With the aim of lending credibility to this account, someone has written a preface to this work, linking it with Jerome (347–420), who reportedly claimed that the original Gospel of Matthew was written in Hebrew. In the Middle Ages this Pseudo-Matthew served as a major source for popular piety about the birth of Jesus, especially for artists and poets who wanted to portray the events surrounding the pregnancy of Mary and the infancy of Jesus.                                       H.K.

**PSYCHICAL RESEARCH.** The scientific study of parapsychological or paranormal phenomena. These are sometimes referred to as parapsychology or EXTRASENSORY PERCEPTION. The areas under consideration include thought transference, foretelling the future, hauntings (appearances of ghosts or moving objects), and messages through mediums from spirits of the dead.

The beginnings of psychical research are to be found in the establishment of the Society for Psychical Research in London in 1882. An American society was formed in 1888, and soon there were societies in a number of European countries and Japan. The universities have been hesitant to enter this field as a valid area of research, but serious work has been done at Duke University in the parapsychology laboratory of J. B. Rhine from the 1930s to the 1960s. Later a similar department was established at the University of Utrecht.

These investigations were encouraged by the rise of the SPIRITUALISM movement in the nineteenth century. British researcher Sir Oliver Lodge was a Spiritualist. Others accepted the reality of psychic phenomena but rejected the religious explanations derived from spiritualism.

Both the methods and findings of psychical research are ignored or rejected by most scientists. Some see possibilities for future research, but few are willing to enter into the search. There are two areas for such research. Cognitive phenomena include clairvoyance, telepathy or precognition, prophecy, and acquisition of facts about one person by another through normal sensory channels (ESP). Physical phenomena include "willing" the dice to fall in a certain way and the moving of objects by poltergeists (psychokinesis). People have believed in the existence of such phenomena for thousands of years, but there has been no agreement on causes, no effective statement of theory, or adequate methods for research. While some investigations have been done, much foundational work still remains.       I.C.

**PSYCHOANALYSIS.** A branch of psychology, a method for studying how the mind works, and a form of treatment, named by SIGMUND FREUD, who developed it over a period of fifty years. Associated with Joseph Breuer in the 1890s, Freud observed the behavior of neurotic patients under hypnosis. He became aware that during a process of free association they brought out hitherto repressed painful memories, usually sexual. Freud theorized that basic to behavior was sexual energy, which he named libido, and that specific defense mechanisms developed as attempts to inhibit such memories. The study of dreams, slips of the tongue, and forgetfulness led to a model of the structure of personality that became basic to psychoanalytic theory and treatment.

According to psychoanalysis the structure of personality is threefold. The *id* is formed in the unconscious instinctual drives, which impel a person to activity. This energy arises from the erotic (libidinal) and aggressive drives. Such drives are important to the emotional life, their purpose being to regulate, control, and discharge instinctual energy. This basic element in the personality is exhibited most fully in infancy. The aim is gratification. Social processes of nurture and education are used to repress and direct these basic drives. Insufficient repression leads to the development of inappropriate behavior patterns. Over-repression leads to anxiety and self-concern, preventing attachment to others. Hence the means to direct the healthy development of libidinal energy is important.

The second aspect of personality is the *ego*, the conscious level of existence. Here the individual becomes related to the environment. Preconscious (but not unconscious) material is available for recall. The ego seeks to gratify instinctual needs but is open to delayed gratification and able to accept a modification of the pleasure principle. One way it builds defenses against anxiety is through identification. Modes of behavior are imitated through parents and other people in situations in which the child lives. Repression (forgetting) is another defense. Reaction formation is another way; the person acts contrary to what is expected in order to prevent psychic discomfort. Kindness may mask aggression; boldness may be a front for submissiveness. These "masks" may not be recognized by the wearer. Or, a person may try isolation, by objectifying feelings. What sounds like the repression of an idea may be in reality a deeply felt wish. Through the method of projection, an individual attributes personal attitudes and feelings to others. By not admitting to having such attitudes, pressures of anxiety, guilt, or hostility may be lessened. Prejudice is a form of projection. Denial of a possibility is another way of handling psychological threat. Finally, it is possible to regress to an earlier stage of development. The ego's task is to mediate between personal needs and environmental pressures in order to steer a course close to reality.

The third element in personality is the *superego*. Beginning to develop between the ages of three and six, this is the ego ideal, concerned with the values and mores of the community. This is conscience, first developed through identification with parents and concern to obey them. Later, teachers and heroes become other persons with whom to identify. In another way, the conversion experience comes out of struggles with the superego toward the formation of a new life-style expressing an understanding of conscience. Overall the superego acts as a censor on the ego in its response to the id.

Psychoanalytic theory highlights the importance of several mechanisms within the personality. Instinctual conflict among id, ego, and superego leads to anxiety. Such normal conflict becomes pathological when it inhibits enjoyment of life. Unconscious mental processes are also important in understanding the personality. While preconscious thoughts can be recalled, unconscious thoughts lie so deep that they can be recalled only with difficulty, if at all, yet are important for understanding behavior, especially when neurotic.

Psychoanalysis has added a dimension to developmental theory, notably through the work of ERIK ERIKSON and his stage theory. The field has also established the fact that there is a relationship between present behavior and childhood experiences.

From his work with adults, Freud established a pattern by which he discerned that persons go through specific stages related to the development of sexuality. The infant in the oral stage seeks instant gratification of physical needs for food and external comfort. In the next stage the child seeks anal satisfaction, expressed as a need to give or withhold, whichever brings gratification. The three-year-old, in the genital stage seeks fulfillment through a relationship to the parent of the opposite sex, later transferring that affection to the parent of the same sex as the one who becomes a role model. It is here that the superego begins to develop. The six-year-old enters a sexually latent stage, free to develop knowledge and skills before the identity struggles of adolescence.

Inevitably, psychoanalysis developed in many directions. Otto Reich, ALFRED ADLER, CARL JUNG, and others developed their own "schools." Psychoanalytic theory has influenced anthropology, sociology, literature, and the visual arts. Psychoanalysis is a descriptive method. It does not provide quantitative data that some forms of research generate. Recently there have been questions concerning the need for guidelines for evaluation. In the face of questions as to the efficacy of psychoanalytic treatment (however acceptable in theory) with reference to the amount of time and money expended, there may be further developments.　　　　　　　　　　　　　　I.C.

**PSYCHOLOGY OF RELIGION.** The ancient Greeks speculated on the meaning of religion, as evidenced in the writings of Plato and Aristotle. The people of the Bible wrote about religious experiences. But the psychology of religion in a technical sense could not arise until psychology itself became a discipline apart from philosophy. This occurred with the laboratory studies of Wilhelm Wundt in 1875. Somewhat earlier, the theologian Friedrich Schleiermacher (1768–1834) had been describing religion as "feeling."

The earliest uses of critical empirical methods were in studies of conversion by Edwin D. Starbuck and E. Stanley Hall and in studies of mysticism. Starbuck's *Psychology of Religion* appeared in 1899 and was followed three years later by William James' *Varieties of Religious Experience*.

During the same period, anthropologists were approaching the study of religious experience from the phenomenological perspective. J. H. Leuba's *Psychological Origin and the Nature of Religion* (1912), Sir James George Frazer's *Golden Bough*, and Emil Durkheim's writings were all influenced by evolutionary theory. Those who study preliterate religions use such terms as "mana" to indicate the essential Spirit, "animism" to indicate life in everything, and "totemism" to symbolize the figure that represents the clan or tribal group and the place of the ancestors in collective life. Further systematization of the field was made through E. S. Ames' *Psychology of Religious Experience* and J. B. Pratt's *Religious Consciousness*.

Studies in early forms of religion, insofar as these

could be uncovered, provided agenda for psychological research. To what extent is religion an individual response and to what extent does the individual respond as participant of a group? In many cultures the relationship to the Other is a delicately ordered expression of the life of the community. This is observed in all religions where group or congregational worship is practiced, whether on a weekly basis, as in the Western religions, or on holy days, as is more characteristic of Eastern religions. The phase of individualism that became distinctive of the Western world during the Renaissance made possible the emphasis on personal sin, redemption, conversion, and commitment, which became characteristic of much of Protestantism.

An understanding of the Transcendent is a phenomenon of all religions. Some understand and deny, as in the origins of Buddhism, or recent secular responses implied in the terms "eclipse of God" or "death of God," and in agnosticism or atheism. The activity of the Other is known only by the responses of believers. A psychology of religion needs to inquire into the nature and meaning of prayer, both individual and collective. Verbal and bodily responses indicate the interrelationships of awe, fear, and love. The nature of praise and petition indicates the believers' understanding of the power of the One worshiped. The occasions on which the community gathers and the objectives of its worship indicate its understanding of and relationship to the Holy One.

This reflects the human understanding of the nature of the numinous, an area studied by psychologists of religion. The numinous evokes awe, as reflected in the care with which the worshiping people approach the Holy One and the way in which they order their existence. In some forms of religion the ethical character of the Divine is an integral part of the holiness, so that approaching the Divine requires righteousness on the part of a community or individuals. Yet in all religions there have been attempts to influence this reality through magic.

Another area in the psychology of religion is the study of the human response to the understanding of the Transcendent. People have always sought meaning for life, whether in community or as individuals. How a particular form of religion regards life after death, or its absence, is one indication of the goal of life. Another basic factor is the life-style a religion sets for its adherents—the values for living and the rewards and/or punishments it declares. This aspect of the study of religious psychology receives strong emphasis in early twentieth-century writings, beginning with George Albert Coe's *Psychology of Religion* (1916). What does one *do*, he asks, in studying a religion? The functioning of religion is a clue to the strength of the beliefs. Religious consciousness includes values, as indicated by individual and group conduct. The human response to the sacred is to be seen in behavior. Those values that a culture holds to be most important reflect its

view of the nature of its god(s). The commands for the ordering of life, whether in oral tradition or written form, as in the Bible and in the Qur'an, are indications of the character of the Transcendent.

Out of an understanding of holiness arises the awareness of sin and, concomitantly, forgiveness. Sin is wrongdoing or a wrong attitude toward the Divine that disrupts a relationship. Some way must be found to restore wholeness. Repentance in some religions has been indicated through forms of a sacrificial system, functioning in behalf of individuals and/or a community. In more individualistic times repentance is demonstrated through personal acts of penance as signs of restoration. Doctrines of redemption, whereby the Other in some way takes the initiative in restoring human beings to favor, are important in studying the nature of a religion. Related to this, and beyond doctrines concerning life after death, are eschatological doctrines concerning the ultimate fulfillment of the purposes of existence and the world itself.

The study of CONVERSION has attracted research workers because it is a complex phenomenon, affecting not only individuals but groups. It arises in various contexts, expresses itself in differing ways, and affects people at any age level. It can be studied through the writings of those who have had this experience, through descriptive histories of revival meetings, and through observation. The study of MYSTICISM has a vast literature, not only in the writings of mystics, but in the books in which writers on the devotional life have tried to explicate the path for those who would follow.

Today, several streams of twentieth-century psychology inform the study of psychology of religion. BEHAVIORISM, with its emphasis on habit formation and the importance of rewards, has given direction to the psychological aspects of worship and the liturgies that support worship. It raises questions about the place of conditioning in developing expected behavior patterns and about the nature of the freely willed response. One could also cite theories and practices in psychotherapy designed for behavioral change.

Developmental psychologists such as ERIK ERIKSON lend insights that have bearing on religious development, through the use of such terms as "basic trust," "initiative vs. guilt," or "self-identity." Developmental psychology has led to recent and continuing studies in moral and religious development: Lawrence Kohlberg in moral development, James Fowler in faith development, and Kenneth Stokes in adult religious development.

An important influence in the study of religious psychology has come through the work of SIGMUND FREUD and CARL G. JUNG. Freud began his studies of religion in *Totem and Taboo*. His delineation of the unconscious facets in behavior have implications for religious belief and practice. The broad understanding of the nature of libido has brought a new dimension into the study of religious experience, the relationship to God, and the response in religious living. Freud's studies on the superego have influenced the understanding of conscience, whether one is dealing with the child's internalization of parental rules, or the adult's struggles among the aspects of self. The concept of projection is a help in understanding guilt and blame. Introversion/extroversion help explain the varieties of religious experience from the deeply personal to the corporate.

Jung's more positive regard for religion has made his writings a welcome addition to the research in religious psychology. In speaking of the anima/animus he points to the complexity of human personality. Individuation indicates the possibility of personal rebirth. In his theory of archetypes he brings the development of myths and symbols into the center of the understanding of religion.

PAUL PRUYSER, in his book *A Dynamic Psychology of Religion* (1968), developed another approach. Wishing to avoid systematization, he describes perceptual processes in religion such as sight, sound, and touch, and intellectual processes such as knowledge, memory, and imagination. He discusses symbolism and religious language, followed by emotional processes and the motor system. He concludes with the areas of relationships to persons, things, ideas, and the self.

Another influence is that of studies in EXTRASENSORY PERCEPTION and related fields. J. B. Rhine at Duke University initiated studies in parapsychology relating to life after death. Huston Smith studied the effects of mind-expanding drugs on religious experience. Morton Kelsey has explored dreams in a biblical-psychological perspective. The area of meditation as a way of self-awareness and relationship to the Transcendent has led to the development of a number of systems, including that of Robert Assagioli. This postdates ABRAHAM MASLOW's "religion . . . and peak experiences," a broader description of how people develop a sense of what is ultimate, or ERICH FROMM's view of a fully humanistic religion.

In less than a century the study of religious psychology has expanded through several disciplines into many areas, all continuous with the phenomena first observed by early researchers.                    I.C.

**PTOLEMY.** A dynasty of Hellenic kings who ruled over Egypt, beginning with the breakup of ALEXANDER THE GREAT's empire in 323 B.C., down to 30 B.C. The founder, Ptolemy (who died about 283 B.C.), was one of Alexnder's most trusted associates and one of seven bodyguards who accompanied Alexander everywhere. Ptolemy married a Persian princess, Artacama. On Alexander's death he became ruler of Egypt, threw out Alexander's officials, conquered Cyrenaica, and later controlled Cyprus and Palestine (318 B.C.). Many wars took place between Alexander's various successors but Ptolemy held his throne in Egypt securely. Ptolemy is remembered

as the founder of the famous library in ALEXANDRIA.

Ptolemy II (also known as Philadelphus, 309–246 B.C.) was not a soldier, but his navy became dominant in the eastern end of the Mediterranean. His court was the height of luxury, and he adopted the Egyptian custom of marrying one's sister. Ptolemy III (also Euergetes, king 246–221 B.C.) made war on the Seleucid (Hellenic) dynasty of Syria and Babylon, invading this empire as far as Babylon itself. Ptolemy IV (also Philopator, king 221–204 B.C.) was a weak, luxury-loving ruler. The decline of the dynasty begins with him. He was ruled by his advisors and mistresses. Ptolemy V (also Epiphanes, king 204–181 B.C.) came to the throne at age five. The government was paralyzed and all overseas possessions, as well as Palestine, were lost. He married Cleopatra, the daughter of his rival, Antiochus III. Ptolemy VI (also Philometor, 181–145 B.C.) became king as an infant. The country was ruled by his mother, Cleopatra. Later the Seleucid King Antiochus IV Epiphanes invaded Egypt and captured Ptolemy VI. Thereupon the city of Alexandria put his younger brother on the throne as Ptolemy VII (also called Physcon, king 146–117 B.C.). When Antiochus withdrew from Egypt, the two brothers ruled as joint-kings. When quarrels broke out between them, appeals were made to Rome, which intervened in Egypt in 168 B.C. Philometer, or Ptolemy VI, emerged the stronger. He invaded the Seleucid realms and conquered them but was mortally wounded in a battle near Antioch in 145 B.C. Ptolemy VIII (known as Lathyros, king 117–107, 89–81 B.C.) and Ptolemy IX (or Alexander I, king 107–89 B.C. ), sons of Ptolemy VII, shared the empire and soon were embroiled in warfare. Ptolemy IX ruled Egypt alone from 104–)9 B.C. He was overthrown by a popular revolt in 89 B.C. and died in a naval battle in 88 B.C. His son was briefly on the throne as Ptolemy X, but was murdered after only twenty days as king. This ended the legitimate Ptolemaic line.          J.C.

**PUBLICANS.** Petty officials who collected minor taxes on salt, duty on goods, tolls on highways and bridges, and on any transaction they could intercept with toll gates or other controls. The term "publican" is derived from the older Roman order of *publicani*, who were contract TAX COLLECTORS, that is, they contracted to derive a certain sum from a territory in the provinces and were allowed to keep as profit any money above that contracted sum. The *publicani* were abolished under the empire and replaced with the *telonai*.

In the RSV the term "tax collector" is regularly used for this office, while the KJV (or Authorized Version) regularly uses "publican." The publicans (or tax collectors) were utterly despised by the Jews in Jesus' time because of their legal, but unjust, extortion of money from the people, as well as their cooperation with Rome. Yet Jesus befriended publicans, as he did other public sinners, offering salvation to them if they repented. Among the publicans who accepted Jesus and changed their lives was Levi, or Matthew, who became an apostle (Matt. 9:9-13; Luke 5:27-31), and Zacchaeus of Jericho, who welcomed Jesus and repaid all he had stolen (Luke 19:6). In Luke 18:9-14, Jesus told the parable of the Pharisee and the publican, which contrasted the humility of the tax collector and the pride of the Pharisee.                                              J.C.

**PUJA.** In BHAKTI Hinduism, puja is worship offered to deities in a temple or a household shrine. Typical features of puja include invocation of the god, bathing and dressing its image, anointing it with sandalwood paste, offering flowers and incense, and waving a lamp in front of it. Food to be eaten by the family or to be distributed to temple worshipers is also presented. In household puja, done every morning in devout homes by the head of the family or a retained priest, the patronal deity is treated as an honored guest. In temples, the emphasis shifts somewhat to make the deity a king in his court. The regimen is based on the daily routine of a maharajah, with times for audience when worshipers may present petitions and simple offerings, usually assisted by ritually pure priests.
                                                                R.E.

**PUL.** TIGLATH-PILESER III, king of Assyria from 745 to 727 B.C., took the name Pul when he ruled Babylon from 729 to 727 B.C. (II Kings 15:19; I Chr. 5:26; in Isaiah 66:19 the KJV has Pul, the RSV has Put). His son Shalmaneser V later ruled Babylon under the name Ululai.                                            B.J.

**PUNNA.** From the Pali word for "merit." In BUDDHISM, punna is the spiritual power, capable of producing certain reward in this or another life, that results from the good KARMA engendered by good actions. Punna can effect present benefits, a postmortem sojourn in a paradisal heaven, or a happy future rebirth. The actions that create punna are (1) donations, especially the giving of gifts to temples and monasteries, such as gilding images of the Buddha or donating food and clothes to monks; (2) morality—the keeping of moral precepts; and (3) the practice of meditation; for while the practice of vipassana—the meditation of analysis—can lead one beyond the karmic realm altogether to the realization of NIRVANA, other "samadhic" meditations generate very refined forms of karma, leading to rebirth in a high, perhaps "formless," heaven.

Understandably, the first two are ways of making punna appeal to the laity, while the third is of greatest interest to monks. The quest for punna is especially popular in THERAVADA Buddhism, where the distinction between lay and monastic spiritual paths is particularly marked, and where making punna is really the central focus of religious life for the great majority of Buddhists.                                R.E.

**PURANA.** In HINDUISM, the Puranas are sacred writings, generally written between A.D. 400 and 1000, which offer popular treatment of such topics as cosmology, the myths of the gods, dynastic histories, and the performance of pilgrimage and ritual. These books were very important for the development of BHAKTI and later types of Hinduism. Themes like the periodic destruction and re-creation of the world, the four YUGAS, the veneration of bhaktic deities, and the importance of CASTE, so characteristic of recent Hinduism, all received great impetus from this literature. MOKSHA, in fact, is less emphasized than the following of DHARMA in the context of life in this world combined with devotion to the gods.

Each Purana is "sectarian" in that it particularly exalts one of the deities, especially VISHNU, SHIVA, or BRAHMA. Tradition names eighteen Puranas as the major ones. Among them, the *Vishnu Purana* is a major source for information on the AVATARS of Vishnu. By far the most popular and influential Purana of all, the *Bhagavata Purana* relates the familiar stories of KRISHNA's childhood and youth, as well as offering rich insights into the meaning of Krishna devotion.                                      R.E.

**PURCELL, HENRY** (1659–95). Outstanding English composer of sacred and secular music, known for his dramatic effects, creativity, realism, and melodic achievements in instrumental and vocal works. Born in London, an apprenticed chorister at the Chapel Royal from an early age, by 1683 Purcell had become composer for King Charles II's string ensemble, organist at Westminster Abbey, Chapel Royal organist, and keeper of the royal instruments. Often called the Father of Anglican Church Music, he composed numerous anthems, organ voluntaries, cantatas, sonatas, and chants, many still widely used. Deeply involved in music for the theater, he wrote partial and full-length scores for over forty dramas by Dryden, Congreve, Beaumont and Fletcher, and others. His single true opera was *Dido and Aeneas* (1689), although *King Arthur, Don Quixote,* and other compositions interspersed dialogue with music. Madrigalist, polyphonist, and instrumentalist, he died at thirty-six, preserver of the past, forger of the future.                                                C.M.

**PURE LAND BUDDHISM.** A popular movement within MAHAYANA BUDDHISM, especially in China and Japan, which emphasizes the saving power of faith in Amitabha (Japanese: *Amida*) Buddha. According to the SUTRAS venerated by the movement, Amida Buddha made a vow that all who called upon his name in faith would be brought into his Buddha paradise, the "Pure Land," after death. From it entry into NIRVANA would be easy; the paradise itself is described in such glowing language as to make it incomparably appealing. Faith is expressed by recitation of what is called (in Japanese) the *Nembutsu: Namu Amida Butsu,* "Hail Amida Buddha."

Devotion to Amida in China goes back as far as the fourth century A.D. but, though adopted by some monasteries, has chiefly a lay character. In Japan, however, teachers such as Hōnen (1133–1212) and Shinran (1173–1262) made it the exclusive basis of powerful denominations with mass appeal. They taught (1) that Amida is really one with the universal Buddha nature, (2) that the Pure Land Buddhism of faith is really closer to the essence of Buddhism than the way of the ascetic because it is more ego-free, and (3) Shinran especially averred that since it is faith alone that counts, even one recitation of the *Nembutsu* by a sinner is sufficient for salvation.     R.E.

**PURGATORY.** In Roman Catholic doctrine the state in which the souls of the dead suffer, through the pain of longing to see the beatific vision of God, until they are purged of unforgiven VENIAL SINS, or the punishment imposed by God for forgiven MORTAL SINS, so they may enter HEAVEN. In popular thought, this suffering involves fire, but this material element is not officially taught by the church and is vigorously denied by the Eastern Orthodox churches, who teach a form of purgatory, yet deny the fully developed Roman Catholic doctrine.

The Catholic faith is that souls in purgatory can be aided by the PRAYERS FOR THE DEAD as well as by the sacrifice of the Mass, hence funeral masses and masses said for the dead, especially on the anniversary of death. Popular piety also allows prayers for the dead in purgatory, requesting them to intercede with God on behalf of the living. All people are considered to go to purgatory on their death, unless they die in mortal sin, which causes their condemnation to hell. No one is considered so free of venial sin that he or she can be declared to go straight to heaven.

Perhaps nowhere is the difference between Catholics and Protestants so pronounced as in the matter of purgatory. Luther declared the whole doctrine and practice wrong, since it is not taught in Scripture. Calvin and the Anabaptists followed Luther in this rejection. Luther saw the whole system of prayers and masses for the dead, indulgences, and the stress on good works as the outgrowth of a doctrine of salvation by works rather than justification by faith alone in Christ through grace. There is no comparable doctrine concerning the souls of the dead in Protestantism. Luther gave his opinion that the souls may sleep until the final judgment. Prayers are not said for the dead in Protestant churches. Protestants in general will mention the dead in prayers only to commend the departed to God's grace and mercy and to give thanks for their lives and works among us. Lutherans and Anglicans commemorate the saints of the early church in their services.     J.C.

**PURIFICATION.** *See* CLEAN AND UNCLEAN.

**PURIM.** The Jewish festival that commemorates the miracle of survival from Haman's plot to kill all the Jews of Persia. The story is told in the biblical book of ESTHER. Haman, chief minister of King Ahasuerus,

plotted to destroy the Jews of Persia. Esther, the king's Jewish queen, at the urging of her older cousin Mordecai, interceded with Ahasuerus, who authorized the Jews to defend themselves on the day marked for their death. They routed their enemies, and celebrated the following day, the fourteenth of the Hebrew month, Adar. Purim means "lots," objects used in deciding a matter by chance, and refers to the lots Haman cast to determine the day for the destruction of the Jews. Purim is thus also called the Feast of Lots.

When the scroll of Esther is read in the synagogue on Purim, congregants make a lot of noise each time Haman is mentioned, thus "drowning out" his name. Other Purim customs are sending gifts to friends, giving food or money to the poor, the Purim feast, merrymaking, drinking, and Purim plays and carnivals. Purim is particularly popular in Israel. In Tel Aviv the festivities take the form of a three-day colorful carnival, called *Adloyada*.     L.K.

**PURITANS.** Those within the CHURCH OF ENGLAND in the 1560s who opposed the ELIZABETHAN SETTLEMENT and wished to further purify the church of all "popish" forms, particularly vestments, and to adhere strictly to the theology of CALVINISM. The Puritans also represented the rising gentry and market capitalism.

Their dissent surfaced again in reaction to the ceremonial uniformity stressed by WILLIAM LAUD, archbishop of Canterbury from 1633. When Laud tried to impose the Scottish Book of Common Prayer in 1637, the Scots responded with the National Covenant repudiating bishops, and with armed force. Charles I had to call the Long Parliament, which was under Puritan leadership. Laud was condemned and executed in 1645. In league with the Scots, Parliament in 1643 agreed to make the Church of England Presbyterian. It convened the WESTMINSTER ASSEMBLY, which drew up the WESTMINSTER CONFESSION, still the basis for Presbyterianism. (*See* PRESBYTERIAN CHURCHES.)

In the civil war between Royalist Cavaliers and Parliamentarian Roundheads, OLIVER CROMWELL emerged. Charles I was executed as a traitor in 1649 after which Cromwell and the Puritans declared England a "Bible Commonwealth," with Cromwell as Lord Protector until his death in 1658. In 1660 Charles II restored the "middle way" of the Church of England. The Act of Uniformity (1662) forced two thousand Puritan ministers out of their churches, and Puritan chapels were illegal until the 1689 Act of Toleration.

Puritans were of many types. In the 1580s Separatist leaders were hanged or exiled to Holland (*see* SEPARATISM). In 1607 one congregation from Scrooby, England, fled to Holland and from there went to Plymouth Colony in 1620. Independents or Congregationalists and Baptists wanted no church hierarchy. Presbyterians favored that form of govern-

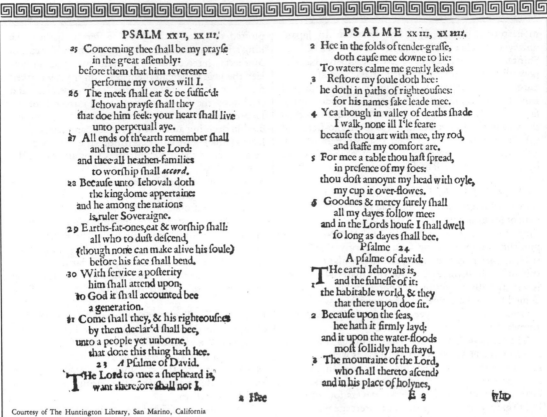

PSALM xx ii, xx iii.

25 Concerning thee shall be my prayse
in the great assembly:
before them that him reverence
performe my vowes will I.
26 The meek shall eat & be suffic'd:
Iehovah prayse shall they
that doe him seek: your heart shall live
unto perpetuall aye.
27 All ends of th'earth remember shall
and turne unto the Lord:
and thee-all heathen-families
to worship shall *accord.*
28 Because unto Iehovah doth
the kingdome appertaine:
and he among the nations
is ruler Soveraigne.
29 Earths-fat-ones, eat & worship shall:
all who to dust descend,
(though none can make alive his soule)
before his face shall bend.
30 With service a posterity
him shall attend upon:
to God it shall accounted bee
a generation.
31 Come shall they, & his righteousnes
by them declar'd shall bee,
unto a people yet unborne,
that done this thing hath hee.
23   A Psalme of David.
THe Lord to mee a shepheard is,
want therefore shall not I.

PSALME xx iii, xx iiii.

2 Hee in the folds of tender-grasse,
doth cause mee downe to lie:
To waters calme me gently leads
3 Restore my soule doth hee:
he doth in paths of righteousnes:
for his names sake leade mee.
4 Yea though in valley of deaths shade
I walk, none ill I'le feare:
because thou art with mee, thy rod,
and staffe my comfort are.
5 For mee a table thou hast spread,
in presence of my foes:
thou dost annoynt my head with oyle,
my cup it over-flowes.
6 Goodnes & mercy surely shall
all my dayes follow mee:
and in the Lords house I shall dwell
so long as dayes shall bee.
Psalme 24
A psalme of david:
THe earth Iehovahs is,
and the fulnesse of it:
the habitable world, & they
that there upon doe sit.
2 Because upon the seas,
hee hath it firmly layd:
and it upon the water-floods
most sollidly hath stayd.
3 The mountaine of the Lord,
who shall thereto ascend?
and in his place of holynes,

Courtesy of The Huntington Library, San Marino, California

*The Bay Psalm Book (1640), the first book printed in Colonial America*

ment. More radical were the democratic LEVELLERS, the agrarian communist Diggers, and the extremely millenarian Fifth Monarchy Men. From the SEEKERS, who awaited direct Spirit inspiration, emerged GEORGE FOX as leader of the QUAKERS, who rejected all external forms.

One estimate is that 85 percent of colonial American churches were Puritan in spirit. In New England they were CONGREGATIONALISTS, who divided into BAPTISTS (Separatists) and Unitarians (*see* UNITARIAN UNIVERSALIST ASSOCIATION) after the First Great Awakening. Quakers settled in Pennsylvania, Presbyterians in the middle colonies, and loyalist Puritans in Virginia.

Puritans hailed the Bible as authority and source for patterns of worship and church polity. A personal conversion experience was requisite for church membership. Ministers were to preach the Word, administer the sacraments, and discipline church members. Puritans gave to America its cultural core: a sense of covenant with God, a millennial hope, a desire for pietistic perfection, a sense of individual piety, a belief in higher law, a commitment to freedom of conscience, and a belief in separation of church and state.   N.H.

*PURUSA.* From the Sanskrit word for "person." In Samkhya and YOGA philosophy, this term refers to

the pure consciousness or "soul" principle awaiting liberation, in contrast to *prakrti* or "matter." In the VEDAS the word also names the creator God when conceived of in human form.   R.E.

PUSEY, EDWARD BOUVERIE (1800–82). Anglican theologian and leader of the OXFORD MOVEMENT, which is also known as Puseyism. Pusey was born August 22, and was educated at Eton and Christ Church College, Oxford (B.A. 1822, M.A. 1825). He was elected a fellow in 1823 at Oriel, where he met John Keble and John Henry Newman. He studied in Germany (1825–27) and then returned to become professor of Hebrew at Oxford in 1828, as well as canon at Christ Church. In 1828 he was ordained and married that same year Maria Catherine Barker.

To the *Tracts of the Times* he contributed one on fasting in 1834, three on baptism in 1835, and several on the Eucharist in 1836. His 1843 sermon "The Holy Eucharist: A Comfort to the Penitent," asserting the Real Presence, resulted in his being suspended from preaching for two years.

His publications included *The Doctrine of the Real Presence* (1855), *The Real Presence* (1857), *The Minor Prophets* (1860), and *Daniel the Prophet* (1864). He instituted the Oxford Library of the Fathers with a translation of Augustine's *Confessions* (1838). Pusey became the visible leader of the Oxford movement because of his defenses of it before bishops, and because he eventually became the only leader left at Oxford. Sympathizers were often called "Puseyites."

N.H.

**PYRRHONISM.** The skeptical philosophy that originated with the Greek thinker Pyrrho of Elis (365–275 B.C.). Pyrrho left no writings, and the main source of his life and thought is Diogenes Laërtius' *Lives of Eminent Philosophers.*

Pyrrho's student, Timon of Phlius, and others insisted that Pyrrho neither engaged in speculation nor taught a body of doctrine. Rather, he offered a way of living, reflecting a radical indifference to the circumstances of life and the opinions of philosophers. The goal of philosophy was, for Pyrrho, happiness based on tranquility of mind. Timon summarized Pyrrhonism in terms of three questions to which Pyrrho gave clear answers. To the question "What is the nature of things?" Pyrrho answered that we cannot know, since we have only the mutually contradictory evidence of our sensations, the evidence of phenomena and not of things in themselves. To the question "What is our relation to phenomena around us?" Pyrrho again answered that we cannot know, that we should acknowledge our ignorance, and suspend all judgment. To the last question, "What will result from such a lack of comprehension and suspension of judgment?" Pyrrho answered, tranquility of mind and happiness. The term Pyrrhonism has come to mean a skeptical approach to thought and life.

J.L.

**PYTHAGOREANISM.** A school of Greek philosophy named after its preeminent member, Pythagoras, an Ionian Greek, born in the sixth century B.C. Pythagoras was one of the most influential of the pre-Socratic philosophers. He founded a famous society in southern Italy, which continued in existence for over a century. It is difficult to distinguish the teachings of Pythagoras from those of his school, since he left no writings, because the society was sworn to secrecy, and the disciples, in esteem for their master, attributed their own ideas to him.

For the Pythagorean school, philosophy was a way of life devoted to the salvation of the soul. The society engaged in many dietary practices and other ascetic activity as a means of purification. The pursuit of knowledge, especially mathematics, which held a mystical significance, was seen as the highest form of purification. Pythagoras taught that by studying the *cosmos*, or the world's orderly perfection, one creates order in the soul. The Pythagoreans saw the nature and order of things in their mathematical structure. Things were observed to be made up of their numbers, just as other pre-Socratics saw the fundamental nature of things as water or fire. The ultimate principles were *limit* and the *unlimited*, which were equated with good and bad, respectively. There followed ten pairs of fundamental opposites, including right and left, male and female, and so forth. The universe was thus perceived as a harmony of opposites. The *cosmos* or order was achieved by the imposition limit, the number series, on the unlimited. The Pythagorean school made important contributions to arithmetic and geometry.

J.L.

**Q (QUELLE).** Q symbolizes the hypothetical document(s) that many students of the NT believe is the "second source" drawn on by Matthew and Luke, in addition to the Gospel of Mark, in the composition of their Gospels. Q stands for *Quelle*, the German term for "well" or "source."

No such document has ever been found, but a close study of the Synoptic Gospels (Matthew, Mark, and Luke) discloses Matthew's and Luke's similar use of almost all of Mark (the "first source" for their Gospels), and a mutual dependence upon a second source in numerous other places. This unknown "second source" is known as Q, and also as the LOGIA or "sayings of Jesus." It is thought that Q might have been a handbook that recorded oral traditions about Jesus that originally circulated in Aramaic as well as Greek. Q may even have been a collection of Jesus' "wisdom" sayings, as it contains many of his discourses.                                          J.C.

**QARMATIANS.** A radical, revolutionary Islamic sect that flourished in the Arab world between the ninth and eleventh centuries A.D. Secretive, based on the doctrines of the Ismaili movement within Shi'a Islam, it sought social reform and the creation of an ideal egalitarian society through revolution and force of arms. Qarmatians under Hamdan Qarmat, after whom the movement was named, seized power in a part of Iraq in A.D. 877, established strongholds through Arabia and North Africa, and ruled the Persian Gulf island of Bahrein from about A.D. 900 to 1077. Qarmatian ideas and practices have had an impact on subsequent Islamic history, particularly in later extremist Ismaili sects such as the Assassins and Druzes.                                          R.E.

**QUAKERS.** *See* FRIENDS, SOCIETY OF.

**QUARTODECIMANS.** Those who disputed the date of EASTER in the early church, which was set by the Council of Nicaea in A.D. 325. There were a number of disputes about this complex computation of the proper day on which to observe the Festival of the Resurrection of our Lord. The Quartodecimans led the first dissent, teaching that Easter should be celebrated on the same day that the Jews observed Passover, the fourteenth of Nisan, on whatever day of the week that observance fell, even if it were not a Sunday. The Nicene fathers believed Easter should always be observed on a Sunday, since the Resurrection took place on the first day of the week. These dissenters took their name from *quattuordecima,* the Latin word for fourteen. Some churches observed Easter in this fashion even after the council's decision, but eventually Nicea prevailed.                                          J.C.

**al-QUDS.** The Arabic name for Jerusalem. A city holy to Islam only after Mecca and Medina, its importance goes back to the Prophet Muhammad, who, seeing its role as a pilgrimage center for the other two monotheistic faiths, Judaism and Christianity, wished to associate Islam with it as well. According to Islamic tradition, the Prophet made a mystical ascent to heaven there from the Temple mount. Later the DOME OF THE ROCK mosque was built on that site.                                    R.E.

**QUEEN OF HEAVEN.** *See* BLESSED VIRGIN MARY.

**QUIETISM.** The term used for a movement in seventeeth-century Roman Catholicism, which is associated especially with Miguel de Molinos. Quietism taught a form of spirituality that called for extreme passivity of the soul and the suppression of all human effort. According to traditional Catholic spirituality, a certain passivity is necessary for the operation of the grace of God in the soul. However, this state of contemplativeness is reached by certain ascetical exercises and virtuous acts. The Quietists, on the contrary, rejected all ascetical and intellectual activity, as well as good works, regarding all attempts to do anything exemplary as an offense against God. They held that spiritual perfection requires the complete extinction of the will and claimed to care neither for heaven, hell, nor salvation but abandoned the soul completely to God. Devotional pictures and mental religious images were rejected, even contemplation of Christ and the Holy Trinity. They refused to engage in acts of mortification, confession, and petition. The Quietists taught that sin is impossible. Since the will is annihilated, all that one does is the work of God. Certain actions may be viewed as sinful, even devilish, by others, but they are not, and must not distract the Quietist's passivity.

In 1675 Molinos published his *Spiritual Guide*, which was at first highly approved but soon was recognized as leading to dangerous tendencies. In 1685 Molinos was arrested, and two years later Quietism was condemned as a heresy by Pope Innocent XI in his bull *Coelestis Pastor*. Sixty-eight of Molinos's writings were condemned. Notable exponents of Quietist spiritual tendencies were Madame GUYON and Fénelon, archbishop of Cambrai. Their teachings ignited the debate over semi-Quietism in the last years of the seventeenth century. Semi-Quietism was condemned by Pope Innocent XII in 1699.
                                                                      J.L.

**QUIRINIUS.** The Roman governor of the province of Syria, to which Judea was attached, during (according to Luke 2:2) the time of Jesus' birth. The governor, or propraetor, was known as "Cyrenius," and his full name was P. Sulpicius Quirinius. It is recorded that he traveled to Judea in A.D. 6 to hold a census and levy taxes. Scholars question Luke's accuracy because he also mentions that Herod the Great was on the throne, and Herod's death date was approximately 4 B.C. The census that supposedly took

Joseph and Mary to Bethelehem from Nazareth is thus ten years after Herod's death. Some scholars believe there may have been an earlier census (about which we know nothing) and Luke confused the earlier census with the historically attested one of Quirinius in A.D. 6. It is known that Quirinius was in the area of Syria before becoming governor, during a war between 10 and 7 B.C.                                                J.C.

**QUMRAN.** The local Arab name for the lower end of a valley down which a seasonal stream flows from Jerusalem to the Dead Sea is the Wadi Qumran. On a plateau overlooking this wadi, about ten miles south of Jericho and about a mile west of the Dead Sea, are the ruins of a fortress, built originally in the seventh or eighth century B.C. and converted into the headquarters for a religious community about 135 B.C. Abandoned temporarily in 31 B.C., it was restored about A.D. 1, and continued to be used until the Romans destroyed it in A.D. 68. In nearby caves were found the DEAD SEA SCROLLS.                     H.K.

*QUODLIBET.* This Latin word means "whatever you please." The term was used among the medieval scholastics for a special kind of disputation held at certain times of the year. The professor, instead of propounding for discussion a question of his own choosing, would offer to discuss any question proposed to him.                                           J.M.

Courtesy of the Museum of Fine Arts, Boston, George Bruce Upton Collection

*Page from a Qur'an*

**QUR'AN.** The Arabic word meaning "recital." The sacred scripture of ISLAM, the Qur'an (sometimes spelled Koran) is comprised of 114 *suras* or chapters;

the entire book is about the length of the Christian NT. The *suras* are arranged in approximate order of length, with the longest first.

The Qur'an is believed to have been delivered by God through the angel Gabriel to the Prophet MUHAMMAD over a period of more than twenty years. The revelations, beginning in a mountain cave around A.D. 610, came through several "modes"—in dreams, in waking deliverance by the angel, and in auditory experience. But in Muhammad's mind they were clearly distinct from any other divine inspiration, part of a unique message of which he was only the medium. In the original Arabic, the Qur'an is undeniably of intense poetic power; Muslims, pointing to the tradition that the Prophet was himself illiterate, say that its deliverance through such a person is itself a miracle, which indicates the book's uniqueness.

*Suras* of the Qur'an are classified as Meccan, Medinan, or combinations of both. This refers to whether they were received during the earlier ministry of the Prophet at Mecca, or the later at Medina, or assemble material from both periods. In general the Meccan *suras*—which, being shorter, tend actually to appear at the end of the volume—speak of God's power and judgment, presenting vivid escha-tological passages, while the Medinan are more legislative, dealing with theological and practical concerns of the emerging Islamic community. But throughout all, the unvarying fundamental themes are apparent: absolute monotheism, the one God being creator of the world and humankind, controller of all destinies, judge of all at the End; God's appeals to humanity through a series of past prophets and in the signs of nature; and the supreme importance of submitting to God's will in all areas of life.

In Muslim belief, the Qur'an is itself the Word of God in the world, in a way that has been compared to Christian belief in Christ as the incarnation of the divine Logos. Not only does it contain God's message to humanity, but its very cadences recall people to God, are the basis of most Muslim prayer, and are said to reflect the actual personality or "style" of God in interaction with humankind. In addition, many assert, particularly in Sufi and Shi'a circles, that the Qur'an contains layer upon layer of hidden meanings. For ritual purposes the Qur'an is always recited in the original Arabic. It is held to be untranslatable; versions in other languages are at best paraphrases, which can hint at its verbal meaning but do not convey the divine power of the original.

R.E.

# Rr

**RABANUS MAURUS** (776–856). Archbishop of Mainz, student of ALCUIN, master of the monastic school in Fulda, and abbot of Fulda (822–842). An excellent scholar and a vigorous abbot, he greatly advanced the monastery until his election as archbishop in 842. He was active in criticizing heresy and in defending orthodox doctrine. He chaired three synods between 847 and 852, including one involving the theologian Gottschalk's doctrines on predestination, Rabanus Maurus was a prolific author, writing a work on grammar, sermons, a martyrology, poetry, and a manual for priests and monks dealing with the sacraments, fasts, and public prayer, called *De institutione clericorum*. He also wrote scriptural commentaries and essays on the church fathers. Later he was proclaimed "the teacher of the Germans."                                                            J.C.

**RABBAH.** A city of Judah, mentioned in Joshua 15:60, whose name means "great." The site of this ancient city has not been positively identified, but some scholars suggest it may have been the same as Beth-shemesh, the capital of Ammon, which is the modern Amman, capital of the Kingdom of Jordan, twenty-four miles east of the Jordan River, in Transjordan.

Beth-shemesh was captured by David (II Sam. 11:1, 12:26; I Chr. 20:1). The prophets Amos, Jeremiah, and Ezekiel condemned the city. Much

later it was rebuilt by Ptolemy II and named Philadelphia. It was one of the cities of the Decapolis in NT times. Herod the Great captured the city in 30 B.C. The Romans completely rebuilt the city, demolishing all ancient remains. Only a few ruins of ancient times have been discovered, among them a late Bronze Age temple and some ruins of the old citadel.                                                            J.C.

**RABBI.** Jewish teacher, preacher, and spiritual leader. The office of rabbi was created in the Middle Ages, when the rabbi was the recognized leader of the community and the official JEWISH legal authority.

From the days of Joshua until the monarchy, the spiritual leaders were the elders, judges, and prophets. During the monarchy, the spiritual and religious authority was divided among the prophets, priests, scholars, and king. From Ezra until the destruction of the Second Temple, A.D. 70, the authority of the scholars increased, while the influence of the priests waned; prophecy had ceased. The term "rabbi" ("my master, my teacher") first came into general use at the end of the first century A.D. It was applied to scholars who had been ordained in Palestine, while the term "Rav" was applied to those in Babylonia. The rabbis of the Talmudic period did not accept any salary from the community, in accordance with the law that prohibits receiving any income or material benefit from the knowledge of the Torah. Thus a rabbi always had another occupation. The situation changed during the Middle Ages.

Formerly, the main duties of a rabbi lay in deciding legal questions in all branches of Jewish law, acting as a judge in civil and criminal cases, and supervising religious institutions. Until the nineteenth century, preaching was of secondary importance. Today the rabbi is a communal official, a congregational leader, whose duties include not only religious activities but also embrace educational, pastoral, social, and interfaith activities. Many rabbis have administrative positions with organizations, teach Judaic studies at universities, and engage in other non-pulpit occupations.

The three major rabbinical seminaries in the United States are the Rabbi Isaac Elchanan Theological Seminary of Yeshiva University (Orthodox); the Jewish Theological Seminary of America (Conservative); and Hebrew Union College–Jewish Institute of Religion (Reform).

L.K.

**RACA.** A word of Aramaic derivation, with the meaning "fool," "wretch," and used as an expletive. The single NT usage is Matthew 5:22, which illustrates the force of this name-calling. A similar Hebrew word is used to imply a moral judgment, that is, a worthless person (Judg. 11:3; II Sam. 6:20).

R.M.

**RACHEL.** A woman from Haran who helped bring the nation of Israel into being. Ruth refers to Rachel and her sister LEAH as those who "built up the house of Israel" (4:11). It was from Rachel's two sons, Leah's six sons, and the four sons of their handmaids that the twelve tribes of Israel arose. Rachel's sons were: Joseph, Benjamin; Leah's: Reuben, Simeon, Levi, Judah, Issachar, Zebulun; their handmaids': Gad, Asher, Dan, Naphtali. Some scholars think it possible that there was a Rachel tribe or clan whose symbol was the ewe, the female lamb (the Hebrew word *rachel* means "ewe"). Such a symbol would have been a good representation of a nomadic group.

When Rachel was of marriageable age, her cousin Jacob came from Palestine to Mesopotamia seeking a wife from among her clan, as his father Isaac had done (Gen. 29:1-13). Rachel's father, Laban, arranged for Jacob to work for him seven years to earn the right to marry her. Seven years later, after the wedding ceremony, Jacob discovered that Laban had tricked him into marrying his older daughter Leah. Jacob then worked another seven years to earn Rachel.

Jeremiah pictures Rachel as weeping at the fate of her children (31:15). This could refer to the northern kingdom represented by Ephraim, Joseph's son, or to the male children two years old or under living in Bethlehem, Rachel's home area, who were ordered killed by King Herod after the wise men spoke of the birth of a new king (Matt. 2:16-18). B.J.

**RACOVINIAN CATECHISM.** An early confession of modern Unitarianism (as distinct from ancient Arianism), dating from 1605. It expresses the theology of Faustus SOCINUS, that the OT and NT are inspired, but revelation is received through human reason alone; Christ is not God although he is not merely a man, rather he was the chosen instrument of God to found Christianity, through which all may find eternal life. Since Jesus is not truly divine (for if he were, he could not have died on the cross), then the doctrine of the Holy Spirit cannot be true. Rather there is only one person in God, the Father. The son is but an instrument, a prophet, and a sacrifice for sin. The Holy Spirit is only the presence of God in the world. The doctrine of original sin is rejected and human beings are said to be born innocent. By the exercise of human reason one may live a godly life and merit eternal life. (*See* UNITARIAN UNIVERSALIST ASSOCIATION.) J.C.

**RAD, GERHARD VON.** (1901–71). German OT scholar and theologian. At the beginning of the twentieth century, OT scholarship had reached a stalemate. The focus for many years had been on seeking the origins of the stories of the OT. Scholars had nearly exhausted the possibilities of discovering more layers of literary sources. Gerhard von Rad felt that the time had come to shift attention to exploring the meaning of the OT in its final form, to look at the OT as a whole and the Bible as a whole. After completing his theological studies in 1925, he began serving as a parish pastor. The growing anti-Semitism of his people, however, led him to request a leave of absence to study problems placed on the Christian church by the OT. Upon completing this further work he began teaching at Leipzig, then at Jena and Heidelberg.

Central to von Rad's work was his belief that three statements of God's saving deeds formed the core of Israel's faith:

Deuteronomy 26:5b-9—Wandering Aramean ancestors, after going down into bondage in Egypt, were brought out by the Lord God and led into a new land.

Deuteronomy 6:20-24—The Lord freed the people from Egypt.

Joshua 24:2b-13—God worked with Israel over the years, from Mesopotamia to Egypt to their own land.

Among von Rad's greatest contributions are his books, including *Deuteronomy, Genesis, Holy War in Ancient Israel, Old Testament Theology* (2 vols.), *The Sacrifice of Abraham,* and *Wisdom in Israel.* B.J.

**RADHAKRISHNAN, SARVEPALLI** (1888–1975). A distinguished modern Hindu, Radhakrishnan enjoyed a varied career as philosopher, educator, diplomat, and, from 1962 to 1967, president of India. His studies of the history of Indian philosophy are standard, and in such works as *An Idealist View of*

*Life* he presents Advaita VEDANTA as a viable philosophical option for the modern world.     R.F.

## RADICAL REFORMATION.

A term used to describe several of the movements that were an early part of the Protestant REFORMATION. Generally speaking, the term "Radical Reformation" is used in contrast to the "Magisterial Reformation" of Luther and Calvin.

One of the first of these movements was led by Andreas Bodenstein von CARLSTADT (or Karlstadt), an early colleague of Luther on the theological faculty at Wittenberg. While Luther was hiding at Wartburg Castle, Carlstadt made reforms on his own that went far beyond Luther's ideas, including the introduction of a vernacular mass, the discarding of vestments and images, and an extreme view of the priesthood of all believers. His anticlerical views led him to renounce his academic degrees and to dress as a peasant, wearing no shoes. He asked people to call him "Brother Andrew."

Carlstadt joined the fanatical group known as "the prophets of Zwickau" who conducted raids on churches and monasteries, claiming direct inspiration from God. THOMAS MÜNZER, one of the "prophets," was involved with the Peasants' Revolt (1524–25) that spread throughout southwestern Germany. This insurrection had no doubt been incited by long-standing oppression. Luther was appalled by the excesses of the revolt. Addressing both rulers and peasants, Luther reproached the former for oppressing the poor, and exhorted the latter to "be subject to the higher powers." When the revolt continued, Luther encouraged the nobility to stamp out the revolt. Münzer was one of those killed in the conflict.

In Zurich, where Zwingli was active in the Swiss Reformation, one of his more radical followers, Conrad Grebel, began to question infant baptism. The Anabaptist movement, so called because they rebaptized adults who had been baptized as infants, was born January 21, 1525, when Grebel baptized Georg Blaurock, who, in turn, baptized others, and a "gathered church" was inaugurated. Blaurock continued his ministry in the Tyrol.

There were numerous leaders in the Radical Reformation: Jacob Hutter, the leader of the HUTTERITES, one of the Anabaptist sects; Kaspar von Ossig SCHWENKFELD, the leader of a movement, still existing, known as the Schwenkfelders; Michael SERVETUS, of Spain, who was influenced by the Anabaptists but violently attacked the traditional views of the Trinity. Subsequently, he carried on a pamphlet war with John Calvin, who was to bear the burden forever, rightly or wrongly, of causing Servetus to be burned at the stake for heresy.

The MENNONITES, who developed in the Netherlands and northeast Germany, are the surviving descendants of the Anabaptist movement. The leader of the Mennonites was a Dutch Roman Catholic priest named Menno Simons who joined the Anabaptists in 1536.     R.H.

## RAHAB.

The woman of faith who saved the lives of the two men sent by Joshua to spy out Jericho.

JOSHUA sent two men secretly to see what the land was like that they were about to enter and take (Josh. 2:1). They lodged that night at the house of Rahab, a harlot. When the king of Jericho heard that spies had entered the city, he ordered a search. Rahab then hid the men in the piles of flax drying on her roof. When the search party arrived, she told them that the men had left. Being a person of faith, Rahab said to the spies of Joshua, "I know that the Lord has given you the land. . . . We have heard how the Lord dried up the water of the Red Sea . . . and what you did to the two kings of the Amorites. . . . The Lord your God is he who is God in heaven above and on earth beneath." She asked the men to promise to protect her family when they attacked the city, and they agreed. She then let them down by a rope through her window, which opened onto the city wall. Later when the city was attacked by the Israelites, she hung a scarlet cord in her window, and her family was spared (Josh. 6:17, 22-25).

The same Rahab may have been the mother of Boaz, the ancestor of Jesus (Matt. 1:5). Rahab is cited as a person whose faith resulted in good works (James 2:25-26 and Heb. 11:31).     B.J.

## RAHNER, KARL.

(1904–84). One of this century's most important theologians and widely considered the most influential Catholic theologian of the middle decades of the century. Rahner was born in Freiburg im Breisgau in Germany. He entered the novitiate of the north German province of the Society of Jesus in 1922. Three years earlier his brother Hugo, a noted theologian, had entered the same novitiate. Rahner pursued philosophical studies at Feldkirch and at Pullach, near Munich, focusing especially on Immanuel Kant and the Catholic philosopher Joseph Marichal, S.J., the father of the Neo-Thomist school known as Transcendental Thomism. This initiated Rahner's sustained effort to reconcile Thomistic epistemology and metaphysics with Kant's critical philosophy.

Rahner contends that God is not merely a regulative idea of pure reason, as Kant thought, but that a transcendental reflection on human knowledge will show God's existence to be an a priori necessary condition of any speculative judgment. Neo-Thomists such as Etienne Gilson, however, consider Rahner's transcendental method a dangerous concession to Kantianism. After a two-year period of practical experience as a Latin teacher, Rahner was sent to Valkenburg, Holland, where he studied theology between 1929 and 1933. In 1934 his superiors sent him to Freiburg for further philosophical training, and there he studied with Martin Heidegger. This initiated a new dialogue with German idealism, especially Hegel, and with Heidegger. Rahner's doctoral dissertation on Thomas Aquinas and theological anthropology was refused by

*Karl Rahner*

his mentor at Freiburg, Martin Honecker, who opposed Transcendental Thomism. However, Rahner was transferred to Innsbruck, where he completed his doctorate in theology in 1936. His Freiburg dissertation was published in 1939 as *Spirit in the World* (Eng. trans. 1968). A second important study, on the foundations of a philosophy of religion, entitled *Hearers of the Word,* was published in 1941 (Eng. trans. 1969). Rahner began his teaching career at the Jesuit theological faculty at Innsbruck in 1938. The faculty was suppressed by the Nazis in 1939, and until 1944 Rahner was largely occupied in pastoral work in Vienna. After the war he resumed his teaching, first at Pullach and then at Innsbruck in 1948. He was appointed to a chair at Munich in 1964 and later taught at the University of Münster.

Rahner was a prolific writer. While his theology is highly coherent, based on a carefully worked out theological anthropology, his practice of presenting his work in short articles and monographs and his prodigious output have not made his work easily accessible or comprehensible beyond the circle of professional theologians. His most important studies have appeared, since 1954, in a series of large volumes of *Theological Investigations*. The range of subjects is extremely wide, including not only creative interpretations of anthropology, the Trinity, Christology, grace, ecclesiology, tradition, and development of dogma, but also ascetical theology and spirituality, moral theology, pastoral theology and practice, and ecumenism. Rahner played an important role in the sessions of the VATICAN COUNCIL II (1962–65) as a consultant and theological adviser. He also served as author or editor of a number of important theological source-books and encyclopedias, including a later edition of Denzinger's *Enchiridion Symboloum,* the multi-volume *Lexikon für Theologie und Kirche,* the series of monographs, *Quaestiones Disputatae,* and *Sacramentum Mundi* (6 vols.). Rahner was also instrumental in inaugurating the international theological review, *Concilium* (1965– ). Rahner's contribution to the advancement of Catholic thinking in the fields of dogmatics, ecclesiology, and moral and practical theology is unique among theologians of the past quarter-century.

The major criticisms of his work tend to focus on ambiguities and difficulties in reconciling his transcendental method and his dependence on Kant and Hegel with traditional Catholic, and especially Thomistic, philosophy and theology. While his many writings initially give the appearance of being themselves rather traditionalist, Rahner's doctrine of God, his teaching regarding "anonymous Christianity," and his advocacy of theological pluralism in the Catholic Church, to mention only a few themes, are often considered progressive and even revolutionary.

J.L.

**RAIKES, ROBERT** (1735–1811). Founder of the Sunday school. He was born September 14 in Gloucester, England, to the daughter of the Reverend R. Drew and a printer named Robert Raikes. He inherited his father's newspaper, the *Gloucester Journal,* and published it until his retirement in 1802. His philanthropic work began with prison reform and concern for the sick. Then noticing that children were unsupervised on Sundays, Raikes hired women to teach them reading and the catechism. After the first school opened in July 1780, the concept spread rapidly in Britain and the United States. In 1785 the Sunday School Society was formed, and in 1803 the Sunday School Union was organized in England.

N.H.

**RAINBOW**. A colorful bow, visible to a person facing away from the sun, produced by the refraction and reflection of sunlight by falling rain. Since it is often seen against the cloud mass of a retreating thunderstorm, the rainbow has become a symbol of a storm that is past. It is like a bow that the Lord has set aside after shooting arrows of lightning (Lam. 2:4; Hab. 3:9-11). As such it becomes a sign of the covenant that God will never again let a flood destroy all flesh (Gen. 9:8-17). Appreciated for its beauty, the rainbow appears in descriptions of the heavenly city (Ezek. 1:28). John saw a throne in heaven surrounded by a rainbow that shown like an emerald (Rev. 4:3; 10:1). The Hebrew word for "bow" can refer to a rainbow, to a bow used with arrows, and possibly to masculine vigor (Gen. 49:22-25).                B.J.

**RAMABAI, PANDITA** (1858–1922). An important early leader among women of India and for the Christian cause in her country. Born of Brahmin parents, she was taught Sanskrit and the wisdom of the Hindus by her father, contrary to the custom of India. Later she married a Bengali lawyer and lived in Calcutta. After a short marriage, she was left a widow with a small child. She then began studying Christianity and was baptized on a trip to England. Her life was spent in helping to raise the status of women in India, especially young widows who by tradition were not allowed to remarry. She started a school to educate women, which met with much opposition. India's learned men gave her the title "Pandita" ("the learned one"), which had not been given to a woman before that time.                W.G.

**RAMADAN.** In Islam, the ninth month of the lunar calendar, and the month of fasting, when Muslims are to abstain from food and drink between sunrise and sunset. This fast is one of the Five PILLARS, or fundamental obligations, of the faith, and is also customarily a time of special religious study and devotion.                R.E.

**RAMAH.** Several cities carry this name.

(1) A border town in the northern tribe of Asher near Tyre. This may be the same as modern Ramia, eleven miles east of Ras en-Naqura.

(2) A town in the tribe of Naphtali, modern er-Rameh, fifteen miles west of Safed. The ancient site may be located beneath the highest point of the modern village.

(3) A town in the tribe of Benjamin, near the frontier between Israel and Judah, a few miles north of Jerusalem.

(4) A town in the tribe of Ephraim, perhaps the modern Rentis, nine miles northeast of Lydda on the west slope of the hill country.

(5) A town in the Negeb, the desert on the southern border of Palestine. Sometimes this Ramah was referred to as "Ramah of the South."

(6) The town of Ramoth-gilead in the land to the east of the River Jordan.                B.J.

**RAMAKRISHNA** (1834–86). Ramakrishna is widely recognized as one of the greatest and perhaps the most influential of the saintly spiritual personalities of modern HINDUISM. Not only an exemplar of the life of the traditional "holy man," Ramakrishna also dealt experientially with religious pluralism, a problem felt acutely in the modern world, and inspired the foundation of an order that has had a unique role in Hindu modernization in India and in introducing that tradition to the West.

Born the son of a poor Brahmin in a Bengali village, he went as a young man with his brother to serve a temple of Kali near Calcutta. An essentially simple and deeply mystical spirit, Ramakrishna was wholly oriented toward religious experience rather than learning. He maintained a profound devotion toward Kali, the Great Mother, and frequently went into samadhic trance. He was initiated into several Hindu paths—Saiva, Vaisnava, Tantric, Advaita—and undertook the experimental practice of Islam and Christianity as well. He became convinced that all led to the same ultimate goal of God-realization. The Ramakrishna Mission, which has done teaching and charitable work in India and the West, was founded by Swami Vivekananda and other of his disciples.                R.E.

**RAMANUJA.** The most important Hindu theologian and philosopher in the Bhakti tradition, Ramanuja rejected the radical nondualism (Advaita) of SAMKARA in favor of a "modified nondualism," which allowed for a personal God and a definite distinction between God and humanity, thus permitting the loving, personal devotion to God central to Bhakti.

Ramanuja's exact dates are a subject of controversy, but it is clear that he did his major work in south India during the twelfth century A.D. A strict adherent of VAISNAVISM, he argued in commentaries on the Upanishads, the Bhagavad Gita, and the Brahma sutras that their right interpretation shows BRAHMAN, or God, to be, not impersonal and objectless consciousness, but personal, aware, and eternal, ruler and redeemer of all selves.                R.E.

**RAMAYANA.** Together with the MAHABHARATA, one of the two great epic poems of Hindu India. The two combined comprise 200,000 lines. The Ramayana is shorter than the other work (48,000 lines), and, unlike it, tells a straightforward story centered on a single character, Rama, a reincarnation of VISHNU. Born as a prince, Rama married the beautiful Sita, traditionally regarded as the ideal of Indian womanhood. But owing to intrigue, Rama is banished and retires to a forest with Sita and his half brother, Laksmana. There Sita is abducted by Ravana, the demon-king of Sri Lanka (Ceylon). To rescue her, Rama makes an alliance with the king of the monkeys. After many adventures, assisted by monkey soldiers and especially their great hero Hanuman, Ravana is vanquished. Rama and Sita return to their capital at Ayodhya, where Rama gains the throne. But because people question the chastity of Sita, since she had dwelt with Ravana, Rama sends her away. She returns with a sage who attests for her, and she asks the earth itself to take her as proof of her virtue; the earth opens and the queen sinks into it on a golden throne. Saddened, Rama leaves the kingdom to his sons and goes to the realm of the gods.

In the earliest version of the Ramayana, that of Valmiki, about A.D. 300, Rama is merely a human prince. Later versions make him an avatar of Vishnu, the epic becoming a major force on behalf of Vaisnavism and BHAKTI. The principals, especially Hanuman and Sita, are characterized by utter loving devotion to the divine Rama, and he plays the avataric role of defeating demonic evil and restoring dharma. Told and retold, known by almost everyone in some form, the Ramayana has been a very influential component of Indian popular culture for centuries. It has been just as influential in Buddhist and Islamic southeast Asia as popular literature.          R.E.

**RAMCARITMANAS.** A literary version of the RAMAYANA, written about 1574 in a Hindi dialect by the great poet Tulsi Das (1532–1623). It emphasizes devotion to Rama as God and makes the chief characters ideals of their social roles.          R.E.

**RAMESES.** The royal residence city in the Egyptian Delta about 1300–1100 B.C., often occupied by kings named Ramses. During their bondage in Egypt, the people of Israel helped build the storage cities of Pithom and Raamses (Exod. 1:11). It was from the residence city of Rameses that they began the Exodus (Exod. 12:37).          B.J.

**RAMOTH-GILEAD.** An important fortress city in Gilead, east of the River Jordan in the tribe of Gad, often referred to simply as Ramah. It was one of the three CITIES OF REFUGE in east Palestine. Tell er-Ramith on the Wadi Shomer may mark the ancient site.          B.J.

**RANK, OTTO** (1884–1939). Internationally known psychologist and author. Rank was associated with SIGMUND FREUD for twenty years but broke with Freud because of his own interests in the conscious mind, as opposed to Freud's psychoanalytic interest in conflicts within the subconscious. Rank, after 1925, called his technique "will therapy" and sought to help his patients reconcile their wills with the environment. Rank received his Ph.D. from the University of Vienna. From 1912 to 1924 he edited two leading European psychoanalytical journals. He founded the International Psychoanalytic Institute in Vienna in 1912 and served as its director until 1924.          J.C.

**RANKIN, JEREMIAH EAMES** (1828–1904). Congregational minister, educator, and hymn writer. Rankin was born January 2 in Thornton, New Hampshire. After his graduation from Middlebury College in Vermont, he attended Andover Theological Seminary. After graduation he was ordained to the ministry in the Congregational Church. He served

congregations in New York, Vermont, and Massachusetts, after which he was called to the First Congregational Church, Washington, D. C. He subsequently was pastor of the Valley Congregational Church, and president of Howard University. Rankin featured gospel singing in his Sunday evening services. He wrote a number of hymns, including "God Be With You Till We Meet Again," published in *Gospel Bells* (1883), which he and others edited. Earlier he had compiled a book of gospel songs entitled the *Gospel Temperance Hymnal* (1878). Some of his original hymns, including, "Laboring and Heavy Laden," appeared in *Songs of the New Life.*          R.H.

**RANSOM.** *See* ATONEMENT, THEORIES OF.

**RANTERS.** A term of derision applied to lay preachers of the antinomian and pantheistic type during the great sectarian upheavals during the English Commonwealth of the mid-seventeenth century. They rejected the Church of England and stressed the INNER LIGHT, considering themselves above the ordinary distinctions between right and wrong.          J.C.

**RAPP, GEORGE** (1757–1847). The founder of the Harmony Society was born November 1 in Württemberg, in what is now West Germany, to Hans Adam and Rosine Berger Rapp. A devout student of the Bible, the Pietists, the mystics, and Emanuel Swedenborg, Rapp led a group of Separatists to Harmony, Butler County, Pennsylvania, where they organized the Harmony Society (1805). Its beliefs were a combination of Lutheran Pietism overlaid with millenarianism. From 1807 they practiced celibacy. From 1814 to 1824 they lived in New Harmony, Indiana, until that land was sold to Robert Owen. Rapp died in a third settlement, at Economy, Pennsylvania.          N.H.

**RAPTURE.** *See* PAROUSIA.

**RAS SHAMRA.** *See* UGARIT.

**RASTAFARI MOVEMENT.** A politico-religious movement that originated among Jamaican blacks in 1930. Their belief is that blacks are the true heirs of biblical Israel, and that Ras (Prince) Tafari, crowned as Emperor Haile Selassie of Ethiopia in the year of the movement's founding, would be their messiah who would repatriate blacks back to Africa. Rastafari has roots in several earlier black prophetic and repatriation movements. The movement is distinguished by its puritanical ethic, its black separatism, its distinctive hairstyle ("dreadlocks"), its religious use of "ganja" or cannabis, and its association with the music known as "reggae." In the 1960s a division began to appear between those Rastafarians who held to the earlier mystical religion and those who were more interested in using the movement as the basis of black social and political action. Rastafari has branches in England, North America, and several Caribbean islands.                    R.E.

**RATIONAL-EMOTIVE THERAPY.** An approach to psychological counseling developed by Albert Ellis in the 1960s and practiced through his Institute for Rational Living.

It is based on the thesis that neurotic fears, angers, and depression may be caused by events, but essentially are the result of how people *think* about these events. People have been in situations of great danger, yet maintained courage. Others are crushed by similar situations. This attitude prevents people from fulfilling their potential.

If the situation cannot be changed, the solution is to help the person view it differently. The patient is encouraged to think rationally about possible meanings in the situation. This brings a non-emotional factor into play to view the situation more objectively. As the person learns to accept a less defensive and subjective interpretation, the result becomes different. The situation can be dealt with from a new perspective and potentially with more positive effect. It is acknowledged that some feelings arise from unconscious factors going back to childhood and require deeper therapy.    I.C.

**RATIONALISM.** A term (from the Latin word *ratio*, "reason") that has been used in reference to a variety of movements in Western philosophy and theology. The word signifies that reason, rather than experience, tradition, or authority, is the final arbiter in matters of knowledge and truth. Rationalism is often contrasted with empiricism, the latter basing knowledge on experience and observation, the former on innate ideas or A PRIORI categories possessed by the mind. Classical philosophical rationalism is associated with certain philosophers of the seventeenth and early eighteenth centuries, particularly DESCARTES, SPINOZA, and LEIBNITZ. These thinkers shared the belief that genuine knowledge is derived from what Descartes called the clear and distinct perceptions of the intellect, and that God is the ultimate guarantor of the possibility of such knowledge.

Philosophical rationalism profoundly influenced Protestant theology in the first half of the eighteenth century, largely through the influence of Christian von Wolff (1679–1754), a follower of Leibnitz. Pursuing the model of mathematics, Wolff developed his theological system deductively from a few simple, self-evident truths. The world mirrors God's perfection, and God's perfect image is found in human reason. Our natural knowledge of God cannot, therefore, be contradicted by revelation. In Germany the tradition of Wolffian rationalism led directly to the critical rationalism of IMMANUEL KANT and is reflected in his *Religion Within the Limits of Reason Alone* (1794).

The term "rationalism" is often associated with the ENLIGHTENMENT and its critique of orthodox Christianity, especially in DEISM. However, the English Deists and the Frenchman VOLTAIRE, in their commitment to the principle of criticism, were influenced not by Descartes but by JOHN LOCKE and the empiricist tradition. They were "rationalists" only in the sense that they appealed to experience and scientific inquiry, rather than to faith and authority, and in their confidence in human nature to increase freedom and human happiness. The rationalists of the seventeenth century were not characteristically anti-religious; in fact, God is the crux of the systems of Descartes, Spinoza, and Leibnitz. On the other hand, the rationalism of the eighteenth century was often, in figures such as Holbach, Helvetius, Reimarus, and Tom Paine, atheist or at least antagonistic to all forms of orthodoxy.

In the nineteenth century the term "rationalism" was used loosely to signify a general commitment to reason as the ultimate arbiter of truth. Again, it often is used to describe the position of those who attacked Christian theology.                    J.L.

**RAUSCHENBUSCH, WALTER** (1861–1918). American theologian who was one of the leading exponents of the SOCIAL GOSPEL. Among his writings were *Christianity and the Social Crisis* (1907) and *A Theology for the Social Gospel* (1917). In the former of these books, he advocated an alliance between the churches and the working class and expressed the view that Christianity is committed to a socialist solution to the problems of industrial society. The purpose of Christianity is to transform this world into the Kingdom of God, conceived as an ideal society. In the second of the books mentioned, he set out to rewrite Christian theology, making the doctrine of the Kingdom of God central and interpreting all the other doctrines so that they articulate organically with the central truth. But Rauschenbusch did not think that he was reducing Christianity to a mere political ideology. "The kingdom of God is divine in its origin, progress, and consummation. It is miraculous all the way, and is the continuous revelation of the power, the righteousness, and the love of God." To make this doctrine central, he held, is simply to return to Jesus' own way of looking at things.                    J.M.

**RE/RA.** Egyptian god associated with the sun who came to have marked preeminence over all the other gods. Frequently represented as a falcon-headed figure topped by the solar disk in his boat, or sometimes by the solar disk alone, Re was said to cross the sky in a solar ship every day, then to make his way during the night back through the underworld to the East. In the course of this journey he had to defeat an evil demon, Apepi. By the Fifth Dynasty (2494–2345 B.C.), Re was the chief god worshiped by the pharaohs, the ruler being considered both a descendant of Re and Re incarnate. Still later, Re was joined with the deity of the temple city of Thebes, Amon, to form the composite creator and sovereign god AMON-RE.                                              R.E.

## REAGAN, RONALD WILSON (1911– ) Forti-
eth president of the United States; former governor of California; former motion picture actor. Born on February 6 to John Edward Reagan and Nellie Wilson Reagan in Tampico, Illinois, he grew up in a succession of northern Illinois towns where his father was employed as a shoe salesman. Ronald did not become a Roman Catholic like his father, but was reared in his mother's faith, the Christian church (Disciples of Christ). When he was nine, the family settled in Dixon, Illinois, where Ronald attended high school and played football and basketball, and was elected president of the student body. There he gained his first acting experience in school plays. He next entered Eureka (Ill.) College, graduating in 1932. After leaving college he became a sports announcer on a Des Moines (Ia.) radio station.

The future president began a successful career as a film actor in 1937 and starred in a number of movies. He was a captain in the Army Air Force during World War II. He later acted in television, appearing regularly until the 1960s. He served as president of the Screen Actors Guild from 1947 to 1952 and again in 1959. Starting out as a liberal Democrat, Reagan switched his party allegiance and became active in the 1964 presidential campaign of Barry Goldwater. Reagan was elected governor of California in 1966 and reelected in 1970. It was after his second term as governor of California that Ronald Reagan became a leading voice of conservative Republicanism, and made a strong bid for the party's 1976 presidential nomination. In 1980 he gained the Republican nomination and won the presidency by a landslide victory over Jimmy Carter.

Once in the White House he followed what he regarded as his mandate for radical change, seeking to end the excessive growth of government bureaucracy, and reducing government spending. Early in his first term he forged a coalition of Republicans and conservative Democrats to enact his economic program, which included the largest budget and tax cuts in United States history. His "new federalism" sought to transfer many federal powers to the states. Yet he increased defense spending, vowing that he would restore the armed forces to their pristine strength.

John W. Hinckley, Jr. attempted to assassinate the president on March 30, 1981. Reagan recovered from his bullet wounds, with a renewed sense of his place in history. His opposition to the Equal Rights Amendment, his pro-government policies in El Salvador, as well as his anti-Sandinista program in Nicaragua, and his efforts to bring peace to the Middle East, especially in Lebanon, aroused bitter criticism.

The president maintained his program, supported heavily by the religious right, opposing abortion, and advocating prayer in public schools and tax relief for families with children in private schools. His long campaign for reelection ended triumphantly when Ronald Reagan was again swept into office for a second term in November 1984, losing only the electoral votes of Minnesota and the District of Columbia.                                              R.H.

REALISM. An assertion of the independence of an object from human perception. Realists believe that there is a reality of things, qualities, or species. Kant used the phrase "thing-in-itself" to denote this quality of inner reality. The realist affirms that the object perceived has an ontological quality and is not simply an ideal or an appearance, as idealists assert. It is more than a name, as the nominalist asserts, and more than a mental concept, as the conceptualist asserts.

Realism has its roots in ARISTOTLE, whose work was the basis for medieval scholastic philosophy. DESCARTES in the eighteenth century, another realist, affirmed "I think, therefore I am." JOHN LOCKE affirmed that sensations have their origins outside the person who feels. Despite the popularity of IDEALISM during much of the nineteenth century, there was a resurgence of interest in realism (or empiricism) with the work of WILLIAM JAMES. PRAGMATISM deals with the concept of reality versus cognition. The neo-realistic position was a defense of the independent existence of things. Realism is one of the basic strands of what has been called the "perennial philosophy."
                                              I.C.

REALITY THERAPY. A treatment developed by William Glasser and G. L. Harrington as an alternative to Freudian-based psychotherapy. Rejecting traditional labels, Glasser substitutes "responsible behavior" for the term "mental health," and "irresponsible behavior" for "mental illness." Although unconscious factors exist, these are not important for the therapeutic process. The past is irrelevant for developing new behavior patterns.

People have two basic needs: to love and to be loved; to have a sense of self-worth and feel that others value them. People love and value those who act responsibly. In this way they fulfill their needs without harming others. Such persons know right from wrong and maintain a standard of behavior consonant with that knowledge. This requires a realistic estimate of the self and a will to self-correction. Normal people know the ethical standards of the society; their need is to learn how to live up to these standards.

Discomfort at not feeling loved or valued may be met in irresponsible ways that hurt others. People who act irresponsibly need a relationship to someone who cares in order that they may become concerned and involved in a process of change. The therapist, by accepting the patient while rejecting the wrong behavior, encourages responsible ways of acting. At the beginning, the patient may deny or evade the behavior or blame the problem on other people. The goal of therapy is to help the person view the self realistically in order to act responsibly.

The process of responsible living can begin in early childhood through responsible parents and teachers who insist on responsible action from children through a process of loving discipline.      I.C.

## REALIZED ESCHATOLOGY. *See* DODD, CHARLES H.

**REAL PRESENCE.** The way in which Christ is understood to be present in the EUCHARIST. The Council of Trent affirmed that Christ is "really, truly, and substantially" present in the Eucharist, that is, the bread and wine actually become the Body and Blood of Christ. This doctrine, called TRANSUB-STANTIATION, is affirmed to continue the tradition found in the ante-Nicene fathers. It also reflects the categories of medieval philosophy, where "substance" designates a reality and "accidents" designate appearances. Hence, after the words of consecration, the bread still appears to be bread but in reality it is transformed into the Body of Christ, an actuality perceived only by faith.

The Reformers rejected this view. Calvin taught that the life-giving power of Christ is present in the Eucharist to those who receive in faith. Luther affirmed CONSUBSTANTIATION—the substance of the Body and Blood of Christ is in, with, and under the bread and wine in a "sacramental" union. Zwingli viewed the Lord's Supper as a "sign" of the presence of Christ without sacramental signification. Anglicans affirm a doctrine of the Real Presence but leave open the way in which this is effected. The division is between those who affirmed "real" to mean the natural (but transformed) Body of Christ, and those who use words such as "in," "under," or "through" to indicate how the Real Presence is known by faith to the believer.      I.C.

**REASON.** *See* RATIONALISM.

**REBEKAH.** A woman of faith who became the mother of Jacob and Esau. When ISAAC reached the age to marry, his father, Abraham, sent a servant to Mesopotamia to find him a wife from among the relatives there who were faithful to the living God (Gen. 24). The servant prayed to the Lord to make known to him which woman this should be. And, as he had asked, a young woman came to the well and offered him water. Rebekah and her family agreed that she should return with the servant. She married Isaac, and, after twenty years of marriage, finally gave birth to Jacob and Esau. When Isaac became old and about to die, he asked his son Esau to go hunting and prepare some savory food for him so that he could

bless him before he died (27:1-4). After Esau went out, Rebekah instructed Jacob to go out to the flock and get two kids to prepare that he might receive the blessing instead. She then dressed Jacob in his brother's best clothes and put the skins of kids over his arms. When Jacob then received the blessing, Esau became so angry that Rebekah sent Jacob to her family home in Mesopotamia. There Jacob met Rachel, and after fourteen years of work, married her (29:1-20).      B.J.

**RECAPITULATION.** From the Greek verb used in Ephesians 1:10 ("to unite [*anakephalaioō*] all things in him"), Christian theology has taken the cue that Christ's cosmic work is to sum up all the disparate elements of the universe into a single whole. In the context of Ephesians the argument seems to run in response to a philosophical question current in the first century. The issue lay in attempting to reconcile the "many" and the "one." Greek philosophers knew that there were many objects of sense-perception in the universe. They strove to seek behind the variety of phenomena the key to all in "the one," a principle of unity. This verse in Ephesians offers the NT answer to this quest. It is in the cosmic Christ.

The term has thus become part of a Christian philosophy of history that seeks to integrate the many facets of human existence and experience into a har-monious end-result, an omega point, as Teilhard de Chardin calls it. The patristic writer who laid the foundation for this notion was Irenaeus. His entire soteriology hinges on his statement that the incarnate Christ "recapitulated" Adam's career as man in order to bring the divine life to humankind. Christ, as the SECOND ADAM, came into human life to repair the consequences of Adam's sinful disobedience (see Rom. 5:12-21) and to restore man to union with his creator.      R.M.

**RECEIVED TEXT.** A phrase directly taken from Erasmus' edition of the Greek NT in 1533, which contained the Latin words: *"Textum . . .receptum"*; "The *text* which [the reader] thus has is now *accepted* by everyone." The term Textus Receptus refers to the standard edition of the text of the Bible of its day and was the basis of the KJV/AV translation of 1611. (*See* BIBLE, TEXT OF.)      R.M.

**RECHABITES.** A group that lived a simple life-style in a rural setting, possibly as a protest against the lack of faith they saw in the cities. They may have been metallurgists or smiths who moved from place to place to find ore and work it (I Chr. 2:55).      B.J.

**RECONCILIATION.** A theological term to denote one aspect of Christ's work in restoring good relations between God and humankind. He is called "our peace, who . . . might reconcile us both to God in one body through the cross, thereby bringing the hostility to an end" (Eph. 2:14-16)—a characteristic

NT statement (it is not an OT word) that includes several elements of the early Christian teaching. First, reconciliation presupposes an ALIENATION between God and humanity, which has a twofold dimension. On God's part, since God is holy, God is distanced from humanity, which is both creaturely finite and morally unfit to be in fellowship with the Creator. On humanity's side, the enmity gives rise to feelings of guilt and bereftness, leading to suspicion and hostility. Second, the initiative in securing reconciliation lies with God, who is always said to be the prime mover and never the one needing reconciliation (II Cor. 5:18-21; Rom. 5:1-10). Yet the cost is great since the process is not easily achieved and God's way of "making peace" entailed both God's own self-giving in Christ and God's absorbing human ESTRANGEMENT in an act of identification and vicarious ATONEMENT. The focus of that "at-one-ment" is the cross, where Jesus' self-sacrifice marks the limit of divine determination to be at one with God's erring creation (Col. 1:20-22). Third, reconciliation has cosmic aspects (notably in Col. 1:15-20), but it is best interpreted as a restoration of personal relations which, once established, need to be worked out in daily living and on a human level (see Matt. 5:24; I Cor. 7:11).

One further dimension of the word is seen in Ephesians 2:11-22. Here the situation described is one of mutual hostility dividing Jews and Gentiles in the ancient world. The enmity was mutual. The Jews regarded themselves as a race apart, by their election and destiny as God's people. The Gentiles despised the Jews for their aloofness and strange customs. Now, the text declares, in the Christian message there is hope to reconcile these alienated factions as they are brought into fellowship with God through Christ and so united in the "one body" of the church. Reconciliation is eminently fitted to be a vehicle of communicating the Christian message in our day for the reasons implied above. (*See also* REDEMPTION; REGENERATION.)      R.M.

## RECONSTRUCTIONIST JUDAISM. *See* JU-DAISM, HISTORY OF.

**RECTOR.** From the Latin word meaning "a ruler." In the Roman Catholic church a priest legally appointed as the head of a parish, church, or other ecclesiastical organization, such as a university. A priest may not be the rector of more than one parish at the same time. The term is also used in the Church of England and the Episcopal Church.      J.C.

**RECUSANCY.** The resistance to Anglican church attendance laws from the reign of ELIZABETH I to George III. Recusants were chiefly Roman Catholics, but a few dissenting Protestants were also prosecuted. The law held that all people must attend the Church of England, and was specifically aimed at "papists," or Roman Catholics. Conviction of recusancy brought large fines, disqualification from public office and from bringing suits at law or acting as a guardian, practicing law, or holding a military commission. Finally, three months after conviction, recusants were to renounce the supremacy of the pope over the Church of England, or failing that, to leave England as exiles. The laws against recusancy were not always enforced, but in the earlier reigns of Protestant monarchs, many martyrs were made among Catholics. The practice of holding secret masses, and of hiding priests, was common among the Catholic gentry and nobility. The secret hiding places, called "priest's holes," can still be seen in some old English country houses.      J.C.

**REDACTION CRITICISM.** *See* BIBLICAL CRITICISM.

**REDEMPTION.** The basic meaning of redemption is "deliverance," with a setting determined by the context in which the word is used. In the OT there are three special areas of interest. First, prisoners in captivity were set free by payment of a ransom or an act of clemency on the part of the ruling authority, as the exiles were restored by Cyrus' decree (Ezra 1; a return celebrated in Second Isaiah's writings, for example, Isa. 45:1-25; 52:3, where Cyrus is the agent of the release of the Babylonian exiles, but God is the redeemer). Second, slaves were liberated by a procedure that entailed the notional payment of money to the Temple or, in Greco-Roman religion, the depositing of money in a sanctuary (notably at Delphi) for the owner to claim. Paul exploits this act of "sacred manumission" in Galatians 4:1–5:1; 6:17, to explain how Christians, in bondage to evil powers, have been ransomed and redeemed (I Cor. 1:30). Third, the most important background, however, is seen in the OT imagery of the Passover, which lies at the heart of Israel's celebration of its national redemption from Egyptian servitude to become the free people of God's covenant. One verse (Exod. 8:23, RSV marg.) neatly sums up the basic Hebrew thought of this episode. Yahweh says "I will set redemption" between Jews and Egyptians, thus claiming Israel as God's own possession. So they are bound to God by covenant obligation and treaty (Exod. 12–24).

The NT writers pick up this idea repeatedly. The wide range of literature on this subject in the NT, with variant idioms and set against diverse backgrounds, is in fact unified by its common indebtedness to the theme of redemption. It sees in Christ's coming and death the action of God to release people from slavery to SIN and to create them as a new covenant community, in succession to old Israel who rejoiced in God as their redeemer from alien political powers and tyranny. The NT, however, goes beneath the outer forms to describe the power of evil from which God in Christ has redeemed creation, as Revelation 21:22, heralds a new world of freedom of humanity's spiritual oppressions (Rev. 21:4; 22:3). The nation of humanity's alienation and enslavement, in the NT, is much more in terms of separation from God (Eph. 2:1; 4:18) and estrangement by reason of sin (see Rom. 6, 7; Col. 1:21). Just on the periphery lies the idea of being set free from political or social bondage (for example, Luke 1:73), but while the NT writers know that slavery is a common reality of life in their society, they say little in terms of emancipation (see I Cor. 7:20-24; Philem.; I Pet. 2:13-38), and redemption or SALVATION is celebrated as a release from humanity's great spiritual enemies: Satan, judgment, fear, and death (Rom. 16:20; Gal. 4:3-7; Rom. 8:1, 2, 14-17; I Cor. 15:54-57). (*See also* RECONCILIATION; REGENERATION.)       R.M.

**RED HAT.** *See* CARDINAL.

**RED SEA.** The body of water that separates Egypt and Ethiopia in Africa on the west from Arabia on the east. The northwest arm of this sea is referred to as the Gulf of Suez, and the northeast arm as the Gulf of Aqaba. These two upper arms form the coasts of the Sinai Peninsula. The Red Sea, also known as the Arabian Gulf, is part of a rift system beginning in the north with the Jordan and the Dead Sea and continuing south through the Arabah and the Gulf of Aqaba. The Gulf of Suez lies in another rift.

In ancient times the name Red Sea was also given to the Persian Gulf on the far side of Arabia and to the Erythrean Sea to the south and the Indian Ocean beyond. In the biblical account of the EXODUS, the Red Sea is referred to in the original Hebrew (Exod. 13:18) as the Sea of Reeds or Sea of Rushes. It is not clear in the story of the Exodus which part of the sea the Israelites crossed. Isaiah refers to the Red Sea as "the tongue of the sea of Egypt" (11:15).

The name Red Sea may have come from the red coral that lines its shores and covers its floor, or from the color of the Arabian mountains that border its east shores, from the glow of the sunset reflected in its waters, or from the name of a king (Erythras, meaning "red") who ruled the area.       B.J.

**REDUCTIONISM.** A philosophical term current in contemporary discussions of the relations between the various sciences. Reductionism implies that one science can be understood and explained, that is, reduced to, the laws and processes of another, more primary science. For example, some would assert that psychology is reducible to physiology, or that biology is reducible to chemistry and physics. Since the Enlightenment, many influential thinkers have used forms of reductionism to interpret religious beliefs and practices. Feuerbach and Freud, for example, viewed religious beliefs as essentially unconscious expressions of psychological wishes, fears, and aspirations. Durkheim interpreted religion as the unconscious institutionalization of powerful sociological needs. Karl Marx and contemporary Marxists see

religion as explainable in terms of material, economic forces.

In the nineteenth century, reductionism was often joined with evolutionism in the search for *the* origin and explanation of religion, for example, in animism or in the worship of natural objects such as the sun. The reductionistic search for a single origin of religion in human psychological or social need today is widely repudiated. Reductionism can be guilty of the *genetic fallacy*, of judging the present truth or value of a science, a belief, or an institution in terms of its primitive beginnings. An example would be to judge the worth of chemistry in terms of its origins in alchemy.       J.L.

**REFORMATION, CHRISTIANITY IN THE.** The sixteenth-century ecclesiastical separations from Roman Catholicism initiated by MARTIN LUTHER's discovery of justification by faith alone and his reliance on the Scriptures as an authority greater than that of the pope in Rome. Luther's search for salvation was intensely personal. He had no desire to start a new church, yet he felt that selling INDULGENCES to cancel out sins was a mockery of faith and repentance. His Ninety-five Theses, October 31, 1517, questioned this lucrative practice. He maintained his view that indulgences were neither helpful, lawful, nor scriptural. Luther's act sent shock waves throughout Europe and stirred up long smoldering desires for change. Repressed resentment of church abuses and calls for reform burst forth. Political, economic, social, and intellectual support developed.

During the events that followed, Luther's understanding of what had happened deepened. In 1520 he ably defended his convictions in three essays basic to PROTESTANTISM. (1) *The Appeal to the German Nobility* declared that elevation of the clergy over laity is wrong. Claims that the PAPACY is superior to the state, that only the pope can interpret Scripture, and that only the pope can call a council are also false. Every Christian is part of the body of Christ by baptism. The parts have different functions, but none is spiritually superior to another. Every vocation is sacred. Christians are a priesthood of believers. All parts contribute to the common good. The baker's job is spiritually equal to the priest's. Luther called on the nobility to function as Christians by curbing abuses of the church. (2) *The Babylonian Captivity* maintained that only baptism and the Lord's Supper are truly SACRAMENTS instituted by Christ. Luther painted transubstantiation and denial of the cup to the laity as captivities to increase the clergy's power. Thus Luther rejected the medieval church's claims to control over society through the sacraments. (3) *The Liberty of a Christian Man* set a basic ethical standard for Protestants. The Christian is both free and bound. He is free because he is saved by faith, not by a multitude of required good works. He is bound because he does good works out of joy and gratitude for what God has done.

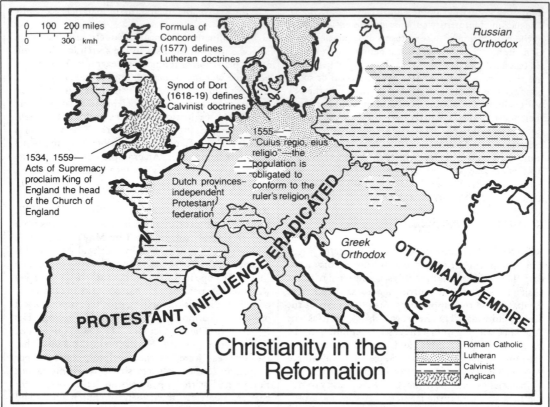

Formula of Concord (1577) defines Lutheran doctrines

Synod of Dort (1618-19) defines Calvinist doctrines

1534, 1559— Acts of Supremacy proclaim King of England the head of the Church of England

Dutch provinces— independent Protestant federation

1555— "Cuius regio, eius religio"—the population is obligated to conform to the ruler's religion

Russian Orthodox

Greek Orthodox

OTTOMAN EMPIRE

PROTESTANT INFLUENCE ERADICATED

## Christianity in the Reformation

Roman Catholic
Lutheran
Calvinist
Anglican

Reprinted with permission of the Macmillan Publishing Company, from *Macmillan Atlas History of Christianity* by Franklin H. Littell. Copyright © 1976 by Carta Ltd.

*Christendom in the late sixteenth century*

Luther already stood excommunicated by the papal bull *Exsurge Domine,* June 15, 1520. After it reached him, he publicly burned it on December 10, 1520, and was summoned to the Diet of Worms, 1521, to justify his actions. Luther declared he would not retract anything unless proved wrong by Scripture and right reason: "Here I stand, so help me God." The Diet of Worms condemned Luther, but sufficient political strength rallied behind him to forestall enforcement. CHARLES V, elected emperor in 1519, was too busy with other affairs to press against Luther.

In 1526 Charles V granted the Lutheran evangelicals freedom to pursue their religious convictions until a council could settle matters. This freedom was withdrawn in 1529. The Lutherans protested, thus acquiring the name Protestants. At the Diet of Augsburg, 1530, with Luther still under excommunication, the Lutherans put forth their classical AUGSBURG CONFESSION, written largely by PHILIP MELANCHTHON. It is Protestantism's fundamental creed. Sympathetic princes used its doctrines in their territories, thus establishing territorial churches in Germany, with the princes as "necessary bishops."

With the Turks threatening Austria and other matters of state pressing, Emperor Charles V did not proceed with force against the Lutheran "heretics" until 1546, the year of Luther's death. The Lutheran

forces surrendered in 1547, but Charles could not force Catholicism on the populace. The Peace of Augsburg, 1555, recognized the right of the ruler, whether Lutheran or Catholic, to establish his religion in his territory. Churches had been formed in Germany, East Prussia, Denmark, Sweden, and Norway; and Lutheran ideas had spread throughout Europe.

With the power of the medieval church weakened in principle and in fact, other forms of Protestantism soon emerged.

*Zwinglianism.* ULRICH ZWINGLI (1484–1531) launched a reform movement in Switzerland. His study of the NT made him critical of Roman Catholic practices as early as 1516. As people's priest of the Great Minster Church in Zurich in 1518, he took the Bible as his guide and preached against indulgences and fasts. By 1522 the civil rulers of Zurich declared all religious customs had to be based solely on the Word of God. Zwingli's Sixty-seven Articles, 1523, broadened the reform. Zurich's rulers declared priests, nuns, and monks could marry and ordered ministers to preach from the Bible. Images were removed from churches; clerical robes were banned. Zwingli's disciples spread these reforms in other Swiss cities. Luther and Zwingli conferred on the Lord's Supper at Marburg, but disagreed. Zwingli held a memorial view of Christ's presence in the bread and wine. Zwinglianism had a proclivity toward HU-MANISM and RATIONALISM and passed into the PURITAN and REFORMED traditions.

*Anabaptism.* Early on Zwingli clashed with some of his co-workers over infant baptism. Conrad Grebel, Felix Manz, and some others closely studied the Bible. They found no infant baptism. They challenged Zwingli. Zwingli won in debate, January 17, 1525, and the civil authorities ordered parents the next day to baptize their infants. A death penalty for rebaptizing adults was passed in 1526, and in January 1527 Manz became Zurich's first victim. At Schleitheim in 1527 the Anabaptists issued a confession. They insisted on adult believer's baptism, separation from worldly activity, congregational polity, non-participation in war and government, and no swearing of oaths. Thousands suffered death from Zwinglian, Lutheran, and Catholic rulers, who regarded separation of church and state as treason. BALTHASAR HUBMAIER wrote the first plea for religious toleration in this period in 1524. This group was severely discredited by extremists at Münster in 1534-35, but continue today as the MENNONITES and HUTTERITES. Separation of church and state, congregational rule, pacifism, and right of conscience in religion are among their legacies.

*Calvinism.* JOHN CALVIN did not initiate reform at Geneva, but with the publication of *The Institutes of the Christian Religion,* 1536, he became the leader. He established a theocracy in Geneva that became a model for Protestants in the Netherlands, West Germany, France, and Scotland. He stressed God's sovereignty, election, predestination, human sinfulness, discipline, and the will of God as he understood them according to the Bible. His logical theology appealed to the revolutionary elements rising in Europe. He made success a sign of God's blessing and strove to make everything glorify God. Calvin's emphasis on vocation as a means of changing the world and glorifying God helped Calvinists to control society. Although entangled with complicated politics, the HUGUENOTS expressed Calvinism in the French wars of religion. JOHN KNOX put Calvinism into nationalistic developments in Scotland, and Dutch Calvinists drew on nationalistic feelings to throw off the yoke of Spain. Calvinism displaced Lutheranism as the international expression of Protestantism.

*Socinianism.* The execution of MICHAEL SERVETUS in Geneva, 1553, caused a reaction to Calvin. Servetus used reason to judge the Bible and rejected the Trinity. Laelius and Faustus Socinus fostered this rationalism, and Faustus and others carried these ideas into Poland and Transylvania. Socinianism appeared in England as Unitarianism (*see* UNITARIAN UNIVERSALIST ASSOCIATION). Theophilus Lindsey founded the first Unitarian Church in London, 1774. The movement is known for individual freedom to seek religious truth through reason.

*Anglicanism.* Desiring royal supremacy, HENRY VIII overthrew the papacy in England, but remained Roman Catholic in doctrine. Protestantism took forward steps with THOMAS CRANMER under Edward VI, but Queen Mary temporarily reestablished Catholicism. Elizabeth I established a national church with her *via media,* a combination of Lutheran, Calvinistic, and Catholic elements. The defeat of the Spanish Armada in 1588 heightened English nationalism and clinched Elizabeth's ERASTIAN settlement.

Many forces converged to make the Reformation possible. The rapid spread of Protestant ideas attests their appeal and widespread discontent with Catholicism. Dissatisfaction had steadily mounted after the reforming COUNCIL OF CONSTANCE (1414–18). Erasmus and other humanists poured scorn on the church's immoralities and abuses. They especially censured popes Alexander VI, Innocent VIII, Julius II, and Leo X, and showed that some major church documents were forgeries. Peasants were restive and desirous of social and economic change, as seen in the Peasants' Revolt, 1524–25. Many scholars sought to return to Greek antiquity and primitive church purity. The church's dominance was deeply resented. By the end of the sixteenth century, a CATHOLIC REFORMATION had countered many Protestant gains and a series of reform-minded popes had strengthened the Catholic image once more.      C.M.

**REFORMED CHURCHES.** The various communions that developed during the Protestant REFORMATION and embraced the theological system and polity of JOHN CALVIN. The churches of this persuasion generally have been called "Reformed" if their origin was on the Continent and "Presbyterian" if they came into being in Scotland or England. "Reformed" refers to the distinctive theology of Calvinism and "Presbyterian" to polity—the form of church government by presbyters, or elders.

Reformed churches emerged in Holland, Germany, Switzerland, France, Hungary, and Scotland and, to a lesser extent, England produced Presbyterian churches. The first Reformed churches in America were established from 1628 onward by Dutch settlers in New Amsterdam. At first these churches were controlled by the Classis of Amsterdam in the Netherlands. The colonial churches did not become self-governing until the middle of the eighteenth century.

In the middle of the nineteenth century waves of Dutch immigrants settled in the Midwest, particularly in Michigan and Iowa. The Reformed churches in the eastern United States welcomed the immigrant groups and assisted them in various ways. Eventually the older and newer settlers formed a single denomination known today as the Reformed Church in America.

The Reformed type of Protestantism, distinguished from the LUTHERAN, became a separate communion in Germany's Palatinate in 1563. Later, other provinces of the Rhineland accepted the Reformed faith and the German Reformed church evolved. The German Reformed church was planted in the United States by German, Swiss, and a sprinkling of Dutch and Huguenot immigrants, who came to Pennsylvania and adjacent colonies in the early part of the eighteenth century. In the first groupings of Reformed churches both Germans and Dutch often were joined.

Through a series of denominational mergers the German Reformed church disappeared as a separate entity. Some German Reformed congregations were absorbed into the Presbyterian Church in the U.S.A., but a major union occurred when the Reformed group merged with the Evangelical Synod of North America in 1934 to form the Evangelical and Reformed church. Then later (1957) this church united with the Congregational Christian churches to form the United Church of Christ in America.

The largest segment of Reformed churches in the United States are the PRESBYTERIAN CHURCHES. As a result of the merger of the United Presbyterian Church in the U.S.A., with the (Southern) Presbyterian Church in the United States in 1982, the new Presbyterian church (U.S.A.) now lists 3¼ million communicants. There are six other Presbyterian bodies with a combined membership of more than 300,000.

The Reformed Church in America, with about 350,000 members, is the largest communion that contains "Reformed" in its official name. It is a vigorous denomination with two seminaries—New Brunswick Theological Seminary in New Jersey and Western Theological Seminary in Michigan and three colleges, Central and Northwestern in Iowa, and Hope in Michigan.

A group of Dutch immigrants settled in Michigan in 1846 and allied themselves with the Reformed Church in America. Unhappy with this relationship, they left it in 1857 and formed the Christian Reformed church, which today boasts a membership of well over 200,000 in the United States and another 80,000 in Canada. Says the noted church historian, Sydney E. Ahlstrom: "With a well supported church-school system and a strong intellectual and theological tradition nourished by Calvin College and Seminary in Grand Rapids, Michigan, the denomination has become the country's most solid and dignified bastion of conservative Reformed doctrine and church discipline."

There are Reformed churches in perhaps eighty nations of the world but the principal countries continuing to promote Calvinistic teaching and church order are the Netherlands, Scotland, Ireland, South Africa, Canada, and the United States.

The WORLD ALLIANCE OF REFORMED CHURCHES was formed in 1875 in London to foster cooperation and understanding between Reformed and Presbyterian churches around the globe. It is the oldest international confessional body, growing out of the revivals and missionary movements of the nineteenth century. In 1970 at Nairobi, Kenya, the alliance united with the International Congregational Council. Now the corporate designation is the World Alliance of Reformed Churches (Presbyterian and Congregational). R.H.

**REFORM JUDAISM.** *See* JUDAISM, HISTORY OF.

**REFUGE, CITIES OF.** Six cities appointed to give sanctuary to those who had killed accidentally: Kedesh, Shechem, and Hebron in Canaan; Bezer, Ramoth-gilead, and Golan across the Jordan to the east (Josh. 20:7-8). The purpose of these cities was to prevent revenge and encourage justice, that the murderer might not die before having faced the congregation for judgment (Num. 35:12).

Those who were found guilty were returned to their home towns to the avenger of blood. Those found innocent were to remain in the city of refuge until the death of the high priest, which was seen as a return of life for life. Those who left the city before the death of the high priest could be killed by the avenger (35:24-28). This detention not only protected the innocent but also atoned for and prevented further bloodguilt. The killing of an innocent person caused the land to be polluted (Deut. 19:10). B.J.

**REGENERATION.** The two occurrences of the word in the KJV are Matthew 19:28 (RSV "the new world") and Titus 3:5, literally "bath of rebirth," referring to Christian BAPTISM. Both texts speak of the new order of existence, both cosmic and personal, that is promised in the new age of Jesus Christ (see II Cor. 5:17). The term is basically a declaration of the new life to which Christians are called, since with Christ's advent a fresh start has been made to world history, in "the fulness of the time" (Gal. 4:4 KJV).

The verb "to be born again" (better, "born from above"; see NEB, which combines the two ideas in John 3:3, 7, by rendering "born over again") gives rise to the term "new birth," elaborated in I John 2:29; 3:9; 4:7; 5:1, 4, 18, thus making regeneration a particularly emphasized Johannine idiom. First Peter 1:3, 23, repeats the same idea. Christians are likened to newly born members of the divine family. Their new life is traced back to their baptism, which marks the death of the "old person" and the ushering of converts to a new way of living.

Paul's teaching is more complex, with more application to the life of the regenerate believers who are expected to act out their new life (Rom. 12:2; Col. 3:10) as part of God's new order (Gal. 6:15). The term "regeneration" corresponds to the NEW MAN of Ephesians 2:15; 4:24, made up of believing Jews and Gentiles based on Christ's RECONCILIATION, and certified in baptism (Tit. 3:5; compare I Pet. 3:21). Romans 6:1-14 is especially significant, with its insistence that Christians as raised to new life are committed to a new allegiance to Christ. They are to deem themselves "dead to sin," but "alive to God" in newness of life.

In theology regeneration has a wide range of meanings, extending from transference to the visible church by the rite of infant baptism (*in foro coeli*, that is, spiritually regenerate) to an admission to the fold of believers. In the former case, the teaching is historically known as baptismal regeneration and rests on the belief that the sacrament, when performed aright, has the power to confer what it signifies, namely regeneration or new birth of the child to God's family. The latter understanding professes to safeguard the sacrament by insisting on the need for faith, whether personal or corporate. If infant baptism as a means of regeneration requires the presence of faith, whether the child's incipient trust or the parents' pledge to bring up their offspring as Christian, the regeneration is treated as *in foro ecclesiae*, that is, baptism regenerates by placing the child within the sphere of the church's influence. The two views of regeneration are thus distinguished. On the one hand, regeneration denotes a real change in a person, although an infant. On the other, the child is placed in a believing atmosphere which, in later life, will ensure his or her full participation in Christ's body.                                                                R.M.

**REGIONAL MINISTER.** This term is employed by the CHRISTIAN CHURCH (Disciples of Christ) to describe the ecclesiastical administrative office of a minister charged with relationships with the pastors and churches of a geographical area. The regions may cover single states or several states as population dictates. In the congregational polity of the Christian Church, the regional minister does not exercise responsibility in a magisterial or authoritarian way. Besides conferring and counseling with churches seeking pastors, the regional minister gives similar help to ministers seeking places of service. The regional minister supports the program of the denomination in such areas as world mission support, leadership development, stewardship, and so forth. Similar nomenclature (regional executive minister) is employed by the United Church of Christ.      R.H.

**REHOBOAM.** King of Judah about 922–915 B.C.; son and successor of Solomon; first king of the southern kingdom. In Hebrew, Rehoboam can mean "may the people become greater." Solomon's son may have taken this name to indicate that he would not exert over his people the harsh kind of power of his father Solomon. Rehoboam became king at forty-one and reigned seventeen years (I Kings 14:21; II Chr. 12:13). But in time he became even harsher than his father, which led to the revolt of the north and the breakup of the kingdom. After the land was attacked by Egypt, Rehoboam began building cities for defense in Judah (II Chr. 11:5-12). For three years Rehoboam followed the teachings of the Lord; then he turned away, and all the people with him. The Lord let Shishak, king of Egypt, come in and take away the treasures of the Lord's house (II Chr. 12:1-12).
                                                                                B.J.

**REINCARNATION.** A belief that the soul, spirit, or essential self, bearing personality traits and one's debit sheet of merit and demerit, passes into another body after death, perhaps after time in an intermediate state. Belief in reincarnation is widespread but is most central to HINDUISM and BUDDHISM, and the smaller religions of India such as JAINISM and SIKHISM. Through Buddhist influence, reincarnation has been important as a belief in China and Japan, including the "new religions" of Japan, but has had to come to terms with indigenous ANCESTOR VENERATION and worship of Shinto KAMI.

Reincarnation is widely held in primitive religion, typically in the simple form of belief that the same souls may be reborn over and over in the same tribe, or that dead children may be reborn as subsequent offspring of the same mother or of relatives. In Hinduism, the JIVA or particularized soul is thought to be reborn lifetime after lifetime in accordance with one's KARMA, until MOKSHA or liberation is finally won. Reincarnation is often viewed as a theoretical rationale for the caste system, since one's status in it is seen as the result of karma carried over from previous lives. It is also seen as an expresson of SAMSARA—the world as fundamentally in a state of transitoriness and flux.

In Buddhism, much the same view of reincarnation as an articulation of karma and samsara obtains. But Buddhism rejects the Hindu caste system and philosophically asserts that there is no actual entity that is reincarnated, but rather an ongoing process of karmic energy. Reincarnation has generally not been accepted by normative Jewish thought, but it has a place in the mystical cabalistic tradition as the concept of *gilgul*, "wave."

In the classical world, reincarnation found expression in Platonic philosophy and in such mystery religions as Orphism. Later it appeared in quasi-Christian Gnosticism and Manichaeism. But although belief in reincarnation was attributed to such highly Hellenistic Christian thinkers as Origen, it has been rejected by normative Christianity. In Islam also reincarnation has been accepted by certain fringe mystical schools, often influenced by Neoplatonism in the West and Hinduism in the East, but not by the main body of believers. Under the influence of movements like Theosophy, interest in reincarnation has shown a remarkable upswing in America and western Europe in the twentieth century.      R.E.

**RELATIVISM.** Relativism is the notion that knowledge and/or values are not absolute but dependent upon related factors. Interrelated forms of relativism are: (1) historical and cultural, (2) epistemological, (3) ethical, and (4) religious.

Historical and cultural relativism emerged from the study of the past and other societies and affirms that human faith and values are conditioned by historical and sociocultural context. Marxist analysis emphasizes economic factors as determinative. Anthropological study shows how different cultural wholes shape the beliefs and actions of various societies.

Epistemological relativism holds that human knowing is conditioned by the viewpoint of the knower. Einstein's theory of relativity, formulated to apply in physics, is the most widely known and influential form of relativism and has served to emphasize the temporal and spatial relativity of all knowing.

Ethical relativism affirms, in parallel fashion, that human goals and rules of conduct are dependent upon the cultural context, and that the goodness and rightness of actions are relative to particular circumstances.

Religious relativism discloses the circular quality of relativism. On the one hand, faith in God, gods, or comparable ultimates emerges within specific sociocultural contexts. On the other hand, ethics, knowledge, and cultural/historical viewpoints are dependent upon the ultimate convictions that shape and validate them. The "personal knowledge" of Michael Polanyi's philosophy, with its fiduciary or tacit dimension, demonstrates appreciation of the circularity of relativism, as does the "theocentric relativism" of H. Richard Niebuhr in theology.

Relativism may be mistakenly identified with the recognition of a plurality of perspectives or with the notion that knowledge is only of relationships. If relativism is held as truth it tends toward an absolutism that is contradictory. (See also SITUATION ETHICS.)                                           C.Mc.

**RELICS.** Bones or personal articles belonging to departed saints, which in Roman Catholic theology are venerated, and with which many miracles of healing or divine help are associated in popular religion. The use of relics in devotion is traced to the solemn dignity given the bones of the martyred Polycarp by Christians in Smyrna in A.D. 156. So popular did relics—in the form of skulls, fingers, hands, and other body parts—become that the corpses of the saints were exhumed and dismembered, first in the East, and then, by the seventh century, in the West, although it was forbidden before that time in Rome. The Council of Nicaea in A.D. 787 legislated the presence of relics as necessary for the consecration of a church. Each altar was constructed with a relic box within it to sanctify it. Although ICONS were more popular in the East, the Council of Constantinople ratified the veneration of relics in A.D. 1084 for the Eastern churches.

Roman Catholics explain the practice of venerating the saints by declaring that it has biblical sanction in II Kings 2:14 and 13:21, which report miracles brought about through Elijah's mantle and even Elisha's bones. In the NT there are reports of people being healed by contact with handkerchiefs that had been on Paul's person (Acts 19:12). This biblical material is similar to the healings and other miracles said to occur through relics throughout Christian history. Catholics argue that since the Lord works miracles through such remains of believers now with God in heaven, then those remains ought to be venerated. Almost every large cathedral contains relics, some of which are only occasionally put on public display for veneration, such as the Shroud of Turin in Italy or the body of St. Francis Xavier in Goa, India.

During the Crusades, thousands of relics were brought back to Europe, many of them counterfeits. Because relics foster superstition, many abuses arose. Perhaps the worst case was the displaying of relics and sale of indulgences in Germany in the early sixteenth century. Martin Luther reacted sharply against these abuses, denouncing them in the Ninety-Five theses. Thus the abuses connected to relics contributed to the coming of the Protestant Reformation. Protestantism rejected the veneration of relics entirely.         J.C.

**RELIGION, STUDY OF.** Since the nineteenth century the study of religion or the "science of religion" has been distinguished from the study of THEOLOGY. The latter frequently refers to inquiry in a particular confessional tradition, for example, Roman Catholic or Lutheran. The former is concerned with the investigation of religion as a universal human phenomenon and with the common religious elements that can be observed in preliterate, archaic, and advanced cultures.

Study of the gods and religious mythology can be traced back to classical Greece. However, the science of religion as we know it today dates from the nineteenth century. Max Müller (1823–1900), the German-educated Oxford Sanskrit scholar and philologist, was responsible for the adoption and present use of the terms "science of religion" and "comparative study of religion." He also is considered the father of the scientific study of religion. Between the 1860s and 1920s there was a great burst of interest in the application of the new sciences to the investigation of religion. Scholars were especially interested in seeking out the origin of religion and its evolutionary development, as well as the comparative study of religious phenomena. This new interest is traceable to several factors: (1) the emergence of such new sciences as sociology, anthropology, and psychology; (2) the sudden availability of valuable new information, including archaeological evidence, which shed light on the religions of ancient Egypt, Greece, Rome, Babylonia, and the Semitic religions of Syria and Palestine; (3) the rapid expansion of the European colonial empires, which brought with it an enormous increase of information concerning the preliterate and archaic cultures and religions of Africa, India, Asia, and Oceana; this new information came to the attention of scholars through the reports of explorers, civil servants, traders, and missionaries; and (4) the availability, for the first time, of translations of many of the important sacred texts of Iran, India, China, and Japan, exemplified in Max Müller's editorship of the fifty-one-volume series, *The Sacred Books of the East,* which was begun in 1870.

The first chair of the History of Religions was founded at Geneva in 1873. In 1876 four chairs were established in Holland at the universities of Amsterdam, Groningen, Leiden, and Utrecht. Dutch scholars have continued as leaders in the field ever since. In 1885 a special faculty for the Religious Sciences was organized at the Sorbonne in Paris. In 1880 the *Revue de l'Histoire des Religions* was founded in Paris. The best-known current journal in the field, *Numen* (1954), is published by the International Association for the History of Religions. The first International Congress for the Sciences of Religion was held in 1897 at Stockholm. Among the earliest reference works and encyclopedias reflecting the influence of this new science were Hastings' *Encyclopedia of Religion and Ethics* (13 vols.; 1908–23) and *Die Religion in Geschichte und Geganwart* (5 vols.; 1909–13).

Due largely to the influence of the evolutionary theories of Auguste Comte and Charles Darwin, many of the pioneers in the science of religion were absorbed by the question of religious origins and development. Among the earliest was Edward Burnett Tylor (1832–1917), whose *Primitive Culture* (1871) proposed animism, or the belief that everything is endowed with a soul, as the origin of religion. Sir James George Frazer, in *The Golden Bough* (1890; 3rd ed. 1907–13, in 12 volumes), suggested that religion emerged as a result of the failure of primitive magic. In 1900, R. R. Marett and others contended that the beginning of religion was to be found in the pre-animistic experience of a pervasive, impersonal force, which the Melanesian natives called *mana.* Andrew Lang (1844–1912) and Wilhelm Schmidt (1868–1954) attacked the theory of animism, but from a different point of view. Both scholars discovered a belief in supreme beings in numerous primitive cultures. Schmidt sought to demonstrate the fact of what he called "primordial monotheism" in *Der Ursprung der Gottesidee (The Origin of the Idea of God,* 12 vols.; 1912–55). The biblical scholar J. Robertson Smith (1846–94), in *The Religion of the Semites* (1889), and the sociologist Emile Durkheim (1858–1917), in *The Elementary Forms of the Religious Life* (1916), claimed that the earliest-known expression of religion is found in the social function of totemism. However, by the second decade of this century, field research had largely discredited these theories and had shown the futility of the search for origins. Interest shifted to the historical, functional, and phenomenological study of religions.

The most important contributions to the scientific study of religion in this century would include the work of the sociologists MAX WEBER and ERNST TROELTSCH, the psychological studies of WILLIAM JAMES and CARL JUNG, and the work of the anthropologists Lucien Levy-Bruhl (1857–1939), Bronislaw Malinowski (1884–1942), Robert Lowie (1883–1957), Paul Radin (1883–1959) and, more recently, E. E. Evans-Pritchard (1902–73) and C. Levi-Strauss (1908–    ).

The phenomenological study of religion has produced some of the most valuable scientific work. This would include Rudolf Otto's (1869–1937) *The Idea of the Holy* (Eng. ed. 1923), Gerardus van der Leeuw's (1890–1950) *Religion in Essence and Manifestation* (Eng. ed. 1938), W. Brede Kristensen's (1867–1953) *The Meaning of Religion* (Eng. ed. 1960), Joachim Wach's (1898–1955) *Types of Religious Experience* (1951) and *The Comparative Study of Religions* (1958), and the numerous works of Mircea Eliade (1907–    ) including *Patterns in Comparative Religion* (1958) and *The Sacred and the Profane* (1959). (See also WORLD RELIGIONS.)                                             J.L.

**RELIGIOUS EXPERIENCE.** Religious experience is usually regarded as personal, involving a relationship to the divine Other, or God. Religious experience includes the whole person, but uppermost is an awareness of the emotions and senses: sight, sound, touch, smell, and taste. Signs made and attitudes assumed express feelings through the senses and heighten experience. The objective is to stir emotions of yearning, guilt, repentance, love, and joy. Reflection on the experience is an intellectual work and helps to form the understanding of who God is and how God acts in relation to the individual and the world.

Religious experience has an individual component but is also known through corporate worship and may be strengthened through the awareness of a religious community's singing, praying, and reenacting rituals. The individual is both strengthened by the group and more closely related to it through shared worship. There is the further possibility of deepened relationships to other individuals and a satisfying integration of the self.

The nature of the relationship sought with the Transcendent varies with the personality of the individual. Some seek a strong authority figure to give reassurance and direction. Others seek a flexible figure who invites openness and exploration. Each person hopes for freedom through a different route. Some, more aware of the dark side of life and the self, struggle in their religious experience against darkness, separation, and even a sense of temporary abandonment while yet believing that God is present. Others, temperamentally attuned to the sunny side of life, develop an uncomplicated trusting relationship to God with little turmoil.

To speculate on the needs out of which the quest for religious experience arises borders on the philosophical. For some there is a yearning for completeness, arising from the awareness of the difference between being human and being empowered by God. Others, overwhelmed by a sense of guilt (which is sometimes pathological), seek forgiveness and reconciliation. VICTOR FRANKL speaks of the search for meaning. ABRAHAM MASLOW speaks of self-actualization as the apex of the values on a ladder of need fulfillment. Some seek a direction for life, motivated not only by a desire for order but from a belief that goodness and self-transcendence in loving service is the basic way to self-fulfillment. Others seek a relationship to God—the saint's desire to know and love God for love's sake alone, without fear of hell or hope for heaven.

For some people religious experience is a discovery. They seek God, sometimes with great difficulty and loneliness, fighting the shadows until the light appears. They take the initiative, and God is both the objective and the fulfillment of their search. Others affirm that their religious experience was initiated by God, revealed through God's action in Scripture, an exemplar, the created world, or some personal sign. Their desire is active, but their response is that of passive waiting. They are found by God rather than seeking God.

One of the most studied aspects of religious experience has been that of CONVERSION, beginning with the work of E. D. Starbuck in 1899 and continued by G. Stanley Hall in his classic study of adolescence. WILLIAM JAMES in *The Varieties of Religious Experience* devotes careful attention to this phenomenon.

Conversion literally means "a turning around" and indicates a change in life direction. Frequently, as a religious experience, it has been a dramatic, even cataclysmic, event of life-shaking proportions to the convert and a source of awed astonishment to onlookers. Some forms of Protestant Christianity have expected this kind of experience as indication of a changed life. In this theology, each person needs to hear proclaimed the gospel that the death and resurrection of Jesus Christ brought redemption from sin. This redemption must be appropriated personally through a conviction of sin, deep remorse, repentance, and full confession. The result is a sense of release and joy that signals entrance into the redeemed life. While this experience can occur in private, it frequently occurs at a public meeting. Repeated personal conversation with a believer will sometimes bring this response. The whole setting of a revival meeting is directed toward this end: singing, preaching, prayer, testimonies, exhortation, and invitation. The result for the convert is a sense of peace with God and acceptance into a community of faith. In surrender to God there is release from the sense of sin and guilt, and a new direction for life. The person is now committed to Jesus Christ for life.

Conversion can also be a gradual process in which a person becomes aware of deeper commitment and/or change of direction only in retrospect. The process is motivated by the same needs for wholeness and relationship. Some of the same factors of personal and group persuasion may be present in a quieter way. Some religious groups consider this the normative form of conversion. Others reject it as not being manifest enough to give witnesses certainty that anything critical has happened.

Religious experience is both developed and expressed through prayer. The primary motivation is for an ever closer relationship to God as the source of life and love. To the believer, strength for everyday living comes through the power given by God. Thanksgiving expresses joy for gifts received and acknowledges that God is the giver of all. Adoration and praise celebrate not only the Being of God but the active divine presence in the life of the believer. Petition and intercession affirm the power of God to act in the lives of people and societies in response to the request of those in need. Some dimensions of prayer are beyond psychological probing. In fact prayer seems odd to a rational world view that affirms a cause and effect universe even while leaving space for indeterminism.

Hence a study of MEDITATION indicates many forms of the art practiced by those with no belief in the Transcendent. Meditation can be self-suggestion, a way of relaxing and reflecting that renews the physical, mental, and emotional powers of the practitioner. Many forms of meditation are currently popular that use classical religious techniques with no divine reference. To the religious person, however, the experience of prayer is deepened through the practice of meditation. Many of the classical writers on prayer have offered methods. Basically these stress ways in which the goal is a self-emptying and an awareness of God that goes beyond speech or image, or ways that imply the visualization of events, or words on which to concentrate in a reaching out toward God. Meditation, while drawing the believer into a deeper awareness of relationship to God, makes the person sensitive to the purposes of God for life, open to strengthening through divine power and clearer direction for action.

Meditation is a widely practiced way of prayer, but the mystical experience lies even deeper. Some people seem able to transcend the self and enter into a sense of union with God that they liken to the union of two persons in marriage, but which is recognized to be a deeply interior experience. In all religions, this is considered the apex of spirituality, differing both in kind and degree from the ordinary experiences of relationship to the Divine through prayer. This is a state of awareness not easily reached and not lightly held. It involves struggle, long periods of waiting, and an awesome sense of being close to the Holy. St. John of the Cross speaks of the "dark night of the soul" during which there is only waiting. Christians have known ever since the witness of the apostle Paul about such experiences. Within Judaism the Hasidic tradition conveys the mystical sense of joyous abandonment to the presence of God. Among

Muslims the Sufis express the mystical dimension. There is also a mystical tradition in both Buddhism and Hinduism.

MYSTICISM includes a sense of the Spirit of God working in the world. The Pentecostal tradition has taken many forms through the centuries and there is a renewed surge today, not only among traditional Pentecostal groups but also in mainline traditions and independent congregations.

Religious experience is also evidenced in techniques for heightened awareness, notably among some cultic groups, in the use of drugs with specifically religious intent and usually within a communal liturgical setting. Parapsychology provides for some another avenue for religious experience, as people seek communication with those who have died, develop an elevated sense of personal immortality, become aware of a power to know events happening elsewhere or that will happen in the future. Some seek deeper understanding of God's will through dreams—a biblical practice recently attracting new interest in some circles.       I.C.

**RELIGIOUS LIBERTY.** *See* LIBERTY, RELIGIOUS.

**RELIGIOUS ORDERS.** *See* ORDERS AND ORDINATION.

**REMISSION OF SINS.** *See* FORGIVENESS.

**REMNANT.** The remaining group of people that continue the life of the community after some traumatic event. Throughout the OT and NT there appears a small remnant remaining faithful to the Lord God.

*Remnant in the Old Testament:*

*Noah.* The earliest reference to a remnant is in the story of the Flood: "He blotted out every living thing. . . . Only Noah was left, and those that were with him in the ark" (Gen. 7:23).

*Lot.* When God indicated that the wicked city of Sodom was about to be destroyed, Abraham asked that the righteous be spared. Only Lot, his wife, and their two daughters were rescued, and his wife lost her life shortly thereafter (Gen. 18:17–19:29).

*Jacob.* When he went to meet Esau after having stolen the birthright many years earlier, Jacob divided his large company of people and animals into two groups so that if Esau's forces attacked one group the other might survive (Gen. 32:6-12).

*Joseph.* When famine struck his land, Jacob sent ten of his sons to Egypt to purchase food, but kept one of his sons, Benjamin, at home in case something should happen to the others (Gen. 42:1-38).

*Moses.* The pharaoh ordered all Israelite male children killed at birth, but Moses' mother hid him in the bulrushes, saving his life (Exod. 1:8–2:10).

*Isaiah.* The prophet, at the Lord's direction, named his son Shear-jashub, "a remnant will return" (from exile, to the Lord) (Isa. 7:3).

*Remnant in the New Testament:*

*John the Baptist.* The forerunner of Jesus called all people to repent (John 1:6-8) but knew that not all might choose to do so (Matt. 3:1-12).

*Jesus.* While he called all to repent and believe the good news (Mark 1:14-15), Jesus knew that not everyone would want to "enter by the narrow gate" (Matt. 7:13-14). The faithful will be a remnant (Matt. 22:14). Jesus said that at the end of time his reapers will separate the weeds from the wheat, and only the wheat will remain (Matt. 13:24-30).

*Paul.* In Romans 9–11 Paul quotes Isaiah: "For though your people Israel be as the sand of the sea, only a remnant of them will return" (Isa. 10:22; Rom. 9:27). There is, Paul says, a remnant, chosen by grace (Rom. 11:5).

*John of Revelation.* In writing to the seven churches, John addresses the faithful remnant at Thyatira (2:24-25) and calls the faithful in Sardis to awake from deadness and stir up the remnant of their faith (3:1-2). In 11:13 he speaks of a remnant surviving a devastating earthquake and giving glory to God; and in 12:17; and 13:11-18 of the persecution of the faithful remnant.       B.J.

**REMONSTRANCE, THE** A theological platform presented by followers of ARMINIUS in 1610. This platform was directed to the Estates of Holland and contained five points rejecting the doctrine of Calvinism on predestination. The Remonstrance claimed predestination is not absolute but conditional on the human response of faith. It denied the concept of the limited atonement, that is, that Christ died only for the elect, and held that Christ died for all, so all could, in theory, be saved. While affirming free will, it held that free will could not choose to do God's will unless it was first given God's grace. This grace is not irresistible, however, so it may be accepted or rejected. (*See* DORT, SYNOD OF.)       J.C.

**RENAISSANCE, CHRISTIANITY IN THE.** The Renaissance (meaning "rebirth") extended roughly from 1350 to 1550, during which time SCHOLASTICISM, feudalism, and church dominance declined, and HUMANISM, individualism, and nationalism emerged as dominant factors in European culture. Centered in Italy, the Renaissance reached spectacular artistic heights in the fifteenth century, was carried by humanist scholars beyond Italy, and then experienced decline as the Protestant Reformation erupted.

The first hundred years of the Renaissance found the papacy, Christendom's highest office, in disarray. NOMINALISM'S Duns Scotus, William of Ockham, and others attacked Aquinas' system by saying abstract eternal forms were simply names, without the reality of particular things, thus impugning all value assertations. French domination during the Babylonian Captivity (1305–77) made claims of papal superiority sound hollow. The Great Schism (1378–1415), with popes at both Avignon and Rome claiming primacy, shattered confidence in papal authority. The reforming Council of Pisa (1409) then elected another pope without unseating the other two, thus embarrassing Christendom with the spectacle of three supreme authorities. JOHN WYCLIFFE and JOHN HUSS raised strong nationalistic voices of protest. Mysticism, a subtler protest, increased in popularity and further eroded ecclesiastical power by stressing simple Christian living and seeking more direct contact with the Divine. Its leaders included MEISTER ECKHART, JOHN TAULER, Henry Suso, Gerhard Groot, and THOMAS À KEMPIS. The Brethren of the Common Life and other semi-mystic groups called for inward transformation and popularized a new devotion (DEVOTIO MODERNA) that emphasized plain, undogmatic Christianity. Conciliarists Conrad of Gelnhausen, Heinrich of Langenstein, Pierre D'Ailley, Jean Gerson, and others clamored for reform through a council, and national states repeatedly challenged papal superiority. Although the Council of Constance (1414–17) unseated Christendom's three popes, elected Martin V, and declared conciliarism the supreme church authority, a buffeted papacy by 1460 had reclaimed power and made appeal to a council cause for excommunication.

Out of this turmoil the Renaissance came. Papal ecclesiasticism was no longer satisfactory. Scholars turned to ancient Greece and Rome for new views and secular values. FRANCESCO PETRARCH (1304–74), who molded the modern Italian language, and Giovanni Boccaccio, author of *The Decameron,* a forerunner of novels that virtually ignored Christianity, are credited with initiating the Renaissance. Petrarch wrote three hundred Italian sonnets to a married woman and collected old manuscripts. Boccaccio ignored Christianity in his frank celebration of worldly joys. Both bypassed medieval Christianity and looked to classical culture for inspiration—a characteristic that proved central in the Renaissance.

The fall of Constantinople to the Turks in 1453 causing Greek refugees to disperse, the invention of printing, new ways of making paper, the discovery of America, the circumnavigation of the globe, the mariner's compass, and new theories from Copernicus and Galileo stimulated intellectual interest not only in the past but in the present. Man as the measure of man gradually dominated, not the church, hence the term "humanism." LORENZO VALLA and NICHOLAS OF CUSA demonstrated that the Donation of Constantine, which gave Western Europe to the church, was a forgery. Perhaps other documents were also spurious. Ancient Greek, Roman, and Hebraic origins promised new beginnings.

With scholars like Lino Salutati (1331–1406), Leonardo Bruni (1369–1444), Marsilio Ficino (1433–99), and others, Florence soon had a complete translation of Plato's works and consciously modeled itself on Greek culture. Other cities followed. Patrons

of art like the Medici in Florence, the Sforza family in Milan, and the dukes of Urbino surrounded themselves with poets, painters, sculptors, architects, and scholars—all vying with one another for Renaissance magnificence. Painting, sculpture, and architecture reached spectacularly creative heights in MICHELANGELO, Raphael, Andrea del Sarto, and LEONARDO DA VINCI. Religious subjects were not neglected, but secular objects gained in prominence, marking a drift toward earthly emphases.

Despite much anticlericalism and worldliness in the Renaissance, the papacy, after weathering its multiple popes and conciliarism, belatedly became an important patron of Renaissance culture. Pope Nicholas V (1447–55) helped found the Vatican Library and commissioned scores of scholars to find manuscripts and make translations. Sixtus IV (1471–84) commissioned the Sistine Chapel with its magnificent acoutrements. Julius II (1503–13) undertook to rebuild St. Peter's and employed such personages as Bramante, Michelangelo, and Raphael. Leo X (1513–21), who never understood the Luther "squabble" in Germany, encouraged Renaissance arts and literature with generous patronage. However, religious dedication was lacking. The papacy, despite its patronage, seemed more concerned to enhance its political prestige and power. The papacy was rife with nepotism, immoralities, political intrigue, financial abuses, wars, and ornate living. Several popes, notably Alexander VI (1492–1503), openly promoted their children's welfare. The Renaissance popes seemed unable to comprehend the widespread discontent with ecclesiastical control and the significance of social changes taking place. Catholic French King Charles VIII, seeing little difference between the papacy and other rulers, invaded Italy in 1494, and Emperor Charles V's Catholic forces sacked Rome in 1527. These invasions diminished Italy's role in the Renaissance, and attention shifted to outside Italy.

During the height of the Renaissance, scores of scholars visited Italy and returned home imbued with zeal for studies of ancient Greece and Rome, soon enlarged to include Christian and Hebraic origins. Johann Reuchlin especially promoted Hebrew in Germanic areas. Among the scholars who visited Italy and returned home were William Grocyn, Thomas Linacre, and John Colet from England; Rudolph Agricola, Conrad Celtis, Ulrich von Hutten, and Albrecht Dürer from Germany; and many others. Biblical and patristic studies tended to predominate outside Italy. Preeminent among northern humanists was ERASMUS of Rotterdam, who combined piety and classical learning to rejuvenate church and society. His Greek NT (1516) sought a purified biblical text as a beginning. His ecclesiastical criticisms attracted international attention, but Erasmus was not a radical reformer. He remained loyal to Roman Catholicism, as did many humanists after the clash with Luther in 1524–25. Nevertheless, humanism laid the intellectual foundations for the Protestant REFORMATION. In some, like Philip Melanchthon, Renaissance-Reformation currents combined, especially in education, but other forces, particularly Luther's justification by faith alone, brought basic reforms. The Renaissance was the Reformation's forerunner.     C.M.

**RENAN, ERNEST** (1823–92). French writer and student of religion who studied for the priesthood but turned away from the church when he became acquainted with biblical criticism. He wrote a series of books on the origins of Christianity, of which one (not the most scholarly) had tremendous popular appeal. This was his *Vie de Jésus (Life of Jesus)*, published in 1863 after a visit to the Holy Land. Though the book is marred in places by sentimentality, and is more a work of the imagination than a properly historical study, Renan does evoke a vivid picture of the human Jesus, first in the happy phase of his ministry in the idyllic surroundings of Galilee, then in the dramatically altered scenes of controversy with the religious establishment, culminating in the death on Calvary. In Schweitzer's judgment, "he offered his readers a Jesus who was alive—there is something magical about the work."     J.M.

**REORGANIZED CHURCH OF JESUS CHRIST OF LATTER-DAY SAINTS.** *See* CHURCH OF JESUS CHRIST OF LATTER-DAY SAINTS.

**REPENTANCE.** A word used mainly by Christians, most frequently by Protestant evangelicals, for personal, religious CONVERSION.

The idea of repentance is expressed in the OT by the word "turn"—turn from all else in order to turn to God. "Turn back from your evil ways; for why will you die?" (Ezek. 33:11; "return" Hos. 2:7; Mic. 7:17). The word "repent" is generally avoided in modern Judaism. Considered in its broadest meaning, repentance, whether the word is used or not, is part of many living world religions whenever better ways of life are shown and people are encouraged to choose these ways and not to follow others.

Jesus' parable of the prodigal son (Luke 15:11-32) gives graphic symbols of repentance and non-repentance. The younger son repented and returned to find his father waiting to restore him to the family. The elder son did not leave home but fostered such an unforgiving and unsympathetic spirit that he was kept from a harmonious relationship with his family.

John the Baptist's preaching and baptism centered on repentance (Matt. 3:8, 11; Mark 1:4; Luke 3:8). Jesus' public preaching began with a call to his hearers to repent (Matt. 11:17; Mark 1:15, also Luke 5:32; 15:7; 24:47). The early church continued calling people to repent (Acts 2:3, 8; 3:19; 17:30; 26:20), using the baptism of repentance (Acts 13:24; 19:4) and striving "that all should reach repentance" (II Pet. 3:9). The Revelation made clear the consequences of non-repentance while sounding the call to repent (2:5, 16; 3:3).

Christians do not view repentance as an end in itself. Rather, it is a requisite for positive belief. Jesus' first preaching was, "Repent, and believe in the gospel" (Mark 1:15). Belief, in this sense, is a positive acceptance of Jesus Christ as Lord, a commitment that enables that good way of living called in the Gospels "fruits that befit repentance" (Matt. 3:8; Luke 3:8).     P.L.G.

**REPHAIM.** A biblical term used in three apparently unrelated ways.

(1) A prehistoric, legendary people associated with such non-Israelite people as Hittites, Perezites, Moabites, Ammonites, and, particularly, with the Anakim. The Rephaim were "a people great and many, and tall as the Anakim" (Deut. 2:21). Og, king of Bashan, is said to be of the Rephaim. His iron bedstead, preserved for a long time, measured 14½ feet by 6 feet (Deut. 3:11). "Bashan is called the land of Rephaim" (Deut. 3:13).

(2) The valley or vale of Rephaim is located southwest of Jerusalem and north of Bethlehem (Josh. 15:8; 18:16; II Sam. 5:18, 22; 23:13; I Chr. 11:5; 14:9; Isa. 17:5 where the growing of grain is mentioned). The valley formed part of the boundary between Benjamin and Judah.

(3) Rephaim as Hebrew "shades," or RSV "the dead" (Ps. 88:10; Prov. 9:18; 21:16; Job 26:5; Isa. 27:14). The connection may be that, in popular Hebrew thought, the Rephaim were a people who lived a long time ago and about whom little was known. There are references in the Ras Shamra texts to the Rephaim both as a clan and as a high-class guild connected with a royal fertility cult.     P.L.G.

**REQUIEM.** A mass, set to music, sung in commemoration of the dead in the Roman Catholic Church. The name "requiem" comes from the Introit, which begins, "Give them rest eternal, O Lord. . . ." The Requiem Mass (and there are many) is officially to be used only at funerals, on the anniversary of the death of the departed (funds are often deposited to pay for such anniversary masses each year), and on All Souls' Day, November 1. Interestingly, because of this limited use, the Requiem Mass was adapted to concert use. Beautiful musical masses were written by many outstanding musicians such as Guiseppe Verdi, and these masterpieces are often played by orchestras in concert. The addition of orchestral accompaniment was completed in the eighteenth century.     J.C.

**RERUM NOVARUM.** The encyclical letter of Pope LEO XIII published on May 15, 1891, which many regard as that pope's most important social pronouncement and the real entrance of the Vatican into the arena espousing social justice. While the letter was directed against certain forms of extant socialism and economic liberalism, the document imparted a strong impulse to the Christian social movement and social thought.

The pope examined the transfer of ownership to the state and rejected it on human, philosophical, and religious grounds. He then set out what he regarded as the true remedy by action of the church, of the state, of employers and employed. He maintained the priority of individuals and their families over the state, and their right by nature to possess property of their own in permanent possession. He asserted the right of workers to a living wage and reasonable comfort. The encyclical advised both employers and workers to organize into mixed and separate associations for mutual help and self-protection.

R.H.

**RESERVATION OF THE EUCHARIST.** The Roman Catholic practice of reserving or keeping the consecrated bread (or Host) from the Mass, originally for purposes of communing the sick, but also for devotional reasons, as in the adoration of the Blessed Sacrament. Reservation is an ancient tradition, as it is discussed by the church father Tertullian of North Africa. Justin Martyr, even earlier, speaks of retaining some of the consecrated elements in order to take Communion to the sick in their homes. Solitary monks and even private Christians reserved the bread in their homes until prohibited by the Council of Saragossa in A.D. 380. The adoration of the Sacrament was a later development, arising after TRANSUBSTAN-TIATION became the general theology of the Eucharist in the High Middle Ages.

At the Reformation, Martin Luther rejected the reservation of the Eucharist, and the practice did not become part of Protestantism. It was briefly permitted in the Church of England but was rejected by 1552 (the second prayer book). In recent years reservation has been revived by Anglicanism.

J.C.

**RESPONSIBILITY.** See FREEDOM; FREE WILL.

**RESTORATION, THE.** Primarily the reinstate-ment of the monarchy in England in 1660 under Charles II. After the Puritan Commonwealth and the protectorate of OLIVER CROMWELL, the monarchy was restored and the Anglican church reestablished. The "Restoration Period" usually includes the reigns of Charles II (1660–85) and James II (1685–88). Literature and science flourished in this period.

Restoration is also a term applied to the movement initiated by Thomas and ALEXANDER CAMPBELL to restore the patterns of primitive Christianity in the church. Their ideas came from two Old Scottish Independents in Scotland, John Glas and Robert Sandeman, who advocated weekly Communion, believers' baptism by immersion, and congregational independence. The Campbells formed the Disciples of Christ and the Churches of Christ.          N.H.

**RESTORATION OF ALL THINGS.** The "res-toration of all things" is an expression that occurs in the NT (Acts 3:21). The word translated "restora-tion" is *apokatastasis*, and it was used in secular contexts in many ways. It could mean, for instance, recovery from sickness or the return of the heavenly bodies to positions that they had occupied at some previous time. In any case, it meant the reversion to some earlier and desirable state of affairs. In the OT, we meet the idea of a return to a Golden Age and, on a more limited scale, the idea of a restoration of the Davidic kingdom. Among early Christian writers, Origen made significant use of the idea of a universal restoration. But while Chistians look in some sense for a final perfecting of the creation of Christ (*anakephalaiosis* is the word used in Eph. 1:10 and also by Irenaeus), the objection has been made that this is not merely a restoration and that what is promised is a *new* heaven and earth. Also the word "restoration" seems to imply that there was an original perfection. It might be replied that the restoration consists in the undoing of the history of sin and the realization of the potentiality that has always been there.          J.M.

**RESURRECTION OF JESUS.** That God raised Jesus from the dead is the central and distinctive claim of the early church, as evidenced in the NT. The earliest surviving witness to this claim is to be found in I Corinthians 15:3-9, where Paul declares that the tradition he received affirmed Jesus' death for the sins of his people and his having been raised from the dead—that is, by God. Although this letter was written in the early fifties A.D., Paul makes clear that he is passing on a set of convictions that had been passed on to. him, presumably at the time of his conversion, which could have been within a year or two of the Crucifixion itself. Similarly, in Philippians 2:9 and in Romans 1:4, Paul is apparently reproducing older hymnic or creedal tradition, which affirms that after Jesus' death on the cross he was exalted by God, and that his resurrection was the means by which God acclaimed Jesus as his Son. Thus the belief in the Resurrection goes back to the earliest years of the church's existence.

Paul further reports that the appearances of the Risen Jesus were not all private, individual experi-ences, but that they took place in groups ranging in size from "the twelve" (I Cor. 15:5) to "more than five hundred" (15:6). His own encounter with the resurrected Christ (15:8) may be identical with the experience he describes in Galatians 1:16, when God "was pleased to reveal his Son to [or in] me." In both the I Corinthians account and this one in Galatians, the appearances of Christ are linked with his being commissioned to carry out the church's mission to the Gentiles. He observes that both the death and the resurrection of Jesus are "in accordance with the scriptures," which is a surprising claim since there is almost no direct mention of the RESURRECTION OF THE DEAD in the OT. The few scriptures to which Paul does make reference in this connection have to do with the exaltation of Jesus, rather than with his resurrection as such. Of paramount importance for Paul is that the resurrection of Jesus makes possible the moral renewal and transformation of God's new people, who are invited to share in the new life of obedience and victory over sin, which Jesus' resurrection has made possible and for which it is a model (Phil. 3:10; Rom. 6:5; II Cor. 4:10).

One striking detail of the resurrection tradition, which Paul draws upon in I Corinthians 15, is the claim that Jesus was raised "on the third day." That tradition may be based on a historical tradition as to when the appearances began, or it may derive from the prophecy of Hosea 6:2 (which predicts that God will restore people "on the third day"), or it may represent an effort to demonstrate that the Resurrection took place in space and time, rather than as a merely inner or spiritual experience. Or it may be a combination of these factors. Unlike Paul, the Gospels all point initially to the emptiness of the tomb of Jesus on the morning after the Sabbath (Mark 16:1, 6; Matt. 28:1, 5, 6; Luke 24:1, 2; John 20:1), which by Jewish calculation would be "the third day."

Another form of pre-Pauline tradition that presupposes Jesus' being restored to life, without actually referring to the Resurrection, is the words of institution of the Lord's Supper, where reference is made to the restoration of fellowship with the disciples in the kingdom of God (Mark 14:25) or to his coming to them in the future (I Cor. 11:26). Apart from this feature of expectation of renewal of fellowship in the Age to Come, and the predictions that God will vindicate him by raising him from the dead (Mark 8:31; 9:31; 10:33, and parallels in Luke and Matt.), the Gospels differ from Paul and among themselves in their portrayal of the appearances of Jesus after his death.

In Mark, in addition to the predictions of his being raised just mentioned, there are promises that Jesus will resume his role as leader of the disciples (14:28; 16:7). His exaltation as SON OF MAN is announced in connection with his prediction of the Temple's destruction (13:26). But there is merely a description of the empty tomb, and no report of a post-Resurrection appearance. In Luke, however, there are several stories of his appearances to groups of followers (24:13-22), in which Jesus stresses that what has happened to him is in fulfillment of Scripture (24:26, 32), and that he is a tangible human being, as demonstrated by his sharing a meal with the disciples—one in which the traditional eucharistic words appear: took, blessed, broke, gave.

In Matthew more attention is given to the miraculous details that accompany the descriptions of the Risen Jesus: the earthquake and angelic visit when the stone is rolled back (28:2), the felling of the Roman guards (28:4). The message of the Resurrection is explicit (28:16-20). There is in addition an apologetic feature that discounts the charge of the detractors of the Christians' belief in the Resurrection by claiming that the followers stole his body from the tomb (28:11-15). In John's Gospel, the Resurrection is no surprise, since Jesus throughout the narrative announces his eternal existence (8:58), his identity as "the resurrection and the life" (11:25), and that his death is to be regarded as his glorification (13:31-33). It is assumed throughout that he will be raised (14:2-3, 19, 28; 17:1, 13), and his appearances are described in detail (20:11-18, 19-28, and in the epilogue, John 21).

In Acts, the Resurrection is appealed to primarily as proof that Jesus, the chosen instrument of God, has been exalted (Acts 1:3, 6:11), that his death was in fulfillment of Scripture (2:22-28), and that God has now glorified Jesus (3:13-15; 7:56; 10:40-41; 13:33-35). In the post-Pauline letters, Jesus' resurrection is described almost entirely in terms of his exaltation as the triumphant agent of God who establishes God's rule in the Creation (Eph. 1:19-23; Col. 2:9-13). In I Peter the Resurrection is the ground of the new birth of Christians (I Pet. 1:3-7), and in Revelation, Christ is depicted as the Lamb that was slain, who is now exalted in the presence of God and who is God's agent to defeat the powers of evil and bring to earth the City of God, in which God dwells in the midst of people (Rev. 21). In spite of the variety of images, therefore, the different NT writers share the conviction that the resurrection of Jesus is both the instrument of and the demonstration of his role as the one through whom God's kingdom is established in the earth.                                        H.K.

**RESURRECTION OF THE DEAD.** The belief in the resurrection of the dead began to develop in Jewish thinking only in the two centuries before the birth of Jesus. The earlier view of human existence assumed that God had animated human beings by a divine breath or Spirit (Gen. 2:7) and that in death the Spirit returned to God and the body was placed in its eternal home (Eccl. 12:5-7). A common way to describe death was joining one's ancestors in sleep, as David (I Kings 2:10), Solomon (I Kings 11:43), and Hezekiah (II Chr. 32:33) had done. There was no notion that these would awaken from that everlasting sleep. The abode of the dead was known as SHEOL, and was pictured as a vast underground tomb, where those who once lived are only shadows, where "maggots are the bed beneath you, and worms are your covering" (Isa. 14:11). This attitude toward the fate of the dead was shared with other cultures in Mesopotamia. Nevertheless, in some of the Psalms there are occasional expressions of hope for a share in the life of God beyond death, as in Psalms 16:10; 73:23-26. These remain undeveloped themes until the second century B.C.

Jewish thinking about the future of human existence was stimulated and challenged by alien religious and philosophical influences as well as the nation's bitter disappointment with the priestly Hasmonean family who, under the Maccabees, had gained political independence and freedom of worship for the Jews, but who had become secular, ruthless, and dependent on foreign powers. This tragic experience raised the questions, Is God just? Does God reward those who seek to obey God's laws, who endure martyrdom rather than dishonor the divine name?

The dominant religion of Persia during the period of Israel's exile in Babylon seems to have been what is now called Zoroastrianism, the doctrines of which included the concept of the supreme god overcoming the powers of evil by establishing the rule of righteousness and vindicating the faithful, who would be restored to life in a renewed creation. The Greek belief in the IMMORTALITY of the soul, in contrast to the decay and disappearance of the body, also had its influence on Jewish thinking in this period. No uniform pattern emerged, however, and it is impossible to determine how widespread interest was in the questions about life beyond death.

In the OT, the only clear statement about resurrection is in Daniel 12:2, where both the righteous and the disobedient are raised, the first group to everlasting life and the second to divine judgment. Less explicit, but seemingly pointing in the same direction, is Isaiah 26:19, which is part of an apocalyptic section of Isaiah in which assurance is offered to those who are suffering for their fidelity to Yahweh, the God of Israel. The period of divine wrath will soon be over and the divine vindication will follow.

Those Jews who were most open to the intellectual appeal of Greek philosophy incorporated the concept of the immortality of the soul into their hopes for future reward, as is most evident in the Wisdom of Solomon, where "blameless souls" are said to have been created in the image of God's own immortality (2:21-24), and where "the souls of the righteous" are to share in God's eternal rule over the Creation (3:1-8). In other Jewish writings of this period there is a clear belief in a bodily resurrection to share in the time of future blessing: II Baruch 50–51, for example, expects the faithful to be temporarily restored to a physical body, which will later be transformed to a body of glory; in some books, only the righteous are raised (Pss. of Sol.; I Enoch 83–90), while in others all humanity is raised for judgment (Sibylline Oracles; II Esdras; Testaments of the Twelve). In some documents, the divine fulfillment occurs on earth, but for others it occurs in paradise; for some it will take place in a Messianic Age, and for others in eternity. An important detail is that bodily, physical resurrection is to be expected by those who suffer a martyr's death (II Macc. 7:14-38; 14:46).

The Pharisees apparently believed in the resurrection, and the Sadducees did not (Mark 12:18), although Josephus' *Wars* describes the Pharisaic concept as though it were the immortality of the soul. The rabbinic teachings from the second century A.D. mingle representations of bodily resurrection with notions of the immortality of the soul. In the Dead Sea

community's Scroll of the Rule (IV, 6–7) there is a belief in life after death for those who "walk in the Spirit," but the text does not specify whether this bliss is in or outside the body. Clearly there was in Judaism in this period a widespread concern for the destiny of humans beyond death, but no clear concept of the form that immortal existence would take.

H.K.

**REUBEN.** The firstborn son of Leah and Jacob, and the tribe named for him.

After working seven years to marry Rachel, Reuben's father, JACOB, was tricked into marrying her older sister Leah (Gen. 29:1-26). Reuben, their first son, is listed first in the twelve tribes of Israel (Jacob). Jacob then worked another seven years to earn Rachel. Reuben found some ripe mandrakes, an herb with an edible root and berry (30:14). Rachel bargained with her sister Leah to have some of these mandrakes in hopes of increasing her (Rachel's) fertility, and later gave birth to Joseph and Benjamin. Reaching adulthood, Reuben lay with Bilhah, his father's concubine, challenging his father (35:22).

One day Reuben's brother JOSEPH came out to show the eleven brothers the coat of many colors their father had given him (37:3-4). When they began plotting to kill Joseph, Reuben convinced them to throw him into a pit instead, from where Reuben intended to rescue him. Without Reuben's knowledge, the brothers then sold Joseph into slavery (37:17b-28).

Later it was Reuben, after he and his brother had gone down to Egypt to get food during a famine, who suggested that their harsh treatment of Joseph earlier was bringing trouble upon them (42:22). It was also Reuben who promised his father Jacob that he would give his own two sons' lives if he did not return Benjamin home safely (42:37). Before he died, Jacob blessed each of his sons. Reuben he called preeminent in pride and power but unstable as water, and warned that Reuben would not have preeminence because he had defiled his father's bed (49:3-4).

Possibly beginning west of the Jordan, the tribe settled east of the Jordan in the land east of the northern part of the Dead Sea. Their strength and numbers dwindled over the years, and Moses blessed them with the words "Let Reuben live, and not die" (Deut. 33:6). The tribe is rebuked in the Song of Deborah for not having taken part in the battle against the Canaanites (Judg. 5:15-16). During the period of the kings the tribe played no further role.

B.J.

**REVELATION, BOOK OF.** The last book of the NT in most Christian canonical lists is called in Greek the Apocalypse, which means "Revelation." The name indicates more, however, than just that some things are revealed in the book to its author. The term "apocalypse" refers to a type of literature prevalent in

*The Seven Churches of Asia*

the period between the OT and the NT, which emphasized the impending end of the world and the triumph of good and light over evil and darkness. The conflict was described in this literature, typically, in bizarre terms that tended to identify good with the color white and tame animals, and bad with the colors black or red and wild animals. A common theme of APOCALYPTICISM is that the sufferings of the righteous are caused not by the punishment of God but by the afflictions of Satan, who seeks to turn the sufferer away from God. The book of Job is an ancient prototype of this teaching. Paul reflects upon this when he says, "Yea, all that live godly in Christ Jesus shall suffer persecution" (II Tim. 3:12), as did Jesus when he said, "Blessed are those who are persecuted for righteousness' sake" (Matt. 5:10).

The book of Revelation is the only book of its type in the NT, but many other examples exist in the period before the NT, in such books as I Enoch and the Testaments of the Twelve Patriarchs, and in the period after the NT in such books as the Ascension of Isaiah and the Apocalypse of Peter. It was a literature of the oppressed who looked for a solution to their plight not on the plane of human history but in God's own action. Apocalyptic literature flourished in the hopes of Jews under oppression. The literature enflamed the Zealots of the first centuries B.C. and A.D., but when both wars of liberation (A.D. 70 and A.D. 135) ended in disaster for the Jewish nation, interest waned in apocalypticism. It seems to have made its way into Jewish Christianity in those early

centuries, however, in the wake of Jewish Christian reaction to the destruction of Jerusalem, which was different from that of non-Christian Jews. Those who were Christian continued to look for an apocalyptic solution in the newly found Messiah, which Judaism had rejected. In this hope apocalyptic thought continued to flourish and the book of Revelation was written.

The date of its composition is not known for certain, but Eusebius dated the exile of the apostle John to Patmos during the reign of Domitian (A.D. 81–96), which is when Irenaeus writing in the second century had dated it. Scholarship over the past century has tended to agree with this, though there is no unanimity of opinion. Recently John A. T. Robinson dated the book to the period before the destruction of Jerusalem in A.D. 70.

The authorship has been equally troublesome to determine, and no final consensus prevails here either. Most have held in recent times that the book was written not by John the Apostle, but by another John who refers to himself in 1:4, 9. Dionysius of Alexandria decided in the third century, on the basis of grammatical style, that there were two different authors for the Gospel and the Apocalypse. Papias declared, in the second century, that the apostle wrote the Gospel and another John, known as "the elder" (see II John 1; III John 1), wrote the Apocalypse. It has become commonplace to attribute the Apocalypse

Courtesy of the Metropolitan Museum of Art. Gift of Junius S. Morgan, 1919

*The Riders on the Four Horses from the Apocalypse, from a sixteenth-century woodcut by Albrecht Dürer*

to this other John, but the evidence has not been strong enough to make the hypothesis a fact. Although many modern commentators are convinced that the grammatical styles of the two books are incompatible, the greatest scholar of the third century, Origen of Alexandria, was not.

The book professes to be written about things that "must soon take place" (1:1), and it seems best to regard it as a revelation about persecutions that the first readers would soon be facing. The latter part of the book (chaps. 20–22) seems to contain references to events in the distant future, however. Envisioned by the author was the divine intervention of God after a great catastrophe had befallen the world, a catastrophe involving supernatural terrors that John is preparing the church to meet and overcome. The major thrust of the book is that the Lamb will conquer the Dragon (Christ will conquer Satan).

The book of Revelation was known and used by authors in the second century (Justin Martyr, Irenaeus, Papias, Melito of Sardis), the third century (Tertullian, Cyprian, Clement of Alexandria, Origen), and the fourth century (Eusebius, Jerome). It was not accepted, however, into the canon of the Syrian church by the fourth century, having been omitted from the influential Peshitta Version, but was incorporated into the Philoxenian translation in the beginning of the sixth century. Under the influence of Jerome and Augustine it was recognized more widely in the West. Portions of the text exist in papyrus manuscripts dating to the third century. (*See also* ESCHATOLOGY.)                           J.R.M.

**REVELATION IN HISTORY.** *See* INSPIRATION AND REVELATION.

**REVISED STANDARD VERSION** (RSV). The International Council of Religious Education, an agency of the major American and Canadian churches, launched the effort to revise the AMERICAN STANDARD VERSION. The project continued after the ICRE became a part of the National Council of the Churches of Christ in the U.S.A.

The translators were to "embody the best results of modern scholarship as to the meaning of Scriptures," and they were to "express this meaning in English diction" suitable "for use in public and private worship." Still the new Revised Standard Version was to retain "those qualities which have given to the King James Version a supreme place in English literature."

While a large segment of the Christian public accepted the new version when the NT appeared in 1946, the OT in 1952, and the Apocrypha in 1957, ultraconservatives in the United States were harshly critical of it. They were suspicious of this translation of the Bible because of its sponsors and also because "young woman" was substituted for "virgin" in Isaiah 7:14. This was regarded as a subtle undermining of the virgin birth of Christ. There were other renderings also that conservatives regarded with suspicion.

A Roman Catholic version was published in 1965, bearing the imprimatur of the church. As a result, the RSV received wide acceptance among Catholics as well as Protestants. A British version had wide acceptance with all stripes of believers, including evangelicals. Soon it was warmly received throughout the English-speaking world.

Due to the proliferation of new translations in contemporary English during the 1970s, sales of the RSV have slumped somewhat. Yet it continues as a preferred version in most of the major denominations in the United States.                           R.H.

**REVISED VERSION** (RV). Since biblical scholarship had advanced by the late part of the nineteenth century and a trove of new biblical manuscripts had been discovered, pressure began to build for a revision of the 1611 translation of the KING JAMES VERSION. Therefore, the Convocation of Canterbury in 1870 voted to undertake "a revision of the Authorized Version of the Holy Scriptures."

It was decided to invite scholars from a wide spectrum of the church and to include both British and Americans on the two committees of OT and NT translators. In due time the Revised Version (RV), sometimes referred to as the English Revised Version (ERV), appeared. The NT was published in 1881 and the entire Bible in 1885.

Because of the strict rules of procedure, the resultant product was regarded by many as too awkward in style for liturgical use. The American scholars later produced their own rendering, which was published in 1901 as the AMERICAN STANDARD VERSION (ASV).                           R.H.

**REVIVALS.** Periods of religious fervor when the faith of Christians is revitalized and non-Christians are converted. While one could refer to such periods as the twelfth-century flourishing of MONASTICISM or the fourteenth-century intensity of devotion as "revivals," the term is usually reserved for the modern phenomenon, which grew out of the PURITAN emphasis on conversion as a personal, emotional commitment and on the necessity of such a conversion for church membership.

Revivals are the Protestant religious corollary of "awakenings" or periods of national/cultural crisis in beliefs and values extending over a generation until reorientation is achieved. Puritanism (1610–40) is the birthplace of American cultural understandings, followed by the First GREAT AWAKENING (1730–60), the Second (1800–30), the Third (1890–1920), and the Fourth (1960–). Revivals have been identified with the work of revivalist preachers such as JONATHAN EDWARDS, GEORGE WHITEFIELD, CHARLES G. FINNEY, Phoebe Palmer, DWIGHT MOODY, BILLY SUNDAY, and BILLY GRAHAM. British revivals include the Evangelical Revival of

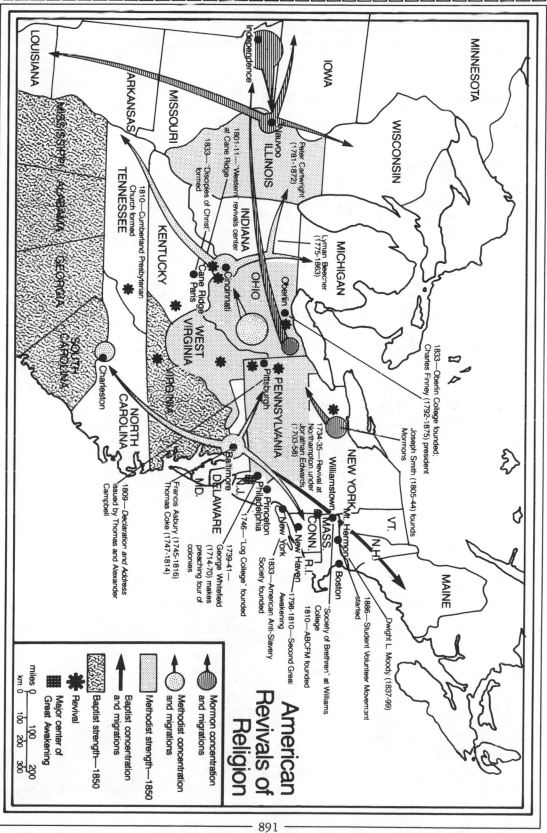

**American Revivals of Religion**

1833—Oberlin College founded; Charles Finney (1792-1875) president

Joseph Smith (1805-44) founds Mormons

1886—Student Volunteer Movement

Dwight L. Moody (1837-99)

"Society of Brethren" at Williams College

1810—ABCFM founded

1798-1810—Second Great Awakening

1833—American Anti-Slavery Society founded

1734-35—Revival at Northampton under Jonathan Edwards (1703-58)

1746—"Log College" founded

1739-41—George Whitefield (1714-70) makes preaching tour of colonies

Francis Asbury (1745-1816) Thomas Coke (1747-1814)

1809—Declaration and Address issued by Thomas and Alexander Campbell

Lyman Beecher (1775-1863)

1801-11—"Western" revivals center

1833—Disciples of Christ" formed

Peter Cartwright (1781-1872)

1810—Cumberland Presbyterian Church formed

LOUISIANA
ARKANSAS
MISSOURI
IOWA
MINNESOTA
WISCONSIN
ILLINOIS
INDIANA
MICHIGAN
OHIO
KENTUCKY
TENNESSEE
MISSISSIPPI
ALABAMA
GEORGIA
SOUTH CAROLINA
NORTH CAROLINA
WEST VIRGINIA
VIRGINIA
PENNSYLVANIA
MAINE
VT.
N.H.
NEW YORK
MASS.
CONN.
R.I.
N.J.
DELAWARE
MD.

Independence
Nauvoo
Cane Ridge
Paris
Cincinnati
Oberlin
Charleston
Pittsburgh
Baltimore
Philadelphia
Princeton
New York
New Haven
Boston
Mt. Hermon
Williamstown

Legend:
- Mormon concentration and migrations
- Methodist concentration and migrations
- Baptist concentration and migrations
- Methodist strength—1850
- Baptist strength—1850
- ✳ Revival
- ▦ Major center of Great Awakening

miles 0  100  200  300
km   0  100  200  300

JOHN and CHARLES WESLEY in the 1740s and the 1859–65 revival, which was linked to America's "laymen's," "prayermeeting," or "holiness" revival. Western missionary efforts have also sparked revivals in such places as Korea and Indonesia.    N.H.

**REWARD.** Pay or return for something done or left undone. Reward is used in many ways, such as in employment where the value for labor is determined by the rights of the laborer or the generosity of the employer.

In ethics, reward and punishment relate to the pleasant or painful consequences of choices made or not made. In religion, reward and punishment have to do with SALVATION. In some religions, rewards and punishments are corporate, individuals being involved solely as parts of the whole society. In still other religions, rewards and punishments are matters for the individual person who, on the basis of choices, will be rewarded or punished in this life or in life after death. The decision of who is rewarded or punished, that is, JUDGMENT, is variously described. In a state or nationalistic religion, rewards are those of a good citizen, punishment is specified in the civil or criminal codes.

In the Bible, rewards may be everyday wages or earnings (Matt. 20:8; Jas. 5:4; I Tim. 6:9; compare Matt. 10:10; Luke 10:7) or may be compensation generally as "they have their reward," spoken by Jesus concerning hypocrites (Matt. 6:2; 5:16); "your reward is great in heaven" (Matt. 5:12); "love your enemies, and do good . . . and your reward will be great" (Luke 6:35).

That good produces good consequences and that evil results in evil is an ethical principle or law essential in biblical thinking. "The wages of sin is death, but the free gift of God is eternal life" (Rom. 6:23). Like the law of gravity, that law is obeyed or people suffer the consequences, for example, Amos' plumb line (7:7) and Jesus' parable of the two houses (Matt. 7:24-27; Luke 6:47-49 and Ezek. 33:11, 12; Mic. 6:15) and "whatever a man sows, that he will also reap" (Gal. 6:7). It is wisdom to follow this, and folly to ignore. Herein is judgment in the realm of practical affairs applicable to nations as well as to individuals.

Judgment is under God's control. God may make rewards greater than those merited (Pss. 100:6; 103:10; Matt. 20:1-16). Or the punishment may be total annihilation as Sodom and Gomorrah (Gen. 19:24). Joseph's fidelity under temptation brought good to him and saved the lives of his family (Gen. 50:20).

As with piety and humility, rewards cannot be striven for directly, they are by-products of commitment. "Seek first God's kingdom . . . and all things shall be yours as well" (Matt. 18:33). Beyond all other rewards is fellowship with God now (Ps. 73:25ff.; Job 42:5) and eternally in the New Jerusalem (Rev. 21:22).    P.L.G.

**REZIN.** (1) Name of the final king of independent Syria, a contemporary of Pekah of Israel and of Jothan and Ahaz of Judah. Tiglath-pileser III took Damascus in 732 B.C. and killed Rezin (II Kings 16:9). The OT mentions Rezin in connection with the attack he and Pekah made on Jerusalem about 735 B.C. (II Kings 15:37; 16:5; Isa. 7:1). Isaiah considered Rezin and Pekah "two smoldering stumps of firebrands" (7:4).

(2) The "sons of Rezin" (Ezra 2:48; Neh. 7:50) were a Jewish family connected with a Temple guild, the Nethinim, who returned with Zerubbabel from Babylon in 536 B.C.    P.L.G.

**REZON.** Son of Eliada and an early supporter of the king of Zobah. He moved to Damascus where, during Solomon's reign, the band of men he gathered about him made him king. He was "an adversary of Israel" who did "mischief"; "he abhored Israel" (I Kings 11:23-25).    P.L.G.

**RHODES.** The easternmost and second largest island in the Aegean Sea, ten miles south of Asia Minor. Its position on the east-west shipping lanes of the Mediterranean made it, through much of history, a major trading center.

Although Rhodes had supported the Roman imperial expansion, Gaius Cassius Longinus, in 43 B.C., in the name of the triumvirate, mercilessly sacked the capital city, Rhodes, confiscated all public and private silver and gold, and transported it and many Rhodian works of art to Rome. This disaster left Rhodes the defeated and impoverished country it was when Paul landed there (Acts 21:1). Whether he stopped at the capital city or elsewhere is not known. Local tradition points to the "Port of Paul," an almost completely enclosed bay on the east side of the island, and north of the acropolis of Lindos. By the shore there is a very old church and monastery commemorating the apostle.    P.L.G.

**RICCI, MATTHEW** (1552–1610). An Italian Jesuit; one of the greatest of the Christian missionaries to China. He entered China via Macao, a Portuguese colony, bringing with him clocks, astronomical and musical instruments, richly bound books, European paintings, and the most astounding to the Chinese, a map of the world. He began early to learn the Mandarin language and the Chinese classics. He showed himself to be a Christian priest, but he adopted Chinese dress and continued his studies of the language and literature of China. Making his way into official circles, by 1601 Ricci was invited by the emperor to visit Peking. There he was asked to remain and teach science at the court. He translated many European works into Mandarin and wrote books in that language about Christian beliefs. His book *True Knowledge of God* (1603) led to the first conversions in Korea. He met with much criticism from more conservative Christians for his acceptance of Chinese culture and customs into his Christian teaching.    W.G.

**RICHARD, TIMOTHY** (1845–1919). A Welsh Baptist missionary whose methods and approach to work in China has been said to be similar to the earlier policies of RICCI, the great Jesuit missionary to China. He was sent to China in 1870. The famine of 1876–79 convinced Richard that a new approach needed to be made to the leaders of China who had refused needed help because they thought Westerners were barbarians. He advocated that colleges be established in every province to help win the thinking upper classes. After troubles during the Boxer Rebellion (about 1900), modern style education spread, and many eventual leaders of China were trained in these Christian institutions. Although Richard was little known outside missionary circles, his policies became accepted as an important part of missionary endeavor in many lands.          W.G.

**RICHARD OF ST. VICTOR.** A twelfth-century Scottish monk and theologian of mysticism. Richard entered the Abbey of St. Victor in Paris, studying under Hugh of St. Victor. He became prior there in 1162. As a theologian he wrote *De Trinitate* and commentaries on Scripture, but he is best remembered for his mystical works *Benjamin Major* and *Benjamin Minor*. Benjamin, the beloved son of Rachel, is a symbol for the contemplative life. Richard calls mysticism "the science of the heart." His rigorous intellect, though disdaining secular learning, digested the older traditions of Plotinus and Dionysius the Areopagite and transmitted them to the medieval world. For the Victorines, MYSTICISM is a proper branch of theology.          N.H.

**RICHELIEU, ARMAND JEAN DU PLESSIS** (1585–1642). Born on September 9, the third son of lesser nobility at Poitou, France, he became chief minister in 1628 to Louis XIII. Richelieu was a prime example of the medieval use of power for both ecclesiastical and secular ends. Though a cleric, he brought about the secularization of politics.

Richelieu was ordained priest and consecrated bishop of Luçon at Rome in August 1607. He was made a cardinal September 5, 1622, by Pope Gregory XV. He rose in power as adviser to Marie de Medici, the mother of Louis XIII, and almoner to Anne of Austria, Louis' child queen. In 1616 he became the king's secretary of state and in 1624 was appointed chief of the royal council.

His political goals were to establish royal absolutism and weaken the power of the nobility. His ultimate goal was to shift the European balance of power from the Hapsburgs of Spain to the Bourbons of France. Though he persecuted the Huguenots, stripping them of constitutional safeguards and defeating them at LaRochelle in 1628, he aligned France with the Protestant powers of Germany and against Spanish interests during the Thirty Years' War. Though it came after his death, Richelieu managed to lay down the lines for the Treaty of Westphalia in 1648, which established the religious map of modern Europe. His power and diplomacy aided the recovery of the Protestant sovereigns and halted the sweep of the Counter-Reformation. A patron of the arts and founder of the French Academy in 1635, Richelieu was buried in a chapel at the Sorbonne following his death on December 4.

N.H.

**RICOEUR, PAUL** (1913– ). French philosopher who has written widely on religion and theology, especially in the areas of phenomenology, the philosophy of language, and hermeneutics. Educated at the University of Paris, Ricoeur has served as professor of philosophy at the University of Strasbourg (1948–56), the University of Paris (1956–65), and the University of Chicago (1965– ), where, since 1976, he has been the John Nuveen Professor of Philosophical Theology. His many books include *Fallible Man* (1965), *History and Truth* (1965), *Freedom and Nature: The Voluntary and Involuntary* (1966), *The Symbolism of Evil* (1967), *Freud and Philosophy* (1970), *Conflict of Interpretations* (1974), and *The Rule of Metaphor* (1978).

Ricoeur's early work explored the phenomenology of the will or volition, especially the themes of freedom, necessity, human finitude, and guilt. These studies in existential phenomenology show the influence of HUSSERL as well as JASPERS and MARCEL. Ricoeur's study of the use of symbolic language in *The Symbolism of Evil* turned his interests to the problem of language, especially the religious use of the indirect language of metaphor and myth. This led in turn to reflection on the more general questions of hermeneutics, or the theory of interpretation. Ricoeur developed the interesting distinction between a reductive hermeneutics of suspicion as found in Freud and Marx and a hermeneutics of recollection in which one seeks to retrieve the original meaning of the religious symbol. This involves a move from a first naïveté through criticism to a second naïveté. Ricoeur's more recent work shows the influence of French structuralism, in which interpretation is more concerned with the objective meaning of the text as distinct from the subjective intention of the author or the appropriation by the reader.          J.L.

**RIGHTEOUSNESS.** As a key biblical idea the term covers two aspects of the divine character: it defines what God is and how God acts in history, and it sets a standard, based on that character, which is expected of God's people, both Israel in the OT and the church of Christ in the NT. There is thus both an ontological-historical dimension and an ethical connotation to the term. Recent discussion, especially seen in John Reumann, *Righteousness in the New Testament* (1982), reports the result of a fruitful dialogue between Lutheran and Catholic scholars who have reached a consensus, namely that at a deeper level righteousness has to be seen as describing a personal relationship within a COVENANT, both the OT covenant of the Exodus and the NT covenant of redemption by Christ. On God's side, that aspect is best designated "saving activity" leading to Israel's calling to be Yahweh's people and the church's inclusion within God's redeeming purposes for the whole of humankind. The human counterpart is spelled out in terms of loyalty as "covenant-behavior," befitting those who enjoy a right relationship with God (see JUSTIFICATION).

*Old Testament.* Yahweh's person is embraced by this term "righteousness" (Isa. 24:16). Yahweh is "righteous" by definition, and so God acts in righteousness, that is, reliably, faithfully, in a trustworthy manner (Jer. 9:24; compare Deut. 32:4; Dan. 9:7). Yahweh speaks the truth (Isa. 45:19) and all Yahweh does is in line with the divinely revealed character. (See Exod. 9:27; Jer. 12:1.)

Two further applications are made of Yahweh's self-chosen conformity to this norm. Yahweh judges by upholding justice in the covenant community (Pss. 9:5; 119:7; Isa. 42:21; 58:2). Second and importantly, Yahweh vindicates the oppressed and delivers the captive, giving victory to the cause of people when they cry for redress and deliverance (Judg. 5:11; Isa. 41:2; 62:1, 2). It follows that "righteousness" shades into salvation, expressing God's gracious enterprise of deliverance (especially in Second Isaiah's prophecies, for example, Isa. 46:13; 51:5, 6, 8; compare 61:10). This may be called the clearest anticipation of the Christian gospel in the OT.

*New Testament.* See Romans 3:24-26; 4:24, 25; II Corinthians 5:18-21; Philippians 3:7-11. These are the three NT books that have preponderant references to righteousness. The unifying themes are that (1) righteousness is God's saving action in Christ; (2) it has a cosmic aspect, possessing the character of both gift and power, and denotes a new world set right with the Creator's plan; (3) its entry into human experience is faith in Christ who as the "righteous one" both makes possible human response and sets the new ethical standards in the gift of the Spirit in the new age (Rom. 8:1-4; Gal. 5:5) to enable believers to be "made righteous" (I Cor. 1:30) and to live in conformity with God's righteous demands (compare Matt. 3:15; Rom. 14:17).

The OT teaching on righteousness as a way of life, from the Davidic king who rules in righteousness (Jer. 23:5) to obedience to the law as a hallmark of covenant relations (Isa. 51:7; Ezek. 18:19, 21), is thus realized in the NT. The locus of this teaching is in the community of the new covenant (Jer. 31:31-34) heralded by Jesus' upper room words (Matt. 26:26-29) and made real in the NT picture of early companies of believers in Jesus Christ who sought to live righteously (Luke 1:75), both in relation to God's purpose and in their mutual life (I John 3:7, 10). No excuse is ever given for indulging in immoral ways, since the calling of the Christian in the NT churches is to be worked out in serious ethical endeavor. In the picturesque idiom of Revelation 19:8, the church of Christ is likened to the bride who is arrayed in white clothes: "fine linen stands for the righteous acts of the saints" (NIV).                R.M.

**RIGHT TO LIFE MOVEMENT.** A descriptive term arising during the anti-abortion struggle in the United States, especially after the Supreme Court legalized abortion (during the first two trimesters of pregnancy) on January 22, 1973.

The Right to Life movement had its origins among Roman Catholics. As early as 1967 the Los Angeles diocese of the Roman Catholic church employed an advertising agency to promote a campaign advancing the Right to Life Leagues. Partisans identified their cause with the Declaration of Independence stating "that the right to life was inalienable." The Massachusetts Citizens for Life was founded in 1970, after Thomas Connelly discovered the number of abortions being performed at the Boston City Hospital. Massachusetts Citizens for Life was given great impetus by the positions taken by the vice president of the organization, Dr. Mildred Jefferson. The first black to graduate from Harvard Medical School, Dr. Jefferson soon became a prestigious national figure. She later became a director of the national Right to Life Committee.

The incident that sharpened the debate was the arrest of Dr. Kenneth Edelin, a highly professional gynecologist and obstetrician on the Boston City Hospital staff, who was indicted for manslaughter, in what was called the abortion of a living infant. Edelin's trial began January 6, 1975. About this time, Richard Viguerie, a conservative Protestant, espoused the Right to Life movement, adding a large new segment of supporters.

Colorado in 1967 was the first state to liberalize its abortion laws. Hawaii and New York followed in 1970. Challenges to similar laws in Georgia and Texas resulted in the Supreme Court's 1973 decision legalizing abortion.                R.H.

**RIG VEDA.** The oldest and most important part of the VEDAS of HINDUISM, the Rig Veda is a collection of hymns addressed to the gods. They probably emerged as an oral tradition among the Aryan (Indo-European) invaders of ancient India around 1400–1200 B.C.                R.E.

**RINKART, MARTIN** (1586–1649). German Lutheran pastor and hymn writer. Rinkart's greatest hymn of thanksgiving, "Now Thank We All Our God," was produced in the crucible of suffering caused by the Thirty Years' War. Born on April 23, in Eilenburg, a village in Saxony, Rinkart was the son of a coppersmith. As a youth he was a chorister at St. Thomas Church in nearby Leipzig. This was the church where later Johann Sebastian Bach was to serve as musical director. Young Rinkart sang to earn money to attend Leipzig University. He was ordained to the Lutheran ministry in his hometown of Eilenburg, serving the parish of that walled city through the suffering, plague, and famine of the long religious and political struggle between Protestant and Catholic forces. Twice Eilenburg was overrun by the Swedish army and once by Austrian troops. It has been erroneously reported that Rinkart composed this famous hymn in celebration of the Peace of Westphalia, but it is more likely that it marked the one hundredth anniversary of the Augsburg Confession. Rinkart wrote many other hymns but none has been as widely sung as *Nun danket alle Gott*. The English-speaking world owes a debt to Catherine Winkworth of Bristol, England, for translating the hymn into English.                                R.H.

## RISSHO KOSEIKAI.

A modern Japanese form of NICHIREN Buddhism, regarded as one of the "new religions" that arose before and after World War II. Like other Nichiren sects it bases its doctrines on the LOTUS SUTRA and uses in its worship the chant *"Namu myo-ho-renge-kyo"* ("I give homage to the marvelous teaching of the Lotus Sutra").

Rissho Koseikai arose in the 1930s under the leadership of a remarkable woman, Myoko Naganuma, and a gifted man, Nikkyo Niwano. Mrs. Naganuma adopted many practices of traditional shamanism, including faith healing. After her death in 1957 the shamanistic practices were deemphasized in favor of more traditional Buddhist beliefs and practices. The concept of compassion for others, connected with the bodhisattva ideal, and the promise of salvation in terms of happiness and material blessing in the present life receive particular emphasis.

Much of Rissho Koseikai's popularity is due to the success of its small-group counseling procedures, known as *hoza*, or "circle of harmony." Many of these groups are composed of women who have moved from the countryside to Tokyo and other cities. Companionship with others from the same rural area helps members deal with loneliness and alienation and affirm traditional values.

Mr. Niwano has been a leader in interfaith discussions and in the search for world peace. He has met with world leaders, including Pope Paul VI. The Great Sacred Hall in Tokyo, headquarters of the sect, is a striking blend of modern and traditional elements. Other buildings nearby include schools and a modern hospital.                              K.C.

## RITSCHL, ALBRECHT (1822–89).

German theologian and historian of Christian doctrine, considered to be the most influential Protestant theologian between F. SCHLEIERMACHER and K. BARTH. Born in Berlin, the son of a prominent Lutheran clergyman, Ritschl studied theology at Bonn, Halle, and Heidelberg but, initially, found most satisfaction at Tübingen under the tutelage of the Hegelian church historian F. C. BAUR. After taking his first teaching position at Bonn, Ritschl renounced Baur and developed his own distinctive interpretation of Christian origins and the history of doctrine. However, Ritschl's most important contribution was in the field of constructive theology which, taking the name of Ritschlianism, dominated Protestant theology in Germany from 1875 to World War I and in the English-speaking world during the early decades of the twentieth century.

Ritschl moved to Göttingen in 1864 and remained there for twenty-five years. Between 1870 and 1874 he published the three volumes of his major work, *The Christian Doctrine of Justification and Reconciliation*, whose themes were the focal point of Ritschl's own constructive interpretation of Christian theology. According to Ritschl, God is known neither by intuitive insight and mystical feeling (Schleiermacher) nor by philosophical speculation (Hegel). Religion is essentially a practical matter—in short, our experience of moral freedom. Religion is the warranty for the attainment of our spiritual victory over bondage to nature's necessity through the help of superhuman, spiritual power, or God. However, belief in God is always a value judgment of faith for Ritschl. God is known only through the effects of the Divine upon the individual, only, that is, as God is revealed to each person as the guarantor of that person's victory over the world.

For the Christian, the goodness and power of God are revealed in the person and work of Christ. However, knowledge of Christ is not based on a purely scientific, historical knowledge; Christ, too, is known only "through his benefits." Christ's divinity, therefore, is found in the service he renders and in the benefits he bestows. Ritschl insists that the Christian is not only justified and liberated from sin and nature's necessity through Christ's moral influence, the Christian is also called to an ethical task of reconciliation, or the upbuilding of the kingdom of God in and through the Christian community, the church. Ritschl's focus on the Christian's ethical vocation, on the *social* dimension of salvation within the Christian community, and on the regulative principle of the kingdom of God as a social ideal, had a profound influence on the SOCIAL GOSPEL and on theologians such as WALTER RAUSCHENBUSCH.
                                                    J.L.

## RITUAL.

Meaningful acts performed in appropriate circumstances and often following strictly prescribed patterns. In this broad sense, ritual pervades the whole of human life. Shaking hands with a friend or saluting an army officer are examples of ritual acts from everyday secular life. However, ritual has especial importance in religion. Every religion requires practice as well as belief from its adherents, and though not all religious practices are ritualistic (for the moral behavior demanded by a religion would not be considered ritual), yet every religion has some ritual dimension, however simple. In Protestantism, for instance, while the more elaborate forms of ritual have been rejected, new and simple rituals have emerged, such as solemnly carrying the Bible into the pulpit before the sermon.

In primitive and archaic religions, ritual was of very great importance. There was as yet no theology. Such religion, wrote anthropologist Marett, "was not so much thought out as danced out." Yet something like an incipient theology was already present in the meaningful actions performed in the ritual. The ritual might be the acting out of a myth or sacred story, and that myth, with its narrative form and its symbolic incidents, could be considered a halfway house between the ritual and its theological explication. These early rituals, then, were like sacred dramas. They might, as in the Greek mysteries, reenact the story of a god or a divine hero; or they might be suggestive of the processes of nature, as in the New Year ceremonies performed in Semitic religions. But these rituals did not just express a story for edification. They were also, as a form of *doing,* believed to be efficacious—they brought about results. Thus those who participated in the mysteries were believed to be united with the god or hero who was being celebrated, and to be made the recipients of power; while the New Year ceremonies were supposed to ensure the fertility of the flocks and fields for the coming year, as if there were an efficacious parallel between the ritual act and events in the world of nature.

Ritual persists into the higher religions. In Christianity, the most obvious examples of ritual are the SACRAMENTS. In baptism, the ritual act of pouring water over the baptized person or immersing in water can be understood as an act of cleansing from sin and, more elaborately, as being buried with Christ and then raised with him. In the Eucharist, the bread and wine become for the worshipers the Body and Blood of Christ, so that in receiving these visible objects, they inwardly receive Christ and are incorporated into him. Most Christians believe that these sacraments are not only *illustrative* of inward meanings but that they are actually *efficacious* in bringing about a new spiritual condition of the believer. There are many other ritual acts in Christianity, such as making the sign of the cross as a tacit affirmation of faith, laying on hands to signify the transmission of an office, kneeling in prayer as a sign of reverence, and so on. Similarly in Judaism, Islam, and the religions of the East, there are many rituals that survive, even though all of these religions have developed profound theologies.

Opinions differ about the value and importance of ritual and ceremonial. As mentioned above, Protestants have greatly reduced or simplified the rituals found among Catholic Christians. In all the great religions are found groups that reduce ritual or even seek to abolish it altogether. This might suggest that once religion has been thought out, it need no longer be danced out; or, to put it in another way, that religion should be completely interiorized. In the Christian tradition, for instance, the Quakers have abolished outward sacraments and have replaced them by acts of silent interior meditation. In Protestantism generally, preaching has become much more important than sacramental action. Religion has become verbalized, and the only kind of action that is encouraged is moral action.

Catholics, however, would contest the view that ritual ought to be phased out as religion becomes more self-consciously theological. It is true that the Anglican "ritualists" of the nineteenth century defended themselves by claiming that in the slum urban areas in which most of them worked, Christianity could be conveyed by ritual acts where it would never be understood through theological formulations. But most Catholics would choose a different ground for the defense of ritual. The human being is a psychosomatic unity, a creature of sense as well as intellect, of sight as well as sound. Hence the full expression of Christian faith and its full communication demand the visible act as well as the spoken word. The traditional High Mass is a multimedia experience, including words, action, music, and even incense. As such, it addresses the whole human being. This view is reinforced by the rise of television in recent decades and the consequent shift in communication from the verbal to the visible.

But even enthusiasts for the enduring importance of ritual would have to acknowledge that many rituals have a tendency to survive even after their significance has been forgotten or opinions have changed about what ought to be signified. Ritual has a built-in tendency to proliferate and then to become frozen and unchangeable. Recent liturgical changes in the Christian churches have tended to simplify the ritual, making it on the whole less fussy but at the same time placing emphasis on the important moments. Also, the strict precision required in the older rites has given way to a measure of flexibility. What is important is not the fact that something has always been done, but that what is done should be understood by the worshipers and should help to communicate to them and realize in them a religious truth.

J.M.

**RIZPAH.** Daughter of Aiah; concubine of Saul. After Saul's death, Abner took up with Rizpah, which amounted to claiming the throne (II Sam. 3:7; I Kings 2:22). When a famine arose later, David offered up two sons of Rizpah (II Sam. 21:1-9). Rizpah then began a heroic vigil by the bodies.

B.J.

**ROBERTS, DANIEL CRANE** (1841–1907). Episcopal clergyman, educator, and hymn writer. Born on November 5, in Bridgehampton, New York, Roberts attended Kenyon College in Ohio. His studies were interrupted when he enlisted as a private in the Civil War. After completing preparation for the ministry, Roberts was ordained as a deacon in the Episcopal Church (1865) and a priest the following year. He served Christ Church, Montpelier, Vermont; St. John's, Lowell, Massachusetts; St. Thomas, Brandon, Vermont; and St. Paul's, Concord, New Hampshire, for nearly thirty years. He wrote the hymn "God of Our Fathers, Whose Almighty Hand" for the local Fourth of July centennial celebration while he was rector in Brandon, Vermont. He served as chaplain of the Grand Army of the Republic in New Hampshire and was active for many years in the New Hampshire State Historical Society. He died at Concord, New Hampshire, on October 31.                    R.H.

**ROBERTS, ORAL GRANVILLE** (1918–  ) Famed faith healer and evangelist; founder of Oral Roberts University and the City of Faith hospital and medical center in Tulsa, Oklahoma. Born in Ada, Oklahoma, on January 24, Oral Roberts was reared by a family well acquainted with poverty. Oral was afflicted by a serious illness that has been described as tuberculosis and was said to have threatened his life at age sixteen or seventeen. Roberts frequently testifies to the manner in which he was healed of this illness by prayer.

For twelve years young Roberts served as pastor to several Pentecostal Holiness churches, the denomi-

*Oral Roberts*

nation in which he was nurtured. He attended Oklahoma Baptist University and Phillips University. In 1947 he began to travel extensively as a healing evangelist and in 1948 founded the Oral Roberts Evangelistic Association. His campaigns, conducted in a huge tent, attracted throngs of people seeking healing and salvation.

The Christian world was surprised when Roberts announced that he was moving his ministerial credentials from the Pentecostal Holiness church to the Methodist church. Then in 1963, he launched the beginning of Oral Roberts University in his home city of Tulsa. Before long ORU attracted attention as a school with high academic standards as well as very competitive athletic teams.

Meanwhile Roberts continued his ministry on television and at one time had the largest viewing audience in the religious field. The format of his television program was changed to feature performances by many performers enlisted from the show business world. Roberts, however, maintained the spiritual content of his TV specials. In 1981, amid controversy, Roberts opened the sixty-story City of Faith, which included a hospital, clinic, medical center, research center, and full-fledged medical school.                    R.H.

**ROBINSON, ROBERT** (1735–90). Baptist minister and hymn writer. Robinson, author of the beloved hymn "Come, Thou Fount of Every Blessing," came from a humble home in the village of Swaffham in the former county of Norfolk, England. He was born on September 27. His mother sent him off to London when he was fourteen to be apprenticed to a barber. Robinson was an undisciplined youth who spent his free time with a group of rowdies. When he was nineteen, he and his pals were on a drinking spree when they encountered a gypsy fortune teller whom they plied with drinks, seeking to obtain a prediction from her. To Robinson, she declared: "Young man, you will live to see your children and grandchildren." This prophetic declaration disturbed Robinson, but later he and his colleagues were bent on mischief as they stopped at an open-air revival meeting. They were there to scoff at "the poor deluded Methodists." However, the speaker, who was none other than George Whitefield, was preaching on Matthew 3:7. To his listeners the great evangelist declared "O generation of vipers, who hath warned you to flee from the wrath to come?"

Robinson was convicted by the message and confessed his faith in Christ. Soon after, John Wesley appointed him to serve as pastor of the Calvinist Methodist Chapel in Norfolk. Subsequently he became an Independent, and for a time a Unitarian, before becoming a Baptist. He served for a number of years as pastor in Cambridge and became a forceful preacher despite his limited formal education. Later he was called to serve a church in Birmingham, but retired on his first night there. The next morning, his host found that he had died in the night. Among Robinson's many publications is *History of the Baptists* (1790).            R.H.

Courtesy of Religious News Service

*Homer Rodeheaver*

**RODEHEAVER, HOMER ALVAN** (1880–1955). Famed gospel song leader and hymnbook publisher. Rodeheaver was born in Hocking County, Ohio. The family moved to Newton, Tennessee, where young Rodeheaver learned to play the cornet. While studying at Ohio Wesleyan University, Rodeheaver also began to play the trombone, which became the symbol of his later ministry as a gospel song leader for evangelists Billy SUNDAY and W. E. Biederwolf. For twenty-five years he headed Rodeheaver Publishers of Sacred Music, which then merged with another concern to be known as the Rodeheaver Hall-Mack Company. Rodeheaver wrote many songs, but he distinguished himself primarily as the promoter of the songs of other people, such as Charles Gabriel's "Brighten the Corner."       R.H.

**ROGERS, CARL RANSOM** (1902– ). Psychologist, psychotherapist, and university professor best known for his "client-centered," non-directive theory of psychotheraphy. Rogers favors what he calls a person-to-person rather than a doctor-patient relationship in counseling. Born on January 8, in Oak Park, Illinois, Rogers attended the University of Wisconsin, thinking perhaps he would enter the ministry. He attended a World Student Christian Conference in China in 1922 but thereafter turned away from the strict religious position in which he had been reared.

"I was forced to stretch my thinking," he says in an autobiographical essay entitled "This Is Me," which appeared in his book *On Becoming a Person* (1961), "to realize that sincere and honest people could believe in very divergent religious doctrines. In major ways I for the first time emancipated myself from the religious thinking of my parents, and realized I could not go along with them."

He was graduated from Wisconsin in 1924 with a Phi Beta Kappa key. He next attended Union Theological Seminary in New York, taking a seminar in which he hoped to resolve "his own religious doubts and questions." But he decided he could not work in a field "where I would be required to believe in some specified religious doctrine." He moved over to Columbia University Teachers College, where he took courses in psychology and psychiatry. He received an M.A. in 1928 and a Ph.D. in 1931 from Columbia, having specialized in child psychology.

Ohio State University called him in 1940 to serve as a full-time professor in clinical psychology. His book *Counseling and Psychiatry* (1942) appeared next. In 1945 he became professor of psychology at the University of Chicago and executive secretary of the University's Counseling Center. He remained at Chicago until 1957, when he accepted professorship in psychology at his alma mater, the University of Wisconsin. From 1964 through 1968 Rogers was appointed a resident fellow of the Western Behavioral Sciences Institute in LaJolla, California. In 1968, he joined the Center for Studies of the Person at LaJolla.        R.H.

**ROMAN CATHOLICISM.** The worldwide ecclesiastical structure—the largest in CHRISTENDOM—known officially as the Holy Catholic and Apostolic church with its headquarters in the Vatican, a tiny enclave within the city of Rome. It is known as the "Roman" Catholic church as an expression of its submission to the bishop of Rome, the POPE, who is said to derive his supreme authority from the apostles and particularly to the primacy of Peter as Vicar of Christ. Without apology, it proclaims itself to be "the Catholic" (universal) church.

The Roman Catholic church, despite contemporary rumblings, still is hierarchical and authoritarian, requiring submission of clergy and laity. The pope exercises his administrative authority through the CARDINALS, who serve as his senate and his advisers. The global outreach of his government is extended through jurisdiction exercised first by archbishops, metropolitans or patriarchs, and then by bishops who direct their dioceses and parish priests at the congregational level. The pope either appoints or confirms the election of bishops and they in turn select diocesan officials and pastors. While there are some beginnings of lay representation in the direction of parishes, the teaching authority of the church has remained with the clergy.

The basic doctrines of the Catholic church are found in the Apostles', Nicene, and Athanasian creeds. After the Protestant REFORMATION the Roman Catholic church reasserted its claims to its unique authority, especially through the actions taken by the COUNCIL OF TRENT (1545-63), which was called during the CATHOLIC REFORMATION. Its disciplinary decrees were intended to reform the structure of the church and to halt the influence of PROTESTANTISM. At this gathering the Niceno-Constantinopolitan Creed was affirmed as a basis of faith: TRADITION and SCRIPTURE were declared as equal sources of the faith, and other positions that sought the revitalization of Catholicism were affirmed or reaffirmed.

The Roman Catholic church is a sacramental church; that is, the church regards itself as being the divinely appointed agent to convey the grace of God to humanity through the sacraments—baptism, confirmation, the Eucharist, penance, extreme unction, orders, and matrimony. The Council of Trent taught that all seven sacraments were instituted by Christ.

While Catholic theologians sometimes employ the Pauline description of the church as the Body of Christ, they have developed the concept of the church as the extension of the Incarnation. In *Mystici Corporis,* the encyclical issued by Pius XII in 1943, the church as imperium, outside of which there is no salvation, and as the continuing Incarnation were melded. Thus the Body of Christ is equated with the Roman Catholic church in which Christ speaks and works as Christ did when he was on earth. The living voice of the church is held to expound infallibly the revealed truths contained in the deposit of faith.

Pope Paul VI in a speech at one of the later sessions of Vatican II said: "We must not think of the church as two substances but a single complex reality, the compound of a human and divine element. . . . The nature taken by the divine Word serves as the living organ of salvation in a union with Him which is indissoluble."

The Catholic position on baptism, which is administered to infants as well as adults, is said to cleanse the individual's original sin and restore original righteousness. The high point of Roman Catholic liturgy is the MASS. The word is derived from the Latin word *missio,* meaning dismiss, referring to the dismissal of catechumens before the Eucharist was celebrated. The Mass still closes with *"Ite, missa est."* Two main ideas are involved in the doctrine of the Mass: (1) the change whereby the bread and wine become the actual Body and Blood of Christ, the teaching known as TRANSUBSTANTIATION; and (2) the concept of the Mass as the reiterated "bloodless sacrifice" of Christ on the altar of the cross.

Vatican II, in its decree on the priestly life, continues the traditional teaching. Priests are "given the power of sacred Order, to offer sacrifice, forgive sin, and in the name of Christ publicly to exercise the office of priesthood in the community of the faithful." The confessional has always played an important part in sacramental teaching. PENANCE, which is allied to penitence, is required of those who have made their confession to a priest.

The veneration of MARY, the mother of the Lord, is a prominent feature of Roman Catholic worship. Even though there are many changes in the practices of contemporary Catholicism, devotion directed to the Blessed Virgin persists throughout the church. It can be traced to the early centuries of the church when her perpetual virginity was first mentioned. The Marian doctrine received considerable impetus at the Council of Ephesus (431), which upheld the title *Theotokos* (God-bearer). The Latin equivalent was *Dei Genetrix* or Mother of God.

Belief in Mary's intercession and directing prayers to her was a very early practice. Ambrose held her to be a type of the church, in that in giving birth to Christ she also brought forth Christians who were formed in her womb with him. The IMMACULATE CONCEPTION, the teaching that Mary was born "free from all stain of original sin," emerged late in the Middle Ages and did not become official church dogma until the bull issued by Pope Pius IX in 1854.

The ASSUMPTION, the belief that Mary at the completion of her earthly life "was taken up in body and soul to heavenly glory," did not become official teaching of the church until 1950. In modern times (nineteenth and twentieth centuries) efforts have been made to obtain a papal definition of Mary as "Mediatrix of All Graces" and "Co-Redemptress." Impetus has been given to Marian dogma by such diverse Catholic leaders as Edward Schillebeeckx, contemporary liberal Catholic theologian, who wrote a book called *Mary, the Mother of Redemption,* and Pope John Paul II, who journeyed to the Portuguese shrine of Fatima to thank Mary for preserving his life after the attempt was made to assassinate him.

Yet the Roman Catholic church cannot be described as a static entity. It is experiencing great internal turmoil on a number of issues. Even at the turn of the century the growth of what was called MODERNISM caused disturbances. Certain Catholic theologians had begun to accept forms of biblical higher criticism and similar teachings that had been embraced by a majority of Protestant scholars. Pius X condemned the movement and imposed an anti-modernist oath on the clergy. But it was the calling of VATICAN II (1962–65) by Pope John XXIII that really unleashed streams of progressive thought that have changed the course, perhaps irrevocably, of the Roman Catholic Church. Said John XXIII at the opening of the council: "The substance of the ancient doctrine of the deposit of faith is one thing, and the way in which it is presented is another."

HANS KÜNG analyzed the concept of papal infallibility (and incidentally biblical infallibility) in his book *Infallible*. In due time he was censured by his bishop and removed from the list of those officially permitted to teach Catholic theology. Other scholars have questioned the teachings of transubstantiation and clerical celibacy.

It is true that Vatican II had many beneficial effects, many observers have thought. The church now encourages Bible study by lay people, the Mass is celebrated in the vernacular, and there are new attitudes toward non-Catholic believers. Yet there are many who feel that in departing from the basis of authority in "sacred tradition, Holy Scripture, and the Church magisterium," progressive Catholic theologians have been too quick to embrace the theories of radical biblical criticism.

The concept that Protestants are heretics has been replaced by fellowship with "separated brethren." Some Catholic progressives look beyond Christian ecumenism to acceptance by Catholics of the non-Christian religions.

In various parts of the world, and especially in Latin America, leading Catholic theologians have turned their backs on the Catholicism that allied itself with despotic regimes, and some have become ardent proponents of LIBERATION THEOLOGY. The leaders in this new concern for the desperately poor and needy have adapted Marxist concepts to Christian ethical teaching. This has divided the church, especially in Latin America, into two camps—the traditionalists and the radical theologians and priests who have heartily embraced the teachings of revolutionary movements such as the Sandinistas of Nicaragua.

In the United States, progressive religious and priests have taken strong stands against the Vatican's official position on the role of women in the church. The diminishing number of candidates for the priesthood and the religious life has been attributed to the church's demands to maintain the regulations on clerical celibacy and what are regarded as limited opportunities for women to serve in more significant places of ministry. Lay people, especially in the United States, have expressed opposition to the Vatican's teaching on contraception, abortion, and divorce. The official Catholic position on nuclear warfare, service in the armed forces, capital punisment, and unbridled free enterprise has changed radically in recent years.

Another phenomenon in the Roman Catholic church has been the emergence of Catholic Pentecostalism or as it prefers to be known, charismatic renewal. What has grown to be a worldwide movement began in 1966 at Duquesne University in Pittsburgh. Influenced by some old-time Protestant Pentecostals, gatherings of Catholic believers reported that they had received gifts of the Spirit such as speaking in tongues, prophetic utterances, and were witnessing miracles of healing. The renewal has been characterized by emphasis on personal faith in Christ, increased interest in Bible study, and evangelistic outreach. To date there has been no tendency on the part of charismatics to leave the church. Many testify to a heightened interest in the Mass and devotion to Mary. It is dificult to assess the full significance of charismatic renewal, but there are indications that spirituality has increased, and there are signs of parish renewal.

There are now more than one billion professing Christians in the world. Of this number more than 600 million are Roman Catholics and more than 350 million are Protestants. Even though Catholics include all baptized believers in their statistics and most Protestants do not, Catholic dominance numerically seems to continue. With more than 50 million communicants listed in the United States, Catholics form the leading denomination, although the many varieties of Protestants total more than 100 million. In the United States there are 31 archdioceses and 131 dioceses, served by 320 bishops and 60,000 priests. Chicago, with a Catholic population of 2½ million, boasts the largest archdiocese. It is followed by Boston, Los Angeles, New York, Newark, and Philadelphia—all cities where the major religion is Roman Catholic. The vast Roman Catholic educational system is very impressive, from parochial grammar and high schools to huge and prestigious universities. No religious group, certainly not in America, has so devoted itself to providing the healing resources of hospitals, institutions that care for the needy, and charities of all descriptions.

The Catholic church proliferated in the United States earlier through large waves of immigrants. In recent decades their numbers have been amplified by millions of Hispanics from all the countries of Latin America and Asiatics from Vietnam, Cambodia (Kampuchea), Korea, and the Philippines. Because of the church's teaching against contraception and abortion, Catholic families have traditionally been large and this has led to a burgeoning Catholic population. Evangelization has augmented the ranks of converts—both blacks and whites—even in traditional Protestant sections of the country.                                         R.H.

**ROMAN CURIA.** From the Latin phrase *curia Romana*, meaning the Roman court. The Curia consists of all the organizations that assist the pope in governing the Roman Catholic church. Such administrative bodies include the twelve Sacred Congregations, the Tribunals, and the Curial offices, along with certain standing commissions. The pope is finally responsible for all the decisions and actions of the Curia, as the administrators are exercising authority delegated from him. Popularly, "the Curia" denotes the pope and the papal family, including the cardinals, bishops, and priests residing in the

Vatican. Particularly prominent parts of the Curia are the Chancery, the Dataria, and the Camera Apostolica, the divisions that make up the Curial offices.

J.C.

**ROMAN EMPIRE.** In the first century B.C. the old Roman republic, weakened by social clashes between the rich and the poor, the corruption of wealthy nobility in the city of Rome as well as of the senate itself, the destruction of both a productive agricultural economy and decent urban life, the ravages of war upon the countryside, famine, taxes, and other factors, gave way to the control of military dictators and the emergence of the empire. Julius Caesar was assassinated in 44 B.C. on March 15, and into this vacuum stepped his adopted son, Octavian, who took control of the army after defeating Mark Antony in 31 B.C. By 27 B.C. he took the title of Augustus CAESAR and became the first emperor of the new Roman Empire. During his reign Jesus Christ was born (Luke 2:1). Augustus established the "Peace of Rome," which prevailed for two centuries, guaranteeing the conditions under which extensive travel might be conducted in peace and safety. This facilitated the spread of the Christian message. Paul refers to this general cultural condition as the "fullness of time" (Gal 4:4). Augustus (27 B.C.–A.D. 14) was followed by several other emperors who ruled during the lifetime of Jesus and the apostles: Tiberius (A.D. 14–37), Caligula (A.D. 37–41), Claudius (A.D. 41–54), and Nero (A.D. 54–68). Jesus died under Tiberius; Paul and Peter almost certainly died under Nero. Citizenship was granted to people in the provinces under certain conditions. Paul, a Jew, was a Roman citizen by birth (Acts 22:28ff.)

Archaeological evidence of the glory of the empire is everywhere present in the Mediterranean world and the Middle East. Stretches of the Egnatian Way and the Appian Way may still be seen in Greece and Italy, among other places. The road system was extensive, well built, and marked by frequent milestones measured from the heart of Rome. Aqueducts bringing water over long distances were built all over the empire and can be seen still today in Spain, Italy, Greece, Turkey, and Israel, among other countries. Roman arches were designed to bear heavy loads, enabling the construction of Roman theaters (and smaller odeia in which municipal business was conducted) in the heart of town. The Greeks had built their theaters into hillsides, usually at the edge of town. Thus town planning changed in the empire due to advanced engineering capabilities. Cities were laid out in orthogonal patterns with intersecting main streets (*cardo*) and secondary streets (*decumanus*), often with a tetrapylon at the central intersection. Architecture reflected the basic Greek patterns—Doric, Ionic, and Corinthian. Art, sculpture, and literature were greatly influenced by the Greeks, being done with occasional flares of creativity. Roman law gave the world a new sense of justice.

The empire in the time of Augustus, Trajan, and Hadrian (first and early second centuries A.D.) extended from Spain in the west to Armenia in the east, and from England (Britannia) in the north to Egypt in the south. Britannia, Mauretania, Dacia, Thracia, Moesia, Armenia, Assyria, Cappadocia, Mesopotamia, and Arabia Petraea were added after the death of Augustus. Some of the provinces, such as Achaia, were governed by proconsuls (Gallio, Acts 18:12) while others, such as Judea, were under procurators (Pilate, Matt. 27:2). In most towns under Roman rule the official positions were held by Romans. Kings, like Herod the Great and his sons, were allowed to govern only under the eye of Roman authority. In the fourth century Constantine, who became at least nominally a Christian, transferred the capital from Rome to Byzantium in the east and renamed it Constantinople. The west deteriorated, and eventually ROME fell to the barbarians. The old pagan Roman Empire then became the Christian Byzantine Empire, in which the power of the church gradually grew until it became a formidable rival to the power of the emperor. Augustine's *City of God* laid the theoretical foundation for the eventual supremacy of the pope over the emperor.

J.R.M.

**ROMAN RELIGION.** The oldest prehistoric religion in the area of ROME was tied to animism, magic, and polydemonism. It consisted of mere ritual, without theology, in its earliest expressions. After the founding of Rome, traditionally in 753 B.C., worship centered around one of the seven hills on which the city stood in later times, the Palatine Hill. During the time of the Etruscan kings pagan temples were built on the Capitoline Hill, but Augustus built his chapel to Apollo on the Palatine below which lay the home of the vestal virgins and the Sacred Way, which was the oldest street in Rome. Beside it were the oldest and holiest structures of the Roman religion. The oldest elements in the religion were often referred to as the "religion of Numa" because Numa Pompilius, the second Etruscan king, was considered the founder of religious law and tradition. The religious rituals of Roman religion, however, are thought to be much older and, since no records of the earliest times survive, they have to be perceived in the pre-Julian calendars dealing with the various festivals that were religiously oriented. They tell of primitive sacrifices of animals, fruit, grain, and wine offered to various gods.

This early agricultural orientation of Roman religion gave way to the temples, statues of gods, divination, and mythology that were introduced by the Etruscans and Greeks. As the state developed, religion was urbanized. The primitive religion was inevitably weakened. Into this instability was injected GREEK philosophy and oriental mythology, creating a religious syncretism. Out of this amalgamation of religious ideas and rituals absorbed by Roman conquest arose a new kind of Roman religion, quite different from the primitive religion of Numa. With the transition from republic to empire the rapid rise of the importance of the emperor contributed to the rising tide of state-centered awareness by the people, promoted by those who stood to benefit by a stronger central, political power. Enhancing that power with religious meaning was a predictable if gradual development.

A state cult emerged with the worship of the emperor, as the representative of the gods, at its center. EMPEROR WORSHIP reached beyond Rome to the empire. Already in the second century B.C. a cult of the genius of Rome had begun in the provinces. A temple erected in honor of the city of Rome was built in Smyrna. But with the rise of the empire the cult of the emperor developed and a temple was built in 29 B.C. to Augustus in Pergamum. By the end of his reign or shortly thereafter, an altar or temple of Rome and Augustus had been set up in most of the Roman provinces. Pergamum eventually had three temples dedicated to Roman emperors and was the center of emperor worship in Asia. The spirit of the religion was political, often commercial, and seldom if ever religious. The emperor was the high priest and head of the state religion, being responsible for maintaining proper relations between humans and gods. He was semidivine while living and a god after death. Conducting the cultic practices, which were purely formal acts of religious ritual, was an essential part of public business, comparable to collecting taxes. There were neither ethical nor doctrinal ramifications to the religion. Questions concerning the nature of God, the character and purpose of human existence, the ultimate destiny of humankind, and the sense of community of belief, such as existed in Judaism and Christianity, were foreign to the cult. Because it lacked those dimensions that were of most concern to its adherents it eventually and inevitably died. Oriental religions took its place.                    J.R.M.

**ROMAN RITE.** The ordinary, traditional Latin Mass of the Roman Catholic church, as contrasted with the several variations of the Latin Mass, such as the Ambrosian, Mozarabic, Carmelite, Carthusian, and Dominican. It was the most widely used Christian liturgy in the world before the authorization of masses in the vernacular of each country by Vatican Council II (1962–65).                    J.C.

**ROMANS, LETTER TO THE.** This letter, written by Paul to the church at Rome in the mid-fifties A.D., has been universally praised as one of the chief books of the NT and as giving the essence of Paul's teaching.

*Setting.* During a winter's respite—when the seas would be closed to navigation—Paul remained at Corinth (Acts 20:2-6), and it is traditionally believed that he wrote this letter while he was in that city. Thereafter, he planned to visit Jerusalem to carry the collection that had been gathered in the Gentile churches for the poverty-stricken Jerusalem Christian

believers in the holy city. He had no prospect of what the future might hold (Rom. 15:31; compare Acts 20:3). So, it is suggested that this document was written as his "last will and testament," ensuring that, even if he never reached Rome—as he longed to do (Rom. 1:10, 13)—or even Jerusalem, there would be a record of his gospel to be sent to the western outpost of the church, for Christians to whom he was something of a stranger (1:13).

Clearly, at this time in his life, Paul had reached a turning point. According to Romans 14–16, especially 15:22-29, he makes it clear that, with his missionary work in eastern Mediterranean lands now concluded (Rom. 15:19, 23), he is ready to turn his face to new opportunities in the West. He is projecting a trip to Spain and wishes to secure the full support of the most influential church in the Christian world, at Rome, to aid him in his missionary outreach. He believes that they can, and will, do this; hence this is one reason for the letter.

Since it was Paul's intention to change the course of his mission and head in a new direction, we can well appreciate why he would want to "sum up" in this formal way the salient features of his preaching.

The tone and style of the earlier chapters (1–8) of his letter gives the impression of being just such a summing-up. Many scholars classify the letter—unlike other pieces of Paul's pastoral correspondence, more occasional in character—as "epistolary catechesis," that is, it is a letter couched in didactic form. It gives the substance of Paul's preaching and teaching for the training of new converts to the faith. It is also argumentative; and it also represents a sample of Paul's debating style, used in synagogue discussions and by the use of diatribe, to answer objections to his gospel from his Jewish compatriots (clearly in chaps. 2, 3). These combined features make the letter unique in Paul's writing to the churches. To be sure, it is a real letter, with addressees who are named (1:7), meant to meet the needs of a real-life, not an imaginary, congregation. But much of the argument is cast in the rhetorical style of exposition, as Paul enters into debate with his Jewish and Christian opponents (for example 3:4, 6, 27; 6:2, 15; 7:13; 9:14; 11:1, 11). These verses illustrate how he refuted false premises and conclusions in his enemies' and detractors' arguments.

The church at Rome sorely needed this statement of Paul's teaching. If chapter 16 is an essential part in the letter and not, as some teach, a detailed note of greeting addressed to Ephesus and tacked onto the copy of the Roman letters that eventually found their way to Ephesus, we can appeal to Romans 16:17-20 for the false ideas current. Even without that chapter, it is still obvious from chapters 14 and 15 that the church was divided over some practical issues, such as dietary rules and the observing of holy days. Two groups—the "strong" and the "weak"—were at loggerheads, and there were several other mediating positions taken on these issues. Paul wrote therefore to settle these churchly disputes.

A much more central concept of Paul in this letter relates to the Gentiles' freedom in the gospel. The position stated and enforced throughout the letter is that Paul's gospel is for all people (3:29), and salvation is designed to embrace all nations (10:12, 13) on the sole condition of human need (3:19-20), and God's grace in Christ offered to faith (3:24-26). New life is given on the basis of God's favor to all. The Jewish law is set on its true basis (3:31) when it is seen as pointing to Christ, who is both its goal and termination as a path of salvation (10:4). Christ is the universal Savior, and his people, whatever their racial origins, should find a center of unity as members in his own body in the one church (12:4-5). "Welcome one another, therefore, as Christ has welcomed you" (15:7) is the force in Paul's logic as well as his pastoral advice given at a distance.

Part of the problem within the church at Rome was evidently a suspicion created by Gentile arrogance, as this faction within multiracial house congregations was overemphasizing its independence of the church's Jewish origins in the OT and becoming forgetful of its indebtedness to historical Israel as God's chosen people (11:28). Paul tackles this issue at length in three chapters (9-11) by showing how Israel's past election, though frustrated by the nation's present disbelief and resistance to his message, will eventually be carried through to success. The outcome will be the salvation of Israel (11:26) as believing Jews will unite with the "wild olive" in Paul's Gentile mission to form one complete tree, and so "all Israel will be saved."

*Plan.* This letter is the most clearly structured of the surviving Pauline epistles. It is traditional to see three main divisions, with an exhortation (1:1-15) and conclusion (15:30–16:27). Paul is wrestling with three basic questions: How can sinful humanity be set right with God? What is the significance of Israel in history? What are the practical evidences in the outworking of Christian life and character? But these are not three unrelated matters. The single idea that binds them is the "righteousness of God," announced in the first chapter (1:16, 17), which then draws on Habakkuk 2:4. The prophet's statement, "The righteous shall live by faith," is sometimes taken to be the overarching text for Paul's treatment of chapters 1–8 in this letter. But the application of that verse in Habakkuk may be wider. Given that "righteousness" carries in this document its OT meaning of God's saving purpose, it then becomes possible to see how Paul is expounding God's salvation in three interconnected areas: (1) in the rescue of sinners from condemnation to new life by way of justification, reconciliation, and holy living (chaps. 1–8); (2) in the restoration of Israel, at least in its believing remnant now as a promise of a fuller response later to divine favor (chaps. 9–11); and (3) in the practical terms of daily living in the Christian society (chaps. 12–15

[16]). The main advantage of this way of seeing the infrastructure of Romans is that one is able to take in all the chapters and refuse to regard chapters 9–11 as an excursus and chapters 12–15 (16) as an appendix. We can also highlight the "center" or "heart" of Pauline theology as human recovery to God's family—for which the best modern term is reconciliation—as he is pleased to act, not only as Judge and Deliverer but most appropriately as Father. It can also be viewed as God's action to restore a fallen, alienated creation and to lead humans from their lostness "in Adam" to their inheritance "in Christ" (5:12-21), who is the first brother in a reconstituted and reconciled family of God (8:29) that embraces Jewish members (11:11-13) as well as Gentiles, and all sentient creatures and nature as well as human beings (8:19-21).                                                         R.M.

**ROMANTICISM.** A complex cultural movement of the late eighteenth and early nineteenth centuries held together by a common reaction against the RATIONALISM, DEISM, and classicism of the late seventeenth and eighteenth centuries. The first pure phase of Romanticism ran from 1780 to 1830. During this period poets and artists such as Byron, Blake, Wordsworth, Coleridge, Beethoven, Chopin, Balzac, Goethe, and Schiller produced the fruits of their genius. The Romantics exalted the emotions, feeling, and the affections. It is quite wrong, however, to think that Romanticism repudiated reason and intellect. Rather, it sought to enlarge the vision of the Age of Reason by stressing both emotion and intellect, spiritual aspiration and feeling, as well as scientific fact.

The Romantics believed that experience involves much that eludes analytical reasoning, including the insights and powers derived from the affections, the will, intuition, and imagination. The Romantics were weary of abstract, rationalistic proofs for and against religion and Christianity in particular. They were unashamed to declare: "My experience is my proof." The essence of religion is in feeling and sentiment, not in abstract ideas. "Evidences of Christianity! I am weary of the word," wrote the poet Coleridge. The French writer Chateaubriand (1768-1848) perfectly represents Romantic sentiment in *The Genius of Christianity* (1802), for this popular apology shifts the argument for Christianity from rational demonstration to aesthetic feeling. The truth of Catholicism is found, according to Chateaubriand, in its symbolization of human aspiration and in its unexcelled beauty.

The Romantic emphasis on experience enhanced the value of individuality, in contrast to what was uniform and universal. Schleiermacher pointed out that nature everywhere aims at diversity and individuality. The Deist search for one universal religion was contrary to nature's multiplicity. The rich diversity of experience attracted the Romantics to past ages, to primitive societies, and to tastes and experiences that appeared to the Age of Reason as superstitious, even barbaric. The Romantics were especially drawn to the Middle Ages because it represented chivalric romance and the unity of religion and culture. Romanticism contributed to our modern historical consciousness and to historicism, in that it recognized that every historical occasion is unique and relative and must be understood and appreciated in terms of its own particular context and time. Attacking the past now seemed childish. This new appeal to history proved to be a two-edged sword for theology. It led to a new appreciation of ancient tradition and the organic development of that tradition over the centuries. This is evident in the work of both the Protestant and Catholic TÜBINGEN SCHOOL. On the other hand, interest in history ushered in a period of intense investigation of the origins and development of Christianity, the results of which often challenged traditional doctrines and practices of the church.

Romantics envisioned nature not as a well-ordered machine, but as an insatiably dynamic and creative process. Behind and within nature they felt a spirit, a vital force, a Demiurge at work. This Spirit or God was not the Deist watchmaker God, wholly removed from creation. God is the vital Spirit immanent in all things, luring all creatures toward the achievement of their creative potential. "Call it Bliss! Heart! Love! God!" wrote Goethe, "I have no name for it. 'Tis feeling all."

Many Romantics found that through communion with nature they achieved an artless wisdom, which surpassed all knowledge and which brought with it spiritual repose. This gave the movement a distinctly religious sensibility. We are, in many respects, living today in a Romantic age.                                      J.L.

## ROME, CHURCHES OF.

Rome, ancient capital of the ROMAN EMPIRE, present capital of Italy, and the location of VATICAN City, the headquarters of the 600-million-member Roman Catholic church, is known as the city of churches. Early Christian tradition links both Peter and Paul with Rome. There was a vigorous church there in the mid-first century A.D., as Paul wrote his Epistle to the Romans during the decades of the fifties A.D.

Rome is the site of ST. PETER'S BASILICA, the largest Christian church in the world, and the seat of the pope. But Rome has several other basilicas and numerous other Roman Catholic churches. Among these are the basilica of St. Maria Maggiore (St. Mary Major), the Church of St. Peter in Chains, the Church of St. Prassede, the basilica of St. John Lateran, the basilica of St. Paul Outside the Walls, the Church of St. Maria in Cosmedin, the Church of St. Maria delle Vittorie, and the Church of St. Maria di Trastevere.

The areas around St. Peter's Basilica, along with three other basilicas—St. Maria Maggiore, St. John Lateran, and St. Paul Outside the Walls—form the Vatican state, a temporal possession of the Roman

Catholic church, ruled by the pope. The first basilica built in Rome was St. John Lateran, which dates back to A.D. 311-314; the second built was St. Peter's (A.D. 326); the third built was St. Paul Outside the Walls (A.D. 386); the fourth built was St. Maria Maggiore, which was begun in 432 and consecrated in A.D. 440.

The four basilicas of Rome have all undergone repairs, restorations, additions, and even complete rebuilding (in the case of St. Peter's, St. John's Lateran, and St. Paul's Outside the Walls) over the centuries. St. Maria Maggiore, also, has been much modified, chiefly in 1676 and 1758. St. Paul Outside the Walls stood intact from 386 until it was completely destroyed by fire in 1823. All of these historic churches and many of the smaller parish churches are full of priceless works of art, sacred relics, and reminders of the long, event-filled history of Western Christianity.

J.C.

## ROME, CITY OF.

Traditionally (according to Titus Livius), Rome was founded April 21, 753 B.C. The original site of the city was some seventeen miles up the Tiber River from the Tyrrhenian Sea, in west

Courtesy of the Italian State Tourist Office, New York

*Air view of the Colosseum and the Arch of Constantine*

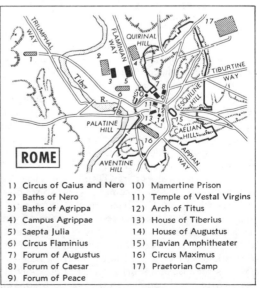

| | |
|---|---|
| 1) Circus of Gaius and Nero | 10) Mamertine Prison |
| 2) Baths of Nero | 11) Temple of Vestal Virgins |
| 3) Baths of Agrippa | 12) Arch of Titus |
| 4) Campus Agrippae | 13) House of Tiberius |
| 5) Saepta Julia | 14) House of Augustus |
| 6) Circus Flaminius | 15) Flavian Amphitheater |
| 7) Forum of Augustus | 16) Circus Maximus |
| 8) Forum of Caesar | 17) Praetorian Camp |
| 9) Forum of Peace | |

From *Bible Atlas* by Emil G. Kraeling. Copyright © 1962 by Rand McNally and Company

*The Arch of Titus, with the Colosseum in the background*

*The Pantheon at Rome*

*The ruins of the Temple of Mars in the Roman Forum*

*The Forum at Rome*

central Italy, on seven hills. Originally a barbarous village ruled by petty kings (according to Tacitus), Rome, through warfare and trade, grew and developed into the Roman Republic by 509 B.C. Rome steadily grew in prominence in Italy and throughout the Mediterranean world until it became an empire (after the assassination of Julius Caesar in 44 B.C. and the civil war between Mark Antony and Octavius, who became Caesar Augustus, the first Roman Emperor). Rome went from glory to glory, conquering the Mediterranean world, western and central Europe, the Middle East and North Africa. Ultimately, external pressures by barbarian tribes,

internal discord, and palace coups brought the fall of Rome in A.D. 410, when it was sacked by the Visigoths. The eastern ROMAN EMPIRE continued, ruled from Constantinople, or Byzantium, until A.D. 1492.

Rome was, and is, a city of glorious architectural structures. It has been built and rebuilt over and over again, beginning in the time of the republic and running down to the 1930s under Mussolini.

It was said that all roads led to Rome, and this was true because the Romans built sturdy roads all over their empire and posted stadia or mileposts along them giving the distance to Rome. A Roman once declared that all the sewers of Antioch (Asia) flowed through the streets of Rome. Indeed every fad, fashion, faith, and superstition from the East did come to Rome, including Judaism and Christianity. Thousands of Jews settled in Rome, and controversies among them (perhaps with Christian Jews) caused the emperor CLAUDIUS to expel many of them in A.D. 49. Paul's Epistle to the Romans (around A.D. 56) shows that a flourishing Christian church was there by that time, with some Christians in the emperor's household. Peter, too, is closely identified with Rome, and the "trophy" (or burial monument) of Peter under St. Peter's Basilica tends to confirm his presence there. Tradition holds that both Paul and Peter were martyred in Rome, under NERO, who had caused the city to be burned in A.D. 64 or 66. Nero destroyed the ghetto-like tenements of Rome's working classes and rebuilt the city, boasting that he found the city brick and left it marble.

The great Forum was begun by Julius Caesar and added to by many emperors. The Circus Maximus, the Colosseum, the baths of Caracala, and many other magnificent public works impressed the ancient world and still have the power to awe visitors almost seventeen centuries after Rome's fall.                      J.C.

## ROOT AND BRANCH.

**ROOT AND BRANCH.** A petition introduced by the PURITANS in the Long Parliament in London December 11, 1640, demanding that the episcopacy "with all its dependencies, roots, and branches, be abolished." The image comes from Malachi 4:1. Parliament did little with the petition initially; its introduction only alienated more moderate supporters. But bishops, deans, and chapters were abolished and church lands confiscated during the Civil War.                                                        N.H.

**ROSARY.** A popular Roman Catholic devotion in the cult of the Virgin Mary. It is a prayer directed to God through Mary, consisting of fifteen sets of ten HAIL MARYS (decades), each set opening with the Lord's Prayer and ending with the phrase, "Glory be to the Father, and to the Son, and to the Holy Spirit." The reciting of these prayers is accompanied by meditation upon the sufferings and glories of our Lord and the Virgin Mary. The rosary itself is similar to the prayer beads used both by Buddhists and Muslims. It is a string of small beads separated from each other by a larger bead, with a crucifix attached. Use of the rosary goes back at least to the twelfth century. Pope Pius V organized the pattern of saying the Rosary that is still followed.                                                      J.C.

**ROSETTA STONE.** An inscribed, irregularly shaped, thick block of basalt (3 feet 9 inches by 2 feet 4½ inches) found in August 1799, near the delta town of Rosetta, Egypt, during the Napoleonic campaigns. The second century B.C. text honors Ptolemy V Epiphanes by recording his benefactions to the Memphis priests.

Following the work by English physicist Thomas Young, Jean François Champollion, a brilliant young French scholar, in 1821–22 published the decipherment of the stone's text. The surface of the stone (now in the British Museum) is divided into three parts. Champollion discovered that the texts of the three parts were identical and were written in two ancient Egyptian scripts (hieroglyphic and Demotic) and in Hellenistic Greek. His conclusion, confirmed in 1866, has been generally accepted. This remarkable discovery allows scholars to translate previously unintelligible, ancient Egyptian writings. Egyptology, thus begun, has contributed much to our knowledge of Egyptian history and literature as well as to biblical backgrounds.                            P.L.G.

**ROSH HASHANAH.** The Jewish New Year. Unlike New Year celebrations of many people, the Jewish New Year is observed with a solemnity that is marked by prayer, contemplation, and soul-searching. Rosh Hashanah begins the pensive ten-day period known as the Days of Awe, which end with Yom Kippur, the DAY OF ATONEMENT. Despite its solemn character, Rosh Hashanah is a festival when Jews pray that "the righteous shall see and rejoice, the upright shall exult, and the devout shall delight in song." As it is written in Nehemiah 8:9-10, "This day is holy to the Lord your God; do not mourn or weep . . . do not be grieved, for the joy of the Lord is your strength."

Traditionally regarded as the first day of Creation, Rosh Hashanah is also called *Yom ha-Zikaron* (Day of Remembrance), and *Yom ha–Din* (Day of Judgment), in which God remembers all creatures and passes judgment on all human beings. Rosh Hashanah is also called *Yom Teruah* (Day of Blowing of the Ram's Horn) as a symbol of God's summons to the people for self-judgment, self-improvement, and atonement.

Prayer, solemnity, and rest from work mark the Jewish New Year. Apples dipped in honey are eaten in anticipation of a sweet and good year. On the first day, traditional Jews go to a body of water for *tashlikh,* the "casting out of sins."

L.K.

**ROSICRUCIANS.** An esoteric society said to have existed since the days of ancient Egypt. Actually its true origins can be traced back to the early sixteenth century and to the writings of a Lutheran pastor, Johan Valentin Andrea (1586–1654). He apparently used the pseudonym Christian Rosenkreunz (rose cross) to author a series of pamphlets between 1614 and 1616. In *Fama Fraternitatis* and *Confessio rosae crucis,* two of the pamplets, he announced the existence of a Rosicrucian fraternity that possessed occult powers. He said that Rosicrucianism had Eastern and Arab origins. It really was not until the eighteenth century, however, that Rosicrucian groups were formed in Germany, Russia, and Poland. The organization was known variously as the Brothers of the Rosy Cross, Rosy-Cross Knights and Rosy-Cross Philosophers. There was an apparent connec-

*Rosetta Stone*

tion with FREEMASONRY. Indeed some Masonic lodges still offer an optional degree called the Rose Croix. The cross and rose symbolically declare the candidate's death and resurrection. In Great Britain this is a trinitarian rite that includes the reading of Isaiah 53. In the United States the same rite has pagan significance.

H. Spencer Lewis founded the Ancient Mystical Order, Rosae Crucis (AMORC), with headquarters in San Jose, California. The Rosicrucian Brotherhood (Fraternitas Rosae Crucis) has headquarters in Quakertown, Pennsylvania, and the Society of Rosicrucians (Societas Rosicruciana in America) has offices in New York City.

AMORC has published the so-called "lost" Book of Jashar, which, it is believed, was written by Jacob

Ilive in 1751. Also published by the same group is a book called *Secret Teachings of Jesus*. American Rosicrucians are proponents of doctrines of THEOSOPHY. There is an emphasis in AMORC on developing psychic powers. The cross represents the human body rather than Christ's atoning death. The rose is said to contain a pure fluid that overcomes human passion.                                                                         R.H.

*Rotas-Sator Square*

**ROTAS-SATOR SQUARE.** A cryptogram called the magic square. It is of uncertain date, origin, and interpretation.

Five Latin words of five letters are arranged in a square so that they can be read from top to bottom or from right to left as a sentence(?): *Sator*, "the sower"; *Arepo*, "with his plow"; *Tenet*, "holds"; *Opera*, "with purpose"; *Rotas*, "the wheels." Where the middle word "tenet" intersects, an equal-armed or Greek cross is formed. The design was first discovered in four copies at Dura–Europos in 1932, dating it to the third century A.D. In 1937, a copy was discovered at Pompeii (destroyed in 79 A.D.), which has raised doubts about its connections with Christianity.
                                                                         P.L.G.

**ROUSSEAU, JEAN JACQUES** (1712–78). The philosopher and political theorist who inspired the French Revolution and ROMANTICISM was born in Geneva, Switzerland, on June 28. After a Calvinist, working-class childhood, he ran away at sixteen, emigrated to Turin, and became a Roman Catholic. From 1733 to 1740 he lived in Chambéry, France.

His first publication was *Dissertation sue la musique moderne* (1743). His essay "Discours sur les sciences et les arts" (1750) created a stir by arguing that the arts and sciences served only the rich. He became friends with the Encyclopedists and contributed to their work. In 1754 he returned to Geneva, and to

Calvinism to some extent. His *Discours sur l'origine et les fondements de l'inegalite parmi les hommes* suggested that primitive people are free and happy, and that society and reason corrupts the "noble savage." He spelled out the educational ramifications in *Émile* (1762). In *Social Contract* (1762), Rousseau outlined a theory of a just state based on the general consent of the populace. Both *Émile* and *Social Contract* were condemned by the parliament in Paris. He published his autobiographical *Confessions* (1781–88), in which he aimed "to show a man in all the truth of nature."

In an age of rationalism, Rousseau advocated a Deism centered in a personal relationship to God through conscience. His is a simple religion of love for God and humankind. Feeling is more important than thought. Nature and humanity are fundamentally good, though people are corrupted by society. He offered a substitute for revealed religion that was intellectually and emotionally satisfying.          N.H.

**ROYCE, JOSIAH** (1855–1916). American idealist philosopher who had a lifelong interest in the problems of religion. In an early writing, *The Religious Aspect of Philosophy* (1885), he acknowledged that it was a religious interest that first drove him to philosophy. The variety of IDEALISM that Royce espoused was that known as "absolute idealism," in which the central reality is a spiritual Absolute. But, unlike some other absolute idealists, Royce did not believe that finite spirits are absorbed into the Absolute. They do indeed live within the Absolute, but the Absolute is "just to the finite aspect of every flying moment," so that the finite spirits are "ethically free individuals who are nevertheless one in God" (quoted from *The World and the Individual*, Royce's Gifford Lectures of 1900–1901). He laid great stress on the virtus of loyalty, defined as "the willing and thoroughgoing devotion of a self to a cause, when the cause is something which unites many selves in one." His last major writing, *The Problem of Christianity* (1912), expounded Christianity as a religion of loyalty, reaching out toward an ideal community that would be the realization of the divine on earth. His concern with loyalty was later to influence Marcel's stress on fidelity in interpersonal existence.                                                                         J.M.

**RUDRA.** From the Sanskrit word meaning literally "the Howler" or "the Red One." A deity of the ancient VEDAS of HINDUISM who is said to inhabit wilderness areas and so to represent the powerful but unpredictable forces of nature. Rudra is an outsider who can sometimes be prevailed upon to heal, but can also be malevolent. He is generally considered to be a precursor of SHIVA in later Hinduism.          R.E.

**RULE OF FAITH** (*regula fidei*). A summary of the Christian faith as handed down from the apostles, through the bishops, used primarily as a standard in catechetical instruction and as a guide for the interpretation of Scripture in preaching.

In contrast to creeds, rules of faith are more flexible in both wording and theological content. They became common before creeds, in the second half of the second century. Examples are found in the works of Justin Martyr, Irenaeus, Tertullian, Clement, and Origen. Tertullian, for example, offers three different forms.

The rule of faith constituted the first summary of Christian TRADITION and was used as authority against the Gnostics. Irenaeus called the rule "the canon of the truth." The early church fathers assumed that the rule was not in contrast to Scripture but condensed the true meaning of Scripture and the apostles' teachings. The rule of faith was more useful than Scripture in theological debates because the Gnostics interpreted Scripture to support their own position and claimed secret traditions. The church fathers claimed that their rule of faith was the one universally accepted by the church. During the third century, tradition became more firmly fixed in the liturgy and developing creeds. Precise wording became more crucial in the emerging theological debates.                                                            N.H.

**RUSSELL, CHARLES TAZE** (1852–1916). Founder of the religious movement now known as JEHOVAH'S WITNESSES. Born in Pittsburgh, Pennsylvania, Russell was employed as a clerk in a dry goods store. He disagreed with the teachings of the Congregationalist church in which he was reared, particularly the doctrine of eternal punishment. A self-taught student of the Bible, Russell began to develop his own set of doctrines. In 1872 he taught that the Second Coming of Christ would occur in 1874 and the end of the world would come in 1914. He refused trinitarian teaching, declaring that the Trinity meant "three Gods in one person." He also taught that Christ was the first created being and not the eternal divine Son of God.

Russell gained a group of followers and established an independent church in 1878, of which he was the pastor. His first book dealing with the Second Coming was entitled *The Object and Manner of Our Lord's Return*. In 1879 he launched a magazine called *Zion's Watchtower and Herald of Christ's Presence*. In 1881 he wrote *Food for Thinking Christians*, which was reissued five years later as *Millennial Dawn*, and later incorporated in his *Studies of the Scriptures*. By 1884 he had founded a publishing house, Zion's Watchtower Tract Society, which issued Russell's six volumes of *Studies in the Scriptures* (1886–1904). After his death a seventh volume on the book of Revelation was written by his followers. These seven volumes comprise the basis for the theology of Jehovah's Witnesses.

In 1909 Russell moved his headquarters to Brooklyn Tabernacle, New York City, where the growing movement of "Russellites" or "Millennial Dawnists" continued to thrive. Russell was a capable writer, with sermons syndicated in fifteen hundred papers. He also continued to travel extensively, and slide films synchronized with sound extended his vast ministry.

The world did not end in 1914, as Russell had predicted, but when World War I broke out, events only increased his popularity. In his works on Daniel and Revelation, similar to other Adventist writing, Russell taught a general revolution of the workers, followed by the resurrection of the dead, the Last Judgment, and the establishment of the messianic Kingdom on earth. Upon Russell's death the new head of the work was a lawyer named J. F. RUTHERFORD.                                                           R.H.

**RUSSIAN ORTHODOX CHURCH.** *See* ORTHODOX CHURCHES.

**RUTH, BOOK OF.** On the face of it, the story of Ruth and her mother-in-law, Naomi, is a story about human loyalty that transcends all bounds of duty and kinship. Ruth was a woman of Moab who married one of the sons of Elimelech and Naomi, Bethlehemites who had settled in her land. After the death of all of the men of the family and in a time of famine, Naomi determined to return to Bethlehem and urged her two daughters-in-law to remain with their kinfolk in Moab. The other woman, Orpah, was persuaded to do so, but Ruth uttered that cry of total human loyalty that has glorified her in all the ages since: "Where you go I will go, and where you lodge I will lodge; your people shall be my people, and your God my God; where you die I will die, and there will I be buried" (Ruth 1:16-17).

In the event, Ruth and Naomi did return to Bethlehem, and there through a series of honorable transactions, Ruth entered into a marriage contract with Boaz, a distant kinsman of Elimelech. Unlike an even closer relative, Boaz was willing to raise up through Ruth a family line for Naomi and her late son, thus fulfilling the law of leviratic marriage (Deut. 25:5-10). Thanks to Boaz' willingness to take the foreigner Ruth in marriage, she became an ancestor of David, according to the end of the book. Christians even acknowledge her as an ancestor of Jesus (Matt. 1:5, 16). Like the book of Jonah, the real purpose of the book of Ruth seems, therefore, to be an affirmation of the universal love of God for human beings and the universal scope of God's saving grace.

Although the book of Ruth is attached to the book of Judges in the Septuagint and in the English Bible tradition, it is commonly held now to have been written in the postexilic period. It is a classic example of the Hebrew narrative art, and some even regard it as the perfect example of storytelling in the Bible.                                                                W.S.T.

**RUTHERFORD, JOSEPH FRANKLIN** (1869–1941). Second head of the JEHOVAH'S WITNESSES, a name he gave to the organization in 1931. Born to a Missouri Baptist family, Rutherford obtained an attorney's license in 1892. For a time he served as a special judge in Missouri and so became known as "Judge" Rutherford. He met CHARLES TAZE RUSSELL through serving him as legal counsel and became a devout follower of his teachings. Thus he became a candidate to succeed Russell in the leadership of the proliferating organization.

Under Rutherford's firm hand the organization took on an increasingly revolutionary thrust. In 1918 he and six others were sentenced to twenty-one years in the federal prison at Atlanta after being charged with insubordination and disseminating propaganda against military service. Rutherford served nine months.

Like his predecessor, Rutherford was a prolific writer and crusader for the doctrines of the group. To give an explanation for Russell's failed prediction that the world would end in 1914, "Judge" Rutherford explained in 1921 that Christ actually returned invisibly in 1914 and had begun to purge his temple in 1918. Since Armageddon had been postponed and the Witnesses had grown well beyond the expected 144,000 (derived from Revelation 14), Rutherford discovered a new class in which many of his followers would be found.                                    R.H.

RUYSBROECK, JAN VAN (1293–1381). Flemish mystic. Raised by a pious uncle who was a canon at St. Gudule in Brussels, Ruysbroeck was ordained in 1317 and became a chaplain there from 1317 to 1343. In 1343, along with two other priests, he moved to a hermitage at Groenendael. As others joined them, they formed an Augustinian abbey in 1349 of which Ruysbroeck became prior. His first mystical work, *The Kingdom of the Lovers of God*, derived much from Hadewych, who also spoke of mysticism's relationship between the soul and God as that between a lover and the beloved. Ruysbroeck's most famous work, *The Spiritual Espousals* (1350), is a commentary on "Behold, the Bridegroom comes." It is a guide for the soul searching for God. He also wrote *The Seven Steps of the Ladder of Spiritual Love* and *The Sparkling Stone*.

Ruysbroeck's spirituality, which anticipated the fifteenth-century *devotio moderna*, deeply influenced John Tauler, Gerard Groote, and Henry Suso. His fusion of the metaphysical and personal earned him the title of "the Ecstatic Doctor." He was beatified in 1908. His feast day is the anniversary of his death, December 2.                                    N.H.

# Ss

**SABAOTH.** Hebrew noun meaning "hosts," often located in the special epithet for Israel's God, "Yahweh of hosts." Aptly highlighting divine sovereignty and splendor, "Yahweh Sabaoth" is sometimes affirmed as God's very name (Amos 5:27; Jer. 10:16). Fundamentally a military term denoting an army of men (Judg. 4:2) or warfare itself (I Sam. 28:1), "Sabaoth" probably originated as a divine epithet at Shiloh, the central sanctuary of eleventh-century B.C. Israel (I Sam. 1:3). Yahweh of hosts is both the creator and commander of the celestial army (sun, moon, stars; Ps. 33:6; Deut. 4:19) and the determiner of historical events involving the subjection of God's wayward people to foreign power (Jer. 6:6) and their ultimate redemption (Isa. 47:4).

J.K.K.

**SABBATARIANISM.** A belief that Sunday should be observed as the OT SABBATH. According to the fourth commandment (Exod. 20:8-11), one should keep it holy and do no work. Constantine made Sunday a day of rest in A.D. 321.

The sabbatarian movement in its strictest form, however, is largely the creation of Scottish and English Reformers during the last two decades of the sixteenth century (it was not an issue on the Continent). Nicholas Bound's book *True Doctrine of the Sabbath* (1595) joined the issue. James I's *Book of Sports* (1618), which allowed sports on Sundays,

provoked political controversy. The Puritan Parliament burned the book in 1643 and enforced strict Sabbath observance.

Puritans and Presbyterians brought the practice to America, where "blue laws" were enacted and continue to our day, though nearly obliterated by urbanization, industrialization, and immigration. Various nineteenth-century organizations tried to stem the tide. In 1828 the General Union for Promoting Observance of the Christian Sabbath mounted a petition campaign against mail delivery on Sunday. Evangelicals protested the opening on Sunday of the 1876 Centennial Exposition in Philadelphia and the 1893 Columbian Exposition in Chicago.

The word "sabbatarianism" is also sometimes applied to groups that consider the Jewish Sabbath, Saturday, as the proper day for Christian worship, that is, Seventh-day Adventists, and Seventh-day Baptists.

N.H.

**SABBATH.** *Jewish.* The weekly day of rest, pleasure, and meditation. Jews acknowledge the period from sunset Friday to nightfall Saturday as their Sabbath. Most Christians observe it on Sunday and Moslems on Friday.

To the Jewish people, the weekly Sabbath is the holiest day in the Hebrew calendar, with the one exception of the Day of Atonement (Yom Kippur).

The first thing in the world that God made holy was not a mountain, not an altar, not a land. It was a day—the Sabbath. "And God blessed the seventh day and made it holy" (Gen. 2:3).

In the Bible, the Sabbath is the only holy day of which observance is mandated in the Ten Commandments—first in Exodus and again in Deuteronomy. The first part of the Fourth Commandment, "Remember the sabbath day, to keep it holy" (28:8 JPS), may show that the Sabbath was well established long before the Israelites stood at the foot of Mount Sinai.

Jews connect the Sabbath to two events: the Creation and the Exodus from Egypt. "And on the seventh day God finished His work which He had made; and He rested on the seventh day from all His work which He had made" (Gen. 2:2 JPS). "And thou shalt remember that thou wast a servant in the land of Egypt, and the Lord thy God brought thee out thence by a mighty hand and by an outstretched arm; therefore the Lord thy God commanded thee to keep the sabbath day" (Deut. 5:7, 15 JPS).

It is for this reason that the kiddush, the blessing over wine that ushers in the holy Sabbath, contains these words: "With loving favor Thou hast given us the heritage of Thy holy Sabbath, a memorial of Thy work of creation. That day is the first of the holy convocations, recalling our going forth from Egypt."

The special status of the seventh day and its name were disclosed to the Jewish people (Israel) in the wilderness. For their food, God supplied their day's portion of manna for five days. On the sixth day, God provided a double portion of manna to last through the seventh day, on which no manna appeared. The Israelites were commanded to go out and collect and prepare each day's portion for the first five days. On the sixth day, they were to prepare for two days. On the seventh day they were not to go out. In this way, they learned that the seventh day is "a holy sabbath unto the Lord" (Exod. 16:23 JPS). The two loaves of Sabbath bread at the Friday night meal are a reminder of the double portion of manna.

*Shabbat,* the Hebrew word for the Sabbath, is related to the verb *shavat,* which means "cease, desist, rest (from work)." While the Bible does not specify all kinds of work forbidden on the Sabbath, it does mention a few, among them buying and selling, traveling, and cooking. The Mishnah, the largest post-biblical collection of Jewish laws, lists, under thirty-nine categories, all acts defined as work in Jewish law and therefore forbidden on the Sabbath. These include plowing, reaping, carrying loads, kindling a fire, writing, sewing, and the like. The prohibition against work on the Sabbath extends to the free and the slave alike and to beasts of burden. ". . . thou shalt not do any manner of work, thou, nor thy son, nor thy daughter, nor thy man-servant, nor thy maid-servant, nor thy cattle, nor thy stranger that is within thy gates" (Exod. 20:10 JPS).

The Sabbath demands more than the stoppage of work, however. It is specifically marked off as a day devoted to God and to the life of the Spirit. It is to be honored by the kindling of lights, eating good food, wearing one's best clothes, worshiping, receiving religious instruction, studying, and demonstrating love for family and friends.

The most important observance of the Jewish Sabbath is in the home. Every home is perceived as a small sanctuary. The family table is the "altar." In the observant home, the mother lights the candles at sundown Friday and recites a blessing over them. The father blesses the children. For boys, the blessing is, "May the Lord make thee as Ephraim and Manasseh"; for girls, the blessing is, "May the Lord make thee as Sarah, Rebecca, Rachel, and Leah." Then he recites the priestly blessing over all their children:

> May the Lord bless thee and keep thee.
> May the Lord cause His countenance to shine upon thee and be gracious unto thee,
> May the Lord lift up His countenance unto thee and give thee peace. Amen.

In honor of his wife, the husband recites "A woman of valor . . ." from Proverbs.

The Sabbath table is covered with the best tablecloth, set with the best dishes, with the kiddush cup, and with two loaves of Sabbath bread. The father says the kiddush over the wine and a blessing over the bread. After the Sabbath meal, blessings are said and joyful songs are sung.

In the synagogue, the Sabbath is welcomed as a bride and bidden farewell as a queen. Sabbath services include reading from the Torah—a scroll of parchment that contains the Five Books of Moses, the Pentateuch, in unvowelled Hebrew—and from the Prophets. There is a period of study and religious instruction in the afternoon. The end of the Sabbath is marked when three stars appear in the sky. The Havdalah ceremony features the lighting of a specially braided candle, blessings over wine, over spices in a special spicebox, and over the candle. Finally, a "separation" blessing praises God "who divides the holy from the ordinary, the light from the darkness."

The beauty of the Jewish Sabbath has been enhanced by a rich embroidery of folklore. The Sabbath, for example, is perceived as a fair and chaste bride descending on the rays of the setting sun to her faithful lover. There is a legend about two angels who accompany each Jew as that person goes home from the synagogue on Friday night. Every devout Jew is said to acquire an additional soul on the Sabbath—an extra measure of spirituality.

Scholars assert that the Sabbath as a universal rest day devoted to God is one of the most important Jewish contributions to civilization.          L.K.

*In the New Testament.* The celebration of the Sabbath is noted in the Gospels, Acts, and also (more negatively) in the Epistles. As a devout Jew, Jesus kept the Sabbath, attending synagogue and helping to lead the service (Luke 4:16-30; Matt. 13:53-58; Mark 6:1-6; Acts 13:14-16). Jesus' devotion, however, was tempered by the view that "the Sabbath is made for man, not man for the Sabbath." Indeed, Jesus' practices sparked controversy with the Pharisees, with Jesus showing that the intent of the Sabbath is to benefit people, rather than being a ritual observance that must not be deviated from (Luke 6:1-11; Matt. 12:1-14; Mark 2:23-28; 3:1-3).

After the Resurrection, which took place on Sunday, the first day of the week, Christians began to celebrate their "sabbath" on Sunday, although the early Jewish Christians apparently continued to honor the Jewish Temple worship and the Sabbath as well (Acts 3:13; 13:14-15; 14:1; 16:16; 17:17; 18:4; 21:26). Indeed, Paul probably lived according to his Jewish upbringing, despite his clear teaching that such observances were not necessary for Christians (Acts 15; Gal. 2:11-21). In the period after the destruction of the Temple (A.D. 70), the widely scattered and increasingly Gentile church dropped the observance of the Sabbath altogether. The LORD'S DAY, the first day of the week, became the Christian day of worship exclusively.                               J.C.

**SABBATICAL YEAR.** An early Israelite institution organized around the final year of a seven-year cycle. Its antiquity is attested in the Covenant Code mandate that the land lie uncultivated every seventh year (Exod. 23:10-11) and that the slave who desires it be liberated after serving six years (21:2-6). Since owners were forbidden to harvest untilled agricultural yields, this humanitarian regulation provided sustenance for the landless poor. Lack of a specific starting date for the sowing cycle implies the existence of field rotation, ensuring that not all land would lie fallow simultaneously.

The Deuteronomic Code makes the sabbatical year an occasion for the remission of debts owed by one Israelite to another (Deut. 15:1-4a). Through this generous addressing of human need, the Deity was honored in this "Lord's release" (v. 2). Writing off indebtedness included the liberation of Hebrews enslaved for nonpayment of debts who had served six years (15:12-18). Deuteronomy's silence about the land's noncultivation implies that the practice had lapsed or that the nation's economy was no longer solely agrarian.

The Holiness Code perceives this institution as a Sabbath, signifying Yahweh's ownership of the land (Lev. 25:2-7). Everything from the agricultural land was to be left untouched. But God promises a yield in the sixth year so extraordinary that it will sustain Israel through the year of fallow and the next year till harvest time (25:19-22). Unlike Deuteronomy, debt cancellation was transferred to the fiftieth or jubilee year (25:13).

Only in Nehemiah 10:31 does the OT offer a lucid historical allusion to sabbatical year observance (see also I Macc. 6:49, 53). The intensity of Israel's religious fervor in any given era surely determined how zealously this institution was upheld.
                                                              J.K.K.

**SABEANS.** A sturdy and tall (Isa. 45:14) Semitic people living "far off" (Joel 3:8) in the southwest Arabian Peninsula, roughly near modern Yemen. They were renowned in the Bible as traders in slaves (Joel 3:8), camels (I Kings 10:2; Isa. 60:6); gold (I Kings 10:4; Ps. 72:10, 15; Isa. 60:6; Ezek. 27:22-23; 38:13); spices (I Kings 10:4; Ezek. 27:22-23; 38:13); precious stones (I Kings 10:4; Ezek. 27:22-23; 38:13); frankincense (Isa. 60:6; Jer. 6:20) and myrrh. Saba (in Hebrew *Sheba*) was the capital city (Job 6:19 and elsewhere). The Sabeans, who had colonies in Ethiopia, traded goods from many lands, much from Africa.                                            P.L.G.

**SABELLIANISM.** *See* MONARCHIANISM.

**SAB'IYYA.** In ISLAM, one of several subdivisions of the Shi'ites. The name, literally meaning "sevener," is generally used to identify the Ismailites, who recognize as IMAMS (divinely inspired leaders) only the first seven successors to MUHAMMAD. It is also sometimes used for only the largest subgroup of Ismailites.

The question of how to transmit authority has always been important in Islam. Who can truly claim to be the successor to the Prophet Muhammad? Shi'ites believe that each imam, beginning with Ali, Muhammad's son-in-law, designated one of his sons as his successor. Ja'far al-Sadiq (died A.D. 765) designated his son Ismail, but he outlived Ismail and then designated another son as successor. Many felt that the designation once made could not be changed, and so they accepted Ismail's son as the seventh imam.

Several popular beliefs came into play at that point: there would be only seven imams; the seventh would not die but would enter a state of seclusion that would last indefinitely; during that time he would rule through special representatives; and finally he would return as Mahdi, a "messianic" figure, and not die until he had conquered the world. Down to the present day there have been various people who claimed to be the Mahdi.

A number of Sab'iyya sects arose. The QARMATIANS were the most shocking. In A.D. 930 they captured Mecca and stole the sacred black stone from the Ka'ba. The Fatimid dynasty ruled Egypt (A.D. 909–1171). And the Assassins dominated the area south of the Caspian Sea from the eleventh to the thirteenth century. They survive today as the Nizarites, governed by Aga Khan IV, with headquarters in Paris.                                              K.C.

**SACERDOTAL.** Having to do with sacred things, with the divine liturgy and the duties of a priest. Sacerdotal means consecrated or sacred; the holy. There are sacerdotal robes or vestments, sacerdotal vessels, such as the chalice and paten, and sacerdotal rites, such as the Mass and the sacrament of baptism.

J.C.

**SACKCLOTH.** A coarse, dark cloth woven from the hair of goats or camels. Literally, the word is used of a sack for grain (Gen. 42:25, 27, 29; Levi. 11:32; Josh. 9:4) and as a garment worn in mourning (II Sam. 3:31; 21:10; I Kings 21:27), as a sign of mental anguish, personal grief (I Sam. 21:10), or national calamity (II Kings 6:30; Neh. 9:1; Esth. 4:2). Sackcloth is associated with the rending of clothing and putting ashes on the head. In Jonah 3:8, the Ninevites covered man and beast with sackcloth. In Judith 4:11 (Apocrypha), sackcloth was put on an altar.

Sackcloth was worn on occasion by prophets (Isa. 2:2) but was not the usual prophetic garment. There is no indication that wearing sackcloth was uncomfortable nor was it a form of penance or self-discipline. The only mention in the Pentateuch is of Jacob (Gen. 37:34). The practice seems to have been mandated by custom rather than by law.                                P.L.G.

**SACRAMENTARY.** A liturgical book containing the canon of the Mass along with proper collects, prefaces, and prayers, used in the Western church until the thirteenth century for celebration of the Mass. Beginning in the tenth century, sacramentaries were gradually replaced by MISSALS.           N.H.

**SACRAMENTS.** A significant rite or action that makes present or effective the sacred or holy. Sacraments are found in all religions in which the divine or the supernatural is made present through the natural. SYMBOLS are images that suggest or present the sacred, while effective action is essential to sacraments. They leave the situation different from what it was before. A classic definition of a sacrament describes it as "an outward and visible sign of an inward and spiritual grace." This would be in accord with the general teaching of the church fathers and the medieval theologians. Augustine defined a sacrament as a "visible sign of an invisible reality," and Thomas Aquinas spoke of a sacrament as "a sign of a sacred thing insofar as it sanctifies men," indicating the importance of its effective action.

The word "sacrament" does not appear in the Bible, although sacramental actions, for example, baptisms and purification rites, common sacred meals, and rites of initiation and confirmation, are found in both the OT and the NT. The Latin *sacramentum* meant an oath of allegiance and, while this had some influence on Christian usage, the word "sacrament" is more closely associated with the Latin NT rendering of the Greek *mysterion* or sacred mystery. In the early and medieval church, the scope of what constituted valid sacraments was not sharply drawn, in part because no clear distinctions were made between, for example, baptism and confirmation. Augustine even applied the word to the creed

and to the Lord's Prayer. Hugh of St. Victor (twelfth century) held that there were as many as thirty sacraments. Peter Lombard (1100–60), in his *Sentences,* established seven sacraments, the number that became traditional and authoritative in the Roman Catholic church, namely, BAPTISM, CONFIRMATION, the EUCHARIST, PENANCE, EXTREME UNCTION, ORDERS, and matrimony. Aquinas accepted these seven, and they were formally affirmed at the councils of Florence (1439) and Trent (1545–63). The Eastern Orthodox churches also accept these seven sacraments, as do many Anglicans. In the latter case, baptism and the Eucharist are given a special rank of importance.

The Reformation brought with it sharp differences regarding the sacraments, especially between the new Protestant churches and the Roman Church, but also among the Protestants. The principal differences were three: (1) *The number of sacraments.* The Protestants accepted only two sacraments as valid—baptism and the Eucharist (or Lord's Supper, Holy Communion)—arguing that they alone are explicitly sanctioned in the NT. The Roman church finds direct or implicit scriptural sanction for the other five sacraments. Catholic theologians argue, for example, that penance derives from the disciples' authority to "bind and to loose," and from the church's responsibility to give fraternal correction (Matt. 18:15). (2) *The Lord's Supper as a sacrifice.* The Reformers also rejected the Catholic teaching that Christ is sacrificed anew, as a genuine expiatory sacrifice for the remission of sins, in the Mass or Eucharist. Protestants have insisted that this detracts from the NT witness to the once-for-all nature of Christ's sacrifice for sin. Therefore Protestant churches have usually viewed the Lord's Supper simply as a commemoration of Christ's sacrifice or as a "sacrifice of praise and thanksgiving." Catholic theologians point to the fact that, while there is a real identity, the sacrifice of the Mass must be understood as a representation of the sacrifice of the cross. Through the ministry of the priest (*in persona Christi*), Christ offers his sacrifice. More recently, Vatican II stressed the active cooperation of the faithful, not only through but with the priest, in the offering of the Eucharist. (3) *The manner in which grace is present and conveyed in the sacraments.* Concerning the Eucharist, all of the Protestant Reformers rejected TRANSUBSTIATION, the doctrine that at the consecration the substance of the bread and wine are changed into the substance of Christ's Body and Blood. However, the Reformers all taught the REAL PRESENCE of Christ in the Holy Communion. Luther taught that Christ is bodily present "in, with, and under" the elements of bread and wine (CONSUBSTANTIATON), while Calvin insisted on Christ's presence, though not "enclosed in the Bread and Wine."

Because of the common emphasis on Christ's Real Presence, it can be misleading to speak of Catholic sacramental theology as *objective* and Protestant as *subjective.* Roman Catholicism insists, for example, that the right disposition of faith must be present, without which the sacrament, while formally valid, is not efficacious. Likewise, Protestant sacramental theology insists that the sacraments must be properly performed in terms of matter (for example, water in baptism) and form (for example, the NT formulas). Keeping this in mind, it is true to say that historically the Catholic doctrine of the sacraments is more objective since it has stressed that, with the right intention and proper conditions, the sacraments convey or even infuse sanctifying grace. That is, their validity is independent of the worthiness of the priest or minister or the recipient, and thus the sacrament mediates or produces grace *ex opere operato.* The emphasis on the real efficient causality of the sacraments is related to the Catholic teaching that they are necessary for salvation and therefore that they must be administered as established by Christ and as entrusted to the church. Historically, the Protestant view has tended to see the sacraments not so much as direct channels of GRACE but, rather, as signs or seals of God's divine favor or promise, which must be received by a lively faith. Like the Word of God, the Reformers viewed the sacraments as proclaiming or showing forth or ratifying God's gracious goodness and, therefore, they were less willing to restrict grace to the sacraments or to claim them as necessary for salvation.

In his encyclical *Mysterium Fidei* (1965), Pope Paul VI reaffirmed the Roman Catholic church's teaching regarding transubstantiation and called for a retention of the traditional sacramental terminology. Nevertheless, Vatican II and actions since then have opened up a new dialogue between Catholics and Protestants on a number of traditional points of contention regarding sacramental theology, especially concerning the Lord's Supper. While differences remain, significant progress has been achieved toward a common understanding of the Real Presence, the Eucharist as a sacrifice, and the relationship of faith and grace in sacramental action. Furthermore, studies in psychology and social anthropology have underlined the important but often unconscious benefits of ritual and sacramental action in the life of both individuals and social groups. This has enhanced the church's awareness of the role of sacramental rites in its ministry of healing.                                                                J.L.

**SACRED.** *See* HOLY.

**SACRED CONGREGATIONS.** The technical name for some Vatican commissions or administrative bodies such as the Sacred Congregation for the Propagation of the Faith. It is equivalent to "Holy Organizations." They are bodies composed of cardinals and officials for the transaction of the headquarter's work of the Roman Catholic church. Before Vatican II there were twelve such congregations.                                                                       J.C.

**SACRED HEART.** Devotion to the Sacred Heart of Jesus, symbolized by paintings, statues, and medals that portray Jesus' heart (usually marked with the letters, IHS, for "Jesus Christ, Savior") on the outside of his robes with one hand pointing to it. This cult, or way of devotion to Jesus, is found only in the Roman Catholic Church. Neither the Eastern Orthodox nor the Protestant churches promote or follow this practice.

Devotion to the Sacred Heart originated in the Middle Ages among contemplative monks or mystics. The Carthusian Order and the Society of Jesus (the Jesuits) took up the cult and promoted it throughout the church. St. Francis de Sales and the Silesian Order also spread the practice, as did St. Margaret Mary Alacoque and the Visitandine Order.

The Sacred Heart movement was not without opposition. The Jansenist movement resisted the cult, claiming that a separation was introduced between Christ's heart and his full divine-human being. The Jansenists, meeting in Pistoia, formalized this objection, which was subsequently condemned by Pope Pius VI on August 28, 1794. Pope Pius IX created a Feast of the Sacred Heart, setting it on the Friday after the octave of Corpus Christi, the third Friday after PENTECOST. There are at least three orders of monks, missionaries, and priests dedicated to the Sacred Heart.                                                  J.C.

**SACRIFICES, HUMAN.** Cultic expressions involving child holocausts permitted in some ancient Near Eastern religions, but officially rejected by Israelite religion.

At one level, Genesis 22:1-19 constitutes an Israelite polemic against child sacrifice. As a unique test, Abraham is divinely commanded to sacrifice Isaac. Having acted obediently, the patriarch is permitted to substitute a ram for his son. First Kings 16:34 reporting that Hiel rebuilt Jericho "at the cost of" two sons during Ahab's reign (869–850 B.C.) is too ambiguous to be decisive. Jephthah's sacrifice of his daughter (Judg. 11:30-40) is undeniably tragic *and* extraordinary; a Hebrew rendition of a widespread folk tale, it does not disclose pervasive Israelite practice. Infant skeletons excavated at Gezer, Megiddo, and Taanach provided no direct evidence of child sacrifice. Infant mortality explains the situation equally well.

Nevertheless, biblical denunciations of human sacrifices suggest significant deviation from the religious norm (Deut. 18:10; Ps. 106:37-38; Jer. 19:5; also Wisd. Sol. 12:5-6). An acutely endangered adult might give up a child in order to induce divine intervention. Three kings behaved thus. Regarding defeat by the Israelites as imminent, Mesha, a ninth-century B.C. king of Moab, sacrificed his son (II Kings 3:27). Similarly, amid threatening international conditions, two Judean kings, Ahaz (735–715) and Manasseh (687–642), made a burnt offering of a son (II Kings 16:3; 21:6). Though Josiah worked to eliminate this pagan rite (II Kings 23:10), prophetic oracles in Jeremiah (7:31-32) and Ezekiel (16:20-21) indicate that precarious Judean existence prior to Jerusalem's destruction (587 B.C.) stimulated its revival.

In Leviticus 18:21; 20:2-5; II Kings 23:10; and Jeremiah 32:35, child sacrifice is linked with Molech. Though an Ammonite deity is named Molech (I Kings 11:7), in Punic, the language of Carthage, *molch* denotes a type of human sacrifice, not a deity. If this bears on the above mentioned texts, as some scholars claim, Israelite children were offered to Yahweh as well as foreign gods. Child sacrifice likely invaded Israel from Phoenicia in an era of religious syncretism. Israel's prophets, priests, and the Deuteronomist loathed it as an alien perversion of proper Israelite religious expression.          J.K.K.

**SACRIFICIAL OFFERINGS.** Diverse rituals that enhance relations between God and humanity. Motivated by the dual need to acknowledge Yahweh's sovereignty with tribute and influence Yahweh's action with gifts, or the desire to strengthen divine-human communion, or the urge to expiate human wrongdoing, people perform these cultic ceremonies to provide a vital continuity in divine-human intercourse. Though strictly speaking, sacrifice in biblical Israel involved the slaughter or burning of an animal, meal and cereal offerings constituted significant accompaniments.

*History.* The Israelites offered sacrifices to Yahweh throughout their history. Since sacrifice is virtually a universal religious phenomenon, biblical procedures often resemble those reflected in extra-biblical texts. Still, whatever the Israelites adopted from the surrounding cultures of Mesopotamia and Canaan was made to serve their own purposes. Several technical names for sacrifices attested in the OT appear in the Ugaritic literature uncovered at Ras Shamra. Thus the antiquity of these sacrifices is obvious.

Various historical, prophetic, and cultic texts in the OT reflect preexilic sacrificial undertakings. First Samuel 1 reports that Elkanah, Samuel's father, made annual sacrifices at Shiloh; Amos 4:4 reveals sacrificial frenzy at Bethel and Gilgal; and Psalm 56:12 mentions sacrificial vows made by the hard-pressed, pious Israelite. The clearest biblical statement regarding sacrificial offerings is found in Leviticus 1–7. Serving as a "memorandum" for priests, Leviticus 1:1–6:7 offers directives when individual Israelites seek participation in sacrificial offerings. It is supplemented by Leviticus 6:8–7:38, a section more specifically concerned with priestly leadership. This postexilic legislation traces back to ritualistic prototypes that are much older.

Since sacrificial offerings incorporated self-evident procedures and symbols for the priestly editors of the Pentateuch, they felt no urge to systematize ritualistic data or to advance a specific theory of sacrifice justifying the existence of the sacrificial cult. While not definitive, biblical sacrifices are probably best classified according to their several functions—as gifts, vehicles of communion with God, and mechanisms facilitating the expiation of sin and guilt.

*Sacrifices as Gift.* The gift aspect of sacrificial offerings rests on the obvious consideration that they all involve the presentation of something to or before God. Two general Hebrew nouns for sacrifice fundamentally convey the idea of gift. One is *minhâ*. In its earliest biblical usage it denotes sacrifices in general, though sometimes it relates to secular expressions of respect (people to a king; I Sam. 10:27) or common personal allegiance (Jacob to Esau; Gen. 32:13). When the *minhâ* later acquired the sense of "cereal offering" (Exod. 29:41), another noun, *qorbān* (linked with the verb *hiqrib*, "to bring near"), imparted the general notion of giving (Lev. 2:1).

The tributary offering of firstlings also falls into this category. It was commonly held that the firstborn of the herd and firstfruits of the ground belong to the Deity; they must be delivered to Yahweh as sacred gifts (Exod. 13:2; 23:19). This regulation did not apply to the firstborn child who was "redeemed" when a young animal served as suitable substitute (13:13). Accordingly, the God who activates animal and plant life is respectfully celebrated as worthy of a portion of that life. The claim of divine ownership is thankfully recognized (Deut. 26:1-11).

The cereal offering (*minhâ*) is another type of sacrificial gift (Lev. 2). Consisting of flour, cakes, or crushed grain, the *minhâ* is placed on the altar along with oil and frankincense. A portion, known as the *'azkārâ*, is burned. Stemming from the verb *zākar* ("to remember"), this noun (meaning "reminiscence"?) may suggest the actual function of the cereal offering, namely, bringing the worshiper to Yahweh's own remembrance.

The burnt offering (commonly called an *'ōlâ*, though sometimes a *kālîl*) is yet another sacrificial gift. It consisted of a bull, ram, goat, or dove (Lev. 1). Probably in order to designate it as his own gift, the offerer laid his hand on the animal's head. The animal was slaughtered, its blood was dashed at the altar's base, and the carcass was cut into pieces and burned in its entirety. No sacramental eating was involved. Though an atoning dimension is ascribed to this sacrifice (1:4), originally that was unlikely the case. In Numbers 28:2 the Deity refers to the *'ōlâ* as "my food for my offerings by fire, my pleasing odor." Whatever be its ancient Near Eastern antecedents, Israelite priests perceived this expression figuratively.

Since sacrificial gifts were basically motivated by the offerer's gratitude, the votive (*neder*), thank (*tôdâ*) and freewill offering (*nedābâ*) also merit mention. Precarious circumstances stimulated the pious to promise the Deity a sacrifice following personal deliverance (Jonah 1:16). The thank offering was a similar expression of gratitude, though it entailed no previous vow (Ps. 107:21-22). Finally, spontaneous thanksgiving is best denoted by the freewill offering that lacked stringent regulations (Lev. 22:23).

*Sacrifice as Communion.* Through the *shelem* sacrifice, worshipers were sacramentally linked with the Deity and one another. Since the Hebrew noun *shālōm* means "peace," *shelem* is often rendered "peace offering." The chief concern, however, is the establishment of full harmony between God and worshipers through a shared banquet. While the biblical legislation (Lev. 3) somewhat resembles that mandated for the burnt offering (*'ōlā*), Yahweh's portion is limited to the poured out blood of the sacrificial animal, along with the fatty parts of the entrails and the kidneys that are burned. The rest of the victim was consumed in a communion meal joyfully eaten by both priests and laity in God's presence (Deut. 12:18).

The same type of sacrifice is sometimes designated by the noun *zebah,* meaning "what is killed" (Exod. 18:12), and is indicative of an early Israelite period when domestic animals were solely slaughtered for the purpose of a meal in which God shared. With its vivid portrayal of one family banqueting in Yahweh's presence, I Samuel 1 highlights the communal aspect of Israelite sacrifice.

*Sacrifice as Expiation.* Whereas spontaneously motivated sacrifices are outlined in Leviticus 1–3, two mandatory sacrifices, the sin offering (*hattā'th*) and guilt offering (*'āshām*), are respectively portrayed in Leviticus 4:1–5:13 and 5:14–6:7. Since the exact distinction between them is never stated, perhaps they constitute two independent, parallel atonement rituals. Both were emphasized during and after the Exile, and both were designed to expiate "unwittingly" committed sinfulness (Lev. 4:2) that ruptures the individual's relation with God and threatens communal well-being. Such wrongdoing involved engagement in real but minor offenses that do not incur expulsion from the covenant community. No sacrificial remedy existed for such presumptuously deliberate sins as murder and apostasy.

Above all, the problem of continuing ritual uncleanness is addressed. Concerning the sin offering, only special portions of the sacrificial victim are destined for "the altar of burnt offering" (4:10). Most of the animal, now contaminated by the sin of the worshiper who placed his hand on it (4:4), is burned outside the camp (4:12). By sprinkling the blood on the horns of the altar, the officiating priest "makes atonement" (4:20) for the individual offering the sacrifice.

Moreover, Leviticus 16 contains legislation for an annual DAY OF ATONEMENT, which provides the Israelite community a solemn occasion for returning to spiritual wholeness. This ceremony distinctively uses a scapegoat that symbolically receives, through the laying on of the hands of the high priest, the nation's transgressions and is driven into the wilderness for Azazel, probably a desert demon.

Financial compensation, not animal sacrifice, is the central factor within the legislative procedures established for the guilt offering. Its place in any discussion of Israelite sacrificial offerings is admittedly peripheral.

*Religious Significance.* Across the centuries, not all Israelites esteemed sacramental offerings identically. In popular thought, sacrifices were often regarded as wielding such automatic power as to render the worshiper's inward involvement irrelevant. Yet the religiously perceptive within Israel argued otherwise. The priesthood did not approach sacrifices mechanically. Though in instituting the sin offering Yahweh favored Israel with an instrument for EXPIATION, humble confession constituted an intrinsic expectation (Lev. 5:5). Sacrifices were serious business to devout Israelites who continuously presented Yahweh with daily offerings of sacrificial beasts, grain, and wine libation (Num. 28:3-8). Indeed, sacrificial offerings might instill reverence within the Israelite community. Rather than badgering Yahweh with new requests for benefits, the Israelite, in a thank offering, might recognize that benefits had already come from God. And voicing a vow might place one under moral obligations capable of enhancing one's spirituality.

Nevertheless, Yahweh would not tolerate flagrant abuse of the sacrificial system. Samuel and Hosea respectively ranked obedience and steadfast love ahead of sacrifice (I Sam. 15:22; Hos. 6:6). Amos railed against the juxtaposition of external sacrificial observance and rampant social injustice (Amos. 5:21-24). Concern for proper human attitude is echoed in Psalm 50, where thank and votive offerings are favorably regarded (v. 14) despite Yahweh's disclosure, "I will accept no bull from your house" (v. 9). Malachi's rebuke of sacrificial negligence (1:6-14) is further reminder that Yahweh welcomes appropriately rendered offerings. They ensure the continuance of a positive relationship between God and people. But the aphorism "The sacrifice of the wicked is an abomination" (Prov. 21:27) admonishes that this relationship is doomed should Israel become manipulative.                                                     J.K.K.

**SADDUCEES.** An aristocratic party or sect of the Jews composed of the high-priestly families, lesser priests, and wealthy persons of rank who participated in the rule of the Jewish homeland from the years following the Maccabean wars of independence to the revolt against Rome, about 160 B.C. to A.D. 70. The Sadducees derived their name from the priest ZADOK (Greek *Saddouk*), whose descendants held office from the time of Solomon and who performed their priestly duties in Jerusalem's Temple (I Kings 1:5-8, 32-40; 2:26-27, 35).

References to the Sadducees in both Jewish and Christian sources chiefly relate to their beliefs and practices, which are opposed to those of the Pharisees.

As controversial as these opposing positions some-times were, both parties found common cause in the face of intermittent threats to the survival of Judaism and its Temple. In the Roman period some priests belonged to the sect of the Pharisees; conversely, some of the Pharisees before A.D. 70 conscientiously adhered to the priestly laws concerning their revenues and sought to extend to their own tables the priest's rules concerning ceremonial purity.

*Early History.* Already in the Persian period, but especially under Ptolemaic rule 323–200 B.C., the power of the priests greatly increased. The HIGH PRIEST was the head of the state, and other leading priests directed the Gerousia (council, later known as the Sanhedrin). The concerns of the priestly aristocracy were therefore political as well as religious. These political concerns led them to become enamored with HELLENISM in the early years of the Seleucid rule of the Jewish state and to adopt an assimilationist posture. When Antiochus Epiphanes, 175–164 B.C., sought to promote the Hellenization of his Jewish subjects he found allies among high-ranking priests. The successful Maccabean wars of independence resulted in the discrediting of the Hellenizing priests (the office of high priest remained vacant for a time) and necessitated the establishment of a new high-priestly line: Simon Maccabeus (142–135 B.C.) and his dynastic successors (I Macc. 14:35, 41-49). During the brief period of Jewish political independence, various sectarian movements developed, distinguished by their differing attitudes toward the Hasmonean priest-kings. Among those who rallied around the Maccabeans were priestly families who traced their ancestry to Zadok. Together with wealthy aristocrats these partisans became known as the Sadducees (*Saddoukaioi*; Mark 12:18).

*The Roman Period.* Information concerning the fortunes of the Sadducees under Roman rule derives from the record in Josephus' *Antiquities* of the succession of high priests in Jersualem. Under the Herods and Roman procurators the powers of the high priests were greatly diminished, and concerted efforts were made to install persons who were subservient and loyal. Josephus reports that there were twenty-eight high priests from the days of Herod the Great to the fall of Jerusalem. Josephus sought to relieve the leading priests as well as the Pharisees of blame for the Jewish war with Rome, but the fact cannot be concealed that Eleazer, the son of the high priest Ananias, by preventing the daily sacrifice to the emperor, provoked the Romans to retaliate. It is probable that a preponderance of the priesthood sided with Eleazer against the Romans and the incumbent puppet high priest. The destruction of Jerusalem's Temple, and the implication of members of their party in the revolt, led to many casualties among the Sadducees. Their (always limited) influence among the populace was eclipsed by the growing prestige of the PHARISEES. With the collapse of the Jewish state the Sadducees disappear from history.

*Distinctive Characteristics of the Sadducees.* Given the scattered, disparaging references of Josephus and the Gospels to the Sadducees, it is difficult to form a coherent picture of their beliefs and practices. Josephus writes that the party contained "persons of the highest reputation," yet they were "influential only with the wealthy," and had no following among the people. In their relationship to each other the Sadducees were "rather boorish in their behavior," in their relationship with their countrymen, "as rude as with aliens."

One could hardly expect religious idealism to flourish among the Sadducees; theirs was the pragmatic stance of expediency. Even after the Hellenizers had been expelled or silenced there was still among the priestly aristocracy a worldly mindedness and the same comparative laxity in their practice of Judaism. Driven to make the most of bad bargains, they maintained that human choices are free and responsible. They held "that all things lie within our own power." The statement of Josephus that the Sadducees "do away with fate altogether" is not to be understood as a flat denial of divine providence, nor should his comparison of them with Epicureans be pressed. The Sadducees stood for the old dogma: God is responsible for the good; humans are responsible for their misfortunes. Yet their emphasis on human freedom promoted self-reliance and represented a lessening of reliance upon God.

A fundamental difference between the Sadducees and other contemporary sects is that these partisans did not regard the observance of "anything besides what the Law enjoins them." The Sadducees refused to be bound by the achievements of the previous centuries in regard to both the interpretation of the Torah and the introduction of religious views derived by inference therefrom. They saw in "the tradition of the elders" an unnecessary limitation of their hereditary, judicial, and doctrinal authority. In their rejection of the legal tradition of the Torah scholars, many of whom belonged to the sect of the Pharisees, they revered the written Torah only. Accordingly, they rejected belief in bodily resurrection and rewards and penalties in the world to come; they also denied the existence of angels and evil spirits (Mark 12:18-27; Acts 23:6-8). Conservative and autocratic tendencies, plus their attraction to Hellenistic cultural advantages, inclined the Sadducees to hold that the progressive religious ideas of the Pharisees were either superfluous or unacceptable. The more insistent the Pharisees were upon the observance of both the oral and written Torah, the more resistant the Sadducees became. Mark's account of Jesus' encounter with the Sadducees may reflect a typical defense: holding up their opponent's beliefs to ridicule (Mark 12:18-27).                    J.L.P.

**SAHABA.** Literally "companions," the closest associates of MUHAMMAD during his career. Most of the HADITH traditions are attributed to them, and their actions and procedures are regarded as standards for orthodox behavior.

Among the companions, the first four caliphs occupy the highest place. Muhammad promised to these four and to six other companions a place in paradise. There are several other groups of companions. The *Muhajirun* are those who migrated from Mecca to Medina before, with, or after Muhammad. The *Ansar,* or helpers, are those believers in Islam in Medina who welcomed and assisted Muhammad. The *Badriyun* took part in the important battle of Badr, where Muhammad defeated a hostile military force.
K.C.

**ST. PAUL'S CATHEDRAL.** One of the two most famous churches in London, along with WESTMINSTER ABBEY. St. Paul's serves as the chief seat of the Church of England in the city. St. Paul's was built by the noted English architect Sir Christopher Wren, who brought the building to completion over a thirty-five year period, 1675–1710. His structure replaced the earlier St. Paul's that had been burned in the great fire of London in 1666. Wren's dome rises 365 feet above the street, where St. Paul's stands on Ludgate hill in the center of the old city of London.

The first church to stand where St. Paul's is now was said to date back to A.D. 604, built by King Aethelberht of Kent and Bishop Mellitus of London. Several churches were destroyed and rebuilt over the centuries before Wren undertook his task in 1675. His building is based on the Gothic plan, in the shape of a Latin cross; but like St. Peter's Basilica, it is dominated by the large central dome. Many sculptures adorn the building, although some have been destroyed by time. There are beautiful choir stalls, a huge baptismal font, artistic ironwork, and a geometrical staircase, thirty-five feet in diameter, in the southwest tower.
J.C.

**ST. PETER'S BASILICA.** The cathedral church of Rome, seat of the Roman Catholic church's pope, in VATICAN City, Rome. St. Peter's, the largest Christian church in the world, is the second church built above the traditional tomb of Peter, the first having been built by the emperor Constantine the Great about A.D. 325. This original basilica signified Constantine's acceptance of Christianity as the religion of the Roman Empire. However, in 1506, Pope Julius II determined to build a new, more magnificent church and had the original one completely demolished. The construction of the present St. Peter's took 150 years, with ten architects directing, and frequently changing, its design. The original architect, Donato Bramante, planned a domed church in the form of a Greek cross (all four arms of equal length). However, in the seventeenth century, the nave was lengthened so that the basilica is now in the shape of a Latin cross. St. Peter's is 210 meters (700 feet) long and 137 meters (450 feet) across at its widest point. It covers 12,960 square

meters (15,500 square yards) of space. The great dome, designed by Michelangelo, is 42 meters (138 feet) in diameter and more than 120 meters (400 feet) high. (See photo on next page.)
J.C.

**ST. SOPHIA.** *See* HAGIA SOPHIA.

**ST. SULPICE, SOCIETY OF.** An order of secular priests, founded in Paris in 1642 by J. J. Olier, devoted to the theological education of parish priests. They are not monks but live in community with their students in order to encourage spiritual formation and growth. Scripture, theology, prayer, and spiritual exercises are encouraged. The Sulpicians received papal endorsement and their own constitution. They spread to Canada and to the newly independent United States. In 1791, the order founded St. Mary's Seminary in Baltimore, the first Roman Catholic seminary in the country and now a pontifical university. It follows that the Sulpicians would produce outstanding theologians. The most distinguished modern American Sulpician is the biblical scholar Raymond Brown.
J.C.

**SAINTS, VENERATION OF.** The practice began in the early church with the belief that martyrs gained immediate entry into heaven and that their intercession with God was particularly effective. Revelation 6:9 indicates that MARTYRS do occupy a special place before God's altar, and the parable of Dives and Lazarus (Luke 16:19-31) suggests that the dead do intercede for the living. Veneration is based on the theory that the saints' goodness makes them closer to God and their humanness makes them more accessible to us.

Veneration of confessors—those who had persevered in the faith under persecution and were not martyred—followed. Gradually bishops, popes, church fathers, ascetics, virgins, and mystics were all included in this veneration. The practice was first limited to celebrations at a person's tomb, but soon became attached also to relics, particularly the person's bones, and then significant places and objects from that person's life. The *Martyrdom of Polycarp* (about A.D. 160) calls his remains "more precious than costly stones and more excellent than gold."

Mention of the saints in the liturgy can be dated from the time of Augustine. In the eighth century it became customary to read from the lives of the saints at matins. Veneration was primarily an act of lay piety; local holy persons were venerated. Gradually the papacy tried to take control, regulating the process through rigorous examinations before allowing beatification and canonization. Everything was strictly defined in canon law. Many people, however, continued to venerate whomever they considered worthy.

Eventually each "official" saint was assigned to a day on the calendar when he or she was especially remembered. Children are often given the name of the

Courtesy of G. E. Kidder Smith

*Interior of St. Peter's (Rome) showing Bernini's Tabernacle*

saint on whose day they are baptized. Because it is sometimes difficult to separate fact from pious fiction in the lives of the saints, Pope Paul VI tried to eliminate many of the more nonhistorial saints, but popular piety continues.

In the Greek church veneration is based on the idea that the saints are instructional examples for us of the Christian life of sanctification. Thus the Eastern church treasures ICONS more than relics. In the West the saints became supernatural helpers in times of need. A perceived need for special protection led cities, countries, guilds, individual people, and so forth, to claim their own patron saints. Patrick, for example, is the patron saint of Ireland; Cecilia is the patron saint of music and musicians.

The Reformation repudiated the veneration of the saints, declaring that all true Christians are saints and that Christ is our only intercessor. In most Protestant churches very little attention is paid to the saints, and thus there is a certain loss of historical perspective and sense of connectedness. Charles Williams in *Descent of the Dove* and several of his fiction works argues that Paul's image of the church as the body of Christ means that all Christians—past, present, and future—cohere in one body and that they can indeed help one another. Worship, then, is reserved for God, but one can still offer reverence to the saints and receive inspiration and comfort from them.    N.H.

**SAIVA SIDDHANTA.** From the Sanskrit word for "wisdom of the Saivas," or worshipers of SHIVA. A school in HINDUISM with a distinctive teaching and body of literature, Saiva Siddhanta expounds Shiva as the supreme lord. In contrast to Advaita Vedanta, it accepts the reality of souls and matter created by MAYA, not illusion, but God's creative energy. However, souls in this real universe are in bondage to KARMA because of ignorance until liberated by the power of Shiva. That is attained by following a spiritual discipline under the direction of an authentic GURU. Saiva Siddhanata has its major center of strength in the Tamil areas of south India.    R.E.

**SALEM.** The name of the place where Melchizedek was king (Gen. 14:18). The word, meaning "completion," is not related to *shālōm* ("peace") or to the name Jerusalem, even though in Psalm 76:2 Salem and Zion are in parallel relationship and Hebrews 7:2 reads "king of Salem, that is, king of peace." The Hebrew word Salem probably preserves the name of the Ugaritic god who completes the day, that is, the Venus star at sunset, Shalem. Yurūshalem thus means "foundation or sacred place of Shalem," the local god of the pre-Israelite city whose name also may be incorporated in Solomon's name.    P.L.G.

**SALEM COLONY.** The first settlement of what became the MASSACHUSETTS BAY COLONY; founded in 1626 by Roger Conant as a successor to a previous settlement at Cape Ann (Gloucester). The settlements were promoted by John White, rector of Holy Trinity Church, Dorchester, England, who got Salem chartered as the New England Company in 1628. He sent John Endecott as leader of a party of forty, who arrived aboard the *Abigail* on September 6, 1628. Originally called Naumkeag, the colony was renamed Salem or "peace" after the resolution of conflict between Endecott and older settlers. Salem was incorporated as a town in 1630. It is most famous as the site of the first Congregational church in the United States, founded August 6, 1629, and as home of the witchcraft trials of 1692.    N.H.

**SALOME.** (1) The daughter of Herodias who danced for Herod Antipas and his guests (Matt. 14:6; Mark 6:22) is unnamed in the Gospels. Josephus (*Antiquities*) names her Salome.

(2) A Galilean woman from Capernaum, wife of Zebedee, a wealthy fisher, and mother of James and John, mentioned mainly in Mark.

The Salome in Mark 15:40 has been thought to be the same person as "the mother of the sons of Zebedee" in Matthew 27:56, and also the same person as "his [Jesus'] mother's sister" in John 19:25. If so, Jesus called James and John, his first cousins, among his earliest disciples (Matt. 4:21-22; Mark 1:20), men he nicknamed "sons of thunder" (Mark 3:17).

Salome may have been among the Galilean followers of Jesus from early in his ministry. She is named among the women "who, when he was in Galilee, followed him, and ministered to him" (Mark 15:40). "The mother of the sons of Zebedee" (Matt. 20:20-22) asked Jesus that her two sons should sit "one at your right hand and one at your left, in your kingdom" and was told that this was not his to grant. Jesus anticipated, probably in her presence, that both James and John would suffer persecution comparable to that of his own. Salome is named (Mark 15:10) as one of the women who witnessed Jesus' crucifixion. The beloved disciple (John 19:26) to whom Jesus committed the care of his mother is thought to be Salome's son John, Jesus' cousin.    P.L.G.

**SALVATION.** A key biblical term to embrace several important aspects of the divine enterprise in restoring humankind to God's family and of the human response to that initiative. The basic meaning of "save" is "to deliver," whether the offending condition is one of danger or disease or death. Hence "to be saved" carries a wide range of meanings, but the three most common are: (1) to be set free from the peril of physical or spiritual dangers that would ensnare and ruin human lives; (2) to be restored to health and wholeness (Heb. *shālōm*; the NT equivalent is "peace" with God or with one's neighbor or oneself); (3) to be rescued from death when the biblical author is faced by mortal peril or when he contemplates the prospect of sin's penalty of separation from God. These are the three major emphases of the word.

*Old Testament.* The Hebrew verb "to save" carries the sense of "space," that is, to be set free from narrow confines and led out to a spacious area (Pss. 18:36; 66:12). It is an easy transition to associate debilitating conditions with one's enemies, such as disease (Isa. 38:16, 20), disaster (Jer. 30:7), or human foes (II Sam. 3:18; Ps. 44:7).

God is known throughout the OT as the author and giver of salvation. God alone is Israel's savior (Hos. 13:4), and when pressed by religious syncretism, Israel's prophet of the Exile denies that there is another savior (Isa. 43:11). With consistency the OT writers look back to Israel's salvation from bondage in Egypt and its REDEMPTION by God's acts in the time of Moses and the Exodus (Exod. 12–15). Moses' song epitomizes the theme: "Yahweh . . . has become my salvation" (Exod. 15:2), a note repeated whenever Israel faced the threat of national invasion by surrounding peoples (for example, Isa. 12:2, 3). The psalmists rehearsed the salvation from Egypt as part of the later Temple worship (Pss. 66:1-7; 106:7-10), which was essentially a "remembrance" of God's mighty deeds. At Passover the same "re-presentation" was set on a domestic level, as Jewish families have always looked back, in their Passover liturgy (based on Exod. 12), to God's saving power as a pledge of future salvation.

The Babylonian exile reinforced these themes, with a new dimension added. Israel's hopes, centered on its newly gained monotheistic belief (seen in Isa. 40–55, and later articulated after the Exile in the Priestly section of the Pentateuch, for example, Gen. 1), were widened to take in a cosmic sweep of salvation. Yahweh was hailed as savior of the entire world, and the creator of a new age set free from SIN and decay and restored to its pristine integrity as a paradise regained. The Jewish apocalyptic writers (second century B.C.–first century A.D.) gave even richer meaning to this eschatological salvation as cosmic and transcendental (for example, Daniel and IV Ezra). Sometimes these hopes were pinned on a special figure (first called messiah in Psalms of Solomon, about 50 B.C.; and the "anointed one" in IV Ezra), but often it was God's own intervention that was celebrated.

*New Testament.* The cultural and religious world of the NT writer was racked by uncertainty. In spite of outward calm there were still political upheavals, economic stresses, and much intellectual ferment. To meet this challenge contemporary religious cults of Greco-Roman society offered "salvation" as a way to inner peace. The term "salvation" may be defined, in the background of the NT, as "escape from the prison-house of bondage," from the pessimism of despair. The blind goddess of change imposed a sense of life's meaninglessness, or else the more philosophical belief that the whole of life was determined by an inevitable link of cause and effect seemed to give no purpose to existence. Both aspects, popular and philosophical, of life in the first century A.D. led to a feeling of hopelessness and "failure of nerve," to use the expressive phrase of Gilbert Murray.

The Jewish elements in that society were caught in this web, with one additional factor compounding their woes. Postexilic Judaism (sixth century B.C. on) became increasingly marked by the fear that God was so far removed from people that contact was difficult and only an intricate system of priestly mediation could assist. This led to the codification of Levitical rules in the final edition of the Pentateuch, made in these centuries; and a heightened sense of guilt, both national and personal, dominated the Jewish mentality.

Two factors, then, made ready for the Christian gospel, which offered salvation as a removal of guilt by Christ's sacrifice on the cross which, in turn, abolished all other sacrifices (Heb. 8–10). This is the primary declaration of salvation that entailed a new start to life based on FORGIVENESS (see Matt. 1:21, 23 for the symbolism of the name "Jesus," which means "God saves," with sin's remission an integral part) and restoration to God's favor (Gal. 4:5ff.; Eph. 1:7, 13; II Cor. 5:18-21).

But salvation was no less real when offered to the members of Greco-Roman society. Paul is greeted at Philippi (Acts 16:17) as one of the servants of the Most High God (a paganized title), "who proclaim to you a way of salvation." Significantly, release came to the girl with the demonic spirit as she was set free from the power of bad religion and superstitious dread. The Philippian jailer, too, asked, "What must I do to be saved?" (Acts 16:30), a reference perhaps to his fear for physical safety, but including for the NT narrator an undertone of religious fear, which Paul addressed: "Believe in the Lord Jesus, and you will be saved, you and your household" (v. 31), that is, he will pass from the loneliness of despair into a new society of "the saved," the eschatological community of the end-time, called the church.

As with the OT, God is universally greeted as the originator of salvation, both personal and cosmic. Indeed, the title Savior is severely restricted in the NT, being used only occasionally of Jesus and more often of God in Luke-Acts and the Pastorals. Nonetheless, God is the agent of salvation, which is God's direct gift in response to faith and obedience (Rom. 10:9, 10; Eph. 2:4-10).

The phases of salvation are clearly demarcated. The past tense is only rare (Eph. 2:5), while the tense that looks back to a point in past time usually refers to baptism as the occasion when the new Christian professed the faith and was welcomed from the alienation of separation from God to the new society (for example, Rom. 10:9, 10; Gal. 3:2; Eph. 1:13, 14). The present tense (I Cor. 1:18) denotes that salvation is an ongoing, progressive experience that must be applied in everyday living. There is an implicit warning against treating salvation as an excuse for continuing evil ways. The future aspect is important for Paul. His teaching makes clear that final salvation is not attained until the PAROUSIA or the glorious return of Christ (Phil. 3:20, 21), when believers will at last be saved (Rom. 8:19-25). Part of the reason here is to encourage Christians to live in anticipation of the final day (I Cor. 4:5); but because Paul's salvation teaching has a cosmic dimension, he can contemplate only in hope the ultimate outworking in God's plan for the universe as well as the church. Salvation will not be achieved until God's purpose is complete—for Jew as well as Gentile (Rom. 11:26-32), for all people as well as believers (I Cor. 15:25-28).                                    R.M.

Courtesy of the Salvation Army, National Communications Department

*General William Booth, founder of the Salvation Army*

**SALVATION ARMY.** This Christian international evangelistic and relief agency was founded in London in 1865 by William Booth, a Methodist lay preacher. He and his wife, Catherine, were moved by compassion for the needy people of London's East End. To achieve their goal they launched the East London Christian Mission, which was renamed the Salvation Army in 1878 when the organization was restructured on a military basis.

With Booth as "General" the "Army" served "territories" that conformed to the national boundaries of various countries. The territories were subdivided into "provinces" and "divisions" headed by various officers—majors, captains, and so forth. All in the Army were expected to offer "unquestioning obedience" to orders that came down from the top.

The doctrinal basis of the Salvation Army reflected Booth's own strongly evangelical and evangelistic background, including an emphasis on personal holiness and free will. In a real sense the Army was and is a denomination that differs from others in its military structure and its refusal to observe the sacraments of baptism and the Lord's Supper.

The Salvation Army relief program is unparalleled in the Christian world. It pioneered in working with released prisoners and homeless men and women, and in providing homes for unwed mothers, and soup kitchens. During World Wars I and II the army set up stations to provide coffee and doughnuts to men and women in the armed forces, and it provided services latterly taken over by other organizations.

Because of its colorful uniforms, its bands, and its open-air street meetings, the Army has become known to most of the civilized world. Despite its emphasis on a wide range of social services, the Army has maintained its evangelistic zeal.

From the start Booth and his associates employed women as officers on an equal basis. Booth's wife, Catherine, was an eloquent preacher. Their daughter, Evangeline, eventually became the commanding general of the entire international organization.

R.H.

**SALVE REGINA.** A prayer to Mary, Queen of Heaven, second in regular use among Roman Catholics only to the Hail Mary. The phrase is from the first words of the fourth antiphon of Our Lady. These antiphons are four chants in honor of Mary, each with a versicle, response, and prayer, which vary with the seasons of the church year. The four antiphons are *Alma Redemptoris Mater, Ave Regina Coelorum, Regina Coeli,* and *Salve Regina.* The antiphon for the season is sung after compline in the divine office. When the office is said in choir, the antiphon of Our Lady is sung kneeling, except on Saturdays, Sundays, and during Lent. In the Dominican liturgy, the antiphon is accompanied by a procession; in the Carmelite liturgy, it is said before the altar steps before the last gospel at mass; and in the Mozarabic rite, before the blessing.

J.C.

**SAMADHI.** From the Sanskrit word meaning "total collectedness." In HINDUISM, the highest state of yogic or meditative concentration of mind. Samadhi is a state of pure consciousness, which has transcended all particular objects or moods as objects of consciousness, and is thus, in VEDANTA, a sharing in the absolute consciousness or BRAHMAN, ultimate reality. In the yoga sutras of Patanjali, samadhi is the last and highest of the "eight limbs of yoga," the state at which PURUSHA or spirit attains full release from the toils of prakriti, matter.

In BUDDHISM, on the other hand, samadhi generally refers to meditation techniques that train the mind in reaching subtle levels of consciousness, but that are not themselves the goal, Nirvana.

R.E.

**SAMARIA/SAMARITANS.** The place-name denotes a city in Israel that became the capital of the northern kingdom after the division of the tribes (I Kings 12:25-33). To replace SHECHEM nearby as capital, it was built by Omri, who settled the site and made it his royal residence (I Kings 16:24), its prominence on a high elevation adding to its prestige. The palace has been excavated to reveal an early Bronze Age and Iron Age fortification. Omri's settlement was the first of many attempts to develop the site. Jeroboam II furbished the palace before it fell to the Assyrians in 722 B.C. The city was restored in Hellenistic times, as Greek pottery finds have shown. The Romans further enlarged the Israelite city and erected a temple to Augustus.

From a religious point of view Samaria became a center for Canaanite worship. Ahab domesticated the deity Melkart under the influence of his wife Jezebel (I Kings 18:19), and Jehu's later reforms aimed to purify worship at Samaria, which the eighth-century prophets regarded as evil and idolatrous (Isa. 9:9; 28:1-4; Hos. 7:1; Mic. 1:6; Amos 3:9–4:3). According to Isaiah and Amos, Samaria was notorious for its commercial greed and social injustice.

The prophets saw divine judgment in successive invasions by the Syrians (I Kings 20:1-21) and especially the Assyrians (II Kings 15:17-22, recounting the invasion of Tiglath-pileser III, which was a prelude to the more successful attacks of the Assyrian Shalmaneser V and Sargon II, who in 721 B.C. deported the inhabitants to denude the city). Some inhabitants did remain (II Kings 17:29), called in the biblical text Samaritans, and formed the nucleus of a later settlement, subsequently to be

From *Atlas of the Bible* (Thomas Nelson & Sons Limited)

*The hill of Samaria, with the modern village of Sebastiyeh on the right.*

destroyed by Alexander the Great, then rebuilt by the Roman general Pompey, and later refurbished as a part of Herod's grandiose building projects. This explains how Samaria takes its place in NT history (Luke 17:11; John 4:4-26, 30-42; Acts 8:4-25).

The Samaritans, as mentioned, appear in II Kings 17:29 as a remnant left in the city, to be joined by others whom the Assyrian king brought in to populate the ravaged area. But the later references to Samaritans in Jewish history are confused, and it is likely that the term strictly belongs to those who lived at or near Shechem, a short distance from the ancient site of Samaria, in the postexilic era. Sychar in John 4:5 is another name for Shechem. The Samaritans formed a distinctive community of Semitic people, with their own holy place (Mount Gerizim; see John 4:20) and customs, especially a distinctive celebration of Passover. In NT times they retained this identity and were not on friendly terms with their Jewish neighbors (see John 4:9 and the setting of Luke 10:20-37; 17:11-20). They were often in trouble with the Roman overlords of Palestine because of their political and religious demonstrations. Pilate massacred many of them, and they were harshly treated by the Romans in the Jewish war of A.D. 66–72, in spite of their earlier support of Rome's cause.

The Samaritans left a literary legacy of an edition of the Pentateuch, which they highly valued, and a creed that included a hope of a second Moses who would restore their fortunes. Their liturgy and beliefs live on into modern times. The many influences that history brought to bear on the Samaritans pose a complex question. They seem to have had contact with the people of the Dead Sea Scrolls, in view of parallels with the ideas common to both groups. Their interest in cosmological matters suggests that they came under the power of Gnostic thinking, especially in its Judaic form. An early Gnostic sect

Courtesy of the Palestine Exploration Fund

*Retaining walls supporting forecourt of temple to the divine Augustus in Herodian Samaria. At the lower level are the remains of casemate walls, which surrounded the citadel of the period of the Israelite kings.*

called Dositheans evidently had some connection with the Samaritans. As a final observation we note the penetration of Islam into Samaritan life in a later century. We can see how Samaritan and Muslim writers agree in their assessment of the Christian story of Jesus, stemming from a shared belief in the unity of God and the high place accorded to Moses. This led to a devaluing of Jesus as the final revelation of God, according to the orthodox Christian position.

The NT writers outline the progress in the Christian message to include Samaria (Acts 1:8; 8:4-25; 9:31), which, in later church history, became regarded as the seat of heresy, mainly because Simon the magician (in Acts 8) was treated as the father of the Gnostic aberration. More plausibly it has been argued that the development of early Christianity was influenced by those teachers, such as Stephen and Philip, who had connections with Samaritan ideas and practices. R.M.

## SAMARITAN PENTATEUCH. *See* PENTATEUCH.

## ŚAMKARA.

Founder of the Advaita VEDANTA school, Śamkara is widely regarded as the most important single philosophical voice within HINDU-ISM and among the most influential of all Indian philosophers. He was born in south India in what is now the state of Karela. His dates remain a subject of debate, but were most likely around A.D. 700-732. According to tradition, Śamkara was a child genius who early mastered Vedic lore, took the garb of an ascetic, and traveled extensively about India study-ing, teaching, and establishing monastic centers. Most accounts have him die at only thirty-two years of age.

Śamkara's basic works are his commentaries on the Brahma sutras, the UPANISHADS, and a few other texts. His fundamental doctrine is the sole reality of Brahman, God, as pure *sat-chit-anada,* "being, knowledge, bliss." All that appears other than Brahman is maya, apparent realities superimposed upon Brahman by ego-consciousness because of AVIDYA or ignorance. This ignorance is overcome not through much learning but by non-attachment and spiritual insight. R.E.

## SAMKHYA.

From the Sanksrit word for "calcula-tion," in the sense of "analysis." One of the darshans or schools of philosophy of ancient HINDUISM, Samkhya emphasized a dualism between matter, prakriti, and spirit, purusha. Matter is composed, in varying degrees, of three *gunas* or attributes: *sattva,* intelligence; *rajas,* active energy; and *tamas,* slug-gishness. Purusha, on the other hand, is scattered throughout the cosmos as an infinite number of "souls" that are motionless, unchanging, and desireless. But purusha draws prakriti to itself, activating it in the process, and out of this process come into being humans and other animate beings.

Entrapped thus in prakriti, the purusha may yearn for KAIVALYA, MOKSHA, or liberation. That liberation is the goal of the classical systems of YOGA, which are considerably influenced by Samkhya philosophy. Samkhya in particular has a close relationship to the yoga sutras of Patanjali and to parts of the BHAGAVAD GITA. R.E.

## SAMOTHRACE.

An island in the northeastern part of the Aegean Sea. On a sea lane linking Greece to the Black Sea, Samothrace was a center for traders, travelers and colonists in the sixth and fifth centuries B.C. From Hellenistic times to the fourth century A.D., the island was a celebrated religious site, comparable to Olympia and Delphi, famous for its Sanctuary of the Great Gods. The island's capital, located on the north coast, had a small harbor that was visited by Paul on his way from Troas to Neapolis (Acts 16:11) and again, probably, on his return journey (Acts 20:6). P.L.G.

## SAMSARA.

From the Sanskrit word meaning literally "going around." In the thought of HINDU-ISM, BUDDHISM, and JAINISM, samsara refers to the "wheel of exitence," the endless rounds of transmi-gration or rebirth in this and other worlds decreed by KARMA, which is the lot of all beings until they attain MOKSHA, KAIVALYA, or liberation into NIRVANA, unconditioned reality by whatever name it is called.

The idea of samsara implies that the jiva or ego, or in Buddhism the accumulated energies of a life, pass through a succession of bodies. Sometimes regarded as fatalistic, the doctrine actually implies, first, that the universe is grounded upon DHARMA or righteous-ness and justice in its eternal ordering, since entities receive the proper fruits of their actions, and second, individual responsibility, in that one's future destiny is determined by the karma one makes or the liberation one seeks here and now. R.E.

## SAMSON.

A Danite judge, famed for his enormous strength and heroic accomplishments against neigh-boring Philistines (Judg. 13–16). Samson's Canaan-ite personal name (meaning "solar," "little sun") has invited the thesis that he was a mythical sun hero. But the proximity of Zorah, his hometown, to Beth-she-mesh ("house of the sun"), with its solar cult, suggests that Samson's name may not have been extraordinary and encourages our reading his bawdy exploits as those of an earthy frontier hero.

*Samson's Career.* Artful biblical narrative initially focuses on Samson's birth (Judg. 13:1-25). The angel of Yahweh informs Manoah's unnamed barren wife that she will bear a son who shall, from birth, be consecrated to Yahweh's service as a NAZIRITE. He must let his hair grow long and avoid wine, strong drink, and unclean food. Following his birth and early development, "the Spirit of the Lord began to stir him" (13:25). The meaning of that inner turmoil becomes evident only in subsequent narrative.

If Judges 13 suggests that Samson will pursue an austere existence, his exploits enumerated in Judges 14:1–16:22 tell otherwise! Willful Samson insists that his parents arrange his marriage to a Philistine maiden of nearby Timnah. A theological notation confers respectability on Samson's request: "it was from the LORD; for he was seeking an occasion against the Philistines" (14:4). After Samson has posed a riddle to the wedding guests (14:14), his bride coaxes out of him its meaning. She informs the Philistines, who solve the riddle. Samson pays the promised reward with the clothing of thirty Philistine victims at Ashkelon. In a rage he returns to Zorah.

When Samson learns that his wife has been given to his best man, he seizes three hundred foxes, ties blazing torches to their tails, and sends them through the Philistine grain fields (15:5). The Philistines burn Samson's wife and father-in-law after learning that they are the source of his rage. Samson then avenges himself on these murderers. Determined Philistines now induce certain Judeans to deliver Samson to them in a bound condition. Samson cooperates. Then with perfect timing, he frees himself and slays a thousand Philistines with the jawbone of an ass, his improvised weapon (15:15). Subsequently recognized while visiting a harlot in Gaza, Samson eludes the ambushers and uproots Gaza's gates, which he triumphantly carries forty miles to Hebron (16:3).

Tragedy soon overtakes Samson. Having won Samson's affection, Delilah obtains the secret of his strength so that the Philistines may seize him. Finally, "he told her all his mind" (16:17). Thereupon Samson's head is shaved as he sleeps on Delilah's lap. The Nazirite vow is violated. The weakened Samson is captured, blinded, and forced to grind meal at Gaza's prison. As Samson's hair begins to grow, his former strength returns. In a final desperate deed, Samson pulls down the pillars of the Philistine temple of Dagon. With the edifice crashing on both the Philistine throng and himself, Samson slays more enemies at his death than he had during his reckless life (16:30).

*Historical and Religious Significance.* Though the deeds of this legendary hero elude historical verification, the Samson narrative is historically significant insofar as it thoroughly reflects mounting Philistine-Israelite border tension during the eleventh century B.C. Though perhaps only sporadic and local, the friction was the harbinger of mounting hostility between the two populations in the years ahead. The narrative's religious import mainly lies in its convincing rendition of Samson as a negative example. Divinely given charismatic talent is wasted on someone susceptible to selfishness and unrestrained passion. His deeds were consistently motivated out of personal revenge, not out of recognition that he might have sacrificially and systematically rescued Dan, his native tribe, from augmenting Philistine pressure. Despite his flawed character,

Samson's story has inspired such noteworthy creations as Saint-Saëns' opera *Samson and Delilah* and Milton's dramatic poem *Samson Agonistes.*                J.K.K.

**SAMUEL.** The OT material presents several portraits of the man Samuel, making it difficult to determine the real identity of the "historical Samuel."

*The Priest-Prophet at Shiloh.* In I Samuel 1:1–4:1a, Samuel is presented as a person born to a barren mother, Hannah. As a consequence of the mother's vow (I Sam. 1:11), the lad is dedicated to the service of God and functions under the priest Eli at the sanctuary in Shiloh. Here he becomes prominent as a prophet while still a youth, condemns the house of Eli, and develops a reputation throughout Israel (I Sam. 3:10–4:1a).

Serious questions have been raised about this portrait of Samuel: (a) The story of the birth plays on the words "asked for" and "lent" (I Sam. 1:20; 2:20). These are the meanings of the name SAUL, not Samuel, which suggests that this birth and dedication story was once told about Saul and only secondarily applied to Samuel. (b) Only in these stories does Samuel have anything to do with SHILOH. Elsewhere in the stories he is associated with other places. (c) The content of Samuel's oracle against Eli's house (I Sam. 3:10-18) is already pronounced by an unnamed man of God in I Samuel 2:27-36, suggesting that the condemnation of Eli's family was originally made by someone other than Samuel.

*The Seer-Prophet from Zuph.* A second portrait of Samuel is found in I Samuel 9:1–10:16. In this account, he is presented as a seer-PROPHET (see 9:9), who at God's direction anoints Saul to rescue Israel from the Philistines. It would seem that Samuel has been introduced also into this story secondarily. At the beginning of the story, the seer is simply an unnamed man of God (9:6) and only later in the story is this character identified with Samuel (9:14). The only other text that associates Samuel with prophecy is I Samuel 19:20, where he is shown presiding over a group of prophets. This story, however, goes on to report a saying about Saul (19:24), which is already found in 10:12.

*The Judge.* A third picture of Samuel is found in I Samuel 7:3–8:22; 10:17-25; 12:1-25; 13:8-15; 15:1-35; 16:1-13. In these materials, Samuel is never called a seer or prophet but is presented as the last judge of Israel who reluctantly presides over the establishment of the monarchy. After aiding in the selection of Saul (10:17-25), he rejects him and moves to make DAVID king. Much of this material has been made to serve the themes of the books of I-II Samuel, namely, kingship as a blessing and curse, the repudiation of Saul, and the exaltation of David. These seem to be more theological and literary concerns used as propaganda than really historical factors.

*The "Historical Samuel."* Probably the portrait of Samuel as judge, king-maker, and king-rejector has more historical accuracy about it than the other two portraits. Samuel seems to have been a revered religious leader in the tribe of Benjamin: "Samuel judged Israel all the days of his life. And he went on a circuit year by year to Bethel, Gilgal, and Mizpah; and he judged Israel in all these places" (I Sam. 7:15-16). He may also have assisted in some fashion in Israel's war with the Philistines (7:1-4). He seems to have been drawn rather reluctantly into the move to make Saul king (I Sam. 8; 10:17-25; 12) and then to have broken with Saul probably over a struggle for power and authority (I Sam. 13; 15). Samuel may have aided David in the latter's struggles against Saul (19:18), but the account of his anointing David (16:1-13) sounds very much like an old folktale told to exalt David and to suggest that he was God's chosen even when an unpretentious lad.    J.H.

**I and II SAMUEL.** The ninth and tenth books in the English Bible that continue the historical narrative of the book of Judges. In the Hebrew Bible, they are counted a part of the "Former Prophets." In the ancient Greek tradition, I-II Samuel were called "first and second kingdoms" and closely associated with I-II Kings, called "third and fourth kingdoms." In Hebrew, the books follow Judges, but in other ancient versions, as in modern English texts, the book of Ruth has been placed between Judges and I-II Samuel.

*Title.* From the early centuries of the present era, the name of SAMUEL has been associated with these two books although his death is described before the end of I Samuel (25:1). In ancient times the two books were considered as a single work. Why the material should be called "Samuel" is unknown except that he does appear as the first important person in the book. First Chronicles 29:29 speaks of the Chronicles of Samuel the seer, which contained "the acts of David." No such work as this is known, but such a reference may have suggested Samuel's name for the books now bearing his name.

*Structure.* One way of looking at the books of Samuel is to see them as the continuation of the book of JUDGES. In the latter book, conditions are described in the early history of Israel, when judges ruled the people and "there was no king in Israel; every man did what was right in his own eyes" (Judg. 21:25). If the books continue the story in Judges, then Samuel's speech in I Samuel 12 would mark the end of the period of the judges (begun in Judg. 2) and introduce the period of the kings (begun in I Sam. 13). The latter period would then extend through the end of II Kings.

If we only focus on the two books themselves and the main characters in the story, the following outline suggests itself: (a) stories about Samuel (I Sam. 1–3; 7:3-17), (b) stories about the ARK OF THE COVENANT (I Sam. 4:1–7:2; II Sam. 6), (c) Samuel and Saul (I Sam. 8–15), (d) Saul and David (I Sam. 16–II Sam. 1), (e) David as king in Hebron (II Sam. 2:1–5:5), (f) David as king in Jerusalem (II Sam. 5:6–20:26), and (g) miscellaneous material about David (II Sam. 21–24). The story about David is not complete until the opening chapters of I Kings, which report David's death and Solomon's ascension to the throne.

*Contents.* In I Samuel 1–7, Samuel is the dominant character. Stories in the first three chapters report his birth and early service in the sanctuary at Shiloh under the direction of the priest ELI. An important theme in these narratives is the downfall of the house of Eli and the loss of prestige by the sanctuary at Shiloh. In I Samuel 4:1b–7:2, Samuel does not even appear. These stories, continued in II Samuel 6, concern the loss (and subsequent return) of the ark. Clearly, the Ark narrative originally had nothing to do with the Samuel narrative but has been included in the story here because it emphasized the loss of prestige by Shiloh, the home of the ark. The last independent Samuel story tells of his presiding over the Israelite triumph over the Philistines (I Sam. 7:3-17).

First Samuel 8–12 describes relationships between Samuel and Saul. In reality, however, these chapters are put together to provide a judgment on the institution of kingship and on Saul (see I Sam. 8:12). The account of Saul's coming to the throne that presents him in a good light (I Sam. 9–11) is sandwiched between two speeches of Samuel that condemn kingship. Again the material that focuses on Saul (I Sam. 13–15) has been edited so that Samuel condemns him in both I Samuel 13 and 15.

Once David enters the picture (I Sam. 16), he tends to dominate the stories even though Saul is the king and David only his servant. As David becomes more successful, Saul becomes more tragically obsessed. Eventually the tension between the two led to David's flight and his stay with the Philistines until their defeat of Saul. Thus I Samuel 16–II Samuel 1 is really not so much about Saul as about David's rise to prominence.

DAVID, of course, is the central character in II Samuel. Here the material can be seen as structured in various ways. First, it presents David under the blessing (II Sam. 2–8), when things work well for him and culminate in his empire. Then David is presented under the curse (II Sam. 9–20), when his reign is tormented by family and political problems. Another way to look at the material is to see II Samuel 2–7 as telling how David came to acquire his great state (I Sam. 8), followed by the account of how that state and its well-being were threatened (II Sam. 9–20).

The miscellaneous materials in II Samuel 21–24, containing stories from various periods in David's career and rule, have not been integrated into the story line of I-II Samuel and thus must be viewed as a catch-all of remaining Davidic stories.

*Themes.* Various themes stand out in the books of Samuel, and to treat these was a primary purpose. (a) Kingship is presented as both a blessing and a curse, as a hope and as a source of despair, a perspective then illustrated in the books of Kings. (b) The fall of the house of Eli and the demise of Shiloh and their replacement by Jerusalem and a new priesthood are stressed. (c) Saul is presented as the first but the forsaken ruler. (d) David and his family are presented as the elect, but even they are not a complete blessing.

J.H.

**SAMURAI.** In Japan, a warrior class characterized by distinct moral and spiritual values. As aristocratic knights or *bushi,* the samurai came to power in the eleventh century and as a class controlled Japanese political and cultural life in the Middle Ages, a period of almost incessant civil war. When the Tokugawa shogunate (1600–1868) established peace, the samurai had little fighting to do, but became a rigorously demarcated caste marked by certain privileges, such as the right to wear swords, and dominating government and education. The samurai way of life, often called BUSHIDO (the way or tao of the warrior), increasingly codified as the centuries of samurai dominance passed, drew inspiration from CONFUCIANISM, ZEN, and SHINTO. It emphasized frugality, courage, indifference to suffering, and utter loyalty to one's lord. If he failed to meet his obligations, a samurai was expected to commit ritual suicide, *seppuku* or *hara-kiri.*

The samurai class, along with other relics of feudalism, was officially abolished after the Meiji restoration of 1868. But its values continued to play a significant role in Japanese life, above all in the mentality of many military people and their supporters until the end of World War II in 1945.

R.E.

**SANBALLAT.** A politician called by Nehemiah (2:10) "the Horonite," that is, from Beth-horon. In a letter from Elephantine in Egypt, dated 407 B.C., Sanballat is called "the governor of Samaria" who had two sons with Hebrew names. Nehemiah 4:2 speaks of Sanballat's "brethren" (political followers) and of "the army of Samaria" as sources of his power. He seems to have been a Persian appointee, located in the city of Samaria, to whom the Persians had given authority over Judah and Jerusalem. TOBIAH, the Ammonite, was his henchman in their attempt to stop the rebuilding of Jerusalem's walls (Neh. 2:10, 19; 4:7; 6:1, 12, 14). Nehemiah "chased . . . from me" (13:28) the unnamed member of a prominent, priestly family in Jerusalem who had married Sanballat's daughter.

P.L.G.

**SANCTIFICATION.** The process of growth in personal sanctity or holiness, following JUSTIFICATION, or acceptance of the sinner as righteous by God on account of the sacrifice of Christ, appropriated by faith. Justification is the initial stage of salvation, which immediately reconciles the sinner to God. This new relationship or turn toward God is then followed by a lifelong process of growth in grace, called sanctification. In both justification and sanctification, all is accomplished by God's free grace, received humbly in faith or trust.

Sanctification is derived from "sanctify," which is from the Latin *sanctus,* or holy. To sanctify directly means "to make holy." Sanctification refers to the ongoing process of becoming HOLY. To be "holy" means "to be identified with God," for only God is holy, according to biblical revelation. God's name is holy; and elements of worship, such as temples and scriptures, are made holy by their relationship to God. Anything used by God becomes holy (Pss. 99:3, 9; 111:9; Exod. 3:5; 20:8, 11; 28:2; 35:2; Josh. 5:15; II Chr. 35:3; I Kings 8:4, 6). Clearly, sanctification means "to be in close relationship with God." Any practice, then, that keeps us near the Divine and available for God's service, such as prayer, works of love and mercy, or sensitivity to the needs of people made in God's image, is conducive to growth in sanctity.

In the OT, holiness means "to be set apart." Thus the Levites (Lev. 20:26; 21:8) were holy because of their separation from ordinary life and their devotion to God. In the NT, as well as in the prophetic writings of the OT, sanctification is more personally and ethically understood. Paul declares in Romans 12:1-2, "Present your bodies as a living sacrifice, holy and acceptable to God, which is your spiritual worship. Do not be conformed to this world but be transformed by the renewal of your mind." Personal holiness or ethical purity is here equated with sanctification. Paul goes on to list humility, generosity, faithfulness, mercy, cheerfulness, love, sincerity, joy, patience, peacefulness, and good deeds as the expression of sanctification in the Christian's life.

J.C.

**SANCTUARY.** A place that is sacred in that it is both consecrated and a place of refuge or asylum. "Sanctuary" is also the term used for the right of asylum, of protection from one's enemies or the power of the law. The Hebrews had cities of REFUGE or sanctuary (Deut. 4:41-42). The area immediately surrounding the altar, in the chancel of a church, is also called the sanctuary. (*See also* SANCTUARY, RIGHT OF.)

J.C.

**SANCTUARY, RIGHT OF.** The sacred character of holy places, the protection provided by the Holy, taboos against shedding blood on holy ground, and fear of the effectiveness of any curses uttered by anyone cornered in a sacred place have combined to make churches asylums for those who have committed crimes.

In Israel, certain cities were designated as places of REFUGE (see Deut. 19:1-13). The first record of the right of sanctuary in Christian churches is found in fourth-century Roman law. The Theodosian and Justinian codes also acknowledge and regulate the practice, which developed in recognition of the bishop as intercessor with the civil government. Both civil and canon law regulated just which offenses would be offered sanctuary and which would not. Sometimes those guilty of violent crimes would be given temporary sanctuary to check blood vengeance, to provide for compensation for the victim or kin, or to gain assurance that the criminal would be tried and not just summarily executed.

In medieval England every church was considered a sanctuary, and other places obtained the right through royal charter. Henry VIII abolished twenty-two such places and substituted seven "cities of refuge" in 1540. James I in 1623 abolished the right of sanctuary for certain crimes, but the practice was not totally eliminated until 1723. On the Continent, the practice survived until the French Revolution. It is the basis today for diplomatic asylum in embassies.

The right of sanctuary was tested in the United States during the 1980s, as churches responded to the plight of refugees from Latin American military dictatorships. The United States government would not grant political asylum to refugees from governments that it supported. Some church leaders risked civil disobedience in claiming the right of sanctuary in order to shelter and help such refugees.

N.H.

**SANCTUS.** The hymn of victory or *tersanctus*, derived from Isaiah 6:3, which appears in the liturgy of the Mass at the end of the preface (to Holy Communion). It consists of the phrase "Holy, holy, holy, Lord God of Hosts. Heaven and earth are full of thy glory." This portion of the Christian liturgy (which also occurs in Holy Communion services of several denominations) is taken from synagogue worship.

J.C

**SANGHA.** From the Pali word for "assembly." In BUDDHISM, the monastic order. Originating in the band of disciples gathered by the Buddha himself, the Sangha is perhaps the oldest existing non-hereditary institution in the world today. Its purpose is the pure practice, conservation, and teaching of the Buddhist path to enlightenment. Those who formally become Buddhists, and those who enter the Sangha, affirm the *Triratna,* "Three Jewels": "I take refuge in the Buddha, the dharma, and the Sangha"—that is, in the Buddha as the supreme example of the enlightened person, in his teaching, and in the organization that perpetuates it.

The Sangha is found in most traditional form in the Theravada Buddhist countries. Here monks are celibate and follow literally such ancient observances of the Vinaya Pitaka, the scripture of monastic discipline—such as no meals after noon—and retreat during the rainy season. Mahayana monks and priests, while part of the Sangha, often follow considerably modified rules.

Everywhere, however, the Sangha has developed from its original ideal as an assembly of wandering teaching monks, the "Sangha of the Four Quarters," to a collection of monastic and temple communities, together with some hermit recluses. Ruled by an abbot, larger monasteries serve as Buddhist educational centers and places of retreat, while village temples with their modest staff of monks are local centers of religious life. In the Theravada countries, except Sri Lanka (Ceylon), boys traditionally spend a year as a member of the Sangha before marriage as part of initiation into manhood.

R.E.

**SANHEDRIN.** The term is a loanword into Hebrew from the Greek word *synedrion* meaning "a council or meeting place." It has specific application to the Jewish senate (Acts 5:21) or "council of elders" (Luke 22:66; Acts 22:5) called in session to determine legal questions for the people according to the rabbinic interpretation of the law, both civil and religious. Joseph of Arimathea is called a counselor (Mark 15:43; Luke 23:50) since he was a member of this body.

The rabbis traced back the genesis of the Sanhedrin to the seventy men appointed to assist Moses (Num. 11:16), and they believed that after the Exile the company of ruling elders was convened by Ezra (see the Mishnah, *Sayings of the Fathers* 1:1 for a statement to this effect). Josephus, however, knows of the Sanhedrin from a decree of Antiochus III (third-second century B.C.) debated by the "senate" of the Jews. Here we meet the composition of the body as consisting of priests and elders under the controlling influence of the high priest. There are several allusions to this governing council in I Maccabees and Josephus, showing that the PHARISEES came to power in this way by becoming a numerous group in the Sanhedrin.

With the Roman occupation of Israel after 63 B.C., when Pompey took over the administration of Palestine, the Sanhedrin's power was restricted, and with Herod the Great's virtual dictatorship in force, the elders were muted or reduced to compliance. A sharp turn of events in A.D. 6, which made Judea a province of Rome, threw the Sanhedrin into prominence, and restored the power and privilege it had enjoyed in the earliest Hasmonean times. During the six decades that span much of the NT (A.D. 6–66, when the great rebellion against Rome broke out) the Sanhedrin was in the seat of authority as the center of religious, judicial, and administrative power in Israel.

In this period the council was dominated by the aristocracy of the SADDUCEES, led by the chief priests with the HIGH PRIEST (known from the Gospels as Annas and his son-in-law Caiaphas; and from the Acts as Ananias at the trial of Paul, Acts 23:2) the leader. Patterned on the reference given in Numbers 11:16 and following, of the "elders of Israel," the number of the senate was fixed at seventy (plus one); the extra person in excess of seventy was the high priest who acted as chairman. The latter office was hereditary, while it seems that the council members elected one another for life. The main credential for membership was a knowledge of the Torah (Moses' Law) and its rabbinical interpretation.

The jurisdiction of the Sanhedrin covered a wide geographical area (including the Dispersion; see Acts 9:1ff.) and it had within its competence to deal with an extensive range of judicial themes and concerns. In particular, it acted as the main *beth din*, "a court of justice," and its speciality was the examination and punishment of heretics, that is, those accused of teaching contrary to the Torah and leading others astray (as in the stories of Acts 4, 5, 22, 24). In this context we must view the "trials" of Jesus and Stephen (Acts 6:9–8:1) as well as the later sentence of death passed on James, the Lord's brother, for alleged transgression against the Law of Moses (compare Paul's defense too, Acts 25:8; 26:2-8). It seems that both Jesus and Stephen were regarded as deviant teachers in Israel, though Jesus' pretension to be a messianic figure was taken to imply that he claimed to share God's throne (Mark 14:62), a bid that the Sanhedrin regarded as blasphemy (Mark 14:64). On Stephen's part, the grievance was similar except for the obvious difference that he claimed to see the exalted Jesus as an occupant of God's throne like Daniel's Son of man (Dan. 7:13; Acts 7:55).

The competence of the Sanhedrin to carry out capital punishments is much debated. John 18:31 clearly indicates that the Romans reserved the right to execute, and there is some independent corroboration of this restriction on the Sanhedrin's power. On the other side, there is a conflicting body of data to show that the Sanhedrin did expect to have the power of life and death in religious cases demanding the death penalty (for example, adultery), and the "executions" of Stephen and James indicate how they brought about the deaths of these men. But these instances were in the nature of mob violence and murder rather than summary execution. Yet again the evidence of John 18:31 is capable of a nuanced interpretation, given John's theological interest, and it may mean: "it is not lawful for us to put any man to death" by crucifixion, the Roman method of execution, a point John wished to emphasize since he regarded the manner of Jesus' death (John 18:32) as both significant and symbolic (Jesus' being "lifted up," John 12:32, 33).

Saul of Tarsus is often thought to have been a Sanhedrin member (Acts 26:10), but this is unlikely, given his youthful age at the time of Stephen's interrogation. R.M.

## SANKEY, IRA DAVID

SANKEY, IRA DAVID (1840-1908). Famed musician and associate of DWIGHT L. MOODY in his evangelistic campaigns. Born in Lawrence County, Pennsylvania, Sankey early demonstrated his gifts as a musician. After having served with the Union troops during the Civil War, he returned to Newcastle,

Courtesy of the Library of Congress

*Ira D. Sankey*

Pennsylvania, where evangelistic singing became his primary interest. He was often a soloist at large Sunday school conventions in the heyday of that movement.

As a delegate to the international convention of the YMCA. in Indianapolis in 1870, he met D. L. Moody for the first time. The evangelist urged Sankey to return to Chicago to work with him, in what was to be an association that was to continue for twenty-five years. Moody did the preaching, and Sankey sa... gospel songs and served as organ accompanist.

Moody and Sankey were involved in a preach... tour of the British Isles that continued from 18... 1875. In the meetings the *Sankey and Moody Book* (published in 1873) was employed to int... to the British public gospel songs, a genre o... then unknown to the more formal British pu... Moody and Sankey traveled through Scotland, and Ireland, the meetings met response from both clergy and lay peopl...

After some revisions, a resultant hymn... *Hymns and Sacred Songs*, published by P... Sankey, appeared in the United States i... was the book used in the great Moody m... Brooklyn Rink, the old Pennsylvania in Philadelphia, and in other cities. nor Sankey benefited personally from... their hymnbook sales. "The new m... even the music halls and were whis... the street" (Louis F. Benson, 1962). Sankey's singing in a b... accompanied himself on a smal... him to a new plane of popula...

**SANSKRIT.** An ancient Indo-European language of India, which is the sacred language of HINDUISM. Sanskrit is often referred to as *devavani*—the language of the gods. Sanskrit literature is of four types: the VEDAS; sastras or guides to conduct, such as the *Laws of Manu*; PURANAS; and poetry, such as the epics MAHABHARATA and RAMAYANA. Of these classes, the first three are believed to be divinely inspired, the Vedas being the fundamental Hindu scriptures. Sanskrit remains the tongue of the most sacred Hindu rituals performed by Brahmins. Important religious texts of BUDDHISM and JAINISM are also in Sanskrit.

R.E.

**SARACENS.** The term first used by late classical authors (first through third centuries A.D.) to refer to an Arab tribe of the Sinai. After the rise of Islam, European Christians used the term to refer to any Muslim subject of the caliphate, whether Arab, Turkish, or some other nationality.          K./M.C.

**SARAH.** (1) The wife of Abraham and mother of Isaac. As Abram's childless wife (Gen. 11:29-30), Sarah, alternately Sarai, meaning "princess, mistress," accompanied him to Canaan (12:5) via Haran (11:31). Believing that Sarai's beauty would endanger him during their emergency sojourn in Egypt, Abram instructed her to pretend that she was his sister (12:13; in 20:12 she is his half sister). Sarai's presence in Pharaoh's house evoked divinely sent plagues. Discerning Sarai's true identity, Pharaoh expelled the couple (12:15–13:1).

Subsequently, Sarai despaired over her inability to provide Abram an heir. Abram accepted Sarai's offer of her Egyptian maid Hagar. Once pregnant, Hagar acted arrogantly. Obtaining Abram's consent, resentful Sarai expelled Hagar (16:1-6), but she returned under divine leading to bear Ishmael (16:7-15).

When God assigned the couple the names "Abraham" and "Sarah" (17:5, 15 [dialectical variants of their former names]), he assured ABRAHAM that this "mother of nations" would bear a son within a year (17:16-21). Hearing that same divine promise at Mamre, ninety-year-old Sarah laughed incredulously (18:10-15).

At Gerar, the uneasy couple made King Abimelech victim of the wife-sister deception. Once Sarah was inside Abimelech's house, God warned the king to return her untouched to Abraham (20:1-7). Abimelech complied, offering Abraham a reprimand, gifts, and an invitation to settle nearby (20:9-16).

When Sarah bore the child of promise, Abraham named him Isaac to commemorate his wife's joyful laughter over his birth (21:1-3, 6-7). At Isaac's weaning feast, Sarah demanded the permanent expulsion of Hagar and Ishmael, who threatened her own son's inheritance (21:8-14). When Sarah died at Kiriath-arba (Hebron) at the age of 127 (23:1-2), Abraham buried her in the cave of Machpelah that he purchased for a family sepulcher (23:3-20). Beyond Genesis, Sarah is mentioned but once in the OT—in Isaiah 51:2 as Israel's ancestress.

NT texts refer to Sarah's protracted barrenness (Rom. 4:19), conception of Isaac (Rom. 9:9), dissimilarity with Hagar (Gal. 4:21-31), faith in God's promise (Heb. 11:11), and submissiveness to Abraham (I Pet. 3:6). A superlative expression of Sarah's beauty appears in the Genesis Apocryphon, a first-century A.D. Aramaic scroll from Qumran.

(2) The daughter of Raguel and bride of Tobias whose story is told in the Apocrypha (Tob. 3:7; 7:13).

J.K.K.

Courtesy of Ahmet Dönmez, archaeologist, Izmir, Turkey

*The temple of Artemis at Sardis*

**SARDIS.** A city in Asia Minor, capital of ancient Lydia and of the Roman province of Lydia, located in the Hermus River valley, near the river Pactolus. In the sixth century B.C., Sardis was one of the most powerful and rich cities in the world. The famed Croesus was one of its prominent and despotic kings. An oriental and geographically well-defended city, its wealth came from agriculture and much commerce and trade. It became the most important Persian city in Asia Minor. The patron deity of the city was Artemis-Cybele, who claimed power to restore life to the dead.

The letter to Sardis (Rev. 3:1-6) is to a church that is nearly dead (v. 2) but that had a few faithful believers (v. 4) to whom the promise is given that their names remain in "the book of life" and will be confessed before God and the angels (v. 5).

P.L.G.

**SARGON.** (1) Sargon of Akkad. As history's first empire-builder, Sargon founded the Semitic Empire of Akkad (about 2360–2180 B.C.). Credited by the Sumerian King List with a fifty-six-year reign, this energetic imperialist ascended to power in Kish, defeated Lugalzaggisi of Erech, and won mastery over all Sumer. His inscriptions also report spectacular

Courtesy of the Oriental Institute, University of Chicago

*Winged bull with human face, once flanking the main entrance to the throne room of Sargon II at Khorsabad*
*(eighth century* B.C.*)*

campaigns throughout Upper Mesopotamia enabling him to command territory spanning the Lower Sea (Persian Gulf) to the Upper Sea (Mediterranean).

At Akkad (near the later Babylon, though still archaelogically unidentified), Sargon established a new capital. He brought sufficient unification to his wide-ranging empire so that, following his death, two sons and an impressive grandson, Naramsin, could hold sway for nearly sixty years. Sargon's birth, rise to kingship, and eventful rule have been vastly embellished by Sumerian and AKKADIAN legend.

(2) Sargon I. A virtually unknown nineteenth-century B.C. monarch standing in twenty-seventh position within the Assyrian King List, whose seal impression is attested on ancient Cappadocian texts.

(3) Sargon II (722–705 B.C.). Son of Tiglath-pileser III, father of Sennacherib, and king of ASSYRIA, who succeeded his brother, Shalmaneser V, after the latter had been murdered during the siege of Samaria. Sargon claimed the throne amid obscure, yet real, internal conflict. He was immediately greeted by extensive anti-Assyrian rebellion. Thus his goal of reestablishing the dimensions of his father's empire was realized only through sustained diligence. For a decade, he successfully waged war against various enemies to the west (Syria and Asia Minor) and north (Urartu). His army even advanced to the Egyptian frontier.

Sargon then engaged in delayed retaliation against Merodach-baladan, a Chaldean prince, who had led Babylonian and allied Elamite rebels against him at the outset of his Assyrian reign. Merodach-baladan, who presently suffered internal problems of his own, fled to Elam. This enabled Sargon to enter Babylon without incident in 709 B.C. and make himself king there.

In 713 Sargon began the ambitious construction of his own new city Dur-Sharrukin (Khorsabad) near Nineveh. It was completed in 707, but never truly inhabited. After Sargon's battlefield death amid a minor engagement in Iran in 705 (which thrust his son Sennacherib into kingship), the city was abandoned.

The extent of Sargon's engagement in Palestinian affairs is somewhat unclear. Whereas the OT seems to credit Shalmaneser with the capture of Samaria (II Kings 17:1-6; 18:9-12), Sargon's annals repeatedly claim that as his own achievement. Moreover, some biblical scholars have equated Sargon with the imprecise "king of Assyria" reference in II Kings 17:6. Since Samaria fell to the Assyrians in the late summer or autumn of 722 and Shalmaneser died late in 722, Samaria's capitulation likely predated Sargon's regal installation. Sargon probably boasted about the event because it happened in his accession year. The reorganization of Samaria into an Assyrian province, however, occurred under Sargon's supervision.

Less than a decade later, Palestinian inhabitants impressed by Egypt's resurgence under its new Twenty-fifth (Ethiopian) Dynasty decided that the time was ripe to stand up to Assyria. In about 714, the Philistine city of Ashdod defied Assyria by withholding tribute. Judah, Edom, and Moab were invited to join an expanding coalition of anti-Assyrian rebels. Isaiah's opposition to Judah's involvement is recorded in Isaiah 20, the only biblical text that

Courtesy of the Oriental Institute, University of Chicago

*Restored painting showing Sargon II (722–705 B.C.) and attendant before the god Ashur, from Khorsabad*

names Sargon (v. 1). Judah's king Hezekiah apparently accepted Isaiah's advice and stood aloof. Busily preparing to overtake Babylon, Sargon dispatched his general, who severely punished Ashdod in 712 and straightaway turned it into an Assyrian province. If Judah escaped disaster, it was forced to recognize that under Sargon, Assyria was a most resourceful military power.                    J.K.K.

**SARTRE, JEAN-PAUL** (1905–80). French philosopher, playwright, novelist, and essayist, best known as one of the leaders of twentieth-century atheistic EXISTENTIALISM. Born in Paris, he entered the Ecole Normale Supérieure in 1924. Sartre did further study in Germany under EDMUND HUSSERL and MARTIN HEIDEGGER. Both were critical influences. From 1931 to 1944, he taught philosophy at lycées in Le Havre, Laon, and Paris. His first novel, *Nausea* (1938), established his reputation in French literary circles. It concretely expresses existentialist themes developed in his philosophical works. Sartre's major work, *Being and Nothingness,* appeared in 1943, the same year as the play *The Flies,* which, with *No Exit* (1944), attracted much attention. In 1945 he co-founded the periodical *Les Temps Modernes.* After the war there appeared a number of novels, plays, and literary studies, including *The Age of Reason* and *The Reprieve* (1945), *Dirty Hands* (1948), *Troubled Sleep* (1949), *The Condemned of Altona* (1956), *Saint Genet* (1961), and a study of Flaubert (1971).

Sartre's life was one of political engagement and disputation. Drawn to Marxism, he later criticized French Communism and identified with Maoist causes. His *Critique of Dialectical Reason* (1960) is an effort to show Marxism's compatibility with existentialism. However, the relationship between his highly individualistic existentialist moral theory and his Marxist and later Maoist views is never clearly resolved. At the center of Sartre's existentialism is an analysis of human consciousness, the crux of which is the anguish of our experience of inescapable freedom. Sartre calls "bad faith" the effort to conceal our freedom by assuming that our situation is determined or inevitable. Sartre insists that authentic existence requires the acceptance of our own freedom and the recognition that we are the sole origin of, and thus responsible for, all our acts. Yet human consciousness is radically contingent, never ontologically self-sufficient. We therefore project this perfection in the idea of God. However, Sartre insists, God does not exist.
                                                           J.L.

**SAT/SATYA.** In SANSKRIT, these terms combine the concepts of being, existence, essence, truth, and that which is morally right. This combination offers a valuable insight into a keynote of HINDUISM: its identification of ontological reality, *sat* or being, with *satya* or truth as expressed through human speech and deed; and with righteous conduct, which is moral both in itself and because it is in accordance with the true nature of the cosmos. In ancient India, telling truth and acting in accord with it at whatever sacrifice was thought to have great sacred potency. In the twentieth century MOHANDAS GANDHI revived the belief in his concept of *satyagraha,* "holding to truth/being," as the principle underlying his tactics of non-violent resistance.                                    R.E.

**SATAN.** The word, meaning simply "adversary," is seldom found in the Hebrew OT, where it refers to David (I Sam. 29:4), the sons of Zeruiah (II Sam. 19:22), and David's enemies (I Kings 5:4), including Hadad the Edomite (I Kings 11:14) and Rezon (11:23). In a few places the term seems to have a special significance equivalent to "the adversary" and apparently refers to that ruler of evil beings who is constantly set in opposition to God's purposes. This seems to be the meaning in I Chronicles 21:1; Job 1:6-12; 2:1-7; and Zechariah 3:1-2. Interestingly, in these passages the Septuagint consistently translates the term by the Greek word for the DEVIL. The Latin Vulgate uses Satan. The paucity of references to Satan in the OT is in striking contrast to the saturation of apocalyptic literature in the intertestamental period with various terms for Satan, such as Asmodeus, Semjaza, Azazel, Mastema, Satanail, and Belial. Whether this influx of teaching on angels and demons is due to Persian cosmology is debated, but the tremendous increase of such teaching after the return from Persia in 538 B.C. is incontrovertible. It may be more likely explained by the transcendentalizing of God by the Jews after the destruction of the Temple and the need to fill the void with intermediary beings, both good and evil.

The NT inherits the tradition of the previous centuries and speaks frequently of the role of Satan and the demons. He is called Satan (II Cor. 12:7; Rev. 12:9), the Devil (Matt. 4:1; 25:41), Beelzebul (Mark 3:22), Belial (II Cor. 6:15), and perhaps Abaddon and Apollyon (Rev. 9:11). In addition, many metaphors are used to describe Satan: the Serpent (Rev. 12:9), the Dragon (Rev. 12:7), the Lion (I Pet. 5:8; II Tim. 4:17), the Strong Man (Matt. 12:29), the Evil One (Eph. 6:16), the Accuser (Rev. 12:10), the Tempter (Matt. 4:3), the Destroyer (I Cor. 10:10), the Adversary (I Pet. 5:8), the Enemy (Matt. 13:25; I Cor. 15:25), an Angel of Light (II Cor. 11:14), the Prince of Demons (Matt. 9:34; 12:24), the Ruler of this World (John 12:31; 14:30; 16:11), the Prince of the Power of the Air (Eph. 2:2), and the God of this World (II Cor. 4:4).

The Bible contains no account of the origin of Satan, although he is already present in the Garden of Eden when the story of humanity begins (Gen. 3:1; II Cor. 11:3). Some find allusions to his origin in Isaiah 14 and Ezekiel 28, though in both passages it is a human ruler who is under primary consideration. In the NT, Jude 6 speaks of the expulsion of angels from their own position and proper dwelling and their consignment to the nether gloom until the Judg-

ment. In II Peter 2:4, angels are said to have sinned and been cast into hell, awaiting judgment in pits of nether gloom. Since Matthew speaks of the devil and his angels (25:41), these verses may have some bearing on the origin of both. The only alternative to strict dualism is the acceptance of Satan as a created being.

Satan is considered the greatest enemy of God and Christ, whose power includes control of the kingdoms of the world (Matt. 4:9; I John 5:19) and death itself (Heb. 2:14). Christ's earthly ministry was viewed as a period of binding the strong man so that he might spoil his goods (Matt. 12:29). The resurrection of Jesus Christ was thus an evident conquest of Satan's ultimate power over death (Heb. 2:14), guaranteeing that both Death and Hades will finally be cast into the lake of fire (Rev. 20:14).                               J.R.M.

**SATI.** This word, meaning in Sanskrit "virtuous woman" or "chaste wife," has two distinct but related denotations. First, Sati is a HINDU goddess, daughter of the sage Daksha. She desired to marry the god SHIVA despite the opposition of her father, who despised Shiva's unkempt appearance and mad behavior. Though uninvited, Shiva appeared at the ceremony in which Sati was to choose her spouse, and the two were united. But when Daksha then failed to invite Shiva to a great sacrifice, Sati in her mortification committed suicide in the sacrificial fire. Shiva wandered the world in sorrow, bearing the corpse of his wife, until to end his mourning the other gods cut the body into many pieces; the place where each piece fell to earth is considered sacred to Sati, and many temples thus attribute their location. Sati is reported to have been reborn as Parvati, Shiva's great consort-goddess.

Second, sati, in this usage often written "suttee," refers to the customary suicide of a Hindu widow at the death of her husband, most commonly by immolation on his funeral pyre. Never universal, though encouraged by the hard lot that often fell to widows, the practice was abolished in British India in 1829.                                                                R.E.

**SATISFACTION.** *See* ATONEMENT, THEORIES OF.

**SATORI.** A Japanese word used in ZEN to indicate enlightenment, meaning literally "surprise." In Zen, satori is the supreme attainment, a complete inexpressible experience of freedom from the fetters of conditioned reality. It is an inward, intuitive realization that cannot be articulated in the language of ordinary rational discourse, but can be demonstrated by an utter joy and spontaneity of being. It is identified with the enlightenment of the Buddha under the bodhi tree.

Satori experiences may be realized repeatedly, both as "little" and "great" satoris. Generally they are attained after a period of intensive Zen practice, often stimulated by a gesture or even slap from a Zen master. The Soto tradition of Zen emphasizes the realization of satori during quiet sitting *(zazen)*, while the Rinzai school employs the more concentrated methods of koan work, harsh interviews, and grueling retreats to bring about the abrupt spontaneous "surprise" of awakening.                               R.E.

## SATYA SAI BABA. (1926– ). Satya Sai Baba is among the most famous of contemporary holy men in HINDUISM. While his personality is dynamic and his preaching simple but effective, it is undeniably the almost endless stories of miracles done by him, from healings to materializations of gems, that has attracted the most attention, laying the foundation of a large religious movement. Many of his followers consider him an avatar.                                      R.E.

## SAUL (meaning asked [of God], or lent [to God]). Son of Kish and first king of Israel (about 1020–1000 B.C.).

*Historical Context.* On Saul fell the uneasy task of governing a people undergoing social transition as they left their loosely organized tribal existence behind and advanced toward statehood. Though some regarded the emergence of monarchy as an affront to Yahweh, who alone was Israel's king, others embraced monarchy as a historical necessity. The Philistine defeat of Yahweh's people at Aphek not long after 1050 B.C. (I Sam. 4:1-11) induced more politically minded Israelites to conclude that Canaan might become a Philistine empire within months. With its army in shambles, the central sanctuary at Shiloh upended, and priestly leadership rendered inadequate, the Israelite confederacy faced grim prospects. Continuing Israelite presence in the Land of Promise required stronger leadership. The Israelite monarchy was thus spawned, and a Benjaminite named Saul was ushered into the regal office.

*Saul's Regal Election.* Since the Chronicler's portrayal of Saul is limited to his battlefield death at the hand of triumphant Philistines (I Chr. 10), we must consult I Samuel to glean information about Saul's regal election and accomplishments. Two variant traditions reporting Saul's choice as king are preserved. The earlier one (I Sam. 9:1–10:16) tells of Kish's lost asses, which "handsome" Saul and a servant were sent to recover. After a lengthy, fruitless search, they decided to consult a seer in a nearby town (presumably Ramah, 7:17; 9:5,6). As they entered, they were met by SAMUEL, a prominent man of God, who informed them that Kish's asses had been recovered and urged their attendance at a cultic sacrifice where the choice portion had been reserved for Saul. Samuel privately anointed Saul to be "prince" over Israel (10:1*a*) and, in a lengthy speech, defined his new function as a charismatic leader capable of delivering Israel from its enemies (10:1*b*-8).

Integrated with this account is the originally separate story of Saul's courageous rescue of the Transjordan city of Jabesh-gilead from Ammonite aggression (I Sam. 11). Threatened by the ultimatum of Nahash the Ammonite, the beleaguered city sent an embassy to Gibeah to solicit help. Just then Saul appeared. Upon hearing the news, "the spirit of God came mightly upon Saul" (11:6). Dramatically he mustered numerous volunteers and conquered the Ammonite enemy. After securing Israel's striking triumph, Saul was publicly acclaimed by the people as king "before the Lord in Gilgal" (11:15).

A later tradition similarly tells of Saul's regal election, but exhibits anti-monarchical overtones (I Sam. 8:1-22; 10:17-27; 12:1-25). Here Samuel is no seer, but a judge who is offended when the people demand, "Appoint for us a king to govern us like all the nations" (8:5). Perceiving that it is Yahweh's will that he both honor their request and warn them of the odious ways of sovereigns, Samuel assembled the people at Mizpah, where Saul is chosen by divinely controlled lot (10:20-21). Taken together, these two traditions aptly reflect Israel's ambivalent attitude toward monarchy. In choosing a king, Israel strode boldly in a new direction that broke with venerable Yahwistic tradition. But how else might the Philistine challenge be met? In light of such ambivalence, Saul's regal career was destined to be troublesome.

*Narrative Bias.* Unlike DAVID, Saul does not enjoy a predominantly favorable biblical portrait. We would do well to recognize Saul's negative "press" before dealing further with his achievements and problems. That Saul's name is not listed among those Israelite heroes celebrated in Ecclesiasticus 44:1–50:24 and Hebrews 11:1-40 is itself indicative of the way he is treated within the detailed Saul traditions preserved in I Samuel 9–31. Samuel largely dominates chapters 9–15 and David chapters 16–31.

Hostility toward Saul is not merely a mark of the Deuteronomic historian who gave I-II Samuel its present shape. Rather, it is indigenous to the traditions he used. In early monarchical Israel, two main factors contributed to a prejudicial attitude toward Saul. First, Samuel and his hawkish support group, the sons of the prophets, kept alive the holy war mentality of premonarchical Israel. Thus they opposed Saul's modern, pragmatic approach, which compromised Israel into becoming like the other nations. Second, at Saul's expense, the Samuel narrative is rife with pro-Davidic sentiment. By setting Saul in an unfavorable light, it intensifies the prestige of David and his Jerusalem-based dynasty. Indeed, the tradition seems more resolute in reporting Saul's emotional imbalance than it is in describing those extremely trying conditions that would have frustrated any able Israelite who might have ruled as Israel's first monarch. With this in mind, let us consider Saul's tragic alienation from Samuel and David.

*Alienation from Samuel.* While the relationship involving Saul, the statesman, and SAMUEL, the prophet, began auspiciously, in time it suffered grave rupture. Saul never forgot that it was Samuel who had conferred him with regal status. Samuel never forgot that the new order that Saul represented merited scrutiny. Their personal rift began as Saul prepared to fight the Philistines at Michmash (I Sam. 13). As holy war required, Saul waited at Gilgal for Samuel, who was expected to offer Yahweh the appropriate sacrifice. With the volunteer army scattering and Samuel's failure to arrive at the appointed time, Saul made the sacrifice himself. At once Samuel did arrive, and with the thundering words, "Your kingdom shall not continue" (13:14), he condemned the monarch. By offering sacrifice in Samuel's absence, Saul had usurped the authority of the old guard militant prophetism that Samuel embodied.

The rupture became permanent when Saul ignored the requirements of holy war during his battle, at Samuel's instigation, against the Amalekites (I Sam. 15). By sparing the king Agag and taking the best of the Amalekite spoils, Saul presumptuously decided to rewrite the rules of Israelite warfare. Saul reasoned expediently: Why should his troops not be allowed to benefit from the spoils of war? Samuel reasoned theologically: Was Saul's insubordination to Yahweh's will not unpardonable? After announcing that Yahweh had rejected Saul in favor of a better person (15:28), Samuel strode off, never to see Saul again. Finally, just prior to Saul's combat with the Philistines at Mount Gilboa, he conversed with Samuel's ghost, which the medium at Endor summoned (28:8-25). The distraught king heard a chilling prediction about Philistine triumph and his own death. Prophetic support for Saul had long vanished.

*Alienation from David.* However David entered Saul's service, be it through his musical talent (I Sam. 16:15-23) or slaying of Goliath (17:31-58), he quickly rose to prominence. Soon he was promoted to army lieutenant (18:5). Enormously jealous of David's popularity, Saul resolved to exterminate him. Saul's attempts at spearing David against the wall failed (18:9-11; 19:9-10), as did his stratagem to demand from David an outlandish marriage present for his daughter Michal that should have made him easy Philistine prey (18:20-27). Unable to persuade Jonathan to kill David (19:1-7), he dispatched servants to David's sleeping quarters only to learn that David had escaped through Michal's assistance (19:11-17). Saul shamelessly ordered the massacre of the priests of Nob because they unwittingly helped David (22:11-19). Rumors of David's whereabouts sometimes reached Saul too late to be useful (23:7-13, 19-25). Twice Saul might have died at David's hand had it not been for the latter's fear of slaying Yahweh's anointed (24:5-7; 26:6-12). Indeed, Saul even confessed his wrong in seeking David's life (26:21).

Throughout, Saul assumed that David coveted the throne for himself (18:8). So suspicious was Saul of conspiracy that he questioned the loyalty of his closest supporters (22:6-8). Saul's obsession with tracking down David cost him dearly, for meanwhile, the Philistines were free to reorganize against Israel.

*Saul's Statecraft.* Like the judges preceding him, Saul became a prominent Israelite leader because he displayed charismatic endowment. This was notably the case in his triumph over Ammon (I Sam. 11). Saul's military victories were many (14:47-48). Speedily limiting Philistine advances into Israel's central highlands, Saul enhanced his own ability to move in a north-south direction within the land (chaps. 13–14). Thus he was able to penetrate deeply into Judah and oust meddlesome Amalekites (chap. 15). Required to devote much of his attention to warfare, Saul drafted recruits into a small standing professional army that Abner commanded (14:50, 52b). Moreover, the inclusion of foreign mercenaries in Saul's militia can be inferred from mention of "Doeg the Edomite" (22:9, 18).

Saul also seems to have been aggressive in setting economic policy. The spoils of war were to be kept alive (15:9), and, paying some homage to feudalism, Saul exercised the right to allocate property to his retainers (22:7). Of course, Saul made no attempt to subvert tribal loyalties, establish an intricate bureaucracy, or spend lavishly on an ambitious building program at Gibeah. Excavations there have shown Saul's fortress to be quite unpretentious.

Saul was well endowed with personal initiative, courage, and piety. The prophetic opposition he incurred troubled him greatly. He was a competent monarch who faced awesome challenges as Israel became a political state. Though his personal life was plagued by emotional instability and his public life by strained relations with the religious establishment, Saul's numerous contributions toward the welfare of his people are worthy of remembrance.

Saul is also the original name of the apostle Paul (Acts 7:58; 13:9).                                    J.K.K.

**SAVIOR.** Both in biblical religion and in the worship of those peoples whose lives had an impact on Jews and Christians, God or the gods (or their earthly agents) were hailed as savior figures. The basic meaning was deliverance or SALVATION from evil, whether physical or moral.

In OT times God is known as the people's rescuer from all manner of troubles, notably invasion, disease, and death. God often worked through human instruments, according to Judges, which chronicles the rise and exploits of leaders such as Deborah, Gideon, Samson (see Judg. 3:9, 15; compare II Kings 13:5; Neh. 9:27; Obad. 21).

In Greco-Roman religion, the cult divinities were invoked as saviors, a title common to Isis, Serapis, and especially Asclepious, the god of bodily healing. Mighty leaders and rulers were similarly regarded as saviors of their people, for example, Ptolemy I. In the Roman principate the title expanded, and later in Hellenistic society the appellation was given to emperors from Nero onward as a mark of veneration, and later, under Domitian, of worship.

The Revelation of John and I John, set in the time period of the last named, were thus engaged in polemic against these claims, as Jesus Christ, the Christian savior, was accorded titles of "King of kings" (Rev. 19:16) and "Savior of the world" (I John 4:14).

But the title "savior" is found earlier, belonging especially to the Luke-Acts sections of the NT (Luke 2:11; Acts 5:31), and in the Pastorals the term is used of Christ and God ten times. Paul's usage is descriptive (Phil. 3:20; compare Eph. 5:23), that is, denoting Christ the Lord as deliverer or preserver.

R.M.

**SAVITRI.** The heroine of a story in HINDUISM recounted in the MAHABHARATA, Savitri is often held up as a model of ideal wifely devotion. A princess of unequaled beauty, Savitri looked long for an acceptable husband before marrying the forest-dwelling son of a deposed king. This prince was fated to have but one more year to live, however. When he died and YAMA, ruler of the dead, claimed his soul, Savitri diligently followed him. Yama, impressed by her faithfulness, granted her several boons, including a hundred children. When Savitri pointed out that this last gift could not be realized without a husband, Yama relented and restored her mate to life.

R.E.

**SAVONAROLA, GIROLAMO** (1452–98). Born September 21, in Ferrara, Italy, the fiery preacher and reformer became a Dominican novice at Bologna in 1475. In 1482 he became a lecturer at the convent of San Marco in Florence, where he was to spend the rest of his life. In 1491 he was made prior.

His denunciation of the corruption of the Medicis and the immorality of his fellow clergy evoked controversy. When the Medicis fell from power in 1494, Savonarola became the leader of Florence and set up a theocracy, burning books, fancy clothes, and other signs of luxury and immorality. Pope Alexander V tried to curb his power by summoning him to Rome on July 21, 1495; forbidding him to preach on October 16, 1495; and even trying to bribe him with a cardinal's hat. When Savonarola ignored these attempts, the pope excommunicated him in May 1497. When the pope put the city under interdict, the people turned on Savonarola. Denounced as a schismatic and heretic, he was tortured, hanged, his body burned, and his ashes thrown in the river. He died on May 23.

N.H.

**SAVOY DECLARATION.** The 1658 statement of faith adopted by English Congregationalists at the Savoy Palace in London. Its full name is *A Declaraction of the Faith and Order Owned and Practiced in the Congregational Churches in England.* The Declaration consists of three parts: a preface, a confession of faith

based on the 1646 WESTMINSTER CONFESSION, and a platform of discipline affirming the autonomy of local congregations. It was drawn up by representatives of 120 churches and was a compilation of what Congregationalists commonly believed, but they did not consider it a binding statement of doctrine.

N.H.

**SAYINGS OF JESUS** *See* LOGIA.

**SAYYID.** A term in Islam that refers to a person with authority. At the popular level, it may be used to refer to any holy person, such as a Sufi. More precisely, it refers to the descendants of MUHAMMAD through FATIMA, beginning with al-Hasan and al-Husayn, and to Muhammad's close relatives, including Ali. Sunni sayyids wear green turbans to mark their status. Shi'ite sayyids wear black turbans. They are forbidden to receive alms but are eligible for part of a special tax called *al-khums* ("the fifth"). Shi'ite piety encourages devotion to and blessings on the sayyids.

K./M.C.

**SCAPEGOAT.** The goat used in Judaism's solemn DAY OF ATONEMENT ritual (Lev. 16) to bear the people's sins before being dispatched into "the wilderness to Azazel" (v. 10). This annual expiation involved two male goats. By the casting of lots, one goat was chosen for Yahweh, and one "for Azazel" (v. 8).

The goat destined for Yahweh was immediately sacrified as a sin offering (v. 15). Still alive, the other goat was set "before Yahweh." Placing his hands on the goat's head, the high priest transferred all of Israel's iniquities to it (v. 21). An attendant led this sin-laden "scapegoat" into the desert. He was readmitted into the community after he had cleansed his body and clothing of impurity acquired from contact with the beast (v. 26).

The personal parallelism in verse 8, "for the Lord . . . for Azazel," invites the conjecture that the name Azazel belongs to a remote desert demon and not to the goat. In its impurity, the goat could be sacrificed neither to Yahweh nor to Azazel. Sinfulness was expiated by virtue of the goat's introduction into Yahweh's powerful presence (v. 10).

J.K.K.

**SCHAEFFER, FRANCIS A., IV** (1912–84). Evangelical theologian, apologist, author, and crusader. Born in Philadelphia, Francis Schaeffer was preparing for the Christian ministry at Princeton Theological Seminary when he became involved in the Fundamentalist-Modernist controversy.

As a young minister, Schaeffer served congregations in St. Louis, Chester, and Grove City, Pennsylvania. Then he and his wife, Edith, moved to Europe in 1949. Their original goal was to be involved in children's work. However, because their ministry was prospering in the Roman Catholic canton of Valais, the Schaeffers were asked to leave.

They moved to the tiny hamlet of Huemoz in the Protestant canton of Vaux. There in a chalet they started the L'Abri Fellowship. In 1955 they began to minister to young people of a lost generation who were seeking answers to their personal problems.

Schaeffer conducted a series of lectures dealing with the relevancy of Christian faith in a hostile culture. These lectures became the basis of twenty-three books Schaeffer later authored. They reached tens of thousands—a far wider audience than he had assembled face to face at L'Abri. One of the first books was *The God Who Is There,* followed by *Escape from Reason.*

In 1979 Schaeffer, though suffering from cancer, conducted a lengthy tour of the country accompanied by Dr. C. Everett Koop, a noted pediatric surgeon, later to be named United States Surgeon General. They had written *Whatever Happened to the Human Race?*—a book that declared that secular humanism had replaced the laws of God as the basis of contemporary ethics. They also presented their views against abortion and euthanasia in a film that had been produced by Schaeffer's son, Franky. In December, 1983, there was a flare-up of the cancerous condition that sent Schaeffer to the hospital in Rochester, Minnesota, where he died on May 15.                                                    R.H.

**SCHAFF, PHILIP** (1819–93). Swiss-born church historian and Mercersburg theologian. In 1837 he began studies at the universities of Tübingen, Halle, and Berlin, where he studied with Johann A. W. Neander. He received the licentiate in theology in 1841. In 1843 he was invited to the Reformed Church's Mercersburg Seminary (Pennsylvania), where his 1845 inaugural address, published as *The Principle of Protestantism,* shocked listeners by viewing the Reformation as a flowering of the best in medieval Catholicism.

During nineteen years at Mercersburg he mediated between German and American scholarship in such monumental works as *What Is Church History?* (1846), *Apostolic Christianity* (1851), *America* (1854), three books on the church to 1073, volumes on the German and Swiss Reformations, and *Creeds of Christendom* (3 vols., 1877). He edited the *Nicene and Post-Nicene Fathers* (28 volumes, 1886–1905), *The Schaff-Herzog Encyclopedia of Religious Knowledge* (3 vols., 1882–84), and the American Church History series (13 vols., 1893–97) for the American Society of Church History, which he helped found. He later taught at Andover and Union seminaries. He strongly supported the Evangelical Alliance and the Alliance of the Reformed Churches.
                                                    N.H.

**SCHELLING, FRIEDRICH W. J. VON** (1775–1854). German idealist philosopher who wrote extensively on religion. He was the son of a Lutheran pastor and destined for the ministry. At the theological seminary at Tübingen he became friends with the philosopher GEORGE HEGEL and the romantic poet Hölderlin. By the age of twenty-three he was professor at Jena, the center of German ROMANTICISM. There he was colleague and friend of JOHANN FICHTE. The two thinkers' subjective IDEALISM, emphasizing the aspiring, unconditioned ego, epitomized German Romanticism. Schelling later taught at Würzburg, Erlangen, Munich, and Berlin. His philosophy has been divided into four rather distinct phases. The first period was dominated by Fichte. The second stage, the philosophy of nature, sought to move beyond the subjective ego to the objective reality of nature. This period produced *Transcendental Idealism* (1800), his most systematic statement. In his third period Schelling developed a pantheistic philosophy of identity. Here BENEDICT SPINOZA and the Protestant mystic Jacob Boehme are influential.

Schelling sees evil as a necessary stage in the becoming of good, as well as a dark or negative principle in God, which exists to be overcome. After 1809 Schelling entered his last philosophical stage, during which he wrote extensively on religion, mythology, and revelation. These last writings introduce themes—the mystery of existence, anxiety, resistance—which resemble EXISTENTIALISM. The theologian PAUL TILLICH was greatly influenced by the later views of Schelling.                     J.L.

**SCHILLEBEECKX, EDWARD.** One of the most influential Roman Catholic theologians of the second half of the twentieth century. Born in Antwerp, Belgium in 1914, he studied at the Dominican houses at Ghent and Louvain and was ordained in 1941. Schillebeeckx continued his studies in Paris in 1945 at the Dominican Theological Faculty of LeSaulchair and at the Sorbonne, completing his doctoral dissertation on sacramental theology in 1951. He taught at the Dominican House of Studies at Louvain from 1943 to 1957. Since 1958 he has served as professor of dogmatic theology at the University of Nijmegen in the Netherlands. Schillebeeckx was a major contributor to the controversial Dutch Catechism; an adviser to the Dutch bishops and to Bernard Cardinal Alfrink; and *peritus,* or theological adviser, to the Second Vatican Council (1962–65). His influence is detected in several of the Council documents.

One of Schillebeeckx's earliest works, *Mary, Mother of the Redemption* (1955), reflects a somewhat conservative Marian piety. His most important early works, however, were in the field of sacramental theology. In *Christ, the Sacrament of the Encounter with God* (Eng. trans., 1963) and *The Eucharist* (Eng. trans., 1968), Schillebeeckx sought to enlarge upon the post-Reformation Roman emphasis on TRANSUBSTANTIATION. While not rejecting the doctrine, Schillebeeckx amplifies it in terms of what he calls "transsignification." The objectivity of Christ's Real Presence in the sacrament is affirmed, but emphasis also is placed on the response of the personal belief of the faithful.

*Edward Schillebeeckx*

Since 1964 Schillebeeckx has written a series of books—*Revelation and Theology* (1967); *God, the Future of Man* (1968); *God and Man* (1969); and *World and Church* (1971)—which reflect his concern for Christianity's witness to the human existential situation, the implications of secularization for Christian belief today, and the responsibilities of the church to the world.

In 1974 Schillebeeckx published *Jesus, the Story of a Life* (Eng. trans., *Jesus—An Experiment in Christology,* 1979), a best-seller. The Roman authorities found the book ambiguous on several christological doctrines, and summoned Schillebeeckx to Rome in 1979 to clarify his views. His most recent study in Christology is *Christ, the Experience of Jesus as Lord* (Eng. trans., 1980).                    J.L.

**SCHISM.** From the Greek verb *schizein* meaning "split" or "cut." A schism is a break in the unity of the church. In NT references such as I Corinthians 1:10 and 11:18, the word refers to division or factionalism within one church or the breaking away of members of one church to establish rival churches. Originally it described divisions caused by nonessentials. Thus schismatic groups are not necessarily guilty of HERESY, though that

distinction becomes less and less clear in Christian history.

The Schism of 1054 refers to the division of Eastern Orthodoxy and the Western, Roman church. In that year pope and patriarch excommunicated each other. The Western Schism of 1378 to 1417 refers to a period in which there were two or sometimes three rival popes. The Protestant Reformation is the major schism in the Western church. According to Roman Catholic canon law, any baptized Christian who does not submit to papal authority is schismatic.

N.H.

**SCHLEIERMACHER, FRIEDRICH D. E.** (1768–1834). Generally considered the father of modern liberal theology and the dominant Protestant theologian between JOHN CALVIN and KARL BARTH. He was nurtured in the fervent piety of the German MORAVIANS, an experience that remained lasting. At the University of Halle he read deeply in PLATO, KANT, and SPINOZA. He moved to Berlin in 1796, where his imaginative powers were kindled through his association with the literary leaders of German ROMANTICISM. This led to his first book, *On Religion: Speeches Addressed to Its Cultured Despisers* (1799). Next came *The Soliloquies* (1800), representing Schleiermacher's most characteristic expression of Romantic spiritual aspiration. In 1804 Schleiermacher became professor of theology at Halle, but in 1809 he returned to Berlin as preacher at Holy Trinity Church. In 1811 he acceded to the chair of theology at the University of Berlin. The crowning achievement of these years was his masterpiece, *The Christian Faith* (1821–22; 1830). His literary remains comprise over thirty volumes of books, lectures, sermons, and letters.

Schleiermacher's contribution to modern theology is best seen in his two greatest works, *On Religion* and *The Christian Faith*. *On Religion* proposed that what the cultured despised wasn't the essence of religion at all. Religion is neither metaphysics (HEGEL) nor morals (Kant). It "cannot be an instinct craving for a mess of metaphysical and ethical crumbs." Religion is essentially a unique form of feeling, "the immediate consciousness of the universal existence of all finite things, in and through the Infinite, and of all temporal things in and through the Eternal." Later Schleiermacher was to define this feeling as "the consciousness of absolute dependence" on God. True religion of feeling cannot be taught by acquiring knowledge. In fact, our religious concepts may be crude and erroneous, but it is "the manner in which the Deity is present to a man in feeling that is decisive."

*The Christian Faith* draws out the implications of this experiential view of religion for a science of theology. Christian doctrine is the formulation in language of the prior Christian feelings. For Schleiermacher, theology presupposes the experience of the Christian community and is meant for the church. It is, therefore, confessional, not apologetic. Since all Christian doctrines are determined by reference to the consciousness of redemption accomplished by Jesus Christ, the Christian's God-consciousness always comes to realization in the experience of sin and redemption through the person of Christ, who is integral to the Christian experience of absolute dependence. According to Schleiermacher, sin is an arrestment of our God-consciousness, made known through Christ by means of the self-communication to us of his unique God-consciousness. Christ is both—the perfect spiritual Exemplar and Redeemer. The church is the community formed by the mind of Christ, whose vocation it is to mediate his unique God-consciousness to others.

Since Schleiermacher, liberal theology finds its authority in experience. Barth and EMIL BRUNNER considered this modern theology's great "false start," since theology appears imprisoned in human self-consciousness and subjectivity. However, recently theology has returned to and vindicated Schleiermacher's experiential method.               J.L.

**SCHMALKALD ARTICLES.** A confession of faith written by Martin Luther in 1536. Pope Paul III had issued a call for a general council of the church to deal with the Reformers. John Frederick I, Elector of Saxony, asked Luther to review several previous statements of faith and to state the essential issues with a view toward negotiation.

Luther wrote out a statement and conferred with his friends. Eight fellow theologians signed the statement and presented it to the elector in January 1537. It was divided into three sections: (1) on the nature of God, divine unity, the Trinity, Christ, the Incarnation, matters in which the Reformers agreed with the church; (2) on Christ and justification by faith, noting how the Reformers differed from the church on this and such issues as the Mass, monasticism, and the papacy; and (3) fifteen articles for discussion on sin, law, sacraments, confession, the ministry, and the definition of the church.

In February 1537 members of the Schmalkaldic League (Protestant secular heads of state) met with theologians at Schmalkalden to discuss the statement and talk about responses to the pope's request. Luther was ill and did not attend. Philipp Melanchthon preferred the AUGSBURG CONFESSION and its Apology, so the group adopted that as their standard.

The Schmalkald Articles, as Luther's statement came to be called, were circulated, however, and signed by forty-four theologians who said the articles represented their views. They were included in the 1580 Book of Concord and remain a historic document of Lutheranism.            N.H.

**SCHOLASTICISM.** The name "scholasticism" meant originally the teaching of the schools, and is applied to the intellectual movement, both philosophical and theological, which dominated Europe from about the seventh century until the emergence of modern philosophy in the sixteenth century, and which has continued to be esteemed especially in the Roman Catholic Church even into the twentieth century. Because of its long persistence, it has been called the *philosophia perennis*, the "perennial philosophy."

*Leading Characteristics.* In Scholasticism, it is difficult to know where philosophy ends and theology begins. This is because of the conviction of most of the Scholastics that faith and reason belong together and that reason will not contradict faith, even if it cannot attain unaided to the truths of faith. In this regard, Scholasticism differs sharply from post-Kantian philosophy, in which faith and reason are kept apart. Since the Scholastics drew both on the revealed truths of the Christian religion and on the resources of classical philosophy, they considered theology to be a science and used logic and reason in their theological constructions.

The types of work that they produced included (1) Commentaries: these had their origin in the practice of reading texts, which were glossed and expounded by the teacher, and these expositions developed into major commentaries. A special case was the "sentences," in which propositions from the Scriptures were arranged and commented upon not in chronological order but in logical order, a step toward the systematic theologies and dogmatics of later times. (2) Questions and disputations. Problems were set up and then answers and objections to the answers were considered in a dialectical fashion. The pattern followed is clearly seen in the writings of Thomas Aquinas. First, the question is put, introduced by the Latin word *utrum*, "whether," for example, "whether God exists." Then there is given a provisional answer, introduced by the words *videtur quod*, "it seems that. . . ." Next, objections are raised to the alleged answer, introduced by *sed contra*, "but, on the other hand. . . ." Finally, the teacher gives his *respondeo*, "I reply," in which he comes down on one side or the other. The arguments for and against are usually appeals to Scripture or to the writings of Christian authors, so that there is a subtle mingling of argumentation and authority. Still, the student does not just accept matters without further thought, but is compelled to face objections and to follow the course of the reasoning. (3) Finally, the *summas* were comprehensive treatments of wide areas of questions in philosophy and theology, conducted on the same dialectical principles.

*History of Scholasticism.* The roots of Scholasticism are usually traced back to Augustine and Boethius, though the period up to the eleventh century is often called "pre-Scholasticism." At this stage, the dominant philosophical influence was that of Plato and Neoplatonism. In the second half of the eleventh century there was a great surge of Scholastic thought. In those days the monasteries were still the major centers of learning, and one of the greatest was the monastery of Bec in Normandy. It was there that

ANSELM (1033–1109) taught, before he became archbishop of Canterbury. He is often called the "father of Scholasticism." His watchword was *Credo ut intelligam*, "I believe in order to understand," and with him the rationalistic character of Scholasticism reached a high level. In a series of writings, he tried to prove the existence of God from reason alone, and then went on to demonstrate the rational necessity of atonement. Karl Barth, however, has argued that even for Anselm, faith remained primary, and reason simply expounds and systematizes the truths of faith. PETER ABELARD (1079–1142) showed the typical interest in dialectics in his *Sic et non* (*Yes and No*), in which he sets side by side contradictory judgments of the Christian fathers and then seeks to reconcile them. He also wrote an important treatise on ethics. Meanwhile the works of Aristotle were being rediscovered, and he became a more important influence than Plato.

Scholasticism reached its highest point with the work of THOMAS AQUINAS (1225–74). His *Summa Theologica*, written in the last years of his life and still unfinished when he died, is still the greatest single work on Christian theology ever written. Yet it was only a part of Thomas's colossal output. Scarcely less impressive is his *Summa contra Gentiles*, a Christian apologetic written in answer to the criticisms of Jewish and Muslim writers. It has been said of his major commentary on Aristotle's *Metaphysics* that even if it had been the only work to survive, it would still have entitled Thomas to a place among the world's great philosophers.

But after Thomas a decline set in. The once fruitful and exciting ways of investigation and argument became increasingly formal and stereotyped. We have reached "Scholasticism" in the bad sense in which the word is often employed, a formal system in which artificial questions are answered by unreal, hair-splitting distinctions. The underlying reason for this decline was a loss of confidence in reason itself, contrasting sharply with what we have seen in Anselm and Aquinas. Duns Scotus (1266–1308) and WILLIAM OF OCKHAM (1285–1347) brought flashes of brilliance to this scene of decay, but the former limited the role of reason in theology while the latter denied that any theological truths at all are rationally demonstrable. Scholasticism was eclipsed by the rise of modern philosophy after Descartes. It still produced an occasional thinker of importance, such as Francisco Suarez (1548–1617), but it was not till the end of the nineteenth century that it was revived by Pope Leo XIII. Cardinal Mercier of Belgium took a leading part in the revival, publishing *A Manual of Modern Scholastic Philosophy* (1916), and in the next generation JACQUES MARITAIN and ETIENNE GILSON were brilliant representatives of a reinvigorated neo-Scholasticism.                                    J.M.

**SCHOOLMASTER.** The Greek word *paidagōgos* is rendered thus in Galations 3:25, KJV (RSV has "custodian") and translates as "guide" in I Corinthians 4:15. In both instances the background is that of Greco-Roman educational systems, which entrusted the elementary training of children to a slave who acted as tutor and disciplinarian. R.M.

**SCHOOLMEN.** *See* SCHOLASTICISM.

**SCHOPENHAUER, ARTHUR** (1788–1860). German philosopher, advocate of a metaphysical and moral pessimism, and one of the important anti-Christian philosophers of the nineteenth century. Schopenhauer studied at Göttingen and Berlin and received a doctorate from Jena in 1819. Scornful of academics, he remained a private scholar. His masterpiece is *World as Will and Idea* (1819).

Schopenhauer was profoundly influenced by IMMANUEL KANT and held that the perceived world is phenomenal appearance, not what is metaphysically ultimate, which he calls Will. Here he departs from Kant and reveals the influence of Oriental and especially Indian philosophy. The world of objects is appearance, or maya, but what lies behind all maya, independent of our perception, is an energy or blind impulse called Will. It is endless striving, or the will to live, which characterizes all life. Knowing no cessation, the will can find no satisfaction or state of peace. Each being strives to assert its own will at the expense of others, hence avarice, cruelty, and war. Humanity creates its own hell. An escape from the futility of desire and striving can be achieved temporarily only through a disinterested contemplation of the beautiful and the sublime. A more lasting release can come, however, through radical renunciation of the will. Here Schopenhauer appeals to the Buddhist ideals of self-denial, mortification, and sympathy for all beings. For him death is simply extinction, and belief in God is infantile desire. Schopenhauer greatly influenced the composer Richard Wagner and the early philosophy of FRIEDRICH NIETZSCHE. He was also successful in stimulating German interest in Oriental philosophy.      J.L.

**SCHWEITZER, ALBERT** (1875–1965). Alsatian theologian, philosopher, musician, and medical missionary. From peasant stock, Schweitzer was born on January 14 in Kayersberg, Alsace, at that time a part of the German Empire. He spent his boyhood in Gunsbach, attended the gymnasium at Mulhausen, and received three degrees from the University of Strassburg; a doctorate in philosophy (1899), a licentiate in theology (1900), and a doctorate in medicine (1913). He also received an honorary doctorate in music. Later he studied at the universities of Paris and Berlin.

In 1899 Schweitzer became the pastor of a church in Strassburg, and in 1903 he was appointed head of the Theological College at Strassburg. His first book was *J. S. Bach* (1905; Eng. trans. 1911), of whom

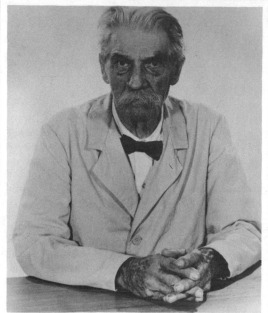

Courtesy of Religious News Service

*Albert Schweitzer*

Schweitzer became an acknowledged authority and a brilliant interpreter at the organ.

In quite another field Schweitzer received international attention by writing the controversial *The Quest of the Historical Jesus* (1906). Earlier (1901) he had written *The Mystery of the Kingdom of God*. In this work Schweitzer argued that Christ's teaching centered on his conviction of the imminent end of the world. His more widely known *Quest* held that Christ believed that the world would soon end, and when this proved a mistake, concluded that he must suffer in order to save his people from the tribulations preceding the last days. In 1911, in *Paul and His Interpreters*, Schweitzer applied the same theological principles in seeking to interpret Pauline teaching.

At the height of his career as a musician and theologian, Schweitzer decided he must give himself to the service of others. After seven years of preparation, he became a medical missionary to Africa. In 1913 he established a hospital at Lambaréné on the Ogowe River in the Gabon Colony of French Equatorial Africa. There he labored for forty years, except for a ten-year interval when as a German subject he was interned in French prison camps during World War II.

The hospital that Schweitzer built mostly with his own hands was supported from the proceeds of organ recitals he gave in Europe, his lecture tours, and book royalties. During his stay in Africa he developed the principle of "reverence for life."

In 1952 Schweitzer was awarded the Nobel Peace Prize, and received the British Order of Merit in 1955. He died on September 4 at Lambaréné.

R.H.

**SCHWENKFELD, KASPAR** (1489–1561). ANA-BAPTIST theologian, writer, and preacher born in Ossig, Lower Silesia. He studied at the universities of Cologne and Frankfurt, and served as a counselor to various courts from 1511 to 1523. In 1518 he experienced a spiritual awakening. Schwenkfeld helped to introduce his form of Lutheran reform, which was called Reformation by the Middle Way, into Silesia in 1522. In 1525 he visited Luther and found they disagreed on the Eucharist. When he published anti-Catholic, anti-Lutheran views on the subject, he was dismissed by the Duke of Liegnitz.

In 1529 he went to Strassburg to confer with Sebastian Franck, Michael Servetus, Ulrich Zwingli, and others. At a synod there in 1533 he defended his views against Martin Bucer. Bucer won. Schwenkfeld went to Ulm, until the Lutherans ran him out in 1539. When he published his *Great Confession* in 1540, the Schmalkaldic League issue an anathema against him, and he became a religious fugitive. He died December 10, in Ulm. Societies he established survive as Pietist sects. The denomination has its headquarters in Pennsburg, Pennsylvania. N.H.

**SCIENCE AND RELIGION.** If, as many Christian thinkers have declared, both revealed religion and science deal ultimately with truth, only harmony should exist between them. Such a view is predicated on the idea that a sovereign God is the author of all truth. Data accumulated through empirical research have provided humankind with vast stores of verifiable knowledge, and the results of such research have been an ongoing boon to civilization in countless areas.

Some would argue that modern science owes much to Christianity and its Jewish antecedent for the idea of a rational universe. Carl F. H. Henry has said: "From the Christian religion western science derived its conviction of a comprehensively rational universe that everywhere bears evidence of one ultimate principle of the explanation" (study note, Holy Bible, RSV, A. J. Holman Co., 1962). Reformed theologians attribute the human propensity to gain understanding of and mastery over certain aspects of the physical world as an integral part of what is called the creation mandate. This stems from the divine instruction to humankind to subdue the earth (Gen. 1:28). It gives those working in scientific research with resultant discoveries an almost limitless work area. "The success of modern science in interpreting and shaping the world we live in stands unrivaled in the history of human achievements," declares Dr. William H. Werkmeister, professor of philosophy at the University of Florida (*Scientific Method*, Collier's Encyclopedia, Vol. 20, Macmillan Educational Corp., 1974).

Science as we know it today is one of the products of the Renaissance, spurred on by the Protestant Reformation. By the sixteenth and seventeenth centuries the scientific method had evolved. Once begun, knowledge of both the animate and inanimate world burgeoned in the eighteenth and nineteenth centuries. In the twentieth century knowledge exploded in every area of learning, aided by the dazzling developments in computer science.

Science has advanced various aspects of Christian faith in such areas as archaeology, anthropology, modern linguistics, and communication techniques—including everything from the printing press to telephones, radio, and television. Yet the development of scientism—the exaggerated trust in the efficacy of the methods of natural science to explain all the pressing problems of humanity—inevitably has brought science and religion into collision.

There are several areas of conflict that still remain unresolved for many people. Probably the most publicized has been the rival explanations for the origin of human beings. The argument was started when CHARLES DARWIN's *The Origin of Species* was published in 1859. This brilliant English scientist was the first to present the concept of organic EVOLUTION, the theory that existing plants and animals developed by a process of gradual, continuous change from previously existing forms. The idea developed popularly, however, that humankind had descended from monkeys. Many religionists immediately declared that this intrusion of science conflicted with the biblical doctrine of CREATION. Today the general concept of some form of evolution has been accepted, rightly or wrongly, by a good share of Christendom. But a vanguard of Christians, particularly in the United States, has waged unceasing warfare against the teaching of evolution in the schools. There are various levels of opposition, but the most vocal in recent years have been the proponents of "scientific creationism." They contend that there is as much scientific evidence to support the biblical account of creation as there is of evolution. Therefore they urge that both explanations be given in biology classes.

There are similar, but less emotional, battles over the relative merits of the biblical versus the several scientific theories of the origin of the universe. Currently in the scientific realm there are two theories vying for universal acceptance—the "big bang" and the "steady state" concepts.

The discovery of nuclear fission, employed as a domestic power source as well as for military weapons that threaten the existence of civilization, has revealed the moral limitations of science. Many critics of modern culture have felt that scientific advance has generated moral paralysis. Sometimes the scientsts who recognize the perilous situation caused by the nuclear arms race warn of imminent doom more eloquently than churchmen. The threat of nuclear extinction has brought protests from a wide range of the world's inhabitants, from the left-wing picketers and marchers of Europe, to normally docile housewives, to those in the religious community.

In the creation of the most sophisticated weapon, a means of complete self-destruction has been devised. Is it possible that human beings may be the agents of a chain nuclear holocaust that will destroy the earth (II Pet. 3:10-12)?

Technology has advanced further in this age than in all previous generations—fission, fusion, radar, television, automation, miniaturization, plastics, jets, rockets, and satellites. An increasing number of thinkers in all realms of modern culture fear that moral and spiritual concern has not advanced as rapidly as amoral scientific progress.          R.H.

**SCIENTOLOGY, CHURCH OF.** In 1950, L. Ron Hubbard, a science fiction writer, produced a book expounding his views on psychology, *Dianetics: The Modern Science of Mental Health*. Ultimately, this book is the basis of the new American religious movement called Scientology, which Hubbard founded in 1954. Hubbard declares that his movement resulted from years of study in philosophy, religion, science, and extensive travel in the Orient and elsewhere. Hubbard says he was concerned by the apparent dominion of death over life and wished to increase life and free people from deathlike circumstances: criminals, the insane, and all who are trapped in their own errors.

By discerning that people need to be freed from spiritual and psychological traumas, which he called "engrams," Hubbard devised a sort of Freudian psychoanalysis called "auditing" in which these "engrams" were uncovered and dissolved. To aid this counseling ("auditing") process, Hubbard devised an "E-meter," a sort of crude "polygraph" (or lie detector) that would register whenever the auditing uncovered a sensitive spot or engram. Hubbard set up the Church of Scientology to teach his religious philosophy and train "auditors" who opened Scientology centers all over the country and overseas as well. The person recruited for auditing is known as a "pre-clear." Once the person has gone through the process, he is called a "clear." After this basic step, many other stages of enlightenment through auditing and training have been worked out and set up by Hubbard. Large sums of money are charged Scientology students for this training through some thirty-eight or more grades, up to what is called "operating thetan" IX. The group is highly controversial and has been involved in many lawsuits.
                                                              J.C.

**SCOFIELD, CYRUS INGERSON** (1843–1921). Lawyer turned Bible teacher and editor of a popular reference Bible. Scofield was born in Michigan but reared in Tennessee. During the Civil War he served with the Southern forces under General Robert E. Lee. For his valor, Scofield was awarded the Confederate Cross of Honor.

He was admitted to the Kansas bar in 1869, served for two years as United States attorney, then set up his own law practice in St. Louis. Much of his life during these years is veiled, but there have been persistent reports that Scofield was a heavy drinker and was involved in domestic discord.

However, when he was converted, Scofield applied himself to Bible study, coming under the influence of those who followed the system of Bible hermeneutics known as DISPENSATIONALISM. This view of Scripture teaches there is much variety in the divine economy in the Bible, that God has dealt differently with people during different eras of biblical history. There are several schools of dispensationalist thought, but Scofield's view of seven dispensations has been widely accepted. He became one of the great popularizers of dispensationalism through the influence of the *Scofield Reference Bible* (1909, 1967), which has had wide distribution. He was ordained as the pastor of a Congregationalist church in Dallas and served there from 1882 to 1895.

At the request of D. L. Moody, Scofield became pastor of the Moody Church in East Northfield, Massachusetts, from 1895 to 1902. Then he returned to serve the church in Dallas again until 1907. That year he began full-time service as a Bible conference teacher in the United States and in the British Isles. During this period he also founded the Central American Mission.                                    R.H.

## SCOPES TRIAL.

Famed legal case involving the teaching of evolution in a public school contrary to Tennessee law. Besides the controversy over biological evolution versus direct creation, the trial attracted worldwide attention because it pitted the talents of William Jennings Bryan against those of Clarence Darrow.

The trial was a test case in June, 1925, involving John T. Scopes, a biology teacher who was tried for teaching in the Dayton (Tenn.) High School a "theory that denies the story of the Divine Creation of man as taught in the Bible and to teach instead that man has descended from a lower order of animals."

Darrow argued that academic freedom was being violated and the legislature had demonstrated a religious preference, violating the separation of church and state. Bryan, aiding the state prosecutor, was unable to present statements of Bible scholars and other evidence because of the presiding judge's ruling. Nevertheless, the jury returned a verdict of guilty and fined Scopes $100. Two years later the Tennessee Supreme Court ruled the law was constitutional but reversed the judgment against Scopes on a technicality, thus preventing an appeal to the United States Supreme Court.        R.H.

## SCRIBES.

Professional TEACHERS of the (Mosaic) Law in the Second Temple period (postexilic Judaism). In Jeremiah 36:26 the term *sōpher* (pl. *sōpherim*) identified a royal "secretary" in charge of legal documents (II Kings 22:3 ff.; Isa. 36:3). The spiritual ancestors of the *sōpherim* in NT times, howver, were the priest-scholars who, during the Babylonian exile, were the collectors, copyists, and

Courtesy of the Library of Congress

*William Jennings Bryan, prosecutor at the Scopes Monkey Trial*

editors of the scriptures (later to become the Hebrew Bible, the OT). Ezra the PRIEST, who is described as "a scribe skilled in the law of Moses," typifies these early Torah scholars (Ezra 7:6, 10; Neh. 8:7; II Chr. 34:13; Ecclus. 39:6-11 is often cited as the classic description of the scribe of this period, early second century B.C.).

At the time of the Maccabean wars of liberation, scribes were among the "devout" (Hasidim) who supported the cause (I Macc. 7:11-17). During the rule of the Hasmonean priest-kings, an influential group of lay scribes emerged, who formed a component of the sect of the Pharisees.

There are numerous references in the NT to scribes (Mark 9:11, 14; 12:28; Matt. 8:19; 13:52; 23:34; Luke 5:17; 7:30; 10:25). In other references scribes are identified as "scribes of the Pharisees" (Mark 2:16; Acts 23:9). Still other references associate scribes with "the elders and the chief priests" (Mark 8:31; 11:27; 15:1; Luke 22:66). Or only with "the chief priests" (Mark 10:33; 11:18; 14:1; 15:31; Matt. 2:4; 21:15; Luke 23:10). From these accounts it is apparent that the pre A.D. 70 scribes were a high-ranking group serving on the SANHEDRIN. Next to the chief priests, the Sanhedrin scribes were leaders in the government of the Jewish nation. Some (possibly all) of them belonged to the sect of the PHARISEES (for example, Gamaliel, Acts 5:34-39).

In Matthew's Gospel the common reference to "the scribes and the Pharisees" appears to have been a stereotypical formula (also John 8:3), representing a later but valid judgment: the specialists in the law exceeded the nonprofessionals in importance in the sect. According to Matthew the formal authority of the scribes was acknowledged by Jesus, but he denounced the example they set (Matt. 23:2-3). One should contrast Jesus' commendation of the scribe, according to Mark 12:28-34. The parallels in Matthew and Luke of this meeting reflect the anticlerical bias of the late first-century churches (Matt. 22:35: Luke 10:25). A balanced perspective must take account of the fact that it was the dedication of the scribes that was chiefly responsible for the preservation of Judaism and of the OT during Greco-Roman times.                                        J.L.P.

**SCRIPTORIUM.** A Latin name for a monastery room dedicated to writing or copying manuscripts, especially books of the Bible. Currently it is associated with such a room excavated at Qumran, where the Dead Sea Scrolls were produced.                                          P.L.G.

**SCRIPTURE, AUTHORITY OF.** All the great world religions possess scriptures that keep them in touch with their origins and provide identity, stability, and continuity through the course of history. Here we are concerned with the authority of scripture in Christianity. By an authority, we understand that which rightfully claims the respect and allegiance of believers. Presently authority in matters of religion is not coercively imposed, like the authority of the state. People in most countries are free to believe or disbelieve, and so any authority in religion needs to justify itself. Reasons have to be given for holding that any book or institution or tradition is to be regarded as authoritative. There are at least three important reasons for ascribing authority to the Bible:

(1) Christians believe that their faith originated in

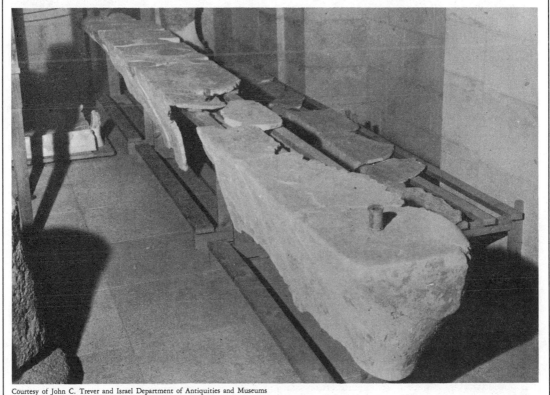

Courtesy of John C. Trever and Israel Department of Antiquities and Museums

*Table and bench with ink wells from the Scriptorium at Qumran*

an act of God in which God was revealed and communicated. The Bible witnesses to this act, so that in some sense (which we must examine more closely) it is or contains the WORD OF GOD and is therefore to that extent authoritative. The Bible is not identical with the Word of God. The primary Word was the living person, Jesus Christ, and the Bible is the Word of God only in the secondary sense, that it points to Jesus Christ and sets him before the reader or hearer as the REVELATION of God, and so he is the one who demands the response of faith. Both the OT and the NT derive their authority from Christ. The OT, of course, has a different ground for its authority among Jews, but for Christians it is authoritative because of its relation to Christ. At one time it was thought that the OT was full of specific prophecies relating to Jesus, and though few scholars would look on it in that way today, it is the OT that supplies the basic theological background assumed in the NT and that also supplies the expectations in terms of which Jesus Christ is interpreted in the NT. The NT itself bears a more direct relation to Jesus Christ. It sets before us his teaching, testifies to his death and resurrection, and also to the experience of salvation that the early Christian community found in him. Because it tells not only of Jesus but of the response to him, some modern writers prefer to speak of it as testifying to the "Christ-event," where this expression includes the complex social event of Jesus and the community that he gathered about him. The fact that the reading or preaching of the Bible today can still evoke the response of faith or bring about the experience of salvation is a ground for believing that it is inspired and may rightly be called the "Word of God."

(2) Apart altogether from its claim to be the Word of God, the Bible possesses the historical authority belonging to any document that records past happenings not too far distant from it in time. Admittedly, the historical authority of the Bible is more questionable today than it once was. It was once believed that Moses himself had written the first five books of the OT, so that they contained a firsthand account of the Exodus and the formative period of Israel's history. That theory of Mosaic authorship has long been abandoned, and we recognize that the books come from several centuries later and that the traditions they contain have been worked over again and again. Likewise, in the NT, many scholars are doubtful if any of the Gospels is an eyewitness account. Even so, the Gospels are quite close in time to the events they record. NT scholarship has moved beyond the extreme skepticism of an earlier period. There is no reason to doubt the general picture of the Christ-event given in the NT.

(3) A third kind of authority belongs to the Bible in virtue of its relation to the church. We say that the books of the Bible are canonical, and by that is meant that out of the great mass of sacred literature that proliferated in ancient times, these particular books were chosen by the church for inclusion in the CANON as the normative Christian books. Many people would say that this selection was made under the guidance of the Holy Spirit, but whether or not one wants to use such language, it can at least be agreed that the canonical status of the biblical writings rests on the collective consideration and judgment of the church, and this gives to these books an authority that cannot be claimed by the judgment or experience of an individual. The authority here is very much like the authority recognized in any science. Students do not begin to learn a science from scratch. They learn what those who have studied the subject before them have discovered, and they begin at that point. They may, of course, come to disagree with the received wisdom, but they will have to produce very good reasons for abandoning it or revising it. Likewise, in the church each individual begins within that collective tradition of faith that finds its principal expression in the Bible, as the church's book.

If the three points mentioned offer reasons for according authority to the Bible, we have to ask how far this authority may have been weakened by BIBLICAL CRITICISM. It needs little thought to realize that any theory of biblical inerrancy is problematic. As already mentioned, the primary Word of God is not a book at all, but the living person, Jesus Christ. Again, as we have seen, questions of dating and authorship have weakened the historical claims of the Bible, so far as they depended on "eyewitness" accounts. Further, to be infallible, the Bible would need to exist in a single universally accepted TEXT, whereas there are many textual variations. It would also need to be free of contradictions and incoherences, but there are several discrepancies on quite important matters, for example, which women discovered the empty tomb. One would also expect an inerrant Bible to be absolutely clear and unambiguous, but there are in fact many obscure and disputed passages. So, although we have seen that there are good reasons for acknowledging the authority of the Bible, this is not an absolute authority but one that has to be critically approached and evaluated on different matters. In any case, there would still be the question of interpreting a Bible pronouncement into the changed concepts and circumstances of the present (see HERMENEUTICS). But when all this is recognized, biblical authority has not been destroyed by critical scholarship. On the contrary, it has become possible to recognize that authority in a more intelligent way.

One further point is to recognize that the Bible is not the *sole* authority recognized by all Christians. TRADITION (including traditional interpretations of the Bible), REASON, and CONSCIENCE all carry weight alongside the biblical teaching when one seeks the answer to some disputed question about Christian belief or behavior.                                              J.M.

**SCRIVEN, JOSEPH MEDLICOTT** (1820–86). Itinerant Plymouth Brethren preacher and poet, the author of "What a Friend We Have in Jesus," one of the most popular hymns in the English language. Scriven had written the poem to comfort his ailing mother in Ireland. He never intended for it to be published, let alone sung as a hymn. Scriven was born to an affluent family in Dublin, Ireland. After graduation from Trinity College, Dublin, Scriven was planning to marry. However, the night before the wedding his fiancée was drowned. Because of his grief and estrangement from his family over his attachment to the Plymouth Brethren, Scriven decided to emigrate to Canada. He took up residence in Port Hope, Ontario, on the northern shore of Lake Ontario, where he became a tutor. He also stayed frequently in the home of James Sackville, in whose home the words of Scriven's famous hymn were written. Subsequently Scriven fell in love a second time and became engaged to Eliza Catherine Roche. However, she contracted tuberculosis and their wedding was called off.

Scriven devoted himself to the poor of the area, giving most of his private income away. He was living with the Sackville family again in 1886 when he was stricken with a fatal illness. Before he died, his host found the poem Scriven had written for his mother. Modestly Scriven told Sackville that "the Lord and I did it between us." Sackville made copies of the hymn and sent one to a publisher. Scriven, delirious from fever, stumbled from his bedroom and went outside. Several yards from the house, he fell into a creek and was drowned.          R.H.

**SCROLL.** Writing material consisting of a long strip of papyrus, leather, or parchment. Though leather scrolls are unattested in the Bible, impressive specimens, widely known as the Dead Sea Scrolls, have been uncovered at Qumran. The celebrated twenty-four-foot-long Isaiah text contains seventeen sheets of sheepskin joined by linen thread. Ancient Egyptian PAPYRUS scrolls consist of a double thickness of strips cut from the stalk of the papyrus plant that have been placed side by side and glued together.

At Jeremiah's dictation (Jer. 36:4), Baruch wrote a relatively brief scroll (thrice read aloud in a single day; 36:10, 15, 21). That it was burned in Jehoiakim's brazier (36:23) suggests that it consisted of papyrus, because the stench of burning leather would have been overwhelming.

A scroll figures significantly in the visionary experiences of Ezekiel, Zechariah, and John. During his prophetic commissioning, Ezekiel perceives a scroll that he is divinely commanded to eat (Ezek. 2:8b–3:3). Its message of divine judgment is so extensive that, contrary to custom, the scroll is covered on both sides. This materializing of God's judgmental word finds further expression in Zechariah's vision of an enormous flying scroll (Zech. 5:1-4). In his visions, John sees a sealed scroll containing God's unalterable secrets about the future

(Rev. 5:1-14) and a scroll of doom that he must eat (10:1-11).          J.K.K.

**SCYTHIANS.** A nomadic people who, in the eighth century B.C., wandered from southern Russia through the Caucasus Mountains into the Near East. They are first mentioned as Assyrian opponents in the annals of Esarhaddon (680–669). In time, Esarhaddon allied himself with the Scythians to buttress his position against other meddlesome Indo-Aryan hordes—the Medes and Cimmerians.

When the power of the Scythians was concentrated on the northern Euphrates (about 640–600), their influence extended in an east-west direction from the Caspian Sea through northern Armenia on to Cappadocia. It is uncertain what role the Scythians played as Assyrian allies when the Assyrian Empire expired before enemy Babylonians and Medes around 610. Also the chronology of the movements of these nomads is inexact. Presumably by 625, some Scythians had pushed into western Asia, swept down the Phoenician coast, and reached the Egyptian border. Bought off by Pharaoh Psammetichus I (664–610), they turned northward. In the early sixth century, the Medes defeated the Scythians and thrust them back into southern Russia.

By referring to the Scythians as Ashkenaz (Gen. 10:3; I Chr. 1:6; Jer. 51:27), the OT links them with populations of Asia Minor and northern Mesopotamia. A decreasing number of scholars maintain that the book of Zephaniah and oracles of Jeremiah referring to the so-called "foe from the north" (for example, Jer. 4:5-31) reflect Palestine's uneasiness regarding possible Scythian incursions. Indeed, the impact of the Scythians on biblical history cannot be readily determined. Employing the name "Scythian" to denote savage behavior (Col. 3:11), Paul knew of Scythian brutality manifested over six centuries earlier (compare II Macc. 4:47).          J.K.K.

**SEA, MOLTEN.** A huge bowl of cast bronze located in the courtyard of Solomon's Temple (I Kings 7:23-26).

Measuring fifteen feet in diameter and over seven feet in height, this object may have weighed nearly thirty tons and held approximately ten thousand gallons of water. Under its outward curving brim were two rows of ornamental gourds. It rested on twelve bronze oxen, so arranged that three each faced the four main points of the compass.

The Chronicler's notation that "the sea was for the priests to wash in" (II Chr. 4:6) does not mean that the men climbed into the bowl. Possibly analogous to the great mosques, this water source simply facilitated the ritual ablutions of TEMPLE entrants. The name "sea" suggests cosmic concerns. It may have been mythically linked with the Mesopotamian *apsu* (subterranean fresh water) from which all life originated, or with the Canaanite god Baal, who triumphed over the chaotic sea. Moreover, the

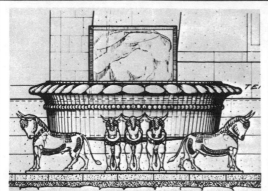

Courtesy of William Morden, the Oriental Institute, University of Chicago

*Reconstruction of the Bronze Sea; made of cast bronze, this fifteen-foot diameter bowl rested on the backs of twelve oxen; estimated weight: twenty-five to thirty tons*

fertility symbolism of the twelve oxen was scarcely subtle. This valuable bronze object finally met disaster. King Ahaz seized the oxen under it to meet Assyrian demand for tribute (II Kings 16:17), and the Babylonians broke up the bowl and carried its fragments homeward after capturing Jerusalem in 587 B.C. (II Kings 25:13). J.K.K.

**SEABURY, SAMUEL** (1729–96). The first bishop of the Protestant Episcopal Church in the United States, Seabury was born November 30 in Groton, Connecticut, to Abigail Mumford and the Reverend Samuel Seabury, a Congregational minister. His father joined the Church of England in 1730 and served the Society for the Propagation of the Gospel as a missionary. Seabury graduated from Yale College in 1748 and studied medicine at the University of Edinburgh. Ordained a priest in 1753, he went to New Jersey, in 1754 as a missionary. Seabury became rector of the church in Westchester, New York, in 1767, where he practiced medicine and ran a school as well. During the Revolution, Seabury sought to keep the colonists loyal and served as chaplain to the British troops. However, in 1783 the Connecticut clergy chose him as their candidate for bishop. He was consecrated by Scottish non-juring bishops in 1784. From St. James Church, New London, he reorganized the church, ordaining priests and confirming communicants. N.H.

**SEAL OF CONFESSION.** The absolute secrecy observed by the Roman Catholic priest in his role as a CONFESSOR and by any others who may have knowledge of anything revealed in the sacrament of penance. The confessor is forbidden to disclose or to use any information gained through confession if such use would harm the person who confessed, even if such use did not involve revealing what was confessed. A priest who reveals anything confessed would automatically be excommunicated. Ecclesiastical superiors may not publicly use information

obtained through confession. Priests are expressly under the obligation not to reveal confessed material if called into a secular court of law. In general, English and American laws have respected the seal of confession, but in neither country is there an absolute law that respects the seal of confession. Some American state courts have recently begun to question the secrecy of material revealed to Protestant ministers, who have usually been accorded the same privileged information status as Catholic priests. J.C.

**SEARS, EDMUND HAMILTON** (1810–76). Unitarian minister and hymn writer. Sears was one of several Unitarian writers who contributed greatly to a vast outpouring of hymns between the 1830s and the Civil War. His greatest contributions were two Christmas carols, "It Came upon a Midnight Clear," and "Calm on the Listening Night." Sears was born in Sandisfield, Massachusetts, on April 6. After attending Westfield Academy, Brattleboro, Vermont, he enrolled at Union College, Schenectady, New York. He studied law briefly, then theology (while on the faculty of the academy), and later was graduated from Harvard Divinity School. Ordained to the Unitarian ministry, he twice served pastorates at Wayland (Mass.), and for a short time at Lancaster (Mass). His final charge was at Weston (Mass.). Sears wrote hundreds of articles, poems, and hymns. He died on January 16, at Weston. R.H.

**SECOND ADAM.** In I Corinthians 15:21-22 and Romans 5:14-19, Christ is described as a second Adam in the sense that Adam brought sin into the world and Christ brought salvation. Adam represents death for all, and Christ, life. Tradition emphasizes these roles of the first and second Adams at the Church of the Holy Sepulchre in Jerusalem when it locates the place of Adam's creation in a chapel directly below the site of the cross, where the blood of the dying Christ could flow through to Adam. T.J.K.

**SECOND COMING OF CHRIST.** See PAROUSIA.

**SECT.** This word derives from the Latin verb *sequi* (to follow), not, as is often thought, from *secare* (to cut). Thus in its proper usage, it emphasizes a group's response to a leader and not its existence as a tiny fraction or section of the whole. Often it refers to a religious body that is gathered or called out of some natural organic group or state church on anti-conformist grounds, sometimes by a charismatic leader or by some principle of greater strictness or more single-minded dedication.

The Protestant Reformation was the progenitor of many sectarian movements. Some of these were rationalistic and anti-trinitarian, some intensely biblical, some described as spiritual. The continental Radical Reformation groups include the Anabaptists and their descendants, the Mennonites, the

Amish, and the Hutterites. Technically, they fall into this category of sects, as do the Pietists who formed a distinct religious movement within existing churches. Many of these groups, such as the Dunkers, the antecedents of the Church of the Brethren, had their origins in Europe but flourished after emigration to America. The Moravian Brethren, influenced by Count Nicholaus Ludwig von Zinzendorf, became one of the most influential of the pietistic sects. The somewhat related Schwenckfelders also became a miniscular example.

According to Sydney E. Ahlstrom, "the term 'sect' refers to a movement, almost necessarily small at the outset, that secedes from or forms the periphery of a more stable, socially adjusted, and often culturally dominant religious group. Sect formation is thus usually an expression of alienation; it is a movement of people who are spiritually, socially, economically, educationally, or in other ways 'disinherited' " (*A Religious History of the American People*, p. 473).

While sects are particularly a phenomenon of post-Reformation history, they have emerged throughout the long life of the church. In a sense Christianity itself was at first a Judaic sect. In the years that followed, sectarian movements, such as Montanism, Novatianism, and Donatism, developed within Christendom. Many sects through the years have become churches. This is particularly true of the vast number of religious groups that have proliferated in the United States. (*See* DENOMINATIONALISM.)

R.H.

**SECULARISM.** From the Latin word *saeculum,* referring to time. The "temporal" is contrasted with the "eternal" and by implication, the worldly with the religious.

Secularism denotes a turn away from an other-worldliness to a worldliness that values human achievement. This development took place in the Western world during the Renaissance, when new learning and discoveries encouraged pride in cultural achievements. Secularism continued to develop during the eighteenth-century Enlightenment, when political theory stressed the potential power of human beings to govern themselves in contrast to the religious theory of the divine right of kings. AGNOSTICISM, a skepticism regarding the activity of God, has been one facet of secularism.

Humanism stresses the value of people and envisions a world order that gives primacy to human welfare. Twentieth-century "secular Christianity" calls Christians to become involved in the world as the arena of God's activity. Secularism is characteristic of a society open to change within itself, interaction with other societies, and a contextual framework for values.

I.C.

**SECURITY OF THE BELIEVER.** *See* PERSEVERANCE.

**SEDER.** The ceremonial feast that takes place on the first two nights of the Jewish festival of PASSOVER (the first night in Israel and among Reform Jews). The Seder starts with the chanting by the leader of the kiddush, a proclamation of the sanctity of the Passover, over a cup of wine. The second step in the order of the service is the washing of hands, without reciting a blessing. Next a small piece of celery or other green vegetable is dipped in salt water and the benediction for vegetables is recited. Many people have associated the vegetable, symbolically, with spring and the salt water with the tears shed by Jews during their slavery in Egypt. The middle of the three matzoth is divided into two. The larger piece, called the afikomen, is then wrapped in a napkin and hidden by the leader. Using the HAGGADAH, the participants in the Seder join in unfolding the drama of the Passover. This includes the chanting of The Four Questions by the youngest person present, the parable of the four sons, blessings, rabbinic lessons, the counting of the ten plagues, the thanking of God through singing "Dayenu," the explanation of the three major Passover symbols, the singing of psalms, and the drinking of the second cup of wine. The next step is to wash the hands, with the appropriate blessing. Following the blessings is the eating of the MATZAH (unleavened bread), the bitter herbs dipped in haroset—the mixture of apples, nuts, cinnamon, and wine symbolizing the mortar out of which the Jewish slaves made bricks—and the sandwich of matzah and bitter herbs. After this, the Passover meal is served. Following this, children search for and find the afikomen, which is distributed and eaten. Grace after meals is recited, the third cup of wine is drunk, and the service is concluded with the chanting of more psalms, the drinking of the fourth cup of wine, a closing poem, and the singing of hymns and songs.

L.K.

**SEEKERS.** A radical PURITAN sect that flourished in the 1640s. They met in small groups to wait on God because they believed there was no true church since the spirit of the Antichrist had gained the upper hand, but that in time God would ordain new apostles and prophets to found another church. In the 1650s many became Quakers and Baptists. ROGER WILLIAMS' mature beliefs resembled theirs.     N.H.

**SEER.** *See* PROPHET/PROPHECY.

**SEICHŌ NO IE.** From the Japanese phrase meaning "house of growth." One of the "new religions" of contemporary Japan, Seichō no Ie was founded by Masaharu Taniguchi (born in 1893), who was a worker for the Omoto faith before inaugurating his own movement. Although influenced by Buddhism and Confucianism as well as Omoto, the ideas that directly sparked Seichō no Ie actually came to Taniguchi through reading a book by an American "New Thought" writer in 1928. In 1930 Taniguchi started a magazine called *Seichō no Ie* to promulgate these teachings. Since then the religion has grown in organizational structure, establishing study groups and centers throughout Japan, but it has always been less a church in the conventional sense than an institution for disseminating Taniguchi's teachings through publications, lectures, and retreats.

The basic doctrine is that human beings are children of God and therefore perfect. Evil has no reality whatsoever of its own. It is only through the mind's false belief in imperfection that the illusions of evil and suffering arise from it, illusions that can be erased through the power of mind. In this way does Seichō no Ie deal with sickness, failure, and all other manifestations of evil. Its worship practices consist in large part of affirmations of perfection and a meditation method called *shinsokan*. It also has texts by Taniguchi, which play the role of Scripture.

Up until 1945, Taniguchi and Seichō no Ie actively supported the extreme nationalism and war effort of that era, unlike many other "new religions," and since then has endorsed causes regarded in Japan as ultra-conservative. Nonetheless, the movement has grown to number several million followers.   R.E.

**SEIR.** A name used of a land, a people, and a mountain.

(1) *The Land.* "The hill country of Seir" (Gen. 36:8, 9; Josh. 24:4), "Mount Seir" (Deut. 1:2; 2:1), and "Seir" (Josh. 11:17; 12:7), all refer to an area of mountains and high plateaus (up to five thousand feet above sea level), which lies east of the Arabah and west of the desert. This land was the scene of the wilderness wanderings: "for many days we went about Mount Seir . . . the territory of your brethren the sons of Esau, who live in Seir" (Deut. 2:1-4). Mount Halak, a term related to Seir, seems to refer to the wooded slope east of the Arabah "that rises toward Seir" (Josh. 11:17; 12:7).

(2) *The People.* Seir was the grandfather of Hori and, thus, the ancestor of the "sons of the Horites" (Gen. 36:20, 21; I Chr. 1:38). The HORITES were the pre-Edomite inhabitants of the land who later assimilated with the Edomites (Num. 24:18), the descendants of Esau (Gen. 33:14, 16; Deut. 2: 4, 5, 12, 22, 29). It is now thought that the Horites may well have been Hurrians, migrants from the second-millennium kingdom of Mitanni in north and northeast Mesopotamia. The "men of Seir" (II Chr. 25:11, 14), whether Horites, Amorites, Edomites, or Idumeans, are considered hostile to Israel (II Chr. 20: 10, 22). Psalm 137:7-9 is perhaps an echo of the Jacob-Esau rivalry. In Isaiah 21:11; Numbers 24:18; Ezekiel 35:2ff. "Mount Seir" is used for the Edomite nation.

(3) *The Mountain.* A mountain, also called Mount Jearim on the north border of Judah, near Beth-she-mesh, about nine miles west of Jerusalem (Deut. 1:44; Josh. 15:10, and, possibly, I Chr. 4:42-43).
P.L.G.

**SELA.** Meaning literally "rocky" or "cliff."

(1) Name of an ancient Edomite fortress-city whose ruins are about 2700 feet above sea level (Isa. 16:1). Amaziah of Judah took the city and renamed it Jokthe (II Kings 14:7). In Obadiah 3, Sela appears in the Hebrew text (RSV, "the rock"). The Nabateans built the city of Petra in a neighboring high valley. The Greek name Petra probably replaced the biblical name Sela.

(2) A place associated with the Amorites (Judg. 1:36).

(3) In Isaiah 42:11, Sela is a distant, unidentified place.                                               P.L.G.

**SELAH.** A signal in poetry calling for a pause or music. Selah appears seventy-one times in thirty-nine psalms and three times in Habakkuk 3. The word, originally in the margin, made its way into the text. It is thought to have alerted the conductor of choir and orchestra to interrupt the even flow of the chanting with a clash of cymbals or a short musical interlude.                                                       P.L.G.

**SELEUCIA IN SYRIA.** One of nine known cities all named Seleucia for one of Alexander's generals, Seleucus I Nicator, who, in 312 B.C., founded the Seleucid Empire. He made Antioch in Syria his western capital, and in 301 B.C. built, at a former Phoenician harbor named Pieria, where the Orontes River meets the sea, a Greek-type city as a guardian fortress and seaport for Antioch, fourteen miles upstream. The city was built on the south side of the mountain Musa Dagh, with walls extending down to enclose the harbor. From the ruins of the city, still to be seen above ground, the city was large and properous.

For more than two centuries, Seleucia served as the Seleucids' Mediterranean port. Throughout the first century A.D. the Romans used it as their main naval base for the eastern Mediterranean. Cyprus is about one hundred miles to the southeast. It could be reached in less than a day's sailing. On a clear day, it can be seen on the horizon.

Barnabas and Saul with John Mark sailed to Cyprus from Selucia (Acts 13:4) on the "first missionary journey." Barnabus and Mark later, probably, did also (Acts 15:39), though this is not stated.
P.L.G.

**SELF.** Psychological study of the self began with the work of William James (1890) but was not really developed until the 1940s with GORDON ALLPORT's research on the individual and Prescott Lecky's *Self-Consistency.*

The self is the sum of the constituent parts of a person, including not only the physical self but one's work, family, and culture. Personal identity is a process, forged from interaction with the physical and social environment. It develops from the moment the infant begins to distinguish the self from the nurturer. Language is an important factor: to name the self and others brings both a cognitive and emotional understanding of selfhood. A stable selfhood depends upon the ability to cope with life situations and to have a realistic perception of relationships to others within a social group. Changes in the self-concept arise during adolescence in the quest for identity (Erikson) and during the stages of adulthood as people determine what is important in their lives and the degree to which they adapt to change.                                                                      I.C.

**SEMINARY.** An institution for the training of candidates for the ministry, priesthood, or the rabbinate. In the United States it is a professional school giving training in religion, especially for men and women preparing for pastoral duties, requiring a college degree for entry, and having a three-year course of study leading to a master of divinity degree. Seminaries also often offer advanced graduate degrees.

In Great Britain the term "seminary" is normally used by Roman Catholic institutions preparing men for the diocesan priesthood, or for membership in a religious order. Commonly such schools offer a course of study comprising typically ten years of secondary, collegiate, and theological training. Some Roman Catholic institutions so named offer four-year courses in theology and other special studies. In Britain theological colleges, often associated with universities, provide the training for young men and women preparing for ministry in Anglican and free churches.

In the earlier half of the nineteenth century in both the United States and Britain, a "seminary for young ladies" was the common designation of a private school for girls.                                                   R.H.

**SEMI-PELAGIANS.** A term used to describe the anti-Augustinian movement that flourished in southern France and North Africa between 429 and 529. Writings of three of its leaders have survived: John Cassian, Vincent of Lérins, and Faustus, bishop of Riez.

Faustus' *De gratia*, ("Concerning Grace"), defined their position. They believed in the universality of original sin as a corruptive force and in the necessity of grace to overcome sin. But they also argued against Augustine that human volition can initiate the process of salvation by desiring it, though grace is needed to achieve it. Later Semi-Pelagians saw divine help not as grace infused in a person but as external prompting through the preaching of divine threats and promises. Their major concern was the justice of God. If human beings are totally incapable of action, then God is a capricious tyrant, arbitrarily saving some and damning others. The Semi-Pelagians were condemned as heretical by the Second Council of Orange in 529. (*See also* PELAGIANISM.)       N.H.

**SEMITES.** Members of any of various ancient and modern peoples originating in southwestern Asia, including Sumerians, Akkadians, Canaanites,

Phoenicians, Hebrews, and Arabs. According to the Bible, Semites, called "sons of Shem" (Gen. 10:22; I Chr. 1:17), have a common ancestor, SHEM, the long-lived, eldest son of Noah (Gen. 5:32; 6:10; 7:13; 10:1, 31; 11:10, 11; I Chr. 1:4, 24). With his brother Japheth, Shem acted honorably toward their father in contrast to their brother Canaan. Noah blessed them (Gen. 9:23, 26-27).       P.L.G.

**SENECA.** Lucius Annaeus Seneca, a Roman statesman and the tutor of the young NERO. Seneca was born in Cordoba in Spain about 4 B.C. and died outside Rome in A.D. 65. Of a noble family, he was educated at Rome for a legal career, studying Cynic, Stoic, and Pythagorean philosophy. When he intrigued with the sister of Caligula to gain control of the throne, he was banned to the island of Corsica. Later the emperor Claudius invited him to return and become the tutor of the eleven-year-old Nero.

A good writer and speaker, more moral than most Romans in positions of power and leadership, he first guided Nero through a glorious five years of rule before Nero plotted with him to help do away with Nero's mother. One of Nero's richest and most powerful friends, Seneca was eventually ordered to cut his veins and take his own life, though when this proved ineffective, he died in a steam bath.

His Latin is clear and precise and was much admired by many of the early fathers of the church. His advice about daily living and attitudes toward one's neighbors was charitable and insightful. Some early Christians counted him as one of their own, a Christian in secret. This belief is based in part on fourteen letters, still extant, which are now almost universally thought to be spurious. His flair for drama, his precise Latin, and the plays he wrote made him popular again in the century of the Reformation.
                                                                                      T.J.K.

**SENNACHERIB.** King of Assyria and Babylonia (704–681 B.C.), son of SARGON II, and father of ESARHADDON

*Initial Challenges.* Sargon's battlefield death brought Sennacherib to the Assyrian throne in uncontested fashion. Though Sennacherib inherited a well-consolidated empire, he soon encountered serious rebellion. With Elamite assistance, Marduk-apaliddina (MERODACH-BALADAN) reestablished himself as king in Babylon. This Chaldean prince had previously asserted his independence against Sargon. Merodach-baladan sought to buttress his position by uniting warring Chaldean and Aramean tribes against Sennacherib and dispatching envoys to Assyria's western vassals to incite their insurrection. HEZE-KIAH, king of Judah, warmly hosted such a delegation (II Kings 20:12-13). Defeating Elamite and Chaldean forces near Kish, Sennacherib took control of Babylonia, appointed Bel-ibni to the throne (702–700), and triumphantly returned with captives and spoil to Nineveh.

Courtesy of the Oriental Institute, University of Chicago

*Sennacherib's prism, a hexagonal clay cylinder on which the Assyrian monarch recorded his various campaigns, including one against Hezekiah of Judah.*

The rebellion of western states against Sennacherib was extensive. The kings of Tyre and Sidon refused to pay Assyria customary tribute. To brace himself against Assyria, Hezekiah negotiated a treaty with Egypt (Isa. 30:1-7; 31:1-3). Also, Sennacherib's annals report that Hezekiah consented to the Jerusalem imprisonment of King Padi of Ekron, one of Assyria's few remaining western allies.

In 701 Sennacherib was free to press westward. Though some historians argue that he made two separate invasions into Judah (the second in about 668), a second invasion is neither readily discernible in the relevant, yet confusing, biblical text (II Kings 18:13–19:37) nor mentioned in Assyrian annals. Accordingly, the following reconstruction is plausible. Sennacherib quickly subdued Tyre and replaced its fleeing king with his own appointment. This induced several western states to submit immediately, but Ashkelon, Ekron, and Judah remained resolute rebels. Sennacherib soon overtook Ashkelon and Ekron, defeated a large Egyptian army allied with Ekron, and overran Judah. According to Sennacherib's report, he seized forty-six of Hezekiah's fortified cities, and by isolating Jerusalem from all outside assistance, confined Hezekiah inside his royal city "like a caged bird." While Sennacherib was still leveling Lachish, Hezekiah sent a message of surrender (II Kings 18:14a). Sennacherib was not lenient. He demanded the return of King Padi to his Ekron throne, the parceling of certain Judean territory to Padi and the loyal heads of Ashdod and Gaza, and Hezekiah's payment of such enormous tribute that he had to lift gold and silver from the Jerusalem Temple and surrender his royal treasuries (18:14b-16).

Presently, the unexpected happened. Rather than conquering Jerusalem, Sennacherib suddenly withdrew from Judah. This may be understood as Sennacherib's response either to a devastating epidemic that crippled his army (19:35, a verse inspiring Lord Byron's well-known poem "The Destruction of Sennacherib," 1815), or, more likely, to a "rumor" that reached him and demanded his attention elsewhere—presumably renewed rebellion in Babylonia (19:7). Jerusalem's much relieved citizens were left to ruminate on Zion's inviolability, and in time, make it national dogma.

*Continuing Babylonian Problem.* With Merodach-baladan still stirring up Babylonian politics, Sennacherib acted decisively in 700 B.C. by placing his own son Asshur-nadin-shum on its throne. Meanwhile, Merodach-baladan fled to Elam. After six years of relative peace, Sennacherib directly faced Elam. Resentful of Elam's tendency to support Babylonia in anti-Assyrian measures, including its granting asylum to defeated rebels, Sennacherib undertook a novel expedition by ship in 694 and overtook Elam's coastal cities. Elamites, however, were able to invade Babylonia, take Sennacherib's son prisoner, and install Nergal-ushezib on Babylon's throne. Once Sennacherib dealt with him, another usurper, Mushezib-Marduk, surfaced. When Sennacherib reasserted himself in 691, he was defeated by a coalition of Elamites, Babylonians, and neighboring tribal confederates. Finally, in 689 Sennacherib mastered Babylon's rebellion. This time an internally distraught Elam was incapable of interfering. Forced to face Sennacherib alone, Babylon was turned into shambles and its citizenry massacred.

Sennacherib's last eight years of rule were mainly tranquil, allowing him to concentrate on palace construction in Nineveh. In 681 he was assassinated by two sons, Adrammelech and Sharezer, who fled (II Kings 19:37). Thus his favorite son, Esarhaddon, moved swiftly to claim Assyria's throne.     J.K.K.

**SENTENCES, BOOKS OF.** The latin word *sententia* originally meant any exposition of thought. In the twelfth century, theologians compiled collections of "sentences," systematized catalogues of teaching from Scripture and earlier church fathers. One of the first was Peter Abelard's *Sic et non*. The most famous was Peter Lombard's *Four Books of Sentences*. The books of sentences became syllabi for the theological education of men like Martin Luther. They marked the transition from monastic education to the Scholastic universities. A master taught his students from the books of sentences, which summarized past opinion, and then gave his own views and judgments.
N.H.

**SEPARATION OF CHURCH AND STATE.** This concept is rooted in the ANABAPTISTS, who favored a congregation of gathered believers and eschewed all entanglements with the state. Many refused to pay taxes, serve in the army, and later to vote. Among English Puritans, the Separatists or BAPTISTS were its most ardent advocates. They opposed conformity of worship and discipline decreed by the crown and particularly that decreed by Archbishop William Laud. They claimed the right of the local congregation to ordain, baptize, worship, and discipline.

In America, Baptist founder ROGER WILLIAMS was undoubtedly its earliest proponent. Separation of church and state was part of the foundation of Rhode Island. Quakers in New Jersey, Delaware, and Pennsylvania worked to the same end. Williams grounded his stand on a doctrine of the church and a belief in liberty of conscience. Separation was recognized in Maryland in the 1630s and during the seventeenth century in the Carolinas, Georgia, and New York.

It was written into the federal Constitution in 1787 and the Bill of Rights in 1791 on the basis of the "rights of man" natural law philosophy and the fact of religious PLURALISM. Though many states then had religious tests, Article 6 of the Constitution prohibited them "as a qualification to any office or public trust." The First Amendment declared that "Congress shall make no law respecting an establishment of religion or prohibiting the free exercise thereof." Due to the work of THOMAS JEFFERSON and JAMES MADISON, the Church of England had been disestablished in Virginia in 1785. The Congregational Church was disestablished in Connecticut 1818, New Hampshire 1819, Maine 1820, and finally Massachusetts 1833.

The concept, while usually lauded as a unique American ideal and achievement, continues to be controversial. Most staunchly upheld by Baptists and such organizations as Americans United for the Separation of Church and State, issues such as prayer in public schools, federal aid to education, draft registration, abortion, and affirmative action against racism and sexism have raised questions about its limits.

Since nineteenth-century controversies over which version of the Bible to read in public schools, some religious groups have tried to keep the government from interfering in their business (such as taxing churches' auxiliary enterprises) while seeking to disseminate their religious ideas to others (such as requiring the Ten Commandments to be posted in public schools or having abortion outlawed by constitutional amendment). Religious pluralism in a democratic state requires, however, at least TOLERATION and a measure of separation.     N.H.

**SEPARATISM.** Separatism is the tendency or impulse for a religious group to separate itself from a mother group in order to purify the group's life or restore its doctrine to a more pristine form. Even though the tendency to come out from among them has roots as old as ancient Israel, the term "separatism" was probably first applied to the followers of ROBERT BROWNE and the INDEPENDENTS, who withdrew from the Church of England and established autonomous local churches. Separatism's classic instance in American religious life was Plymouth Colony, whose pilgrims established a city set upon a hill amidst a howling wilderness. There the "visible saints" could truly re-create primitive Christianity. Separatism was subsequently an important impulse in early Baptist and Congregational history.     W. G.

**SEPHARDIM.** Hebrew term applied to Jews of Spanish and Portuguese origin and to their descendants, as distinct from ASHKENAZIM, or Jews whose origins go back to central Europe. After the Jews were expelled from Spain in 1492, the term "Sephardim" was given a wider connotation because of the influence of the Jews from Spain on the culture and traditions of the Jewish communities of North Africa and the Middle East. Sephardim also refers to a Jew belonging to a community that has adopted the Sephardic rite, whether or not the community is of Spanish origin.

The Sephardi Jews made great contributions to Jewish learning. They developed their own institutions and congregations, and had great rabbis, poets, and other famous personalities. Some of the works of their poets have become an integral part of the daily and Sabbath liturgy.

While they do not differ in the basics of Judaism from their fellow Jews, their ritual, traditions, customs, food, and language do differ. In the Sephardic synagogue, for example, the chants are simpler than in the Ashkenazic synagogue, the Torah is raised and shown to the worshipers before the public reading rather than after, the procedures and arrangements are different, and terms for religious services and objects are dissimilar. Babies are named for living relatives in the Sephardic tradition. The Sephardic pronunciation of Hebrew is different. On Passover, rice is permitted, and lettuce is used instead of horseradish to symbolize the bitter herbs.

The first Jewish settlers in the United States were Sephardim, and the Spanish and Portuguese synagogue (Congregation Shearith Israel) in New York is the oldest in America, dating back to 1654. After 1900, there was a wave of Sephardic immigrants from the Balkans, Asia Minor, Syria, and Turkey. After World War II, more came from Morocco, Egypt, Iraq, Syria, Iran, Israel, and Cuba (after 1959). Sephardim are divided into three language groups: Judeo-Spanish, Greek, and Arabic.          L.K.

**SEPHARVAIM.** A city of disputed location conquered by the Assyrians. With Israel's fall to Assyrian forces in 722 B.C., Samaria became an Assyrian province. When Sargon II later sought to confer on Samaria a more permanent organization, he dispatched inhabitants of Sepharvaim to colonize it (II Kings 17:24). If consonantal confusion in the Hebrew text may be assumed, these colonists may have been the Median inhabitants of Sepharad whom Sargon conquered in 716 B.C.          J.K.K.

**SEPTUAGINT.** The name of the earliest Greek translation of the Hebrew Torah. Ultimately it encompassed the entire OT and the Apocrypha. The undoubtedly spurious Letter of Aristeas, composed about 125 B.C., reports that Ptolemy II Philadelphus (285–246 B.C.) was persuaded by his librarian to have a translation of the Jewish Law prepared for his magnificent library in ALEXANDRIA. He contacted the high priest Eleazer in Jerusalem, who dispatched seventy-two men (six from each tribe) to Egypt. Isolated on the island of Pharos, they completed their task in seventy-two days. The version was thus called the Septuagint (translation of the seventy), and is designated by the numerals LXX.

This legend was both accepted and embellished by early Christians in advocating the inspiration and reliability of their favorite version, a factor causing it to fall into disfavor among Jews. Mention that several savants shared this task, that the Torah was the first to be translated, and that it was officially authoritative are the main historical kernels within the legend. Actually the Septuagint emerged to answer the desire of Greek-speaking Jews of the DIASPORA to comprehend the OT in their native tongue. Presumably, by the third century B.C., nearly a million Jews inhabited Alexandria. With the Greek translation of Jewish Scripture, communication between Jew and Gentile intensified. Also Judaism began appropriating Greek thought with greater enthusiasm.

Manuscripts discovered at Qumran demonstrate that the Septuagint had a long, complex prehistory. Following the relatively uniform and accurate rendering of the Torah into Greek in about 250 B.C., other books were translated during the next century.

Some of the translation of I Samuel–II Kings is slavish to the Hebrew, and some is far better Greek, though paraphrastic. Shifts in the narrative sequences in I Kings provide Solomon and Ahab a more sympathetic press. The Proverbs text has been expanded to include Greek ethical and metaphysical instruction. Throughout, the Septuagint introduces anti-anthropomorphisms (thus, the Hebrew of Exod. 24:10, "they saw the God of Israel," is rendered in Greek, "they saw the place where the God of Israel stood"). Also the Septuagint differs from the Hebrew canon in its arrangement of the individual books into three categories—historical, poetic, and prophetic. Most OT quotations within the NT are drawn from the Septuagint.          J.K.K.

**SERAPHIM.** Heavenly beings mentioned only in Isaiah 6:2, 6, associated with the throne of God. The word "seraphim" is now thought to derive from the Hebrew word meaning "to burn," not, as previously thought, "to be bright," that is, "shining ones."

The description of the seraphim's impressive appearance emphasizes the six wings. Each seraph had two wings covering his face, two covering the "feet" (a euphemism for male sex organs), and two for flying. A representation of a six-winged female or smooth-shaven male figure has been found at Tell Halaf (Gozan in ancient Assyria) on a relief dated a century before Isaiah's time.

The seraphim are attendants and servants of God. They have voices for speaking, singing, or chanting, and hands capable of managing tongs. The seraphim show humility and modesty. They demonstrate intelligence and character by celebrating "the Holy One of Israel" in song and by serving as agents of divine purgation and forgiveness, thus preparing for the Lord's call to Isaiah to be sent and to go as the Lord's prophet. The "living creatures"or CHERUBIM of Ezekiel 10 and of Revelation 4:8 are in some way related to the seraphim of Isaiah's vision (*compare* ANGEL).          P.L.G.

**SERMON ON THE MOUNT.** The collection of teachings that Jesus is reported in Matthew 5–7 to have delivered to the crowds that were following him are commonly known as the Sermon on the Mount. The name derives from the vantage point that he chose from which to address them, according to Matthew 5:1. These chapters read more like a series of excerpts from his teaching than a unified address such as a modern sermon might be. Luke 6:17-49 describes Jesus as delivering a similar discourse, though it is shorter than in Matthew and is said to have been given "on a level place" (Luke 6:17). The variations in detail between these two "sermons" are significant.

Throughout his Gospel, Matthew has grouped the teaching of Jesus into a series of discourses, most of which conclude with the remark "when Jesus had finished . . ." (7:28; 11:1; 13:53; 19:1; 26:1). At least one discourse section, however, does not have this stylized conclusion (23:1-39). Since Matthew in the Sermon on the Mount contrasts the teaching of Jesus with the LAW of Moses (referring indirectly to Moses in such phrases as "you have heard it was said to the men of old," Matt. 5:21, 27, 31, 33, 38, 43), it is possible that the editorial marking off of these five discourses is intended as a contrast with the Pentateuch, or Five Books of Moses (Gen. to Deut.). In this way Jesus stands over against Moses as the giver of the New Law. Whether the fivefold division of the material is intended or not, the links and contrast between Jesus and the interpretation of Mosaic Law that seem to have been current in Jesus' time are explicit in Matthew 5:17-20. Although Paul asserts that "no human being will be justified in his [God's] sight by works of the law" (Rom. 3:20), Paul is in apparent agreement with Jesus that the Christian should and can fulfill what the Law justly requires (Rom. 8:4; Matt. 5:17).

The first cluster of sayings in the Sermon is widely known as the BEATITUDES (5:3-12), from the Latin word for blessed, *beatus*. In contrast to Luke's "Blessed are *you* poor" (Luke 6:20), Matthew quotes Jesus in such a way as to convert statements in which are depicted those who are in literal need (such as poverty or hunger) into general statements about spiritual or moral deprivation: "Blessed are the poor in spirit"; and "Blessed are those who hunger and thirst for righteousness" (Matt. 5:3, 6). In each of Matthew's versions of the Beatitudes, there is a contrast between the present difficult spiritual conditions for the faithful and their future reward and vindication by God. It is those presently experiencing oppression or difficulties who already share in the Kingdom. The Greek term *makarios* means much more than "happy," although several modern translations render it that way. It implies, rather, a special condition of humans beings as a result of their close relationship to God, through which they are privileged beneficiaries of God's actions. The last two Beatitudes, however (Matt. 5:10-11), warn of suffering and persecution "for righteousness' sake" and "on my account," so that the blessed state of the faithful includes courage to endure suffering and even martyrdom, rather than a life of tranquil withdrawal. They are urged to fulfill their mission: as "salt of the earth" and as "light of the world," they are to give taste and seasoning to life and to share the light of God's grace with others (5:13-16).

Next in the Sermon comes an extended section in which Jesus shows what attitude his followers should take toward the Law of Moses. His outlook is phrased in a series of contrasts with the then-current views among Jews, especially those of the Pharisees (5:17-48). Linking the Law and the Prophets (5:17), Jesus declares that it is his mission from God to bring to fulfillment the scriptural demands, not to do away with them. Indeed, not the smallest letter (*iota*) or punctuation mark (dot) in Scripture will disappear until all its demands and promises have been realized.

The charge against the Pharisees and those who spend their time in interpretation of the Scriptures ("scribes") is not that they are too strict, but that through pretended piety they evade the true obligations laid down in Scripture (5:19-20). From the specific examples that follow, however, it is clear that what Jesus is demanding is not simple, literal conformity to the Law. What is demanded by him is not merely avoidance of murder, but taking the initiative in reconciliation with those with whom one is in conflict (5:21-26); not simple abstinence from adultery, but self-discipline to root out even the inclination to sexual promiscuity (5:27-30). Divorce, though allowed by the Law (Deut. 24:1), is not to be practiced, except in case of infidelity on the part of one's spouse (5:31-32). Oaths are to be avoided in favor of direct, unequivocal statements (5:33-37). Retaliation is to be replaced by initiative toward one's antagonist by acting in generosity toward those who abuse or threaten. What Jesus here represents God as expecting from people is nothing less than complete obedience to God's will (5:38-48).

On the three aspects of piety that seem to have been especially important for Jews in the first century— almsgiving, fasting, and prayer—Jesus has demanding requirements. Alms are to be given solely out of personal, human concern, never as a means of gaining public recognition of one's generosity (6:1-4). Similarly, prayer is grounded in one's personal commitment to God's will and must include an appeal for sensitivity concerning injustices done to others (6:5-15). Fasting is a form of private discipline, rather than a pious mode of showing off (6:16-18). In this section, the so-called LORD'S PRAYER appears in a version that reflects how it had developed as a liturgical form, in contrast to Luke's much simpler version (compare Luke 11:2-4).

The rest of the Sermon concerns questions of personal values: whether one's top priority is the accumulation of transitory earthly treasures or the devotion of one's energies to works of mercy that will be rewarded by God (6:19-21); whether the light of the knowledge of God is allowed to illumine the whole of one's inner life (6:22-23); whether the final standard in life is God's will or the acquiring of wealth (6:24); whether one lives life in total reliance upon God's purpose or is preoccupied with anxieties about appearances, achievements, and acquisitions (6:25-34); whether one devotes time and energy in criticism of others or to self-examination (7:1-5). What is called for is unconditional reliance upon God (7:7-11), which involves treating others as one would want to be treated (7:12), self-discipline in preparation for entering the life of the age to come (7:13-14), discernment so as to differentiate false from true agents of God (7:15-20), and active devotion to doing God's will (7:21-23). Only the adoption of these values will enable one to withstand the difficulties of life and the divine judgments that will bring this age to a close (7:24-27). The Sermon graphically describes what are the privileges and the costs of discipleship for those who see in Jesus the agent for the coming of God's Rule.

H.K.

**SERPENT.** A scaly, limbless, elongate reptile of the genus *Serpentes.*

In various religions the serpent is widely used as a symbol of both beneficent and hostile supernatural and sacred power. With the Canaanites, the symbol for disruptive and destructive chaos was the dragon. Figurines of Asherah, the fertility goddess, are often draped with snake representations, as were her altars also. Nehushtan, the name of the bronze serpent destroyed by King Hezekiah (II Kings 18:4), may have been the name of a Canaanite serpent-nature deity. In the Hebrew wilderness wanderings, the Israelites encountered deadly "fiery serpents" (Num. 21:6-8). To counteract their poison, Moses made a brazen or BRONZE SERPENT (Num. 21;9), which is said to have been preserved. (For a Christian reference to the bronze serpent, see John 3:14.)

In Palestine, especially in the Negeb, snakes are common, thirty species being known. A small number of these are poisonous, a few deadly. The situation was probably much the same in biblical times. Snakes were abhorrent to writers of the Bible. They viewed serpents as dangerous and vicious. This is reflected in the record of Moses' use in Pharaoh's court of a rod that became a serpent and then a rod again (Exod. 4:3; 7:9-15). Snakes have sharp tongues (Ps. 140:3) in which is poison (Ps. 58:4); they bite (Prov. 23:32; Eccl. 10:11) and follow mysterious ways (Prov. 30:19).

The serpent in the Garden of Eden narrative (Gen. 3:1, 2, 4, 13, 14) is well informed and most crafty (Matt. 23:33), as well as critical of the Creator. He tempts Eve successfully but, in the end, loses his place in paradise (Gen. 3:14-15). In postexilic thought, when SATAN came to be considered responsible for all evil in the world, the Genesis serpent was understood either as an agent of Satan or Satan himself. This is most graphically expressed in Revelation 12:9-15; 20:2.

P.L.G.

**SERPENT, BRONZE.** *See* BRONZE SERPENT.

**SERVANT OF THE LORD.** A title assigned to the highly idealized figure whose career is portrayed in four "Servant Songs" within Second Isaiah.

*The Servant Songs.* Displaying a vocabulary and message largely representative of Second Isaiah, these lyrics presumably encompass Isaiah 42:1-4; 49:1-6; 50:4-9; and 52:13–53:12. Yahweh speaks in 42:1-4, and depicts the servant as God's chosen agent who faithfully extends justice to the nations. The servant speaks in 49:1-6. He discloses his prenatal divine appointment. Confidence in Yahweh has overtaken his despair about obstacles so that he might pursue a universal mission benefiting distant peoples and

Israel. As a light mediating salvation "to the end of the earth" (49:6), his identity is puzzling. He is charged with returning Israel to God (49:5), but the servant designation is also attached to Israel itself (49:3).

The servant speaks in 50:4-9. He declares that having been taught daily by Yahweh, he teaches others. Though forced to endure shame, he resolutely pursues his mission and confidently anticipates divine vindication. Yahweh and the nations speak in 52:13–53:12. Yahweh announces the future exaltation of God's innocent servant. Looking on this disfigured "man of sorrows" (53:3), astonished nations declare, "He was wounded for our transgressions" (53:5). Giving his life as a sin offering for many, the servant will know that in his endeavors, Yahweh's will has triumphed.

*The Servant's Identity.* (1) *As an individual.* While consensus is impossible, various proposals have recognized the servant's individual, corporate, and quasi-corporate existence. The servant's striking personal characteristics have led to his identification with known historical persons (for example, Moses, Jeremiah, Cyrus), the ideal monarch (Messiah), and Second Isaiah himself. But no known historical figure fits the servant's description completely, though the law-giving Moses and tormented Jeremiah are sometimes recalled. Moreover, suffering coordinates poorly with the messianic office. If referring to himself, Second Isaiah appears grossly immodest.

(2) *As Israel.* Perhaps the servant symbolizes the nation Israel. The two are equated in 49:3. Outside these lyrics, Second Isaiah applies the servant label to Israel (42:19; 43:10; 48:20). The nation itself is regarded as Yahweh's agent of universal righteousness and salvation chosen from the womb and equipped with God's spirit. Also in the servant's humiliation, Israel might perceive its own humiliation in Babylonian exile. This interpretation is likewise problematic. The servant Israel is deaf and blind to Yahweh's purpose (42:19). Israel often meets suffering with complaint. And significantly, the servant is charged to return Israel to Yahweh (49:5).

(3) *As individual and nation.* The coalescence of individual and corporate realities in Hebrew thinking may apply here. If Abraham embodies Israel (51:2), why not the servant? Perhaps Second Isaiah sketched the servant figure with deliberate fluidity. Accordingly, the servant is the called people of Yahweh, its faithful remnant purged through Babylonian exile, and, notably in the fourth servant song, an individual representing the nation. This interpretation may be the most viable, for it properly esteems the capacity of these lyrics to portray the true Israel and the true Israelite as radically engaged in Yahweh's redemptive world mission.

J.K.K.

**SERVETUS, MICHAEL** (1511–53). Learned Spanish physician and early UNITARIAN. After studying at Saragossa and Toulouse, Servetus's study of the Bible led him to deny a fundamental tenet of the classic doctrine of the Trinity, that is, that the Son was eternal with the Father. After studying medicine in Paris, he was physician to the archbishop of Vienne for twelve years (1541–53), during which time he carried on a secret correspondence with JOHN CALVIN. After Servetus published his repudiation of the Trinity, the divinity of Christ, the cult of the saints, purgatory, and predestination, he was imprisoned by the Vienne Inquisition. He escaped to Geneva, where Calvin, who had violently disagreed with him, had him arrested. Tried for denying the Trinity and infant baptism, both capital offenses under the Justinian Code, he was burned at the stake as a heretic. (*See also* SOCINIANS).          W. G.

**SESSION.** In the polity of PRESBYTERIAN and REFORMED churches, the session is the lowest court in the denomination, concerned with the oversight of a particular congregation and made up of elders, including the minister. The elders, as representatives of the people, along with the pastor, are responsible for the nurture and discipline of the congregation. Both ministers and elders are ordained for life, although there is a recognized distinction in ordination to the pulpit ministry. The end to which ordination is directed determines the character of the rite. Sometimes ministers are referred to as teaching elders and the others as ruling elders. The elder has been regarded as a representative of the people, though not appointed by or responsible to the people in the ordering of church affairs.

R.H.

**SEVEN CHURCHES OF ASIA.** In Revelation, the city of ROME, built on seven hills (17:9), symbolizes the anti-Christian character of the Roman Empire and its emperor worship. Seven is the Hebrew number that symbolizes completeness. Thus the churches in seven cities of the province of Asia symbolize the conquering power of Christ and of his ecumenical church over all evil. The seven cities are:

(1) *Ephesus*—an economic, postal, and administrative center of the province. The site of a temple of Artemis or Diana.

(2) *Smyrna*—second most important city and seaport of Asia.

(3) *Pergamum*—cultural and religious center.

(4) *Thyatira*—in the province of Lydia, renowned for its purple dye industry (Acts 16:14).

(5) *Sardis*—political, commercial river city with a noted temple of Artemis.

(6) *Philadelphia*—joined by river and road to Sardis.

(7) *Laodicea*—commercial and industrial center on the international highway from Ephesus to the Orient.          P.L.G.

**SEVEN CHURCHES OF ROME.** *See* the place-names.

**SEVEN DEADLY SINS.** *See* CARDINAL SINS/CARDINAL VIRTUES.

**SEVEN GIFTS OF THE HOLY SPIRIT.** A list derived from Romans 12:6-8. The seven gifts are: prophecy, service, teaching, exhortation, liberality, zeal, and mercy with cheerfulness. Comparable lists are found in I Corinthians 12:8-10, with nine items; I Corinthians 12:28-30, with eight items; and Ephesians 4:11, with five items. (See also Isa. 11:2.)

P.L.G.

**SEVEN LAST WORDS.** The phrase describes the seven statements made by Jesus from the cross, as recorded in the Gospels. It is impossible to place the statements in precise chronological order because they derive from different narratives. In the traditional order listed below the first three sayings concern other people at the scene; the last four concern Jesus' own mission.

"Father, forgive them; for they know not what they do" (Luke 23:24). In his hour of intense suffering Jesus prays for his oppressors—both the Roman soldiers and all who had a part in the Crucifixion.

"Truly, I say to you, today you will be with me in Paradise" (Luke 23:43). One among several views of the afterlife in Judaism understood paradise (an elaborate garden or park) to be the realm where the souls of the righteous go at death. Jesus mediates forgiveness to the repentant criminal crucified near him.

"Woman, behold, your son!" "Behold, your mother!" (John 19:26-27). Jesus demonstrates his filial concern for his mother by entrusting her to the care of the beloved disciple.

"Eloi, Eloi, lama sabachthani? My God, my God, why hast thou forsaken me?" (Mark 15:34; Matt. 27:46). Jesus quotes the Aramaic version of Psalm 22:1, which becomes both his cry of abandonment by the Father and his confession of faith in the midst of suffering.

"I thirst" (John 19:28). Jesus' final request is itself a fulfillment of the Scriptures (see Ps. 69:21).

"It is finished" (John 19:30). Jesus, thoroughly obedient to the Father's will, utters a cry of completion and so of victory. God's plan is accomplished.

"Father, into thy hands I commit my spirit!" (Luke 23:46). This commital of himself to God evokes from a nearby centurion a testimony to Jesus' innocence.

C.B.C.

**SEVEN PENTITENTIAL PSALMS.** *See* PENITENTIAL PSALMS.

**SEVEN/SEVENTH/SEVENTY.** The Hebrew people's interest in mathematics was ordinarily in utilitarian arithmatic. For anything beyond that, the systems developed in Egypt and/or Mesopotamia were available. As in those older cultures certain NUMBERS had symbolic significance beyond numbers as such, indeed, perhaps as all numbers once had. Seven, seventh, and seventy, together with their multiples, have been called "sacred" numbers by reason of their relation to the furnishings and decorations of the tabernacle and Temple (Ezek. 40:22, 26; Exod. 25:31-37; I Kings 6:38; 7:17; 8:2; Zech. 4:2, 10). In Egypt, seven was a holy number in religion, magic, and medicine. In Mesopotamia, where the seven-day week was developed, seven is found in reference to religious festivals and observances, perhaps related to the seven planets known to that culture.

In the Bible, seven was associated with vengeance and punishment (Lev. 26:18; Dan. 4:16, 23, 25), with angels (Ezek. 9:2; Zech. 4:10*b*; Rev. 15:1, 6-8), with evil spirits and infirmities (Luke 8:2; 11:26), with healings (II Kings 5:10), with the ideal number of sons (Ruth 4:15; Job 1:2; II Macc. 7; Acts 19:14), with famine and years of great plenty (Gen. 41:26-27; II Kings 8:1), and with wedding festivals and defilements (Lev. 15:19, 28; Num. 19:11, 14, 16).

Matthew's genealogy of Jesus is divided into three sections of fourteen (7 x 2) generations (Matt. 1:1-17). Seventy is also often used as an approximate number (Gen. 50:3; Luke 10:1, 17). The forgiveness to be given seventy times seven times, which Jesus recommended, means an undetermined, large number (Matt. 18:22).

There are numerous sets of seven items in both the OT and the NT: seven qualities of the Lord's Spirit in people (Isa. 11:2); the seven petitions of the Lord's Prayer (Matt. 6:9-13); Christ's post-Resurrection appearance to seven disciples (John 21:2); and SEVEN GIFTS OF THE HOLY SPIRIT (Rom. 12:6-8).

The Revelation uses seven throughout the book beginning with letters to the SEVEN CHURCHES (chaps. 2–3). Seven marks the culmination of a series, as in the seventh seal (8:1), the seventh trumpet (11:15), and the seventh bowl (16:17). It is difficult to identify a single symbolic meaning for the numerous usages of seven, but perhaps "completeness" comes closest. (*See also* TWELVE.)

P.L.G.

### SEVENTH-DAY ADVENTISTS. *See* ADVENTIST CHURCHES.

### SEVEN VIRTUES. According to Roman Catholic moral theology, the four CARDINAL VIRTUES: prudence, justice, fortitude, and temperance, plus the three THEOLOGICAL VIRTUES or supernatural gifts: faith, hope, and charity (that is, love). The concept of virtue means the perfection of something, a state, condition, or habitual mode of thinking and action. A virtue is a lasting disposition of the soul, aiming its powers toward good. As opposed to vice, a virtue is a good habit—not an action—for it is the intention and tendency of one's thoughts and habits that are virtuous or not virtuous. There are intellectual virtues or perfections of the mind, including wisdom,

understanding, and knowledge, along with prudence and artfulness in action. However, the four cardinal virtues are the basis for all righteous action and for the practice of religion. These moral virtues relate to our duties as people and only indirectly to God. They are infused in the soul just as the three theological virtues are, that is, they are supernatural gifts that perfect our natural powers, and do not arise out of human habits and the repetition of good acts. They are infused, given directly by God. The infused theological virtues enable people to attain their final aim, to become one with God, and members of God's kingdom.

J.C.

### SEVEN WORKS OF MERCY. Traditionally, in the Roman Catholic church, the good works to which Christians, and particularly the religious and priests, should devote themselves. These include the conversion of sinners, the instruction of the ignorant, the counseling of the wavering and doubting, the comfort of the sorrowful, bearing ills patiently, forgiving wrongs, and praying for the living and the dead. The seven works of mercy are also known as the spiritual works of mercy.

J.C.

### SEX. A biological phenomenon, an adaptation of the physical structures of living beings to enable and enhance the reproduction of the species and thus the continuation of life itself. What began as a biological development and fundamentally natural activity has become, in every age and culture, a generating point for customs, traditions, moral codes, religious beliefs, and the great themes of literature, drama, music, and art.

Sex among the peoples of the Bible, which reports human experiences from about 1800 B.C. to A.D. 150, as among all peoples everywhere in all ages, was more than the relief of physical tension, engagement in pleasure, or even the creation of new life. Rather sex and its expression became the framework for the organization of social life and a mainstay of moral codes.

It is natural and reasonable to expect that such a deep human drive, and biological necessity, should form a major component of religious concern, thought, law, and symbolism. When we consider the wide area of religious activity in the world and point out the sexual elements in religious life everywhere, the expectation is more than met. Religions have honored sex, denigrated sex, encouraged sex, forbade sex, regulated sex, even worshiped the Divine through sex. From the polygamy of the Hebrew patriarchs and the early Mormons to the strict monogamy of the early Christian church to the sacred prostitution of Baal worship in Canaan that infiltrated Hebrew worship itself, sex is a paramount theme in religion, the Bible, and theology. This article will consider sex in three parts: in religion generally, in the Bible (first in the OT, then in the NT), and in Christian theology, as it has historically developed. In the case of the Bible and theology, the negative influence of the prophetic reaction against the lure of Baalism in ancient Israel must be especially noted.

*Sex in Religion: Ancient.* Much of early religion developed as an explanation of natural phenomena (why do some things happen?) and elaborated rituals to influence or control the necessary conditions for life. This is called etiology and is illustrated in the story of the Fall (Gen. 3), when the pain of childbirth and feminine sexual attraction to the male are explained as the result of sin. Ancient people entertained a belief in life after death and in the essential "livingness" of all that is—fields, stones, hills, trees. This ANIMISM or spiritism explains why trees were prayed to, why food and weapons were placed in the grave with the dead, and why sexual intercourse was often practiced in fields soon after planting. Such a practice illustrates "sympathetc magic," that is, it aims to encourage the spirits or gods also to have intercourse and so make the fields fertile. These beliefs and practices seem to have been spread worldwide, and such beliefs played a strong role in Israelite history after the invasion of Canaan in the thirteenth century B.C.

Sex, in animism, was identified clearly with life—the power of life itself. It was, therefore, closely monitored. Taboos against intercourse at various times, for example, before battle, during a woman's menstrual period, or at holy seasons, developed. This belief system, for example, that sexual intercourse before a sports competition is ill-advised, still exists in developed countries today.

Because sex was identified so closely with the power of life, the sexual organs were often objects of veneration, if not outright worship. While the representation of the male phallus (penis) figures in ancient (as well as modern) Hindu rituals, the female breasts and vulva play an even larger role. Throughout Europe and the Middle East many examples of female sex worship (or "the Mother Goddess") are found. These take their name from an early discovery in Germany, "the Venus of Wilhelmsdorf." "Venus" is a crude, almost round lump with exaggerated large breasts and buttocks and a clearly defined vulva. There is no neck, head, arms, or legs, just a torso.

But sex seen as so powerful caused opposite reactions as well. CELIBACY, the restraint of the sexual impulse, also played a role in ancient religion (and still is practiced today). Here the retention of strength was the dominating idea. The identification of spiritual power and wisdom with celibacy, and its association with the priest, may stem from this idea.

Much has been written recently about possible matriarchal (mother dominated) societies in ancient times. Some tribal peoples in the past had some such system, which explains the Amazon myth among the Greeks. However, the widespread worship of "the Mother Goddess" (Venus), which probably forms the background of most Mesopotamian religion, and that of the Canaanites, was found along with patriarchal (father dominated) societies. The real interest of Jew and Christian in the sexual elements of ancient religion lies precisely here, in the religious matrix of the Mesopotamian and Canaanite areas, into which the people of the Exodus came, bearing Yahweh worship and Yahweh's Sinaitic covenant. The bald facts are that the Canaanites worshiped the Mother Goddess, engaged in sexual practices in their religion (including sacred "prostitution," which was actually priestly, not profane, work), and the Canaanites were a patriarchal society.

*Sex in the Bible: Old Testament.* The Hebrews who appear in history symbolized by Abraham (probably the eighteenth century B.C.) wandered in Canaan for generations, then at least some of them entered Egypt. Perhaps some Hebrews (or "river crossers," that is, nomads) regularly wandered from Canaan and the Sinai into Egypt. These nomads were patriarchal (male dominated) and polygamous (one man, many wives) and also held lesser wives or concubines. Many stories illustrating all these practices are found in Genesis and throughout the Pentateuch as well as in Judges and in the historical books, I and II Samuel and I and II Kings. Since they were nomads, the earliest (or proto-) Hebrews seemed immune from Canaanite sex (BAAL) worship. The story of Joseph, tempted by the Egyptian's wife, shows the high moral standards (with a polygamous world view) that characterize not only the Hebrews but the nomadic peoples of the Middle East in general.

After the Exodus (probably thirteenth century B.C.) and the Sinai wandering, the Hebrews probably joined the (first in Sinai, later in Canaan) other clans and tribes of "Hebrews" and began a long struggle of attrition against the Canaanite (and Philistine) city-states already in place in the area. This was a difficult struggle as the Canaanites were far more technologically advanced. For centuries (the period of the Judges) the Hebrews occupied the rough hilly sections and were kept out of the fertile valleys and the Canaanite cities that guarded them. As long as this was the case the Hebrews retained a comparatively pure worship of Yahweh. But, over time, they acquired bronze, and then iron weapons and great war chiefs, and conquered Canaanite and Philistine cities. Settling into an urban life-style (under Saul and David), the Hebrews culturally assimilated the Canaanite agriculture, architecture, literature, technology, and many religious practices. Here Baal and the ASHTORETH—the golden bulls and sacred poles that represented fertility—entered Hebrew religion in force. The stories of Solomon building Temples to foreign gods in Jerusalem, to satisfy his many foreign-born wives, illustrate this development. Later, after the breakup of Solomon's kingdom on his death in 931 B.C., the prophet Hosea, writing in the northern kingdom, Israel, portrayed sacred PROSTITUTION as part of the temple worship in Samaria. All the prophets in Judah as well identify the Hebrews (and later, the Jews, in the remaining southern kingdom) as adulterous, meaning idolatrous, as they forsook Yahweh, Israel's true husband, for the Baals.

It was this experience of the dilution of Yahweh worship with Baalism and its pansexuality, under Canaanite cultural influences, that led to the most negative attitudes toward sex and sexuality, and toward women and feminine sexuality in particular, among the Jews (that is, those Hebrews who survived the defeat of the nation and exile in 586 B.C.). This negative reaction to Baalism also is read back into the patriarchal stories and the law codes included in the Pentateuch as the Pentateuch and the historical books were reworked and brought into their present state during and after the Babylonian exile (ended in 538 B.C.).

With this in mind, we may examine examples of sexuality and regulations on sexual conduct in the OT.

*Marriage.* The patriarchs were polygamous, and indeed, polygamy was not banned among Jews until A.D. 1030, by Rabbi Gershom ben Judah. Christians who adopted the monogamy of the Greeks and Romans in the first century A.D. thereby signalized their break with Judaism. Marriages were arranged by parents and generally were businesslike affairs. However, love could be present as in Jacob and Rachel's match (Gen. 29:1-35).

*Concubines.* Although a man could have as many wives as he could support (later the Talmud, and still later, the Qur'an, limited this to four wives), he could also have lesser wives or CONCUBINES. Concubines were not prostitutes but members of the FAMILY circle.

*Prostitution.* Commercial prostitution was practiced by non-Israelites in the cities and towns of Canaan and throughout the Middle East. Prostitutes served the nomadic foreigners who traveled from place to place. In earlier times, they were not without some recognized social standing (Deut. 23:17-18).

*Sex Outside of Marriage.* FORNICATION was not looked upon as negatively as ADULTERY. The major restriction on such activity was that it could render a young woman unmarriageable. If the man married the woman, all was well. If not, a fine would be levied by the courts (Exod. 22:16-17).

*Masturbation.* This was considered an unnatural act, since the life force—here the semen—was wasted. Perhaps this was condemned so harshly because of its possible connection with Baal worship or with homosexuality.

*Homosexuality* (Male). This was condemned because it apparently was connected with Baal worship. Guilds of male cult prostitutes (called "dogs" by the OT writers) were known at cult shrines, perhaps including Samaria and Jerusalem. Once again, this practice was seen as wasting the life force and was unholy as well as unnatural. There is no factual basis for the recent claim that the OT condemned HOMOSEXUALITY because it was connected with degrading prisoners taken in war. Rape of women was usual in war.

(Female). Female homosexuality seems unknown in the OT. It is not condemned. This probably is the case because of the situation of many wives in a harem as well as because the practice involved no loss of the life force (semen) and contained no danger of illegitimate offspring to threaten the family line.

*Divorce.* This was allowed by ancient Hebrew law (Deut. 24:1-4), but it is mentioned only in the sermon attributed to Moses in Deuteronomy (a later document); it is not specifically mentioned in the Covenant Code, Exodus 21–23. The Hebrews did practice DIVORCE, which was initiated by the husband, not the wife. The wife had no power to refuse the divorce once the husband wrote out a letter of dismissal and gave it to her (Deut. 24:3-4), and the husband could not take her back if she remarried. (Consequently, remarriage after divorce was allowed for both men and women by the ancient Hebrews.) Isaiah 50:1 and Jeremiah 3:8 both mention decrees or bills of divorce.

*Bestiality.* Sexual contact with animals was severely condemned as unnatural, a waste of the life force and an affront to human dignity, which represents the image of God (Exod. 22:19; Deut. 27:21).

*Adultery.* This was condemned specifically in the Decalogue at Sinai (Exod. 20:14). The integrity of the family was jeopardized by such conduct. A man could not be sure that his son was really his son if his wife was unfaithful. Economic and social conditions within a patriarchal society dictated this rigidly enforced law. Adultery breaks up the family, not just the marriage.

*Incest.* Sex between parents and children, among siblings, and among close relatives was not unknown (Gen. 19:30-38). Indeed, Lot is said to have had intercourse with his daughters, although this may reflect an earlier Middle Eastern story taken over by the Hebrews (Deut. 22:30). Incest was condemned.

*Levirate Marriage.* Because of the strong patriarchal stress on family and the veneration of ancestors (the patriarchs), a cult of the dead arose. If a man died without sons, the OT law held that his brother must take the dead brother's wife and beget sons, who would be counted as the sons of the dead brother (Deut. 25:5-10; compare Num. 27:1-11). They could then venerate their "father" on the appropriate anniversaries and holy days. The prophets later criticized ancestor veneration, which was common to the Orient and best known in China and Japan.

*Sex in the Bible: New Testament.* Since the NT's earliest writings date from shortly before A.D. 50 (Paul's earliest letters) and originated in the cosmopolitan Roman Empire, and later writings (for example, Luke-Acts, as well as all of Paul's letters and the other letters attributed to Paul) also consciously were produced with audiences in Greece, Asia Minor, and even Italy (Romans) in mind, it is natural that the NT attitude toward sex reflects the most moral attitudes of Greco-Roman society.

Like the OT, the NT considers sex good. It is not denigrated, although its expression is regulated. Through Paul, as well as Jesus, many of the Jewish attitudes and background beliefs (for example, the sacred quality of semen, in the prohibitions against anything but male-female contact within marriage were preserved. However, two developments, neither foreign to Judaism in Judea in the first century A.D.., are explicitly brought out in the NT: monogamy (I Tim. 3:2, 12; Tit. 1:6) and the beginnings of celibacy (I Cor. 7). In both of these developments, Paul—and his disciples who probably wrote the Pastoral Letters in his name—led the way. In one other area, the NT also departs from the OT, in the matter of divorce. According to a probably genuine Jesus tradition Jesus forbade divorce. Of course, other evangelists softened this prohibition, adding "except for adultery" (Matt. 5:31-32; 19:8-9; Luke 16:18; compare Mark 10:2, 4).

Paul was inclined toward celibacy, which is demonstrated in several clear passages (I Cor. 7:1, 6-9, 25-40). Of course, the reason for this teaching (which he was willing to relax for those not able to bear it—I Cor. 7:8-9, 36-38) was Paul's earlier belief in the imminent return of the Lord to judge the earth. Since the last days were upon the Christians, it was better to concentrate all one's energies on evangelism and prayer rather than on starting a family. There are strong indications that Paul later modified his eschatology, and it is certain that his disciples did, and also the subapostolic church, during the period the NT was being written. Paul's disciples, in the Pastoral Letters, clearly state the early church's monogamous tradition: A bishop must be "the husband of one wife" (Tit. 1:6). In later centuries, under the influence of Stoic and Neoplatonic ideas that stressed asceticism, celibacy would become more and more recommended for the higher clergy. However, clerical celibacy for all was not the rule in the early and even medieval church, as the Greek Orthodox custom of allowing a man to marry as long as he gives up all hope of becoming a bishop (who must be celibate) shows.

*Christian Theological Developments.* No discussion of the NT's attitude toward sex would be complete without mention of the VIRGIN BIRTH narratives in Matthew and Luke and the resulting stress on the virginity of Mary. It must be borne in mind that Mark begins with Jesus' baptism, John begins with the Logos hymn followed by Jesus' baptism by John the Baptizer, and Paul nowhere shows any knowledge of the virgin birth story.

The virgin birth account (Luke 1:26-38; Matt. 1:18-25) undoubtedly reflects an influence from the larger Greco-Roman world. Although much of the birth narrative is grounded (as is the Passion narrative) in a creative weaving together of OT passages, virgin births play no part in Hebrew religion. The passage in Isaiah 7:14 KJV, "Behold a virgin shall conceive . . ." (see Luke 1:27), has been conclusively shown to be mistranslated by the Septuagint (LXX) translators in the second century B.C. The Hebrew word *almah,* translated as *parthenos* in the LXX and in the NT, actually means "young woman," not "virgin." *Almah* is even used to refer to young women who were prostitutes, so nothing pertaining to sexual status other than being a young female is implied in the word. The NT narrative rests, at least here, on a mistranslation.

The concept of virgin birth, however, stems from the Egyptian and Middle Eastern tendency to divinize rulers and heroes. Legends arose, for example, that Alexander the Great was born of a virgin. Of course, after receiving divine honors upon his conquest of Egypt, Alexander considered himself a god. Something of the same corruption by popular religion in Asia Minor, Egypt, and the Middle East later affected the Roman emperors. In all events, the virgin birth doctrine spread in Christianity under the influence of Neoplatonism, a form of idealism that depreciated the material world, including the body. The same influence encouraged ASCETICISM, which was strong in Egypt by the late third century, as well as celibacy. The councils of the church that drew up the orthodox creeds had to combat this influence (which was a large part of the Gnostic movement) and undergird the real humanity of Jesus, so that his "perfect manhood" would not be swallowed up in his divinity. Interestingly, most of the great heresies attacked by the Nicene Creed were those that denied the full humanity of Jesus, not (as Fundamentalism implies) attacks on Jesus' divinity. The stress on the virgin birth, as well as the influence of Neoplatonism and the rise of Gnostic systems (as in Arianism), made such heresies probably inevitable.

The growing cult of the BLESSED VIRGIN MARY resulted in her confirmation as "Theotokos," the "God-bearer" or "the Mother of God" by the orthodox ecumenical councils. Over time, Mary became more and more prominent in the personal piety of the people, especially among women. In particular, after Christianity became a favored—and later the official—religion in the Roman Empire, devotion to Mary spread as the church crowded out the pagan shrines devoted to Isis or other Greek or Roman representations of the Mother Goddess ("the Earth Mother" or Venus). In this way, the FEMININE element that was ruthlessly criticized by the prophets and suppressed by the reforms of Ezra and the priests of the Second Temple (after the Exile and return, 538 B.C.) came back, in purified form, into popular Christianity. During the medieval period devotion to Mary spread and became more and more institutionalized. The Protestant Reformers removed all Mariolatry from the evangelical churches while affirming the ecumenical creeds with their emphasis on the virgin birth and on Mary as "Theotokos."

In the twentieth century, the Roman Catholic church has both formally declared certain doctrines long held in popular piety to be the teachings of the church as well as, later, undergoing the thorough reformation of Vatican Council II (1962–65). It has, however, on a more conservative note, continued its theological objections to artificial birth control and to most abortions, as well as to homosexuality, despite more liberal developments among most mainline Protestants. The Neo-Fundamentalist movement of the past decade has stressed male dominant, anti-abortion positions in reaction to the major Protestant churches, mirroring the Catholic position.

J.C.

**SHADDAI.** A divine term meaning "the mountain one" (assuming its derivation from the Akkadian word *shadū* ["mountain"]). It was linked with *'ēl*, the dominant name for "god" in Semitic, to form *'ēl shadday*. Ordinarily this compound is translated "God Almighty" in deference to an early rabbinic etymology ("self-sufficient").

The Priestly account of the call of Moses claims that in patriarchal times the Deity was known as "God Almighty" (Exod. 6:3). This name appears in Genesis 17:1; 28:3; 35:11; 43:14; and 48:3, where it is associated with the covenant that the Deity establishes with Abraham's line. In Jacob's testament (Gen. 49:25) and Balaam's oracles (Num. 24:4, 16) it is situated in early poetic tradition. In Numbers 1:6, 12, within an ancient name list, the "Shaddai" element surfaces in the personal names Zurishaddai and Ammishaddai. "Shaddai" may locate the patriarchal EL in mountainous territory or associate El's self-revelation with the mountain storm (congenial with Yahweh's stormy theophany on Sinai; Exod. 19). Accordingly, Shaddai resembles Hadad, the Amorite storm god.

In later usage, "Shaddai" and "Yahweh" were sometimes synonymous (Ruth 1:20-21; Pss. 68:14; 91;1; Ezek. 1:24; 10:5). For Job, however, this name so highlighted divine omnipotence that it transcended uniquely Israelite connotations. It appears thirty-one times in Job. With one exception (II Cor. 6:18), its Greek counterpart, PANTOKRATOR, is limited to the book of Revelation (for example, 1:8; 11:17; 21:22).                      J.K.K.

**SHADRACH, MESHACH, ABEDNEGO.** Daniel's three companions whose Babylonian names always occur together (Dan. 1:7; 2:49; 3:12-30).

The names conferred on these youths by Nebuchadnezzar's chief eunuch replaced their Hebrew names (Hananiah, Mishael, Azariah) compounded with *-el* ("God") and *-iah* ("Yahweh"). Jews in foreign service were customarily assigned foreign names. These new names presumably distort those of Babylonian gods. Perhaps in "Shadrach" and "Meshach" a fractured form of the name "Marduk" (Babylon's patron deity) is concealed. "Abednego" is a corruption of "Abdi-nabu," meaning "servant of Nabu" (Babylonian wisdom deity).

The story of DANIEL's companions deservedly stands within a larger narrative collection (Dan. 1–6)

designed to buttress the faith of Palestinian Jews suffering under Seleucid oppression around 165 B.C. Their courageous fidelity to Jewish tradition is exemplary. As "youths without blemish, handsome and skilful in all wisdom . . . and competent to serve in the king's palace" (1:4), they and Daniel abstain from eating the king's food, which fails to meet Jewish dietary regulations. Yet after a ten-day fare of vegetables and water, they appear healthier than Nebuchadnezzar's other trainees (1:15). And their divinely given wisdom eclipses that of Babylon's court magicians (1:20).

Without mention of Daniel, chapter 3 reports that the youths would rather be thrust into a furnace than worship the king's golden image. Their reply to Nebuchadnezzar demonstrates that they rate religious integrity above concern for personal safety (3:17-18). Astonished that the divinely protected youths are completely spared from the fire, the king commands their release, legitimizes their religion, and rewards them with regal advancement (3:26-30).

J.K.K.

**al–SHAFI'I** (767–820). The first great systematizer of Islamic law and founder of one of its four major schools. Though born at Gaza in Palestine, he was a member of the clan to which MUHAMMAD belonged, and his mother took him to Mecca to be educated. After finishing the mosque school there he lived with a Bedouin tribe and learned a pure form of Arabic that distinguished all his speaking and writing.

Since Islam is a comprehensive system, touching on all aspects of life, law is also comprehensive. Al-Shafi'i carefully studied the two schools of law already existing and tried to go beyond them and provide a truly scientific approach to law.

He taught that there are four sources of Islamic law. The most important is the QUR'AN, the words of God. Next is the practice of Muhammed, as preserved in the HADITH (traditions). Since not all questions can be answered from these two sources, he also recognized the importance of laws agreed on by the consensus of the Muslim community as expressed by the jurists. And finally, he affirmed the validity of reasoning by analogy to existing laws. He believed that in this way a scholar could reach conclusions that avoided the errors that result from relying only on individual opinions.

In A.D. 815 (year 199 of the Muslim era) al-Shafi'i moved to Egypt. Many hailed him as the restorer of Islam, whom God had promised to send at the beginning of each new century.          K.C.

**SHAKERS.** The United Society of Believers in Christ's Second Coming, or the Millennial church, traces its lineage back to the French Camisards who proclaimed illumination of the Holy Spirit and a return to NT simplicity. Their beliefs were taken up by the Shaking QUAKERS, whose leaders James and Jane Wardley were instrumental in the conversion of

Courtesy of the American Antiquarian Society

*Shaker mode of worship*

Ann Lee Stanley. Persecuted and imprisoned for her beliefs, "Mother" Ann and at least seven followers emigrated to America in 1774. In New York City she and her husband encountered marital problems and separated. She had borne him four children, but they all died in infancy.

The Shakers regrouped in 1776 near Albany and organized a Christian socialistic community. In 1779 they were joined by a group of New Light Baptists. They grew rapidly with converts from the Second GREAT AWAKENING, particularly CANE RIDGE, and by 1830 numbered more than six thousand in nineteen settlements in eight states.

They were intensely biblical, millennial, revivalistic; universalists, perfectionists, and spiritualists. They regarded Ann Lee as a female incarnation of Jesus. Their worship featured personal testimony, group dancing, and speaking in tongues (GLOSSOLALIA). A period of enthusiasm (1837–45) included séances and visions. Their celibate and segregated communities were models of male-female equality and functional efficiency which is evident in their highly prized furniture. They are credited with the invention of the buzz saw and nail cutter (both invented by women), the screw, propeller, rotary harrow, clothes pins, apple parer, and the threshing machine.                                                    N.H.

**SHALMANESER.** The name of five kings of the Assyrian Empire.

The objective of this empire's southward expansion was Egypt. The small kingdoms of Syria-Palestine, among them Israel and Judah, had first to be brought under submission. ASSYRIA deserved its reputation for savage and brutal warfare, yet it developed an imperial administration that more closely interrelated its world and was a model for the subsequent empires of Persia, Greece, and Rome.

(1) Shalmaneser I (1274–1245 B.C.), son of Adad-nirari I, began Assyria's rise to power. He founded and fortified Kalah.

(2) Shalmaneser II (1031–1020 B.C.) was not an active imperialist.

(3) Shalmaneser III (858–824 B.C.), son of Ashurnasirpal II, was the first Assyrian king to make direct contact with Israel. From his first year, he began what turned out to be three decades of almost yearly Assyrian campaigns in Syria-Palestine.

In 853 B.C. at Qarqar, Shalmaneser's army was confronted by a confederated army put together by kings of territories from Cilicia to Ammon. Shalmaneser recorded that the opposing army numbered 63,000 men, and that Ahab had supplied 10,000 foot soldiers and 2,000 chariots. Shalmaneser claimed the victory, but he withdrew from the area and did not

Courtesy of the Oriental Institute, University of Chicago

*A cast of the Black Obelisk of Shalmaneser III of Assyria; in the second panel from the top, Shalmaneser receives tribute of "Jehu, son of Omri," king of Israel, who is on his hands and knees, his face to the ground. The original of the Black Obelisk is in the British Museum.*

*A relief of Ashurnasirpal II (father of Shalmaneser III) killing lions.*

*Upper part of bas-relief on bronze band shows the war chariots of Shalmaneser III. Lower bas-relief depicts the storming of the town of Hazor.*

come again for eight years. In 845 B.C. Shalmaneser returned with an immense army of 115,000 men; they defeated the king of Damascus at Mount Hermon.

In 841 B.C., the kings of Tyre and Sidon along with Jehu, the king of Israel, brought heavy tribute to Shalmaneser, the first of such payments made by the kings of Israel and Judah. This event is reported on Shalmaneser's Black Obelisk (in the British Museum), where Jehu is pictured groveling abjectly before Shalmaneser.

From 839 B.C. to 828 B.C., Shalmaneser was campaigning in northwest Syria. In 835 B.C., he waged a punitive raid on Damascus. He left his name and figure carved on a cliff beside Dog River, north of Beirut, Lebanon, and a record of his military exploits on the Balawat Gates (now in the British Museum).

(4) Shalmaneser IV (783–774 B.C.), son of Adad-nirari III. Throughout his reign, he was concerned with domestic affairs and defense against attack from nearer enemies. This was the Golden Era

for Israel under Jeroboam II (786–746 B.C.) and for Judah under Uzziah (783–742 B.C.).

(5) Shalmaneser V (726–722 B.C.), son of TIGLATH-PILESER III, who, by the time of his conquest of Damascus in 732 B.C., had either defeated or received surrender from nearly all of the Syria-Palestine kingdoms. He had taken Gilead and much of Galilee and had exiled their people and put Hoshea on the throne of Israel as an Assyrian appointee. When Tiglath-pileser III died, Hoshea, with Egypt's backing, rebelled. Shalmaneser responded at once. In 725 B.C., he captured Shechem. The next year, he surrounded Samaria and took Hoshea prisoner. Samaria held out more than two years under siege. (Tyre's siege, at the same time, lasted five years.) Shalmaneser's records show that after he had destroyed the city in 722 B.C, he deported 27,290 people from Samaria and resettled them in such places as Gozan, Harran, Media, Halah, and Nineveh (II Kings 17:6). Whether Shalmaneser V died in battle or was murdered is not clear. His successor, Sargon II, claimed the victory over Samaria (see II Kings 17:1-6, 24).                     P.L.G.

**SHALOM.** Popularly translated from the Hebrew as "peace" and used in greeting or taking leave of someone. "Shalom," however, has little in common with its English equivalent. Shalom does not mean merely the absence of strife. It connotes totality, health, wholesomeness, harmony, success, and the completeness and richness of living in a wholesome social environment. When persons meet or part, they wish each other "shalom," or they inquire about each other's shalom. The ideal of peace is considered so important in Jewish tradition that the sages of old took Shalom to be one of the names of the Lord.

L.K.

**SHAMANISM.** This term, derived through Russian from the Siberian Tungusic language, refers to a distinctive class of religious specialists, shamans, and their practices. Interpreted somewhat broadly, shamanism can be found among preliterate peoples in a wide variety of places. Its practitioners include not only Siberians, but also Native Americans, Eskimos, Native Australians, and tribalists of South and Southeast Asia. Shamanism survives in the popular religion of China, Korea, and Japan, where female shamans are most typical.

Shamanism is not itself a religion, but a pattern of roles and practices that can exist within the context of ANIMISM's belief in many spirits, both natural and ancestral, and usually belief also in a sacred cosmology with other realms where spirits and gods dwell and to which souls may depart. In this world the shaman emerges as a "man of power," able to control spirits and travel to the other spheres.

The most distinctive feature of shamanism is the specialist's call and initiation. Although sometimes shamanism is hereditary or learned through apprenticeship, characteristically the candidate is a young person of unstable or epileptic traits, who "hears voices" and seems beset by spirits. The person undergoes, either alone or with the help of a senior shaman, a strenuous initiation including isolation, visions, and mystical death and restructuring of mind and body. Through this process the person gains control of the spirits, being able now to use them as assistants in healing and marvelous flight.

Courtesy of the Department of Library Services, American Museum of Natural History

*A Northwest American Coast Indian shaman's wooden mask*

Illness is commonly interpreted in shamanistic cultures as caused either by infestation of foreign evil or by separation of the sick person's soul from the body. In the first case the shaman may send his (or her) spirit aide into the body to identify the alien entity, then expel it by magical means. In the second the shaman may, entranced, journey far in search of the lost soul, then bring it back with great fanfare. For these scenarios the shaman typically wears elaborate garb, often ornamented with bells, mirrors, and feathers. The shaman employs a drum, and the performance may include such seemingly miraculous phenomena as spirit voices and the extraction of a visible noxious substance from the sick person's body. While on one level the performance may partly depend on ventriloquism and sleight of hand, undoubtedly it enables many patients to interpret the disease in a way congruent with their world view, to become assured a therapeutic process is underway, and to open themselves to healing energies. Shamans also serve as psychopomps, or guides of departed souls.

Shamanism has very ancient roots in human culture. Some authorities believe that the shamanistic experience played a major part in the emergence of human religion, and that much of human culture, including song, poetry, and art, has ultimate roots in the entranced utterances and the accoutrements of the shaman. Conversely, a residue of the shamanistic paradigm of call, initiation, healing power, and magical journeying can be seen in the myths and sacred biographies of later cultures. (*Compare* WITCHCRAFT.)                                                    R.E.

**SHAMGAR.** A non-Israelite who, before 1125 B.C., by a single exploit, delivered Israel from an enemy, killing six hundred of them with an "ox goad," a long pole tipped with metal (Judg. 3:31). The enemy was somewhat like the Philistines but did not likely have that name. Shamgar, a Hurrian name, is called Son of Anath, that is, from Beth-anath, a fortified Canaanite town in Galilee (Josh. 19:38; Judg. 1:33). The effect of Shamgar's heroism was to clear the roads temporarily of bandits and to make them safe for travelers and caravans (Judg. 5:6). Shamgar's story is comparable to Samson's (Judg. 15:14-16). His name is similar to Shammah, one of David's "mighty men" who also "slew the Philistines" (II Sam. 23:11-12). Shamgar is not said to have served Israel as a judge.
                                                                    P.L.G.

**SHAMMAI.** (1) In I Chronicles 2:28, 32, a descendant of Jerahmeel. His father was Onam and his sons were Nadab and Abishur. His brother was Jada. (2) First Chronicles 2:44-45 lists a Shammai as a descendant of Caleb. His father was Rekem and his son was Maon. (3) A descendant of Caleb, the son of Jephunneh the Kenizzite (I Chr. 4:17; Num. 32:12). His father was Mered and his mother was "Bithiah, the daughter of Pharaoh."

All these men appear to have non-Israelite ancestry. In sound, the name is similar to other Hebrew names, but Shammai does not appear to have been given to any man of Judah or of Israel.

P.L.G.

**SHAPHAN.** The name of two OT figures. (1) The secretary and financial officer to JOSIAH. Shaphan received from Hilkiah the newfound "book of the law" (substantially the book of Deuteronomy), which had been discovered during the reconstruction of the Temple, and delivered it to King Josiah (II Kings 22:3-13; II Chr. 34:8-20). Friends and supporters of Josiah's reforms, Shaphan and his sons Ahikam, Elasah, and Gemariah, also supported Jeremiah (Jer. 26:24; 29:3; 36:10-12; 39:14; 40:5).

(2) Father of Jaazaniah (Ezek. 8:11).     W. G.

**SHARIA.** The path of true religion that a MUSLIM is to follow. Although *sharia* is sometimes translated as law, it includes all the aspects of the proper way of life, morality as well as law. As revealed truth it has been contrasted to theological speculation or human endeavor. More recently it has been used to designate the traditional Muslim law, in contrast to the modern civil law.

*Sharia* includes law in the narrow sense (*fiqh*), moral and religious regulations, mystical thought, and personal piety. Some actions are neither prohibited nor required but are classified as worthy of praise or as deserving God's disfavor. From early times the *sharia* has been interpreted and enforced by an organized judiciary system. Various schools developed that differ from one another in interpretation and strictness of enforcement. Shi'ite law differs considerably from Sunnite law, largely because of the role of the imams, who, according to Shi'ite belief, are divinely inspired and thus able to speak for God, the great Lawgiver. Specific areas of legislation include penal law, laws governing commercial transactions, family law, the law of succession and inheritance, and matters of procedure and the taking of evidence.

Under the impact of modernization and urbanization many changes have been introduced into the laws of Muslim countries. The status of women has been a particular concern of the modernizers. But in rural areas and in countries such as the Islamic Republic of Iran, where traditional values are emphasized, the old principles are enjoying new popularity.     K.C.

**SHARON.** The "level place" or "plain" in the central coastal area of Palestine stretching from Joppa north to south of Mount Carmel, about fifty miles long and from eight to ten miles wide. It was well watered with three perennial and two seasonal streams. With marshes, sand dunes, and no natural ports, in OT times the area was relatively undeveloped. The one known settlement was north of Joppa, Tell Qasile, founded about 1200 B.C. In the east, toward the hill country, there once were forests of oaks. When weather conditions were favorable, sheep herding and farming were possible. This gave Sharon a reputation for fertility (Isa. 65:10, "pasture for flocks"). "The Way of the Sea," a part of the international trade route leading from Mesopotamia through Damascus, entered Sharon by way of Megiddo and ran southward by Joppa and Gaza, ultimately to Egypt.

Generally speaking, Sharon was thought of in the OT as a forbidding, rather than an inviting area: "Sharon is like a desert" (Isa. 33:9), a "rose of Sharon," a crocus (Song of S. 2:1). Sharon was not a center of strength in OT times. Several events that are significant in Christian history took place in Sharon, however, and are connected with Joppa and, especially, Caesarea Maritima.     P.L.G.

**SHAVUOT.** Hebrew name of the Feast of Weeks, one of the three Jewish pilgrimage festivals. It is also known as PENTECOST, since it takes place on the fiftieth day after the completion of the counting of the *omer* (sheaf of new barley), which begins on the second day of PASSOVER. The festival is also called the Festival of the Firstfruits because of the wheat, which is harvested after the barley. Shavuot is also commemorated as the time that God gave the Ten Commandments on Mount Sinai, and the holy day thus has another name—the Season of the Giving of Our Torah. The book of Ruth, relating Ruth's acceptance of the Jewish faith, is read in the synagogue. Confirmation and consecration services are generally held on this festival.     L.K.

**SHEBA, QUEEN OF.** A ruler of a kingdom located in southwest Arabia that is known biblically as Sheba but is otherwise known as Saba, its citizens being the SABEANS. The kingdom lay in the territory of modern Yemen.

The accounts in I Kings 10:1-13 and II Chronicles 9:1-12 of the lady's twelve-hundred-mile desert trek to visit the rich and proverbially wise King SOLOMON has given this unnamed monarch universal fame. The queen's kingdom was situated geographically to become wealthy through trade in Arabian products, especially the lucrative incense business, exchange goods imported from Asia and Africa, and perhaps slaves.

Archaeological investigation has been made of this area. The notable queen has not yet been attested, but available evidence corroborates the biblical account. The gifts that the queen brought to Solomon are things that could have come from Saba, products of the Red Sea commerce, gold, precious stones, "algum" wood and spices, as well as incense and perfume.

What prompted the queen of Sheba to make the arduous journey to Jerusalem and return? Recent interpreters have stressed economics as the motive. She did what her neighboring kingdoms in South Arabia had not yet undertaken, that is, to establish a trade agreement for an exchange of goods with

Solomon, first by means of the recently domesticated camel and later by the fleet of ships Solomon and Hiram developed (I Kings 10:22; II Chr. 9:21).

The I Kings 10:1-10, 15 account, exactly copied in II Chronicles 9:1-9, 12, reports that after she had observed and admired Solomon's "affairs" and "wisdom," and also his answers to her questions, she said, "the half was not told me" (I Kings 10:6-7). "When the queen of Sheba had seen all . . . there was no more spirit in her" (I Kings 10:4-5); that is, it took her breath away. The Hebrew phrase translated "she came to Solomon" is translated in Genesis 19:34 "go in and lie with him," that is, for purposes of sexual relations. Another expression, Solomon gave the queen of Sheba "all that she desired" or "whatever she asked" (v. 13) has been taken to mean the same thing. Arabic legends give considerable detail along these lines. It is known that the Sabeans had colonies in Ethiopia and that the Abyssinians' royal line claims to have originated from relations between Solomon and the queen of Sheba.                                   P.L.G.

**SHECHEM.** An old Canaanite city near Mount Gerizim that became a significant regional, Israelite religious and political center. Currently it is thought that the name, meaning "shoulder," relates to the city's location, near both Mount Ebal and Mount Gerizim (Deut. 27–28). The name was previously associated with a certain man named Shechem, identified as the son of Hamor (Gen. 33:18-19).

The name Shechem appears in Egyptian texts as early as the nineteenth century B.C. "Sychar" in John 4:5 is thought to be a later name for the OT Shechem. Excavations have identified Shechem with Tell Balatah, about 1½ miles east of the pass between Mounts Gerizim and Ebal and near "Jacob's well" which is east of the tell.

Shechem, according to excavators, was occupied from about 4000 B.C. and reached the height of its prosperity in the patriarchal age. It declined in the times of the Hebrew conquest but was rebuilt in the Hellenistic era and was occupied from then until about 100 B.C. Abundantly supplied with water and located in a fertile plain, where major north-south and east-west highways met, at times Shechem was a wealthy and powerful city, walled and conquerable only through ambush (Judg. 9:34-35). Abraham (Gen. 12:6-7) and Jacob (Gen. 33:18-20) were at Shechem. Dinah was raped there (Gen. 34:1-24). Joseph visited his brothers there (Gen. 37:12-24), and later his bones were buried there (Josh. 24:32). Shechem flourished throughout the history of the northern kingdom but suffered under the Assyrians (724–722 B.C.) From about 325 to 107 B.C., the Samaritan period, Shechem regained its status as a city related to the Samaritan temple, which was built on Mount Gerizim. Shechem suffered its death blow under John Hyrcannus in 107 B.C.

The numerous sanctuaries and temples found in and around Shechem through archaeological excava-tions and built at various periods of the city's long history support the Bible's connection of Shechem with religious ceremony and covenant-making (Gen. 12:6; 33:18-20; 35:4; Deut. 27–28; Josh. 8:30-35; 24:1-28; Judg. 9:1-40). Shechem's reputation as a place of religious significance to the Samaritans remained in NT times (John 4:5-6, 20).     P.L.G.

**SHEEN, FULTON JOHN** (1895–1979). Roman Catholic archbishop, noted radio and television personality described as one of the most persuasive voices for the Catholic faith in America, and author.

Bishop Sheen was born on May 8, in El Paso, Illinois. His father, Newton Morris Sheen, a farmer, and his mother, Delia Fulton Sheen, moved to Peoria when Fulton was a small child. He attended St. Mary's School and Spalding Institute in Peoria, then enrolled in St. Viator College in Bourbonnais, Illinois, where he was a member of the debating team and an editor on the staff of the college newspaper. He received a B.A. in 1917 and an M.A. in 1919 from St. Viator. In 1919 he attended St. Paul Seminary in St. Paul, Minnesota, and was ordained a priest in the Diocese of Peoria on September 20, 1919. Subsequently he earned S.T.B. and J.C.B. degrees from the Catholic University of America, Washington, D.C., in 1920. He received a Ph.D. from the University of Louvain in Belgium (1923) and attended the Sorbonne in Paris and the Collegio Angelico in Rome (D.D.; 1924). In 1925 Louvain made him an *agrégé en philosophie* for his dissertation, "God and Intelligence." For this he earned the Cardinal Mercier International Prize for Philosophy.

*Archbishop Fulton J. Sheen*

After serving for a brief period as a parish priest at St. Patrick's Church, Peoria, Sheen in 1926 joined the faculty of the Catholic University of America as an instructor in philosophy of religion. Monsignor Sheen became the speaker on the NBC radio network "Catholic Hour" on March 2, 1930. Before long his audience of both Catholics and Protestants reached many millions. Later he was featured on a television program called "Life Is Worth Living." Many experts in the field rated him as the most eloquent preacher in the United States. His broadcasts formed the basis for a number of books that became best sellers. A series of prominent people were converted to the Catholic faith through contact with the soft-spoken radio priest. Monsignor Sheen was appointed national director of the Society for the Propagation of the Faith in 1950 and was consecrated as a bishop the following year. He died on December 10.                          R.H.

**SHEKEL.** From the Hebrew word meaning "to weigh." The shekel was an OT measure of weight before it became a primary unit of money. The substances most often weighed were silver (Gen. 23:15, "four hundred shekels of silver" for a piece of land), gold (Num. 7:86; Josh. 7:21; II Chr. 3:9), iron (I Sam. 17:7), and bronze (I Sam. 17:5). The weights used were of stone. The Hebrew word translated "weight" is "stone." (Prov. 16:11: "A just balance and scales are the Lord's, all the weights in the bag are his work.") There were different sizes of shekel weights. Most often mentioned in scripture is "the shekel of the sanctuary" (Lev. 5:15), which was a half shekel, and a shekel "by the king's weight" (II Sam. 14:26). The weights of silver plates (130 shekels) and basins (70 shekels) are listed (Num. 7:13). Until after the Babylonian exile, shekels as money represented uncoined metal.                          P.L.G.

**SHEKINAH.** A Hebrew word meaning "to dwell." The word "shekinah" is not used in the Bible but appears frequently in post-biblical, Jewish writings representing the presence or immanence of God. The word is associated with bright light. Moses on Mount Sinai could see Yahweh's "goodness" and "back" but not Yahweh's face "for man shall not see me and live" (Exod. 33:12-23). The presence of the risen Christ to Paul on the road to Damascus was "a light from heaven, brighter than the sun" (Acts 26:13). In rabbinical writings, the lamps of the Temple's Holy Place are witnesses "that the Shekinah abides in the midst of Israel" (*Shab.* 22*b*). And, the windows of the Temple were made "to let the light of the Shekinah illumine the world" (*Num. Rab.* 15:2).

The concept of God present with people and nations occurs frequently in the OT, for example, Jerusalem, where Yahweh has chosen to put the divine "name" (I Kings 11:36). In the NT, the significance of shekinah is taken by the more detailed doctrine of the Holy Spirit. In the OT the nearest approach to the NT doctrine of the Holy Spirit is the idea of the shekinah. In a sense, shekinah became, like Word (Ps. 18:30 KJV), Spirit (Isa. 63:10), Wisdom (Prov. 8:22-33), and Name, a substitute for the Divine Name (Deut. 12:5; I Kings 8:16), the pronunciation of which was avoided.

GLORY is a term related to shekinah, the glory of God to be seen in nature (Ps. 1: 11 ff.), on Mount Sinai (Exod. 24:16), in the tabernacle (Exod. 29:43; 40:34), and in the Temple (I Kings 8:11). Glory is used in Paul's letters almost as a title, for example, "Lord of glory" (I Cor. 2:8). God has made the light to shine out of darkness "to give the light of the knowledge of the glory of God in the face of Christ" (II Cor. 4:6).                          P.L.G.

**SHELDON, CHARLES M.** (1857–1946). Author of *In His Steps,* Sheldon was born February 26 in Wellsville, New York, to Sarah Ward and Stewart Sheldon, a Congregational minister. He studied at Phillips Academy, Brown University (1883), and Andover Theological Seminary (1886). Ordained a Congregationalist, he pastored the church in Waterbury, Vermont, before becoming pastor of Central Congregational Church in Topeka, Kansas (1889–1919).

He began to expound the SOCIAL GOSPEL in stories, of which he read a chapter each Sunday evening to his congregation. *In His Steps*—stories of how members of a middle-class congregation followed the teachings of Jesus by asking in each situation "What would Jesus do?"—was written in this way. It appeared serially in *The Advance,* a Chicago magazine, and in book form in 1897. Estimates of its sales run as high as thirty million. It continues in print today, and has been translated into twenty-three languages, as well as becoming a movie in 1936. In 1919 Sheldon became editor of the *Christian Herald.* He wrote fifty other books dealing with slums, class tensions, political corruption, corporate dishonesty, and labor turmoil. He also crusaded for prohibition, pacifism, and ecumenism.                          N.H.

**SHEM.** Possibly from a Hebrew root word meaning "hear" or from a Babylonian word meaning "name" or "son." Shem was the first named and thus considered the oldest of NOAH's three sons (Gen. 10:21), Ham being named second, and Japheth the third (Gen. 5:32; 9:18; see also 10:1). Biblical tradition describes all the peoples of earth as lineal descendants of Noah through one of his three sons. Thus, all share in the covenant God made with Noah (Gen. 9:9, 12-17; 10:32).

The term "Semite" is applied to some of Shem's descendants, who are called Semites after his name. According to Genesis 10:22, Shem was also the father of several non-Semitic peoples. The division of nations by Noah's sons seems to have been based on geography. All of Shem's "children" appear to have occupied lands to the northeast of Palestine, that is, "Elam, Asshur, Arpachshad, Lud, and Aram" (Gen.

10:22). Shem is mentioned specifically as the ancestor of the Hebrews through Eber (Gen. 10:21), a name that has been found in the Elba tablets. Genesis 11 concludes the narrative of Shem's progeny by naming Terah as the father of Abraham, thus introducing the more detailed accounts of the patriarchs and how they became residents of the land of Canaan.

When Noah became drunk on wine and lay "uncovered" in his tent, Ham "saw the nakedness of his father" (Gen. 9:20 ff.). Shem, along with Japheth, covered Noah with "a garment," but in such a way that they did not see his nakedness (Gen. 9:23). Noah, awake, blessed the kind ones but cursed Canaan, a son of Ham (9:24-25; 10:6). The blessing of Shem made Canaan his slave (Gen. 9:26).

P.L.G.

**SHEMA.** The heart of the Jewish service. The worshiper who recites it proclaims allegiance to the kingdom of heaven and joyful submission to God's laws and commandments. The Shema is a proclamation of the existence and unity of God; of Israel's complete loyalty to God and God's commandments; the belief in divine justice; the remembrance of the liberation from Egypt; and the election of Israel as God's people. The opening verse, "Hear, O Israel; the Lord our God is One Lord," sounds the keynote of all Judaism: God is One because there is no other God than he; God is also One because he is wholly unlike anything else in existence.

The Shema commands undivided allegiance to and total love of God. It bids the worshiper to teach God's commandments "diligently unto thy children, and [thou] shalt talk of them when thou sittest in thine house, and when thou walkest by the way, and when thou liest down, and when thou risest up." The middle of the Shema teaches the doctrine of Divine Righteousness. The third section indicates how God's teachings are constantly to be kept before the eyes of the worshipers and their children by means of an outward expression of an inward thought, the fringes on the prayer shawl. The Shema is the first prayer of innocent childhood and the last utterance of the dying.

L.K.

**SHEOL.** A Hebrew word of uncertain meaning, signifying the abode of the dead. It appears sixty-five times in the OT and is variously translated in the KJV, transliterated consistently in the RSV.

The Hebrew people generally shared with Semites the view that after DEATH, people survived but in an underworld place of darkness, dust, and inactivity, from which none escaped. Few details are given, but Sheol is pictured as a walled place with stout gates. Life there is shadowy and characterized by eternal thirst. The horror of such existence is that it is without hope or any communication with God (Ps. 6:5; 88:4 ff; Isa. 38:18). Synonyms used for Sheol include: the ditch or pit, the realm of death, the earth, and perdition. Sheol is not a place for

punishment of the wicked. In classical Greek, as in NT Greek, Sheol is translated "Hades."

In late OT times, some taught that, even in Sheol, Yahweh rules people and would work their vindication (Pss. 49:14 ff; 139:8; Job 19:26 ff.). In a few passages mention is made of liberation from Sheol through resurrection of the righteous to bliss and the wicked to shame (Isa. 26:19; Dan. 12:2). Such notions were rejected by most of Judaism so that no consistent doctrine of the subject developed.

The whole concept of life after death was changed for Christians by the RESURRECTION of Christ. His body did not see corruption in Hades (Acts 2:31) for he has "the keys of Death and Hades" (Rev. 1:18).

The NT knows a place of punishment for the dead, GEHENNA, a term rarely used in the NT. It is used most often in the teachings of Jesus as a place of the final sufferings of the wicked and unrepentant. In II Peter 2:4, the word translated "hell" is Tartarus, which to Greeks was the place where the wicked were punished. It was thought to be located in the bowels of the earth, far deeper than Hades. Such subjects are treated in the NT but with restraint and always with the intent to warn and to awaken responsibility.

P.L.G.

**SHEPHERD.** In Palestine in ancient times the shepherd was a prominent figure. Along with agriculture, herds of sheep and cattle represented the prime means of wealth. Sheep provided wool, meat, clothing, material for tents, and were regularly used for sacrifices in the cultic system. Sometimes the owner tended the flocks, sometimes his sons, and sometimes paid servants. Their job included supervision of the herd, protection from animals of prey and thieves, searching for stray sheep, caring for the sick, leading the flock to adequate land for grazing, and regularly contending for the scarce sources of water (for example, Gen. 26:19-22). The story of the conflict between Cain and Abel in Genesis 4 illustrates the tension that often existed between farmer and shepherd.

As a conspicuous person in the society the shepherd came to be widely used symbolically in the literature of Israel and the early church. (1) *As a Figure for God.* Repeatedly in the OT God is depicted as the shepherd of the flock Israel. The familiar Psalm 23 links the image of the shepherd with that of the Oriental host. Psalm 80 begins, "Give ear, O Shepherd of Israel, thou who leadest Joseph like a flock!" The tender, protective care God shows Israel is movingly affirmed in Isaiah 40:11: "He will feed his flock like a shepherd, he will gather the lambs in his arms, he will carry them in his bosom, and gently lead those that are with young."

(2) *As a Figure for Jesus.* In the NT God as shepherd is missing, except in the parables of Jesus (for example, Luke 15:3-7). Instead, Jesus is "the great shepherd of the sheep" (Heb. 13:20), to whom the straying members of the flock have turned (I Pet.

2:25). In John 10 the image is developed in a striking way. Jesus as the shepherd knows the sheep by name and goes before them on their wanderings. The good shepherd is distinguished from the mercenary in that the shepherd will not flee when thieves or wild beasts attack. "I am the good shepherd. The good shepherd lays down his life for the sheep" (10:11). The flock is extended beyond the bounds of Israel: "And I have other sheep, that are not of this fold; I must bring them also, and they will heed my voice" (10:16).

(3) *As a Figure for Leaders and Ministers*. Ezekiel 34 describes the kings of Israel as shepherds who, instead of feeding the sheep, have fed themselves and have exploited the flock. They have abdicated their pastoral role like mercenaries, and thus the sheep have scattered to become a prey for wild beasts. The only hope for Israel is that God will search them out, rescue them, and bring them to green pastures.

In the NT the figure of the shepherd is never used in a negative or judgmental fashion as in Ezekiel, except perhaps Mark 6:34, where it is said that Jesus had compassion on the crowds, "because they were like sheep without a shepherd." In Ephesians 4:11 the word translated in the RSV as PASTORS is the same Greek term translated elsewhere as "shepherds" (for example, Luke 2:8). They function as tenders of the flock under "the chief Shepherd" and are warned about the temptation to grow rich at the expense of those in their care and the temptation to domineer them (I Pet. 5:2-4).                C.B.C.

**SHEPHERD OF HERMAS.** The writer of this treatise is Hermas, a fairly unknown APOSTOLIC FATHER. He had been a slave at Rome, but had been set free to become a farmer. He lived at the same time as Clement of Rome, around A.D. 100; yet the one outside reference to him—in the Muratorian Canon, where authoritative books of the church are listed— dates his writing at a time when his brother Pius was bishop of Rome (about A.D. 140–154). Modern scholars see his composition as the work of more than one person; its composition is not the work of a single author but is spread over several decades.

*The Shepherd* is made up of five *Visions*, twelve *Mandates*, and ten *Similitudes*. The sources of these visions are an old woman of youthful beauty—a figure of the church—and a shepherd-angel who instructs Hermas on the nature of the Christian life. The genre of Hermas' treatise is apocalyptic, that is, revealing divine truths from the heavenly world, couched in figurative or allegorical idiom. The teaching is centered on the possibility of repentance after baptism, and probably reflects the author's own family experience since his sons had abandoned the faith in time of persecution. The call of the book is ethical, exhorting to purity and limiting the chance of post-baptismal forgiveness, a rigorous doctrine to be seen in view of the impending end of the world, which is expected soon.

The value of *The Shepherd* is the light it throws on a species of Jewish Christianity as it became domiciled at Rome. The book was prized as possessing quasi-canonical status, especially in the Eastern sector of Christendom, and was regularly included in the list of the church's sacred scriptures. Athanasius' Festal Letter of A.D. 367 shows that the *Shepherd* was being used for training converts in his day. But its pessimistic outlook, which adopted a narrow view of God's forgiveness for penitent sinners, and its otherworldly apocalyptic genre made it an unpopular treatise, and it soon lost any appeal it had.

R.M.

**SHESHBAZZAR.** A Babylonian name meaning "Sin (the moon god) protects the father." Sheshbaz- zar, "the prince of Judah" (Ezra 1:8), grew up in Babylon, where his father, Jehoiachin, the exiled king of Judah, was in prison. ZERUBBABEL was the grandson of Jehoiachin, and thus a nephew to Sheshbazzar (Ezra 3:2, 8; 5:2; Hag. 1:1, 12, 14; 2:2, 23; Matt. 1:12; Luke 3:27). We hear of Sheshbazzar first when he was selected by Cyrus I, the king of Persia, to lead the first group of Babylonian Jews to Jerusalem, with royal authority and support, to rebuild the city and its Temple (Ezra 1:8). To Sheshbazaar the king entrusted a collection of valuables from Jews of Babylonia together with the Temple gold and silver vessels that Nebuchadnezzar had carried away to Babylon after he had sacked the city in 587 B.C. Sheshbazzar, like Zerubbabel after him, was called "governor" of Judah (Ezra 5:14; Hag. 1:1, I Esdras 6:18), and is credited with having laid the foundations of the house of the Lord, that is, Zerubbabel's Temple (Ezra 5:16; I Esdras 6:20).

P.L.G.

**SHEVAT.** *See* HEBREW CALENDAR.

**SHIBBOLETH.** As a consequence of the part that this word played in the narrative of Judges 12:1-6, it has an acquired meaning as a test word used to distinguish a particular group or class of people.

The "mighty warrior" Jephthah lived in Gilead on the east bank of the Jordan River (Judg. 11:1-6). Since his mother was a harlot, Jephthah was rejected by the clan's leader as heir to his father's estate (Judg. 11:2). He fled to the wilderness, where he became the leader of a band of "worthless fellows." When the Ammonites, southern neighbors of Jephthah's tribe, threatened war, the Gileadite chieftains offered Jephthah leadership over the tribe in exchange for his successfully making war on their enemies. Jephthah accepted the offer and prevailed in battle. After this, armed men from Ephraim came from the west bank of the Jordan and complained to Jephthah that he had not invited them to join the battle with him. Jephthah replied that he had waited for them to defend Gilead from Ammon but, since they took no action, he initiated the battle and "the Lord gave them into my hand" (Judg. 12:2).

At this, the Ephraimites attacked Jephthah and his men but were defeated. They attempted to retreat westward to their territory, crossing the Jordan. But Jephthah's men had seized control of the fords and, as a test of his identity, required each fleeing man to pronounce the word "shibboleth." The text explains that since Ephraimites "could not pronounce it right," they were killed. Apparently, the Ephraimites had a peculiarity in pronunciation that made it difficult for them to make the "sh" sound (12:6). This narrative has given to shibboleth its acquired meaning as a test or password used for identification purposes.  P.L.G.

**SHI'ITE.** The "separate party" of Islam, a collection of diverse groups and movements that arose in opposition to Abu Bakr, Umar, and Uthman, the first three caliphs. The Shi'ites believe that Ali, the fourth caliph, was the mandated successor to MUHAMMAD the prophet. In their view, the first three caliphs were usurpers. (The Sunni majority of Islam honor all four caliphs.) Since the time of the civil war of A.D. 656, which established Ali, Shi'ites have divided into a bewildering array of splinter groups and messianic sects, following various lines of IMAMS. These imams traced descent from Muhammad through Ali and Ali's son al-Husayn. The Druzes and BAHA'I also arose from Shi'ite groups.

The imam in Shi'ism fills both a religious and a political role. Thus the history of Shi'ite religious movements is also a history of political disaffection and revolt. Born in the civil war of A.D. 656, the Shi'ite movement has almost always been in opposition to the dominant political power. Although they held power in the Fatimid dynasty in tenth- to twelfth-century Egypt, and are now in power in the Islamic Republic of Iran, they have traditionally been downtrodden.

The movement gained its greatest solidarity in the eighth century under the imam Ja'far al-Sadiq, who provided it with a distinctive ideology. Even before this, however, the movement had suffered divisions between extremists and moderates, and the Zaydiyya, who form the majority in Yemen, had already split off. In 750 the Shi'ites overthrew the Umayyad dynasty, but the leaders of the revolution embraced Sunnism and established the ABBASID caliphate, which was hostile to Shi'ites.

Ja'far al-Sadiq designated one of his sons, Isma'il, to succeed him in the imamate, but Isma'il died before his father. Some Shi'ites believed that he had not died, but rather had gone into a state of "occultation," or concealment, and would return as the Mahdi (messiah). This group gave rise to the large number of sects known as ISMA'ILYYA, including the Nizari sect called Assassins. The Isma'ilyya count seven imams from Ali and therefore are also known as Seveners (SAB'IYYA). Other Shi'ites believe in twelve imams and are called Twelvers or IMAMIYYA.

Shi'ism as a reform movement has received much support through the centuries from non-Arabs, who often felt discriminated against in the Arab-dominated areas. It carries, however, an elitist message—that only the descendants of Ali have legitimate political and religious authority. The difficulty here may not be as great as it seems, since individuals as far from Arabia as Iran have claimed descent from Ali.

The number of groups increased throughout the Middle Ages as leadership disputes divided and subdivided the Shi'ites. Among those who look for the coming of the Mahdi, some expect the return of the seventh imam and some the twelfth. A number of men have declared themselves to be the Mahdi, and some have attracted large numbers of followers. Others have claimed to be a new imam, including the Iranian leader Ruhollah Khomeini, formerly recognized only as an AYATOLLAH.  K./M.C.

**SHILOH.** (1) A site (Seilûn) in ruins nine miles north of Bethel, nine miles south of Shechem, east of the main road from Shechem to Jerusalem, just off the "Highway of the Patriarchs," which follows the crest of the north-south ridge of Palestine.

Throughout the period of the Judges, Shiloh was Israel's most important political and religious city (Judg. 18:31). Previously the site may have had a Canaanite high place. The narratives of "the daughters of Shiloh" who danced at a feast (Judg. 21:21), the behavior of Eli's "worthless" sons (I Sam. 2:12, 22-23), and the "base" women at Shiloh (I Sam. 1:16) suggest that Shiloh was the scene of an early encounter of Israel in Palestine with the fertility cult of the Canaanites.

At Shiloh the people of Israel assembled at the completion of the conquest (Josh. 18:1), at the casting of lots in the division of the land (Josh. 18:8-10; 19:51) and, possibly, annually (I Sam. 1:3). Great religious festivals and pilgrimages were held at Shiloh (Judg. 21:19-21; I Sam. 1:3). Special meetings of the tribes were held there to settle difficult matters (Josh. 22:12 ff.).

Religiously, Shiloh was distinguished as the place where the tabernacle with the Ark of the Covenant rested after the conquest. The phrase "the doorpost of the temple of the Lord" (I Sam. 1:9) has been taken to suggest that the desert tabernacle had been replaced at Shiloh by a more permanent structure. When the Ark was seized in battle by the Philistine overlords (I Sam. 4:11), Shiloh lost its prominence. The priesthood of Shiloh fled to Nob, a site probably on the slopes of Mount Scopus overlooking Jerusalem. The thought that Shiloh was destroyed by the Philistines about this time is supported by the findings in excavations by Danish expeditions in 1926, 1929, and 1932.

(2) A personal name that appears in Genesis 49:10, Jacob's blessing on Judah, ". . . until Shiloh come. . . ." (KJV). The RSV here chooses to treat Shiloh not as a place or personal name. This has disappointed some interpreters who had taken Shiloh

here to be a code name for the Messiah, the son of David, of the house of Judah.                      P.L.G.

**SHIMEI.** An abbreviated form of the Hebrew word for "Yahweh has heard." A popular Hebrew personal name for men, especially in Levitical circles. Of the many men who possessed this name, of only a few do we have details other than the name. They do not seem to have been connected other than by name. The most important Shimei was a son of Gera, a Benjaminite, belonging to Saul's family. As David fled Jerusalem from Absalom's revolt, Shimei stoned and cursed David, "You are a man of blood" (II Sam. 16:5-8). After the revolt was quelled, David gave Shimei royal clemency. The time came when, on his deathbed, David charged Solomon to bring death to Shimei (I Kings 2:8-10) and this was done (I Kings 2:39-46).                      P.L.G.

**SHINAR.** A Hebrew name for a large part, if not the whole, of ancient Babylonia. Genesis 10:9-10 speaks of Nimrod, "a mighty hunter," as king over Shinar, a land that included the cities of Babel (Babylon), Erech (ancient Uruk, modern Warka) and Accad (ancient Akkade, near Babylon and modern Baghdad). The town of Babel (Gen. 11:9) was built in Shinar. Amraphel, otherwise unknown, is named "king of Shinar" in Genesis 14:1, 9.                      P.L.G.

**SHINTO.** From the Japanese word meaning "The Way (Tō, from Chinese tao) of the Gods." Shinto as a religion represents a perpetuation, with some modification, of the worship of the indigenous KAMI or gods of Japan that existed before the coming of Buddhism in the sixth century A.D.

The most important of these deities were the *ujigami,* patronal gods of particular *uji* or clans. Accounts of the deities of the imperial house and other noble families are given, together with the Shinto creation myth, in the earliest extant Japanese books,

Courtesy of the Japan National Tourist Organization

*The Great Torii of Shinto Shrine of Miyamjima Island*

the *Kojiki* (A.D. 712) and the *Nihonshoki* (720). However, these works should not be taken as comprehensive Shinto scriptures; the gods of a large number of shrines are not presented in them.

Theologically, Shinto is polytheistic, perhaps the only unambiguous polytheism to be found in a modern, advanced society. Some contemporary Shinto spokesmen have endeavored to develop the ramifications of this "pluralistic" view of the spiritual universe with interesting results. However, what can be expressed doctrinally is not the most significant aspect of Shinto experience. What most Japanese appreciate in Shinto is probably its traditionalism, which affords a link to the past, and the clean, simple, rustic atmosphere of the shrines in which its gods are honored. The latter quality suggests an important feature of Shinto, the distinction it makes between purity and pollution. Shrines, worship, and worshipers should be clean and pure.

Shinto worship is of two kinds. First, individuals approach shrines at all times to clap the hands twice, then offer a short prayer. Second, offerings of food and sometimes other objects are formally presented by priests periodically. The most important offerings are given at *matsuri,* shrine festivals, which will also include carnivals and highly colorful and diverse traditional dances, processions, and ceremonies.

Sociologically, Shinto remains a religion of the particular, centering on the *ujigami* of particular lineages or communities to which people feel a special relation. But certain shrines, above all the Grand Shrine of ISE, dedicated to the divine ancestress of the imperial house, evoke the loyalty of larger groups or of the nation as a whole.

Shinto has had a checkered history. After the introduction of BUDDHISM, a pattern of assimilation between the two religions emerged. In various ways, the kami and the Buddhas and bodhisattvas were viewed as different expressions of the same spiritual essences and were often worshiped together. But with the Meiji restoration of 1868, Shinto was seized upon by the new government as a uniquely Japanese institution. It was thoroughly separated from Buddhism, and emphasis was put on the legitimation of imperial rule by Shinto mythology and on participation in Shinto as an expression of patriotism. As extreme nationalism took stronger hold in Japan until the end of World War II in 1945, this often cynical use of Shinto only increased. Since then Shinto has largely resumed a more traditional role as the cultus of community shrines.                      R.E.

**SHISHAK.** The biblical name of a pharaoh who in Egypt was known as Sheshonq I (935–914 B.C.). Shishak rose to power as a Libyan chieftain-warrior and became so widely respected that he was received with royal honors at Thebes. He became ruler of all Egypt with his capitol in the Delta. His son was made high priest of Amun at Thebes. Shishak made a substantial addition to the great temple of Amun at

Karnak on one wall of which he recorded an account of his victories in Judah and Israel in the fifth year after the death of Solomon (about 918 B.C.) It has been proposed that he was Gezer's destroyer and Solomon's father-in-law, but by current Egyptian chronology this now seems unlikely.

The biblical accounts of Shishak's raid (I Kings 14:25; II Chr. 12:2-12) are concerned only with his plundering the palace and the Temple of Jerusalem. Shishak could have considered the Temple's Ark of the Covenant to be the unique throne of Rehoboam's kingdom, the container for the national deity, and, therefore, he seized it to show his sovereignty over the nation by taking the Ark to Egypt as a prize of war. At any rate, after Shishak's raid, the Bible tells nothing more about the Ark.

Shishak's campaign was not intended to destroy as much as to demonstrate Egypt's military and political power. For some 250 years before (1552–1300 B.C.) Egypt was without question the dominant empire of the world. At that time Egyptian armies repeatedly swept over Palestine. Thutmosis III (about 1490–1436) made more than a dozen such campaigns. It appears that in the thirteenth century B.C., after the Sea Peoples had destroyed Megiddo and Beth-shan, the Egyptians rebuilt those walled cities and established Philistine caretakers for Egypt in them. Merneptah is said to have left at Lachish marks of his raiding in 1223 B.C. Egypt had a long memory. Shishak may have considered his military action in Palestine as a reassertion of Egypt's imperial claims on that territory.

There is another indication of how confident Shishak may have been of his right to act in Palestine's political affairs. This was his welcoming JEROBOAM, son of Nebat, when he was forced under threat of death to flee from Jerusalem (I Kings 11:40). When Jeroboam returned from Egypt (with Shishak's backing?), he became the first king of Israel (I Kings 12:20). (The LXX [Septuagint] has a supplement at I Kings 12:24 ff. and 19:18 ff. according to which, during the years that Jeroboam was a guest in Shishak's court, he married Shishak's sister-in-law, who bore a son named Abia. These facts, if true, suggest that Shishak may have continued to support Jeroboam as one of Egypt's client-kings. Jeroboam's wife and son are mentioned in I Kings 14:1-17.)

Shishak's successors lacked his imperial interests. It would be two centuries after Shishak's time before Egypt would be involved again in political and military affairs in Palestine.                      P.L.G.

**SHITTIM.** From the Hebrew word meaning "acacia." (1) Acacia was the only kind of wood used in the construction of the tabernacle and its furnishings (Exod. 25:10). Two kinds of acacia grow in the Sinai and Negeb desert valleys, *acacia spyrocarpa* and *acacia raddina*. The latter is distinguished by its umbrella-like top, which provides a deep shade.

(2) A place name, Israel's final campsite on the east bank of the Jordan before crossing the river (Josh. 3:1; Mic. 6:5). From this place spies were sent into Jericho (Josh. 2:1). Two sites have been suggested for Shittim. They are located near each other and about six miles northeast of where the Jordan River empties into the Dead Sea: Tell el-Hammon, favored by W. F. Albright, N. Glueck, and G. E. Wright; and Tell el-Kefrein, a little to the northwest.

(3) "The valley of Shittim" (Joel 3:18), which was watered by a stream issuing from the Jerusalem Temple, probably should be understood as "the valley of acacias."                      P.L.G.

*Shiva Nataraja*

**SHIVA.** With VISHNU, Shiva is one of the two major deities of HINDUISM. He is worshiped throughout the Hindu world, his "family" of gods including his "great mother" consort, who is known by such names as Parvati, Durga, and Kali, and his sons Skanda and the elephant-headed GANESHA.

Shiva himself can be traced back to the Vedic deity RUDRA. In myth and art he is represented in various ways: as the great yogin seated on Mount Kailas in Tibet, whose meditations sustain the world; as the erotic lover of Parvati; as the lord of the dance, who tramples time and enacts the destiny of the universe; as the uncouth ascetic who dwells in cemeteries and cremation grounds. Most commonly, however, Shiva is worshiped in shrines as the simple quasi-phallic pillar known as the *lingam*. In these symbols, as well as in more philosophical expressions of Saivism, the Great God is seen as the timeless, absolute consciousness that underlies the cosmos, before which universes rise and fall in their immense cycles of creation and destruction. The destructive aspect of Shiva is, in fact, particularly emphasized. He is the destroyer of worlds in this cosmos of impermanence and, on a deeper level, the destroyer of illusion. Shiva is worshiped in simple puja rites by all classes of society and is the patron of certain sects such as the LINGAYATS, as well as of the large number of Saiva yogis and ascetics.                                    R.E.

**SHOFAR.** The horn of an animal, most often a ram, prepared for use as a musical instrument in the Jewish synagogue. It is sounded during the month of Elul, on Rosh Hashanah (the Jewish New Year), and at the end of Yom Kippur (the Day of Atonement). The Bible refers to two kinds of sounds to come from the shofar: *teki'ah* and *teru'ah* (Num. 10:5-8). Since doubt arose as to whether *teru'ah,* a wavering blast, was a moaning sound or an outcry, a third set of sounds was instituted—that of *shevarim* (broken sounds). The final great blast of *teki'ah* (a long single note) is explained as a sign of the removal of the Divine Presence, deduced from Exodus 19:13: "When the trumpet sounds a long blast, they shall come up to the mountain."                                           L.K.

Courtesy of Religious News Service

*Sounding the Shofar*

**SHOWBREAD.** From the Hebrew word meaning "bread of the face" thus "bread of the Presence" (RSV) or "shewbread" (KJV), an English expression apparently traceable to William Tyndale.

In many grain-oriented societies, bread is considered a suitable SACRIFICIAL OFFERING to a deity along with other gifts and sacrifices of food. The original notion was probably providing food for the gods or of worshipers sharing a meal with the gods as a symbol of good will and friendship between them: "he was made known to them in the breaking of the bread" (Luke 24:35). In this way, bread so used became special or holy. Careful preparation of such bread was required. Worshipers who ate the bread were made holy through ceremonial purifications. The practice is found in ancient Egypt and in ancient Babylonia where cakes of bread were laid out before various deities in twelves or in multiples of twelve. (See Jer. 7:18; 44:19, cakes offered to the queen of heaven.) In Ugaritic writings, the gods are said to eat bread. Bread offerings were also common in Greek and Roman rituals.

The passage in I Samuel 21:4-6 relating to David and his men eating the bread of the Presence calls it "the holy bread." The bread had been made to be a holy offering to the holy God. The priest required that the partakers themselves must be in a state of holiness. In Numbers 4:7 and II Chronicles 2:4, showbread is called "continual" bread.

In Israel's tabernacle-temple arrangements, the number twelve is a symbol, as when reference is made to the twelve cakes of holy bread that are put on the table in two rows, six in a row. This suggested to R. de Vaux that the bread offering was "a pledge of the covenant between the twelve tribes and Yahweh" (compare Lev. 24:5-6). The number twelve may also refer to the twelve months of the year, Yahweh being thanked for providing food the year around.

The law concerning the preparation of the bread of the Presence is given in Leviticus 24:5-9. The bread was made in the ordinary way but without leaven and of fine meal or flour. Such bread was fit to set before angels (Gen. 18:6) and daily before Solomon (I Kings 4:22). The bread was to be prepared and presented by the Kohethites "every sabbath" (Lev. 24:8). The holy bread shared the table with cups of pure frankincense, which is "a memorial portion" (Lev. 24:1-7). The incense was offered by being burned on the nearby altar of incense. "Drink offerings" or libations were also made (Num. 4:7).

The bread of the Presence ceremonies were presumably maintained in the tabernacle and temples throughout Hebrew history, except after Antiochus Epiphanes defiled the Temple of Zerubbabel in 169 B.C. and before Judas Maccabeus revived the practice in 165 B.C. at the time of the rededication of the Temple. Josephus states that at Herod's Temple, the showbread was made of unleavened flour, was baked on Friday and brought into the Temple on Saturday morning and was placed on the table in two rows of six each, "one loaf leaning against another."

A number of the religious meanings of the OT bread of the Presence carry over into the Christian sacrament of Communion or the Lord's Supper. Jesus often said, "I am the bread of life" (John 6:35, 48). At his last supper, Jesus "took bread, and blessed, and broke it, and gave it to the disciples and said, Take, eat; this is my body' " (Matt. 26:26), "do this in remembrance of me" (I Cor. 11:24).          P.L.G.

**SHRINE.** From the Latin word *scrinium*, meaning a box containing writing materials. Originally, a shrine was a reliquary, a container for the bones and/or possessions of a departed saint, shaped like a writing box. In wider use, it refers to a sacred image to which devotion is given, such as a statue of the Virgin Mary, or to a holy place, particularly the resting place of a saint.          J.C.

Courtesy of Religious News Service

*The Shroud of Turin*

**SHROUD OF TURIN.** An ancient linen cloth, which is dimly imprinted—to the naked eye—with the image of a man. For centuries, many Christians have believed that the shroud is the linen burial cloth in which Joseph of Arimathea and Nicodemus wrapped the body of Jesus before laying him in the tomb. It is now in the Cathedral in Turin, Italy, and only rarely is put on public display.

Interestingly, unlike many religious relics, the shroud becomes more fascinating as scientists study it. In 1898, it was photographed for the first time, and the print on the cloth was found to be negative, that is, its light and dark areas were reversed when it was developed on film. This photography showed a very detailed picture of a man who appeared to have been crucified, crowned with thorns, and pierced by a sharp instrument through the side. The person whose picture was mysteriously imprinted on the shroud suffered and died in the same way Jesus' passion and death is reported by the Gospels.

In 1978, a team of scientists founded the Shroud of Turin Research project, which rephotographed the shroud using modern techniques, and also performed tests on threads of the material. They announced that the image was not painted on the cloth, but could offer no explanation for the phenomenon.          J.C.

**SHUNNING.** The avoidance of flagrant and unrepentant sinners after they have been "banned" or excommunicated—a part of church discipline practiced particularly among the AMISH and MENNONITES. It amounts to almost complete social ostracism, including the avoidance of marital and familial contact. Based on Matthew 18:15-17; I Corinthians 5:11; Romans 16:17; II Thessalonians 3:14; and II John 10, if a person is found in sin, admonished by the elders, disciplined by the church, and still persists in sin, that person is banned, and thereafter shunned.

Strict shunning was introduced by Obbe Philips of the Netherlands about 1533–35. MENNO SIMONS joined the group in 1536 and taught the idea in *Loving Admonition* (1541), *A Fundamental Doctrine or an Account of Excommunication, Ban, Exclusion* (1541), and *A Kind Admonition . . . Concerning the Shunning and Separation of the Unfaithful Brethren* (1558). Shunning is accorded an article in the Dordrecht Confession (1632).

Most rigorously practiced today by Old Order Amish, it includes refusal to eat at the same table, exchange social courtesies, or work together. It is imposed by a bishop with consent of a congregation. Often practiced between factional groups, it has been challenged in court as a boycott.          N.H.

**SHUR, WILDERNESS OF.** A desert-like region in the northwest part of the Sinai Peninsula. Its northern border was the Mediterranean coastal plain, with its "way of the land of the Philistines" (Exod. 13:17). Its western boundary was the route of the present Suez canal. To the east was the Wadi el-Arish or "the river of Egypt," the border between ancient Israel and Egypt. Through its southern portion ran an important east-west caravan route called "the way to Shur" (Gen. 16:7). It led from Egypt via Beersheba, Hebron, and Jerusalem, finally to Damascus and Mesopotamia.          P.L.G.

**SHURTLEFF, ERNEST W.** (1862–1917). Congregational minister and hymn writer. Shurtleff is best remembered for "Lead On, O King Eternal," which he wrote for his graduating class at Andover Theological Seminary in 1883. Born in Boston on April 4, he received training at Boston Latin School, then entered Harvard, and later Andover. At the time of his seminary graduation Shurtleff was already an accomplished organist and had published two books of verse, including many hymns. He served churches in California, Massachusetts, and Minnesota. He and his family went to Europe in 1905. He organized the American Church in Frankfurt and later was in charge of student ministry for the Academy Vitti in Paris. He died in the French capital on August 29.

R.H.

**SHUSHAN.** The Hebrew name for the Persian city Susa. Susa is an unoccupied site near the modern village in Iran named Shūsh. The place is in the district of Khuzistan, near the Iraq border, some 175 miles north of the Persian Gulf. The ancient city was situated in a fertile plain abundantly supplied with water from four nearby rivers. From June through October, the area is intolerably hot, with temperatures reaching 140 degrees fahrenheit. During the winter, even in the January-February rainy season, the weather is pleasant. The kings of ancient Persia used it as their winter capital. Easy access from Susa southeast to the Mesopotamian Valley and northeast to the Persian plain made it a crossroad of international trade, war, and politics.

Aside from the many times Susa is named in the book of Esther, Susa is mentioned in the OT in Nehemiah 1:1 (Nehemiah was in Susa when he first got word of conditions in Jerusalem) and Daniel 8:2 (Susa was the locale of one of Daniel's visions). In today's Shūsh, there is a mosque where the tomb of Daniel is venerated.

P.L.G.

**SIBYLLINE ORACLES.** This name covers a widely disparate collection of writings whose dates are from the second century B.C. to the seventh century A.D. The title derives from the Sibyl who is described as an old woman who gave out prophecies in a trance-like state. The name is generic, since there were as many soothsayers as there were shrines where the oracles were given. The most famous were at Erythrea in Asia Minor and at Cumae in Italy.

The literature that is labelled Sibylline Oracles is cast in the form of Greek hexameter verse, and the themes are all connected with prognostications of doom awaiting the human race. Especially at Rome a collection of such predictions was highly regarded, and they were consulted especially in time of war and crisis. The oracles were also propaganda pieces that in the hands of Virgil the poet were exploited to magnify the accomplishments of the emperor Augustus, and to forecast a utopia under his rule. Augustus, however, was suspicious of the oracles since they seemed to portend a rival empire as a challenge to his principate, and he had two thousand of the oracles destroyed. The religious overtone also is obvious, since the shrines of Apollo were supported by the oracles, and in days of stress people flocked to gain assurance from, the Sibyl.

Jewish and Christian writers in later centuries edited these documents in their own interests and used the eschatological hopes in the oracles to their advantage. Beliefs in judgment, resurrection, and the afterlife were enlisted, and the notion of a new world, purified by fire, is common to Persian, Stoic, Jewish, and Christian apocalyptic (see II Pet. 3:10-13).

Christian influence is especially seen in Oracles 2, 7, and 8, where the prospect of the afterlife is set in terms of the Christian hope. The fathers of the church quoted copiously from these books and chapters, and their influence on medieval thought, art, and liturgy (for example, in the *Dies Irae*, "Day of Wrath," in the various Requiems and Masses) was considerable. Michelangelo often brought the Sibyls into his paintings alongside OT prophets and Christian figures.

R.M.

**SIDDHARTHA.** From the Sanskrit phrase meaning "he who attains the goal." The personal name of the BUDDHA, whose family name was Gautama and clan name Sakya. The hero of the famous novel *Siddhartha* by Hermann Hesse, while a contemporary of the Buddha, was another spiritual seeker of ancient India.

R.E.

**SIDDHI.** From the Sanskrit word meaning "attainment, perfection." In YOGA, siddhis are extraordinary psychic powers the yogin attains at advanced stages of his practice, as a consequence of withdrawal of attachment to sense-objects (*pratyahara*) and complete control (*samyama*). The list includes clairaudience, clairvoyance, and the ability to disappear or assume whatever form one wishes. In SANKHYA, siddhis are attitudes conducive to spiritual growth, such as studiousness and detachment.

R.E.

**SIDDIM, VALLEY OF.** A battleground hosting the triumph of Chedorlaomer and three other allied Mesopotamian kings over five local rulers of the lower Jordan Valley (Gen. 14:1-12). Since this bituminous region is explicitly equated with the Salt (Dead) Sea (14:3), it was likely situated in what is presently the shallow portion of the Dead Sea, south of the el-Lisan ("tongue") peninsula.

J.K.K.

**SIDDUR.** The Jewish daily and Sabbath prayer book. The liturgical expression of the hopes and convictions of the Jewish people as a whole, the siddur is of paramount importance to Jews. Its phrases and teachings are either culled from Scripture and the rabbinic writings or are a devotional paraphrase of them. The siddur is preoccupied with the One Eternal Lord. It engages in direct speech with God and exhausts the resources of language in songs of praise, in utterances of loving gratitude, and in rejoicing at God's nearness in natural outpourings of grief for sin.

The siddur includes the three daily services: *Shaharit* (morning service); *Minhah* (afternoon service); and *Ma'ariv* (evening service), followed by the

Sabbath service. The structure of the classic Jewish prayer book and its inspiration derive from the Bible, especially the Psalms, and rabbinic creativity throughout the ages. The oldest prayers included in the siddur are the SHEMA, which was recited daily in the Second Temple, and the *Amidah,* or *Shemoneh Esreh* (the Eighteen Benedictions). Many other prayers composed by famous personalities were added to the daily liturgy. Most Jewish prayer books include blessings for a variety of occasions, such as the recovery from an illness, a prayer for a safe trip, and the like. They include blessings for other festivals, although special prayer books carry the full service for the High Holy Days and festivals. The basic prayers of the liturgy are recorded in the Talmud.

L.K.

**SIDON.** An ancient Phoenician city situated on the Mediterranean seacoast twenty-five miles north of TYRE. The Amarna Letters (thirteenth century B.C.) disclose that Sidon's loyalty toward Egypt was more formality than fact. Nevertheless, trade relations between Egypt and Phoenicia persisted.

The city's political influence is symbolized in biblical genealogies that refer to Sidon as Canaan's "first-born" (Gen. 10:15; I Chr. 1:13). The nouns "Sidon" and "Sidonians" frequently denote all Phoenicia and its inhabitants (Judg. 3:3; 10:6; I Kings 5:6; 16:31). Israel felt anxious about "Sidon the Great" (Josh. 19:28), which lay just beyond the tribal border of Asher (Judg. 1:31). Hence, prophetic texts eagerly await the destruction of Sidon and its increasingly dominating neighbor, Tyre (Isa. 23:1-18; Jer. 27:3-7; Joel 3:4).

During the first millennium B.C., Sidon experienced Assyrian, Babylonian, and Persian invasions. Assyria's king Esarhaddon destroyed Sidon in 677. The city reemerged only to be captured by the Babylonians under Nebuchadnezzar in 593. Later, the Persians enlisted Sidon's fleet in warfare against the Greeks. Still smarting from its abortive revolt against Persia's king Artaxerxes III Ochus (351), Sidon surrendered to Alexander the Great in 333 without incident. Rome under Pompey claimed Sidon in 64. Jesus and Paul each visited Sidon (Matt. 15:21; Acts 27:3), and Sidonians journeyed southward into Galilee to receive Jesus' message and healing (Luke 6:17).

J.K.K.

**SIGER OF BRABANT.** A thirteenth-century professor of philosophy at the University of Paris, he was a leading exponent of radical Aristotelianism and defended the independence of philosophy from theology. In 1270 the bishop of Paris condemned thirteen errors in his teaching. In 1277 the same bishop condemned 219 more propositions. Aquinas' *De Unitate Intellectus contra Averroistas* was directed against him. Summoned by the Inquisition, Siger and two colleagues fled to Italy, where he was fatally stabbed by a mad cleric.

Dante admired him and placed him with eleven others in the Heaven of Light. Fourteen authentic works by Siger survive along with six probable ones. He taught Aristotle's thought, whether or not it agreed with church doctrine. Main points of controversy centered around the eternity of the world and the unity of all human intellect, which involved the denial of individual immortality and rewards and punishments.

N.H.

**SIGN.** Something that represents something else, often with a related purpose or identity, a mark, a SYMBOL, a quality, a trace, as smoke is a sign of fire.

In the OT, the much-used word "sign" had many meanings: an identifying mark, a statement, a proof, an omen, a lesson, a testimony, an assurance, a warning. God put the rainbow in the sky as a sign that God would not again destroy the earth in a flood (Gen. 9:12-13). God gave the people the rite of circumcision so that they would be marked with a divine sign. God marked Cain. The blood on the lintels of the Israelite homes was a sign of God's mercy toward the chosen people, as the plague of grasshoppers was a sign of God's might before the Egyptian court.

In the NT, John the Baptist was expected to provide signs by which the Messiah could be identified. Christ himself condemns those who demand signs, for example signs in the heavens (Matt. 12:39; Luke 11:29) and refuses to supply any. Yet the angels had provided at least descriptive signs of where the infant Jesus had been laid. Christ argues that the demand for signs springs from lack of faith. Yet in a sense his miracles—giving the blind sight, casting out devils, helping the lame walk—are in fact signs to those who have faith, even if he often says, "Go and tell no man." In the church some of the most meaningful acts of worship, such as baptism and the Lord's Supper, like Passover in the OT, are signs loaded with history, association, and meaning.

T.J.K.

**SIGN OF THE CROSS.** The act of making the outline of the cross on one's upper body during worship services in the Orthodox, Roman Catholic, Episcopal, and many Lutheran churches. It accompanies the benediction at the end of divine services and in the sacrament of baptism and the rite of confirmation.

J.C.

**SIGNS AND WONDERS.** In the first three Gospels the phrase "signs and wonders" is almost a catchword for Christ's demonstrations of the power of God among people. John, on the other hand, leans toward the "signs" that demonstrate God's "glory." The Greek words involved are *dunamis* (miracles), *terata* (wonders), *semeia* (signs), and *doxa* (glory).

Either in the NT or the OT, God is seldom revealed full-blown without accompanying wonders and miracles. Often those revelations are described as mighty acts, miracles, wonderful deeds, signs, marvels, great wonders, mighty doings. They create awe, respect, admiration, appreciation, thanksgiving, and faith (Exod. 3:20; Josh. 3:5; Mark 6:5; Acts 2:22). In general these signs and wonders can be described as miraculous events that seem to contravene the normal laws of nature. Yet God is a provident and loving God who normally makes use of the normal patterns of creation in the world, such as life and death, seedtime and harvest, in order to improve the lot of people.

The use of signs and MIRACLES is continually addressed to people who have faith. In Exodus 3:12, God assures Moses, from Sinai, "This shall be the sign for you"—the giving of the commandments. In the NT, the single most signifiant *dunamis*, as Paul continues to insist, is the raising of Christ from the dead. Without that, there could be no faith in any of the other signs and wonders. Not only believers but also Christ's enemies accepted the reality of his miracles (Mark 3:22). Thus the work of Christ, through his signs and miracles, through his preaching, and through his relationships with people, became further witness of the person and work in the plan of salvation.    T.J.K.

## SIHON.

An Amorite king whose story is mainly told in Numbers 21:21-31. He wrested Heshbon from the Moabites and made it his capital. As the Israelites advanced northward in Transjordan en route to Canaan, Sihon inhospitably denied them permission to cross his territory. When warfare erupted, Sihon met defeat, and the triumphant Israelites seized his kingdom. Impressed by its good pasturage, the tribes of Gad and Reuben subsequently settled there (Josh. 13:8-28).    J.K.K.

## SIKHISM.

From a Pali/Sanskrit word meaning "disciple." The religion now numbers about ten million adherents, who largely live in the Punjab province of India. It was inaugurated by NANAK in the late fifteenth century A.D. Growing out of the Hindu Bhakti tradition and also influenced by Sufi Islam, Sikhism is centered on a monotheistic belief in one Creator, who is formless and beyond all human comprehension. Karma and reincarnation are also accepted. The Sikh God can be worshiped anywhere by means of simple prayers and hymns that focus on the "True Name" (*Sat Nam*) of God, such as those employed in the attractive morning devotions or JAPJI.

From the time of Nanak, Sikhism was guided by a succession of ten GURUS until the death of the last in 1708. From then on, the only authority has been the Sikh scriptures, called the Adi Granth. It was compiled by the fifth Guru in the succession, Arjun, who served as Guru from 1581 to 1606. It was the

Courtesy of the United Nations

*The Golden Temple at Amritsar, which houses the Holy Granth, the Sikh scriptures*

martyrdom of this guru by the Muslim Mogul rulers of north India that brought about bad feelings between Sikhs and Muslims and began the celebrated Sikh military tradition, culminating in a Sikh state, which lasted until subjugated by the British in the nineteenth century. The last Guru, Govind, created the Khalsa, a Sikh military order, in 1699.

Sikh worship consists of hymns, prayers, sermons, and reading from the Granth, which is given great symbolic honor, and is followed by a communal meal. Sikh community identity, enhanced by such practices of the Khalsa as refusing to cut the hair and wearing a turban, is very strong.    R.E.

## SILAS.

A friend and companion of Paul. The name Silas, which might be either Hebrew or Greek, occurs only in Acts. In the Pastoral Epistles (I and II Tim. and Tit.) this same individual is called Silvanus (see also II Cor. 1:19; I Thess. 1:1; I Pet. 5:12). Acts 16:37 reports that Silas, like Paul, held Roman citizenship. Doubtless he came from a Jewish background, because he is described as one of the "leading men among the brethren" at Jerusalem (Acts 15:22).

Once the great council at Jerusalem had met, Silas was designated as a "prophet" or missionary to bring the report of that convention to the church at Antioch, where he remained for a considerable time. Later he was chosen as Paul's companion for the second missionary journey, taking the place of Barnabas. At Philippi he and Paul were beaten because they had driven out evil spirits from a girl who was possessed, but they escaped from prison after an earthquake. Instead of departing, they converted the family of the jail keeper. They would not quietly go on their way, insisting that they be properly treated as Roman citizens. They continued to evangelize in Thessalonica and Berea.

Silas remained in Berea with Timothy after Paul moved on to Athens. Later they rejoined him in Corinth. At this point Silas apparently no longer traveled with Paul, who continued to praise the work of Silas while Paul was on his third missionary journey (II Cor. 1:19). Later Silas seems to have served as scribe, perhaps even as coauthor, and messenger of the First Epistle of Peter, probably working closely with him. Tradition made him the first bishop of Corinth and a favorite saint in the Greek world.     T.J.K.

**SILOAM.** A spring, a tunnel, a collecting cistern, and a village, all with a significant part in the history of Jerusalem, both among the Jebusites and the Isrealites. The spelling of this location sometimes varies—Siloe, Siloam, and Shiloah, or in Arabic, Silwan. The place so named borders on the lower valley of the Kidron, a usually dry wadi that in its upper area runs between the present eastern wall of Jerusalem and the Mount of Olives. On the village side, to the east, there are thousands of Jewish and Arabic graves. Atop this hill Solomon built a temple to Chamos for the Moabite wives in his harem. For this reason the hill is also sometimes known as the Mount of Scandal. A tomb near the valley floor is known by tradition as that of Solomon's favorite wife, a daughter of the pharaoh.

Herbert G. May

*The Pool of Siloam*

At the bottom of the western slope of the wadi is the spring of Gihon, which feeds its water into the Pool of Siloam through an ancient tunnel. Another spring farther down the Kidron, Ain Rogel, probably gets its water from the same flow under Jerusalem that supplies Gihon. Other names for Gihon are the Fountain of the Virgin or the Fountain of Steps.

The Jebusites once sealed off this spring and conducted its water into a well inside the city walls, where they hauled up water for pre-Israelite Jerusalem by ropes and buckets, to keep attackers from cutting off the supply of water. It was up this fifty-foot shaft that David's commandos climbed one dark night, after the city gates were closed, to conquer Jerusalem for Israel (II Sam. 5:8).

To make the waters of Gihon and the Pool of Siloam even more reliable during the Assyrian sieges, King Hezekiah cut a 1,730-foot tunnel through the limestone under the city (II Kings 20:20; Ecclus. 48:17). The tunnel was picked out from both ends, and despite a broad S-curve, finally did come together. Among energetic tourists the wade through Hezekiah's unlighted tunnel to the Pool of Siloam is still a highlight of a tour of Jerusalem. One of the oldest long inscriptions of ancient Hebrew was discovered in the cave in 1880, describing how the two teams pierced through the rock and finally met. The tower of Siloam (Luke 13:4), the King's garden (Neh. 3:15), and the place where a blind man waited for Christ (John 9) are all closely connected with the Siloam area, as are many other stories.

T.J.K.

**SILVANUS.** *See* SILAS.

**SIMEON.** The name of several biblical figures. (1) The second son of JACOB and LEAH (Gen. 29:33). In the story of JOSEPH in Egypt, Simeon was retained as a hostage by Joseph, who sent back the other brothers for young Benjamin (Gen. 42:24, 36; 43:23). Simeon and his brothers Reuben, Levi, and Judah were not highly regarded by the writers of the Jacob-Joseph stories. Simeon's six sons (with the exception of Ohad) each headed a tribe (Gen. 46:10; I Chr. 4:24; Num. 26:12-14), although by the time of the judges (Judg. 5) the Song of Deborah does not mention the tribe of Simeon, which is an indication of its fallen status.

(2) The "righteous and devout" man of Jerusalem who recognized Jesus as the Messiah (Luke 2:22-35). At Jesus' presentation Simeon blessed God in the words that have become known as the Nunc Dimittis.

(3) An ancestor of Jesus (Luke 3:30).

(4) A name of Simon Peter in the KJV (Acts 15:14).

(5) A prophet and teacher in Antioch (Acts 13:1).

W.G.

**SIMEON STYLITES** (about 390–459). First of the stylites or pillar saints. After some time as a monk,

Simon became a hermit in northern Syria, near Antioch, when he was about twenty years old. Ten years later he mounted a pillar, first a low one and then higher ones. He lived the remainder of his life sixty to seventy feet off the ground, never coming down. His ascetic example was widely emulated. His feast day is January 5.                                    N.H.

**SIMON.** (1) *Magus.* One of Philip's converts in a village of Samaria (Acts 8:9-24). Simon Magus (magician, exorcist, necromancer, charlatan) attempted to buy from the apostles Peter and John the right to confer the Holy Spirit and to perform miracles. For this Peter condemned him, saying not even Philip had such ability. Ever since, in the history of the church, simony has meant the buying and selling of church offices.

In the popular tradition of the early church, Simon set himself up as a deity to be worshiped, together with his consort Helena. Church fathers like Eusebius, Irenaeus, and Justin condemned his teachings, which later became mixed with Gnosticism. One account says he was worshiped with sacrifices, incense, images, and libations. Generally, the confusion and the wild stories about Simon Magus reflect an age that was fascinated by mystical signs, miracles, and wonders.

(2) *The Zealot.* Simon Zelotes, Simon the Canaanite, and Simon the Zealot are different names for the same individual in the NT (Mark 3:18; Matt 10:14). He was apparently active against the Roman occupiers of his country, and became one of the twelve disciples, even though the Scriptures are almost completely silent about his activities as a disciple.

T.J.K.

**SIMON MACCABEUS.** *See* MACCABEAN REVOLT.

**SIMON PETER.** *See* PETER, APOSTLE.

**SIMONS, MENNO.** *See* MENNONITES.

***SIMUL IUSTUS ET PECCATOR.*** From the Latin phrase meaning "simultaneously justified and a sinner." It is MARTIN LUTHER's phrase to explain how he understood the justification of sinful humanity by a righteous God.

This was possible because God imputed the perfect righteousness of Christ to those who were redeemed. Christ died on the cross for sinners, but God sees there the human beings for whom Christ died. JUSTIFICATION is made possible through the work of the Holy Spirit. Human beings, although still capable of falling into sin, are freed from the fear of judgment. They are also freed from the sin of pride, because they know that justification is not their own work but solely that of a gracious God who in Christ suffered on their behalf. Good works become evidences of the redeemed life, and not ways of obtaining salvation.

Paul speaks of being "in Christ" and says that such people are a new creation.                                 I.C.

**SIN.** *A Religious Concept.* In ordinary speech, the word "sin" is commonly used of any moral fault. This obscures the fact that it is primarily a religious concept. Sin is basically an offense against God. This is clear when we think of primitive and archaic religion, where sin was usually understood in ceremonial terms as the transgression of some rule connected with the cultus, though this rule might have no moral import. In the higher religions, however, sin is usually a moral as well as a religious matter. We sin against God by breaking the moral law. Our duty to God is closely related to our duty to the neighbor, and when we injure the neighbor, we thereby sin against God.

The essence of sin has been variously understood. The notion of lawbreaking or transgression has already been mentioned and is appropriate where God is understood as Lawgiver. In Greek, the word for sin was *hamartia,* "missing the mark," and the Greek philosophers often equated sin with ignorance. They believed that no one would sin who really understood what he or she was doing. But although some sin does arise from ignorance, this hardly accounts for deliberate sin. The notion of sin as stain or pollution is also common, and is important in the OT. This certainly emphasizes the personal nature of sin, which enters into and disfigures the person of the sinner. Some such notion of sin lies behind the ceremonial practices of washing and those ideas of ATONEMENT that stress the cleansing blood of Christ. In much modern theology, sin is understood as separation from God, a deep ESTRANGEMENT reflected in the sinner's ALIENATION from others and even from the self. Each of these ideas contributes something to the complex notion of sin.

*Original and Corporate Sin.* The universality of sin in human life has led to various theories of ORIGINAL SIN. In the crudest form of such theories, it is believed that the first sin of Adam and Eve produced in them an inward corruption and tendency toward sin that was hereditarily transmitted to their descendants, down to the present time. Though this view has been largely abandoned, the universality of sin remains as an observable fact of human life, and there is a residual truth in the doctrine of original sin. Most theologians today would be content to say that sin has so distorted human life that every new individual born into this world absorbs something of the sinful attitude. Original sin is, in the words of Schleiermacher, "in each the work of all, and in all the work of each." No doubt there is an ORIGINAL RIGHTEOUSNESS that is more original than original sin, for it is that original ideal of a humanity made in the IMAGE OF GOD. But actual humanity has everywhere departed from that archetype.

The words of Schleiermacher, just quoted, draw attention to the corporate nature of sin. We are too inclined to think of sin in individualistic terms. More frightening than any individual sin is the massive distortion of human society through injustice and evil passions, with its resultant damaging consequences for individual lives. These corporate dimensions of sin are far more stubborn than sin in the individual, as Reinhold Niebuhr pointed out. No one seems responsible, so no one's conscience is troubled. But Niebuhr may have been too pessimistic, for sometimes vast corporate sins have been overcome. The classic instance is slavery, and the same might happen with war.

*Sin and Sins.* At the heart of sin is an attitude of the whole person—the attitude of turning away from God in resentment and revolt. All actual sins follow from this basic attitude, and it is with the basic attitude that theologians have been primarily concerned, since only if it can be changed will specific sins be overcome. However, there is a danger that theologians will simply condemn all human actions as sinful without making distinctions. Calvin's statement, "Everything proceeding from the corrupt nature of man is damnable," is a judgment that can easily become anti-human. Niebuhr believed that Barth too was indiscriminate in his condemnation of sin, and that one has to acknowledge that there are relativities. All sin is bad, but some sins are worse than others.

Moral theologians have for a long time distinguished different sins and tried to analyze the specific nature of each. Broadly speaking, a division is made between sins of indulgence and sins of the spirit. The former—sloth, lust, gluttony, and so on—are the grosser and more obvious sins, and perhaps the ones that attract most popular disapproval. Among Christians, for instance, there has been undue preoccupation with sins connected with sex. On the other hand, as Niebuhr and before him Augustine believed, the most serious sins are spiritual rather than bodily—such sins as pride, arrogance, and the desire for domination. The original temptation in the garden of Eden was: "You will be like God." All sin is turning from God, but perhaps the most deadly is the attempt to take over from God. A turning from God, however, is also a turning to the creature, that is to say, an IDOLATRY or putting some finite being in place of God. Paul sees this as characteristic of the Fall of human beings: "They worshiped and served the creature rather than the Creator" (Rom. 1:25). This links the sins of indulgence and pride, since both can be considered forms of idolatry.

*Forgiveness and Punishment.* The Bible attributes to God two responses to the sins of human creatures—forgiveness and punishment. We put forgiveness first, because it is God's affirmative response by which God seeks to overcome the damage that sin has done to the Creation. God's covenant and promise to Israel and to the whole creation stands in spite of human sin. So every falling away is met with forgiveness and the possibility of a new beginning. This culminates in the NT message of RECONCILIATION between God and humanity, effected by the work of Christ. Fallen human beings, who are unable to save themselves from sin, are offered the GRACE of forgiveness and renewal.

The alternative to forgiveness is punishment, and this remains as at least a hypothetical possibility. We need not think of God as a vengeful executioner, though God has sometimes been represented in this way. But we can envisage the possibility that the sinner will obstinately refuse the gifts of forgiveness and grace (and there is no "irresistible" grace that would violate personal being). If we suppose that people persist in sin, what then? Even in that case, their punishment is not something arbitrarily imposed by God; it is simply the unchecked working out of sin to its conclusion. When death was threatened as the punishment of sin, this was not some external punishment, but simply the dissolution of the sinner's being brought about by the ravages of sin itself. To indulge in lust and anger is to be inwardly torn apart by these passions, to be proud and arrogant is already to lapse into a coldness that freezes the springs of life, to be alienated from God is to be like a branch cut off from the vine that gives it life.

*Sin and Finitude.* It is important not to confuse sin with finitude. People cannot be blamed for not being God. Their finitude, however, makes it essential for their well-being that their lives should be lived in dependence on and companionship with God. We could say, however, that it is finitude that makes sin possible, perhaps even inevitable. Kierkegaard explored this question when he showed how finitude gives rise to an anxiety that issues in the sinful act. Other writers have tried to be more specific in linking finitude to sin. William Temple believed that it is the fact that each human being is an individual, seeing the world from one's own point of view, that gives an initial tendency toward self-centeredness. Leibnitz claimed more generally that all finitude implies imperfection; for instance, in the human being it implies imperfect knowledge and thus mistakes. Sin is not a fate, but it is perhaps inevitable in the development of the human being, who combines both freedom and finitude, and in the end it makes possible a more mature relation between redeemed humanity and God than would have been possible if that relation had never advanced beyond the immediacy of what has been called "dreaming innocence." This helps to explain why the sin of the garden of Eden came to be called by Christian theologians the *felix culpa* or "happy fault."                         J.M.

**SIN, WILDERNESS OF.** The desert region between Elim and Mount Sinai through which the Hebrews passed during their EXODUS from Egypt (Exod. 16:1; 17:1; Num. 33:11-12). Though its name resembles that of Sinai, the itinerary of the Hebrews offered in both Exodus and Numbers assumes two distinct regions. Presumably, the Wilderness of Sin is situated at the western edge of the Sinai Peninsula. Likely the ancient equivalent of modern Debbet er-Ramleh, it should not be confused with the Wilderness of Zin, located directly south of Judah.                                          J.K.K.

## SIN AGAINST THE HOLY SPIRIT.

A particular sin of an attitude opposing God described, among other places, in Mark 3:28; Matthew 12:31-32; and Luke 12:10; sometimes called BLASPHEMY against the Holy Spirit, or the UNFORGIVABLE SIN.

The sayings of Jesus about the sin against the Holy Spirit have always proved troublesome to commentators, whether Augustine, the Scholastics of the Middle Ages, the Reformers, or present-day theologians. Mark describes this sin as a denial of Christ's work and that of the Holy Spirit, crediting it instead to an evil spirit.

The sin is basically a denial of God and of God's authority. Yet Christianity has long taught the possibility of forgiveness and of faith up till the time of death, even as Christ forgave the penitent thief on the cross, since only sin against the Holy Spirit cuts one off from God. If one can ever confess faith in Christ as Savior and Messiah, however, there is no longer any chance of being guilty of blasphemy against the Holy Spirit.

Christ constantly pointed to the Pharisees as examples of those who had lost all power to retrace their steps and had therefore cut themselves off permanently from God's forgiveness. These sayings of Jesus should not trouble concerned seekers after God, since by their very seeking they demonstrate they have not reached this state.               T.J.K.

## SINAI, MOUNT.

The name of the sacred mountain before which the Israelites encamped during the EXODUS. The same site is called "Horeb" in Deuteronomy. Thus Moses is summoned at "Horeb, the mountain of God" (Exod. 3:1), and there Elijah experiences Yahweh's presence (I Kings 19:8). Lacking geographical distinctiveness, Sinai and Horeb are presumably the same site.

*Israel's Encounter with God.* At Sinai (Exod. 19–24) Israel experienced Yahweh's self-revelation and joined Yahweh in covenantal relationship based on the Law imparted through Moses, the unique mediator representing the people to God (19:8; 20:21) and God to the people (19:3, 7; 24:3). Following covenant ratification (24:3-8), Moses returned to Sinai's summit for forty days (24:18). Audible and visual elements forcefully signaling Yahweh's august presence included thunder and lightning (19:16; 20:18), cloud (24:15), fire (19:18; 24:17), smoke (20:18), and thick darkness (20:21).

*Sinai's Location.* Given the disparate biblical evidence, the locus of Mount Sinai is debated. Traditionally it has been equated with Jebel Mûsā

Courtesy of the Israel Government Tourist Office, Houston, Texas

*Traditional Mount Sinai with St. Catherine's Monastery at the base*

(Arabic: "Mount of Moses"), a 7,500-foot summit situated in the southern apex of the Sinai Peninsula.

Two alternatives merit mention. Those who interpret the Exodus 19 portrayal of Yahweh's self-revelation historically claim that volcanic activity is reflected. They favor territory east of the Gulf of Aqaba in Midian, where extinct volcanoes exist. They also note that after fleeing Egypt, Moses married into a priestly family of Midianites (Exod. 3:1; 18:1). This proposal, however, establishes a much greater distance between Egypt and Sinai than the biblical narratives imply. Moreover, the Midianites were not confined to northwest Arabia. The family Moses joined was part of the Kenite clan of roving smiths. Consequently, this group would have ample motive to visit Sinai's copper mines. Reference to the quaking mountain (Exod. 19:18) is metaphorical and no more conducive to literal appropriation than, say, the disclosure in Psalm 29:6a that Yahweh's powerful voice "makes Lebanon to skip like a calf." Manifestations of God typically embrace awesome natural phenomena as evidence of Yahweh's marvelous presence (Ps. 18:7-15 offers a superb example).

Others locate Mount Sinai at Jebel Helal west of Kadesh, a northern oasis on the Sinai Peninsula. Kadesh enjoyed prominence in the Israelite memory about wilderness wandering, and is near Seir and Paran, regions poetically associated with Sinai (Deut. 33:2; Judg. 5:4-5; Hab. 3:3). Moreover, Exodus 15:22 and Judges 11:16 imply a direct trek from Egypt to Kadesh. Nevertheless, the poetic texts lack sufficient precision to settle the issue. Certainly the

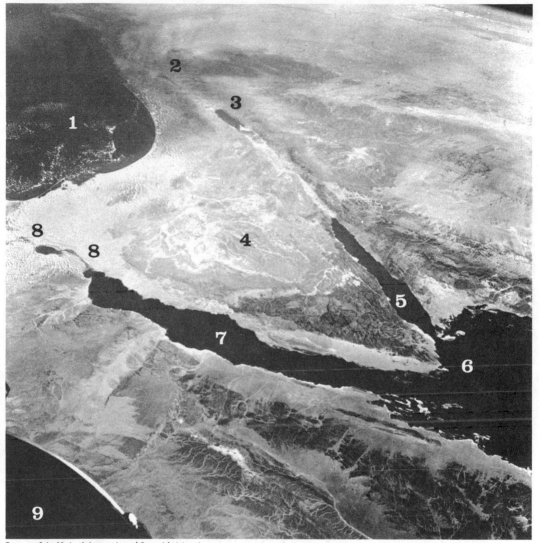

Courtesy of the National Aeronautics and Space Administration

*The Sinai Peninsula and related areas, looking north: (1) Mediterranean Sea; (2) Sea of Galilee; (3) Dead Sea; (4) Sinai Peninsula; (5) Gulf of Aqaba; (6) Red Sea; (7) Gulf of Suez; (8) Suez Canal; (9) space capsule*

notation in Deuteronomy 1:2 that Mount Horeb (Sinai) and Kadesh are separated by an eleven-day journey embarrasses this proposal.

The view that Sinai is distant from Kadesh (likewise assumed by Num. 33:2-49) plays no havoc with the traditional view, advanced since the fourth century A.D., locating the sacred mountain at Jebel Mûsâ. The present Monastery of Saint Catherine situated on its northwestern slope can be traced to A.D. 527. Legend claims that after her martyrdom, angels carried Catherine of Alexandria to the top of the mountain now bearing her name (Jebel Katarin, adjacent to Jebel Mûsâ's summit). From the monastery it is a ninety-minute climb to Jebel Mu-sā's summit. That this location has been inaccessible and dangerous for

pilgrims across the centuries itself speaks for the antiquity and authority of the tradition. Moreover, the regularly unpatrolled Egyptian copper mines of Serābît el-Khâdim located nearby might have attracted Moses' Kenite associates. The traditional identification, albeit unprovable, *is* attractive.

*Conclusion.* Biblical Israel was far more taken with the content of the event than its location. The theophany, Law, and covenant linked with Mount Sinai truly facilitated Yahweh's becoming the God of Israel and Israel's becoming the people of Yahweh.

J.K.K.

**SINAITICUS, CODEX.** Codex is a name for a writing in book form where the pages (or leaves) are

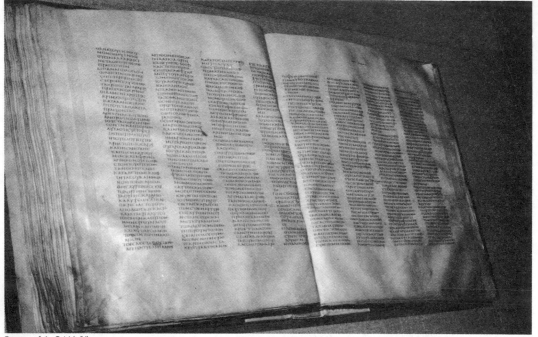

*Codex Sinaiticus (fourth century* A.D.*), the only early Greek manuscript containing the entire NT. Sheets are of high quality vellum, probably made from antelope skins.*

bound together within covers. The adjective "Sinaiticus" is given to the manuscript, comprising virtually the entire Bible, discovered by L. F. K. von Tischendorf in 1844 in the monastery on Mount Sinai. It is now in the British Library, London. The extant copy contains most of the biblical books plus some parts of the OT Apocrypha, including some extra-canonical works such as the letter of Barnabas and the *Shepherd of Hermas*. The first edition of the Codex, abbreviated by the Hebrew letter Aleph or S (Sinaiticus), is fourth century in origin, with scribal copies of later date. These copies are labeled by Aleph with an upraised small letter such as *a, b,* or *c* to denote scribal correctors. The textual evidence of Aleph is regarded as important, especially where it agrees with B (Codex Vaticanus), mainly in the Synoptic Gospels and Pauline letters. (*See* BIBLE, TEXT OF.)                                    R.M.

## SIRACH, WISDOM OF JESUS BEN. *See* ECCLESIASTICUS.

**SISERA.** The leader of the Canaanite confederacy presumably allied with Aegean elements that unsuccessfully competed against the Israelites for mastery over the Esdraelon Plain (about 1125 B.C.). Though Judges 4 identifies Sisera as the army commander of King Jabin of Hazor (4:2), Judges 5, containing the archaic Song of Deborah, presents

Sisera as the head of a coalition of Canaanite monarchs and omits mention of Jabin. Forced to flee from Israel's foot soldiers when the flooding waters of the Kishon bogged down the Canaanite chariots, Sisera sought refuge with Heber the Kenite, with whom he was on good terms. Heber's wife Jael, a deadly hostess, killed Sisera unawares, thereby parading her loyalty to Israel (4:18-21; 5:24-27).          J.K.K.

**SISTINE CHAPEL.** Famous chapel decorated by Michelangelo in the VATICAN during the reign of Pope Sixtus IV (1471–84), for whom it was named. It was originally a chapel and also a fortification (or keep), but later other walls were built and it lost its defensive function. It contains the outstanding paintings of the Creation on its ceiling and of the Last Judgment on the altar wall.          J.C.

**SITUATION ETHICS.** Situation ethics is often referred to as the "new morality," a movement in contemporary Christian ethics initiated by Joseph Fletcher in an article entitled "A New Look in Christian Ethics" (1959). The view was given prominence in the chapter on ethics in Bishop John A. T. Robinson's best-selling *Honest to God* (1963). Joseph Fletcher expanded his position in *Situation Ethics: the New Morality* (1966).

In contrast to LEGALISM or antinomianism, Fletcher proposes the situational method for making moral decisions. This method is pragmatic, relativistic, positivistic (that is, based on faith), and personal. Christian ethics interprets the situation and utilizes the situational method within the context of Christian faith and love. Fletcher's method is informed by six propositions: (1) only love is always good; (2) the ruling norm of Christian decision is love alone; (3) love includes justice, which is love distributed; (4) love does not depend upon liking a person; (5) love as the end justifies the means; and (6) decisions in love are to be made in particular circumstances.

Situation ethics evoked a storm of controversy in the 1960s and continues as a subject of discussion. Proponents emphasize its focus upon people and actual cases as a means for overcoming rigid legalism and prepackaged answers in Christian ethical reflection. Critics point to the utilitarian tendency of situation ethics, the imprecision of movement from loving intentions to loving consequences, the lack of clarity in relating the facts of particular cases to value judgments, and the limited view of the situation among adherents of situation ethics.

In spite of the difficulties of situation ethics, the movement has served as a corrective to certain tendencies in contemporary Christan ethics. For example, H. Richard Niebuhr held that the reduction of ethics to TELEOLOGY and deontology is inadequate. These two types must be supplemented by responsibility in context to form a threefold method in Christian ethics. Situation ethics has in some measure made up for the lack that Niebuhr saw, though its corrective has, in the view of many, focused too narrowly on the immediate situation rather than on the comprehensive context intended by Niebuhr. In similar fashion, situation ethics has also served to correct the tendencies in recent decades toward excessive emphasis in Christian ethics on rules and on rationalism. (*See also* RELATIVISM.)          C.Mc.

*SITZ IM LEBEN.* The German phrase for "the setting in life," a term used in biblical criticism to refer to the situation in which a biblical passage was written. Used in redaction (editorial) criticism, it aims to demonstrate the prevailing conditions in the life of a group that caused the biblical writer to present an idea (for example, the teachings of Jesus) in a certain way.          J.C.

**SIVAN.** *See* HEBREW CALENDAR.

**SIX HUNDRED AND SIXTY-SIX.** *See* BEAST.

*SKANDHAS.* From the Sanksrit word for "bundles." In the philosophy of BUDDHISM, the entities that comprise a human being. Themselves aggregates or bundles of the primordial particles, *dharmas,* the human *skandhas* are five in number: physical form, senses, perceptions, reactions (for example, an emotional response), and consciousness. The *skandha* concept emphasizes the composite and hence imper-

manent (that is, *anatman* or "no self") nature of the human being.          R.E.

**SKEPTICISM.** Skepticism denotes: (1) a general attitude of doubt, (2) a philosophical tradition originating in ancient Greece that questions the possibility of authentic knowledge, and (3) the doubting of particular religious, scientific, or societal convictions.

The term derives from *skepsis,* a Greek word originally meaning "inquiry" or "speculation" in a reflective manner, especially related to sense perception. Further developing Socrates' questioning method, Pyrrho (about 360–270 B.C.) and thinkers of the third century B.C. in Plato's Academy initiated skepticism as a philosophy that challenged the reliability of sense perception and proposed to doubt the truth of all assertions.

AUGUSTINE (A.D. 354–430) sought to refute skepticism, affirming that doubt presupposes faith and that philosophy is faith seeking understanding. Medieval and Reformation thinkers tended to use skepticism to show the inadequacy of reason and the need for revelation and faith.

DESCARTES (1596–1650) developed a rigorous skepticism to strip away the dubious, leaving "clear and distinct" ideas as a basis for knowledge. The skepticism of David Hume (1711–76) about all knowledge provoked IMMANUEL KANT (1724–1804) to formulate his critical philosophy. In this perspective, only natural scientific knowledge is certain, while religious convictions rest on mere faith or moral certainty. Much philosophy and theology in the twentieth century have been preoccupied with the problems posed by the critical separation of objectivity from subjectivity and of knowledge from faith.

Michael Polanyi (1891–1976) illustrates the emergence of a post-critical attitude toward skepticism, holding that all knowing takes place within a communal context of faith. When skepticism ignores this tacit dimension of knowing, it destroys the possibility of knowledge in every area, including the natural sciences. Doubting presupposes a background of believing that defines the meaning and limits of skepticism. Skepticism, therefore, provides correctives to inherited dogmas—scientific, societal, religious—but has no meaning apart from communities of interpretation and commitment. (*See also* RELATIVISM.)          C.Mc.

**SKINNER, B. F.** *See* BEHAVIORISM.

**SLAVERY.** An institution, involving one person's legal ownership of another, widely embraced in the biblical world as essential to the social order.

Just as slavery is addressed by such second-millennium B.C. Mesopotamian documents as the Laws of Eshnunna, the Lipit-Ishtar Law Code, the Code of Hammurabi, and the Middle Assyrian Laws, so it is addressed by biblical legislation in Exodus 21,

Leviticus 25, and Deuteronomy 15. Slaves were obtained by wartime capture (Num. 31:9; II Chr. 28:8), purchase from slave owners (Gen. 17:27), and self sale, when there was no other way for the poor to meet financial indebtedness (Lev. 25:47) or the thief to make restitution (Exod. 22:3). Biblical narratives refer to defaulting debtors fleeing from their creditors (I Sam. 22:2), parents agitated that they might have to sell their children (Neh. 5:1-5), and the creditor preparing to seize the offspring of his deceased debtor (II Kings 4:1). Some slaves taken in war became the property of either the sanctuary (Josh. 9:27) or the crown (II Sam. 12:31), but most slaves served as domestics in the homes and fields of their masters.

Though biblical Israel did not question this institution, memory of its own enslavement in Egypt led to a humanitarian treatment of slaves who were valued as human beings as well as chattel. A slave wounded by his master was granted freedom (Exod. 21:26-27). Sabbath rest was mandated for both slaves and masters (Exod. 20:10). Slaves were entitled to freedom after six years of service, and masters were urged to be generous when liberating them (Deut. 15:12-14). The fugitive slave escaping from his master in a foreign land was to be granted asylum in Israel (Deut. 23:15-16 [the Code of Hammurabi decrees the death penalty for such harboring]). Ecclesiastes recommends leniency toward the slave who curses his master (Eccl. 7:21-22).

With population statistics yielding a slave-freedman ratio of one to five throughout the Roman Empire, the presence of slaves in the early church was, of course, accepted without incident. Nevertheless, the NT epistles advocate a brotherly interaction between master and slave (Philem. 16) and affirm that slave and free are one "in Christ" (Gal. 3:28; I Cor. 12:13). Masters are admonished to treat their slaves fairly (Col. 4:1; Eph. 6:9). Slaves, in turn, are urged to be respectful (I Tim. 6:1-2), to work conscientiously (Col. 3:22-23), and to strive for integrity (Tit. 2:10). The Gospels attest the slave as a stock figure in the teachings of Jesus (Matt. 25:14-30; Mark 10:43-45; Luke 14:16-24) and portray Jesus healing servants who were the property of the centurion (Matt. 8:5-13) and high priest (Luke 22:50-51).

J.K.K.

**SMITH, JOSEPH** (1805–44). Mormon founder and prophet. He was born on December 23 in Sharon, Vermont, to Joseph and Lucy Mack Smith. In 1816 the family moved to Palmyra, New York. Joseph experienced his first vision in the spring of 1820, followed by similar ones in 1823, in which the angel Nephi (later called Moroni) appeared to him. The angel said that no sect on earth represented God's will, that the church of Christ had been withdrawn, and that Smith was chosen to restore it.

On September 22, 1827, Smith was shown plates of gold at Hill Cumorah, Ontario County, New York, which recorded the "true" history of the church

Courtesy of the Library of Congress

*Joseph Smith*

in America. His three-year translation of the plates was published in July 1830 as the *Book of Mormon*. Along with *A Book of Commandments* (1833) and *Doctrine and Covenants* (1835), it forms the basis of Mormonism. Smith founded the CHURCH OF JESUS CHRIST OF LATTER-DAY SAINTS on April 6, 1830. The church was at once millennial, restorationist, and perfectionist.

On June 18, 1827, Smith married Emma Hale of Harmony, Pennsylvania. She bore him five children, including Joseph Smith (1832–1914). Smith (the father) allegedly had as many as twenty-seven other wives and in 1843 declared that polygamy was a part of Mormon belief and practice. In 1831 Smith moved his flock to Kirtland, Ohio, in 1838 to Missouri, and in 1839 they were forced to Commerce, Illinois, which Smith renamed NAUVOO. There the Mormons grew and prospered. In 1844 Smith even announced he would run for the presidency. His destruction of his critics' press, however, gave outsiders an excuse for revenge. He and his brother were imprisoned in Carthage, Illinois, and were taken out and shot.

N.H.

**SMITH, SAMUEL FRANCIS** (1808–95). Baptist minister, linguist, author, and hymn writer. Smith gained his greatest fame as the one who penned the words for "America," which was introduced on July 4, 1832, by Lowell Mason's children's choir at Park Street Congregational Church, Boston. Educated at Boston Latin School and Harvard College (where Oliver Wendell Holmes was a classmate), Smith received his ministerial training at Andover Theological Seminary. His first church was in Waterville, Maine, where he also taught modern languages at Colby College. Later Smith was called to the Baptist Church at Newton, Massachusetts, from which he resigned to become secretary of the American Baptist Missionary Union. He and Baron Stow compiled *The Psalmist: A New Collection of Hymns* (1843), a widely known Baptist hymnal. His deep missonary interest is reflected in "The Morning Light Is Breaking." His immersionist convictions are contained in "Down to the Sacred Wave." Smith died at Newton Center, Massachusetts, on November 16.          R.H.

**SMYRNA.** The present-day Turkish city of Izmir on the shores of the Aegean Sea. It was one of the SEVEN CHURCHES addressed by John in the book of Revelation; he encouraged it to remain faithful during the Roman persecutions. Perhaps the most beautiful city of Asia Minor, rivaled only by Ephesus, this seaport had a large Jewish colony. One of its early bishops was the church father Polycarp.     T.J.K.

**SNAKE HANDLING.** This is a phenomenon that has been practiced by a small group of Pentecostals, mostly outlawed congregations of the Church of God, in Appalachia. During the course of fervent services the snake handlers pass poisonous snakes, usually rattlers or copperheads, from one member of the congregation to another. This is done in observance of the phrase in Mark 16:18, "they shall take up serpents" (KJV).

The initiator of the practice was "Little" George Hensley, who in 1909 climbed White Oak Mountain, which rims Grasshopper Valley (Tenn.), in search of a large rattlesnake. A few days later, while conducting evangelistic services at nearby Sale Creek, Hensley quoted the Markan passage, thrust the rattlesnake at the people, and challenged them to take it up as a test of their faith.

Thereafter the practice of snake handling continued, until Garland Defriese, one of Hensley's converts, was bitten. In the summer of 1938 three members of the Pine Mountain Church of God were arrested for a breach of the peace—reptile handling. Later they were acquitted. Bona fide figures on the number of groups that practice snake handling are impossible to track down, but reports indicate that the phenomenon continues.     R.H.

**SOBORNOST.** The Russian Orthodox term for synod or church assembly, akin to the Greek concept of koinonia. In Orthodoxy, there is a mystical sense to the sobornost, a union or henosis between priests and laypeople that expresses itself in the traditional liturgy. This unity is considered superior to the polity of Catholicism and Protestantism.     J.C.

**SOCIAL DARWINISM.** A term for the use of evolutionary ideas, drawn from the writings of CHARLES DARWIN and HERBERT SPENCER, and applied to ethics, social theory, and history. Social Darwinism was prevalent in England, Europe, and especially in America between the 1880s and World War I. The Social Darwinists were particularly taken with the Darwinian idea of development from simple, homogeneous forms of life to higher, more complex forms. They also accepted Spencer's evolutionary optimism with regard to society, based on the view that the "struggle for existence" has a beneficial effect on the progress of the human race by ensuring the "survival of the fittest." They assumed that pressure of subsistence on human populations encourages the development of skill, intelligence, and adaptability.

Acceptance of Lamarck's theory of the inheritance of acquired characteristics by Social Darwinists gave impetus both to competition and to social planning and eugenics. Social Darwinism thus produced contradictory social theories. Some emphasized Darwinian natural selection through the struggle *among* members of the species to justify extreme views of laissez-faire political economy. Others argued, on the basis of natural selection as a struggle *between* species and races, for imperialistic policies based on national and racial superiority. One of the most dangerous twentieth-century offshoots of this vogue of Social Darwinism was the myth of Aryan supremacy and the prominence of anti-Semitic theories derived, for example, from the popular writing of Houston Stewart Chamberlin.     J.L.

**SOCIAL ETHICS.** *See* ETHICS.

**SOCIAL GOSPEL.** This term, often used imprecisely and pejoratively, refers to the general teaching arising in the late nineteenth and early twentieth centuries that sought to relate the Christian gospel to the social environment as well as to individuals.

The Social Gospel was a product of liberal Protestantism that for a time exercised the dominant influence on United States Christianity. The German-American WALTER RAUSCHENBUSCH (1861–1918), who was moved by the dislocations in society caused by industrialization, gained the title "Father of the Social Gospel in America." Essentially, the Social Gospel movement was a transitory phase of Christian social thought, a submovement within religious liberalism. Because of its optimistic view of human nature, many of its critics believe the Social Gospel did not prepare Christians for two world wars and the depression. The Social Gospelers were crusaders who believed in social progress and the essential goodness of people.

The Social Gospel movement was given formal expression in 1908, when the Federal Council of the Churches of Christ in America was formed. Many of its ideals were embodied in the New Deal legislation of the 1930s.

The Social Gospel is an identifiable development in American religious thinking. While it did emerge from liberal interpretations of the faith, it cannot be denied that it stressed the truth of the gospel's relationship to the world in which Christians are called upon to witness.

In the intense struggle of FUNDAMENTALISM and MODERNISM in the early part of the twentieth century, orthodox believers tended to speak disparagingly of the Social Gospel with its liberal origins. The Fundamentalists moved defensively into a position of declaring that the unique—the only—task of the church was the preaching of the gospel. Only toward the end of the twentieth century did Evangelicals reassert their concern for people's social as well as spiritual needs.                                        R.H.

## SOCIETY FOR PROMOTING CHRISTIAN KNOWLEDGE (SPCK).

In response to pleas from colonists in Maryland, the bishop of London commissioned Thomas Bray to find them Bibles, Christian books, and pastoral help. He and others founded SPCK in 1698. It was given a royal charter in 1701 and continues to be a major English publisher today. SPCK initially provided free libraries for the colonies. Many Christian schools and teacher training colleges were founded in Britain and on various British mission fields around the world under its auspices.                                        N.H.

## SOCIETY FOR THE PROPAGATION OF THE GOSPEL IN FOREIGN PARTS.

The SPGFP was founded by the Reverend Thomas Bray in 1701. Bray had been sent from England to inspect the state of church life in the American colonies. The purpose of the society was to minister to English settlers overseas and also among the Indians. The first missionaries were sent to North America, but soon afterward the work of the society spread to several other outposts of British colonialism such as India, Burma, South Africa, and even to other territories such as Japan, North China, Korea, and Polynesia. In 1965 the SPGFP united with the Universities Mission to Central Africa to form the United Society for Promoting the Gospel, under which name it continues its missionary endeavors.

W.G.

## SOCIETY OF JESUS. *See* JESUITS.

## SOCINIANS/SOCINUS.

A sixteenth-century religious group, precursors of UNITARIANISM. They accepted Jesus as God's revelation but considered him primarily human, and divine only by office, not by nature.

The group originated in Italy with the work of Laelius Socinus (1525–62) and his nephew Faustus (1539–1604). (Socinus is the latinized form of Sozzini.) Laelius, trained in law at Padua, was a friend of John Calvin and Philipp Melanchthon. Faustus'

anti-trinitarian views were denounced by the Inquisition in 1559. He published them anyway in 1562 and in 1563 denied human immortality. He fled to Poland, where the Polish Brethren, under his leadership, grew to three hundred congregations. Their center was Rakow, where Socinian views were taught in the university and propagated by its press, until forced to close in 1638 by Jesuit persecution. In 1658 the Polish Diet offered the Socinians their choice of exile or conformity. Some fled to Transylvania, the Netherlands, and Germany, where they were gradually absorbed by other groups.

N.H.

## SOCIOBIOLOGY.

A new field of science that emerged during the 1970s that proposes to apply the findings of evolutionary biology and genetics to human behavior in areas previously dealt with by anthropology, sociology, and ethics. Much controversy has surrounded sociobiology because of claims such as those by zoologist Edward O. Wilson (*Sociobiology: the New Synthesis,* 1975; *On Human Nature,* 1978) that the new discipline will be able to displace the dying social sciences by "biologizing" them.

The analytical methods of evolutionary biology have made remarkable advances in recent decades in dealing with certain adaptive patterns of animal and insect behavior. For example, worker ants that produce no offspring apparently have evolved to provide for the progeny of the queen ant and thus serve the purposes of the community. Their behavior in the ant society can be explained on the basis of biological programming to ensure not the survival of the individual insect but of the group and its genes. Building on this success in explaining nonhuman behavior, sociobiologists first offered genetic explanations of such forms of human behavior as sexual relationships and orientation, war, religion, and the design of architecture, and subsequently developed an explanatory model based on genetic/cultural coevolution.

Sociobiologists do not assert that human social behavior is totally dependent upon or determined by biological factors, specifically genetic programming. However, when there is a choice between two alternative patterns of behavior, for example, between monogamy and polygamy, rules representing genetic predisposition condition the outcome. These theories suggest the possible importance of genetic engineering and gene-splicing.

Critics of sociobiology point to its insufficiency for clear results, to its overly complex biological analyses of simple human behavioral issues, and to its tendency toward theological comprehensiveness rather than scientific precision. The accusation is also made that sociobiology can easily become a successor to SOCIAL DARWINISM, a movement of the late nineteenth century claiming that the socially rich and powerful must be the fittest and the best. Many fear that sociobiology will provide the basis for continued discrimination against people of particular races and those who are socially disadvantaged.

Though these criticisms must be kept in mind, sociobiology gives promise of throwing new light on human behavior and relating the natural sciences more closely to the social sciences and humanities. Some of its claims seem exaggerated, but it deserves continuing attention and careful evaluation.

C.Mc.

## SOCIOLOGICAL STRUCTURALIST CRITICISM. *See* BIBLICAL CRITICISM.

## SOCIOLOGY OF RELIGION.
The term "sociology" was invented by the French philosopher AUGUSTE COMTE (1795–1857) as a designation for a grand synthesis of knowledge of humanity. Its methods were to be "positivistic": observation, experimentation, and comparison. In the spirit of the later eighteenth and early nineteenth centuries, Comte sought to free human thought from traditional religious authority in order to explore and understand human origins and human culture. Earlier thinkers, whose work anticipated the aims of Comte, had sought to trace statistically the changes in human society through population and migration studies, but the focus of sociology soon shifted to political and cultural factors. These lines of inquiry were greatly facilitated by detailed studies of primitive societies in lands newly accessible to the West, or seriously analyzed for the first time and in their own terms. An important ingredient in these investigations, which paved the way for anthropology, was what was known as "folk psychology"—how members of a particular society viewed the world, their origins, their destiny. Akin to this was the analysis of the social process itself: individual and group behavior patterns, societal structures, including class stratification and development of leadership, and the perception of group identity. Strongly influential in the development of these methods were the theories of evolution, which gave rise to such notions as the survival of the fittest and inevitable progress.

In the later nineteenth and early twentieth centuries, scholars interested in ancient cultures— both those of Greece and Rome and those of the ancient Near East—turned to archaeological, literary, and inscriptional sources, with the aim of performing analyses similar to those of the sociologists and anthropologists. The aim in most cases was to discern universal patterns of human behavior, individually and corporately. Meanwhile sociological theoreticians were seeking to discover the general laws of human social behavior and societal development in order to understand the past and to predict the future. Inevitably, these lines of inquiry affected the study of religion, which is a common feature of all societies. Those who wanted to place biblical religion in a framework of universal religious experience were eager to utilize the new methods, whether to classify the biblical evidence in the general categories of religion, as in the studies by E. B. Tylor (1932–1917), or in the still widely utilized approach of JAMES G. FRAZER (in *The Golden Bough*), whose encyclopedic study treats the variety of world religions as variations on a basic theme of a dying and rising divinity. Those who wanted to affirm the special character of biblical religion understandably held aloof from the sociological enterprise with its drive toward generalizations.

Thinkers who were seeking to trace patterns of historical development, on the other hand, including the emergence of early Christianity, are exemplified by the so-called Tübingen School in Germany, which took its cue from G. W. F. HEGEL'S theory that human history moves by a dialectical process in which an idea (thesis) evokes a counter-idea (antithesis), from which then emerges a new, higher synthesis. For example, Paul's law-free gospel (thesis) is attacked by Judaizing Christians (antithesis), from which there emerges early catholic Christianity (synthesis). KARL MARX, on the other hand, regarded history as moving on through the actions and reactions of economic and social forces, rather than of ideas. Responding to Marx's theory, MAX WEBER proposed that the history of any society is shaped by the network of values, convictions, and aspirations that it shares. In addition to his study, *The Protestant Ethic and the Spirit of Capitalism*, in which he directly takes issue with Marxist theory, Weber undertook detailed studies of religious traditions in the Middle and Far East to show how they are constitutive for their respective societies. The most significant of these for biblical studies was *Ancient Judaism*. In this work Weber sought to show how Israel had changed historically from a loose aggregation of tribes among whom spontaneous ("charismatic") leaders emerged in time of crisis, to a unified nation, with institutionalized political and religious powers and with a common central shrine under a king.

Perhaps because both liberal and evangelical Protestants were preoccupied with their own respective forms of religious individualism, the potential of Weber's sociological approach for the study of biblical history went largely unrealized. There were some short-lived efforts at the University of Chicago in the 1920s and 1930s to use this resource as support for the Social Gospel by reconstructing the social setting of primitive Christianity. And in Germany, the form-critics M. Dibelius and R. Bultmann talked about the life situation (*Sitz im Leben*) of the oral traditions later incorporated into the Gospels, but their focus was almost solely on the ideas of the Gospel material rather than on the specifics of the social structures and dynamics. Similarly, in the OT field, archaeologists, such as W. F. Albright, were seeking to assemble and assess for historical purposes the mass of archaeological and inscriptional evidence from the ancient Near East, with its enormous potential for aiding historical reconstruction of ancient Israelite society. And a century and more of classical studies, as well as the discovery of quantities of writings from the Greco-Roman period, including personal and commercial records, shed new light on social details of the culture of this period during which Pauline and the other NT writings were produced in the Roman world. But apart from pointing out parallels or general similarities between specific ideas and practices in the Bible and those in the ancient world, little systematic use was made of this evidence for sociological analysis. Efforts at historical reconstruction in the OT period at the turn of this century include the work of Julius Wellhausen (1884–1918), whose analysis of the oral and literary forms embedded in the biblical material and whose empathy for the poetic and mythic elements in the Bible (in contrast to his skepticism about historical reconstruction) evidenced a closer kinship to sociologists than to historians. Only since the 1970s has a broad-based effort been made by biblical scholars to utilize sociological methods for biblical history and interpretation; yet nearly the entire range of those methods and theory has been put to use.

Sociology concerns itself with social organization, social psychology, and social change. Akin to these, but emphasizing description and classification of data rather than tracing patterns of development, is anthropology, within which may be distinguished ethnology (comparative study of customs), social anthropology (comparison of social organizations), and ethnography (gathering evidence about human societies), which is assisted by archaeology (material remains of ancient cultures). In recent years a kindred undertaking is sociology of knowledge, which builds on Max Weber's concept of values as forming the basis of a society. The concern of social anthropologists for the social function of phenomena, as distinguished from mere description, meshes well with sociology of knowledge and with sociology of literature (the analysis of the social function of a writing). For example, the social function of an exorcism in one society may be the display of magical power, while in another (the gospel tradition), an exorcism is a sign of the coming of God's rule (Luke 11:20).

In OT studies, some of the major areas of interest for sociological inquiry have been whether the tribal structure of ancient Israel in the period before the monarchy is to be seen as a loose confederation around a common shrine (Martin Noth) or a peasants' revolt (George Mendenhall, and from a Marxist perspective, Norman Gottwald); what was the social function of the prophets and what is the historical significance of the genealogies (Robert R. Wilson); what was the social situation that gave rise to Jewish apocalyptic (Paul D. Hanson). On the NT side, traditional sociological questions and methods that treat of class and economic distinctions appear in the significant work of Gerd Theissen of Heidelberg, who has published illuminating analyses of the Jesus move-

ment and of the Pauline churches. Wayne Meeks of Yale has produced an important study of *The First Urban Christians*, working from socio-economic evidence both within and outside of the NT. As noted above, in OT studies Robert R. Wilson of Yale has provided valuable insight into the social dynamics of Israel's history and religion through his use of sociological methods. Some attempts have been made by exponents of liberation theology to reconstruct the origins of Israel and of the church by the use of Marxist sociology, with results that are heavily ideological and not historically persuasive to most.

In France and to a lesser extent in North America the attempt has been made to use the anthropological theories of Claude Lévi-Strauss in NT studies, especially his notion that all human thought may be reduced to patterns of "binary opposition," such as good/evil, real/unreal, literal/figurative. By this method both the historical development evident in the Bible and the intentions of the authors are dismissed as unimportant, in favor of timeless patterns present universally in the human mind. Like the methods of the history of religions school and the psychologists of religion (of Jungian persuasion) who want to discern eternal mental models of religious experience, the results are counterproductive for the historical study of the Bible.

Of all the anthropologists whose work has been utilized in biblical studies, the one whose contribution has been the greatest and the most direct is Mary Douglas, whose studies of purity and boundaries that demarcate social and religious communities has a direct and immensely fruitful contribution to make in both OT and NT studies. Her own work on Levitical purity makes the links explicit.

Some scholars have been content to draw on anthropology primarily to provide categories for classifying biblical phenomena, but their work ignores the distinctiveness of the changing historical contexts in which the biblical people lived and wrote. By contrast, the most significant work being done in the biblical field combines insights from the anthropological methods and studies wih sociology of knowledge, as represented by the work of Peter Berger, Thomas Luckmann, and Alfred Schutz. This method takes fully into account the view of the world shared by a distinct segment of society and constitutive of its values, its hopes and anxieties, its leadership, and its social structure. By raising these kinds of questions concerning the changing world of the biblical writers, in both OT and NT times, the distinctive features and the diversity that is there represented may be discerned and illuminated. Since in the biblical tradition the Word of God is always addressed to human beings in human terms, and since human existence is always societal in nature, it is essential that the social dimensions of the Bible be taken into account in interpreting the biblical message and reconstructing its history.

Introductory manuals for using sociological

methods in biblical interpretation include Robert R. Wilson's *Sociological Approaches to the Old Testament* (1984) and Howard C. Kee's *Christian Origins in Sociological Perspective* (1980).                    H.K.

**SOCRATES** (about 470–399 B.C.). Greek thinker, regarded as the father of Western philosophy and perhaps the greatest figure in the history of Greek thought. Socrates turned Greek philosophy away from the pre-Socratic interest in cosmology to the concerns of human conduct. There is little agreement on what can be known of the historical Socrates or of his specific contributions to philosophical doctrine. Living at the time of Athens' splendor, he was known for his physical robustness and endurance and distinguished himself for bravery in the Peloponnesian War. Historians have long been engaged by the "problem of Socrates," or determining his actual philosophical teaching. The sources—Xenophon's Socratic works (*Memorabilia* and *Symposium*), PLATO's dialogues, and statements in ARISTOTLE and Aristophanes's *Clouds*—give contradictory evidence. Xenophon makes him out to be a popular ethical teacher, while Plato portrays Socrates as a sophisticated metaphysician.

Socrates's method of philosophizing, it is agreed, was "dialectical" or conversational. He would engage a companion and profess ignorance on a subject, for example, the meaning of courage. When the companion offered a definition, Socrates would raise a few questions, exposing the inadequacy of the companion's response. In this way he would lead his companion to a more adequate, universal definition. Some found Socrates's method irritating and humiliating, but his aim was to discover truth and the good life. Socrates believed in the unity of knowledge and virtue, that is, that clear knowledge of truth is essential for a virtuous and happy life. Furthermore, he believed that knowledge and virtue are one in that the man who *knows* what is right will *do* what is right.

This ethical rationalism is criticized by some who would claim that Socrates didn't take into account the irrational character of the human will. Socrates insisted, nevertheless, that virtue is teachable and he certainly practiced what he preached. About 400 B.C. Socrates was accused by the court of King Archon of (1) not worshiping the gods of the State and (2) corrupting the youth (by instilling in them the spirit of criticism). He refused to go into exile or to make special appeal to the court. Rather, he made light of the charges. He was sentenced to death and refused to escape when it was arranged by his friends. He died of his own hand by taking the poison hemlock. The nobility of his last day and death is recounted by Plato in the *Phaedo*.                    J.L.

**SODOM.** Like its twin, GOMORRAH, the legendary city of Sodom is described in Genesis 10:19 as lying at the southeastern border of Canaan. It is identified with LOT, the nephew of Abraham, in Genesis

Courtesy of the American Schools of Oriental Research

*Pillar of salt on Jebel Usdum ("Mount of Sodom"), located on the shore of the Dead Sea near Sodom*

13:1-13, where the stage is set for Sodom's abiding image as Sin City: "Now the men of Sodom were wicked, great sinners against the Lord." In Genesis 14 Sodom is one of the five cities that fight a losing battle in the region of the Dead Sea against the four kings of the East. Attempts to locate Sodom either alongside or under the southern end of the Dead Sea have not, however, brought any trace of it to light.

Genesis 18:16-33 is the famous account of Abraham's bargaining session with Yahweh over the fate of Sodom. The Lord agrees to spare the city if as few as ten righteous people can be found there, but chapter 19 reveals that not even that small number can be reached. Sodom's fate is sealed when the two angels who had visited Abraham and Sarah in the previous chapter are trapped in Lot's house by the men of that place who demand that they be brought forth for the purpose of homosexual abuse (known in our criminal codes as "sodomy"). Yahweh urges Lot and his household to flee from the impending destruction of Sodom. When Lot's wife looks back at the spectacle of Sodom's demise she immediately becomes a pillar of salt.

In the majority of the ensuing biblical references, Sodom is used together with Gomorrah as a metaphor for utter human depravity. In a curious reversal, however, the prophet Ezekiel favorably compares Sodom with her "sisters" Samaria and the harlot Jerusalem, to provide a standard against which the even greater wickedness of his contemporary community could be dramatized. Similarly, Jesus warns the cities in which his miracles had been performed that "if the mighty works done in you had been done in Sodom, it would have remained until this day" (Matt. 11:23).

In Luke 17:29-30, the destruction of Sodom by fire and brimstone is an analogy for the day of the coming of the Son of man. That analogy is echoed in another way in Jude 7, where the fire that punished Sodom and Gomorrah is called "eternal."                    W.S.T.

**SOJOURNER.** *See* FOREIGNER.

**SOKA GAKKAI.** The Japanese term for "Value Creation Society." Founded in 1937 by Tsunesaburo Makiguchi (1871–1944) as the Soka Kyoiku Gakkai, this lay organization was originally a small group for the discussion of educational philosophy, particularly from the point of view that it should emphasize benefit rather than abstract truth. But Makiguchi, who died in prison during the war, was a strong believer in NICHIREN Shoshu, a Buddhist tradition that also has an aspect favoring this-worldly benefits. When Soka Gakkai was revived in 1945 by Josei Toda (1900–58), a dynamic leader, it was as a lay auxiliary to Nichiren Shoshu.

Possessing many features of the "new religions" of Japan, it grew phenomenally during the 1950s and 1960s. Its convert-winning tactics were often criticized, but served to make Nichiren Shoshu the largest single religious institution in Japan, with some sixteen million members by the early 1980s. (Membership in Soka Gakkai and Nichiren Shoshu is now coextensive.) Soka Gakkai is known for its elaborate organization, its lavish conventions, its sponsorship of many cultural activities, and the Kokeito political party founded by Soka Gakkai members.                                                        R.E.

**SOLA FIDE.** From the Latin phrase for "faith alone." This is MARTIN LUTHER's translation of Romans 3:28, "A man is justified by faith apart from works of law." The word "alone" was not in the original text of Scripture, but Luther felt that the intention was there and used it to balance the contemporary stress on justification by works. The doctrine as stated is an effort to emphasize the fact that being made just in the sight of the holy God can come only through an act of God. This act was the death and resurrection of Jesus Christ. Faith is a gift of God that brings a person into a new relationship with God. Faith is also the appropriate human response to God's prior gift of salvation. Only by trusting God can a person appropriate salvation, the new life that makes one a new creature.                                      I.C.

**SOLA GRATIA.** From the Latin phrase "grace alone." The Greek equivalent means "gift." The theological term means that human beings are saved only by the unmerited grace of God. God's love for all creation is so full that in spite of human sinfulness, God desires people to respond to divine love. Because God is totally good and loving, human beings can fulfill this relationship only by being freed from the sinfulness that alienates them from God. The grace or love of God enables people to accept the righteousness offered through Christ (justification) and be saved.

Good works flow from grace and are an expression of the love of God in people's lives.                      I.C.

**SOLA SCRIPTURA.** The expression used for the teaching that Scripture alone is decisive in settling questions of doctrine or practice. This teaching is one of the fundamental principles of PROTESTANTISM and is common to all Protestant denominations, though held with varying degrees of rigor. It was formulated in opposition to the Roman Catholic teaching that there are two sources of doctrine, Scripture and TRADITION, the latter understood as a deposit of unwritten truths that have been transmitted in the teaching of the church. In its broadest sense, *sola scriptura* simply means the sufficiency of the Scriptures, the claim that they contain everything that is necessary for salvation. Some theologians who believed this were willing to allow certain beliefs and practices that are neither forbidden nor expressly permitted in Scripture, on the ground that they were matters of indifference or "adiaphora." The much stricter view was that nothing is to be believed or practiced that is not explicitly authorized by Scripture. However, it was virtually impossible to adhere to this strict view. Vatican II abandoned the teaching about two sources and claimed instead that Scripture and tradition are like two streams rising from a common wellspring. The sharp difference that *sola scriptura* was supposed to emphasize has become blurred at the present time.                          J.M.

**SOLOMON.** Israel's third king (about 961–922 B.C.) and son of DAVID and Bathsheba. Through Nathan's revelation, he was named Jedidiah ("beloved of Yahweh"). But David named him Solomon (meaning "peaceful"), hoping that his son's reign would be more tranquil than his (II Sam. 12:24-25; see I Chr. 22:9).

During an era of relative peace, Solomon worked diligently to bring international esteem to Israel. No major world power existed to bother Solomon, and commercial alliances and military surveillance enabled him to dominate lesser neighboring nations. Solomon obtained political advantage with Egypt through a nameless pharaoh of the impotent Twenty-first Dynasty (I Kings 3:1). Agreements with Hiram I, king of TYRE (5:1, 10-11), and the queen of Sheba (10:1-10, 13), respectively, cemented ties with northern Phoenicians and the Sabeans of Arabia. This was Israel's golden age, one further enriched by unprecedented intellectual and cultural attainments. Yet when Solomon died, so did Israel's united monarchy.

The Deuteronomic presentation of Solomon in I Kings 1–11 demands careful reading. Schematically arranged, good news about Solomon prefaces bad news. Tenacious about divine retribution, the Deuteronomist judged Solomon's basic flaw to be his toleration of the gods of his foreign wives that triggered Yahweh's wrath (11:1-13). The Deuteronomist favorably portrays Solomon's demonstration of wisdom, far-reaching commercial enterprises, and building program. Objectionable aspects of Solomon's reign are summarized in I Kings 11 to imply their emergence during Solomon's last years when "his wives turned away his heart after other gods" (11:4). During this dark hour, Solomon is said to have lost territory to Hadad the Edomite and Rezon of Damascus, whom Yahweh raised up against him (11:14, 23). Actually, Hadad troubled Solomon much earlier (11:21). With this chronological shift, the Deuteronomist claims that Solomon received his just deserts.

One source behind these chapters, the book of the acts of Solomon (I Kings 11:41), is a legendary biography indiscriminately celebrating the king's splendor. Representative of its content are Solomon's dream at Gibeon, where he intently prayed for wisdom (3:3-15), and his brilliant decision regarding the two harlots contesting possession of one child (3:16-28). The accolade that under Solomon, "Judah and Israel were as many as the sand by the sea; they ate and drank and were happy" (4:20) suppresses consideration of Israelite commoners disgruntled that urban civilization and social stratification were rapidly dominating. The biblical witness that the Israelites were masters and not slaves (9:22) is refuted by the disclosure that "Solomon raised a levy of forced labor out of all Israel" (5:13). If Solomon astutely stablized the sound administrative policy innovated by David, many Israelites would finally rebel against his repressive approach (I Kings 12:1-16).

*Solomon's Enthronement.* Aging David's indecision regarding his successor provoked palace intrigue. David's military commander Joab and his priest Abiathar supported Adonijah, David's eldest living son. But Solomon was favored by Bathsheba, the royal guard Benaiah, the priest Zadok, and the prophet Nathan. Certain that Adonijah's seizure of the throne was imminent (I Kings 1:9-11), Bathsheba and Nathan successfully influenced David's decision for Solomon. Escorted by Davidic troops, Solomon was publicly anointed by Zadok (1:38-40).

After David's death, Solomon swiftly strengthened his position. When ADONIJAH expressed his continued craving for the throne by asking for Abishag, David's concubine, Solomon ordered his execution (I Kings 2:23-25). While ABIATHAR, Solomon's priestly opponent, was spared, owing to previous support of David, he was sent home to Anathoth (2:26). Unhesitatingly, Solomon honored David's command to assassinate Joab so that his murders of Abner and Amasa might be avenged (2:5-6, 31-34). Solomon rewarded his supporters by making Benaiah commander of the army and Zadok chief priest (2:35). Truly, "the kingdom was established in the hand of Solomon" (2:46).

*Administrative Achievements.* (1) *Provincial reorganization.* To obtain firmer control, Solomon reorganized the nation into twelve administrative districts that generally ignored tribal boundaries (I Kings 4:7-19). Each was charged with delivering a month's provisions to the burgeoning court (4:22-23). This demanded enormous Israelite energy, as did Solomon's ambitious building program. When compulsory labor from conquered peoples proved insufficient, Solomon instituted the *corvée*, including the enrollment of his own people for a third of the year. Thus, unpaid labor gangs penetrated Lebanon for timber (5:13-14). Others worked in Jerusalem, where Solomon's building program was concentrated. Since Adoram, the director of Solomon's forced labor, was lynched by Israelites (12:18), presumably the *corveé* included freeborn Israelite draftees.

(2) *Military policy.* Solomon's military machine boasted 1,400 chariots and 12,000 horsemen (I Kings 10:26). The king strengthened Jerusalem's fortifications, and along the nation's perimeter established a band of military centers, including Hazor, Megiddo, Gezer, Beth-horon, Baalath, and Tamar (9:15-19). Solomon appreciably enhanced Israel's capacity to repel military attacks.

(3) *Foreign policy.* Solomon's amicable relations with foreigners led to international alliances. Typically confirmed by marriage, they expanded Solomon's harem (I Kings 11:1-3). Through marriage to Pharaoh's daughter, Solomon acquired the Canaanite city of Gezer, tentatively an Egyptian holding (3:1; 9:16). Also Solomon's alliance with Tyre supported his architectural and maritime ambitions.

(4) *Commerce and industry.* Assisted by Phoenician sailors, Solomon established a trade program centered at Ezion-geber on the Gulf of Aqaba (I Kings 9:26-28; 10:11-12, 22). Solomon's engagement in caravan trade with the Sabeans of Arabia is attested by his audience with the visiting queen of Sheba (10:1-10, 13). Moreover, the king turned a profit as middleman in the horse and chariot business (10:28-29). Of necessity, chariots constructed in Egypt and horses bred in Cilicia traversed Israelite territory.

(5) *Building program.* Among those sites hosting Solomonic architecture, Gezer, Hazor, and Megiddo have yielded impressive four-entry-way gate systems. Relying on Phoenician technology (5:1-12), Solomon built an impressive administrative complex in Jerusalem (7:1-8). Supplementing the palace itself

Herbert G. May

*Solomon's pool, south of Bethlehem*

were "the House of the Forest of Lebanon" (dual armory and treasury), judgment hall, and residence for Pharaoh's daughter. Details about the construction and dedication of the Jerusalem Temple, both a royal dynastic chapel and national sanctuary, are offered in I Kings 5–8.

*Solomon and Wisdom.* In this culturally productive era, much Israelite myth, legend, and history achieved literary fixation. Moreover, impressed by Egypt's long-standing example, Solomon fostered a court-centered wisdom movement. Three canonical wisdom books are attributed to Solomon—PROVERBS, ECCLESIASTES, and the SONG OF SOLOMON. Though the latter two postdate him, perhaps Proverbs contains a Solomonic nucleus. Yet immodest statements that Solomon "was wiser than all other men," spoke 3,000 proverbs, and composed 1,005 songs discourage literal acceptance (I Kings 4:31-32).

*Final Assessment.* Having inherited much from Saul and David, Solomon properly recognized that his main political task involved holding the Israelite state together. Though temporarily successful, his grandiose governmental programs drained his subjects. Expenses regularly outdistanced income. Solomon inspired social stratification repugnant to loyal Yahwists whose faith had been nourished by a Mosaic covenant embracing all Israelites as equals before God. Because his statecraft often manifested more dazzle than substance, at Solomon's death, Israelite elders understandably pleaded for more tolerant rule.

J.K.K.

**SOLOMON, ODES OF.** *See* PSEUDEPIGRAPHA.

**SOLOMON, PSALMS OF.** *See* PSEUDEPIGRAPHA.

**SOLOMON'S PORTICO.** A three-story, roofed building with an impressive, first-floor colonnade on the south side of a cloister-like quadrangle in Herod's Temple. Architecturally, the enclosure resembled the portico of the Bethsaida pool (John 5:2; KJV, porch).

The whole complex of Herod's TEMPLE had taken forty-six years to build and was not completely finished in Jesus' lifetime (John 2:20). It is not known when Solomon's portico was erected, but before the first century A.D., Josephus states that Solomon's first-floor portico had four rows of columns, one row "interwoven into the wall." The height of each first-floor column was twenty-seven feet, and its circumference such "that three men might with their arms extended, fathom it round, and join hands again." The columns were fashioned with bases and capitals in the Corinthian style. An upper, open, columned gallery, with an enclosed "attic" above, ran the length of the portico.

Inside the enclosed space, which Solomon's portico faced, were stalls for merchants and money changers. When Jesus entered the Temple and was teaching and preaching in Solomon's portico, during Tuesday of Holy Week, he could see where, the day before, he had driven out the merchants and overturned the money changers' tables (Matt. 21:12-13; Mark 11:15-19; Luke 19:45-48). When the Temple authorities saw Jesus on Tuesday, they asked, perhaps pointing to the enclosure, "By what authority are you doing these things?" (Matt. 21:23; Mark 11:27; Luke 20:1-2).

Solomon's portico was the traditional meeting place for the scribal schools and for learned men to hold debates. Here is where twelve-year-old Jesus must have been when Mary and Joseph found him (Luke 2:46). Solomon's portico was Jesus' favorite place in Jerusalem to teach (Luke 19:17; John 10:23). Here, later, people saw the man lame from birth, healed in the name of Jesus, "walking and leaping and praising God" (Acts 3:8).

P.L.G.

**SOMA.** From the Sanskrit word meaning literally "pressed." A sacred plant and its pressed-out juice offered to the gods and consumed ritually in the religion of VEDIC HINDUISM. Many hymns of the RIG-VEDA are devoted to the praise of Soma, personified as a god, and to the drink's exalting effect. Probably hallucinogenic, the plant from which soma was produced has been identified by one modern theory with the *Amanita muscaria* or fly-agaric mushroom. As early as the BRAHMANAS, around 800 B.C., other plants of non-psychedelic effect were beginning to be substituted for the original soma, as they are now in the rites of the BRAHMINS.

R.E.

**SONG OF SOLOMON.** An anthology of approximately two dozen pastoral lyrics affirming the pleasure and power of human sexual love. As one of the five MEGILLOTH (festival scrolls), this OT book was read at Passover as an allegorical reflection on Yahweh's relation with Israel since the Exodus.

*Literary Aspects.* Although clear-cut structure and movement are lacking, this book contains a variety of songs extolling the love of man and maiden. Among the literary types employed are the descriptive song (*wasf*) advertising the physical charms of the beloved (4:1-7), the song of yearning (1:2-4), and the boast (8:11-12). The book swarms with accomplished imagery exhibiting an obvious rural orientation. The repeated phrase, "O daughters of Jerusalem" (1:5; 2:7; 3:5; 5:8, 16; 8:4) and the presence of two lovers throughout confer a lyric unity upon the whole. In terms of anonymity, dialogical style, and rural atmosphere, Egyptian love songs from the mid-second millennium B.C. offer the closest extra-biblical parallels.

*Authorship and Date.* The tradition that Solomon composed many songs (I Kings 4:32) and use of his name in Song of Solomon 1:5; 3:7-11; and 8:11-12 ineptly inspired the Solomonic reference in the title (1:1). The presence of Persian and Greek loanwords plus many Aramaisms suggest the third century B.C. for the final editing. These lyrics span a wide chronology and geography with the oldest tracing to the early monarchical period.

*Interpretation.* (a) *Allegorical.* This poetry has evoked widely differing interpretations. Early on, the clear wording of the erotic lyrics was overlooked by a Jewish allegorical approach, which maintained that the Song reflects God's mystical love for Israel. Similarly, Christian commentators claimed this book celebrates a mutual love involving Christ (bridegroom) and the church (bride). This once popular interpretation attracts few adherents today.

(b) *Dramatic.* Since these poems reveal no monologue, two major Greek manuscripts affixed character headings that denote as speakers the bride, bridegroom, and companions. Eventually some scholars saw an intricate plot involving a beautiful maiden, her shepherd lover to whom she remains faithful, and King Solomon. But the absence of any conflict in the canonical text argues against a dramatic interpretation. Too much must be read between the lines.

(c) *Cultic.* Could these lyrics have originally fulfilled a fertility cult function in accord with the Babylonian Tammuz festival or the Baal cycles of Canaanite mythology? This approach views the bride as a goddess seeking her lost lover, who has descended to the underworld. Once rejoined, their sexual union restores fertility and wholeness to the world. While ancient Near Eastern fertility customs may lie behind this poetry, the dying-rising god motif is lacking in the text. Moreover, in dissociating the poems from human love, the cultic interpretation is itself an allegorization.

(d) *Syrian wedding analogy.* Parallels have been adduced from week-long wedding celebrations in present-day Syria wherein the couple is enthroned as king and queen. The descriptive song portraying the bride's beauty is particularly significant. But biblical Israel's link with modern Syrian customs is necessarily remote. Moreover, only 3:6-11 indisputably depicts a wedding celebration. Even if some of the lyrics were sung at ancient Jewish weddings, the text preserves more love songs than wedding songs.

(e) *Lyrical.* Since the eighteenth century, this book has increasingly been regarded as an assemblage of artful poems celebrating the mysteries of prenuptial and nuptial human love. This approach excels in its capacity to grasp the poetry on its own terms and to appreciate it as a product of high literary merit commensurate with the sophistication and education of its composers.                                J.K.K.

**SONG OF SONGS.** *See* SONG OF SOLOMON.

**SON OF GOD.** In the OT "son of God" is used as a designation for Israel, for kings, and occasionally for special messengers of God. In the NT it is used primarily for JESUS.

Preeminently, Israel is God's son whom God has chosen "out of Egypt" (for example, Hos. 11:1; Exod. 4:22-23). As such, Israel is the object of God's

election and owes God absolute obedience. In a derivative sense the king is described as God's son, a fact that may have been stressed in the coronation ritual (for example, II Sam. 7:14; Pss. 2:7; 89:26-27). Further, from time to time a messenger of God, usually a heavenly being sent for a special function, is called a son of God (for example, Gen. 6:2; Job 1:6).

Jesus is universally recognized as God's unique Son, though the understanding of that designation varies somewhat from writer to writer. For Mark the title, used not often but in key locations, is central to the understanding of who Jesus is (1:1). Jesus is acknowledged by God as the chosen Son at his baptism (1:11) and at his transfiguration (9:7). The demons respect Jesus' power over them as they confess him to be "Son of the Most High God" (5:7; compare 3:11). Yet it is in his obedience unto death that the Roman centurion perceives the truth about Jesus: "Truly this man was the Son of God!" (15:39; compare 12:1-11). Election, authority, and obedience are the hallmarks of Mark's CHRISTOLOGY.

In the Gospel of John the understanding of the Son of God is somewhat different. He has been sent by the Father into the world (3:17; 6:40-46; 8:42) and represents the Father in his words and actions (5:19-30; 7:16). Since Jesus is one with the Father and does the Father's works, he is entitled to be called "the Son of God" (10:30-38; 17:20-23). In his farewell discourse the Son, who has come from the Father, anticipates returning to the Father (13:1; 14:28; 16:5, 28). For John, then, the Son of God is a preexistent divine being who in his incarnation reveals the person and purpose of the Father and whose authority and obedience are presented in the cause of revelation.

Elsewhere in the NT the Son of God becomes a basic confession of Jesus by the early church (1 John 4:15; Heb. 4:14; Rom. 1:3-4), and in light of that confession Christians are invited to address God with the striking words, "Abba! Father!" (Gal. 4:6; Rom. 8:15-16).

Though the NT writers describe the intimate relationship between the Father and the Son, it is something of a jump from the first century to the third, fourth, and fifth centuries, when the ancient church used the title Son of God to designate the Son's identity of substance with the Father. (*See also* SON OF MAN.)                                C.B.C.

**SON OF MAN.** A term used in the Bible in three basic ways: for a human being, for an exalted apocalyptic figure, and for Jesus.

*For a Human Being.* Several times in the Psalms "son of man" appears in a parallel construction with the ordinary Hebrew word for human being.

What is man that thou art mindful of him
  and the son of man that thou dost care for him

(Ps. 8:4).

In Ezekiel the prophet is repeatedly addressed as "son of man," probably stressing the insignificance of the creature in contrast to the majesty of God.

*For an Exalted Apocalyptic Figure.* In Daniel 7:13-14 "one like a son of man" with the clouds of heaven is presented to the Ancient of Days and receives from him "dominion and glory and kingdom." In the apocryphal book of II Esdras (chap. 13) and the pseudepigraphal book of Ethiopic Enoch (chaps. 37–71), "son of man" is developed further in apocalyptic contexts.

*For Jesus.* The term appears approximately eighty-one times in the Gospels, in each case as a self-designation of Jesus, and in Acts 7:56. The sayings can be classified according to three types:

(a) those that speak of the coming of the Son of man in the glory of the Father with the clouds of heaven (for example, Mark 8:38; 14:62);

(b) those that predict the passion, death, and resurrection of the Son of man (for example, Mark 8:31; 9:31; 10:33-34);

(c) those that describe the earthly activity of the Son of man (for example, Mark 2:10, 28).

The scholarly community has debated vigorously a number of issues surrounding the uses of "Son of man" in the Gospels. How widely known was the term in Judaism of the first century A.D., and what did it imply? To what extent did the OT uses and/or the uses in II Esdras and Ethiopic Enoch shape the NT uses? Did Jesus actually use the term for himself, and if so, why? Could Jesus have spoken of the Son of man as an apocalyptic figure who was to come, which the early church then identified with Jesus in light of his resurrection from the dead? Are the uses of the term that describe Jesus' earthly ministry meant to be substitutes for "I" or "me"? Do the writers of the Gospels employ "Son of man" in the same way (compare John 1:51; 3:14-15)? However these questions are answered, "Son of man," when used for Jesus, designates not merely his humanity, but more importantly his authority on earth and in the age to come. (*See* CHRISTOLOGY and SON OF GOD.)

C.B.C.

**SOPHERIM.** Hebrew scribes, starting with Ezra in the mid-fifth century B.C. They were a professional class that preserved, interpreted, and applied the oral traditions that supplemented the written TORAH. The scribes are considered the initiators of the "Jewish" as distinct from the "Israelite" period of history. From their ranks came the men of the Great Assembly, whose contributions to Judaism were in liturgy, the preservation of Scripture, and the oral Law. The scribes were active for two centuries after Ezra. *Sopherim* also applies to those people occupied in the writing of the scrolls of the Torah, as well as prayers and passages that go into *mezuzot* and *tephillin* (phylacteries).

L.K.

**SOPHIA.** Greek for "wisdom." The ultimate wisdom of the OT was seeking after God (Prov. 4:5). In the NT Paul identifies Christ as wisdom become flesh (I Cor. 1:24, 30; Col. 2:3), just as John does with Christ as the word LOGOS. Not related to Greek philosophy, the doctrine of Christ as wisdom was especially alive among the Greek church fathers. Thus in Constantinople the most significant church of early Christendom could be named Hagia Sophia, Holy Wisdom, dedicated to Christ.

T.J.K.

**SOSTHENES.** Sosthenes is mentioned as a co-worker of Paul, perhaps his scribe when the apostle wrote to the church at Corinth (I Cor. 1:1). He is not mentioned, however, in I Corinthians 16:17-19, when Paul lists his companions there in Ephesus. The same or a different Sosthenes appears as the head of the synagogue at Corinth (Acts 18:17), who turned Christian and was later beaten by a hostile crowd. Clement of Alexandria identifies him as one of the seventy disciples. Chrysostom says he was the same person as Crispus. By tradition Sosthenes served as bishop of Colophon in Greece.

T.J.K.

**SOTERIOLOGY.** The doctrine of SALVATION or REDEMPTION. It explains how humans are reconciled to God. However, the explanation has varied through the centuries. Early theologians emphasized redemption as illumination through Christ, his victory over sin and death, or the liberation of the human race from the power of Satan. Other explanations stress expiation, mediation, and reconciliation. Contemporary theologians stress the role not only of the cross but also of the Resurrection, Ascension, and sending of the Holy Spirit in the salvation event.

I.C.

**SOUL.** The English word "soul" is much richer and broader in meaning than its Hebrew or Greek equivalents, *nephesh* and *psyche*. In either of the two biblical languages the roots include the concept of breath and breathing. Thus Genesis 2:7: The Lord God formed man of dust from the ground, and breathed into his nostrils the breath of life (*nephesh*); and man became a living being.

In OT usage the word that we most often translate as soul, especially in the KJV, normally should be translated as LIFE. The word usually refers to the entire living being, to the whole individual, body and soul, in fact, even to living animals. It is the word *ruach* or SPIRIT that the OT writers more often use when they want to refer to what we think of as the soul, that part of a human being that relates to God, that trusts, that believes. Soul as *nephesh* normally does not exist apart from a living person. To say in our terms that the "soul" of the loved one has departed to be with the Lord or to speak of the "immortal soul" would simply not be understandable in the culture of the OT.

Among philosophers and interpreters of Scripture there have been long discussions whether the individual human being consists of two parts, that is, body and soul, or of three parts, body, soul, and spirit. The believer in the OT viewed the self as a single entity, with the soul intertwined as part of the material body, for as long as one lived. Thus one did not possess or inhabit a body but consisted of a living, breathing body and soul, which were inseparable. Both the life force or soul and the body emanated from the Creator. Relationships to and trust in this Creator were manifested through the spirit, which the Creator had breathed into one, not merely as a life force but as a living proof that one was made after the image and with the life force of the Creator.

The whole concept of soul or *nephesh* in the OT is extremely complex, in all of its changing cultural implication, making translation difficult. It is further complicated by a Hebrew view that assumed that the thinking process occurred within the heart, not the head. Many of the proof texts about the life of the soul before or after death occur in poetic and prophetic passages.

In the NT the word *psyche* for soul is perhaps equally limited, in a still different cultural setting. *Psyche* also refers more to life than to spirit, as in Matthew 6:25 or John 10:11. *Pneuma* or spirit comes closer to the present concept of soul, but must also be carefully distinguished from those instances where it refers to the Holy Spirit. In some passages, however, *pneuma* and *psyche* actually appear to be synonymous, as if soul and life were identical.

Sometimes spirit (*pneuma*) and life (*psyche*) are both contrasted to the material elements of the BODY, the sarx or soma. In I Corinthians 15:42-50 and 2:14-15, Paul uses the adjective *psychikos* or "living element" to contrast what is natural, human, or non-spiritual with that which is spiritual. In fact, so many overtones of meaning have crept into the various Hebrew and Greek words sometimes translated as "soul," as demonstrated also in English in the poetry of Milton or Shakespeare, that the English word "soul" is equally difficult to define with exactness.

T.J.K.

**SOURCE CRITICISM.** *See* BIBLICAL CRITICISM.

**SOVEREIGNTY OF GOD.** *See* PREDESTINATION.

**SPEAKING IN TONGUES.** *See* GLOSSOLALIA.

**SPENCER, HERBERT** (1820–1903). English philosopher and early sociologist, known for applying evolutionary theory to all branches of learning. Essentially self-taught, he early worked as an engineer, in journalism, and in 1848 he became subeditor of *The Economist*. His *Social Statics* (1850) attracted wide attention. This was followed by *Principles of Psychology* (1855), which was later incorporated into his ten-volume *Synthetic Philosophy*, which also included *First Principles* (1862), *Principles of Biology* (Vol. 1, 1864; Vol. 2, 1867), *Principles of*

*Sociology* (Vol. 1, 1876; Vol. 2, 1882), and *Principles of Ethics* (Vol. 1, 1892; Vol. 2 1893).

In ethics Spencer was a utilitarian. He believed that agnosticism was the only reasonable religious position, since theism assumes a knowledge of that which lies beyond observable phenomena. Spencer proposed the worship of what he called the Unknowable. He held that the origin of religion is traceable to fear of spirits or ghosts, which then evolved into polytheism and eventually to monotheism. Spencer accepted Lamarck's belief in the inheritance of acquired characteristics and invented the term "survival of the fittest." He advocated an extreme individualism and laissez-faire economics and opposed welfare programs, which, he felt, impeded natural selection, hence social progress. Spencer was a leading proponent of SOCIAL DARWINISM, and his views were extremely influential in the late nineteenth century. Today he is read largely for historical interest.

J.L.

**SPENER, PHILIPP JAKOB** (1635–1705). The founder of German PIETISM. Spener was born at Rappoltsweiler in Upper Alsace. He was early influenced by the devotional writings of the English Puritans. His concern to reform the German Lutheran Church was further strengthened during a visit to Geneva, where he came under the influence of the pietistic reformer Jean de Labadi. Spener studied theology at the University of Strassburg (1651–53) and was appointed preacher at the church there in 1663. He became chief pastor of the Lutheran church at Frankfurt am Main in 1666. There he introduced the *Collegia Pietatis*, or small devotional meetings, which met twice weekly to encourage personal piety and Bible study.

In 1675 he published *Pia desideria* or *Heartfelt Desires for a God-pleasing Reform of the True Evangelical Churches*, which outlined his program of evangelical reform. The book increased Spener's reputation throughout Germany and stimulated pietistic reform in Lutheranism. In 1686 Spener was appointed first court chaplain at Dresden, a highly valued position. However, disagreement with the elector John George III caused him to move to Berlin as rector of the St. Nicholas' Church in 1691. There he found the support of the elector of Brandenburg and was able to carry out many reforms. In 1694 the University of Halle was founded through Spener's influence. It became a center of Pietism under Spener's disciples, A. C. FRANCKE and Christian Thomasius. At the time of Spener's death, Pietism was well established in Germany.

J.L.

**SPINOZA, BENEDICT DE** (1632–77). Philosopher and foremost representative of modern RATIONALISM and PANTHEISM. Born in Amsterdam of Portuguese-Jewish parents, Spinoza had an early rabbinical training. However, in 1656 he was excommunicated from the synagogue for unorthodox views. He was compelled to leave Amsterdam and, after some moving about, settled in The Hague, where he earned a living grinding lenses. He was a tenacious defender of freedom of speech and thought and refused a pension from Louis XIV and a professorship at Heidelberg for fear that they might limit his freedom. His principal works include the *Theological-Political Treatise* (1670) and the posthumous *Ethics* (1677).

For Spinoza philosophy begins with a discussion of substance as the ultimate reality and causality. He rejects Descartes's dualism of God and world, mind and body, for if substance is that which exists by itself, then there is only one infinite substance, whose essence implies its existence, God or Nature *(Deus sive Natura)*. Such an infinite being has an infinite number of attributes, of which only two, thought and extension, are known to the human mind. All things are modes of these two attributes, that is, either ideas or bodies. Since God and Nature are the same, the goal of religion and philosophy is the same: what Spinoza called "the intellectual love of God." To love God is at the same time to know the infinite causal system of Nature. To know God is to conceive things under the species of eternity *(sub specie aeternitatus)*, which is the highest human pleasure.

For Spinoza the life of reason is also the life of virtue, for to understand is to be freed from the servitude of the emotions. For example, hatred is a mere passion, for once we understand that others act out of a certain necessity we overcome our hatred of them. A consequence of Spinoza's pantheism is his denial of a personal God and the immortality of the soul. He is one of the fathers of the modern historical-critical study of the Bible. Spinoza's greatest influence was in Germany in the nineteenth century.                                                      J.L.

**SPIRIT.** From the Latin *spirare*, "to breathe"; that which is immaterial or of the spirit; SOUL, personality, life force, will, consciousness, feeling, thought, existence, as distinguished from that which can be touched or measured.

The word "spirit," occurring more than five hundred times in the Bible, is almost indefinable. Its common form in Hebrew is *ruach* and in Greek, *pneuma*. Both basically mean "breath," "wind," or "life force," as in Job 34:14 or Genesis 6:17. Particularly in the OT, spirit can be associated with the life that originated with God, a breath breathed into humanity by the Creator, so that giving up one's spirit meant to die. Life itself was godlike in origin. Spirit often also occurs as the site of human experience and emotion—joy, dejection, anger, frustration (see Josh. 2:11; Gen. 26:34). Even more significantly it appears as a contrast to the part of a human being that decays and passes away, the flesh. On the other hand that part of human life that more narrowly relates to the life principle and to breathing, *nephesh*, often is

inseparable from the body in Hebrew thought and dies when the body dies, even though this word too is sometimes translated as spirit or soul.

The concept of a disembodied spirit that stays alive after death, that is, a ghost, does not occur until relatively late in OT writings, as in the story of Saul and the witch at Endor, or in the evil spirits that came to trouble Saul in I Samuel 16:14. In general, spirit comes from God, provides life and breath, makes people human, sometimes gives special strength or insight, and occasionally persists after death.

In the NT, the word "spirit" appears to have adopted many added meanings from the Greco-Roman world and at least a few from Persian or Zoroastrian thought. Basically it still means "breath" or "principle of life." But human spirit, soul, or personality now continues to live after death (Luke 8:55). It is the seat of emotion (II Cor. 2:13). It eventually goes to heaven or hell (Heb. 12:23; I Pet. 3:19). Paul often contrasts the flesh with the spirit. And evil or unclean spirits are described as invading human personality during Jesus' ministry, or existing as a whole hierarchy of angels, demons, powers, principalities, and other ethereal spirits, as they did in Persia.                                                      T.J.K.

**SPIRITS IN PRISON.** This quotation from I Peter 3:19 refers to the story of Christ's DESCENT INTO HELL (Hades) and how he preached there, either to the spirits of people who had died or to the fallen angels. The Hades and descent into hell stories are common themes in Oriental mythology. The Christian account was very popular in medieval legend and epic, though the scriptural evidence is extremely limited.
                                                      T.J.K.

**SPIRITUAL EXERCISES, THE.** A series of meditations and rules for helping a soul conquer its passions and give itself to God. Written by IGNATIUS OF LOYOLA, the *Exercises* originated in his own experience in 1521 and were written during a stay at Manresa in 1522. Throughout his life he revised and expanded the work. The book offers four "weeks" of meditations: (1) on sin and its consequences, (2) on Christ's life on earth, (3) on Christ's Passion, and (4) on the risen life in Christ. The work was given papal approval by Paul III in 1548 and is still widely used by Christians in various traditions.          N.H.

**SPIRITUAL GIFTS.** *See* GIFTS, SPIRITUAL.

**SPIRITUALISM.** The philosophical doctrine that holds to the reality of spirit as well as matter in the universe. An extreme view, called IDEALISM, holds that only spirit or mind is real. This absolute idealism was taught by Bishop GEORGE BERKELEY of Ireland. All forms of idealism or spiritualism oppose MATERIALISM.

However, the term has more specific—and negative—reference to the beliefs and practices of those who believe it is possible to communicate with the spirits of the dead (necromancy). This practice traditionally was called "spiritism," and is still so termed in German, French, and Italian use. In America, where the practice arose and flourished in the nineteenth century, it has always been called spiritualism, and it was institutionalized in several Spiritualist churches and associations.

Spiritualism makes use of people who supposedly have the power to allow the dead to speak through them. Table rapping, Ouija boards, trances, and séances are used in such practices, and these occult forms are subject to abuse and fraud. According to traditional Christian doctrine, all such attempts to contact the spirits of the departed are wrong since spiritualism involves the danger of communication with evil spirits, or, at least, the sin of superstition. The Roman Catholic church forbids its members to attend séances and Spiritualist meetings.    J.C.

**SPIRITUALITY.** The condition of spiritual-mindedness, or devotion to God and the things of the spirit; also a disciplined approach to the spiritual life, opposed to materialism, secularism, and sensuality (hedonism). Spirituality may involve ascetic practices such as voluntary poverty, chastity (including complete celibacy), and entire obedience to the laws of the church.

Spirituality, or spiritual formation, is the theme of the Christian life after justification (either through infant baptism or by way of conversion and baptism for the Free churches), and, theologically, falls under the head of SANCTIFICATION. The formation of the Christian character is biblically described as being more and more conformed to the image of Christ. This metaphor is based upon the practice of pressing a signet ring into hot wax. The content or matter of the sanctified life is, then, Jesus Christ. Obedience to him and imitation of his absolute obedience to God and compassionate love for all people is a major element of sanctification. The concept of imitating Christ stems from Paul, who told his fellow believers to imitate him as he imitated Christ (Phil. 3:17; I Cor. 4:16; 11:1)

This inspirational idea was widely taught and practiced (however imperfectly) in the ancient and medieval church. A famous treatise, *The Imitation of Christ*, was written by Thomas à Kempis. After the Reformation, Luther reacted negatively to the concept of imitation because of its misuse in teachings that implied salvation by (or partially by) good works. Calvin later was more open to the concept of imitation as he stressed Christian discipline in his adaptation of Luther's Reformation teachings. For this reason, there has been a historically different development of the understanding of sanctification, that is, of spirituality, in Lutheranism and the Reformed churches. Nevertheless, PIETISM, a far-reaching movement of Protestant spirituality, grew out of late seventeenth-century Lutheranism, which fertilized

the several sects that arose in Lutheran and Reformed circles in Europe and America; sects that often stressed Christian discipline and spirituality. The third force of the Reformation, the Anabaptists, stressed spiritual life, especially the distancing of the Christian from the secular world. Mennonite churches soon suffered a split and the world-denying Amish movement arose and migrated to America. Anabaptist spirituality chiefly consists in attempts to live a "primitive" or simple life, remote from the cities of the modern world, and rejective of modern science and technology. Houses without central heat, running water, and electricity, and church services held in a barn, along with the speaking of German dialect, the use of horses and buggies, and strict morality characterize the Amish, the Anabaptist ideal. Of course, the Mennonites adapted to the modern world, and like the Quakers exhibit a socially liberal attitude to the world that portrays a genuine spirituality of love.

In the mainline Protestant churches, the concept of spirituality or sanctification received little attention during the middle decades of the twentieth century. Social action, based on devotion to the justice of God, took preeminence for many years. However, the resurgence of evangelicalism in the 1970s made all churches reexamine the Christian's obligation to pursue spirituality. The concept of the people of God was adopted by several Protestant denominations and became the watchword of the post-Vatican II Roman Catholic Church. The neo-Fundamentalist movement, promoted by the Moral Majority, does, of course, endorse a spirituality of its own although it is legalistic and culturally conformist.

The media prominence of this movement has made spirituality, especially the stress on sexual purity, a topic of national interest and discussion in America. Spirituality—becoming more like Christ, expressing his love for others, trusting him more and more—is the very meaning of becoming a Christian.    J.C.

**SPIRITUALS.** (1) Those practices that belong to priests. These include honoraria such as stole fees and fees for masses. Sometimes these practices are called spiritualities. These are also spiritual works of mercy, which consist of the work of converting sinners, instructing the ignorant, counseling those with problems, comforting the sorrowful, bearing ills patiently, forgiving wrongs, and praying for both the living and the dead.

(2) Black (Afro-American) spirituals make up one of the largest bodies of American folk songs to survive into the twentieth century. Spirituals are also the most widely known of American folk songs. These beautiful songs, hymns, and choir arrangements originated in the black Protestant congregations of the American South. For a long time, the spirituals were not recorded. Colonel Thomas Higginson of the Union Army in the 1860s did record the songs he heard his black soldiers singing and published these

works in 1870. Black spirituals typically follow the form of an alternating line and refrain, which permits a wide display of extemporization. While there is some African influence on them, the spirituals seem to be creations of Afro-Americans rather than retentions from Africa.

J.C

**SPRINKLING.** *See* BAPTISM.

Courtesy of Southern Baptist Historical Library and Archives

*Charles Spurgeon*

**SPURGEON, CHARLES HADDON** (1834–92). Reared as a Congregationalist, Spurgeon became a Baptist preacher in 1850. In 1852 he was named pastor of a church at Waterbeach, Cambridgeshire, England. In 1854 he moved to New Park Street Chapel in Southwark, London. Soon he was preaching to crowds of as many as ten thousand. Eventually his congregation built the Metropolitan Tabernacle at Newington Causeway, which became his pulpit. He founded a seminary in 1856 and an orphanage in 1867. His collected sermons run to fifty volumes.

Theologically conservative, he distrusted science and the higher criticism of the Bible. In 1887 he left the more liberal Baptist Union. A friend of D. L. Moody, he was admired by many American Evangelicals and Fundamentalists. One of his successors, as pastor of the London Tabernacle, was Amzi Clarence Dixon, chair of the editors of the *Fundamentals*.

N.H.

**SRADDHA.** From the Sanskrit word for "act of faith." In HINDUISM, offerings presented to departed ancestors through rituals based upon VEDIC rites. These usages consist of ritually building a spiritual body for the deceased after death, then of presenting food offerings (usually balls of rice) at regular intervals to sustain its life in celestial realms, where it awaits eventual rebirth. The rituals, among the most ancient widely observed in popular Hinduism, serve to establish family identity among participants as well as links between living and dead. Certain pilgrimage centers, especially Banaras and Gaya on the Ganges, are particularly visited as places to perform *sraddha*.

R.E.

**SRAMANA.** From the Sanskrit word for "one who exerts effort." *Sramana* ("one who sees all things equally") is often used interchangeably. In ancient India, *sramanas* were wandering ascetics and spiritual teachers. They are contrasted in classical writings with the hereditary priestly BRAHMIN caste. Sramanas rejected caste, ritual, Vedic authority, and the gradual progression to the renunciant state through the stages of life *(ashramas)* inculcated by the Brahmins. They advocated instead the sudden giving up of worldly life at any point, and thenceforward seeking MOKSHA or liberation entirely through inward ascetic and meditative means. The BUDDHA and MAHAVIRA, both of Kshatriya rather than Brahmin caste, together with their followers, were outstanding examples of the *sramana* type in early India.

R.E.

**SRI VAISNAVA.** A BHAKTI or devotional movement within HINDUISM found in south India and directed toward VISHNU and his avatars. The earliest movement to combine VEDIC and popular religious elements under the direction of BRAHMINS, it took shape in the ninth century A.D. Sri Vaisnava accepts the priestly leadership of Brahmins, yet employs the hymns of the ALVARS and other post-Vedic material as equal in worship and scriptural authority with the Vedas. Later, the great theologian RAMANUJA provided a strong intellectual foundation for Sri Vaisnava belief in a personal God, the importance of loving devotion and good works, and the power of God's grace. On the Brahminical side, Sri Vaisnavas adhere strictly to rules of caste and diet and highly value scholarship. They are now split into two groups. The "Southern" upholds more the Alvar heritage, while the "Northern" emphasizes Vedic texts.

R.E.

**STAR OF DAVID.** *See* MAGEN DAVID.

**STATION DAYS.** A Roman Catholic custom in which the priests and people of Rome meet together and processed to a certain church where the pope, or a representative of the pope, sang mass. These station days include all of Lent, ember days, the Sundays in

Advent, and other feast days, a total of eighty-four days.                                                               J.C.

## STATIONS OF THE CROSS.

A series of fourteen pictures or symbols representing incidents in Christ's walk from his condemnation by Pilate to the cross. The tradition of walking from one picture or station to another during Lent was begun by the Franciscans. The custom of observing the Stations of the Cross has spread from Roman Catholics to Anglicans. A route through the old city of Jerusalem has been mapped out and marked by the Stations of the Cross. Thousands of pilgrims follow this route during Holy Week. The present order of the Stations and the accompanying liturgy were established in the nineteenth century.

The fourteen events commemorated are: Jesus' condemnation; taking the cross; Christ falls down; Christ meets Mary, his mother; Simon of Cyrene carries the cross; Veronica wipes Christ's face; Christ falls again; he tells the women of Jerusalem not to weep for him; Christ falls a third time; he is stripped; nailed to the cross; Christ's death; his body is taken from the cross; and his body is placed in the tomb.
J.C

## STENNETT, SAMUEL

(1727–95). Baptist clergyman and hymn writer. Samuel Stennett was born in Exeter, England. His father, Dr. Joseph Stennett, was a distinguished Baptist minister, who served for many years at Little Wild Street Church in London. In 1748 Samuel became an assistant in the church and ten years later succeeded his father as the pastor. The son became known throughout the land as an evangelical preacher; he became confidant to many of the country's statesman, including King George III. Stennett, like his grandfather and father before him, attained a wide reputation as a hymn writer. Two of his best known hymns are "Majestic Sweetness Sits Enthroned," and "On Jordan's Stormy Banks I Stand." Most of the thirty-nine hymns he wrote appeared in John Rippon's *Selection of Hymns* (1787). Stennett served the Little Wild Street Church for thirty-seven years, never holding another pulpit. He died in London on August 24.                          R.H.

## STEPHEN.

The first of the Christian martyrs, whose name means "wreath" or "crown," was stoned to death in Jerusalem about A.D. 33. Since his name is Greek and since he was the first of seven deacons chosen by the church in Jerusalem to look after the overlooked widows and orphans of Greek background, his roots may well have been from the world outside Jerusalem. Acts 6:5 describes him as a "man full of faith and of the Holy Spirit," and later as "full of grace and power," who "did great wonders and signs among the people."

In an age of much insurrection among the Jews against the Romans, when many of the Christians were already fleeing for safety across the Jordan to Pella, Stephen drew the ire of the Hellenic Jews from the free men's synagogue for what they termed his blasphemy against Moses and against God. Luke reports that his opponents hired false witnesses against him. At his defense before the Sanhedrin, Stephen argued that from the beginning of history the people of Israel had stubbornly resisted the workings of God. The arguments are well summarized in the book of Acts. The climax of Stephen's speech was that the Jews had brazenly rejected Christ and even slain him, just as their fathers had wiped out the prophets. This so enraged the court and the people that in a fit of mob anger they took him out and stoned him, even though under Roman law they had no such authority.

Stephen's death proved to be the turning point in splitting apart those Jews who accepted the work and sayings of Christ and those who did not. As the first MARTYR, his importance is marked by the great number of boys who were named after him in the early church and for centuries thereafter, by the great number of churches that bore his name, and by the position of his feast day on the day after Christmas—as if the church considered him more important than any individual in the NT other than Christ.

T.J.K.

## STEWARD/STEWARDSHIP.

In the biblical world a steward was one who controlled the working of the household, directing the domestic affairs of the establishment, controlling the finances and supervising the servants and workers. Thus Joseph had a steward (Gen. 43:19) as did Abraham (Gen. 15:2), and on a larger scale, the kings of Israel, whose function was more largely financial.

In the NT, the commonest word for steward is *oikonomos*, the one who sets rules for the household. Bishops are stewards of the things of God (Tit. 1:7). In fact, every Christian is a steward of God's mysteries (I Cor. 4:1; Gal. 4:2). Stewardship is not limited merely to money or material goods. Stewardship before God involves everything God has provided—ability, talents, time, emotions, even life itself. When the Law tells us that the earth is the Lord's, and when the Lord places us in it as stewards, then stewardship becomes practical indeed. Biblical stewardship includes protection of the earth and all that is in it—animals, forests, land, people. In fact the charge to be stewards really puts the human race back in the position of Adam and Eve, to care for the creation as its guardians and custodians. Both the spiritual and material well-being of one's neighbors are necessary concerns for those who practice biblical stewardship, in the fullest sense of the word (Jas. 2:17; I John 3:17).                                T.J.K.

## STICHOMETRY.

This term refers to a method of arranging a text into hypothetical lines and stanzas on the assumption that its original literary form was poetic. The criteria are syllabic length and meter based on the kinds of vowels used. The method has been used extensively to reconstruct Hebrew poetry, especially in the Psalms. In the NT one of the clearest examples of a trochaic meter is Ephesians 5:14, giving rise to a two- or three-line "hymn" (see RSV and NEB for different versification).                    R.M.

**STITES, EDGAR PAGE** (1836–1916). Ship builder and hymn writer. A New Jersey native, Stites was attending a Methodist camp meeting about 1875 at Ocean Grove, New Jersey, when he wrote the words of his hymn "Beulah Land," with its famous opening words, "I've reached the land of corn and wine." The text was based on Isaiah 35:10. Ira Sankey said the famous number was sung most frequently at funerals. Not much is known of Stite's life. He was a cousin of another hymn writer, Eliza E. Hewitt.
R.H.

**STODDARD, SOLOMON** (1643–1729). The "Pope" of Connecticut Congregationalism was one of fifteen sons of Anthony and Mary Downing Stoddard. A graduate of Harvard, he served the Northampton, Massachusetts, church from November 1669 until his death in February 1729. While there his grandson JONATHAN EDWARDS became his associate. Stoddard let professing Christians enjoy privileges of full membership even if they were uncertain of their state of grace. His sermons stressing judgment led to several revivals.                    N.H.

**STOICISM.** A philosophical movement that arose in ancient Athens and remained important for five hundred years. It was one of the most influential of the ancient philosophical schools, but only fragments of its early writings remain. The Stoics' aim was to understand the universe as macrocosm and human life and culture as microcosm. Heraclitus of Ephesus was the forerunner with his doctrines concerning the creative nature of reason in people and the universe, the subordination of the individual to the laws of nature, and the fact that all things are in a process of change.

The Stoics take their name from the Painted Colonnade *(stoa)* from which Zeno their founder lectured in Athens around 300 B.C. He emphasized the centrality of human character as evidenced in ethical and political action. He divided philosophy into three parts: logic, physics (cosmogony) and ethics. During the middle period, second and third centuries B.C., the movement was centered in Rome, where Diogenes lectured. There was at this time a modification in theme from the ascetic ideal of the wise person to the idea of the potential for moral progress in all people.

The late Stoic period, A.D. 100–200, is distinguished by the life and writings of SENECA, EPICTETUS, and the emperor Marcus Aurelius, whose *Meditations* are still accessible. He realized that Stoicism and Christianity were rivals and opponents in their appeal as the bases for popular life-styles. The

stress now was less on natural science and more on moral philosophy: inward self-control and exemplary citizenship. Finding truth was both the desire and goal of the Stoics. They defined the formative creative power of the world—God—as LOGOS, Providence, and Order. They understood the course of the universe to be cyclical and timeless. In this universe God and world are autonomous and orderly. Those who live in harmony with this order will develop peace and well-being. This state could be achieved through virtue (which includes intelligence—knowing good from evil), bravery, justice, and self-control. All people, including slaves, have the divine spark, and the goal of each person should be service to others.

Stoicism has influenced Christianity, Judaism, and Islam. It influenced medieval political theory and the Renaissance tradition of Christian humanism. Its themes are still important for modern definitions of moral living.                    I.C.

**STONE, BARTON W.** (1772–1844). One of the early pioneers of the CHRISTIAN CHURCHES (Disciples of Christ), Stone was born on December 24 near Port Tobacco, Maryland. Ordained by the Presbyterian church in 1768, he was pastor at CANE RIDGE during the revival there. In 1803 he and four others formed the Springfield Presbytery. In 1804 they dissolved it, resolving to have no name but Christian, no creed but the Bible. In 1832 he agreed with Alexander Campbell to act as one of his disciples.                    N.H.

**STONE, SAMUEL JOHN** (1839–1900). Anglican clergyman, conservative apologist, and hymn writer. Stone was born in Whitmore, England. After his graduation from Oxford University, Stone served two English parishes—one at Windsor and one in the East End (London), where he ministered to the poor and needy. While Stone was a twenty-seven-year-old curate at Windsor, a controversy erupted in the Anglican communion over the writings of Bishop John Colenso of Natal, South Africa, who is said to have questioned several articles of the Christian faith. Colenso was forced from the church by his superior, the metropolitan, Bishop Robert Gray. Stone, a member of the High Church party, supported Gray and wrote a collection of twelve hymns, *Lyra Fidelium*, based on the Apostles' Creed. That association with the church inspired Stone to write his most enduring number, "The Church's One Foundation."                    R.H.

**STOWE, HARRIET BEECHER** (1811–96). Noted American author, abolitionist, and hymn writer. Harriet Beecher Stowe was the daughter of LYMAN BEECHER, New England Congregationalist minister, and a sister of the famed HENRY WARD BEECHER. Born on June 14 in Litchfield, Connecticut, she was four years old when her mother died. At thirteen she was sent to Hartford to attend a girls' school. She moved to Cincinnati in 1832, where her father became head of Lane Theological Seminary. She was employed there as a teacher in the Western Female Institute in Cincinnati, which had been founded by her sister, Catherine. About this time Harriet began her writing career and became an ardent abolitionist. In 1836 she married Calvin Ellis Stowe, professor of biblical literature at Lane Seminary. Later her husband received a call to a professorship at Bowdoin College, Brunswick, Maine. After the birth of her seventh child, Mrs. Stowe began to write *Uncle Tom's Cabin*, which appeared serially in an antislavery paper, the *National Era*. She wrote a number of books and hymn texts. Among her best-known hymns are "Still, Still with Thee," "Abide in Me, O Lord, and I in Thee," and "When Winds Are Raging." Mrs. Stowe died on July 1 in Hartford, Connecticut.

R.H.

**STRANGER.** *See* FOREIGNER.

**STRAUSS, DAVID FRIEDRICH** (1808–74). German theologian. Born in Ludwigsburg, Strauss studied theology and philosophy at Tübingen and Berlin, where he was influenced by F. D. E. Schleiermacher and Georg W. F. Hegel. His *Das Leben Jesu* (*The Life of Jesus*, 1835–36) applied "myth theory" to the life of Christ. He saw the Gospels as "historical garb fashioned for primitive Christian ideas by naïve poetic mythmakers and consolidated in an historical personality." The book brought about his dismissal as a professor at Tübingen. In later life he rejected Christianity entirely in favor of scientific materialism.

N.H.

**STRONG, AUGUSTUS** (1836–1921). Author of *Systematic Theology* (three vols. 1907–09), Strong was born August 3 in Rochester, New York. A graduate of Yale College (1857) and Rochester Theological Seminary (1859), he was ordained (1861) to serve the Baptist church in Haverhill, Massachusetts. From 1865 to 1872 Strong served First Baptist Church in Cleveland. He then became professor of biblical theology and president of Rochester Seminary, until his retirement in 1912. He also helped establish the University of Chicago.

N.H.

**STRONG, JOSIAH** (1847–1916). Social reformer and prophet of the SOCIAL GOSPEL. He was born January 19 in Naperville, Illinois. He graduated from Western Reserve College in 1869 and attended Lane Theological Seminary. Ordained in 1871, he served the Congregational church in Cheyenne, Wyoming, for two years. Returning to Western Reserve College as chaplain in 1873, he took a pastorate in Sandusky, Ohio, in 1876. Strong served as secretary of the Congregational Home Missionary Society and as pastor of Central Congregational Church, Cincinnati. He was secretary of the American EVANGELICAL ALLIANCE until he resigned in 1898. His most famous book, *Our Country* (1885), was sympathetic to labor

and critiqued capitalism. *The New Era* (1893) discussed the ideal society as Christ's kingdom.

N.H.

**STRUCTURAL CRITICISM.** *See* BIBLICAL CRITICISM.

**STUDENT CHRISTIAN MOVEMENT (SCM).** The British member of the World Student Christian Federation. The SCM began in 1892 with the "Cambridge (University) Seven." It drew students with a "desire to understand the Christian faith and live the Christian life" into study groups, conferences, and camps. An integral part of the movement was the Student Volunteer Missionary Union. Originally supported by the British Evangelicals, it reached out to High Church students and Liberals, paving the way for the modern ecumenical movement. Leaders included H. J. Oldham, William Temple, and Nathan Soderblom. Eventually more conservative members withdrew to form the Cambridge Inter-Collegiate Christian Union in 1910. To publish literature for students the group formed SCM Press, Ltd., London, in 1929, which continues to be a major British religious publisher.

N.H.

**STUDENT VOLUNTEER MOVEMENT.** The Student Volunteer Movement for Foreign Missions began in the U.S.A. in 1866, and from it emerged in 1892 the Student Volunteer Missionary Union in Britain. The SVM slogan "The evangelization of the world in this generation," stated its aim—to enroll university students for worldwide missionary work. The SVM helped shape Protestant missions from 1890 to 1940, drew various churches together in mission, and became an important factor leading to the Edinburgh Conference on missions in 1910. Among the volunteers in the movement who became leaders in mission endeavors were Robert P. Wilder, John R. Mott, and Robert E. Speer. By 1939 SVM had recruited 25,000 missionaries, most of whom were from North America, and the majority went to Africa and Asia.

W.G.

**STUPA.** In BUDDHISM, a domed building serving as a place of pilgrimage and worship. The oldest style of Buddhist edifice, the stupa was originally a place of burial for holy people and a reliquary housing remains of the Buddha and other saints. While this use has never been lost, the stupa later came to be venerated also for its symbolic significance. The traditional stupa of India and Southeast Asia first consists of a round base with a path outside it for walking around, a major devotional practice. Atop the base is a rounded dome, capped by a square structure. From the center of the square rises a pole bearing three horizontal discs or umbrellas.

The basic symbolic interpretation of the stupa is that the base represents the earth, the dome the sky,

the cap the transcendent heavens, and the pole with its three discs the path of the Buddha, who has passed beyond all levels of conditioned reality, even the heavens. The stupa at Sanchi, India, built by Ashoka, with its rich carvings, is among the earliest and a classic example. The most imposing temple based on the stupa idea is probably the celebrated one at Borobudur in Java. The Tibetan *chorten* and the East Asian pagoda are further developments of the stupa.
R.E.

**SUBDEACON.** In the Roman Catholic church, a person in the lowest of the two major orders leading to priesthood. Subdeacons arose in the early Catholic Church in the mid-third century A.D. Until the thirteenth century, it was a minor order, understood as instituted by the church. At that time it became a major order. Subdeacons are required to accept perpetual celibacy and to recite the divine office daily.
J.C.

**SUBDEAN.** One who assists a dean in parish supervision. A dean is a clergyman appointed by the bishop (Roman Catholic church) or elected by the clergy (Lutheran) to supervise a district of the diocese (Roman Catholic) or synod (Lutheran). In the Catholic tradition, the office of rural dean or *vicar forane* dates to 1565.
J.C.

**SUBORDINATION.** A teaching about the Godhead or the Trinity that regards the Son as subordinate to the Father and the Holy Spirit as subordinate to both. This was a strong temptation in the first three centuries of Christian theology, but all forms of subordination within the Trinity were explicitly rejected in the resolutions of the Arian and Pneumatomachi controversies.

In more recent times some otherwise orthodox Christians have resurrected subordinationist trinitarian formulations to buttress arguments for male supremacy and female subordination. Confusing the image of head and body with structures of authority, they interpret such passages as I Corinthians 11:13 (see especially the TEV) to mean that all women should be subordinate to all men because Christ is subordinate to God. Subordination is also often confused with submission, which is a voluntary act of servanthood. Just as there is mutual submission at times between the coequal persons of the Trinity, so the NT repeatedly calls for mutual submission among all Christians (for example, Eph. 5:21).
N.H.

**SUBSTANCE.** An important word in the history of philosophy since Aristotle and in Christian theologies of the Incarnation and the Eucharist. According to Aristotle, the substance of a thing is what makes it what it is, its form or essence. The Greek term *ousia*, meaning what is underlying or basic, was rendered in Latin as *substantia*. *Substantia* is the permanent reality of a thing in contrast to its mutable, visible accidents.

These Aristotelian distinctions were taken up by the Scholastic philosophers and especially Thomas Aquinas. For Aquinas the reality of a thing is its substance, the source of a thing's unity and the subject of all predicates—that which sustains all accidents. For Descartes substance is that which needs nothing else for its existence, God being absolute substance in contrast to created substances. Spinoza taught that there is only one eternal, infinite substance, God or Nature, the things that make up the universe being God's finite modes.

In Christian theology the term "of one substance" was used in the NICENE CREED to express the relationship of the Father and the Son in the Godhead. In the Middle Ages the word "substance" was also used in Eucharistic theology to distinguish the substance of the species bread and wine from their mere accidents. The Council of Trent authorized TRANSUBSTANTIATION, or the change of the whole substance of bread and wine into the whole Body and Blood of Christ in the Eucharist, with only the accidents of bread and wine remaining.
J.L.

**SUCCOTH.** (1) A city of Gad (Josh. 13:27) in Transjordan. Its name, meaning "booths," probably derives from a Canaanite harvest festival, though Genesis 33:17 associates "Succoth" with booths Jacob erected for his cattle as he returned from Paddan-aram. In the Judges era, its seventy-seven elders scornfully refused Gideon's request for food for his famishing army as it pursued Midian. On his triumphant return, Gideon severely punished them (Judg. 8:5-7, 14-16). Moreover, bronze equipment for Solomon's Temple was cast near Succoth (I Kings 7:46). The site is identified with Tell Deir 'Alla, situated along the course of the Jabbok as it turns northward to meet the Jordan. Presumably, "the Vale of Succoth" (Pss. 60:6; 108:7) denotes the fertile area dominated by this tell.

(2) An Egyptian city listed in Exodus 12:37; 13:20; and Numbers 33:5-6 as the first encampment of the Hebrews in the Exodus from Egypt. Ordinarily it is identified with modern Tell el-Maskhutah, a border fortress in the Wadi Tumeilat.
J.K.K.

**SUFFERING.** *See* EVIL.

**SUFFERING SERVANT.** *See* SERVANT OF THE LORD.

**SUFFRAGAN.** An assistant bishop in Roman Catholic polity, but also the bishop of a diocese who is subject to the authority of a superior bishop or metropolitan.
J.C

**SUFISM.** Islamic MYSTICISM. The name "Sufi" is derived from the Arabic word meaning "wool clad," from the ascetic clothing worn by the mystics. A broad movement, Sufism embraces ascetic hermits, protest movements, theological schools, and international brotherhoods. Sufis practice total reliance on God and have expressed their love for him in many ways, including meditation, poetry, dance, music, and recitation of the QUR'AN.

Sufism arose in the early days of Islam. The earliest Sufis practiced poverty (see FAKIR). They praised God through repetition of his name and through listening to poetry and music. The movements of the Umayyad and ABBASID dynasties, especially in politics, influenced early Sufism, and some Sufis may have drawn inspiration from Monophysite Christianity, Buddhism, Hinduism, and Zoroastrianism. Sufism began to coalesce in the late tenth century A.D., when various writers attempted to bring together the differing strands of the movement. In Sufism's medieval period (about A.D. 1000–1500), philosophers such as al-Ghazzali (who died in 1111) helped the movement gain recognition as a legitimate form of Islamic piety. Poetry gained increasing importance in that period, especially in the work of Jalal ad-Din Rumi, founder of the DERVISHES.

Sufism reached its peak of popularity in the time of the Mogul and Ottoman empires, about A.D. 1500–1800. The movement helped to expand the borders of Islam in Africa and Asia. Sufi missionaries brought Islam to West Africa, where today it competes with Christianity, and to Southeast Asia, particularly Indonesia, where it competes with Hinduism and Buddhism. The movement began to lose strength, however, during the time of Western colonialization. Wahhabiya, a movement requiring strict adherence to the Qur'an, rejected many aspects of Sufism: separate traditions, veneration of saints, and ecstatic communion with God. Wahhabis blamed Sufis for the weakened state of the Islamic world. Nevertheless, Sufism did remain strong in some areas, providing organization for resistance to colonialism. Both Sufism and Wahhabiya sought liberation from Western rule, and in nineteenth-century North India the *mujahidin* (holy warriors, see JIHAD) managed to combine the movements.

Today Sufism has little support. From a high point, when it was accepted as legitimate by perhaps 80 percent of all Muslims, Sufism has fallen to a small minority. Schools survive in seclusion and on the peripheries of the Muslim world. Westerners have heard about the movement through Indries Shah and others, and Western scholars have recently published several works on Sufism.

A major reason for hostility to Sufism is that the mystics have often said and done things that shock and infuriate the orthodox. One Sufi saint stared into the sun as a form of meditation. A Sufi saying is that God is an atheist, because he believes in no higher deity. Sufis have invited persecution and even martyrdom through such sayings and remarks that are regarded as even greater blasphemies, for example, "I am God." Sufis have also postulated a godhead, immutable and passive, behind or above Allah. Other Sufis reject all metaphysical speculation and therefore criticize the schools of Islamic philosophy that followed Greek thought.

Sufism's great spread in time, space, and philosophy defies generalization. The earliest Sufis, to whom later teachers looked for authority, most likely did not recognize themselves as members of a separate school. When the movement came to think of itself as distinct from other schools of thought it became divided through differences in temperament and varying degrees of borrowing from other religions. Persecution took its toll on membership and reputation. Though Sufi influence lingers on, it no longer commands widespread loyalty.        K./M.C.

**SUKKOT.** A Jewish festival held during the fall season, which commemorates the time the Israelites lived in booths in the wilderness. Known as both the Feast of Booths and the Feast of Tabernacles, it was from ancient times one of the most important festivals of the Israelites. The Bible calls it "the feast of the Lord" (Lev. 23:39). It is observed for seven days in Israel (and by Reform Jews) and for eight days by Conservative and Orthodox Jews outside Israel. Temporary booths are constructed, and Jews are supposed to live in them for the entire festival so "that your generations may know that I made the people of Israel dwell in booths when I brought them out of the land of Egypt" (Lev. 23:43). Jews also recite blessings over the "fruit of goodly trees (a citron called *etrog*), branches of palm trees *(lulav)*, boughs of leafy trees, and willows of the brook; and you shall rejoice before the Lord your God . . ." (Lev. 23:40). A harvest festival, Sukkot is also known as the "feast of ingathering." It is one of the three pilgrimage festivals, the other two being PASSOVER and SHAVUOT. (See also JEWISH HOLIDAYS.)        L.K.

**SULLIVAN, HARRY STACK** (1892–1949). Founder of the practice of psychiatry as the study of interpersonal relations. Sullivan was born in Norwich, New York, on February 21. He became a doctor in 1917, studied psychiatry at St. Elizabeth's Hospital in Washington, D.C., 1919–1923, and did clinical research at Sheppard and Enoch Pratt Hospital in Towson, Maryland, 1923–30. From this research he developed his idea that psychiatric disorders arose out of disturbances in the person's interpersonal relationships, particularly with the mother. This disturbance causes anxiety in the infant and the child develops a life-style designed to reduce this anxiety. Sullivan died in Paris, France on January 14.        J.C.

**SULPICIANS.** See ST. SULPICE, SOCIETY OF.

**SUMER.** The land situated in the Tigris-Euphrates plain of Lower Mesopotamia, spanning modern Baghdad and the Persian Gulf. At history's dawn, its Sumerian inhabitants fashioned a remarkable civilization.

*Historical Overview.* The Ubaidians were Sumer's original inhabitants (about 4000–3300 B.C.). Their culture is attested at Tell al-Ubaid and in the lowest strata of numerous villages that ultimately became substantial urban centers. As they prospered, they sustained infiltrations of western Semitic nomads. The Sumerians arrived about 3300–3000. Speaking a unique language, they blended with the native population and spawned a culture rich in technological, religious, and literary achievements. Especially significant was the Sumerian invention of a cuneiform system of writing.

During Sumer's early dynastic period (about 3000–2360), such city-states as Kish, UR, and Erech vied for dominance, though none permanently unified the land. Sumer's kings included Enmebaraggesi of Kish, founder of the Nippur temple of Enlil, Sumer's chief deity; Mesannepadda of Ur, founder of a dynasty noted for its exquisite tombs; and Gilgamesh of Erech, whose exploits made him the focus of legend. Sumer yielded to Semitic rule when SARGON established the Akkad Empire (about 2360–2180). Encompassing most of western Asia, it collapsed when Sargon's grandson, Naram-Sin, was overwhelmed by Guti barbarians who loosely controlled Sumer for approximately one dark century.

The Sumerians gradually revived. Presumably, toward the end of Gutian dominance, Gudea advanced his city, Lagash, by sponsoring effective programs in trade, temple building, visual arts, and literature. Utu-hegal, king of Erech, liberated Sumer from the Guti yoke, but was overthrown by Ur-nammu, founder of the Third Dynasty of Ur (about 2060–1950). Through his law code, Ur-nammu corrected various social abuses. Sumer likewise prospered under his son Shulgi, but was soon overrun by Semitic nomads, the Amurru (biblical Amorites). Elam's destruction of Ur (about 1950) induced rival Amorite dynasties to assert themselves. Babylon claimed the victory when Hammurabi defeated Rim-sin of Larsa (about 1720). Thus ancient Sumer expired.

*Sumerian Society.* Though agrarian in economy, Sumerian society was predominantly urban. The typical Sumerian city-state hosted, as the property of its patron deity, a large, walled city featuring as its outstanding edifice a mud brick temple with enormous tower (*ziggurat*). Surrounding land belonged to the temple and private citizens. The city's governor (*ensi*) and an assembly of free citizens determined local policy. Emergencies evoked by barbarian incursions and city-state rivalries inspired the institution of kingship. Most Sumerians were free citizens devoted to private enterprise. They farmed, fished, traded, and engaged in various crafts. Thousands of clay tablets attest the importance of writing. Though most served economic and legal interests, some contain literary expressions of myth, epic, hymn, lament, and proverb. Sumer's schools ensured the education of professionals and general

Courtesy of the Oriental Institute, University of Chicago

*Group of statues, from the Abu temple at Tell Asmar*

advancement of learning. Its artists excelled in music, sculpture, and cylinder seal engraving (small stone cylinders creating geometric and scene impressions when rolled over wet clay).

*Sumerian Religion.* In their cosmology, the Sumerians spoke of a heaven vaulting over an earth disk, all of which was surrounded by primordial water. A pantheon of inscrutable, immortal deities supervised the universe. Four were particularly prominent—Enlil, An, Ki, and Enki (deities of atmosphere, heaven, earth, and water). Sumerian perspectives about the nature and destiny of humanity were sober. Determined to concentrate on divine pursuits, the gods created humanity from clay to meet their needs for food, drink, and lodging. Through cultic rituals, the most crucial being the New Year festival, humanity served and placated the gods. Abject existence was plagued by uncertainty. When tragedy struck, the day's order was not complaint but confession of moral and ritual offense against the gods. At death humanity entered a netherworld dismally reflecting previous earthly existence.

J.K.K.

**SUMMA.** Originally the medieval title of any compendium of a subject such as theology, philosophy, or canon law. Summas superseded SENTENCES as handbooks for schools. The best known is Thomas Aquinas' *Summa Theologica.*          N.H.

***SUMMA CONTRA GENTILES.*** *See* AQUINAS, THOMAS.

***SUMMA THEOLOGICA.*** *See* AQUINAS, THOMAS.

**SUN.** The daytime luminary that God created under the designation "the greater light" (Gen. 1:16) to avoid any mythological association with the Mesopotamian and Canaanite sun-gods, Shamash and Shapsh, with whose names *shemesh*, the Hebrew noun for "sun," is cognate.

*Diverse Literary Usage.* Solar biblical references define space and time: east ("from the rising of the sun"; Deut. 11:30), west ("toward the going down of the sun"; Isa. 45:6; 59:19), the whole earth ("from the rising of the sun to its setting"; Pss. 50:1; 113:3; Mal. 1:11); morning ("when the sun rises"; Ps. 104:22), midday ("until the sun is hot"; Neh. 7:3), and evening ("the sun went down"; Judg. 19:14). The frequent phrase "under the sun" in Ecclesiastes (1:3, 9, 14) indicates mundane existence. The sun is mentioned in expressions denoting shameful public exposure (Num. 25:4; II Sam. 12:11-12), sunstroke (Ps. 121:6), the just ruler (II Sam. 23:4), dynastic permanence (Ps. 89:36), Yahweh's creative power (Pss. 19:4; 74:16; 136:8; Ecclus. 43:2), and the transfiguration of Jesus (Matt. 17:2). Folkloristic allusions appear in Joshua 10:12-13, where postponed sunset ensures Joshua's military triumph, and II Kings 20:8-11 (Isa. 38:7-8), where the sun's receding shadow on a sundial signals Hezekiah's recovery from severe illness.

*Solar Idolatry.* Israelite involvement in the Palestinian solar cult, whose appeal is betrayed by the place-names Beth-shemesh ("house of the sun"; I Sam. 6:9) and En-shemesh ("spring of the sun"; Josh. 15:7), was prohibited by Yahweh (Deut. 4:19; 17:3). Nevertheless, King Manasseh (687–642 B.C.) legitimized the worship of "all the host of heaven" (II Kings 21:3, 5), in which many Judeans presumably participated (Jer. 8:2). Though Josiah's reform (622 B.C.) abolished its priesthood and horse-and-chariot paraphernalia (II Kings 23:5, 11), its survival soon thereafter (Ezek. 8:16) again jeopardized Yahweh's incomparability.

*Final Judgment and Blessing.* Several prophetic texts declare that with the cessation of the present era on the Day of Yahweh, the world will confront a sun "dark at its rising" (Isa. 13:10), one covered "with a cloud" (Ezek. 32:7; see Joel 2:10, 31). Jesus speaks similarly in his portrayal of the end of the age (Matt. 24:29; Mark 13:24). The faithful, however, are marvelously reassured. With Yahweh's ultimate triumph, either the sun will shine with sevenfold brightness (Isa. 30:26), or in the new Jerusalem, their future home, the resplendence of God's indwelling glory will render the sun irrelevant (Isa. 60:19; Rev. 21:23).                                                       J.K.K.

**SUNDAY.** The first day of the week, and by ancient tradition of the church, the chief day of Christian worship. In the OT the people of God had worshiped, instead, on the seventh day of the week, Saturday. But Christ's resurrection from the dead on EASTER Day established a new day for worship, as did his appearances to the women, the disciples, the two men on their way to Emmaus, and later to Thomas, all on Sunday, and still later, his sending of the Holy Spirit on Pentecost Sunday. It was almost as if Christ had picked Sunday over Saturday.

The SABBATH day had been both a day of worship and a day of rest. In the Greco-Roman world there was no fixed pattern for a weekly day of rest. Christians

therefore often worshiped either before or after the working day. As for the Mosaic Law, Christ disregarded a Pharisaical interpretation of the Law when he healed the crippled and harvested wheat on the Sabbath. Sunday almost immediately became the cornerstone of Christian worship. As several fathers of the early church wrote, every Sunday became a little Easter. In fact, the replacement of Saturday with Sunday as the chief day of worship was almost automatic, even for a die-hard loyalist to the laws of Moses like Simon Peter. What few references the NT provides almost all point to Sunday as the normal day of worship, whether reported by Luke, Paul, or John. In Acts 20, for example, Luke writes of the visit to Troas and how Paul preached "on the first day of the week, when we were gathered together to break bread" (v. 7). This is the service in a private house or apartment, not in a synagogue, at which Eutychus fell asleep on the window sill and crashed to the street below. The service was apparently held at night.

Paul further exhorts the Corinthians to gather an offering for Jerusalem when they gathered on the first day of the week. He says he had given similar instructions to the churches in Galatia. John, in Revelation 1:10, terms Sunday as the "Lord's day" as if the term were already understood by everybody.

Paul normally refers to Sunday as the first day of the week. By the time John was a prisoner in exile on Patmos, the "first day" had universally assumed the new name, "the day of the Lord." In Greek this is *kyriake*, and means simply "the Lord's" or "pertaining to the Lord." The Latin equivalent is *dominicale*, a word that has given us the name for Sunday in most of the Romance languages—those based on Latin. Even in the twentieth century we have such forms as *domingo* (Portuguese), *domenica* (Italian), and *dimanche* (French). The other days of the week continued to be named after Roman gods— Luna, Mars, Mercury, Jupiter, Venus, and Saturn. In northern Europe, where the biggest family of languages was the Germanic one, the names of the days of the week remained pagan. The deities honored were the sun, the moon, Tiu, Woden, Thor, Freia, and Saturn. Even so pious a monk as the Venerable Bede in his monastery in England could write that Christians should not be disturbed to worship on a day, Sunday, whose name honored the sun god. After all, should not Christians make some concessions to the lack of knowledge of the unconverted heathen? And did Christians not also mark the resurrection of the Lord on Easter, also a pagan rather than a Christian name?
                                                                          T.J.K.

**SUNDAY, WILLIAM (BILLY) ASHLEY** (1862–1935). Colorful American evangelist who left a career in professional baseball. Born in Ames, Iowa, Sunday for a time worked as a fireman on the Chicago and Northwestern Railroad between baseball seasons. Soon after his conversion at Chicago's Pacific Garden Mission in 1886, Sunday left baseball. From 1891 to

Courtesy of Religious News Service

*William A. (Billy) Sunday*

1893 he served as an assistant secretary of the Chicago YMCA. Then for two years he served with J. Wilbur Chapman in his evangelistic campaigns.

Sunday began his independent career as an evangelist in 1896. He developed an organization of co-workers including HOMER RODEHEAVER, the trombone-playing song leader. Sunday developed the idea of conducting city-wide campaigns, enlisting the support of all the churches in an area. Often his meetings were conducted in wooden tabernacles especially built for his meetings.

Sunday became famous for his humorous rhetoric and unorthodox preaching style. Since sawdust covered the ground in the tabernacles, the converts resulting from his meetings were described as "hitting the sawdust trail." Sunday always found opportunity to strike hard against evolution and "Demon Rum." He was heard by more people—some one hundred million—than any preacher up to his time.                                                                          R.H.

**SUNDAY SCHOOLS.** Newspaper editor ROBERT RAIKES of Gloucester, England, in 1780 hired women to teach poor children to read and recite their catechism in an effort to "check the deplorable profanation of the Sabbath." The concept spread throughout England. A Sunday School Society was formed in 1785, and the British Sunday School Union in 1803. Promoted by the Clapham sect, it changed from a secular charity into a vehicle for Christian education. The Sunday School Institute was formed in 1843 to ensure Church of England teaching; it became the National Sunday School Union in 1903, and the National Christian Education Council in 1966.

The concept was promoted in the United States by Isabella Marshall Graham and her daughter and son-in-law Joanna and Divy Bethune, who first started a class for adults in 1792. In 1804 some Philadelphia women formed a Sabbath school to teach poor girls. A landmark decision by the Superior Court in 1808 declared them as women "citizens of the commonwealth" and thus eligible for incorporation. Whereas British teachers had been paid, American schools became entirely a voluntary enterprise.

Joanna Bethune formed the Female Union for the Promotion of Sabbath Schools in 1816. Patterned after the Edinburgh Gratis Sabbath-School Society, its constitution was borrowed from a Bristol society. The executive committee included Presbyterian, Baptist, Methodist, and Dutch Reformed women. The Bethunes also organized the New York Sunday School Union and in 1824 the American Sunday School Union. In 1829 its mission became the evangelization of the nation; in 1833 the "Valley Campaign" to save the Midwest from Roman Catholicism; in 1834 the "Southern Enterprise" to promote Sunday schools from Maryland to Florida; and in 1835 to win the world.

Begun as an ecumenical effort by women, Sunday schools were perceived by some as an intrusion on parents' educational responsibilities. Others said it infringed on the pastor's teaching office and was a violation of Sabbath rest. In the work of Dwight L. Moody and in many conservative churches today, the Sunday school remains a form of evangelistic outreach. Children of the poor and unchurched are bussed to church in hopes that parents will eventually join.

In 1872 Moody convinced the ASSU to adopt the "uniform lesson plan," in which all age levels studied the same text. This ecumenical venture, an important part of the Evangelical United Front, encouraged interdenominational publishing and teacher training. The Sunday school became an integral part of the American church, sometimes more important to its members than worship services.                    N.H.

**SUNNA.** The Arabic word meaning "way, course of action, manner of acting." In Islam, Sunna refers to the decrees of God and the precedents of the prophet Muhammad, taken as models for the faithful. The term Sunni is commonly used for the majority body of Islam, which emphasizes the Sunna of the Prophet, tradition, legal precedent, and the consensus of believers. The other major party is the Shi'a.                                                     R.E.

**SUNNI/SUNNITE.** The majority party in Islam, so called because it follows the SUNNA, or traditional forms of faith and practice, in contrast to the SHI'ITE movement, the party loyal to Ali.                 K.C.

**SUNYATA.** From the Sanskrit word for "emptiness." In BUDDHISM, a term used to describe the phenomenal world and the world of thought that stems from it as ultimately empty or void. It is most prominently used in the Mahayana thought of NAGARJUNA (about A.D. 200), for whom emptiness was the most appropriate metaphor for a universe in which all is in flux, and there is nothing to which to cling, neither god nor abiding self, in the realm of conditioned reality. What is unchanging is NIRVANA, not different from the void, the indescribable opposite of the conditioned realm yet also one with it, since Nirvana and Sunyata are in no other place and time than the here and now. Sunyata or emptiness, in other words, is simply the ordinary world seen with the eye of enlightenment, which sees it as it really is: transitory, with no place for attachment, but also where liberation can be realized in the midst of ordinariness by those who so view it.       R.E.

**SUPER EGO.** *See* FREUD, SIGMUND.

**SUPEREROGATION, WORKS OF.** Traditionally, in Roman Catholic moral theology, good works that go beyond those strictly obligatory on Christians. Those who voluntarily take upon themselves the counsels of perfection (celibacy, poverty, obedience) are considered to practice good deeds beyond the call of a believer's duty. Any extraordinary act, such as the work of a missionary in dangerous areas, serving the sick in an epidemic, or voluntarily identifying oneself with the oppressed would be considered a work of supererogation.

In Protestantism, generally, the concept of WORKS of supererogation is rejected. Luther saw such a notion as resting on works righteousness, the belief that one cooperates with God in salvation, or somehow wins a reward from God for one's ascetic life-style. Of course, legalism and an emphasis on good works developed in some Protestant sects. In the case of John Wesley's early teachings on the possibility of Christian perfection, Wesley—and the later Methodists—found it helpful to deny the need for works of supererogation.                 J.C.

**SUPERNATURAL.** *See* TRANSCENDENCE.

**SUPREMACY, ACTS OF.** The first, passed in 1534, confirmed to HENRY VIII and his successors the title "the only supreme head on earth of the Church of England." As enforced by Thomas Cromwell, it gave the king and his agents precedence over the entire episcopacy. The act was later repealed by Queen Mary. A second Act of Supremacy, passed in 1559, named ELIZABETH I "the only supreme governor . . . as well in all spiritual or ecclesiastical things or causes as temporal." This act set limits on the government's ability to judge heresy and made Parliament a more equal partner in the church's governing. An oath affirming the sovereign's supremacy was required of all clergy and public officials.                 N.H.

**SUSANNA, BOOK OF.** Apocryphal addition to the book of DANIEL. In the story Susanna refused to have sexual relations with two elders who approached her in her garden pool. Accused of adultery, she maintained her innocence in an ensuing trial. Daniel, in an attempt to defend her, confronted and cross-examined the two elders who contradicted each other's testimony. Susanna was acquitted and in accordance with the law of Deuteronomy 19:18-21, the two elders were executed. The apocryphal books of JUDITH and TOBIT are similar to the book of Susanna in showing how God vindicates the righteous and punishes the wicked.                 W.G.

**SUTRA.** From the Sanskrit word for "thread." In HINDUISM, a sutra is a short saying or aphorism, often collected into a text, as are the "Yoga Sutras" of Patanjali. In BUDDHISM, the much longer SANSKRIT scriptures of Mahayana are called sutras.       R.E.

**SUTTA PITAKA.** From the Pali phrase meaning "Basket of Discourse." The second of the three collections of texts that make up the Tripitaka, "Three Baskets," the Pali scriptures of BUDDHISM that alone are authoritative in the Theravada tradition. The Sutta Pitaka is important for its presentation of basic Buddhist teaching on the origin of suffering and the way to liberation, its instruction on meditation, and its account of the Buddha's last days. Its discourses, mostly attributed to the Buddha himself, tend to be in concrete stories or lists that make for easy memorization.                 R.E.

**SUZUKI, DAISETZ TEITARO** (1870–1966). The person far more responsible than anyone else for the considerable cultural and spiritual influence enjoyed by ZEN Buddhism in Europe and America. A scholar, writer, and Buddhist layman, Suzuki was religiously trained in a Zen monastery in Kamakura. Fluent in English, he resided in the United States (1897–1909) as editor and translator for the Open Court Publishing Company. He subsequently made several lecture tours of the West, the most important being an extended stay in America in the early 1950s, which did much to make Zen an important motif in the "Beat" literature and art of that decade. Suzuki made a lasting impression on such Western expounders of Zen as Christmas Humphreys and Alan

Watts, as well as on psychologists and philosophers like Erich Fromm.

In his many books, Suzuki engagingly discussed Zen monastic life and the relation of Zen to Japanese culture. However, Zen, as he presented it, was not bound to any particular discipline or culture. Instead, it offers the profound freedom of overcoming the dualities that trap the mind, through non-attachment to specific routines or sets of ideas. Suzuki's gift lay in his ability to present Zen in language that spoke to the West's spiritual quest.                          R.E.

## SWEDENBORG, EMANUEL (1688–1772). The
father of the Church of the NEW JERUSALEM was born to Jesper Swedberg, a professor of theology at Uppsala, Sweden, and bishop of Skara. Having studied natural science at Uppsala and served on the Board of Mines (1716–47), Swedenborg is sometimes called the father of "crystallography." Between 1743 and 1745 he became ever-conscious of the spiritual world. In *The Worship and Love of God* he explained that in a vision God told him to explain the "spiritual sense of the Scripture." Thus he published the *Arcana Coelestia* (1749–56), an eight-volume commentary on Genesis and Exodus. Thirty more volumes followed.

Swedenborg asserted human freedom. His self-assured optimism influenced transcendentalism, spiritualism, communitarianism, faith healing, mesmerism, perfectionism, and millenarianism. He believed in three orders of being: the natural world of mineral, vegetable, or animal "ultimates," the spiritual order, and the celestial realm. Everything on the natural level corresponds to something on higher levels. Swedenborg argued that his interpretations of the spiritual meaning of Scripture constituted Christ's Second Coming or the New Jerusalem as prophesied in Revelation 21:2.

Swedenborg's works include *The Earths in the Universe* (1758), *The New Jerusalem and Its Heavenly Doctrine* (1758), *Heaven and Hell* (1758), *Divine Love and Wisdom* (1763, perhaps his central work), *The Apocalypse Revealed* (1766), and *The True Christian Religion* (1771).                          N.H.

## SWEETMAN, JAMES WINDROW (1891–1966).
Entering the Methodist ministry in 1915, Sweetman spent much of his life (1919–46) in India, where he worked on a Christian approach to Muslims, a task for which he prepared himself through private study. He concentrated on a sympathetic understanding and effective communication with Islam. In 1947 he took up the chair of Islamics at Selly Oakes College in Birmingham, England, where he fostered interreligious sensitivity and introduced missionary candidates to the priority for Christian mission to Muslims. He also wrote several articles and books, the major one being a three-volume work, *Islam and Christian Theology*, a study of Islamic theology in its relationship with Christian thought.          W.G.

## SYCHAR. A city of Samaria visited by Jesus. The
site of Jacob's well, it was situated "near the field that Jacob gave to his son Joseph" (John 4:5-6). This surely recalls Jacob's gift to Joseph of "one mountain slope" (Hebrew *shekem* ["shoulder"]) reported in Genesis 48:22. Presumably, "the sons of Hamor, Shechem's father" had earlier sold this field to Jacob (Gen. 33:18-19).

Sychar's proper identity turns on the question of whether Sychar and SHECHEM refer to the same locality. Though the best ancient manuscripts attest "Sychar" in John 4:5, "Shechem" appears in a Syriac witness, and Jerome equates Sychar with Shechem. The once popular identification of Sychar with the Arab village of 'Askar, located approximately a mile northeast of Jacob's well, no longer appears persuasive. At best, the similarity of name is uncertain. Also this equation plays havoc with the narrative. The presence of a decent well at 'Askar calls into question the Samaritan woman's lengthy journey to Jacob's well (John 4:7), which is doubtless situated just beyond the southeastern edge of Tell Balatah (biblical Shechem). Thus "Sychar" is most likely a textual error displacing "Shechem," the reading intended by the biblical writer.                          J.K.K.

## SYLLABUS OF ERRORS. Pope Pius IX in 1864
issued *Syllabus Errorum,* condemning eighty theses. An accompanying encyclical *Quanta cura* appeared to make the Syllabus dogmatically binding. Among other things the Syllabus condemned rationalism, indifferentism, socialism, communism, naturalism, freemasonry, separation of church and state, freedom of the press, and freedom of religion as practiced in many democratic countries. The document culminated in the rejection of any suggestion that "the Roman pontiff can and ought to reconcile himself and reach agreement with progress, liberalism and modern civilization."

Most understood the documents as a direct attack on Americanism, a liberal Catholic movement in the United States, and Catholic Liberalism on the Continent. Others, however, argued that the pope was surprised by the hostile reaction because he sought merely to attack ideas basic to the current Italian Liberal attack on his temporal power. One can also see in it the temporary triumph of ultramontanism. Much of it was reiterated in the dogmatic constitution "De Fide Catholica" of VATICAN I in 1870.                          N.H.

## SYMBOL. A symbol is something that, because of its
natural properties, historical associations, or mere convention, has come to be understood as referring beyond itself to some other reality. Symbols are very common in both secular and religious life. A ruler of a country may use the lion as a symbol of courage; Christianity uses the cross as a symbol of the sacrificial love of Christ. Virtually anything can become a symbol, not only objects but actions and gestures.

In religion, a special importance belongs to the symbolic use of words. In a sense, all referring words are symbols, since they refer to realities beyond themselves. But when we speak of symbolic language, we mean that the reference of the words is not to be taken in the literal or dictionary sense, but has been transferred to some other reality, perhaps in itself difficult to understand, yet now illuminated in some respects by the use of the symbol. For instance, if one says that God is a strong tower, it is obvious that the expression "strong tower" is not to be taken literally—God is not a building. But the words suggest that God can be trusted for protection against evil, just as a strong tower can be trusted. The infinite and eternal being of God must inevitably be beyond human comprehension and cannot be directly grasped by our minds. Hence, virtually all language about God is symbolic or indirect. We take items from everyday human experience and apply them to God, though we understand that they do not apply directly but at most suggest what we believe God to be like. This is the case even when we say "God exists," for we know what it means to exist as a finite being in the world, but we cannot grasp what would be the fullness of being that transcends the world and gives existence to everything in the world. Thus, although Aquinas named God "He who is," the mystical theologians were perhaps wiser when they declared God to transcend even being.

Though symbolic language is indirect, it should not be despised, for it has a flexibility of outreach that makes it in some situations superior to precise conceptual language, just as poetry can express meanings that cannot be put into prose. Paul Tillich warned against thinking of language as "only symbolic," and claimed that the power of symbolic language surpasses that of nonsymbolic language. Tillich mentioned six characteristics of a symbol: (1) It refers beyond itself to the reality that it is intended to illuminate. (2) It participates in that reality, in the sense that it shares some deep affinity, which it brings to light. (3) In doing so, it opens up a level of reality that has hitherto been closed and that cannot be opened up in any other way. (4) At the same time it opens up new dimensions of perception within ourselves, making us sensitive to realities that we had previously missed. (5) Symbols are not produced intentionally or at will—they grow up in human experience and perhaps have their roots in the unconscious. (6) Symbols not only come into being and grow, they eventually wither and die if, in changed historical circumstances, they can no longer perform their work as they did in the past. This is one reason why religions rise and fall.

Thomist scholars have been critical of symbolic theories of religious language because, they believe, such theories have surrendered the cognitive element in religion and reduced religion to emotional response. They contrast with the symbolic theories their own theory of ANALOGY. But these criticisms

seem unjust. While symbols do have emotional appeal, they are also cognitive, and in fact no hard and fast line can be drawn between symbols and analogues.

On the other hand, some philosophers (Hegel is an example) have held that symbols or images produced by the religious consciousness are only stages on the way to the rational concepts of the absolute philosophy. But the question here concerns the reach of human reason. A god who could be grasped in precise concepts would surely be less than God, and God's ultimate mystery is respected rather in symbols that are content to hint at God's being.

Unfortunately, the religious have a tendency to absolutize their symbols and to take them literally. When this happens, the symbols distort rather than illuminate the divine reality, and they become objects of idolatry rather than pointers to God.          J.M.

**SYMBOLICS.** A symbol is a statement of faith or CREED, therefore, symbolics is the area of study of the doctrines of various churches. The great symbols of the Christian faith include the Nicene Creed, which is technically known as the Nicene-Constantinopolitan Creed, written by the councils at Nicaea, in A.D. 325 and 387, the Apostles' Creed, and the Athanasian Creed.          J.C.

**SYNAGOGUE.** A Jewish house of worship. Traditionally, it has had three functions: a place of prayer, a place of study, and a place of assembly. The term is from the Greek and referred to the congregation rather than the site or building. It is used interchangeably with temple.

It evolved from antiquity, appearing as a fully grown and firmly established institution around the first century of the Christian Era. Some scholars say that it originated in the Babylonian Exile. They reason that the exiles, deprived of the TEMPLE in Jerusalem, felt the need to meet from time to time and read the Scriptures. Ezekiel repeatedly refers to the assembly "of the elders" (Ezek. 8:1; 14:1; 20:1).

*Model of an ancient synagogue at Capernaum, built in the third century* A.D.

Some customs and rites of the Temple in Jerusalem were transferred to the synagogue, although some rituals were restricted to the Temple and could not therefore be assumed by the synagogue. Prayer was regarded as the substitute for sacrifice. The service, functions, and officials of the synagogue have remained remarkably consistent throughout the 2,500 years of its history. To the officials were added the professional CANTOR, unknown in early times; the *ba'al keriah,* who reads the Torah portions, where previously the person called up read his own portion; and, particularly in Western countries, the RABBI of the synagogue as distinct from the rabbi of the community.

Synagogues are oriented toward Jerusalem. According to Jewish law, the synagogue must have windows, a requirement stemming from Daniel 6:10-11, which describes how Daniel prayed by windows facing toward Jerusalem. The Torah scrolls are placed in a closet, called the Holy Ark, which is supposed to be on the side facing Jerusalem. The reader's desk was placed immediately in front of the ark. The Eternal Light burns over the ark. The Torah was read, and in many cases still is, from the *bimah,* an elevated platform surrounded by a railing and located so that the entire congregation can hear the Torah reading. The requirement of special accommodations for women is based on a strict interpretation of the existence of women's galleries in the "women's court" of the Temple in Jerusalem. There is no stipulation in Jewish law about the exterior of synagogues, and therefore they range from the simple Hasidic *shteiblech* to impressive edifices of virtually every architectural style. Symbols used in the structure include the MENORAH, SHOFAR (a ram's horn), symbols of the Jewish festivals, the Ten Commandments, the Star of David, fruits of the land of Israel, the Lions of Judah, and the like.

The ritual of the Temple in Jerusalem was conducted inside the sanctuary by only the priests. The rest of the worshipers were kept at a distance. By contrast, the synagogue was a new type of religious building. It was based on the full participation of people in collective acts of worship conducted around a focal point inside the building.                L.K.

## SYNERGISTIC/SYNERGISM.

These terms have (1) the general meaning of cooperating and working together so that separate energies are combined and enhanced, and (2) a theological meaning referring to the doctrine that human wills work together with God's grace to effect regeneration.

The general meaning appears in contemporary group work. Here synergism refers to the way the interacting energies of individuals can enhance each other so that cooperation produces a resultant whole greater than the sum of the parts.

The theological meaning appears especially in controversies during the post-Reformation period. Both the Lutheran and Reformed traditions taught that regeneration from sin is solely by God's grace, revealed and imparted through Jesus Christ and accomplished through the work of the Holy Spirit. In opposition to Protestant teaching, the Roman Catholic Council of Trent, following Thomas Aquinas, affirmed that humans through PREVENIENT GRACE consent to the work of God and cooperate with God for justification. This synergistic tendency is strengthened by the general acceptance of the theology of the Jesuit Luis Molina and the condemnation of the Jansenist attempts to reaffirm the Augustinian teaching. In the Reformed tradition, Arminian tendencies toward synergism were rejected by the SYNOD OF DORT, while the federal stream of Reformed thought maintained the meaning of human responsibility within the covenant of God.

C.Mc.

**SYNOD.** From the Greek word *synodos,* meaning "a meeting." A synod is an ecclesiastical council. Ecumenical, plenary, national, provincial, and diocesan councils are all called "synods" in Roman Catholic practice, as well as in Eastern Orthodox practice. However, in modern times, the term is usually reserved for a diocesan assembly. Such a diocesan meeting is not technically a council, since it does not make laws for the whole church or decide on the orthodoxy of doctrine. The term "synod" is used by the Lutheran church for the major governing unit of their polity. In the United States, a Lutheran synod is often territorially the same as a state, although a state may contain several synods in heavily populated areas, and several less-populated states may form a synod. In Presbyterian churches, the term "synod" is used for a larger governing unit, made up of a number of presbyteries, and often includes the territory of a number of states in the United States.

J.C.

**SYNOPTIC GOSPELS.** The first three canonical Gospels, traditionally ascribed to MATTHEW, MARK, and LUKE. They are known as the Synoptic Gospels, since they share a generally common presentation of the events of Jesus Christ's life, death, and resurrection. In spite of important differences, these three Gospels share a basic structural core, running from Jesus' baptism at the hands of John the Baptist to the report of the women who found the tomb of Jesus empty. The term "synoptic" comes from the Greek words *syn* (with or together) and *optos* (seeing), meaning that these Gospels "see events together or alike." In contrast, the Fourth Gospel, John, diverges from the other three Gospels in sequence and in content (In John, for example, Jesus drives out the money changers from the Temple early in his ministry; in the Synoptics, the cleansing of the temple takes place in the last week of Jesus' life and is the last straw that forces the chief priest to act against him.).

But despite the general similarity of the Synoptics, the dissimilarities among them cause difficulties in interpretation and understanding that together are called "the Synoptic problem." Among these dissimilarities are the different ways the Synoptics begin and end. Only Matthew and Luke have birth narratives; Mark does not, nor does John. Yet the birth stories are very different in Matthew and Luke. More perplexing, the oldest manuscripts of Mark contain no resurrection appearances of Jesus to the disciples. Moreover, long sections of Mark (whose general outline and even wording Matthew and Luke share) are not found in Matthew and Luke, or else the material is found in one Gospel but not the other. In other places, Matthew and Luke share a common outline and verbal presentation; yet this material (generally discourses by Jesus) is not found in Mark at all.

Because of these content similarities in Matthew and Luke, and the fact that both longer Gospels follow Mark, but Mark does not follow either of them, the four-document theory of the composition of the Synoptic Gospels was devised by early modern NT scholars. Briefly, the theory of Gospel development and composition is that from the beginning the sayings of Jesus and reports of his healings and miracles circulated among the disciples in oral form. These ORAL TRADITIONS may have been in Aramaic and in Greek. Later, as Jesus' expected imminent return did not materialize, the reports of his life were written down. The first "gospel" was Mark, which tradition says is dependent upon Peter. Additionally, a "sayings source" or LOGIA, which recorded Jesus' teaching and preaching, was written, probably as a guide for Christian preaching and evangelism. Biblical scholars called the logia Q for *Quelle*, the German term for source. The later evangelists, Matthew and Luke, used Mark as their major source and supplemented Mark with Q. They both also included additional traditions (especially the birth narratives), which are called "M" in Matthew, and "L" in Luke. Mark, Q, M, and L thus form the four documents underlying the Synoptic Gospel tradition.

Newer biblical origins theories suggest that all three Synoptics may have been created out of units of tradition that circulated independently (the FORM CRITICISM theory) or that the various evangelists were actually theologians who personally selected and shaped the materials they found in earlier oral and written sources into coherent theological statements (REDACTION CRITICISM).

Each of the Synoptic Gospels presents Jesus in a slightly different way. Matthew shows us Jesus as the Messiah, the fulfillment of every OT prophetic prediction. Mark is the Gospel of action, showing us Jesus in dynamic activity. For Mark, Jesus is the Son of man. Luke reflects the humanity of Jesus and stresses his journey from Galilee to Jerusalem.

J.C.

**SYRIA.** A Greek noun applied, since Herodotus (fifth century B.C.), to extensive Aramean territory north-northeast of Israel.

*Geopolitical Considerations.* Never a precise political entity, Syria possessed vague frontiers. Syria's interior consisted of wide-ranging mountains separating the Syro-Arabian desert plateau from the Mediterranean. Boasting many natural harbors, Syria's coast was particularly valuable. Primarily settling into Syria's sparsely populated inland, Aramean tribes developed into such states as Zobah (II Sam. 8:3), Damascus (8:5), Beth-rehob, Maacah, Tob (10:6), and Geshur (15:8). As Syria's dominant state during the ninth-eighth centuries B.C., Damascus regularly plagued Israel. In NT times, Syria was a Roman province, with ANTIOCH as its capital.

*Biblical Events.* Augmenting their leverage against David (about 1000–961 B.C.), the Ammonites hired Syrian troops from Beth-rehob, Zobah, Maacah, and Tob (II Sam. 10:6). After Israel's triumph in two phases of battle, Syria transferred allegiance to David (10:19). In another campaign, David so overwhelmed Zobah and Damascus that they proclaimed their vassalage (8:3-8). Though Solomon (about 961–922) prospered in horse and chariot trade with Syria (I Kings 10:29), his influence there suffered reduction when Rezon seized the throne of DAMASCUS (11:23-25).

During Israel's dual monarchy, Syria ordinarily enjoyed the advantage. When Asa of Judah (913–873) felt pressured by Baasha of Israel (900–877), he bribed BEN-HADAD I of Syria (about 885–870) to betray his ally Baasha. Ben-hadad's invasion forced Baasha's withdrawal from Judah and intensified Syria's control over a crucial Galilean caravan route linking Damascus with the Mediterranean (I Kings 15:18-21). Nevertheless, Ben-hadad II (about 870–842) endured Israelite resurgence under AHAB (869–850). His forces failed twice at overtaking Samaria, and Ben-hadad was captured. On condition that Syria would restore to Israel border cities previously taken and allow Israel a trading street in Damascus, Ahab released Ben-hadad (I Kings 20:1-34). But Ahab could not wrest Ramoth-gilead from Syria and died in the attempt (22:29-37). Under Hazel (about 842–806), Syrian troops wounded Israel's king Joram (849–842) in warfare (II Kings 8:28-29), seized its Transjordanian territories (10:32-33), and spared Jerusalem only because Joash (837–800) raised enormous tribute (12:17-18). Nevertheless, Jehoash (802–786) reclaimed Israelite cities from Ben-hadad III (13:24-25). Inflicting Assyrian retaliation against Syrian defiance in 732, Tiglath-pileser III (745–727) destroyed Damascus, killed its king Rezin (about 740–732), and transformed its territory into four Assyrian provinces (16:7-9).

Syria is rarely mentioned in the NT. Summarizing Jesus' Galilean activities, Matthew reports that "his fame spread throughout all Syria" (Matt. 4:24), and Luke states that Syria's churches were strengthened by Paul's missionary endeavors (Acts 15:41).

J.K.K.

## SYROPHOENICIA.

The territory along the Mediterranean around Tyre and Sidon, now Lebanon, was the original Phoenicia, a part of the Roman province of Syria. It is to be distinguished from the colony in North Africa, sometimes also known as Phoenicia, which is now Libya. Jesus healed the daughter of a Syrophoenician woman near Tyre and commended the woman's persistence and faith. Mark (7:26) describes her as "Greek," or Gentile, probably because she was Greek-speaking, as one might expect in a merchant seaport, but Matthew (15:22) uses the older name Phoenicians employed in speaking of themselves, "Canaanite."

                                                    T.J.K.

## SYSTEMATIC THEOLOGY.

The attempt to present the entire body of Christian beliefs as a system of truth in which each doctrine is related to every other doctrine. The presupposition is that there is one fundamental truth—the truth of God in Jesus Christ. When that truth is put into words, it has to be broken up into many propositions. The systematic theologian seeks to show how these propositions cohere with each other and mutually imply each other as elements within the one inclusive truth.

Some systematic theologians employ a philosophical framework. The use of the basic categories of a philosophical system is employed to bring out the unified character of theological truth, as these categories are applied to the several Christian doctrines. In the nineteenth century, Hegelianism was sometimes used as the philosophical framework for a systematic theology. In the twentieth century, one of the most notable examples has been PAUL TILLICH's *Systematic Theology,* which employs the whole German philosophical tradition. The danger in such forms of PHILOSOPHICAL THEOLOGY is that the distinctively theological element may become subordinated to the philosophical, and the latter may have the effect of distorting Christian teaching as it fits it into its own framework.

This explains why KARL BARTH rejected the idea of "systematic theology" (he had in mind especially the work of Tillich). Barth himself preferred to speak of "dogmatics," and although he sharply distinguished dogmatics from systematic theology, many writers have equated these two terms. If indeed we accept the definition of systematic theology given at the beginning of this article, then Barth's dogmatics can be considered as an example of systematic theology, for here is an attempt, unrivaled in modern times, "to present the entire body of Christian beliefs as a system of truth in which each doctrine is related to every other doctrine." Barth's carefully articulated system is held together not by a philosophical framework but by tracing all the Christian doctrines back to the fundamental datum: the Word of God. God has spoken, communicated, and revealed, and from this follow in order the triune being of God and the doctrines of creation, reconciliation, and redemption.

There are, of course, several possible starting points for systematic theology, besides the WORD OF GOD. In a secular age, it may be wiser to begin (as Tillich does) with the human condition (*see* CORRELATION, METHOD OF). This anthropological approach has been common since the time of SCHLEIERMACHER.

It has sometimes been objected that the idea of a systematic theology is too ambitious, and that acceptance of a system may result in a frozen dogmatism that discourages further inquiry. But the best systematic theologians have never fallen into this error. KARL RAHNER tells us that every conclusion is the springboard for fresh investigation, while Schleiermacher was explicit about the provisional character of any system of dogmatics: "Dogmatic theology is the science which systematizes the doctrine prevalent in a Christian church at a given time."                                    J.M.

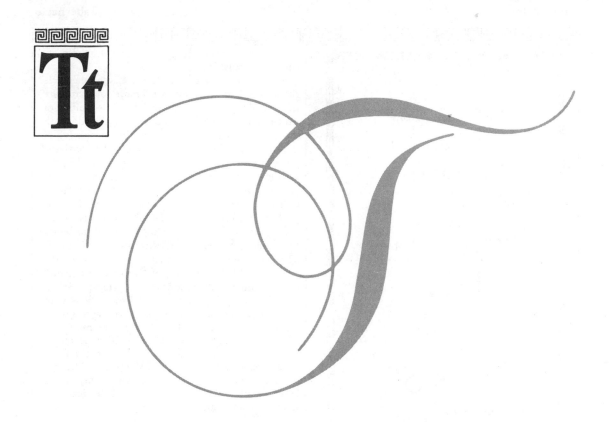

# Tt

TAANACH. A royal Canaanite city overlooking the plain of Esdraelon, about five miles south of Megiddo, mentioned at least eight times in the OT. The walled city controlled several trade routes, especially one that left the Way of the Sea and cut across the valley to Tiberias and Damascus. Taanach long remained in Canaanite control even after the Hebrew conquest. Deborah's Song (Judg. 5:19) mentions it as the site of the battle between Sisera and Barak, "at Taanach, by the waters of Megiddo." The city is also mentioned in the Tell el-Amarna Letters. Solomon made it a twin fortress to MEGIDDO.                                          T.J.K.

TABERNACLE. From the Hebrew word for "tent." The portable, earliest, and distinctive Israelite sanctuary, made at Mount Sinai. It represented the abiding presence (SHEKINAH) of Yahweh in the midst of the people and celebrated the Sinai covenant bond between Yahweh and Israel.

Theologically, the tabernacle was an architectural answer to a basic question in religious thought, "Oh, that I knew where I might find him [God], that I might come even to his seat" (Job 23:3). Israel's unique response to that was the holy tabernacle. Yahweh said to David, "In all places where I have moved with all the people of Israel, did I speak a word, . . . 'Why have you not built me a house of cedar?' " (II Sam. 7:7). In the same oracle, the promise is given to David that an offspring of his,

after the kingdom is firmly established, "shall build a house for my name" (II Sam. 7:13). Here, as in I Chronicles 17:3-14, the tabernacle is not regarded as Israel's final sanctuary but is a first step, valid for as long as Israel has no "peace" and "rest," that is, a nationhood. Then, the tabernacle is to be replaced with "a house of cedar," that is, a sanctuary with a fixed location, a TEMPLE. In history, this anticipation was realized in Solomon's Temple and its successor Temples, Zerubbabel's and Herod's. The floor plans and furnishings of each would correspond to those of the tabernacle. Metaphorically, the psalmists called the Jerusalem Temple "the tent" (Pss. 15:1; 27:5; 43:3; also Lam. 2:6, "booth").

The ALTARS to Yahweh established in sacred places by the patriarchs were forerunners of the Temple. The long biblical history of Israel's "holy place" tradition makes understandable the texts' minute concern for every small detail, including the priests' costumes (Exod. 28:1-43; 39:1-31), how the unleavened SHOWBREAD was to be made, the directions for preparing the food for consecration (Exod. 29:31-37), the incense (Exod. 30:1-10), and the holy oil (Exod. 30:22-25).

Interpretations of Exodus have implied that cultic influences from the Canaanite or Midianite "high places" and temples were present in the tabernacle. It would be surprising if some borrowing of this sort took place, together with memories of Egyptian

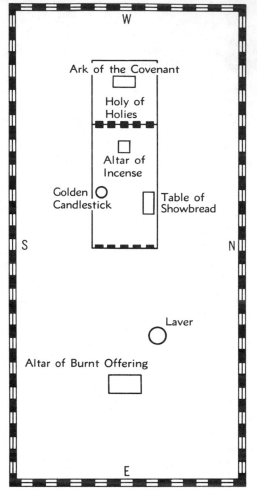

Courtesy of the American Schools of Oriental Research

*Plan of the tabernacle and its courts*

monumental shrines and temples. Israel had left Egypt less than a year before the tabernacle was constructed (Exod. 40:17). Borrowings from others are evident but in this, as in other regards, Israel had ways of supplying meanings distinctive to its own particular religion. The tabernacle, together with its successor temples, was a monument of remembrance of Israel's primary religious tradition of monotheism as established through the covenant of Sinai.

All the materials, except the gold, used to build the tabernacles—Sinai, Shiloh, and Jerusalem—were perishable. It is hardly to be expected that any of these parts, including the ark, have survived since biblical times and could be recovered. Some cultural parallels to the tabernacle have been studied. Recently (1959-73) excavations at Timnah, eighteen to twenty miles north of Elath, have discovered a Midianite-Kenite sanctuary. The Timnah find, contemporary with the tabernacle and in a desert adjacent to Sinai, is

the closest evidence comparable to the tabernacle currently available.

*The Tabernacle in Exodus.* In the eleven tabernacle chapters of Exodus, there is reference to a structure that is easily confused with the tabernacle, neither of which were halls where audiences gathered. Both names signify a place for the dwelling or meeting of Yahweh. Both are associated with Moses and with the pillar of cloud. But the tabernacle-tent stood in the middle of the camp with its sacred enclosure, the place for priestly rituals. The other tent, which Moses called "the tent of meeting" (Exod. 33:7 ff.), was pitched "far off from the camp" and served as an oracle-place where Yahweh "used to speak to Moses face to face, as a man speaks to his friend" (Exod. 33:11). Aaron and the Levites had charge of the tabernacle. "Joshua the son of Nun, a young man," was custodian of the tent of meeting (Exod. 33:11).

More than half of the book of Exodus deals with Israel's experiences at SINAI. Of those chapters more than half, eleven, deal with the tabernacle, its construction and furnishings, and with arrangements for its priesthood. These data are presented three times over, the last, 40:1-33, Moses' actual assembling of the tabernacle parts and equipment, giving fewer details. The parallels between the first and second accounts are:

| 25:1–31:17 | 35:1–39:43 |
|---|---|
| The offering—25:1-9 | 35:4-29;33:24-31 |
| The ark—25:10-22 | 37:1-9 (I Kings 6:19) |
| The table—25:23-30 | 37:10-16 |
| The lampstand—25:31-40 | 37:17-24 |
| The tabernacle—26:1-37 | 36:8-38 |
| The wooden structure—26:15-30 | 36:20-34 |
| The veil and the screen—26:31-32 | 36:35 |
| The bronze altar—27:1-8 | 38:1-7 |
| The tabernacle court—27:9-19 | 38:9-20 |
| Oil for the lamp—27:20-21 | 39:1-31 |
| The priesthood and its dress—28:1-43 | 39:1-31 |
| The consecration of priests—29:1-36a | |
| The great altar—29:36b-42a | 38:1-7 (I Kings 8:64) |
| The unleavened bread—29:2 | (1 Sam. 21:3) |
| The altar of incense—30:1-10 | 37:25-28 (I Kings 6:20, 28) |
| The brass laver—30:17-21 | 38:8 |
| The holy oil—30:22-33 | |
| The incense recipe—30:24-38 | |
| The Sabbath—31:12-17 | 35:1-3 |
| Conclusion— | 39:32-43 |

The first of the six chapters of the first account of the tabernacle in Exodus begins, "The Lord said to Moses . . ." (Exod. 25:1), comparable to "God spoke all these words, . . ." the introduction to the Ten Commandments (Exod. 20:1). To the Exodus writers, the plans for the tabernacle, down to the smallest details, are as much spoken commands of the

Lord of the covenant as are the Ten Commandments. Further, the divine orders were given visually. The heavenly prototype of the tabernacle was "shown" to Moses "on the mountain" (Exod. 25:40). To the writers, the tabernacle's every detail was "holy," the "holy" bread as sacred as the "holy" ark. The tabernacle as a whole was a copy of a heavenly reality. It was to be built in strict adherence with God's specific commands and with the heavenly vision God gave to Moses.

Exodus seems to share the view of Numbers 2:3, 17, that the tents of the Israelites were arranged so as to encircle the tabernacle. Next to the tabernacle court were the tents of the Levites, the priests of the tabernacle. The tabernacle court was a sacred enclosure 150 feet by 75 feet. A wall of linen curtains separated it from the people. The court's dimensions made two squares 75 feet by 75 feet. (A sacred precinct in the Amarna Letters is called "city of God.") At the center of the tabernacle's outer square stood the altar of burnt offering or the bronze altar 7½ feet square by 4½ feet high, made of wood and overlaid with bronze. Between it and the tabernacle was a laver of bronze with a base; it held water for purification.

The tabernacle itself stood at the center of the inner square of the tabernacle enclosure and was a structure consisting of wooden, ladder-like pieces, which were joined together and stood, like walls, on three sides of the structure, 45 feet by 15 feet. Over these was placed a series of coverings ("a tent over the tabernacle," Exod. 26:7). The innermost covering was the most "heavenly," made of fine linen embroidered with blue, purple, and scarlet material and embroidered with cherubim designs. The other coverings protected the interior from the weather.

The interior of the tabernacle was divided by a curtain in two parts: an outer, rectangular room (30 feet by 15 feet), the Holy Place, and the inner room, the square Holy of Holies (15 feet by 15 feet). The Holy Place had an altar for incense, a table for holy bread, and a highly ornate lampstand made of gold. The inner sanctuary was reserved for the ARK OF THE COVENANT alone. This sacred box, which contained the tablets of the Law, was covered by a "mercy seat," a slab of pure gold 45 inches by 27 inches; cherubim figures guarded the throne of the invisible Divine Presence.

To the Exodus writers, there were zones of holiness in the wilderness camp, ranging from the least holy, the peoples' tents, through the tabernacle court with its altar, to the ark. The final word in Exodus about the tabernacle is that, after it was erected and dedicated, "the cloud," "the glory of the Lord," so filled the tabernacle that Moses was not able to enter it (40:34-35).

*The Plausibility of the Exodus Tabernacle.* Comments have been made that the Exodus tabernacle "never actually existed. It is the product of the priestly imaginary structure" (J. Coert Rylaarsdam). The entire description "is a mere reflection of the temple at Jerusalem" (M. Burrows). Such judgments reflect conclusions based on Wellhausen's documentary hypothesis of sources within the Pentateuch. According to this theory *P* (for priestly) is the last strand of Pentateuchal material to be composed, dated to a time during or after the Babylonian exile. Since the Exodus tabernacle chapters manifest a strong priestly interest, this block of material, chapters 19–40, has been assigned to the P document. On literary considerations alone, the conclusion has been reached that the Exodus tabernacle account cannot be historically factual but is to be understood as a product of priestly, devoted imagination, reflections on what was known or had been heard of Solomon's Temple.

Roland de Vaux's conclusion is representative of more recent opinion: "However amply influenced by Solomon's temple," the Exodus description of the desert sanctuary "did preserve an authentic tradition" (*Ancient Israel*, 1961). The shift in opinion is traceable generally to more recent, nonliterary, cultural and archaeological investigations. Admittedly, we have few evidences of sanctuaries comparable to the Exodus tabernacle in its time and geographical setting. The nearest approach to this is the desert sanctuary at Timnah. This, however, is not inconsiderable in view of its proximity in time and location and the fact that the Timnah sanctuary was constructed by Midianites and Kenites, Semites and near relatives of the Israelites. Moses' father-in-law, Jethro, was a Midianite priest (Exod. 3:1).

In the Egyptian Delta, where the Hebrews were slaves, temples and shrines and gold-covered god-boxes were carried in sacred, festal processions. In Tutankhamen's tomb a gold-covered box was found that contained some of the pharaoh's treasures. It was equipped with carrying poles that fit into sockets located beneath the base.

Given the desert environment and the fact that the Israelites were less than a year away from the land of Goshen, there is nothing essentially impossible in the Exodus description of the tabernacle. The materials needed were at hand. Acacia wood was readily available nearby, perhaps then more than now in the sizes required. The fabrics, the precious and non-precious metals, could have been obtained through trade or through offerings from the people (Exod. 32:1-3; 35:20-29; compare 12:35-36). Workmen like Bezalel and Oholiab (Exod. 31:1-6; 36:2), skilled craftsmen in many building arts, were available to do the work and to train others (Exod. 31:6). The symmetrical proportions of the tabernacle, with its rectangular rooms, all aligned on a longitudinal axis, and the most holy place at the rear of the structure, was an architectural pattern regularly observed in Egyptian temples, a style with which the Israelites could have been familiar.

The Exodus tabernacle was made for a people who involuntarily had had to become nomads. All that they possessed they had to carry from one camp to another. Question may be raised how the outer court, bronze lampstand, and the bronze laver, each of which must have weighed well over a hundred pounds, could be carried, and also about the forty wooden "frames," which were 15 feet long and 27 inches wide, and must have been awkward to carry. But, with abundant manpower available, this probably could be managed. More than 1,200 years before this, the Egyptian slaves had built the Pyramids, a much more difficult undertaking. Students of the ancient Near East have discovered traveling tents for gods or god-emblems in Assyria as well as in Egypt.

*David's Jerusalem Tent.* At the end of II Samuel (24:18-24), David is directed by a prophet to erect an altar on the threshing floor of Araunah the Jebusite. After the land was purchased, David built "the altar of burnt offering for Israel" (I Chr. 22:1) there and offered sacrifices. David designated this threshing floor as the site for the future house of the Lord. The place is widely accepted to be somewhere within the Haram es Sherif in Jerusalem, not far from the Islamic shrine, the Dome of the Rock. This means the site David chose was high ground, a short distance from the walled city of the Jebusites to the south. The "threshing floor" may have been used previously by the Jebusites as a "high place" and thus was "sacred ground" before being used as such by Israelites.

On the threshing floor, David pitched a tent for the ark (II Sam. 6:17; I Chr. 16:1), which stood isolated on the mountaintop. David's palace and other buildings were inside the walled city below. The erection of Yahweh's tabernacle or tent on this prominent spot or acropolis set Yahweh's seal upon the city and upon the kingdom of which it had become the capital. David's tent was a monument of political and religious significance, plainly evident for all who had eyes to see.

Roland de Vaux and others have remarked that perhaps it was David's tent on the "high place" of Jerusalem that was the remembered prototype of P's Exodus description of the Sinai tabernacle. That depiction features items of pure gold, gold-plated things and foundation bases of silver and gold, all of which would seem perhaps more readily available to David with his wealth than to Moses. "The wealth of the Davidic court and the important part which the tabernacle played in David's political strategy would lead us to believe that the Davidic tabernacle was richly and ornately fabricated, in which case it would agree well with the Priestly descriptions" (Frank M. Cross, "The Priestly Tabernacle," *BA Reader I,* 1961).

*The Tabernacle in the History of Religions.* Ikhnaton (or Akh-en-ton), pharaoh of Egypt (about 1369–1353 B.C.) is popularly regarded as the world's first monotheist, perhaps more accurately, monalatrist, since what distinguished him was his enthusiastic preoccupation with the worship of Aton, the sun god. It was this concern that motivated his revolution, not

a denial of the existence of other deities. There is no evidence that Moses was aware of Ikhnaton's "reformation," but it is posible that, in his Egyptian education, he could have heard something of it (Acts 7:22). What is clear from the biblical text and from Jewish tradition is that Moses was completely devoted to Yahweh alone, the one and only God. Ethical monotheism underlies biblical religion fundamentally. According to Exodus, the Sinai tabernacle was (and is) the unique, architectural monument to ethical monotheism, Moses' grand legacy to the world's religious thought and life.

P.L.G.

**TABERNACLES, FEAST OF.** See SUKKOT.

**TABITHA.** See DORCAS.

**TABOO.** A prohibition for magical or religious reasons. Taboos can apply to a place, person, object, or action. They arouse fear of the sacred or supernatural or fear of contamination. They can preserve a culture's separateness (*see* KOSHER) or express mystic identity with a TOTEM. Many, like the incest taboo, serve to maintain the structure of the society.

K./M.C.

**TABOR, MOUNT.** A limestone peak rising about 1,840 feet above sea level five miles south of Nazareth. In the OT it is often associated with the prophets, and in the NT as one of the possible sites of Christ's transfiguration. Its Arabic name is Jebel el Tor. It often served as a place of refuge. The armies of Naphtali and Zebulun gathered here before fighting Sisera (Judg. 4:6). Two Midianite kings killed Gideon's brothers on Tabor. From the conelike summit of the steep slopes there are good views down on several trade routes and toward the Sea of Galilee. The mountain where the Transfiguration occurred is not named in the accounts in Matthew, Mark, and Luke. Nonetheless the emperor Constantine's mother, Helena, ordered a memorial church built atop the moutain early in the fourth century, with shrines to Jesus, Moses, and Elijah. The fact that a town existed there in Christ's time does not mark it as a likely place where he might have taken his disciples for solitude.

T.J.K.

**TADMOR.** A desert town, perhaps named from the Hebrew *tamar,* meaning "a palm tree." It was fortified by Solomon to control a trade route in the eastern desert. Tadmor, later known by its Greek name of Palmyra, lay east of Damascus, a distant outpost of Solomon's vast kingdom. By scribal error Tadmor east of Damascus and Tamar south of the Dead Sea were sometimes confused with "Tamar in the wilderness" described in I Kings 9:18.

T.J.K.

**TAGORE, RABINDRANATH** (1861–1941). A Hindu poet and the first Asian to win the Nobel Prize in literature. Tagore did much to focus the cultural renaissance and growing national awareness of India in the first half of the twentieth century. He came from a wealthy, educated, and active family; his father, Debendranath Tagore, was prominent in the reformist Brahmo Samaj. Tagore's Hindu religion was by no means narrow and dogmatic, but expressed a universal spiritual quest for a God found everywhere, above all in the ordinary daily lives of India's millions. He was much influenced by the fervent, yearning, formless mysticism of the Bauls, wandering minstrels of Bengal. He also wrote passionately of India as a nation, yet Tagore's nationalism was more cultural and spiritual than political. Nonetheless, he renounced the knighthood Britain had given him in protest against the Amritsar massacre, and it was he who first called Mohandas K. Gandhi, spiritual leader of the independence movement, Mahatma or "Great Soul."

Besides poetry, Tagore wrote short stories, novels, dramas, and essays; he was also an accomplished artist and musician, and took an active role in improving education. It was the English translation (by himself) of *Gitanjali,* a collection of his Bengali mystical poems, however, that won him the Nobel Prize in 1913. This event, rightly seen by British-ruled Indians as vindication of their native culture and spirituality, brought him immense popularity. Tagore's contribution to rising nationalism is symbolized by the fact that the national anthems of both India and Bangladesh are from songs of his, yet his greatest work has a universal spirituality that has appealed to people of many lands.          R.E.

**T'AI CHI.** From the Chinese term for "Great Ultimate." In Chinese philosophy, especially Neo-Confucianism, T'ai Chi represents the cosmic unity through which the Tao or universal way expresses itself and becomes the two primordial forces, YIN and YANG, and then the phenomenal world.          R.E.

**TAIZÉ.** An ecumenical monastic community founded in 1940 in Burgundy, France, by Rogert Schutz. Schutz had envisioned the need for a monastic order within Protestantism while preparing his dissertation at the University of Lausanne. He became the first prior in a house established in Taizé, France. His first act of service was to harbor Jewish and other refugees, but this activity was halted shortly by the Gestapo. In 1942 he returned with three newly appointed brothers and began to live the monastic life. Taking a vow of celibacy and common property, the small band grew gradually until it reached seventy in the 1970s. While the brothers wear white, hooded robes in church, they wear no distinctive garb at other times. They have been joined by Franciscan and Eastern Orthodox monks who are accepted as equals in the community. Their principal work is devoted to the promotion of Christian unity, but they also operate a large cooperative farm and dairy. Some of the brothers undertake missions to other countries, especially to Africa and Latin America.          R.H.

**TAJWID.** The recitation of the QUR'AN. Although manuals of recitation exist that are sufficient for the average MUSLIM, *tajwid* can occupy a lifetime of learning. Experts study not only different styles of chanting, but also textual variants, the exact pronunciation of words and letters, and the ritual acts demanded in the performance. Performers study with a master in the art who can trace his training back through a line of master reciters to Muhammad and the archangel Gabriel. Master reciters can build up a devoted following as they perfect their chanting. Three distinct styles exist: slow and deliberate chanting for examination of the text; rapid recitation, used to acquire merit; and an intermediate speed. Some reciters use melodies; others reject them.          K./M.C.

**TALISMAN.** An object believed to bring divine protection or good fortune and drive away evil influences. Usually small, fabricated of wood, stone, metal, or bone, and worn on the person or placed in the home, talismans are common in most religious traditions, especially on the popular level.          R.E.

**TALLIS, THOMAS** (about 1505–85). English composer and organist; the "father of English cathedral music." He was organist at Waltham Abbey until its dissolution in 1540. Tallis became a gentleman of the Royal Chapel, where he remained all his life. He and William Byrd, another great composer, were jointly granted by Queen Elizabeth a twenty-one-year monopoly to print music. Most of this was vocal music set to Latin words. Tallis' "Responses" are his best-known compositions. Some of the hymn tunes he composed still appear in contemporary hymn books. His "Lamentations" and office hymns are greatly appreciated by critics. His motet, *Spem in alium,* was written in five parts to be sung by eight choirs. His "If Ye Love Me," composed for the English service, is still greatly loved.          R.H.

**TALMUD.** A vast and varied work geared toward an understanding of a Jew's legal and moral responsibilities as set forth in the Bible and discussed, commented upon, and interpreted by rabbis and scholars over a period of about seven hundred years—roughly between 200 B.C. and A.D. 500. Almost every conceivable area of human interest is dealt with. Comprising more than thirty large volumes, the Talmud is a treasure-trove of ethics, religion, folklore, and jurisprudence. The Talmud ranks next to the sacred Scriptures in significance as a source for religious insight, inspiration, and practice.

In early biblical Judaism, except for the Bible,

there was a ban on committing to writing anything handed down by tradition. Scholarly discussions and opinions were transmitted by word of mouth, from scholar to disciple, teacher to pupil, father to son. Because it was transmitted orally, it was called the Oral Law, while that which was written down—the Bible—was called the Written Law. When the ban against committing the discussions, opinions, and commentaries was lifted, the vast mountain of centuries of learning that had been transmitted by word of mouth was finally put into written form.

The MISHNAH, a collection of Jewish legal material, is one part of the Talmud; the GEMARA, or commentary on the Mishnah, is the other part. The Mishnah is divided into six sections, called Orders. They deal with (1) the laws of agriculture and prayers; (2) laws of the Sabbath and the festivals; (3) laws pertaining to marriage, divorce, and family relationships; (4) civil and criminal statutes and court procedures; (5) laws of sacrifice and the Temple cult; and (6) laws of ritual uncleanliness.

The Gemara proceeds by way of question and answer and generally follows the method of analogy and association. A discussion may thus cover a wide range of subjects and often ends up with a completely different subject than it started with. Very seldom does the Talmud give a direct answer to a problem when there is a variety of opinions on a subject.

In the evolution of Judaism, the Talmud is the sequel to the Bible. The study of its contents has been the basis of Jewish religious life. Since the study of the Mishnah was actively pursued in two centers of learning, Palestine and Babylon, two Talmuds emerged, the Palestinian Talmud (sometimes referred to as the Jerusalem Talmud) and the Babylonian Talmud. The Babylonian Talmud has been accepted as the authoritative one.

The text of the Talmud consists of some 2.5 million words, on 5,894 folio pages. Roughly one third is halakhah and two thirds is aggadah. Halakhah embraces two areas of prescribed conduct; one relates to the rules of ritual and religion, the other pertains to the rights and obligations of people in civil society. Aggadah covers whatever is excluded from Halakhah. This includes countless norms of conduct, moral but unenforceable in courts of law, reflections on the cosmos and its Prime Mover, impressions of the character and manners of the rabbis of the Talmud, views on the economy of nature, scientific observations, passages illuminating the religious experience and social life of the Jews and their association with non-Jews, and much else.    L.K.

**TAMAR.** (1) In Genesis 38, Tamar was a Canaanite woman who was left childless in turn by two of the sons of Judah, Er and Onan. Under the levitical laws she was also promised to a third son, Shelah, but her father-in-law never met this obligation. Frustrated, Tamar put on the clothes of a prostitute and tricked her father-in-law Judah into giving her children, the twin boys Perez and Zerah (Gen. 38:6-30). Tamar belongs to the genealogical line of the ancestors of Christ, as cited in Ruth 4:12 and Matthew 1:3.

(2) A daughter of King David; the beautiful sister of Absalom (II Sam. 13:1). Her half brother Amnon was so taken by her charms that he raped her. As she wept in shame he drove her out of the palace. Her brother Absalom got revenge by ordering the killing of Amnon.

(3) The beautiful daughter of Absalom, probably named after his sister of the same name (II Sam. 14:27). According to the Septuagint version of the OT, this Tamar married King Rehoboam and became queen. Her name also appears as Maacah (I Kings 15:2).

(4) According to Ezekiel 47:19 and 48:28, Tamar was the boundary fortress in the extreme southeast corner of Solomon's kingdom. South of the Dead Sea, it lay on the trade route to King Solomon's mines in the Arabah. About fifty miles from Jerusalem, Tamar (palm tree or oasis) had a mystical, legendary meaning for the Israelites, not unlike neighboring Kadesh, where they had spent their sojourn in the wilderness after leaving Egypt. Often Tamar served as a watering spot and as a garrison town, both for the Israelites and later for the Romans. The exact site cannot be determined, but the place was mentioned by Ptolemy.    T.J.K.

**TAMIL.** A language of the Dravidian group spoken by about forty million people in south India and Sri Lanka. The word "Tamil" evokes a racial and cultural heritage as well as a tongue. The Tamil areas of India centering around Madras have long been a heartland of traditional HINDUISM, even though originally non-Indo-European in language and culture, and only gradually penetrated by SANSKRIT BRAHMIN, and VEDIC Hinduism, beginning in the early centuries A.D. Much correlation of indigenous and mainstream Hindu gods and institutions took place; for example, the popular Tamil deity Murukan, originally a lord of the hills and of hunters, came to be seen as a son of SHIVA.

Since entering the major Hindu current, the Tamil area has been a source of much creativity in that tradition. BHAKTI or devotionalism, with its overtones of resistance to excessivism Brahminism and caste, received a powerful early impetus from the ALVARS, seventh-to ninth-century Tamil-area poets of devotion to VISHNU, and the Nayanars, singers from about the same period of devotion to Shiva. The greatest theologian of Bhakti, RAMANUJA, was born of a Brahmin family living in the Tamil area. At the same time, the appeal of ascetic and non-dualist spirituality is shown by the early success of JAINISM and Advaita in the Tamil lands, and by the recent Advaita sage Ramana Maharshi (1879-1951).    R.E.

**TAMMUZ.** See HEBREW CALENDAR.

**TANTRISM.** A set of systems for attaining enlightenment and spiritual power in HINDUISM and BUDDHISM. The term has been used broadly to embrace any path outside such "orthodox" ways as Patanjali Yoga and Vedanta, or regular Theravada and Mahayana Buddhism. However, the more common usage restricts Tantrism to a particular set, which stresses arduous initiations, rigorous gurus, considerable use of mantras and mudras, and antinomian practices (some sexual, like much Tantric symbolism) reputedly of great power. Tantric adepts are said to be persons of great wizard-like ability, but fierce and unconventional, and Tantrism has often cultivated an aura of secrecy and mystery. The word comes from *tantra,* literally "thread," the name of a class of Tantric texts.

Some characteristics of Hindu Tantrism are:

(1) Practice is invariably considered more important than doctrine in Tantrism. However, certain ideas that particularly uphold the practice are taught. The belief that the Absolute—BRAHMAN, or SHIVA—is all is stressed, for Tantrism brings home that this means the flesh and the passions, as well as the mind and spirit, are divine, and capable of realizing divinity in their own way. For the initiated adept the body and passions can be used as means to liberation, even though to attempt such a thing would be dangerous for the untrained.

(2) The polarity of Shiva, the Absolute, and his consort, Shakti, representing the phenomenal world, is central to much of Hindu Tantrism. In the sexual ritual, the male identifies with Shiva and his partner with Shakti, making it thus an enactment of the ecstatic union of God and the world.

(3) The role of the guru and of initiation is very important, since the great danger of Tantric practice without proper empowerment and guidance is emphasized. The only absolute for a Tantric practitioner is usually his guru's instruction, which may not always conform to conventional morality.

(4) Intense ritual activity, the use of quasi-magical mantras and mudras, and the evocation of deities with whom the adept may identify, are important. Yantras, mystical diagrams, and MANDALAS, diagrammatic arrangements of gods, are also significant in Tantrism's "spiritual technology."

(5) The use of "forbidden things," such as meat, alcohol, and illicit sex, whether actually or symbolically, is important in part of the Tantric tradition as a sort of "shock therapy" technique by which one's conventional, socially conditioned personality structure is broken down to make room for reshaping as a new person of power and oneness with the Absolute.

(6) The yogic theory and practice connected with raising the *kundalini* energy up the spine to open the cakras or centers of psychic power in the body are closely associated with Tantrism.

In Hinduism today, Tantric groups are small and secretive, well outside the mainstream. But Tantrism has had a considerable influence on Hindu symbolism, art, and ritual.

Buddhist Tantrism, on the other hand, in the form of VAJRAYANA, the "Diamond Vehicle," is the dominant form of Buddhism in Tibet, Mongolia, and the Himalayan area, and is represented by the influential Shingon denomination in Japan. Vajrayana and Shingon emphasize Tantric Buddhist deities, mandalas, mantras, initiations, and evocational rites, treating the sexual aspects only symbolically. Buddhist Tantrism differs from Hindu in making the feminine principle represent the Absolute, and the masculine the Buddha or bodhisattva, who demonstrates attainment of it.          R.E.

**TAOISM.** An important tradition in Chinese philosophy and religion, Taoism is composed of several related but not identical strands: the naturalistic philosophy of LAO-TZU and CHUANG-TZU; Neo-Taoism, with its emphasis on spontaneity and its close ties to poetry and art, yogic and alchemical practices designed to produce immortality; popular religion involving the ministration of Taoist priests; and new religious movements with overtones of social protest.

The word Taoism (Chinese: *Tao-chiao,* "Teaching on the Tao") comes from *Tao* (pronounced dow). *Tao* literally means "way," in the sense of a road or path, but in philosophy it has acquired a broader meaning, as the supreme Way or the Great Path down through which the universe is moving. It has been translated not only as Way, but also as Nature, as Existence, even as God, and each of these English words suggests something of its significance. If the Tao is ultimate reality, then clearly the greatest human good ought to be to live in harmony with it. The major Chinese philosophical traditions agree on this, and the term is used by both CONFUCIANISM and Taoism. But while the former emphasize that for humans the Tao is to be found in human nature and human relationships, Taoists stress the corruption and artificiality of society, telling us that the Way is best found by one who seeks it instead in nature and mystical experience.

Taoism has always looked to the non-rational, poetic, and imaginative aspects of consciousness as revelatory; over against Confucian rationalism and this-worldliness it has played a role comparable to that of Romanticism in the West. Thus, though generally tolerated except in extreme manifestations, Taoism has usually had a "non-establishment" character in China over against the Confucian-based moral, political, educational, and family systems. This "other side" quality is really what unifies the highly diverse philosophical, ritual, and sociological strands that go under the name of Taoism. They all in some way meet individual needs, or needs of classes disadvantaged by the system, not wholly fulfilled by the sober Confucian "work ethic" for personal solace and the alleviation of fear, for expression of inner feeling and fantasy, for the acquisition of spiritual power, or for protest. This quest for meeting personal needs, even if that means going "outside the system," rather than offering values that simply help one fit into society effectively, has been a dominant theme that has produced practices ranging from nature mysticism to occultisms of many sorts, although at times Taoism has also inculcated political perspectives. It should not, however, be thought that Taoism and the Confucian "system" need be mutually exclusive. Religion in China was not generally thought of as exclusive, and most traditional Chinese had some relation to all three major traditions, Taoism, Confucianism, and BUDDHISM. It was said that Chinese officials were Confucian at work and Taoist in retirement.

Major components of the Taoist tradition include the following:

The *Tao te ching*. This ancient Taoist classic, whose name means "The Book of the Way and Its Power," is usually dated by scholars at somewhere around 300 B.C. Its author is said to be Lao-tzu, but that name simply means "The Old Man," and despite traditional identifications the work is essentially anonymous. The *Tao te ching* is the earliest known source in which the concept of Tao receives its full cosmic, metaphysical meaning. Main themes of the book include (1) the Tao as the underlying, ever-changing, ever-productive unity of the universe, beyond all human words and concepts, for "the Tao that can be named is not the real Tao"; (2) feminine and maternal imagery for the Tao, for it or an expression of it is "the mother of all things," its creativity is compared to giving birth, and one adhering to it to an infant nursing at the breast; (3) comparisons are invidious, for seeming good and bad, life and death, are like the high and low notes of music, and each is to be lived as something to animate in its time, but not to cling to; (4) the *Tao te ching* contains attacks on rule-bound morality of the Confucian sort, preferring a wordless intuitive approach to the conduct of life; (5) the Tao is acquired by creative "unlearning," forgetting the superficial so that one can be close to the wellsprings of life; (6) the Tao is to be lived by *wu wei*, "not doing," which means not sheer idleness but doing that which is in accord with the way the Tao is going, and so sustained by its inexhaustible energy; (7) the political ideal of a small state composed of people who live simply, close to the earth, without reading and writing, guided by leaders so subtle they govern without being known as rulers. These themes enunciated in the *Tao te ching* have been important to philosophical Taoism down through the centuries.

*Chuang-tzu*. Second in importance only to the *Tao te ching* in philosophical Taoism, the book attributed to the sage Chuang is believed by many modern scholars to have been written, in its major parts, at about the same time as the book of Lao-tzu. Like the other Taoist, Chuang-tzu emphasized that the Tao is beyond words and cannot be understood conceptually. But Chuang-tzu approached his literary task with brilliant and imaginative originality. Through unforgettable images he led the reader to see that in the Tao "all things are equal," whether they seem to us large or small, good or bad, important or trivial. By means of such perceptions one can lead a life of genuine freedom, both in one's mind and in one's relations with the world.

*Neo-Taoism*. A modern term for what was traditionally known as Hsuan-hsueh, Dark (that is, esoteric) Learning, a revival of philosophical Taoism in roughly A.D. 220–420. Its adherents honored Confucius and were in intellectual interaction with Buddhism. Major spokesmen like Kuo Hsiang taught that the Tao, as ultimate reality, is "non-being," and what happens flows out of it with free, ever-changing, unplanned spontaneity. The person who would live with the Tao must live with the same radical freedom and flexibility. Taoism in this period developed important links to the world of artists, poets, and intellectuals, many of whom attempted to live the "free" wandering or retired life its emphasis on spontaneity inculcated.

At the same time, Taoism was acquiring links to popular and sectarian religion among the masses. As early as the second century A.D., a shamanistic figure called Chang Ling inaugurated a popular healing movement, which quickly became a state within the state in western China. The *Tao te ching* was a scripture of the movement, and Chang was said to have received an empowering vision of Lao-tzu. However, his cause had millenarian and magical overtones, replete with spells and recipes for immortality that went beyond philosophical Taoism. Other comparable Taoist sects stem from about the same period or later. But Chang's, known as the Teaching of Right Unity, has remained a major force in religious Taoism to the present. Chang took the title T'ien Shih, "Celestial Teacher" or "Heavenly Master," to which his descendants succeeded. Their authority was recognized by the emperor in 1016, and the hereditary court established on Dragon and Tiger Mountain in Kiangsi. There, as Taoist "pope," the Celestial Teacher regulated the priesthood under his control, blessed charms, and performed quasi-magical rites. A Celestial Teacher, claimed to be in direct line of descent from Chang Ling, holds office today in Taiwan.

Undoubtedly its anti-establishment character contributed to its service as a motif for sectarianisms. But whether for political reasons or out of conviction, rulers have from time to time come to terms with Taoism, particularly in the form of its own religious establishments. In the wake of the Right Unity and the Dark Learning movements, Taoism prospered along with Buddhism under the T'ang dynasty (A.D. 618–907). Its most fervent supporter was the emperor Hsuan Tsung (reigned 712–56), who ordered a Taoist temple in every city and a copy of the *Tao te ching* in every noble home. Sovereigns of the Sung dynasty (A.D. 960–1280) made a mutually beneficial covenant with the Celestial Teacher. It was during this period, aided by the Sung rulers' penchant for naming deities on a large scale, that the lavish Taoist pantheon took shape. Headed by Yu Huang, the Jade Emperor, identified with the Pole Star and cosmic sovereign, it embraces a vast heavenly bureaucracy parallel to that which administered the empire below, colonies of immortals on distant islands or in mountain recesses, and innumerable gods of special functions and localities brought into tenuous relationship with it. The *Tao Tsung*, or Taoist Canon, containing some 1120 volumes, was collected and published in the Sung period, in 1019.

*The Taoist Priesthood.* It would be misleading to say that the great mass of Chinese people are Taoist, in the sense that Spaniards are traditionally Catholic, for most Chinese have had a non-exclusive relation with the three major traditions and above all with a basic popular religion of local gods and ancestrism. But religious specialists who are definitely Taoists play an important part in popular religion. Taoist specialists fall into two categories: those who are monastics or recluses, often celibate, who practice meditation, asceticism, and perhaps yogic activities like those to be discussed below, and who relate only to those who seek them out; and Taoist priests of orders like that under the Celestial Teacher. These priests are generally married and pass their office to their children, and indeed are often not full-time clericals. They work among the people, performing religious functions such as divinations, exorcisms, funeral and memorial services for fees, or selling charms and amulets. Often SHAMANS and mediums are associated with them. Their most important rite is the *chiao*, a lengthy liturgy requiring many priests and enacted in a community temple on the occasion of a major festival to petition the gods on behalf of that community.

Some outside observers, following the example of Chinese Confucian scholars, have dismissed religious Taoism and its priests as superstitious and degenerate. Undoubtedly, like any religion catering to belief in the mystical and miraculous, it is open to much abuse. But it should be noted that, first, there is no small amount of elitism involved in such judgments, and, more important, that although operating on an unphilosophical level religious Taoism remains consistent with many of the fundamental principles of the tradition: belief that in alignment with the Tao and its derivative forces is all power, belief that the non-rational faculties of the mind can be in touch with important realities and that therefore divine beings and occult forces may have reality, belief in the importance of meeting personal spiritual needs. The *chiao* rite seeks to raise the officiants step by step, through hierarchical rank after rank of evoked gods, to the presence of the great Tao itself.

*Yoga and Alchemy.* The major purpose of these practices, and related ones such as marking merit by good deeds, is the attainment of personal immortality. Taoism seeks immortality not so much through the liberation of the soul from mortal flesh, as by the transformation of the body itself into a refined, incorruptible vessel. This is done by perfectly harmonizing its energies so that it can in no way be broken and there is no place for death to enter. The yin and yang forces, respectively feminine and masculine powers of the universe, and the five elements, earth, air, fire, water, and wood, must be harmonized within the microcosm of the self for it to share the immortality of the universal Tao.

Taoist alchemy was concerned with the production of elixirs of immortality, based on the right balancing of these elements. Among its important texts are the writings of the Taoist/Confucian philosopher Ko Hung (A.D. 284–343); he makes it clear that, as was the case with Western alchemy, the practice of this art involved a combination of spiritual and chemical work. The adept was to prepare with fasting and worship and to regard these operations as symbolic of inner transformation. The same principle of psycho-physiological balance applied to dietary and exercise techniques widely engaged in by Taoists. Foods and medicinal herbs were taken or abstained from in accordance with beliefs about their energies corresponding to cosmic energies. The senses, as gateways potentially letting in discordant forces, were carefully controlled.

Circulation of breath, or more precisely *ch'i*, the life-energy closely associated with it, was very important as an exercise for self-regeneration in hope of immortality. It involved deeply breathing in energies from the five directions and major celestial bodies. A further stage was the circulation of breath in the body. Through a combination of gymnastics, "embryonic breathing" (soft breathing like that of an infant), and holding the breath, *ch'i* or breath-energy was circulated through all parts of the body.

One ultimate purpose of the circulation was to unite the breath with the semen to produce a spiritual embryo, which eventually would provide a vehicle for the adept's immortal existence. Esoteric Taoism embraced other sexual techniques as well. Certain practices of sexual union allowed male and female fluids, and so energies, to be exchanged, balancing the yin and yang forces that lay behind them, preparing for immortality.

Though immensely varied, Taoism, an inseparable component of traditional Chinese culture, has as its basis the individual finding of union with the ultimate Unity.

R.E.

**TAO TE CHING.** *See* LAO-TZU.

**TAPAS.** From the Sanskrit word meaning literally "heat." In HINDUISM, tapas refers to practices of

**TAXES.** Taxation was an integral part of society in the various parts of the Bible, though the purpose of tax gathering was diverse. The tabernacle and the Solomonic Temple were supported by levies on the people for the upkeep of the priests (Deut. 18:1-5); hence "tithes," a tenth portion, were extracted (Deut. 14:22-29). This levy was obviously open to abuse when the priesthood fell into unscrupulous hands (see I Sam. 2:12-17, 29).

The warnings given in I Samuel 8:11-18 relate to the actions of Israel's monarchy in imposing taxes for the king's greater glory, and this indication points to Solomon, who financed both his building schemes and his foreign campaigns by taxing the nation (I Kings 4:7-34: the glowing account puts a good face on Solomon's policies, but the truth lies rather in the outcome of protest against Solomon's economic oppression seen in I Kings 12:4, 16, 17). Levies required to stave off foreign invasion and to raise tribute paid to invaders were also a feature of Israel's history occasioned by its geographical situation on the main military routes in the Fertile Crescent (see II Kings 15:19, 20; 23:35).

Religious taxes were renewed after the Exile (Neh. 10:32-39), and the complaint of Haggai and Malachi in their preaching was that the people were becoming slack in payment (Hag. 2:8; Mal. 1:6-14). The later legacy of this tax was the imposition of a half-shekel tax required to finance the Temple services and levied on all Jews, including those living in the Dispersion (see Matt. 17:24-27 for an allusion to this).

The NT references to taxation are dominated by Rome's custom to get money from its provinces. So, in the birth stories of the Gospels, there is a census to ensure that all residents were on the roll (Luke 2:1-5). Jesus lived in a society in which payment of Roman taxes was an accepted part of the way of life. The taxes were variously levied as income tax, a sales tax, a poll tax, a land tax. Such taxes were all part of Jewish society and equally hated by loyal, patriotic Jews, especially the Zealots who resented Rome's presence in the holy land of Israel. TAX COLLECTORS, like Matthew (Matt. 9:9) and Zacchaeus (Luke 19:1-10) were common, and known to be rapacious. Jesus was faced with the patriotic issue in Mark 12:13-17, as Paul was at a later time (Rom. 13:6, 7). The issue was a delicate one: Is it right for Jews and Christians to pay taxes to Rome? Both teachers accepted in principle the right of governments to tax their subjects, but reserved the believer's higher allegiance for devotion to God in the Kingdom. Another view of Rome, with its merchantile commerce, which brought gain not least by taxation, is seen in Revelation 18:2-18, a passage reflecting Rome's role as persecutor of the church. Then in A.D. 96 when the Revelation of John was written, submission to Rome had become impossible since the empire had turned hostile.

R.M.

**TAYLOR, JAMES HUDSON** (1832–1905). Born in Yorkshire, England, Taylor underwent a deep conversion experience at the age of seventeen, followed by a call to China—at that time a virtually closed empire. While evangelizing among the poor in London, Taylor trained to become a doctor but sailed as the first agent of the short-lived Chinese Evangelization Society. Later he returned to complete his studies and again in 1866 sailed for China with a company of skilled workers, the core of the new CHINA INLAND MISSION. Against extraordinary odds, the missionaries penetrated into the inland provinces. By 1895 the CIM had about half the Protestant force in China (over 600 missionaries). The CIM example led others to penetrate into other provinces. Taylor became a great influence in Chinese missions through his writing and speaking, his example of faith, and his unselfish promotion of interdenominational missions.          W.G.

**TAYLOR, JEREMY** (1613–67). The Anglican bishop and devotional writer was born to Nathaniel and Mary Dean Taylor. He attended Gonville and Caius colleges, Cambridge. Sponsored by Archbishop Laud, he received a fellowship at All Soul's College, Oxford, in 1630, and received an M.A. from University College in 1635.

In *The Rule and Exercise of Holy Living* (1650) and *The Rule and Exercise of Holy Dying* (1651), he taught an ordered life of devotion, which requires self-discipline in the care of one's time, purity of intention, and practice of the presence of God. In *Holy Dying* he suggested that life must be a preparation for death.

With the Restoration, Taylor was made bishop of Down and Connor and vice-chancellor of Dublin University. At St. Patrick's Cathedral, Dublin, he also became bishop of Dromore (1661), where he was buried.          N.H.

**TAYLOR, NATHANIEL W.** (1786–1858). The architect of the New Divinity was born June 23 in New Milford, Connecticut, to Nathaniel and Anne Northrop Taylor. He was graduated from Yale in 1807, and was ordained in 1812. Taylor served as minister of First Church, New Haven, from 1811 to 1822 and then became Dwight Professor of Didactic Theology at Yale Divinity School until his death. His 1828 sermon "Concio ad Clerum" announced his revision of Jonathan Edwards' theology. He declared that people are not depraved by original sin except by their own actions: "Sin is in the sinning." Sin is "original" only in the sense of being "universal." Inevitable, it is not causally necessary. People always have "power to the contrary."          N.H.

**TEACHER.** There is little speculative interest in knowledge for its own sake in the biblical books. What little there is may be traced to the influence of Greek moral philosophy on the wisdom writers and their schools.

WISDOM, defined as the knowledge of God and God's law with an application to everyday-life situations, is the object of both study and communication by Israel's teachers (see Job 28; Prov. 1:2-33; 2–5, and later in the book of ben Sirach, a preeminent teacher in early Judaism). Israel's sages stood in a succession of prophetic figures who instructed the people from Samuel onward. In Elisha's time we read of "schools of the prophets," which, however, were more like guilds than places of teaching and learning (II Kings 2:15; 9:1). After the Exile, with the birth of the SYNAGOGUE, teaching was set on a firm basis as part of the Sabbath and weekday liturgy. The rise of "wise men" whose work it was to interpret the law for the community gave impetus to the importance of the teacher; hence the term SCRIBE found in the Gospels, used of such professional students and teachers. Nonetheless, it must be remembered that Judaism has always given pride of place to teaching in a domestic setting, and Hebrew parents are charged to light the lamp of truth in the minds of their offspring, a duty going back to Deuteronomy 4:9-10; 6:7, 20-25; 11:19; 32:46 (see also Prov. 6:20-23).

The NT church perpetuated the teaching office, taking a cue from its Jewish roots but also from the legacy left by its head, Jesus, who is often called Teacher in the Gospel records. While Jesus was no trained scribe, he is sometimes greeted as RABBI meaning "my great one" or "teacher," an honorific title accorded to a person in Judaism (John 1:38, 49; 3:2; 6:25). Jesus as a teacher possessed charismatic authority (Mark 1:27-28), and modern opinion classifies his role in first-century Jewish life as that of a teacher-holy man-healer, of whom we have other specimens in Galilean Judaism. As such a leader, he drew the inspiration of his teaching less from the Mosaic Law (the Torah) than from his immediate apprehension of divine truth, his mission as the agent of God's rule, which he claimed to embody, and (it may be) his filial awareness of being God's Son (see Matt. 11:25-30). On that basis he taught his followers in a way that set him apart from Israel's teachers (see Matt 23:1-12). The Sermon on the Mount (Matt. 5–7) epitomizes his message, along with the parables of the kingdom of God (Matt. 13; Mark 4; Luke 15: these are chapters that collect such examples of teaching methods).

In the early congregations the office of teacher was honored. Gifted people were charged to interpret the divine will for young converts and for community life (Acts 13:1, 5 [John Mark is a catechist]; I Cor. 12:28; Rom. 12:7; Jas. 3:1). Gradually the office became regularized with an exalted status given to it as part of Christ's legacy to the church (Eph. 4:11), and the apostles were regarded as authoritative teachers (II Tim. 1:11), who in turn were to instruct others (II Tim. 2:1-2). Teachers like Timothy (I Tim. 4:11-16) set a model, which in due course became taken up into the office of BISHOP, so that in the pre-Nicene church (before A.D. 325), the bishop was essentially a "prophet-teacher."                                    R.M.

## TEACHER OF RIGHTEOUSNESS.

A specific title, found in the documents of the Qumran sect, the DEAD SEA SCROLLS. It refers to the leader of the community as a man of exemplary character ("righteous teacher") or, more likely, as the person raised up in the community to point the way to God's will (called righteousness) for those who had emigrated in obedience to the call of Isaiah 40:3. Attempts to identify the historical personage behind the name are all speculative, though we can describe him as a priest who in turn was the community's founder and inspiration. He was despised, persecuted, and exiled by the Jerusalem Temple hierarchy. His life is to be dated in the mid-second century B.C.
R.M.

## TEACHING OF THE TWELVE APOSTLES. See DIDACHE.

## TE DEUM LAUDAMUS.

The title of a psalm-type hymn sung at matins as the last response on all feast days, and on all Sundays except in Advent and in the Lenten season. The Latin name is from the opening words, "You are God; we praise you." It is often sung as a thanksgiving hymn and is sometimes referred to as the Ambrosian hymn. It is generally thought to have been composed by Niketas of Remesiana, who died about A.D. 414.         J.C.

## TEFILLIN. See PHYLACTERY.

## TEILHARD DE CHARDIN, PIERRE (1881–1955).

Jesuit priest, theologian, and paleontologist, known for his interpretation of Christianity in the perspective of cosmic evolution. Born into a family of the landed gentry of Sarcenat in the province of Auvergne, France, Teilhard entered the Jesuit novitiate in 1899. He took his first vows in 1901, at a time when the French government's anticlerical crusade was at its zenith. The Jesuit order was soon outlawed in France, and Teilhard and his classmates and teachers went to the island of Jersey. He studied philosophy in Jersey for two years, at the same time making a geological study of the island. He then taught physics and chemistry at a Jesuit school in Cairo for three years. In 1908 Teilhard moved to Hastings in Sussex, England, for his theological training. He was ordained in 1911. In 1912 he began work in paleontology at the Museum of Paris. This was an especially rich period intellectually, for he came under the influence of Bergson's *Creative Evolution* and the Bergsonian philosopher-scientist and Catholic modernist Edouard LeRoy. At the same time Teilhard worked with the abbé Henri Breuil, discoverer of the Cro-Magnon cave culture of the Dordogne valley. Evolution then became the crux of Teilhard's scientific and spiritual reflection.

Teilhard served as a stretcher-bearer for four years on the front during World War I, for which he earned a *Croix de guerre* and a *médaille militaire*. He returned to Paris in 1919 and received his doctorate in paleontology from the Sorbonne in 1922. During this period he taught geology at the Institut Catholique, where his evolutionary ideas were already under suspicion. In 1924, while working with E. LeRoy and teaching at the Collège de France, Teilhard privately circulated a paper on original sin, which was denounced. His superiors ordered him to resign his post, and he was sent to China where, in virtual exile, he remained for over twenty years until 1946. In China he worked on the stratigraphy and paleontology of northern China and Asia and participated in the discovery of the famous *Sinanthropus* skull. He published scores of scientific papers, but during these years he was forbidden to publish religious works, such as *The Divine Milieu* (1960) and, later, *The Phenomenon of Man* (1959). These and *The Appearance of Man* (1966), *The Future of Man* (1964), and *Letters from a Traveller* (1962) appeared posthumously. From 1946, Teilhard lived in France, South Africa, and New York City, where he died on Easter Day.

Teilhard portrays the cosmos as energy in the process of an evolutionary movement toward greater systems of complexity, involving three stages or "critical points," each marked by profound changes. The first threshold was the emergence of inorganic matter; the second, the appearance of life, the encircling of the earth's surface with a covering, or "biosphere." The third critical threshold was the appearance of mind, or the "noosphere," the movement from instinct to thought or "hominization," the emergence of humans. Evolution now can follow a conscious direction. Teilhard believes that the future will exhibit a progressive extension of this higher consciousness, or "noogenesis." The first stage of human evolution exhibited a kind of centrifugal force, making for increased individuality and personal freedom. The next stage will be centripetal and will result in greater intercommunion and socialization on a planetary scale. Teilhard envisions a new convergence of humankind toward what he calls the Omega point—or Christogenesis—the goal of the evolutionary process. At the Omega point all things reach a suprapersonal unity in God in which agape, or self-transcending love, reigns.

Critics disagree as to whether Teilhard considers the Omega point *as* God or the point at which all things are brought into perfect unity with God. The latter, more orthodox view, appears to be his view. In any case, the Christian perceives the Omega as given in foretaste in the person of Christ, the divine *Logos* incarnate. Some scientists have dismissed Teilhard's evolutionary scheme as pure speculation, beyond all scientific evidence; other scientists have been sympathetic. Teilhard's theology has similarly been both praised and reviled by Catholic theologians and ecclesiastical authorities. At the height of Teilhard's

extraordinary popularity, the Holy Office issued a *monitum*, or simple warning, on June 30, 1962, against uncritical acceptance of his views. Today Teilhard's writings do not appear to elicit the wide interest that they enjoyed in the sixties.

J.L.

**TEKOA.** A deserted village in the highlands of Judea ten miles south of Jerusalem. Sometimes also spelled Tekoah and Thecoe, it once held an important place in the commerce and defense of Israel. From its height of about 2,800 feet one could easily see nearby Herodium or Bethlehem, both somewhat lower, and even the hills of Jerusalem. A few springs in the area made it a good place to grow crops, so close to the edge of the desert.

It was once the home of the prophet Amos, who was later called to prophesy in the northern kingdom. The church father Eusebius writes of a cave in Tekoa in which Amos was buried, and where a monastery was located. This monastery, the New Laura, is known in church history as a center for spreading the teachings of Origen. It was also to Tekoa that Absalom fled when he was under sentence of death for killing his brother Amnon.

When Israel was under attack from Assyria, Rehoboam named Tekoa as one of the significant fortresses that should be rebuilt to withstand the invaders. Jeremiah suggested a trumpet call from the towers of Tekoa as a warning of the enemy's approach. Tekoa, because of its height and because the limestone soil made tracking difficult or impossible, was often a place of refuge. Cisterns stored water during the dry season. The houses of the village, the churches, and the monasteries did not fall into complete disuse until after the Crusader period.

T.J.K.

**TELEOLOGICAL ARGUMENT.** *See* GOD'S EXISTENCE, ARGUMENTS FOR.

**TELEOLOGY.** From the Greek word *telos* meaning "end," and carrying a sense of finality or completion. Although the idea is traceable to Aristotle and Thomas Aquinas, the word was first used by Christian von Wolff in 1728. It includes the idea of purposive structure within an organism and the theory that ends are inherent in the nature of things. Paley's *Evidences* affirmed that the universe is under the dominion of a purposeful, intelligent being who is also the final cause. Such thinking arises by analogy from the observation that human beings have the capacity to plan and pursue rational goals. Teleological thinking in the twentieth century stems from inquiry into problems of structure and function. This teleological approach differs from that of Darwin, who viewed life as a process evolving by natural selection.

Teleology raises the question of the reality of evil. If all things are developing toward an end, can evil be considered a form of completion? Christian eschatology is a form of teleology affirming that life is not cyclical but is directed by God toward completion of the divine plan: the reign or kingdom of God. In John's Gospel, Jesus' statement at his death, "It is completed," signifies the fulfillment of his *telos* in God's purpose. The movement of biblical history is teleological because the history of Israel is viewed as God's way of working in the life of a nation toward the fulfillment of divine purposes.

I.C.

**TELL.** A "heap" (KJV) or "mound" (RSV, except Josh. 8:28). A characteristic feature of Near Eastern topography is the appearance of numerous rounded hills, some natural and some made by people. The Arabic word "tell" has come into common use to distinguish it from the former (tel). The Hebrew Bible uses the word "tel." How much awareness the biblical writers had of the tel's nature is difficult to say. From references such as Joshua 8:28; Deuteronomy 13:16; and Jeremiah 49:2, it would appear that they had perhaps more understanding than the archaeologists did at the beginning of Palestinian investigation around 1850.

Surface surveys, such as those of Edward Robinson and Eli Smith beginning in 1838, called attention to the phenomenon of the tell. But it was not until Sir Flinders Petrie at Tell el-Hesi in 1890 demonstrated stratigraphic excavation and pottery chronology that tells attracted scientific diggers to these "mounds of buried cities." From those early beginnings and continuing until today, excavation techniques have been refined to the point that the trained archaeologist can be confident in "reading" a tell, that is of tracing its material cultural history from the surface to bedrock. In 1963 P. Lapp estimated that excavations of about 150 tells, including 26 major ones, had been made, out of about 5,000 known tells. Since 1963, about 2,000 more tells have been identified and more are to be expected.

A tell is produced when groups of people in successive periods of history, separated in time by decades or centuries, choose to build settlements on the same geographic spot, each, after the first, living on top of the remains of its predecessors. The first settlement may have been prompted by geographical position, by a spring or stream of water, by a nearby caravan route or junction of such routes, by fertile land surrounding the site, or by ease of defense against attack. As the tell "grows," the added height provides vantage points in observing the approach of enemies as well as comfort in summer heat by catching refreshing winds, an added advantage in threshing grain.

The technique of excavation on a Near East tell is the same as that used elsewhere. The difference lies in the time-span involved. Elsewhere "trash heaps" are often of one or two periods of occupation. The antiquity of the Near Eastern civilizations makes it possible that the lower levels of the tell may go back to prehistoric times, while the uppermost level may have been laid down recently.

The final objective of ARCHAEOLOGY is to describe, as far as material remains and written records permit, life as it was at the several periods of a tell's occupation. A basic concern is accuracy and completeness of record keeping. For every object uncovered, in what stratum it was found and just where within the stratum must be recorded. To this end, surveying the tell to establish elevation and grid points is a first step in setting up those kinds of records that will be used throughout the excavation. Once the workers are organized, slow and deliberate removal of earth is begun with constant care to conserve every object of significance. Of prime importance is every piece of pottery. Rarely are pieces found unbroken. But each small fragment means something to the trained pottery expert. From these pieces, their quantity and kinds, the historical time period of the stratum is established.

Archaeologists usually will not be able to uncover a whole stratum of the tell at one time. They choose what seems to be a promising spot and stick to that spot as long as the digging there proves productive, hopefully down to bedrock. Stratum levels are determined by the uncovering of pavements and floors or by destruction levels with thick layers of ash or an accumulation of airborne dirt blown in over a long period when no one lived at the place.

Once data from the excavation begin coming in and a rough indication of the occupation dates of the first level is obtained, the archaeologist begins to compare the findings with the findings of other archaeologists who have worked with comparable material. This sort of "comparative stratigraphy" goes on level by level. In this way, the tell's story fits in with and makes a contribution to our knowledge of its particular periods of human history.

Sometimes digging a tell brings to light an important or even unique item, such as an Egyptian scarab, a cuneiform tablet, an inscribed piece of pottery, or even a statue with the name of a king, and possibly, but not usually, some evidence of the name of the place. These finds make news, but of greater interest to the archaeologist is what each level of the tell can contribute to knowledge of what human life was like at its time in history.

P.L.G.

**TELL EL-AMARNA.** *See* AMARNA, TELL EL-.

**TEMPLE.** The idea of a temple developed from people discovering places where they met satisfactorily with a deity (for example, a "Garden of Eden"). "Do not come near; put off your shoes from your feet, for the place on which you are standing is holy ground" (Exod. 3:5). "It is well that we are here; let us make three booths" (literally tent, dwelling, habitation; and, hence, tabernacle, Holy Place and Holy of Holies, Mark 9:5; Heb. 9:1-4, 11). In Greek

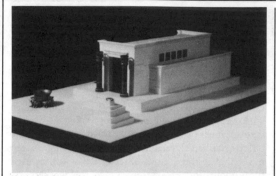

Howland-Garber model of Solomon's Temple, Agnes Scott College, Decatur, Georgia

*A view of a model of Solomon's Temple from the right corner*

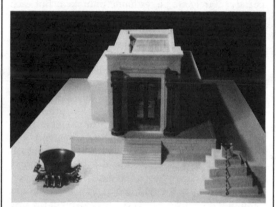

Howland-Garber model of Solomon's Temple, Agnes Scott College, Decatur, Georgia

*Front view of a model of Solomon's Temple, with "molten sea" at left and altar of burnt offering at right*

there is a specific word for temple; In Hebrew there is none. When reference is made to a temple, it is a "house of . . ." either a deity or person. This Semitic usage is reflected in NT Greek in "house of God" (Matt. 12:4) and "my Father's house" (John 2:16).

The location of the three Jerusalem Temples was the same, the hill to the north of Jebus. Second Chronicles 3:1 calls it Mount Moriah, thus linking it to "the land of Moriah" (Gen. 22:2), where Abraham attempted to sacrifice Isaac. Second Samuel 24:16 and following refers to the hill as "the threshing floor of Araunah the Jebusite" (he is called Ornan in I Chr. 21:15). There David met "the angel of the Lord," erected an ALTAR to the Lord, and purchased the threshing floor for a quantity of silver. He had previously brought the TABERNACLE and the ARK OF THE COVENANT into Jerusalem (II Sam. 6:12-19).

A threshing floor is generally a cleared, flat, large, rock surface at such an elevation that, during threshing, the winds can drive away the chaff (Pss. 1:4; 35:5; Hos. 13:3). When not used for threshing, such places were useful for public gatherings and as HIGH PLACES for community worship. Hence, it has

been suggested that Araunah's threshing floor could have been "holy ground" for residents of the area from time immemorial. Holes in the rock beneath the Dome of the Rock may be understood as places for libations, or liquid sacrifices, of blood, wine, oil, or water, to honor the earth-gods of fertility.

*Relation to the Tabernacle.* The wilderness sacred tent, erected first in Moses' time, was the portable sanctuary for Israel from Sinai to Solomon's Temple (Exod. 25–31; 35–40). Once in Palestine, the tabernacle, with the ark, is said to have remained in SHILOH for some three hundred years, from Joshua to David. In I Samuel 1, "the house of the Lord" (v. 7) is also described as "the temple of the Lord" (v. 9), suggesting that, while preserving parts of the Mosaic tent and some of its furnishings, the Shiloh sanctuary had become a more permanent structure. Other provincial sanctuaries housed at least pieces of the tabernacle or its furnishings and existed along with Shiloh: Nob (I Sam. 21:1-6) and Kiriath-jearim (I Sam. 7:1-2). Gibeon, according to I Chronicles 21:29 and II Chronicles 1:3, 5, at some time had custody of the tabernacle and its bronze altar. The sanctuaries at Laish-Dan and at Bethel are regarded in parts of the OT as heretical.

*The Temple of Solomon.* Solomon's Temple, the "First" Temple, was Israel's earliest Jeusalem sanctuary. Thanks to the details in I Kings and less extensive references in II Chronicles, Jeremiah, and Ezekiel, more is known of Solomon's structure than of either of the others—Zerubbabel's and Herod's, together considered the "Second Temple."

Israel did not have the skilled technicians required to erect a temple as grand as Solomon's. The Israelites had manpower, and they could be trained by the foreign workers (I Kings 5:13-16). The professional builders, as well as imported materials, came by way of an international treaty initiated by King Hiram of Tyre (986-933 B.C.), who was a friend of David (II Sam. 5:11) and a business partner of Solomon in several enterprises (I Kings 9:11-12; 9:27; 10:11-12). Archaeological findings at Palestinian sites where Phoenicians also worked (for example, Megiddo and Samaria), as well as sites in Phoenicia itself, provide valuable information for an understanding of the construction and decoration of Solomon's buildings in Jerusalem, including the Temple.

Solomon's Temple had a separate courtyard, adjacent to and connected with areas that contained the king's residence and other governmental buildings. The Temple was begun in the fourth year of Solomon's reign (about 957 B.C.) and completed and dedicated seven years and nine months later. It took thirteen years to finish the whole complex (I Kings 7:1).

The measurements of the Temple, given in cubits (I Kings 6:2-3), are interior figures. (The ordinary cubit is estimated at around 18 inches. The "royal" cubit is ½ meter and a little more, around 20 inches.) The entry way was 10 x 20 x 15; the Holy Place was

40 x 20 x 15; the Holy of Holies was 20 x 20 x 20, a cube. An estimate of the outside dimensions would be 102 cubits (153 ft.) long x 49 cubits (73½ ft.) wide or approximately the size of the Parthenon at Athens, not counting its outer colonnades. Like the Parthenon at Athens, the Temple of Solomon stood on the city's highest ground, readily seen from nearly every direction. (Compare the centrality of the Dome of the Rock in present-day Jerusalem.) Unlike later Jerusalem Temples, Solomon's stood surrounded by open space rather than by adjacent structures which, as in Herod's Temple, crowded in on the later Temples.

Howland-Garber model of Solomon's Temple, Agnes Scott College, Decatur, Georgia

*A model of the Brazen Sea*

Before the House were three features symbolic of the created universe. (1) The Altar of Burnt Offering (II Chr. 3; Ezek. 43:13-17) was the place for the central ceremonial in the Temple ritual, the offering by fire of animal sacrifices. It was built in stages like a Babylonian temple-tower (ZIGGURAT), with a ramp around the pyramidal sides leading to the altar with "horns" at the top (Ezek. 43:14 calls it "mountain of God"). (2) The Brazen Sea. A very large bowl holding almost ten thousand gallons of water, represented the seas of the earth as the altar represented the mountains. Under the sea were twelve larger-than-life, copper-bronze statues of bull calves, arranged in triads, each three facing a major point of the compass. Several suggestions have been made as to their significance. They were not objects of worship. (3) The Pillars: Jachin (beauty) and Boaz (strength) (I Kings 7:15-22; Ps. 96:6). Nothing parallels these in the tabernacle. Temples of the ancient Orient typically had two such columns or statues flanking the temple doorways as guardians to keep out evil influences. Jachin and Boaz had carved stone bases, shafts made to resemble solid metal. There were capitals at the top that have been thought to function as braziers, pillars of fire by day and cloud by night (Exod. 13:21). The description in I Kings 7:16-20 is nearly matched by a wall fresco in color excavated in the Solomonic strata at Megiddo. The columns have been interpreted as representing celestial "props" (the

Greeks called them Pillars of Hercules), which the ancient peoples thought kept the inverted bowl of the heavens from falling upon the flat earth. If so, heaven is implied by the pillars and earth by the altar and laver together to symbolize that the Lord of this Temple is the Creator God of the cosmos, a thought distinctively Israelite in character.

The walls of the Temple and of the 7½ foot raised basement were made of gleaming white limestone in huge blocks, 12 to 15 feet long and approximately 1½ feet high. Excavations show that a particular pattern of headers and stretchers was the style of Phoenician masonry in Solomon's time (I Kings 5:6, 18). Such stones could be obtained from quarries inside the solid limestone mountain upon which the Temple was erected. The stones were carefully shaped at the quarry and fitted together on the site without mortar. The "Giblite" (Byblos) carpenters were also Phoenicians (I Kings 5:18). "Neither hammer nor axe nor any tool of iron was heard in the Temple, while it was being built" (I Kings 6:7). The great double doors of the Temple were sheltered by a liwan type porch, a three-sided room. The porch was roofed. Its fourth side had an open doorway.

"The House" as used in I Kings, designates the Temple's two rooms, the Holy Place and the Holy of Holies, in the same arrangement as those of the tabernacle but twice the dimensions. Around these were placed side rooms on three floors with entrances from the inside of the Holy Place. The function of these chambers is not given in the text. It is thought that they served not only as storage for priestly things but also as "safety deposit vaults" (see "the treasures of the house of the Lord"; I Kings 7:51; 14:26; 15:18; II Kings 18:15; 20:13, 15; 24:13). They had no outside doors or windows, and the walls were 5½ feet of solid masonry.

The Holy Place had tall and narrow, double, two-leaved doors to the Temple on its short side, facing east. The wood carving of the walls, to a height of 7½ feet above the floor, consisted of cherubim facing each other with a palm tree between and a border of open flowers (I Kings 6:32; Ezek. 41:18-20). The design of the cherubim was provided by the sarcophagus of Hiram of Byblos (about 1000 B.C.). The important furnishings, the table of showbread (I Sam. 21:6 KJV) and the incense altar, came from the tabernacle. There were five lampstands and seven-wicked, clay, bowl-like, oil lamps on each side of the room—the Temple's only artificial light. Inserted in the wall paneling were ten "pillars," probably pilasters made of algum wood, thought to be East Indian sandalwood. These were 3½ feet wide and reached the 45-foot ceiling, where they terminated in volute capitals often called "proto-Ionic" or "proto-Aeolic" after later Greek designs.

The Holy of Holies was a cube room, 20 cubits on a side. Its floor was elevated 7½ feet above that of the Holy Place, its doorway being approached by a short flight of steps. The inner shrine was visually dominated by two statue cherubim, 15 feet high, each with a 15-foot wingspread. The design was Phoenician, of a heavenly creature, which was widely considered a guardian, companion, and bearer-through-the-air of deified kings and deities. Here they were covered with gold. Between them was the tabernacle Ark of the Covenant. With its "mercy seat," a gold-plated lid, the ark became the throne or "footstool" (Pss. 99:5; 132:7) for Yahweh who, at times of sacrifices and prayer, came in invisible presence to receive and respond to the people's petitions.

The Temple of Solomon was plundered in 597 B.C. by NEBUCHADNEZZAR II of Babylon. Ten years later, in August 587 B.C., the Temple, along with the city, was burned down by the same enemy (I Kings 24:13). "By the waters of Babylon, there we . . . wept, when we remembered Zion" (Ps. 137:1).

Visual reconstructions of Solomon's Temple have been produced from as early as A.D. 1720; more than thirty were produced in the nineteenth century, including a widely published model by Conrad Schick (1896). Twentieth-century archaeology has transformed the Temple's looks in more recent efforts. Two that took archaeological findings seriously are a drawing by Stevens under the direction of G. Ernest Wright (1955) and the Howland-Garber scale-model reconstruction, begun in 1945 and finished in 1950, which shows the Temple's interior as well as its exterior.

*The Second or Zerubbabel's Temple.* The site of Solomon's Temple had lain desolate ("jackals prowl over it," Lam. 5:18), for fifty years, when the Second Temple, often called ZERUBBABEL's, was begun in March/April 537 B.C. It was finished in March 515 B.C. This construction was made possible by a decree of King Cyrus of Persia, quoted in Ezra 1:2-4 (see also 6:3-5; II Chr. 36:22-23). The year was 538 B.C., as it is known from the Cyrus Cylinder, a barrel-shaped, engraved stone that Hormazd Rassamin discovered at Babylon about 1880. Cyrus restored to the various exiled peoples in Babylon their "sacred things" that the Babylonians had taken away from their conquered lands. At government expense, Cyrus ordered the rebuilding of the devastated temples.

Many, though not all, of the Jews in Babylon accepted Cyrus' offer to return home. By September 538 B.C., those who had returned to Jerusalem had set up an altar on the Temple mount. The foundations of the Temple were laid the following year and, after several long interruptions the Temple was finished and dedicated, seventy-two years after the First Temple had been destroyed.

Although those younger people who had grown up in Babylon rejoiced greatly in the accomplishment, the few older people who remembered the glory of Solomon's Temple "wept with a loud voice" (Ezra 3:11-12; Hag. 2:3).

The records of Cyrus cited in Ezra 6:3 give the Temple dimensions: "its height shall be sixty cubits [90 feet] and its breadth sixty cubits [90 feet], with three courses of great stones and one course of timber." If, as one assumes, the Second Temple was similar in plan and appearance to the First, these dimensions are puzzling. They do suggest a relatively large building. Ezra 3:7 states that it was constructed with the help of Sidonians and Tyrians, as was Solomon's Temple (I Kings 5:1-18). The Second Temple stood for nearly five hundred years, compared to less than one hundred for Herod's Temple.

The Second Temple was not connected with a palace. It stood in an inner court, which was surrounded by a larger court and its side rooms.

Some of the Temple furnishings are listed in I Maccabees 1:21: golden altar, lampstand, table of bread of the Presence, cups, censers, along with the gold decoration for the front of the Temple. These must have been those treasures that Antiochus Epiphanes took away "to his own land" in 169 B.C. (I Macc. 4:49-51). For the rededication in 164 B.C. of the "purified" Temple, the Maccabees made new holy vessels to replace those never recovered from the Seleucids.

Nehemiah (2:8) refers to "the fortress of the temple," indicating that the Second Temple, like Herod's but unlike Solomon's, had a role to play in times of war. First Maccabees 6:7 states that Alexander the Great tried unsuccessfully to take Jerusalem. Simon II, the high priest in Jerusalem, repaired the house, and in his time fortified the Temple with "high double walls," "high retaining walls for the temple enclosure" (Sirach 50:1-2). So the Temple became a stronghold of the Jews against the foreign troops that occupied the *Birah,* a nearby tower, later known as *Baris,* which overlooked the Temple. In Sirach 50:5-24 there is an admirable word-picture of what it was like to share in a worship service at the Second Temple in the times of Simon II.

Little did those who wept at the dedication of Zerubbabel's Temple know that it would stand through nearly five hundred turbulent years of Israel's history. Its reputed inferiority when compared with Solomon's Temple may have been exaggerated. The compiler of II Maccabees claims that the Second Temple was the most famous and most sacred shrine in the world (2:19, 22; 3:12; 5:15; 14:31; 15:18). Haggai and Zechariah, the two prophets of the Second Temple, seem to have offered early messianic prophecies (Hag. 2:20-23; Zech. 6:9-15).

*Herod's Temple.* Herod began his reign in 37 B.C.; he began the Temple in about 20 B.C. He finished the Temple itself in 1½ years, but the work on elaborate, adjacent structures continued and was still being done in Jesus' time (John 2:20). The work is said not to have been entirely completed when the whole was destroyed in A.D. 70. He had already begun his miniature Rome, Caesarea Maritima, and its fortresses. In Jerusalem he had built a theater, a neighboring amphitheater, a stadium, and his own royal palace, guarded by three strong towers and a

Herbert G. May

*The Temple area with Jerusalem in the background, from the Mount of Olives*

huge fortress, named Antonia, for Mark Antony. But still the Zerubbabel Temple, ancient and in looks contrasting badly with all Herod's new Greco-Roman structures of white marble and gold, dominated the skyline of the city. Josephus calls Herod's Temple "the most glorious of his actions." In rabbinic literature, it is said that "one who has not seen Herod's Temple has never seen a beautiful building." Herod's Temple was part of his ambition to bring Jerusalem up-to-date, a city to match other cities of Caesar's realm. He seems to have hoped that his gift of the Temple would make the Jews accept him.

The site was the same as that of previous Temples, the arrangement of major rooms the same, but, otherwise, the Temple was almost completely a new structure, as was required by the Hellenistic-Roman style of architecture. Colonnaded courtyards and supplementary buildings called for an enlargement of the Temple mount. The total area covered nearly all of the present-day el-Haram esh-Sharif ("the Noble Sanctuary" or "the glorious holy place") plus the adjoining fortress of Antonia. The Temple itself, like its predecessors, faced East and was built over or near today's Dome of the Rock. The whole walled area was a square, 600 feet on each side, oriented to the points of the compass. To provide this space, it was necessary to put up walls of great stones (usually 15 feet long and 3 to 4 feet high) and then fill in the area where needed. Some of these Herodian walls can be seen today, for example, the West or Wailing Wall. The southeast corner of the Haram wall with its dizzying drop-off from the top seems to be "the pinnacle of the temple" (Matt. 4:5; Luke 4:9).

The enclosure was terraced so that the Court of the Gentiles was lowest; the Women's Court five steps higher; and, at another five steps, the Court of the Priests, with the Temple towering above it on a still higher elevation. The area was walled in with a double colonnade on the inner side. The columns were 27 feet high and about 17 feet in circumference. Gates were provided: one (Golden Gate) on the east, one on the

north, two on the south leading to the City of David, and four entries from the Upper City to the west, including one that led directly to Herod's palace. The largest area was the Court of the Gentiles; the smallest was the Court of the Priests. The Women's Court served as a passageway to both the Court of Israel and the Court of the Priests. It was clearly not exclusively a gallery for women. The Levitical choir sang from this court. Thirteen chests with inverted trumpets received offerings (Mark 12:41-44). The Beautiful Gate (Acts 3:2, 10) was probably in the east wall of the Women's Court. Its high doors of bronze were imported from Corinth and were called the Corinthian Gates.

The Court of the Gentiles (literally Nations) was open to all. Here were the extensive finance offices of the merchants and money changers. Because of the heavy tax, the Temple was the wealthiest of Jerusalem's institutions. Jesus and other teachers gathered people here to listen to what they had to say. Here, also, the handicapped gathered to ask for alms, and scholars debated with one another (Matt. 21:23-23:30; Mark 11:27-12:40; Luke 20:1-47).

A marble fence about 10 feet high, with a number of openings, surrounded the inner sanctuary. On the fence were carved notices in Latin and Greek warning foreigners to go no farther, for they would die (see Acts 21:28). Two of the Greek inscriptions have been found. Steps led to the courts surrounding the Temple with gates at the top. One court was for men, the Court of Israel. In the other, the Court of Priests, stood the altar for burnt offerings.

The Temple floor plan was that of the Temples of Solomon and Zerubbabel. The only difference was in the Temple porch, which Herod made 100 cubits (or about 150 feet) wide and 100 cubits (or about 150 feet) high, an arrangement that gave opportunity for much Greco-Roman decoration, as with some of the tomb façades at Petra. A restrained reconstruction appears in the Holy Land hotel scale model of Jerusalem. The Herodian Temple's height made possible an "upper room" above the Holy Place and the Holy of Holies, not part of the earlier sanctuaries.

The Arch of Titus in Rome portrays some of the sacred furnishings taken from the Temple before its destruction in A.D. 70: the golden lampstand, the golden table of showbread, and two silver trumpets. The function and appearance of the whole Herodian construction was that of a stout, defensive bastion supplementing the strength of the Antonia tower. So it proved to serve in Titus' battle against Jerusalem. After all else in the city had been taken, the Romans, at the end of June, laid siege to Antonia and the Temple area. Antonia soon fell and was razed, but, until August 28, the city defenders within the Temple area held out against the might of Rome. Titus had given orders to save the Temple but, in the tumult of battle, fire entered and consumed the Temple. Legend has it that Titus himself rescued the Temple's sacred furnishings.                P.L.G.

**TEMPLE, WILLIAM** (1881–1944). Archbishop of Canterbury (1942–44), theologian, philosopher, and noted preacher. Son of Frederick Temple, who also had been archbishop of Canterbury, the younger Temple was educated at Rugby, then at Balliol and Queen's colleges, Oxford. Ironically, he was refused ordination in 1906 by Bishop Henry Luke Paget, who felt that Temple was weak in his declaration of the Virgin Birth and Resurrection. Two years later he was ordained by Randall Thomas Davidson, with Paget's consent.

In 1910 Temple was appointed headmaster of Repton and in 1914 chosen as rector of St. James, Piccadilly. In 1919 he was made canon of Westminster. He was consecrated bishop of Manchester in 1921, archbishop of York in 1929, and archbishop of Canterbury in 1942.

From his earliest years, William Temple was interested in social, economic, and international issues. He became active in Faith and Order and the Life and Work Movements that developed into the World Council of Churches. His books included *Mens Creatrix; Christus Veritas; Nature, Man and God; Readings in St. John's Gospel;* and *Christianity and Social Order.*                R.H.

**TEMPLES.** From the Hebrew word for "house," any location where it is believed deity or deities reside or visit, where people offer worship and petitions. Nearly every religion has "holy places," some more sacred than others. The idea of a temple is more important than place or structure. These matters are determined often by a particular theology, history, and ritual. Temples in biblical Palestine, Israelite and Canaanite, their physical arrangements, furniture, utensils, and ritual practices, resemble each other so closely that archaeologists often find it difficult to distinguish one from the other. Yet, as the biblical records clearly indicate, there were, related to these temples, two distinctly different kinds of theology

and motives for worship. The contrast in ideologies was so fundamental that committed followers of Yahweh could not, or, it was thought, should not, practice both religions simultaneously. The necessary decision is illustrated by Joshua's call, "Choose this day whom you will serve" (Josh. 24:15), and by Elijah's demand, "If the Lord is God, follow him; but if Baal, then follow him" (I Kings 18:21).

Here are the beginnings of the exclusivism that is characteristic of monotheism as it was later in Zoroastrianism, Judaism, Christianity, and Islam. Exclusivism is no issue in polytheistic religious systems. Worshipers in these are at liberty to practice as many different religious rites, rituals, and commitments as may suit their individual tastes. Temples are to be found in many different physical forms, with the form reflecting different traditions, histories, physical and material environments. To survey forms of temples in various religions is not intended here. What is attempted is an illustrative survey of characteristic non-Israelite sanctuaries in biblical Syria-Palestine as known from literary and archaeological sources. The data are selected to compare the material similarities of non-Israelite temples to those of Israel.

There were non-Israelite temples in Syria-Palestine during the times of the Gospels and Acts. These were mainly temples of Greco-Roman religions and architecture. Examples would be the temples at Samaria and Caesarea Maritima and the one at Caesarea Philippi. The surviving monuments at Nabatean Petra give an informative representation of what that architecture was like.

*The Patriarchal Shrines.* The devotional practices of the patriarchs accord with the simple, ancient, Semitic religious shrine practice. The progenitors of the Israelites are said to have founded worship of Yahweh at Shechem (Gen. 12:6-7; 33:18-20), Bethel (Gen. 12:8; 28:18-22; 31:13), Mamre (Hebron, Gen. 13:18), and Beer-sheba (Gen. 21:33; 26:23-25). Typical features of such installations are altars, raised stones, a sacred tree or trees, and a well or cistern of water. (Gen. 28:18-22). Bethel was a place that was made "holy" for Jacob by his dream there of "angels of God" "ascending and descending" on "a ladder," the top of which reached to heaven (v. 12) and by a theophany of Yahweh (v. 13), who gave Jacob a blessing (vv. 13-17). Here Jacob set up a "pillar" stone, which he anointed and named "God's house" (v. 22). He gave the place, previously called Luz, a new name, Beth-el, that is, "God's house" and "the gate of heaven" (v. 17). In Genesis 31:13, Yahweh is spoken of as "the God of Bethel."

Since patriarchal Bethel was on, or near, a well-used travel route, the place became for passersby a wayside shrine. Except for Jerusalem, Bethel is the city name most used in the OT. Its character as a temple site was enhanced when it became one of the two royal, border sanctuaries of the northern kingdom.

A number of the patriarchal shrines were maintained for centuries, popular with Israelites making pilgrimages. In Amos, there are references to Gilgal as a "winter house" and to Bethel as a "summer house" (3:15; 4:4), to Beer-sheba (5:5; 8:14), Samaria, and Dan (8:14).

*The High Places.* This expression in English Bible translations represents a single Hebrew word, *bamah*. By reason of the prophets' denunciation of the HIGH PLACES as locations where Israelites compromised their loyalty to Yahweh, *bamah* became a derogatory, technical term. It signifies a non-Israelite, traditional, open-air shrine or sanctuary. Sometimes these installations were deliberately located on high ground or hilltops which, being physically nearest heaven, Canaanites considered to be the home of the gods. Note Hosea 4:10-14, "They sacrifice on the tops of the mountains, and make offerings upon the hills, under oak, popular, and terebinth, because their shade is good" (v. 13). Also Psalm 121:1-2 (TEV) "I look to the mountains; where will my help come from? My help will come from the Lord, who made heaven and earth."

A *bamah* site, however, was not always on a hilltop. Archaeology has demonstrated that such sanctuaries could be located on low ground (Gezer) or by the sea (Byblos and Ugarit). A textual description of a mountaintop *bamah* is Mount Peor (Num. 23:28), identified as a sanctuary of the Moabites at Shittim (Num. 25:1-9). The account implies that a high place's rituals included eating, drinking wine, dancing, mass sexual intercourse, possibly suggesting sacred prostitution, male and female—all typical of imitative magic, dramatic presentations designed to urge the deity to provide fertility. The OT characterizes such worship as "harlotry." The very name Peor was long remembered as a symbol of Israel's defection from Yahweh, "the sin at Peor" (Josh. 22:17; Num. 25:18; 31:16).

The past half century of archaeology in Palestine has given information about Canaanite worship practices that has altered previous opinion. It was once thought that Canaanites worshiped only at high places. Now it is known that they erected monumental temple buildings from early times onward. These often were functioning at the same time as the high places and in the same communities.

*Illustrative Non-Israelite Temples.* (1) *Syrian.* Temples in two excavations in Syria demonstrate cultural continuity with Canaan in temple building. Ebla, about thirty miles south of Aleppo, was the capital of an empire that for about eight centuries, beginning about 2500 B.C., the age of the Egyptian pyramids, commercially dominated lands between Mesopotamia and Egypt. During Ebla's most prosperous era it had an estimated population of 260,000. As many as five hundred god-names appear in the Ebla tablets. Of the many city sanctuaries, the largest, near the

the royal palace on the city's acropolis, was Temple D. This was a solidly constructed, enclosed building about 93 feet by 37 feet. Its three rooms, porch, nave, and cella, were arranged along a longitudinal axis with entrance on the south side. The innermost room was the largest (about 40 feet long). Within the rear wall, a niche was provided presumably for a god emblem. Except for the niche, the floor plan generally, even the size approximately, bears striking resemblance to the Temple of Solomon, even though Ebla's temple was erected fifteen hundred years earlier. The temple was dedicated to a god named Davar, which is the Hebrew for "word," as in "the word of Yahweh."

Ugarit was near the sea about sixty miles southwest of Ebla, at the junction of the north-south coastal highway from Egypt to Asia Minor and a trade route leading to Aleppo, Mari, and Babylon. The city flourished, and its temples were built, in the Middle Bronze Age, 2100-1500 B.C. Ugarit had twin temples situated on the highest spot in the city, visible from the harbor and the sea. These structures, identical in size and floor plan, were, except for the palace, which was located elsewhere, the largest buildings in Ugarit. Each temple consisted of two rooms, a nave, and a cella, where, in a corner, the god emblem was displayed. The entrance, flanked by pillars, was on the south side and faced an open-air courtyard, which had a large, stepped altar at its center.

The twin temples of Ugarit were dedicated to Baal and Dagon. According to the Ugaritic texts, Dagon was an associate of El, the senior god. Baal was the son of Dagon, the young fertility and warrior god. After he had defeated enemies of the gods, he demanded and received from them a high social rank and a "house" (temple) of his own.

(2) *Midianite.* At Timnah, about fifteen miles due north of Elath in the Arabah Valley and near the Edomite boundary, a copper mining center was excavated (1969). From the fourteenth to the twelfth century B.C., Egyptians operated the center with local Midianite and Kenite labor. Egypt abandoned the center after an earthquake but the laborers reopened it. Under the Egyptians, a temple to Hathor, "the Lady of Turquoise," had been erected. Out of the ruins, the Midianites made their own kind of sanctuary. It consisted of a low stone wall enclosing an area about 26 feet square with a single entrance on the south side. On the east wall was a row of standing stones. Inside the south wall, on either side of the entrance, were low benches for offerings. On the west rear portion of the area, there was an elevated masonry structure containing a niche for the god emblem, possibly the bronze serpent with the gilded head found by the excavators. The whole of the enclosure was covered with a cloth awning or tent of skins. The pole holes were found. Outside the structure was a small room, possibly for the priests.

This find is our best available counterpart to the

Sinai tabernacle. It was built by desert-dwelling Midianites. Moses' father-in-law, Jethro, was a Midianite nomad who lived in the Sinai Desert, an area adjacent to the Arabah.

At Amman, when the site was being cleared for the present airport in the mid-1950s, a temple of about 1400 B.C. was discovered and was excavated in 1966. The temple is located in the same area as Timnah. It consists of stone walls forming a small square within a larger square. Evidence of humans' being burned as foundation deposits was found (Josh. 6:26). At the center of the open-air inner square, there was a "pillar" base made up of two flat, circular stones, one on top of the other, thought to be a base for a god-emblem such as a wooden tree trunk. Between the inner and outer squares, partitions with open doorways formed rooms that adjoined each other and were probably roofed over with tent material. This provided what has been interpreted as a covered walkway for ceremonial processions to circumambulate the inner square. The temple is far removed from any known ancient settlement and seems to have belonged to nomadic tribes. Nomadic justice and treaty formation required witnesses by or before the gods. This structure seems well arranged for such special occasions.

A temple dated about 1600 B.C., also in an isolated spot and on the slopes of Mount Ebal, some distance from Shechem, was first discovered in 1931 and excavated in 1962. The plan and function of the Mount Ebal sanctuary duplicate almost exactly those of the Amman temple, both open and part-covered sanctuaries. Covenant-making is associated also with this locale. The great temple of Shechem was dedicated to Baal-berith, Lord of the covenant (Judg. 8:33; 9:4).

(3) *Egyptian*. During those times when Egyptians held active control over the Esdraelon area, both at Megiddo and at Beth-shan, they built temples for worship by themselves and for the Canaanite natives. These were not the kind of temples that were built in Egypt. They were, rather, simply series of irregularly shaped rooms strung out along a natural ridge; some were open-air, others roofed. Mekal was the city-god of Beth-shan, a local form of Reshef, god of lightning, whom the Egyptians identified with their god Seth. To these gods several Beth-shan temples were dedicated. Others nearby were devoted to Ashtoreth (I Sam. 31:10), or Anat, whom the Egyptians equated with Antit. In these were found models of multistoried temples that were decorated with molded figurines of naked human beings, serpents, and doves. Another temple belonged to Dagon (I Chr. 10:10), an old Semitic deity who was popular with the Philistines (Judg. 16:23 ff.). The Philistine clients of Egypt celebrated their victory over Saul by exhibiting on the temple and city walls his head, body, and armor (I Sam. 31:10; I Chr. 10:10).

It is not likely that the Egyptian-built "foreign" temples at Beth-shan and Megiddo influenced the architecture of Canaanite temples even though the rites and ceremonies held in them may have resembled Canaanite practices.

(4) *Philistine*. These non-Semitic folk, who rivaled and, at times, dominated the Israelites for possession of the land of Canaan, erected in their cities temples with another kind of "foreign" architecture. If the Philistines worshiped deities of the Aegean, from which area it is supposed they came, the Bible does not mention it. According to biblical records, the Philistines in Canaan worshiped gods with Semitic names, Dagon and his consort Tanit in Gaza and Ashdod (Judg. 16:23; I Sam. 5:1-5), Ashtoreth or Asherah-Anat in Ashkelon, and Baalzebub in Ekron (II Kings 1:16).

The Philistines appear to have used their temples for festivals involving large gatherings of people (Judg. 16:27). This may suggest worship practices similar to those of the Canaanite high places—eating, drinking, and carousing (compare "their hearts were merry," Judg. 16:25).

The first unmistakably Philistine temple ever discovered was excavated in 1972 at Tell Qasile, now in the northern part of Tel Aviv. Tell Qasile may have been the port through which David received the cedars of Lebanon from Tyre for the building of his palace, and Solomon for the Jerusalem Temple. The Tell Qasile temple consists of a well-planned complex of a number of units with its entrance to the west, that is, the temple faced the Mediterranean Sea. The rooms followed a "bent axis" plan, not unknown in Mycenaean Greece. Worshipers, entering the open courtyard, had to make a right-angle turn in order to face the altar, which stood in front of the temple proper. This rectangular room, 57 feet by 45 feet, had, on stone bases, two interior columns to support the roof. It has been suggested that these columns were shaped like those at Mycenaean Knossus on Crete, that is, broad at the top, tapering to a narrow point at the base. If so, it is understandable that Samson, standing between "the two middle pillars" "upon which the house rested" could have pulled down the Philistine-built house of Dagon at Gaza (Judg. 16:27).

(5) *Canaanite*. It was once thought that Palestinian Canaanites did not build temples but that the high places were their only sanctuaries. The only architectral evidence that was then available seemed to be the ninth-century B.C. palace-chapel at Tell Tainat in remote northern Syria. Excavations since that time have provided abundant evidence of Canaanite temple building in Palestine. Those that have been found date from Early Bronze Age to the divided kingdom and have been found throughout the land. For example, at Megiddo, a series of three temples were built at different periods on the same location. At Hazor, in a "holy of holies" shrine, a remarkable row of standing stones was found, which were flanked by the figure of a man seated and by a beautifully carved stone figure of a crouching lion. The central standing stone had

carved upon its top a pair of praying hands with a crescent moon encircling a sun disk above and between them. There was a three-roomed temple at Hazor also, in plan not unlike the Temple of Solomon.

At Lachish, in a location just outside the city gate, a series of three superimposed temples have been reported, the earliest from about 1600 to 1200 B.C. and the latest, destroyed possibly by the Israelites, about 1200 B.C. In pits near the temples, bones of sheep, goats, oxen, and gazelles—all young—were identified; many right forelegs and shoulders were included (see Lev. 7:32).

At Ai (Tell et-Tell) there was a small Early Bronze (before 2000 B.C.) temple consisting of two rooms built against the inner facing of the city wall. Two steps led to the roofed, rectangular first room (25 feet by 18 feet). Benches for offering and incense stands were found along two walls. A narrow door led into the second room, about the same size but irregular in shape. In the corner was a masonry structure thought by the excavators to be an altar.

At Nahariya, five miles north of Acre on the shore, a structure, dated about 1800 B.C., was found (1953-54). It consisted of a long, stone building with a square room at the east end. Like the Tell Qasile, the Philistine temple, this one faced the sea and had its cella at the east end. There was a vestibule at the west end, the single room. Incense burners, pottery, and a silver figurine of a female deity were found together with a number of clay figurines of doves, probably indications that the temple belonged to Asherah-Anat.

An unusual design for a Canaanite temple was used for the temple of Baal-berith at Shechem. Its floor plan was not unusual. It provided for a single, rectangular room (33 feet by 40 feet), the space divided by two rows of three columns each, with stone bases. The door was protected by a porch that incorporated a single column. On either side of the porch were entrances to stairs that led to a second floor with, possibly, a balcony on four sides and then to the flat roof. There were no windows on the ground floor but inside lighting was provided by windows on the second floor, just under the roof. Flanking the porch and just outside the porch were two standing stones. This, with its great altar in the courtyard outside, was the Shechem temple of the Lord of the covenant built about 1600 B.C. (Judg. 9:4).

The outside walls of this temple were made of exceptionally thick, solid masonry. The roof was flat and is thought to have been surrounded by a crenelated wall. All of this has led to a conclusion that this temple building, unlike any other Canaanite temple thus far known, was designed to serve the city not only as a place for worship in peacetime and/or for public gatherings (Judg. 9:27), but also as a refuge and fortress to which the population could retire for safety in case the city came under enemy attack.

*Noteworthy Israelite Temples.* From the excavations (1962–74) of Tell Arad and Beer-sheba, eighteen miles apart, it has been realized that throughout the kingdom period, the southernmost border of Judah was guarded by a chain of defensive fortress settlements of which Beer-sheba and Arad are examples. Furthermore, each of these had temples with altars at central locations. The tenth-century B.C. Arad temple, built over an elevation on the summit of the mound (a *bamah*?), consisted of a rectangular building, 65 feet by 49 feet, with entry on the east and the "holy of holies" toward the west. The inner room was elevated by three broad steps on which were stone incense altars flanking the entrance. These were well finished; some of the final incense offerings were still on the tops. One altar had YHWH written on it in ink, a unique find in Palestinian archaeology. Around the walls of the outer room were plastered benches probably for offerings and cult vessels. Outside the temple doors were two stone slabs, probably bases for pillars, comparable to the Jachin and Boaz of the Solomonic Temple. East of the house was an altar for burnt offerings, square and built of earth and small field stones (see Exod. 20:24-25). Throughout its history, the temple was approached directly from the city gate. Ostraca with priestly Hebrew names were found in some of the side rooms. Strikingly, the Arad resembles Solomon's Temple in orientation and plan, as well as furnishings.

The temple at Beer-sheba, which may have been as fine as the one at Arad, the excavator thinks was destroyed to make room for a later residential development. The stone altar was discovered, dismantled but with all its pieces. This has been reconstructed and measures 7½ feet by 7½ feet by 4½ feet high.

At the northernmost border of Israelite territory, not far from the foothills of Mount Herman, stood Dan, which has been under excavation from 1966 and continues until now. The place was strongly fortified, with a freely flowing spring in its midst, one of the sources of the Jordan River, and with a large and well-preserved city gate. Its "temple" was a *bamah*, pre-Israelite and Israelite, about 60 feet square. The enclosure wall was made of dressed limestone blocks laid in "ashlar" construction, which was typical of the way Phoenician masons made walls. In its center was a small horned altar 16 inches by 16 inches by 14 inches high. Monumental steps, 26 feet wide, led from the city up to the high place.

Jereboam I established Dan and Bethel as fortress towns at Israel's north and south borders to mark off and defend them (I Kings 12:26-33; II Chr. 13:8-9). Bethel had walls 11 feet thick and other defensive features. Amaziah, its priest in Amos' day, referred to its sanctuary (not yet located) as "the king's sanctuary" and "a temple [along with that of Dan?] of the kingdom" (Amos 7:13).

*Conclusion.* The Canaanites and the Israelites both had temples, some open air, some architectural structures, which in outer appearances looked very much alike. What went on in these places of worship differed sharply.

The Canaanites worshiped with a gathering of peoples to eat, drink, dance, and carouse, all for the pleasure of gods who, it was thought, would respond with the increase of families, food, and flocks. The focus of Canaanite ritual, as was true also of their stories of the gods, was focused on the ways of nature, their great festival days determined by the agricultural calendar.

The Israelite worship was conducted in quarters isolated from crowds, participated in by qualified personnel, joined at crisis times by political leaders, and conducted largely in silent places, except for the outer court sacrificial ceremonials where music and spoken word might be provided. The focus of Israelite worship was the remembrance of past history, deliverance from bondage in Egypt, the covenant made at Sinai, wilderness wanderings, and the gift of their own land. Such worship bound the society more closely together as a people through thoughtful contemplation rather than by action. The festivals observed, though held at times of year similar to the festal times of the Canaanites, emphasized historical and theological meanings. Canaanite and Israelite worshipers in their sanctuaries both used the word El for God and employed outwardly similar acts of sacrifice but in different atmospheres and with different meanings.

P.L.G.

**TEMPTATION.** The state of being enticed, especially to do wrong. God allows people to be tempted by Satan in order that they may grow in faith and be better prepared to follow the Lord. Temptation is part of God's process of TESTING people.

God permitted Satan to afflict Job (1:6-22; 2:1-7) so that Job would decide what place God had in his life. He allowed Satan to incite David to take a census in Israel (I Chr. 21:1-4). And God allowed a "lying spirit" (I Kings 22:19-23) to entice King Ahab through his prophets.

God permitted Jesus to be led by the Holy Spirit into the wilderness to be tempted by Satan to prepare him for his ministry (Matt. 4:1-11; Mark 1:12-13; Luke 4:1-13). In the Lord's Prayer we pray, "Lead us not into temptation" (Matt. 6:13). These words echo those Jesus prayed in the Garden of Gethsemane while the disciples slept: "Watch and pray that you may not enter into temptation" (Matt. 26:41). We are assured that God is faithful and will not let anyone be tempted beyond one's strength, but will provide a way of escape, that a person may be able to bear it (I Cor. 10—13). The Lord, who has been tempted as we are, is able to help those who are tempted (Heb. 4:15; 2:18). When someone is tempted and falls, that person can have God's forgiveness (Col. 1:13), for God has conquered all the forces of evil (Col. 2:13-15).

B.J.

**TEMPTATION OF JESUS.** God allowed Satan to tempt Jesus to prepare him for his ministry. God tempts no one, nor can God be tempted (Jas. 1:13). But Jesus, who not only was the Son of God but also came to earth as a fully human person, could be tempted.

After Jesus was baptized by John the Baptist in the River Jordan, God arranged for him to be tempted. The Gospel writers Matthew (4:1-11), Mark (1:12-13), and Luke (4:1-13) state that Jesus was led out into the wilderness by the Holy Spirit to be tempted by Satan. For forty days Jesus fasted. Then the tempter came to him and tried to get him to: turn a stone into bread; hurl himself down from the pinnacle of the Temple; and worship him, Satan. Jesus responded with words from Scripture: We do not live by bread alone, but by every word that proceeds from the mouth of God; we should not test the Lord our God; and we should worship the Lord and serve only the Lord. Jesus then was ready to begin his ministry, and to help all those who are tempted (Heb. 2:18, 4:15) because he had been through TEMPTATION himself.

B.J.

**TEN COMMANDMENTS.** The summary of the agreement between Jehovah and the Hebrew people at Mount SINAI, known in Hebrew as the ten words or ten statements. In only slightly differing versions in Exodus 20 and Deuteronomy 5, the laws were first stated directly and orally by God to the people in the desert.

First God was identified as the author when he stated, "I am the Lord your God, who brought you out of the land of Egypt, out of the house of bondage." Later Moses is made the go-between on Mount Sinai to receive the Decalogue in its written form. Exodus 32:15-16 makes it clear that Jehovah had shaped and inscribed the two tablets on which the commandments were written. After forty days in the presence of Jehovah, Moses descended the mountain, presumed to be Jebel Musa in the Sinai peninsula. Finding the people had deserted both him and Jehovah for a golden calf, he dashed the tablets to pieces.

Later Jehovah ordered Moses to go back up the mountain, bringing blank tablets on which Jehovah once again inscribed the "ten words." This time Moses successfully delivered them to the people. The stone tablets were then safeguarded within the Ark of the Covenant (Deut. 10:1-5). First Kings 8:9 states that the ark's sole purpose was to house these two tablets of the Law. The oldest Jewish tradition is that Jehovah engraved the commandments on the stone, and that Moses was merely the courier. On the other hand a second tradition, supported by Exodus 34:27-28, makes Moses the scribe.

Scripture itself gives no clue for how to divide or number the commandments. Generally they are thought of as falling into two parts: those that relate to one's relationship to God and those that relate to one's relationship to one's neighbor. Christ also divided them into these two groups. Traditionally the Jews generally count the statement, "I am the Lord your God" as the First Commandment. Most later practices count this statement rather as an introduction.

Since the time of Augustine, the Western church has placed three commandments in the first table and seven in the second, nor counting the commandment about graven images as a separate one and splitting out the final commandment(s) on coveting as nine and ten. This is still the practice of the Roman Catholics and Lutherans. The Jews, Greek Orthodox, Anglican, and Reformed generally make the commandment about images a separate one. Except for the Jews, they place four commandments in the first table and six in the second. Since the time of the Reformation the numbering has been very confused. From a Jewish interpretation, the commandment to honor one's parents is a religious obligation one really owes to God, not merely to one's parents, and this places it logically in the first table. Thus under the Jewish system there are five commandments in each table.

Many scholars think that the original form of the commandments, in whatever language Jehovah gave them, was a strong negative followed by a verb. Such a form in English is preserved in "Don't kill," "Don't steal," "Don't covet." The first of the commandments dealt with problems the Hebrews faced in Egypt and among the Canaanite tribes in the desert: worshiping many gods other than Jehovah, worshiping those gods in the form of idols, misusing the name of God, and honoring and revering God's name in worship and obedience. Whether the commandment to honor one's parents belongs to the first table or the second will probably never be solved, but the role of the parent as one's first influence in life, almost godlike, does make it a good transition between the commandments that deal with God and those that deal with one's neighbor. The commandment against killing is primary to humanity's ability to live in community with others. Apparently Deuteronomy 19:1-10 and Numbers 35:1-15 allow for killing in time of war and for capital punishment. The commandment on adultery protects the integrity of the family, and in fact Deuteronomy 22:22-27 makes adultery a capital offense. Stealing likewise was a serious offense in a society of wandering shepherds, often away from their families, tents, and animals. Testifying falsely before a court, lying or ruining the reputation of one's neighbor, was also a serious matter, and the establishment of a court and judicial system at Kadesh about the same time as the giving of the Decalogue emphasizes the importance of legal testimony and the wrongness of perjury. The last commandment(s) had to do with coveting. As in contemporary Arabic, *house* included everything that belonged to the house—wives, servants, flocks, household goods.

The spectacular theophany of Jehovah to Moses and to the people of Israel both before and after the giving of the Decalogue helped establish its importance in the COVENANT relationship. Exodus reports that the people trembled when they saw the mountain smoking and the lightning flashing, or when they heard the sound of thunder and blasts of the trumpets. They begged Moses to ask God not to speak to them in person but instead that he act as God's spokesman.

After the account of the giving of the Law on Mount Sinai in the biblical record come chapter after chapter of the detailed code of conduct, which the Ten Commandments had merely summarized. Taking up a great portion of the Pentateuch, the five books of Moses, these detailed laws about the building of the tabernacle, about sacrifices, about farming, and about dealing with one's neighbor differ from other social codes of the Near East only in degree. In general, the Ten Commandments in Exodus are only loosely connected historically with the setting of the text. Their repetition in Deuteronomy appears to be a teaching tool for the training of priests. Psalm 81 is probably a hymn extolling the giving of the commandments and the making of the covenant.

Physically, the tablets of the Law followed the people of Israel wherever they wandered. The Ark of the Covenant seems to have belonged most closely to the tribe of Ephraim, and soon became an object of reverence, even of worship, as the dwelling place of Jehovah. Even when captured by the Philistines, however, or later kept safely hidden at Kiriath-jearim because David had not yet been able to subdue Jerusalem, it was still an object of great importance. According to one Talmudic legend, the ark contained not merely the two tablets of the Law but also the fragments of the two others that Moses had smashed. When Christ makes reference to "the commandments" in the NT (for example Mark 10:19), he does so without the phrase "the *ten* commandments." In any case, the commandments sum up the relationships between a loving God and what God expects of loving people.                                                 T.J.K.

**TENDAI.** A Japanese word from the Chinese term *T'ien T'ai* meaning literally "heavenly terrace," the name of the mountain and monastery where it originated. A school of MAHAYANA BUDDHISM brought to Japan by the monk Saicho (Dengyo Daishi) early in the ninth century A.D., Tendai had immense influence on the development of Japanese Buddhism and remains an influential denomination in Japan.

Based on the LOTUS SUTRA as the supreme expression of truth, Tendai asserts that all other scriptures represent accommodations for different audiences at different stages of this ministry. It is thus able to affirm a vast number of teachings and practices as partial but valid, and a salient characteristic of Tendai has been its openness to diversity. In Japan, within it were nourished (before they became separate movements) ZEN meditation, PURE LAND devotionalism, esotericism borrowed from Shingon, and worship of bodhisattvas, such as Kannon and Jizo. Philosophically Tendai has emphasized the presence of the Absolute as the Sunyata, Emptiness, Buddha-nature, in the transitory phenomenal world just as it is. It teaches "Three thousand realms in a single instant," that is, that all states of existence from the heavens of the gods to the hells, including the path of bodhisattvahood and Buddhahood, can be experienced here in this life in every moment of thought.

In Japan, Tendai is headquartered at Mount Hiei just outside of Kyoto. In the Middle Ages this great monastery exercised considerable cultural and political power. The leaders of most of the important new Buddhist movements of the Kamakura period (1185-1333), such as Nichiren, Honen and Shinran of Pure Land, and Eisai and Dogen of Zen, were trained at Mount Hiei. Several "new religions" of modern Japan have received indirect inspiration from Tendai.                                                    R.E.

**TENEBRAE.** The name of the special matins and lauds services of the liturgical churches celebrated on Maundy Thursday, Good Friday, and Holy Saturday. These services are so called from the Latin word *tenebrae* meaning "darkness." They are held as a mourning service and a reenactment of the terrible events surrounding the death of Christ, enacted by means of candles, darkness, and noise as part of the ceremony.

The first lessons read during Tenebrae are all from Jeremiah and Lamentations, and the psalms and antiphons have references to the passion of Christ. There are fifteen lighted candles, and one is put out after every psalm, while the last lighted candle is hidden behind the altar. Prayers are then said in darkness; during this period noise is made by shuffling prayer books and hand clapping, and the congregation disperses in silence. This noise symbolizes the convulsion of nature at the death of Christ on the cross. The single remaining light is the Light of the World. In Protestant churches a simpler service, also called Tenebrae, which ends in silence and darkness is often held on Good Friday and/or Holy Saturday.                                                         J.C.

**TENNENT, GILBERT** (1703–64). The Presbyterian revivalist was born February 5 in Ireland, the eldest son of William and Catharine Kennedy Tennent. Licensed by the Philadelphia Presbytery in May 1725, he was ordained in New Brunswick, New Jersey, in 1726. During the FIRST GREAT AWAKENING he followed George Whitefield to New England in 1740–41. His 1739 sermon "The Danger of an Unconverted Ministry" caused a 1741 schism between New Side and Old Side. Tennent served as moderator when the church reunited seventeen years later. In 1743 he accepted a call to Second Presbyterian Church in Philadelphia, where he was buried.                                                            N.H.

**TENNYSON, ALFRED** (1809–92). English poet and hymn writer. Commonly known as Alfred, Lord Tennyson, he was the first Baron Tennyson. Born at Somersby, Lincolnshire, he was the son of an Anglican rector. He first was educated by his father, then at Louth Grammar School, and Trinity College, Cambridge. There he was part of a group known as "the Apostles." On the death of Arthur Hallam, his good friend and his sister's fiancé, Tennyson wrote *Two Voices* and began *In Memoriam*. In the year 1850, he published this completed elegy and was married to Emily Smallwood. That same year he succeeded Wordsworth as poet laureate. Tennyson wrote the *Charge of the Light Brigade* in 1854, and *Idylls of the King* in 1859. Some of his poems have become hymns, including parts of *In Memoriam*, "Strong Son of God," "Crossing the Bar," and "Ring Out, Wild Bells." Tennyson became a baron in 1884. He was buried by the side of Robert Browning in Westminster Abbey.                                                                    R.H.

**TENRI-KYO.** The Japanese words for "religion of divine wisdom." One of the oldest of the "new religions" of Japan, Tenri-kyo was founded by Nakayama Miki (1798–1887). In 1838, in the course of a shamanistic healing rite, she was possessed by a deity who declared himself the "true and original God," the monotheistic God now most commonly known in Tenri-kyo as Oyagami, "God the Parent." During the remainder of her long life Nakayama practiced spiritual healing, taught dancing rituals, and penned the scriptures called *Ofudesaki*. All these are still basic features of the religion.

Tenri-kyo, a cheerful, optimistic faith, centers on belief that God originally created humankind to live a joyous life. God is eagerly calling us back to that primal purpose. This divine work commenced in the ministry of the founder and is expressed in Tenri-kyo's main rite, a dance enacting the Creation. In its amplest form, this ritual is performed at the religion's main temple, near Nara, Japan, around a pillar said to represent the spot where the Creation began. Tenri-shi, the headquarters city built by the main temple, draws many pilgrims and includes a university, museum, library, hospital, and extensive administrative facilities. The religion is well organized, actively missionary, and in the 1980s numbered several million adherents in Japan and abroad.                                                                  R.E.

**TEFILLIN.** *See* PHYLACTERY.

**TERAPHIM.** A Hebrew word, plural in form but singular in meaning, translated in English as IDOLATRY (I Sam. 15:23), "image" (I Sam. 19:13, 16), and "household GODS" (Gen. 31:19, 34, 35). No one form, shape, or size of the teraphim has been identified. Rachel concealed the teraphim she stole from her father in her camel's saddle and sat upon it (or them) (Gen. 31:19, 34, 35). Michal took a human-sized teraphim, gave it goat's hair, and covered it with bed clothing to look like a sick David (I Sam. 19:13, 16). In Judges 17:5; 18:14-20; Ezekiel 21:21; and Zechariah 10:2, the teraphim is associated with the ephod in divination. Employing it for such purposes was condemned in the OT, as in Josiah's reformation (II Kings 23:24); yet clearly the teraphim appears to have been used by some Israelites from the period of the Judges to the times of Zechariah, who states, "The teraphim utter nonsense" (10:2).                                P.L.G.

**TERESA OF AVILA** (1515–82). Renowned Spanish Carmelite nun and mystic, reformer of the CARMELITE order, and part of the Catholic Reformation. Descended from an old Spanish family, Teresa was born in Avila, received a modest education from Augustinian nuns, and in 1535 joined the Carmelites. After passing twenty years in lukewarmness, negligence, and frequent illness, Teresa experienced a true conversion in 1555. A picture of the wounded Christ and Augustine's *Confessions* brought her to an ecstatic vision of Christ. She surrendered completely to God's will. Discovering that the original Carmelite rule had been strict, she resolved to establish a monastery with strict rules. Strong opposition came from townspeople, groups within the church, and officials in her own order, but she presented everyone with a reformed convent in 1562. Criticized and pressured not to do anything further, she nevertheless perservered until she founded sixteen reformed Discalced (barefoot) branches of the Carmelite order for women and fourteen for men. Saint JOHN OF THE CROSS (1542–91), who wrote *Dark Night of the Soul,* zealously assisted her in administration. After her conversion to perfection, Teresa spent her life in intense devotions, ascetic exercises, self-mortification, and reforming efforts. Her *Spiritual Autobiography* (1562) scrutinizes her life and gives directions for achieving genuine prayer. She also wrote *The Way to Perfection, Foundations,* and *The Interior Castle,* giving classic guidelines for prayer. Gregory XV in 1622 canonized Teresa as the "seraphic virgin," and in 1970 Paul VI declared her a Doctor of the Church.
C.M.

**TERTULLIAN** (about 145–220). Born Quintus Septimus Florens Tertullianus, he was the "father of Latin theology," who established the West's trinitarian doctrine, wrote its earliest plea for religious liberty, realized that culture religion compromises worship of God, and defended Christianity against pagans and heretics. Tertullian's exact dates are not known, making chronology uncertain. He was born in Carthage, North Africa, received a good pagan education in literature and philosophy, and practiced law in Rome. When about fifty he accepted Christianity, returned to Carthage, and rose to presbyter. Rigorist and legalistic in his views, he rejected Catholicism's lax clergy and joined strict MONTANISM in about 207.

Tertullian's *Against Praxeas* explains the Trinity of Father, Son, and Holy Spirit as one person in three functions, thus arguing that Christ was not less than God, and that Christ was fully human and fully divine, thus setting the West's orthodox view. Shortly after his conversion, Tertullian wrote his *Apology,* which defends Christians as honorable, peaceful people who contribute to society; yet in court they are not given privileges accorded to murderers. He demands equality and toleration as God-given inalienable rights.

*Prescriptions against Heretics,* written before Tertullian joined the Montanists, maintains that Christian authority rests on the faithful transmission of Christ through canon, creed, and clergy, and that heretics and outsiders have no right to interpret Scripture. After joining the Montanists, Tertullian held that Rome's morally lax clergy had compromised Christianity and forfeited authentic guidance. He saw more validity in the Montanists, who relied on the Spirit for guidance, than in institutionalized apostolic succession.

*On Idolatry* calls for a full break with the world because Scripture forbids idolatry, and participation in the world's affairs involves idolatrous customs and ceremonies, thus compromising loyalty to God. Tertullian's *Testimony of the Soul* maintains that the soul will tend upward to God if not frustrated by earthly matters.

Tertullian's many works also include *On the Resurrection of the Flesh, On the Flesh of Christ, Scorpiace,* and numerous ascetic writings: *On Baptism, On Penance, On Patience, On Women's Dress, The Soldier's Crown, On Fasting, Monogamy, On Flight in Persecution,* and *Exhortation to Chastity.*                                C.M.

**TESTAMENT.** From the Latin word *testamentum,* meaning an "oath" or "covenant." Generally, what is meant by the term "testament" in the names "Old Testament" and "New Testament" is conveyed by the word COVENANT. A testament, so understood, is a religious order or epoch of divine revelation. In the Christian understanding, the later testament (NT) is the fulfillment of promises made by God in the former testament (OT). The OT concept of testament (or covenant) is that of *berith,* the ceremony of making an agreement or treaty. Yahweh's covenant with Israel was a particular kind of *berith,* a suzerainty treaty, whereby vassals are bound to loyalty by a conquering monarch.

Jeremiah the later prophet, speaking near the destruction of Judah (586 B.C.), tells us God will make a new covenant (testament), written on people's hearts (Jer. 31:31). This idea is taken up by the NT writers. In Hebrews we read of a new covenant made in Jesus Christ (Heb. 7:1-22; 8:8 ff.). This new testament is primarily seen in the Eucharistic meal shared by Jesus with his disciples before his death, and recelebrated every Lord's Day by the emerging Christian church. Paul, in Galatians 4:21-28, connects the original testament (covenant) of God's promises made to Abraham and the new testament made in Jesus, showing the primacy of PROMISE over the LAW given to Moses in the covenant at Sinai.

J.C.

**TESTAMENTS OF THE TWELVE PATRIARCHS.** *See* PSEUDEPIGRAPHA.

**TESTEM BENEVOLENTIAE.** This ENCYCLICAL by Pope Leo XIII, issued January 22, 1899, condemned Americanism, a liberal Catholic movement. It referred to the French translation of Walter Elliott's *Life of Father ISAAC HECKER* and declared certain doctrines to be in error without saying that either Hecker or other American theologians actually taught them.

N.H.

**TESTIMONY.** The offering of evidence or the bearing of WITNESS, either in a court proceeding or in the context of preaching or prophesying. The RSV translation—and most other English translations of the OT—use "testimony" for three Hebrew words that all share the radical (or three-letter root, in Hebrew), *UDH*, meaning "to bear witness" or "to testify." In the NT, similarly, there are three Greek terms that are translated as "testimony." In both testaments, "testimony" refers to prophetic witness, as in Isaiah 8:16, 20 and Matthew 8:4 (KJV). In Ruth 4:7 (KJV), "testimony" refers to evidence in a business contract. In I Corinthians 1:6 and II Timothy 1:8, it refers to witnessing to the salvation made possible through Christ. Hebrews 11:5 (KJV) uses "testimony" to refer to prophecy given by Enoch.

J.C.

**TESTING.** God tests individuals and groups to know what is in their hearts (Deut. 8:2), to motivate them to grow as Christian people (Jas. 1:2-4), and to prepare them for Christian service (Matt. 4:1-17). God allows Satan to tempt people in order that they may grow (Matt. 4:1). But God tempts no one (Jas. 1:13).

In the OT God tests individuals: Abraham (Gen. 22:1), Hezekiah (II Chr. 32:31); nations: Israel (Exod. 15:25; Deut. 33:8); and objects: a sword (I Sam. 17:39) or a reputation (I Kings 10:1).

In the NT God tests Jesus through the TEMPTATION by Satan to prepare him for his ministry (Luke 4:1-13). The faithful can also expect to be tested (I Pet. 4:12-13). The NT also speaks of the final testing that is to come upon the whole earth (Rev. 3:10).

In both the OT and NT the concept of testing is closely linked with the promises of God. Abraham was encouraged to go through a series of tests by the promise of a land, an heir, many descendants, and a blessing to come to all nations. Testing thereby becomes an important way in which God works with people.

B.J.

**TETRAGRAMMATON.** *See* YAHWEH.

**TETRARCH.** In Greek, the ruler of a fourth part of a land or territory. A tetrarch may once have been of lower status than an ethnarch, which was in turn lower than a king. When Herod the Great died in 4 B.C., his lands went to three sons. Of these, Herod Antipas and Philip were usually referred to as tetrarchs, and Archelaus as an ethnarch. But all these words were generally interchangeable in common use. How significant a petty ruler was, and what he was called, often depended on his territory, wealth, education, and status. In Roman histories Herod the Great is often called tetrarch and equally often king. Usually in the NT Herod the Tetrarch means Herod Antipas, as in Matthew 14:1, Luke 3:1, and other passages. But in Mark 6:14 and Matthew 14:9 the same Antipas is styled king. Luke 3:1 cites two other tetrarchs, Herod Philip, the brother of Antipas, and Lysanias.

T.J.K.

**TEVETH.** *See* HEBREW CALENDAR.

**TEXT OF THE BIBLE.** *See* BIBLE, TEXT OF.

**TEXTUAL CRITICISM.** *See* BIBLICAL CRITICISM.

**TEXTUS RECEPTUS.** *See* RECEIVED TEXT.

**THADDAEUS.** One of the twelve disciples of the Lord, often called Judas, but not Judas Iscariot. The KJV of the Bible describes him as a brother of James, but the RSV lists him as the son of James. Luke usually calls him Judas (Luke 6:16; Acts 1:13), but in Matthew 10:3 and Mark 3:18 his name appears in the usual sequence with the other disciples as Thaddaeus. In some variant readings of the older Bible manuscripts his name also appears as "Lebbaeus whose surname was Thaddaeus." He is also sometimes confused in early Christian writing with Addai (Thaddaeus' name in Syriac is Taddai), one of the seventy disciples who brought Christianity to the area of the Black Sea.

T.J.K.

**THEBES.** One of the best-known national capitals in the ancient world. It lies on both sides of the Nile about four hundred miles south of Cairo. Throughout much of Egypt's long history, Thebes was the nation's well-fortified (Nah. 3:8) military, political, and religious center. Thebes is mentioned in the OT only in the late books of Jeremiah, Ezekiel, and Nahum. The reason for this is that Israel's earlier dealings with Egypt and its pharaohs were with monarchs who

Courtesy of Trans World Airlines

*Massive columns in the temple of Karnak at Thebes*

Courtesy of Trans World Airlines

*Avenue of the sphinxes, temple of Karnak*

Courtesy of Trans World Airlines

*The temple of Luxor, at Thebes*

chose capitals or alternate capitals in Egypt's delta region, far nearer to the Palestine border, which these pharaohs were eager to defend.

The city of Thebes is divided into two parts: Karnak, situated on the east bank, the city of the living, with palaces, temples, shops, offices, and residences; and Luxor, on the west bank, the city of the dead, with funeral temples and elaborate tombs for royal and wealthy persons.

The ancient name of the city was Wase or Wo'se, dating from the age of the Pyramids. The place became Egypt's capital about 2040 B.C. and was known as Nowe or Nuwe, "the city of Amun." That name appears in Hebrew as "No'Amun" or "No" (Jer. 46:25). It was the Greeks who named the city after their own Thebes in Boeotia. Luxor at that time was called Ta-ope, which sounded to the Greeks like Thebes.

Like Rome, Thebes is noted for its monumental temples and tombs. Pharaoh after pharaoh exhausted the riches of the nation in erecting, adding to, or embellishing these enduring buildings, which were intended to memorialize their builders' names as well as to be gifts to the gods, chiefly Amun. Amun's temple at Karnak was and is the centerpiece of Thebes. Its ruins cover an immense area and consist of a complex of temples in an incoherent plan. There are ten pylons, a number of processional gateways, and an avenue of sphinxes two miles long. The most imposing part is a pillared hall, dedicated to AMON-RE, king of the gods, with fourteen enormous columns 78 feet high and a clerestory to admit light and air. There are 140 other columns in the temple. Its walls are covered with reliefs and inscriptions showing and telling the victories of the pharoahs; some of them recount Seti's and Sheshonq's triumphs in Palestine as well as Ramses II defeating the Hittites at Kadesh in Syria (about 1299 B.C.).          P.L.G.

**THEISM.** The basic religious doctrine of Christians, Jews, and Muslims that GOD exists. This God who is, is spirit, personal and intentional, omnipotent, omnipresent, omniscient, perfectly good, eternal, and the creator and preserver of the universe. Only this one God is the worthy subject of human worship and obedience.                              J.C.

**THEOCRACY.** From the Greek word *theokratia* meaning "the rule of God." In a theocracy the people or tribes are thought to be ruled directly by God, as in ancient Israel, in Calvin's commonwealth at Geneva, in early New England, or in some parts of Islam. The word is first used in Josephus, who contrasts it to monarchy or democracy, to describe the system of government at the time of Moses. He writes of the nomadic shepherd's need to be completely free of human interference, but yet to depend on the guidance and leadership of a divine being, to live out a fulfilled life.

God can express leadership in many ways, perhaps through leaders like Moses and Aaron, perhaps through a judge like Gideon or Deborah, perhaps even through a Nazirite like Samson. Yet it is not these individuals who are governing, but God, through human agents. Such a theocratic government was first established at Sinai. God demanded pledges of the people, and God was committed to their welfare and support. Even the annual COVENANT meal emphasized once again the importance of this theocratic relationship (Exod. 24:3-11). The basic ingredient if such a state is to succeed is the loyalty and trust of the people. God's symbolic presence in the tabernacle, between the cherubim, was the assurance of God's continued guidance and direction, as was the system of the twelve tribes, the burnt offerings, and the ark.

The medieval concepts of feudalism and of the divine right of kings adopted much of their philosophy from that of the OT theocracy, except that the intermediaries of God's authority were now dukes, barons, bishops, and kings.          T.J.K.

**THEODICY.** *See* EVIL.

**THEODORET** (about 393–466). Able Antiochene theologian and bishop of Cyrus near Antioch, deeply involved in the fifth-century controversies over Christ's nature. Born in Antioch and educated in monastery schools, Theodoret gave away his property, became a monk around 415, and bishop about 423. Friend and ex-classmate of Nestorius, Theodoret resented Cyril of Alexandria's railroading of Nestorius and wrote against Cyril before and after the COUNCIL OF EPHESUS (431), which condemned and deposed Nestorius in a brief session. In 433 Cyril, hoping to ease tensions, accepted a faith statement written by Theodoret, but Dioscorus, Cyril's successor, denounced Theodoret's alleged division of Christ into two sons. Theodoret's new faith statement asserted Christ's unity and condemned anyone who rejected *Theotokos* (Mary as the "Mother of God"), even the NESTORIANS. Dioscorus continued harassing Theodoret and influenced the "robber" Ephesian council in 449 to depose him. Summoned to the Council of Chalcedon (451), Theodoret was acquitted and restored, after condemning Nestorius. However, in the aftermath of Chalcedon, Theodoret was again condemned by the Council of Constantinople (553). Although few have survived, Theodoret wrote numerous defenses of Christianity, biblical treatises, theological tomes, and historical works. He continued Eusebius' *Ecclesiastical History* to 428, still extant.
                                                                          C.M.

*THEOLOGICA GERMANICA* ("German Theology"). A German mystical work from the late fourteenth century that influenced Luther and later Pietism with its subtle denigration of external works. Although of unknown authorship, the book came from near Frankfurt am Main, probably written by one or more people associated wth the Friends of God, which a layman, Ruleman Merswin of Strassburg (1703–82), apparently founded. Reflecting MEISTER ECKHART and JOHANN TAULER, the work stressed inward transformation, love, and complete surrender to God's will. Scripturally oriented, the "German Theology" identified sin as inordinate self-will—claiming for oneself what truly comes from God. It emphasized spiritual pride and lawless freedom as self-will's chief fruits. Those who aim for perfection wish only to be used by God. Union with God is effected not by creaturely works, exercises, or cunning flowing from self-will but by surrender to divine will. Luther republished the book in 1516 and 1518.                              C.M.

**THEOLOGICAL VIRTUES.** In Christian tradition, especially in Roman Catholicism, there are three theological virtues: faith, hope, and love (charity).

These three virtues, identified by Paul in I Corinthians 13, were added to the four CARDINAL VIRTUES of prudence, temperance, justice, and fortitude, which were derived from Greek philosophy. Faith, hope, and love are said to be infused into the person by God.                                                J.C.

**THEOLOGY.** *See* SYSTEMATIC THEOLOGY.

**THEOLOGY OF GLORY.** The Latin expression *theologiae gloriae*, meaning "theology of glory," was used by Luther, Barth, and others as the opposite of *theologia crucis*, THEOLOGY OF THE CROSS. Whereas the latter looks only to the humiliated and suffering Christ for the knowledge of God, the theology of glory claims that there is a direct knowledge of God accessible through the exercise of reason in natural theology. The advocates of a theology of the cross deny that there is any such direct route to the knowledge of God, which lies beyond the reach of finite and sinful creatures and is given only in the divine condescension in Jesus Christ.       J.M.

**THEOLOGY OF THE CROSS.** The Latin expression *theologia crucis*, meaning "theology of the cross," is associated chiefly with Luther. In opposition to the Scholastic teaching that there is a "natural" knowledge of God open to all human beings, Luther held that we know God only in the humiliation and passion of Jesus Christ. In the condescension of the Incarnation, God is veiled so as to be communicated to our creaturely spirits. In recent times Karl Barth has revived the expression *theologia crucis*. He called for theological obedience to the revelation in Christ, and denounced what he considered to be the arrogance of natural theology as the creature's attempt to grasp at God. (*See also* THEOLOGY OF GLORY.)       J.M.

**THEONOMY.** From the Greek words *theos* (God) and *nomos* (law) meaning "the law of human reason united with its ultimate ground, or God." The term was brought into current usage by the theologian PAUL TILLICH, who contrasts theonomy with autonomy and heteronomy in his writings on religion and culture.

AUTONOMY is the obedience of the individual to the law of reason, which one finds within one's own mind or conscience. Autonomy was the ideal of the ENLIGHTENMENT. HETERONOMY (from *heteros* or strange) is a law of reason or conscience commanded from outside. It represents an alien law, religious or secular, imposed upon the mind. The history of thought and religion reveals the continuous struggle and fluctuation between autonomous and heteronomous reason and authority. Both claim to speak in the name of what is unconditional or ultimate. However, individual autonomy often is empty and illusory, while heteronomy denies personal freedom and easily becomes totalitarian.

Theonomy is autonomous reason united with its ultimate ground or depth, that is, God. In a theonomous culture, individual reason actualizes itself in obedience to its divine ground. The late Middle Ages was a theonomous age, when religion and culture were one. Tillich insists that there is, however, no complete theonomy under the conditions of historical existence. He sees the yearning for theonomy, for the union of individual reason and its unconditional ground, as the quest for revelation or the KAIROS.       J.L.

**THEOPHANY.** From the Greek words *theos* (god) and *phainein* (appear). A temporary showing, REVELATION, or appearance of God to people, not unrelated to epiphany. In the OT there are frequent examples of theophany, especially in the times before the Babylonian Captivity. Sometimes the Lord seems to appear bodily, in visible form, sometimes as an angel or messenger, often in a cloud or fire relating to a glorious and majestic presence. Some of the best known of these many appearances are the ones to Abraham at the oaks of Mamre (Gen. 18:1; very popular as a subject for Orthodox icon painting), to Moses in the burning bush (Exod. 3), or to the prophet Elijah in the cave at Horeb (I Kings 19:9-14).

The most frequent and awesome theophanies are those related to the Ten Commandments, the Ark of the Covenant, and the tabernacle. Usually these incidents reflect God's glory and majesty, as when God appeared at a distance to the people in smoke, fire, lightning, and the sound of trumpets. Many passages of the OT (Exod. 3:6 or 33:20) insist that no one can see God and live. Yet there is an equal amount of testimony about those who actually did see God and did survive (Gen. 32:30; Judg. 6:22-23; Deut. 4:33). Moses sometimes appears to have seen God face to face, sometimes only from the back.

In the NT, Christ became "flesh and dwelt among us, . . . we have beheld his glory, glory as of the Son of the Father," a kind of living theophany. Appearances such as those at Christ's baptism, the angel that freed Peter from prison, or the fiery tongues at Pentecost are probably not theophanies in the most normal sense. One other use of theophany is the appearance of Christ at his Second Coming.

T.J.K.

**THEOPHILUS.** The name, meaning a "person loved by God," attached to the addressee of Luke's two-volume work (Luke 1:3; Acts 1:1). Evidently Luke saw some significance in this fact, since both his writings underline the wide embrace of the Christian message to include the Gentile world as "loved by God."

The name may well be generic and designate the world of Luke's interest. Against this is the adjective "most excellent," which rather suggests an honorific title of a man highly placed in Roman circles as enjoying rank, such as Felix and Festus, who were procurators of Judea (Acts 23:26; 24:3; 26:25).

According to this view, Luke had some well-known representative of Roman officialdom in his mind, and from Luke 1:4 it seems this man professed an initial interest in the Christian gospel by becoming an inquirer or catechumen. He was in need of further instruction (see Luke 1:4, "that you may know the truth") and possibly required to be steered away from misconceptions of Christianity that he had entertained. No certain clue to his precise identity is found.          R.M.

**THEOSOPHY.** A religious movement fostered by the Theosophical Society founded by Helena Petrovna Blavatsky and others in 1885. Emphasis is placed on finding deeper spiritual reality, mystical experience, and inner, hidden spiritual meaning. There is also an interest in occult phenomena. Theosophy is monistic, asserting a unity of mind and spirit that tends to negate the objective reality of evil. Theosophists believe in a basic eternal principle beyond human understanding. They seek to investigate unexplained powers and laws in the universe.

The American section has split several times over questions of leadership. The Indian section developed through the work of Annie Besant. Although small, the Theosophical Society has been influential in popularizing Asian religion and philosophy in the West and has stimulated a revival of Buddhism and Hinduism in Asia.          I.C.

**THEOTOKOS.** *See* MOTHER OF GOD.

**THERAVADA BUDDHISM.** *See* BUDDHISM.

**I AND II THESSALONIANS.** Written by the apostle Paul, with Silvanus and Timothy, to the church in THESSALONICA shortly after its foundation. The common view is that these two letters are the earliest in the Pauline collection. Beyond doubt I Thessalonians is an authentic writing of the apostle, for while he speaks of his colleagues as active partners in the nurture of these recent converts, he also shares himself, as well as the gospel, with the Thessalonians, for they "had become very dear" to him (I Thess. 2:7-12, 17-20). The origin of II Thessalonians is less certain. It lacks the affectionate tone of I Thessalonians. Its apocalyptic passage, II Thessalonians 2:1-12, details events that will occur before the return of Jesus, whereas I Thessalonians states that no predictable signs will be given heralding the End.

Various attempts have been made to explain these and other differences: (a) II Thessalonians antedates I Thessalonians; (b) II Thessalonians is a pseudonymous letter; (c) II Thessalonians was addressed to Jewish Christians; I Thessalonians to Gentiles in the church. It may be that (a) eases some problems. Paul's letters in the NT are placed in a descending order according to their length. The letter's pseudonymity (b) is unlikely since those who have advanced this premise have provided no satisfactory motive for its composition. It is also unlikely (c) that Paul would have fostered separations in the church between Christians

of Jewish and Gentile origins. Note I Thessalonians 5:27. It is probable that Paul wrote II Thessalonians soon after I Thessalonians and addressed both letters to the same persons. First Thessalonians was dispatched from Corinth during Paul's first visit to this major city and shortly after Timothy's return from Macedonia (I Thess. 3:1-12; Acts 18:5). Adopting the date usually given for Paul's first mission in Corinth, one may conclude that I Thessalonians was written within the year A.D. 50-51; II Thessalonians shortly afterward. References in both letters to the founding of the church and subsequent developments imply a somewhat longer ministry than the notice in Acts implies.

*The Form of I Thessalonians.*

A. Greeting, 1:1
B. Thanksgiving for the Thessalonians' endurance and progress, 1:2-10
C. Opposition: insidious aspersions concerning Paul's motives and conduct; the apostle's defense, 2:11-16
D. Post-campaign events recalled, 2:17–3:10
E. A prayer for the church, 3:11-13
F. Deficiencies in the church's life and thought:
  1. Moral injunctions, 4:1; 5:12
  2. Encouragement concerning the "coming" of Christ—life today in the light of this event, 4:13–5:22
G. Final prayer and farewell, 5:23-28

It is noteworthy that Paul is not drawn into doctrinal disputes in I Thessalonians, and that no references are made to a specific form of opposition. Therefore some of the major themes of the apostle's polemical theology are not treated: justification by faith; dying and rising with Christ; the church as the Body of Christ, etc. Paul had many reasons to commend this congregation. It had had a good beginning (I Thess. 1:9-12; 2:13; compare II Thess. 1:3-4, 11). The church's members had stood fast in the midst of persecutions (I Thess. 3:1-8; compare II Thess. 1:3). What was needed most was encouragement, not rebuke; a deepening understanding of the gospel they had welcomed, not new instruction (I Thess. 3:12; 4:1-2, 9-10; compare II Thess. 2:5; 3:4). There were, however, some shortcomings. Paul prayed for the opportunity to "supply what was lacking" by means of a face-to-face encounter, but some matters were of such urgency that he could not wait (I Thess. 3:9-10; 4:13; compare II Thess. 2:1-12).

*Paul's Eschatological Teaching in I Thessalonians.* According to Paul's response it is clear that unresolved grief, occasioned by the death of loved ones, was deeply troubling some members of the church. It was feared that those who had "fallen asleep" were precluded from salvation, that God willed to deny them that final blessedness to be enjoyed by those who live to experience the coming (PAROUSIA) of Christ. The apostle's teaching contains traditional and distinctively Pauline elements.

First of all, the apostle cites the common creed of the early church: "we believe that Jesus died and rose again" (I Thess. 4:14; Paul's usual statement is that Jesus *was raised*, I Cor. 6:14; 15:4, 12-14). The apostle then appeals to "a word of the Lord": procedural priority shall be given those who have fallen asleep, the dead in Christ shall come with him (I Thess. 4:15-17; compare I Cor. 15:51-52). Perhaps this assurance was given to Paul in a post-resurrection appearance (note Gal. 1:12; 2:2). The apostle next employs a metaphor used by Jesus to declare the unpredictability of the coming Day of the Lord— "like a thief in the night" (I Thess. 5:2. compare Matt. 24:43-44; Luke 12:39-40). This element of surprise causes Christ's own no dread, for they already belong to "the day": they are not destined for wrath but to obtain salvation through him (I Thess. 5:5-10). For Paul, the coming of the Day of the Lord was not only a future event, but a present reality; a lasting union with Chist had already been established, a union indissoluble even in death (I Thess. 5:10; compare Rom. 8:31-39). In the meantime the three theological virtues—faith, love, and hope—provide the best equipment for the warrior who is not able to know in advance when and how Christ's final victory will be shared.

*The Form of II Thessalonians.*

A. Greeting, 1:1-2
B. Thanksgiving for the progress of the church; a prayer for those being persecuted; assurances of recompense, 1:3-12
C. Concerning the Day of the Lord, and the man of lawlessness:
    1. The rebellion comes first, 2:1-2
    2. The apocalyptic scenario, 2:3-12
D. Paul's conviction concerning the election of his converts; prayers for them and theirs for him, 2:13–3:5
E. A command concerning "the idle" among the brethren, 3:6-15
F. Closing prayer; signature, 3:16-18

*The Eschatological Teaching in II Thessalonians.*

It is probable that the actions of the emperor Gaius (Caligula) provide the background for Paul's allusions to "the man of lawlessness." In A.D. 40, Gaius had given orders to set up a statue to him in Jerusalem's Temple. The emperor's decree was withdrawn at the last moment, but this crisis forewarned Jews and Christians of a real and lasting threat, and may have contributed to Paul's dreaded expectancy (II Thess. 2:8-10; compare Mark 13:14-23). The restraining factor, if not the critical role of Paul's mission to the Gentiles, may be a reference to Roman law and order, embodied in Gaius' successor, the emperor Claudius.

In no other letter does Paul draw so extensively upon APOCALYPTICISM. Did he come to realize the limited value of this opaque imagery for a faithful exposition of the Christians' hope, which was based upon the passion, death, and resurrection of Jesus the Christ?     J.L.P.

**THESSALONICA.** When the apostle Paul established a church in this principal city of Macedonia (Acts 17:1-9), it was a thriving commercial center and maritime base. The site of several ancient settlements, Thessalonica was refounded by Cassander, king of Macedonia, in 315 B.C., who named it after his wife, a stepsister of Alexander the Great. After the conquest of the Romans, Pompey made this city the headquarters for his campaigns in the East. In the power struggles among the successors of Julius Caesar, the Thessalonians sided with the victors. Octavian designated Thessalonica a "free city" and assigned its government to five or six *politarches*. Luke's accuracy in identifying the city's authorities by this title is corroborated by an inscription on a local arch (Acts 17:6, 8).

Paul came to Thessalonica overland via the Egnatian Way about A.D. 49. For three Sabbaths he preached in the synagogue, the result being that "some [Jews] . . . a great many of the devout Greeks [Godfearers] and not a few of the leading women" became believers (Acts 17:2-4; compare I Thess. 1:8). Paul's ministry was terminated when some of the synagogue authorities stirred up the populace and charged Paul with politically subversive activities. The charge was a serious one, since Jewish communities in several regions were at this time in a restive, militant mood. Remaining cool, the authorities arrested Jason and some others (Paul's hosts), making them go bail for Paul's good behavior. Out of consideration for his recent converts Paul left Thessalonica under cover of darkness, an action that susequently left him open to accusations of not caring (I Thess. 2:1-12, 17-18). According to I Corinthians 16:5, Paul later revisited Macedonia (Acts 20:1-3). Two letters in the Pauline collection are addressed to the THESSALONIANS.     J.L.P.

**THIELICKE, HELMUT** (1908 – ). German Lutheran pastor and theologian whose writings have had considerable influence within evangelical Protestantism in Europe and North America in recent decades. Thielicke was educated at Greifswald, Marburg, Erlangan, and Bonn. He served as a parish minister at Ravensburg, and as head of the Theological Office of the Württemberg Church. His theological work is closely related to the concerns of the church and preaching, and he was first introduced to the English-speaking world through his sermons.

Thielicke was removed from his university post and interned by the Nazi government during World War II. The war experience is reflected in his prolific output of sermons, essays, speeches, radio talks, articles, and books in the years following the war. Thielicke served as professor at Heidelberg (1936–40), Tübingen (1945–54), and Hamburg (1954–74), and as rector of both Tübingen (1951) and Hamburg (1960) universities. He was a popular teacher and lectured to packed halls of students. His two most

Courtesy of Wm. B. Eerdmans Publishing Company

*Helmut Thielicke*

important works are his *Theological Ethics* (4 vols.; Eng. trans. 1964–69), a three-thousand-page work, perhaps the most extensive analysis of Christian ethics in Protestantism since the Reformation, and a three-volume systematic theology, *The Evangelical Faith* (1968–78; Eng. trans. 1974–82). The *Ethics* treats foundational questions in Christian ethics, issues of politics, church and state, and sexual ethics. Many of the traditional Lutheran themes—law and gospel, the orders of creation, Luther's two kingdoms, and the discussion of Catholic natural law—are prominent in Thielicke's ethical analysis. Among his other works, available in English, are *Between Heaven and Earth, Faith and Action, Nihilism, The Silence of God,* and *Man in God's World.*                    J.L.

**THIGH.** The leg bone joining the hip to the knee, the longest bone of the human body. The numerous biblical references to thigh may literally refer to the bones of animals or a human. The phrase to put "sword on thigh" means "to fight" (Judg. 3:16; Ps. 45:3; Song of S. 3:8; Ezek. 21:4). When the Hebrew word for thigh is translated "shaft," it refers to the riser of lampstands (Exod. 25:31; 37:17). To "smite upon the thigh" refers to a gesture of shame or sorrow (mentioned only in Jer. 31:19). Thigh is also translated "side," as in north side, south side, right side, or left side (Exod. 32:27; 40:22-24). The translation "thigh" or "loins" is a substitute for penis, the male organ (Gen. 24:2, 9; 47:29). Thigh in Judges 8:30 appears in the KJV as "sons of his body (thigh)." In Exodus 1:5 (KJV), reference is made to "all the souls that came out of the loins (thigh) of Jacob." Thus, oaths taken "under" the patriarch's "thigh" may be understood as in contact with his penis, the rationale being: (1) that the oath is rendered serious by being witnessed by the superior seat of life, and (2) that the descendants of the superior are honor bound to enforce obedience to the oath and to act in vengeance if the oath is broken. The practice is mentioned only of Abraham (Gen. 24:2, 9) and of Jacob (Gen. 47:29; Exod. 1:5).          P.L.G.

**THIRD ROME.** A theory of Moscow's divine election to protect Christianity. Philotheos (early sixteenth century) argued that Rome became heretical, Constantinople (second Rome) compromised with Rome's heresy at Florence (1439) only to fall in 1453, and Moscow became third Rome when Russia, through Ivan the Great's marriage (1472), assumed Christianity's protection.          C.M.

**THIRTY-NINE ARTICLES.** The doctrinal formulas of the Church of England, also used by Protestant Episcopal and Methodist churches. Although not a creed, they are short summaries of dogmatic tenets on a variety of issues occasioned by the theological controversies of the sixteenth century. Since 1865 clergy of the CHURCH OF ENGLAND have been required to give only general assent to them.

The Thirty-nine Articles began as Ten Articles issued in 1536, to parallel the Lutherans' Wittenberg Articles. In 1538 Thomas Cranmer and a group of colleagues agreed with a group of Lutherans on a series of Thirteen Articles based on the Augsburg Confession. In 1549 Cranmer drew up a code to be signed by clerics wishing to be licensed. From May 1552 a version of these was discussed by the bishops, who in October 1552 referred the matter to a committee of six, including John Knox.

Edward VI approved the resulting Forty-two Articles in 1553. With excisions and additions these became ELIZABETH I's Thirty-nine Articles (1571). JOHN WESLEY reduced them to twenty-four, which with one addition asserting the autonomy of the new American nation, have survived in the Methodist *Discipline.* The Articles are decisively Protestant, declaring a commitment to belief in original sin (IX) and justification by faith (XI). On election their approach is supralapsarian. The Article on the Lord's Supper (XXVIII) is more of a compromise than a theological consensus.          N.H.

**THOMAS, ACTS OF.** One of a collection of writings known as the Apocryphal Acts, purporting to retell the doings of the apostles after the birth of the church, but almost certainly a product of Gnostic Christianity. The traits that characterize the Acts of Thomas as Gnostic are (1) a view of redemption that is world-denying, ascetic, and based on secret lore, and (2) a myth that recounts, in poetic idiom, the visitation of the redeemer. In the "Wedding Hymn" (chap. 6 ff.) the redeemer's relation to his people is akin to a bridal one, typical of Valentinian religion, a second-third-century system of GNOSTICISM. The document also contains the celebrated "Hymn of the Pearl" (chaps. 108–113), which is an extended allegory based on the tale of a prince sent to Egypt to recover a pearl. He is enticed by the luxuries of Egypt and sidetracked from his mission by falling into a stupor, until he is aroused by a message from home. Thus bestirred, he executes his mission and returns home to receive again the beautiful robe he had left there. Clearly the story is a parable of the soul's fall into the obliviousness that would lead to ruin unless it had been stirred up by the Gnostic appeal. Then it regains its high honor, being clothed with splendor on its reascent to the heavenly region. There is also the possibility that the allegory cloaks a mission of the Gnostic redeemer on his visit to earth and subsequent return to the Father of all.

The Acts of Thomas exists in two versions: Greek and Syriac. Its origin is evidently in Syria, at Edessa, and may be dated in early third century. It was highly valued at one time by orthodox Christians, but its use by the Manichaeans, a second-third-century group of ascetics, who claimed it and interpreted it in line with their teaching, meant it lost its appeal.

Its main story line is of THOMAS, who is appointed apostle to India. His exploits there are told, with stress on his miracles and his celibate life, thus praising the single state and condemning marriage and the home life of orthodox Christians.     R.M.

## THOMAS, APOSTLE.

THOMAS, APOSTLE. One of the Twelve whom Jesus called to follow and serve him (Matt. 10:3; Mark 3:18; Luke 6:15; Acts 1:13). In the Fourth Gospel he is further identified as the Twin (John 11:16; 20:24; 21:2), with a textual and ecclesiastical variant that makes his full name Judas Thomas, otherwise known as Judas the Twin, that is, the twin brother of Jesus, being the same person as in Mark 6:3. This information is given in the apocryphal ACTS OF THOMAS, and in the Syriac versions of John 14:22.

Thomas' character can only be partially pieced together from a few references to him, mainly in the Fourth Gospel. He appears in dialogue with Jesus (John 11:16; 14:5), suggesting both a courageous zeal, "Let us also go, that we may die with him," but also a weak grasp of who Jesus was. Jesus is said to have corrected him (John 14:6-7), and the trait of skepticism is further illustrated in John 20:24-25, where, since Thomas was absent from a resurrection appearance on Easter Day, he doubted the reality of Jesus' rising again and wanted tangible proof. So the

proverb "doubting Thomas" was created; but his full faith is seen in his confession, a week later (John 20:28). His return to a fisherman's trade is recorded in John 21:1-14; and he is again with the apostolic band in the upper room according to Acts 1:12-14.

Later church tradition makes much of Thomas' missionary exploits, assigning him a sphere of service in Parthia (so Eusebius), and in India (according to the Acts of Thomas), where he is revered as church founder and martyr. Documents are extant—such as the *Martyrdom of St. Thomas in India*—that are claimed by the present-day Mar Thoma church in southwest India as part of the wide group of Malabar Christians. Other traditions locate his missionary work and death in Edessa on the Syrian border.
R.M.

## THOMAS, GOSPEL OF.

THOMAS, GOSPEL OF. There is an Infancy Gospel of Thomas, extant in several languages, which tells some fabled stories of the miracle-working childhood and boyhood of Jesus as an infant prodigy. His use of miracle-power is bizarre, such as the ability to lengthen a beam of wood, his turning models of clay birds into live ones that fly off, and the striking dead a playmate in the village. All this is docetic in tone, that is, it denies the full human life of Jesus in the interests of promoting his divine powers.

By contrast, the Coptic Gospel of Thomas is a compendium of sayings, 114 in number, most beginning with "Jesus said." There is hardly any narrative to frame the sayings. The logia are of various kinds; many are gnostic in flavor, insinuating that Jesus came to enlighten the elect and to abolish death, thereby releasing the soul held in bondage. Some are parallel with the canonical Gospels' record, especially in the Synoptic Gospels and notably in the common sayings source called Q found in the OXYRHYNCHUS papyri, but the full gospel was discovered as part of the NAG HAMMADI Coptic library, which was disclosed in Egypt in 1956. The material was published in translated form in 1959, and has been commented on with great interest since then. Some have argued that this document reveals a gospel used by Syrian Christians, and others have traced a continuing influence on the development of early wisdom Christology, that is, Christ is presented as a "wise teacher," instructing believers with proverbs and sagacious sayings.     R.M.

**THOMAS À KEMPIS.** *See IMITATION OF CHRIST.*

**THOMAS AQUINAS.** *See AQUINAS, THOMAS.*

**THOMAS CHRISTIANS.** A group of Christians in Kerala, South India, who believe on the basis of a third-century document (Acts of Thomas) that their Christian community was founded by the apostle THOMAS, sent to India by Jesus. The story is accepted by many Roman Catholic authorities. Most sober historians say that the story is credible, but that it lacks actual confirmation. This community in India was governed for centuries by bishops from Syria, uses Syriac in worship, and is often referred to as a Syrian church. The first Europeans to contact the church in modern times were the Portuguese in 1599. W.G.

**THOMISM.** This is the name given to the teaching of THOMAS AQUINAS (1225–74) and of his many followers. Thomism is both a philosophy and a theology—a philosophy that draws its categories and procedures from ARISTOTLE and other classical writers, and a theology that expounds Christian faith with the aid of these philosophical categories. Pope Leo XIII initiated a revival of Thomistic studies in 1879, giving to this philosophy something like an official status in the Roman Catholic Church. The revival, sometimes called neo-Thomism, produced such distinguished thinkers as JACQUES MARITAIN and ETIENNE GILSON. More recently, Thomism has moved on to the new phase of "transcendental" Thomism. In this form, it has confronted the transcendental philosophy of Kant and developed a dynamic concept of the human being. Leaders of the new development of Thomism include Joseph Maréchal, KARL RAHNER, and Bernard Lonergan. J.M.

**THOREAU, HENRY DAVID** (1817–62). The essayist, poet, and transcendentalist was born July 2 in Concord, Massachusetts, to John and Cynthia Dunbar Thoreau. Graduating from Harvard in 1837, he began his famous *Journal* in 1834 and continued it until his death from tuberculosis. He and his brother John took a thirteen-day vacation in September 1839, which became the basis for *A Week on the Concord and Merrimack Rivers.* In 1838 Thoreau gave the first of his almost annual lectures to the Concord Lyceum on "Society."

In 1841 he went to live with Ralph Waldo Emerson. The two became life-long friends and leading members of the Transcendental Club. In March 1845 Thoreau began to build a hut on Walden Pond, where he lived from 1845 to 1847. His stay and reflections on it became *Walden, or Life in the Woods,* published in 1854.

His concern for slavery led him to help a fugitive slave in 1851 and to defend John Brown in *A Plea for Captain John Brown* (1860). During his life he published a number of essays including "Civil Disobedience" (1849), "Slavery in Massachusetts" (1854), "Life without Principle" (1863). A number of other works were published posthumously including *Excursion in Field and Forest* (1863), *The Maine Woods* (1864), *Cape Cod* (1865), and *A Yankee in Canada* (1866). N.H.

**THUMMIM.** *See* URIM AND THUMMIM.

**THURNEYSEN, EDUARD** (1888–1974). Swiss Protestant pastor and theologian, best known for his

association with KARL BARTH and the beginnings of NEO-ORTHODOXY or dialectical theology. He was pastor successively at Leutwil in Aargau, Bruggen near St. Gall, and the Münster at Basel. His study of Dostoevsky (1921) had a significant influence on his fellow theologians. His other writings include *Come, Holy Spirit* (sermons, in collaboration with K. Barth, 1924); *Christoph Blumhardt* (1926); and *The Word of God and the Church* (1927). Thurneysen was an editor, with Barth, of the periodical *Zwischen den Zeiten* (*Between the Times,* 1923). Unlike EMIL BRUNNER and RUDOLF BULTMANN, Thurneysen never broke with Barth, and his correspondence with him is an important source of information about the early years of dialectical theology. J.L.

**THYATIRA.** A city in the Roman province of Asia on the main road from Pergamum to Sardis and on a tributary of the Hermus River, about sixty miles from Smyrna (modern Izmir). Thyatira is situated at the junction of two river valleys, a borderline fortress town. Ak-Hissar, its modern name, means "white castle."

In NT times, Thyatira had developed into a regional manufacturing and commercial center and was celebrated for its elaborately organized trade guilds. The bronze workers' guild may be reflected in Revelation 2:18. The dyers' guild had produced a special and famous purple dye (Turkish or Turkey red) made from the madder root grown in the region. The Phoenician purple dye came from murex shellfish. Lydia, a woman "from the city of Thyatira" whom Paul converted in Philippi (Acts 16:14), was "a seller of purple goods." Her name may have meant "woman of Lydia" since Thyatira, on the Lydia-Mysia border, was spoken of sometimes at the one and at other times at the other.

The trade guilds were closely allied to the city's pagan religious establishments, Apollo and Artemis mainly. Members were expected to join in the rituals, celebrations, and feasts with the "immorality" (Rev. 2:20-21) that a "Jezebel" type woman in the church seems to have practiced and to have encouraged other Christians to continue from their pagan past. Thus, Thyatira has a NT connotation of syncretism and compromise even though it was recognized that many in the church were not holding to Jezebel's "teaching" or had "learned what some call the deep things of Satan" (Rev. 2:24). P.L.G.

**TIBERIAS.** A city on the west bank of the Sea of Galilee, seven hundred feet below sea level. Its founder was the tetrarch Herod Antipas, who named it after Emperor Tiberius, made it his capital, and forced Jews to help construct it and live in it. Because of an earlier graveyard there, Jews considered the place ritually unclean. Christ frequently passed it by on the road, and it is mentioned in the NT only in connection with the Sermon on the Mount. There is good arable land along the shore, and Christ's own

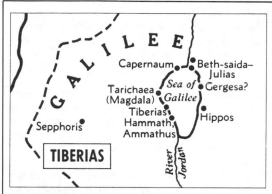

TIBERIAS

disciples demonstrated that the neighboring waters were good fishing grounds. From the natural rise of land at Tiberias there are fine views eastward five miles across the lake to Gergesa and Hippos, and northward to Magdala and Capernaum. Thermal baths made it a resort and a place of healing in Roman times.

After the destruction of Jerusalem, it became one of the most important cities among the Jews, once a leading rabbi had declared most of it ritually clean. It became the home of the supreme court or Sanhedrin. The Masoretic vowel-pointing of the OT was developed in Tiberias. It is the burial place of Maimonides, the prince of Jewish scholars. During the Inquisition in the fifteenth and sixteenth centuries many Jews from Spain fled there. Because of its warm climate it remains a favorite Jewish winter resort even now.          T.J.K.

TIBERIUS. The successor of AUGUSTUS as Roman emperor, appointed by the senate in A.D. 14. The Gospel of Luke dates the beginning of Jesus' ministry in the fifteenth year of Tiberius' reign (Luke 3:1). Other references in the Gospels to "Caesar" allude to Tiberius. His was "the likeness and superscription" on the coin presented to Jesus, who commented, "Render to Caesar the things that are Caesar's, and to God the things that are God's" (Mark 12:13-17 and parallels; John 19:12-15).

Tiberius refused to accept divine honors in Italy, but in Eastern provinces worship was accorded him. He encouraged the veneration of Augustus and sought to preserve the traditions of governance established by his illustrious predecessor. Tiberius showed little interest in religions and violently suppressed the Isis mystery cult following a scandal in a temple raised in her honor.

Intrigue brought Tiberius to power, and his late years were marred by intrigue. A praetorian prefect, Sejanus, conspired to depose the emperor, but the conspiracy was exposed and Sejanus was executed. It is thought that Sejanus was responsible for the appointment in A.D. 26 of Pontius Pilate as prefect of Judea, and that his anti-Semitism provoked the rioting that led Tiberius to order the expulsion of Jews from Rome around A.D. 19. The emperor died on March 16, A.D. 37, in his self-imposed exile at Capri, after an illness that left him deranged.          J.L.P.

TIBETAN BUDDHISM. See BUDDHISM.

T'IEN T'AI. See TENDAI.

TIGLATH-PILESER III. King of ASSYRIA and under the name by which he was known in biblical history, Pul, he was also King of Babylon (745–727 B.C.). He was the son of Adadnirari III and the father of SHALMANESER V. One of the most

*Tiglath-pileser III, from Nimrud*

active and important Assyrian kings for Israel and Judah. In 842 B.C., Jehu paid tribute to campaigning Shalmaneser III in Lebanon. Assyria's armies were occupied elsewhere until Tiglath-pileser III's first campaign (740 B.C.), which resulted in the conquest of Arpad in northern Syria, tribute to the Assyrian king being brought from Tyre, Damascus, Cilicia, Carchemish, and others (II Kings 19:13; Isa. 37:13). Tiglath-pileser III's next effort (734 B.C.) posed a threat to Damascus and Israel, but the invader was satisfied with receiving tribute from Menahem of

*Inhabitants of a conquered city being deported; from a bas-relief from the palace of Tiglath-pileser at Calah*

Israel (II Kings 15:19), Rezon of Damascus, and others, including Zabibi, queen of the Arabs.

In about 733 B.C. Tiglath-pileser III became aware that Damascus was rallying the anti-Assyrian forces of the Levant against him. He characteristically avoided a direct assault. He advanced through Phoenicia and as far down the coastline as Gaza, whose king fled to Egypt. Tiglath-pileser returned to accept Ahaz's tribute (II Kings 16:10) and the surrender of Pekah of Samaria (II Kings 15:29). When Tiglath-pileser III did finally attack Damascus, it fell (732 B.C.) without an ally. King Hoshea of Israel paid tribute, as did Ashkelon, Tyre, and others. Damascus was no longer a political power, and Assyria was free to organize Syria-Palestine into an Assyrian province. In each area, Assyrian inspectors were installed to check on the loyalty to Assyria and performance of the local administrators. Messengers with fresh horses stationed on the highways brought reports to Tiglath-pileser III's capitol at Calah, about twenty miles south of Nineveh. News of the slightest rebellion brought swift retribution. By 729 B.C. Tiglath-pileser III had become king of Babylon. The stage was set, as Egypt fully realized, for an extension of Assyrian rule southward beyond Syria-Palestine. This was left for Tiglath-pileser III's successors to accomplish.

P.L.G.

From *Atlas of the Bible* (Thomas Nelson & Sons Limited)

*The Tigris River emerging from the mountains near Ibn 'Omar*

**TIGRIS.** Known as Hiddekel in the OT, this was both one of the four rivers of Eden in Genesis 2:14 and the scene of one of the great visions of the prophet Daniel (Dan. 10:4). The eastern source of the Tigris rises near Lake Van in the Armenian highlands (now eastern Turkey), only a few miles from the source of its sister river, the EUPHRATES. It flows in a southeasterly direction and enters the great flood plain (Mesopotamia), which it shares with the Euphrates some 460 miles north of the Persian Gulf.

Along its total length of 1150 miles, the Tigris flows by the major centers of the ancient Mesopotamian cultures, including the Assyrian capital, Nineveh, and cult center, Assur. Even in times less ancient, the Parthians and Sassanians maintained their capital at Ctesiphon, on its banks; the Hellenistic rulers of the Middle East built a capital nearby at Seleucia; and the Abbasid caliphs founded Baghdad on the Tigris in A.D. 762.

W.S.T.

**TILLICH, PAUL** (1886–1965). One of the most creative and influential Protestant theologians of the twentieth century. Born in Starzeddel, Germany, son of a Lutheran pastor, Tillich studied at several universities, including Berlin, Tübingen, and Halle. He received the degree of Doctor of Philosophy from Breslau in 1911 with a dissertation on FRIEDRICH W. J. VON SCHELLING. He served as an army chaplain for four years during the First World War. After the war, Tillich taught at Berlin and later was professor of theology at Marburg, Dresden, and Leipzig. In 1929 he became professor of philosophy at Frankfurt. At this time he was active in the Religious Socialist movement (*see* KAIROS), and his opposition to Hitler and national socialism resulted in his dismissal from his university chair. He left Germany in 1933 and settled in New York, where he served as professor of philosophical theology at Union Theological Seminary until 1955, also teaching at Columbia University. He was university professor at Harvard (1955–1962) and Nuveen professor of theology at the divinity school at the University of Chicago (1962–65).

Tillich was a prolific writer. His *Systematic Theology* (3 vols.; 1951–64) is one of the great works of constructive theology in this century. Among his other writings are *Interpretation of History* (1936), *The Protestant Era* (1948), *Courage to Be* (1952), *Love, Power, and Justice* (1954), *Dynamics of Faith* (1958), and three volumes of popular sermons: *Shaking of the Foundations* (1948), *The New Being* (1956), and *The Eternal Now* (1963).

The sources of Tillich's thought are many and complex. They include Platonism; the late medieval Christian mystics, such as Jacob Boehme; the German idealist philosophers, especially Schelling; and the existentialists, from KIERKEGAARD to HEIDEGGER. His writings reveal a unique joining of biblical, ontological, and existentialist language and concepts. Tillich says that theology must concern itself both with Christian truth *and* the human situation. He calls this the METHOD OF CORRELATION. Unlike the philosopher, the theologian stands within a community of faith or a "theological circle." The theologian analyzes the situation out of which the human existential questions arise and then seeks to demonstrate that the symbols used in the Christian message are the answers to these questions. Theology always begins with commitment, with an existential decision concerning the object of one's ULTIMATE CONCERN. Existential analysis reveals that finite existence is marked by a sense of estrangement symbolized by the Fall. Humanity's finite freedom, the source of anxiety, drives us from a state of "dreaming innocency," of undecided potentialities,

Courtesy of the University of Chicago Press, from Paul Tillich, *Systematic Theology* (University of Chicago Press, 1967).

*Paul Tillich*

to the actualization of freedom and existential estrangement. In the state of estrangement we seek salvation (*salvus*, meaning "healthy" or "whole") but cannot save ourselves.

Only God, the ground and power of all being, can save us from the forces that threaten our finite existence and can create a new being. Jesus Christ is the New Being, for he is essential God-personhood under the conditions of existential estrangement. In Jesus Christ the ground and power of being is revealed concretely, overcoming the forces that threaten creaturely existence. Those who participate in Christ are "new creatures," new beings. However, while living under the conditions of existential estrangement human beings are never fully healed. Hence the Christian hope for the ultimate communion of all beings in the eschatological new creation, the kingdom of God.

Tillich's analysis of the spiritual malaise of twentieth-century life, his understanding of religion as the depth-dimension of all human aspiration, and his existentialist reinterpretation of the themes of classical Christian theology form an unparalleled theological achievement in this century, and he has had a wide influence, both within and outside the church and theology.                                    J.L.

**TIME.** One of the great enigmas of philosophy, which seems to elude the grasp of thought. It is not an object of human experience that can be objectively studied, but is rather the form and condition of all human experience. Time, of course, can be measured objectively. We make clocks, based on that natural

clock which is the solar system, giving rise to the succession of days and months and years. This successiveness, that all things stand to one another in relations of "before" and "after," is one of the fundamental characteristics of time. Here we notice too a basic difference between time and space. Though scientists talk of space time, the distinction is that we can move in any direction in space and come back to the starting point; time is like a one-way street. The order of before and after is irreversible. We can develop these ideas a little further by contrasting time as we experience it in ourselves with time as we objectively measure it in the world.

Clock time is pure succession. Day follows day and year follows year. Human experience too is successive, but is not just pure succession. Indeed, we find pure succession rather frightening, as the past swallows up one moment after another, and the future remains veiled in uncertainty. Human beings, through memory and anticipation, are able to transcend mere successiveness. They live in a "span" of time rather than in a knife-edge instant. They have even visualized the possibility ("eternal life") of an experience in which past and future are gathered up in a present enjoyment that includes both—what Boethius called "the whole, simultaneous and complete fruition of a life without bounds." Perhaps the divine experience is like this, so that, as the psalmist supposed, a thousand years are to God like a day or a watch in the night. "Eternal life" then would not mean a life infinitely prolonged through time, but our participation in the divine experience of perfect simultaneous fruition, free from the tyranny of successiveness.

A further difference between clock time and humanly experienced time is this: clock time is uniform—as the seconds tick by, each one is like all the others, for they are all quantitatively defined. For the human being, time is qualitative as well as quantitative. There are times in life that seem to drag slowly, because they are empty, and times that are so full that they flash by. These are the times of crisis and decision, both in individual lives and the history of the race. Some biblical scholars have made a distinction between *chronos* (uniform time) and KAIROS (a time of crisis or fulfillment). This linguistic distinction has been challenged, but in any case we can recognize what is meant by the biblical expression, the FULLNESS OF TIME, a conjunction when the course of affairs has come to a decisive turning point.

Another question is whether time has a beginning or an end. In Christianity, it has generally been believed that there is both a beginning and an end, the time of creation and the time of consummation. In the nineteenth century, such ideas might have seemed utterly unscientific or anti-scientific. Nowadays, however, cosmologists can visualize certainly a beginning and possibly an end, and though their speculations have little to do with theological beliefs about CREATION and ESCHATOLOGY, they at least show that to talk of a beginning and an end is not an obvious absurdity.                                     J.M.

**TIMOTHY.** This man is mentioned in both Acts and the letters of Paul as a trusted colleague of the apostle and is the recipient of two letters sent to him when he fulfilled a role as church leader in Ephesus (I Tim. 1:3).

He was the son of a marriage that united two cultures. His Jewish Christian mother Eunice (II Tim. 1:5) and father, a Greek (Acts 16:1), represented the two streams of influence on his young life. His contact with Paul arose out of the latter's missionary journeys (Acts 13–14), which brought Paul to Timothy's native place, Lystra, in Asia Minor (Acts 16:2). The commendation of the church fellowship enabled Paul to enlist Timothy on the return visit to Lystra, perhaps as a replacement for John Mark, who had deserted the apostolic party earlier and was not deemed worthy to rejoin the group. At all events Timothy was sure to prove a valued member of the apostolic entourage, having been set apart for the work of ministry (I Tim. 1:18; 4:14; II Tim. 1:6).

Timothy's various commissions took him to Thessalonica and to Corinth (II Cor. 1:19). He was delegated to visit Corinth as Paul's envoy (I Cor. 4:17), but without much success. He was Paul's travel companion to Jerusalem and then to Rome (Acts 20:4-5) en route to the Holy City. We know of Timothy's association with Paul in Rome only from the so-called Captivity Epistles, especially Philippians, assuming these emanate from Rome. If Paul was released from Roman imprisonment, it would be possible that he then appointed Timothy to Ephesus while he headed west to Spain. But this is conjectural. At some point in his life Timothy shared an imprisonment (Heb. 13:23).

His character references are impeccable (Phil. 2:19-24; I Cor. 16:10; compare II Tim. 1:5-7), even if he was nervously fearful (II Tim. 1:7) and sickly (I Tim. 5:23).                                          R.M.

**I AND II TIMOTHY.** These two NT letters, addressed on their face to Timothy, Paul's junior colleague, along with Titus are called the PASTORAL EPISTLES.

*I Timothy.* Its features are a singular absence of personal information given to Timothy and they reflect very little of the writer's own circumstances. Timothy is evidently a church leader in Ephesus (1:3), and he is counseled to attend to his office as minister (4:11-14) with a backward glance to his ordination. The call he must heed is to remain loyal to the apostolic standards (6:20-21) given in the Pauline teaching.

The letter is notable for (a) its exposé of the false doctrine Timothy must resist (1:3-11, 18-20; 4:1-4: a type of Jewish GNOSTICISM seems to lie at the heart of these descriptions), and (b) its clear instructions or

directions for the recruitment, selection, maintenance, and disciplining of ministerial orders (3:1-16: overseers, deacons, deaconesses; 4:12–6:19: widows and elders in particular).

*II Timothy.* The writer is known to be a prisoner (1:8) and the prospect for his release is not good (in spite of a remarkable deliverance he has had, 4:6-8, 16-18). In the light of his impending martyrdom he writes to encourage Timothy, who is spoken to in personal terms, revealing his family background (1:3-7) and calling for his assistance in a moving plea (4:1-22).

In the face of aberrant teaching (2:1-3, 7; 3:10-11) Timothy is to remain committed to his task as an exponent of Paul's doctrine and draw an example for Paul's life (3:10-17). The presence of a block of material reflecting Paul's own plea and his autobiographical details has been argued for, with some cogency, in this letter; and this would explain the warmth and intimacy of many personal allusions.

R.M.

**TINDAL, MATTHEW** (1657–1733). A leading English rationalist and Deist. Educated at Oxford, Tindal briefly accepted Roman Catholicism but returned to the Church of England in 1688. Two early works, *The Rights of the Christian Church* (1706) and *Defence of the Rights of the Christian Church* (1709), aroused heated controversy. He attacked papalism and defended DEISM, rationalism, and Erastianism. His reputation rests on *Christianity as Old as the Creation* (1730), often called "the Deists' bible." Tindal argues that natural religion is all that is needed, and God has given human beings reason to apprehend it. The law of nature preceded revealed law, and God being immutable and perfect, revealed law can add nothing to the natural law. God's supreme gift to humankind is reason that rejects all superstitions and miracles. To advocate revelation is to insult God's perfectly ordered, mechanical universe. True Christianity is not new; it is as old as creation.                                                C.M.

**TIRHAKAH.** King of Ethiopia and Egypt, the third king of the Ethiopian dynasty, born about 709 B.C. Throughout his reign (690–644 B.C.), he was active in opposition to the Assyrian presence in Palestine. Tirhakah established his first capital in the delta to be nearer those he regarded as his vassals in Philistia, Phoenicia, and Syria-Palestine. Second Kings 19:9 states that Tirhakah was king of Ethiopia at the time of the Assyrian attack on Jerusalem in 701 B.C., and that he offered military support for Hezekiah's resistance to the Assyrians. Tirhakah was eight years old then. It is possible that Sennecherib invaded Egypt in 688 B.C., when Tirhakah was king of Egypt. At that time he was forced to flee to Thebes. Tirhakah continued the struggle and regained control. But, two years later, Ashurbanipal sent an expedition to Egypt, and Tirhakah had to flee from the delta to

Thebes a second time. Tirhakah died before Thebes fell to the Assyrians in 633 B.C. (Nah. 3:8).

P.L.G.

**TIRTHANKARA.** The Sanskrit word meaning "crossing maker." In JAINISM, one of a series of twenty-four great ascetics and teachers who aid persons in "crossing over" ordinary life and attaining liberation. Their cultus is central to Jain worship. While they are not gods, their memory and spiritual energy are invoked with simple offerings and chants. Most Tirthankaras are nonhistorical, but the last, MAHAVIRA, is accounted the founder of the present Jain religion.

R.E.

**TIRZAH.** Meaning "delight." (1) The last named daughter of Zelophehad, a descendant of Joseph through Manasseh. He had no son. Tirzah and her sisters were involved in a significant judicial decision dealing with women's rights to inherit property (Num. 26:33; 27:7; 36:2, 6, 10-11).

(2) A city in Samaria that for about forty years was the second capital of Israel. Its location on the road from Shechem to Beth-shan gave it a traditional reputation for beauty (Song of S. 6:4). It was, however, the scene of some of the ugliest episodes in Israel's political history: Elah was slain while drunk (I Kings 16:9-10), Zimri burned the palace down over himself (I Kings 16:18), and Menahem made a revolution (II Kings 15:14, 16).

P.L.G.

**TISHBE.** The name of a place, not precisely located, but in the hill country of Gilead about six or seven miles east of the Jordan River, perhaps modern Khi Lisdib. The name is associated with the prophet Elijah, who is called "the Tishbite," an inhabitant of Tishbe (I Kings 17:1; 21:17, 28; II Kings 1:3, 8; 9:36).

P.L.G.

**TISHRI.** *See* HEBREW CALENDAR.

**TITHE.** From ancient times, the tenth part of a person's income and/or property devoted to religious use as an offering, or to political use as a tax or tribute. Across the Middle East and Mediterranean world, in every center of civilization, and among nomadic peoples, the concept of the tithe, as a person's obligation to Deity (sometimes to the king reverenced as a deity) prevailed. The Assyrians, Babylonians, Romans, and Hebrews all knew and practiced, in various ways, the tithe.

Interestingly, the Covenant Code, much of which dates from the time of the Decalogue (the thirteenth century B.C.), does not mention a tithe for Yahweh. Rather OFFERINGS (Exod. 23:16, 19) are commanded. The much later Deuteronomic Code (622 B.C.) speaks specifically of tithing the firstfruits of grain and other crops. Undoubtedly, the tithe, in different forms in different historical contexts, was

practiced by the Hebrews long before the seventh century B.C. Under David and Solomon a tenth of one's income was the usual national tax (I Sam. 8:15-17). The usual exploitation of conquered people (and the Hebrews were oppressed and conquered many times, from the times of the Judges to the final fall of Jerusalem in A.D. 70) by the invading power was a tenth of every subject's possessions.

In the ongoing Hebrew tradition of tithes and offerings, one concept stands out—only the best, the virgin oil pressed from the olive, the perfectly formed healthy sheep or calf, and the finest wheat were to be offered to God as the tithe. God's portion is to come first, not last.

In the course of Hebrew history, the tithe became a sign of reverence for God by way of showing love and mercy for God's children. The tithe, by various arrangements (as in the third and sixth years of the seven-year cycle of feasts and offerings) was made into a social welfare program to support widows and orphans and even stateless nomadic people dwelling in the land. The book of Ruth illustrates how the grain that was hard to gather was left in the field for the poor and helpless to gather as a tithe due to God's creatures. Sharing was stressed, unselfishness taught, by way of the tithe. Additionally, the costs of the temple (and shrines) cultus and the support of the priests and Levites were gathered by way of the tithe (Deut. 12:17, 19; 14:22-29; Lev. 27:32; Neh. 10:36; Num. 18:26-28; Deut. 26:12; Neh. 10:37).

The tithe was the general rule among the Jews in Jesus' time. A temple tax was paid by all adult male Jews for the support of the cultus and the upkeep of the sanctuary. Among the stricter Pharisees (to whose theological outlook Jesus inclined, and which Paul embraced), the tithe was practiced scrupulously. Jesus made sarcastic references to the hypersensitivity of the Pharisees to tithing even the mint leaves from their garden, but nonetheless taught the appropriateness of the tithe as the believer's normal act of gratitude to God (Luke 11:42).

Throughout Christian history, the tithe has been taught as an ideal of Christian giving. Old English law collected the tithe of the crops and stored them in tithe barns. Although not practiced by the majority of Christians, the ideal of the tenth that belongs to God is a living reality in all the churches.

J.C.

**TITUS.** This man's name (strangely) does not appear in Acts, but from Paul's letters we know him to have been a loyal assistant and a person meriting Paul's trust. At the Jerusalem Council (Acts 15), if we assume Galatians 2:1-10 refers to this same event, he was a test case since, as a Gentile, he had not been circumcised. It is uncertain whether Paul agreed to his circumcision or not (Gal. 2:3 is not clear).

Titus' mission responsibility was especially to Corinth, to whose church he had gone to raise the "offering for the saints" (II Cor. 9:1). At a crucial time in Paul's dealing with the Corinthians, Titus played a vital role, succeeding where Timothy failed in representing Paul's mind and carrying the "letter of reproof" (II Cor. 2:4), which led the church to penitence (II Cor. 7:8-9). Titus met Paul in Macedonia with the news of the end of the church's disaffection (II Cor. 7:5-7; compare 2:13)—at least for the time being. Paul's writing contained in II Corinthians 1–7, which rejoices over this reconciliation, was evidently taken by Titus to Corinth. And in a subsequent note (II Cor. 10–13) addressing a further outbreak of the church's rebellion, Titus again is a link person (II Cor. 12:18).

Paul's mission preaching to Crete is not evidenced in our records, but Titus' appointment to that charge is (Tit. 1:5ff.), and Eusebius' *Church History,* the first full-length, continuous narrative written by a Christian, has Titus remaining there as bishop. The letter, ostensibly written by Paul to Titus (*see* PASTORAL EPISTLES), describes how Titus is to conduct his ministry at Crete, with exhortations to oppose false, Gnosticizing notions (Tit. 1:10-16), to appoint faithful leaders (2:1-15), and to remain true to Paul's message.        R.M.

*Bronze sestertius commemorating Titus' capture of Judea. The reverse side reads IVDAEA CAPTA ("Judea captured")*

**TITUS, EMPEROR.** Son and successor of the emperor VESPASIAN. After military training and billets in Germany and Britain, Titus assisted his father in the suppression of the Jewish revolt in A.D. 66. The Arch of Titus in the Roman Forum celebrates the subjection of Judea in A.D. 70. During his brief reign Titus ordered the construction of costly public works.        J.L.P.

**TOBIAH.** A leader in Ammon, modern Amman in the kingdom of Jordan, who was at least half Jewish. Tobiah, whose name means "Yahweh is good," was a worshiper of Yahweh and, along with the Samaritans (descendants of the conquered Israelites, who also worshiped Yahweh), offered to help Nehemiah and the returned exiles rebuild Jerusalem in the mid-sixth century B.C. NEHEMIAH, reacting from the developing sense that Judaism must purify itself and keep all other elements at arm's length, rejected the offer of help made by Sanballat the Samaritan and Tobiah the Ammonite (Neh. 2:10; 4:3, 7; 6:1-19). However, Tobiah, who apparently was governor of Ammon

under the Persians, moved into Jerusalem and took a room located in the ancient Temple area. This happened during a trip Nehemiah made back to Babylon (Neh. 13:6). On his return, Nehemiah threw Tobiah and his belongings out and had the room ritually purified (Neh. 13:6-9).

Ezra 2:60 mentions that the Tobiah family was one that had been exiled in Babylon and returned to Palestine. Tobiah may have made this return himself but found the growing exclusiveness of the Jews under Ezra and Nehemiah offensive. Tobiah then became the enemy of Nehemiah's reconstruction.

       J.C.

**TOBIT, BOOK OF.** The book of Tobit, also sometimes called Tobias, as in the Latin Vulgate, is one of the most interesting and revealing books of the APOCRYPHA. Polycarp, Ambrose, and Augustine argued that it should be part of the Bible, whereas Jerome, Athanasius, and Luther considered it just a rollicking good story. It was probably written sometime between the third and first centuries B.C. It exists in a variety of ancient manuscripts—Greek, Latin, Aramaic, and Syriac.

The story reads like a novel, except that the setting is the Hellenistic/Semitic world. Tobit is a pious Jew of the tribe of Naphtali. He, his wife Hannah, and his son Tobias are taken as prisoners of war to Nineveh by the Babylonians. Tobit distinguished himself by giving food to the poor and giving proper burial to the dead. Tobit had to flee, but was later allowed to return to Nineveh. Unclean from burying the dead, he had to sleep outside the house. At night birds blinded him with their droppings. He prayed for the return of his sight.

At the same time there was a young woman in Ecbatana by the name of Sarah who was praying at exactly the same time as Tobit. Seven times she had married, and seven times on her marriage night her husbands had been murdered by an evil spirit named Asmodaeus. When God heard the prayers of Sarah and Tobit, he sent his angel Raphael to help them. Thinking he was near death, Tobit sent his son Tobias to Ecbatana to recover a loan. Raphael accompanied him, along with a pet dog. As they camped along the river, a large fish jumped from the water as if to bite Tobias. Tobias caught the fish, saving the gall, liver, and heart to be used for medical purposes.

Tobias was the only eligible kinsman left for Sarah to marry, under levirate law. To drive away the evil spirit and escape death, Tobias burned the fish's heart on the incense stand of his new wife. He got the money he came for, used the gall bladder of the fish to cure his father's blindness, and learned that Raphael was really an angel. He and his whole family lived happily ever after, to a ripe old age.

The extended story of Tobias is a well-told tale, encouraging Jewish virtues, faith, and morals at a time when the Jews were being persecuted and scattered throughout the world, and for centuries was popularized in painting, song, and legend.    T.J.K.

**TOCQUEVILLE, ALEXIS DE** (1805–59). Born in Paris on July 29, de Tocqueville was a political scientist, historian, and politician. With his friend Gustave de Beaumont, he spent nine months in America (1831–32), which resulted in a joint work on the American penal system and the first part of de Tocqueville's *Democracy in America* (2 vols.; 1835, 1840), which focused on America's social equality. In 1839 he was elected to the Chamber of Deputies. After the French Revolution in 1848, he was elected to the Constituent Assembly and helped write the Constitution for the Second Republic. Deprived of all positions by Napoleon III's coup, he wrote *The Old Regime and the Revolution* in 1856. He died in Cannes.
N.H.

**TODAY'S ENGLISH VERSON (TEV).** *See* GOOD NEWS BIBLE.

**TOLAND, JOHN** (1670–1722). English Deist, philosopher, political pamphleteer, and biblical critic. Born a Roman Catholic near Londonderry, Ireland, he became a Protestant at sixteen. In 1690 he received the M.A. at Edinburgh University, studied at Leiden for two years, and settled in Oxford in 1694. Then followed a stream of mostly anonymous or pseudonymous books and pamphlets on a wide range of subjects. Politically, Toland was a Whig and a strong defender of toleration. Philosophically and religiously, he was influenced by Lord Herbert of Cherbury, the Cambridge Platonists, and JOHN LOCKE. Religiously, Toland advocated RATIO-NALISM, freethought, and latitudinarianism.

His most influential work, *Christianity not Mysterious, Or a Treatise Showing That there is nothing in the Gospel Contrary to Reason, Nor above it: And that no Christian Doctrine can be properly call'd A Mystery*, was published in 1696. It is one of the great treatises of DEISM and elicited over fifty attempted refutations. The book was condemned by Parliament. The title nicely sums up its central theme: Christianity cannot be contrary or above reason. Revelation may give us knowledge that we otherwise might not apprehend; but once known, revelation must be entirely reasonable—not mysterious. Toland ends the book: "I acknowledge no Orthodoxy but the Truth." Toland's exploration of the origins of religion appears to anticipate David Hume's *Natural History of Religion*, as does his naturalistic interpretation of the biblical miracles preview the biblical criticism of Enlightenment thinkers.    J.L.

**TOLERATION, RELIGIOUS.** *See* LIBERTY, RELIGIOUS.

**TOLSTOY, LEO.** (1828–1910). Russian nobleman and author of such world-famous novels as *War and*

*Peace* (1866) and *Anna Karenina* (1875–77). He was also a social reformer, inspired by Christian principles. Already during the time he was writing his novels he was engaged in improving the lot of the Russian peasantry, and after 1877 he devoted himself wholly to developing his religious and social ideas. He lived in a very simple manner, and his theology was also stripped down to the barest essentials. It resembled in fact the kind of theology that Harnack was teaching at the same time, that is to say, it put at the center not the doctrines of the person and work of Christ but Jesus' own proclamation of the kingdom of God and the conduct that he commanded in the Sermon on the Mount. But whereas Harnack was conservative in politics, Tolstoy was liberal and also commended nonviolence. He was excommunicated from the Orthodox Church in 1901, became estranged from his family because of his religious and social preoccupations, and died on his way to a monastery.    J.M.

**TOMB.** A building or other masonry structure, such as a pyramid, used for the burial of the dead. In Palestine, natural caves also were used as tombs. Perhaps the most famous Christian tombs were caves, such as Lazarus' tomb at Bethany (John 11:38), and Jesus' tomb at Jerusalem (Matt. 27:60), which was a

Courtesy of the Oriental Institute, University of Chicago

*Royal tombs, carved out of the rock, of Darius I, Artaxerxes I, and Darius II; at Naqsh-i-Rustam in Iran*

From *Atlas of the Bible* (Thomas Nelson & Sons Limited)

*Tomb cut in the rock, in Palestine*

*The so-called Garden Tomb at Jerusalem*

man-made cave hewn out of the rock at the direction of Joseph of Arimathea. Abraham and the other patriarchs and their wives were probably buried in the cave of Machpelah, in a field near Hebron. Abraham bought the field from Ephron the Hittite for just this purpose (Gen. 23:10 ff.).

The most famous tombs of ancient times were not caves, however, but huge masonry constructions, the great pyramids of Egypt at Gizeh near modern Cairo. These included the Fourth Dynasty pyramid of Mycerinus (or Menkaure), the pyramid of Chephren (or Khafre), and the Great Pyramid of Cheops (or Khufu). Actually, there were older pyramids than these. A Second Dynasty pyramid at Sakkara is 6,500 years old, the world's oldest stone structure. However, for sheer size—and the wonder of the ages—nothing surpasses Cheops' Great Pyramid, which covers 13.1 acres, and contains 2,300,000 stone blocks that weigh, on average, two and one-half tons each. This tomb is over 481 feet high, and the four sides of the base are roughly 756 feet each.

The Persians buried nine of their emperors in the hills near Persepolis. Cyrus the Great, who permitted the Jews to return to Jerusalem, was buried in a small, freestanding stone tomb near Pasargadae.
J.C.

**TONGUES, GIFT OF.** *See* GLOSSOLALIA.

**TONGUES OF FIRE.** One of the metaphors describing the reception of the Holy Spirit by the disciples of Jesus gathered in the upper room in Jerusalem on the Day of Pentecost after Jesus' resurrection (Acts 2). The passage reads: "Cloven tongues like as of fire" (KJV) descended and rested on the faithful resulting in their all being "filled with the Holy Ghost." They then "began to speak in other tongues, as the Spirit gave them utterance," that is, they exhibited *xenoglossia*, or the ability to speak languages that were real but hitherto unknown to them. This outpouring of the Spirit and tongue-speaking experience was not the GLOSSOLALIA Paul discusses in I Corinthians 12–14, and that modern Pentecostals and contemporary neo-Pentecostals practice (Acts 2:3 ff., 6-18; 10:46). The disciples saw their experience as the fulfillment of Joel's prophecy, that the old would dream dreams and the young see visions (Joel 2:28; Acts 2:16 ff.).
J.C.

**TONSURE.** From the Latin word *tondere*, meaning "to shave." A shaving of part of the hair of the head, prescribed by canon law for all Catholic priests, except in countries like Britain and the United States, where it is out of harmony with public custom. It symbolizes the clerical state and reminds one of Christ's crown of thorns.
J.C.

**TOPHETH.** Meaning "fireplace" or "hearth." A place in the valley of Hinnom that bounds Jerusalem on the southwest. The name has associations with cremation as a punishment (Deut. 32:22; Isa. 33:14; Isa. 30:33, where the RSV reads Topheth as "burning place") and with the Phoenician and Moabite practice of child sacrifice or passing of children through fire (II Kings 23:10; II Chr. 28:2-3; 33:6).
P.L.G.

**TOPLADY, AUGUSTUS MONTAGUE** (1740–78). English clergyman, theologian, and hymn writer. Born in Farnham, Surrey, England, Toplady was educated at Westminster School, London, and Trinity College, Dublin. Converted through the influence of a Methodist layman, he was ordained to the Anglican priesthood. Subsequently, after serving as pastor of the French Calvinist Church in London, he became a bitter antagonist of John Wesley and Methodism and a stout defender of Calvinism. He outlined his position in *Historic Proof of the Doctrinal Calvinism of the Church of England*. However, he is probably best known for his hymns: "Rock of Ages," "A Debtor to Mercy Alone," "A Sovereign Protector I Have," and "From Whence This Fear and Unbelief?"
R.H.

**TORAH.** Scroll of the law and teaching, read in the synagogue on the Jewish Sabbath, Mondays and Thursdays, and on Jewish holy days. The scroll of the Torah is made up of separate leaves of specially treated parchment sewn together with threads made from the tendons of ritually clean animals. On the parchment are the words, in unvocalized and unaccented Hebrew, of the five books of Moses, the PENTATEUCH, hand-lettered by a special copyist, known in Hebrew as a *sofer* ("scribe"), who must be devout and learned. The scroll is rolled on two wooden staves called in Hebrew *Etz Hayim* ("tree of life"), topped by an ornamental headpiece or crown. The scroll is tied by a sash and covered with an embroidered mantle, over which a breastplate hangs. A pointer *(yad)*, in the form of a tiny hand with a pointing finger, is used to keep the place in the reading of the Torah. When not in use, the scrolls of the Torah are kept in a closet called the Holy Ark *(Aron ha-Kodesh)*. During services when the ark is opened, worshipers rise and remain standing until it is closed. When the Torah is carried, the congregation stands, and those nearest to it kiss its mantle as it goes past. On Simhat Torah, the "Rejoicing of the Law" festival, all scrolls are taken from the ark and carried in procession seven times around the synagogue.

In rabbinic literature, "Torah" also refers to the Pentateuch as distinct from the other two sections of the Hebrew Bible—the Prophets and the Writings—and indeed to all the teachings of Judaism, its laws, doctrines, ethics, philosophy, and customs and ceremonies.

The study of Torah is considered a major religious duty and its fulfillment the highest goal of piety and virtue. God's command to Joshua (Josh. 1:8), "This book of the Torah shall not depart from thy mouth, but thou shalt meditate on it day and night," was interpreted as an exhortation to devote one's whole life to the study of the Torah. The daily prayers include a blessing to God for the commandment to occupy oneself with the study of Torah. The blessing preceding the reading of the SHEMA praises God for giving the Torah. The rabbinic passage setting forth those things the fruit of which the individual enjoys in this world while the main reward is reserved for the world to come ends with "but the study of the Torah is equivalent to them all." The idea that the Torah is the source of life of the Jewish people is expressed in many parables and homilies but especially in the prayer: "Blessed is our God, who hath created us for His glory and hath separated us from them that go astray, and hath given us the Torah and thus planted everlasting life in our midst. May He open our heart unto His Torah."                                                L.K.

**TORAH READING CYCLE.** Since study is an integral part of prayer in Jewish life, public religious services on the Sabbath, festivals, Mondays and Thursdays and the new moon include the reading of a portion of the TORAH scroll. The Torah, containing the five books of Moses in unvowelled Hebrew on parchment, is divided into portions and read in annual cycles. The public recitation of the Torah is usually followed by the reading of a supplementary portion from the Prophets, called the *Haftarah*. The Torah portions are subdivided, and the subdivisions on Sabbath mornings number seven. Different congregants are called up to the Torah to pronounce the blessings before and after the reading of each *parashah* (subdivision).                          L.K.

**TORII.** The Japanese word meaning literally "bird-roost." A distinctive gateway marking the entrance to the precincts of a Shinto shrine. Typically made of two round, upright pillars and two crossbeams, the torii is a distinctive mark of a Shinto shrine and its "sacred space."                 R.E.

**TOTAL DEPRAVITY.** *See* ORIGINAL SIN.

**TOTEM.** In primitive religion, a natural object, commonly a particular species of animal, believed to have a special sacred or symbolic relationship to a social group, such as a tribe. Early anthropology and psychoanalysis made much of totemism in its theories of religious origins, but modern thought has tended to give it less importance and to point to considerable diversity in its practice.

A totem animal is often present in mythology as the primal ancestor of its people. In some cases eating it may be taboo, although in others the animal is eaten but usually only in special ritual circumstances in which the act is a sort of Holy Communion. Totemism at its most intense presents a significant link between the human and the natural order, and makes the totem creature an objectification of the people's sacred corporate identity. It is, however, usually not the central motif of a society's religion and may have little more significance than as a way of reckoning kinship or as a touchstone of emotional identity, like its modern survival in team mascots and the bears and eagles that are the emblems of contemporary nations.                              R.E.

**TRACHONITIS.** An area of ancient Palestine south of Damascus, north of Hauran, east of Bashan, and north of Galilee, now part of Israel, Syria, and the kingdom of Jordan. It was ruled by the tetrarch Herod Philip (Luke 3:1), and, at a later date, by Herod Agrippa I. Caesarea Philippi was in that region.                                             J.C.

**TRACTARIAN MOVEMENT.** *See* OXFORD MOVEMENT.

**TRADITION.** The word "tradition" comes from the Latin *traditio*, meaning "handing over." The corresponding Greek word, used in the NT, is *paradosis*. This is the word used by Paul when he writes, "Hold to the traditions which you were taught by us" (II Thess. 2:15). Tradition pervades virtually all the departments of human activity. In government, education, family life, and so on there are recognized principles and practices that are passed on from one generation to another. Even in the sciences, tradition is important. Each new investigator joins a scientific community in which there is already a body of received opinion on the science concerned and recognized ways of conducting research. Even the most acute and innovative researcher builds on what is already there and owes far more to the legacy received than he or she is likely ever to contribute to the science concerned. Tradition is especially important in religion and theology, and it is to the place of tradition in these areas that we now turn.

*The Structure of Tradition.* In a religious tradition, it is possible to distingish three constitutive elements: first, the origin, the truth or insight or event from which the tradition took its rise and which it is intended to pass on and to perpetuate; second, the transmission, the actual process of passing on or handing over; and, third, the reception and appropriation of what is passed on by those living at a particular point in time. The origin of an entire religious tradition (as distinct from minor traditions within the mainstream of tradition) is usually a REVELATION, an event that brings a new spiritual insight so profound that it serves as the foundation on which an entire religion is built up. We must notice, however, that even the originating event is not an isolated happening but already belongs in traditions that reach further back. The originating event from which the Christian tradition came was the life, death, and resurrection of Jesus Christ, but these were understood in the light of the Jewish tradition with its messianic expectations and so on. The process of transmission is effected by quite specific vehicles in the Christian church. Preaching is the most fundamental, and has gone on since the time of the apostles. Alongside preaching, we may set teaching (didache), especially the instruction of catechumens. The earliest preaching and teaching antedated the composition of written SCRIPTURES—indeed, it is now generally believed that the Synoptic Gospels were constructed out of units of teaching circulating in the church. But when the Scriptures did emerge, they obviously became a very important vehicle for transmitting and stabilizing the traditions about Jesus. The sacraments constituted a further vehicle for the transmission of the tradition, in the dramatic liturgical forms of baptism and the Eucharist. The community itself, and especially the ordained ministry, played an indispensable part in the work of transmission. Finally, tradition needs to be received and appropriated. Where the reception is only outward or formal, the tradition becomes lifeless and even meaningless, and this of course does sometimes happen. If the tradition is alive, it must be received in such a way that the recipient participates in something of the power and illumination of the original event.

*Tradition and Development.* There are two opposed ways in which tradition may be understood: as static or dynamic. In the first case, tradition is understood as a body of truths and practices given at the beginning and then to be kept pure and unchanged from generation to generation. There is a hint of this view in a late writing of the NT that speaks of "the faith which was once for all delivered to the saints" (Jude 3). This is sometimes called the "deposit of faith." On a more dynamic view of tradition, it is recognized that there may be development of both practices and doctrines. Such development may be simply an unfolding of what is implicit in the original given, or it may be due to the pressures of social or intellectual developments, for instance, belief in the authority of scripture has to be rethought in the light of historical criticism. The question then arises, What is legitimate development? Clearly there must be a demonstrable continuity, or else the tradition may be abandoned altogether. An acorn must change and develop as it grows into a tree, but it does not grow into just any tree, but into an oak. In a living tradition there is both development and continuity. Vincent of Lerins seemed to be favoring the static view when he urged Christians to hold to "that which has been believed everywhere, always, and by all," but he also declared that there should be "a great increase and vigorous progress in understanding as the ages and centuries march on."

*Catholic and Protestant Views of Tradition.* The discussion of tradition and development brings us to consider the sharp opposition that prevailed for many years between Catholics and Protestants over the place of tradition. Protestants claimed that the Bible alone is authoritative (the principle of SOLA SCRIPTURA), and that tradition can have no binding force. Catholics, on the other hand, seemed to recognize tradition as a separate source of revealed truth. But in recent years the views of both Catholics and Protestants have changed, and tradition is no longer the contentious matter it once was. In view of biblical criticism, Protestants acknowledge that the Gospels are collections of traditions about Jesus that circulated for a long time before they were written down, and that the CANON of the NT was decided by the church, largely on the grounds of what were judged to be writings that continued the tradition of the apostles. On the Catholic side, tradition is now seen not as a separate source from scripture but as intimately joined to it. The Constitution on Divine Revelation of Vatican II suggests that tradition and scripture flow along in dynamic interaction like a river: "Sacred tradition and sacred scripture, then, are bound closely together and communicate one with the other. For both of them, flowing out from the same divine wellspring, come together in some fashion to form one thing, and move toward the same goal."

J.M.

**TRADITION CRITICISM.** *See* BIBLICAL CRITICISM.

**TRADUCIANISM.** Sometimes called "generationalism" because it is a doctrine about the beginnings of the human soul. Some theologians speculate that the soul comes from the parents through the act of generation and was in the embryo at conception. Others theorize that the soul of the parent generated the soul of the infant as a separate process. The doctrine entered Christian thought from Stoicism through Tertullian (second century) as an effort to explain the transmission of sin through Adam. I.C.

Courtesy of G. E. Kidder Smith

*Lower portion of the Column of Trajan, Rome*

**TRAJAN.** Roman Emperor from A.D. 98 to 117. An exchange of letters in A.D. 111–112 between the emperor and the younger Pliny, proconsul of Bithynia and Pontus, reflects the imperial position toward the profession and practice of Chistianity at this time. Some scholars see a correspondence between the situation revealed in these letters and that presupposed in I Peter, but many assign an earlier date to this writing.                                    J.L.P.

**TRANCE.** *See* MYSTICISM.

**TRANSACTIONAL ANALYSIS.** A school of psychology originating in the work of Eric Berne, popularly known for his book *Games People Play,* to shorten the therapeutic process required by conventional psychotherapy. Noting that people reveal themselves through interaction, Berne devised a system of group therapy by which people could help one another see themselves more clearly. Building on SIGMUND FREUD's analysis of the continuous struggle between ego-id-superego and the discoveries by neurosurgeon Wilder Penfield that all memories, including feelings, are stored in the brain, Berne constructed a method to explore the interaction

of any two persons as stimulator and responder. He called this Transactional Analysis (TA). These "games" reveal the past through present transactions.

The key terms are "Parent," "Adult," and "Child," but these words do not hold the common meanings attributed to them. Every individual incorporates each "person." Parent may mean nurturer or conscience; child may mean dependency or creativity; adult may mean a way of processing the other two "persons" maturely, or it may include an overload of conflicting stimuli that cause inappropriate behavior. When behavior is analyzed by correlating action with memories, a person can begin to sort out the reasons for these actions and begin to modify behavior. Transactional Analysis is popularly outlined in the book *I'm OK—You're OK* by Thomas A. Harris.                                    I.C.

**TRANSCENDENCE.** The word derives from the Latin phrase *trans scandere,* meaning to "climb over." The term may refer (1) to being above and apart from or (2) to transcending by rising above and beyond. Transcendence is contrasted with IMMANENCE, understood as indwelling and abidingly pervasive.

Transcendence, as applied to God by theologians and philosophers, distinguishes God as Creator and Ruler, external to the universe, from God as immanent within the world. Aristotle depicts God as the transcendent Unmoved Mover, final cause of the world but unaware of it. The Neoplatonists, and Augustine following them, affirm the immanence of God as the source and sustainer of Being, yet transcending it. The transcendence of God has been stressed by medieval nominalists, by critical philosophers from Descartes to Kant, by Deists, by existentialists, and by Neo-orthodox theologians.

IMMANUEL KANT (1724–1804) gives "transcendental" a highly specialized meaning referring to the a priori of experience and knowledge: the Transcendental Aesthetic as the a priori of sensory experience, the Transcendental Logic as the a priori in thought, and the Transcendental Unity of Apperception as the self.

New England TRANSCENDENTALISM is a literary movement led by Ralph Waldo Emerson (1803–82), deriving from Kant the notion of a transcendence based on intuition, but giving it a meaning akin to Romantic idealism.                                    C.Mc.

**TRANSCENDENTALISM.** This American contribution to philosophy and theology, an outgrowth of German idealism and the English Romantic movement, represents an intellectual, aesthetic, and spiritual ferment. Transcendentalism began in 1836 with publication of RALPH WALDO EMERSON's *Nature* and the first meeting in September of the Transcendental Club at the home of George Ripley. Attending were Bronson Alcott, Orestes Brownson, Emerson, and other leading UNITARIAN ministers.

Prominent members over the next four years included HENRY DAVID THOREAU, Theodore Parker, Margaret Fuller, and Elizabeth Palmer Peabody. They published the *Dial* from 1840 to 1844.

An affront even to Unitarian orthodoxy, transcendentalism represented an attack on historic Calvinism, tradition in general, a belief in miracles specifically, and an acceptance of German critical scholarship including that concerning the historical Jesus. Affirmatively transcendentalists believed that the universe was centered in one mind, one will, and the Oversoul, which was active in all nature, awakening in human beings religious sentiment and happiness. Their optimistic views rooted in a pantheistic concept of the universe, represented a post-Kantian IDEALISM with a dash of the mystic SPIRITUALISM of Emanuel Swedenborg and Eastern religions. They tended to ignore such problems as evil, sin, pain, and death. A complementary creed to the optimism of Jacksonian democracy, it influenced American culture through such literary giants as Emerson, Thoreau, and Nathaniel Hawthorne. Many of its members were involved in the communitarian experiments at Brook Farm and Fruitlands.

N.H.

**TRANSCENDENTAL MEDITATION.** A technique from the Hindu tradition brought to the Western world by Mahareshi Mahesh Yogi. It is a process of turning inward to transcend thought and expand consciousness, in order to get in touch with creative intelligence. The procedure is used twice daily for fifteen- to twenty-minute periods while the person, comfortably seated with eyes closed, sinks into the deeper levels of mind. Breathing and pulse rate are reduced, muscles relax, and a stillness is felt. The alternation of daily activity and meditation is designed to bring strength and perspective in order to gain enlightenment and self-realization through self-awareness. Transcendental Meditation (TM) recognizes five stages: waking, dreaming, deep sleep, temporary pure awareness, and permanent pure awareness. Beyond this are two states seldom reached: that in which one sees the world as transformed, and one in which it is realized that the self is not only an inner but an outer reality.

I.C.

**TRANSEPT.** From the Latin words *trans septum*, meaning "across wall," denoting a projection between the nave and choir of a cruciform (cross-shaped) church. It is the aisle or hall that crosses right in front of the nave, extending to both sides.

J.C.

**TRANSFIGURATION.** An important episode in the Gospel story and life of Jesus, according to the Synoptic Gospels. John 12:27-30 is sometimes thought to be a recast version of the incident, without any specific setting so typical of the threefold account (see John 1:14).

The center of interest is the transformation of Jesus' appearance to resemble a shining being (presumably angelic), with the appearance of two OT characters, Moses and Elijah, adding to the drama and the scenario (Matt. 17:1-8; Mark 9:2-8; Luke 9:28-36). The usual interpretation is that OT figures witness to the presence of the Messiah, whom the Father's voice from heaven greets as "my Son." Peter's action in wishing to erect three booths was evidently intended to make the event memorable and to prolong it, though it is more likely that it represents a plea for Jesus to act in a nationalistic way and bring in the divine kingdom as patriotic leader (Lev. 23:39-43 tells of the erecting of booths, a feast that in first-century Judaism carried strong national overtones).

As the evangelists use the incident, it stands in some relation to the promise given in Mark 9:1 that the Twelve will see God's kingdom come in power. This is taken to refer to either the RESURRECTION (in which case some think the Transfiguration is a predated Resurrection appearance) or the PAROUSIA (in which case the story anticipates the final glory of Christ). The memory of this tradition is seen in II Peter 1:16-18, which suggests a setting in the Parousia (v. 19).

R.M.

**TRANSGRESSION.** *See* SIN.

**TRANSLATIONS.** *See* BIBLE TRANSLATIONS, ENGLISH.

**TRANSUBSTANTIATION.** The word means "the change of one substance into another" and refers to the Roman Catholic dogma that in the EUCHARIST the substance of the elements of bread and wine are changed into the substance of the Body and Blood of Jesus Christ. Early medieval theologians used terms such as "transform" and "transfigure" to refer to the change of the Eucharistic elements. However, by the thirteenth century the doctrine and term "transubstantiation" were well established and frequently used, for example in the words of Thomas Aquinas: "The whole substance of the bread is changed into the whole substance of Christ's body, and the whole substance of the wine into the whole substance of Christ's blood. Hence this conversion . . . may be designated by a name of its own, transubstantiation." Martin Luther opposed transubstantiation, while teaching the Real Presence of Christ "in, with, and under" the bread and wine (consubstantiation).

To counter Luther's teaching, the Council of Trent issued its teaching on transubstantiation (1551), which has remained authoritative in Roman Catholicism to the present day: "It has always been the conviction of the Church of God and this holy Council now again declares that by the consecration of the bread and wine a change takes place in which the entire substance of the bread is changed into the substance of the body of Christ our Lord and the entire substance of the wine into the substance of his blood." This dogma often has been misunderstood, due largely to a confusion over the word "substance." Using an Aristotelian and Thomistic distinction, some theologians have taught that it is the substantial form of the bread and wine, the reality that underlies their appearance or accidents, which is changed, and not their species, which are perceptible to the senses. The Roman church does not, however, sanction any particular philosophical interpretation of substance, and Catholic theologians continue to disagree on the precise nature of the conversion of the elements. Recently Catholic theologians have entered into serious dialogue with Anglicans and Lutherans on the interpretation of transubstantation.               J.L.

**TRAPPISTS.** The popular name of Roman Catholic monks belonging to the Order of Cistercians of the Strict Observance. The CISTERCIAN order was founded in 1098 by Saint Robert Molesmes at the monastery of Citeaux in France. In 1664 Armand Jean LeBouthillier de Rance, abbot of LaTrappe, a Cistercian abbey in Normandy, instituted a movement to reform the order. One of the strictest monastic communities, the Trappists demand absolute silence; emphasize liturgical worship including observance of the divine office for seven hours daily; and forbid the eating of meat, fish, and eggs. The monks spend their days in liturgical prayer and contemplation, theological study, and manual labor. Since Vatican Council II, the Trappists have abolished the position of lay brothers. Nuns of the Strict Observance are called Trappistines. The expulsion of monks during the French Revolution was responsible for Trappists' establishing monasteries in Europe, China, Japan, and the United States. In 1817 they returned to LaTrappe.               R.H.

**TREE OF KNOWLEDGE/TREE OF LIFE.** Genesis 2:9 reports that "the Lord God made to grow every tree that is pleasant to the sight and good for food, the tree of life also in the midst of the garden, and the tree of the knowledge of good and evil." The tree of knowledge was the tree whose fruit ADAM AND EVE were forbidden to eat; the tree of life was to promote continuing life to those who ate its fruit. The Genesis account does tell that Adam and Eve ate of the one tree, but leaves silent the question of the other. Eating of the tree of knowledge traditionally thought of as an apple tree, probably incorrectly, was a direct challenge by the human race to Jehovah's judgment about what is right and wrong. In church iconography, only one tree, not two, is ordinarily depicted in Paradise. In some passages in the OT the phrase "knowledge of good and evil" has sexual overtones (Deut. 1:39; II Sam. 19:35), and some scholars think it also does here.               T.J.K.

**TRENT, COUNCIL OF** (1545–63). Nineteenth ecumenical council and Roman Catholicism's doctri-

nal response to sixteenth-century Protestantism, which set the doctrine for Roman Catholicism until VATICAN COUNCIL II (1962–65). Despite opposition and delays, Pope Paul III convoked the Council of Trent, which opened December 13, 1545. Interruptions were frequent: session 1–8 at Trent and 9–11 at Bologna took place under Pope Paul III (1534–49), sessions 12–16 at Trent under Julius III (1550–55), and sessions 17–25 at Trent under Pius IV (1559–65). Middle and lower clergy and university representatives were not invited; they had abetted conciliarism earlier. Fifty theologians and fifty canonists acted as consultants without official voice. Only archbishops, bishops, influential abbots, and heads of religious orders could vote. A few scattered Protestants attended only briefly. Luther refused to go unless the council was free of papal domination and Scripture was accorded final authority. Some 255 prelates finally signed Trent's conclusions, but only 60 to 70 attended the various sessions. Jesuits Salmeron and Lainez, known for their papal loyalty, spoke first and last on all proposals, and only they were allowed to preach. Heated debate and even fighting marked some sessions.

Trent declared Scripture and tradition equal for faith and morals; sanctioned the Apocrypha as biblical; made Jerome's Latin Vulgate translation the official Catholic Bible; defined justification by grace as a joint effort by God and man in which good works have merit and increase faith; reaffirmed and defined the seven sacraments (baptism, the Lord's Supper, confirmation, penance, ordination, marriage, and extreme unction); declared the Mass a propitiatory sacrifice and ordination indelible; made Latin official for the Mass; reaffirmed transubstantiation and withholding of the cup; said celibacy and chastity were better than marriage; asserted the efficacy of indulgences; and approved the honoring of relics, invocation and veneration of saints, and masses for the dead. More preaching, restraints on pluralities, and less concubinage were urged, and an index of prohibited books was established, but reforms were noticeably missing. Office by divine right was denied all bishops except the pope, and no concessions were made to the Protestants. (See also CATHOLIC REFORMATION.)               C.M.

**TRESPASS.** See SIN.

**TRIAL OF JESUS.** Jesus' trial followed his arrest on the Mount of Olives by Roman soldiers directed by Judas. This occurred in the evening hours of Nisan 14, as the day began at twilight (roughly 6:00 P.M.). Actually, Jesus had not one but several trials that were brought about by the rising fear and dislike of Jesus as an authoritative leader by the religious powers of Judea. The problem of convicting Jesus of anything grew out of the overlapping political jurisdictions and the supremacy of Roman power in Judea.

Jesus' trial (or trials) began with an interview

before Annas, former high priest and father-in-law of Caiaphas, the present high priest (John 18:13). Then he was taken to Caiaphas' house and forced to undergo an illegal (because it was held at night) grand jury investigation by some Sanhedrin members (Matt. 26:69-75; Mark 14:55; Luke 22:54-64). At dawn, Jesus was tried by the Sanhedrin (Luke 22:66), and on his tacit admission that he was the Son of God, he was condemned to death. Because the Romans had a monopoly on the death sentence, Jesus was then taken to Pilate, the governor, at the Praetorium. The charged lodged was not blasphemy, but treason, for it was said he claimed to be King of the Jews (Luke 23:1-3). Pilate, uncomfortable with this process, sent Jesus to Herod Antipas, tetrarch of Galilee and Peraea, since Jesus was a Galilean (Luke 23:6). Herod examined and mocked Jesus but found him not guilty and sent him again to Pilate (Luke 23:15). Pilate, at the second interview, tried to release Jesus, but the crowd, stirred up by the priests, demanded the release of Barabbas, a convicted murderer, as their Passover favor, instead of Jesus, as Pilate had suggested (Luke 23:16-18). Pilate, afraid of a riot, and of a letter to Rome by the priests suggesting that he was easy on traitors, washed his hands to symbolize his innocence of Jesus' blood and handed him over to an execution squad for crucifixion—the punishment for treason (Matt. 27:24; Mark 15:15-20).                J.C.

**TRIBES OF ISRAEL.** According to the final editing of the OT, based on an idealized vision of Israel's early history (which is also reflected in the later prophets like Ezekiel [chap. 48] and the NT), there were twelve tribes of Israel. However, a close reading of the OT reveals a wide variation of names and in the number of the tribes. The Song of Deborah (Judg. 5) names only ten tribes, and completely omits Judah. The Blessing of Moses (Deut. 33) names only eleven tribes, omitting Simeon. The Blessing of Jacob (Gen. 49) lists twelve. Indeed, one of Jacob's sons, Joseph, was represented, as early as Genesis 41, by not one but two tribes, named after his half-Egyptian sons, Ephraim and Manasseh. This gives a list of thirteen tribes: Reuben, Simeon, Levi, Judah, Issachar, Zebulun, Ephraim, Manasseh, Benjamin, Gad, Asher, Dan, and Naphtali. Later, the territory of Canaan was divided into twelve areas since Levi received no territory because of their devotion to the service of the tabernacle, and later the Temple in Jerusalem. Much later, Solomon entirely disregarded the old tribal boundaries and divided the kingdom into twelve administrative districts (I Kings 4:7-19). Some scholars surmise that later editors projected back twelve tribes in Israel's early history on the basis of Solomon's districts. Whatever is the case, it is clear that the number of tribes was fluid in early Israelite history, reflecting the varied peoples that ultimately came to form Israel.

The idealized twelve tribes were said to be descended from the grandson of Abraham, Jacob. The twelve sons were born of two of Jacob's wives, Leah and Rachel, and two of his concubines, Zilpah and Bilhah. The sons of Jacob by Leah were Reuben, Simeon, Levi, Judah, Issachar, and Zebulun. The sons by Rachel were Joseph and Benjamin. By Zilpah, they were Gad and Asher. By Bilhah, they were Dan and Naphtali.

The tribal system did not survive the monarchy of Solomon. Indeed, it may have been the intention of the imperial-minded Solomon to break forever the residual tribal loyalties that threatened national unity. Indeed, those tribal loyalties burst into flames of revolt at Solomon's death, when ten of the tribes broke away from David's monarchy and the northern kingdom of Israel was established (922 B.C.). In fact, Jeroboam, who was made king, was given his power by the ten tribes joined in solemn assembly. Folklore and pride in ancestry kept the tribal ideal alive down through the NT period, when frequent allusions were made to Jesus' descent from David, and Paul gloried in his identity as a Benjamite. The twelve apostles were told by Jesus, too, that they would sit in judgment on the twelve tribes of Israel. The Epistle of James even refers to Christians as "the twelve tribes."

Judges 1 describes the territory conquered—or not conquered—by the various tribes, doing this in terms of the Canaanite peoples who formerly inhabited the land, and in many instances continued to live there. Joshua 15–19 gives precise boundaries for the tribes. Judah stretched from Edom to the Wilderness of Zin to the south end of the Dead Sea to Kadesh-barnea to the Brook of Egypt and then to the sea. On the north, Judah touched Jerusalem, ran up to Ekron, and ended at the sea. The Joseph tribes (Ephraim and Manasseh) occupied the land from the Jordan River by Jericho to Bethel to Beth-horon to Gezer and the sea.

Gad and Reuben and some of Manasseh received land east of the Jordan. Benjamin received land within the original territory of Judah, to the east and south of Jerusalem. Simeon also received land in the area of Judah, as Judah could not occupy all of it. Zebulun received twelve cities with their villages. Issachar settled in the north near Mount Tabor. Asher settled near Mount Carmel and bordered on Tyre. Naphtali received nineteen cities in the north. Dan settled near Joppa but lost his land and captured Leshem, renaming it Dan.                J.C.

**TRIBULATION, THE GREAT.** The term has acquired something of a technical significance in a type of biblical interpretation known as DISPENSA-TIONALISM. This is an attempt to see the prophetic passages of the Bible as detailed and chronological descriptions, with specific reference, of the end times, the fate of the world, the future of the Jewish people, and the experience of Christians in those final generations.

So the phrase in Daniel 12:2, "a time of trouble" (compare Jer. 30:7), is thought to be elaborated in the reported saying of Jesus (Matt. 24:21; compare Mark 13:19, 24) concerning "the great tribulation." The term here relates to the bitter experiences to befall the followers of Christ at the onset of the Jerusalem war of A.D. 66, which in turn led to their migration to Pella. Dispensational interpreters, however, view the historical setting of A.D. 66 as mirroring the greater trial to occur in the events, both historical and on a cosmic scale, prior to the PAROUSIA or Second Coming of Christ. The debate is joined on the issue whether the church of that period will escape the tribulation by being taken out of history by God's intervention (either as an entire generation of Christians or as a remnant of faithful believers, the elect ones: the technical expressions are "total" or "partial rapture," based on I Thess. 4:17, which describes a catching up or seizure from earth to the Lord's presence). The alternative is that the church will be compelled to enter this dark experience and suffer martyrdom in the tribulation period, often associated with the reign of evil, called the rule of ANTICHRIST. Some verses point in the direction of Christians having to suffer: Acts 14:22; II Thessalonians 2:1-12; Revelation 7:14.

Modern biblical scholarship sees the term as a figurative expression for (1) what occurred historically in the events of A.D. 66–70, and (2) the solemn reminder that the church's lot in this world is always to encounter suffering and trial, as the Johannine Christ foretold (John 16:33). There is, most modern scholars hold, no futuristic specificity to "the great tribulation," aside from the warning that good and evil will be in fierce contention until the ultimate denouement of history when God's universal kingdom comes, and God will be "all in all" (I Cor. 15:28 KJV).                                                                  R.M.

**TRIBUTE.** A general term to cover the objects, mainly money or precious metals, paid in TAXES usually imposed by a monarch or an alien world power. With the setting up of the Israelite monarchy, it was expected that the people would be called on to maintain its support, as in Samuel's warning (I Sam. 8:10-18). Gifts as tribute were also rendered to the king as a sign of vassalage (I Sam. 10:27).

As Israel was exposed to the dominance of foreign powers, it was open to direct levies in the form of ransom money and taxes; but in the Davidic phase of the monarchy the reverse was true, and various peoples brought tribute to David's court (II Sam. 8:6) and to his son Solomon (I Kings 4:21), who ruled much like an Oriental potentate. Other Israelite kings such as Ahab (II Kings 3:4-5) and Jehoshaphat (II Chr. 17:11) received gifts from neighboring states.

A weakened country, divided into two kingdoms, was unable to resist the might of rising empires, such as Syria (II Kings 12:17, 18) and Assyria, which under Tiglath-pileser III and Shalmaneser V (II Kings 16:8; 17:3), imposed tribute on Israel and Judah. Hezekiah's willingness to concede the right of the Babylonian king to levy this tribute is a notable example of Judah's vulnerability (II Kings 20:12-15).

The southern kingdom was forced to accept the suzerainty of both Egypt and Babylon (II Kings 25:13-17).

Rome's presence in the Syrian Levant in the second and first centuries B.C. meant that Palestine came under its jurisdiction and control for taxation purposes. In the NT, tribute is expected to be paid to Rome whether as head tax (Matt. 22:17, 19; Mark 12:13-17) or a tax levied on the land of the provinces (so Luke 23:2, which uses the term *phoros* in possible allusion to the Roman *tributum soli*, that is, land tax). Paul also recognized the duty of paying tribute to Rome (Rom. 13:6-7) in return for the benefits of the *pax Romana* of Roman civilization with the peace and security it maintained throughout the world in the Iulio-Claudian period.

A religious tribute is mentioned in Matthew 17:24-25, namely the levy of the half-shekel Temple tax on all male adult Jews, whether living in Israel or the Dispersion. After the fall of Jerusalem in A.D. 70, the money thus raised was channeled by the Romans into a poll tax for the upkeep of the pagan temple of Jupiter Capitolinus in Rome (this is the *fiscus iudaicus*).                                                                R.M.

**TRINITY.** Meaning literally "threeness," this term is used especially of the Christian doctrine that GOD is three persons in one substance, or one substance in three persons—three in one and one in three. Strictly speaking, the word "triunity" is preferable to the word "trinity," since "triunity" emphasizes the unity as much as it does the trinity. But even to say this is to show where the difficulty of the doctrine lies. How does one reconcile the paradox of unity and trinity? Why was it first considered necessary to get into the paradox? Theologians have oscillated between an emphasis on the unity of God, which leads into unitarianism and the virtual abandonment of the Trinity, or else they have so emphasized the distinctness of the three persons that they have moved toward tritheism, a belief in three Gods.

*Origins and Levels of Meaning.* Perhaps the origins of the doctrine of the triune God were simply linguistic, and at one level the formula may be regarded as the distinctively Christian name or designation of God. After all, "God" is not a specifically Christian word. Many gods have been worshiped in the course of human history, and Christians found it necessary to say *which* God they worshiped. We see this early problem very clearly expressed in a passage written by Paul, where he says: "Although there may be so-called gods in heaven or on earth—as indeed there are many 'gods' and many 'lords'—yet for us there is one God, the Father, from whom are all things and for whom we exist, and one Lord, Jesus Christ, through whom are all things and through whom we exist" (I Cor. 8:5-6). Here is one of the earliest attempts to specify the Christian God and to distinguish that God from the many "gods" and "lords" worshiped in the pagan world.

Two points may be noted about this early statement by Paul. The first is the introduction of Jesus Christ. Christians believed that Christ had brought them a signal revelation of God, and so from then on one could not speak of God without reference to Christ, or of Christ without reference to God, even if there was still no developed CHRISTOLOGY and still less a doctrine of the triunity of God. The second point is that Paul mentions only the Father and the Son, without naming the Spirit. He distinguishes only two persons who are significant for understanding the object of Christian worship, so that this might seem to be an incipient "binitarianism," rather than a trinitarianism. It is indeed the case that the understanding of the Holy Spirit developed only later, so that in the early period one sometimes finds "binitarianism," but this is not a considered doctrine (as it would be in a modern writer who advanced it) but a stage on the way to trinitarianism.

The next level of understanding beyond the Trinity as linguistic convention is the so-called "economic" Trinity, that is to say, the recognition of a threefold action or function of God toward creatures. This reflects the Christian experience of God in salvation history. God has been known as the Father, the God of Israel who created heaven and earth and spoke to people by the prophets; God has been known in Jesus Christ, the Son, through whom, Christians believed, God had spoken and acted in a new and decisive way; God has been known also in the Holy Spirit, who, from the day of Pentecost onward, was guiding and inspiring the church (though here we have to notice that, to begin with, no clear distinction was made between the Holy Spirit and the risen Christ). But if God's self-revelation as given in the Judeo-Christian experience is true, then must not one proceed from the economic Trinity to what is called the "imma-nent" or "essential" Trinity, that is, the doctrine that not only has God been known in a threefold action but that God in God's self is three in one and one in three? Obviously this brings us into a much more speculative region, for how can we know God's self? Yet the very paradox of three in one and one in three may be thought to preserve the ultimate mystery and incomprehensibility of the divine being.

*History of the Doctrine.* The doctrine of the triune God is not found explicitly in the NT, but the raw

*Traditional Symbols for the Trinity*

materials, so to speak, are undoubtedly there, and the later formulations are legitimate developments from the NT sources. As we have noted already, there already appears in the NT an accidental or incidental binitarianism, through the close association of Christ with God. Here it should be noted that the word "God" *(theos)* is in the NT almost invariably applied to the Father of trinitarian terminology, to the God of Israel or the ultimate Source, though in a very few cases (John 1:1; 20:28; Heb. 1:8) Jesus Christ is called God. However, the close association between God and Christ in many passages, especially the greetings at the beginning and end of some of the Epistles, is indicative of how these early Christians were thinking. Even if this is "binitarian," the important point is that one has departed from undifferentiated monism in thinking of God, and the way is open to trinitarianism as the next stage, once the theology of the Holy Spirit has been developed. In a few cases the full trinitarian formula appears: "The grace of the Lord Jesus Christ and the love of God and the fellowship of the Holy Spirit be with you all" (II Cor. 13:14); "Go therefore and make disciples of all nations, baptizing them in the name of the Father and of the Son and of the Holy Spirit" (Matt. 28:19)—though these words are unlikely to come from Jesus, and the earliest formula was probably baptism in the name of Jesus.

The development of trinitarian doctrine from the NT proceeds hand in hand with the development of Christology, and to a large extent the two doctrines share the same terminology. A high Christology inevitably encouraged a differentiated understanding of Godhead. In the earliest period, Jesus was often considered subordinate to God, but the tendency was more and more to declare him equal to the Father. At Nicaea (325) he was declared to be "of one substance" (HOMOOUSIOS) with the Father, in opposition to the Arians, who maintained a form of subordinationism. Meanwhile, ATHANASIUS developed a theology of the Holy Spirit, so completing the Trinity.

In the West, theological thought began from the unity of the Godhead, conceived as one substance or being, and then differentiated the persons. Already in TERTULLIAN (about A.D. 200) we find the classic language of "substance" and "persons." But when the emphasis on the substantial unity was pushed to extremes, the persons might be reduced to mere temporary "modes" of the one God, or it might even be maintained that it was the one God (the Father) who was incarnate and suffered in the Son—the heresies of modalism and patripassianism respectively. The East, like the NT, began from the three persons, God (the Father), the Son or Logos, and the Spirit. Here the principle of unity was God the Father, the origin of all. God is not derived from anything other than God's self, God is "ingenerate" or "unbegotten." The Son, on the other hand, is "begotten" of the Father. The Spirit also derives from the Father, but is said to "proceed," a word used in

John's Gospel. When pushed to extremes, this Eastern view could come close to a belief in three Gods. The difference is made clear by the different models or analogies used in West and East. In the West, Augustine illustrated the three-in-oneness of the Deity from the threefold unity of the human mind, for example, as memory, understanding, and will. In the East, Basil used the analogy of a society of three persons, Peter, James, and John. The continuing difference between East and West over the question of whether the Holy Spirit proceeds from the Father alone or from the Father *and* the Son (FILIOQUE) reflects these deeper theological differences.

*Non-Christian Trinities.* It is interesting to note that in many non-Christian religions one finds views of God that have some analogy to trinitarianism. The mystical philosopher PLOTINUS (about A.D. 250) visualized a divine Triad, consisting of the ineffable One who is the Source of all, the Mind or Logos, and the Psyche or World-soul, which indwells the entire universe. Although these three were hierarchically arranged, each being lower than the one above it from which it "emanated" or proceeded, there is at least a remote resemblance to the Christian doctrine of the Trinity. In Indian religion, the three Gods, Brahma the creator, Vishnu the preserver, and Shiva, often called the "destroyer" but performing many other functions, form together the Trimurti or "Three Powers," and each may be also represented as threefold in itself. The older theologians saw in such phenomena *vestigia trinitatis* or traces of the Trinity, and believed that they go back to some primeval revelation, vaguely remembered in all religions. Few would take that view nowadays, but the fact that trinitarian views of God are widespread perhaps indicates that some such understanding of God belongs to NATURAL THEOLOGY and is not only part of the Christian revelation. If that is so, then all serious reflection about God leads in a trinitarian direction. In spite of his insistence on the specifically Christian revelation, Barth seems to lend tacit support to the view expressed here, for he holds that the doctrine of the triune God follows immediately from any revelation on the ground that revelation itself has a threefold structure—revealer, revealed, and revealedness.                                                    J.M.

**TRINITY SUNDAY.** The Festival of the Holy Trinity or the Octave of Whitsunday (that is, the Sunday after Pentecost), a late developing festival of the Christian liturgical year. The church in Gaul founded that day as a festival in honor of the Holy Trinity in the tenth century A.D. It was approved by the pope only in A.D. 1334. There is no such festival in the Orthodox churches.

                                                    J.C.

**TRISAGION.** From the Greek words *tris* and *hagion* meaning "thrice holy." A prayer that forms part of the liturgy of the catechumens in the Orthodox churches. Its text is: "Holy God, Holy Mighty, Holy Immortal, have mercy upon us." Sometimes the liturgical refrain, "Holy, Holy, Holy" (the Sanctus) of the old Lutheran Communion service is incorrectly called the Trisagion.                                                    J.C.

**TROAS.** A seaport and standard port of call of northwest Asia Minor near the site of ancient Troy. It revolted against the Roman Empire in the second century B.C. and for a time was ruled by Syria. At Troas, Paul had a vision of a man calling him to preach in Macedonia. Paul visited and preached at Troas a number of times (Acts 20:6).                                                    T.J.K.

**TROELTSCH, ERNEST** (1865–1923). German Protestant theologian also noted as a social philosopher active at the turn of the century. Born on February 17 at Augsburg, he died on February 1. Troeltsch's higher education was at Erlangen and Göttingen. He taught systematic theology at Bonn (1892-94), systematics and the philosophy of religion at Heidelberg (1894-1914), and philosophy of religion and philosophy in Berlin (1914-19). He was a Prussian government official for church and educational affairs from 1919 to 1921.

Troeltsch was a forerunner in the developing field of the philosophy of religion. He was deeply interested in the history of religions (*religionsgeschichte Schule*). A major influence on him was ALBRECHT RITSCHL. Ritschl and Troeltsch are often mentioned together as the highest development of German Protestant liberalism. Troeltsch rejected supernatural revelation and understood Christianity as a historically developing phenomenon. He saw the church as involved in a social evolution that forces the institution to adjust itself again and again to the new social environment it finds itself part of. The core of Christianity is the piety Jesus exhibits in the Gospels, Troeltsch felt. He believed that all religion grew, not out of revelation, but out of inner feelings.    J.C.

**TRUEBLOOD, DAVID ELTON** (1900–   ). American QUAKER theologian, educator, and author. Born on December 12, in Pleasantville, Iowa, to devout Quaker parents, Elton was reared on a family farm. He attended William Penn College in Oskaloosa. Both studious and involved in extracurricular activities, Trueblood played varsity football, edited the yearbook, and was a member of the debating team. Majoring in history, he was graduated in 1922 with a B.A. degree. Subsequently Trueblood studied a year at Brown University and another at Hartford School of Theology, before entering Harvard Divinity School. After his graduation he was appointed assistant professor of philosophy and dean of men at Guilford College in North Carolina. He completed work on a Ph.D. degree at Johns Hopkins University in 1934. For three years he served as assistant professor of philosophy at Haverford College

Courtesy of Yokefellows International

*D. Elton Trueblood*

in the suburbs of Philadelphia. From 1936 to 1945 he was professor of philosophy at Stanford University, and for a year he was on the faculty of Garrett Biblical Institute in Illinois.

It was in 1946 that Trueblood began his long career at Earlham College, a Quaker school in Richmond, Indiana. Trueblood's first book was *The Essence of Spiritual Religion* which was followed by a number of others. He interrupted his long career at Earlham for the better part of two years, starting in 1954, when he served as chief of religious policy for an information agency. In 1956 Trueblood founded the Earlham School of Religion. He also was president of the Yokefellow Association, which he had started.

R.H.

**TRUST.** *See* FAITH.

**TRUTH.** This word has different meanings in different kinds of discourse. The truth of a mathematical proposition and that of an empirical proposition are obvious examples of different kinds of truth. Similarly, there are different criteria for testing different truths. In the case of what claims to be a mathematical truth, we check whether it is deducible from the fundamental axioms of the mathematical system in which it appears. In the case of an empirical

proposition, there are many possible procedures, some very simple, some highly complex. If someone asserts, "It is raining," the matter can be simply settled by looking out of the window. If it is claimed that Julius Caesar was assassinated on the ides of March, this calls for much more complicated procedures. Perhaps we could say in every case, however, that a proposition is true if it shows us things *as they really are.*

Religious and theological statements claim to be true. Here the first move is to ascertain the meaning of what is being asserted, for religious language is frequently symbolic or even mythological. It may look like empirical assertion, but may be quite different, so that the first task in any assessment is a hermeneutical one. Suppose someone asks, "Is it true that Jesus rose from the dead?" This looks at first sight as if it referred to an event of past history, like Caesar's assassination, but from Paul onward many Christian theologians have not regarded the Resurrection as the empirical matter of the raising of a corpse. In that case, it is up to them to say what resurrection does mean, and to indicate what considerations would be relevant to the truth or falsity of the claim that Jesus rose from the dead.

Let us take another example: "In the beginning God created the heaven and the earth." This too looks like an assertion about the past. But what meaning is to be given to the phrase "in the beginning"? Or how is one to understand the verb "created," a strange metaphysical verb without parallels in ordinary experience? If the interpretation of religious assertions is the first step toward assessing their truth, the second must be the development of a religious EPISTEMOLOGY. This implies that the question of truth in religion or theology has to be put in the context of an entire PHILOSOPHY OF RELIGION.

J.M.

**TÜBINGEN SCHOOL.** A term used to refer to a school of Protestant historians and theologians and to a school of Catholic theologians, both attached to the University of Tübingen in Germany during the first half of the nineteenth century. The Protestant Tübingen School was founded by F. C. BAUR, who, influenced by HEGEL's dialectical view of history, insisted that theology be approached historically, both in terms of its development and by means of the historico-critical method. The school saw the early church as divided between Petrine (Jewish) and Pauline (Gentile) Christianity, which reached a synthesis in second-century Caholicism. This view was later discredited by the work of the Ritschlians, especially Adolf Harnack. The Catholic Tübingen School is associated with J. S. Drey and J. A. Möhler, who were influenced by German ROMANTICISM and IDEALISM. They emphasized religious experience and the evolution of tradition, stressing Catholicism's diversity within an organic unity. Their influence was felt in later liberal Catholicism.                    J.L.

**TURIN.** *See* SHROUD OF TURIN.

**TWELFTH NIGHT.** The twelfth evening after Christmas, and the eve of Epiphany. According to the Julian calendar (before 1752), this day (twelfth day) was Christmas, and certain Christmas-related ancient customs still cling to it in many countries. In England, Christmas decorations are removed from the church and the home on the twelfth day.   J.C.

**TWELVE.** In the OT and NT NUMBERS are often used symbolically or with hidden meanings. Some numbers were especially sacred or laden with symbolic significance. Among these were one, three, four, seven, ten, twelve, forty, seventy, and one thousand.

"Twelve" early took on importance in astrology and other occult arts among the Mesopotamian civilizations as the Sumarians divided the year into twelve months, based on the lunar cycle. Twelve functions symbolically in Genesis as the number of the sons of Jacob (Gen. 35:22), and consequently of the tribes of Israel (Num. 1). The tribes of Ishmael are also said to be twelve. In the NT, Jesus called twelve of his disciples to be apostles (Mark 3:14). An added note, from the Fourth Gospel, tells us there were twelve baskets of food left over after the miraculous feeding of the crowd (John 6:13).   J.C.

**TWELVE, THE.** *See* APOSTLE.

**TWO SWORDS.** The doctrine of the two swords, in Roman Catholicism, signifies that God gave the church power to loose and bind on earth and in heaven (Matt. 16:13-20), thus giving Rome spiritual and temporal rule, which the church may delegate. Christianity gained legal toleration in 313 and became the only legal religion in the Roman Empire in 380. By 416 only Christians could serve in the Roman army. During this period Rome began asserting primacy over both swords. Pope Leo I (440–461) manifested the theory against the invading Huns and Vandals, and Pope Gelasius I (492–496) boldly claimed priestly power is above kingly power, setting the stage for the struggle between church and state through the Middle Ages. The greatest manifestations of the theory came during the pontificates of Gregory VII and Innocent III. Modern nationalism has made the theory virtually impossible to implement, but Roman Catholicism has not officially abandoned it. (*See also* SEPARATION OF CHURCH AND STATE.)   C.M.

**TYCHICUS.** A Greek name meaning "fortunate." A native of the Roman province of Asia and a traveling companion of Paul on the journey to Jerusalem (Acts 20:4). Tychicus traveled to Troas from Greece in advance of Paul to prepare the way. Together with Onesimus, he is the bearer of the Letter to the Colossians. He later served at Ephesus after being diverted from Crete (Tit. 3:12).   T.J.K.

**TYNDALE, WILLIAM** (about 1494–1536). English Reformer and Bible translator. Born between 1490 and 1495 in England near the Welsh border, Tyndale was educated at both Oxford and Cambridge. At the latter university he became interested in reading the Greek NT. Finding both clergy and laity ignorant of the Scriptures, he set out to translate the NT into English. Failing to enlist the help of the bishop of London, Tyndale went to Wittenberg, Germany, where he met Martin Luther. Driven from Cologne, when his translation was partly printed, he published his first edition in Worms in 1525. This was widely distributed in England before the authorities discovered it and burned it. In 1534 Tyndale printed a revised version of the NT in a style said to have formed the basis of the KING JAMES VERSION. Betrayed by one he regarded as a friend, Tyndale was imprisoned at Vilvorde, near Brussels, where he had translated the first five books of the OT. He was tried, condemned, and on October 6 was burned at the stake.   R.H.

**TYPOLOGY.** A comparison of events or persons in an earlier portion of Scripture to a later portion, for example, of an OT event to an NT event, or even to something in the Christian church. Thus typology sees types as moving across the scale of time, and is an effort to understand later revelation or acts of God historically, and to see foreshadowings or predictions of such events as the Incarnation of Christ, the Crucifixion, and Resurrection, in the OT.

Generally, typology is distinguished from ALLEGORY, which makes no historical claims but uses earlier events or persons as signs of eternal, philosophical truths. Typology is considered basic to the internal consistency and unity of the OT and NT, as one Bible, while allegory, though present in both testaments, is not. This neat distinction is not fully accepted by biblical scholars today, however, because of the contemporary insights of literary criticism, including rhetorical criticism, into the biblical materials.

Types are ideals, in the traditional form of biblical exegesis followed by rabbis in Judaism, as well as by Roman Catholics and Protestants. Paul used typology in comparing the ideal person of Adam to the ideal person of Christ, and drew an analogy between Adam's sin and Christ's redemption. (Rom. 5:12-21).   J.C.

**TYRANNUS.** Tyrannus is mentioned only in Acts 19:9. On first coming to Ephesus, Paul taught for three months at the synagogue, but when opposed, "he withdrew . . . taking the disciples with him, and argued daily in the hall of Tyrannus." Tyrannus may have been a Jewish scribe, a Greek teacher of rhetoric or philosophy, or even someone long dead, whose name was still associated with the school or the building where Paul taught.   T.J.K.

From *Atlas of the Bible* (Thomas Nelson & Sons Limited)

*Aerial view of Tyre*

**TYRE.** An important city in Phoenicia, bordering on the shores of Israel. Tyre, meaning "rock," lies about halfway up the coast of the Mediterranean Sea between Carmel and Beirut. Originally the city lay on the mainland, and even there it was protected by rugged promontories, known in history as the Ladder of Tyre. Later the city was rebuilt on an island just off shore. The historian Herodotus dates its age from about 3000 B.C., and Josephus from about 1200 B.C. Isaiah 23:7 describes Tyre as an "exultant city whose origin is from days of old."

Tyre is frequently mentioned in the Bible and in the Tell el-Amarna letters. King HIRAM of Tyre had dealings with David and provided Solomon with architects and materials to build the Temple in Jerusalem. At home he built the new city on the island and rebuilt the old one on the mainland. He constructed fabulous new harbors and breakwaters that were the envy of the ancient world, connecting two harbors with a canal. He traded for grain in the Crimea, mined gold and lead in Spain, copper in Cyprus, and tin in Cornwall, and established colonies in North Africa, Sicily, and Crete. His traders appear to have sailed around Africa and ventured out into the Atlantic. During the wars with Assyria, Tyre was able to buy off the invaders several times by paying tribute money. When Alexander the Great laid siege to the city, Tyre resisted. He built a causeway two hundred feet wide between the mainland and the island, and after the conquest, slaughtered, crucified, or sold into slavery all the survivors.

T.J.K.

**TYRRELL, GEORGE.** (1861–1909). The leading representative of Catholic Modernism in the British Isles. Originally an Anglican, he became a Jesuit priest in 1891, and declared his aim to be the synthesis of the truth of religion with the truth of Modernity. He believed that the principal source of theology is the evolving experience of Christians, and that the test of its truth is the pragmatic one of whether it fosters moral and spiritual development. He was expelled from the Jesuits and virtually excommunicated in 1907. He continued to regard himself as a Catholic but also continued to be a severe critic of the church, especially of the efforts then being made by Cardinal Mercier to revive Scholastic philosophy. At his death, he was refused a Catholic burial.

J.M.

# Uu

UGARIT. An important seaport of the Canaanite period, about seven miles north of Latakia (in Syria), the biblical Laodicea. The city lay half a mile from the sea on a navigable river. The tell from which the ruins rise is about seventy feet above the landscape. Another name for Ugarit is Ras Shamra, "the hill of the fennel plants." The tablets and writings found at Ras Shamra probably shed more light on the CANAANITE culture in which the people of Israel found themselves at the time of the conquest than any other site in the history of archaeology.

Ugarit was an active city from about 5000 B.C. to about 120 B.C., when it was destroyed by the sea peoples. The gold bowls found there are among the finest samples of the goldsmith's art anywhere in the ancient world. An ivory trumpet two feet long was made from a single tusk, and other pieces of ivory found there are large and impressive, both in the

From C. F. A. Schaeffer, *Cuneiform Texts of Ras Shamra-Ugarit*. (Courtesy of the British Academy, Schweich Lectures, 1937)

*Air view of Ras Shamra (Ugarit), with the mound outlined in black and showing excavated areas on the mound*

From C. F. A. Schaeffer, *Cuneiform Texts of Ras Shamra-Ugarit*. (Courtesy of the British Academy, Schweich Lectures, 1937)

*El seated on a throne accepting an offering from the king of Ugarit; from Ras Shamra (fourteenth century* B.C.*)*

intricate Egyptian-style carvings and in basic design. Scores of bronze tools and weapons have been found, often in a single workshop or warehouse, many with cuneiform inscriptions. The collection of pottery from Ugarit demonstrates the importance of the city from a standpoint of trade, and most of the pieces are of the highest workmanship. One caravan route led along the coast from Asia Minor to Egypt, and another toward the east to Mari and Babylon. Copper articles from Crete were common, but Ugarit itself seems to have been a center for the making of tools and weapons from bronze.

The buildings are no less impressive than the artifacts. Even the graves were much more sophisticated than those in other parts of the world, king-size tombs of cut stone, in the style of Crete and Mycenae. The huge temple dedicated to Baal had much the same design as Solomon's Temple in Jerusalem. The main palace had sixty-seven rooms, in a building considerably bigger than a football field. This contained living quarters for the high priest and a huge collection of cuneiform tablets. Apparently it also served as a library and a writing school for scribes. Of the three largest buildings, roughly of the same size, two were temples to Baal and Dagon. The images of the gods appeared to have been kept in an inner room, a "holy of holies," even as Jehovah held such a spot in Jerusalem.

What makes Ras Shamra more remarkable than any other Canaanite site are the thousands and thousands of tablets found there. Some were in languages or forms of writing that had not previously been known—Hurrian, Hittite, Sumerian, Akkadian, Egyptian, Cretan-Minoan, and Ugaritic. The Akkadian ones alone number well into the thousands. These are in part history, in part business records, in part private letters, and very largely religious, mythological, and cultural. They describe the whole pattern of Canaanite gods and their relationships, as complex a hierarchy as what we know of the Greek gods and goddesses of Mt. Olympus. Many of the references shed significant light on obscure passages of the OT, previously not well understood, such as the one about cooking a kid in its mother's milk. Some are interesting for their cultural values, in the style of *Poor Richard's Almanac*, such as "Don't tell your wife where you keep your wallet."

The tablets give a very lively picture of the involvement of Baal and Anath in the doings of human beings. The king of the gods is El, the father of all. Often he is depicted as a bull. Here we also meet Baal, the son of Dagon, and the Prince of the Sea. The count of the gods and goddesses numbered well into the hundreds, each with individual functions and cults. In fact, the collection of tablets found at Ras Shamra since 1929 will keep scholars, linguists, and students of Near Eastern religion busy for many generations, and we are fortunate to have so many parallel insights into the world of the OT.

T.J.K.

**ULAMA.** The Arabic word plural of *'ālim,* meaning "an authority, a scholar." A collective term for the religious scholars of Islam who, having received a traditional education in Arabic, the Qur'an, the Hadith, and Islamic law, constitute an elite group competent to teach religion and interpret it authoritatively. Their role, combining that of the preacher, the professor, and the lawyer in other traditions, is a recognized one throughout Islam. Serving as theologians, judges, and officials in traditional Muslim states, members of the ulama have wielded great power. For this reason states have at various times sought the support of the ulama or to control or limit its power. In particular, modernizers within the Islamic world in recent centuries have often found themselves at odds with the usually highly conservative ulama, a conflict that lay behind the Iranian revolution of 1979. R.E.

**ULTIMATE CONCERN.** A term used by PAUL TILLICH to describe the existential basis and object of religion and the criteria for any authentic theology. For Tillich, religion is the depth dimension in all human cultural and spiritual life. By the metaphor "depth" Tillich means that the religious dimension of life points to what is ultimate and unconditional in a person's life—that which both gives meaning to that life and sustains its being. Hence a person's ultimate concern is that person's religion. Such a concern can manifest itself in any aspect of life—in the moralist's unconditional demand of conscience or in the scientist's passionate, unflinching search for truth. According to Tillich, only those propositions that deal with their object insofar as it can become a matter of ultimate concern for us are theological. It is obvious, however, that often the object of ultimate concern is not truly ultimate. A genuine ultimate concern must have the power to determine our being or nonbeing. That is, it must actually possess saving power. 								J.L.

**ULTRAMONTANISM.** Meaning "beyond the mountains"; a catchword symbol for belief in the absolute supremacy of the papacy over all clerical and civil matters throughout the world. Although Ultramontanism has rootage in the ancient claims of the papacy to primacy in church and state, seen especially in the pontificates of Leo I, Gregory VII, Innocent III, and Boniface VIII, it reached a pinnacle and is commonly associated with Pius IX's (1846-78) rejection of modernism. Historically it was a nineteenth-century reaction to the French Revolution, which outlawed traditional Catholicism and instituted the worship of reason. Ultramontane papal superiority over church and state was preeminently affirmed by Pius IX's *Immaculate Conception of Mary* (1854) and *Syllabus of Errors* (1864), a sweeping rejection of progress and liberalism; by Vatican I's (1870) dogmatism of papal infallibility; by Pius X's (1903-14) condemnation of modernism in *Lamentabili* and *Pascendi* (1907); and excommunication of Alfred Loisy and George Tyrrell for biblical liberalism. 								C.M.

**UMMA.** The entire community of ISLAM, the ideal unity of all Muslims, regardless of the religious and political factors that divide them. This concept derives from the position of Muhammad as the Prophet around whom the community centered. Today most Muslims are non-Arabs, live outside the Middle East, speak a great variety of languages, differ widely from one another in culture, and live under a wide range of political systems. Yet the ideal of an all-embracing community persists. It is strongest when Islam faces threats to its traditional values and standards of conduct. 								K.C.

**UNAM SANCTUM.** *See* INNOCENT III.

**UNBELIEF.** *See* ATHEISM.

**UNCLEAN.** *See* CLEAN AND UNCLEAN.

**UNCTION OF THE SICK.** The sacramental anointing with oil of the sick. In the Roman Catholic Church, such anointing is counted as one of the seven sacraments. It was formerly called extreme unction because it was given only at the approach of death, but since Vatican II the adjective "extreme" has been dropped, and the anointing is now regarded not as a

preparation for death but as part of the church's ministry of HEALING. There are similar practices in the Anglican and Eastern Orthodox churches. The oil used is consecrated each year by the bishop on Maundy Thursday and then distributed to the parishes of the diocese. The anointing is often accompanied by LAYING ON OF HANDS and a PRAYER for the recovery of the sick person.

The practice is very ancient in the Christian church. The disciples of Jesus "anointed with oil many that were sick and healed them" (Mark 6:13), while the apostle James advises the sick person to "call for the elders of the church, and let them pray over him, anointing him with oil in the name of the Lord" (Jas. 5:14). The rite is to be understood within the larger concept of the church's ministry of healing, itself closely connected in the NT with the forgiveness of sins. The renewed interest in recent years in the ministry of healing, which goes with the modern understanding of the human being as a psychosomatic unity, has led to a corresponding renewal of interest in the sacrament of unction. 								J.M.

**UNDERHILL, EVELYN** (1875–1941). Writer, lecturer, spiritual director, and mystic who encouraged the rediscovery of Christian MYSTICISM. Her *Mysticism* (1911) is still the definitive treatment. Born December 6, the only child of Lucy Ironmonger and Sir Arthur Underhill, she was not reared in a religious home. She studied at King's College, London, where she later was made a Fellow (1927). Her father was a Deist, a lawyer, and a yachtsman, as was Hubert Stuart Moore, whom she married in 1907. Confirmed in the Church of England in 1891, she was deeply attracted to Roman Catholicism. However, her spiritual director, BARON FRIEDRICH VON HÜGEL, whom she met in 1911, advised her against changing. Under his influence she became increasingly Christocentric and devoted to the sacraments. From 1924 she conducted frequent retreats at Pleshey and served as spiritual director to many, including her devoted friend and literary executor Lucy Menzies. She died on June 15, and is buried at St. John's, Hampstead. Her writings include *Practical Mysticism* (1915), *The Essentials of Mysticism* (1920), and *Worship* (1938). 								N.H.

**UNFORGIVABLE SIN.** Resistance to the Holy Spirit, so that God's offered forgiveness cannot be received, hence the sin of sins, making pardon impossible. This concept is based on Scripture, both OT and NT, but is not expressly stated in the Bible. It is, above all, BLASPHEMY and a SIN AGAINST THE HOLY SPIRIT, that is, on God, as God communicates grace to people. In Matthew 12:24-32, Jesus condemned the action of certain Pharisees who accused him of casting out demons by use of the power of the chief of demons, Beelzebub, rather than acknowledging that God's cleansing power was working through Jesus to overcome Satan and his demons. The unforgivable sin, then, is to call evil good, and good evil, along with rejecting God's offer of forgiveness.

In the OT, the concept is far different, although there, also, the rejection of God is the basic idea. In Numbers 15:30, doom is pronounced on the person who willfully rejects God's law. Such a wicked person is separated from Yahweh's grace, and so lost forever. The unpardonable sin is more popularly known as the unforgivable sin.                                    J.C.

**UNIATE CHURCHES.** A general term to identify various churches connected historically with the Eastern rite that have separated from the parent body and are now in communion with the Roman Catholic church. Many of them in early times accepted the teachings of Eutyches and Nestorius and were cut off from Christendom for over five hundred years by the Muslims. While under the authority of Rome, Uniate churches generally have kept some distinctive practices: married clergy, leavened bread, both bread and wine in Communion, Greek or other languages in the liturgy, and baptism by immersion. The variations, not necessarily the same for all, reflect agreements made with Rome when the unions took place, from as early as 1182 to modern times. Among the most important groups of Uniate churches are the Maronites; Armenians; Ruthenian Ukrainians, Hungarians, Podcarpathians, and Yugoslavs; Copts; Ethiopians; Melkites; and some Bulgars, Albanians, and St. Thomas Christians. A few have rescinded their unions.                                               C.M.

**UNIFICATION CHURCH.** The worldwide movement founded by the Reverend Sun Myung Moon in Korea in 1954 as the Holy Spirit Association for the Unification of World Christianity (HSAUWC), whose members are known informally as "Moonies." In the United States the movement is officially known as the Unification Church of America, and its president is Dr. Mose Durst. There are also Unification churches in Korea, Japan, a number of European countries, Canada, South America, and Africa. The Unification Church (U.C.) is much in the news due to charges by many parents of youthful members that their sons and daughters were "brainwashed" or recruited by forms of mind control; a number of kidnappings of members who were then "deprogrammed" or—it is claimed—freed of mind control; and the conviction and imprisonment of Rev. Moon by United States courts for income tax evasion.

The U.C. began, according to Unificationist accounts, when Rev. Moon, a Presbyterian minister in North Korea, was imprisoned by Communist authorities in the late 1940s because of his successful religious work. Opponents claim that Moon was actually imprisoned for adultery. Moon was a prisoner in a forced labor camp near Hung Nam, North Korea, in October 1950, when the United Nations forces landed at nearby Wonsan and overran the camp. Moon then fled south to Pusan in South

Korea and built a small chapel in Seoul and founded the HSAUWC. After a few years, the movement spread to Japan and prospered. Somewhat later, missionaries (among then, Mrs. Durst) carried the movement to the United States.

Starting in California, the U.C. grew by conversions on college campuses and in places frequented by questioning youth. It spread across the country both by evangelism and by way of Rev. Moon's "I Love America" crusades in dozens of United States cities. Disillusioned youth, tired of the radicalism of the 1960s and the anti-Americanism of the anti–Vietnam war movement, found Moon's blend of Christian fundamentalism, Asian cultural religion, fervent patriotism, and anti-Communism very attractive. Some 35,000 young Americans had committed themselves to Moon by the 1980s.           J.C.

**UNION OF AMERICAN HEBREW CONGREGATIONS** (UAHC). The network of and major leadership service organization for about 750 Reform Jewish congregations in the Western hemisphere. The life ambition of Rabbi ISAAC MAYER WISE was to establish a seminary to train American Jewish youth for service as American rabbis. On July 8, 1873, he gained his first major objective when the UAHC was organized in Cincinnati, Ohio, at a conference of congregational representatives. The constitution of the newly established Union declared "it is the primary object . . . to establish a Hebrew Theological Institute." Two years later Hebrew Union College was opened. Other provisions of that constitution were "to encourage and aid the organization and development of Jewish congregations; to promote Jewish education and enrich and intensify Jewish life . . . and to foster other activities for the perpetuation and advancement of Judaism." Originally "unalterably opposed to political ZIONISM," the UAHC in 1942 underwent an ideological transformation. It is headquartered in the House of Living Judaism in New York City.                                       L.K.

**UNITARIAN UNIVERSALIST ASSOCIATION.** A liberal Protestant denomination formed in 1961 by the merger of the American Unitarian Association and the Universalist Church of America. Arising in the late eighteenth and early nineteenth centuries, both groups shared common concerns and a common history. In 1953 the two groups had formed the Council of Liberal Churches. The merged group is characterized by Congregational polity, creedlessness, commitment to social and ethical issues, love for freedom of religious belief, a quest for truth, belief in human dignity, a humanistic Christology, acceptance of religious humanists and agnostics as well as theists into fellowship, and a desire for an ecumenical, interfaith community.

Most members of the association have come to it from other denominations. In 1983, there were 935 churches, with 131,844 members. The association belongs to the International Association for Liberal Christianity and Religious Freedom. Its lack of a creed precludes membership in the National Council of Churches or the World Council of Churches.

J.C.

## UNITAS FRATRUM. See MORAVIAN BRETHREN.

## UNITED BIBLE SOCIETIES.

A world fellowship of sixty-four national Bible societies, founded in 1946, which coordinates the efforts of Bible societies in more than one hundred countries.

The first Bible society developed from the concerns of the Pietist movement in Germany when the Van Canstein Bible Society was formed. The modern movement was launched in 1804, when the British and Foreign Bible Society (BFBS) was organized in London. Shortly after, the AMERICAN BIBLE SOCIETY was formed in 1816 in New York City. Then came the Russian Bible Society in 1819. The BFBS grew rapidly and by the end of the nineteenth century had developed a worldwide network of Bible distribution. Likewise, the ABS grew at an equal pace. This resulted in duplication of effort in many areas.

In the early decades of the twentieth century, leaders of the two major Bible societies recognized that there was need for greater coordination of their efforts. Joint agencies were set up as a first step in solving the problem. But it was not until after World War II that the United Bible Societies organization was established at a conference of sixteen member societies at Haywards Heath, England. In 1947 Olivier Beguin was appointed as the first UBS secretary.

The UBS has functional subcommittees on translation, production, distribution and fund raising, and the World Service Budget. Specialized consultants work at the World Service centers in New York and London and others in four regional centers: Africa's in Nairobi; Asia's in Singapore; America's in Mexico City; and Europe's in Basserdorf, Switzerland. The UBS headquarters is now located in Stuttgart, Germany.

The UBS organizes training institutes and publishes technical helps for translators, seeks means of achieving the most economical means of producing Bibes, stimulates new methods of Bible distribution, and aids millions of new literates in Bible reading. The UBS Council meets at least once every ten years. Its general committee meets every three years and supervises the executive committee, which meets at least once a year. Through the World Service Budget pooled funds are appropriated for the worldwide program of UBS.

R.H.

## UNITED BRETHREN IN CHRIST.

A denomination formed in 1800 by Philip William Otterbein (1726–1813), who had been a German Reformed minister, and Martin Boehm (1725–1812), of Swiss Mennonite ancestry.

Boehm had served a Mennonite congregation in Lancaster County, Pennsylvania, but he lost favor with the Mennonites when he conducted revival meetings in English. He continued to preach, and in 1768 he met Otterbein at an evangelistic service near Lancaster. After the meeting, Otterbein embraced Boehm and declared: "We are brethren."

Otterbein, who earlier had been called to serve as minister of a German Reformed congregation in Lancaster, struggled to find a more vital experience of his faith. When this occurred, he began to preach with greater power. He stressed the need for his converts to experience a new birth. Like Boehm, Otterbein worked cooperatively with ministers of other denominations. He participated in the consecration of Francis Asbury as a bishop in the newly formed Methodist Episcopal church.

In this framework Boehm and Otterbein, both of whom had moved to a pietistic and revivalistic stance, formed their new Methodist-type denomination, which was evangelical, Arminian, and perfectionist in doctrine. They became the first two bishops of the United Brethren church. Otterbein nevertheless served as minister of the German Evangelical Reformed church in Baltimore from 1774 until his death.

Two parties developed in the United Brethren— one held closely to the original constitution, and another sought to revise it to meet what they considered were changed conditions. When a new constitution was adopted in 1889, the minority group separated and became the United Brethren in Christ (Old Constitution). In 1946 the parent body joined with the Evangelical church, another German-speaking Arminian pietistic group that had been formed in 1807 by Jacob Albright (1759–1808), a former Lutheran turned Methodist. The resulting Evangelical United Brethren church merged with the Methodist church in 1968 to form The United Methodist church.

R.H.

## UNITED CHURCH OF CANADA.

A Protestant church formed by the merger of the Congregational, Methodist, and Presbyterian churches in the Dominion of Canada, negotiated between 1908 and 1925. The United Church of Canada resulted from a deliberate effort to reverse the fragmentation of the Protestant church into smaller and smaller sects. Each one of the churches that initiated the United Church was also itself the product of mergers.

A Basis of Union was established by 1908, giving the polity and doctrine of the proposed new church. About three thousand local unions of congregations took place before the formal merger in June 1925. Since 1925, several other Protestant churches have joined the merger. The Evangelical United Brethren are the last group to join.

Doctrinally, the Bible is declared to be supreme authority but tradition is also acknowledged, especially the ancient creeds and the confessions of the Reformed churches. A careful balance has been achieved between the Calvinism of the Presbyterians and the Arminianism of the Methodists. Those seeking ordination are asked to be only in essential agreement with the church's doctrine. There are two sacraments, baptism—generally infant baptism—and the Lord's Supper, which is celebrated a minimum of four times a year. Worship is ordered by the *Book of Common Order,* adopted by the UCC in 1932. A common Protestant emphasis upon Bible reading and preaching is observed. The UCC is a leader in the struggle to remove sexism from church life. All church offices are open to women as well as men. The UCC is a member of the World Council of Churches, the World Methodist Council, the World Alliance of Reformed Churches, and the International Congregational Council.

J.C.

**UNITED CHURCH OF CHRIST** (UCC). An American Protestant denomination formed June 25, 1957, and completed with the adoption of a constitution in July 1961. The UCC is a merger of the Congregational Church, the Christian Church, the Evangelical Synod, and the Reformed Church. The Congregationalists and the Christians merged in 1931 and the Evangelical Synod and Reformed Church merged in 1934. Total membership of the UCC in 1985 was 1,701,513 in 6,427 churches.

The UCC seeks to express more fully the oneness in Christ of the churches composing it, to make more effective their common witness to Jesus and to serve his kingdom in the world. The UCC has a statement of faith, adopted at Oberlin, Ohio, in July 1959, but it is a testimony rather than a test of faith. The doctrines and theological positions of the four churches now within the UCC remain established. It stands as a tribute to the faith, charity, and understanding of the merged churches.

The UCC is an unusual union of congregational local church government and presbyterian polity in larger church, district, and synod matters. The UCC is mainstream Protestant in overall theology, although it generally leans toward the more liberal side of the centrist position. It affirms the responsibility of the church to make the historic faith of Christianity its own in every generation. It recognizes two sacraments—baptism (usually of infants) and the Lord's Supper. The UCC is committed to ecumenicity. It belongs to the National Council of Churches, the World Council of Churches, and the World Alliance of Reformed Churches. At the present there is talk that it may be considering a merger with the Community churches and the Christian churches (Disciples of Christ).

J.C.

**UNITED METHODIST CHURCH.** *See* METHODIST CHURCHES.

**UNITED PRESBYTERIAN CHURCH IN THE U.S.A.** *See* PRESBYTERIAN CHURCHES.

**UNITED STATES CATHOLIC CONFERENCE.** The secretariat, or civil arm, of the National Conference of Catholic Bishops. Since the NCCB is the highest ecclesiastical authority of the Roman Catholic church in the United States, the USCC renders an important service in such areas as social justice and family life. Strategically located in its headquarters in Washington, D.C., the USCC conducts its work through seven major departments: education, legislation, immigration, social action, lay organizations, youth, and press. The USCC traces its origins to the National Catholic War Council, formed during World War I. In 1919 the War Council became the National Catholic Welfare Conference, which in turn was succeeded by the launching of the USCC on January 1, 1967.

R.H.

**UNITY.** *See* ECUMENICAL MOVEMENT.

**UNIVERSALISM.** The doctrine that in the end all souls (human, angelic, and even demonic) will be saved by God's grace. Some NT scholars claim that this teaching is already found in Paul's belief that Christ "must reign until he has put all enemies under his feet" (I Cor. 15:25). It clearly emerges in some of the patristic writers, especially ORIGEN, who used the word *apocatastasis* (*compare* RESTORATION OF ALL THINGS). The term meant the return of the heavenly bodies to their original positions and was used by Origen to mean the return of all things to an original perfection. "We think," he wrote, "that indeed the goodness of God through his Christ may recall all his creatures to one end, even his enemies being conquered and subdued." Though universalism was rejected by Augustine and the Reformers, it has been revived by liberal theologians who have found the idea of eternal punishment repellent. Karl Barth too has taught a form of universalism, holding that the entire human race has been elected in Jesus Christ. A doctrine of universalism seems to accord very well with belief in a God of love. How could such a God rest until every soul had been saved? But there are difficulties about universalism. Salvation cannot be forced on people, so must there not always remain open the possibility that some people or angels will steadfastly refuse the divine grace? There is another serious objection: the Christian proclamation is good news or gospel only on the assumption that there is some peril from which it offers deliverance; but if it has already been decided that all will be saved, the gospel ceases to have any force. If there is nothing but salvation, then Christ offers us nothing that is not already assured to us, whatever we may do or believe. This is as fatalistic as the extreme forms of PREDESTINATION. J.M.

**UNIVERSALS.** Those things that can be possessed by everyone, a cause with many effects, or a thought so broad that many people can grasp the idea. A universal can be an idea deduced by abstraction. Several philosophical schools define universals. The conceptualists accept mental constructs or ideas as universal. Nominalists view words as universals. Idealists view the ideal as universal. Realists accept only intellectual ideas as universals. Linguistic analysts assert that definition is a language issue; for that reason universals do not really exist. Existentialists are not interested in universals because such a theory obstructs for them the real need, which is to understand human existence.

The idea of a universal finds little place in a thought world where the emphasis is on inductive reasoning, finding particularity, or being aware of differences. When the emphasis is on variety and distinctiveness, the universal seems too abstract to be useful. In popular terms, however, the word is used to frame broad categories, although even within such categories there will be exceptions.                  I.C.

## UNKNOWN GOD, ALTAR TO AN.

In Acts 17:23, Luke's narrative of Paul's experiences in Athens says that he pointed to an altar on Mars Hill inscribed "To an unknown god." Paul then used this as a springboard to proclaim the true God, Yahweh, whom they did not know. Paul's sermon (considered a Lukan composition) also makes reference to two Stoic poets in terms that stress the fatherhood of God. The King James (Authorized) Version says "The Unknown God," but the Greek uses the indefinite article, so that the expression means not any one specific god but any of the many gods who inadvertently might have been overlooked. There is historical evidence that the Greeks did dedicate altars to anonymous gods. The biography of the philosopher Apollonius (written in the third century A.D.) speaks of the practice. The phrase "an unknown god" is used by the philosopher Hegel in his religious writings.
                                                      J.C.

## UNLEAVENED BREAD.

Bread baked without leaven (hops or yeast) and associated with the Passover meal from the time of the Exodus according to the accounts in the Pentateuch. The term also applies to the week-long Feast of Unleavened Bread which formed the greater part of the Passover season.

One of three great traditional festival times among the Hebrews, PASSOVER, which commemorates the miraculous deliverance of the Hebrews from Egyptian slavery in the Exodus (about 1290 B.C.), is celebrated in the first month of the liturgical year, Nisan (March-April), on the fourteenth day of the month. This is followed on the fifteenth of Nisan by the Feast of Unleavened Bread.

Scholars believe that Passover was originally a nomadic or sheepherders' festival held during the lambing season. Certainly there is some evidence that the Passover ritual is older than the time of Moses. The text of the Pentateuch explains the use of unleavened bread as the result of the haste in which the Hebrew slaves prepared the Passover as they were awaiting the imminent sign from Yahweh to escape from Egypt (Exod. 12:14-20; 13:6-10). The "leaven" was symbolic, also, of sin, and the casting out of the old leaven from Hebrew homes during this season represented the searching of one's soul for sins and repentance of them.                  J.C.

## UNMOVED MOVER. See PRIME MOVER.

## UNTOUCHABLES.

This term was formerly used for those people in India considered outside the four major caste groups of HINDUISM, and therefore especially polluting to people of CASTE. They were referred to by Mohandas K. Gandhi as "Harijan," "children of God," an expression widely used, and are officially spoken of as "scheduled castes." Their social and economic position has generally been highly depressed. In the modern Republic of India both the term and the enforcement of restrictions on people because of "untouchable" background has been illegal, and the government has taken vigorous steps to improve their lot. However, discrimination persists, especially in rural areas.                  R.E.

## UPANISHADS.

From the Sanskrit phrase meaning literally "to sit down near to," meaning "instruction" such as a master would give privately to his closest disciples. Since the eighth century A.D. this term has referred to the latest section of the VEDIC scriptures of HINDUISM, a series of philosophical treatises that technically serve as commentaries on the earlier ritual-oriented texts. Despite many diversities of point of view, the major Upanishads present a reasonably consistent philosophical position which, together with the Brahma Sutras and the Bhagavad Gita, has been the basis of the VEDANTA philosophical Darshana, above all the Advaita Vedanta associated with Samkara. Although 108 Upanishads are counted in all, thirteen are considered most important; they were composed over about five hundred years, beginning around 400 B.C.

The basic theme of the Upanishads is BRAHMAN, the Universal, and its relation to Atman, the soul, spirit, or true self of the individual. The various texts tell us that Brahman pervades and is all things, taking many different forms like the flames of a fire. Thus Brahman and Atman are one; our true nature is none other than the divine Universal. This deep wisdom, the Upanishads insist, is not known through reason or study, but can only be acquired by a diligent student practicing meditation under the guidance of a sage who already has it. For the true self cannot be perceived objectively, any more than the eye can see itself, for it is itself the source of awareness. It can only be realized through inner experience.

Other themes of the Upanishads include the five "sheaths" that surround the Atman in the human being: joy, intellect, mind, vital energy, and physical form. Vedanta philosophers correlated these with the three states of consciousness also presented in the Upanishads: physical form with waking, the middle three with dream consciousness, and joy with deep sleep without dreams, when one is united with Brahman. The Upanishads also discuss reincarnation and the emergence of the world from Brahman, together with the idea that the phenomenal world is to be understood as MAYA. The most persistent notion of the Upanishads, however, is the supreme reality of Brahman and the realization of it as the supreme value of human life.                                                    R.E.

**UPPER ROOM.** In connection with Jesus' last meal in Jerusalem and the venue of the first Christians after the Resurrection, mention is made of a locale called the upper room (Mark 14:15; Luke 22:12; Acts 1:13). Palestinian dwellings were made with a room (usually large) set above street level to avoid the noise and heat of ground activity (II Kings 1:2, "upper chamber"; II Kings 4:10, a "small roof chamber," set for the prophet Elisha).

The place where Jesus gathered the disciples is sometimes equated with the home of Mary, mother of John Mark (Acts 12:12), but this cannot be shown (but see Acts 1:14 for the presence of women in the apostolic party). Other possibilities include the location of the upper room at the home of one of the disciples, "whom Jesus loved" (John 13:23); again a guess. Also uncertain is the present-day identification of the NT upper room of the Last Supper with the *coenaculum*, near the Benedictine monastery (the Dormition church) on Mount Zion in Old Jerusalem. Evidence points to this site as a medieval foundation (fourteenth century), though the tradition that here is located David's tomb is older, possibly reaching back on historical and archaeological grounds to Herod's time. But this is disputed. The one strand of evidence is that the historian Epiphanius in the fourth century refers to the emperor Hadrian's visit made in A.D. 135 to this building as to the "upper room." But no attempt was made to perpetuate this tradition.
                                                                                    R.M.

**UR.** Also known as Uru, Uri, Urim, or Ur kasdim, "Ur of the Chaldees." Ur was an important Babylonian city on the lower Euphrates, from which ABRAHAM's family emigrated to HARAN. It lay about 150 miles from the head of the Persian Gulf in present-day Iraq. The city was occupied from about 4000 to 500 B.C. and reached the peak of its riches and influence about 2600 B.C. The phrase "Ur of the Chaldees" occurs four times in the OT. It gives rise to scholarly questions of priestly editing in the OT, since the word for Chaldees is not used elsewhere until the ninth century.

After seventy-five years of preliminary exploration, serious archaeology began at Ur in 1922, under Sir Leonard Woolley, for the British Museum and the University of Pennsylvania. Ur yielded valuable

Courtesy of The University Museum, University of Pennsylvania

*Statuette of a he-goat standing by a tree; made of gold, silver, lapis lazuli, and white shell on a wooden core; from Ur, early dynastic period*

Courtesy of The University Museum, University of Pennsylvania

*Headdress of the Lady Pu-abi from the royal tombs of Ur (about 2650–2550 B.C.)*

Courtesy of The University Museum, University of Pennsylvania

*Gold cup and lamp, from Ur royal tombs, early dynastic period*

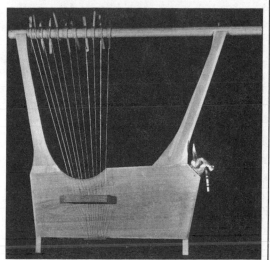

Courtesy of The University Museum, University of Pennsylvania

*Lyre with gold and lapis bull's head from the death pit at Ur*

Courtesy of The University Museum, University of Pennsylvania

*Gold helmet from the tomb of Mes-kalam-dug; found at Ur, early dynastic period*

artifacts and texts from the life of the ancient Near East, especially in the age of the patriarchs. The excavations revealed harbors along the river, storehouses, private houses, palaces, a huge ziggurat or temple, and hundreds of valuable artifacts in gold, jewelry, and ivory. The base of the three-storied step pyramid, a ziggurat, was about the size of a football field. The walls were of dried brick, but faced with fired brick. From the uppermost courtyard rose a temple to the moon god Nanna, also known as Sin. A long, open stairway, not unlike some seen among the Inca and Aztec ruins, rose directly through the three levels of the ziggurat. A huge gate at the first level was later converted into a separate place of worship. Raised platforms probably at one time contained images of the moon god and his companion gods. A vast network of other rooms supported the temple complex—kitchens, workshops, storerooms.

Perhaps the most revealing discoveries at Ur relate to Sumerian burial customs of the period 2700 to 2500 B.C. For example, in the tomb of Shubad (not a queen but certainly a noblewoman) are buried seventy-four of her attendants. Apparently they followed her voluntarily into death, probably by taking poison. In this and other tombs were found fully outfitted soldiers, charioteers, musicians, grooms, dressers, courtiers, cooks. Evidence for the burial of living attendants has not been found elsewhere in the Middle East, but is born out by an ancient Sumerian poem, the Gilgamesh Epic.

The leading role of Ur in the Tigris-Euphrates Valley continued to decline gradually over the centuries, after its heyday in the time of the moon god. The major temples were partially restored by Nebuchadnezzar about 1700 B.C. and again by Cyrus the Great about 535 B.C.                              T.J.K.

***URBI ET ORBI.*** Latin for "to the city and the world," a special papal blessing for Rome and the world given traditionally following the pope's election, but also on other celebrative occasions. Although usually bestowed from St. Peter's, it has also come from the balconies of other Roman basilicas.                                    C.M.

**URIAH.** An officer in David's army of Hittite background who served loyally and well. Uriah or Urijah ("Yahweh is light") was a worshiper of Yahweh, as his name indicates. His professionalism and dedication to duty was outstanding. Granted leave by David, he refused the comforts of his own home while his comrades were still in the field (II Sam. 11 and 12). Uriah served in the wars with Syria and Ammon, but rather than honoring him, David shamed him and treacherously committed him to death because of David's overwhelming passion for Uriah's wife, BATHSHEBA.

David wished to cover his adultery with Bathsheba, which had left her pregnant, by bringing Uriah home on leave. Uriah's devotion to duty frustrated this plan, so David misused his power as comander in chief, ordering his officers to put Uriah in the most exposed front rank, in the battle at Rabbah-Ammon, then fall back so that Uriah would be killed. Nathan the prophet condemned David for this and foretold disasters that would afflict David's house because of this sin.

Others named Uriah (or Urijah) included a high priest in the monarchy of Ahaz of Judah; a prophet who predicted the destruction of Jerusalem and was tracked down and killed in Egypt (Jer. 26:20-23); and two priests during the times of Ezra and Nehemiah (Ezra 8:33; Neh. 3:4; 8:4).          J.C.

**URIEL.** The name of two men, and of an angel, in the OT and OT Apocrypha. In I Chronicles 6:24; 15:5, 11, Uriel, whose name means "my light is El," is a Levite who helped moved the Ark of the Covenant from Obed-edom's home to Jerusalem. In II Chronicles 13:2, Uriel is a man from Gibeah, the grandfather of King Abijah of Judah. In II Esdras 4:1-11, Uriel is an angel.          J.C.

**URIM AND THUMMIM.** Two objects of unspecified material that were used by Israel's priests as instruments of discovering the divine will. They were kept in the high priest's "breastpiece" (RSV) or "breastplate," in the case of Aaron, so that he could "bear the judgment of the people of Israel upon his heart before the Lord continually" (Exod. 28:30). It is thought that each of these objects must have had a "yes" side and a "no" side. The inquirer (as Saul in I Sam. 28:6 and David in I Sam. 30:7-8) framed the question in a form so that it could be answered with a yes or no. The priest took or tossed out of the breastpiece Urim and Thummim. Two objects with yes showing would be an affirmative answer; two with no, a negative answer; one yes and one no would mean no answer (I Sam. 28:6). H. H. Rowley suggests that since "thummim" means "perfect things," it was the yes symbol, leaving Urim to be the no. The Pentateuch and records of the early monarchy show use of the Urim and Thummim. No further mention is made of this practice until the brief references in Ezra and Nehemiah (Ezra 2:63; Neh. 7:65). (See EPHOD.)          P.L.G.

**URSULINES.** The oldest teaching order for women in the Roman Catholic church. The formal title of the order is the Company of Saint Ursula. It was founded by St. Angela Merici at Brescia, Italy, in 1535, for the purpose of reforming society through the education of girls. At first young women were to aid in accomplishing this goal while living in their own homes. In 1566, Archbishop Charles Borromeo revised the rules of the order to permit community life. By 1612 the Ursulines of Paris were raised to the status of a religious order with solemn vows and strict enclosure. The order spread to North America when Marie Guyard founded a convent at Quebec in 1639.

Today there are sixty-five autonomous communities in the world. In 1900 representatives of communities from various countries met in Rome to form the Roman Union, now the central governing body of the order.          R.H.

**USSHER, JAMES** (1581–1656). Irish prelate, born at Dublin and educated at Trinity College in that city, where subsequently he was appointed professor of divinity and cathedral chancellor (1607). His ecclesiastical and theological position was that of Calvinism, which he sought to make a powerful influence in the Irish church. This is seen in his advocacy of the Lambeth Articles of 1595. Later, he became a bishop, then archbishop of Armagh. His visit to England in 1640 was destined to become a permanent stay and led to an absence from his native land. In the English Civil War (1642–49) he associated himself with the royalistic cause, but the protector Oliver Cromwell treated him well, granting him on his death a burial niche in Westminster Abbey.

His writings include a history of Western Christianity and various ecclesiastical treatises. But his fame was made by his drawing up a scheme of biblical chronology in which he concluded that the world was made in 4004 B.C. Allied with the KJV, this chronology became very popular until the rise of biblical criticism, though Ussher's name stands out as one who first attempted a chronological chart of the Bible's history.          R.M.

**UTILITARIANISM.** The theory that arose during the late eighteenth and early nineteenth centuries through the English philosophers Jeremy Bentham and John Stuart Mill. The theory of utilitarianism is that right action is one that brings the best possible consequences. No action is in itself morally right or wrong but becomes so when the consequences are known. The "best" consequence is one that brings the greatest happiness for the greatest number of people. This is based on the theory that people live on pleasure-pain motivation and that happiness is the balance of pleasure over pain. There is a utilitarianism of act, which looks for the consequences of each human act; and a utilitarianism of rule, which judges actions within principles. (It might be right, in general, to be truthful in order that people can trust one another, but in a specific situation a person might cause less pain or give more pleasure to another by a lie.) G. E. Moore, twentieth-century linguistic analyst, broadened the concept "happiness" to include love, knowledge, and beauty. Some have asked whether the elimination of suffering might be a more important consequence for action than that of striving after the achievement of happiness.

Utilitarianism has become a guiding principle in several areas of public life. In law it has affected the theory of punishment to focus its purpose on reform rather than retribution. The validity of a government is based on whether or not it promotes the general interest. Economists debate the relative balance of government or private enterprise on the basis of which better promotes the general welfare. Under this theory, there are no good actions to be praised and rewarded, but only good consequences that justify the action. In today's world, however, when the consequences of an action may not be known until many years later, the definition of a utilitarian act in advance is problematic.         I.C.

**UTOPIANISM.** A view of an ideal or imagined world or society. The term was first used by Sir Thomas More in *Utopia* (1516; Eng. trans. 1551) and is derived from the Greek meaning "no place" but by a play on words is connected with "eutopia" meaning "good place." Descriptions of such a society where harmony reigns through beneficent institutions may be found in literary forms such as novel, story, poetry, and essay. It also appears in political theory, such as Plato's *Republic.* Philosophies of history, such as those of Hegel, Spencer, and Marx in the nineteenth century grow out of a theory of inevitable progress that envisions the possibility of a just society. Anthropological philosophies such as those of Marcuse or Arendt describe utopia in terms of the fulfillment of genuinely human values in individuals and societies. Finally there are utopias growing out of the prophecies of MILLENARIAN religious groups who predict a cataclysmic end to the world and of political revolutionaries who affirm that tearing down the old foundations is necessary to building new and better political and social structures.

Utopian theories arise partly as a critique of a present society and as an encouragement to reform. They are based on the belief that humans have the knowledge and power to change society. This implies a will to know and to do the good, the possibility of modifying human behavior, and some agreement on what constitutes a good social order. Utopian concepts also arise from an effort at moral clarity—defining an ideal—and from the impulse in a creative mind to think freely and imaginatively about the future.         I.C.

**UZZIAH.** Also known as Azariah, meaning "Jehovah is my might," or "Jehovah is my strength." A king of Judah who ruled from about 783 to 742 B.C. He came to the throne at age sixteen and according to the biblical record ruled for fifty-two years. External evidence would prefer forty-two. Judah prospered mightily under his reign. Along the coast he conquered Philistia and exacted tolls from the camel caravans (II Chr. 26:6). He built his own fortresses after demolishing Gath, Jabneh, and Ashdod. To the southeast he overran Moab, Edom, and Petra, building the city of Elath and restoring the land to Judah (II Kings 14:22). At Jerusalem he raised stronger defense towers. He strung fortresses across the Negeb, apparently to control the trade routes from Arabia. His military skills included developing new weapons, probably catapults (II Chr. 26:8). He ordered new cisterns and water systems for irrigation. According to Chronicles, however, he depended too much on his own powers and forsook God. He entered the Temple "to burn incense on the altar of incense," a duty strictly reserved for priests (II Chr. 26:16-18). As a result he was stricken with leprosy. He moved to a "separate house," where he was isolated, and stepped aside from his role as ruler. Uzziah was probably more grandiose and successful than any other king except Solomon.

Of the two other Uzziahs mentioned in the OT, one was the father of Jonathan, one of David's stewards, and the other a priest from the tribe of Levite, a Kohathite.         T.J.K.

# Vv

**VAIROCANA.** From the Sanskrit word for "The Illuminator." In MAHAYANA BUDDHISM, the supreme cosmic Buddha. As Mahavairocana, "Great Illuminator," he is the personification of the primordial enlightened reality, the Adi-Buddha. In other instances, Vairocana is simply the first of the "self-born" Dhyani ("meditation") Buddhas, who personify transcendent aspects of nature and Buddha virtues. Vairocana is particularly important in the VAJRAYANA Buddhism of Tibet; he holds the central position in the MANDALA that underlies the well-known *Bardo Thodol,* or "Tibetan Book of the Dead."
R.E.

**VAISNAVISM.** In HINDUISM, the worship of the deity VISHNU, or one of his avatars such as Rama and KRISHNA. A major form of modern Hinduism, Vaisnavism is textually based on the BHAGAVAD GITA and certain of the PURANAS, and represents a consummate expression of BHAKTI or devotionalism. More like the God of Christianity than his counterpart Shiva, in the other great theistic tradition of India, Vishnu is a benign deity who creates, upholds the moral order, comes into the world in human form whenever righteousness declines to combat evil, and is linked only to subordinate and highly decorous goddesses. In Vaisnava doctrine Vishnu, or Krishna, is bound to the devotee in an intense relation of love and grace; the fervent love of the worshiper for God calls forth a response in divine grace, which deepens it still more and burns away all karma. This enables the worshiper to escape the cycle of birth and death and live eternally in the heavenly presence of Vishnu.

Vaisnavism has inspired important philosophical work, such as that of the great theologian of bhakti, RAMANUJA; no less important is its rich treasure of devotional poetry, including that of the ALVARS and of such major writers as Tulsidas and Mira Bai. With its emphasis on deep subjective fervor, it is not surprising that it has also evoked a number of revival and sectarian movements, down to the HARE KRISHNA movement of today.
R.E.

**VAJRAYANA.** From Sanskrit, "vehicle of the Vajra," the word "vajra" meaning both "diamond" and "thunderbolt." The Tantric form of BUDDHISM, Vajrayana is the form of the religion traditionally prevalent in Tibet, Mongolia, Nepal, and Bhutan, and has influenced Chinese and Japanese Buddhism, especially the Shingon denomination of Japan. Deriving from Mahayana, its philosophical, symbolic, and practical forms of expression are deep and complex. Grounded in belief in the power of mind to create its own reality, they center around mantras and evocations of Buddhas designed to awaken enlightenment, putting much stress on initiation and the master-disciple relationship. The MANDALA is central to the distinctive Vajrayana iconography, and such implements as the vajra, or ten-pronged wand, and the bell are common in its rites.                    R.E.

## VALENTINIAN GNOSTICISM. *See* GNOSTICISM.

**VALLA, LORENZO** (about 1405–57). Italian Renaissance humanist, opponent of Scholasticism, often called the father of modern HISTORICAL CRITICISM, famed for demonstrating the falsity of the DONATION OF CONSTANTINE. Born in Rome, he received a thorough humanistic education, and was ordained a priest in 1431. That same year he wrote a dialogue, *De voluptate*, extolling sensual pleasure (published later). Critical of monastic vows and inferior Latin, he shared the humanists' ideal that pure language would lead to reform, expressed in *De Elegantia Latinae Linguae*. His *Declamatio* (1440) not only attacked the pope's temporal power but showed the falsity of documents in which Constantine purportedly gave the church Western Europe. As early as 1435 Valla, dissatisfied with contentions in Rome, took employment with King Alfonso V of Aragon, who shielded him in 1442 from the Inquisition. His *Collatio Novi Testamenti* (1444), published by Erasmus (1505), advanced historical criticism with a sharp comparison of the Vulgate Latin and Greek NTs. About 1447 Pope Nicholas V, a friend of humanists, invited Valla to Rome, where in 1450 he became professor of eloquence. However, his erudition and critical views aroused opposition and suspicion of heresy. Luther considered him an eminent Christian scholar.                    C.M.

**VALUES CLARIFICATION.** A movement made up of various techniques of teaching and content analysis in contemporary religious education, including Roman Catholic catechetics. Values clarification aims at understanding people's behavior, especially that of children, with an aim to understanding just what elements of moral education the person is capable of learning. Of course, the techniques of values clarification are applied to adults as well. A value is the relationship of the self as it relates to other people in the environment through the feelings, ideas, behavior and intellect of the individual, in such a way as to enhance that person's creative growth.

Values have to do with the priorities we maintain in our lives. Questions of values always have to do with the relationship of the self to other people, so they have to do with societal relations. The value process is one in which the self, in responding to the various environments in which it finds itself (people, things, institutions), selects its priorities and expresses them through the behavior, feelings, and ideas of the person in such a way as to creatively enhance that person's total development.

Values clarification always begins with the human experience, but for religious education it has a theological bias. Religious values clarification holds that "we believe in the sacredness of human life." Values clarification makes understandable the stance of the person to the environment. According to some catechists, it makes no difference whether the educator starts from human experience and moves to the Word of God, or starts with Scripture and doctrine and moves to human experience. Values clarification makes the human experience more receptive to the events in which God is revealed and is a way that enables the teacher to examine his or her own experience and the setting and the system at hand, so that the environment may be ordered and made sacred to the person. Religious instruction, then, consists of that environment, people, teachers, and educational system that permits students to make meaning and to order their priorities in such a way as to maximize their creative and spiritual development. Christian education, above all, seeks to promote spiritual growth and especially the person's relationship to God.

Values are clarified by an inductive growth process, that is, a give-and-take session in which people discover themselves, their attitudes, desires, relationships, hopes, and dreams. Students in such an open session learn to make choices and to take responsibility for their choices. They also learn to rank their values. Over time, the members of the session evolve into a community; it is hoped into a caring, Christian community. Values clarification is thus a learning process that searches into the reasons for our choices and commitments and explores the effects those choices have on ourselves and on others. Religious education further measures those choices and effects on the environment in terms of Scripture, doctrine, and Christian moral teaching. Catechists see a need for the theologian and the religious educator to continually engage in the process of values clarification, constantly confronting people with the presence of Christ in the world.

                                                        J.C.

**VAN DYKE, HENRY** (1852–1933). United States Presbyterian minister, educator, diplomat, and author. Born in the Germantown section of Philadelphia, Van Dyke was educated at Princeton University and Princeton Theological Seminary. After his ordination, Van Dyke served as minister of Brick Presbyterian Church, New York (1883–99). He served as professor of English literature at Princeton University (1899–1913; 1919–23). He was U.S. minister to the Netherlands and Luxembourg from 1913 to 1916 and was chaplain (lieutenant commander) in the U.S. Navy from 1917 to 1919. He authored many books, including *The Reality of Religion* (1884), *Little Rivers* (1885), and *The Story of the Other Wise Man* (1896). Van Dyke wrote poetry, short stories, essays, and attained considerable reputation as a literary critic. He died on April 10 in Princeton, New Jersey.                    R.H.

## VAN EYCK, HUBERT

**VAN EYCK, HUBERT** (or Huybrecht; about 1366–1426) and **JAN** (about 1390–1441). Flemish painters. The van Eyck brothers presumably were born in Maeseyck (modern Maaseik), Belgium, on the Meuse River. Founders of the Flemish school of painting, the van Eycks were the reputed originators of a process of oil painting employing a drying varnish. They introduced a new realism into painting that had not been attained by earlier artists.

Facts about the gifted brothers are sketchy. Their famed Ghent altarpiece, a twelve-by-nineteen-foot work representing scenes from the Apocalypse, was created for the church of Saint Bavon in Ghent. The inscription: "Hubert van Eyck, the greatest painter who ever lived, began this work, which his brother Jan, the second in art, finished at the order of Jodocus Vyd." The masterpiece was completed in 1432. The center and largest panel of the altarpiece represents the *Adoration of the Lamb*. Hubert is considered by many experts to have been the painter of the *Three Marys at the Sepulchre*, now to be seen in the Van Beuningen Collection in Rotterdam.

Jan's life is documented from 1422. Painter and diplomat, he first served John, count of Holland, and Philip the Good of Burgundy. Jan was known for his scrupulous attention to detail.   R.H.

**VASHTI.** The queen of Persia, wife of Xerxes I (or Ahasuerus), mentioned in the book of Esther (Esth. 1:9, 11, 12, 15-17; 2:1, 17). Vashti refused to come before Ahasuerus and show her beauty to the court, so she was demoted from her position. This led to Esther's becoming queen (Esth. 2:17).   J.C.

**VATICAN.** The residence of the POPE, the head of the Roman Catholic Church, located in the city of the Vatican, an autonomous, independent, though tiny, state, which lies on Vatican hill, one of the seven hills of Rome.

The palace of the Vatican, is, in effect, the international headquarters of the Western or Roman Catholic Church. The pope's private living quarters are located here, and additionally, the palace contains the apartments of cardinals and other officials, staff, the secretary of state; a number of chapels, including the famous Sistine Chapel; the archives of the church; art galleries; five museums; a printer's establishment; and an astronomical observatory. This vast palace, with its gardens that go back to the time of Nero, plus the great plaza of St. Peter's Cathedral and St. Peter's itself, form the independent state of Vatican City. The pope once ruled over large territories in Italy (the papal states), which were absorbed into the unified Italian state in the nineteenth century. In 1929, the government of Mussolini negotiated the Lateran Treaty, which recognized the "extraterritoriality" or independence of the Vatian city-state. This "state" comprises an area of less than one square mile, with a population of some five hundred people. The ruler of the state is the pope and, during a papal vacancy, the college of cardinals. Also recognized as "extraterritorial" and under the complete control of the pope are the basilicas of St. John Lateran, St. Mary Major, St. Paul Outside the Walls; the churches of Sant' Andrea-della-Valle and San Carlo-ai-Catarine, plus the palaces of San Callisto and Castel Gandolfo.

In a figurative sense, the term "Vatican" stands for the pope or the official position of the Roman Catholic Church. It can even be used to symbolize the whole church itself.   J.C.

**VATICAN COUNCILS.** Two widely important church-wide councils held by the Roman Catholic Church, in 1869–70 (and not completed) and in 1962–65 (under Pope John XXIII, with its completion under Pope Paul VI).

According to Roman Catholic reckoning, Vatican I was the twentieth ECUMENICAL COUNCIL. It opened December 8, 1869, and was adjourned in October 1870, when the Italian army captured Rome from papal forces. Some six hundred cardinals, bishops, and patriarchs attended, and a constitution on the Catholic faith was written. The third session dealt with the primacy of the pope; the fourth session declared it to be Christian doctrine that the pope is infallible when making pronouncements, as the successor to St. Peter and the head of the Catholic church, in matters of faith and morals. The vote on this doctrine was 433 for, 2 against: there were 55 in opposition who did not vote. Because of the political situation the council was able to do only a fraction of the work planned for it. The decree on papal infallibility resulted in the defection of 150,000 believers who became "Old Catholics." Actually, however, the popes have made little use of the power given, and only one doctrine has been so defined. Pope Pius XII pronounced the Assumption of the Blessed Virgin Mary into heaven a dogma in 1950.

Vatican II was announced by Pope John XXIII in January 1959. Upon requests for agenda, twelve volumes of Catholic self-criticism were assembled. There were 2,540 bishops and superiors of religious orders in attendance at the opening session on October 11, 1962, making it one of the largest councils in church history, including forty observers from the Orthodox and Protestant churches. The first session debated five major issues: the liturgy, sources of revelation, the communications media, church unity, and the nature and structure of the church. The council recessed on December 8, 1962, until September 1963. Tragically, John XXIII died on June 3, 1963, before the second session could begin. But the newly elected and more conservative Pope PAUL VI reconvened the council. It opened again on September 29. Paul VI announced himself as a firm supporter of the renewing, reforming work of the council begun by Pope John. The second session was more open than the first and ran smoother, completing its work on December 4, 1963. Decrees on the liturgy and on the communications media were promulgated by session two.

The third session opened September 14, 1964, with even more observers from the Greek Orthodox Church, Protestants, and Catholic laypersons, as well as nuns and parish priests in attendance. Decrees on the dogmatic constitution of the church and on the pastoral office of the bishop were passed, as well as a declaration of freedom of religion and "on the church's attitude toward non-Christian religions." Further decrees on the Eastern rite Catholic churches and on ecumenism were passed but left changes in marriage legislation to the decision of the pope. The council closed on November 21, 1965.

Both Vatican councils were courageous and timely responses to the real changes in the church's position in society and on social problems in the modern world. While fault might be found with the decree on papal infallibility of Vatican I, in the main, the decisions of both councils were practical and genuinely responsive to real issues that affected the whole Christian church. No general council had been held since the Council of TRENT (1545–63) at the time of the Counter-Reformation. Vatican I responded to the rise of rationalism (the Enlightenment), liberalism (social democracy and the breakdown of the older monarchical orders in European nations), and materialism. Some or all of these systems of thought denied basic Christian doctrines such as revelation, the existence of God, and the immortality of the soul. The council met largely to condemn such errors, as well as to clarify the church's position on the pope's infallibility. While many bishops and lay Catholics already firmly believed in papal infallibility, the issue caused discontent in Germany, France, and England. Eventually, this discontent resulted in the Old Catholic schism but also in a great strengthening of the Catholic Church.

Vatican Council II stands undoubtedly as one of the greatest episodes, if not the greatest, in Roman Catholic history. If Vatican I dealt with an array of problems built up over two centuries, Vatican II had even more problems, which had accumulated during the suffering, toil, and rapid social change of one century. World Wars I and II, the rise of Communism and its triumph over half the world, the new morality, the ever-present threat of nuclear war, and vast strides in medical science that enabled the prolongation of life and birth control through many techniques, all raised issues that challenged the traditional Catholic faith. Vatican II tackled many of these issues and others, too, including Christian attitudes towards Jews in the light of the Nazi holocaust, the status of women, and the church's relations with the other great, non-Christian religions.

If the attempt was courageous, in the best spirit of Christian faith, hope, and love, then the initial credit for Vatican II must go to the popular Pope JOHN XXIII. But, in even larger measure, credit must go to the council fathers who stoutly defended the faith while freely and openly admitting mistakes and striving to accommodate the church's practice, organization, and outlook to the late twentieth-century world. The reforms of the church initiated by Vatican II have continued to develop and unfold among Catholics. The use of the vernacular in the Mass, the deepening involvement of the laity in the church as the people of God, improved relationships with Protestants (including many ongoing theological talks with Baptist, Presbyterian, Reformed, Lutheran, Anglican, and Orthodox bodies), and a new respect between Catholics and Jews, all stem from Vatican II beginnings. Even the involvement of the church in the welfare of Christians behind the Communist Iron Curtain, so promoted by the election of the non-Italian, Pope John Paul II, a Pole and confronter of Communist power, has its roots in the heroic efforts of the fathers of Vatican I and II to make the faith relevant to the problems of the here and now.        J.C.

**VAUGHAN WILLIAMS, RALPH** (1872–1958). English composer. Born in Down Ampney, Gloucestershire, on October 12, Vaughan Williams received his musical education at Trinity College, Cambridge, and the Royal College of Music, London. Subsequently, he pursued advanced study under Max Bruch in Berlin and Maurice Ravel in Paris. After serving four years with the British Army in Macedonia and France, he became a professor of composition at the Royal College of Music. He continued on that faculty until 1940. Although Vaughan Williams spent some time teaching, he spent even more on composition. He led a very active life up to the time of his death on August 26.

Religiously Vaughan Williams was a sort of agnostic, yet he produced significant religious music, including the oratorio "The Holy City," and his Christmas cantata "Hodie." He was a coeditor of *Songs of Praise* and *The Oxford Book of Carols*. Some of his other works bordered on religious themes, such as the music for George Herbert's "Mystical Songs," the Tallis Fantasia for string orchestra, and the "Fantasia on Old 104th Psalm Tune" for piano, chorus, and orchestra.

Early in his career Vaughan Williams was interested in English folk song, which shaped his later compositions. He was both an adventurous and a precise composer, who many feel had the greatest impact on religious music in the twentieth century. His major works include Mass in G Minor (1923), Sonata Civitas (1926), Five Tudor Portraits (1936), Serenade to Music (1938). He also composed two operas, *Sir John in Love* (1929) and *The Pilgrims' Progress* (1951).        R.H.

**VEDANTA.** This term, meaning in Sanskrit "end of the VEDAS," in the sense of their completion or fulfillment, is the most influential of the six traditional DARSANAS or schools of philosophy in HINDUISM. The name indicates that it is thought by its followers to present the truest or highest philosophical interpretation of the ancient Vedic scriptures.

Vedanta is not a single philosophical position, but rather a tradition and family of philosophical schools that have developed in interaction with one another, but which show some very marked differences. For the entire tradition, however, the most important authority is the UPANISHADS, the latest and most metaphysical section of the Vedas. The teachings of the Upanishads are themselves not entirely consistent, but overall emphasize such themes as these, which have also been major themes of Vedanta: the oneness of Brahman, God or the Absolute; the possibility and importance of liberation from the world of SAMSARA, life and death and subjection to KARMA, through inwardly realized union with or love for God; that liberation is attained through discipline, attention to spiritual rather than material things, and the following of true teachers or GURUS.

After the Upanishads, the most important classic Vedanta text is the Brahma sutras of about 200 B.C.–A.D. 200, attributed to Badarayana. They are brief, cryptic comments on various Upanishadic passages, virtually unintelligible without the commentary that later philosophers gave them in turn, each according to his own school.

Because of its immense popularity in the Hindu world, the BHAGAVAD GITA is also often regarded as a classic text for Vedanta and has been much commented on by Vedantists, although the Gita itself shows evidence of considerable influence from Samkhya, another of the traditional six schools.

The best-known Vedanta school, especially outside of India, is Advaita Vedanta, "Non-dualist Vedanta." Its greatest spokesman was Samkara (eighth century A.D.). Advaita teaches the unreality of all appearances other than Brahman, and hence of all duality or multiplicity, including our own apparent existence as separate individual selves. Such appearances are the realm of maya, which means, in its "strong" sense, the "creative energy of God," but negatively, the illusion of seeing the world as other than Brahman. Contrary to what is sometimes thought, Advaita Vedanta does not teach that the world is illusion, but that it is seen in an illusory way if it is seen as anything other than Brahman. Such misperception is the product of avidya, ignorance or not seeing, in turn the result of one's misplaced identification with the individual self. For the true self is the Atman, the ultimate principle within the self not different from Brahman; the other parts of the human being, which Vedanta describes as a series of "sheaths" around the Atman—joy, intellect, mind, life-energy, and physical form—are contingent upon the reality represented by the Atman. Liberation, in the Advaita Vedanta tradition, is fundamentally a matter of right seeing, rightly distinguishing between the real and the unreal, and so is based on right knowledge more than right action or right feeling. However, it is strongly emphasized that mere intellectual knowledge of truth is insufficient. Liberation requires *prajna,* deep wisdom or insight that comes only with meditation and freeing the spirit from sensory attachments.

Another Vedantic school is Visista Advaita Vedanta, "modified non-dualist Vedanta." Its most important teacher was RAMANUJA (twelfth century A.D.). This school, closely linked to the BHAKTI movement, stressed the personal theism that makes devotionalism real. It vehemently criticized Samkara and the Advaita school for its teaching that Brahman is ultimately without attributes, and for its failure to make any real distinction between the Creator and souls dependent upon the Creator. Visista Advaita Vedanta asserted instead that God really has qualities such as truth, awareness, and eternity, and that human souls can be united with God in love but not in absolute identity.

Another school, Dvaita Vedanta, was founded by Madhava (1238–1317). Related like Ramanuja's system to devotionalism, this "dualistic Vedanta" stressed the distinctions between God, self, and world, teaching that while all is dependent upon God, God is separate from them, and salvation must depend solely on God's grace.

Other schools of Vedanta have tried to find middle ground between Advaita and the requirements of theistic experience. Since tension between the philosophical drive toward unity and the theistic experience of divine otherness expressed through God's love and grace has been a central dynamic of Hinduism, the Vedanta tradition, concerning itself with these issues, has come to be the religion's intellectual mainstream.                    R.E.

**VEDAS.** The Vedas, "knowledge," are the ancient sacred scriptures of HINDUISM. More properly, they should be called sacred songs and chants, since they were preserved only in oral tradition until comparatively recently, together with ritual and philosophical commentary.

The premier portion of these scriptures is the RIGVEDA, probably from 1500–1200 B.C., the era when the Indo-European or Aryan people whose priests recited them invaded India. The RigVeda consists of hymns, often of great beauty and vigor, chanted by BRAHMIN priests while sacrifices are being presented. They are addressed to various gods: the sovereign deities of the sky, Varuna and Mitra; the atmospheric Indra; the gods of the sacrifice itself, Agni, fire, and Soma, the sacred drink. Others such as Aditi, the mother of the gods, and Uma, the dawn, may also be praised; all the deities tend to be simply honored as bright, shining, and beneficent, though some hints of their mythology also appear.

Other Vedas of the same order as the RigVeda are the YajurVeda, MANTRAS recited by priests; the SamaVeda, mostly chants from the RigVeda but for a different group of priests; and the AtharvaVeda, a collection of more popular hymns and magical spells.

The scriptural Vedic literature is then completed by the BRAHMANAS, Aranyakas, and UPANISHADS, extensive commentaries on the four books of the original order of Vedas. The Brahmanas and Aranyakas ("forest books") contain much ritual instruction, together with mythological and philosophical commentary. The Upanishads, the most philosophical of the Vedas, deal chiefly with ultimate metaphysical truths.                                    R.E.

**VEDIC RELIGION.** Sometimes used to refer to the religion of the ancient Indian Indo-Europeans before the rise of BHAKTI and other new developments in the early centuries B.C. In that case, the word HINDUISM is reserved for Indic religion in the latter period and after; in it different gods are most prominent, and the whole style of spiritual life has many quite different characteristics. But it should be borne in mind that we know relatively little of popular religion, and religion of non-Indo-European background (apart from its probable manifestation in BUDDHISM and JAINISM), in the period covered by Brahmanism, although they are undoubtedly the soil out of which much of later Hinduism grew. Brahmanism is essentially a religion of the priestly Brahmin caste and their upper-caste, Indo-European associates.

Major features of Brahmanism are (1) the authority of the Brahmin priests, (2) the authority of the Vedic scriptures, (3) the centrality of the sacrificial rites, (4) as time went on, increasing emphasis given to TAPAS—spiritual power produced by ASCETICISM, and (5) increasing metaphysical speculation, especially that centering around the concept of Brahman (originally the holy power associated with the sacrifice and an amorphous vital force invoked by it, but later the underlying universal Reality of which all things are merely diverse forms, and which the UPANISHADS identify also with the ATMAN, the innermost self or "soul" of a human being). The gods of Brahmanism are those of the Vedic hymns, sovereign Varna and Mitra, heroic Indra, and so forth. In what might be called its "classic" period, the early centuries of the first millennium B.C. when the BRAHMANAS were composed, special attention was given to Agni, the fire-god who is the heart of the sacrifice, and Brahma, the creator-god and source of wisdom, ultimately to be superseded by Brahman, the more impersonal version of the same name and vital Reality.

Brahmanism upheld a social order based on caste and patriarchal family, and put much emphasis on such ethical virtues as truth-telling and the keeping of compacts. But it was a religion ostensibly heavily centered on priesthood and ritual sacrifice. These were thought to have correspondences with the great universe itself, by which the latter could be adjusted and manipulated. But the practitioners of these rites, who loved delving deeper and deeper into their meaning and that of the forces they evoked, could not in the end resist the conclusion, published in the Upanishads, that the ultimate locus of the sacrifice, the power, and the Reality behind them was within—in the sacrifice of asceticism, the spiritual power it generated (*tapas*), and in the universe in the self as Brahman in the Atman.                       R.E.

**VEIL OF THE TEMPLE.** (See Matt. 27:51; Mark 15:38; and Luke 23:45.) A door hanging (or "curtain," RSV) that covered the opening between the Holy Place and the Holy of Holies in Herod's Temple and perhaps in Zerubbabel's Temple also. It is reported to have been torn in two (Matt. 27:51 and Mark 15:38, which add "from top to bottom"; Luke 23:45) at the time of Jesus' death on the cross. Hebrews 10:20 takes the torn curtain to represent the torn "flesh" of Jesus, thus concluding that Jesus' death opened for Christians a "new and living way" to the presence of God.

No mention of such a curtain is made in the I Kings description of Solomon's Temple. Exodus 26:31 states that in the tabernacle a textile partition separated the two rooms of the tent and that it was made "of blue and purple and scarlet stuff and fine twined linen; in skilled work [embroidery?] shall it be made, with cherubim." Second Chronicles 3:14 quotes this verse almost verbatim and applies it to Solomon's Temple. When such a curtain or veil was installed in the temple, it would seem an effort to magnify the transcendent otherness of God by keeping even priests, performing sacred duties in the Holy Place, from seeing the Ark of the Covenant and its guardian cherubim.                       P.L.G.

**VENERATION.** *See* WORSHIP.

**VENIAL SIN.** A term used in Roman Catholic theology to distinguish between the nature and effects of certain forms of sin. Venial sin is distinguished from MORTAL SIN. Neither term is found in Scripture, and the Protestant Reformers rejected such distinctions. However, the early church fathers did posit two classes of sin, and the modern distinctions between mortal and venial sin were established by the Scholastic theologians, especially THOMAS AQUINAS. According to Thomas, while mortal sin is a deliberate turning away from God and merits an eternal punishment, venial sin is a disorder of the soul, a sickness that is reparable, and thus merits only a temporal penalty. Venial sin can be declared in confession before taking the Sacrament, but this need not be done. Venial sin can be expiated by other means. Unlike mortal sin, venial sin does not directly cause a loss of charity or deprive the soul of sanctifying grace. The distinctions between mortal and venial sin were approved at the Council of Trent.          J.L.

**VENIAMINOV, INNOKENTI** (1797–1879). The Russian Orthodox metropolitan noted as a missionary to Alaska and Siberia. He was born John Popov but took the name Veniaminov after his first bishop. He went to the Aleutians in 1823 as a missionary, studied the local language, and in 1829 extended his missionary activity to Alaska. In 1839 he was commissioned as bishop of Kamchatka and Russian America. He founded many mission stations and organized the work of the church in the region. As metropolitan of Moscow, he urged his church to its missionary responsibility. His best-known book is *A Guide to the Kingdom of Heaven.* His collected works and letters have been published in several volumes.                                                                W.G.

**VENI CREATOR SPIRITUS.** Latin for "Come, Creator Spirit," the opening line of a hymn invoking the Holy Spirit, used at vespers during Pentecost (or Ordinary Time) in the Roman Catholic Church. It is also sung at ordinations, consecrations of bishops, dedications of churches, and at the opening of synods and before elections.                                J.C.

**VERBAL INSPIRATION.** *See* INSPIRATION AND REVELATION.

**VERONICA.** The traditional name of a woman who is supposed to have shown mercy on Jesus as he was carrying his cross to Golgotha by wiping his face with her handkerchief. Tradition says Jesus' face was imprinted on her handkerchief. This handkerchief or veil is preserved at St. Peter's in Rome, where it can be handled and shown to the faithful for veneration only by a canon of the basilica. This veil is itself known as the Veronica; a name that may be formed of the Latin and Greek words for true (*vera*) and image (*eikon*).

Nothing is known of Veronica. She is not a saint in the Roman martyrology but is said to have been the wife of a Roman officer and in other places is spoken of as the same woman mentioned in Mark 5:25-34, who was healed of an issue of blood.                J.C.

**VERSIONS OF THE BIBLE.** *See* BIBLE VERSIONS, NON-ENGLISH; BIBLE TRANSLATIONS, ENGLISH.

**VESPASIAN.** Titus Flavius Vespasianus, Roman Emperor from A.D. 69 to 79; founder of the Flavian dynasty. After receiving a customary military training, Vespasian became a *praetor* in the reign of Gaius, commanded a legion under Claudius, and became proconsul of Africa in A.D. 66. In that year he was assigned three legions to quell the Jewish revolt in Judea.

After NERO's death, Vespasian aspired to succeed him. Already Josephus, the Jewish historian who sought asylum with Vespasian, had predicted his accession. Egypt's legions swore their allegiance, and the emperor-designate picked up more supporters en route to Rome. Vespasian left his son, TITUS, to pursue the war with the Jews.

Vespasian proved himself an able administrator. He ridiculed the notion that he was a god or would become one. There is no record of persecutions of Jews

*Silver shekel dated from the Jewish revolt against Rome (A.D. 66). The inscription reads "Jerusalem the holy."*

or Christians during his reign, but Cynic and Stoic philosphers were banished for allegedly promoting sedition. Judea remained a part of the imperial estate, and the head tax of two drachmas, paid to the Temple by every male Jew before its destruction by Titus, was transferred to the temple of Jupiter Capitolinus. Vespasian died on June 24, A.D. 79, and was succeeded by his son, Titus.                J.L.P.

**VESPERS.** The normal evening service in Roman Catholic churches of the Latin rite, as well as in monastic, cathedral, and collegiate churches. It is sung daily between 3:00 P.M. and 6:00 P.M. In Protestant churches it is the normal evening service (usually, but not limited to, Sundays). In the Byzantine rite the service is called *Hesperinos.*                J.C.

**VESTMENTS.** Vestments are the liturgical garments worn at church services by the clergy and their assistants. Originally, Christian ministers wore the street dress of Roman men, a long tunic. As styles changed, the church retained this earlier dress and elaborated upon it.

Vestments included the ALB, or white linen robe; the surplice, or loose white outer garment that originated in the cold churches of northern Europe (where it was worn over a fur coat); the maniple and stole, derived from the Roman handkerchief and napkin; the chasuble, or outer Eucharistic vestment, which is often ornately decorated; and the cape, or warm black overcoat, usually worn at the church door or in out-of-doors processions.

There are variations in vestments according to ecclesiastical rank, from DEACON to PRIEST (or PASTOR) to BISHOP, as well as according to the various services of the church, from preaching to officiating at Holy Communion. Generally, in the ancient and medieval church, the minister celebrating Communion wore the alb, the stole, and the chasuble. He also wore the amice, a linen protective cloth worn over the shoulders, and the maniple, a narrow linen strip that was hung on the left forearm. The stole, a narrow scarf in colors to match the liturgical colors of the church year, was worn about the neck and secured at the waist by a cincture, or rope. The chasuble covered everything. At baptisms and confession ministers wore the surplice and stole. Essentially, the surplice was a widened, shortened alb.

In earlier days, the minister or priest also wore, as his distinctive garment, the cassock, a robe that was usually black and reached to his feet. This had a standing collar—the origin of today's clerical collar.

Clergy of higher ranks than priests wore much more elaborate vestments, both for everyday use and for worship. Deacons were identified by wearing their stoles crossed over their chests, in the shape of St. Andrew's cross (X). Priests wore their stoles hanging straight down. This practice is still followed in the Roman Catholic and Anglican churches. Bishops, archbishops, and cardinals were, and still are, marked by such items as the dalmatic, gloves, the miter, the pallium, and the pectoral cross.                J.C.

### VIA ANALOGIA. See ANALOGY.

### VIA DOLOROSA.
The traditional route Jesus Christ followed through the streets of Jerusalem from the praetorium, or judgment hall of Pontius Pilate, to Calvary. It is also known as the Way of the Cross or the Way of Sorrows. Today pilgrims to the Holy City often follow a full-sized wooden cross in a procession through the ancient streets, singing a passiontide hymn, and pausing to pray at the nine Stations of the Cross on the way to the Church of the Holy Sepulchre. Most of the older communions regard the church as the true site of Calvary. The last five stations are within the church itself.                R.H.

### VIA MEDIA.
The expression, Latin for the "middle way," has been applied to Anglicanism, understood as pursuing a middle course between Roman Catholicism on the one side and Protestantism on the other. The idea goes back to the Anglican Reformation, but it was given eloquent expression by JOHN HENRY NEWMAN and other Tractarians.        J.M.

### VIA NEGATIVA. See NEOPLATONISM.

### VICAR.
In Roman Catholic polity, a clergyman who exercises an ecclesiastical office in the place of another, acting in the other's name and with his authority. Examples include the vicar apostolic, who acts for the pope in missionary countries, and parochial vicars, who assist the rector or chief pastor of a parish. It is used among Lutherans to signify seminarians on internships and among Anglicans as a title for a parish priest, usually an assistant.                J.C.

### VICAR APOSTOLIC.
A titular bishop, that is, one without a territorial diocese, cathedral, or chapter of canons. The vicars apostolic rule territories as delegates of the pope, for example, the church in England was ruled in this way until 1850. Such vicars apostolic have seats and vote in the general councils of the church.                J.C.

### VICAR GENERAL.
A deputy administrator appointed by a diocesan bishop to help with the governing of the diocese. The vicar general exercises the bishop's full power but must do so according to the bishop's wishes. He takes precedence over all clergy in the diocese but loses this rank on the death or move of the bishop.                J.C.

### VICAR OF CHRIST.
The title applied to the pope, the bishop of Rome, by the Roman Catholic Church. The pope is the visible head of the church, which is the mystical or sacramental body of Christ, and so is the representative of Christ on earth and the supreme authority of the church.                J.C.

### VIDYA.
In Hinduism *vidya* (knowledge) is not knowledge gained through the senses or through reflection. That knowledge only leads us to draw distinctions, and all distinctions are illusion, quite unreal. Therefore such knowledge is really ignorance, *avidya*. True *vidya* must overcome all distinctions.

*Avidya* is the normal state of human beings and is the reason we cannot escape KARMA (our actions and their results). Karma makes us prisoners of SAMSARA, a cycle of rebirth time after time after time. Actions, no matter how good or wise, cannot free us from the burdensome necessity of this rebirth. But knowledge can. Paradoxically both *vidya* and *avidya* are hidden within Brahman, ultimate reality. *Avidya* is perishable, while *vidya* is immortal, and if we control both of them we can transcend them and escape samsara.

To the Western mind distinctions are real, and the distinction between the one who knows and the object of knowledge is basic. In Hinduism, especially the Vedanta philosophy of Samkara (eighth century A.D.), that basic distinction is the worst illusion of all and the hardest to overcome. Ultimate reality (Brahman) is the only thing worth knowing. But Brahman contains no distinctions. Therefore the one who knows Brahman has true knowledge, but as a result becomes one with Brahman. The self ceases to exist; in fact, it has always been merely an illusion, *avidya* or ignorance. Thus karma and samsara are overcome. Distinctions are no more. Everything is one.
                K.C.

### VIENNE, COUNCIL OF.
Fifteenth ecumenical council in Roman Catholicism (October 16, 1311–May 6, 1312) which condemned the wealthy Order of Templars and dealt with controversies over Franciscan poverty. Pope Clement V (1305-14), who moved the papacy to Avignon, France, called the council to meet at Vienne in southeast France in 1308, only to have it delayed until 1311. King Philip IV of France was already brutally suppressing the Templars and seizing their properties. The council majority believed the charges of heresy and immorality against the Templars lacked evidence, but Philip IV intimidated Templar sympathizers by bringing his army to Vienne early in 1312. About a month later Pope Clement V suppressed the Templars in his bull *Vox clamantis*, with the council acceding on April 3. Other

council actions sanctioned strict Franciscan poverty, encouraged Raymond Lull to establish university centers for missionaries to learn Oriental languages, and granted tithes for six years to Philip IV for a crusade that he never made. However, Philip, with papal aid, managed to seize most of the Templars' property and execute most of their leaders as heretics. Vienne's decrees on reform were eventually incorporated in the "Clementines" published by Pope John XXII.                                                                    C.M.

**VIGIL.** From the Latin word meaning "a watching." A vigil is the day preceding certain feasts, and is equivalent to the eve of the feast. It is observed as a preparation for the celebration of the festival. In early times, a fast was observed as part of the vigil. Festivals that have vigils in the Roman Catholic Church include Easter; Christmas; Pentecost; Ascension Day; the Assumption of Mary; the Feasts of St. John the Baptist, of St. Lawrence the Martyr, and of saints Peter and Paul. The vigils of Pentecost, the Assumption, and Christmas are fast days, unless they fall on a Monday. The Orthodox churches also observe vigils called *proeorita* ("preparations"). Vigils arose from overnight services held to prepare for feast days, such as the Easter vigil service and the midnight Mass at Christmas. Among some Protestants, a "Watch-night" service on New Year's Eve is held.          J.C.

**VIHARA.** A dwelling for Buddhist monks; a monastery. In earliest Buddhism monks spent the annual rainy season in caves or in free-standing structures called *viharas*. With the development and growth of the monastic orders, large buildings were constructed for the use of monks. The usual monastery was a group of buildings for various purposes. In addition to living quarters for monks there were buildings for daily and special services, for study, and for other uses.

In India many ancient *viharas* were built of brick. From country to country the use of materials, the style of architecture, and the types of specialized buildings have varied greatly. In China, Korea, and Japan most monastery buildings are of wood. Some buildings were set aside for the use of the laity, and others were built as devotional chapels. During periods when the laity gave generously to the support of monasteries, magnificent structures were built and were lavishly decorated. By the fifth century A.D. in China, many monasteries had accumulated so much wealth that they aroused the greed of the state. Over the next several centuries periodic persecutions involved the confiscation of monastery property, the forced return of monks and nuns to lay life, and the melting down of images made of precious metals.

One of the best-known monastic buildings is the great Potala palace in Lhasa, Tibet. Until the country was occupied by the Peoples' Republic of China, it served as the center of Tibet's theocratic government, headed by the Dalai Lama.

In Japan the history of Buddhism can be traced in the development of the major temples. In Nara, the first major center of Japanese Buddhism, and Kyoto, capital of the nation for a thousand years, monasteries have preserved priceless art treasures and bear witness to changing styles in architecture. At a Nichiren temple in Yamanashi Prefecture, a contemporary treasury for relics was built entirely of aluminum, but in traditional style.                                             K.C.

**VIMALAKIRTI.** The hero of a MAHAYANA Buddhist scripture probably written in the first century A.D. As a layman, married and the father of children, Vimalakirti was especially popular in China because he demonstrated that it was possible to achieve enlightenment (bodhi) without becoming a monk or being celibate. His highly moral character was close to the Chinese ideal.                              K.C.

**VINAYA PITAKA.** The first of three collections (known as "Three Baskets") of sacred Buddhist writings in the Pali language. It deals principally with the rules governing the monastic order of BUDDHISM. The rules are traditionally believed to have been given by the Buddha (sixth century B.C.) but some of them may be as late in origin as the first century B.C.                                                        K.C.

**VINCENT DE PAUL** (about 1581–1660). French Roman Catholic priest, devoted to helping the poor, who founded the missionary order of Lazarists and Sisters of Charity. Born in Ranquine in Gascony, he studied theology at Toulouse, receiving ordination when about twenty years old. Seized by Turkish pirates in 1605, he was enslaved in Tunisia for two years. Eventually escaping, he went to Paris where he worked among the poor. About 1610 he vowed to devote his life to charitable works, a few years later founding at Chatillon-les-Dombes the first of several confraternities of charity for both men and women. He founded the Congregation of Priests of the Mission in 1624, commonly called Lazarists. Approved by Pope Urban VIII, Vincent extended his missions for the poor throughout Europe. About 1632 he established Sisters of Charity specifically to care for the sick and poor. He was canonized in 1737.
                                                                   C.M.

**VINCENTIAN CANON.** A Roman Catholic rule for determining the validity of doctrines, based on the criticism of Augustine's predestination advanced by Vincent of Lérins in his *Commonitorium* in 434, four years after Augustine's death. To distinguish truth from heretical views one should look for that faith "which has been believed everywhere, always, and by all" (*Commonitorium*). Vincent, a monk at Lérins, urged this three fold test of universality, tradition, and consent to avoid what he believed was novel teaching in Augustine's writings, namely predestination and irresistible grace. He explained universality as what the whole church confesses, tradition or antiquity as what was held by holy ancestors and fathers, and consent as definitions and determinations of all or at least most priests and doctors. Vincent thought Augustine's views threatened motivation for doing good works and undercut human responsibility.                                                              C.M.

**VIRGIL.** Publius Vergilius Maro (70–19 B.C.), classical Roman poet, often considered a Christian prophet, who influenced Dante, Chaucer, and Milton. Born near Mantua, of middle-class parents, Virgil studied literature, rhetoric, and philosophy at Cremona, Milan, Rome, and Naples. He abandoned politics for poetry and spent most of his life near Naples, where he knew Octavian (later emperor Augustus) and the poet Horace. His three masterpieces were the ten *Eclogues*, the *Georgics*, and the *Aeneid*. The *Eclogues* (37 B.C.) were pastoral poems invested with real Italian people, places, and events, both directly and allegorically. The fourth *Eclogue* extolled the birth of a child destined to usher in a Golden Age of peace and prosperity. The Middle Ages regarded this as a prophecy of Christ's birth. The highly artistic Latin of the *Georgics* (36–29 B.C.), in four books, feelingly depicted country life and became famous for its description of bee life, the plague, and the significance of sacrifice. Virgil's unfinished twelve books of the *Aeneid* (29–19 B.C.) was a mythological, national epic about the origins of Rome and the glories of Romans under emperor Augustus. The *Aeneid* depicted the wanderings of Aeneas from Troy to Italy, including an underworld trip where Aeneas' father revealed the unborn heroes of Roman history. In the Middle Ages Christians found hidden, prophetic meanings in this epic. They often imitated Virgil's style and altered Vergil to Virgil, linking him with Christ's virgin birth. (Virgil's nickname, Parthenias, connoted "virgin.") Jerome and Augustine objected to Christianizing Virgil, yet he influenced Christian writing for sixteen hundred years.                                                     C.M.

**VIRGIN BIRTH.** The Gospels of Matthew and Luke agree in reporting that Mary conceived Jesus without having had sexual intercourse (Matt. 1:18-21; Luke 1:26-38). In both accounts Joseph and Mary were betrothed, but had not had sexual relations at the time Jesus was born. They disagree about where the holy family lived: Matthew locates it in Bethlehem, from which they moved to Nazareth by way of Egypt. Luke locates them from the outset in Galilee, with the journey to Bethlehem occurring just before Jesus is born. But on the miracle of his conception they are in agreement.

Such a claim is not evident, however, in the rest of the NT. Paul refers to Jesus as simply "born of woman," thereby implying an ordinary human birth. Mark 6:3 identifies Jesus as "son of Mary," which might imply that he had no legitimate father, since

personal identity among Jews was always in terms of X, son of his father, Y, as the abundant references to Jacob and his twelve sons show. John 1:45 goes even farther in describing Jesus as "son of Joseph."

A problem for those who accept the virgin conception of Jesus as literal, historical fact is the evidence in Mark that his family did not want to accept his claims of divine authority, but considered him to be mad, as a literal reading of Mark 3:21 (compare 3:31-34) makes clear. If they had had knowledge of his supernatural birth, it seems wholly unlikely that they would have evaluated in such a manner his mission and sense of destiny. This way of understanding the passage in Mark about his family thinking he is crazy is confirmed by the fact that both Matthew and Luke—who have the virgin birth theme—omit that passage from Mark when they tell the story that it introduces in Mark (compare Matt. 12:22-30; Luke 11:14-23). Since there are no birth stories in either Mark or John, one cannot infer from these sources alone that Jesus was virginally conceived.

A related paradox is that Matthew and Luke, while denying that Joseph is the actual father of Jesus, take care to trace his genealogy back through Joseph to David, although each Gospel writer follows a different genealogical route (Matt. 1:2-17; Luke 3:23-38). In John, however, Jesus' descent from the Davidic line is directly called into question (John 7:40-43).

As confirmation of his account of the miraculous birth of Jesus, Matthew appeals to Scripture (Matt. 1:22-23; Isa. 7:14) to show how the divine plan, which is to be achieved through Jesus, is prepared for supernaturally by his virginal conception: "Behold, a virgin shall conceive, and bear a son, and shall call his name Immanuel" (which means "God with us"). Matthew quotes the passage from the Greek version used by early Christians (the Septuagint), where the word PARTHENOS can mean "virgin," but can also refer to a young woman of marriageable age. In the original Hebrew, however, the word for a young woman, *almah*, means only the latter, and appears in contexts describing ordinary sexual relationships between young men and young women (Prov. 30:19). In Isaiah 7:14 the point of the prophecy is not the extraordinary nature of the child's conception or birth but that the period of her pregnancy—that is, less than nine months—will see the problem posed by the invasion of Judah resolved. Hence the child is to be given the symbolic name for the people's deliverance from foreign occupation, "God with us."

In second-century writings that attack Christianity the charge is made that Jesus was really the son, not of *parthenos*, the virgin, but of Pantheros, a Roman soldier. Thus instead of virgin born he is the illegitimate son of a soldier.

Various explanations have been offered for the rise of these traditions about Jesus' virginal conception: (1) It was a matter of historical recollection that Jesus had been virginally conceived and miraculously born. (2) Mary's period of gestation was unusually short, with the result that the charge arose that she must have had premarital sexual relations or was sexually promiscuous. (3) Jesus was indeed illegitimate, as the designation in Mark 6:3 may be read as implying. (4) The wishes of the early Christians to heighten the significance of Jesus by the story of his virgin birth were joined with the desire to demonstrate that this event had taken place in fulfillment of Scripture.

Although, as noted above, Paul and the other NT writers do not make this claim in behalf of Jesus, they do share with other NT writers the conviction that God's purposes were revealed to and for humanity in a human being, who entered the world by physical birth rather than in a heavenly or an angelic being who merely masqueraded as human, as other religions of that epoch claimed. For all of these NT writers the important emphasis is on the fact of his human birth rather than on the virginal conception that Matthew and Luke claim brought it about.

H.K.

**VIRGIN MARY.** *See* MARY, MOTHER OF JESUS; BLESSED VIRGIN MARY.

**VIRTUES, CARDINAL.** *See* CARDINAL VIRTUES.

**VIRTUES, SEVEN.** Ancient Greek philosophy spoke of four CARDINAL VIRTUES: prudence, justice, temperance, and fortitude. Aristotle in his *Ethics* defined virtue as a "disposition which makes a man good and causes him to do his own work well." To live in such a virtuous state makes the person happy or blessed. The exercise of a virtue is due to the virtuous person's disposition to choose the mean, the middle way, between extremes. Courage thus is the path of moderation between being cowardly and being rash. A virtue is therefore an excellence of one's character.

In Christianity, the word for virtue (*arete*) occurs only four times in the NT, and three of these occurrences are in II Peter 1:3, 5. Only in Philippians 4:8 does Paul use the term, and this is generally translated as "excellence," as in the RSV. Later theologians added the three THEOLOGICAL VIRTUES taken from I Corinthians 13, faith, hope, and love (charity), to the four cardinal virtues and produced the teaching device of the seven virtues.

J.C.

**VIRTUES, THEOLOGICAL.** *See* THEOLOGICAL VIRTUES.

**VISHNU.** One of the two highest gods of HINDUISM, equal in importance to SHIVA. He played a small role in the Vedic period (second and first millennia B.C.). His major importance lies in the veneration given to him in devotional or BHAKTI Hinduism. In the overall Hindu pantheon, Vishnu is the protector and maintainer of world order—a role complementary to that of Shiva, the destroyer. Vishnu, like many gods, is also the focus of a sect, in his case VAISNAVISM . Vaisnavas worship Vishnu as the supreme god of the universe, not only the preserver, but also the creator and destroyer. They focus their worship on his AVATARS, or incarnations.

*The main temple at Angkor Wat, Cambodia. This temple was originally dedicated to the Hindu god Vishnu. It shows sculptures and reliefs of Vishnu in his various avatars and scenes from the Ramayana.*

In the mixture of the Aryan religion and that of the Indus Valley, which gave birth to the many forms of Hinduism, Vishnu does not play a major role. The Vedas mention the three strides he took to cross the earth, atmosphere, and heaven. They picture him in his heavenly abode, "the highest place." The later BRAHAMANAS identify him with the Vedic sacrifice, which was still the center of Hindu religion at the time. The Brahamanas refer to him as the highest god. However, his greatest importance came after the Bhagavatas identified their god, Vasudeva-Krishna, as the incarnation of Vishnu. The Bhagavad Gita, part of the Mahabharata epic, tells the story of Vishnu's incarnation as Lord KRISHNA. It advances the concept of avatar and the idea of a supreme personal God. From these developments arose the cult of the Vaisnavas.

The Vaisnavas gained power after the fourth century A.D. because Hindu rulers began to see Vishnu the preserver as the cosmic equivalent of a king. Just as Vishnu maintained the cosmic order, kings maintained the social order. These kings became devotees of Vishnu's avatars. Many demigods became identified as avatars of Vishnu. The list of avatars eventually became limited to ten names. Krishna and Rama are two important avatars. Gautama the Buddha has been considered an avatar who diverted the unworthy into another religion. Non-human avatars include the fish that rescued the Hindu first man, Manu, from the great Flood, and a boar which raised the earth from the waters.

In later times, the Hindus elevated Vishnu to the role of creator, overseer, and destroyer of the entire universe. He is portrayed as floating on the cosmic ocean, asleep in the coils of the cobra Sesa. At the beginning of each age he awakens, and a lotus issues from his navel. The god Brahma comes forth from the lotus to create the world. Vishnu's avatars enter the world to maintain it, but eventually Vishnu, in the form of RUDRA, destroys the world. Beyond the immeasurable and incomprehensible world of Vishnu and the cosmic ocean lies only the formless and indifferent creator Bhagavan. The world we perceive was created from the innate creativity, or *lila* ("sport") of Bhagavan, and it will eventually dissolve back into the blessed state of unity.        K./M.C.

**VISIBLE CHURCH.** *See* CHURCH: Visible and Invisible.

**VISION.** *See* BEATIFIC VISION.

**VITELLIUS.** A personal name shared by two distinct, though related, historical personages. Lucius Vitellius was legate of Syria in the time of Roman occupation (A.D. 35–37). He arranged a truce with a rebellious Parthian king, Artabanus III, at the instigation of Emperor Tiberius. Herod Antipas appears on the scene as the one who relayed the news of the settlement to the emperor, an act to which Vitellius took exception. It later formed the occasion on which he got his own back, and refused to press an invasion on the Jewish enemy, Aretas, in A.D. 37. He replaced Caiaphas by another high priest, Jonathan, whom he later replaced by Theophilus, since he acted as successor to Pontius Pilate. He permitted the stoning of Stephen.

His son, who also bore the name Vitellius, briefly became a Roman emperor in competition with Otho in the "year of the Four Emperors," A.D. 69. In fact, he ruled only from April to December that year and was executed by Vespasian on December 21.

R.M.

**VOCATION.** In the religious sense, a feeling of being called by God into service. In a general way, the concept of vocation or CALLING applies to all Christians, who are called to faith in Christ (I Pet. 2:9). According to Roman Catholic teaching, this vocation (calling) is to all human beings, even to those remote from the church, for vocation is a prevenient grace, in which all people have sufficient grace to be saved. The calling of God cannot be restricted to those who respond in acceptance, as was done by the Reformed Synod of Dort, which taught a limited atonement, that is, that Christ died only for the elect, which is to say, only for those who accept his calling to salvation.

Vocation, in the broad sense, implies the way one makes one's living in the world. This includes secular as well as religious professions and duties. Paul declared: "Everyone has his own vocation (calling), in which he has been called; let him keep to it" (I Cor. 7:20). Any human activity that is wholesome, no matter how humble in the eyes of society, may be the object of a vocation from God. Brother Lawrence thought of his position as dishwasher as a divine vocation, and indeed, was able to minister to others through it.

More specifically, the term "vocation" has been reserved for the sense of divine calling to the ministry or the religious life, as to the priesthood or to a monastic order. The actual presence of a vocation in one's life is demonstrated by a fitness or suitability in the person for the religious (that is, monastic) life, or for the priestly life, which has the same requirements plus an actual attainment of holiness of life. In the Catholic Church, the call of the bishop to a man to become a priest is the decisive element in a priestly vocation. In the Protestant churches, the concept of vocation to being a Christian (the PRIESTHOOD OF ALL BELIEVERS) is the same as in Catholicism. The concept of vocation to the ministry is similar, also, with the external call exercised by the Roman Catholic bishop generally exercised by the synod, district, or conference, except among Baptists, where it is usually exercised by the local congregation. All Protestants generally accept the need for a demonstration of fitness or aptitude (the inner call) on the part of the candidate for ordination, which is usually expressed in the ability to pursue academic and theological education successfully, plus the affirmation of the external call of the synod or other ecclesiastical body.                                    J.C.

**VOID.** Emptiness or nothingness. In mystical religious thought it suggests an emptying of the mind. There is a psychological quality as well as an ontological meaning to emptiness. Nothingness is a nihilistic concept, but self-emptying has a positive meaning by the implication of fulfillment through the divine life. Genesis describes the world as void before the divine Word brought order from chaos.
                                                                I.C.

**VOODOO.** A syncretistic religion combining Roman Catholic and African, particularly Dahoman, elements. It developed among slave populations of the new world, especially in Haiti and Brazil. In it African deities are associated with Catholic saints. African and Catholic ritual have combined to form a new religion, often equated with WITCHCRAFT by white observers. Voodooists believe in one supreme God, but interact with the lesser gods, known as *loa*. The *loa* possesses ("mount") their devotees and perform sacred dances. Possession can be used for healing, protection from evil influences, and bringing good or evil fortune to others. Particular *loa* become attached to individual families or priests. A male priest is called a *hungan* and a female priest a *mambo*. Each priest organizes a congregation.        K./M.C.

**VOLTAIRE** (1694–1778). French philosopher, polemicist, and man of letters, born François Marie Arouet. Voltaire had a very great influence on the European thought of his own and subsequent times. He wrote history, biography, novels, tragedies, essays, and pamphlets, and carried on an extensive correspondence with the leading men and women of his age, including Frederick II of Prussia. His best-known work is the philosophical romance, *Candide* (1759). In it Voltaire attacks the optimism and abstract speculation made fashionable by the philosopher Leibnitz and concludes with the practical advice, "Let us cultivate our garden."

Voltaire is the best representative of French DEISM. While skeptical of religious dogma, he was firmly convinced that reason and the order of nature justify belief in a creator God. He attacked the materialism and atheism of his fellow philosophers Holbach and Helvetius. Before 1751, Voltaire refrained from assailing orthodox Christianity. He limited his religious writings to praise of natural religion and pleas for religious toleration. However, for twenty years after 1751 he issued a torrent of books and pamphlets denouncing Christianity. His battle cry was *Ecrasez l'infâme*—"Crush the infamous thing"— by which he meant Christianity in all its orthodox, ecclesiastical forms, both Catholic and Protestant.

Typical of Voltaire's writing in this period is the *Sermon of the Fifty* in which he pokes fun at the outmoded science, the historical incongruities, and primitive morals that he finds in the Bible. His attack seldom varied, but he spared his readers tedium by lighting up long, tendentious passages with brilliant and outrageous humor. What drove Voltaire was his conviction that organized Christianity supported superstition, which inevitably led to fanaticism. He wanted to purify religion of these dangers and replace orthodoxy with a rather vague and emotional Deism. Doctrine would consist of belief in one God, whose service was the practice of virtue. At the time of his death, Voltaire was a national hero. In 1791 his remains were buried in the Pantheon in Paris.
                                                                J.L.

**VOLUNTARISM.** Contrary to the European practice of state churches, churches in America are "voluntary," that is, dependent on the voluntary support of members who choose to affiliate with them. It is a consequence of freedom of religion and the SEPARATION OF CHURCH AND STATE.

Voluntarism is a typically American arrangement, often accompanied by a tendency toward democratically governed local churches opposed to or in tension with national hierarchies, a concern for practical achievements rather than doctrinal purity (support is based on the popularity of the minister and program, thus success is measured by numbers and budgets), and rotating ministers obliged to please their congregations. The voluntary system emphasizes religious experience (conversion is sometimes required to join), the priesthood of all believers, and ethical distinctives (the strictest churches appear to be most attractive), and downplays the sacraments and the authority of the minister. The voluntary system also carries over into charitable work and cultural efforts, much of which depends on volunteers rather than being supported by the state. (*See* DENOMINATIONALISM.)                                        N.H.

**VOLUNTEERS OF AMERICA.** A religious and social welfare organization incorporated in New York City on November 6, 1896. The Volunteers came into being as a result of a dispute between General William Booth of the SALVATION ARMY and his son Ballington Booth, who wanted to inject more democratic procedures in the army. The Volunteers under Ballington Booth continued to operate much as the Salvation Army. The organization today holds evangelistic services and Bible classes and conducts numerous social services such as family aid, day nurseries, hospices for working girls, maternity homes, and ministries to needy older people. There is a major service to prisoners in state institutions called the Volunteers Prisoners League. Headquarters of the Volunteers is located in New York City.        R.H.

**VON HÜGEL.** *See* HÜGEL, BARON FRIEDRICH VON.

**VOTIVE MASS/OFFICE.** A mass that differs from the formal office of the day in that it is celebrated for a special intention or wish. Its name comes from the Latin *votum*, "a wish." These intentions may include a wish for the blessing of a marriage, for the repose of a soul (at a funeral mass), or for some other worthy cause, at the choice of the priest. Among these causes, votive masses may be said for the election of a pope, for the removal of the separation between churches, for a good death, for peace, for the sick, or for the evangelization of the world. Private votive masses may be said using any mass in the Roman missal, as well as from the special votive offices or masses found in the missal. There are special rubrics that govern when such private votive offices may be said, as well as rubrics on nuptial and funeral masses.          J.C.

**VOWS.** A solemn promise made to God freely, without coercion, with due deliberation, to do some task or enter some particular state such as becoming a priest, monk, or nun. Vows may be public (as are the vows of monks) or private. Bishops and other ordinaries can dispense persons from their vows if the request is based on a just cause, except for those vows reserved to the pope. In Roman Catholicism vows are impediments to marriage; that is, anyone under the vows of monasticism or of the major orders (subdeacons, deacons, priests, bishops) and those of first profession in the Jesuit order, is ineligible to marry and only rarely is dispensed; to marry without dispensation results in excommunication.

The vows of religion are the three vows of poverty, chastity, and obedience, which all religious (that is, monks and nuns) take. These are the evangelical counsels that are seen as steps to Christian perfection. These vows are taken at profession. Sometimes a fourth, special vow is added by the person making profession.          J.C

**VULGATE.** This venerable Latin translation of the Holy Scriptures was the work of JEROME, a fourth-century scholar. Jerome set an example for future translators by working from the original languages. Probably no other Bible has left a greater impact on the church. Even in 1546 the Council of Trent declared it to be the only authentic Latin text of the Scriptures. Until recently the Roman Catholic Church would permit no other basis for vernacular translations.

Jerome began his work on the Vulgate in 382 and completed it in 404. His scholarship and linguistic ability towered above others in the early church, yet the completed translation met opposition from those who felt their own renditions were superior. But the sheer excellence of Jerome's scholarship ultimately won acceptance for this great version. The Vulgate was the version of the Bible that became the first to be printed on Gutenberg's press in 1456.          R.H.

# Ww

**WAHHABIYAH.** The name given to a puritanical movement in ISLAM, derived from the name of its founder Muhammad ibn 'Abd al-Wahhab (1703–92). It was given to its followers by others; they call themselves *muwahhidun* ("Unitarians") because of their emphasis on the unity of Allah.

Al-Wahhab was born near Riyadh in present-day Saudi Arabia and achieved his greatest success in collaboration with the tribal leader Muhammad ibn Sa'ud. After dominating Arabia for nearly a century, the movement declined in the nineteenth century, but regained its position with the establishment of the modern kingdom of Saudi Arabia in the early 1930s.

The Wahhabis reject anything that might compromise the sovereignty and unity of God. They condemn veneration of saints, the building of mausoleums for them, and even celebration of the Prophet's birthday. They believe in literal interpretation of the Qur'an and following the theology and legal theory of the conservative thinkers Ahmad ibn Hanbal and ibn Taymiyya. The only authorities for belief and behavior are the Qur'an, Sunna (customary practice established by the example of Muhammad), and the four orthodox Sunni schools of legal thought (*Fiqh*). Any other practice or belief constitutes "innovation" or heresy. Targets of the displeasure of the Wahhabs include the mystical Sufis.

K./M.C.

**WAHY.** From the Arabic word for "inspiration." In Islam, divine inspiration or revelation. In pre-Islamic times, the term referred to the inspiration of poets, particularly those who gave utterance out of a trance-like state. But in Islam, it is restricted generally to NABI and *rasul*—prophets and emissaries of God—and above all to the inspired revelation that God delivered through the Prophet MUHAMMAD. However, the QUR'AN itself, the vehicle of that revelation, refers to other *wahy* as well: to that of angels, to other prophets, to the mother of Moses. An angel can also be the bearer of God's revelation, as was Gabriel for Muhammad. The process of receiving *wahy* was, for Muhammad, often excruciating: he would shake, be in pain, perspire heavily, and fall into a trance. But the result, the Qur'an, is said by believers to be inimitable.

R.E.

**WAILING WALL.** Known in Hebrew as *Kotel Maaravi*, which means "Western Wall," the Wailing Wall is the last remnant of the Temple complex in Jerusalem. Throughout the centuries it was a place of "wailing" and religious pilgrimages and prayers. It is about 160 feet long and 60 feet high. Arabs and Jews have had frequent arguments about its use by the Jews as a place of worship, despite the fact that the Western Wall came under the protection of the British during their administration in Palestine. After the Arab riots

1096

Courtesy of the Israel Government Tourist Office, Houston, Texas

*The Wailing Wall of Jerusalem*

in 1929, the League of Nations guaranteed the Jews access to the Western Wall under British protection. Following the establishment of the State of Israel and the War of Liberation in 1948, the old city of Jerusalem was occupied by Jordan. Contrary to the provisions of the armistice between the State of Israel and Jordan for free access to the Western Wall, the approach to it was forbidden to Jews. With the Six-Day War in 1967, Israel regained the old city, and Jews could once again go to the Western Wall.

L.K.

**WALDENSES.** A Protestant communion that still survives, particularly in the valleys of northwest Italy, and traces its roots back at least to the twelfth century. The name of the movement derives from Peter Waldo (properly Valdes), a merchant of Lyons, who adopted a life of apostolic poverty in 1173 and organized the Poor Men of Lyons to spread the vernacular Scriptures. Later, they were more generally called Vaudois. Some historians seek to trace the Waldenses back to the days of the apostle Paul and others to the time of Constantine in the fourth century. There are those who trace the etymology of the name Waldenses to the Latin word for valley (vallis), but their twelfth-century origin and Peter Valdes as their founder is more likely correct.

The Waldenses sought to be strictly orthodox, but after a time they ignored the church's insistence that they preach only when permitted by the clergy. Soon their own clergy (*barbis*) conducted an itinerant

ministry that spread their influence all over Europe. They doubted the validity of the sacraments when they were administered by unworthy priests. The Waldenses were ascetics who believed in visions, prophecies, and spirit possession. They also were committed to millenarian views. Prayers for the dead and veneration of the saints and relics were on their proscribed list.

During the Inquisition, the Waldenses suffered persecution, and their numbers were reduced. But they survived in the mountain valleys of the Savoy and Piedmont. After contact with Geneva, early in the sixteenth century, the Waldenses accepted the major doctrines of the Reformed faith. In 1532 they convened a synod at Chanforans at which they adopted the Genevan Confession of Faith, which included the doctrine of predestination. They also renounced their ties with the Roman church.

General J. C. Beckwith, a British officer, lived with the Waldenses in the nineteenth century and exerted a strong influence on them. He prevailed upon them to give up French as their language and to speak Italian. With Beckwith's encouragement, they established 120 schools.

Today the Waldenses enjoy freedom of worship and respect in both Roman Catholic and Protestant circles. They operate a theological seminary in Rome.

R.H.

**WALI.** A Muslim saint. In its original meaning of "friend," the term was used of those especially close to

God. In time the people applied it to the Sufi mystics, many of whom were regarded as saints while still alive. A system of graded ranks of saints developed, and devout followers collected stories of the lives of the saints. Many saints have had only a local following, but others are revered widely. In time the tombs of saints attracted pilgrims who made vows to the saints and prayed to them as intermediaries between humans and God. The veneration of saints was the occasion by which non-Muslim practices came to be observed.

In India and other parts of the world, incidents from the lives of the saints were popular subjects for artists. One of the saints often portrayed by Indian Muslims was Ibrahim ibn Adhan, known in English literature through the poem "Abu Ben Adhem" by Leigh Hunt. Orthodox theologians regarded such veneration as contrary to Islam. The Wahhabi reform movement, especially influential in Saudi Arabia, destroyed many tombs of saints and declared that worship at tombs was idolatry (*shirk*).                K.C.

**WAR.** Refers primarily to armed conflict among nation-states or between contending forces within a nation-state, to the military actions and violence associated with such conflict, and to the condition of open and declared hostility that is the context of intra- or international conflict and violence. The term is used also in a secondary, metaphorical sense to refer to any condition of continuing hostility and strife, as in the "war of the sexes" or "class war." It is an end to war in the primary meaning that the prophetic heritage of the Hebrew and Christian faiths affirms: "Nation shall not lift up sword against nation, neither shall they learn war any more" (Isa. 2:4). It is the primary meaning that Carl von Clausewitz uses in his classic *Vom Kriege* (1933; Eng. trans. *On War*, 1873) when he defines war as a rational, limited instrument of national policy, as calculated acts of violence designed to force the actions of others into line with that national policy.

*The Causes of War.* In varied forms, war has been a pervasive element in human interaction as far into the past as historical memory reaches. While means as diverse as marital alliances, political and diplomatic strategems, economic pressures and lures, and threats of violence have been used by rulers to attain their ends, war has remained one of the most powerful ways to enforce the will of governments. The causes of war, therefore, occupy the same spectrum as those goals that have at particular times motivated leaders of states and nations. Among the most prominent of these are: the accumulation of more power; the acquisition of additional wealth, especially territory, productive lands, taxable people, and profitable economic rights and enterprises; the desire for honor, status, and glory that wars once provided in abundance; and for attaining the security of space to live and food to eat or for the maintenance of security by defending the group and its resources against attack. As human conditions and capabilities have changed over the centuries, the valence and mix of these causes have altered, but so has war itself and its problems for society.

*War as an Escalating Problem.* War has always been a problem for those who were victims of its violence and cruelty. For rulers and military leaders, however, it has usually been regarded as providing opportunities for glory, wealth, and power as well as absolutely essential for defense. In recent centuries, and especially in recent decades, changes have occurred in war that have magnified its problems so greatly as to render meaningless most benefits it has traditionally been thought to offer. The most significant of these changes are these:

(a) The shift to total war is one striking change that has occurred. War for the empires and kingdoms of the past was a concern mainly of rulers and soldiers. Alexander the Great assembled his army, marched off to war, fought a succession of armies, and, with the defeat of each army and its leader, conquered yet another empire. War could bring a different ruler and at times impinge violently on a sector of the people, but for the most part it was peripheral to ordinary life and did no more than decide which oppressive tyrant would occupy the throne. In the modern world, the entire populace has been increasingly involved in war. First, a large number and a broader cross-section of people became part of the armies as more egalitarian weapons like the longbow and then the musket replaced the more elite weaponry of an armored knight on horseback. Second, the increasing economic and political power of the emerging middle class meant wider participation in the decisions regarding war. Third, the industrial revolution produced improved weaponry and vehicles for warfare, requiring revised strategy and tactics that combined armies, navies, political economies, and, later, air power for a new type of conflict involving total societies in waging war and in enduring attacks by the enemy. War in the twentieth century has become relentlessly more total. By World War II this process had developed to the point where it was possible to speak of total war in the sense of the war effort and the consequences of the struggle reaching into every sector of the nation. The saturation bombing of cities at times made it safer to be in the armed forces than at home.

(b) The development of nuclear weapons has been even more decisive in escalating the problems of war and, indeed, turning war into a mortal peril for culture, human life, and perhaps for all forms of life on planet Earth. Weaponry changed very slowly in the ancient and medieval worlds but developed with alarming rapidity in the nineteenth and twentieth centuries. First, rifling made it possible to fire greater distances with accuracy. Second, larger guns and improved vehicles increased the firepower of weapons and the rapidity for delivering devastating explosives. Third, the development of nuclear devices, combined with jet aircraft, rockets, and computerized control for long-distance, rapid, and accurate delivery, now provides the capability for the total destruction of nations and human life. These changes mean that war is no longer a pervasive and troublesome phenomenon on the periphery of society but has become a threat to entire peoples and nations through its total involvement and because of its capability of total destruction. The violence of war, always massive, has now, with the advent of nuclear weaponry, made the end of human history a clear and present danger.

*Ethics and War.* Reflection on the moral significance of war has taken place through much of human history in social contexts where conflict and violence were accepted elements of the customs and mores. Teachings that have provided increasingly critical perspectives on war have emerged gradually, in response to human suffering, from religious faith, and based on the perceived dangers of war.

(a) Emerging criticism appears gradually from multiple sources. The teaching of Taoism, though not directly critical of war, include the notion of *wu-wei* as a pattern of non-action leading to inward balance and peace. Jainism, emerging from Hinduism in the fifth century B.C., developed the ethical concept of *ahimsa* as non-violence toward living creatures, a notion that has been influential in Buddhism and Hinduism and, through exemplars like Gandhi, in the global community. In the Hellenic period, exhaustion from the wars among Greek city-states led to ideas of escape from violence and of benevolence toward others. The Hellenistic period witnessed the development of the practice of amnesty toward conquered peoples and the emergence of the notion of universal humanity. Though war is condoned in ancient Hebrew ethics, the OT contains strong admonitions for mercy and justice toward the oppressed and also a powerful understanding of God's covenant developing in history toward conditions of greater peace and with justice. The ethical teachings of the NT, especially Jesus' emphasis on turning the other cheek and loving one's enemies, have fueled growing opposition to war in Western society. The critique of war emerging around the globe from diverse communities, combined today with the massive threat of nuclear weapons, has produced broad-based and powerful movements opposed to war and to the policies of nations that lead toward war.

(b) Ethical perspectives on war resulting from these developments can be delineated with the following patterns: (1) Conventions governing the way war is waged that mitigate its violence but accept its existence. In ancient days, such conventions were minimal and often not observed. During the medieval period, the customs associated with knighthood dealt with the methods of fighting and the appropriate behavior of victor and vanquished. In recent centuries, customs governing warfare have been formulated and ratified by nations and international bodies such as the Red Cross, designated to oversee compliance. Under the League of Nations and the United Nations a body of international law related to war has been shaped. (2) PACIFISM holds that war is wrong and must be rejected as a means of settling human conflicts or attaining collective goals. A significant minority movement in both the Hindu/Buddhist and Christian traditions, pacifism has become much more widespread and influential in the twentieth century through the work of leaders like Mahatma Gandhi and Dr. Martin Luther King, Jr. (3) The just war ethic, based on Roman thought, is the traditional Roman Catholic position, though it has been widely influential beyond the bounds of that church. The just war ethic lays down criteria for war: just cause, declared and waged by legitimate political authority, begun as a last resort, just methods in waging war, reasonable expectation of successful outcome, results less evil than if not undertaken, just intentions, and carried out as a path to a better condition of peace. (4) The view of war as crusade, to be carried out as religious duty, can be based upon a few passages in the OT but appears most prominently in the Islamic view of war and in the view held by Christian leaders of the Middle Ages who initiated and encouraged the Crusades against the Muslims. (5) The position of political realism holds that all social collectivities, including nations, act only out of motives charged with interests of survival, power, and acquisitiveness. The use of force and the waging of war are inevitable and must be brought insofar as possible under the control of justice by means of the balance of power. (6) Nuclear pacifism affirms that the tremendous peril of nuclear war requires that it be rejected. This does not mean, however, that limited wars, that is, wars not using nuclear weapons, are unacceptable and even unnecessary. Under no circumstances, due to its destructive potential fo all, can nuclear war serve the national interest of any nation.

*War and the Future.* Given the escalation of weaponry and the probability that all parties would be annihilated in a nuclear war, it would be easy to suppose that war is now impossible. Not at all. Instead the superpowers continue to produce more and more nuclear warheads and increasingly larger and faster means to deliver them to enemy territory. Nuclear weapons exist in sufficient numbers not only to destroy the entire world a hundred times over but with enough left over "to make the rubble bounce," as Winston Churchill phrased it. In addition, there is the problem of the proliferation of nuclear weapons and the possibility of nuclear bombs falling into the hands of terrorists. The situation has a desperate quality that makes such positions as the just war ethic with its rational calculations seem quaint. With reference to war today, reality has walked off the ethical maps of the past.

As never before, war and the future are opposed to each other. If there is to be a future for humans, it will be because war as it can now be waged has been avoided and the causes of war contained within social structures. The dimensions of the problem are at last emerging with clarity.

Karl Barth has placed war in perspective for the Christian community in *Church Dogmatics*. According to Barth, the traditional and continuing view that war is a normal and acceptable way to pursue the policies of nations has become, given the possibilities of war today, "an increasingly unbearable perversion of Christian truth." War now involves total civil communities so that all suffer and inflict suffering. War now makes enemies of people and communities because of differing national loyalties, not because some are guilty and others innocent. And war now is total because its possibilities of destruction are total and because it involves not only killing but all other sins as well. War means killing without glory, without dignity, without chivalry, without restraint, and without reserve, and it just as surely means also to steal, ransack, fornicate, burn, lie, deceive, and dishonor, Barth says. And there are no longer mitigating values sufficient to begin balancing its evil.

Beyond clear perspective on the danger and evil of war, what can be done? So preoccupied with the number, complexity, and destructive potential of weaponry have many become that the only solutions are seen to be in terms of unilateral or multilateral reduction in arms, especially nuclear arms. While such reduction is undoubtedly desirable and eventually necessary, it will only come about when the means for reducing tension and building a fabric of relations based on justice and respect is achieved. Neither war nor peace is "natural" or "normal" among people either individually or collectively. Tensions and some forms of conflict are inevitable. The crucial issue is whether situations of tension can be mitigated or resolved to prevent escalation of conflict, whether agreed-upon means for adjudication of differences can be developed that will lead toward higher levels of justice, and whether covenants of shared interests and goals that transform relations toward peace can be built and reinforced.     C.Mc.

**WARDEN.** A lay officer in Anglican and Episcopal churches. Wardens (generally two to a parish) have been appointed in Anglican churches since the Middle Ages to care for the maintenance and furnishings of the church building. Historically, churchwardens are responsible for public order in the church and church yard and so had the power of arrest in England until the nineteenth century.     J.C.

**WARFIELD, BENJAMIN B.** (1851-1921). Old School theologian and refiner of Princeton theology, Warfield was born near Lexington, Kentucky. He attended Princeton University (B.A. 1871; M.A. 1874) and studied (1876-77) at the University of Leipzig. After serving as assistant minister at First

Presbyterian Church, Baltimore, he taught at Western Theological Seminary in Pittsburgh (1878-87).

In 1887 he became professor of didactic and polemical theology at Princeton Seminary, where he shaped the doctrine of scriptural INERRANCY. In an article with A. A. Hodge titled "Inspiration" in the *Princeton Review* (1881), he argued that Scripture was inerrant in the original autographs. Warfield contributed to *The Fundamentals* and also wrote *An Introduction to the Textual Criticism of the New Testament*. Published posthumously were *Revelation and Inspiration, Studies in Tertullian and Augustine, Calvin and Calvinism,* and two volumes on *Perfectionism*.

N.H.

**WARING, ANNA LAETITIA** (1820–1910). Welsh hymn writer who lived her entire life—ninety years—in Neath, a town located on the river of the same name in southeastern Wales. As one of several gifted women writers belonging to the evangelical wing of the Church of England, Miss Waring compiled her *Hymns and Meditations* (1850, 1863) under the wider influence of the Oxford movement. Critics praised her hymns, which combined great lyric virtues with devotional warmth. Miss Waring's most famous hymn no doubt is "In Heavenly Love Abiding," which many regard as one of the best hymns of the nineteenth century. Another is "My Heart Is Resting, O My God."     R.H.

**WARNACK, JOHANNES** (1867–1944). Missionary with the Batak Church in Sumatra. Born in Germany, Warnack went in 1892 as a pioneer missionary to the island of Samosir. Later he became a teacher and in 1898 director at the Rhenish Mission seminary for preachers in Sipoholon. In 1908 he was appointed to the home staff with responsibility for the mission's work in Indonesia. He went back to Sumatra as a successor to the pioneer missionary LUDWIG NOMMENSEN in 1920, and led the church there until 1931. He is known for his research into the language and primitive beliefs of the Indonesian people. He was a prolific writer and greatly influenced the public in central Europe to interest in missionary endeavors in Indonesia.     W.G.

**WARNECK, GUSTAV** (1834–1910). Generally regarded as the founder of the Protestant science of missions. Born in Naumburg, Germany, Warneck became professor of the science of missions at the University of Halle in 1896. One of his contributions to missions was the founding of the journal *Allgemeine Missionszeitschrift* in 1874. This journal promoted the scientific discussion of missions and was influential in the field. Warneck also influenced missions through other publications, particularly his *Sketch of the History of Protestant Missions from the Reformation to the Present Day,* first published in 1892 and reprinted ten times.

W.G.

**WARNER, ANNA BARTLETT** (1824–1915). American hymn writer and novelist. The author of "Jesus Loves Me, This I Know" was a daughter of a prosperous New York lawyer. Anna was born on August 31 in New York City. When there were reverses in the family fortune, the Warners moved to their summer home on Constitution Island in the Hudson River off West Point. Anna and her sister, Susan, turned to writing as a means of making up for their reduced circumstances. Susan wrote novels, one of which, *Wide, Wide World*, was a great success. This was followed by *Queecky*, which was almost as popular.

For fifty years the sisters devoted their Sunday afternoons to Bible classes they conducted in their home for West Point cadets. The future officers were rowed to the island and back by the Warners' hired man. Susan was the teacher of the classes until her death in 1885, and Anna took her place.

Under the pseudonym Amy Lothrop, Anna also wrote novels, including the six-volume *Stories of Vinegar Hill* (1873), *Say and Seal* (1860), and *Fourth Watch* (1872). She also wrote several books on gardening. However, her name will live longest for the always popular children's hymn "Jesus Loves Me," which first appeared in her novel *Say and Seal*. "We Would See Jesus" first appeared in another of her novels, *Dollars and Sense*. "One More Day's Work for Jesus" was published in her volume *Wayfaring Hymns, Original and Translated*. Anna Warner also compiled *Hymns of the Church Militant* (1858).     R.H.

**WASHINGTON, BOOKER T.** (1856–1915). Educator and social reformer, Washington was born April 5 on the James Burroughs plantation near Roanoke, Virginia, to a slave, Jane Furguson. After the Civil War he moved to Malden, West Virginia, where he worked in the salt furnaces and coal mines. From 1872 to 1875 he studied at Hampton (Virginia) Institute and Industrial School, to which he returned in 1879. In 1881 he was chosen by Hampton founder Samuel C. Armstrong to head the Tuskegee Normal School and Industrial Institute in Alabama.

Washington gained national recognition as an educational leader of black people in the United States and was counted among the ablest speakers of his time. He felt that blacks could stay in the South if they accepted segregation and worked on their own to gain a solid social and financial base. In 1900 he founded the National Negro Business League. His Cotton States Exposition speech in 1895 in Atlanta advocated cooperation between the races, a bold concept for the times among blacks or whites. Washington died at Tuskegee in 1915.     N.H.

**WATCHTOWER BIBLE AND TRACT SOCIETY.** *See* JEHOVAH'S WITNESSES.

**WATER FOR IMPURITY.** Water played many ritual roles in the Hebrew law. Above all, water's use as a cleanser made it the symbol of purification from those conditions that made a person ceremonially unclean. The cleansing of lepers (Lev. 14:8) was done with water. Elisha sent Naaman the Syrian to bathe as part of his cure of leprosy. Uncleanliness brought on by illness was cleansed with water, and also the unclean state that was caused by eating unclean animals (Lev. 15:5-8; 10–13; 17:25 ff.). The "water of bitterness" was made of water and dust from the tabernacle's floor. A person suspected of adultery was forced to drink it, with the belief that the unfaithful would be revealed (Num. 5:11-31). The "water of separation" (Num. 19) was a mixture of fresh running water and the ashes of a perfect, reddish-brown heifer. It was sprinkled with a sprig of hyssop on a person who had become unclean by touching a dead body, on the third and seventh days after the contact. After a bath and clean clothes, the person was declared clean.     J.C.

**WATER OF BITTERNESS.** *See* JEALOUSY, ORDEAL OF.

**WATSON, RICHARD** (1781–1833). Early Methodist theologian. Born in Lincolnshire, England, Watson was a Methodist traveling preacher from 1796 to 1801. From 1803 to 1809 he was secretary of the New Methodist Connexion conference. Committed to Wesleyan orthodoxy and Arminianism, Watson wrote against both special election and predestination. In his *Theological Institutes* (1823) Watson held that Christ died for all—for those who finally obtain salvation as well as for those who by rejecting Christ fail to be saved. The *Institutes'* systematic presentation of Wesley's thought was influential for British and American Methodism until the turn of the twentieth century.     W.G.

**WATTS, ISAAC** (1674–1748). Hymn writer and clergyman; the "father of English hymnody." A son of a Dissenting schoolteacher, Watts was born on July 17, in Southhampton, England. Although a friend offered him a university education, Watts chose to attend the Dissenting Academy at Stoke Newington. In 1702 he became pastor of the Independent Church at Mark Lane, London, a post he held all his life. One of the most influential of the British hymn writers, Watts composed a total of six hundred hymns, many of which are still sung today. He first published *Hymns and Spiritual Songs* in 1707, which was revised in the subsequent sixteen editions. His writing gave strong impetus to hymn singing in worship services, which up to that time had chiefly employed metrical psalms. Some of his great numbers are "When I Survey the Wondrous Cross," "O God, Our Help in Ages Past," "There Is a Land of Pure Delight," and "Jesus Shall Reign."     R.H.

**WAVE OFFERING.** An early Hebrew festival practice, undoubtedly begun after the invasion and settlement of Canaan. The first sheaves of grain to be harvested were waved before the altar as a sacrifice to Yahweh, seen as Lord of the Harvest (Lev. 23:10-15). Along with the waving of the sheaves before the altar by the priest, the farmer was also to offer a year-old male lamb, without blemish, as a burnt OFFERING. A cereal (or grain) offering of flour, oil, and wine was to be offered along with the lamb. No one was to eat of the grain harvest until this offering was made.

J.C.

**WAY, THE.** An international religious movement founded by Victor Paul Wierwille (1917–85), a former Evangelical and Reformed minister, with headquarters in New Knoxville, Ohio.

The movement resulted from youth gatherings that were addressed by Wierwille, who took to the road in 1968 on a Harley-Davidson motorcycle at the age of fifty-one. A charismatic personality, Wierwille attracted many of the youth of the JESUS PEOPLE era. Thousands attended his "Rock of Ages Festivals."

Wierwille was a capable organizer and from "the trunk" of his Ohio headquarters grew "branches" in twenty state organizations, which in turn grew "twigs" (churches) on which "leaves" (disciples) sprouted. Newcomers are enrolled in Wierwille's "Power for Abundant Living" course, which consists of twelve three-hour sessions.

While much of what the Wierwille organization teaches has an orthodox ring to it, since 1977, at least, the founder insisted that "Christ is not God." In fact, his most strident attack on the doctrine of the Trinity is contained in his book, *Jesus Christ Is Not God* (1975). He also stressed the necessity for a recruit to speak in tongues, declaring that one is not regenerate unless one can do this.

Young converts, after pledging allegiance to The Way, are encouraged to leave home in order to make their full commitment. They sign up as WOW ambassadors, pledging themselves to a year's service in the movement. Wierwille's leadership trainees are enlisted in The Way Corps. Persistent reports indicate that these elite disciples are trained in military strategy, including the use of weapons.

Followers of The Way are assured that salvation will bring them successful living. One of the posters advertising Wierwille's course reads: "You Can Have Whatever You Want." Beside the 150-acre Ohio headquarters, The Way has two colleges, one in Emporia, Kansas, and one in Rome City, Indiana, as well as a mountain retreat in Colorado, and survival camps in New Mexico and Colorado, in addition to dozens of smaller properties. Estimates of the number of The Way disciples ranges from 40,000 to 100,000. Assets of The Way have been estimated at $50 million.

R.H.

**WAY OF DEVOTION.** See BHAKTI.

**WAY OF KNOWLEDGE.** See VIDYA.

**WAY OF WORKS.** See KARMA MARGA.

**WEATHERHEAD, LESLIE DIXON** (1893–1976). British Methodist preacher and author. Weatherhead was born on October 14 in London. He was educated at Newton Secondary School in Leicester, Richmond Theological College, Manchester University, and London University. Serving with the Indian army in World War I, Weatherhead rose to staff captain, and after the Armistice he became an army chaplain. His first pastorate was in Madras, India. Returning to Britain in 1922, he ministered to Methodist churches in Manchester and Leeds. In 1936 he was called to serve the prestigious City Temple in London and continued in that pulpit until 1960. Thereafter for many years he was pastor emeritus.

Weatherhead wrote thirty books, many of them on the relationship of religion and psychology. In 1966 *The Christian Agnostic* was published. In that work Weatherhead acknowledged the difficulty of drawing a hard line between belief and unbelief. Long before it became popular, Weatherhead supported the Campaign for Nuclear Disarmament. He criticized the United States for being involved in the Vietnam war, and argued in favor of mercy killings. Weatherhead died at Bexhill, England, on January 3.

R.H.

**WEBER, MAX** (1864–1920). German sociologist and economist. Born in Erfurt, Germany, on April 21, Weber was educated at the University of Heidelberg and later in Berlin and Göttingen. A professor at Berlin, Freiburg, Munich, and Heidelberg, Weber pioneered in developing a methodology for social science. He opposed the Marxian view that economics is the determinant factor in social causation, insisting that the dynamic factors were much more complex than that. He stressed the role of religious values and ideologies and the place of charismatic leaders in shaping societies.

In Weber's major work, *Protestant Ethic and the Spirit of Capitalism* (1920), he developed a thesis concerning the intimate connection between the ascetic ideal fostered by Calvinism and the rise of capitalistic institutions. He advocated that Germany establish a democratic form of government similar to the American model. Other works by Weber include *Theory of Social and Economic Organization* and *Methodology of the Social Sciences*.

R.H.

**WEEKS, FEAST OF.** One of the three great holy days of the Jews, the Feast of Weeks is also known as the Day of Firstfruits, the Feast of Harvest, the Assembly, the Completion, Pentecost, and the Feast of the Reaping. Originally this festival of harvest had probably been a typical Canaanite agricultural celebration that the Hebrews adopted as their own, a time to celebrate the end of the barley reaping.

In ancient Israel the time probably varied from place to place and from year to year, depending on the locale and the weather. Later the date settled down, seven weeks after the OFFERING of a sheaf of barley at the Feast of Unleavened Bread (Exod. 23:16). When the Feast of Unleavened Bread later merged into the Passover, the date apparently became fixed throughout the country, no matter when the harvest was completed. At the Feast of Unleavened Bread the ritual was to offer at the altar two loaves without leaven, but at the Feast of Weeks, the two loaves from the new crop were required to be like those of the daily diet—leavened (Lev. 23:17). Exodus 34:18 refers to a pilgrimage of weeks, as people brought forward their individual offering of loaves.

This was traditionally a time of merriment and celebration, with the assurance there would again be bread for the coming year. The Priestly Code (Lev. 23:15-23) also required sacrifices of seven lambs, two young bulls, and a ram. During the rites God was honored as the provider of the land, a land overflowing with milk and honey. The males did a liturgical dance around the altar, now a form of worship nearly extinct except in the rites of ancient Christian Copts and Amharics. This was also the occasion for chanting the great Hallel or hallelujah, as found in Psalms 113–118. After the religious ceremonies there was a huge FEAST for everyone in the neighborhood, including the poor, the travelers, the non-Jews, and the strangers. Sometimes local villages continued to offer individual gifts of loaves until the time of the Feast of the Booths.

Associating the modern Christian festival of Pentecost and its outpouring of the Holy Spirit with the Feast of Weeks, some authorities say, is not justified, even if both occurred historically at the same time. In nineteenth-century Germany several Jewish rabbis developed for the first time the concept of celebrating Jewish confirmation, bar mitzvah and bat mitzvah, on this feast, perhaps to conform to Christian custom. This pattern is now fairly common among many Jews.                                    T.J.K.

**WEIL, SIMONE** (1909–43). French philosopher, mystic, and writer on socio-political and religious topics. Her brilliant, passionate, uncompromising, and often enigmatic life and writings have accorded her the reputation of both genius and saint. Born in Paris into a well-to-do and intellectual Jewish family, Simone Weil's academic career was a brilliant success. She taught in a number of secondary schools and became engaged in left-wing politics.

Throughout her short life she fought for the weak and the oppressed but never joined a political party. Taking leave from her teaching, she worked as a farm laborer and for a year in a Renault auto factory, but this came to an end because of illness.

The years 1936 to 1943 were a period of intense religious speculation and personal agony of soul. She was drawn to the Catholic Church and its spirituality but refused to be baptized. She was intensely Jewish but castigated Judaism and rejected much of the OT. She lived in exile at the time of the German occupation but sought unsuccessfully to return from London to join the forces of the Resistance. Denied this, she sought to share in the privations of her countrymen. She allowed herself to die of hunger while a tuberculosis patient at the Ashford Sanatorium, Kent, at the age of thirty-three. Among her posthumously published books are *Gravity and Grace* (Eng. trans., 1952), *The Need for Roots* (1952), *Waiting for God* (1951), and *The Notebooks of Simone Weil*, 2 vols. (1956).

J.L.

**WELLHAUSEN, JULIUS** (1844-1918). Famous German Lutheran biblical scholar and Orientalist, born in Hameln on May 17. Wellhausen is widely known for his studies on the documentary theory of the composition of the Hexateuch (the first six books of the OT).

Wellhausen's chief works are the *Prolegomena* and the *Komposition des hexateuchs*, at one time the standard texts in all scientific biblical study. Every student of the OT came to know Wellhausen's view on *J, E, D, P*, the basic documents he believed underlay the received texts of Genesis, Exodus, Leviticus, Numbers, Deuteronomy, and Joshua. Much of Wellhausen's more startling theories have been modified by later scholars but, in the main, the DOCUMENTARY HYPOTHESIS—though often challenged by conservatives—remains a major element in biblical study and exegesis. Wellhausen's higher education was at Göttingen. He taught at Greifswold, Halle, and Marburg. From 1892 to 1918 he taught at Göttingen. His works are extensive; some of the more important are *Israelitische und Judische Geschichte; Reste arabischen Heidentums; Das Evangelium Marci; Das Evangelium Matthai; Das Evangelium Lucae;* and *Das Evangelium Johannis*. Wellhausen died at Göttingen on January 7.                                    J.C.

**WELTANSCHAUUNG.** The German term for "world view" or basic unexamined philosophical outlook. The term is widely used with reference to attempts to understand the way biblical writers viewed the world around them, especially in the work of Rudolf Bultmann and his school, who sought to "demythologize" the NT.

J.C.

**WESLEY, CHARLES** (1707–88). The co-founder of Methodism and a most prolific hymn writer. The eighteenth child of Samuel and Susanna Wesley, Charles was born on December 18, at Epworth, a symbol of his parents' reconciliation. At age nine he followed his older brothers Samuel and John to Westminster School in London. In 1726 he enrolled at Christ Church College, Oxford. There he drew together a group of friends into a "Holy Club," which

Portrait of Frank O. Salisbury's painting, from the World Methodist Museum, Lake Junaluska, North Carolina

*Charles Wesley*

was eventually dubbed "Methodist." John joined the group later.

In 1735 Charles was ordained a priest of the CHURCH OF ENGLAND and joined General James Oglethorpe's expedition to Georgia. There Charles served as secretary to Oglethorpe and chaplain to Ft. Frederica. After a brief but stormy stint, Charles returned to England.

After John's return from Georgia in 1738, the brothers came under the influence of MORAVIAN Peter Bohler. Charles experienced conversion on May 21, three days before John's Aldersgate experience. Despite a reprimand from the archbishop of Canterbury, he joined his brother and their friend GEORGE WHITEFIELD in preaching the Wesleyan revival.

In 1748 Charles married Sarah Gwynne in Wales. They had a daughter and two sons, Charles and Samuel, both of whom were musical prodigies. Samuel became a Roman Catholic. A fiery preacher but a mediocre organizer, Charles the senior gave up the itinerary in 1756 and settled in Bristol. In 1771 he returned to London, where he lived until his death on March 29, 1788. He is buried in the churchyard of St. Marylebone.

It is said that one can sing the theology of John in the hymns of Charles. Between 1737 and 1742 they published six volumes of hymns. The United Methodist *Book of Hymns* contains seventy-three of his songs, the Episcopal *Hymnal* eighteen, and the Presbyterian *Worshipbook* ten. His best-known hymns include "And Can It Be?"; "Christ the Lord Is Risen Today"; "Christ, Whose Glory Fills the Skies"; "Come, Holy Ghost, Our Hearts Inspire"; "Come, Thou Long Expected Jesus"; "Hark! The Herald Angels Sing"; "Love Divine, All Loves Excelling"; and "O for a Thousand Tongues."    N.H.

**WESLEY, JOHN** (1703–91). The founder of Methodism was born on June 17 in Epworth, England, the fifteenth child and second son of Samuel and Susanna Annesley Wesley. In 1709 John was saved when angry parishioners set fire to the Epworth rectory, and thereafter John always considered himself "a brand plucked out of the burning."

In 1714 he entered Charterhouse school in London, and in June 1720, he enrolled at Christ Church College, Oxford. Wesley was ordained a deacon in 1725, elected a fellow at Lincoln College, Oxford, in 1726, and a priest in 1728. After a period as curate for his father in Wroot, he returned to Oxford in 1729 as a tutor and leader of the HOLY CLUB, founded by his brother CHARLES WESLEY. In 1733 John preached on "The Circumcision of the Heart," signaling his own growing belief that a personal experience of God's grace was essential.

During his 1735 trip to Georgia, he met a group of Moravians, who caused him to question his own faith. He was appointed rector of Christ Church, Savannah, and served there until he "ran away" in 1737. His return to England was due in part to a failed love affair with a young woman named Sophy Hopkey and also disillusionment over the lack of spiritual discipline among his parishioners.

Portrait of Frank O. Salisbury's painting, from the World Methodist Museum, Lake Junaluska, North Carolina

*John Wesley*

The year 1738 has been called "the year of grace" in Wesley's life. On February 7 he met Moravian Peter Bohler, who encouraged him to "preach faith until you have it." During a meeting of a small group at Aldersgate on May 24, Wesley found his "heart was strangely warmed" during the reading of Martin Luther's *Preface to the Epistle to the Romans*. That summer he visited the Moravians in Germany and met COUNT NICHOLAS VON ZINZENDORF. He later (1740) rejected Moravian teaching and separated from their Fetter Lane Society.

Influenced by reading Jonathan Edwards' *Faithful Narrative*, Wesley agreed to succeed George White-field in preaching to the miners near Bristol in April 1739. In 1739 he preached on "Free Grace" at Bristol and for the first time at the Foundry in London, which became the Methodist headquarters. United societies were organized in 1739, and the first official Methodist society was formed in July 1740 with the first annual conference in June 1744. The Articles of Religion were drawn up at this conference and were based to a considerable extent on the Thirty-nine Articles of the Church of England.

About the same time Wesley began to hear reports of people who believed that they were "saved from all sin." He published his *Plain Account of Christian Perfection* first in 1766, with the fourth and definitive edition published in 1777. Influenced by mysticism, he concluded that one could begin a process of sanctification after one was converted, and that one could attain entire sanctification or Perfect Love before death. Wesley, however, never claimed to have attained it himself, though many of his followers did so claim.

Wesley was unlucky in matters of the heart. In 1748 he was nursed back to health by Grace Murray in Newcastle and announced his intentions to marry her. But interference by Charles resulted in her marriage to John Bennet. In February of 1751 John Wesley married Mary Vazeille, a marriage that was marked by discord until her death in 1781.

Having initially encouraged the American Revolution, Wesley appointed THOMAS COKE and FRANCIS ASBURY as superintendents of the American work in 1784. He tried to keep his followers within the Church of England but did not succeed. Wesley's major writings are his *Journals, Explanatory Notes Upon the New Testament,* the *Standard Sermons* (4 vols.), and voluminous letters. A writer who developed his theology in the midst of his preaching, he emphasized universal atonement and human freedom to respond affirmatively to the gospel. Well-versed in church history, Wesley had a reverence for classical spirituality and the liturgy of the Church of England. A traditionalist, he hesitated, yet felt compelled by circumstances, to license and ordain lay people.

N.H.

**WESLEYAN CHURCH.** *See* METHODIST CHURCHES.

**WESTCOTT, BROOKE FOSS** (1825–1901). English prelate and NT scholar. His education at Cambridge brought him into close touch with men who subsequently were to be his collaborators, especially J. B. LIGHTFOOT and F. J. A. Hort, the so-called Cambridge trio. He moved along well-worn paths of preferment and advancement in the English public school system and church offices, proceeding first to Harrow School, where he was a teacher. He moved to a residentiary canonry at Peterborough cathedral, and thence back to Cambridge as professor of divinity. He became a Fellow at King's College, Cambridge (1882), a canon of Westminster (1884), and bishop of Durham (1890). One of the interests he showed, in addition to his academic and administrative innovations, was in a school for the training of the ministry, later to become Westcott House, a seminary for episcopal ordinands.

His switch from the academe to the high office in the Church of England as bishop of Durham came in succession to Lightfoot. At Durham he showed continued interest in ordination candidates as well as the social well-being of men and women in a depressed area of the English northeast. In 1892 he was instrumental in settling a miners' strike.

His literary work brought him into close liaison with Hort; together they published in 1881 a new scientifically prepared text of the Greek Testament, which gave preference to the manuscripts Sinaiticus (Aleph) and Vaticanus (B). This edition lay at the basis of the Revised Version translation of 1895. Westcott's work as a biblical commentator is especially valuable, with important writings on the Gospel of John, the Johannine Epistles, and the Letter to the Hebrews. His knowledge of the early church fathers was extensive, and with Lightfoot and Hort he shared a theological position of enlightened conservatism and churchly allegiance.

R.M.

**WESTMINSTER ABBEY.** One of the great shrines of the Church of England and of the English nation. Its official name is the Collegiate Church of St. Peter in Westminster. The precise date of the founding of the abbey is unknown, but it was rebuilt and restored by King Edward the Confessor, who died in 1066 and whose remains are buried in the abbey. A new rebuilding of the church began in 1245 and went on intermittently for several centuries. In 1540 the monastery was dissolved, and a collegiate church under a dean and canons was set up as a royal peculiar, independent of the bishop of London. The abbey contains the coronation chair, and here the kings and queens of England have been crowned for many centuries. The tombs of many of them are also within the abbey, as are memorials to many famous Britons. (See photo on next page.)

J.M.

**WESTMINSTER ASSEMBLY.** During the struggle between king and Parliament in England,

Courtesy of Religious News Service

*Westminster Abbey*

Parliament summoned an assembly of divines in 1643, and charged them with the task of reforming the church in a PURITAN direction. The Assembly was overwhelmingly Presbyterian in its composition, but it was not, strictly speaking, a church synod but a creation of Parliament. The Assembly continued to meet for about ten years. The place of meeting was Westminster Abbey, from which the body became known as the Westminster Assembly. Its principal work was to draw up various documents for the projected national Presbyterian church of the future. These documents included not only the well-known WESTMINSTER CONFESSION of Faith and the WEST-MINSTER CATECHISMS, but also the Directory for the Public Worship of God, and the Form of Presbyterial Church Government. The Assembly was never officially dissolved. Its work gained full acceptance only in Scotland, though only a tiny minority of its members were Scottish and they attended only part of the proceedings.

J.M.

**WESTMINSTER CATECHISMS.** There are two Westminster Catechisms, the Larger Catechism and the Shorter Catechism, both produced by the WESTMINSTER ASSEMBLY in 1647. The Larger Catechism is a more popular version of the teaching of the WESTMINSTER CONFESSION of Faith. The Shorter Catechism is much better known because it was widely taught to children and is still in use in some Presbyterian churches. The first question and answer are very well known: "What is the chief end of man?" "Man's chief end is to glorify God and to enjoy him for ever."

J.M.

**WESTMINSTER CONFESSION.** This was the Confession of Faith produced by the WESTMINSTER ASSEMBLY and was intended to become the standard of doctrine for the whole of the British Isles. In fact, it had lasting influence only in the (Presbyterian) Church of Scotland, a strange irony since only eight out of the 159 members of the Assembly were from Scotland. However, the Westminster Confession has continued to be the standard of doctrine (after the Bible) in the Church of Scotland and in many of the Presbyterian churches of the English-speaking world.

The Confession consists of thirty-three short chapters. The first asserts the authority of the Scriptures, understood as the canonical books of the OT and NT, and each point of doctrine is supported by one or more references to so-called "proof texts" from the Bible. The second chapter treats of God, conceived in a strongly monarchical way, while the third goes on immediately to the eternal decree of predestination, whereby "some men and angels are predestinated unto everlasting life, and others foreordained to everlasting death." In the words of G. S. Hendry, "The Gospel is construed in the framework of a gigantic drama, which begins when God in his eternal decree separates the elect from the reprobate, and ends at the last judgment when he separates the righteous from the wicked for all eternity; and at every stage of the drama as it unfolds, the Confession seeks the motif in the separation that is going on beneath the surface (where they are mixed up together) between the good and the bad." The stress on double predestination is perhaps even more extreme than is found in Calvin. Another related emphasis is the sharp distinction between the visible and the invisible church.

With the liberalizing of theology in the nineteenth century, the Confession became increasingly an embarrassment to the churches that subscribed to it. Some of them have revised or replaced it, but because of the difficulty of doing this, a more common practice has been to modify the terms of assent required of ministers. In the Church of Scotland, what is required is acceptance of "the fundamental doctrines of the Christian faith contained in the Confession of Faith of this Church, recognizing liberty of opinion on such points of doctrine as do not enter into the substance of the faith." But just what "the substance of the faith" comprises is not stated.

J.M.

**WHITE, ELLEN GOULD HARMON** (1827–1915). Prophetess and pioneer leader of the Seventh-day Adventist Church. Although Ellen White cannot properly be called the founder of Seventh-day Adventism, she is revered greatly as one of its significant figures.

Ellen was born in Gorham, Maine, to devout Methodist parents, followers of WILLIAM MILLER, a Baptist minister who had predicted that the Lord's Second Coming would occur in 1844. Ellen was a teenager when she had her first vision, shortly after the Great Disappointment (the wave of feeling that followed the failure of Miller's prediction regarding the time of Christ's return).

After marrying James White, an Adventist elder, in 1846, Ellen continued to experience visions or revelations—about two thousand in her lifetime. She wrote forty-five books and four thousand articles. One of her works, *Steps to Christ*, reached a circulation of 5 million copies and appeared in eighty-five languages. Another important volume dealing with Adventist doctrines was entitled *In Defense of the Faith*.

In 1855 the Whites moved to Battle Creek, Michigan which became the headquarters of the burgeoning church. Although her prophetic utterances formed much of the doctrinal basis of the Seventh-day Adventist Church, Ellen recoiled from a leadership role. In 1903 the church headquarters was moved to Takoma Park in Washington, D.C.

Besides prophecies dealing with doctrine, Ellen also had many visions dealing with health and diet, which has long been emphasized by ADVENTISTS. Her vegetarian protege, Dr. John H. Kellogg, made Battle Creek the nation's breakfast cereal center.

R.H.

**WHITE FATHERS.** The Society of Missionaries of Africa commonly known as White Fathers because of their hooded capes and white robes. The society was founded by the archbishop of Algiers, Charles Lavigerie, in 1868. Its priests and brothers come from Europe, the United States and Canada. The order, first founded to care for thousands of homeless Arab children in Algiers, eventually conducted missionary work throughout the African continent. The White Fathers have concentrated their attention on the training of African clergy.                    W.G.

**WHITEFIELD, GEORGE** (1714–70). The primary evangelist of the first GREAT AWAKENING and colleague of JOHN and CHARLES WESLEY was born December 16 in Gloucester, England, to Thomas and Elizabeth Edwards Whitefield. In 1732 George entered Pembroke College, Oxford, where he shortly met Charles Wesley and joined the HOLY CLUB. During an illness in the spring of 1735 he experienced "new birth." Recuperating in Gloucester, he converted friends, started a religious society, and was ordained deacon in Gloucester Cathedral (1736). He received his B.A. from Oxford in June 1736.

Already well known as a preacher, he traveled to Georgia, landing in Savannah in May 1738 and returning in September. Criticized as an enthusiast and as one who drew "the wrong crowd," he was forced to preach out-of-doors, beginning in 1739 to the colliers (coal miners) near Bristol and later to the well-to-do at summer resorts. It is said that as many as twenty thousand people were reached by Whitefield in one setting. In August 1739 he again sailed for America to erect Bethesda, an orphanage near Savannah. He preached from Georgia to Massachusetts, mostly in Presbyterian and Congregational churches, including those of Jonathan Edwards and Gilbert Tennent.

He returned to England in 1741 and became engaged in a controversy with the Wesleys over predestination and free grace. A chapel on Tottenham Court Road in London became the center of his activity. In 1741 he was made perpetual moderator of the Welsh Calvinistic Methodist Conference. In August 1744 he again sailed for America, landing in York, Maine, and spending the next year in New England and two years in the South. In 1748 he returned to England, via Bermuda, and was named chaplain by Selina, Countess of Huntingdon. After four more visits to America, he died of asthma while ministering in Newburyport, Massachusetts.

N.H.

**WHITEHEAD, ALFRED NORTH.** *See* PROCESS THEOLOGY.

**WHITING, WILLIAM** (1825–78). British educator and hymn writer. In the work *Hymns and Human Life*, Erik Routley, a British hymnologist, calls William Whiting's "Eternal Father, Strong to Save" "a national possession." Actually, it was the only hymn Whiting ever wrote. It is still known to worshipers in the church today by its famous tune *Melita* by J. B. Dykes. Whiting served as master of the Winchester College Choristers' School for more than thirty-five years (1842–78). His single contribution to Christian hymnody was created under the influence of the Tractarian movement in the Anglican Church, which sought to maintain the beauty of ancient liturgy. Whiting's great work first appeared in *Hymns Ancient and Modern* (1868).        R.H.

**WHITMAN, WALT** (1819–92). American poet, born May 31 on Long Island to Walter and Louisa Van Velson Whitman, who were Hicksite Quakers. In 1823 the family moved to Brooklyn, New York. With very little education, Whitman at age eleven became an office boy. At thirteen he became a printer's devil, beginning three decades in newspaper offices as a typesetter, printer, writer, reporter, and editor.

Over a seven-year period he wrote his most notable work, *Leaves of Grass,* first published in 1855 with twelve poems. It was revised and expanded in nine editions (1856–92); its two great themes were love and death. The work reflects his loneliness, his isolation, and his struggle to understand himself as a human being. During the Civil War he moved from New York to Washington, where he worked in military hospitals as a volunteer and later as a clerk in the Department of the Interior. After a stroke in January 1873 he returned to Camden, New Jersey, to live with his brother George. Lionized in Europe, he was regarded by American critics as too innovative in his poetic techniques. His other works include *Drum Taps* (1865), *Passage to India* (1871), and the prose work *Democratic Vistas* (1870).        N.H.

**WHITSUNDAY.** White Sunday or the Day of Pentecost. The term is from English popular usage from the twelfth century to the present. The name derives from the white baptismal garments of the babies traditionally baptized on this festival. There is also Whitsun Eve, the eve of Pentecost.        J.C.

**WHITTIER, JOHN GREENLEAF** (1807–92). American Quaker poet and abolitionist. Born on December 17 on a farm near Haverhill, Massachusetts, Whittier developed a love for nature and rural life. Although his formal education was limited, he became an insatiable reader. He was early influenced by the poetry of Robert Burns, which started him on his own poetical career. His first verse was published in 1831.

Early in his life, Whittier met William Lloyd Garrison, the great abolitionist, whose influence plus his own ancestral Quakerism caused him to embrace the antislavery cause. Garrison, then editor of the Newburyport *Free Press*, published Whittier's first poetry in 1826. The turning point in Whittier's life

was the publication in 1833 of his *Justice and Expediency*, a powerful abolitionist document. That same year he entered politics and by 1834 had been elected to the Massachusetts legislature. He broke with Garrison in 1843 but continued in politics and was active in the formation of the Republican party. He supported Abraham Lincoln's campaign for the presidency.

After the Civil War, Whittier withdrew from political life that had brought him much persecution and settled in Amesbury (Mass.), to spend the rest of his life writing poetry. His verse can be described in four categories: religious poetry, antislavery poems, rhymed legends and historical ballads, and poems of nature and rural life—especially emphasizing the glories of New England. Probably his best known work was *Snowbound* (1866).

It is ironic that a Quaker who attended services where hymns are never sung should have authored so many verses that became popular Protestant hymns. Some of the most familiar hymns are: "Dear Lord and Father of Mankind," "Immortal Love, Forever Full," "I Know Not What the Future Hath," and "All Things Are Thine."

Whittier died on September 7 in Amesbury.        R.H.

**WHOLLY OTHER.** *See* BARTH, KARL.

**WIDOW.** The surviving female spouse of a deceased man. In biblical times widows were treated with respect and pity and protected by the covenant laws (Deut. 16:11; 26:12; 27:19). Widows had special privileges in gathering the remainder of the crops (Deut. 24:19 ff.) and taking part in sacrifices and feasts (Deut. 14:29). The third-year tithe was divided with widows.        J.C.

**WIEMAN, HENRY NELSON** (1884–1975). American philosopher and theologian associated with the "Chicago School" of Protestant modernism, especially influential between 1910 and 1940. Wieman graduated from Park College in Missouri; San Francisco Theological Seminary; studied in Jena and Heidelberg in Germany; and completed his doctorate in philosophy at Harvard. He taught at Occidental College and at the Divinity School of the University of Chicago from 1927 until his retirement in 1949. The greatest intellectual influence on Wieman was the scientific experimentalism and instrumentalism of JOHN DEWEY. Among Wieman's most important religious writings are *Religious Experience and Scientific Method* (1926), *The Wrestle of Religion with Truth* (1927), *Source of Human Good* (1946), and *Directive in History* (1949).

Wieman insists that knowledge of God is subject to scientific experiment and is derived from our experience of those qualities, events, and processes that constitute the natural world. For Wieman, God is the source of creative good, that process or event which endures, through frustration and destructive conflict, to enhance the qualitative meaning of life. Wieman calls God the creative event. Humans do not create their own good but are called upon to commit themselves to God, the source of creative good. Wieman's particular form of naturalistic theology has few adherents today, but its influence can perhaps be seen in the return to a more empirically based theology.                                                      J.L.

## WILBERFORCE, WILLIAM (1759–1833). The politician and philanthropist was born August 24 in Hull, Yorkshire. He attended Cambridge University and entered the House of Commons in 1780, a supporter of parliamentary reform and Roman Catholic political emancipation. From 1787 on he worked to abolish the slave trade and then slavery itself in the British colonies. Wilberforce was a leader of the Proclamation Society, a society founded in 1787 for the "reformation of manners," and the Society for Effecting the Abolition of the Slave Trade, which after 1823 was called the Society for the Mitigation and Gradual Abolition of Slavery Throughout the British Dominions. Despite disheartening opposition Wilberforce and his associates went on to form the Anti-Slavery Association in 1823. They were often called the Clapham Sect.

Their first success was abolition of the slave trade in the British West Indies in 1807. Their goal was finally accomplished in 1833, when all slavery was abolished in the West Indies. Wilberforce, however, had retired from Commons in 1825. A month after his death the Emancipation Bill was passed.
                                                        N.H.

## WILDERNESS WANDERINGS. The uncertain movements of the Israelites who escaped from Egyptian bondage under the leadership of Moses, after the plagues and the Passover culminated in the crossing of the Sea of Reeds, and their entry into the Sinai Peninsula. This forty-year pilgrimage took place in the four "wilderness" (or desert) areas of the Sinai and the wilderness areas to the east and north in the Transjordan region. The wildernesses of Sinai include the wildernesses of Shur, Sin, Paran, and Zin. The experiences of the Israelites are recorded in Exodus, Numbers, and Deuteronomy. These biblical books include a rather detailed list of spots visited by the Israelites (Num. 33 contains a list), but many of them are not yet identified by scholars. Indeed, at least two routes through the Sinai are considered probable, so it is not clear that we will ever know the exact route.

Some forty-four different sites, towns, and natural phenomena, such as mountains and oases, are mentioned in the OT as being visited during the wilderness wanderings. Traditionally, the EXODUS was across the north end of the Red Sea, but modern scholars have shown that the "Red Sea" (Exod. 13:18; 14), or *yam suph* in Hebrew, was the "Sea of Reeds" or the Lake of Reeds north of the modern city of Suez. The crossing of the sea was, then, across the present Suez Canal area. The wandering, then, was south, toward the apex or end of the Sinai Peninsula, where Mount Sinai (or Gebel Musa, the mountain of Moses) was probably located. The Israelites then turned north and east along the Gulf of Aqaba and proceeded north up the Arabah to skirt the east side of the Dead Sea. They entered Canaan from the Transjordan area and pushed west into the Promised Land. However, a northern route, along the Egyptian military road that linked Egypt with the Philistine cities of the Canaanite coast, has also been suggested.      J.C.

## WILFRID (634–709). English missionary, bishop of York, advocate of papal authority who turned England toward Roman Catholicism. A native of Northumbria, Wilfrid was educated in the Celtic monastery at Lindisfarne, but was drawn toward Roman Christianity. Between 653 and 658 he journeyed to Rome and spent three years at Lyons, France, where he learned Benedictine monasticism and received the tonsure. Returning to England, he was made abbot of Ripon, where he established the rule of Saint Benedict. At the Celtic-Roman synod of Whitby (664), he persuaded King Oswy to switch to Rome's dating of Easter and the Benedictine tonsure for monks, popular symbols of differences between Roman and Celtic Christianity. Years of struggle between the old Celtic and Roman forms of religion followed. Regarding Celtic Christianity as non-apostolic, Wilfrid received consecration as bishop of York from twelve Frankish bishops. Twice he lost possession of his bishopric and was once briefly imprisoned, but was restored on personal appeal to Rome. In the interims, he evangelized in Frisia (679) and missionized pagans in Sussex (681–686). He spent the last years of his life in a monastery at Ripon. In the long Celtic-Roman struggle in Britain, Rome contributed order and liturgy, and Celtic Christianity missionary zeal and learning.        C.M.

## WILLARD, FRANCES. *See* WOMEN'S CHRISTIAN TEMPERANCE UNION.

## WILLIAM OF OCKHAM (1285–1347). English philosopher and theologian, studied and taught at Oxford University in the declining years of medieval SCHOLASTICISM. On several occasions his controversial views brought him into conflict with the authorities, and he died out of communion with the church. He was a nominalist, holding that universals have no real existence and are simply names invented by the human mind. The real things of the world are the individual entities. He did not share the confidence in reason that had been shown by earlier Scholastics, and believed that the propositions of theology cannot be established by reason and depend only on revelation. At a later time, this teaching was taken up by Luther and other Protestant Reformers.

Ockham's views are also seen as pointing the way toward later empiricism. His famous dictum, "Entities are not to be multiplied beyond what is necessary" (*entia non sunt multiplicanda praeter necessitatem*), is known as "Ockham's razor," and has been revived in modern times by naturalists and positivists who claim that there is no need ever to invoke supernatural agencies. In ethics, William of Ockham denied natural law, just as he had denied NATURAL THEOLOGY, and claimed that morality depends not on the divine nature but on the will and command of God.         J.M.

**WILLIAMS, JOHN** (1796–1839). Pioneer missionary to the South Pacific Islands. Williams, with little formal education, was apprenticed to an ironmonger in London at the age of fourteen. He experienced an intense conversion four years later, just at the time the churches were beginning to hear of the mission to the Pacific Islands. His conversion experience plus his reading of the voyages of Captain Cook stirred his missionary ambition. He was ordained into the Congregational ministry in 1816 and sailed for Tahiti, where a strong Christian movement was in progress. He began his work on the island of Raiatea and later traveled to other islands, teaching, evangelizing, and training the native workers. He also did linguistic work. On one of these voyages he was murdered by cannibals. His martyrdom inspired many others to take up the Christian cause in the South Pacific.       W.G.

**WILLIAMS, ROGER** (about 1604–83). Regarded as the founder of the BAPTISTS in America, Williams was born in London to James and Alice Pemberton Williams. He entered Charterhouse in 1621, received a B.A. from Pembroke College, Cambridge, in January 1627, and took holy orders shortly thereafter. In December of 1629 he married Mary Barnard, and in December of 1630 they sailed for New England. A NONCONFORMIST, he criticized Boston PURITANS as an "unseparated people." Though called to the Salem church, because of interference he went to Plymouth. Two years later he returned to Salem as an assistant and in 1634 became the church's pastor over the objections of the general court. He consistently protested Puritan treatment of the Indians and moved the Salem church toward democratic policies. In 1635 the general court banished him from Massachusetts.

In 1636 he founded the first settlement in Rhode Island, Providence, a community whose government was planned as a pure democracy—a safe harbor to Jews and Quakers, complete religious LIBERTY, and SEPARATION OF CHURCH AND STATE. Williams' spiritual quest led him to become a Baptist and by 1639 a Seeker. In 1644 Williams published *The Bloudy Tenet of Persecution,* followed in 1651 by *The Bloudy Tenet Yet More Bloudy* in which he argued that religious liberty was a natural right.    N.H.

**WILLIAMS, WILLIAM** (1717–91). Welsh hymn writer and itinerant Methodist minister. This prolific author of some eight hundred hymns in Welsh and more than one hundred in English is probably best known for "Guide Me, O Thou Great Jehovah."

Born in the village of Cefn-y-coed, near Llandovery, Wales, on February 11, Williams was a son of an elder in the Congregational church. He was enrolled at the Dissenting Academy at Llwynllwyd, where he was converted through the witness of Howell Harris, the founder of Welsh Calvinistic Methodism. Williams later became an important agent in the Evangelical Revival, along with Christmas Evans and John Elias.

Williams joined the Church of England and was ordained as a deacon in 1740, but he was refused ordination as a priest in 1743. Serving for a time as a Anglican curate, he identified himself more closely with the Methodist Revival. His hymns contributed greatly to the Revival. He was the author of two long poems—"View of Christ's Kingdom" (1756, 1764) and "Life and Death of Theomemphus" (1764, 1781). Altogether he produced twenty-four hymnbooks.    R.H.

**WILL OF GOD.** The imposition of the will of God upon the affairs of people is a prevalent teaching in Middle Eastern religions and those of the Far East but less evident in the Western world. John Calvin rooted his theology in the idea of the sovereignty of God and its implications for PREDESTINATION in the created order. Most Calvinistic forms of Christianity have this in common. The Bible, however, is not as clear on the question of the exercise of that sovereignty as this system of thought might imply. A basic assumption in the Bible's discussion of human responsibility and accountability is the FREEDOM to make the choice to sin (Ezek. 18:1 ff.). God "judges each one impartially according to his deeds" (I Pet. 1:17). God's will is not seen in the inability of people to exercise their own will but in the encouragement of people to do the will of God: "It is God's will that by doing right you should put to silence the ignorance of foolish men" (I Pet. 2:15). God's will is not always imposed upon us: "He is forbearing toward you, not wishing that any should perish, but that all should reach repentance" (II Pet. 3:9; compare Matt. 18:14). And yet "If the righteous man is scarcely saved, where will the impious and sinner appear?" (I Pet. 4:18). Those who "suffer according to God's will" (I Pet. 4:19) are evidently those who suffer as Christians (4:16) rather than those who are predestined to suffer.

Jesus declared that those who enter the kingdom of heaven will be the ones who do "the will of my father who is in heaven" (Matt. 7:21). He said, "Whoever does the will of my father who is in heaven is my brother, and sister, and mother" (Matt. 12:50). One's capacity to do God's will is emphasized by Jesus in John 7:17: "If any man's will is to do his will, he shall know whether the teaching is from God or whether I am speaking on my own authority." Jesus came to do the will of God (John 4:34; 5:30; 6:38 ff.), and yet he was capable of exercising his own will in the temptations of Satan (Matt. 4:1; Heb. 4:15; 5:8). Paul speaks often about the will of God in his own life and in that of the believer. He considers his own call to apostleship as the will of God (I Cor. 1:1; II Cor. 1:1; Gal. 1:1-4; Eph. 1:1) and emphasizes that God "accomplishes all things according to the counsel of his will" (Eph. 1:11). One should try to understand what the will of the Lord is (Eph. 5:17) and try to live by it. In order to "prove what is the will of God" one must be transformed in mind and no longer conform to the world (Rom. 12:2). It is the "will of God in Christ Jesus" to rejoice, pray, and give thanks in all circumstances (I Thess. 5:18). Clearly, then, one can and should learn what the will of God is and do "the will of God from the heart" (Eph. 6:6).

There is a meaning of the term "will of God," however, that suggests *Heilsgeschichte* (redemptive history), suggesting that God's purposes for humankind are firm and unalterable (Rom. 3:3-4; Eph. 1:5; Acts 22:14) as is God's purpose for the Jews (Rom. 11:5, 11). There is no contradiction in the realization that God's purposes for humankind will come to fruition and the recognition that this does not nullify human freedom in the working out of that divine will.                                                  J.R.M.

**WILL TO BELIEVE.** A phrase used by WILLIAM JAMES in one of his essays on pragmatism. The implication is moral: one makes a deliberate effort not to rest on opinions or think about options but to make a decision. The will to believe involves a commitment to someone or something beyond the self. The element of choice and decision is based on a hypothesis of freedom of the will. This assumes the existence of a power in the universe that supports and sustains those who make this commitment. "Believe" includes the element of "faith in" and represents a step beyond what is reasonably acceptable, although the rational faculty is involved in the decision to make the commitment; this is itself a moral stance. Existentialists, on the contrary, would define the will to believe as a solitary free-floating decision with no guarantee that anyone or anything in the universe would sustain the person.                                    I.C.

**WILL TO POWER.** This expression, from the German phrase *Wille zun Macht*, is associated above all with the philosophy of FRIEDRICH NIETZSCHE. It was used as the title of a posthumous volume consisting of fragments and aphorisms collected and edited by his sister, but though this was claimed to be his greatest work, modern scholars believe that it was edited in a distorting manner and does not truly represent Nietzsche's thought. Will to power is a metaphysical principle, the universal striving for preservation and enhancement of being. It is therefore a philosophical interpretation of the becoming of the

universe, or, in Heidegger's words, "a richer name for the overused and vacuous term 'becoming.'" Heidegger has associated will to power with contemporary NIHILISM and the rise of technology. Earlier attempts to associate it with militarism (for example, by Bertrand Russell) are now generally regarded as mistaken.                                                   J.M.

**WILSON, WOODROW** (1856–1924). The twenty-eighth president of the United States was born December 28 in Staunton, Virginia, to Janet (Jessie) Woodrow and Joseph Ruggles Wilson, a Presbyterian minister. After his childhood in Augusta, Georgia, and Columbia, South Carolina, where his father became a seminary professor and pastor of First Presbyterian Church, and a year at Davidson College, he enrolled at Princeton, where he received a B.A. in 1879. He attended the University of Virginia law school and completed his Ph.D. at Johns Hopkins University in 1886, with a dissertation on "Congressional Government."

Wilson taught at Bryn Mawr (1885–88) and Wesleyan University (1888–90) before returning in 1890 to Princeton as professor of jurisprudence and political economics. In June of 1902 he was elected university president but resigned in 1910 to become governor of New Jersey, where he passed sweeping reform measures within ten months. Nominated by the Democratic party in 1912, he defeated Theodore Roosevelt and William Howard Taft by advocating "New Freedom." His adminstration instituted the federal income tax and the Federal Reserve System, created the Federal Trade Commission and passed the Clayton Anti-Trust Act.

When war broke out in Europe, Wilson attempted to keep America neutral. He was reelected in 1916 on the slogan "He kept us out of war." However, German submarine warfare forced the United States to declare war on April 6, 1917. On January 8, 1918, Wilson delivered his famous "Fourteen Points" speech, which became the basis for peace negotiations, after the armistice was signed on November 11. Although he was able to make the League of Nations part of the Versailles Treaty, he was not able to get Congress to pass it. In the fall of 1919, after a national tour to gain support for the treaty, he collapsed and was paralyzed. Incapacitated by his illness, he could neither engineer nor accept compromise. The Republicans won the presidency, and Wilson died three years later in his sleep.                            N.H.

**WINTHROP, JOHN** (1588–1649). First governor of the MASSACHUSETTS BAY COLONY, born in Edwardstone, England, to Adam Winthrop and his second wife, Anne Browne. Winthrop entered Trinity College, of Cambridge, in 1603 but left without a degree. In 1605 he married Mary Forth, who died in 1615 after bearing six children. Their eldest child, John, was later governor of Connecticut. Winthrop was admitted to Gray's Inn in 1613 and practiced law in London, eventually being admitted to the Inner Temple. A PURITAN, he was part of the group granted a charter for Massachusetts in 1628. A year later he became its first governor, serving a dozen one-year terms. He was also the first president of the New England confederacy. The most serious disruption of his career involved the antinomian controversy surrounding ANNE HUTCHINSON.                    N.H.

**WISDOM.** A search for the ideal way to think and live, with guidelines granted to humankind both from the wisdom of God and from the individual's own powers of intellect.

*Near East.* The search for God and for God's wisdom to achieve both an idealized life-style and an understanding of one's self and of one's environment is certainly not restricted to biblical writings. The sacred literature of ancient India, China, Canaan, and Mesopotamia all emphasize the search for wisdom and truth, whether divinely revealed or self-discovered. Thus proverbs like "Know thyself" and "Nothing to excess" were bywords of those who trekked to garner wisdom from the oracle at Delphi. Those who sought learning, wisdom, and inspiration pilgrimaged elsewhere in Greece to drink of the Castalian and Pierian springs. King Minos of Crete kept open house for the travelers who came seeking knowledge. The reverence paid to Ea, the Babylonian goddess of wisdom, typified the search for human understanding. Pallas Athene, Greek goddess of wisdom, ruled the acropolis in Athens from her temple, the Parthenon. The queen of Sheba traveled for months to discover if Solomon was really as wise as his reputation made him out to be.

*Old Testament.* The concept of wisdom in the OT relates not just to knowledge and skill but most of all to spirituality, goodness, kindness, and usefulness to society. Thus the coming Messiah is characterized in Isaiah 9:6 and 11:2 as a "Wonderful Counselor" and the one on whom "the Spirit of the Lord shall rest, . . . the spirit of wisdom and understanding, the spirit of counsel and might, the spirit of knowledge and the fear of the Lord."

Wise men were often found at royal courts, or at what in the ancient world were called academies (now universities), though not exclusively. Others who are cited in the Bible for their wisdom included musicians, architects, goldsmiths, and even midwives. But the usual place to look for a "wise man" was at a royal court, where kings vied to recruit them. Thus Daniel (2:12-14) in Babylon was described as one "skilful in all wisdom, endowed with knowledge, understanding learning, and competent to serve in the king's palace." Other classes of wise men would include astrologers, soothsayers, sorcerers, magicians, and magi.

The story of Moses and Aaron before the court of the pharaoh in Egypt also provides some understanding of the functions of wise men at court, contrasted in this case with the court-appointed Egyptian ones.

And the story of Joseph (Gen. 39:21) in Potiphar's household sheds further light on the practical role of a wise man in the proper running of a courtly household, in the interpretation of dreams, and eventually in running the whole kingdom of Egypt.

The whole OT is alive with the overlying concept of wisdom as a major factor in humankind's search for truth and life. Individual after individual is cited as "wise" as if this were the highest compliment one could bestow—Moses, David, Ethan, Darda, Joseph, Joshua, Bezalel, and most of all, Solomon, to cite only a few. Jeremiah (9:23) urges the wise not to glory in their wisdom. The author of Proverbs urges one to accept good advice (12:15), avoid evil (14:16), keep sobriety (20:1), and save money (6:6). The wise were expected to speak with care, restrain their emotions, not be proud, know how to address kings, desire good rather than evil, and seek to lead others in the paths of wisdom.

The epitome of wisdom in the OT is King Solomon, whose influence and dominion extended further than those of any other of the kings of Israel, when everyone lived peaceably "under his vine and under his fig tree." "And God gave Solomon wisdom and understanding beyond measure, and largeness of mind like the sand on the seashore, so that Solomon's wisdom surpassed the wisdom of all the people of the east, and all the wisdom of Egypt. For he was wiser than all other men, wiser than Ethan the Ezrahite, and Heman, Cacol, and Darda, the sons of Mahol; and his fame was in all the nations round about. He also uttered three thousand proverbs; and his songs were a thousand and five. He spoke of trees, from the cedar that is in Lebanon to the hyssop that grows out of the wall; he spoke also of beasts, and of birds, and of reptiles, and of fish. And men came from all peoples to hear the wisdom of Solomon, and from all the kings of the earth, who had heard of his wisdom" (I Kings 4:29-34).

Particularly in the OT, as the above quotation suggests, wisdom developed its own vast library of "wisdom literature," which at the very least included categories like proverbs, fables, oracles, dreams, riddles, sayings, poetry, myth, and epic. Some of the best examples of this wisdom literature, in the canonical books of the OT, would include Job, Proverbs, Ecclesiastes, and some of the Psalms, along with many other non-canonical books like the Wisdom of Solomon, Ecclesiasticus, and IV Maccabees.

*New Testament.* As one would expect, the significance of wisdom literature and of the search to find one's self in relationship to God and the world continued from the Hebraic culture of the OT to that of the NT world. In a Jewish-oriented society, the concept of wisdom was simply inescapable, as when Luke records a proverb like "Physician, heal yourself" (4:23). Probably the most significant continuation of the concept of wisdom from the OT is the effort to show Jesus as a teacher of wisdom and to make his "sayings" like those of Solomon (Matt. 23:24; Luke 11:49). "Take my yoke upon you, and learn from me" (Matt. 11:29). "Behold, something greater than Solomon is here" (Luke 11:31).

The emphasis on wisdom and all its aspects is equally important in the letters of Paul, as in Romans 11:33, which echoes with such a phrase as "the depth of the riches and wisdom and knowledge of God." Colossians, Corinthians, and Ephesians also offer wisdom concepts and phrases relating directly to those of the OT. James is probably the only NT book that really measures up completely to the best of the wisdom books of the OT, and perhaps to a lesser degree the book of Revelation, where insight and knowledge characterize the eschatological realm of the glorified Lamb.

In short, the whole concept of wisdom in the Bible is an integral part of the world of both the OT and the NT.      T.J.K.

**WISDOM OF SOLOMON.** This book from the APOCRYPHA belongs to the wisdom literature, like Proverbs, Ecclesiastes, Job, Sirach, and many of the Psalms. It takes its cue from the incident in which the Lord appeared to Solomon in a dream and said, "Ask what I shall give you" (I Kings 3:5). Solomon responded, "Thy servant is in the midst of thy people whom thou hast chosen, a great people, that cannot be numbered or counted for multitude. Give thy servant therefore an understanding mind to govern thy people." Its author claims to be Solomon, a man who is a king and the son of a king, a rich man, a wise man, a judge, a builder of the Temple, and a man whose reputation for practical know-how and accomplishment ranged so far afield that it attracted even the queen of Sheba and an Egyptian princess.

The book appears to have been composed about 100 B.C., probably by a Hellenistic Jew living in the significant Jewish colony at Alexandria on the mouth of the Nile. The writer is intimately knowledgeable about the writings of Moses, from which he continually quotes passages and incidents. He is equally learned, however, in the subtleties of the Greek philosophers of the Hellenistic age, as one often finds them in Paul and in the Epistles. His views offer a meaningful insight into the troubled world of the intertestamental Jews, trying to accommodate their faith to the quickly changing culture of their times, cut off from the umbilical cord they had known when they lived in their homeland.

The book begins as Solomon chides secular rulers for abandoning God, for their impiety and their idolatry, and praises those who remain faithful. He insists that in the long run only the godly can expect earthly and heavenly rewards, despite appearances to the contrary. WISDOM for Solomon comes only from identifying with God. Human wisdom reflects that of God, almost like a ray of light or an emanation. That is why wisdom brings joy to the believer, even as it has from the time God first created the human race.

Wisdom, which is identical with God, makes the world go round and constantly renews it.

The last half of the book goes into detail about how God dealt with people during the time of the Exodus, with many chapters given to the foolishness of people who worship false idols, either in the time of their wandering in the desert or in the current Mediterranean world of Greece and Rome.      T.J.K.

**WISE, CARROLL A.** (1903– ). A graduate of the Boston University School of Theology, Wise served for a time as a counselor for the YMCA and for a Minneapolis Methodist church before becoming professor of pastoral psychology and counseling at Garrett Theological Seminary. The author of numerous articles on pastoral counseling, his particular focus has been on the duties of the supervisor in the clinical practice of pastoral psychotherapy. His more important books include *Religion in Illness and Health* (1942), *Pastoral Counseling: Its Theory and Practice* (1951), *Psychiatry and the Bible* (1956), *The Meaning of Pastoral Care* (1966), and *Pastoral Psychotherapy: Theory and Practice* (1980).      J.C.

**WISE, ISAAC MAYER** (1819–1900). A pioneer of REFORM JUDAISM in America. Born in Bohemia in

Courtesy of the American Jewish Archives, Cincinnati Campus, Hebrew Union College—Jewish Institute of Religion

*Isaac Mayer Wise*

1819, Wise studied for the rabbinate in Prague. He came to America in 1846 and became rabbi of the Orthodox Beth El Synagogue in Albany, New York. He shocked the congregation there when he introduced his first reforms in the ritual, which led to a congregational split. Wise next became rabbi in Cincinnati, which started him on his amazing career as teacher, orator, editor, author, reformer, organizer, and administrator.

Wise dedicated his life to the creation of an informed and progressive laity and an American-trained rabbinate. He founded and edited the *American Israelite,* through which he promoted his ideas for Reform Judaism. In 1855, he opened the short-lived Zion College in Cincinnati, the earliest attempt to create a Jewish university in the United States. In 1873, Wise and the leaders of thirty-four synagogues founded the UNION OF AMERICAN HEBREW CONGREGATIONS. Two years later, he achieved another goal—the founding of Hebrew Union College, the first permanent American rabbinical seminary. In 1889, Wise brought into being the Central Conference of American Rabbis, the first permanent body of Jewish religious leaders.

L.K.

**WISE MEN.** *See* MAGI.

**WITCHCRAFT.** Generally defined by anthropologists as the practice of magic for harmful, destructive ends, witchcraft has found credence in a very wide range of premodern societies. Undoubtedly, in traditional cultures in which belief in the power of spells and fetishes to work supernatural good or ill prevails, individuals have not seldom resorted to those means to harm others they regard as enemies or against whom they wish to avenge a wrong.

However, observers have noted that often witchcraft serves chiefly as an explanatory device to interpret otherwise unintelligible evil. Humankind would usually prefer to affirm any depth of iniquity than to leave an evil simply unexplained; for once it is interpreted in a way rationally consistent with one's world view, it can be dealt with either practically or symbolically or at least accepted with resignation. Death, sickness, or misfortune, then, can be fitted into a universe of meaning by attributing them to witchcraft. Sometimes the general explanation is sufficient, the witches being vague, almost mythical entities; in certain African societies, for instance, almost all sickness or death seems to be laid at the witch's door in this manner.

But in other cases the charge of witchcraft is aimed at particular individuals, commonly "weird," abberrant, unpopular people, or people against whom the victim or victim's family has a grudge. If the community in general accepts the accusation, the "witch" may be tried, often by ordeal, such as with poison or hot coals. If found guilty, the witch was customarily killed. In many primitive societies, a witch may be of either sex, but in the major traditional civilizations was most often female.

That was certainly the case in Europe during the era of notorious persecution of alleged witches for a period of about two centuries after 1480. Estimates vary widely, but undoubtedly the number of people who lost their lives—after unspeakable torture in innumerable cases—was in the millions and was mostly women. It seems beyond doubt that most of the elaborate witchcraft these unfortunate people were made to confess under torture, with its nocturnal assemblies and pacts with the Devil, existed only in their tormentors' twisted and misogynist imaginations. It is another example of the projection of evil onto the witch, in this case a deep-seated anxiety and social malaise engendered by Europe's wrenching transition from the medieval to the modern world.

In more recent times the term "witchcraft," or its putative root "wicca," has been used in a positive sense to refer to the practice of benign or "white" magic. In the twentieth century witchcraft or wicca groups have appeared as part of a small neo-pagan movement in England and America. Often associated with an affirmation of feminine spirituality, they practice rites in the tradition of pre-Christian European religion. (*See also* SHAMANISM)

R.E.

**WITHERSPOON, JOHN** (1723–94). Presbyterian minister, signer of the Declaration of Independence, and president of the College of New Jersey (now Princeton), Witherspoon was born on February 5 to the Reverend James and Anne Walker Witherspoon near Edinburgh, Scotland. At age thirteen he entered the University of Edinburgh, receiving an M.A. in 1739 and a B.D. in 1743. He was licensed to preach in 1743 and ordained in 1745. From 1757 to 1768 he served as pastor in Paisley and became leader of the conservative Popular Party. His diatribe *Ecclesiastical Characteristics* (1753) censured certain "paganized Christian divines." He also argued for the "right of personal conscience" and the right of the people to choose their own ministers. In 1759 he became moderator of the Synod of Glasgow and Ayr.

In 1768 he became president of the College of New Jersey, which prospered until the Revolution curtailed its growth. In 1776 he was chosen as a delegate to the Continental Congress and urged adoption of the Declaration of Independence. He served in Congress until November 1782. From 1782 to 1794 he attempted to rebuild the college, also serving in the New Jersey state legislature in 1783 and 1789. From 1785 to 1789 he organized a national Presbyterian church, drafting its catechism, confessions of faith, directory of worship, form of government, and discipline. In May 1789 he became the moderator of its first general assembly.

N.H.

**WITNESS.** The OT setting for the majority of the places where this word or its equivalent,

TESTIMONY, occurs is the rudimentary legal system of the Hebrews, especially in the books of Exodus and Leviticus. The Ten Commandments (Exod. 20:1-17) are referred to as "the two tables of the testimony" (Exod. 31:18; 32:15-16). This reference gives an orientation to the OT usage of witness: it is a pointer to a particular event and provides evidence for it. In the case cited it is the covenant Yahweh instituted with Israel and their acceptance of it. Other objects served the same purpose, even when the events in Israel's life are different and diverse. For example, the "tent of meeting" as a portable reminder of God's presence with the migrating tribes en route to Canaan is called the "tent of testimony," a witness to Yahweh's nearness especially when the "ark of the testimony" is also mentioned (Exod. 31:7). Otherwise "witness" includes monuments set up by patriarchs (Gen. 31:44) or tribes (Num. 32; Josh. 22:26-34, where the tribes of Reuben, Gad, and half of Manasseh opt to remain on the east side of the Jordan River and set up a "memorial altar," called witness, that they will abide by the terms of this arrangement) or individuals such as Absalom (II Sam. 18:18, Absalom's pillar is erected as a witness to his family name, since he had no male offspring to perpetuate it).

Witness also plays a significant role in legal disputes, whether of property (Ruth 4:9 ff.) or persons (Gen. 31:44 ff.). A person's own integrity is stated with an appropriate summons to a witness (I Sam. 12:3-5). Yahweh's role as a witness is often invoked, since it is believed that Yahweh's character as righteous judge will vouch for the uprightness of the person who so calls on God to attest (Job 16:19-21; Ps. 89:34-37). A lying witness is treated as unmitigated evil in Israel (especially in Prov. 12:17, 19; 14:4, 25). Isaiah (8:2) makes certain to secure "reliable witnesses." In Second Isaiah's thought such need for sound witness is applied to the nation as Israel is called to bear Yahweh's name to the nations and must be true; hence "you are my witnesses" (Isa. 43:10, 12; 44:8) is Israel's vocation, epitomized in the servant of Yahweh who is a missionary and witness to the world (Isa. 49:1-6).

Since witness-bearing involves loyalty to the truth and one's own convictions, the logical step is taken in times when Israel has to be faithful under persecution. In the mid-second-century B.C. Maccabean age, faithful Jews were called to suffer for their faith, and herein lies the birth of the idea of witness as martyrdom (especially in Daniel and the books of Maccabees, for example, IV Macc. 18:11-19, and the Martyrdom of Isaiah; and Heb. 11:32-40).

In the NT the major OT themes of integrity in speech as bearing witness to the truth and preparedness to suffer for it are continued. The need for witnesses in solemn oath-making (Deut. 19:15) is renewed (Matt. 18:16; John 8:17; Heb. 10:28). Paul will appeal to his honesty as an apostle and witness that he is not lying in protestations of his own defense (II Cor. 1:20-23; 13:1; compare I Tim. 5:19), and his role as witness is especially important in attesting to the resurrection of Jesus (I Cor. 15:15) as the locus of his apostolic call (I Cor. 9:1). What he proclaims as the kerygma is nothing less than the witness of God (I Cor. 2:1; II Thess. 1:10), a thought taken up in I John which emphasizes the apostolic community as a witness to God's revelation in Christ (I John 5:6-12).

In the Johannine literature, witness becomes a key concept; in fact, "witness" takes the place of "preaching the gospel," a phrase absent from this body of literature. The Johannine Jesus comes as a "witness" (John 18:37), and other figures bear witness to him (John 1:6-7; 3:25-36; 5:30-39; 10:25; 15:26-27; 21:24,; III John 12).

The transition from witness to MARTYR, which is the same Greek word, is made in the Revelation (2:13; 11:3-8; 12:11, 17), but the prototype is Stephen in his role as both a preacher of the truth (Acts 6:8–7:51) and a witness who sealed his testimony with his blood (Acts 7:54–8:1; compare Acts 22:20). The hymnic *Te Deum* celebrates the "noble army of martyrs," with Tertullian's adage in mind: the blood of the martyrs is the seed of the church.

R.M.

**WITTGENSTEIN, LUDWIG.** *See* LOGICAL POSITIVISM.

**WOLSEY, THOMAS** (about 1474–1530). English Roman Catholic cardinal, papal legate, controversial chancellor, and opponent of Lutheranism. Born into a butcher's family in Ipswich, Wolsey studied at Oxford and received ordination in 1498. He rose rapidly to power. After three minor appointments, Wolsey became chaplain to Henry VII (1507), privy councilor to HENRY VIII (1511), bishop of Lincoln and Tournai and archbishop of York (1514), cardinal and Lord Chancellor of England (1515), and papal legate (1518). He virtually ran England from 1515 to 1529. Wolsey adroitly handled England's foreign policy to make England the balancing factor in European politics. A secret treaty with Emperor Charles V to elect Wolsey pope fizzled in 1521 and 1523. Wolsey's life-style, arrogance, and ruthless tax collecting engendered widespread anticlericalism. He held multiple offices and had five hundred household servants and enormous wealth. His young son Thomas Wynter received numerous church offices, and in 1521 and 1523 Wolsey directed massive burnings of Luther's works in London. Unable to maneuver Henry VIII's divorce from Catherine, Wolsey incurred Henry's disfavor in 1529, forfeited his posts and wealth, and was accused of treason for breaking the law of Praemunire (1353). He died while on his way to London to stand trial.

C.M.

**WOMEN.** To outline the role of women during biblical times is a difficult and uncertain task because the Bible covers a span of several thousand years and various cultures, most of which we know little about. The place of women in a given culture also varies according to social class. Thus Esther, queen of Persia in the fifth century B.C., lived a quite different life from that of Rhoda, a maid in the home of Mary the mother of John Mark in first-century Jerusalem (Acts 12:12-17).

One generalization that can be made is that most of these cultures were highly patriarchal. While Israel's neighbors Sumer and Assyria originally worshiped female deities and held women in high esteem, the position of women gradually deterioriated as male deities gained ascendance in the region. Men were dominant, women subordinate, no matter what their social status. MARRIAGES were arranged at early ages, so that most women moved from being under the authority of their father to the authority of their husband. Even widows were under the authority of their sons or brothers.

In Israel women were essentially considered property (note the command against coveting, Exod. 20:17), and were of lesser value (fifty shekels of silver for a man, thirty for a woman, Lev. 27:1-7). Polygamy was the rule, with multiple wives, concubines, and servants (women were men's sexual property as well). A woman could be divorced at the will of her husband. All the sexual taboos listed in Leviticus are stated in terms of male activity (except the prohibition of bestiality). Adultery and fornication were interpreted as one man's crime against another man's property. Children were the property of their fathers. Thus a childless widow was required to submit to the right of levirate and marry her husband's brother in order to produce male offspring to bear the family name and inherit her late husband's property (see Deut. 25:5 ff.). Women could not inherit tribal lands (the daughters of Zelophehad were an exception in Num. 27:5-8; 36:1-9), and they were not considered competent witnesses in legal matters. As Roland de Vaux has noted, "the social and legal position of an Israelite wife was . . . inferior to the position a wife occupied in the great countries round about."

Indeed one could argue that only a male was truly a Jew: only men were circumcised to indicate their membership in the Hebrew community; only sons were required to be taught the Law (Deut. 6:8); first-born males were to be dedicated to God; and only males were members of the Aaronic priesthood. Women could participate in all the great religious festivals and often did, but unlike men they were not required to do so. They were exempt because such female functions as menstruation and childbirth made them ritually impure for periods of time. However, mothers were to be honored (Exod. 20:12; Lev. 19:3); children who struck or cursed either parent were to die (Exod. 21:15, 17). Likewise Exodus 21 lists penalties for anyone who hurt or killed slaves of either gender.

Babylonian women, by contrast, had a fairly high status. They could own property, conduct their own business, appear in public, plead their own cases in court, even hold public office, and witness contracts. Women's property remained theirs after their marriage and was passed to their children. Marriage was a contract between husband and wife as well as the sale of a woman to a man by her father. Divorced women retained custody of their children.

The women of ancient Egypt also enjoyed a relatively high status. The land of Egypt belonged to its queen; the king was the man who married the daughter of his predecessor. As late as the Ptolemies, marriage contracts frequently assigned a man's property to his wife. Either spouse might be the owner of house and lands. Mutual respect was expected between spouses. Jewish women in the colony at Elephantine in the fifth century B.C. seemed to have enjoyed the same privileges. Women still were not considered the social equals of men, however, and men were dominant in public life.

The status of women in Greek culture also varied. Plato felt that women in the ideal republic should share the appropriate tasks of their class, while Aristotle viewed women's nature as inherently defective (a view Aquinas later wrote into Scholastic theology). Demosthenes summed up women's roles: "We have hetaerae for the pleasure of the spirit, concubines for sensual pleasure, and wives to give us sons." Wives were secluded and regarded as perpetual minors, though loved and respected. Hetaerae were cultured, artistic, educated, and intellectual women, often foreigners, single women, forbidden to marry Greek citizens.

Likewise in Roman culture women held a variety of positions. During the republic women had few legal rights; but during the empire, marriage laws were changed, giving wives greater rights and more mutual responsibility for children and property. This growing emancipation disturbed many people (see the *Satires* of Juvenal and the *Epigrams* of Martial). Upper-class women were well educated and retained their own property and inherited that of their husbands. The early Christian church benefited greatly from their liberal giving.

In interpreting Scripture, one must be cautious about projecting our own twentieth-century assumptions about sex role stereotypes on the preindustrialized world of the Bible. It is safer to assume that their customs were different from ours than that they were the same. Many are totally foreign to us (for example, there is no consensus among scholars about what customs may have been behind Paul's discussion of proper hairstyle or head covering for women who pray and prophesy in the Corinthian church, I Cor. 11:2-16). We should also be wary about generalizing from early Hebrew customs of the Pentateuch to the Greco-Roman world of the post-Pauline letters, or vice versa. Another temptation is to denigrate Jewish customs regarding women in an attempt to make

Christianity appear as their social salvation, which it was not. Indeed, Christian women of the Middle Ages had much less freedom and autonomy than upper-class women of the Roman Empire or ordinary women in the earliest Christian communities. (*See also* FEMININE DIMENSIONS OF THE SACRED and FEMINIST THEOLOGY.)                                                    N.H.

## WOMEN, ORDINATION OF.

Women in the early church participated in various forms of ministry, including those inaugurated by the laying on of hands. These included the offices of widow, deacon, and presbyter. One tomb bears the mosaic inscription *Theodora episcopa*—"Theodora, bishop"—over the head of a veiled woman; the words are repeated on a nearby marble slab. Medieval abbesses also exercised certain clerical and episcopal functions. Gradually, however, the liturgical service of women was eliminated and their other ministries severely limited.

The first woman officially ordained in the United States was Antoinette Brown (Blackwell), who became the pastor of a Congregational church in 1853. The first woman ordained by a denomination was Universalist Olympia Brown in 1863. The Disciples of Christ began ordaining women in the 1880s. In the late nineteenth century many women were ministers in the growing Holiness denominations, which continue to ordain them.

Among mainline Protestants, the Methodist and Presbyterian churches began ordaining women to full ministry in 1956. In 1964 the Presbyterian church U.S. followed suit. In 1970 the Lutheran church in America and the American Lutheran church ordained women. The Episcopal church admitted women to the diaconate in 1970 and the priesthood in 1976. However, the hierarchies of the Southern Baptist Convention, the Eastern Orthodox, and the Roman Catholic churches still oppose women's ordination.

The number of women in ministry has grown steadily in the past decade, though they still experience difficulty in placement and advancement. Among the United Methodists, however, women have advanced to the positions of district superintendent and bishop. In mainline seminaries female enrollment is approaching 50 percent.

The chief arguments against women's ordination are the lack of a positive tradition in church history; the supposed NT prohibitions found in I Corinthians 14:34 and I Timothy 2:11-12; the example of the Twelve (male) apostles; and the fact that Jesus was male, and thus women do not bear a physical resemblance to him.

Those who favor it argue that women were involved in the ministry of the early church (for example, Phoebe, the "deaconess" in Rom. 16:1-2, and other women co-workers of Paul, Rom. 16:3, 6, 15; Phil. 4:3, and so on). They interpret the NT passages cited as merely attempts to order worship (I Cor. 14:40; see 11:5) and to silence uneducated or unorthodox

women (I Tim. 3:11; Tit. 2:3-5). They note that women exhibiting gifts for ministry should be allowed to exercise those gifts (I Cor. 12:11-13, 27-31; Eph. 4:11-12). They point out that Peter recognized the prophecy of Joel (2:28-32) that daughters as well as sons were to prophesy (Acts 2:17-18), as being fulfilled in the church. Proponents of women's ordination argue that in the ministry of the church there is to be no regard for gender (Gal. 3:28) since both men and women were created in the image of God (Gen. 1:26-27) and are re-created in Christlikeness (Phil. 2:1-9; Gal. 5:22-23).    N.H.

**WOMEN AND RELIGION.** *See* FEMININE DIMENSIONS OF THE SACRED.

## WOMEN'S CHRISTIAN TEMPERANCE UNION (WCTU).

This organization came into being in 1874, during the course of the temperance crusade that swept the United States. It was founded in Cleveland, Ohio, as a means of upgrading the country's moral condition, and total abstinence was a major goal.

Frances Willard, a New York-born feminist, was president of the Evanston (Ill.) College for Ladies when she became involved in the burgeoning battle against the use of alcohol. In the excitement of the hour, bands of women invaded saloons to sing hymns and kneel in prayer. As an activist Miss Willard envisaged the temperance crusade as a means of advancing the cause of women's rights and as a vehicle to demonstrate their ability in politics.

Miss Willard soon became president of the Chicago WCTU and then was elevated to the post of president of the national work in 1879 and the world organization in 1883. Today the WCTU has branches in seventy countries. Miss Willard used the organization to advance the cause of women's suffrage. In 1882 she helped organize the Prohibition Party.

The WCTU has long worked for public education against the use of alcohol and campaigned for legislation to prohibit its sale. Lately, the movement has been involved in research in the field of drug abuse. While the WCTU is not as great a force as it once was, it still had a following of 250,000 members in the 1970s.                                                    R.H.

## WOOLMAN, JOHN (1720–72).

This QUAKER leader and proponent of abolition was born October 19 to Samuel and Elizabeth Burr Woolman in Rancocas, New Jersey. In 1749 he married Sarah Ellis. Originally a surveyor, he drew up wills, taught school, and published a primer. Profoundly religious from his youth, at age twenty-three he felt called to the Quaker ministry. For thirty years he traveled the East Coast from North Carolina to New Hampshire. Having executed bills of sales for slaves, he became convinced that the practice was wrong. While visiting slave-trade centers such as Perth Amboy and Newport, and during a 1746 visit to Virginia, he witnessed the corruption slavery brought to society.

In 1776 he convinced the Philadelphia yearly meeting to disown members who kept slaves. He published his ideas in *Some Considerations on the Keeping of Negroes* (1754) and in his *Journal,* published posthumously in 1774. His *A Plea for the Poor* (1763) also argued against exploitation by the wealthy. He died in York, England, while laboring among the poor.                                                           N.H.

**WORD, THE.** A title for the preincarnate Lord who became human, in Johannine theology. Another term is LOGOS, which is Greek for "word." Various backgrounds for the term, which is restricted to the NT literature associated with JOHN, have been proposed. In Greek philosophy the Word was regarded as a divine principle underlying the cosmos. Marcus Aurelius speaks of the "reason (*logos*) that governs the universe." Indeed according to Stoic thought, Logos was another name for Zeus or God or fate. The setting is metaphysical and cosmological, and it is not likely that Johannine use that relates the Word to the incarnate life of the Son of God (John 1:14) is directly drawing from philosophical categories. The "Word," we should observe, is not identical to God, though sharing in the divine life (John 1:1).

In Philo we see how Logos in Stoic religion did influence his understanding of the OT; with Philo Logos is a mediator between God and the raw stuff of creation—an idea possibly seen in John 1:1-3. But again John has a clearly personal idea of the Word, a notion not seen in the Jewish philosopher.

More promising is the OT-rabbinic setting of the Word. In two ways the WORD OF GOD was given personalized existence either as an attribute of God active in creation (Prov. 8:22-31; Ecclus. 24; Wis. Sol. 7–9) or as personification of God in revelation, chiefly through the Law, the Torah, wisdom, or the Prophets (Prov. 1:1-33; 4:7-9; Isa. 55:11; IV Ezra 6:38). These two ideas as media of God's activity in the created order (Ps. 33:6, 9; Gen. 1:1-5) and in God's prophetic word of revelation (compare Heb. 1:1-3) lie at the center of the OT teaching on the Word, and form the most plausible backdrop to the NT usage. In the prologue to the Fourth Gospel Jesus is depicted in both his preincarnate and incarnate existence. To the Word are ascribed activities in creation (John 1:1-3) and in revelation (John 1:17), with the fulcrum of Johannine Christology clearly established at the pivot of the "becoming-man" of the preexistent, heavenly being who is set on a par with God (1:1; see John 1:14). The incarnate Word thus embodies the full and final revelation of God (1:18), and the revelation comes in the person who claims ultimacy as a revealer of the Father (14:9), akin in idiom but hardly in substance to the later Gnostic claim that divine secrets are made known through a heavenly revealer figure.

The later Johannine writings (for example, I John 1:1-2) explain how the Word was truly incarnate in the human being Jesus, probably as a counter-thrust to the incipient Gnostic teaching that God cannot really be seen and known in human terms.

Just as our words are a gateway to our true self insofar as we are willing to disclose it to others, so Jesus as the Word is the medium by which we see what God is really like, "his essence all-divine" (John Henry Newman).                                                R.M.

**WORD OF GOD.** A fundamental theological concept in the Judeo-Christian tradition. In Hebrew, "word" is *dabar,* which has a variety of meanings, not only "word," but also "deed," "thing," and so forth. In the Greek of the NT, "word" usually translates LOGOS, but the connotations of Logos in the NT are much closer to those of the OT *dabar* than to the Logos of Greek philosophy, where the term had taken on the significance of a "rational principle" and came to be understood as a kind of hypostasis proceeding from God, yet remaining in closest union with God. Logos came to have this sense in patristic theology. In the prologue to John's Gospel we probably see the beginning of a transition from the traditional sense of the Hebrew *dabar* in the direction of a more philosophical and Hellenistic understanding of the term, but this is a matter of controversy.

The presupposition of talking about a "Word of God" is that "God speaks." Perhaps in the earliest times it was supposed that God literally speaks, and that human beings can hear God's word (or words) directly. In later times God's speaking was not understood in such a literal and anthropomorphic way. God speaks in the sense of communicating, and the very notion of speaking or uttering a word implies that the speaker reveals what has hitherto been hidden in the mind. God releases the divine word into the world, but it is still God's word and, in a sense, an extension of God's own personal being.

The Bible itself is reticent about the precise mode of the divine speech or communication. A common expression in the OT is: "The Word of the Lord came to Jeremiah" (or some other prophet). In Jeremiah's case, it might be seeing some common object, for example, an almond tree in blossom, that triggered the word in his mind. In the case of ecstatic prophets, it may have been some intense inward experience that gradually resolved itself into words. In the NT, it is the human personal life of Jesus Christ that is the Word of God incarnate, God's fullest self-communication.

Karl Barth distinguished three basic forms of the Word of God. First, there is Jesus Christ, the living and incarnate Word; second, there is the Bible, the witness to Jesus Christ expressed in human words; third, there is the proclaimed word, the church's proclamation of Jesus Christ in its preaching and other forms of witness. Raymond F. Collins distinguishes seven "different but interrelated" meanings of the expression "Word of God" in his *Introduction to the New Testament* (1983).      J.M.

**WORDS OF INSTITUTION.** *See* INSTITUTION, WORDS OF.

**WORDSWORTH, WILLIAM** (1770–1850). English Romantic poet, born April 7 to John and Ann Cookson Wordsworth. His mother died when he was eight, his father when William was thirteen. Wordsworth attended St. John's College, Cambridge, on scholarship and graduated in January 1791. His first works published were *An Evening Walk* and *Descriptive Sketches* (both in 1793), the latter being an account of a walking tour in the Alps.

In October 1795 he set up housekeeping in Dorsetshire with his sister Dorothy. There he wrote *The Borderers*, a blank-verse tragedy. In the summer of 1795 he met SAMUEL COLERIDGE, and around 1797 William and Dorothy moved to Alfoxden Park in Somerset to live near him. In 1798 Wordsworth and Coleridge published *Lyrical Ballads*, which included "Lines Composed a Few Miles Above Tintern Abbey." In 1798 the three friends went to Germany. In 1799 the Wordsworths returned to Dove Cottage, Grasmere, in the Lake District, and in October 1802 he married Mary Hutchinson. He completed an autobiographical poem, *The Prelude*, in 1805, but it was not published until after his death. Other works by Wordsworth are: "Ode to Duty," "Intimations of Immortality," and "The Excursion." Wordsworth was named poet laureate in 1843 and is buried at Grasmere.

N.H.

**WORK.** *See* VOCATION.

**WORKS.** Few words in moral theology have such a conflict-filled past as the term "works." While great strides toward theological reconciliation have come for Protestants and Roman Catholics since Vatican II, nonetheless the two branches of the Christian church still disagree in principle (if not in practice) on works. Protestants, at least the majority, believe that people are saved by faith in God through Christ alone, without works; while Catholics follow the decisions of the Council of Trent that declared both FAITH and works necessary for salvation. Luther's stout rejection of religious works or even good works as a basis (total or partial) of human salvation is well known.

This controversy turns on a complex development in biblical religion, which gives grounds for disagreement about the relation of faith and works, as is illustrated in the Epistle of James: "Show me your faith apart from your works, and I by my works will show you my faith" (Jas. 2:18).

These elements include the development of doctrine within the OT, from the view that God will reward everyone according to one's works, good or bad, to the recognition that all people are sinful (Prov. 24:12; Pss. 62:12; 143:2; Eccl. 7:20; Matt. 16:17; Rom 2:6; 3:23; Rev. 2:23). Then, the book of Job, overturned the simple bookkeeping idea that

good people are rewarded with prosperity, heightening the "mystery of evil" even more. Within Hebrew thought, and in Christianity, faith as trust in God came to be seen as the basis for reconciliation with God (Isa. 28:16; Hab. 2:4; also see Heb. 11).

Paul saw that faith as trust, a faith reckoned to the sinner from before the foundation of the world (predestination) was the grounds of JUSTIFICATION, and not any work of religious merit, although he continued to observe the Jewish Law.

Augustine attempted to solve the problem of the relation of faith and works by declaring that God imputes righteousness to the sinner and infuses righteousness into those so justified, so they can do works worthy of salvation. Luther and Calvin followed Augustine's first doctrine, and the Council of Trent elected to follow the second.        J.C.

**WORKS OF GOD.** In Latin *opus dei*, a term for the Divine Office (or daily worship of God) in the Roman Catholic Church. Benedict gave it this title in his famous *Rule*. He held that monks were to prefer nothing to the work of God, that is, to worshiping the Lord. In a monastery it is the most important activity to be performed, although men must work and study also.

On a larger scale biblical theology understands the Bible as the record of God working in history as "the God who acts." The faithful are called to participate in God's work by witnessing to God's grace. But, as Luther pointed out, God calls people to their secular vocations also. As we fulfill our roles in society we also aid in the work of God. However, our calling and participation does not earn our salvation. No one is saved by works; justification is by faith through grace. Augustine believed he settled the tension between faith as the basis of salvation and the need to do good works—the work of God—by holding that God not only imputes righteousness to sinners so that they are accounted as righteous, but also imparts (infuses) righteousness to sinners so that they actually can do good works.        J.C.

**WORLD ALLIANCE OF REFORMED CHURCHES.** *See* REFORMED CHURCHES.

**WORLD COUNCIL OF CHURCHES.** The surge of feeling for church unity across Christendom in the early part of the twentieth century developed into what has come to be known as the ECUMENICAL MOVEMENT. The formal organization of the World Council of Churches occurred in Amsterdam in 1948, when its first general assembly convened.

Church historians trace the origin of the WCC to the missionary-oriented Edinburgh Conference in 1910. During the course of this ten-day gathering, the need became apparent that a representative organization should be formed to coordinate missionary cooperation, an authoritative body that could be a mouthpiece to governments. Within weeks an international agency was formed called Faith and Order, which sought to further some of the visions presented at Edinburgh.

Meanwhile another international, interchurch movement, Life and Work, concerned with social and political action by the churches, met in Stockholm in 1925 and again at Oxford in 1937. In the latter conference proposals were acted on recommending that a World Council of Churches be formed. This information was passed along to the conveners of the Faith and Order Conference being held at Edinburgh the same year. When both conferences had approved the proposal, a joint committee was appointed to bring the WCC into being. World War II prevented the initial assembly being held until 1948.

The International Missionary Council was formed in 1921 at Lake Mohonk, New York. The leaders of the IMC were told about the plans to form the WCC, but they decided that the missionary organization should be maintained as a cooperative but separate organization. However the IMC joined the WCC at the New Delhi WCC Assembly in 1961. Today the WCC is the principal agency of the ecumenical movement with a membership of nearly three hundred churches of the Protestant, Anglican, Orthodox, and Old Catholic traditions.      R.H.

**WORLD MISSIONARY CONFERENCES.** Ten major world missionary conferences from 1860 to 1963 provide a useful measure of the church's self-understanding and methodology in mission and of its worldwide growth in a century of revolutionary change. Three of these conferences stand out as being specially significant.

*Edinburgh 1910.* The beginning of the organized ECUMENICAL MOVEMENT was marked at this conference. The one significant result of this conference was the organization of the international committee that became the INTERNATIONAL MISSIONARY COUNCIL in 1921 and that had a large influence on foreign missions.

*Jerusalem 1928.* A small group gathered at the Mount of Olives to reexamine the Christian mission. The Christian and non-Christian encounter in an increasingly industrialized world was the major concern of this conference.

*Madras, 1938.* This conference meeting ten years later looked at the meaning of mission in relation to the growth of the "younger churches" as the churches of the Third World began to make a larger contribution to mission and to urge the need for unity and union among the churches. Madras produced a brief statement of faith, outlining three new world religions: Communism, Nationalism, and Scientific Skepticism.      W.G.

**WORLD RELIGIONS.** The great religions that number their adherents in the millions, which may be composed of several different traditions or denominations, and which, even if confined to one culture area,

have been of major historical and cultural importance to the world as a whole. These large religious families fall into distinct groupings: HINDUISM, predominant in India; BUDDHISM, which has spread over much of Southeast and East Asia; Chinese and JAPANESE RELIGION, an amalgam of usually non-exclusive practices of CONFUCIANISM, TAOISM, Buddhism, SHINTO and traditional ancestral and agricultural rites; and the interrelated Western monotheistic faiths of Semitic origin, JUDAISM, CHRISTIANITY, and ISLAM. It may be noted that most of these religions trace their origin to a single founder, or at least a "founding era," when its distinctive sacred writings and doctrines were defined, generally in the period the philosopher Karl Jaspers has called the "axial age," the era from roughly 600 B.C. to A.D. 600, when writing became widespread and the classical civilizations took shape. Of the world religions, only Buddhism, Christianity, and Islam are transcultural on a large scale, having spread across many cultural areas and serving as the religious bases of a number of otherwise often different societies. We will summarize the status of the major world religions in the 1980s. For their basic character, see their respective articles.

Although it is not strictly a world religion, what is called primitive religion, or better primal or basic religion, should not be left out of the account. This is the religion of nonliterate tribal societies, characterized by ANIMISM, archaic hunting and agricultural rites, tribal initiations, and often SHAMANISM. It is now in considerable decline due to modernization and the missionary efforts of major religions throughout the world, but is still practiced in isolated areas and rather widely in syncretism with major religions.

*Hinduism.* The traditional religion of India, in its great variety of strands, despite some secularizing influences, continues to flourish in its homeland and to provoke interest around the world in its philosophies and practices, such as yoga.

*Buddhism.* This religion has been severely afflicted in numbers and influence in some of its traditional homelands, owing to Marxist revolution in China, Tibet, and Indochina, but continues to teach freely in other centers such as Japan, Thailand, Burma, and Sri Lanka, and to attract growing interest in the West.

*Chinese Religion.* Little is known definitely of the status of the traditional religious pattern among the one-fourth of the world's people living in the People's Republic of China, but undoubtedly its practice is much diminished from before the 1949 revolution. Traditional Chinese religion continues in such places as Taiwan, Hong Kong, and Singapore.

*Japanese Religion.* Despite the pressure of secularization in affluent modern Japan, Buddhism, Shinto, and the "new religions" of Japan continue to draw a significant following.

*Judaism.* This numerically small but worldwide and immensely important faith suffered devastating

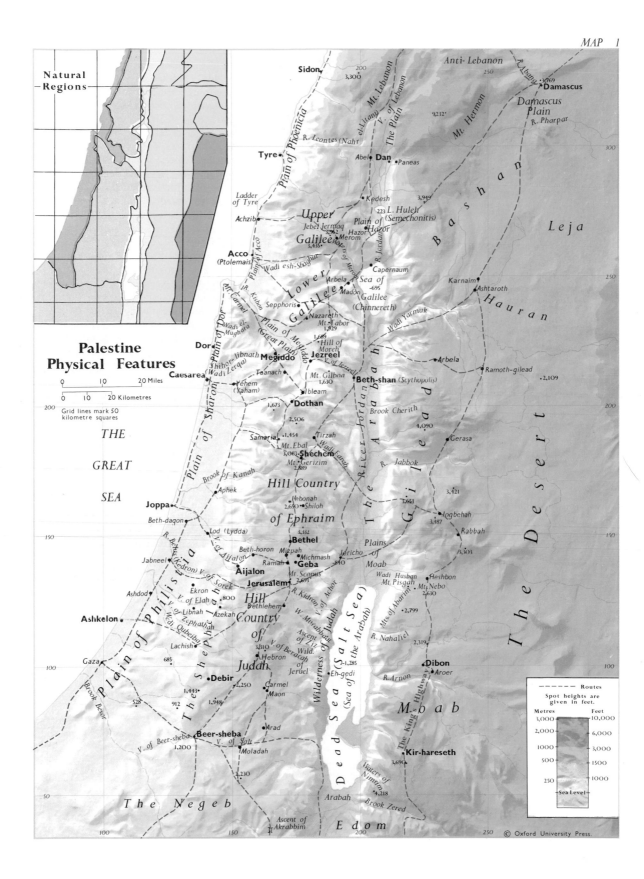

MAP 1

Natural Regions

Sidon
Anti-Lebanon
200
3,300
R. Abana
3,769
Damascus
Damascus Plain
R. Pharpar
Mt. Lebanon
V. of Lebanon
The Plain
250
9,232
Mt. Hermon
300

R. Leontes (Nahr
el-Litany
Tyre
Plain of Phoenicia
Abel  Dan  Paneas
Kedesh
3,949
Bashan
Leja

Ladder of Tyre
Achzib
Upper Galilee
Jebel Jermaq
3,962
Galilee
3,435
223 L. Huleh (Semechonitis)
Hazor
Plain of Hazor
Merom
Waters of Merom
R. Jordan
250

Acco (Ptolemais)
Plain of Acco
Wadi esh-Shaghur
Lower Galilee
Arbela
Capernaum
Karnaim
Ashtaroth
Hauran

Mt. Carmel
Plain of Dor
R. Kishon
Sepphoris
Arbela
Madon
Sea of Galilee (Chinnereth)
-695
Nazareth
Mt. Tabor
1,929
Wadi Yarmuk

Dor
Wadi el-Mughara
Plain of Megiddo (Great Plain)
libnath
Megiddo
Jezreel
1,689
Hill of Moreh
R. Jordan
Arbela
Ramoth-gilead
2,109

Caesarea
Shihor-libnath
Wadi Zerqa
Taanach
Yehem (Yaham)
Ibleam
Mt. Gilboa
1,630
V. of Jezreel
Beth-shan (Scythopolis)

THE
Plain of Sharon
1,673
Dothan
2,506
Brook Cherith
4,090
The Arabah
Gilead

GREAT
Samaria
1,454
Tirzah
Wadi Farah
Mt. Ebal
3,083
Shechem
Mt. Gerizim
2,889
R. Jabbok
Gerasa
3,421
200

SEA
Brook of Kanah
Aphek
Hill Country
Nebonah
2,690  Shiloh
3,651
3,487
Jogbehah
Rabbah

Joppa
Beth-dagon
of Ephraim
3,332
Bethel
Plains of Moab
3,303

R. Beth (Kedron) V. of Aijalon
Lod (Lydda)
Beth-horon  Mizpah
Michmash
Jericho
840
150

Jabneel
Plain of Philistia
V. of Sorek
Raman
Geba
Wadi Husban
Mt. Pisgah
Heshbon
Mt. Nebo
2,630

Aijalon
Mt. Scopus
2,693
Jerusalem
R. Kidron of Achor
The Desert

Ashdod
Ekron
V. of Elah
800
Hill
Bethlehem
W. Mukhmas  to Jericho (the Arabah)
2,799

Libnah
V. of Zephathah
Azekah
Country
Ascent of Ziz
R. Nahaliel
2,319

Wadi Qubeiba
Lachish
of
Wild. of Jeruel
Dead Sea (Salt Sea) (Sea of the Arabah)
Eh-gedi
-1,285

Gaza
The Shephelah
685
Judah
3,810 V. of Beracah
Dibon
Aroer

Debir
2,250
Hebron
Carmel
Maon
R. Arnon

1,443
1,948
Moab

528
912
Arad
Kir-hareseth

Beer-sheba
V. of Beer-sheba
1,200
V. of Salt
Moladah
Waters of Nimrim
3,690

3,230
Brook Besor
The Negeb
Arabah
Brook Zered
4,218

Ascent of Akrabbim
Edom

Palestine
Physical Features

0    10    20 Miles
0    10    20 Kilometres

Grid lines mark 50 kilometre squares

--- Routes
Spot heights are given in feet

| Metres | Feet |
|---|---|
| 3,000 | 10,000 |
| 2,000 | 6,000 |
| 1000 | 3,000 |
| 500 | 1500 |
| 250 | 1000 |
| Sea Level | |

© Oxford University Press.

MAP 2

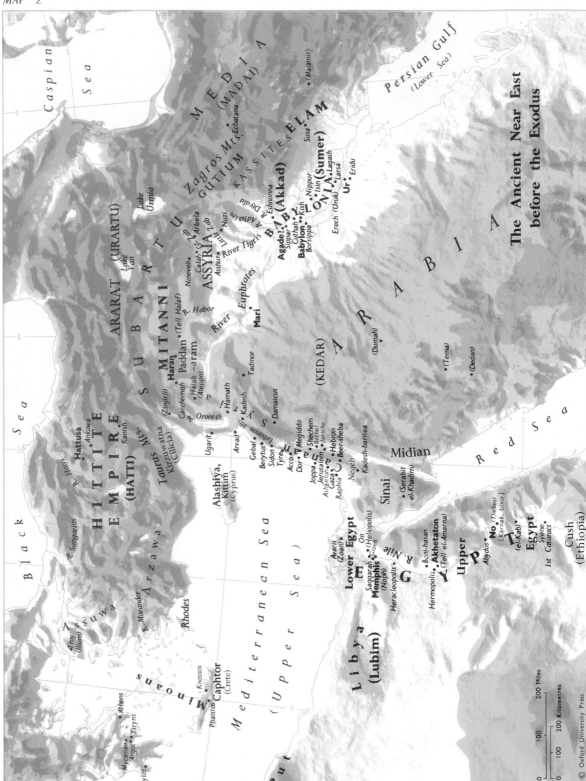

The Ancient Near East
before the Exodus

Caspian
Sea

MEDIA
(MADAI)

Persian Gulf
(Lower Sea)

•(Malamir)

Zagros Mts.•Ecbatana
GUTIUM
ELAM
KASSITES
•Susa

Lake
Van
ARARAT (URARTU)
Lake
Urmia

SUBARTU
•Eshnunna
R. Adhaim
R. Diyala
Agade?•
Sippar•  Kish• Nippur
BA(BYLONIA (Sumer)
Cuthah• Babylon• Isin•Lagash
Borsippa•  Erech (Uruk)• Larsa•
Ur•  Eridu•

ASSYRIA
Calah•  Arbela•
Asshur•  Nuzi•
Nineveh•
Upper Zab
Lower Zab
River Tigris

MITANNI
Paddan-aram
Harran•
(Zinjirli)•
Carchemish•
Halab-aram
•(Aleppo)
R. Habor
Euphrates
River
Mari•

ARABIA
(KEDAR)
(Dumah)•
•(Tema)
•(Dedan)

Black
Sea

HITTITE
EMPIRE
(HAITI)
Hattusa•
Ankuwa•
Kanish•
R. Halys
Taurus Mts.
Kizzuwatna
(Cilicia)

Arzawa
R. Maeander
R. Sangarius
Assuwa
•Troy (Ilium)

Tadmor•
•Kadesh
Hamath•
R. Orontes
Lebanon Mts.
•Damascus
Ugarit•
Arvad•
Gebal•
Berytus•
Sidon•
Tyre•
Acco•
Dor•  •Megiddo
Joppa•  Shechem•
Jerusalem•  Bethel•
Ashkelon•  Jericho•
Gaza•  Hebron•
Raphia•  Beer-sheba•
Negeb
Kadesh-barnea•

Midian

Red Sea

Alashiya,
Kittim
(Cyprus)

Rhodes

Mediterranean Sea
(Upper Sea)

Minoans
Caphtor
(Crete)
Knossos•
Phaistos•

Athens•
Mycenae•
Argos•  Tiryns•
Pylos•

Sinai
(Serabit
el-Khadim)•

Avaris
(Zoan)•
On
Lower Egypt  (Heliopolis)•
Goshen
Memphis•
(Noph)
Saqqarah•
Heracleopolis•

No (Thebes)
[Karnak, Luxor]
Abydos•  •T•
Hermopolis•  (el-Kab)•
Beni-hasan•  Egypt
Akhetaton•  Syene•
(Tell el-Amarna)  1st Cataract•
Upper

Cush
(Ethiopia)

R. Nile

Libya
(Lubim)

Put

EGYPT

200 Miles
0      100      200 Kilometres

© Oxford University Press

MAP 3

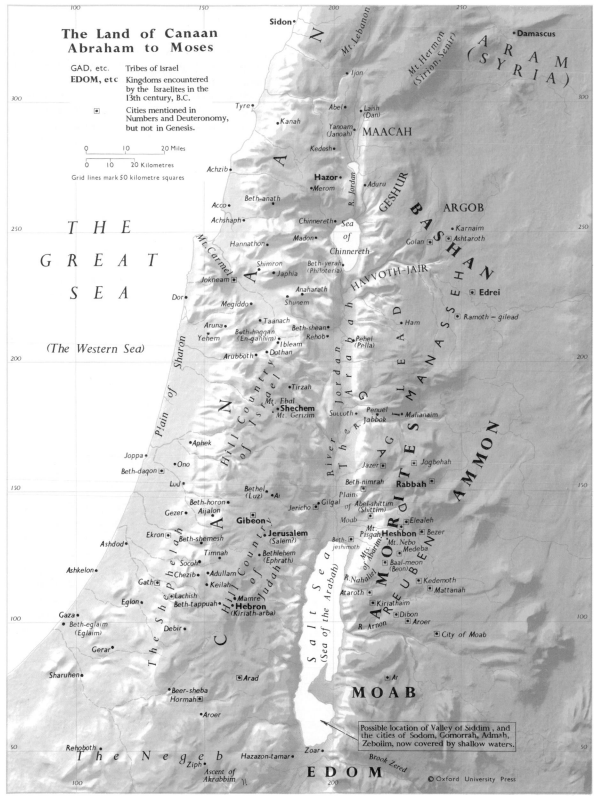

# The Land of Canaan
# Abraham to Moses

GAD, etc.   Tribes of Israel

**EDOM, etc**   Kingdoms encountered by the Israelites in the 13th century, B.C.

▣   Cities mentioned in Numbers and Deuteronomy, but not in Genesis.

0    10    20 Miles

0    10    20 Kilometres

Grid lines mark 50 kilometre squares

THE
GREAT
SEA

(The Western Sea)

Sidon

Damascus

A R A M
(S Y R I A)

Mt. Lebanon

Mt. Hermon
(Sirion, Senir)

Ijon

Tyre

Abel

Laish
(Dan)

Kanah

Yanoam
(Janoah)

MAACAH

Kedesh

Achzib

Hazor

Aduru

Merom

R. Jordan

GESHUR

Acco

Beth-anath

ARGOB

Achshaph

Chinnereth

Sea
of
Chinnereth

BASHAN

Karnaim

Golan

Ashtaroth

Hannathon

Madon

Mt. Carmel

Shimron

Beth-yerah
(Philoteria)

HAVVOTH-JAIR

MANASSEH

Edrei

Jokneam

Japhia

Dor

Anaharath

Shunem

Ramoth – gilead

Megiddo

Taanach

Ham

Aruna

Beth-shean

Pehel
(Pella)

Yehem

Beth-haggan
(En-gannim)

Rehob

Plain of Sharon

Arubboth

Ibleam

Dothan

Tirzah

Mt. Ebal

Shechem

Mt. Gerizim

Succoth

Penuel

Jabbok

Mahanaim

HILL Country of Israel

River Jordan

The Arabah

GILEAD

AMMON

Aphek

Jazer

Jogbehah

Joppa

Ono

Beth-dagon

Lud

Beth-nimrah

Rabbah

Bethel
(Luz)

Ai

Plains
of
Moab

Abel-shittim
(Shittim)

Beth-horon

Jericho

Gilgal

Gezer

Aijalon

Gibeon

Elealeh

Heshbon

Bezer

Ekron

Beth-shemesh

Jerusalem
(Salem?)

Beth-
jeshimoth

Mt.
Pisgah

Mt. Nebo

Medeba

Ashdod

Timnah

Bethlehem
(Ephrath)

Mts.
of Abarim

Baal-meon
(Beon)

Socoh

AMORITES

REUBEN

Ashkelon

Chezib

Adullam

Keilah

Gath

Lachish

R. Naholi

Kedemoth

Mattanah

Eglon

Beth-tappuah

Mamre

Hebron
(Kiriath-arba)

Ataroth

Kiriathaim

Gaza

Beth-eglaim
(Eglaim)

Debir

R. Arnon

Dibon

Aroer

City of Moab

The Shephelah

HILL Country of Judah

Gerar

Sharuhen

Arad

Ar

Beer-sheba

Hormah

M O A B

Aroer

Salt Sea
(Sea of the Arabah)

Possible location of Valley of Siddim, and the cities of Sodom, Gomorrah, Admah, Zeboiim, now covered by shallow waters.

Rehoboth

The Negeb

Ziph

Hazazon-tamar

Zoar

Brook Zered

Ascent of
Akrabbim

E D O M

© Oxford University Press

MAP 4

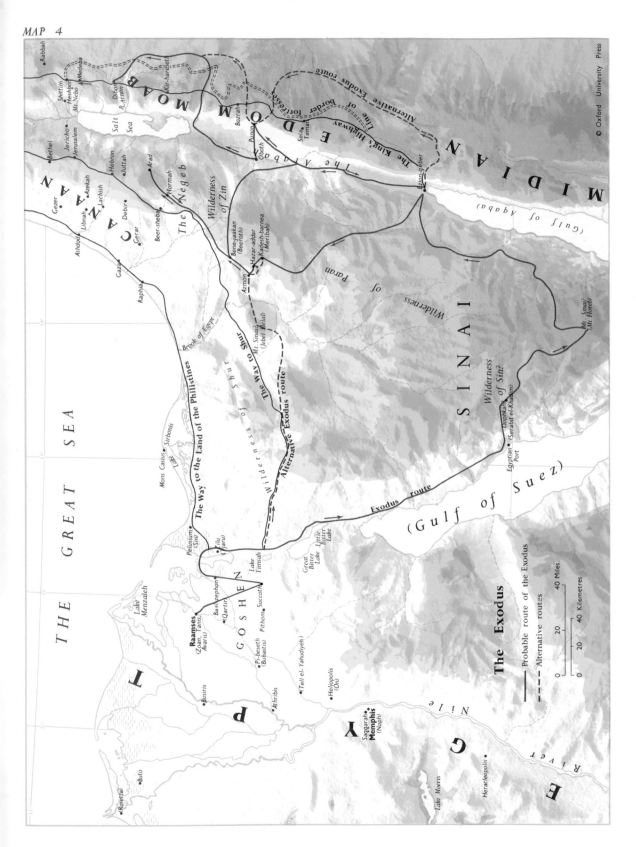

© Oxford University Press

**The Exodus**

—— Probable route of the Exodus
---- Alternative routes

0     20     40 Miles
0     20     40 Kilometres

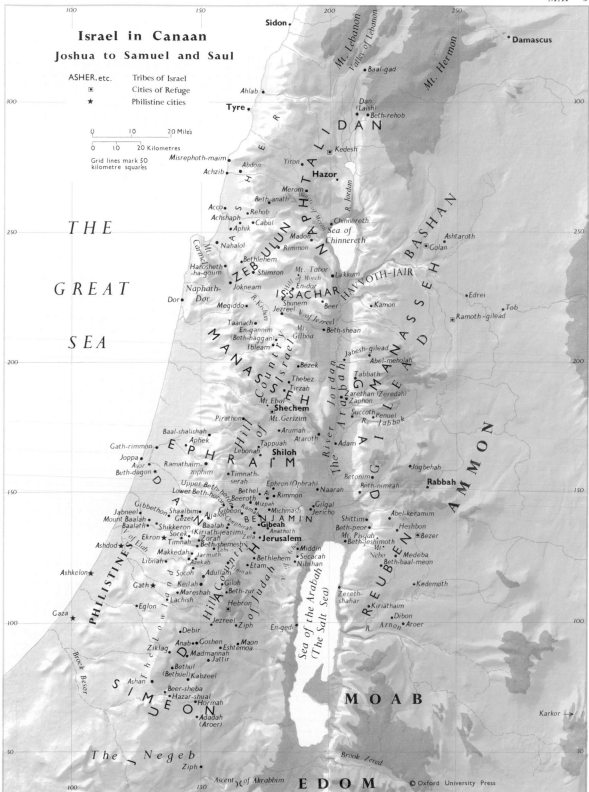

MAP 5

Israel in Canaan
Joshua to Samuel and Saul

ASHER, etc.   Tribes of Israel
⊡   Cities of Refuge
★   Philistine cities

0   10   20 Miles
0   10   20 Kilometres
Grid lines mark 50
kilometre squares

Sidon

Damascus

Mt. Lebanon
Valley of Lebanon
Mt. Hermon
Baal-gad

Ahlab
Tyre
Dan
(Laish)
Beth-rehob

DAN

Misrephoth-maim
Abdon
Achzib
Yiron
Kedesh
Hazor

Merom
Beth-anath
Acco
Rehob
Achshaph
Cabul
Aphik
Nahalol
Madon
Rimmon

THE
GREAT
SEA

Chinnereth
Sea of
Chinnereth

NAPHTALI
BASHAN

Ashtaroth
Golan

ZEBULUN
Bethlehem
Shimron
Mt. Tabor
Hill of Moreh
Lakkum
En-dor

Harosheth
-ha-goiim
Mt. Carmel
Joknean
ISSACHAR
Shunem
Beer
Kamon

Naphath-
Dor
Edrei
Tob
Ramoth-gilead

Dor
Megiddo
R. Kishon
Jezreel
V. of Jezreel
Beth-shean
HAVVOTH-JAIR
MANASSEH

Taanach
En-gannim
(Beth-haggan)
Ibleam
Mt.
Gilboa

Jabesh-gilead
Abel-meholah

Country of Israel
Bezek
Tabbath
Zarethan (Zeredah)
Zaphon

Thebez
Tirzah
Mt. Ebal
Shechem
Mt. Gerizim
Succoth
Penuel
R. Jabbok

GILEAD
MANASSEH

Pirathon
Arumah
Ataroth
Adam

Baal-shalishah
Aphek
Tappuah
Lebonah
Shiloh
Jogbehah

Gath-rimmon
Joppa
Asor
Ramathaim-
zophim
EPHRAIM
Betonim
Beth-nimrah

AMMON
Rabbah

Beth-dagon
Timnath-
serah
Ephron (Ophrah)
Naarah

Upper Beth-horon
Lower Beth-horon
Bethel
Ai
Rimmon
Beerotth
Mizpah
Gilgal
Jericho

Gibbethon
Shaalbim
Gibeon
Michmash
Abel-keramim
Heshbon

Jabneel
Mount Baalah
Gezer
Aijalon
Chephirah
Ramah
Shittim
Beth-peor
Mt. Pisgah
Beth-jeshimoth

Baalath
Shikkeron
Baalah
BENJAMIN
Bezer

Ekron
Sorek
Timnah
Zorah
Kiriath-jearim
Gibeah
Anathoth
Zela
Mt.
Nebo
Medeba
Beth-baal-meon

Ashdod
Beth-shemesh
Jerusalem
REUBEN

Makkedah
Jarmuth
Lehi
Timnah
Middin
Secacah
Nibshan

Ashkelon
Libnah
Azekah
Bethlehem
Etam

PHILISTINES
V. of Elah
Socoh
Adullam
Timnah
Beth-zur
Kedemoth

Gath
Keilah
Giloh
Hill Country of Judah
En-gedi

Mareshah
Lachish
Hebron
Sea of the Arabah
(The Salt Sea)

Eglon
Gaza
Jezreel
Ziph
Zereth-
shahar
Kiriathaim

Debir
Anab
Goshen
Maon
Dibon
Aroer
R. Arnon

Ziklag
Eshtemoa
Jattir
Madmannah

The Shephelah
Bethul
(Bethuel)
Kabzeel

Ashan
Hill
Beer-sheba
Hazar-shual
Hormah
Adadah
(Aroer)

SIMEON

MOAB

Karkor →

Brook Besor

The Negeb
Ziph

Brook Zered

Ascent of Akrabbim
EDOM

© Oxford University Press

JUDAH
GAD
The Arabah
R. Jordan
Waters of Merom
R. Jordan
DAN

MAP 6

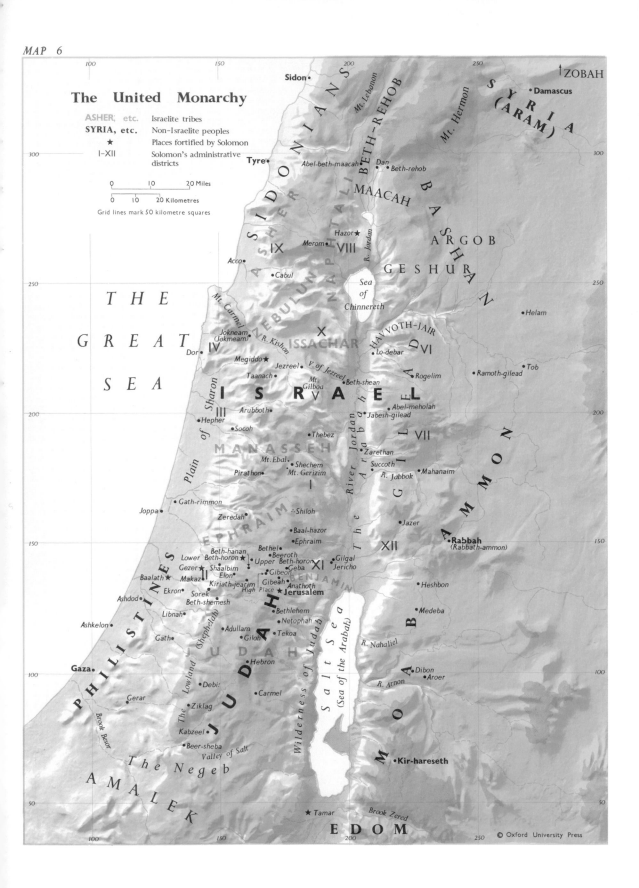

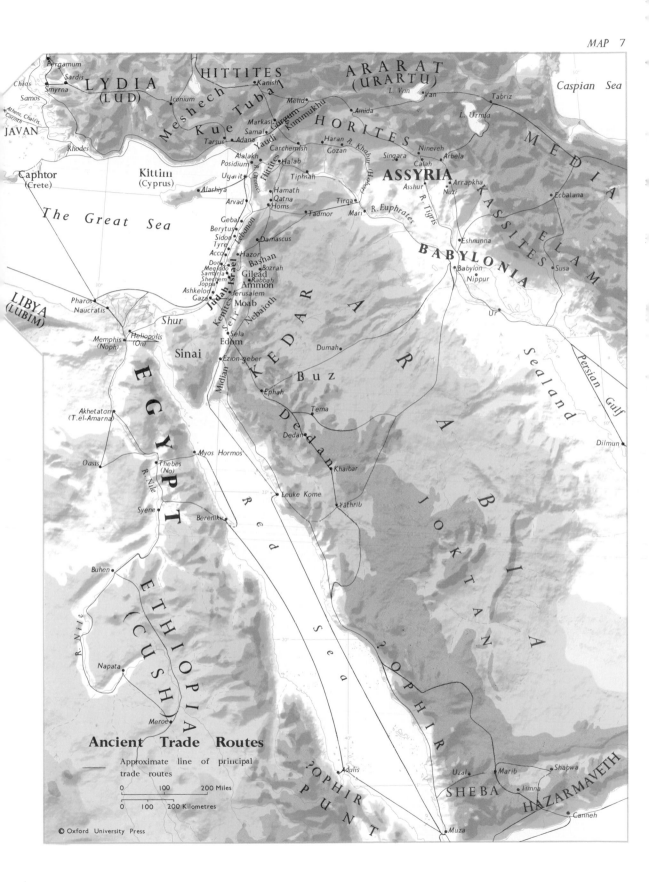

MAP 8

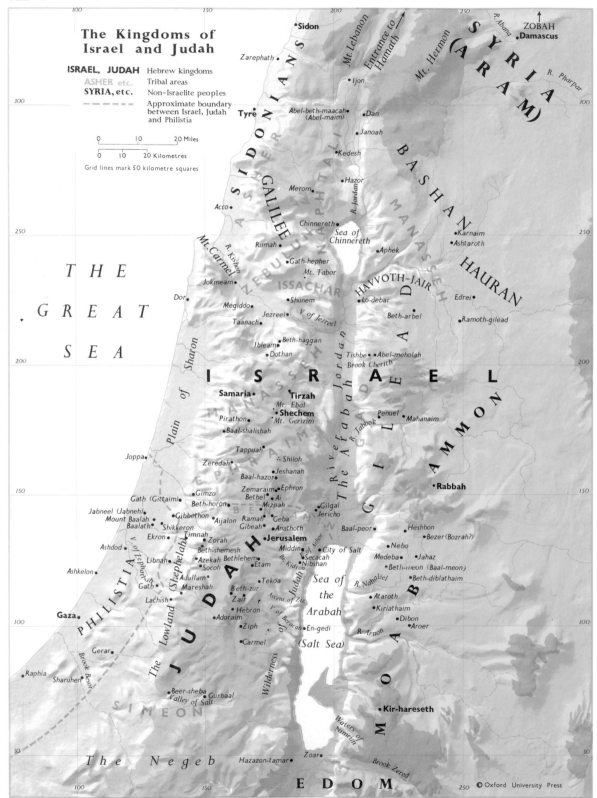

## The Kingdoms of Israel and Judah

**ISRAEL, JUDAH**   Hebrew kingdoms
ASHER etc.   Tribal areas
**SYRIA, etc.**   Non-Israelite peoples
– – – –   Approximate boundary between Israel, Judah and Philistia

0    10    20 Miles
0    10    20 Kilometres
Grid lines mark 50 kilometre squares

ZOBAH
•Damascus
R. Abana
R. Pharpar

•Sidon
Zarephath
Mt. Lebanon
Entrance to Hamath
Mt. Hermon
SYRIA (ARAM)

•Ijon
Tyre
Abel-beth-maacah (Abel-maim)
•Dan
•Janoah
•Kedesh
BASHAN
HAURAN

SIDONIANS
GALILEE
ASHER
NAPHTALI
Merom
•Hazor
R. Jordan
Acco•
Chinnereth
Sea of Chinnereth
•Karnaim
•Ashtaroth
Rumah•
•Aphek
•Edrei
MANASSEH

Mt. Carmel
R. Kishon
•Gath-hepher
Mt. Tabor
ISSACHAR
HAVVOTH-JAIR
•Lo-debar
•Ramoth-gilead
GILEAD
Dor•
Jokmeam•
•Shunem
V. of Jezreel
•Beth-arbel
Megiddo•
Jezreel•
•Taanach
•Ibleam
•Beth-haggan
•Dothan
•Tishbe •Abel-meholah
Brook Cherith

THE GREAT SEA

Plain of Sharon
ISRAEL
MANASSEH
Samaria•
•Tirzah
Mt. Ebal
•Shechem
Mt. Gerizim
•Penuel
•Mahanaim
Pirathon•
•Baal-shalishah
R. Jabbok
Joppa•
•Tappuah
❖Shiloh
EPHRAIM
Zeredah•
•Jeshanah
•Baal-hazor
•Ephron
Zemaraim•
•Ai
•Rabbah
AMMON
Gath (Gittaim)•
•Gimzo
Bethel• •Mizpah
Beth-horon•
•Gilgal
•Jericho
Jabneel (Jabneh)•
BENJAMIN
Gibbethon•
Ramah•
•Geba
Mount Baalah•
Aijalon•
•Gibeah •Anathoth
•Baal-peor
•Heshbon
Baalath•
•Shikkeron
•Timnah
•Zorah
•Jerusalem
•Bezer (Bozrah?)
Ekron•
Beth-shemesh•
Middin•
•Nebo
Ashdod•
Libnah•
•Azekah Bethlehem•
•Etam
Secacah
•Nibshan
City of Salt
Medeba•
•Jahaz
•Beth-meon (Baal-meon)
Ashkelon•
Gath•
•Socoh
•Adullam
•Mareshah
Zair•
•Beth-zur
•Tekoa
JUDAH
Ascent of Ziz
Br. Kidron
Valley of Achor
R. Nahaliel
•Beth-diblathaim
•Ataroth
•Kiriathaim
Lachish•
•Hebron
V. of Beracah
•Dibon
•Aroer
Gaza•
•Adoraim
•Ziph
•En-gedi
R. Arnon
•Carmel
Sea of the Arabah (Salt Sea)
MOAB
Gerar•
Wilderness
•Raphia
Sharuhen•
Brook Besor
Beer-sheba•
•Gurbaal
Valley of Salt
•Kir-hareseth
SIMEON
Waters of Nimrim
The Negeb
Hazazon-tamar•
•Zoar
Brook Zered
EDOM
© Oxford University Press

MAP 9

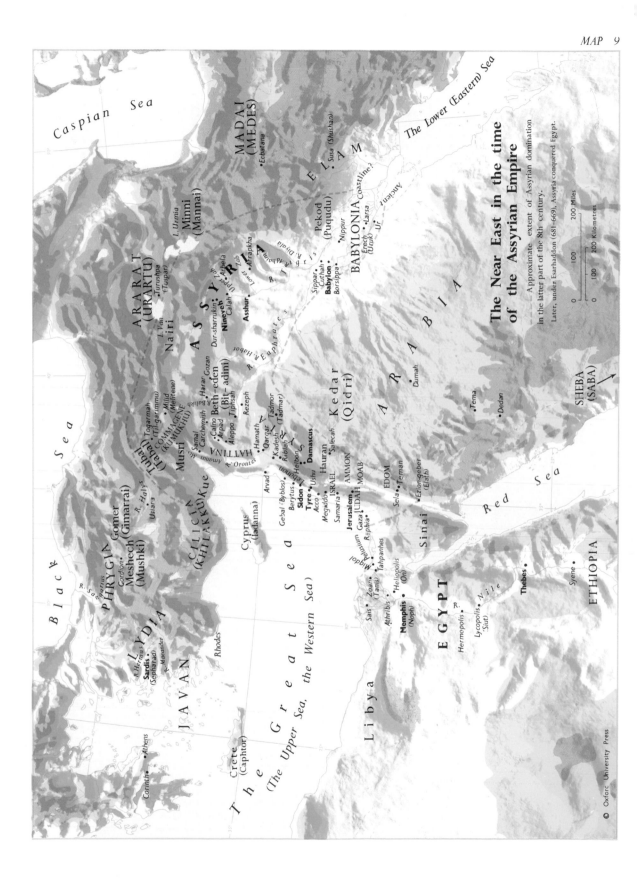

**The Near East in the time of the Assyrian Empire**

Approximate extent of Assyrian domination in the latter part of the 8th century.

Later, under Esarhaddon (681–669), Assyria conquered Egypt.

0    100    200 Miles

0    100    200 Kilometres

Caspian Sea

MADAI (MEDES)

Ecbatana

The Lower (Eastern) Sea

ELAM

Susa (Shushan)

ARARAT (URARTU)

L. Urmia

Minni (Mannai)

Turushpa (Tushpa)

L. Van

Nairi

Pekod (Puqudu)

BABYLONIA

Ancient coastline?

ASSYRIA

Upper Zab

Arbela

Lower Zab

R. Tigris

R. Adhaim

Sippar

Cuthah

Babylon

Borsippa

Nippur

Erech (Uruk)

Larsa

Ur

Dur-sharrukin

Nimeveh

Calah

Asshur

Afrapkha

R. Gozan

R. Habor

R. Euphrates

Togarmah (Til-garimmu)

COMMAGENE (KUMMUKHU)

Milid (Melitene)

Musri

Mts.

Tubal (Tibal)

Harar

Beth-eden (Bit–adini)

Calno

Carchemish

Balikh

Rezeph

Arpad

Tiphsah

Samal

Aleppo

Tadmor (Tadmar)

A R A B I A

Kedar (Qidri)

Dumah

Tema

Dedan

SHEBA (SABA)

PHRYGIA

Gomer (Gimarrai)

Gordion

Meshech (Mushki)

R. Halys

Uiara

CILICIA (KHILAKKU)

Kue

Ammanus Mts.

R. Orontes

Hamath

Qarqar

Kadesh

Riblah

HAMATH

Helbon

Damascus

Hauran

Salecah

AMMON

MOAB

Arvad

Gebal (Byblos)

Berytus

Sidon

Tyre

Ushu

Acco

Megiddo

ISRAEL

Samaria

Jerusalem

JUDAH

Gaza

Raphia

Lachish

EDOM

Teman

Sela

Ezion-geber (Elath)

Red Sea

Sinai

Black Sea

R. Sangarius

LYDIA

Sardis (Sepharad)

R. Hermus

R. Maeander

JAVAN

Rhodes

Crete (Caphtor)

T h e   G r e a t   S e a

(The Upper Sea, the Western Sea)

Corinth

Athens

Pelusium

Migdol

Tahpanhes

Zoan (Tanis)

Sais

Athribis

Heliopolis (On)

Memphis (Noph)

E G Y P T

Hermopolis

Lycopolis (Siut)

R. Nile

Thebes

Syene

ETHIOPIA

Libya

© Oxford University Press

MAP 10

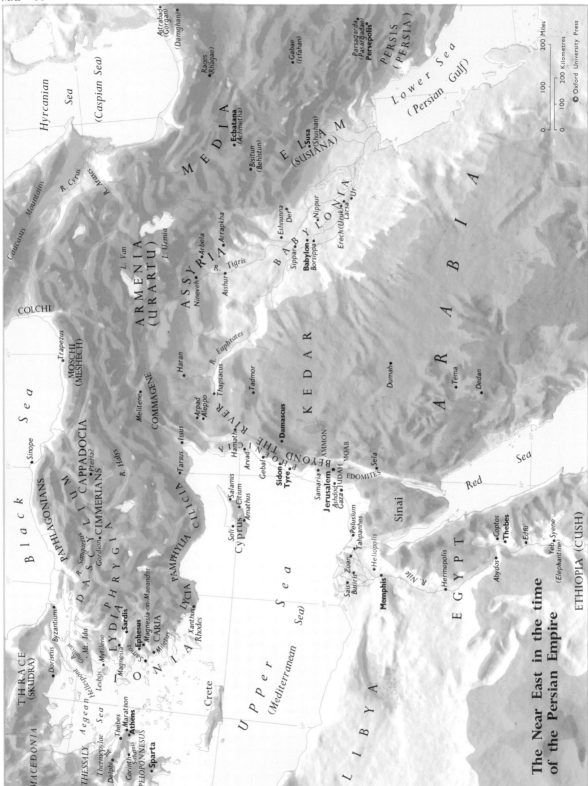

The Near East in the time
of the Persian Empire

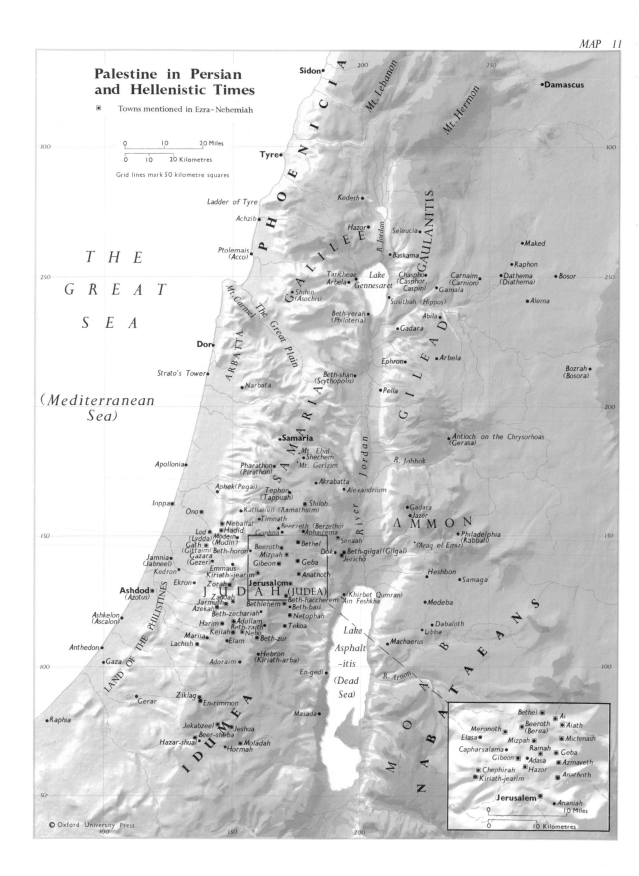

MAP 11

# Palestine in Persian and Hellenistic Times

⊡ Towns mentioned in Ezra–Nehemiah

0   10   20 Miles
0   10   20 Kilometres
Grid lines mark 50 kilometre squares

THE GREAT SEA

(Mediterranean Sea)

Sidon
•Damascus

PHOENICIA
Mt. Lebanon
Mt. Hermon

Tyre•

Ladder of Tyre
Achzib•
Kedesh
GALILEE
GAULANITIS
Hazor
Seleucia
•Maked
Ptolemais (Acco)
R. Jordan
Baskama
•Raphon
Taricheae
Lake
Chaspho (Casphor, Caspin)
Carnaim (Carnion)
•Dathema (Diathema)
•Bosor
Arbela
Gennesaret
Gamala
Shihin (Asochis)
Susithah (Hippos)
•Alema
Mt. Carmel
Beth-yerah (Philoteria)
Abila
Dor•
The Great Plain
•Gadara
Arbela•
ARBATTA
Bozrah (Bosora)
Strato's Tower
Ephron•
Beth-shan (Scythopolis)
GILEAD
Narbata
•Pella
SAMARIA
Apollonia•
•Samaria
Antioch on the Chrysorhoas (Gerasa)
Mt. Ebal
Shechem
Jordan
Pharathon (Pirathon)
Mt. Gerizim
Aphek(Pegai)
•Akrabatta
•Alexandrium
Ioppa•
Tephon (Tappuah)
R. Jabbok
Ono
Shiloh
Kathanin (Ramathaim)
•Gadara
Jazer
•Timnath
AMMON
Lod (Lydda)
Neballat
Beerzeth (Berzetho)
Hadid
Gophna
Aphairema
•Philadelphia (Rabbah)
Modein (Modin)
Senaah
('Araq el Emir)
Gath (Gittaim)
Beth-horon
Bethel
Dok•
Gazara (Gezer)
Beeroth
Beth-gilgal (Gilgal)
Jamnia (Jabneel)
Mizpah
Jericho
Emmaus
Gibeon
•Geba
Heshbon
Kedron
Kiriath-jearim
•Anathoth
•Samaga
Ekron•
Zorah•
Jerusalem•
JUDAH (JUDEA)
(Khirbet Qumran)
Ashdod (Azotus)
Zanoah
Beth-haccherem
'Ain Feshkha
•Medeba
Jarmuth
Bethlehem
•Beth-basi
Ashkelon (Ascalon)
Azekah
Beth-zechariah•
•Netophah
Harim
Adullam
Tekoa
Dabaloth
Marisa•
Beth-zaith
Keilah
Nebo
Libba
Anthedon•
Lachish•
Elam
Beth-zur
Lake Asphaltitis (Dead Sea)
•Machaerus
•Gaza
Adoraim
Hebron (Kiriath-arba)
En-gedi
R. Arnon
NABATAEANS
•Raphia
Ziklag•
En-rimmon
Masada•
Gerar
Jekabzeel
Jeshua
Hazar-shual
Beer-sheba
Moladah
Hormah
IDUMEA
MOAB

© Oxford University Press

### Inset

Bethel ⊡   ⊡ Ai
Beeroth (Berea) ⊡   ⊡ Aiath
Meronoth ⊡   ⊡ Michmash
Elasa ⊡   Mizpah ⊡
Capharsalama ⊡   Ramah ⊡   ⊡ Geba
Gibeon ⊡   ⊡ Adasa   ⊡ Azmaveth
Chephirah ⊡   ⊡ Hazor   ⊡ Anathoth
Kiriath-jearim ⊡
Jerusalem ⊡   ⊡ Ananiah

0   10 Miles
0   10 Kilometres

MAP 12

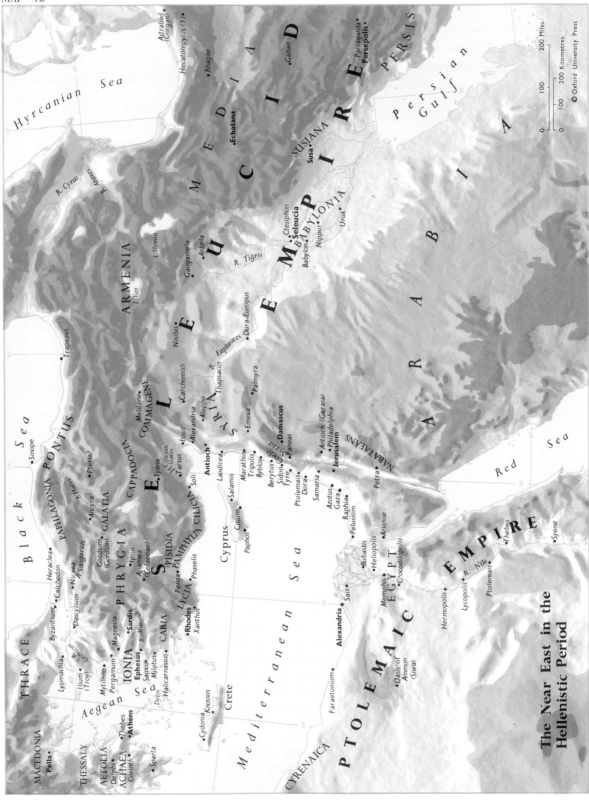

Hyrcanian Sea

MEDIA

SELEUCID EMPIRE

PERSIS

Persian Gulf

200 Miles

200 Kilometres

100

© Oxford University Press

Astrabad (Gorgan?)

Hecatompylus (?)

Khagae

Gabae

Parsagarda

Persepolis

R. Maxes

R. Cyrus

Ecbatana

SUSIANA

Susa

ARABIA

ARMENIA

L. Van

L. Urmia

Ctesiphon

Seleucia

BABYLONIA

Babylon

Nippur

Uruk

Gaugamela

Arbela

R. Tigris

Trapezus

Nisibis

Dura-Europus

Euphrates

Carchemish

Aleppo

R. Euphrates

Thapsacus

Palmyra

Melitene

COMMAGENE

Alexandria

Issus

Antioch

Laodicea

Emesa

Damascus

Coele-Syria

Antioch (Gerasa)

Philadelphia

Paneas

NABATAEANS

PONTUS

Sinope

Black Sea

PAPHLAGONIA

R. Halys

Pteria?

CAPPADOCIA

Tyana

Cilician Gates

Tarsus

CILICIA

Soli

Marathus

Tripolis

Byblos

Berytus

Sidon

Tyre

Ptolemais

Dora

Samaria

Jerusalem

Azotus

Gaza

Raphia

Pelusium

Petra

Heraclea

Calchedon

Nicaea

Gordium (Gordion)

Ancyra

GALATIA

R. Sangarius

Ipsus

Apamea (Celaenae)

PHRYGIA

PISIDIA

PAMPHYLIA

Perga

Phaselis

Cyprus

Salamis

Citium

Paphos

Red Sea

Bubastis

Heliopolis

Arsinoe

EMPIRE

Thebes

Syene

Byzantium

Dascylium

Lysimachia

Granicus

Ilium (Troy)

Mytilene

Pergamum

Magnesia

Sardis

IONIA

Ephesus

Samos

Miletus

Halicarnassus

CARIA

R. Maeander

Rhodes

Xanthus

THRACE

Aegean Sea

Delos

Cnidos

Crete

Cydonia

Knossos

Mediterranean Sea

Alexandria

Sais

Memphis

EGYPT

R. Nile

Crocodilopolis

PTOLEMAIC

Hermopolis

Lycopolis

Ptolemais

Faraetonium

Oasis of Ammon (Siwa)

CYRENAICA

MACEDONIA

Pella

THESSALY

AETOLIA

Delphi

ACHAEA

Thebes

Athens

Corinth

Sparta

The Near East in the
Hellenistic Period

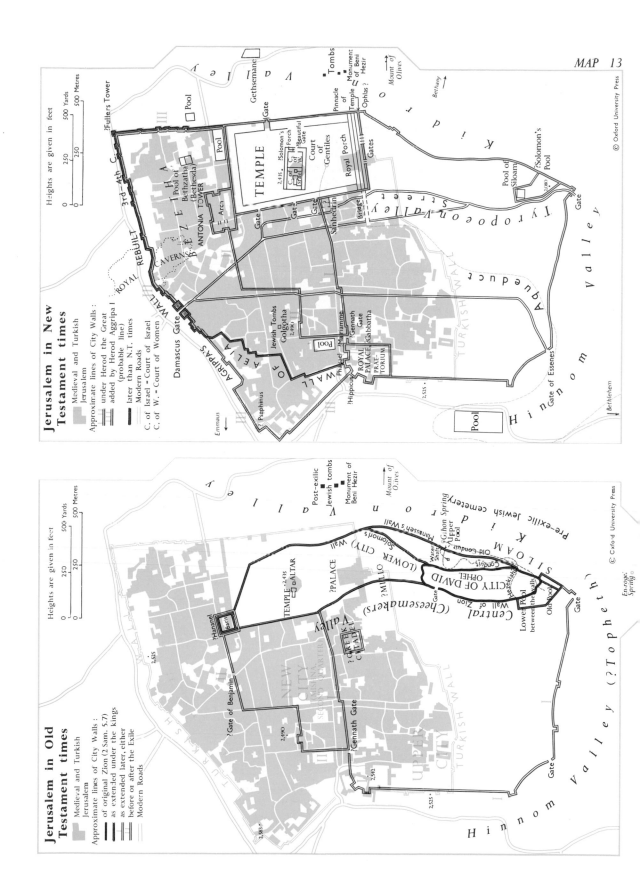

MAP 13

© Oxford University Press

**Jerusalem in New Testament times**

Medieval and Turkish Jerusalem

Approximate lines of City Walls:
— under Herod the Great
—‖‖‖ added by Herod Agrippa I (probable line)
— later than N.T. times
— Modern Roads

C. of Israel = Court of Israel
C. of W. = Court of Women

Heights are given in feet

0    250    500 Yards
0    250    500 Metres

Kidron Valley
Mount of Olives
Bethany
Gethsemane
?Tombs
?Monument of Beni Hezir
Ophlas
?Solomon's Pool
Pool of Siloam
Tyropoeon Valley
Pinnacle of Temple
?Solomon's Porch
Beautiful Gate
Court of Gentiles
Royal Porch
Gates
Bridge
Sanhedrin
TEMPLE
C. of I.
C. of W.
Pool
?Bethzatha (Bethesda)
Pool of Bethzatha
ANTONIA TOWER
Arch
CAVERNS
BEZETHA
3rd–4th C.
ROYAL REBUILT
WALL
?Fullers Tower
Gate
Pool
Damascus Gate
AELIA
AGRIPPA'S
WALL OF
Jewish Tombs
Golgotha 2,490
Pool
?Gennath Gate
?Kabbatha
?Mariamne
?Phasael
?Hippicus
ROYAL PALACE
PRAE-TORIUM
Turkish Wall
Aqueduct
Hinnom Valley
Gate of Essenes
Gate
Pool
2,525
Emmaus
?Psephinus
Bethlehem

**Jerusalem in Old Testament times**

Medieval and Turkish Jerusalem

Approximate lines of City Walls:
— of original Zion (2 Sam. 5.7)
—‖‖‖ as extended under the kings
— as extended later, either before or after the Exile
— Modern Roads

Heights are given in feet

0    250    500 Yards
0    250    500 Metres

© Oxford University Press

Kidron Valley
Mount of Olives
Post-exilic Jewish tombs
Monument of Beni Hezir
Pre-exilic Jewish cemetery
Gihon Spring
Upper Pool
SILOAM
Solomon's Wall
Manasseh's Wall
Water Shaft
Old conduit
Conduit
OPHEL
CITY OF DAVID
(LOWER CITY)
Hezekiah's
Gate
between the walls
Lower Pool
Old Pool
Gate
Central Valley
Wall of ?Zion
?MILLO
(Cheesemakers)
(Valley
?PALACE
TEMPLE 2,435
ALTAR
?Hananel
Baris
?Gate of Benjamin
2,490
NEW CITY
SECOND QUARTER
GREEK CITADEL
?Cennath Gate
2,542
UPPER CITY
TURKISH WALL
Hinnom Valley (?Topheth)
Gate
2,525
En-rogel Spring
2,581
2,525

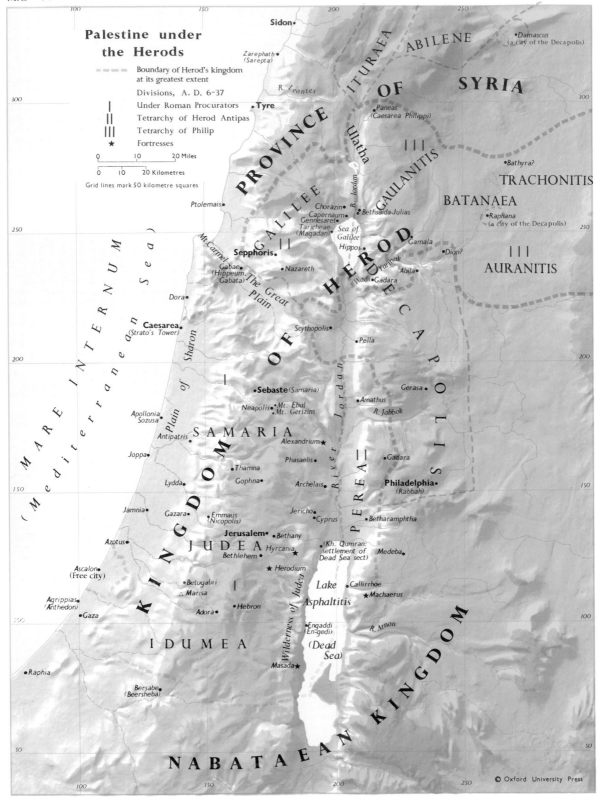

MAP 14

Sidon

**Palestine under the Herods**

- – – – Boundary of Herod's kingdom at its greatest extent

Divisions, A. D. 6-37

Ⅰ — Under Roman Procurators
Ⅱ — Tetrarchy of Herod Antipas
Ⅲ — Tetrarchy of Philip
★ — Fortresses

0    10    20 Miles
0    10    20 Kilometres

Grid lines mark 50 kilometre squares

Zarephath (Sarepta)

•Damascus (a city of the Decapolis)

R. Leontes

**ABILENE**

**ITURAEA**

**PROVINCE**

**OF**

**SYRIA**

**Tyre**

Paneas (Caesarea Philippi)

Ulatha

Ptolemais•

**GALILEE**

Chorazin•
Capernaum•  •Bethsaida-Julias
Gennesaret
Taricheae (Magadan)
Sea of Galilee
Hippos•

**GAULANITIS**

**BATANAEA**

**TRACHONITIS**

•Bathyra?

•Raphana (a city of the Decapolis)

Mt. Carmel

**Sepphoris.**
Gabae (Hippeum, Gabata)

The Great Plain

•Nazareth

**HEROD**

Gamala

Wadi•Gadara
Yarmuk
Abila•

•Dion?

**AURANITIS**

Dora•

Plain of Sharon

**Caesarea.** (Strato's Tower)

**OF**

Scythopolis•

R. Jordan

•Pella

**DECAPOLIS**

**MARE**
**INTERNUM**

(Mediterranean Sea)

Ⅰ

**Sebaste** (Samaria)

Neapolis•  •Mt. Ebal
•Mt. Gerizim

•Amathus
R. Jabbok

Gerasa•

Apollonia
Sozusa•

Plain of Sharon

Antipatris•

**SAMARIA**

Alexandrium★

**KINGDOM**

Joppa•

•Thamna
•Gophna

Phasaelis•

Archelais•

River Jordan

**PEREA**
Ⅱ
•Gadara

**Philadelphia**• (Rabbah)

Lydda•

Jamnia•   Gazara•

•Emmaus (Nicopolis)

Jericho•
•Cyprus

•Betharamphtha

Azotus•

**Jerusalem**• •Bethany

**JUDEA**  Hyrcania★
Bethlehem•

•(Kh. Qumran: settlement of Dead Sea sect)

•Medeba

Ascalon (Free city)

•Betogabri
.: Marisa

Ⅰ

★ Herodium

Lake

•Callirrhoe
•Machaerus

Agrippias (Anthedon)•

•Gaza

•Hebron
Adora•

Asphaltitis

**IDUMEA**

Wilderness of Judea

•Engaddi (En-gedi)

R. Arnon

(Dead Sea)

•Raphia

Masada★

**NABATAEAN**

Bersabe (Beersheba)•

**KINGDOM**

© Oxford University Press

MAP 15

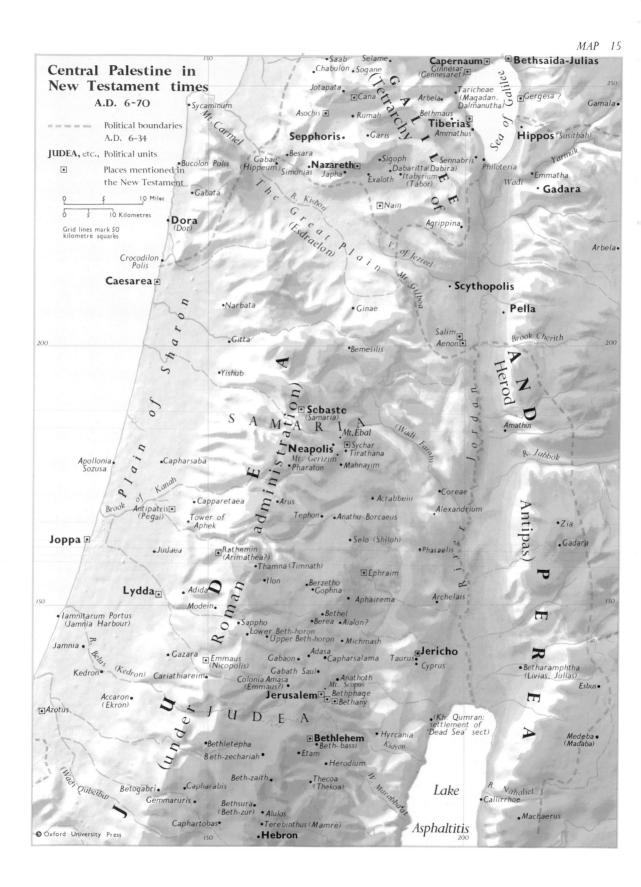

# Central Palestine in New Testament times

## A.D. 6-70

- - - - Political boundaries
      A.D. 6-34

**JUDEA**, etc., Political units

⊡ Places mentioned in the New Testament

0        5        10 Miles
0    5      10 Kilometres

Grid lines mark 50
kilometre squares

*Saab*  Selame.  **Capernaum**⊡  ⊡**Bethsaida-Julias**
*Chabulon*  Sogane  *Ginnesar* (*Gennesaret*)

150

*Sycaminum*  *Jotapata*  ⊡*Cana*  Arbela.  *Taricheae* (*Magadan,* *Dalmanutha*)  *Gergesa?*  250

*Asochis*⊡  *Rumah*  *Bethmaus*  *Gamala*.

*Mt. Carmel*  **Sepphoris**.  *Garis*  **Tiberias**  *Ammathus*  **Hippos** (*Susithah*)

*Gabae* (*Hippeum*)  *Besara*  *Sigoph*  *Sennabris*  *Yarmuk*

*Bucolon Polis*  *Simonias*  **Nazareth**⊡  *Dabaritta* (*Dabira*)  *Philoteria*  *Emmatha*

*Gabata*  *Japha*.  *Exaloth*  *Itabyrium* (*Tabor*)  *Wadi*  **Gadara**

The  *R. Kishon*  ⊡*Nain*

**Dora** (*Dor*)  *Great*  *Agrippina*.  *Arbela*.

*Crocodilon Polis*  *Plain*  (*Esdraelon*)  *Mt. Gilboa*  **Scythopolis**

**Caesarea**⊡  *V. of Jezreel*  **Pella**

*Narbata*.  *Ginae*  *Salim*  *Brook Cherith*

200  *Gitta*.  *Bemesilis*.  *Aenon*⊡  200

*Plain of Sharon*  *Yishub*.  **Herod**

*(administration)*  **SAMARIA**  *(Wadi Farah)*

*Apollonia Sozusa*  *Capharsaba*.  **Sebaste** (*Samaria*)  *Mt. Ebal*

*Brook of Kanah*  ⊡*Sychar*  *Amathus*.  **AND**

*Antipatris*⊡ (*Pegai*)  *Capparetaea*.  **Neapolis**  *Tirathana*  *R. Jabbok*

*Tower of Aphek*  *Mt. Gerizim*  *Pharaton*.  *Mahnayim*

**Joppa**⊡  *Arus*.  *Acrabbein*.  *Coreae*.  *Zia*.

*Judaea*  *Tephon*.  *Anathu Borcaeus*.  *Alexandrium*.

⊡*Rathamin* (*Arimathea?*)  *Selo* (*Shiloh*)  *Gadara*.

*Thamna* (*Timnath*)  *Phasaelis*.

150  **Lydda**⊡  *Ilon*.  *Berzetho*  ⊡*Ephraim*  150

*Adida*.  *Gophna*.  *Aphairema*.  *Archelais*.  **P**

*Modein*.  *Bethel*.  **E**

*Iamnitarum Portus* (*Jamnia Harbour*)  *Sappho*.  *Berea*  *Aialon?*  **R**

*Jamnia*  *R. Belus* (*Kedron*)  *Lower Beth-horon*.  *Michmash*  **E**

*Gazara*.  *Upper Beth-horon*  *Adasa*  *Taurus*.  **Jericho**⊡  **A**

*Kedron*.  ⊡*Emmaus* (*Nicopolis*)  *Gabaon*.  *Capharsalama*  *Cyprus*.  *Betharamphtha* (*Livias, Julias*)

*Cariathiaraim*.  *Gabath Saul*.  *Anathoth*  *Esbus*.

*Accaron* (*Ekron*)  *Colonia Amasa* (*Emmaus?*)  *Mt. Scopus*  *Bethphage*

⊡*Azotus*  **Jerusalem**⊡  ⊡*Bethany*

**U**  **J U D E A**  *(Kh. Qumran: settlement of 'Dead Sea' sect)*  *Medeba* (*Madaba*)

**D**  **(under**  *Hyrcania*  *Kidron*

*Bethletepha*.  ⊡**Bethlehem**  *Beth-bassi*

**Roman**  *Beth-zechariah*.  *Etam*.  *Herodium*.

*Betogabri*  *Beth-zaith*  *Thecoa* (*Thekoa*)  *Lake*

*(Wadi Qubeiba)*  *Caphatabis*.  *W. Murabbat*  *R. Nahaliel*  *Callirrhoe*.

**J**  *Gemmaruris*.  *Bethsura* (*Beth-zur*)  **Asphaltitis**  *Machaerus*.

*Caphartobas*.  *Alulos*.  *Terebinthus* (*Mamre*)

© Oxford University Press  150  **Hebron**  200

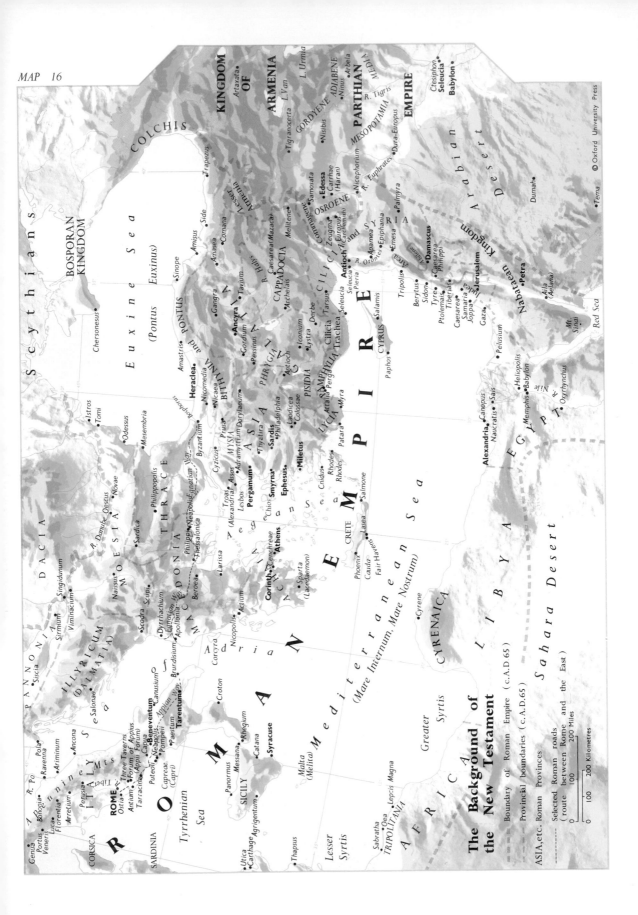

MAP 16

© Oxford University Press

**The Background of the New Testament**

losses in the Holocaust of the Nazi era in Europe but has since established its own state in Israel.

*Christianity.* In the twentieth century, the largest of the world religions has grown significantly in Africa and parts of Asia but has experienced practical losses to Marxism and secularization in Europe.

*Islam.* This faith has experienced more growth in both numbers (as percent of world's population) and influence in the twentieth century than any other major world religion and has been swept by revitalization movements.

The following chart provides comparative figures and percentages of the world's population for the world religions in 1900 and 1980, based on the best data and estimates available, together with a projection of these figures for A.D. 2000.

Numbers in millions and as % of world population

| Religion | 1900 | % | 1980 | % | 2000 | % |
|---|---|---|---|---|---|---|
| Christianity | 558 | 34.4 | 1433 | 32.8 | 2020 | 32.3 |
| Non-religious | 3 | .2 | 911 | 20.8 | 1334 | 21.3 |
| Islam | 200 | 12.4 | 723 | 16.5 | 1201 | 19.2 |
| Hinduism | 203 | 12.5 | 583 | 13.3 | 859 | 13.7 |
| Buddhism | 127 | 7.8 | 274 | 6.3 | 359 | 5.7 |
| Chinese popular religion | 380 | 23.5 | 198 | 4.5 | 158 | 2.5 |
| Primitive religion | 118 | 7.3 | 103 | 2.4 | 110 | 1.8 |
| "New Religions" | 6 | .4 | 96 | 2.2 | 138 | 2.2 |
| Judaism | 12 | .8 | 17 | .4 | 20 | .3 |
| Other* | 13 | .8 | 36 | .8 | 61 | 1.0 |

*Includes Sikhism, Confucianism, Shinto, Baha'i, Jainism, Spiritism, and Zoroastrianism.

This chart is based on that of David B. Barrett, ed., *World Christian Encyclopedia.* (Oxford University Press, 1982), p. 6; and the summary of its findings in *Time* magazine, May 3, 1982, p. 66.          R.E.

**WORLD VIEW.** *See* WELTANSCHAUUNG.

**WORLD VISION INTERNATIONAL.** An evangelical interdenominational service agency that supports the work of child care, community development, evangelism, leadership development, and many related ministries.

This international work evolved from the concerns of Robert (Bob) Willard Pierce, former Nazarene pastor and missionary to China. Pierce, whose methods were as unorthodox as they were effective, began his ministry in Los Angeles as a youth worker and evangelist. He later became one of the co-founders of Youth for Christ International and the director of Los Angeles Youth for Christ. Colleagues of his Youth for Christ days included Billy Graham, Torrey Johnson, Robert Cook, Robert Evans, and many others.

His free-wheeling tours to cities of Asia confronted Pierce with the tragic plight of hordes of orphans, especially in Korea. The formal organization of World Vision, Inc., occurred in 1950, primarily to serve as a support agency for the work among orphans. Eventually this operation spread to nineteen countries. Impressed by the needs of Asia, Pierce produced motion picture films on China and Korea that had great impact on Christian audiences in America. For many years he conducted a radio program and later produced television specials.

One of the most significant aspects of Pierce's ministry was to impress on United States evangelicals the importance of combining concern for both physical and spiritual needs. Pierce was a major factor in reestablishing the importance of wedding evangelism and social action.

In India, and subsequently in other lands, World Vision sponsored pastors' conferences designed to revitalize the vision of indigenous leaders. In 1978 World Vision International was formed of the original United States work plus World Vision of Canada and other World Vision entities.          R.H.

**WORLDWIDE CHURCH OF GOD, THE.** Originally named the Radio Church of God, this contemporary religious group is the creation of Herbert W. Armstrong, who founded it in Eugene, Oregon, on radio station KORE in 1934. Today, this most successful variant of "British-Israelitism" has 250 churches with some 75,000 members in North America, Europe, Africa, and Asia, and distributes 4.3 million copies of its magazine, *The Plain Truth.* The church largely consists of the public speaking efforts of the elderly Mr. Armstrong (since he removed his son, Garner Ted Armstrong, from the church in 1978) on 100 radio stations and 150 television stations each week. Additionally, the group maintains two college campuses (Ambassador College), in Pasadena, California, and in Texas, and a vast publishing enterprise that produces and mails 80,000 Bible lessons every month.

The Worldwide Church of God is based on a number of sectarian—or cultic—ideas that were not invented by Armstrong, but were taken up by him and widely and successfully propagated for the first time. Briefly, these ideas include Sabbatarianism (that the only legitimate day of worship for Christians as well as Jews is Saturday—the OT Sabbath); a rejection of Christian liturgical festivals and fasts, especially the Nativity (Christmas) and Easter; a rejection of the observance of birthdays in general; legalism (the belief that the OT Law is binding, and OT festivals and fasts, like Pentecost, are binding on Christians); and British-Israelitism (Anglo-Israelism), the claim (made since the eighteenth century by some British sectarians) that the British people, along with their Germanic relations, the Angles and Saxons, are the descendants of the "Ten Lost Tribes of Israel." Armstrong mixes all these elements together, along with others, and uses them to denounce the Roman Catholic and Protestant churches as teaching a "counterfeit gospel." Armstrong, along with previous sectarians, identifies this "demonization" of the gospel with the destruction of the temple in A.D. 70 and the eventual embrace of Christianity by the Roman Empire under Constantine the Great in A.D. 312.                                    J.C.

**WORMS (DIET AND DISPUTATION).** *See* LUTHER, MARTIN; DIET OF WORMS.

**WORSHIP.** The word derives from the Saxon term "worthship" and is used to indicate an attitude of homage. It is used in English to translate a Hebrew term in the OT that means "to bow or prostrate oneself," and a Greek term in the NT that means the same but derives from a root meaning "to kiss." The posture indicated refers to the practice of bowing to kiss the hand or foot of the person or thing to which homage is being paid. The idea of emotional and spiritual emptiness in the presence of the HOLY lies at the heart of the experience of worship. It is significant that no noun conveying this thought is found in the OT or the NT. The inevitable conclusion that must be reached is that worship is viewed in the Bible as an action rather than a state or condition. Even though a noun form of the verb *proskuneo* exists in classical Greek, in more than one form, it does not appear in the NT. The words that do appear and are sometimes translated "worship" are different Greek words that refer to the external services and ministries involved in the religious life (Rom. 9:4; Col. 2:18; Heb. 9:1, 21; 12:28) rather than the essence of intellectual, spiritual, and emotional expression proceeding from the inner self (Matt. 4:9, 10; Rev. 4:10).

*Old Testament.* In the patriarchal period, worship was individual rather than corporate, except where families were involved. Jacob set up a stone as an altar and poured oil upon it (Gen. 28:18). The mountain where Moses saw the burning bush (Exod. 3:2) was later called the mountain of God (Exod. 4:27). Abraham built an altar on a mountain where he offered sacrifice (Gen. 22:9, 13). Noah built an altar after the ark landed, and SACRIFICIAL OFFERINGS were made to God (Gen. 8:20). There was no written law before Moses according to which the Hebrews conducted their lives and performed their acts of worship. Rather, they seemed to conduct themselves according to the life and teaching of Abraham, who experienced theophanies that provided him with divine instruction (Gen. 12:1; 13:14; 15:12). This revelatory experience was passed on by tradition and combined with further theophanies and dreams to his descendants: Isaac (Gen. 26:24), Jacob (Gen. 28:10; 32:25; 48:3), Joseph (Gen. 37:5), and Joseph's brothers (Gen. 50:24-25). The condemnation of Adam presupposes a prior revelation that he violated (Gen. 3:17), as does the unacceptability of Cain's sacrifice (Gen. 4:4-5). Abel's sacrifice was accepted because it was offered by faith (Heb. 11:4) and faith requires an awareness of the will of God by which divine approval may be obtained (Heb. 11:2). Thus, the ancients worshiped by the revealed will of God, transmitted to them in various ways (Heb. 1:1).

The nations among which the Hebrews lived were polytheistic and worshiped idols. When the Israelites moved into Canaan they established sanctuaries as fixed places of worship, as the Canaanites had done, for example, at Shiloh, Bethel, and Shechem. They eventually adopted some Canaanite practices including idolatry and cult prostitution connected with these "high places," practices which Josiah, king of Judah, corrected during his reign in 621 B.C. (II Kings 23:4-20). The Israelites were supposed to have offered worship only in the places God designated and in the way God prescribed (Deut. 12:5-7), but their violation of this, due partly to Canaanite influence, led to the eventual downfall of the northern kingdom of Israel in 722 B.C. and the southern kingdom of Judah in 587 B.C.

In Canaan the Israelites celebrated three major agricultural festivals that are still recognized, with varying degrees of interest, in the several forms of modern Judaism. The PASSOVER and unleavened bread, celebrated in the spring during the barley harvest, was the beginning of the religious year (Exod. 12:2). The purpose of the Passover observance was to remind the Israelites of God's miraculous intervention on their behalf, when God passed over their firstborn and destroyed the firstborn of Egypt (Exod. 12:17; 13:8-9). The Feast of WEEKS (Pentecost, Acts 2:1) was observed fifty days later (Deut. 16:9) at the time of the wheat harvest. It was also called Feast of the Firstfruits (Num. 28:26) or the Feast of Harvest (Exod. 23:16). This was a one-day feast during which the poor were not to be forgotten (Lev. 23:22). The final festival of the religious year was the Feast of TABERNACLES (Ingathering, Exod. 23:16; 34:22; Lev. 23:39), observed in the fall when the olives, grapes, and grain harvests were completed. The Israelites lived in tents during this seven-day festival (Exod. 23:16) and remembered the period of their wilderness sojourn when they had lived in tents for forty years. Yards and porches in modern Jerusalem are still dotted with tabernacles during this week each fall. The most solemn occasion of the entire religious year was Yom Kippur, the DAY OF ATONEMENT (Lev. 16:1-34; 23:26-32; Num. 29:7-11), observed also in the fall. Contrary to the others it was a day of solemn fasting and holy convocation. It was a Sabbath day and the only one on which fasting was obligatory according to the Law of Moses. It is still the most solemn day in modern Israel, when virtually everything under Jewish control is shut down. It was a day for solemn reflection on one's sins and those of the nation; a day when the high priest went into the Holy of Holies in the tabernacle or Temple and made a blood offering for the sins of the nation. This is the only time of the year when anyone was allowed in this holiest place in the nation, the place where the very presence of the Lord was felt (Exod. 40:34-38; Lev. 16:11-19).

When the Israelites became a nation and entered into covenant relationship with God at Mount Sinai, where they received the Law of Moses, they were given a sacrificial system as an integral part of their worship experience (Lev. 1–7). Four kinds of sacrifice involved the shedding of blood. The burnt offering was a lamb that was sacrificed each morning and evening, reminding Israel of its devotion to God (Exod. 29:38-42; Num. 28:3-8). The complete dedication of the worshiper to God was indicated by the fact that the whole animal was consumed on the altar (Lev. 1:5-17). Paul probably alludes to this in Romans 12:1. The second offering, the peace offering, was made to indicate living communion between God and humans. This was a voluntary sacrifice, and any animal, except a bird, could be offered. The primary feature of this offering was the sacrificial meal in which one's family and friends might participate (Lev. 3:1-17; Deut. 12:6-7). The sin offering was a third kind of sacrifice that was offered for specific sins intentionally or inadvertently committed (Lev. 4:1-35; 6:24-30; 12:6-8; 14:19-31). If one could not afford a sheep or a goat, two turtledoves or pigeons could be substituted (Lev. 5:7). The fourth type of sacrifice was the trespass offering, which involved the legal rights of a people and their property, whether in relation to God or people (Lev. 5:14–6:7; 7:1-7). Failure to offer the tithe, firstfruits, or other required offerings necessitated this sacrifice of a ram, a very costly retribution.

After the Jews of Judah were carried into captivity in Babylonia in the sixth century B.C., the exiles were forced to build local places of study and worship, since they no longer had access to the TEMPLE. These they called SYNAGOGUES. The exact date of their origin is unknown, but they must have been built rather soon after the Jews attained some measure of freedom under the Persians late in the sixth century B.C. Synagogues were built throughout the Diaspora and served as cultural centers for the preservation of the Jewish way of life, not just as places of worship. However, worship was an important part of the function of the synagogue. The ruler of the synagogue (Acts 18:8; Mark 5:22) was in charge of worship and selected those who led prayers, read from the Law, and preached (Luke 4:16 ff.; Matt. 4:23; Acts 13:15). The services, held on Sabbath days, consisted of psalms, benedictions, recitation of the Shema (Deut. 6:4) and the Eighteen Benedictions, reading from the Law and the Prophets, and a sermon (Luke 4:16-27). There is evidence that the reading of the Law followed a triennial cycle. It was read in its entirety over a three-year period. Later, selections from the Prophets (Haftorah) were added to the readings from the Torah. Eventually, the Babylonian cycle was adopted, allowing the completion of the reading in one year. The passage was read in Hebrew and then translated into Aramaic, one verse at a time. Sacrifice was not performed in the synagogues, nor associated with them. By A.D. 70, when the Temple in Jerusalem was destroyed by the Romans, it is estimated that four to seven million Jews in the Diaspora had more than a thousand synagogues.

*New Testament.* Worship was a matter of private conviction with Jesus, who refused to bow down before Satan and worship him (Matt. 4:9). He rebuked some of the Pharisees who came to him for replacing the word of God with tradition in their external expressions of worship (Matt. 15:1-9). Since Jesus forbade his disciples to preach to Gentiles (Matt. 10:5) and did not make a special effort to go to them himself (Matt. 15:24), he and his disciples worshiped in synagogues and in the Temple (Luke 4:16-22; Mark 11:15-19; Luke 21:37; 24:53; Acts 2:46; 3:1). After Gentiles were admitted to the church (Acts 10) Paul spoke to both Jews and God-fearing Greeks in synagogues throughout the Diaspora (Acts 17:1-4; 18:4). He charged the Greeks in Athens with worshiping in ignorance through their IDOLATRY and taught them to seek after the one true God in whom we "live and move and have our being" (Acts 17:22-34).

In his letters, Paul used a variety of Greek terms to discuss the external expressions of worship in the religious life of the believer (Rom. 9:4; I Cor. 10:14; Col. 2:18; II Thess. 2:4). Similar terms are also found in Hebrews (9:1-2; 12:28). In almost all other NT references, however, the concept of worship is conveyed with the verb meaning "to prostrate oneself " in the presence of the object of worship, whether physically or spiritually (Matt. 2:2; John 4:20; Acts 8:27; 17:23; 19:27; Heb. 11:21; Rev. 19:10). There is no uniform posture for worship in the Bible. Jesus prayed on the cross (Luke 23:34). Stephen prayed while he was being stoned to death (Acts 7:59). Jesus prayed lifting his eyes to heaven (John 17:1), but the tax collector would not lift his eyes to heaven as he prayed (Luke 18:13). Paul and Christians from Ephesus knelt and prayed on the beach at Miletus (Acts 20:36). Moses took off his shoes in the presence of God (Exod. 3:5), as did Joshua, who "fell on his face to the earth, and worshiped" (Josh. 5:14).

The NT does not give a full description of early Christian worship, but a survey of various passages shows the following components of worship: PRAYER (I Cor. 11:4; 14:15; I Tim. 2:1-8; Phil. 4:4-8); singing (Col. 3:16; Eph. 5:19; I Cor. 14:15, 26); teaching or PREACHING (Acts 20:7; I Cor. 14:26-33; I Tim. 4:13); reading of scripture (I Tim. 4:13); observance of the LORD'S SUPPER (I Cor. 11:2-16) on the first day of the week (Acts 20:7); and giving of their money for benevolent and other needs during these assemblies (I Cor. 16:2), although giving was not limited to these occasions (Gal. 6:10). Some of these acts of worship were performed charismatically (I Cor. 14), but the principle that was to be kept uppermost in mind during these services was that they should "let all things be done for edification" (I Cor. 14:4, 26). In these assemblies men lifted up "holy hands" in prayer, indicating a lack of anger and quarreling (I Tim. 2:9-15). A public "amen" was given to the thanksgiving (I Cor. 14:16), which apparently was a part of the prayer service (I Tim. 2:1; Phil 4:6).

*Post-New Testament Period.* Evidence from the second century indicates that this type of worship was continued into that century. Justin Martyr, in the second century, described essentially this same kind of service. Christians met on Sunday at one place and read the writings of the apostles and the prophets, following which there was a sermon of exhortation. The congregation prayed and then observed the Lord's Supper, after which a contribution was taken up and sent to the needy by the deacons. The congregation said the Amen at the conclusions of the prayers and thanksgivings. Christian worship in modern times perpetuates essentially these same elements found in early centuries with slight modification among the various branches of Christendom. The Roman Catholic and Episcopal traditions, along with most forms of Eastern Orthodoxy, highlight the liturgical aspects of worship, while the Protestant and Evangelical traditions tend to highlight the place of preaching, due largely perhaps to the Reformation inheritance.                                                      J.R.M.

**WRATH OF GOD.** The justifiable and righteous anger of God against sin, mentioned many times in the OT. God's wrath is the expression of divine holiness as it comes into contact with the evils wrought by people, especially by those God has called into covenant. The divine wrath is seen in God's reaction to Moses (Exod. 4:14), to Miriam and Aaron (Num. 12:9), against Sodom and Gomorrah (Gen. 19), against those who opposed the children of Israel as they went up to occupy Canaan (Joshua), and against Israel many times as the people broke the covenant and followed other gods. Ultimately, Yahweh's wrath against Israel's sin led to the destruction of both Israel (Samaria, 722 B.C.) and Judah (Jerusalem, 586 B.C.). Yet God's wrath is but the opposite side of God's love. God wishes people to turn from sin, and if they persist in it, then God punishes them to bring them to repentance. This is the message of all the great prophets from Amos to the Isaiah of the Exile (Second Isa.; Isa. 40–55).

Even in visiting wrath on humankind, Yahweh tempered anger with mercy. God is slow to show anger because God is full of *chesid*, or steadfast love. God is said to have wrath, to be angry, and to hate certain actions and situations in the OT (Deut. 11:17; Exod. 4:14; Ps. 85:4; Hos. 9:15). Related to God's wrath is the jealousy of God (Exod. 20:5). God's jealousy is displeasure with Israel's sinfulness. In the NT God is also said to have wrath against a present sin (Rom. 1:18), but generally, the wrath of God means the punishment of sinners at the Last JUDGMENT. In general, the NT ideas about God's wrath are similar to those of the OT.

The concept of God's wrath has been under attack since the first century A.D. Philo of Alexandria had to defend the OT against Stoic criticisms. The Stoics did not believe in divine punishment. The heretic Marcion accepted this view and taught that there were two Gods—the OT God, who had wrath, and the Christian God, who only loved. The church condemned him. Schleiermacher rejected God's wrath and thus hell. Ritschl later agreed. Some sectarians and cultists, such as the Jehovah's Witnesses, also deny the wrath of God and the reality of hell and eternal punishment. Obviously, the concept of universal salvation is opposed to the concept of God's wrath.                                        J.C.

**WRITING AND WRITING MATERIALS.** Apart from some verses in Daniel (2:4-7, 28) and Ezra (4:8–6:18; 7:12-26), which are written in Aramaic, the writing of the Bible is in either HEBREW or GREEK. There are a few exceptions to this: Genesis 41:43 has an Egyptian loanword, *abrek* (RSV "bow the knee!"), and both Hebrew and Aramaic equivalents of the English rendering "heap of witness" are given in Genesis 31:47.

The LANGUAGE of the NT is *koinē* Greek, that is, the language common among the populace in first-century Greco-Roman society, though this older view of *koinē* stated in classic form by A. Deissmann needs to be qualified in two directions. First, recent studies have shown the strong influence of the OT in Greek, the so-called Septuagintal style, on NT authors; and the Aramaic influence from the spoken dialect of Palestine has been successfully noted on many NT passages, thanks to the work of Matthew Black, Nigel Turner, and Klaus Beyer. Second, in modern times it has been argued—with some cogency—that especially the NT writers of the apostolic church (Paul, Peter) have command of a literate, sophisticated, and urbane manner of composition to suit their audiences in the higher strata of society, which is more professional and upper class than artisan. Allusions to classical Greek authors are rare (for example, I Cor. 15:33, citing Menander's comedy *Thais*), but the point made by E. A. Judge is that Paul was at home with the upper levels, both educationally and in his written style and language, of middle-class society in the large Hellenistic cities, such as Ephesus, Corinth, and Rome, where he founded and ministered to congregations.

*Writing.* References to writing are as wide and continuous as the story of biblical history. Writing has been in existence at least from the third millennium B.C., so it is not surprising that the early figures of Israel's history are said to have left written compositions (Moses, Exod. 17:14), especially those parts of the OT that later Judaism prized so highly as God's law or Torah (Exod. 24:12; 34:27), the "words of Yahweh" (Exod. 24:4) engraved on stone tablets (Exod. 32:16; compare Job 19:24 for this material used for inscriptions). Moses was evidently assisted by a body of scribes whose work codified the judicial rules (Deut. 16:18; Jos. 8:33; I Chr. 23:4). Thereafter, in the narrative sequence of the OT story,

From *They Wrote in Clay*, The University of Chicago Press

*A clay tablet in its envelope*

| | A | B | C | D | E |
|---|---|---|---|---|---|
| | Original pictograph | Pictograph in position of later cuneiform | Early Babylonian | Assyrian | Original or derived meaning |
| 1 | | | | | bird |
| 2 | | | | | fish |
| 3 | | | | | donkey |
| 4 | | | | | ox |
| 5 | | | | | sun day |
| 6 | | | | | grain |
| 7 | | | | | orchard |
| 8 | | | | | to plow to till |
| 9 | | | | | boomerang to throw to throw down |
| 10 | | | | | to stand to go |

From Henri Frankfort, *The Birth of Civilization in the Near East*, Indiana University Press

*Table showing the development of cuneiform signs*

leaders of Israel wrote down their deeds (I Sam. 10:25), sent letters (II Sam. 11:14), and corresponded with surrounding heads of state (II Chr. 2:11), using court officials as amanuenses (I Chr. 24:6).

The prophets of the eighth and seventh centuries wrote (Isa. 8:1; 30:8), sometimes dictating to a trusted secretary like Baruch (Jer. 30:2; 36:27; 45:1). Postexilic leaders were familiar with the art of writing, and Zerubbabel and later Nehemiah had much correspondence with their patrons in Persia (Ezra 4:6, 7), while Ezra, a contemporary figure, is given the epithet, "the scribe" (Ezra 7:6).

Interestingly, Jesus Christ left no book, and occasional allusions (John 8:6) are more tantalizing than informative (Rev. 2–3: letters of Christ to the seven churches of Asia, which are said to have been transcribed by John for these congregations, Rev. 1:11). Not much is recorded of writing in the Gospel accounts, since they reflect the traditional Jewish method of teaching by word of mouth or ORAL TRADITION. In the apostolic age, however, the scene changed, and Paul in particular found it essential to keep open regular lines of communication with his churches by letter-writing habits. He regarded his letters as his alter ego, sending them at such times as he was unable to travel because of imprisonment (Phil. 2:12; Col. 2:5; 4:18) or other circumstances (I Cor. 5:1-13). His writings were evidently effective (II Cor. 10:10), and he expected a wide circulation for them (I Thess. 5:27; Philem. 1-2; Col. 4:16), adding a postscript in his own handwriting (I Cor. 16:21; Gal. 6:11; II Thess. 3:17, especially when there were forgeries being circulated, II Thess. 2:2). Paul used amanuenses, one of whose names we know as Tertius (Rom. 16:22), as Peter appears to have enlisted Silvanus to help in the composition of I Peter (5:12). As we observed, the letters of Paul are artistically shaped and to be classified as elegant prose compositions, however much they were occasioned ad hoc by the needs of his readers. Letters of commendation formed one special type of writing (II Cor. 3:1-3; compare Acts 18:27). In the later NT books the claim is registered that written compositions of the apostles, like those of the OT prophets, are under the inspiration of the Spirit (II Tim. 3:15, 16; II Pet. 3:15, 16).

*Writing Materials.* The earliest form of writing material was stone or rock, on the surface of which marks or alphabetic letters were chiseled (Job 19:24) by an iron stylus (Jer. 17:1). Stone altars were a permanent witness to this type of inscription (Josh. 8:32; Deut. 27:2-8). Of less durability but far more convenient were wooden boards, used by the prophets of Israel (Isa. 30:8; Hab. 2:2), and this type of material was popular in Greco-Roman schools and in Jewish homes (Luke 1:63). Clay tablets made of baked brick are also mentioned (Ezek. 4:1), especially for legal documents where the object is to be deposited and not subject to the wear and tear of constant use.

*Hieroglyphs on a limestone fragment from a tomb wall, Twenty-sixth Dynasty in Egypt (663–525 B.C.)*

*Hieroglyphs from the temple of Sesostris (about 1950 B.C.)*

Finds of CUNEIFORM tablets at Elba and Ugarit are on clay.

PAPYRUS was perfectly suited to fill the need for convenient, inexpensive, and durable writing material. The papyrus plant is native to Egypt, growing

*Egyptian scribal outfit consisting of a slate palette with restored water jug and a brush case with a rush pen*

especially in the marshes of the Nile Delta since it grows with its roots in water. The plant grows ten to fifteen feet high, which is adequate for preparation into a writing surface. The sections of the stem are cut, and strips are laid side by side to form a narrow mat. The layers are joined by hammering and pressing. The sheets are trimmed, with the surface polished smooth, and then glued together to form a continuous roll. Not surprisingly this simple yet profound invention gave a monumental impetus to writing and supplied the English language with the word "paper."

While papyrus is not explicitly mentioned in the OT, papyrus scrolls were found among the cache at Qumran (the Dead Sea Scrolls), and the inexpensive cost and durability of papyrus in the first and second centuries A.D., according to C. H. Roberts and T. C. Skeat, led to the Christian use of this material for their first compositions. A number of these survive as NT textual papyri, on which selected Gospels and other NT books are written (for example, P52, a fragment of John 18, the John Rylands manuscript, going back to the early second century A.D.). The transition from the common practice of using papyrus in a roll (as a scroll to be unwound, as in Luke 4:17, 20; Rev. 5:1-7; 10:2, 8-10) to a codex form, that is, like a book with leaves to be turned over, is a matter for debate between experts. One possible suggestion is that Christians found it easier to locate passages of a text when the writing was in page form. See II Timothy 4:13 for some brief allusion to these materials and the suggestion that parchment notebooks were a Roman invention.

The next important change came with the shift from papyrus to PARCHMENT. The turning point was in A.D. 301, when an edict of Emperor Diocletian clamped down on high wages paid to scribes who wrote on parchment, a leather-like substance drawn from the hides of sheep, goats, and calves (its invention derives from the kings of Pergamum in the second century B.C.), suitably tanned, shaved, and polished. Later (A.D. 312) the Christian emperor Constantine ordered fifty Bibles in vellum (a kind of parchment) to be placed in churches. This shows how popular the parchment codex had become. The evidence survives in our two finest specimens of parchment codices, Sinaiticus and Vaticanus.

Earlier scribes used a pen made of reed sharpened to a point (Jer. 8:8; III John 13). The ink was a mixture of gum and carbon in the form of lampblack. The absence of an acid base made the writing erasable, and it could easily be washed or scraped off; in the course of time it faded (see Col. 2:14 for illustration of this fact). The later addition of iron sulfate to ink caused the lettering to eat into the writing material, so that it became permanent.                          R.M.

**WYCLIFFE, JOHN** (1328–84). English theologian and church reformer, the "Morning Star of the Reformation." Born in Hipswell, Yorkshire, he was educated at Oxford and lived there during most of his life, winning notice as a philosopher-theologian. Wycliffe grew increasingly skeptical of prevailing church conditions: the papacy moved from Rome to Avignon causing the Babylonian Captivity (1305–77), and Christendom was soon embarrassed by two popes during the Great Schism (1378–1417). Wycliffe turned to Augustine, the Bible, and early church fathers for inspiration. He gave lectures on the entire Bible to complete his doctoral degree and gradually developed a view of the church contrasting the earthly institution with the invisible, ideal church. He was rector at Fillingham and Ludgershall before Lutterworth (1374–84), where he gained fame as a radical critic of the church and especially monasticism, which he regarded as religiously bankrupt. He expected a plush appointment from the pope in view of his scholarship at Oxford, and when that did not happen, he entered the service of King Edward III, who appointed him to Lutterworth. He represented the king in a dispute with the pope, who still claimed England as a fief and was demanding tribute (based on the "Donation of Constantine"). Wycliffe appealed to English law and developed a

doctrine of righteous stewardship, which runs throughout his works. He held that everything belongs to God and that we are but stewards who can lose our stewardship through unworthy service.

*On Divine Lordship* (1375) and *On Civil Lordship* (1376) maintained that every creature, whether priest or king, is a servant of God the Creator, and that human stewardship (lordship) is neither unlimited nor permanent. Since lordship is by grace, one not in grace can be replaced. Priests and rulers are but stewards and if unfit should lose their stewardships. Wycliffe rejected the use of force but was accused of fomenting the Peasants' Uprising in 1381. He thought the church should institute radical reform, but that secular powers might do so if the church did not.

*On the King's Office* anticipated a national church as realized under Henry VIII. In 1377 Pope Gregory XI issued five bulls against Wycliffe and demanded his arrest, an order resisted by Wycliffe's political protectors. *On the Pastoral Office* (1378) called for clerical poverty and non-support of immoral and negligent clergy by the withholding of funds and attendance. *On the Eucharist* (1380) rejected transubstantiation as biblically, historically, and philosophically invalid and argued that the elements remain bread and wine after consecration. In 1381 Oxford repudiated this view, and the Blackfriars Council (1382) condemned ten of his views as heretical. Wycliffe spent his last years writing pamphlets against opponents. Wycliffe's LOLLARD followers extended and spread his ideas, preaching and circulating the Bible in English, but were condemned by Parliament in 1401 and forced underground. They fostered an ethos that later prepared England for the REFORMATION. Wycliffe's views were further condemned by the Council of Constance in 1415.

C.M.

**WYCLIFFE BIBLE TRANSLATORS.** Working through eighteen national sending agencies, WBT is the world's largest organization involved in translating the Scriptures into the languages of tribal peoples. To accomplish its goals, Wycliffe sponsors the work of 1,781 North Americans overseas as well as 658 linguists and aides from other parts of the world. These figures do not include the North American administrative staff of 200 nor 466 short-term personnel. WBT has two major affiliates: the Summer Institute of Linguistics and the Jungle Aviation and Radio Service.

The ministry of WBT was conceived by W. Cameron Townsend and L. L. Legters, missionaries to Latin America. Their vision was to translate the Bible into every tongue on earth. In 1917 Townsend was peddling Bibles in Central America. When he realized that 60 percent of the people of Guatemala could not read the Spanish edition of the Bible he was selling, he quit his job, joined another mission and started on a seventeen-year task of translating the

Scriptures into Cakchiquel, the language of one of the Indian tribes. In 1934 Townsend launched Camp Wycliffe in Arkansas as a training school for linguists. Eventually this work evolved into the Summer Institute of Linguistics. In 1935 members of this group started field work among the larger tribes of Mexico. By 1942 Wycliffe Bible Translators, Inc., was established.

Today linguists are working in primitive tribes of the continents of both North and South America, Asia, and Africa. The task is not yet complete. Even as late as 1959 Ethel E. Wallis and Mary A. Bennett wrote the significant book *Two Thousand Tongues to Go.*

R.H.

# Xx

**XAVIER, FRANCIS.** *See* FRANCIS XAVIER.

**XERXES.** The Greek name of two Persian emperors, called Ahasuerus in Hebrew (Esth. 1:1 ff.; 4:6), and, in the original Persian, Khshayarsha. Both emperors belong to the Achaemenid dynasty. The king who figures in the romantic—and late—story of ESTHER is considered to be Xerxes I. His father was the famous Darius, and his grandfather was Cyrus the Great.

Xerxes I ruled the Persian Empire from 486 to 465 B.C. He was at first a very vigorous king, suppressing revolts in Egypt and pacifying Babylonia by abolishing Babylon as a separate kingdom and removing the images of Marduk (Bel, Merodach) that were needed for a king of Babylon to be legitimatized. This caused two revolts that he put down.

Xerxes I then turned to the Greeks who had defeated Darius at Marathon. In 483 B.C. he began his western campaign. He bridged the Hellespont and raised a vast fleet. In 480 B.C., he conquered Athens. Then the tide turned. The Greek navy defeated the larger Persian fleet at Salamis (Sept. 28, 480 B.C.). Xerxes withdrew, and his Greek expeditionary force was defeated by the combined Greek armies at Plataca (479 B.C.). He then degenerated to the type of king portrayed in Esther.                                    J.C.

**XIMENÉZ DE CISNEROS.** *See* JIMENÉZ DE CISNEROS.

Courtesy of the Oriental Institute, University of Chicago

*Darius (522–486 B.C.) on the throne, with Xerxes (486–465) behind him and the symbol of Ahura-Mazda above him; from the Council Hall at Persepolis*

# Yy

**YADIN, YIGAEL** (1917–84). Often hailed as Israel's most celebrated biblical archaeologist, Yadin was born with the family name of Sukenik. His father, Eliezer Sukenik, played a prominent part in the publishing of the first Dead Sea Scrolls in 1947, having arrived in Palestine as an emigré from Poland. His son Yigael was required to take a code name as a member of the anti-British Haganah or Jewish defense force, which protested the British mandate. Thus Yadin was given him, a name taken to mean "he will be redeemed." And this name has remained.

Yadin's role in Israeli history was first as a leader in the national defense army, where he served as chief of staff. He was active in the first Israeli-Egyptian war, and was a member of the delegation that secured a cease-fire. In 1952 he returned to his initial interest in biblical and Israeli archaeology, cooperating, as his father had done, with others in the securing of the Dead Sea Scrolls for the State of Israel. The documents are now housed in the splendid Shrine of the Book museum, thanks to Yadin's advocacy. He edited two of the seven major scrolls—the War Scroll and the Genesis Apocryphon Scroll.

Between 1956 and 1958 Yadin was the principal excavator in the site of Hazor. Not only did this important site receive expert and scientific attention, but Yadin used the operation to train what became a rising generation of Israeli archaeologists. In the 1960s he turned to Masada, where Herod the Great had built his summer place and where the last resistance stand of the Zealots against the Roman armies was made until the outpost fell in A.D. 73. Yadin's book on his work made Masada a well-known name of Jewish patriotic history, and he publicized the small sherds on which were written the names of the freedom fighters who ended their lives in a mass suicide pact.

He entered politics in 1977 to head a new party in the Knesset. His influence gave impetus to the coming to power of Menachem Begin, whose first government had Yadin as its deputy prime minister. Not fully successful as a political figure, he returned to archaeology in 1981, with further publications on the art of warfare in Bible lands and the discoveries found in the caves of Bar Kochba's time (A.D. 132–135) adding to his reputation. His work on the Temple Scroll from Qumran found in 1976 was one of his latest and most spectacular enterprises (his book appeared in English translation in 1983).     R.M.

**YAHWEH.** The personal name for the Israelite national Deity, usually translated "the LORD" in modern versions. Both the exact pronunciation and meaning of the name are uncertain. Ancient Hebrew texts in which only consonants and not vowels were written reproduce the name, the so-called Tetragrammaton, as YHWH. Since the name was later not pronounced, except on special occasions by the high priest, substitutes such as ADONAI ("my Lord") or SHEMA ("the name") were used instead. Thus the exact pronunciation was lost. Evidence supplied by ancient church fathers suggests the form Yahweh.

The meaning of the name is uncertain although it may have never been anything more than a proper noun. Exodus 3:14 suggests that it may have been connected with the verb "to be," but here the author may have been offering a late, uncertain folk etymology. According to Genesis 4:26, people have worshiped Yahweh since the earliest days of human history. According to Exodus 6:2, however, the name was not revealed until the time of Moses. These different views probably reflect different literary and theological traditions in ancient Israel. Yahweh was worshiped by other than Israelites according to Exodus 18, where Moses' father-in-law, a Midianite or Kenite, is depicted as a devotee. (*See* JEHOVAH.)
J.H.

**YAMA.** From the Sanskrit word for "restrainer, punisher," or "twin." In the mythology of Hinduism, the god of death who rules over the underworld. He was the first man, who, being therefore also the first to die, established his realm in the place where departed souls go. He is presented in the Vedas as less grim than a jovial, majestic figure, green but wearing red robes, who gathers ancestors to himself and bestows upon them the immortality whose secret he discovered. Later, however, Yama became more terrifying. He personified the dread aspect of death and was the *Dharmaraja,* the judge of righteousness who weighs the deeds of the deceased and has the wicked punished in the hells. In this form he passed into the lore of Buddhism, and so into the mythology of Tibet, China, and Japan.
R.E.

**YEAR, CHRISTIAN.** *See* CHRISTIAN YEAR.

**YIDDISH.** One of two major languages of the Jewish people. Printed and written in Hebrew characters, Yiddish became the language of the Jewish masses. Before the Holocaust, Yiddish was spoken by about twelve million people.

According to some authorities, the history of Yiddish dates back to the tenth or eleventh century, when in the German provinces of the Rhineland, Jews speaking the local German dialects intermingled Hebrew expressions. Yiddish has since undergone its own development. In addition to the Hebrew elements—estimated at about 20 percent—contained in Yiddish, some other elements from the languages of the countries where Jews lived (mainly Slavic words) were gradually adopted. The term "Jewish" when applied to "Yiddish" is wrong. In modern times, Yiddish became the medium of expression of many outstanding writers—Sholem Aleichem among them—who created a great modern Yiddish literature. Like Hebrew, Yiddish is written and printed from right to left.
L.K.

**YIGDAL.** A Hebrew hymn based on the thirteen Articles of Faith formulated by MOSES MAIMONIDES. "Yigdal," which opens the hymn, means "Magnified be (the Living God)." Sung to a variety of tunes, it is one of two hymns often chanted at the conclusion of the Sabbath and festival evening services. Among Ashkenazi Jews, it is also recited before the daily morning service. The tune for Tabernacles was used by Isaac Nathan in 1815 as the air for one of Lord Byron's "Hebrew Melodies," being set by him to the verses of "The Wild Gazelle."
L.K.

*The I Ching trigrams with yin-yang symbol in the middle*

**YIN/YANG.** In Confucianism and Taoism, complementary cosmological principles that emanate from the Supreme Ultimate (T'ai Chi) and whose interplay underlies the movement of the world. Yin is earth, feminine, dark, and passive, embodied in valleys and streams, and emblemed by the tiger and the color orange. Yang is heaven, male, light, active, and sovereign, embodied in mountains and sky, and represented by the dragon and the color azure. Yin and yang thinking goes back at least to cosmological theories of the third century B.C. and is basic to countless Chinese rituals, art motifs, and the geomancy used to orient a house or grave properly between yin and yang lines of force. The first half of the year, for example, is yang, being the growing season and the time of lengthening days; it is inaugurated by dragon dances on New Year's Day. At the summer solstice, tiger dances usher in the time of increasing dark and ingathering. Yin and yang, portrayed respectively by broken and unbroken lines put into trigrams and hexagrams, are fundamental to the divination of the celebrated I CHING. Although yang may be favored in popular religion, it is important to note that theoretically yin and yang do not represent good or evil but symbolize complementary forces that should be kept balanced.
R.E.

**YM and YWHA.** A voluntary organization that provides group experiences to people who use its facilities. Unlike the Christian YMCA and YWCA, which are separate for men and women, the Jewish Ys are combined and provide a wide variety of activities for all age groups—from the preschooler to the older adult. These activities include physical fitness, Jewish culture and education, recreation, classes, discussion groups, lounge programs, and the like. Whereas in New York most of these institutions are known as YM & YWHAs, in most of North America they are called Jewish Community Centers. They originated in America, unlike other Jewish institutions that were brought over from other countries. Their memberships include Orthodox, Reform, Conservative, and unaffiliated. The Jewish Welfare Board (JWB) is the network of and central service agency for 275 Jewish Community Centers, YM & YWHAs, and camps in North America serving one million people.

L.K.

**YMCA/YWCA.** Two parallel but separate international organizations ministering to young men and women and seeking to aid them through activities that develop their powers of body, mind, and spirit. The organizations employ a triangle—red for men, blue for women—as a symbol of their programs.

George Williams (1821–1905), a London dry goods merchant, is credited with the founding of the YMCA in 1844. When he arrived in London, he was appalled by the working conditions he found there. He was concerned for the spiritual welfare of working-class young men and coupled with this a recreational program. The YWCA, originally two separate organizations, was founded in London in 1855. The two British groups were joined in 1877. The first United States organization was formed in New York City in 1858 under the name of the Ladies' Christian Association. The YMCA began as a pronouncedly evangelical movement, and Williams early sponsored Bible classes and other meetings designed to win young men for Jesus Christ. Leading evangelicals of the day, such as Lord Shaftesbury, sponsored the movement. Soon the YMCA spread to the Continent, to the United States, and to the British Empire. The American YMCA was founded in Boston in 1851. During the Civil War, Dwight L. Moody, the famed evangelist, served the troops as a YMCA worker.

Local YMCAs are autonomous corporations voluntarily affiliated with national councils in the various countries they serve and with the World Alliance of YMCAs, which has its headquarters in Geneva, Switzerland. Like the YMCA, the work of the YWCA was strengthened by the Second Evangelical Awakening. The program of the YWCA closely parallels that of the YMCA with internationalism and interdenominationalism promoted strongly. Both the YMCA and YWCA, as active participants of the United Service Organizations (USO), served the men in uniform during World War II. The YMCA has served the United States military forces in four wars.

R.H.

**YOGA.** Literally "discipline." A term that includes a variety of beliefs and practices in Hinduism. A person who practices yoga is a yogi (or yogin). In the United States the feature best known is a set of physical exercises, with emphasis on proper posture and disciplined breathing. In the Bhagavad Gita the term "yoga" is used to designate three ways of conducting the religious life: bhakti-yoga, or the life of devotion to deity; karma-yoga, the doing of one's duty in the world without attachment to the results of one's actions; and jnana-yoga, the gaining of true knowledge. To distinguish these ways from what is most widely thought of as yoga, many writers prefer to speak of them as *marga* (path). Scholars have pointed out yoga-like practices in ancient Taoism and medieval Christianity.

*Classic Yoga.* Various features of early Hinduism have been regarded as forerunners of yoga, but many scholars see its true beginnings in the Yogasutra of Patanjali. Those who believe that the author of the sutra is the great grammarian Patanjali date its origin to around 200 B.C. Because of the philosophical ideas in the sutra, however, many scholars feel that around A.D. 300 is a preferable date, and that the author was another person with the same name as the grammarian.

Patanjali's system of yoga is the basis for one of the six *darshanas*, or accepted philosophical systems of orthodox Hinduism. It is close to the system known as samkya, and like samkya teaches a dualism of matter and soul. These two, matter and soul, are eternally separate and distinct. Yoga seeks to free the soul from dependence on material reality. In this it draws on the help of a soul that, unlike all other souls, has never been involved in matter. This soul, Ishvara, is, in effect, a god and can serve as an object of MEDITATION and thus as an aid toward salvation. Salvation is not viewed, however, as involving a state of oneness with the god.

The Yogasutra consists of four sections. The first stresses true consciousness as prior to and more important than mere awareness of our common sense world. This consciousness is the real self, and yoga is the method by which one comes to freedom apart from ordinary awareness. Second, under the guidance of a guru one learns the practices that lead to that goal. Third is the gaining of paranormal powers. These powers, however, may actually hinder the yogi from the final goal and must be used with great care. Fourth is the attainment of *kaivalya*, the final liberation of the person or soul. Classic Patanjali yoga is also known as *raja* or "royal" yoga.

*Hatha Yoga* is a system of rigorous physical practices accompanying meditation and designed to achieve the goals of royal yoga. *Ha* or "sun" refers to the "breath" that circulates through the upper half of the body, and *tha* or "moon" refers to the "breath" that circulates from the abdomen to the feet. Thus the yogi strives to coordinate the life forces in the body. Also involved is an ancient theory of the human self that teaches that there are channels (*nadi*) running from the base of the torso to the head, and that there are centers of energy (*chakra*) from the base of the spine to the top of the head. Although these channels and centers cannot be discovered by a surgeon, they are considered more real than the physical body. They represent within the body real cosmic forces that the yogi can activate through Tantric practices. One important method for doing this is the use of mantras, or sacred words and phrases full of spiritual power. The practice of yoga is believed to arouse the dormant energy latent in the individual and make it move upward along the central channel through the various *chakras*.

*Kundalini Yoga* is the term used in Tantric meditation to describe the awakening of the dormant energy. This energy is known as *kundalini* or "serpent power" because it is pictured as coiled at the base of the central channel. There it rests in the lowest *chakra*, situated between the genitals and the anus. When it is awakened it rushes upward like lightning to the highest *chakra* within the brain and causes a state of complete absorption in the experience (samadhi). The person thus gains "liberation." Tantric yoga differs from other forms of yoga in that it does not reject or renounce sensuous experiences. Instead it places great emphasis on them and is in sharp contrast to the ascetic life-style.

A side effect of awakening the *kundalini* is the generation of paranormal powers. These powers are quite dangerous. Anyone not meditating under the supervision of a qualified guru may be harmed, and even a competent yogi may find them so distracting as to interfere with the true goal—liberation.

*The Self-Realization Fellowship.* Yoga was introduced to North America in 1920 by a gifted and dynamic teacher named Mukunda Lal Ghosh, who was born near Calcutta in 1893. He took as his religious name Paramahansa (that is, Master Yogi) Yogananda. His life and teachings have become well known through his informative and highly readable book, *The Autobiography of a Yogi*, which is distributed by the Self-Realization Fellowship.

Lively and enthusiastic as a boy, he visited a great number of holy men, many of whom could perform paranormal acts that impressed their followers. He recounts these experiences in his book, including his encounter with a holy woman who had solved the perennial problem of the food chain by being able to draw nourishment directly from the air without any need of photosynthesis or other material process. He finally chose as his master the family guru, who had been instructed by another guru from a long line of gurus, beginning with one who had been living in the Himalayas for many centuries.

After coming to America, Yogananda quickly gathered a following. His teachings combine the traditional *kundalini* beliefs and practices with a variety of other ways of thought. One of his concerns was to demonstrate the universal validity of yoga philosophy. He borrowed heavily from the vocabulary of modern science and of Christianity, and taught that Jesus, Paul, and other spiritual masters throughout the ages had essentially the same message that he proclaimed.

The technique he used was termed *kriya* ("applied") yoga. By meditation, yogic exercises, and the use of the powerful syllable "Om" the practitioner can concentrate his or her own life-energy and draw it away from outward concerns to spiritual centers within. In the opposite of the upward movement of the *kundalini* energy, the brain serves as the source of power and sends power coursing downward to open up the *chakras*. If rightly done, this action enables the individual to speed up the course of evolution and perhaps even control death.

Branches of the Fellowship, called Churches of all Religions, exist in many countries, including India. California has about a fourth of the branches in the United States. There are two classes of members, laity and more advanced members called renunciants. Worship services are simple and low key. Christian scriptures are used, along with the Bhagavad Gita and Yogananda's writings.

Yogananda died in the United States in 1952. It is reported that his body remained incorruptible until his casket was closed for the last time, twenty days after his death.

*The International Sivananda Yoga Society.* Named for a prominent modern teacher of yoga (Sivananda) in India, this movement was brought to the United States in the early 1960s by Swami Vishnu-Devananda. He is described as an extrovert and is the first yoga teacher to be licensed as an airplane pilot. His specialty is hatha yoga (described above).

The most striking feature of yogic practice is the control that can be achieved over the body and its normal functions. The lungs, heart, and other internal organs can be subjected to the will of the yogi, and physical health can be enhanced. Claims of paranormal powers, however, have not been verified. Powers of levitation, if demonstrated, would probably convince skeptics. Such claims are part of the Indian tradition that austerity can create power so great that an ascetic can threaten even the gods. Also a part of the tradition is the belief that mystical experience itself is the supreme goal of religion, far more important than the worship of supernatural beings.                                                    K.C.

**YOM KIPPUR.** *See* DAY OF ATONEMENT.

**YOUNG, BRIGHAM** (1801–77). The second president of the Mormon church and colonizer of Utah was born June 1 in Whitingham, Vermont, to John and Abigail Howe Young. When Brigham was three, they moved to New York's "burned-over district." With little education, he became a house painter and glazier. At twenty-two Young joined the Methodist church, but when *The Book of Mormon* appeared, he studied it for two years before being baptized in 1832. In July 1833 he led a group to Kirtland, Ohio, where in 1834 he married Mary Ann Angell. Later they led "Zion's Army" to Missouri.

In February 1835 he became third in seniority among the quorum of the Twelve Apostles and in 1838 its senior member. He later directed the group's removal to Nauvoo, Illinois, where he acted as chief financial officer. Following JOSEPH SMITH's murder, he was elected president in 1847. He led the exodus to the Great Salt Lake Valley, founding Deseret. A colonizing genius, Young scientifically planned the cities and sent colonists into every fertile valley with specialists to ensure viable communities. A Perpetual Emigration Fund helped settle immigrants converted by the Mormon missionaries. He had little interest in theology, confined church power to the ruling oligarchy, and stifled charismatic tendencies. When Congress passed the Utah Territory Act in 1850, Young became its first governor.

N.H.

**YOUTH FOR CHRIST INTERNATIONAL.** An interdenominational organization that specializes in teenage evangelism. Youth for Christ began in the United States during the large youth rallies of the early 1940s, and was organized in 1945. It soon spread rapidly to foreign countries. It now ministers in fifty-four nations. Its major emphases are (1) Saturday night youth rallies conducted to instill commitment to Christ; (2) on-campus activities designed to help teenagers reach their peers; (3) national youth magazines and other literature aimed at both Christian evangelism and growth; (4) Lifeline ministries to delinquents; (5) leadership training in evangelism methods; (6) overseas outreaches by teen teams; and (7) camps and conventions. Its headquarters is in Wheaton, Illinois.

W.G.

**YUGA.** In Hinduism "an age," an extremely long period of time, part of a vast calendar of time on a cosmic scale. The concept can be traced back to the Vedic period (about 1000–600 B.C.) and was developed in later periods. Four *yugas* covering more than five million human years are believed to be at the center of a complex system of rendering time. It is linear, since it moves forward, but it is also circular, as eventually the universe will dissolve and the whole cycle will begin over again.

The system involves two Hindu deities: BRAHMA, whose lifetime is the same length as created time, and VISHNU, who descends to earth in various forms. It is also believed that each of the *yugas* is shorter and less virtuous than the one before it. The present age, the Kali Yuga, last of the four, is 420,000 human years in length and is the most wicked of all. Humans are morally too weak to live virtuously without the restraints of law.

K.C.

**ZACCHAEUS.** According to Luke 19:1-10, a man from Jericho who followed Jesus, after showing his deep interest in Jesus by climbing up into a sycamore tree to see his entry into the town. Zacchaeus (whose name means "pure") is said to have been a short man who could not see Jesus over the heads of the crowd. He was a tax collector of Jericho, who had become wealthy through his profession. Apparently, his conscience troubled him, and he was looking for the power of forgiveness to change his life. Jesus recognized this and invited himself to Zacchaeus' house. At dinner, Zacchaeus was converted and declared that any unjust gains he had made would be repaid with interest.

J.C.

**ZADOKITE FRAGMENTS.** The fragments of two medieval copies of a Jewish sectarian manual, written in Hebrew, discovered in the Ibn-Ezra Synagogue in the old city of Cairo, Egypt, during 1896–97. These fragments describe a Jewish sect that leaves Judea and goes to Damascus and there enters into a new covenant. This may be symbolic of the group's leaving orthodox Judaism. Solomon Schechter, a Jewish scholar and educator, edited these fragments in 1910 and named them the Zadokite Fragments because he believed them to be from a Zadok book. However, later, some other portions of the same work were found at the monastery at

Qumran, near where the Dead Sea Scrolls were found. Now scholars believe the work arose out of the same monastic, apocalyptic sect that produced the Manual of Discipline and the Book of the War of the Sons of Light and the Sons of Darkness. While this Qumran group is often called the ESSENES (who are described in Josephus), there is no certainty that these celibate sectarians, who looked for two messiahs, were Essenes. The Zadokite Fragments are now generally called the Damascus Document fragments. The contents of the document are rules for living and reflections on the history of the group.

J.C.

**ZADOK THE PRIEST.** The high priest of Israel during the reign of King David. Zadok lived in Jerusalem during the monarchies of David and Solomon and first shared priestly rank with Abiathar, but, because of his loyalty to Solomon as heir to the throne, became chief priest (I Kings 2:35).

Zadok was the father of Ahimaaz and Jerushah and the grandfather of Jotham (II Sam. 18:19 ff.; II Kings 15:32-33). Zadok played a role in protecting David's throne during Absalom's rebellion, guarding the ark (II Sam. 15:24 ff.). On Absalom's death, Zadok supported Solomon and anointed him as king. He was awarded with preeminence among the priests, a rank and privilege held by his descendants for centuries. Zadok's descendants were numerous and highly placed in the restored Temple after the return from Babylonian exile (I Chr. 24:2 ff.; 27:17; 29:22). Indeed, the prophet of the Exile, Ezekiel, believed that Zadok's descendants were the only legitimate priests (Ezek. 40:46; 43:19; 44:15; 48:11).

Zadok was also the name of four men in Jerusalem during the time of Nehemiah. Ezra 7:25 and Nehemiah 11:11 also mention a high priest named Zadok.                                                                                   J.C.

**ZARATHUSTRA.** *See* ZOROASTRIANISM.

**ZAREPHATH.** A Phoenician city controlled by the city-state of Sidon, where Elijah stayed with a widow during a famine and raised her son from the dead (I Kings 17:8 ff.). Zarephath was located on the coast of Lebanon eight miles south of Saida. It had two harbors. The prophet Obadiah (v. 20) spoke of Zarephath as the northern boundary of the restored kingdom.                                                                          J.C.

**ZARETHAN.** A city in the Jordan Valley near where the Israelites under Joshua crossed the Jordan River "on dry foot" (Josh. 3:16). The description in I Kings 4:12 indicates that it was not far from Beth-shean. It was at Zarethan that Hiram, Solomon's artificer, cast the bronze vessels for Solomon's Temple (I Kings 7:45-46). The site of Zarethan is not absolutely known, but it is thought to be one mile east of the Jordan halfway between the Dead Sea and the Sea of Galilee.                                                                      J.C.

**ZAYDIYYA.** One of the three main branches of the Shi'a in ISLAM; important in Yemen to the present day. Like all SHI'ITES, the Zaydites consider the first three caliphs inferior to Ali. Ali's sons, al-Hasan and al-Husayn, are regarded as imams (religious heirs of MUHAMMAD'S authority). Zaydites differ from other Shi'ites in their support of the revolt led by Zayd ibn Ali, al-Husayn's grandson, in the city of Kufa in A.D. 739. They believe that it is not necessary to have an imam in every age, and they reject the principles of "clear designation" and "infallibility" as prerequisites for being an imam.

The Zaydiyya early divided into two groups, the compromisers and the revolutionaries. The compromisers, unlike all other Shi'ites, consider the first two caliphs legitimate, although inferior to Ali. Thus they tried to find a compromise between the Shi'a and the Sunnis, who acknowledge all the first four caliphs. This branch died out after the ninth century A.D. The revolutionary Zaydiyya are more like other Shi'ites, and their only connection with the compromisers is their shared name. The revolutionaries hold that all who did not acknowledge the imamate of Ali became unbelievers.                                                              K./M.C.

**ZEALOTS.** Members of the several sects of Jews in the first century A.D. that Josephus called "the fourth philosophy," distinguishing them from the Pharisees, Sadducees, and Essenes. The Zealots were Jewish patriots who deeply resented foreign domination of their country. In the first century A.D. that was the Roman Empire. It was unlikely that the Zealots were fanatics or guerrilla fighters, although such people and groups existed. Judas of Galilee revolted against Rome when Quirinius, governor of Syria, began a census of the Jews. John of Gischala terrorized the territory in A.D. 66 and that resulted in the tragic Roman-Jewish war of A.D. 67-70.

One of Jesus' disciples, Simon, is called the Zealot in Luke 6:15 and Acts 1:13, but is called the Cananaean in Matthew 10:4 and Mark 3:18. Probably this distinguishing title is given to keep him from being confused with Simon Peter.                                  J.C.

**ZEBAH AND ZALMUNNA.** Kings of Midian who were pursued beyond the Jordan by Gideon (Judg. 8:4-28). Gideon captured them in a surprise raid east of Nabah and executed them at Succoth (Judg. 8:21). This caused the Israelites to offer Gideon a kingship over them, but he refused it (Judg. 8:23).                                                                                    J.C.

**ZEBEDEE.** The father of James and John, two of Jesus' twelve apostles (Matt. 4:21; Mark 3:17). Zebedee, whose name means "Yahweh has given," was married to Salome (Mark 15:40; Matt. 27:56). Zebedee was a fisherman with his sons and many hired workers. Jesus, setting out on his ministry, called James and John to follow him, and they did. There is no further information about Zebedee in the NT.
                                                                                                J.C.

**ZEBULUN.** The sixth son of Leah and Jacob; Jacob's tenth son. Zebulun was a full brother to Reuben, Simeon, Levi, Judah, and Issachar (Gen. 30:20; 35:23). He had three sons: Sered, Elon, and Jahleel (Gen. 46:14), who went into Egypt with the tribes of Jacob while Joseph was prime minister there. The tribe of Zebulun was allotted territory in Canaan (Gen. 49:13) near Sidon, including a part of the Plain of Esdraelon and the region of the later village of Nazareth. The important "way of the sea" commercial route ran through Zebulun's territory. Many of the tribe were carried into Assyrian captivity and lost to history.                                                                              J.C.

**ZECHARIAH, BOOK OF.** One of the Minor Prophets in the OT; the eleventh in the "Book of the Twelve." Zechariah's ministry (about 520 B.C.) was contemporaneous with HAGGAI, but is reflected only in chapters 1–8 (First Zechariah). Chapters 9–14 represent a much later time, the third century B.C. (Second Zechariah).

Both Haggai and First Zechariah deal with the Jews in Jerusalem under DARIUS, emperor of Persia. Conditions were unsettled, and the Temple reconstruction begun by the returned exiles was at a standstill (Hag. 2:6-9; Zech. 2:6 ff.; 6:15; 8:9).

Haggai and First Zechariah urged the people to complete the Temple, with Zechariah's preaching occurring around 520–518 B.C., over a two-year period (Zech. 1:1; 7:1). This reconstruction must be accompanied by repentance on the part of the Jews, Zechariah declared. Much of his message seems influenced by Ezekiel, although First Zechariah shows his later development of doctrine by speaking of angels, in terms similar to the princpalities and powers of Paul. These angels control the fate of human groups. Both Haggai and First Zechariah held messianic beliefs, and both prophets supported the Jewish governor (a descendant of David), Zerubbabel, as the Messiah (Hag. 2:23; Zech. 6:9-15). These pretensions were discovered by the Persians, and Zerubbabel disappeared from history. A non-Jew was then made governor in Judah. The Temple restoration was allowed by the authorities, and it was completed in 515 B.C. The renewing of the Temple cultus was one of Zechariah's major concerns.

First Zechariah was an apocalyptic visionary, who recorded his calls for repentance in a series of eight highly imaginative visions. These include the vision of the horseman (1:7-17); the four horns and four smiths (1:18-21); the measuring line (2:1-5); the high priest, Joshua, clad in filthy clothes (3:1-10); the candlestick and the olive trees (4:1-3); the flying scroll (5:1-4); the woman inside a basket (5:5-11); and the four chariots (6:1-8).

In chapter 6, Zechariah's coronation of Zerubbabel as the Messiah is recorded. Some scholars believe that originally the text said Joshua, the high priest, was recognized as the Messiah. The passage seems to be corrupt either through accident or censorship.

Chapters 9–14 (Second Zechariah) come from the time of Alexander the Great's Hellenistic empire. The oracles or messages of some unknown prophets were attached to Zechariah by the editors of the OT books. Three prophetic sections were added, two to Zechariah and one entitled Malachi (1:1). Second Zechariah consists of prophecies on the coming of the Greeks (chap. 9); the restoration of Israel to the land (chap. 10); a parable of the shepherds (chap. 11); and a series on Israel's promised future (chaps. 12–14). Much of the material here is apocalyptic and has heavily influenced Christian eschatology. Some of these ideas were used by the Gospel writers to underscore the belief in Jesus' messiahship. From Zechariah 11:12, Matthew drew the prophecy that the Christ would be betrayed for thirty pieces of silver.                                      J.C.

**ZEDEKIAH.** The name of four men in the OT, chief of whom was the last king of Judah, reigning 597-587 B.C. The other men of this name were (1) one of Ahab's four hundred court prophets, who was burned because of blasphemies and crimes (I Kings 22:11, 24; II Chr. 18:10-23); (2) a prophet who was deported to Babylon and who also was executed (II Kings 24:12-16; Jer. 29:21-23); and (3) a prince in the time of Jehoiakim, king of Judah (Jer. 36:12).

Zedekiah's reign is extensively recorded in II Kings 24–25; II Chronicles 36; and Jeremiah 39 and 52, as well as in some passages in Ezekiel (chaps. 17 and 19). He was the son of King Josiah and became king after his older brothers and nephew, Jehoahaz II, Jehoiakim, and Jehoiachin had briefly occupied the throne. When the Babylonians conquered Jerusalem in 597 B.C., the king, Jehoiachin, was deported to Babylon (Jer. 27:20; II Kings 25:27; Ezek. 1:2) and Zedekiah was made a puppet king (Jer. 37:11). His name was changed from Mattania to Zedekiah, and he was forced to swear loyalty to Nebuchadnezzar. He violated this oath and the Babylonians returned to attack Jerusalem again. In 587 B.C., the city was captured and destroyed. Zedekiah was carried before the Babylonian king. His sons were murdered before his eyes; he was then blinded and taken to Babylon in chains (Jer. 39:1-5; II Kings 24:17-20; 25:1-7; II Chr. 36:11-21; Jer. 39:6-14; 52:11).        J.C.

**ZEN.** A form of Mahayana BUDDHISM that arose in China sometime around A.D. 500 and spread to Korea and Japan. It developed into the form in which it is best known in the West today around the eighteenth century in Japan. The name is derived from the Sanskrit word *dhyana* ("meditation") by way of the Chinese name for the sect, Ch'an.

*Early History.* Although traditions teach that there was a long line of Zen patriarchs before the time of Bodhidharma, he is the first that is clearly identifiable. The stories about him are largely legendary, but they indicate that he arrived in Canton, China around A.D. 520. He is said to have sat before a wall for nine years, deep in meditation. A would-be disciple, desperate to catch Bodhidharma's attention, cut off his own arm. Seeing this, the master accepted him as a disciple. Another story, often depicted in art, relates that Bodhidharma crossed the Yangtze River standing on a single reed. Black ink paintings show him with fierce eyes and stern face.

During this early period Buddhism was influenced by TAOISM, and the two religions were regarded as nearly identical, though in time the differences became clear. Zen shows many signs of Taoist influence. While other Buddhist schools stressed ultimate reality, Zen placed primary emphasis on mind. Zen taught that NIRVANA is identical with the original Buddha mind or Buddha nature, and that this nature is in everyone. Therefore it is possible to see one's nature and as a result to become Buddha. Reading scriptures, reciting the name of Buddha, joining the monastic order, and other religious practices are unnecessary. This teaching led in time to such extreme statements as, "If you meet the Buddha, kill him." That is, the Buddha is no help toward enlightenment, but is only a hindrance. It all depends on the individual.

The most significant early Zen document is the Platform Scripture. It relates the story of how a simple country boy from southern China, Hui-neng, perceived the true nature of Buddhism, to the amazement of the then patriarch, who at once chose him as his successor. The succession was passed in secret, and this secrecy resulted in a dispute between followers of Hui-neng and a rival claimant. Separate schools in the north and the south of China were the result.

*Medieval China.* During the T'ang dynasty, A.D. 618-907, Buddhism gained its greatest influence, but also met with fierce opposition from the government. Monasteries had accumulated power and wealth, arousing both envy and greed. Zen monks fared better than those of other orders because they worked with their own hands and thus earned the respect of the people. Several schools of Zen thought and practice developed in this period. The two schools that have been dominant to the present, especially in Japan, are the Lin-chi (Rinzai), and the Ts'ao-t'ung (Soto). Rinzai is known for its use of the koan (see below) and for *zazen,* sitting in silent meditation.

*Features of Zen Life.* A *roshi,* or Zen teacher, is responsible for guiding a novice to enlightenment (satori). In formal interviews the teacher seeks to help the novice break free of conventional thinking and suddenly awaken to one's own true nature, the Buddha mind. The teacher might use slaps, shouts, symbolic and enigmatic actions, and traditional sayings, or koans. A koan might be a classic saying from ancient China, or a contemporary question to which there is either no one correct answer, or at best a seemingly illogical one. This illustrates the inadequacy of ordinary thought processes in the search for enlightenment. One famous koan is: "What is the meaning of the coming of Bodhidharma from the West? The cypress tree is in the garden." And another is: "What is the pure Dharmakaya (Buddha as absolute reality)? The hedge around the privy."

Monastic life is carefully regulated. "Meditation in movement has a thousand times more value than meditation in stillness," is a traditional statement. The movements of the monk include such things as the daily routine of rising, washing, and using the toilet, gathering for morning services, chanting scriptures, cooking food, waiting on tables, cleaning the garden, begging in the streets, and visiting in the homes of the laity.

*Zen in Japan.* Although Buddhism was introduced to Japan in A.D. 552, Zen did not become a major influence until the Kamakura period (1185–1333). Features of other sects were often included in Zen practice. One example is the repeated chanting of the name of Buddha (*nembutsu*). Zen became popular among the ruling class, especially the samurai, and had patriotic overtones well into modern times.

After a period of decline, Zen was revived by Hakuin Ekaku (1685–1768), a Rinzai monk. He is greatly admired for his calligraphy and his painting in black ink, a distinctive Zen style. He wrote about his enlightenment experiences and gave new vitality to the use of the koan in discipline and training.

Zen exerted strong influence on a number of distinctive features of Japanese culture. One of these is the tea ceremony. The preparation and the drinking of tea take place in a refined and formal setting of simple beauty. A rustic hut in a carefully planned garden, special teapots and bowls, special instruments, all add to the charm of the ceremony and help create an atmosphere of calm contemplation. Each step of the ceremony has its tradition and its significance.

The form of Japanese poetry most widely known and most imitated in other countries, the haiku, is closely associated with Zen, and many of the greatest poets have been monks. A haiku consists of seventeen "sound units" (roughly equivalent to seventeen syllables) arranged in three lines of 5, 7, 5 units. The haiku has been described as Zen directed to certain selected natural phenomena, the simple, often overlooked things of everyday life. War, sex, harmful plants, hostile animals, floods, plagues, and earthquakes are omitted as being menacing to human life. By contrast, sunrise and sunset, plum blossoms, rain, a lake, the autumn full moon, stubble in a cold rice field, signs of the Buddha's presence in the world of nature, are typical themes in the poetry of Basho (1644-94), one of the greatest writers of haiku.

*Zen in the Modern World.* Because of its close connection with the warrior class in Japan, Zen declined after World War II, while new religions and new sects of Buddhism dominated the popular religious scene. It is, however, too distinctively Japanese a form of religion, too deeply spiritual, too sublimely aesthetic ever to vanish entirely, and it has regained vitality. Propagated by creative teachers, it attained considerable popularity in the United States, and a number of Zen monasteries were built here. Writers have drawn parallels between Zen and aspects of Roman Catholic spirituality. Most of those interested in Zen have preferred its gentler features connected with its view of life and have not undertaken the rigid monastic way of life with its austere discipline and its slaps and beatings.

K.C.

## ZEPHANIAH, BOOK OF.

Zephaniah, son of Cushi, was a descendant of King Hezekiah, and was probably a citizen of Jerusalem. His prophetic ministry can only be located historically by conjecture, but it is likely that he preached before the sweeping religious reforms of King JOSIAH (622 B.C.) occasioned by the discovery of the Deuteronomic code during the remodeling of the Temple. This would make Zephaniah a contemporary of the young Jeremiah (about 630–625 B.C.). His book is ninth in the "Book of the Twelve," the shorter writing or Minor Prophets.

Zephaniah is full of harsh judgments on the syncretistic and morally corrupt religious life of Jerusalem. He declares God's judgment on the whole world (1:2 ff.), but specifically on Jerusalem and

Judah (1:4–2:3). Jerusalem is condemned for mixing the worship of Yahweh and false gods and for social evils and the mistreatment of the poor (1:7-13). Zephaniah calls for repentance before the soon to come Day of Yahweh's Wrath.

He goes on to pronounce judgment on the surrounding nations, including Assyria (2:4-5). Then his text returns to more judgments on Jerusalem (3:1-13). The people's apostasy from true worship and their rejection of God's prophets (3:5-7) mean defeat for Judah but ultimately restoration in the faithful remnant (3:11-13). For Zephaniah, doom for Jerusalem was certain, yet he praises the Lord for overthrowing enemies and for ultimately redeeming the people. Zephaniah's book, however, remains one of the darkest—and clearest—expressions of the terrible Day of God's Wrath (1:14-18) that awaited Judah. Zephaniah went beyond Amos and First Isaiah, and visualized the Day of Yahweh as the final judgment of the world. In his view, God's patience has been stretched to the limit, and the long delayed and fully deserved punishment of a disobedient people was about to come. Because of this strong emphasis on judgment, some scholars believe the notes of hope, especially that of the righteous remnant (3:13), were added in later times.          J.C.

**ZERUBBABEL.** The grandson of Jehoiakim, who was carried into Babylonian exile as a prisoner, although a well-treated one. Zerubbabel (whose name means "offspring of Babylon") was son of Shealtiel (Ezra 3:2, 8; Hag. 1:1) and was rightly king of Judah. He was permitted to return to Jerusalem by the liberal policies of Cyrus the Great upon the defeat of Babylon by Persia (539 B.C.). Returning with the first band, Zerubbabel and Joshua, the high priest, set up an altar and began the sacrificial cultus in the ruins of the Temple, observed the Feast of Tabernacles, and began planning the rebuilding of the Temple (Ezra 3).

Opposition from the Samaritans and the local Jews brought on a period when nothing was done to restore the Temple. The preaching of Haggai and the First Zechariah in 520–518 B.C. inspired the people to complete the Temple by 515 B.C. During this time Zerubbabel was the Persian governor of Jerusalem. Both Haggai and First Zechariah declared Zerubbabel to be the Messiah, the Davidic king promised of old. However, the Persians apparently removed Zerubbabel, and Joshua, the high priest, became the leading Jewish authority, with temporal power in Persian hands. The second Temple is, nonetheless, often called Zerubbabel's Temple.          J.C.

**ZEUS.** Chief god of the ancient Greek pantheon, father of Apollo, Artemis, Athena, Hermes, Ares, Dionysus, and several demigods. His father was Cronus, king of the Titans and son of Heaven (Uranus) and Earth (Ge). According to one myth, Cronus swallowed his children for fear of being dethroned, but Zeus was saved by his mother, Rhea. Zeus later overthrew the Titans, took control of the heavens, and ruled over the sky and the weather. He assigned the underworld to his brother Hades, and the sea to his brother Poseidon. Zeus was the god of justice and the protector of property and strangers, but his power was universal, while other gods, such as Athena, were locally of greater importance.

Zeus had oracles at Dodona in Epirus, at Olympia, and at the oasis of Siwas in Libya. His great festivals were the Dipolieia, the Pandia, or the festival of "All Zeus," and the Diasia, which celebrated Zeus Meilichios, an early fertility god.

Courtesy of Bildarchiv Preussischer Kulturbesitz

*The West Front of the Altar of Zeus at Pergamum (restored)*

Zeus was famous in legend for his love affairs with mortal women. He probably became identified with heroes of pre-Hellenic cults, and in many legends he took the form of an animal such as the bull. His infidelity and promiscuity presented an ethical dilemma for later Greeks.

K./M.C.

**ZIDON.** *See* SIDON.

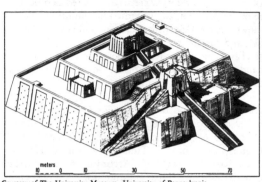

Courtesy of The University Museum, University of Pennsylvania

*Isometric projection of the ziggurat of Ur-Nammu (restored)*

**ZIGGURAT.** Square-based, stepped towers used as temples in ancient Mesopotamia. Ziggurats had no interior rooms but possessed exterior stairways or ramps. As exemplified by the famous Hanging Gardens of Babylon, the terraces were often landscaped. The largest were over three hundred square feet and perhaps approached two hundred feet in height. They obviously represent artificial mountains, created for deities worshiped on high peaks before their devotees moved to the flat plains of the Valley of the Two Rivers.

R.E.

**ZIMRI.** The descendant of King Saul mentioned in I Chronicles 9:36-42. Zimri is said to be the father of Moza. There are four other men named Zimri in the OT, including a chariot captain who killed King Elah and became king of Israel for seven days (I Kings 16:8-10; 15). He was killed by Omri, who became king.

J.C.

**ZIN, WILDERNESS OF.** One of four distinct wilderness regions of the SINAI Peninsula that should not be confused with another region, the wilderness of Sin. Zin is located to the south and west of the Dead Sea, directly across the Arabah (or Wadi) from Edom. The oasis of Kadesh-barnea was located at the edge of this desolate region (Josh. 15:1; Num. 33:36; 34:3). Moses sent spies into Canaan through this wilderness area (Num. 13:21). Perhaps the most famous biblical event there was the murmuring (or complaining) of the Israelites against Yahweh while passing through the hardships of the wilderness of Zin (Num. 27:14).

J.C.

**ZINZENDORF, COUNT NICHOLAS LUDWIG VON** (1700–60). The founder of the MORAVIANS was born May 26 in Dresden, Germany. His maternal grandmother, Henriette von Gersdorf, was a friend of Jakob Spener, who became the boy's godfather. A brilliant pupil at Halle from 1710 to 1716, Zinzendorf attracted attention from Pietist August Francke. Zinzendorf had begun to seek God at age four, and by age ten he founded the Order of the Mustard Seed, which eventually numbered such men as the archbishop of Canterbury and General James Oglethorpe among its members.

In 1722 Zinzendorf inherited a small estate at Beethelsdorf, Saxony, from his grandmother, which housed a party of refugees from Bohemia or Moravia led by Christian David. In 1727 the Brotherly Agreement of Herrnhut established an ecumenical community. To stop growing citicism of their work, Zinzendorf was ordained as an orthodox Lutheran pastor in 1734. However in 1736 Saxony banished them from the estate; they did not return until 1747. In 1737 they consecrated Zinzendorf bishop in order to give him more authority in his missionary journeys to Holland, the Baltics, the West Indies, England, and finally to America (1741–43). Zinzendorf, author of such hymns as "Jesus, Thy Blood and Righteousness," "O Thou, to Whose All-Searching Sight," and "Jesus, Still Lead On," was buried in Herrnhut.

N.H.

**ZION.** The rock outcropping at the southern tip of the ridge between the Kidron and Tyropoeon valleys in Jerusalem. This rock, now covered by the mosque of Omar, supposedly was the site of Abraham's attempted sacrifice of Isaac and, later, of Mohammed's ascent into heaven. On this rock David set up an altar of sacrifice, and Solomon built Yahweh's Temple. The second Temple, reared by Ezra and Nehemiah, and beautified by Herod the Great in Jesus' time, also stood on Mount Zion. As the city of Jerusalem grew, the entire eastern ridge (David's city) was called Zion, and later the whole old city of Jerusalem became known as Zion, the City of God.

J.C.

**ZION, DAUGHTER OF.** A term referring to Jerusalem and to Judah (or Israel, in the broad sense); the people of the Mosaic Covenant and believers in the Royal Covenant theology that developed in Jerusalem from the time of Nathan the prophet to the First Isaiah. According to this theological view, Jerusalem was sacred to Yahweh, and most especially the southern tip of the ridge between the Kidron and the Tyropoeon Valley, at the top of which stood Zion (or "Citadel"), the ancient rock outcropping called Mount Moriah. On this ancient natural-rock threshing floor, David built an altar of sacrifice and Solomon later built the Temple.

This royal David theology further held that God would never allow David's kingly line to fail—there would always be a king descended from him on the throne in Jerusalem. Since Zion, even in relatively ancient times, formed only a small portion of the city of Jerusalem, the city (and by extension, the nation and the people of the Jews) came to be called the Daughter of Zion. J.C.

**ZIONISM.** The belief in the restoration of the Jewish people to Zion, the poetic name for both Jerusalem and the land of Israel. The wish to return to Zion has been a part of Jewish prayers for centuries.

Political Zionism, first promulgated by THEODOR HERZL in 1897, aimed to create for the Jewish people a home in Palestine secured by public law. After more than half a century, in 1948, the State of Israel was established.

Cultural Zionism saw Palestine as a "spiritual center" from which would come new cultural influences to revive the spirit of the Jewish people outside the Promised Land. The founder of cultural Zionism was Ahad Ha'Am.

Labor Zionism, promoted by Aaron David Gordon, emphasized the importance of the return of the Jewish people to the soil. Gordon believed that the Jewish people could be "reborn" through the reeducation and moral conduct of the Jewish individual and through love of the soil of the Holy Land, or work, and of one's fellow human beings.

Religious Zionism projected a concept of religious nationalism, which asserted that "the thought-image of Jewish nationality lay in the unity of the Jewish people with its Torah and its faith." L.K.

**ZOAN.** The capital of the Twenty-first Dynasty of Egypt, situated on the northeast frontier of Egypt on the Tanaitic branch of the Nile River and northeast of Cairo. Known as Tanis in Greek, this area was the dwelling place of the Hebrews during their sojourn in Egypt. It may be that Zoan-Tanis is the same city as Avaris and the biblical Rameses. J.C.

**ZOAR.** One of the five cities of the plain known to Lot in Genesis 19:20-23, situated on the east side of the Dead Sea. Zoar was a city in Moab during the eighth century B.C. and was mentioned by Isaiah (15:5) and Jeremiah (48:34). In the Christian Era, Zoar's site was moved to the southern end of the Dead Sea. The original site may be below the present Dead Sea. J.C.

**ZOHAR, THE.** In Hebrew, the Zohar means "the [Book of] Splendor." It is not a book so much as a collection of Jewish occult literature; the major deposit of writings on the KABBALAH. Throughout history, the Zohar has had many names, including Midrash ha-Zohar, Midrash Yehi Or, and the Menorat Ha-ma'or.

The Zohar is a collection of several books, each of which contains short midrashic statements, long sermons, and miscellaneous discussions. Most of these writings are said to be teachings of Simeon ben Yohai and his colleagues. The printed version consists of five books, three under the name Sefer ha-Zohar al ha-Torah; one is entitled Tikunei ha-Zohar, and one is called Zohar Hadash. The books are unified around the fiction that Simeon ben Yohai and his companions (ten men in all) are joined together in study and discussion. The writings purport to come from Palestine, but scholars declare that internal evidence shows they arose in Spain. J.C.

**ZOROASTRIANISM.** The religion of ancient Iran ("land of the Aryans") from soon after the Aryan migrations from central Asian down to the Islamic conquest (A.D. 651). Today there are only about 150,000 followers, of whom 120,000 live in and around Bombay, India.

*History.* There are many different accounts of the history of Zoroastrianism, and because of lack of adequate data any history of the religion must be regarded with some skepticism. "Zoroaster" is the Greek form of the name "Zarathustra" or "Zarathushtra," a prophet of Iran. Some time around 600 B.C. seems the probable date of his birth, based on linguistic evidence, but some scholars place him as early as 1200–1500 B.C.

Zoroaster was a reformer who abolished some of the more distasteful aspects of Indo-Aryan religious practice and established a new morality, details of which are not clear. His influence spread slowly throughout Iran, probably during the sixth through the fourth centuries B.C. He left behind a collection of hymns, the AVESTA, which was gradually expanded and constantly edited until the Islamic conquest. Related languages of the area around the Aral Sea are Modern Afghan and Sogdian, in which Buddhist and Manichaean texts are still preserved today.

Zoroastrian contact with the Middle East began under the West Iranian Achaemenid dynasty, founded by Cyrus in 550 B.C. (see II Chr. 36:22). His successors expanded westward, coming into contact and conflict with Babylonians, Assyrians, Egyptians, and Greeks. The Jews, who had been conquered by Babylonia, welcomed the coming of the Persians and prospered under their rule. At that time, what we call Zoroastrianism was the official religion of the empire, but Zoroaster was rarely mentioned. Devotion centered around AHURA MAZDA (the "Wise Lord"), but included a host of nature and tribal deities. Most likely, popular religion was little changed from the original beliefs of the Iranians. This period of rich cross-fertilization with ancient empires hopelessly muddled the picture of Iranian religion. Further interchange came after 331 B.C. with the conquest of Iran by Alexander the Great (356–323 B.C.). The Parthians (a west Iranian tribe) regained their independence and reasserted Zoroastrianism under the Arsacid dynasty (250 B.C.–A.D. 226). During this time there was extensive contact with Rome. Mithraism, a Zoroastrian cult, became for a time as popular as Christianity within the Roman Empire. During the Sassanian dynasty (A.D. 226–651) the figure of Zoroaster gained greater importance in the official religion. The rulers fought against the inroads of Christianity and Manichaeism. Iran fell to Arabian armies in 651, and most Zoroastrians converted to Islam. Although officially regarded as "People of the Book," Zoroastrians were not treated as well as Jews or Christians. Perhaps Zoroastrians seemed more dualistic because of the position they gave to the powerful evil spirit Ahriman, or perhaps their tradition was further removed from Islam than either Judaism or Christianity. In any case Zoroastrianism declined precipitously.

A great exodus to India began in the eighth century, but some few Zoroastrians remained in remote villages in Iran. Official persecution ended in the 1920s under the Pahlavi dynasty, and Zoroastrians flourished. Many moved to Tehran and other cities, and their numbers increased to about twenty thousand. Like other religious minorities they have suffered under the Islamic republic.

In India Zoroastrians cluster around Bombay in the Gujarat region, where they are successful businessmen and merchants. Due to their wealth they enjoy influence out of proportion to their numbers and consequently are resented by their less wealthy neighbors. Overseas, large communities live in London and Toronto.

*Beliefs and Practices.* The practices of the Iranian Zoroastrians (known as Gabars) and those in India (Parsis) differ, due to their long separation. In addition, differences of calendar split the Parsis into two groups. Common characteristics include, first of all, the use of the Avesta and its commentary, the Zand. Central symbols in Zoroastrian practice are fire and binding. Fire symbolizes life, royalty, truth, and justice, and all fire is regarded as sacred. Initiates are given a sacred shirt and sacred belt, which they wear at all times except when bathing. This is similar to the sacred thread worn by high caste Hindus. Bride and groom are ceremonially bound together at their wedding. Sacred fires are maintained in fire temples. Since, however, Zoroastrians form communities but not congregations, they do not gather together at these temples. The Zoroastrian concept of the nimbus of fire around royal or holy people spread into Buddhism, Christianity, and Islam. The dead are ceremonially cleansed, clothed with their sacred shirt and belt, and exposed to carrion-eating birds in "Towers of Silence." Corpses are disposed of in this way so that earth, fire, and water will not be defiled. The main ceremony of the hereditary priesthood is the sacrifice of *haoma (soma)*, the holy liquor, to the sacred eternal fire. Priests offer the sacrifice on behalf of a worshiper, receiving a fee for the performance.

Zoroastrians seek to uphold two principles: to maintain life and to combat evil. To maintain life, one must marry and have children, and if possible, work the land and maintain food animals. Asceticism and celibacy, which are contradictory to life, are discouraged. The struggle against evil means to work for the victory of Ahura Mazda (later called Ormazd) and his angels and archangels over Ahriman (Angra Mainyu) and his demons and archfiends. While this may seem to be a dualistic world view, it has been interpreted in a variety of ways. Early views, apparently, were explicitly dualistic, with Ormazd and Ahriman equal. The actions of humans were seen as tipping the balance in one direction or another. During the Sassanian dynasty, a higher power or principle was contemplated. This was called Zurvan, the name for the highest deity or "god of time" in some sects of both Zoroastrianism and Manichaeism. Finally, the current view is that good has an inherent advantage. As in Christianity, the ultimate triumph of good is assured. This resemblance is more than coincidence.

*Relation to Other Religions.* Zoroastrianism occupies a pivotal position in the history of world religions. On the west it interacted with the great religions that were born in the Middle East, and on the east it shares roots with Hinduism and its offshoot, Buddhism. Thus it stands amid five religions, which together embrace well over half the world's population. The clearest influences can be seen in the figures of Satan and the Messiah in Judaism and Christianity. In early Jewish tradition Satan was the servant of God (for example, in the book of Job). Under Persian influence after the Babylonian captivity, Satan came to be regarded as the cosmic enemy of God, parallel to Ahriman in Zoroastrianism. In Islam Satan is the personification of evil, a fallen angel who tempts humans to sin. But even in hell he will continue to be God's servant. Angels and archangels, as conceived of in late Judaism and post-biblical Christianity, are drawn from Zoroastrian myths. The demon Asmodeus in the book of Tobit in the OT Apocrypha is derived from the *daeva* Aeshma. A parallel can be drawn between Philo Judaeus' six powers of God and the Zoroastrian equivalent, six "Holy Immortals," such as Cosmic Order, Good Mind, the Kingdom and others. Judaism's world ages with final judgment and redemption bear a strong resemblance to Zoroastrianism's cosmology. Beyond the similarities speculation can run wild, but hard evidence is lacking.

In addition to Zoroastrian elements borrowed by Judaism, Christianity picked up from Zoroastrianism the idea of guardian angels and the heavenly journey of the soul. Belief in the heavenly book of record, bodily resurrection, paradise, and the transformation of the earth show further parallels between Judaism and Christianity on the one hand and Zoroastrianism on the other. But there is no evidence that these elements were borrowed, or, if so, which religion did the borrowing. The Zoroastrian practice of prayer five times a day seems to have been borrowed from Islam, but it could be the other way around. Similarities between Parsis and Hindus that are not shared by Iranian Zoroastrians are probably borrowings from

Hinduism, but since the two religions have common Indo-Aryan roots, these features may represent parallel developments.

Modern pressures make many religious practices, such as the exposure of the dead in the Tower of Silence, difficult to perform, but a religion that has survived so many crises and threats to its existence clearly has the power to adapt, while maintaining its essential nature.

K./M.C.

**ZWICKAU PROPHETS.** *See* MÜNZER, THOMAS.

*Ulrich Zwingli*

**ZWINGLI, ULRICH** (1484–1531). Humanist-biblical Swiss reformer, noted for his "memorial" view of the Lord's Supper. Born at Wildhaus, Switzerland, Zwingli received educational guidance from his uncle, a local priest. He became skilled in music and pursued humanistic studies at Berne, Vienna, and Basel. In 1504 and 1506 he acquired B.A. and M.A. degrees from Basel, where he also taught classics for four years. In 1506 Zwingli received Roman Catholic ordination and served as parish priest at Glarus, 1506–16. He diligently studied Greek classics, early church fathers, and the Greek NT, and he also served as an army field chaplain but vigorously opposed recruitment of Swiss mercenaries for any but the pope. From 1516 to 1519 he was priest at Einsiedeln, where he preached an Erasmian philosophy of Christ and combatted the selling of indulgences. On January 1, 1519, he became chief pastor at Great Minster Church, Zurich. Taking the Bible as his basic authority, he expounded the entire NT, verse by verse, by 1525. His preaching attracted large audiences and soon led to changes.

In 1522 Zwingli challenged the validity of fasts, and before the year ended the Zurich Council declared all religious practices had to conform to the Bible. In 1522 he and ten other priests petitioned the bishop of Constance to allow priests to marry. That same year he married Anna Reinhart, a marriage kept secret until 1524. In 1523 he successfully defended his Sixty-seven Articles against Roman Catholic opponents.

Zwingli upheld biblical authority, salvation by faith, the Mass as a remembrance, and the right of priests and nuns to marry. He said good works do not merit salvation, rejected prayer to saints, and opposed any religious rules contrary to the Bible. The council enacted these views into law, virtually completing the REFORMATION in Zurich. By the end of 1523 the council had forbidden images and the Mass. A commemorative love feast replaced the Mass. Zwingli abandoned robes, tapestries, frescoes, relics, crucifixes, candles, bell-ringing, chanting, and organ-playing as creaturely items that distract from worship of God the Creator. In 1525 Zwingli published *Commentary on True and False Religion*, his best theological work. He accepted the Bible for faith and practice, God's foreordination and election, and those things expressly enjoined in Scripture. He repudiated original sin and held that the Holy Spirit had inspired men like Socrates.

In 1525 Zwingli successfully debated against some co-workers who said infant baptism was not biblical. By 1526 Anabaptist co-workers were under the death penalty for rebaptizing adults. Felix Manz was martyred in Zurich (1527), the first Anabaptist executed by Protestant authorities. Other Swiss cities—Basel, Berne, St. Gallen, Schaffhausen, Mülhausen—adopted Zwingli's reforms. At the Marburg Colloquy (1529), LUTHER and Zwingli agreed on fourteen religious issues but not on the Lord's Supper. Luther insisted on Christ's physical presence: "This is my body" (Matt. 26:26). Zwingli insisted the elements "signify" Christ's presence (John 6:48-63). This disagreement blocked political and theological union. In a brief battle at Kappel between Protestant and Catholic Swiss cantons, Zwingli was killed.

C.M.

This listing of selected books will be helpful in locating further information on any of the text found in the entries in the Dictionary.

## I. BIBLE

*Abingdon Bible Handbook,* Edward P. Blair (Nashville: Abingdon Press, 1975).

*The Anchor Bible,* general eds. William Foxwell Albright and David Noel Freedman (44 vols.; Garden City: Doubleday, 1964–).

*Daily Study Bible,* William Barclay (Philadelphia: The Westminster Press, 1952–).

*Dictionary of the Bible,* ed. John L. McKenzie (Milwaukee: Bruce Publishing Company, 1965).

*Eerdman's Handbook to the Bible,* eds. David Alexander and Pat Alexander (Grand Rapids: Wm. B. Eerdmans, 1983).

*Encyclopedia of Religion and Ethics,* ed. James Hastings (12 vols.; New York: Charles Scribner's Sons, 1908–27; 1959).

*An Expository Dictionary of Biblical Words,* W. E. Vine; eds. Merril F. Unger and William White, Jr. (Nashville: Thomas Nelson, 1984).

*Handbook of Biblical Criticism,* Richard N. Soulen (2nd. ed.; Atlanta: John Knox Press, 1984).

*Harper's Bible Dictionary,* general editor Paul J. Achtemeier (New York: Harper & Row, 1985).

*International Standard Bible Encyclopedia,* general editor Geoffrey W. Bromiley (revised ed.; Grand Rapids: Wm. B. Eerdmans, 1983).

*The Interpreter's Bible,* general editor George Buttrick (12 vols.; Nashville: Abingdon Press, 1952–57).

*The Interpreter's Concise Commentary,* ed. Charles M. Laymon (8 vols.; Nashville: Abingdon Press, 1983).

*The Interpreter's Dictionary of the Bible* and *Supplementary Volume* (5 vols.; Nashville: Abingdon Press, 1962, 1976).

*The Interpreter's One-Volume Commentary on the Bible,* ed. Charles M. Laymon (Nashville: Abingdon Press, 1971).

*The Jerome Biblical Commentary,* eds. R. E. Brown, J. A. Fitzmyer, and R. E. Murphy (Englewood Cliffs: Prentice-Hall, 1968).

*Nelson's Complete Concordance of the New American Standard Bible* (Nashville: Thomas Nelson, 1977).

*Nelson's Complete Concordance of the RSV Bible,* compiler John W. Ellison (New York: Thomas Nelson & Sons, 1957).

*New Bible Commentary,* eds. Donald Guthrie and J. A. Motyer (Grand Rapids: Wm. B. Eerdmans, 1970).

*New Bible Dictionary,* ed. James D. Douglas (Grand Rapids: Wm. B. Eerdmans, 1962).

*New Catholic Commentary on Holy Scripture*, eds. Reginald C. Fuller, Leonard Johnston, and Conleth Kearns (Nashville: Thomas Nelson, 1969).

*New Century Bible*, general editors Ronald E. Clements and Matthew Black (London: Oliphants, 1967–).

*The New International Version Complete Concordance*, compiled by Edward W. Goodrick and John R. Kohlenberger III (Grand Rapids: Zondervan, 1981).

*Oxford Bible Atlas*, ed. Herbert G. May (3rd ed.; New York: Oxford University Press, 1984).

*Strong's Concordance of the Bible*, James Strong (Nashville: Abingdon, 1980).

*A Theological Word Book of the Bible*, Alan Richardson (New York: Macmillan, 1950).

*The Westminster Historical Atlas to the Bible*, G. Ernest Wright and Floyd V. Filson (Philadelphia: The Westminster Press, 1956).

## A. OLD TESTAMENT

*The Ancient Near East*, ed. James B. Pritchard (Princeton: Princeton University Press, 1969).

*Ancient Near Eastern Texts in Pictures Relating to the Old Testament*, ed. James B. Pritchard (Princeton: Princeton University Press, 1950).

*Apocrypha and Pseudepigrapha of the Old Testament*, ed. R. H. Charles (2 vols.; New York: Oxford University Press, 1913).

*The Dead Sea Scrolls in English*, ed. G. Vermes (Baltimore: Pelican Books, 1968).

*From the Stone Age to Christianity*, W. F. Albright (Garden City: Doubleday, 1957).

*Handbook to the Old Testament*, Claus Westermann (Minneapolis: Augsburg, 1967).

*A Hebrew and English Lexicon of the Old Testament*, Francis Brown, S. R. Driver, and Charles A. Briggs (Oxford: Clarendon Press, 1957).

*A History of Israel*, John Bright (3rd. ed.; Philadelphia: The Westminster Press, 1981).

*The History of Israel*, Martin Noth (2nd ed.; New York: Harper & Row, 1960).

*An Introduction to the Apocrypha*, Bruce Metzger (New York: Oxford Univeristy Press, 1957).

*Old Testament Theology*, Gerhard von Rad (2 vols.; New York: Harper & Row, 1962).

*The People of Ancient Israel*, J. Kenneth Kuntz (New York: Harper & Row, 1974).

*The Prophets*, Abraham J. Heschel (2 vols.; New York: Harper & Row, 1969).

*Theological Dictionary of the Old Testament*, eds. G. Johannes Botterweck and Helmer Ringgren (Grand Rapids: Wm. B. Eerdmans, 1974–).

*Theological Wordbook of the Old Testament*, eds. R. Laird Harris, Gleason L. Archer, and Bruce K. Waltke (2 vols.; Chicago: Moody Press, 1980).

*The Tyndale Old Testament Commentaries*, ed. D. J. Wiseman (London: Inter-Varsity Fellowship, 1974–).

*Understanding the Old Testament*, Bernhard W. Anderson (4th. ed.; Englewood Cliffs: Prentice-Hall, 1986).

## B. NEW TESTAMENT

*Gospel Parallels*, Burton H. Throckmorton, Jr. (4th ed.; Nashville: Thomas Nelson, 1979).

*A Greek-English Lexicon of the New Testament and Other Early Christian Literature*, ed. Walter Bauer (2nd. ed.; Chicago: University of Chicago Press, 1979).

*Handbook to the New Testament*, Claus Westermann (Minneapolis: Augsbur)1977).

*Introduction to the New Testament*, Werner G. Kümmel (Nashville: Abingdon Press, 1966).

*Jesus of Nazareth*, Gunther Bornkamm (New York: Harper & Brothers, 1960).

*New International Commentary on the New Testament*, general editor F. F. Bruce (Grand Rapids: Wm. B. Eerdmans, 1951–).

*New International Dictionary of New Testament Theology*, ed. Colin Brown (3 vols.; Grand Rapids: Zondervan, 1975–78).

*The New Testament: An Introduction*, Norman Perrin and Dennis C. Duling (2nd. ed.; New York: Harcourt Brace Jovanovich, 1982).

*New Testament Apocrypha*, ed. Wilhelm Schneemelcher (2 vols.; Philadelphia: The Westminster Press, 1963).

*New Testament Introduction*, Donald Guthrie (Downers Grove, IL.: Inter-Varsity Press, 1971).

*Paul*, Gunther Bornkamm (New York: Harper & Row, 1969).

*Theological Dictionary of the New Testament*, ed. Gerhard Kittel (10 vols.; Grand Rapids: Wm. B. Eerdmans, 1964–76).

*Theology of the New Testament*, Rudolph Bultmann (2 vols.; New York: Charles Scribner's Sons, 1951).

*The Tyndale New Testament Commentaries*, general editor R. V. G. Tasker (10 vols.; Grand Rapids: Wm. B. Eerdmans, 1957–74).

*Understanding the New Testament*, Howard C. Kee (4th ed.; Englewood Cliffs: Prentice-Hall, 1983).

## II. HISTORY OF CHRISTIANITY

*American Catholicism*, John Tracy Ellis (2nd. ed.; Chicago: University of Chicago Press, 1969).

*American Judaism*, Nathan Glazer (Chicago: University of Chicago Press, 1957).

*The Black Experience in Religion*, C. Eric Lincoln (New York: Doubleday, 1974).

*Christendom*, Roland H. Bainton (2 vols.; New York: Harper & Row, 1966).

*Documentary History of Religion in America*, Edwin S. Gaustad (2 vols.; Grand Rapids: Wm. B. Eerdmans, 1982).

*Documents of the Christian Church*, ed. Henry Bettenson (New York: Oxford University Press, 1963).

*Early Christian Doctrines*, J. N. D. Kelly (revised ed.; New York: Harper & Row, 1978).

*Eerdman's Handbook to Christianity in America*, ed. Mark A. Noll (Grand Rapids: Wm. B. Eerdmans, 1983).

*Here I Stand*, Roland H. Bainton (Nashville: Abingdon Press, 1950).

*Historical Atlas of Religion in America*, Edwin S. Gaustad (New York: Harper & Row, 1976).

*A History of the Christian Church*, Williston Walker (4th ed.; New York: Charles Scribner's Sons, 1985).

*A History of Christianity in the World*, Clyde L. Manschreck (2nd ed.; Englewood Cliffs: Prentice-Hall, 1985).

*A History of the Expansion of Christianity*, Kenneth S. Latourette (7 vols.; New York: Harper & Brothers Publishers, 1937–45).

*Macmillan Atlas History of Christianity*, Franklin H. Littell (New York: Macmillan Publishing Co., 1976).

*A Nation of Behavers*, Martin E. Marty (Chicago: University of Chicago Press, 1976).

*The Negro Church in America*, E. Franklin Frazier (New York: Schocken Books, 1964).

*The New International Dictionary of the Christian Church*, ed. J. D. Douglas (Grand Rapids: Zondervan, 1978).

*Oxford Dictionary of the Christian Church*, ed. F. L. Cross (2nd ed.; New York: Oxford University Press, 1974).

*The Pelican History of the Church*, ed. Henry Chadwick (6 vols.; Baltimore: Penguin Books, 1962–70).

*Pilgrims in Their Own Land*, Martin E. Marty (Boston: Little, Brown, & Co., 1984).

*Protestant-Catholic-Jew*, Will Herberg (New York: Doubleday, 1955).

*The Protestant Ethic and the Spirit of Capitalism*, Max Weber (New York: Scribner's, 1930).

*The Public Church*, Martin E. Marty (New York: Crossroads, 1981).

*The Reformation of the Sixteenth Century*, Roland H. Bainton (Boston: Beacon Press, 1952).

*A Religious History of America*, Edwin S. Gaustad (New York: Harper & Row, 1974).

*A Religious History of the American People*, Sydney E. Ahlstrom (New Haven: Yale University Press, 1972).

*Social and Religious History of the Jews*, Salo W. Baron (12 vols.; New York: Columbia University Press, 1952–67).

## III. THEOLOGY OR CHRISTIAN DOCTRINE

*Baker's Dictionary of Christian Ethics*, ed. Carl F. H. Henry (Grand Rapids: Baker Book House, 1973).

*A Catholic Dictionary of Theology*, ed. H. F. Davis (New York: Thomas Nelson, 1962–).

*Christian Ethics*, eds. Waldo Beach and H. Richard Niebuhr (New York: Ronald Publishing Co., 1955).

*A Dictionary of Christian Ethics*, ed. John Macquarrie (Philadelphia: The Westminster Press, 1967).

*Documents of Vatican II*, Austin P. Flannery (Grand Rapids: Wm. B. Eerdmans, 1975).

*Encyclopedia of Bioethics*, ed. Warren T. Reich (4 vols.; New York: Macmillan, 1967).

*Evangelical Dictionary of Theology*, ed. Walter A. Elwell (Grand Rapids: Baker Book House, 1984).

*From Hegel to Nietzche*, Karl Löwith (New York: Holt, Rinehart, and Winston, 1964).

*A Handbook of Christian Theologians*, eds. Martin E. Marty and Dean Peerman (revised ed.; Nashville: Abingdon Press, 1984).

*A Handbook of Christian Theology*, ed. Arthur Cohen (Nashville: Abingdon Press, 1980).

*A Handbook of Theological Terms*, Van A. Harvey (New York: Macmillan, 1964).

*A History of Philosophy*, Frederick Copleston (9 vols.; Garden City: Doubleday, 1962).

*History of Christian Philosophy in the Middle Ages*, Étienne Gilson (New York: Random House, 1955).

*Introduction to Scholastic Philosophy*, Maurice Dewulf (New York: Dover Publications, 1956).

*Modern Christian Thought*, James C. Livingston (New York: Macmillan, 1971).

*Principles of Christian Theology*, John Macquarrie (2nd ed.; New York: Scribner's, 1977).

*Protestant Thought: From Rousseau to Ritschl*, Karl Barth (New York: Harper & Row, 1959).

*Twentieth Century Religious Thought*, John Macquarrie (New York: Charles Scribner's Sons, 1981).

*The Westminster Dictionary of Christian Theology*, eds. Alan Richardson and John S. Bowden (Philadelphia: The Westminster Press, 1983).

## IV. WORLD RELIGIONS

*Abingdon Dictionary of Living Religions*, ed. Keith Crim (Nashville: Abingdon, 1981).

*A Dictionary of Comparative Religion*, ed. S. F. G. Brandon (New York: Charles Scribner's Sons, 1970).

*A Dictionary of Non-Christian Religions*, ed. E. G. Parrinder (Philadelphia: The Westminster Press, 1973).

*Eerdman's Handbook to the World's Religions* (Grand Rapids: Wm. B. Eerdmans, 1982).

*The Historical Atlas of the Religions of the World*, eds. Isma'il Ragi al Farqui and David E. Sopher (New York: Macmillan, 1974).

*The Idea of the Holy*, Rudolf Otto (2nd ed.; New York: Oxford University Press, 1950).

*Man's Religions*, John B. Noss (7th ed.; New York: Macmillan, 1984).

*Many Peoples, Many Faiths*, Robert S. Ellwood (Englewood Cliffs: Prentice-Hall, 1982).

*The Meaning and End of Religion*, W. C. Smith (New York: New American Library, 1963).

*The Myth of the Eternal Return*, Mircea Eliade (Princeton: Princeton University Press, 1954).

*The Religious Experience of Mankind*, Ninian Smart

(3rd. ed.; New York: Charles Scribner's Sons, 1984).

*The Sacred and the Profane,* Mircea Eliade (New York: Harcourt, Brace and World, 1959).

*The Sacred Books of the East,* F. Max Müller (51 vols.; New York: Oxford University Press, 1879–1910).

## V. CONTEMPORARY RELIGION

*American Hymns Old and New,* eds. Albert Christ-Janer, Charles W. Hughes, and Carleton Sprague Smith (2 vols.; New York: Columbia University Press, 1980).

*Christian Symbols Ancient and Modern,* Heather Child and Dorothy Colles (New York: Charles Scribner's Sons, 1971).

*Concise Dictionary of the Christian World Mission,* eds. Stephen Neill, Gerald H. Anderson, and John Goodwin (Nashville: Abingdon Press, 1971).

*A Dictionary of Hymnology,* ed. John Julian (New York: Charles Scribner's Sons, 1907).

*The Encyclopedia of the Jewish Religion,* eds. R. J. Zwi Werblowsky and Geoffrey Wigoder (New York: Holt, Rinehart and Winston, 1966).

*Encyclopedia Judaica* (16 vols.; New York: Macmillan, 1971).

*The Encyclopedia of the Lutheran Church,* ed. Julius Bodensieck (3 vols.; Minneapolis: Augsburg, 1965).

*Encyclopedia of Southern Baptists* (3 vols.; Nashville: Broadman Press, 1958, 1971).

*The Encyclopedia of World Methodism,* ed. Nolan B. Harmon (2 vols.; Nashville: The United Methodist Publishing House, 1974).

*Handbook of Denominations,* Frank S. Mead and Samuel S. Hill (9th. ed.; Nashville: Abingdon Press, 1985).

*Handbook of Symbols in Christian Art,* eds. J. G. Davies and Gertrude G. Sill (New York: Macmillan, 1975).

*The Jewish Encyclopedia,* ed. Isidore Singer (12 vols.; New York: Funk and Wagnalls, 1903–06).

*The Mennonite Encyclopedia* (4 vols.; Scottsdale, PA.: Mennonite Publishing House, 1955–59).

*The New Catholic Encyclopedia* (17 vols.; New York: McGraw-Hill, 1967–78).

*New Grove's Dictionary of Music and Musicians,* ed. George Grove (20 vols.; 6th ed.; New York: Macmillan, 1979).

*The New Standard Jewish Encyclopedia,* eds. Cecil Roth and Geoffrey Wigoder (5th ed.; New York: Doubleday, 1977).

*Profiles in Belief,* Arthur C. Piepkorn (4 vols.; New York: Harper & Row, 1977–79).

*The Seventh-day Adventist Encyclopedia* (Washington, D.C.: Review and Herald Publishing Association, 1966).

*The Universal Jewish Encyclopedia,* ed. Isaac Landman (10 vols.; New York: KTAV Publishing House, 1969).

*The Westminster Dictionary of Worship,* ed. J. G. Davies (Philadelphia: The Westmister Press, 1979).

*World Christian Encyclopedia,* ed. David Barrett (New York: Oxford University Press, 1982).

*Yearbook of American and Canadian Churches,* ed. Constant H. Jacquet, Jr. (Nashville: Abingdon Press, 1985).